WEST'S
BUSINESS
LAW TEXT&
CASES

WEST'S BUSINESS LAW

TEXT&CASES

KENNETH W. CLARKSON
University of Miami School of Law

ROGER LeROY MILLER
University of Miami School of Law

BONNIE BLAIRE
Sparber, Sevin, Rose, Shapo, and Heilbroner
Miami Florida

WEST PUBLISHING COMPANY
St. Paul   New York   Los Angeles   San Francisco

COPYRIGHT © 1980 By WEST PUBLISHING CO.
50 West Kellogg Boulevard
P.O. Box 3526
St. Paul, Minnesota 55165

Library of Congress Cataloging in Publication Data

Miller, Roger LeRoy.
     West's business law.

     Includes index.
     1.   Commercial law—United States—Cases.
     2.   Business law—United States.
     I.   Clarkson, Kenneth W., joint author.
     II.   Blaire, Bonnie, joint author.
     III.   West Publishing Company, St. Paul.   IV.   Title.
KF888.M52   1980   346'.73'07   79-26505
ISBN 0-8299-0295-3

A student workbook has been developed to assist you in mastering the concepts presented in this text. The workbook includes fill-in-the-blanks, multiple choice, and essay questions with answers as well as instructions on how to brief a case and suggestions for pre-law students and CPA candidates. This workbook is available from your local bookstore under the title *Student Workbook to Accompany West's Business Law: Text and Cases* prepared by Barbara Behr.

If you cannot locate it in your bookstore, ask your bookstore manager to order it for you.

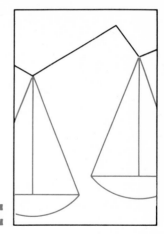

PREFACE

The average business man or woman is now, more than ever before, practically inundated with possible legal problems. So, too, is the average consumer. We are clearly witnessing a trend in American society in which the law is taking on more importance. It is with this underlying fact in mind that we have written this text. Familiarity with the legal process and specific laws can only benefit today's business student whether or not he or she continues a career in the world of commerce. We have written this text to present with maximum accuracy the legal realities facing business men and women of today.

While we cannot in any way dictate how business law should be taught, we can and have attempted to present a text that allows maximum flexibility to the instructor. To that end, you will find this text to be extremely comprehensive. Instructors can choose those areas of the law that they wish to emphasize rather than depending on our, the authors', personal preferences.

OTHER SPECIAL FEATURES OF THIS TEXT

In addition to being comprehensive and, we believe, accurate, our text provides some unique features for the student and the instructor.

1. Cases fully integrated: Cases follow the legal point that they either substantiate or illustrate rather than appearing at the back of each chapter.

2. Cases have a unique format: The case cite is fully presented in the margin. *Background and Facts* are first given in italics and then the actual case excerpts are presented in roman face to differentiate them. Following the excerpts is a *Judgment and Remedy* section, again in italics. Finally, in some cases, a *Comments* section follows.

3. Vocabulary stressed: Each time a new word of importance is introduced, it is presented in bold face. A further explanation of bold faced terms is given in a glossary at the end of the text.

4. Easy to read and learn from: The text is written in an easy-to-read manner that is liberally broken up with appropriate subheadings of four different levels. This greatly eases the learning process and allows for easier outlining by the student reader.

5. Case questions and problems: At the end of every chapter, there are approximately ten questions and case problems. The majority of these are taken out of important cases for which full and correct cites are given. Complete answers to these end-of-chapter problems and questions are given in a separate booklet which instructors may order to put on reserve in their libraries. The answers to these end-of-chapter problems and questions constitute a complete review of the law.

UNIQUE CHAPTERS

In keeping with the trends in today's law, we have added several unique chapters that we believe many professors will want to use. They cover **Special Partnerships** (including limited partnerships), **Special Corporate Forms** (including subchapter S corporations), and **Private Franchises.** We have also added an entire unit on government regulation which includes chapters on **Regulation and Administrative Agencies, Consumer Protection, Environmental Law, Antitrust,** and **Trade Regulation.** Finally, since many students taking this course will use some of the law they have learned in their own personal lives, we have included a final chapter on **Trusts, Wills, and Estates.**

APPENDICES

Because many students keep their texts as a reference source, we have decided to include a full set of appendices. They are as follows:
reference source, we have decided to include a full set of appendices. They are as follows:

1. The Uniform Commercial Code, fully updated.
2. The Uniform Consumer Credit Code.
3. The Uniform Partnerhsip Act.
4. The Uniform Limited Partnership Act.
5. The Revised Uniform Limited Partnership Act.
6. The Model Business Corporation Act.

SUPPLEMENTAL MATERIALS

We realize that most business law teachers face a difficult task in finding the time to teach all of the materials they are required to teach during each term. We have developed, with several colleagues, supplementary materials which will ease both the students' and instructors' jobs.

STUDENT WORKBOOK

Professor Barbara Behr of Bloomsburg State College has put together what we believe to be the most comprehensive, informative, and helpful *Student Workbook* for business law students that exists. It is directly aimed at allowing the student to comprehend not only "black letter" law, but also some of the subtleties behind the legal process. Basically, though, it is designed to allow the student to comprehend each chapter in such a way that exam time will not be a moment of panic. The student workbook contains:

1. A "things to keep in mind" section.
2. An outline of the chapter.
3. A set of fill-in questions (a type of program learning device).
4. A set of multiple choice questions.
5. The answers to the fill-in and multiple choice questions.

INSTRUCTOR'S MANUAL
AND TEST BANK

Testing is an inevitable part of teaching business law. With the help of William Auslen and Stephen Chaplin, we have put together approximately 600 multiple choice questions that instructors can use to make up their exams. We have also included in the **Instructor's Manual** the answers to the end-of-chapter questions and case problems. As mentioned above, these answers also appear in a separately-bound booklet which can be put on reserve in your library.

ACKNOWLEDGEMENTS

Literally hundreds of individuals have participated in one way or another on this project. While it is impossible for us to mention all of them here, we would like to thank a number of individuals for the extraordinary jobs they have done in helping us. In particular, Barbara Behr of Bloomsburg State College, the author of the *Study Guide*, has been a consistent, never-tiring critic of our work. She read the second and third drafts of the manuscript and made extensive comments throughout, helping us refine our presentation and the correctness of the law. Stephen Chaplin, the co-author of the *Instructor's Manual* and also the author of the end-of-chapter questions and case problems, has worked with us well beyond the call of duty. He has made extensive comments at various stages of our project and has helped us immensely. We have had helpful research assistance from Joseph Krabacher, Andrew Caverly, Randy Chartash, Robert Staaf, and others at the University of Miami School of Law. We were also able to impose on other colleagues at the University of Miami School of Law without them complaining too loudly. In particular, we wish to thank Professors Daniel E. Murray, Richard A. Hausler, Irwin Stotzky, and Patrick O. Gudridge. Finally, we wish to acknowledge valuable secretarial assistance from Linda Craig, Mary Gilmore, and Sharon Marsh.

Since we firmly believe that this book should be the most accurate of any published, we have relied on in-house help from the staff at West Publishing Company. Additionally, we have had numerous reviewers throughout the country. They are: Robert D. McNutt, San Fernando Valley State; Roger E. Meiners, Texas A & M University; James E. Moon, Meyer, Johnson & Moon, Minneapolis; William Auslen, San Francisco City College; Barbara Behr, Bloomsburg State College - Pennsylvania; Donald Cantwell, University of Texas at Arlington; Frank Forbes, University of Nebraska; Bob Garrett, American River College - California; Thomas Gossman, Western Michigan University; Charles Hartman, Wright State University, Ohio; Robert Jesperson, University of Houston; Susan Liebeler, Loyola University; Robert D. McNutt, California State University, Northridge; Gerald S. Meisel, Bergen Community College - New Jersey; Bob Morgan, Eastern Michigan University; Arthur Southwick, University of Michigan; Raymond Mason Taylor, North Carolina State; Edwin Tucker, University of Connecticut; Gary Victor, Eastern Michigan University; Gary Watson, California State University, Los Angeles.

Needless to say, we do not hold any of the above-mentioned individuals responsible for any errors that might exist in this text. We do ask, however, that instructors who believe that they have found an error to write us about it. It is only through the help of concerned teachers of business law that we can continue to improve upon our product and make it even more well-suited for today's student of business law.

CONTENTS IN BRIEF

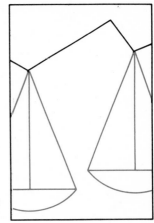

Preface v

Table of Cases xxi

UNIT I The Legal Environment of Business   1

1. Introduction to the Law 2
2. Courts and Procedures 11
3. Torts 29
4. Criminal Law 51

UNIT II Contracts   67

5. Nature, Form and Terminology 68
6. Agreement 79
7. Consideration 104
8. Contractual Capacity 124
9. Legality 140
10. Genuineness of Assent 157
11. Writing and Form 172
12. Third Party Rights 189
13. Performance and Discharge 205
14. Breach of Contract and Remedies 227

UNIT III Personal Property and Bailments   247

15. Personal Property 248
16. Bailments 261

UNIT IV Commercial Transactions and the Uniform Commercial Code   279

17. Sales/Introduction to Sales Contracts and Their Formation 280
18. Sales/Title, Risk, and Insurable Interest 302
19. Sales/Performance and Obligation 319
20. Sales/Introduction to Sales Warranties 336
21. Sales/Products Liability 356
22. Sales/Remedies of Buyer and Seller for Breach of Sales Contracts 367
23. Commercial Paper/Basic Concepts of Commercial Paper 387

24. Commercial Paper/Negotiability 395
25. Commercial Paper/Transferability
    and Negotiation 406
26. Commercial Paper/Holders In Due Course 417
27. Commercial Paper/Liability, Defenses,
    and Discharge 432
28. Commercial Paper/Checks
    and Banking System 452
29. Secured Transactions/Introduction 474
30. Secured Transactions/Liens, Priorities,
    and Remedies 490

UNIT V Creditor's Rights and Bankruptcy   505

31. Rights of Debtors and Creditors 506
32. Bankruptcies and Reorganization 526

UNIT VI Agency and Employment   543

33. Creation and Termination of Agency
    Relationships 544
34. Duties of Agents and Principals 560
35. Liability of Principals and Agents 570

UNIT VII Business Organizations   589

36. Forms of Business Organization 590
37. Partnerships/Creation and Termination 596
38. Partnerships/Operation and Duties 614
39. Partnerships/Limited Partnerships 627
40. Corporations/Nature and Formation 637
41. Corporations/Corporate Powers
    and Management 656

42. Corporations/Special Corporate Forms
    and Benefits of Incorporating 670
43. Corporations/Corporate Financing
    and Securities Regulation 682
44. Corporations/Rights and Duties of Directors,
    Managers, and Shareholders 702
45. Mergers, Consolidation, and Termination 715
46. Franchises 730

UNIT VIII Government Regulation   743

47. Regulation and Administrative Agencies 744
48. Consumer Protection 772
49. Environmental Law 791
50. Antitrust 806
51. The Federal Trade Commission
    and Trade Regulation 827

UNIT IX Protection of Property and Other Interests   847

52. Nature and Ownership of Real Property 848
53. Future Interests, Nonpossessory Interests,
    and Land Use Control 870
54. Insurance 885
55. Wills, Trusts, and Estates 907

Appendixes
A. Uniform Commercial Code 929
B. Uniform Consumer Credit Code 1055
C. Uniform Partnership Act 1109
D. Uniform Limited Partnership Act 1121
E. Revised Uniform Limited Partnership Act 1129
F. Model Business Corporation Act 1143
Glossary 1199
Index 1219

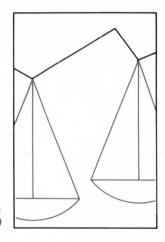

CONTENTS

Preface v

Table of Cases xxi

1 Introduction to the Law 2
What is the Law? 2
Schools of Legal, or Jurisprudential, Thought 3
History and Sources of American Law 4
Sources of the Law Today 5
The Uniform Commercial Code 7
Classification of Law 8
What is to Follow 10

**UNIT I
The Legal
Environment
of Business
1**

2 Courts and Procedures 11
Jurisdiction 11
The State Court System 12
The Federal Court System—Cases and Controversies 14
Federal Court Jurisdiction 16
Which Cases Reach the Supreme Court? 17
Judicial Procedures—Following a Case Through the Courts 18
How to Find the Law 24
A Constitutional Law Case 25

3 Torts 29
The Scope of Tort Law 30
The Elements of Every Tort 30
Kinds of Torts 34
Intentional Torts: Wrongs Against the Person 34
Intentional Torts: Wrongs Against Property 39
Business Torts 42
Negligence 44
Strict Liability 47

4 Criminal Law   51

The Nature of Crime   51
The Essentials of Criminal Liability   53
Defenses to Criminal Liability   54
Criminal Procedure   59
Crimes Involving and Affecting Business   60

UNIT II
Contracts
67

5 Contracts/Nature, Form and Terminology   68

Some Perspectives   68
Nature and Types of Contracts   70
Types of Contracts Explained   70

6 Contracts/Agreement   79

Mutual Assent   79
Essential Contract Terms   80
Requirements of the Offer   80
Termination of the Offer   94
Acceptance   98

7 Contracts/Consideration   104

Requirements of Consideration   104
Situations Where Consideration is not Present   109
Special Consideration Questions   113

8 Contracts/Contractual Capacity   124

Minors   124
Nonvoidable Contracts   132
Intoxicated Persons   133
Insane Persons   136
Convicts   136
Aliens   137
Married Women   137

9 Contracts/Legality   140

Contracts Contrary to Statute   140
Contracts Contrary to Public Policy   145
Effect of Illegality   154

10 Contracts/Genuineness of Assent   157

Mistakes   157
Fraud   161
Undue Influence—Fiduciary Relationships   168
Duress   168
Adhesion Contracts and Unconscionability   169

11 Contracts/Writing and Form   172
Contracts That Must be in Writing   173
Contracts for the Sale of Goods   183
Sufficiency of the Writing   184
The Parol Evidence Rule   184

12 Contracts/Third Party Rights   189
Third Party Beneficiary Contracts   189
When the Rights of a Third Party Vest   192
Assignment of Rights and Delegation of Duties   193

13 Contracts/Performance and Discharge   205
Conditions   205
Discharge By Performance   207
Discharge By Agreement   211
Discharge By Operation of Law   215
Discharge By Breach of Contract   216
Discharge By Impossibility of Performance   221

14 Contracts/Breach of Contract and Remedies   227
Damages   227
Rescission and Restitution   234
Specific Performance   235
Reformation   237
Recovery Based on Quasi-Contract   238
Election of Remedies   240
Waiver of Breach   241
Contract Provisions Limiting Remedies   242

15 Personal Property   248
The Nature of Personal Property   248
The Expanding Nature of Personal Property   249
Acquiring and Transferring Ownership of Personal Property   249
Will or Inheritance   253
Accession   253
Confusion   253
Mislaid, Lost, and Abandoned Property   254
Patents   258
Trademarks   258
Copyrights   258

UNIT III
Personal Property
and Bailments
247

16 Bailments   261
Elements of a Bailment   261
Types of Bailments   266

Rights and Duties of a Bailee (Bailee's Responsibilities)   267
Rights and Duties of a Bailor   271
Special Bailments   274

UNIT IV
Commercial
Transactions
and the Uniform
Commercial Code
279

**17 Sales/Introduction to Sales Contracts and
Their Formation   280**
Historical Perspective   280
The Uniform Commercial Code   281
The Scope of Article 2: The Sale of Goods   281
Formation of a Sales Contract   286

18 Sales/Title, Risk, and Insurable Interest   302
Passage of Title   303
Risk of Loss   304
Sales by Nonowners   312
Insurable Interest   316

19 Sales/Performance and Obligation   319
Duty of Good Faith and Commercial Reasonableness   319
Performance of a Sales Contract   321
Concurrent Conditions of Performance   321
Seller's Obligation of Tender of Delivery   321
The Perfect Tender Rules   323
Buyer's Obligations   329

20 Sales/Introduction to Sales Warranties   336
Warranty of Title   337
Warranties of Quality   338

21 Sales/Products Liability   356
Warranty Theory   356
Liability Based on Negligence   357
The Doctrine of Strict Liability   361
The Consumer Product Safety Act   363

**22 Sales/Remedies of Buyer and Seller for
Breach of Sales Contracts   367**
Remedies of the Seller   367
Remedies of the Buyer   372
Statute of Limitations   379
Contractual Provisions Affecting Remedies   379

23 Commercial Paper/Basic Concepts of Commercial Paper 387
Functions and Purposes of Commercial Paper 387
Types of Commercial Paper 388
Other Ways of Classifying Commercial Paper 390
Parties to Commercial Paper 391

24 Commercial Paper/Negotiability 395
The Requirements of Negotiability 395
Omissions That Do not Affect Negotiability 404

25 Commercial Paper/Transferability and Negotiation 406
Assignments and Negotiation 406
Indorsements 407

26 Commercial Paper/Holders in Due Course 417
Contract Law Versus The Law of Commercial Paper 417
Holder 418
Holder in Due Course 418
Holders Through a Holder in Due Course 429

27 Commercial Paper/Liability, Defenses, and Discharge 432
Liability Based on Signatures 432
Defenses 442
Discharge 447

28 Commercial Paper/Checks and the Banking System 452
Checks 452
The Bank-Customer Relationship 457
Duties of the Bank 457
Accepting Deposits 468

29 Secured Transactions/Introduction 474
The Law Before the UCC 475
Article 9 of the UCC 475
Definitions 475
Creating a Security Interest 476
Purchase Money Security Interest 477
Perfecting a Security Interest 478
Other Ways to Perfect 487

30 Secured Transactions/Liens, Priorities, and Remedies 490

Parties that Prevail Over the Unperfected Security Interest 490
The Range of Perfection and the Floating Lien Concept 491
Priorities 492
Exceptions to Perfection Priority Rules 493
The Rights and Duties of Debtors and Creditors Under the UCC 495
Default 496
Termination 501

**UNIT V
Creditor's Rights
and Bankruptcy
505**

31 Rights of Debtors and Creditors 506

Laws Assisting Creditors 506
Bulk Sales Law—Article 6 of the UCC 515
Protection of the Debtor 515

32 Bankruptcies and Reorganization 526

The Bankruptcy Reform Act of 1978 526
Goals of Bankruptcy Law 527
Types of Bankruptcy 527
Bankruptcy Procedures 528
Debts and Claims 531
Defining the Bankrupt's Estate 536
Non-Liquidation Proceedings 537

**UNIT VI
Agency and
Employment
543**

33 Creation and Termination of Agency Relationship 544

The Nature of Agency 544
Kind of Agents 545
Formation of the Agency Relationship 551
Legal Capacity 553
Agency Power Coupled with an Interest 553
Termination of an Agency 553

34 Duties of Agents and Principals 560

The Agent's Duty to the Principal 560
Principal's Remedies for Agent's Violation of Fiduciary Duty 567
Principal's Duties to Agent 567
Agent Remedies Against Principal 567

35 Liability of Principals and Agents 570

Principal's Liability for Contracts 570
Agent's Liability for Contracts 578
The Principal's Liability for Torts of an Agent 581
Employer's Liability for Employee's Intentional Torts 586

36 Forms of Business Organization   590
Sole Proprietorship   590
Partnership   590
Business Corporations   591
Other Forms of Business Organization   591
The Advantages and Disadvantages of a Sole Proprietorship   593
Comparing a Partnership with a Corporation   593

37 Partnerships/Creation and Termination   596
Characteristics of a Partnership   597
Formation of a Partnership   598
Property Rights   604
Property Rights of Partners   605
Limited Partnerships   605
Termination   605

38 Partnerships/Operation and Duties   614
Rights Among Partners   614
Duties and Powers of Partners   620

39 Partnerships/Limited Partnerships   627
Definition of Limited Partnership   627
History of Limited Partnerships   628
Formation   628
The Use of a Limited Partnership   633
Dissolution   633
Limited Partnership Associations   634

40 Corporations/Nature and Formation   637
A Brief History of the Corporation   637
The Nature of a Corporation   638
Formation of a Corporation   641
Disregarding the Corporate Entity   648
Separation of Personal and Corporate Interest   651

41 Corporations/Corporate Powers and Management   656
Corporate Powers   656
Corporate Management: Shareholders   661
Corporate Management: Directors   666

42 Corporations/Special Corporate Forms and Benefits of Incorporating   670
The Subchapter S Corporation   670
Close Corporations   671

UNIT VII
Business Organizations
589

Professional Service Associations—Professional Corporations   674
Foreign Corporations   675
Nonprofit Corporations   677
Corporate Formation and Its Costs   678

43   Corporations/Corporate Financing and Securities Regulation   682

Characteristics of Bonds   682
Characteristics of Stocks   683
Dividends   686
Federal Securities Regulations   689
State Securities Laws   699

44   Corporations/Rights and Duties of Directors, Managers, and Shareholders   702

The Role of Officers and Directors   702
Liabilities of Corporate Officers   706
Rights of Corporate Officers and Other Management Employees   706
Duties and Liabilities of Major Shareholders   706
Rights of Directors   706
Shareholder Rights   706
Shareholder Liabilities   713

45   Corporations/Merger, Consolidation, and Termination   715

Mergers and Consolidation   716
Termination   725

46   Corporations/Private Franchises   730

The Law of Franchising   731
Types of Franchises   731
Advantages of the Franchise System   731
The Franchise Agreement   732
Regulation of the Franchising Industry   738

UNIT VIII
Government
Regulation
743

47   Government Regulation/Regulation and Administrative Agencies   744

Increasing Regulations   745
Administrative Agencies   746
Regulatory Powers and Procedures   746
Overlapping Regulation   752
Types of Regulation   752
Regulated Activities   759
Public Review of Regulation   767

48 Government Regulation/Consumer Protection 772
Consumer Protection Sources   773
Advertising   774
Certification   779
Sales   780
Credit   781
Warranties   788

49 Government Regulation/Environmental Law   791
Historical Background   791
Regulation By Administrative Agencies   792
Environmental Protection Agency   792
Private Litigation   795
Air Pollution   796
Water Pollution   798
Noise Pollution   800
Toxic Substances   801
Pesticide Control   801
Waste Disposal   801
Judicial Limits   804

50 Government Regulation/Antitrust   806
Common Law Actions   806
The Beginning of U.S. Antitrust Law   807
The Development of Per Se Violations   813
The Clayton Act   822
Exemptions from Antitrust Laws   822

51 Government Regulation/The Federal Trade Commission and Trade Regulations   827
Commission Resources and Authority   827
FTC Activities   834
Vertical Restraints   837
Horizontal Restraints   840
Conglomerate Mergers   841
Industry-Wide Matters   843
Exemptions to FTC Regulation Activities   844

52 Nature and Ownership of Real Property   848
Nature of Real Property   848
Ownership Interest in Real Property—Estates in Land   850
Relationship of Landlord and Tenant   855
Concurrent Ownership   856
Transfer of Ownership   858

UNIT IX
Protection of Property and Other Interests
847

53 Future Interests, Nonpossessory Interests, and Land Use Control   870

Future Interests   870
Land Use Control   877

54 Insurance   885

The Nature of Insurance   885
Indemnity   889
The Right of Subrogation   889
Other Insurance Clauses   889
State Regulation of Insurance   890
The Insurance Contract   890
Interpretation   892
Cancellation of Insurance Policies   893
Defenses Against Payment to the Insured   894
Rebuttal of the Defenses of the Insurance Company   895
Types of Insurance   895
Two Basic Types of Life Insurance   896
Home, Property, and Liability Insurance Policies   898
Automobile Insurance   899
Accident and Health Insurance   903

55 Wills, Trusts, and Estates   907

Origins of Inheritance Laws   908
Purposes of Inheritance Laws   908
Wills   908
Formal Requirements of a Will   913
Fraud, Undue Influence, and Mistake   914
Revocation of Wills   914
Rights Under a Will   917
Statutes of Descent and Distribution   918
Trusts   919
Estate Administration   920
The Taxation of Estates   923
The Numbers are Small   923
State Inheritance and Estate Taxes   924

Appendixes

The Uniform Commercial Code   929
The Uniform Consumer Credit Code   1055
The Uniform Partnership Act   1109
The Uniform Limited Partnership Act   1121
The Revised Uniform Limited Partnership Act   1129
The Model Business Corporation Act   1143

Glossary   1199

Index   1219

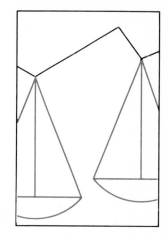

TABLE OF CASES

The principal cases are in italic type. Cases cited or discussed are in roman type.

ABC Trans, etc. v. Aeronautics Forwarders, Inc., 561

Abell Co. v. Skeen, 588

Abernathy, State v., 260

Adams v. Lindsell, 101

Adams v. United States Distributing Corp. 728

Adams v. Wilson, 179

Addyston Pipe & Steel Co., United States v., 807, 814, 816

Adolph Coors Co. v. Federal Trade Comm., 771

Aero Drapery of Kentucky, Inc. v. Engdahl, 714

Aetna Casualty & Surety Co. v. Traders National Bank and Trust Co., 471

Alex, Brown and Sons v. Latrobe Steel Co., 713

Alexopoulos v. Dakouras, 569

Allegheny College v. National Chautauqua County Bank of Jamestown, 119

Allen v. Steinberg, 635

All-State Industries of North Carolina, Inc. v. Federal Trade Comm., 777

Alport & Son, Inc., A v. Hotel Evans, Inc., 405

Alyeska Pipeline Service Co. v. The Wilderness Society, 774

American Can Co. v. Oregon Liquor Control Comm., 802

American Container Corp. v. Hanley Trucking Corp., 354

American Mail Line Ltd. v. Federal Maritime Comm., 845

American Oil Co. v. McMullen, 826

American Petroleum v. Occupational Safety and Health Administration, 804

American Sand & Gravel, Inc. v. Clark and Fray Constr. Co., 301

Appalachian Coals, Inc. v. United States, 819

Application of (see name of party)

Arizona Public Service Co. v. Federal Power Comm., 793

Armory v. Delamire, 255

Armour & Co. v. Celic, 113

Aryeh v. Eastern International, 430

Asher v. Herman, 524

Ashgrove Cement Co. v. Federal Trade Comm., 838

Asphalt Roofing Mfg. Ass'n v. ICC, 804

Associated Creditors Agency v. Dunning Floor Covering, 524

Atlantic Richfield Co. v. Razumic, 733

Atlantic Richfield Co. v. United States, 799

Autry v. Republic Productions, 224
Avis Plumbing and Heating Contractors Corp. v. McCormick Theological Seminary, 244

Bagby Land and Cattle Co. v. California Livestock Comm. Co., 187
Baisch v. Publishers' Typographic Service, Inc., 260
Baldwin, In re Estate of, 569
Balon v. Cadillac Automobile Co. of Boston, 493
Bank of Louisville Royal v. Sims, 473
Bank of West v. Wes-Con Development Co., 416
Barber v. Kimbrell's, Inc., 517, 789
Barker v. Allied Supermarket, 365
Barnes v. Euster, 208
Barnes-King Development Co. v. Corette, 714
Barthuly v. Barthuly, 625
Bartus v. Riccardi, 334
Bates v. State Bar of Arizona, 754
Beck and Pauli Lithographing Co. v. Colorado Milling and Elevator Co., 224
Beco, Inc. v. Minnechaug Golf Course, Inc., 384
Bell v. Herzog, 625
Bennett v. United States Fidelity and Guaranty Co., 422
Bentall, F.M. v. Koenig Brothers, Inc., 657
Bickford v. Mattocks, 251
Billetter v. Posell, 243
Bishop v. Ellsworth, 260
Black v. Schenectady Discount Corp., 502
Blanchard v. Calderwood, 177
Borg-Warner Acceptance Corp. v. Wolfe City National Bank, 502
Botwin v. Central Structural Steel Co., 681
Boulevard National Bank of Miami v. Air Metal Industries, Inc., 204
Bower, United States v., 57
Bowles v. City National Bank and Trust Co., 489
Boyd v. Aetna Life Ins. Co., 160
Brackenbury v. Hodgkin, 102
Bragg v. Johnson, 612
Brainard v. Commissioner, 926
Brind v. International Trust Co., 253
British Wagon Co. v. Lea & Co., 204
Brooks v. Scoville, 226
Brown v. Brown, 635
Brown v. Lober, 860
Brown-Crummer Inv. Co. v. Arkansas City, 92
Budget Rent-A-Car Corp. of America v. Fein, 147
Buford v. American Finance Co., 790
Bunge Corp. v. London and Overseas Ins. Co., 905

Bunker, Estate of, 926
Bunny Bear, Inc. v. Peterson, 771
Burbank v. Lockheed Air Terminal Inc., 801
Burchett v. Allied Concord Financial Corp., 443, 446
Butler v. Frontier Telephone Co., 849
Butterfield v. Forrester, 50

Cain v. Country Club Delicatessen of Saybrook, Inc., 484
Cal Distributing Co. v. Bay Distributors, Inc., 824
California State Auto v. Barrett Garages, Inc., 242
Callano v. Oakwood Park Homes Corp., 239
Callarama v. Associates Discount Corp. of Delaware, Inc., 786
Cambridge Trust Co. v. Carney, 472
Campbell v. Miller, 612
Campbell v. Pollack, 331
Campbell v. Vose, 722
Campbell Soup Co. v. Wentz, 235
Canal v. Bank of Albany, 450
Capezzaro v. Winfrey, 264
Carpenter v. Alberto Culver Co., 354
Carpenter v. Mason, 241
Carroll v. Protection Maritime Ins. Co., Ltd., 844
Casey v. Kastel, 553
Cash Register Co. v. Townsend Grocery Store, 170
Catania v. Brown, 346
Causby, United States v., 849
Central Trust and Safe Co. v. Respass, 613
Chalet Ford, Inc. v. Red Top Parking, Inc., 262
Chaplin v. Hicks, 245
Chemical Bank of Rochester v. Ashenburg, 632
Chiarella, United States v., 701
Childers v. United States, 611
Childs v. Philpot, 654
Chrysler Credit Corp. v. Malone, 502
Cintrone v. Hertz Truck Leasing and Rental Service, 272
Circle v. Jim Walter Homes, Inc., 405
Citizens Against Toxic Sprays, Inc. v. Bergland, 804
Citizens State Bank v. Rausch, 587
City of (see name of city)
Clark v. Campbell, 926
Clarke Memorial College v. Monaghan Land Co., 668
Clearlake Apartments, Inc. v. Clearlake Utilities Co., 884
Clemens v. Commissioner of Internal Revenue, 681
Coleman v. Plantation Golf Club, Inc., 713
Collins v. Smith, 540

Colorado Pump and Supply Co. v. Feb-co, Inc., 844

Columbus Cosmetic Corp. v. Shoppers Fair of South Bend, 883

Commercial Discount Corp. v. Milwau-kee Western Bank, 489

Commercial Savings Bank v. G & J Wood Products Co., 449

Commonwealth v. _____ (see oppos-ing party)

Comstock v. Great Lakes Distributing Co., 729

Conner v. Herd, 880

Consolidated Bottling Co. v. Jaco Equipment Corp., 317

Container Corp. of America, United States v., 826

Continental Ore Co. v. Union Carbide and Carbon Corp., 809

Cook v. Johnson, 73

Corcoran v. Lyle School Dist. No. 406, Klickitat County Washington, 94

Craig v. Hamilton, 625

Crane Ice Cream Co. v. Terminal Freezing Co., 202

Crawford v. DiMicco, 565

Crisan Estate, In re, 77

Crittendon v. State Oil Co., 558

Crocker v. Winthrop Laboratories, Div. of Stirling Drugs, Inc., 361

Crystal, Inc., David v. Ehrlich-Newmark Trucking Co., 277

Cummings General Tire Co. v. Volpe Constr. Co., 524

Dalsis v. Hills, 804

Danielson v. Roberts, 258

Davis v. Pioneer Bank and Trust Co., 611

Davis v. State, 65

Davis v. Western Union Telegraph Co., 416

Decatur Cooperative Ass'n v. Urban, 283, 295

Deesen v. Professional Golfers Ass'n of America, 825

Delaney v. Fidelity Lease Ltd., 636

Delaware Racing Ass'n, Application of, 728

Delmar Bank v. Fidelity & Deposit Co., 416

Delta Oxygen Co. v. Scott, 365

Den Gre Plastics Co. v. Travelers In-dem. Co., 883

Denkin v. Sterner, 385

Diamond Match Co. v. Roeber, 156

Dickinson v. Dodds, 103

Dinkler Management Corp. v. Stein, 588

Dodge v. Ford Motor Co., 708

Domestic Loan, Inc. v. Peregoy, 225

Dorf v. Tuscarora Pipeline Co., 857

Dorin v. Occidental Life Ins. Co., 569

D'Orio v. Startup Candy Co., 142

Dorton v. Collins & Aikman Corp., 293

Double Eagle Lubricants, Inc. v. Feder-al Trade Comm., 845

Douglas v. Citizens Band of Jonesboro, 472

Downey v. Moore's Time-Savings Equipment, Inc., 365

Duilio v. Senechal, 447

Earle v. Fiske, 868

Eastern Airlines, Inc. v. Stuhl, 137

Edward & Associates, Charles v. Eng-land, 541

Eglee, Estate of, 915

Electric Regulator Corp. v. Sterling Extruder Corp., 305

Ellingson v. Walsh, O'Connor and Bar-neson, 626

Embry v. Hargadine, McKittrick Dry Goods Co., 102

Erdman v. Johnson Brothers Radio and TV Co., 385

Ernst & Ernst v. Hochfelder, 701

Ertag, Inc. v. Lehigh Valley Mills, Inc., 385

Escott v. Barchris Constr. Corp., 690

Estate of (see name of party)

Ethyl Corp. v. Environmental Protec-tion Agency, 796

Evans v. American National Bank and Trust Co. of Chattanooga, 524

Evergreen Amusement Corp. v. Mil-stead, 244

Exchange National Bank of Tampa v. Alturas Packing Co., 300

Fabian v. Wasatch Orchard Co., 187

Fair Finance Co. v. Fourco, Inc., 441

Fairfield Lease Corp. v. Radio Shack Corp., 587

Faretta v. California, 18

Farny v. Bestfield Builders, Inc., 40

Farris v. Glen Alden Corp., 720

Faulkenberry v. Springs Mills, Inc., 36

Faulkner, Regina v., 65

Fedders Corp. v. Federal Trade Comm., 845

Federal Trade Comm. v. Colgate-Palmolive Co., 774

Federal Trade Comm. v. Consolidated Foods Corp., 838

Federal Trade Comm. v. Procter & Gamble Co., 841

Feinberg v. Pfeiffer Co., 122

Felch v. Findlay College, 244

Ferguson v. Coleman, 156

Fernandez v. Arizona Water Co., 825

Ferri v. Sylvia, 405

Fetting Mfg. Jewelry Co. v. Waltz, 868

Finch v. Warrior Cement Co., 728

Fink v. Cox, 104

First County National Bank and Trust Co. v. Canna, 488

First Federal Savings and Loan Ass'n v. Branch Banking and Trust Co., 405
First Flight Associates, Inc. v. Professional Golf Co., 558
First National Bank v. Anderson, 431
First Western Mortgage Co. v. Hotel Gearhart, Inc., 609
Fisher v. Carrousel Motor Hotel, Inc., 49
Fletcher v. Hurdle, 884
Flynn v. Reaves, 626
F-M Potatoes, Inc. v. Suda, 269
Foakes v. Beer, 112
Fong v. Miller, 158
Frances Hosiery Mills, Inc. v. Burlington Industries, Inc., 300
Free For All Missionary Baptist Church, Inc. v. Southeastern Beverage and Ice Equipment Co., 669
Friedhoff v. Engberg, 138
Frigaliment Importing Co. v. B.N.S. International Sales Corp., 89

GAC Finance Corp. v. Burgess, 525
Gaines & Sea v. R.J. Reynolds Tobacco Co., 80
Galler v. Galler, 672
Ganley Brothers, Inc. v. Butler Brothers Building Co., 188
Garfield v. Strain, 700
Gast v. Petsinger, 636
Gastonia Personnel Corp. v. Rogers, 128
Gateway Co. v. Charlotte Theaters, Inc., 300
Gendron v. Pawtucket Mutual Ins. Co., 887
General Foods Corp. v. Bittinger Co., 334
General Motors Acceptance Corp. v. Colwell Diesel Service and Garage, Inc., 502
General Motors Corp., United States v., 819
Gentry, Estate of, 911
Gentry v. Hanover Ins. Co., 905
Ger-Ro-Mar, Inc. v. FTC, 741
Giberson v. Ford Motor Co., 363
Gilberton Contracting Co. v. Hook, 260
Gindy Mfg. Corp. v. Cardinale Trucking Corp., 355
Ginsburg v. Bull Dog Auto Fire Ins. Ass'n. of Chicago, 204
Girard Bank v. Haley, 613
Girard Trust Corn Exchange Bank v. Warren Lepley Ford, Inc., 488
Glaire v. La Lanne-Parris-Health Spa, Inc., 786
Glover v. Jewish War Veterans of the United States, Post No. 58, p. 92
Goddard v. Ishikawajima-Harima Heavy Industries Co., 335
Goldberg v. Rothman, 420

Goldstein v. Stainless Processing Co., 334
Gomes, Commonwealth v., 63
Gonzalez v. Schmerler Ford, 790
Goodson Steel Corp., Matter of, 384
Goody, Inc., Sam v. Franklin National Bank of Long Island, 455
Gordon v. Portland Trust Bank, 926
Grace v. Grace Institute, 662
Grana v. Security Ins. Group, 277
Granite Equipment Leasing Corp. v. Hempstead Bank, 459
Granite Management Services, Inc. v. Usry, 170
Graphic Arts Finishers, Inc. v. Boston Redevelopment Authority, 123
Gray, Matter of the Estate of, 559
Gray v. Martino, 122
Great American Indemnity Co. v. Berryessa, 151
Great American Ins. Co. v. Penn, 276
Greenberg v. A & D Motor Sales, Inc., 412
Greenspon's Sons Iron and Steel Co., Joseph v. Pecos Valley Gas Co., 668
Grey v. European Health Spas, Inc., 790
Griffin v. Ellinger, 434
Griggs v. Duke Power Co., 763
Groban v. S.S. Pegu, 906
Groening v. Opsata, 170
Gruenberg v. Goldmine Plantation, Inc., 726
Guarino v. Mine Safety Appliance Co., 45
Gulf Chemical & Metallurgical Corp. v. Sylvan Chemical Corp., 325
Gulf Refining Co. v. Williams, 50
Gunn v. Schaeffer, 549

H & R Block, Inc. v. Lovelace, 742
Hadley v. Baxendale, 231
Halsey v. Choate, 625
Hamer v. Sidway, 105
Hanberry v. Hearst Corp., 779
Hanigan v. Wheeler, 199
Hanks v. McNeil Coal Corp., 139
Haragan v. Union Oil Co., 365
Hardesty v. Andro Corp.-Webster Div., 365
Harestad v. Weitzel, 626
Harker v. Ralston Purina Co., 669
Harlo Products Corp. v. J.I. Case Co., 676
Harrison, City of v. Wilson, 884
Hartman v. San Pedro Commercial Co., 206
Hartung v. Architects Hartung/ Odle/Burke, Inc., 714
Haven v. Randolph, 558
Haverty Co., Thomas v. Jones, 225
Hawkins v. McGee, 81
Hayden v. Hoadley, 188

Haydocy Pontiac, Inc. v. Lee, 130
Hebrew University Ass'n v. Nye, 259
Hecht v. Harris, Upham and Co., 569
Heggblade-Marguleas-Tenneco, Inc. v. Sunshine Biscuit, Inc., 296
Heinicke Instruments Co. v. Republic Corp., 489
Henningsen v. Bloomfield Motors, Inc., 150, 349
Herrin v. Sutherland, 849
Hessler, Inc. v. Farrel, 681
Hicks v. Miranda, 18
Hidell v. International Diversified Investments, 655
Hill v. Grat, 181
HML Corp. v. General Foods Corp., 568
Hochester v. De La Tour, 217
Hodgeden v. Hubbard, 50
Hoffman v. Howmedica, Inc., 365
Hoffman v. Red Owl Stores, Inc., 117
Hogue v. Wilkinson, 138
Hohenberg Brothers Co. v. Killebrew, 587
Holly v. First National Bank, 113
Holly Hill Acres, Ltd. v. Charter Bank of Gainesville, 398
Holzman v. De Escamilla, 630
Hopkins v. United States, 810
Hotchkiss v. National City Bank of N.Y., 80
Hotman, In re, 533
Howard v. Nicholson, 225
Hudiburg Chevrolet, Inc. v. Ponce, 316
Hudson Supply and Equipment Co. v. Home Factors Corp., 204
Humber v. Morton, 869
Hunt v. Perkins Machinery Co., 355

In re (see name of party)
Industrial Leasing Corp. v. Sabetta, 488
Industrial National Bank of Rhode Island v. Leo's Used Car Exchange, Inc., 424
Ingham Lumber Co. v. Ingersoll & Co., 221
Ingle v. Marked Tree Equipment Co., 334
International Film Center, Inc. v. Graflex, Inc., 844
Interstate Commerce Comm., United States v., 760
Intertherm, Inc. v. Olympic Homes Systems, Inc., 651
Isbrandtsen Co. v. Local 1291 Longshoremen, 203

Jack Dev., Inc. v. Howard Eales, Inc., 508
Jackson v. Kusmer, 524
Jacob & Youngs v. Kent, 209

Jagger Brothers, Inc. v. Technical Textile Co., 384
Jemison v. Tindall, 204
Joel v. Morison, 584
Johnson v. Nychyk, 654
Johnson & Johnson v. Colgate-Palmolive Co., 771
Joint Traffic Ass'n., United States v., 810
Jones v. Adams, 25
Jones v. Bank of Nevada, 503
Jones v. Grow Investment and Mortgage Co., 869
Jones v. Hartmann, 654
Jones & Laughlin Supply v. Dugan Production Corp., 479
Joseph v. Norman's Health Club, Inc., 789

Kademenos v. Equitable Life Assurance Society, 568
Kaiser v. Northwest Shopping Center, 473
Kaiser Trading Co. v. Associated Metals and Minerals Corp., 385
Kampman v. Pittsburgh Contracting and Engineering Co., 181
Kanan, People v., 66
Kaplan v. Odd Lot Corp., 317
Kaufman v. Jaffee, 166
Keane v. Pan American Bank, 450
Keddie v. Beneficial Ins. Inc., 891
Kendall Yacht Corp. v. United California Bank, 458
Kentile Floors, Inc. v. Winham, 541
Kerr Steamship Co. v. Radio Corp. of America, 244
Kesler and Sons Constr. Co. v. Utah State Div. of Health, 751
Kichler's Inc. v. Persinger, 225
Kiefer v. Fred Howe Motors, Inc., 137
Kingston v. Preston, 207
Kirksey v. Kirksey, 122
Kittredge v. Langley, 631
Klebanow v. New York Produce Exchange, 634
Klor's Inc. v. Broadway-Hale Stores, Inc., 826
Kloster-Madsen, Inc. v. Tafi's Inc., 523
Knight, Co., E.C., United States v., 809
Knotts v. Safeco Ins. Co. of America, 317
Koczwara, Commonwealth v., 66
Kortz v. American National Bank of Cheyenne, 909
Kowal v. Sportswear by Revere, Inc., 225
Kruger v. Gerth, 729
Kuchta v. Allied Builders Corp., 740

La Gasse Pool Constr. Co. v. Fort Lauderdale, 225

Laemmar v. J. Walter Thompson Co., 170

Lair Distributing Co. v. Crump, 317

Lamb v. Leroy Corp., 728

Lamb Enterprises, Inc. v. Toledo Blade Co., 825

Lambert v. Home Federal Savings and Loan Ass'n., 174

Lamson v. Commercial Credit Corp., 409

Lane v. Honeycutt, 313

Lanfier v. Lanfier, 110

Lange v. United States, 114

Langeveld v. LRZH Corp., 451

Lanners v. Whitney, 373

Lantz International Corp. v. Industria Termotecnica Compana, 431

Lawrence v. Fox, 190

Lefkowitz v. Great Minneapolis Surplus Store, Inc., 83

Lefkowitz v. Slowek, 655

Levine v. British Overseas Airways Corp., 558

Lewis v. Michigan Millers Mutual Ins. Co., 905

Lichfield v. Dueitt, 317

Lichtyger v. Franchard Corp., 629, 635

Lincoln Stores v. Grant, 714

Lindenfelser v. Lindenfelser, 857

Lionberger v. United States, 558

Little Rock & Ft. Smith Railway Co. v. Eubanks, 150

Lloyd, Town of v. Kart Wheelers Raceway, 884

Loeb & Co. v. Schreiner, 301

Losner v. Union Bank, 541

Loveless v. Yantis, 795

Lubitz v. Wells, 50

Lucas v. Hamm, 191

Lucy, W.O. and J.C. Lucy v. A.H. Zehmer and Ida S. Zehmer, 133

Lumber Sales, Inc. v. Brown, 307

Lumbermens Mutual Cas. Co. v. Borden Co., 905

Lumley v. Gye, 44

Lux v. Lux, 873

M.F.A. Mutual Ins. Co. v. United States, 546

MacPherson v. Buick Motor Co., 358

McAvoy v. Medina, 260

McCallum v. Gray, 681

McCloskey and Co. v. Minweld Steel Co., 225

McConnell v. Commonwealth Pictures Corp., 150

McCrea, In re, 922

McCutcheon v. United Homes Corp., 868

McDonald v. Davis, 555

McDonald Constr. Co. v. Murray, 203

McGlynn v. Schultz, 927

McLouth Steel Corp. v. Jewell Coal and Coke Co., 78

McMeekin v. Gimbel Brothers, Inc., 354

McMichael v. Price, 122

McNair v. Capital Electric Ass'n, 668

McQuade Travel Agency, Inc., E.A. v. Domeck, 588

McVay v. McVay, 260

Maas v. Dreher, 366

Macke Co. v. Pizza of Gaithersburg, Inc., 197

Macy Corp. v. Ramey, 642

Mann v. Clark Oil and Refining Corp., 541

Manufacturers and Traders Trust Co. v. Murphy, 430

Maras v. Stilinovich, 606

Marble Card Electric Corp. v. Maxwell Dynamometer Co., 354

Marbury v. Madison, 5

Marine Midland Bank-New York v. Graybar Electric Co., 415

Marshall v. Barlow's Inc., 761

Martin v. American Express, Inc., 525, 781

Martin v. Houck, 49

Marvin v. Marvin, 145

Mascioni v. J. B. Miller, Inc., 224

Mason v. Blayton, 405

Massachusetts Gas & Electric Light Supply Corp. v. V-M Corp., 320

Massachusetts Mutual Life Ins. Co. v. Central Penn National Bank, 558

Master Homecraft Co. v. Zimmerman, 405

Masterson v. Sine, 185

Matter of (see name of party)

May, State v., 66

May Dept. Stores Co. v. Pittsburgh National Bank, 414

Mellen v. Johnson, 81

Melms v. Pabst Brewing Co., 867

Mendelson-Zeller Co. v. Joseph Wedner & Son Co., 289

Merchants and Farmers Bank v. Harris Lumber Co., 668

Merritt v. Railroad Co., 126

Michelson v. Duncan, 659

Michigan National Bank v. American National Bank and Trust Co., 472

Mid-State Homes, Inc. v. Berry, 572

Millard v. Littlewood, 155

Miller v. City Bank & Trust Co., N.A., 601

Miller v. Fox, 510

Miller v. Plains Ins. Co., 166

Miller v. Preitz, 365

Millman v. State National Bank, 431

Mills v. Kopf, 138

Mills v. Wyman, 123

Mills, State v., 66

Mineral Park Land Co. v. Howard, 224

Minneapolis v. Republic Creosoting Co., 221

Minor v. Bradley, 244
Minton v. Cavaney, 650
Miranda v. Arizona, 60
Mishara Constr. Co. v. Transit-Mixed Concrete Corp., 327
Mitchell v. Reynolds, 807
Mobil Oil Corp. v. Hurwitz, 623
Mobil Oil Corp. v. Rubenfeld, 740
Mogul Steamship Co. v. McGregor Gow & Co., 807
Monroe, State v., 66
Moog Industries Inc. v. Federal Trade Comm., 751
Moon Over the Mountain, Ltd. v. Marine Midland Bank, 473
Moore v. Copeland, 416
Morad v. Coupounas, 704
Morris, In re Estate of, 927
Moureau v. Leaseamatic, 529
Mourning v. Family Publications Services, Inc., 789
Multiplastics, Inc. v. Arch Industries, Inc., 310
Munchak Corp. v. Cunningham, 204
Mutual Savings Life Ins. Co. v. Noah, 904
Myzel v. Fields, 701

Nassar v. Smith, 277
Nation-Wide Check Corp. v. Banks, 405
National-Dime Bank v. Cleveland Brothers Equipment Co., 488
Natural Resources Defense Council Inc. v. Morton, 793
Neese v. Brown, 669
New Liberty Medical and Hospital Corp. v. E.F. Hutton and Co., 654
New York Times Co. v. Sullivan, 38
Nichols v. Arthur Murray, Inc., 741
Nicholson's Mobile Home Sales, Inc. v. Schramm, 502
Nixon, United States v., 5
Nolan v. Williamson Music, Inc., 194
Norfolk Dev. Corp. v. St. Regis Pulp and Paper Corp., 366
North Star Coal Co. v. Eddy, 613
Northern Securities Co. v. United States, 810
Northside Building and Investment Co. v. Finance Co. of America, 416
Norwood, People v., 393
Nu-Way Services, Inc. v. Mercantile Trust Co. National Ass'n, 465

O'Brien v. Bickett, 625
O'Callaghan v. Waller and Beckwith Realty Co., 171
Okamoto, In re, 541
O'Keefe v. Lee Calan Imports, Inc., 102
Olsen v. Hawkins, 136
Orr v. Orr, 25, 27

Ortelere v. Teachers' Retirement Bd., 136
Orzeck v. Englehart, 728
Ouachita Air Conditioning, Inc. v. Pierce, 170
Overbeck v. Sears, Roebuck and Co., 156

P. S. & E., Inc. v. Selastomer Detroit, Inc., 559
Pace Carpet Mills, Inc. v. Life Carpet and Tile Co., 680
Palsgraf v. Long Island Railroad Co., 31, 33
Paluch, Appellate Court of Illinois, People v., 66
Pankas v. Bell, 138
Pansica, Inc., P. J. v. Llobell, 450
Paramount Paper Products Co. v. Lynch, 334
Pareira v. Wehner, 245
Park City Corp. v. Watchie, 654
Park County Implement Co. v. Craig, 317
Parker v. Arthur Murray, Inc., 221
Parker v. Brown, 147, 823
Parker, People v., 729
Paset v. Old Orchard Bank & Trust Co., 255
Peddy v. Montgomery, 138
Peerless Glass Co. v. Pacific Crockery Co., 158
People v. _____ (see opposing party)
Permalum Window and Awning Mfg. Co. v. Permalum Window Mfg. Corp., 333
Petersen v. Pilgrim Village, 87
Peterson v. Peterson, 513
Peterson v. Rowe, 187
Pfizer and Co., Charles v. Federal Trade Comm., 770
Phillips v. City of New York, 276
Phillips v. Cook, 626
Phillips Home Furnishings, Inc. v. Continental Bank, 472
Phillipsburg National Bank, United States v., 845
Piper v. Morris, 868
Plasteel Products Corp. v. Helman, 629
Plotnick v. Pennsylvania Smelting & Refining Co., 371, 378
Pollack v. Commissioner of Internal Revenue, 681
Portal Gallaries, Inc. v. Tomar Products, Inc., 384
Prevost v. Gomez, 588
Priebe and Sons v. United States, 244
Probert v. American Gypsum Div., 568
Procter & Gamble Distributing Co. v. Lawrence American Field Warehouse Corp., 278
Provident Tradesmens Bank & Trust Co. v. Pemberton, 300
Pym v. Campbell, 102

Quality Motors, Inc. v. Hays, 126
Quantum Dev. v. Joy, 411

Raffles v. Wichelhaus and Another, 158
Ramsey v. Gordon, *563*
Rapoport v. 55 Perry Co., 612
Rea and 22 Ford, Inc. v. Ford Motor Co., 736
Real Estate Development Corp., United States v., 587
Reed v. Washington Trailer Sales, Inc., 790
Regina v. _____ (see opposing party)
Rehrig v. Fortunak, 433
Reich v. Helen Harper, Inc., 187
Reliance Cooperage Corp. v. Treat, 217
Reliance Electric Co. v. Emerson Electric Co., 701
Reynolds v. Armstead, 229
Reynolds v. Penhow, 122
Rhodes v. Wilkins, 184
Ricchetti v. Meister Brau, Inc., 824
Richards Co., Enoch C. v. Libby, 853
Ricketts v. Scothorn, 116
Riely, United States v., 687
Robertson v. King, 137
Robinson v. Mann, 541
Rollins, State v., 170
Romitti, United States v., 588
Rose v. Lurvey, 108
Roseman v. Retail Credit Co., 790
Rosen v. Deporter-Butterworth Tours, Inc., 579
Ross Transport, Inc. v. Crothers, 714
Roy v. Allstate Ins. Co., 892
Royal Indemnity Co. v. Westinghouse Electric Corp., 244
Royal Ins. Co. v. Sisters of Presentation, 906
Royal Store Fixture Co. v. Bucci, 286
Rozmus v. Thompson's Lincoln-Mercury Co., 375
Runyan v. Pacific Air Industries, Inc., 742
Ruth v. Crane, 635
Rutkin Electric Supply Co. v. Burdette Electronics, Inc., 488
Rybicki, United States v., 65
Rylands v. Fletcher, 50

S.W. Neighborhood Assembly v. Eckard, 805
Saka v. Sahara-Nevada Corp., 430
Salinas, City of v. Sousa & McCue Constr. Co., 165
Samples v. Trust Co. of Georgia, 473
Sanders v. Pottlitzer Brothers Fruit Co., 102
Sanders Inc. v. Chesmotel Lodge Inc., 165
Save the Bay Committee, Inc. v. Mayor, etc., of the City of Savannah, 792

Schaefer v. Smith, 540
Schaefers v. Apel, 883
Schilling v. Waller, 259
Schrier v. Home Indemnity Co., 318
Sears, Roebuck & Co. v. Seven Palms Motor Inn, 868
Seaver v. Ransom, 203
Securities and Exchange Comm. v. Children's Hospital, 700
Securities and Exchange Comm. v. Koenig, 701
Securities and Exchange Comm. v. Texas Gulf Sulphur Co., 693
Securities and Exchange Comm. v. W. J. Howey Co., 700, 739
Security Trust Co. v. First National Bank, 472
Semple v. State Farm Mutual Automobile Ins. Co., 317
Shackleton v. Food Machinery and Chemical Corp., 155
Shakey's Inc. v. Martin, 742
Shelley v. Kraemer, 878
Shepard v. Glick, 71
Shuey v. United States, 102
Sigrol Realty Corp. v. Valcich, 868
Simeon Management Corp. v. Federal Trade Comm., 835
Simpson v. Compagnie Nationale Air France, 569
Singleton v. Commissioner of Internal Revenue, 18
Skouras v. Admiralty Enterprises, Inc., 710
Slaughter v. Jefferson Federal Savings and Loan Ass'n, 430
Sloane v. Dixie Gardens, Inc., 883
Smith v. Gentilotti, 405
Smith, Co., Maurice C. v. Fisher Plastics Corp., 338
Smith, Inc., L.B. v. Foley, 502
Smith's Sons Co., John E. v. Lattimer Foundry & Machine Co., 354
Socony Vacuum Oil Co., United States v., 819
Southern Baptist Hospital v. Williams, 399
Southern Pacific Co. v. Loden, 275
Spaulding v. New England Furniture Co., 138
Springstead v. Nees, 122
Sprogis v. United Airlines, Inc., 771
Standard Brands, Inc. v. Zumpe, 569
Standard Oil Co. of New Jersey v. United States, 810
Stanspec Corp. v. Jelco, Inc., 212
Star Corp. v. General Screw Products Co., 668
Starks v. Orleans Motors, Inc., 785
State v. _____ (see opposing party)
Stauth v. Stauth, 619
Steele v. J.I. Case Co., 380
Steigler v. Insurance Co. of North America, 894

Stephens v. Bowie National Bank of Bowie, 430

Sterling Finance Co. v. Thornhill, 790

Sterling National Bank and Trust Co. v. Fidelity Mortgage Investors, 450

Stevens v. Cook and Stevens, 612

Stewart v. Thornton, 431

Stilson v. Moulton-Niguel Water Dist., 559

Stone, In re, 511

Stoops v. Smith, 188

Stott v. Stott Realty Co., 668

Street Auto Wrecking, John v. Motors Ins. Corp., 353

Strevell-Paterson Finance Co. v. May, 481

Strong v. Repide, 701

Stuart v. Overland Medical Center, 598

Sullivan v. Creed, 50

Sullivan County Wholesalers, Inc. v. Sullivan County Dorms, 450

Summers v. Dooley, 625

Sun Pipe Line Co. v. Altes, 716

Surchin, Application of, 714

Sweedler v. Oboler, 416

Sylvestre v. Minnesota, 98

Tallahassee Bank and Trust Co. v. Raines, 416

Tampa Electric v. Nashville Coal Co., 845

Tate v. Short, 52

Taunton v. Allenberg Cotton Co., 333

Taute v. Econo-Car International, Inc., 741

Tennessee Valley Authority v. Hill, 746

Texas Kenworth Co. v. First National Bank, 503

Theodore, United States v., 655

Thomas v. Estate of Eubanks, 251

Thompson v. Occidental Life Ins. Co., 904

Thompson v. Reedman, 357

Thompson Crane & Trucking Co. v. Eyman, 169

Timmermann v. Timmermann, 612

Town of (see name of town)

Tracy v. Vinton Motors, Inc., 354

Transatlantic Financing Corp. v. United States, 224, 334

Trans-Missouri Freight Ass'n, United States v., 810, 814

Travco Corp. v. Citizens Federal Savings & Loan Ass'n, 416

Travelers Ins. Co. v. Coleman E. Adler, Inc., 277

Trenton Potteries Co., United States v., 816

Troop v. St. Louis Union Trust Co., 260

Troutman v. Southern Railway Co., 156

Turk v. St. Petersburg Bank & Trust Co., 498

Turner v. General Motors Corp., 363

Tuttle v. Buck, 42

Undergraduate Student Ass'n v. Peltason, 795

Union Marine and General Ins. Co. v. American Export Lines, Inc., 277

Union Motors, Inc. v. Phillips, 385

United National Life Ins., People v., 781

United Refrigerator Co. v. Applebaum, 438

United States v. _____ (see opposing party)

United States Finance Co. v. Jones, 431

Universal C.I.T. v. Foundation Reserve Ins. Co., 886

Universal C.I.T. Credit Corp. v. Ingel, 405

Utah Pie Co. v. Continental Baking Co., 829

Valley Loan Ass'n. v. United States, 681

Vermillion, City of v. Stan Houston Equipment Co., 501

Vickrey v. Sanford, 462

Vinylweld, Inc. v. Metropolitan Greetings, Inc., 681

Vlases v. Montgomery Ward Co., 354

Vodopich v. Collier County Development, Inc., 654

Vokes v. Arthur Murray, Inc., 162

Von's Grocery Co., United States v., 831

Waagen v. Gerde, 615

Walkovszky v. Carlton, 648

Walls v. Morris Chevrolet, Inc., 401

Walraven v. Ramsay, 631

Walters Estate, Re, 926

Waltman Appliance Buyers Credit Corp., In re v. Stikes, 489

Warnet v. Texas & P. Railway Co., 178

Washington Tent and Awning Co. v. 818 Ranch, Inc., 188

Wat Henry Pontiac Co. v. Bradley, 340

Watertown Federal Savings and Loan v. Spanks, 415

Watson, In re Estate of, 927

Watson v. United States Fidelity and Guaranty Co., 905

Weaver v. Bank of America, 231

Webster v. Blue Ship Tea Room, 343

Weil v. Beresth, 668

Weil v. Diversified Properties, 635

Weilersbacher, Distributor v. Pittsburgh Brewing Co., 301

Welding Engineers, Inc. v. Aetna-Standard Engineering Co., 318

Welmaker v. W.T. Grant Co., 789

Wetterow v. White, 378

Wheeless v. Eudora Bank, 503
White v. Jeffrey Galion, Inc., 366
White v. Smyth, 869
White Birch Park, Inc., Matter of, 538
White, State v., 54
Whitehead v. Bishop, 926
White-Sellie's Jewelry Co. v. Goodyear Tire and Rubber Co., 488
Widmer v. Gibble Oil Co., 214
Wilco Forest Machinery, Inc., In re, 653
Wild v. Brewer, 638
Williams v. Burrus, 608
Williams v. Illinois, 52
Williams v. Walker-Thomas Furniture Co., 155, 773
Williams v. Welch, 883
Williams & Associates v. Ramsey Products Corp., 188
Willred Co. v. Westmoreland Metal Mfg. Co., 384
Wilson v. Zimmerman, 741
Winegardner v. Burns, 574
Wing v. Lederer, 587
Wishing Well Club v. Akron, 141
Witlin, Estate of, 621

Wolfe's Will, In re, 926
Wolter, State v., 62
Womack v. Maner, 78
Wood v. Holiday Inns, Inc., 558
Wood v. Lucy, Lady Duff-Gordon, 116
Wood v. Willman, 431
Wyatt v. Mount Airy Cemetery, 431
Wydel Associates v. Thermasol, Ltd., 576

Yarborough v. Harkey, 742
Yommer v. McKenzie, 47
Young, Inc., Roy v. Delcambre, Inc., 277
Young Lumber Co., United States v., 612
Younger v. Plunkett, 524
Youse v. Employers Fire Ins. Co., 906

Zabriskie v. Lewis, 700
Zalis v. Blumenthal, 156
Zorotovich v. Washington Toll Bridge Authority, 278

WEST'S BUSINESS LAW TEXT& CASES

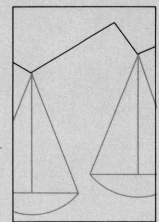

UNIT I

The Legal
Environment
Of Business

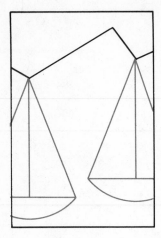

1

Introduction
to the Law

WHAT IS THE LAW?

Oliver Wendell Holmes contended that the law was a set of rules that allowed one to predict how a court would resolve a particular dispute—"the prophecies of what the courts will do in fact, and nothing more pretentious, are what I mean by the law." Aristotle saw the law as a rule of conduct. Plato believed it was a form of social control. Cicero contended that it was the agreement of reason and nature, the distinction between the just and the unjust. The British jurist, Sir William Blackstone, described the law as "a rule of civil conduct prescribed by the supreme power in a state, commanding what is right, and prohibiting what is wrong."

There have been and will continue to be different definitions of the law. We can begin to understand something about the nature of law by looking at two different approaches to the study of it. The *traditional approach* sees the law as a body of principles and rules that courts apply in deciding disputes. The study of law is the study of these rules and the general principles of right and wrong on which the rules are based. Reason and logic tell how the rules should be applied in specific cases. The traditional approach is based on the idea that the principles of right and wrong are unchanging even though society changes. This approach fulfills one of the important functions of law—to provide stability and continuity so that people can be sure of how to order their affairs.

The *environmental approach* sees the law as only one part of the total environment of society. The law is the institution that specializes in social control, and other parts of society act upon and influence it. Studying the process by which the broader society shapes the rules is part of the study of law. In the legal world this approach is known as sociological juris-prudence. The environmentalist emphasizes how social change is accomplished by using the legal system and how the law functions to provide an orderly process for social change. The environmentalist believes that if the law fails to adapt to changes in technology, attitude, and organization, social change may become violent.

Most of the material in this book takes the traditional approach. It presents the rules of law that apply to the business world and the princi-ples on which they are based. Remember, however, that outside forces in the environment *do* shape the rules. The interplay between logic and social pressure and the tension between stability and change act on the law and the courts.

SCHOOLS OF LEGAL, OR JURISPRUDENTIAL, THOUGHT

The court opinions in this book show that judges will often refer to custom, logic, history, or a philosophy of what is right in making a decision. Sometimes, however, they may seem to ignore custom and history, to stretch their logic to the breaking point, and to depart from previous notions of what is right. It would be easy to shrug one's shoulders, say "that's legal reason-ing," and dismiss the majority of judges as scoundrels. However, there are reasons for deciding a case one way as opposed to another. Part of the study of law, or **jurisprudence,** is discovering what these reasons are.

All legal philosophers would agree that custom, history, logic, and ideals have in-fluenced the development of the law in some way. They disagree, however, on the impor-tance that each of these influences should have in shaping the law, and their disagreements have produced different schools or philosophies of jurisprudence.

The Natural Law School

The natural law philosopher assumes that there is an ideal state of being, either inherent in the nature of humanity or derived from a divine source. This ideal state, or *natural law*, presup-poses a definite right and wrong. The purpose of a legal system is to order society toward the ideal of natural law. People do not create this natural law; they discover it through the use of reason and the knowledge of good and evil. The natural law school emphasizes ethics as the source of the law's authority. It uses basic philosophical values to make legal decisions. Documents such as the Magna Carta, the Declaration of Independence, the U.S. Consti-tution, and the U.N. Declaration of Human Rights reflect natural law ideals in phrases like: "We hold these truths to be self-evident, that all men are created equal, that they are endowed by their creator with certain inalienable rights . . . ."

The Historical School

The historical school emphasizes the evolution-ary process of law. It concentrates on the origin and history of the legal system and looks to the past to discover what the principles of con-temporary law should be. The legal principles that have withstood the passage of time—those that have worked in the past—should be used to shape present laws. Thus, law develops in and with the social environment. The law's legit-imacy and authority come from adhering to the principles that historical development has shown to be workable.

The Analytical School

The analytical school uses logic to shape the law. A legal analyst examines the structure and subject matter of a legal code and uses logical analysis to extract the principles that underlie it. By analyzing cases and rules, analysts formulate general principles, and these principles become the starting points for legal reasoning. In-dividual laws are judged on the basis of whether they are in logical agreement with these starting points. The law's legitimacy and authority come from the fact that it is commanded and enforced by the legal institutions in society.

The Legal Realists

Legal realism is based on the idea that the law is shaped by social forces and is an instrument of social control. It stresses the pragmatic and empirical sides of the law. Legal realists see the law as a means to a social end, and they desire to predict and influence lawmaking. They believe that, despite moral law, historical development, and logical analysis, the same conclusion will not always follow from the same set of facts. A reviewing court may view facts differently than a lower court. For the legal realist, the legitimacy of law and of legal institutions is measured by how well they serve the needs of society.

HISTORY AND SOURCES OF AMERICAN LAW

Because of our colonial heritage, much of American law is based on the English legal system. Understanding this heritage is necessary to understanding the nature of our legal system today.

The Establishment of Courts of Law

In 1066 the Normans conquered England, and William the Conqueror and his successors began the process of unifying the country under their rule. One of the means they used to this end was the establishment of the *Curia Regis*, or king's court. Before the Conquest, disputes had been settled locally according to local custom. The king's court sought to establish a common or uniform set of customs for the whole country. The body of rules that evolved under the *Curia Regis* was the beginning of the **common law.** As the number of courts and cases increased, the more important decisions of each year were

gathered together and recorded in year books. Judges settling disputes similar to ones that had been decided before used the year books as the basis for their decisions. If a case was unique, judges had to create new laws, but they based their decisions on the general principles suggested in earlier cases. The body of judge-made law that developed under this system is still used today and is known as the common law.

Stare Decisis

The practice of deciding new cases with reference to former decisions eventually became a cornerstone of the English and American judicial systems. It forms a doctrine called **stare decisis** ("to stand on decided cases"). It means that judges will follow the *precedent* established by the decisions of the past.

The rule of *stare decisis* performs many useful functions. First, it helps the courts to be more efficient. It would be very time-consuming if each judge had to reason out the policies for deciding what the law should be for each case brought before a court. Instead, the judge can rely on precedent to help make a decision.

Second, *stare decisis* makes for a more just system. All courts follow precedent, and thus, different courts will use the same rule of law. There is no incentive to shop around for a favorable court. Also, the rule of precedent tends to neutralize the personal prejudices of individual judges. Whatever their personal feelings may be, judges are obligated to use precedent as the basis for their decision.

Third, the rule makes the law stable and predictable. Someone bringing a case to court can rely on the court to make a decision based on what the law has been.

Finally, *stare decisis* reflects the experience of the past and is based on the wisdom of the past.

Sometimes a court will depart from the rule of precedent because it has decided that the precedent is incorrect. Several factors can lead to such a decision. If changes in technology, business practice, or society's attitudes necessitate a change in the law, courts might depart from precedent. Judges are reluctant to overthrow precedent, and whether they do or not will depend on how strong the precedent is and how radical the change in society is.

Sometimes there is no precedent on which to base a decision, or there are conflicting precedents. In these situations, a court will: (1) refer to past decisions that may be similar to the current case and decide the case by reasoning through analogy; (2) look at social factors—changes in the status of women, for example—that might influence the issues involved; (3) examine historical trends that indicate a direction for a decision; and (4) consider the question of justice and what the fairest result would be.

Cases that overturn precedent often receive a lot of publicity, and it might seem that they are fairly common. In reality, the vast majority of cases are decided according to precedent by the rule of *stare decisis*.

SOURCES OF THE LAW TODAY

Much law has been made since the officials of the king's court made decisions with reference to the year books. Today, courts have sources other than precedent to consider when making their decisions.

Constitutions

The federal government and the states have constitutions that set forth the general organization, powers, and limits of government. The U.S. Constitution is the supreme law of the land. A law in violation of the Constitution, no matter what the source, will not be enforced by the courts. Similarly, the state constitutions are supreme within their respective borders.

The U.S. Constitution defines the powers and limitations of the federal government. All powers not retained by the federal government reside in the states or the people. For example, the Constitution gives the federal government the power to regulate *interstate* commerce. The states retain the power to regulate *intrastate*

commerce. The Constitution also delineates how federal powers are divided among the three government branches, establishing a system of checks and balances. Thus, the legislative power (power to make laws) is vested in the Congress; the executive power (power to see that laws are carried out) is vested in the president; and the judicial power (power to determine what the law is and whether laws are valid) is vested in the courts.[1]

The judiciary did not always have the power to decide whether a law was contrary to the mandates of the Constitution. The authority to make such determinations, known as *judicial review*, is of great importance in the system of checks and balances. It was first established in the famous case, Marbury v. Madison. The court determined that:

It is emphatically the province and duty of the Judicial Department to say what the law is. Those who apply the rule to a particular case, must of necessity expound and interpret that rule. If two laws conflict with each other, the courts must decide on the operation of each.

So if the law be in opposition to the Constitution, if both the law and the Constitution apply to a particular case, so that the court must either decide that case conformably to the law, disregarding the Constitution; or conformably to the Constitution, disregarding the law; the court must determine which of these conflicting rules governs the case. This is of the very essence of judicial duty.

If, then, the courts were to regard the Constitution and the Constitution is superior to any ordinary Act of the Legislature, the Constitution, and not such ordinary Act, must govern the case to which they both apply.[2]

In another famous case, United States v. Nixon, the court again exercised its authority to interpret the Constitution with respect to President Nixon's claim of executive privilege. In 1974, a grand jury indicted seven individuals for

---

1. State governments are generally established and organized the same way as the federal government.
2. 5 U.S. (1 Cranch) 137, 2 L.Ed. 60 (1803). How to read case citations is explained at the end of Chapter 2.

obstruction of justice and conspiracy to defraud (among other things). President Nixon was ordered by the special prosecutor to produce tapes, memoranda, papers, and transcripts. The president attempted to avoid the subpoena on the ground of executive privilege, but this ground was denied him by the district court. The Supreme Court eventually heard the case, denied the claim of executive privilege that was the heart of the controversy, and affirmed the order of the district court. Among other things, the court pointed out that:

* * * The Sixth Amendment explicitly confers upon every defendant in a criminal trial the right "to be confronted with the witnesses against him" and "to have compulsory process for obtaining witnesses in his favor * * * " It is the manifest duty of the courts to vindicate those guarantees and to accomplish that it is essential that all relevant and admissible evidence be produced.

    * * * [T]he allowance of the privilege to withhold evidence that is demonstrably relevant in a criminal trial would cut deeply into the guarantee of due process of law and gravely impair the basic function of the courts. * * *[3]

Statutes and Ordinances

Another source of law in the United States is the statutes enacted by the Congress and the various state legislative bodies (statutory law). In addition, cities and counties pass ordinances, none of which can violate the U.S. Constitution or the relevant state constitution. Because the states retain many powers, Congress can pass only the legislation that falls within the range of power granted to it by the U.S. Constitution.[4] Today, legislative bodies and regulatory agencies have assumed an ever-increasing share of lawmaking. A large part of the work of modern courts is interpreting what the rulemakers meant when the law was passed and applying it to a present set of facts. In large part, statutory law has replaced the common law.

---

3. 418 U.S. 683, 94 S.Ct. 3090 (1974).

4. Given in Article I, Section VIII; there are eighteen specific powers given to Congress. Amendment X gives all other powers to the states or to the people.

Administrative Agency Regulations

An administrative agency is created when the executive or legislative branch of the government delegates some of its authority to an appropriate group of persons. Administrative agencies exercise legislative, executive, and judicial power—in their rulemaking, they are using legislative power; in their regulation and supervision, they are using executive power; and in their adjudication procedures, they are wielding judicial power.

    Government agencies have proliferated in the United States. Federal agencies include the Federal Communications Commission, the Civil Aeronautics Board, the Federal Aviation Administration, the National Labor Relations Board, the Consumer Product Safety Commission, the Environmental Protection Agency, the National Highway Safety Transportation Administration, and the Interstate Commerce Commission. There are also state boards and agencies—for example, environmental agencies and state labor agencies.

    Administrative law is the branch of public law concerned with the executive power and actions of administrative agencies, their officials, and their workers. When an individual has a dispute with such an agency, administrative law comes into play. The scope of administrative law has expanded enormously in recent years, and the scope of administrative agencies has increased so much that their activities have come to be called administrative process, in contrast to judicial process. *Administrative process* involves the administration of law by nonjudicial agencies, whereas *judicial process* is the administration of law by judicial bodies (the courts). Because administrative bodies are quasi-judicial, appeals from their rulings can be taken directly to the courts after administrative remedies have been exhausted.

    Federal administrative agencies have expanded the number of their rulings at what appears to be an exponential rate. Some observers believe that the United States is in danger of having an overly bureaucratic government.

Case Law and Common Law

Case law comprises the rules of law announced in court decisions. It is sometimes called judge-made law. In most instances, case law is an interpretation of the other sources of law noted above. Once a court has interpreted a statute, a regulation, or a constitution, the interpretation becomes part of the authoritative law on the subject.

Much of the common law has been either included in legislation or changed by it, but there are still areas of law that legislation does not cover. In those areas, courts still refer to the common law. The history and circumstances of the various states differ, and this has given rise to differences in the common law in each state. Even where legislation has been substituted for common law, courts rely on common law rules to interpret the legislation and the judicial methodology used in making decisions has its origins in common law.

THE UNIFORM COMMERCIAL CODE

In the interests of uniformity and reform, the legal profession, under the leadership of the American Law Institute, has suggested comprehensive codes of laws to be adopted by the states. The most important of these to business students is the Uniform Commercial Code, which is the basis of many chapters in this book. Its origins will be briefly examined here.

Commercial Law

The body of laws that pertain to commercial dealings is commonly referred to as commercial law. It includes most of the topics in this text—partnerships, corporations, agency, and contracts, for example.

The Law Merchant

A system of mercantile courts existed in England well before the advent of the common law courts. These courts administered a law known as *Lex Mercatoria,* or the Law Merchant. This law was based on customs of the merchants, many of whom traveled from place to place to do business. The law merchant was important during the Middle Ages when the fair, or market, was an important commercial event. In fact, the Magna Carta made special provisions for merchants. Section 41, for example, states that all merchants should "have safe and secure conduct, to go out of, and to come into England, and to stay there, and to pass as well by lands as by water, for buying and selling by the ancient and allowed customs."

The Operation of Merchant Courts

From the very beginning, there was an attempt to get cases in and out of the merchant courts as quickly as possible. Law merchant courts operated from hour to hour. One of the most common types was called the piepoudre court. The words *pied* and *poudre* together mean dusty feet. In principle, justice was administered in such courts even before dust could fall from the litigant's feet. Piepoudre courts were courts of record (they kept a written record of their proceedings). They had jurisdiction over mercantile, or commercial, wrongs and minor offences that occurred at a particular fair or marketplace. Even in these early courts, there was an ideal that it was fairer to resolve disputes in the way they had been resolved before (*stare decisis*). The law merchant eventually became part of the common law and was incorporated into American law.

Codification of Commercial Law

The National Conference of Commissioners on Uniform State Laws started to meet in the late 1800s to draft uniform statutes. Once these uniform codes were drawn up, the commissioners urged each state legislature to adopt them. The first such code, or act, was the Negotiable Instruments Act, finally approved in 1896 and ultimately adopted in every state.

Afterwards, other acts were drawn up in a similar manner; they included the Uniform Sales Act, the Uniform Warehouse Receipts Act, the Uniform Bills of Lading Act, and the Uniform Stock Transfer Act. Recently, a Uniform Probate Code was prepared. The most ambitious uniform act of all, however, is the Uniform Commercial Code.

The Uniform Commercial Code (UCC)

The National Conference of Commissioners on Uniform State Laws and the American Law Institute sponsored and directed the preparation of the Uniform Commercial Code. These two organizations were assisted by literally hundreds of law professors, businesspersons, judges, and lawyers. The work on the UCC began in 1942, and the finished draft was completed in 1952. The complete text of the Code can be found in Appendix A in this book. All fifty states, the District of Columbia, and the Virgin Islands have adopted the Uniform Commercial Code.[5]

The UCC consists of ten articles:
1. General Provisions
2. Sales
3. Commercial Paper
4. Bank Deposits and Collections
5. Letters of Credit
6. Bulk Transfers
7. Documents of Title
8. Investment Securities
9. Secured Transactions
10. Effective Date and Repealer

When each of the states adopted the Code, it repealed numerous statutes, such as the Uniform Sales Act, the Uniform Bills of Lading Act, the Uniform Warehouse Receipts Act, the Uniform Negotiable Instruments Act, the Uniform Conditional Sales Act, the Uniform Trust Receipts Act, the Uniform Stock Transfer Act, the Bulk Sales Act, and the Factors Lien Act.

The Code does not change the basic principles of commercial law derived from the law merchant and common law but expands and codifies them in order to modernize, clarify, and liberalize the rules. The Code also helps state the legal relationship of the parties in modern commercial transactions. The Code is designed to help determine the intentions of the parties to a commercial contract and to give force and effect to their agreement.

CLASSIFICATION OF LAW

Much of the study of law involves the process of classification—taking the whole mass of law and putting it into categories in order to make sense of it. Different approaches to the law and the different sources of law have already been classified. This section will consider some other ways of classifying the law.

Substantive versus Procedural Law

Substantive law includes all those laws that define, regulate, and create legal rights and obligations. A rule stating that promises are enforced only where each party receives something of value from the other party is part of substantive law. So, too, is a rule stating that a person who injures another through negligence must pay damages.

Procedural law establishes the methods of enforcing the rights that are established by substantive law.[6] Questions about how a lawsuit should begin, what papers need to be filed, which court the suit should go to, which witnesses can be called, and so on are all questions of procedural law. In brief, substantive law tells us our *rights;* procedural law tells us *how to get the benefit of them.*

Exhibit 1-1 classifies law in terms of its subject matter, dividing it into law covering substantive issues and law covering procedural issues. Most of this text concerns substantive law.

---

5. Louisiana has adopted only Articles 1, 3, 4, and 5, however.

---

6. Sometimes procedural law is called adjective law.

EXHIBIT 1-1 SUBJECT MATTER DIVIDED INTO SUBSTANTIVE AND PROCEDURAL[a]

SUBSTANTIVE	PROCEDURAL
Agency	Evidence
Commercial Paper	Civil Procedure
Contracts	Criminal Procedure
Corporation Law	Administrative Procedure
Property	Appellate Procedure
Torts	
Taxation	
Sales	
Real Property	
Personal Property	
Partnerships	
Trusts and Wills	
Criminal Law	
Constitutional Law	
Administrative Law	

Public versus Private Law

Public law affects the relationship between individuals and their government; *private law* involves direct dealings between individuals. Criminal, constitutional, and administrative law are generally called public law because they deal with individuals and their relationships to government. Criminal acts are acts that individuals commit against society as a whole. They are prohibited by the governments themselves. (The violation of a criminal law may also violate a private right.) Constitutional law involves questions of whether the government—federal, state or local—has the *power* to act. In other words, governments receive their power from the Constitution. Additionally, constitutional law limits the exercise of governmental power in certain ways usually designed to protect the life, liberty, or property of individuals from governmental action. Administrative law details the procedures that govern the activities of various government commissions and administrative agencies. Other areas

---

a. The importance of this distinction is more than academic; the *result* of a case may well depend upon the determination that a rule is substantive rather than procedural.

of the law, such as contract rights and duties, fall within the private law category. (See Chapters 5 through 14.)

Civil versus Criminal Law

Civil law spells out the duties that exist between individuals. Contract law, for example, is part of civil law. The whole body of tort law, which has to do with the infringement by one person of the legally recognized rights of another, is an area of civil law. (Tort law is treated in Chapter 3.)

Criminal law is concerned with a wrong committed against the public as a whole. Criminal acts are proscribed by local, state, or federal government by statute. (Criminal law is treated in Chapter 4.)

Remedies in Law versus Remedies in Equity

The distinction between law and equity is primarily of historical interest, but it has special relevance to students of business law. In the early king's courts, the kinds of *remedies* (legal means to recover a right or redress for a wrong) that the courts could grant were severely restricted. If one person wronged another in some way, the king's court could award one or more of the following: (1) land, (2) items of value, or (3) money as compensation. The courts that awarded these compensations became known as *courts of law.* The three remedies were called *remedies at law.* Such a system introduced uniformity in the settling of disputes, but when *plaintiffs* (parties suing) wanted a remedy other than economic compensation, the courts of law could do nothing, so "no remedy, no right."

GOING TO THE KING FOR RELIEF When individuals could not obtain their preferred remedy in a court of law, they petitioned the king for relief. Most of these petitions were decided by an adviser of the king called the chancellor. When the chancellor thought that the claim was a fair one, new and unique remedies were granted. Thus, a new body of chancery rules and reliefs, or remedies, came into being. Finally, formal chancery courts were established. These were known as *courts of equity.* Thus, two distinct systems were created, each having a different set of judges. There were two bodies of rules and remedies that existed at the same time, *remedies in law* and *remedies in equity.* Plaintiffs had to specify whether they were bringing an "action at law" or an "action in equity," and they chose their courts accordingly.

DECREES OF SPECIFIC PERFORMANCE
plaintiff might come into a court of equity asking it to order a defendant to perform within the terms of a contract. A *court of law* could not order specific performance because its remedies were limited to payment of money or property as compensation for damages. A *court of equity,* however, could issue a decree of *specific performance*—an order to perform what was promised.

INJUNCTIONS If a person wanted certain activity prevented, he would have to go to the chancellor in equity to ask that the person doing (or about to do) the wrongful act be ordered to stop. The order was called an *injunction*—a court order requiring that a person either do something or stop doing something.

Today the distinction between courts of law and courts of equity has largely disappeared. Trial courts normally can grant remedies in law or in equity. The distinction is important to the student of business law because of the types of remedies available.

WHAT IS TO FOLLOW

This introductory chapter is meant to give the reader a feel for the nature of law, its origins, and the way it is classified. The rest of this introductory unit will cover the courts and the judicial system in the United States today (Chapter 2); torts—wrongs committed against individuals that are not criminal acts (Chapter 3); and, finally, criminal law (Chapter 4).

QUESTIONS AND CASE PROBLEMS

1. What is the difference between common law and statutory law? Should judges have the same authority to overrule statutory law as they have to overrule common law?
2. What is the difference between common law and *stare decisis?* Should judges have the same power to change the common law as they do to depart from *stare decisis?*
3. The law draws a distinction between substantive law and procedural law. Is there any reason for this distinction?
4. Note that *evidence* is included in procedural law. What is evidence all about? One rule of evidence, called the *hearsay rule,* states that in a trial one cannot introduce second-hand evidence of statements or writings that were made outside the courtroom to prove the truth of the matter asserted. That is, evidence that does not proceed from the *personal* knowledge of the witness is not admitted. What is the reason for such a rule?
5. The concept of *equity* was mentioned in this chapter. Courts of equity tend to follow general rules or maxims rather than following the common law or *stare decisis* as courts of law do. Some of those maxims are: "He who seeks equity must do equity"; "For one to seek the aid of equity courts he must come to the court with 'clean hands,' "; and "Equity does not lie for one who sits on his laches" (that is, one who does not pursue a remedy within a reasonable time). Why would equity courts give more credence to such maxims than to a hard and fast body of law?
6. The United States Constitution is a document in which the people of the United States give up to the government the "power to govern." Yet the Constitution was written by a handful of men who represented the aristocracy of the time. Surprisingly, this group of aristocrats wrote a document giving more freedoms to common people than any other constitution in existence. Name some of the basic guarantees found in the Constitution.
7. The Uniform Commercial Code took years to develop and has only recently been adopted by all of the states (although Louisiana did not adopt all the articles). The UCC attempts to establish uniformity throughout the states in every conceivable area of commercial law. What are some of the advantages of such a document?

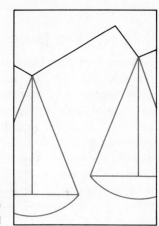

2

Courts
and Procedures

The United States has a dual court system that includes the various state systems and one federal system. This chapter will look at the state system first and the federal system second. Then it will follow a typical case from beginning to end. Using the courts is part of the process of adjudication, that is, determining which rules apply to the facts in the case. The rules can be substantive or procedural. They can come from several sources and can cover several areas of the law.

The word *court* comes from the Latin word *cors*, meaning an open space near the king's palace. This is where disputants came to have their differences adjudicated by the king or by his representatives. Today courts settle controversies between persons or between persons and the state. Note that throughout the legal literature, the term *court* frequently is used synonymously with the term *judge*.

JURISDICTION

Juris means "law"; *diction* means "to speak." Thus, the power to speak the law is the literal meaning of the term *jurisdiction*. Before a court can decide a case, it must have jurisdiction, the power to decide that case. Otherwise it cannot exercise any authority in the case. In order for a court to exercise valid authority, it must have both jurisdiction over the subject matter of the case and jurisdiction over the person against whom the suit is brought.

Subject Matter Jurisdiction

Subject matter jurisdiction is a limitation on types of cases a court can hear. For example, probate courts—courts that handle only matters relating to wills and estates—are a common example of limited subject matter jurisdiction. The subject matter jurisdiction of a court is usually defined in the statute or constitution creating the court. A court's subject matter jurisdiction can be limited by the amount of money in controversy, by whether a case is a felony or misdemeanor, or by whether the proceeding is a trial or an appeal.

Jurisdiction over the Person

In order to consider a case, a court must also have power over the person or, in some cases, the property of the person against whom a suit is brought. Jurisdiction over the person is known as *in personam* jurisdiction. Generally, a court's power is limited to the territorial boundaries of the state in which it is located. Therefore, a court has jurisdiction over the person of anyone who can be served with a summons within those boundaries. Additionally, if a person is a resident of the state or does business within the state, there will be *in personam* jurisdiction. Finally, in some cases where an individual has committed a wrong, such as an automobile injury or the sale of defective goods within the state, a court can exercise jurisdiction using the authority of a *long-arm statute* even if the individual is outside the state. A court can exercise *in personam* jurisdiction over a corporation in the state where it is incorporated, in the state where it has its main plant or office, and in any state where it does business.

If an individual owns property within a state, and the property is the subject of the suit, a court can exercise jurisdiction by virtue of its authority over property within the state even if the owner is outside the state. This is known as an action *in rem* as opposed to an action *in personam*. A court can also use property within a state to help satisfy a general debt. This is known as an action *quasi in rem*.

In all cases where a court exercises jurisdiction, the parties must be served either with actual notice that they are involved in a suit (usually by service of a summons) or, where the parties cannot be located, by publication of notice in a manner defined by statute.

Venue

Jurisdiction is concerned with whether a court has authority over a specific subject matter or individual. *Venue* is concerned with the particular geographic area within a judicial district where a suit should be brought.

Basically, the concept of venue reflects the policy that a court trying a suit should be in the neighborhood where the incident leading to the suit occurred or where the parties involved in the suit reside. That neighborhood is usually the county where the incident occurred or where the parties live. The correct venue for a suit is defined by statute.

THE STATE COURT SYSTEM

There are variations among the court systems of the several states, but there is a general pattern to the hierarchy of courts within each state. Exhibit 2-1 illustrates a hypothetical state judicial system with four levels of courts: (1) inferior or trial courts of limited jurisdiction, (2) trial courts of general jurisdiction, (3) intermediate reviewing courts, or appellate courts, and (4) a final appellate court, usually called the supreme court of the state. In many states there is no intervening appellate court. The appeal goes directly from the court of original jurisdiction to the highest court.

Inferior Trial Courts

Every state has some type of trial court that has limited jurisdiction of subject matter. Some typical inferior trial courts are domestic relations courts, which handle only divorce actions and child custody; local municipal courts, which handle mainly traffic cases; probate courts, which handle the execution of wills and estate settlement problems; and small claims and justice-of-the-peace courts. These are sometimes called inferior courts because they have limited, specialized jurisdiction.

Trial Courts of General Jurisdiction

Cases involving state law most often originate in the general jurisdiction trial courts of that state. These courts can hear all cases arising under state law except those assigned expressly by statute to the inferior courts discussed above. (Sometimes jurisdiction is concurrent.) Many important cases involving business originate in these general trial courts. Thus, cases involving corporate law, contract law, and criminal law will start here. They can be called district courts, common pleas courts, or, in a few locations, superior courts. (This is a misnomer

because they are clearly not at the top of the hierarchy of state courts. In New York, the general jurisdiction courts are called *supreme courts*, which is even more of a misnomer.) General jurisdiction courts typically exist in at least every county of every state. In some counties, because of the heavy demand, there is more than one court. Conversely, in lightly populated areas, a judge will serve several counties and be in one county only at stated times. General jurisdiction courts are also called courts of record because a written report of the proceedings, taken by a court stenographer, is kept.

Appellate Courts, or Courts of Appeal and Review

In each state, there is at least one court of review, or appellate court. The subject matter jurisdiction of these courts is limited to hearing

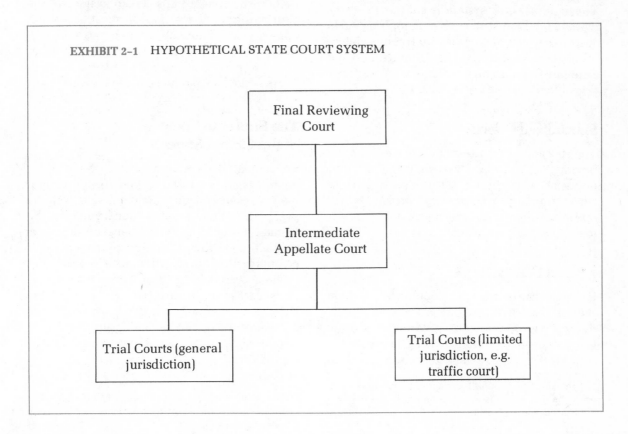

EXHIBIT 2-1   HYPOTHETICAL STATE COURT SYSTEM

Final Reviewing Court

Intermediate Appellate Court

Trial Courts (general jurisdiction)

Trial Courts (limited jurisdiction, e.g. traffic court)

appeals. In many states, there are intermediate reviewing courts and then one supreme court. The intermediate appellate, or review, court, is often called the court of appeals. The highest court of the state is normally called the supreme court (in New York it is called the Court of Appeals). Appellate courts do not try cases. They examine the record of the case on appeal and determine whether the trial court committed an error. They look at questions of law and procedure, not questions of fact.[1] The decisions of each state's highest court in all questions of state law are final. It is only when questions of federal law are involved that a state's highest court can be overruled by the Supreme Court of the United States.

THE FEDERAL COURT SYSTEM—CASES AND CONTROVERSIES

The federal court system is similar in many ways to a typical state court system. It includes specialized courts, general trial courts, intermediate review, or appellate, courts, and the Supreme Court. Exhibit 2-2 shows the organization of federal courts.

Specialized Courts

The specialized courts are the courts of limited jurisdiction. There is, for example, a U.S. court of claims, a tax court, a customs court, a bankruptcy court, and a court of customs and patent appeals. Congress has the constitutional power to establish specialized courts.

District Courts

Congress has divided the country into federal judicial districts. These districts contain federal district courts, which are analogous to state general jurisdiction trial courts. The number of judicial districts can vary over time. Congress

has established at least one in each state, but some states need, and have, more. Thus, an entire state can comprise a single district, or a state can be divided into several districts. With one exception, the districts do not cross state lines.[2] United States district courts are often called federal trial courts. Most federal cases originate in these courts. Whenever there are two or more district courts within a single state, there is limited geographical jurisdiction in each court. The state of Florida, for example, has district courts for northern, middle, and southern Florida.

Intermediate Courts of Review

The first level of review in the federal court system is the federal appellate courts, which are called U.S. circuit courts of appeal. Congress has established eleven judicial circuits that hear appeals from the district courts located within their respective circuits. The decisions of the courts of appeal are final in most cases, but appeal to the Supreme Court is possible. Appeals from federal administrative agencies, such as the Federal Trade Commission, are also made to the U.S. circuit courts of appeal.

The Supreme Court of the United States

The nation's highest court is the Supreme Court; it consists of nine justices, who, like all federal judges, receive lifetime appointments from the president. (They must be confirmed by the Senate, however, and their behavior is always subject to review.) The Supreme Court was created by the U.S. Constitution. Although it has original, or trial, jurisdiction in some cases, most of its work is as an appeals court. The Supreme Court can review any case decided by any of the federal courts of appeal, and it also has appellate authority over some cases decided in the state courts.

---

1. The only time an appellate court tampers with the trial courts findings of fact is when the finding is clearly erroneous, that is, when it is contrary to the evidence presented at trial.

---

2. The one exception is the District of Wyoming, which includes sections of Yellowstone National Park located in Montana and Idaho.

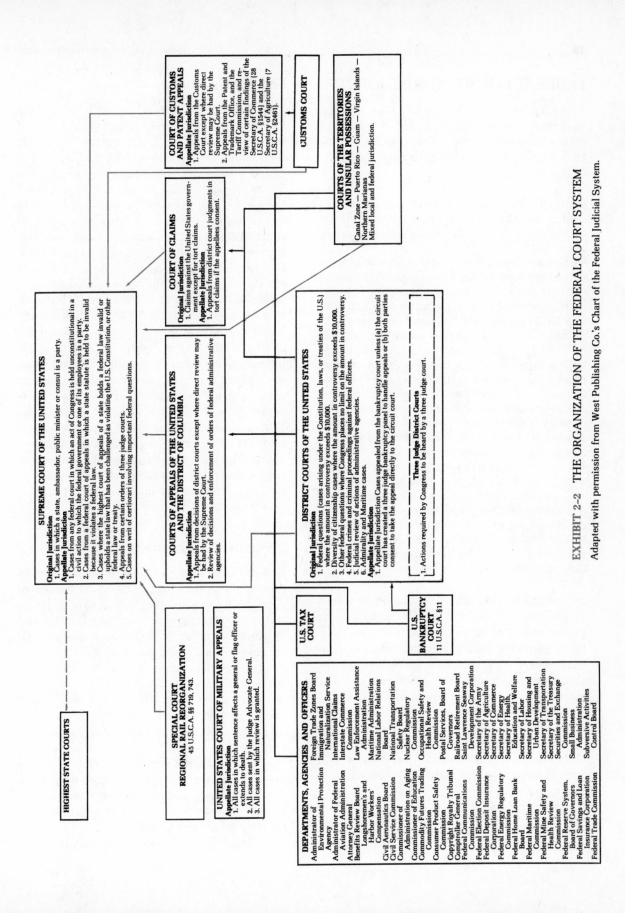

EXHIBIT 2-2 THE ORGANIZATION OF THE FEDERAL COURT SYSTEM

Adapted with permission from West Publishing Co.'s Chart of the Federal Judicial System.

FEDERAL COURT JURISDICTION

Since the federal government is a government of limited powers, the jurisdiction of the federal courts is limited. Article III of the U.S. Constitution established the boundaries of federal judicial power:

Section 1. The judicial power of the United States shall be vested in one supreme Court and in such inferior Courts as the Congress may from time to time ordain and establish. * * *

Section 2. The judicial power shall extend to all Cases, in Law and Equity, arising under this Constitution, the Laws of the United States, and Treaties made, or which shall be made, under their Authority; —to all Cases affecting Ambassadors, other public Ministers and Consuls;—to all Cases of admiralty and maritime Jurisdiction;—to Controversies to which the United States shall be a Party;—to Controversies between two or more States; between a State and Citizens of another State;[3]—between Citizens of different States;—between Citizens of the same State claiming Lands under the Grants of different States, and between a State, or the Citizens thereof, and foreign States, Citizens or Subjects.

In all Cases affecting Ambassadors, other public Ministers and Consuls, and those in which a State shall be a Party, the supreme Court shall have original Jurisdiction. In all the other Cases before mentioned, the supreme Court shall have appellate Jurisdiction, both as to Law and Fact, with such Exceptions, and under such Regulations as the Congress shall make.

In line with the checks and balances system of the federal government, Congress has the power to control the number and kind of inferior courts in the federal system. Except in those cases where the Constitution gives the Supreme Court original jurisdiction, Congress can also regulate the jurisdiction of the Supreme Court. Therefore, although the Constitution sets the outer limits of federal judicial power, Congress can set other limits on federal jurisdiction. Furthermore, the courts themselves can promulgate rules that limit the types of cases they will hear.

---

3. Amendment XI, passed in 1798, prohibits any exercise of federal judicial power in cases brought against a state by citizens of another state.

Federal Questions

"The Judicial Power shall extend to all cases * * * arising under this Constitution, the laws of the United States and Treaties made * * * under their authority." Whenever a plaintiff's cause of action is based, at least in part, on the United States Constitution, a treaty, or a federal law, then a *federal question* arises, and the case comes under the judicial power of federal courts. People whose claims are based on rights granted by an act of Congress can sue in a federal court. People who claim that their constitutional rights have been violated can originate their suits in federal court. However, Title 28, Section 1331, of the United States Code limits the federal question jurisdiction of the district courts. Unless the suit is brought against the federal government or one of its employees, the amount in controversy in a federal question case must exceed $10,000, or else the district court will not have jurisdiction. Of course, if the suit does not meet the $10,000 requirement, the plaintiff can always begin the suit in a state court. There is no dollar amount requirement where federal courts have exclusive jurisdiction, that is, where the suit cannot be brought in a state court.

Diversity of Citizenship

Another basis for federal district court jurisdiction is *diversity of citizenship*. Diversity of citizenship cases involve (1) citizens of different states, (2) a foreign country as plaintiff and citizens of a state, or different states, and (3) citizens of a state and citizens or subjects of a foreign country. As in federal question suits, under Title 28, Section 1332, the amount in controversy must be $10,000 before a federal court can take jurisdiction. For purposes of diversity of citizenship jurisdiction, a corporation is a citizen of the state where it is incorporated and of the state where it has its principal place of business. Diversity cases starting out in a state court can be *removed*, or transferred, to a federal court if the defendant is not a citizen of the state where the case begins.

Diversity jurisdiction originated in 1789

with the authors of the Constitution, who felt that a state might be biased toward its own citizens. The option of moving to a federal court provided by diversity jurisdiction was thought to protect the out-of-state party. A large percentage of the 70,000 cases filed in federal courts each year are based on diversity of citizenship grounds. Consider some examples: Smith is driving from his home state, New York, to Florida. In Georgia, he runs into a car owned by Abel, a citizen of Georgia. Abel's new Mercedes is demolished, and he is out of work for six months; thus the case in question involves more than $10,000 worth of damages. Georgia gains *in personam* jurisdiction through a long arm statute, but Smith can have the suit removed to a federal district court on the basis of diversity of citizenship.

Jones, who resides in Texas, is owed $25,000 by Corporation XYZ, which is incorporated and has its principal place of business in Louisiana. XYZ does enough business in Texas to allow Texas courts to exercise *in personam* jurisdiction over it. Since, for purposes of diversity of citizenship jurisdiction, XYZ is a citizen of Louisiana, Jones can begin her suit in a federal district court in Texas.

Concurrent versus Exclusive Jurisdiction

Even though a case involves a federal question or diversity of citizenship, state courts can still hear the case. Federal jurisdiction is available, but it is not required. When both federal and state courts have the power to hear a case, jurisdiction is *concurrent*. When cases can be tried only in federal courts, jurisdiction is *exclusive*. Federal courts have exclusive jurisdiction in cases involving federal crimes, bankruptcy, patent, and copyright cases; in suits against the United States; and in some areas of admiralty law.

WHICH CASES REACH THE SUPREME COURT?

Many people are surprised to learn that in a typical case, there is no absolute right of appeal to the United States Supreme Court. The Supreme Court is given original, or trial court, jurisdiction in a small number of situations. In all other cases, its jurisdiction is appellate "with such Exceptions, and under such Regulations as the Congress shall make." Today the exceptions and rules set by Congress and some rules that the court has set for itself are quite complex. Over 4,500 cases are filed with the Supreme Court each year; yet it hears an average of only 300.[4] There are basically two procedures for bringing a case before the Supreme Court: by *appeal* or by *writ of certiorari*.

Appeal

Under rules set out by Congress, the Supreme Court must review a decision (that is, an individual has a right to appeal) in the following situations:

1.   When a federal court of appeals holds a state statute to be invalid because it violates federal law.
2.   When the highest state court of appeals holds a federal law invalid or upholds a state law that has been challenged as violating federal law.
3.   When a federal court holds an act of Congress unconstitutional and the federal government or one of its employees is a party.
4.   When the hearing under appeal is for an injunction in a civil (as opposed to criminal) action that Congress requires a district court of three judges to determine.

Theoretically, the Supreme Court is required to hear any appeal that falls within one of these four categories, but it can decide which of these cases require full consideration, including written briefs from the lawyers and oral arguments before the Court. The Court will give full consideration only if four of the nine justices vote to do so. Otherwise the case will be

4.   There has been some discussion about establishing a new national appellate court to relieve the Supreme Court's workload. The new court would take cases that the Supreme Court felt it should not spend its time deciding so that it could take on more cases that had important public policy implications.

dismissed. A case can be dismissed because the Court agrees with the lower court's decision, because the federal question presented is not a substantial one, or on some other procedural ground. When a case is dismissed for reasons of substantive law—that is, when the higher court agrees with the lower court or when a substantial federal question is lacking—the Court's decision has value as precedent, and the dismissal can be cited in later cases.[5]

Writ of Certiorari

With a **writ of certiorari,** the Supreme Court orders a lower court to send it the record of a case for review. Parties whose cases do not fall into one of the appeal categories can petition the Supreme Court to issue a writ of certiorari, but whether the Court will issue one is entirely at its discretion. In no instance is the Court required to issue a writ of certiorari.

The following situations indicate when the Court can issue a writ, although they are not a limit on the Court's discretion:

1.   When a state court has decided a substantial federal question that has not been determined by the Supreme Court before, or the state court has decided it in a way that is probably in disagreement with the trend of the Supreme Court's decisions.
2.   When two federal courts of appeal are in disagreement with each other.
3.   When a federal court of appeals has decided an important state question in conflict with state law, has decided an important federal question not yet addressed by the Court but which should be decided by the Court, has decided a federal question in conflict with applicable decisions of the Court, or has departed from the accepted and usual course of judicial proceedings.

Most petitions for writs of certiorari are denied. A denial is not a decision on the merits of a case; nor does it indicate agreement with

the lower court's opinion. Therefore, it has no value as precedent.[6] The court will not issue a writ unless at least four justices approve of it. This is called the "rule of four." Typically, only the petitions that raise the possibility of important constitutional questions are granted writs of certiorari.

JUDICIAL PROCEDURES— FOLLOWING A CASE THROUGH THE COURTS

American and English courts follow the *adversary system of justice.* The judge's role is viewed as nonbiased and mostly passive. The lawyer functions as the client's advocate, presenting the client's version of the facts in order to convince the judge or the jury (or both) that they are true. Judges do not have to be entirely passive. They are responsible for the appropriate application of the law. They do not have to accept the legal reasoning of the attorneys. They can base a ruling and a decision on a personal study of the law. Judges sometimes ask questions of witnesses and even suggest types of evidence to be presented. For example, if an indigent defendant chooses to act as his own counsel, the judge will often play less of a passive role and more of an advocate role, intervening during the trial proceedings to help the defendant.[7]

Procedure

Procedure involves the way disputes are handled in the courts. A large body of law, procedural law, establishes the rules and standards for determining disputes in courts. The rules are very complex, and they vary from court to court. There is a set of federal *rules of procedure,* and there are various sets of procedural rules in the state courts. Rules of procedure differ in criminal and civil cases.

We will now follow a civil case through the

───────────────

5.   Hicks v. Miranda, 422 U.S. 332, 95 S.Ct. 2281 (1975).

6.   Singleton v. Commissioner of Internal Revenue, 439 U.S. 940, 99 S.Ct. 335 (1978).

7.   See Faretta v. California, 422 U.S. 806, 95 S.Ct. 2525 (1975).

state courts. The case involves an automobile accident in which Jones, driving a Cadillac, has struck Adams, driving a Ford. The accident has occurred at an intersection in New York. Adams has suffered personal injuries, incurring medical and hospital expenses as well as four months of lost wages. Jones and Adams are unable to agree on a settlement, and Adams sues Jones. Adams is the *plaintiff,* and Jones is the *defendant.* Both have lawyers.

The Pleadings

Adams's suit or action against Jones will commence when her lawyer files a *complaint* (sometimes called a petition or declaration) with the clerk of the general trial court that has jurisdiction and venue. The complaint will contain: (1) a statement alleging the facts necessary for the court to take jurisdiction, (2) a short statement of the facts necessary to show that the plaintiff is entitled to a remedy, and (3) a statement of the remedy the plaintiff is seeking.

First, Adams's complaint will be filed with a court of general jurisdiction in the county where the accident has occurred. The complaint will state that Adams was driving her Ford through a green light at the specified intersection, exercising good driving habits and reasonable care, when Jones carelessly drove his Cadillac into the intersection from a cross street and struck Adams, causing serious personal injury and property damage. The complaint will go on to state that she is entitled to $85,000 to cover medical bills, $10,000 to cover lost wages, and $5,000 to cover property damage to the car.

After the complaint has been filed, the sheriff or a deputy of the county will serve a summons and a copy of the complaint on the defendant Jones. The *summons* notifies Jones that he is required to prepare an answer to the complaint and file a copy with both the court and the plaintiff's attorney within a specified time period (usually thirty days after the summons has been served). The summons also informs Jones that failure to answer will result in a judgment by default for the plaintiff. Rules governing the service of a summons vary, but

usually *service* is made by handing the summons to the defendant personally or by leaving it at the defendant's residence or place of business. In a few states, a summons can be served by mail. When the defendant cannot be reached, special rules sometimes permit serving the summons by leaving it with a designated person, such as the secretary of state.

Upon receiving the summons and complaint, the defendant must file a document with the court and with the plaintiff. The document either admits the statements set out in the complaint or denies them and sets out any defenses the defendant may have. Appropriately enough, this document is called an *answer.* If Jones admits all of Adams's allegations in his answer, judgment will be entered for Adams. If Jones denies Adams's allegations, the matter will proceed to trial. Jones can deny Adams's allegations and set forth his own claim that Adams was negligent and owes Jones money for damages to the Cadillac. This is called a *counterclaim.* If Jones files a counterclaim, Adams will have to answer it with a document that is normally called a *reply.* Jones can also admit the truth of Adams's complaint but raise *new* facts that will result in dismissal of the action. This is called raising an *affirmative defense.* For example, Jones can admit that he was negligent but plead that the time Adams had to raise the claim has passed and that her complaint must therefore be dismissed.

The complaint and answer (and the counterclaim and reply) taken together are called the *pleadings.* The pleadings inform each party of the claims of the other and specify the issues involved in the case. Pleadings remove the element of surprise from a case. They allow lawyers to prepare better arguments, and they increase the probability that a just and true result will be forthcoming from the trial.

Dismissals and Judgments before Trial

Many actions for which pleadings have been filed never come to trial. There are numerous procedural avenues for disposing of a case without a trial. Many of them involve one or the other party's attempts to get the case dismissed through the use of pretrial *motions*.

MOTION TO DISMISS, OR DEMURRER The defendant can present to the court a *motion to dismiss*, or *demurrer*, instead of an answer. (The rules of civil procedure in many states do not use the term *demurrer;* they use only *motion to dismiss*.) The motion to dismiss is an allegation that even if the facts presented in the complaint are true, their legal consequences are such that there is no reason to go further with the suit and no need for the defendant to present an answer. It is a contention that the defendant is not legally liable even if the facts are as the plaintiff alleges. If, for example, Adams's complaint alleges facts that exclude the possibility of negligence on Jones's part, Jones can move to dismiss, and he will not be required to answer because his motion will be granted.

If Adams wishes to discontinue the suit because, for example, an out-of-court settlement has been reached, she can likewise move for dismissal. The court can also dismiss on its own motion.

MOTION FOR JUDGMENT ON THE PLEADINGS After the pleadings are closed— after the complaint, answer, and any counterclaim and reply have been filed—either of the parties can make a *motion for a judgment on the pleadings*. This motion is basically an argument that the court can decide the case just by looking at the pleadings without having to consider any evidence. A judgment on the pleadings will be granted if the complaint is insufficient to allow any remedy or if the answer admits the allegations of the complaint or fails to deny them and no affirmative defense is pleaded. If, for example, Jones admits all of the facts alleged in Adams's complaint—admits that, in fact, he was negligent—the court can grant a motion for judgment on the pleadings and grant Adams her remedy.

MOTION FOR SUMMARY JUDGMENT A lawsuit can be shortened or a trial can be avoided if there are no disagreements about the facts in a case and the only question is which laws apply to those facts. Both sides can agree to the facts and just ask the judge to apply the law to them. In this situation, it is appropriate for either party to move for *summary judgment*. Summary judgment will be granted when there are no genuine issues of fact in a trial and the only question is one of law. In a pretrial setting, one party can bring in a sworn statement that refutes the other party's claim. Unless the second party brings in affidavits of conflicting facts, the first party will receive summary judgment. Jones, for example, can bring in the sworn statement of a witness that Jones was in California at the time of the accident. Unless Adams can bring in other statements raising the possibility that Jones was at the scene of the accident, Jones will be entitled to dismissal on a motion for summary judgment. Motions for summary judgment can be made before or during a trial, but they will be granted only if it is plain that there are no factual disputes.

Discovery

Before a trial begins, the parties can use a number of procedural devices to obtain information and gather evidence about the case. Adams, for example, will want to know how fast Jones was driving, whether he had been drinking, whether he saw a red light, and so on. The process of obtaining information from the opposing party or from other witnesses is known as **discovery.** Discovery serves several purposes. It preserves evidence from witnesses who might not be available at the time of the trial or whose memories will fade as time passes. It can pave the way for summary judgment if it is found that both parties agree on all facts. It can lead to an out-of-court settlement if one party decides that the opponent's case is too strong to challenge. Even if the case does go to trial, discovery prevents surprises by giving parties access to evidence that might otherwise be hidden, and it serves to narrow the issues so that trial time is spent on the main questions in the case. The federal rules of civil procedure and similar rules in the states set down the guidelines for discovery activity. Discovery includes gaining access to witnesses, documents, records, and other types of evidence.

DEPOSITIONS AND INTERROGATORIES Discovery can involve the use of depositions or interrogatories, or both. *Depositions* are sworn testimony by the opposing party or any witness, recorded by a court official. The person deposed appears before a court officer and is sworn. That person then answers questions asked by the attorneys from both sides. The questions and answers are taken down, sworn to, and signed. These answers will, of course, help the attorneys prepare their cases. They can also be used in court to impeach a party or witness who changes testimony at the trial. Finally, they can be used as testimony if the witness is not available at trial. Depositions can also be taken with written questions from both sides prepared ahead of time.

Interrogatories are a series of written questions for which written answers are prepared and then signed under oath. The main difference between interrogatories and depositions for written questions is that the former are directed to a party, not to a witness, and the party can prepare answers with the aid of an attorney. The scope of interrogatories is broader because parties are obligated to answer questions even if the answer requires disclosing information from their records and files. Interrogatories are also less expensive than depositions.

REQUEST FOR ADMISSIONS A party can serve a written request to the other party for an admission of the truth of matters relating to the trial. Any matter admitted under such a request is conclusively established for the trial. For example, Adams can ask Jones to admit that he was driving at a speed of forty-five miles an hour. A request for admission saves time at trial because parties will not have to spend time proving facts on which they already agree.

DOCUMENTS, OBJECTS, AND ENTRY UPON LAND A party can gain access to documents and other items not in the party's possession in order to inspect and examine them. Likewise, the party can gain entry upon land to inspect the premises. Jones, for example, can gain permission to inspect and duplicate Adams's medical records and repair bills.

PHYSICAL AND MENTAL EXAMINATION Where the physical or mental condition of a party is in question, a party can ask the court to order a physical or mental examination. If the court is willing to make the order, the party can obtain the results of the examination. It is important to note that the court will make such an order only when the need for the information outweighs the right to privacy of the person to be examined.

The rules governing discovery are designed to make sure that a witness or party is not unduly harassed, that privileged material is safeguarded, and that only matters relevant to the case at hand are discoverable.

Pretrial Hearing

Either party or the court can request a pretrial conference or hearing. Usually the hearing consists of an informal discussion between the judge and the opposing attorneys after discovery has taken place. The purpose of the hearing is to identify the matters that are in dispute and to plan the course of the trial. The pretrial hearing is not intended to compel the parties to settle their case before trial, although judges may encourage them to settle out of court if circumstances suggest that a trial would be a waste of time.

Jury Trials

A trial can be held with or without a jury. If there is no jury, the judge decides the truth of the facts in the case. The Seventh Amendment guarantees the right to a jury trial for cases at law in federal courts. Most states have similar guarantees in their own constitutions, although many states put a minimum dollar amount restriction on the guarantee. For example, Iowa requires the dollar amount of damages to be at least $1,000 before there is a right to a jury trial.

The right to a trial by jury does not have to be exercised, and many cases are tried without one. In most states and in federal courts, one of the parties must request a jury or the right is presumed to be waived.

In the case between Adams and Jones, both parties want a jury trial. The jurors are questioned by the judge and by both attorneys to ensure that their judgment will be impartial. After the jurors are selected, they are sworn, and the trial is ready to begin.

The Trial

Both attorneys are allowed to make *opening statements* concerning the facts that they expect to prove during the trial. Since Adams is the plaintiff and has the burden of proving that her case is correct, Adams's attorney begins the case by calling the first witness for the plaintiff and examining (questioning) the witness. (For both attorneys, the type of question and the manner of asking are governed by the rules of evidence.) This examination is called *direct examination.* After Adams's attorney is finished, the witness will be questioned by Jones's attorney in *cross-examination.* After that, Adams's attorney has another opportunity to question the witness in *redirect examination,* and Jones's attorney can then follow with *recross-examination.* When both attorneys have finished with the first witness, Adams's attorney will call the succeeding witnesses in the plaintiff's case, each of whom is subject to cross-examination (and redirect and recross, if necessary).

At the conclusion of the plaintiff's case, the defendant's attorney has the opportunity to ask the judge to direct a verdict for the defendant on the ground that the plaintiff has presented no evidence that would justify the granting of the plaintiff's remedy. This is called a *motion for a directed verdict.* In considering the motion, the judge will look at the evidence in the light most favorable to the plaintiff and will grant the motion only if there is insufficient evidence to raise an issue of fact. Motions for directed verdicts are seldom granted. An experienced attorney will not take a case to court unless there is enough evidence to ensure the possibility of a favorable verdict.

The defendant's attorney will then present the evidence and witnesses for the defendant's case. Witnesses are called and examined. The plaintiff's attorney has a right to cross-examine them, and there is a redirect and recross if necessary. At the end of the defendant's case, either attorney can again move for a directed verdict, and the test will again be whether the jury can, under any reasonable interpretation of the evidence, find for the party against whom the motion is made.

After the defendant's attorney has finished the presentation of evidence, the plaintiff's attorney can present additional evidence to refute the defendant's case in a *rebuttal.* The defendant's attorney can meet that evidence in a *rejoinder.* After both sides have rested their cases, the attorneys each present a *closing argument,* urging a verdict in favor of their respective clients. The judge instructs the jury (assuming it is a jury trial) in the law that applies to the case. The instructions to the jury are often called *charges.* Then the jury retires to the jury room to deliberate a verdict. In a case like Adams v. Jones, the jury will not only decide for the plaintiff or for the defendant but will also make a finding on the amount of money to be paid to the plaintiff.

JUDGMENT N.O.V. (NOTWITHSTANDING THE VERDICT) If Adams wins, Jones's attorney can make a motion for a *judgment n.o.v. (notwithstanding the verdict).* In other words, Jones can state that even though the jury found for the plaintiff, none of the evidence presented at the trial supported such a verdict. If the judge finds this to be correct or decides that the law requires the opposite result, the motion will be granted. This occurrence is rare indeed. Assume here that this motion is set aside, and Jones appeals the case. (If Adams wins but receives a smaller money award than she sought she can appeal also.) These events are illustrated in Exhibit 2-3.

The Appeal

A notice of appeal is filed with the clerk of the trial court within the prescribed time. Jones then becomes the *appellant*. His attorney files in the reviewing court (or court of appeal) the record on appeal, which contains the following: (1) the pleadings, (2) a transcript of the testimony, (3) the judge's rulings on motions made by the parties, (4) the arguments of counsel, (5) the instructions to the jury, (6) the verdict, (7) the posttrial motions, and (8) the judgment order from which the appeal is taken.

Jones's attorney is required to prepare a condensation of the record, known as an *abstract*. The abstract, the brief, and the argument are filed with the reviewing court. The brief contains (1) a short statement of the facts, (2) a statement of the issues, (3) the rulings by the trial court that Jones contends are erroneous and prejudicial, (4) the grounds for reversal of the judgment, (5) a statement of the applicable law, and (6) an argument on Jones's behalf. The attorney for the *appellee*, Adams, must now file an answering brief and argument. Jones's attorney can now file a reply (although this is not required). The reviewing court then considers the case.

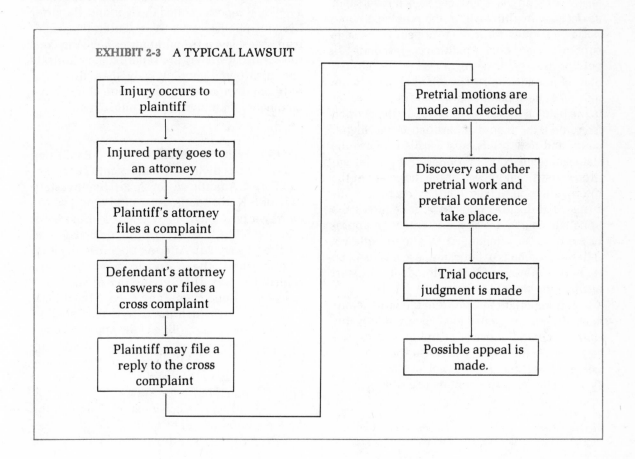

EXHIBIT 2-3   A TYPICAL LAWSUIT

Injury occurs to plaintiff

Injured party goes to an attorney

Plaintiff's attorney files a complaint

Defendant's attorney answers or files a cross complaint

Plaintiff may file a reply to the cross complaint

Pretrial motions are made and decided

Discovery and other pretrial work and pretrial conference take place.

Trial occurs, judgment is made

Possible appeal is made.

NO EVIDENCE HEARD Appeals courts do not hear any evidence. They take the case upon the abstracts, the record, and the briefs. The attorneys can present oral arguments, after which the case is taken under advisement. When the court has reached a decision, the decision is written. It contains the opinion (the court's reason for its decision), the rules of law that apply, and the judgment. If the reviewing court believes that the trial court was correct, it affirms the judgment. If the reviewing court believes that a reversible error was committed during the trial, the judgment will be reversed. Sometimes the case will be *remanded* (sent back) for a new trial.

HIGHER APPEALS COURTS If the reviewing court is an intermediate appellate court, the losing party (in that court) can seek a reversal of its decision by filing within the prescribed time period a petition for leave to appeal to the state supreme court.[8] Such a petition corresponds to a petition for a writ of *certiorari* in the United States Supreme Court. The winning party in the intermediate appellate court can file an answer to the petition for leave to appeal. If, the petition is granted, the record is certified to the higher court, and new briefs must be filed before the state supreme court. Whenever the state supreme court concludes that the judgment of the intermediate appellate court is correct, it affirms. If it decides otherwise, it reverses the appellate court's decision and enters an appropriate order of remand. At this point, unless a federal question is at issue, the case has reached its end. If a new trial is ordered, it will start again at the court of origin.

It is important to know that the vast majority of disputes are settled out of court mainly due to the time and expense of trying a case. Furthermore, of those cases that go to trial, about 97 percent are decided at the trial level as relatively few trial court decisions are changed on appeal.

─────────────
8. In some states, the appeal from the court of original jurisdiction to the state supreme court is a matter of right.

HOW TO FIND THE LAW

Most trial court decisions are not published. Except for the federal courts and New York and a few other states that publish selected opinions of their trial courts, decisions in trial courts are merely filed in the office of the clerk of the court, where they are available for public inspection.

On the other hand, the written decisions of appellate courts are published and distributed. Virtually all the cases in this book have been taken from these decisions. It is therefore important to understand the case reporting system.

The reported appellate decisions are published in volumes called *Reports*, which are numbered consecutively. State court decisions are found in the state reports of that particular state. Additionally, many state reports appear in a regional reporter called the *National Reporter System*, published by West Publishing Company. Most lawyers and libraries have the West reports because they are reported more quickly and distributed more widely than the state-published reports. In fact, some states have eliminated their own reports altogether.

GEOGRAPHICAL AREAS West Publishing Company has divided the states into geographical areas: Atlantic (A. or A.2d), Southeastern (S.E. or S.E.2d), Southwestern (S.W. or S.W.2d), Northwestern (N.W. or N.W.2d), Northeastern (N.E. or N.E.2d), Southern (So. or So.2d), and Pacific (P. or P.2d). After an appellate decision is published, these opinions or *cases* are referred to (cited) by giving the name of the case; the volume, name, and page of the official state report in which the case is published (if any); and the date of filing of the appellate court decision. Alternatively, cases can be cited by giving the name of the case and the volume, name, and page of the particular set and series of the *National Reporter System*.

Federal court decisions are found in the *Federal Reporter* (F. or F.2d), *Federal Supplement* (F.Supp.), *Federal Rules Decisions*

(F.R.D.), *United States Supreme Court Reports* (U.S.), *Supreme Court Reporter* (S.Ct.), and the Lawyer's Edition (L.Ed.).

In reading the title of a case such as Adams v. Jones, the v. or vs. stands for versus, which means against. In the trial court, Adams was the plaintiff—the person who filed the suit. Jones was the defendant. When the case is appealed, however, the appellate court will sometimes place the name of the party appealing the decision first, so that the case will be called Jones v. Adams. Since some appellate courts retain the trial court order of names, it is not possible to distinguish between the plaintiff and the defendant from the title of a reported appellate court decision.

A CONSTITUTIONAL LAW CASE

The following case involves issues of constitutional law.

BRENNAN, Justice.

* * *

The question presented is the constitutionality of Alabama alimony statutes which provide that husbands, but not wives, may be required to pay alimony upon divorce. [footnote omitted]

On February 26, 1974, a final decree of divorce was entered, dissolving the marriage of William and Lillian Orr. That decree directed appellant, Mr. Orr, to pay appellee, Mrs. Orr, $1,240 per month in alimony. On July 28, 1976, Mrs. Orr initiated a contempt proceeding in the Circuit Court of Lee County, Ala., alleging that Mr. Orr was in arrears in his alimony payments. On August 19, 1976, at the hearing on Mrs. Orr's petition, Mr. Orr submitted in his defense a motion requesting that Alabama's alimony statutes be declared unconstitutional because they authorize courts to place an obligation of alimony upon husbands but never upon wives. The Circuit Court denied Mr. Orr's motion and entered judgment against him for $5,524, covering back alimony and attorney fees. Relying solely upon his federal constitutional claim, Mr. Orr appealed the judgment. On March 16, 1977, the Court of Civil Appeals of Alabama sustained the constitutionality of the Alabama statutes, 351 So.2d 904 (1977). On May 24, the Supreme Court of Alabama granted Mr. Orr's petition for a writ of certiorari, but on November 10, without court opinion, quashed the writ as improvidently granted. 351 So.2d 906 (1977). We noted probable jurisdiction, 436 U.S. 924, 98 S.Ct. 2817, 56 L.Ed.2d 767 (1978). We now hold the challenged Alabama statutes unconstitutional and reverse.

* * *

In authorizing the imposition of alimony obligations on husbands, but not on wives, the Alabama statutory scheme "provides that different treatment be accorded ... on the basis of ... sex; it thus establishes a classification subject to scrutiny under the Equal Protection Clause," Reed v. Reed, 404 U.S. 71, 75, 92 S.Ct. 251, 253, 30 L.Ed.2d 225 (1971). The fact that the classification expressly discriminates against men rather than women does not protect it from scrutiny. "To withstand scrutiny" under the equal protection clause, " 'classifications by gender must serve important governmental objectives and must be substantially related to achievement of those objectives.' " Califano v. Webster, 430 U.S. 313, 316-317, 97 S.Ct. 1192, 1194, 51 L.Ed.2d 360 (1977). We shall, therefore, examine the

ORR v. ORR
Supreme Court of the United States, 1979.
——U.S.——99 S.Ct. 1102.

* * * governmental objectives that might arguably be served by Alabama's statutory scheme.

Appellant views the Alabama alimony statutes as effectively announcing the State's preference for an allocation of family responsibilities under which the wife plays a dependent role, and as seeking for their objective the reinforcement of that model among the State's citizens.

[T]he "old notion" that "generally it is the man's primary responsibility to provide a home and its essentials," can no longer justify a statute that discriminates on the basis of gender. "No longer is the female destined solely for the home and the rearing of the family, and only the male for the marketplace and the world of ideas," *id*, at 14-15, 95 S.Ct., at 1378. See also Craig v. Boren, 429 U.S., at 198, 97 S.Ct., at 457. If the statute is to survive constitutional attack, therefore, it must be validated on some other basis.

The opinion of the Alabama Court of Civil Appeals suggests other purposes that the statute may serve. Its opinion states that the Alabama statutes were "designed" for "the wife of a broken marriage who needs financial assistance," 351 So.2d, at 905. This may be read as asserting either of two legislative objectives. One is a legislative purpose to provide help for needy spouses, using sex as a proxy for need. The other is a goal of compensating women for past discrimination during marriage, which assertedly has left them unprepared to fend for themselves in the working world following divorce. We concede, of course, that assisting needy spouses is a legitimate and important governmental objective. We have also recognized "[r]eduction of the disparity in economic condition between men and women caused by the long history of discrimination against women * * * as * * * an important governmental objective," Califano v. Webster, 430 U.S. at 317, 97 S.Ct., at 1194. It only remains, therefore, to determine whether the classification at issue here is "substantially related to achievement of those objectives."
* * *

Under the statute, individualized hearings at which the parties' relative financial circumstances are considered *already* occur. There is no reason, therefore, to use sex as a proxy for need * * * since individualized hearings can determine which women were in fact discriminated against vis à vis their husbands, as well as which family units defied the stereotype and left the husband dependent on the wife.
* * *

Having found Alabama's alimony statutes unconstitutional, we reverse the judgment below and remand the cause for further proceedings not inconsistent with this opinion.
* * *

Reversed.

Mr. Justice REHNQUIST, with whom THE CHIEF JUSTICE joins, dissenting.

In Alabama only wives may be awarded alimony upon divorce. In Part I of its opinion, the Court holds that Alabama's alimony statutes may be challenged in this Court by a divorced male who is demonstrably not entitled to alimony even if he had, and who contractually bound himself to pay alimony to his former wife and did so without objection for over two years. I think the Court's eagerness to invalidate Alabama's statutes has led it to deal too casually with the "case and controversy" requirement of Art. III of the Consitution.

* * *

This Court has long held that in order to satisfy the injury in fact requirement of Art. III standing, a party claiming that a statute unconstitutionally withholds a particular benefit must be in line to receive the benefit if the suit is successful.

---

1. The name of the case, also known as the *style,* is Orr v. Orr. William Orr and Lillian Orr were the parties involved; but one cannot tell, without reading the opinion closely, which was the plaintiff and which was the defendant at the trial court level.

2. The court that heard this case was the Supreme Court of the United States, the highest court of appeal in the United States. That this was a Supreme Court opinion can be determined from the citation discussed below.

3. The justice who delivered the opinion of the court was Mr. Justice Brennan. Members of the Supreme Court are known as justices; persons who preside over other courts in the United States are known as judges. The Supreme Court has a total of nine members—a chief justice and eight associate justices.

4. The numbers and letters found below the case name or party names, such as 99 Supreme Court 1102 (1979), constitute the citation. This is what lawyers use to locate the case. This case can be found in volume 99 of the *Supreme Court Reporter,* a West publication, on page 1102. The case was decided in 1979.

5. The *opinion* usually begins with a recital of the facts followed by a discussion of the law.

6. The triple asterisks (* * *) indicate that the authors of this book have deleted part of the opinion (a few words or even paragraphs) to make the case more concise and readable. Where an opinion cites another case, the citations to the referenced case have been omitted without leaving asterisks in the interest of saving space and helping readability.

7. This case came to the Supreme Court of the United States in the following way. Mrs. Orr initiated a contempt proceeding in the Circuit Court of Alabama, which is a trial court. The Circuit Court found against Mr. Orr, who then appealed from this judgment to the Court of Civil Appeals of Alabama—the intermediate appellate court in Alabama. (Note that the opinion of this case is reported on page 904 of volume 351 of the *Southern Second Series Reporter.*) Mr. Orr then appealed to the Supreme Court of Alabama by a writ of *certiorari.* At first, the Supreme Court of Alabama granted Mr. Orr's writ (in other words, agreed to hear this case) but later, the court decided not to hear it. Mr. Orr then appealed to the United States Supreme Court. One can appeal from the highest state court to the Supreme Court of the United States whenever a constitutional issue is involved. Here, the issue arose under the equal protection clause of the Fourteenth Amendment.

8. In this case, the majority of the Supreme Court decided to reverse the judgment of the lower courts. Often, not all the appellate justices hearing a case agree. In this case, Justice Rehnquist and Chief Justice Burger disagreed, or *dissented.* Note from their dissenting opinion that they did not disagree with the majority view that the Alabama statute was unconstitutional because it discriminated on the basis of sex. Rather, the two dissenting justices felt that the Supreme Court had no *jurisdiction* in the matter.

The Supreme Court has jurisdiction only when there is a case or controversy in front of it. This means that persons must sustain actual injury before they will be permitted to go before the Supreme Court and seek redress. For example, if your best friend is rejected for a job because of racial discrimination, *you* will not be allowed to sue on his behalf, regardless of the injustice that you think has been committed. In such a case, the Court will say that you lack *standing.* Similarly, in this case, Justice Rehnquist and Chief Justice Burger held that, since Mr. Orr was well-off financially, he would not be able to collect alimony from his wife regardless of Alabama's statute.

9. Throughout the case, Justice Brennan cites other cases that support his opinion as precedent for what he is saying now. The constitutional issue involved in this case arose from the Fourteenth Amendment of the United States Constitution, part of which reads as follows: "No state shall * * * deny to any person within its jurisdiction the equal protection of the laws." In this case, Mr. Orr claimed that Alabama's alimony statute was unconstitutional: Since the obligation of alimony could never fall upon wives under Alabama's statute, the statute denied equal protection of Alabama's laws to males as opposed to females. When people claim that they have been denied equal protection of the laws, they must show that they are a member of a class that has been discriminated against. In this case, the class of which Mr. Orr claimed to be a member was the male gender. Since Mr. Orr showed that his class had been discriminated against, the burden of proving some rational basis for this discrimination fell upon the state of Alabama. Alabama could not prove any basis for the discrimination that satisfied the majority of the Supreme Court. Therefore, the Court held that the law was unconstitutional.

QUESTIONS AND CASE PROBLEMS

1. The American system of government is unique in that it has essentially two sets of governments—state and federal. This is called the dual, or federal, system. One problem that arises in a federal system is that each government tends to duplicate the other's efforts. Can you see any way to avoid such problems of duplication?

2. How does the Constitution attempt to categorize the respective powers of the state and federal governments so that duplication of effort is avoided?

3. When a person commits an act that violates both state and federal law, quite often both the federal and the state government have jurisdiction. What problems do you see here?

4. The Constitution says that a person cannot be tried twice for the same crime. Does this problem arise when both the federal and the state government try the same person for the same crime? Explain.

5. a. Before two parties go to trial, there is an involved process called pleadings and discovery. Until recently, pleadings were very formal, and trials often turned on elements of surprise. For example, a plaintiff would not necessarily know until the trial what the defendant's defense was going to be. Does this seem like a fair way to conduct a trial?

b. Within the last twenty years, new rules of pleadings and discovery have substantially changed all this. Now, each attorney can discover practically all the evidence that the other will be presenting at trial. However, certain information is still not available to the parties—namely, each attorney's work product. *Work product* is not a clear concept. Basically, it includes all the attorney's thoughts on the case. Can you see any reason why such information should not be made available to the opposing attorney?

6. Quite often, trials are concluded before they are ever begun. If the parties do not dispute what the facts are, they simply relate those facts to the judge, and then, through motions on the pleadings, they simply ask the judge to decide what the law is, given this basic set of facts. How is it possible that two parties can agree on the facts yet disagree that one party is liable to the other party?

7. If a judge enters judgment on the pleadings, the losing party can usually appeal but cannot present evidence to the appellate court. Does this seem fair? Explain.

8. Once a case is appealed, most appellate courts do not have the power to enter judgment or to award damages to a party who should have received them at trial. Thus, if the appellate court disagrees with the trial court's decision, it will reverse and remand, in effect, ordering the trial court judge to change the judgment. Why should an appellate court not take a judge's word as final?

9. Sometimes on appeal there are questions of whether the facts presented in a trial support the conclusion reached by the judge or the jury. The appellate court will reverse on the basis of the facts only when so little evidence was presented at trial that no reasonable person could have reached the conclusion that the judge or jury reached. Appellate courts normally defer to a judge's decision with regard to the facts. Can you see any reason for this?

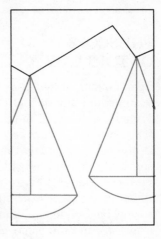

3

Torts

Part of doing business today and, indeed, part of everyday life is the risk of being involved in a lawsuit. A normal and ever-increasing business operating cost is the cost of liability insurance to protect against lawsuits. The list of possible circumstances in which businesspeople can be sued is long and varied. An employee injured on the job may attempt to sue the employer because of an unsafe working environment. The consumer who is injured while using a product may attempt to sue the manufacturer because of a defect in the product. The patient who has received negligent treatment may attempt to sue the doctor. The issue in all of these examples is alleged wrongful conduct by one person that causes injury to another. Such wrongful conduct is covered by the law of torts.

Tort law has its origin in early common law. Even today, when most other areas of the law have been codified in statutes, tort law is found primarily in the reports of court opinions. A **tort** can be simply defined as wrongful conduct by one individual that results in injury to another. However, this definition does not say much about the specific nature of torts, what wrongs are considered torts, and what injuries find a remedy in tort law. It is difficult to find a more exact definition because there are so many different torts, and torts cover such a broad area. Other areas of the law are more readily defined. Contract law, for example, covers the area of mutual promises and their enforcement. Criminal law deals with activities which contravene the rights of society as a whole. (Note, however, that a criminal act can also be a tort.) Tort law is a broad, almost all-encompassing area of law covering the whole range of human activity.

THE SCOPE OF TORT LAW

Two notions serve as the basis of all torts: wrongs and compensation. The word *tort* is French for "wrong" and derives from the Latin for "twisted." Tort law recognizes that some acts are wrong because they cause injury to someone. The actor is to blame or bears the fault for these injuries. There are, of course, different types of wrongs. A crime involves conduct society has defined as wrongful, but a crime and a tort are not the same. A crime is an act so wrong that it is considered to be a wrong against the state or against society as a whole as well as a wrong against the individual victim. Therefore, the state prosecutes the criminal. A tort is a civil action in which one person brings a suit of a personal nature against another, and the state is not involved as a party to the suit. On the other hand, there are some acts which you or I might consider morally wrong that are not "wrongs" for purposes of tort law. You or I might consider it wrong to be rude or ungrateful or to shirk our responsibilities. Yet, this type of wrongful conduct does not constitute a tort.

Tort law also recognizes that the victims of wrongs should be compensated. Criminal law and the law of torts are both concerned with wrongful conduct, but criminal law punishes the culprit. The function of torts, on the other hand, is to provide the injured party with some remedy. The law of torts is used to decide when victims must bear the loss of their injuries themselves and when the responsibility belongs to someone else. One quick way of recognizing a tort is by asking whether the injury done is of the type that deserves compensation from another.

THE ELEMENTS OF EVERY TORT

A tort has been committed when someone has suffered injury caused by the failure of another to live up to a required duty of care. There are three key elements in this definition: (1) injury, (2) causation, and (3) breach (failure) of duty of care.

Injury

In order for a tort to have been committed, there must be a recognizable injury to the plaintiff. The plaintiff must have suffered some loss, harm, wrong, or invasion of a protected interest to recover damages (that is, to receive compensation). The reason for the requirement of injury is obvious. Without an injury of some kind, there can be no compensation. Remember that the purpose of torts is to *compensate* for injuries resulting from wrongful acts, not to *punish* the act.

Tort law covers a broad variety of injuries. Society recognizes an interest in personal physical safety, and tort law provides a remedy for acts causing physical injury or interfering with physical security and freedom of movement. Society recognizes an interest in protecting personal property, and tort law provides a remedy for acts causing destruction or damage to property. Society recognizes other more intangible interests in such things as personal privacy, family relations, reputation, and dignity. Tort law provides a remedy for invasion of protected interests in these areas. Tort law is constantly changing and growing with society. Although many torts have their origin in the old common law, new torts protecting new interests develop in step with social change.

Causation

The second element necessary to a tort is causation. If a person fails in a duty of care and someone suffers injury, the wrongful activity must have caused the harm for a tort to have been committed. In deciding whether there is causation, the court must actually address two questions:

1. Is there factual causation?
2. Was the act the proximate cause of the injury?

FACTUAL CAUSATION   Did the injury occur because of the defendant's act or would it have occurred anyway? If an injury would not have occurred without the defendant's act, then there is *factual causation*. If X carelessly leaves a campfire burning, and the fire burns down the rest of the forest, there is factual causation. If X carelessly leaves a campfire burning, but it burns out, and then lightning causes a fire that burns down the forest, there is no factual causation. In both cases there is a wrongful act and damage. In the second case, however, there is no causal connection and, thus, no liability. Factual causation can usually be determined by use of the *but for* test: But for the wrongful act, the injury would not have occurred.

In some cases, factual causation is difficult to determine. What if X's campfire did spread, but at the same time, lightning also started a fire. In this type of situation, the courts apply the *substantial factor* test. If X's conduct was a substantial factor in bringing about the damage, X will be held liable.

Determining factual causation involves examining the facts portrayed in evidence in a trial. The plaintiff has the burden of proving factual causation and other elements such as damages. The plaintiff need not prove factual causation beyond a reasonable doubt but must prove only that the causal connection is more likely than not.

PROXIMATE CAUSATION   How far should a defendant's liability extend for a wrongful act that was a substantial factor in causing injury? For example, X's fire not only burns down the forest but also sets off an explosion in a nearby chemical plant that spills chemicals into a river, killing all the fish for a hundred miles downstream and ruining the economy of a tourist resort. Should X be liable to the resort owners? To the tourists whose vacation was ruined? These are questions about the limitation of liability, which is the second element in the general issue of causation. The courts use the term **proximate cause** (or sometimes legal cause) to describe this element. Proximate cause is a question not of fact but of law. The question is whether the connection between an act and an injury is strong enough to justify imposing liability. Probably the most cited case on proximate cause is the *Palsgraf* case.

BACKGROUND AND FACTS   *The plaintiff, Palsgraf, was waiting for a train on the station platform. A man carrying a package was rushing to catch a train that was already moving away from a platform across the tracks from Palsgraf. As the man attempted to jump aboard the moving train, he seemed unsteady and about to fall. A railroad guard on the car reached forward to grab him, and another guard on the platform pushed him from behind to help him on the train. In the process, the man's package fell upon the railroad tracks and exploded because it contained fireworks. There was nothing about the package to indicate its contents. The repercussions of the explosion caused decorative scales to fall from the ceiling and walls around the train platform. One of these scales struck Palsgraf, causing injuries for which she sued the railroad company. At the trial, the jury found that the railroad guards were negligent in their conduct.*

PALSGRAF v. LONG ISLAND RAILROAD COMPANY

Court of Appeals of New York, 1928.
248 N.Y. 339, 162 N.E. 99.

CARDOZO, Chief Justice.
* * *

The conduct of the defendant's guard, if a wrong in its relation to the holder of the package, was not a wrong in its relation to the plaintiff, standing far away. Relatively to her it was not negligence at all. Nothing in the situation gave notice that the falling package had in it the potency of peril to persons thus removed.

Negligence is not actionable unless it involves the invasion of a legally protected interest, the violation of a right. "Proof of negligence in the air, so to speak, will not do." [Emphasis added.]

* * * If no hazard was apparent to the eye of ordinary vigilance, an act innocent and harmless, at least to outward seeming, with reference to her, did not take to itself the quality of a tort because it happened to be a wrong, though apparently not one involving the risk of bodily insecurity, with reference to some one else. "In every instance, before *negligence* can be predicated of a given act, *back of the act must be* sought and found a *duty to the individual complaining,* the observance of which would have averted or avoided the injury." [Emphasis added.]

A different conclusion will involve us, and swiftly too, in a maze of contradictions. A guard stumbles over a package which has been left upon a platform. It seems to be a bundle of newspapers. It turns out to be a can of dynamite. To the eye of ordinary vigilance, the bundle is abandoned waste, which may be kicked or trod on with impunity. Is a passenger at the other end of the platform protected by the law against the unsuspected hazard concealed beneath the waste? If not, is the result to be any different, so far as the distant passenger is concerned, when the guard stumbles over a valise which a truckman or a porter has left upon the walk? The passenger far away, if the victim of a wrong at all, has a cause of action, not derivative, but original and primary. His claim to be protected against invasion of his bodily security is neither greater nor less because the act resulting in the invasion is a wrong to another far removed. In this case, the rights that are said to have been violated, the interests said to have been invaded, are not even of the same order. The man was not injured in his person nor even put in danger. The purpose of the act, as well as its effect, was to make his person safe. If there was a wrong to him at all, which may very well be doubted it was a wrong to a property interest only, the safety of his package. Out of this wrong to property, which threatened injury to nothing else, there has passed, we are told, to the plaintiff by derivation or succession a right of action for the invasion of an interest of another order, the right to bodily security. The diversity of interests emphasizes the futility of the effort to build the plaintiff's right upon the basis of a wrong to someone else. The gain is one of emphasis, for a like result would follow if the interests were the same. Even then, the orbit of the danger as disclosed to the eye of reasonable vigilance would be the orbit of the duty. One who jostles one's neighbor in a crowd does not invade the rights of others standing at the outer fringe when the unintended contact casts a bomb upon the ground. The wrongdoer as to them is the man who carries the bomb, not the one who explodes it without suspicion of the danger. Life will have to be made over, and human nature transformed, before prevision so extravagant can be accepted as the norm of conduct, the customary standard to which behavior must conform.

* * * What the plaintiff must show is "a wrong" to herself; i. e., a violation of her own right, and not merely a wrong to some one else, nor conduct "wrongful" because unsocial, but not "a wrong" to any one. * * * This does not mean, of course, that one who launches a destructive force is always relieved of liability, if the force, though known to be destructive, pursues an unexpected path. "It was not necessary that the defendant should have had notice of the particular method in which an accident would occur, if the possibility of an accident was clear to the

ordinarily prudent eye." Some acts, such as shooting are so imminently dangerous to any one who may come within reach of the missile however unexpectedly, as to impose a duty of prevision not far from that of an insurer. Even to-day, and much oftener in earlier stages of the law, one acts sometimes at one's peril. * * * Here, by concession, there was nothing in the situation to suggest to the most cautious mind that the parcel wrapped in newspaper would spread wreckage through the station. If the guard had thrown it down knowingly and willfully, he would not have threatened the plaintiff's safety, so far as appearances could warn him. His conduct would not have involved, even then, an unreasonable probability of invasion of her bodily security. Liability can be no greater where the act is inadvertent.

* * * One who seeks redress at law does not make out a cause of action by showing without more that there has been damage to his person. *If the harm was not willful, he must show that the act as to him had possibilities of danger so many and apparent as to entitle him to be protected against the doing of it though the harm was unintended.* [Emphasis added.] * * * The victim does not sue derivatively, or by right of subrogation, to vindicate an interest invaded in the person of another. * * * He sues for breach of a duty owing to himself.

* * * [To rule otherwise] would entail liability for any and all consequences, however novel or extraordinary.

Palsgraf's complaint was dismissed. The railroad could not be said to have been negligent toward her because injury to her was not foreseeable.

JUDGMENT AND REMEDY

FORESEEABILITY Since the decision in the *Palsgraf* case, the courts have used *foreseeability* as the test for proximate cause. The railroad guards were negligent, but the railroad's duty of care did not extend to Palsgraf because she was an unforeseeable plaintiff. If the consequences of the harm done or the victim of the harm are unforeseeable, there is no proximate cause. Of course, it is foreseeable that people will stand on railroad platforms and that objects attached to the platforms will fall as the result of explosions nearby. However, this is not a chain of events against which a reasonable person will normally guard. It is difficult to predict when a court will say that something is foreseeable and when it will say that something is not. This difficulty stems from the fact that proximate cause is tied up with the notion of duty. (This point is obvious from Chief Justice Cardozo's opinion.) How far a court stretches foreseeability will be determined in part by how far the court stretches the defendant's duty of care.

Breach of Duty of Care

The final element in a tort can also be broken up into a two-part question:

1. Is there a duty of care?
2. Did the defendant's action breach (fail to live up to) that duty?

DUTY OF CARE Basically, the concept of duty arises from the notion that, if we are to live in society with other people, some actions can be tolerated and some cannot, some actions are right and some are wrong, and some actions are reasonable and some are not. The basic rule of duty is that people are free to act as they please as long as their actions do not interfere with and infringe on the interests of others.

Tort law measures duty by a standard of

reasonableness—the *reasonable person standard*. In determining whether a tort has been committed, the courts will ask how a reasonable person would have acted in the same circumstances. The reasonable person standard is objective. It is not necessarily how a particular person would act. It is society's judgment on how people should act. If the reasonable person existed, he or she would be the most careful, most conscientious, most even-tempered, and most honest of people.

BREACH OF DUTY When someone fails to live up to the standard of reasonableness, a tortious act has been committed (but not necessarily a completed tort since that will depend on whether there is damage and proximate cause). Failure to live up to the standard of care may be an act (setting fire to a building) or an omission (forgetting to put out a fire). It may be an intentional act, a careless act, or a careful but dangerous act that results in injury.

Whether or not a person's act or failure to act is unreasonable depends on the interaction of a number of factors. One factor is the nature of the act. Some actions—spitting on someone, for instance—are so outrageous that the actor should pay for what has been done regardless of physical damage. Other acts, like blasting with dynamite, are so dangerous that any damage they cause should be paid for. Another factor in determining whether damages should be paid is the manner in which an act is performed. Intentionally hitting someone on the back probably should be paid for; accidentally doing so probably should not be. A third factor is the nature of the injury—whether it is serious or slight, extraordinary, or simply part of everyday life. Two other factors are whether the activity causing the injury was socially useful and how easily the injury could have been guarded against. Finally, when all other factors hang in the balance, the determining factor may be the ability to suffer the loss. For instance, a large corporation can shoulder a loss more easily than an individual victim because the corporation will be able to spread the loss to all its customers by raising prices.

KINDS OF TORTS

Determining whether or not some action is a tort basically involves drawing a conclusion about the way that losses in an increasingly complex society should be allocated. As such, it is a decision on social policy, and it requires the balancing of many social factors. Legal commentators traditionally divide torts into three categories: intentional torts, negligence, and strict liability. Intentional torts, as the name implies, are concerned with intentional acts. Negligence concerns careless acts, and strict liability concerns liability without regard to fault.

INTENTIONAL TORTS: WRONGS AGAINST THE PERSON

An intentional tort is one in which the defendant wished to perform the tortious act or knew with substantial certainty that an injury would result. Note that it is intent with respect to the act that is important. The nature of the damage caused is irrelevant in determining whether there was intent. If I intentionally push you, and you fall to the ground and break your arm, it does not matter that I had no intention of breaking your arm. I did intend to push you, and that in itself is the tortious act for which I am liable for damages, including the injury to your arm.

Battery

A battery is harmful or offensive physical contact done with the intent of making the contact. If I intentionally punch someone in the nose, it is a battery. The interest this tort protects is the right to personal security and safety. The contact can be harmful, or it can merely be offensive. There is no necessity for actual physical injury. The contact can be to any part of the body or anything attached to it—for example, a hat or other clothing, a purse, a chair, or an automobile one is sitting in. Whether the contact is offensive or not is determined by the reasonable person standard. The contact can be made by the defendant or by some force that the defendant sets in motion—for example, a rock thrown, food poisoned, or a stick swung.

There is no need to prove special damages. If the plaintiff shows that there was a contact, and the jury agrees that the contact was offensive, that is enough to have a right to some compensation. Furthermore, there is no need to show that the defendant acted out of malice. He or she could have been joking or playing. The defendant's motive does not matter.

Assault

Any intentional act which creates a reasonable apprehension or fear of immediate harmful or offensive contact is an assault. The apprehension of contact must be a reasonable one, but apprehension is not the same as fear. The plaintiff may be unafraid, but if he or she believes the contact is coming, there is apprehension. At the same time, the apprehended contact must be such that a reasonable person would want to avoid it.

The interest protected in assault is the interest in being free from having to expect harmful or offensive contact. The arousal of the apprehension is enough to justify compensation. Of course, the *completion* of the act which threatens harm causing apprehension in another is a battery, discussed above. For example, A threatens B with a gun, then shoots him. The pointing of the gun at B is an assault, the firing of the gun is a battery.

DEFENSES TO ASSAULT AND BATTERY
Assault and battery have certain legally recognized defenses. A person who voluntarily signs up for a touch football team implicitly consents to the *normal* physical punishment that takes place during such activities. People who use reasonable force in attempting to remove intruders from their homes can use the excuse of **defense of property** to counter tort lawsuits for assault or battery or both. The same is true for people who are defending their lives or their physical well-being. This is called **self-defense.**

False Imprisonment

False imprisonment, sometimes called false arrest, is defined as the intentional confinement or restraint of another person. It involves interference with the freedom to move without restraint. The confinement can be accomplished through the use of physical barriers, physical restraint, or threats of physical force. Moral pressure or future threats are not a restraint sufficient to constitute false imprisonment. It is essential that the person being restrained not comply with the restraint willingly. On the other hand, a person is under no duty to risk personal harm in trying to escape.

Businesspeople are often confronted with suits for false imprisonment after they have attempted to confine a suspected shoplifter for questioning. Consider, for example, the case in which a store detective locks an alleged shoplifter in one of the store's offices. An hour later, the manager returns and is told of the act. If the customer can prove his or her innocence, the store can be sued for false imprisonment.

The loss to business from shoplifting is estimated to exceed 10 billion dollars a year. Almost all states have adopted so-called merchant protection legislation, which allows a merchant to detain any suspected shoplifter, provided that there is reasonable cause for suspicion and provided that the confinement is carried out in a reasonable way. However, the risk of real injury to an innocent person is great. Educational programs are often offered to all employees; these programs explain the exact procedures to be followed when a customer is suspected of shoplifting. Harm to reputation and the mental distress from a wrongful imprisonment are believed by the law to be so real that damages are presumed and need not be proven to make a case.

A merchant can use the defense of probable cause to justify delaying a suspected shoplifter, but the delay must be *reasonable*. The following case provides a good example.

**FAULKENBERRY v.
SPRINGS MILLS, INC.**
Supreme Court of South
Carolina, 1978. 247 S.E.2d 445.

BACKGROUND AND FACTS   *Barbara Faulkenberry brought this action against her employer, Springs Mills, Inc., for false imprisonment. On two separate occasions, fellow employees had reported to supervisory personnel that Faulkenberry had been seen secreting cloth in her pocketbook. After the second report, her supervisors and some plant security guards delayed her for about fifteen minutes at the mill gatehouse as she attempted to leave work. The delay was to investigate whether she had any cloth in her possession.*

Faulkenberry refused to open her pocketbook at the request of her supervisors. After some discussion and her continued refusal to open her pocketbook to reveal its contents, she left the mill gatehouse without further hindrance. Subsequently, she filed this action for false imprisonment based upon the delay at the gatehouse.

The trial court found the employer guilty of false imprisonment.

LEWIS, Chief Justice.
* * *

We stated in [a prior case] that the essence of the tort of false imprisonment consists in depriving the plaintiff of his or her liberty without lawful justification.

Since we conclude that the actions of appellant's [Springs Mills's] agents were done with legal justification we need not determine whether the delay or restraint of respondent at the gatehouse as she left work constituted the restraint required to make out false imprisonment. If appellant was legally justified in restraining respondent, she is not entitled to recover. The following from 32 Am.Jur.2d, False Imprisonment, Section 74, soundly states the applicable principles:

> Ordinarily the owner of property, in the exercise of his inherent right to protect it, is justified in restraining another who seeks to interfere with or injure it where the restraint or detention is reasonable in time and manner. Thus, where a person has reasonable grounds to believe that another is taking his property, he is justified in detaining the suspect for a reasonable length of time for the purpose of making an investigation in a reasonable manner. In such cases, probable cause is a defense, even though the injury which is about to be inflicted constitutes only a misdemeanor, for it is the existence of a reasonable ground to suppose that one's property is in danger which gives right to the protection. It follows that the owner of a store or other premises has a right to detain a customer or patron, for a reasonable time for a reasonable investigation, whom he has reasonable grounds to believe has not paid for what he has received, or is attempting to take goods without payment * * * Moreover, the right to detain the person suspected of wrongdoing exists only during commission of the offense, and does not arise where the offense was completed at some prior time.

Probable cause is * * * a defense * * * to actions arising from a merchant's delay of suspected shoplifters. [State law] provides:

> In any action brought by reason of having been delayed by a merchant or merchant's employee or agent on or near the premises of a mercantile establishment for the purpose of investigation concerning the ownership of

any merchandise, it shall be a defense to such action if: (1) The person was delayed in a reasonable manner and for a reasonable time to permit such investigation, and (2) reasonable cause existed to believe that the person delayed had committed the crime of shoplifting.

We find no sound reason to deny the * * * defense, * * * to employers who reasonably delay employees in an attempt to determine the ownership of property. Such actions, of course, must be supported by probable cause; and the delay must be reasonable in time and manner and can only be justified during the commission of the suspected wrongdoing.

Appellant's [Springs Mills's] actions met the requirements of the foregoing rule. The evidence conclusively shows probable cause or legal justification for the restraint of [respondent, Barbara Faulkenberry]. Appellant's supervisory personnel acted only after the second report from an eyewitness that respondent was seen placing cloth in her purse. She was detained immediately thereafter at the gatehouse for the purpose of investigating the report that she was removing appellant's property from the Mill, an act which the information indicated was then in progress.

Respondent was not physically restrained, but was asked to come into the gatehouse so that the security officer could talk to her. The gatehouse was respondent's intended destination to complete her work check-out sheet. When she had completed "checking out" from work, she was asked to open her pocketbook and was told the reason for the request. She refused the request and after about twenty minutes discussion left without hindrance.

The record conclusively shows that respondent was delayed by appellant's security officers for only about twenty minutes for the purpose of making the legitimate inquiry into the charge that respondent was then in the act of unlawfully taking appellant's property. The information from fellow employees (eyewitnesses), upon which appellant acted in making the inquiry of respondent, was properly deemed reliable. The inquiry or investigation made was reasonable in nature, consisting solely of requests that respondent open her pocketbook.

The legal justification for the investigation by appellant into the alleged taking of its property by respondent is conclusively shown. The evidence therefore fails to sustain the finding of false imprisonment.

JUDGMENT AND REMEDY

The state supreme court reversed the trial court's finding of false imprisonment. Springs Mills had legal justification for stopping Faulkenberry to investigate the reports that she was stealing from her employer. Hence, Faulkenberry was not entitled to recover on her action for false imprisonment. The case was reversed and then remanded to the trial court for entry of a judgment in favor of the appellant, Springs Mills.

Infliction of Mental Distress

Recently the courts have begun to recognize an interest in freedom from mental distress as well as an interest in physical security. The tort of mental distress can be defined as an intentional act that amounts to extreme and outrageous conduct resulting in severe emotional distress to another. For example, a prankster telephones an individual and says that the individual's spouse has just been in a horrible accident. As a result, the individual suffers intense mental pain or anxiety. Extreme and outrageous conduct is defined as conduct that is outside the bounds of decency accepted by society. This test is measured by the reasonable person standard.

Defamation

The protection of a person's body is involved in the torts of assault, battery, and false imprisonment. **Defamation** of character involves wrongfully hurting a person's good reputation. The law has imposed a general duty on all persons to refrain from making defamatory, false statements about others. Breaching this duty orally involves the tort of **slander;** breaching it in writing involves the tort of **libel.**[1]

The basis of the tort is the publication of a statement or statements that hold an individual up to contempt, ridicule, or hatred. *Publication* here means that the defamatory statements are made to or within the hearing of persons other than the defamed party. If Thompson writes Andrews a letter accusing him of embezzling funds, that does not constitute libel. If Peters calls Gordon dishonest, unattractive, and incompetent when no one else is around, that does not constitute slander. In neither case was the message communicated to a third party. Interestingly, the courts have generally held that dictating a letter to a secretary constitutes publication. Moreover, if a third party overhears defamatory statements by chance, the courts have generally held that this also constitutes publication. Note further that any individual who republishes or repeats defamatory statements is liable even if that person reveals the source of such statements. Most radio stations have instituted seven-second delays for live broadcasts such as talk shows to avoid this kind of liability.

Whenever libel is concerned, there is a presumption of damages unless the written statement is not defamatory on its face. On the other hand *slander* is not actionable (i. e., no grounds for a lawsuit) without proof of damages unless the statements can be classed as

defamatory per se. The common law defines four types of false utterances that are torts per se:

1. A statement that another person has a loathsome communicable disease.
2. A statement that another person has committed improprieties while engaging in a profession or trade.
3. A statement that another person has committed or has been imprisoned for a serious crime.
4. A statement that an unmarried woman is unchaste.

DEFENSES AGAINST DEFAMATION Truth is normally an absolute defense against a defamation charge. Furthermore, there may be a privilege involved. For example, statements made by attorneys and judges during a trial have an *absolute privilege* against a defamation charge. Members of Congress making statements on the floor of Congress have an absolute privilege. Legislators have complete immunity from liability for false statements made in debate, even if they make such statements maliciously—that is, knowing them to be untrue. In general, false and defamatory statements that concern public figures and are published in the media are privileged if they are made without malice.[2] Under this rule of privilege, public figures are defined as those who "thrust" themselves into the forefront of public controversy. A plaintiff needs to show that the defendant either has actual knowledge of falsity or has engaged in a reckless disregard of the truth in order to show malice.

The tort law of slander and libel will continue to change as federal and state courts continue to expand or constrict the free speech guarantees of the federal and state constitutions.

Slander of Title and Disparagement of Goods

A tort that is related to defamation involves harm or injury resulting from false statements

---

1. This distinction between oral and written defamation is becoming less meaningful.

2. New York Times Co. v. Sullivan, 376 U.S. 254, 84 S.Ct. 710 (1964).

made about one's product, business, or title to property. Thus, any type of property interest that is legally protected can be the subject of disparagement, which can consist of false statements about leases, land, patents, or literary property. False statements can relate to the character of a business or a product. Again, publication is required for the tort of disparagement of goods to have occurred. Furthermore, actual damages must result. For example, if Myers owns a bakery and Smith falsely claims to a third party that Myers puts rat poison in the flour, Myers can sue for damages only if the third party indeed no longer patronizes the shop.

Defamation by Computer

A computer can contain erroneous information about a person's credit standing or business reputation. When such information is given out, it can seriously damage the ability of that person to obtain credit in the future. Who is liable to the injured person under such circumstances—the data bank operator or the company that owns the information? Whichever one acted negligently is liable. (If both were negligent, both are liable.) The tort involved has been given the distinctive but misleading name of defamation by computer. Such liability can arise also under the federal Fair Credit Reporting Act of 1970 when the individual affected is a consumer. Furthermore, the federal Credit Card Act of 1970 gives further protection against defamation by computer.

Invasion of the Right to Privacy

A person's right to solitude and to freedom from prying public eyes is the interest protected by the tort of invasion of privacy. Four different acts qualify as an invasion of privacy:

1. The use of a person's name or picture for commercial purposes without permission.
2. Intrusion upon an individual's affairs or seclusion.
3. Publication of information that places a person in a false light. This could be a story

attributing to the person ideas that are not held or actions that were not taken. (Publishing such a story could involve the tort of defamation as well.)
4. Public disclosure of private facts about an individual. The private facts that are made public must be facts that an ordinary person would find objectionable.

Misrepresentation (Fraud, Deceit)

The tort of misrepresentation involves the use of fraud and deceit for personal gain. It includes several elements:

1. Misrepresentation of facts or conditions with knowledge that they are false or with reckless disregard for the truth.
2. Intent to induce another to rely on the misrepresentation.
3. Justifiable reliance by the deceived party.
4. Damages suffered as a result of reliance.
5. Causal connection between the misrepresentation and the injury suffered.

In general, the reliance must be upon a statement of fact. Reliance on a statement of opinion is not justified unless the person making the statement has a superior knowledge of the subject matter. A lawyer's opinion of the law, for example, is an example of superior knowledge.

INTENTIONAL TORTS: WRONGS AGAINST PROPERTY

Wrongs against property include (1) trespass to land and to personal property, (2) conversion, and (3) nuisance. The wrong is against the individual who has legally recognized rights with regard to land or personal property.

Trespass to Land

Any time a person enters onto land that is owned by another, or causes anything to enter onto the land, or remains or permits anything to remain on it, such action constitutes a **trespass to land.** Note that *actual* harm to the land is not an essential element of this tort, because the tort is designed to protect the right of an owner to exclusive possession. Clearly, though, if no harm is done, usually only nominal damages (such as $1) can be recovered by the landowner. Examples of common types of trespass to land include walking or driving on the land, shooting across it with a gun, throwing rocks or spraying water on a building in the possession of another, building a dam across a river that causes water to back up on someone else's land, and placing part of one's building on the adjoining landowner's property.

In the past, the right to land extended from "the center of the earth to the heavens," but this rule has been relaxed. Today, reasonable intrusions are permitted. Thus, aircraft can normally fly over privately owned land. In other words, the temporary invasion of the air space over such land is often privileged by the aircraft owner.

DEFENSES AGAINST TRESPASS TO LAND
Trespass to land involves wrongful interference with another person's real property rights. But if one can show that the trespass was warranted, a complete defense is given. Another defense is to show that the purported owner did not actually have the right to the possession of the land in question.

Some situations carry a measure of damages for trespass to land, especially when the trespasser damages or wrongfully destroys items of value on the land. For example, land purchasers can recover the value of destroyed trees when avoidable errors caused construction crews to knock them down. The following case provides a good example.

FARNY v. BESTFIELD BUILDERS, INC.
Superior Court of Delaware, New Castle County, 1978.
391 A.2d 212.

BACKGROUND AND FACTS *The plaintiffs, James F. and Doris O. Farny, appealed an award of the Court of Common Pleas (the trial court) allowing them only $1 and costs for damages in their lawsuit against a builder whose workers destroyed trees on their property during the construction of their home. In a clause added to the contract of sale, the defendant, Bestfield Builders, Inc., assured Mr. and Mrs. Farny that all healthy trees would remain on the property and that none would be lost as a result of the construction.*

At the trial, the plaintiffs presented uncontroverted expert testimony that the value of the trees that were lost as a result of avoidable errors made by the construction crew was $3,358 and that the replacement cost would involve an additional amount of 50 percent of the value, for a total of $5,037. The trial court determined that the measure of damages should be the value of the property with the trees less the value of the property without them. Since that before and after value was not entered into evidence, the lower court awarded only nominal costs.

STIFTEL, President Judge.
* * *

Generally, in Delaware, the measure of damages for trespass of land is the difference between the value of the land before the trespass occurred and the value of the land after the trespass. In [Jordan v. Delaware & A. Telegraph & Telephone Co.,] plaintiff brought an action for the loss of several maple trees and a pear tree on her property across the street from her dwelling. Several contemporary cases followed this general rule where the measure of damages would be expressed in terms parallel to a loss in commercial value of timber.
* * *

The *Jordan* doctrine is still alive in this State. However, in the appropriate case, the jury may properly consider both the costs of restoration and the before and after valuation of the land itself. In instances where the costs of replacement are unreasonable or excessive in relation to the damage to the land itself, the Court will, in its discretion, allow the jury to consider more than one measure of damage in order to permit flexibility and achieve a just and reasonable result.

* * *

The application by the Court below of the before and after value that produced a judgment of $1.00 appears to be disproportionate to the reasonable damages suffered by the plaintiffs as a consequence of contract non-performance. However, the claim of plaintiffs for judgment of $5,037.00 also appears to be unreasonable and unduly excessive for the amount of damage suffered. The Court below may consider whether the plaintiffs Farny as reasonable owners would well have replaced the dead trees, perhaps then fully matured, in light of the fact that their replacement cost may unreasonably exceed their marginal aesthetic value; or whether the plaintiffs Farny would have replaced the lost trees with less mature trees of a somewhat lower replacement cost but with an aesthetic value near to that of the lost trees.

* * *

Nevertheless, we are persuaded that it is the better rule that where trees and shrubbery have aesthetic value to the owner as ornamental and shade trees or for purposes of screening sound and providing privacy, replacement cost may be considered to the extent that the cost is reasonable and practical. Of course, the defendant may always show by way of rebuttal that the effect on the value of the land as a whole is minimal, and it is for the jury to balance these elements of damages in arriving at a just and reasonable award. There are situations where it is conceivable that from a practical point of view, because of the size of the trees, they cannot be replaced without costs which are wholly disproportionate to the damage inflicted. Under such circumstances, it cannot be expected that restoration or replacement will exactly duplicate what was damaged or destroyed.

JUDGMENT AND REMEDY *The judgment was reversed, and the case was remanded to the Court of Common Pleas so that it could consider the proper measure and amount of damages, including in its assessment reasonable restoration costs and the decline in the market value of the land.*

Trespass to Personal Property

Whenever any individual unlawfully injures the personal property of another or otherwise interferes with the personal property owner's right to exclusive possession and enjoyment of that property, **trespass to personalty** occurs. Trespass to personal property involves intentional meddling. If a fellow student takes your business law book as a practical joke and hides it so that you are unable to find it for several days prior to your final examination, the student has engaged in a trespass to personal property. (Today, this is called conversion, which is discussed below.)

DEFENSES AGAINST TRESPASS TO PERSONAL PROPERTY   If it can be shown that trespass to personal property was warranted, then a complete defense has been made. Many states, for example, allow hotel owners to retain the personal property of guests who refuse to pay for their lodgings.

Conversion

Whenever personal property is taken and kept from its rightful owner or possessor, the act of **conversion** has occurred. Conversion is the civil side of the crimes relating to stealing.[3] A bank clerk who steals money from the bank commits a crime and a conversion at the same time. A person who unlawfully takes goods is liable for the tort of conversion even if the person mistakenly believed that he or she was entitled to them. In other words, good intentions are not a defense against conversion, and conversion can be an entirely innocent act. If I mistakenly deliver your groceries to someone else, and that person eats them, I have committed a conversion even though I did not intend to commit such an act. (The recipient of the groceries has also committed a conversion.)

Whoever suffers a conversion is generally entitled to recover the reasonable value of the goods that have been lost. If you enter a china shop, pick up a $500 vase, and drop it, you owe the store owner the value of the vase (and value can be different from price).

DEFENSES AGAINST CONVERSION   If one can show that the purported owner has no superior title or right to possess, then that can be a successful defense against the charge of conversion.

Nuisance

It is possible to commit a tort and be liable because of unreasonable use of your own

---

3.   Theft requires intent, but conversion does not.

property. A **nuisance** is an improper activity that interferes with another's enjoyment or use of his or her property. Nuisances can be either public or private. A public nuisance disturbs or interferes with the public in general, whereas a private nuisance interferes with the property interest of only one individual. Reasonable limitations are placed on the use of the property in all situations. Such limitations prevent the owner from unreasonably interfering with the health and comfort of neighbors or with their right to enjoy their own private property. Those who suffer from nuisances can seek redress in the courts through an injunction, an equitable remedy whereby the undesirable activity is prohibited by court order.

BUSINESS TORTS

Many torts that have arisen in recent years can be classified as business torts. They involve the disparagement of goods and slander of title mentioned above as well as infringement on trademarks. A **trademark** is a word, name, device, or symbol used by a manufacturer or seller to distinguish his or her goods from those of others. Infringements of *patents* and *copyrights* are also business torts. The term *unfair competition* covers a variety of business torts. Such unlawful conduct is normally reported to various government agencies, such as the Federal Trade Commission.

Malicious injury to business is a tort that occurs when an individual engages in a business venture for the sole purpose of injuring an established business.[4]

---

4.   The existence of a tort in this situation depends on the motive of the party.

BACKGROUND AND FACTS   *The plaintiff, a barber, filed suit against the defendant for malicious interference with his business. The plaintiff had owned and operated a barbershop for the previous ten years and had been able to maintain himself and his family comfortably from the income of the business.*

The defendant was a banker in the same community. During the past twelve months, the defendant had "maliciously" established a competitive barbershop, employed a barber to carry on the business, and used his personal influence to attract customers from the plaintiff's barbershop. Apparently, the defendant had circulated false and malicious reports and accusations about the plaintiff and had personally solicited, urged, threatened, and otherwise persuaded many of the plaintiff's patrons to stop using the plaintiff's services and to use the defendant's shop instead. The plaintiff charged that the defendant undertook this entire plan with the sole design of injuring the plaintiff and destroying his business, not for serving any legitimate business interest or as fair competition.

ELLIOTT, Justice.

* * *

For generations there has been a practical agreement upon the proposition that competition in trade and business is desirable, and this idea has found expression in the decisions of the courts as well as in statutes. But it has led to grievous and manifold wrongs to individuals, and many courts have manifested an earnest desire to protect the individuals from the evils which result from unrestrained business competition. The problem has been to so adjust matters as to preserve the principle of competition and yet guard against its abuse to the unnecessary injury to the individual. So the principle that a man may use his own property according to his own needs and desires, while true in the abstract, is subject to many limitations in the concrete. Men cannot always, in civilized society, be allowed to use their own property as their interests or desires may dictate without reference to the fact that they have neighbors whose rights are as sacred as their own. The existence and well-being of society requires that each and every person shall conduct himself consistently with the fact that he is a social and reasonable person. The purpose for which a man is using his own property may thus sometimes determine his rights. "If there exists, then, a positive duty to avoid harm, much more, then, exists the negative duty of not doing willful harm, subject, as all general duties must be subject, to the necessary exceptions. The three main heads of duty with which the law of torts is concerned, namely, to abstain from willful injury, to respect the property of others, and to use due diligence to avoid causing harm to others, are all alike of a comprehensive nature." Pollock, Torts, (8th Ed.) p. 21.

To divert to one's self the customers of a business rival by the offer of goods at lower prices is in general a legitimate mode of serving one's own interest, and justifiable as fair competition. But when a man starts an opposition place of business, not for the sake of profit to himself, but regardless of loss to himself, and for the sole purpose of driving his competitor out of business, and with the intention of himself retiring upon the accomplishment of his malevolent purpose, he is guilty of a wanton wrong and an actionable tort. In such a case he would not be exercising his legal right, or doing an act which can be judged separately from the motive which actuated him. To call such conduct competition is a perversion of terms. It is simply the application of force without legal justification, which in its moral quality may be no better than highway robbery.

<table>
<tr>
<td>JUDGMENT
AND REMEDY</td>
<td>The plaintiff's cause of action was recognized under Minnesota law. The Supreme Court of Minnesota concluded that modern business requires certain protection against abusive business practices. The plaintiff then returned to the trial court to prove his case. From that point forward, Minnesota recognized a cause of action for tortious interference with business relations.</td>
</tr>
</table>

Interference with Contractual Relations

Tort law relating to *intentional interference with contractual relations* has increased greatly in recent years. A landmark case in this area involved an opera singer, Joanna Wagner, who was under contract to sing for a man named Lumley for a specified period of years.[5] A man named Gye, who knew of this contract, nonetheless "enticed" Wagner to refuse to carry out the agreement, and Wagner began to sing for Gye. Gye's action constituted a tort because it interfered with the contractual relationship between Wagner and Lumley. In principle, any lawful contract can be the heart of an action for interference with contractual relations. The plaintiff must prove that the defendant actually induced a breach of contractual relationship, not merely that the defendant reaped the benefits of a broken contract. If Jones has a contract with Smith that calls for Smith to mow Jones's lawn every week for a year at a specified price, Jones cannot sue Miller when Smith breaches the contract merely because Miller now receives gardening services from Smith.

NEGLIGENCE

Unlike intentional torts, negligence does not involve a mental state. In negligence, the actor neither wishes to bring about the consequences of the act nor believes that they will occur. The actor's conduct creates a *risk* of such consequences. Without the creation of a risk there can be no negligence, and the risk must be foreseeable; that is, it must be such that a reasonable person would be likely to anticipate it and guard against it. By the standard of the reasonable person, the negligent person should have foreseen the risk.

In examining a question of negligence, five questions should be asked:

1. What did the person do (act)?
2. Did the act create a foreseeable risk of harm (breach of duty of care)?
3. Was harm done (damages)?
4. Did the act cause the harm (causation in fact)?
5. At what point should liability cease (proximate cause)?

Many of the actions discussed in the section on intentional torts would constitute negligence if they were done carelessly without intent. For instance, carelessly bumping into someone who falls and breaks an arm constitutes negligence. Likewise, carelessly, as opposed to intentionally, flooding someone's land constitutes negligence. In a sense, negligence is a way of committing a tort rather than a distinct category of torts.

Negligence involves the allocation of loss between an innocent plaintiff and an innocent, but careless, defendant. In all torts, but especially in negligent torts, the extent of duty and liability is determined by social policy—for example, by the extent to which the injurious activity is socially useful or by the extent to which the injuring party can spread the cost.

Defenses to Negligence

There are three basic defenses in negligence cases: (1) superseding, intervening forces; (2) assumption of risk; and (3) contributory and comparative negligence.

---

5.   Lumley v. Gye, 118 Eng.Rep. 749 (1853).

SUPERSEDING, INTERVENING FORCES A superseding, intervening force breaks the connection between a wrongful act and damage to another. It cancels out the original, wrongful act. For example, if I have a can of gasoline in the trunk of my car, this creates a foreseeable risk and is, thus, a negligent act. If lightning strikes my trunk, exploding the can and injuring passing pedestrians, the lightning supersedes my negligence as a cause of the damage if it was not foreseeable. This example illustrates that the doctrine of superseding forces is also a question of proximate cause and legal duty.

An act of God, such as a lightning bolt, if it is not foreseeable, is a superseding force. If one person creates a potentially dangerous condition, and the gross negligence of a second person causes the condition to result in damage, the second person's act can be a superseding force. Criminal acts or intentional torts by other persons, if not foreseeable, constitute superseding forces.

In other situations, the intervention of a force may not relieve liability. If medical maltreatment of an injury aggravates the injury, the person who orginally caused the injury by negligence is not relieved of liability. If subsequent disease or a subsequent accident is proximately caused by the original injury, the person who caused the *original* injury will be liable for the injury caused by the disease or subsequent accident. Where negligence endangers property, and the owner is injured in an attempt to protect the property, the negligent party will be liable for the injury. Finally, rescuers are considered a foreseeable intervening force, and a negligent party will be liable for injuries to them.

In negligence cases the negligent party will often attempt to show that some act has intervened after his or her action and that this second act was the proximate cause of injury. Typically, in cases where an individual takes a defensive action, such as attempting to escape by swerving or leaping from a vehicle, the original wrongdoer will not be relieved of liability even if the injury actually resulted from seeking to escape. The same is true under the so-called "rescue doctrine." Under this doctrine, if Smith commits an act that endangers Jones, and Brown sustains an injury trying to protect Jones, then Smith will be liable for Brown's injury. Rescuers can injure themselves, or the person rescued, or even a stranger, but the original wrongdoer will still be liable. The following case illustrates this doctrine.

BACKGROUND AND FACTS *This case arose out of an accident that killed three men and seriously injured five others. All were sewage treatment workers. After correcting a water leakage problem in a New York City sewer, one of the workers, Rooney, was fatally stricken by lethal gas present in the sewer when the oxygen-type protective mask he was wearing failed to operate properly. A companion worker shouted for help. Two other workers responded to the cries for help and were fatally stricken by the gas when they entered the sewer tunnel without masks.*

The plaintiffs sued the manufacturer of the oxygen masks to recover damages for injuries they sustained in attempting to rescue a member of the sewer repair crew whose oxygen mask had malfunctioned.

GUARINO v. MINE SAFETY APPLIANCE CO.

Court of Appeals of New York, 1969.
25 N.Y.2d 460, 306 N.Y.S.2d 942, 255 N.E.2d 173.

JASEN, Judge.
* * *

Here the defendant committed a culpable act against the decedent Rooney, by manufacturing and distributing a defective oxygen-producing mask * * * By virtue of this defendant's culpable act, Rooney was placed in peril, thus inviting his rescue by the plaintiffs who were all members of Rooney's sewage treatment crew. There was no time for reflection when it became known that Rooney was in need of immediate assistance in the dark tunnel some 30 to 40 feet below the street level. These plaintiffs responded to the cries for help in a manner which was reasonable and consistent with their concern for each other as members of a crew. To require that a rescuer answering the cry for help make inquiry as to the nature of the culpable act that imperils someone's life would defy all logic.

We do not believe that the theory of the action, whether it be negligence or breach of warranty, is significant where the doctrine of "danger invites rescue" applies. A breach of warranty and an act of negligence are each clearly wrongful acts. Both terms are synonymous as regards fixation of liability, differing primarily in their requirements of proof.

As Judge Cardozo so eloquently stated in Wagner v. International Ry. Co.: "Danger invites rescue. The cry of distress is the summons to relief. * * * The *wrong* that imperils life is a wrong to the imperiled victim; it is a wrong also to his rescuer." [emphasis added].

"* * * [T]he rescue doctrine [is] a concept unaffected by the exact label put upon the wrong which created the danger to the imperilled victim. For the same reason, the rescuer's status as a user or non-user of the defective instrumentality is not directly relevant to our analysis. It is enough that the plaintiffs attempted to rescue a user with respect to whom a breach of warranty or 'tortious wrong' had been committed."

We conclude that a person who by his culpable act, whether it stems from negligence or breach of warranty, places another person in a position of imminent peril, may be held liable for any damages sustained by a rescuer in his attempt to aid the imperilled victim.

* * *

JUDGMENT AND REMEDY *The manufacturer of the malfunctioning oxygen mask was held liable for damages resulting from the death or injury sustained by the plaintiffs who sought to rescue the individual overcome by sewer gas when the mask failed.*

ASSUMPTION OF RISK A plaintiff who voluntarily enters into a risky situation knowing the risk involved will not be allowed to recover. This is the defense of **assumption of risk.** For example, a driver who enters a race knows that there is a risk of being killed or injured in a crash. The driver has assumed the risk of injury. The two requirements of this defense are: (1) knowledge of the risk and (2) voluntary assumption of the risk.

The risk can be assumed by express agreement, or the assumption of risk can be implied by the plaintiff's knowledge of the risk.

Of course, the plaintiff does not assume a risk different from or greater than the risk normally carried by the activity. Risks are not deemed to be assumed in situations involving emergencies. Neither are they assumed where a statute protects a class of people from harm and a member of the class is injured by the harm.

CONTRIBUTORY AND COMPARATIVE NEGLIGENCE All individuals are expected to exercise a reasonable degree of care in looking out for themselves. Failure to do so, combined with the negligence of another, which results in an injury, prevents either party from recovering for their injuries. Thus, recovery for negligence is barred by the defense of **contributory negligence.** Each party has been negligent, and their combined negligence has contributed to cause the injury. When one party sues the other in tort for damages for negligence, the defendant can claim contributory negligence, which is a complete defense under common law rules. (Contributory negligence is not, however, a defense to intentional torts or to suits based on strict liability, a topic that will be covered later.)

There is a trend toward narrowing the scope of the defense of contributory neglience. Instead of allowing contributory negligence to negate a cause of action *completely,* an increasing number of states allow recovery based on the doctrine of **comparative negligence.**[6] Comparative negligence is the proportional sharing between the plaintiff and the defendant of compensation for injuries based on the relative negligence of the two. In jurisdictions that follow the contributory negligence doctrine, negligence on the part of the plaintiff will bar any recovery of damages. In comparative negligence jurisdictions, however, the plaintiff will be able to recover the percentage of damages that was due to the defendant's negligence.

If a person has a last chance to avoid injury and could have avoided it by doing what a reasonable person in the circumstances would have done, many jurisdictions will deny recovery to the injured party. This is known as the doctrine of *last clear chance.* There must be proof that the injured party discovered the situation and had the time to prevent the injury.

STRICT LIABILITY

The final category of torts is called **strict liability** or *liability without fault.* Intentional or negligent torts involve an act that departs from a reasonable standard of care and causes an injury. Under the theory of *strict liability,* liability for injury is imposed for reasons other than fault.

Abnormally Dangerous Activities

Strict liability for damages proximately caused by abnormally dangerous activities is one application of strict liability. Abnormally dangerous activities have three characteristics:

1. The activity involves potential harm of a serious nature.
2. The activity involves a high degree of risk that cannot be completely guarded against by reasonable care.
3. The activity is not commonly performed in the community or area.

Strict liability is applied because of the extreme risk of the activity. Although the activity is performed with all reasonable care, there is still a risk of injury. Balancing that risk against the potential for harm, it is fair to ask the person engaged in the activity to pay for injury caused. Although there is no fault, there is still responsibility because of the nature of the activity.

---

6. Comparative negligence has been adopted in about half the states.

BACKGROUND AND FACTS *The Yommers operated a grocery store and gasoline station. In December 1967, their neighbors, the McKenzies, noticed a smell in their well water, which proved to be caused by gasoline in the well water. McKenzie complained to the Yommers, who arranged to have one of their underground storage tanks replaced. Nevertheless, the McKenzies were unable to use their water for cooking or bathing until they had a filter and water softener installed. At the time of the trial*

YOMMER v. McKENZIE
Court of Appeals of Maryland, 1969.
255 Md. 220, 257 A.2d 138.

in December 1968, they were still bringing drinking water in from an outside source.

The McKenzies sued the Yommers for nuisance and recovered damages of $3,500. The Yommers appealed the verdict on the grounds that the McKenzies did not prove that there was any negligence.

SINGLEY, Judge.

* * *

The argument that the McKenzies must prove negligence in order to recover fails to take into account the doctrine of strict liability imposed by the rule of Rylands v. Fletcher which has been adopted by our prior decisions.

* * *

The black letter of new § 520 sets out the definition:

"520.   *Abnormally Dangerous Activities*

In determining whether an activity is abnormally dangerous, the following factors are to be considered:

(a)   Whether the activity involves a high degree of risk of some harm to the person, land or chattels of others;

(b)   Whether the gravity of the harm which may result from it is likely to be great;

(c)   Whether the risk cannot be eliminated by the exercise of reasonable care;

(d)   Whether the activity is not a matter of common usage;

(e)   Whether the activity is inappropriate to the place where it is carried on; and

(f)   The value of the activity to the community."

We believe that the present case is clearly within the ambit of this definition. Although the operation of a gasoline station does not of itself involve "a high degree of risk of some harm to the person, land or chattels of others," the placing of a large underground gasoline tank in close proximity to the appellees' residence and well does involve such a risk, since it is not a matter of common usage.* The harm caused to the appellees was a serious one, and it may well have been worse if the contamination had not been detected promptly.

Although there is no evidence of negligence on the part of the Yommers (indeed such a showing is not required as will be discussed below), it is proper to surmise that this risk cannot, or at least was not, eliminated by the exercise of reasonable care.

The fifth and perhaps most crucial factor under the Institute's guidelines as applied to this case is the appropriateness of the activity in the particular place where it is being carried on. No one would deny that gasoline stations as a rule do not present any particular danger to the community. However, when the operation

---

*   "An activity is a matter of common usage if it is customarily carried on by the great mass of mankind, or by many people in the community. * * * Gas and electricity in household pipes and wires [are examples of common usage], as contrasted with large gas storage tanks or high tension power lines." Restatement, Torts 2d, *supra*, comment on clause (d) at 65-66.

of such activity involves the placing of a large tank adjacent to a well from which a family must draw its water for drinking, bathing and laundry, at least that aspect of the activity is inappropriate to the locale, even when equated to the value of the activity.

* * *

We accept the test of appropriateness as the proper one: that the unusual, the excessive, the extravagant, the bizarre are likely to be non-natural uses which lead to strict liability.

* * *

It is apparent to us that the storage of large quantities of gasoline immediately adjacent to a private residence comes within this rule and relieved the McKenzies of the necessity of proving negligence. * * *

The Yommers' appeal was rejected. There was no need to prove negligence in the case because the nature of the activity and the location of the tank caused the Yommers to be held strictly liable for the gasoline seepage.

JUDGMENT AND REMEDY

Other Applications of Strict Liability

There are other applications of the strict liability principle, most notably in the workmen's compensation acts and in the area of products liability. Liability here is a matter of social policy, and it is based on two factors: (1) the ability of the employer and manufacturer to better bear the cost of injury by spreading it out to society through an increase in the cost of goods and services and (2) the fact that the employer and manufacturer are making a profit from their activities and therefore should bear the cost of injury as an operating expense. Products liability will be considered in depth in Chapter 21.

QUESTIONS AND CASE PROBLEMS

1. Fisher was standing in line waiting to be served at a buffet luncheon when a waiter grabbed a plate from his hand, shouting that Negroes could not be served in that restaurant. The waiter never struck Fisher; nor did he threaten to strike him. Given that the definition of a battery is "the intentional unprivileged touching of another," decide whether a battery has been committed. [Fisher v. Carrousel Motor Hotel, Inc., 424 S.W.2d 627 (Texas 1967)]

2. A local department store caught fire and was ransacked by a number of people. Jones was suspected of having taken a pair of shoes from the store during the fire. The next night, Smith, a police officer, and two deputies went to Jones's house and told him that he was under arrest. Smith did not have a warrant for Jones's arrest. At first, Jones refused to go, but later he agreed. Smith then told Jones that if he would agree to come to town voluntarily the next day, he would not have to go with the police that night. Jones promised to do this, and the next day he went into town but was never indicted (charged) for the crime. Can Jones recover from Smith for false arrest? [Martin v. Houck, 141 N.C. 317, 54 S.E. 291 (1906)]

3. Hodgeden purchased a stove from Hubbard's warehouse in Montpelier, Vermont. Hubbard was not in the store at the time of the purchase. Hodgeden gave Hubbard's clerk a promissory note for the stove payable in six months. When Hubbard learned of the purchase and of Hodgeden's irresponsibility about paying his debts, he started in pursuit of Hodgeden and overtook him about two miles outside of Mont-

pelier. Hodgeden refused at first to give back the stove, claiming that he had paid good money for it. Hubbard, who had brought an employee along with him, drew a knife, and his employee held Hodgeden back. Then Hubbard took the stove, put it into his own wagon and told his employee to let Hodgeden go. Hodgeden sued Hubbard for assault and battery. Hubbard claimed as a defense that since the goods were fraudulently purchased he could use such force as was necessary to recover them. Is he right? [Hodgeden v. Hubbard, 18 Vt. 504 (1846)]

4. Roger owned a large home in a residential area outside the city of New York. Roger's four children all left their toys scattered around the house, throughout the hallways, and on the stairways. On October 1, Steven, the youngest child, left his toy dump truck just inside the front door. Late that night, Dan the Man, a local cat burglar, gained entry into Roger's home by picking the lock on the front door. As Dan entered the home, he stepped on the cab of Steven's dump truck, slipped, fell, and suffered severe head injuries. Dan sued Roger. Can he recover?

5. a. A father who was an avid golfer left one of his golf clubs in the backyard behind his home. Later that day, his five-year-old son picked up the golf club and swung it, hitting a neighbor. Is the father liable for the injury sustained by the neighbor on the grounds of negligence? Was the son's act foreseeable? [Lubitz v. Wells, 19 Conn.Sup. 322, 113 A.2d 147 (1955)]

b. Another time, a father left a loaded gun alongside a fence at the edge of his yard. Later that day, a boy who lived in the neighborhood picked up the gun and fired it, injuring Jones. The boy who picked up the gun had not known that it was loaded. Is the father liable in this case? Was the injury foreseeable? [Sullivan v. Creed, 2 Ir. R. 317 (K.B. 1904)]

6. Gulf sold a drum of gasoline to Williams for use in Williams's farm tractor. When Williams attempted to open the drum, he found that the bung hole cap was stuck because the threads were in disrepair. When Williams attempted to loosen the cap by banging on it, he produced a spark that caused an explosion and a fire. When Williams sued Gulf, Gulf admitted that it knew that the threads in the bung cap were in a state of disrepair because the drum had been used for a number of years, and bung caps had always been replaced by repeated hammering. Gulf claimed, however, that it should not be held liable for the injury sustained by Williams because it was so unusual that it was not reasonably foreseeable. Is Gulf correct? [Gulf Refining Company v. Williams, 183 Miss. 723, 185 So. 234 (1938)]

7. Hank Johnson, a frozen food delivery man, was employed by Clarkson and Company. Bubba Clarkson was both president and general manager of the company. On Tuesday morning, Clarkson sent Johnson out on a regular run to a local grocery store about six miles from Clarkson's warehouse, instructing him to take the regular route to the grocery store, which was straight up Hwy. 1. Clarkson knew that Johnson's girlfriend lived just half a mile off Hwy. 1 along the route to the grocery store, and he told Johnson to go directly to the grocery store, to return directly, and not to engage in any "funny business" along the way. On his return trip, since he was running a little bit ahead of schedule, Johnson turned off Hwy. 1 to visit his girlfriend. About halfway there, he negligently struck a young boy who was in the middle of the road. Most courts today hold employers liable for the negligent acts of their employees if the acts are committed within the "scope of the employee's employment." Employers are generally not held liable if the employee has gone on a "frolic of his own." Is Clarkson liable for Johnson's misconduct?

8. On a Friday evening at about dusk, Butterfield was riding his horse at a "swift rate of speed" down the road. Shortly before this, Forrester, who was making some repairs to his home, laid a long pole partially across the road. Because of the speed at which he was riding, Butterfield did not see the pole. The horse collided with it, and Butterfield was thrown many feet from his horse and injured. At trial, evidence showed that the pole could be seen from approximately a hundred yards away at that time of night. The facts also showed that Butterfield would have seen the pole and could have avoided hitting it if he had been riding at a normal rate of speed. If the court finds that both Butterfield and Forrester were negligent, can Butterfield collect any damages at all? [Butterfield v. Forrester, 11 East 60, 103 Eng.Rep. 926, Huntsey (1809)]

9. Fletcher owned and operated a mill that needed a large reservoir of water to operate. Fletcher dug a large surface reservoir and filled it with water. A number of mines operated within the general area of the reservoir. Eventually, water started to leak through the ground into an underground mine shaft owned and operated by Rylands. Rylands sued Fletcher for the damage that Fletcher's reservoir had caused to Rylands's mining operation. Rylands, however, did not allege that Fletcher had been negligent in constructing or in operating his reservoir or mill. Can Rylands sue Fletcher without claiming that Fletcher has been negligent in any way? [Rylands v. Fletcher, L.R. 3 H.L. 330 (1868)]

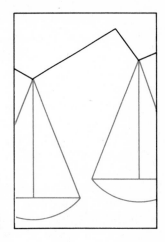

4

Criminal Law

Businesspeople are concerned with crimes for two reasons. First, businesses are often the target of criminals. The crimes of embezzlement, passing bad checks, shoplifting, and theft, for example, are costly for both businesses and consumers. Second, some criminal law applies directly to the activities of businesses and those who run them. For example, the Sherman Antitrust Act contains specific criminal sanctions. The Great Electrical Conspiracy of the 1960s resulted in several top officials from various electric companies serving time in jail for price fixing.

THE NATURE OF CRIME

Crimes are distinguished from other wrongful conduct in that they are offenses against society as a whole. Certain acts hurt not only the individual against whom they are committed but all other members of the community as well. For this reason, crimes are prosecuted by a public official and not by their victims.

In addition, criminals are punished. Tort remedies are generally intended to compensate the injured, but criminal law is directly concerned with punishing the wrongdoer. The act of punishment is intended to accomplish four aims:

1. Punishment is supposed to deter not only the wrongdoer in a particular instance but also all other members of society who might commit a similar wrong.

2. Punishment protects society by incapacitating the criminal through imprisonment.

3. Punishment serves as a substitute for private vengeance.

4. Punishment is supposed to rehabilitate criminals by showing them the error of their ways. Programs for treatment and education are part of the American penal system.

A final distinguishing factor is that the source of criminal law is primarily statutory. Both the acts that constitute crimes and the resulting punishments are formally set out in statutes. A **crime** can thus be defined as a wrong against society proclaimed in a statute and punishable by society if committed.

Classifications of Crimes

FELONIES AND MISDEMEANORS Crimes are classified as felonies or misdemeanors according to their seriousness. **Felonies** are more serious than misdemeanors and are punishable by death or by imprisonment in a federal or state penitentiary for more than a year. The definition of a felony derives from the common law crimes of arson, rape, grand larceny, and murder. Felonies can be divided into degrees of seriousness. The Model Penal Code, for example, provides for four degrees of felony: capital offenses where the maximum penalty is death, first degree felonies punishable by a maximum penalty of life imprisonment, second degree felonies punishable by a maximum of ten years imprisonment, and third degree felonies punishable by up to five years imprisonment. (It is important to note that these are maximum penalties. The actual sentence served can be less than the maximum.)

Misdemeanors are crimes punishable by a fine or by confinement for up to a year.[1] Misdemeanors are also sometimes defined as offenses where incarceration takes place in a local jail instead of in a penitentiary. In prac-

tice, the jail confinement is usually for no more than a year. Disorderly conduct and trespass are common misdemeanors. Some states have different classes of misdemeanors. For example, in Illinois there are Class A misdemeanors (confinement for up to a year), Class B (not more than six months), and Class C (not more than thirty days).

Whether a crime is a felony or a misdemeanor can determine whether the case is tried in a magistrate court or a general trial court.

Another kind of wrong is termed a petty offense and often is not classified as a crime. Petty offenses include traffic violations or violations of building codes. Even for petty offenses, a guilty party can be put in jail for a few days, or fined, or both.

MALA IN SE AND MALA PROHIBITA Crimes are also classified by whether they are inherently evil or wrong simply because the law says so. **Crimes *mala in se*** are immoral in themselves. Murder, arson, larceny, and any other acts involving moral turpitude are crimes *mala in se*. **Crimes *mala prohibita*** are acts that are wrong because they are prohibited by law, but they are not inherently evil. Parking in a no parking zone is an example. The distinction between the two types of crime is a very old one, but it can still be important today, especially where intent to harm is an element required for conviction.

Crimes *mala prohibita* change through time as laws change; and to a lesser extent, crimes *mala in se* change as social mores change. The fact that the definition of criminal conduct changes over time does not negate the continuity of criminal law. Virtually all societies have considered murder, theft, and treason as crimes, but the severity of the penalty and, indeed, the nature of the crime itself have varied. Today, in the United States, publishing criticism of the government does not constitute treason; but elsewhere in the world, it does.

FEDERAL AND STATE CRIMES Criminal law is primarily the province of the states, but the federal government also has a criminal code.

---

1. The Constitution prohibits sending to jail an offender who cannot pay a fine. Tate v. **Short,** 401 U.S. 395, 91 S.Ct. 668, 28 L.Ed.2d 130 (1971). Williams v. Illinois, 399 U.S. 235, 90 S.Ct. 2018, 26 L.Ed.2d 586 (1970).

Federal crimes relate to federal government functions or involve federal personnel or institutions. Counterfeiting, unlawful immigration, spying, robbing a federally insured bank, or assaulting a federal officer are examples of federal crimes. In other instances, the federal government can use its general regulatory powers to aid state law enforcement agencies in combating crimes that have a national impact. Transporation of stolen vehicles across state lines, kidnapping, and civil rights violations are areas that fall under federal criminal law.

CLASSIFICATION BY NATURE Crimes can be classified according to their nature. For example, there are crimes against property (theft, burglary, arson), crimes against the person (murder, assault, rape), and crimes against the government (perjury, bribery). These classifications are used to group crimes within a statutory code.

In addition, there are sociological classifications of crimes. These classifications may not have any legal consequence, but they are helpful in describing different types of crime. *Organized crime*, for example, is characterized by organization, continuity, a broad scope of operations, and the use of public corruption. It is involved in such activities as gambling, prostitution, labor rackets, and narcotics. In *victimless crime*, such as prostitution, gambling, and drug abuse, the participants consent to acts defined as criminal. They can also harm themselves, and their criminal acts can lead them to commit crimes against unwilling victims. For example, an addict may have to steal to support a habit. *White collar crime* refers to crimes committed in the course of business by employees (white collar workers). It includes crimes committed for the benefit of the business, such as price fixing, and crimes committed against the business, such as embezzlement.

THE ESSENTIALS OF CRIMINAL LIABILITY

Three elements are necessary for a person to be convicted of a crime: (1) the performance of a prohibited act, (2) a specified state of mind or intent on the part of the actor, and (3) the absence of circumstances that the law recognizes as excusing actions that would otherwise be criminal.

Prohibited Acts

Every criminal statute prohibits certain behavior, called the *actus reus*, or guilty act. Most crimes require an act of commission; that is, the criminal must do something. In some cases an act of omission can be a crime, but only if what is omitted is a legal duty. Failure to file a tax return is an example of an omission that is a crime.

The *guilty act* requirement is based on one of the premises of criminal law—that a person is punished for *harm done* to society. Thinking about killing someone or about stealing a car may be wrong, but these thoughts do no harm in themselves until they are translated into action. Of course, a person can be punished for attempting murder or robbery, but only if substantial steps toward the criminal objective have been taken.

Completion of the act will not complete the crime, however. A court must also find that the required state of mind was present.

State of Mind

In addition to the act, there is also a mental element called the *mens rea*, or evil intent, required for criminal liability. Without a wrongful mental element, the actor is not truly guilty. Both the *actus reus* and the *mens rea* vary from crime to crime. Thus, for murder, the *actus reus* is the taking of a life, and the *mens rea* is the intent to take life. For theft, the *actus reus* is the taking of another person's property, and the *mens rea* involves both the knowledge that the property belongs to another and the intent to deprive the owner of it. Without the mental state required by law, there can be no crime.

The *mens rea*, or mental state, in which a particular act is committed can vary in the degree of its wrongfulness. The same act— shooting someone—can be committed with varying mental states. It can be done coldly after premeditation. It can be done in the heat of passion or can be the result of negligence. In each of these situations, the law recognizes a different degree of wrongfulness, and the punishment varies accordingly.

The Model Penal Code recognizes four categories of *mens rea*: (1) purpose or intent, (2) knowledge (both formerly covered under the term *specific intent*), (3) recklessness, and (4) negligence (both formerly covered by the term *general intent*).

DEFENSES TO CRIMINAL LIABILITY

The law recognizes certain conditions that will relieve a defendant of criminal liability. These conditions are called defenses, and the most important of them are infancy, intoxication, insanity, mistake, consent, duress, entrapment, statute of limitations, and justifiable use of force. A criminal defendant can also gain immunity from prosecution.

Infancy

In the common law, children up to seven years of age were considered incapable of committing a crime because they did not have the moral sense to understand that they were doing wrong. Children between the ages of seven and fourteen were presumed to be incapable of committing a crime, but this presumption could be rebutted by showing that the child understood the wrongful nature of the act. Today, states vary in their approaches, but all retain the defense of infancy as a bar to criminal liability. Most states retain the common law approach, although age limits vary from state to state. Other states have rejected the rebuttable pre-

sumption and simply have a minimum age required for criminal responsibility. All states have juvenile court systems that handle children below the age of criminal responsibility who commit crimes. Their aim is reform rather than punishment. In states that retain the rebuttable presumption approach, children who are beyond the minimum age but are still juveniles can be turned over to the criminal courts if the juvenile court judges that they should be treated as adults.

Intoxication

The law recognizes two types of intoxication, whether from drugs or from alcohol: voluntary and involuntary. Involuntary intoxication occurs when a person is either physically forced to inject an intoxicating substance or is unaware that a substance contains drugs or alcohol. Involuntary intoxication is a defense to crime if its effect was to make a person either incapable of understanding that the act committed was wrong or incapable of obeying the law.

Voluntary intoxication is a defense where intoxication precludes having the required *mens rea*. Thus, if Johnson shoots Peters while too drunk to know what she is doing, she cannot be convicted of *murder* because she did not have the required intent to kill when she shot Peters. Voluntary intoxication, however, does not serve as a defense for crimes requiring recklessness or negligence. The law requires that people be aware that intoxication can make it impossible to behave as a reasonable person. Therefore, becoming intoxicated and committing a reckless or negligent act is a crime. In the example above, Johnson could be convicted of *manslaughter*.

STATE v. WHITE
Supreme Court of
South Dakota, 1978.
269 N.W.2d 781.

BACKGROUND AND FACTS   *The defendant, White, was convicted of burglary. He contended, among other things, that he had been drinking heavily the night of the alleged burglary, that he had fallen asleep, and that he had no recollection of the event occurring. In short, he claimed that voluntary intoxication precluded him from forming the specific intent needed to commit burglary. The jury concluded that White was guilty. In reviewing the conviction, the appellate court addressed the issue of whether the evidence sustained a rational theory of guilt.*

PORTER, Justice.

* * *

The totality of this evidence is sufficient to support the verdict. It was not necessary for the State to prove precisely how defendant participated. Since a rational hypothesis of guilt is supported by this evidence, the conviction must be affirmed.

The State's evidence tended to show a joint effort in committing the burglary. The amount of activity at the burglary scene permits an inference that several persons participated. The fact that defendant and his party fled the scene before the first officers arrived (abandoning the tape player, and some of the beer) together with the fact that the burglars inside could not see toward Sisseton, supports an inference that one or more lookouts participated. It was shown that the occupants of the car were closely associated with each other. Defendant admitted that he had been with the occupants of his car for several hours before the burglary. He was found sitting in the front seat and his brother was in the driver's seat.

The evidence also points to defendant's individual participation in the crime. Keys and change from the burglarized property were found in the snow where defendant and German were subdued. Although an officer involved thought the keys probably came from German, the jury could have reasonably found otherwise. The car used in the crime was owned by defendant. Beer found in the trunk of that automobile was of the same type as that missing from the Pub. Finally, defendant resisted violently when he was arrested. This allows an inference that defendant was aware of his implication since ordinarily one being extricated from a car stuck in a snowbank in midwinter would have no reason to resist, particularly since he recognized the officers as police.

Defendant's explanation was that he had drunk large quantities of intoxicants and had passed out before the burglary. Defendant asserts that this version is "uncontroverted" and shows that he neither participated in the crime nor had the requisite specific intent to aid in the commission thereof. We have already concluded, however, that the State's evidence was sufficient to prove at least aiding and abetting.

Upon the issue of whether a specific intent to aid or abet had been proven beyond a reasonable doubt, the jury was properly instructed that they could consider whether from the evidence defendant was unable to form a specific intent because of his claimed state of intoxication. It was for the jury to weigh the circumstantial evidence as against defendant's testimony. The jury saw and heard all the witnesses and the issue of witness credibility, including a defendant's credibility is peculiarly within the jury's province in a trial by jury.

Defendant also argues that since only three sets of footprints were found leaving the Pub, not more than three persons participated in the burglary. However, the State presented evidence from which the jury could reasonably infer the need for one or more lookouts. Most importantly, the jury could find that defendant aided and abetted by permitting use of his car in the burglary. Because of the remote location of the Pub and the severe winter weather, the vehicle was practically indispensable to the carrying out of the burglary.

*The conviction was upheld because the appellate court found reasonable support for the jury's finding that White had committed the burglary or at least **had aided and abetted** in committing it.*

JUDGMENT AND REMEDY

Insanity

Just as a child is judged incapable of the state of mind required to commit a crime, so also is someone suffering from mental illness. Thus, insanity is a defense to a criminal charge. The law has had difficulty deciding what the test for legal insanity should be, and psychiatrists are critical of the tests used. Almost all federal courts and some states use the standard in the Model Penal Code:

A person is not responsible for criminal conduct if at the time of such conduct as a result of mental disease or defect he lacks substantial capacity either to appreciate the wrongfulness of his conduct or to conform his conduct to the requirements of the law.

Other states use the M'Naghten test, which excuses a criminal act if a mental defect makes a person incapable of appreciating the nature of the act or incapable of knowing that it was wrong. Some states that follow the M'Naghten rule have also adopted the irresistible impulse test. A person operating under an irresistible impulse may know that an act is wrong but may still be unable to keep from doing it. Even if a mental illness is not grave enough to serve as a complete defense, it may render a person legally incapable of certain crimes if the illness precludes the possibility of the required *mens rea*.

Mistakes

Everyone has heard the saying "ignorance of the law is no excuse." It may seem harsh to presume that everyone knows or should know the law, but imagine what the result of a different rule would be. Ordinarily, ignorance of the law or a mistake about what the law requires is not a valid defense. In some states, however, that rule has been modified. A person who claims that he or she honestly did not know that a law was being broken may have a valid defense if: (1) the law was not published or reasonably made known to the public or (2) the person relied on an official statement of the law that was erroneous. An official statement is a statute, judicial opinion, administrative order, or statement by someone responsible for administering, interpreting, or enforcing the law. Statements in newspapers or textbooks are not official statements.

A mistake of fact, as opposed to a mistake of law, will operate as a defense if it negates the required *mens rea*. If, for example, John Jones mistakenly drives off in Mary Thompson's car because he thinks that it is his, there is no theft. Theft requires knowledge that the property belongs to another.

Consent

What if a victim consents to a crime or even encourages a criminal to commit it? The law will allow consent as a defense if the consent cancels the harm that the law is designed to prevent. In each case, the question is whether the law forbids an act against the victim's will or forbids the act without regard to the victim's wish. The law forbids murder, prostitution, and drug use whether the victim consents to it or not. Consent operates as a defense most successfully in crimes against property since one can always give away one's property. Of course, if the act operates to harm a third person who has not consented, there will be no escape from criminal liability. Consent or forgiveness given after a crime has been committed is not really a defense, though it can affect the likelihood of prosecution.

Duress

A person who is asked or instructed to commit a crime is not excused from criminal liability, but committing a crime under duress is a valid defense. The courts use a number of requirements to measure duress. First, the threat must be of serious bodily harm or death. A person who was threatened with failing a course or losing a job cannot plead duress as a defense. Second, the harm that is threatened must be greater than the harm that will be caused by the crime. A threat to shoot a woman's husband unless she robs a bank would be sufficient; a threat to hit her over the head would not be. The third requirement is that the threat must be immediate and inescapable. Finally, people who plead duress as a defense must have gotten into the situation through no fault of their own. If, for example, a person committing a burglary forces an accomplice to kill someone, the accomplice cannot use duress as an excuse. Participating in the burglary in the first place carries with it the possibility of being forced to commit a greater crime. The situation is the accomplice's fault.

The threat in a duress defense can be to the person under duress or to someone close to him or her, like a spouse. One crime that cannot be excused by duress is murder. It is difficult to justify taking a life even if the threat is to one's own life.

Justifiable Use of Force

Probably the most well-known defense to criminal liability is self-defense. But there are other situations that justify the use of force: the defense of one's dwelling, the defense of other property, and the prevention of a crime. In all of these situations, it is important to distinguish between the use of deadly and nondeadly force. Deadly force is likely to result in death or serious bodily harm. Nondeadly force is force that reasonably appears necessary to protect against the imminent use of criminal force.

Generally speaking, persons can use the amount of nondeadly force that seems necessary to protect themselves or their dwelling or other property or to prevent the commission of a crime. Deadly force can be used in self-defense if there is a reasonable belief that imminent death or grievious bodily harm will otherwise result, if the attacker is using unlawful force (e. g., not a police officer), and if the person has not initiated or provoked the attack. Deadly force can be used to defend a dwelling only if the unlawful entry is violent, and the person believes that deadly force is necessary to prevent imminent death, great bodily harm, or, in some jurisdictions, the person believes deadly force is necessary to prevent commission of a felony in the dwelling.

In defense of other property, the use of nondeadly force is justified to prevent or end the criminal's attempt to take away or otherwise interfere with the property. Deadly force usually is justifiable only when used in self-defense.

Force reasonably necessary to prevent a serious crime is permissible, but in the modern view, deadly force can be used to prevent only crimes that involve a substantial risk of death or great bodily harm.

Entrapment

Entrapment is a defense designed to prevent the police or other government agents from encouraging criminal acts in order to apprehend criminals. In the typical entrapment case, an undercover agent suggests that a crime be committed and somehow pressures or induces an individual to commit it. The agent then arrests the individual for the crime. Both the suggestion and the inducement must take place. The defense is not intended to prevent the police from setting a trap for an unwary criminal. It is intended to prevent them from pushing the criminal into it. The crucial issue is whether a criminal was predisposed to commit the crime or committed the crime because the agent induced it. This is often a question of fact.

BACKGROUND AND FACTS   *This case involves a cocaine transaction that ultimately led to the defendant's conviction for selling the narcotic to a paid government informer. The informer initiated a relationship with the defendant, who supplied the informer with narcotics. The informer encouraged the defendant to supply a quantity of cocaine to an out-of-town buyer. Ultimately, the defendant agreed to meet the buyer*

UNITED STATES v. BOWER
United States Court of Appeals, Fifth Circuit, 1978.
575 F.2d 499.

*and make the exchange. The buyer was a Drug Enforcement Adminis-
tration (DEA) agent posing as a buyer. The agent met with the defendant
at the defendant's apartment. After the defendant delivered the cocaine
to the agent, the agent arrested him. The defendant was subsequently
found guilty on various charges, including possession and distribution of
cocaine. The defendant claimed entrapment on the part of the government officials.*

RONEY, Circuit Judge.

* * *

Entrapment

Defendant contends the evidence established an entrapment as a matter of law. In
support of this claim, defendant relies primarily on his own trial testimony that he
had agreed to participate in the criminal enterprise in a moment of extreme
depression. Defendant had recently turned 30 and, reflecting upon an uneventful
past and contemplating a similar future, had decided to return to college and
finish his education. Unfortunately, a year of voluntary unemployment had so
depleted his personal finances that he could not return to school without working
at least part time. Having hoped to be able to focus his undivided attention on his
studies, defendant began to recognize Clegg's proposals as an opportunity to
finance his schooling. His depression at this time was heightened by the fact that
he and his girlfriend had recently severed their long-standing relationship.
Consequently, although he had repeatedly rejected Clegg's earlier entreaties, he
could no longer resist the temptation of the promised "exorbitant gains" to be
reaped from a single cocaine sale.

Since Clegg did not testify at trial, defendant's account of Clegg's repeated
attempts to persuade defendant to procure narcotics is uncontradicted. The record
nevertheless contains evidence weighing against the contention that defendant
was "an innocent seduced by a government agent." Defendant admitted that he
saw the sale as a source of "easy money" and that he expected to make a $1,000
profit on the transaction. He purchased the cocaine from a nongovernment source
who trusted defendant enough to defer payment until defendant had resold the
drug. Indeed, while negotiating the actual exchange, defendant assured DEA
agent Sylvestri that he could handle Sylvestri's future cocaine needs if the
amounts were not too large. Both agent Sylvestri and defendant testified that
during the transaction, defendant received a telephone call from his source.
Defendant interrupted his telephone conversation to ask Sylvestri if he was
interested in buying another four ounces of cocaine. When the DEA agent
expressed interest, defendant requested his source "not to lock up the other four"
and offered to produce the additional cocaine for Sylvestri in 30 minutes.

On this evidence, the trial court did not err in submitting the entrapment issue
to the jury. The crucial issue in entrapment cases is whether the defendant was
predisposed to commit the crime. The Government's provision of aid, incentive,
and opportunity for commission of the crime amounts to an entrapment only if it
appears that the defendant has done that which he would never have done were it
not for the inducement of Government operatives. Although the record contains

evidence upon which a jury might conclude that defendant was induced by a Government informer to commit a crime that he was not otherwise predisposed to commit, the evidence was not "so overwhelming that it was 'patently clear' or 'obvious' that [defendant] was entrapped as a matter of law".

The appellate court affirmed the defendant's conviction. A defense of entrapment was not permitted because the defendant was already predisposed to committing the crime.   JUDGMENT AND REMEDY

Statute of Limitations

An individual can be excused from criminal liability by a statute of limitations. Such statutes provide that the state has only a certain amount of time to prosecute a crime. If it does not do so within the allotted time, it has lost its opportunity, and the suspect is free from prosecution. The idea behind these statutes is that people should not have to live under the threat of criminal prosecution indefinitely. Also, if prosecution is delayed for too long, it becomes difficult to find out what the truth is because witnesses die or disappear and evidence is destroyed.

Time limits vary from state to state. Felonies usually have a longer time period than misdemeanors, and there is no time limitation placed on murder. For all other crimes, the time limit runs from the time the crime is committed, unless it is a crime that is difficult to discover. In those cases, the time begins to run when the crime is discovered. A time limitation will be suspended, however, if the suspect leaves the state or hides. Normally, statutes will provide for subtraction of time if the suspect cannot be found or is not available to stand trial.

Immunity

At times, the state may wish to obtain information from a criminal. Criminals, of course, have an absolute right against self-incrimination and are understandably reluctant to give information if it will be used to prosecute them. In these cases, the state can grant immunity from prosecution or agree to prosecute for a less serious offense in exchange for the information.

CRIMINAL PROCEDURE

Our criminal justice system operates on the premise that it is far worse for an innocent person to be punished than for a guilty person to go free. A person is innocent until proven guilty, and guilt must be proven beyond a reasonable doubt. The procedure of the criminal law system is designed to protect the rights of the individual and preserve the presumption of innocence.

Constitutional Safeguards

Criminal law brings the weighty force of the state, with all its resources, to bear against the individual. Recognizing this fact, the Founding Fathers provided specific safeguards for the accused criminal in the Constitution. The Supreme Court has ruled that most of these safeguards apply not only in federal but also in state courts by virtue of the due process clause of the Fourteenth Amendment. The safeguards include:

1.   Fourth Amendment protection from unreasonable searches and seizures.
2.   Fourth Amendment requirement that no warrants for a search or an arrest can be issued without probable cause.
3.   Fifth Amendment requirement that no one can be deprived of "life, liberty, or property without due process of law."
4.   Fifth Amendment prohibition of double jeopardy, or trying someone twice for the same offense.
5.   Sixth Amendment guarantees of a speedy

trial, by jury, a public trial, the right to confront witnesses, and the right to a lawyer.

6. Eighth Amendment prohibitions against excessive bails and fines and cruel and unusual punishment.

In recent years, the Supreme Court has been active in interpreting these rights. Some of the cases are widely known. The *Miranda* decision, for example, established the rule that individuals who are arrested must be informed of their right to remain silent, of the fact that anything they say can be used against them in court, of their right to have a lawyer present, and of the duty of the state to provide lawyers if individuals cannot pay for them.[2]

Criminal Process

A criminal prosecution differs significantly from a civil case in several respects. These differences reflect the desire to safeguard the rights of the individual against the state.

ARREST Before a warrant for arrest can be issued, there must be a finding that there is probable cause to believe that the individual has committed a crime. **Probable cause** can be defined as a substantial likelihood that the individual has committed or is about to commit a crime. Note that probable cause involves a likelihood, not just a possibility. Arrests are sometimes made without a warrant when there is no time to get one, but the action of the arresting officer is still judged by the standard of probable cause.

INDICTMENT Individuals must be formally charged with specific crimes before they can be brought to trial. This is called an **indictment** if issued by a grand jury and an **information** if issued by a magistrate. Before a charge can be issued, the grand jury or the magistrate must determine that there is sufficient evidence to justify bringing the individual to trial. The

2. Miranda v. Arizona, 384 U.S. 436, 86 S.Ct. 1602 (1966).

standard used to make the judgment varies in different jurisdictions. Some courts use the probable cause standard. Others use the preponderance of evidence standard, which is a belief based on evidence provided by both sides that it is more likely than not that the individual committed the crime. Still another standard is the *prima facie* case standard, which is a belief based only on prosecution evidence that the individual is clearly guilty.

TRIAL At the trial, the accused criminal does not have to prove anything. The entire burden of proof is on the prosecution (the state). Guilt is judged on the basis of the **reasonable doubt** test. The prosecution must show that, based on all the evidence, the defendant's guilt is established beyond all reasonable doubt. Note that a verdict of not guilty is not the same as a statement that the defendant is innocent. It merely means that there is not enough evidence to prove guilt beyond all reasonable doubt.

CRIMES INVOLVING AND AFFECTING BUSINESS

Forgery

The fraudulent marking or alteration of any writing that changes the legal liability of another is **forgery**. If Smith signs Brown's name to the back of a check made out to Brown, Smith has committed forgery. Forgery also includes changing trademarks, falsifying public records, counterfeiting, and, in fact, the alteration of any legal document.

Most states have a special statute, often called a *credit card statute*, to cover the illegal use of credit cards. Thus, the prosecuting attorney can prosecute a person who misuses a credit card for violating either the forgery statute or the special credit card statute.

Robbery

At common law, **robbery** is defined as forcefully and unlawfully taking personal property of any value from another. The use of force or fear is usually necessary for an act of theft to be considered a robbery. Thus, pickpocketing is not robbery because the action is unknown to the victim. Typically, states have more severe penalties for *aggravated* robbery—robbery by use of a deadly weapon.

Burglary

The common law defines **burglary** as breaking and entering a dwelling at night with the intent to commit a felony. Originally, the offense was aimed at protecting a person's home and its occupants. Most state statutes have eliminated the requirements of the common law definition. Thus, the time at which the breaking and entering occurs is usually immaterial, state statutes frequently omit the element of breaking, and some states do not require that the building be a dwelling. Aggravated burglary, which is defined as burglary with the use of a deadly weapon, or burglary of a dwelling or both incurs a greater penalty.

Larceny

The wrongful or fraudulent taking and carrying away by any person of the personal property of another is **larceny**. It includes the fraudulent intent to permanently deprive an owner of property. Many business-related crimes entail fraudulent conduct.

The place from which physical property is taken is generally immaterial. However, statutes usually prescribe a stiffer sentence for property taken from buildings such as banks or warehouses. Larceny is differentiated from robbery by the fact that the latter involves force or fear. Therefore, pickpocketing is larceny, not robbery.

DISTINGUISHING BETWEEN GRAND AND PETIT LARCENY

The common law distinction between grand and petit larceny depends on the value of the property taken. Many states have abolished this distinction, but in those that

have not, grand larceny is a felony and petit larceny a misdemeanor.

WHAT CONSTITUTES PROPERTY?

As society has grown more complex, the definition of the property that is subject to statutes of larceny has been expanded. Stealing computer programs now constitutes larceny, even though they consist of magnetic impulses. Trade secrets can be subject to larceny statutes. Stealing the use of telephone wires by the device known as a "blue box" is subject to larceny statutes. So, too, is the theft of natural gas.

Embezzlement

The fraudulent conversion of property or money owned by one person but entrusted to another is **embezzlement**. Typically, it involves an employee who fraudulently appropriates money. Banks face this problem, and so do a number of businesses in which corporate officers or accountants "jimmy" the books to cover up the fraudulent conversion of money for their own benefit. Embezzlement is not a larceny because the wrongdoer does not physically take the property from the possession of another, and it is not a robbery because there is no taking by use of force or fear.

It does not matter whether the accused takes the money from the victim or from a third person. If, as the comptroller of a large corporation, Saunders pockets a certain number of checks from third parties that were given to her to deposit into the account of another company, Saunders has committed embezzlement.

MISAPPLICATION OF TRUST FUNDS

Often the owner of property will remit money to a contractor specifically for the contractor to pay various persons who worked on the owner's building. The contractor who does not use the money for this purpose commits a special form of embezzlement called misapplication of trust funds. The funds were entrusted to the contractor for a specific purpose and that trust has been violated. The fact that the accused intended to return the embezzled property does not constitute a sufficient defense. Practically speaking, though, an embezzler who returns what has been taken will not ordinarily be prosecuted because the owner usually will not testify.

Some states have laws with both a civil and a criminal side, and a person can be prosecuted for both the civil and the criminal violation. In the following case, a state has a criminal statute covering the crime of theft by a contractor and a civil statute governing the offense of theft by fraud. These two statutes prohibit the same behavior. The only difference between them is that the criminal action required the element of wrongful intent.

STATE v. WOLTER
Court of Appeals of Wisconsin,
1978.
85 Wis.2d 353, 270 N.W.2d 230.

BACKGROUND AND FACTS *The defendant, Wolter, appealed his conviction for improper use and misappropriation of money. Wolter and his wife were the sole owners and stockholders of Warjo Construction Company. Wolter was also its chief operating officer. The company was primarily engaged in purchasing and developing land, arranging for financing the construction of various units, acting as general contractor, and selling units upon completion. Wolter, as the owner and prime contractor and as the trustee of construction mortgage funds, did not use these funds to pay for the material and labor supplied by subcontractors and materials suppliers on a construction project. His action constituted the civil offense of theft by contractor under state law. Wolter refused to deliver any money, and, according to a similar criminal statute in the state code, his refusal to pay these trust monies upon demand to those entitled to receive them was prima facie evidence of a criminal intent to convert the money for his own personal use. At the time the lawsuit was brought, some money remained in the corporate account, but it was not nearly enough to complete the construction project.*

Wolter attempted to convince the appellate court that he should not have been prosecuted under the criminal statute for theft by a contractor but instead should have been prosecuted under the civil statute.

MOSER, Judge.
* * *

[There] is a criminal statute, creating the crime of theft by contractor * * * [which] also creates civil liability. The two statutes are *in pari materia* and should be read and harmonized where it is possible to do so. It is the duty of the court to construe these statutes, making both operative.

Aside from the differing burdens of proof in the civil and criminal actions for theft by contract, the only difference between them is the additional element of wrongful intent required in the criminal action.

Wolter argues that since he is an owner/prime contractor, [the criminal statute] is inapplicable to him. He asserts that as the owner described in that section of the statute he cannot steal from himself. He concludes that the only remedy against an owner/prime contractor is the civil remedy. * * *

The failure of this argument is that * * * [the criminal, not the civil statute] creates the crime of theft by contract. [The civil statute] is only the conduit through which the crime of theft by contract becomes operative. * * * These statutes must be harmonized.

Mortgage money was given by Heritage to Wolter, as prime contractor and president of Warjo, only for improvements to the Granville land to pay for labor and materials until all claims were paid. The trial record unequivocally demonstrates that the Heritage mortgage money was used for other corporate purposes, such as office rent, utilities, salaries, interest due on other corporate obligations and real estate taxes on other corporate properties. The jury found that $65,200 in claims for materials and labor were outstanding at the time of trial. * * * The use of the Heritage mortgage funds by Wolter, the president of Warjo and the owner/prime contractor, for any other purpose until all claims for materials and labor had been paid is theft by contractor.

No * * * vagueness exists in [the criminal statute], which creates the crime of theft by contract as it gives fair notice and proper standards for adjudication. It is clear notice to any citizen of this proscribed crime of theft by fraud. This statute can be easily harmonized with [its civil counterpart] as the conduit through which the criminal sanctions * * * are operative. Wolter, the owner/prime contractor, is a trustee of the Heritage construction mortgage funds owed to material and labor suppliers. [His use of funds for any other purpose than paying all outstanding claims for materials and labor is theft by the contractor.]

Wolter's next assignment of error is that he as "owner" of the land cannot be equated with [a] "trustee" * * * who intentionally uses, conceals, or retains possession of money without the "owner's" consent contrary to his authority, and with intent to convert to his own use. The "trust" herein is money paid by the mortgagee, Heritage, to Wolter (Warjo), to be used only in payment of material and labor claims on the Granville project. [The criminal statute] establishes the test not only for the protection of the owner but also for the protection of materialmen and labor suppliers. Here Wolter never paid the material or labor suppliers named in the criminal complaint and used the mortgage proceeds for other corporate purposes in violation of the criminal [statute which is] punishable under [the civil statute]. The parties protected by this statute are the mortgagee, the owner, and the material and labor suppliers. Any or all of these parties can seek the criminal sanctions of the statute. In this case it was the mortgagee and the material and labor suppliers.

Wolter was found both criminally and civilly liable for the crime of theft by a contractor. The civil and criminal statutes were construed together, and penalties were applied under both statutes.

JUDGMENT AND REMEDY

The constitutional protections applicable in criminal prosecutions do not apply equally to civil matters. For example, the warnings required under Miranda *have been deemed inapplicable to civil commitments.[3]*

COMMENTS

3. See, for example, Commonwealth v. Gomes, 355 Mass. 479, 245 N.E.2d 429 (1969).

Arson

The willful and malicious burning of a building (and in some states personal property) owned by another is the crime of **arson**. At common law, arson applied only to burning down the dwelling house of another. Such law was designed to protect human life. Today, arson statutes apply to other kinds of buildings. Also, if someone is killed as a result of an arson fire, the act is murder by the application of the murder-felony rule. This rule states that any killing that is committed in the course of a dangerous felony is a first degree murder, whether it is intentional or not.

BURNING TO DEFRAUD INSURERS Every state has a special statute that covers burning a building in order to collect insurance. If Allison owns an apartment building that is falling apart and pays someone else to set fire to it, Allison is guilty of burning to defraud insurers.

Obtaining Goods by False Pretenses

It is a criminal act to obtain goods by means of false pretenses—for example, buying groceries with a check, knowing that there are insufficient funds to cover it. Statutes covering such illegal activities vary widely from state to state.

Receiving Stolen Goods

It is a crime to receive stolen goods when there is knowledge of that fact and there is intent to deprive the owner of those goods. It does not matter that a third party has presented the goods to the ultimate possessor. Moreover, it does not matter whether the ultimate receiver knows the true identity of the owner or the thief.

Use of the Mails to Defraud

It is a federal criminal act to use the mails to defraud the public. Illegal use of the mails must involve (1) mailing or causing someone else to mail a writing for the purpose of executing a scheme to defraud and (2) a contemplated or organized scheme to defraud by false pretenses. If, for example, Johnson advertises the sale of a cure for cancer that he knows to be fraudulent because it has no medical validity, he can be prosecuted for fraudulent use of the mails. Federal law also makes it a crime to use a telegram to defraud.

False Measures, Labels, and Weights

Numerous federal and state regulations have been adopted to prevent and prosecute those who cheat, defraud, or mislead the public by using false labels, false measures, or false weights.

Lotteries

In general, lotteries are illegal even if they appear to be a legitimate form of business or advertising or are called by some other name. There are three necessary elements for a lottery to exist: a prize, a lot by chance, and payment of something of value in order to have the opportunity to win. Often, contest advertisements will say that participants can send in either a box top (or label) or a facsimile. This keeps the contest from being a lottery because contestants can enter without paying anything.

Some Specialized Crimes

The list of specialized crimes is very long indeed. It includes (1) misrepresentation, which is defined as failing to disclose knowledge of the commission of a felony; (2) subornation of perjury, which is defined as inducing or knowingly permitting another to commit perjury; and (3) false pretenses, which is the obtaining of the title to the personal property of another by an intentional false statement of past or existing fact with intent to defraud the other.

Other Crimes Affecting Businesses

The list of crimes affecting businesses could be extended for many pages. It includes swindles and confidence games, counterfeiting, criminal libel, civil disorders, riots, the making of false credit statements, false advertising, and so on. Undoubtedly, the list will continue to grow as society continues to insist on greater protection in the marketplace.

Corporate Crimes

Corporations are "artificial" persons created by law. Clearly, they cannot harbor the criminal intent that is required for conviction of a crime, but their officers can. The modern tendency is to hold corporations criminally responsible for their acts or omissions if the penalty provided for is a fine and intent either is not an element of the crime or can be implied.

Obviously, a crime such as perjury cannot be committed by a corporation but can be committed by a natural person, such as an officer of the corporation. Furthermore, crimes punishable by imprisonment or corporal punishment cannot be committed by corporations. However, when a statute allows a fine in addition to, or in the place of, these penalties, a corporation can be convicted of that crime. If, for example, a statute requires that adequate safety equipment be installed on machines, and a corporation fails to do so—and if the result is the death of a worker—the corporation can be fined for committing criminal manslaughter. In addition, officers of the corporation can be jailed for their conduct.

QUESTIONS AND CASE PROBLEMS

1. Civil trials and criminal trials are conducted under essentially the same format. There are, however, several important differences. In criminal trials, the defendant must be proven guilty beyond all reasonable doubt, whereas in civil trials, the defendant need only be proven guilty by a preponderance of the evidence. Can you see any reason for this difference?

2. In a criminal trial, but not in a civil trial, the defendant has the right to remain silent. In both civil and criminal cases, the defendant has a right to a trial by jury; and in civil cases, the plaintiff has the same right. Can you see any reason for this?

3. Davis, who had been married for a number of years, suspected that his wife and a neighbor by the name of Noe were having an affair. In fact, the two had never been intimate, but Davis, acting under an insane delusion, murdered Noe. Even though Davis was under a delusion, the jury found that he was able to distinguish between right and wrong at the time he committed the murder. Can the defense of insanity be invoked when it has been sufficiently shown that Davis was acting under an insane delusion at the time he murdered Noe? [Davis v. State, 161 Tenn. 23, 28 S.W.2d 993 (1930)]

4. Faulkner was a seaman on the ship Zemindar. One night while on duty, Faulkner went in search of the rum that he knew the ship was carrying. He found it and opened one of the kegs, but because he was holding a match at the time, he inadvertently ignited the rum and set fire to the ship. Faulkner was criminally prosecuted for setting fire to the ship. At the trial, it was determined that even though he had not intended to set fire to the rum, he had been engaged in the unlawful act of stealing it. Does Faulkner's theft of the rum make him criminally liable for setting fire to the ship? [Regina v. Faulkner, 13 Cox C.C. 530 (Ireland 1877)]

5. In 1965, Rybicki failed to pay the complete amount of income tax he owed the federal government. Attempts by the IRS to collect the tax proved fruitless. Therefore, the IRS, through lawful means, obtained a tax lien on Rybicki's personal property, which included his truck. In October 1967, while sitting in his living room, Rybicki heard somebody slam the doors of his truck in the driveway. Rybicki went to his front door wielding a shotgun and told the two men who were attempting to take his truck that he would shoot them if they did not get off his property. Rybicki did know that the two men were IRS agents. Subsequently, the federal government indicted Rybicki for obstructing justice. Can Rybicki be held criminally liable when he did not know that he was obstructing justice? [United States v. Rybicki, 403 F.2d 599 (6th Cir. 1968)]

6. Pennsylvania makes it unlawful for any person or his or her agent to sell liquor to minors. This statute does not require that the sales be made knowingly, willfully, or intentionally. Koczwara, who owned a bar in Pennsylvania, was accused of having sold liquor to minors. Although Koczwara owned the bar, he had no knowledge of such sales; nor had he ever given his permission that liquor be sold to minors. Should Koczwara be held absolutely liable for the

acts of the bartenders he employed? [Commonwealth v. Koczwara 397 Pa. 575, 155 A.2d 825 (1959)]

7. Kanan was accused of writing several checks on an account that had been closed for over a month. It was unclear whether Kanan knew that his bank account had been closed, since his bank statements had never been delivered to him. In a criminal prosecution for passing bad checks, the judge instructed the jury that when a person writes checks, the law presumes that he knows whether his checking account has sufficient funds to cover the checks. Is this a proper instruction? [People v. Kanan, 186 Colo. 255, 526 P.2d 1339 (1974)]

8. For several years Horrocks had loaned money to May. With each loan, however, Horrocks had required May to seek his father's signature as a cosigner on the note. In October, May sought a further loan of $4,000 from Horrocks. As usual, Horrocks requested that May have his father cosign the note. That evening May cosigned his father's name without ever showing his father the note. The next day Horrocks loaned May the $4,000. Several years later, the state of Idaho indicted May for forging the note with the intent to defraud. The state contended that intent to defraud need not be specifically proven in this case but can be inferred from the fact that May had the forged note in his possession and passed it to Horrocks. Is this sufficient to prove intent to defraud? [State v. May, 93 Idaho 343, 461 P.2d 126 (1969)]

9. Monroe sold a certain quantity of croton oil to Horn. Horn in turn placed some of the oil in a piece of candy and gave it to Barrett, who ate the candy and suffered a physical injury. The state of North Carolina charged Monroe with criminal assault and battery. At trial Monroe admitted that he sold the oil to Horn and that he knew Horn's reputation for playing practical jokes. Was there adequate intent to commit an assault and battery on Monroe's part for him to be found guilty? [State v. Monroe, 121 N.C. 677, 28 S.E. 547 (1897)]

10. The state of Illinois prohibits the attempt to practice barbering without a license. Paluch, while in a barbershop one morning, invited Pinkston into the shop. Paluch then put on a barber smock, walked over to the barber chair, and asked Pinkston if he wanted to sit down. Paluch was unaware that Pinkston was a member of the local barber's union. When Pinkston demanded to see Paluch's license, Paluch at first refused but then admitted that he did not have one. Paluch was later tried for practicing barbering without a license. At the trial, in addition to the above facts, the state also proved that Paluch had possession of certain barber tools and a key to the barbershop into which he had invited Pinkston. Paluch denied that he had ever engaged in barbering and contended that he had never serviced Pinkston. Paluch further claimed that he had only prepared to serve Pinkston but had never completed any act that could be considered illegal. Is Paluch's contention valid? [People v. Paluch, Appellate Court of Illinois, 78 Ill.App.2d 356, 222 N.E.2d 508 (1966)]

11. Pivowar agreed to loan Mills approximately $10,000, and Mills agreed to repay the loan and further agreed that the loan would be secured by two houses that he owned. Mills showed Pivowar the two houses but falsely represented that Pivowar was to get a first mortgage on the houses. Pivowar later learned that the mortgages he held were not on the two houses but on two vacant lots and, further, that the mortgages were second mortgages and not first mortgages, as Mills had promised. Can Mills be prosecuted criminally for false pretenses if he contends that he intended to pay back the loan and that Pivowar never demanded payment on the note? [State v. Mills, 96 Ariz. 377, 396 P.2d 5 (1964)]

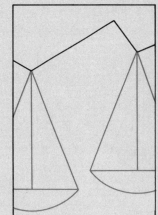

UNIT II

Contracts

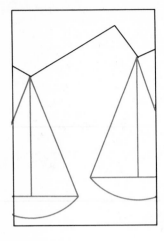

5 _____

Contracts
Nature, Form, and Terminology

SOME PERSPECTIVES

Contract law governs the relationships between people and those to whom they make promises. The use of similar concepts dates back thousands of years. Very early in history, the importance of contracts was clearly recognized, and they were given legal effect. That is, certain promises were enforced by the courts. The following chapters will explain how contracts are formed, how they are discharged, and what results when they are not performed. The laws and rules relating to the formation, discharge, and breach of legally enforceable promises are called "the law of contracts."

Society could make all promises binding, but it does not. The law of contracts establishes when they are binding and when they are not as well as the parties' remedies in case of breach.

Why do we need contracts? Countless commodities are regularly bought and sold by the use of contracts. People who rent apartments and open bank accounts all enter into contracts, even though the contracts are not all written or even explicit. In short, we could not order our daily activities without them.[1] They help us predict the future because they look to the future.

_____

1. The Soviet Union attempted to eliminate the need for contracts by dispensing with the private ordering of activities. The state required everyone to engage in certain specified activities—work, education, recreation—in the hope of redistributing wealth according to

The Function of Contracts

Contract law assures the parties to private agreements that the promises they make will be enforced. When a promise is kept, however, it is not necessarily because the **promisor** (the person making the promise) is conscious of the rules of contract law. People routinely keep social and business engagements because of a sense of duty and, perhaps more importantly, because it is to the mutual self-interest of the parties to go through with the deal and keep the goodwill of customers or suppliers. Nevertheless, the rules of contract law are often followed in an apparent attempt to avoid potential problems if and when a party does not live up to the promises.

Since contract law provides procedures for the enforcement of private agreements, it also provides an essential condition for the existence of a market economy. Without a framework for reasonably assured expectations within which to plan and venture, businesspersons would be able to rely only on the good faith of others. Duty and good faith are usually sufficient, but when price changes or adverse economic factors make it costly to comply with a promise, these elements are not enough. Contract law is necessary in order to assure compliance with a promise or to entitle the innocent party to some form of relief.

Contract law provides a foundation upon which more specialized areas of law are built. The sale of goods (Chapters 17 to 22); the transfer and negotiation of checks, notes, and drafts (Chapters 23 to 28); the giving of security in goods or land (Chapters 29 to 30); the rights of debtors and creditors (Chapter 31); the rights of agents, employees, and their employers (Chapters 33 to 35); the creation, operation, and termination of partnerships and corporations (Chapters 36 to 46); the regulation of trade and monopolies (Chapters 47 to 51); and the transfer of property (Chapters 52 and 55) all require a basic understanding of contract law.

Contract law underlies virtually all business relationships. Knowledge of it is essential to avoid costly mistakes. Additionally, studying contract law introduces the student to lawyers and how they think. Since businesspersons must often deal with lawyers, this understanding is of great practical value.

Freedom of Contract and Freedom from Contract

Contract law recognizes almost everyone's ability to enter freely into contractual arrangements. This recognition is called *freedom of contract,* and this freedom is protected by the U.S. Constitution in Article I, Section 10. As the character of institutions and society changes, however, the functions of contract law and its enforcement must also change. This change can be perceived today in the fact that not all agreements are valid and enforceable. For example, illegal bargains, agreements in restraint of trade, and "adhesion contracts" made by parties who have inordinate amounts of bargaining power are not enforced. In addition, certain contracts with consumers, as well as certain clauses within those contracts, are not enforceable. (See Chapter 10 for details.) Public policy, fairness, and justice do not allow these contracts to be enforced. The law of contracts is moving to place new controls on the manner of contracting and on the allowable terms of agreements. These controls are referred to as *freedom from contract,* and they serve to protect certain members of society from the contracts they make.

The Elements of a Contract

In order to comprehend the many topics that follow in this unit on contracts, an understanding of the basic requirements of a contract and the process by which it is created is needed. The

---

administrative standards and norms. The experiment failed, and Lenin explicitly recognized this when he wrote in 1921, "The private market proved to be stronger than we [thought]. * * * We ended up with ordinary * * * trade." Ultimately, contracts were reintroduced, and contract law was codified along traditional lines. See Loeber, "*Plan and Contract Performance in Soviet Law*", reprinted in LaFave, *Law in the Soviet Society,* Wayne R. LaFave, ed. Urbana, University of Illinois Press (1965).

following list is a brief description of the elements of a contract. The full explanations of these elements will come in later chapters.

1. **Agreement:** An agreement includes an offer and an acceptance. A party must offer to enter into a legal agreement, and another party must assent to the terms of the offer.
2. **Consideration:** Any promises made by the parties must be supported by legally sufficient consideration—something of legal value.
3. **Contractual capacity:** Both parties entering into the contract must have the contractual capacity to do so; they must be recognized by contract law to possess characteristics qualifying them as competent parties.
4. **Legality:** The contract must be made to accomplish some goal that is legal.
5. **Reality of assent:** Apparent consent of both of the parties must be genuine.
6. **Form:** The contract must be in whatever form the law requires.

NATURE AND TYPES OF CONTRACTS

In order for the detailed elements of a contract to be understood, certain terms and certain types of contracts must be defined. When reading the following chapters, refer to the definitions given in this chapter. This effort will reinforce the understanding of the language of contract law.

Definition of a Contract

A **contract** is simply any agreement that can be enforced in a court of law or equity. It is formed by two or more parties who agree to perform or refrain from performing some act.[2] Essentially, a contract is a promise that must be fulfilled. A promise is an undertaking either that something shall happen or that something shall not happen in the future. (Courts sometimes enforce

---

2. As defined by the American Law Institute, a contract is "a promise or a set of promises for the breach of which the law gives a remedy, or the performance of which the law in some way recognizes as a duty." Restatement, Second, Contracts (tentative draft), Section 1.

promises that are *not* contracts.) If the promise is not fulfilled, the party who made it is subject to the sanctions of a court of law or equity. The party may be required to pay money damages for failing to perform or may be required to perform the promised act.

TYPES OF CONTRACTS EXPLAINED

This section will explain the various types of contracts by comparing them to each other. They are: (1) express versus implied; (2) bilateral versus unilateral; (3) executed versus executory; (4) valid versus void, voidable, and unenforceable; and (5) formal versus informal contracts.

Express versus Implied Contracts

An **express contract** is one in which the terms of the agreement are fully and explicitly stated in words, oral or written. A signed lease for an apartment or house is an express written contract.[3] If a classmate calls you on the phone and agrees to buy your textbooks from last semester for $50, an express oral contract has been made.

A contract that is implied from the conduct of the parties is called an **implied-in-fact contract,** or an implied contract. Implied-in-fact contracts differ from express contracts in that the conduct of the parties, rather than their words, creates and defines the terms of the contract. For example, suppose you need a tax consultant or an accountant to fill out your tax return this year. You look through the phone book and find both an accountant and a tax consultant at an office in your neighborhood, so you drop by to see them. You go into the office and explain your problem; and they tell you what their fees are. The next day you return, leaving the secretary all of the necessary information such as cancelled checks, W-2 copies, and so on. You say nothing expressly to the secretary; rather, you walk out the door. Nonetheless, you have entered into an implied-in-fact contract to pay the tax consultant and accountant their usual and reasonable fees for

---

3. Leases historically were not contracts, although they are in most places today.

their services. The contract is implied from your conduct and from the tax preparers' conduct. They expect to be paid for helping you file your tax return, and by bringing in all of the necessary records that will allow them to do so, you *appear* to be intending to pay them for their work.

OBJECTIVE THEORY OF CONTRACTS   In the above example, *apparent intentions* rather than personal or subjective intentions are the controlling factor. You may have been thinking to yourself, "I really don't want tax help; I'm just leaving off all my tax records at their office because I can't think of a better place to keep them." However, a theory that runs through all aspects of the law of contracts—the **objective theory of contracts**—is illustrated by the tax preparation example. The theory says that a party's intention to enter into a contract is judged by outward, objective facts rather than by the party's own secret, subjective intentions. Objective facts include: (1) what the party said when entering into the contract, (2) how the party acted or appeared, and (3) the circumstances surrounding the transaction.

Courts need verifiable evidence in order to determine whether a contract has been made, so they usually rely only on objective facts when passing judgment on a contract dispute. Using this approach, they often determine that the parties have entered into contracts that are *implied-in-fact*. In other words, courts examine all the objective facts, conduct, and circumstances surrounding a particular transaction in order to determine if the parties have made a contract.

BACKGROUND AND FACTS   *In this case, a plumber, Shepard, sued a widow, Glick, for the cost of installing a sewer line into the Glick home. The services were contracted for by Glick's husband, who subsequently died. The widow claimed that the oral agreement for installation of the sewer line was between her deceased husband and Shepard and that she had no part in it. Hence, she denied ever promising to pay Shepard for his labor and for the other charges for the sewer hookup.*

SHEPARD v. GLICK
Court of Appeals of Missouri, 1966.
404 S.W.2d 441.

MAUGHMER, Judge.
* * *

The sole issue on appeal is whether or not Mrs. Glick was a party to the oral contract under which plaintiff agreed to and did connect the Glick premises to the sewer. [Emphasis added.] On appeal defendant contends that she was not a party to the contract and the verdict and judgment [in the trial court] should have been in her favor, that there is no evidence that she promised to pay, that her husband was the contracting party and that "proof of a joint contract does not support a definite and certain contract between plaintiff and defendant."
    * * *

It is true as defendant contends on appeal that in order for a contract to arise under the laws of Missouri, there must be a definite meeting of the minds and the nature and extent of the obligations must be certain. [The Court quotes from a legal treatise on Contract Law:]

"Neither a written offer and acceptance nor oral counterparts are essential to establish a contractual relationship, for unambiguous conduct of one party toward another under such circumstances as clearly to manifest an intention that one party perform and that the other party compensate for such performance is sufficient."
    * * *

"(1) ' "Implied contract" is one dictated by reason and justice, and which the law presumes from the relation of the parties.'

"(2) An 'implied contract' is inferred from the conduct, situation, or mutual relations of parties, and enforced by the law on the ground of justice."

In the case before us it is undisputed that a contract was entered into with Mr. Glick. Under it plaintiff was to connect the property to the sewer, to cut through the rock and provide drainage of the spring water from the basement. It is undisputed that his compensation was to be cost plus 10 percent, and there is no contention but that on this basis the judgment is for the correct amount. Therefore, there was a meeting of the minds and the agreement is definite as to the work to be done and the price to be paid. All parties concede that such an agreement with plaintiff was made by Mr. Glick. The disputed issue and the only disputed issue is whether or not Mrs. Glick was a contracting party. The trial court found that she with her husband, was a contracting party. *What evidence is there from which such a conclusion should be drawn? We shall list the chief points as they appear to us* [emphasis added]: (1) Mrs. Glick owned at least a wife's share in the property; (2) she wanted to "hook on" to the sewer. She knew it was necessary to go through rock and drain the springs in order to stop the basement floodings. She said she wanted these things done; (3) she called plaintiff to come to their home and discuss the Post easement; (4) she paid plaintiff $25 on this account with her personal check. Plaintiff had done work for the Glicks before. He discussed and entered into the oral contract in their home. These factual conclusions appear from defendant's own testimony and, standing alone, are possibly sufficient to establish liability.

However, in addition we have the affirmative testimony of the plaintiff. He says Mrs. Glick was present on all occasions when the matter was discussed and that she took part as a principal in the contract negotiations and agreement; that she promised to pay the bill, tried to get a loan from the Laurel Bank to pay it and when that effort failed, told plaintiff she would get a loan elsewhere. The Laurel Bank's Vice President and Cashier said Mrs. Glick personally consulted him and tried to secure a $1,000 loan from the bank and told him the proceeds were to be used to pay plaintiff for the sewer connection work and supplies. If the trial court believed this testimony and it quite evidently did believe it, then there was direct, substantial evidence that Mrs. Glick was and became a party to the contract. In addition, defendant's denials as a witness do not read very impressively. She did not so much deny, as fail to remember.

* * *

We believe there was *substantial, credible evidence* upon which the trial court could find *that defendant was a party to the oral contract sued upon and is liable thereunder. In addition, the conduct, general situation, mutual relations and unambiguous acts all support such a result.* [Emphasis added.] We agree with that conclusion. * * *

JUDGMENT AND REMEDY   *The trial court's judgment was affirmed. Glick had to pay Shepard the reasonable and proper charges for the work performed.*

Bilateral versus Unilateral Contracts

Every contract involves at least two parties. When one party promises to perform some act if the other party *actually performs* some act, a **unilateral contract** is formed. With a unilateral contract, only the party who makes the promise is bound to perform. Therefore, only that person can break the promise (that is, breach the contract). A **bilateral,** or **reciprocal, contract** binds both parties. Both parties expressly enter into mutual engagements. An unconditional promise is exchanged for an unconditional promise.

An important problem arises in unilateral contracts when the promisor attempts to revoke the promise after the promisee has begun performance. Since acceptance can occur only upon full performance and since offers are normally revocable until accepted, the question arises whether the promisor can revoke after the promisee has started performance. The modern view is that the offer becomes irrevocable once performance begins.

The classic illustration of a unilateral contract is the situation where A says to B, "If you walk across the Brooklyn Bridge, I'll give you $10." A *promises* to pay if B walks the entire span of the bridge. Only then does B accept A's offer to pay $10. If B does not walk, there are no legal consequences.

The distinction between bilateral and unilateral contracts shows which party to a contract is bound by a promise and which party is not bound (because no promise was made by that party). Beyond this, the distinction has no significant value. The Uniform Commercial Code and the Restatement, Second, Contracts avoid using the terms, since they doubt the utility of the distinction.[4]

The following case provides a good example of how the characterization of unilateral or bilateral can mean the difference between an enforceable promise to pay or proceeding at one's own risk in the hope of being paid after the work is done.

---

4. Section 12 of the Restatement, Second Contracts (tentative draft), was eliminated because of this doubt. See Reporter's Note, Restatement, Second (tentative draft), Contracts, Section 12.

BACKGROUND AND FACTS *Sometime during the fall of 1947, Fulton Cook sold a ranch in Idaho to L. D. Johnson. The ranch was located in the lowlands, and the drainage ditch had become clogged. After the sale, Cook, who owned a dragline, agreed to clean out and extend the ditch for Johnson. While Johnson was negotiating with Cook to do the ditch work, he was also negotiating to sell the ranch to Harry Fink. But Johnson never told Cook about the potential sale; nor did he indicate to Cook to hold off doing the ditch work.*

In January 1948, Johnson sold the ranch to Fink under a conditional sales contract and then left for California. Shortly thereafter, Cook learned of the sale but could not contact Johnson because he did not know where in California Johnson had gone.

Nevertheless, in the early part of April, Cook moved his ditch-digging equipment onto the ranch. An unusually heavy frost had kept the work from beginning in January.

Cook did the work after Fink had agreed that he should go ahead with it. He wanted to be paid and did not care whether it was Fink or Johnson who paid. The lower court concluded that Johnson and Cook never had had a valid contract even though letters describing the work to be done on the ditches had been exchanged.

COOK v. JOHNSON
Supreme Court of Washington,
Department 1, 1950.
37 Wash.2d 19, 221 P.2d 525.

SCHWELLENBACH, Justice.

* * *

The law recognizes, as a matter of classification, two kinds of contracts—bilateral and unilateral. A bilateral contract is one in which there are reciprocal promises. The promise by one party is consideration for the promise by the other. Each party is bound by his promise to the other. A unilateral contract is a promise by one party—an offer by him to do a certain thing in the event the other party performs a certain act. The performance by the other party constitutes an acceptance of the offer and the contract then becomes executed. Until acceptance by performance, the offer may be revoked either by communication to the offeree or by acts inconsistent with the offer, knowledge of which has been conveyed to the offeree. An example of this class of contract is the offer of a reward.

The letters between the parties indicate that they had negotiated for some time with reference to appellant cleaning out and extending the ditches. Those negotiations culminated in an offer by respondent to pay upon performance by appellant and upon appellant's submission of a bill to him. Up to that point appellant was not obligated to perform. He could have accepted the offer by performance. But he went further than that and promised to do the work. The promises of the two men thereby became reciprocal and binding, each upon the other. The two letters constitute a binding reciprocal agreement between the parties. There was a definite proposal by respondent which was unconditionally accepted by appellant. The minds of the parties met.

* * *

In a unilateral contract the offer may be revoked by the offeror before acceptance by performance by the offeree. [Emphasis added.] But such an offer may not be revoked by either party to a bilateral contract. *A bilateral contract may be rescinded, but only with the consent of both parties.* [Emphasis added.] That was not done here.

Respondent contends that it became appellant's duty, after learning of the conditional sale to Fink, coupled with Fink's possession of the property, to contact respondent before performing—that, under the circumstances, he proceeded with the work at his peril. *That might have been true if the contract were unilateral.* [Emphasis added.] However, we are here considering the reciprocal promises of the parties, each to the other—a bilateral contract. It was respondent's duty, if he wished to be relieved of his obligation to pay for the work, to contact appellant and attempt to have him agree to a rescission [cancellation]. Furthermore, although the testimony as to what transpired at the meeting in Spokane between respondent and Fink is so conflicting as to make it impossible to determine what was said, respondent then knew that appellant was on the ranch ready to perform and that he had not performed up to that time. He did nothing to stop performance or to protect any rights which he might have claimed under the contract.

* * *

We do not feel that the correspondence between the parties in June, 1948, showed an intention on appellant's [Cook's] part to relieve respondent [Johnson] of his obligation and look to Fink for payment. He merely stated that he did not care who paid for the work; but he most certainly did not release * * * [Johnson from payment].

Here the appellant [Cook] discharged his obligation by performance in accordance with the terms of the agreement between the parties.

Johnson was held liable to Cook for $1,790 for the work Cook had performed in extending and cleaning the ditches. The appellate court explained that the law recognizes two categories of contracts, bilateral and unilateral, and gave its opinion that in this case a bilateral contract existed and could be enforced by Cook.

JUDGMENT AND REMEDY

Bilateral contracts are complete when two mutual promises have been exchanged for one another. In essence, a bilateral contract is "a promise given for a promise." A unilateral contract consists of a promise and an act—the promise that something will be done in return for an act. In a unilateral contract, once the party is in the midst of the act requested, the other party cannot, in fairness, withdraw the promise. In such cases, the courts will normally prevent injustice to the party performing the act by holding the other party liable for the reasonable value of the benefits received.

COMMENTS

Formal versus Informal Contracts

Formal contracts are contracts that require a special form or method of creation (formation) to be enforceable. They include: (1) contracts under seal, (2) recognizances, and (3) negotiable instruments and letters of credit. **Contracts under seal** are formalized writings with a special seal attached.[5] The significance of the seal has been almost entirely eroded, although about ten states require no consideration when a contract is under seal. (See Chapter 7 for details.) A **recognizance** is an acknowledgment in court by a person who agrees to pay a certain sum if a certain event occurs. The most common form of recognizance is the surety bond or criminal recognizance bonds. Negotiable instruments and letters of credit are special methods of payment that are designed for use in many commercial settings. **Negotiable instruments** include checks, notes, drafts, and certificates of deposit. **Letters of credit** are agreements to pay contingent on the purchaser's receipt of invoices and bills of lading. Negotiable instruments and letters of credit are discussed at length in subsequent chapters.

Informal contracts include all other contracts. (Such contracts are also called *simple contracts*.) No special form is generally required (unless the contract *must* be in writing), as the contracts are usually based on their substance rather than their form. Informal contracts can be written or oral, bilateral or unilateral, executory or executed.

Quasi-Contracts, or Contracts Implied-in-Law

Quasi-contracts, or **contracts implied-in-law,** should be distinguished from contracts *implied-in-fact*. Quasi-contracts are not really contracts at all. They arise in order to achieve justice rather than from a mutual agreement between the parties. A quasi-contract is imposed on the parties in order to avoid *unjust enrichment*. The doctrine of unjust enrichment holds that people should not be allowed to profit or enrich themselves inequitably at the expense of others. The doctrine is equitable rather than contractual in nature.

In contrast to quasi-contracts, a contract implied-in-fact is a true contract. The parties express their agreement to the terms of the contract by conduct. When a quasi-contract is imposed on the parties, it is imposed despite their actual or apparent intentions. Equity and

---

5. A seal is usually an impression made on a thin wafer of wax firmly affixed to the writing. In some instances, the word *seal* or the letters *L.S.* appear at the end of the document. *L.S.* stands for *locus sigilli* and means "the place for the seal."

fairness require one party to pay for benefit received from another party, even if the parties had no true or explicit contract. Under a quasi-contract, the party receiving the benefit is required to pay for the reasonable value of that benefit, usually equal to the fair market value of the benefit.

Suppose A enters into an oral agreement with B and agrees to work with B for two years in developing a noise reduction turbine for fixed-wing commercial jets. B agrees to pay A a "fair share of the profit" derived from the sale of the device. After working six months on the project and making considerable headway, B tells A she will not pay her anything because the terms of the contract are too indefinite and the contract must be in writing. Assuming B is correct, A cannot sue on the contract itself, since there is no contract. Instead A sues on the theory of quasi-contract for the reasonable value of her services. Obviously, it would be unfair to allow B to pay nothing for A's work, so the court will imply a quasi-contract. Thus, B will be required to pay A a fair wage for the six months of work.

Executed versus Executory Contracts

Contracts are also classified according to their stage of performance. A contract that has been fully performed on both sides is called an **executed contract.** (Strictly speaking, it is not a contract.) A contract that has not been *fully* performed on either side is called an **executory contract.** If one party has fully performed but the other has not, the contract is said to be executed on one side and executory on the other (and is still called an executory contract). For example, assume you agree to buy ten tons of coal from the Wheeling Coal Company. Further assume that Wheeling has delivered the coal to your steel mill, where it is now being burned. At this point, the contract is executed on the part of Wheeling and executory on your part. After you pay Wheeling for the coal, the contract will be executed on both sides.

Valid versus Void, Voidable, and Unenforceable Contracts

A valid contract is one that has all the necessary elements; it entitles the parties to enforcement of the contract in court. The elements necessary for a valid contract include an offer and an acceptance and legally sufficient consideration. These elements are discussed in detail in the following chapters.

A **void contract** is no contract at all. The terms *void* and *contract* are contradictory, since a void contract is one that never existed. It produces no legal obligations by any of the parties. A contract can be void because one of the parties was adjudged legally insane or because the purpose of the contract was illegal, for example.

A **voidable contract** is one in which one of the parties has the option of avoiding his or her legal obligations. The party having this option can elect either to avoid any duty to perform or to *ratify* the contract. If the contract is avoided, both parties are released from it. If it is ratified, both parties must fully perform their respective legal obligations.

As a general rule, and subject to many qualifications, contracts made by minors are voidable at the option of the minor. (See Chapter 8 for details.) Contracts entered into under fraudulent conditions are voidable at the option of the defrauded party. (See Chapter 10 for details.) In addition, some contracts entered into because of mistakes and all contracts entered into under legally defined duress are voidable.

An **unenforceable contract** is one that cannot be enforced. It remains in existence, but certain legal defenses make enforcement impossible. Contracts barred by a statute of limitations, for example, are unenforceable contracts.[6] Likewise, oral contracts under the Statute of Frauds are unenforceable.[7] In brief,

---

6. A statute of limitations prevents a party from suing on a contract after a certain period of time has elapsed.

7. The Statute of Frauds requires certain contracts to be in writing in order to be enforceable.

an unenforceable contract is one that satisfies all the requirements of a contract except at least one, and this makes it unenforceable.

A Limitation on the Quasi-Contract

The principle underlying quasi-contractual obligations is based on the notion of "unjust enrichment." Nonetheless, there are situations in which the party obtaining the "unjust enrichment" is not liable. Basically, the quasi-contractual principle cannot be invoked by the party who has conferred a benefit on someone else unnecessarily or as a result of misconduct or negligence. Consider the following example. You take your car to the local car wash and ask to have it run through the washer and to have the gas tank filled. While it is being washed, you go to a nearby shopping center for two hours. In the meantime, one of the workers at the car wash has mistakenly believed that your car is the one that he is supposed to hand wax. When you come back, you are presented with a bill for a full tank of gas, a wash job, and a hand wax. Clearly, a benefit has been conferred on you. But this benefit has been conferred because of a mistake by the car wash employee. You have no liability. You have not received an *unjust* benefit under these circumstances. People cannot normally be forced to pay for benefits "thrust" upon them.

Also, the doctrine of quasi-contract cannot be used when there is a contract that covers the area in controversy. For example, X delivers a stove to a building project and does not get paid. Contractor Y goes bankrupt. X cannot collect from Z—the owner of the building—in quasi-contract because X has a contract with Y already.

QUESTIONS AND CASE PROBLEMS

1. Suppose Felix, a local businessman, is a good friend of Miller, the owner of a local candy store. Every day at his lunch hour Felix goes into Miller's candy store and usually spends about five minutes looking at the candy. After examining Miller's candy and talking with Miller, Felix usually buys one or two candy bars. One afternoon, Felix goes into Miller's candy shop, looks at the candy, picks up a $1 candy bar, and, seeing that Miller is very busy at the time, waves the candy bar at Miller without saying a word and walks out. Is there a contract? If so, classify it within the categories presented in this chapter.

2. Sosa Crisan, an eighty-seven-year-old widow of Roumanian origin, collapsed while shopping at a local grocery store. The Detroit police took her to the Detroit city hospital. She was admitted, and she remained there fourteen days. Then she was transferred to another hospital, where she died some eleven months later. Crisan had never regained consciousness after her collapse at the local grocery store. After she died, the city of Detroit sued her estate to recover the expenses of both the ambulance that took her to the hospital and the expenses of her hospital stay. Is there a contract between Sosa Crisan and the hospital? If so, how much can the Detroit hospital recover? [In Re Crisan Estate, 362 Mich. 569, 107 N.W.2d 907 (1961)]

3. Air Advertising employed Red, a World War II flying ace, to fly its advertisements above Long Island Sound beaches. Burger Baby restaurants engaged Air Advertising to fly an advertisement above the Connecticut beaches that offered $1,000 to any person who could swim from the Connecticut beaches to Long Island across Long Island Sound in less than a day. On Saturday, October 10, at 10:00 a.m., Red flew a sign above the Connecticut beaches that read: "Swim across the Sound and Burger Baby pays $1,000." Upon seeing the sign, Davison dove in. About four hours later, when he was about halfway across the Sound, Red flew another sign over the Sound that read: "Burger Baby revokes." Is there a contract between Davison and Burger Baby? Can Davison recover anything?

4. Womack was a well-known gambler in Saline County. Judge Maner, a friend of Womack, not only knew of Womack's gambling enterprises, but approved of them. From time to time over a period of several years, Womack paid money to the judge to ensure that he would not be prosecuted. As a result of this long-standing agreement, Womack paid the judge

a total of $1,675. Womack then claimed that the consideration for his paying the judge was void and unlawful at the time the contract was entered into as well as at the present time. Therefore, Womack sued Judge Maner to rescind the contract and to get back the $1,675 he had paid. Should Womack recover? [Womack v. Maner, 277 Ark. 786, 301 S.W.2d 438 (1957)]

5.   On April 1, 1969, McLouth Steel Corporation entered into a contract with Jewell Coal Company under which Jewell agreed to supply all McLouth's coal requirements for the next thirty years. The contract mentioned no specific quantities. The price was set at $100 a ton for the first year and was subject to an "escalation clause" whereby each subsequent year the original price would be increased by the cost increases encountered by Jewell. Five years later Jewell found that even with the cost increases that it had added onto the price it charged McLouth, the price it could receive in the open market was far greater. Jewell stopped shipping coal, claiming that the contract was invalid because the price and quantity under the contract were too indefinite to be enforced. Jewell admitted in court, however, that it had performed under this agreement for the past five years. Is the contract executory or nonexecutory? Is the contract enforceable or unenforceable? [McLouth Steel Corp. v. Jewell Coal and Coke Co., United States Court of Appeals, Sixth Circuit (1978), 570 F.2d 594]

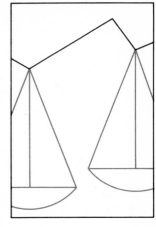

6

Contracts
Agreement

A contract is a legally enforceable *agreement* creating rights between two or more individuals. The agreement need not be in writing (unless required by statute), but each of the parties must assent to it.[1] The judicial system enforces contracts that are assented (agreed) to by the parties,[2] supported by legally sufficient consideration,[3] not illegal,[4] and entered into freely by parties with contractual capacity.[5]

MUTUAL ASSENT

Ordinarily, assent is established by an **offer** and an **acceptance.** In other words, one party offers a certain bargain to another party, who then accepts that bargain. The parties are required to manifest to each other their **mutual assent** to the same bargain.[6] Because words often fail to

---

1. Under early English and American law, many contracts were not enforced unless they complied with rigid legal standards requiring a writing and in many cases a seal or impression made on wax, which was firmly affixed to the writing. Today, some contracts must still be in writing (see Chapter 11). The seal has been almost entirely done away with. [UCC, Sec. 2-203]

2. See discussion *infra.*

3. See Chapter 7.

4. See Chapter 9.

5. See Chapter 8.

6. Restatement, Second, Contracts (tentative draft,) Section 22.

convey the precise meaning intended, the law of contracts generally adheres to the objective theory of contracts, as discussed in Chapter 5. Under this theory, a party's words and conduct are held to mean what a reasonable person would think they mean. The court will give words their usual meaning even if "it were proved by twenty bishops that [the] party * * * intended something else."[7]

ESSENTIAL CONTRACT TERMS

Certain terms are *essential* to the contract and must be either expressed or capable of reasonable implication from the agreement. These terms are: (1) identification of the parties; (2) subject matter—goods, services, money loaned, and so on; (3) the time for performance; and (4) the price. If these terms are expressly stated, the contract is definite and enforceable. If absolutely no mention is made of the terms, some courts today will often *imply* reasonable terms, as long as the terms are consistent with the parties' intentions. If the contract mentions the terms, but does so in a vague or ambiguous manner, the terms may *not* be implied, and the contract will fail for indefiniteness.

For example, assume Gaines agrees to sell tobacco leaves to R. J. Reynolds Company. The leaves are to be delivered at the beginning of the following month. If a price is mentioned, then the contract is reasonably definite and may be enforced in a court of law. If no price is mentioned in the contract, a court may imply a reasonable price, which ordinarily will be equal to the fair market value of the tobacco leaves. If the parties say the price will be "cost plus a fair profit," no price term may be implied, and the contract will fail for indefiniteness because no definite proportion of the cost to be added as profit is mentioned. "Cost plus 10 percent" would, however, be sufficiently definite.[8]

---

7. Learned Hand in Hotchkiss v. National City Bank of N.Y., 200 F. 287 (2nd Cir. 1911), aff'd 231 U.S. 50, 34 S.Ct. 20, 58 L.Ed. 115 (1913).
8. Gaines & Sea, v. R. J. Reynolds Tobacco Co., 163 Ky. 716, 174 S.W. 482 (1915).

Uncertainty or indefiniteness of *incidental, or collateral, terms* will not cause the contract to be unenforceable. Incidental terms include all other terms besides: (1) the parties, (2) the subject matter of the contract, (3) the time for performance, and (4) the price. The reason for enforcing contracts with uncertain incidental terms is that a party should not be deprived of a bargain merely because some minor aspect is overlooked. This is especially important in extremely complex and detailed contracts. If the parties were required to spell out every last detail explicitly, the negotiations process would be slowed, and contracts would encumber business instead of aiding it.

REQUIREMENTS OF THE OFFER

Most contracts are formed by one party, the **offeror,** who makes an offer or proposal to another party, the **offeree.** An **offer** is a promise or commitment to do or refrain from doing some specified thing in the future. Three elements are necessary in order for an offer to be effective: (1) there must be an *intention* (or, under the objective theory of contracts, an appearance of an intention) to become bound by the offer; (2) the terms of the offer must be reasonably *certain* or definite, so that the parties and the court can ascertain the terms of the contract; and (3) the offer must be *communicated* to the offeree. Once an effective offer has been made, the offeree has the power to accept the offer. If the offeree does so, the offer is transformed into a binding legal agreement.

Intention

The first element of an effective offer, intention, can best be explained by distinguishing between offers and various kinds of non-offers. None of the following statements or actions— expressions of opinion; preliminary negotiations; statements of intention; or advertisements, catalogues, and circulars—are effective offers because they all fail to meet the legal requirement of intention.

EXPRESSIONS OF OPINION   An expression of opinion is not an offer. It does not evidence an intention to enter into a binding agreement. Hawkins took his son to McGee, a doctor, and asked McGee to operate on the son's hand. McGee said the boy would be in the hospital three or four days and that the hand would probably heal within a few days afterward. The son's hand did not heal for a month, but the father did not win a suit for breach of contract. The court held that McGee did not make an offer to heal the son's hand in three or four days. He merely expressed an opinion as to when the hand would heal.[9]

PRELIMINARY NEGOTIATIONS   A request or invitation to negotiate is not an offer. It only expresses a willingness to discuss entering into a contract. Included are statements such as "Will you sell Blythe Estate?" or "I wouldn't sell my car for less than $1,000." A reasonable person would not conclude that these state-

---

9.   Hawkins v. McGee, 84 N.H. 114, 146 A. 641 (1929).

ments evidence an intention to enter into a binding obligation. Likewise, when construction work is done for the government and private firms, contractors are invited to submit bids. The *invitation* to submit bids is not an offer, and a contractor does not bind the government or private firm by submitting a bid. (The bids that the contractors submit *are* offers, however, and the government or private firm can bind the contractor by accepting the bid.)

STATEMENTS OF INTENTION   If Henry says "I *plan* to sell my stock in Ryder Systems for $150 per share," a contract will not be created if Fred "accepts" and tenders the $150 per share for the stock. Henry has merely expressed his intention to enter into a future contract for the sale of the stock. No contract is formed because a reasonable person would conclude that Henry was only thinking about selling his stock, not promising to sell, even if Fred accepts and pays the $150 per share. Henry is stating a future contractual intent, not a present one. The next case further illustrates this point.

BACKGROUND AND FACTS   *The defendant, Johnson, is the owner of real estate. Johnson's real estate agent wrote a letter to the plaintiff, Mellen, indicating that certain seashore property that Mellen had expressed an interest in purchasing would be placed on the market. The letter further indicated that several other people who had expressed an interest in purchasing the property were also being informed at the same time before the property went on the open market. Mellen interpreted the letter as an "offer" and promptly "accepted." Mellen, thinking he was entitled to buy the property, sued Johnson to force her to go through with the sale (specific performance). The trial court upheld Mellen's position that the letter was an offer.*

MELLEN v. JOHNSON
Supreme Judicial Court of
Massachusetts, Essex, 1948.
322 Mass. 236, 76 N.E. 2d 658.

WILKINS, Justice.
* * *

The defendant is the owner of two parcels of land with the buildings thereon at 74 and 75 Willow Road, Nahant. On March 27, 1947, the defendant's son-in-law, Edward Hicks, who was her agent to sell the property, wrote the following letter to the plaintiff's brother-in-law, who was his agent as to this subject matter: "You will perhaps remember that we spent a pleasant visit * * * on the break water at Nahant last summer. On that occasion either you or your brother-in-law expressed an interest in my Mother's property which is the Johnson cottage. I told you that I would contact you if and when my Mother expressed a desire to dispose of her property. Well, that time has arrived and her health is such that she will not be able to open the cottage this year. She has, therefore, decided that it will be best to place the property on the market, however, before turning it over to the real estate agents, I am writing the several people, including yourself, who have previously expressed an interest in the property. Our price is $7,500. This property consists of the lot and cottage on the south side of Willow Road, and also a very large plot on which a two car garage is situated running from Willow Road clear through the block to the next street. Just how much property there is in this tract, I cannot tell you at the moment. I can say, however, that it is a large tract which would offer possibilities for further building. The price of $7,500 would include the entire property on both sides of Willow Road. The cottage is in very good condition. There are three rooms downstairs with a large entry hall, and a sun porch, also three good sized bedrooms upstairs, with bath. Hardwood floors throughout, hot water heat and is suitable for all year round occupancy if desired. The oil burner is in good condition and the house is far better built than most of the new constructions of today. *I will be interested in hearing from you further if you have any interest in this property, for as I said before, I am advising those who have asked for an opportunity to consider it.* [Emphasis added.] I might just add that the property would be available for immediate occupancy. By that I mean within such time as the present furnishings could be removed and title transferred."

On March 28 Hicks received a telegram from the plaintiff's brother-in-law which read: "We are interested in your offer. Will look at house tomorrow. Communicate with you first of week." On the same day shortly after the telegram was received Hicks telegraphed the plaintiff's brother-in-law: "Have heard from three interested buyers tonight which means we must accept highest bid for Nahant property. Suggest you wire or phone us Elmsford N. Y. 7292 Saturday your best offer on cash basis." Before this was received the plaintiff's brother-in-law telegraphed Hicks: "I accept your offer on Nahant cottage. Letter in mail."

It is unnecessary to recount the subsequent communications of the parties other than to state that the defendant entered into a written contract to sell the property to someone other than the plaintiff. This sale has not been completed pending this suit.

* * *

The letter of March 27 was not an offer. It expressed "a desire to dispose of" the property. It announced that the agent was "writing the several people, including yourself, who have previously expressed an interest in the property." Its conclusion, in part, was, "I will be interested in hearing further from you if you have any interest in this property, for as I said before, I am advising those who have asked for an opportunity to consider it." The recipient could not reasonably understand this to be more than an attempt at negotiation. It was a mere request or suggestion that an offer be made to the defendant.

JUDGMENT AND REMEDY

The trial court was found in error; its decision was reversed. The court of appeals decided that the letter was merely a negotiation, and Johnson was not required to sell the property to Mellen.

It is often difficult to distinguish an actual "offer" from preliminary negotiations, or what lawyers call "invitations to offer." The key distinction between preliminary negotiations and offers is that an offer is a definite commitment, whereas a preliminary negotiation is non-commital.

COMMENTS

ADVERTISEMENTS, CATALOGUES, AND CIRCULARS In general, advertisements, mail order catalogues, price lists, and circular letters are not offers to contract but invitations to negotiate. Suppose Loeser & Co. advertises a used paving machine. The ad is mailed to hundreds of firms and reads, "Used Case Construction Co. paving machine. Builds curbs and finishes cement work all in one process. Price $11,250 firm." If Star Paving calls Loeser and says, "We accept your offer," no contract is formed. No reasonable person would conclude that Loeser was promising to sell the paving machine; the conclusion would have to be that Loeser was attempting to solicit offers to buy it.

The same result occurs when a new car dealership advertises "New Lincoln Continentals; loaded with options; now only $13,899." The ad is intended to draw customers who will make offers. If Bill Weinberg goes to the dealership with a check for $13,899, the dealership is not legally bound to sell the Lincoln. (However, federal and state statutes prohibit "false and misleading advertising" that is intended only to draw customers to the retail outlet.)

Advertisements are not offers because the seller never has an unlimited supply of the goods. If advertisements were offers, then everyone who "accepted" after the retailer's supply was exhausted could sue for breach of contract. Suppose you had put a "For Sale" sign on your home and seven people had called and "accepted" your "offer" before you could take it down. If the sign were an offer, you would be bound on seven contracts to sell your home. Since initial advertisements are treated as invitations to make offers, you would have had seven offers to choose from, and you could have accepted the best one without incurring any liability for the six you rejected. Moreover, your sign lacked an element of a successful offer—the identity of the offeree. (However, rewards can be offers even though there is no predetermined and specified offeree.)

Sometimes offers are worded such that they can be accepted only by performance, as opposed to verbal or written acceptance. A unilateral contract requires a person to accept by performing the requested acts. In the following case, the court had to decide whether a newspaper advertisement announcing a "special sale" in a department store should be construed as an offer, the acceptance of which would complete a contract.

BACKGROUND AND FACTS *Plaintiff read a newspaper advertisement offering certain items of merchandise for sale on a first come-first served basis. Plaintiff went to the store twice and was the first person to demand the merchandise and indicate a readiness to pay the sale price. On both occasions, the defendant department store refused to sell the merchandise to the plaintiff, saying that the offer was intended for women only, even though the advertisement was directed to the general public. Plaintiff sued the store for breach of contract, and the trial court awarded the plaintiff damages.*

LEFKOWITZ v. GREAT MINNEAPOLIS SURPLUS STORE, INC.
Supreme Court of Minnesota, 1957.
251 Minn. 188, 86 N.W. 2d 689.

MURPHY, Justice.

* * *

This case grows out of the alleged refusal of the defendant to sell to the plaintiff a certain fur piece which it had offered for sale in a newspaper advertisement. It appears from the record that on April 6, 1956, the defendant published the following advertisement in a Minneapolis newspaper:

"Saturday 9 A.M. Sharp
3 Brand New
Fur
Coats
Worth to $100.00
First Come
First Served
$1
Each"

On April 13, the defendant again published an advertisement in the same newspaper as follows:

"Saturday 9 A.M.
2 Brand New Pastel
Mink 3-Skin Scarfs
Selling for $89.50
Out they go
Saturday. Each $1.00
1 Black Lapin Stole
Beautiful,
worth $139.50 . . . .$1.00
First Come
First Served"

The record supports the findings of the court that on each of the Saturdays following the publication of the above-described ads the plaintiff was the first to present himself at the appropriate counter in the defendant's store and on each occasion demanded the coat and the stole so advertised and indicated his readiness to pay the sale price of $1. On both occasions, the defendant refused to sell the merchandise to the plaintiff, stating on the first occasion that by a "house rule" the offer was intended for women only and sales would not be made to men, and on the second visit that plaintiff knew defendant's house rules.

* * *

The defendant contends that a newspaper advertisement offering items of merchandise for sale at a named price is a "unilateral offer" which may be withdrawn without notice. He relies upon authorities which hold that, where an advertiser publishes in a newspaper that he has a certain quantity or quality of goods which he wants to dispose of at certain prices and on certain terms, such advertisements are not offers which become contracts as soon as any person to whose notice they may come signifies his acceptance by notifying the other that he will take a certain quantity of them. Such advertisements have been construed as an invitation for an offer of sale on the terms stated, which offer, when received, may be accepted or rejected and which therefore does not become a contract of sale until accepted by the seller; and until a contract has been so made, the seller may modify or revoke such prices or terms.

* * *

[However] * * * [t]here are numerous authorities which hold that a particular advertisement in a newspaper or circular letter relating to a sale of articles may be construed by the court as constituting an offer, acceptance of which would complete a contract. * * *

The test of whether a binding obligation may originate in advertisements addressed to the general public is "whether the facts show that some performance was promised in positive terms in return for something requested."

The authorities above cited emphasize that, where the offer is clear, definite, and explicit, and leaves nothing open for negotiation, it constitutes an offer, acceptance of which will complete the contract.

* * *

Whether in any individual instance a newspaper advertisement is an offer rather than an invitation to make an offer depends on the legal intention of the parties and the surrounding circumstances. We are of the view on the facts before us that the offer by the defendant of the sale of the Lapin fur was clear, definite, and explicit, and left nothing open for negotiation. The plaintiff having successfully managed to be the first one to appear at the seller's place of business to be served, as requested by the advertisement, and having offered the stated purchase price of the article, he was entitled to performance on the part of the defendant. We think the trial court was correct in holding that there was in the conduct of the parties a sufficient mutuality of obligation to constitute a contract of sale.

The defendant contends that the offer was modified by a "house rule" to the effect that only women were qualified to receive the bargains advertised. The advertisement contained no such restriction. This objection may be disposed of briefly by stating that, while an advertiser has the right at any time before acceptance to modify his offer, he does not have the right, after acceptance, to impose new or arbitrary conditions not contained in the published offer.

* * *

The only evidence of value was the advertisement itself to the effect that the coats were "Worth to $100.00," how much less being speculative especially in view of the price for which they were offered for sale. With reference to the offer of the defendant on April 13, 1956, to sell the "1 Black Lapin Stole * * * worth $139.50 * * *" the trial court held that the value of this article was established and granted judgment in favor of the plaintiff for that amount less the $1 quoted purchase price.

JUDGMENT AND REMEDY

The Supreme Court affirmed the trial court's order for judgment, awarding the plaintiff the sum of $138.50 in damages for breach of contract against the defendant department store.

OTHER NON-OFFER SITUATIONS In other cases, what appears to be an offer is not sufficient to serve as the basis for formation of a contract.

Auctions In an auction, a seller "offers" goods for sale through an auctioneer. This is not, however, an offer for purposes of contract. The seller is really only expressing a willingness to sell. He or she may withdraw the goods at any time before the auctioneer closes the sale and may even refuse the highest bid. There is no obligation to sell. The bidder is actually the offeror. The auctioneer accepts a bid and completes a contract by knocking the hammer. A bidder can retract an offer while the auctioneer sings "going once, going twice, third and last call." If the bid is not withdrawn and the hammer falls, the contract is formed.[10]

Social Affairs Invitations to attend social affairs are not offers. If a friend asks you to dinner, and you arrive at the specified time but no one is home, you cannot bring suit. The invitation created a social obligation, not a legal one.

Agreements to Agree Agreements to agree are not contracts and cannot be enforced. Suppose Zahn Consulting gets together with Leon Construction Company to discuss plans for designing a shopping mall. Zahn and Leon agree further to meet in a month and work out the terms of the contract. The agreement to agree "or make a contract at a future time" is not enforceable. There is nothing to enforce in an agreement to agree because the terms have not yet been agreed upon.

Sham Transactions A sham transaction is entered into by two parties in order to deceive a third person and is unenforceable. For example, a sham transaction might involve the alleged sale or transfer of a house to make one party's net worth appear larger than otherwise. Let's say Sneed is trying to get a loan to buy a new BMW. In order to increase his unimpressive net worth on paper, he agrees in a personal letter to a close friend to sell his power boat for $50,000 (it's actually worth only about $25,000), and his friend agrees in a letter to pay that much. In filling out his net worth statement, Sneed claims that his boat is worth $50,000, and, if questioned, he can produce a personal letter from his friend to show that that is the price at which it will be sold. Sneed and his friend entered into the sham transaction knowing that they were not actually going to perform their respective obligations. Sneed cannot attempt now to enforce that transaction by requesting payment of $50,000 for his boat.

Definiteness

An offer must have reasonably definite terms so that a court can determine if a breach has occurred and can give an appropriate remedy.[11] An offer may invite an acceptance that supplies the necessary terms to make that contract reasonably definite. For example, assume D'Onfro contacts your corporation and offers to sell "from one to ten sheet metal presses for $1,750 each, state number desired in acceptance." Your corporation agrees to buy two presses. If the quantity had not been specified in the acceptance, the contract would be unenforceable because the terms of the contract would have been indefinite. But since the acceptance stated that your corporation wanted two presses, the contract is definite and capable of enforcement.

Will an employment contract that provides for a salary plus "a share of the profits" be too vague and indefinite for a court to enforce? The following case tells the plight of a plaintiff, Victor Petersen, who worked first as construction supervisor and then as manager for the Pilgrim Village Company, the defendant.

---

10. See UCC Sec. 2-328. At auctions announced as "without reserve," goods must be sold to the highest bidder.

11. Restatement, Second, Contracts (tentative draft), Section 32.

BACKGROUND AND FACTS *Petersen was employed by Pilgrim Village for nearly ten years. His contract of employment provided that he was to be paid a stated salary. Petersen claimed that Pilgrim told him when he began work that he would share in the profits of the corporation and promised him repeatedly throughout the term of his employment that he would share in the profits.*

When Petersen left Pilgrim Village, Pilgrim paid him all but $666.67 of his salary for the time he had worked the previous year.

Petersen sued Pilgrim for the back salary of $666.67 and for $20,000, which he declared was his "reasonable" share of corporate profits. Pilgrim agreed to pay Petersen the salary but objected to paying any amount based on Petersen's claim that he was entitled to "a share of the profits." The trial court allowed the jury to award Petersen whatever part of the $20,000 they thought corresponded to "the reasonable value of services" Petersen had rendered to Pilgrim. The jury decided on $8,000. Pilgrim appealed, arguing that the parties had never come to any definite agreement as to what, if any, the percentage of profits was to be. The Supreme Court of Wisconsin reviewed Pilgrim's arguments.

FRITZ, Chief Justice.

* * *

As stated in Restatement of the Law on Contracts, sec. 32, pp. 40, 41.

"An offer must be so definite in its terms, or require such definite terms in the acceptance, that the promises and performances to be rendered by each party are reasonably certain.

"Comment:

"a. Inasmuch as the law of contracts deals only with duties defined by the expressions of the parties, the rule stated in the Section is one of necessity as well as of law. The law cannot subject a person to a contractual duty or give another a contractual right unless the character thereof is fixed by the agreement of the parties. A statement by A that he will pay B what A chooses is no promise. A promise by A to give B employment is not wholly illusory, but if neither the character of the employment nor the compensation therefor is stated, the promise is so indefinite that the law cannot enforce it, even if consideration is given for it.

"b. Promises may be indefinite in time or in place, or in the work or things to be given in exchange for the promise. In dealing with such cases the law endeavors to give a sufficiently clear meaning to offers and promises where the parties intended to enter into a bargain, but in some cases this is impossible."

As stated in 12 Am.Jur. sec. 70, p. 561, "The general rule is that price is an essential ingredient of every contract for the transfer of property or rights therein or for the rendering of services. Accordingly, an agreement must be definite as to compensation. In order that an executory agreement may be valid, it is generally necessary that the price must be certain or capable of being ascertained from the agreement itself. By this is not meant that the exact amount in figures must be stated in the agreement; however, where that is not the case, the price must, by the terms of the agreement, be capable of being definitely ascertained. An agreement leaving the price for future determination is not binding. * * * (p. 562) Although there is some authority to the contrary, a promise to pay a reasonable sum for

PETERSEN v. PILGRIM
VILLAGE

Supreme Court of Wisconsin,
1950.
256 Wis. 621, 42 N.W. 2d 273.

goods or services is generally held valid. * * * On the other hand, a promise to pay a fair share of profits has been held too indefinite to be valid."

In Varney v. Ditmars, supra, the employer promised to pay plaintiff $40 a week and "the first of January next year I will close my books and give you a fair share of my profits." The court said:

"The statement alleged to have been made by the defendant about giving the plaintiff and said designer a fair share of his profits is vague, indefinite, and uncertain, and the amount cannot be computed from anything that was said by the parties or by reference to any document, paper, or other transaction. The minds of the parties never met upon any particular share of the defendant's profits to be given the employes or upon any plan by which such share could be computed or determined. The contract so far as it related to the special promise or inducement was never consummated. It was left subject to the will of the defendant or for further negotiation. It is urged that the defendant by the use of the word 'fair,' in referring to a share of his profits, was as certain and definite as people are in the purchase and sale of a chattel when the price is not expressly agreed upon, and that if the agreement in question is declared to be too indefinite and uncertain to be enforced, a similar conclusion must be reached in every case where a chattel is sold without expressly fixing the price therefor. The question whether the words 'fair' and 'reasonable' have a definite and enforceable meaning when used in business transactions is dependent upon the intention of the parties in the use of such words and upon the subject-matter to which they refer. In cases of merchandising and in the purchase and sale of chattels the parties may use the words 'fair and reasonable value' as synonymous with 'market value.' * * *

"The contract in question, so far as it relates to a share of the defendant's profits, is not only uncertain, but it is necessarily affected by so many other facts that are in themselves indefinite and uncertain that the intention of the parties is pure conjecture. * * * The courts cannot aid parties in such a case when they are unable or unwilling to agree upon the terms of their own proposed contract." * * *

Consequently, * * * plaintiff's [claim] * * * was merely that he was to be paid "some share of the profits," and as the parties never came to any definite agreement as to what that percentage of the profits was to be, the [trial] court erred.

JUDGMENT AND REMEDY

Petersen left the appellate court without any of the $8,000 in "reasonable profits" the trial court jury had awarded him originally. Even assuming Petersen had been offered some share of the profits, the parties never showed that they had come to any definite agreement as to what that percentage of the profits ought to be. Note, however, that the appellate court allowed Petersen a new trial to establish sufficient evidence that he was entitled to payment of "the reasonable value" of any additional services he had rendered to Pilgrim over and above what he had been paid in his actual salary.

COMMENTS

Because an offer must be definite, a court can determine and award a monetary remedy if the offer is accepted and thus becomes a contract that is subsequently breached. The terms of the agreement forming the contract between the parties must be specific and firm enough for the court to measure which damages are directly related to the breach of the contract in question.

RELAXATION OF DEFINITENESS UNDER THE UNIFORM COMMERCIAL CODE

Contract law is designed to aid business, not to hinder it. Thus, the Uniform Commercial Code has liberalized the requirement of definiteness as to essential terms. Contract law, however, continues to be much stricter than the Uniform Commercial Code. The UCC allows such terms as "according to custom and usage" in order to fill in indefinite terms in an otherwise valid agreement. Following are a few ways in which the UCC fills in missing terms. Even though one or more terms are left open, a contract for sale does not fail for indefiniteness if the parties have intended to make a contract and there is a reasonably certain basis for giving an appropriate remedy [UCC Sec. 2-204]. If no price is stated, or if the price is left open to be agreed on, "the price is a reasonable price at the time for delivery" [UCC Sec. 2-305]. If no place of delivery is specified, then delivery is to occur at the seller's place of business [UCC Sec. 2-308(a)].[12] If the time for shipment or delivery is not provided for, then the time shall be a reasonable time after the contract is formed [UCC Sec. 2-309]. If the time for payment is not specified, then payment is due at the time and place of delivery [UCC Sec. 2-310(a)].

In addition, under the UCC, omitted terms may be supplied by custom and usage in trade and by prior dealings. If the parties have dealt with each other previously, their past conduct may be used to supply the omitted terms. For example, assume John's Poultry has purchased spring chickens from Robinson Farms for the last ten years, and the chickens have always been paid for on credit. John's Poultry then enters into a contract to buy 150 chickens, but no mention is made of the terms of payment. Due to prior dealings, John's may pay on credit, since the understandings of the past may be implied in the current contract.

Indefiniteness may be cured by *part performance*, that is, by performance that has already begun. Assume Brown-Crummer, Inc., agrees to buy beans at $4 per bushel from Arkansas Grains. Arkansas Grains, however, has four different grades of beans. This is an indefinite contract since its subject matter is insufficiently described. But if Arkansas Grains ships No. 3 beans and Brown-Crummer accepts them, the indefiniteness is cured. This contract becomes enforceable when Brown-Crummer accepts the beans because Brown-Crummer's acceptance (part performance) identifies the subject matter of the contract [UCC Sec. 2-306].

In the following case, when plaintiff bought "chicken," he meant broiling and frying chickens—not stewing chickens. The defendant contended that a chicken is a chicken. The following case illustrates how a federal district court applied New York law to decide the weighty question "What is a chicken?"

12. But if both parties know the goods are elsewhere when the contract is formed, then the place of delivery is the place where the goods are located.

BACKGROUND AND FACTS *A buyer of fresh frozen chicken brought this action for breach of contract against the seller. The plaintiff, purchaser, sued for breach of warranty, claiming that the goods sold did not correspond to the contract description.*

Plaintiff, a Swiss corporation, bought chicken from defendant, a New York sales corporation. The two contracts involved were negotiated predominately through an exchange of cablegrams written for the most part in German but using the English word "chicken." Both contracts were identical except that there were different prices quoted for the 2½ to 3 pound chickens and the 1½ to 2 pound chickens. When the initial shipment arrived in Switzerland, plaintiff found that the birds were not young chickens suitable for broiling and frying but were stewing chickens or "fowl." Plaintiff protested, but more and more "birds" were shipped.

FRIGALIMENT IMPORTING CO. LTD. v. B.N.S. INTERNATIONAL SALES CORP.

United Stated District Court of New York, 1960. 190 F. Supp. 116.

FRIENDLY, Circuit Judge.
* * *

The issue is, what is chicken? Plaintiff says "chicken" means a young chicken, suitable for broiling and frying. Defendant says "chicken" means any bird of that genus that meets contract specifications on weight and quality, including what it calls "stewing chicken" and plaintiff pejoratively terms "fowl." Dictionaries give both meanings, as well as some others not relevant here. To support its [claim], plaintiff sends a number of volleys over the net; defendant essays to return them and adds a few serves of its own. Assuming that both parties were acting in good faith, the case nicely illustrates Holmes' remark "that the making of a contract depends not on the agreement of two minds in one intention, but on the agreement of two sets of external signs—not on the parties' having *meant* the same thing but on their having *said* the same thing." The Path of the Law, in Collected Legal Papers, p. 178. * * *

Two contracts are in suit. In the first, dated May 2, 1957, defendant, a New York sales corporation, confirmed the sale to plaintiff, a Swiss corporation, of

"US Fresh Frozen Chicken, Grade A, Government Inspected, Eviscerated
2½-3 lbs. and 1½-2 lbs. each
all chicken individually wrapped in cryovac, packed in secured fiber cartons or wooden boxes, suitable for export
75,000 lbs. 2½-3 lbs. ....@$33.00
25,000 lbs. 1½-2 lbs. ....@$36.50
per 100 lbs. FAS New York"

The second contract, also dated May 2, 1957, was identical save that only 50,000 lbs. of the heavier "chicken" were called for, the price of the smaller birds was $37 per 100 lbs.

The initial shipment under the first contract was short but the balance was shipped on May 17. When the initial shipment arrived in Switzerland, plaintiff found, on May 28, that the 2½-3 lbs. birds were not young chicken suitable for broiling and frying but stewing chicken or "fowl"; indeed, many of the cartons and bags plainly so indicated. Protests ensued. Nevertheless, shipment under the second contract was made on May 29, the 2½-3 lbs. birds again being stewing chicken. Defendant stopped the transportation of these at Rotterdam.

This action followed. * * *

Since the word "chicken" standing alone is ambiguous, I turn first to see whether the contract itself offers any aid to its interpretation. Plaintiff says the 1½-2 lbs. birds necessarily had to be young chicken since the older birds do not come in that size, hence the 2½-3 lbs. birds must likewise be young. This is unpersuasive—a contract for "apples" of two different sizes could be filled with different kinds of apples even though only one species came in both sizes. Defendant notes that the contract called not simply for chicken but for "US Fresh Frozen Chicken, Grade A, Government Inspected." It says the contract thereby incorporated by reference the Department of Agriculture's regulations, which favor its interpretation; I shall return to this after reviewing plaintiff's other contentions.

[A]n exchange of cablegrams * * * preceded execution of the formal contracts. Plaintiff stresses that, although these and subsequent cables between plaintiff and defendant, which laid the basis for the additional quantities under the first and for all of the second contract, were predominantly in German, they used the English word "chicken"; it claims this was done because it understood "chicken" meant young chicken whereas the German word, "Huhn," included both "Brathuhn" (broilers) and "Suppenhuhn" (stewing chicken), and that defendant, whose officers were thoroughly conversant with German, should have realized this.

* * *

Plaintiff's * * * contention is that there was a definite trade usage that "chicken" meant "young chicken." Defendant showed that it was only beginning in the poultry trade in 1957, thereby bringing itself within the principle that "when one of the parties is not a member of the trade or other circle, his acceptance of the standard must be made to appear" by proving either that he had actual knowledge of the usage or that the usage is "so generally known in the community that his actual individual knowledge of it may be inferred." Here there was no proof of actual knowledge of the alleged usage; indeed, it is quite plain that defendant's belief was to the contrary. In order to meet the alternative requirement, the law of New York demands a showing that "the usage is of so long continuance, so well established, so notorious, so universal and so reasonable in itself, as that the presumption is violent that the parties contracted with reference to it, and made it a part of their agreement."

Plaintiff endeavored to establish such a usage by the testimony of three witnesses and certain other evidence. Strasser, resident buyer in New York for a large chain of Swiss cooperatives, testified that "on chicken I would definitely understand a broiler." * * * Niesielowski, an officer of one of the companies that had furnished the stewing chicken to defendant testified that "chicken" meant "the male species of the poultry industry. That could be a broiler, a fryer or a roaster," but not a stewing chicken; * * * Dates, an employee of Urner-Barry Company, which publishes a daily market report on the poultry trade, gave it as his view that the trade meaning of "chicken" was "broilers and fryers." * * *

Defendant's witness Weininger, who operates a chicken eviscerating plant in New Jersey, testified "Chicken is everything except a goose, a duck, and a turkey." * * * Its witness Fox said that in the trade "chicken" would encompass all the various classifications. Sadina, who conducts a food inspection service, testified that he would consider any bird coming within the classes of "chicken" in the Department of Agriculture's regulations to be a chicken:

"*Chickens.* The following are the various classes of chickens:

(a) Broiler or fryer . . .	(d) Stag . . .
(b) Roaster . . .	(e) Hen or stewing chicken or fowl . . .
(c) Capon . . .	(f) Cock or old rooster . . ."

Defendant argues, as previously noted, that the contract incorporated these regulations by reference.
* * *
When all the evidence is reviewed, it is clear that defendant believed it could comply with the contracts by delivering stewing chicken in the 2½-3 lbs. size.

JUDGMENT
AND REMEDY
The plaintiff's complaint was dismissed. The court held that plaintiff failed to sustain the burden of proving that the word "chicken" in the contract referred only to chickens suitable for broiling and frying and did not include stewing chickens.

OUTPUT AND REQUIREMENT CONTRACTS

The Uniform Commercial Code also validates output and requirements contracts.[13] **Output contracts** are agreements to sell all production during a specified period to a certain party. **Requirements contracts** are agreements to buy all production needs "or requirements" during a specified period from a certain party. These contracts do not specifically state the quantity of output or requirements, but the quantity is definitely ascertainable, within reasonable limits. The courts have a reasonably certain basis for giving an appropriate remedy if either type of contract is breached.

Communication

An effective offer must be *communicated* to the offeree because one cannot agree to a bargain without knowing that the bargain exists. Sup-

pose Emerman advertises a reward for the capture of her lost dog. Baldwin, not knowing of the reward, finds the dog and returns it to Emerman. Baldwin cannot recover the reward because he did not know it was offered.[14]

REWARDS   A reward is a special kind of contract, for it is unilateral. It can be accepted only by performance. Another element to the reward contract is that one who claims a reward must have known that it was offered. Otherwise there can be no contract. This rule follows because it is impossible to have an acceptance under contract law unless the offeree knows the existence of the offer. The following case is one of the classic "reward" cases in the common law.

---

13.   Brown-Crummer Inv. Co. v. Arkansas City, 125 Kan. 768, 266 P. 60 (1928).

---

14.   A few states will allow recovery of the reward but not on contract principles. Since Emerman wanted her dog returned, and Baldwin returned it, these few states allow Baldwin to recover. It would be unfair to deny him the reward just because he did not know about it.

GLOVER v. JEWISH
WAR VETERANS OF
THE UNITED STATES,
POST NO. 58
Municipal Court of Appeals for
the District of Columbia, 1949.
68 A.2d 233.

BACKGROUND AND FACTS   *The Jewish War Veterans of the United States offered a reward of $500 in a newspaper "to the person or persons furnishing information resulting in the apprehension and conviction of the persons guilty of the murder of Maurice L. Bernstein." A day or so after the notice appeared, one of the men suspected in the crime was arrested and the police received information that the other murderer was the "boyfriend" of a daughter of Mary Glover, the plaintiff and claimant in the present case. That evening, the police visited Mary Glover. She provided names and addresses and possible locations where her daughter and the suspect might be found. The suspect was arrested at one of the places suggested by Mary Glover, and all suspects were subsequently convicted of the crime.*

Mrs. Glover claimed the $500 reward from the Jewish War Veterans, arguing that the information she gave to the police officers led to the arrest and conviction of the murderers. But there was some *question as to whether Mrs. Glover was entitled to the reward. At the time she gave the information to the police officers, she did not know that any reward had been offered for information leading to the arrest and conviction of the guilty persons. In fact, Mrs. Glover did not learn about the reward until several days afterward. The trial court denied Mrs. Glover the $500 reward. The appellate court reviewed the law of contracts concerning rewards.*

CLAGETT, Associate Judge.

* * *

While there is some conflict in the decided cases on the subject of rewards, most of such conflict has to do with rewards offered by governmental officers and agencies. So far as rewards offered by private individuals and organizations are concerned, there is little conflict on the rule that questions regarding such rewards are to be based upon the law of contracts.

Since it is clear that the question is one of contract law, it follows that, at least so far as private rewards are concerned, *there can be no contract unless the claimant when giving the desired information knew of the offer of the reward and acted with the intention of accepting such offer* [emphasis added]; otherwise the claimant gives the information not in the expectation of receiving a reward but rather out of a sense of public duty or other motive unconnected with the reward. "In the nature of the case," according to Professor Williston, "it is impossible for an offeree actually to assent to an offer unless he knows of its existence." After stating that courts in some jurisdictions have decided to the contrary, Williston adds, "It is impossible, however, to find in such a case [that is, in a case holding to the contrary] the elements generally held in England and America necessary for the formation of a contract. If it is clear the offeror intended to pay for the service, it is equally certain that the person rendering the service performed it voluntarily and not in return for a promise to pay. If one person expects to buy, and the other to give, there can hardly be found mutual assent. These views are supported by the great weight of authority, and in most jurisdictions a plaintiff in the sort of case under discussion is denied recovery."

The American Law Institute in its Restatement of the Law of Contracts follows the same rule, thus: "It is impossible that there should be an acceptance unless the offeree knows of the existence of the offer." The Restatement gives the following illustration of the rule just stated: "A offers a reward for information leading to the arrest and conviction of a criminal. B, in ignorance of the offer, gives information leading to his arrest and later, with knowledge of the offer and intent to accept it, gives other information necessary for conviction. There is no contract."

The trial court judgment was affirmed. The Jewish War Veterans did not have to pay the reward to Mrs. Glover. No contract existed because Mrs. Glover did not know about the offer at the appropriate time.

JUDGMENT AND REMEDY

COMMENTS *In this case, the court indicated that there is some conflict concerning rewards offered by government officers and agencies. Some courts provide a remedy when a government body offers a reward on the theory that the government is benefited equally whether or not the claimant gave it the information while knowing about the reward. The public good is served regardless. Another rationale is that knowledge of government actions is imputed. Whichever theory the courts use, the result is the same—the government pays the reward.*

TERMINATION OF THE OFFER

The communication of an effective offer to an offeree creates a power in the offeree to transform the offer into a binding legal obligation (a contract). This power of acceptance, however, does not continue forever. It can terminate by operation of law or by an act of the parties. The power may be terminated by *operation of law* through: (1) lapse of time, (2) destruction of the subject matter of the contract, (3) death or incompetency of the offeror or offeree, and (4) supervening illegality of the proposed contract. The power may be generally terminated by *action of the parties* through: (1) revocation of the offer, (2) counter-offer by the offeree, and (3) rejection of the offer by the offeree.

Termination by Operation of Law

LAPSE OF TIME An offer terminates when the period of time specified in the offer has passed. For example, suppose A offers to sell his boat to B if B accepts within twenty days. B must accept within the twenty-day period or the offer will lapse (terminate). The period of time specified in an offer begins to run when the offer is *actually received* by the offeree, not when it is sent or drawn up. When the offer has been delayed, the period begins to run from the date the offeree *would have* received the offer, but only if the offeree knew or should have known the offer was delayed.[15] For example, if A had used improper postage when mailing the offer to B, but B knew A had used improper postage, the offer would lapse twenty days after the day B would ordinarily have received the offer had A used proper postage.

If no time for acceptance is specified in the offer, the offer terminates at the end of a *reasonable* period of time. In order to determine what a reasonable period of time is, the subject matter of the contract, business and market conditions, and other relevant circumstances must be taken into account. An offer to sell farm produce, for example, will terminate sooner than an offer to sell farm equipment because farm produce is perishable and subject to greater fluctuations in market value. The question of reasonable period of time arises in the next case.

------

15. Restatement, Second, Contracts (tentative draft), Section 51.

CORCORAN v. LYLE SCHOOL DISTRICT NO. 406, KLICKITAT COUNTY, WASHINGTON
Court of Appeals of Washington, Division 3, Panel Four, 1978.
20 Wash.App. 621, 581 P.2d 185.

BACKGROUND AND FACTS *Bradley T. Corcoran, plaintiff, appealed his dismissal from the Lyle School District for his failure to accept his employment contract for the 1976-1977 school year in a timely manner. Corcoran is a certified teacher. He received an unsigned copy of his proposed employment contract on June 4, 1976. It provided: "If this contract is not signed by said employee and returned to the Secretary of the school district on or before June 14, 1976, the Board reserves the right to withdraw this offer."*

In addition, the superintendent of schools personally called Corcoran's attention to the time provision contained within the contract. At that time, Corcoran informed the superintendent that he was considering other employment. In any event, Corcoran did not return the contract with his signature on it until June 16. Two days later, he received a letter from the superintendent stating that the school board had decided not to accept any contracts returned after the June 14 deadline. Therefore, Corcoran would not be rehired for the forthcoming school year.

McINTURFF, Judge.
* * *

Beyond the statutory rights contained in the continuing contract law, the relationship between the school district and its employees is a contractual one governed by general principles of law. *It is well settled that an offeror may require acceptance within a specified reasonable time and that failure of the offeree to so accept constitutes a rejection of the offer.* By his failure to timely return the contract in the face of express written and personal notice that such conduct could result in the school board's rejection of its offer, Mr. Corcoran effectively waived his continuing contract rights. [Emphasis added.]

While certified teachers who have not been given notice of non-retention are entitled to contracts containing terms and conditions substantially identical to those of the previous year, they may not desire such employment. If they fail to accept or reject those contracts within a reasonable time, school districts should be released from their obligations to rehire them under their former contracts. Unless a reasonable contract-return deadline is established and enforced, school districts, as a practical matter, may not know until classes begin how many of their retained teachers will return to the classroom each fall.

Mr. Corcoran does not contend the 10-day contractual limit was unreasonable, nor has he alleged any circumstances which would have prevented him from returning his signed contract within the time established. Therefore, we need not determine the reasonableness of the 10-day return provision.
* * * [B]y his own conduct Mr. Corcoran foreclosed the potential contractual relationship between himself and the school district. * * *

Judgment of the lower court was affirmed. The school district was not required to rehire Corcoran.	**JUDGMENT AND REMEDY**

DESTRUCTION OF THE SUBJECT MATTER

An offer is automatically terminated if the subject matter is destroyed before the offer is accepted. For example, if Watts offers to sell her race horse to Teagle, but the horse dies before Teagle can accept, the offer is automatically terminated. Likewise, an offer to sell a par-ticular lathe is terminated if the lathe is destroyed in a fire before the offer is accepted.

DEATH OR INCOMPETENCY OF THE OFFEROR OR OFFEREE

An offeree's power of acceptance is terminated when the offeror or offeree dies or is deprived of legal capacity to enter into the proposed contract.[16] An offer is personal to both parties and cannot pass to the decedent's heirs, guardian, or estate. Furthermore, this rule applies whether or not the other party had notice of the death or incompetency of the party. For example, on June 4, Manne offers to sell Clark a rowboat for $300, telling Clark that he, Manne, needs the answer by June 20. On June 10, Manne dies. On June 18, Clark informs the executor of Manne's will that he has accepted the offer. The executor can refuse to sell the rowboat because the death of the offeror has terminated the offer.

SUPERVENING ILLEGALITY OF THE PROPOSED CONTRACT A statute or court decision that makes an offer illegal will automatically terminate the offer. If Barker offers to loan Jackson $20,000 at 15 percent annually, and a usury statute is enacted prohibiting loans at interest rates greater than 14 percent before Jackson can accept, the offer is automatically terminated. If in the above hypothetical case, the usury statute had been passed *after* Jackson accepted the offer, a valid contract would have been formed, but the contract would be discharged. (Note that most state constitutions and the federal Constitution prohibit the government from passing laws that affect the already existing rights and duties of contracting parties.)

Termination by Action of the Parties

REVOCATION OF THE OFFER BY THE OFFEROR An offer may be terminated by the offeror if a revocation is communicated to the offeree *before* the offeree accepts. Revocation may be accomplished by expressly repudiating the offer (such as "I withdraw my previous offer of October 17") or by acts inconsistent with the existence of the offer (where, for example, the

---

16. Restatement, Second, Contracts (tentative draft), Section 48.

offeree discovers the offeror has sold the property that was the subject matter of the offer).

The revocation must be communicated to the offeree before acceptance, or the revocation will be ineffective and a valid contract will be formed. The general rule followed by most states is that a revocation is effective only upon actual receipt by the offeree or that person's agent of the revocation. Therefore, a letter of revocation that is deposited in a mailbox on April 1 and that arrives at the offeree's residence or place of business on April 3 becomes effective on April 3. If the offeree accepts the offer on April 2, a valid contract will be formed, and the contract will be enforceable in a court of law.

Alternatively, communication to the offeree exists if the offeree indirectly discovers that the offer is revoked. This indirect discovery may be through a third person who tells the offeree that the offeror has revoked prior to offeree's acceptance. In addition, the revocation may be communicated indirectly where the offeree learns that the subject matter of the contract has been sold to a third party.

Offers made to the general public may be revoked by communicating the revocation in the same manner in which the offer was communicated. For example, suppose Macy's offers a $10,000 reward for anyone giving information leading to the apprehension of the persons who burglarized Macy's downtown store. The offer is published in three local papers and in four papers in neighboring communities. In order to revoke the offer, Macy's must publish the revocation in all seven papers for the same number of days as it published the offer. The revocation will then be accessible to the general public, even though some particular offeree did not know about it.

Option Contracts As a general rule, offerors may revoke their offers even if they expressly agreed to hold them open for a specified period of time. When an offeror promises to hold an offer open for a specified period of time, however, and the offeree pays for the promise (gives consideration), an **option contract** is created. An option contract takes away the offeror's power to revoke the offer for the period of time specified in the option. If no time is specified, then a reasonable period of time is implied, just as in offers.

For example, suppose Brennan offers to sell one hundred shares of stock in Texas Instruments to Columbus for $189 per share. Brennan promises to keep the offer open for thirty days. After fourteen days Brennan calls Columbus on the telephone and says that the offer is revoked. If Columbus has not given any consideration (say $25 in cash) for the offer, Brennan may revoke the offer even though he promised to keep it open for thirty days. If Columbus has given some consideration for the offer, Brennan cannot revoke the offer for thirty days, and his attempt to do so will be ineffective. In the latter case, even if Brennan attempted to revoke after fourteen days, Columbus could still accept the offer and force Brennan to sell the Texas Instruments stock for $189 per share. This particular option contract (for the purchase of common stock) is becoming increasingly popular, and similar options are traded publicly on the Chicago Board Options Exchange.

Death or Incompetency of Offeror or Offeree
When the offer is in the form of an option and the decedent was not required to perform an essential part of the contract, the offer survives the death or incompetency of the offeror.[17] For example, assume Vendrick executes an option to Carney entitling Carney to purchase Vendrick's hundred-acre ranch in Costa Rica. Carney pays $750 for the option, but before he can exercise it, Vendrick dies. Carney can still exercise the option against Vendrick's estate, since Vendrick is not required to perform the act of conveying the ranch to Carney personally. In sum, option contract rights and duties are not discharged by the death of either party unless

performance is of a personal nature—that is, consists of personal services.

Firm Offers   Under the Uniform Commercial Code, certain offers may be irrevocable even if no consideration is given. These are called **firm offers.**[18] If a merchant makes a written, signed offer to buy or sell goods and states that the offer is not revocable, the offer cannot be revoked regardless of the lack of consideration. The offer will remain open for the period of time specified in the offer, but the period of irrevocability cannot exceed three months. Note the various elements necessary for a firm offer: (1) the offer must be for the purchase or sale of goods; (2) the offer must be made by a merchant dealing in those goods; (3) the offer must be written and signed by the merchant; and (4) the offer must give assurance that it will be held open for some period of time. (If the offer makes such assurances but does not state a period of time, a reasonable period of time not in excess of three months is assumed.)

Detrimental Reliance on the Offer   A growing number of courts are refusing to allow an offeror to revoke the offer when the offeree changes position in justifiable reliance on the offer. In such cases, revocation would be unjust to the offeree. Consider an example. Feinberg has worked for Pfeiffer for thirty-five years. Pfeiffer tells her that whenever she quits, she will be paid $150 a month for the rest of her life. There is no indication by Pfeiffer that she should quit now. In fact, she works for a couple more years. She quits and Pfeiffer starts sending her checks every month for $150. Five years later, Pfeiffer dies and his son takes over the business. The son says the $150 checks are ridiculous and attempts to avoid the promise. He will not be able to do so because Feinberg has been relying on the promise to pay her $150 a month. Had the promise not been made, she

17.   Restatement, Second, Contracts (tentative draft), Section 35A.

18.   Restatement, Second, Contracts (tentative draft), Section 24A.

would have rearranged her affairs to obtain other retirement funds. This is a case of a detrimental reliance on a promise and therefore cannot be revoked.

Revocation of Offer for Unilateral Contract   In a unilateral contract, the offer invites acceptance only by *full* performance or forbearance. The offer of a unilateral contract cannot be accepted by promising to perform; only full performance will suffice. Obviously, injustice can result if an offeree expends time and money in part performance and then the offeror revokes the offer before full performance is complete. Therefore, many courts will not allow the offeror to revoke after the offeree has performed some substantial part of his or her duties.[19] In effect, part performance changes the offer into an option, and the offeree has reasonable time to complete performance.

REJECTION OF THE OFFER BY THE OFFEREE   The offer may be rejected by the offeree, in which case the offer is terminated and may not subsequently be accepted by the offeree. Any subsequent attempt to accept will be construed as a new offer, giving the original offeror (now the offeree) the power of acceptance. A rejection is ordinarily accomplished by words or conduct evidencing an intent to reject the offer.

As in the case of revocation of the offer, rejection is effective only when actually received by the offeror or the offeror's agent. (The only difference is the party to whom the communication is made.)

Suppose you offer to sell Procter & Gamble twenty-five tons of linseed oil at thirty-five cents per pound. Procter & Gamble could reject your offer by writing or telephoning you, expressly rejecting the offer (perhaps by saying, "We are sufficiently stocked in linseed oil and do not need any more"). Alternatively, the company could mail your offer back to you, evidencing an intent to reject the offer. Or it could offer to buy the oil at twenty-three cents per pound, which would operate as a counter-offer, necessarily rejecting the original offer.

COUNTER-OFFER BY THE OFFEREE   A counter-offer—a change in one or more terms of the original offer—by the offeree will terminate the original offer. It is treated as a rejection. Suppose X offers to sell his home to Y for $70,000. Y then offers to buy the house for $65,000. Y's offer is termed a counter-offer and terminates X's original offer. At common law, the "mirror image" rule requires the offeree's acceptance to match the offeror's offer exactly— to mirror the offer. Any change in, or addition to, the terms of the original offer automatically terminates that offer and substitutes the counter-offer, which, of course, need not be accepted. The original offeror can, however, accept the terms of the counter-offer and create a valid contract.

In a contract for the sale of goods, now governed by the Uniform Commercial Code, an acceptance that varies from the terms of an offer does not always terminate that offer. An acceptance can add terms to the offer or change its terms.[20] Between merchants, the new or changed terms become part of the contract automatically unless: (1) the original offer expressly required acceptance of its terms, (2) the new or changed terms materially alter the contract, or (3) the offeror rejects the new or changed terms.

ACCEPTANCE

Acceptance is a voluntary act (either words or conduct) by the offeree that shows assent (agreement) to the terms of the offer. The acceptance must ordinarily be made in the manner requested by the offeror.[21] In addition, the acceptance must be unequivocal and communicated to the offeror.

---

19.   UCC Sec. 2-205.

20.   E.g., Sylvestre v. Minnesota, 289 Minn. 142, 214 N.W. 2d 658 (1973). See UCC, Sec. 2-207.

21.   The UCC has changed the common law in this area. [UCC Sec. 2-206(1)(a)].

Who Can Accept?

Ordinarily, only the person to whom the offer is made (the offeree) can accept the offer and create a binding contract. If the offer is an option contract, however, the right to exercise the option is generally considered a contract right and as such assignable or transferable to third persons (with exceptions—see Chapter 12). If the offeree is an agent for an undisclosed principal, the acceptance may be made by the principal and will bind both the principal and the offeror (see Chapter 34).

Suppose Black & Decker offers to sell John Rushmore a combination power saw/grinder for $335. If Rushmore has not given consideration for the offer, only he can accept it. He cannot let his neighbor, Sam Ullman, accept the offer because Black & Decker assented to sell the power saw/grinder to Rushmore only. If he has paid $5 for the option to buy the power saw/grinder during the next thirty days, he can accept the offer. Additionally, he can sell his option contract to Ullman which will entitle Ullman to accept the offer from Black & Decker. Suppose further that Rushmore is the agent of Janet Blackstone, an undisclosed principal. Here, Blackstone can direct Rushmore to accept, and Black & Decker will be bound on a valid contract with Blackstone.

Unequivocal Acceptance

In order to exercise the power of acceptance effectively, the offeree must accept unequivocally. If the acceptance is subject to new conditions, or the terms of the acceptance change the original offer, the acceptance may be a counter-offer, implicitly rejecting the original offer. An acceptance may be unequivocal even though the offeree expresses dissatisfaction with the contract. For example, "I accept the goods, but I wish I could have gotten a better price" will operate as an effective acceptance. So, too, will "I accept, but can you shave the price?" On the other hand, the statement "I accept the goods, but I want to pay on ninety days credit" is not an unequivocal acceptance and operates as a counter-offer, rejecting the original offer.

CONDITIONS Certain conditions, when added to an acceptance, will not qualify the acceptance sufficiently to reject the offer. Suppose Childs offers to sell her sixty-five-acre cotton farm to Sharif. Sharif replies, "I accept your offer to sell the farm, provided you can supply a good title." This condition (providing of good title) does not make the acceptance equivocal. A warranty of good title is normally implied in every offer for the sale of land, so the condition does not add any new or different terms to the offer.

Or suppose that in response to an offer to sell a motorcycle, the offeree replies, "I accept; please send written contract." This does not make the acceptance ineffective. The request for a writing is not necessary or conditioned upon the acceptance. Therefore, the acceptance is effective. However, if the offeree replies, "I accept *if* you send a written contract," the acceptance is *expressly* conditioned on the request for a writing, and the statement is not an acceptance but a counter-offer.

As noted above, under the Uniform Commercial Code, an acceptance that varies in insignificant ways from the terms of the offer, can, nonetheless, operate as an acceptance. The additional or changed terms are treated as proposals for *additions* to the contract.[22] If both parties are merchants, the proposals become part of the contract unless the offer expressly limits acceptance to the terms of that offer, or the proposals materially alter the contract, or the offeror objects to the proposals within a reasonable time. Terms treated as proposals for addition to a contract between persons when one or both are not merchants must be agreed to by the original offeror.

Silence as Acceptance

Ordinarily, silence cannot be acceptance, even if the offeror states, "By your silence and inaction you will be deemed to have accepted this offer." This general rule applies because an offeree should not be put under a burden to act affirmatively in order to reject the offer.

---

22. Restatement, Second, Contracts (tentative draft), Section 52 and UCC Sec. 2-207.

Silence can operate as an acceptance when, for example, an offeree takes the benefit of offered services with an opportunity to reject them and knowledge that they were offered with the expectation of compensation. Suppose Sarah Holmes watches while her daughter is given piano lessons. The piano instructor has not been requested to give the daughter lessons but plans to give a series of fifteen. Holmes knows the instructor plans to be paid but lets the lessons continue nonetheless. Here, her silence constitutes an acceptance, and she is bound to pay a reasonable value for the lessons. This rule applies only to services and goods if they are used by the offeree.

A second situation arises when the offeree, due to prior dealings with the offeror, notifies the offeror only if the offer is rejected. To illustrate: X, a salesman, has previously ordered goods from Y and paid without notifying Y of his acceptance. Whenever X receives a shipment from Y, he sells it and simply sends a check to Y. Only if the goods are defective does X notify Y. The last shipment, however, has been neither paid for nor rejected. Nonetheless, X is bound on a contract and must pay Y for this last shipment of goods.[23]

A third and final situation arises when an offeror sends goods to an offeree and the parties have had no prior dealings. Here, silence does not constitute an acceptance *unless* the receiver exercises control over the goods. The most common example of this is when books or magazines are sent to an individual through the mails. The individual did not order the books or magazines and is under no duty to reship them to the seller. Under the common law, if the individual uses the books or magazines he or she will have accepted them and must pay reasonable value for them. This common law rule of contract law has been chaged by statute. The Postal Reorganization Act of 1970 provides that unordered merchandise sent by mail may be retained, used, discarded, or disposed of in any manner deemed appropriate, without the individual incurring any obligation to the sender.[24] In addition, the mailing of unordered merchandise (except for free samples) constitutes an unfair trade practice and is not permitted. (Exceptions are mailings by charitable agencies and those made by mistake.)

Communication of Acceptance

Whether the offeror must be notified of the acceptance depends on the nature of the contract. In a unilateral contract, notification or communication is not necessary. Since a unilateral contract calls for the *full* performance of some act, acceptance is not complete until the act has been fully performed. Therefore, notice of acceptance is unnecessary. To illustrate: Beta offers to pay Gamma $150 to paint Beta's garage. Gamma can accept only by painting the garage. Once the garage is completely painted (and hence the acceptance is complete), notification of the acceptance is superfluous. Certain exceptions do exist. When the offeror requests notice of acceptance or has no adequate means of determining whether the requested act has been performed, notice of acceptance is necessary.

In a bilateral contract, notification of acceptance is necessary because acceptance is in the form of a promise (not performance), and the contract is formed when the promise is made (rather than when the act is performed). The offeree must use reasonable efforts to communicate the acceptance to the offeror. In a bilateral contract, however, notification of acceptance is not necessary if the offer dispenses with the requirement. In addition, if the offer can be accepted by silence, no communication or notification is necessary.

Under the Uniform Commercial Code, an order or other offer to buy goods for prompt shipment may be accepted by either a promise to ship or by actual shipment.[25]

---

23. Restatement, Second, Contracts (tentative draft), Section 72 and Illustration 1.

24. 39 USCA, Sec. 3009, and state statutes.
25. UCC Sec. 2-206(1)(b).

When an Acceptance Becomes Effective

The general rule is that an acceptance becomes effective when the offeree assents to the same terms as the offeror by way of a reasonable and appropriate communication. If an offeree accepts by mail, the acceptance is effective when the letter is dropped in the mailbox. This is the so-called "mailbox rule,"[26] and it applies to any situation where: (1) no means of acceptance is specified in the offer and (2) acceptance is made in the same manner as the offer was made. For example, if an offer is made by telegraph, then the acceptance is made when the offeree gives a message to a telegraph operator. If the acceptance is not properly dispatched, it will not be effective until it is actually received by the offeror. Note that this rule involves two separate elements.

First, the acceptance must be properly dispatched. When the mails are involved, this simply means that the letter must be properly addressed and have the correct postage. If the acceptance is not properly dispatched, it will not be effective until the offeror actually receives it.[27] If the letter is delayed in the mails, the offer may lapse or be revoked in the meantime.

Second, the acceptance must be made via a reasonable means of communication. At common law, this requires the offeree to use the particular means used by the offeror or some faster means. If the offer is conveyed by the mails, then the acceptance can be sent by mail, telegraph, or telephone. If the offer is conveyed by telegraph, the use of the mails to accept is not authorized (since the mails are usually much slower than the telegraph). Naturally, if the offeror requires the use of some particular means, that means has to be used or the acceptance will not become effective until the offeror actually receives it.

Recall that rejections or revocations of offers are not effective until actually received, and then study the following hypothetical situations:

1.   On January 1, A mails an offer to B. On January 2, A decides to revoke the offer and sends B a letter to that effect. On January 3, B receives the offer and accepts it, putting a letter of acceptance in the mail. On January 4, B receives the letter of revocation. On January 5, A receives the letter of acceptance. Has a valid contract been formed? Yes, because B's acceptance was effective when it was dropped in the mail (on January 3). The revocation cannot become effective until B actually receives it (on January 4), which in this case was subsequent to the acceptance.

2.   On January 1, A mails an offer to B. On January 2, B receives the offer and mails a rejection letter to A. On January 3, B changes his mind, wires A, and accepts the offer. On January 4, A receives the letter of rejection. Has a valid contract been formed? Yes. Since the rejection was not effective until received, and the offer was accepted (on January 3) prior to A's receipt of the rejection letter (on January 4), a valid contract has been formed. This is a special situation in which the contract is valid upon receipt, not mailing, because of intervening attempted rejection.

---

26.   Adams v. Lindsell, 106 Eng.Rep. 250 (K.B. 1818).

27.   Restatement, Second, Contracts (tentative draft), Section 68.

QUESTIONS AND CASE PROBLEMS

1.   McKittrick Co. employed Embry under a written contract at a fixed annual salary. Just before the contract expired, Embry approached McKittrick's president, seeking to have his employment contract extended another year. The president did not make any firm commitments to Embry, and Embry continued working. A week after his contract had run out, Embry again approached the president, this time threatening to quit if his contract was not extended. The president responded, "Go ahead, you're all right, and don't let that worry you." Two months later

Embry was laid off. Can Embry recover his salary under the contract for the entire year? [Embry v. Hargadine, McKittrick Dry Goods Co., 127 Mo.App. 383, 105 S.W. 777 (1907)]

2. Calan Imports advertised a 1964 Volvo station wagon for sale in the *Chicago Sun-Times*. The newspaper erroneously stated the price as $1,095. Calan had instructed the newspaper to advertise the price at $1,795. Upon reading the advertisement, O'Brien visited Calan's showroom and told one of the salesmen that he wished to purchase the car. At first the salesman agreed, but upon learning of the advertising error, he refused to sell the car at that price. Can O'Brien recover for breach of contract? [O'Keefe v. Lee Calan Imports, Inc., 128 Ill.App.2d 410, 262 N.E.2d 758 (1970)]

3. A widow wrote to her daughter: "If you come and live with me on my farm and support me for the rest of my life you may have the use of the farm during my lifetime and the farm will be yours when I have passed away." Without responding to the letter, the daughter and her husband sold their home and moved across the country onto the widow's farm. The daughter and husband lived with the widow until she died. Before she died, the widow sold the farm to her son instead. Can the daughter claim the farm? [Brackenbury v. Hodgkin, 116 Me. 399, 102 A. 106 (1917)]

4. Jones was an inventor. Pym held exclusive rights to the invention. Campbell, who desired to purchase Pym's rights to the invention, entered into negotiations with Pym. On the day set for contract negotiations Campbell told Pym that he, Campbell, would agree to buy the invention if his friend Abernathie, an engineer, gave a favorable opinion of it. Since Abernathie was not able to be present at the negotiations, it was proposed that Pym and Campbell draw up a contract and sign it. But if Abernathie did not approve the invention, the contract was to be ineffective. Subsequently, Abernathie disapproved the invention. Pym contended that the contract they signed was a valid agreement. Is he correct? [Pym v. Campbell Q.B. 1856, 6 Ellis & Blackburn 370]

5. On October 28, 1891, Sanders submitted the following proposition to Pottlitzer Bros.: "We offer you ten car loads of apples, 175 to 200 barrels per car, to be shipped as follows: 1st car by December 15th, 2nd car by December 30th and one car each ten days after January 1." To this Pottlitzer Bros. replied: "We accept your proposition on apples, provided you will change it to read — car every eight days from January first, none in December." On the same day, Sanders

responded that he could not accept Pottlitzer's changes and had to insist on the original offer. Several days later, Pottlitzer Bros. wrote a detailed letter to Sanders explaining why the requested changes were important and reiterating that it could not do business on Sanders's terms. Sanders then responded: "Letter received. Will accept conditions. If satisfactory, answer, and will forward contract." Pottlitzer Bros. replied by telegraph: "All right. Send contract as stated in our message." Sanders sent the contract as modified by Pottlitzer Bros. But Pottlitzer refused to accept the contract unless it also included a provision that Sanders furnish stoves on the carrier to protect the apples from freezing. Can Sanders enforce the agreement as originally modified? [Sanders v. Pottlitzer Bros. Fruit Co., 144 N.Y. 209, 39 N.E. 75 (1894)]

6. John H. Surratt was one of John Wilkes Booth's alleged accomplices in the murder of President Lincoln. On April 20, 1865, the Secretary of War issued and caused to be published in newspapers the following proclamation: "$25,000 reward for the apprehension of John H. Surratt and liberal rewards for any information that leads to the arrest of John H. Surratt." On November 24, 1865, President Johnson revoked the reward and published the revocation in the newspapers. Shuey learned of the reward but left for Rome prior to its revocation. In Rome, Shuey discovered Surratt's whereabouts; and, in April of 1866, unaware that the reward had been revoked, he reported this information to United States officials. Pursuant to receiving this information, the officials were able to arrest Surratt. Should Shuey have gotten the reward? If so, was he entitled to the full $25,000? [Shuey v. United States, 92 U.S. 73, 23 L.Ed. 697 (1875)]

7. Dodds signed and delivered to Dickinson the following memorandum on Wednesday, June 10:

> "I hereby agree to sell to Mr. George Dickinson the whole of the dwelling houses, garden ground, stabling, and outbuildings these to belonging, situated at Croft, belonging to me, for the sum of £800. As witness my hand this tenth day of June, 1874.
> "£88 [signed] John Dodds."
> "P.S. this offer to be left over until Friday, 9 o'clock A.M. 12th June, 1874."
> [Signed] J. Dodds."

The next afternoon (Thursday) Dickinson learned that Dodds was negotiating with a man named Allan. That evening Dickinson went to the house of Dodds' mother-in-law and left her a written acceptance. This document never reached Dodds. The next morning, at 7 A.M., Dickinson's agent gave Dodds a copy of the acceptance. Dodds replied that it was too late as he had already sold the property. Was the memorandum signed by Dodds a binding contract? If it was merely an offer, was Dickinson's acceptance sufficient to form a binding contract? [Dickinson v. Dodds, 2 Div. 463 (1876)]

8. For about the past two weeks Wilfred, a tall, good-looking college fraternity man, has been trying to get a date for fraternity Greek night. Wilfred has had his heart set on Melinda from the first day he saw her. Every night at 8:30 Wilfred calls Melinda to ask her to Greek fraternity night. Every night Melinda tells Wilfred that she does not like him and does not want to go anywhere with him. On Thursday, the evening before Greek fraternity night, Wilfred again calls Melinda at the usual time. This time he pleads with Melinda, "I promise if you go with me I'll never bother you again." Melinda promises to go with him, but the next night she stands Wilfred up. Wilfred goes to his attorney, Schiester, and asks him to bring a lawsuit against Melinda. Is there a breach of contract?

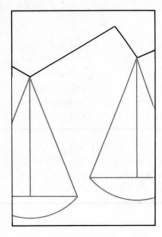

7

Contracts
Consideration

In order to create a legally binding promise, one or more of the parties must give legally sufficient consideration. **Consideration** is something that is intentionally exchanged for something else and is required in nearly every contract. The courts will not enforce a promise against a breaching party unless the party seeking enforcement has resorted to a proper form of agreement or has given up a valuable legal right.

Two elements constitute consideration: (1) something must be given, and (2) there must be a bargained-for exchange. Essentially, the parties must bargain together and trade something for something, that is, a *quid pro quo*.

Suppose Earl says to his son, "In consideration of the fact that you are not as wealthy as your brothers, I will pay you $500." This promise is not enforceable because Earl's son has not given any consideration to support it.[1] Earl has simply stated his motive for giving his son a gift.

REQUIREMENTS OF CONSIDERATION

Legal Sufficiency

To create a binding contract, the consideration must exist, and it must be legally sufficient. In order to be **legally sufficient,** *consideration* for a

---

1. Fink v. Cox, 18 Johns 145, 9 Am. Dec. 191. (1820).

promise must be either legally *detrimental to the promisee* or legally *beneficial to the promisor*, or both.[2] (The promisor makes a promise; the promisee receives it.) Legal detriment is doing or promising to do something that there was no prior legal duty to do. It also includes refraining or promising to refrain from doing something that there was no prior legal duty to refrain from doing. Conversely, legal benefit is obtaining something that there was no prior legal right to obtain. *Legal* detriment or benefit is not synonymous with *actual* (economic) detriment or benefit. In most cases, the promisor's legal benefit is the same as the promisee's legal detriment. However, the existence of *either* a legal detriment or a legal benefit constitutes legally sufficient consideration.

Suppose Myers owns a brickhouse that causes considerable air pollution in and around his property. Myers is thinking about getting out of the brick-making business since he is not making much profit and his property is constantly enveloped in a thick layer of smoke. Bernard, his neighbor, is sick of the smoke and pollution and offers Myers $1,500 to stop making bricks (and thus stop the smoke). Myers agrees. The consideration flowing from Myers to Bernard is the promise to refrain from doing an act that Myers is legally entitled to do, that is, to earn a living by making bricks. The consideration flowing from Bernard to Myers is the promise to pay a sum of money that is not otherwise legally required to be paid.

On the other hand, assume X owes Y $100 and Y promises to discharge the debt if X pays $50. Consideration is not legally sufficient in this example because X had a prior legal obligation to pay Y the $100. This is known as X's pre-existing duty, a subject that will be discussed later in the chapter.[3]

In one of the classic cases in contract law, the court found that refraining from certain behavior at the request of another was sufficient consideration to support a promise to pay a sum of money.

---

2. The whole concept of sufficient consideration is losing its force. Restatement, Second, Contracts (tentative draft) drops the idea. Basically, one either meets the requirements of consideration outlined in Section 75 or does not. Nothing additional is needed. The modern way seems to be to talk simply in terms of "bargained-for" consideration.

3. The reasoning is limited to obligations that are or can be reduced to specific dollar amounts.

BACKGROUND AND FACTS *William E. Story, Sr., was the uncle of William E. Story, II. In the presence of family members and guests invited to a family gathering, Story, Sr., promised to pay his nephew $5,000 if he would refrain from drinking, using tobacco, swearing, and playing cards or billiards for money until he became 21. The nephew agreed and fully performed his part of the bargain. When he reached 21, he wrote and told his uncle that he had kept his part of the agreement and was thereby entitled to $5,000. The uncle replied that he was pleased with his nephew's performance, writing, "I have no doubt but you have, for which you shall have five thousand dollars, as I promised you. I had the money in the bank the day you was twenty-one years old that I intend for you, and you shall have the money certain."*

The letter went on to describe how the uncle had worked hard to earn his money and how he hoped that his nephew, Willie, would make good use of the money and not squander it. The uncle also indicated that he had bought his nephew fifteen sheep twenty-one years before and that every four years the sheep were put out to pasture and doubled their numbers. Now, there were between five hundred and six hundred sheep.

HAMER v. SIDWAY
Court of Appeals of New York, Second Division, 1891.
124 N.Y. 538, 27 N.E. 256.

They were worth quite a bit of money, and the uncle wanted his nephew to have these as well. He wrote, "You can consider this money on interest."

The nephew received his uncle's letter and thereafter consented that the money should remain with his uncle according to the terms and conditions of the letter. The uncle died about two years later without having paid his nephew any part of the $5,000 and interest. The executor of the uncle's estate (the defendant in this action) did not want to pay the $5,000 (with interest) to the nephew, claiming that there had been no valid consideration for the promise.

The court disagreed with the executor and reviewed the doctrine of detriment-benefit as valid consideration under the law.

PARKER, Justice.
* * *

The defendant contends that the contract was without consideration to support it, and therefore invalid. He asserts that the promisee, by refraining from the use of liquor and tobacco, was not harmed, but benefited; that that which he did was best for him to do, independently of his uncle's promise,—and insists that it follows that, unless the promisor was benefited, the contract was without consideration,—a contention which, if well founded, would seem to leave open for controversy in many cases whether that which the promisee did or omitted to do was in fact of such benefit to him as to leave no consideration to support the enforcement of the promisor's agreement. Such a rule could not be tolerated, and is without foundation in the law. The exchequer chamber in 1875 defined "consideration" as follows: "A valuable consideration, in the sense of the law, may consist either in some right, interest, profit, or benefit accruing to the one party, or some forbearance, detriment, loss, or responsibility given, suffered, or undertaken by the other." Courts "will not ask whether the thing which forms the consideration does in fact benefit the promisee or a third party, or is of any substantial value to any one. It is enough that something is promised, done, forborne, or suffered by the party to whom the promise is made as consideration for the promise made to him. In general a waiver of any legal right at the request of another party is a sufficient consideration for a promise. Any damage, or suspension, or forbearance of a right will be sufficient to sustain a promise."
* * *

Now, applying this rule to the facts before us, the promisee used tobacco, occasionally drank liquor, and he had a legal right to do so. That right he abandoned for a period of years upon the strength of the promise of the testator that for such forbearance he would give him $5,000. We need not speculate on the effort which may have been required to give up the use of those stimulants. It is sufficient that he restricted his lawful freedom of action within certain prescribed limits upon the faith of his uncle's agreement, and now, having fully performed the conditions imposed, it is of no moment whether such performance actually proved a benefit to the promisor, and the court will not inquire into it; but, were it a proper subject of inquiry, we see nothing in this record that would permit a determination that the uncle was not benefited in a legal sense.

The court ruled that the nephew had provided legally sufficient consideration by giving up smoking, drinking, swearing, and playing cards or billiards for money, until he became twenty-one and was therefore entitled to the money.

The Hamer v. Sidway case has provided incentive for many young law students to strike bargains with wealthy family members. It must be remembered, however, that although the court found that the benefit-detriment bargain was sufficient consideration to support the promise to pay, the only reason the nephew was actually permitted to collect the money from the executor was because the court went on to find that the uncle had established a trust to hold the money for the benefit of the nephew. Without that, the Statute of Limitations would have barred the nephew's claim.

"Good Consideration" and Legal Sufficiency

Sometimes people feel a moral obligation to make a promise to loved ones. A father may promise to pay $10,000 to his daughter "in consideration of the love and affection that I have for you." An employer may promise to give a sum of money to a trusted employee "in consideration of the many acts of kindness and thoughtfulness over the years" that the employee has performed. This is generally called "good consideration." It is founded on natural duty and affection or on a strong moral obligation. Good consideration is not legally sufficient consideration, however. Therefore, promises made in exchange for it are unenforceable.

Adequacy of Consideration

Adequacy of consideration refers to the fairness of the bargain. If B agrees to pay $2 for S's motorcycle, B's consideration is legally sufficient since B was under no prior legal duty to pay out the money. However, the consideration is far from adequate, since S is not getting a very fair bargain.

In general, a court of law will not question the adequacy of consideration if the consideration is legally sufficient. Under the doctrine of freedom of contract, parties are normally free to bargain as they wish. If people could sue merely because they entered into an unwise contract, the courts would be overloaded with frivolous suits. In extreme cases, a court may look to the amount or value (the adequacy) of the consideration because inadequate consideration can indicate fraud, duress, or undue influence. Suppose Lansky has a house worth $25,000, and he sells it for $5,000. The consideration would be legally sufficient but not very adequate. The $5,000 sale could indicate that the buyer pressured Lansky into selling or that Lansky was defrauded into selling at far below market value.

In an equity suit, courts will question the adequacy of consideration. (Remember from Chapter 1 that actions at law allow for remedies that consist of some form of compensation. Actions at equity allow for remedies that involve a specific performance or an injunction.) The parties in an equity suit must show that the transaction was fair and that substantially equivalent consideration was exchanged. For example, a suit to compel specific performance is equitable and requires the losing party actually to perform the contract duties rather than pay damages for breach of contract. Assume McMichael agrees to sell land worth $45,000 to Price for only $7,500. After signing the contract, McMichael refuses to deliver possession, and Price sues for specific performance. The court may now look at the relative values of the consideration exchanged and may refuse to allow specific performance since the consideration is inadequate. Today, law and equity cases are no longer handled by separate courts.

As a general principle of contract law, the courts will not ordinarily look into the adequacy of the consideration in an agreed exchange. However, in the following case, the court would not allow "peace of mind" and $1.05 to constitute adequate consideration for a $12,000 land sale.

ROSE v. LURVEY
Court of Appeals of Michigan,
1972.
40 Mich. App.230, 198 N.W.2d
839

BACKGROUND AND FACTS *When the Rose family ran into marital difficulties, Robert Rose sought the advice and help of his sister, Norma Lurvey. Robert's estranged wife, Barbara, had failed to make several mortgage payments, and the family home was in danger of default as well as being in arrears on taxes. Norma Lurvey suggested to Robert that her son (his nephew), Wyman Lurvey, might assist financially.*

Robert and Wyman discussed transferring the house, but no price was ever mentioned. Wyman agreed that following such a transfer, he would make the back mortgage payments and pay the taxes that were owing. An attorney drew up the necessary papers. The instruments were executed despite the fact that they failed to specify a sale price. The only money mentioned was $1.05 recited as consideration in the documents. Subsequently, Robert and Barbara Rose reconciled and continued to live in the house, anticipating that Wyman would be paying them some additional money. Wyman instead served them with notice to vacate the premises. The Roses ignored the notice. A month or so later, Robert Rose entered the hospital. During the short time the house was unoccupied, Wyman moved in and began remodeling the interior.

The Rose family (plaintiffs) contended that the quit claim deed and the contract assigning the land to Wyman Lurvey (defendant) should be thrown out because the consideration was so grossly inadequate as to shock the conscience.

LESINSKI, Chief Judge.
* * *

It is a general principle of contract law that courts will not ordinarily look into the adequacy of the consideration in an agreed exchange. Equity will, however, grant relief where the inadequacy of consideration is particularly glaring. Thus the Michigan Supreme Court stated the rule that:

"Mere inadequacy of consideration, unless it be so gross as to shock the conscience of the court, is not ground for rescission."

In the case at bar [the one under consideration], the trial judge found that plaintiffs received more than just the $1.05 recited consideration from defendants. This additional consideration was said to have been the peace of mind plaintiffs obtained from knowing that they did not have to worry about the ramifications of defaulting on the land contract. This Court believes that this finding of additional consideration was erroneous. What the trial court mistakenly referred to as consideration was in actuality nothing more than the inducements and motives which influenced plaintiffs into making the contract. Inducements and motives are merely the subjective manifestation of plaintiffs' own desires. They are not that bargained for exchange or legal detriment to defendants which is necessary to establish a legally valid contract.

"*The motive which prompts one to enter into a contract and the consideration for the contract are distinct and different things.* [Emphasis added.] Parties are led into agreements by many inducements, such as the hope of profit, the expectation of acquiring what they could not otherwise obtain, the desire of avoiding a loss, etc. These inducements are not, however, either legal or equitable consideration, and actually compose no part of the contract."

In light of the fact that $1.05 represented the entire consideration for the transfer of an equity in the property worth approximately $12,000, we find ourselves called upon to decide whether such consideration was so grossly inadequate as to "shock the conscience of the court." We believe it was.

The South Carolina Supreme Court * * * stated:

" 'Grossly inadequate consideration does not mean simply less than the actual value of the property. It means a consideration so far short of the real value of property as to shock a correct mind.' "

The Virginia Supreme Court of Appeals cited * * * grossly inadequate consideration as:

" 'An inequality so strong, gross and manifest that it must be impossible to state it to a man of common sense without producing an exclamation at the inequality of it,' * * *."

This Court reaches the conclusion that the transfer of an equity in property worth $12,000 for $1.05 exhibited an inequality so strong as to amount to a gross inadequacy of consideration.

"Inadequacy of price paid for real property is not sufficient alone to authorize a court of equity to set aside a deed of conveyance, unless it is so gross as to shock a conscientious person; but, if the inadequacy is so great as to shock a conscientious person, it alone may furnish sufficient ground for annulling the conveyance."

The court held that the gross inadequacy of the consideration mandated the cancellation of the quit claim deed and the contract of assignment. Wyman Lurvey was required to vacate the house. A new trial was ordered to determine whether Wyman owed the Roses rent for the time he occupied the house and whether the Roses owed Wyman the amount of back taxes and mortgage payments he had made on their behalf.

JUDGMENT AND REMEDY

SITUATIONS WHERE CONSIDERATION IS NOT PRESENT

The element of exchange is absent whenever: (1) a promise is given in exchange for a past occurrence or transaction, (2) there is a pre-existing duty, (3) there is a moral obligation, (4) an illegal act is involved, and (5) there is an illusory promise.

Past Consideration

Past consideration is not consideration. Therefore, a promise given for something that has already been done is not enforceable. Suppose a father tells his son, "In consideration of the fact that you named your son after me, I promise to pay you $1,000." The promise is unenforceable since no present consideration supports it. There was no exchange.

Suppose instead that the father tells his son, "In consideration of your promise to name your next child after me, I promise to pay you $1,000." The son's next child is named after the father. Here, there is an exchange. Hence, legally sufficient consideration supports the father's promise to pay $1,000. (Note that in some jurisdictions, past consideration may serve as consideration if in writing.)

A familiar legal maxim says, "Love and affection do not constitute sufficient considera-tion to support a contract." This rule takes into account the so-called moral consideration that occurs when there is no expectation on the part of either party at the time the promise is made that it will be carried out. Thus, in the following case, the court reiterates that past or moral consideration is not sufficient to support an executory contract.[4]

---

4. For an exception, see Restatement, Second, Contracts (tentative draft), Section 89A.

LANFIER v. LANFIER
Supreme Court of Iowa, 1939.
227 Iowa 258, 288 N.W. 104.

BACKGROUND AND FACTS   *This suit concerned title to certain real property. The plaintiff-appellee was a minor bringing suit through his father. The defendants were the heirs of August Schultz and the administratrix of his estate. The case came to court on the basis of an oral contract allegedly made between Schultz and the plaintiff (through the plaintiff's mother).*

Schultz agreed to give the plaintiff certain real estate if plaintiff's mother would name plaintiff after him. He also agreed to reserve to the plaintiff's parents a life estate in that real estate. The plaintiff's parents accepted the proposal and named plaintiff after Schultz. Schultz neglected to perform his oral contract and never arranged for title to the property to pass to plaintiff. However, he did deliver possession of the real estate to plaintiff's parents, who held possession for about twelve years. Among other things, the plaintiff wanted the court to adjudge him the absolute owner of the real estate.

The administratrix of Schultz's estate and the other beneficiaries challenged plaintiff's right to the property. The trial court awarded the property to the plaintiff based on the alleged oral contract between decedent and plaintiff's mother.

MILLER, Justice.
* * *

"The general principle of the law of contracts, that to be valid and legally enforceable, as between the parties thereto an agreement or undertaking of any kind must be supported by a consideration, is too elementary to call for citation of authorities.

Under the record herein, there is a total absence of any evidence of a legal consideration to support the alleged contract plaintiff seeks to enforce. The evidence is undisputed that plaintiff was born on December 17, 1925, and, two days later, December 19, 1925, he was named August Dwayne Lanfier. He was named August after his grandfather, the decedent herein.

There is no evidence of any request on the part of the decedent that plaintiff be named after him until the latter part of March, 1926, over three months after plaintiff had been named. There are several witnesses who testified to conversations between plaintiff's mother and the decedent at that time, the substance of which was that, if plaintiff's mother would name plaintiff after the decedent, decedent would make a will and would thereby devise to plaintiff the real estate in question, subject to a life estate in plaintiff's parents. At the time these conversations were had, plaintiff and his parents were already in possession of the property, as tenants of the decedent.

Counsel for plaintiff assert that the contract was supported by sufficient consideration, in that the prior naming of the plaintiff for the decedent constituted a past or moral consideration, and further that the contract should be supported on the basis of love and affection being good consideration. The contentions of counsel are without merit.

This court has repeatedly held that past or moral consideration is not sufficient to support an executory contract. If the services are gratuitous, no obligation, either moral or legal, is incurred by the recipient. No one is bound to pay for that which is a gratuity. No moral obligation is assumed by a person who receives a gift. Suppose the plaintiff had given the defendant a horse, was he morally bound to pay what the horse was reasonably worth? We think not. In such case there never was any liability to pay, and therefore a subsequent promise would be without any consideration to support it.

* * *

The contentions of counsel to the effect that love and affection constitute sufficient consideration to support the contract here asserted are likewise without merit. No such consideration is expressed in the contract, and we seriously doubt that the record supports any claim that such might have been consideration for the alleged contract. However, in any event, the proposition of law contended for by counsel has no support in the decisions of this court or in the courts generally.

* * *

"Although love and affection is a 'good' consideration, it is not a sufficient consideration for a promise. Promises or contracts made on the basis of mere love and affection, unsupported by a pecuniary or material benefit, create at most bare moral obligations, and a breach thereof presents no cause for redress by the courts."

Plaintiff was not awarded title to the property. Love and affection are not legally sufficient consideration to support a promise, and thus breach of such a promise presents no legally recognizable cause of action.

JUDGMENT AND REMEDY

In rare cases, courts are willing to recognize a moral obligation of the promisor as a substitute for consideration where the promisor receives a material benefit and subsequently expresses a promise to pay for it. For example, in Webb v. McGowin, 27 Ala.App. 82, 168 So. 196 (1935), Webb was maimed for life when he diverted the course of a falling block of wood that otherwise would have killed McGowin. McGowin was so grateful to Webb that he agreed to send him $15 every two weeks for the remainder of Webb's life. But McGowin died before Webb. Ultimately, the court ruled that McGowin's estate was responsible for continuing to pay Webb the $15 every other week. McGowin's promise became a valid and enforceable contract.

COMMENTS

Performing a Pre-existing Duty

Under most circumstances, a promise to do what one already has a legal duty to do is not legally sufficient consideration because no legal detriment or benefit has been incurred.[5] The pre-existing legal duty may arise out of a previous contract or may be imposed by law. A sheriff cannot collect a reward for information leading to the capture of a criminal if the sheriff is under a duty to capture the criminal. Similarly, assume Healey agrees to hire Brewster for one year at $175 per week. Brewster begins working. After two months, Healey agrees orally to increase the wages to $195 per week. Healey's promise is unenforceable because it is not supported by legally sufficient consideration. Brewster was under a pre-existing duty to work for one year, and the performance of that duty cannot be consideration for the wage increase.

The harshness of the pre-existing duty rule is evident. In the examples above, the sheriff is denied a reward that anyone else could have received, and Brewster, the employee, can be denied his pay raise. Therefore, the courts are ready to find *any* legal detriment or benefit, no matter how small or insignificant, so that the promise will be enforceable. Hence, if Brewster was required to perform any *extra* duties, the promise modifying his employment contract would be enforceable.

Incurring a Moral Obligation

Promises based on moral duty or obligation are not enforceable because a moral obligation is not legally sufficient consideration. Suppose your friend is injured in a distant city and a grocer takes care of him during his injury. Thereafter, feeling a moral obligation to help your friend and aid the grocer, you promise the grocer to pay for your friend's expenses. The promise is unenforceable since it is supported only by your moral obligation, and a moral obligation cannot be legally sufficient consider-

ation. Other examples of promises made out of a moral obligation include promises to pay the debts of one's parents or promises to pay for the care rendered to relatives one was under no duty to support. A minority of states enforce promises supported only by a moral obligation— but only to the extent of the actual obligation or of the services or care rendered.[6]

Performing an Illegal Act

A promise to perform an illegal act is not legally sufficient consideration. If it were, then an illegal act could be enforced in a court of law. Public policy requires the consideration to be for the performance of a legal act.

Making an Illusory Promise

An illusory promise is actually no promise at all. It may sound like a promise, but close examination reveals that the promisor has actually agreed to do nothing. For example, if I promise to buy "whatever supplies I *may want* during August and September," I have not really *promised* to buy anything. Therefore, I suffer no legal detriment, and the promise is unenforceable. (Note the difference here between the above promise, which is unenforceable, and a promise to buy "all the supplies I will need," which is enforceable.)

Illusory contracts do not unconditionally bind anyone. A contract under which X promises to buy from Y all the natural gas that X "might wish" over the next year with Y promising to sell that quantity at a specified price per thousand cubic feet is no contract at all. X is not bound to buy any quantity of natural gas and has thus incurred no detriment. Neither promisor is liable to the other. If X wishes to buy natural gas later on, he can buy it anywhere. Furthermore, if X orders natural gas from Y under this agreement, Y has no duty to supply it under the terms of the contract.

---

5. Foakes v. Beer, 9 App.Cas. 605.

6. For example, see California Civil Code, Sec. 1606.

SPECIAL CONSIDERATION QUESTIONS

Settlement of Debts

When a debt is disputed and the dispute has some merit, payment of part of the debt can be satisfaction of the whole debt. Courts view the debtor's relinquishing of contentions (reasons for the dispute) as legally sufficient consideration, and the entire debt is thereby discharged or satisfied.

A **liquidated debt** is one in which the amount owing is not disputed and can be expressed as a certain sum of money. (The term "liquidated" means ascertained, fixed, settled, and determined.) An **unliquidated debt** cannot be expressed as a certain sum. The debt in question may be either liquidated or unliquidated and may involve a dispute as to the existence or amount of the debt.

When both parties agree to discharge a debt for a lesser amount, and part payment is accepted by the creditor as *payment in full,* the debt is discharged if it was disputed or unliquidated. This discharge is usually accomplished by the parties first reaching a settlement agreement, then by sending the creditor a check marked "payment in full." Suppose you hire a painter to paint your apartment at $10 an hour plus materials costs. He finishes the job and presents you with a bill for $1,000. You contend that the job is only worth $500. The painter agrees to settle for $700, and you write a check for $700. The painter cannot come back later and sue you to recover the difference between $700 and $1,000. Why? Because his acceptance of the $700 is an implied promise to release you from the debt. Your payment to the painter constitutes a detriment to you because you can no longer go to court to contend that the debt was only $500. The painter cannot obtain a ruling in his favor that the debt was not completely paid. This is particularly true if you write "payment in full" on the back of the check, and the check is cashed by the painter. If the debt is liquidated and not disputed, payment of part of the debt will *not* discharge the entire amount. This is due to the pre-existing legal duty to pay the full amount. (Under the Uniform Commercial Code no consideration is necessary to discharge a liquidated and undisputed debt.[7] The discharge can be accomplished by a written waiver or renunciation signed and delivered to the debtor.)

Construction Contracts

Suppose Bauman-Bache, Inc., begins construction on a seven-floor office building and after three months demands an extra $75,000 on its contract or it will stop working. The owner of the land, having no one else to complete construction, agrees to pay the extra $75,000. The agreement is not enforceable because it is not supported by legally sufficient consideration; Bauman-Bache was under a pre-existing duty to complete the building. Some courts, however, have held such a modifying agreement enforceable. The conflicting policies are two: (1) people should be able to modify their legal relations; and (2) modification in some cases will resemble duress, as in the Bauman-Bache example.

Most of the time, a promise to modify a construction contract will not be enforced, but in some cases it will be. In those minority of cases, courts have said that the original contract was rescinded and replaced with the new agreement.[8] Other courts have said the original consideration carries over into the new agreement.[9]

As was pointed out, a promise to do something that a party is already under a legal obligation to do is not valid consideration sufficient to support a contract. However, sometimes a party runs into some unforeseen or substantial difficulty in the performance of a contract that could not have been anticipated when the contract was entered into. If this casts an additional burden not contemplated by the parties, an additional promise to pay extra compensation will be valid consideration. Such is the situation in the following case.

---

7. UCC Sec. 1-107.
8. Armour & Co. v. Celic, 294 F.2d 432 (2d Cir. 1961).
9. Holly v. First Nat. Bank, 218 Wis. 259, 260 N.W. 429 (1935).

LANGE v.
UNITED STATES
United States Court of Appeals,
Fourth Circuit, 1941.
120 F.2d 886.

BACKGROUND AND FACTS *Lange Bros. (appellant) entered into a contract to construct a laundry building at the United States Naval Academy at Annapolis, Maryland. Prior to submitting a bid as general contractors, Lange Bros. obtained estimates from various subcontractors on the costs of numerous projects involved in the construction. In particular, the construction and installation of a laundry chute was to be undertaken by C. M. Wilkinson & Company (appellee). The entire work on the chute was to be done in strict accordance with the plans and specifications of the government architect and was subject to the approval and acceptance of both Lange Bros. and the government. After signing the government contract, Lange Bros. mailed to Wilkinson the particular page of the General Government Specification applicable to the clothes chute appellee was to install under the subcontract.*

The original contract price was $347; to comply with specifications would cost $1,071. After much discussion, appellee and appellant entered into a second contract that was practically identical to the original subcontract except that the second contract provided for a higher price. Lange Bros. contended that the second contract was unenforceable because it lacked new consideration—appellee was merely doing what he was already under a legal obligation to do—that is, install a laundry chute.

DOBIE, Circuit Judge.
* * *

An outstanding fact in this record that impresses us is the very wide spread, or variance, that exists between the agreed prices in the first and second contracts.
* * *

On the strength of this single factor we would be strongly tempted to conclude that there was, in fact and law, no real contract under the agreement of March 1st; for the rule seems to be well-settled that an offeree may not snap up an offer that is on its face manifestly too good to be true.
* * *

We are of the opinion that with the exception of the provision for a higher price, the second contract was practically identical with the first.
* * *

[A]dherence is given to "the general rule that a promise to do, or actually doing, that which a party to a contract is already under legal obligation to do, is not a valid consideration to support the promise of the other party to the contract to pay additional compensation for such performance."

But to this rule the Court of Appeals of Maryland admits an exception. The exception relates to unforeseen difficulties in the performance of the contract, and is thus expressed in Linz v. Schuck, "[W]here the party refusing to complete his contract does so by reason of some unforeseen and substantial difficulties in the performance of the contract, which were not known or anticipated by the parties when the contract was entered into, and which cast upon him an additional burden not contemplated by the parties, and the opposite party promises him extra pay or benefits if he will complete his contract, and he so promises, the promise to pay is supported by a valid consideration."

The contract in Linz v. Schuck called for the digging of a cellar under a store to a depth of seven feet. The house stood on a hard crust of earth three feet thick, through which the foundation did not extend. When the contractor proceeding with the work got through the crust, he found soft muddy material, and it was impossible to go on without much unexpected labor and expense to provide proper footing for the building. The contractor refused to go on until he was promised additional compensation; and this promise was held by the court to be supported by sufficient consideration and to be enforceable. It is important to note, in considering the facts of that case, that the condition of the earth beneath the house, although unknown to the parties, could have been ascertained by tests before the first contract was signed. And such tests are not uncommonly made by building contractors before they enter into building contracts.

The same element of surprise existed as to the actual nature of the work to be done under the contract in [this] suit. [Emphasis added.] We do not suppose that appellants were aware that appellee had made an obvious mistake when he agreed in the first contract to a price that was less than one-third of the cost of installing the chute. Otherwise, the case might be decided against appellants under the rule already referred to. But there is substantial foundation in the evidence for the finding that neither party to the contract realized that the document referred to under the symbol 47S20a in the government specifications required a kind of material that could not possibly be installed for the price named in the contract.

* * *

But both parties were careless in ascertaining the facts relating to the chute, just as in Linz v. Schuck the parties might by tests have ascertained the nature of the ground beneath the house. The circumstances which might make it equitable and fair to increase the contract price, and the nature of the difficulties encountered, are not the same in the two cases; but the cases are alike in that, in each, both parties were taken by a surprise which might have been avoided had either party taken the necessary precautions. We, therefore, are of the opinion that the pending case falls within the principle and spirit of the exception set out in Linz v. Schuck.; * * *.

Wilkinson was entitled to be paid the second contract price of $1,071. The court felt that this was a situation in which an unforeseen and substantial difficulty unknown and unanticipated by the parties required an exception to be made.

JUDGMENT AND REMEDY

The settlement of a disputed claim must be made in good faith. There must be actual disagreement over the existence or the amount of the debt.

COMMENTS

Output and Requirements Contracts

An output contract requires a seller to sell the entire amount of goods produced over a specified period to another party. A requirements contract obligates a party to purchase all requirements from another party. For example, if U.S. Steel agreed to sell all I-beams produced during March to Boeing Aircraft, an output contract would be made. If U.S. Steel agreed to buy all coal needed during March from West Virginia Coal Company, a requirements contract would be made. These promises are not illusory. They obligate U.S. Steel to sell all output or buy all requirements, whatever they may be.

The Uniform Commercial Code imposes a *good faith limitation* on output and requirements contracts. The quantity under such contracts is the amount of output or the amount of requirements that occur during a *normal production year*. Therefore, if U.S. Steel produced 1,500 tons of I-beams last March and required 4,500 tons of coal, it could not sell 10,000 tons of I-beams or purchase 15,000 tons of coal under the contracts. The actual quantity sold or purchased cannot be unreasonably disproportionate to normal or comparable prior output or requirements.

Exclusive Dealing Contracts

An **exclusive dealing contract** requires a buyer to carry only products made by the seller. Wood agrees to market fabrics, millinery, and dresses upon which Lucy, Lady Duff-Gordon, places her endorsement. Lady Duff-Gordon receives no promise that Wood will market any dresses, but she gives Wood an exclusive right to market whatever number is deemed appropriate. At first blush, Wood's promise appears illusory. He has not agreed to sell anything. However, as in the output and requirements contracts, Wood is under a duty to use his "best efforts" to market the dresses.[10] This duty or obligation is consideration for the promise to either supply or sell.

Consider another example, that of a real estate broker who has obtained a thirty-day exclusive contract from the seller of a house. The broker has the duty to perform his or her best efforts in selling the house within thirty days and in dealing with a potential buyer.

Promises Enforceable Without Consideration

Certain promises, either by statute or court decision, can be fully or partially enforceable without consideration.

PROMISSORY ESTOPPEL   A promise given by a party that induces another party to act may be enforceable without consideration. When the promisor (the person making the promise) can reasonably expect the promisee (the person receiving the promise) to act on the promise, and injustice cannot be avoided any other way, the promise will be enforced.[11] Additionally, the promisee must act with justifiable reliance on the promise.

The promise is enforced by refusing to allow the promisor to set up the defense of no consideration. This is called estoppel. The promisor is estopped from asserting the lack of consideration. The estoppel arises from the promise, hence **promissory estoppel.** (This doctrine is *not* used in some jurisdictions.)

Imagine that your grandfather tells you, "I'll pay you $75 per week so you won't have to work anymore." Then you quit your job, and your grandfather refuses to pay. You can enforce the promise since you have justifiably relied on it.[12]

Traditionally, promissory estoppel has been applied only to gratuitous promises, that is, when the parties are not bargaining in a commercial setting. The trend, however, is to apply it in any situation if justice so requires (as shown in the next case).

---

10.   Wood v. Lucy, Lady Duff-Gordon, 222 N.Y. 88, 118 N.E. 214 (1917).

11.   See UCC Sec. 2-306. Also Restatement, Contracts, Section 90 provides: a promise which the promisor should reasonably expect to induce action or forbearance of a definite and substantial character on the part of the promisee and which does induce such action or forbearance is binding if injustice can be avoided only by enforcement of the promise.

12.   Ricketts v. Scothorn, 57 Neb. 51, 77 N.W. 365 (1898).

BACKGROUND AND FACTS   *Red Owl Stores, Inc. (defendant), induced the Hoffmans (plaintiffs) to give up their current business and run a Red Owl franchise. The Hoffmans relied on the representations of Red Owl, and when the deal ultimately fell through because of Red Owl's failure to keep its promise concerning the operation of the franchise agency store, the Hoffmans brought this suit to recover their losses.*

HOFFMAN v. RED OWL STORES, INC.
Supreme Court of Wisconsin, 1965.
26 Wis. 2d 683, 133 N.W.2d 267.

CURRIE, Chief Justice.
* * *

Recognition of a Cause of Action Grounded on Promissory Estoppel.
    Sec. 90 of Restatement, 1 Contracts, provides (at p. 110):
    "A promise which the promisor should reasonably expect to induce action or forbearance of a definite and substantial character on the part of the promisee and which does induce such action or forbearance is binding if injustice can be avoided only by enforcement of the promise."
* * *

    Because we deem the doctrine of promissory estoppel, as stated in sec. 90 of Restatement, 1 Contracts, is one which supplies a needed tool which courts may employ in a proper case to prevent injustice, we endorse and adopt it.

Applicability of Doctrine to Facts of this Case.
    The record here discloses a number of promises and assurances given to Hoffman by Lukowitz in behalf of Red Owl upon which plaintiffs relied and acted upon to their detriment.
    Foremost were the promises that for the sum of $18,000 Red Owl would establish Hoffman in a store. After Hoffman had sold his grocery store and paid the $1,000 on the Chilton lot, the $18,000 figure was changed to $24,100. Then in November, 1961, Hoffman was assured that if the $24,100 figure were increased by $2,000 the deal would go through. Hoffman was induced to sell his grocery store fixtures and inventory in June, 1961, on the promise that he would be in his new store by fall. In November, plaintiffs sold their bakery building on the urging of defendants and on the assurance that this was the last step necessary to have the deal with Red Owl go through.
    We determine that there was ample evidence to sustain the answers of the jury to the questions of the verdict with respect to the promissory representations made by Red Owl, Hoffman's reliance thereon in the exercise of ordinary care, and his fulfillment of the conditions required of him by the terms of the negotiations had with Red Owl.
    There remains for consideration the question of law raised by defendants that agreement was never reached on essential factors necessary to establish a contract between Hoffman and Red Owl. Among these were the size, cost, design, and layout of the store building; and the terms of the lease with respect to rent, maintenance, renewal, and purchase options. This poses *the question of whether the promise necessary to sustain a cause of action for promissory estoppel must embrace all essential details of a proposed transaction* between promisor and promisee so as to be the equivalent of an offer that would result in a binding contract between the parties if the promisee were to accept the same. [Emphasis added.]

Originally the doctrine of promissory estoppel was invoked as a substitute for consideration rendering a gratuitous promise enforceable as a contract. In other words, the acts of reliance by the promisee to his detriment provided a substitute for consideration. If promissory estoppel were to be limited to only those situations where the promise giving rise to the cause of action must be so definite with respect to all details that a contract would result were the promise supported by consideration, then the defendants' instant promises to Hoffman would not meet this test. However, sec. 90 of Restatement, 1 Contracts, does not impose the requirement that the promise giving rise to the cause of action must be so comprehensive in scope as to meet the requirements of an offer that would ripen into a contract if accepted by the promisee. Rather the conditions imposed are:

(1) Was the promise one which the promisor should reasonably expect to induce action or forbearance of a definite and substantial character on the part of the promisee?

(2) Did the promise induce such action or forbearance?

(3) Can injustice be avoided only by enforcement of the promise?

We deem it would be a mistake to regard an action grounded on promissory estoppel as the equivalent of a breach of contract action. As Dean Boyer points out, it is desirable that fluidity in the application of the concept be maintained. While the first two of the above listed three requirements of promissory estoppel present issues of fact which ordinarily will be resolved by a jury, the third requirement, that the remedy can only be invoked where necessary to avoid injustice, is one that involves a policy decision by the court. Such a policy decision necessarily embraces an element of discretion.

We conclude that injustice would result here if plaintiffs were not granted some relief because of the failure of defendants to keep their promises which induced plaintiffs to act to their detriment.

JUDGMENT AND REMEDY *Trial court's judgment was affirmed. Hoffman was awarded damages, the exact amount to be determined when the case was returned to the trial court. The Supreme Court concluded that injustice would result if Hoffman were not granted some relief because of the failure of Red Owl Stores to keep its promises concerning the operation of the franchise agency store.*

COMMENTS *Promissory estoppel does not mean that each and every gratuitous promise will be binding merely because the promisee has changed position. Liability is created only when there is "justifiable reliance on the promise." The promisor must have known or had reason to believe that the promisee would likely be induced to change position as a result of the promise.*

CHARITABLE SUBSCRIPTIONS Ordinarily, a promise to make a gift is not enforceable since it is not supported by legally sufficient consideration. Exceptions have been made, however, where a charitable organization solicits subscriptions for donations. A subscription is a written pledge of some specific amount of money that is signed by the person making the donation. Charitable institutions covered by this exception include churches, colleges, and hospitals or other religious, educational, or charitable organizations.

Promises to make charitable subscriptions are exempted from the necessity of consideration because the promisee (usually a church school or charitable foundation) often changes its position on the basis of the subscription. A church may solicit donative subscriptions to build a new church on a different property. On the basis of the total pledges and amounts received, it employs architects, makes contracts, and in many other ways changes its position. Such changes are held to be either the equivalent of consideration or a substitute for it. Another way the courts have looked at it is that, by accepting the subscription, the trustees of the charity imply a promise to complete the proposed undertaking.

BACKGROUND AND FACTS *The plaintiff, Allegheny College, inaugurated a fund raising drive to secure an endowment of $1,250,000. Mary Yates responded to the request to contribute and signed the following writing:*

> "Estate Pledge, Allegheny College Second Century Endowment.
> "Jamestown, N.Y., June 15, 1921.
> "In consideration of my interest in Christian education, and in consideration of others subscribing, I hereby subscribe and will pay to the order of the treasurer of Allegheny College, Meadville, Pennsylvania, the sum of five thousand dollars; $5,000.
> "This obligation shall become due thirty days after my death, and I hereby instruct my executor, or administrator, to pay the same out of my estate. This pledge shall bear interest at the rate of _____ per cent. per annum, payable annually, from _____ till paid. The proceeds of this obligation shall be added to the Endowment of said Institution, or expended in accordance with instructions on reverse side of this pledge.
> "Name: Mary Yates Johnston,
> "Address: 306 East 6th Street, Jamestown, N.Y.
> "Dayton E. McClain, Witness,
> "T. R. Courtis, Witness,
>   "To authentic signature."
> On the reverse side of the writing is the following indorsement:
> "In loving memory this gift shall be known as the Mary Yates Johnston memorial fund, the proceeds from which shall be used to educate students preparing for the ministry, either in the United States or in the Foreign Field.
> "This pledge shall be valid only on the condition that the provisions of my will, now extant, shall be first met.   Mary Yates Johnston."

The subscription was not payable by its terms until thirty days after the death of the promisor. However, the sum of $1,000 was paid while the promisor was still alive. The college then set aside the money to be held as a scholarship fund for the benefit of students preparing for the ministry. Three years after pledging the subscription, Mary Yates repudiated the promise. She gave notice to the college that she was not going to make the complete $5,000 gift.

Mary Yates died, and the college sought to have her estate held liable for the unpaid balance of the subscription.

ALLEGHENY COLLEGE v. NATIONAL CHAUTAUQUA COUNTY BANK OF JAMESTOWN
Court of Appeals of New York, 1927.
246 N.Y. 369, 159 N.E. 173.

CARDOZO, Chief Justice.

* * *

The promisor wished to have a memorial to perpetuate her name. She imposed a condition that the "gift" should "be known as the Mary Yates Johnston Memorial Fund." The moment that the college accepted $1,000 as a payment on account, there was an assumption of a duty to do whatever acts were customary or reasonably necessary to maintain the memorial fairly and justly in the spirit of its creation. The college could not accept the money and hold itself free thereafter from personal responsibility to give effect to the condition. More is involved in the receipt of such a fund than a mere acceptance of money to be held to a corporate use. The purpose of the founder would be unfairly thwarted or at least inadequately served if the college failed to communicate to the world, or in any event to applicants for the scholarship, the title of the memorial. By implication it undertook, when it accepted a portion of the "gift," that in its circulars of information and in other customary ways when making announcement of this scholarship, it would couple with the announcement the name of the donor. The donor was not at liberty to gain the benefit of such an undertaking upon the payment of a part and disappoint the expectation that there would be payment of the residue. If the college had stated after receiving $1,000 upon account of the subscription, that it would apply the money to the prescribed use, but that in its circulars of information and when responding to prospective applicants it would deal with the fund as an anonymous donation, there is little doubt that the subscriber would have been at liberty to treat this statement as the repudiation of a duty impliedly assumed, a repudiation justifying a refusal to make payments in the future. Obligation in such circumstances is correlative and mutual.

* * *

We think the duty assumed by the plaintiff to perpetuate the name of the founder of the memorial is sufficient in itself to give validity to the subscription within the rules that define consideration for a promise of that order. [Emphasis added.]

JUDGMENT AND REMEDY

The estate was required to pay the full amount owing on the pledge to Allegheny College.

COMMENTS

There are two major theories used to "find" consideration in charitable subscription cases. These theories are promissory estoppel and mutual promises. The case presented here is Justice Cardozo's classic example of the promissory estoppel doctrine. The second theory is that the promise of each subscriber is given in exchange for the promise of each other subscriber such that these promises interrelate and mutually support one another.

Exceptions to Consideration under the Uniform Commercial Code

The Uniform Commercial Code has expressly eliminated the requirement of consideration in several situations. The UCC is treated extensively in Unit IV, so only a brief review of some salient points is given here.

FIRM OFFERS A signed written offer by a merchant to buy or sell goods is not revocable for lack of consideration. The offer, termed a firm offer (defined in the previous chapter), is irrevocable for the time stated in the offer (but for no longer than three months). If no time is stated, the offer remains irrevocable for a reasonable time (UCC Sec. 2-205). The law of firm offers is analogous to the option contract, but by statute the firm offer does not require consideration.

WAIVER OR RENUNCIATION OF CLAIM
Any claim or right arising out of an alleged breach can be discharged in whole or in part without consideration by a written waiver or renunciation signed and delivered by the aggrieved party (UCC Sec. 1-107). By the use of such a waiver, the repayment of $50 on a $100 debt can discharge the entire debt, notwithstanding the pre-existing duty rule.

COMMERCIAL PAPER Special rules apply to commercial paper. For a detailed discussion, see Chapter 26.

MODIFICATION An agreement modifying a contract for the sale of goods needs no consideration to be binding [UCC Sec. 2-209(1)].

LETTERS OF CREDIT No consideration is necessary to establish a letter of credit. In addition, no consideration is necessary to modify or enlarge the terms of a letter of credit (UCC Sec. 5-105).

New Promises to Pay Barred Debts

DEBTS BARRED BY THE STATUTE OF LIMITATIONS Statutes of limitations in all states require a creditor to sue within a specified period to recover debts. If the creditor fails to sue in time, recovery of the debt is barred by the statute of limitations. A debtor who promises to pay a previous debt barred by the statute of limitations makes an enforceable promise. *The*

promise needs no consideration. (Some states, however, require that it be in writing.) In effect, the promise extends the limitations period, and the creditor can sue to recover the entire debt. The promise can be implied if the debtor acknowledges the barred debt by making a partial payment.

Suppose you borrow $5,000 from First National Bank of San Jose. The loan is due in November 1980. You fail to pay, and the bank does not sue you until December 1985. If California's statute of limitations for this debt is five years, recovery of the debt is barred. If you then agree to pay the loan off, First National Bank can sue for the entire amount. This is an example of an express promise, which extends the limitations period. Likewise, you can make a monthly payment and implicitly acknowledge the existence of the debt. Again First National Bank can sue you for the entire debt. This is an example of acknowledgment. Suppose instead that you expressly promise First National Bank to pay it $2,500. This promise is enforceable only to the extent of $2,500 (and usually must be in writing).

DEBTS DISCHARGED BY BANKRUPTCY A promise to pay a debt previously discharged by bankruptcy proceedings needs no consideration to be binding (but it must be in writing). The promise must be clear and definite. For example, if D says, "I promise to pay you what I can if I make some money this year," the promise is not enforceable because it is not a definite promise.

Unlike debts barred by the statute of limitations, part payment of a debt discharged in bankruptcy will not implicitly acknowledge the existence of the debt. Therefore, if you make a monthly payment on the loan received from First National after the loan has been discharged in bankruptcy, you are not liable for the entire amount of the loan.[13]

---

13. The revisions of the Bankruptcy Act recently passed by Congress, make revival of debts discharged in bankruptcy very difficult, and in the case of consumer loans, virtually impossible.

QUESTIONS AND CASE PROBLEMS

1. Gray is a special police officer in Atlantic City. Martino, who lost a significant amount of her jewelry during a burglary of her home, offered a reward for the recovery of the property. Incident to his job, Gray possessed certain knowledge concerning the theft of Martino's jewelry. When Gray informed Martino of his knowledge of the theft, Martino offered Gray $500 to help her recover her jewelry. As a result of police work, the diamonds and jewelry were recovered and returned to Martino. Gray sued Martino for the reward he claimed she promised him. Was there a valid contract between Gray and Martino? [Gray v. Martino, 91 N.J.L. 462, 103 A.24 (1918)]

2. McMichael agreed to furnish Price all the sand of various grades and qualities that Price could "sell for shipment to various and sundry points outside of the city of Tulsa." McMichael agreed to furnish the sand upon Price's written or oral request within a reasonable time after the request was made. At the time of the agreement, Price was not engaged in the business of selling sand. The agreement was to run for a ten-year period. After about five months, McMichael refused to deliver any more sand to Price. Was McMichael in breach of contract? [McMichael v. Price, 177 Okl. 186, 58 P.2d 549 (1936)]

3. Feinberg was secretary to the president of Pfeiffer Company. After she had worked there for eighteen years, the board of directors, in recognition of her "long and faithful service," passed a resolution whereunder she would be paid $200 a month for the rest of her life at any time she decided to retire. Shortly thereafter, Feinberg retired and for several years received the $200 per month as promised. The president of Pfeiffer eventually died and was succeeded by his son, who cut off all subsequent money to Feinberg. Feinberg sued Pfeiffer Company. Was she able to recover under contract theory? [Feinberg v. Pfeiffer Company, 322 S.W.2d 163 (Mo. App. 1959)]

4. Reynolds refused to pay Penhow the $500 he owed him, and Penhow sued. Prior to judgment, in an attempt to work out their differences, Reynolds and Penhow agreed that Reynolds could pay off the debt in full settlement for $400. Later, after the parties had already agreed to this arrangement, judgment was entered in favor of Penhow for the full $500. Instead of accepting $400 from Reynolds as full payment of the debt, Penhow insisted that Reynolds pay according to the full force of the judgment. Was the settlement agreement entered into between Penhow and Reynolds supported by adequate consideration? [Reynolds v. Penhow, Cro.Eliz. 429 (1595)]

5. Kirksey wrote a letter to his widowed sister-in-law, "Sister Antillico," inviting her to come live with him. The letter, in part, stated: "If you will come down and see me, I will let you have a place to raise your family." Within a month or two after receiving this letter, Sister Antillico abandoned her home and moved her family sixty miles to Kirksey's residence. She and her family lived with Kirksey for two years, when he notified her that she was to remove all her possessions and leave. Unenforceable gift or enforceable contract? [Kirksey v. Kirksey, 8 Ala. 131 (1845)]

6. Star Furniture Company manufactured summer lawn furniture. Its sole product consisted of webbed aluminum frame furniture used mainly on outdoor patios and on beaches. As of October 1, Star Furniture was heavily indebted to its three main suppliers—Aluminum Pole, Inc., Plastic Webbing, Ltd., and The Little Steel Rivet Company. Star owed each of these suppliers approximately $10,000. Star's president met individually with the presidents of each of the three suppliers to work out some arrangement whereby the company could avoid declaring bankruptcy. Since all the parties desired that Star Furniture not go bankrupt, the president of each supplier company agreed to accept $7,000 in full payment of all outstanding debts as of October 1. Was this agreement enforceable?

7. Nees owned two parcels of land. One parcel, located on Atlantic Avenue, he held exclusively in trust for two of his children, Sophia and George. The other parcel, known as the Sackett Street property, passed to all four of Nees's children upon Nees's death. None of the children learned that only Sophia and George were to receive the Atlantic Avenue property until they were informed by Nees's attorney at the time the attorney opened Nees's strongbox. Sophia and George, seeing that their brothers and sisters were disappointed that none of them had gotten any interest in the Atlantic property, promised to give them their share in the Sackett Street property, "if you don't bother us on the Atlantic Avenue house." Was this promise enforceable against Sophia and George? [Springstead v. Nees, 125 App.Div. 230, 109 N.Y.S. 148 (1908)]

8. Wyman was suddenly taken ill on a voyage. Mills, a nurse, took him in since he had no money and no place to go. Mills cared for Wyman over a consider-

able period of time and expended substantial sums of money in reviving him. After all the expenses had been incurred, Wyman's mother wrote a letter to Mills thanking her for taking care of her son and promising to repay all the expenses Mills had incurred on his behalf. Later, Wyman's mother refused to repay the expenses. Was Mills able to recover? Was there adequate consideration? [Mills v. Wyman, 20 Mass. (3 Pick.) 207 (1825)]

9. In the early 1960s the city of Boston was engaged in extensive redevelopment. In October of 1961, the Boston Redevelopment Authority (BRA) agreed to pay the expenses of relocating Graphic Arts Finishers, a business displaced by the Government Center Urban Renewal Project. BRA's promise to pay Graphic Arts' total moving expenses was given in exchange for performance of certain promises by Graphic Arts. The company promised: (1) to depart the premises peacefully and expeditiously, without requiring the BRA to resort to legal actions; (2) to relocate its business elsewhere and not liquidate; and (3) to induce its landlord to consider wiring, plumbing, and other property as the plaintiff's personal property so that the landlord would not claim greater damages from the BRA. Graphic Arts' moving expenses amounted to approximately $130,000. The BRA refused to pay. Did Graphic Arts give any consideration for BRA's promise? [Graphic Arts Finishers, Inc. v. Boston Redevelopment Authority, 357 Mass. 40, 255 N.E.2d 793 (1970)]

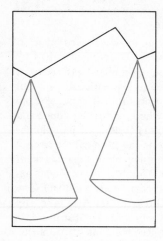

8

Contracts
Contractual Capacity

Some people, like minors and the mentally impaired, lack the capacity to make an enforceable contract, regardless of whether they understand its terms.

MINORS

At common law, a minor was defined as a male who had not attained the age of twenty-one or a female who had not attained the age of eighteen. Today, in most states, the age of majority (when a person is no longer a minor) has been changed by statute usually to eighteen years for both sexes.[1] In addition, some states provide for the termination of minority upon marriage. Subject to certain exceptions, the contracts entered into by a minor are avoidable at the option of that minor. A **voidable contract** is one in which the minor may avoid legal obligations by exercising the option to disaffirm the contract. On the other hand, an adult who enters into a contract with a minor cannot avoid his or her contractual duties on the ground that the minor can do so. Unless the minor exercises the option to avoid the contract, the adult party is bound by it.

---

1. While the age of majority applicable in contracts has been changed to eighteen in many states, it may still be twenty-one for some purposes, including the purchase and consumption of alcohol. The word "infant" is used synonymously with the word "minor."

Minors' Rights to Disaffirm

A minor's contract is not entirely void, despite the option to avoid the contract. A minor exercising the power to avoid a contract *disaffirms* it and *releases* both parties from their legal duties. A minor's voidable contract can become binding, however, if the minor *ratifies* or approves it. However, ratification cannot occur before the minor attains majority, since ratification is also voidable.

DISAFFIRMANCE IN GENERAL   In order for a minor to exercise the option to avoid a contract, he or she need only manifest an intention not to be bound by it. The infant "avoids" the contract by "disaffirming" it. The technical definition of *disaffirmance* is the legal avoidance, or setting aside, of a contractual obligation. Words or conduct may express this intent. Suppose James Caldwell, a seventeen-year-old, enters into a contract to sell his car to Joseph Reed, an adult. Caldwell can avoid the contract and avoid his legal duty to deliver possession of the car to Reed by either telling Reed that he refuses to abide by the contract or by selling the car to a third person. In other words, Caldwell can disaffirm the contract by expressing his intention in words or by acting inconsistently with his duties under the contract.

The contract can ordinarily be disaffirmed at any time during minority or for a reasonable time after the minor comes of age. However, an exception exists in the case of a contract for the sale of land by a minor. Here a minor cannot disaffirm the contract until he or she reaches majority.

If a minor fails to disaffirm a contract in a reasonable time after reaching majority, the contract can be deemed ratified due to the minor's failure to disaffirm. This is almost always true where the contract has been executed by the other party. For example, suppose Susan Taylor enters into a contract to buy a pool table from Snooker, Inc. She takes delivery of the table while she is a minor, and the contract is thereby executed by Snooker, Inc. By keeping the pool table when she reaches majority, Susan ratifies the contract and is bound to fulfill her legal duty to pay the full purchase price.

In some states, common law and statutes require minors to disaffirm their contracts within a reasonable time after reaching majority or they lose the right to avoid their legal duties. When the contract is executory—in other words, when neither party has fully performed their contractual obligations—some states require the minor to expressly affirm the contract. Other states deem the executory contract ratified for failure to disaffirm within a reasonable time after majority.

DUTY OF RESTORATION   When a contract has been executed, minors cannot disaffirm without returning whatever they have received (or making an offer to do so). This is called the minor's *duty of restoration*. Although many states recognize this duty, most place certain limitations on it. Under the majority view, the minor need only return the goods (or other consideration), provided they are in the minor's possession or control. Suppose Pat Boland, another seventeen-year-old, purchases a used Ford Fairmont from Jane Crow, an adult. Boland is a bad driver and runs the car into a telephone pole on his grandfather's farm. The next day he returns the car to Crow and disaffirms the contract. Under the majority view, this return fulfills Boland's duty even though the auto is now wrecked.

On the other hand, a few states, either by statute or by court decision, have placed an additional duty on the minor—the *duty of restitution*. The theory is intended to return the adult to his or her position before the contract was made. The duty of restitution requires Boland to pay Crow for the damage done to the car in addition to returning it. Some states do not require full restitution. A minor must pay a "reasonable" amount for the use of the property or to compensate the adult for the reasonable wear and tear to the property.

A minor must disaffirm the *entire* contract. The minor cannot decide to keep part of the goods and return the remainder. When a minor disaffirms, all property that the minor has transferred can be recovered even if it is then in the hands of a third party. If the property itself cannot be returned, the other party must pay the minor its equivalent value. Under UCC Sec. 2-403, the rule about recovering property does not apply if the transfer was a sale subject to the provisions of the UCC and if the transfer was to a bona fide purchaser.[2] (Note that the sale of land continues to be governed by common law—which often has specific rules for real

estate. Therefore, when a minor contracts to sell real estate and ultimately disaffirms the contract, even a bona fide purchaser will be required to return the land to the minor. For example, if Mary sells real estate to a broker who in turn sells it to Carol, Mary can disaffirm the contract and recover the land from Carol.)

In the following case, a minor's father brought an action to disaffirm the minor's purchase of an automobile and to recover the purchase price. The court reviewed the contract with the minor and took into account the fact that the seller knew the buyer was a minor when the contract was made.

2. Defined as "a purchaser for a valuable consideration paid or parted with in the belief that the vender had a right to sell, and without any suspicious circumstances to put him on inquiry." (Merritt v. Railroad Co., 12 Barb., N.Y. 605).

QUALITY MOTORS, INC. v. HAYS
Supreme Court of Arkansas,
1949.
216 Ark. 264, 225 S.W.2d 326.

BACKGROUND AND FACTS *Johnny Hays, the plaintiff, was a sixteen-year-old minor. He went to Quality Motors, Inc. (the defendant), to inspect and test a car. When the Quality Motors salesman raised the question of Hays's age, he was told that Hays's father in New York had sent him the money to buy the car. The salesman refused to sell the car unless the purchase was made by an adult. Hays left the salesman and returned shortly with a young man of twenty-three, whom he had met that day for the first time.*

The salesman then accepted Hays's cashier's check in payment for the car. The bill of sale was made out to the twenty-three-year-old. The salesman then recommended a notary public to prepare the necessary papers for transfer of the title to Hays, and he drove the two into town for this purpose. The young man did transfer title, and the car was delivered by the salesman to Hays at his college.

When Hays's father, Dr. D. J. Hays, learned of the transaction, he called Quality Motors and asked it to take the car back. The company refused to do so. Dr. Hays was unable at that time to tender the car back to Quality Motors, since his son had taken it out of town. However, the next day, Dr. Hays retrieved the car from his son and once again called Quality Motors to ask it to take the car back. It again refused. Dr. Hays then went to his attorney's office and, through his attorney, once more attempted to have the company accept the car back. The company refused but said it would try to sell the car for the Hays's if it could. The car was put into storage.

The following week this lawsuit was filed. Plaintiff's attorney indicated in writing to the defendant that the return of the automobile had been refused but that the automobile was now in storage and would be turned over to the defendant any time it would be accepted. Meanwhile, the son found the keys to the car and the bill of sale, took the car out of state, and damaged it in two accidents. At the time of trial, the car was subject to various repair bills and was not in running condition. The defendant continually refused to take the car back.

The special chancellor in the trial court found that for all intents and purposes, the defendant sold the car to the plaintiff, knowing the plaintiff was a minor. The use of a third person adult was merely a sham.

DUNAWAY, Justice.

* * *

Johnny M. Hays [plaintiff], by his [father], Dr. D. J. Hays, brought this suit to disaffirm his purchase of a Pontiac automobile and recover the purchase price of $1,750 from defendant Quality Motors, Inc.* * *

In the case at bar Johnny Hays testified positively that he desired to disaffirm his purchase and return the car to the seller.* * *

The law is well settled in Arkansas that an infant may disaffirm his contracts, except those made for necessaries, without being required to return the consideration received, except such part as may remain in specie in his hands.

We do not find any merit in [Quality Motors's] contention that no proper tender of the car was made when [Johnny Hays through his father] sought to disaffirm his purchase. The undisputed testimony shows that Dr. Hays and his attorney offered to return the car on several occasions, but were informed that [defendant] would not accept it. That it was not actually delivered to Quality Motors when the suit was filed, is [defendant's] own fault. The law does not require that a tender be made under circumstances where it would be vain and useless.

[Quality Motors's] most serious contention is that the plaintiff is liable for damages to the car which occurred while he was driving over the country, after he had slipped the car from its storage place and while the suit to disaffirm was pending. In order to obtain any relief on this score, it must be shown that plaintiff was guilty of conversion in taking the automobile. [See Chapter 3 on torts.] Conversion is the exercise of dominion over property in violation of the rights of the owner or person entitled to possession. In advancing this argument [defendant] is in an inconsistent position. In its answer, [defendant] denied selling the car to [plaintiff] and was stoutly insisting that it did not have to take the car back. If that was true [defendant] was not the owner of nor entitled to possession of the car. Until the court decreed return of the car and recovery of the consideration paid, plaintiff still had title to the car. One cannot be liable for conversion in taking his own property.

[I]n the instant case Quality Motors, Inc. was insisting at the time of the alleged conversion by Johnny Hays, that it did not have to accept return of the car. Ebbert, one of the owners of Quality Motors, Inc., testified that during his conversation with his employees in regard to keeping the car in the shop after the first wreck, he told them they could not make Johnny leave it. "Well, it's not our car," was his statement at that time. In these circumstances it certainly cannot be said [plaintiff's] possession was that of a bailee or trustee.

[Defendant] knowingly and through a planned subterfuge sold an automobile to a minor. It then refused to take the car back. Even after the car was wrecked once, it was in [defendant's] place of business, and [defendant] was still resisting disaffirmance of the contract. The loss which [defendant] has suffered is the direct result of its own acts.

JUDGMENT
AND REMEDY

The court affirmed the minor's right to avoid the contract. The plaintiff, Johnny Hays, was ordered to return the car to the defendant within seven days. When the wrecked car was returned, plaintiff was allowed to recover the purchase price from the defendant.

COMMENTS

Minors comprise a particular category of persons the law protects from economic exploitation. A minor is not compelled to "avoid" contracts made before attaining majority. Rather, the minor has the option of keeping the bargain or avoiding it.

LIABILITY FOR NECESSARIES A minor who enters into a contract for "necessaries" may disaffirm the contract but does remain liable for the reasonable value of the goods. The legal duty to pay a reasonable value does not arise from the contract itself but is imposed by law on a theory of quasi-contract. The theory is that the minor should not be *unjustly* enriched and should therefore be liable for those things that fulfill basic needs, such as food, clothing, and shelter.

Note, though, that the minor is liable only for the reasonable value of the goods (because there is no contract and therefore no contract price to which the court can refer). Suppose Hank Olsen, a minor, purchases a suit that is list priced at $150. After wearing the suit for several weeks, Olsen wants to disaffirm his contract with the clothier. He can do so, but he is liable for the reasonable value of the suit. If the value is actually $115, then the clothier can recover only that amount, even if this deprives the clothier of all profit on the sale.

Necessaries include items absolutely necessary for the minor's existence, like food, clothing, shelter, medicine, and hospital care. In order to determine whether an item is a necessary, all the facts and circumstances must be taken into account. Therefore, a minor's station in life or financial and social status will be taken into account to determine if an item is a necessary. Necessaries may include services that are reasonably necessary to enable a minor to earn a living, such as an employment agency fee in obtaining a job.

GASTONIA
PERSONNEL
CORPORATION v.
ROGERS
Supreme Court of North
Carolina, 1970.
276 N.C. 279, 172 S.E.2d 19.

BACKGROUND AND FACTS *Bobby L. Rogers, defendant, was nineteen years old, married, and nearing completion of his associate of arts degree when he went to the office of plaintiff, an employment agency, and signed a contract for assistance in obtaining suitable employment. The contract contained the following provision:*
"If I ACCEPT employment offered me by an employer as a result of a lead (verbal or otherwise) from you within twelve (12) months of such lead even though it may not be the position originally discussed with you, I will be obligated to pay you as per the terms of the contract."

Under the contract, the defendant was otherwise free to continue his own quest for employment. He became obligated to the plaintiff only if he accepted a job to which the plaintiff agency had referred him.
After several telephone calls to prospective employers, the employment agency arranged an interview with an employer who ultimately hired the defendant. The service charge to defendant of $295 was never paid. Plaintiff attempted to collect its fee. Defendant

attempted to disaffirm the contract on the theory that services of a professional employment agency are not "necessaries" and hence can be disaffirmed. The trial court agreed with the defendant.

BOBBITT, Chief Justice.

* * *

Under the common law, persons, whether male or female, are classified and referred to as *infants* until they attain the age of twenty-one years. [Under modern law, the age is lowered to eighteen years.]

An early commentary on the common law, after the general statement that contracts made by persons (infants) before attaining the age of twenty-one "may be avoided," sets forth "some exceptions out of this generality," to wit: *"An infant may bind himselfe to pay for his necessary meat, drinke, apparell, necessary physicke, and such other necessaries, and likewise for his good teaching or instruction, whereby he may profit himselfe afterwards."* (Our italics.) Coke on Littleton, 13th ed. (1788), p. 172.

* * *

If the infant married, "necessaries" included necessary food and clothing for his wife and child.

In accordance with this ancient rule of the common law, this Court has held an infant's contract, unless for "necessaries" or unless authorized by statute, is voidable by the infant, at his election, and may be disaffirmed during infancy or upon attaining the age of twenty-one.

* * *

The nature of the common law requires that each time a rule of law is applied it be carefully scrutinized to make sure that the conditions and needs of the times have not so changed as to make further application of it the instrument of injustice.

In general, our prior decisions are to the effect that the "necessaries" of an infant, his wife and child, include only such necessities of life as food, clothing, shelter, medical attention, etc. In our view, the concept of "necessaries" should be enlarged to include such articles of property and such services as are reasonably necessary to enable the infant to earn the money required to provide the necessities of life for himself and those who are legally dependent upon him.

The evidence before us tends to show that defendant, when he contracted with plaintiff, was nineteen years of age, emancipated, married, a high school graduate, within "a quarter or 22 hours" of obtaining his degree in applied science, and capable of holding a job at a starting annual salary of $4,784.00. To hold, as a matter of law, that such a person cannot obligate himself to pay for services rendered him in obtaining employment suitable to his ability, education and specialized training, enabling him to provide the necessities of life for himself, his wife and his expected child, would place him and others similarly situated under a serious economic handicap.

In the effort to protect "older minors" from improvident or unfair contracts, the law should not deny to them the opportunity and right to obligate themselves for articles of property or services which are reasonably necessary to enable them to provide for the proper support of themselves and their dependents. The minor should be held liable for the reasonable value of articles of property or services received pursuant to such contract.

JUDGMENT
AND REMEDY

The services of a professional employment agency were construed to be a "necessary." The case was remanded to the lower court for a new trial. The defendant could be expected to pay the reasonable value of the services rendered to him pursuant to the employment contract.

COMMENTS

Although the doctrine of voidability of a minor's contract often seems necessary for the protection of the young person, there are situations in which such a result is unjust. This is consistent with the policy of law that promotes business by allowing contracts to develop between parties whenever possible. Some states allow the parties to submit a proposed contract to a court that removes a minor's right to disaffirm if the court finds the particular contract to be fair or just.

THE EFFECT OF A MINOR'S MISREPRESENTATION OF AGE

Suppose a minor tells a seller that she is twenty-one years old when she is actually only seventeen. Ordinarily, the minor can still disaffirm the contract, even though she has acted fraudulently. However, since the other party has been induced by the minor's fraudulent misrepresentation to enter into the contract, the other party also has the option to avoid the contract. (See Chapter 10 on lack of real assent.) In the above example, the seller can therefore disaffirm the contract. In addition, the seller has the option of electing to seek a remedy under a tort action.

In certain circumstances a minor can be bound by a contract when a misrepresentation of age has been made. First, several states have enacted statutes prohibiting minors from disaffirming contracts when they have made a false representation of age. Some of these statutes prohibit disaffirmance by a minor who has engaged in business as an adult.[3]

Second, some courts refuse to allow minors to disaffirm executed contracts unless they can return the consideration received. The combination of misrepresentation by minors and the unjust enrichment if they are allowed to keep the property received, has persuaded several courts to estop (prevent) minors from asserting contractual incapacity.

Third, some courts allow a misrepresenting minor to disaffirm the contract but hold the minor liable for damages in tort. Here, the defrauded party may sue the minor for misrepresentation or fraud. A split in authority exists on this point, since some courts have recognized that allowing a suit in tort is equivalent to the indirect enforcement of the minor's contract.

In the following case, an Ohio appellate court reviewed the trial court's decision regarding a purported disaffirmation of a purchase contract by a minor. The court was impressed mainly by the fact that the contract had been induced by a false representation of the age of the minor in question.

———————————

3. See, for example, statutes in Iowa, Kansas, Utah, and Washington.

HAYDOCY PONTIAC,
INC. v. LEE

Court of Appeals of Ohio,
Franklin County, 1969.
19 Ohio App.2d 217, 250 N.E.2d
898.

BACKGROUND AND FACTS *The plaintiff is Haydocy Pontiac, a seller of automobiles. The defendant, Lee, was twenty years of age when she contracted to purchase the automobile, but she represented to the plaintiff, seller, that she was twenty-one years old. The defendant purchased the car by making a trade-in and financing the rest of the purchase price. She executed a note for the unpaid purchase price, including financing charges and insurance charges. The total amount of the note was approximately $2,000.*

Immediately following delivery of the automobile, Lee turned the car over to a third person. She never at any time thereafter had possession of the automobile. She made no further attempt to make payment on the contract, and she attempted to rescind it. She did not return the automobile to the plaintiff-seller; nor did she offer to return it. She merely announced that she was a minor at the time of purchase, that she had not ratified the agreement to purchase the car, and that she was repudiating her contract and would not be bound by it. The trial court applied the general rule of law permitting a minor to avoid a transaction without being required to restore the consideration received.

STRAUSBAUGH, Judge.

* * *

To allow infants to avoid a transaction without being required to restore the consideration received where the infant has used or otherwise disposed of it causes hardship on the other party. We hold that where the consideration received by the infant cannot be returned upon disaffirmance of the contract because it has been disposed of the infant must account for the value of it, not in excess of the purchase price, where the other party is free from any fraud or bad faith and where the contract has been induced by a false representation of the age of the infant. *Under this factual situation the infant is estopped [prevented] from pleading infancy as a defense where the contract has been induced by a false representation that the infant was of age.* [Emphasis added.]

The necessity of returning the consideration as a prerequisite to obtaining equitable relief is still clearer where the infant misrepresents age and perpetrated an actual fraud on the other party. The disaffirmance of an infant's contract is to be determined by equitable principles, whether sought in a proceeding in equity or a case at law.

The common law has bestowed upon the infant the privilege of disaffirming his contracts in conservation of his rights and interests. Where the infant, 20 years of age, through falsehood and deceit enters into a contract with another who enters therein in honesty and good faith and, thereafter, the infant seeks to disaffirm the contract without tendering back the consideration, no right or interest of the infant exists which needs protection. The privilege given the infant thereupon becomes a weapon of injustice.

JUDGMENT AND REMEDY

Judgment of the trial court was reversed. The Ohio Appellate Court allowed the seller, Haydocy Pontiac, Inc., to recover the fair market value of the automobile from the defendant, Lee. The only restriction imposed by the court was that the fair market value could not be in excess of the original purchase price of the automobile.

COMMENTS

The theory behind protecting minors is that a young person lacks the maturity of judgment and experience to be able to avoid the pitfalls of the marketplace. Yet, the magical age of eighteen years is no longer an indication of contractual maturity that has its basis in fact or in public policy.

INSURANCE AND LOANS Traditionally, insurance has not been viewed as a *necessary*, so minors can ordinarily disaffirm their contract and recover all premiums paid. However, some jurisdictions limit the right to disaffirm—for example, when minors contract for life or health insurance on their own lives. Other jurisdictions allow a minor to disaffirm but limit recovery to the value of premiums paid less the insurance company's actual cost of protecting the minor under the policy. Suppose Bob Berzak takes out an automobile insurance policy and pays $125 in premiums. Bob has an accident for which his insurance company, State Farm, pays a claim of $85. In states following the traditional rule, Bob's recovery upon disaffirmance will be $125, the full value of the premiums. In states limiting his recovery, Bob can recover only $40, the excess of the value of the premiums over State Farm's actual cost under the policy.

In and of itself, a loan is seldom viewed as a necessary, even if the minor spends the money on necessaries. However, if the lender makes a loan for the express purpose of enabling the minor to purchase necessaries, and the lender personally makes sure the money is so spent, the minor is normally obligated to repay the loan.

Ratification

Ratification is an act or expression of words by which a minor, upon reaching majority, indicates an intention to become bound by the contract. As noted above, ratification must necessarily occur after the individual comes of age, since any attempt to become legally bound prior to majority is no more effective than the original contractual promise. This protects the minor and is consistent with the theory that the contracts of a minor are voidable at his or her option.

EXPRESS RATIFICATION Suppose John Lawrence enters into a contract to sell a house to Carol Ogden. At the time of the contract Carol is a minor. Naturally, Carol can avoid her legal duty to pay for the house by disaffirming the contract. Imagine, instead, that Carol reaches majority and writes a letter to John stating that she still agrees to buy the house. Carol thus ratifies the contract and is legally bound. John can sue for breach of contract if Carol refuses to perform her part of the bargain. This is an example of *express* ratification.

IMPLIED RATIFICATION The contract can also be ratified by *conduct*. Suppose, after reaching majority, Carol lives in the house. This conduct evidences an intent to abide by the contract and is a form of *implied* ratification. Again, Carol is legally bound, and John can sue her for breach of contract if she fails to perform her duty to pay the purchase price. Another example of implied ratification occurs when an individual, after reaching majority, continues to use property purchased as a minor. The continued use is inconsistent with disaffirmance and implicitly indicates an intention to be bound by the contract.

In general, any act or conduct showing an intention to affirm the contract will be deemed to be ratification. However, silence alone after reaching the age of majority will not constitute ratification of an executory contract in most situations. If Carol had said nothing to John and had not entered into possession, she would not have ratified the contract, since she had expressed no intention to abide by it. On the other hand, the minor may have a duty to speak in some circumstances. Suppose that after coming of age, a minor fails to act while purchaser makes improvements on property of which the minor was the vendor. If the vendor knows of the improvements being made and says nothing, the vendor cannot disaffirm the contract.

NONVOIDABLE CONTRACTS

Minors

Many states have passed statutes restricting the ability of minors to avoid certain contracts. Loans for education or medical care received by minors create binding legal duties that they cannot avoid.[4]

In addition, certain statutes specifically require minors to perform legal duties. Suppose James Dornan, a minor, wants to attach the property of Davis Snowden for default of a loan. In some states, Dornan is required to file a bond before the legal attachment can occur. After filing the bond, Dornan cannot avoid the obligations of the bonding agreement, since the bond is a legal duty imposed by state statute. In such situations, a minor cannot rely on the common law rule that the bonding contract is voidable. Similar legal duties are imposed on minors with respect to bank accounts and transfers of stocks.

Parents' Liability

As a general rule, parents are not liable for the contracts made by their minor children. Due to this fact, businesses will ordinarily require parents to sign any contract made with a minor. Parents who sign such contracts then become personally obligated to perform the conditions of the contract, even though their child can or actually does avoid liability.

If the parents have neglected their minor child, they will be liable for the reasonable value of necessaries supplied to the child, even if they do not expressly agree to pay for such products. In other words, if a child purchases shoes because his parents refuse to give him

---

4. New York Education Laws, Sec. 281; Pennsylvania, 35 Pa.S., Sec. 10101.

something to wear on his feet, the parents can be held liable for the reasonable value of the shoes.

INTOXICATED PERSONS

A contract entered into by an intoxicated person can be either voidable or valid. If the person was drunk enough to be *non compos mentis*, then the transaction is voidable at the option of the intoxicated person even if the intoxication was purely voluntary. In order to be *non compos mentis*, all reason and judgment must be impaired, so that the intoxicated party does not realize he or she is entering into a valid contract. If a party is slightly intoxicated but still comprehends the legal consequences of entering into a contract, the contract will be valid and can be enforced by the other party. Simply because the terms of the contract are foolish or largely in favor of the other party does not mean that the contract is voidable (unless the other party fraudulently induced the person to become intoxicated). Problems often arise in determining whether a party was drunk enough to avoid legal duties. Many courts will not inquire into the intoxicated party's mental state in order to determine the degree of intoxication. Instead, they look at objective indications to determine whether the contract is voidable.

The following case shows an unusual business transaction in which boasts, brags, and dares "after a few drinks" resulted in a binding sale and purchase transaction.

BACKGROUND AND FACTS *W. O. Lucy and J. C. Lucy filed suit against A. H. Zehmer and Ida Zehmer, the defendants, to compel the Zehmers to perform a contract by which it was alleged that the Zehmers had sold to the Lucys their property known as the Ferguson Farm for $50,000. The transaction had come about in a most unusual manner. Lucy had known Zehmer for fifteen or twenty years and for the last eight years or so had been anxious to buy the Ferguson Farm from Zehmer. One night, Lucy stopped in to visit with the Zehmers in the restaurant, filling station, and motor court they operated. While there, Lucy tried to buy the Ferguson Farm once again. This time he tried a new approach.*

W. O. LUCY AND J. C. LUCY v. A. H. ZEHMER AND IDA S. ZEHMER

Supreme Court of Appeals of Virginia, 1954.
196 Va. 493, 84 S.E.2d 516.

According to the trial court transcript, Lucy said to Zehmer, "I bet you wouldn't take $50,000 for that place." Zehmer replied, "Yes, I would too; you wouldn't give fifty."

Throughout the evening the conversation returned to the sale of the Ferguson Farm for $50,000. At the same time, the parties continued to drink whiskey and engage in light conversation. The conversation repeatedly returned to the subject of the Ferguson Farm. Eventually, Lucy enticed Zehmer to write up an agreement to the effect that Zehmer would agree to sell to Lucy the Ferguson Farm for $50,000 complete. Zehmer first wrote that out on the back of a restaurant check. He tore up the first copy because he had written "I do hereby agree" and thought it had better read "we" because Mrs. Zehmer would have to sign it too. Zehmer rewrote the agreement and asked Mrs. Zehmer to sign it. She agreed.

Lucy sued Zehmer to go through with the sale. Zehmer argued that he was drunk and that the offer was made in jest and hence was unenforceable. The trial court agreed with the Zehmers.

BUCHANAN, Justice.
* * *

The instrument sought to be enforced was written by A. H. Zehmer on December 20, 1952, in these words: "We hereby agree to sell to W. O. Lucy the Ferguson Farm complete for $50,000.00, title satisfactory to buyer," and signed by the defendants, A. H. Zehmer and Ida S. Zehmer.

A. H. Zehmer admitted that * * * W. O. Lucy offered him $50,000 cash for the farm, but that he, Zehmer, considered that the offer was made in jest; that so thinking, and both he and Lucy having had several drinks, he wrote out "the memorandum" quoted above and induced his wife to sign it; that he did not deliver the memorandum to Lucy, but that Lucy picked it up, read it, put it in his pocket, attempted to offer Zehmer $5 to bind the bargain, which Zehmer refused to accept, and realizing for the first time that Lucy was serious, Zehmer assured him that he had no intention of selling the farm and that the whole matter was a joke. Lucy left the premises insisting that he had purchased the farm.
* * *

The discussion leading to the signing of the agreement, said Lucy, lasted thirty or forty minutes, during which Zehmer seemed to doubt that Lucy could raise $50,000. Lucy suggested the provision for having the title examined and Zehmer made the suggestion that he would sell it "complete, everything there," and stated that all he had on the farm was three heifers.

Lucy took a partly filled bottle of whiskey into the restaurant with him for the purpose of giving Zehmer a drink if he wanted it. Zehmer did, and he and Lucy had one or two drinks together. Lucy said that while he felt the drinks he took he was not intoxicated, and from the way Zehmer handled the transaction he did not think he was either.
* * *

The defendants insist that * * * the writing sought to be enforced was prepared as a bluff or dare to force Lucy to admit that he did not have $50,000; that the whole matter was a joke; that the writing was not delivered to Lucy and no binding contract was ever made between the parties.

It is an unusual, if not bizarre, defense.

* * *

In his testimony Zehmer claimed that he "was high as a Georgia pine," and that the transaction "was just a bunch of two doggoned drunks bluffing to see who could talk the biggest and say the most." That claim is inconsistent with his attempt to testify in great detail as to what was said and what was done.

* * *

The record is convincing that Zehmer was not intoxicated to the extent of being unable to comprehend the nature and consequences of the instrument he executed, and hence that instrument is not to be invalidated on that ground.

* * *

The appearance of the contract, the fact that it was under discussion for forty minutes or more before it was signed; Lucy's objection to the first draft because it was written in the singular, and he wanted Mrs. Zehmer to sign it also; the rewriting to meet that objection and the signing by Mrs. Zehmer; the discussion of what was to be included in the sale, the provision for the examination of the title, the completeness of the instrument that was executed, the taking possession of it by Lucy with no request or suggestion by either of the defendants that he give it back, are facts which furnish persuasive evidence that the execution of the contract was a serious business transaction rather than a casual, jesting matter as defendants now contend.

* * *

Not only did Lucy actually believe, but the evidence shows he was warranted in believing, that the contract represented a serious business transaction and a good faith sale and purchase of the farm.

In the field of contracts, as generally elsewhere, *"We must look to the outward expression of a person as manifesting his intention rather than to his secret and unexpressed intention.* [Emphasis added.] 'The law imputes to a person an intention corresponding to the reasonable meaning of his words and acts.' "

* * *

Whether the writing signed by the defendants and now sought to be enforced by the complainants was the result of a serious offer by Lucy and a serious acceptance by the defendants, or was a serious offer by Lucy and an acceptance in secret jest by the defendants, in either event it constituted a binding contract of sale between the parties.

JUDGMENT AND REMEDY

The Supreme Court of Virginia determined that the writing was an enforceable contract and reversed the lower court. The Zehmers were required by court order to carry through with the sale of the Ferguson Farm to the Lucys.

COMMENTS

If a joke is so successful that the promisee, as a reasonable person under the circumstances, reasonably believes that an offer has been made and that person therefore accepts, then, under the objective theory of contracts the parties have entered into a valid contract. On the other hand, if the promisee should reasonably be aware that the promisor is joking or making a promise in the heat of excitement, then there is no offer to be accepted, and hence no contract arises.

Avoidance of Ratification

If a contract is held to be voidable due to a person's intoxication, that person has the option of disaffirming (avoiding) it—the same options available to a minor. Like a minor, an intoxicated person may ratify expressly or implicitly. An example of implied ratification is where a person enters into a contract while drunk and fails to disaffirm the contract within a *reasonable* time of becoming sober. Also, acts or conduct inconsistent with an intent to disaffirm will ratify the contract—for example, where the person continues to use property purchased under a voidable contract.

In addition, contracts for necessaries are voidable (as in the case of minors), but the intoxicated person is liable in quasi-contract (implied-in-law contract) for the reasonable value of the consideration received. Restitution must also be made, and the courts tend to require it more often than in the case of minors. In fact, it is usually necessary for the intoxicated person to return the full consideration before being permitted to disaffirm an executed contract. For example, a person may agree to purchase a set of encyclopedias while drunk. If the books are delivered, the purchaser can disaffirm the executed contract only by returning the encyclopedias.

The lack of contractual capacity due to intoxication while the contract is being made must be distinguished from capacity (or the lack thereof) of an alcoholic. If a contract is made while an alcoholic is sober, there is no lack of capacity.[5]

INSANE PERSONS

The contracts made by insane persons can be either void, voidable, or valid. If a person has been adjudged insane by a court of law and a guardian has been appointed, any contract made by the insane person is void—no contract at all. Only the guardian can enter into binding legal duties on behalf of the insane person.

Insane persons not so adjudged by a court may enter into *voidable* contracts if they do not know they are entering into the contracts or if they lack the mental capacity to comprehend the subject matter, nature, and consequences of the contracts. In such situations, the contracts are avoidable at the option of the insane person, although the other party does not have this option.[6]

The contract may be disaffirmed or ratified. Ratification must occur after the person is mentally competent or after a guardian is appointed and ratifies the contract. As in the case of minors and intoxicated persons, insane persons are liable in quasi-contract for the reasonable value of necessaries they receive.

A contract entered into by an insane person may also be valid. If the person understands the nature and effect of entering into a contract, the contract will be valid. Of course, here the person is not really insane and therefore has the contractual capacity to make a binding agreement.

In some circumstances, a substantial number of states refuse to allow disaffirmance of a contract entered into by an insane person. If the contract is fair and reasonable and the other party had no knowledge or reason to believe the person was insane, the contract will be enforced. However, the majority of states allow disaffirmance even here, provided the insane person restores any consideration received and makes restitution to the other party.[7]

CONVICTS

Persons convicted of a major criminal offense (a felony or treason) often lack full contractual capacity. Laws pertaining to their ability to contract vary from state to state. In some states, the convicted felon can make a valid transfer of his or her property while in prison. In other states, the convicted felon is typically under partial or total disability to contract during the period of incarceration.

5.   Olsen v. Hawkins, 90 Idaho 28, 408 P.2d 462 (1965).

6.   This applies to all voidable contracts.

7.   Modern courts no longer require a person to be *legally* insane to disaffirm contracts. See Ortelere v. Teachers' Retirement Bd., 25 N.Y.2d 196, 303 N.Y.S.2d 362, 250 N.E.2d 460 (1969). The court sets out what the tests for mental incompetency are.

ALIENS

An alien is a citizen of another country who resides in this country. Generally, aliens who are legally in this country have the same contractual rights as U.S. citizens. They may be sued and they may sue in the courts in order to enforce their contractual rights. Some states restrict the right of an alien to own real property. In virtually all cases, an enemy alien during time of war will not be able to enforce a contract, although the contract can be held in abeyance until the war is over.

MARRIED WOMEN

At common law, a married woman could not make binding contracts even if she lived apart from her husband. In other words, married women's contracts were *void* rather than voidable. Even after the death of the husband, the married woman was incapable of ratifying a previously drawn up contract because that contract was invalid from the beginning. Virtually all states have abolished common law restrictions on the contractual capacity of married women.[8] A number of restrictions do remain in certain states, although many of them will be eliminated if the Equal Rights Amendment is passed.

_____

8. These statutes are normally called Married Women's Property Acts.

QUESTIONS AND CASE PROBLEMS

1. Robertson, a minor, entered into a conditional sales agreement whereby he purchased a pickup truck from Julian Pontiac Company for the agreed price of $1,743.85. Robertson traded in a passenger car for which he was given a credit of $723.85 on the purchase price, leaving a balance of $1,020, which he agreed to pay in twenty-three monthly installments. Robertson had already paid one of the installments when the pickup truck began to experience electrical wiring difficulties. Less than a month after the purchase of the truck, Robertson turned eighteen. About two weeks later, as a result of the electrical wiring defects, the truck caught fire and was practically destroyed. Robertson refused to make any further payments under the installment agreement. Julian Pontiac Company sued Robertson for the balance of the installments. Was it able to recover? [Robertson v. King, 225 Ark. 276, 280 S.W.2d 402 (1955)]

2. Kiefer, a minor, purchased an automobile from Howe Motors, Inc. in December 1968. At the time he made the purchase, he had been living away from his parents for about six months. Several months after the purchase, Kiefer attempted to rescind the deal by returning the automobile to Howe Motors and requesting the company to return the purchase price to him. Howe Motors refused. Kiefer sued the company to recover payments made on the purchase of the automobile. Was he able to recover? [Kiefer v. Fred Howe Motors, Inc., 39 Wis.2d 20, 158 N.W.2d 288 (1968)]

3. Stuhl was an entrepreneur at age seventeen. He had flown to seven major cities, all for the purpose of entering into profitable business deals. On each trip, Stuhl flew his favorite airline, Eastern Airlines. Stuhl liked Eastern because it always took his checks, even though his checks always bounced. About five months after Stuhl's twenty-first birthday, Eastern Airlines instituted an action to collect on Stuhl's dishonored checks. The action was instituted in the state of New York, where the majority age is twenty-one. In his response to the lawsuit filed by Eastern Airlines, Stuhl disaffirmed the contract he had made with Eastern. Was Eastern able to recover? [Eastern Airlines, Inc. v. Stuhl, 65 Misc. 2d 901, 318 N.Y.S.2d 996 (1970)]

4. Pankas was the owner and operator of a hair styling boutique in downtown Pittsburgh, Pennsylvania. He had maintained his shop in the same location for a number of years and had built up a substantial clientele. In October 1962, Pankas hired Bell, who was about twenty and one-half years old at the time. Part of Bell's employment included an agreement that he would not thereafter leave Pankas's employ and work at another beauty parlor within a ten-mile radius of downtown Pittsburgh. Shortly after his twenty-first birthday, Bell left Pankas's employ and, along with another Pankas employee, opened a beauty shop only a few blocks away from Pankas's business. In addition, Bell

advertised the fact that he and his partner were former employees of Pankas. Pankas sued Bell to enjoin him from further breach of their restrictive covenant. Bell claimed that as a minor he could rescind the agreement. Was he correct? [Pankas v. Bell, 413 Pa. 494, 198 A.2d 312 (1964)]

5. Peddy and Montgomery entered into a contract under which Montgomery agreed to sell a certain parcel of her land to Peddy. At the time of the transaction, Montgomery was a resident of the state of Alabama. Alabama, by statute, prohibited married women from selling real estate without the consent of their husbands. Montgomery's husband refused to consent to the deal, and Montgomery in turn refused to transfer the land to Peddy. Montgomery claimed that because of the statute she was not obligated under the contract since the contract was invalid from the beginning. Peddy responded that the statute violated the equal protection clause of the Constitution since it treated men and women differently with no reasonable basis for the difference in treatment. Was the contract between Montgomery and Peddy void or voidable? What do you think of the Constitutional claim? [Peddy v. Montgomery, 345 So. 2d 631 (Ala. 1977)]

6. Hale, age eighteen, was employed by Ghost Canyon Ranch as a "wrangler" for the summer of 1965. Ghost Canyon Ranch was located in South Dakota, where the age of majority is twenty-one. One of Hale's duties was to drive camp children on trips. On one of these trips Hale rounded a curve on the wrong side of the road and ran into an approaching car. The accident resulted in injuries to Friedhoff, who was a passenger in the car that Hale was driving. Immediately after the accident, Hale returned to his employer all the compensation the employer had paid him and disaffirmed the employment contract. About a month later, Friedhoff sued Hale to recover for the injuries he had suffered in the accident caused by Hale. Under South Dakota's guest statute, a passenger in a car cannot sue the driver for the driver's negligence unless: (1) the passenger pays compensation, and (2) the driver receives some benefit from the compensation. Hale claimed that because he rescinded the contract, he received no compensation from the passenger. Therefore, Hale argued, the guest statute effectively prevented Friedhoff from suing him. Was this argument valid? [Friedhoff v. Engberg, 82 S.D. 522, 149 N.W.2d 759 (1967)]

7. Gordon, a minor, loved exotic animals. In fact, he loved them so much that he paid Hogue $1,150 for a

pair of chinchillas. A month later, he purchased a second pair of chinchillas from Hogue, this time for $700. The chinchillas, having nothing better to do, doubled in number within a year. About a year and a half after Gordon had purchased the original chinchillas, he attempted to disaffirm both purchase contracts by returning the remaining chinchillas to Hogue. At the time he attempted to return the chinchillas, two had died due to his negligence. Hogue refused to return the purchase price. Gordon sued. By the time the case came to trial, four more of the chinchillas had died, again due to Gordon's negligence. Was Gordon able to rescind? [Hogue v. Wilkinson, 291 S.W.2d 750 (Tex.Civ.App.1956)]

8. Spaulding, a minor, was married and living with his wife and child when he entered into a contract with New England Furniture Co. for the purchase of bedroom furniture. The purchase included a three-piece bedroom set that was priced significantly higher than most other three-piece bedroom sets. After making several payments on the new furniture, Spaulding defaulted, disaffirmed his contract, and allowed the company to remove all the furniture. New England Furniture, however, refused to return the money that Spaulding had already paid. Was Spaulding able to recover these payments? [Spaulding v. New England Furniture Co., 154 Me. 330, 147 A.2d 916 (1959)]

9. Mr. Mills died in an automobile accident. Thereafter a dispute arose as to who was the intended beneficiary under an insurance contract on Mr. Mills's life. The parties to the dispute, Mrs. Mills and Mary Kopf, entered into an agreement whereby they would share the proceeds of the insurance. Later, Mary Kopf attempted to rescind the contract, claiming that she was insane at the time she made it. At trial, Kopf produced an expert witness who testified to her insanity at the time she had entered into the agreement with Mrs. Mills. Mrs. Mills also produced an expert witness who testified that Mary Kopf had been sane. Did the judge have to accept the testimony of Mary Kopf's witness over the testimony of Mrs. Mills's witness? [Mills v. Kopf, 216 Cal.App. 2d 780, 31 Cal.Rptr. 80 (1963)]

10. In 1937, Hanks entered into an agreement whereby he sold to McNeil Coal Corp. a large tract of land for coal mining. Three years later he was adjudicated insane. About a year after this, his son brought a suit on his behalf to rescind the sale of the coal mining land. To support a claim of insanity at the time the transaction was entered into, Hanks's son introduced evidence that Hanks had grown quite ill around the year 1937, that Hanks had joined several

religious cults at about that time, and that Hanks had concocted an odd medicine for the cure of horse disease that contained powdered glass and was to be poured into the animals' ears. McNeil Coal Corp. introduced the testimony of several local businessmen who had had dealings with Hanks around 1937. They testified that Hanks had acted rationally at all times and that there had been nothing unusual in the way he had conducted his business affairs. Was Hanks's son able to rescind on behalf of his father? [Hanks v. McNeil Coal Corp., 114 Colo. 578, 168 P.2d 256 (1946)]

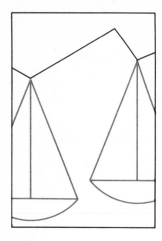

9

Contracts
Legality

In order for a contract to be enforced in court, the contract must call for the performance of a legal act. A contract is illegal if either its formation or its performance is criminal, tortious, or otherwise opposed to public policy.[1] The first part of this chapter will consider what makes a bargain illegal—when the contract is contrary to state or federal statutes and when the contract is contrary to public policy. The second part will consider the *effects* of an illegal bargain. Such contracts are often void—that is, they really are not contracts.

CONTRACTS CONTARY TO STATUTE

Usury

Every state has statutes that set the maximum rates of interest that can be charged for different types of transactions, including ordinary loans. A lender who makes a loan at an interest rate above the lawful maximum is guilty of **usury**. The maximum rate of interest varies from state to state but is usually between 10 and 15 percent.

In order to determine the amount of interest being charged on a loan, many states require service charges, credit insurance, and "points"

---

1. Restatement, Contracts, Section 512.

to be included in the calculation. For example, suppose you are charged $60 per year to borrow $1,000. In addition, the lender charges you $15 in service charges and requires you to take out credit insurance that costs another $15. The true annual rate of interest is then 9 percent (the total of $90 in charges divided by the principal amount of $1,000). A discount from the principal amount (points) is also included in the calculation. If you receive only $970 for the $1,000 loan, you are paying $30 in points. Points are prorated over the life of the loan and then added to the other charges to determine the true rate of interest. Paying $30 in points on your loan increases the true interest rate from 9 to 12 percent.

EXCEPTIONS Because usury statutes place a ceiling on the allowable rates of interest, exceptions have been made in order to facilitate business transactions. For example, many states exempt corporate loans from the usury laws. In addition, almost all states have adopted special statutes allowing interest rates up to 36 percent on small loans. Such high rates of interest are allowed because many borrowers simply cannot get loans at interest rates below the lawful maximum and will otherwise be forced to turn to loan sharks.

INSTALLMENT SALES Sales made on an installment basis, generally calling for payment for goods on a monthly basis, with interest rates of 1.5 percent per month, sometimes have been exempted from usury statutes by court decision or legislative enactment. For example, purchases on a revolving credit account or purchases made with Visa or Master Charge credit cards usually call for interest payments of 1.5 percent per month on the outstanding balance. Courts have interpreted these transactions as not being "loans of money" and therefore not subject to the usury laws. Some states have passed installment sales statutes that expressly permit such practices.

The effects of a usurious loan differ from state to state. A number of states allow the lender to recover the principal of a loan along with interest up to the legal maximum. In effect, the lender is denied recovery of the excess interest. In other states the lender can recover the principal amount of the loan but not the interest. In a few states, a usurious loan is a void transaction, and the lender cannot recover *either* the principal *or* the interest.

Gambling

In general, wagers, lotteries, and games of chance are illegal. All states have statutes that regulate gambling—defined as any scheme for the distribution of property by chance, among persons who have paid a valuable consideration for the opportunity to receive the property.[2] Gambling is the creation of risk for the purpose of assuming it. A few states do permit gambling as long as the prizes or winnings do not exceed $100 to $500.[3] In addition, a number of states have recognized the substantial revenues that can be obtained from gambling and have legalized state-operated lotteries and those for charitable purposes.

Often it is difficult to recognize a gambling contract. Suppose Adams takes out a life insurance policy on Ziegler, naming himself as beneficiary under the policy. At first blush, this may seem entirely legal; but further examination shows that Adams is simply gambling on how long Ziegler will live. In order to prevent this type of practice, insurance contracts can be entered into only by someone with an **insurable interest.** An insurable interest, discussed in Chapter 54, is a property or ownership right in the thing being insured. Adams cannot take out an insurance policy on Ziegler's home or auto because Adams does not have an insurable interest in Ziegler's property. But if Adams has a mortgage on Ziegler's house, he can take out an insurance policy because he has a property interest in the house.

Futures contracts, or contracts for the future purchase or sale of commodities such as

2. See Wishing Well Club v. Akron, 112 N.E.2d 41 (1951).
3. Iowa and Florida are two such states.

corn and wheat, are not illegal gambling contracts. It might appear that a person selling a futures contract is essentially gambling on the price of the commodity. However, since the seller can purchase the commodity elsewhere and deliver the commodity as required in the

futures contract, courts have upheld the legality of such contracts.

Gambling comes in many forms. In the following case, a Utah court held that the game of checkers was not a game of chance prohibited by the state lottery law, but a game of skill.

D'ORIO v. STARTUP CANDY CO.

Supreme Court of Utah, 1928.
71 Utah 410, 266 P. 1037.

BACKGROUND AND FACTS *The plaintiff, D'Orio, brought an action for damages against the defendant, Startup Candy Company, to recover the reasonable value of certain goods plaintiff sold to defendant. Part of the goods consisted of checker boards and checkers. Although the defendant admitted that he purchased these goods from the plaintiff, he took the position that the merchandise was for use in games of gambling or lottery and that such games were prohibited by the laws of Utah. He argued that the consideration was illegal and the contract was therefore void. Hence, he refused to pay the plaintiff.*

At trial, the court found for the plaintiff, holding that the defendant did purchase the goods and did not pay for them.

THURMAN, Chief Justice.

* * *

[The defendant invented a game in which players paid a sum of money to punch a board and obtain a checker problem. If the players solved the problem, they got a prize. All the checker problems were solvable if a player had sufficient skill. The court described the game.]

[T]he face of each board * * * [is] a regular standard checker board, and the squares used in the checker problem are numbered. Upon the board there are 300 or more holes perforated through the board, in each of which there is a small slip of paper, and upon the board is a list of 10 or more names, and opposite these names appears the color of the checkers, and after every color appear the numbers upon which these respective checkers are to be placed. The customer pays 10 cents to purchase one of the slips of paper. Upon this slip of paper appears one of the names which appear on the face of the board. That the customer then places the checkers upon the checker board, as is indicated after the name which appears upon his slip of paper. Then he is to move both colored checkers—the dark-colored checkers to be moved first. If the customer can then move the checkers in such a way that the dark-colored checkers win over the light-colored checkers, the customer receives a prize. That the slips of paper which the customer has received are good and apply upon the purchase price of merchandise, which is advertised on the face of the board. That in all problems that appear upon the board, the dark-colored checkers can win if the player moves the checkers in the proper way. That in every problem, therefore, the dark-colored checkers can win over the light-colored checkers, if the person playing the game has sufficient skill as a checker player to move his checkers skillfully.

If the player plays the game in good faith and has the dark-colored checkers win over the light-colored checkers, he receives one of the boxes of candy displayed with the board.

* * *

Was the operation and use of the [checker board games] a lottery, game of chance, or gift enterprise? This is the question presented * * * for our determination.

[T]he Laws of Utah * * * define a lottery as follows:

"A lottery is any scheme for the disposal or distribution of property by chance, among persons who have paid or promised to pay any valuable consideration for the chance of obtaining such property or a portion of it, or for any share, or any interest in such property, upon any agreement, understanding, or expectation that it is to be distributed or disposed of by lot or chance, whether called a lottery, raffle, or gift enterprise, or by whatever name the same may be known."

[The court then distinguished between games of chance and games of skill, giving some examples.]

[E]xamples of games of chance, [are] throwing dice and playing at cards, dealing with the face down. On the other hand, * * * chess, checkers, billiards, and bowling [are] games of skill. The distinction is clear. In [cards or throwing dice] chance is the dominating element. Such, manifestly, is not the case in games of chess, checkers, billiards, bowling, and other games of skill. It was [only] games of chance that the Legislature intended to prohibit.

* * *

[Checkers] is a game of skill. In fact, skill is not only the dominating element, but it appears that nothing whatever is left to chance. The customer or patron of the device plays the game alone. There are 300 holes, any one of which the player may select. These holes contain a slip of paper upon which is the name of a checker problem. There are ten problems which are described on the board. When the player selects a hole and punches out the slip of paper therein, he then knows the problem he has to solve. The slip of paper indicates how the checkers shall be placed on the checker board which is in front of the player. The checkers are divided into black and white. The player plays the black against the white and must win in order to solve the problem. In some of the problems an equal number of black and white checkers are played on the board; in others there are more of one kind than the other. From the limited number of checkers used in each problem and their location on the board it has the appearance of a game which has been partly played. Some of the problems are more difficult to solve than others. This cannot be determined until the player punches out the problem. For this reason it is contended by appellant that here is an element of chance. But * * * *"any of said games can be won if the person playing has sufficient skill as a checker player to move his checkers skillfully."* [Emphasis added.] * * * It is unquestionably a game of skill * * * without any element of chance. The fact that one player may be less skillful than another or that one of the games may be more difficult than another does not make it a game of chance. If it can certainly be won by a skillful player it is not a game of chance. Checker playing is universally held by the authorities to be a game of skill. The fact that one of the players may be more skillful than the other does not alter the nature of the game. It is nevertheless a game of skill.

JUDGMENT AND REMEDY *The court disagreed with defendant's theory that the subject matter of the contract was illegal. The plaintiff was awarded damages in the amount of the contract price for the goods, wares, and merchandise. Defendant was required to pay.*

COMMENTS *It is a general principle of public policy that when an agreement is illegal, neither party can sue the other for breach and neither can recover for performance rendered. However, some exceptions exist. The following people can sue for breach: (1) persons induced to enter into an illegal contract through fraud, duress, or undue influence; (2) persons unaware or ignorant of facts that make the agreement illegal; (3) persons who withdraw from an illegal agreement before the transaction is performed; and (4) persons protected by statutory law.*

Sunday Laws

Statutes in some states prohibit the formation or performance of certain contracts on a Sunday. (These are often called Sunday laws.) At common law, contracts entered into or contracts to be performed on a Sunday were illegal. The statutes today vary greatly in scope and applicability. Some make all contracts entered into on Sunday illegal. Others prohibit only the sale of merchandise, particularly alcoholic beverages, on a Sunday. (These are often called Blue laws.) A number of states have laws that forbid the carrying on of "all secular labor and business on 'The Lord's Day'." In such states, it would appear that all contracts made on a Sunday are illegal and unenforceable *as long as they remain executory.*

Exceptions to Sunday laws permit works of necessity and works of charity to be performed on Sundays. In addition, a contract entered into on a Sunday that has been fully performed (that is, an *executed* contract) cannot be rescinded or cancelled. Active enforcement of Sunday laws also varies from state to state and even among communities within a particular state. Many do not enforce the Sunday laws, and many such laws have been held to be unconstitutional.

Licensing Statutes

All states require members of certain professions or callings to obtain licenses allowing them to practice. Doctors, lawyers, real estate brokers, construction contractors, electricians, and stockbrokers are but a few of the people who must be licensed. Some licenses are obtained only after extensive schooling and examinations. Others require only that the particular person be of good moral character.

When a person enters into a contract with an unlicensed individual, the contract may or may not be enforceable. By looking at the statute itself, one can often tell if a contract is enforceable. Some statutes expressly provide that the failure to obtain a license will bar enforcement of any contracts entered into by the unlicensed individual. If the statute does not expressly state whether or not the contracts are enforceable, one must look to the underlying purpose of the licensing requirements. If the underlying purpose is to protect the public from unauthorized practitioners, then the contract will be illegal and unenforceable. For example, if you enter into a contract with an unlicensed chiropractor, the chiropractor cannot enforce the contract. The licensing of chiropractors is designed to protect the public from persons who are not capable (or who have not shown their capability) of practicing their trade. On the other hand, if the underlying purpose of the licensing statute is to raise revenues, contracts entered into with an unlicensed practitioner will be enforceable.

The sanction instead will be a fine on the unlicensed practitioner.

Assume you live in a state where anybody can be a television repairman. The only requirement for a license is the payment of $15 a year. Since there are no restrictions on who can get a license, it obviously is used only to raise revenue. If Hyde has his television fixed in a reasonable manner by Jenkins and is charged a reasonable price, Hyde cannot escape his contractual liability to pay Jenkins simply because Jenkins does not have a valid license.

CONTRACTS CONTRARY TO PUBLIC POLICY

Although contracts are entered into by private parties, some are not enforceable because of the negative impact they would have on society. These contracts are said to be *contrary to public policy*. In the following case, a famous movie star is party to a most unusual suit brought to enforce an oral contract for property and support growing out of a nonmarital relationship.

BACKGROUND AND FACTS *Michelle Marvin lived with Lee Marvin for seven years without marriage and then brought suit to enforce an alleged oral contract existing between them. Michelle Marvin, the plaintiff, claimed that, according to their agreement, she was entitled to half the property that had been acquired in Lee Marvin's name during the seven years, and she sought support payments.*

The aspect to be dealt with here is the Supreme Court of California ruling that a court can enforce a contract between nonmarital parties unless the contract was explicitly founded on the consideration of meretricious sexual services, which are illegal.

MARVIN v. MARVIN

Supreme Court of California, 1976.
18 Cal.3d 660, 134 Cal.Rptr. 815, 557 P.2d 106.

TOBRINER, Justice.
* * *

During the past 15 years, there has been a substantial increase in the number of couples living together without marrying.[1] Such nonmarital relationships lead to legal controversy when one partner dies or the couple separates. Courts of Appeal, faced with the task of determining property rights in such cases, have arrived at conflicting positions. * * * We [the Supreme Court] take this opportunity to resolve that controversy and to declare the principles which should govern distribution of property acquired in a nonmarital relationship.
* * *

Although the past decisions hover over the issue in the somewhat wispy form of the figures of a Chagall painting, we can abstract from those decisions a clear and simple rule. *The fact that a man and woman live together without marriage, and engage in a sexual relationship, does not in itself invalidate agreements between them relating to their earnings, property, or expenses.* [Emphasis added.] Neither is such an agreement invalid merely because the parties may have contemplated the creation or continuation of a nonmarital relationship when they entered into it. Agreements between nonmarital partners fail only to the extent that they rest upon a consideration of meretricious sexual services.

---

1. "The 1970 census figures indicate that today perhaps eight times as many couples are living together without being married as cohabited ten years ago." [Comment, *In re Cary: A Judicial Recognition of Illicit Cohabitation* (1974) 25 Hastings L.J. 1226.]

In summary, we base our opinion on the principle that adults who voluntarily live together and engage in sexual relations are nonetheless as competent as any other persons to contract respecting their earnings and property rights. Of course, they cannot lawfully contract to pay for the performance of sexual services, for such a contract is, in essence, an agreement for prositution and unlawful for that reason [because the action is illegal; hence the contract would be illegal and void]. But they may agree to pool their earnings and to hold all property acquired during the relationship in accord with the law governing community property; conversely they may agree that each partner's earnings and the property acquired from these earnings remains the separate property of the earning partner. So long as the agreement does not rest upon illicit meretricious consideration, the parties may order their economic affairs as they choose, and no policy precludes the courts from enforcing such agreements.

In the present instance, plaintiff alleges that the parties agreed to pool their earnings, that they contracted to share equally in all property acquired, and that defendant agreed to support plaintiff. The terms of the contract as alleged do not rest upon any unlawful consideration. We therefore conclude that the complaint furnishes a suitable basis upon which the trial court can render declaratory relief. * * * We conclude that the judicial barriers that may stand in the way of a *policy based upon the fulfillment of the reasonable expectations of the parties to a nonmarital relationship should be removed.* [Emphasis added.] As we have explained, the courts now hold that express agreements will be enforced unless they rest on an unlawful meretricious consideration. We add that in the absence of an express agreement, the courts may look to a variety of other remedies in order to protect the parties' lawful expectations.

The courts may inquire into the conduct of the parties to determine whether that conduct demonstrates an implied contract or implied agreement of partnership or joint venture or some other tacit understanding between the parties. * * * Finally, a nonmarital partner may recover in quantum meruit for the reasonable value of household services rendered less the reasonable value of support received if he can show that he rendered services with the expectation of monetary reward.

JUDGMENT AND REMEDY *The court recognized that a contract can exist between nonmarital parties with regard to their earnings and property rights and that such an agreement can be enforced by the court as long as it is not explicitly founded on the consideration of sexual services. The case was sent back to the trial court for its determination as to the terms of the implied contract between the parties.*

Contracts in Restraint of Trade

An example of contracts that adversely affect the public are contracts in restraint of trade. Public policy favors competition in the economy. Contracts in restraint of trade usually violate one or more federal statutes.[4] However, prior to the adoption of these federal statutes, case law prohibiting certain contracts that had the effect of restraining trade had developed.

---

4. Some of these statutes are the Sherman Antitrust Act, the Clayton Act, and the Federal Trade Commission Act. Antitrust and contracts in restraint of trade are fully discussed in Chapters 50 and 51.

AGREEMENTS NOT TO COMPETE *Agreements not to compete* are often contained in contracts for the sale of an ongoing business. The seller agrees not to open up a new store within a certain geographical area surrounding the old store. When agreements not to compete are accompanied by the sale of an ongoing business, the agreements are usually upheld as legal if they are "reasonable." The seller has built up an established clientele, and the buyer pays for this goodwill or reputation when purchasing the ongoing business. Thus the seller should not be able to open up a similar business right down the block and draw away the buyer's customers.

If the agreement not to compete is made without an accompanying sales agreement, it is void. When no business is being sold, there is no reason for a person to agree not to compete in a certain geographical area. Such an agreement tends to restrain trade and is contrary to public policy.

Even when ancillary to a primary agreement, agreements not to compete can be contrary to public policy if they are unreasonably broad or restrictive. Suppose Orian Capital sells its San Francisco loan and finance business to Bankers Life Company. If Orian Capital agrees not to open another business in the whole state of California, the agreement not to compete is unreasonably broad. After all, the threat of losing customers to Orian is not very severe in San Diego. On the other hand, if the agreement covers only the San Francisco Bay area, it will probably be upheld.

Ancillary agreements not to compete can also be held contrary to public policy if they last for an unreasonably long period of time. In the above example, if Orian agrees not to compete for a hundred years, the contract will be con-trary to public policy. On the other hand, a five-year agreement is reasonable and enforceable.

Agreements not to compete can be ancillary to employment contracts. It is common for many middle and upper level management personnel to agree not to work for competitors or not to start a new business for a specified period of time after terminating employment. If such an agreement is not ancillary to an employment contract, it is illegal. If ancillary, it is legal if it is not excessive in scope or duration. (The courts are reluctant to enforce these contracts, however.)

RESALE PRICE MAINTENANCE AGREEMENTS Another contract in restraint of trade is the resale price maintenance contract between a manufacturer and a dealer or a set of dealers. The dealer or dealers agree not to sell a product at a price below some specified minimum, thereby assuring a certain price level for the product. Between 1937 and 1977, manufacturers could require resale price maintenance on the part of dealers throughout the country (subject to state control). Today, however, such laws (called fair trade laws) are against public policy as expressed by federal statute. They are illegal.[5]

The reasonableness of a "restraint of trade" covenant was the subject of the court's opinion in the following case.

_____

5. There are exceptions, however. The states can regulate the sale of alcoholic beverages in virtually any way they wish, and many have resale price maintenance for alcoholic beverages. Additionally, in certain instances, if state laws regarding resale price maintenance comply with the "state action" doctrine expressed in Parker v. Brown, 317 U.S. 341, 63 S. Ct. 307 (1942), then those laws are allowed to stand.

BACKGROUND AND FACTS *Budget Rent-A-Car, the plaintiff, franchises and services operators in the discount automobile rental business. Budget brought this lawsuit to enforce a restrictive covenant not to compete against Fein, the defendant.*

Defendant Fein was a prospective purchaser of a Budget franchise. It is standard practice for Budget to require prospective purchasers to sign a standard agreement with many provisions, among them "not to

BUDGET RENT-A-CAR CORPORATION OF AMERICA v. FEIN
United States Court of Appeals, Fifth Circuit, 1965.
342 F. 2d 509.

enter into any daily discount automotive rental business in the western hemisphere for a period of two years" without the written permission of Budget. The agreement also prevents the franchisee from disclosing any information about the operational aspects of the business to any other business or organization.

After Fein signed the standard agreement, Budget divulged to him much of its confidential literature describing its operating technique. Budget believed its knowledge of how to start and operate a local rental agency successfully was akin to a trade secret. Consequently, when the franchise deal between Fein and Budget fell through and Fein acquired another franchise from a competitor, Budget charged that Fein was operating his agency similarly to a Budget agency, apparently using some of the confidential information he had seen after signing the agreement.

BROWN, Circuit Judge.

* * *

[A]s a matter of public policy, * * * this restrictive covenant would be unenforceable—primarily because of the "unreasonable" breadth of the territorial restriction. * * *

Of course the equitable doctrine of restrictive covenants is the law's reflex to the needs of the businessman and the commercial world. Consequently it is the business judgment on the value of the relationship, the nature of acquired trade confidences, the uniqueness of skills and the like which counts for much. In that process it is not for Judges, certainly not initially, to determine independent of the practical appraisal of business what is reasonably necessary to protect these several interests. These practical judgments carry great weight. But in the final analysis a court has to evaluate the competing factors to determine whether the legal sanction sought unduly interferes with personal economic freedom of individuals or the flow of goods and services free of monopolistic restraints.

For the covenantee to obtain judicial relief, he must show more than the mere promise of the covenantor. He must bare the soul of the business, or parts of it, even though this breaches for a time or a limited extent the confidences, trade secrets, etc. sought to be protected.

* * *

Before the law will foreclose economic opportunity to an individual for a long period of time because of a covenant exacted as a prelude to the consideration of whether a new relationship is to come into being, it is obvious that what is to be revealed has to be something which is of demonstrable value and deserving of protection.

* * *

Nothing in this record met that test.

* * *

There is another important aspect. *Budget, by extracting this covenant from everyone it talks turkey with, deleteriously affects a far wider range of people than a covenant ancillary to a sale of business where only two parties—the seller and the buyer—are involved.* [Emphasis added. Here the court is saying that true ancillary restrictive agreements are acceptable.] Of course Budget can say that there are only two parties to this particular agreement. The difference is that when a business changes hands, a transaction economically beneficial to the community occurs, but when an individual signs the Budget agreement, looks the deal over, and then does not buy, the only result of economic significance to the community—here the wide, wide world, or at least the half wide world—is that one less individual is free to choose how he will make his living.

* * *

If Fein had actually bought the franchise and this covenant pertained to the eventuality of his selling out and thereafter competing, * * * a much stronger argument could be made for the enforceability of the covenant. But such is not this case.

* * *

Obviously this [covenant] has an anti-competitive effect since anyone talking to Budget is nailed down for two years—anywhere in the western hemisphere. Business necessities justifying such a consequence are not revealed in this record.

Another basis—independent of those already mentioned—why this covenant cannot be enforced is that *the territory encompassed is unreasonably large.* [Emphasis added.]

* * *

Since Budget does not do· business throughout the western hemisphere and the papers utterly fail to demonstrate that there is any reasonably foreseeable likelihood that it will in the near future, it follows that the territorial limitation is unreasonably broad. The covenant is therefore unenforceable.

JUDGMENT AND REMEDY

Both the trial court and the appellate court agreed that the restrictive covenant was unenforceable. Budget could not prohibit Fein from engaging in the rental car franchise business.

COMMENTS

The current view of restraints of trade is that reasonable restraints contained in an employment agreement are enforceable if the purpose of the restraint is to protect a property interest of the promisee (usually the employer) and the conditions of the restraint are reasonable in terms of geographical limitations, duration, and so on. In addition, where confidential or secret information is involved, the courts will occasionally imply a noncompetition agreement where one is not expressly provided.

Unconscionable Contracts and Exculpatory Clauses

Ordinarily, a court will not look at the fairness or equity of a contract. Persons are assumed to be reasonably intelligent, and the courts will not come to their aid just because they have made an unwise or foolish bargain. In certain circumstances, however, bargains are so oppressive that the courts will relieve innocent parties of their duties. Such bargains are called **unconscionable contracts**.

Contracts attempting to absolve parties of negligence are often held to be unconscionable. For example, suppose Jones and Laughlin Steel Company hires a laborer and has him sign a contract stating:

Said employee hereby agrees with employer, in consideration of such employment, that he will take upon himself all risks incident to his position and will in no case hold the company liable for any injury or damage he may sustain, in his person or otherwise, by accidents or injuries in the factory, or which may result from defective machinery or carelessness or misconduct of himself or any other employee in service of the employer.

Such clauses, called **exculpatory clauses**, are defined as clauses that have one party free the other party of all liability in the event of monetary or physical injury no matter who is at fault. This contract provision attempts to remove Jones and Laughlin's potential liability for injuries occurring to the employee, and it can be contrary to public policy.[6]

Contracts entered into because of one party's vastly superior bargaining power are sometimes held to be unconscionable. For example, if every auto manufacturer inserts an exculpatory clause (a clause freeing the manufacturer from liability for personal or monetary damage) in contracts for the sale of autos, consumers will have no chance to bargain for the elimination of the clause. Essentially, the consumer can take it or leave it. In order to combat such clauses, courts have recently held them to be unconscionable.[7] The consumer has no choice, so the contract is contrary to public policy.

Both the Uniform Commercial Code (UCC) and the Uniform Consumer Credit Code (UCCC) have embodied the unconscionability concept—the former with regard to the sale of goods[8] and the latter with regard to consumer loans and the waiver of rights.[9]

Contracts for the Commission of a Crime or Tort

Contracts that require either party to commit a crime are illegal. The courts will not come to the

aid of someone who entered into a contract to commit a crime.[10]

In addition, contracts that require a party to commit a civil wrong or a tort are illegal. Remember that a *tort* is an act that is wrongful to another individual in a private sense, even though it may not necessarily be criminal in nature.

Contracts Injuring Public Service

Contracts that interfere with a public officer's duties are contrary to public policy. For example, contracts to pay legislators for favorable votes or judges for favorable rulings are obviously harmful to the public. Often, a fine line is drawn between lobbying efforts and agreements to influence voting. When a lobby group provides certain factual information in order to influence the outcome of legislation, the lobby is not engaging in an illegal activity. But if the lobby enters into a contingency fee agreement, where the legislator receives a certain amount of money if a certain bill is passed or a certain contract is awarded, the agreement is illegal as contrary to public policy. In the United States, people are not entitled to buy and sell votes. Therefore, agreements having that effect are illegal.

Agreements that involve a *conflict of interest* are often illegal. Public officers cannot enter into contracts that cause conflict between the officers' duties as representatives of the people and the officers' private finances. Statutes require many public officers to liquidate their interests in private businesses before serving as elected representatives. Other statutes merely require them to put their businesses in blind trusts, so that private and public responsibilities remain separate.

Suppose Ladd is a county official in charge of selecting land for the building of a new courthouse. He makes a contract for the state to

---

6. For a case with similar facts, see Little Rock & Ft. Smith Railway Company v. Eubanks, 48 Ark. 460, 3 S.W. 808 (1887).

7. See Henningsen v. Bloomfield Motors, Inc., 32 N.J. 358, 161 A. 2d 69 (1960)

8. See, for example, UCC Secs. 2-302 and 2-719.

9. See, for example, UCCC Secs. 5.108 and 1.107.

---

10. See, for example, McConnell v. Commonwealth Pictures Corp., 7 N.Y. 2d 465, 199 N.Y.S. 2d 483, 166 N.E.2d 494 (1960). In this famous case, the majority view and the dissent clearly showed two different ideas about illegality.

buy land that he happens to own. This is a conflict of interest. If the state discovers later that Ladd owned the land, it can normally use this information to show a conflict of interest and to void the contract.

Agreements
Obstructing Legal Process

Any agreement that intends to delay, prevent, or obstruct the legal process is illegal. For example, an agreement to pay some specified amount if a criminal prosecution is terminated is illegal. Likewise, agreements to suppress evidence in a legal proceeding or to commit fraud upon a court are illegal. Tampering with a jury by offering jurors money in exchange for their votes is illegal.

In a trial, most witnesses (except expert witnesses) are paid a flat fee to compensate them for their expenses. Offering to pay one witness more than another is contrary to public policy, since the extra payment can provide an incentive for the witness to lie.

A promise to refrain from the prosecution of a criminal offense in return for a reward is voidable because it is against public policy. A reward given under the threat of arrest or prosecution is also voidable. In the following situation, in order to cover up an embezzlement, a promissory note was given for the amount embezzled in return for the promise that criminal prosecution would not be pursued. Such consideration was illegal and therefore insufficient to support the note. The Supreme Court of Utah explained the situation as it related to the defenses of duress and illegal consideration.

BACKGROUND AND FACTS *The Great American Indemnity Company, appellant, sought enforcement of a promissory note in this suit against the Berryessas, joint obligors on the note. Berryessa argued that the note was unenforceable, pleading duress and lack of consideration as defenses.*

The underlying transaction involved a father and son. The son had misappropriated some of his employer's funds. When the father first learned of this, it was thought that the sum was approximately $2,000. The father agreed to repay this amount of money by giving a promissory note to the son's employer for that amount to cover the shortage. But before the note became due, it was discovered that the shortage would probably amount to over $6,000. The father, upon learning this, realized that he could not pay the larger sum of money. It was decided between the father and the employer that the employer's bonding company should be advised of the shortage. Thereafter, the employer did not try to collect the note from the father, apparently expecting the bonding company to reimburse it for the entire shortage.

After the bonding company was notified, its agent had several conferences with the Berryessas, both father and son, and with the employer to ascertain the precise amount of the shortage. Once the amount was determined, the son signed a statement indicating that he had misappropriated that amount of money. The total shortage amounted to $6,865.28. At a subsequent meeting between the Berryessas and the bonding company agent, arrangements were made whereby the entire debt would be paid off.

The Berryessas alleged that the bonding company agent ordered

GREAT AMERICAN INDEMNITY CO. v. BERRYESSA

Supreme Court of Utah, 1952.
122 Utah 243, 248 P.2d 367.

them to pay $2,000 in cash and sign a promissory note for $4,865.20, payable at the rate of $50 a month. In return, the agent agreed that the son would not be prosecuted. However, both father and son had to sign the note or the son would be prosecuted.

The Berryessas gave the agent a cashier's check for $1,500 and a personal check for $500 as payment for the $2,000, but they refused to make the monthly payments. Thereupon, the bonding company sued to collect the note.

The trial court ruled for the Berryessas, holding the note invalid. The bonding company challenged the legal accuracy of the instructions the court gave the jury. The Supreme Court reviewed the jury instructions and the law involved.

WADE, Justice.

* * *

The [trial] court in its Instruction No. 1 told the jury:

"You are instructed that the defendant, W. S. Berryessa [the father], admits signing the note sued upon but raises two defenses to his liability thereon. The first defense is that his signature was obtained as a result of the duress upon him of the plaintiff's agent, J. G. Hagman Jr., that if defendant, W. S. Berryessa, did not sign the note his son, Frank Berryessa, would be criminally prosecuted and sent to jail. The second defense is that even if it should be determined that such duress has not been proven, nevertheless the only consideration for his signing the note was the promise of plaintiff's agent, J. G. Hagman, Jr., that if he would sign Frank Berryessa would not be criminally prosecuted, and that such consideration is illegal and insufficient to support the note. You are instructed that either of these defenses, if established by preponderance of the evidence is a sufficient and adequate defense to plaintiff's action against the defendant, W. S. Berryessa."

In Instruction No. 6, the jury were told:

"You are instructed that the note sued upon by the plaintiff is invalid against the defendant, W. S. Berryessa, if not supported by a valuable consideration. A promissory note given for the suppression of a criminal prosecution is against public policy and cannot be enforced between the parties, and it is immaterial whether the individual as to whom the criminal prosecution is suppressed was guilty or innocent. Accordingly, if you believe from a preponderance of the evidence that the defendant, W. S. Berryessa, signed the note sued upon by the plaintiff in consideration of plaintiff's promise through its agent, J. G. Hagman, Jr., that Frank Berryessa would not be criminally prosecuted for his defalcations, the note is invalid as to the defendant, W. S. Berryessa, and you must so find.

"The burden of proof is on the defendant in this case to prove that the consideration for which the defendant signed the note was the suppression of a criminal prosecution against defendant's son."

It will be noted that these instructions correctly placed the burden of proving their defenses of duress or illegal consideration upon the Berryessas.

It is well settled that a note given to suppress a criminal prosecution is against public policy and is not enforceable between the parties.

"It is conceded that a note or mortgage given on promise to refrain from the prosecution of a person for a felony, or under threats of arrest or prosecution, would be void as against public policy; * * *."

In this case respondent relied on two separate defenses, duress and illegal consideration, either one of which is sufficient to nullify this note. So if the jury found that the note was the result of duress or that respondent signed the note because appellant promised to refrain from criminal prosecution of his son, either one would be sufficient to invalidate the note and would constitute a defense thereto.

The bargain was illegal, and the bonding company could not recover on the note.

JUDGMENT AND REMEDY

The preceding case establishes the rule that a bargain is illegal if either promised performance or the consideration for a promise involves concealing or compounding a crime or alleged crime. However, private restitution can be a strongly desirable public policy. One of the judges in the preceding case wrote a dissenting opinion that pointed out an interesting commentary found in the Restatement, Contracts, Section 548:

COMMENTS

[2] Where an act is a crime and also creates a claim for damages, a bargain for the settlement of that claim is not illegal whether or not the prosecution has begun.

The following illustration is included:

A embezzles money from his employer B. A's father C, gives B a note for the amount embezzled in consideration of B's promise not to prosecute A. The bargain is illegal and neither party can recover for its breach. If C had given the note in satisfaction of B's civil rights against A in the hope that B would not prosecute but *without any agreement to that effect,* C's note would not be illegal, although B refrains from prosecuting as a consequence of receiving it. [Emphasis added.]

The dissenting judge observed that it is difficult to determine when the maker of a note gives it in consideration of a promise not to prosecute or when it is given merely in the hope that prosecution will not occur. Nevertheless, private restitution is a means of inducing settlement of a civil claim.

FORUM SELECTION AND ARBITRATION CLAUSES Agreements that do not obstruct the legal process include agreements for the preselection of a forum or agreements for the arbitration of a dispute. *Forum selection clauses* are often contained in contracts where the parties are large multinational firms. For example, a contract for the sale of construction machinery made between a French corporation and a Colombian corporation can provide for the resolution of disputes in London, England. Agreements to preselect a forum are usually upheld unless they are designed to discourage litigation (for example, where a consumer in

Florida buys an auto from General Motors Corp. and the contract contains a forum selection clause requiring any lawsuit to be brought in Detroit, Michigan).

Arbitration is the negotiation of a dispute before a certain panel of arbitrators. Both sides present their stories, and the arbitrator makes the decision. Essentially, arbitration is similar to a trial, although formal rules of pleading, discovery, and evidence are not recognized. After arbitration, the losing party usually can appeal the arbitrator's decision to a court of law. **Arbitration clauses** (clauses in the contract calling for the settlement of disputes through arbitration) are generally upheld today, although courts previously invalidated such clauses as interfering with the jurisdiction of the court.

Discriminatory Contracts

Contracts providing that parties must discriminate in terms of color, race, religion, national origin, or sex are contrary to statute and contrary to public policy.[11] A contract stating that a property owner will not sell the property to a member of a particular race is unenforceable. Public policy underlying these prohibitions is very strong. People should be treated equally, and the courts are quick to invalidate discriminatory contracts.

EFFECT OF ILLEGALITY

In general, an illegal contract is void. That is, the contract is deemed never to have existed, and the courts will not aid either party. This holds true whether the contract is executory or executed. Suppose Sonatrach, Algeria's national oil company, contracts to sell oil to Tenneco. Algeria has a law that prohibits the export of oil without government approval. Therefore, the contract is illegal and unenforceable. If Tenneco sues to enforce delivery of the oil, the suit will be dismissed since the contract is void. Even if Tenneco has paid for some of the oil, the contract cannot be enforced. Tenneco cannot even get back the money it paid under the illegal contract. The courts take a hands off attitude toward illegal contracts in order to discourage future illegality. Under certain circumstances, however, an illegal contract can be enforced.

Severable Contracts

If a contract is severable into legal and illegal portions, and the illegal portion does not go to the essence of the bargain, the legal portion can be enforced.[12] A *severable contract* consists of distinct parts, performance of which can be

accomplished in installments, with separate consideration provided for each portion.

Suppose Norman Harrington contracts to buy ten pounds of bluegrass seed for $25 and five gallons of herbicide for $30. At the time, Harrington does not know that the Food and Drug Administration has banned sale of the herbicide and that the contract for its sale is therefore illegal. Here, the contract is severable because a separate consideration was stated for the bluegrass seed ($25) and the herbicide ($30). Therefore, the portion of the contract for the sale of bluegrass seed is enforceable; the other portion is not.

Members of Protected Classes

An illegal contract can be enforced by a member of a group of persons specifically protected by statute. When a statute is clearly designed to protect certain classes of people, a member of that class can enforce an illegal contract even though the other party cannot. A statute that prohibits employees from working more than a specified number of hours per month is designed to protect those employees. An employee who works more than the maximum can still recover for those extra hours of service. Flight attendants are subject to a federal statute that prohibits them from flying more than a certain number of hours every month. Even if an attendant exceeds the maximum, the airline must pay for those extra hours of service.

Another example of statutes designed to protect a particular class of people concerns **"Blue Sky" laws,** legislation that regulates and supervises investment companies for the protection of the community. Typical "Blue Sky" laws are intended to stop the sale of stock in fly-by-night concerns like visionary oil wells and distant gold mines. Investors are protected as a class and can sue to recover the purchase price of stock issued in violation of such laws.

Most states also have statutes regulating the sale of insurance. If the insurance company violates a statute when selling insurance, *the purchaser can nevertheless enforce the policy.* For example, assume Indemnity Insurance

---

11. Federal Civil Rights Act of 1964; 42 U.S.C.A., Sec. 2000, *et seq.*

12. Restatement, Contracts, Section 606.

Company is not qualified to sell insurance in Montana but does so anyway. A purchaser who buys a policy to insure his auto has an accident and seeks to recover. The insurer cannot resist payment under the policy, even though the contract is illegal. The statutes regulating insurance companies are designed to protect policyholders, so the buyer can recover from the insurer.

Parties Not Equally at Fault

In most illegal contracts both parties are considered to be equally at fault—in *pari delicto.*

In such cases, the contract is void. If executory (not yet fulfilled), neither party can enforce it. If executed, there can be neither contractual nor quasi-contractual recovery.[13]

When one of the parties is relatively innocent, that party can often obtain restitution or recovery of benefits conferred in a partially executed contract. In this case, the courts will not enforce the contract but will allow the parties to return to their original position.

_____

13.   Restatement, Contracts, Section 598.

QUESTIONS AND CASE PROBLEMS

1.   During the time that Mr. and Mrs. Littlewood were legally married, Mr. Littlewood agreed to marry Millard. Millard did not know that Mr. Littlewood was married. Thereafter Mr. Littlewood informed Millard that he was married, and refused to keep his promise to marry her. Millard brought a suit for breach of contract against Mr. Littlewood, claiming as damages that she had not married another man since she believed that she would marry Mr. Littlewood. Could she collect damages? [Millard v. Littlewood, 5 Exchq. 755 (Eng.)]

2.   In October 1928, Laude Sells entered into an agreement with her two sons to sell the Food Machinery Company, a family-owned business, to her sons, Augden Miller and Neil Sells. The main business of Food Machinery Company was the manufacture of corn husking machines. Part of the agreement between Mrs. Sells and her sons obligated the new owners to pay her $25 for each corn husking machine sold during her lifetime. Upon her death the same royalties were to be paid thereafter to her daughter, Dorothy, provided that she (Dorothy) did not remarry. About a year before Mrs. Sells's death, Dorothy remarried. Upon Mrs. Sells's death, the company refused to pay any royalties to Dorothy, since she had violated the remarriage clause of the agreement. Dorothy sued to have the agreement enforced. Was she able to recover? [Shackleton v. Food Machinery and Chemical Corp., 166 F.Supp. 636, C.D.Ill. (1958)]

3.   Williams, a woman of limited education who was separated from her husband and living on welfare, entered into a series of installment contracts with Walker-Thomas Furniture Company. During the period 1957 to 1962 she purchased various items from Walker-Thomas, including curtains, rugs, chairs, mattresses, a washing machine, and a stereo set. With each purchase, she paid part in cash and signed an installment agreement for the balance. Included in the installment agreement was a paragraph, in extremely fine print, that provided that payments, after the first purchase, were to be prorated on all purchases then outstanding. In other words, each time Williams made an additional purchase from Walker-Thomas under an installment agreement, her payments were credited against the total of all outstanding installment purchases from the company. This had the effect of keeping a balance due on every item until the total bill was paid. Prior to her final purchase, Williams had reduced her outstanding balance to $164. The last purchase, a stereo, increased her balance due to $678. After making several more payments, Williams defaulted. Walker-Thomas attempted to enforce the installment provision allowing it to repossess all the goods previously purchased by Williams. Was this contract enforceable? [Williams v. Walker-Thomas Furniture Company, 198 A.2d 914 (D.C.App.1964)]

4.   In 1970, Overbeck received a Sears credit card. In 1974, he charged several purchases on the credit card. If Overbeck had paid for each purchase within thirty days, no service charge would have been added to the outstanding balance. But he chose to let the account "revolve." Therefore, under the credit card agreement between Overbeck and Sears, a service charge of 1.5 percent (18 percent annually) was added each month. Overbeck claimed that the 18 percent annual interest was usurious and contrary to the laws of Indiana that set the maximum legal rate at 6

percent. Was Overbeck correct? [Overbeck v. Sears, Roebuck and Company,   Ind. App.   , 349 N.E.2d 286 (1976)]

5.   In 1963, the Interstate Commerce Commission issued an order increasing the rates charged by railroad grain shippers by about 16 percent. Southern Railway Company, whose business was primarily dependent on grain shipping, stood to lose millions of dollars if the order were enforced. Southern Railway hired Troutman, an attorney, to fight the order. It knew that Troutman had little experience in Interstate Commerce Commission matters, but it hired him because of his political connections with President John F. Kennedy. Southern Railway anticipated that Troutman could use his influence to gain access to the president and persuade him to use his power to stop enforcement of the ICC's order. Troutman prevented the rate increase, but when he attempted to recover a legal fee, Southern Railway refused to pay. Was the contract between Troutman and Southern Railway in violation of public policy? [Troutman v. Southern Railway Company, 441 F.2d 586 (5th Cir. 1971)]

6.   Mr. and Mrs. Fong entered into an agreement with Miller, who owned and operated a bar and restaurant known as The Gate Inn. Under the contract, the Fongs agreed to manage the restaurant for a five-year period in return for all the profits from the restaurant plus a percentage of profits derived from certain "amusement machines" located near the bar. Essentially, these amusement machines were gambling devices. Gambling was illegal under California law. Shortly after the agreement was made, a dispute arose between Miller and the Fongs. Thereafter, Miller refused to allow the Fongs to operate the restaurant or to collect revenues under the agreement. Could the Fongs enforce this agreement? [Fong v. Miller, 105 Cal.App. 2d 411, 233 P.2d 606 (1951)]

7.   Ferguson and Coleman entered into an agreement for the sale of land to be used for growing cotton. The agreement stated two alternative prices. The land was to be sold for $900 "if cotton should rise to 8¢ by the first of November . . ." If cotton did not rise to the price of 8¢, the selling price was to be $500. Before the first of November, cotton rose to 8½¢, but Coleman refused to pay $900 for the land. Was this an illegal gambling contract? Do you see any possible usury here? What if the contract had read: "Price of the land $500 if Russia lands a man on the moon by the first of November, otherwise price $900"? [Ferguson v. Coleman, 3 Rich. 99, 45 Am.Dec. 761.]

8.   Roeber and Diamond Match Company were both engaged in the business of manufacturing matches. Diamond desired to purchase Roeber's business, which was quite lucrative and essentially national in scope. Pursuant to the sale agreement between Diamond and Roeber, Roeber agreed not to engage in the match business in any state in the United States other than Nevada and Montana for ninety-nine years. Was the contract enforceable? [Diamond Match Company v. Roeber, 106 N.Y. 473, 13 N.E. 419 (1801)]

9.   Riggs Realty entered into a contract with Zalis to pay Zalis a finder's fee of $15,000 for Zalis's services in seeking a buyer for certain farmland. Riggs had received a $45,000 commission on the sale. Thereafter, Riggs refused to pay Zalis his finder's fee, claiming that since Zalis was acting as a real estate broker without a broker's license the contract was unenforceable. Could Zalis collect his finder's fee? [Zalis v. Blumenthal, 254 Md. 265, 254 A.2d 692 (1969)]

10.   The Constitution provides for the separation of church and state. The government can in no way support or affiliate itself with any particular religion or group of religions. (Note that across-the-board legislation, such as tax exemptions for religious organizations, is not prohibited by this constitutional provision) Illinois enacted a law requiring all non-food retailers to remain closed on Sunday. A local retailer challenged the law as a violation of the constitutional provision calling for separation of church and state. Do you think such a "Sunday closing law" is unconstitutional?

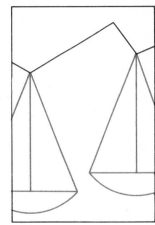

10

Contracts
Genuineness of Assent

When there is no *genuine assent* to the terms of a contract because of the existence of a mistake, fraud, undue influence, or duress, the contract is voidable. The innocent party is able to rescind the contract and avoid the legal obligations it imposes.

MISTAKES

It is important to distinguish between mistakes *as to facts* and mistakes *in judgment as to value or quality*. Only the former have legal significance. Suppose Jane Simpson plans to buy ten acres of land in Montana. If she believes the land is worth $10,000, and it is worth only $4,000, her mistake is one of value or quality. However, if she believes the land is the ten acres owned by the Boyds of Helena, and it is actually the ten acres owned by the Deweys, her mistake is one of fact. Only a mistake as to fact allows a contract to be avoided.

   Mistakes occur in two forms—*unilateral* and *mutual* or *bilateral*. A unilateral mistake is made by only one of the contracting parties; a mutual mistake is made by both.

Unilateral Mistakes

A unilateral mistake involves some *material fact* that is important to the consideration of the contract. If the party had not made the mistake, the

157

contract would probably not have been formed. However, in general, a unilateral mistake does not afford the mistaken party any right to relief from the contract.[1] According to the objective theory of contracts, the subjective intent of the contracting parties is irrelevant. If a party mistakenly believes something a reasonable person would not believe, the contract is enforceable, except when the other party knows or should have known of the mistake.

For example, Odell Construction Co. made a bid to install the plumbing in a proposed apartment building. When Herbert Odell, the president, added up his costs, his secretary forgot to give him the figures for the pipe fittings. Because of the omission, Odell's bid was $6,500 below that of the other bidders. The prime contractor, Sunspan Inc., accepted Odell's bid. If Sunspan was not aware of Odell's mistake or could not reasonably have been aware of it, the contract would be enforceable, and Odell would be required to install the plumbing at the bid price. However, if Odell's secretary had mentioned her error to Sunspan, the contract could be rescinded because Sunspan would have known of the mistake. Similar-ly, if Odell's bid was so far below the others' that, as a contractor, Sunspan should reasonably have known of a mistake, the contract could be rescinded. Sunspan would not be allowed to accept the offer knowing it was made by mistake.[2] The law of contracts protects only *reasonable* expectations.

Mutual Mistakes of Material Fact

When both parties are mistaken as to a material fact, the contract can be rescinded by either party.[3] The mistake must be about a material fact—that is, a fact that is important and central to the contract.

The classic case on mutual mistake of fact involved a ship named "Peerless" that was to sail from Bombay with certain cotton goods on board. However, more than one ship named "Peerless" sailed from Bombay that winter. The mistake was mutual, and it was about a material fact.

---

1. Restatement, Contracts, Section 503.
2. Peerless Glass Co. v. Pacific Crockery Co., 121 Cal. 641, 54 P. 101 (1898).
3. Restatement, Contracts, Section 502.

RAFFLES v. WICHELHAUS AND ANOTHER
2 H. & C. 908, 1864.

BACKGROUND AND FACTS   *The defendant purchased a shipment of Surat cotton from the plaintiff "to arrive ex 'Peerless' from Bombay." The defendant expected the goods to be shipped on the Peerless sailing from Bombay in October. The plaintiff expected to ship the goods on another Peerless, which sailed from Bombay in December. By the time the goods arrived and the plaintiff tried to deliver them, the defendant was no longer willing to accept them.*

* * *

Declaration. For that it was agreed between the plaintiff and the defendants, to wit, at Liverpool, that the plaintiff should sell to the defendants, and the defendants buy of the plaintiff, certain goods, to wit, 125 bales of Surat cotton, guaranteed middling fair merchant's Dhollorah, to arrive ex "Peerless" from Bombay; and that the cotton should be taken from the quay, and that the defendants would pay the plaintiff for the same at a certain rate, to wit, at the rate of 17¼d. per pound, within a certain time then agreed upon after the arrival of the said goods in England. Averments: that the said goods did arrive by the said ship from Bombay in England, to wit, at Liverpool, and the plaintiff was then and there ready, and willing and offered to deliver the said goods to the defendants, &c. Breach: that the defendants refused to accept the said goods or pay the plaintiff for them.

Plea. That the said ship mentioned in the said agreement was meant and intended by the defendants to be the ship called the "Peerless," which sailed from Bombay, to wit, in October; and that the plaintiff was not ready and willing and did not offer to deliver to the defendants any bales of cotton which arrived by the last mentioned ship, but instead thereof was only ready and willing and offered to deliver to the defendants 125 bales of Surat cotton which arrived by another and different ship, which was also called the "Peerless", and which sailed from Bombay, to wit, in December.

* * *

There is nothing on the face of the contract to shew that any particular ship called the "Peerless" was meant; but the moment it appears that two ships called the "Peerless" were about to sail from Bombay there is a latent ambiguity, and parol evidence may be given for the purpose of shewing that the defendant meant one "Peerless," and the plaintiff another. That being so, there was no consensus ad idem, and therefore no binding contract.

The judgment was for the defendants.

JUDGMENT AND REMEDY

The effect of a mistake upon the formation of a contract is a difficult area of law to understand. In order to find mutual assent, the courts employ the following objective test: Persons are bound by the reasonable impressions they create in the mind of the other party, regardless of whether that impression is the same as their subjective intentions.

COMMENTS

Two Common Types of Mutual Mistakes

A mutual mistake as to some incidental aspect of the contract does not entitle the parties to rescission (cancellation) or reformation (a rewording of the contract). Mutual mistakes usually occur in two types of cases. In the first, the parties erroneously believe the contract can be performed when it actually cannot. For example, suppose Adams contracts to buy Bender's race horse, and the night before the sale, unknown to either, the horse dies. Since both parties mistakenly assumed the horse would be alive, either can rescind the contract.

The second type of mistake usually involves the identity of the subject matter of the contract. For example, suppose you are the purchasing agent for Estner Cosmetics. You visit Sandra Imports one day and see four boxes marked No. 4 Red Dye. You ask Sandra to ship them to your plant. However, when they arrive, you discover that blue dye has been delivered in red dye boxes. Since both you and Sandra Imports believed that the boxes contained red dye, the contract can be rescinded or reformed.

Distinguish carefully between a mistake *in identity* and a mistake *in value*. Suppose Daniel Murray looks at Beverly Beale's violin and buys it for $250. Later, Murray discovers that the violin is a Stradivarius, built in 1717. Here there is no mistake that will warrant rescission or reformation. Both parties knew what the subject matter of the contract was — the violin that Murray had seen. Both Murray and Beale mistook the value of that particular violin. Therefore, the contract cannot be rescinded.

Modern courts still apply the "Peerless" theory of mutual mistake in evaluating whether or not a contract exists. In the following case, the court applied the mutual mistake doctrine to a situation where a contract was cancelled and the cancellation accepted on the basis of a mutual mistake of fact.

BOYD v. AETNA LIFE INSURANCE CO.
Appellate Court of Illinois,
Fourth District, 1941.
310 Ill.App. 547, 35 N.E.2d 99.

BACKGROUND AND FACTS   *The plaintiff, Christine Boyd, was named beneficiary in a policy insuring her husband's life. The policy, issued by Aetna Life (the defendant), contained a provision for payment of benefits in the event of the husband's permanent total disability. The couple separated, but the policy was still in force, and Mrs. Boyd continued to pay the premiums. However, she eventually agreed to surrender the policy. She did not know the whereabouts of her husband and was uninformed about his state of health. After she surrendered the policy, Mrs. Boyd learned that her husband had become disabled. His disability had occurred before she surrendered the policy, and had she known about it, she would not have surrendered the policy. She asked the court to rescind her surrender agreement with the Aetna Life Insurance Co. and to pay her the disability (and death) benefits due under the policy on the ground of "mutual mistake of fact."*

STONE, Presiding Justice.

* * *

The decisive and practically sole question for the consideration of this court is whether the facts alleged in the amended complaint, set forth a sufficient mistake of fact, in the legal acceptation of the term, as to justify the intervention of a court of equity, and relieve against the consequences of that alleged mistake of fact, in the entering into the contract of recision.

"Mistake of fact" has been defined to be a mistake, not caused by the neglect of a legal duty on the part of the person making the mistake, and consisting in an unconscious ignorance or forgetfulness of a fact past or present material to the contract, or belief in the present existence of a thing material to the contract which does not exist, or in the past existence of a thing which has not existed. [Emphasis added.]

* * *

[A]t the time of cancellation plaintiff had a perfectly valid claim, but she and the company were both at that time, * * * ignorant of the fact that there was a claim in existence, due to the total permanent disability of insured. The supposed element of doubt as to the health of Boyd never entered into the contemplation of either party, nor did it form any part of the consideration for the cancellation and surrender of the policy. It would be quite natural that they would assume as they evidently did, that the insured was in good health. As matter of fact such is the express allegation of the amended conplaint.

* * *

In the instant case, the insured's state of health was not merely incidental, nor was it a matter that would merely enhance the amount of damages. The subject matter of the mistake was intrinsic to the transaction. As set forth in plaintiff's amended complaint, "if she had known the true facts as to said Jimmie Boyd's total permanent disability * * * she would not have surrendered same (the policy) to the defendant." This policy was in full force and effect at the time of total permanent disability. Upon that contingency coming to pass the liability of defendant was fixed. The cancellation was not intended to reach back and absolve defendant from any liability which it had already incurred.

Aetna was held liable to Mrs. Boyd as a beneficiary for payment of benefits under the policy, since she had been paying the policy up to and including the point when her ex-husband became disabled. At the time of his disability, Aetna became indebted to Mrs. Boyd as beneficiary for those payments. Therefore, there was indeed a mutual mistake of fact, since neither she nor Aetna knew of her ex-husband's disability entitling her to payment. The court permitted Mrs. Boyd to rescind her surrender agreement with Aetna and ordered Aetna to pay her the disability benefits.

JUDGMENT AND REMEDY

FRAUD

The five elements of **fraud** are: (1) a misrepresentation of facts, (2) the misrepresenting party's knowledge that the facts are false, (3) an intent to deceive, (4) the innocent party's justifiable reliance on the misrepresentation, and (5) injury to the innocent party.

When a party consents to a contract with fraudulent terms, the contract can be voided because the party has not voluntarily consented to its terms.[4] In addition, fraud entitles the innocent party to recover damages caused by the fraud. The party can either rescind the contract and be restored to his or her original position or can enforce the contract and seek damages for any injury incurred from the fraud.

Today, courts find fraud more easily. Also, government standards of fraud, such as those used by the Federal Trade Commission in its litigation, are much less stringent than those of the common law.

Misrepresentation

In order to prove fraud, the innocent party must first show that a past or present fact has been misrepresented. The misrepresentation can be words or actions. For example, the statement "This sculpture was made by Michelangelo" is an express misrepresentation of fact if the statue was made by a local artisan.

Suppose Quid contracts to buy a horse from Ray. The horse is blind in one eye, but when Ray shows the horse, he skillfully keeps its head turned so that Quid does not see the defect. The concealment constitutes fraud because of Ray's *conduct*. Likewise, if a salesperson shows a sample from the top of a large box, but does not show the inferior samples at the bottom, a misrepresentation *by conduct* has occurred if there is a marked difference in quality between the top and the bottom.

Representations of future facts (predictions) or statements of opinion are generally not subject to a claim of fraud. Every person must exercise care and judgment when entering into contracts, and the law will not come to the aid of one who simply makes an unwise bargain. For example, statements that "This land will be worth twice as much next year" or "This car will last for years and years" are statements of opinion, not fact. Hence, contracting parties should recognize them as such and not rely on them. An opinion is usually subject to contrary or conflicting views; a fact is objective and verifiable.

In certain cases, however, opinions as to value may entitle the innocent party to rescission or reformation. These cases always involve some sort of "expert" giving a naive purchaser some opinion, and they are decided on equitable grounds. The courts usually hold it to be unfair to allow an expert to take advantage of a novice, especially if the expert knows the novice is relying on the expert's opinion.

---

4. Restatement, Contracts, Section 476; when there is fraud in the execution of the contract, it is void.

VOKES v. ARTHUR MURRAY, INC.

District Court of Appeal of
Florida, Second District, 1968.
212 So.2d 906.

BACKGROUND AND FACTS *The defendant, Arthur Murray, Inc., operated dancing schools throughout the nation through local franchised operators, one of whom was the defendant. The plaintiff, Audrey E. Vokes, a widow without family, wished to become "an accomplished dancer" to find "a new interest in life." In 1961, she was invited to attend a "dance party" at J. P. Davenport's "School of Dancing." Vokes went to the school and received elaborate praise from her instructor for her grace, poise, and potential as "an excellent dancer." The instructor sold her eight half-hour dance lessons for $14.50, to be utilized within one calendar month.*

Subsequently, over a period of less than sixteen months, Vokes bought a total of fourteen dance courses, which amounted to 2,302 hours of dancing lessons for a total cash outlay of $31,090.45, all at Davenport's school.

PIERCE, Judge.

* * *

These dance lesson contracts and the monetary consideration therefor of over $31,000 were procured from her by means and methods of Davenport and his associates which went beyond the unsavory, yet legally permissible, perimeter of "sales puffing" and intruded well into the forbidden area of undue influence, the suggestion of falsehood, the suppression of truth, and the free exercise of rational judgment, if what plaintiff alleged in her complaint was true. From the time of her first contact with the dancing school in February, 1961, she was influenced unwittingly by a constant and continuous barrage of flattery, false praise, excessive compliments, and panegyric encomiums, to such extent that it would be not only inequitable, but unconscionable, for a Court exercising inherent chancery power to allow such contracts to stand.

She was incessantly subjected to overreaching blandishment and cajolery. She was assured she had "grace and poise"; that she was "rapidly improving and developing in her dancing skill"; that the additional lessons would "make her a beautiful dancer, capable of dancing with the most accomplished dancers"; that she was "rapidly progressing in the development of her dancing skill and gracefulness", etc., etc. She was given "dance aptitude tests" for the ostensible purpose of "determining" the number of remaining hours instructions needed by her from time to time.

At one point she was sold 545 additional hours of dancing lessons to be entitled to award of the "Bronze Medal" signifying that she had reached "the Bronze Standard", a supposed designation of dance achievement by students of Arthur Murray, Inc.

Later she was sold an additional 926 hours in order to gain the "Silver Medal", indicating she had reached "the Silver Standard", at a cost of $12,501.35.

At one point, while she still had to her credit about 900 unused hours of instructions, she was induced to purchase an additional 24 hours of lessons to participate in a trip to Miami at her own expense, where she would be "given the opportunity to dance with members of the Miami Studio".

She was induced at another point to purchase an additional 126 hours of lessons in order to be not only eligible for the Miami trip but also to become "a life member of the Arthur Murray Studio", carrying with it certain dubious emoluments, at a further cost of $1,752.30.

At another point, while she still had over 1,000 unused hours of instruction she was induced to buy 151 additional hours at a cost of $2,049.00 to be eligible for a "Student Trip to Trinidad", at her own expense as she later learned.

Also, when she still had 1100 unused hours to her credit, she was prevailed upon to purchase an additional 347 hours at a cost of $4,235.74, to qualify her to receive a "Gold Medal" for achievement, indicating she had advanced to "the Gold Standard".

On another occasion, while she still had over 1200 unused hours, she was induced to buy an additional 175 hours of instruction at a cost of $2,472.75 to be eligible "to take a trip to Mexico".

Finally, sandwiched in between other lesser sales promotions, she was influenced to buy an additional 481 hours of instruction at a cost of $6,523.81 in order to "be classified as a Gold Bar Member, the ultimate achievement of the dancing studio".

All the foregoing sales promotions, illustrative of the entire fourteen separate contracts, were procured by defendant Davenport and Arthur Murray, Inc., by false representations to her that she was improving in her dancing ability, that she had excellent potential, that she was responding to instructions in dancing grace, and that they were developing her into a beautiful dancer, whereas in truth and in fact she did not develop in her dancing ability, she had no "dance aptitude", and in fact had difficulty in "hearing the musical beat". The complaint alleged that such representations to her "were in fact false and known by the defendant to be false and contrary to the plaintiff's true ability, the truth of plaintiff's ability being fully known to the defendants, but withheld from the plaintiff for the sole and specific intent to deceive and defraud the plaintiff and to induce her in the purchasing of additional hours of dance lessons". It was averred that the lessons were sold to her "in total disregard to the true physical, rhythm, and mental ability of the plaintiff". In other words, while she first exulted that she was entering the "spring of her life", she finally was awakened to the fact there was "spring" neither in her life nor in her feet.

* * *

It is true that "generally a misrepresentation, to be actionable, must be one of fact rather than of opinion". But this rule has significant qualifications, applicable here. It does not apply where there is a fiduciary relationship between the parties, or where there has been some artifice or trick employed by the representor, or where the parties do not in general deal at "arm's length" as we understand the phrase, or where the representee does not have equal opportunity to become apprised of the truth or falsity of the fact represented.

> "* * * A statement of a party having * * *superior knowledge may be regarded as a statement of fact although it would be considered as opinion if the parties were dealing on equal terms."

It could be reasonably supposed here that defendants had "superior knowledge" as to whether plaintiff had "dance potential" and as to whether she was noticeably improving in the art of terpsichore. And it would be a reasonable inference from the undenied averments of the complaint that the flowery eulogiums heaped upon her by defendants as a prelude to her contracting for 1944 additional hours of instruction in order to attain the rank of the Bronze Standard, thence to the bracket of the Silver Standard, thence to the class of the Gold Bar Standard, and finally to the crowning plateau of a Life Member of the Studio, proceeded as much or more from the urge to "ring the cash register" as from any honest or realistic appraisal of her dancing prowess or a factual representation of her progress.

* * *

"* * * [W]hat is plainly injurious to good faith ought to be considered as a fraud sufficient to impeach a contract", and that an improvident agreement may be avoided * * * because of surprise, or mistake, *want of freedom, undue influence, the suggestion of falsehood, or the suppresion of truth"*. (Emphasis supplied.)

JUDGMENT AND REMEDY

Vokes's complaint, which had originally been dismissed from the trial court, was reinstated, and the case was returned to the trial court to allow Vokes to prove her case.

COMMENTS

Fraud is an ambiguous concept in law. It includes various degrees of misrepresentation that can be separated into three tort categories: (1) intentional behavior, (2) negligent behavior, and (3) strict liability for certain behavior. In all cases involving the tort of misrepresentation and the contract defense of fraud, the defendant must misrepresent a fact or facts, and the plaintiff must believe the misrepresentation to be true and must rely on it with resulting damages.

MISREPRESENTATION OF LAW Misrepresentation of law does not ordinarily entitle the party to relief from a contract. For example, S has a parcel of property that she is trying to sell to B. S knows that a local ordinance prohibits building anything on the property higher than three stories. Nonetheless, S tells B, "You can build a condominium fifty stories high if you want to." B buys the land and later discovers that S's statement is false. Normally B cannot avoid the contract because at common law people are assumed to know state and local law where they reside. Additionally, a layperson should not rely upon a statement made by a nonlawyer about a point of law.

Exceptions to this rule occur when the misrepresenting party pursues a profession that requires greater knowledge of the law. The courts are recognizing an increasing number of persons whose clients can expect them to know the law in their specific area of expertise. For example, real estate brokers are expected to

know the law governing real estate sales, land use, and so on. If S, in the example above, were a lawyer or a real estate broker, her misrepresentation of the area's zoning status would probably constitute fraud.

CONCEALMENT AND SILENCE Ordinarily, neither party to a contract has a duty to come forward and disclose facts. Therefore, a contract cannot be set aside because certain pertinent information is not volunteered. For example, assume that General Corporation is involved in a dispute with Henderson Air Conditioning. The two companies have been doing business for ten years, but General is not satisfied with Henderson's performance on one large contract. Finally, General and Henderson enter into a settlement agreement of their differences. Henderson believes that the long-standing business relationship with General will continue after the dispute is settled. General, on the other hand, has decided to do no further business with Henderson. If Henderson does not question General about this issue, General has no duty to make a full statement of this material fact.

Certain exceptions to this rule exist. When a defect or potential problem exists that a buyer cannot reasonably be expected to discover, the seller often has a duty to speak. When a house is infested with termites, the owner/seller is obliged to disclose this fact to potential buyers (and this is usually spelled out in real estate contracts). When the foundation of a factory is cracked, creating a potential for water damage, the seller must reveal this fact. Likewise, when a city fails to disclose to bidders subsoil conditions that will cause great expense in constructing a sewer, the city is guilty of fraud.[5]

In addition, failure to disclose important facts will constitute fraud when the parties have a relationship of trust and confidence. In such a relationship, if one party knows any facts that materially affect the other's interests, they must be disclosed. For example, an attorney has a duty to disclose material facts to a client. Other such relationships include partners in a partnership, directors of corporations and the shareholders, and guardians and wards.

Knowledge of the Fact's Falsity

The second element of fraud is knowledge on the part of the misrepresenting party that facts have been falsely represented.[6] Proof of such knowledge is not limited to direct testimony, but may be *inferred* from the circumstances surrounding the transaction. For example, suppose Roper has owned a 1976 Oldsmobile for two years and suddenly, for no apparent reason, quits driving it. Roper then puts the auto up for sale. Chipper asks Roper how the engine runs, and Roper says, "This Olds runs like a Swiss

watch; there's nothing wrong with it." So Chipper buys the Olds, only to discover that the engine block is cracked. Here, a court can *infer* that Roper knew the block was cracked (at least in the absence of another explanation from Roper), since he suddenly quit driving the car and put it up for sale.

Some states do not require actual knowledge of falsity, but hold that statements made with a reckless disregard for the truth will satisfy the knowledge requirement.[7] For example, a salesman who tells a customer, "This air conditioner will cool your whole house," without knowing the size of the customer's house, is acting with reckless disregard. A real estate broker who assures a customer that a particular house is insulated, when the broker does not know if it is insulated or not, is acting with reckless disregard.

An Intent to Deceive

The third element of fraud is an intent to deceive. Since this intent is very difficult to prove directly, circumstances surrounding the transaction are usually used *to infer* the intent. Often, courts combine this element with the second element of fraud, knowledgeable misrepresentation, and conclude that the act of misrepresentation combined with the knowledge of its falsity constitute an intent to deceive.

INNOCENT MISREPRESENTATION If a person makes a statement honestly, and it misrepresents material facts, that person is guilty not of fraud, but only of an *innocent misrepresentation*. When an innocent misrepresentation occurs, the aggrieved party can rescind the contract but usually cannot seek damages caused by the misrepresentation (because there was indeed a lack of knowledge).

Reliance on the Misrepresentation

Another element of fraud is reasonably *justified reliance* on the misrepresentation of fact. The

---

5. City of Salinas v Souza & McCue Constr. Co., 66 Cal.2d 217, 57 Cal.Rptr. 337, 424 P.2d 921 (1967).

6. Note, however, that where fraud is inferred from silence (where there is a duty to disclose) proof of this type of knowledge is irrelevant. Rather, the focus will be upon the party's knowledge of a particular defect or problem regarding the subject matter of the contract, not on the fact that there was no disclosure of the problem.

---

7. E. g., Sanders Inc. v. Chesmotel Lodge Inc., 300 S.W.2d 239 (Ky.1957).

reliance must be justified but need not be the only reason for entering into the contract. As long as the innocent party relies on the misrepresentation, and the misrepresentation is a major factor inducing the party to enter into the contract, the requirement of reliance will be satisfied.

Reliance is not justified if the innocent party knows the true facts or relies on extremely extravagant statements. For example, suppose a used car dealer tells you, "This old Cadillac will get fifty miles to the gallon." You would not normally be justified in relying on the statement. Or suppose Phelps, a bank director, induces Scott, a co-director, into signing a guarantee that the bank's assets will satisfy its liabilities, stating, "We have plenty of assets to satisfy our creditors." If Scott knows the true facts he will not be justified in relying on Phelps's statement. However, if Scott does not know the true facts and has no way of finding them out, he will be justified in relying on the statement. The same rule applies to defects in property sold. If the defects are obvious, the buyer cannot justifiably rely on the seller's representations. If the defects are hidden or latent, however, the buyer can rely on the seller's statements.

Injury to the Innocent Party

The final element of fraud is injury to the innocent party. The courts are divided on this issue, and some do not require a showing of injury when the action is to rescind or cancel the contract. Since rescission returns the parties to the position they were in prior to the contract, showing injury to the innocent party has been held to be unnecessary.[8]

In an action to recover damages caused by the fraud, proof of an injury is universally required. The measure of damages is ordinarily equal to what the value of the property would have been if it had been delivered as represented, less the actual price paid for the property. In effect, this gives the innocent (nonbreaching) party the benefit of the bargain, rather than reestablishing the party's position prior to the contract.

In the next case, Hazel Gales applied for auto insurance, stating falsely that she had not been in an auto accident in the past five years and had not received a ticket for a moving violation in the past three years. The defendant, Plains Insurance Co., claimed that such false representations made her policy void from the very beginning (void *ab initio*). The company contended that it would not have sold the policy at the specified rate and perhaps would not have sold it at all if Gales had provided true information about her driving record. Thus, the insurance company did not engage in a genuine assent (that is, there was no reality of consent).

---

8. E. g., Kaufman v. Jaffee, 244 App.Div. 344, 279 N.Y.S. 392 (1935).

MILLER v. PLAINS INSURANCE COMPANY
Springfield Court of Appeals, Missouri 1966.
409 S.W.2d 770.

BACKGROUND AND FACTS   *The plaintiff in this action, D. C. Miller, is suing the insurance company of the owner and driver of the automobile in which his wife was killed. The owner and operator of the automobile, Hazel Gales, also perished in the crash. She was insured by Plains Insurance Company, the defendant. The policy provided, among other things, $500 medical expense coverage and up to $10,000 uninsured motorists coverage.*

At the trial, Miller was awarded both $500 in medical expenses and $10,000 under the uninsured motorists provision. On appeal, the defendant argued that had it known the representations were untrue, it would not have undertaken the risk in insuring Gales, who had a record for moving traffic violations and, in particular, for hazardous driving.

TITUS, Judge.

* * *

What is a material misrepresentation? A misrepresentation that would likely affect the conduct of a reasonable man in respect to his transaction with another is material. [Emphasis added.] Materiality, however, is not determined by the actual influence the representation exerts, but rather by the possibility of its so doing. A representation made to an insurer that is material to its determination as to what premium to fix or to whether it will accept the risk, relates to a fact actually material to the risk which the insurer is asked to assume. The word "risk" does not relate to an actual increase in danger but to a danger determined by the insurer's classification of the various circumstances affecting rates and insurability. That the fact misrepresented has no actual subsequent relation to the manner in which the event insured against occurred, does not make it any the less material to the risk. Thus, whether a misrepresentation is material in an application for an automobile insurance policy, is determined by whether the fact, if stated truthfully, might reasonably have influenced the insurance company to accept or reject the risk or to have charged a different premium, and not whether the insurer was actually influenced.

* * *

It is a well-known fact insurance companies rely on expense, loss, and other statistical data to measure differences among risks and thus ascertain rates to be charged for individual risks in accordance with standards for measuring variations in hazards. This is recognized and, to some extent, controlled by our statutes. Questions as to traffic violations of prospective insureds and as to previous accidents in which they have been involved are legitimate fields of research for insurance companies, for these are not only rate-determining facts but may also determine if the risk will even be insured. In consideration of the authorities previously cited, * * * we are of the opinion the misrepresentations involved in this case might reasonably be expected to have influenced the insurance company to have accepted or rejected Mrs. Gales as an insured or to have charged her a different premium for issuing her a policy. As the only evidence in this case is that if defendant had known the truth it would have declined the risk, we are drawn to the conclusion the misrepresentations were material and should permit defendant to avoid its liability under the policy.

The trial court was reversed. The defendant, Plains Life Insurance Company, did not have to pay the estate of D. C. Miller the $10,000 uninsured motorists claim or the $500 medical expense coverage because of the material misrepresentation of fact made by Hazel Gales when she filled out the application on which her insurance policy was issued. In essence, the court decided there was no true assent by the insurance company to insure Gales under that premium for that policy. No insurance contract ever came into existence.

JUDGMENT AND REMEDY

UNDUE INFLUENCE—FIDUCIARY RELATIONSHIPS

A contract entered into under the excessive or **undue influence** of another is voidable.[9] Undue influence arises from special kinds of relationships in which one party can greatly influence another party. Minors and elderly people are often under the influence of guardians. If the guardian induces a young or elderly ward to enter into a contract that benefits the guardian, undue influence is likely being exerted. There is no genuine assent (reality of consent) to the terms of the contract if the contract is entered into because of another's excessive influence. Undue influence can arise from a number of fiduciary or confidential relationships: attorney-client; doctor-patient; guardian-ward; parent-child; husband-wife; or trustee-beneficiary. The essential feature of undue influence is that the party being taken advantage of does not, in reality, exercise free will in entering into a contract.

In the final analysis, to determine undue influence, the court must ask to what extent the transaction was induced by influencing a competent judgment or by dominating the mind or emotions. The weakness or dependence of the person in question will often show to what extent the persuasion from an outside influence was "unfair".

Courts often presume that in legally challenged contracts between, for example, guardians and their wards, the advantage is taken by the guardians. Thus, the guardian has to rebut this presumption in such cases. To rebut successfully, the guardian has to show that full disclosure was made to the ward, that consideration was adequate, and that the ward received independent and competent advice before completing the transaction.

In cases where the relation is one of trust and competence, such as between an attorney and a client, the dominant party (the attorney) is held to extreme or utmost good faith in dealing with the subservient party. A long-time attorney for an elderly man who induces him to sign a contract for the sale of some of his assets to a friend of the attorney at below-market prices has engineered a voidable contract. The attorney has not upheld good faith in dealing with the man.

DURESS

Assent to the terms of a contract is not genuine if one of the parties is *forced* into agreement. Recognizing this, the courts allow that party to rescind the contract. Forcing a party to enter a contract under the fear of threats is legally defined as **duress**.[10] For example, if Pirranha Loan Co. threatens to harm you or your family unless you sign a promissory note, Pirranha is guilty of using duress. In addition, threatening blackmail or extortion to induce consent to a contract constitutes duress. Duress is both a defense to the enforcement of a contract and a ground for rescission or cancellation. Therefore, the party upon whom the duress is exerted can choose to carry out the contract or to avoid the entire transaction. (This is true in most cases in which assent is not real.)

Generally, the threatened act must be wrongful or illegal. Therefore, a husband's nagging to get a new car does not constitute duress unless he pulls a gun and demands one. Threatening civil litigation does not constitute duress, but threatening a criminal suit does. Suppose that Donovan injures Jones in an auto accident. Donovan has no automobile insurance, but she has substantial assets. Jones is willing to settle the potential claim out of court for $3,000. Donovan refuses. After much arguing, Jones loses her patience and says, "If you don't pay me $3,000 right now, I'm going to sue you for $35,000." Donovan is frightened and gives Jones a check for $3,000. Later in the day she stops payment on the check. Jones comes back to sue her for the $3,000. Donovan argues that she was the victim of duress. However, the threat of a civil suit is normally not duress.

---

9. Restatement, Contracts, Section 497.

10. Restatement, Contracts, Section 492.

Suppose Nelson and Dice belong to a fashionable social club. Nelson watches Dice cheating in a game of bridge and threatens to expose him unless Dice agrees to sign a contract with Nelson. In fear of being expelled from the club, Dice signs. Since Nelson's actions are wrongful, the contract is entered into under duress.

Economic need is generally not sufficient to constitute duress, even though one party exacts a very high price for an item the other party needs. However, if the party exacting the price also creates the need, duress may be found. For example, the Internal Revenue Service assessed a large tax and penalty against Sam Thompson. Thompson retained Earl Eyman to resist the assessment. The last day before the deadline for filing a reply with the Internal Revenue Service, Eyman declined to represent Thompson unless he signed a very high contingency fee agreement. The agreement was unenforceable.[11] Although Eyman had threatened only to withdraw his services, something that he was legally entitled to do, he was responsible for delaying the withdrawal until the last day. Since it would have been impossible to obtain adequate representation elsewhere, Thompson was forced into either signing the contract or losing his right to challenge the IRS assessment.

ADHESION CONTRACTS AND UNCONSCIONABILITY

Modern courts are beginning to strike down terms that are dictated by one of the parties with overwhelming bargaining power. **Adhesion contracts** arise when one party forces the other party to adhere to dictated terms or go without the commodity or service in question. Adhesion contracts usually contain copious amounts of fine print disclaiming the maker's liability for everything imaginable. Standard lease forms are often called adhesion contracts. Formerly, many automobile retailers used contracts containing several pages of fine print when selling a car. In the past, nearly every company excluded liability for personal injuries suffered as a result of using the product. The average consumer, out to buy a five or six thousand dollar car, was in no position to bargain for personal injury coverage. The consumer could either go without an automobile or take the auto risking personal injury.

Standard form contracts are used by a variety of businesses and include life insurance policies, residential leases, loan agreements, and employment agency contracts. In order to avoid enforcement of the contract or of a particular clause, the aggrieved party must show substantially unequal bargaining positions and show that enforcement would be "manifestly unfair" or "oppressive."[12] If the required showing is made, the contract or particular term is deemed *unconscionable* and not enforced. Technically, unconscionability under the Uniform Commercial Code applies only to contracts for the sale of goods. Many courts, however, have broadened the concept and applied it in a number of situations. For example, provisions disclaiming liability, confessing judgment in the event of a breach, and consenting to repossession for trivial breaches have been stricken as unconscionable.

Unconscionability is not a strict legal doctrine, but it enables courts to exercise great discretion in validating or striking down particular contract provisions. As a result, some states have not adopted the appropriate Section 2-302 of the Uniform Commercial Code. In some of those states, the legislature and the courts prefer to rely on traditional notions of fraud, undue influence, and duress. In one respect, this gives certainty to contractual relationships, since parties know they will be held to the exact terms of their contracts. But on the other hand, public policy can dictate that there be some limit on the power of individuals and businesses to dictate terms of a contract. At a minimum, individuals and certain businesses should not be allowed to dictate terms to "powerless" consumers.

---

11.   Thompson Crane & Trucking Co. v. Eyman, 123 Cal. App.2d 904, 267 P.2d 1043 (1954).

---

12.   See UCC Sec. 2-302.

QUESTIONS AND CASE PROBLEMS

1. Jones was a salesman for Cash Register Company. Over the years he had sold cash registers to a number of retail establishments. Jones approached Townsend, a retail merchant, to sell him a cash register. Jones told Townsend that he would save the full cost of a bookkeeper and half the cost of a sales clerk if he bought a machine. Relying on this, Townsend bought the cash register. After several months, he realized that the cash register was not bringing about the savings that Jones had promised. Can Townsend rescind the agreement? [See Cash Register Co. v. Townsend Grocery Store, 137 N.C. 652, 50 S.E. 306 (1905)]

2. Pierce's home was equipped with a four-ton York air-conditioning system that had been installed by a York distributor. When the unit began to malfunction, Pierce contacted Walters, whom he thought was a York serviceman. Walters said that he was no longer in the air-conditioning repair business and suggested that Pierce contact a man named Lawler. Walters told Pierce that Lawler was experienced in repairing York units. Subsequently, Lawler and Pierce negotiated a price for the replacement of the condenser in Pierce's unit. Neither party ever mentioned the brand that was to be used to replace the old condenser, and Lawler installed a new condenser that was not made by York. When Pierce learned this, he demanded that Lawler replace it. Lawler refused. Can Pierce rescind? [Ouachita Air Conditioning, Inc. v. Pierce, 270 So.2d 595 (La.App.1972)]

3. Granite Management Services leased ice-making machines. Don Poag, one of Granite's leasing agents, convinced Usry to lease several Granite machines. Before Usry signed the lease agreement, Poag asked him to sign a document stating that the machines would be serviced free of charge by B Manufacturing Company throughout the lease period. Usry later signed a lease agreement that did not provide for free services. The contract did state, however, that "this contract constitutes the entire agreement between the lessor and lessee and that no representation or statement made by any representative of the lessor or the supplier not stated herein shall be binding." Shortly after Usry received the machines, they broke down and failed to work properly thereafter. Granite never supplied free services for the machines as represented by Poag. Usry discontinued payments under the lease agreement. Can Granite sue? [Granite Management Services, Inc. v. Usry, 130 Ga.App. 667, 204 S.E.2d 362 (1974)]

4. Laemmar was an employee of J. Walter Thompson Co. During the years of his employment, he purchased shares of common stock from the company. Laemmar's stock was subject to repurchase by the company if Laemmar quit. The officers and directors of the company decided to increase their control and demanded that Laemmar and several other employees sell their stock back or lose their jobs. Although Laemmar did not wish to sell his stock, he did so to keep his job. The officers and directors never made any physical threats or suggestions of physical harm to Laemmar. Several years later Laemmar instituted a lawsuit to rescind his sale of the stock. Can Laemmar rescind? [Laemmar v. J. Walter Thompson Co., 435 F.2d 680 (7th Cir. 1970)]

5. Groening wanted to purchase Opsata's home, which was located half way up the side of a small, steep hill overlooking Lake Michigan. The lake came up to the very foot of the hill. Groening, concerned about erosion of the hill and possible damage to the residence, inquired whether the proximity of the house to the lake could result in damage to the home. Opsata responded, "You don't have to have no fear; it is perfectly safe." Groening later purchased the home. Shortly after the purchase, the bottom of the hill eroded completely as a result of the waves in Lake Michigan. Groening sought to rescind the sale on the basis of fraud. Can Groening rescind? [Groening v. Opsata, 323 Mich. 73, 34 N.W.2d 560 (1948)]

6. Rollins was an inmate in the State Prison of Rhode Island. During a prison riot, several of the institution's employees were taken hostage, and a number of demands were made to improve conditions. One of the final demands was that none of the inmates, including Rollins, be prosecuted for any of the illegal acts committed during the riot. Rollins was later prosecuted for holding prison personnel hostage. Rollins claimed that he had a binding contract with the Rhode Island attorney general promising him immunity from prosecution. Is Rollins's defense valid? [State v. Rollins, 116 R.I. 528, 359 A.2d 315 (1976)].

7. Howard, an archeologist and collector of ancient Greek treasures, purchased a vase from Take It or Leave It Antique Company. Take It or Leave It told Howard that the vase had been found in the tomb of a

famous Egyptian king. In reality, Take It or Leave It had purchased the vase for $2 from a local resident. Take It or Leave It sold the vase to Howard for $9,000. Howard later discovered that the vase had not in fact belonged to a famous Egyptian king but was instead the work of the famous sculptor Juan Reynaldo, whose vases sold for over $10,000. Howard seeks to rescind the sale. Must Take It or Leave It return Howard's money?

8.   W & B Realty Company owned and operated an apartment building in Chicago and rented one of the apartments to O'Callaghan. O'Callaghan signed a lease with a clause relieving W & B from all liability for any injuries that O'Callaghan might sustain anywhere on the premises of the apartment area, regardless of any negligence by W & B Realty. One evening, while crossing the courtyard, O'Callaghan fell because the pavement in the courtyard had been inproperly maintained. O'Callaghan sued W & B for her injuries. W & B claimed that it was not liable because of the exculpatory clause contained in the lease. Is W & B correct? [O'Callaghan v. Waller and Beckwith Realty Co., 15 Ill.2d 436, 155 N.E.2d 545 (1958)].

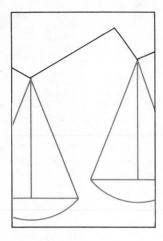

11

Contracts
Writing and Form

I agree to mow your lawn. You agree to pay me $25. I mow your lawn. You give me $15. I threaten to sue. After all, we did have an *oral* contract. Is it enforceable? In most cases, it is, but the party seeking to enforce it must establish the existence of the contract as well as its actual terms. Naturally, when the parties have no writing or memorandum about the contract, only oral testimony can be used in court to establish the existence of the terms of the contract. The problem with oral testimony is that parties are sometimes willing to perjure themselves in order to win lawsuits. At early common law, parties to a contract were not allowed, therefore, to testify. This led to the practice of hiring third party witnesses. As early as the seventeenth century, the English recognized this practice as a problem and enacted a statute to help deal with it. The statute was known as "An Act for the Prevention of Frauds and Perjuries."[1] The act required *certain* types of contracts to be in writing and signed by the party to be charged. By requiring a writing, the act prevented unscrupulous parties from committing fraud and giving perjured testimony. In order to be enforceable, certain types of contracts had to be in writing, or evidenced by a written memorandum. Otherwise, neither party could sue on the contract.

---

1. The English Parliament passed the act in 1677.

CONTRACTS THAT MUST BE IN WRITING

Today, almost every state has a Statute of Frauds, modeled after the English act. The actual name of the Statute of Frauds is misleading since it neither applies to fraud nor invalidates any type of contract. Rather, it denies enforceability to contracts that do not comply with its requirements. Although the statutes vary slightly from state to state, they all require the following types of contracts to be in writing or evidenced by written memorandum:[2]

1. Contracts for the sale of land.
2. Contracts involving lessor interests in land.
3. Contracts which cannot *by their terms* be performed within one year.
4. Collateral contracts such as promises to answer for the debt or duty of another and promises by the administrator or executor of an estate to pay a debt of the estate personally.
5. Promises made in consideration of marriage.
6. Contracts for the sale of goods above a specified dollar amount.

Contracts for the Sale of Land

A contract calling for the sale of land or for the sale of any interest in land will not be enforceable unless it is in writing. Land is real property and includes all physical objects that are permanently attached to the soil. Thus, land includes buildings, crops, trees, and the soil itself. The Statute of Frauds operates as a *defense* to the enforcement of an oral contract for the sale of an interest in land. Therefore, even if *both* parties acknowledge the existence of an oral contract for the sale of land, under many circumstances the contract will still not be enforced.[3] If S contracts orally to sell Blackacre to B but later decides not to sell, B cannot enforce the contract. Likewise, if B refuses to

2. Restatement, Second, Contracts (tentative draft), Section 178.
3. However, the contract will be enforced if the parties admit to the existence of the oral contract in court or admit to its existence pursuant to discovery before trial.

close the deal, S cannot force B to close by bringing a lawsuit. The Statute of Frauds is a defense to the enforcement of this type of oral contract.[4]

Ordinarily a contract for the sale of land involves the entire interest in the property. It is necessary to distinguish between real property, which is affixed to the land, and personal property, which previously was real property. Suppose Collins Pine agrees to sell timber to Seabrook, Incorporated. If the timber is still standing, the contract is for the sale of an interest in land and must therefore be in writing. On the other hand, if Collins Pine has already cut the timber down, the contract is for the sale of personal property and may or may not fall under the Statute of Frauds.[5]

Contracts Involving Lessor Interests in Land

LIFE ESTATES The Statute of Frauds requires written contracts for the sale of an interest in land. Interests in land include life estates, real estate mortgages, easements, and leases. A **life**

4. In the majority of cases, contracts are fully performed by both parties without any problems and it does not matter if the contract is in writing. Most people in business feel a moral duty to perform contracts, and the strength of their word is sufficient to assure that the contract will be performed. However, unforeseen problems do arise, and when they do, a written contract is an absolute necessity. So in order to provide the extra reassurance, a written contract is always advisable. Even when the contract is not within the Statute of Frauds, it is wise to write down its essential terms. If problems do arise, it is much easier to settle them in court.
5. If the contract is for the sale of already cut timber worth more than $500, it has to be in writing. Under UCC Sec. 2-201, the contract for the sale of goods (personal property) worth more than $500 must be in writing. Note that under the Uniform Commercial Code, the contract for the sale of timber, minerals, structures, or materials is a contract for the sale of goods if the items are to be severed from the land *by the seller*. Once severed, they cease to be real property and become personal property or goods subject to the Uniform Commercial Code. [UCC Sec. 2-107] If the *buyer* is to sever the items from the land, the contract is for the sale of an interest in land and must be in writing. If growing crops are sold and they can be severed from the land without material harm to the land, then the contract is for the sale of goods whether the seller or the buyer severs the crops. [UCC Sec. 2-107(2)]

estate is an interest in land that lasts for a person's lifetime. For example, if Sally Manne sells Edenfarm to Mary Johnson "for life, then after Johnson's death, to Nancy Smole," Johnson has a life estate in the farm. When Johnson dies, Smole will have a full estate in the farm— that is, she will own it entirely.[6]

MORTGAGES A real estate **mortgage** is a conveyance of an interest in land as a security for repayment of a loan. If Nancy Smole, now full owner of Edenfarm, wants to borrow money from First National Bank, First National will require collateral for the loan. By giving conditional title of Edenfarm to the bank, Smole can get the loan.[7] When Smole pays off the debt, Edenfarm will be hers once again.

---

6. Full ownership like Nancy Smole's, is called a fee simple absolute. See Chapter 52.

7. Technically, only in "title" states will Nancy Smole be required to convey title to First National Bank. In "lien" states, she can enter into a mortgage giving the bank a lien against the farm. Today, all the distinctions between title states and lien states have essentially been eliminated.

LAMBERT v. HOME FEDERAL SAVINGS AND LOAN ASSOCIATION

Supreme Court of Tennessee, 1972.
481 S.W.2d. 770.

BACKGROUND AND FACTS *The Lamberts (plaintiffs) brought suit against Home Federal Savings and Loan Association and Marx & Bensdorf (defendants) for breach of a promise to make a long-term loan of $2,910,000. The Lamberts were constructing ninety-six apartment units. Marx & Bensdorf, Home Federal's agent, made a construction loan of $672,000. This loan was evidenced by a one-year note in trust deed, which, by its terms, became null and void in October 1968 upon payment and release. Clearly, by the terms of the construction loan, it in no way involved the $2,910,000 permanent loan that was to follow, even though the permanent loan was to be made by the same organization.*

When the Lamberts tried to obtain the $2,910,000, the defendants refused to make the loan. The Lamberts claimed that the permanent loan was tied into the construction loan, and they alleged that there were memoranda indicating the terms of the permanent financing transaction sufficient to satisfy the Statute of Frauds. Thirteen documents were produced at the trial, none of which had any bearing on the permanent loan. The lower court dismissed the case, finding that neither Home Federal nor Marx & Bensdorf had made any commitment to lend that money to the Lamberts.

The Lamberts tried to convince the appellate court that the original construction loan was evidenced by a writing sufficient to satisfy the Statute of Frauds. Furthermore, they argued that since the permanent loan was related to the construction loan, testimony about discussions and negotiations should be permitted to show the court the relationship between the loans and permit the original construction loan agreement to be modified to include the permanent loan.

HUMPHREYS, Justice.
* * *

To meet the requirements of the Statute of Frauds, the Lamberts produced memoranda which they contended would, when considered in connection with this [original construction] mortgage to Marx & Bensdorf, furnish written memoranda of the transaction which would satisfy the Statute of Frauds.

The memoranda relied on by the Lamberts consists of thirteen documents which, considered separately, and collectively, made no commitments whatsoever by Home Federal or Marx & Bensdorf to lend [an additional $2,910,000 of] money to the Lamberts and take a trust deed as security. Nor is any commitment made by the Lamberts to Home Federal and Marx & Bensdorf to accept such a loan and to give a trust deed to secure the same on any described real property. [In other words, there was no written document specifically showing a bilateral agreement, or a "promise for a promise."]

Marx & Bensdorf is not involved in the memoranda other than by the note and deed of trust for the construction loan of $672,000.00 [Moreover], this deed of trust by its terms became null and void upon payment and release, which was and done October 1, 1968; and contains no terms which considered alone or with the thirteen instruments satisfies the statute.

The deed of trust does not, and could not, under its terms, secure any greater amount than the $672,000.00 for which it was intended to furnish security. No other amounts are mentioned in the instrument and there is no language therein indicating any intention that it shall apply to any other loan than the single one mentioned.

A mortgage, or a deed of trust, in its legal aspect is a conveyance of an estate or an interest in land and as such within the meaning of the Statute of Frauds. A mortgage or deed of trust of land cannot be made by parol [orally]. A promise to make another the owner of a lien or charge upon land is equivalent to sell him such an interest therein, and is within the statute.

* * * It is * * * the rule that a mortgage cannot be modified or extended by an oral agreement to secure further indebtedness.

On the basis of this authority the Lamberts' contention that the trust deed to Marx & Bensdorf to secure the single $672,000.00 loan can be looked to as memorandum satisfying the Statute of Frauds must be rejected.

The rule by which the thirteen instruments exhibited to the bill as memoranda satisfying the Statute of Frauds must be tested is well stated thusly: "The general rule is that the memorandum, in order to satisfy the statute, must contain the essential terms of the contract, expressed with such certainty that they may be understood from the memorandum itself or some other writing to which it refers or with which it is connected, without resorting to parol evidence. A memorandum disclosing merely that a contract had been made without showing what the contract is, is not sufficient to satisfy the requirement of the Statute of Frauds that there be a memorandum in writing of the contract."

Considered in the light of this statement of what is required of memoranda to satisfy the statute, the conclusion is unavoidable that the memoranda does not satisfy the statute.

The appeal was dismissed. The Lamberts could not enforce the loan contract for $2,910,000. The court required that in order to satisfy the Statute of Frauds, the writing had to include the essential terms of the contract.

JUDGMENT AND REMEDY

COMMENTS   *The writing should specify the parties, subject matter, and any special conditions or terms with certainty. Documenting consideration is a matter of state law. Some states require it; some do not. If the writing consists of several pages, each page should be signed separately and clearly identified as part of the same transaction.*

EASEMENTS   An **easement** is a legal right to use land without owning it. Easements are created expressly and implicitly. An express easement arises when the owner of land expressly allows another person to use the land, and it must be in writing. Implied easements can arise from the past conduct of the parties. For example, when a farmer has used a certain path to reach the back forty acres of his farm for ten years, and the path goes across a neighbor's property, the farmer has an *implied* easement across the neighbor's property. Implied easements need not be in writing and rarely are because of the way they are created. Another example of an implied easement involves the ownership of adjacent properties by one person. The owner establishes an apparent and permanent use of, say, a road through one property to the other. He then sells that property without specifying the easement. It is implied nonetheless.

LEASES   A **lease** is a conveyance of real property for a certain period of time.[8] Most states have statutes dealing specifically with leases apart from the Statute of Frauds and exempt leases of less than one year from the writing requirements. Thus, any lease lasting more than one year must be in writing. Some states extend this period. For example, Indiana allows leases to be oral for up to three years.

PARTIAL PERFORMANCE   Since the Statute of Frauds is a defense against the enforcement of an oral contract for the sale of land, problems arise when an oral contract has been partially performed. For example, the buyer may have paid part of the purchase price and then taken possession of the premises or made permanent improvements to the property.[9] If the parties cannot be returned to their status quo, the courts are likely to grant *specific performance* of the oral contract (if they enforce it at all). When the purchase price has been paid, but the buyer has not taken possession, the parties can be returned to their original positions, so the courts will not grant specific performance. When the buyer has paid part of the purchase price and entered into possession, some states allow enforcement of the contract since the parties cannot be restored to their status quo. When part of the purchase price is paid, possession has been taken by the buyer, and permanent improvements have been made to the land, most states allow enforcement of the contract. Once these three things have been done, the courts can be fairly sure there was actually a contract in existence, even if it was an oral contract. Otherwise the parties would not have taken the steps they did. Furthermore, it would be unfair to allow the seller to retake possession after a substantial part of the purchase price had been paid and the buyer had made valuable improvements.[10]

The following case involves a promise to leave property in a will. Unless the promise is in fact embodied in a will, it is unenforceable because of the Statute of Frauds.

8.   While a lease is technically a conveyance of an interest in land, it is usually accompanied by a contract. This contract, though loosely referred to as a "lease," is not really a lease at all but merely a contract entered into pursuant to a lease.

9.   Executed contracts—that is, contracts that have been fully performed—are not subject to the Statute of Frauds.
10.   In some states, mere *reliance* on an oral contract is enough to remove it from the Statute of Frauds.

BACKGROUND AND FACTS *The plaintiffs, Winifred and Isaac Blanchard, attempted to enforce an alleged oral promise made by the defendant, Ernest Calderwood to leave all of his property to the plaintiffs. The plaintiffs furnished Calderwood with personal and financial assistance, attending to his affairs under a power of attorney given to Isaac Blanchard. Calderwood died intestate (without a valid will), leaving both real and personal property. The Blanchards alleged that his property was theirs because he had promised it to them in return for the services they had rendered him during the last seven and one-half years of his life.*

BLANCHARD v. CALDERWOOD

Supreme Court of New Hampshire, 1969.
110 N.H. 29, 260 A.2d 118.

DUNCAN, Justice.
* * *

The statute of frauds requires that in order to be enforceable a "contract for the sale of land," or some memorandum thereof, shall be in writing. In Lemire v. Haley, 91 N.H. 357, 19 A.2d 436, it was held that an oral promise that "everything I have shall be yours when I'm gone" was wholly unenforceable under the statute, where the promisor's estate at his decease consisted of both real and personal property.
* * *

It follows that in the absence of the writing required by the statute, the plaintiffs are restricted to their rights to recover in *quantum meruit* for the fair value of the services rendered, "disassociated from the alleged contract to make a will."
* * *

Relying upon the opinion in Lemire v. Haley, * * * neither evidence of the oral contract nor of the value of the decedent's estate was admissible under the count in *quantum meruit*. This was a proper application of the principles laid down in the last cited *Lemire* opinion; but we are asked to overrule it, upon the ground that it will unjustly deprive the claimants of the benefit of the value placed upon their services by the oral agreement of the parties. We agree that evidence of the oral contract may be received when it is contended that services were rendered gratuitously, not for the purpose of "fixing" their value, but to establish that they were intended to be for compensation; and, in a proper case, as evidence to be considered in determining their value. But the holding [final decision] of the case was that the contract should not be admitted in evidence, since as in the case before us, the defendant there conceded that the services were not gratuitous. There as here, the alleged promise of the decedent was thought to imply no admission of the value of the services, since the extent to which they would be required was problematical when the agreement was made, and there was no indication that recompense in the strict sense of the term was in the minds of the parties. The right of the plaintiff Isaac in *quantum meruit* "is only to obtain what equitably belongs to him * * * he may not recover by way of damages for the loss of his bargain."

JUDGMENT AND REMEDY

The plaintiffs could not recover on any oral promise to convey property made by the deceased. However, the case was remanded to the trial court for a new trial so that the plaintiffs could establish the worth (fair value) of the services they had rendered to the decedent before he died. The court recognized their right to recover the fair value of the services they had provided, in quantum meruit.

COMMENTS

The Statute of Frauds requires a writing to enforce an executor's or an administrator's promise to pay the decedent's outstanding debts out of personal funds. This provision is consistent with the provision of the Statute of Frauds requiring a writing to enforce a promise to pay the debts of another.

Contracts That Cannot Be Performed Within One Year

Contracts that cannot, by their own terms, be performed within one year must be in writing to be enforceable. Since disputes over such contracts are unlikely to occur until some time after the contracts are made, the disputes will be too difficult to decide if the contracts are oral.

In order for a particular contract to fall into this category, it must be possible (even if highly improbable) to perform it in less than one year. If so, it is not within the Statute of Frauds and need not be in writing. Suppose Bankers Life contracts to loan $40,000 to Janet Lawrence "as long as Lawrence and Associates operates its financial consulting firm in Omaha, Nebraska." Assume further that Lawrence has just opened up the firm and plans to operate the company for at least five years. The contract is not within the one-year provision of the Statute of Frauds, for Lawrence and Associates may go out of business in less than one year. If the firm ceases operations, the loan will come to an end, and the contract will be fully performed in less than one year. Although this is quite unlikely, it could happen, and that possibility removes the contract from the Statute of Frauds.[11] On the other hand, suppose Bankers Life agrees to loan the money to Lawrence "for a period of two years."

Lawrence and Associates may go out of business in less than one year, but the terms of the contract cannot be performed in less than one year, so it is subject to the Statute of Frauds and must be in writing. Next assume that the contract states that the loan will last for two years "terminable at the end of six months subject to review of Lawrence and Associates' financial condition." Here the contract is not subject to the Statute of Frauds because, by the terms of the contract, it can be fully performed (by termination) within one year.

The one-year period begins to run the day after the contract is made.[12] Suppose Shearson, Hayden Stone, Incorporated agrees on May 31 of year one to hire Paul Simpson for the summer of year two. Performance of the contract will take place over three months. Counting from the day following May 31 until the last day of performance, it is apparent that the contract will take over one year to perform. Therefore it must be in writing.

Suppose instead that Shearson, Hayden Stone, Incorporated contracts on May 31 to hire Paul Simpson for one year, effective immediately. This contract is not subject to the Statute of Frauds (and need not be in writing) because counting from the day following May 31 until the last day of performance, it will take exactly one year to perform.

---

11. See *Warner v. Texas & P. Railway Co.*, 164 U.S. 418, 17 S.Ct. 147, 41 L.Ed. 495 (1896).

12. 2 Corbin on Contracts, Sec. 444.

The test under the one-year rule of the Statute of Frauds is not whether an agreement is *likely* to be performed within a year from the date of making the contract but whether performance within a year is *possible*. Conversely, when performance of an oral contract is *impossible* during a one-year period, this provision of the Statute of Frauds will bar recovery.

BACKGROUND AND FACTS   *This suit involved the enforceability of an oral contract to purchase a one-third interest and become a partner in an accounting firm. Robert C. Wilson and Vernon Robbins, both Certified Public Accountants, formed an accounting firm as a partnership in 1956. Ten years later, the firm employed the defendant, Thomas H. Adams, Jr., also a Certified Public Accountant. Adams desired to become a partner. After much discussion, the two partners, Robbins and Wilson, agreed to permit Adams to purchase a one-third interest in the partnership.*

By the terms of the oral purchase agreement, Adams was to pay a total of $30,000 for his interest—$20,000 to be paid immediately ($10,000 each to Wilson and Robbins) and the remaining $10,000 to be paid from Adams's earnings in any fiscal year (June 1 to May 31) that his earnings exceeded $20,000. Adams was then admitted as a member of the partnership.

Subsequently, the partnership was dissolved. Wilson asked Adams what he was going to do about the $5,000 Adams still owed him. Adams also owed Robbins $5,000, but Robbins made no demand for it.

After the dissolution of the partnership, Robbins and Adams formed a new partnership and continued in the accounting business. Meanwhile, Wilson filed this action against Adams to recover $5,000, alleging that it was part of the purchase price of the one-third interest in the old partnership. Adams refused to pay the $5,000, claiming, among other arguments, that recovery by Wilson was barred by the Statute of Frauds because the oral contract was unenforceable.

The trial court ruled against Adams's contention that his obligation was unenforceable under the Statute of Frauds as a contract not to be performed within a year.

ADAMS v. WILSON
Court of Appeals of Maryland,
1971.
264 Md. 1.284 A.2d 434.

BARNES, Judge.

* * *

Section IV, Clause 5 of the Statute of Frauds, 29 Car. II C. 3 (enacted 1676, effective 1677), Alexander's British Statutes (Coe ed. 1912), in force in Maryland subsequent to July 4, 1776, by the provisions of Article 5 of the Declaration of Rights of the Maryland Constitution, requires a memorandum signed by the party to be charged for the enforcement of contracts "not to be performed within the Space of one Year from the making thereof."

Adams contends that in view of the finding that the oral contract in regard to the deferred payment of $10,000 was conditioned upon his share of the profits from the partnership exceeding $20,000 *in any one year*, the contract was within the meaning of Section IV, Clause 5 of the Statute of Frauds.

* * * There are two answers to this contention. The first answer is that, as construed by the English Courts and by this Court, it is only when performance of the oral contract is *impossible* during the year period will this provision of the Statute of Frauds bar recovery.

The second answer is that Adams testified at the hearing that this was a provision of the oral contract, and this is sufficient memorandum to satisfy the Statute of Frauds. As Chief Judge Brune stated, for the Court, in Pollin v. Perkins, 223 Md. 532, 539-540, 165 A.2d 908, 911 (1960):

"[T]he admissions of a party in the form of testimony constitute sufficient "memoranda" or "writings" under the Statute of Frauds, for recorded testimony is regarded as equivalent to signed depositions."

JUDGMENT AND REMEDY *Adams had to pay Wilson the $5,000. Not only was the oral contract performable during the one-year period, but Adams's testimony at a prior legal proceeding constituted sufficient legal "memoranda" to satisfy the Statute of Frauds.*

COMMENTS *The year is measured from the time the agreement is made, not from the time performance begins. Note the court's very narrow interpretation of the one-year rule. Courts in England and in the United States have been notorious for choosing the narrowest possible meaning for this rule.*

Promises to Answer for the Debt or Duty of Another

Promises made by one person to pay the debts or discharge the duties of another if the latter fails to perform are subject to the Statute of Frauds and must be in writing. This rule applies only if the promise is made to a creditor or obligee by one who is not presently liable for the debt in order to discharge the present or future obligations of a third party. Suppose a vice-president of European Cavenham Limited says that if Occidental Petroleum will send 40,000 barrels of crude oil to Husky Oil Company, European will pay for the oil if Husky does not. If the promise to pay is not in writing, it is not enforceable. The nature of European's liability is *secondary*. That is, European is liable only if Husky Oil does not pay. Only when the promise creates secondary liability will it fall under this section of the Statute of Frauds. Suppose instead that Husky Oil Company has already ordered the barrels of crude oil, and

European Cavenham Limited says, "We will pay your debt to Occidental Petroleum." If the agreement is oral and supported by legally sufficient consideration, it is valid.[13] In this case, European's liability is *primary*. It is obligated to Husky Oil Company to pay Husky's debt to Occidental Petroleum.

This section of the Statute of Frauds is not applicable if the primary contract is between the party making the promise and the creditor or obligee (buyer). Suppose European Cavenham Limited tells Occidental Petroleum to "send 40,000 of crude oil to Husky Oil Company and send the bill to us." Now European Cavenham Limited has entered into a contract with Occidental Petroleum with Husky Oil Company as a third party beneficiary.[14] This contract is not subject to the Statute of Frauds and therefore need not be in writing to be enforced.

13. Restatement, Second, Contracts (tentative draft), Section 184.
14. See Chapter 12 for a full discussion of third party beneficiaries.

Another exception to the writing requirement is a contract where the promisors' main purpose in contracting to guarantee the obligation or debt of another is to obtain a benefit. This type of contract need not be in writing.[15] Suppose the General Contracting Corp. agrees to build a home for Oswald. General Contracting subcontracts part of the work to Ace Construction Company. After several weeks, Ace refuses to supply further labor or materials because General is in a shaky financial condition, and Ace is worried about being paid. Orally, Oswald agrees to pay General's debts if General fails to pay. Oswald's oral promise is enforceable because the primary, or main, purpose in making the guarantee was to get the house built.[16]

The promise to answer for the debt of another requires a written document under the Statute of Frauds; however, in certain circumstances such a promise is "taken out" of the statute when the promisor gains some benefit from making the promise.

_____

15. Restatement, Second, Contracts (tentative draft), Section 184.
16. Kampman v. Pittsburgh Contracting and Engineering Company, 316 Pa. 502, 175 A. 396 (1934).

BACKGROUND AND FACTS *The plaintiff lent $400 jointly to Rubenstein and the defendant, and both promised to repay with interest. Rubenstein gave the plaintiff a promissory note. The defendant failed to repay because he went bankrupt. In order to clear himself of the debt, the defendant made an oral agreement with the plaintiff that if she would release Rubenstein from the $400 debt, he (the defendant) would see that she got repaid. The plaintiff agreed. She discharged and cancelled the debt as it applied to Rubenstein. At the same time, she received $100 as partial payment. A $300 debt was therefore outstanding. The defendant, at his own request, was the sole person responsible for repaying the $300 to the plaintiff. The defendant attempted to get out of the debt by claiming that it was a "promise to pay the debt of another," namely Rubenstein. Therefore, it had to be in writing to be valid under the Statute of Frauds. The court did not agree. The debt for $300 was a completely new transaction between the plaintiff and the defendant; it was not at all part of the original loan of $400 from the plaintiff to the defendant and Rubenstein. Thus, no writing was necessary to make it valid.*

HILL v. GRAT
Supreme Judicial Court of Massachusetts, Worcester, 1923.
247 Mass. 25, 141 N.E. 593.

BRALEY, Justice.
* * *

[T]he plaintiff * * * lent to the defendant and [to] one Rubenstein $400, which both promised to repay, with interest, and that Rubenstein also gave his promissory note for the amount. The defendant having been adjudicated [declared in court] a bankrupt, he promised the plaintiff, at the first meeting of creditors, that if she would release Rubenstein from his obligation to pay "the $400 which she had loaned them.
* * *

[H]e (the defendant) would pay her the balance." The plaintiff, pursuant to the promise, released Rubenstein, proved her claim, received the dividend [a partial payment] of "$100," and delivered the note to the defendant. The defendant, however, who duly obtained his discharge, repudiated [refused to acknowledge as valid] the agreement, and this action is brought to recover the difference between the amount of the note and the dividend. * * * [The defendant tries to argue that] no action shall be brought "to charge a person upon a special promise to answer for the debt * * * of another, * * * unless the promise, contract or agreement upon which such action is brought, or some memorandum or note thereof, is in writing and signed by the party to be charged therewith or by some person thereunto by him lawfully authorized." If in any aspect the defendant's promise could be held to include his original obligation for money lent, the promise was not in writing signed by him, and his discharge is a complete bar.

It is settled, as the defendant contends, that *under a collateral promise the agreement is not taken out of the [S]tatute [of Frauds] unless the controlling purpose and effect of the whole transaction enabled the promisor to gain by his promise some benefit from the plaintiff, the promisee.* [Emphasis added.] But in reliance upon the promise, the debt of Rubenstein had been relinquished and canceled by the plaintiff, and he no longer could be held as principal. The defendant at his own request had been substituted for Rubenstein and the promise therefore was an independent, original agreement to pay his own debt contracted after the bankruptcy proceedings were begun. The agreement not being repugnant to the statute, nor barred by the discharge can be enforced in the present action. * * *

By the terms of the report judgment is to be entered for the plaintiff "for $300 and interest from the date of the writ."

So ordered.

JUDGMENT AND REMEDY   *The court found that a completely new transaction had occurred between the plaintiff and the defendant. Therefore, the defendant had to pay the plaintiff the $300 plus interest.*

Promises Made in Consideration of Marriage

A unilateral promise to pay a sum of money or to give property in consideration of a promise to marry must be in writing. If Bill MacAdams promises $10,000 to Bruce Coby if Coby promises to marry Sally MacAdams, MacAdams's promise must be in writing. The same rule applies to *prenuptial agreements* (agreements made before marriage), which define the ownership rights of each partner in the other partner's property. For example, a prospective husband may wish to limit the amount his prospective wife could obtain if the marriage ended in divorce. Prenuptial arrangements must be in writing to be enforceable, and there must be consideration. (Some states do not require consideration—Florida, for example.)

Promises by the Administrator or Executor of an Estate to Pay the Debts of the Estate Personally

The administrator (or executor) of an estate has the duty of paying the debts of the deceased and distributing any remainder to the deceased's heirs. The administrator can contract orally on behalf of the estate. A writing is required only when the administrator promises to pay the debts of the estate personally. Suppose Edward Post (administrator) contracts with Martha Lynch for legal services. If Post contracts on behalf of the estate, an oral contract is valid, and the estate is bound to pay Lynch for her legal services. But if Post agrees to pay Lynch's legal fees personally, the contract must be in writing. Otherwise it is not enforceable, and Lynch cannot recover.

CONTRACTS FOR
THE SALE OF GOODS

The Uniform Commercial Code contains several Statute of Frauds provisions that require a writing in certain circumstances. Section 2-201 contains the major provision, which generally requires a writing or memorandum for the sale of goods priced at $500 or more.[17] A writing that will satisfy the Code requirement need only state the quantity term, and that need not be stated accurately. The contract will not be enforceable, however, for any quantity greater than that set forth in the writing. In addition, the writing must be signed by the person to be charged—that is, the person who refuses to perform. Beyond these two requirements, the writing need not designate the buyer or seller, the terms of payment, or the price.

Exceptions

There are four general exceptions to the writing requirements contained in Section 2-201. First, if the buyer pays the purchase price, the contract can be enforced even though it was not originally in writing. Second, if the goods are made for a particular buyer, if they are of a type not suitable for sale to others, and if the seller has started to manufacture them or has made commitments for procuring them, then no writing is required. Third, if the seller has delivered the goods to the buyer, the contract can be enforced even though it is not in writing.

---

17. UCC Sec. 2-201, reads in part:

[A] contract for the sale of goods for the price of $500 or more is not enforceable by way of action or defense unless there is some writing sufficient to indicate that a contract for sale has been made between the parties and been signed by the party against whom enforcement is sought. * * * A writing is not insufficient because it omits or incorrectly states a term agreed upon but the contract is not enforceable under this paragraph beyond the quantity of goods shown in the writing. * * *

A contract which does not satisfy the requirements of subsection (1) but which is valid in other respects is enforceable * * * with respect to goods for which payment has been made and accepted or which have been received and accepted.

Fourth, if the party admits in pleading testimony or otherwise in court that the contract was for sale, then the contract is enforceable.

PARTIAL PERFORMANCE The Statute of Frauds provides that a contract will become enforceable if the buyer accepts or actually receives part of the goods sold. For example, Windblown Sailboats makes an oral contract with Sunset Sails to have Sunset make 750 specially designed sails for Windblown's new nineteen-foot Day Sailer. Windblown repudiates the agreement after the sails have been made and after two dozen have been delivered. Although Sunset might be able to sell the sails elsewhere, the contract is enforceable because Windblown has accepted part of the order.

GOODS MADE SPECIALLY TO ORDER Even if the seller has not completed the manufacture of the goods, the contract is enforceable to the extent that actions have been taken. In each situation the action must be completed before the seller learns that the buyer has repudiated the oral agreement. Thus, if Sunset Sails had ordered the material and cut the sailcloth but had not begun to put the sails together, the agreement would still have been enforceable to the extent of the work performed.

RECEIPT OF CONFIRMATION Oral contracts will be enforced between merchants if, within a reasonable time, either party sends a written confirmation of the contract. The party receiving the confirmation must have knowledge of its contents, and it must satisfy the requirements of Section 2-201. Under these circumstances, the contract will be enforced unless written notice of objection is given within ten days after the confirmation is received.

ADMISSIONS If a party to a normal contract "admits" in "pleading testimony or otherwise in court that a contract for sale was made," the contract will be enforceable. Thus, if the president of Windblown Sailboats admits under testimony that an oral agreement was made, the agreement will be enforceable.

Other Provisions

The Uniform Commercial Code has three other Statute of Frauds provisions: (1) all contracts for the sale of securities (bonds, stocks) must be in writing to be enforceable regardless of amount [UCC Sec. 8-319]; (2) security agreements under Article 9 must be in writing—see Chapter 29 [UCC Sec. 9-203]; and (3) contracts for the sale of personal property that do not fall under the other categories must be in writing if over $5,000 [UCC Sec. 1-206(1)]. This provision applies mainly to sales of intangibles, such as rights to royalties, which are not covered by the "sale of goods" provision of the Uniform Commercial Code.

SUFFICIENCY OF THE WRITING

To be safe, all contracts should be fully set forth in a writing signed by all the parties. This assures that if any problems arise concerning performance of the contract, a written agreement that can be introduced into court is available. The Statute of Frauds and the Uniform Commercial Code require only a written contract or a written memorandum signed by the party to be charged. In other words, any confirmation, invoice, sales slip, check, or telegram can constitute a writing sufficient to satisfy the Statute of Frauds.[18] The signature need not be placed at the end of the document. It can be in the body of the writing or can even be an initial identifying the person to be charged.

Since only the party to be charged need sign the writing, one party may be able to enforce a contract, while the other party cannot. Suppose AT&T negotiates via telephone with General Electric Corp. for the purchase of radio transistors for a telecommunications satellite. AT&T decides to buy the transistors, and its vice-president of purchasing signs a confirming telegram setting forth the terms of the agreement. Here General Electric can force

---

18. Remember that even if the Statute of Frauds is satisfied, the existence and terms of the contract must be proven in court.

AT&T to buy the transistors because AT&T is the party to be charged, and AT&T has signed the memorandum. AT&T cannot, however, force General Electric (the party to be charged) to sell because General Electric has signed no writing or memorandum.

A memorandum evidencing the contract need only contain the essential terms of the contract. Under the Uniform Commercial Code, the writing need only name the quantity term and be signed by the party to be charged. Under other provisions of the Statute of Frauds, the writing must ordinarily name the parties, subject matter, consideration, and quantity. Contracts for the sale of land are exceptions. The memorandum must state the *essential* terms of the contract with sufficient clarity to allow the terms to be determined from the memo itself, without reference to any outside sources.[19]

THE PAROL EVIDENCE RULE

The **parol evidence rule** prohibits the introduction of words (parol) that contradict or vary the terms of certain written contracts. The written contract is ordinarily assumed to be the complete embodiment of the parties' agreement. Courts are reluctant to allow oral or other written evidence of prior or contemporaneous agreements that conflict with the terms of the written agreement. If courts allow contradictory oral evidence, the utility of the Statute of Frauds will be lost. Parties will once again be encouraged to commit frauds and perjuries in order to win their lawsuits. Therefore, courts assume that all prior negotiations and oral agreements are embodied in the written contract.

Due to the rigidity of the parol evidence rule, courts make several exceptions. First, when the parties modify the written agreement orally, evidence of the modification can be introduced into court. Since courts assume all prior negotiations and oral agreements are merged in the written contract, there is no reason to forbid changes in the written contract

---

19. Rhodes v. Wilkins, 83 N.M. 782, 498 P.2d 311 (1972).

when they occur after the writing. Second, oral evidence can be introduced in all cases to show that the contract was voidable or void (for example, induced by mistake, fraud, or misrepresentation). In this case, one of the parties was tricked into agreeing to the terms of a written contract, so oral evidence attesting to fraud should not be excluded. Courts frown upon bad faith and are quick to allow such evidence when it establishes fraud. Third, when the terms of a written contract are ambiguous, oral evidence is admissible to show the meaning of the terms. Fourth, oral evidence is admissible when the written contract is incomplete. Here not all the essential terms are included in the writing, so courts allow oral evidence to fill in the gaps. Fifth, under the Uniform Commercial Code, oral evidence can be introduced to explain or supplement a written contract by showing a prior course of dealing or usage of trade. When buyers and sellers deal with each other over extended periods of time, certain customary practices develop. They are often overlooked when writing the contract, so courts allow the introduction of oral evidence to show how the parties have acted in the past.

The parol evidence rule applies only to an "integrated" contract, that is, one in which the parties have indicated within the terms of the writing that the writing is the complete statement of the agreement between them. When there is such an *integration clause*—often called a merger clause—in an agreement, no parol evidence of any other agreement will be permitted to vary, change, alter, or modify any of the terms or provisions of that written agreement.

BACKGROUND AND FACTS *Masterson sold his ranch to Sine, his brother-in-law. Their contract of purchase included a clause giving Masterson a ten-year option to repurchase the ranch for the same price plus a percentage of the cost of any improvements Sine might have made over the course of the years. Masterson went bankrupt sometime after the sale. His trustee in bankruptcy attempted to exercise this option clause to repurchase the ranch to obtain funds to satisfy Masterson's debts. The trial court refused to allow Sine to introduce extrinsic evidence showing the meaning the parties attached to the option clause, specifically that it was personal to Masterson. Thus, the trial court permitted the trustee to enforce the option to repurchase on Masterson's behalf. Defendant Sine appealed.*

MASTERSON v. SINE
Supreme Court of California, 1968.
68 Cal.2d 222, 65 Cal.Rptr. 545, 436 P.2d 561.

TRAYNOR, Chief Justice.
* * *

When the parties to a written contract have agreed to it as an "integration"—a complete and final embodiment of the terms of an agreement—parol evidence cannot be used to add to or vary its terms. * * * When only part of the agreement is integrated, the same rule applies to that part, but *parol evidence may be used to prove elements of the agreement not reduced to writing.* [Emphasis added.]
* * *

The crucial issue in determining whether there has been an integration is whether the parties intended their writing to serve as the exclusive embodiment of their agreement. The instrument itself may help to resolve that issue. It may state, for example, that "there are no previous understandings or agreements not contained in the writing," and thus express the parties' "intention to nullify antecedent understandings or agreements." Any such collateral agreement itself must be examined, however, to determine whether the parties intended the subjects of negotiation it deals with to be included in, excluded from, or otherwise affected by the writing. Circumstances at the time of the writing may also aid in the determination of such integration.

* * *

In formulating the rule governing parol evidence, several policies must be accommodated. One policy is based on the assumption that written evidence is more accurate than human memory. This policy, however, can be adequately served by excluding parol evidence of agreements that directly contradict the writing. Another policy is based on the fear that fraud or unintentional invention by witnesses interested in the outcome of the litigation will mislead the finder of facts.

Legal authorities have suggested that the party urging the spoken as against the written word is most often the economic underdog, threatened by severe hardship if the writing is enforced. [This] view [of] the parol evidence rule arose to allow the court to control the tendency of the jury to find through sympathy and without a dispassionate assessment of the probability of fraud or faulty memory that the parties made an oral agreement collateral to the written contract, or that preliminary tentative agreements were not abandoned when omitted from the writing. [It] recognizes, however, that if this theory were adopted in disregard of all other considerations, it would lead to the exclusion of testimony concerning oral agreements whenever there is a writing and thereby often defeat the true intent of the parties.

Evidence of oral collateral agreements should be excluded only when the fact finder [the judge or the jury] is likely to be misled. The rule must therefore be based on the credibility of the evidence. One such standard, adopted by section 240(1)(b) of the Restatement of Contracts, permits proof of a collateral agreement if it "is such an agreement as might *naturally* be made as a separate agreement by parties situated as were the parties to the written contract." The draftsmen of the Uniform Commercial Code would exclude the evidence in still fewer instances: "If the additional terms are such that, if agreed upon, they would *certainly* have been included in the document in the view of the court, then evidence of their alleged making must be kept from the trier of fact." [UCC Sec. 2-202] (italics added.)

The option clause in the deed in the present case does not explicitly provide that it contains the complete agreement, and the deed is silent on the question of assignability. Moreover, the difficulty of accommodating the formalized structure of a deed to the insertion of collateral agreements makes it less likely that all the terms of such an agreement were included. The statement of the reservation of the option might well have been placed in the recorded deed solely to preserve the grantors' rights against any possible future purchasers and this function could well be served without any mention of the parties' agreement that the option was personal. There is nothing in the record to indicate that the parties to this family transaction, through experience in land transactions or otherwise, had any warning of the disadvantages of failing to put the whole agreement in the deed. This case is one, therefore, in which it can be said that a collateral agreement such as that alleged "might naturally be made as a separate agreement." *A fortiori,* the case is not one in which the parties "would certainly" have included the collateral agreement in the deed.

Since the writing did not have an integration clause, extrinsic evidence could be used to show that the option was personal to the grantors and, therefore, not assignable. Therefore, the trial court judgment was reversed because that court had excluded parol evidence improperly.

JUDGMENT AND REMEDY

In numerous situations, the parol evidence rule does not apply: (1) when obvious and gross clerical or typographical errors exist; (2) when a written offer is verbally accepted and nothing further is reduced to writing; (3) when the underlying contract is voidable, unenforceable, or never arose because of lack of capacity of a party, fraud, duress, illegality, or a condition precedent that failed; and (4) when supplemental materials do not change the terms of the contract by evidence of custom and usage.

COMMENTS

QUESTIONS AND CASE PROBLEMS

1. In December 1965, Kaplin ordered 11,000 yards of madras at seventy-five cents a yard from Reich. The order was made over the telephone. On January 9, 1966, Reich sent Kaplin a bill that included a statement of the quantity that Reich had sent Kaplin. On February 18, 1966, Kaplin wrote to Reich, stating:

Replying to your letter of the 18th, please be advised that we examined a few pieces of merchandise that were billed to us against your invoice No. 10203, and found that it was not up to our standard. We are, therefore, unable to accept this shipment. * * * Very truly yours, (signed) Isador Kaplin.

Reich sued Kaplin for payment owed under the contract. Kaplin defended on the grounds that the contract was entered into over the telephone and therefore failed to meet Statute of Frauds requirements. Is Kaplin's argument convincing? [Reich v. Helen Harper, Inc., 3 UCC Rep. 1048 (1966)]

2. After lengthy discussions by its board of directors, Holiday Inn decided to build a new sixteen-story motel on Key Largo, Florida. On April 1, 1979, Holiday Inn and Lyonel Construction Company reached an oral agreement that Lyonel would build the motel according to Holiday Inn specifications. Lyonel agreed to begin work on May 15, 1979, and finish by January 1, 1980. Holiday Inn promised to pay Lyonel $200,000 for the job. Are the parties bound under this oral agreement?

3. In October 1968, Bagby entered into an oral contract with Livestock Company under which he was to sell the company 2,000 head of cattle, all to be delivered by January 15, 1969. Bagby delivered only 222 of the 2,000 head and refused to deliver any more. Can Livestock Company enforce the rest of the agreement? [Bagby Land and Cattle Company v. California Livestock Commission Company, 439 F.2d 315 (Tex.1971)]

4. Wasatch Orchard Company entered into an oral agreement with Fabian to have him sell its canned asparagus. Wasatch agreed to pay Fabian a 2.5 percent commission on all sales he made in the East. Within six months Fabian had secured orders totaling $30,000. Thereafter, Wasatch refused to honor its oral commitment. Can Fabian sue under the oral agreement? What, if anything, can Fabian recover? [Fabian v. Wasatch Orchard Company, 41 Utah 404, 125 P. 860 (1912)]

5. On July 26, 1955, William Rowe was admitted to General Hospital, suffering from the effects of a severe gastric hemorrhage. On the day Rowe was admitted, Rowe's son informed an agent for the hospital that his father had no financial means but that he would pay for his father's medical services. Subsequently, the son stated, "Well, we want you to do everything you can to save his life, and we don't want you to spare any expense because whatever he needs, Doctor, you go ahead and get it, and I will pay you." After Rowe was discharged from the hospital, his son refused to pay the medical bills. Can the hospital enforce the son's oral promise? [Peterson v. Rowe, 63 N.M. 135, 314 P.2d 892 (1957)]

6. Hoadley and Peck entered into the following agreement with Hayden:

We, the said Hoadley and Peck, in consideration of the said Haydens having this day conveyed to us their farm * * * have this day conveyed to the Haydens certain land and premises situated on the westerly side of North Street * * * and for additional consideration for such exchange of properties, bind ourselves and agree to make, without expense to said Haydens, the following repairs * * *: straighten up and shingle the barn on said premises; repair and paint the roof, and paint the same back of said house; and install a pump in said house.

Hayden later sued Hoadley and Peck for noncompliance with their agreement. At the trial, Hoadley and Peck attempted to show that an oral agreement had been entered into at the same time as the written agreement by which all parties agreed that repairs were not to exceed $60. Is this oral agreement admissible at trial? [Hayden v. Hoadley, 94 Vt. 345, 111 A. 343 (1920)]

7. Butler Brothers were the main contractors for a highway construction project near Minneapolis. Butler hired another contractor, Ganley Brothers, to perform some of the highway construction work. At the time the contract was formed, Ganley made several false representations to Butler. If Butler had known Ganley's statements were fraudulent, Butler would never have entered into the contract. The written contract between Butler and Ganley included the following clause: "The contractor [Butler] has examined the said contracts * * * and is not relying upon any statement made by the company in respect thereto." In light of this clause, can Butler introduce evidence of Ganley's fraudulent misstatements at trial? [Ganley Brothers, Inc. v. Butler Brothers Building Co., 170 Minn. 373, 212 N.W. 602 (1927)]

8. Rimshot, director of a local basketball camp, wished to increase his business by advertising his camp. He discussed with Lyal, a local printer, the possibility of Lyal printing up flyers about the camp. Rimshot told Lyal that not only did he want Lyal to print the flyers, he wanted him to distribute them to local merchants. Lyal said that he usually distributed about 20 flyers to each one and charged a small publication fee. Subsequently Lyal and Rimshot entered into a written agreement under which Lyal agreed to print 1,000 flyers for Rimshot and to "publish the same locally." Lyal printed the flyers but distributed them to only four merchants, giving 250 to each. After the poorest turnout in his basketball

camp's history, Rimshot sued Lyal for breach of contract. Can he introduce parol evidence concerning Lyal's statements about how he normally distributed flyers? [See Stoops v. Smith, 100 Mass. 63, 97 Am.Dec. 76 (1868)]

9. Washington Tent and Awning Company entered into a contract with 818 Ranch, Inc., under which Washington Tent was to manufacture and install a canopy in front of Ranch's restaurant. After Washington made the canopy, it called Ranch to set up a date for installation. Ranch told Washington that not only did it not want the canopy installed, but it had not wanted the canopy in the first place. Washington sued Ranch for payment for the canopy. At the trial, Ranch attempted to introduce evidence that the installation of the canopy depended on the approval of Ranch's landlord and that this had been discussed with Washington. Should this evidence be admitted? [Washington Tent and Awning Company v. 818 Ranch, Inc., 248 A.2d 126 (D.C.App.1968)]

10. Ramsey Corporation, a manufacturer, entered into negotiations with Williams & Associates, architects, to design a new factory for Ramsey. After several days of negotiations, Ramsey and Williams signed a contract under which Williams promised to design the factory. The contract was brief, containing a short description of the type of plant as well as the number of offices that Ramsey wanted. Over the next several months Williams drew up plans for a new factory that would cost about $500,000. Since this was about twice what Ramsey expected to pay, Ramsey officials changed their minds and refused to compensate Williams for his plans. Williams sued Ramsey to recover for his services. Ramsey wished to defend Williams's claim on the ground that Williams had not performed the contract as agreed to by the parties. Specifically, Ramsey wanted to introduce evidence about an oral agreement made before the written contract, which said that Williams would design a building costing about $250,000. Since the building Williams had actually designed would cost $500,000, Williams had breached his contract. Can Ramsey introduce this evidence? [Williams & Associates v. Ramsey Products Corporation, 19 N.C.App. 1,198 S.E.2d 67 (1973)]

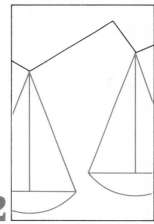

12

Contracts
Third Party Rights

Once it has been determined that a valid and legally enforceable contract exists, attention can be turned to the rights and duties of the parties to the contract. Usually, two parties promise to perform certain acts. *Third parties* have no right to enforce the promises of either of the original parties except in two special situations. The first is a *third party beneficiary contract.* Here, the rights of a third party against the promisor arise from the original contract, and the parties to the original contract make it in order to benefit the third party. The second situation is an **assignment of rights** or **delegation** of duties. Here, one of the original parties transfers contractual rights or obligations to a third party.

THIRD PARTY BENEFICIARY CONTRACTS

In Exhibit 12-1, A offers to pave B's driveway if B promises to pay C $375. A is the promisee (since she has received B's promise); B is the promisor (since she has made the promise); and C is the third party beneficiary (since she is benefiting from B's promise).

In general, the law recognizes three types of beneficiaries—creditor, donee, and incidental.[1] The courts will usually uphold B's promise if C is a creditor or donee beneficiary but not if C is an incidental beneficiary. In order to determine whether the third party beneficiary contract is valid, the intent of Promisee A in the above diagram must be examined.

---

1. Restatement, Second, Contracts (tentative draft), Section 133. This is the traditional terminology used to describe the various types of third party beneficiaries. Under the Restatement of Contracts (tentative draft), the term, "intended beneficiary" replaces "creditor beneficiary" and "donee beneficiary." However, a majority of state courts still distinguish between donee and creditor beneficiaries, so the traditional terms will be used here, too.

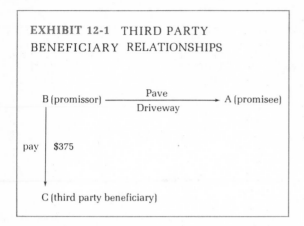

EXHIBIT 12-1 THIRD PARTY
BENEFICIARY RELATIONSHIPS

Creditor Beneficiaries

If a promisee's main purpose in making a contract is to discharge a duty he or she already owes to a third party, then the third party is a *creditor beneficiary.*[2] Suppose, for example, that several months ago, Duval Copper Company delivered 75,000 pounds of copper cathode to Pensoil Corporation. Pensoil still owes Duval $24,000, so Pensoil arranges to sell some of the copper cathode to Kennecott Copper Corp. Kennecott, in turn, agrees to pay the $24,000 purchase price to Duval. In terms of the diagram above, Pensoil (A) agrees to sell cathode to Kennecott (B) if Kennecott will pay the purchase price to Duval (C). Duval is a creditor beneficiary and can enforce payment of the $24,000 against Kennecott.

The following case is a classic illustration of third party beneficiary theory.

_____

2.   Restatement, Contracts, Section 133 (1)(A).

LAWRENCE v. FOX

Court of Appeals of New York,
1859. 20 N.Y. 268.

BACKGROUND AND FACTS   *Holly owed the plaintiff $300. The defendant suggested that Holly give him the money and promised to pay it to the plaintiff to discharge Holly's debt. (Sufficient consideration was present in this transaction to create a contract between Holly and the defendant.) The defendant never paid the plaintiff, so the plaintiff sued the defendant, considering himself a third party beneficiary of the contract between Holly and the defendant. The court decided that the plaintiff had a legal right to sue the defendant for failing to pay the $300 as promised, even though the plaintiff was never "in privity;" that is, he was never a direct participant or party to the contract.*

H. GRAY, Justice.

* * *

In this case the promise was made to Holly and not expressly to the plaintiff; * * * As early as 1806 it was announced by the Supreme Court of this State, upon what was then regarded as the settled law of England, "That where one person makes a promise to another for the benefit of a third person, that third person may maintain an action upon it." *Schermerhorn v. Vanderheyden* (1 John. R., 140), has often been re-asserted by our courts and never departed from.

* * *

In *Hall v. Marston* the court [said]: "It seems to have been well settled that if A promises B for a valuable consideration to pay C, the latter may maintain assumpsit [the agreement] for the money;" and in *Brewer v. Dyer*, the recovery was upheld, as the court said, "upon the principle of law *long recognized and clearly established*, that when one person, for a valuable consideration, engages with another, by a simple contract, to do some act for the benefit of a third, the

latter, who would enjoy the benefit of the act, may maintain an action for the breach of such engagement; that it does not rest upon the ground of any actual or supposed relationship between the parties as some of the earlier cases would seem to indicate, but upon the broader and more satisfactory basis, that the law operating on the act of the parties creates the duty, establishes a privity, and implies the promise and obligation on which the action is founded."
* * *

In this case the defendant, upon ample consideration received from Holly, promised Holly to pay his debt to the plaintiff; the consideration received and the promise to Holly made it as plainly his duty to pay the plaintiff as if the money had been remitted to him for that purpose, and as well implied a promise to do so as if he had been made a trustee of property to be converted into cash with which to pay.
* * *
No one can doubt that he [Holly] owes the sum of money demanded of him, or that in accordance with his promise it was his duty to have paid it to the plaintiff; nor can it be doubted that whatever may be the diversity of opinion elsewhere, the adjudications in this State, from a very early period, approved by experience, have established the defendant's liability * * * "

The judgment should be affirmed.

Judgment was for the plaintiff. The defendant was required to pay the   **JUDGMENT**
plaintiff $300 to fulfill his original contract with Holly.   **AND REMEDY**

ASSUMPTION OF A MORTGAGE The *assumption of a mortgage* is a very common type of third party beneficiary contract. Here one person buys real estate from another, and the real estate is encumbered by a mortgage. In the diagram above, suppose A is the original owner of a lawn and garden supply store. B wants to buy the store, which is subject to a mortgage held by C, City National Bank. When A and B make a contract for the sale of the store, A will agree to convey the store if B promises to pay A's debt to City National Bank. City National Bank is the creditor beneficiary of this third party beneficiary contract and can enforce payment against B.

Donee Beneficiaries

If a promisee's main purpose in making a contract is to confer a gift upon a third party, then the third party is a *donee beneficiary*.[3] A donee

beneficiary can enforce the promise of a promisor (B in the diagram) just as a creditor beneficiary can. To illustrate: Suppose A goes to her attorney, B, and enters into a contract in which B promises to draft a will naming C as A's heir. C is a donee beneficiary, and if B does not prepare the will properly, C can sue B.[4] Or suppose A offers to paint B's house if B pays $750 to C. A does not owe C any money, but C is a close friend of A's, and A wants to give the money to C. Again, C is a donee beneficiary and can enforce B's promise to pay $750.

The most common third party beneficiary contract involving a donee beneficiary is a life insurance contract. A, the promisee, pays premiums to B, a life insurance company, and B promises to pay a certain amount of money upon A's death to anyone A designates as

---

3.   Restatement, Contracts, Section 133 (1)(B).

4.   Lucas v. Hamm, 56 Cal.2d 583, 15 Cal.Rptr. 821, 364 P.2d 685 (1961); although the Lucas decision follows Restatement, Second, Contracts (tentative draft), it is not clear that all courts will agree.

beneficiary. The beneficiary, C, is a donee beneficiary under the life insurance policy and can enforce payment against the insurance company upon A's death.

Incidental Beneficiaries

The benefit that an *incidental beneficiary* receives from a contract between A and B is unintentional. Therefore, an incidental beneficiary cannot enforce a contract against the promisor, B. Several factors must be examined to determine whether a party is an incidental beneficiary. The presence of one or more of the factors listed below strongly indicates an *intended* (rather than an incidental) benefit to the third party.

1. Performance rendered directly to the third party.
2. The rights of the third party to control the details of performance.
3. Express designation in the contract.

The following are examples of incidental beneficiaries. The third party has no rights in the contract and cannot enforce against the promisor.

1. B contracts with A to build a factory on A's land. B's plans specify that Ad Vest Company pipe fittings must be used in all plumbing. Ad Vest Company is an incidental beneficiary and cannot enforce the contract against B by attempting to require B to purchase its pipe.
2. B contracts with A to build a recreational facility on A's land. Once the facility is constructed, it will greatly enhance the property values in the neighborhood. If B subsequently refuses to build the facility, C, a neighboring property owner, cannot enforce the contract against B by attempting to require B to build the facility.
3. B is a water company and contracts with city A to supply water throughout the city. The water is supposed to have 145 pounds of constant pressure. One day, in a local suburb, C, the owner of a pickle factory, discovers a fire in her receiving warehouse. C quickly calls the fire department, but because the water pressure is only 64 pounds, the fire hoses do not work correctly, and C's warehouse burns down. If C sues city A's water company, alleging that she is a third party beneficiary of the contract between the water company and the city, she will lose. She is an incidental beneficiary to the contract to supply water at a certain pressure level, so she cannot sue for breach of that contract in most courts.[5]

WHEN THE RIGHTS OF A THIRD PARTY VEST

Until the rights of a third party *vest*, the third party cannot enforce a contract against the original parties. The rights of a third party vest when the original parties cannot rescind or change the contract without the consent of the third party. Older cases distinguish between vesting in the case of a donee beneficiary and a creditor beneficiary, but modern courts no longer do so.[6]

The rights of a third party beneficiary (donee or creditor) vest (and the power of the original contracting parties to change, alter, or rescind the contract terminates) whenever one of the following three things happen:

1. The third party learns of and consents to the contract.[7]
2. The third party brings suit upon the contract.

---

5. The basis of liability can be in tort, and C can recover in tort, but the courts are split on this issue.

6. According to the original Restatement and Contracts as well as a number of courts (some of which make these distinctions), a donee beneficiary's rights vest immediately upon the creation of a contract, and knowledge or assent to the contract is unnecessary. Creditor beneficiaries, on the other hand, must have relied on a contract detrimentally or must bring suit upon the contract in order for their rights to vest.

7. Restatement, Second, Contracts (tentative draft), Section 142(3) says that the promisor and the promisee have to request assent.

3. The third party materially alters his position in detrimental reliance on the contract.

Suppose, for example, that C learns of B's intention to pay $375 to C after the driveway is paved. Before C agrees to accept the payment, however, B decides to make payment elsewhere. C's rights to the payment will not have been vested since C did not assent prior to the contract revision.

If the contract expressly reserves the right to cancel, rescind, or modify the contract, the third party takes his or her rights subject to such rights. In such a case, the vesting of the third party's rights will not terminate the power of the original contracting parties to alter their legal relationships.[8]

ASSIGNMENT OF RIGHTS AND DELEGATION OF DUTIES

Third parties can acquire rights or assume duties arising from a contract to which they were not parties. The rights are transferred to them by *assignment*. Duties are transferred by *delegation*. Assignment or delegation should be distinguished from third party beneficiary contracts. In a third party beneficiary contract, the rights of the third party arise from the original contract. Assignment, or delegation, occurs after the original contract is made, when one of the parties transfers an interest in the contract to another party.

A distinction must also be made between assignment, or delegation, and *novation* (see Chapter 13). A novation is an agreement entered into by *all* the parties whereby one party is substituted for another party. One party is completely dismissed from the contract, and another is substituted. The dismissed party is no longer liable under the original contract. In an assignment, or delegation, the original party remains liable on the contract.

8. Defenses raised against third party beneficiaries are given in Restatement, Second, Contracts (tentative draft), Section 140.

Assignments

Every bilateral contract has corresponding rights and duties. One party has a *right* to require the other to perform some task, and the other has a *duty* to perform it. The transfer of rights to a third person is known as an *assignment*. When rights under a contract are assigned unconditionally, the rights of the assignor (the party making the assignment) are extinguished.[9] The third party (the assignee, or party receiving the assignment) has a right to demand performance from the other original party to the contract (the obligor, or buyer). This can best be illustrated by Exhibit 12-2.

Once A has assigned his or her rights under the original contract with B to C, C can enforce the contract against B if B fails to perform.

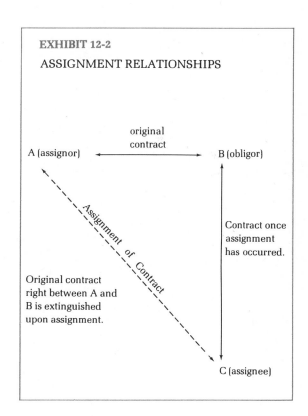

EXHIBIT 12-2

ASSIGNMENT RELATIONSHIPS

A (assignor) ←→ B (obligor)
original contract

Assignment of Contract

Contract once assignment has occurred.

Original contract right between A and B is extinguished upon assignment.

C (assignee)

9. Restatement, Second, Contracts (tentative draft), Section 163.

**NOLAN v.
WILLIAMSON MUSIC,
INC.**

United States District Court,
Southern District of New York,
1969. 300 F.Supp. 1311.

BACKGROUND AND FACTS *The plaintiff in this case was Robert
Nolan, who composed the song "Tumbling Tumbleweeds." Nolan
entered into an agreement with the Sam Fox Publishing Company
whereby he conveyed his interest in the song to the publisher, Sam Fox,
and the publisher's successors and assigns. The agreement stated that it
was Nolan's intention to transfer to the publisher all rights of every kind,
nature, and description (including the rights generally known in the field
of literary and musical endeavor as the moral rights of the authors)
throughout the world. No right of any kind, nature, or description was to
be reserved by the composer.*

*In consideration of this agreement, Sam Fox agreed to pay Nolan
certain royalties on a pre-agreed schedule. Sam Fox Publishing
Company published and exploited the song "Tumbling Tumbleweeds."
Several years later, the company assigned all of its rights and interests in
the song to the defendant, Williamson Music, Inc. Sam Fox never
notified Nolan that the assignment had been made. When Nolan
subsequently learned of the assignment, he attempted to rescind the
contract.*

EDELSTEIN, District Judge.

* * *

Nolan also seeks:

(a) an injunction permanently enjoining defendants from asserting any rights
in or to the song;

* * *

The assignment to Sam Fox Publishing Company was dated July 11, 1934, and
it provided, *inter alia*, that the "Composers" (defined as Nolan, Walker and Hall)
conveyed to the "Publisher (defined as Sam Fox Publishing Company), its
successors and assigns forever, all the right, title and interest of every kind, nature
and description, including the copyright therein, throughout the world, of the
Composers in 'Tumbling Tumbleweeds.' " This agreement also recites that it was
the intention of the parties:

to transfer to the Publisher all rights of every kind, nature and description
(including the rights generally known in the field of literary and musical endeavor
as the moral rights of the authors) throughout the world which the Composers
have, own and possess in and to the said musical composition and no right of any
kind, nature or description is [to be] reserved by the Composers.

The "Composers" also agreed to renew the copyright on the song and then to
assign the renewal term to the "Publisher."

In consideration of these undertakings, the "Publisher" agreed to pay to the
"Composers" royalties[.]

* * *

Subsequently, by an agreement dated January 28, 1946, Sam Fox assigned all
of its right and interest in and to the song to defendant, Williamson Music, Inc.,

(Williamson) and agreed to use its best efforts to obtain the renewal copyright of the song and then to assign the renewal term to Williamson.

* * *

The instant action followed a letter dated May 29, 1963, which Nolan sent to Fox and Williamson seeking to terminate any and all agreements relating to "Tumbling Tumbleweeds" between Nolan and Fox.

* * *

The basic claim which plaintiff has urged in this suit is that he had the legal right to, and, in fact, did rescind his agreements with Fox by the May 29, 1963, notice. Plaintiff argues that rescission is justified in this case because over the years Fox has allegedly committed the following breaches:

* * *

assignment of the copyright and its renewal term to Williamson; payment of royalties by Fox based only on Fox's receipts from Williamson;

* * *

In addition * * * plaintiff argues that Fox has generally acted fraudulently towards plaintiff and that in particular it was fraudulent not to have revealed to plaintiff Fox's relationship with Williamson.

The court finds that it was not a breach of contract for Sam Fox to assign the copyright to Williamson. The 1934 transfer from plaintiff to Sam Fox of "all rights of every kind, nature and description" which plaintiff had in the copyright was clearly absolute on its face. Furthermore, the agreement specifically provided that the conveyance was to the "Publisher, its successors and assigns." Whether a contract is assignable or not is, of course, a matter of contractual intent, and one must look to the language used by the parties to discern that intent. Clearly the language just quoted contemplated that the agreement was to be assignable.

The plaintiff, by citing Paige v. Faure, seems to be saying, however, that this contract involved such personal elements of trust and confidence that it was not assignable without the consent of the parties despite the clear language to the contrary. This argument, though, is not premised upon any reliable evidence adduced at the trial which would demonstrate that Nolan entered into his agreement with Fox because of any personal trust and confidence which he placed in Fox. Further, rescission of copyright exploitation agreements much like the one in issue in the case at bar was also sought in the case of In re Waterson, Berlin & Snyder Co. when the original assignee of the copyrights at issue there attempted to assign them to other publishers. The District Court granted rescission in that case on the ground that the agreements were not assignable because of the degree of personal trust involved in them. The Court of Appeals, however, reversed that decision and held that the copyrights could be assigned further.

Plaintiff's assertions of fraud are based in part upon the allegation that Fox concealed from plaintiff its relationship with Williamson by never giving plaintiff actual notice of the assignment. The evidence, however, does not support a finding of fraud in this regard. It is true that Fox never gave plaintiff actual notice of the assignment, but the court has already held that the contract was assignable without Fox's first having to obtain the plaintiff's consent.

JUDGMENT
AND REMEDY

An injunction was denied. The court declared that Sam Fox had every right under the terms of the contract to make the assignment to Williamson Music, Inc. Nolan had no right to rescind the contract or refuse to comply with its terms.

COMMENTS

The law favors the right of a person to assign contractual benefits. This is consistent with the principle of free alienability of rights that we, as citizens, enjoy under the Constitution.

STATUTE OF FRAUDS   In general, an assignment can take any form, oral or written. Naturally, in the event of a dispute, it is more difficult to prove the occurrence of an oral assignment. Therefore, it is practical to put all assignments in writing.

Assignments covered by the Statute of Frauds, however, must be in writing to be enforceable. As noted in Chapter 11, assignments of an interest in land, contracts not to be performed within one year, promises to answer for the debts of another, promises in consideration of marriage, and promises of an administrator or an executor to personally pay the debts of an estate must also be in writing. In addition, most states require contracts for the assignment of wages to be in writing.[10]

CONSIDERATION   An assignment need not be supported by *legally sufficient consideration* to be effective. A gratuitous assignment is just as effective as an assignment made for money. However, the absence of consideration becomes significant when the assignor wants to revoke the assignment. If the assignment was made for consideration, the assignor cannot revoke it. If no consideration is involved, the assignor can revoke, thereby revoking the right of the third party to demand performance or to sue for failure to render that performance.[11] Gratuitous assignments can be revoked by:

1. The subsequent assignment of the same right to another third party.
2. The death of the assignor.
3. The bankruptcy of the assignor.
4. A notice of revocation given to the assignee.

RIGHTS THAT CAN BE ASSIGNED   Except in a few special situations, all rights can be assigned. If a state statute expressly prohibits assignment, the particular right in question cannot be assigned. If a contract stipulates that the rights cannot be assigned, then, ordinarily, they cannot be assigned.[12] When a contract is personal in nature, the rights under the contract cannot be assigned. Finally, a right cannot be assigned if assignment will materially increase or alter the burdens of the obligor.

To illustrate these rules, recall the diagram showing A the assignor, B the obligor, and C the assignee. Suppose B owes A $50, and A assigns the right to receive the $50 to C. Here valid assignment of a debt exists, and B must pay the $50 to C, or C will be entitled to enforce payment in a court of law.

Next, suppose B agrees to build a house for A. The contract between A and B states: "The contract cannot be assigned by A. Any assign-

---

10.   See, for example, California Labor Code Sec. 300.
11.   Restatement, Second, Contracts (tentative draft), Section 164.

12.   Several exceptions to this rule exist. First, a contract cannot prevent assignment of the right to receive money. This exception exists to encourage the free flow of money and credit in modern business settings. Second, the assignment of rights in real estate cannot be prohibited because this would be contrary to public policy. Such prohibitions are called *restraints against alienation*. Third, the assignment of negotiable instruments cannot be prohibited.

ment renders this contract void and all rights hereunder will thereupon terminate." A then attempts to assign his rights to C. C cannot enforce the contract against B by trying to get B to build the house, since the contract expressly prohibits the assignment of rights.

Suppose B signs a contract to be a tutor for A's children. A then attempts to assign her right in B's services to C. C cannot enforce the contract against B because the contract called for the rendering of a personal service.[13]

Finally, assume A takes out an insurance policy on her hotel with B, an insurance com-

pany. The policy insures against fire, theft, floods, and vandalism. A then attempts to assign the insurance policy to C, who also owns a hotel. The assignment is ineffective because it alters B's *duty of performance* substantially. Insurance companies evaluate the particular risk of a certain party and tailor their policies to fit the exact risk of that party. If the policy is assigned to a third party, the insurance risk will be materially altered. Therefore, the assignment will not operate to give C any rights against B.

The following case illustrates the assignment of rights that materially changed the performance of obligations under the agreement.

---

13. Restatement, Second, Contracts (tentative draft), Section 149 and Section 150.

BACKGROUND AND FACTS *The Pizza of Gaithersburg (the Pizza Shop) arranged to have cold drink machines installed in several of its pizza establishments. The Pizza Shop (appellee) originally contracted with Virginia Coffee Service, Inc., to install the vending machines. The Macke Company (appellant) bought out the Virginia Company's assets and took over its vending operations. The Pizza Shop wanted to rescind the contracts. It argued that the assignment amounted to such a "material change" in the performance of the obligations under the agreements that it resulted in a breach of the contract. The lower court agreed with the Pizza Shop and granted it the right to rescind the contract, but the appellate court held that the assignment was permissible under the terms of the contract.*

MACKE COMPANY v. PIZZA OF GAITHERSBURG, INC.
Court of Appeals of Maryland, 1970.
259 Md. 479, 270 A.2d 645.

SINGLEY, Judge.
* * *

In the absence of a contrary provision—and there was none here—rights and duties under an executory bilateral contract may be assigned and delegated, subject to the exception that duties under a contract to provide personal services may never be delegated, nor rights be assigned under a contract where *delectus personae* was an ingredient of the bargain.[1] [It has been] held that the right of an individual to purchase ice under a contract which by its terms reflected a knowledge of the individual's needs and reliance on his credit and responsibility could not be assigned to the corporation which purchased his business. [It has been] held that an advertising agency could not delegate its duties under a contract which had been entered into by an advertiser who had relied on the agency's skill, judgment and taste.

---

1. Like all generalizations, this one is subject to an important exception. Uniform Commercial Code § 9-318 makes ineffective a term in any contract prohibiting the assignment of a contract right: *i. e.*, a right to payment. Compare Restatement, Contracts § 151(c) (1932).

We cannot regard the agreements as contracts for personal services. They were either a license or concession granted Virginia by the appellees, or a lease of a portion of the appellees' premises, with Virginia agreeing to pay a percentage of gross sales as a license or concession fee or as rent and were assignable by Virginia unless they imposed on Virginia duties of a personal or unique character which could not be delegated.

The appellees earnestly argue that they had dealt with Macke before and had chosen Virginia because they preferred the way it conducted its business. Specifically, they say that service was more personalized, since the president of Virginia kept the machines in working order, that commissions were paid in cash, and that Virginia permitted them to keep keys to the machines so that minor adjustments could be made when needed. Even if we assume all this to be true, the agreements with Virginia were silent as to the details of the working arrangements and contained only a provision requiring Virginia to "install * * * the above listed equipment and * * * maintain the equipment in good operating order and stocked with merchandise." We think the Supreme Court of California put the problem of personal service in proper focus a century ago when it upheld the assignment of a contract to grade a San Francisco street:

> "All painters do not paint portraits like Sir Joshua Reynolds, nor landscapes like Claude Lorraine, nor do all writers write dramas like Shakespeare or fiction like Dickens. Rare genius and extraordinary skill are not transferable, and contracts for their employment are therefore personal, and cannot be assigned. But rare genius and extraordinary skill are not indispensable to the workmanlike digging down of a sand hill or the filling up of a depression to a given level, or the construction of brick sewers with manholes and covers, and contracts for such work are not personal, and may be assigned."

* * *

Restatement, Contracts § 160(3) (1932) reads, in part:

> "Performance or offer of performance by a person delegated has the same legal effect as performance or offer of performance by the person named in the contract, unless,
>
> (a) performance by the person delegated varies or would vary materially from performance by the person named in the contract as the one to perform, and there has been no * * * assent to the delegation * * *."

As we see it, the delegation of duty by Virginia to Macke was entirely permissible under the terms of the agreement. [T]he Pizza Shops had no right to rescind the agreements.

JUDGMENT AND REMEDY	*Pizza of Gaithersburg could not rescind the vending machine contracts without being liable to Macke for damages.*

ANTI-ASSIGNMENT CLAUSES As part of the terms of their agreement, parties can stipulate that the contract or certain rights under the contract are not assignable. However, anti-assignment clauses bring up public policy concerns. For example, when an anti-assignment clause restrains the alienation of property, courts will sometimes refuse to enforce it. Thus, anti-assignment clauses are subject to judicial review.

BACKGROUND AND FACTS *This case centered around an anti-assignment clause in an agreement for a franchise business that required the consent of the area franchise-holder before the business could be transferred. The proceeding was brought for a declaratory judgment. (In a declaratory judgment, a court merely declares the rights and duties of parties without awarding damages. Such judgments are given to prevent disputes from arising.)*

The appellant, George Hanigan, entered into a "Dairy Queen Store Agreement" with the appellee, Eileen A. LeMoines. The contract contained a provision that read as follows: "Second Party shall not assign or transfer this Agreement without the written approval of First Party." Subsequently, the LeMoines entered into a deposit and receipt agreement with Wheeler for the sale of the Dairy Queen franchise as well as the real property located at and built specifically for the franchise.

A few days later, Hanigan was told about the sale, and an attempt was made to gain his approval. Hanigan refused to approve the sale. He stated that the price of $90,000 was too high and that, in his experience, an inflated sale price was detrimental to the Dairy Queen business. Hanigan also stated that the Wheelers were inexperienced in business and that they were too young to run the franchise properly. (Mr. Wheeler was a dentist, and Mrs. Wheeler was a housewife.) The trial court declared that the clause disallowing assignment without Hanigan's consent was unenforceable as against public policy. The franchise holders, the LeMoines, appealed.

HANIGAN v. WHEELER
Court of Appeals of Arizona,
Division 2, 1972.
19 Ariz.App. 49, 504 P.2d 972.

HOWARD, Judge.

* * *

The primary question dispositive of this appeal is whether the trial court erred in determining that the contract provision precluding the franchise transfer without the area franchise holder's approval is unenforceable as against public policy. A review of the record and the relevant law leads us to answer this question in the affirmative. Given the instant fact situation, the law in this area does not warrant the trial court's order requiring Hanigan to consent to the subject transaction:

> "As a general rule, a contract is not assignable where the nature or terms of the contract make it nonassignable, [footnote omitted] unless such provision is waived. * * * The parties may in terms, by a provision in the contract, prohibit an assignment thereof, * * *" 6 C.J.S. Assignments § 24.b (1937).

> "Provisions in bilateral contracts which forbid or restrict assignment of the contract without the consent of the obligor have generally been upheld as valid and enforceable when called into question, [footnote omitted] although the meaning of such terms becomes a matter of interpretation. * * *" 6 Am.Jr. 2d Assignments § 22 (1963).

These general statements are in accord with the Restatement of the Law of Contracts § 151, which reads as follows:

"A right may be the subject of effective assignment unless, * * *
(c) the assignment is prohibited by the contract creating the right."
* * *

A leading case stated the law as follows:

* * * we think it is reasonably clear that, while the courts have striven to uphold freedom of assignability, they have not failed to recognize the concept of freedom to contract. In large measure they agree that, where appropriate language is used, assignments of money due under contracts may be prohibited. When 'clear language' is used, and the 'plainest words * * * have been chosen' parties may 'limit the freedom of alienation of rights and prohibit the assignment.'

* * *

In opposition to the above principles, appellees contend that more than a contract right is involved in the case at bench in that the subject clause restricting assignment without Hanigan's approval serves as an unreasonable and unlawful restraint on the right of alienation of property, since the Store Agreement provides no guidelines by which the area franchise holder is to base his approval or disapproval of potential buyers, and that hypothetically, through the whim or arbitrariness of the holder, the LeMoines could be prevented from ever selling their franchise and the property associated with the franchise.

We accept the fundamental principle that one of the primary incidents inherent in the ownership of property is the right of alienation or disposition. However, this right is not limitless. The right to make an assignment of property can be defeated where there is a clear stipulation to that effect. The current state of the law in this area appears to be that a restraint on the alienation of property may be sustained when the restraint is reasonably designed to attain or encourage accepted social or economic ends.

* * *

We also perceive that despite the restriction on assignment of the store agreement, the LeMoines are not entirely powerless. Where a contract contains a *promise* to refrain from assigning, an assignment which violates it would not be ineffective. "The promise creates a *duty* in the promisor not to assign. It does not deprive the assignor of the *power* to assign and its breach, therefore, would simply subject the promisor to an action for damages while the assignment would be effective. * * *"

In summary, we hold that the law as set forth above demonstrates that the contract limitation against assignment of the Store Agreement without the approval of the area franchise holder is proper and valid. The trial court erred in concluding that the provision limiting assignability was unenforceable as against public policy. The court also erred in ruling that defendants had a duty to consent to the franchise sale, for this is contrary to the manifested intention of the parties to the contract. The general proposition is that " 'a covenantor [promisor] is not to be held beyond his undertaking and he may make that as narrow as he likes.' "

JUDGMENT AND REMEDY *The trial court was incorrect. The appellate court declared that it was the right of the area franchise-holder to consent or refuse to consent to the sale (assignment) of a franchise.*

The trial court had ordered Hanigan to consent to the transaction. **COMMENTS**
Hanigan wanted the appeals court to declare affirmatively that, as a matter of law, he was not required to approve the transfer. The court had to use a declaratory judgment because no sale had occurred yet. A declaratory judgment is a "declaration of rights" between parties or of a particular party in a situation. It enables the parties to know ahead of time whether their intended actions will be legal.

NOTICE OF THE ASSIGNMENT Once a valid assignment of rights has been made to a third party, the third party should notify the obligor (B in the diagram) of the assignment. This is not legally necessary because an assignment is effective immediately, whether or not notice is given, but it protects all of the parties. The following examples illustrate some of the problems that can arise when a third party fails to give notice of an assignment.

First, suppose A delivers eight ounces of high grade uranium to B, a nuclear energy cooperative. B is to pay a specified sum for the uranium. Before B pays, A assigns the right to receive payment for the uranium to C, one of A's suppliers in South Africa. C fails to notify B of the assignment, and B makes the payment to A. Since C failed to give notice of the assignment, C lost the right to collect the money from B. Before notice of the assignment, B is free to fulfill its obligation by paying A directly. If C had given notice of the assignment to B, B would have been required to pay C instead of A.

Second, suppose further that, after A assigned the right to receive payment to C, A also assigned the right to receive payment to D. Further assume that D then notified B of the second assignment. Many states will allow D to recover the money from B because of timely notification. Suppose several days after D notified B of the second assignment, C notified B of the first assignment. Here B is in a touchy situation, since it has received notice from two different people that payment is to be made to each. In this case, a majority of states will require payment to be made to D. D gave notice first and should be entitled to prevail over C, who was delinquent. However, some states

would allow C to recover the money even though C failed to give notice before D.[14]

Delegation of Duties

Just as a party can transfer rights under a contract through an assignment, a party can also transfer duties. Duties are not assigned, however. They are "delegated." Normally, a delegation of duties does not relieve the party making the delegation of the obligation to perform in the event that the party who has been delegated the duty fails to perform.

FORM OF THE DELEGATION No special form is required to create a valid delegation of duties. As long as the delegator (the party delegating the duty) expresses a present intention to make the delegation, it will be effective. The delegator need not even use the word "delegate."

DUTIES THAT CAN BE DELEGATED As a general rule, any duty can be delegated. However, when performance depends on the personal skill or talents of the obligor, or where special trust has been placed in the obligor, or when performance by a third party will vary

---

14. At common law, there were three different rules. The first rule was called the English rule. Second assignees prevailed in every case in which they had paid value, had taken the assignment without notice of the prior assignment, and had given the *obligor* notice of the assignment before the first assignee gave such notice. The next rule was called the New York rule: first in time, first in right. Finally, the third rule was called the Massachusetts rule. The first assignee prevailed provided the first assignment was not revokable at the time the second assignment was made.

materially from the expectancy of the obligee under the contract, the duty cannot be delegated.

Suppose B contracts with A to tutor A in the various aspects of financial underwriting and investment banking. B is an experienced businessman who is well known for his expertise in finance. Further, assume that B wants to delegate his duties to teach A to a third party, C. This delegation would be ineffective since B has contracted to render a service to A which is founded upon B's expertise. It is a change from A's expectancy under the contract. Therefore, C cannot perform B's duties.

Suppose B, an attorney, contracts with A, a bank, to advise A on a proposed merger with a savings and loan association. B wishes to delegate her duty to advise the bank to C, a law firm across town. Services of an attorney are personal in nature. B's delegation will be ineffective.

Finally, assume that B contracts with A to pick up and deliver heavy construction machinery to A's property. B then delegates this duty to C, who is in the business of delivering heavy machinery. The delegation is effective. The performance required is of a routine and non-personal nature and does not change A's expectancy under the contract. Exhibit 12-3 illustrates this relationship.

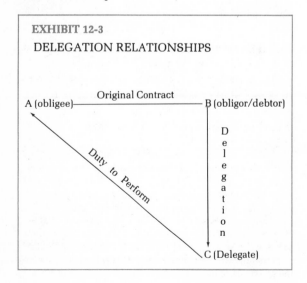

EXHIBIT 12-3

DELEGATION RELATIONSHIPS

A (obligee) —— Original Contract —— B (obligor/debtor)

Duty to Perform

D
e
l
e
g
a
t
i
o
n

C (Delegate)

EFFECT OF A DELEGATION OF DUTIES If a delegation of duties is legitimate, the obligee (A in the diagram) must accept performance from the delegate. The obligee can refuse performance from the delegate if the duty is one that may not be delegated. A valid delegation of duties does not relieve the delegator (B in the diagram) of obligations under the contract.[15] If the delegate (C in the diagram) fails to perform, the delegator is still liable to the obligee.

The liability of the delegate to the obligee depends on whether the agreement between delegate and delegator is interpreted as a "mere delegation" or a delegation plus an "assumption of duty" by the delegate. Where the delegate has made no promise to perform the duty *for the benefit of the obligee,* there is a "mere delegation." In these cases, the obligee cannot compel the delegate to perform or hold the delegate liable for non-performance. Common examples are cases where the delegate is an employee or a subcontractor of the obligor.

Where the delegate does make a promise to perform the duty for the benefit of the obligee, there is an "assumption of duty." The obligee is then in the position of third party creditor beneficiary and can hold the delegate liable for non-performance.

Suppose B contracts to build a house for A. B is the obligor. A is the obligee. B then contracts with C for C to supply the necessary construction materials. C fails to deliver. A can sue B, but cannot sue C. This is a clear case where C's promise to deliver the materials was for the benefit of the obligor, B, but not for the benefit of the obligee, A.

Suppose A and B have the same contract. B is unable to build the house so B contracts with C to build the house for A. C does not build the house. Here, the delegate, C, entered into a contract for the benefit of the obligee, A. A can sue both B and C.

When a party makes an assignment of a contract, the question of whether a delegation of

---

15.   Crane Ice Cream Co. v. Terminal Freezing Co., 147 Md. 588, 128 A. 280 (1925).

duties and assumption of duties were not also intended will sometimes arise. For example, B assigns a contract with the words "I assign this contract to C." C has not expressly assumed any duties. Is C liable to perform the duties?

The traditional view was that under this assignment, C did not assume any duties. This view was based on the theory that the acceptance of the benefits of the contract was not sufficient to imply a promise to assume the duties of the contract. Modern authorities, however, take the view that the probable intention in using such general words was to create both an assignment of rights and an assumption of duties.[16] Therefore, when general words are

used (e. g., "I assign the contract" or "all my rights under the contract") the contract is construed as implying both an assignment of rights and an assumption of duties. Naturally, this result occurs only when the parties have not expressly provided otherwise. When the agreement making the assignment and delegations specifically states that the delegate is not assuming the duties, the delegate cannot be sued for failure to perform those duties.

Suppose in the contract for the sale of B's boutique to C, it stated, "B does hereby sell, transfer, and assign to C all of B's rights with regard to the Honneywell Boutique." Under the traditional view, C would not be obligated to pay B's business debt to A. In the modern view, a promise to pay B's debt to A would be implied, and A could require C to pay.

---

16. UCC Sec. 2-210 (where there is a general assignment of a contract for the sale of goods). Restatement, Second, Contracts (tentative draft), Section 160.

QUESTIONS AND CASE PROBLEMS

1. Beman wrote out his wife's will as she was about to die. When he read the will to her, she said that it was not the way she wanted it and that she wanted to leave her house to her niece, Seaver. Beman offered to write her another will, but she said she was afraid she would not hold out long enough to sign it. Beman told her that if she would sign the will, he would leave Seaver the house in his will. When Beman died, no provision was made for Seaver to receive the house. Seaver brought an action against Beman's estate, claiming a contract right in the house. What result? [Seaver v. Ransom, 224 N.Y. 233, 120 N.E. 639 (1918)]

2. Murray contracted with McDonald Construction Company to build an addition to a building Murray owned. Murray intended to rent part of the addition to Queen Anne News, and McDonald knew this. The terms of the contract between Murray and McDonald called for McDonald to complete the addition within 75 days. However, completion was delayed an additional 164 days. Queen Anne News sued McDonald for damages resulting from the delay in construction. Can Queen Anne recover? [McDonald Construction Company v. Murray, 5 Wash.App. 68, 485 P.2d 626 (1971)]

3. Isbrandtsen Company chartered a ship to transport paper pulp. Isbrandtsen hired Livano Shipping Company to unload the ship. After the ship was partially unloaded, the longshoremen's union, of which Livano's employees were members, went on strike in violation of their union contract. As a result, part of the pulp shipment was damaged. Isbrandtsen sued the longshoremen for breach of the union contract. Can Isbrandtsen recover? [Isbrandtsen Co. v Local 1291 Longshoremen, 204 F.2d 495 (3d Cir. 1953)]

4. Christopher wrote a letter to Daniel claiming that Daniel owed him $3,000 for the shipment of string bikinis that Christopher had sent him three months before. Daniel wrote back, saying that the bikinis were defective and that therefore he refused to pay. Christopher wrote back that his lawyer had advised him that it was questionable whether Daniel had informed him of the defect in time. Therefore Christopher felt that he might have a valid claim for the purchase price of $3,000. About a month later, Daniel wrote back to Christopher informing him that Jones, who owed Daniel $3,000 from a previous contract, had agreed with Daniel to make the payment to Christopher. Thereafter, Jones failed to make the payment to Christopher. Can Christopher sue Jones?

5. For several years, Eastern Company and Hudson Company had made a number of purchases and sales to each other on account. By January 1963, Eastern owed Hudson $2,200, and Hudson owed Eastern

$1,300. Eastern assigned the accounts Hudson owed it to Home Factors Corporation. Home Factors attempted to collect the $1,300 debt from Hudson, but Hudson refused to pay because of the $2,200 debt Eastern owed it. Is this a valid defense? [Hudson Supply and Equipment Co. v. Home Factors Corp., 210 A.2d 837 (D.C.App.1965)]

6. Mrs. Jemison hired Tindall and two other men, Miller and Cohen, to help her sell her farm and agreed in writing to pay them a $300 commission. When the men procured the sale, Mrs. Jemison paid the $300 commission to Tindall, who was supposed to divide the money among the three. Tindall, however, concealed the commission from the other two men. When they learned of this fact, Miller and Cohen brought suit against Mrs. Jemison instead of against Tindall to recover the $200 owed them for their commissions. After she paid them the $200, Mrs. Jemison took back an oral assignment of their claims against Tindall. Mrs. Jemison then sued Tindall to recover the commissions of Cohen and Miller. Can she collect? [Jemison v. Tindall, 89 N.J. 429, 99 A. 408 (1916)]

7. D'Alassandro had an insurance policy with Bull Dog Insurance Company that protected against loss of an automobile by theft. On January 17, D'Alassandro's automobile was stolen and was never recovered. D'Alassandro's insurance policy provided that "no assignment of interest under this policy shall be or become binding upon the association unless the written consent of the attorney is endorsed thereon and an additional membership fee is paid." D'Alassandro assigned his claim under the policy to Ginsburg without complying with this policy provision. Ginsburg claimed D'Alassandro's insurance proceeds from BullDog Insurance Company. Bull Dog refused to pay Ginsburg, and Ginsburg sued. Can Ginsburg recover? [Ginsburg v. Bull Dog Auto Fire Insurance Association of Chicago, 328 Ill. 571, 160 N.E. 145 (1928)]

8. An obligor owed Tompkins $10,000. On January 1, Tompkins assigned his rights to the $10,000 to a bank. On January 10, Tompkins assigned the same rights to the $10,000 to an insurance company. On February 1, the insurance company notified the obligor of Tompkins's assignment. On February 15, the bank notified the obligor of Tompkins's assignment. On March 15, the obligation came due. Both the bank and the insurance company claimed the entire $10,000. Who wins? [Boulevard National Bank of Miami v. Air Metal Industries, Inc., 176 So.2d 94 (Fla1965)]

9. Southern Sports Corp., owned and operated by James Gardner, was the owner of the Cougar's Basketball Franchise. Cunningham had a four-year contract with Southern Sports to play with the Cougars. In 1971 Southern Sports assigned the basketball franchise, along with Cunningham's contract to play with the franchise, to Munchak. Cunningham thereafter refused to play, claiming that the assignment was invalid without his consent. Must Cunningham play for the new owners? [Munchak Corp. v. Cunningham, 457 F.2d 721 (4th Cir. 1972)]

10. Lea and Parkgate entered into a lease agreement whereby Lea rented certain wagons from Parkgate for a number of years. Part of the rental agreement provided that Parkgate would keep the wagons in good repair. During the term of the lease, Parkgate decided to liquidate its business. With several years left in the lease agreement, Parkgate assigned the rights and delegated the duties under its contract with Lea to British Wagon Company. When Lea learned of the transfer, it claimed that Parkgate had no right to sell the contract to British Wagon and that it did not have to accept services from British Wagon. Can British Wagon enforce the contract? [British Wagon Company v. Lea & Company, 5 Q.B. 149 (1880)]

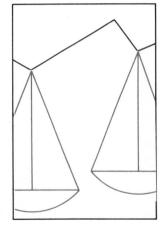

13

Contracts
Performance and Discharge

The **discharge** (termination) of a contract is ordinarily accomplished when both of the contracting parties perform those acts promised in the contract. For example, the buyer of goods pays the seller for the goods, and the seller gives up possession to the buyer. Discharge can also occur in other ways. The parties can agree to terminate the contract, or one party can **breach** the contract—that is, fail to perform the acts promised in the contract. A breach discharges the duties of the nonbreaching party. In addition, the law can operate to terminate or discharge a contract. Finally, performance of the promised acts can be excused if the acts become impossible or extremely impractical to perform or if the purpose for which the contract was created is frustrated.

CONDITIONS

A condition is inserted into a contract for the protection of the promisor. A *condition* is any operative event, the occurrence or nonoccurrence of which modifies, limits, precludes, or must occur prior to the existence of a duty to be performed under a contract. The occurrence or nonoccurrence of a condition can also terminate an existing obligation under a contract. The more conditions attached to a promise, the less content the promise has. Thus, promises made by a person entering into a contract are either absolute or conditional. An absolute promise is one that must be performed, or the party promising the act will be in breach of contract. There is a fundamental distinction between the breach or performance of an absolute promise and the failure or nonoccurrence of a condition. A breach of contract subjects the promisor to liability and can excuse performance of the other party's duty under the contract. The occurrence or nonoccurrence of a condition, on the other hand, prevents the promisee from acquiring a right or deprives the promisee of a right. It does not, however, subject the promisee to liability (unless he or she has promised that the condition will or will not happen).

For example, suppose you promise to buy a corn futures contract from Merrill Lynch if the price of No. 2 yellow corn reaches $2.25 per bushel. The condition to your promise to buy is that the price of No. 2 yellow corn will reach $2.25 per bushel. If there is a failure of that condition—if No. 2 yellow corn never reaches $2.25 per bushel and, therefore, you do not buy—the contract is not breached. However, once the price of corn does reach $2.25, your promise to buy becomes absolute, and if you do not buy, the contract is breached.

Types of Conditions

Three types of conditions can be present in any given contract—conditions *precedent*, conditions *subsequent*, and conditions *concurrent*.

CONDITIONS PRECEDENT   A condition that must be fulfilled before a party's promise becomes absolute is a **condition precedent.**[1] The condition precedes the absolute duty to perform. For example, if Craig promises to pay Davis $500 if Davis installs a tile roof on Craig's house, Craig's promise is subject to the condition precedent of Davis's installing the tile roof. Or if Fisher promises to contribute $1,000 to the Salvation Army if Calvin completes college, Fisher's promise is subject to the condition precedent of Calvin's completing college. Until the conditions are fulfilled or satisfied, Craig's promise to pay Davis and Fisher's promise to donate to charity do not become absolute.

CONDITIONS SUBSEQUENT   When a condition operates to terminate a party's absolute promise to perform, it is called a **condition subsequent.**[2] The condition follows, or is subsequent to, the absolute duty to perform. If the condition occurs, the party need not perform any further. For example, if Hartman promises to work for the San Pedro Company for one year unless he is called into military service, the absolute duty to work is conditioned upon not being drafted. Hartman's promise to work for San Pedro continues to be absolute until he is drafted or otherwise inducted. Once Hartman is drafted, the absolute duty to work for San Pedro ends, and Hartman is released from the contract.[3]

CONCURRENT CONDITIONS   Where each party's absolute duty to perform is conditioned on the other party's absolute duty to perform there are **concurrent conditions.** Concurrent conditions occur only when the parties are to perform their respective duties simultaneously. For example, if a buyer promises to pay for goods if they are delivered by the seller, each party's absolute duty to perform is conditioned upon the other party's absolute duty to perform. The buyer's duty to pay for the goods does not become absolute until the seller either delivers or tenders the goods.[4] Accordingly, the seller's duty to deliver the goods does not become absolute until the buyer tenders or actually makes payment.[5]

EXPRESSED AND CONSTRUCTIVE CONDITIONS   Conditions can also be classified as: (1) express, (2) implied-in-fact, and (3) implied-in-law. Express conditions are provided for by

1.   Restatement, Contracts, Section 250(a).

2.   Restatement, Contracts, Section 250(b). It is possible that a condition may be subsequent in form but precedent in fact. Further, if there is any difference at all between the two, it is as to burdens of proof and pleading. For this reason, the draft of the Restatement, Second, Contracts drops the distinction between the two.
3.   Hartman v. San Pedro Commercial Co., 66 Cal.App.2d 935, 153 P.2d 212 (1945).
4.   Tender means offering to deliver the goods or making the goods available for the buyer to take delivery.
5.   This is in accord with UCC Secs. 2-503 and 2-511.

the parties' agreement. An express condition is usually prefaced by "if," "provided," "after," or "when." Conditions implied-in-fact are similar to expressed conditions because they are understood to be part of the agreement, but they are not expressly found in the language of the agreement. They can be inferred from the promise, however. Finally, implied-in-law, or constructive, conditions are imposed by the law in order to achieve justice and fairness. They are not contained in the language of the contract or even necessarily implied.[6] Suppose Silverman and Lyon enter into two agreements. The first states, "Silverman promises to pay Lyon $1,500 if Lyon delivers 100 cases of oranges to Silverman's business office. Lyon promises to deliver 100 cases of oranges to Silverman's business office if Silverman pays $1,500 for the oranges." The second agreement states, "Silverman promises to pay $1,500 for 100 cases of Lyon's oranges to be delivered at Silverman's business office." In the first agreement, Silverman's promise to pay is expressly conditioned on Lyon's promise to deliver. Also, Lyon's promise to deliver is expressly conditioned on Silverman's promise to pay. As noted above, these are *concurrent conditions*. In the second agreement, Silverman's promise to pay is *constructively* conditioned on Lyon's promise to deliver, and Lyon's promise to deliver is *constructively conditioned* on Silverman's promise to pay. The conditions are *implied* (the promises are construed as conditional) in order to achieve justice and fairness. The conditions are implied-in-fact because they are necessarily inferred from the promise contained in the contract. In other words, it is obvious from custom and context that the duties here are conditional.

Suppose neither Silverman nor Lyon perform their promises under the second agreement. If the promises were not constructively conditioned on the other party's performance, both parties could sue for breach of contract without attempting to perform themselves (since the promises would be absolute and not subject to any conditions). By creating

constructive conditions, this problem is eliminated. *In order to sue for breach of contract (that is, breach of an absolute promise to perform), the suing party must fulfill his or her respective condition(s) (or those conditional promises must be excused).*[7] Silverman must tender payment to Lyon before suing for breach of contract. Likewise, Lyon must tender delivery to Silverman before suing for breach of contract.

Now consider some examples of condition implied-in-law. A contract in which a builder is supposed to build a house for a buyer can leave silent when the buyer is supposed to pay the builder. Nonetheless, the court will infer an implied condition that the buyer is not obliged to pay the builder until the house is completed. This is done because the buyer should not be compelled to perform unless the builder has performed. (If the builder performs substantially, such as finishing everything except the hook-up for an outside water faucet, the court will allow the builder to recover the agreed price less the amount necessary to cover the cost of hooking up the outside water faucet.)

The following sections discuss some of the most important (and common) ways in which contracts are discharged.[8]

DISCHARGE BY PERFORMANCE

The great majority of contracts are discharged by performance. The contract comes to an end when both parties fulfill their respective duties by performing the acts they have promised to do. Performance can also be accomplished by tender. **Tender** is an unconditional offer to perform by one who is ready, willing and able to do so. Therefore, a seller who places goods at the disposal of a buyer has tendered delivery and can demand payment. A buyer who offers to pay for goods has tendered payment and can demand delivery of the goods. Once performance has been tendered, the party making the

---

6. Restatement, Contracts, Section 253.

7. See Kingston v. Preston, 2 Doug. 684 (K.B.) and followed in the Restatement, Contracts, Section 266.
8. Looking at all of them would take an entire book. For example, Restatement, Contracts, Section 385, presents twenty-five distinct ways a contract can be discharged.

tender has done everything possible to carry out the terms of the contract. If the other party then refuses to perform, the party making the tender can consider the duty discharged and sue for breach of contract.

The Degree of Performance Required

In most contracts, the parties will fulfill their respective duties completely. Sometimes, however, a party will fulfill most of the duties under the contract but not all of them. Or a party may complete all the duties but do so in a way that departs from the precise requirements of the contract. In order to determine whether all conditions have been fulfilled or whether the contract has been breached, the express and constructive conditions of the contract must be scrutinized.

EXPRESS CONDITIONS AND FULL PERFORMANCE Conditions that are expressly stated normally must be fully performed in all respects. For example, a contract stating that "Mason, the builder, will be paid $750 when he installs three-eighth inch DuPont asbestos covering on the welding work benches in Nie Company's Fort Lauderdale plant" expressly requires the installation of DuPont asbestos. If Mason installs Pennecott asbestos, he will not be fulfilling the express condition precedent to payment and will not be entitled to payment. Likewise, if Cowles Inc. agrees to buy two tanks of butane fuel from Oneida Company for $1,750 and tenders a check for $1,749.95, the express condition precedent will not be fulfilled, and Cowles will not be entitled to delivery of the butane fuel.

BARNES v. EUSTER
Court of Appeals of Maryland, 1965.
240 Md. 603, 214 A.2d 807.

BACKGROUND AND FACTS *In the following case, a contract for the sale of a tract of land by the appellee (seller) to the appellant (buyer) was subject to a condition precedent that certain zoning variances be obtained. Generally, applications for zoning can be filed only during each of two specified months of the year, six months apart. The parties had included in their contract a provision that "this sale [is] subject to the obtaining of necessary zoning for the erection of general offices for use of doctors within the next zoning application term." The parties had further agreed that the provision meant the six-month period following the first day of the month in which zoning applications could be filed after the signing of the contract.*

The zoning application was timely filed (that is, within the legal, necessary, or reasonable period) but not obtained "within the next zoning application term." The sellers then notified the buyer in writing that the contract was terminated and the buyer's 10 percent deposit was being returned. The land was sold to another purchaser. The buyer (appellant) attempted to obtain damages from the seller (appellee) for having sold the land to another purchaser. The buyer took the position that the contract was still in force.

HAMMOND, Judge.
* * *

Although the contract did not expressly make time of the essence, it may well be, as appellees contend, that by reason of the condition as to rezoning, the contract was like a unilateral contract, such as an option, in which the law makes time of the essence and *that time ran out with the expiration of the then current "zoning*

application term," and the contract then ended, * * * without further obligation on either party. [Emphasis added.]
* * *

The contract provision was that it was "subject" to the specified rezoning being obtained within the current zoning application term, and "where a contractual duty is subject to a condition precedent, whether express or implied, there is no duty of performance and there can be no breach by nonperformance until the condition precedent is either performed or excused." Here it was not performed, and, if the further assumption be made that the condition * * * was for the protection only of the buyer, it could have been excused or waived by him as being a provision for his benefit, but the excusing or waiving would have had to be done before the expiration of the current zoning application term or within a reasonable time thereafter.
* * *

In mid-1960 the buyer knew the condition had not been met, but it was not until three years later, * * * that he first indicated by word or act that he was willing to excuse or waive the condition and take the land as it was. Some sixteen months after the last day of the critical zoning application term, when the sellers wrote that the contract had terminated, he took the position it was still in force, subject to the condition.
* * *

His delay in excusing or waiving the condition was unreasonable as a matter of law in light of the notification of termination by the sellers and the rapidly rising prices of real estate. * * *

The appellate court affirmed the trial court order. The prospective buyer had no right to damages from the seller for sale of the land to another purchaser since the condition precedent had never been fulfilled.

JUDGMENT AND REMEDY

CONSTRUCTIVE CONDITIONS AND SUBSTANTIAL PERFORMANCE Conditions that are constructive (that is, imposed by law to achieve justice and fairness) can be fulfilled by *substantial performance* rather than full performance. In order to qualify as substantial, the performance must not vary greatly from the performance promised in the contract. If the performance is substantial, the constructive condition is satisfied and the other party's duty to perform becomes absolute.

Suppose you are a construction contractor and you contracted to build a meatpacking plant for Wilson & Company. Certain specifications for construction materials were set forth in the contract. One of them stated, "All wrought iron pipe must be well-galvanized, lap welded pipe of the grade known as 'standard pipe' of Reading Manufacture." After the plant was complet-

ed, Wilson & Company discovered that Cohose pipe was used and refused to pay anything for the plant, alleging that you had not fulfilled the constructive condition precedent of using Reading pipe. If you were required to use Reading pipe, you would not have fulfilled the condition, Wilson & Company's promise to pay would not become absolute, and you would not be paid. In order to avoid this harsh result, courts hold that substantial performance of a constructive condition precedent (or concurrent condition) is sufficient to satisfy or fulfill that condition.[9] Otherwise, Wilson & Company would be unjustly enriched, and you would forfeit all the time and expense put into building the meatpacking plant. However, if you installed Read-

9.   For an excellent analysis of substantial performance see Judge Cardozo's opinion in Jacob & Youngs v. Kent, 230 N.Y. 239, 129 N.E. 889 (1921).

ing pipe, but the pipe was not galvanized and the seams were butt-welded, the performance would not be substantial. You would not be paid since the constructive condition precedent would not be satisfied or fulfilled.

Substantial performance does not operate to eliminate any breach of contract arising from less than full performance. *It operates only to satisfy or fulfill constructive (implied) conditions.* In the above example, if you installed Cohose pipe, Wilson & Company would still be entitled to recover damages caused by the less than full performance. If the meatpacking plant were worth $1,000 less because of the substitution of Cohose for Reading pipe, you, the builder would be allowed to recover the price of the building, less $1,000.

PERFORMANCE TO THE SATISFACTION OF ANOTHER Contracts will often state that completed work must satisfy one of the parties or a third person. This satisfaction then becomes a condition precedent to the parties' duty to perform. The question that always arises is whether the performance must actually satisfy that person or whether performance that would satisfy a "reasonable" person will be sufficient.

When the subject matter of the contract is personal, contracts to be performed to the satisfaction of one of the parties must actually satisfy that party. For example, contracts for portraits, works of art, medical or dental work, and tailoring are considered personal. Therefore, only the personal satisfaction of the party will be sufficient to fulfill the condition. Suppose Williams agrees to paint a portrait of Hirshon's daughter for $500. The contract provides that Hirshon must be satisfied with the portrait. If Hirshon is not, she will not be required to pay for it. The only requirement imposed on Hirshon is that she act honestly. If she expresses dissatisfaction only to avoid paying for the portrait, the condition of satisfaction is excused, and her duty to pay becomes absolute.

Contracts that involve mechanical fitness, utility, or marketability need only be performed

to the satisfaction of a reasonable person unless they expressly state otherwise. For example, construction contracts or manufacturing contracts are *not* considered to be personal, so the party's personal satisfaction is normally irrelevant. As long as the performance will satisfy a reasonable person, the condition is fulfilled. For example, assume Duplex Safety Boiler Company agrees to rebuild Garden's boiler "to Garden's satisfaction." After rebuilding the boiler, it operates properly, but Garden is dissatisfied and refuses to pay for the repair work. If a reasonable person would be satisfied with the boiler's operation, Duplex is entitled to be paid for the repair work.[10]

At times, contracts also require performance to the satisfaction of a third party (not a party to the contract). For example, assume you contract to pave several city streets. The contract provides that the work will be done "to the satisfaction of Phil Hopper, the supervising engineer." In this situation, the courts are divided. A minority of courts require the personal satisfaction of the third party, here Phil Hopper. If Hopper is not satisfied, you will not be paid, even if a reasonable person would be satisfied. Again, the personal judgment must be made honestly or the condition will be excused. A majority of courts require the work to be satisfactory to a reasonable person. So even if Hopper were dissatisfied with the cement work, you would be paid, as long as a reasonable supervising engineer would have been satisfied.

Time for Performance

If no time for performance is stated in the contract, a reasonable time is implied. If a specific time is stated, the parties must usually perform by that time. However, unless time is expressly stated to be vital, a delay in performance will not destroy the performing party's right to payment. When time is expressly stated to be vital, or when "time is of the essence," the time

---

10. If, however, the contract specifically states that it is to be fulfilled to the "personal" satisfaction of one or more of the parties, and the parties so intended, the outcome will probably be different.

for performance must be strictly complied with. For example, a contract for the sale of soybeans without stating more, must be performed within a reasonable time. A contract for the sale of soybeans "on or before April 1" may be performed by April 2 or 3. (But the party rendering late performance will have to pay for any damages caused by the delay.) A contract for the sale of soybeans "on or before April 1—necessary for immediate shipment abroad on April 2" must be performed by April 1. Time is of the essence because the buyer plans on immediate resale. Delivery after April 1 will prevent the buyer from exporting the soybeans.

DISCHARGE BY AGREEMENT

Any contract can be discharged by agreement of the parties. The agreement can be contained in the original contract, or the parties can form a new contract for the express purpose of discharging the original contract.

Discharge by Rescission

Rescission is the process whereby the parties cancel the contract and return to the positions they occupied prior to forming it. In order to rescind a bargain, the parties must make another agreement, which must also satisfy the legal requirements for a contract. There must be an *offer*, an *acceptance*, and *consideration*. Ordinarily, if the parties agree to rescind the original contract, their promises not to perform those acts promised in the original contract will be legal consideration for the second contract.

Where one party has fully performed, however, an agreement to call off the original contract will not normally be enforceable. Because the performing party has received no consideration for the promise to call off the original bargain, additional consideration will be necessary. To illustrate: Suppose Beatrice Foods Company contracts to buy forty truckloads of oranges from Tropicana Products Inc. Later, representatives of Beatrice and Tropicana get together and decide to call off the deal or rescind the original contract. This agreement, without more, is enforceable since neither party

has yet performed. The consideration for Tropicana calling off the deal is not having to perform that which it was legally bound to perform under the contract—that is, not having to deliver the forty truckloads of oranges. The consideration for Beatrice calling off the deal is not having to pay for the oranges, an obligation it otherwise had to honor. On the other hand, if Tropicana had already delivered the oranges, an agreement to call off the deal would not normally be enforceable. Since Tropicana had already performed, it had received no consideration for its promise to call off the deal. In sum, contracts that are *executory* on *both* sides (contracts where neither party has performed) can be rescinded by agreement without more.[11] But contracts that are *executed on one side* (contracts where one party has performed) can be rescinded only if the party who has performed receives consideration for the promise to call off the deal.

Discharge by Novation or Substituted Agreement

The process of novation substitutes a new party for one of the original parties. Essentially, the parties to the original contract and one or more new parties all get together and agree to substitute the new party for one of the original parties. The requirements of novation are: (1) an agreement among all parties to discharge the original contract, (2) the substitution of a new party, and (3) a new contract that is valid. Suppose Union Carbide Corp. decides to sell its petrochemical business in Europe. Union Carbide contracts with British Petroleum Company to sell Bakelite Xylonite Ltd. stock to British Petroleum for $200 million in cash. The contract is signed by both parties. After British Petroleum consults its tax and securities experts, it decides to substitute BP Chemicals as the

11. Note that certain sales made to consumers at their homes can be rescinded by the consumer within three days for no reason at all. This three-day "cooling-off" is designed to aid consumers who are susceptible to high-pressure door-to-door sales tactics. See Chapter 48 and 15 USC Sec. 1635(a).

purchaser instead. In order to accomplish this, the parties agree to a novation. Union Carbide, British Petroleum, and BP Chemicals all get together and agree that BP Chemicals will buy the Bakelite Xylonite stock from Union Carbide. As long as the new contract is supported by consideration, the novation will discharge the original contract (between Union Carbide and British Petroleum) and replace it with the new contract (between Union Carbide and BP Chemicals).

A substituted agreement is a new contract that expressly or impliedly revokes and discharges a prior contract. The parties involved may simply want a new agreement with somewhat different terms. So they *expressly* state in a new contract that the old contract is now discharged. They can also make the new contract without expressly stating that the old contract is discharged. If the parties do not expressly discharge the old contract, it will be *impliedly* discharged due to the change or different terms of the new contract. For example, suppose Triangle Pacific Corp. contracts to sell its lumber manufacturing facilities in Slocan, British Columbia to a Canadian investor group for $7.9 million in cash and $800,000 in five-year subordinated debentures. Before the sale is closed, however, Triangle Pacific Corp.

decides that it wants $6.9 million in cash and $1.8 million in five-year subordinated debentures. The Canadian investor group agrees, and the parties draw up a new contract with these terms of sale. If the second agreement states, "Our previous contract to accept payment of $7.9 million in cash, balance in five-year subordinated debentures is hereby revoked," the original contract will be expressly discharged by substitution. If the second agreement does not state this, the original contract will nevertheless be discharged by implication. Triangle Pacific Corp. cannot sell the same lumber manufacturing facilities under two different terms of payment. Since the terms are inconsistent, a court will enforce the terms that were decided upon most recently. In this case, the sale would be for $6.9 million in cash and $1.8 million in five-year subordinated debentures.

A compromise or settlement agreement that arises out of a bona fide dispute over the obligations under an existing contract will be recognized at law. Such an agreement will be substituted as a new contract, and it will either expressly or impliedly revoke and discharge the obligations under any prior contract. In the following case, a long history preceded an ultimate compromise settlement.

STANSPEC CORPORATION v. JELCO, INCORPORATED

United States Court of Appeals, Tenth Circuit, 1972. 464 F.2d 1184.

BACKGROUND AND FACTS *This action was brought by a seller, Stanspec Corporation, against a buyer, Jelco Incorporated, to recover the unpaid balance of the purchase price under an equipment supply contract. Jelco bid for and was awarded a contract to do the mechanical and electrical work for the Straight Creek Tunnel Project in Colorado. In preparing its bid, Jelco requested bids from suppliers of bulkhead hoists. One of the suppliers contacted was Plant Equipments Company of Denver, which in turn obtained a written proposal for the manufacture and delivery of the hoists from the plaintiff, Stanspec. A representative of Plant Equipment Company obtained the specifications from the Colorado State Department of Highways and supplied Stanspec with the specifications for its use in preparing the proposals. For some unknown reason, the specifications did not include certain amendments and revisions, one in particular relating to the type of electrical system to be used in the hoists.*

For reasons unrelated to the suit, Stanspec prepared a second proposal for Plant Equipment to submit to Jelco. For the second time, a Plant Equipment representative obtained the "current" specifica-

tions—this time from Jelco. Although Jelco had received revisions and amendments, they were not given to Plant Equipment's representative. Stanspec developed a second proposal based on incomplete specifications. When the second proposal was rejected, it became apparent that both proposals had been prepared on the basis of incomplete specifications.

In May 1968, Stanspec submitted a third proposal to Jelco—one designed to meet the specifications that included the revisions and amendments. This proposal required a higher price for the hoists under the revised description. However Jelco rejected the third proposal, claiming that it was Stanspec's responsibility to provide equipment conforming to the new specifications but at the original contract price.

Jelco attempted to locate another supplier of the hoists but was unable to do so. It finally agreed to purchase the hoists from Stanspec. In November, Stanspec and Jelco entered into an agreement whereby Stanspec would supply Jelco the specified hoists at an agreed price. The contract was consummated, and Stanspec performed. Jelco withheld a portion of the final payment essentially equivalent to the price difference between the May and November contracts. Stanspec filed this suit against Jelco for the unpaid balance of the purchase price under the November contract.

SETH, Circuit Judge.
* * *

At trial Stanspec contended that the November 10, 1969, agreement was the only effective contract, and maintained that it would not have entered into this November contract had it been aware of Jelco's intention to reserve its rights under the earlier contract. In this regard it urges that Jelco fully appreciated Stanspec's position at the time. Jelco, on the other hand, maintains that the November 10th agreement was not the solution to the dispute, but on the contrary, maintains that it entered the contract with Stanspec only to facilitate prompt and equitable mitigation of its damages under the initial contract. Jelco further urges that Stanspec was expressly bound under the original contract to furnish equipment in conformity with existing specifications.

The trial court found that the November 10th contract represented an agreed compromise of the dispute, and was binding on the parties. Thus no rights remained under the first contract. The court further found as a matter of law that an out-of-state supplier of equipment and materials has no duty to inquire into changes in or addenda to the specifications furnished by a bidding subcontractor.

An agreement which compromises a bona fide dispute as to the duties under an existing contract is of course enforceable and binding if the dispute as to those duties and obligations is not founded on bad faith. [Emphasis added.] The law actively encourages compromise and settlement of disputes.

A damaged party entitled to the benefit of a contract is under a duty to mitigate his damages, and generally speaking his rights are not diminished if the circumstances force him to deal with the party in default. However, Jelco maintains that because it had no real choice in this regard, and because of its obligation to mitigate damages, its acceptance of the terms of the second contract cannot be construed as a waiver of its rights under the earlier contract.

JUDGMENT
AND REMEDY

The trial court ruling was affirmed. Jelco was held liable for the amount of the contract price it tried to withhold from Stanspec. Jelco was bound by the November contract and could not try to argue that the prior contract was still in force. The agreed compromise extinguished the prior contract.

Discharge by Accord and Satisfaction

For a contract to be discharged by accord and satisfaction, one or both of the parties must agree to accept performance different from the performance originally promised. An *accord* is defined as an executory contract (that is, one that has not yet been performed) to perform some act in satisfaction of an existing contractual duty.[12] A *satisfaction* is the performance of the accord agreement. An **accord and** its **satisfaction** (performance) discharge the original contractual obligation. However, an accord is not binding until the satisfaction is made. Thus, either party can revoke an accord before payment or performance has been made.

An accord can also be used to settle disputed debts. Suppose, for example, that Andrew Matthews obtains a judgment against Elizabeth

Brown for $3,000. Both parties agree that the judgment can be satisfied if Brown pays $2,000 in cash and transfers her automobile to Matthews in lieu of the $1,000 balance. Brown pays $2,000 in cash and then offers the car to Matthews, but he refuses it. The subsequent agreement for $2,000 in cash and the transfer of the automobile is the accord. However, the satisfaction does not occur, and the debt is not discharged until it is completed by both parties. As long as any part of the accord and satisfaction remains to be performed, it does not constitute payment of the debt.

Accord and satisfaction occur when the parties to a contract agree that a substitute performance will be rendered in satisfaction of the original obligation, and the substituted performance is accepted. A disputed amount and the consent to accept less must be involved before there can be an accord and satisfaction.

---

12.   Restatement, Contracts, Section 417.

WIDMER v. GIBBLE OIL
COMPANY
Supreme Court of Arkansas,
1967.
243 Ark. 735, 421 S.W.2d 886.

BACKGROUND AND FACTS   *The creditor, Gibble Oil Company, brought the following action against Carl Widmer, the defendant and debtor. Gibble attempted to collect the $67.80 due on Widmer's credit card account. Widmer sent a check to Gibble Oil Company for $9.01 and marked on the check "full payment of all accounts to date." Because Gibble cashed the check, Widmer contended that Gibble had accepted the $9.01 check in full payment of his bill.*

HARRIS, Chief Justice.
* * *

Gibble Oil Company instituted a suit on November 23, 1966, asking judgment for $67.80, plus costs and interest, from the appellant. On November 30, 1966, Widmer sent his check to appellee in the amount of $9.01, the check being marked, "Full payment of all accounts to date." Gibble then cashed the check. This is the only factual difference between this case and Widmer v. Price Oil Company, for in that case, the check sent in a less amount (than that owed) was not cashed. This fact, however, is immaterial. As pointed out in *Price*, there must be a disputed amount involved, and a consent to accept less than that amount in settlement of the whole before there can be an accord and satisfaction.
* * *

This holding is in accord with 6 Corbin on Contracts, Section 1277, Page 123, where it is said:

"It is not enough for the debtor merely to write on a voucher or on his check such words as 'in full payment' or 'to balance account,' where there has been no such dispute or antecedent discussion as to give reasonable notice to the creditor that the check is being tendered as full satisfaction."

In addition, we have held that a dispute or controversy about the amount of an account must be made in good faith, i. e., there must be a *bona fide* dispute. In [a similar case this court said]:

" 'While it is not necessary that the dispute or controversy should be well founded, it is necessary that it should be made in good faith.' "

As stated in *Price*, there is no evidence that Widmer denies that he actually owed the full amount demanded. In fact, it is stipulated that "as of November 23, 1966, the defendant Carl Widmer owed the amount of $67.80 to the Gibble Oil Company as a result of credit card purchases made by said defendant from the plaintiff." Further, that "prior to November 30, 1966 [the date of the sending of the check], no communication was exchanged between plaintiff, Gibble Oil Company, and defendant, Carl Widmer, in regard to the correctness or validity of said account."

The trial court judgment was affirmed. The $9.01 check was not deemed "accord and satisfaction" of Widmer's debt to Gibble Oil Company.   **JUDGMENT AND REMEDY**

DISCHARGE BY OPERATION OF LAW

Alteration of the Contract

In order to discourage parties from altering written contracts, the law operates to discharge an innocent party when the other party has materially altered a written contract without consent. For example, contract terms such as quantity or price might be changed without the knowledge or consent of all parties. If so, the party who was unaware of the change can treat the contract as discharged or terminated.[13]

Statute of Limitations

Statutes of limitations limit the period of time during which a party can sue on a particular

cause of action. A cause of action is a cause or reason for suing or bringing an action. After the applicable limitations period has passed, suit can no longer be brought in a court of law or equity. For example, the limitations period for oral contracts is usually two to three years; for written contracts, four to five years; for recovery of judgments, ten to twenty years. Technically, the running of a statute of limitations bars access only to *judicial* remedies; it does not extinguish the debt or the underlying obligation. The statute precludes access to the courts for collection. But if the party who owes the debt or obligation agrees to perform (that is, makes a new promise to perform) the cause of action barred by the statute of limitations will be revived. For example, suppose Burlington Northern Railroad contracts for sixty-three new miles of track to be laid between Dalhart and Amarillo, Texas. Martin Marietta Corp. supplies four tons of cast iron railway for the project and is paid $22,000 of the $30,000 purchase price. Texas's statute of limitations for collection of this debt is five years, and Martin

---

13. The innocent party can also treat the contract as in effect, either on the original terms or on the terms as altered. A buyer who discovers that a seller altered the quantity of goods in a sales contract from 100 to 1,000 by secretly inserting a zero can purchase either 100 or 1,000 of the items.

Marietta Corp. fails to collect the debt or sue for collection during that five-year period. Therefore, Martin Marietta Corp. can no longer sue. It is barred by the statute of limitations. But if Burlington Northern Railroad agrees, in writing, to pay the remaining $8,000, or if it actually pays part of the $8,000, Marietta Corp. can again sue to collect the debt. The statute of limitations is no longer a bar, and the cause of action for recovery of the debt is revived. (The Statute of Frauds in some states requires a writing here.)

Bankruptcy

Bankruptcy will ordinarily bar enforcement of a debtor's contract. (Bankruptcy is fully discussed in Chapter 32.) It can be entered into voluntarily or involuntarily. The essence of bankruptcy is that the debtor owes more than he or she owns, or is unable to pay debts as they come due. A proceeding in bankruptcy attempts to allocate the assets the debtor owns at bankruptcy to the creditors in a fair and equitable fashion. Once the assets are allocated, the bankrupt receives a **discharge in bankruptcy.** The discharge is not really a discharge of the debt but operates like a statute of limitations in barring a suit for collection of the debt. As with statutes of limitations, the debts of a bankrupt can be revived by a new promise to pay (that must be in writing). Partial payment of a debt barred by bankruptcy will not revive the entire debt (unlike partial payment of a debt barred by a statute of limitations).

DISCHARGE BY BREACH OF CONTRACT

Duties of the non-breaching party can be discharged by material breach of contract or by anticipatory repudiation of the contract by the other party.

Material Breach of Contract

A **breach of contract** is the nonperformance of a contractual duty. When the breach is *material,* the nonbreaching party is excused from the performance of contractual duties and has a cause of action to sue for damages caused by the breach. If the breach is *minor* (not material), the nonbreaching party's duty to perform can

sometimes be suspended until the breach is remedied but is not entirely excused. Once the minor breach is cured, the nonbreaching party must then resume performance of the contractual obligations undertaken. Any breach entitles the nonbreaching party to sue for damages, but only a material breach discharges the nonbreaching party from the contract. The policy underlying these rules allows contracts to go forward when only minor problems occur but terminates them if major problems occur.

Suppose Raytheon Corp. contracts with the United States government to build an all-weather tactical strike force system and to test equipment for the Hawk missile system. Raytheon is to complete the project in two years and has certain schedules to meet for each stage of the production. Every six months Raytheon is to receive $3.8 million of the total $15.2 million contract price. If Raytheon is four months late in completing the first stage of production, the government will be entitled to treat the contract as discharged. Taking ten months to complete a stage that was scheduled for six months is a material breach of contract. In addition, the government can sue Raytheon for breach of contract and recover damages caused by the four-month delay. If, on the other hand, Raytheon is two days late in completing the first stage, the government will not be entitled to treat the contract as discharged. Two days is only a minor breach. However, the government can sue Raytheon for damages caused by the minor delay.

A nonbreaching party need not treat a material breach as a discharge of the contract. Instead, the party can treat the contract as being in effect and sue for damages caused by the material breach. In the above example, if Raytheon delays four months on the first stage, the government can treat the contract as still being in effect and simply sue for damages caused by the delay.

Anticipatory Breach (Anticipatory Repudiation)

Before either party to a contract has performed, one of the parties may refuse to perform the contractual obligations. This is called **anticipatory breach,** or **repudiation.** For example, De La Tour made a contract with Hochester in March to employ Hochester as a courier for three months—June, July, and August. On April 1, De La Tour told Hochester, "I am going abroad this summer and will not need a courier." This is an anticipatory breach of the employment contract. Since De La Tour repudiated the contract, Hochester could treat the act as a present, material breach.[14] Furthermore, he could sue to recover damages *immediately,* without having to wait until June 1 to sue.[15]

There are two reasons for treating an anticipatory breach as a present, material breach:

1. The nonbreaching party should not be required to remain ready and willing to perform when the other party has already repudiated the contract.

2. The nonbreaching party should have the opportunity to seek a similar contract elsewhere.

Hochester should not be required to remain ready to serve as De La Tour's courier until June 1 since that would be a waste of time. In the meantime, Hochester could be working elsewhere.

_____

14. Restatement, Contracts, Section 318, and UCC Sec. 2-610.

15. The doctrine of anticipatory breach first arose in the landmark case of Hochester v. De La Tour, 2 Ellis and Blackburn Reports 678 (1853) when the English court recognized the delay and expense inherent in a rule requiring a nonbreaching party to wait until the time for performance to sue on an anticipatory breach.

BACKGROUND AND FACTS   *Often, cases of anticipatory breach, or repudiation, arise when a sharp fluctuation in market prices make a contract price either very favorable to the buyer or very favorable to the seller. In the case that follows, the market price of "white oak bourbon staves" rose sharply, and the sales contract called for a fixed price for the staves. As the market price rose, the seller tried to improve his position by informing the buyer that he would not deliver the staves under the agreement unless the buyer agreed to pay whatever the market price was when the deliveries were made. The trial court found the seller liable for breach by anticipatory repudiation, but the buyer appealed the trial courts judgment with regard to damages.*

RELIANCE COOPERAGE CORP. v. **TREAT**

United States Court of Appeals, Eight Circuit, 1952.
195 F.2d 977.

SANBORN, Circuit Judge.

* * *

The parties to this action entered into a contract which, so far as pertinent, reads as follows:

"This Agreement entered into in St. Louis, Missouri this 12th day of July, 1950 by and between Reliance Cooperage Corporation, an Illinois corporation, Party of the First Part, and A. R. Treat, of Marshall, Arkansas, Party of the Second Part; Witnesseth:

"Party of the First Part hereby agrees to purchase and Party of the Second Part hereby agrees to sell a quantity of staves sufficient to aggregate three hundred thousand (300,000) white oak bourbon staves of four and one-half average width, to be produced by, or purchased by, Second Party in Arkansas, Missouri, or

Oklahoma, upon the following terms and conditions:

"1. Said staves when shipped shall be not less than 90% bourbon grade. Production shall commence as soon as possible and shall be completed not later than December 31, 1950. First Party agrees that on each final inspection, not more than 3% of the bourbon staves shall be less than two inches in width and none shall be less than one and one-half inches in width. The price to be paid Second Party by First Party shall be $450.00 per thousand for said bourbon grade staves of four and one-half inch average width, and $40.00 per thousand for oil grade staves of four and one-half inch average width, all f.o.b. freight cars nearest millsite where staves were produced, * * *.

* * *

"4. This agreement shall be governed by the laws of the State of Missouri."

Treat [the defendant] produced and delivered no staves to the Reliance Cooperage Corporation. After the time for performance specified in the contract had expired, the Corporation brought this action against Treat to recover the difference between the contract price of the staves and their market price at the time delivery was due under the contract. This difference was alleged to be $90,000. Treat, the defendant, admitted having entered into the contract, but denied that his nonperformance had caused the plaintiff any damage.

* * *

The evidence indicated that there had been, between the date of the contract and the date when performance was due, a rise in the market price of staves.

* * *

It was admitted that the defendant had on August 12, 1950, sent to Ralph Ettlinger, an officer of the plaintiff, the following letter:

"Marshall, Arkansas
August 12, 1950

"Dear Mr. Ralph Ettlinger:

"I have been trying to get a letter to you for some time but they return to me. I went to Harrison yesterday and got Tom Burns Co. adress [sic] trying to get in touch with you. We got a mill at Hallaster, Mo. trying to get started. Have a few Bolts will have a time getting any more. I can't make these staves up there or any where else at the price I haft to pay for Bolts. Every one else are paying $475.00 to $500.00 per M. You see I can't compete with them so if you want those staves I will haft to get around what ever the market is from time to time. You can see your seff that I can get bolts say 70¢ a price when others paying $100.00 per foot. I think the boys can make a lot of staves fast up there if they can pay as much as others are paying if not they will haft to quit. Now you can see where I am at. The other to co. that I am making for with my other 3 mills have raised from $75.00 to $100.00 on the 1000 4½" staves and said they would cancel out as the market raises. So you do just what you want to. I can't make them unless I can buy the timber so let me hear at once. I will have a car before long.

"Yours as ever,
A. R. Treat."

* * *

The following letter written by the plaintiff to the defendant, which he admitted having received, was introduced in evidence:

"October 6, 1950

"Mr. A. R. Treat
Marshall, Arkansas.
Dear Mr. Treat:

"Last week you advised our Mr. Ralph Ettlinger that you would not deliver staves under our agreement with you dated July 12, 1950, until he came down to Marshall and talked to you about revising the price at which the staves are to be sold to us.

"Under date of August 14, 1950, we wrote you requesting that you reconsider your decision, stated in your letter of August 12, 1950, not to deliver staves under our agreement unless we would pay 'whatever the market is from time to time.' We have not had a formal reply to our letter of August 14, 1950, and the substance of your phone conversation with Mr. Ralph Ettlinger certainly does not permit us to feel confident that you will perform in accordance with your agreement.

"We want to make it very clear to you at this point that we are looking forward to your strict compliance with all of the obligations which you have undertaken in your agreement with us. Over two months have elapsed since we met in St. Louis and worked out the terms of our present contract and to this date you have not advised us that you have produced a single stave for delivery to us under this agreement.

"Information reaching us discloses that you are cutting staves in several different locations. There is, therefore, no reason at all why you cannot deliver to us the staves contracted for in accordance with the terms of our agreement. Please let us hear from you at once on the matter of our agreement or we shall be obliged to take some action to protect our rights in the matter.

"Very truly yours,
"Reliance Cooperage Corp.,
By Adolf Loeb.

"AL:vg"
* * *

In [a prior case], this Court said: "The general doctrine of anticipatory breach by repudiation has, however, been clearly recognized in that state [Missouri]." The leading case on the general subject adopted the views which are expressed in part as follows: "The man who wrongfully renounces a contract into which he has deliberately entered cannot justly complain if he is *immediately* sued for a compensation in damages by the man whom he has injured [emphasis added]; and it seems reasonable to allow an option to the injured party, either to sue immediately, or to wait till the time when the act was to be done, still holding it as prospectively binding for the exercise of this option, which may be advantageous to the innocent party, and cannot be prejudicial to the wrongdoer."
* * *

" * * * The law is that, where the promisor before the time of performance expressly renounces his contract, the promisee is thereby entitled either to treat the contract as broken and sue at once for its breach without averring an offer or readiness to perform, or he may wait until the time of performance has expired, and then sue for the consequences of nonperformance."

[W]hile as a general rule an action upon an executory contract [one that has still not been performed] cannot be maintained until the time for performance has expired, the repudiation of the contract by one of the parties before that time gives to the other party the option to treat the contract as ended and to sue for the damages resulting from the anticipatory breach. In other words, unless the injured party chooses to treat the contract as breached by the anticipatory repudiation, his claim for damages does not accrue until the expiration of the time for performance.

There is no doubt that a party to an executory contract such as that in suit may refuse to accede to an anticipatory repudiation of it and insist upon performance, and, if he does so, the contract remains in existence and is binding on both parties, and no actionable claim [cause of action] for damages arises until the time for performance expires.

It is our opinion that, under the undisputed facts in this case, the unaccepted anticipatory renunciation by the defendant of his obligation to produce and deliver staves under the contract did not impair that obligation or affect his liability for damages for the nonperformance of the contract, and that the measure of those damages was no different than it would have been had no notice of renunciation been given by the defendant to the plaintiff. If there had been no anticipatory repudiation of the contract, the measure of damages for nonperformance by the seller would have been the difference between the contract price and the market price of the staves on the date when delivery was due, and that is the measure which should have been applied in assessing damages in this case.

Moreover, the measure of damages would have been the same had the plaintiff accepted the anticipatory repudiation as an actionable breach of the contract. The plaintiff would still have been entitled to recover what it had lost by reason of the defendant's failure to produce and deliver by December 31, 1950, the staves contracted for, namely, the difference between the market price and the contract price of the staves on that date. The Comment in Restatement of the Law of Contracts, § 338, Measure of Damages for Anticipatory Breach, contains the following statement (page 549): "The fact that an anticipatory repudiation is a breach of contract (see § 318) does not cause the repudiated promise to be treated as if it were a promise to render performance at the date of the repudiation. Repudiation does not accelerate the time fixed for performance; nor does it change the damages to be awarded as the equivalent of the promised performance."

* * *

The doctrine of anticipatory breach by repudiation is intended to aid a party injured as a result of the other party's refusal to perform his contractual obligations, by giving to the injured party an election to accept or to reject the refusal of performance without impairing his rights or increasing his burdens. Any effort to convert the doctrine into one for the benefit of the party who, without legal excuse, has renounced his agreement should be resisted.

* * *

The plaintiff is entitled to recover as damages the amount by which on December 31, 1950, the market price of the staves contracted for exceeded their contract price. What the market price of such staves was on that date is a question of fact [to be determined at the new trial].

A new trial, in which the market price of wooden staves on the date in question was to be established, was ordered. The difference between that market price and the contracted for market price times the number of staves in question would determine the actual damages to be awarded the plaintiff, Reliance Cooperage Corp.

JUDGMENT AND REMEDY

DISCHARGE BY IMPOSSIBILITY OF PERFORMANCE

After a contract has been made, performance may become impossible. One of the parties may die, the subject matter of the contract may be destroyed, or a change in law may make performance illegal. This is known as *impossibility of performance* and may discharge the contract.[16] It is necessary to distinguish between impossibility and a mistake. A mistake occurs if the contract was always impossible to perform. Impossibility occurs if the contract was possible to perform when it was formed but became impossible to perform *at some later time.*

Normally, a duty to perform will be discharged when a change in circumstances makes performance impossible, impractical, or unreasonably expensive, provided the risk of loss due to impossibility has not already been allocated: (1) expressly by the contract, (2) by custom, or (3) due to one party's negligence. Thus, subject to these qualifications, impossibility where *no one* can possibly perform the contractual duties will discharge the contract. Impossibility where someone can perform the contractual duties, but where the party who has promised to perform the duties cannot, will not normally discharge a contract. Examples of the latter type of impossibility include contracts to deliver goods that cannot be delivered on time due to freight car shortages[17] or contracts to pay money where the party cannot pay because the bank has closed.[18] In effect the party is saying "It is impossible for *me* to perform," not "It is impossible for *anyone* to perform." Accord-

ingly, such excuses will not discharge the contract, and the nonperforming party will normally be held in breach of contract.

Three types of cases generally qualify as impossibility and discharge the contract: (1) where one of the parties to a personal service contract dies;[19] (2) where the subject matter of a contract is destroyed;[20] and (3) where a change in law makes performance illegal.[21] Here it is impossible for anyone to perform, and the contract is therefore discharged. Examples of the first type include contracts to paint portraits where the painter dies or contracts to perform in Broadway plays where the actor or actress dies. Examples of the second type include a contract to lease a building where the building is destroyed by fire or a contract to sell oil from a particular well where the well goes dry. Examples of the third type include a contract to loan money at 15 percent where the usury rate is changed to make loans in excess of 12 percent illegal or a contract to build an apartment building where the zoning laws are changed to prohibit the construction of residential rental property.

In the following case, the defendant invoked the doctrine of impossibility even though the contract specified that it was not cancellable.

16. Restatement, Contracts, Section 457.
17. Minneapolis v. Republic Creosoting Co., 161 Minn. 178, 201 N.W. 414 (1924).
18. Ingham Lumber Co. v. Ingersoll & Co., 93 Ark. 447, 125 S.W. 139 (1910).
19. Restatement, Contracts, Section 459.
20. Restatement, Contracts, Section 460.
21. Restatement, Contracts, Section 458.

BACKGROUND AND FACTS *In November 1959, the plaintiff, Parker, went to the Arthur Murray Dance Studio to redeem a certificate entitling him to three free dance lessons. At the time, Parker was a thirty-seven-year-old college-educated bachelor who lived alone in a one-room attic apartment. During the free lessons, the instructor told Parker that*

PARKER v. ARTHUR MURRAY, INC.

Appellate Court of Illinois, Second Division, First District, 1973. 10 Ill.App.3d 1000, 295 N.E.2d 487.

he had exceptional potential to become an accomplished dancer and generally encouraged him to take more lessons. Parker signed a contract for seventy-five hours of lessons at a cost of $1,000. At the bottom of the contract, "NON-CANCELLABLE NEGOTIABLE CONTRACT" was printed in boldface type.

Parker attended lessons regularly. He was praised and encouraged by the instructors despite his lack of progress. Contract extensions and new contracts for additional instructional hours were executed. Each contract and each extension contained the same boldface words: "NON-CANCELLABLE CONTRACT." Some of the agreements contained the statement, "I UNDERSTAND THAT NO REFUNDS WILL BE MADE UNDER THE TERMS OF THIS CONTRACT," also in boldface.

On September 24, 1961, Parker was seriously injured in an automobile collision. The accident rendered him incapable of continuing his dance lessons. By that time, he had contracted for a total of 2,734 hours of lessons for which he had paid $24,812.80. Despite repeated written demand, the defendants, the Arthur Murray Dance Studio, refused to return any of Parker's money. This lawsuit ensued.

STAMOS, Presiding Justice.
* * *

The sole issue raised by defendants is whether the terms of the contracts barred plaintiff from asserting the doctrine of impossibility of performance as the basis for seeking recision.
* * *

Plaintiff was granted recision [by the trial court] on the ground of impossibility of performance. The applicable legal doctrine is expressed in the Restatement of Contracts, § 459, as follows:

A duty that requires for its performance action that can be rendered only by the promisor or some other particular person is discharged by his death or by such illness as makes the necessary action by him impossible or seriously injurious to his health, unless the contract indicates a contrary intention or there is contributing fault on the part of the person subject to the duty.

Similarly, § 460 of the Restatement states:

(1) Where the existence of a specific thing or person is, either by the terms of a bargain or in the contemplation of both parties, necessary for the performance of a promise in the bargain, a duty to perform the promise . . . (b) is discharged if the thing or person subsequently is not in existence in time for seasonable performance, unless a contrary intention is manifested, or the contributing fault of the promisor causes the nonexistence.

In Illinois impossibility of performance was recognized as a ground for recision in Davies v. Arthur Murray, Inc., 124 Ill.App.2d 141, 260 N.E.2d 240, wherein the court nonetheless found for the defendant because of the plaintiff's failure adequately to prove the existence of an incapacitating disability.
* * *

Defendants do not deny that the doctrine of impossibility of performance is generally applicable to the case at bar. Rather they assert that certain contract provisions bring this case within the Restatement's limitation that the doctrine is inapplicable if "the contract indicates a contrary intention." It is contended that such bold type phrases as "NON-CANCELLABLE CONTRACT," "NON-CANCELLABLE NEGOTIABLE CONTRACT" and "I UNDERSTAND THAT NO REFUNDS WILL BE MADE UNDER THE TERMS OF THIS CONTRACT" manifested the parties mutual intent to waive their respective rights to invoke the doctrine of impossibility. This is a construction which we find unacceptable. Courts engage in the construction and interpretation of contracts with the sole aim of determining the intention of the parties. We need rely on no construction aids to conclude that plaintiff never contemplated that by signing a contract with such terms as "NON-CANCELLABLE" and "NO REFUNDS" he was waiving a remedy expressly recognized by Illinois courts. Were we also to refer to established tenets of contractual construction, this conclusion would be equally compelled. An ambiguous contract will be construed most strongly against the party who drafted it. Exceptions or reservations in a contract will, in case of doubt or ambiguity, be construed least favorably to the party claiming the benefit of the exceptions or reservations. Although neither party to a contract should be relieved from performance on the ground that good business judgment was lacking, a court will not place upon language a ridiculous construction. We conclude that plaintiff did not waive his right to assert the doctrine of impossibility.

Defendants have also contended, albeit indirectly, that plaintiff failed to establish the existence of an incapacitating disability. In contrast to Davies v. Arthur Murray, Inc., *supra*, wherein the plaintiff relied solely upon his own uncorroborated testimony, plaintiff in the case at bar produced both lay witnesses and expert medical testimony corroborating the severity and permanency of his injuries. That testimony need not be recited; suffice it to say that overwhelming evidence supported plaintiff's contention that he was incapable of continuing his lessons.

The trial court ruling that impossibility of performance was grounds for recision was upheld. Parker was entitled to recover the prepaid sums of money representing unused lessons.

JUDGMENT AND REMEDY

A closely allied theory is the doctrine of frustration of purpose. In principle, a contract will be discharged if supervening circumstances make it impossible to attain the purpose both parties had in mind when making the contract. The origins of the doctrine lie in the old English "coronation cases." A coronation procession was planned for Edward VII when he became king of England following the death of his mother, Queen Victoria. Hotel rooms along the coronation route were rented at exhorbitant prices for that day. When the king became ill and the procession was cancelled, the purpose of the room contracts was "frustrated." A flurry of lawsuits resulted. Hotel and building owners sought to enforce the room rent bills against would-be parade observers and would-be parade observers sought to be reimbursed for rental monies paid in advance on the rooms. It was from this situation that the court developed its theory of recovery known as frustration of purpose.

COMMENTS

Temporary Impossibility

An occurrence or event that makes it temporarily impossible to perform the act for which a party has contracted will operate to suspend performance until the impossibility ceases. Then, ordinarily, the parties must perform the contract as originally planned. However, if the lapse of time and the change in circumstances surrounding the contract make it substantially more burdensome to perform the promised acts, the parties will be discharged. The leading case on this subject, Autry v. Republic Productions,[22] involved an actor who was drafted into the army in 1942. Being drafted rendered his contract temporarily impossible to perform, and it was suspended until the end of the war. When the actor got out of the army, the value of the dollar had so changed that performance of the contract would have been substantially burdensome for him. Therefore, the contract was discharged.

Commercial Impracticability

There is a growing trend of allowing parties to discharge contracts in which the performance that was originally contemplated turns out to be extremely different or more expensive than anticipated. This is known as the doctrine of commercial impracticability.[23]

In order to invoke this doctrine, the anticipated performance must become extremely difficult or costly. In a leading case, the California Supreme Court held that a contract was discharged because it would cost ten times more than the original estimate to excavate a certain amount of gravel.[24] In another case, commercial impracticability was not found where a carrier of goods was to deliver wheat from the West Coast of the United States to a safe port in Iran.[25] The Suez Canal, the usual route, was nationalized by Egypt and closed, forcing the carrier to travel around Africa and the Cape of Good Hope, through the Mediterranean and on to Iran. The added expense was approximately $42,000 above and beyond the contract price of $306,000, and the original journey of 10,000 miles was extended by an additional 3,000 miles. Nevertheless, the court held that the contract was not commercially impracticable to perform. Therefore, caution should be used when attempting to invoke commercial impracticability. The added burden of performing must be extreme—about ten times the original cost.

---

22. 30 Cal.2d 144, 180 P.2d 888 (1947).
23. Restatement, Contracts, Section 454.
24. Mineral Park Land Co. v. Howard, 172 Cal. 289, 156 P. 458 (1916).
25. Transatlantic Financing Corp. v. United States, 363 F.2d 312 (D.C. Cir. 1966).

QUESTIONS AND CASE PROBLEMS

1. Miller, a general contractor, contracted with Village Apartments, Inc., to build a number of apartments. Miller hired a subcontractor, Mascioni, to construct certain walls and agreed to pay him $.55 per cubic foot for the walls. The contract between Miller and Mascioni contained the following clause: "Payments to be made as received from the owner." In compliance with his contract with Miller, Mascioni completed construction of the walls. However, the owner never paid Miller, and Miller therefore refused to pay Mascioni. Mascioni sued Miller. What judgment? [Mascioni v. I. B. Miller, Inc., 261 N.Y. 1, 184 N.E. 473 (1933)]

2. Beck Lithographing Company agreed in a contract with Colorado Milling Company to furnish 10,000 business cards and 5,000 checks, letterheads, noteheads, billheads, and envelopes bearing Colorado Milling's logo. Beck was to design and deliver these items to Colorado Milling within one year of the signing of the contract. Beck failed to tender or deliver the items contracted for until six or eight days after the expiration of the year. Colorado Milling refused to accept them and refused to pay any part of the contract price. Was Colorado Milling justified in doing this? [Beck and Pauli Lithographing Company v. Colorado Milling and Elevator Company, 52 F. 700 (10th Cir. 1892)]

3. Minweld, a steel producer, agreed to furnish McCloskey with the steel he needed for a hospital he had contracted to build. The contract between McCloskey and Minweld indicated that time was of the essence. After several letters were exchanged between McCloskey and Minweld concerning Minweld's shipment schedule, Minweld finally wrote to McCloskey explaining that it would have difficulty obtaining steel because of the war in Korea. Minweld also suggested to McCloskey that since the hospital was a state hospital, the state should attempt to use its influence to help Minweld obtain steel to fulfill its obligation under the contract. McCloskey felt that Minweld's letter to it constituted an anticipatory repudiation. Do you agree? [McCloskey and Company v. Minweld Steel Company, 220 F.2d 101 (3d Cir. 1955)]

4. Prince had been employed as a salesman by Sportswear, Inc., for over twenty-two years. Each year Prince and Sportswear entered into a one-year contract that described the way Prince would receive commissions for his sales. The last contract was dated January 2, 1962. Under it, Prince was allowed to employ persons to assist him, provided that their work was "consistent with the achievement of the result contracted for." Thus, Prince's obligation, if he hired an assistant, was in a supervisory capacity. At the beginning of the year, Prince hired Nadler as his sales assistant. Prince died on August 22, 1962. A dispute later arose over whether Prince's estate should receive the commissions on sales obtained prior to Prince's death and commissions on orders obtained by Nadler after Prince's death. What judgment? [Kowal v. Sportswear by Revere, Inc., 351 Mass. 541, 222 N.E.2d 778 (1967)]

5. Jones hired Haverty to install a plumbing and heating system in a building that Jones was constructing. Jones made a number of payments to Haverty during the period of construction, but when construction was completed, he still owed Haverty about $10,000. Jones refused to pay because Haverty had not completed his work according to the contract. Specifically, Haverty had used a number of inferior quality plumbing couplings and had substituted cheaper three-quarter-inch pipe for one-inch pipe in a few places. The damage to the building as a result of these and other deviations from the contract by Haverty amounted to about $2,000. Should Jones pay Haverty $8,000 or nothing at all? [Thomas Haverty Company v. Jones, 185 Cal. 285, 197 P. 105 (1921)]

6. Nicholson hired Howard Construction Company to build a building for use as a bridal salon. At the time, Nicholson had arranged that Honey's International would be the tenant. Once built, the building would be suitable only for a bridal salon. After Nicholson and Howard had entered into their contract but before construction had begun, Honey's International went bankrupt. Nicholson thereafter refused to pay Howard to go through with the contract since Nicholson's intended tenant was no longer in existence. Howard sues Nicholson for breach of contract. Can Howard recover? [Howard v. Nicholson, 556 S.W.2d 477 (Mo.App.1977)]

7. The city of Fort Lauderdale hired La Gasse Pool Company to renovate a swimming pool owned and operated by the city. When La Gasse was about three-quarters finished, the pool was vandalized. The damage to the pool required La Gasse to redo part of its work. Thereafter, La Gasse completed the renovation project. Who should pay for the extra work caused by the vandalism? [La Gasse Pool Construction Company v. Fort Lauderdale, 288 So.2d 273 (Fla. App.1974)]

8. Persinger engaged Kichler to do certain interior decorating for Persinger's bedroom. Kichler was given the appropriate measurements for making a bedspread and was required to match this bedspread with valances and shades, which he was also supposed to supply. When Kichler delivered the bedspread, shade, and valances, several problems arose. First, the bedspread was two inches short. To remedy this, Kichler added a ruffle around the edge. In addition, the shades and valances did not match the bedspread. Persinger rejected Kichler's performance and demanded her money back. Kichler refused, claiming that he had substantially performed the contract. What result? [Kichler's Inc. v. Persinger, 24 Ohio App.2d 124, 53 O.O.2d 337, 265 N.E.2d 319 (1970)]

9. Peregoy owed Domestic Loan, Inc. a little over $500 on a promissory note. Peregoy refused to pay, and Domestic Loan brought an action and obtained a judgment for $509. Shortly thereafter, Peregoy voluntarily went into bankruptcy, and his obligation to Domestic Loan for $509 was extinguished. After Peregoy went bankrupt, the two parties entered into a revivor agreement in which Peregoy acknowledged the previous debt of $509 and agreed to pay $250. Peregoy failed and refused to pay Domestic Loan any money at all. What does Peregoy owe Domestic Loan—$509, $250, or nothing at all? [Domestic Loan, Inc. v. Peregoy, 116 Ohio App. 381, 22 O.O.2d 208, 184 N.E.2d 457 (1962)]

10. On June 10, 1927, Scoville sold certain shares of

stock to Brooks. At the time of the sale, Scoville promised to repurchase the stock from Brooks at Brooks's request at any time within one year from the date of the purchase by Brooks. On November 1, Brooks notified Scoville that he wanted Scoville to repurchase the stock according to the terms of the agreement of June 10. On several occasions after November 1, Brooks again demanded that Scoville repurchase the stock. Each time Scoville agreed to repurchase the stock but failed to carry out his promise. Brooks claimed that each time he contacted Scoville, he was "ready and willing" to deliver the stock to Scoville. Brooks never made a *formal* tender of the stock. Is Scoville in breach of contract? [Brooks v. Scoville, 81 Utah 163, 17 P.2d 218 (1932)]

14

Contracts
Breach of Contract and Remedies

Whenever a party fails to perform part or all of the duties under a contract, that party is in *breach of contract*. Breach of contract is the failure to perform what a party is under an absolute duty to perform.[1] Once a party fails to perform or performs inadequately, the other party—the nonbreaching party—can choose one or more of several remedies. A *remedy* is the relief provided for an innocent party when the other party has breached the contract. It is the means employed to enforce a right or redress an injury. Strictly speaking, "remedy" is not a part of a lawsuit but the result thereof, the object for which the lawsuit is presented and the end to which all litigation is directed. The most common remedies available to a nonbreaching party include: (1) damages, (2) rescission and restitution, (3) specific performance, and (4) reformation.

DAMAGES

A breach of any contract entitles the nonbreaching party to sue for money damages. *Damages* are designed to compensate the nonbreaching party for the loss of the bargain. When a party loses the benefit of the bargain or contract, the breaching party must make up this loss to the nonbreaching party. Often, courts say that innocent parties are to be placed in the position they would have occupied had the contract been fully per-

---

1. Restatement, Contracts, Section 312.

formed. The nonbreaching party is entitled to the benefit of the bargain.[2]

Types of Damages

There are numerous types of damages. This chapter will discuss (1) compensatory, (2) consequential, (3) punitive, and (4) nominal damages.

COMPENSATORY DAMAGES Damages compensating the nonbreaching party for the loss of the bargain are known as **compensatory damages.** These damages compensate the injured party only for the injuries sustained. They simply make good or replace the loss caused by the wrong or injury. In a breach of contract, compensatory damages are usually the only damages recoverable. When a breach of contract places the innocent party in a *better* position, the party is not entitled to anything other than **nominal damages**—a trivial amount for the technical breach of the contract. For example, suppose that Jackson contracts to buy potatoes from Stanley at fifty cents a pound. Stanley breaches the contract and does not deliver the potatoes. If Jackson then buys the potatoes on the open market at half the price, he is clearly better off because of Stanley's breach.

Sale of Goods The standard or ordinary measure of damages depends on the type of contract involved. In a contract for the sale of goods the usual measure of damages is an amount equal to the difference between the contract price and the market price.[3] Suppose Chrysler Corporation contracts to buy ten model UTS 400 computer terminals from Sperry Rand Corporation for $8,000 apiece. If Sperry Rand fails to deliver the ten terminals, and their price rises to $8,150, Chrysler's measure of damages in this case is $1,500 (10 times $150).

Sale of Land The measure of damages in a contract for the sale of land is ordinarily the same as the measure in contracts for the sale of goods—that is, the difference between the contract price and the market price of the land. The majority of states follow this rule regardless of whether it is the buyer or the seller who breaches the contract. A minority of states, however, follow a different rule when the seller breaches the contract and the breach is not deliberate.[4] In such a case, these states allow the prospective purchaser to recover any down payment plus any expenses incurred (such as fees for title searches, attorneys, and escrows). This minority rule effectively places purchasers in the position they occupied *prior* to the sale. Purchasers do not get the benefit of their bargains as they would if the measure of damages equaled the difference between the contract price and the market price.

Construction Contracts The measure of damages in a building or construction contract varies depending upon which party breaches and at what stage the breach occurs. The owner can breach at three different stages of the construction: (1) before performance begins, (2) during performance, and (3) after performance is complete. If the owner breaches before performance begins, the contractor can recover only the profits that would have been made on the contract (that is, the total contract price less the cost of materials and labor). If the owner breaches after performance begins, the contractor can recover the profits plus the costs incurred in partially constructing the building. If the owner breaches after the construction is complete, the contractor can recover the entire contract price.[5] To illustrate: Goodyear Tire & Rubber Co. wants to build an international

---

2. Restatement, Contracts, Section 329, and UCC Sec. 1-106(1).
3. At the time and place where the goods were to be delivered. See UCC Secs. 2-708 and 2-713.

4. A deliberate breach includes the vendor's failure to convey the land because the market price has gone up. A nondeliberate breach includes the vendor's failure to convey the land because an unknown easement rendered title unmarketable. See Chapter 52.
5. Actually, this is true for most contracts; the nonbreaching party is normally owed the contract profit plus the cost of performance.

research center at its industrial and film products plant in Craigavon, Northern Ireland. Goodyear makes a contract for the 54,000-square-foot center with your corporation. The contract price is $5 million, and your company plans to spend $4.3 million in materials and labor. However, before construction begins, Goodyear's president calls you and unequivocally repudiates the contract. Your measure of damages is $700,000. Alternatively, assume you begin the work, but after you spend $1.2 million, Goodyear throws your crews off the land and refuses to allow any more construction to go on. Your measure of damages is $1.9 million ($700,000 of lost profit plus $1.2 million in costs). Next assume you are able to complete the research center, but Goodyear breaches the contract by refusing to pay. Your measure of damages is $5 million (the full contract price). Note that the result is ultimately the same in each example. You are able to recover the $700,000 profit and are reimbursed for your actual costs.

When the construction contractor breaches the contract by stopping halfway through the project, the measure of damages is the cost of completion. If the builder substantially performs, the courts may use the cost of completion formula, but only if there is no substantial economic waste in requiring completion.[6] If the builder finishes late, the measure of damages

_____

6. Economic waste occurs when the cost of additional resources to finish the project exceeds any conceivable value placed on the additional work done. For example, if a contractor discovers that it will cost $10,000 to move a large coral rock eleven inches as specified in the contract, and the change in the rock's position will alter the appearance of the project only a trifle, full completion will involve an economic waste.

will be the *loss of use*. As examples, assume three situations:

1. The builder of a house quits working after the foundation is built.
2. The builder of a house completes the construction, but the paneling is one-quarter-inch thick instead of five-sixteenths-inch thick.
3. The builder completes the house one week late.

In situation 1 the measure of damages equals the cost of getting another builder to complete the house. In situation 2 the cost to complete the house includes the cost of tearing out the walls and installing the thicker paneling. This additional cost is economic waste and a needless expense (which the owner probably would not incur anyway), so the courts will usually give the owner the difference between the value of the house as it is and the value of the house if it had been completed as promised. If the house is worth $2,000 less due to the thinner paneling, that will be the amount of damages recoverable. In situation 3 the measure of damages is the cost incurred by the owner to live elsewhere for a week.

Often, the party suing for compensatory damages has failed to perform completely his or her part of the bargain. Faced with this situation in the following case, two courts arrived at the same figure for damages but used different theories. The trial court used the theory of *substantial performance*; the appellate court insisted that the proper action was *quantum meruit* (recovery of fair value). In either event, a contractor who did not live up to the requirements of his contract was not entitled to full payment of the contract price.

BACKGROUND AND FACTS *Armstead Masonry Company brought this action against Roper (and Reynolds), the defendants, to collect $267.62 in damages for nonpayment of an oral contract whereby Roper agreed to pay Armstead to do some brick veneer work on Roper's house. The record showed that the parties entered into this oral contract, and Armstead expressly promised to use new brick matching as closely as*

REYNOLDS v. ARMSTEAD

Supreme Court of Colorado, 1968.
166 Colo. 372, 443 P.2d 990.

*possible the color and appearance of the existing brick on Roper's house.
Armstead failed to use brick that conformed reasonably to Roper's
existing brick work, although Armstead's veneer work was sound in all
other respects.*

*Since work was completed, Armstead was entitled to a certain
amount of payment on the contract. However, both the trial court and
the appellate court agreed that Armstead was certainly not entitled to the
entire $535.25, the original contract price.*

MOORE, Chief Justice.

* * *

The question presented here, however, is whether as a matter of law Armstead
substantially performed his contract with Roper, and therefore became entitled to
a recovery on the contract. Our authorities judiciously decline to state a formula
determining with mathematical certainty what constitutes substantial performance, but instead rely upon the application of general principles. Thus, in Morris
v. Hokosona, supra, we stated:

" * * * substantial performance permitting a recovery on the contract means an
attempt in good faith to strictly and fully perform and is not satisfied unless there
has been only slight or inadvertent omissions or departures which have not
affected the value of the structure and which are capable of remedy and for which
the employer may be compensated by a reduction of the contract price."

"Substantial compliance with reference to contracts, means that although the
conditions of the contract have been deviated from in trifling particulars not
materially detracting from the benefit the other party would derive from a literal
performance, he has received substantially the benefit he expected, and is,
therefore, bound to pay."

* * *

This court has repeatedly held that a contractor may recover the agreed price
for substantial performance of his contract, subject to a deduction for damages for
the contractor's failure to adhere to the contract in minor details.

In the instant case the trial court, in legal effect, found that there had not been
a substantial compliance with the terms of the contract, and that to the extent of
fifty per cent of the contract price there was a failure to perform. Armstead's
failure to install brick which reasonably matched the existing veneer damaged the
appearance of Roper's house to the extent of half the value of the contract. The
parties entered into their agreement with the acknowledged intent that
Armstead's brickwork should be aesthetically, as well as functionally, acceptable.
Consequently, we hold that as a matter of law Armstead's breach was material and
cannot be deemed a "slight and trivial defect" "not materially detracting from the
benefit the other party would derive from a literal performance."

Armstead's failure to substantially perform his contract deprived him of the
right to recover under the "theory" of express contract.

* * *

Upon a "theory" of quantum meruit the plaintiff, under the evidence, was
entitled to the judgment entered by the trial court.

The trial court's judgment was affirmed. Armstead was entitled to collect **JUDGMENT**
for the work he did, but his failure to perform in compliance with the **AND REMEDY**
terms of his agreement with Roper resulted in a substantial reduction in
the amount of money he could collect from Roper.

CONSEQUENTIAL (SPECIAL) DAMAGES Damages resulting from a party's breach of contract are called *consequential damages*. They differ from compensatory damages in that they are caused by special circumstances beyond the contract itself. They flow only from the consequences or results of a breach. For example, if a seller fails to deliver goods that a buyer is planning to resell *immediately*, consequential damages will be awarded for the loss of profit from the planned resale. The buyer will also recover compensatory damages for the difference between the contract price and the market price of the goods.

In order to recover consequential damages, the breaching party must know (or have reason to know) that special circumstances will cause the nonbreaching party to suffer an additional loss. The rationale here is to give the nonbreaching party the whole benefit of the bargain, provided the breaching party knew of the special circumstances when the contract was made. For example, suppose Leed sends a vital part of her printing press to be repaired, and the part is properly repaired. Leed tells the shipper who is to return the part that she must receive it by Monday or she will not be able to print her paper and will lose $750. If the shipper is late, Leed can recover the consequential damages caused by the delay (that is, the $750 in lost profits). Likewise, when a bank wrongfully dishonors a check, and the drawer (the person writing the check) is arrested, the drawer can recover consequential damages (that is, damages from the harm to the drawer's reputation).[7] An ice company that is supposed to deliver ice to keep a butcher's meat cold can be held liable for meat spoilage if it does not deliver the ice on time.

A leading case on the necessity of giving notice of "consequential" circumstances is *Hadley v. Baxendale*, decided in 1854. The case involved a broken crankshaft used in a mill operation. In the mid-1800s, it was very common for large mills, such as the one the plaintiffs operated, to have more than one crankshaft in case the main one broke and had to be repaired, as it did in this case. Also, in those days it was common knowledge that flour mills had spares. It is against this background that the parties argued whether or not the damages resulting from lost profits while the crankshaft was out for repair were "too remote" to be recoverable.

---

7. Weaver v. Bank of America, 59 Cal.2d 428, 30 Cal.Rptr. 4, 380 P.2d 644 (1963). A checking account is a contractual arrangement.

BACKGROUND AND FACTS   *The plaintiffs ran a flour mill in Glouces-*
ter. The crankshaft attached to the steam engine broke, causing the mill
to shut down. The shaft had to be sent to a foundry located in Greenwich
so that the new shaft could be made to fit the other parts of the engine.
The defendants were common carriers, who transported the shaft from
Gloucester to Greenwich. The plaintiffs claimed that they had informed
the defendants that the mill was stopped and that the shaft must be sent
immediately. The freight charges were collected in advance, and the
defendants promised to deliver the shaft the following day. They did not
do so, however. As a consequence, the mill was closed for several days.

HADLEY v.
BAXENDALE
9 Exch. 341, 156 Eng.Rep. 145,
1854.

The plaintiffs sued to recover their lost profits during that time. The defendants contended that the loss of profits was "too remote." The court held for the plaintiffs, and the jury was allowed to take into consideration the lost profits. The Court of Exchequer ordered a new trial.

ALDERSON, B

* * *

We think that there ought to be a new trial in this case; but, in so doing, we deem it to be expedient and necessary to state explicitly the rule which the Judge, at the next trial, ought, in our opinion, to direct the jury to be governed by when they estimate the damages.

* * *

Now we think the proper rule in such a case as the present is this:—Where two parties have made a contract which one of them has broken, the damages which the other party ought to receive in respect of such breach of contract should be such as may fairly and reasonably be considered either arising naturally, i.e., according to the usual course of things, from such breach of contract itself, or such as may reasonably be supposed to have been in the contemplation of both parties, at the time they made the contract, as the probable result of the breach of it. Now, if the special circumstances under which the contract was actually made were communicated by the plaintiffs to the defendants, and thus known to both parties, the damages resulting from the breach of such a contract, which they would reasonably contemplate, would be the amount of injury which would ordinarily follow from a breach of contract under these special circumstances so known and communicated. But, on the other hand, if these special circumstances were wholly unknown to the party breaking the contract, he, at the most, could only be supposed to have had in his contemplation the amount of injury which would arise generally, and in the great multitude of cases not affected by any special circumstances, from such a breach of contract. For, had the special circumstances been known, the parties might have specially provided for the breach of contract by special terms as to the damages in that case; and of this advantage it would be very unjust to deprive them. Now the above principles are those by which we think the jury ought to be guided in estimating the damages arising out of any breach of contract.

* * *

Now, in the present case, if we are to apply the principles above laid down, we find that the only circumstances here communicated by the plaintiffs to the defendants at the time the contract was made, were, that the article to be carried was the broken shaft of a mill, and that the plaintiffs were the millers of that mill. But how do these circumstances show reasonably that the profits of the mill must be stopped by an unreasonable delay in the delivery of the broken shaft by the carrier to the third person? Suppose the plaintiffs had another shaft in their possession put up or putting up at the time, and that they only wished to send back the broken shaft to the engineer who made it; it is clear that this would be quite consistent with the above circumstances, and yet the unreasonable delay in the delivery would have no effect upon the intermediate profits of the mill. Or, again, suppose that, at the time of the delivery to the carrier, the machinery of the mill had been in other respects defective, then, also, the same results would follow. Here it is true that the shaft was actually sent back to serve as a model for a new one, and that the want of a new one was the only cause of the stoppage of the mill, and that the loss of profits really arose from not sending down the new shaft in proper time, and that this arose from the delay in delivering the broken one to serve as a model. But it is obvious that, in the great multitude of cases of millers sending off broken shafts to third persons by a carrier under ordinary circumstances, such consequences would not, in all probability, have occurred; and these special circumstances were here never communicated by the plaintiffs to the defendants. It follows, therefore, that the loss of profits here cannot reasonably be considered such a consequence of the breach of contract as could have been fairly and reasonably contemplated by both the parties when they made this contract.

JUDGMENT AND REMEDY

The Court of Exchequer ordered a new trial. According to the court, the special circumstances that caused the loss of profits had never been sufficiently communicated by the plaintiffs to the defendants. The plaintiffs would have to have given express notice of these circumstances in order to collect consequential damages.[8]

COMMENTS

In awarding damages, compensation is given only for those injuries that the defendant could reasonably have foreseen as a probable result of the usual course of events following a breach. If the injury complained of is outside the usual and foreseeable cause of events, it must be shown specifically that the defendant had reason to know the facts and foresee the injury.

In this case, the plaintiff claimed that he gave express notice to the carrier's clerk that the shaft was needed immediately because "the mill was stopped." Today this would be considered adequate notice. At the time that the case was decided, however, notice to the clerk of the common carrier was not considered to be notice to the common carrier.

---

8. See Restatement, Contracts, Section 330.

PUNITIVE DAMAGES Punitive, or exemplary, damages are generally not recoverable in a breach of contract action. *Punitive damages are designed to punish a guilty party and to make an example of the party in order to deter similar conduct in the future.* Such damages are also intended to give solace to the plaintiff from mental anguish, shame, and other aggravations of the original wrong. (These damages are also called "smart money.") Punitive damages have no real place in contract law since society does not punish a person for breaching a contract. Society compensates the other person for the loss of the bargain, no more and no less. In certain cases, however, punitive damages are available, but not on a contractual theory of recovery. Some breaches of contract are also torts (see Chapter 3) and the nonbreaching party may be able to recover compensatory and consequential damages for the breach of contract as well as punitive damages for the tort.[9]

---

9. For example, if a bus driver negligently swerves the bus so that a passenger is injured, the passenger can sue for breach of the contract for safe carriage and in tort for negligence.

NOMINAL DAMAGES When no financial loss is involved because of a breach of contract, the court may award nominal damages to the innocent party. Nominal damage awards are often trifling, but they do establish that the defendant acted wrongfully.

Mitigation of Damages

Whenever a breach of contract occurs, the injured party should take reasonable steps to mitigate the damages. In a literal sense, the nonbreaching party is under no duty to mitigate damages, but a nonbreaching party who does not mitigate damages will recover less as a remedy. For example, if goods are in the process of manufacture, and the buyer repudiates the contract, the seller must stop production. The seller can recover only for the time, effort, and resources expended up to the time of repudiation. Similarly, an employee who is discharged before the end of an employment contract must seek similar employment elsewhere. A discharged employee is under no duty to accept dissimilar employment, but if he or she does, the pay received will be deducted from damages otherwise recoverable.

Liquidated Damages and Penalties

A **liquidated damages** provision in a contract specifies a certain amount to be paid in the event of a default or breach of contract. For example, a provision requiring a construction contractor to pay $100 for every day he is late in completing the construction is a liquidated damages provision. Liquidated damages differ from penalties. **Penalties** specify a certain amount to be paid in the event of a default or breach of contract and are designed to *penalize* the breaching party. Liquidated damage provisions are enforceable; penalty provisions are not. In order to determine if a particular provision is for liquidated damages or for a penalty, two questions must be answered. First, were the damages difficult to estimate when the contract was entered into? Second, was the amount set as damages a reasonable estimate and not excessive?[10] If both answers are yes, the provision will be enforced. If either answer is no, the provision will not be enforced. In a construction contract, it is difficult to estimate the amount of damages caused by a delay in completing construction, so liquidated damage clauses are often used. On the other hand, the damage caused by failure to pay rent is easily estimated, so in leases, liquidated damage clauses are not used. As to the reasonableness of the estimate, a liquidated damage provision that requires a construction contractor to pay $500 for every day's delay when the rental value of the property is $100 per day is clearly unreasonable and excessive. But if the provision requires the construction contractor to pay $110 or $90 per day, the provision is reasonable and not excessive.[11]

The amount that a nonbreaching party can recover from a breach of contract depends upon whether the provision is held to be a liquidated damage provision or a penalty. A liquidated damage provision is enforceable, and the nonbreaching party can recover the amount specified in the provision, even if the actual damages are less than the specified amount. If the provision is determined to be a penalty, it is not enforceable (no matter what it is called in the contract). Therefore, the nonbreaching party can recover only the actual damages. Actual damages are compensatory and consequential damages, as defined above.

RESCISSION AND RESTITUTION

Rescission is essentially an action to undo, or cancel a contract—to return the contracting parties to the places they occupied prior to the transaction.[12] Where fraud, a mistake, duress, or

10.   Restatement, Contracts, Section 339.
11.   But to learn how inconsistent the courts are, see K. W. Clarkson, R. L. Miller, and T. J. Muris, "Liquidated Damages vs. Penalty: Sense or Nonsense?" *Wisconsin Law Review*, Spring 1978.
12.   The rescission discussed here refers to *unilateral* rescission where only one party wants to undo the contract. In mutual rescission, both parties agree to undo the contract. Mutual rescission discharges the contract; unilateral rescission is generally available as a remedy for breach of contract.

failure of consideration are present, rescission is available. (See Chapter 9.)[13] The failure of one party to perform entitles the other party to rescind the contract. The rescinding party must give prompt notice to the breaching party. In order to rescind a contract, both parties must make **restitution** to each other. Essentially, they must return whatever they have received under the contract. If the goods or property received can be restored *in specie*—that is, if the actual goods or property can be returned—they must be. If the goods or property have been consumed, restitution must be made in an equivalent amount of money.

SPECIFIC PERFORMANCE

The remedy of *specific performance* calls for the performance of the act promised in the contract. This remedy is quite attractive to the nonbreaching party since it provides the exact bargain promised in the contract. It also avoids some of the problems inherent in a suit for money damages. First, the nonbreaching party need not worry about collecting the judgment.[14] Second, the nonbreaching party need not look around for another contract. Third, the actual performance may be more valuable than the money damages.

Although the equitable remedy of specific performance is often preferable to other remedies, specific performance will not be granted unless the party's legal remedy (money damages) is inadequate. For example, contracts for the sale of goods rarely qualify for specific performance. The legal remedy, money damages, will ordinarily be adequate in such a situation because substantially identical goods can be bought or sold in the market. If the goods are unique, however, a court of equity will decree specific performance. For example, paintings, sculptures, or rare books are so unique that money damages will not enable a buyer to obtain substantially identical substitutes in the market.

The situation in the following case seemed to be suited for a decree of specific performance, but the court would not enforce the contract because it concluded that the agreement was an unconscionable bargain.

---

13. States often have statutes allowing consumers to rescind unilaterally contracts made at home with door-to-door salespersons. Rescission is allowed within three days for any reason or for no reason at all. See, for example, California Civil Code, Sec. 1689.5.

14. Courts enter judgments as final dispositions of cases. The judgment, of course, must be collected. Collection, however, poses problems. For example, the judgment debtor may be broke or have only a very small net worth.

BACKGROUND AND FACTS *Campbell Soup Company, the plaintiff, entered into a contract for the sale of carrots with farmers who grew and produced the particular variety of carrots used in the company's canned goods. Under the terms of the contract, a farmer was required to cut, clean, and bag the produce. When the carrots were delivered, the company determined if they conformed to company specifications. Another provision in the contract excused the company from accepting carrots under certain circumstances but retained the right to prohibit the sale of those carrots elsewhere unless the company agreed. The carrots involved in this case were Chantenay red carrots.*

Campbell Soup made a written contract with the defendant, Wentz, a Pennsylvania farmer. Wentz was to deliver all the Chantenay red carrots he grew on his fifteen-acre farm that year for $30 per ton. During the year, the market price of the carrots rose sharply to about $90 per ton, and Chantenay red carrots became virtually unobtainable. The defendant told a Campbell representative that he would not deliver his carrots at the contract price. Then, he sold the rest of his carrots to a neighboring farmer. Campbell bought about half the shipment from the neighboring

CAMPBELL SOUP CO. v. WENTZ
United States Court of Appeals, Third Circuit, 1948.
172 F.2d 80.

farmer and then realized that it was purchasing its own "contract carrots." Campbell refused to purchase any more and sought an injunction against both the defendant and the neighboring farmer to prohibit them from selling any more of the contract carrots to others. In addition, Campbell sought to compel specific performance of the contract against Wentz. The trial court denied the equitable relief requested by Campbell.

GOODRICH, Circuit Judge.

* * *

We think that on the question of adequacy of the legal remedy the case is one appropriate for specific performance. It was expressly found that at the time of the trial it was "virtually impossible to obtain Chantenay carrots in the open market." This Chantenay carrot is one which the plaintiff uses in large quantities, furnishing the seed to the growers with whom it makes contracts. It was not claimed that in nutritive value it is any better than other types of carrots. Its blunt shape makes it easier to handle in processing. And its color and texture differ from other varieties. The color is brighter than other carrots. The trial court found that the plaintiff failed to establish what proportion of its carrots is used for the production of soup stock and what proportion is used as identifiable physical ingredients in its soups. We do not think lack of proof on that point is material. It did appear that the plaintiff uses carrots in fifteen of its twenty-one soups. It also appeared that it uses these Chantenay carrots diced in some of them and that the appearance is uniform. The preservation of uniformity in appearance in a food article marketed throughout the country and sold under the manufacturer's name is a matter of considerable commercial significance and one which is properly considered in determining whether a substitute ingredient is just as good as the original.

* * *

Judged by the general standards applicable to determining the adequacy of the legal remedy we think that on this point the case is a proper one for equitable relief. There is considerable authority, old and new, showing liberality in the granting of an equitable remedy. We see no reason why a court should be reluctant to grant specific relief when it can be given without supervision of the court or other time-consuming processes against one who has deliberately broken his agreement. Here the goods of the special type contracted for were unavailable on the open market, the plaintiff had contracted for them long ahead in anticipation of its needs, and had built up a general reputation for its products as part of which reputation uniform appearance was important. We think if this were all that was involved in the case specific performance should have been granted.

* * *

The trial court denied equitable relief. We agree with the result reached, but on a different ground from that relied upon by the District Court.

* * *

The reason that we shall affirm instead of reversing with an order for specific performance is found in the contract itself. We think it is too hard a bargain and too one-sided an agreement to entitle the plaintiff to relief in a court of conscience. For each individual grower the agreement is made by filling in names and quantity and price on a printed form furnished by the buyer. This form has quite obviously been drawn by skilful [sic] draftsmen with the buyer's interests in mind.

The provision of the contract which we think is the hardest is paragraph 9 * * *. It * * * [provides] that Campbell is excused from accepting carrots under certain circumstances. But even under such circumstances the grower, while he cannot say Campbell is liable for failure to take the carrots, is not permitted to sell them elsewhere unless Campbell agrees. This is the kind of provision which the late Francis H. Bohlen would call "carrying a good joke too far." What the grower may do with his product under the circumstances set out is not clear. He has covenanted not to store it anywhere except on his own farm and also not to sell to anybody else.

We are not suggesting that the contract is illegal. Nor are we suggesting any excuse for the grower in this case who has deliberately broken an agreement entered into with Campbell. We do think, however, that a party who has offered and succeeded in getting an agreement as tough as this one is, should not come to a chancellor and ask court help in the enforcement of its terms. That equity does not enforce unconscionable bargains is too well established to require elaborate citation.

Campbell Soup Company's petition for an injunction and for specific performance was denied by both the trial court and the district court. The court recognized that, if the contract had not been unconscionable, specific performance would have been available to the company. The unique nature of the product involved meant that there was no adequate legal remedy.	**JUDGMENT AND REMEDY**

Sale of Land

Specific performance is generally granted in a contract for the sale of land. The legal remedy for breach of a land sales contract is inadequate because every piece of land is considered to be unique. Money damages will not compensate a buyer adequately because the same land cannot be obtained elsewhere.

Contracts for Personal Services

Personal service contracts require one party to work personally for another party. Courts of law and equity uniformly refuse to grant specific performance of personal service contracts. The remedy at law may be adequate if substantially identical service is available from other persons (for example, if you hire someone to mow your lawn). On the other hand, it may be inadequate if no one of the same quality is available elsewhere (say, where a specific actress is to perform). In either event, courts are very hesitant to order specific performance by a party because public policy strongly discourages involuntary

servitude.[15] Moreover, the courts do not want to have to monitor a continuing service contract.

Specific performance will be denied if it is impossible or impractical to enforce performance. Courts do not want to become entangled in complex business transactions and will not decree specific performance if supervision will be prolonged or difficult. For this reason, courts refuse to order specific performance that requires the exercise of personal judgment or talent. For example, if you contract with an eccentric artist for a portrait of your mother, and the artist refuses to paint it, a court will not compel the artist to do so. There is no way the court can assure meaningful performance. Similarly, courts refuse to order specific performance of a construction contract because they are not set up to operate as construction supervisors or engineers.

---

15. The Thirteenth Amendment to the United States Constitution prohibits involuntary servitude, but *negative* injunctions (i. e. prohibiting rather than ordering certain conduct) are possible.

REFORMATION

Reformation is an equitable remedy used when the parties have *imperfectly* expressed their agreement in writing. Reformation allows the contract to be rewritten to reflect the parties' *true* intentions. It applies most often where fraud or mutual mistake is present. If B contracts to buy a certain piece of land from C, but both parties are mistaken about what piece of land is to be sold, a mutual mistake has occurred. Accordingly, a court of equity will reform the contract so that B and C can agree on which piece of land is being sold.

Reformation is frequently utilized to make use of another remedy. For example, a contract for the sale of goods can be reformed in order for one of the parties to show that the contract has been breached. Or it can be reformed to show that one of the parties is entitled to rescission, restitution, or specific performance. Before a court will grant reformation, one or both of the parties must present clear and convincing evidence of either fraud or mutual mistake.

RECOVERY BASED ON QUASI-CONTRACT

As stated in Chapter 5, a quasi-contract is not a legal contract but an equitable theory *imposed* on the parties to obtain justice. Hence, a quasi-contract becomes an equitable basis for equitable relief. The contract arises because the law *implies* a promise to pay for benefits received by a party. Essentially, when one party has conferred a benefit on another party, justice requires the party receiving the benefit to pay the reasonable value of it. The party receiving the benefit should not be unjustly enriched at the other party's expense.

In order to recover on a quasi-contract, the party seeking recovery must show that: (1) a benefit has been conferred on the other party; (2) the benefit was conferred with the expectation of being paid; (3) the party seeking recovery did not act as a volunteer in conferring the benefit; and (4) retention of the benefit without being paid would result in unjust enrichment of the party receiving the benefit. Quasi-contractual recovery is useful where one party has *partially* performed under a contract that is unenforceable. It can be used as an alternative to a suit for damages and will allow the party to recover for the reasonable value of the partial performance. For example, suppose Abrams contracts to build two oil derricks for the Texas Gulf Sulfur Co. The derricks are to be built over a period of three years, but the parties do not make a written contract. Enforcement of the contract will therefore be barred by the Statute of Frauds.[16] If Abrams completes one derrick before Texas Gulf Sulfur tells him that the contract is unenforceable, Abrams can sue in quasi-contract.

First, a benefit has been conferred on Texas Gulf Sulfur, since one oil derrick has been built. Second, Abrams built the derrick (conferred the benefit) expecting to be paid. Third, Abrams did not volunteer to build the derrick; he built it under an unenforceable oral contract. Fourth, allowing Texas Gulf Sulfur to retain the derrick would enrich the company unjustly. Therefore, Abrams should be able to recover. Abrams is entitled to recover the reasonable value of the oil derrick (under the theory of *quantum meruit*). This is ordinarily equal to the fair market value of the derrick.

Benefits conferred as a result of fraud, mistake, or duress are recoverable by the use of the quasi-contractual theory of recovery. Quasi-contractual relief is generally available where some benefit has been conferred on a party and where the party conferring the benefit cannot sue on the contract itself.

Quasi-contractual relief and quasi-contractual liability are doctrines formulated and applied by the courts to prevent unjust enrichment. In the following situation, the plaintiff provided goods and services and was not paid. Although, as the court points out, the plaintiff sued the wrong defendant, the plaintiff's theory of recovery is a valid one.

---

16. Contracts which by their terms cannot be performed within one year must be in writing to be enforceable. See Chapter 11.

BACKGROUND AND FACTS   *The plaintiff, Callano, operated a nursery. Oakwood constructed a housing development and contracted to sell a certain lot with a house on it to a purchaser named Pendergast. Before the house was finished, Callano delivered and planted shrubbery pursuant to a contract with Pendergast. A representative of Oakwood knew about the planting.*

Pendergast never paid Callano the invoice price of $494.95 for the shrubbery. A short time after the shrubbery was planted, Pendergast died. Thereafter, Oakwood and the Pendergast estate cancelled the contract of sale for the house. At that time, Oakwood had no knowledge of Pendergast's failure to pay Callano. Subsequently, Oakwood sold the Pendergast property, including the shrubbery, to a third party.

Callano sought payment of the invoice price for the shrubbery from Oakwood.

CALLANO v. OAKWOOD PARK HOMES CORP.

Superior Court of New Jersey,
Appellate Division, 1965.
91 N.J.Super. 105, 219 A.2d 332.

COLLESTER, J. A. D.

* * *

The single issue is whether Oakwood is obligated to pay plaintiffs for the reasonable value of the shrubbery on the theory of *quasi*-contractual liability. Plaintiffs contend that defendant was *unjustly* enriched when the Pendergast contract to purchase the property was cancelled and that an agreement to pay for the shrubbery is implied in law. [Emphasis added.] Defendant argues that the facts of the case do not support a recovery by plaintiffs on the theory of *quasi*-contract.

Contracts implied by law, more properly described as *quasi* or constructive contracts, are a class of obligations which are imposed or created by law without regard to the [mutual] assent of the party bound, on the ground that they are dictated by reason and justice. They rest solely on a legal fiction and are not contract obligations at all in the true sense, for there is no agreement; but they are clothed with the semblance of contract for the purpose of the remedy, and the obligation arises not from consent, as in the case of true contracts, but from the law or natural equity. Courts employ the fiction of *quasi* or constructive contract with caution.

In cases based on *quasi*-contract liability, *the intention of the parties is entirely disregarded, while in cases of express contracts and contracts implied in fact the intention is of the essence of the transaction. In the case of actual contracts the agreement defines the duty, while in the case of quasi-contracts the duty defines the contract.* [Emphasis added.] Where a case shows that it is the duty of the defendant to pay, the law imparts to him a promise to fulfill that obligation. The duty which thus forms the foundation of a *quasi*-contractual obligation is frequently based on the doctrine of unjust enrichment. It rests on the equitable principle that a person shall not be allowed to enrich himself unjustly at the expense of another, and on the principle of whatsoever it is certain a man ought to do, that the law supposes him to have promised to do.

The key words are *enrich* and *unjustly*. To recover on the theory of quasi-contract the plaintiffs must prove that defendant was enriched, *viz.*, received a benefit, and that retention of the benefit without payment therefor would be unjust.

It is conceded by the parties that the value of the property, following the termination of the Pendegast [sic] contract, was enhanced by the reasonable value of the shrubbery at the stipulated sum of $475. However, we are not persuaded that the retention of such benefit by defendant before it sold the property to the Grantges was inequitable or unjust.

Quasi-contractual liability has found application in a myriad of situations. However, a common thread runs throughout its application where liability has been successfully asserted, namely, that *the plaintiff expected remuneration from the defendant* or if the true facts were known to plaintiff, he would have expected remuneration from defendant, at the time the benefit was conferred. [Emphasis added.]

* * *

It is further noted that *quasi*-contract cases involve either some direct relationship between the parties or a mistake on the part of the person conferring the benefit.

In the instant case the plaintiffs entered into an express contract with Pendergast and looked to him for payment. They had no dealings with defendant, and did not expect remuneration from it when they provided the shrubbery. No issue of mistake on the part of plaintiffs is involved. Under the existing circumstances we believe it would be inequitable to hold defendant liable. Plaintiffs' remedy is against Pendergast's estate, since they contracted with and expected payment to be made by Pendergast when the benefit was conferred.

Recovery on the theory of *quasi*-contract was developed under the law to provide a remedy where none existed. Here, a remedy exists. Plaintiffs may bring their action against Pendergast's estate. We hold that under the facts of this case [this particular] defendant was not unjustly enriched and is not liable for the value of the shrubbery.

JUDGMENT AND REMEDY *The superior court reversed the trial court's judgment. The housing developer was not a proper defendant in this case. The court explained that the nursery firm had entered into a contract with an individual purchaser and had had no dealings with the housing developer. Plaintiff's remedy, if any, must be against the deceased purchaser's estate.*

COMMENTS *Note that in a lawsuit between Callano and Pendergast (or his estate), there would be a direct claim for damages based upon an underlying contract that had occurred between the parties. Hence, the theory of quasi-contract would be inapplicable in such a lawsuit.*

ELECTION OF REMEDIES

In many cases, a nonbreaching party will have several remedies available, and they may be inconsistent. The party must choose which remedy to pursue. For example, a person who buys a fradulently represented car can sue either to cancel (rescind) the sales contract or to recover damages. Obviously, these remedies are inconsistent. An action to rescind undoes the contract; an action for damages affirms it. The purpose of the *election of remedies* doctrine is to prevent double recovery. Suppose McCarthy agrees to sell his land to Tally. Then McCarthy changes her mind and repudiates the contract. Tally can sue for damages or for specific performance. If she receives damages caused by the breach, she should not be able to get specific performance of the sales contract, since failure to deliver possession of the land was the cause of the injury for which she received damages. If Tally could seek damages *and* specific performance, she would recover twice for the same breach of contract. The doctrine of election of remedies requires Tally to choose the remedy she wants, and it eliminates any possibility of double recovery.

Unfortunately, the doctrine has been applied in a rigid and technical manner, leading to some harsh results.[17] The nonbreaching party is required to choose a remedy fairly early in the lawsuit, and the choice is then irrevocable even if no prejudice will result to the other party from allowing the nonbreaching party to change remedies. The election can be made by conduct, and the party does not have to be aware that a certain remedy is being elected. Therefore, the doctrine of election of remedies has been eliminated in contracts for the sale of goods. The Uniform Commercial Code expressly rejects the doctrine. (See UCC Secs. 2-703 and 2-711.) Remedies under the UCC are essentially cumulative in nature and include all the available remedies for breach of contract. Whether the pursuit of one remedy bars another depends entirely on the facts of the individual case. In other words, if double recovery is possible, only

one remedy can be chosen in the final analysis. However, this remedy need not be chosen until absolutely necessary to decide the case.

WAIVER OF BREACH

Under certain circumstances, a nonbreaching party may be willing to accept a defective performance of the contract. This knowing relinquishment of a legal right (that is, the right to require satisfactory and full performance) is called a **waiver**.[18] When a waiver of a breach of contract occurs, the party waiving the breach cannot take any later action on the theory that the contract was broken. In effect, the waiver erases the past breach; the contract continues as if the breach had never existed. Of course, the waiver of breach of contract extends only to the matter waived and not to the whole contract. Businesspersons often waive breaches of contract by the other party in order to get whatever benefit possible out of the contract.

Scope of a Waiver

Ordinarily the waiver by a contracting party will not operate to waive *subsequent* breaches of contract. This is always true when the subsequent breaches are unrelated to the first breach. For example, an owner who waives the right to sue for late completion of a stage of construction does not waive the right to sue for failure to comply with engineering specifications. However, subsequent breaches in the form of late performance can be waived by prior waivers.

Suppose the construction contract above was to be completed in six stages, each two months apart, spanning a period of one year. The question is whether the waiver of the right to object to lateness in stage 1 will operate as a waiver of the time requirements for stages 2 through 6. If only stage 1's time requirements have been waived, the waiver will not extend to the other five stages. However, if the first five stages were all late (and the right to object to the lateness was always waived), the waivers will extend to stage 6.

---

17. For example, in a Wisconsin case, Carpenter was fraudulently induced to buy a piece of land for $100. He spent $140 moving onto the land and then discovered the fraud. Instead of suing for damages, Carpenter sued to rescind the contract. The court denied recovery of the $140 because the seller, Mason, did not receive the $140 and was therefore not required to reimburse Carpenter for his moving expenses. So Carpenter suffered a net loss of $140 on the transaction. If Carpenter had sued for damages, he could have recovered the $100 and the $140. See Carpenter v. Mason, 181 Wis. 114, 193 N.W. 973 (1923).

---

18. Restatement, Contracts, Sections 297 and 298.

A waiver will be extended to subsequent defective performance if a reasonable person would conclude that similar defective performance in the future will be satisfactory. Therefore, a *pattern of conduct* that waives a number of successive breaches will operate as a continued waiver. In order to change this result, the nonbreaching party should give notice to the breaching party that full performance will be required in the future. In the example above, the owner can simply notify the builder that each stage must be completed on time in the future.

A waiver of the right to full performance waives only the requirement of full performance. The party who has rendered defective or less than full performance remains liable for the damages caused by the breach of contract. In effect, the waiver operates to keep the contract going. The waiver prevents the nonbreaching party from calling the contract to an end or rescinding the contract. The contract continues, but the nonbreaching party can recover damages caused by defective or less than full performance.

CONTRACT PROVISIONS LIMITING REMEDIES

A contract can include provisions stating that no damages can be recovered for certain types of breaches or that damages must be limited to a maximum amount. Exhibit 14-1 is an example of this. In addition, the contract can provide that the only remedy for breach is replacement, repair, or refund of the purchase price. Provisions stating that no damages can be recovered are called *exculpatory clauses*. (See Chapter 3.) Provisions that affect the availability of certain remedies are called *limitation of liability clauses*.

Mutual Assent Required

Initially, a court must determine if the provision has been made a part of the contract by offer and acceptance. In order for a term or provision to become part of a contract, both parties must consent to it. Therefore, courts will analyze whether the provision was noticed by the parties—whether, for example, the provision was in fine print or on the back of a lengthy contract. If either party did not know about the provision, it will not be a part of the contract and will not be enforced. For example, motorists often park their cars in lots and receive a small ticket stub that excludes liability for damages to cars parked in the lot. If a reasonable person would have noticed such an exculpatory clause, it will be enforced. If the clause is not conspicuous and a reasonable person would not have noticed it, the clause will not be enforced, and the motorist can sue for damage caused to his or her car.[19]

Type of Breach Covered

Once it has been determined that the provision or clause is part of the contract, the analysis must focus on the type of breach that is exculpated. For example, a provision excluding liability for fraudulent or intentional injury will not be enforced. Likewise, a clause excluding liability for illegal acts or violations of law will not be enforced. On the other hand, a clause excluding liability for negligence will be enforced in appropriate cases. When an exculpatory clause for negligence is contained in a contract made between parties with roughly equal bargaining positions, the clause will be enforced.

For example, assume Delta Airways buys six DC-9s from Douglas Aircraft. In the contract for sale, a clause excludes liability for errors in design and construction of the aircraft. The clause will be upheld because both parties are large corporations with roughly equal bargaining positions. The equality of bargaining power assures that the exculpatory clause was not dictated by one of the parties and forced upon the other.

---

19. See California State Auto v. Barrett Garages, Inc., 257 Cal.App.2d 84, 64 Cal.Rptr. 699 (1967).

Adhesion Contracts

If the parties do not have equal bargaining positions, exculpatory clauses will usually be stricken or held unenforceable. This problem of unequal bargaining positions arose earlier in Chapter 10 in the context of adhesion contracts. In an adhesion contract, a party with greatly superior bargaining power dictates the terms of the contract and forces the other party to adhere to those dictated terms.

Limited Remedies

Under the Uniform Commercial Code, in a contract for the sale of goods, remedies can be limited, but rules different from those discussed above apply. First, in order to make a certain remedy the only remedy available, the contract must state that the remedy is exclusive. Suppose you buy an automobile, and the sales contract limits your remedy to repair or replacement of defective parts. Under the Uniform Commercial Code, the sales contract must also state that "the sole and exclusive remedy available to the buyer is repair and/or replacement of the defective parts." If the contract states that the remedy is exclusive, then the specified remedy will be the only one ordinarily available to the buyer (provided the contract is not unconscionable).

When circumstances cause an exclusive remedy to fail of its essential purpose, then it will not be exclusive. [See UCC Sec. 2-719(2).] In the above example, if your car breaks down several times, and the dealer is unable to fix or replace the defective parts, the exclusive remedy fails of its essential purpose. Then all the other remedies under the UCC become available.

Under the Uniform Commercial Code, a sales contract may limit or exclude consequential damages, provided the limitation is not *unconscionable*.[20] Where the buyer is a consumer, the limitation of liability for personal injury is *prima facie* unconscionable and will not normally be enforced. Where the buyer is not a consumer and the loss is commercial in nature, the limitation of liability for personal injuries is not necessarily unconscionable. In the above example, if the sales contract excludes all liability for personal injuries caused by defects in the design or the construction of the automobile, the provision will not be enforced because it is *prima facie* unconscionable. However, if you buy the car as a company car, the limitation will not necessarily be unconscionable, although if it were proven to be unconscionable, it would be unenforceable.

—————————————

20. See Chapter 10 for a discussion of unconscionability.

QUESTIONS AND CASE PROBLEMS

1. On July 1, 1946, Billetter and Posell entered into an oral contract whereby Posell employed Billetter as a designer for a period of one year commencing from the date of the contract. The salary agreed upon was $75 per week. On December 31, Posell fired Billetter without cause. Posell told Billetter that the company had decided to hire another designer and suggested that Billetter take a position as a floor lady at a salary of $55 per week. Billetter was unwilling to accept such a reduction in salary. For the remainder of the contract, Billetter was unable to find comparable employment, although she made a good faith effort to do so. During this period of unemployment, Billetter received payments from the state unemployment and compensation fund. In Billetter's suit against Posell, Posell defended on the ground that Billetter should have mitigated her damages by accepting the position as floor lady. Posell also argued that he should be allowed to deduct the unemployment payments Billetter received from her damages. What result? [Billetter v. Posell, 94 Cal.App.2d 858, 211 P.2d 621 (1949)]

2. The United States, acting through the Department of Agriculture, entered into a contract with Priebe and Sons for the purchase of dried eggs. The contract called for delivery by Priebe and Sons on May 18 or any day within a ten-day period thereafter at the option of the United States. Priebe and Sons was also required under the contract to have the eggs inspected prior to delivery. Finally, the contract contained a

liquidated damage clause providing that "failure to have specified quantities of dried egg products inspected and ready for delivery by the date specified" will be cause for payment of liquidated damages. The contract between Priebe and Sons and the United States was entered into pursuant to the country's war effort. By May 18, the eggs had neither been delivered nor inspected. Inspection was completed on May 22. The United States did not call for delivery of the eggs until May 26. Priebe and Sons made timely shipments pursuant to this May 26 demand. The United States then attempted to sue Priebe and Sons under the liquidated damage clause for not having the eggs ready for shipment by the agreed upon date. Will the United States be successful in its suit? [Priebe and Sons v. United States, 332 U.S. 407, 68 S.Ct. 123, 92 L.Ed. 32 (1947)]

3. Avis Plumbing and Heating entered into a contract with McCormick to do plumbing and heating duct installation in McCormick Seminary. The contract expressly provided that if Avis breached its contract with McCormick, the general contractor could complete the work in any expedient manner. Thereafter, Avis did breach its contract, and the general contractor hired a subcontractor to complete Avis's work, relying on a subcontractor with whom it had had previous dealings. The general contractor made no attempt to select the lowest bidder to replace Avis. McCormick sued Avis Plumbing and Heating to recover the excess cost incurred in hiring a second subcontractor to complete Avis's work. Avis counterclaimed that McCormick's general contractor failed to mitigate damages. Is Avis's counterclaim correct? [Avis Plumbing and Heating Contractors Corp. v. McCormick Theological Seminary, 13 Ill.App.3d 484, 300 N.E.2d 542 (Ill.App.1973)]

4. Westinghouse entered into a contract with New Jersey Electric to manufacture and install a turbine generator for producing electricity. The contract price was over $10 million. The parties engaged in three years of negotiations and bargaining before they agreed on a suitable contract. The ultimate contract provided, among other things, that Westinghouse would not be liable for any injuries to the property belonging to the utility or to its customers or employees. Westinghouse warranted only that it would repair any defects in workmanship and materials appearing within one year of installation. After installation, part of New Jersey Electric's plant and several of its employees were injured because of a defect in the turbine. New Jersey Electric sued Westinghouse, claiming that Westinghouse was liable for the damages because the exculpatory provisions in the contract were unconscionable. What result? [Royal Indemnity Company v. Westinghouse Electric Corp., 385 F.Supp. 520 (D.C.N.Y.1974)]

5. Findlay College had employed Felch as a member of its faculty for a number of years. One of the provisions of Felch's employment contract was that Findlay College would not be allowed to dismiss Felch unless Felch were given an adequate hearing. In August 1961, Findlay College dismissed Felch without a hearing. Felch sought an injunction, requesting that the college be ordered to continue him as a member of its faculty. Should the court grant Felch the relief he requests? [Felch v. Findlay College, 119 Ohio App. 357, 200 N.E.2d 353 (1963)]

6. Bradley put his cow and 400 pounds of hay up for bid at an auction. The cow was present at the auction, but the hay was back at Bradley's farm. Minor successfully bid $17 for the cow and the hay. He paid the $17, received the cow, and later demanded the hay. Bradley was unable to deliver the hay since it had already been used. Can Minor retain the cow but sue for the price of the hay? [Minor v. Bradley, 22 Pick. 457 (Mass.1839)]

7. Kerr Steamship Company delivered to RCA a twenty-nine-word coded message to be sent to Kerr's agent in Manila. The message included instructions on loading cargo onto one of Kerr's vessels. Kerr's profits on the carriage of the cargo were to be about $6,600. RCA mislaid the coded message, and it was never sent. Kerr sued RCA for the $6,600 in profits that it lost because RCA never sent the message. Can Kerr recover? [Kerr Steamship Company v. Radio Corp. of America, 245 N.Y. 284, 157 N.E. 140 (1927)]

8. Evergreen Amusement Corporation purchased a parcel of land for use as a drive-in movie theater. Evergreen contracted with Milstead to have the lot cleared and graded according to specifications that would make it adequate for a drive-in theater. Milstead was supposed to complete the work by June 1, and Evergreen planned to open the theater at about that time. However, Milstead did not finish clearing and grading the lot until the third week in August. Evergreen sued Milstead, claiming as damages the profits that it could have made on the drive-in theater had it been in operation. Are lost profits the proper measure of damages here? [Evergreen Amusement Corp. v. Milstead, 206 Md. 610, 112 A.2d 901 (1955)]

9. Chaplin was a contestant in the Miss America Beauty Contest. The bathing suit competition was to begin at 8:00 Sunday evening, August 5. Hicks, Chaplin's agent, inadvertently forgot to inform her

that the bathing suit competition was to begin at that hour. As a result, Chaplin missed that competition. Twelve prizes were offered in the competition, and because Chaplin missed it, she lost all chance of winning any of the prizes. Chaplin sued Hicks for failing to inform her of the bathing suit segment of the competition, in breach of Hicks's contract. Can Chaplin recover anything? If so, how would a jury determine the amount of the award? [See Chaplin v. Hicks, 2 Kings Bench 786 (1911)]

10. Pareira and Wehner entered into a contract for the sale of land that Wehner intended to develop into a housing project. The contract called for payment in installments. Before Wehner took possession of the land, he drew up plans for the housing project. Shortly after the contract was formed, Wehner realized that the land was four acres smaller than Pareira had said. Because of this difference in size, Wehner was forced to hire a surveyor to replot the housing project. Wehner refused to make any further payments on the land. Pareira filed suit. What kinds of damages can Wehner claim in defending the suit by Pareira? [Pareira v. Wehner, 133 Vt. 74, 330 A.2d 84 (1974)]

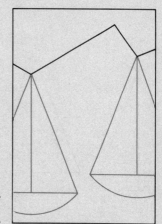

UNIT III

Personal Property and Bailments

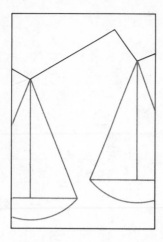

15

Personal Property

Property is the legally protected rights and interests a person has in anything with an ascertainable value that is subject to ownership. Property would have little value (and the word would have little meaning) if the law did not define the right to use it, to sell it, and to prevent trespassing upon it. In the United States, the ownership of property receives unique protection under the law. The Bill of Rights states that "no person shall . . . (by any Act of Congress) be deprived of life, liberty, or property, without due process of law; nor shall private property be taken for public use, without just compensation." The Fourteenth Amendment provides that "no State shall . . . deprive any person of life, liberty, or property, without due process of law."

THE NATURE OF PERSONAL PROPERTY

Personal property is a right or interest in personal things that are moveable. Immovable property, like land or houses, is called *real property*. (See Chapters 52 & 53.) Personal property and real property differ significantly, so the law has developed different sets of rules to deal with their acquisition and the transfer of their ownership.

Personal property can be tangible or intangible. *Tangible personal property*, like a TV set, heavy construction equipment, or a car, has physical substance. *Intangible personal property* represents some set of rights and duties, but it has no real physical existence. Stocks and bonds are intangible personal property.

Attorneys sometimes refer to all personal property as **chattel**, a more comprehensive term than *goods* because it includes living as well as inanimate property. Often, instead of saying personal property, the law will refer to goods and chattel.

THE EXPANDING NATURE OF PERSONAL PROPERTY

In a dynamic society, the concept of personal property must expand to take account of new types of ownership rights. For example, gas, water, and telephone services are now considered property for the purpose of criminal prosecution when they are stolen or used without payment. Federal and state statutes protect against the copying of musical compositions. It is a crime now to engage in "bootlegging"— illegal copying for resale—of records and tapes. The theft of computer programs is usually considered a theft of property.

ACQUIRING AND TRANSFERRING OWNERSHIP OF PERSONAL PROPERTY

Possession

The old saying, "possession is nine-tenths of the law," in certain respects is true. Possession is the most basic property right in personal property. It involves a certain amount of *control* over the property and the intention of excluding others from possession. It gives the possessor certain rights: (1) the right to enjoy the use of the property without interference from anyone except the true owner (if there is one) and (2) the right to recover the property if any person (except the true owner) wrongfully takes it. Of course, if the possessor is not the true owner, the latter can retrieve the property.

A third person cannot attempt to take personal property away by alleging that the possessor is not the true owner. Suppose Mary Bloomingthal has a Mack truck that she has been using in her hauling operation. One of her employees believes that the truck really belongs to his friend, Scott Lambert. The employee decides to take the truck and store it in his garage for Lambert. When he returns to work, his boss wants to know where the Mack truck is, and the employee says: " That truck is not yours. My friend, Scott Lambert, owns it. I am going to keep it for him." Bloomingthal immediately fires the employee and brings suit to recover the truck. Bloomingthal will recover the truck plus any damages she has sustained. The former employee will not prevail at trial unless Lambert comes in and proves that he owns the truck. It is not a defense to claim that a third person has *better* title than a possessor.

WILD ANIMALS Acquisition is a means of acquiring ownership rights over wildlife. (Technically, this is called *occupation*.) Suppose you are on a fox hunt in Lancashire, England. Your dogs do a tremendous job, almost entrapping the fox. Then suddenly, out of nowhere, another hunter shoots the fox and takes it for himself. If you sue to recover the fox, you will lose. Merely being in hot pursuit of wild animals will not normally give you title to them. An animal has to be captured, or capture has to be certain, before title to the animal can be obtained. If you attempt to take the fox away from the other hunter, you will be liable to that hunter.[1]

Wild animals belong to no one in their wild state, and the first person to take possession of a wild animal normally owns it. Generally, the killing of a wild animal amounts to assuming ownership of it. (This rule, however, is superseded by laws relating to trespass. If Sneed hunts deer on Williams's land, and Williams finds Sneed dragging off freshly killed deer, Williams can demand that the deer be given to him. Any wild animals captured by a trespasser are the property of the landowner, not the captor.)

_____

1. Today, many state and federal statutes regulate the hunting of wildlife. If wildlife is killed in violation of these statutes, the owner does not obtain title to the animal.

Purchase

Purchase is one of the most common means of acquiring and transferring ownership of personal property. The purchase or sale of personal property is covered in depth in Chapters 17 to 22 on the Uniform Commercial Code. The first step in solving problems with the purchase and sale of personal property is to determine which laws apply. Article 2 of the UCC governs the sale of goods. Intangible personal property like notes, checks, drafts, and certificates of deposit is governed by Articles 3 and 4. Other intangibles, such as stocks and other investment securities are dealt with in Article 8.

Production

Production—the fruits of labor—is another means of acquiring ownership of personal property. Nearly everyone in the United States today is involved in some sort of production. For example, writers, inventors, and manufacturers all produce personal property and thereby acquire title to it.

Gifts

A **gift** is another fairly common means of both acquiring and transferring ownership of real and personal property. A gift is essentially a *voluntary* transfer of property ownership. It need not be supported by legally sufficient consideration since the very essence of a gift is giving without consideration. A gift must be transferred in the present rather than in the future. For example, suppose your aunt tells you she is going to give you a new Mercedes Benz for your next birthday. This is simply a *promise* to make a gift. It is not enforceable unless you give some consideration for the promise. Then it becomes a binding contract.

THE REQUIREMENTS OF AN EFFECTIVE GIFT There are three requirements of an effective gift—delivery, donative intent, and acceptance by the donee.

Delivery Delivery is obvious in most cases, but some objects cannot be relinquished physically. Then the question of delivery depends upon the surrounding circumstances. When the physical object cannot be delivered, a symbolic or **constructive delivery** will be sufficient. Constructive delivery does not confer real possession of the object in question. It is a general term for all those acts that the law holds to be equivalent to acts of real delivery. Suppose you want to make a gift of various old rare coins that you have stored in a safety deposit box. You certainly cannot deliver the box itself to the donee, and you do not want to take the coins out of the bank. Instead, you can simply deliver the key to the box to your donee. This is symbolic, or constructive, delivery of the contents of the box.

Delivery of intangible personal property must be accomplished by symbolic or constructive delivery. Stocks and bonds are represented by certificates, and delivery of the certificate entitles the holder to income of dividends or interest. Other examples of intangible personal property that must be constructively delivered include insurance policies, contracts, promissory notes, and chattel mortgages.

An effective delivery also requires giving up *complete dominion and control* (ownership rights) over the subject matter of the gift. Cases often turn on the retaining or relinquishing of control over the subject matter of the gift. The Internal Revenue Service scrutinizes transactions between relatives when one relative has given away income-producing property. A relative who does not relinquish complete control over a piece of property will have to pay taxes on the income from the property. Under the tax laws, it is illegal to assign or give away income while retaining control over the property that produces the income.

Delivery can be accomplished by means of a third person. The third person may be the agent of the donor or the donee. If the person is the agent of the donor, the gift is effective when the agent delivers to the donee. If, on the other hand, the third person is the agent of the donee, the gift is effective when the donor delivers to the donee's agent.[2] Where there is doubt as to whose agent the third party is, he or she is generally presumed to be the agent of the donor. Naturally, no delivery is necessary if the gift is already in the hands of the donee. All that is necessary to complete the gift in such a case is the required intent and acceptance by the donee.

Donative Intent   Donative intent is determined from the language of the donor and the surrounding circumstances. For example, when a gift is challenged in court, the court may look at the relationship between the parties and the size of the gift in relation to the donor's other assets. A gift to an arch enemy will be viewed with suspicion. Likewise, when people give

_____
2.   Bickford v. Mattocks, 95 Me. 547, 50 A. 894 (1901).

away a large portion of their assets, the courts will scrutinize the transaction to determine whether there is any fraud or duress.

Acceptance   The final requirement of a valid gift is acceptance by the donee. This rarely presents any problems since most donees readily accept their gifts. The courts generally assume acceptance unless shown otherwise.

In the following case, the Supreme Court of Mississippi dealt with an issue involving a certificate of deposit made payable to the order of two persons. Because the certificate was made payable *in the alternative*, the question arose whether it was actually the depositor's property at the time she died and therefore an asset of her estate or whether it was the property of the individual to whom it was payable in the alternative.

BACKGROUND AND FACTS   *On April 6, 1973, Ruby Eubanks deposited $14,000 with the Mechanics Bank of Water Valley, Mississippi. The bank issued a certificate of deposit in the amount of $14,000 payable as follows:*

THOMAS v. ESTATE OF EUBANKS

Supreme Court of Mississippi, 1978. 358 So.2d 709.

> Mrs. Ruby Eubanks has deposited in this bank $14,000 payable to the order of herself or Doyle Thomas in current funds twelve months after date on the return of this certificate properly indorsed with interest at 5 per cent per annum.

At the time of Eubanks's death, the certificate of deposit was still in her possession. The administratrix of her estate cashed the certificate on April 6, 1974, and retained the proceeds pending further court order about their distribution. The proceeds of the certificate thus passed from the bank, which had no further liability because it had paid the proceeds to the administratrix.

Eubanks's estate was closed out in November 1974. However, the administratrix continued to hold the proceeds of the certificate pending a court decision about their ownership. The following year, Doyle Thomas filed this lawsuit. The trial court held that the certificate of deposit was part of Eubanks's estate and that there had been no completed gift to Thomas. The Supreme Court of Mississippi based its decision upon the major elements of a gift: donative intent, delivery, and acceptance.

SUGG, Justice, for the Court.

* * *

Thomas contends that he was entitled to the certificate of deposit. It is well settled that a person may make a gift in severalty to another by making a deposit of the subject of the gift in a bank to the credit of the donee provided the donor in so doing retains no such control over the deposit as will enable him to withdraw it for his own personal uses or purposes. If he retains a control such as mentioned, and as was retained in the present case, the transaction will be ineffective as a gift in severalty and the deposit will remain the property of the depositor.

It is equally well settled that a person may make a gift in joint tenure by making a deposit of the subject of the gift in a bank in such a manner that it shall stand to the credit, as joint owners, of the donor and the donee, as where, for illustration, John Doe makes a deposit to the credit of 'John Doe or Richard Roe,' which * * * would raise the presumption that the deposit was intended to be in joint ownership, and by the further force of the statute, subject to withdrawal by either of the joint owners. Precise form is not essential if and when formal deficiencies are supplied by definite proof; so that when the facts, well proved, are sufficient to disclose that there was a clear intention to create a right which embraces the essential elements of joint ownership and survivorship in respect to the particular bank deposit, or account, the intention so proved will be given effect and the survivor held entitled to the fund.

* * *

Negotiable instruments payable to two or more persons in the alternative, in this case the certificate of deposit, may be negotiated, discharged, or enforced by the holder. * * *

At the trial it was stipulated that the certificate of deposit was in the possession of Mrs. Eubanks at the time of her death. It had not been negotiated by her to Thomas. It was in her possession as a holder in due course therefore it was her property when she died and became an asset of her estate.

[Thomas's second contention was that Eubanks had tendered the certificate of deposit to Thomas during her lifetime. He did not accept possession of it at the time. Moreover, Thomas had witnesses to whom Eubanks had stated on two separate occasions that the proceeds of the certificate were intended for Thomas. Thomas argued that this evidence showed donative intent and constructive delivery of the certificate to him during Eubanks lifetime.]

"* * *[O]ne of the essentials of a valid gift *causa mortis*, as well as a gift *inter vivos*, is that the property must be delivered in such manner that the donor retains no control or dominion over it."

[T]ender by Mrs. Eubanks of the certificate of deposit would not constitute delivery and relinquishment of control by her. Neither would proof that Mrs. Eubanks told a disinterested third party that the proceeds of the certificate were the property of Thomas constitute delivery and relinquishment of control by her. [Such] testimony was not sufficient to show either a valid gift *inter vivos* or *causa mortis*.

JUDGMENT AND REMEDY *The Supreme Court of Mississippi affirmed the trial court's ruling that the proceeds of the certificate of deposit were payable to Eubanks's estate. Thomas failed to show that actual or constructive delivery had been made during Eubanks's lifetime; therefore, no valid gift was completed.*

INTER VIVOS GIFTS AND CAUSA MORTIS GIFTS **Inter vivos gifts** are made during one's lifetime.[3] **Causa mortis gifts** are made in contemplation of imminent death. *Causa mortis* gifts do not become absolute until the donor dies from the illness or disease that was contemplated. The donee must survive to take the gift, and the donor must not have revoked the gift prior to death. A *causa mortis gift* is revocable at any time up to the death of the donor and is automatically revoked if the donor recovers. Suppose Stevens is to be operated on for a serious tumor. Before the operation, he delivers an envelope to a close business associate. The envelope contains a letter saying "I realize my days are numbered and I want to give you this check for $1,000,000 in the event of my death from this operation." It also contains a check for $1,000,000. The surgeon begins the operation and decides not to remove the tumor. Stevens recovers from the operation but dies several months later. If Stevens's personal representative tries to recover the $1,000,000, she will succeed. The *causa mortis gift* is automatically revoked if the donor recovers. The specific event that was contemplated in making the gift was death from a particular operation. Since Stevens did not die, the gift is revoked and the $1,000,000 passes to Stevens's personal representative when Stevens dies.[4]

WILL OR INHERITANCE

Ownership of property can also be passed by *will* or under *inheritance laws.* Both methods are statutory (property must be passed by will in accordance with specific statutory rules) and are discussed in Chapter 55.

ACCESSION

Literally, **accession** means "adding on" to something. *Accession* occurs when someone puts labor into a piece of property or adds materials to it. When a carpenter comes on an owner's land and builds a front porch with materials supplied by the owner, accession has occurred. There is usually no dispute about who owns the property after accession has occurred. The owner of the house in the example above can simply pay the carpenter for the improvements and leave it at that. However, disputes can arise over ownership of the property, especially when one party has expended a great deal of labor or materials. In general, whenever one party has wrongfully caused accession, that party is liable to the other party for the damage caused. For example, if Winkler wrongfully enters onto the land of Ames and makes improvements, Winkler cannot claim title to the property and is liable to Ames for any damage caused by the trespass.

In some situations the person making the addition or accession will be allowed to claim title to the property added to. For example, suppose Angelo is walking in a large field and discovers a huge marble stone that is shaped approximately like the Lone Ranger's horse, Silver. Angelo comes back for twenty-seven weeks and transforms the stone into an exact replica of Silver. Angelo's artist friends are very impressed and convince him to move the stone horse to a gallery. Subsequently, it is sold to an eccentric Arab, who wants to paint it red and put it in front of his Beverly Hills mansion. The owner of the field where Angelo found the stone now wants to claim title to it. Normally, the courts will give Angelo title to the stone because the changes he made caused it to increase in value. But Angelo will have to pay the owner of the field for the reasonable value of the stone before it was altered.

CONFUSION

When the personal property of two persons becomes intermingled, this is called **confusion**. Confusion is defined as the comingling of goods such that one person's property cannot be distinguished from another's. For example, if two farmers put their number 2 grade winter

3. When a person dies and his or her will leaves property to anyone, there is technically no gift. Instead, the giving of the property is termed a bequest, devise, or inheritance.
4. Brind v. International Trust Co., 66 Colo. 60, 179 P. 148 (1919).

wheat in the same silo, confusion will occur. Under the confusion of goods doctrine, if one person wrongfully and willfully mixes goods with those of another in order to render them indistinguishable, the innocent party acquires title to the total.

On the other hand, the doctrine of confusion does not apply when confusion occurs by (1) agreement, (2) an honest mistake, or (3) the act of some third party. When one or more of those three events occurs, the owners all share ownership of the whole equally. Suppose you enter into a cooperative arrangement with six other farmers in your local community of Midway, Iowa. Each fall everyone harvests nearly the same amount of number 2 yellow corn. The corn is stored in silos that are held by the cooperative. Everyone owns one-sixth of the total corn in the silos.[5] If anything happens to the corn, each will bear the loss in equal proportions of one-sixth.

Often, though, each owner will not have an interest equal to the other owners. In such a case, the owners must keep careful records of their respective proportions. If a dispute over ownership arises, the courts will presume that everyone has an equal interest or proportion of the goods. So you must be prepared to prove that you own more than an equal part. As a practical matter, whenever you are dealing with goods that can easily be comingled, you should be aware of the special problems that can arise. Therefore, be sure to maintain accurate records of the goods you or your company owns. Suppose you own two-thirds of the corn in the Midway Co-op silos above. Further assume that the silos are partially damaged by a tornado and thunderstorm. How much have you lost of your total if one-half of the corn is blown away by the storm? You have lost one-half of your two-thirds, or one-third. When corn is stored by several owners, each owning a different proportion of the total, any loss is suffered proportionally.

Intentional, or Negligent, Confusion

Confusion that results from intentional wrong-

doing or negligent conduct creates a different problem. The person responsible for the comingling must bear the entire loss if any of the goods are lost, stolen, or destroyed. However, if the wrongdoer can show that no injury occurred and can show the specific portion contributed to the whole, then the wrongdoer can recover that portion.

Suppose you are the vice-president in charge of purchasing for a salad oil company. You buy 10,000 gallons of high grade salad oil and have it delivered to a field warehouse and company. The warehouse and company stores many grades of oil, and your oil is negligently mixed with a much lower grade of oil. The oil was worth $.64 per gallon before it was confused, but now it is worth only $.32 per gallon. Here you should be entitled to claim your 10,000 gallons of oil and sue the warehouse for damages caused by the negligent confusion. On the other hand, suppose the grades of oil were exactly the same but you wanted your oil stored in a separate bin? Here you have no reason to complain and you cannot recover any damage.[6]

MISLAID, LOST, AND ABANDONED PROPERTY

Mislaid Property

Property that has been placed somewhere by the owner voluntarily and then inadvertently forgotten is **mislaid property**. Suppose you go to the theater and leave your gloves on the concession stand. The gloves are mislaid property, and the theater owner is entrusted with the duty of reasonable care for the goods. Whenever mislaid property is found, the finder does not obtain title or possession to the goods.[7] Instead, the owner of the place where the property was

---

5. As tenants-in-common. See Chapter 52.

6. Unless, of course, you had a warehousing contract with a storage firm. Then you could sue for breach of contract, provided the contract required the warehouser to store in a separate bin. As a matter of commercial reality, very few, if any, warehouses contract for storage in separate facilities. If they did, many people would want separate facilities for fear of confusion. This would negate the savings in warehouse storage. Here we are really dealing with *fungible* goods.

7. The finder is an involuntary bailee. See Chapter 16.

mislaid becomes the caretaker of the property because it is highly likely that the true owner will return.[8]

Lost Property

Property that is *not* voluntarily left and forgotten is **lost property**. A finder of lost property can claim title to the property against the whole world, *except the true owner*. If the true owner demands that the lost property be returned, the finder must do so. However, a third party cannot fraudulently assert that title lies with another person in an attempt to take possession of the lost property from a finder. The finder is guilty of a tort, or civil wrong known as *conversion* (see Chapter 3), if he or she knows who the true owners of the property are and fails to return it to them. In addition, many states require the finder to make a reasonably diligent search to locate the true owner of lost property.

Suppose Arnolds works in a large library at night. In the courtyard on her way home, she finds a piece of gold jewelry that looks like it has several precious stones in it. Arnolds decides to take it to a jeweler to have it appraised. While pretending to weigh the jewelry, an employee of the jeweler removes several of the stones. If Arnolds brings an action to recover the stones from the jeweler, she will win because she found lost property and holds valid title against

everyone *except the true owner*. Since the property was *lost* and not *mislaid,* the owner of the library is not the caretaker of the jewelry. Instead, Arnolds acquires title good against the whole world (except the true owner).[9]

Estray Statutes   Many states have **estray statutes** to encourage and facilitate the return of property to its true owner and then to reward a finder for honesty if the property remains unclaimed. Such statutes provide an incentive for finders to report their discoveries by making it possible for them, after passage of a specified period of time, to acquire legal title to the property they have found. The statute usually requires the county clerk to advertise the property in an attempt to enhance the opportunity of the owner to recover what has been lost.

There are always some preliminary questions to be resolved before the estray statute can be employed. The item must be *lost property,* not merely mislaid or abandoned property. When the situation indicates that the property was probably lost, not mislaid or abandoned, as a matter of public policy loss is presumed and the estray statute applies. Such a situation occurs in the following case.

---

8.   He or she is a bailee with right of possession against all except the true owner. See Chapter 16.

9.   See Armory v. Delamire, 1 Strange 505. However, if Arnolds had found the jewelry during the course of her employment, her employer would be the involuntary bailee. Further, many courts now say that lost property recovered in a private place allows the owner of the place, *not* the finder, to become the bailee (even if the finder is not a trespasser).

BACKGROUND AND FACTS   *A safety deposit box subscriber brought this action against a bank seeking a declaratory judgment that the state estray statute applied to her finding $6,325 on a chair in the examination booth in the bank's safety deposit vault area. The money was not claimed within the statutory time period of one year. Hence, the plaintiff petitioned the court to grant her ownership of the money. The trial court entered an order refusing to determine ultimate ownership of the money.*

PASET v. OLD ORCHARD BANK & TRUST CO.
Appellate Court of Illinois, First District, Third Division, 1978.
62 Ill.App.3d 534, 19 Ill.Dec. 389, 378 N.E.2d 1264.

SIMON, Justice.
On May 8, 1974, the plaintiff, Bernice Paset, a safety deposit box subscriber at the defendant Old Orchard Bank (the bank), found $6,325 in currency on the seat of a chair in an examination booth in the safety deposit vault. The chair was partially

under a table. The plaintiff notified officers of the bank and turned the money over to them. She then was told by bank officials that the bank would try to locate the owner, and that she could have the money if the owner was not located within 1 year.

The bank wrote to everyone who had been in the safety deposit vault area either on the day of, or on the day preceding, the discovery, stating that some property had been found and inviting the customers to describe any property they might have lost. No one reported the loss of currency, and the money remained unclaimed a year after it had been found. However, when the plaintiff requested the money, the bank refused to deliver it to her, explaining that it was obligated to hold the currency for the owner.

The bank's position is that the estray statute is not applicable because the money was not lost in the sense the word "lost" is used in that statute. The bank contends that, under the common law, the money was mislaid by its owner rather than lost, and that the estray statute does not apply to mislaid property. In the alternative, the bank argues that the money was discovered not in a public place, but in a private area with access restricted to safety deposit box subscribers. The bank claims, therefore, that the money always was in its constructive possession or custody, either as owner of the premises or as bailee for an unknown and unidentified safety deposit box subscriber, and that property in someone's constructive possession or custody cannot be lost. As against the plaintiff, the bank claims to have the superior right to hold the money indefinitely, and in fact is required to do so until the true owner puts in his appearance. * * * The estray statute provides in [relevant part]:

"If any person or persons find any lost goods, money, bank notes, or other choses in action, of any description whatever, such person or persons shall inform the owner thereof, if known.

"* * * If the value thereof exceeds the sum of $15, the county clerk, within 20 days after receiving the certified copy of the judge's order shall cause an advertisement to be set up on the court house door, and in 3 other of the most public places in the county, and also a notice thereof to be published for 3 weeks successively in some public newspaper printed in this state and if the owner of such goods, money, bank notes, or other choses in action does not appear and claim the same * * * within one year after the advertisement thereof as aforesaid, the ownership of such property shall vest in the finder."

* * *

Traditionally, the common law has treated lost and mislaid property differently for the purposes of determining ownership of property someone has found. Mislaid property is that which is intentionally put in a certain place and later forgotten; at common law a finder acquires no rights to mislaid property. The element of intentional deposit present in the case of mislaid property is absent in the case of lost property, for property is deemed lost when it is unintentionally separated from the dominion of its owner. The general rule is that the finder is entitled to possession of lost property against everyone except the true owner. We are not concerned in this case with abandoned property where the owner, intending to relinquish all rights to his property, leaves it free to be appropriated by any other person. Although at common law the finder is entitled to keep abandoned property, the plaintiff has not taken the position that the money here was abandoned.

[W]e do not accept the bank's initial argument that the money was mislaid rather than lost. It is complete speculation to infer, as the bank urges, that the money was deliberately placed by its owner on the chair located partially under a table in the examining booth, and then forgotten. If the money was intentionally placed on the chair by someone who forgot where he left it, the bank's notice to safety deposit box subscribers should have alerted the owner. The failure of an owner to appear to claim the money in the interval since its discovery is affirmative evidence that the property was not mislaid.

Because the evidence, though ambiguous, tends to indicate that the money probably was not mislaid, and because neither party contends that the money was abandoned, we conclude that the ambiguity should, as a matter of public policy, be resolved in favor of the presumption that the money was lost. * * * Accordingly, we conclude that the money was "lost," and so encompassed by the Illinois estray statute.

* * *

We also reject the bank's alternative argument that the money, having been found in a place from which the general public was excluded, was always in the bank's constructive custody or possession, and therefore could not have been "lost," as that word is used in the estray statute. * * * The bank's record of its safety deposit box subscribers who visited the vault on the day of or the day preceding the plaintiff's discovery gave the bank the opportunity to search for the owner among this limited group. The bank also had sufficient time to contact any subscriber who had not been in his box since the date the plaintiff discovered the money. Consequently, in view of the opportunities the bank had to search out the owner of the money among this limited group, of the notice the bank gave to that group and of the plaintiff's undisputed compliance with the estray statute, vesting the ownership of the money in the finder is a more pragmatic and sensible solution than having the bank continue to hold the money indefinitely.

The appellate court decided that the estray statute should be applied and that the ownership of the money should be vested in the finder.	**JUDGMENT AND REMEDY**

Abandoned Property

Property that has been discarded by the true owner with no intention of claiming title to it is **abandoned property**. Someone who finds abandoned property acquires title to it, and such title is good against the whole world, *including the original owner*. If, however, a finder is trespassing and finds abandoned property, title does not become vested in the finder. This is also true of lost property.

Suppose C employs A and B to clean out a henhouse. C has recently purchased a home that previously had changed hands a number of times. A and B find a tin can full of gold buried in a corner of the henhouse. The can is extremely old and rusty, suggesting that it has been buried there for quite some time. C, the owner of the land, takes the coins from A and B and claims that they belong to her. A and B bring suit to recover the coins. A and B can recover the coins because they were lost articles found concealed in the earth. Such articles, commonly known as *treasure trove*, are usually coin, gold, or silver found hidden in the earth or other private place. In England, treasure trove belongs to the crown, but in the United States, it is treated like lost property and becomes the property of the finder, subject to the rights of the true owner. Note in this example that A and B are not trespassers. If they were trespassers, they would not be entitled to retain the title to the treasure trove.[10]

PATENTS

A patent is a grant from the government that conveys and secures to an inventor the exclusive right to make, use, and sell an invention for seventeen years. Patents are typically given for new articles, but *design patents* are given for manufactured articles that have been changed in a way that will enhance their sale. *Plant patents* are given to individuals who invent, discover, or reproduce a new variety of plant. Patent law has been evolving with respect to computer programs. Initially, computer programs could not be patented, but the commercial necessity of protecting them has led to a revised view.

TRADEMARKS

A trademark is a distinctive mark, model, device, or emblem that manufacturers stamp, print, or otherwise affix to the goods they produce so that the goods can be identified in the market and their origin can be vouched for. Federal statute allows a trademark to be registered by its owner or user. Exclusive use of the trademark can be perpetual. Protection depends on adoption and use; if the owner continues use, no one can infringe upon the trademark. International protection can also be afforded by various registrations. Registration is made before using the trademark in most other countries.

A trademark must be distinctive in order to be registered. It is not enough to merely describe an article or to name a city. For example, it would be hard to register the trademark New

York Clothes. Exceptions to this rule, of course, exist. When particular words have been used for such a long time that the public identifies them with a particular product and its origin, then those words can be registered as a trademark. The same holds for geographic terms that have acquired a meaning other than their location.

Trademarks can grow so common that they become generic names. For example, "Thermos" was originally a brand name for a thermal food-storage container. Now the term has become synonymous with such containers and therefore can no longer be used solely as one company's trademark.

COPYRIGHTS

A copyright is an intangible right granted by statute to the author or originator of certain literary or artistic productions. With a copyright, the owner is vested for a limited time period with the sole and exclusive privilege of reproducing copies of the work for publication and sale.

At common law, any author or compiler of data who prevented others from using the work without permission by keeping it secret had a common law copyright. Such a copyright ended when the work was published. (Publication meant any communication to others, not necessarily in written or printed form.) Federal statutes now govern virtually all copyright law in this country.

Copyright Law

On January 1, 1978, a new copyright law became effective, completely replacing Title 17 of the United States Code, which had been used since 1909. The new law is divided into eight different chapters, beginning with a discussion of the subject matter and scope of copyright. It includes chapters relating to copyright duration, notice, deposit and registration requirements, infringement, manufacturing requirements, administration, and the like. The new copyright law has four essential purposes:

---

10.   Danielson v. Roberts, 44 Or. 108, 74 P. 913 (1904). But the court will distinguish between finding "treasure" in the course of employment and finding it strictly in a private place. In the latter case, if the treasure trove is "embedded-in-the-soil", the landowner will normally prevail, *not* the finder.

1. To maximize the availability of creative works to the public.

2. To give creators of copyrighted works a fair return and to provide users of copyrighted works with a fair income.

3. To balance the interest of copyright users and owners.

4. To minimize any negative impact on industries regulated by change in the copyright law.

Copyright Duration

Works created after January 1, 1978, are given statutory copyright protection for the life of the author plus fifty years. Pseudonymous and anonymous publications, as well as those done "for hire" (ghosted) have a copyright term of seventy-five years from publication or one hundred years from creation, whichever is shorter. For those works already under copyright protection, their present term of twenty-eight years from date of first publication will remain. If a renewal is asked for, the second term will be increased to forty-seven years.

Exclusive Use of Copyright

The copyright holder is entitled to the exclusive use of all those materials that are copyrighted subject to a number of exceptions, such as fair use and library reproduction.

FAIR USE Some copying is allowed without payment of fees or permission of the copyright holder under the doctrine of "fair use". "Fair use" allows reproduction of copyrighted material without permission if the use of the material is reasonable and not harmful to the rights of the copyright owner. Section 107 of the new copyright law mentions permissible purposes such as criticism, comment, news reporting, teaching (including multiple copies for classroom use), scholarship, or research. Four criteria are used in considering whether a particular use is reasonable: (1) the purpose and character of the use, including whether it is of a nonprofit, educational nature or of a commercial nature; (2) the amount and importance of the material used in relation to the work as a whole; (3) the nature of the copyrighted work; and, (4) the effect of the use on the potential market or value of the copyrighted work.

LIBRARY REPRODUCTION Libraries and archives can reproduce single copies of certain copyrighted items for noncommercial purposes without violating the copyright law. Notice of copyright on the library or archive reproduction is necessary, however. Wholesale copying of periodicals is not permitted.

QUESTIONS AND CASE PROBLEMS

1. Ethel Yahuda had an extensive library of rare books and manuscripts. Several years before her death, Yahuda announced at a public luncheon attended by a head of state that she was donating her library to Hebrew University. Her public announcement was accompanied by the delivery of an itemized memorandum of the books and manuscripts contained in her library. Hebrew University Association accepted the list. No books were ever tendered by Yahuda to the university. Is there a completed gift? [Hebrew Univ. Assn. v. Nye (executors of estate of Ethel S. Yahuda), 26 Conn.Sup. 342, 223 A.2d 397 (1966)]

2. Waller dabbled for a number of years in the stock market, keeping most of his stocks in a safe deposit box to which there were two keys. On June 1, Waller gave one of these keys to his wife. On June 5, Waller died during an exploratory operation that had been scheduled on June 2. Is there a valid *causa mortis gift* here? Is there a valid *inter vivos gift*? [Schilling v. Waller, 243 Md. 271, 220 A.2d 580 (1966)]

3. Lucille and Earl McVay were married in 1947, and their marriage ended in divorce. After the divorce, Earl took possession of the 1971 Buick automobile that he and Lucille owned jointly. Earl refused to return the automobile to Lucille and refused to pay her for her half of the value of the car. In an action by Lucille against her ex-husband for her share of the value of the car, she also claimed the value of the car's tires, which she herself had purchased. Assuming that Lucille presents adequate

proof at trial that the tires were purchased with her own money, can she recover the full value of the tires in addition to half the value of the automobile? [McVay v. McVay, 318 So.2d 660 (La.App.1975)]

4. In 1963 the Rhoads Coal Company leased a large parcel of land and coal mining plant that it intended to take over for mining operations. The land was owned by Gilberton. As a result of Rhoads's mining operations, large piles of silt built up on various portions of the land. At one point during its coal mining operations, Rhoads sold a large amount of the silt to a zinc company. Thereafter, due to financial difficulties, Rhoads Coal Company ceased mining the parcel of land and vacated the premises. About a year later, in an attempt to collect back taxes owed by Rhoads, the United States government attempted to place a lien on the remaining piles of silt. Gilberton, the owner of the land, claimed that the piles of silt belonged to him since Rhoads had abandoned them. Was there an abandonment? [Gilberton Contracting Co. v. Hook (District Director of Internal Revenue), 255 F.Supp. 687 (D.C.Pa.1966)]

5. Dukes and Abernathy had been good friends for many years. Dukes, an elderly man who lived alone, died on November 8, 1966. Just before he died, and knowing that he did not have much time to live, he told a friend, Stewart, that he wished to give a number of his personal items to his good friend, Abernathy. Dukes instructed Stewart to place certain items in an envelope and deliver them to Abernathy. Stewart followed Dukes's instructions and delivered the items to Abernathy, who gratefully accepted them. After Dukes died, his heirs claimed the items in the envelope as part of their inheritance. In a suit between Abernathy and the heirs, who will win? [State v. Abernathy, 431 S.W.2d 359 (Tex.Civ.App. 1968)]

6. McAvoy owned a barbershop. Medina, a regular customer, spotted a pocketbook lying on one of the tables where McAvoy kept magazines for his customers. Medina pointed out the pocketbook to McAvoy. McAvoy put the purse aside and told Medina that he would hold it until its owner returned. Several weeks passed, and no one claimed the pocketbook. Medina returned to the barbershop and claimed that, since the pocketbook was lost property and he was the finder, and since the owner had not reclaimed it, it was his. Who should get possession of the pocketbook—McAvoy or Medina? [McAvoy v. Medina, 93 Mass. (11 Allen) 548 (1866)]

7. Troop and Rust were partners in an oil and gas operation. Troop owned a three-fourths interest in the operation, and Rust owned a one-fourth interest.

After eight years of operation, a dispute arose as to whether Rust had contributed his share of the expenses. As a result of the dispute, the partnership was dissolved. In attempting to divide up the oil, Rust learned that Troop had comingled the partnership's oil with oil from another lease that Troop owned. At trial, Troop was unable to show how much of the comingled oil had come from his other operation. How much of the oil should each of the parties receive? [Troop v. St. Louis Union Trust Co., 25 Ill. App.2d 143, 116 N.E.2d 116 (1960)]

8. Mark and Jeff Ellsworth and David Gibson, three small boys, entered Bishop's salvage yard without his permission and, while there, happened upon a bottle, partially embedded in the earth, which contained $12,590 in U.S. currency. The boys took the money to the police chief, who deposited it with the Canton State Bank. Bishop initiated suit against the three boys, claiming that since the boys found the money on his property, it was rightfully his. Who is entitled to the money? [Bishop v. Ellsworth, 91 Ill.App.2d 386, 234, N.E.2d 49 (1968)]

9. Hall Printing Company entered into a contract with Publishers' Typographic Service, Inc., in which Publishers' agreed to typeset some books that Hall wished to have printed. Hall requested that Publishers' keep its type intact for six months after the first publication of Hall's book. Publishers' refused to agree to this unless Hall would agree to supply all of the metal used in the typesetting. Thereafter, Hall agreed to supply twenty-five tons of metal for purposes of typesetting. The contract provided that all metal that was shipped to Publishers' was to remain Hall's property. The contract also explicitly required that Publishers' keep all the metal that Hall shipped to Publishers' separate and apart from Publishers' other property so that it could be identified as property belonging to Hall. In spite of this contractual obligation, Publishers' mixed Hall's metals with other metals belonging to Publishers' and melted all of them down for reuse. About two years after the contract was entered into, Publishers' went into bankruptcy. Hall, knowing that Publishers' had 23,000 pounds of its metals, demanded the metals or their dollar value from the receiver in bankruptcy. The receiver refused to return either the metals or their dollar value to Hall since, in bankruptcy, all creditors divide up the bankrupt's total assets and each receives a share proportionate to the debt that the bankrupt owed it at the time of bankruptcy. Can Hall claim under the doctrine of confusion? [Baisch v. Publishers' Typographic Service, Inc., 70 N.J.Super. 340, 175 A.2d 485 (1961)]

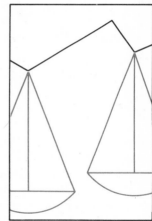

16

Bailments

A **bailment** is an agreement in which the owner of personal property temporarily delivers it to another person for a particular purpose (loan, lease, storage, repair, or transportation). Later the property is returned to the owner or disposed of as directed. Some common bailments are lending a lawn mower to a neighbor, leasing a U-Haul, leaving clothes at the dry cleaner or tailor for repair, storing goods in a warehouse, and checking a coat at a restaurant. The owner of personal property who delivers the goods to another in a contract of bailment is the **bailor**. The person accepting temporary possession for a specific purpose is the **bailee**.

ELEMENTS OF A BAILMENT

Not all transactions involving the delivery of property from one person to another create bailments. The following sections will examine each of the general requirements necessary to create a bailment.

Personal Property Requirement

A bailment involves *personal* property. Bailments involving *tangible* items like jewelry, cattle, or automobiles are more frequent than bailments of *intangible* personal property like promissory notes and shares of corporate stock.

Delivery of Possession

Delivery of possession must transfer the possession of property to the bailee in such a way that: (1) the bailee is given *exclusive* possession and control over the property and (2) the bailee must *knowingly* accept the personal property.[1] Suppose, for example, that Stevenson is in a hurry to catch his plane. He has a package he wants to check at the airport. He arrives at the airport check-in office, but the man in charge has gone on a coffee break. Stevenson decides to leave the package in a corner. This does not constitute delivery, even though there has clearly been physical transfer of the package. The person in charge of the check-in station did not knowingly accept the personal property. Or consider a

woman checking a coat at a restaurant. In the coat pocket is a $20,000 diamond necklace. By accepting the coat, the bailee does not *knowingly* accept the necklace.

If either delivery of possession or knowing acceptance is lacking, there is no bailment relationship. To illustrate: Valet parking constitutes a bailment, but self-park parking does not. The difference is found in the control of the car keys. When a car owner is required to leave the car keys with the parking attendant, the owner transfers a sufficient amount of control over the car to the parking company to constitute a bailment. When the car is parked and locked and the keys retained by the owner, the parking garage is merely a *lessor* of space and the car owner a lessee. This distinction is illustrated in the next case.

1. We are dealing here with *voluntary* bailments.

CHALET FORD, INC. v. RED TOP PARKING, INC.

Court of Appeals of Illinois, 1978. 62 Ill. App.3d 270, 19 Ill. Dec. 573, 379 N.E. 2d 88.

BACKGROUND AND FACTS *The plaintiff, Chalet Ford, sued Red Top Parking after the plaintiff's automobile was stolen from a parking facility operated by the defendant. The car was a demonstrator driven by Hall, the sales manager of Chalet Ford. Hall parked his car in the defendant's lot and went to a hockey game at the Chicago Stadium. When he returned, the automobile had been stolen.*

MEJDA, Justice.

* * *

Hall testified that on the night his car was stolen, he pulled into the parking lot, left the motor running, paid $4 to the attendant and left. The car keys were left in the possession of the attendant, who was to park the car and, after the game, warm it up and move it close to the exit so that Hall could leave easily. After the game Hall could not find the car and was told by the attendant where the latter had parked it.

Hall had been parking at the lot for approximately four years in attending various hockey games and this was the same procedure he had followed during that time. The same attendants normally worked at the lot and Hall had never received a claim check from them. The actual fee for parking was $2.50, and the remaining $1.50 was paid as a gratuity.

Hall described the lot as being mostly unpaved dirt, with no building on it and with some lighting. He recalled signs identifying the lot and agreed that there was also a sign which read: "Attendants have no authority to accept keys." Hall did not recall any sign saying that the attendants would warm up cars, but had seen other cars being warmed up in the same way his was and agreed with the characterization that it was a "reasonably common practice." Hall said he had never informed

defendant's management of the tipping and warm-up practice and also stated he had never been informed that defendant would not sanction the practice.
* * *

Defendant first contends that no bailment relationship existed between the parties. *A bailment is created by an agreement, whether express or implied, and requires both delivery by the bailor and acceptance by the bailee so that the bailee may exercise exclusive control of the bailed property.* [Emphasis added.] In the instant case, plaintiff's car and car keys were left with an attendant in one of defendant's parking lots. Based upon a pattern established over a period of four years, the attendant was to park the car in defendant's lot while Hall, the driver, attended a hockey game. After the game the attendant was to return the car to Hall. Clearly, a bailment was created. The sole question to be resolved is whether the bailment is binding upon the defendant, the owner of the lot.
* * *

During [the past] four years, the same attendants were generally at the parking lot, regularly performing acts in contradiction of the signs that stated they had no authority to do so. Although a person dealing with an agent has a duty to use reasonable diligence to determine the scope of an agent's authority, it was reasonable under the circumstances here for Hall to believe that the attendant's actions were authorized and that the signs were disregarded by those who ran the parking lot, as well as by its patrons.
* * *

Defendant cannot insulate itself from liability arising from its employees' acts by claiming those acts were against its policies when its regular practices contradicted its policies. Defendant's business was operated in such a way that it knew, or should have known, that the attendants at its lots did not act in accordance with their employer's policies. Defendant's failure to repudiate the actions of its employees thus constituted a ratification of the attendants' acts and defendant is bound by them. The trial court's conclusion that the attendant had the authority to bind defendant is amply supported by the record and a bailment did therefore exist between plaintiff and defendant. Plaintiff established its prima facie case and raised a presumption of defendant's negligence by showing that the car had been left with the attendant in good condition and was not returned upon Hall's demand.
* * *

We therefore conclude that the trial court's finding that defendant is liable for damages resulting from the theft of plaintiff's automobile was proper.

The trial court's decision was affirmed. Red Top Parking was held liable and had to pay damages resulting from the theft of plaintiff's automobile.	**JUDGMENT AND REMEDY**

EXCLUSIVE POSSESSION A similar distinction is made between a restaurant patron who checks a coat with an attendant and the patron who hangs it on a coatrack. The coat given to the attendant constitutes a bailment. The attendant (hence the restaurant) has exclusive possession and control over the retention and removal of the coat. By contrast, the self-hung coat can be removed at any time by the patron or anyone else so inclined. The restaurant does not have substantial control over the property and is not considered a bailee.

KNOWING ACCEPTANCE   A second aspect of the delivery of possession requirement is that the bailee knowingly accept the property. Consider this situation. An auto repair shop accepts a car for body work. The shop owner does not know, nor does the owner reveal, that some expensive jewelry is in the glove compartment. A contract for bailment exists for the car *but not for the valuables* in the glove compartment.

CONSTRUCTIVE DELIVERY   There are two further points that should be made about delivery of possession. First, *actual delivery* means the physical transfer of the property itself; however, *constructive delivery* can be sufficient to support a bailment. For example, X owns a boat that she loans to Y for the weekend. It is moored at a municipal marina. X gives Y the boat registration papers so that the harbor master will allow Y to board the boat. X has made constructive delivery of the boat to Y.

Second, there are certain unique situations in which a contract of bailment is found despite the apparent lack of the requisite elements of control or knowledge. In particular, safe deposit box rental is usually held to constitute a bailor-bailee relationship between the bank and its customer, despite the bank's lack of knowledge of the contents and its inability to have exclusive control of the property.[2]

A bailee may be liable if the goods being held or delivered are given to the wrong person. Hence, a bailee must be satisfied that the person to whom the goods are being delivered is the actual owner or has authority from the owner to take possession of the goods. Should the bailee be in error, particularly when the bailee knows the goods are stolen or that there is another claim of ownership against the goods, then the bailee may be liable for conversion or misdelivery. The following case presents an example of this principle.

---

2.   By statute or by express contract, however, a safe deposit box may be a lease of space or license depending on the jurisdiction or the facts or both.

CAPEZZARO v. WINFREY

Superior Court of New Jersey, 1977.
153 N.J.Super. 267, 379 A.2d 493.

BACKGROUND AND FACTS   *The plaintiff was a robbery victim who sued the city and its police officers after the police arrested a suspect who the plaintiff claimed had stolen money. During their apprehension of the suspect, the police had removed the money from the suspect's clothing, and the police department kept it.*

When the suspect was released from custody, she went to the police station and demanded return of the money. The police officers gave it to her. The robbery victim claimed to be the rightful owner of the money and sued the city for negligence because police officers in the city's employ had released the money.

The jury found for the robbery victim, and the police officers and the city appealed this judgment.

LORA, SEIDMAN and MILMED, Judges.
PER CURIAM
* * *

It has been said that a constructive bailment or a bailment by operation of law may be created when a person comes into possession of personal property of another, receives nothing from the owner of the property, and has no right to recover from the owner for what he does in caring for the property. Such person is ordinarily considered to be a gratuitous bailee, liable only to the bailor for bad faith or gross negligence.

Where possession has been acquired accidentally, fortuitously, through mistake or by an agreement for some other purpose since terminated, the possessor, "upon principles of justice," should keep it safely and restore or deliver it to its owner. Under such circumstances, the courts have considered the possessions *quasi*-contracts [implied contracts created by law] of bailment or constructive and involuntary bailments.

Here the police seized and obtained custody of the money which was found in Winfrey's [the robbery suspect's] girdle during a search in her cell after her arrest on the robbery charge and after plaintiff claimed Winfrey had stolen it from him. It is undisputed that the money was being kept by the police as evidence for use in Winfrey's prosecution. It follows, then, that the City of Newark, through its police department, was holding the money for its own benefit as well as for the benefit of its rightful owner.

Ordinarily, a person who has possession of property may be presumed by another to be the rightful owner thereof in the absence of any knowledge to the contrary. However, here the police were fully aware of plaintiff's adverse claim, but notwithstanding such knowledge and without notice to plaintiff turned the money over to Winfrey.

In view of the mutual benefit attendant upon custody of the money in the case before us, we find no error in the trial judge's refusal to charge that the police department was a gratuitous bailee.

Defendants further contend that when the indictment was dismissed any claim by plaintiff lost its validity and they were obligated to return the monies in question to Winfrey as bailor. We disagree. A bailee with knowledge of an adverse claim makes delivery to the bailor at his peril, and only if he is ignorant of such a claim will he be protected against a subsequent claim by the rightful owner. The position of a bailee in such situation and his possible courses of action are set forth in 9 *Williston on Contracts* (3 ed. 1967), § 1036 at 897-898:

* * *

If a bailee knows goods are stolen, or that the bailor is acting adversely to a clearly valid right, even though the true owner has as yet made no demand for them, the bailee will be liable to him for conversion if delivery is made to the bailor. In case, therefore, that the bailee knows or has been notified of an adverse claim, he will deliver to the bailor at his peril. The bailee must, for his own protection, choose one of two courses:

First, he may satisfy himself of the validity of one of the two claims and obtain authority from the owner of the claim to refuse delivery to all other claimants. In such a case he may plead at law to an action by any but the rightful owner the title of the latter, or the right of one having a superior right to immediate possession. If this title or right can be proved, a perfect defense is established.

Second, if no actual adverse claim has been made, but the bailee knows of the existence of an adverse right, or if the bailee cannot determine which of two claimants has the better title, and neither claimant will give a bond indemnifying the bailee from all damage caused by delivery to him, the only course open to the bailee is to file a bill of interpleader against the several possible owners, praying a temporary injunction against actions against himself until the true ownership of the goods is determined. And it should be added that a bailee who redelivers the goods to the bailor, or upon his order, in ignorance of his lack of title, is fully protected against subsequent claims of the rightful owner.

The police returned the money to Winfrey after being informed by the warden of the county jail that the indictments had been dismissed. They did not contact plaintiff before doing so, even though they were on notice of his adverse claim. The dismissal of the indictment for the reasons here present did not vitiate plaintiff's adverse claim to the money. Inherent in the jury's verdict is a finding that defendants were negligent in releasing the money without a determination of the validity of the adverse claim. Such finding and the verdict are amply supported by the evidence.

JUDGMENT AND REMEDY   *The judgment of the trial court was affirmed. The police officers and the city were liable to the robbery victim, the rightful owner of the stolen money.*

The Bailment Agreement

A bailment agreement can be *express* or *implied*. Although a written agreement is not required (that is, the Statute of Frauds does not apply), it is a good idea to have one, especially when valuable property is involved. However, if there is a writing that appears to be *complete*, missing terms cannot be proven by parol evidence because of the parol evidence rule. (See Chapter 11.)

RETURN OF SPECIFIC PROPERTY AND THE FUNGIBLE GOODS EXCEPTION The bailment agreement presupposes that the bailee will return the *identical goods* originally given by the bailor. However, in bailment of *fungible goods*—uniform identical goods—or bailments with the option to purchase, only *equivalent* property must be returned.

Fungible goods are defined in UCC Sec. 1-201 as units of goods that are by nature equivalent to one another—for example, grain or gasoline. The UCC in Sec. 7-207(1) states clearly, "Fungible goods may be commingled." For example, Smith, Basen, and Kerlly each store 1,000 pounds of grain in Sam's Warehouse every year, and each receives receipts. When Smith returns to reclaim "his grain," Sam's Warehouse is obligated to give him 1,000 pounds of wheat grain—but not necessarily the particular kernels he originally deposited. Smith cannot claim that Sam's Warehouse is

guilty of conversion in not returning him the exact wheat that he put into storage. As long as it returns goods of the same *type, grade,* and *quantity*, Sam's Warehouse—the bailee—has performed its obligation.

TYPES OF BAILMENTS

Bailments are either "ordinary" or "special" ("extraordinary"). There are three types of ordinary bailments. The distinguishing feature among them is *which party receives a benefit from the bailment.* Ultimately, the courts will use this factor to determine the standard of care owed by the bailee handling the goods or chattel (personal property), and this factor will dictate the rights and liabilities of the parties. However, modern courts tend to use reasonable standards of care regardless of the type of bailment arrangement in effect.

Bailments for the Sole Benefit of the Bailor (Gratuitous Bailments)

When one person holds something for safe-keeping as a favor to another, a bailment for the sole benefit of the *bailor* is in effect. It is a *gratuitous bailment* for the convenience and *benefit* of the bailor. In such a situation, the bailee is expected to use *slight care* to preserve the bailed property. Consider an example. Michael is leaving for a two-week trip to

Jamaica. He asks Susan if he can store his Ford Mustang II in her garage. He gives her the keys. She promises not to use the car for personal use. She is not paid any rent. One day, her children happen to be playing in the garage when Michael's car is there, and they accidentally dent its fender. When Michael returns, he complains that Susan should pay for the repair of the fender. She probably will not have to unless he can prove that she was guilty of gross negligence. Letting her children play in the garage would not normally be considered gross negligence.

Bailments for the Sole Benefit of the Bailee

The loan of an article to a person (the bailee) solely for that person's convenience and *benefit* is the essence of a *bailment for sole benefit of the bailee.* Under such circumstances, the bailee must use *great care* to preserve the bailed item from damage. If your best friend loans you a car so you can go out on a date, you must exercise great care in driving that car. If the car gets scratched because you parked it in a crowded parking lot, you will have trouble proving that you used great care, and, normally, you will be liable.

Bailments for the Mutual Benefit of the Bailee and the Bailor (Contractual Bailments)

Mutual benefit bailments are by far the most common kind, and they involve some form of compensation (although not necessarily money) between the bailee and the bailor for the service provided—for example, repair work, transporting goods, storing items, renting goods, or holding property.

A mutual benefit bailment need not involve the payment of a fee. All that is required is that both bailor and bailee receive a benefit. For example, many corporations provide locker and cloakroom facilities for their employees' personal belongings because employees are not permitted to bring these items into the work area. The employee (bailor) benefits by receiving storage facilities. The employer (bailee) benefits by keeping the work area uncluttered, thus decreasing the chances of minor accidents.

RIGHTS AND DUTIES OF A BAILEE (BAILEE'S RESPONSIBILITIES)

Rights of the Bailee

The bailee takes possession of personal property for a specified purpose after which that property is returned (in the same or prespecified altered form). Thus, implicit in the bailment contract is the right of the bailee to take possession, to utilize the property in accomplishing the purpose of the bailment, and to receive some form of compensation (unless the bailment is intended to be gratuitous). Depending upon the nature of the bailment and the terms of the bailment contract, these bailee rights are present (with some limitations) in varying degrees in all bailment transactions.

RIGHT OF POSSESSION Temporary control and possession of property that ultimately is to be returned to the owner is the hallmark of a bailment. The meaning of "temporary" depends upon the terms of the bailment. If a specified period is expressed, then the bailment is continuous for that time period. Earlier termination by the bailor is a breach of contract, and the bailee can recover damages from the bailor. If no duration is specified, the bailment ends when either the bailor or the bailee so demands.

A bailee's right of possession, even though temporary, permits the bailee to recover damages from any third persons for damage or loss to the property. For example, No Spot Dry Cleaners sends all suede leather garments to Cleanall Company for special processing. If Cleanall loses or damages any leather goods, No Spot has the right to recover against Cleanall. (The customer can also recover from No Spot.)

If goods or chattel are stolen from the bailee during the bailment, the bailee has a legal right to regain possession (recapture) of the goods or obtain damages from any third person who has wrongfully interfered with the bailee's possessory rights.

RIGHT TO USE BAILED PROPERTY Naturally, the extent to which bailees can use the goods or chattel entrusted to them depends upon the terms of the bailment contract. Where no provision is made, the extent of use depends upon how necessary it is to have the goods at the bailee's disposal in order to carry out the ordinary purpose of the bailment. For example, when leasing drilling machinery, the bailee is expected to use the equipment to drill. On the other hand, in long-term storage of a car, the bailee is not expected to use the car because the ordinary purpose of a storage bailment does not include use of the property.

RIGHT OF COMPENSATION In nonrental bailments, the bailor is expected to compensate the bailee for the safekeeping of or service to the property.[3] Most common nonrental bailments involve repair or transportation of goods and chattel. The amount of compensation is often expressed in the contract. For example, a moving company contract would ordinarily specify "moving and storage fees for 9,000 pounds of furniture loaded at point X and unloaded at point Y to be delivered on or about 30 days from this date . . . for $1,000." When the amount is not specified, the law provides that the bailee is entitled to "reasonable value for services rendered."

Duties of the Bailee

The bailee has two basic responsibilities: (1) to take proper care of the property and (2) to surrender the property at the end of the bailment. The bailee's duties are based on a mixture of tort law and contract law. The duty of care involves the standards and principles of tort law discussed in Chapter 3. A bailee's failure to exercise appropriate care in handling the bailor's property incurs tort liability for the bailee. The duty to relinquish the property at the end of the bailment is grounded in contract law principles. Failure to return the property is a breach of contract, and, with one exception, the bailee is liable for damages. The exception to this contractual liability exists when the obligation is excused because the goods or chattel have been lost or stolen through no fault of the bailee (or claimed by a third party with a superior claim).

DUTY OF CARE Bailees must exercise proper care over the property in their possession to prevent its loss or damage. The three types of bailments demand different degrees of care, although the trend is toward a uniform standard of care. When a bailment exists for the sole benefit of the bailee, great care, or the highest level of care, is required. When the bailment exists for the mutual benefit of the bailor and the bailee, reasonable care is the standard. When the bailment exists for the sole benefit of the bailor, slight care, or something less than ordinary or reasonable care, is expected.

PRESUMPTION OF NEGLIGENCE At the end of the bailment, a bailee has the duty to return the bailor's property in the condition it was received (allowing for ordinary wear and aging). In some cases, the bailor can sue the bailee in tort (as well as contract) for damages or lost goods on the theory of *negligence*. But often it is not possible for the bailor to discover and prove the specific acts of negligence committed by the bailee that caused damage to the property.[4] Thus, the law of bailments recognizes a rule whereby a bailor's proof that damage or loss to the property has occurred will, in and of itself, raise a presumption that the bailee is guilty of negligence. Once this is shown, the bailee must prove that he or she was *not* at fault. A bailee

_____

3.   In a rental bailment, the bailee pays the bailor for the use of the property—for example, rental of furniture or a car.

4.   The basic formula for finding negligence requires proof that (1) a duty exists, (2) a breach of that duty occurred, and (3) the breach is the proximate cause of damage or loss.

who is able to *rebut* (contradict) the presumption of negligence is not liable to the bailor. When damage to goods is normally of the type that results only from someone's negligence, and the bailee had full control of the goods, it is more likely than not that the damage was caused by the bailee's negligence. Therefore, the bailee's negligence is presumed.

Determining whether a bailee exercised an appropriate degree of care is usually a question of fact. This means that the trier-of-fact (a judge or a jury) weighs the facts of a particular situation and concludes that the bailee did or did not exercise the requisite degree of care at the time the loss or damage occurred. The failure to exercise appropriate care is *negligence*, and the bailee is liable for the loss or damage in tort. On the other hand, if the bailee has exercised sufficient care, then loss or damage to the property falls upon the bailor.

BACKGROUND AND FACTS *The plaintiff, F-M Potatoes, Inc., sued the defendant, Paul Suda, asserting that Suda owed F-M $6,500 pursuant to an oral contract for air conditioned storage of a large number of potatoes from October 1974 through March 1975. The storage agreement provided for a reasonable rental rate in the F-M warehouse facilities. Each storage bin contained a fan, heater, and humidifying equipment. The temperature and ventilation of each bin was controlled by a thermostat. Such conditioning capabilities permit the warehouse to store potatoes for about twelve months. The potatoes that Suda stored with F-M were to be used for potato chips. Therefore, during the conditioning process at the warehouse, they were to be kept at a temperature higher than normal to change the proportion of sugars to starches within each potato.*

Starting in December 1974, Suda's potatoes were taken to a laboratory for testing; they never attained an acceptable potato chip color shade. Thus, no buyer would purchase them. In March 1975, F-M hauled Suda's potatoes from its warehouse and disposed of them. Suda claimed at the trial that the potatoes were not marketable because F-M failed to provide proper air conditioned storage. F-M asserted that the potatoes were not marketable because of other factors.

F-M POTATOES, INC. v. SUDA
Supreme Court of North Dakota, 1977.
259 N.W.2d 487.

PAULSON, Judge.

* * *

Prior to discussing the issues raised by F-M on this appeal, it is necessary to determine whether the legal relationship which existed between Suda and F-M, pursuant to the oral storage agreement, was that of landlord-tenant or that of bailor-bailee. " '* * * [T]he test is whether the person leaving the property has made such a delivery to the owner of the premises as to amount to a relinquishment, for a time, of his exclusive possession, control, and dominion over the property, so that the latter can exclude, within the limits of the agreement, the possession of all others. If he has, the general rule is that the transaction is a bailment. If there is no such delivery and relinquishment of exclusive possession, and control and dominion over the goods is dependent in no degree upon the co-operation of the owner of the premises, and access to the goods is in nowise subject to the latter's control, it is generally held that the owner of the goods is a tenant or lessee of the space upon the premises where they are left.' "

In the instant case, F-M agreed to provide conditioned storage for Suda's potatoes and to control all of the mechanical equipment for maintaining the temperature and other conditioning factors. F-M received an additional 30¢ per cwt. for conditioned storage which it would not have received if it had simply rented to Suda unconditioned storage space.

* * *

Under these facts, we conclude that the agreement between Suda and F-M created a bailment for hire and that they were in the relationship of bailor-bailee.

Duty of care—Contractual limitation of warehouseman's liability.—1. A warehouseman is liable for damages for loss of or injury to the goods caused by his failure to exercise such care in regard to them as a reasonably careful man would exercise under like circumstances but unless otherwise agreed he is not liable for damages which could not have been avoided by the exercise of such care. Although a warehouseman is not an insurer of the stored goods, he must exercise the degree of skill and care that a reasonable man would exercise requisite to the operation of the business in which he is engaged. [UCC Sec. 7-204.] F-M contracted to provide Suda "conditioned storage" for his potatoes. Modern day conditioned storage of potatoes is a complicated process requiring the proper combinations of temperature, humidity, and ventilation to condition the potatoes for market while at the same time preventing deterioration of the potatoes. F-M was required, therefore, to exercise the degree of skill and care that a reasonable warehouseman would have exercised in providing conditioned storage for potatoes. [Several instances of negligent care were cited by the court.]

* * *

F-M * * * failed to exercise the degree of care in providing conditioned storage for Suda's potatoes that a reasonable warehouseman would have exercised under like circumstances.

JUDGMENT AND REMEDY   *The Supreme Court of North Dakota affirmed the trial court's findings that F-M acted negligently in providing storage for Suda's potatoes. F-M had to compensate Suda for 75 percent of the damaged potatoes.*

DUTY TO RELINQUISH PROPERTY   At the end of the bailment, the bailee normally must relinquish the identical undamaged property (unless it is fungible) to either the bailor or someone the bailor designates or otherwise dispose of it as directed. This is a *contractual* duty arising from the bailment agreement (contract). Failure to give up possession at the time the bailment ends is breach of a contract term.

As noted before, there are recognized exceptions from tort law that will excuse contract liability. If the bailee does not or cannot return the property at the end of the bailment because it has been lost, stolen, or damaged *through no negligence* (fault) on the part of the bailee, then the contractual obligation to return the property is excused. (There are a number of exceptions to this rule that concern common carriers, public warehouse companies, and innkeepers. They are discussed below.) They usually cannot limit liability except as provided by statute because they have a higher duty of care. Also, if a third party with a superior claim takes the property, the bailee normally is not liable.

RIGHTS AND DUTIES OF A BAILOR

Rights of a Bailor

The bailor's rights are essentially a complement to each of the bailee's duties. A bailor has the right to expect the following:

1. The property will be protected with reasonable care while in the possession of the bailee.
2. The bailee will utilize the property as agreed in the bailment contract (or not at all).
3. The property will be relinquished at the conclusion of the bailment according to directions given by the bailor.
4. The bailee will not convert (alter) the goods.
5. In cases of rental or lease bailments, all agreed-upon payments will be made.
6. Repairs or service on the property will be completed without defective workmanship.

Many bailees attempt to contract against liability for negligence; for example, they disclaim liability on a claim check for any harm to property due to their negligence. Courts nonetheless often protect the rights of the bailor by considering disclaimer clauses as against public policy, especially where the clause is in very fine print or where there is great disparity in the relative bargaining strength of the parties.

Duties of a Bailor

A bailor has a single, all-encompassing duty to provide the bailee with goods or chattel that are free from hidden defects that could cause injury to the bailee. This duty translates into two rules:

1. In a *mutual benefit bailment*, the bailor must notify the bailee of all *known defects* and any *hidden defects* that the bailor could have discovered with reasonable diligence and proper inspection.
2. In *bailments for the sole benefit of the bailee*, the bailor must notify the bailee of all *known defects only*.

The bailor's duty to reveal defects is based on a negligence theory of tort law. A bailor who fails to give the appropriate notice is liable to the bailee and to any other person who might reasonably be expected to come into contact with the defective article. To illustrate: Rentco (bailor) leases four tractors to Hopkinson. Unknown to Rentco (but discoverable by reasonable inspection), the brake mechanism on one of the tractors is defective at the time the bailment is made. Hopkinson uses the defective tractor not knowing of the brake problem and injures herself and two other field workers when the tractor rolls out of control. Rentco is liable on a negligence theory for injuries sustained by Hopkinson and the two employees. This is the analysis: Rentco has a *duty* to notify Hopkinson of the discoverable brake defect. Rentco's failure to notify is the *proximate cause* of injuries to farm workers who might be expected to use or have contact with the tractor. Therefore, Rentco is *liable* for the resulting injuries. (Rentco normally could not escape liability by including a disclaimer in the rental contract. Disclaimers are normally unenforceable unless both parties are privy to the contract and are often unenforceable even with privity of contract because they are against public policy.)

A bailor can also incur *warranty liability* based on contract law for injuries resulting from bailment of defective articles. Property leased by a bailor must be *fit for the intended purpose of the bailment*. The bailor's knowledge or ability to discover any defects is immaterial. Warranties of fitness arise by law in sales contracts and by judicial interpretation in the case of bailments "for hire."

CINTRONE v. HERTZ TRUCK LEASING AND RENTAL SERVICE
Supreme Court of New Jersey, 1965.
45 N.J.Super. 434, 212 A.2d 769.

BACKGROUND AND FACTS *Cintrone, an employee of the lessee of a truck brought this action against the defendant, Hertz (the bailor). The plaintiff alleged that the defendant negligently maintained the truck, which had a brake failure, causing the plaintiff to be injured. The trial court dismissed the warranty claim, and the jury found for the defendant. The plaintiff appealed.*

FRANCIS, Justice

* * *

The nature of the U-drive-it enterprise is such that a heavy burden of responsibility for the safety of lessees and for members of the public must be imposed upon it. The courts have long accepted the fact that defective trucks and cars are dangerous instrumentalities on highways. They present great potentiality for harm to other highway users as well as to their own drivers and passengers. Therefore the offering to the public of trucks and pleasure vehicles for hire necessarily carries with it a representation that they are fit for operation. This representation is of major significance because both new and used cars and trucks are rented.

* * *

The nature of the business is such that the customer is expected to, and in fact must, rely ordinarily on the express or implied representation of fitness for immediate use.

A bailor for hire, such as a person in the U-drive-it business, puts motor vehicles in the stream of commerce in a fashion not unlike a manufacturer or retailer. In fact such a bailor puts the vehicle he buys and then rents to the public to more sustained use on the highways than most ordinary car purchasers. The very nature of the business is such that the bailee, his employees, passengers and the traveling public are exposed to a greater *quantum* of potential danger of harm from defective vehicles than usually arises out of sales by the manufacturer.

* * *

When the implied warranty or representation of fitness arises, for how long should it be considered viable? Since the exposure of the user and the public to harm is great if the rented vehicle fails during ordinary use on a highway, the answer must be that it continues for the agreed rental period. The public interests involved are justly served only by treating an obligation of that nature as an incident of the business enterprise. The operator of the rental business must be regarded as possessing expertise with respect to the service life and fitness of his vehicles for use. That expertise ought to put him in a better position than the bailee to detect or to anticipate flaws or defects or fatigue in his vehicles. Moreover, as between bailor for hire and bailee the liability for flaws or defects not discoverable by ordinary care in inspecting or testing ought to rest with the bailor just as it rests with a manufacturer who buys components containing latent defects from another maker, and installs them in the completed product, or just as it rests with a retailer at the point of sale to the consumer. And, with respect to failure of a rented vehicle from fatigue, since control of the length of the lease is in the lessor, such risk is one which, in the interest of the consuming public as well as of the members of the public traveling the highways, ought to be imposed on the rental business.

Accordingly, we are of the opinion (1) that the leasing agreement gave rise to a continuing implied promissory warranty that the leased trucks would be fit for plaintiff's employer's use for the duration of the lease, (2) that the nature of the U-drive-it business is such that the responsibility of Hertz may properly be stated in terms of strict liability in tort[.] * * * Strict liability in tort does not make an insurer of the person subject to the duty to provide a truck safe for use. Happening of an accident without more, would not establish liability. There must be proof of such a failure of the truck as shows a breach of the warranty or breach of the duty to supply a vehicle fit for the agreed period of use. For example, if a rented vehicle was driven around a curve at such an excessive rate of speed that the driver lost control and struck a pole, the cause would not be failure of the vehicle, but failure of the driver. Here, as we have said, a factual issue exists as to whether the brakes were defective and the collision and plaintiff's injuries resulted from the defect. The jury must pass upon the credibility of the various witnesses; they must resolve the factual conflicts in the testimony about the condition of the brakes and whether a defective braking mechanism was repaired after the accident; and they must decide whether the collision was occasioned by defective brakes[.]
* * *

For the reasons stated, the trial judge should have submitted the issue of breach of implied warranty of fitness to the jury for determination. His refusal to do so constituted reversible error. * * *

The trial court's judgment was reversed, and the case was remanded to the trial court for a new trial. The trial judge should have acknowledged the legal theory that the lease agreement gave rise to an implied warranty that the leased truck would be fit for ordinary use for the duration of the lease.

JUDGMENT AND REMEDY

Exculpatory Clauses

Exculpatory clauses in contracts of bailment purport to "hold (one) absolutely harmless" from any and all risks of loss, damage, or injury. Courts regularly find them illegal and against public policy.

The classic illustration of an exculpatory clause is found on parking receipts: "We assume no risk for damage to or loss of automobile or its contents regardless of the cause. It is agreed that the vehicle owner assumes such risks." Whatever the language of such a clause, the result is normally the same—it is illegal and unenforceable. This is especially true in the case of bailees providing a quasi-public service. The "take it or leave it" message implicit in the exculpatory provision is normally located on the reverse side of a parking receipt, which most people are unaware of; and these clauses are generally in very fine print. The public policy violated, therefore, is one of *unfair surprise.*

Certain bailees can limit their liabilities by contract with the bailor, but such limitation must be brought to the bailor's attention. In particular, professional bailees, such as repair garages, are subject to this rule. A sign on Joe Brown's Garage indicating that the garage is "not responsible for anything that happens to any car left here" does not ordinarily come to the attention of the bailor. The bailee must show the writing to the bailor and inform the bailor that it limits or varies the bailee's liability. (The bailee is *not* required to read and interpret the limitation or variation to the bailor.)

Termination of Bailment

Bailments for a specific term end when the stated period lapses. When no duration is specified, the bailment can be terminated any time by the following events:

1. The mutual agreement of both parties.
2. A demand by either party.
3. The completion of the purpose of the bailment.
4. An act by the bailee that is inconsistent with the terms of the bailment.
5. The operation of law.

SPECIAL BAILMENTS

Most of this chapter has concerned itself with ordinary bailments. Special, or extraordinary, bailments include (1) common carriers, (2) warehouse companies, and (3) innkeepers or hotel keepers.

Common Carriers

Common carriers are publicly licensed to provide transportation services to the general public. They are distinguished from private carriers who operate transportation facilities for a select clientele. A private carrier is not bound to provide service to every person or company making a request. The common carrier, however, must arrange carriage for all who apply, within certain limitations.[5] The delivery of goods to a common carrier creates a *bailment relationship* between the shipper (bailor) and the common carrier (bailee). The common carrier contract of transportation creates a

mutual benefit bailment. But, unlike ordinary mutual benefit bailments, the common carrier is held to a standard of care based on *strict liability* rather than reasonable care in protecting the bailed personal property. This means that the common carrier is absolutely liable for all loss or damage to goods except damage caused by one of the five common law exceptions: (1) an act of God, (2) an act of a public enemy, (3) an order of a public authority, (4) an act of the shipper, or (5) the inherent nature of the goods.

Common carriers are treated as if they were absolute insurers for the safe delivery of goods to the destination but really, they are not. They cannot contract away this liability for damaged goods, but, subject to government regulations, they are permitted to limit their dollar liability to an amount stated on the shipment contract.[6]

Except for the five exceptions given, any damage to goods in shipment, even that caused by the willful acts of third persons or sheer accident, do not relieve the common carrier from liability. Thus, a common carrier trucking company moving cargo is liable for acts of vandalism, mechanical defects in refrigeration units, or a dam bursting if any of these acts result in damage to the cargo. But damage caused by acts of God—earthquake or lightning striking, for example—are the shipper's loss.

There are many interesting cases concerning what constitutes an "act of God." The following extract is from a case in which a common carrier learned that a flood was *not* necessarily enough of an "act of God" to excuse liability:

The only acts of God that excuse common carriers from liability for loss or injury to goods in transit are those operations of the forces of nature that could not have been anticipated and provided against and that by their super human force unexpectedly injure or destroy goods in the custody or control of the

---

5. A common carrier is not required to take any and all property anywhere in all instances. Public regulatory agencies, such as the Interstate Commerce Commission, govern commercial carriers, and carriers can be restricted to geographical areas. They can also be limited to carrying certain kinds of goods or to providing only special types of transportation equipment.

---

6. For example, federal laws and Interstate Commerce Commission regulations require common carriers to offer shippers the opportunity to obtain higher dollar limits for loss by paying a higher fee for the transport.

carrier. Extreme weather conditions which operate to foil human obligations of duty are regarded as acts of God. However, every strong wind, snowstorm, or rainstorm cannot be termed an act of God merely because it is of unusual or more than average intensity. Ordinary, expectable, and gradual weather conditions are not regarded as acts of God even though they may have produced a disaster, because man had the opportunity to control their effects.[7]

SHIPPER'S LOSS   The shipper bears any loss occurring through its own faulty or improper crating or packaging procedures. For example, if a bird dies because its crate was poorly ventilated, the shipper bears the loss, not the carrier.

CONNECTING CARRIERS   Where connecting carriers are involved in transporting goods, the shipper can recover from the original carrier or any connecting carrier. In all cases of carrier liability, the shipper must prove that the cargo was in good condition at the time it was shipped. Normally, the *last* carrier is presumed to have received the goods in good condition.

Warehouse Companies

Warehousing is the business of providing storage of property for compensation. A warehouse company is a professional bailee whose responsibility differs from an ordinary bailee in two important aspects. First, a warehouse company is empowered to issue documents of title, in particular, warehouse receipts.[8] Second, warehouse companies are subject to an extraordinary network of state and federal statutes and Article 7 of the Uniform Commercial Code (as are carriers).

---

7. Southern Pacific Co. v. Loden, 508 P.2d 347 (Arizona App.1972)

8. Document of title is defined in UCC Sec. 1-201 (15) as any "document which in the regular course of business or financing is treated as adequately evidencing that the person in possession of it is entitled to receive, hold, and dispose of the document and the goods it covers. To be a document of title, a document must purport to be issued by or addressed to a bailee and purport to cover goods in the bailee's possession * * *."

Like ordinary bailees, a warehouse company is liable for loss or damage to property and possession resulting from *negligence* (and therefore does not have the same liability as a common carrier). The duty is one of reasonable care to protect and preserve the goods. A warehouse company can limit the dollar amount of liability, but the bailor must be given the option of paying an increased storage rate for an increase in the liability limit.

A warehouse company accepts goods for storage and issues a warehouse receipt describing the property and the terms of the bailment contract. The warehouse receipt can be negotiable or nonnegotiable depending on how it is written. (Negotiable and nonnegotiable instruments are discussed in Chapter 24.) The warehouse receipt is negotiable if its terms provide that the warehouse company will deliver the goods "to the bearer" of the receipt, or "to the order of" a person named on the receipt.

The warehouse receipt serves multiple functions. It is a receipt for the goods stored; it is a contract of bailment; it also represents the goods (that is, it indicates title) and hence has value and utility in financing commercial transactions. Thus, Oakner, a rancher, delivers 6,000 head of buffalo to Abel, the owner of a warehouse. Abel issues a negotiable warehouse receipt payable "to bearer" and gives it to Oakner. Oakner goes to the ranchers' market and ultimately sells the entire herd of buffalo to Jones and Smith, buffalo investors. Oakner delivers the warehouse receipt to Jones and Smith. They are now the owners of the buffalo and have the right to obtain them from Abel. Jones and Smith present the warehouse receipt to Abel, who in return releases the 6,000 buffalo to them.

Most states have special laws relating to the warehousing industry. In addition, if the warehouse company operates in interstate commerce, federal regulations impose other controls on business operations. Article 7 of the Uniform Commercial Code is involved only with the rights and liabilities relating to documents of title.

Innkeepers

At common law, innkeepers, hotel owners, or similar operators were held to the same strict liability as common carriers with respect to bailed personal property. Now, only those who provide lodging to the public for compensation as a *regular* business are covered under this rule of strict liability. The rule further applies to those lodgers who are "guests". To be a guest, a person must be a traveler, not a permanent lodger. Courts and statutes are tending to reduce the strict liability of the common law.

STATUTORY CHANGES In many states, inn-keepers can avoid strict liability for loss of guests' valuables and money by providing a safe in which to keep them. Each guest must be clearly notified of the availability of such a safe. Various statutes dictate the requirements for such notices. When articles are not kept in the safe, or when they are of such a nature that they are not normally kept in a safe, statutes will often limit innkeepers' liability.

Consider an example covering personal property that cannot be put in a safe. Jackson stays for a night at Hideaway Hotel. When he returns from eating breakfast in the hotel restaurant, he discovers that the people in the room next door have forced the lock on the door between the two rooms and stolen his suitcase. Jackson claims that the hotel is liable for his loss. The hotel denies liability due to the lack of negligence on its part. At common law, inn-keepers are actually insurers of the valuables of their guests. In states where this common law liability prevails, the hotel will be liable. In some states, though, the hotel will not be liable at all in the absence of negligence. In others, the liability of the hotel in the absence of negligence will be limited to a fairly small sum.

GUESTS' AUTOMOBILES Normally, the inn-keeper assumes no responsibility for the safety of a guest's automobile because the guest usually retains possession and control. If, on the other hand, the innkeeper provides parking facilities, and the guest's car is entrusted to the innkeeper or to an employee, the innkeeper will be liable under the rules that pertain to parking lot bailees.

QUESTIONS AND CASE PROBLEMS

1. Pal lent his best friend, Penn, a crane that Penn intended to put to his own personal use. Penn tied the crane to the back of his truck with several chains. After he drove a short distance, he checked the chains. They were loose, and he tightened them. During the transport of the crane, Penn checked the chains two other times. Penn made several sharp turns with his truck between his last inspection of the chains and the truck's destination. Just before Penn reached his destination, the crane fell off the truck while he was driving down an interstate highway exit ramp. Even though the crane was extensively damaged, Penn claimed that he was not negligent. Can Pal recover for damage to his crane? [Great American Ins. Co. v. Penn, 275 So.2d 221 (La.App.1973)]

2. In the early 1970s, New York City was engaged in extensive urban renewal, and many people were forced to relocate. Phillips, a resident of a large apartment building that the city planned to tear down, was forced to move his belongings to an apartment that was not yet ready for occupancy. After Phillips had moved his belongings, but while he was staying with some friends, a number of his belongings were stolen. Phillips attempted to sue New York City for his lost property, but the trial court judge dismissed the case, stating that the city owed no duty to Phillips. Is the trial court judge correct? [Phillips v. City of New York, 71 Misc.2d 861, 337 N.Y.S.2d 303 (1972)]

3. The Mid-Top Restaurant, located in downtown Hartford, Connecticut, required its waitresses, as part of their work, to wear waitress uniforms. Mid-Top provided a rack and lockers adjacent to the wait-resses' dining room in which they could change into their uniforms and get ready for work. On November 13, 1970, a fire destroyed most of the Mid-Top Restaurant. Sandra Grana, a waitress at the Mid-Top, sued the restaurant to recover for the destruction of

the personal property that she had left in her locker. Mid-Top claimed that, since the locker room was always left unlocked, it was not holding Grana's personal property in storage and, therefore, was not a bailee. Is this argument convincing? [Grana v. Security Ins. Group, 72 Misc.2d 265, 339 N.Y.2d 34 (1972)]

4. During a dark November night in 1966, Adler and Sons, one of the largest jewelry stores in New Orleans, was burglarized. The burglars cut a hole in the roof and brought in special tools, including an acetylene torch, which they used to cut through the solid steel door on the vault. Even though an alarm system connected to the doors, windows, vents, and vault was activated by an employee before he left for the night, the burglars successfully completed their task and escaped without capture. One of the jewelry store's customers had left over $100,000 worth of jewelry with Adler for repair that morning. All of the customer's jewelry was stolen in the burglary. Can the customer recover from Adler? [Travelers Ins. Co. v. Coleman E. Adler, Inc., 285 So.2d 381 (La.App. 1973)]

5. Dunham owned and operated a business that included the selling of sand and gravel, which he obtained through a dredging operation. On July 20 Dunham informed his friend Roy Young, president of Roy Young, Inc., that the engine on one of Dunham's dredges had become inoperative. Dunham told Young that he wanted to borrow one of Young's engines for a few days until his own could be repaired. Young agreed to loan a diesel engine to Dunham under the condition that Dunham would pay for repairs if the engine became damaged. The parties never agreed that any consideration would be paid for the use of the engine. When Dunham returned the engine to Young, it was damaged. Must Young prove that Dunham was negligent, or is Dunham presumed to have been negligent? [Roy Young, Inc. v. Delcambre, Inc., 233 So.2d 612 (La.App. 1970)]

6. Cook Company contracted with American Export Lines for American to carry certain cargo. Cook also contracted with McRoberts for McRoberts to provide storage and security for the cargo once it was placed in McRoberts's "safe room." American shipped the cargo belonging to Cook Company and unloaded it at the pier as provided in the contract. While the cargo was being unloaded, several of McRoberts's security guards were at the scene observing the operation. After the goods were unloaded onto the pier, but before they were transported into McRoberts's "safe room," the goods were stolen. In a suit by Cook Company against McRoberts, can Cook Company successfully claim that McRoberts was a bailee of the cargo? [Union Marine and General Ins. Co. v. American Export Lines, Inc., 274 F.Supp. 123 (D.C.N.Y. 1966)]

7. Ehrlich-Newmark Truck Company was a common carrier. It entered into a contract with David Crystal Inc. for the transportation of some garments from North Carolina to New York City. When Ehrlich-Newmark's truck arrived in New York, it was highjacked. All of the garments were stolen, and the truck was never retrieved. David Crystal sued Ehrlich-Newmark for the price of the garments. Ehrlich-Newmark conceded that there was a bailment, but defended on the grounds that the highjacking was the act of a "public enemy" and that therefore it was not responsible for the loss. Is this a valid defense? [David Crystal Inc. v. Ehrlich-Newmark Trucking Co., 64 Misc.2d 325, 314 N.Y.S.2d 559 (1970)]

8. Tire City, Inc., was in the business of whitewalling and recapping tires. Smith, a tire dealer, entered into a contract with Tire City to have four dozen of Smith's tires white-walled. Smith sent Tire City four dozen black-walls on May 1. On May 3, Tire City acknowledged receipt of the forty-eight tires. Soon thereafter, the tire business became somewhat deflated, and Tire City's financial situation steadily worsened. Shortly after Tire City received the shipment from Smith, one of Tire City's creditors obtained a lien on Smith's four dozen tires. If Tire City does not object to its creditor taking possession of the tires, can Smith stop the creditor? [Nassar v. Smith, 21 Ill.App. 3d 462, 315 N.E.2d 692 (1974)]

9. Procter & Gamble was a distributor of soybean oils. Soybean oil production is seasonal, and Procter & Gamble's inventory was usually very high in the summer, decreasing gradually over the months that followed. The seasonal nature of oil production meant that Procter & Gamble had to store large quantities of oil for a long period of time. In 1962 the company began utilizing the storage facilities of Field Warehousing Corporation. Procter & Gamble shipped oil to Field Warehousing, which stored the oil in its own storage tanks. In exchange for the oil, Field Warehousing gave Procter & Gamble "warehousing receipts." This allowed Procter & Gamble to sell the oil by merely selling the receipt (which was evidence of title to the oil). Thus, Procter & Gamble did not have to ship any of the oil in order to make a sale. About six months after it began storing oil at Field Warehousing, Procter & Gamble sold a large number of its warehouse receipts to Allied Oil Refining Corp. When Allied attempted to get the oil, it found that the

storage tanks were filled nine-tenths with water and one-tenth with oil. Allied rescinded its contract with Procter & Gamble, and Procter & Gamble in turn sued Field Warehousing. After a year-long investigation, neither Field Warehousing nor Procter & Gamble could determine how the oil disappeared. Who is liable for the missing oil? [Procter & Gamble Distributing Co. v. Lawrence American Field Warehousing Corp., 16 N.Y.2d 344, 266 N.Y.S.2d 785, 213 N.E.2d 873 (1965)]

10. Washington Toll Bridge Authority operated a ferry service in Port City, Washington. The ferry was docked at the far end of a pier several hundred feet in length. Tickets were sold by the Toll Bridge Authority at the near end of the pier. While waiting to buy a ticket to ride the Washington ferry, Zorotovich was struck by a vehicle being driven across the dock platform. Zorotovich sued Washington Toll Bridge Authority, claiming that the Toll Bridge Authority was liable to him as a passenger of the Washington ferry. Washington Toll Bridge Authority claimed that it was not liable. Who wins? [Zorotovich v. Washington Toll Bridge Authority, 80 Wash.2d 106, 491 P.2d 1295 (1971)]

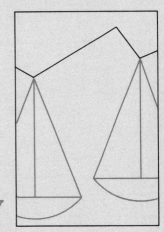

UNIT IV
Commercial Transactions and the Uniform Commercial Code

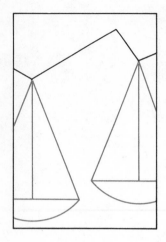

17

Sales

Introduction to Sales Contracts and Their Formation

Every day of our lives we make purchases—the daily newspaper, groceries, clothes, textbooks, a stereo, a car, and so on. Most of our purchases are of "goods" rather than real property. Thus, studying the law of sales of goods is relevant to our daily lives.

The people from whom we buy our goods are, to us, "sellers." But our "sellers" are in turn "buyers" from their suppliers, who are in turn, "buyers" from manufacturers. The law of sales is the study of the rights and responsibilities of those in the purchase-and-sale of goods chain, from the original maker of the item to the ultimate user. A **sale** is a contract that, by its terms, transfers goods from a seller to a buyer for a price in current money (or a promise of payment).

HISTORICAL PERSPECTIVE

Today's law of sales originated centuries ago in the customs and traditions of merchants and traders. The *Lex Mercantoria* (Law Merchant) was a system of rules, customs, and usages self-imposed by early commercial traders and merchants to settle disputes and to enforce obligations among themselves. (See Chapter 2.)

By the end of the seventeenth century, the principles of the Law Merchant were widely accepted and quite naturally became part of the common law. From that time on, judges, not merchants, refined the principles of mercantile law into the modern commercial law of sales.

Numerous attempts were made in the United States to produce a uniform body of laws relating to commercial transactions. Two major enactments, the Uniform Negotiable Instruments Law (1896) and the Uniform Sales Act (1906), were followed by several other "uniform acts," none of which were widely adopted by the states. In the 1940's the need to integrate the half-dozen or so uniform acts covering commercial transactions into a single, comprehensive body of statutory law was recognized. Accordingly, the Uniform Commercial Code (UCC, or simply "the Code") was developed to serve that purpose.

THE UNIFORM COMMERCIAL CODE

The UCC is the single, most comprehensive codification of the broad spectrum of laws involved in a total commercial transaction. It views the entire "commercial transaction for the sale of and payment for goods" as a single legal occurrence having numerous facets. Consider a consumer who buys a refrigerator from an appliance store and agrees to pay for it on an installment plan. Article 2 of the Code treats the contract of sale. If a check is given as the down payment on the purchase price, it will be negotiated and ultimately passed through one or more banks for collection. This process is the subject matter of Article 3, Commercial Paper, and Article 4, Bank Deposits and Collections. The appliance store extends credit to the consumer through the intallment plan, and it retains a right in the refrigerator (collateral). This is the subject matter of Article 9, Secured Transactions. Suppose the appliance company must first obtain the refrigerator from its manufacturer's warehouse, after which it is to be delivered by common carrier to the consumer. The storage and shipment of goods is the subject matter of Article 7, Documents of Title. When the appliance company arranges to pay the manufacturer located in another state for the refrigerator supplied, a letter of credit, which is the subject matter of Article 5, may be used. Every phase of commerce is involved in the seemingly simple sale of and payment for goods. The Code attempts to provide a consistent and integrated framework of rules to deal with all the phases *ordinarily arising* in a commercial sales transaction from start to finish.[1]

THE SCOPE OF ARTICLE 2: THE SALE OF GOODS

No body of law, and certainly not the Code, operates in a vacuum removed from other principles of jurisprudence. A sales contract is governed by the same common law principles applicable to all contracts—offer, acceptance, consideration, and capacity—and these principles should be re-examined when studying sales. The law of sales, found in Article 2 of the UCC, is a part of the law of contracts.

Two things should be kept in mind. First, Article 2 deals with the sale of *goods*, not real property (real estate), services, or intangible property such as stocks and bonds. Second, in some cases, the rules will vary quite a bit, depending upon whether the buyer or seller is a *merchant* or a consumer.

It is always a good idea to note the subject matter of a dispute and the kind of people involved. If the subject is goods, then the UCC will govern. If it is real estate or services, then the common law alone will apply. If one of the people involved is a merchant, certain rules apply. If both are, another rule applies. If neither is, still a different rule applies.

---

1. Two articles of the Uniform Commercial Code seemingly do not fit into the "ordinary" commercial sales transaction. Article 6, Bulk Transfers, involves merchants who sell off the major part of their inventory, (often pocketing the money and disappearing, leaving creditors unpaid). Since such "bulk sales" do not "ordinarily arise" in a commercial transaction for the sale of goods, they are treated separately. Article 8, Investment Securities, deals with negotiable securities (stocks and bonds), transactions that do not fall within the concept of sale of or payment for *goods*. However, the subject matter of Articles 6 and 8 was considered by the Code's drafters to be related closely enough to ordinary commercial transactions to warrant inclusion in the Uniform Commercial Code.

What Is a Sale?

Article 2 applies to the "sale of goods", but Section 2-102 states that Article 2 applies to "*transactions* in goods", indicating a broader scope that includes, for example, leases and gifts. However, for the purposes of this Chapter (and most authorities and courts will agree), Article 2 applies only to an actual *sale*.

The word "sale" is a shorthand way of saying "a sales contract which by its terms transfers goods from seller to buyer for a price." A sale is officially defined "... as the passing of title from the seller to the buyer for a price". [UCC Sec. 2-106(1)] The price may be payable in money or in other goods, services, or realty (real estate).

What Are Goods?

To be characterized as a *good*, an item must be *tangible*, and it must be *movable*.

A tangible item has physical existence—it can be touched or seen. Thus, intangible property such as corporate stocks and bonds, promissory notes, bank accounts, patents and copyrights, or ordinary contract rights have only conceptual existence and do not come under Article 2.

A *movable* item can be carried from place to place. Hence, real estate is excluded from Article 2. However, goods "*associated with real estate*" fall under Article 2. Section 2-107 provides the following rules:

1. A contract for the sale of minerals or the like (including oil and gas) or a structure (such as a building) is a contract for the sale of goods *if severance is to be made by the seller*. If the buyer is to sever them from the land, the contract is considered a sale of real estate governed by the principles of real property law, not the UCC. To illustrate: S agrees to sell B a quantity of oil that is located under S's property. If B is to drill the wells to remove the oil, the contract is a sale of real estate. If the agreement provides that S is to drill the wells to obtain the oil, the transaction is a sale of goods. Similarly, S agrees to sell B an old barn located on S's farm. If the

agreement requires B to remove the barn, it is a contract for the sale of real estate. If S is to remove the barn, the contract is characterized as a sale of goods under UCC Article 2.

2. A sale of growing crops or timber to be cut is a contract for the sale of goods regardless of who severs them.

3. Other "things attached" to realty but capable of severance without material harm to the land are considered goods regardless of who severs them.[2] Examples of such things are a furnace or window air-conditioner in a house or counters and stools in a luncheonette. The test is whether removal will cause *material harm* to the realty to which the item is attached. Removal of a window air-conditioner would be a sale of goods, but removal of a central air-conditioning system or an in-ground swimming pool would probably do a great deal of damage and hence would be treated as a sale of real estate. When the parties do not envision any items being removed (severed) from the realty, such as in the sale of "ten acres of corn fields", then the transaction is characterized as the sale of real estate.

GOODS VERSUS SERVICES   Courts have disagreed over whether a particular transaction involves the sale of goods or the rendering of a service. For example, is the blood furnished to a patient during an operation a "sale of goods" or the "performance of a medical service"? Some courts say "a good"; some say "a service." The same kind of "mixed transaction" problem is encountered when a beautician applies hair dye to a customer in a beauty shop. The Code does not provide the answer, and court decisions are in conflict. The Code does stipulate, however, that serving food or drink to be consumed either on or off restaurant premises is the "sale of goods", at least for the purpose of an implied warranty of merchantability. [UCC Sec. 2-312(1)] Whether the transaction in question involves the sale of goods or services is important because the majority of courts treat services as being excluded by the UCC.

---

2.   The Code avoids using the word "fixtures" here because of the numerous definitions of this term. (See Chapter 52.)

SPECIAL CLASSIFICATIONS   The Code refers to several special cases that it explicitly characterizes as "goods":

1.   The unborn young of animals are goods.
2.   Rare coins and other forms of money as a commodity are goods (but money as a form of payment is not).
3.   Items specially manufactured for a particular buyer are goods. Even though the "special order" might be construed as a contract for "special services", the Code clearly categorizes these transactions as a sale of goods.

Who Is a Merchant?

Article 2 governs the sale of goods in general. It applies to sales transactions between all buyers and sellers. In a limited number of instances, however, the Code presumes that, in certain phases of sales transactions between *professional merchants*, special business standards ought to be imposed because of the merchants' degree of commercial expertise.[3] Such standards do not apply to the casual or inexperienced seller or buyer. Section 2-104 defines three ways that *merchant* status occurs:

1.   A merchant is a person who *deals in goods of the kind* involved in the sales contract. Thus, a retailer, a wholesaler, or a manufacturer is a

---

3.   The provisions that apply only to merchants deal with the Statute of Frauds, firm offers, confirmatory memoranda, warranties, and contract modification. These special rules reflect expedient business practice, commonly known to merchants in the commercial setting. They will be discussed in the materials presented later in this chapter on sales contract formation.

merchant of those goods sold in the business. A merchant for one type of goods is not necessarily a merchant for any other type. For example, a sporting equipment retailer is a merchant when buying tennis equipment but not when buying stereo equipment.

2.   A merchant is a person who, by occupation, *holds himself or herself out as having knowledge and skill peculiar to the practices or goods involved in the transaction.* This is a broad definition that can include banks or universities as merchants.

3.   A person who employs a merchant as a broker, agent, or other intermediary has the status of merchant in that transaction. Hence, if a "gentleman farmer" who ordinarily does not run the farm hires a broker to purchase livestock, the farmer is considered a merchant in the livestock transaction.

In summary, a person can be considered to have the professional status of "merchant" by having specialized knowledge of the business or the goods, by employing a merchant to conduct a particular transaction, or by holding him- or herself out to be a merchant. These provisions apply only when a merchant is acting in a mercantile capacity.

Is a farmer a merchant? The answer depends upon the particular goods involved, the transaction, and whether, in the particular situation, the farmer is held out as having special knowledge concerning the goods involved in the transaction. The following case illustrates how the courts decide whether or not a person is a merchant and therefore subject to the UCC version of the Statute of Frauds.

BACKGROUND AND FACTS   *A cooperative grain association sued a wheat farmer who was a member of the association to enforce an oral contract for the sale of 10,000 bushels of wheat. The wheat farmer prevailed at the trial, and the cooperative association appealed.*

The appellant owned and operated a grain elevator. Its principal business was the purchase of wheat and other grains from area farmers, which it then marketed to larger, regional grain dealers.

The appellant never speculated on the price of grain. Therefore, as soon as it purchased about 2,000 bushels of grain from its supplying

DECATUR COOPERATIVE ASS'N. v. URBAN
Supreme Court of Kansas, 1976.
219 Kan. 171, 547 P.2d 323.

farmers, it placed a phone call to a terminal elevator and orally sold the grain to that elevator at the prevailing price. Thereafter, the terminal elevator sent a written confirmation of sale to the cooperative. This procedure was a well-established and well-known method of handling and marketing grain in Kansas.

The appellee, Urban, had been a wheat farmer for about twenty years and was a member of the cooperative. Urban was engaged solely in the farming business, and had sold wheat and other grains he grew to the appellant and to other elevators in the area.

The controversy underlying this lawsuit arose when Urban supposedly called the cooperative and asked to speak to the assistant manager. The assistant manager was not available. Later that afternoon, Urban placed a second call to the cooperative office and allegedly agreed to sell 10,000 bushels of wheat at $2.86 per bushel to the cooperative, to be delivered on or before September 30, 1973. Urban later denied that any contract of sale was made during this phone call.

The cooperative disagreed with Urban's version, claiming that, during the conversation, there was a discussion of a written memorandum of sale to be prepared and later sent to Urban. The cooperative always sent such written confirmations of sale to the seller immediately after oral conversations and claimed that it did in fact send such a confirmation to Urban. This confirmation was signed by the cooperative's assistant manager and was binding against the cooperative. Urban received the confirmation within a reasonable time, read it, and did not give written notice of objection to its contents within ten days after it was received. The cooperative argued that the confirmation to which Urban made no objection became a binding contract under the provisions of the Uniform Commercial Code. [BACKGROUND AND FACTS essentially as stated by the court.]

HARMAN, Commissioner.

* * *

This action was brought to obtain possession of 10,000 bushels of wheat allegedly purchased under an oral contract, or alternatively, for damages for failure to deliver the wheat. The primary issue is whether the alleged seller, a farmer, was a "merchant" within the meaning of the uniform commercial code so as to remove the oral contract from operation of the statute of frauds.

K.S.A. [Kansas Statutes Annotated] 84-2-104 contains the following definitions:

"(1) 'Merchant' means a person who deals in goods of the kind or otherwise by his occupation holds himself out as having knowledge or skill peculiar to the practices or goods involved in the transaction or to whom such knowledge or skill may be attributed by his employment of an agent or broker or other intermediary who by his occupation holds himself out as having such knowledge or skill.

"(3) 'Between merchants' means in any transaction with respect to which both parties are chargeable with the knowledge or skill of merchants."

The official UCC comment states:

"*Purposes:*

"1. This Article assumes that transactions between professionals in a given field require special and clear rules which may not apply to a casual or inexperienced seller or buyer. It thus adopts a policy of expressly stating rules applicable 'between merchants' and 'as against a merchant', wherever they are needed instead of making them depend upon the circumstances of each case as in the statutes cited above. This section lays the foundation of this policy by defining those who are to be regarded as professionals or 'merchants' and by stating when a transaction is deemed to be 'between merchants'.

"2. The term 'merchant' as defined here roots in the 'law merchant' concept of a professional in business. The professional status under the definition may be based upon specialized knowledge as to the goods, specialized knowledge as to business practices, or specialized knowledge as to both and which kind of specialized knowledge may be sufficient to establish the merchant status is indicated by the nature of the provisions. * * *"

From the foregoing it appears there are three separate criteria for determining merchant status. A merchant is (1) a dealer who deals in the goods of the kind involved, or (2) one who by his occupation holds himself out as having knowledge or skill peculiar to the practices or goods involved in the transaction, even though he may not actually have such knowledge, or (3) a principal who employs an agent, broker or other intermediary who by his occupation holds himself out as having knowledge or skill peculiar to the practices or goods involved in the transaction. Professionalism, special knowledge and commercial experience are to be used in determining whether a person in a particular situation is to be held to the standards of a merchant.

* * *

In our opinion the facts here disclose that appellee neither "deals" in wheat, as that term is used in 2-104, nor does he by his occupation hold himself out as having knowledge or skill peculiar to the practices or goods involved in the transaction. The concept of professionalism is heavy in determining who is a merchant under the statute. The writers of the official UCC comment virtually equate professionals with merchants—the casual or inexperienced buyer or seller is not to be held to the standard set for the professional in business. The defined term "between merchants", used in the exception proviso to the statute of frauds, contemplates the knowledge and skill of professionals on each side of the transaction. The transaction in question here was the sale of wheat. Appellee as a farmer undoubtedly had special knowledge or skill in raising wheat but we do not think this factor, coupled with annual sales of a wheat crop and purchases of seed wheat, qualified him as a merchant in that field. The parties' stipulation states appellee has sold only the products he raised. There is no indication any of these sales were other than cash sales to local grain elevators, where conceivably an expertise reaching professional status could be said to be involved.

We think the trial court correctly ruled under the particular facts that appellee was not a merchant for the purpose of avoiding the operation of the statute of frauds.

JUDGMENT AND REMEDY

The trial court correctly ruled that the appellee was not a merchant. However, the Supreme Court of Kansas ultimately based its decision on the theory of promissory estoppel. Since the cooperative had relied on Urban to sell the grain, and Urban knew that the cooperative was relying on him, the court would not allow the farmer to avoid all responsibility under the contract.

EXHIBIT 17-1 UCC RULES FOR CONTRACTS FOR THE SALE OF GOODS

	RULE	SECTION OF UCC
OFFER AND ACCEPTANCE	1. The acceptance of unilateral offers can be made by a promise to ship or by shipment itself.	2-206 (1) (b)
	2. Not all terms have to be included in negotiation for a contract to result.	2-204
	3. Particulars of performance can be left open.	2-311 (1)
	4. Firm written offers by *merchants* for three months or less cannot be revoked.	2-205
	5. Acceptance by performance requires notice within a reasonable time; otherwise the offer can be treated as lapsed.	2-206 (2)
	6. The price does not have to be included to have a contract.	2-205
	7. Variations in terms between the offer and the acceptance may not be a rejection but may be an acceptance.	2-207
	8. Acceptance can be made by any reasonable means of communication; it is effective when deposited.	2-206 (1) (a)
CONSIDERATION	1. A modification of a contract for the sale of goods does not require consideration.	2-209 (1)
	2. Adding a seal has no effect on the validity of the contract.	2-203
ILLEGALITY	1. Unconscionable bargains will not be enforced.	2-302
VOIDABLE CONTRACTS	1. Revocation of acceptance does not prevent a lawsuit for monetary damages.	2-721
	2. A person with voidable title has power to transfer a good title to a good faith purchaser for value.	
FORM OF THE AGREEMENT	1. The Statute of Frauds covers: (a) All sales of goods for a price in excess of $500. (b) Written confirmations between merchants. (c) Specially manufactured goods. (d) Memoranda that do not include all the agreement terms. (e) Goods for which payment has been made and accepted; goods which have been received and accepted. (f) Admission in pleadings or court proceedings that a contract for sale was made.	2-201
RIGHTS OF THIRD PARTIES	1. Delegation of duties is included when a contract, or the rights under a contract, are assigned.	2-210 (4)
PERFORMANCE OF CONTRACTS	1. Tender of payment is a condition precedent to a tender of delivery, unless a credit sale was agreed upon.	2-511
	2. Anticipatory breach cannot be withdrawn if the other party gives notice that it is final.	2-616, 2-611
	3. Claims and rights can be waived without consideration.	1-107
DISCHARGE	1. The statute of limitations is four years. Mutual agreement can reduce it to not less than one year.	2-725

FORMATION OF A SALES CONTRACT

The policy of the Uniform Commercial Code is to recognize that the law of sales is part of the general law of contracts. The Code often restates general principles or is silent altogether. In those situations, the common law of contracts and applicable state statutes govern. The following sections summarize the ways that UCC provisions change the effect of the general law of contracts. Exhibit 17-1 summarizes the special rules for contracts of sale of goods and the Code section out of Article 2 that applies. All these rules will be treated in this chapter and in Chapters 18 through 22.

Offer

In general contract law, the moment a definite offer is met by an unqualified acceptance, a binding contract is formed. In commercial sales transactions, the verbal exchanges, the correspondence, and the actions of the parties may not reveal exactly when a binding contractual obligation arises. The Code states that an agreement sufficient to constitute a contract can exist even if the moment of its making is undetermined. [UCC Sec. 2-204]

OPEN TERMS   According to contract law, an offer must be definite enough for the parties (and the courts) to ascertain its essential terms when it is accepted. The UCC states that a sales contract will not fail for indefiniteness even if one or more terms are left open as long as: (1) the parties intended to make a contract and (2) there is a reasonably certain basis for the court to grant an appropriate remedy.

The Code provides numerous *open term* provisions that can be used to fill in the gaps in a contract. Two factors should be kept in mind. The more terms left open, the less likely the courts will find that the parties *intended* to form a contract. As a general rule, if the *quantity* term is left open, the courts will have no basis for determining a remedy, and the sales contract will fail. If the contract is for all of one's needs, it is a requirements contract and is valid even though it has, in a sense, an open quantity term.

Open Price Term   If the parties have not agreed on a price, the court will determine "a reasonable price at the time for delivery." [UCC Sec. 2-305(1)] If either the buyer or the seller is to determine the price, it means a price fixed in good faith. [UCC Sec. 2-305(2)]

Sometimes the price fails to be fixed through the fault of one of the parties. In that case, the other party can treat the contract as cancelled or fix a reasonable price. For example, Axel and Beatty enter into a contract for the sale of goods and agree that Axel will fix the price. The agreement becomes economically burdensome to Axel, and Axel refuses to fix the price. Beatty can either treat the contract as cancelled, or he can set a reasonable price. [UCC Sec. 2-305(3)]

Although the UCC has radically changed the requirements for definiteness of essentials in contracts of sale, it has not obviated the common law requirement that the contract must at least be definite enough to allow the court to identify the agreement either for the purpose of enforcing it or for awarding appropriate damages if it is breached. In the following case, the language of the contract, even under the liberal standards of the UCC, was insufficient to identify the subject of the agreement of the parties.

BACKGROUND AND FACTS   *Bucci, the defendant, purchased some land, intending to build a combination restaurant and delicatessen on it and contacted several contractors and suppliers for estimates. Bucci ultimately made a written agreement with the Royal Store Fixture Co., the plaintiff, "to purchase the store fixtures and refrigeration equipment required" for the new store. Subsequently, the plaintiff submitted various*

ROYAL STORE FIXTURE CO. v. BUCCI
Pennsylvania County Court, 1969. 7 UCC Rep. Serv. 1193.

proposals for an equipment layout to the defendant. The defendant also received bids from other companies and ultimately purchased the required equipment from one of the plaintiff's competitors. The plaintiff insisted that the defendant was bound by the writing—that is, by a valid agreement to buy all store fixtures and equipment requirements through the plaintiff at competitive prices. The defendant argued, on the other hand, that the document signed by the parties was too vague and indefinite to be a binding contract.

MEADE, Judge.
* * *

The Uniform Commercial Code * * * (UCC) §2-204. * * * provides that "(3) Even through one or more terms are left open a contract for sale does not fail for indefiniteness if the parties have intended to make a contract and there is a *reasonably certain basis for giving an appropriate remedy* ." (Italics supplied.)

The commentary to the code * * * points out that, as to contract rules "The prime test is simply that the parties intended to make a contract and that 'there is a reasonably certain basis for giving an appropriate remedy'. It is specifically provided that the price, particulars of performance, the time for performance and the duration of the contract must not necessarily be fixed by the agreement of the parties." The authors of the code itself point out in the comment to §2-204 that "The more terms the parties leave open, the less likely it is that they have intended to conclude a binding agreement, but their actions may be frequently conclusive on the matter despite the omissions."

The subject matter in the case sub judice [the case at bar or the case under study] is described only as "store fixtures and refrigeration equipment." This description is wholly inadequate to give the requisite clarity to the agreement so as to make it an enforceable contract.
* * *

Nor do we believe that the price of the unspecified store fixtures and refrigeration equipment could ever be reduced to reasonable certainty. While §2-305 of the UCC dealing with "open price term", has been construed to call for a reasonable price (Kuss Machine Tool & Die Co. v. El-Tronics, Inc., 393 Pa 353 (1958)), this may not necessarily be the same as the "competitive prices" called for in the writing. The testimony is clear that the parties left open the term of price, because it was to be agreed upon at a later date. Whether the court could arrive at a "reasonable" price is doubted in view of plaintiff's testimony on that question.
* * *

For the foregoing reasons, we hold that the instrument signed by the parties was not an enforceable agreement. * * *

Judgment must be entered in favor of defendant and against plaintiff.

JUDGMENT AND REMEDY *Judgment was for the defendant. Bucci was allowed to purchase store fixtures and refrigeration equipment from another supplier. The sales contract, or agreement, was too vague because it did not state the price of the unspecified goods that were to be sold, and, more importantly, it was not possible for the court to determine exactly what goods Bucci was to purchase under the "agreement."*

Open Delivery Term   When no delivery terms are specified, the buyer normally takes delivery at the seller's place of business. [UCC Sec. 2-308(a)] If the seller has no place of business, then the seller's residence is used. When goods are located in some other place and both parties know it, then delivery is made there. When the time for shipment or delivery has not been clearly specified in the sales contract, the court will infer a "reasonable" time under the circumstances for performance. [UCC Sec. 2-309(1)]

BACKGROUND AND FACTS   *The dispute here concerned 400 cartons of lettuce.*

The contract provided that the lettuce would be shipped from El Centro, California, on January 18 and that lemons would be loaded at Yuma, Arizona. The parties estimated that delivery to Pittsburgh, Pennsylvania, would be in time for the market of Monday morning, January 22, 1968.

Mendelson-Zeller, the defendant, shipped the lettuce on January 18, 1968, at 9:40 P.M. from El Centro, California, and the lemons on January 19, 1968, at 4:30 A.M. from Yuma, Arizona, in a truck. The truckload of produce arrived at Wedner & Son's (the plaintiff's) place of business at 12:30 P.M., January 22, 1968. Wedner's docking superintendent refused to unload the truck and instructed the driver to return the next morning at 2:00 A.M. to have the truck unloaded for Tuesday's market. The driver locked the truck and did not return until 6:30 A.M. on Tuesday. Thus, the produce was delivered on the scheduled delivery date, but, according to Wedner, it arrived 9½ hours late. Wedner claimed that the agreement indicated that the goods would arrive between 2:00 and 3:00 A.M. so they would be available when the produce market opened. Mendelson-Zeller claimed that neither the time of loading nor the time of arrival was guaranteed.

Wedner eventually sold the lettuce and remitted the net proceeds of $1,028.93 to Mendelson-Zeller along with the net proceeds from the consignment sale of the lettuce. Mendelson-Zeller sued for the difference between the contract price and the amount remitted.

MENDELSON-ZELLER CO., INC. v. JOSEPH WEDNER & SON CO.

U.S. Department of Agriculture, 1970.

7 UCC Rep. Serv. 1045.

THOMAS J. FLAVIN, Judicial Officer.

* * *

There is evidence that the trucker was under some pressure to get the lettuce to respondent [Wedner & Son] for Monday morning's market.

It is evident * * * that [seller] * * * distinguishes between an estimated delivery time and a delivery time which is specified as a part of the contract terms. Neither party submitted a broker's memorandum covering the sale which would presumably show whether there was a specified contract delivery time. In addition the bill of lading does not disclose a specified arrival time though a blank space is provided in which such information can be entered. All of the statements relevant to arrival time other than [buyer] Wedner's statement can be interpreted to mean estimated or anticipated arrival time rather than a time specified as a contract condition. * **

Respondent [Wedner] as the party alleging that a specified arrival time was a part of the contract of sale had the burden of proving by a preponderance of the evidence that its allegation was true. In view of the foregoing discussion we conclude that respondent has not met its burden of proof.

Section 2-309(1) of the Uniform Commercial Code provides that the time for delivery in the absence of an agreed time shall be a reasonable time. Section 2-503(1) provides that tender of delivery must be at a reasonable hour. The evidence shows that the truck left Yuma at 4:30 a.m. January 19 and arrived at respondent's warehouse at 12:30 p.m. January 22. Although the trucker offered to pay overtime for unloading, respondent's docking superintendent refused to unload. Wedner testified that he thought the truck arrived well after business hours. However, he also testified that respondent's office hours are 9 a.m. to 5 p.m. and the hours at its warehouse and terminal on Mondays are 4 a.m. to anywhere from 11:30 to 12:30 p.m. There is no evidence as to the exact time the warehouse closed on January 22. It is unnecessary to resolve whether the tender on January 22 was within a reasonable hour or whether, as complainant contends, respondent accepted delivery by ordering the truckers to return the next morning. The load was tendered and accepted at 6:30 a.m. January 23, about 97 hours after the truck left Yuma. Although there was some testimony indicating that the normal transit time is 72 hours, the trucking company states that this is an impossibility in the winter time. The truck was actually in transit about 80 hours between Yuma and Pittsburgh. Under the circumstances, we are unable to say that delivery on January 23, was not within a reasonable time.

JUDGMENT AND REMEDY *Judgment is held for the seller, Mendelson-Zeller Co. The delivery was made in reasonable time; hence Wedner's failure to pay the full contract price of the lettuce was a breach of contract. The court awarded Mendelson-Zeller damages plus interest on the amount owing.*

Duration of an Ongoing Contract In other situations parties undertake an *ongoing* contractual relationship whereby one party supplies goods to the other party. A single contract might specify successive performances, but may not indicate how long the parties are required to deal with one another. In such a case principles of good faith and sound commercial practice normally call for reasonable notification before termination of the ongoing contractual relationship so as to give the other party reasonable time to seek a substitute arrangement. [UCC Sec. 2-309(3)]

Options and Cooperation Regarding Performance When shipping arrangements have not been made but the contract contemplates shipment of the goods, the *seller* has the right to make these arrangements in good faith, using commercial reasonableness in the situation. [UCC Sec. 2-311]

When terms relating to the assortment of goods are omitted from a sales contract, the *buyer* can specify the assortment. For example, A and B contract for the sale of 1,000 pens. B, the buyer, opts to take 600 blue pens and 400 green pens. B must make the selection in good faith and must use commercial reasonableness. [UCC Sec. 2-311]

Open Payment Term When parties do not specify payment terms, payment is due at the time and place at which the buyer is to receive the goods. Generally, cash, not credit, is used. [UCC Sec. 2-310(a)] The buyer can tender payment using any commercially normal or proper means, such as a check or credit terms. If the seller demands payment in cash, however, the buyer must be given a reasonable time to obtain it. [UCC Sec. 2-511(2)]

MERCHANT'S FIRM OFFER The merchant's firm offer is in the special category of rules applicable only to *merchants*. Under regular contract principles, an offer can be revoked any time before acceptance. The major common law exception is an option contract in which the offeree pays consideration for the offeror's irrevocable promise to keep the offer open for a stated period.

The UCC creates a second exception that applies only to *firm offers* for the sale of goods made *by a merchant* (regardless of whether or not the offeree is a merchant). If the merchant gives assurances in a signed writing that the offer will remain open for a stated period of time not to exceed three months, the *merchant's firm offer* is irrevocable without the necessity of consideration.[4] [UCC Sec. 2-205] To illustrate: Daniels, a used-car dealer, writes a letter to Peters on January 1 stating, "I have a 1974 Dodge Dart which I'll sell to you for $2,200 any time between now and the end of the month." By January 18, Daniels has heard nothing from Peters so he sells the Dodge Dart to another person. On January 23, Peters tenders $2,200 to Daniels and asks for the car. When Daniels tells him the car has already been sold, Peters claims that Daniels has breached a good contract. Peters is right. Since Daniels is a merchant of used cars, he is obligated to keep his offer open until the end of January. Since he has not done so, he is liable for breach.

It is necessary, however, that the offer be both *written and signed* by the offeror.[5] Where a firm offer is contained in a form contract prepared by the offeree, a *separate* firm offer assurance must be signed in addition. The purpose of the merchant's firm offer rule is to give effect to a merchant's deliberate intent to be bound to a firm offer. If the firm offer is buried in one of the pages of the offeree's form contract amid copious language, the offeror might inadvertently sign the contract without realizing it, thus defeating the purpose of the rule.

Acceptance

METHODS OF ACCEPTANCE The general common law rule is that an offeror can specify a particular method of acceptance. This is still true under the Code. Where the offeror has said nothing about the manner in which acceptance must be made, however, the Code provides that acceptance can occur in any manner and by any means of communication reasonable under the circumstances. [UCC Sec. 2-206(1)]

For example, X phones Y to make an offer that X will keep open for five days. If Y telegraphs or mails an acceptance two days later, will there be a valid contract? The answer depends on which form of communication was commercially reasonable under the circumstances.

The UCC permits acceptance of an offer to buy goods for current or prompt shipment by either a promise to ship or prompt shipment of the goods to the buyer. The Code permits the seller to ship out "nonconforming goods" as an accommodation, as long as the seller notifies the buyer that the shipment is offered only as an accommodation. [UCC Sec. 2-206(1)(a)] For example, X orders 1,000 blue widgets from Y. Before the goods arrive, Y notifies X that black widgets have been sent as an accommodation instead of blue widgets. If accepted by X, the shipment is a counteroffer, and a valid contract for the purchase of black widgets will result.

If, however, Y has shipped 1,000 black widgets instead of blue, but does not notify X that the goods are being shipped *as an accommodation*, Y's shipment acts as both an acceptance of X's offer and a *breach* of the resulting contract. X may sue Y for any appropriate damages.

At common law, a unilateral contract in-

---

4. If the offeree pays consideration, then an *option contract* and not a *merchant's firm offer* is formed.

5. "Signed" includes any symbol executed or adopted by a party with present intention to authenticate a writing. [UCC Sec. 1-201(39)]

vites acceptance by a performance. The offeree need not notify the offeror of performance unless the offeror would not otherwise know about it. The UCC is more stringent than common law, stating that "Where the beginning of requested performance is a reasonable mode of acceptance an offeror who is not notified of acceptance within a reasonable time may treat the offer as having lapsed before acceptance." [UCC Sec. 2-206(2)] To illustrate: Johnson writes the Scroll Bookstore on Monday, "Please send me a copy of *West's Book of Business Law* for $20, C.O.D., as soon as possible." Signed "Johnson." Scroll receives the request on Tuesday. The owner does nothing until the following month, when she ships the book for $20 C.O.D. Johnson receives the book and rejects it, indicating that the book has arrived too late to be of value. In this case, since Johnson heard nothing from Scroll for a month, he was justified in assuming that the store did not intend to deliver *West's Book of Business Law.* Johnson could consider that the offer lapsed due to the length of time.

ADDITIONAL TERMS Under traditional common law, if X makes an offer to Y and Y in turn accepts but adds some slight qualification, there is no contract. The so-called "mirror-image rule" of offer-to-acceptance makes Y's action a rejection of and a counteroffer to X's offer.

The UCC generally takes the position that if the offeree's response indicates a *definite* willingness to accept the offer, it will be recognized as an effective acceptance even if it includes terms in addition to or different from the original offer. [UCC Sec. 2-207(1)] The additional terms are construed as "proposals for addition" to the contract when ordinary buyers and sellers are involved. [UCC Sec. 2-207(1)] For example, X offers to sell his car to Y. Y replies, "I accept, but I would like you to put new tires on it". This is a contract. X is not bound to put new tires on the automobile. However, if Y says, "I accept, but only on the condition that you put new tires on the car," there will be no contract unless X agrees to put on the new tires.

Rules Between Merchants The Code rule for additional terms in the acceptance is a little different when the transaction occurs *between merchants* (that is, when both buyer and seller are merchants). Additional terms do not become part of the contract between ordinary buyers and sellers—they are merely proposals. *Between merchants* the additional proposed terms *automatically* become part of the contract unless:

1. They materially alter the original contract.
2. The offer expressly states that no terms other than those in the offer will be accepted.
3. The offeror has already objected to the particular terms.

If the new terms make no material change and the offeror does not object to them, they will become part of the contract. [UCC Sec. 2-207] To illustrate: X and Y are merchants. X offers to sell 20,000 pens to Y at $10 each plus freight. Y responds: "I accept. Price is $10.01 each, including freight." There is a contract because the difference in total cost is only $200 out of a $200,000 contract. The change is probably not material and will automatically become part of the contract unless X objects. If X does object, there is a contract on X's original terms only. In the same situation, suppose Y replies: "Will take if you make the price $10.10 including freight." There is no contract here. This is merely a counteroffer since there is no definite expression of acceptance on the part of Y. Now suppose X offers to sell Y "20,000 pens at $10 each plus freight. No changes." Y replies: "I accept. Price is $10.10 each, including freight." There is no contract. The offer expressly limits Y's acceptance to the terms as stated. Finally, suppose that X offers to sell Y "20,000 pens at $10 each" and Y replies, "Accept. But I only need 10,000 pens at $10 each." There is no contract since Y's response materially alters X's offer.

In this next case, the court grapples with the question of whether a carpet manufacturer's written confirmation of a carpet dealer's oral orders for carpet was an "acceptance expressly conditioned on the buyer's consent to additional terms" (specifically, an arbitration provision), which would bring their situation within UCC Sec. 2-207(1), or whether the written confirmation between merchants automatically became part of the contract unless they "materially altered it", which would bring the action within the provisions of UCC Sec. 2-207(2).

BACKGROUND AND FACTS   *The Carpet Mart was a carpet dealer, and Collins & Aikman Corp. was a carpet manufacturer. Typically, the parties did business orally, followed with acknowledgment forms that were generally recognized as confirmations of prior oral agreements. In this particular instance, Collins & Aikman attempted to introduce in their confirmation form an additional term concerning an arbitration provision. The court was not able to resolve who should prevail because a final decision required additional findings of fact from the trial court. So, the court merely provided a framework within which the trial court could proceed after the additional information had been gathered. The case should be read for an understanding of the law.*

DORTON v. COLLINS & AIKMAN CORP.
United States Court of Appeals, Sixth Circuit, 1972.
453 F.2d 1161.

CELEBREZZE, Circuit Judge.

* * *

Under the common law, an acceptance or a confirmation which contained terms additional to or different from those of the offer or oral agreement constituted a rejection of the offer or agreement and thus became a counter-offer. [Emphasis added.] The terms of the counter-offer were said to have been accepted by the original offeror when he proceeded to perform under the contract without objecting to the counter-offer. Thus, a buyer was deemed to have accepted the seller's counter-offer if he took receipt of the goods and paid for them without objection.

Under Section 2-207 the result is different. This section of the Code recognizes that in current commercial transactions, the terms of the offer and those of the acceptance will seldom be identical. Rather, under the current "battle of the forms", each party typically has a printed form drafted by his attorney and containing as many terms as could be envisioned to favor that party in his sales transactions. Whereas under common law the disparity between the fine-print terms in the parties' forms would have prevented the consummation of a contract when these forms are exchanged, Section 2-207 recognizes that in many, but not all, cases the parties do not impart such significance to the terms on the printed forms.

* * *

Assuming, for purposes of analysis, that the arbitration provision was an addition to the terms of The Carpet Mart's oral offers, we must next determine whether or not Collins & Aikman's acceptances were "expressly made conditional on assent to the additional * * * terms" therein, within the proviso of Subsection 2-207(1).

Because Collins & Aikman's acceptances were not expressly conditional on the buyer's assent to the additional terms within the proviso of Subsection 2-207(1), a contract is recognized under Subsection (1), and the additional terms are treated as "proposals" for addition to the contract under Subsection 2-207(2). Since both Collins & Aikman and The Carpet Mart are clearly "merchants" as that term is defined in Subsection 2-104(1), the arbitration provision will be deemed to have been accepted by The Carpet Mart under Subsection 2-207(2) unless it materially altered the terms of The Carpet Mart's oral offers.

JUDGMENT AND REMEDY   *If Collins & Aikman's acknowledgments are in fact acceptances and the arbitration provision is additional to the terms of Carpet Mart's oral orders, the contracts will be recognized under the provisions of UCC Sec. 2-207(1). The arbitration clause will then be viewed as a "proposal" under UCC Sec. 2-207(2), and it will be deemed to have been accepted by Carpet Mart unless it materially altered the oral agreement.*

Consideration

The Uniform Commercial Code radically changes the common law rule that contract modification must be supported by new consideration. Section 2-209(1) of the UCC states that "an agreement modifying a contract needs no consideration to be binding." Of course, contract modification must be sought in good faith. [UCC Sec. 1-203] Modifications *extorted* from the other party are in bad faith and, therefore, unenforceable. For example, Hal agrees to manufacture and sell certain goods to Betty for a stated price. Subsequently, a sudden shift in the market makes it difficult for Hal to sell the items to Betty at the given price without suffering a loss. Hal tells Betty of the situation, and Betty agrees to pay an additional sum for the goods. Later Betty reconsiders and refuses to pay more than the original price. Under Section 2-209(1) of the UCC, Betty's promise to modify the contract needs no consideration to be binding. Hence, Betty is bound by the modified contract.

In the example above, a shift in the market provides an example of a *good faith* reason for contract modification. In fact, Section 1-203 states that "Every contract or duty within this act imposes an obligation of good faith in its performance or enforcement." Good faith in the case of a merchant is defined to mean honesty in fact and the observance of reasonable commercial standards of fair dealing in the trade. [UCC Sec. 2-103(1)(b)] But what if there really were no shift in the market, but Hal knew that Betty needed the goods immediately and refused to deliver unless Betty agreed to pay an additional sum of money? This sort of extortion of a modification without a legitimate commercial reason would be ineffective because it would violate the duty of good faith. Hal would not be permitted to enforce the higher price.

WHEN MODIFICATION WITHOUT CONSIDERATION REQUIRES WRITING   There are situations in which modification without consideration must be written in order to be enforceable. According to Section 2-209(2), a contract that, by its terms, prohibits modification or rescission (cancellation) except by a signed writing, must be written in order to be enforceable. However, if a consumer (nonmerchant buyer) is dealing with a merchant, *and* the merchant supplies the form that contains a prohibition against oral modification, the consumer must sign a separate acknowledgment of such a clause.

Statute of Frauds

Section 2-201(1) of the UCC contains a Statute of Frauds provision that applies to contracts for the sale of goods. The provision requires a writing for the contract to be enforceable if the price is $500 or more. The parties can have an initial oral agreement, however, and satisy the Statute of Frauds by having a subsequent written memorandum of their oral agreement. In each case the writing must be signed by the party against whom enforcement is sought.

BETWEEN MERCHANTS—WRITTEN CONFIRMATION Once again the Uniform Commercial Code provides a special rule for a contract for the sale of goods between merchants. Merchants can satisfy the requirements of a writing for the Statute of Frauds if, after the parties have agreed orally, one of the merchants sends a signed written communication to the other merchant. The communication must indicate the terms of the agreement. The merchant receiving the confirmation must have reason to know of its contents, and, unless written notice of objection to its contents is given within ten days after receipt, the writing will be sufficient against the receiving merchant. (see *Decatur Cooperative Ass'n v. Urban,* page 283 above.)

RELAXED REQUIREMENTS The Uniform Commercial Code has greatly relaxed the requirements for the sufficiency of a writing to satisfy the Statute of Frauds. A written contract, a memorandum, or even an unsigned confirmation between merchants will be sufficient as long as all the essential terms of the agreement are reflected. The single term that must be included in the writing is the quantity (except in the case of output and requirements contracts). All other terms can be proved in court by oral testimony. Often, terms that are not agreed upon can be supplied by the open term provisions of Article 2 itself.

EXCEPTIONS Section 2-201 defines three exceptions to the Statute of Frauds requirement. A contract, if proved to exist, will be enforceable despite the absence of a writing and even if it involves a sale of goods for over $500 if:

1. *The oral contract is for specially manufactured goods for a particular buyer* and: (a) these goods are not suitable for resale to others in the ordinary course of the seller's business, and (b) the seller has substantially started to manufacture the goods or made commitments for the manufacture of the goods. In this situation, once the seller has taken action, the buyer cannot repudiate the agreement. To illustrate: Archer ordered a unique, strangely-styled cabinet from Collins, a cabinetmaker. The price of the cabinet is $1,000, and the contract is oral. Collins finishes the cabinet and tenders delivery to Archer. Archer refuses to pay for it even though the job is completed on time. Archer claims that he is not liable because the contract is oral. Clearly, if the style of the cabinet is so strange that Collins cannot find another buyer, or if it is not suitable for sale to Collins's ordinary customers, then Archer is liable to Collins. An oral contract for the manufacture of nonresalable goods is enforceable, even if the contract price is $500 or more, as long as the manufacturer has "made a substantial beginning of their manufacture. * * *"

2. *A party to a contract can admit in pleadings (written complaints), testimony, or other court proceedings that a contract for sale was made.* In this case the contract will be enforceable even though it was oral. To illustrate: By telephone Archer orders 50 gallons of gas from Collins for 75 cents a gallon. Collins agrees to deliver the next day, but Collins thinks that Archer has ordered 500 gallons of gas, and that is what he delivers. Archer refuses to accept or pay for *any* of the gas. Collins, who is certain that Archer ordered 500 gallons, sues Archer for breach of contract for the sale of 500 gallons. Archer's defense will be that he ordered only 50 gallons. Since Archer has admitted that he ordered 50 gallons only, that is the only damages that Collins can recover. The parties agree that a contract was made; therefore the contract is enforceable to the extent of the quantity of goods admitted by Archer, since there is no writing.

3. *An oral agreement will be enforceable to the extent that payment has been made and accepted or to the extent that goods have been received and accepted.* For example, suppose that X orally agrees to sell Y ten chairs at $100

each. Before X delivers them, Y sends X a check for $500, which X accepts. X then attempts to dishonor the contract. Under the UCC, Y can enforce the oral contract to the extent of $500. Similarly, if Y had made no payment but X had made a partial shipment of five chairs that Y accepted, an oral contract against Y for $500, the price of five chairs, would be enforceable.

Parol Evidence

If the parties to a contract set forth its terms in a confirmatory memorandum (a writing expressing offer and acceptance of the deal) or in a writing intended as their final expression, the terms of the contract cannot be contradicted by evidence of any prior or contemporaneous oral or written agreements. Such terms, however, can be explained or supplemented by consistent additional terms, or by *course of dealing, usage of trade,* or *course of performance.*

CONSISTENT ADDITIONAL TERMS If the court finds an ambiguity in a writing that is supposed to be a complete and exclusive statement of the agreement between the parties, it may accept evidence of consistent additional terms to clarify and remove the ambiguity. The court will not, however, accept evidence of contradictory terms. This is the rule under both the Code and the common law of contracts.

COURSE OF DEALING AND USAGE OF TRADE In construing a commercial agreement, the court will assume that the course of prior dealing between the parties and the usage of trade were taken into account when the

agreement was phrased. [UCC Secs. 2-202 and 1-201(3)] The Code states, "A course of dealing between the parties and any usage of trade in the vocation or trade in which they are engaged or of which they are or should be aware give particular meaning to [the terms of an agreement] and supplement or qualify the terms of [the] agreement." [UCC Sec. 1-205(3)]

The Code has determined that the meaning of any agreement, evidenced by the language of the parties and by their action, must be interpreted in light of commercial practices and other surrounding circumstances.

Usage of trade is defined as any practice or method of dealing having such regularity of observance in a place, vocation, or trade as to justify an expectation that it will be observed with respect to the transaction in question. [UCC Sec. 1-205(2)] Further, the expressed terms of an agreement and an applicable course of dealing or usage of trade will be construed to be consistent with each other whenever reasonable. However, when such construction is unreasonable, the expressed terms in the agreement will prevail. [UCC Sec. 1-205(4)]

A *course of dealing* is a sequence of previous conduct between the parties to a particular transaction that establishes a common basis for their understanding. [UCC Sec. 1-205(1)] Course of dealing is restricted, literally, to the sequence of conduct between the parties that has occurred prior to the agreement in question.

In the following case, the court permitted the introduction of evidence of usage and custom in the trade to explain the meaning of quantity figures that the parties took for granted when the contract was formed.

**HEGGBLADE-
MARGULEAS-
TENNECO, INC. v.
SUNSHINE BISCUIT, INC.**

Court of Appeals of California,
5th District, 1976.
59 Cal. App.3d 948, 131
Cal.Rptr. 183.

BACKGROUND AND FACTS *Heggblade-Marguleas-Tenneco (HMT) entered into two contracts with Sunshine Biscuit (referred to in this opinion as Bell Brand). Under the terms of the contract, HMT was to supply Bell Brand with potatoes to be used in the production of potato-snack foods, such as chips and french fries. It was understood that the amount of potatoes to be supplied would vary because of HMT's commitments to its other customers. HMT was a newly-merged company. One of its constituent companies had been engaged in the business of marketing agricultural products, and the other had grown* potatoes but never marketed them. HMT had no prior marketing experience with this type of potato processing. HMT did, however, conduct a market study concerning the feasibility of growing, marketing, and processing potatoes. Based on the results of this study, it decided to plant between one and two thousand acres of potatoes.

HMT informed Bell Brand that, after analyzing its needs and obligations to other customers, it would probably be able to supply Bell Brand with 100,000 sacks of potatoes to start. A Bell Brand potato buyer read HMT's estimates and became concerned that the quantity was too high. HMT hired an expert with over twenty years experience in the potato processing industry to obtain more marketing contacts and to assist in selling the potatoes HMT was planning to grow.

Because of the decline in demand for Bell Brand products from May to July 1971, Bell Brand's sales for the late spring and summer of 1971 went down substantially, and its need for potatoes was severely reduced. Bell Brand prorated this reduced demand among its suppliers, including HMT, as fairly as possible. By the end of the harvest season, Bell Brand was able to take only 60,105 hundredweight sacks out of the 100,000 estimated by HMT on the contracts in dispute.

HMT sued Bell Brand for damages on the difference between the 100,000 estimated and 60,105 actual sacks of potatoes purchased. The trial court held for Bell Brand on the basis that it was understood and agreed "* * * as is customary in the potato processing industry, that the numbers of potatoes specified in each of said contracts were reasonable estimates of the respective requirements of [Bell Brand] only during said period, and did not constitute the exact number of potatoes to be ordered by [Bell Brand] * * * and delivered by plaintiff under said contracts."

FRANSON, Acting Presiding Justice.
* * *
California Uniform Commercial Code section 2202 states the parol evidence rule applicable to the sale of personal property:

"Terms with respect to which the confirmatory memoranda of the parties agree or which are otherwise set forth in a writing intended by the parties as a final expression of their agreement with respect to such terms as are included therein may not be contradicted by evidence of any prior agreement or of a contemporaneous oral agreement but may be explained or supplemented "(a) By course of dealing or usage of trade (Section 1205) * * *;"

California Uniform Commercial Code section 2202, subdivision (a), permits a trade usage to be put in evidence "as an instrument of interpretation." The Uniform Commercial Code comment to subdivision (a) of section 2202 states that evidence of trade usage is admissible " * * * in order that the true understanding of the parties as to the agreement may be reached. Such writings are to be read on the assumption that * * * the usages of trade were taken for granted when the document was phrased. Unless *carefully negated* they have become an element of the meaning of the words used. Similarly, the course of actual performance by the parties is considered the best indication of what they intended the writing to mean."

A case factually similar to the instant case is *Columbia Nitrogen Corporation*

v. *Royster Company* (4th Cir. 1971), 451 F.2d 3. There the seller sued the buyer for breach of contract for the purchase of a specified quantity of phosphate. The buyer's defense was a trade usage which imposed no duty to accept at the quoted prices the minimum quantity stated in the contract. The trial court had excluded this evidence because " * * * 'custom and usage * * * are not admissible to contradict the express, plain, unambiguous language of a valid written contract, which by virtue of its detail negates the proposition that the contract is open to variances in its terms. * * *' " The Court of Appeal interpreted Virginia Uniform Commercial Code section 2-202, which is identical to California Uniform Commercial Code section 2202(a), as meaning that where the contract does not expressly state that trade usage cannot be used to explain or supplement the written terms, the evidence of trade usage should be admitted to interpret the contract. "The contract is silent about adjusting prices and quantities to reflect a declining market. It neither permits nor prohibits adjustment, and this neutrality provides a fitting occasion for recourse to usage of trade and prior dealing to supplement the contract and explain its terms."

We find *Columbia Nitrogen Corporation* persuasive. Under subdivision (a) of section 2202, established trade usage and custom are a part of the contract unless the parties agree otherwise. Since the contracts in question are silent about the applicability of the usage and custom, evidence of such usage and custom was admissible to explain the meaning of the quantity figures.

Appellant's [HMT] argument that the evidence of custom should not have been considered by the jury in interpreting the contracts because the officers of HMT were inexperienced in the marketing of processing potatoes and lacked knowledge of the custom is similarly without merit. Mr. Hoffman was knowledgeable in the processing potato business and was aware of the trade custom. Since appellant pleaded that the contracts had been entered into on October 15, 1970, and Hoffman had been employed by HMT on October 1, 1970, his knowledge was imputed to HMT.

Moreover, persons carrying on a particular trade are deemed to be aware of prominent trade customs applicable to their industry. The knowledge may be actual or constructive, and it is constructive if the custom is of such general and universal application that the party must be presumed to know of it. Because potatoes are a perishable commodity and their demand is dependent upon a fluctuating market, and because the marketing contracts are signed eight or nine months in advance of the harvest season, common sense dictates that the quantity would be estimated by both the grower and the processor. Thus, it cannot be said as a matter of law that HMT was ignorant of the trade custom.

We conclude that the trial court properly admitted the evidence of usage and custom to explain the meaning of the quantity figures in the contracts.

JUDGMENT AND REMEDY *The trial court judgment was affirmed. Bell Brand did not have to pay HMT for the difference between the 100,000 estimated hundredweight sacks of potatoes and the 60,105 actual sacks of potatoes that were purchased.*

COMMENTS *Parol evidence of usage and custom that is not inconsistent with the terms of the written agreement can be introduced in situations where both* *parties knew or should have known of the existence of the particular custom or usage in that industry in that locality. Such evidence is supplemental and shows the meaning that the parties attach to the particular language. It does not alter or change the contract terms. Just as a previous course of dealing between parties can be regarded as establishing a common basis for interpreting their expressions and conduct [UCC Sec. 1-205(1)], so, too, a usage of trade is a regularly observed practice or method of dealing that is normally accepted and followed in a place, vocation, or trade and that establishes a common basis for interpreting expressions or conduct. [UCC Sec. 1-205(2)]*

COURSE OF PERFORMANCE Course of performance is the conduct that occurs under the terms of a particular agreement. The course of performance actually undertaken is the best indication of what the parties to an agreement intended it to mean. Presumably, the parties themselves know best what they meant by their words, and their action under that agreement is the best indication of what they meant. [UCC Sec. 2-208]

To illustrate: Lumber Company A contracts with B to sell B a specified number of "2-by-4s". The lumber in fact does not measure 2 inches by 4 inches but rather 1⅞ inches by 3¾ inches. If B objects to the lumber delivered, A can prove that "2-by-4s" are never exactly 2 inches by 4 inches by using usage of trade or course of prior dealings or both. A can show in previous transactions that B took 1⅞ inch by 3¾ inch lumber without objection. In addition, A can show that, in the trade, 2-by-4s are commonly 1⅞ inches by 3¾ inches. Both usage of trade and course of prior dealings are relevant in determining and explaining what the parties meant by 2-by-4s.

Using the same example, suppose that A agrees to deliver the lumber in five separate deliveries. The fact that B has accepted lumber without objection in three previous deliveries under the agreement (course of performance) is relevant in determining that the words 2-by-4 actually mean 1⅞ by 3¾.

The Code provides *rules of construction.* Express terms, course of performance, course of dealing, and usage of trade are to be construed together whenever consistent with one another. When such construction is unreasonable, how-ever, the following order of priority controls: (1) express terms, (2) course of performance, (3) course of dealing, and (4) usage of trade. [UCC Secs. 1-205(4) and 2-208(2)]

Unconscionability

An unconscionable contract is one that is so grossly unfair and one-sided that it would be unreasonable to enforce it. Section 2-302 allows the court to evaluate a contract or any clause in a contract, and if the court deems it to be unconscionable *at the time it was made,* the court can (1) refuse to enforce the contract, or (2) enforce the remainder of the contract without the unconscionable clause, or (3) limit the application of any unconscionable clauses to avoid an unconscionable result.

The court, in determining whether a contract or clause is unconscionable, uses a basic test that evaluates whether, in light of general commercial practice and the commercial needs of the particular trade involved, the clauses are so one-sided as to be unconscionable under the circumstances at the time the contract was made. In this day of consumer law, consumer sales contracts are increasingly coming under attack for unconscionability. Typical cases involve high pressure salespersons and uneducated consumers who may pay contract prices several times the market value of the goods. In general, the courts have concluded that unequal bargaining power, coupled with unscrupulous dealings by one party, will result in an unenforceable, unconscionable contract.

CASE PROBLEMS AND QUESTIONS

1. Article 2 of the Uniform Commercial Code applies to "transactions in goods." Which of the following transactions is covered by Article 2?

a. the contract for the sale of a large fishing boat
b. the sale of an aircraft
c. a contract between two private individuals for the sale of investment bonds
d. a contract for the sale and installment of tile by a professional tile setter
e. the sale of a laundry and dry cleaning business
f. the sale of a central heating and air-conditioning system in a home (pursuant to the sale of the home)

2. Pemberton went to Tradesmens Bank to secure a loan to buy a car. The bank would loan Pemberton the money only under the conditions that the car would serve as collateral for the loan, that the car would be insured, and that the car dealer who was to sell the car to Pemberton would guarantee payment of the loan if Pemberton defaulted. Both Pemberton and the car dealer agreed to these conditions, and Pemberton secured the loan and purchased the car. Shortly thereafter, Pemberton was involved in an accident. After the insurance company paid the claim, it cancelled his insurance policy. The bank, after learning that the insurance was cancelled, failed to notify the car dealer, even though it was the local business custom for banks to give such notice. Shortly thereafter, Pemberton was involved in another accident that totally wrecked the car. Pemberton's financial situation was such that he could not pay the balance of the loan. Therefore, the bank sued the car dealer based on the guarantee that the car dealer had given under the loan agreement. At trial, the car dealer defended on the grounds that it was not liable under the guarantee because the bank had failed to give the car dealer notice of the cancellation of the insurance. The bank claimed that it was under no obligation to give notice to the car dealer because such a term was not included in the written loan guarantee agreement. In light of the parol evidence rule, can the car dealer prove that there was an implied promise on the part of the bank to give notice of cancellation of insurance? [Provident Tradesmens Bank & Trust Co. v. Pemberton, 196 Pa. Super. 180, 173 A.2d. 780 (1961)]

3. Frances and Burlington engaged in the purchase and sale of yarn for a number of years. Frances normally placed its orders for yarn over the telephone. Each time Burlington shipped yarn to Frances, it sent a contract along with the yarn. Included in the contract was a clause providing for arbitration of all disputes in New York. Frances was located in North Carolina. Frances never signed or returned any of these contracts but never rejected them or the yarn. After several years of uninterrupted dealings, Frances rejected one of Burlington's shipments, stating that the yarn was defective, and refused to pay for it. Burlington sought to enforce the arbitration clause contained in the contracts that it sent to Frances, but Frances said that it was not bound by the clause. Who is right? [Frances Hosiery Mills, Inc. v. Burlington Industries, Inc., 19 N.C. App. 678, 200 S.E.2d. 668 (1973)]

4. After several weeks of negotiation, Valley Electric and Heating Service orally agreed to sell and install an air-conditioning system in a theater owned by Charlotte Theaters, Inc. Valley Electric then put the terms of the agreement in writing and sent two copies to Charlotte Theaters. Charlotte retained one copy for itself and returned the other copy to Valley Electric after inserting a clause calling for completion of the work by a specified date. Along with the copy of the contract, Charlotte Theaters also sent a cover letter that mentioned the specified completion date. Valley Electric proceeded to install the air-conditioning system but was unable to complete work by the date specified by Charlotte Theaters. Is Valley Electric in breach of contract? [Gateway Co. v. Charlotte Theaters, Inc., 297 F.2d. 483 (1st Cir. 1961)]

5. For a period of years, Exchange National Bank lent money to Citrus Incorporated to finance Citrus's orange growing operations. Shortly after the beginning of the growing season, Citrus sold all of its crops then growing to Alturas Packing Company. After the sale, but before the orange crop was harvested, Exchange National Bank sued Citrus for nonpayment of several outstanding loans. Exchange National Bank obtained a judgment against Citrus and, pursuant to the judgment, obtained a levy on the citrus crops. Under the applicable state law, Exchange National's levy against the crops would fail if and only if the sale of the orange crop to Alturas was deemed a sale of real estate instead of a sale of goods. Was this a sale of goods within the meaning of Article 2? [Exchange Nat. Bank of Tampa v. Alturas Packing Co., 269 So.2d 733 (Fla. App. 1972)]

6. In 1961, Clark and American Sand & Gravel

discussed the possibility of a purchase by Clark of 25,000 tons of sand at 45 cents per ton. Although both parties found the terms of the possible sale agreeable, no sale was ever made. About eighteen months later, Clark requested American Sand & Gravel to deliver 1,500 tons to one of Clark's construction sites. American Sand & Gravel made the delivery, but no purchase price was ever mentioned. Subsequently, American charged Clark 55 cents per ton for the sand. Is there a contract between American and Clark? If so, what price can American charge for the sand? [American Sand & Gravel, Inc. v. Clark and Fray Constr. Co., 2 Conn. Cir. 284, 198 A.2d 68 (1964)]

7. Loeb & Company entered into an oral agreement with Schreiner, a farmer, whereby Schreiner was to sell Loeb 150 bales of cotton. Shortly thereafter, Loeb sent Schreiner a letter confirming the terms of the oral contract. Schreiner neither acknowledged receipt of the letter nor objected to its terms. When delivery came due, Schreiner ignored the oral agreement and sold on the open market because the price of cotton had more than doubled (from 37 cents to 80 cents per bale) since the oral agreement was made. In a lawsuit by Loeb & Company against Schreiner, can Loeb & Company recover? [Loeb & Co. v. Schreiner, 294 Ala. 722, 321 So.2d 199 (1975)]

8. Pittsburgh Brewing Company and Weilersbacher had a long-standing business arrangement under which Weilersbacher sold Pittsburgh Brewing the malt that Pittsburgh Brewing used in making beer. In 1963 Weilersbacher and Pittsburgh orally agreed to a particular price schedule based upon the varying qualities of malt sold. No agreement was made as to how long the price schedule would be in effect or how long the parties would be bound under the contract. About a year later, Weilersbacher informed Pittsburgh Brewing that it would no longer honor the oral agreement and thereafter refused to make any more shipments of malt. Can Pittsburgh Brewing force Weilersbacher to continue performing under the contract? [Weilersbacher, Distributor v. Pittsburgh Brewing Co., 421 Pa. 118, 218 A.2d 806 (1966)]

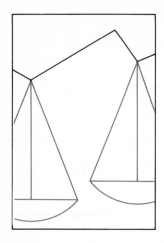

18

Sales

Title, Risk,

and Insurable Interest

The sale of goods transfers ownership from seller to buyer. Often a sales contract will be signed before the actual goods are available. For example, a sales contract for oranges is signed in May, but the oranges are not ready for picking and shipment until October. Any number of things can happen between the time that a sales contract is signed and the time that the goods are actually transferred to the buyer's possession. Fire, flood, or frost can destroy the orange groves. The oranges may be lost or damaged in transit. The parties may want to obtain casualty insurance on the goods. The government may levy a tax on the oranges.

Before the UCC, *title*—right of ownership—was the central concept in sales law, controlling all issues of rights and remedies of the parties to a sales contract. However, it was difficult to determine when title actually passed. Therefore, the UCC divorced the question of title as completely as possible from the question of the rights and obligations of buyers, sellers, or third persons (such as subsequent purchasers, creditors, or the tax collector).

In some situations title is still relevant under the Code, and the UCC has special rules for locating title. These rules will be discussed in the materials that follow. In most situations, however, the Code replaces the concept of title with three other concepts: (1) identification, (2) risk of loss, and (3) insurable interest.

PASSAGE OF TITLE

Sales Contracts and Contracts to Sell

A *sales contract* (or contract for sale) must pertain to specific goods already existing before any interest in them can pass. [UCC Sec. 2-105] *Contracts to sell* deal with future goods, such as crops not yet planted; but until the crops are actually growing, no title to them can pass to the buyer. [UCC Sec. 2-105(2)] Thus, the first condition to passage of title is that the goods be in existence.

Identification

A further condition for the passage of title is that the goods must be identified in a way that will distinguish the particular goods to be delivered under the sales contract from all other similar goods.[1] **Identification** is a designation of goods that are the subject matter of the sales contract. It is significant because it gives the buyer the right to obtain insurance (insurable interest) on the goods and the right to recover from third parties who damage the goods. In certain circumstances, identification allows the buyer to get the goods from the seller. In other words, the concept is easier to understand if one looks at the consequences of identification.

Parties can agree to when identification will take place in their contract; but if they do not specify, the following rules apply:

1. Identification takes place at the time the contract is made *if the contract calls for the sale of specific and ascertained goods already existing.*

---

1. According to Section 2-104, each provision of Article 2 "with respect to the rights, obligations, and remedies of the seller, the buyer, purchasers or other third parties applies irrespective of title to the goods except where the provisions refer to such title." These provisions referring to title include: Section 2-312, warranty of title by seller; Section 2-326(3), consignment sales; Section 2-327(1)(a), sale on approval and "risk of loss"; Section 4-403(1), entrustment; Section 2-501(2), insurable interest in goods; and Section 2-722, who can sue third parties for injury to goods.

2. If the sale involves unborn young animals that will be born within twelve months from the time of the contract, or if it involves crops to be harvested within twelve months (or the next harvest season occurring after contracting, whichever is longer), identification will take place, in the first case, when the young are conceived and, in the second case, when the crops are planted or begin to grow.
3. In other cases, identification takes place when the goods are marked, shipped, or somehow designated by the seller as the particular goods to pass under the contract. The seller can delegate the right to identify goods to the buyer.

When Title Passes

Once goods exist and are identified, the provisions of UCC Sec. 2-401 provide the rules relating to the passage of title.

BY AGREEMENT Parties can expressly agree to the conditions under which title will pass to the buyer and to the time. In virtually all subsections of UCC Sec. 2-401, the words "unless otherwise explicitly agreed" appear, meaning that any explicit understanding between the buyer and the seller will determine when title passes.

WHEN THE SELLER COMPLETES THE DUTIES OF DELIVERY Unless another agreement is explicitly made, title passes to the buyer at the time and the place the seller performs the *physical* delivery of the goods. [UCC Sec. 2-401(2)] The delivery arrangements determine when this occurs.

Shipment Contracts Under shipment contracts, the seller is required only to deliver the goods into the hands of a carrier (like a trucking company), and title passes to the buyer at the time and place of shipment.

Destination Contracts With destination contracts, the seller is required to deliver the goods to a particular destination, usually directly to the buyer but sometimes to the buyer's designate. Title passes to the buyer when the goods are tendered at that destination.

Contracts Where Documents of Title Are Involved   Where the contract of sale does not call for delivery the passage of title depends on whether the seller must deliver a document of title, such as a bill of lading or a warehouse receipt, to the buyer. When a document of title is required, title passes to the buyer *when and where the document is delivered.* Thus, if the goods are stored in a warehouse, title passes to the buyer when the appropriate documents are delivered. The goods never move. In fact, the buyer can choose to leave the goods at the same warehouse for a period of time, and the buyer's title to those goods will be unaffected.

Non-Document of Title Cases   When no documents of title are required, and delivery is made without moving the goods, title passes at the time and place the sales contract was made, if the goods have already been identified. If the goods have not been identified, then title does not pass until identification occurs. Consider an example: Fein sells lumber to Ozo. It is agreed that Ozo will pick up the lumber at the yard. If the lumber has been identified (segregated, marked, or in any other way distinguished from all other lumber), title will pass to Ozo when the contract is signed. If the lumber is still in storage bins at the mill, however, title will not pass to Ozo until the particular pieces of lumber to be sold under this contract are identified.

RISK OF LOSS

Under the UCC, several concepts replace the concept of title in determining the rights and remedies of parties to a sales contract. The risk of loss does not necessarily pass with title. The question of who suffers a financial risk if goods are damaged, destroyed, or lost before or during

shipment is resolved under Sections 2-509 and 2-319. Risk of loss depends on whether or not a sales contract has been breached at the time of loss. [UCC Sec. 2-510]

Passage of Risk of Loss Absent a Breach of Contract

BY AGREEMENT   Risk of loss can be assigned through an agreement between both parties, preferably in writing.

CARRIER CASES—SALES REQUIRING DELIVERY BY MOVEMENT OF GOODS Assuming that there is no specification in the agreement, the following rules will apply to so-called carrier cases.

Shipment Contracts   In a shipment contract, the seller is required to ship the goods by carrier but is not required to deliver them to a particular destination. Risk of loss passes to the buyer when the goods are duly delivered to the carrier. [UCC Sec. 2-509(1)(b)] For example, a seller in New York sells 10,000 tons of sheet metal to a buyer in California, F.O.B. New York (free on board in New York—that is, buyer pays the transportation charges from New York). The contract authorizes a shipment by carrier; it does not require the seller to tender the metal in California. Risk passes to the buyer when the goods are placed in the possession of the carrier. If the goods are damaged in transit, the loss falls on the buyer. (Actually, buyers have recourse against carriers, subject to tariff rule limitations, and they usually insure the goods from the time they leave the seller.)

Destination Contracts   In a destination contract, the seller is required to deliver the goods at a particular destination. The risk of loss passes to the buyer when the goods are tendered to the buyer at that destination. In the above example, if the contract had been F.O.B. California, risk of loss during transit to California would have fallen on the seller.

In the following case the court reviewed UCC Sec. 2-509(1) as it relates to passage of the risk of loss. Under the Code, an F.O.B. term indicates whether the contract is a "shipment" contract or a "destination" contract, with the risk of loss passing at different times in each of these contracts. The F.O.B. terminology controls. In the following case a "shipment" contract shifted the risk of loss to the buyer when the goods were delivered to a carrier. The fact that there was a "ship to" address had no significance in changing the UCC presumption that the contract was a "shipment" contract.

BACKGROUND AND FACTS   *The buyer (defendant) sent orders to the seller (plaintiff), and upon these orders, contracts were made and goods were delivered. The contracts were F.O.B. Norwalk, Connecticut, the seller's location. The buyer, however, supplied the seller with "ship to" addresses, designating where the goods were to be shipped. When the goods were damaged in shipment, the seller argued that the risk of loss had passed to the buyer because these contracts were "shipment" contracts using an F.O.B. seller's place of shipment.*

ELECTRIC REGULATOR CORP. v. STERLING EXTRUDER CORP.
United States District Court
D. Connecticut, 1968.
280 F. Supp. 550.

TIMBERS, Chief Judge.
* * *

Defendant recognizes the significance of risk of loss but argues that the risk of loss was not transferred to defendant in Connecticut. There cannot be any serious disagreement in this respect, however, as to that part of the purchased equipment shipped directly to defendant's customers in Connecticut, since these goods never left the state; risk of loss necessarily was shifted to defendant at one point or another in Connecticut. As to the equipment shipped out of the state, while the question is more open to dispute, nevertheless the Court finds, from the exhibits and undisputed facts, that risk of loss was transferred to defendant when plaintiff put the goods in possession of the carriers in Connecticut.
* * *

Section 2-509(1) of the Uniform Commercial Code, in force in Connecticut as Conn.Gen.Stat. § 42a-2-509(1), and also in force in New Jersey, provides:

> "Where the contract requires or authorizes the seller to ship the goods by carrier (a) if it does not require him to deliver them at a particular destination, the risk of loss passes to the buyer when the goods are duly delivered to the carrier * * * but (b) if it does require him to deliver them at a particular destination and the goods are there duly tendered while in the possession of the carrier, the risk of loss passes to the buyer when the goods are there duly so tendered as to enable the buyer to take delivery."

Defendant contends that plaintiff was required to deliver the equipment at particular destinations. But defendant does not dispute the fact that the parties contemplated shipment of the goods F.O.B. Norwalk, Connecticut, as the invoices show. Conn.Gen.Stat. § 42a-2-319(1) (Uniform Commercial Code § 2-319(1)) provides that:

> "Unless otherwise agreed the term F.O.B., which means 'free on board,' at a named place, even though used only in connection with the stated price, is a delivery term under which (a) when the term is F.O.B. the place of shipment, the seller must at that place ship the goods in the manner provided in section 42a-2-504 and bear the expense and risk of putting them into the possession of the carrier; or (b) when the term is F.O.B. the place of destination, the seller must at his own expense and risk transport the goods to that place and there tender delivery of them in the manner provided in section 42a-2-503; * * *"

Thus, an F.O.B. term must be read to indicate the point at which delivery is to be made unless there is specific agreement otherwise and therefore it will normally determine risk of loss. See W. Hawkland, Sales and Bulk Sales 93-94 (2 ed. 1958). Here the term used was F.O.B. Norwalk, Connecticut, indicating that these contracts were "shipment" contracts, as opposed to "destination" contracts, with risk of loss passing when plaintiff carried out the duties imposed upon it by Conn.Gen.Stat. §42a-2-504 (Uniform Commercial Code §2-504). Any doubt to the contrary is disposed of by Official Comment 2 to Uniform Commercial Code §2-509(1) which explains that this section on risk of loss must be construed parallel to comparable language in Sections 2-503 and 2-504. Conn.Gen.Stat. §42a-2-504 (Uniform Commercial Code §2-504), covering "shipment" as opposed to "destination" contracts, requires the seller to:

> "(a) put the goods in the possession of * * * a carrier and make such a contract for their transportation as may be reasonable having regard to the nature of the goods and other circumstances of the case; and (b) obtain and promptly deliver or tender in due form any document necessary to enable the buyer to obtain possession of the goods or otherwise required by the agreement by usage of trade; and (c) promptly notify the buyer of the shipment."

Since it is undisputed that the plaintiff accomplished all of this while the goods were still in Connecticut, risk of loss passed to defendant in this state.

The only evidence cited by defendant to support its position that the contracts here involved were "destination" contracts rather than "shipment" contracts is the fact that there are "ship to" addresses on defendant's purchase order forms. However, "ship to" addresses must be supplied to a seller if he is to make arrangements for shipment as required by Conn.Gen.Stat. §42a-2-504(a) (Uniform Commercial Code §2-504(a)). They have no significance in determining whether a contract is a shipment or destination contract. But even if the "ship to" addresses had significance they would be inadequate to upset the Uniform Commercial Code's presumption in favor of "shipment" contracts, particularly in view of the fact that defendant does not dispute that the equipment was properly shipped F.O.B. Norwalk, Connecticut [the seller's location].

JUDGMENT AND REMEDY _The risk of loss passed to the buyer when seller delivered the goods to the carrier. The F.O.B. term rather than the "ship to" addresses controlled._

NON-CARRIER CASES—DELIVERY WITHOUT MOVEMENT OF GOODS In non-carrier cases, goods are delivered without being moved. Sometimes the goods remain in the warehouse, or they are held by a bailee (the person to whom they are entrusted). [UCC Sec. 2-509(2)]

Merchant Seller If the seller is a merchant, risk of loss passes to the buyer when the buyer actually takes physical possession of the goods. [UCC Sec. 2-509(3)] For example, a merchant sells goods to a buyer who is supposed to pick them up. Risk of loss does not pass to the buyer until the goods are actually picked up. (Tender is not enough.)

Non-Merchant Seller If the seller is not a merchant, the risk of loss passes to the buyer upon *tender of delivery*. To illustrate: Suppose that Jones and Farber negotiate a contract on May 1 concerning a pile of firewood that Jones has in his yard. At the time of their contract, Jones tells Farber that he can take the wood with him on that day if he wishes. Farber tells Jones to keep the wood until May 15, so that he, Farber, can arrange for a place to keep it after taking possession. The firewood burns up three days later through no fault of Jones's. Jones claims that Farber is obligated to pay for the wood, even though it has been destroyed. Jones is right. When goods are in the possession of a non-merchant seller, and they are not to be shipped by carrier, the risk of their loss passes when the seller tenders delivery, in the absence of any agreement to the contrary. Jones tendered delivery when he offered to let Farber take the wood with him on May 1. The question of tender of delivery arises in the following case.

BACKGROUND AND FACTS *The court provided a concise statement of the facts as follows.*

PURYEAR, Judge.
* * *

The uncontroverted evidence shows that during the early morning hours of November 27, 1968, the Louisville and Nashville Railroad Company, to which we will hereinafter refer as the carrier, placed a boxcar loaded with lumber consigned to the defendant on this siding at track location 609-A.

This boxcar was designated as NW54938 and it was inspected by an employee of the carrier between 8:00 A.M. and 8:30 A.M. on November 27, 1968, at which time it was found loaded with cargo and so designated upon the carrier's records.

At 11:07 A.M. on November 27, 1968, the carrier notified one of defendant's employees that the carload of lumber had been delivered at track location 609-A.

At approximately 4:00 P.M. on that same day an employee of the carrier again inspected this boxcar at track location 609-A, found one of the seals on it to be broken and resealed it at that time. The evidence does not show whether the car was still loaded with cargo at that time or not.

The following day, November 28th, was Thanksgiving Day and the record does not disclose that the carrier inspected the boxcar on that date. But on November 29, 1968, between 8:00 A.M. and 8:30 A.M. an employee of the carrier inspected the car and found it empty.

LUMBER SALES, INC. v. **BROWN**
Court of Appeals of Tennessee, 1971.
63 Tenn. App. 189, 469 S.W.2d 888.

* * *

The particular Code Section applicable here is Sub-section (1) of [the Tennessee Code] as follows:

"47-2-509. *Risk of loss in the absence of breach.*—(1) Where the contract requires or authorizes the seller to ship the goods by carrier (a) (this portion not applicable) (b) if it does require him to deliver them at a particular destination and the goods are there duly tendered while in the possession of the carrier, the risk of loss passes to the buyer when the goods are there duly so tendered as to enable the buyer to take delivery."

* * *

Counsel for defendant argues that the lumber in question was not duly *so tendered as to enable the buyer to take delivery"* as required by [UCC Sec. 2-509(1)(b)]

However, this argument seems to be based upon the premise that it was not convenient for the defendant to unload the lumber on November 27th, the day on which it was delivered at track location 609-A and defendant was duly notified of such delivery.

This was an ordinary business day and the time of 11:07 A.M. was a reasonable business hour. If it was not convenient with the defendant to unload the lumber within a few hours after being duly notified of delivery, then he should have protected himself against risk of loss by directing someone to guard the cargo against loss by theft and other hazards.

To hold that the seller or the carrier should, under the circumstances existing in a case of this kind, continue to protect the goods until such time as the buyer may find it convenient to unload them would impose an undue burden upon the seller or the carrier and unnecessarily obstruct the channels of commerce.

The language of subsection (1)(b) of [the Tennessee Code] does not impose such a burden upon the seller, in the absence of some material breach of the contract for delivery, and we think a reasonable construction of such language only requires the seller to place the goods at the buyer's disposal so that he has access to them and may remove them from the carrier's conveyance without lawful obstruction, with the proviso, however, that due notice of such delivery be given to the buyer.

JUDGMENT AND REMEDY *The trial court judgment was affirmed. Risk of loss had passed to the buyer, and the buyer was liable to the seller for the contract price of the carload of lumber. Basically, the UCC and the court indicated that the buyer should have provided insurance in kind by having someone physically protect the lumber, or he should have purchased a regular insurance policy against theft.*

CASES INVOLVING BAILEES When a bailee is holding goods for a person who has contracted to sell them, and the goods are to be delivered without being moved, the risk of loss passes to the buyer when: (1) the buyer receives a negotiable document of title for the goods, or (2) the bailee acknowledges the buyer's right to possess the goods, or (3) the bailee receives a non-negotiable document of title or other written direction to deliver the goods, unless the buyer objects within a reasonable period of time. [UCC Sec. 2-509(2) and Sec. 2-503(4)(b)] To illustrate, McKee stores goods in Hardy's warehouse and takes a negotiable warehouse receipt for them. On the following day, McKee endorses and sells the receipt to Byne for cash. The day after that, Hardy's warehouse burns down, and the goods are completely destroyed. At the time of the fire, Hardy had not been informed of the sale of the warehouse receipt. The risk of loss is on Byne because it accompanies the negotiable warehouse receipt that gave him title to the goods.

SALE ON APPROVAL AND SALE OR RETURN CONTRACTS

Contracts for *sale on approval* or *sale or return* are distinct from other kinds of sales transactions. Under these contracts, the seller undertakes a particular business risk to enable the prospective buyer to obtain the goods on a trial basis.

Sale on Approval

If a buyer can return delivered goods even though they conform to the contract, the transaction is a "sale on approval" if the goods were originally delivered for use. [UCC Sec. 2-326(1)(a)] Goods held on approval are not subject to the claims of the buyer's creditors until acceptance.

A sale on approval contract can have a time limit. Both title and risk of loss are on the seller until "approval" or acceptance of the goods by the buyer. Upon approval, title passes to the buyer, who then becomes liable to the seller for the price of the goods.

Sale or Return

If a buyer can return delivered goods even though they conform to the contract, the transaction is a "sale or return" if the goods were originally delivered for resale. [UCC Sec. 2-326(1)(b)] Goods held on sale or return are subject to the claims of the buyer's creditors while they are in the buyer's possession. The risk of loss is on the buyer, who has title until the

goods are returned. The return of the goods is at the buyer's risk and expense.

It is often difficult to determine from the facts of a particular transaction whether there is a sale on approval or a sale or return. The consequences are drastically different, though, with risk of loss and transfer of title. The Code states that (unless otherwise agreed) if the goods are for the buyer to use, the transaction is a sale on approval; if the goods are for the buyer to resell, the transaction is a sale or return.

Risk of Loss in a Breached Sales Contract

There are many ways to breach a sales contract; for example, the delivered goods may be defective. The transfer of risk operates differently, depending on whether the seller or the buyer breaches.

SELLER'S BREACH

If the goods are so defective that the buyer has the right to reject them, the risk of loss will not pass to the buyer until the defects are cured or until the buyer accepts the goods in spite of their defects (thus waiving the right to reject). For example, a buyer orders blue widgets from a seller, F.O.B. seller's plant. The seller ships black widgets, giving the buyer the right to reject. The widgets are damaged in transit. The risk of loss falls on the seller, although the risk would have been on the buyer if blue widgets had been shipped under a shipment contract. [UCC Sec. 2-510]

If a buyer accepts a shipment of goods and later discovers a defect, acceptance can be revoked. For example, B orders $100,000 of frozen pies from S and insures them for $75,000. The pies are destroyed when the railroad carrying them loses its refrigeration, and B revokes his acceptance. B's insurance will cover $75,000, and S's insurance will cover the remaining $25,000. If B had no insurance, then S's insurance would cover the entire loss. Conversely, if B's insurance covered the entire value of the shipment, S's insurance company would not be liable at all. [UCC Sec. 2-510(2)]

BUYER'S BREACH The general rule is that when a buyer breaches a contract, the loss *immediately* shifts to the buyer. There are three important limitations to this rule:

1. The seller must have already identified the goods under the contract. (Regardless of the delivery arrangements, the risk will shift.)
2. The buyer will bear the risk for only a *reasonable time* after the seller learns of the breach.

3. The buyer will be liable only to the extent of any *deficiency* in the seller's insurance coverage. [UCC Sec. 2-510(3)]

The following case is a good example of the disastrous effect a buyer's breach can have when it results in a shift of the risk of loss for a shipment that becomes a total loss when fire destroys the seller's plant.

MULTIPLASTICS INC. v. ARCH INDUSTRIES, INC.

Supreme Court of Connecticut, 1974. 166 Conn. 280, 348 A.2d 618.

BACKGROUND AND FACTS *A manufacturer of plastic pellets (the plaintiff) brought this action against a buyer (the defendant) for breach of contract to purchase plastic pellets. The buyer breached its contract by failing to accept the goods when acceptance became due after the seller had made a proper tender of delivery. The seller was entitled to acceptance of the goods and to payment in accordance with the contract terms. However, the buyer failed to provide delivery instructions. The buyer sent the seller a confirming order containing the following notation: "Make and hold for release. Confirmation."*

The seller had manufactured 40,000 pounds of brown polystyrene plastic pellets within two weeks of the order and had requested release orders from the buyer. The buyer repeatedly refused to issue these release orders, citing labor difficulties and vacation schedules.

The buyer finally agreed to issue the release orders on August 20, 1971, but never actually released them. On September 22, 1971, the seller's plant, which contained the pellets manufactured for the buyer, was destroyed by fire, and the seller's fire insurance did not cover the loss of the pellets. The seller then brought this action against the buyer to recover the contract price. The buyer argued that, because the risk of loss had not passed, the seller could not recover the contract price.

The trial court concluded that the seller had made a valid tender of delivery and that the buyer had repudiated and breached the contract by refusing to accept delivery on August 20, 1971. Moreover, the trial court found that the month between August 20 and September 22, 1971, was not a "commercially unreasonable time" for the seller to treat the risk of loss as having shifted to the buyer. Hence, the trial court concluded that the seller was entitled to recover the contract price plus interest from the buyer.

ROGDANSKI, Associate Justice.
* * *

General Statutes §42a-2-510, entitled "Effect of breach on risk of loss," reads, in pertinent part, as follows: "(3) Where the buyer as to conforming goods already identified to the contract for sale repudiates or is otherwise in breach before risk of their loss has passed to him, the seller may to the extent of any deficiency in his effective insurance coverage treat the risk of loss as resting on the buyer for a commercially reasonable time."

* * *

* * * The defendant does not claim that the destroyed pellets were not "conforming goods already identified to the contract for sale," as required by General Statutes §42a-2-510(3).

* * *

The defendant contends that §42a-2-510 is not applicable because its failure to issue delivery instructions did not constitute either a repudiation or a breach of the agreement. * * * The plaintiff's requests for delivery instructions cannot be said to have misled the defendant into thinking that the plaintiff did not consider their contract breached. In fact, General Statutes §42a-2-610, entitled "Anticipatory repudiation," specifically provides that the aggrieved seller may "resort to any remedy for breach as provided by section 42a-2-703 * * *, even though he has notified the repudiating party that he would await the latter's performance and has urged retraction." Although the present case is not governed by General Statutes §42a-2-610, that section does demonstrate that the plaintiff's conduct after the defendant refused to accept delivery was not inconsistent with his claim that the contract was breached.

The remaining question is whether, under General Statutes §42a-2-510(3), the period of time from August 20, 1971, the date of the breach, to September 22, 1971, the date of the fire, was a "commercially reasonable" period within which to treat the risk of loss as resting on the buyer. The trial court concluded that it was "not, on the facts in this case, a commercially unreasonable time," which we take to mean that it was a commercially reasonable period. The time limitation is designed to enable the seller to obtain the additional requisite insurance coverage. 2 Anderson, op. cit. §2-510:6. The trial court's conclusion is tested by the finding. Although the finding is not detailed, it supports the conclusion that August 20 to September 22 was a commercially reasonable period within which to place the risk of loss on the defendant. As already stated, the trial court found that the defendant repeatedly agreed to transmit delivery instructions and that the pellets were specially made to fill the defendant's order. Under those circumstances, it was reasonable for the plaintiff to believe that the goods would soon be taken off its hands and so to forego procuring the needed insurance.

We consider it advisable to discuss one additional matter. The trial court concluded that "title" passed to the defendant, and the defendant attacks the conclusion on this appeal. The issue is immaterial to this case. General Statutes §42a-2-401 states: "Each provision of this article with regard to the rights, obligations and remedies of the seller, the buyer, purchasers or other third parties applies irrespective of title to the goods except where the provision refers to such title." As one student of the Uniform Commercial Code has written: "The single most important innovation of Article 2 [of the Uniform Commercial Code] is its restatement of * * * [the parties'] responsibilities in terms of operative facts rather than legal conclusions; where pre-Code law looked to 'title' for the definition of rights and remedies, the Code looks to demonstrable realities such as custody, control and professional expertise. This shift in approach is central to the whole philosophy of Article 2. It means that disputes, as they arise, can focus, as does all of the modern law of contracts, upon actual provable circumstances, rather than upon a metaphysical concept of elastic and endlessly fluid dimensions."

JUDGMENT AND REMEDY	*The trial court was correct. The risk of loss had passed to the defendant buyer. The plaintiff seller was entitled to recover the full contract price plus interest from the defendant because the seller had no insurance to offset the loss.*

The court of appeals ignored entirely any dispute that the parties tried to raise over who had clear title to the merchandise. Under the Code, the passage of title does not determine who is responsible for the risk of loss.

Bulk Transfers

Special problems arise when a major portion of a business's assets are transferred. This is the subject matter of Article 6, Bulk Transfers, which are defined as any large transfers of a major part of the material, supplies, merchandise, or other inventory not made in the ordinary course of the transferor's business. [UCC Sec. 6-102(1)] Problems arise, for example, when a business owing numerous creditors sells a substantial part of its equipment and inventories to third parties. [UCC Sec. 6-102(2)] If the merchant uses the proceeds to pay off debts, no problems arise. But what if the merchant spends the money on a trip around the world, leaving the creditors without payment? Can the creditors lay any claim to the goods that were transferred in bulk to the buyer? To prevent this problem from arising, Article 6 lays out certain requirements for bulk transfer:

1.   Anyone engaging in a bulk transfer must furnish a list of creditors to the buyer. Both the buyer and the seller must prepare a list of the property to be sold. The buyer must notify the seller's creditors of the bulk sale at least ten days before taking possession or paying for the goods (whichever is first).
2.   Any buyer who fails to comply with this advance notice requirement does not have effective claim to the purchased goods against the claims brought by the seller's extant creditors before (but not after) the sale takes place. Existing creditors, under such circumstances, can still treat the goods as belonging to the seller.
3.   The buyer, on the other hand, can transfer

good title to the goods to a bona fide purchaser. Existing creditors of the seller presumably cannot lay claim to the goods that are in the possession of a bona fide purchaser.

SALES BY NONOWNERS

Special problems arise when persons who acquire goods fraudulently attempt to resell them. UCC Sec. 2-403 governs the power to transfer, the good faith purchase of goods, and entrusting—all of which involve sales by nonowners.

Imperfect Title

VOID TITLE   A buyer acquires whatever title the seller has to the goods sold. A buyer may unknowingly purchase goods from a seller who is not the owner of the goods. If the seller is a thief, the seller's title is *void*—legally, there is no title at all. Thus, the buyer acquires no title, and the real owner can reclaim the goods from the buyer.

For example, if X steals goods owned by Y, X has *void title* (no legally recognized title) to those goods. If X sells the goods to B, Y can reclaim them from B even though B acted in good faith and honestly had no knowledge that the goods were stolen.

VOIDABLE TITLE   A seller will have a *voidable title* if goods are obtained by fraud; paid for with a check that is later dishonored; or purchased on credit, when the seller later learns that the buyer is insolvent. If a seller discovers that an insolvent buyer has received goods on credit, the seller will have only ten days from the time the buyer has received the goods to void the buyer's title and reclaim the goods. If the buyer, however, made a misrepresentation of solvency in writing to that owner within three months before delivery, then the ten-day limit to void the title and reclaim the goods does not apply. [UCC Sec. 2-702(2)] Purchasers of goods acquire all title that their transferors either had or had the power to transfer. However, a purchaser of a limited interest acquires rights only to the extent of the interest purchased. A seller with *voidable title* has power, nonetheless, to transfer a good title to a good faith purchaser for value. This means that the real owner cannot recover the goods from a good faith purchaser for value. [UCC Sec. 2-403(1)] If the buyer of the goods is not a good faith purchaser for value, then the actual owner of the goods can reclaim them from the buyer (or from the seller if the goods are still in the seller's possession).

The defendant in the following case had some warning that there was something suspicious about the transaction in which he was participating.

BACKGROUND AND FACTS   *The plaintiff was engaged in the business of selling boats, motors, and trailers. He sold a new boat, motor, and trailer to a person who called himself John W. Willis. Willis took possession of the goods and paid for them with a check for $6,285. The check was later dishonored.*

About six months later, the defendant bought the boat, motor, and trailer from a man identified as "Garrett," who was renting a summer beach house to the defendant that year. The defendant had known Garrett for several years.

The plaintiff sought to recover the boat, motor, and trailer from the defendant. The defendant's sole defense was that he was a good faith purchaser, and therefore the plaintiff should not be able to recover from him.

LANE v. HONEYCUTT

Court of Appeals of North Carolina, 1972.
14 N.C.App. 436, 188 S.E.2d 604.

VAUGHN, Judge.
* * *

The question * * * which we consider to be determinative of this appeal is whether there is any evidence to support the following findings of fact by the court. "(2) The Defendant, Jimmy Honeycutt, did not purchase the boat, motor and trailer in good faith."
* * *

Plaintiff has been engaged in the business of selling boats, motors and trailers in Carteret County for a number of years. On 21 February 1970, he sold a new 20-foot Critchfield boat, a new 120 hp motor and a new 1970 Cox boat trailer to a person who represented himself as John W. Willis. The purchaser took possession of the goods in exchange for a check in the amount of $6,285.00. The check was later dishonored. Contrary to the contentions of plaintiff, we hold that the goods were delivered under a transaction of purchase and that the consequences of this purchase are governed by G.S. [General Statutes] §25-2-403, which, in part, is as follows:

"*Power to transfer; good faith purchase of goods; 'entrusting.'*—(1) A purchaser of

goods acquires all title which his transferor had or had power to transfer except that a purchaser of a limited interest acquires rights only to the extent of the interest purchased. A person with voidable title has power to transfer a good title to a good faith purchaser for value. When goods have been delivered under a transaction of purchase the purchaser has such power even though
(a) the transferor was deceived as to the identity of the purchaser, or
(b) the delivery was in exchange for a check which is later dishonored, or
(c) it was agreed that the transaction was to be a 'cash sale,' or
(d) the delivery was procured through fraud punishable as larcenous under the criminal law."

[Next, the court carefully reviewed the defendant's testimony concerning "Mr. Garrett," who had sold the defendant a boat, motor, and trailer worth over $6,000 for a mere $2,400.]

"Mr. Garrett first approached me about buying his house on the beach that I was staying in, and told me he wanted $50,000.00 for it, and I told him I couldn't afford anything like that. He said, 'Well, let me sell you a boat out there.' And I said, 'Well, I couldn't afford that either.' * * *"
* * *

"* * * As to whether or not, in other words, this boat looked like it was fairly expensive, well, I thought it would be a little more than it was. He told me the price and I was very pleasantly surprised.... * * *...(H)e sells fishing tackle and stuff of that nature, and beer. He also sells gasoline for boats. Yes, sir, that is about all he sells down there. He rents small fishing boats and motors too. No, he doesn't sell them, he doesn't sell boats as far as I know.... * * *"

Garrett told defendant he would let defendant have the boat for $2500. Defendant then paid Garrett a deposit of $100. Garrett had nothing to indicate that he was the owner of the boat, motor or trailer. Garrett told defendant he was selling the boat for someone else. "This guy comes down, you know, and does some fishing."

Two weeks later defendant returned to Garden City, South Carolina, with $2400, the balance due (on a boat, motor and trailer which had been sold new less than six months earlier for $6,285.00). On this occasion,

"Mr. Garrett had told me—well, he always called him, 'this guy' see, so I really didn't know of any name or anything, but he told me, 'this guy does a lot of fishing around here, but I can't seem to get ahold of him.' He said, 'I've called him, but I can't get ahold of him, so since you have the money and you're here after the boat' * * * '(s)ince you have the money and I can't seem to find him,' he said, 'I don't believe he would object, so I'll just go ahead and sign this title for you so you can go on and get everything made out to you.' He then signed the purported owner's name on the documents and he signed the title over to me then."

The so-called "document" and "title," introduced as defendant's exhibit No. 8, was nothing more than the "certificate of number" required by G.S. §75A-5 and issued by the North Carolina Wildlife Resources Commission. This "certificate of number" is not a "certificate of title" to be compared with that required by G.S. §20-50 for vehicles intended to be operated on the highways of this State. Upon the change of ownership of a motor boat, G.S. §75A-5(c) authorizes the issuance of a new "certificate of number" to the transferee upon proper application. The application for transfer of the number, among other things, requires the seller's *signature*. A signature is "the name of a person written with his own hand."

Webster's Third New International Dictionary (1968). Defendant observed Garrett counterfeit the signature of the purported owner, John P. Patterson, on the exhibit. Following the falsified signature on defendant's exhibit No. 8, the "date sold" is set out as "June 12, 1970" and the buyer's "signature" is set out as "George (illegible) Williams." There was no testimony as to who affixed the "signature" of the purported buyer, George Williams, and there is no further reference to him in the record.

* * *

We hold that the evidence was sufficient to support the court's finding that defendant was not a good faith purchaser.

The trial court ruling was affirmed. The defendant was not a good faith purchaser. The plaintiff was determined to be the owner and was entitled to immediate possession of the boat, motor, and trailer. The plaintiff was also awarded damages against the defendant for wrongful detention of the property.

JUDGMENT AND REMEDY

ENTRUSTMENT According to Section 2-403(2), entrusting goods to a merchant *who deals in goods of that kind* gives the merchant the power to transfer all rights to a *buyer in the ordinary course of business. Entrusting* includes both delivering the goods to the merchant and leaving the purchased goods with the merchant for later delivery or pickup. [UCC Sec. 2-403(3)] A "buyer in the ordinary course" is a person who buys in good faith from another person, who deals in goods of the kind. The buyer cannot have knowledge that the sale violates the ownership rights of a third person. For example, X leaves her watch with a jeweler to be repaired. The jeweler sells the watch to Y, who does not know that the jeweler has no right to sell it. Y gets *good title* against X's claim of ownership.

The good faith buyer, however, obtains only those rights that the person entrusting the goods has. For example, X's watch is stolen by Z. Z leaves the watch with a jeweler for repairs. The jeweler sells the watch to L, who does not know that the jeweler has no right to sell it. L gets good title against Z, the entrustor, but not against X, who neither entrusted the watch to Z nor authorized Z to entrust it. Another example: X leaves a watch with a jeweler for repairs. The jeweler borrows money from a bank, using X's

watch as collateral. X can recover the watch from the bank. The bank is not a buyer; it is a "purchaser," but the "entrusting" provision of Section 2-403 protects only the "buyer in the ordinary course." [UCC Secs. 1-201(9) and 1-201(33)]

SELLER'S RETENTION OF SOLD GOODS Ordinarily, sellers do not retain goods in their possession after the goods are sold. [UCC Sec. 2-402(1)] A seller who retained goods after they were sold could mislead creditors into believing that the seller's assets were more substantial than they really were.

The Code, in Section 2-402(2), recognizes that it is not necessarily a fraud upon creditors if a merchant seller retains possession in good faith for a "commercially reasonable time" in order to accomplish some legitimate purpose (for example, repairs or adjustments). In such situations, the seller's unsecured creditors cannot void the sale.

A seller can defraud creditors by selling items at something substantially less than "fair consideration," thereby depleting the seller's assets. This is fraud on the seller's creditors if the seller is insolvent at the time of the sale, is made insolvent by the sale, or actually intended to defraud or delay creditors. Assets sold at less than "fair consideration" often are sold to a friend or relative of the seller. Such sales are considered sham transactions used to conceal assets. For example, suppose that FL Boat Company is on the verge of bankruptcy. Many of the loans that FL's owner had taken out were personally secured by him, so his creditors can go after his personal assets to recover what he owes them. Knowing this, FL's owner sells several expensive cars to his father for only $3,000 apiece, and he sells his personal yacht to his brother-in-law for $10,000 (when it is worth $110,000). He has an implicit understanding with his father and his brother-in-law that he will retain control over these assets but that they will have title. At bankruptcy, if the creditors find out about the sham transactions, they can void the sales.

INSURABLE INTEREST

Buyers and sellers often obtain insurance policy coverage to protect against damage, loss, or destruction of goods. But any party purchasing insurance must have a "sufficient interest" in the insured item to obtain a valid policy. Insurance laws—not the Code—determine "sufficiency." (See Chapter 54.) However, thc Code is helpful because it contains certain rules regarding a buyer's and a seller's insurable interest in goods on a sales contract.

Buyer's Insurable Interest

Buyers have an insurable interest in *identified* goods. This enables them to obtain necessary insurance coverage for goods that are the subject of a sales contract even before the risk of loss has passed. [UCC Sec. 2-501(1)] Consider an example: In March, a farmer sells a cotton crop he hopes to harvest in October to a buyer. After the crop is planted, the buyer insures it against hail damage. In September, a hailstorm ruins the crop. When the buyer files a claim under his insurance policy, the insurer refuses to pay the claim, asserting that the buyer has no insurable interest in the crop. The insurer is not correct. The buyer acquired an insurable interest in the crop when it was planted, since he had a contract to buy it. The rule in UCC Sec. 2-501(1)(c) indicates that a buyer obtains an insurable interest in the goods by identification, which occurs "when the crops are planted or otherwise become growing crops * * * if the contract is * * * for the sale of crops to be harvested within twelve months or the next normal harvest season after contracting, whichever is longer."

Seller's Insurable Interest

Sellers have an insurable interest in goods as long as they retain title to the goods. However, even after title passes to a buyer, a seller who has a "security interest" in the goods (a right to secure payment) still has an insurable interest and can insure the goods. [UCC Sec. 2-501(2)]

Hence, both a buyer and a seller can have an insurable interest in identical goods at the same time. In all cases, one must sustain an actual loss in order to have the right to recover from an insurance company.

QUESTIONS AND CASE PROBLEMS

1. In January 1961, James purchased an automobile from Hudiburg Chevrolet, Inc., an Oklahoma car dealer. Under the purchase contract, James was not to take the car outside the state of Oklahoma without the express permission of Hudiburg. James paid for the car with his personal check. Subsequently, the check was dishonored, and, when Hudiburg attempted to repossess the automobile, it found that James had taken it first to Georgia and then to Wisconsin. In both states James had obtained a certificate of title under a fictitious name. By the time Hudiburg caught up with the car, it was in the hands of Ponce, who had purchased it from a Milwaukee car dealer in good faith and for value. Who has title to the car? [Hudiburg Chevrolet, Inc. v. Ponce, 17 Wis.2d. 281, 116 N.W.2d 252 (1962)]

2. Craig, interested in purchasing a chassis-cab

combination vehicle, approached a salesman for Park County Implement Co. about ordering such a vehicle. Park's salesman told Craig that Park did not have the vehicle in stock but that it could purchase one for Craig from another dealer. The salesman then informed Craig that it would be cheaper for Craig to pick up the vehicle in Billings, Montana, than for it to be shipped to Wyoming, where Park was located. Subsequently, Craig did pick up the vehicle in Billings and brought it back to Wyoming, where he began installing a hoist and dump bed on it. Before Craig had finished installing this equipment, the vehicle was destroyed by fire. Craig refused to pay Park Company for the vehicle, claiming that, since he never received a certificate of title for the vehicle (none was ever issued), the sale was incomplete. Is Craig's argument valid? [Park County Implement Co. v. Craig, 397 P.2d. 800 (Wyo. 1964)]

3. Crump, a TV fanatic, purchased a TV antenna and antenna tower from Lair Company. The antenna was guaranteed to pick up any TV station within a 550-mile radius. Crump purchased the antenna and tower under a ten-year conditional sales contract that obligated him to make monthly payments. The sales contract provided that Lair Company would retain title until Crump had completed all payments under the contract. The purchase contract stated, among other things, that Crump was not to move or tamper with the antenna during the ten-year payment period. About a year later, lightning struck and destroyed Crump's new antenna. At Crump's request, Lair Company performed extensive repairs on the antenna. Crump refused to pay, claiming that risk of loss or damage resulting from the lightning should be borne by Lair Company. Will Lair be successful in a suit for the cost of its repairs? [Lair Distributing Co. v. Crump, 48 Ala. App. 72, 261 So.2d. 904 (1972)]

4. Dueitt, an industrial construction contractor, owned a large crane for his construction business. Dueitt took the crane, which was badly in need of repair, to Small, who was in the business of both selling and repairing heavy duty equipment. Small told Dueitt that the repair work would take two months, but one week after Dueitt left the crane with Small, Small sold it to Lichfield, who, in good faith paid a reasonable price. Can Dueitt recover the crane from Lichfield? [Lichfield v. Dueitt, 245 So.2d. 190 (Miss. 1971)]

5. Consolidated Bottling Company agreed to purchase a used can-filling machine from Jaco Equipment. The contract provided that delivery of the machine was to be made "f.o.b. purchaser's truck." The parties agreed that Consolidated would send its truck to pick up the machine on the last day of June. On June 15 vandals broke into Jaco's warehouse where the machine was kept and did extensive damage to it. Who bears the risk of loss for the damage caused to the machine? [Consolidated Bottling Co. v. Jaco Equipment Corp., 442 F.2d. 660 (10th Cir. 1971)]

6. On August 15 Kaplan entered into an agreement with Odd Lot Corp. for the purchase and sale of 10,000 pieces of odd fabrics. Included in the contract between Kaplan and Odd Lot was the phrase "goods held at buyer's risk." Odd Lot, the seller, was to retain possession of the goods for fifteen days before Kaplan was to pick them up. During the fifteen-day period, while the goods were still in Odd Lot's possession, much of the material suffered water damage. Who must absorb the cost of the damage to the material— Kaplan or Odd Lot? [Kaplan v. Odd Lot Corp., 16 UCC Rptg. Serv. 704 (N.Y. 1975)]

7. S agreed to sell his car to B. The two arranged over the telephone to meet at B's place of business to complete the sales transaction. At the time agreed upon, S arrived at B's place of business, parked his car, and met with B to close the deal. S gave B the keys to the car along with an unnotarized certificate of title, and B paid S the full purchase price. Under local law, a certificate of title was not validly transferred until it was notarized, so the parties agreed to meet the next day and have the title officially transferred in front of a notary. That evening, on his way home, B injured a person while driving S's car. When the injured person attempted to sue B, B in turn sued S's insurance company, claiming that he was driving the car with S's permission, and it was therefore covered under the "permission clause" included in S's policy. Has title passed to B so that S's insurance company is not liable under S's policy? [Semple v. State Farm Mutual Auto Ins. Co., 215 F.Supp. 645 (E.D. Pa. 1963)]

8. As one of the benefits of working with A&Z Motor Company, Knotts received a model car to use both for family and business purposes. Knotts was to be the sole user of the car, and A&Z retained the certificate of title. The car was insured by Safeco Insurance Company, and Knotts was named in the policy as the owner of the car. Several weeks after A&Z gave Knotts the use of the car, he had an accident. Knotts sued the insurance company to recover for damages, which were covered by the insurance policy. Safeco refused to pay, claiming that Knotts was not the owner of the car and that, since A&Z was the owner, the insurance policy necessarily ran in favor of it. Can Knotts recover from Safeco? [Knotts v. Safeco Ins. Co. of America, 78 N.M. 395, 432 P.2d. 106 (1967)]

9. In a patent infringement suit brought by a Delaware corporation against an Ohio corporation, the court, for purposes of determining where the suit should be brought, had to decide in what jurisdiction the Ohio corporation "sold" its goods. The court found that the Ohio corporation manufactured its goods in Ohio and shipped them to buyers in Michigan "F.O.B. Warren, Ohio." The court also found that the Ohio corporation had its main business office in Pennsylvania. This office controlled production policies and had the power to veto all sales. Where were the Ohio corporation's goods sold? [Welding Engineers, Inc. v. Aetna-Standard Engineering Co., 169 F.Supp. 146 (W.D. Pa. 1958)]

10. Jones purchased an automobile from Phillips Chevrolet in January 1978. Less than a year later, the car was stolen. After filling out the appropriate forms, Jones collected the full price of the car from his insurance company, Home Indemnity Company. When he was reimbursed, Jones assigned all his interest in the automobile to Home Indemnity. Subsequently, the thief sold Jones's car to an automobile wholesaler, who in turn sold it to a retail car dealer. Schrier purchased the automobile from the car dealer without knowledge of the theft. Home Indemnity Insurance Company sued Schrier to recover the car. Can Home Indemnity recover? [Schrier v. Home Indemnity Co., 273 A.2d. 248 (D.C. App. 1971)]

19

Sales

Performance and Obligation

DUTY OF GOOD FAITH AND COMMERCIAL REASONABLENESS

To understand the performance that is required of a seller and a buyer under a sales contract, it is necessary to know the duties and obligations each party has assumed under the terms of their contract. Keep in mind that "duties and obligations" under the contract here include the agreement, the custom, and the Code. Sometimes the sales contract leaves open some particulars of performance and permits one of the parties to specify them. The obligations of "good faith" and "commercial reasonableness" underlie every sales contract within the UCC. They are objective obligations, and they can form the basis for a breach of contract suit later on. These standards are read into every contract, and they provide a framework in which the parties can specify particulars of performance. "Any such specification must be made in good faith and within limits set by commercial reasonableness." [UCC Sec. 2-311(1)]

The duty of cooperation between the parties required by Section 2-311 must be read along with the Code's "good faith" provision, which can never be disclaimed. "Every contract or duty within this Act imposes an obligation of good faith in its performance or enforcement." [UCC Sec. 1-203] "Good faith" in the case of a merchant means honesty in fact *and* the observance of reasonable commercial standards of fair dealing in the trade. [UCC Sec. 2-103(1)(b)] Thus, when one party delays specifying particulars of performance for an unreasonable period of time or fails to cooperate with the other party, the innocent party is excused from any resulting delay in performance. In addition, the innocent party can proceed to perform in any reasonable manner. If the innocent party has performed as far as is reasonably possible under the circumstances, then the other party's failure to specify or lack of cooperation can be treated as a breach of contract.

Good faith can mean that one party must not take advantage of another party by manipulating contract terms. Good faith applies to both parties, even the nonbreaching party. The principle of good faith applies through both the performance and the enforcement of all agreements or duties within a contract. Good faith is a question of fact for the jury. In the following case, good faith was a major issue in determining the damages flowing from a breach of contract.

MASSACHUSETTS GAS & ELECTRIC LIGHT SUPPLY CORP. v. V-M CORP.

United States Court of Appeals,
First Circuit, 1967.
387 F.2d 605.

BACKGROUND AND FACTS *The plaintiff, a distributor of phonographs, tapes, records, and other appliances, entered into a distributorship agreement with the defendant, a manufacturer. Their agreement contained a thirty-day cancellation option that could be exercised upon written notice. Under the contract, the manufacturer promised to provide the distributor with a reasonable inventory for current sales. The distributor's normal inventory was about a hundred units.*

When the distributor learned that the manufacturer was going to exercise the thirty-day cancellation option, it placed an extraordinarily large order—enough to meet its estimated needs for six months. The manufacturer refused to fill the order, so the distributor sued the manufacturer for damages for an alleged breach of contract in refusing to fill the order.

ALDRICH, Chief Judge.
* * *

[I]t might well be that defendant would have been required to fill an order, made on June 28, to maintain a *reasonable* inventory through the coming month. [Emphasis added.] We could not construe defendant's obligation to be any greater than this. Moreover, when we consider a further paragraph, plaintiff is in difficulties even here. Under paragraph 14 of the agreement, at the option of the defendant exercised at any time within 30 days after termination, plaintiff was obliged to return, at essentially the price paid, plus freight, all goods purchased from the defendant and then unsold. Had the defendant filled the June 28 order in its entirety, in the light of the above-quoted findings which are fully supported in the record, the clear purport of which is that no part of these goods would have been sold, the defendant could have required the return of the entire order.

An interest defeasible at the option of the defendant cannot support a claim for damages. In the light of paragraph 14 it may be said that the substance of the plaintiff's case is that it had a right to carry defendant's products terminable in all respects in 30 days. Such a contract cannot justify a claim for damages for a longer period than 30 days even it if was prematurely breached. * * * On this basis plaintiff's loss must be predicated only on the number of additional units it could have sold by August 3 had the order been filled, which, so far as appeared, was none.

Alternatively, even if whatever detriment plaintiff may be thought to suffer by reason of paragraph 14 be disregarded, the maximum June 28 order which defendant should have had to respect was to maintain an appropriate inventory through July. Plaintiff's order was not a good faith attempt to accomplish this, see U.C.C. §§1-203, 2-103(1) (b), 2-306, but an effort to nullify the termination clause. And when defendant offered to take plaintiff's possible termination difficulties into consideration and fill a part of the June 28 order, plaintiff took the position, to quote the language of the district court, that it "wanted the whole order or nothing." Of these alternatives the court gave it nothing. We agree.

The appellate court affirmed the trial court's ruling. The distributor took nothing. The court in part rested its decision on the finding that the distributor's final order was so excessive as to amount to a breach of its duty of good faith.

JUDGMENT AND REMEDY

PERFORMANCE OF A SALES CONTRACT

A *seller* has the basic obligation to *transfer and deliver conforming goods.* According to the terms of the sales contract, the *buyer* has the obligation to *accept and pay for the goods.* Overall performance of a sales contract is controlled by the agreement between the buyer and the seller. When the contract is unclear, or when terms are indefinite in certain respects and disputes arise, the Code provides built-in standards and rules for interpreting their agreement.

CONCURRENT CONDITIONS OF PERFORMANCE

The delivery of goods by the seller and the payment of the purchase price by the buyer are said to be *concurrent conditions*—those that are mutually dependent and are to be performed at the same time. The theoretical assumption is that delivery and payment can occur simultaneously. In reality this rarely, if ever, happens.

Section 2-301 of the Code provides that "the obligation of the seller is to transfer and deliver and that of the buyer is to accept and pay *in accordance with the contract.*" (Emphasis added.) If the contract expressly provides that the seller must first deliver the goods before receiving payment or that the buyer must pay before receiving the goods, then the terms of the contract control. However, where the agree-

ment does not specifically provide, both the buyer and the seller can be "ready, willing, and able" to perform. But who goes first? The Code charges both parties with the duty to proceed. In other words, in order for either party to maintain an action against the other for breach, the party bringing suit must put the other party in default by performing. This is accomplished in one of three ways—through: (1) performance according to the contract, (2) tender of performance according to the contract, or (3) excuse from tender of performance.[1]

For example, Laval agrees to deliver goods to Boyd on September 1, and Boyd agrees to pay on September 15. If Laval fails to deliver the goods, Boyd can sue Laval on or after September 2. Since Laval is in default, Boyd can proceed without first tendering the purchase price.

SELLER'S OBLIGATION OF TENDER OF DELIVERY

Tender of Delivery

Tender of delivery requires that the seller have and hold *conforming* goods at the buyer's disposal and give the buyer whatever notification is reasonably necessary to enable the buyer to take delivery. [UCC Sec. 2-503(1)]

---

1. To tender is to offer or make available money or property in pursuance of a contract in such a way that nothing further remains to be done to fulfill the obligation of the party tendering.

Tender must occur at a *reasonable hour* and in a *reasonable manner.* In other words, a seller cannot call the buyer at 2:00 A.M. and say, "The goods are ready. I'll give you twenty minutes to get them." Unless the parties have agreed otherwise, the goods must be tendered for delivery at a reasonable time and must be kept available for a reasonable period of time in order to enable the buyer to take possession of them. [UCC Sec. 2-503(1)(a)]

All goods called for by a contract must be tendered in a single delivery unless the parties agree otherwise [UCC Sec. 2-612] or the circumstances are such that either party can rightfully request delivery in lots. [UCC Sec. 2-307] Hence, an order for 1,000 shirts cannot be delivered two at a time. If seller and buyer contemplated, though, that the shirts would be delivered in four orders of 250 each as they are produced, for summer, winter, fall, and spring stock, and the price can be apportioned accordingly, it may be commercially reasonable to do so.

Place of Delivery

NON-CARRIER CASES   If the contract does not designate where the goods will be delivered, and the buyer is expected to pick them up, the place of delivery is the *seller's place of business* or, if the seller has none, the *seller's residence.* [UCC Sec. 2-308] If the contract involves the sale of *identified goods* (see Chapter 18 for a discussion of such goods), and the parties know when they enter into the contract that these goods are located somewhere other than at the seller's place of business (such as at a warehouse or in the possession of a bailee), then the *location of the goods* is the place for their delivery. [UCC Sec. 2-308] For example, Laval and Boyd live in San Francisco. In San Francisco, Laval contracts to sell to Boyd five used railroad dining cars, which both parties know are located in Atlanta. If nothing more is specified in the contract, the place of delivery for the railroad cars is Atlanta.

Assume further that the railroad cars are stored in a warehouse and that Boyd will need some type of document to show the warehouse (bailee) in Atlanta that Boyd is entitled to take possession of the five dining cars. The seller "tenders delivery" without moving the goods. The seller "delivers" either by giving the buyer a *negotiable document of title* or by obtaining the *bailee's* (warehouse's) *acknowledgment* that the buyer is entitled to possession.[2]

CARRIER CASES   There are many instances, resulting either from attendant circumstances or from delivery terms contained in the contract, when it is apparent that the parties intended that a carrier be used to move the goods. There are two ways a seller can complete performance of the obligation to deliver the goods—through a shipment contract or a destination contract.

Shipment Contracts   Under a shipment contract, the seller is authorized to send the goods to the buyer, but the contract does not obligate the seller to be responsible for the goods all the way to the buyer. [UCC Secs. 2-509 and 2-319] The seller must:

1.   Put the goods into the hands of the carrier.
2.   Make a contract for their transportation that is reasonable according to the nature of the goods and their value.
3.   Obtain and promptly deliver for tender to the buyer any documents necessary to enable the buyer to obtain possession of the goods from the carrier.
4.   Promptly notify the buyer that shipment has been made. [UCC Sec. 2-504]

If the seller fails to complete *any* of these requirements, and a *material loss* of the goods or a *delay* results, the buyer can reject the shipment. Of course, the parties can agree that a lesser amount of loss or a delay will be grounds for rejection.

---

2.   If the seller delivers a nonnegotiable document of title or merely writes instructions to the bailee to release the goods to the buyer without the bailee's *acknowledgment* of the buyer's rights, this will also be a sufficient tender, unless the buyer objects. [UCC Sec. 2-503(4)]

Destination Contracts   Under destination contracts, the seller agrees to see that the goods are actually delivered to the buyer at a particular destination. Once the goods arrive, the seller must tender the goods at a reasonable hour and hold conforming goods at the buyer's disposal for a reasonable length of time, giving appropriate notice. The seller must also provide the buyer with any documents of title necessary to enable the buyer to obtain delivery from the carrier. This is often done by tendering the documents through ordinary banking channels.

F.O.B. Contracts   In contracts specifying that the goods, price, or delivery are F.O.B. to a particular point, the F.O.B. point is the delivery point. [UCC Sec. 2-319(1)]

If the F.O.B. point is the seller's place of shipment, then it is a *shipment contract*, and the seller incurs only the risk and expense of putting the goods into the hands of the carrier under the four conditions described above. If the F.O.B. point is at a particular destination, then it is a *destination contract*, and the responsibilities to the seller are the same as those under any destination contract. [UCC Sec. 2-319]

If the vehicle of transportation at the F.O.B. point is referred to, then the seller must pay the expense of loading the goods on board the vehicle. For example, "F.O.B. car X23JM, Balt. RR yard, Baltimore" means that the seller transports the goods to the carrier (Baltimore Railroad) at the railroad yard in Baltimore and loads the goods onto car X23JM.

F.A.S. Contracts   F.A.S. contracts involve transportation by ship or other seagoing vessel. In contracts specifying that the goods, price, or delivery are F.A.S. (free alongside ship), the seller must deliver the goods alongside the vessel, usually on a dock designated by the buyer. In effect, this is a *shipment contract*. The seller has no responsibility for loading the goods onto the vessel. The seller must obtain and tender a receipt, which is delivered to the buyer, ordinarily through banking channels. Once delivered, the F.A.S. contract is complete;

the consigner (seller) is then relieved of any liability for the goods. [UCC Sec. 2-319(2)]

Ex-ship Contracts   If the contract specifies ex-ship, then the seller is responsible for loading the goods onto the vessel. In effect, ex-ship, which means "from the carrying vessel," is a *destination contract*, and it includes the shipper's obligation to *unload the goods at the port of destination*. The words "ex-ship" do not constitute a condition of the contract but are inserted for the benefit of the seller.

C.I.F. Contracts   Contracts specifying C.I.F. (a maritime term meaning "cost, insurance, and freight") indicate that the buyer's purchase price includes the *cost* of the goods, *insurance* during transit, and *freight* charges. If a contract is merely C&F, then only the cost and freight charges, not insurance, are included in the purchase price. Both C.I.F. and C&F contracts require the seller to load the goods on board the vessel, and in both cases the risk of loss in transit is borne by the buyer, who will be the insured under a C.I.F. contract. [UCC Secs. 2-320 and 2-321]

THE PERFECT TENDER RULE

As previously noted, the seller has an obligation to tender *conforming goods*, and this entitles the seller to acceptance by and payment from the buyer according to the terms of the contract. The so-called *perfect tender rule* of Section 2-601 of the UCC states that "if goods or tender of delivery fail, *in any respect,* to conform to the contract" the buyer is not obliged to accept them. (Emphasis added.) Such a rigid rule seems uncharacteristic of the Code's philosophy of finding and preserving a contract whenever possible.

Exceptions to the Perfect Tender Rule

AGREEMENT OF THE PARTIES   If the parties have agreed, for example, that defective goods or parts will not be rejected if the seller is able to repair or replace them within a reasonable time, then the perfect tender rule does not apply.

CURE The term **cure** is not specifically defined in the Code, but it refers to the seller's right to repair, adjust, or replace defective or nonconforming goods. Some courts allow a money allocation to be sufficient cure—for example, when conforming goods are tendered after delivery is overdue—but a price allowance is made for late delivery. [UCC Sec. 2-508]

The seller's right to cure substantially restricts the buyer's right to reject. If the buyer refuses a tender of goods as nonconforming but does not disclose the nature of the defect to the seller, the buyer cannot later assert the defect as a defense if the defect is one that the seller could have cured. The buyer must act in good faith and state specific reasons for refusing to accept the goods. [UCC Sec. 2-605] When any tender or delivery is rejected because of *nonconforming goods* and the time for performance *has not yet expired,* the seller can notify the buyer promptly of the intention to cure and can then do so *within the contract time for performance.* [UCC Sec. 2-508] For example, Horn sells Gill a white refrigerator, to be delivered on or before September 15. Horn delivers a yellow refrigerator on September 10, and Gill rejects it. Horn can cure by notifying Gill that he intends to cure and by delivering a white refrigerator on or before September 15.

Once the time for performance under the contract has *expired,* the seller can still exercise the right to cure if the seller had *reasonable grounds to believe that the nonconforming tender would be acceptable to the buyer.* For example, Demsetz has been supplying auto body paint to Hall Body, an auto body paint shop, for several years. Demsetz and Hall have a contract for R-Z type paint. In the past, when Demsetz could not obtain R-Z type paint, he substituted R-Y type paint, and Hall accepted without any objection. Hall signs a new contract for R-Z type paint to be delivered on April 30. Demsetz realizes that, with the paint supply on hand, only half the order can be filled with R-Z type paint, so he completes the other half of the

order with R-Y type paint. The order is delivered on April 30. Hall rejects. Demsetz, knowing from their prior course of dealing that R-Y had always been an acceptable substitute, has "reasonable grounds to believe" that R-Y will be acceptable. Therefore, Demsetz can cure within a reasonable time, even though conforming delivery will occur after the actual time for performance under the contract.

INAPPROPRIATE SHIPPING ARRANGEMENTS In a *shipment contract,* the seller's failure to make a reasonable contract of carriage for the particular goods with an appropriate carrier or the seller's failure to notify the buyer that the goods have been shipped is a *defect in tender.* This is grounds for a buyer to reject, but *only if material delay or loss results.* [UCC Sec. 2-504]

SUBSTITUTION OF CARRIERS Where an agreed manner of delivery (berthing, loading, or unloading facilities) becomes impracticable or unavailable through no fault of either party, but a commercially reasonable substitute is available, this substitute performance is sufficient tender to the buyer. [UCC Sec. 2-614(1)] For example, a sales contract calls for the delivery of a number of tons of oil "F.O.B. Stanley Steamer at New York." War breaks out, and the shipping line is prohibited from sailing to New York due to an embargo. The buyer will be entitled to make a reasonable substitute tender, perhaps by rail. Note that the seller here is responsible for any additional shipping costs, unless contrary arrangements have been made in the sales contract.

INSTALLMENT CONTRACTS An **installment contract** is a single contract that permits delivery in two or more separate lots to be accepted and paid for separately. In an installment contract, a buyer can reject an installment *only if the nonconformity substantially impairs* the value of the installment and cannot be cured. [UCC Secs. 2-612(2) and 2-307]

The entire installment contract is breached

only when one or more nonconforming install-ments substantially impair the value of the *whole contract*. If the buyer subsequently accepts a nonconforming installment and fails to notify the seller of cancellation, then the contract is reinstated, however. Also, if the buyer brings an action with respect only to past installments or demands performance as to future installments, the aggrieved party has reinstated the contract. [UCC Sec. 2-612(3)]

BACKGROUND AND FACTS *This case arose from a dispute between a buyer and a seller for the purchase and sale of goods to be delivered on an installment contract basis. The contract provided for the goods to be delivered in three separate lots. The seller delivered the first installment of goods, but the buyer failed to pay for it, and the seller failed to deliver the remaining two installments. The seller then sought to have the court declare the value of the whole contract impaired and hold the buyer in breach, relieving the seller of its obligation to continue performing under the contract.*

GULF CHEM. & METALLURGICAL CORP. v. SYLVAN CHEM. CORP.
New Jersey Superior Court, 1973.
12 UCC Rep.Serv. 117.

VAN TASSELL, Judge.
* * *

It is clear that the contract in question is an installment contract as defined by NJS [New Jersey Statutes] 12A:2-612(1) which states:

"An 'installment contract' is one which requires or authorizes the delivery of goods in separate lots to be separately accepted, even though the contract contains a clause 'each delivery is a separate contract' or its equivalent."

It is undisputed that this action arose as a result of a series of negotiations culminating in one contract which contemplated the delivery of the goods in three separate lots to be separately accepted. This was evidenced by three purchase orders sent by the defendant to the plaintiff together on the same date.

NJS 12A:2-709, dealing with an action for the price states that:

"(1) When the buyer fails to pay the price as it becomes due the seller may recover, together with any incidental damages under the next section, the price
"(a) of goods accepted * * *."

[The buyer accepted the first shipment of goods. The goods delivered were not the size specified in the contract, but since the defendant accepted the goods, the court considered that the defendant had made a valid express waiver as to size. Subsequently, the parties made a good faith modification of the contract that reduced the buyer's obligation for the goods delivered in the first installment. Nonetheless, the buyer failed to pay for the first installment of goods. As a result, the seller failed to deliver the two remaining installments. In the absence of proof that the buyer's failure to pay for the first installment subsequently impaired the value of the whole contract, the seller was not relieved of its obligation to continue performing under the contract.]

There is, however, a New Jersey case which is in point and, though decided prior to the adoption of the Uniform Commercial Code is consistent with current New Jersey law. In Empire Rubber Mfg. Co. v. Morris, 77 NJL 498 (E&A 1909) the seller claimed that the refusal of the buyer to pay for goods already shipped pursuant to an installment contract released the seller from any obligation of further performance on their part. The court in that case states the rule that, "when the seller has agreed to deliver the goods sold in installments, and the buyer has agreed to pay the price in installments which are proportioned to and payable on delivery of each installment of goods, then the default by either party with reference to any one installment will not, ordinarily, entitle the other party to abrogate the contract." The current policy of New Jersey wih respect to the above rule is reflected in the Uniform Commercial Code's section dealing with installment contracts.

NJS 12A:2-612(3) states:

"(3) Whenever non-conformity or default with respect to one or more installments substantially impairs the value of the whole contract there is a breach of the whole. But the aggrieved party reinstates the contract if he accepts a non-conforming installment without seasonably notifying of cancellation or if he brings an action with respect only to past installments or demands performance as to future installments."

That this subsection is in line with the rule as expressed in Empire Rubber Mfg. Co. v. Morris, supra, with respect to the continuance of an installment contract is demonstrated by Uniform Commercial Code Comment (6) to NJS 12A:2-612:

"This subsection is designed to further the continuance of the contract in the absence of an overt cancellation. Whether the non-conformity in any given installment justifies cancellation as to the future, depends, not on whether such non-conformity indicates an intent or likelihood that the future deliveries will also be defective, but whether the non-conformity substantially impairs the value of the whole contract. (As indicated further in the Comment, 'prior policy is continued, putting the rule as to buyer's default on the same footing as that in regard to seller's default'). If only the seller's security in regard to future installments is impaired, he has the right to demand adequate assurances of proper future performance but has not an immediate right to cancel the entire contract."

In order for the seller to relieve itself of its obligation to continue the contract, there must be a showing by the plaintiff-seller, that the defendant's failure to pay for the first installment "substantially impaired" the value of the whole contract. There is no such proof in this case. Furthermore there was never an overt cancellation of the entire contract by the seller. Therefore the plaintiff is liable to the defendant for non-delivery of purchase orders 8640 and 8641.

JUDGMENT AND REMEDY   *The plaintiff seller was not relieved of its obligation to continue performing under the contract. Hence, the plaintiff was held liable to the defendant for the nondelivery of the last two of the three installments.*

COMMERCIAL IMPRACTICABILITY When-ever unforeseen occurrences that neither party contemplated when the contract was made make performance commercially impractic-able, the rule of perfect tender no longer holds. According to UCC Sec. 2-615(a), delay in delivery or nondelivery in whole or in part is not a breach when performance has been made impracticable "by the occurrence of a contin-gency the nonoccurrence of which was a basic assumption on which the contract was made * * *."

However, the seller must notify the buyer as soon as it is practicable to do so that there will be a delay or nondelivery.

The notion of commercial impracticability is derived from contract law theories of impos-sibility and frustration of purpose. Does a picket line at a job site cause a party's performance to become so "impracticable" that the excuse of "impossibility" becomes a valid defense to performance?

BACKGROUND AND FACTS *The plaintiff, Mishara Construction Com-pany, Inc., was a general contractor. Mishara was under contract with the Pittsfield Housing Authority for the construction of Rose Manor, a housing project for the elderly. In September 1966, Mishara negotiated with the defendant, Transit-Mixed Concrete Corp., for the supply of ready-mixed concrete to be used on the project. An agreement was reached that Transit would supply all the concrete needed on the project at a price of $13.25 per cubic yard, with deliveries to be made at the times and in the amounts ordered by Mishara. The two parties signed a purchase order on September 21, 1966. The purchase order identified the Rose Manor project and indicated that delivery was to be made as required by the Mishara Construction Company. Performance under this contract was satisfactory to both parties until April 1967.*

In that month a labor dispute disrupted work on the job site. Although work resumed on June 15, 1967, a picket line was maintained on the site until the project was completed in 1969. Throughout this period, with very few exceptions, Transit delivered no concrete, despite frequent requests by Mishara. After notifying Transit of its intention, Mishara purchased the balance of its concrete requirements elsewhere. Mishara then sought damages for the additional cost of the replacement concrete and for the expenses it incurred in locating an alternate source of ready-mixed concrete.

MISHARA CONSTR. CO., INC. v. TRANSIT-MIXED CONCRETE CORP.

Supreme Judicial Court of Massachusetts, 1974.
310 N.E.2d 363.

REARDON, Justice.
* * *

The principal issue in the case was the defendant's claimed excuse of impossibili-ty of performance. The determination of that issue depended on facts and circumstances which were for the jury to decide.
* * *

The excuse of impossibility in contracts for the sale of goods is controlled by the appropriate section of the Uniform Commercial Code, * * * § 2-615. That section sets up two requirements before performance may be excused. First, the performance must have become "impracticable." Second, the impracticability must have been caused "by the occurrence of a contingency the non-occurrence of which was a basic assumption on which the contract was made." This section of the Uniform Commercial Code has not yet been interpreted by this court. Therefore it is appropriate to discuss briefly the significance of these two criteria.

With respect to the requirement that performance must have been impracticable, the official Code comment to the section stresses that the reference is to "*commercial* impracticability" as opposed to strict impossibility. [Emphasis added.] G.L. c. 106, § 2-615, comments 3-4. This is not a radical departure from the common law of contracts as interpreted by this court. Although a strict rule was originally followed denying any excuse for accident or "inevitable necessity," e. g., Adams v. Nichols, 19 Pick. 275 (1837), it has long been assumed that circumstances drastically increasing the difficulty and expense of the contemplated performance may be within the compass of "impossibility." By adopting the term "impracticability" rather than "impossibility" the drafters of the Code appear to be in accord with Professor Williston who [prior to enactment of the UCC] stated that "the essence of the modern defense of impossibility is that the promised performance was at the making of the contract, or thereafter became, impracticable owing to some extreme or unreasonable difficulty, expense, injury, or loss involved, rather than that it is scientifically or actually impossible."

The second criterion of the excuse, that the intervening circumstance be one which the parties assumed would not occur, is also familiar to the law of Massachusetts. The rule is essentially aimed at the distribution of certain kinds of risks in the contractual relationship. By directing the inquiry to the time when the contract was first made, we really seek to determine whether the risk of the intervening circumstance was one which the parties may be taken to have assigned between themselves. It is, of course, *the very essence of contract that it is directed at the elimination of some risks for each party in exchange for others. Each receives the certainty of price, quantity, and time, and assumes the risk of changing market prices, superior opportunity, or added costs.* [Emphasis added.] It is implicit in the doctrine of impossibility (and the companion rule of "frustration of purpose") that certain risks are so unusual and have such severe consequences that they must have been beyond the scope of the assignment of risks inherent in the contract, that is, beyond the agreement made by the parties. To require performance in that case would be to grant the promisee an advantage for which he could not be said to have bargained in making the contract. "The important question is whether an unanticipated circumstance has made performance of the promise vitally different from what should reasonably have been within the contemplation of both parties when they entered into the contract. If so, the risk should not fairly be thrown upon the promisor." Williston, Contracts (Rev. ed.) § 1931 (1938). The emphasis in contracts governed by the Uniform Commercial Code is on the commercial context in which the agreement was made. The question is, given the commercial circumstances in which the parties dealt: *Was the contingency which developed one which the parties could reasonably be thought to have foreseen as a real possibility which could affect performance?* [Emphasis added.] Was it one of that variety of risks which the parties were tacitly assigning to the promisor by their failure to provide for it explicitly? If it were, performance will be required. If it could not be so considered, performance is excused. The contract cannot be reasonably thought to govern in these circumstances, and the parties are both thrown upon the resources of the open market without the benefit of their contract.

With this backdrop, we consider Mishara's contention that a labor dispute which makes performance more difficult never constitues an excuse for nonperformance. We think it is evident that in some situations a labor dispute would not meet the requirements for impossibility discussed above. A picket line might constitute a mere inconvenience and hardly make performance "impracticable." Likewise, in certain industries with a long record of labor difficulties, the nonoccurrence of strikes and picket lines could not fairly be said to be a basic assumption of the agreement. Certainly, in general, labor disputes cannot be considered extraordinary in the course of modern commerce. See Restatement: Contracts, § 461, illustration 7 (1932). Admitting this, however, we are still far from the proposition implicit in the plaintiff's requests. Much must depend on the facts known to the parties at the time of contracting with respect to the history of and prospects for labor difficulties during the period of performance of the contract, as well as the likely severity of the effect of such disputes on the ability to perform. From these facts it is possible to draw an inference as to whether or not the parties intended performance to be carried out even in the face of the labor difficulty. *Where the probability of a labor dispute appears to be practically nil, and where the occurrence of such a dispute provides unusual difficulty, the excuse of impracticability might well be applicable.* [Emphasis added.] * * * "Rather than mechanically apply any fixed rule of law, where the parties themselves have not allocated responsibility, justice is better served by appraising all of the circumstances, the part the various parties played, and thereon determining liability."

The plaintiff was successful in obtaining damages from the defendant. The court was not persuaded that a labor dispute would be considered a commercial impracticability under the Uniform Commercial Code. Therefore, the defendant was not excused from performing under the terms of the contract. **JUDGMENT AND REMEDY**

DESTRUCTION OF IDENTIFIED GOODS The Code provides that when a casualty occurs that totally destroys *identified goods* under a sales contract through no fault of either party and *before risk passes to the buyer*, the seller is excused from performance. [UCC Sec. 2-613(a)] However, if the goods are only *partially* destroyed, the buyer can inspect them and either treat the contract as voided or accept the damaged goods with an allowance off the contract price.

Mary Murphy contracts to sell lumber to Nancy Jones. If the lumber is destroyed by fire before identification and risk of loss pass to Jones, then Murphy must not only stand the loss of the fire, she must still perform by delivering the lumber to Jones. If the lumber is destroyed by fire *after risk of loss* has passed to Jones (for example, in a shipment contract when the lumber is already en route to Jones), then Jones must still pay because Murphy has completed performance (that is, she has put the lumber into the hands of the carrier). If the lumber is destroyed by fire *after* it has been identified and *before* risk of loss has passed to Jones (in a destination contract or in a shipment contract *before* lumber has been given to the carrier), then Murphy is excused from performance, but she must bear the fire loss.

BUYER'S OBLIGATIONS

Once the seller has adequately tendered delivery, the buyer is obligated to accept the goods and pay for them according to the terms of the contract. In the absence of any specific agreements, the buyer must:

1.   Furnish facilities reasonably suited for receipt of the goods. [UCC Sec. 2-503(1)(b)]

2.   Make payment at the time and place the buyer *receives* the goods even if the place of shipment is the place of delivery. [UCC Sec. 2-310(a)]

Payment

When a sale is made on credit, the buyer is obliged to pay according to credit terms (for example, 60, 90, or 120 days), *not* when the goods are received. The credit period begins on the *date of shipment*. [UCC Sec. 2-310(d)]

Payment can be made by any means agreed between the parties. Cash can be used, but the buyer can also use any other method generally acceptable in the commercial world. If the seller demands cash when the buyer offers a check, then the seller must permit the buyer reasonable time to obtain legal tender. [UCC Sec. 2-511]

Right of Inspection

The buyer's right to inspect the goods allows the buyer to verify before making payment that the goods tendered or delivered are what were contracted for or ordered. If the goods are *not* what the buyer ordered, there is no duty to pay. *An opportunity for inspection is therefore a condition precedent to the seller's right to enforce payment.* [UCC Sec. 2-513(1)]

C.O.D. SHIPMENTS   If a seller ships goods to a buyer C.O.D. (collect on delivery), the buyer can rightfully refuse to accept them (unless the contract expressly provides for a C.O.D. shipment). Since C.O.D. does not permit inspection by the consignee, the effect is a denial of the buyer's right of inspection. It is a breach on the part of the seller to arrange shipment that will deprive the buyer of the right to inspect the goods. But when the buyer has agreed to a C.O.D. shipment in the contract or has agreed to pay for the goods upon the presentation of a bill of lading, no right of inspection exists because it was negated by the agreement. [UCC Sec. 2-513(3)]

PAYMENT DUE—DOCUMENTS OF TITLE   Under certain contracts, payment is due on the receipt of the required documents of title even though the goods themselves may not have arrived at their destination. With C.I.F. and C&F contracts, payment is required upon receipt of the documents unless the parties have agreed to the contrary. Thus, payment is required prior to inspection, and it must be made unless the buyer knows that the goods are nonconforming. [UCC Secs. 2-310(b) and 2-513(3)]

Acceptance

The buyer can manifest assent to the delivered goods in different ways:

1.   The buyer can expressly accept the shipment by words or conduct. For example, there is an acceptance if the buyer, after having reasonable opportunity to inspect, signifies agreement to the seller that either the goods are conforming or that they are acceptable despite their nonconformity. [UCC Sec. 2-606(1)(a)]

2.   Acceptance will be presumed if the buyer has had a reasonable opportunity to inspect the goods and has failed to reject them within a reasonable period of time. [UCC Secs. 2-606(1)(b) and 2-602(1)]

3.   The buyer accepts the goods by performing any act inconsistent with the seller's ownership. For example, any use or resale of the goods will generally constitute an acceptance. Limited use for the sole purpose of testing or inspecting the goods is not an acceptance, however. [UCC Sec. 2-606(1)(c)]

Revocation of Acceptance

A buyer who accepts goods and then fails to discover and notify the seller of any breach of contract within a reasonable time will be barred from any remedy. The burden is on the buyer to establish a breach of contract once the goods are accepted. [UCC Sec. 2-607(3)]

After a buyer accepts a lot or a commercial unit, acceptance can still be revoked if nonconformity substantially impairs the value of the goods and if acceptance was predicated on the reasonable assumption that the nonconformity would be cured, and it has not been cured within a reasonable period of time. [UCC Sec. 2-608(1)(a)] Acceptance can be revoked even if the buyer does not discover the nonconformity if acceptance was reasonably induced either by the difficulty of discovering the nonconformity before acceptance or by the seller's assurances. [UCC Sec. 2-608(1)(b)]

In the following case, the court made clear that "substantial impairment of the value to the buyer" is the test of whether revocation of purchased goods can occur once a buyer has "accepted" the goods.

BACKGROUND AND FACTS   *The plaintiff purchased the contents of an automatic car wash facility from the defendant. The defendant owned the contents only, not the building. The plaintiff intended to build and operate a car wash in another location. Thus the machinery and equipment were important to him; he did not want or intend to use the building. At the time the sale was taking place, the defendant assured the plaintiff that he (the defendant) owned everything within the four walls of the building except the soft-drink machine. The contract of sale was drawn up to include "everything within the walls of the building." As it turned out, not quite everything was in fact included. The boiler, hot air blowers, and fluorescent lighting could not be removed from the premises because the landlord declared that these were part of the building. In addition, a conveyor chain used to move cars through the washing process could not be taken because the chain was embedded in the floor.*

The plaintiff notified the defendant by letter that because he could not obtain these items, which the defendant had previously assured him would be included in the purchase, the plaintiff was "rejecting his acceptance" and demanding rescission of the contract. The plaintiff claimed that his inability to procure these items substantially impaired the value of the contract to him (in light of the fact that he was building a car wash). The defendant attempted to argue that the dollar value of these items was small when compared to the total purchase price and thus did not represent a "substantial breach" of the contract.

CAMPBELL v. POLLACK
Supreme Court of Rhode Island, 1966.
101 R.I. 223, 221 A.2d 615.

KELLEHER, Justice.
* * *
This transaction between plaintiff and defendants is governed by the uniform commercial code, G.L. 1956, title 6A (P.L. 1960, chap. 147). [This statute corresponds to Article 2, Sales, of the Uniform Commercial Code. This abbreviation means General Law, passed in 1956, Volume 6A; Public Law passed (or amended) in 1960.] The defendants, however, maintain that despite the enactment of the code, the law of recission is unchanged.
* * *
Section 6A-2-106(2) states that *goods conform to the contract when they are in accordance with the obligations of the contract. The warranty of title is one of those obligations.* [Emphasis added.] The assurance * * * that plaintiff was to have everything within the four walls certainly places this transaction within the purview of § 6A-2-608(1)(b).
* * *

While defendants use the term substantial breach, an examination of § 6A-2-608 shows no such phrase. The words of the section are "substantially impair its value to him * * * ." We will use these words and point out that the mathematical legerdemain [sleight of hand or trick] of defendants is not the basis for a determination as to whether the seller's nonconformity has substantially impaired the buyer's purchase. The car-wash business of today is no longer the warm-weather week-end endeavor it was years ago. The proliferation of car-wash stands which one observes throughout our communities is the best witness to the fact that the car-wash business is a year-round activity. Heat and adequate lighting play an important part in the efficient operation of any such enterprise. A car-wash establishment in the middle of winter in Rhode Island without heat and light would be a strange place indeed. *Here plaintiff expected to obtain everything within the four walls of the building and this he did not receive. The superior court's finding that the inclusion of these articles was a sufficiently important part of the entire sale as to make the omission material was well warranted. Implicit in this finding was the fact that their omission substantially impaired the value of the sale to the buyer.* [Emphasis added.]

APPENDIX

§ 6A-2-608. Revocation of acceptance in whole or in part.

(1) The buyer may revoke his acceptance of a lot or commercial unit whose non-conformity substantially impairs its value to him if he has accepted it

(a) on the reasonable assumption that its non-conformity would be cured and it has not been seasonably cured; or

(b) without discovery of such non-conformity if his acceptance was reasonably induced either by the difficulty of discovery before acceptance or by the seller's assurances.

(2) Revocation of acceptance must occur within a reasonable time after the buyer discovers or should have discovered the ground for it and before any substantial change in condition of the goods which is not caused by their own defects. It is not effective until the buyer notifies the seller of it.

(3) A buyer who so revokes has the same rights and duties with regard to the goods involved as if he had rejected them.

JUDGMENT AND REMEDY   *The plaintiff was entitled to rescind the contract. The defendant was held liable to the plaintiff to refund the purchase price of $8,000.*

NOTICE OF REVOCATION REQUIRED Revocation of acceptance will not be effective until notice is given to the seller, and that must occur within a reasonable time after the buyer either discovers *or should have discovered* the grounds for revocation. The rule also provides that revocation must occur before the goods have undergone any substantial change that was not caused by their own defects (such as spoilage). [UCC Sec. 2-608(2)]

PARTIAL ACCEPTANCE If some of the goods delivered do not conform to the contract, and if the seller has failed to cure completely and part of the goods are still nonconforming, the buyer can make a *partial* acceptance. [UCC Sec. 2-601(c)] The same is true if the nonconformity was not reasonably discoverable before acceptance. A buyer cannot accept less than a single *commercial unit*, however. According to Section 2-105, "commercial unit" means a unit of goods that, by commercial usage, is viewed as a "single whole" for purposes of sale, division of which would materially impair the character of the unit, its market value, or its use. A commercial unit can be a single article (such as a machine), or a set of articles (such as a suite of furniture or an assortment of sizes), or a quantity (such as a bale, gross, or carload), or any other unit treated in the trade as a single whole.

Anticipatory Repudiation

The buyer and the seller have *concurrent* conditions of performance. But, what if before the time for either performance, one party clearly communicates to the other the intention not to perform? Such an action is a breach of the contract by *anticipatory repudiation*. When this occurs, the aggrieved party can, according to UCC Sec. 2-610:

1. For a commercially reasonable time await performance by the repudiating parties.
2. Resort to any remedy for breach even if the

aggrieved party has notified the repudiating party that he or she awaits the latter's performance and has urged retraction.

3. In either case, *suspend performance* or proceed in accordance with the provisions of this Article on the seller's right to identify goods notwithstanding breach or to salvage unfinished goods. [Emphasis added.]

Sometimes the situation is unclear. One party may have reason to feel insecure about the other party's willingness or ability to perform when the time comes. Under these circumstances, a party who has a reasonable basis for feeling insecure can demand, in writing, to receive adequate assurance of due performance. Until such assurance is received, the insecure party can suspend any performance for which the agreed-upon return has not already been received, if it is commercially reasonable to do so. [UCC Sec. 2-609(1)] Failure to provide this assurance in response to a justified demand within a reasonable time not exceeding thirty days constitutes a repudiation of the contract. [UCC Sec. 2-609(4)]

QUESTIONS AND CASE PROBLEMS

1. Taunton entered into a contract to sell Allenberg Cotton Company three hundred bails of cotton. Taunton had not yet harvested the cotton but had planted it two months before. Both parties were aware that the cotton would be harvested at some later date. The contract specifically stated that the price of the cotton was $3.50 a bale, but it did not state either a time or a place for delivery. Subsequently, when the bottom dropped out of the cotton market, Allenberg attempted to avoid its contractual obligation. At the trial, Allenberg claimed that, since the contract failed to state a time or a place for performance, it was too indefinite and too vague to be enforced. Will Allenberg succeed in avoiding its liabilities under the contract? [Taunton v. Allenberg Cotton Co., Inc., 378 F.Supp. 34 (M.D.Ga. 1973)]

2. New York Window and Awning Company entered into a contract with Louisville Manufacturing Company to furnish Louisville with certain raw

materials that Louisville needed for its window manufacturing operation. The agreement between the parties provided that New York Company would ship the raw materials "FOB New York." Pursuant to this agreement, New York Company prepared the raw materials and put them aboard a railroad car to Louisville. The railroad in turn gave New York Company the documents of title (bills of lading), and New York Company promptly mailed them to Louisville Company. Shortly after it mailed the documents, New York Company sent a telegram to Louisville Company informing it that the shipment had been made. When the goods arrived, the railroad notified Louisville Company. Louisville refused to accept the goods, claiming that New York Company was supposed to deliver the materials directly to Louisville Company's manufacturing plant. If Louisville Company refuses to pay, can New York Company recover? [Permalum Window and Awning Mfg. Co. v. Permalum Window Mfg. Corp., 412 S.W.2d 863 (Ky.App.1967)]

3. Riccardi needed a hearing aid and consulted his physician to determine the best model for his particular needs. After the doctor advised him that an R3

would be best, Riccardi contracted with Bartus to purchase one. Bartus placed an order for the R3 model but two weeks later received the R3X, an improved model of the R3. Bartus informed Riccardi that this was not the model that Riccardi had ordered, but it was an improved version. Bartus then proceeded to fit Riccardi with the new hearing aid. Shortly thereafter, Riccardi complained that the new model was noisy and gave him headaches. Bartus at this point offered to obtain the older model for Riccardi, but Riccardi neither consented to the offer nor refused it. About two weeks later, Riccardi returned the hearing aid and refused to make any further payments on it. Can Bartus recover the price of the hearing aid? [Bartus v. Riccardi, 55 Misc.2d 3, 284 N.Y.S.2d 222 (1967)]

4. Lynch, a candy distributor, ordered 100,000 cellophane bags from Paramount Paper Products. Lynch submitted a sample bag with his order, requesting that the 100,000 bags conform to the sample. The bags were delivered to Lynch's place of business while Lynch was out of town, and approximately 25,000 were used before he returned. Upon his return, Lynch discovered that the bags did not conform to the sample and stopped using them. Lynch immediately notified Paramount that the bags were unsuitable and that he wanted to return the unused ones. Must Paramount return the purchase price of the bags? If so, for how many of the bags must Paramount give Lynch a refund? [Paramount Paper Products Co. v. Lynch, 182 Pa. Super. 504, 128 A.2d 157 (1956)]

5. On October 1, Ingle purchased a combine to use on his farm from Marked Tree Equipment Company. The combine was delivered, and Ingle used it for about twelve days and then stopped. Later, during the month of November, Ingle attempted to use the combine approximately fifteen times. When Ingle's first payment came due on December 1, he told the salesperson that he would not pay until the machine worked. Marked Tree sued Ingle for the balance of the purchase price. Will Marked Tree recover? [Ingle v. Marked Tree Equipment Co., 244 Ark. 1166, 428 S.W.2d 286 (1968)]

6. Pursuant to its contract with General Foods Corporation, Bittinger Company made a large shipment of frozen corn to General Foods. Bittinger included in the shipment a copy of General Food's order, which was for six hundred pounds of grade A frozen cut corn. Unknown to General Foods, half the corn was grade A and the other half was grade B. When the corn was unloaded and placed in General

Food's freezers, however, all the grade A corn was placed in front, and all the grade B corn was placed in back. Four months after the delivery, General Foods opened and used the boxes containing grade B corn. Four months after that, General Foods notified Bittinger that the second half of the shipment had been grade B instead of grade A as General Foods had ordered. Must Bittinger return the purchase price paid by General Foods? [General Foods Corp. v. Bittinger Co., 31 D.&C.2d 282 (Pa. 1962)].

7. After lengthy telephone negotiations, Goldstein and Stainless Processing Company entered into an agreement whereby Stainless Processing agreed to sell Goldstein 20,000 pounds of nickle cathodes at $4.60 per pound. To secure the deal, Goldstein promised to send Stainless Processing a check for $20,000, which Stainless Processing was to hold in escrow until the nickle cathodes were ready for shipment. About a month later, Goldstein sent a letter confirming the oral negotiations and enclosed a $20,000 check as a "good faith deposit." Goldstein also indicated in his letter that the check was to be held in escrow awaiting preparation of the nickle cathodes. When Stainless Processing attempted to deposit Goldstein's $20,000 check in an escrow account, it was rejected by the bank because Goldstein had stopped payment on it. Stainless Processing immediately ceased production of the nickle cathodes. Subsequently, Goldstein purchased 20,000 pounds of nickle cathodes on the open market at a price substantially higher than the price it had contracted to pay Stainless Processing. Goldstein then sued to recover this difference in price. How can Stainless Processing defend against Goldstein's suit? [Goldstein v. Stainless Processing Co., 465 F.2d 392 (7th Cir. 1972)].

8. On October 2, 1956, the United States entered into a contract with Transatlantic under which Transatlantic promised to carry 10,000 tons of wheat from a port in the Gulf of Mexico to Iran. No route was specified in the contract. A month later, while en route to Iran, Transatlantic received notice that Egypt had just closed the Suez Canal. Transatlantic's anticipated route had been through the Suez, so it immediately changed its course and went to Iran by passing around the Cape of Good Hope. Transatlantic then sued the United States for the additional costs (15 percent) that it had incurred. The United States refused, claiming that no route was ever specified in the agreement between the parties. Can Transatlantic recover? [Transatlantic Financing Corp. v. United States, 363 F.2d 312 (D.C.Cir. 1966)].

9. Goddard and Ishikawajima Industries entered into a contract on December 1 under which Ishikawajima agreed to furnish Goddard with as many boats as Goddard would require. Over a period of several years, Goddard submitted numerous written orders to Ishikawajima requesting delivery of numerous boats of different sizes. Ishikawajima satisfactorily complied with all these orders. On January 28, 1965, Goddard sent a written order to Ishikawajima for three dozen boats. On February 17, 1965, just after Ishikawajima had begun manufacturing the boats, its plant was completely destroyed by fire. Goddard was therefore forced to purchase its boats on the open market at a far greater price than Ishikawajima had promised to charge. Is Ishikawajima liable to Goddard for the difference? [Goddard v. Ishikawajima-Harima Heavy Industries Co., 29 A.D.2d 754, 287 N.Y.S.2d 901 (1968)]

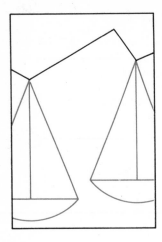

20

Sales

Introduction to
Sales Warranties

Until recently, *caveat emptor*—let the buyer beware—was the prevailing philosophy in sales contract law. In twentieth century America, however, this outlook has given way to a more enlightened consumer approach (although many sellers argue that today's standards of liability are unrealistic and excessive). This chapter will review the concept of product warranty as it occurs in a sales contract under the Uniform Commercial Code.

The concept of *warranty* is based upon the seller's assurance to the buyer that the goods will meet certain standards. The UCC designates five types of warranties that can arise in a sales contract:

1. Warranty of title. [UCC Sec. 2-312]
2. Implied warranty of merchantability. [UCC Sec. 2-314]
3. Implied warranty of fitness for particular purpose. [UCC Sec. 2-315]
4. Express warranty. [UCC Sec. 2-313]
5. Implied warranty arising from the course of dealing or trade usage. [UCC Sec. 2-314(3)]

In the law of sales, since a warranty imposes a duty upon the seller, a breach of warranty is a breach of the seller's promise, and a buyer can sue to recover damages against the seller. Also, a breach can allow the buyer to rescind the agreement.[1]

---

1. The word *rescind* carries two meanings. It can refer either to rejection of goods before acceptance or to revocation by the buyer after acceptance.

WARRANTY OF TITLE

The title warranty arises automatically in most sales contracts. Under Section 2-312, the Code imposes three types of warranties of title.

Good Title

In most cases, sellers warrant that they have good and valid title to the goods sold and that transfer of the title is rightful. [UCC Sec. 2-312(1)] For example, A steals goods from O and sells them to B, who does not know that they are stolen. If O discovers that B has the goods, then O has the right to reclaim them from B. Under this Code provision, however, B can then sue A for breach of warranty because a thief has no title to stolen goods and thus cannot give good title in a subsequent sale. Yet, under sales law, when A sold B the goods, A *automatically* warranted to B that the title conveyed was valid and that its transfer was rightful. Obviously this was not in fact the case, so A has breached the warranty of title imposed by UCC Sec. 2-312(1)(a).

No Liens

A second warranty of title provided by the Code protects buyers who are unaware of any encumbrances (claims or liens) against goods at the time of the contract. [UCC Sec. 2-312(1)(b)] This warranty protects buyers who, for example, unknowingly purchase goods that are subject to a creditor's security interest. (See Chapters 29 and 30.) If a creditor reclaims the goods from a buyer who *had no actual knowledge of the security interest,* then the buyer can recover from the seller. Of course, the buyer who has *actual knowledge* of a security interest has no recourse against the seller. Now consider an example: Henderson buys a used color TV from Sneed for cash. A month later Reynolds repossesses the set from Henderson, proving that she, Reynolds, has a valid security interest in it that was duly recorded with the proper county clerk and that Sneed had missed five payments on the set. Henderson demands his money back from Sneed after he gives the set to Reynolds. Under Section 2-312(2)(b), Henderson will be able to recover because the seller of goods warrants that the goods shall be delivered free from any security interest or other lien of which the buyer has no knowledge.

No Infringements

A third, and special, category of title warranty is the warranty against infringement. A merchant is also deemed to warrant that the goods delivered are free from any patent, trademark, or copyright claims of a third person.[2] [UCC Sec. 2-312(3)] If this warranty is breached and the buyer is sued by a third person, the buyer *must notify the seller* of litigation within a reasonable time to enable the seller to decide whether to defend the lawsuit. If the seller decides to defend and agrees to bear all expenses, including that of an adverse judgment, then the buyer must let the seller undertake litigation; otherwise the buyer loses all rights against the seller if any infringement liability is established. [UCC Sec. 2-607(3)(b)] To illustrate: X buys a machine from Y, a manufacturer of such machines, for use in his factory. Three years later, Z sues X for damages for patent infringement. Z claims that he has a patent on the machine and that it cannot be used without his permission. At once, X informs Y of this suit and demands that Y take over the defense. Y refuses to do so, claiming that Z is crazy and has no case. X goes to court and loses. Z obtains a judgment against X, which X pays off. X now demands that Y reimburse him for the amount. Y must reimburse X because merchant sellers of goods warrant to buyers that the goods they regularly sell are free of infringement claims by third parties.

This infringement warranty does not apply to buyers who furnish specifications for the goods to be made in a particular way. In fact, it

---

2. Recall from Chapter 17 that a *merchant* is defined in UCC Sec. 2-104(1) as a person who deals in goods of the kind involved in the sales contract or who, by occupation, holds himself or herself out as having knowledge or skill peculiar to the practices of goods involved in the transaction.

is the buyer who must hold the seller harmless (i. e., not liable) against any third person's claims of infringement arising out of the goods manufactured to the buyer's specifications. [UCC Sec. 2-312(3)] The same requirements of notice apply to a seller who is sued for breach of an infringement warranty for which the buyer is answerable by virtue of the "hold harmless" agreement. [UCC Sec. 2-607(6)] To illustrate: X orders a custom-made machine from Y, who is a manufacturer of such machines. It is built strictly to X's specifications. While the machine is being built, Z files a suit against Y for patent infringement. Y immediately informs X in writing of this suit and demands that X take over the expense of the litigation. X refuses to do so. Y settles with Z out of court by paying Z modest damages. Y now wishes to be reimbursed by X. Y will be able to collect because a buyer who orders custom-built goods from a seller and who furnishes the seller with the specifications warrants to the seller that there are no patent infringements on the specifications.

DISCLAIMER OF TITLE WARRANTY In an ordinary sales transaction, the title warranty can be disclaimed or modified only *by specific language* in a contract. For example, sellers assert that they are transferring only such rights, title, and interest as they have in the goods.

In certain cases, the circumstances of the sale are sufficient to indicate clearly to a buyer that no assurances as to title are being made. The classic example is a sheriff's sale, where buyers know goods have been seized to satisfy debts and it is apparent that the goods are not the property of the person who is selling them. [UCC Sec. 2-312(2)]

WARRANTIES OF QUALITY

Express Warranties

A seller can create an **express warranty** by making representations concerning the quality, condition, description, or performance potential of the goods. Under Section 2-313, express warranties arise when a seller indicates that:

1. The goods will conform to any *affirmation or promise* of fact that the seller makes to the buyer about the goods. Such affirmations or promises are usually made during the bargaining process and can include such statements as "These drill bits will *easily* penetrate stainless steel—and without dulling"
2. The goods will conform to any *description* of them. For example, "Crate contains one 150-horsepower diesel engine."
3. The goods will conform to any *sample or model.*

BASIS OF THE BARGAIN The Code requires that for any express warranty to be created, the affirmation, promise, description, or sample must become part of the "basis of the bargain." Just what constitutes the basis of the bargain is hard to say. The Code does not define the concept, and each case presents a question of fact to determine whether a representation came at such a time and in such a way that it induced the buyer to enter the contract.

A Federal court in Massachusetts held that a statement of fact made *after* title to the goods had passed to the buyer could not be construed as an express warranty relating back to the time of the sale, as illustrated in the next case.

MAURICE C. SMITH CO. v. FISHER PLASTICS CORP.
District Court Massachusetts, 1948. 76 F.Supp. 641.

BACKGROUND AND FACTS *The plaintiff, a manufacturer, decided to experiment in making a boot with plastic instead of leather or rubber for the outer covering. The plaintiff ordered vinyl plastic sheeting from a supplier, the defendant, without indicating the particular purpose for which it was intended. About a week before the goods were to be delivered, the plaintiff called the defendant to ask what temperature ranges the vinyl resin would withstand. The plaintiff never revealed the* *reason for the question or the intended use of the plastic. The defendant said that the vinyl material would withstand any temperature between 50 degrees below zero and 250 degrees above zero Fahrenheit and confirmed this information in a letter a short time later.*

The plastic was delivered, the boots were manufactured, and they were sold throughout the United States, primarily in the northern areas and in Alaska. They proved to be totally unsatisfactory. The outer covering made from the plastic vinyl cracked on exposure to the cold temperatures, and the plaintiff was forced to recall all the boots.

The plaintiff attempted to sue the defendant to recover damages on a breach of either an express warranty or an implied warranty of fitness, or both. The court rejected the implied warranty claim—at no time until after he recalled the boots that had been sold did the plaintiff inform the defendant of the particular purpose for which the plastic was to be used. The court acknowledged that the defendant knew that the plaintiff produced boots and shoes. However, plastic used in the manufacture of footwear had previously been restricted to imitating patent leather and to ornamenting parts of shoes. The defendant could reasonably expect the plastic to be used on dress shoes. Since there was no way for the defendant to have known the purpose of the plastic, no implied warranty of fitness arose.

The court also rejected the plaintiff's second claim—that an express warranty was created when the defendant indicated the temperature ranges that the plastic could withstand.

SWEENEY, Judge.

* * *

The plaintiff alleges the breach of an express warranty based upon the representation by the defendant's salesman that the goods would withstand temperatures as low as -50° F. The difficulty with this claim is that the representation was made after title to the goods had passed to the plaintiff, and could not have been an inducing representation. In the absence of an intent on the part of these contracting parties to have title pass at the time of payment or at the time of delivery, it actually passed in July at the time when the contract was made. This is in conformity with [the] General Laws of Massachusetts. I [as Judge] find that the plaintiff has not sustained the burden of showing that the representations as to temperature were made prior to the time when the contract of sale was entered into. General Laws of Massachusetts define a warranty as an " * * * affirmation of fact * * * relating to the goods * * * if the natural tendency of such affirmation * * * is to induce the buyer to purchase the goods, and if he purchases the goods relying thereon." A statement of fact made after the title to the goods has passed to the buyer cannot be construed as a warranty relating back to the time of the sale.

The plaintiff has failed to sustain the *burden of proving that the representations as to temperature were the inducing cause of the sale, or that the defendant was aware at any time during the negotiations of the purpose for which the plaintiff was buying the plastic.* [Emphasis added.]

Conclusions of Law

On the basis of the foregoing I must conclude and rule that there were no warranties attached to the sale of the defendant's product to the plaintiff and that, consequently, there has been no breach of a warranty by the defendant.

JUDGMENT AND REMEDY

Judgment was entered for the defendant. No express warranty was created when the defendant indicated certain temperature ranges that the plastic could reasonably be expected to withstand because the statement was made after the contract had been entered into.

STATEMENTS OF OPINION AND VALUE— USE OF FORMAL WORDS NOT REQUIRED

According to Section 2-313(2), "It is not necessary to the creation of an express warranty that the seller use formal words such as 'warrant' or 'guarantee' or that he has a specific intention to make a warranty * * *." It is necessary only that the buyer regard the representation as part of the basis of the bargain.

On the other hand, if the seller merely affirms that the value of the goods is such and such or makes a statement of opinion or recommendation about the goods, the seller is not creating an express warranty. [UCC Sec. 2-313(2)] For example, a seller claims, "This is the best used car to come along in years; it has four new tires, a 350-horsepower engine just rebuilt this year." The seller has made several *affirmations of fact* that can create a warranty: The automobile has an engine; it is a 350-horsepower engine; it was rebuilt this year; there are four tires on the automobile; the tires are new. But the seller's *opinion* that it is "the best used car to come along in years" is known as "puffing" and creates no warranty. (Puffing is an expression of opinion by a seller that is not made as a representation of fact.) A statement relating to the value of the goods, such as "it's worth a fortune" or "anywhere else you'd pay $10,000 for it," will not normally create a warranty.

The ordinary seller can give an *opinion* that is not a warranty. However, if the seller is an expert and gives an opinion as an expert, then a warranty can be created. For example, S is an art dealer and an expert in seventeenth century painting. If S states to B, a purchaser, that a particular painting is definitely a Rembrandt, and B buys the painting, S has warranted the accuracy of his opinion.

Sometimes statements made by a seller cross the fine line between mere opinion and express warranty—for example, in the following case, where a dealer of secondhand automobiles assures a buyer that an automobile is in top mechanical condition.

WAT HENRY PONTIAC CO. v. BRADLEY

Supreme Court of Oklahoma, 1949. 202 Okl. 82, 210 P.2d 348.

BACKGROUND AND FACTS *This action was brought to recover $324.56 in damages for breach of an express oral warranty made by a used car dealer. The dealer (defendant) assured his customer (the plaintiff) that the automobile was in fine mechanical condition and that it would take the plaintiff anywhere she wanted to go. The trial court held that such an assertion was more than an expression of mere opinion. It constituted a warranty.*

The plaintiff alleged that on October 22, 1944, she purchased a used Buick automobile from the defendant, paying $890 in cash. At that time, the defendant assured her orally that the vehicle was in first-class condition, usable and serviceable in every respect. The plaintiff relied on that representation and purchased the vehicle. But as it turned out, the car was not in first-class usable condition. In fact, it was necessary to have the vehicle repaired and have parts replaced. Ultimately, the plaintiff spent $249.56 in repair and replacement and suffered damages, expenses, and inconvenience in the sum of $75.

The defendant argued, in the first place, that the expression was mere opinion and did not constitute a warranty and, in the second place, that no implied warranty of quality or fitness is ever present in the sale of a secondhand automobile.

JOHNSON, Justice.

* * *

We now consider defendant's proposition one: "Generally, no implied warranty of quality or fitness is present in sale of a secondhand automobile, but doctrine of caveat emptor applies."

This is the general rule as to implied warranties however, the plaintiff in this case does not rely on an implied warranty, but upon an express verbal warranty, and the rule of caveat emptor does not apply where there is an express warranty of condition, and does not apply to hidden defects which are not open to discovery by the buyer.

[The court thus found that the rule of *caveat emptor* did not apply in this case. The court looked next at the defendant's other contention—that he had not asserted a warranty but merely stated an opinion.]

The salesman who sold the car testified in substance that he had been an auto mechanic for about twelve years before becoming a salesman; that he was engaged in demonstrating and selling cars; that he did not warrant the car, but explained to the buyer that the sale was without a warranty, but did state that after the deal was closed that he told plaintiff, "I would not be afraid to start, and I wouldn't have been afraid to start any place in the car, because it run as nice as you would expect a car that age to run. There wasn't anything to indicate to me that there was anything wrong with the car, if there was anything wrong with it."

The evidence adduced as to the issues involved was in conflict, each side having witnesses to substantiate their theory. Now, did these facts as stated by plaintiff, if true, constitute an oral warranty?

The rule is that to constitute an express warranty no particular form of words is necessary, and any affirmation of the quality or condition of the vehicle, not uttered as a matter of opinion or belief, made by a seller at the time of sale for the purpose of assuring the buyer of the truth of the fact and inducing the buyer to make the purchase, if so received and relied on by the buyer, is an express warranty.

This court * * * [has stated the rule of law as follows:]

" 'Warranty' is a matter of intention. A decisive test is whether the vendor assumes to assert a fact of which the buyer is ignorant, or merely states an opinion, or his judgment, upon a matter of which the vendor has no special knowledge, and on which the buyer may also be expected to have an opinion and to exercise his judgment. In the former case there is a warranty; in the latter case there is not.

* * *

"The buyer knew nothing about the capacity of the automobile purchased. The seller was an expert in the handling of automobiles, and was engaged in the business of demonstrating and selling the same. Held, a statement made by the seller that the automobile could be driven over the roads in a certain vicinity satisfactorily constituted a warranty and was not the expression of a mere opinion."

The facts in this case bring it squarely within the above well-settled principles of law, and the jury was justified in finding that there was an oral warranty.

JUDGMENT AND REMEDY *The court held that the defendant's statements about the mechanical condition of the car constituted a warranty. The defendant was liable to the plaintiff, who was awarded $324.56 in damages for breach of the express oral warranty of the used car.*

MAGNUSON-MOSS WARRANTY ACT The Magnuson-Moss Warranty Act was designed to prevent deception in warranties by making them easier to understand.[3] The Magnuson-Moss Warranty Act is usually enforced by the Federal Trade Commission (FTC). Additionally, the attorney general or a consumer who has been injured can enforce the Act if informal procedures for settling disputes prove to be ineffective. The Magnuson-Moss Warranty Act modifies UCC warranty rules to some extent where personal sales transactions are involved. However, the UCC remains the primary codification of warranty rules for industrial and commercial transactions.

No seller is *required* to give a written warranty for consumer goods sold under the Warranty Act. But if a seller chooses to make an express written warranty, then it must be either a full or a limited warranty.

A *full warranty* binds the seller (but not others in the distribution chain) to meet rigid federal standards for certain types of products costing $10 or more. Full warranty requires free repair or replacement of any defective part; if it cannot be repaired within a reasonable time, the consumer has the choice of either a refund or a replacement without charge. The full warranty does not have a time limit on it. Any limitation on consequential damages must be *conspicuously* stated.

A *limited warranty* arises when the written warranty fails to meet one of the minimum requirements for a full warranty. The fact that a seller is giving only a limited warranty must be conspicuously designated. If it is only a time limitation that distinguishes a limited warranty from a full warranty, then the warranty act allows the seller to indicate it by such language as "full 12-month warranty."

Creating an express warranty under the warranty act differs from creating one under the Uniform Commercial Code.[4]

1.   An express warranty is *any written promise* or *affirmation of fact* made by the seller to a consumer indicating the quality or performance of the product and affirming or promising that the product is either free of defects or will meet a specific level of performance over a period of time. For example, "this watch will not lose more than one second a year."
2.   An express warranty is a written agreement to refund, repair, or replace the product if it fails to meet written specifications. This is typically a service contract.

---

3.   15 U.S.C.A. Secs. 2301-12.

4.   For example, express warranties created by description or sample or model will continue to be governed under UCC provisions because only written promises or affirmations of fact are covered by the Magnuson-Moss Warranty Act.

Implied warranties do not arise under the Magnuson-Moss Warranty Act. They continue to be created according to the Uniform Commercial Code provisions. In the case of an express warranty in a sales contract or a combined sales and service contract (where the service contract is undertaken within ninety days of the sale), the Magnuson-Moss Warranty Act prevents sellers from disclaiming or modifying the implied warranties of merchantability and fitness for a particular purpose. The time limit that a seller imposes on the duration of an implied warranty has to correspond with the duration stated in the express warranty.[5]

Implied Warranties

An *implied warranty* is one that *the law derives* by implication or inference from the nature of the transaction or the relative situation or circumstances of the parties. For example: Kaplan buys an axe at Enrique's Hardware Store. The first time she chops wood with it, the axe handle breaks, and Kaplan is injured. She immediately notifies Enrique. Examination shows that the wood in the handle was rotten but that the rottenness could not have been noticed by either Enrique or Kaplan. Nonetheless, Kaplan notifies Enrique that she will hold him responsible for the medical bills. Enrique is responsible because a merchant seller of goods warrants that the goods he sells are fit for normal use. This axe was obviously not fit for normal use.

IMPLIED WARRANTY OF MERCHANT-
ABILITY   An **implied warranty of merchant-**

5. The time limit on an implied warranty occurring by virtue of the seller's express warranty must, of course, be reasonable, conscionable, and set forth in clear and conspicuous language on the face of the warranty.

ability arises in every sale of goods made *by a merchant* who deals in goods of the kind sold. [UCC Sec. 2-314] Thus, a retailer of ski equipment makes an implied warranty of merchantability every time she sells a pair of skis, but a neighbor selling skis at a garage sale does not.

Goods that are *merchantable* are "reasonably fit for the ordinary purposes for which such goods are used." They must be of at least average, fair, or medium-grade quality—not the finest quality and not the worst. The quality must be comparable to quality that will pass without objection in the trade or market for goods of the same description. Some examples of nonmerchantable goods include: light bulbs that explode when switched on, pajamas that burst into flames upon slight contact with a stove burner, high heeled shoes that break off under normal use, or shotgun shells that explode prematurely.

The implied warranty of merchantability imposes *absolute* liability for the safe performance of their product upon merchants when dealing in their line of goods. It makes no difference that the merchant did not know of a defect or could not have discovered it. (Of course, merchants are not absolute insurers against *all* accidents arising in connection with the goods. For example, a bar of soap will not be unmerchantable merely because a user can slip and fall by stepping on it.) In an action based on breach of warranty, it is necessary to show: (1) the existence of the warranty; (2) that the warranty was broken; and, (3) the breach of warranty was the proximate cause of the injury sustained.

The serving of food or drink on the premises of a restaurant is recognized by the UCC as a sale of goods subject to the warranty of merchantability. [UCC Sec. 2-314(1)] "Merchantable" food means food that is fit to eat.

BACKGROUND AND FACTS   *Webster brought the following action against the Blue Ship Tea Room for personal injuries she sustained when consuming a bowl of their fish chowder. Her theory was breach of implied warranty of merchantability.*

WEBSTER v. BLUE SHIP TEA ROOM
Supreme Judicial Court of Massachusetts, 1964.
347 Mass. 421, 198 N.E.2d 309.

REARDON, Justice.

* * *

This is a case which by its nature evokes earnest study not only of the law but also of the culinary traditions of the Commonwealth [Massachusetts] which bear so heavily upon its outcome. It is an action to recover damages for personal injuries sustained by reason of a breach of implied warranty of food served by the defendant in its restaurant.

On Saturday, April 25, 1959, about 1 P.M., the plaintiff, accompanied by her sister and her aunt, entered the Blue Ship Tea Room operated by the defendant. The group was seated at a table and supplied with menus.

This restaurant, which the plaintiff characterized as "quaint," was located in Boston "on the third floor of an old building on T Wharf which overlooks the ocean."

The plaintiff, who had been born and brought up in New England (a fact of some consequence), ordered clam chowder and crabmeat salad. Within a few minutes she received tidings to the effect that "there was no more clam chowder," whereupon she ordered a cup of fish chowder. Presently, there was set before her "a small bowl of fish chowder." She had previously enjoyed a breakfast about 9 A.M. which had given her no difficulty. "The fish chowder contained haddock, potatoes, milk, water and seasoning. The chowder was milky in color and not clear. The haddock and potatoes were in chunks" (also a fact of consequence). "She agitated it a little with the spoon and observed that it was a fairly full bowl * * * . It was hot when she got it, but she did not tip it with her spoon because it was hot * * * but stirred it in an up and under motion. She denied that she did this because she was looking for something, but it was rather because she wanted an even distribution of fish and potatoes." "She started to eat it, alternating between the chowder and crackers which were on the table with * * * [some] rolls. She ate about 3 or 4 spoonfuls then stopped. She looked at the spoonfuls as she was eating. She saw equal parts of liquid, potato and fish as she spooned it into her mouth. She did not see anything unusual about it. After 3 or 4 spoonfuls she was aware that something had lodged in her throat because she couldn't swallow and couldn't clear her throat by gulping and she could feel it." This misadventure led to two esophagoscopies at the Massachusetts General Hospital, in the second of which, on April 27, 1959, a fish bone was found and removed. The sequence of events produced injury to the plaintiff which was not insubstantial.

We must decide whether a fish bone lurking in a fish chowder, about the ingredients of which there is no other complaint, constitutes a breach of implied warranty under applicable provisions of the Uniform Commercial Code,[1] the annotations to which are not helpful on this point. As the judge put in his charge, "Was the fish chowder fit to be eaten and wholesome? * * * [N]obody is claiming that the fish itself wasn't wholesome. * * * But the bone of contention here—I don't mean that for a pun—but was this fish bone a foreign substance that made the fish chowder unwholesome or not fit to be eaten?"

---

1. "(1) Unless excluded or modified by section 2-316, a warranty that the goods shall be merchantable is implied in a contract for their sale if the seller is a merchant with respect to goods of that kind. Under this section the serving for value of food or drink to be consumed either on the premises or elsewhere is a sale. (2) Goods to be merchantable must at least be such as * * * (c) are fit for the ordinary purposes for which such goods are used * * * ." G.L. c. 106, §2-314.

* * * It is not too much to say that a person sitting down in New England to consume a good New England fish chowder embarks on a gustatory adventure which may entail the removal of some fish bones from his bowl as he proceeds. We are not inclined to tamper with age old recipes by any amendment reflecting the plaintiff's view of the effect of the Uniform Commercial Code upon them. We are aware of the heavy body of case law involving foreign substances in food, but we sense a strong distinction between them and those relative to unwholesomeness of the food itself, e.g., tainted mackerel (Smith v. Gerrish, 256 Mass. 183, 152 N.E. 318), and a fish bone in a fish chowder. Certain Massachusetts cooks might cavil at the ingredients contained in the chowder in this case in that it lacked the heartening lift of salt pork. In any event, we consider that the joys of life in New England include the ready availability of fresh fish chowder. We should be prepared to cope with the hazards of fish bones, the occasional presence of which in chowders is, it seems to us, to be anticipated, and which, in the light of a hallowed tradition, do not impair their fitness or merchantability. While we are bouyed up in this conclusion by Shapiro v. Hotel Statler Corp., 132 F.Supp. 891 (S.D.Cal.), in which the bone which afflicted the plaintiff appeared in ''Hot Barquette of Seafood Mornay,'' we know that the United States District Court of Southern California, situated as are we upon a coast, might be expected to share our views. We are most impressed, however, by Allen v. Grafton, 170 Ohio St. 249, 164 N.E.2d 167, where in Ohio, the Midwest, in a case where the plaintiff was injured by a piece of oyster shell in an order of fried oysters, Mr. Justice Taft (now Chief Justice) in a majority opinion held that ''the possible presence of a piece of oyster shell in or attached to an oyster is so well known to anyone who eats oysters that we can say as a matter of law that one who eats oysters can reasonably anticipate and guard against eating such a piece of shell * * * .''

The court ''sympathized with a plaintiff who has suffered a peculiarly New England injury,'' but the case against the defendant was dismissed.	**JUDGMENT AND REMEDY**

IMPLIED WARRANTY OF FITNESS FOR A PARTICULAR PURPOSE The implied warranty of fitness for a particular purpose arises when *any seller* (merchant or non-merchant) knows the particular purpose for which a buyer will use the goods *and* knows that the buyer is relying upon the seller's skill and judgment to select suitable goods. [UCC Sec. 2-315]

A ''particular purpose of the buyer'' differs from the ''ordinary purpose for which goods are used'' (merchantability). Goods can be merchantable but still not fit for the buyer's particular purpose. For example, house paints suitable for ordinary walls are not suitable for painting over stucco walls. A contract can

include both a warranty of merchantability *and* a warranty of fitness for a particular purpose, which relates to the specific use or special situation in which a buyer intends to use the goods. For example, a seller recommends a particular pair of shoes, *knowing* that a customer is looking for mountain climbing shoes. The buyer purchases the shoes *relying* on the seller's judgment. If the shoes are found to be suitable only for walking, not for mountain climbing, the seller has breached the warranty of fitness for a particular purpose.

A seller does not need ''actual knowledge'' of the buyer's particular purpose. It is sufficient if a seller ''has reason to know'' the purpose.

However, the buyer must have *relied* upon the seller's skill or judgment in selecting or furnishing suitable goods in order for an implied warranty to be created. For example, Josephs buys a shortwave radio from Radio Shack, telling the salesperson that she wants a set strong enough to pick up Radio Luxemburg. Radio Shack sells Josephs a Model XYZ set. The set works, but it will not pick up Radio Luxemburg. Josephs wants her money back. Here, since Radio Shack is guilty of a breach of implied warranty of fitness for the buyer's particular purpose, Josephs will be able to recover. The salesperson knew specifically that she wanted a set that would pick up Radio Luxemburg. Furthermore, Josephs relied upon the salesperson to furnish a radio that would fulfill this purpose. Radio Shack did not do so. Therefore, the warranty was breached.

In the next case, a seller helped a buyer solve a painting problem and became the defendant in a lawsuit for breach of an implied warranty of fitness.

CATANIA v. BROWN

Circuit Court of Connecticut,
Appellate Division, 1967.
4 Conn.Cir. 344, 231 A.2d 668.

BACKGROUND AND FACTS *The defendant, Brown, was engaged in the retail paint business. Catania, the plaintiff, asked Brown to recommend a paint to cover the exterior stucco walls of his house. Brown recommended and sold to Catania a certain brand of paint called "Pierce's Shingle and Shake" paint. Brown also advised Catania how to prepare the walls before applying the paint and how to mix the paint in proper proportion to the thinner. Catania followed Brown's instructions, but the paint blistered and peeled soon after it was applied.*

JACOBS, Judge.
* * *

Under the statute governing implied warranty of fitness for a particular purpose (§42a-2-315), two requirements must be met: (a) the buyer relies on the seller's skill or judgment to select or furnish suitable goods; and (b) the seller at the time of contracting has reason to know the buyer's purpose and that the buyer is relying on the seller's skill or judgment. "It is a question of fact in the ordinary case whether these conditions have been met and the warranty arises."
* * *

"The raising of an implied warranty of fitness depends upon whether the buyer informed the seller of the circumstances and conditions which necessitated his purchase of a certain character of article or material and left it to the seller to select the particular kind and quality of article suitable for the buyer's use. * * * So when the buyer orders goods to be supplied and trusts to the judgment or skill of the seller to select goods or material for which they are ordered, there is an implied warranty that they shall be reasonably fit for that purpose."

"Reliance can, of course, be more readily found where the *retailer* selects the product or recommends it."
* * *

[T]he buyer, being ignorant of the fitness of the article offered by the seller, justifiably relied on the superior information, skill and judgment of the seller and not on his own knowledge or judgment, and under such circumstances an implied warranty of fitness could properly be claimed by the purchaser.

The plaintiff prevailed on the theory of implied warranty of fitness for a particular purpose. The defendant had created and breached a warranty of fitness by recommending the particular paint as suitable for stucco walls.

JUDGMENT AND REMEDY

Overlapping Warranties

Sometimes two or more warranties are made in a single transaction. An implied warranty of merchantability or of fitness for a particular purpose, or both, can exist in addition to an express warranty. For example, where a sales contract for a new car states that "this car engine is warranted to be free from defects for 12,000 miles or 12 months, whichever occurs first," there is an express warranty against all defects and an implied warranty that the car will be fit for normal use. The rule of Section 2-313 is that express and implied warranties are construed as *cumulative* if they are consistent with one another. If the warranties are *inconsistent*, the courts will usually hold that: (1) *express* warranties will displace inconsistent *implied* warranties other than implied warranties of fitness for a particular purpose, (2) samples will take precedence over inconsistent general descriptions, and (3) technical specifications will displace inconsistent samples or general descriptions. [UCC Sec. 2-317] Say that when Josephs buys a shortwave radio at Radio Shack, the contract of sale states that the radio's maximum range is 4,000 miles. She tries to pick up Radio Luxemburg, which is 8,000 miles away, but the set cannot do it. Josephs claims that Radio Shack is guilty of breach of warranty of merchantability because the set is unfit for normal use. She does not have a good complaint because the contract contained an *express* warranty about the range of the set. This express warranty will take precedence over any implied warranty that a shortwave set would pick up any station anywhere in the world. On the other hand, if Josephs had specified to the salesperson that she wanted to pick up Radio Luxemburg, and if the salesperson had sold her that same radio, Josephs has a good claim. In a case of inconsistency between an express warranty and

a warranty of fitness for buyer's particular purpose, the warranty of fitness for buyer's particular purpose prevails. [UCC Sec. 2-317(c)]

Warranty Disclaimers

Each warranty is created in a special way, and the manner in which each one can be disclaimed or qualified varies also.

EXPRESS WARRANTIES Any affirmation of fact or promise, description of the goods, or use of samples or models by a seller will create an express warranty. A seller can scarcely be expected to sell goods without somehow describing them, thereby affirming some fact about them—although selling goods without description is one way to exclude an express warranty under Section 2-316(1).

Express warranties can be excluded if the seller has carefully refrained from making any promise or affirmation of fact relating to the goods, or describing the goods, or selling by means of a sample model. [UCC Sec. 2-313] The seller can also disclaim an express warranty by clear, specific, and unambiguous language to that effect in the contract. [UCC Sec. 2-316(1)]

IMPLIED WARRANTIES Generally speaking, and unless circumstances indicate otherwise, implied warranties (merchantability and fitness) are disclaimed by expressions like "as is," "with all faults," or other similar expressions that in common understanding call the buyer's attention to the fact that there are no implied warranties. [UCC Sec. 2-316(3)]

The fitness disclaimer must be in *writing* and *conspicuous*, but it can be a general statement. According to the Code, it is sufficient if, for example, the disclaimer states, "There are no warranties that extend beyond the description on the face hereof."

A *merchantability disclaimer* must be more specific; it must mention merchantability. It need not be written; but if it is, the writing must be *conspicuous*. According to UCC Sec. 2-201(10):

A term or clause is conspicuous when it is so written that a reasonable person against whom it is to operate ought to have noticed it. A printed heading in capitals is conspicuous. Language in the body of a form is conspicuous if it is in large or other contrasting type or color.

Consider the example used above. When Kaplan buys an axe from Enrique's Hardware Store, Enrique tells Kaplan that he (Enrique) is not responsible for any defects of the axe. The axe breaks when Kaplan uses it for the first time. Enrique is not liable because merchant sellers can orally disclaim the warranty of merchantability when they sell goods under an oral contract of sale. As long as Enrique uses words in the disclaimer that make it clear to a reasonable person that he is disclaiming all warranties as to the quality of the goods, the disclaimer is valid. Enrique has to make clear, though, that he is disclaiming the warranty of merchantability by using that specific word.

However, under UCC Sec. 2-316(2), "to exclude or modify any implied warranty of *fitness* the exclusion must be by a writing and conspicuous."

BUYER'S REFUSAL TO INSPECT   If a buyer examines the goods (or a sample or model) as fully as desired before entering a contract or if the buyer *refuses* to examine the goods at all, *there is no implied warranty with respect to defects that a reasonable examination will reveal.* Suppose that the defect in Kaplan's axe could easily have been spotted by normal, careful inspection. Kaplan inspects the axe before buying it but somehow does not notice the defect. After being hurt by the defective axe, she will not be able to hold Enrique for breach of warranty of merchantability because she

could have or should have spotted the defect during her inspection. [UCC Sec. 2-316(3)(b)]

Failing to examine the goods is not a refusal to examine them; it is not enough that the goods were merely available for inspection, and the buyer simply never did it. A "refusal" occurs when the seller makes a *demand* upon the buyer, *notifying* the buyer that the goods must be examined or the buyer will assume the risk of the defects that the examination might have revealed. Of course, the seller always remains liable for all latent (hidden) defects that ordinary inspection will not normally reveal. [UCC Sec. 2-316, Comment 8]

USAGE OF TRADE   The Code recognizes in Section 2-314(3) that implied warranties can arise (or be excluded or modified) from course of dealing, course of performance, or usage of trade. [UCC Sec. 2-316(3)(c)] In the absence of evidence to the contrary, when both parties to a sales contract have knowledge of a well-recognized trade custom, the courts will infer that they both intended that custom to apply to their contract. For example, in the sale of a new car, where the industry-wide custom includes lubricating the car before delivery, a seller who fails to do so can be held liable to a buyer for resulting damages on a theory of breach of implied warranty.

Unconscionability and Warranty Disclaimers

The Code sections dealing with warranty disclaimers do not refer specifically to unconscionability as a factor. Eventually, however, the courts will test warranty disclaimers with reference to the unconscionability standards of Section 2-302. Such things as lack of bargaining position, "take it or leave it" choices, and failure of a buyer to understand a warranty disclaimer provision will become relevant to the issue of unconscionability. Note in the following landmark decision the court's recognition of the consumer's "bargaining" position with respect to large auto manufacturers.

BACKGROUND AND FACTS   *This case involves the recovery of damages from an automobile manufacturer for injuries sustained by the owner and driver of a new car manufactured by Chrysler. The standard form purchase order used in the transaction contained an express warranty by which the manufacturer warranted the vehicle free from defects in material or workmanship. If any defects were found, the manufacturer promised to correct them without cost to the purchaser for a ninety-day period or four thousand miles, whichever occurred first. In addition, the purchase order contained a disclaimer in fine print, of any and all other express or implied warranties. The disclaimer purported to absolve Chrysler and the dealer from all liability for the implied warranty of merchantability against injuries suffered because of negligent manufacture. The standard form purchase order became part of the Chrysler contract when a consumer purchased an automobile. Hence, the express warranty that was offered instead of all other warranties, express or implied, was intended to provide the limits of Chrysler's liability.*

HENNINGSEN v.
BLOOMFIELD
MOTORS, INC.
Supreme Court of New Jersey,
1960.
32 N.J. 358, 161 A.2d 69.

FRANCIS, Justice.
* * *

Plaintiff Clause H. Henningsen purchased a Plymouth automobile, manufactured by defendant Chrysler Corporation, from defendant Bloomfield Motors, Inc. His wife, plaintiff Helen Henningsen, was injured while driving it and instituted suit against both defendants to recover damages on account of her injuries. The complaint was predicated upon breach of express and implied warranties and upon negligence.
* * *

The facts are not complicated, but a general outline of them is necessary to an understanding of the case.

On May 7, 1955 Mr. and Mrs. Henningsen visited the place of business of Bloomfield Motors, Inc., an authorized De Soto and Plymouth dealer, to look at a Plymouth. They wanted to buy a car and were considering a Ford or a Chevrolet as well as a Plymouth. They were shown a Plymouth which appealed to them and the purchase followed. The record indicates that Mr. Henningsen intended the car as a Mother's Day gift to his wife. He said the intention was communicated to the dealer. When the purchase order or contract was prepared and presented, the husband executed it alone. His wife did not join as a party.

The purchase order was a printed form of one page. On the front it contained blanks to be filled in with a description of the automobile to be sold, the various accessories to be included, and the details of the financing. The particular car selected was described as a 1955 Plymouth, Plaza "6", Club Sedan. The type used in the printed parts of the form became smaller in size, different in style, and less readable toward the bottom where the line for the purchaser's signature was placed. The smallest type on the page appears in the two paragraphs, one of two and one-quarter lines and the second of one and one-half lines, on which great stress is laid by the defense in the case. These two paragraphs are the least legible and the most difficult to read in the instrument, but they are most important in the evaluation of the rights of the contesting parties. They do not attract attention and there is nothing about the format which would draw the reader's eye to them. In fact, a studied and concentrated effort would have to be made to read them. De-emphasis seems the motive rather than emphasis. More particularly, most of the printing in the body of the order appears to be 12 point block type, and easy to read. In the short paragraphs under discussion, however, the type appears to be six point script and the print is solid, that is, the lines are very close together.

The two paragraphs are:

"The front and back of this Order comprise the entire agreement affecting this purchase and no other agreement or understanding of any nature concerning same has been made or entered into, or will be recognized. I hereby certify that no credit has been extended to me for the purchase of this motor vehicle except as appears in writing on the face of this agreement.

"I have read the matter printed on the back hereof and agree to it as a part of this order the same as if it were printed above my signature. I certify that I am 21 years of age, or older, and hereby acknowledge receipt of a copy of this order."
* * *

The testimony of Claus Henningsen justifies the conclusion that he did not read the two fine print paragraphs referring to the back of the purchase contract. And it is uncontradicted that no one made any reference to them, or called them to his attention. With respect to the matter appearing on the back, it is likewise uncontradicted that he did not read it and that no one called it to his attention.

The reverse side of the contract contains 8½ inches of fine print. It is not as small, however, as the two critical paragraphs described above. The page is headed "Conditions" and contains ten separate paragraphs consisting of 65 lines in all. * * * In the seventh paragraph, about two-thirds of the way down the page, the warranty, which is the focal point of the case, is set forth. It is as follows:

"7. It is expressly agreed that there are no warranties, express or implied, *made* by either the dealer or the manufacturer on the motor vehicle, chassis, or parts furnished hereunder except as follows.

" 'The manufacturer warrants each new motor vehicle (including original equipment placed thereon by the manufacturer except tires), chassis or parts manufactured by it to be free from defects in material or workmanship under normal use and service. Its obligation under this warranty being limited to making good at its factory any part or parts thereof which shall, within ninety (90) days after delivery of such vehicle *to the original purchaser* or before such vehicle has been driven 4,000 miles, whichever event shall first occur, be returned to it with transportation charges prepaid and which its examination shall disclose to its satisfaction to have been thus defective; *this warranty being expressly in lieu of all other warranties expressed or implied, and all other obligations or liabilities on its part,* and it neither assumes nor authorizes any other person to assume for it any other liability in connection with the sale of its vehicles. * * *.' " [Emphasis added.]

After the contract had been executed, plaintiffs were told the car had to be serviced and that it would be ready in two days.
* * *

The new Plymouth was turned over to the Henningsens on May 9, 1955. No proof was adduced by the dealer to show precisely what was done in the way of mechanical or road testing beyond testimony that the manufacturer's instructions were probably followed. Mr. Henningsen drove it from the dealer's place of business in Bloomfield to their home in Keansburg. On the trip nothing unusual appeared in the way in which it operated. Thereafter, it was used for short trips on paved streets about the town. It had no servicing and no mishaps of any kind before the event of May 19. That day, Mrs. Henningsen drove to Asbury Park. On the way down and in returning the car performed in normal fashion until the accident occurred. She was proceeding north on Route 36 in Highlands, New Jersey, at 20-22 miles per hour. The highway was paved and smooth, and contained two lanes for north-bound travel. She was riding in the right-hand lane. Suddenly she heard a loud noise "from the bottom, by the hood." It "felt as if something cracked." The steering wheel spun in her hands; the car veered sharply to the right and crashed into a highway sign and a brick wall. No other vehicle was in any way involved. A bus operator driving in the left-hand lane testified that he observed plaintiffs' car approaching in normal fashion in the opposite direction; "all of a sudden [it] veered at 90 degrees * * * and right into this wall." As a result of the impact, the front of the car was so badly damaged that it was impossible to determine if any of the parts of the steering wheel mechanism or workmanship or assembly were defective or improper prior to the accident. The condition was such that the collision insurance carrier, after inspection, declared the vehicle a total loss. It had 468 miles on the speedometer at the time.

I.

The Claim of Implied Warranty against the Manufacturer.

In the ordinary case of sale of goods by description an implied warranty of merchantability is an integral part of the transaction. If the buyer, expressly or by implication, makes known to the seller the particular purpose for which the article is required and it appears that he has relied on the seller's skill or judgment, an implied warranty arises of reasonable fitness for that purpose. The former type of warranty simply means that the thing sold is reasonably fit for the general purpose for which it is manufactured and sold

Of course such sales, whether oral or written, may be accompanied by an express warranty. * * * [A]ny affirmation of fact relating to the goods is an express warranty if the natural tendency of the statement is to induce the buyer to make the purchase. [A] question of first importance to be decided is whether an implied warranty of merchantability by Chrysler Corporation accompanied the sale of the automobile to Claus Henningsen.
* * *

Chrysler points out that an implied warranty of merchantability is an incident of a contract of sale. It concedes, of course, the making of the original sale to Bloomfield Motors, Inc., but maintains that this transaction marked the terminal point of its contractual connection with the car. Then Chrysler urges that since it was not a party to the sale by the dealer to Henningsen, there is no privity of contract between it and the plaintiffs, and the absence of this privity eliminates any such implied warranty.
* * *

Under modern conditions the ordinary layman, on responding to the importuning of colorful advertising, has neither the opportunity nor the capacity to inspect or to determine the fitness of an automobile for use; he must rely on the manufacturer who has control of its construction, and to some degree on the dealer who, to the limited extent called for by the manufacturer's instructions, inspects and services it before delivery. In such a marketing milieu his remedies and those of persons who properly claim through him should not depend "upon the intricacies of the law of sales. The obligation of the manufacturer should not be based alone on privity of contract."

* * *

Accordingly, we hold that under modern marketing conditions, when a manufacturer puts a new automobile in the stream of trade and promotes its purchase by the public, an implied warranty that it is reasonably suitable for use as such accompanies it into the hands of the ultimate purchaser. [Emphasis added.] Absence of agency between the manufacturer and the dealer who makes the ultimate sale is immaterial.

II.
The Effect of the Disclaimer and Limitation of Liability Clauses on the Implied Warranty of Merchantability.

* * *

In a society such as ours, where the automobile is a common and necessary adjunct of daily life, and where its use is so fraught with danger to the driver, passengers and the public, the manufacturer is under a special obligation in connection with the construction, promotion and sale of his cars. Consequently, the courts must examine purchase agreements closely to see if consumer and public interests are treated fairly.

What influence should these circumstances have on the restrictive effect of Chrysler's express warranty in the framework of the purchase contract? As we have said, *warranties originated in the law to safeguard the buyer and not to limit the liability of the seller or manufacturer.* [Emphasis added.]

* * *

But does the doctrine that a person is bound by his signed agreement, in the absence of fraud, stand in the way of any relief?

* * *

The traditional contract is the result of free bargaining of parties who are brought together by the play of the market, and who meet each other on a footing of approximate economic equality. * * * But in present-day commercial life the standardized mass contract has appeared. It is used primarily by enterprises with strong bargaining power and position.

* * *

The warranty before us is a standardized form designed for mass use. It is imposed upon the automobile consumer. He takes it or leaves it, and he must take it to buy an automobile. No bargaining is engaged in with respect to it. In fact, the dealer through whom it comes to the buyer is without authority to alter it; his function is ministerial—simply to deliver it. The form warranty is not only standard with Chrysler but, as mentioned above, it is the uniform warranty of the Automobile Manufacturers Association.

* * *

The gross inequality of bargaining position occupied by the consumer in the automobile industry is thus apparent. * * * Having in mind the situation in the automobile industry as detailed above, and particularly the fact that the limited warranty extended by the manufacturers is a uniform one, there would appear to be no just reason why the principles of all of the cases set forth should not chart the course to be taken here.

* * *

Courts keep in mind the principle that the best interests of society demand that persons should not be unnecessarily restricted in their freedom to contract. But they do not hesitate to declare void as against public policy contractual provisions which clearly tend to the injury of the public in some way.

[W]e are of the opinion that Chrysler's attempted disclaimer of an implied warranty of merchantability and of the obligations arising therefrom is so inimical to the public good as to compel an adjudication of its invalidity. [Emphasis added.]

* * *

III.
The Dealer's Implied Warranty.

The principles that have been expounded as to the obligation of the manufacturer apply with equal force to the separate express warranty of the dealer. This is so, irrespective of the absence of the relationship of principal and agent between these defendants, because the manufacturer and the Association establish the warranty policy for the industry. The bargaining position of the dealer is inextricably bound by practice to that of the maker and the purchaser must take or leave the automobile, accompanied and encumbered as it is by the uniform warranty.

For the reasons set forth in Part I hereof, *we conclude that the disclaimer of an implied warranty of merchantability by the dealer, as well as the attempted elimination of all obligations other than replacement of defective parts, are violative of public policy and void.* [Emphasis added.]

The court upheld the right of the plaintiff, Henningsen, to recover damages for injuries notwithstanding the attempted warranty disclaimer on the part of the defendants, Chrysler Corporation and Bloomfield Motors, Inc.	**JUDGMENT AND REMEDY**

QUESTIONS AND CASE PROBLEMS

1. While driving home from a fraternity dance, Peabody drove his 1979 Firebird off an embankment and into a tree, causing severe damage to the car. Peabody's insurance company, Motors Insurance Corp., paid Peabody under the insurance policy, and, in return, Peabody gave the insurance company title to the car. Motors Insurance then sold the car to John Street Auto Wrecking, a dealer in auto parts. John Street subsequently sold the car to Gullible, who hoped to restore the car to its original condition. About three weeks later, the police seized the car from Gullible as a stolen vehicle. Can Gullible recover from John Street? If so, can John Street in turn recover from Motors Insurance? [John Street Auto Wrecking v. Motors Ins. Corp., 56 Misc.2d 232, 288 N.Y.S.2d 281 (1968)]

2. Hanley and Herschel entered into a contract under which Herschel was to sell Hanley a used semitrailer. Hanley received the semitrailer and used it for sixteen months. Then it was impounded by the state police on the basis of a report that it had been stolen. Hanley immediately notified Herschel of the seizure and of his decision to rescind the contract.

Shortly thereafter the police informed Hanley that the proper owner of the vehicle was unclear and that the person who claimed to be the owner had questionable title. Can Hanley still rescind his contract with Herschel instead of first going to court to determine rightful ownership? [American Container Corp. v. Hanley Trucking Corp., 111 N.J. Super. 322, 268 A.2d. 313 (1970)]

3. Lattimer Foundry & Machine Company entered into a contract with Smith to manufacture and sell iron castings for use in Smith's manufacture of sausage-stuffing machines. Lattimer knew how the castings were to be used. Under the contract, the castings were to conform to samples that Lattimer had manufactured in accordance with blueprints drawn up by Smith. Before Lattimer started manufacturing the iron castings, it submitted the samples to Smith, and Smith approved them. Describe the warranties that resulted from the transaction between Lattimer and Smith. [John E. Smith's Sons Co. v. Lattimer Foundry & Machine Co., 19 F.R.D.379 (M.D. Pa. 1956)]

4. Carpenter entered Discount Drugs to purchase some hair dye. One of Discount's clerks told Carpenter that her personal favorite was Alberto. The clerk further stated that Carpenter "would get very fine results" with Alberto. When Carpenter used the hair dye, however, she suffered an adverse skin reaction. Carpenter sued both Discount Drugs and Alberto Culver Company for breach of warranty. Carpenter also sued Discount Drugs for breach of the express warranties that Carpenter alleged that Discount's salesclerk had made to her. Were any express warranties made to Carpenter? [Carpenter v. Alberto Culver Co., 28 Mich.App. 399, 184 N.W.2d 547 (1970)]

5. In August 1961, McMeekin purchased a lawnmower from Gimbel Brothers. In June of the next year, while McMeekin was mowing his lawn, his son was struck in the eye by an unknown object and subsequently lost sight in the eye. In a suit filed by McMeekin on behalf of his son against Gimbels, McMeekin sought recovery on the theory that Gimbels had breached its warranty of merchantability. McMeekin claimed that "somehow, part of the lawnmower broke off and flew into my son's eye." Can McMeekin recover? [McMeekin v. Gimbel Brothers, Inc., 223 F. Supp. 896 (W.D. Pa. 1963)]

6. Montgomery Ward sold Vlases a number of one-day-old chicks. Vlases intended to raise them in his newly constructed chicken coop. Several weeks after Montgomery Ward sold the chickens to Vlases, they developed leukosis, and all of them died. Vlases demanded his money back from the company. Montgomery Ward refused, and Vlases brought suit, claiming breach of implied warranty of merchantability. Montgomery Ward claimed that it was not liable since no amount of knowledge, skill, or foresight on its part would have enabled it to detect the sickness. Assuming Montgomery Ward's claim is true, is this a valid defense? [Vlases v. Montgomery Ward Co., 377 F.2d 846 (3rd Cir. 1967)]

7. Tracy purchased a used car from Vinton Motors, Inc., on April 9. At the time of the purchase, one of Vinton's salespeople told Tracy that "this baby is good for years." Subsequently, Tracy paid cash for the car and signed a written contract that stated on its face that any express warranties accompanying the sale were effective for only thirty days or 1,000 miles, whichever came first. About six weeks later, Tracy noticed that the exterior paint on the car was peeling and demanded that Vinton Motors repaint it. Vinton Motors refused, and Tracy brought suit. What will be the result? [Tracy v. Vinton Motors, Inc., 130 Vt. 512, 296 A.2d 269 (1972)]

8. Maxwell Dynamometer Company sent the following purchase order to Marble Card Electric Corp.: "1 30/15 H.P. Induction Motor Drip Proof 3600/1800 RPM single winding, constant torque, 220 volt A.C. 60 cycle, 3 phase Frame 365. Shaft end to be tapered and threaded as per sketch forwarded to factory, Gladstone, Mich." Marble sent Maxwell the motor, but Maxwell failed to pay for it. Marble sued Maxwell to recover the purchase price of the motor. Maxwell defended on the ground that Marble breached its warranty of fitness for a particular purpose. Under the facts given, how valid is Maxwell's claim? [Marble Card Electric Corp. v. Maxwell Dynamometer Co., 10 Chest. 145 (Pa. 1961)]

9. Hunt, a fisherman, placed an order with Perkins Machine Company for a new engine for his fishing boat. When the engine arrived, Perkins called Hunt in to pick it up. Hunt paid cash for the engine and signed a written form contract from a pad of contracts as evidence of the sale. On the front of the contract was the following statement in boldface print: "Both this order and its acceptance are subject to 'terms and conditions' stated in this order." On the reverse side the words "terms and conditions" appeared at the top of the page. Below this was the following statement, also printed in boldface: "Seller makes no warranties including any warranties as to merchantability or fitness either express or implied." From about a week after Hunt purchased the new engine, it was in constant need of repair. Perkins made several attempts to repair it, but it still did not work properly,

and Perkins refused to make further attempts to fix it. Hunt demanded his money back, but Perkins refused. In a lawsuit by Hunt against Perkins, can Hunt successfully claim that Perkins has committed breach of warranty? [Hunt v. Perkins Machinery Co., 352 Mass. 535, 226 N.E.2d 228 (1967)]

10. For the past twenty years Cardinale Trucking Corp. and Gindy Manufacturing Corp. have done business with each other, buying and selling semitrailers. It is customary in the semitrailer trade for sellers of semitrailers to assume responsibility for any manufacturing defects that might occur within a reasonable time after the sale. In July 1969, Gindy sold Cardinale twenty-five semitrailers, and Cardinale signed one of the written contracts supplied by Gindy. The contract stated that the new semitrailers were sold "as is." Shortly thereafter Cardinale learned that the semitrailers were defective and requested that Gindy repair them. Gindy refused, and Cardinale refused to pay for the trucks. In a suit by Gindy against Cardinale for the purchase price, what will be the result? [Gindy Mfg. Corp. v. Cardinale Trucking Corp., 111 N.J.Super. 383, 268 A.2d 345 (1970)]

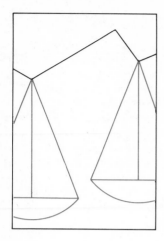

21

Sales
Products Liability

Often retailers serve simply as go-betweens, selling the manufacturer's goods to consumers in prepackaged, sealed containers. Retailers are still liable to purchasers on express or implied warranties, even though the retailers cannot always examine the goods prior to resale. Today, liability has been extended to manufacturers through the application of new principles of the law.

Manufacturers and sellers of goods can be held liable to consumers, users, and bystanders for physical harm or property damage that is caused by the goods. This is called *products liability* and it encompasses tort theories of *strict liability* and *negligence* and the contract theory of *warranty*. It should be noted that these theories of recovery are *not* mutually exclusive.

WARRANTY THEORY

As we learned in Chapter 20, consumers and other purchasers of goods can recover *from any seller* for losses resulting from breach of implied or express warranty. Thus, since a manufacturer is a *seller*, a person who purchases goods from a retailer can recover either from the retailer or the manufacturer if the goods are not merchantable. This was not always the case. Until enactment of the UCC, *privity of contract* was required for a purchaser to bring an action for breach of warranty against a manufacturer.

Privity of Contract

Privity of contract is the connection or relationship that exists between two or more contracting parties because of the fact that they entered into a contract. Privity must exist between a plaintiff and a defendant with respect to the matter under dispute in order to maintain any action based upon a contract. At common law, the retailer making a sale was solely responsible to the consumer of defective goods. The UCC has broadened the basis of liability and therefore modified the notion of privity of contract as the basis for lawsuits.

Third-Party Beneficiaries of Warranties: Express or Implied

There is sharp disagreement over *how far* warranty liability should extend. In order to satisfy opposing views of the various states, the drafters of the Uniform Commercial Code proposed three alternatives for liability under UCC Sec. 2-318. Accordingly, some states have adopted alternative A; others, alternative B; and still others, alternative C. All three alternatives are intended to eliminate the privity requirement with respect to certain enumerated types of injuries (personal versus property) for certain beneficaries (e.g., household members, bystanders).

ALTERNATIVE A   All sellers' warranties (express or implied) extend to any *natural person* in the buyer's family or household or to anyone who is a guest in the home, when it is reasonable to expect that such persons will use, consume, or be affected by the goods or be personally injured because of a breach of the warranty. Consider an example. Anderson buys an electric washing machine from E-Z Appliances. One month after the purchase, Anderson's mother-in-law, who has been living with his family for a year, receives a severe electric shock from a defective wire while using the machine. Anderson's mother-in-law claims damages from E-Z Appliances for breach of warranty of merchantability. She can recover

because the defective wire made the washing machine unfit for normal use. Since she was living with Anderson's family, she naturally would use the washing machine if she helped with housekeeping chores. Anderson's mother-in-law therefore qualifies as a third-party beneficiary of the warranty. Note the restriction in this alternative—the guest has to be in the person's home. In one case, a federal court, applying Pennsylvania law, held that under the provision adopted in Pennsylvania, the warranty protection did not extend to a guest injured while riding in the purchaser's new automobile since it was not the buyer's home.[1]

ALTERNATIVE B   Alternative B extends the seller's warranty (express or implied) to any *natural person* who can reasonably be expected to use, consume, or be affected by the goods and who suffers personal injury because of the breach of warranty. This is a broader basis for liability than alternative A since protection is not limited to family or household members. Note the restrictions here. As with alternative A, the seller's warranty extends only to persons, not corporations. It also limits the right of recovery to personal injury damages and therefore eliminates the possibility of suing for property damages. A seller may not exclude or limit the warranties given under alternative A or B.

ALTERNATIVE C   Alternative C offers the broadest coverage of all. It extends to *any* person, and provides recovery for either personal or property injury. It does not allow the seller to exclude or limit the operation of liability for personal injury of an individual to whom the warranty extends.

LIABILITY BASED ON NEGLIGENCE

Chapter 3 defined *negligence* as omitting to do something that a *reasonable person* would do, guided by the considerations that ordinarily

1.   Thompson v. Reedman, 199 F. Supp. 120 (D.C. Pa. 1961).

regulate human affairs, or doing something that a reasonable and prudent person would not do. The failure to exercise reasonable care in the circumstances that cause an injury is the basis of liability for negligence. Thus, the manufacturer of a consumer product must exercise "due care" to make that product safe to be used as it was intended. Due care must be exercised in designing the product, in selecting the materials, in using the appropriate production process, in assembling and testing the product, and in placing adequate warnings on the label of dangers of which an ordinary person might not be aware. The duty of care extends to the inspection and testing of purchased products used in the final product sold by the manufacturer.

The opposite of due care is negligence. In the following case, the New York court dealt with the liability of a manufacturer who failed to use due care in manufacturing a finished product.

MACPHERSON v. BUICK MOTOR CO.

Court of Appeals of New York, 1916.

111 N.E. 1050, 217 N.Y. 382.

BACKGROUND AND FACTS *The MacPherson case is the classic products liability case. Its subject matter, defectively manufactured wooden wheels for automobiles, is dated, but the principles involved are not.*

The defendant, Buick Motor Company, was sued by Donald C. MacPherson, the plaintiff, who suffered injuries while riding in a Buick automobile that suddenly collapsed because one of the wheels was made of defective wood. The spokes crumbled into fragments, throwing MacPherson out of the vehicle and injuring him.

The wheel itself had not been made by Buick Motor Company; it had been bought from another manufacturer. There was evidence, however, that the defects could have been discovered by reasonable inspection and that inspection had not taken place. Although there was no charge that Buick knew of the defect and willfully concealed it, MacPherson charged Buick with negligence for putting a human life in imminent danger.

Keep in mind that MacPherson sued the manufacturer directly, despite the fact that the automobile was purchased from a retail Buick dealer.

CARDOZO, Justice.

* * *

The question to be determined is whether the defendant owed a duty of care and vigilance to any one but the immediate purchaser.

The foundations of this branch of the law, at least in this state, were laid in Thomas v. Winchester, 6 N.Y. 397, 57 Am.Dec. 455. A poison was falsely labeled. The sale was made to a druggist, who in turn sold to a customer. The customer recovered damages from the seller who affixed the label. "The defendant's negligence," it was said, "put human life in imminent danger." A poison, falsely labeled, is likely to injure any one who gets it. *Because the danger is to be foreseen, there is a duty to avoid the injury.* [Emphasis added.]

* * *

Thomas v. Winchester became quickly a landmark of the law. In the application of its principle there may, at times, have been uncertainty or even error. There has never in this state been doubt or disavowal of the principle itself.

* * *

These early cases suggest a narrow construction of the rule. Later cases, however, evince a more liberal spirit. First in importance is Devlin v. Smith, 89 N.Y. 470, 42 Am.Rep. 311. The defendant, a contractor, built a scaffold for a painter. The painter's servants were injured. The contractor was held liable. He knew that the scaffold, if improperly constructed, was a most dangerous trap. He knew that it was to be used by the workmen. He was building it for that very purpose. Building it for their use, he owed them a duty, irrespective of his contract with their master, to build it with care.

From Devlin v. Smith we * * * turn to the latest case in this court in which Thomas v. Winchester was followed. That case is Statler v. Ray Mfg. Co., 195 N.Y. 478, 480, 88 N.E. 1063. The defendant manufactured a large coffee urn. It was installed in a restaurant. When heated, the urn exploded and injured the plaintiff. We held that the manufacturer was liable. We said that the urn "was of such a character inherently that, when applied to the purposes for which it was designed, it was liable to become a source of great danger to many people if not carefully and properly constructed."

It may be that Devlin v. Smith and Statler v. Ray Mfg. Co. have extended the rule of Thomas v. Winchester. If so, this court is committed to the extension. The defendant argues that things imminently dangerous to life are poisons, explosives, deadly weapons—things whose normal function it is to injure or destroy. But whatever the rule in Thomas v. Winchester may once have been, it has no longer that restricted meaning. A scaffold (Devlin v. Smith, supra) is not inherently a destructive instrument. It becomes destructive only if imperfectly constructed. A large coffee urn (Statler v. Ray Mfg. Co., supra) may have within itself, if negligently made, the potency of danger, yet no one thinks of it as an implement whose normal function is destruction. * * *

We hold, then, that the principle of Thomas v. Winchester is not limited to poisons, explosives, and things of like nature, to things which in their normal operation are implements of destruction. If the nature of a thing is such that it is reasonably certain to place life and limb in peril when negligently made, it is then a thing of danger. Its nature gives warning of the consequences to be expected. If to the element of danger there is added knowledge that the thing will be used by persons other than the purchaser, and used without new tests, then, irrespective of contract, the manufacturer of this thing of danger is under a duty to make it carefully. * * * It is possible to use almost anything in a way that will make it dangerous if defective. That is not enough to charge the manufacturer with a duty independent of his contract. * * * There must also be knowledge that in the usual course of events the danger will be shared by others than the buyer. Such knowledge may often be inferred from the nature of the transaction. But it is possible that even knowledge of the danger and of the use will not always be enough. The proximity or remoteness of the relation is a factor to be considered. We are dealing now with the liability of the manufacturer of the finished product, who puts it on the market to be used without inspection by his customers. If he is negligent, where danger is to be foreseen, a liability will follow.

We are not required, at this time, to say that it is legitimate to go back of the manufacturer of the finished product and hold the manufacturers of the component parts. To make their negligence a cause of imminent danger, an independent cause must often intervene; the manufacturer of the finished product must also fail in his duty of inspection. It may be that in those circumstances the negligence of the earlier members of the series is too remote to constitute, as to the ultimate user, an actionable wrong. * * * There is here no break in the chain of cause and effect. In such circumstances, the presence of a known danger, attendant upon a known use, makes vigilance a duty.

From this survey of the decisions, there thus emerges a definition of the duty of a manufacturer which enables us to measure this defendant's liability. Beyond all question, the nature of an automobile gives warning of probable danger if its construction is defective. This automobile was designed to go 50 miles an hour. Unless its wheels were sound and strong, injury was almost certain. It was as much a thing of danger as a defective engine for a railroad. The defendant knew the danger. It knew also that the car would be used by persons other than the buyer. This was apparent from its size; there were seats for three persons. It was apparent also from the fact that the buyer was a dealer in cars, who bought to resell. The maker of this car supplied it for the use of purchasers from the dealer just as plainly as the contractor in Devlin v. Smith supplied the scaffold for use by the servants of the owner.
* * *

It is true that * * * "an automobile is not an inherently dangerous vehicle." The meaning, however, is that danger is not to be expected when the vehicle is well constructed. The court left it to the jury to say whether the defendant ought to have foreseen that the car, if negligently constructed, would become "imminently dangerous." Subtle distinctions are drawn by the defendants between things inherently dangerous and things imminently dangerous, but the case does not turn upon these verbal niceties. If danger was to be expected as reasonably certain, there was a duty of vigilance, and this whether you call the danger inherent or imminent.
* * *

We think the defendant was not absolved from a duty of inspection because it bought the wheels from a reputable manufacturer. It was not merely a dealer in automobiles. It was responsible for the finished product. It was not at liberty to put the finished product on the market without subjecting the component parts to ordinary and simple tests. The obligation to inspect must vary with the nature of the thing to be inspected. The more probable the danger the greater the need of caution. * * *

JUDGMENT AND REMEDY   *The New York Court of Appeals, the highest court in the New York state system, affirmed the judgment of the original trial court and the intermediate review court that the defendant, Buick Motor Company, was liable in damages to Donald C. MacPherson for the injuries he sustained when he was thrown from the vehicle.*

PRIVITY OF CONTRACT NOT REQUIRED An action based upon negligence does not require privity of contract between the injured plaintiff and the negligent defendant-manufacturer. Section 395 of the Restatement, Second, Torts states:

A manufacturer who fails to exercise reasonable care in the manufacture of a chattel [movable good] which, unless carefully made, he should recognize as involving an unreasonable risk of causing substantial bodily harm to those who lawfully used it for a purpose for which it was manufactured and to those whom the supplier should expect to be in the vicinity of its probable use, is subject to liability for bodily harm caused to them by its lawful use in a manner and for a purpose for which it is manufactured.

Basis of Liability—Violation of Statutory Duty

Numerous federal and state laws impose duties upon manufacturers of cosmetics, drugs, foods, toxic substances, and flammable materials. These duties involve appropriate description of contents, labeling, branding, advertising, and selling. The statutes include the Federal Flammable Fabrics Act; the Federal Food, Drug, and Cosmetics Act; and the Federal Hazardous Substances Labeling Act. In a civil action for damages (tort), a violation of statutory duty is often held to constitute negligence per se. Consider an example: Jason Manufacturing Company produces pipe fittings for use in the construction of homes in Monroe County. The fittings do not comply with county building codes. One of the pipe fittings bursts in a home, allowing hot water to spray on the homeowner. The homeowner can bring a negligence action for personal damages on the ground that failure to comply with the building codes is a breach of the manufacturer's duty of reasonable care. Of course, the homeowner has to show proximate cause.

Fraudulent and Nonfraudulent Misrepresentation

When a fraudulent misrepresentation has been made to a user or consumer, and that misrepresentation ultimately results in an injury, the basis of liability may be the tort of **fraud.** Examples are the intentional mislabeling of packaged cosmetics or the intentional concealment of a product's defects. A more interesting basis of liability is nonfraudulent misrepresentation, when a merchant *innocently* misrepresents the character or quality of goods.

A famous example involved a drug manufacturer and a victim of addiction to a prescrip-

tion medicine called Talwin. The manufacturer, Winthrop Laboratories, a division of Stirling Drug, Inc., innocently indicated to the medical profession that the drug was not physically addictive. Using this information, a physician prescribed the drug for his patient, who developed an addiction that turned out to be fatal.Even though the addiction was a highly unusual reaction resulting from the victim's highly unusual susceptibility to this product, the drug company was still held liable.[2]

THE DOCTRINE OF STRICT LIABILITY

A recent development of tort law is the revival of the old doctrine of strict liability, under which people are liable for the results of their acts regardless of their intentions or the degree of their negligence. For example, a company that uses dynamite to blast for a road is strictly liable for any damages that it causes, even if it takes reasonable and prudent precautions to prevent such damages. In essence, the blasting company becomes the insurer for any personal injuries it causes.

The English courts accepted the doctrine of strict liability for many years. Any persons whose conduct resulted in the injury of another were held liable for damages, even if they had not intended to injure anyone and had exercised reasonable or even great care. This approach was abandoned around 1800 in favor of the *fault* approach. An action was considered tortious only if it was wrongful or blameworthy in some respect. Strict liability was reapplied to manufactured goods in several landmark cases in the 1960s and has since become a common method of holding manufacturers liable. The purchaser of a product who is injured has a cause of action against the manufacturer simply by showing (1) that the product was defective, (2) that the defect made the product unreasonably dangerous, and (3) that the defect was the proximate cause of the injury.

---

2. Crocker v. Winthrop Laboratories, Div. of Stirling Drugs, Inc., 514 S.W.2d 429 (Tex. 1974).

The Restatement of Torts

The Restatement, Second, Torts designates how the doctrine of strict liability should be applied. It is a precise and widely accepted statement of the liabilities of sellers of goods (including manufacturers) and deserves close attention. Section 402A of Restatement, Second, Torts states:

(1)   One who sells any product in a defective condition unreasonably dangerous to the user or consumer or to his property is subject to liablity for physical harm thereby caused to the ultimate user or consumer or to his property, if

> (a) the seller is engaged in the business of selling such a product, and
> (b) it is expected to and does reach the user or consumer without substantial change in the condition in which it is sold.

(2) The rule stated in Subsection (1) applies although

> (a) the seller has exercised all possible care in the preparation and sale of his product, and
> (b) the user or consumer has not bought the product from or entered into any contractual relation with the seller.

Thus, liability is imposed by law as a matter of public policy. It does not depend on privity of contract or on proof of negligence. The manufacturer's liability to an injured party is virtually unlimited. The injured party does not have to be the buyer or a third-party beneficiary, as required under contract warranty theory. [UCC Sec. 2-318] Indeed, this liability in law is not governed by the provisions of the Uniform Commercial Code.

Requirements of Strict Liability

The five basic requirements of strict liability are:

1.   The defendant must sell the product in a defective condition.
2.   The defendant must normally be engaged in the business of selling that product.
3.   The product must be unreasonably danger-ous to the user or consumer because of its defective condition.
4.   The plaintiff must incur physical harm to self or property by use or consumption of the product.
5.   The defective condition must be the proximate cause of the injury or damage.

Thus, in any action against a manufacturer or seller, the plaintiff does not have to show why or in what manner the product became defective. The plaintiff does, however, have to show that at the time the injury was sustained, the condition of the product was essentially the same as it was when it left the hands of the defendant manufacturer or seller.

Limitations on Recovery

Some courts have limited the application of the strict liability doctrine to cases in which personal injuries have occurred. Thus, when a defective product causes only *property damage*, the seller may or may not be liable under a theory of strict liability, depending on the law of the particular jurisdiction. Note, however, that recovery for *breach of warranty* may be available, depending upon the type of injury and which alternative section of UCC Sec. 2-318 is in effect. Finally, recovery under negligence theory may be possible, but negligence of the manufacturer may be difficult to prove.

Defenses

In some cases, manufacturers have proven as a defense that a product was being misused at the time of the injury or that it was used in a manner for which it was not made. Also, there have been recent legislative attempts to limit the application of the doctrine of strict liability to new goods.

Assumption of risk can be used as a defense in an action based on strict liability in tort. Whenever consumers or users use goods improperly under unreasonable circumstances, they assume the risk of injury. In order for such a defense to be established, the defendant must show (1) that the plaintiff voluntarily engaged in the risk while realizing the potential danger, (2) that the plaintiff knew and appreciated the risk created by the defect, and (3) that the plaintiff's decision to undertake the known risk was unreasonable.

Strict Liability to Bystanders

Some courts extend the strict liability of manufacturers and other sellers to injured bystanders, although the drafters of Restatement, Second, Torts, Section 402A did not take a position on bystanders. For example, the manufacturer of an automobile was held liable for injuries caused by the explosion of the car's motor while in traffic. A cloud of steam that resulted from the explosion caused multiple collisions because other drivers could not see well.[3]

Crash-worthiness Doctrine

Certain courts have adopted the doctrine of crash-worthiness, which imposes liability for defects in the design or construction of motor vehicles that increase the extent of injuries to passengers if an accident occurs. The doctrine holds even when the defects do not actually cause the accident.[4] By accepting the crash-worthiness doctrine, the courts reject the argument of automobile manufacturers that involving a car in a collision does not constitute "ordinary use" of a car. There are in fact, strong differences of opinion among the courts on this issue.

Strict Liability of Suppliers of Component Parts and Lessors

Under the rule of strict liability in tort, the basis of liability has been expanded to include suppliers of component parts and lessors of mov-

able goods. Thus, if General Motors buys brake pads from a subcontractor and puts them in Chevrolets without changing their composition, and those pads are defective, both the supplier of the brake pads and General Motors will be held strictly liable for the damages caused by the defects.

Liability for personal injuries caused by defective goods extends to those who lease such goods. Section 408 of the Restatement, Second, Torts states that:

One who leases a chattel as safe for immediate use is subject to liability to those whom he should expect to use the chattel, or to be endangered by its probable use, for physical harm caused by its use in a manner for which and by a person for whose use it is leased, if the lessor fails to exercise reasonable care to make it safe for such use or to disclose its actual condition to those who may be expected to use it.

Some courts have held that a leasing agreement gives rise to a contractual *implied warranty* that the leased goods will be fit for the duration of the lease. Under this view, if Hertz Rent-a-Car leases a Chevrolet that has been improperly maintained, and a passenger is injured in an accident, the passenger can sue Hertz. (Liability is based on the contract theory of warranty, not tort.)

THE CONSUMER PRODUCT SAFETY ACT

One of the newest federal agencies designed to protect the consumer is the Consumer Product Safety Commission (CPSC). Established in 1972, it was given sweeping powers to regulate the production and sale of potentially hazardous consumer products. The agency's staff will eventually be over a thousand, which will make it one of the major federal regulatory agencies for consumer protection.

Consumer product safety legislation began in 1953 with the enactment of the Flammable Fabrics Act. Between 1953 and 1972 Congress enacted legislation regulating specific classes

---

3. Giberson v. Ford Motor Co., 504 S.W.2d 8 (Mo.1974).
4. Turner v. General Motors Corp., 514 S.W.2d 497 (Texas Civ. App. 1974).

rather than broad categories of consumer products. Finally, as a result of 1970 recommendations of the National Commission on Product Safety, the Consumer Product Safety Act was passed in 1972, creating the CPSC to regulate all potentially hazardous consumer products.

Products Subject to the Act

The 1972 Act states that "* * *any article, or component part thereof produced or distributed for sale to a consumer for use in or around a permanent or temporary household or residence, a school, in recreation or otherwise, or for the personal use, consumption or enjoyment of a consumer" shall be subject to regulation by the CPSC. As further evidence of how comprehensive the act is, the authority to administer other acts is transferred to the CPSC. These acts include the Federal Hazardous Substance Act, the Child Protection and Toy Safety Act, the Poison Prevention Packaging Act, the Flammable Fabrics Act, and the Refrigerator Safety Act.

Purposes of the Act

As stated in the act, the Consumer Product Safety Commission was created:

1. To protect the public against unreasonable risk of injury associated with consumer products.
2. To assist consumers in evaluating the comparative safety of consumer products.
3. To develop uniform safety standards for consumer products and to minimize conflicting state and local regulations.
4. To promote research and investigation into causes and prevention of product-related deaths, illnesses, and injuries.

Form and Functions of the CPSC

The commission was set up to conduct research on product safety and maintain a clearinghouse to "collect, investigate, analyze, and dissemi-

nate injury data, and information, relating to the causes and prevention of death, injury, and illness associated with consumer products * * *" To this end, the CPSC immediately started gathering data on the two hundred most hazardous consumer products in the nation. The commission required emergency wards to indicate the particular cause of any injury, illness, or death related to a consumer product. The initial CPSC survey found that the most hazardous consumer product was the bicycle. The CPSC hoped that the data obtained and the resulting hazard index for consumer products would move manufacturers to improve their most hazardous products voluntarily and to warn consumers about them.

Powers of the CPSC

Not only can the CPSC set safety standards for consumer products, it can also ban the manufacture and sale of any product deemed hazardous to consumers. The commission has the authority to remove from the market products that are deemed imminently hazardous. It can require manufacturers to report information about any products already sold or intended for sale that have proven hazardous.

Impact of the CPSC

Congress sought to create an agency with broad powers to regulate the sale and manufacture of all consumer products. The CPSC is likely to have increasingly profound effects upon the consumer products industry. At the very least, if it continues its present effectiveness, it will give consumers more information about the safety of the products that they buy.

CPSC regulations have resulted in safer but more expensive products. Recently, regulations for power mowers were challenged by certain government agencies because they would raise the price of the mowers too much. This involves the thorny problem of weighing the costs of safety against the benefits. In other words, how much safety do people want to pay for?

QUESTIONS AND CASE PROBLEMS

1.   Howmedica, Inc., manufactured and distributed artificial replacements for human bones and joints. Hoffman, who was injured in a serious automobile accident, underwent surgery for repair to her injured hip. As part of the surgery, her doctor implanted a hip prosthesis. Several months later, Hoffman's hip fractured, causing serious injury. At trial, Howmedica, Inc., conceded that it had been negligent in manufacturing and testing the hip and that it had breached its warranty of merchantability. But Howmedica contended that it was not liable to Hoffman under UCC Sec. 2-318 (Alternative B) since Hoffman and Howmedica were not in privity of contract. Is this a sound argument? [Hoffman v. Howmedica, Inc., 364 N.E.2d 1215 (Mass.1977)].

2.   While shopping in an Allied Supermarket store, Barker placed two bottles of soda in his shopping cart and thereafter paid for them. While Barker was pushing the cart out the exit door, one of the bottles exploded, and a sliver of glass flew into Barker's eye. Barker sued both Allied Supermarket and B&B Bottling Company, the manufacturer of the soda, but not until two years had passed, so he was no longer able to bring a tort action. Assuming Barker can prove breach of a warranty of merchantability, and assuming the jurisdiction in which he brings suit follows alternative A of UCC Sec. 2-318, can Barker recover against Allied Supermarket? Against B&B Bottling? [Barker v. Allied Supermarket, 20 U.C.C. Rptg. Serv. 6 (Okla. 1976)]

3.   James Welding Company purchased from Delta Oxygen Company a cylinder filled with oxygen to be used in welding operations. Scott, who had worked for James Welding Company for a number of years, was attempting to connect the cylinder to an acetylene torch when a leak in the cylinder caused an explosion to occur. Scott was seriously burned and was hospitalized as a result of the explosion. In an action by Scott for breach of implied warranty against Delta Oxygen Company, Scott relied on UCC Sec. 2-318. What result? [Delta Oxygen Co. v. Scott, 238 Ark. 534, 383 S.W.2d 885 (1964)]

4.   Miller purchased a vaporizer-humidifier from Rexall Drug Company. While she was using the humidifier in her home, it suddenly shot boiling water on her nephew. The incident resulted in the nephew's death. Miller's nephew did not live in Miller's home; he lived next door. Will an action brought against Rexall Drug Company on behalf of Miller's nephew be successful in a jurisdiction in which UCC Sec. 2-318 (alternative A) is in effect? [Miller v. Preitz, 422 Pa. 383, 221 A.2d. 320 (1966)]

5.   Hardesty, the owner of an apartment building, contracted with a subcontractor to install a central air-conditioning system in the building. After the subcontractor had properly installed the air-conditioning system, it failed to work because the chiller unit of the system was defective. As a result of the defect and because the system failed to work, Hardesty was unable to rent many of the apartment units in his building. Hardesty sued the manufacturer of the units, from whom the subcontractor had purchased them, for damages for breach of warranty under UCC Sec. 2-318. Can he recover? [Hardesty v. Andro Corp.—Webster Div., 555 P.2d. 1030 (Okl. 1976)]

6.   Downey owned a mechanical rug washer that he had purchased from a local retailer. The manufacturer was Moore's Time-Saving Equipment, Inc. While using the rug washer, Downey was struck in the eye and injured when the cam lift handle counter-rotated after Downey failed to turn it the required 180 degree arc. Downey was aware that such counter-rotation was common on these types of rug washers because he was experienced in the use of these machines. Downey wished to recover for his eye injury from Moore's Equipment, Inc., on a theory of strict liability. Can he recover? [Downey v. Moore's Time-Sav. Equipment, Inc., 432 F.2d. 1088 (C.A. Ind. 1970)]

7.   Union Oil Company was engaged in drilling operations off the Alaskan coast. As a part of its operations, Union installed gas protection systems in its offshore drilling rigs. Over a period of less than a year, the salt water and spray caused the internal parts of the detection system to corrode, resulting in a failure in the system. Subsequently, because of an undetected gas leak, an explosion killed one of Union's employees, Jones. Jones's representative sued Haragan, the manufacturer and seller of the gas detection system. Can Jones's representatives recover on a theory of strict liability? How would they argue that there was a defect? [Haragan v. Union Oil Co., 312 F.Supp. 1392 (D.C. Alaska, 1970)]

8.   White, a bystander, was injured when a coal

mining ram car with a defective steering valve struck an air line, which in turn struck White. Assuming that the steering mechanism was defective at the time the manufacturer sold it to the mining company, what problems will White have bringing suit under a theory of strict liability in tort? Look closely at the wording of Restatement, Second, Torts, Section 402A. [White v. Jeffrey Galion, Inc., 326 F.Supp. 751 (D.C. Ill. 1971)]

9. In July 1971, St. Regis Paper Corp. purchased a compressor from Norfolk Development Corp. for use in its paper-producing plant. Several weeks later the compressor exploded, resulting in a fire that caused extensive damage to the purchaser's manufacturing plant. The explosion was caused by a defect in the manufacture of the pistons. St. Regis sought to recover from Norfolk for damage done the plant and for the profits it lost while the plant was closed for repairs. What results? [Norfolk Dev. Corp. v. St. Regis Pulp and Paper Corp., 338 F.Supp. 1213 (D.C. Neb. 1972)]

10. Dreher purchased a plastic waste container from Maas for use in her home. After she brought the container home, she found that the lid had been improperly manufactured and did not fit on the top of the container. Dreher purposely hit the corner of the lid with her hand in an attempt to make it fit properly and suffered a deep gash in her hand when she hit the lid. She sought to recover for the injury from Maas, the seller, but Maas refused to compensate her. In a suit by Dreher against Maas, can Dreher successfully recover on a theory of strict liability? [Maas v. Dreher, 10 Ariz. App. 520, 460 P.2d. 191 (1969)]

22

Sales

Remedies of Buyer and Seller
for Breach of Sales Contracts

When a sales contract is breached, remedies are provided to the non-breaching party not only for *damages* but also to enable the nonbreaching party to retain physical possession of the goods. [UCC Secs. 2-711 and 2-703] The general purpose of these remedies is to put the aggrieved party "in as good a position as if the other party had fully performed." [UCC Sec. 1-106(1)]

REMEDIES OF THE SELLER

The remedies available to an unpaid seller under the Uniform Commercial Code include: (1) the right to withhold delivery of the goods, (2) the right to stop a carrier or bailee from delivering goods to an insolvent buyer, (3) a limited right to reclaim goods in the possession of an insolvent buyer, (4) the right to identify and resell goods to the contract after the buyer has breached, (5) the right to recover the purchase price plus incidental damages, (6) the right to recover damages for the buyer's nonacceptance or repudiation of the contract, and (7) the right to cancel the sales contract.

Seller's Lien

In certain circumstances, a seller has a lien, or legal interest, in goods being sold. Technically, a lien is a right incident to the sale rather than a remedy for breach of contract. A lien enables the seller to retain possession of the goods until the buyer pays for them.

The seller's lien can be waived or lost by: (1) express agreement, (2) acts inconsistent with the lien's existence, (3) payment or tender of payment by the buyer, or (4) voluntary and unconditional delivery of the goods to a carrier or other bailee or to the buyer or an authorized agent of the buyer.

The seller's right to retain possession of the goods until the buyer pays the purchase price can be waived by express agreement in the sales contract. If the sales agreement provides for an extension of credit to the buyer, the seller has no lien on the goods, since the act of extending credit is inconsistent with the existence of the lien. The seller will have a lien on the goods, however, if the buyer becomes insolvent or if the credit period expires while the goods are still in the seller's possession. The tender of payment or the actual payment of the debt that the lien secures will ordinarily discharge the lien. This occurs when the buyer pays the full price for the goods and the seller gives up possession. When the buyer gives a promissory note, the lien will ordinarily not be discharged until the note is paid even if the seller relinquishes possession of the goods. Finally, sellers lose their liens when they voluntarily deliver possession of the goods to the buyer or to an authorized agent of the buyer. The lien is not lost, though, where delivery is qualified or where the buyer obtains possession fraudulently.

Consider the following illustration. Williams, the plaintiff, sold his Chevrolet sedan to the Greers, the defendants. The defendants paid $90 by check and $235 in cash. After the Greers received possession of the Chevy, they stopped payment on the check. Williams went to court to regain possession of the auto by enforcing his seller's lien. The court upheld his complaint, allowing him to regain possession of the auto and to keep it until the Greers paid the $90. Essentially, the Greers had obtained possession fraudulently; therefore, title had not passed to them. Since Williams had legal possession, he could validly enforce his lien.

The Right to Withhold Delivery of the Goods

In general, sellers can withhold or discontinue performance of their obligations under a sales contract when buyers breach. If a seller discovers that the buyer is insolvent, the seller can refuse to deliver the goods unless the buyer pays in cash. [UCC Sec. 2-702] If a buyer has wrongfully rejected, revoked acceptance, failed to make proper and timely payment, or repudiated a part of the contract, the seller can withhold delivery of the particular goods in question. Furthermore, the seller can withhold the entire undelivered balance of the goods if the buyer's breach is material. [UCC Sec. 2-703]

The Right to Stop a Carrier or Bailee from Delivering Goods to an Insolvent Buyer

An unpaid seller can stop a carrier from delivering goods in transit to a buyer whenever the seller learns of the buyer's insolvency. The seller can also stop delivery if the buyer repudiates or behaves in any other way that gives the seller the right to withhold or reclaim the goods when the quantity involved is at least a carload, a truckload, or a planeload. [UCC Sec. 2-705(1)]

Consider an example. On January 1, Beel orders a carload of onions from Sneed. Sneed is to ship them on January 8, and Beel is to pay for them on January 10. Sneed ships on time, but Beel does not pay. As soon as Sneed learns of this, she orders the carrier to stop the carload in transit. Since the carload is still on its way to Beel's city, the carrier stops shipment. Beel cannot claim that Sneed and the carrier have performed a wrongful act by stopping the shipment, for a seller can always stop a carload of goods in transit when a buyer commits some breach of contract that gives the seller the right to withhold or reclaim the goods.

In order to stop delivery, the seller must _timely notify_ the carrier or other bailee that the goods are to be returned or held for the seller. If the carrier has sufficient time to stop delivery, then the goods must be held and delivered according to the instructions of the seller, who is liable to the carrier for any additional costs incurred. If the carrier fails to act properly, it will be liable to the seller for any loss. [UCC Sec. 2-705(3)]

The right of the seller to stop delivery is lost when: (1) the buyer obtains possession of the goods, (2) the carrier acknowledges the buyer's rights by reshipping or storing the goods for the buyer, (3) a bailee of the goods other than a carrier acknowledges that he or she is holding the goods for the buyer, or (4) a negotiable document of title covering the goods has been negotiated to the buyer. [UCC Sec. 2-705(2)]

The Right to Reclaim Goods in the Possession of an Insolvent Buyer

The seller can demand that an insolvent buyer return the goods if the demand is made within ten days after the buyer has received them. However, the seller can demand and reclaim the goods at any time if the buyer misrepresented his or her solvency in writing within three months prior to the delivery of the goods.

The seller's right to reclaim, however, is subject to the rights of a good faith purchaser or other buyer in the ordinary course of business who purchases the goods from the buyer before the seller reclaims.[1]

The Right to Identify Goods to the Contract after the Buyer Has Breached

Sometimes a buyer may breach or repudiate a sales contract while the seller is still in posses-

---

1. *A buyer in the ordinary course of business* is a person who, in good faith and without knowledge that the sale violates the ownership rights or security interest of a third party, buys in ordinary course from a person (other than a pawnbroker) in the business of selling goods of that kind. [UCC Sec. 1-201(9)]

sion of some finished or partially manufactured goods. The seller can identify the conforming goods that are still in his or her possession or control even if they were not identified at the time of the breach. Then the seller can sue for the purchase price and resell the goods, holding the buyer liable for any loss.

Unfinished goods that were supposed to be used to fulfill a particular sales contract can be treated in two ways. First, the seller can cease manufacturing the goods and resell them for scrap or salvage value. [UCC Sec. 2-704] Second, the seller can complete the manufacture, identify the goods to the contract, and resell them, holding the buyer liable for any deficiency. In choosing between these two alternatives, the seller must exercise reasonable commercial judgment in order to mitigate the loss and obtain maximum realization of value from the unfinished goods. [UCC Sec. 2-704, Comment 2]

The Right to Resell the Goods

When buyers breach sales contracts by wrongfully rejecting goods, by revoking acceptance, by failing to pay, or by repudiating the contract, sellers can resell goods that remain in their possession or goods that they have reacquired, say, by stopping delivery. The resale must be made in good faith and in a commercially reasonable manner. The seller can recover any deficiency between the sales price and the contract price along with incidental damages. [UCC Sec. 2-706(1)] (The seller is *not* liable to the buyer for any profits made on the resale.) [UCC Sec. 2-706(6)] Consider an example. On Monday, S contracts to sell four thousand heads of romaine lettuce to B for thirty cents per head, delivery and payment to be due on Friday. On Wednesday, S has fourteen thousand heads of romaine lettuce in her inventory, but she has not yet identified the four thousand she means to sell to B. On that day, B telephones S to inform her that he will not accept or pay for the lettuce. B claims that, since the four thousand heads of romaine lettuce for his contract have not yet been identified, S cannot resell and recover damages from B. B is incorrect here. S has the right to identify the four thousand heads of romaine lettuce for B's contract. Under UCC Sec. 2-704(1), S has the right to resell the lettuce at private sale and to recover damages of the contract price of thirty cents per head, less the resale price, plus expenses.

The resale can be private or public, and the goods can be sold as a unit or in parcels. A seller planning to use a private sale must give the original buyer reasonable notice of the intention to sell. If a public sale is anticipated, the seller must give the buyer reasonable notice unless the goods are perishable or will rapidly decline in value. [UCC Secs. 2-706(2) and 2-706(3)] A bona fide purchaser in a resale takes the goods free of any of the rights of the original buyer, even if the seller fails to comply with the requirements of the Uniform Commercial Code regarding resales. [UCC Sec. 2-706(5)]

The Right to Recover the Purchase Price Plus Incidental Damages

Before the Uniform Commercial Code was adopted, a seller could not sue for the purchase price of the goods unless title had passed to the buyer. Under the Code, an unpaid seller can bring an action to recover the purchase price and incidental damages in three situations: (1) when the buyer has accepted the goods and has not revoked acceptance, (2) when conforming goods have been lost or damaged after the risk of loss has passed to the buyer, and (3) when the buyer has breached after the goods have been identified to the contract and the seller is unable to resell at a reasonable price. [UCC Sec. 2-701(1)] This remedy is distinct from an action to recover damages for breach of the sales contract and is available to the seller only in the situations described above.

If sellers sue for the contract price of undelivered goods that they have been unable to resell, they must hold the goods for the buyer. The seller can resell at any time prior to the collection of the judgment from the buyer, but the net proceeds of the sale must be credited to the buyer. The following example illustrates these points. The Rubin Glass Company sells glass strips to the Clearview Window Corporation, which uses them in manufacturing jalousie windows. Part of the merchandise is delivered, and the purchase price for the delivered order is paid. When Rubin attempts to tender the remainder of the order to Clearview, the order is refused. Rubin has two alternatives. First, it can sell the remaining glass and sue for the difference between the contract price with Clearview and the price that the glass will bring on the open market. Second, it can keep the glass and sue for any difference between the contract price and the fair market value of the glass on the date of delivery. However, Rubin will be allowed to sue for recovery of the full contract price only if it is never able to sell the glass as scrap. [UCC Sec. 2-709(1)(b)]

If a buyer repudiates a contract or wrongfully refuses to accept the goods, a seller can maintain an action to recover the damages that were sustained. Ordinarily, the amount of damages will equal the difference between the contract price and the market price (at the time and place of tender of the goods). If the difference between the contract price and the market price is too small to place the seller in the position that he or she would have been in if the buyer had fully performed, the proper measure of damages is the seller's lost profits, including a reasonable allowance for overhead and other incidental expenses. [UCC Sec. 2-708(2)]

The Right to Cancel the Sales Contract

A seller can cancel a contract if the buyer wrongfully rejects or revokes acceptance of conforming goods, fails to make proper payment, or repudiates the contract in part or in whole. The contract can be canceled with respect to the goods directly involved, or the entire contract can be canceled if the breach is material. A material breach is one that substantially impairs the value of the entire contract. [UCC Sec. 2-703]

The seller must notify the buyer of the

cancellation, and at that point, all remaining obligations of both the buyer and the seller are discharged. The seller, however, retains the right to a remedy for a breach on the part of the buyer if it occurred before the contract was canceled. [UCC Sec. 2-106(4)] If the seller's cancellation is not justified, then the seller is in breach of the contract, and the buyer can sue for appropriate damages.

In the following case, the seller attempted to cancel an installment sales contract because the buyer had been unreasonably slow in making payment. At the same time, the buyer sued the seller for damages in a cross-claim, which is the equivalent of a defendant's complaint. (See Chapter 2.) The buyer claimed that the seller's rescission (cancellation) was unjustified.

BACKGROUND AND FACTS *The seller was a Canadian company that supplied lead products, and the buyer was a Pennsylvania company. The contract in question was the last in a series of contracts that had been mutually agreed upon and fully performed with no apparent disputes. The contract reviewed by the court provided for numerous deliveries totaling 200 tons of battery lead. The parties agreed to delivery dates and to the price. They also agreed that at least 63 percent of the price was to be paid after each delivery and that the balance was to be paid within four days after the delivery.*

Although there had been no apparent disputes over the earlier contracts, the seller had complained orally that the payments were untimely, and the buyer had complained frequently that the shipments were not made at the times required by the contract. Nonetheless, the parties continued to deal with each other and apparently felt that full performance was being made.

Under the contract in question, three installment deliveries of lead had already been made (about 14.5 tons remained to be delivered out of 200 tons). The third delivery had been made after the contract period had expired. The buyer had been prodding the seller for more lead for some time. Finally, the buyer notified the seller that, unless the balance of the lead was delivered within thirty days, the buyer would purchase the lead on the open market and charge the price differential to the seller. The seller responded by pointing out that the buyer had neglected to pay for the third delivery of lead. Therefore, the seller considered the contract canceled.

PLOTNICK v.
PENNSYLVANIA
SMELTING &
REFINING CO.
United States Court of Appeals,
Third Circuit, 1952.
194 F.2d 859.

HASTIE, Judge.
* * *

[The court began by quoting the Pennsylvania Sales Act] "Where there is a contract to sell goods to be delivered by stated instalments, which are to be separately paid for, and * * * the buyer neglects or refuses to * * * pay for one or more instalments, it depends in each case on the terms of the contract, and the circumstances of the case, whether the breach of contract is so material as to justify the injured party in refusing to proceed further * * * or whether the breach is severable, giving rise to a claim for compensation, but not to a right to treat the whole contract as broken."
* * *

We are dealing, therefore, with a situation in which the controlling statute explicitly makes the circumstances of the particular case determine whether failure to pay the price of one shipment delivered under an installment contract justifies the seller in treating his own obligation with reference to future installments as ended.

First, non-payment for a delivered shipment may make it impossible or unreasonably burdensome from a financial point of view for the seller to supply future installments as promised. Second, buyer's breach of his promise to pay for one installment may create such reasonable apprehension in the seller's mind concerning payment for future installments that the seller should not be required to take the risk involved in continuing deliveries. If any such consequence is proved, the seller may rescind.

* * *

In this case there is no evidence that the delay in payment for one carload made it difficult to provide additional lead. To the contrary, seller admits that throughout the period in controversy he had sufficient lead on hand for the full performance of this contract. He could have delivered had he chosen to do so. His excuse, if any, must be found in reasonable apprehension as to the future of the contract engendered by buyer's behavior.

The substantiality of this alleged apprehension must be judged in the light of the uncontroverted finding that no impairment of buyer's credit had been shown. Moreover, the market was rising and all of the evidence indicates that buyer needed and urgently requested the undelivered lead.

* * *

Throughout the controversial period the seller, with a stock of lead on hand adequate for the full performance of this contract, was using this lead in a rising market for sales to other purchasers at prices higher than agreed in the present contract. The inference was not only allowable but almost inescapable that desire to avoid a bad bargain rather than apprehension that the buyer would not carry out that bargain caused the seller to renounce the agreement and charge the buyer with repudiation. Recission for such cause is not permissible.

JUDGMENT AND REMEDY   *Judgment was for the buyer. The seller was not entitled to rescind the contract, and the buyer was entitled to recover damages caused by the seller's unjustified rescission. (Note that this case was decided before the Uniform Commercial Code was adopted.)*

Repossession of Goods

An unpaid seller does not have any inherent right to repossess goods that are in the possession of a buyer.[2] In modern business practice, however, when goods are sold on an installment basis, a provision allowing the seller to re-possess is ordinarily included in the security agreement. This enables the seller to retake the goods if the buyer defaults in payment. Security agreements will be discussed in Chapters 29 and 30.

REMEDIES OF THE BUYER

Under the Uniform Commercial Code, the remedies available to the buyer include: (1) the

---

2. Except where the buyer is insolvent and the seller reclaims within ten days of delivery.

right to reject nonconforming or improperly delivered goods, (2) the right to revoke acceptance of the goods, (3) the right of *cover*, (4) the right to recover damages for nondelivery or repudiation by the seller, (5) the right to recover damages for breach in regard to accepted goods, (6) the right to recover identified goods upon the seller's insolvency, (7) the right to obtain specific performance, (8) the right to replevy the goods, (9) the right to retain and enforce a security interest in the goods, (10) the right to cancel the contract, and (11) remedies for fraud by the seller.

The Right to Reject Nonconforming or Improperly Delivered Goods

If either the goods or the seller's tender of the goods fail to conform to the contract in any respect, the buyer can reject the goods. If some of the goods conform to the contract, the buyer can keep them and reject the rest. [UCC Sec. 2-601]

TIMELINESS AND REASON FOR REJECTION REQUIRED Goods must be rejected in a reasonable time. Furthermore, the buyer must designate particular defects that are ascertainable by reasonable inspection. Failure to do so precludes the buyer from using an unstated defect to justify rejection or to establish breach when the seller could have cured the defect if it had been stated reasonably. [UCC Sec. 2-605] After rejecting the goods, the buyer cannot exercise any right of ownership over them. If

the buyer acts inconsistently with the seller's ownership rights, the buyer will be deemed to have accepted the goods. [UCC Sec. 2-602]

The Right to Revoke Acceptance

A buyer who accepts goods can later revoke that acceptance, but only under limited circumstances. First, the defect in the goods must *substantially* impair their value to the buyer. Second, if the buyer accepted the goods without knowledge of the nonconformity (because the defect was not discoverable or because the seller assured the buyer that the goods were conforming), the buyer can revoke acceptance. Third, if the buyer accepted the goods knowing of their defect but reasonably believing that the seller would cure the problem, the buyer can revoke acceptance if the seller fails to cure.

In addition, the buyer must notify the seller of the revocation within a reasonable time after the defect is discovered or *should have been discovered*. If proper notice is given, the revocation of acceptance becomes effective, and the buyer need not make an immediate return of the goods. Ultimately, however, the buyer must return the goods to the seller. [UCC Sec. 2-608] (The right of a buyer to revoke acceptance is seldom used because the Code severely restricts buyers from claiming under it.)

Revocation after acceptance must be done within a reasonable time after delivery. Otherwise, failure to reject nonconforming goods will constitute an acceptance. The following case involves a dispute over whether and when a buyer has the right to revoke acceptance.

BACKGROUND AND FACTS *Lanners agreed to purchase a 1955 Beechcraft Bonanza airplane from Whitney, the seller. An F.A.A. mechanic inspected the aircraft and found it to be in airworthy condition. After the plane was delivered, Lanners discovered that it burned oil, overheated, and had abnormally high cylinder pressure. Lanners attempted to repair the aircraft, but then he sought to revoke his acceptance.*

LANNERS v. WHITNEY
Supreme Court of Oregon,
1967.
247 Or. 223, 428 P.2d 398.

REDDING, Justice.

* * *

Failure to reject nonconforming goods within a reasonable time after delivery or tender constitutes an acceptance thereof. Nevertheless, such acceptance may be revoked where the nonconformity of the goods to the contract substantially impairs the value of the goods to the buyer, if the buyer's acceptance was without discovery of the nonconformity and his acceptance was reasonably induced either by the difficulty of discovery before acceptance or by the seller's assurances that the goods conformed to the contract.

[W]e conclude that the unairworthy condition of the airplane materially impaired its value to plaintiff. We further hold that defendant's assurances that the aircraft was airworthy were reasonably relied upon by plaintiff and that he was induced thereby to accept it without first inspecting it to determine whether it in fact conformed to the contract.

[Oregon law] provides that after acceptance of goods, a buyer " * * * must within a reasonable time after he discovers or should have discovered any breach notify the seller of breach or be barred from any remedy * * *." Notice of *any* breach preserves the buyer's remedy of damages if given within a reasonable time after the breach was or should have been discovered. Plaintiff preserved his remedy of damages by notifying defendant on September 7, 1964, that he had encountered unanticipated difficulty with the aircraft and that "it couldn't go on this way." Revocation of acceptance which is involved here, however, is not accomplished by notice of "any" breach, but requires that notice be given of a nonconformity in the goods *materially impairing their value* to the buyer, and must be given within a reasonable time after the buyer discovers or should have discovered *such* nonconformity.

Notice that a party intends to consider a contract at an end or terminated amounts to a revocation of acceptance, and preserves to the plaintiff [certain] remedies, including that of cancellation. We hold that plaintiff's notice of "rescission" to which we have referred, reasonably informed defendant of his intent to terminate the contract and was sufficient to constitute a revocation of acceptance.

We must next determine whether the notice which was otherwise adequate was given within a reasonable time after the nonconformity warranting cancellation was or should have been discovered. What is a reasonable time is a question to be determined on the facts of each case. The authors of the UCC comment that since revocation of acceptance will usually occur only after the buyer has ascertained that adjustments cannot be made, a reasonable time for revocation of acceptance will extend ordinarily beyond the time in which notice of breach must be given.

With respect to the question of reasonable notice, the evidence showed that on September 7, one day after plaintiff returned to Portland from Chicago, plaintiff Lanners notified defendant of the difficulty encountered with the Beechcraft and was in communication with him thereafter about the airplane. One week later, on the 14th of September, inspection of the craft was made for plaintiff Lanners by Bancroft. On the 18th, both Bancroft and Evans inspected it and found it unairworthy. Prior to these inspections conducted at plaintiff's request, he had no certain knowledge of the extent of the nonconformity of the airplane to the contract. Less than three weeks later, plaintiff Lanners, through his attorney, notified defendant of his decision to cancel the contract. Plaintiff was not required to notify the defendant of his intention to revoke his acceptance until he was reasonably certain that the nonconformity substantially impaired the value of the airplane to him. His mere suspicions prior to inspection were not sufficient to require notice. Plaintiff was entitled to and did inspect the aircraft and make attempts to adjust the differences between the parties prior to revoking his acceptance. Considering all the circumstances, we hold the delay of less than three weeks, between September 18, when the unairworthy condition of the Beechcraft became known, and October 6, the date on which notice was given defendant of his intention to rescind, was not an unreasonable delay.

JUDGMENT AND REMEDY

The plaintiff was entitled to cancel the contract and recover as much of the purchase price as he had paid, including the value of a Cessna airplane that he had given to the defendant as a trade-in on part of the purchase price.

Lanners was not required to notify Whitney of his intention to revoke acceptance of the aircraft until Lanners was reasonably certain that the nonconformity substantially impaired the value of the airplane to him. Therefore, the delay of three weeks between the time Lanners discovered the defect and the time he notified Whitney was not unreasonable.

OPPORTUNITY FOR CURE REQUIRED Before a buyer can successfully revoke acceptance of the goods, the seller must be given a reasonable opportunity to cure the defects. Revocation of acceptance can be a hazardous remedy if done unsuccessfully. For example, B traded in his old car and purchased a new car from S. The car developed loud, thumping noises, and B returned it to S. S cured the defect in forty minutes, but B demanded a replacement auto or a refund. B left S's shop and refused to pay for the auto. The auto was repossessed. At trial the court held that B had improperly revoked acceptance and had entered into a valid contract. B's unsuccessful attempt to revoke acceptance lost him both his new car and his old one.[3] Therefore, this remedy should be used with caution.

The Right to Recover for Nondelivery or Repudiation

If a seller repudiates the sales contract or fails to deliver the goods, the buyer can sue for

damages. The measure of recovery is the difference between the contract price and the market price of the goods at the time that the buyer learned of the breach. The market price is determined at the place where the seller was supposed to deliver the goods. In appropriate cases, the buyer can also recover incidental and consequential damages less the expenses that were saved as a result of the seller's breach. [UCC Sec. 2-713] Note that the damages here are based upon the time and place a buyer would normally obtain cover.

THE RIGHT OF COVER In certain situations, buyers can protect themselves by obtaining cover, that is, by substituting goods for those that were due under the sales contract. This option is available to a buyer who has rightfully rejected goods or revoked acceptance. It is also available where the seller repudiates the contract or fails to deliver the goods. In obtaining cover, the buyer must act in good faith and without unreasonable delay. [UCC Sec. 2-712]

After purchasing substitute goods the buyer can recover from the seller the difference between the cost of cover and the contract price.

---

3. Rozmus v. Thompson's Lincoln-Mercury Co., 209 Pa. Super. 120, 224 A.2d 782 (1966).

The buyer can also recover incidental and consequential damages less the expenses that were saved as a result of the seller's breach. [UCC Secs. 2-712 and 2-715]

Consider the following illustration. Jefferson Island Salt Mining Company orders 5 million salt cartons made of a special moisture-proof cardboard from Empire Box Corporation. Empire delivers 1 million of the cartons but refuses to deliver the balance of the order. Jefferson purchases the remaining 4 million cartons in a distant market and sues Empire for the difference between the cover price—the price of purchasing the cartons in a distant market—and the contract price. The court will hold that Jefferson acted in good faith in purchasing the cartons in a distant market only if no close market was available in which it could fulfill its needs.

Buyers are not required to cover, and failure to do so will not bar them from using any other remedies that are available under the Uniform Commercial Code. [UCC Sec. 2-712(3)] But a buyer who fails to cover will not be able to recover the consequential damages that could have been avoided by purchasing substitute goods. [UCC Sec. 2-715(2)(a)] For example, if a wholesaler is supposed to supply a grocer with eggs, and the wholesaler is unable to deliver them, the grocer has the option of covering. If the grocer covers, he or she can recover any lost profits resulting from the wholesaler's breach of the contract. If the grocer does not cover, however, and has no eggs to sell, he or she cannot recover lost profits. The Code's remedies for buyers are designed to encourage them to cover since their recovery will normally be about the same whether they choose to cover or not.

The Right to Recover Damages for Breach in Regard to Accepted Goods

A buyer who has accepted nonconforming goods must notify the seller of the breach within a reasonable time after the defect was or should have been discovered. Otherwise, the buyer cannot complain about defects in the goods. [UCC Sec. 2-607(3)] In addition, the parties to a sales contract can insert a provision requiring the buyer to give notice of any defects in the goods within a certain prescribed period. Such a requirement is ordinarily binding on the parties.

MEASURE OF DAMAGES IF A WARRANTY IS BREACHED When the seller breaches a warranty, the measure of damages equals the difference between the value of the goods as accepted and their value if they had been delivered as warranted. The buyer can recover all damages resulting from the breach of warranty as well as incidental and consequential damages. [UCC Sec. 2-714] If the buyer is entitled to recover damages and the seller is notified, then the buyer can deduct the amount of the damages from the balance due on the sales contract. [UCC Sec. 2-717]

SUIT BY A BUYER'S CUSTOMER RESULTING FROM THE SELLER'S BREACH OF WARRANTY When a buyer resells defective goods that were originally sold by a breaching seller, the buyer's customer can sue the buyer. Under these circumstances the buyer has two alternatives:

1. The buyer can notify the seller of the pending litigation. The notice should state that the seller can come in and defend, and it should also state that the seller will be bound by the buyer's action if the seller does not come in and defend after reasonable receipt of the notice. [UCC Sec. 2-607(5)(a)]
2. The buyer can also defend against the customer's suit and later bring an action against the original seller. This situation arises most frequently where there is a manufacturer-dealer arrangement—for example, where a car dealer sells a defective automobile and the customer sues the dealer but not the manufacturer.

The Right to Recover Identified Goods from an Insolvent Seller

If a buyer pays for goods that remain in the possession of the seller, the buyer can recover the goods if the seller becomes insolvent within ten days after receiving the first payment as long as the goods are identified to the contract. To exercise this right, the buyer must tender to the seller any unpaid balance of the purchase price. [UCC Sec. 2-502]

The Right to Obtain Specific Performance

A buyer can obtain specific performance of a sales contract when the goods are unique or when the buyer's remedy at law is inadequate. [UCC Sec. 2-716(1)] Ordinarily, a suit for money damages will be sufficient to place a buyer in the position he or she would have occupied if the seller had fully performed. However, when the contract is for the purchase of a particular work of art, patent, copyright, or similarly unique item, money damages may not be sufficient. Under these circumstances, the equity side of the court will require the seller to perform exactly (a remedy of specific performance) by delivering the particular goods identified to the contract. To illustrate: Casey contracts to sell an antique car to Smith for $30,000, delivery and payment due on June 14. Smith tenders payment on June 14, but Casey refuses to deliver. Can Smith force delivery of the car? Probably she can because the antique car is unique. Therefore, Smith can obtain specific performance of the contract of the sale from Casey.

The Right to Replevy the Goods

Replevin is similar to specific performance. It is an action to recover specific goods in the hands of a breaching party who is unlawfully withholding them from the other party. The buyer can replevy goods identified to the contract if the seller has repudiated or breached the contract. Additionally, buyers must show that they were unable to cover for the goods after a reasonable effort.

Consider the following example. On July 1, S contracts to sell her tomato crop to B, delivery and payment due on August 10. By August 1, it is clear that the local tomato crop will be bad and that the price of tomatoes is going to rise. S

therefore contracts to sell her tomato crop to X for a higher price and then informs B that she will not deliver on August 10 as agreed. B indicates that cover is unavailable and that he is therefore going to bring a replevin action against S to force her to deliver her tomatoes to B on August 10. This replevin action will succeed. Although a tomato crop is not unique, a buyer of scarce goods for which no cover is available has a right to a replevin. In a normal tomato year, cover would probably have been available. Under such circumstances, B would be limited to an action for damages.

The Right to Retain and Enforce a Security Interest in the Goods

Buyers who rightfully reject goods or who justifiably revoke acceptance of goods that remain in their possession or control have a security interest in the goods. The security interest encompasses any payments the buyer has made for the goods as well as any expenses incurred with regard to inspection, receipt, transportation, care, and custody of the goods. [UCC Sec. 2-711(3)] A buyer with a security interest in the goods is a "person in the position of a seller." This gives the buyer the same rights as an unpaid seller. Thus, the buyer can resell, withhold delivery, or stop delivery of the goods. A buyer who chooses to resell must account to the seller for any amounts received in excess of the security interest. [UCC Secs. 2-711(3) and 2-706]

The Right to Cancel the Contract

When a seller fails to make proper delivery or repudiates the contract, the buyer can cancel or rescind the contract. In addition, a buyer who has rightfully rejected or revoked acceptance of the goods can cancel or rescind. Under these circumstances, the buyer can cancel or rescind that portion of the contract directly involved in the breach. If the seller's breach is material and substantially impairs the value of the whole contract, the buyer can cancel or rescind the whole contract. Upon notice of cancellation, both parties are relieved of any further obligations under the contract. The buyer is entitled to a return of any part of the purchase price that was paid. The cancellation has no effect on the buyer's right to recover for any breach occurring prior to the cancellation. [UCC Sec. 2-711(1)] (Recall the case of Plotnick v. Pennsylvania Smelting earlier in this chapter.)

The right to cancel or rescind a sales contract can be lost or waived if the buyer delays in exercising it. So too, a buyer who refuses to allow the seller to make repairs or one who acts inconsistently with the intent to cancel can lose or waive the right to rescind.

WETTEROW v. WHITE

Supreme Court of Idaho, 1951.
71 Idaho 372, 232 P.2d 973.

BACKGROUND AND FACTS *The plaintiffs (the Wetterows) entered into a contract to purchase a business known as the Kendrick Beer Tavern and Cafe from the defendants (the Whites). The plaintiffs paid part of the purchase price and took possession of the tavern. Shortly thereafter, they learned of certain fraudulent misrepresentations that had been made about the business in the course of the transaction. The plaintiffs filed a lawsuit to rescind the contract against the defendants. However, once the suit was filed, the plaintiffs continued in possession of the property and continued to operate the business. Eventually, nearly eighteen months later, the case came to trial, at the defendants' insistence. Throughout the entire period, the plaintiffs ran the business and did not account to the defendants for any profits or make any further payment on the contract.*

TAYLOR, Justice.
* * *

In other words, although their action was commenced promptly, the plaintiffs apparently made no effort to get the case disposed of on its merits, and appeared by counsel only after a date was fixed for the trial on the petition of the defendants. Yet in their complaint and upon the trial * * * [the plaintiffs] sought *the remedy of rescission, to obtain which the law requires that they act promptly upon the discovery of the grounds therefor, and * * * restore, or offer to restore, to the other party that which * * * [the plaintiffs had] received under the contract.* [Emphasis added.] Instead of making such restoration or in good faith seeking to do so, the plaintiffs remained in possession of the business and continued to operate the same from October, 1948, when they claimed to have discovered the fraud, until July 1, 1950, on which date Wetterow testified he closed the business. But, they were still in possession on the day of the trial. During this period of possession and operation of the business they refused to make any payments upon the contract and made no further offer or attempt to deliver the property or business [back] to the defendants, or to account for any profits derived therefrom. Having thus remained in possession of the property and the business, operating it and treating it as their own during this period of nearly two years, the plaintiffs waived any right they had to rescission of the contract, or to a recovery of the payments made.
* * *

Since the plaintiffs had continued to operate the business but had not accounted for any profits or made any further payment on the contract, the court thought that they had acted inconsistently with their intent to rescind. In order to rescind a contract, possession of the goods must be given to the seller. Therefore, judgment was affirmed for the defendants. They were restored to the property, and the plaintiffs forfeited that part of the purchase price already paid.

JUDGMENT
AND REMEDY

Remedies for Fraud of the Seller

Independent of any remedies provided by the Uniform Commercial Code, the buyer can sue the seller for fraud. This remedy can be asserted even if the buyer is barred from all other remedies under the Code. Since the general principles of law remain in force under the Code, sellers can also be held liable for the fraudulent acts of their agents. This remedy, however, is not always the best solution for an aggrieved buyer, since fraud is generally difficult to prove.

STATUTE OF LIMITATIONS

In the case of breach of a sales contract, a statute of limitations limits the period of time during which an action can be brought. The interval depends upon the type of action, the jurisdiction, and the circumstances of the case.

Actions Brought under the Uniform Commercial Code

An action brought by a buyer or seller for breach of contract must be commenced under the Code *within four years after the cause of action accrues*. A cause of action accrues for breach of warranty when the seller makes tender of delivery. This is the rule even if the aggrieved party is unaware that the cause of action has accrued. [UCC Sec. 2-725(1)] In addition to filing suit within the four-year period, an aggrieved party must ordinarily notify the breaching party of a defect within a reasonable time. [UCC Sec. 2-607(3)(a)]

Future performance warranties (those that take effect in the future) are not breached until the time for performance begins. The statute of limitations also begins to run at that time. For example, B purchases a central air-conditioning unit for her restaurant. The unit is warranted to keep the temperature below a certain level. The unit is installed in the winter, but when summer comes, the restaurant does not stay cool. Therefore, this warranty was breached in the summer and not when the unit was delivered in the winter. The statute of limitations did not begin to run until the summer.

Actions Not Falling within the Uniform Commercial Code

When a buyer or seller brings suit on a legal theory unrelated to the Code, the limitations periods specified above do *not* apply, even though the claim relates to goods. For example, B buys tires for his automobile. The tires prove to have an inherently dangerous defect. Four years and one month after purchasing the tires, B loses control of the car and injures several passengers as well as himself. B can bring a suit against the tire manufacturer based on strict liability in tort. The suit will not be governed by the Code's statute of limitations, but rather by the state's tort statute of limitations.

CONTRACTUAL PROVISIONS AFFECTING REMEDIES

The parties to a sales contract can vary their respective rights and obligations by contractual agreement. Certain limitations are placed upon the ability of parties to contract around the requirements of the UCC, but the common provisions include: (1) the liquidation or limitation of damages, (2) the limitation of remedies, and (3) the waiver of defenses.

Liquidated Damages and Limitation of Damages

The parties to a sales contract can provide that a specified amount of damages will be paid in the event that either party breaches. These damages, called **liquidated damages,** must be reasonable in amount and approximately equal to the anticipated or actual loss caused by the breach. If the provision is valid, the aggrieved party is limited to recovering only that amount of damages. If the amount of liquidated damages is unreasonably large, the provision is void as a penalty. [UCC Sec. 2-718]

Consider as an example the sale of a car. S contracts with B to sell a car for $8,000. The contract contains a liquidated damages clause that holds the breaching party liable for $5,000 in case of a breach by either party. Payment and delivery of the car are due on January 1. B tenders payment on that date, but S refuses to deliver for no valid reason. Can B demand $5,000 in damages? If the car is an antique, B will probably be able to recover. S's breach might cause B a loss of $5,000. If the car can easily be acquired on the open market, B will probably not be able to recover $5,000. The normal measure of damages will be the market price of the car less the contract price. The liquidated damages clause would in essence be imposing a penalty upon S and therefore would be void. [UCC Sec. 2-718(1)]

A buyer often makes a down payment when a contract is executed. If the buyer defaults and the contract contains a liquidated damages provision, the buyer can recover only the amount by which the down payment exceeded the amount that was specified as liquidated damages. The buyer is entitled to this sum as restitution. If the contract contains no provision for liquidated damages, the seller's damages are deemed to be 20 percent of the purchase price or $500, whichever is less. [UCC Sec. 2-718(2)(b)] The amount by which the buyer's down payment exceeded this sum must be returned to the buyer. If the seller can prove that his or her actual damages are higher, the buyer can recover only the excess over the seller's actual damages.

For example, B pays $1,250 down on a $10,000 lathe. B then breaches, and S offers no proof of the actual damages. In the absence of a liquidated damages clause, B is entitled to restitution of $750 ($1,250 less $500). If B had put $350 down on a $500 lathe, she would be entitled to $250 ($350 less $100, which is 20 percent of the purchase price).

Limitation of Remedies

A seller and a buyer can expressly provide for remedies in addition to those provided in the Code. They can also provide remedies in lieu of those provided in the Code, or they can change the measure of damages. The seller can provide that the buyer's only remedy upon breach of warranty will be repair or replacement of the item, or the seller can limit the buyer's remedy to return of the goods and refund of the purchase price. A remedy that is so provided is in addition to remedies provided in the Code unless the parties expressly agree that the remedy is exclusive of all others.

If the parties state that a remedy is exclusive of all other remedies, then it is the sole remedy. [UCC Sec. 2-719(1)] But when circumstances cause an exclusive remedy to fail of its essential purpose, the remedy will no longer be exclusive. [UCC Sec. 2-719(2)] For example, a sales contract that limits the buyer's remedy to repair or replacement fails of its essential purpose if the item cannot be repaired and no replacements are available. This situation is illustrated in the next case.

STEELE v. J. I. CASE CO.

Supreme Court of Kansas, 1966.
197 Kan. 554, 419 P.2d 902.

BACKGROUND AND FACTS   *This action was brought to recover crop damage that resulted from a breach of an express warranty given on the purchase of three new farm combines. The plaintiff-buyer, Dale Steele, was a western Kansas farmer who owned and operated a large wheat and* *barley farm. The defendant-seller was the J. I. Case Company, a corporation engaged in the manufacture, distribution, and servicing of farm machinery.*

Steele took delivery of three new combine machines in June 1960. The purchase order contract was a standard printed form furnished by Case. On the reverse side, it contained a printed warranty with various provisions. First, Case warranted the quality of its product. Second, Case warranted that if the machine should contain a defect, the company "would see to it that the defect was remedied." Third, if the defect could not be remedied, Case had the option to replace the machine or refund the purchase price, but "no further claim shall be made." (Emphasis added.) Finally, Case attempted to exclude all other express, implied, or statutory warranties by adding the following limitation on damages in the event of breach:

The Company's liability for any breach of this warranty is limited to the return of cash and/or notes actually received by it on account of the purchase price of said product or part.

The machines delivered in June 1960 were to be used for the harvest that began shortly thereafter. From the beginning, the combines failed to work properly, and the numerous mechanical defects that they developed resulted in the loss of a disproportionate amount of grain. Steele made several complaints, and Case dispatched various employees and representatives in an effort to correct the defects. Case's frequent attempts to repair the combines failed. Throughout the thirty days during which Case attempted to repair the machines, Case representatives insisted that the machines could be made to work. The company categorically refused Steele's several demands for a return of his purchase price.

Steele and Case had several conferences concerning the problems that had arisen from the faulty machines. Because of the many delays and the faulty performance of the combines, Steele's crops were harvested some ten to fourteen days later than normal, and they were materially damaged by adverse weather conditions. As a result, the present action was instituted to recover the consequential damages resulting from the delays.

Case ultimately agreed to supply Steele with new combines, but not until the following year.

FONTRON, Justice.

* * *

[T]he new machines were not to be delivered until on or about *June 1, 1961,* or as soon thereafter as they could be furnished. Certainly a replacement in kind on *that* date was not contemplated by Mr. Steele when he purchased the combines for use in the 1960 harvest. His 1960 crops had to be harvested in 1960—not 1961. It is well known by those who live or do business on the High Plains that wheat must be cut when it matures, lest it fall victim to storms and other vagaries of nature which often cause havoc. Delays can, indeed, prove disastrous; stands of ripened grain can be ruined and farmers wiped out in a matter of minutes.

The provisions of [the warranty] * * * which gave Case an option, after failing to remedy defects, either to furnish other machines or to return the purchase money and which forbade further claims, are to be construed in the setting under which the machines were purchased. Case representatives who were involved in the sale of the combines to Steele either were at the time or had been connected with the company dealership at Dodge City, in the heart of the wheat belt, and must have been fully as cognizant of the hazards of wheat farming, as was the plaintiff himself. The company, as well as Steele, knew the machines were to be used in the 1960 harvest and both parties must have been equally aware of the damage which might well be sustained by Steele if the combines proved defective and occasioned delays in the harvesting of his grain crops.

The seller of a piece of machinery would be wrong to suppose that he could fully fulfill a warranty * * * by first taking an inordinately long time in an effort to remedy the defect and then, failing in his attempt, by furnishing a substitute machine a year after special damages had accrued. We believe such is not the law.

In Allen v. Brown, 181 Kan. 301, 310 P.2d 923, this court was confronted by a somewhat comparable situation, and we there said:

"Where, as in this case, the express warranty contemplates that the seller's liability for a breach of warranty does not attach until he has had an opportunity to remedy the defects, his failure or refusal to act, where such opportunity is afforded the seller, fixes his liability. Under these circumstances the following is quoted from 77 C.J.S. Sales §340, p. 1235:

" ' * * * An unsuccessful effort to remedy the defects renders the seller liable on his warranty; and the buyer is not bound to allow him a second opportunity, or to permit him to tinker with the article indefinitely in the hope that it may ultimately be made to comply with the warranty. * * *' " (p. 308, 310 P.2d p. 928.) [Emphasis added.]

* * *

[Thus, the court held that Case's failure to repair the combines constituted a breach of the warranty of quality. The court went on to decide whether the remedy limitation included in another provision of the warranty would operate to prevent the award of consequential and special damages growing out of the breach.]

We deem the rule to be well settled in this jurisdiction, as well as in a majority of others, that in the absence of valid provisions limiting the extent of a vendor's liability upon its warranty, special or consequential damages may be recovered where they proximately result from a breach of warranty and may reasonably be regarded as having been within the contemplation of the contracting parties. [Emphasis added.]

The general rule in this regard is stated in 77 C.J.S. Sales §374 b, pp. 1318, 1319:

"Where there are special circumstances, the buyer is entitled to recover any special or consequential damages he has suffered, which are the natural and direct result of the breach of warranty, and which are the proximate result of the breach of warranty, and which may reasonably be considered as within the contemplation of the parties at the time of the contract as the result of a breach."

However, the question presented in *this action is whether the limitation contained * * * [under the warranty] precludes recovery of consequential damages of the character shown here, damages which, we hasten to add, we think must be within the contemplation of every person dealing in harvesting equipment who is familiar with the exacting demands of a Kansas harvest.* [Emphasis added.]

In this case, also, the seller knew the combines were purchased for use in the 1960 harvest and must be deemed to have known, through its representatives, the urgency of harvest on the High Plains and the dangers consequent upon any stoppage in operations after the grain has ripened and is ready to cut. And in this case, despite such knowledge, the seller wasted thirty crucial days in attempting to remedy defects and to get the machines working, refusing during this critical time either to replace the machines with others which would operate or to repay the purchase price, even though such was demanded.

Under the conditions outlined, we conclude that it would be unfair and inequitable to give effect to the provisions of limitation encompassed in * * * the warranty.

The court affirmed the rights of the buyer, Steele. Steele was permitted to recover consequential and special damages for his lost crops. After all, Case knew how urgent it was to harvest the wheat and barley crops after the grain ripened. Despite this knowledge, Case wasted thirty days attempting to repair the combines.

JUDGMENT AND REMEDY

LIMITING CONSEQUENTIAL DAMAGES A contract can limit or exclude consequential damages provided the limitation is not unconscionable. When the buyer is a consumer, the limitation of consequential damages for personal injuries resulting from a breach of warranty is *prima facie* unconscionable. The limitation of consequential damages is not necessarily unconscionable where the loss is commercial in nature—for example, lost profits and property damage.

Waiver of Defenses

A buyer can be precluded from objecting to a breach of warranty by a seller in certain situations. For example, when a buyer purchases on credit, the seller usually assigns the note or account to a financial institution in order to obtain ready cash. In order to facilitate the assignment of these notes or accounts, the seller will include a waiver of defense clause in the sales contract. By entering into the contract, the buyer agrees not to assert against the assignee defenses that may apply to the seller. In essence, the buyer must complain directly to the seller, and the buyer cannot withhold payment for breach of warranty. If the financial institution is a holder in due course of the buyer's note, no defenses can be asserted against the institution even if the contract contains no waiver of defense clause. In such a case buyers are in the same position they would be in if they had signed a waiver.

QUESTIONS AND CASE PROBLEMS

1. As a result of inquiries by Sumitomo, a steel manufacturer, Goodson supplied Sumitomo with a written statement of its solvency on February 7, 1968. On February 25, 1968, Goodson and Sumitomo entered into a contract for the sale of steel to be shipped from Japan. Goodson received the steel on June 24, 1968, about two months after Sumitomo had shipped it. On July 30, 1968, Sumitomo learned that Goodson was insolvent and had been insolvent for the entire month of February 1968. The same day, Sumitomo attempted to reclaim the steel from Goodson's trustee in bankruptcy. Will Sumitomo succeed? In the matter of Goodson Steel Corp., (citation omitted) (S.D. Tex. 1968).

2. Portal Gallaries, Inc., entered into a contract with Tomar Products to sell Tomar certain paintings. Pursuant to the contract, Portal delivered some of the paintings, worth $23,000, and Tomar made a partial payment for them. Portal withheld shipment of the remaining paintings until Tomar tendered the balance of the original payment. However, Tomar decided that it did not wish to purchase any more paintings and notified Portal of its desire to cancel the contract. After receiving notice of the cancellation, Portal resold the paintings at a public auction but did not notify Tomar of the resale. Portal then claimed that Tomar owed it the balance due for the original shipment of paintings as well as the difference between the contract price and the price that the remaining paintings brought at auction. What damages is the court likely to award Portal Gallaries? [Portal Gallaries, Inc. v. Tomar Products, Inc., 60 Misc.2d 523, 302 N.Y.S.2d 871 (1969)]

3. Jagger Brothers and Technical Textile Company entered into a contract for the purchase and sale of 20,000 pounds of yarn at $2.15 per pound. Delivery was to be made in a number of shipments and was to be completed by December 31, 1960. On August 12, 1960, the buyer, Technical Textile, repudiated the contract. On that date the market price for yarn was $2.35 per pound. Jagger Brothers immediately brought suit, but the case did not come to trial until nearly two years later. At the time of trial, the price of yarn was $2.80 per pound. Jagger Brothers had not manufactured any of the yarn at the time Technical Textile repudiated the contract. Therefore, Jagger Brothers claimed that Technical Textile owed it the difference between the contract price ($2.15 per pound) and the market price for yarn at the time of trial ($2.80 per pound). Technical Textile argued that it was liable only for the difference between the contract and the market price at the time and place of repudiation ($2.35 per pound). Who is correct? [Jagger Brothers, Inc. v. Technical Textile Co., 202 Pa. Super. 639, 198 A.2d. 888 (1964)]

4. Beco, Inc., entered into a contract with Minnechaug Golf Course to supply Minnechaug with certain restaurant equipment. Beco delivered the restaurant equipment to Minnechaug on June 24, 1966. After using it for two months, Minnechaug attempted to return the equipment, making a vague claim that it did not work properly. Beco repeatedly offered to cure any defects, and Minnechaug refused to accept any cure. Beco then demanded payment for the equipment, and Minnechaug refused. At trial, the issue arose as to whether damages should be based upon the difference between contract price and market price at the time and place of tender or whether Minnechaug should pay the purchase price. What is the proper measure here? [Beco, Inc. v. Minnechaug Golf Course, Inc., 5 Conn. Cir. 444, 256 A.2d. 522 (1968)]

5. Westmoreland Metal Manufacturing Company made school furniture. In 1955, Willred Company entered into a contract with Westmoreland to be the latter's exclusive distributor of school furniture in the metropolitan New York area. Under this contract, Westmoreland made a number of shipments of furniture to Willred, which Willred resold to the New York Board of Education. The distributorship contract between Willred and Westmoreland was to end in December 1957, but Westmoreland, without legal justification, terminated the contract in February 1956. Just before Westmoreland breached the contract, it made a large shipment of furniture to Willred that amounted to about half the furniture that Willred had just ordered from Westmoreland. Much of the furniture was shipped in damaged condition, requiring Willred to repair it extensively before it could be resold. In addition, Willred was forced to purchase a large quantity of school furniture on the open market to satisfy a current contract with the New York Board of Education. Finally, Willred had to rent a small amount of furniture in order to satisfy its contractual obligations to the New York Board of Education. Which of these expenditures, if any, can Willred recoup from Westmoreland? [Willred Co. v.

Westmoreland Metal Mfg. Co., 200 F. Supp. 59 (E.D. Pa. 1961)]

6. Phillips, who was in the market for a new car, visited Union Motors, Inc., a local Dodge dealer. When Phillips saw some of the prices that the new cars were going for, he approached one of the salespersons and stated, "That's too darn much to spend on a new car. You got anything any cheaper?" Thereupon the salesperson showed Phillips what appeared to be a slightly used 1966 Dodge and stated that the car was a "demonstrator with 2,000 miles on it, that it was like a brand new one, and that it had been handled with kid gloves." Relying on this statement, Phillips purchased the car, but later he learned that the car had been in a bad accident and had been poorly repaired. Has there been any breach here? If so, what would be the proper measure of damages? [Union Motors, Inc. v. Phillips, 241 Ark. 857, 410 S.W.2d. 747 (1967)]

7. Lehigh Valley Mills, a producer of various types of seeds, sold several hundred pounds of grass seed to Ertag, Inc., a distributor to retail outlets and retail customers. Ertag sued Lehigh for breach of warranty, claiming that the grass seed was several years old and therefore would not germinate as warranted. Ertag proved at trial that a number of its customers were municipal golf courses. They had already done their spring planting, and they learned of the breach at a time that caused them to lose several weeks of business. While none of these golf courses had yet brought suit against Ertag, Ertag claimed as damages against Lehigh the projected losses that would result from suits that might be brought by its customers. If the court is convinced that such lawsuits against Ertag are imminent, should it allow Ertag to recover against Lehigh for these damages? [Ertag, Inc. v. Lehigh Valley Mills, Inc., 29 Leh.L.J. 487 (Pa.1962)]

8. Erdman purchased a color television set from Johnson Brothers Radio and TV Company and experienced difficulties with it from the start. Erdman immediately called Johnson, and Johnson sent two repairmen to attempt to fix the set. Johnson's repairmen were unsuccessful on the first trip and on approximately twenty subsequent trips. Erdman continued to use the set during the four weeks that Johnson attempted to repair it. After it had been on for two hours one evening, the set began to smoke and spark. At first, Erdman ignored the smoke and sparks but later left the room to call Johnson again. While he was making the call, a fire began behind the TV set and subsequently destroyed his house. Erdman sued Johnson for breach of warranty of merchantability, claiming as consequential damages the destruction of his house. Can Erdman recover? [Erdman v. Johnson Brothers Radio and TV Co., Inc., 260 Md. 190, 271 A.2d 744 (1970)]

9. In a contract between Associated Metals and Minerals Corp. and Kaiser Trading Company, Associated promised to deliver to Kaiser 4,000 tons of cryolite over the next sixteen months. After Associated had delivered about one-eighth of the cryolite to Kaiser, it repudiated the contract. Kaiser sought to enforce the contract and requested the court to grant it specific performance against Associated. Kaiser presented convincing proof at trial that only a few hundred tons of cryolite were available on the open market and that Kaiser needed the 4,000 tons that Associated had promised to deliver in order for Kaiser to fulfill its contractual obligations to a number of other industrial companies. Should the court grant specific performance in this case? [Kaiser Trading Co. v. Associated Metals and Minerals Corp., 321 F. Supp. 923 (N.D. Cal. 1970)]

10. Denkin manufactured refrigeration equipment. Sterner entered into a contract with Denkin to purchase refrigeration equipment that was needed for a new grocery store. The contract included a clause allowing Denkin to retake all the goods that it had delivered to Sterner and to recover the entire price if Sterner breached the contract. Sterner signed the contract but later found that a number of other manufacturers could supply refrigeration equipment at far lower prices than Denkin. In a suit by Denkin against Sterner, can Denkin enforce the liquidated damages provisions stated above? [Denkin v. Sterner, 10 D.&C.2d. 203 (Pa. 1956)]

23

Commercial Paper

Basic Concepts of
Commercial Paper

Commercial paper can be defined as any written promise or order to pay a sum of money. Drafts, checks, and promissory notes are typical examples. Commercial paper is transferred more readily than ordinary contract rights, and persons who acquire it are normally subject to less risk than the ordinary assignee of a contract right.

FUNCTIONS AND PURPOSES
OF COMMERCIAL PAPER

Commercial paper has two basic functions. It is a substitute for money, and it is a credit device.

A Substitute for Money

Commercial paper is used when a debt is paid by check. Debtors can use cash, but for convenience and safety, they use commercial paper. The substitute for money function of commercial paper developed in the Middle Ages. Merchants began to deposit their precious metal with bankers to avoid the dangers of loss or theft. When they needed funds to pay for the goods that they were buying, they gave the seller a written order addressed to the bank. This authorized the bank to deliver part of the precious metal to the seller. These orders were called *bills of exchange* and were sometimes used as a substitute for money. Today people use mainly checks, but they also use drafts and promissory notes that are payable either on demand or at some specified date in the future. That some commercial paper is a substitute for money is further indicated by the fact that the Federal Reserve's official definition of what is called the "narrow" money supply (M_1) is currency (dollar bills and coins) in the hands of the public and demand deposits (that is, checking account balances).

A Credit Device

Commercial paper creates credit. When a buyer gives a seller a promissory note by which the buyer agrees to pay in sixty days, the seller has essentially extended sixty days credit to the buyer. The credit aspect of commercial paper was also developed in the Middle Ages soon after bills of exchange began to be used as substitutes for money. Merchants were able to give to sellers bills of exchange that were not payable until a future date. Since the seller would wait until a maturity date to collect, this was a form of extending credit to the buyer.

DISCOUNTING   The holder of a promissory note payable in sixty or ninety days who wishes to sell this instrument to a third party can do so for immediate cash in return. Typically, banks buy these instruments and wait until their maturity date to receive payment. In order to induce a bank to buy a promissory note, the holder of the instrument accepts a discount of, say, 5, 10, or 15 percent of the face amount. In effect, the bank pays less than the amount it will eventually collect as a way of charging interest.

The Law of Commercial Paper

Some historians believe that promissory notes were used more than two thousand years ago. In any event, by the thirteenth century, bills of exchange were used extensively, particularly in conducting foreign trade. In the earlier Middle Ages, English courts were not empowered to enforce commercial agreements. Therefore, merchants created their own methods for en-

forcing rights. Part of these methods were a form of the Law Merchant, discussed in Chapter 1.

By the eighteenth and nineteenth centuries, English and American courts recognized Law Merchant principles relating to commercial paper. In England in 1882, a Bills of Exchange Act that codified the common law on the subject was passed. In 1896, the Uniform Negotiable Instruments Law (NIL) was presented by the American Bar Association to the states, and all of them passed it eventually. Article 3 of the Uniform Commercial Code superseded the Uniform Negotiable Instruments Law. Every state has enacted Article 3, which is quite similar to the Uniform Negotiable Instruments Law.

TYPES OF COMMERCIAL PAPER

Section 3-104 of the Uniform Commercial Code specifies four types of instruments—drafts, checks, certificates of deposit, and notes.

Drafts

A draft, negotiable draft, or bill of exchange is an unconditional written order. The party creating it (the *drawer*) orders another party (the *drawee*) to pay money to a third (the *payee*). Exhibit 23-1 shows a typical draft (bill of exchange). The drawee must be obligated to the drawer either by agreement or through a debt relationship before acceptance can occur. (Acceptance occurs when the drawee signs the draft agreeing to honor it as presented.)

TIME AND SIGHT DRAFTS   A time draft is a draft which is payable at a future time. A sight draft is payable on sight, that is, when the holder presents it for payment, or at a stated time after sight.

TRADE ACCEPTANCES   The **trade acceptance** is a time draft that is ordinarily used in the sale of goods. The seller is both drawer and payee on this draft. Essentially, the draft orders the buyer to pay a specified sum of money to the seller at a stated time in the future. To illustrate: Good Yard Company sells $50,000 of fabric to Lane Dresses, Incorporated, each fall on terms requiring payment to be made in ninety days. One year Good Yard needs cash, so it draws a *trade acceptance* that orders Lane to pay $50,000 to the order of Good Yard Company ninety days hence. Good Yard presents the paper to Lane. Lane *accepts* by signing the face of the paper and returns it to Good Yard. Lane's acceptance creates an enforceable promise to pay the installment when it comes due in ninety days. Good Yard can sell the trade acceptance in the commercial money market more easily than it can assign the $50,000 account receivable. Thus, trade acceptances are the standard credit instruments in sales transactions. Exhibit 23-2 shows a trade acceptance.

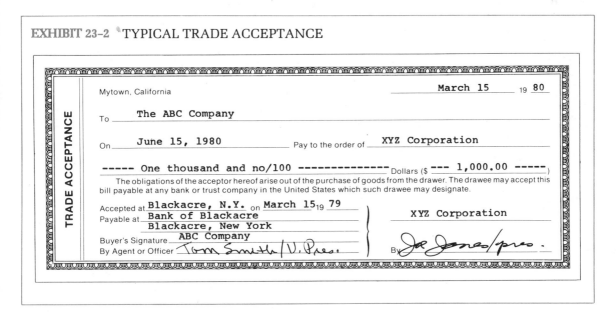

EXHIBIT 23-1   TYPICAL BILL OF EXCHANGE

F 501

Saint Paul, Minn. __January 16__ 19 80 $ 1,000.00 ------

__Ninety days after above date__ ------------ PAY TO THE ORDER OF **The First National Bank** 22-1
OF SAINT PAUL, MINNESOTA

------- One thousand and no/100 --- Dollars

VALUE RECEIVED AND CHARGE THE SAME TO ACCOUNT OF

To __Bank of Warren__   ~~CANCELLED~~
__Warren, Michigan__   Stephen L. Eastman

EXHIBIT 23-2   TYPICAL TRADE ACCEPTANCE

TRADE ACCEPTANCE

Mytown, California   __March 15__   19 __80__

To __The ABC Company__

On __June 15, 1980__   Pay to the order of __XYZ Corporation__

----- One thousand and no/100 -------------- Dollars ($ --- 1,000.00 -----)

The obligations of the acceptor hereof arise out of the purchase of goods from the drawer. The drawee may accept this bill payable at any bank or trust company in the United States which such drawee may designate.

Accepted at __Blackacre, N.Y.__ on __March 15__ 19 79
Payable at __Bank of Blackacre__   __XYZ Corporation__
__Blackacre, New York__
Buyer's Signature __ABC Company__
By Agent or Officer __Tom Smith/V. Pres.__   By __Joe Jones/pres.__

BANK DRAFTS   A bank draft is an instrument drawn by one bank upon another bank. Clearly, the first bank must have money on deposit with the drawee bank. The bank draft is often used for the same purpose as a cashier's check.

Checks

A **check** is a distinct type of draft, drawn on a bank and payable on demand. Checks are discussed more fully in Chapter 28. Note here, however, that on certain types of checks, the bank is both the drawer and the drawee. For example, cashier's checks drawn by the bank on itself are payable on demand when issued. Traveler's checks are drawn on the bank or on a financial institution, but they require the payee's authorized signature before becoming payable.

Promissory Notes

The **note** is the simplest form of commercial paper. It is a promise between two parties in which one person (the maker) promises to pay a sum of money to another person (the payee). Notes can be payable at a definite time or on demand. Note paper can name a payee or merely be payable to bearer. Whenever there are only two parties to the note it is commonly called a **promissory note.**

Notes are used to extend credit in business in many ways. For example, in real estate transactions, a buyer executes a promissory note for the unpaid balance on a house, secured by a mortgage on the property being purchased. This is called a *mortgage note*. A note which is secured by personal property is called a *collateral note*. A sample promissory note is shown in Exhibit 23-3.

Certificates of Deposit

A certificate of deposit is an acknowledgment by a bank of receipt of money with an engagement to repay it. [UCC Sec. 3-104(2)(c)] Certificates of deposit in small denominations are often sold by savings and loan associations, savings banks, and commercial banks. They are called small CDs and are for amounts up to $100,000. Certificates of deposit for amounts over $100,000 are called large CDs.[1] Exhibit 23-4 shows a typical small CD.

OTHER WAYS OF CLASSIFYING COMMERCIAL PAPER

The four-way classification of commercial paper presented above follows the language of the Uniform Commercial Code. There are numerous other ways in which to classify commercial paper, two of which are treated here.

Demand Instruments and Time Instruments

Commercial paper can be classified as demand instruments or as time instruments. A demand instrument is payable on demand, that is, whenever the holder—a possessor *to whom the instrument runs*—chooses to present it to the maker in the case of a note or the drawee in the case of a draft. (Instruments payable on demand include those payable on sight or on presentation, and in which no time for payment is stated.) [UCC Sec. 3-108] Time instruments are payable at a future date. All checks are demand instruments because, by definition, they must be payable on demand. Checking accounts are called demand deposits.

Orders to Pay and Promises to Pay

Commercial paper can be promises to pay or orders to pay. Every instrument involving the payment of money is one or the other. Promises to pay are typically classified as notes; orders to pay are typically classified as drafts. Under this classification, a check is a draft or order to pay.

---

1.   Large CDs are included in certain definitions of the money supply because they are fully negotiable and because the interest they pay is not regulated by the Federal Reserve. Large CDs may, however, be subject to regulation by the state banking authority of the state in which they are issued.

A certificate of deposit and a promissory note are, on the other hand, promises to pay.

PARTIES TO COMMERCIAL PAPER

To review, notes have two original parties—the maker and the payee, and drafts or checks have three original parties—the drawer, the drawee, and the payee. Sometimes two of the parties to a draft can be the same person (drawer/drawee; drawer/payee). Once an instrument is issued, additional parties can become involved. The following sections describe the various parties to commercial paper after the instrument has been issued.

EXHIBIT 23–3 TYPICAL PROMISSORY NOTE

☐ OTHER ☐ SAVINGS 2. CONSUMER GOODS 3. EQUIP. ☐ INSURANCE ☑ SECURITIES ☐ SEC. AGREEMENT 1. INV. & ACCTS.

$ ---3,000.00 ---- Saint Paul, Minnesota April 30, 19 80 Due 6/20/80

-------- Sixty days -------------------------------------- after date,

for value received, the undersigned jointly and severally promise to pay to the order of **THE FIRST NATIONAL BANK OF SAINT PAUL** at its office in Saint Paul, Minnesota, $ --- Three Thousand and no/100 Dollars

with interest thereon from date hereof at the rate of - 15 - per cent per annum (computed on the basis of actual days and a year of 360 days) as indicated in No. 7 below.

[7] INTEREST IS PAYABLE AT MATURITY
[8] INTEREST IS PAID TO MATURITY
[9] INTEREST IS PAYABLE ______ BEGINNING ON ______
☐ ______

CANCELLED

The holder of this note may at its option without notice declare this note immediate[illegible] the entire [illegible] principal hereof plus accrued interest hereon upon or at any time after the occurrence of any of the following events: any default in the payment of this note; any default unde[illegible] security agreement or other note, obligation, instrument, undertaking or agreement concurrently herewith or heretofore or hereafter given to or acquired and held by the holder hereof to which [illegible] indorser, surety or guarantor hereof is a party; if the holder hereof deems itself insecure; or if there is such a change in the condition or affairs, financial or otherwise, of any maker, co-maker, [illegible] guarantor hereof as in the opinion of the holder hereof increases the risk.

Each maker, co-maker, indorser, surety and guarantor hereof jointly and severally agre[illegible] note and guarantees payment hereof and waives demand, presentment, protest and notice of dishonor, and consents to any extensions and renewals hereof without notice, and consents to the release by [illegible] holder hereof with or without consideration of any of them, and exonerates the holder hereof from all duty and obligation to make demand on anyone for payment of any collateral now or hereafter securing this note or to give notice to anyone of non-payment thereof or to collect or sell the same and consents to the extension, renewal, exchange, surrender or release by the holder hereof with or without consideration of any such collateral, and agrees that when or at any time after this note becomes due the holder hereof may without notice offset or charge this note against any bank account or other account then maintained by any of them with the holder hereof or then existing between any of them and the holder hereof and to pay any deficiency, and agrees in case of any default to pay all costs of collection, including reasonable attorneys' fees and the maximum interest or late charges permitted by law. The note shall be deemed a contract made under, and this note and the rights, obligations and duties of the parties hereto shall be governed by, the laws of the State of Minnesota.

SIGNATURE Lawrence E. Roberts SIGNATURE Margaret P. Roberts

SIGNATURE ______ SIGNATURE ______

32-364 (8-71)

NO. 096-85-710
OFFICER Clark
BY RM
ACCRUAL /
☑ NEW ☐ REN'L
☑ SECURED
☐ UNSECURED

EXHIBIT 23–4 TYPICAL SMALL CD

THE FIRST NATIONAL BANK OF SAINT PAUL 22-1/960 Number 3999
NEGOTIABLE CERTIFICATE OF DEPOSIT

SAINT PAUL, MINNESOTA, February 15, 19 80

THIS CERTIFIES to the deposit in this Bank of the sum of $ 5,000.00 -------

----- Five thousand and no/100 ---------------------------------- DOLLARS

which is payable to bearer on the 15th day of July, 19 80, against presentation and surrender of this certificate, and bears interest at the rate of 7 3/4 % per annum, to be computed (on the basis of 360 days and actual days elapsed) to, and payable at, maturity. No payment may be made prior to, and no interest runs after, that date. Payable at maturity in federal funds, and if desired, at Manufacturers Hanover Trust Company, New York.

THE FIRST NATIONAL BANK OF SAINT PAUL

BY [signature] CANCELLED [illegible] SIGNATURE

54-610

Indorsers

The payee of a note or draft can transfer it by signing (indorsing) it and delivering it to another person. By doing this, the payee becomes an indorser. For example, Carol receives a graduation check for $25. She can transfer the check to her mother (or anyone) by signing it on the back. Carol is an indorser.

Indorsees

The person who receives the indorsed instrument is the indorsee. In the example above, Carol's mother is the indorsee. She is entitled to the $25 payment by virtue of Carol's indorsement, and she can indorse the check to someone else or to a bank and thus become an indorser as well.

Holders

The term **holder** includes any person in possession of an instrument that runs to him or her, for example, named payees in possession of order instruments.[2] To illustrate: A check made to the order of John Doe in his possession makes John Doe a holder. So, too, if a promissory note written by Sam Smith promising to pay a sum of money to the order of Tom Jones, is in Jones's possession, then Jones is a holder. If Jones signs the back of the note and transfers (negotiates) it to Adam White, the note becomes bearer paper, and White becomes the holder.

The holder and the owner of negotiable paper can often be the same person, but not necessarily. For example, a thief who steals a bearer instrument is a *holder* under commercial law principles (but obviously the thief is not the owner). Nonetheless, the thief can legally transfer (negotiate) the bearer instrument to another person, who then becomes a *holder*.

HOLDER IN DUE COURSE Under UCC Sec. 3-302, a holder in due course (HDC) is a person who acquires an instrument for value in a good faith transaction without knowing it is defective. It is easier for an HDC to collect payment on an instrument than it is for an assignee of a nonnegotiable contract to collect payment. The assignee is subject to all outstanding defenses of prior parties; the HDC is protected from all but a few defenses.[3]

HOLDER THROUGH A HOLDER IN DUE COURSE An ordinary holder whose manner of acquisition fails to meet the requirements of a holder in due course can still be afforded HDC protection by proving that any prior holder qualified as a holder in due course. [UCC Sec. 3-201(1)]

Makers

A **maker** is the person who issues a promissory note in which he or she promises to pay a certain sum of money to a payee. The maker's signature must appear on the face of the promissory note for the maker to be liable on the note.

Drawers and Drawees

When a check or other draft is issued, the person who issues it, known as the **drawer,** orders the **drawee** (who is a bank in the case of a check) to pay a certain sum of money to a payee (or to the bearer of the instrument). To illustrate: Acme purchases 2,000 ball bearings from J & L Co. Acme issues a draft (at about the same time it ships the ball bearings) ordering J & L Co. to pay $600 in payment of the goods. When J & L receives the draft, it acknowledges its obligation to pay by signing the draft. The draft was made payable to "Acme Co. or its order." Thus, Acme is the *drawer* and *payee* of the draft and J & L Co. is the *drawee*.

---

2. UCC Sec. 1-201(17) defines *holder* as "a person who is in possession of a document of title or an instrument or an investment security drawn, issued, or indorsed to him or to his order or to bearer or in blank."

3. The HDC is subject to real defenses. These generally involve the validity of the instrument, for example, legal capacity or fraud. [UCC Sec. 3-305] An HDC is free from all personal defenses between prior parties, for example, breach of contract.

QUESTIONS AND CASE PROBLEMS

1. Adam Smith, a college student, wished to purchase a new component stereo system from John Locke Stereo, Inc. Since Smith did not have the cash to pay for the entire stereo system, he offered to sign a note promising to pay $150 per month for the next six months. Locke Stereo, anxious to sell the system to Smith, agreed to accept the promissory note as long as Smith had one of his professors sign it. Smith did this and tendered a note to John Locke Stereo that stated, "I, Adam Smith, promise to pay John Locke Stereo or its order the sum of $150 per month for the next six months." The note was signed by Adam Smith and his business law professor. About a week later, John Locke Stereo, which was badly in need of cash, signed the back of the note and sold it to Fidelity Bank. How are each of the four parties designated in commercial paper parlance?

2. Larson and Adkins were partners in a law firm. Larson had just won a case for her client, Brown, against Bill Bucks. When Larson went to collect the judgment from Bucks, Bucks wrote out a check that read: "Pay to the order of Larson and Adkins $6,000,000. Signed Bill Bucks." On the top of the check were the words "Hanover Trust." When Larson went to deposit the check in the trust account that she had set up for her client, she signed the back of the check "L. Larson." How are each of these parties designated in commercial paper law?

3. Negotiable instruments play an important part in commercial transactions. Different needs can be fulfilled by using different types of instruments in certain ways. For instance, many insurance companies use a form of draft instead of a check to remit insurance benefits. The insurance company is both the drawer and the drawee; the beneficiary (the person receiving the money) is the payee; and the draft is made payable through a named bank in which the insurance company maintains a large account. What are the advantages of using such a draft?

4. Often when two parties to a sale are strangers to each other, and the sale is for a substantial amount of money, the selling party will insist that the purchaser make payment with a cashier's check. A cashier's check is a check for which the bank is both the drawer and the drawee. To purchase a cashier's check, a person goes to a bank teller, tenders the amount of money for which the check is to be payable, and supplies the teller with the name of the person who is to be the payee of the check. Once the payee's name is inscribed on the check, only the payee (or a person to whom the payee negotiates the check) will be able to receive money for the check. What problem might arise if a seller asks a prospective buyer of goods to make payment with a cashier's check, and the buyer purchases the check, naming the seller as the payee? How can this problem be avoided?

5. A California statute makes possession of a check with intent to defraud a crime. Norwood had in his possession an instrument that had the following title in the upper right-hand corner: "AUDITOR CONTROLLER'S GENERAL WARRANT COUNTY OF LOS ANGELES." Below this the instrument stated, "The treasurer of the County of Los Angeles will pay to the order of John Norwood $5,000." At trial the district attorney proved that Norwood had intended to defraud the County of Los Angeles of $5,000 while in possession of the above instrument. You are Norwood's attorney, and you are now appealing the case. What arguments would you make to have Norwood's conviction overturned? [People v. Norwood, 26 Cal.3d 148, 103 Cal. Rptr. 7 (1972)]

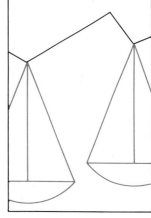

24

Commercial Paper
Negotiability

This chapter will examine a special type of commercial paper—the negotiable instrument. The basic difference between a negotiable instrument and an ordinary contract is that negotiable instruments must have a specific form.

Whenever a dispute arises over the enforceability of an instrument, it is of vital importance to know whether it is negotiable. If it *is* negotiable, all disputes are resolved under Article 3 of the Uniform Commercial Code. If it is *not* negotiable, disputes must be resolved under ordinary contract law. The holder-in-due-course doctrine is recognized only under Article 3. Thus, anyone attempting to utilize this doctrine in enforcing an instrument must show that the instrument is negotiable.

Furthermore, commercial paper is relatively worthless as a substitute for money unless it is freely transferable—that is, unless a prospective purchaser is willing to accept it routinely.

THE REQUIREMENTS OF NEGOTIABILITY

Section 3-104(1) of the UCC specifies the requirements of negotiability. A negotiable instrument must:

1. Be in writing.
2. Be signed by the maker or drawer.
3. Be an unconditional promise or order.
4. Contain a specific sum of money.
5. Be payable on demand or at a definite time.
6. Be payable to order or to bearer.
7. Exclude any other promise, order, obligation, or power.[1]
8. Identify the drawee specifically if the instrument is a third-party instrument.

A Writing

Negotiable instruments must be in *written form*. Clearly, an oral promise can create the danger of fraud or make it difficult to assign liability. Negotiable instruments must possess the quality of certainty that only formal written expression can give.

PRACTICAL LIMITATIONS ON THE WRITING There are certain practical limitations concerning the writing and the substance on which it is placed.

1. The writing must be on material that will lend itself to *permanence*. [UCC Sec. 1-201(46)] Negotiable instruments have been written on the sides of cows, carved in blocks of ice, and recorded on other impermanent surfaces. However, these forms remain written for only a relatively short period of time. For example, if Mary writes in the sand, "I promise to pay $100 to the order of Tom," this is not a writing because it lacks permanence.
2. The writing must have *portability*. This is not a legal requirement, but if an instrument is not movable, it cannot meet the requirement that it be freely transferable. A promise to pay written on the side of a cow is formally correct, but a cow cannot easily be transferred in the ordinary course of business.

Signed by the Maker or the Drawer

For an instrument to be negotiable, it must be signed by the maker if it is a note or by the

1. But see UCC Sec. 3-112.

drawer if it is a draft or check. [UCC Sec. 3-104(1)(a)] Extreme latitude is granted in determining what constitutes a signature. Section 1-201(39) of the UCC defines the word *signed* as "[including] any symbol executed or adopted by a party with present intention to authenticate a writing." Section 3-401(2) expands upon this: "A signature is made by use of name, including any trade or assumed name, upon an instrument, or by any word or mark used in lieu of a written signature." Thus, initials, an X, or a thumbprint will suffice. A trade name or an assumed name is sufficient even if it is false. Parol evidence is admissible in identifying the signer. When the signer is identified, the signature becomes effective. [UCC Sec. 3-104, Comment 2] Also, a rubber stamp bearing a person's name, when used by that person or an authorized agent, constitutes a signature.

PLACEMENT OF THE SIGNATURE The location of the signature on the document is unimportant. The usual place is the lower right-hand corner, but this is not required. A handwritten statement on the body of the instrument, such as "I, Mary Jones, promise to pay John Doe," is sufficient. [UCC Sec. 3-401, Comment 2]

There are virtually no limitations on the manner in which a signature can be made, but it is necessary to be careful when receiving an instrument that has been signed in an unusual way. The burden of proving the genuineness of a signature rests on the recipient. Furthermore, an unusual signature clearly decreases the marketability of an instrument because it creates uncertainty.

Unconditional Promise or Order

The terms of a promise or order have to be included in the writing on the face of a negotiable instrument and must not be conditioned upon the happening or failure to happen of some collateral agreement. [UCC Sec. 3-105(2)(a)]

PROMISE OR ORDER In order for an instrument to be negotiable, it must contain an express order or promise to pay. A mere acknowledgment of the debt, which might logically *imply* a promise, is not sufficient under the Uniform Commercial Code because the promise must be an *affirmative* undertaking. For example, the traditional I.O.U. is only an acknowledgment of indebtedness. Therefore, it is not a negotiable instrument. [UCC Sec. 3-102 Comment 2] But if such words as *to be paid on demand* or *due on demand* are added, the need for an affirmative promise is satisfied. For example, if a buyer executes a promissory note using the words, "I promise to pay $1,000 to the order of the seller for the purchase of goods X, Y, Z," then the requirement for a negotiable instrument is satisfied.

A certificate of deposit is different. Here, the requisite promise is satisfied because the bank's acknowledgment of the deposit and the other terms of the instrument clearly indicate a promise.

An order is usually associated with three-party instruments, such as trade acceptances, checks, and drafts. An order directs a third party to pay the instrument as drawn. The order is mandatory even if it is written in a courteous form with words like *please pay* or *kindly pay*. However, precise language must be used. An order stating, "I wish you would pay," does not fulfill the requirement of precision. [UCC Sec. 3-102(1)(b)] In addition to being precise, an effective order must specifically identify the drawee (the person who must pay). A bank's name printed on the face of a check, for example, sufficiently designates the bank as drawee.

UNCONDITIONAL

A negotiable instrument's utility as a substitute for money or as a credit device would be dramatically reduced if it had *conditional* promises attached to it. It would be expensive and time-consuming to investigate such conditional promises, and, therefore, the free transferability of negotiable instruments would be greatly reduced. There would be substantial administrative costs associated with processing conditional promises. Furthermore, the payee would risk the possibility of the condition not occurring. If X promises to pay Y $10,000 only if a certain ship reaches port safely, anyone interested in purchasing the promissory

note would have to investigate whether the ship arrived. Additionally, the facts that the investigation disclosed might be incorrect. To avoid such problems, the UCC provides that only unconditional promises or orders can be negotiable. [UCC Sec. 3-104(1)(b)] However, the Code expands the definition of *unconditional* in order to make sure that certain conditions do not render an otherwise negotiable instrument nonnegotiable.

FACTORS NOT AFFECTING NEGOTIABILITY Many problems in interpreting unconditionality are resolved by Section 3-105 of the UCC:

A promise or order otherwise unconditional is not made conditional by the fact that the instrument (a) is subject to implied or constructive conditions; or (b) states its consideration * * * or the transaction which gave rise to the instrument * * *; or (c) refers to or states that it arises out of a separate agreement * * *; or * * * (e) states that it is secured, whether by mortgage reservation or title or otherwise; or (f) indicates a particular account to be debited or any other fund or source from which reimbursement is expected; or (g) is limited to payment out of a particular fund or the proceeds of a particular source, if the instrument is issued by a government or governmental agency unit; or, (h) is limited to payment out of the entire assets of a partnership, unincorporated association, trust or estate * * *.

Implied or Constructive Conditions Without the rule allowing implied or constructive conditions, no instrument could be negotiable. Implied conditions, such as good faith and commercial reasonableness appear in virtually every example of a negotiable instrument.

Statements of Consideration Many instruments state the terms of the underlying agreement as a matter of standard business practice. Somewhere on its face, the instrument refers to the transaction or agreement for which it is being used in payment. The policy of the Uniform Commercial Code is to integrate standard trade usages into its provisions. For example, the words *as per contract* or *this debt arises from the sale of goods X and Y* do not render an instrument nonnegotiable. If James Quinta writes, "On July 14, 1980, I promise to pay to the order of Louis Sneed $100 in full payment for the TV set that Louis Sneed will deliver to me on July 2, 1980, signed James Quinta," this can be a negotiable instrument. The statement concerning the TV set is not a condition. It describes the consideration for which the note is given.

Reference to Other Agreements The UCC provides that mere *reference* to another agreement does not affect negotiability. If, on the other hand, the instrument is *made subject* to the other agreement, it will be nonnegotiable. A reference to another agreement is normally inserted for the purpose of keeping a record or giving information to anyone who may be interested. Notes frequently refer to separate

agreements that give special rights to a creditor for an acceleration of payment or to a debtor for prepayment. References to these rights do not destroy the negotiability of the instrument. For example, an instrument states, "On January 23, 1981, I promise to pay to the order of Patricia Senior $1,000, this note being secured under a security agreement and lien upon my 1974 Dodge Dart, noted upon the title certificate thereof, signed Henry Winn." This instrument is negotiable. A statement that an instrument's payment is secured by collateral will not render an otherwise negotiable instrument nonnegotiable. [UCC Sec. 3-105, Comment 5]

In the following case, a promissory note that incorporated and was made *subject to* another agreement was rendered nonnegotiable.

HOLLY HILL ACRES, LTD. v. CHARTER BANK OF GAINESVILLE

District Court of Florida, 1975.
314 So.2d 209.

BACKGROUND AND FACTS *A promissory note and purchase money mortgage were executed by the appellant, Holly Hill Acres, and given to a third party, Rogers and Blythe. Subsequently, Rogers and Blythe assigned the promissory note and mortgage in question to the appellee, Charter Bank of Gainesville, to secure its own note. Ultimately, the Holly Hill note went into default. The bank sued both Holly Hill and Rogers and Blythe to recover payment on the note. The trial court allowed the bank to recover. Holly Hill appealed that ruling, claiming that the note contained a stipulation that rendered it nonnegotiable. Hence, Holly Hill's defense against paying Rogers and Blythe was equally effective as a defense against paying the bank.*

The bank argued that it was a special type of assignee called a holder in due course because the promissory note was a negotiable instrument. On this basis, the bank claimed the unhampered right to recover on the note despite any underlying disputes between Holly Hill and Rogers and Blythe. (A holder in due course takes a negotiable instrument free of most claims of other parties when negotiable commercial paper is involved. See Chapter 26.) Hence, the key to the bank's claim for recovery was that the promissory note was negotiable.

The trial court ruled that the note was negotiable and that the bank could recover. Holly Hill appealed this ruling, claiming that because the note was made subject to the mortgage agreement, it was nonnegotiable.

SCHEB, Judge.
* * *

The note, executed April 28, 1972, contains the following stipulation:

This note with interest is secured by a mortgage on real estate, of even date herewith, made by the maker hereof in favor of the said payee, and shall be construed and enforced according to the laws of the State of Florida. *The terms of said mortgage are by this reference made a part hereof.* [Emphasis added.]

The note having incorporated the terms of the purchase money mortgage was not negotiable. The appellee Bank was not a holder in due course.

* * *

The note, incorporating by reference the terms of the mortgage, did not contain the unconditional promise to pay required by [U.C.C. Sec. 3-104(1)(b)]. Rather, the note falls within the scope of [U.C.C. Sec. 3-105(2)(a)]. Although negotiability is now governed by the Uniform Commercial Code, this was the Florida view even before the U.C.C. was adopted.

Mere reference to a note being secured by mortgage is a common commercial practice and such reference in itself does not impede the negotiability of the note. There is, however, a significant difference in a note stating that it is "secured by a mortgage" from one which provides, "the terms of said mortgage are by this reference made a part hereof." In the former instance the note merely refers to a separate agreement which does not impede its negotiability, while in the latter instance the note is rendered non-negotiable.

The appellate court reversed the trial court's ruling, holding that the note was rendered nonnegotiable because it incorporated another instrument (the mortgage). Any defense against payment that Holly Hill could assert against Rogers and Blythe applied equally to the bank because the note was nonnegotiable. Principles of contract law, not the UCC, determined the rights of the parties.

JUDGMENT AND REMEDY

Secured by a Mortgage   A simple statement in an otherwise negotiable note, indicating that the note is secured by a mortgage, does not destroy its negotiability. Actually, such a statement might make the note even more acceptable in commerce. Note that the statement that a note is secured by a mortgage does not stipulate that the maker's promise to pay is subject to the terms and conditions of the mortgage.

Indication of Particular Funds or Accounts   If a particular fund out of which reimbursement is to be made or a particular account to be debited with the amount is indicated, this does not affect negotiability. Consider the following examples. A note dated March 3, 1979, reads, "Gilbert Corporation promises to pay to the order of the Miami Herald $150 on demand, charged to advertising expense, signed Harold Henry, Treasurer, Gilbert Corporation." This is negotiable. The phrase "charged to advertising expense" is merely a posting instruction to the corporation's accounting department. If a note

states that "Jones plans to liquidate real estate to pay this obligation," the note is still considered negotiable.[2] On the other hand, if the instrument states that it is payable *only* from a particular fund or source, it then becomes conditional. For example, an instrument that states, "Payment of obligation only from a collection of accounts receivable," will be nonnegotiable. [UCC Sec. 3-105(2)(a)] The two exceptions to this rule are instruments issued by government agencies that are payable out of particular revenue funds and instruments limited to partnership, estate, or trust assets.

PROVISIONS NOT PERMITTED   Subsection 2 of Section 3-105 lists two specific provisions that render a writing conditional and therefore nonnegotiable. A promise or order is conditional if the instrument states that (1) it is subject to or governed by any other agreement or (2) it is to

2.   Southern Baptist Hospital v. Williams, 89 So.2d 769 (La. App. 1956).

be paid only out of a particular fund or source except as provided elsewhere in this section.

Instruments subject to other agreements have already been the subject of some of our discussion above. If the language indicates that promises or orders are subject to some other agreement, they are nonnegotiable. These instruments are typically unmarketable because prospective purchasers of such interest will not search out the other agreements to see what their actual provisions are.

Instruments payable only out of a specified fund are normally nonnegotiable. Such a promise or order is impliedly conditioned upon the fund being in existence on the date of maturity. Note, however, as discussed above that merely naming the fund from which payment is to be made, without use of such words as "only" do *not* render an instrument nonnegotiable.

Sum Certain in Money

Negotiable instruments must state the amount to be paid in a *certain sum of money*. This requirement promotes clarity and certainty in determining the value of the instrument. [UCC Sec. 3-104(1)(b)] Any promise to pay in the future is risky because the value of money (purchasing power) fluctuates. Nonetheless, the present value of such an instrument can still be estimated with a reasonable degree of accuracy by financial experts. If the instrument's value were stated in terms of goods or services, it would be too difficult to ascertain the value of those goods and services at the time the instrument was to be discounted.[3]

The UCC mandates that negotiable commercial paper be paid wholly in money. For example, a promise to pay $100 and deliver 10,000 chairs made out of wicker on January 1, 1982, is not a negotiable instrument; neither is a promise to perform 1,000 hours of skywriting.

SUM CERTAIN The term *sum certain* means an amount that is ascertainable from the in-

strument itself without reference to an outside source. A demand note payable with 8 percent interest meets the requirement of sum certain because its amount can be determined at the time it is payable. Section 3-106(1) of the UCC states that the sum is not rendered uncertain by the fact that it is to be paid

(a) with stated interest or by stated installments; or (b) with stated different rates of interest before or after default or a specified date; or (c) with a stated discount or addition if paid before or after the date fixed for payment; * * *

Thus, when the payee calls for payment and the amount due is certain, any such commercial paper will be freely transferable and commercially acceptable.

Instruments that provide for payment of interest at prevailing bank rates are generally nonnegotiable because bank rates fluctuate. In international trade, notes that are to be paid in another currency satisfy the "sum certain" requirement. If X promises to pay 1,000 French francs, this note meets the certainty requirement even though the parties must refer to exchange rates that are not embodied in the instrument. The Code, therefore, makes an exception to its own general rule because of the realities of international trade. [UCC Sec. 3-107]

Often, instruments have provisions authorizing court costs and attorneys' fees upon default. In Section 3-106(1)(e), the UCC indicates that an instrument with such provisions still meets the sum certain requirement and is therefore still negotiable. Providing for collection costs and attorneys' fees lessens some of the costs and risks that a bank (or other institution) dealing in commercial paper would otherwise incur. Note, though, that some states have invalidated such provisions either by statute or by judicial decision. In states where such provisions are legal, the fees must be reasonable, or the clause will be voided as against public policy.

The elements that determine negotiability must be present on the face of the instrument. In the following case, the amount of a finance charge was not apparent from the face of the note.

---

3. Discounting means transferring an instrument for which payment by the maker or drawer is not yet due to another party in exchange for face value of the instrument in cash, less some interest charge.

BACKGROUND AND FACTS *This transaction involved a consumer credit sale in which a note and a security agreement, written on the same sheet of paper, were executed. The note provided that any unearned finance charges would be refunded if the consumer prepaid the full credit amount. The court had to determine whether the note and the security agreement, when read together, constituted a negotiable instrument. The answer was particularly important to the defendant, a merchant, because taking a negotiable instrument in conjunction with a consumer credit sale violated a state law and carried a costly penalty. Hence, the merchant took the position that the note was nonnegotiable because it lacked a sum certain. The consumer took the position that a sum certain could be ascertained by looking at the note and the security agreement, which were contained on the same piece of paper.*

WALLS v. MORRIS CHEVROLET, INC.
Court of Appeals of Oklahoma, 1973.
515 P.2d 1405.

BAILEY, Presiding Judge.

* * *

First, both parties assume that the note, considered by itself, is not negotiable. So do we. The sum payable from the face of the note does not appear to be a sum certain because of the privilege stated in the note of refund of any unearned finance charge upon prepayment of the balance. The amount of the finance charge is not apparent from the face of the note and therefore the sum to be paid is uncertain in the event of prepayment. Under [U.C.C. Sec. 3-106]: "(1) The sum payable is a sum certain even though it is to be paid * * * (c) with a stated discount * * * if paid before * * * the date fixed for payment * * *." In this instance the amount of the discount is not stated in the note and cannot be computed from its face. As is stated in the Uniform Commercial Code Comment to this section: "A stated discount or addition for early or late payment does not affect the certainty of the sum so long as the computation can be made * * * from the instrument itself * * *."

To overcome the absence of a sum certain on the face of the note, the plaintiff argues that the amount of the finance charge appears in the accompanying security agreement, that the security agreement and the note should be considered one instrument because on the same sheet of paper, that so construed the missing term is supplied and both note and security agreement are negotiable.

* * *

We have been cited to no case, nor have we found one, in which a note on its face non-negotiable has been found to be negotiable by reference to an attached security agreement.

It is our opinion that a note cannot depend upon another agreement for elements of negotiability whether that agreement is attached to the note or separate from it except in those rare instances where such an incorporation is sanctioned by the Uniform Commercial Code expressly or by neccessary implication. Negotiable notes are designed to be couriers without excess luggage under both the prior law and under the Code and so negotiability must be determined from the face of the note without regard to outside sources (with rare exceptions) so that the taker may know that he takes a negotiable instrument with the insurance of collectability provided by the Code and not an ordinary contract subject to the possibility of all defenses by the maker.

JUDGMENT
AND REMEDY

The note was not negotiable on its face. A separate agreement cannot supply the elements of negotiability to a note, which from its very nature must be either negotiable or not from its face. Therefore, the merchant prevailed.

MONEY AND NO OTHER PROMISE The Uniform Commercial Code in Section 3-104(1)(b) provides that a sum certain is to be payable in "money and no other promise." The Code defines money as "a medium of exchange authorized or adopted by a domestic or foreign government as a part of its currency." [UCC Sec. 1-201(24)]

If, in consideration of a loan, Y promises to deliver fifty liters of 1964 Chateau Lafite, this is not sufficient for the instrument to be negotiable because the note is not payable in money. If Y then promises to pay $1,000 and deliver the wine, the instrument is still not negotiable because it is not payable *entirely* in money. X can promise to pay 50,000 Spanish pesetas in return for a loan because the instrument specifies a recognized foreign currency. The UCC has a special provision for such notes. [UCC Sec. 3-107(2)] Any instrument payable in the U.S. with a face amount stated in a foreign currency can be paid in the equivalent in U.S. dollars at the due date, unless the paper expressly requires payment in the foreign currency. Consider an instrument that is drafted in Guatemala City, is payable in Miami, Florida, and expressly calls for payment in 100 Guatemalan *quetzales*. The instrument will be deemed payable in money.

On the other hand, an instrument payable in U.S. government bonds or in shares of IBM stock is not negotiable because neither bonds nor stocks are a medium of exchange recognized by the U.S. government.

Payable on Demand or at a Definite Time

Section 3-104(1)(c) of the Uniform Commercial Code requires that a negotiable instrument "be payable on demand or at a definite time." Clearly, in order to ascertain the value of a negotiable instrument, it is necessary to know

when the maker or acceptor can be compelled to pay. It is also necessary to know when the obligations of secondary parties—drawers, indorsers and guarantors—will arise. Finally, it is necessary to know the time during which the instrument will be valid before it expires by operation of the law, through the statute of limitations. With an interest-bearing instrument, it is necessary to know the exact interval during which the interest will accrue in order to determine the present value of the instrument.

PAYABLE ON DEMAND Instruments that are payable on demand usually contain the words *payable at sight* or *payable upon presentment*. No time for payment is specified, and the drawee must pay money for the instrument whenever it is tendered. [UCC Sec. 3-108]

PAYABLE AT A DEFINITE TIME To be negotiable, time instruments must be payable at a definite time that is specified on the face of the instrument. The maker or drawer is under no obligation to pay until the specified time has elapsed.

Many time instruments contain additional terms that seem to conflict with the definite time requirement. In Section 3-109, the Uniform Commercial Code attempts to clear up some of these potential problems:

(1) An instrument is payable at a definite time if by its terms it is payable
(a) on or before a stated date or at a fixed period after a stated date; or
(b) at a fixed period after sight; or
(c) at a definite time subject to any acceleration; or
(d) at a definite time subject to extension at the option of the holder, or to extension to a further definite time at the option of the maker or acceptor or automatically upon or after a specified act or event.
(2) An instrument which by its terms is otherwise payable only upon an act or event uncertain as to time of occurrence is not payable at a definite time even though the act or event has occurred.

Consider an example that relates to Subsection (2). An instrument is dated June 1, 1979, and states, "One year after the death of my grandfather, James Taylor, I promise to pay to the order of Henry Winkler $500. Signed Mary Taylor." This is nonnegotiable. Because the date of the grandfather's death is uncertain, the maturity date is uncertain.

Consider Subsections (a) and (b) of Section 3-109(1). When an instrument is payable on or before a stated date, it is clearly payable at a definite time, although the maker has the option of paying before the stated maturity date. This uncertainty does not violate the definite time requirement. If Lee gives Zenon an instrument dated May 1, 1981, which indicates on its face that it is payable on or before May 1, 1982, it satisfies the requirement. On the other hand, an instrument that is undated and made payable "one month after date" is clearly not negotiable. There is no way to determine the maturity date from the face of the instrument. Drafts stating that they are payable at a fixed period after sight are considered payable at a definite time. [UCC Sec. 3-109(1)(b)] The term *sight* means the moment that the draft is accepted by the drawee. The Code further requires that such instruments be presented for acceptance to the drawee in order to determine the maturity date. [UCC Sec. 3-501(1)(a)] Presenting an instrument for acceptance to the drawee establishes the sight and the time period, which runs from the date the instrument is presented.

ACCELERATION CLAUSES   An **acceleration clause** is one which allows a payee or other holder of an instrument to demand payment of the entire amount due, with interest, if some event occurs, usually a default in payment or in other performance. For example, X lends $1,000 to Y. Y makes a note promising to pay $100 per month for eleven months. The note can contain a provision that permits X to accelerate all of the payments plus interest if Y fails to pay in any given month. If, for example, Y fails to make the third payment, the note will be due and payable. If X accelerates the unpaid balance, Y will owe X the remaining principal plus interest.

Under Section 109(1)(c), instruments which include acceleration clauses are negotiable because the exact value of the instrument can be ascertained. The instrument will be absolutely payable on a fixed date, however, if the event allowing acceleration does not occur. Thus, the fixed date is the outside limit used to determine the value of the instrument. Furthermore, the payee or holder cannot accelerate the instrument even if it contains an acceleration clause unless it is done in good faith. Section 1-208 indicates that the acceleration clause "* * * shall be construed to mean that * * * [the holder of the instrument] shall have the power * * * [to accelerate] only if he in good faith believes that the prospect of payment or performance is impaired." But the burden of proving a lack of good faith is on the borrower— that is, the maker of the note.

EXTENSION CLAUSES   The reverse of an acceleration clause is an extension clause, which allows the date of maturity to be extended into the future. To keep the instrument negotiable, the interval of the extension must be specified if the right to extend is given to the maker of the instrument. If, on the other hand, the holder of the instrument can extend it, the maturity date does not have to be specified. Consider some examples:

1.   A note reads, "The maker [obligor] has the right to postpone the time of payment of this note beyond its definite maturity date of January 1, 1983. However, this extension shall be for no more than a reasonable time." Any note with this language is not negotiable because it does not satisfy the definite time requirement. The right to extend is the maker's, and the maker has not indicated when the note will become due after the extension.
2.   A note reads, "The holder of this note at the date of maturity, January 1, 1983, can extend the time of payment until the following June 1 or later, if the holder so wishes." This is a negotiable instrument. The length of the extension does not have to be specified because the option to extend is solely that of the holder.

Payable to Order or to Bearer

A negotiable instrument must clearly indicate that the maker or drawer intends the instrument to be fully transferable to someone other than the person to whom it was originally issued. Section 3-104(1)(d) states that the instrument must be "payable to order or to bearer." These are considered words of negotiability.

ORDER INSTRUMENT Section 3-110(1) defines an instrument as an order to pay "when by its terms it is payable to the order * * * of any person therein specified with reasonable certainty * * *." This section goes on to state that an order instrument can be payable: (1) to the maker or the drawer; (2) to the drawee or a payee who is not a maker, drawer, or drawee; (3) to two or more payees together; (4) to the representative of an estate, trust, or fund; or (5) to a partnership or unincorporated association. Any time the words appear as "pay to the order of Jim Jones" or "pay to Sam Smith or order," the instrument is an order instrument. If the instrument states "pay John Smith," the Code provides that it can be *negotiated* (transferred from one party to another), but no holder of it can ever qualify as a holder in due course. (See Chapter 26 for details.)

BEARER INSTRUMENT Section 3-111 defines a bearer instrument as one that does not designate a specific payee. The term *bearer* means the person in possession of an instrument that is payable to bearer *or* indorsed in blank. [UCC Sec. 1-201(5)]

Any instrument containing the following terms is a bearer instrument: "Payable to the order of bearer," "Payable to Sam Sneed or bearer," "Payable to bearer," "Pay Cash," or "Pay to the order of cash." An instrument stating that it is "payable only to Mr. Smith" is not payable to bearer.

COMPARING ORDER INSTRUMENTS AND BEARER INSTRUMENTS

1. A check payable to cash is a bearer instrument. [UCC Sec. 3-111(c)]
2. A note payable to the order of Melinda Higgins, which has been indorsed and signed by Melinda Higgins, is a bearer instrument because it is an instrument indorsed in blank. A blank indorsement is made by merely signing the back of the instrument. [UCC Sec. 3-204(2)]
3. A note "payable to bearer" and indorsed "Pay to the order of Leroy Jones, signed by George Porsche," is an order instrument because the indorsement names the person to whom the instrument is being made payable. [UCC Sec. 3-204(1)] See Chapter 25 for a discussion of all types of indorsements.

OMISSIONS THAT DO NOT AFFECT NEGOTIABILITY

UCC Sec. 3-112 lists the following terms and omissions that do not affect negotiability:

1. The omission of a statement of any consideration.
2. The omission of the place where the instrument is drawn or payable.
3. The promise or power to maintain or protect collateral or to give additional collateral.
4. The term in a draft indicating that the payee, by indorsing or cashing the draft, acknowledges full satisfaction of the obligation of the drawer.

QUESTIONS AND CASE PROBLEMS

1. Between 1971 and 1974, a number of Oklahoma residents purchased homes from Jim Walter Homes, Inc. Each purchaser made a down payment and signed a promissory note promising to pay the balance in monthly installments over a number of years. The promissory notes were ordinary in every way, including the payment provisions, which named the exact sum due each month over a specified period of years. A number of persons who signed these notes brought a class action suit against Jim Walter Homes to recover certain credit and financing charges that

they claimed were in violation of the Uniform Consumer Credit Code (UCCC). In order to win their case, the plaintiffs had to prove that the promissory notes were negotiable instruments. Jim Walter Homes contended that they were not negotiable because the UCCC allows all consumers to prepay loans such as those at issue here and to deduct from the balance due all proportional amounts of credit and finance charges associated with any prepayments made. The company argued that because of this statutory provision, the promissory notes were no longer for a sum certain as required by the UCC. Is this a valid argument? [Circle v. Jim Walter Homes, Inc., 535 F.2d. 583 (10th Cir. 1976)]

2. In December 1965, Joseph Smith drew a check on a bank payable on demand to his son, Edward Joseph Smith Gentilotti. Smith postdated the check by fifteen years; that is, he dated the check December 1, 1980. On the back of the check, Smith wrote, "For Edward Joseph Smith Gentilotti, my son, if I should pass away, the amount of $20,000 shall be taken from my estate at death." Joseph Smith signed and dated this indorsement. Is this a negotiable instrument? [Smith v. Gentilotti, 371 Mass. 839, 359 N.E.2d. 953 (1977)]

3. Ingel entered into a contract with Allied Aluminum Associates, Inc., to have aluminum siding put on his home. Ingel executed a promissory note naming Allied as payee, and, at the same time, both Ingel and the Allied representative signed a completion certificate that bound Allied to complete the job satisfactorily. The completion certificate was not mentioned in nor attached to the promissory note. Allied Aluminum Associates later negotiated the promissory note to Universal C.I.T. Credit Corp. Allied never finished the aluminum siding work and was never heard from again. In a suit by Universal to collect on the note, Ingel's defense turned on whether the promissory note was negotiable. Ingel contended that it was not negotiable since it was accompanied by a completion certificate that contained promises other than the promise merely to pay a sum certain in money. Will Ingel's argument succeed? [Universal C.I.T. Credit Corp. v. Ingel, 347 Mass. 119, 196 N.E.2d. 847 (1964)]

4. Robinson purchased forty-three $100 money orders from Nation-Wide Check Corp. The amount was stamped on each money order at the time of the purchase. The only other writing on the instrument was "payable to_____" and "from _____." Robinson was to fill in the names on the instrument later. Are money orders, such as the typical one presented above, negotiable instruments? [Nation-Wide Check

Corp. v. Banks, 260 A.2d. 376 (D.C. App. Ct. 1969)]

5. Mason, a trucking company, owed to Blayton, a lessor, $3,000 for the rental of certain trucking equipment. Blayton informed the president of Mason that unless he issued his personal check for $3,000 immediately, Blayton would sue Mason. Blayton promised to hold onto the check for two weeks to allow Mason time to pay the arrearages, but when it received Mason's check, it negotiated it to another party. Mason claimed that the check was subject to a condition—Blayton's promise to hold onto the check—and that therefore the check was not negotiable. Assuming that Blayton's agreement not to cash the check was first made orally over the phone and later put in writing, will this affect the negotiability of the check issued by Mason's president? [Mason v. Blayton, 119 Ga. App. 203, 166 S.E. 2d. 601 (1969)]

6. Hotel Evans, Inc., issued two promissory notes, as maker, to A. Alport & Son, Inc., payee. One note contained a promise by Hotel Evans to pay Alport $1,600 "with interest at bank rates." The other note, for $900, had "bank rates" typed in after the printed word "interest." Are either of these promissory notes negotiable? [A. Alport & Son, Inc. v. Hotel Evans, Inc., 65 Misc. 2d. 374, 317 N.Y.S. 2d. 937 (1970)]

7. Zimmerman entered into a contract with Master Homecraft Company for the remodeling of Zimmerman's home. In payment for the remodeling, Zimmerman executed a promissory note in the amount of $9,747. The note contained unused blanks for installment payments. It did not contain a maturity date; nor did it indicate whether Zimmerman would be liable for interest. Is this promissory note negotiable? [Master Homecraft Co. v. Zimmerman, 208 Pa. Super. 401, 222 A.2d. 440 (1966)]

8. On May 25, 1963, John Sylvia executed the following note: "I, John Sylvia, promise to pay $3,000 to N. Ferri or his order, within ten years." Is this note payable at a definite time within the meaning of Section 3-109(1)(c)? When would Ferri have the right to collect on the note? [Ferri v. Sylvia, 100 R.I. 270, 214 A.2d. 470 (1965)]

9. In October 1970, Hall issued a draft that included the following: "Pay to L. Westmoreland and B. Bridges or order $1,000 on demand." Before he handed it to Bridges, Hall scratched out the words *or order* with his pen. Does the fact that the draft is payable to two payees destroy its negotiability? Does the scratching out of the words *or order* destroy the draft's negotiability? [First Federal Sav. and Loan Ass'n v. Branch Banking and Trust Co., 282 N.C. 44, 191 S.E. 2d. 683 (N.C. 1972)]

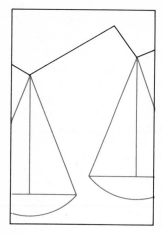

25

Commercial Paper
Transferability
and Negotiation

Commercial paper must be freely transferable. Once a negotiable instrument circulates beyond the original parties, the commercial law principles of *negotiation* come into play.[1] The method of transfer that is used to pass a negotiable instrument from person to person determines the rights and duties that are passed with it.

ASSIGNMENT AND NEGOTIATION

Once issued, a negotiable instrument can be transferred by *assignment* or by *negotiation*.

Assignment

Recall from Chapter 12 that under general contract principles, a transfer by assignment to an assignee gives the assignee only those rights that the assignor possessed. Assignment is a transfer of rights under a contract. Any defenses that can be raised against an assignor can be raised against the assignee.

---

1. The first delivery of a negotiable instrument to a holder occurs when the maker or drawer "issues" the instrument. [UCC Sec. 3-102 (1) (a)] Since a payee is a holder, the issuance of a negotiable instrument is, strictly speaking, negotiation. However, in commercial practice, the term *negotiation* is used to identify those transfers occurring once an instrument has been issued.

Negotiation

Negotiation is the transfer of an instrument in such form that the transferee becomes a holder. [UCC Sec. 3-202 (1)] Under UCC principles, a transfer by negotiation creates a holder who, at the very least, receives the rights of the previous possessor. [UCC Sec. 3-201 (1)] Unlike an assignment, a transfer by negotiation can make it possible for a holder to receive more rights in the instrument than the prior possessor. [UCC Sec. 3-305] (A holder who receives greater rights is known as a *holder in due course.* See Chapter 26.)

NEGOTIATING ORDER PAPER   There are two methods of negotiating an instrument so that the receiver becomes a holder. If the instrument is *order paper*, it is negotiated by delivery with any necessary indorsements. For example, the Transco Company issues a payroll check "To the Order of Jane Smith." Smith takes the check to the supermarket, signs her name on the back (an indorsement), gives it to the cashier (a delivery), and receives cash. Smith has negotiated the check to the supermarket. [UCC Sec. 3-202 (1)] Note that the payroll check, which began as *order* paper was converted to *bearer* paper when Smith indorsed it in blank.

NEGOTIATING BEARER PAPER   If the instrument is payable to bearer, then it is negotiated by delivery — that is, by physically being handed into another person's possession. [UCC Sec. 3-202 (1)] The use of *bearer paper* involves more risk than the use of order paper. Assume Bob Brown writes a check "Payable to Cash" and hands it to Debbie Myers (a delivery). Brown has negotiated the check (as a bearer instrument) to Myers. Myers places the check in her billfold, which is subsequently stolen. The thief has possession of the check. At this point, negotiation has not occurred since delivery must be voluntary on the part of the transferor. If the thief "delivers" the check to an innocent third person, negotiation will be complete. All rights to the check will be passed *absolutely* to that third person, and Myers will lose all right to

recover the proceeds of the check from that third person. [UCC Sec. 3-305] Of course, she can recover her money from the thief if the thief can be found.

The method used for negotiation depends upon the character of the instrument at the time the negotiation takes place. For example, a check originally payable to "Cash", but subsequently indorsed "Pay to X", must be negotiated as order paper (by indorsement and delivery) even though it was previously bearer paper. [UCC Sec. 3-204 (1)]

INDORSEMENTS

Indorsements are made by the holder—that is, the person to whom the instrument is payable either as payee or by indorsement or the person in possession of bearer paper. An indorsement is a signature with or without additional words or statements. It is most often written on the back of the instrument itself. If there is no room on the instrument, indorsements can be written on a separate piece of paper called an **allonge**. The allonge must be "so firmly affixed" to the instrument "as to become a part thereof." [UCC Sec. 3-202(2)] Pins or paper clips will not suffice. Staples are preferable.

One purpose of an indorsement is to effect the negotiation of order paper. Sometimes the transferee of bearer paper will request the holder-transferor to indorse. This is done to impose contractual liability on the indorser. The liability of indorsers will be discussed later in Chapter 27.

Once an instrument qualifies as a negotiable instrument, the form of indorsement will have no effect on the character of the underlying instrument. Indorsement relates to the right of the holder to negotiate the paper and the manner in which it must be done.

Types of Indorsements

The following sections will examine three categories of indorsements: (1) blank versus special, (2) qualified versus unqualified, and (3) restrictive versus nonrestrictive.

BLANK INDORSEMENTS A blank indorsement specifies no particular indorsee and can consist of a mere signature. [UCC Sec. 3-204(2)] Hence, a check payable "To the Order of Rosemary White" can be indorsed in blank simply by having her signature written on the back of the check. Exhibit 25-1 shows a blank indorsement.

EXHIBIT 25-1 BLANK INDORSEMENT

Rosemary White

An instrument payable to order and indorsed in blank becomes payable to bearer and can be negotiated by delivery alone. [UCC 3-204(2)] In other words, a blank indorsement converts an order instrument to a bearer instrument, which anybody can cash. If De Wert indorses a check payable to her order in blank and then loses it on the street, Jones can find it and sell it to Smith for value without indorsing it. This constitutes a negotiation because Jones makes delivery of a bearer instrument (which was an order instrument until it was indorsed).

SPECIAL INDORSEMENTS A **special indorsement** indicates the specific person to whom the indorser intends to make the instrument payable; that is, it names the indorsee. [UCC Sec. 3-204(1)] No special words of negotiation are needed. Words such as "Pay to the Order of Wilson" or "Pay to Wilson" followed by the signature of the indorser are sufficient.[2] When an instrument is indorsed in this way, it is order paper.

To avoid the risk of loss from theft one may convert a blank indorsement to a special indorsement. This returns the bearer paper to order paper. Section 3-204(3) allows that "the holder may convert a blank indorsement into a special indorsement by writing over the signa-

ture of the indorser in blank any contract consistent with the character of the indorsement." For example, Ellen Gordon may wish to insert the words "pay to Ellen Gordon" over the signature of the indorser. Because Gordon is now identified as the indorsee, the check cannot be negotiated further without her indorsement. In this manner, Gordon converts a blank indorsement into a special indorsement. (Special indorsements are discussed below.)

EXHIBIT 25-2 SPECIAL INDORSEMENT

Pay to Wilson
Arthur Engles

QUALIFIED VERSUS UNQUALIFIED INDORSEMENTS Generally, an indorser, *merely by indorsing*, impliedly promises to pay the holder, or any subsequent indorser, the amount of the instrument in the event that the drawer or maker defaults on the payment. [UCC Sec. 3-414(1)] A **qualified indorsement** is used by an indorser to disclaim or limit this contractual liability on the instrument. In this form of indorsement, the notation *without recourse* is commonly used. A sample is shown in Exhibit 25-3.

EXHIBIT 25-3 QUALIFIED INDORSEMENT

Without recourse
Arthur Engles

A qualified indorsement is often used by persons acting in a representative capacity. For instance, insurance agents sometimes receive checks payable to them that are really intended as payment to the insurance company. The agent is merely indorsing the payment through to the principal and should not be required to make good on the check if it is later dishonored. The "without recourse" indorsement absolves the agent. If the instrument is dishonored the

---

2. Had the words "Pay to Wilson" been used on the face of the instrument to indicate the payee, the instrument would not have been negotiable; it would only have been assignable.

holder cannot obtain recovery from a person who has indorsed "without recourse" unless the indorser has breached one of the warranties listed in UCC Sec. 3-417(2). However, a person who indorses an instrument will be liable on the instrument in the absence of a qualified indorsement.

RESTRICTIVE VERSUS NONRESTRICTIVE INDORSEMENTS The **restrictive indorsement** requires indorsees to comply with certain instructions regarding the funds involved. Restrictive indorsements come in many forms. Section 3-205 categorizes four separate types.

Conditional Indorsements When payment is dependant on the occurrence of some specified event, the instrument has a conditional indorsement. [UCC Sec. 3-205(a)] For example, Ted Smith indorses a note to read:

EXHIBIT 25-4 CONDITIONAL INDORSEMENT

Pay to Bob Block, provided he complete renovations on building number 23 by September 1, 1982.

Ted Smith

The indorsement is enforceable (except against intermediary banks as defined below), but neither Bob Block nor any subsequent holder has the right to enforce payment on the note before the condition is met. [UCC Sec. 3-206(3)] Read the example carefully and notice that Ted Smith is an *indorser*, not the maker of the note. Indorsers are permitted to condition rights of indorsees without affecting the negotiability of the instrument. However, if the conditional language had appeared on the face of the instrument, it would *not* have been negotiable because it would not have met the requirement of an unconditional order or promise to pay.

Indorsements Prohibiting Further Indorsement An indorsement such as, "Pay to Bill Jones Only, (signed) X," does not destroy negotiability. Jones can negotiate the paper to a holder just as if it had read "Pay to Bill Jones, (signed) X." [UCC Sec. 3-206(1)] This type of restrictive indorsement has the same legal effect as a special indorsement. It is rarely used. [UCC Sec. 3-205(b)]

Indorsement for Deposit or Collection Indorsements that read "For Deposit Only" or "For Collection Only" have the effect of making the indorsee (almost always a bank) a collecting agent of the indorser. In particular, a "Pay Any Bank or Banker" indorsement has the effect of locking the instrument into the bank collection process. Only a bank can acquire rights of a holder following this indorsement unless it is specifically indorsed to a person and not to a bank. [UCC Sec. 4-201(2)]

Here again, the depositary bank has a special responsibility to act consistently with the restrictive indorsement, and the intermediary banks are not liable if the depositary bank fails to comply.

BACKGROUND AND FACTS *Defendant Commercial Credit Corporation issued two checks payable to the order of Rauch Motor Co. Rauch Motor indorsed the checks in blank and deposited them in its account with University National Bank. University National stamped the checks "Pay Any Bank" and sent them through the collection process. The checks were subsequently returned to University National marked "Payment Stopped". Several months later University National assigned the checks to Lamson who sued Commercial Credit Corp. for the face amount of the checks.*

LAMSON v.
COMMERCIAL CREDIT
CORPORATION
Colorado Court of Appeals,
1974.
521 P.2d 785.

ENOCH, Judge.

* * *

Defendant contends that the trial court erred in finding that plaintiff was a "holder" of the checks. We agree.

The Uniform Commercial Code defines a "holder" as: "a person who is in possession of . . . an instrument . . . drawn, issued, or indorsed to him or to his order or to bearer or in blank." [UCC Sec. 1-201(20)].

When payee deposited the checks, he indorsed them in blank, thereby transforming them into bearer paper. *See* [UCC Secs. 1-201(5) and 3-204(2)]. However, when the bank initiated the collection process, it stamped the checks "Pay Any Bank." No further indorsements appear on the checks. After an item has been indorsed with these words, "only a bank may acquire the rights of a holder: (a) Until the item has been returned to the customer initiating collection; or (b) Until the item has been specially indorsed by a bank to a person not a bank." [UCC Sec. 4-201(2)]. Plaintiff is neither the customer initiating collection nor a bank, and the checks were not specially indorsed to him.

* * *

Plaintiff argues that even if he did not become a holder, he is entitled to recover on the instruments under Section 3-201(1), which states that "[t]ransfer of an instrument vests in the transferee such rights as the transferor has therein . . ." Plaintiff's transferor, the bank, was a holder and plaintiff claims that he suceeded to the bank's rights in the checks. However, absent a special indorsement, Section 4-201 (2) not only precludes plaintiff from becoming a holder but also from "acquiring the rights of a holder." Where provisions in Articles Three and Four of the Code conflict, Article Four governs. [UCC Sec. 4-102(1)]. Therefore, plaintiff may not recover either as a holder or as the transferee of a holder.

This result may appear to place a hypertechnical construction on the requirements of Section 4-201, particularly in light of Section 3-201(3), which gives a transferee for value the right to require the unqualified indorsement of his transferor. However, if the drawer were required to pay a nonbank transferee on the checks as presently indorsed, the payment would be made in a manner not consistent with the restrictive indorsement, *i. e.,* "Pay Any Bank." Therefore, the drawer would not be discharged on the checks [UCC Sec. 3-603(1)(b)], or on the underlying obligation [UCC Sec. 3-802(1)(b)]. A special indorsement is essential to protect the drawer from double liability.

* * *

JUDGMENT AND REMEDY *The appellate court reversed the trial court's judgement which was in favor of Lamson. The appellate court held that the restrictive indorsement "Pay Any Bank" precluded Lamson from becoming a holder.*

Trust or Agency Indorsement Indorsements that are for the benefit of the indorsee or a third person are trust, or agency, indorsements. For example, "Pay to Ann North in Trust for Johnny North, (signed) R. P. North." Or, "Pay to Marge, as Agent of XXO, (signed) XXO." The indorsement results in legal title vesting in the original indorsee. To the extent that the original indorsee pays or applies the proceeds consistently with the indorsement (for example, "in Trust for

Johnny. . .''), the indorsee is a holder and can become a holder in due course. (See Chapter 26). [UCC Secs. 3-205(d) and 3-206(4)]

The fiduciary restrictions on the instrument do not reach beyond the original indorsee.[3] Any subsequent purchaser can qualify as a holder in due course unless he or she has actual notice that the instrument was negotiated in breach of the fiduciary duty.[4]

Bank's Liability for Restrictive Indorsements
Banks handling commercial paper in the normal course of *collection* are called intermediary banks [UCC Sec. 4-105(c)], and banks paying on commercial paper are called payor banks. [UCC Sec. 4-105(b)] Neither bank is bound by any restrictive indorsements of any person except the immediate holder who transfers or presents the instrument for payment. [UCC Sec. 3-206(2)] This means that only the first bank to which the item is presented for collection must pay in a manner consistent with any restrictive indorsement. [UCC Sec. 3-206(3)] This bank is called the depository bank. [UCC Sec. 4-105(a)] This is true even if the depository bank is also the payor bank (that is, where only one bank is involved).

To illustrate: Elliot writes a check on his New York bank account and sends it to Barton. Barton indorses the check with a restrictive indorsement that reads, "For Deposit into Account #4921 Only." A Miami bank is the first bank to which this check is presented for payment (the depository bank), and it must act consistently with the terms of the restrictive indorsement. Therefore, it must credit account #4921 with the money or be liable to Barton for conversion. Elliot's check leaves the Miami bank indorsed "For Collection." As the check moves through the collection network of inter-

mediary banks to Elliot's New York bank for payment, each intermediary bank is only bound by the preceding bank's indorsement to collect. The division of responsibility between types of banks is necessary. Collecting banks process huge numbers of commercial instruments, and there is no practical way for them to examine and comply with the effect of each restrictive indorsement. Therefore, the only reasonable alternative is to charge the depository bank with the responsibility of examining and complying with any restrictive indorsements.

Forged or Unauthorized Indorsements

People cannot be liable to pay on negotiable instruments unless their signatures appear on the instruments. Hence, a forged or *unauthorized signature* is wholly inoperative and will not bind the person whose name is forged.[5]

The forged indorsement rule of the Uniform Commercial Code places the burden of loss on the party who first accepted the forged indorsement, often the bank that cashes the instrument for the forger. In the following situations, the forged indorsement rule does not apply, and the loss resulting from forgery falls on the drawer or maker: (1) when the imposter induces the maker or drawer of an instrument to issue it to the imposter or to a confederate in the name of the payee or (2) when the imposter signs as or on behalf of a maker or drawer, intending that the payee will have no interest in the instrument, and an agent or employee of the maker or drawer has supplied the imposter with the name of the payee, also intending the payee to have no such interest. [UCC Sec. 3-405(1)] These situations often involve an employee who wishes to swindle an employer by padding bills or payrolls.

An *unauthorized indorsement* of a payee's name can be as effective as if the real payee had signed. The *imposter rule* of Section 3-405 of the

---

3. Compare this to the rule governing conditional indorsements. A conditional indorsement binds all subsequent indorsers (except certain banks) and primary parties to see that the money is applied consistently with the condition. Agency or trust indorsements limit this responsibility only to the original indorsee. Subsequent parties are not encumbered with this restriction.

4. See Quantum Dev. v. Joy, 397 F. Supp. 329 (D.C. Virgin Is. 1975).

5. On the other hand, a drawee is charged with knowledge of the *drawer's* signature, and the drawee cannnot recover money paid out on a negotiable instrument bearing a forged drawee's signature.

UCC provides that an imposter's indorsement will be effective — that is, not a "forgery." This occurs when an imposter induces the maker or drawer to issue an instrument in the name of an impersonated payee to the imposter or to an accomplice who is impersonating the payee. For example, an imposter goes to a bank, forges a withdrawal slip on X's account, and requests the bank to issue a check in X's name for the amount. The bank agrees, handing the imposter the check payable to X, thinking she really is X. When the imposter indorses X's name on the back of the check, the unauthorized indorsement will be effective to negotiate the check. Who bears the loss? In this case the drawer bank must bear the loss for being misled into delivering the check to an imposter.

The following case illustrates how a court applied the *imposter rule* which was later adopted in the Uniform Commercial Code.

GREENBERG v. A & D MOTOR SALES, INC.
Appellate Court of Illinois, 1950.
341 Ill.App. 85, 93 N.E.2d 90.

BACKGROUND AND FACTS *A person who purported to be Wallace Gloss sold a car (which he apparently did not own) to A & D Motor Sales. A & D gave the person a check issued to Wallace Gross, and the person later cashed it at a currency exchange operated by Greenberg. The check was dishonored and Greenberg now seeks to recover as a holder against A & D, the drawer.*

FRIEND, Presiding Justice.

* * *

The only witness upon the hearing was the plaintiff, Max Greenberg, whose currency exchange at 750 East 51st street was only a few doors from the place of business of the defendant, A & D Motor Sales, Inc. Greenberg testified that on August 25, 1948 "a party came in to cash the check and made himself known by various identifications, a driver's license. He stated his name was Wallace Gross and asked me to cash the check. I told him he would have to show identifications and that I would have to call further. I telephoned David Eisenstein who was the signer of the instrument. I know Mr. Eisenstein for some time and knew I was talking to him. I told him I had a check for $700.00 and asked him if the check was good and told him it was presented for cashing. He said he had bought a car and that the check was good and that it was all right to cash the check. I then required further identification and made notes on the back of the check. The check was endorsed in my presence and delivered to me and I paid him the face value of the check, $700.00 minus my fee of $3.37. I deposited the check for collection in my bank. It was paid. It was returned a few days later and my account charged with $700.00."

From the brief record and testimony presented upon the hearing, it appears that a person who made himself known as Wallace Gross sold an automobile to defendant, for which he received a check payable to Wallace Gross for $700.00. Defendant was undoubtedly under the impression that the person to whom it delivered the check payable to Wallace Gross, bore that name, and it intended that he have the proceeds thereof. Almost immediately after the check was drawn, it was presented at the currency exchange for cashing, and plaintiff, subsequent to talking with one of defendant's agents and securing his approval to cash that particular check, cashed it. Plaintiff had no knowledge of any irregularities.

Defendant stresses the point that no reply was filed to its amended answer, and that no evidence was offered at the trial to rebut the defense of forgery. Examining the abstract, we find in plaintiff's statement of claim the allegation that "defendant issued to a certain person purporting to be Wallace Gross, its certain check number 14229 in the amount of $700.00; that on said date, and subsequent to its delivery to said person allegedly Wallace Gross, plaintiff became the holder in due course of said check, for value, and without knowledge of any defenses between the parties thereto, nor of any defects thereof." In its original answer defendant admitted that on "August 25, 1948, it issued a certain check to Wallace Gross in the sum of $700.00, but denies that on said date, or any subsequent date thereto, the plaintiff became the holder in due course of said check for value and without knowledge of any defense between the parties nor of any defects thereof." The amended answer contains substantially the same averments. It thus appears that defendant at no time denied the important allegation that it had issued a check to "a certain person *purporting* to be Wallace Gross," and that "subsequent to its delivery to said person *allegedly* Wallace Gross, plaintiff became the holder in due course of said check." There being no denial of this material allegation, it was not necessary for plaintiff to reply to the amended answer; upon the face of the pleadings it stands admitted that the person to whom defendant issued the check which was later cashed by plaintiff, was an impostor; and this is important because the statute and the ordinary rules applicable to forgery of negotiable instruments are not applicable to the circumstances of this case, as will hereinafter appear. That the person who received the check from defendant and who cashed it at plaintiff's currency exchange was an impostor also appears from the following testimony of plaintiff: "I saw the person who made the statement it was a forged endorsement. He was not the person who delivered the check to me." Under the "imposter rule," "* * * where the drawer delivers a check, draft, or bill of exchange to an impostor as payee supposing that he is the person he has falsely represented himself to be, the impostor's endorsement in the name by which the payee is described is regarded as a genuine endorsement as to subsequent holders in good faith." * * * "[W]here the drawer delivers a check to an imposter as payee supposing that he is the person he had falsely represented himself to be, the impostor's subsequent endorsement of the paper in the name by which the payee is described is to be regarded as a genuine endorsement between the drawer and the drawee who pays the paper on such endorsement."

The defense is predicated chiefly on the contention that since the endorsement on the check was a forgery, plaintiff is precluded from recovery under [state statute] which provides that "Where a signature is forged or made without authority, it is wholly inoperative, and no right to retain the instrument or to give a discharge thereof, or to enforce payment thereof against any party thereto, can be acquired through or under such signature, unless the party against whom it is sought to enforce such right is precluded from setting up the forgery or want of authority." However, the authorities are fairly in accord in holding that, under the circumstances presented in the case at bar, the impostor's endorsement in the name by which the payee is described *is to be regarded as a genuine endorsement between the drawer and the drawee who pays the paper on such endorsement—and is not a forgery.*

* * *

The consequences of the mistake should fall upon the drawer rather than on the purchaser, since the mistake is primarily the former's, whether he has himself been deceived or has deliberately tried to shift the burden of identification by giving the impostor a negotiable instrument instead of cash. The fraud upon the drawer facilitated a fraud upon the purchaser.

* * *

JUDGMENT AND REMEDY *The trial court, which had held that Wallace Gross' forged signature was effective to pass title to Greenberg under the imposter rule, was affirmed.*

FURTHER EXAMPLES Assume that the Revco Company gives its bookkeeper, Sam Snyde, general authority to issue checks in the company name drawn on Second Federal Bank so that Snyde can pay employees and pay other corporate bills. Snyde decides to cheat Revco out of $10,000 by issuing a check payable to Fanny Freid, an old acquaintance of his. Snyde does not intend Freid to receive any of the money and Freid is not an employee or creditor of the company.

Snyde indorses the check in Freid's name, naming himself as indorsee. Snyde cashes the check with a local bank, which collects payment from the drawee bank, Second Federal. Second Federal then charges Revco's account $10,000.

Revco discovers the fraud and demands that its account be recredited. Who bears the loss? Neither the local bank that first accepted the check nor Second Federal are responsible. The rule of UCC Sec. 3-405 provides the answer. Since Snyde's indorsement in the name of a payee with no interest in the instrument is "effective," there is no "forgery." Hence, the collecting bank is protected in paying on the check, and the drawee bank is protected in charging Revco's account. It is the employer-drawer, Revco, that bears the loss.[6]

The Code makes no distinction in result when a dishonest employee does not actually sign the check, but merely supplies his employer with names of fictitious creditors or with true names of creditors having fictitious debts.

6. May Dept. Stores Co. v. Pittsburgh Nat. Bank, 374 F.2d 109 (3rd Cir. 1967).

For example, Ned Norris draws up the payroll list from which employee checks are written. Norris fraudulently adds the name Sue Swift (a fictitious person) to the payroll, thus causing checks to be issued to her. Again, it is the employer-drawer who bears the loss because the employer is in the best position to prevent such fraud.

Miscellaneous Indorsement Problems

NO STANDARD CATEGORY Sometimes an indorsement does not seem to fit into any of the standard categories. For example, the indorsement can read: "I hereby assign all my right and title and interest in this note, (signed) XXO." The signature is an effective indorsement despite the additional language of transfer. Use of the word *assign* does not change the negotiation into a mere assignment. Clearly XXO did not intend to limit the rights of the person to whom he was transferring the instrument. [UCC Sec. 3-202(4)]

CORRECTION OF NAME An indorsement should be identical to the name that appears on the instrument. The payee or indorsee whose name is misspelled can indorse with the misspelled name, or the correct name, or both. [UCC Sec. 3-203] For example, Susan Lock receives a check payable to the order of "Susan Locke." She can indorse the check either "Susan Locke" or "Susan Lock." The usual practice is to indorse the name as it appears on the instrument and follow it by the correct name.[7]

BANK INDORSEMENTS When a customer deposits a check with a bank and fails to indorse it, the bank has the right to supply any necessary indorsement for its customer unless the instrument specifically prohibits it. For example, Bob Adams deposits his government check with First National Bank and forgets to indorse it. Since government checks typically state, "Payee's Indorsement Required," the bank will not supply the indorsement. The check will be returned to Adams for his signature.

Ordinarily, checks do not specifically require the payee's indorsement. The bank merely stamps or marks the check, indicating that it was deposited by the customer or credited to the customer's account. [UCC Sec. 4-205]

Commercial paper must move rapidly through banking channels. In the process of clearing through collection, a check can be transferred between banks using any agreed-upon method of indorsement that identifies the transferor bank. [UCC Sec. 4-206] For example, a bank can indorse using its Federal Reserve number instead of its name.

MULTIPLE PAYEES An instrument payable to two or more persons *in the alternative* (for example, "Pay to A or B") requires the indorsement of *either* payee. [UCC Sec. 3-116(a)] However, if an instrument is payable to two or

7. Watertown Federal Sav. and Loan v. Spanks, 346 Mass. 398, 193 N.E.2d 333 (1963).

more persons *jointly* (for example, "Pay C and D" or "Pay G, H"), then *both* indorsements are necessary for negotiation. [UCC Sec. 3-116(b)]

UNINDORSED ORDER PAPER If order paper is transferred without indorsement, it is a transfer by assignment, not by negotiation. The receiver is merely a transferee, not a holder, and can never qualify as a holder in due course. If, however, the transfer is made for value given, the unqualified indorsement of the transferor can be compelled by law unless the parties have agreed otherwise. The effect is the negotiation of the instrument. The transferee becomes a holder and can negotiate the instrument further. [UCC Sec. 3-201(3)]

The rule is a little different for banks. With one exception, a depositary bank receiving a check from its customer has the power to supply its customer's indorsement under UCC Sec. 4-205. Thus the bank is a holder and can negotiate the instrument.

AGENTS OR OFFICERS A negotiable instrument can be drawn payable to a legal entity such as an estate, a partnership, or an organization. For example, if a check reads "Pay to the Red Cross," an authorized representative of the Red Cross can negotiate it.

Similarly, negotiable paper can be payable to a public officer. For example, checks reading "Pay to the Order of the County Tax Collector," or "Pay to Larry White, Receiver of Taxes," can be negotiated by whoever holds the office. [UCC Sec. 3-110(1)(b)]

QUESTIONS AND CASE PROBLEMS

1. Graybar Electric Company and Marine Midland Bank had a long-standing agreement under which Marine Midland received checks payable to Graybar and transferred them to other parties, usually other banks. Graybar never saw the checks. They were made out to Graybar's order and delivered directly to

Marine Midland. Marine Midland stamped the backs of the checks with Graybar's name and insignia and transferred them. Within the meaning of the UCC, is the act of sending checks to Marine Midland Bank a negotiation? Is Marine Midland's transfer of the checks to other parties a negotiation? [Marine Midland Bank-New York v. Graybar Electric Co., 41 N.Y. 2d 703, 363 N.E.2d 1139 (1977)]

2. Wes-Con Development Company was a general contractor involved in building a large office building in San Francisco. Wes-Con hired Phillips as its

plumbing subcontractor. As construction progressed, Phillips experienced financial difficulties, and Phillips's plumbing supplier informed Wes-Con that it was hesitant to supply any more materials. Wes-Con therefore promised the supplier that the next allotment check to Phillips would be made out to the supplier and Phillips as joint payees. One month later, Wes-Con made out a joint check and gave it to Phillips. Phillips signed the back of the check and delivered it to another creditor. Was the check properly negotiated by Phillips? Why or why not? [Bank of West v. Wes-Con Dev. Co., Inc., 15 Wash. App. 238, 548 P.2d 563 (1976)]

3. In May 1964, Northside Building and Investment Company issued a note, as maker, to the order of Citizens Bank. Citizens later indorsed the note to the order of Bankers Finance Company, and Bankers indorsed it to the order of Stockbridge. Several months later, Stockbridge gave the note to Finance Company of America as collateral for a loan. Is Finance Company of America a holder? [Northside Bldg. and Investment Co. v. Finance Co. of America, 119 Ga. App. 131, 166 S.E.2d. 608 (1969)]

4. At one of the weekly auctions that Sweedler conducted, a purchaser bid for and received merchandise worth approximately $300. In return, the purchaser gave Sweedler a cashier's check that was payable to the purchaser. However, he failed to indorse the check, and Sweedler inadvertently failed to request the indorsement. Without the indorsement, the bank refused to pay Sweedler. The purchaser also refused to indorse the check because he was dissatisfied with the merchandise. If, at a trial between Sweedler and the bank, the purchaser admits that he gave Sweedler the cashier's check in exchange for certain merchandise, will Sweedler be allowed to recover against the bank? [Sweedler v. Oboler, 65 Misc. 2d 789, 319 N.Y.S. 2d. 89 (1971)]

5. Over several years, Vinson made a number of business investments for which he had to borrow substantial sums of money from his bank. As collateral for these loans, Vinson gave his bank several thousand shares of stock in XYZ company. Then, Vinson's business investments began to go sour, and XYZ company's stock dropped significantly in value. The bank therefore demanded that Vinson deliver additional collateral. Vinson gave the bank five $10,000 notes payable to his order. Instead of indorsing the notes on the back, Vinson made the indorsements on separate sheets of paper, which he then stapled securely to each note. Has Vinson made a proper negotiation of the notes to his bank? [Tallahassee Bank and Trust Co. v. Raines, 125 Ga. App. 623, 187 S.E. 2d. 320 (1972)]

6. John Copeland owned a small apartment complex in Houston, Texas. Thelma Moore leased one of Copeland's apartments for a number of years. When the rent for March 1970 came due, Moore wrote out a check payable in the appropriate amount to "Mrs. Copeland" rather than "Mr. Copeland." If John Copeland later signs the check on the back "Mr. John Copeland" will this operate as a valid indorsement of the check? [Moore v. Copeland, 478 S.W. 2d. 573 (Tex. Civ. App. 1972)]

7. Davis, student at Baltic University, often ran out of money and phoned his father to wire him extra cash. Davis's roommate watched Davis do this a number of times and later got very proficient at imitating Davis's voice over the phone. One night, the roommate phoned Davis's father and requested that he wire him $1,000 the next morning at 10:00. The father wired a money order at the prearranged hour to the Western Union office at Baltic University. The office wired back asking the father if he wished to have the person present in the office officially identified as his son. The father declined because he believed that it had been his son who had arranged to receive the money order. Later, when the father learned of the roommate's impersonation, he demanded his money back from Western Union. Western Union declined. Should the father recover? [Davis v. Western Union Telegraph Co., 4 D.&C. 2d. 264 (Pa. 1956)]

8. During a two-year period, Young, an employee of General American Life Insurance Company, caused twenty checks to be drawn on First National Bank payable to the order of a fictitious policyholder. Young then took the checks, forged the policyholder's name, and cashed them. When General American learned of the fraud, it demanded that First National Bank reimburse its account. First National Bank refused, and a lawsuit followed. Who will prevail? [Delmar Bank v. Fidelity & Deposit Co., 300 F. Supp. 496 (E.D. Mo. 1969)]

9. F. Mitchell, assistant treasurer of Travco Corporation, caused two checks payable to a fictitious company, L. and B. Distributors, to be drawn on the corporation's account. Mitchell took both checks to his personal bank, indorsed them "F. Mitchell," and gave them to the teller. The teller cashed them. When the bank attempted to collect from Travco, Travco refused to pay. The bank contended that, under the rule concerning fictitious payees and imposters, Mitchell's indorsement was valid and that, therefore, the bank should be allowed to collect. Is the bank's contention true? [Travco Corp. v. Citizens Federal Sav. & Loan Ass'n, 42 Mich. App. 291, 201 N.W.2d. 675 (1972)]

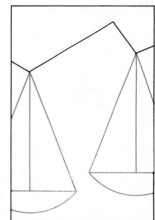

26

Commercial Paper
Holder in Due Course

Since commercial paper is not money itself, but payable in money, commercial paper litigation results when there is a dispute about who should be paid. Litigation issues usually turn on which party can obtain payment on an instrument when it is due or on whether some defense can be asserted to discharge or cancel liability on an instrument.

A holder in due course takes a negotiable instrument free of all claims of other parties. That means that the holder in due course has the right to collect payment on that instrument, and this right will take priority over the claims of other parties.[1]

CONTRACT LAW VERSUS
THE LAW OF COMMERCIAL PAPER

The basic principles of contract law govern when simple contract rights are assigned to a third party (assignee), when a nonnegotiable instrument is transferred to a third party (transferee), or when a negotiable instrument is improperly negotiated to a third party (transferee). The contract rights of assignees and transferees are burdened with every legal

---

1. UCC Sec. 3-505(2) specifically sets forth the very limited number of real *defenses* that defeat payment to a holder in due course. A holder in due course takes commercial paper free from personal (as opposed to real) defenses. These are discussed more thoroughly in Chapter 27.

defense that existed between prior parties regardless of the extent of their knowledge of them. Persons who transfer or assign contractual or nonnegotiable rights pass on only the rights that they had.

The body of rules contained in Article 3 of the UCC govern a party's right to payment of a check, draft, note, or certificate of deposit.[2] The third party is characterized as either an ordinary *holder* or a *holder in due course*. (The party can also be a transferee according to UCC Sec. 3-201.) Our discussion of holders in due course will primarily be concerned with *negotiable* instruments which have been negotiated.

HOLDER

A **holder** is a person who has possession of a negotiable instrument that is "drawn, issued, or indorsed" to that person or to that person's order, or to bearer, or in blank.[3] [UCC Sec. 1-201(20)] The holder is entitled to receive payment of the instrument. Either an original party or a third party can qualify as a holder. The manner in which possession of a negotiable instrument is acquired will determine whether or not a person qualifies as a *holder*. Negotiation is a special form of transfer in which the transferee becomes a *holder*. [UCC Sec. 3-202] (See Chapter 25.)

Order Paper

If the paper is an order instrument, the initial holder is the payee. Thus, Sam Smith is the holder of a check payable to him that is in his possession. If Smith indorses the check to Jane Brown and gives it to her, Brown will become the holder. Order paper is negotiated by delivery and indorsement. [UCC Sec. 3-202] The check payable to Sam Smith is issued when it is delivered to him. Smith's acts of indorsing and delivering the check into Brown's possession constitute negotiation to Brown.

Bearer Paper

If the paper is bearer paper, the holder is the person who is in physical possession of the instrument. Bearer paper can be negotiated only by delivery, but the transferor can indorse it. [UCC Sec. 3-202] Assume that a negotiable promissory note reads "Pay to Bearer the Sum of $100.00." Whoever the instrument is delivered to, whether or not that person is the real owner, is a holder.

Rights of a Holder

The holder of a negotiable instrument has the power to negotiate it to another party. The holder has the right to demand payment of the instrument in his or her own name. Similarly, with certain exceptions, a holder can cancel or discharge the obligation on an instrument whether or not he or she is the original owner. [UCC Sec. 3-301]

A holder has the status of an assignee of a contract right. A transferee of a negotiable instrument who is characterized merely as a holder (as opposed to a holder in due course) obtains only those rights that the predecessor-transferor had in the instrument. In the event that there is a conflicting, superior claim or defense to the instrument, an ordinary holder will not be able to collect payment.

HOLDER IN DUE COURSE

A holder in due course (HDC) is a special-status transferee of a negotiable instrument who, by meeting certain acquisition requirements, takes the instrument free of most defenses or adverse claims to it. Stated another way, an HDC can normally acquire a higher level of immunity to

---

2. The rights and liabilities on checks, drafts, notes, and certificates of deposit are determined under Article 3 of the Uniform Commercial Code. Other kinds of commercial paper, such as stock certificates or bills of lading and other documents of title, meet the requirements of negotiable instruments, but the rights and liabilities of the parties on these documents are covered by Articles 7 and 8 of the Code.

3. A holder, as the term is used in Article 3 of the Uniform Commercial Code, applies here only in the context of negotiable instruments.

defenses against payment on the instrument or claims of ownership to the instrument by other parties.

Requirements for Holder-In-Due-Course Status

The basic requirements for attaining HDC status are set forth in UCC Sec. 3-302. An HDC must first be a holder of a negotiable instrument. Then the holder must take the instrument (1) for value, (2) in good faith, and (3) without notice that it is overdue, or that it has been dishonored, or that any person has a defense against it or a claim to it.

The underlying requirement of "due course" status is that a person must first be a holder on that instrument. Review the qualifications of a holder because, regardless of other circumstances surrounding acquisition, only a holder has a chance to become an HDC.

Value

An HDC must have given *value* for the paper. [UCC Sec. 3-303] A person who receives an instrument as a gift or who inherits it has not met the requirement of value. In these situations, the person becomes an ordinary holder and does not possess the rights of an HDC.[4]

The concept of value in the law of negotiable instruments is not the same as the concept of consideration in the law of contracts. An executory promise (a promise to give value in the future) is clearly valid consideration to support a contract. [UCC Sec. 1-201(44)] However, an executory promise does not normally constitute the "value" (agreed consideration performed) that is necessary for holder-in-due-course status under UCC Sec. 3-303. If the holder plans to pay for the instrument later on or perform the required services at some future date, the holder has not yet given value. Suppose Ted Green draws a $500 note payable to Roger Evans in payment for goods. Evans negotiates the note to Irene Franks, who promises to pay him for it in thirty days. During the next month, Franks learns that Evans breached the contract by delivering defective goods and that Green will not honor the $500 note. Franks can return the note to Evans. She has suffered no out-of-pocket loss because she has not given value. A purchaser of a note or draft who has merely promised to pay or to perform an act but has not yet done so can rescind the transaction and avoid it if he or she learns of a defense.[5]

Once a holder has given value, it may not be possible to rescind the deal. The holder in due course needs protection that permits recovery on the instrument from the primary party regardless of any personal defenses arising between the original parties. Reconsider the last example. Assume this time that Irene Franks pays Roger Evans for the note on the spot. Franks is a holder for value once the agreed consideration is performed. She has "paid" for holder-in-due-course protection. This means she is entitled to collect payment of the $500 note against Green regardless of any personal defenses that Green may have against Evans (for example, breach of contract). The rights between Irene and Ted on the note are governed by Article 3 of the UCC. The rights between Ted and Roger on the contract are governed by contract law and by Article 2.

The following case takes up the question of value. Donald Goldberg sold his interest in a corporation to Rothman and others for $7,500. Upon Goldberg's request the buyers made four promissory notes payable to Ethel Goldberg, his wife.

There is no apparent reason why Donald Goldberg designated the payee as his wife nor is there any indication that Ethel Goldberg received the notes for value as defined by UCC 3-303.

---

4. There is one way an ordinary holder who fails to meet the value requirement can qualify as a holder in due course. The "shelter provision" of the Code allows an ordinary holder to succeed to HDC status if any prior holder was an HDC. This exception is discussed later in the chapter. [UCC Sec. 3-201(1)]

5. Rescission is allowed under the theory that breach of warranty by the transferor is a defense. [UCC Sec. 3-417] Warranty liability is discussed in Chapter 27.

GOLDBERG v.
ROTHMAN
Civil Court of the City of New
York, 1971.
66 Misc.2d 981, 322 N.Y.S.2d
931.

BACKGROUND AND FACTS   *The plaintiff, Ethel Goldberg, sought to recover the sum of $7,500 on four promissory notes in which she was designated the payee. The notes were executed by six individual defendants. At the time the notes were made, the plaintiff's husband, Donald Goldberg, and the defendants, were all stockholders in a corporation known as 86th Street Bay 40th Corporation. The notes were given in consideration for the sale of Donald Goldberg's interest in the corporation to the defendants. At Donald Goldberg's request, the notes were made payable to his wife, the plaintiff, who otherwise had no interest in or connection with the corporation.*

The defendants alleged that they had a valid cause of action that they should be able to assert against Donald Goldberg and against Ethel Goldberg as payee on the promissory notes because, at the time the notes were executed, Donald Goldberg specifically said that certain monies would be paid for goods that had been sold pursuant to a business deal in which the corporation was involved.

The defendants claimed that a balance of $7,643.33 was due as a result of this other business deal and that they should be able to bring an action against Donald Goldberg as a counterclaim, or, at least, as a setoff against the plaintiff's cause of action. [Background and Facts substantially as stated by the court.]

BOYERS, Justice.
* * *

There is no explanation or reason as to why plaintiff was designated payee of the subject notes other than it was done in compliance with Donald Goldberg's request. Nor does it appear that plaintiff took the instruments for "value" as that term is defined by §3-303 of the Uniform Commercial Code. For ought that appears Donald Goldberg gave these notes as a gift to the plaintiff, but such a determination is not relevant to the issues herein. It is clear that a payee may be a holder in due course (see §3-302, Uniform Commercial Code), but since the plaintiff herein did not take the instruments for value she is an ordinary holder. Nonetheless she has the rights of a holder and may enforce payment in her own name (§3-301, Uniform Commercial Code). * * * [T]he court feels the merits or lack of merits of defendants' contention of an assignment and the promise of Donald Goldberg that the debt owing to Caliber could be set off against the notes is not relevant to plaintiff's cause of action for reasons hereafter set forth.

Under §3-306, Uniform Commercial Code, plaintiff not having the rights of a holder in due course takes the instrument here, the notes in question, "subject to (b) all defenses of any party which would be available in an action on simple contract."
* * *

Plaintiff sues herein in her own right. Defendants have not shown that any defenses exist against her in relation to the validity of the notes nor have they established that they have any right of setoff because of an alleged claim against plaintiff's husband.

The court held that Ethel Goldberg was entitled to recover $7,500 from the defendants. However, her award did not prejudice any cause of action the defendants had against Donald Goldberg. The court made it clear that the plaintiff's right to recover was independent of her husband's possible liability in another lawsuit.

JUDGMENT AND REMEDY

AGREED CONSIDERATION PERFORMED A holder takes an instrument for value to the extent that agreed consideration has been performed. In the typical situation, the holder is a purchaser for money. For example, Morris executes a $300 note payable to the order of Paulson. Paulson sells the note to a bank which pays Paulson $285 (a discount is usual). The bank has given value for Morris's note.

Performance of agreed consideration can also include an act such as the delivery of goods. Harper holds a note from Barton and agrees to negotiate the note to Thompson in payment for a purchase of goods. Delivery of the goods is Thompson's agreed performance, that is, the value given for the note.

Section 3-303(a) of the Code provides that a holder takes an instrument for value only to the extent that the agreed-upon consideration has been performed. For example, Arnolds negotiates a $1,000 note to Raymonds for a total price of $950 with $700 payable now and $250 due in thirty days. Raymonds is immediately an HDC to the extent of $700, and when she completes payment of $250, she will become an HDC for the full $1,000 face amount of the note.

Do not be confused when the value of the agreed consideration differs from the face amount of the instrument. When a time instrument is sold, it is usually discounted to allow for transfer costs, collection costs, and interest charges. Thus, a $1,000 note due in ninety days may be sold for $950 cash to a financial institution. The requirement of agreed consideration is satisfied by the $950 payment. If the discrepancy between the purchase and face value is great, however, it can be taken with other factors to indicate a lack of good faith on the part of the purchaser. The good faith element will be discussed later in the chapter.

A holder takes an instrument for value to the extent that the holder acquires a security interest or lien on the instrument.[6] Normally, an instrument is given as security for a loan or other obligation. If, for example, Norris issues a $1,000 note payable to Lomond, Lomond can use the note to secure a $700 loan from Hilton. (Lomond gets $700 cash, Hilton holds the note.) Hilton's $700 loan qualifies her as a holder for value. If Lomond does not repay the $700, Hilton can collect the note. But what if Norris has a personal defense against Lomond? Hilton, as an HDC, is free and clear of the defense, but *only to the extent of $700.* Hence, the rule is, "a purchaser of a limited interest can be a holder in due course only to the extent of the interest purchased." [UCC Sec. 3-302(4)]

ANTECEDENT CLAIM When an instrument is given in payment of an **antecedent claim** (or as security for an antecedent, or prior, debt), the value requirement is met.[7] [UCC Sec. 3-303(b)] Here, again, commercial law and contract law produce different results. An antecedent debt is not valid consideration under general contract law, but it does constitute value sufficient to satisfy the requirement for HDC status in commercial law.

Assume Cary owes Dwyer $2,000 on a past due account. If Cary negotiates a $2,000 note to Dwyer and Dwyer accepts it to discharge the overdue account balance, Dwyer has given value for the instrument.

NEGOTIABLE INSTRUMENT IS VALUE Merely promising to pay money or to perform an act in the future does not constitute giving

---

6. A holder does not become an HDC of an instrument by purchasing it at a judicial sale or by taking it under legal process. [UCC Sec. 3-302(3)(a)]

7. The antecedent claim (or debt) discharged may be one against any person, not just the transferor of the instrument whether or not the claim is due.

value. However, if a purchaser's promise to pay money is made in the form of a negotiable instrument (for example, a check or an irrevocable letter of credit), the requirement of value is met. Section 3-303(c) of the Code provides that a holder takes the instrument for value "when he gives a negotiable instrument for it, or makes an irrevocable commitment to a third person." For example, Tillman writes a check to Samson for the purchase of a ninety-day note that Samson is holding. Tillman gives value when he issues the check to Samson.

A negotiable instrument has value when issued, not when the underlying money is finally paid. In the example above, if later that day but before the check is cashed, Tillman learns that the maker of the note has a personal defense against Samson, Tillman knows that he has the protection of HDC status. Commercial practicality requires this rule because a negotiable instrument, by its nature, carries with it the possibility that it might be negotiated to a holder in due course. If it is, the party that issued it cannot refuse to pay. [UCC Sec. 3-303]

A holder can also take for value by acquiring a lien on the instrument through an agreement rather than through operation of law. For example, a payee of a note pledges it to a bank as security for a loan. The terms of the pledge agreement give the bank a lien on the instrument. The bank is a holder for value to the extent of its lien.

There are various ways a holder can take a negotiable instrument for value and thus become a holder in due course. Section 3-303 of the Code includes within the definition of taking for value either taking an instrument in payment of or as security for an antecedent claim, or making an irrevocable commitment to a third person.

In the following case, the plaintiff tried to fall within the meaning of the definition of taking for value so that he could retain the proceeds of a check.

BENNETT v. UNITED STATES FIDELITY AND GUAR. CO.
Court of Appeals of North Carolina, 1973.
19 N.C. App. 66, 198 S.E.2d. 33.

BACKGROUND AND FACTS *Bennett, the plaintiff, sued to recover $4,400, the amount of a check issued by an insurance company in settlement of an automobile damage claim. The plaintiff's mother, Mabel, owned the car. The plaintiff had possession of it, and he allowed his friend, Wilbur Prince, to borrow it. While driving the car, Prince wrecked it. He reported the accident to his insurance company, the defendant, United States Fidelity and Guaranty Company.*

The insurance company negotiated a settlement for $4,400. It issued a check jointly payable to its insured, Prince, and to the owner of the car, Mabel Bennett. The two indorsed the check to the plaintiff, who then deposited it in his bank account, intending to use the money to purchase a new car.

During the time it took the check to clear, the insurance company issued a stop payment order because it discovered that the insurance policy did not cover collision damage for nonowned vehicles. The plaintiff took the position that he was a holder in due course and had the right to recover from the insurance company, notwithstanding the company's dispute with Prince and Mabel.

MORRIS, Judge.
* * *

Plaintiff [Bennett] contends that he is entitled, under [UCC Sec. 3-302], to the amount of the draft. [UCC Sec. 3-302] defines a holder in due course as one who takes an instrument for value, and in good faith, and without notice that it is overdue or has been dishonored or of any defense against or claim to it on the part of any person.

The undisputed evidence discloses that plaintiff was without notice of the defense of the issuer and that he took the instrument in good faith and for the purpose of purchasing an automobile to replace the one wrecked by defendant's insured. The only question about which the parties disagree is whether plaintiff took the check for value.

[UCC Sec. 3-303] defines taking for value as follows:

"A holder takes the instrument for value (a) to the extent that the agreed consideration has been performed or that he acquires a security interest in or a lien on the instrument otherwise than by legal process; or (b) when he takes the instrument in payment of or as security for an antecedent claim against any person whether or not the claim is due; or (c) when he gives a negotiable instrument for it or makes an irrevocable commitment to a third person."

Plaintiff earnestly contends that he comes within the purview of the definition for two reasons.

He first contends that the evidence discloses that he took the check in payment of an antecedent claim against Wilbur Lee Prince and, therefore, he took the check for value. There is no dispute about the fact that the car was registered in the name of plaintiff's mother. Plaintiff, therefore, had no claim against Prince for the damage to the car. * * * On appeal he says, however, that he had a claim against Prince for damage to personal property in the car at the time of the wreck. A close examination of the record, and particularly the deposition and affidavit of plaintiff, reveals absolutely no evidence of whether plaintiff had any property in the car and if so, what it was. In his affidavit, plaintiff said: "The value given by him to Wilbur Lee Prince was full settlement of any claim that he might have against Wilbur Lee Prince for the loss of any personal property Wilbur Lee Prince was responsible for when the Datsun automobile was damaged," but nowhere does he contend that he did in fact have any personal property in the car. Plaintiff has failed to present any evidence which would tend to show any legal claim against either payee, which plaintiff had and relinquished.

He also contends that he gave value by virtue of the provisions of [UCC Sec. 3-303(c)] in that he made an irrevocable commitment to a third person. Plaintiff contends and the evidence reveals that he intended to use the amount of the check for the purchase of a new car. He stated in his deposition that the insurance draft was delivered to him; that he carried it to his mother and to Prince for endorsement and then deposited it in his checking account at Wachovia Bank and Trust Company; that he was told at the time he made the deposit that it would take "a couple of days to clear"; that he then called the insurance agent who suggested that he postdate the check he was to give in payment for the car he was buying; that he then went to the dealer and followed this suggestion.

The official comment to [UCC Sec. 3-303(c)] is as follows:

"Paragraph (c) is new, but states generally recognized exceptions to the rule that an executory promise is not value. A negotiable instrument is value because it carries the possibility of negotiation to a holder in due course, after which the party who gives it cannot refuse to pay. The same reasoning applies to any irrevocable commitment to a third person, such as a letter credit issued when an instrument is taken."

We are of the opinion that the wording of the statute contemplates a simultaneous transaction—a commitment to a third person made when the holder takes the instrument. We do not construe it to include a commitment made subsequent to the taking of the instrument. We hold, therefore, that plaintiff's subsequent reliance on the payment of the draft does not constitute a taking for value necessary to put plaintiff in the position of holder in due course.

The undisputed facts establish that plaintiff is not a holder in due course.

JUDGMENT AND REMEDY   *Bennett was unable to recover the $4,400, since the appellate court found that he was not a holder in due course of the insurance company's check.*

CHECK DEPOSITS AND WITHDRAWALS

Occasionally, a commercial bank can become an HDC when honoring other banks' checks for its own customers. Assume that Pat Stevens has $100 in her checking account at First National Bank. On Monday, after depositing her payroll check of $250 drawn on the Second National Bank, First National Bank cashes a check on her account for $150. The First National Bank has given value to Stevens for the check, making it an HDC to the extent of $50. The first $100 is presumed to come from the money already in Stevens' account—based on the Code's first-money-in, first-money-out approach. [UCC Sec. 4-208(2)]

Good Faith

The second requirement for HDC status is good faith. [UCC Sec. 3-302(1)(b)] The requirement of good faith means that the purchaser/holder acts honestly in the process of acquiring the instrument. **Good faith** is defined in UCC Sec. 1-201(19) as "honesty in fact in the conduct or transaction concerned."

The good faith requirement *applies only to the purchaser.* It is immaterial whether the transferor acted in good faith. Thus, a person who in good faith takes a negotiable instrument from a thief can be an HDC. The reason is simple. An inherent characteristic of negotiable paper is that any person in possession of an instrument that runs to him or her by its terms is a holder. Also, anyone can deal with the possessor as a holder.

The good faith requirement asks whether or not the purchaser, when acquiring the instrument, honestly believed the instrument was not defective. If a person purchases a $10,000 note for $100 from a stranger on a street corner, the issue of good faith can be raised on the grounds of the suspicious circumstances *and* the grossly inadequate consideration. The Code does not provide clear guidelines to determine good faith.

INDUSTRIAL NAT. BANK OF RHODE ISLAND v. LEO'S USED CAR EXCHANGE, INC.

Supreme Judicial Court of Massachusetts, 1973.
362 Mass. 797, 291 N.E.2d. 603.

BACKGROUND AND FACTS   *Frederick Villa presented two checks for the purchase of used automobiles at an auction. The checks were cashed and sent through the bank collection process. However, a stop payment was issued by Leo's Used Car Exchange, and it was determined that a third party claimed to hold security interest in the purchased cars. Checks cashed at Industrial National Bank had to be approved by the manager. However, the management cashed checks for corporations if it knew the person and his or her business. The question before the court was did the failure to obtain the bank manager's approval constitute a lack of good faith?*

HENNESSEY, Justice.
* * *

We summarize the relevant evidence. On October 9, 1968, an agent of the defendant [Leo's] attended a car auction in the State of Connecticut, and purchased three cars from Frederick Villa, for which he gave the two checks described above. The defendant subsequently resold the cars at a profit.

Frederick Villa was a customer of the plaintiff bank and had a corporate account there under the name of Villa Auto Sales, Inc. The manager of the Centerville Branch of the plaintiff bank in Providence, Rhode Island, was personally acquainted with Frederick Villa. Corporate authority stating that Frederick Villa was the president and treasurer of Villa Auto Sales, Inc., and that he was authorized to sign or indorse any check held by the corporation, was on file with the bank. [Footnotes omitted.]

Frederick Villa presented both checks to the plaintiff bank on October 10, 1968, and as was his practice, asked the teller to cash them and give him the cash since he was going to another auction and needed it. The checks were cashed and sent through the bank collection process. Meanwhile, the defendant stopped payment on the checks at the Security National Bank in Springfield, Massachusetts, following a telephone call from an officer of the Rhode Island Hospital Trust Company which claimed to hold security interests in the cars he purchased. Consequently, the checks were not honored when presented, and were returned to the plaintiff bank.

There was also evidence of a rule at the plaintiff bank that any corporate checks drawn on another bank must be approved by the manager before being cashed by a teller. In this case, the teller did not obtain the manager's approval before he cashed both checks. However, the manager would cash a check for a corporation if he knew the person cashing the check and knew his business. * * * [The court examines the issue of whether the failure to obtain the manager's approval constituted a lack of good faith.]

A holder in due course is a holder who takes the instrument for value, in good faith, and without notice that it is overdue or has been dishonored or of any defense against or claim to it on the part of any person. [UCC Sec. 3-302(1)]. To the extent that a holder is a holder in due course he takes the instrument free from all claims to it on the part of any person, and all defences [sic] of any party to the instrument with whom the holder has not dealt (personal defences) except specifically enumerated "real defences."
* * *

The defendant argues that the plaintiff failed to exercise ordinary care in this transaction by violating the plaintiff's own rule of management when its teller cashed these checks without managerial approval. The defendant points to this as evidence of lack of good faith, which would support the judge's finding. Since there is no other evidence in the report which even arguably goes to the issue of good faith, we conclude that there was no evidence to support a finding of lack of good faith, and therefore both the District Court judge and the Appellate Division were in error.

"Good faith" is defined as "honesty in fact in the conduct or transaction concerned." Nothing in the definition suggests that in addition to being honest, the holder must exercise due care to be in good faith.
* * *

The rights of a holder of a negotiable instrument are to be determined by the simple test of honesty and good faith, and not by a speculative issue as to his diligence or negligence.

JUDGMENT AND REMEDY   *The plaintiff prevailed since the evidence disclosed no dishonesty.*

Notice

The third requirement for HDC status involves notice. [UCC Sec. 3-304] A person will not be afforded HDC protection if he or she acquires an instrument knowing, or having reason to know, that it is defective in any one of the following ways: [UCC Sec. 3-302(1)(c)]

1. It is overdue.
2. It has been dishonored.
3. There is a defense against it.
4. There is another claim to it.

The main provisions of UCC Sec. 3-304 spell out the common circumstances that, as a matter of law, constitute notice of a claim or defense and notice of an overdue instrument. In addition, Section 3-304(4) specifies certain facts that a purchaser might know about an instrument. These facts, in and of themselves, do not constitute notice of a defense or claim and do not disqualify the purchaser from HDC status.

NOTICE OF A FACT   Notice of a fact involves (1) actual knowledge of it, or (2) receipt of a notice about it, or (3) reason to know that a fact exists, given all the facts and circumstances known at the time in question. [UCC Sec. 1-201(25)]

OVERDUE OR DISHONORED INSTRUMENTS   All negotiable paper is either payable at a definite time (time instrument) or payable on demand (demand instrument). What will constitute notice that an instrument is overdue or has been dishonored will vary depending upon whether a person takes demand or time paper.

Time Instruments   A purchaser of a time instrument who takes the paper the day after its expressed due date is "on notice" that it is overdue. Nonpayment by the due date should indicate to any purchaser that the primary party has a defense to payment. Thus, a promissory note due on May 15 must be acquired before midnight on May 15. If it is purchased on May 16, the purchaser will be an ordinary holder, not an HDC.

Sometimes instruments read "payable in thirty days." A note dated December 1 payable in thirty days is due by midnight on December 31. But, what if the note were dated December 2 payable in thirty days? When is it due? If the payment date falls on a Sunday or holiday, the instrument is payable on the next business day so the note is due on January 2.

A large debt is often broken down into successive payments. The debt can be evidenced by a single, large-denomination note payable in installments, or there can be a series of notes in smaller denominations issued, each identified as part of the same indebtedness. In the case of an installment note, notice that the maker has defaulted on any installment of principal (but not interest payments) will prevent a purchaser from becoming an HDC. [UCC 3-304(3)(a)] The same result occurs when a series of notes, each with successive maturity dates, is issued at the same time for a single indebtedness. An uncured default in payment of any one note of the series will constitute overdue notice for the entire series. Prospective purchasers then know that they cannot qualify as HDCs.

Suppose a note reads, "Payable May 15, but may be accelerated if the holder feels insecure." A purchaser, unaware that a prior holder has elected to accelerate the due date on the instrument, buys the instrument. In Section 3-304(3)(b), the Code indirectly provides that such a purchaser can be a holder in due course unless he or she has reason to know that the acceleration has occurred.

Demand Instruments A purchaser has notice that a demand instrument is overdue if he or she takes the instrument knowing that demand has been made or takes it an unreasonable length of time after its issue. "A reasonable time for a check drawn and payable within the states and territories of the United States and the District of Columbia is presumed to be 30 days." [UCC Sec. 3-304(3)(c)]

Naturally, there can be no notice if a purchaser honestly does not know and has no reason to know from the circumstances that an instrument is overdue or that it has been dishonored. For example, Burton holds a demand note dated March 1 on Kayto, Inc., a local business firm. On March 19, she demands payment, and Kayto refuses (that is, dishonors the instrument). On March 20, Burton negotiates the note to Reynolds, a purchaser who lives in another state. Reynolds does not know and has no reason to know that the note has been dishonored so Reynolds can become an HDC.

CLAIMS AGAINST OR DEFENSES TO AN INSTRUMENT Knowledge of claims or defenses can be imputed to the purchaser in certain situations because (1) they are apparent from an examination of the face of the instrument or (2) they are extraneous to the instrument but apparent from the facts surrounding the transaction.

Incomplete Instruments A purchaser cannot expect to become an HDC when an instrument is so incomplete on its face that an element of negotiability is lacking (for example, name of the payee on order paper is missing, or the amount is not filled in). Minor omissions are permissible because these do not call into question the validity of the instrument. For

example, omission of connective words, such as the "on" in "pay to Smith on order," does not affect negotiability and neither does omission of the date from a check that has the month and year. [UCC Secs. 3-304(1)(a) and 3-114(1)]

When a person accepts an instrument without knowing that it is incomplete, then that person can take as an HDC and enforce the instrument as completed. To illustrate: Stuart Morgan asks Joan Nelson to buy a textbook for him when she goes to the campus bookstore. Morgan writes a check payable to the campus store, leaves the amount blank, and tells her to fill in the price of the textbook. Assume the textbook costs $15.50 in each of the following situations.

1. If Nelson gives the store the check with the amount entirely blank, the check is so incomplete that it is neither negotiable (no certain amount) nor enforceable.

2. If the cashier sees that the check is blank, watches Nelson complete the amount as $65.50, and then gives her $50 in change, the store will probably still be an HDC if the cashier is without notice that the filling in of the amount is improper. [UCC Sec. 3-304(4)(d), comment 10]

3. If Nelson fills in the check for $65.50 before she gets to the bookstore, the store sees only a properly completed instrument. Therefore it will take the check as an HDC and can enforce it for the full $65.50. The unauthorized completion is not a sufficient defense against the store in this situation. [UCC Secs. 3-407 and 3-115]

Irregular Instruments Any noticeable irregularity on the face of an instrument that should indicate to a purchaser that something is wrong with the paper will bar HDC status. For example, a note bearing a payee's signature that has been lined through with bold strokes with the second name penciled above it is highly irregular and will disqualify a taker from HDC status. [UCC 3-304 (1)(a)]

On the other hand, a note that is otherwise negotiable containing a notation "Payable at Newark" will not be the subject of inquiry because such notation does not raise questions essential to the terms, ownership, or validity of the note, nor does it create an ambiguity as to who is the party required to pay. [UCC Sec. 3-304(1)(a)]

Different handwriting used in the body of a check and in the signature will not normally make an instrument irregular. Postdating or antedating a check or stating the amount in digits but failing to write out the numbers will not make a check irregular. [UCC Sec. 3-114(2)] Visible evidence of forgery or alterations to material elements of negotiable paper will disqualify a purchaser from HDC status. Conversely, a careful forgery or alteration can go undetected by reasonable examination, and therefore, the purchaser can qualify as an HDC. [UCC Sec. 3-304(1)(a)] However, losses that result from careful forgeries usually fall on the party to whom the forger transferred the instrument (assuming, of course, that the forger cannot be found).

Voidable Obligations   It stands to reason that a purchaser who knows that a party to an instrument has a defense that entitles that party to avoid the obligation in any way cannot be a holder in due course. At the very least, good faith requires honesty in fact of the purchaser in a transaction. For example, a potential purchaser who knows that the maker of a note has breached the underlying contract with the payee cannot thereafter purchase the note as an HDC. [UCC 3-304(1)(b)]

Knowledge of one defense precludes a holder from becoming an HDC with respect to all other defenses. Jones, knowing that the note he holds was previously forged, presents it to the maker for payment. The maker refuses to pay on the grounds of breach of the underlying contract by the payee, Smith. The maker can assert this defense against Jones even though Jones had no knowledge of the breach because his knowledge of the forgery alone prevents him from being an HDC in *all* circumstances.

Knowledge that a fiduciary has wrongfully negotiated an instrument is sufficient notice of a claim against the instrument to disqualify HDC status. Suppose Jordan, a trustee of a university,

improperly writes a check on the university trust account to pay a personal debt. Farley actually knows that the check has been improperly drawn from university funds, but she accepts it anyway. Farley cannot claim to be an HDC. When a purchaser actually knows that a fiduciary is acting in breach of trust, HDC status is denied. [UCC Sec. 3-304(2)]

There is a strong policy against *imputing* notice to an otherwise good faith purchaser on a negotiable instrument. Not all knowledge charges the purchaser with notice of a claim or defense. Section 3-304(4) of the UCC contains a list of specific facts that do not in themselves constitute notice of a defense or claim. The list can be reviewed in the full text of the Code contained in Appendix A. In short, the Code's position is that certain kinds of information about the instrument or about parties to it can raise some suspicion regarding the ultimate enforceability of the paper, but the information falls short of indicating a defense or claim. For example, mere knowledge that an instrument is bought at a good discount off the face value is insufficient information to constitute notice of an adverse claim or defense.

Finally, a public notice, for example newspapers or official records, are not imputed to a purchaser—the information must actually have been read. [UCC Sec. 3-304(5)]

Recall that the basic test of good faith is honesty in fact. The key concern is whether this particular purchaser honestly knew or had reason to know something was wrong with that particular instrument at the time it was acquired.

Payee as HDC   Under certain circumstances, a *payee* may qualify as an HDC. [UCC Sec. 3-302(2)] A payee must be in good faith, give value and take the instrument without notice of a defense or claim. Logic dictates that in the majority of instances, if there are defenses to the instrument, the payee will know or have reason to know about them. To illustrate: Baker Painters contracts with Amex Company to paint the exterior of its new office building for $2,000. Amex issues a negotiable promissory note to Baker Painters for $2,000, due thirty days later.

When the note comes due, Baker tries to collect the $2,000 from Amex. Amex refuses to pay the note, claiming that the paint was defective; it washed off during a rainstorm. Since Baker Painters obviously knows about the defective paint, Baker Painters is not an HDC. Amex can disavow liability on the note based on the breach of contract. Baker Painters has no recourse in commercial law based on its responsibility for the defect.

HOLDERS THROUGH A HOLDER IN DUE COURSE

A person who does not qualify as a holder in due course but who derives title through a holder in due course can acquire the rights and privileges of a holder in due course. According to UCC Section 3-201(1):

Transfer of an instrument vests in the transferee such rights as the transferor has therein, except that a transferee who has himself been a party to any fraud or illegality affecting the instrument or who as a prior holder had notice of a defense or claim against it cannot improve his position by taking from a later holder in due course.

This has also been called the *shelter provision*. This rule seems to detract from the basic holder-in-due-course philosophy. It is, however, in line with the concept of marketability and free transferability of commercial paper (as well as contract law, where assignees acquire the rights of assignors). The transfer rule extends the holder-in-due-course benefits, and it is designed to aid the HDC to dispose of the instrument readily. Since any instrument in the hands of an HDC is free from personal defenses (by definition), an HDC should reasonably have the privilege of transferring all rights in the instrument.

Consider an example: By fraud, Jensen induces Bonanza to write her a check payable to her order. Later Jensen negotiates the check to Gonzales, an HDC. Still later, Gonzales indorses it specially to Adams for value, but Adams knows of the original fraud. Adams is not an HDC but is a holder through an HDC and has the same rights as an HDC. Normally, a person who acquires an instrument from an HDC or from someone with HDC rights gets HDC rights on the principle that the transferee of an instrument gets at least the rights that the transferor had.

Limitations of the Shelter Provision

The second part of Section 3-201(1) explicitly indicates that persons who formerly held instruments cannot improve their positions by later reacquiring them from HDCs. An HDC should be able to market paper freely, but if a holder was a party to fraud or, as a prior holder, had notice of a claim or defense against an instrument, that holder should not be allowed to improve his or her status by repurchasing from a later HDC. In other words, a person is not allowed to "launder" the paper by passing it into the hands of an HDC and then buying it back. To illustrate: Bailey and Zopa collaborate to defraud Manor. Manor is induced to give Zopa a negotiable note payable to Zopa's order. Zopa then specially indorses the note for value to Adams, an HDC. Bailey and Zopa split the proceeds. Adams negotiates the note to Stanley, another HDC. Stanley then negotiates the note for value to Bailey. Bailey, even though he got the note through an HDC, is not a holder through an HDC, for he participated in the original fraud and can never acquire HDC rights in this note.

Special Cases

In a few exceptional circumstances, a purchaser can take an instrument for value but still not be accorded HDC status. UCC Sec. 3-302(3) specifies the following situations:

1. Purchase at a judicial sale (for example, a bankruptcy sale) or taking under legal process.
2. Acquisition when taking over an estate (as administrator).
3. Purchase as part of a bulk transfer (for example, a corporation buying the assets of another corporation).

This provision limits the rights of the purchaser to that of an ordinary holder.

QUESTIONS AND CASE PROBLEMS

1. Murphy paid Stephens for some goods with a personal check. The check was drawn on the First National Bank of Pennsylvania. Stephens took the check to the Manufacturers and Traders Trust Company and exchanged it for a cashier's check made out to his order. Before Manufacturers Trust gave Stephens the cashier's check, one of its tellers called the First National Bank to make certain that there were sufficient funds to cover it. After it gave Stephens the cashier's check, Manufacturers Trust attempted to collect on Murphy's check. Since Murphy had a personal defense, he ordered his bank to stop payment on the check. Manufacturers Trust sued Murphy to recover. Murphy claimed that Manufacturers could not recover since it was not a holder in due course. Is Murphy correct? [Manufacturers and Traders Trust Co. v. Murphy, 369 F.Supp. 11 (W.D.Pa. 1974)]

2. Stephens was the maker of a promissory note in which Ford was named the payee. Ford placed the note with Bowie National Bank as his collection agent. For the first twelve months that the note was outstanding, Stephens made numerous late payments to which Ford never objected. Subsequently, Ford decided to foreclose on the note, and, at the bank's suggestion, he sold the note to the bank for the specific purpose of foreclosing on it. The bank knew about Stephens's late payments because it had been Ford's collection agent. After the bank became owner of the note, it gave the note over to its attorney for acceleration and foreclosure. Is Bowie National Bank a holder in due course? Is the bank's attorney a holder in due course? If Bowie National Bank is not a holder in due course, it takes as a transferee the rights of its transferor. What right might Bowie National Bank be prohibited from exercising? [Stephens v. Bowie Nat. Bank of Bowie, 517 S.W.2d 686 (Tex.Civ.App. 1974)]

3. Manchester Company entered into an executory contract with Aryeh under which Aryeh was to perform certain construction services over a twelve- to fifteen-month period. Manchester issued a check to Aryeh in prepayment for the services. The check was postdated by fifteen months so that Aryeh could not cash it until he had performed under the contract. Aryeh immediately indorsed the check to Eastern International Finance Company. It soon became apparent to Manchester that Aryeh was not going to perform its part of the original contract properly. Manchester placed a stop order with its bank so that the check could not be cashed. A year and a half later, Eastern International tried to recover on the check. Is Eastern International a holder in due course? [Aryeh v. Eastern Int'l, 54 A.D.2d 850, 388 N.Y.S. 2d. 286, (1976)]

4. Saka spent his first three months in America in the famed Sahara Motel. Each night Saka ordered a bottle of champagne and an expensive crystal drinking glass and had a nightcap. As was customary in his native Japan, Saka then threw his glass against the fireplace in his room and yelled "Hail to the Emperor" in Japanese. Since this ritual was customary, Saka assumed that when he paid for the champagne, the price of the crystal was included. When Saka checked out of the Sahara Motel after his three-month stay, he was handed a bill for $3,046 for the broken crystal. Saka refused to pay and immediately left the U.S. for Japan. The Sahara-Nevada Corporation demanded payment, but Saka refused. Later, however, Saka gave his agent a check made out to the Sahara-Nevada Corporation and signed by Saka to his agent. He instructed his agent to make the check out for $800 and give the cash to the Sahara Motel. Instead, the agent made the check payable for $3,046, the amount claimed by the motel, and delivered it to the motel's manager without mentioning the instructions. Is the Sahara Motel, the payee, a holder in due course? [Saka v. Sahara-Nevada Corp., 92 Nev. 703, 558 P.2d. 535 (1976)]

5. By making several fraudulent misrepresentations, a builder induced several homeowners in Washington, D.C. to sign contracts authorizing home improvements. The homeowners obtained financing to pay the builder's fees from Jefferson Federal Savings and Loan Association, a local lending institution. In exchange for the financing, the homeowners each issued promissory notes to Jefferson. The builder's fees were exorbitant, and the promissory notes were issued by the homeowners in the exact amounts of the fees charged. In addition, it was the builder's agent who introduced the homeowners to the loan manager of Jefferson Savings and Loan. The loan manager was aware of the fact that this person was the builder's agent. About a month later, after the homeowners realized that the prices for the home improvements were exorbitant, they stopped payment on the notes held by Jefferson. If Jefferson qualifies as a holder in due course, it will have every right to payment. Does Jefferson qualify? [Slaughter v. Jefferson Federal Sav. and Loan Ass'n, 538 F.2d. 397 (D.C. Cir. 1976)]

6.   On May 23, 1971, Stewart signed an agreement to purchase a lot from Cochiss College Park, Inc. At the time of the sale, Stewart executed a promissory note and mortgage on the lot for $5,000. Cochiss was the named payee. Two days later Stewart rescinded the transaction as she was entitled to do under the Interstate Land Sales Full Disclosure Act. Under this act, a purchaser of land can rescind within forty-eight hours of the purchase. That same day, Cochiss sold the note to Thornton for $3,550, a one-third discount. Is Thornton a holder in due course? [Stewart v. Thornton, 116 Ariz. 107, 568 P.2d. 414 (1977)]

7.   Which of the following parties has given value such that the party would be deemed a holder in due course under the UCC: (a) A bank that takes a negotiable promissory note from a payee as collateral for a loan. [Millman v. State Nat. Bank, 323 A.2d. 723 (D.C. Ct. App. 1974)]; (b) A bank that receives a draft and then uses the draft to credit the transferor-customer's account toward advances previously made. [Lantz Int'l Corp. v. Industria Termotecnica Campana, S.P.A., 358 F. Supp. 510 (E.D.Pa. 1973)]; (c) A bank that takes a promissory note as security on an overdrawn account of one of it's customers; (d) A legatee who inherits a promissory note from his father? [Wyatt v. Mount Airy Cemetery, 209 Pa. Super. 250, 224 A.2d. 787 (1966)]

8.   Jones signed a mortgage in order to obtain a note for $2,575 so that Bell Company would repair her home. Bell Company sold the note to United States Finance Company before it had finished repairs. When the work was eventually completed, it was inadequate. For example, in place of aluminum siding, Bell Company put tar paper on both sides of the house and sprayed it with aluminum paint. Over the previous two years, Bell had sold more than thirty such promissory notes to United States Finance Company. Jones wanted to avoid her obligation to pay on the promissory note. Can it be argued that United States Finance Company was not a holder in due course? [United States Finance Co. v. Jones, 285 Ala. 105, 229 So.2d. 495 (1969)]

9.   Anderson entered into a contract with Atlantic Storm Window Company for the installation of storm windows in his home. He signed a promissory note and a contract. They were stapled together, and neither had any dollar amounts filled in. Atlantic Storm Window had orally agreed with Anderson that the price would be $744, but later filled in both the contract and the promissory note for $895. Shortly thereafter, Atlantic sold the promissory note with the contract still attached to First National Bank. Atlantic failed to install any storm windows in Anderson's home. If First National Bank qualifies as a holder in due course, Anderson will be obligated on the promissory note. What result? [First Nat. Bank v. Anderson, 7 D. & C. 2d 661 (Pa. 1956)]

10.   Willman was the maker of four promissory notes naming Lucas the payee, each for $2,062.50. Lucas indorsed the notes to Wood and gave them to Wood as collateral for a $50,000 loan to Lucas. All but $458 of the loan was then repaid. Lucas refused to pay the balance, and Wood attempted to collect from Willman, the maker on the notes. Can Wood be considered a holder in due course of all four notes? [Wood v. Willman, 423 P.2d. 82 (Wyo. 1967)]

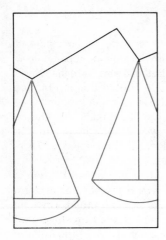

27

Commercial Paper
Liability, Defenses, and Discharge

Once issued, a negotiable instrument can be circulated from person to person. Consider what happens when a check is written to X, who indorses it to Y, who in turn indorses it to Z, who then deposits it in a bank for collection. If the check bounces, can Z recover from X, or must Z look only to Y for reimbursement? What can Z do if X's indorsement was forged by F? The material in this chapter will discuss the liability of drawers of checks and drafts, makers of notes, indorsers of negotiable instruments, accommodation parties, and guarantors of instruments. Since liability is not always absolute on a negotiable instrument, even for a holder in due course, the chapter will then consider the defenses available to prevent liability, and it will conclude by reviewing the various ways a person can be discharged from an obligation on a negotiable instrument. Note that the focus here is on liability *on the instrument itself* or *on warranties connected with transfer or presentment of the instrument* as opposed to liability for the underlying contract.

LIABILITY BASED ON SIGNATURES

The key to liability on a negotiable instrument is a **signature** which is defined in UCC Sec. 3-401(2) as "any name, including any trade or assumed name, upon an instrument, or * * * any word or mark used in lieu of a written signature." [See also UCC Sec. 1-201 (39)] Signature has its origin in the Law Merchant and is based simply on the need to know whose obligation the instrument represents. The UCC in Section 3-401(1) states the general rule: "No person is liable on an instrument unless his [or her] signature appears thereon."

The few exceptions to the general rule are contained in UCC Sec. 3-404, covering unauthorized signatures:

1. Any unauthorized signature is wholly inoperative as that of the person whose name is signed *unless* that person ratifies it or is precluded from denying it. For example, a signature made by an agent exceeding the scope of either actual or apparent authority can be ratified by the principal. A Pennsylvania court held that a wife's acceptance and retention of benefits from a promissory note constituted ratification of an otherwise unauthorized signature made by her husband.[1] For example, a person who writes and signs a check, leaving blank the amount, or the payee, or both can be estopped (prevented) from denying liability for its payment. [UCC Secs. 3-115, 3-407, and 4-401(a)]

2. An unauthorized signature operates as the signature of the unauthorized signor in favor of an HDC. For example, a person who forges a check can be held personally liable to an HDC. [UCC Secs. 3-404 and 3-401(2)]

A signature can be handwritten, typed, or printed; or it can be made by mark, by thumbprint, or in virtually any manner. According to UCC Sec. 1-201(39), "signed" means any symbol executed or adopted by a party with the "present intention to authenticate a writing." A signature can be made in any name, including an alias, a trade name, or even a fictitious name. [UCC Sec. 3-401(2)] The critical element in a signature is a "present intention to authenticate a writing." Parol evidence can be used to identify the signor, and, once identified, the signature is effective against the signor no matter how it is made.

Agent's Signatures

The general law of agency applies to negotiable instruments. Agents can sign negotiable in-

struments and thereby bind their principals (see Chapter 34). [UCC Sec. 3-403(1)] Without such a rule, all corporate commercial business would stop. As Chapter 44 will show, every corporation can and must act only through its agents. However, because of the critical function a signature plays in determining liability on a negotiable instrument, this chapter will go into some detail concerning the potential problems in agents' signatures.

Even an authorized agent will not normally bind a principal on the instrument unless the agent indicates that he or she is signing on behalf of a *clearly named* principal. The agent must write out the principal's name (by signature, mark, or some symbol) and his or her own, or the agent can supply only the principal's signature.[2]

If an authorized agent signs just his or her own name, the principal will not be bound on the instrument. The agent will be personally liable. In these situations, form prevails over intent.

Under Section 3-403(2)(a), when an agent carelessly signs just his or her own name, the agent is *personally* liable on the instrument even though the parties know of the agency relationship. The parol evidence rule precludes the introduction of evidence to establish that the signature was made for a principal (see Chapter 11).

Under Section 3-403(2)(b), two other situations in which an agent is held personally liable on a negotiable instrument can arise. If the instrument is signed in both the agent's name and the principal's name—"John Jones, Bob Smith"—but nothing on the instrument indicates the agency relationship, the agent cannot be distinguished from the principal. In such a case, the form of the signature binds the agent (and it can also bind the principal). Since inclusion of both the agent's and the principal's names without indicating their relationship is

---

1. Rehrig v. Fortunak, 39 D. & C.2d 20, (Pa. 1966).

2. If the agent signs the principal's name, the Code presumes that the signature is authorized and genuine. [UCC Sec. 3-307(1)(b)]

ambiguous, parol evidence is admissable *as between the original parties* to prove the agency relationship and release the agent from personal liability.

Another situation envisioned under Section 3-403(2)(b) occurs when an agent signs a negotiable instrument and indicates agency status but fails to name the principal— for example, "Barry Scott, agent." Against any subsequent holder the agent is *personally* liable, but the unnamed principal cannot be held on the instrument. But, since the indications of agency status without naming the principal is ambiguous, parol evidence is admissable as between the original parties to prove the agency relationship, absolve the agent of liability and establish the liability of the unnamed principal. [UCC Sec. 3-403(2)(b)]

GRIFFIN v. ELLINGER
Supreme Court of Texas, 1976.
538 S.W.2d. 97.

BACKGROUND AND FACTS *O. B. Ellinger, doing business as Ellinger Paint and Dry Wall, sued Percy Griffin on three checks drawn on the account of Greenway Building Company and signed by Griffin, the company president. The checks, totaling $3,950, were issued to Ellinger in payment for labor and materials furnished to Greenway for a construction project. Greenway was the prime contractor for the project, and Griffin was authorized to sign checks as president of the company. The bank refused to honor the checks because of insufficient funds in the Greenway account.*

The major question before the court was whether Griffin's signature on a corporate check, without any indication of his representative capacity, obligated him personally and individually for the amount of the check.

DOUGHTY, Justice.

The question presented by this case is whether a corporate officer who signs a check on a corporate account without designating the capacity in which he signs is personally liable as the drawer of the check. * * *
* * *
[Defendant] contends that the drafts show conclusively on their face that he was signing in a representative capacity only. Second, petitioner contends that extrinsic evidence establishes as a matter of law that the parties understood his signature to be in a representative capacity. * * * To determine whether an authorized representative is personally liable on an instrument which he signs on behalf of his principal, we must look to Section 3-403 of the Code. * * *

Each of the three drafts signed by Griffin were in essentially the same form. A copy of one of the drafts is reproduced below.

The first question is whether the draft shows on its face that Griffin signed in a representative capacity only. Although the draft clearly names the person represented, it does not show that Griffin signed only in his capacity as president of Greenway. Griffin contends, however, that considering the instrument as a whole, and taking into account the normal business usage of personalized checks, it should be apparent from the instrument itself that Griffin signed only as an authorized agent of Greenway. We disagree. We recognize that it is unusual to demand the individual obligation of a corporate officer on checks drawn on the corporate account, and that the more usual way of obtaining the personal obligation of an officer on such a check would be by endorsement. Business practice and usage are proper factors to be considered in construing the particular instrument under consideration. We also recognize that an instrument may disclose on its face that a signature was executed only in a representative capacity even though the particular office or position of the signer is not disclosed thereon. * * *

[W]e can find nothing on the face of the checks in the present case to show that Griffin intended to sign only in a representative capacity. [Defendant] points out that each check is stamped by a "check protector," which imprinted not only the amount of the draft but also the company's name. Although the stamp clearly reveals the name of the principal, it does not aid [Defendant] because it gives no information as to the capacity in which *he* signed the instrument.

The fact that the name of the corporation appears on the check indicates that the account drawn upon is that of the corporation and that the funds in the account are the corporation's. While the drawer of a check is ordinarily the owner of the funds in the account drawn upon, the Code does not require that this be so. Under Section 3.413, *any person* who signs a draft engages that, upon dishonor, he will pay the amount thereof to the holder. Indeed, under Section 3.404, the signer of a draft who has no authority to draw upon the account is nevertheless liable upon his contract as drawer to any person who takes the instrument in good faith for value.

[Defendant] points out that, since a corporation can only act through its agents, a personal signature is always required to authorize withdrawal of funds from a corporate account. Under Section 3.403, however, one signing an instrument is personally liable thereon even though he is authorized to and does in fact bind his principal, if he does not disclose that he is signing only in a representative capacity. In short, the burden is on the signer to relieve himself of personal liability by disclosing his agency. The fact that the instrument is an authorized draft drawn on a corporate account is not enough to disclose the representative character of the signature thereon. Section 3.403(c) expressly provides that the signer of an instrument may avoid personal liability by disclosing both the name of the organization of which he is an agent and the office he holds with the organization. Absent such a disclosure or its equivalent, the signer is personally liable on the instrument according to its terms, unless "otherwise established between the immediate parties" under subsection (b)(2). We hold that the checks in question do not show on their face that Griffin signed only in a representative capacity. * * *

The plaintiff, Ellinger, was able to collect the $3,950 from Griffin personally because Griffin failed to disclose the representative character of his signature.

JUDGMENT AND REMEDY

SAMPLE SIGNATURES Section 3-403 of the UCC applies only to the signature of a representative agent whose authority to sign for the principal has been established. It does not cover unauthorized signatures made by unauthorized agents. Assuming that Mary Night is a principal and Arthur King is her agent, a negotiable instrument can bear the following signatures (after each signature, the effect on each person is indicated):

1. "Mary Night, Incorporated." A signature in this form does not bind the agent, Arthur King, if the agent is authorized. [UCC Secs. 3-401 and 3-404]
2. "Arthur King." A signature written this way personally obligates the agent, and parol evidence will be inadmissible to undo the obligation on the instrument.
3. "Mary Night by Arthur King, agent." This is a clear, unambiguous signature indicating that Arthur King has signed on behalf of Mary Night. The named agent indicates the fact of agency and the name of the principal.
4. "Arthur King, agent." In some courts, an agent using this form of signature can introduce parol evidence *between immediate parties* to prove that the signature was rendered in a representative capacity.
5. "Mary Night, Arthur King." Again, as in (4) above, parol evidence can be admitted in litigations arising between the immediate parties on the instrument to prove that the agent signed in a representative capacity. Both (4) and (5) are covered under Section 3-403(2)(b). However, in either case, if the instrument has been negotiated the agent will be personally liable on the instrument.

When a negotiable instrument is signed in the name of an organization, and the organization's name is preceded or followed by the name and office of an authorized individual, the organization will be bound; the individual who has signed the instrument in the representative capacity will not be bound. [UCC Sec. 3-403(3)]

UNAUTHORIZED SIGNATURE If a person's name is signed to a negotiable instrument by a person who has no authority to sign, that signature is wholly inoperative and does not bind the person named. Such a signing is a forgery. However, the signor can be held liable. For example, a thief steals Dana's checkbook and signs Dana's name to a check. Dana is not liable on the check because the thief had no authority to sign her name. The thief is liable because she signed Dana's check with "present intent to authenticate a writing." If the check is negotiated to an HDC, the thief is liable because the thief signed it. [UCC Secs. 3-404 and 3-401(2)]

Assume once again that Mary Night is the principal and Arthur King is her agent. Arthur King signs a note as follows: "Mary Night, Incorporated, by Arthur King, agent." This signature clearly binds Mary Night, Incorporated, if Arthur King is an authorized representative. However, if King's signature is unauthorized, is Mary Night, Incorporated, bound, or is Arthur King bound? The answer is found in Section 3-404 of the Code. Any unauthorized signature is wholly inoperative as that of the person whose name is signed (in this case, Mary Night, Incorporated) unless it is ratified by the person whose name is signed or that person is precluded from denying it. [UCC Sec. 3-406] The signature will operate as the signature of the unauthorized signor, Arthur King, in a lawsuit by an HDC. [UCC Sec. 3-404]

Contractual Liability

PRIMARY AND SECONDARY LIABILITY Every party to a negotiable instrument is either primarily or secondarily liable for payment of that instrument when it comes due. If a person is primarily liable on a negotiable instrument, then that person is absolutely required to pay the instrument, subject to certain real defenses. [UCC Sec. 3-305(a)] Only *makers* and *acceptors* are primarily liable. [UCC Sec. 3-413(1)]

The liability of a party who is secondarily liable on a negotiable instrument is similar to that of a surety in a simple contract. Drawers and indorsers have secondary liability. (See Chapter 30.) Secondary liability is "contingent liability." In the case of notes, an indorser's secondary liability does not arise until the maker who is primarily liable has defaulted on the instrument.[UCC Secs. 3-413(2) and 3-414]

With regard to drafts and checks, a drawer's secondary liability does not arise until the drawee fails to pay. Note, however, that a drawee is *not* primarily liable. Makers of notes promise to pay, but drawees are ordered to pay. Therefore, the drawee is not primarily liable unless he or she promises to pay—for example, by certifying a check. Nor is a drawee even secondarily liable on an instrument. Unless the drawee *accepts*, its only obligation is to honor its drawer's orders.

Contract Theory   The parties to a negotiable instrument are bound by all of the terms of the contract that are implied by their signatures by operation of law. Once it is established that a party signed the instrument (or that it was signed by that party's authorized agent), the Code defines the party's liability. The liability is contractual in the sense that each party voluntarily incurs it and can modify it by agreement. First, the liability of the primary parties to a negotiable instrument (makers of notes and acceptors of drafts or notes) will be examined. For purposes of this discussion, assume that no defenses against the holder can be asserted to prevent liability.

PRIMARY LIABILITY OF THE MAKER OR ACCEPTOR   The maker of a note promises to pay the note. The words "I promise to pay" embody the maker's contract to pay the instrument according to the terms as written at the time of the signing. If the instrument is incomplete when the maker signs it, then the contract is to pay it as completed, assuming that the instrument is properly completed. [UCC Secs. 3-413(1) and 3-115]

A maker guarantees that certain facts are true by signing a promissory note. In particular, Section 3-413(3) specifies that a maker admits to all subsequent parties that the payee in fact exists and that the payee has current capacity to indorse the note (for example, the payee is not a minor at the time the note is signed).

The drawee/acceptor is in virtually the same contractual position as the maker of a note. [UCC Secs. 3-413(1) and (3)] A drawee owes a contractual duty to the drawer to pay in accordance with the drawer's orders, but a drawee owes no duty to either the payee or any holder.

For example, X buys goods costing $2,000 from Y. These goods will be shipped to arrive on September 1. Instead of giving Y cash, X draws a draft on Finance Company for $2,000 payable to Y on September 1. At this point, Finance is not liable on the draft, and it will not become liable on that particular instrument unless and until it "accepts" the draft.

A check is a special type of draft that is drawn on a bank and is payable on demand. Acceptance of a check is called certification. Certification is not necessary on checks, and a bank is under no obligation to certify. (See Chapter 28 for details.)

A draft which is due on a certain date, or is payable a certain time after sight *may* be presented to the drawee for acceptance. A drawee who refuses to accept such a draft has dishonored the instrument. Similarly, a maker or drawee who refuses to pay an instrument when due (and presented for payment) has dishonored the instrument. Dishonor triggers the liability of secondary parties on the instrument—that is, the drawer, "unqualified indorsers" and accommodation indorsers.[3] The sections that follow will discuss secondary liability.

SECONDARY LIABILITY   Secondary parties on a negotiable instrument promise to pay on that instrument only if:
1.   The instrument is properly and timely presented.
2.   The instrument is dishonored.
3.   Notice of dishonor is timely given to the secondary party.[4]
These requirements must be satisfied in order for a secondary party to have contractual liability on a negotiable instrument, but they are not necessary to hold a secondary party to warranty liability (discussed in one of the following

3.   A "qualified" indorser—one who indorses "without recourse," undertakes no obligation to pay. A qualified indorser merely assumes warranty liability which is discussed later in this chapter.

4.   An instrument can be drafted to provide a waiver of the presentment, dishonor, and notice of dishonor requirements. Presume for simplicity's sake that such waivers have not been incorporated into the instruments described in this chapter.

sections). [UCC Secs. 3-414, 3-501, and 3-502]

Section 3-413(2) provides that "upon dishonor of the draft and any necessary notice of dishonor * * * [the drawer] will pay the amount of the draft to the holder or to any indorser who takes it up." For example, Nancy Jones writes a check on her account at Third National Bank payable to the order of Joel Andrews. If Third National does not pay the check when Andrews presents it for payment, then Jones is liable to Andrews on the basis of her secondary liability. Drawers are secondarily liable on drafts unless they disclaim their liability by drawing the instruments "without recourse." [UCC Sec. 3-413(2)] Since drawers are secondarily liable, their liability does not arise until presentment and notice of dishonor have been made properly and timely. If improperly made, however, the drawer is relieved of liability only when the drawee bank becomes insolvent. Since the days of the Great Depression, the insolvency of banks has become a rather rare phenomenon.

An unqualified indorser contracts that in the event of presentment, dishonor, and notice of dishonor, the indorser will pay the instrument. Thus, the liability of an indorser is much like that of a drawer, with one major exception: Indorsers are *relieved* of their liability to the holder of the instrument by (1) improper (late) presentment or (2) late notice or failure to notify the indorser of dishonor. [UCC Secs. 3-414, 3-501, and 3-502]

When an indorser has actively caused an instrument to be dishonored, the requirements of presentment and notice of dishonor are excused. [UCC Sec. 3-511(2)(b)]

ACCOMMODATION PARTY An **accommodation party** is one who signs an instrument for the purpose of lending his or her name to another party in credit to the instrument. [UCC Sec. 3-415(1)] Accommodation parties are one form of security against nonpayment on a negotiable instrument. For example, a bank about to lend money, a seller taking a large order for goods, or a creditor about to extend credit to a prospective debtor all want some reasonable assurance that the debts will be paid. A party's uncertain financial condition or the fact that the parties to a transaction are complete strangers can cause a creditor to be reluctant to rely solely on the prospective debtor's ability to pay. To reduce the risk of nonpayment, the creditor can require the joining of a third person as an accommodation party on the instrument.

If the accommodation party signs on behalf of a *maker*, he or she will be an *accommodation maker* and will be primarily liable on the instrument. If the accommodation party signs on behalf of a payee or other holder (usually to make the instrument more marketable), he or she will be an accommodation indorser and will be secondarily liable.

In the following case, two corporate officers owning all the stock of the corporation executed a note and deposited the proceeds into the corporation's account to pay corporate debts. The corporate officers were comakers. The note was paid by one of the comakers, who then sued the other comaker for contribution. The defendant insisted that he was an accommodation maker and therefore not liable to the plaintiff.

UNITED REFRIGERATOR CO. v. APPLEBAUM
Supreme Court of Pennsylvania, 1963.
410 Pa. 210, 189 A.2d. 253.

BACKGROUND AND FACTS *The Applebaums issued a number of checks to United Refrigerator Company. They signed the checks in their capacity as officers of Economy Home Food Service, Inc., and indorsed them as individuals. The checks were returned to United Refrigerator when the bank refused payment for insufficient funds. The defendants claimed that they had indorsed the checks solely to accommodate United Refrigerator, and because they had not received any value, they claimed that they had no liability. The question before the court was whether there was sufficient proof that the signing on the back of the checks was an accommodation indorsement.*

COHEN, Justice.

* * *

Herbert and Judith Applebaum, officers of the Economy Home Food Service, Inc. (Maker), issued several checks bearing the name of the Maker to appellant United Refrigerator Company (Payee). Appellees signed the face of these checks in their capacity as officers of the Maker and indorsed the back of the checks as individuals.

Payee brought an action * * * against [defendants] in their capacity as individuals, alleging that appellees endorsed said checks for value received; that the checks were presented to the Maker's banks which refused payment because of insufficient funds; that notice of presentment and dishonor was given to [defendants] and demand for payment made; and that [defendants] have refused to make payment.

[Defendant's] answer to the complaint averred, inter alia, that they had "endorsed [among other things] * * * said checks *solely as an accommodation endorser for the benefit of [Payee]*, and that * * * [they] did not receive any value or consideration whatsoever.* * *'' (Emphasis supplied). Payee's motion for judgment on the pleadings [ruling prior to a trial based on the complaint, answer, reply, if any] was denied and an appeal to this Court followed.

Section 3-415 of the Uniform Commercial Code provides that:

"(1) An accommodation party is one who signs an instrument in any capacity for the purpose of lending his name to another party to it. * * *

"(5) *An accommodation party is not liable to the party accommodated* * * *."

Under section 3-415(5) of the Code, if Payee is found to be the party accommodated then appellees, as accommodation parties, would not be liable to Payee on the instrument. * * *

---

1. Some of the checks were indorsed by Herbert Applebaum and some by Judith Applebaum. None of them were jointly indorsed.

The appellate court affirmed the lower court ruling that an accommodation party is not liable to the party accommodated. If, at trial, the Applebaums can prove that they made accommodation indorsements on the checks for the benefit of United Refrigerator, then they will prevail and not be liable to United Refrigerator for the amount of the checks. Conversely, if United Refrigerator can show that the Applebaums indorsed the checks as accommodation parties for the benefit of Economy Home Food Service (the drawer), then United Refrigerator can hold them liable for payment on the dishonored checks.

JUDGMENT AND REMEDY

Warranty Liability of Parties

In addition to the contractual liability discussed in the preceding sections, transferors make certain implied warranties regarding the instruments that they are negotiating. Liability under these warranties is not subject to the conditions of proper presentment, dishonor, and notice of dishonor. These warranties arise even when a transferor does not indorse the instrument (as in delivery of bearer paper). [UCC Sec. 3-417] Often it is more expedient to compel a transferor to take back an instrument on the basis of breach of warranty than it is to prove a case of contractual liability as a holder in due course against the maker or drawer. Warranties fall into two categories, those that arise upon the *transfer* of a negotiable instrument and those that arise upon *presentment*.

TRANSFER WARRANTIES   The five *transfer warranties* are described in UCC Sec. 3-417(2). They provide that any person who indorses an instrument and receives consideration warrants to all subsequent transferees and holders who take the instrument in good faith that:

1.   The transferor has good title to the instrument or is otherwise authorized to obtain payment or acceptance on behalf of one who does have good title.
2.   All signatures are genuine or authorized.
3.   The instrument has not been materially altered.
4.   No defense of any party is good against the transferor.[5]
5.   The transferor has no knowledge of any insolvency proceedings against the maker, the acceptor, or the drawer of an unaccepted instrument.

THE EXTENT OF TRANSFER WARRANTIES   Finally, the manner of transfer and the negotiation that is used determine how far and to whom a transfer warranty will run. Transfer by indorsement and delivery of order paper extends warranty liability to any subsequent holder who takes the instrument in good faith. However, the warranties of a person who transfers without indorsement (by delivery of bearer paper) will extend only to the immediate transferee. [UCC Sec. 3-417(2)] For example, F takes a bearer note that is apparently made by M. F negotiates the note to G by delivery only. In turn, G negotiates the note by delivery to H. If

5.   A qualified indorser who indorses an instrument "without recourse" limits this fourth warranty to a warranty that he or she has "no knowledge" of such a defense. [UCC Sec. 3-417(3)]

M's signature turns out to be a forgery, H can hold G (the immediate transferor) liable for breach of warranty that all signatures are genuine. H cannot hold F, a prior transferor, liable. Hence, the distinction between transfer by indorsement and delivery of order paper and transfer by delivery of bearer paper is important. (It should be noted that if G must pay damages to H arising out of the breach of warranty action, G has the right to hold F liable because F's warranty runs to G.)

PRESENTMENT WARRANTY   **Presentment warranties** arise when a person presents an instrument for payment or acceptance to a maker or drawee. This warranty operates to protect the person to whom the instrument is presented. As a general rule, when payment or acceptance of an instrument is made, it is final in favor of a holder in due dourse or any person who in good faith has changed a position in reliance on that payment. [UCC Sec. 3-418] This general rule is subject to three exceptions, which are often referred to as the presentment warranties under Section 3-417(1). These warranties provide the following:

1.   The party presenting has good title to the instrument or is authorized to obtain payment or acceptance on behalf of a person who has good title.
2.   The party presenting has no knowledge that the signature of the maker or the drawer is unauthorized.
3.   The instrument has not been materially altered.

The second and third warranties do not apply in certain cases where the presenter is a holder in due course. It is assumed, for example, that a drawer or maker will recognize his or her own signature or that a maker or acceptor will recognize whether an instrument has been materially altered. Thus, the second and third warranties do not arise when an instrument is presented by a holder in due course acting in good faith.

Both transfer and presentment warranties attempt to shift liability back to a wrongdoer or to the person who dealt face to face with a wrongdoer and thus was in the best position to prevent the wrongdoing.

In the following case, the court had to settle a dispute between the holder of a note (the plaintiff) and a qualified indorser (the defendant) who transferred the instrument by qualified indorsement without recourse.

BACKGROUND AND FACTS *A maker issued a promissory note to Fourco, Inc., the appellee. Fourco sold the note to Fair Finance Company, the appellant, and indorsed it without recourse. When the note came due, Fair Finance sought to collect from the maker. It was discovered that, in the transaction between Fourco and Fair Finance, Fourco had computed the interest incorrectly. The amount due on the note was actually $1,361.96 less than the amount that had been represented to Fair Finance at the time of purchase. Consequently, Fair Finance had paid $1,361.96 more for the note than it was actually able to collect. Neither Fourco nor Fair Finance realized that the computation was improper at the time of the sale, so fraud was not an issue. Fair Finance claimed that Fourco made an "unintentional misrepresentation" and sought to recover from Fourco the amount of the overpayment. The trial court denied recovery to Fair Finance, but the appellate court was asked to reverse the decision.*

FAIR FINANCE CO. v. **FOURCO, INC.**

Court of Appeals of Ohio, 1968.
14 Ohio App.2d 145, 237
N.E.2d. 406.

HUNSICKER, Judge.
* * *

Is this * * * a matter which is provided for in the Uniform Commercial Code?

Section 1303.53, Revised Code (U.C.C. 3-417), says, in part:

''* * *

"(B) Any person who transfers an instrument and receives consideration warrants to his transferee and if the transfer is by indorsement to any subsequent holder who takes the instrument in good faith that:

''* * *

"(4) no defense of any party is good against him; and

'''* * *

"(C) By transferring 'without recourse' the transferor limits the obligation stated in division (B) (4) of this section to a warranty that he has no knowledge of such a defense."

* * * This claim of misrepresentation arises from the fact that interest on the note was calculated by the vendor, Fourco, Inc., at the beginning of the interest period and taken in advance instead of at the end of the interest period.

Is the claim of "unintentional misrepresentation" such that it is exempt from the provisions of Section 1303.53(B) (4) and (C), Revised Code, set out above? * * *

* * *

The vendor in the instant case, Fourco, Inc., used its own printed note to obtain the written promise of the maker. The terms of that note concerning the computation of interest were its handiwork. The computation of interest was not made by the maker but by the vendor of the note who now wishes, because of its own error and improper computation of interest, to be relieved of liability because of the endorsement "without recourse." Is this such a lack of knowledge of a defense as releases the vendor-endorser from liability? We think it is not, for we believe that where an endorsement of a promissory note "without recourse" is made by a vendor-payee, who computes the interest incorrectly in determining the face value of that note at the time of sale, and where the form of note and terms thereof are those of the vendor-payee, such vendor-payee has knowledge of that wrongful computation, and the defense arising therefrom, within the terms of Section 1303.53(C), Revised Code. * * *

JUDGMENT AND REMEDY   *The appellate court disagreed with the trial court's view that the defendant, having transferred the instrument by qualified indorsement, was not liable to the plaintiff for the balance of the interest. Therefore, Fourco, Inc. was held liable to Fair Finance Company for the amount that it had paid because of Fourco's improper computation of interest.*

DEFENSES

Depending upon whether a holder or an HDC (or a holder through an HDC) makes the demand for payment, certain defenses will be effective to bar collection from persons who would otherwise be primarily or secondarily liable on an instrument.

Defenses fall into two general categories—personal defenses and real, or universal, defenses. Personal defenses are used to avoid payment to an *ordinary holder* of a negotiable instrument. [UCC Sec. 3-306] Real, or universal, defenses are used to avoid payment to all holders of a negotiable instrument (including an HDC or a holder through an HDC). [UCC Sec. 3-305(2)] (In all of these discussions, reference to an HDC includes a holder through an HDC.)

Personal Defenses

BREACH OF CONTRACT When there is a breach of the underlying contract for which the negotiable instrument was issued, the maker of a note can refuse to pay it or the drawer of a check can stop payment. Breach of the contract can be claimed as a defense to liability on the instrument. For example, P purchases several

cases of imported wine from W. The wine is to be delivered in four weeks. P gives W a promissory note for $1,000, which is the price of the wine. The wine arrives; but many of the bottles are broken, and several bottles that are tested have turned to vinegar. P refuses to pay the note on the basis of breach of contract and breach of warranty. (Under sales law, a seller promises that the goods are at least merchantable; see Chapter 18.) If the note is no longer in the hands of the payee/seller but is presented for payment by an HDC, the maker/buyer will not be able to plead breach of contract as a defense against liability on the note.

FRAUD IN THE INDUCEMENT A person who issues a negotiable instrument based on false statements by the other party will want to avoid payment on that instrument. For example, P agrees to purchase S's slightly used tractor. S assures P that it is in complete working order, that the tires are new, and that it has been used for only one harvest. P issues a promissory note to S for the price of the tractor, but it turns out that the tractor is four years old and has been used in four harvests. P can refuse to pay the note if it is held by an ordinary holder; but if S has negotiated the note to an HDC, P must pay the HDC. Of course, P can then sue S directly.

BACKGROUND AND FACTS   *Mr. and Mrs. Burchett signed a contract with Kelly to install aluminum siding on their home. The original offer (made orally and accompanied by a written statement) indicated that the Burchetts' house would serve as a show house for advertising purposes and that they would receive $100 credit on each contract sold in a specific area of their town. The Burchetts agreed and signed a contract without reading it. In a few days, the first installment of the contract that they had actually signed—a mortgage contract that had been recorded against their property—came due. At that point, the Burchetts realized the nature of the contract they had signed. The trial court determined that since the notes and mortgages were obtained fraudulently, Allied Concord Financial Company could not recover.*

BURCHETT v. ALLIED CONCORD FINANCIAL CORP.

Supreme Court of New Mexico, 1964.

74 N.M. 575, 396 P.2d. 186.

CARMODY, Justice.

* * *

Following the explanation by Kelly, both families agreed to the offer and were given a form of a printed contract to read. While they were reading the contract, Kelly was filling out blanks in other forms. After the appellees had read the form of the contract submitted to them, they signed, *without reading*, the form or forms filled out by Kelly, assuming them to be the same as that which they had read and further assuming that what they signed provided for the credits which Kelly assured them they would receive. Needless to say, what appellees signed were notes and mortgages on the properties to cover the cost of the aluminum siding, and contracts containing no mention of credits for advertising or other sales.

* * *

Within a matter of days after the contracts were signed, the aluminum siding was installed, although in neither case was the job completed to the satisfaction of appellees. Sometime later, the appellees received letters from appellant, informing them that appellant had purchased the notes and mortgages which had been issued in favor of Consolidated Products and that appellees were delinquent in their first payment. Upon the receipt of these notices, appellees discovered that mortgages had been recorded against their property and they immediately instituted these proceedings.

* * *

[The] trial court found that the notes and mortgages, although signed by the appellees, were fraudulently procured. The court also found that the appellant paid a valuable consideration for the notes and mortgages, although at a discount, and concluded as a matter of law that the appellant was a holder in due course.

* * *

* * *The only real question in the case is whether, under these facts, appellees, by substantial evidence, satisfied the provisions of the statute relating to their claimed defense as against a holder in due course.

In 1961, by enactment of ch. 96 of the session laws, our legislature adopted, with some variations, the Uniform Commercial Code. The provision of the code applicable to this case is as follows:

"To the extent that a holder is a holder in due course he takes the instrument free from

"* * *

"(2) all defenses of any party to the instrument with whom the holder has not dealt except

"* * *

"(c) such misrepresentation as has induced the party to sign the instrument with neither knowledge nor reasonable opportunity to obtain knowledge of its character or its essential terms; and * * *"

The test of the defense here stated is that of excusable ignorance of the contents of the writing signed. The party must not only have been in ignorance, but also have had no reasonable opportunity to obtain knowledge. In determining what is a reasonable opportunity all relevant factors are to be taken into account, including the age and sex of the party, his intelligence, education and business experience; his ability to read or to understand English, the representations made to him and his reason to rely on them or to have confidence in the person making them; the presence or absence of any third person who might read or explain the instrument to him, or any other possibility of obtaining independent information; and the apparent necessity, or lack of it, for acting without delay.

"Unless the misrepresentation meets this test, the defense is cut off by a holder in due course."

* * *

Applying the elements of the test to the case before us, Mrs. Burchett was 47 years old and had a ninth grade education, and Mr. Burchett was approximately the same age, but his education does not appear. Mr. Burchett was foreman of the sanitation department of the city of Clovis and testified that he was familiar with some legal documents. Both the Burchetts understood English and there was no showing that they lacked ability to read. Both were able to understand the original form of contract which was submitted to them.

* * *

The Burchetts had never had any prior association with Kelly and the papers were signed upon the very day that they first met him. There was no showing of any reason why they should rely upon Kelly or have confidence in him. The occurrences took place in the homes of appellees, but other than what appears to be Kelly's "chicanery," no reason was given which would warrant a reasonable person in acting as hurriedly as was done in this case. None of the appellees attempted to obtain any independent information either with respect to Kelly or Consolidated Products, nor did they seek out any other person to read or explain the instruments to them. As a matter of fact, they apparently didn't believe this was neccessary because, like most people, they wanted to take advantage of "getting something for nothing." There is no dispute but that the appellees did not have actual knowledge of the nature of the instruments which they signed, at the time they signed them. Appellant urges that appellees had a reasonable opportunity to obtain such knowledge but failed to do so, were therefore negligent, and that their defense was precluded.

We recognize that the reasonable opportunity to obtain knowledge may be excused if the maker places reasonable reliance on the representations. The difficulty in the instant case is that the reliance upon the representations of a complete stranger (Kelly) was not reasonable, and all of the parties were of sufficient age, intelligence, education, and business experience to know better. In this connection, it is noted that the contracts clearly stated, on the same page which bore the signatures of the various appellees, the following:

"No one is authorized on behalf of this company to represent this job to be 'A SAMPLE HOME OR A FREE JOB.' "
* * *

Although we have sympathy with the appellees, we cannot allow it to influence our decision. They were certainly victimized, but because of their failure to exercise ordinary care for their own protection, an innocent party cannot be made to suffer. * * *

The finance company, as holder in due course, took the instrument free from the defenses claimed by the Burchetts. Thus, the Burchetts were liable for the amount of the note.

JUDGMENT AND REMEDY

ILLEGALITY Certain types of illegality constitute personal defenses. Other types constitute real defenses; the latter will be explained below. Some transactions are prohibited under state statutes or ordinances, and some of these applicable statutes fail to provide that the prohibited transactions are void. If a statute provides that an illegal transaction is voidable, the defense is personal. If a statute makes an illegal transaction *void*, the defense is a *real* defense and can successfully be asserted against an HDC.

ORDINARY DURESS OR UNDUE INFLU-ENCE Duress involves threats of harm or force. Ordinary duress—for example, the threat of a boycott—is a personal defense. When the threat of force or harm becomes so violent and overwhelming that a person is deprived of his or her will (aggravated duress), it becomes a real, or universal, defense, good against all holders and all HDCs. [UCC Sec. 3-305, Comment 6]

MENTAL INCAPACITY There are various types and degrees of incapacity. Incapacity is ordinarily only a personal defense. If a maker or drawer is so extremely incapacitated that the transaction becomes a nullity, then the instrument is void. In that case, the defense

becomes real, or universal, and it is good against an HDC as well. [UCC Sec. 3-305(2)(b)]

DISCHARGE BY PAYMENT OR CANCELL-ATION If commercial paper is paid before its maturity date, the maker will ordinarily request the return of the instrument itself or will note on the face of the instrument that payment has been made. Otherwise, it is possible for the instrument to continue circulating. If it comes into the hands of an HDC who demands payment at maturity, the defense of discharge by payment, which is merely a personal defense, will allow the maker to avoid paying a second time on the same note. [UCC Secs. 3-601(1)(a) and 3-602]

UNAUTHORIZED COMPLETION OF AN IN-COMPLETE INSTRUMENT It is unwise for a maker or drawer to sign any negotiable instrument that is not complete. For example, X signs a check, leaves the amount blank, and gives it to A, an employee, instructing A to make certain purchases and to complete the check "for not more than $500." A fills in the amount as $5,000 *contrary to instructions*. If X can stop payment in time, X *may* be able to assert the defense of unauthorized completion and avoid liability to an ordinary holder. However, if the check is negotiated to an HDC, the instrument is payable as completed. [UCC Secs. 3-115, 3-407, 3-304(4)(d), and 4-401(2)(b)]

NONDELIVERY If a bearer instrument is lost or stolen, the maker or drawer of the instrument has the defense of nondelivery against an ordinary holder. Recall that delivery means "voluntary transfer of possession." [UCC Sec. 1-201(14)] This defense, however, is not good against an HDC. [UCC Sec. 3-305. Compare UCC Sec. 3-306(c)]

Real, or Universal, Defenses

Real, or universal, defenses are valid against *all* holders.

FORGERY Forgery of a maker's or a drawer's signature cannot bind the person whose name is used (*unless* that person ratifies the signature or is precluded from denying it). [UCC Secs. 3-401 and 3-404(1)] Thus, when a person forges an instrument, the person whose name is used has no liability to pay any holder or any HDC the value of the forged instrument. In addition, a principal can assert the defense of unauthorized signature against any holder or HDC when an agent exceeds his or her authority to sign negotiable paper on behalf of the principal. [UCC Sec. 3-403] (Forgery is discussed in Chapter 25, and unauthorized signatures have been discussed earlier in this chapter in the section on liability.)

FRAUD IN THE EXECUTION (IN FACTUM) A person can sign a negotiable instrument because he or she is deceived about what the paper actually is. For example, a consumer unfamiliar with the English language signs a paper given by a salesperson who tells the consumer that it is merely a request for an estimate for roof repair. In fact, it is a promissory note. Even if the note is negotiated to an HDC, the consumer has a valid defense against payment. This defense cannot be raised, however, when a reasonable inquiry would have revealed the nature and terms of the instrument.[6]

MATERIAL ALTERATION An alteration is material if it changes the contract terms between the original parties in any way. Examples of material alterations are (1) a change in the number or relations of the parties, (2) the completion of an instrument in an unauthorized manner, or (3) adding to the writing as signed or removing any part of it. [UCC Sec. 3-407(1)] Thus, cutting off part of the paper of a negotiable instrument or any change in the amount, the date, or the rate of interest—even if the change is only one penny, one day, or 1 percent—is material. But it is not a material alteration to correct the maker's address, to have a red line drawn across the instrument to indicate that an auditor has checked it, or to correct the total final payment due when a mathematical error is discovered in the original computation. If the alteration is *not material*, any holder is entitled to enforce the instrument according to its original terms.

Material alteration is a *complete* defense against an ordinary holder but only a *partial* defense against an HDC. An ordinary holder can recover nothing on an instrument if it has been materially altered. An HDC can enforce the instrument according to its original terms *if* the alteration is so skillfully done that it is not readily apparent. [UCC Sec. 3-407(3)] If it is readily apparent, then obviously the holder has notice of some defect or defense, and such a holder cannot be an HDC. [UCC Secs. 3-302(1)(a) and 3-304(1)(a)]

DISCHARGE IN BANKRUPTCY Discharge in bankruptcy is an absolute defense on any instrument regardless of holder because the purpose of bankruptcy is to settle all of the insolvent party's debts *finally*. [UCC Sec. 3-305(2)(d)]

ILLEGALITY When the law declares that an instrument is *void* because it has been executed in connection with illegal conduct, then the defense is absolute against both an ordinary holder and an HDC. If the law merely makes it *voidable*, as in the personal defense of illegality

---

6. Burchett v. Allied Concord Financial Corp., 74 N.M. 575, 396 P.2d 186 (1964)

discussed above, then it is still a defense against a holder, but not against an HDC. The courts are sometimes prone to treat the word *void* in a statute as meaning "voidable" in order to protect a holder in due course.[7]

MENTAL INCAPACITY If a person is adjudicated mentally incompetent by state proceedings, then any instrument that person issues is null and void. The instrument is *void ab initio* (from the beginning) and unenforceable by any holder or any HDC.

EXTREME DURESS When a person signs and issues a negotiable instrument under such extreme duress as an immediate threat of force or violence (for example, at gunpoint), the instrument is *void* and unenforceable by any holder or HDC. (Ordinary duress, discussed above, is only a personal defense.)

DISCHARGE

In addition to discharge by payment, discharge on a negotiable instrument can occur by cancellation, or it can result from a material alteration of the instrument. Discharge can also occur if a party reacquires an instrument, if a holder impairs another party's right of recourse, or if a holder surrenders collateral without consent. [UCC Sec. 3-601] When a party reacquires an instrument, all those who indorsed it between

---

7. Hawkland, *Commercial Paper and Bank Deposits and Collections,* (Brooklyn: Foundation Press, 1979) p. 249.

8. This is true even if the payment is made "with knowledge of a claim of another person to the instrument unless prior to such payment or satisfaction the person making the claim either supplies indemnity deemed adequate by the party seeking the discharge or enjoins payment or satisfaction by order of a court of competent jurisdiction in an action in which the adverse claimant and the holder are parties." [UCC Sec. 3-603(1)]

the holder's original and current possession are discharged.

Discharge by Payment

According to Sections 3-601(1)(a) and 3-603, all parties to a negotiable instrument will be discharged when the party primarily liable on it pays to a holder the amount due in full.[8] The same is true if the drawee of an unaccepted draft or check makes payment in good faith to the holder. In these situations, all parties on the instruments are usually discharged. By contrast, such payment made by any other party (for example, an indorser) will discharge only the indorser and subsequent parties on the instrument. The party making such a payment still has the right to recover on the instrument from any prior parties.

INSTRUMENTS ACQUIRED BY THEFT OR RESTRICTIVELY INDORSED A party will not be discharged when paying in bad faith to a holder who acquired the instrument by theft or who obtained the instrument from someone else who acquired it by theft (unless, of course, the person has the rights of a holder in due course). [UCC Sec. 3-603(1)(a)] Finally, a party who pays on a restrictively indorsed instrument cannot claim discharge if the payment is made in a manner inconsistent with the terms of the restrictive indorsement. [UCC Sec. 3-603(1)(b)]

Once payment or satisfaction is made to the holder in return for the surrender of the instrument, the liability of the maker or drawer is discharged and the transaction comes to an end. There are numerous acts by which makers or drawers can fulfill payment or satisfaction. In the following case, a dishonored check was satisfied when the purchaser returned to the seller the automobile for which the check had been given.

BACKGROUND AND FACTS *The defendant, Senechal, wished to purchase a 1959 Ford automobile from the plaintiff, a dealer. Senechal borrowed $500 from his credit union and gave his promissory note for the repayment of the loan. The credit union issued a check in the amount of $500 payable to the order of Senechal and American Auto Sales, the*

DUILIO v. SENECHAL
Massachusetts, 1969.
7 UCC Rep. Serv. 222.

plaintiff's trade name. Thereafter, Senechal indorsed and delivered the check to the plaintiff together with his 1954 truck as a trade-in.

The plaintiff then transferred ownership of the 1959 Ford automobile to Senechal by bill of sale and possession. Neither the plaintiff nor the credit union had a security interest in the car.

The credit union then learned that Senechal had been fired from his job and stopped payment on the check. Accordingly, when the plaintiff presented the check to the bank for payment, it was dishonored. Thereupon, as a result of the plaintiff's efforts to restore the parties to the status quo, Senechal agreed to return the car to the plaintiff, who accepted it. However, Senechal did not return the bill of sale to the plaintiff because he mistakenly believed that the credit union held a security interest in it.

This lawsuit followed because the plaintiff took the position that the mere exchange of the automobile for the dishonored check was not satisfaction. The trial court found that the plaintiff was not entitled to any damages because the car had been returned to him, title could be perfected, and the car could be sold in satisfaction of the purchase price.

COX, Justice

* * *

In this action of contract the plaintiff seeks to recover, as a holder in due course, five hundred dollars, being the amount of a check he received from the above named defendant Credit Union in connection with the sale of a 1959 Ford automobile to the defendant Senechal.

The plaintiff claims as a holder in due course to be entitled to the amount of the check. He contends that he did not take title to the 1959 Ford and therefore was not made whole.

The plaintiff, contrary to his contention, received not only possession but also a good title to the vehicle, notwithstanding redelivery was not accompanied by a bill of sale. The findings show that Senechal clearly intended a retransfer to the plaintiff of such title as he had, and because in fact there was no security interest outstanding, the title was unencumbered and was good. [UCC Sec. 2-401(2),(3)(b)]. Whether the 1959 Ford was taken back by the plaintiff in satisfaction of the check presented a question of fact.

The conclusion is warranted that the check in the plaintiff's possession had been satisfied and therefore that the plaintiff may not recover the amount thereof. It is provided by [UCC Sec. 3-603], that "(1) The liability of any party is discharged to the extent of his payment or satisfaction to the holder . . ." and "(2) Payment or satisfaction may be made with the consent of the holder by any person including a stranger to the instrument."

The finding was warranted, if not required, that satisfaction of the check was made with the consent of the plaintiff as holder and that the liability of the defendant as drawer was thereby discharged.

Whether the plaintiff is a holder in due course is inconsequential, so far as recovery of the amount of the check is concerned, and there was no prejudicial error in denying the plaintiff's requested rulings to the effect that he is holder in due course or in allowing that of the defendant that he is not. It is enough that he is a holder, and that, as such, satisfaction was made with his consent, as the Uniform Commercial Code provides. [UCC Secs. 3-202(1); 3-301; 3-603(1),(2)]. The plaintiff has obtained restitution [loss value has been restored] by being restored to the position he formerly occupied by the return of the 1959 Ford sedan which he formerly had.

The trial court ruling was affirmed. The plaintiff was not awarded any further recovery, and Senechal was not required to pay any damages because he had restored the plaintiff to his former position.

JUDGMENT AND REMEDY

Discharge by Cancellation

The holder of a negotiable instrument can discharge any party to the instrument by cancellation. Section 3-605(1)(a) of the UCC explains how cancellation can occur: "The holder of an instrument may even, without consideration, discharge any party in a manner apparent on the face of the instrument or the indorsement, as by intentionally cancelling the instrument or the party's signature by destruction or mutilation, or by striking out the party's signature." For example, to write the word *paid* across the face of an instrument constitutes cancellation. Tearing up a negotiable instrument cancels the instrument. Crossing out a party's indorsement cancels that party's liability and the liability of subsequent indorsers who have already indorsed the instrument, but not the liability of any prior parties.

Destruction or mutilation of a negotiable instrument is considered cancellation only if it is done with the intention of eliminating obligation on the instrument. [UCC Sec. 3-605(1)(a)]

Thus, if destruction or mutilation occurs by accident, the instrument is not discharged, and the original terms can be established by parol evidence. [UCC Sec. 3-804]

Discharge by Reacquisition

A person reacquiring an instrument that he or she held previously discharges all intervening indorsers against subsequent holders who do not qualify as holders in due course. [UCC Secs. 3-208 and 3-601(3)(a)]

Discharge by Impairment of Recourse of Collateral

Sometimes a party to an instrument will post or give collateral to secure that his or her performance will occur. When a holder surrenders that collateral without consent of the parties who would benefit from the collateral in the event of nonpayment, those parties to the instrument are discharged. [UCC Sec. 3-606(1)(b)]

QUESTIONS AND CASE PROBLEMS

1. G & J Wood Products Company had a longstanding relationship with its bank, American Bank. G & J's president, Emerick, and American Bank's president were personal friends. In October 1969, Emerick obtained a loan from American Bank and in return signed a promissory note that provided for repayment in monthly installments over a ten-year period. The note was signed "G. Emerick." About a year later, American Bank sold the note to Commercial Savings Bank. Emerick subsequently resigned from G & J Wood Products and could not be located. Can the new holder of the promissory note, Commercial Savings Bank, enforce the note against G & J Wood Products? [Commercial Sav. Bank v. G & J Wood Products Co., 46 Mich. App. 133, 207 N.W.2d. 401 (1973)]

2. P. J. Pansica, president of Pansica, Inc., signed two promissory notes as follows: "P. J. Pansica, president and agent for P. J. Pansica, Inc." Llobell, the payee of the note, then requested Pansica to sign the reverse sides of the notes but without specifying any representative capacity. Pansica complied, but only after Llobell assured him that Llobell would not seek payment from Pansica personally. Thereafter, P. J. Pansica, Inc., was liquidated in bankruptcy, and Llobell sought to enforce the promissory notes against Pansica personally. Is Pansica's personal signature on the reverse side of the note an indorsement? Will Pansica be allowed to introduce evidence of Llobell's promise not to seek payment from him? [P. J. Pansica, Inc., v. Llobell, 19 U.C.C. Rptg. Serv. 564 (N.Y. Sup. Ct. 1976)]

3. Sullivan County Dorms entered into a contract to purchase certain goods from Sullivan County Wholesalers, Inc. Dorms' president, James V. Holt, signed the note "J. Holt." On the face of the note, both at the top and at the bottom, appeared the name of Holt's company, Sullivan County Dorms, and the company's insignia. About two month later, Sullivan County Dorms went out of business. Sullivan County Wholesalers then attempted to collect from Holt personally. Can Holt present parol evidence that he signed the note only in his representative capacity and thus avoid liability? [Sullivan County Wholesalers, Inc. v. Sullivan County Dorms, 59 A.D.2d 628, 398 N.Y.S.2d 180 (1977)]

4. In January 1971, the law firm of Harkavy, Moxley, and Keane was dissolved. Keane left the firm, which continued under the names of the other two partners. Prior to its dissolution, the law firm maintained a business account at Pan American Bank in which the signature of any one of the partners was sufficient for the deposit or withdrawal of funds. After dissolution of the firm, the account was kept open to take care of the former firm's receivables. In May 1971, a check payable to Keane and Moxley in the amount of $16,500 was received by Harkavy for business carried on by the former firm. The check was deposited in the former firm's account after the bookkeeper had rubber-stamped the check with a facsimile of Harkavy's signature. The $16,500 was thereafter withdrawn by Harkavy and Moxley and deposited into the account of the new firm. If the stamping of the check is deemed to be an improper indorsement, then Keane can recover from Pan American Bank. Can Keane recover? [Keane v. Pan American Bank, 309 So.2d. 579 (Fla. App. 1975)]

5. In June 1973, Hemmingway purchased a new home for which he made a small down payment and signed a promissory note and mortgage. The note provided for interest at the rate of 9¼ percent per year. On the face of the note were the words "post maturity rate" followed by a blank line. The seller of the house immediately transferred the note and mortgage to Fidelity Mortgage Investors. Later on, Fidelity wished to sell the note to Sterling National Bank. Before it did so, one of Fidelity's officers penciled in the notation "9¼" on the face of the promissory note to indicate that the postmaturity rate of interest was equal to the prematurity rate. This accorded with standard bank practices in that locality, and the person who made the notation reasonably believed that the holder would be entitled to this rate. Fidelity then sold the note and mortgage to Sterling. What effect did the notation of "9¼" have on each of the parties to the promissory note? [Sterling Nat. Bank and Trust Co. v. Fidelity Mortgage Investors, 510 F.2d. 870 (2d Cir. 1975)]

6. Daniel had a checking account in the Valley Bank of New York. Through no fault of his own, one of Daniel's checks was stolen by Theodore. Theodore made the check out for $333, payable to the Sound Galore Stereo Shop, and signed Daniel's name. Sound Galore then negotiated it to its bank, the Barnett Bank, which gave Sound Galore cash for the check. Barnett Bank obtained payment from Valley Bank, and Valley Bank debited Daniel's account. Daniel then learned of the whole episode and sought recovery. Who will recover from whom, and who will take the loss?

7. In January 1839, Canal Bank drew a check on the Bank of Albany payable to the order of E. Bently, Jr. Two months later, it was presented by the Bank of New York to the Bank of Albany for payment. At the time of presentment, the check appeared to contain the indorsements of Bently and another individual named Budd. The Bank of New York indorsed the check to the Bank of Albany, which paid it. The Bank of Albany then debited Canal Bank's account. Subsequently, it was learned that the indorsement purporting to be that of Bently was a forgery. Who will suffer the loss here, and why? [Canal v. Bank of Albany, 1 Hill 287 (Sup. Ct. N.Y. 1841)]

8. The LRZH Corporation loaned money to Arlington in exchange for Arlington's promissory note and a third mortgage on his property. LRZH also required Arlington to obtain the signature of a reputable party to act as surety. Before LRZH loaned the money, Arlington had his friend Langeveld sign the face of the note as follows: "L. Langeveld, for the accom-

modation of Arlington." LRZH then advanced Arlington the money in exchange for the note and mortgage but failed to record the mortgage as required under state law. There were two prior mortgages in existence on the property at the time. Six months later, Arlington defaulted on the loan, and the same two mortgages were still outstanding. When the property was liquidated at foreclosure, the amount received was sufficient to cover only the first mortgage and a portion of the second. LRZH now seeks to recover from Langeveld. Can it recover? What defense does Langeveld have, if any? [Langeveld v. LRZH Corp., 130 N.J. Super. 486, 327 A.2d. 683 (1974)]

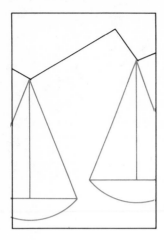

28

Commercial Paper
Checks and the
Banking System

The check is probably the most familiar variety of commercial paper. Checks, credit cards, and charge accounts have replaced cash as a means of payment in almost all transactions for goods and services. It is estimated that Americans write over 35 billion checks each year, transferring about $30 trillion of checkbook dollars around the nation.[1] This means that more than 100 million checks are issued every business day. Checks are more than a daily convenience; checkbook money is an integral part of the economic system.

This chapter will identify the legal characteristics of checks and the legal duties and liabilities that arise when a check is issued. Then it will consider the check deposit and collection process—that is, the actual procedure by which checkbook money moves through banking channels, causing the underlying cash dollars to be shifted from bank account to bank account.

CHECKS

A **check** is a special type of draft that is drawn on a bank, ordering it to pay a sum of money on demand. [UCC Sec. 3-104(2)(b)] The person who writes the check is called the drawer and is usually a depositor in the

---

1. Federal Reserve Bank of New York Publication Department, *The Story of Checks*, 6th ed. (New York: Federal Reserve Bank of New York, 1975), p. 13.

bank on which the check is drawn. The person to whom the check is payable is the payee. The bank or financial institution on which the check is drawn is the drawee. If Anne Gordon writes a check from her checking account to pay her school tuition, she is the *drawer*, her bank is the *drawee*, and her school is the *payee*.

The payee can indorse the check to another person, thereby making that receiver a holder. Recall from Chapter 26 that a holder is a person who is in possession of an instrument that is drawn to that person's order (or drawn to bearer) or that is indorsed to that person (or in blank). [UCC Sec. 1-201(20)] The *holder* of a check has the right to transfer or negotiate it or to demand its payment in his or her own name.

Negotiability

In order for checks to perform their credit function effectively, they must be freely transferable—that is, negotiable. Negotiability is solely a matter of form, which is determined by inspecting the face of the check. According to UCC Secs. 3-104(1) and (2)(b), in order for a check to meet the minimum requirements for negotiability it must:

1. Be signed by the drawer or someone duly authorized to sign on the account.
2. Contain an unconditional order to pay a sum certain in money.
3. Be payable on demand.
4. Be payable to order or to bearer.

Cashier's Checks

Checks are usually three-party instruments, but on certain types of checks, the bank can serve as both the drawer and the drawee. For example, when a bank draws a check upon itself, the check is called a **cashier's check**, and is a negotiable instrument upon issue (see Exhibit 28-1). In effect, with a cashier's check, the bank lends its credit to the purchaser of the check, thus making it available for immediate use in banking circles. (The drawee is treated like an acceptor.) A cashier's check is therefore an acknowledgment of a debt drawn by the bank upon itself.

Traveler's Checks

A traveler's check is always an instrument on which a financial institution is both the drawer

EXHIBIT 28-1   CASHIER'S CHECK

and the drawee. (It is not always a check since a bank is not always the drawee.) On traveler's checks, however, there is an additional requirement that the payee must provide his or her authorized signature in order for it to become a negotiable instrument. A traveler's check has the characteristics of a cashier's check from the issuing bank. It is drawn by the issuer upon itself. (See Exhibit 28-2.)

Certified Checks

A personal check is only as good as the credit of the drawer. When a person writes a check, it is assumed that he or she has money on deposit to cover that check when it is presented for payment. To insure against dishonor for insufficient funds, a check can be certified by the drawee bank. A **certified check** is recognized and accepted by a bank officer as a valid appropria-

EXHIBIT 28-2   TRAVELER'S CHECK

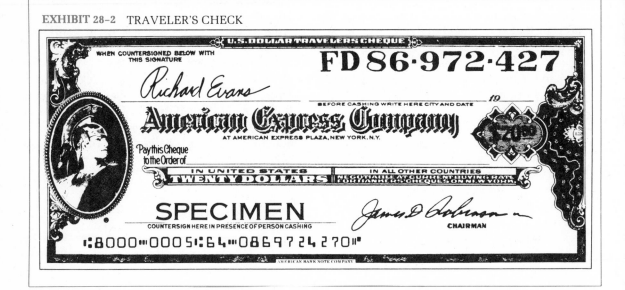

EXHIBIT 28-3   CERTIFIED CHECK

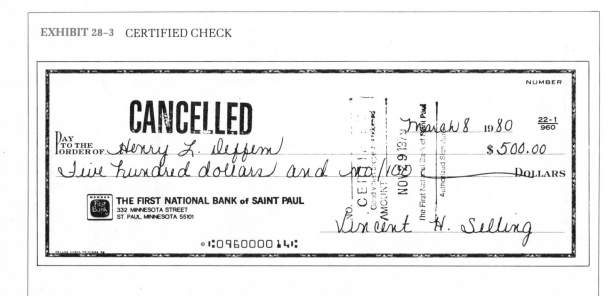

tion of the specified amount that is drawn against the funds held by the bank. (See Exhibit 28-3.) The usual method of certification is for the cashier or teller to write across the face of the check over the signature a statement that it is good when properly indorsed. The certification of a check prevents the bank from denying liability. It is a promise that sufficient funds are on deposit and *have been set aside* to cover the check. Certified checks are used in many business dealings, especially when the buyer and seller are strangers. Sometimes, certified checks are the required form of payment under state law—for example, in purchases at a sheriff's sale.

When a bank agrees to certification, it immediately charges the drawer's account with the amount of the check and transfers those funds to its own certified check account. In effect, the bank is agreeing in advance to accept that check when it is presented for payment and to make payment from those funds reserved in the certified check account. [UCC Sec. 3-411]

DRAWER'S REQUEST FOR CERTIFICATION

The legal liability of the drawer differs on the basis of whether the certification is requested by the drawer or the holder. The drawer who obtains certification remains *secondarily liable* on the instrument if for some reason the certifying bank cannot or does not honor the check when it is presented for payment. For example, Epstein buys Stiple's car for $500. Epstein writes out a check for that amount and takes it to the bank to be certified. In the unlikely event that the bank fails to honor the check when it is presented for payment, Stiple can hold Epstein liable for payment of the $500. [UCC Sec. 3-411]

HOLDER'S REQUEST FOR CERTIFICATION

If the check is certified at the request of the holder, then the drawer and any indorsers prior to certification are completely discharged. A holder's request for certification is viewed as an affirmative choice for the bank's promise to pay over the drawers and any indorsers. In this situation, the holder can look only to the bank for payment. In the example above, Epstein writes a $500 check to Stiple, but Stiple takes the check to the drawee bank for certification. At this point, Epstein is released from all liability, and Stiple can look only to the bank for his $500. [UCC Sec. 3-411(1)]

REVOCATION OF CERTIFICATION

The bank's ability to revoke certification is extremely limited. If a good faith holder has changed position in reliance on that certification, the bank cannot revoke. Furthermore, since certification constitutes acceptance of an instrument under the Uniform Commercial Code, a bank can never revoke certification against a HDC regardless of whether or not the HDC has changed position in reliance on the certification. [UCC Sec. 3-418]

ALTERATION OF A CERTIFIED CHECK

A bank will be liable for payment of an altered check only if the check was altered prior to certification. In the following case, a certified check was altered, and when it was presented to the bank, it was dishonored because of the alteration. The check had been certified at the request of the drawer and subsequently given in payment to a third party. The third party was unsuccessful in its attempt to hold the bank liable for the full amount of the instrument.

BACKGROUND AND FACTS *The Franklin National Bank (defendant) certified a check payable to Sam Goody, Inc., in the amount of $16. The certification stamp of the defendant bank did not show the amount for which the check was certified. The check had been presented to the defendant bank for certification by either the depositor or an accomplice. After the certification was procured, the amount of the check was altered from $16 to $1,600. The check was later presented to the plaintiff, Sam Goody, Inc., in payment for merchandise. The customer who presented the check represented that it was a bonus check. The customer*

SAM GOODY, INC. v. FRANKLIN NAT. BANK OF LONG ISLAND
Supreme Court of New York, 1968.
57 Misc. 2d 193, 291 N.Y.S.2d 429.

had ordered the merchandise on the previous day and had stated that he would secure from his employer a certified check drawn directly to the plaintiff, Sam Goody, to pay the balance owing. Subsequently, the bank refused to honor the check because of the alteration. The plaintiff sued the bank for the full $1,600. The bank asserted that it was responsible only for the amount it had certified originally—that is, $16.

THOMAS P. FARLEY, Justice.

* * *

The unusual facts of this case give rise to the application of law that is rarely invoked.

* * *

The fraudulent scheme perpetrated in this case was obviously made possible by the knowledge that the certification stamp of the defendant Bank would not disclose the amount for which the check was certified. The plaintiff claims the negligence of the Bank in this respect caused the loss and that the Bank is estopped from asserting the defense of alteration under section 3-406 of the Uniform Commercial Code.

* * *

A bank, when certifying a check, does no more than to affirm the genuineness of the signature of the maker, that he has funds on deposit to meet the item, and that the funds will not be withdrawn to the prejudice of the holder. The certification constitutes an acceptance of the check to this extent (U.C.C., §3-411), but the bank by its certification does not guaranty the body thereof * * * and engages only to pay the item according to its tenor at the time certification is procured (U.C.C., §3-413). Furthermore, a holder of a check, by having it certified, is deemed to have warranted to the bank that the instrument has not been materially altered. The Code makes one exception to this rule by providing that the same warranty is not given by a holder in due course whether the alteration is made before or after certification (U.C.C., §§3-417 subd. (1) [c. iii, iv]; 3-413). Consequently, under the Code, where a check is certified *after the amount has been altered*, the bank runs the risk of sustaining the loss if the instrument passes into the hands of a holder in due course. [Emphasis added.] The Code in this respect changes the law which previously obtained in New York (National Reserve Bank of the City of New York v. The Corn Exchange Bank, supra).

The rule, however, is otherwise where the certification of the check is procured by the maker. In such case, the bank does not incur the risk of an alteration prior to its acceptance, and only agrees to pay the instrument according to its tenor at the time of certification even as to a holder in due course (U.C.C., §3-413[1]).

The evidence in this case does not disclose whether the maker or his accomplice procured certification of the check, but the controlling fact that alteration occurred after certification of the instrument is not disputed. The bank, in checking its records, discovered the alteration and refused payment. Under these circumstances, the negligence of the bank, if any, is not a substantial or proximate cause of the loss, and in accordance with the rules mentioned above, it is not liable to the plaintiff except for the amount for which the check was originally drawn.

The defendant, Franklin National Bank, was liable for only $16, the original amount of the certified check.   **JUDGMENT AND REMEDY**

THE BANK-CUSTOMER RELATIONSHIP

The bank-customer relationship begins when the customer opens a checking account and deposits money that will be used to pay for checks written. The rights and duties of the bank and the customer are contractual and depend upon the nature of the transaction.

Article 4 of the UCC is a statement of the principal rules of modern bank deposit and collection procedures. It governs the relationship of banks with one another as they process checks for payment, and it establishes a framework for the deposit and checking agreement between a bank and its customer.

Article 3 of the UCC, dealing with the use of commercial paper, sets forth the requirements for negotiable instruments. The extent to which any party is either charged or discharged from liability on a check is established according to the provisions of Article 3. Note that a check can fall within the scope of Article 3 as a negotiable instrument and yet be subject to the provisions of Article 4 while it is in the course of collection. In the case of a conflict between Articles 3 and 4, Article 4 controls. [UCC Sec. 4-102(1)]

A creditor-debtor relationship is created between a customer and a bank when, for example, the customer makes cash deposits into a checking account or when final payment is received for checks drawn on other banks.

A principal-agent relationship underlies the check collection process. A check does not operate as an immediate legal assignment of funds between the drawer and the payee. [UCC Sec. 3-409] The money in the bank represented by that check does not move from the drawer's account to the payee's account; nor is any underlying debt discharged until the drawee bank honors the check and makes final payment. To transfer checkbook dollars among different banks, each bank acts as the agent of collection for its customer. [UCC Sec. 4-201(1)]

DUTIES OF THE BANK

A commercial bank serves its customers primarily in two ways:

1. Honoring checks for the withdrawal of funds on deposit in its customers' accounts.
2. Accepting deposits in U.S. currency and collecting checks written to or indorsed to its customers that are drawn on other banks.

Honoring Checks

When a commercial bank provides checking services, it agrees to honor the checks written by its customers with the usual stipulation that there be sufficient funds available in the account to pay each check. When a drawee bank wrongfully fails to honor a check, it is liable to its customer for damages resulting from its refusal to pay under breach of contract principles. [UCC Sec. 4-402] When the bank properly dishonors a check for insufficient funds, it has no liability to the customer. On the other hand, a bank may charge against a customer's account a check which is payable from that account even though the account contains insufficient funds to cover the check. The charging of overdrafts will be discussed later in this chapter.

The customer's agreement with the bank includes a general obligation to keep sufficient money on deposit to cover all checks written. The customer is liable to the payee or to the holder of a check in a civil suit if a check is not honored. If intent to defraud can be proved, the customer can also be subject to criminal prosecution for writing a bad check.

Once a bank makes special arrangements with its customer to accept overdrafts on an account, the payor bank can become liable to its customer for damages proximately caused by its wrongful dishonor of overdrafts.

KENDALL YACHT
CORP. v. UNITED
CALIFORNIA BANK

Court of Appeals of California,
1975.
50 Cal.3d 949, 123 Cal.Rptr. 848.

BACKGROUND AND FACTS *Lawrence and Linda Kendall were officers and the principal shareholders of a corporation formed to build yachts upon special order from customers. The corporation had never issued stock and was undercapitalized.*

The corporation had a payroll checking account and a general business checking account with United California Bank. When the corporation ran into some financial problems, Mr. Kendall spoke with Ron Lamperts, a loan officer at the bank, in an effort to obtain financing for the corporation.

The bank agreed to honor overdrafts on the corporate account until such time as the corporation was out of the woods. The Kendalls continued to write checks for supplies, payroll, and other operating expenses of the corporation from about mid-October through December. The corporate bank account was badly overdrawn, and a number of the checks had been dishonored by the bank.

The Kendalls brought this lawsuit against United California Bank, charging that its wrongful dishonor of checks that it had initially agreed to accept as overdrafts caused damage to the Kendalls' personal and credit reputation.

McDANIEL, Associate Justice.

* * *

During October, November, and December, the Bank honored overdrafts of the Corporation totaling in excess of $15,000. There were also a number of overdrafts written during these months which were not honored by the Bank. Some of these were to suppliers and others were payroll checks to employees. In addition, the Bank failed to honor a check written to Insurance Company of North America to cover a premium for workmen's compensation insurance. The Kendalls were not aware that this check had been "bounced" until after one of their employees had been injured and they had been notified by Insurance Company of North America that their insurance had been terminated for nonpayment of premium.

After the collapse of the business, the Kendalls understandably had a number of enemies in the community. They were accused of having breached the trust of their former suppliers and employees and of having milked the Corporation of its funds and placed them in a Swiss bank account. They were repeatedly threatened with legal action and physical harm; they suffered acts of vandalism such as eggs and oil being thrown at their cars. Mr. Kendall's subsequent employer was contacted and threatened by creditors of the Corporation. Criminal charges were brought against Mrs. Kendall for writing checks against insufficient funds; the charges were dismissed shortly before she was brought to trial on them. The Kendalls were required to appear and answer charges in administrative proceedings involving dishonored payroll checks and the Corporation's failure to carry workmen's compensation insurance. Each testified to experiencing severe emotional distress and humiliation as a result of these matters. They also testified to marital problems which were allegedly caused by the stress brought on by the failure of the business.

* * *

The Bank contends first that under Commercial Code section 4402 the wrongful dishonor of a check of a *corporation* does not give a cause of action for damages to individual officers and shareholders of the corporation. Commercial Code section 4402, which represents section 4-402 of the Uniform Commercial Code, reads as follows: "A payor bank is liable to its customer for damages proximately caused by the wrongful dishonor of an item. When the dishonor occurs through mistake liability is limited to actual damages proved." [Footnote omitted.]

[It] was entirely foreseeable that the dishonoring of the Corporation's checks would reflect directly on the personal credit and reputation of the Kendalls and that they would suffer the adverse personal consequences which resulted when the Bank reneged on its commitments.

* * *

[It] has been held in this state that a cause of action for wrongful dishonor of a check sounds in tort as well as in contract (*Weaver v. Bank of America*, 59 Cal.2d 428, 431, 30 Cal.Rptr. 4, 380 P.2d 644), and "if the conduct is tortious, damages for emotional distress may be recovered despite the fact that the conduct also involves a breach of contract."

The court awarded the Kendalls $26,000 each as compensatory damages for the bank's wrongful dishonor of the checks.

JUDGMENT AND REMEDY

Stale Checks

The bank's responsibility to honor its customers' checks is not absolute. A bank is not obliged to pay a noncertified check that is more than six months old. [UCC Sec. 4-404]. Commercial banking practice regards a check outstanding for longer than six months as *stale*. Section 4-404 of the UCC gives a bank the option of paying or not paying on a **stale check**. The usual banking practice is to consult the customer, but if a bank pays in good faith without consulting the customer, it has the right to charge the customer's account for the amount of the check.

BACKGROUND AND FACTS *Granite Equipment Leasing Corporation issued a check to Overseas Equipment Company. After five days, Overseas indicated that the check had not been received. Granite ordered payment on the check stopped and wired the funds to Overseas. Approximately one year later, the check cleared and Granite's account was charged. Granite sued the bank for return of the funds to its account, maintaining that the bank had a duty to inquire into the circumstances of the stale check. The bank based its defense on the premise that the stop payment order had expired and that it had acted in good faith.*

GRANITE EQUIPMENT LEASING CORP. v. HEMPSTEAD BANK
Supreme Court of New York, 1971.
68 Misc.2d 350, 326 N.Y.S.2d 881.

BERTRAM HARNETT, Justice.

* * *

Under the Uniform Commercial Code, does a bank have a duty of inquiry before paying a stale check? Does it matter that the stale check had been previously stopped under a stop payment order which expired for lack of renewal? So this case goes.

Granite Equipment Leasing Corp. kept a checking account with Hempstead Bank. On October 10, 1968 Granite drew a check payable to Overseas Equipment Co., Inc. Five days later, after Overseas advised that the check had not been received, Granite wrote the Bank on October 15, 1968 to stop payment on the check. On that same day Granite authorized the Bank to wire the payee funds in the same amount as the stopped check and the Bank did so. Granite never renewed its stop payment order between October 1968 and November 10, 1969. On November 10, 1969, without notice or inquiry to Granite, the Bank accepted the original check to Overseas which had been stopped the year before, paid the indicated funds to a collecting bank, and charged Granite's account.

Granite now seeks to recover from the Bank the amount charged because of the check paid to Overseas in November 1969. The Bank defends on the ground that under UCC §4-403 the stop payment order had expired for want of renewal, and that acting in good faith it was entitled under UCC §4-404 to pay the stale check.

There is no doubt the check is stale. There is no doubt the stop payment order was properly given at the outset, and that it was never renewed. Granite essentially maintains the Bank had a duty to inquire into the circumstances of that stale check, and should not have paid in face of a known lapsed stop order without consulting its depositor.

The Uniform Commercial Code, which became effective in New York on September 27, 1964, provides that:

"(1) A customer may by order to his bank stop payment of any item payable for his account * * * (2) * * * A written [stop] order is effective for only six months unless renewed in writing". UCC §4-403.

* * *

Granite cannot be permitted to predicate liability on the part of the Bank on its failure to inquire about and find a stop payment order which had become terminated in default of renewal.

* * *

Neither may Granite predicate a claim of liability upon the Bank's payment of a stale check. The legal principles applicable to this circumstance are codified in UCC §4-404, which provides that:

"[a] bank is under no obligation . . . to pay a check, other than a certified check, which is presented more than six months after its date, but *it may charge its customer's account for a payment made thereafter in good faith*". (Emphasis added.) * * *

There is no obligation under the statute of the Bank to search its records to discover old lapsed stop payment orders. The Bank does not have to pay a stale check, but it may pay one in "good faith". Significantly, UCC §1-201(19) defines "good faith" as "honesty in fact in the conduct or transaction concerned". In the absence of any facts which could justify a finding of dishonesty, bad faith, recklessness, or lack of ordinary care, in the face of circumstances actually known, or which should have been known, the Bank is not liable to Granite for its payment of the check drawn to Overseas.

Granite's complete remedy lies in its pending Florida action against Overseas to recover the extra payment.

The court dismissed the complaint and entered judgment in favor of the bank, which was not required to pay Granite Equipment the amount of the check. The court ruled that Hempstead Bank had acted in good faith.

JUDGMENT
AND REMEDY

Death or Incompetence of a Customer

Section 4-405 of the UCC provides that if, at the time a check is issued or its collection has been undertaken, a bank does not know of an adjudication of incompetence, an item can be paid and the bank will not incur liability. Neither death nor incompetency revokes the bank's authority to pay an item until the bank knows of the situation and has had reasonable time to act. Even when a bank knows of the death of its customer, for ten days after the date of death, it can pay or certify checks drawn on or prior to the date of death unless a person claiming an interest in that account, such as an heir or an executor of the estate, orders the bank to stop all payment. Otherwise banks would constantly be required to verify the continued life and competency of their drawers.

Stop Payment Orders

Only a customer can order his or her bank to pay a check, and only a customer can order payment to be stopped. This right does not extend to holders—that is, payees or indorsees—because the drawee bank's contract is only with its drawers. A stop order must be received in reasonable time and in reasonable manner to permit the bank to act on it. [UCC Sec. 4-403] A stop order can be given orally, usually by phone, and it is binding on the bank for fourteen calendar days unless it has been confirmed in writing.[2] (See Exhibit 28-4.) Then it becomes effective for six months. A written stop order must be renewed every six months, or it will lapse. [UCC Sec. 4-403]

_____

2. Some states do not recognize *oral* stop payment orders.

EXHIBIT 28-4 STOP ORDER

TO THE FIRST NATIONAL BANK
OF SOUTH MIAMI
SOUTH MIAMI, FLORIDA

DATE OF ORDER   ACCOUNT NUMBER

Please STOP PAYMENT on my (or our) check drawn on your bank, described as follows:

NO:	DATED:	PAYABLE TO:	AMOUNT: $

REASON: DUPLICATE ISSUED?

THIS REQUEST IS MADE WITH THE UNDERSTANDING THAT THE BANK WILL USE REASONABLE PRECAUTION IN FOLLOWING YOUR INSTRUCTION, BUT IN CONSIDERATION OF THE ACCEPTANCE OF THIS REQUEST IT IS EXPRESSLY AGREED THAT THE BANK WILL IN NO WAY BE LIABLE IN THE EVENT THE CHECK IS PAID. IF PAID THE SAME DAY YOUR ORDER IS RECEIVED OR IF PAID BY OVERSIGHT OR INADVERTENCE OR IF BY REASON OF SUCH PAYMENT OTHER CHECKS DRAWN BY THE UNDERSIGNED ARE RETURNED FOR INSUFFICIENT FUNDS. AND THE UNDERSIGNED FURTHER AGREES TO INDEMNIFY THE BANK AGAINST ALL EXPENSES AND COSTS THAT IT MIGHT INCUR BY REASON OF REFUSING PAYMENT ON SAID CHECK

EXPIRATION DATE

IT IS HEREBY AGREED AND UNDERSTOOD THAT THIS ORDER WILL REMAIN IN EFFECT FOR A SIX MONTH PERIOD UNLESS OTHERWISE DIRECTED AND THE BANK WILL CHARGE $5.00 FOR EACH SIX-MONTH PERIOD OR PORTION THEREOF THAT THIS ORDER IS IN EFFECT. THE BANK MAY CHARGE MY ACCOUNT WITH THIS AMOUNT

ORDER RECEIVED BY	IN PERSON	BY LETTER	SIGNATURE OF MAKER

BANK NOT LIABLE IF CHECK HAS BEEN CASHED IN THE SAME DAY THIS ORDER WAS ACCEPTED.

For example, Pat Davis orders one hundred used typewriters at $50 each from Jane Smith. Davis pays in advance for the goods with her check for $5,000. Later that day, Smith tells Davis that she is not going to deliver any type-writers. Davis immediately calls her bank and stops payment on the check. Two days later, in spite of this stop order, the bank inadvertently honors Davis's $5,000 check to Smith for the undelivered typewriters. The bank will be liable to Davis for the full $5,000. The result would be different if Smith had delivered ninety-nine typewriters. Since Davis would have owed Smith $4,950 for the goods delivered, she would have been able to establish actual losses of only $50 due to the bank's payment over her stop order. The bank would be liable to Davis for only $50.

A stop payment order has its risks for a customer. The drawer must have a *valid legal ground* for issuing a stop order; otherwise the holder can sue the drawer for payment. More-over, defenses sufficient to refuse payment against a payee may not be valid grounds to prevent payment against a subsequent holder in due course. [UCC Sec. 3-305]

A person who wrongfully stops payment on a check will not only be liable to the payee for the amount of the check, but might also be liable for *special* damages which result to the payee on account of the wrongful stop payment order. Special damages, however, must be separately pleaded and proven at trial.

VICKREY v. SANFORD

Court of Appeals of Texas, 1974. 506 S.W.2d 270.

BACKGROUND AND FACTS *Sanford was fired from a restaurant by his supervisor, Vickrey. Vickrey gave him a number of checks for wages due along with a check for $720 to reimburse him for shares of stock that he had purchased in one of Vickrey's other companies. After depositing the checks, Sanford returned to the restaurant and verbally insulted and threatened Vickrey. Following the incident, Vickrey stopped payment on the check for $720. Sanford sued Vickrey for $720 plus interest.*

BREWSTER, Justice.

* * *

On the occasion when Vickrey had given the $720.00 check to Sanford, Sanford had advised Vickrey that he needed the money to pay up bills and to get to Las Vegas, Nevada, at which place he could get a job.

After Sanford had done the cursing at the "Sirloin Stockade", he, on the same day, left for Las Vegas, Nevada, and was there hired at the Golden Nuggett as a dealer and to work at the roulette wheel.

A few days later Sanford called home and was told by his wife that payment had been stopped on the $720.00 check and that Mr. Allen, a vice-president of Denton County National Bank, where he had cashed it, wanted to get in touch with him. He called Allen and Allen wanted him to sign a note for the $720.00.

* * *

Sanford sought in this case to recover the amount of the check ($720.00) plus interest thereon, plus the expenses that he incurred in making the two trips back to Denton, plus exemplary [punishment] damages.

* * *

[The court had no trouble deciding that Vickrey was responsible for paying the $720 plus interest. It was Sanford's most unusual request for the cost of traveling between Nevada and Texas to straighten out the mess that gave the court cause for concern.]

If plaintiff, Sanford, is legally entitled to recover for expenses incurred in making the two trips from Nevada back to Texas plus the loss of salary due to losing his job, it would only be on the theory that they were special damages that were within the contemplation of the parties at the time the contract was executed. This is a necessary element if the expenses sought to be recovered are in the category of special damages.

* * *

There was no evidence tending to show that the entire transaction with reference to Sanford signing the note to the Bank could not have been handled by mail, thus rendering both of Sanford's trips to Texas unnecessary. There was no evidence offered to the effect that it was necessary that this note be signed in Denton.

The court permitted Sanford to recover only the amount of the $720 check in damages. The court held that there was insufficient evidence to uphold Sanford's claim for special damages.	**JUDGMENT AND REMEDY**

Overdrafts

When the bank receives an item properly payable from its customer's checking account, but there are insufficient funds in the account to cover the amount of the check, the bank can either dishonor the item or pay it and charge the customer's account even though an overdraft is created. [UCC Sec. 4-401(11)] The bank can subtract the difference from the customer's next deposit because the check carries with it an enforceable implied promise to reimburse the bank.

When a check bounces, a holder can resubmit the check, hoping that at a later date sufficient funds will be available to pay it. The holder must notify any indorsers on the check of the first dishonor; otherwise they will be discharged from liability. A holder of a noncertified check cannot claim against the bank for dishonoring a check. A holder can sue only the drawer, and any unqualified indorser.

Payment on a Forged Signature of the Drawer

A forged signature on a check has no legal effect as the signature of a drawer. [UCC Sec. 4-404] Banks require signature cards from each customer who opens a checking account. The bank is responsible for determining whether the signature on a customer's check is genuine. The general rule is that the bank must recredit the customer's account when it pays on a forged signature. [UCC Sec. 4-401]

CUSTOMER NEGLIGENCE When the customer's negligence contributes to forgery, the bank will not normally be obliged to recredit the customer's account for the amount of the check. Suppose Axelrod Corporation uses a mechanical check-writing machine to write its payroll and business checks. Axelrod discovers that one of its employees used the machine to write himself a check for $10,000 and that the bank subsequently honored it. Axelrod requests the bank to recredit $10,000 to its account for incorrectly paying on a forged check. If the bank can show that Axelrod failed to take reasonable care in controlling access to the check-writing equipment, Axelrod cannot require the bank to recredit its account for the amount of the forged check. [UCC Sec. 3-406]

TIMELY EXAMINATION REQUIRED A customer has an *affirmative duty* to examine monthly statements and cancelled checks promptly and with reasonable care and to report any forged signatures promptly. [UCC Sec. 4-406(1)] A customer who fails to report a forged signature within one year from the date that the statement and cancelled checks containing the forgery were received loses the right to sue the bank for recredit. [UCC Sec. 4-406(4)

A customer who fails to examine and report any unauthorized signatures within fourteen calendar days of receipt of his or her bank statement and cancelled checks will be liable for subsequent forgeries made by the same wrongdoer. [UCC Sec. 4-406(2)(b)] When a series of forgeries are committed and a customer does not discover the initial forgery, he or she could lose more than the price of one forged check. Middletown Bank sends out monthly statements and checks on the last day of each month. Bradley, owner of a small store, received his April statement and cancelled checks on May 1. Bradley put the unopened envelope near his checkbook which he kept on top of his desk in the storage room. Unknown to Bradley, one of his salesmen, Harry, who had seen the checkbook lying around, had removed a check and forged Bradley's signature. Harry cashed check number 1 earlier that month. Harry forged check number 2 on May 5 and check number 3 on May 12 and cashed them at Middletown Bank. Bradley received his May statement and cancelled checks on June 1, but did not look at them. Meanwhile, Harry continued to forge Bradley's signature, cashing check number 4 on June 7 and check number 5 on June 15. On July 1 Bradley received another bank statement and cancelled checks for the month of June. On July 10, Bradley reviewed his statements and cancelled checks for the months of April, May, and June. He discovered the forgeries and notified the bank that same day.

Can Bradley demand the bank recredit his account for all five forged checks? Probably not. Bradley's deadline for reporting alterations or forgeries on the April checks (which includes forged check number 1) was fourteen days after receipt of his statement—May 15. Liability for any checks forged by Harry and honored by Middletown Bank after May 15 shifts from the

bank to Bradley. Thus, the bank is not required to recredit Bradley on check numbers 4 and 5. Check numbers 1, 2, and 3 may be Middletown Bank's responsibility, since each of them was honored before the reasonable time period had elapsed. Note, however, that the bank may still deny liability on the basis of Bradley's failure to use reasonable care in securing his checkbook in a safe place. If the bank proves that Bradley's negligence substantially contributed to the forgery, Bradley—not the bank—will be liable on check numbers 1, 2, and 3. [UCC Secs. 4-406 and 3-406]

Payment on a Forged Instrument

A bank that pays a customer's check that bears a forged indorsement must recredit the customer's account or be liable to the customer-drawer for breach of contract. [UCC Sec. 4-401(1)] For example, B issues a $50 check "to the order of T." L steals the check, forges T's indorsement and cashes the check. When the check reaches B's bank the bank pays it and debits B's account. Under Sec. 4-401, the bank must recredit B's account $50 because it failed to carry out B's order to pay "to the order of T." [B's bank will in turn recover from the bank which cashed the check under breach of warranty principles. See UCC Sec. 4-207 (1) (a).]

By comparison, the bank has no right to recover from a holder who, without knowledge, cashes a check bearing a *forged drawer's signature*. The holder merely guarantees that he or she has no knowledge that the signature of the drawer is unauthorized. Unless the bank can prove such knowledge, its only recourse is against the forger. [UCC Secs. 3-417(1)(b) and 4-207(1)(b)]

CUSTOMER'S DUTY TO DISCOVER AND REPORT UNAUTHORIZED SIGNATURE OR ALTERATION The customer is never relieved of the duty to examine the returned checks and statements received from the bank and to report forged indorsements within a reasonable time. [UCC Sec. 4-406(1)] If careless-ness that can be traced to the customer results in a loss to the bank, the loss will be borne by the customer. [UCC Sec. 4-406(2)(a)] Also, the customer has the duty to report any unauthor-ized signature or alteration within one year from the time he or she receives the bank statement and the items in question. Any un-authorized indorsement must be reported with-in three years. [UCC Sec. 4-406(4)] In the follow-ing case, the customer's duty to discover and report an unauthorized signature was at issue.

BACKGROUND AND FACTS   *Nu-Way is the customer-drawer in this case and Mercantile Trust Company is the drawee bank. Nu-Way has sued Mercantile Trust for reimbursement for numerous altered and forged checks which the latter paid. The court gives a detailed rendition of the events leading up to this lawsuit.*

NU-WAY SERVICES, INC. v. MERCANTILE TRUST CO. NAT. ASS'N
Missouri Court of Appeals, 1975. 530 S.W.2d 743.

GUNN, Judge.
* * *
Nu-Way, a truck repair company, maintained a checking account with Mercan-tile. The signature card for Nu-Way's president, Mariano Costello, was kept on file by the bank. Each month, Nu-Way wrote approximately 175 checks on its account, and Mercantile sent Nu-Way a monthly statement indicating the fluctuating checking account balance as each check was charged against the account with the cancelled checks being returned with the statement.

In an altruistic gesture designed for the rehabilitation of a former convict, Mr. Costello hired James Ussery as night manager for Nu-Way. Part of Ussery's duties entailed obtaining automotive parts from parts companies. Mr. Costello would on occasion date and sign checks and fill in the name of the payee (always a parts company) for payment of parts used by Nu-Way, and the amount of the check would be left blank for Ussery to fill in when the cost of the parts was determined at the time they were picked up by him. On seven such checks which Mr. Costello had signed, Ussery made alterations to substitute his name as payee and cashed the checks for his own benefit. Ussery also had unauthorized access to Nu-Way's checkbook and removed a substantial number of blank checks therefrom. Ussery made use of 43 of the blank checks by forging Mr. Costello's signature on them after making himself the payee. The dates on the altered and forged checks were from July 29, 1971 to January 13, 1972.

Each of the forged checks was returned to Nu-Way by Mercantile along with an itemized statement of account at the end of each month the checks were cashed. And each month Mr. Costello would have a company clerk compare the amount of the checks with the statements. At Mr. Costello's direction the bookkeeping employee merely compared the amount of the checks with the statements looking only for mathematical computation errors by Mercantile. None of the Nu-Way employees, including Mr. Costello, examined any of the checks for forgeries or alterations nor compared the checks with the company checkbook. Ultimately, one of Nu-Way's vendors called Mr. Costello's attention to a check made payable to Ussery, and an investigation revealed the alterations and forgeries. Mercantile was notified of the irregularities and subsequently reimbursed Nu-Way for $231 to cover the amount of the first check altered by Ussery. Nu-Way brought suit to recover the amount paid out on its checking account on the forged and altered checks.

* * *

In its argument that it has no liability to Nu-Way for the payments made on the altered and forged checks, Mercantile relies on [UCC Sec. 4-406] which in pertinent part provides:

"(1) When a bank sends to its customer a statement of account accompanied by items paid in good faith in support of the debit entries or holds the statement and items pursuant to a request or instructions of its customer or otherwise in a reasonable manner makes the statement and items available to the customer, the customer must exercise reasonable care and promptness to examine the statement and items to discover his unauthorized signature or any alteration on an item and must notify the bank promptly after discovery thereof.

"(2) If the bank establishes that the customer failed with respect to an item to comply with the duties imposed on the customer by subsection (1) the customer is precluded from asserting against the bank

(a) his unauthorized signature or any alteration on the item if the bank also establishes that it suffered a loss by reason of such failure; and

(b) an unauthorized signature or alteration by the same wrongdoer on any other item paid in good faith by the bank after the first item and statement was available to the customer for a reasonable period not exceeding fourteen calendar days and before the bank receives notification from the customer of any such unauthorized signature or alteration.

"(3) The preclusion under subsection (2) does not apply if the customer establishes lack of ordinary care on the part of the bank in paying the items." Nu-Way concedes that under the facts of this case that §400.4-406(3) places the burden upon it of proving that Mercantile lacked ordinary care in paying on the altered and forged checks. We find as a matter of law that Nu-Way failed in this case in its proof of lack of ordinary care by Mercantile as to the 43 forged checks

* * *

* * *The fundamental rule in the Uniform Commercial Code regarding unauthorized signatures is stated in [UCC Sec. 3-404(1)] as follows:

"Any unauthorized signature is wholly inoperative as that of the person whose name is signed unless he ratifies it or is precluded from denying it . . ." It is accepted that Ussery's forgeries of Mr. Costello's signature were unauthorized and would therefore be "wholly inoperative" as to Nu-Way unless Nu-Way is "precluded from denying it." [UCC Sec. 4-406] relates directly to the relationship between depositor and bank and affords an apt guide for determining whether a basis exists for precluding Nu-Way's denial of the signatures.

Initially, we find that Nu-Way failed to meet its obligation under subparagraph (1) of [UCC Sec. 4-406], in that it did not "exercise reasonable care and promptness to examine the statement and items to discover [the] unauthorized signature * * * on an item." In accordance with Mr. Costello's instructions, the

Nu-Way clerk in charge of examining the bank statements examined Mercantile's statements to check the accuracy of the mathematics. The "items"—the cancelled checks—were not examined at all. Mr. Costello readily admitted that the checks were not scrutinized for forgeries as required by statute nor was reasonable notice given to Mercantile of any wrongdoing after the first check and statement was made available to Nu-Way within the meaning of [UCC Sec. 4-406(2)(b). Hence, Nu-Way failed in its duties to discover and report the forgeries under [UCC Sec. 4-406(2)] and is precluded from recovering against Mercantile * * *

After Mr. Costello notified Mercantile that there had been payments made on some forgeries and alterations, the clerk responsible for examining Nu-Way's account and her two supervisors made comparison between the authorized signature card and all Nu-Way's checks for the period covered by the forgeries and alterations and were unable to differentiate between the forgeries and the authorized signature. The forgeries were sufficiently adroit so as to escape detection even under the supervisors' scrutiny. However, the clerk was reprimanded for allowing the alterations to pass, as erasures appearing on the altered checks were perspicuous. [sic]
* * *

[We] have determined as a matter of law that the recovery against Mercantile on the 43 forged checks is precluded by [UCC Sec. 4-406].

Nu-Way was unable to recover against Mercantile on the forty-three forged checks.	**JUDGMENT AND REMEDY**

Payment on an Altered Check

The face amount of a check is the customer's instruction to the bank to pay an exact amount of dollars and cents to the holder. The bank must examine each check before making final payment. If it fails to detect an alteration, it is liable to its customer for the loss because it did not pay as the drawer-customer ordered. The loss is the difference between the original amount of the check and the amount actually paid. Suppose a check written for $11 is raised to $111. The customer's account will be charged $11 (the amount the customer ordered it to pay). The bank will be responsible for the $100 [UCC Sec. 4-401(2)(a)]

The bank is entitled to recover the amount of loss from the transferor who, by presenting the check for payment, warrants that the check has not been materially altered. No customer or collecting bank or other holder in due course

who acts in good faith gives this warranty to: (1) the maker of a note, (2) the drawer of a draft, (3) the acceptor of an item with respect to an alteration made prior to the acceptance if the holder in due course took the item after the acceptance, or (4) the acceptor of an item with respect to an alteration made after the acceptance. [UCC Sec. 4-207(1)(c) and 3-417(1)(c)]

A customer's negligence can shift the risk of loss. A common example occurs when a person carelessly writes a check, leaving large gaps around the numbers and words so that additional numbers and words can be inserted. (See, for example, Exhibit 28-5.)

Similarly, a person who signs a check and leaves the dollar amount for someone else to fill in is barred from protesting when the bank unknowingly and in good faith pays whatever amount is shown. [UCC Sec. 4-401(2)(b)] Finally, if the bank can trace its loss on successive altered checks to the customer's failure to discover the initial alteration, then the bank can alleviate its liability for reimbursing the customer's account.[3] [UCC Sec. 4-406]

In every situation involving a forged drawer's signature or alteration, a bank must observe reasonable commercial standards of care in paying on a customer's checks. [UCC Sec. 4-406(3)] The customer's contributory negligence can be asserted only if the bank has exercised ordinary care.

ACCEPTING DEPOSITS

A second fundamental service a commercial bank provides for its checking account customers is to accept deposits of cash and checks. Cash deposits made in U.S. currency are received into the customer's account without being subject to further collection procedures. This section will focus on the check after it has been deposited. In the vast majority of cases, deposited checks are from parties who do business at different banks, but sometimes checks are written between customers of the

same bank. Either situation brings into play the bank collection process as it operates within the statutory framework of Article 4 of the Uniform Commercial Code.

Definitions

The first bank to receive a check for payment is the **depository bank**.[4] When a person deposits his or her IRS tax refund check into a personal checking account at the local bank, the bank acts as a *depository* bank. The bank on which a check is drawn (the drawee bank) is also called the **payor bank**. Any bank except the payor bank and the depository bank handling a check during some phase of the collection process is a **collecting bank**. During the collection process, any bank can take on one or more of these roles.

Check Collection Process

A buyer in New York writes a check on her New York bank and sends it to a seller in San Francisco. The seller deposits the check in her San Francisco bank account. The seller's bank is both a *depository bank* and a *collecting bank*. The buyer's bank in New York is the *payor*

---

3. The bank's defense is the same whether successive payments were made on either a forged drawer's signature or an altered check. The bank must prove that prompt notice would have prevented its loss. For example, notification might have alerted it to stop paying further items or enabled the bank to catch the forger.

4. All definitions in this section are found in UCC Sec. 4-105.

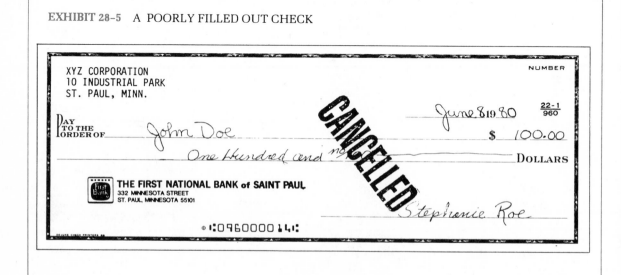

EXHIBIT 28–5   A POORLY FILLED OUT CHECK

bank. As the check travels from San Francisco to New York, any collecting bank (other than the depository bank and the payor bank) handling the item in the collection process is also called an **intermediary bank**.

CHECK COLLECTION BETWEEN CUSTOMERS OF THE SAME BANK An item that is payable by the depository bank that receives it is called an "on-us item." If the bank does not dishonor the check by the opening of the second banking day following its receipt, it is considered paid. [UCC Sec. 4-213(4)(b)] For exam-

ple, Harriman and Goldsmith each have a checking account at First National Bank. On Monday morning, Goldsmith deposits into his own checking account a $300 check from Harriman. That same day, First National issues Goldsmith a "provisional credit" for $300. When the bank opens on Wednesday, Harriman's check is considered honored and Goldsmith's provisional credit becomes a final payment.

CHECK COLLECTION BETWEEN CUSTOMERS OF DIFFERENT BANKS Millions of checks circulate throughout the United States

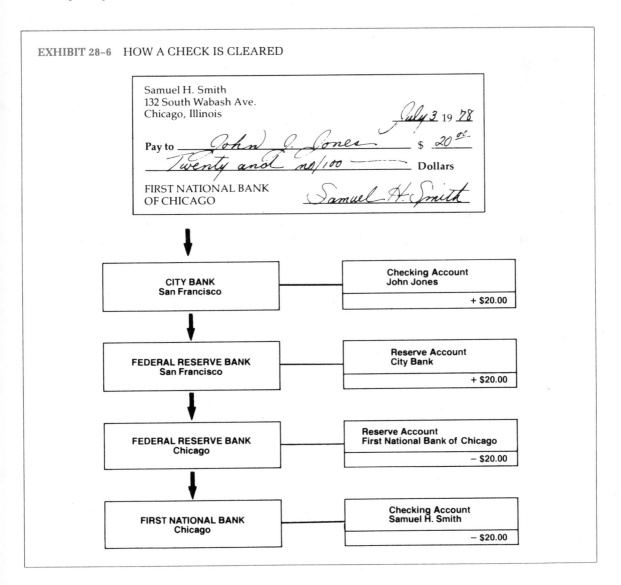

EXHIBIT 28-6   HOW A CHECK IS CLEARED

each day, and every check must be physically transported to its payor bank before final payment is made. Once a depository bank receives a check, it must arrange to present it either directly or through intermediary banks to the appropriate payor bank. Each bank in the collection chain must pass the check on before midnight of the next banking day following its receipt. [UCC Sec. 4-202]

The bank has a duty to use ordinary care in performing its collection functions. [UCC Sec. 4-202(1)] This duty requires banks to conform to general banking usage as established in the Uniform Commercial Code, Federal Reserve regulations, clearing house rules, and so on.[5] [UCC Sec. 4-103] Banks also have a duty to act seasonably. This means that a bank is generally required to take appropriate action before the midnight deadline following the receipt of a check, a notice, or a payment.[6] So, for example, a collecting bank that receives a check on Monday must forward it to the next collection bank prior to midnight on Tuesday.

THE FEDERAL RESERVE SYSTEM CLEARS CHECKS The Federal Reserve System has greatly simplified the clearing of checks—that is, the method by which checks deposited in one bank are transferred to the banks on which they were written. Smith of Chicago writes a check to the Jones family in San Francisco. When the Joneses receive the check in the mail, they deposit it in their bank. Their bank then deposits the check in the Federal Reserve Bank of Chicago. That Federal Reserve Bank then sends the check to Smith's bank, where the amount of the check is deducted from Smith's account. Exhibit 28-6 illustrates this process.

Check Clearing Technology in Banking Operations

The present basis of the payment-collection process is the check, but banks are finding it increasingly more difficult to cope with these trillions of pieces of paper that evidence funds. New systems of automatic payments and direct deposits, known as electronic funds transfer systems (EFTS), promise to rid banks of the problem of moving money by moving mountains of paper. There are basically three parts to an EFTS system: (1) teller machines, (2) point-of-sale systems, and (3) automated clearinghouses.

TELLER MACHINES A recent EFTS development has involved teller machines, which are also called customer bank communication terminals or remote service units. They are located either on the bank's premises or in stores such as supermarkets or drugstores. Automated teller machines receive deposits, dispense funds from checking or savings accounts, make credit card advances, and receive payment. The devices are connected on-line to the bank's computers.

POINT-OF-SALE SYSTEMS Point-of-sale systems allow the consumer to transfer funds to merchants in order to make purchases. On-line terminals are located at check-out counters in the merchant's store. When making a purchase, the customer's card is inserted into the terminal, which reads the data encoded on it. The computer at the customer's bank verifies that the card and identification code are valid and that there is enough money in the customer's account. After the purchase is made, the customer's account is debited for the amount of the purchase.

AUTOMATED CLEARINGHOUSES Automated clearinghouses are similar to ordinary clearinghouses in which checks are cleared between banks. The main difference is that entries are made in the form of electronic signals; no checks are used. These systems are not for further automating the handling of paper checks; they are replacements. Such systems are especially useful to businesspersons for recurrent payments, such as payroll, social security, or pension fund payments.

---

5. The Code is explicit that "the obligations of good faith, diligence, reasonableness and care * * * may not be disclaimed. * * *" [UCC Sec. 1-102(3)]

6. UCC Sec. 4-104(1)(h)

There are some serious consumer concerns over such systems. For example:

1. It is impossible to issue stop payment orders.
2. Fewer records are available.
3. The possibilities for tampering and lack of privacy are increased.
4. "Float"—or the time between the writing of a check and its deduction from an account—is lost.

The Bank's Liability in EFTS

In response to customer concern over EFTS, Congress has passed legislation affecting the liability of both customers and banks. These new rules relate to electronic funds transfer accounts that are operated by telephone, automatically, or by using a customer debit card that is presented to merchants when making purchases. Some of the major rules that apply are:

1. If a customer's debit card is lost or stolen and used without his or her permission, the customer has to pay only $50. However, the customer must notify the bank of the loss or theft within two days of learning about it. Otherwise, the liability increases to $500. The customer is liable for more than $500 if the unauthorized use is not reported within sixty days after it appears on the customer's statement. (Even the $50 limit does not apply if the customer gives his or her card to someone who uses it improperly or if fraud is committed.)

2. Any error on the monthly statement must be picked up by the customer within sixty days, and the bank must be notified. The bank then has ten days to investigate. If the bank takes longer than ten days, it must return the disputed amount of money to the customer's account until the error is found. If there is no error, the customer has to give the money back to the bank.

3. The bank must furnish receipts for transactions made through computer terminals, but it is not obliged to do so for telephone transfers.

4. A monthly statement must be made for every month in which there is an electronic transfer of funds. Otherwise, statements must be made every quarter. The statement must show the amount and date of the transfer, the names of the retailers involved, the location or identification of the terminal, and the fees. Additionally, the statement must give an address and phone number for inquiries and error notices.

5. Any authorized prepayment for utility bills and insurance premiums can be stopped three days before the scheduled transfer.

6. There are certain limitations to the federal government's access to these financial records, but a bank is not prohibited from giving the customer's records to a retailer who might want information on the customer's spending habits.

All of the above information must be given to the customer who opens an EFTS account.[7]

---

7. The $50 limit on consumer liability went into effect February 10, 1978. The other provisions of this new law take effect in May 1980.

QUESTIONS AND CASE PROBLEMS

1. Aetna Insurance Company received an insurance claim from Betty Johnson and drew a draft on itself payable to Johnson or her order. On the face of the draft appeared the words "payable through Traders National Bank and Trust." When she received the draft, Johnson negotiated it to Karen Bentley, her doctor. Bentley indorsed the draft "for deposit only, Karen Bentley," and gave it to her secretary, Mark Upton, to take to the bank. Upton took the check to the Elkstown Bank, which credited Bentley's savings account that evening and passed it on to the Federal Reserve Bank the next morning. Almost immediately, the Federal Reserve Bank transferred the draft to Traders National Bank and Trust. Pursuant to Aetna's instructions, Traders National paid the check from funds that Aetna kept in its account with Traders. What are each of the parties in the above transaction called under Article 4 of the UCC? [Aetna Cas. & Sur.

Co. v. Traders Nat. Bank and Trust Co., 514 S.W.2d. 860 (Mo. Ct. App. 1974)]

2.   Mr. and Mrs. Carney had a joint account in the Cambridge Trust Company. When they opened it, they both signed an agreement that allowed either of them to draw on the account individually and that stated that each would indemnify the bank against overdrafts made by the other. During a three-month period, Mr. Carney issued several large checks, each creating an overdraft in the account. Each time, Mrs. Carney reimbursed the account. Finally, Mrs. Carney instructed the bank that if any further large overdrafts were made, the bank was not to pay. Two weeks later, Mr. Carney again issued a check that overdrew the account by a large amount. The bank honored the check and then sought to recover for the overdraft from Mrs. Carney. Can the bank recover? [Cambridge Trust Company v. Carney, 115 N.H. 94, 333 A.2d. 442 (1975)]

3.   On June 16, 1973, Max Schectman prepared a bank deposit of $5,669 in receipts from his business, Phillips Home Furnishings, Inc. He then proceeded to Continental Bank and properly placed his deposit in the bank's night depository safe. Five days later, not having received confirmation of his deposit, he phoned the bank, which informed him that it had no record of his deposit. In response to Schectman's inquiries, the Continental Bank showed him a copy of the "night deposit agreement" that he had signed in 1972, which placed the risk of loss on the bank's customers. Discuss whether such an agreement ought to be validated by the courts. [Phillips Home Furnishings, Inc. v. Continental Bank, 231 Pa. Super. 174, 331 A.2d. 840 (1974), rev'd 354 A.2d 542 (Pa. 1976)]

4.   Security Trust was the holder of a check drawn on an account at the American National Bank. Security Trust forwarded the check for payment. It arrived on November 28, was processed manually, and was stamped "insufficient funds" on November 29. Notice of dishonor was not sent until December 3. Prior to the end of November, American National had used a manual system of bookkeeping, but a total conversion to computer bookkeeping was made during the last week of November and the first week of December. The last of the manual bookkeeping was done on about November 29. The next day, there was a problem with the computer, and repairs were not completed for another forty-eight hours. When the repair delay became apparent, American National made use of another bank's computer and therefore was able to send notice of dishonor of the above check by December 3. What is the effect, if any, of the

delay in giving the notice of dishonor? [Security Trust Co. v. First Nat. Bank, 79 Misc.2d 523, 358 N.Y.S. 2d. 943 (1974)]

5.   On July 12, 1968, Larsen drew a check for $10,000 on his account at Michigan National Bank and mailed it to the payee. The check was deposited in the account of a customer other than the payee by the Americal National Bank and Trust, which was the depository bank. American National then sent the check to the Federal Reserve Bank for collection. The check was presented for payment by the Federal Reserve Bank to Michigan National Bank and was paid on July 18. The payee notified Larsen in February 1970 that his check had never arrived. Larsen then examined his cancelled checks but did not notify Michigan National Bank of the possibly forged indorsement until August 1970, six months later. In January 1971, Michigan National Bank reimbursed Larsen and sued the Federal Reserve Bank on its warranty of good title and guarantee of prior indorsements. The Federal Reserve Bank filed a suit joining American National on the same grounds. Can the drawee bank, Michigan National, recover? Do you see any possible defenses that the collecting banks—American National and the Federal Reserve Bank—might assert against Michigan National Bank? [Michigan Nat. Bank v. American Nat. Bank and Trust Co., 34 Ill. App. 3d 30, 339 N.E.2d. 375 (1975)]

6.   Rees Plumbing Company, Inc., and Weldon Douglas both maintained checking accounts at the Citizens Bank of Jonesboro. On August 19, 1966, Rees drew a check payable to Douglas in the amount of $1,000 and delivered it to Douglas. On that same day Douglas presented the check to Citizens Bank for deposit in his own checking account. Deposit slips were prepared, and a teller of the bank stamped the back of the check with the August 19 date, and a statement, "pay to any bank—prior indorsement guaranteed, Citizens Bank of Jonesboro, Jonesboro, Arkansas." On August 20, 1966, the bank dishonored the check because of insufficient funds and debited the amount of the check from Douglas's account. Did the bank, by stamping the indorsement upon the check deposited by Douglas and by delivering a deposit slip to Douglas, "accept" the check? Assume that instead of giving Douglas a provisional credit to his account, the Citizens Bank had cashed the check. Could it then have debited Douglas's account upon dishonor of the check? [Douglas v. Citizens Bank of Jonesboro, 244 Ark. 168, 424 S.W.2d. 532 (1968)]

7.   Nancy Sims deposited a check for $756, drawn on an out-of-town bank, into her checking account with

CHECKS AND THE BANKING SYSTEM _____ **473**

the Bank of Louisville Royal. In order to permit the check to clear, it was customary for the bank to delay crediting its customers' accounts for a period of three days. By mistake, however, one of the bank clerks posted a ten-day hold on this particular check. Thus, during a two-week period, Nancy Sims's checks were dishonored and returned with the notation "drawn against uncollected funds." Nancy Sims had some difficulty getting the whole matter straightened out and sued the Bank of Louisville for damages for wrongful dishonor of two small checks. She claimed as damages $1.50 for a telephone call, $130 for two weeks' lost wages, and $500 for "illness, harassment, embarrassment, and inconvenience." At trial she testified that she had been so embarrassed, humiliated, and mortified that the whole matter gave her a case of "nerves" resulting in her doctor advising her to take a two-week leave of absence from work, which she did. Can Nancy Sims recover for these damages? [Bank of Louisville Royal v. Sims, 435 S.W.2d. 57 (Ky. App. 1968)]

8. Samples received a check drawn on the Trust Company of Georgia. He indorsed the check and received payment from another bank, which sent the check for collection to the Trust Company of Georgia and received payment. One week later, the Trust Company of Georgia discovered that the drawer of the check did not have an account with it. Apparently, Trust Company had mistaken the signature on the check for the signature of one of its customers with a similar name. The Trust Company of Georgia then sought to recover the amount paid on the check from Samples. Will it recover? Does Samples have any defense? [Samples v. Trust Co. of Georgia, 118 Ga. App. 307, 163 S.E.2d. 325 (1968)]

9. Moon Over the Mountain, Ltd., was a resort in the mountains of upper New York State. It advertised luxurious rooms overlooking a crystal blue lake and seven moonlit evenings of dining and dancing for the low price of $500. The $500, however, had to be paid in advance and by cashier's check. Harvey, seeing this ad, rushed to his bank, the Marine Midland Bank, and gave the teller $500 cash in exchange for Marine Midland's cashier's check. The next week, Harvey went to the Moon Over the Mountain resort only to find a small rundown cottage overlooking Hudson Bay. Harvey handed over his cashier's check when he arrived and spent the night but then decided that he had been taken. Harvey contacted Marine Midland Bank ten minutes after it opened the following morning and requested it to place a stop payment order on the check. Can Harvey order Marine Midland Bank to stop payment? [Moon Over the Mountain, Ltd. v. Marine Midland Bank, 87 Misc.2d. 918, 386 N.Y.S. 2d. 974 (1976)]

10. Northwest Shopping Center owned and operated a shopping center in Texas. Kaiser was one of its tenants. Pursuant to the rental agreement, Kaiser paid a monthly rent of $500 with a check that it mailed to Northwest. Northwest retained one of these rent checks for over nine months before presenting it to the bank for payment. If Northwest now presents to Kaiser's bank for payment, must the bank pay? If the bank refuses to pay, is Kaiser still liable? [Kaiser v. Northwest Shopping Center, 544 S.W.2d. 785 (Tex. Civ. App. 1976)]

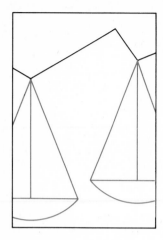

29

Secured Transactions
Introduction

The concept of a secured transaction is as basic to modern business practice as the concept of credit. Few purchasers (manufacturers, wholesalers, retailers, consumers) have the resources to always pay cash for inventory. To a limited extent, consignment arrangements enable a retailer to maintain an adequate stock of goods without always advancing capital (cash), but credit is the most feasible and most common method used.

There are many credit devices available, such as securing credit with a chattel mortgage (tangible personal property) or a lien, giving a promissory note, or making an installment or time payment arrangement. Regardless of the credit method chosen, when the debtor-creditor relationship arises, the creditor often requires the debtor to provide some type of security beyond a mere promise that the debt will be paid. A credit transaction coupled with security is known as a **secured transaction.** The creditor has two major concerns if the debtor defaults on the obligation to repay:

1. Can the debt be satisfied from some *specific property offered as security* (collateral) by the debtor?
2. Will satisfaction of that particular debt from that collateral be given *priority* over the claims of other creditors?

These concerns form the basis for the law of secured transactions.

Virtually any transaction that is the subject of commercial financing when a security interest arises comes within the body of law known as "secured transactions." For example, secured transactions are often involved in the sale of goods when a retailer purchases goods for inventory on credit or when a business purchases equipment on credit or when a consumer buys merchandise on a credit plan. The law of secured transactions tends to favor the rights of creditors, but, to a lesser extent, it offers debtors some protection too.

THE LAW BEFORE THE UCC

Prior to the adoption of the UCC, the law relating to secured transactions was concerned with the person who had title to the property and with the form of the transaction. The law of secured transactions was mystifying, and the terminology was unwieldy because of the large number of methods of obtaining a security interest in goods. The methods most commonly used were chattel mortgages, trust receipts, conditional sales, and pledges.

ARTICLE 9 OF THE UCC

The UCC eliminated the distinctions among the various forms of financing outlined above and simplified the terminology. Article 9 of the UCC provides a framework for the law of secured transactions, and, regardless of the terms used in a security agreement (e.g. use of the term "chattel mortgage" instead of "security interest"), the creditor still has a "security interest" as defined by Article 9. The following sections will be concerned with the vocabulary of secured transactions. This terminology is unique to Article 9 of the Code and to secured transactions themselves.

DEFINITIONS

Under the UCC, not only has the terminology been simplified, but the particular credit devices used are irrelevant to determining the rules for establishing rights and priorities of creditors in the event of a default. The terminology used under the Code is now uniformly adopted in all documents drawn in a secured transaction situation:

1. **Security interest.** Every interest "in *personal property* or *fixtures* (emphasis added) which secures payment or performance of an obligation" is a security interest. [UCC Sec. 1-201(37)]
2. **Secured party.** A lender, seller, or any person in whose favor there is a security interest, including a person to whom accounts[1] or chattel paper[2] have been sold, is a secured party. [UCC Sec. 9-105(1)(m)]
3. **Debtor.** The party who owes payment or performance of the secured obligation, whether or not that party actually owns or has rights in the collateral, is a debtor. The term *debtor* includes sellers of accounts or chattel paper. When the debtor and owner of the collateral are not the same person, the term *debtor* refers to the actual owner of the collateral or describes the obligor on an obligation or *both,* depending upon the context in which the term is used. [UCC Sec. 9-105(1)(d)]
4. **Security agreement.** The agreement that creates or provides for a security interest between the debtor and a secured party is called a security agreement. [UCC Sec. 9-105(1)(l)]
5. **Collateral.** The property subject to a security interest, including accounts and chattel paper that have been sold, is collateral. [UCC Sec. 9-105(1)(c)]

There are four general *classifications of collateral* recognized in Article 9:

1. **Goods.** "All things which are *movable* at the time the security interest attaches or which are *fixtures*" (emphasis added) come under the general category of goods. Goods include standing timber that is to be cut and removed, the unborn young of animals, and growing crops. [UCC Sec. 9-105(1)(h)] They do not include money, documents, instruments, accounts, chattel paper, general intangibles, minerals

---

1. *Account* refers to any right to payment for goods sold or leased or for services rendered; in effect, it is the ordinary commercial accounts receivable.
2. " 'Chattel paper' means a writing or writings which evidence both a monetary obligation and a security interest in or a lease of specific goods, * * *" [UCC Sec. 9-105(1)(b)]

before extraction, or the like. These fall into other categories of collateral discussed in the items that follow.

Article 9 classifies "goods" as (a) consumer goods, (b) equipment, (c) farm products, and (d) inventory.

a. *Consumer goods.* Goods are consumer goods if they are used or bought for use primarily for personal, family, or household purposes—for example, household furniture. [UCC Sec. 9-109(1)]

b. *Equipment.* Goods are equipment if they are used or bought for use primarily in business—for example, a delivery truck. [UCC Sec. 9-109(2)]

c. *Farm products.* Crops or livestock or supplies used or produced in farming operations are farm products. Also the products of crops or livestock in their unmanufactured state (such as ginned cotton, maple syrup, milk, eggs) are farm products. Farm products must be in the possession of a debtor engaged in farming operations. [UCC Sec. 9-109(3)]

d. *Inventory.* Goods held for disposition (that is, for sale or lease) and materials used or consumed in the course of business (raw materials, for example) are all considered inventory. [UCC Sec. 9-109(4)]

2. **Chattel paper.** A writing that evidences both a *monetary obligation and a security interest* in specific goods or leased goods is chattel paper. For example, when a security agreement relates to specific equipment, it is called chattel paper. When any transaction is evidenced both by a security agreement and by instruments evidencing the debt obligation, the group of writings put together constitutes chattel paper. For example, a retail installment contract plus a signed note is chattel paper. [UCC Sec. 9-105(1)(b)]

3. **Accounts and general intangibles.** An *account* is any right to payment for goods sold or leased or for services rendered that is not evidenced by an instrument or chattel paper, whether or not it has been earned by performance. [UCC Sec. 9-106] For example, a retailer sells goods to a consumer on an open account.

The consumer has sixty days in which to pay. The retailer can assign the account receivable in an outright sale or use it to secure a loan. The transaction between the retailer and the lender based on this security is one type of *secured transaction.* The lender is the secured party, the retailer is the debtor, and the consumer is an account debtor.[3] The definition of **general intangibles** is "* * * any personal property (including things in action) other than goods, accounts, chattel paper, documents, instruments, and money." [UCC Sec. 9-106]

4. **Documents of title.** Documents of title include bills of lading, dock warrants, dock receipts, warehouse receipts, and any other documents that in the regular course of business or financing are treated as adequate evidence that the person in possession of them is entitled to receive, hold, and dispose of them and the goods they cover. [UCC Secs. 9-105(1)(f), 1-201(15) and 7-201]

5. **Financing statement.** A financing statement is a document that is filed with a state government office (usually the secretary of state) to give notice to the world that a security interest exists in particular collateral in the possession of the debtor. [UCC Sec. 9-402]

6. **Perfection.** Perfection refers to those procedures that are required under the UCC in order for a secured creditor to validly protect a security interest against other creditors. The sections that follow will discuss creating a security interest and the steps that must be taken to *perfect* that security interest.

CREATING A SECURITY INTEREST

The first concern in dealing with security interests is to determine whether the transaction falls within Article 9. Was there financing in the

---

3. The account debtor is the person who is obligated on the account, chattel paper, or general intangible. [UCC Sec. 9-105(1)(a)] So, for example, when the account of a third person (the user) is assigned to the bank, the dealer becomes a debtor, the bank is the secured party, and the third party is the account debtor.

transaction? Did the parties intend to create a security interest? Are the collateral or the transaction items covered by Article 9? Article 9 applies to any transaction that is intended to create a security interest in personal property or fixtures. It also applies to any sale of accounts or chattel paper. Transactions that are excluded from Article 9 are real estate mortgages, landlords' liens, mechanics' liens, claims arising out of judicial proceedings, wage or salary claims, and so on. [UCC Sec. 9-104] In general, these transactions have been excluded because of their extensive treatment in other areas of the law. For example, landlords' liens against tenants who have defaulted are governed by rules of property law.

Requirements for Attachment

Assuming that the transaction comes within the scope of Article 9, a businessperson must meet three requirements in order to have an enforceable security interest. There must be an agreement in writing. The secured party must give value to the debtor. The debtor must have rights in the collateral. Once these requirements are met, the creditor's rights are said to "attach" to the collateral. This means that the creditor's security interest is *enforceable*. Attachment insures that the security interest between the debtor and the secured party is effective. [UCC Sec. 9-203]

WRITTEN AGREEMENT   Unless the collateral is in the possession of the secured party, there must be a *written security agreement* describing it and signed by the debtor. The security agreement creates or provides for a security interest. For example, it might read "Debtor hereby grants to secured party a security interest in the following goods. * * *" There are three requirements for the agreement to be valid:

1.   The agreement must be signed by the debtor.
2.   The agreement must contain a description of the collateral.

3.   The description must reasonably identify the collateral. [UCC Secs. 9-203(1) and 9-110]

VALUE GIVEN TO DEBTOR   The secured party must give *value*. According to UCC Sec. 1-201(44), value is any consideration that supports a simple contract. In addition, value can be security given for a preexisting (antecedent) obligation or any binding commitment to extend credit. Normally, the value given by a secured party is in the form of a direct loan, or it involves the sale of goods on credit.

DEBTOR HAS RIGHTS IN COLLATERAL   The debtor must have *rights* in the collateral; that is, the debtor must have some ownership interest or right to obtain possession of that collateral. The debtor's rights can represent either a current or a future legal interest in the collateral.

PURCHASE MONEY SECURITY INTEREST

The **purchase-money security interest** occurs when two things happen:

1.   The security interest is retained or taken by the seller of the collateral in order to secure part or all of its price; or
2.   The security interest is taken by a person who, by making advances or incurring an obligation, gives something of value that enables the debtor to acquire rights in the collateral or to use it. [UCC Sec. 9-107]

In either case, a lender or seller has essentially provided a buyer with the "purchase money" to buy goods. For example, Beasley borrows money from Frankel and uses it to purchase furniture. Beasley automatically has a security interest in the furniture. The security interest will last until the loan is repaid.

The importance of the distinction between a purchase money security interest and other types of security interests will be discussed in

Chapter 30. In short, a purchase money security interest ordinarily has priority over a nonpurchase money security interest.

PERFECTING A SECURITY INTEREST

A creditor has two main concerns if the debtor defaults—satisfaction of the debt out of certain predesignated property and priority over other creditors. The concept of *attachment*, which establishes the criteria for creating an enforceable security interest, deals with the former concern; the concept of *perfection* deals with the latter. Even though a security interest has attached, the secured party *must* take steps in order to protect its claim to the collateral over claims that may exist in third parties, such as other secured creditors, general creditors, trustees in bankruptcy, and purchasers of the collateral that is the subject matter of the security agreement. Essentially, the security agreement binds the secured party to the debtor without the need for perfection. But the secured party must go through the process of perfection in order to protect his or her interest in the collateral against third parties, such as other creditors of the debtor. [UCC Sec. 9-301] Perfection represents the legal process by which a secured party protects itself against the claims of third parties who may wish to have their debts satisfied out of the collateral.

Methods of Perfection

There are basically three methods of perfection:

1. *By transfer of collateral.* The debtor can transfer possession of the collateral itself to the secured party. This occurs, for example, when the debtor gives the secured party stocks or bonds, or even a piece of jewelry, provided that it is collateral securing the debt. This type of transfer is called a **pledge.** [UCC Sec. 9-302(1)(a)]

2. *By purchase money security interest in consumer goods.* In certain circumstances, the security interest can be perfected automatically at the time of a credit sale—that is, at the time that the security interest is created under a written security agreement. Note that this *automatic perfection rule* with regard to purchase money security interests applies only when the goods are *consumer goods.* The seller in this situation need do nothing more to protect his or her interest. There are exceptions to this rule, however, that cover security interests in fixtures and in motor vehicles. [UCC Sec. 9-302(1)(d)]

3. *By filing.* The third and perhaps most common method of perfection is by filing a *financing statement.* The UCC requires a financing statement to have: (a) the signature of the debtor, (b) the addresses of both the debtor and the creditor, and (c) a description of the collateral by type or item.[4] [UCC Sec. 9-402(1)] Filing is the means of perfection to use in all cases unless, of course, the collateral is the kind that a secured party can merely take possession of in order to perfect (such as a money pledge), or unless the goods are of the consumer variety. Collateral does not have to be described as precisely in a financing statement as it does in a security agreement.

Both the security agreement and the financing statement must contain a description of the collateral which the secured party has a security interest in. The legal purposes for including a description in each of these documents differ. However, the description contained in each is usually the same. This is true because the secured party often merely files a copy of the security agreement with the secretary of state (in order to perfect). This practice of using a copy of the security agreement as the financing statement is generally valid.

The UCC requires that the security agreement include a description of the collateral because no security interest in goods could

---

4. Certain types of collateral—crops, timber to be cut, minerals, accounts, or goods that are to become fixtures—require more than mere description. [UCC Secs. 9-402(1), 9-103(5), and 9-313]

exist unless the parties agree on which goods are subject to the security interest and then describe these goods in writing. On the other hand, the purpose of including a description of collateral in a financing statement is to put persons who might later wish to lend to the debtor on notice that certain goods in the debtor's possession are already subject to a security interest. The following case demonstrates these different objectives for including a description of collateral in the security agreement and the financing statement.

BACKGROUND AND FACTS *The defendants, Dugan Production Corporation (Dugan) and George McDonald (McDonald), purchased oil drilling equipment at a sheriff's sale. The equipment was previously owned by Lucky Drilling Company, but Jones & Laughlin Supply, the plaintiff, held a security interest in these items. The plaintiff (Jones) claimed that the property purchased at the sheriff's sale was subject to the security interest. The defendants, Dugan and McDonald, argued that the disputed items were not listed in the security agreement. Jones argued that it had given a loan to the Lucky Drilling Company and in return had taken a perfected security interest on all of the company's equipment through a security agreement and a filed financing statement. The language used in the security agreement differed from the language used in the financing statement.*

JONES & LAUGHLIN SUPPLY v. DUGAN PRODUCTION CORP.
Court of Appeals of New Mexico, 1973.
85 N.M. 51, 508 P.2d 1348.

LOPEZ, Judge.
* * *

The case arose out of a sheriff's sale in which certain pieces of equipment belonging to Lucky Drilling Company were sold to the defendants [Dugan and McDonald]. At the sheriff's sale, Dugan * * * purchased the Whealand rotary table in question. The defendant, George McDonald, purchased the Waukesha gasoline engine. Prior to the sheriff's sale, Lucky Drilling Company mortgaged certain equipment to plaintiff and plaintiff took a security agreement and mortgage. * * * A review of the record reveals that this security agreement, together with an unsigned financing statement with exhibits was filed on April 27, 1970 in the office of the County Clerk of San Juan County, New Mexico and on April 24, 1970 in the office of the New Mexico Secretary of State.

* * * [T]he two items in question were not specifically described in the security agreement or in the financing statement. * * * The financing statement was not signed by the debtor or the secured party as required by [UCC Sec.] 9-402.

The financing statement contains the wording: " * * * all hand tools, drill collars, drill pipe, equipment, accessories, parts, exchanges, substitutions, additions, accretions, betterments, supplies and items that Debtor may now have or hereafter acquire and use with or as part of such collateral or in connection therewith. * * *" The financing statement further contains the wording: "Debtor's seven complete rotary drilling rigs identified as No. 1 * * *" through "No. 7 * * *, including all components as described on Exhibit 'A' and Exhibit 'B' attached hereto. * * *" This financing statement is not signed by the debtor or the mortgagee.

The security agreement which is signed by all the parties contains the wording: "Debtor's seven rotary drilling rigs Nos. 1 thru 7 including all components as described on Exhibit 'A' (6 pages) and Exhibit 'B' (7 pages), both of which are attached hereto and made a part hereof by this reference, * * *, together with all hand tools, drill collars, drill pipe and together with all equipment, accessories, parts, exchanges, additions, betterments, and appliances that Debtor may hereafter acquire and use with or as a part of the above described goods. * * *" *The security agreement does not contain the language "equipment, parts, supplies and items which the Debtor may now have" as does the financing statement.* [Emphasis added.]

The undisputed testimony is that the Whealand rotary table in question had been bought with Rig No. 2 originally and prior to the giving of the security agreement had been replaced by a Brewster rotary table. The Whealand rotary table was returned to the parts inventory in the Bloomfield yard and never used again. The inventory mentioned in the Exhibits "A" and "B" lists the Brewster rotary table as a component part of the V-12 gasoline Waukesha engine, the testimony reveals that this engine was purchased with Rig No. 3 and later on was replaced by V-12 Waukesha diesel engine before the security agreement was executed. The inventory mentioned in the Exhibits "A" and "B" shows the V-12 diesel engine as a component of Rig No. 3 and not the engine in question.

Plaintiff would have the two disputed items included within the security agreement on the basis of the "used with" language of the security agreement and on the basis of similar language included in certain of the exhibits referred to in the security agreement. This argument is without merit for two reasons. First, the "used with" phrase in the security agreement applies only to after-acquired property and the disputed items are not in that category. Second, the "used with" phrase in the exhibits applies only to rigs 4 through 7, and the evidence is undisputed that the disputed items were not used with those rigs. The disputed items cannot be included in the security agreement on the basis of "used with" language in the security agreement or the exhibits.

The financing statement was not signed pursuant to the provisions of [UCC Sec.] 9-402. There is a conflict in the language of the security agreement and the financing statement. We follow the reasoning in the Anderson Uniform Commercial Code, Vol. 4 at 124 (2d Ed. 1971) referring to Uniform Commercial Code which states:

"* * * §9-110:17.—Conflicting descriptions in security agreement and financing statement:

"When there is a conflict between the financing statement on file and the security agreement as to the property involved, the latter prevails for the reason that no security interest can exist in the absence of a security agreement, and therefore a financing statement which goes beyond the scope of the agreement has no effect to that extent." * * *

Thus, the "may now have" language of the unsigned financing statement does not provide plaintiff with a security interest in the disputed items.

Plaintiff contends the disputed items were included within the security agreement because they were reasonably described therein. [UCC Sec.] 9-110. Plaintiff contends this reasonable description is provided by "external evidence." This "external evidence" consists of the unsigned financing statement and evidence at trial to the effect that Lucky Drilling Company mortgaged and plaintiff took, pursuant to the mortgage, security on *all* of the equipment of Lucky Drilling Company.

* * * Plaintiff's security agreement neither refers to "now owned equipment" or to "all" equipment of Lucky Drilling Company.

A security agreement is effective according to *its* terms. [UCC Sec.] 9-201. A security interest is not effective against third parties unless the debtor has signed a security agreement which contains a description of the collateral. [UCC Sec.] 9-203(1)(b). The disputed items cannot be included within the security agreement by the "outside evidence" relied on by plaintiff because the disputed items are not described in the security agreement. * * *

* * * We hold that the security agreement did not cover the two disputed items.

JUDGMENT AND REMEDY

The plaintiff, Jones, did not have a security interest in the Whealand rotary table purchased by Dugan or in the Waukesha gasoline engine purchased by McDonald. The defendants had the right to these items bought at the sheriff's sale, and the plaintiff had no claim against them.

In the following case, a security agreement was executed to cover the sale of a guitar and an amplifier that were used by the buyer to perform in nightclubs. Hence they were not consumer goods. (Compare UCC Secs. 9-109(1) and (2).) The seller's perfection of the security interest required the filing of a security agreement and a financing statement. Imperfections in the security agreement did not trouble the court, but the absence of the seller's address on the financing statement was fatal.

BACKGROUND AND FACTS *The plaintiff in this case was a secured party who sold a guitar and amplifier to Elverio Chavez, to be used primarily in the performance of nightclub acts. Hence the goods were not consumer goods. The sale was made on credit, and a "conditional sales agreement" covering the transaction was executed. The sales agreement was entitled "chattel mortgage." Although the terminology was incorrect under the new terminology used in the UCC, the court found that the denomination "chattel mortgage" was immaterial and that a security agreement did exist between the seller and the buyer.*

The buyer took the goods with him on the day of purchase and ultimately defaulted on the credit payments. The seller attempted to recover the guitar and amplifier, but the buyer had pawned them to the defendant pawnshop. The plaintiff obtained possession of pawn tickets representing the guitar and amplifier and presented them to the defendant pawnshop, who refused to deliver the guitar and amplifier because they had been sold to a third party. The plaintiff claimed that he had a valid security interest in the property and that the interest was properly perfected before the goods had been pledged to the pawnshop. Thus, the plaintiff claimed that he had a right to possession of the guitar and amplifier.

STREVELL-PATERSON FINANCE CO. v. MAY
Supreme Court of New Mexico, 1967.
77 N.M. 331, 422 P.2d. 366.

E. T. HENSLEY, Jr., Chief Judge.

* * *

At the outset we note that filing is not necessary to perfect a security interest taken or retained by a seller or other person who finances the actual purchase of consumer goods, [UCC Sec.] 9-302(1)(d). Here the guitar and amplifier, however, were not "consumer goods" as they were primarily used by Chavez to perform in night clubs and are "equipment", [UCC Sec.] 9-109(2). Consequently, perfection by filing of the security agreement was required.

* * *

The fact that an agreement offered for filing is denominated a "chattel mortgage" is immaterial. The traditional forms of security agreements in use before the enactment of [UCC Sec.] 9-203, and [UCC Sec.] 9-102, supra, may continue to be used after their enactment. Uniform Commercial Code, §9-101, comment 2. A "security agreement" is defined as "an agreement which creates or provides for a security interest. * * *" [UCC Sec.] 9-105(1)(h). A "security interest" is defined as "* * * an interest in personal property or fixtures which secures payment or performance of an obligation. * * *" [UCC Sec. 1-201(37). It is clear that the old form "chattel mortgage" meets the definition of a "security agreement." [UCC Sec.] 9-402(1), specifically provides that a copy of the security agreement is sufficient as a financing statement if it is signed by the debtor and secured party, gives an address of the secured party from which information concerning the security interest may be obtained, gives a mailing address of the debtor and contains a statement indicating the types, or describing the items of collateral. Thus, an instrument denominated as a "chattel mortgage" may be filed as a financing statement so long as it contains the necessary information. We must now determine whether the instrument contained the information required by [UCC Sec.] 9-402(1).

[Defendant] contends that since the secured party did not sign the instrument that [UCC Sec.] 9-402(1), * * * was not satisfied. We note that the Uniform Commercial Code is to be construed liberally and applied to promote its underlying purposes and policies [UCC Sec.] 1-102(1). Professor Gilmore, Security Interests in Personal Property, supra, says:

> "Confusingly, and unnecessarily, the formal requisites of the security agreement (§9-203) and the formal requisites of the financing statement (§9-402) are not the same. Under §9-203, all that is required in the 'security agreement' is the debtor's signature and a description of the collateral * * * Under §9-402, however, the 'financing statement' must contain the signatures of both the secured party and the debtor and must also give addresses for both of them. The financing statement must also contain descriptions of collateral * * *."

Professor Gilmore's reasoning, page 347, in resolving the conflict is persuasive:

> "* * * There is no sensible reason for the discrepancies between the formal requisites of §9-203 and §9-402. With respect to signatures §9-203 seems to be right: the debtor's signature on a document binding him to liability is obviously essential; there seems to be no reason for the secured party's signature to be required on either 'agreement' or 'statement' * * *."

We conclude that the lack of the secured party's signature does not make the instrument defective within the meaning of [UCC Sec.] 9- 402 (1). The defendant had due notice even though the secured party did not sign the instrument.

The lack of the secured party's address is more difficult. [UCC Sec.] 9-402(1) says:

> "A financing statement is sufficient if it * * * gives an address of the secured party from which information concerning the security interest may be obtained * * *."

As in the situation of no signature by the secured party, which we have already resolved, there is a conflict between [UCC Sec.] 9-203 and [UCC Sec.] 9-402. The latter requires the address of the secured party while the former does not.

> Professor Gilmore, Security Interest in Personal Property, 347, supra, notes:
> "The addresses are required in the document which is filed for record and, for simplicity's sake, might as well be included in the underlying 'agreement' * * * "

In this case, the plaintiff's name appears only on the cover of the instrument of July 12, 1963. We cannot say that the plaintiff substantially complied with the requirements of [UCC Sec.] 9-403(1). * * * Consequently, the instrument of July 12, 1963, is defective as financing statement and did not give notice to the defendant of the plaintiff's security interest in the guitar and amplifier.

Our conclusion is not inconsistent with the intent of the Uniform Commercial Code to adopt a system of "notice filing." Section 9-402, Uniform Commercial Code, comment 2 says:

> "* * * The notice itself indicates merely that the secured party who has filed may have a security interest in the collateral described. Further inquiry from the parties concerned will be necessary to disclose the complete state of affairs. * * *"

If the secured party's address does not appear it would be an undue burden on the person seeking such information to find him. The filing system will perform its intended function only if secured party substantially complies with the requirements of [UCC Sec.] 9-402(1).

* * * The plaintiff did not perfect its security interest and cannot maintain an action against the pawnshop in conversion.

JUDGMENT AND REMEDY

Judgment was for the defendant, the pawnshop. The plaintiff failed to perfect his security interest and was not able to maintain a claim against the pawnshop, who had sold the guitar and amplifier to a third party.

WHERE TO FILE Depending upon the type of collateral, filing is done either with the secretary of state or with the county clerk or other official, according to state law. In general, financing statements for consumer goods or farm goods should be filed with the county clerk. Most other kinds of collateral require filing with the secretary of state. [UCC Sec. 9-401]

The following case illustrates the importance of the time and the place of filing in order to perfect a security interest priority over other creditors. This case involves a clause in a contract stating that "all property hereinafter acquired" is collateral. This means that even though property will be acquired by the debtor in the future, the creditor's security interest in it will automatically be perfected without a new filing.

CAIN v. COUNTRY CLUB DELICATESSEN OF SAYBROOK, INC.

Superior Court of Connecticut, 1964.
25 Conn. Sup. 327, 203 A.2d. 441.

BACKGROUND AND FACTS _The defendant, Country Club Delicatessen of Saybrook, opened its restaurant business in Old Saybrook on July 26, 1962. At that time it was fully equipped. On August 16, 1962, the defendant borrowed $35,000 from First Hartford, giving a promissory note secured by a security agreement covering "All goods, personal property, equipment, machinery, fixtures, inventory, leasehold rights, including, but not limited to, the property described below, including all after acquired property of like kind." (Attached was a Schedule A listing all specific items included.)_

The previous day, August 15, 1962, First Hartford had filed a financing statement with the secretary of state, Uniform Commercial Code division, showing the defendant as debtor and First Hartford as the secured party. This financing statement had the same description of property as did the security agreement. It also contained a provision covering after-acquired property and a description of the real estate and other data relating to the requirements as to fixtures, in the event any of the property was fixtures. Also, on August 15, 1962, First Hartford executed another financing statement, a duplicate of the one filed in the office of the secretary of state, and filed it with the town clerk of the town of Old Saybrook. The description of the property was exactly the same as in the financing statement filed with the secretary of state. Both these financing statements were executed by the defendant corporation.

On August 30, 1962, approximately fifteen days later, the defendant corporation and Hewitt executed a conditional sales contract covering certain property sold by Hewitt to the defendant. Some of this property was expressly mentioned in the financing statement and security agreement that First Hartford had filed. The defendant was in the process of purchasing property that it simultaneously gave as security for the First Hartford loan. Hewitt also filed a financing statement with the town clerk of the town of Old Saybrook showing Hewitt as the secured party, and General Electric Credit Corporation as an assignee of Hewitt and the defendant corporation as debtor. The description of the types of items of property covered by Hewitt's security agreement was of "complete restaurant and delicatessen including kitchen equipment and display equipment." No financing statement by Hewitt or General Electric was ever filed with the secretary of state, Uniform Commercial Code division. Hewitt filed only with the town clerk of Old Saybrook approximately fifteen days after First Hartford had filed its financing statement with the town clerk. [Background and Facts essentially as stated by the court.]

PASTORE, Judge.

* * *

No financing statement of either Hewitt Engineering, Inc., or General Electric was on file with either the secretary of state, Uniform Commercial Code division, or the town clerk of Old Saybrook against defendant corporation up to the time on

August 15, 1962, when First Hartford first filed its financing statements respectively in both of said offices. Also, no financing statement of said Hewitt or General Electric was on file with the secretary of state up to September 23, 1962, when the instant proceeding was started.

Some of the property specifically mentioned in the conditional sale contract of Hewitt, assigned to General Electric, appears also in the description of the property covered by the financing statement and security agreement of First Hartford.

The position of First Hartford is that it was first to file, that it filed with the secretary of state so as to cover itself with respect to personal property, that it filed with the town clerk of Old Saybrook so as to cover itself as to fixtures (if any be involved), and that General Electric, by failing to file with the secretary of state, does not have priority as to the personal property, and by filing when it did with said town clerk, acquired no rights superior to those of First Hartford in any fixtures, if any there were.

The claim of General Electric is that the evidence shows that as of August 15, 1962, when the financing statement of First Hartford was filed, and as of August 16, 1962, when its security agreement was made, the debtor defendant corporation had only possession of the property subsequently bought from Hewitt, the assignor of General Electric; that there is no evidence showing that as of those dates and within the meaning of [UCC Sec.] 9-204(1) either a "security interest" had been created or the defendant corporation had acquired any "rights" in the property which defendant debtor bought from Hewitt, rights which defendant attempted as for that time to give to First Hartford. [Footnote deleted.] The proper place of filing in order to perfect a security interest in goods which at the time the security interest attaches "are or are to become fixtures" is in the office where a mortgage on the real estate concerned would be filed or recorded; and in all other cases, in the office of the secretary of state. [UCC Sec.] 9-401(1). Thus, the recording or filing with respect to fixtures would be in the town clerk's office of the town where the affected real estate was located, and as to personal property, the filing would be in the office of the secretary of state.

Under [UCC Sec.] 9-204(1), a debtor must have "rights in the collateral" before a security interest may be created. The code does not clearly establish the meaning of this phrase, as for instance whether such rights arise when the debtor enters into a contract to buy goods, or only when he has an interest in the goods when identified with a contract under the Uniform Commercial Code, article 2, "Sales" [Secs.] 2-101 [and] 2-725.

In the instant case, while it is shown that the personal property bought August 30, 1962, from Hewitt, called here the Hewitt goods for convenience, was in the possession of the defendant debtor by July 26, 1962, and at least before August 19, 1962, and that the conditional sale contract between defendant and Hewitt was executed August 30, 1962, there is no showing as to the circumstances or arrangement whereby the defendant had this possession. No legal authority has come, or been brought, to the notice of this court that such mere possession may constitute such "rights in the collateral." An inference that defendant was an unconditional owner of the Hewitt goods on August 15, 1962, would be speculation.

The claim of First Hartford that the Hewitt goods came under the coverage of its financing statement as of August 15, 1962, by virtue of [UCC Sec.] 9-312(5)(a) and (b) is not sustained. Those provisions deal with the "priorities among conflicting security interests in the same collateral." As of August 15 or 16, 1962, there was not yet any security interest existing respecting Hewitt, and the Hewitt goods had not yet become "collateral." Since there was no security interest favoring Hewitt in the Hewitt goods until August 30, 1962, when the conditional sale contract was executed between the defendant debtor and Hewitt, it follows that as of August 15 or 16, 1962, there was no security interest in the Hewitt goods to conflict with any other respecting them.

The conditional sale contract of August 30, 1962, between defendant corporation and Hewitt created a security interest in favor of Hewitt which attached to the property thereby sold. [UCC Sec.] 9-204(1). To perfect this security interest, a financing statement was required to be filed [UCC Sec.] 9-302(1), which, as to goods which at the time the security attached were or were to become fixtures, would be filed in the office where a mortgage on the real estate would be filed, and in all other cases would be filed in the office of the secretary of state. [UCC Sec.] 9-401(1).

Hewitt failed to file in the office of the secretary of state; its financing statement was filed only in the office of the town clerk. * * * [It] is plain that, Hewitt not having filed at all with the secretary of state and First Hartford having done so August 15, 1962, and perfected its security interest on August 16, 1962, First Hartford has priority over General Electric as to this portion of the personal property of the debtor within the coverage of the security agreement of First Hartford. [UCC Sec.] 9-301(1)(a), [UCC Sec.] 9-312(5)(a). Included in this priority of First Hartford are such non-Hewitt goods as might be fixtures as of August 16, 1962, as to which First Hartford filed with the town clerk on August 16, 1962, and Hewitt and General Electric not until August 30, 1962.

JUDGMENT AND REMEDY
The secured claim of First Hartford was filed and perfected and hence given priority over any claim of General Electric Credit Corporation.

CLASSIFICATION OF COLLATERAL DETERMINES WHERE TO FILE The classification of collateral is important in many situations. In determining the place of filing for goods, goods must be classified as consumer goods, equipment, farm products, or inventory. The classes of goods are mutually exclusive; *the same property cannot at the same time and to the same person be both equipment and inventory.* Is a physician's car equipment or a consumer good? Is a farmer's jeep equipment or a consumer good? The principal *use* to which the property is put determines its classification. If the physician uses the car primarily for personal use, then it is a consumer good; if it is used primarily for medical practice, then it is equipment. If a farmer's jeep is necessary for farming operations and is used primarily for that, then the jeep is classified as equipment. But the car and jeep can never be categorized as both equipment and inventory. [UCC Sec. 9-109]

Goods can fall into different classes at different times. For example, a CB radio is *inventory* when it is in the hands of a dealer.

[UCC Sec. 9-109(4)] But when it is purchased by a consumer to use in a private car, it becomes a *consumer good*. [UCC Sec. 9-109(1)] When it is bought and then put in a patrol car, it is *equipment*. [UCC Sec. 9-109(2)] Under the Code, the classification and filing are based on the primary use being made of the collateral. According to Section 9-401, once the security agreement is properly filed, any change in the use of that collateral will not endanger the security interest of the secured party. State laws other than the UCC control where filing is done for each category of collateral.

OTHER WAYS TO PERFECT

Possession

When a creditor has possession of collateral, this is a form of security interest known under common law as a pledge. Possession gives rise to perfection of a security interest. The security interest is perfected from the time possession takes place and continues as long as possession continues. [UCC Sec. 9-305] The creditor can also maintain possession and, hence, perfect the security interest if the collateral is in the hands of a third party, such as a warehouse company. The creditor must inform the warehouse company of the security interest in the collateral, however. [UCC Sec. 9-305]

Consider an example. Ulster borrows $2,000 from Levine, giving Levine possession of three antique guns as collateral for the loan. Several months later, before Ulster has repaid the loan, a creditor obtains a judgment against Ulster. The creditor seeks to have the sheriff take the valuable antique guns away from Levine. Even though no financing statement has been filed, the creditor cannot touch the antique guns because Levine perfected his security interest in them when he took possession of them.

A security interest in *goods* can be perfected either by taking possession of the goods or by filing a financing statement, whereas a security interest in *negotiable instruments* can be perfected only by taking possession of them. The policy is to promote the free transferability of negotiable instruments by not requiring transferees of such instruments to search through financing statements filed with the secretary of state before accepting them.

Automatic Perfection

Under some circumstances, perfection is automatic. One of them is the "purchase-money security interest" in consumer goods. [UCC Sec. 9-302(1)(d)] Otherwise, filing offices would be overwhelmed with financing statements because of the large number of such transactions. A security interest is also automatically perfected when the secured party takes possession of the collateral. A third instance of automatic perfection occurs when a person assigns a small portion of his or her accounts receivable—usually to a collecting agent known as a "factor." Perfection is automatic as long as the assignment does not by itself or in conjunction with other assignments to the same assignee constitute a transfer of a significant part of the outstanding accounts of the debtor. Other situations where perfection is automatic (but which are somewhat less important) are listed in UCC Sec. 9-302(1).

Temporary Automatic Perfection: Proceeds

If a debtor disposes of collateral, a creditor with a perfected security interest in that same collateral has an automatically perfected security interest in the proceeds of the sale of the collateral for ten days after the receipt of those proceeds by the debtor. [UCC Sec. 9-302(1)(b)] A creditor who wants a perfected security interest in those proceeds after ten days must (1) perfect the security interest before ten days, or (2) include coverage of the proceeds in the original financing statement that covered the original collateral. [UCC Sec. 9-306(3)]

QUESTIONS AND CASE PROBLEMS

1. Canna loaned Diodato a sum of money for the purchase of an automobile. Diodato signed a promissory note and procured a title certificate for the automobile. The title certificate included a typed notation designating Canna as a secured party. First County National Bank sued Diodato for money that Diodato owed the bank. The bank obtained a judgment against Diodato and attempted to levy execution upon the automobile. When it did, it became aware of Canna's claim of a prior lien. The bank then attempted to have Canna's lien set aside. Did Diodato and Canna create a valid security interest in the automobile in Canna's favor? [First County Nat. Bank and Trust Co. v. Canna, 124 N.J. Super. 154, 305 A.2d. 442 (1973)]

2. Sabetta entered into an agreement with Industrial Leasing Corp., under which Industrial Leasing was to furnish Sabetta with certain machinery for a five-year period. The agreement provided for regular monthly payments by Sabetta and for all repair work to be provided free of charge by Industrial Leasing. At the end of the five-year term, the machinery was to be returned to Industrial Leasing. Industrial Leasing filed a copy of the agreement with Connecticut's secretary of state. The description of the equipment contained in the agreement was of "all presently owned and hereafter acquired tangible personal property." Does Industrial Leasing have a security interest in the machinery? [Industrial Leasing Corp. v. Sabetta, 16 U.C.C. Rptg. Serv. 195 (D. Conn. 1974)]

3. Henry Reitz obtained a loan from National-Dime Bank in exchange for which he gave a security interest in a tractor and shovel that he owned. National-Dime drew a security agreement describing the collateral as "5/8 yd. shovel, diesel unit, booms, drag bucket." National-Dime then made a copy of the agreement, which both it and Reitz signed, and filed it with the secretary of state. National-Dime then procured Reitz's signature on the original security agreement and put it in its files without an officer of the bank ever signing it. Has National-Dime a security interest in the tractor and shovel attached (that is, is it enforceable)? Is it perfected? [National-Dime Bank v. Cleveland Brothers Equipment Co., 20 D.&C.2d. 511 (Pa. 1959)]

4. Rutkin Electric Supply Company advanced money to Burdette Electronics, Inc., and received in exchange a promissory note secured by an assignment of an account receivable. As evidence of the security interest, the parties signed a financing statement and filed it with the secretary of state. Rutkin notified the account debtor of the arrangement he had made with Burdette. What is the state of Rutkin's security interest in the account receivable? Has it attached? Is it perfected? [Rutkin Electric Supply Co. v. Burdette Electronics, Inc., 98 N.J. Super. 378, 237 A.2d. 500 (1967)]

5. Ford Motor Company shipped thirteen cars by common carrier to Lepley Ford with instructions to the common carrier not to deliver the cars to Lepley except for cash or certified check. The common carrier disregarded this order when it accepted an uncertified check by Lepley Ford that was subsequently dishonored. Ford now is attempting to recover the cars from a receiver in bankruptcy; it offers the following two arguments: Ford points to the written agreement between it and Lepley that provided that "title to each company product shall remain with Ford Motor Company until receipt by the company in cash of the full purchase price." The agreement also stated that Ford Motor Company "shall have the right to retake possession of and resell each company product until title to such product shall have passed to the dealer." Ford Motor Company claims that under the above agreement it still has title to the cars. Ford also argues that the above agreement constitutes an enforceable security agreement and that because cars are consumer goods, its security interest as a result of the agreement is automatically perfected. Discuss the validity of the two arguments made by Ford Motor Company. [Girard Trust Corn Exchange Bank v. Warren Lepley Ford, Inc., 12 D.&C.2d. 351 (Pa. 1957)]

6. Goodyear sold several television sets to Redding on an installment basis, retaining a security interest in them. Redding quickly resold the sets to White-Sellie's, a pawnbroker shop, which sold the sets to customers. Goodyear never recorded its interest, and White-Sellie's had no knowledge of any such interest. Redding later defaulted on the installment contracts and left town. Under the law, if Goodyear can prove that it had a valid security interest in the televisions while they were in White-Sellie's hands, it can sue White-Sellie's for conversion. With what result? [White-Sellie's Jewelry Co. v. Goodyear Tire and Rubber Co., 477 S.W.2d. 658 (Tex. Civ. App. 1972)]

7. City National Bank made a loan to Bowles in the amount of $10,000. In return for the loan, Bowles signed a promissory note and entered into a security agreement whereby City National Bank took a security interest in Bowles's assets, his accounts receivable, and two promissory notes payable to him. City National Bank immediately filed a financing statement that described in detail all of the above items. Does City National Bank have a perfected security interest in all of the above described items? [Bowles v. City Nat. Bank and Trust Co., 537 P.2d 1219 (Okl.Ct.App. 1975)]

8. Block purchased shares of stock in Republic Corporation. These shares had not yet been issued, and there was a delay in their approval by the stock exchange. Before their issuance, Block assigned the stock to Bergman as security for a loan. Is there any way for Bergman to perfect his security interest in the unissued shares of stock? What would your answer be if the shares of stock had already been issued? Do you think the manner of perfection would be different? [Heinicke Instruments Co. v. Republic Corp., 543 F.2d 700 (9th Cir. 1976)]

9. A borrower executed a security agreement granting Waltman Appliance Buyers Credit Corporation a security interest in an automobile that he purchased. The borrower also obtained an insurance policy on the car. He later filed a voluntary petition in bankruptcy. Subsequently, his automobile was "totaled." The automobile insurer issued a check in settlement of the claim. Both the trustee in bankruptcy and Waltman claim the insurance proceeds. Waltman argues that since both the security agreement and the financing statement it filed give Waltman an interest in "any proceeds from the automobile," it is entitled to the insurance check. Is Waltman's argument a valid one? [In re Waltman Appliance Buyers Credit Corp. v. Stikes, 18 U.C.C.Rptg.Serv. 576 (S.D.Ala. 1975)]

10. The Simplex Shoe Company borrowed $240,000 from Milwaukee Bank in return for which Simplex gave the bank its promissory note. Simplex also had two checking accounts with Milwaukee Bank. Prior to this loan, Commercial Discount Corporation made a large loan to Simplex and perfected a security interest in Simplex's "accounts receivable and all proceeds therefrom." When the bank loan came due, Simplex failed to pay, and the bank simply charged the amount of the loan against Simplex's checking accounts. Has Milwaukee Bank contravened Commercial Discount's security interest? [Commercial Discount Corp. v. Milwaukee Western Bank, 61 Wis.2d 671, 214 N.W.2d 33 (1974)]

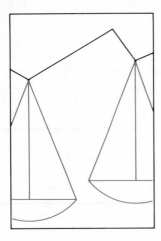

30

Secured Transactions
Liens, Priorities, and Remedies

Under UCC Sec. 9-301, an unperfected security interest is not of much value when challenged by certain parties. Consider an example. James loans money to Ike, who gives James a written security agreement that gives James a security interest in Ike's antique car collection. James files no financing statement. Before Ike repays James, he files voluntary bankruptcy. The person in charge of Ike's bankruptcy (known as the trustee) claims that the antique cars are part of Ike's estate, free and clear of James's security interest. The trustee is right because James's security interest in the antique cars is unperfected.

PARTIES THAT PREVAIL OVER THE UNPERFECTED SECURITY INTEREST

According to UCC Sec. 9-301, three categories of persons prevail over the unperfected security interest: (1) persons who have a perfected security interest in the same collateral; (2) lien creditors—that is, creditors who acquire a lien on property by attachment or levy (judicial process), including trustees in bankruptcy; and (3) buyers in the ordinary course. A *lien* is a claim against property for payment of some debt. Thus, a *lien creditor* is one whose debt or claim is secured by a lien on a particular property, as distinguished from a general creditor who has no such security. Buyers in the ordinary course are persons who purchase goods from a person in the business of selling goods of that kind (excluding pawnbrokers). But the purchasers must not know that their purchase *is in violation* of the ownership rights or security interest of another.

THE RANGE OF PERFECTION AND THE FLOATING LIEN CONCEPT

A security agreement can cover various types of property in addition to collateral already in the debtor's possession—the proceeds of sale, after-acquired property, and future advances.

Proceeds

Proceeds include whatever is received when collateral is sold, exchanged, collected, or disposed of. Perfection of the proceeds of the sale of collateral is available automatically for ten days after the sale. One way to extend the ten-day automatic period is to provide for such coverage in the original security agreement. This is typically done when the collateral is the type that is likely to be sold. [UCC Sec. 9-306(3)(a)]

After-acquired Property

After-acquired property of the debtor is property acquired after the execution of the security agreement. The security agreement itself can provide for coverage of after-acquired property. [UCC Sec. 9-204] This is particularly useful for inventory financing arrangements. An after-acquired property clause normally does not allow for attachment of a security interest in consumer goods "unless the debtor acquires rights in them within 10 days after the secured party gives value." [UCC Sec. 9-204(2)] Presumably, this protects consumers from encumbering all their present and future property.

Consider a typical example. Anderson buys factory equipment from Blonsky on credit, giving as security an interest in all of her factory equipment—both what she is buying and what she already owns. The security interest with Blonsky contains an after-acquired property clause. Six months later, Anderson pays cash to another seller for more equipment. Six months after that, Anderson goes out of business before she has paid off her debt to Blonsky. Blonsky claims to have a security interest in *all* of Anderson's equipment, even the equipment bought from the other seller. Blonsky is correct.

Future Advances

Often a debtor will have a continuing *line of credit* under which the debtor can borrow intermittently. The security agreement can provide that future advances are covered. In such cases, it is not necessary to execute and perfect a new security agreement each time an advance is made to the debtor. [UCC Sec. 9-204(3), amended in 1972]

The Floating Lien Concept

When a security agreement includes proceeds, after-acquired property, and future advances, it is typically called a **floating lien.** Floating liens generally arise in the financing of inventory. A creditor is not interested in specific pieces of inventory because they are constantly changing. Exhibit 30-1 illustrates a typical floating lien,

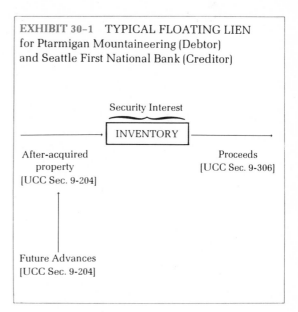

EXHIBIT 30-1   TYPICAL FLOATING LIEN for Ptarmigan Mountaineering (Debtor) and Seattle First National Bank (Creditor)

which involves future advances, after-acquired property, inventory, and proceeds.

Suppose that Ptarmigan Mountaineering, a cross-country ski dealer, has a line of credit with Seattle First National Bank to finance an inventory of cross-country skis. Ptarmigan and Seattle First enter into a security agreement that provides for coverage of proceeds, after-acquired property, and future advances. One day, Ptarmigan sells a new pair of the latest nonwaxable cross-country skis, for which it receives a used pair in trade. That same day, it purchases two new pairs of skis from a local manufacturer with an additional amount of money obtained from Seattle First. Seattle First gets a perfected security interest in the used pair of cross-country skis under the proceeds clause, has a perfected security interest in the two new pairs of skis purchased from the local manufacturer under the after-acquired property clause, and has the new amount of money advanced to Ptarmigan secured by the future-advance clause. All of this is done under the original perfected security agreement. The various items in the inventory have changed, but Seattle First still has a perfected security interest in Ptarmigan's inventory, and hence it has a floating lien on the inventory.

The concept of a floating lien also applies to a shifting stock of goods. Under Section 9-205, the lien can start with raw materials and follow them as they become finished goods and inventories and as they are sold, turning into accounts receivable, chattel paper, or cash.

Collateral Moved to Another Jurisdiction

In general, collateral perfected in one jurisdiction that has been moved to another remains perfected for the time that it would have been perfected in the original jurisdiction or for four months, whichever expires first. [UCC Secs. 9-103(1)(d) and 9-103(3)(e)] The biggest problems here arise with automobiles. The general rule applies to automobiles with one difference. If either the new or the original jurisdiction requires a certificate of title as part of its

perfection process, perfection does not automatically end after four months. Instead, it ceases as soon as the automobile is registered again after the end of the four-month period and a "clean" certificate of title is obtained.

The Effective Time of Perfection

A filing statement is effective for five years from the date of filing. [UCC Sec. 9-403(2)] If a continuation statement is filed within six months prior to the expiration date, the effectiveness of the original statement is continued for another five years, starting with the expiration date of the first five-year period. [UCC Sec. 9-403(3)] The effectiveness of the statement can be continued in the same manner indefinitely.

PRIORITIES

The consequences of perfection and nonperfection are important in determining priorities among parties having conflicting interests in the *same* collateral. As a general rule, perfection protects the interest of a secured party against all lien creditors of the debtor, against all unperfected secured parties, and against all *later* perfected, nonpurchase-money secured parties of that debtor. [UCC Sec. 9-312]

The first question is always whether an *enforceable* security agreement (that is, an agreement in writing, with value given, and with the debtor having interest in collateral) exists. The second question is to determine if and when the secured party's interest has been perfected. Assuming a party has an enforceable security interest, his or her priority will depend upon the time when the security interest attached (became enforceable) or the time when it became perfected or both, according to the following rules:

1. *Conflicting perfected security interest.* When two or more secured parties have perfected security interest in the same collateral, the first to perfect (file or take possession of collateral) wins.
2. *Conflicting unperfected security interest.*

As long as conflicting security interests are unperfected, the first to attach has priority.

EXCEPTIONS TO PERFECTION PRIORITY RULES

Under certain circumstances, the perfection of a security interest will *not* protect a secured party against certain other third parties having claims to the collateral.

Buyers in the Ordinary Course of Business

Since buyers should not be required to find out if there is an outstanding security interest on a merchant's inventory, the Code provides that a person who buys "in the ordinary course of business" will take the goods free from any security interest in the merchant's inventory. [UCC Sec. 9-307] This is true even if the consumer knows at the time of purchase that there is a security interest in the inventory. Of course, if the buyer knows that the sale of goods is *in violation* of the specific terms of the security agreement, the sale is invalidated; but this is a very rare occurrence.

For example, R operates a furniture store, needs money, and seeks a loan from B Bank, using her inventory of furniture as security for the loan. B Bank makes the loan to R, perfecting its security interest in the furniture (collateral) by filing a financing statement with the secretary of state. Assume that a consumer purchases one of the pieces of furniture subject to the security interest. The consumer is a purchaser "in the ordinary course" and will take the property free of the bank's security interest unless he or she knows that the purchase violates a specific prohibition in the dealer's security agreement with the bank.

Secondhand Goods: Goods Sold by a Consumer to a Consumer

C is a consumer who purchases a refrigerator on credit because she cannot pay the full purchase price. The seller takes a "purchase money security interest" in the consumer goods under this type of credit plan. Further, the seller need not file a financing statement because, when a purchase money security interest is taken in consumer goods, perfection occurs automatically. [UCC Sec. 9-302(1)(d)] Later, C sells the refrigerator to her next door neighbor, N, who purchases it for home use without any knowledge of the credit arrangements between C and the original seller. Subsequently, C defaults on the credit payments to the seller. What are the seller's rights? The seller had a perfected purchase money security interest in the refrigerator when it was held by C. However, under Section 9-307(2), the perfection is not good against the next door neighbor.

Section 9-307(2) requires that the purchase take place *before* the secured party files a financing statement. In this case, recall that the seller took a purchase money security interest, which is perfected automatically. No filing was required. Hence, the next door neighbor purchased the refrigerator free and clear before the seller had filed a financing statement. The seller could have avoided this possibility simply by filing a financing statement, even though a purchase money security interest had been perfected.

In the following case, automobiles remained "consumer goods" in the hands of a dishonest consumer-purchaser who later resold them to other consumers. The subsequent buyers were protected by UCC Sec. 9-307(2) because the automobiles were deemed consumer goods both in their hands and in the hands of various sellers.

BACKGROUND AND FACTS *Saia fraudulently purchased two Cadillac automobiles from Cadillac Automobile Company of Boston. Saia told the salesman that he was purchasing the cars on behalf of two friends named Deluca and Russell when in fact Deluca and Russell were fictitious persons. The price of each car was $5,300. Saia paid $1,000 down on each*

BALON v. CADILLAC AUTOMOBILE CO. OF BOSTON
Supreme Court of New Hampshire, 1973. 113 N.H. 108, 303 A.2d. 194.

car and had two friends posing as "Deluca" and "Russell" sign contracts for the balance. Shortly thereafter, Saia resold the cars (still new) to Gibert and Balon for $4,300 (cash) each. Only one payment was made to Cadillac Automobile Company. Neither Gibert nor Balon was aware of Saia's fraudulent scheme.

Cadillac Automobile Company now sues to recover the cars from Gibert and Balon, claiming a purchase money security interest in them.

LAMPRON, Justice.

* * *

[UCC Sec.] 9-307, insofar as material here, reads as follows: (1) "A buyer in the ordinary course of business * * * takes free of a security interest created by his seller even though the security interest is perfected and even though the buyer knows of its existence. (2) In the case of consumer goods * * * a buyer takes free of a security interest even though perfected if he buys without knowledge of the security interest, for value and for his own personal, family or household purposes * * * unless prior to the purchase the secured party has filed a financing statement covering such goods." Under Massachusetts law the secured interest of Cadillac Automobile was perfected when the agreement of the parties was executed. [UCC Sec.] 9-302. However the security agreements covering these two automobiles were never filed. [UCC Sec.] 9-403.

The buyer protected by §9-307(1) is one who purchases in the ordinary course of business from a person in the business of selling goods of the kind involved. §1-201(9). Hence §9-307(1) applies primarily to purchases from the inventory of a dealer in the type of goods sold. The buyer protected under §9-307(2) is one who purchases goods for consumer use, that is, for personal, family or household purposes, from a consumer seller. In order to fall within the protection of this section the goods *must be consumer goods in the hands of both the buyer and the seller.* [Emphasis added.]

The company maintains, however, that the only conclusion which can be reached on the evidence is that Balon and Gibert "could not have conceivably held honest convictions that these transactions were legitimate." In support it cites §1-201(19) which provides: " 'Good faith' means honesty in fact in the conduct or transaction concerned." By its terms this is a subjective standard of good faith, that is, whether the particular purchaser believed he was in good faith, not whether anyone else would have held the same belief. The test is what the particular person did or thought in the given situation and whether or not he was honest in what he did.

There was evidence that Gilbert had known Saia, who made the approaches which culminated in these sales, in a social way for about fifteen years. His wife had known him all her life. Balon knew him also and had purchased a 1963 Cadillac from him without any untoward incidents. Balon and Gibert learned from inquiries made to dealers known to them that the asking price of $4300 was consistent with prices at which such cars could be bought. The explanation advanced that these convertibles sold in September, when the new models were due, could be found by them plausible reasons for the price quoted.

* * * There was no evidence that they had actual knowledge of the status of the title to these cars. The fact that others might have acted differently, made more inquiries, or been more suspicious does not require a conclusion that they lacked good faith when they purchased these cars. The evidence is clear that they paid value and bought for personal, family, or household purposes.

We hold that the trial court properly found and ruled that Balon and Gibert were good faith consumer buyers for value from a consumer seller without knowledge of Cadillac Automobile's security interest which had not been filed. [UCC Sec.] 9-402. Consequently they were entitled to the protection of [UCC Sec.] 9-307(2).

The plaintiffs, Balon and Gibert, are protected from any claims against the automobiles by the defendant, Cadillac Automobile. Balon and Gibert were good faith purchasers of consumer goods and hence are protected by the Uniform Commercial Code.	**JUDGMENT AND REMEDY**

Buyers of Chattel Paper

A third category of purchaser who is not subject to a secured party's interest despite perfection is the purchaser of chattel paper. This protection is provided by Section 9-308(a). Chattel paper is defined as a writing or writings that evidence both a monetary obligation and a security interest in specific goods. Chattel paper is a very important class of collateral used in financing arrangements, especially in automobile financing. When it is sold by a creditor, the creditor can deliver it over to the assignee, who is then responsible for collecting the debt directly from the debtor. This arrangement is known as "notification" or "direct collection." As an alternative, a creditor can sell chattel paper to an assignee with the understanding that the creditor will retain the chattel paper, make collections from the debtor, and then remit the money to the assignee. This kind of transaction is "nonnotification" or "indirect collection." The chattel paper is usually not delivered to the assignee. The widespread use of both methods of dealing with chattel paper is recognized by the Code, and hence the Code permits perfection of a chattel paper security interest either by filing or by taking possession.

Problems arise when perfection is made by filing only. If the chattel paper is thereafter sold to another purchaser who gives *new value* and takes possession of the paper in the ordinary course of business without knowledge that it is subject to a security interest, the new purchaser usually will have priority over the secured creditor.

THE RIGHTS AND DUTIES OF DEBTORS AND CREDITORS UNDER THE UCC

The security agreement itself determines most of the rights and duties of the debtor and the creditor. The UCC, however, imposes some rights and duties that are applicable in the absence of a security agreement to the contrary.

Information Request by Creditors

Under optional Section 9-407(1), a creditor making the filing can ask the filing officer to make a note of the file number, the date, and the hour of the original filing on a copy of the financing statement. The filing officer must send this copy to the person making the request. Under Section 9-407(2), a filing officer must also give information to a person who is contemplating obtaining a security interest for a prospective debtor. The filing officer must give a certificate that provides information on possible perfected financing statements with respect to the named debtor.

Assignment, Amendment, and Release

Whenever desired, a secured party of record can release part or all of the collateral described in a filed financing statement. This ends his or her security interest in the collateral. [UCC Sec. 9-406] A secured party can assign part or all of the security interest to another, called the assignee. That assignee becomes the secured party of record if, for example, he or she either makes a notation of the assignment somewhere on the financing statement or files a written statement of assignment. [UCC Sec. 9-405]

It is also possible to amend a financing statement that has already been filed. The amendment must be signed by both parties. The debtor has to sign the security agreement, the original financing statement, and the amendments. [UCC Sec. 9-402]

Reasonable Care of Collateral

If a secured party is in possession of the collateral, he or she must use reasonable care in preserving it. Otherwise, the secured party is liable to the debtor. [UCC Sec. 9-207] If the collateral increases in value, the secured party can hold this increased value or profit as additional security unless it is in the form of money, which must be remitted to the debtor or applied toward reducing the secured debt. [UCC Sec. 9-207(2)(c)] Additionally, the collateral must be kept identifiable unless it is fungible. [UCC Sec. 9-207(2)(d)] Finally, the debtor must pay for all reasonable charges incurred by the secured party in preserving, operating, and taking care of the collateral in possession. [UCC Sec. 9-207(2)(a)]

The Status of the Debt

During the time that the secured debt is outstanding, the debtor may wish to find out the status of the debt. To do so, he or she need only sign a statement that indicates the aggregate amount of the unpaid debt at a specific date (and perhaps a list of the collateral covered by the security agreement). The secured party must then approve or correct this statement in writing. [UCC Sec. 9-208] The creditor must comply with the request within two weeks of receipt; otherwise, the creditor is liable for any loss caused to the debtor by the failure to do so. One such request is allowed without charge every six months. For each additional request, the secured party can require a fee not exceeding $10 per request.

DEFAULT

Part 5 of Article 9 defines the rights and remedies of a secured party and the debtor. It encompasses alternatives that are available to secured lenders in the event of a default. It prescribes certain duties for a secured party to follow. Should the secured party fail to comply with its duties, the debtor is afforded particular rights and remedies. As mentioned before, while Article 9 tends to stress the rights of creditors, it also protects the rights of several kinds of purchasers of secured goods.

The topic of default is one that is of great concern to secured lenders and to the lawyers who draft security agreements. Default triggers the secured creditor's rights under part 5 of Article 9. However, what constitutes default is not always very clear. In fact, Article 9 does not define the term. Thus, parties are encouraged in practice and by the Code to include in their security agreements certain standards to be applied in the event that default actually comes about. Parties can stipulate the conditions that will constitute a default. [UCC Sec. 9-501(1)] Typically, because of the unusual disparity in the bargaining position between a debtor and creditor, these critical terms are shaped with exceeding breadth by the creditor to arrive at some sense of security. The ultimate terms, however, cannot run afoul of the limitations imposed by the good faith requirement of Section 1-208 and the unconscionability doctrine.

Common Events of Default

Default occurs most commonly when the debtor fails to meet the scheduled payments that the parties have agreed upon or when the debtor becomes bankrupt. If the security agreement covers equipment, the debtor may have warranted that he or she is the owner of the equipment or that no liens or other security interests are pending on that equipment. Breach of any of these representations can result in default.

Basic Remedies

According to Section 9-501, upon default, a secured creditor can reduce a claim to judgment, foreclose, or enforce a security interest by any available judicial process. Where the collateral consists of documents of title, a secured party can proceed against either the documents or the underlying goods.

A secured party's remedies can be divided into two basic categories:

1. A secured party can relinquish a security interest and proceed to judgment on the underlying debt, followed by execution and levy [UCC Sec. 9-501(1)] or
2. A secured party can take possession of the collateral covered by the security agreement. [UCC Sec. 9-503] Upon taking possession, the secured party can retain the collateral covered by the security agreement for satisfaction of the debt ("strict foreclosure") [UCC Sec. 9-505(2)] or can resell the goods and apply the proceeds toward the debt. [UCC Sec. 9-504]

The rights and remedies under Section 9-501(1) are cumulative; therefore, if a creditor is unsuccessful in enforcing rights by one method, another method can be pursued. The Uniform Commercial Code does not require election of remedies between an action on the obligation or repossession of the collateral.[1]

When a security agreement covers both real and personal property, the secured party can proceed against the personal property in accordance with the remedies of Part 5 of Article 9. On the other hand, the secured party can proceed against the entire collateral under procedures set down by local real estate law, in which case the Code does not apply. [UCC Sec. 9-501(4)] This situation occurs when the security interest on a corporate loan can apply to the manufacturing plant (real property) and also to the inventory (personal property). Determining whether a particular collateral is personal or real property can prove difficult, especially when dealing with fixtures—things affixed to real property. Under certain circumstances, the Code allows the removal of fixtures upon default; however, such removal is subject to the provisions of Part 5 of Article 9. [UCC Sec. 9-313]

The Secured Party's Right to Take Possession

The secured party has the right to take possession of the collateral upon default unless the security agreement states otherwise. As long as there is no breach of the peace, the secured party can use self-help to repossess the collateral. Otherwise the secured party must resort to judicial process. [UCC Sec. 9-503]

What constitutes a breach of the peace is of prime importance to both parties, for such an act can open the secured party to liability under Section 9-507 and to tort liability. The Code does not define *breach of the peace*. Therefore, parties must resort to state law to determine it.

Generally, the creditor or the creditor's agent cannot enter a debtor's home, garage, or place of business without permission. Consider a situation where an automobile is collateral. If the repossessing party walks onto the debtor's premises, proceeds up the driveway, enters the vehicle without entering the garage, and drives off, it probably will not amount to a breach of the peace. However, in some states, an action for wrongful trespass could meet the threshold test and start a cause of action for breach of the peace. (Most car repossessions occur when the car is parked on a street or in a parking lot.)

---

1. See White and Summers, *Uniform Commercial Code*, (St. Paul: West Publishing Co., 1972) pp. 964-968.

REASONABLE CARE OF THE COLLATERAL REQUIRED   Once the secured party comes into possession of the collateral after breach by repossession, or where the collateral has been pledged as security and is already in the possession of the secured party, there are certain rights, remedies, and duties provided by Section 9-207. The main requirement of that section calls for the secured party to exercise "reasonable care" in the custody and preservation of any collateral in its possession.

This duty cannot be disclaimed, and any exculpatory clause will be unenforceable. [UCC Sec. 1-201(3)] Reasonable limitations as to what will be required, however, can be agreed upon by the parties. Where the collateral is instruments or chattel paper, reasonable care extends to taking necessary steps to preserve rights against prior parties unless otherwise agreed. Should the secured party fail to meet its obligations as prescribed in Section 9-207, he or she will be liable for any damages occasioned by such failure. The secured party does not, however, lose the security interest for failure to exercise reasonable care.

ASSEMBLING THE COLLATERAL   Section 9-503 provides authorization for security agreements to require that, upon default, the debtor assemble the collateral and make it available to the secured party at a location designated by that party. The location must be reasonably convenient to both parties. This provision is important to a creditor when the collateral is located in several locations or when the debtor is in a better position to assemble it.

The Code also recognizes the inherent practical problems involved in removal and disposition of collateral when it is heavy equipment. Removal and storage costs could quickly reach an impractical level. The Code therefore authorizes the secured party to render such equipment "unusable" and to dispose of the collateral on the debtor's premises. [UCC Sec. 9-503] This authorization does not permit unreasonable action by the secured party, because every aspect of the repossession and disposition must comply with the standards of commercial reasonableness of Section 9-504.

Disposal of Collateral

Once default has occurred, the secured party is faced with several alternatives to secure payment of the debt. The party can, for example, retain the collateral in satisfaction of the debtor's obligation; this is called *strict foreclosure*. [UCC Sec. 9-505(2)] The party can also sell, lease, or otherwise dispose of the collateral in any commercially reasonable manner. [UCC Sec. 9-504(1)] Any sale is always subject to procedures established by state law. In addition, the UCC requires that notice be given before the collateral is sold.

TURK v. ST. PETERSBURG BANK & TRUST CO.
District Court of Appeal of Florida, 1973.
281 So.2d. 534.

BACKGROUND AND FACTS   *The defendant, Irving Turk, president of Bob King, Inc., obtained floor plan financing for automobiles that Bob King, Inc., was selling. Turk, Bob King, and Bob King, Inc., together executed a note for $35,000 along with a security agreement; and the bank, St. Petersburg Bank & Trust Company, took certain automobiles belonging to Bob King, Inc., as security.*

The defendant, Turk, ceased to be active in the corporation during the existence of this agreement. However, prior to his separation from Bob King, Inc., Turk went to the bank with Bob King and sought to have the total obligation reduced to $20,000. They advised Applegate, the assistant vice-president and loan officer at the bank, that they wished to reduce their liability to $20,000. Applegate agreed to this and had a new note in the amount of $20,000 prepared.

After the execution of the $20,000 note, the bank continued to advance monies on the note until, at one point, the indebtedness reached $36,336. The bank became concerned for its collateral and, after investigation, sought to take action. It advised Bob King, Inc., that it was going to take possession of the automobiles, and it did so. It then sold the automobiles for the sum of $17,881.52. The bank alleged that, at the time of repossession, the total outstanding indebtedness was $32,861. The bank sued Turk for the difference between the $17,881.52 recovered and the total outstanding indebtedness of $32,861. This portion is known as the "deficiency," and in this case, it amounted to $15,540.92 plus interest.

LILES, Acting Chief Judge.

* * *

[T]his transaction was governed by the Uniform Commercial Code, and particularly Section 9.504(3), which reads as follows:

> "(3) Disposition of the collateral may be by public or private proceedings and may be made by way of one or more contracts. Sale or other disposition may be as a unit or in parcels and at any time and place and on any terms but every aspect of the disposition including the method, manner, time, place and terms must be commercially reasonable. Unless collateral is perishable or threatens to decline speedily in value or is of a type customarily sold on a recognized market, *reasonable notification* of the time and place of any public sale or reasonable notification of the time after which any private sale or other intended disposition is to be made *shall be sent by the secured party to the debtor,* and except in the case of consumer goods to any other person who has a security interest in the collateral and who has duly filed a financing statement index ed in the name of the debtor in this state or who is known by the secured party to have a security interest in the collateral. [Emphasis added.] The secured party may buy at any public sale and if the collateral is of a type customarily sold in a recognized market or is of a type which is the subject of widely distributed standard price quotations he may buy at private sale."

[T]he language is clear that before a secured party (in this instance the bank) can obtain a deficiency against a debtor (in this instance Turk) the debtor must be given notice of what is about to occur. This is as it should be because the debtor in this instance, Turk, could have done many things. He could have purchased the automobiles himself; he could have paid the extent of the liability, i.e., $20,000; he could have secured purchasers for the automobiles. He was not afforded the opportunity to do anything. If the bank in this instance wanted to dispose of the collateral without judicial process or notice to the debtor as the statute provides, it may do so; but it is not then entitled to a deficiency against any debtor not so notified. The record reflects that notice was given to Bob King, Inc., but the statute prevents the bank from securing a deficiency against Irving Turk.

In the absence of a required notice by the secured creditor pursuant to [UCC

Sec.] 9.504(3), F.S.A., the creditor forfeits his right to any deficiency against any debtor not so notified.

The bank is at liberty to seek repayment from Bob King, Inc. The corporation was presumably the benefactor of the extension of financing over and above the $20,000; and the bank may choose to go against it, but they may *not*, because of the testimony adduced, as well as failure to comply with the U.C.C., now go against Turk for what is obviously the collectible judgment. [Emphasis added.]

JUDGMENT AND REMEDY *The bank is precluded from seeking a deficiency judgment against Turk, but it can obtain a deficiency judgment against Bob King, Inc., because notice had been given to that party.*

RETENTION OF COLLATERAL BY SECURED PARTY AFTER DEFAULT The Code recognizes that parties are often better off if they do not sell the collateral. Therefore, a secured party can retain collateral, but this general right is subject to several conditions. The secured party must send written notice of the proposal to the debtor if the debtor has not signed a statement renouncing or modifying his or her rights after default. With consumer goods, no other notice has to be given. In all other cases, notice must be sent to any other secured party from whom the secured party has received written notice of a claim of interest in the collateral in question. If within twenty-one days after the notice is sent the secured party receives an objection in writing from a person entitled to receive notification, then the secured party must dispose of the collateral under UCC Sec. 9-504. If no such written objection is forthcoming, the secured party can retain the collateral in satisfaction of the debtor's obligation. [UCC Sec. 9-505(2)]

CONSUMER GOODS When the collateral is consumer goods and the debtor has paid more than 60 percent of the cash price, then the secured party must dispose of the collateral under Section 9-504 within ninety days. Failure to comply opens the secured party to an action for conversion or other liability under UCC Sec. 9-507(1) unless the consumer-debtor signed a written statement after default renouncing or modifying the right to demand the sale of the goods. [UCC Sec. 9-505(1)]

DISPOSITION PROCEDURES A secured party who does not choose to retain the collateral, must resort to the disposition procedures prescribed under Section 9-504. The Code allows a great deal of flexibility with regard to disposition. The only real limitation is that it must be accomplished in a commercially reasonable manner. Section 9-507(2) supplies some examples of what does or does not meet the standard of commercial reasonableness:

(2) The fact that a better price could have been obtained by a sale at a different time or in a different method from that selected by the secured party is not of itself sufficient to establish that the sale was not made in a commercially reasonable manner. If the secured party either sells the collateral in the usual manner in any recognized market therefore or if he sells at the price currently in such a market at the time of sale or if he has otherwise sold in conformity with reasonable commercial practices among dealers in the type of property sold, he has sold in a commercially reasonable manner.

Any time before the secured party disposes of the collateral or enters into a contract for its disposition, or before the debtor's obligation has been discharged through the secured party's retention of the collateral, the debtor or any other secured party can exercise the right of *redemption* of the collateral. The debtor can do this by tendering performance of *all* obligations secured by the collateral, by paying the expenses reasonably incurred by the secured party, and by retaking the collateral and maintaining its care and custody. [UCC Sec. 9-506]

A secured party is not compelled to resort to public sale to dispose of the collateral. The party is given the latitude under the Code to seek out the best terms possible in a private sale. [UCC Sec. 9-504] Generally, no specific time requirements must be met; however, the time must ultimately meet the standard of commercial reasonableness.

Except when the collateral is perishable or threatens to decline speedily in value or is of a type customarily sold on a recognized market, notice must be sent by the secured party to the debtor if the debtor has not signed a statement renouncing or modifying the right to notification of sale after default. For consumer goods, no other notification need be sent. In all other cases, notification must be sent to any other secured party from whom the secured party has received written notice of a claim of an interest in the collateral. [UCC Sec. 9-504(3)]

PROCEEDS FROM DISPOSITION Proceeds from the disposition must be applied in a certain order:

1.   Reasonable expenses stemming from the retaking, holding, or preparing for sale are covered first. Where authorized by law and if provided for in the agreement, this can include reasonable attorneys' fees and legal expenses.

2.   The satisfaction of the debt is covered second.

3.   Subordinate security interests whose written demand has been received prior to the completion of distribution of the proceeds are covered third. [UCC Sec. 9-504(1)]

4.   Treatment of any surplus depends upon the nature of the underlying transaction and the existence of specified agreements between the parties. [UCC Sec. 9-504(2)]

TERMINATION

When a debt is paid, the secured party files a termination statement with the filing officer to whom the original financing statement was given. If the financing statement covers consumer goods, the termination statement must be filed within one month after the debt is paid. If, on the other hand, the debtor requests the termination statement in writing, it must be filed within ten days after the debt is paid. [UCC Sec. 9-404(1)] In all cases, the termination statement must be filed or furnished to the debtor within ten days after a written request is made by the debtor. Any failure by the secured party to comply with this rule makes the party liable for $100 and for any loss caused by the failure to provide the termination statement.

QUESTIONS AND
CASE PROBLEMS

1.   The city of Vermillion brought a declaratory judgment action to have a court determine to whom the city should pay the proceeds of a construction contract between the city and a bankrupt contractor. Shortly after the contract was formed, the contractor assigned its interest in the proceeds from the contract to the First National Bank as security for a loan. The contract was the contractor's sole account receivable. Subsequently, the IRS filed notice of a tax lien upon all property of the contractor. On January 15, 1970, the contractor filed for bankruptcy. The IRS renewed its tax lien, and the trustee in bankruptcy claimed all the contractor's assets. Does the First National Bank's claim to the proceeds from the construction contract have priority over either the IRS tax lien or the trustee in bankruptcy? [City of Vermillion v. Stan Houston Equipment Co., 341 F.Supp. 707 (D.C.S.D. 1972)]

2.   On October 9, 1964, Schwab Brothers, Inc., purchased two trailers from L. B. Smith, Inc., under a conditional sales contract. (Under a conditional sales contract, the seller retains title to the goods.) L. B. Smith failed to file a financing statement with respect to the two vehicles. Subsequently, Schwab Brothers defaulted on the contract. Shortly thereafter, the United States filed a tax lien against the two vehicles,

and L. B. Smith attempted unsuccessfully to repossess them. Whose interest has priority in the vehicles? Would it make a difference if L. B. Smith had been successful in repossessing the trucks before the government filed its tax lien? [L. B. Smith, Inc. v. Foley, 341 F.Supp. 810 (W.D.N.Y. 1972)]

3. Chrysler Credit Corporation held a perfected security interest in the inventory of Local Chrysler Dealer (floor plan). Local owed Malone $10,000 and gave Malone a check for $5,000 as part payment. The same day, Malone returned to Local and indorsed the check back to Local in payment for an automobile in which Chrysler Credit held a security interest. Should Malone take free of Chrysler Credit's security interest? [Chrysler Credit Corp. v. Malone, 502 S.W.2d 910 (Tex.Civ.App. 1973)]

4. Schenectady Corp. financed the sale of mobile homes by NuTrend, a dealer, taking a security interest in NuTrend's inventory. Since Schenectady filed its security interest, it had a perfected security interest in each of the mobile homes in NuTrend's inventory. During the first week of March, NuTrend sold two mobile homes. The first it sold to Clothiers, who paid cash for it. When NuTrend later defaulted on its inventory loan with Schenectady, Schenectady sought to repossess the mobile home from Clothiers. NuTrend sold the second mobile home to Welch. The original buyer of this mobile home held the certificate of title, but the buyer had surrendered possession of the home to NuTrend due to default under a retail installment contract. Under the contract, the original buyer gave a promissory note to Schenectady and entered into a security agreement with Schenectady that Schenectady perfected. Upon the original buyer's default, Schenectady also sought to repossess this mobile home from Welch. Can Schenectady recover from Clothiers? Can it recover from Welch? [Black v. Schenectady Discount Corp., 31 Conn. Sup. 521, 324 A.2d 921 (1974)]

5. Rafferty purchased a truck under a retail installment contract from a local General Motors dealer. The contract was then assigned to General Motors Acceptance Corporation, which perfected a security interest in the truck. Rafferty took the truck to Colwell Diesel Service for repairs and was unable to pay the repair bill. Shortly thereafter, Rafferty also defaulted on his retail installment contract. General Motors Acceptance Corporation attempted to repossess the truck, but Colwell refused to give up possession until somebody paid the repair bill. Is Colwell legally justified in retaining possession? [General Motors

Acceptance Corp. v. Colwell Diesel Service and Garage, Inc., 302 A.2d. 595 (Me. 1973)]

6. Mr. and Mrs. Schramm operated a mobile home park. In 1968, Mr. Schramm agreed to allow John Applewhite to locate two mobile homes on his property for a fixed rental. In late 1969, the mobile homes remained unoccupied on Schramm's property. Schramm filed a "Notice of Intent to Hold Hotel-keepers' Lien" on these mobile homes for the amount of unpaid rentals. This notice was also sent to Bloomington National Bank, which was the holder of the perfected security interest in the two homes. (Applewhite had also failed to make payment to the bank.) In late 1970, one of the two homes was taken from the park by an agent of the bank without notice to Schramm. A few days later, several more of the bank's agents returned to the park to take away the remaining mobile home. When they did so, two of them assaulted Mrs. Schramm, who objected to the removal. If under local law, a hotelkeepers' lien has priority over a perfected security interest, what will the Schramms be allowed to recover from the bank? If hotelkeepers' liens are subordinate to perfected security interests, what can the Schramms recover? [Nicholson's Mobile Home Sales, Inc. v. Schramm, 330 N.E.2d. 785 (Ind. Ct. App. 1975)]

7. In 1972, Borg-Warner executed a security agreement with David Brown Tractor Company to secure loans to David Brown for the purchase of inventory to be used in its business. Borg-Warner filed a financing statement with the secretary of state, describing the collateral as "all inventory." In January 1974, Wolfe City National Bank advanced money to David Brown Tractor Company for the purchase by David Brown of additional inventory. Wolfe City executed a security agreement covering the additional inventory, but it did not file a financing statement and did not give Borg-Warner notice of its security interest. When David Brown defaulted on its loan from Wolfe City, Wolfe City took possession of the inventory and sold it. Can Borg-Warner recover the proceeds of the sale? [Borg-Warner Acceptance Corp. v. Wolfe City Nat. Bank, 544 S.W.2d. 947 (Tex. Civ. App. 1976)]

8. In March 1969 Kenworth sold to Sewell four trucks for which four separate security agreements were executed and perfected. In April 1971, First National Bank loaned Sewell money and took a security interest in all equipment owned or thereafter acquired by Sewell. The security agreement was perfected by filing. About two months later, Sewell

finished paying for the four trucks and thus was no longer in debt to Kenworth. A year later, Kenworth loaned more money to Sewell and took a security interest in the four trucks and other equipment belonging to Sewell. Kenworth also perfected this security interest. On Sewell's default to both Kenworth and First National Bank, who will recover the trucks? [Texas Kenworth Co. v. First Nat. Bank, 564 P.2d. 222 (Okl. 1977)]

9. In 1969, Wheeless purchased a car. In order to obtain the money, he executed a promissory note to the bank and gave the bank a security interest covering the automobile that the bank thereafter perfected by filing. About a year later, Wheeless defaulted on his loan, and the bank took possession of the car. At the time it repossessed the car, Wheeless asked the bank what it intended to do with it. An officer of the bank informed Wheeless that the bank intended to sell it. About two weeks later, the car was sold without Wheeless's knowledge. When Wheeless learned the price for which the bank had sold the car, he protested the sale. Does Wheeless have a legal right to protest? [Wheeless v. Eudora Bank, 256 Ark. 644, 509 S.W.2d. 532 (1974)]

10. In 1969, Jones and Percell executed a promissory note and a security agreement covering a converted military aircraft built in the 1950s. Upon default, the Bank of Nevada repossessed the aircraft. After providing the required notice, the bank placed advertisements in several trade journals as well as in major newspapers in several large cities. In addition, the bank sent 2,000 brochures to 240 sales organizations. A sales representative was hired to market the aircraft. The plane was later sold for $71,000 to an aircraft broker, who in turn resold it for $123,000 after spending $33,000 on modifications. Can Jones and Percell object to the bank's manner of resale? [Jones v. Bank of Nevada, 91 Nev. 368, 535 P.2d. 1279 (1975)]

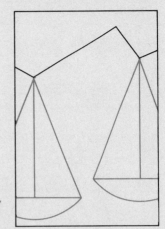

UNIT V

Creditor's Rights
and Bankruptcy

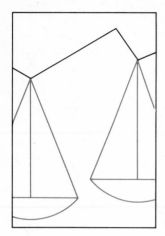

31

Rights of
Debtors and Creditors

The law of debtor-creditor relations has undergone various changes over the years. Throughout history, debtors and their families have been subjected to terrible punishment for their inability to pay debts, including involuntary servitude, imprisonment, and dismemberment. The modern legal system has moved away from a punishment philosophy in dealing with debtors. In fact, many people say that it has moved too far in the other direction, to the detriment of creditors. Nonetheless, this area of consumerism and consumer protection is designed to aid and protect the debtor and the debtor's family.

This chapter deals with various rights and remedies available through statutory laws and under common law to assist the debtor and creditor in resolving their disputes. The next chapter discusses bankruptcy as one possible way to resolve debtor-creditor problems.

LAWS ASSISTING CREDITORS

Mechanic's Lien on Real Property

When a consumer contracts for labor, services, or material to be furnished for the purpose of making improvements on real property but does not immediately pay for the improvements, a special type of debt called a **mechanic's lien** is created. The real estate itself becomes the subject of security for the lien (debt). For example, a roofer repairs a leaky roof at the request of a homeowner. The homeowner owes the roofer the agreed price for the materials, labor, and services performed. If the homeowner cannot pay or pays only a portion of the charges, a mechanic's lien against the property is created. The roofer is the lienholder, and the real property is encumbered with a mechanic's lien for the amount owed. If the homeowner does not pay the lien, the property can be sold to satisfy the debt.

The procedures by which a mechanic's lien is created are controlled by state statutory law. Generally, the lienholder must file a written notice of lien against the particular property involved. The notice of lien must be filed within a specific time period, measured from the last date that materials or labor were provided (usually within 60 to 120 days). Failure to pay the debt entitles the lienholder to foreclose on the real estate where the improvements were made and sell it in order to satisfy the amount of the debt. Of course, the lienholder is required by statute to give notice to the owner of the property prior to foreclosure and sale. If there are any surplus proceeds after the debt and the costs of the legal proceedings are paid, the former owner receives them.

Artisan's Liens on Personal Property

An **artisan's lien** is a security device, created by statute, similar to a mechanic's lien but used to charge personal property with the payment of a debt for labor done, for value added, or for caring for the personal property (bailee or warehousing costs). For example, A leaves her watch at the jeweler's to be repaired and to have her initials engraved on the back. The jeweler can keep the watch if A fails to pay for the repairs and services that the jeweler provides. In that case, the jeweler can obtain a lien on A's watch for the amount of the bill and sell the watch in satisfaction of the lien. Money in excess of the debt and costs of the sale will be returned to A.

An artisan's lien is a *possessory lien*. The lienholder ordinarily must have retained possession of the property and have agreed to provide the services on a cash, not a credit, basis. Usually the lienholder retains possession of the property. When this occurs, the lien remains as long as the lienholder maintains possession and terminates once possession is voluntarily surrendered—unless the surrender is only temporary. If it is a temporary surrender, there must be an agreement that the property will be returned to the lienholder. Even with such an agreement, if a third party obtains rights in that property while it is out of the possession of the lienholder, the lien is lost. The only way a lienholder can protect a lien and surrender possession at the same time is to record notice of the lien in accordance with state lien and recording statutes.

Modern statutes permit the holder of an artisan's lien to foreclose and sell the property subject to the lien in order to satisfy payment of the debt. As with the mechanic's lien, the lienholder is required to give notice to the owner of the property prior to foreclosure and selling. If there are any surplus proceeds after the debt is satisfied and the costs of the sale are paid, the former owner of the property receives them.

Writ of Execution

A debt must be past due in order for a creditor to commence legal action against a debtor. If the creditor is successful, the court awards the creditor a judgment against the debtor (usually for the amount of the debt plus any interest and legal costs incurred in obtaining the judgment). If the debtor still does not or cannot pay the judgment, the creditor is entitled to go back to the court and obtain a **writ of execution.** This writ is an order, usually issued by the clerk of the court, directing the sheriff to seize (levy) and sell any of the debtor's nonexempt real or personal property that is within the court's geographic jurisdiction (usually the county in which the courthouse is located). The proceeds of the sale are used to pay off the judgment and costs of the sale. Any excess is paid to the debtor. The debtor can pay the judgment and redeem the nonexempt property any time before the sale takes place.

Attachment and Garnishment

Attachment is a court-ordered seizure and taking into custody of property that is in controversy over a debt. Attachment rights are created by state statutes. Attachment is normally a prejudgment remedy. It occurs either at the time of or immediately after the commencement of a lawsuit but before the entry of a final judgment. Under some statutes, the restrictions and requirements about when a creditor can attach before judgment are very specific. However, the statutory grounds for attachment before judgment are very limited. The Due Process Clause of the 14th Amendment to the Constitution limits courts' power to authorize seizure of debtors' property without notice to the debtor or a hearing of the facts. In recent years, a number of state attachment laws have been held to be unconstitutional.

In order to use attachment as a remedy, the creditor must follow certain procedures. He or she must file with the court an affidavit stating that the debtor is in default and stating the statutory grounds under which attachment is sought. A bond must be posted by the creditor to cover court costs, value of the loss of use of the good suffered by the debtor, and the value of the property attached. When the court is satisfied that all the requirements have been met, it issues a **writ of attachment.** This writ is similar to a writ of execution in that it directs the sheriff or other officer to seize nonexempt property. If the creditor prevails at trial, the seized property can be sold to satisfy the judgment.

The following case illustrates that because a writ of attachment operates against a debtor's property simply on the strength of the creditor's sworn statement that a debt is owed, strict compliance with every specific procedure established by the state's attachment statute is required before the property is subject to an enforceable writ of attachment.

JACK DEVELOPMENT,
INC. v. HOWARD
EALES, INC.

388 A.2d 466 (D.C. App. 1978).

BACKGROUND AND FACTS *Corcoran was the owner of a large building in Washington, D.C. In April 1976, Eales, a creditor of Corcoran, obtained a prejudgment "writ of attachment" from a Washington, D.C. court against the building. In June 1976, notice of the writ was posted on the building. In October 1976, Corcoran conveyed the building to Jack Development, Inc. Up to this time, Eales had been unable to serve notice on Corcoran as required by Washington D.C. statute. In the alternative, the statute allowed the notice requirement to be fulfilled by three week publication of the writ in a local newspaper. Eales first published notice of the writ in February 1977. Jack Development argues that it is the owner since title was transferred to it before the writ "attached," that is, before the statutory notice requirements had been fulfilled. Eales argues that the writ "attached" when notice was posted on the building, and therefore Corcoran was unable to transfer clear title.*

PER CURIAM: [By the Court—an opinion of the whole court].
* * * The sequence of relevant events therefore was:
April 15, 1976—Writ of attachment before judgment issued by trial court against defendant's realty [real estate].
June 21, 1976—Marshal posts realty with writ.
October 19, 1976—Defendant conveys realty to Jack Development, Inc., by quitclaim deed [a deed passing title, but not professing that the title is valid or not containing any warranty for title].

December 10, 1976—Quitclaim deed to realty recorded by Jack Development, Inc.

February 2, 1977—Marshal signs and files the indorsement on the writ of attachment before judgment which he had posted on the realty the previous June.

February 28, 1977—First date of service of process on defendant by publication.

* * *

Appellant Jack Development argues that it acquired title to the property at 1718 Corcoran Street, N.W., free of the writ of attachment before judgment which had been issued against the transferor, since the defendant transferred his interest *prior to service upon the transferor of the writ of attachment and the indorsement and notice,* as required by D.C.Code 1973, §§16-502, -508.

Initially, we note that because a writ of attachment before judgment is a harsh and drastic remedy, strict compliance with the procedures established by the statute is required. In this case, the delivery of the writ of attachment before judgment to the marshal did create an inchoate [contingent] lien on the defendant's property. The mere posting of the property did *not* comply, however, with the notice procedures mandated by D.C.Code 1973, §§16-502, -508.

[The code in Washington, D.C., provides that if a debtor cannot be found within the district, the creditor must obtain a court order granting permission to inform the debtor by publication (for three consecutive weeks) that said debtor must appear and show cause why the property conditionally attached should not be subject to final attachment and sale.]

* * *

The statutory requirements were not completed in this case until three weeks after the first date of publication on February 28, 1977. At that time, the attachment normally would relate back to the date of the delivery of the writ to the marshal, *i.e.,* April 15, 1976. Here, however, the defendant during the intervening period had transferred the property by quitclaim deed to Jack Development and appellant had recorded its deed on December 10, 1976—all such dates being prior to appellee's full compliance with the attachment statute.

* * *

Here, a valid transfer occurred before the defendant himself had been given notice of a sufficiently levied writ of attachment in compliance with the statute. D.C.Code 1973, §16-508. Jack Development therefore took the property free of the writ of attachment which had been sought against the transferor.

The appellate court quashed the writ of attachment. Jack Development kept title to the property free and clear. The judgment of the trial court was reversed.

JUDGMENT AND REMEDY

Attachment does not always prevent a subsequent transfer of the attached property. If the attachment has been perfected under statutory requirements, the transferee takes the property subject to the terms and conditions of the attachment and its underlying lien.

COMMENTS

ENFORCEABLE RIGHT REQUIRED Attachment is one way that personal property in the debtor's possession that is capable of manual delivery can be taken into custody and held until the creditor's claim is adjudicated in a court of law. But not only must the creditor follow the statutory requirements, he or she must also have an enforceable right to payment of the debt under law. Otherwise, the creditor can be liable for damages for wrongful attachment with malice, as the following case illustrates.

MILLER v. FOX

Supreme Court of Montana,
1977.
__Mont.__, 571 P.2d 804.

BACKGROUND AND FACTS *Miller and Fox entered a contract for the sale of stud horses. The full contract price was not paid at the time of the transaction. Four and a half years later, the plaintiff, Miller, sued the defendant, Fox, for the unpaid balance due on the contract and also obtained a writ of attachment against the defendant's property. The writ was subsequently enforced.*

The court found that the sale of the horses was never completed due to the plaintiff's own failure to perform a condition precedent—that is, to produce stud papers for a particular horse involved in the proposed sale.

The plaintiff's attachment action that was obtained was based on a state statute that allowed prejudgment attachment only upon contracts "for direct payment of money." In this case, the condition precedent was still unfulfilled by the plaintiff who sought the attachment writ.

HATFIELD, Chief Justice.

* * *

Plaintiff also claims that the district judge erred in finding that plaintiff had wrongfully attached defendant's property. [Montana statute], allows prejudgment attachments only in actions upon contracts for the "direct payment of money." In this case, the trial judge found the contract did not call for direct payment of money, but required further performance (presentation of stud horse registration paper) as a condition to payment. Plaintiff's attachment therefore did not meet the statutory requirements and was wrong.

* * *

Plaintiff maintains that even if the attachment was wrongful it was not done with the malice necessary * * * to sustain an award of exemplary damages. Malice necessary for an award of exemplary damages need not consist of spite or hatred; it is sufficient proof of malice in a wrongful attachment action that the defendant knew when the attachment was made that it was wrongful. In this case, plaintiff stated in his affidavit for attachment that the action was on a "contract for the direct payment of money now due", and that the payment of the contract obligation "has not been secured by any mortgage or lien upon real or personal property." Plaintiff, however, knew when he filed the affidavit that the money was not "now due" until he showed defendant the stud registration paper and that defendant's contract debt was "secured" by plaintiff's retention of that registration paper.

For the reasons stated, the judgment of the district court as to plaintiff's liability for wrongful attachment is affirmed. The district court's judgment that defendant was not in breach of contract until the time of trial is affirmed, and the case is remanded to determine the amount on the contract price defendant owes plaintiff for a stud horse whose registration papers were not presented until the time of trial, nine years after the contract was made.

* * *

JUDGMENT AND REMEDY

The trial court's ruling was affirmed, but the case was remanded to the trial court to determine the amount of the contract price that the defendant owed the plaintiff for a stud horse, the money value of the damages that the defendant incurred as a result of the wrongful attachment, and the money value of the exemplary damages for the plaintiff's malicious action in seeking a wrongful attachment.

The original contract for the sale of the horses was enforced between the parties, although it was left to the trial court to determine a fair amount for the contract price, considering the number of years that had passed since the parties had made their agreement.

The wrongful writ of attachment was punishable in both actual damages and exemplary damages, both of which the plaintiff had to pay to the defendant.

GARNISHMENT *Garnishment* is similar to attachment except that it is a collection remedy that is directed not at the debtor but at a third person. The third person, the *garnishee*, owes a debt to the debtor or has property that belongs to the debtor. The typical garnishee is an employer. The wages an employer owes to the debtor-employee are subject to garnishment. As will be discussed later, both state and federal laws, however, permit only a limited portion of the debtor's wages to be garnished.[1]

The legal proceeding for a garnishment action is governed by state law. As a result of a garnishment proceeding, the debtor's employer is ordered by the court to turn over a portion of the debtor's wages to pay the debt. However, garnishment operates differently from state to state. According to the laws in some states, the judgment creditor needs to obtain only one order of garnishment that will then continuously apply to the judgment debtor's weekly wages until the entire debt is paid off. In other states, the judgment creditor must go back to court for a separate order of garnishment for each pay period. In the following case, the Colorado Supreme Court was asked to clarify whether, under its state statute, a writ of garnishment operated continuously or had to be renewed each pay period.

---

1. Some states (for example, Texas) do not permit garnishment of wages by private parties.

BACKGROUND AND FACTS *The judgment creditor (plaintiff) had obtained a judgment against the debtor (defendant) for $16,168.10. The plaintiff sought to execute on the judgment by garnishing the defendant's wages. The defendant received regular salary payments on the fifteenth and last day of each month. The plaintiff wanted the court to grant a single order allowing a continual garnishment against the defendant's wages until the entire debt was paid off. The defendant opposed such an order, saying that the Colorado statute required the plaintiff to undertake a separate garnishment procedure for each regular payment of salary or wages.*

IN RE STONE
Supreme Court of Colorado, 1977.
573 P.2d 98.

KELLEY, Justice.

* * *

This case is here for a determination of a question certified to us pursuant to C.A.R. 21.1 by the United States District Court for the District of Colorado. The question reads:

"Under Colorado Rule of Civil Procedure 103, and in particular, subsections (b), (j), (t) and (z) thereof, may the trial court, upon application by the judgment creditor, issue a writ in the nature of a continuing garnishment against an employer of the judgment debtor requiring the employer to pay into the Registry of the Court the appropriate portion of each regular paycheck or wage payment to the judgment debtor, as it becomes due, without the necessity of serving a separate Writ of Garnishment directed to each such wage payment?

"Alternatively stated, the question might be posed as follows: Where a judgment debtor receives payments of salary or wages at regular intervals from his employer, must a judgment creditor, in effecting execution of his judgment, undertake a separate garnishment procedure against each such regular payment of salary or wages, or may a Writ of Continuing Garnishment, containing appropriate instructions and safeguards for the interests of the judgment debtor, issue from the Trial Court in order to obviate the necessity of a series of individual garnishments against the same employer?"

We answer the question in the negative.

On March 24, 1976, the Bankruptcy Court of the United States District Court for the District of Colorado entered a default judgment in the amount of $16,168.10 against the defendant, Joseph R. Stone (hereinafter defendant). The United States District Court for the District of Colorado affirmed on appeal the judgment of the Bankruptcy Court and the denial of the defendant's motion to set aside the default judgment.

[The Colorado statute] provides for garnishment if "[t]he answer of the garnishee shows that he has *personal property* of any kind in his possession, or under his control, *belonging to the defendant. . .*" and "[i]f the answer shows that the garnishee *is indebted* to the defendant . . . ." (emphasis added). It is well settled in this jurisdiction that garnishment is not available to reach debts that are not due and payable since the garnishee's liability is contingent.

Future earnings are contingent because they depend upon future performance. The employee cannot sue his employer for wages due before the employee has fulfilled his employment contract. At that stage, prospective earnings are hypothetical. Thus, future wages cannot be said to be an indebtedness which is due.

JUDGMENT AND REMEDY

The Colorado garnishment statute does not allow continuing writs of garnishment against future wages. The plaintiff (judgment creditor) could not obtain a continuing writ of garnishment against the defendant's wages but had to secure a separate writ on the fifteenth and last days of each month in order to collect the debt owed.

COMMENTS

Both garnishment and attachment procedures are governed by state law. Both procedures require that the debtor's constitutional right to due process be scrupulously preserved.

FURTHER GARNISHMENT ISSUES The court must always be sure that it is the debtor's property that is actually being taken in a garnishment or attachment proceeding.

BACKGROUND AND FACTS *The plaintiff and the defendant were divorced. The defendant was delinquent in making child support payments, and the plaintiff obtained a judgment against him. The plaintiff then sought a writ of garnishment against funds deposited in a checking account held in the defendant's name. The defendant was successful in having the garnishment writ set aside by establishing in the lower court that the funds in the garnished account were not his but belonged to his second wife.*

PETERSON v.
PETERSON
Supreme Court of Utah, 1977.
571 P.2d 1360.

WILKINGS, Justice.

* * *

At the hearing on defendant's motion to set aside the garnishment execution, the evidence demonstrated that the garnished account was held in defendant's name; that only his name was on the bank's signature card and, therefore, only he was authorized to write checks against the account. However, defendant had not worked for over a year, and the funds in the account were almost exclusively derived from the paychecks of defendant's present wife; and these checks were routinely endorsed to the defendant by her and deposited by him. During the course of the year, defendant did deposit some of his funds in the account, but they amounted to less than $1,000. The money in the account was used for defendant's child support payments to plaintiff, totaling $1,200, as well as for the general living expenses of defendant and his wife. The defendant and his wife each considered the money in the account to be the wife's money though the defendant withdrew for his personal obligations more than he contributed to the account. On the basis of these facts, the District Court found that none of the money belonged to the defendant and all of the funds remaining in the account belonged to defendant's wife, and were not subject to garnishment for the defendant's debts.

* * *

[The plaintiff insisted that her former husband had the burden of proof to show by clear and convincing evidence he had no ownership rights to the money in the checking account.]

Among the classes of cases to which this special standard of persuasion (clear and convincing proof) has been applied are the following: (1) charges of fraud, and undue influence, (2) suits on oral contracts to make a will, and suits to establish the terms of a lost will, (3) suits for the specific performance of an oral contract, (4) proceedings to set aside, reform or modify written transactions or official acts on grounds of fraud, mistake or incompleteness, and (5) miscellaneous types of claims and defenses, varying from state to state, where there is thought to be special danger of deception, or where the court considers that the particular type of claim should be disfavored on policy grounds.

We agree with plaintiff that persuasion by defendant of a clear and convincing nature is required in this matter, believing that there is a "special danger of deception" in cases such as this one but hold that the defendant sustained that burden and the evidence below was sufficient to support the Court's finding, especially in view of the fact that both defendant and his present wife testified that defendant had not been working and earning money for a year because of his medical problems and plaintiff presented no evidence to rebut that testimony.

JUDGMENT AND REMEDY *The judgment was affirmed. The wrongful garnishment was correctly set aside by the lower court.*

Guaranty and Suretyship

When one person becomes responsible for the debt of another, a relationship that insures that the debt will be paid to the creditor results. Such arrangements are of two types. One is called a contract of suretyship and the other a contract of guaranty.

SURETY A contract of suretyship is a promise made by a third person to be responsible for the debtor's obligation. Suretyship is an express contract between the surety and the creditor. The surety is *primarily* liable for the debt of the principal. The creditor can demand payment from the surety from the moment that the principal is in default. A suretyship is not a form of indemnity; that is, it is not merely a promise to make good any loss that a creditor may incur as a result of the debtor's failure to pay. A suretyship makes the surety liable to the creditor at any time the principal debtor defaults in performance on the debt obligation. The creditor need not exhaust all legal remedies against the principal debtor before holding the surety responsible for payment. A surety agreement must always be in writing.

GUARANTY A guaranty contract is similar to a suretyship in that it includes a promise to answer for the debt or default of another. With suretyship, however, the surety is primarily liable for the debtor obligation of the principal. With a guaranty arrangement, the guarantor—the third person making the guarantee—is *secondarily liable*. The guarantor cannot be immediately required to pay the obligation after the debtor defaults. The creditor must first attempt to collect from the principal debtor.

RIGHTS OF THE SURETY A creditor must take care that certain actions that will release the surety from the obligation do not occur. Any material change that is made in the terms of the original contract between the principal debtor and the creditor, including the awarding of an extension of time for making payment without first obtaining the consent of the surety, will discharge the surety. When a creditor discharges the principal debtor (or debtors), discharge of any one of them releases the surety from any obligation unless the surety agrees to the discharge. Naturally, if the principal obligation is paid by the debtor or by another person on behalf of the debtor, the surety is discharged from obligation. Similarly, if valid tender of payment is made and the creditor for some reason rejects it, then the surety is also released from any obligation on the debt. Generally, any defenses available to a principal debtor can be used by the surety to avoid liability on the obligation to the creditor; the defenses that cannot be used are insolvency, bankruptcy, and the statute of limitations. The ability of the surety to assert any defenses the debtor may have against the creditor is the most important concept in suretyship, since the only defenses available to the surety are those of the debtor.

Mortgage Foreclosure on Real Property

A mortgage agreement provides that when the **mortgagor** (debtor/borrower) *defaults* in making payment in accordance with the terms of the agreement, the **mortgagee** (creditor/lender) can declare that the entire mortgage debt is due immediately. The mortgagee/creditor can enforce payment in full by a legal action called **foreclosure.**

In this action, the real estate that is covered by the mortgage is sold at a judicial sale.[2] If the proceeds of the sale are sufficient to cover both the costs of the foreclosure and the mortgaged debt, any surplus is paid over to the debtor. If, on the other hand, the sale proceeds are insufficient to cover the foreclosure costs and the mortgaged debt, the mortgagee can seek to recover the difference from the mortgagor by obtaining a *deficiency judgment.* This type of judgment represents the "deficiency amount"— that is, the difference between the mortgaged debt and the amount actually received from the proceeds of the foreclosure sale. A deficiency judgment is obtained in a separate legal action that is pursued subsequent to the foreclosure action. It entitles the creditor to recover from other property owned by the debtor. However, only nonexempt property can be used to satisfy a deficiency judgment.

For a period of time established by state law, prior to the sale of land, a mortgagor can redeem the property by paying the full amount of the debt plus any interest costs that have accrued. This right of the debtor is known as *equity of redemption.*

BULK SALES LAW— ARTICLE 6 OF THE UNIFORM COMMERCIAL CODE

A bulk transfer, or sale, is the sale of a substantial portion of the assets of a business. It usually includes sale of inventory, equipment, furniture, and fixtures used in the business. A bulk sale usually involves the entire assets of the business, but it can involve just the *major*

portion of the business assets. In either case, the purpose of Article 6 of the Uniform Commercial Code is to protect the rights of creditors who have presumably extended credit on the strength of the inventory, equipment, furniture, fixtures, or other assets of the business. The business owner should not be permitted to sell all the assets, pocket the proceeds, and leave town, thereby avoiding paying creditors. By the same token, a purchaser should not be allowed to purchase a business and reincorporate, thereby leaving creditors of the prior corporation no recourse against the prior corporation's assets.

To avoid this situation, the Code imposes two basic requirements in the event of a bulk sale. First, Article 6 requires that the *seller* draw up a list of the property being sold and a list of all the creditors and that these lists be given to the potential buyer. Second, the buyer is given responsibility for notifying each of the seller's creditors of the proposed sale date. The notice and publication requirements are very specific. A potential purchaser must notify each of the seller's creditors individually and personally to inform them of the potential sale. Creditors must act within a specific time period to inform the potential buyer of the extent of their claims. If a potential buyer fails to follow the UCC procedures, the transfer will be ineffective, and creditors can use any appropriate remedy to collect the debt from the property purchased by the buyer. If the Code procedures have been followed, the transfer is effective, and creditors will lose any rights they failed to pursue at the time of notification. In that case, a purchaser who buys for value and in good faith can obtain the property free and clear of any claims of creditors.

PROTECTION OF THE DEBTOR

Exemptions

In most states, certain types of real and personal property are exempt from debts. Probably the most familiar of these exemptions is the

---

2. This is true even if the property is the debtor's homestead. A mortgage is one debt that is *not* subject to the homestead statutory exemption that exempts the homestead from execution of any general debts of a householder or head of a family.

homestead exemption. Commonly, state statutes provide that the family home of a debtor can be sold in order to satisfy a judgment debt. A specified amount of the sale price, however, will be exempt—that is, reserved for the debtor to provide money to obtain shelter for the family. For example, Daniels owes Carey $20,000. The debt is the subject of a lawsuit, and the court awards Carey a judgment of $20,000 against Daniels. To satisfy the **judgment debt,** Daniels's family home is sold at public auction for $20,000. Assume the homestead exemption is $5,000. The proceeds of the sale are distributed as follows:

1.   Daniels is paid $5,000 as his homestead exemption.
2.   Carey is paid $15,000 toward the judgment debt, leaving a $5,000 deficiency judgment (that is, "leftover debt") that can be satisfied (paid) from any other nonexempt property (personal or real) that Daniels may have.

In many states, statutes permit the homestead exemption only if the judgment debtor has a family. The policy behind this type of statute is to protect the family. If a judgment debtor does not have a family, a creditor can be entitled to collect the full amount realized from the sale of the debtor's home.

State exemption statutes usually include both real and personal property. Personal property that is most often exempt from satisfaction of judgment debts includes:

1.   Household furniture up to a specified dollar amount.
2.   Clothing and certain personal possessions, such as family pictures or a Bible.
3.   Pension or bonus monies based on military service and received from the government (also protected by federal statute).

Federal laws and state laws limit the amount of money that can be garnished from a debtor's weekly take-home pay. Typically, a garnishment judgment will be served on a person's employer so that part of the person's usual paycheck will be paid to the creditor. Federal law provides a minimal framework to protect debtors from losing all their income in order to pay judgment debts.[3] State laws also provide dollar exemptions, and these amounts are often larger than those provided by federal law. State and federal statutes can be applied together to help create a pool of funds sufficient to enable a debtor to continue to provide for family needs while also reducing the amount of the judgment debt in a reasonable way.

Garnishment of an employee's wages cannot be grounds for dismissal of an employee because federal law prohibits _any_ employer from discharging an employee who has been involved in one garnishment proceeding.

Consumer Credit Protection Act (CCPA)

The Consumer Credit Protection Act (CCPA) is commonly called the Truth-in-Lending Act. (It is discussed again in Chapter 48, which deals with consumer protection.) It is basically a "disclosure law," administered by the Federal Reserve Board, that requires sellers and lenders to disclose credit terms or loan terms so that a debtor can shop around for the best financing arrangements.

DISCLOSURE REQUIREMENTS UNDER THE TRUTH-IN-LENDING ACT   The disclosure requirements of the Truth-in-Lending Act apply to any installment sales contract in which payment is to be made in more than four installments. The following is a breakdown of the disclosure requirements as they would apply to the sale of a stereo on such an installment plan:

1.   The cash price of the stereo.
2.   The down payment or trade-in allowance if any.

---

3.   For example, the federal Consumer Credit Protection Act, 15 USCA 1601 et seq., provides that a debtor can retain either 75 percent of the disposable earnings per week or the sum equivalent to thirty hours of work paid at federal minimum wage rates, whichever is greater.

3.   The unpaid cash price (cash price minus the down payment).

4.   The finance charge, which includes interest, points, service charges, lender's fee, finder's fee, fee for investigation of credit, credit life insurance premium, accident insurance premium, and so on.

5.   Charges not included as part of the finance charge.

6.   The total amount to be financed.

7.   The annual percentage rate of finance charge.

8.   The date that the finance charge begins to accrue.

9.   The number, amounts, and due dates of payments.

10.   The penalties in case of delinquency or other late payment charges.

11.   A description of the security interest (see Chapters 29 and 30).

12.   A description of the prepayment penalty charge.

13.   Sometimes a comparative index of credit costs to give the purchaser an idea of how much credit will cost on this account. [CCPA Sec. 127]

WHO IS SUBJECT TO TRUTH-IN-LENDING? Only certain creditors or lenders and only certain types of transactions are subject to the Truth-in-Lending Act. It applies to persons who, in the ordinary course of their businesses, lend money or sell on credit or arrange for the extension of credit. For this reason, sales or loans made between two consumers do not come under the act. Only debtors who are *natural* persons are protected by this law; corporations or other legal entities are not. Transactions involving purchases of property (real or personal) for personal, family, household, or agricultural use come within the terms and provisions of the act if the price is less than $25,000. Transactions covered by the act typically include retail and installment sales and installment loans, car loans, home improvement loans, and certain real estate loans.

The act distinguishes between the information that must be disclosed in real estate loans and personal property loans. For example, in the latter case, a creditor must provide information about the amount financed, the finance charge (interest rate and all other charges), the annual percentage rate, and the amount and number of payments.

A creditor who fails to comply with the disclosure requirements may be liable to the consumer for twice the amount of the finance charge. In no event will that penalty be less than $100 or more than $1,000 for a violation against an individual consumer. The consumer has one year from the date of the violation to bring suit against a creditor who has failed to provide the disclosure statement or who has failed to discover and correct an error in the disclosure statement provided.

In the following case, a creditor furniture store failed to comply with several of the disclosure provisions of the Truth-in-Lending Act in its retail installment contracts. Within a year after making a credit purchase, the consumer-plaintiff sued on behalf of herself and all other persons who had entered into similar installment contracts with the defendant within the year. The plaintiff was permitted to proceed in a class action suit (a lawsuit initiated or defended by a person on behalf of all persons similarly situated and notified). If the defendant was found guilty, it would be liable to every person in the class for statutory damages.

BACKGROUND AND FACTS   *For herself and for a class of 740 consumers, the plaintiff sued the defendant, Kimbrell's Furniture Store, for violating certain disclosure requirements set forth in the Truth-in-Lending regulations. The District Court ruled that Kimbrell's was liable under the act to the plaintiff and to members of the class and Kimbrell's appealed.*

BARBER v. KIMBRELL'S, INC.

United States Court of Appeals, Fourth Circuit, 1978.
577 F.2d 216.

WINTER, Circuit Judge.

* * *

On July 16, 1973, plaintiff entered into a retail installment contract with Kimbrell's, Inc. for the purchase of various items of household furniture totalling $592.70. Because she already owed Kimbrell's $65.00 from a previous credit purchase, the July 16th agreement consolidated both the old and new balance and required repayment of the combined debt in twelve equal monthly installments. The written contract reflecting this agreement purported to disclose credit information as to both the new and combined transactions.

[On May 3, 1974, the plaintiff filed her action as an individual. Later the court certified that a plaintiff class existed, consisting of those persons who had entered into retail installment contracts at Kimbrell's between July 16, 1973 and May 3, 1974. This class numbered approximately 740 persons.

The Appellate Court reviewed the District Court's (trial court's) findings and agreed that Kimbrell's had indeed violated the act. Next the court considered the appropriate damages to be awarded to the plaintiff class.]

In determining the maximum recovery in a class action under the Act, we look to the purposes of the Act and the history of its various enforcement provisions. These, we think, provide the answer to the issue we must decide.

The Truth in Lending Act was enacted by Congress to serve two purposes: (1) to promote the full disclosure of credit terms in consumer credit transactions, and (2) to prescribe a uniform method for stating these terms better to enable the consumer to compare "the various credit terms available to him and avoid the uninformed use of credit." 15 U.S.C. §1601. As enacted in 1968, the Act provided for both administrative enforcement, 15 U.S.C. §1607, and enforcement by private litigation, 15 U.S.C. §1640. As an incentive to private enforcement, the Act allowed a successful plaintiff to recover statutory damages of twice the amount of the finance charge imposed in the transaction (but not less than $100 nor more than $1,000), plus reasonable attorneys' fees and court costs.

While the private enforcement scheme envisioned by the original Act worked well enough in individual suits, it soon became evident that the scheme was not equally well-suited to class actions. Since a class recovery consisted of simply an aggregation of individual statutory damages, with each class member being entitled to a minimum recovery of $100, courts soon recognized that a recovery of statutory damages by a large plaintiff class had the potential of visiting financial disaster upon a defendant creditor. As a consequence, courts became increasingly reluctant to certify class actions.

To strike an appropriate balance between the advantages of the class action as a vehicle of private enforcement and the need of creditors to avoid financial ruin, Congress in 1974 amended [the act] as it related to class recoveries of statutory damages. The amendment (1) eliminated any minimum recovery requirement as to individual class members, (2) placed a ceiling on the total class recovery so that a creditor's total liability for statutory damages would be no more than "the lesser of $100,000 or 1 per centum of the net worth of the creditor," and (3) made the award of statutory damages in the class context discretionary rather than a matter of right as it had been before the amendment and as it continued to be with regard to individual actions.

* * *

[The Appellate Court concluded that, based on an inaccurate computation of "1% of the net worth" of Kimbrell's, the District Court improperly determined the maximum class recovery allowable by statute.]

Thus, that part of the District Court's judgment relating to the penalty fees and other recoverable fees was vacated (stricken), but the part of its judgment that found violations of the act was affirmed. The case was returned to the District Court for the purpose of recomputing the damages against the defendant.

JUDGMENT AND REMEDY

The Truth-in-Lending Act attempts to prevent misinformation. It requires that the seller or lender disclose financing charges and arrangements so that the potential debtor can make an informed decision about credit or loan terms before deciding to accept the financing arrangements. The law is liberally construed to protect potential consumer debtors before they undertake financing arrangements.

COMMENTS

   Not all violations of the Truth-in-Lending Act provide grounds for recovery. When a creditor fails to comply with some requirement of the act that does not impede or confuse the consumer's understanding of the terms of the credit arrangement, the consumer should not recover damages. There must be a demonstrated relationship between the violation of the act and the congressional purposes of insuring meaningful disclosure of credit terms and the informed use of credit.[4]

---

4.   Dzadovsky v. Lyons Ford Sales, Inc., 452 F. Supp. 606 (W.D. Pa. 1978)

The Uniform Consumer Credit Code (UCCC)

Another legislative attempt to protect consumers by utilizing full disclosure of credit information to buyers is the Uniform Consumer Credit Code proposed in 1961. This code is a state statute and has been enacted in only a few states. Where it has been adopted, it applies to practically every transaction involving credit terms.

   One of the focuses of the UCCC is to set ceilings on interest rates. In addition, the statute has detailed provisions regarding credit service charges, prepayments, delinquencies, deferrals, and other financing and refinancing costs. The provisions of the law are exceedingly detailed. The UCCC is, however, similar to the Truth-in-Lending Act in that it requires written disclo-

sure of facts pertinent to the financing arrangements and it keys into the annual percentage rate that a buyer will be paying for the privilege of using a credit payment plan.

   Some specific provisions of the Uniform Consumer Credit Code are discussed in Chapter 48, and these will not be reviewed here. Some of the remedy and penalty portions of the UCCC are, however, relevant to the subject matter of this chapter. For example, the code limits the amount of a debtor's take-home wages that can be subjected to garnishment. It prohibits garnishment *before* judgment has been rendered by a court of law, and it imposes stringent restrictions on deficiency judgments. Similar to the Truth-in-Lending Act, the UCCC prohibits an employer from discharging an employee merely because the employee is subject to a garnishment proceeding.

PENALTIES Violation of the UCCC can result in criminal as well as civil penalties. The major civil penalty arises from improper finance charges—those in excess of rates allowed by the act. If the debtor has paid a rate in excess of the allowable rate, the debtor is entitled to recover the *total* amount of the credit service charge or *ten times* the excess charge (whichever is greater) from the creditor. If a creditor deliberately charges excessive rates, the penalty can be recovered, and the creditor cannot escape liability merely by offering to repay the debtor the amount of the excess. Other kinds of violations can occur under the UCCC. When a debtor can show, for example, violations of advertising requirements or improprieties involving home solicitation sales, the debtor is entitled to recover an amount not in excess of *three times* the finance charge. In addition, the UCCC governs referral sale schemes by which a seller offers a rebate or a discount to a buyer who will furnish the names of other prospective purchasers. The UCCC prohibits these schemes even if they are not fraudulent, and when they are fraudulent, the victim is entitled to punitive as well as actual damages.

PAYMENT BY CHECK REQUIRED A provision of the UCCC that deserves special mention is the requirement that a seller or lessor in a consumer credit sale or lease agreement can accept only a check from the debtor rather than another type of negotiable instrument, such as a promissory note. A holder is treated as not exercising good faith if he or she accepts a negotiable instrument other than a check, in violation of this provision. [UCCC Sec. 2-403] The provision negates the special holder-in-due-course status of the Uniform Commercial Code when a consumer credit sale or lease is involved. The trend in consumer law is toward the elimination of the holder-in-due-course doctrine. The effect is to recognize more legal reasons for a consumer to avoid payment to a third party holding the instrument when merchandise and services ordered on credit either are not received or are defective.

ALTERATION OF THE HOLDER-IN-DUE-COURSE DOCTRINE Historically, the holder-in-due-course doctrine barred a consumer from asserting most defenses against a third party who had purchased negotiable paper. In addition, many installment sales contracts contained provisions saying that if the contract was assigned to a third person, any defenses that might have been available to a debtor could not be used against that third person (referred to as "waiver of defense" clauses).[5] The result was that consumers were often required to pay for defective merchandise and then to seek remedy against the seller. For example, a consumer purchasing aluminum siding would enter a contract known as a **retail installment sales agreement**, which contained provisions whereby the consumer would make monthly installment payments until the entire sales price and financing charges were paid. Most sellers did not wait for the entire installment period to run its course to be paid. Instead, they sold the installment sales contract to others who paid them immediately. The consumer then had to make payments to the third party even if the aluminum siding was defective or never, in fact, installed by the original seller.

After a long history of substantial abuses inflicted upon consumers, many states enacted statutes that prohibit the use of contract clauses that cut off consumer defenses against a third party. Many states require that the words *consumer paper* be printed on the face of any contract or other paper that represents a consumer's indebtedness based upon the sale of consumer goods or services on credit between a retail seller and a retail buyer. In these situations, the paper is nonnegotiable as a matter of law. This means that any purchaser of the paper cannot become a holder in due course. Any defenses to payment the consumer has against

---

5. UCC Sec. 9-206 accepts waiver of defense clauses whenever the assignee takes the assignment for value in good faith and without notice of a claim or defense "except as to defenses of a type which may be asserted against a holder-in-due-course of a negotiable instrument under the Article on Commercial Paper (Article 3)."

the original retailer carry over and apply to any assignee of the contract.

Another alternative provided by some state laws is that the seller assigning the paper must give *written notice* of the assignment to the debtor. The consumer-debtor then has a period of time, usually three months, during which he or she can assert any defenses such as defective merchandise or nondelivery against the assignee-third party. Of course, once the statutory period passes, the consumer-debtor must then make payments. The consumer's only remedy thereafter is against the seller.

Credit Cards

In 1974, Congress passed an amendment to the Truth-in-Lending Act called the Fair Credit Billing Act.[6] Basically, under the rules set up pursuant to this act, a purchaser can withhold payment until a dispute over a faulty product that was purchased and paid for by credit card is resolved. It is up to the credit card issuer to intervene and attempt a settlement between the credit card user and the seller. A purchaser does not have an *unlimited* right to stop payment. Good faith effort to get satisfaction from the seller must first be exercised. The purchaser does not need to notify the credit card company that payment for that item is being cut off. The purchaser can wait for the issuer to act. It is probably a good idea, however, to advise the company.

Other provisions of this act relate to disputes over billing. If the debtor thinks there is an error in a bill, the credit card company must investigate and suspend payments until it does so. The card holder simply writes to the company within sixty days of receipt of the bill and briefly explains the circumstances and why he or she thinks there is an error. Under the law, the company must acknowledge the letter within thirty days and solve the dispute within ninety days. During that period, the debtor does not have to pay the amount of the dispute or any

minimum payment from the amount of dispute. The creditor cannot impose finance charges during that period for unpaid balances in dispute; nor can it close the account. However, if it turns out that there was no error, the creditor can then attempt to collect finance charges for the entire period for which payments were not made.

LOST OR STOLEN CREDIT CARDS The Truth-in-Lending Act contains two important provisions regarding credit cardholders. One provision limits the liability of a cardholder to $50 per card when the creditor has been notified that the credit card has been stolen or lost. The second prohibits a credit card company from billing a consumer for unauthorized charges, say if the company issues an unsolicited card.

Jones loses his Master Charge credit card in the street. Bilas finds it and buys $200 worth of goods with the card. The next day Jones informs Master Charge of his loss. Master Charge later bills Jones for the $200 worth of goods that Bilas bought. Clearly, Master Charge can collect only $50 (or nothing if Jones notified it of the loss before the card was used by Bilas) because that is the maximum liability imposed on the loser of a credit card.

Now consider that Master Charge mails a credit card to Farmer, who has not applied for a card or held one in the past. The envelope is stolen out of Farmer's mailbox, and the thief signs the card and buys $200 worth of goods. Master Charge bills Farmer for the $200. Farmer does not have to pay anything at all, not even $50, because Master Charge performed a prohibited act by sending an unsolicited card.

Credit Reports and Collection Practices

There has been much concern over the years that government is watching every citizen. One major source of information that has increasingly come under attack is investigative reports done on consumers' credit status. One serious

_____
6.   15 USCA Sec. 1681.

drawback to the collection of such information has been that consumers have no access to the contents of the reports or any way to control their use. Inaccuracies, once reported, have been almost impossible to uncover, much less to correct.

The Truth-in-Lending Act provides that consumers are entitled, upon request, to be informed of the nature and scope of a credit investigation, the kind of information that is being compiled, and the names of persons who will be receiving the report. They must make the request within specific time limits, however. Consumers have the right to require that any inaccurate or misleading material be reinvestigated and, if not verified, be removed from the file. If there is a dispute about the accuracy of certain parts of the reports, consumers have the right to include their own one hundred word statement in the file to set forth their position with regard to disputed matters. Such statements become part of the permanent record.

The law also provides for updating information that is obsolete. For example, any bankruptcy adjudication that has occurred more than fourteen years prior to the report can be removed. Lawsuits or judgments that are more than seven years old or for which the statute of limitations has expired (whichever is longer) can be removed. In general, any information unfavorable to consumers that is more than seven years old can also be removed.

Although the law provides that consumers have the right to be informed of the contents of their files, the Act limits that access for others. A person who wishes to obtain information contained in a consumer's credit file must have either a court order or a legitimate business need for the information or must have the permission of the consumer to obtain access to the information. Consumer reporting agencies must inform the consumer when an investigative report is being compiled and of the right to disclosure. A consumer credit reporting agency that fails to comply with the terms of the act can be held liable not only for actual damages but for punitive damages and attorneys' fees resulting from a lawsuit brought by the consumer.

DEBT COLLECTION   Many states have passed legislation that prohibits the use of abusive techniques such as harassment in bill collection. Bill collectors have been known to telephone consumer-debtors at all hours of the night, making threats about the personal safety of the consumer as well as to the consumer's family. Another abusive technique is to telephone or appear at the debtor's place of employment and verbally harass the debtor. States that have enacted collection practice legislation prohibit these kinds of practices but do not prohibit *all* phone calls. Many states provide penalty provisions that include levying a flat penalty fee against the creditor and the collector and that permit damages for emotional distress. Although debtors have always been able to use traditional tort law to protect themselves from creditor abuse, clearly the trend of the law, at the state and federal levels, is toward limiting abusive action by creditors in the debt collection process.[7]

Congressional concerns about improper debt collection practices led to the passage in 1977 of the Fair Debt Collection Practices Act. This act prohibits the following:

1.   Contacting the consumer at his or her place of employment if the employer objects.
2.   Contacting the consumer at inconvenient or unusual times, such as 3 o'clock in the morning, or contacting the consumer at all, if he or she is represented by an attorney.
3.   Contacting third parties other than parents, spouses, or financial advisers about the payment of a debt unless the court so authorizes.
4.   Using harassment and intimidation, such as abusive language, or using false or misleading information, such as posing as a policeman.
5.   Communicating with the consumer after receipt of notice that the consumer is refusing to pay the debt, except to advise the consumer of further action to be taken by the collection agency.

---

7.   Federal statutes also ban certain debt collection techniques. See 15 USCA Sec. 1692. The Federal Trade Commission prosecutes overly zealous debt collectors under federal regulations for unfair and deceptive trade practices.

The enforcement of this act is the responsibility of the Federal Trade Commission. The act limits the damages and penalties that can be recovered for violation, including attorneys' fees.

Real Estate Transactions

The federal government has passed regulations designed to prevent fraudulent sales in real estate transactions. The Interstate Sales Full Disclosure Act (1968) has as its objective disclosure to potential sellers. The act is administered by the Department of Housing and Urban Development (HUD), and its focus is to furnish facts and information to potential buyers so they can make intelligent decisions about whether or not to purchase land.

Land sale abuses have been occurring for years. Everyone has heard about purchasers who invest their life savings in one hundred acres of land for a $10 down payment and $10 a month only to find that the land is under ten feet of water. Federal law does not prohibit land under water from being sold; it merely requires that the seller inform the buyer that it is under water.

As notions of consumer protection expand, so too does the law. In the case of new construction, the purchase and sale of new units are becoming increasingly subject to certain warranty requirements. For example, many states recognize that there is an implied warranty of habitability. A new house or condominium has to be fit to live in. The statutes are new and changing rapidly, and many of the concepts that apply to other consumer transactions are now being applied to the sale of real estate.

THE REAL ESTATE SETTLEMENT PROCEDURES ACT   A recent federal law requires that all closing costs be specifically outlined before a person buys a home. The 1976 revisions of the Real Estate Settlement Procedures Act make the following stipulations about buying a house and borrowing money to pay for it:

1.   Within three business days after a person applies for a mortgage loan, the lender must send a booklet, prepared by the U.S. Department of Housing and Urban Development, that outlines the applicant's rights and explains settlement procedures and costs.
2.   The lender must give an estimate of most of the settlement costs within that three-day period.
3.   The lender must clearly identify individuals or firms that the applicant is required to use for legal or other services, including title insurance and search.
4.   If the loan is approved, the lender must provide a truth-in-lending statement that shows the annual percentage rate on the mortgage loan.
5.   Lenders, title insurers, and others involved in the real estate transaction cannot pay kickbacks for business referred to them.

QUESTIONS AND CASE PROBLEMS

1.   Kloster-Madsen, Inc., a general contractor, entered into a contract with the owner of a building to do certain remodeling work. About a month later, pursuant to the contract, an electrical subcontractor proceeded to remove several light fixtures from one of the ceilings, cutting four holes in the ceiling and placing the removed light fixtures in the holes. Immediately after this work was begun, a new owner, Tafi's, Inc., purchased the building. Several thousand dollars' worth of material and labor was expended before Tafi's informed the general contractor that it did not wish to have the building remodeled. Can Kloster-Madsen impose a mechanic's lien on the building even though the building contract was entered into with a different owner? [Kloster-Madsen, Inc. v. Tafi's, Inc., 303 Minn. 59, 226 N.W.2d. 603 (1975)]
2.   On Wednesday, Plunkett, who was in the towing business, received two telephone calls. The first was from a policeman requesting Plunkett to tow a car from the scene of an accident. This towing was totally at the policeman's discretion, since the driver of the

car was unconscious at the time. The second phone call requested Plunkett to tow a car from private property on which it had been parked. This call was made by the property owner. The owners of the two cars then wished to retrieve their cars, but Plunkett claimed that he had a lien on the cars and refused to give up possession unless the owners paid the towing charges. Does Plunkett have a lien on these two vehicles? [Younger v. Plunkett, 395 F. Supp. 702 (E.D. Pa. 1975)]

3. Jackson, the owner of a trailer with a refrigeration unit, brought the trailer to North Broadway Service Station for repairs. When the service station owner finished the repairs, Jackson was unable to pay. He pleaded with the owner to permit him to use the trailer to enable him to earn the money necessary to pay the repair bill. The owner kindheartedly returned the trailer to Jackson. Shortly thereafter, the trailer was repossessed by the Trailer Refrigeration Company, which held a mortgage on the trailer on which Jackson had defaulted. The service station owner then attempted to enforce an artisan's lien against the trailer, claiming priority over Trailer Refrigeration Company's mortgage. Will he succeed? What if the owner of the service station had obtained a written memorandum from Jackson at the time he released the trailer to him, stating that he retained an artisan's lien on the trailer and was releasing it only to enable Jackson to earn the money to pay the repair bill? Would the results be different? [Jackson v. Kusmer, 411 S.W.2d. 257 (Mo. App. 1967)]

4. One of the ways in which a plaintiff can collect a money judgment from a defendant is by garnishing a debt that is due from a garnishee to the defendant. Garnishment is allowed only where the debt due from the garnishee is unconditional. With this in mind, discuss the following situation. Cummings Company sued C & E Excavating Company. C & E had a contract with Volpe Construction Company to do certain excavating work for Volpe. Can Cummings garnish the money owed under this contract? What must be known about the contract in order to answer this question? [Cummings General Tire Co. v. Volpe Constr. Co., 230 A.2d. 712 (D.C. App. 1967)]

5. Asher entered into a contract with Herman for the sale of land. The contract provided that in the event that the vendors were unable to convey title, the vendors' sole liability would be to refund the purchaser's deposit. Subsequently, the contract fell through, but the escrow agent, who was holding the deposit made by the purchaser, embezzled the money. Under rules of escrow, the loss fell on the

purchasers since it was their money. Can the purchasers argue that under the provision in the contract mentioned above the vendors could be deemed guarantors of the deposit money? Explain. [Asher v. Herman, 49 Misc. 2d. 475, 267 N.Y.S. 2d. 932 (1966)]

6. Evans Motors sold James Perry an automobile under an installment sales contract. The contract required the buyer of the automobile to procure and maintain insurance on it at all times. Evans then sold the installment contract to the American National Bank. Before the bank took the installment note, it required Evans to sign as an accommodation party (surety). Evans and American National had done business together for a number of years, and it was customary that if the bank received notice of cancellation of insurance on an automobile covered by an installment note, it would immediately notify Evans. Shortly after the bank purchased the installment note from Evans, it learned of cancellation of Perry's insurance. However, it failed to notify Evans of this fact, and it failed to make any other arrangements for insurance. Several months later, the automobile was totally destroyed in a collision. Since Perry was insolvent, American National Bank was unable to collect further payments from him and looked to Evans Motors as an accommodation party. Does Evans have any defense? [Evans v. American Nat. Bank and Trust Co. of Chattanooga, 116 Ga. App. 468, 157 S.E.2d. 816 (1967)]

7. Dunning Floor Covering, Inc., owed Raymond Darrah $7,500. In settlement of this debt, Dunning transferred about half of its floor covering inventory and some miscellaneous fixtures to Darrah. The items transferred had a value of $7,500. Darrah later resold the merchandise to a third party for $4,000. Glidden Company, one of Dunning's business creditors, claimed that since it had not received notice of the transfer of the merchandise, Article 6 of the UCC was violated. Is Glidden correct? Why? If Glidden's argument is correct, for what amount will Raymond Darrah be liable to Glidden? Will the third party to whom Darrah sold the goods be liable to Glidden? [Associated Creditors Agency v. Dunning Floor Covering, 265 Cal. App. 2d. 558, 71 Cal. Rptr. 494 (1968)]

8. In the summer of 1972, Robert Martin applied for and was issued an American Express credit card. Approximately three years later, in April 1975, Martin gave his card to a business associate named E. L. McBride and orally authorized McBride to charge only up to $500 on the credit card. However, in June 1975, Martin received a statement from Amer-

ican Express indicating that the amount owed on his credit card account was approximately $5,300. Under the Truth-in-Lending Act, for how much will Martin be liable to American Express? [Martin v. American Express, Inc., 361 So.2d. 597 (Ala. Civ. App. 1978)]

9. GAC Finance Corporation was the holder of a promissory note in which Tom Burgess was the maker. When the note came due, Burgess refused to pay, and GAC brought suit against him. Burgess claimed that the note was in violation of the Truth-in-Lending Act since delinquent charges were designated in the note as .53 instead of $.53. Burgess contended that the amount of the delinquent charge was so unclear that it violated the act. He further contended that, regardless of whether he won or lost against GAC, GAC had to pay his attorney's fees. Discuss Burgess's contentions. [GAC Finance Corp. v. Burgess, 16 Wash. App. 758, 558 P.2d. 1386 (1977)]

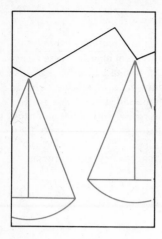

32

Bankruptcies and Reorganization

The U.S. Constitution provides that "The Congress shall have the power
* * * to establish * * * uniform laws on the subject of bankruptcies
throughout the United States."[1] Bankruptcy proceedings are therefore
rooted in federal laws; bankruptcy courts are special federal courts; and
bankruptcy judges are federally appointed.

The original Bankruptcy Act was enacted in 1898, amended by the
1938 Chandler Act, and the last major revision occurred in 1978. The 1898
act as amended covers every form of bankruptcy procedure available to
individuals and organizations, including certain special categories of
organizations for railroads, banks, insurance corporations, municipal
corporations, and building and loan associations.

THE BANKRUPTCY
REFORM ACT OF 1978

The Bankruptcy Reform Act of 1978 made several changes in bankruptcy
laws. It created courts that are staffed by bankruptcy judges appointed by
the president for fourteen-year terms.[2] The jurisdiction of the new
bankruptcy courts is broader than that of the old courts in that they are
given subject matter jurisdiction over all controversies affecting debtors
or their estates.[3] Previously, the bankruptcy court had jurisdiction only

1. Article I, Section 8, Clause 4.
2. 28 USCA Secs. 151-152.
3. 28 USCA Sec. 1471.

where it had possession of the thing in controversy or where the adverse claimant consented to the jurisdiction.

GOALS OF BANKRUPTCY LAW

Bankruptcy law is designed to accomplish two main goals. The first is protection of debtors. Bankruptcy procedure protects against frivolous suits by creditors where the debtor is still able to recover. The second major goal of bankruptcy law is to provide a fair means of distributing a debtor's assets among all creditors. Bankruptcy law establishes priorities among creditors and prohibits the debtor from favoring one creditor over another.

Bankruptcy is an area of *concurrent jurisdiction* for federal and state laws. States are permitted to enact bankruptcy laws as long as they do not conflict with federal law. The discussion in this chapter will deal primarily with federal bankruptcy law.

TYPES OF BANKRUPTCY

Within the category of ordinary bankruptcy, there are basically two types of bankruptcy—**voluntary bankruptcy** and **involuntary bankruptcy**.

Voluntary Bankruptcy

A voluntary petition in bankruptcy is brought by the debtor, who files official forms that are designated for that purpose. Any "person"—a natural person, a firm, an association, or a corporation—can file a petition for voluntary bankruptcy. But voluntary bankruptcy is prohibited for five business organizations: banking corporations, building and loan associations, insurance corporations, municipal corporations, and railroad corporations. These enterprises are subjected to special laws relating to liquidation and reorganization.

When a partnership files a petition for bankruptcy, the proceedings apply to the partnership as a firm. The petition is not on behalf of the individual partners. If individual partners intend to obtain individual discharges in bankruptcy, each one must file a separate, personal bankruptcy petition. A partnership in voluntary bankruptcy must show that it is insolvent—that liabilities exceed assets. Other "persons" do not need to show that they are insolvent to petition successfully for bankruptcy. Insolvency will be discussed below.

The voluntary petition in bankruptcy has four parts, or schedules:

1. A list of both secured and unsecured creditors, their addresses, and the amount of debt owed to each.
2. A statement of the financial affairs of the bankrupt.
3. A list of all property and assets owned by the bankrupt.
4. A list of all property the bankrupt claims to be exempt from creditors.

The voluntary bankruptcy petition is filed on official forms in special federal courts. These forms must be completed accurately, sworn to under oath, and signed by the debtor. To conceal assets or knowingly supply false information on these schedules is a crime under the bankruptcy laws.

Generally, a person can declare bankruptcy only once within a six-year period. If the voluntary petition for bankruptcy is found to be proper, the filing of the petition itself will constitute an order for relief in bankruptcy.[4] A voluntary bankruptcy petition for a partnership requires that the petition be signed by all the partners.

Involuntary Bankruptcy

Involuntary bankruptcy occurs when the debtor's creditors force the debtor into bankruptcy proceedings by filing a petition alleging proper cause. Certain groups, such as farmers and nonbusiness corporations, are exempt from

4. If a debtor repays 70 percent of the debts under a debt consolidation plan (Chapter 13 of the 1978 act), the six-year wait does not apply.

involuntary bankruptcy.[5] Any natural person or any business or corporation (besides the exceptions mentioned above) owing $5,000 or more can be petitioned into involuntary bankruptcy by creditors. When there are three or more creditors whose unsecured claims total $5,000 or more, they can commence an involuntary petition. When there are fewer than twelve creditors, only one need sign the petition, and any creditor who has an unsecured claim totaling $5,000 or more can sign. No creditor holding a secured claim, no relative of the debtor, and no other biased creditor can be counted in determining the number of creditors required to sign the petition. As long as the debtor is generally "not paying such debtor's debts as such debts become due,"[6] involuntary bankruptcy can be initiated.

BANKRUPTCY PROCEDURES

Order for Relief

The U.S. Code specifies that a voluntary bankruptcy case is commenced when an eligible debtor files a petition under the relevant chapter. The filing constitutes the *order for relief* in the case. In all involuntary bankruptcy cases, the debtor is entitled to a trial and has the right to challenge the proceedings. At the conclusion of involuntary bankruptcy proceedings, the judge makes a determination. A debtor who is adjudicated bankrupt by the court is then required to complete the same schedules as a debtor in voluntary proceedings. (The contents of the schedules were discussed in the section on voluntary bankruptcy.)

NAMING A RECEIVER Once a debtor has been adjudicated a bankrupt, the debtor's property becomes subject to the jurisdiction of the bankruptcy court. From this point forward, the proceedings in voluntary and involuntary bankruptcy are the same. The court notifies

each creditor of the date by which all the claims are to be filed, and the court calls the creditors' first meeting with the debtor. This meeting must be called within a reasonable time after the order for relief. Under the Bankruptcy Act of 1978, after the petition for bankruptcy has been filed, the court appoints an interim trustee, who is chosen from a panel of private trustees.

A *receiver* is a temporary officer who is designated to take care of the debtor's property until a trustee in bankruptcy is elected by the creditors at their first meeting. If the court appoints a receiver, the creditors must post a bond to cover any possible loss the debtor may sustain to the property or business as a result of the receiver's actions and in case the debtor is not judged bankrupt. In addition, the receiver is required to post a bond to insure honest performance.

THE CREDITORS' FIRST MEETING The first meeting of creditors is called by the court. Assuming a bankrupt has some assets, the creditors elect a *trustee in bankruptcy*, who then takes title of all nonexempt property (real and personal) owned by the bankrupt at the time the petition was filed. The trustee, who is required to post a bond, has a duty to take over the nonexempt assets of the debtor and to sell these assets and distribute the proceeds to the creditors. The property to which the trustee takes title includes the following:

1. All property owned by the bankrupt on the date the petition was filed.
2. All property inherited by the bankrupt within 180 days after the filing of the petition.

Any other property received by the bankrupt after a petition has been filed is not subject to these bankruptcy proceedings. Likewise, any personal property purchased by an innocent third party from the bankrupt after the filing of the petition and before the trustee or receiver takes possession of the property will be upheld as a valid transfer to that third person. A debtor's property can also include contract rights, tort claims, and leases. Finally, property owned by the bankrupt at the time the petition was filed can include property transferred to credi-

---

5. A *farmer* is anyone tilling the soil, raising poultry or livestock and their products, or operating a dairy who expects to derive 80 percent of his or her income from farm work.
6. Bankruptcy Reform Act of 1978 Sec. 303(h)(1).

tors during the 90 days prior to filing of the petition.[7]

The bankrupt is required to attend the first meeting of creditors. Under the 1978 Act the bankruptcy judge may not attend this first meeting. An unexcused absence from this meeting constitutes a waiver of the debtor's discharge in bankruptcy. Typically, the debtor is anxious to have his or her obligations discharged, so it is to the bankrupt's advantage to appear at the meeting. During this meeting, the creditors and the referee can question and examine the debtor concerning the location of the debtor's property and any matters that are relevant to the right of a debtor to have his or her obligations discharged.

MATTERS RAISED AT THE FIRST MEETING OF CREDITORS

At the first meeting of the creditors, essential matters affecting the rights of the creditors are raised. Creditors must file their claims for payment against the bankrupt within a reasonable period, and in some cases creditors can file an objection to the discharge of the debts owed them.

After the proceedings of the first meeting, creditors file, in a formal written statement, *provable claims* that are deemed allowable unless objected to by an interested party. The principles of law involved in determining what are provable claims and what are valid objections to a bankrupt's discharged debts will be discussed in the sections that follow.

The first creditors' meeting is extremely important. Of equal importance, perhaps, are the schedules filed by the bankrupt that list all creditors and the addresses and amounts owed to each. Creditors who are not listed or who do not learn of the proceedings in time to file claims will not have their claims discharged. In such cases, the bankrupt remains liable for the debts. The bankrupt has the burden of proof to establish that nonlisted creditors actually had knowledge that the proceedings were occurring. In rare cases, the courts will permit the bankrupt to amend or correct errors in the schedule, but this is at the discretion of the court. A bankrupt should not rely on the possibility of amendment. Unless it can be shown that unlisted creditors received actual notice and ample time to protect their rights, the debts will not be discharged. This is illustrated in the next case.

---

7. The Bankruptcy Reform Act of 1978 makes several changes in the trustee's power to avoid prebankruptcy transactions. The so-called strong arm clause enables the trustee to set aside unperfected security interests and transfers that would be invalid against the levying creditor under state law. The new act, unlike the old one, gives the trustee the status of a bona fide purchaser with respect to the transfer of real property at the time the case begins. The new act also allows the trustee to recover payments on old unsecured, or partially secured, debt upon proving that: (1) the payment or transfer was made within 90 days of the filing of the petition, (2) the transfer occurred when the debtor was insolvent, and (3) the effect of the transfer was to give preference to the creditor.

BACKGROUND AND FACTS *Moureau defaulted on a lease to Lease-amatic, and Leaseamatic obtained a judgment for the total amount due. Subsequently, Moureau filed a voluntary petition in bankruptcy but failed to inform the court of his indebtedness to Leaseamatic. At the time the petition was filed, Leaseamatic had repeatedly made formal demands for payment. Nevertheless, Moureau did not disclose the leased equipment, the indebtedness, or the identity of Leaseamatic to the bankruptcy judge. The judge ultimately granted Moureau's application for discharge in bankruptcy. Moureau then attempted to use this discharge to prevet Leaseamatic from recovering against him. Lease-amatic's position was that its debt was nondischargeable because it was never notified of the bankruptcy proceedings, and its indebtedness was never made part of the proceedings.*

MOUREAU v. LEASEAMATIC

United States Court of Appeals, Fifth Circuit, 1976.
542 F.2d 251.

The district court agreed with Leaseamatic that the debt was nondischargeable and awarded Leaseamatic a judgment including interest, attorney's fees, and costs against Moureau. Moureau appealed to the higher court, challenging the order and the judgment in favor of Leaseamatic.

TJOFLAT, Circuit Judge.

* * *

The basic facts are not in dispute. * * * On March 4, 1974, Moureau's voluntary petition in bankruptcy was filed. * * * Though at the time the petition was filed formal demand under the lease had repeatedly been made on him, Moureau did not disclose the leased equipment or the indebtedness, [or] the identity of Leaseamatic. * * * On April 25, 1974, the judge granted Moureau's application for discharge * * *.

On July 25, 1974, Leaseamatic moved the bankruptcy court to revoke the discharge. Leaseamatic alleged, *inter alia*, that Moureau had deliberately attempted to foreclose its right to present its claim in bankruptcy and that, by the time it received actual notice of the proceedings and discharge, so little time remained as to preclude its effective participation as a creditor in the estate of the bankrupt. Moureau resisted the motion, asserting that Leaseamatic received actual notice of the proceedings in sufficient time for proof and allowance of its claim within the meaning of Section 17(a) of the Bankruptcy Act, 11 U.S.C. § 35 (1970), which provides:

"A discharge in bankruptcy shall release a bankrupt from all his provable debts, whether allowable in full or in part, except such as * * * (3) have not been duly scheduled in time for proof and allowance, with the name of the creditor if known to the bankrupt, unless such creditor had notice or actual knowledge of the proceedings in bankruptcy * * *."

Following an evidentiary hearing, the bankruptcy judge, relying on the Supreme Court's decision in *Birkett v. Columbia Bank*, granted the motion, declared Moureau's debt to Leaseamatic non-dischargeable and gave it judgment in the total amount of $9,171.82. The district court affirmed, and this appeal followed.

We are inclined to the view that the *Birkett* decision controls the present case. In *Birkett* the bankrupt failed to schedule a note which he knew was due and payable to the Columbia Bank. He was subsequently discharged. Two months later the bank received its first notice of the bankruptcy proceedings. There was still enough time for the Bank to prove its claim and to move to revoke the discharge; yet the Court said:

> Actual knowledge of the proceedings contemplated by the section is *a knowledge in time to avail a creditor of the benefits of the law—in time to give him an equal opportunity with other creditors—not a knowledge that may come so late as to deprive him of participation in the administration of the affairs of the estate or to deprive him of dividends (section 65). The provisions of the law relied upon by plaintiff in error are for the benefit of creditors, not of the debtor.* That the law should give a creditor remedies against the estate of a bankrupt, notwithstanding the neglect or default of the bankrupt, is natural. The law would be, indeed, defective without them. *It*

would also be defective if it permitted the bankrupt to experiment with it—to so manage and use its provisions as to conceal his estate, deceive or keep his creditors in ignorance of his proceeding without penalty to him. It is easy to see what results such looseness would permit—what preference could be accomplished and covered by it. (emphasis added).

In view of these considerations it has long been held that the debtor must take great care in the scheduling of creditors. His failure to do so will make the unscheduled debt non-dischargeable unless it is clear that the creditor had actual notice in ample time fully to protect his rights. *See e. g., id.; In re Computer Utilization, Inc.,* 508 F.2d 673 (5th Cir. 1975). These cases make it clear that a debtor may not take lightly his obligation to schedule all his creditors, and a court will not read the actual notice exception to the scheduling requirement so broadly that the rights of unlisted creditors are compromised.

Turning to the present case, we find that, as in *Birkett,* notice of the discharge was provided two months after the fact. Furthermore, we cannot ignore Moureau's neglect to list the Leaseamatic debt in any of his schedules—despite its repeated demands for payment * * *. While these facts do not establish fraudulent intent, they do indicate Moureau's complete disregard for the obligations imposed by the statute. Under these circumstances, to hold that the Leaseamatic debt was discharged would be to allow Moureau to "keep his creditors in ignorance of his proceeding without penalty to him." *Birkett, supra.* We therefore hold that the debt was not discharged.

Leaseamatic's judgment was upheld, and Moureau had to pay the debt with interest as well as costs and attorney's fees. **JUDGMENT AND REMEDY**

DEBTS AND CLAIMS

Provable Claims

Certain claims are considered provable under law and entitle the creditor to share in the estate of the bankrupt. The following are the most common types of provable claims:

1. *Fixed liabilities evidenced by a judgment.* A judgment held by any creditor that is delivered against a bankrupt any time before discharge occurs can qualify as a provable claim. As with any provable claim, it must be filed by the creditor within a reasonable time after the date of the first creditors' meeting.

2. *Instruments in writing, such as commercial paper.* These documents create an absolute obligation even though they are not immediately due. When making a claim based on a written instrument, the document itself must accompany the claim unless it has been lost or stolen, in which case a sworn affidavit to that effect will be sufficient.

3. *Any claim that is liquidated or that is for a sum certain.* Although tort claims (intentional torts) are not usually provable, they can be if they have been reduced to judgment prior to the petition in bankruptcy. An exception exists for negligence suits instituted prior to and pending at the time the petition in bankruptcy is filed. For example, in an action for an intentional tort such as assault and battery, brought by A against B, if the case has not proceeded to judgment when B files a petition in bankruptcy, A cannot file a claim or share in B's bankrupt estate. Keep in mind, however, that A's claim is not discharged. Should B acquire any new assets after the date of filing the petition of bankruptcy (except for an inheritance occurring within a

reasonable period), then A can enforce a judgment against any of the new assets that B acquires. If, however, A sues B for negligence, and the suit is instituted prior to B's petition for bankruptcy and is still pending, then A can file a "timely" provable claim and share in the estate of the bankrupt.[8] Note that if A fails to file the negligence suit prior to the time B files a petition in bankruptcy, the claim is not provable and therefore not dischargeable in the bankruptcy proceedings.

4. *Workmen's compensation awards.* These claims are permitted against a bankrupt's estate even though they are not liquidated and the sum is not ascertained.

5. *Breach of contract action on an unexpired lease.* A landlord can file a claim for all past due rents and for any damages caused by the bankrupt's breach of the lease agreement. However, the landlord's claim is limited to the amount of rent due up to the date of surrender plus future rent of up to one year on the remaining lease period.

6. *Open accounts and enforceable contracts.* Provable claims can also be based on open accounts or on any enforceable contract, express or implied, including a claim for anticipatory breach of an executory contract.

7. *Costs incurred in lawsuits.* Claims for costs incurred in lawsuits (started either by the bankrupt or against him or her) are provable claims if the suit is filed by the time the petition for bankruptcy is filed.

A provable claim is entitled to share in the bankrupt's estate. Payment made by the trustee to a creditor for his or her share in the estate is called a **dividend**. Not all claims are provable, and not all provable claims are also dischargeable. Nonprovable claims or nondischargeable claims are not considered within the jurisdiction of the bankruptcy court, and these debts can therefore continue after the bankruptcy proceedings have concluded.

Once a provable claim is filed, it can be challenged by the bankrupt or by the trustee. If

---

8. The 1978 act refers only to timely claims. See Section 501.

the challenge to the claim is upheld by the court, the creditor does not share in the bankrupt's estate. If the challenge is denied by the court, then the claim is considered a provable claim, and is paid out of whatever assets in the estate are available. If there are insufficient assets in the estate to satisfy the entire amount of any provable claims allowed, the unpaid portions of such claims will be discharged.

Provable Claims That Are Not Discharged

Certain claims can be provable but not dischargeable because of either the nature of the claim or some conduct of the debtor/bankrupt that occurs before the proceedings begin or while they are in process. Some common provable claims that will not be discharged are:

1. Claims for back taxes occurring within three years prior to the bankruptcy.
2. Claims based on fraud, embezzlement, misappropriation, or defalcation against the bankrupt acting in a fiduciary capacity.
3. Alimony and child support.
4. Intentional tort claims.
5. Claims against property or money obtained by the bankrupt under false pretenses or by fraudulent representations.

Denying a Bankrupt a Discharge

The preceding section reviewed the typical kinds of provable claims that are not discharged because of the nature of the claim. In other instances, provable claims are not discharged in bankruptcy because the bankrupt has committed some act that serves to deny him or her the privilege of a discharge. A discharge in bankruptcy releases the bankrupt from all provable debts whether or not the person's assets are sufficient to satisfy the claims of the creditors. When a discharge is denied, the assets that exist are still distributed among the creditors, but the debtor remains liable for the unpaid portions of all claims. An application for discharge for all scheduled debts will be granted in bankruptcy unless:

1. A bankrupt waives the right to discharge.
2. A bankrupt fails to appear at the first creditors' meeting.
3. A bankrupt fails to participate in proceedings involved with objections raised to the application for discharge.

The bankruptcy act also provides that a discharge will be denied to any bankrupt who has:

1. Committed a bankruptcy crime punishable by imprisonment—that is, a crime specified by the bankruptcy act, such as taking a false oath or concealing assets.
2. Destroyed, mutilated, falsified, concealed, or failed to keep accounting records from which his or her financial and business condition can be ascertained, unless unusual circumstances justify such acts or failure.
3. Obtained money or property on credit by making a materially false written statement with respect to his or her financial position.[9]
4. Within a twelve-month period immediately

prior to the filing of the petition in bankruptcy, transferred, removed, destroyed, or concealed any property owned with the intent to defraud creditors.
5. Refused to obey any lawful order or to answer any material question of the court occurring in the course of any proceeding under the act.

Any of the objections to permitting a bankrupt a discharge that are mentioned in the bankruptcy act or that are deemed to be waivers can be made by the creditors or by the trustee in bankruptcy when authorized by the creditors. When there is reasonable cause to believe that the bankrupt has performed any of the acts that will bar discharge, the burden shifts to the bankrupt to prove that he or she has not done so. Additionally, as the next case illustrates, a debt cannot be discharged if it is fraudulent.

_____

9. The false statement prevents discharge of the *particular debt* arising out of the transaction in which the fraud occurred.

BACKGROUND AND FACTS *The Houtmans, the appellant bankrupts, had a $55,000 judgment rendered against them in state court. They subsequently declared bankruptcy and listed the judgment creditors on the proper schedules as unsecured creditors. The Manns (the judgment creditors) objected to the discharge of the debt owed them. The bankruptcy judge ultimately declared that the debt was nondischargeable because of fraud. The case was then appealed to the U.S. District Court, which affirmed the nondischargeability of the debt. Then the Houtmans attempted to have the Circuit Court set aside the findings and conclusions of the two lower courts. They asked the court to find the debt dischargeable because they claimed that state court standards of "knowledge" of the statements that constituted fraud differed from bankruptcy court standards.*

IN RE HOUTMAN
United States Court of Appeals,
Ninth Circuit, 1978.
568 F.2d 651.

HUFSTEDLER and SNEED, Circuit Judges, and RENFREW, District Judge.
* * *

III. *The Meaning of Scienter Under Section 17(a)(2).*

There remains but one possible error of law by the bankruptcy judge which we should consider. That is whether the type of fraud on which the judgment debt rests is that described in section 17(a)(2) of the Bankruptcy Act. We have adopted a five-part test for determining when a debt is nondischargeable under this provision. That test is:

> "(1) the debtor made the representations;
> (2) *That at the time he knew they were false;*
> (3) That he made them with the intention and purpose
> of deceiving the creditor;
> (4) that the creditor relied on such representations;
> (5) that the creditor sustained the alleged loss and damage as the proximate result of the representations having been made." [Emphasis added.]
> *In re Taylor*, 514 F.2d 1370, 1370 (9th Cir. 1975).

The bankruptcy judge looked at the jury instructions given in the state court trial as indicative of the specific facts found by the jury. These instructions put all five issues specified in the *Taylor* test before the jury. However, the instructions given in the state case allowed the jury to convict if the representation was "known to be false or recklessly made without knowing whether it is true or false." The bankruptcy judge accepted this as an appropriate formulation of the knowledge element, and, as indicated above, accepted "the contention that the obligation is nondischargeable because of the finding of fraud." Therefore, we must decide whether the second element of the *Taylor* test can be satisfied only by actual knowledge or whether reckless disregard for the truth also satisfies this requirement. * * * [The court cites another case.] There the court actually applied a reckless disregard standard. An illiterate bankrupt was accused of making a false representation on the basis of a statement prepared by his wife which he signed. The court found that there was no evidence of recklessness in Sweet's reliance on his wife. The clear implication is that a showing of recklessness would have been sufficient to make the debt nondischargeable even if the bankrupt had had no actual knowledge of the falsity.

The Supreme Court decision in *Morimura, Arai & Company v. Taback*, provides further support for our holding. In that case the Court held that "reckless indifference to the actual facts, without examining the available source of knowledge which lay at hand, and with no reasonable ground to believe that it was in fact correct" was sufficient to establish the knowledge element under a provision of the Bankruptcy Act then current which completely barred a discharge of all debts if the bankrupt had made a materially false statement in order to obtain property on credit. Since the 1960 amendment to the Bankruptcy Act, use of a materially false statement in order to obtain credit is no longer a complete bar to discharge for individual bankrupts, but is included in § 17(a)(2) along with false representations as one of the grounds which will render an individual debt nondischargeable. The close statutory relationship of these two concepts now suggests that a similar definition of knowledge would be appropriate. Further, a strict reading of the knowledge element of the false representation exception would have the incongruous effect of imposing a stricter standard for exempting a single debt from discharge than formerly was required to completely bar discharge of all debts.

In addition, the scienter requirement [defendant knowing or having guilty knowledge] in the tort of misrepresentation generally has been interpreted to include recklessness. *See* W. Prosser, Torts, § 701 (4th Ed. 1971). The reasons for inclusion, *viz.* the difficulty in distinguishing knowledge from reckless disregard, and to discourage the shunning of truth to preserve the defense of no scienter, are applicable with equal force in the bankruptcy context.

* * *

We recognize that exceptions to dischargeability are to be strictly construed. *Gleason v. Thaw*, 236 U.S. 558, 35 S.Ct. 287, 59 L.Ed. 717 (1915). A canon of interpretation adjuring strictness is not, however, a justification for abandoning good sense. It makes good sense to hold that either actual knowledge of the falsity of a statement, or reckless disregard for its truth, satisfies the scienter requirement for nondischargeability of a debt under § 17(a)(2). We so hold.

The court of appeals affirmed the lower court's holdings. The debt had to be paid by the Houtmans. It was nondischargeable.   **JUDGMENT AND REMEDY**

PRIORITY OF PAYMENT OF CLAIMS   Creditors are either *secured* or *unsecured.* (The rights of secured creditors were discussed in Chapter 30.) Basically, a secured creditor has a security interest in collateral that secures the debt. The secured creditor can enforce the security interest either by accepting the property in full satisfaction of the debt or by foreclosing on the collateral and using the proceeds to pay off the debt. If the secured creditor chooses to foreclose, and if the total value of the property is less than the amount of the debt, the secured creditor becomes an unsecured creditor for the difference. If the proceeds from the collateral exceed the value of the debt, the secured creditor is paid in full, and any excess is used by the trustee to satisfy the claims of unsecured creditors.

Bankruptcy law establishes an order or priority for classes of debts owed to *unsecured creditors*, and they are paid in the order of their priority. Each class of debt must be fully paid before the next class is entitled to any of the proceeds—if there are sufficient funds to pay the entire class. If not, the proceeds are distributed *proportionately* to each creditor in a class, and all classes lower in priority on the list receive nothing. The order of priority among classes of unsecured creditors is as follows:

1.   All costs and expenses for preserving and administering the bankrupt's estate, including such items as court costs and receiver, trustee, and attorney fees and costs incurred by the receiver or trustee during the administration of the bankrupt's estate, such as rental fees and appraisal fees.

2.   Unsecured claims in an involuntary case arising in the ordinary course of the debtor's business after commencement of the case but before the appointment of a trustee or the issue of an order for relief.

3.   Claims of wage earners up to an amount of $2,000 per claimant, provided that the wages were earned within 90 days of the filing of the petition in bankruptcy. Any claims in excess of $2,000 are treated as the "claims of general creditors" (listed as number 7 below). Wage earners include workers, clerks, servants, and salespersons who receive commissions.

4.   Unsecured claims for contributions to employee benefit plans arising under services rendered within 180 days before filing the petition and limited to the number of employees covered by the plan multiplied by $2,000.

5.   Unsecured claims for money deposited (up to $900) with the bankrupt before the filing of the petition in connection with purchase, lease or rental of property or services that were not delivered or provided.

6.   Taxes legally due and owing within three years of the petition in bankruptcy.

7.   Claims of general creditors. These debts have the lowest priority and are paid on a pro

rata basis it and only if funds remain after all the debts having priority are paid in full. Any remaining balance is returned to the bankrupt debtor.

DEFINING THE BANKRUPT'S ESTATE

Exempt Property

Property is exempt from the bankrupt's estate if it falls within an exemption provided under either the laws of the state of the bankrupt's domicile or the laws of the United States. The bankruptcy act provides, however, that property that is ordinarily exempt will be disallowed if the bankrupt has transferred or concealed it and it is recovered ultimately by the trustee for the estate. Moreover, the debtor will lose an exemption for any property he or she has failed to claim on the schedules filed with the petition for bankruptcy.

Bankruptcy laws exempt certain property of the bankrupt debtor from satisfying claims of creditors because otherwise a bankrupt would be left with no resources and would become a burden on society.

Beginning in October 1979, the following property became protected by federal law:

1. Up to $7,500 in equity in a home and burial plot.
2. Interest in a motor vehicle up to $1,200.
3. Interest, up to $200 for any single item, in household goods and furnishings, clothes, appliances, books, animals, crops, and musical instruments.
4. Interest in jewelry up to $500.
5. Any other property worth up to $400 plus any unused part of the $7,500 homestead exemption.
6. Interest in implements, books, or tools of trade up to $750.
7. Professionally prescribed health aids.
8. Social security and veterans' benefits.
9. Unemployment compensation.
10. Alimony and child support.
11. Disability benefits.

12. Payments from pension, profit-sharing, and annuity plans.

If a husband and a wife file bankruptcy jointly, the dollar limits listed above double.

Voidable Transfers

A trustee in bankruptcy takes title to all of the bankrupt's nonexempt property. In the usual course of the proceedings, this property is sold by the trustee, and the proceeds are distributed to creditors whose claims are proven and allowed by the court. The trustee must evaluate all of the bankrupt's property to be sure that no property has been transferred to a third person. The trustee must also determine if any of the creditors have attached liens on the property, thereby reducing the overall amount of property available to be sold. With this in mind, the law permits the trustee to bring a lawsuit to set aside such transfers or avoid (cancel) certain liens. There are various categories of so-called voidable transfers.

VOIDABLE RIGHTS   A trustee steps into the shoes of the debtor. Thus, any reason that a debtor can use to obtain return of his or her property can be used by the trustee as well. These grounds include fraud, duress, incapacity, and mutual mistake. For example, B sells his boat to F. F gives B a check, knowing that there are insufficient funds in the bank account to cover the check. F has committed fraud. B has the right to avoid that transfer and recover the boat from F. Once B has been adjudicated a bankrupt, the trustee can exercise the same right to recover the boat from F.

PREFERENCE   A debtor should not be permitted to transfer property or make a payment that favors one creditor over all others. One of the objectives of bankruptcy proceedings is to distribute a bankrupt's assets equitably among *all* the unsecured creditors. Thus, the trustee is allowed to recover payments made to one creditor in preference to another.

To constitute a preference that can be recovered, an insolvent debtor must have transferred property: for an antecedent debt; within 90 days of the filing of the petition in bankruptcy; and the transfer must give the creditor receiving it a greater share in the bankrupt's estate than other creditors in the same class. Thus, not all transfers and conveyances are preferences. For example, if a creditor receives payment in the ordinary course of business or receives payment for a fully secured transaction the payment cannot be recovered by the trustee in bankruptcy. If a preferred creditor has sold the property to an innocent third party, the property cannot be recovered from the party, but under certain circumstances the creditor can be held accountable for the value of the property.

Mortgages or pledges are often subject to attack as recoverable preferences. A mortgage obtained within 90 days prior to filing a petition for bankruptcy for the purpose of securing a *previous debt* that was incurred 45 days or more before recording can be avoided. (The 90-day period runs from the date the mortgage is recorded, not the date it is signed.) However, a mortgage given to secure a new debt will not be set aside because the transfer has been made for *present* consideration, not prior indebtedness.

LIEN ON DEBTOR'S PROPERTY Any legal, equitable, or contract lien obtained on the debtor's property *while the debtor was insolvent* and *obtained within 90 days* of the petition in bankruptcy can be set aside. Statutory liens cannot be avoided by the trustee if they became effective after the debtor became insolvent (even though they were unenforceable on the date of filing bankruptcy) if such liens are against a bona fide purchaser or if they are for rent. Thus, a trustee will often be unable to avoid an artisan's or mechanic's lien but can avoid any judicial lien (one obtained by court judgment) or judicial sale obtained or conducted within 90 days of the filing of the petition of bankruptcy if such lien or sale occurred while the debtor was insolvent.

FRAUDULENT CONVEYANCE Any fraudulent transfer of property by the debtor is void *ab initio* (from the beginning) and can be set aside by the trustee. Under federal law, a fraudulent conveyance is any transfer made within one year of filing the petition in bankruptcy that is intended (either actually or implicitly) to hinder, delay, or defraud creditors. Under state bankruptcy laws, the period can be longer—usually two to five years within the date of filing the petition. Fraudulent intent can also be implied when a transfer is made for less than full and adequate consideration, when the transfer results in insolvency, or when the conveyance is made to a relative or friend without fair consideration. Solvency or insolvency at the time the transfer is made is a significant factor, but it does not by itself, determine whether fraudulent intent exists.

NON-LIQUIDATION PROCEEDINGS

Some provisions of the bankruptcy act provide for court-approved plans that give the debtor additional time to pay the debts or give the creditors a role to play in assisting the debtor to manage his or her business and financial affairs. These so-called debtor relief provisions are designed to assist debtors in resolving their financial difficulties and to provide creditors with some amount of payment.

Individual Repayment Plans

Debtors who are insolvent and recognize that they may become bankrupt can devise plans for settling the claims of unsecured creditors or extending the time of payment to them. The bankrupt must file a petition for confirmation of this plan with the bankruptcy court. The unsecured creditors can either accept or reject it. If they all accept the plan in writing, and if the debtor is in a position to deposit an amount of money sufficient to cover the plan, the court will approve the arrangement, assuming that it is offered in good faith. If not all the creditors accept the plan, the court can still confirm it as long as a majority of the creditors have accepted it and the court is satisfied that the plan is offered in good faith and is reasonable. In addition, the debtor cannot have committed any act that would bar discharge in bankruptcy.

Corporate Reorganization

When a debtor corporation realizes that it will become insolvent or will be unable to pay its debts as they mature, it can petition for reorganization. Such a petition can be filed by the debtor. If the debtor does not file a plan within 120 days after the order for relief, or if the plan is not accepted within 180 days after the order for relief, a plan can be filed by any indenture trustee, creditor, or creditors' committee. The petition must be filed before the corporation is adjudicated bankrupt.

The debtor corporation normally is permitted to continue business operations under court supervision until some plan of reorganization is approved by two-thirds of the creditors. If the corporation is insolvent at the time a petition for reorganization is filed, a majority of the share-holders must also approve of the plan. The court will approve of any plan agreeable to the creditors (and to the corporate shareholders if the corporation is insolvent) as long as the plan is made in good faith. If agreement cannot be reached, then the court will supervise liquidation proceedings for the corporation as in any other situation of bankruptcy.

Adjustments of Debts of an Individual with a Regular Income

Any insolvent debtor who is a wage earner (earns wages, salary, or commission) can formulate and file a plan with the court that provides the debtor with additional time to pay off unsecured creditors. The debtor's plan must provide that future earnings will be subject to the supervision and control of the trustee until these debts are satisfied. A plan made in good faith and acceptable to the unsecured creditors will be confirmed by the court. Should the wage earner ultimately be unable to pay the debts, liquidation is still an available alternative.

MATTER OF WHITE BIRCH PARK, INC.
United States District Court of Michigan, 1978.
443 F.Supp. 1342.

BACKGROUND AND FACTS *Bus White and Doris Marie White filed a joint petition for bankruptcy in July 1976. The debtors listed their occupations as trailer court manager and office worker, respectively. Bus White claimed a weekly salary of $387.60, and Doris Marie White claimed a weekly salary of $170. These salaries were paid by White Birch Park, a corporation principally owned by Bus White that was involved in a Chapter XI reorganization under bankruptcy law. The debtors submitted $200 per week of their combined salaries to the supervision and control of the bankruptcy court as part of their Chapter XIII wage earner plan (under the Bankruptcy Act of 1978, called "adjustment of debts of an individual with regular income").*

A creditor challenged the propriety of the debtors' claim to wage earner status, contending that the debtors were drawing income from the corporation undergoing a Chapter XI reorganization in order to pay their individual debts by claiming wage earner status and participating in what was then called a wage earner plan. The creditor insisted that the debtors were not legitimate wage earners of White Birch Park Corporation but were merely asserting such status in order to obtain money from the corporation to pay individual debts to the detriment of the corporate creditors.

The bankruptcy court did not agree with the creditor's analysis, and the creditor appealed to the federal district court.

HARVEY, Judge.

* * *

[T]he debtors in the instant case claim to be employees of a corporation [White Birch Park] which is principally owned by them, which is currently proceeding in Bankruptcy Court under a Chapter XI arrangement [called reorganization under the 1978 bankruptcy act] and which is maintained and controlled by them as debtors in possession. The debtors, prior to the filing of the Chapter XI petition, did not draw a salary from White Birch Park. But, upon the institution of Chapter XI proceedings, debtor Bus White claimed a salary of $387.60 per week or an annual salary of $20,155.20 from the Chapter XI estate for his services to White Birch Park. Debtor Doris Marie White, upon the institution of Chapter XI proceedings, claimed a salary of $170.00 per week or an annual salary of $8,840.00 from the Chapter XI estate for her services to White Birch Park. The debtors also claimed $490.00 per month or an annual sum of $5,880.00 additional income from other real property interests.

The total joint income of $34,875.20 is the sum represented to the Bankruptcy Court as the annual gross wages available to the Chapter XIII estate. The sum is a marked increase over the joint gross income of $14,000.00 which the debtor claimed to have earned in the prior calendar year. The increased income of the debtors upon the institution of the Chapter XI proceedings is suspect for a number of reasons. The debtors had ceased construction of new mobile home pads in December, 1974; thus, the number of units to operate and maintain remained constant. As no mobile home pads were constructed, the debtors ceased selling new mobile homes and lost a source of revenue from their commissions on such sales; thus the debtors were more dependent upon White Birch Park for their income. Further, debtor Bus White ceased operating and maintaining his excavating business; thus the debtors lost another source of income and became even more dependent upon White Birch Park for their income.

It is apparent that the debtors began to receive a sizeable income from White Birch Park, a business in serious financial trouble, at a point in time when the debtors themselves were contributing fewer personal services to it and becoming more and more dependent upon it for their livelihood. It is entirely possible that the debtors, as debtors in possession and in control of the Chapter XI estate, could pay out salaries to themselves and not render any services to White Birch Park.

Upon these facts and circumstances, it is the opinion of this Court that the debtors are not wage earners within the definition of the Bankruptcy Act, as the source of their income is not derived from wages, salary or commissions but rather it is derived from and is a return of their invested capital in White Birch Park. It is contrary to the purpose of a * * * Wage Earner Plan to permit a debtor to seek relief and rehabilitation when the debtor is not dependent upon his or her own individual labor or effort as a source of income. See *Hallenbeck v. Penn Mutual*

Life Insurance Co., supra; In Re Reed, supra. Further, it is contrary to the purpose of the Bankruptcy Act to permit a debtor, especially a debtor in possession of a Chapter XI estate, to draw from and to deplete the assets of the Chapter XI estate to satisfy personal debts and to make feasible his or her own wage earner plan. * * *

JUDGMENT AND REMEDY

The decision of the bankruptcy court was reversed. Bus and Doris White were not "wage earners" and were not entitled to draw upon the assets of their corporation, White Birch Park (also in bankruptcy under Chapter XI), to satisfy their own personal debts or to file their own wage earner plan.

COMMENTS

Arrangements, real property arrangements, and reorganizations are now consolidated into a single chapter, Chapter XI, entitled "Reorganization." Under the 1978 act, wage earner plans are now called "adjustment of debts of an individual with regular income." The new act recategorizes proceedings under the bankruptcy act; however, the underlying concepts and principles have not changed.

QUESTIONS AND CASE PROBLEMS

1. In order to sell certain shares of stock, Schaefer entered into a sales contract with Smith. Smith paid $5,000 for the stock, and Schaefer promised to repurchase the stock if, after three years from the date of sale, Smith had not realized an agreed-upon rate of return. One year before this three-year period ended, Schaefer was adjudicated bankrupt, and at the time of the bankruptcy, he had no assets whatsoever. Smith, not wanting Schaefer's obligation to him to be discharged by the bankruptcy, petitioned the court to find his contract with Schaefer not "allowable" since it was a contingent claim. In other words, Smith argued that, since it was uncertain whether Schaefer would be bound under the repurchase agreement, Smith's claim should be deemed not allowable and therefore not dischargeable by the bankruptcy. Section 57d of the bankruptcy act provides that contingent claims shall not be "allowed" if the court determines (1) that they are not capable of liquidation or (2) that such liquidation would unduly delay the administration of the estate. In light of the above facts, should Smith's claim be deemed "allowable"? What will be the consequences to Smith and to Schaefer if the claim is allowable? If it is not allow-

able? [Schaefer v. Smith, 469 F.2d. 1256 (10th Cir. 1972)]

2. In February 1970, a husband and a wife were divorced, and a divorce decree was entered by a court. As part of the decree, the wife was awarded "as and for alimony and maintenance, the furniture used by the parties during their marriage and the 1967 Chevrolet two-door sedan * * * [the husband] is ordered to deliver to [the wife] a good and clear title to the 1967 Chevrolet [free from] any debts or obligations that may be against furniture or automobile." Several months later the husband was adjudicated bankrupt. The husband thereafter refused to make the payments on the furniture or the automobile, claiming that they were discharged in bankruptcy. The wife was therefore forced to make the payments and sought to recover the amounts she had paid from the husband. Is the husband obligated to pay? [Collins v. Smith, 26 Ohio Misc. 231, 55 O.O. 370, 270 N.E.2d. 377 (1971)]

3. a. Edward Kline, owner of a small service station, went out of business on December 4, 1967. On that same date, Kline, who owed Clark Oil Company approximately $2,000, transferred the petroleum products remaining at his station (approximately $1,800 worth) to Clark Oil. Would a bankruptcy court deem this a preferential transfer?

b. Assume that Kline did not transfer the gas to Clark Oil but instead retained ownership and signed a security agreement that gave Clark Oil a security interest in the gas. Clark Oil then filed the security agreement, giving it a perfected security interest in Kline's gas. Is this a voidable transfer? [Mann v. Clark Oil and Refining Corp., 425 F.2d. 736 (8th Cir. 1970)]

4. On June 8, 1964, Losner filed a voluntary petition in bankruptcy and was adjudicated bankrupt on the same date. Losner admitted that, about six months previously, he withdrew about $1,000 from his checking account and carried the money on his person, in cash. Subsequently, he used the money to purchase cashier's checks with which to pay several of his creditors. The payments to his creditors were made more than four months before filing the petition in bankruptcy. Losner also admitted that he withdrew the money and carried it on him because he knew he was about to go bankrupt and did not want all of the money attached through the bankruptcy action. Can any of Losner's creditors who were not paid with the $1,000 object to Losner's actions? [Losner v. Union Bank, 374 F.2d. 111 (9th Cir. 1967)]

5. Kentile Floors, Inc. and Winham's Floor Coverings had a long-standing business relationship through which Kentile sold Winham floor covering goods. Kentile's sales were on a credit basis, and Winham made timely payments throughout the first several years of their business relationship. Beginning in 1965, however, Winham's payments became sporadic, and for the next year Winham had difficulty making payments. In January 1966, Kentile insisted that Winham supply it with a financial statement before Kentile would make further sales to Winham on credit. Before it received any financial statements from Winham, however, Kentile extended approximately $96,000 more in credit to Winham. The financial statements that Kentile finally received from Winham were false. Moreover, Winham's accounts payable on the financial statement were less than the $96,000 that it owed Kentile. Nevertheless, Kentile continued to extend credit to Winham. Shortly thereafter, Winham went into bankruptcy. Kentile objected to being discharged in the bankruptcy because of the false financial statement. What will be the result? [Kentile Floors, Inc. v. Winham, 440 F.2d. 1128 (9th Cir. 1971)]

6. Charles Edward & Associates, a partnership, was adjudged bankrupt in an involuntary proceeding. During the proceeding, it was revealed that the partners failed to keep records of their business transactions so that the bankruptcy court's administration of the bankrupt partnership was severely hindered. Should the partnership be granted a discharge in bankruptcy? Should the individuals who make up the partnership be granted a discharge in bankruptcy in their individual capacities? [Charles Edward & Associates v. England, 301 F.2d. 572 (9th Cir. 1962)]

7. On June 1, 1961, Mann conveyed his home to his three children. At the time, his home was worth $15,000 and was his only asset. At the same time, Mann's debt exceeded $30,000. Five months later, Mann filed a voluntary petition in bankruptcy. Will Mann's creditors be able to levy against the home? Would the answer be different if Mann's liabilities on June 1 had been only $5,000? [Robinson v. Mann, 339 F.2d. 547 (5th Cir. 1964)]

8. The XYZ Corporation went into bankruptcy with $100,000 in assets. Ten of its employees each claimed $5,000 in wages due. N claimed a judgment of $4,000 for injuries received because of XYZ's negligence. XYZ has two classes of stockholders—preferred and common. The preferred stockholders held $60,000 in preferred stock, and the common stockholders owned $500,000 worth of common stock. Costs of administering the bankrupt's estate totaled $20,000. Who will receive what from XYZ's estate?

9. Okamoto had liabilities of about $10,000, assets worth less than $1,000, and a total of nineteen creditors, each of which was unsecured. Okamoto owed Hornblower and Weeks more than $6,000. Of the remaining eighteen creditors, eight were owed amounts less than $65 each, and none was owed more than $150. Hornblower and Weeks filed a petition to have Okamoto declared bankrupt. Okamoto responded that, since he had more than twelve creditors, the petition could not be filed by only one creditor. Will Hornblower and Weeks be successful if it argues that the other creditors should not be counted since the debt owed to it exceeds the total of all other debts owed by Okamoto? [In re Okamoto, 491 F.2d. 496 (9th Cir. 1974)]

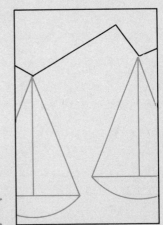

UNIT VI
Agency and Employment

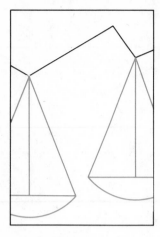

33

Agency and Employment
Creation and Termination of Agency Relationships

In **agency** relationships between two parties, one of the parties, called the agent, agrees to represent or act for the other, called the principal, subject to the principal's right to control the agent's conduct in matters entrusted to the agent. More formally, the Restatement, Agency, Second, defines *agency* as "the fiduciary relation which results from the manifestation of consent by one person to another that the other shall act in his behalf and subject to his control, and consent by the other so to act."[1] In general, the law of agency is based on the Latin maxim *qui facit per alium, facit per se* ("one acting by another is acting for himself"). Agency involves a person acting for and in the place of a principal.

THE NATURE OF AGENCY

Using agents, one individual can conduct multiple business operations simultaneously in various locations. Real estate brokers and corporate officers who serve in a representative capacity for principals are familiar examples of agents.

Agency law is essential to the existence and operation of a corporate entity because only through its agents can a corporation function and enter into contracts. Partnership law is a special application of agency law—that is, mutual agency. Partnership and corporation law are discussed in Unit VII.

---

1. Restatement, Agency, Second, Section 1(1).

Purpose

An agency relationship can be created for any *legal* purpose. One created for an illegal purpose or contrary to public policy is unenforceable. If X (as principal) contracts with Y (as agent) to sell illegal narcotics, the agency relationship is unenforceable because it is a felony and therefore against public policy to sell narcotics illegally. It is also illegal for medical doctors and other licensed professionals to contract unlicensed agents to perform professional actions.

Rights and Duties

The representative relationship created by agency law establishes certain *rights* and *duties*, which are similar to those that arise from the law of torts and contracts. Thus, when one individual acts on behalf of another, the legal impact can be felt in various ways.

DUTIES OF THE AGENT TO THE PRINCIPAL Agents must act with reasonable care and exercise skill and knowledge typical to the place where they are to perform. In addition, they must exercise any particular skills that they possess. Failure to meet these standards allows a principal to bring an action against the agent in either tort or contract.

Generally, agents must act exclusively for the benefit of their principals in all matters within the scope of the agency. This duty obliges agents not to use unfairly any information or property that they have acquired by virtue of the agency.

DUTIES OF THE PRINCIPAL TO THE AGENT The principal must pay the agent the agreed-upon compensation for the services that he or she has performed. The principal must also provide a suitable place for the agent to work and must use reasonable care to prevent injury to the agent.

KINDS OF AGENTS

The first step in analyzing an agency relationship is to determine whether or not such a relationship exists. Traditional analysis in the law of agency distinguishes three types of relationships: (1) principal and agent, (2) master and servant, and (3) employer and independent contractor.

Principal-Agent

In a principal-agent relationship, the parties have agreed that the agent will act *on behalf of and instead of* the principal in negotiating and transacting business with third persons. This relationship will affect the principal's rights and duties. Thus, an agent is empowered to perform legal acts that are binding on the principal. For example, an agent can bind a principal in a contract with a third person. An agent has *derivative authority* to use a degree of independent discretion in carrying out the principal's business.[2] For example, Earl is hired as a booking agent for a rock group—Harry and the Rockets. As the group's agent, Earl can negotiate and sign contracts for the rock group to appear at concerts. The contracts will be binding and thus legally enforceable against the group.

Master-Servant

Today's law defines *servant* as an agent employed by a master to perform services; the servant's physical conduct is controlled or is subject to the right to control by the master. Thus, a servant is now a species of agent. However, the term *master-servant relationship* is anachronistic. Accountants, truck drivers, and business managers are not referred to as servants. For that matter, employers are not called masters. The more current terminology to describe a master-servant relationship is that of employer-employee.

The term *employee* held no significance to common law rules of agency. However, with the industrial revolution and recent social legislation, the term has come into prominence. An employee is an agent (other than an independent contractor) who has an appointment or

---

2. But an agent is not an independent contractor, described below.

contract for hire. In essence, only those agents or servants who work for pay can qualify as employees.

For example, Dana owns a dress shop. She employs Sandy, Sheila, and Sue as sales people. Dana is the employer/master; the women are the employees/servants. The key feature of the employer/employee relationship is that the employer controls, or at least has the right to control, the employee in the performance of the physical tasks involved in the employment. The employees do not have *independent* business discretion. The dress shop sales people can sell dresses, but they cannot sell the dress shop.

Independent Contractor

Independent contractors are not agents because they cannot make contracts with third persons for their employers, and they are not employees (servants) because their employers have no control over the details of their physical performance. The following factors are relevant in determining the status of independent contractors:

1. What is the extent of control that the employer can exercise over the details of the work?
2. Is the employed person engaged in an occupation or business distinct from that of the employer?

3. Is the work usually done under the employer's direction, or is it done by a specialist without supervision?
4. Does the employer supply the tools at the place of work?
5. How long is the person employed?
6. What is the method of payment—by time or at the completion of the job?
7. What is the degree of skill required by the person employed?

Building contractors and subcontractors are independent contractors, and a property owner does not control the acts of either of these professionals. Truck drivers who own their equipment and hire out on an ad hoc basis are independent contractors; however, truck drivers who drive company trucks on a regular basis are usually employees (servants). A collection agency is another example of an independent contractor.

A TAX QUESTION The federal government requires employers to deduct taxes from the wages of employees but not from the payments to independent contractors. In the following case, an insurance company paid taxes to the Internal Revenue Service but later attempted to characterize the particular employees as "independent contractors" and sought to recover the taxes it had paid to the government.

M.F.A. MUTUAL INS. Co. v. UNITED STATES

United States District Court, Western District of Missouri, Central District, 1970. 314 F.Supp. 590.

BACKGROUND AND FACTS *The plaintiff, an insurance company, hired "agents" to sell its insurance policies and to service its clients. The company had a special program for new agents, called an "Agent Financing Agreement," whereby the company guaranteed a monthly salary to each agent in lieu of a commission. The agreement was to last for one year, during which the agents were specially supervised, were fully compensated for expenses incurred, and received instruction and training. The Agent Financing Agreement specifically characterized these agents as "independent contractors."*

From 1962 to 1965, the company paid the employment taxes that were required under the Social Security Act for all of its employees, including its "financed agents." Later, the company questioned whether it was responsible for paying employment taxes and argued that it should be able to recover the tax money that it had paid to the Internal Revenue Service on the ground that the financed agents were not employees within the meaning of the Internal Revenue Code definition, but rather were independent contractors. Therefore, the company had no responsibility to pay federal employment taxes for them. The IRS refused to return the money that the company had paid, claiming that the financed agents were in fact employees and that the company was responsible under the Social Security Act for paying employment taxes for them.

OLIVER, Judge.
* * *

MEMORANDUM OPINION

The parties have stipulated [formally agreed] that the questions of law and fact presented are whether plaintiff's financed agents are:

(a) Employees for purposes of the Federal Insurance Contributions Act * * * and the Federal Unemployment Tax Act, * * * ; and

(b) If they are employees * * * then whether they are remunerated solely by way of commission * * *.

There is no real dispute about the principles of law to be applied. The parties agree that common law principles [of agency] are applicable.

[T]here is no shorthand formula or magic phrase that can be applied to find the answer, but all of the incidents of the relationship must be assessed and weighed with no one factor being decisive. What is important is that the total factual context is assessed in the light of the pertinent common-law agency principles.
* * *

[The court proceeded to evaluate the factual circumstances involved between the company and the financed agents.]

(a) Plaintiff could and did exercise by way of concrete suggestions and required procedures, a considerable amount of control over the details of the work of its financed agents, particularly as evidenced by its demand for daily reports concerning the full time activities of its financed agents and by the presence of its absolute power of termination.

(b) The financed agents were engaged in the business of selling plaintiff's insurance policies. Such an occupation or business cannot fairly be said to be distinct from that of plaintiff's business; indeed, the sale of insurance policies is but one phase of plaintiff's business.

(c) The work usually done by the financed agents could, in one sense of the word, be done by a "specialist without supervision." But such a view would ignore the fact that the work of a financed agent could just as well be done by a salaried employee under the direction of the employer. A financed agent, * * *, was in a process of training which required that much of his work be done under the direction and supervision of plaintiff's district sales manager.

(d) No specialized skill other than of a salesman was required to become a financed agent. An insurance salesman must, of course, as must any other salesman, learn something about the product he is selling. But the occupation of an insurance salesman does not involve the sort of specialized skill required * * *

(e) Plaintiff supplied many forms and business "tools," such as forms of policies, and the like, to its financed agents. A financed agent's place of work, as any insurance salesman, was among members of the public wherever he may catch them. The circumstance of whether an insurance salesman's desk, typewriter, filing cabinet, adding machine, and the like, are located in his home or in an office furnished by the insurance company * * * is not a particularly weighty factor in the determination of the relationship question because it is obvious that sales of insurance policies infrequently occur at either place.

(f) Plaintiff's financed agents were employed for a year but plaintiff retained complete control over the employment tenure of a financed agent; he could be discharged at any time for any or no reason at all.

(g) A financed agent was, in effect, given a guaranteed draw and the amount of money received was not related to the job performed. The money was paid to obtain the full time services of the financed agent; indeed, the system of reporting was designed to make certain that plaintiff received what it paid for. As long as plaintiff did not elect to terminate, the financed agent was entitled to be paid the amount specified in his agreement. The fact that plaintiff's right to terminate was in no way restricted to how its financed agents performed a specific and particular job (in the sense of selling a particular insurance policy to a particular prospect) is totally inconsistent with the basic concept of an independent contractor relationship.

(h) The sales work performed by the financed agents was a regular part of the general insurance business of the plaintiff. Such work could as well be performed by a salaried employee as by a financed agent.

(i) The contract recited a relationship of independent contractor, but, under all the cases, this single factor is not controlling.

(j) Plaintiff, of course, is in the insurance business, a part of which includes the sale of its policies.

* * * [W]e conclude that plaintiff's financed agents are employed to perform sales services in plaintiff's affairs under circumstances in which the performance of those services is subject to plaintiff's right of control. None of the separate factors are fully supportive of plaintiff's contention that its financed agents are independent contractors. All the facts and circumstances, when considered as a whole, make it clear that plaintiff has retained the requisite right, on a full time basis, to control the details and means by which its financed agents are to conduct their sales activity.

JUDGMENT AND REMEDY   *The court concluded that the company's financed agents were employees within the meaning of the statutes and regulations involved. Thus, the company's claim for a refund was rejected. A judgment was entered in favor of the defendant on its counterclaim in accordance with the stipulation of the parties.*

COMMENTS   *In this case, labeling by the parties did not determine that an agency relationship existed. In fact, labeling by the parties is never decisive.*

Scope of Employment

The liability of an employer for the acts of an employee is limited to those acts performed within the scope of employment. The term *scope of employment* is not susceptible to any precise definition; nevertheless, two factors are usually present before it will be found in any given situation. First, the activity of the employee must be motivated at least in part by an intent to serve the employer's purpose rather than his or her own. Second, the manner, place, and time in which the act is performed must not vary substantially from that authorized or from that which is normal. In addition, the employer must have the right to control the activities of the employee. Taken together, an employer is liable only for those torts that would not have occurred except for the fact of the employer-employee relationship.

A very familiar agency relationship occurs in the real estate business. A real estate broker can hire several real estate salespersons who obtain listings, find buyers or sellers, and handle the actual sales transactions. In some states, only the broker obtains a license. Hence, the broker is identified as a principal, and the sales personnel are agents for the broker. In such a relationship, the broker is responsible for the acts of the sales agents.

ACTUAL VERSUS APPARENT AUTHORITY

The following case reviews the concepts of actual authority and apparent authority. A principal will be bound by all acts of a general agent whenever they come within the course and scope of the business entrusted to the agent. However, in some cases, the principal cannot be bound by the agent's acts, especially if they are beyond the ordinary and usual course of the business.

BACKGROUND AND FACTS *The tenants of an apartment complex sued the apartment owners to recover money fraudulently borrowed by the apartment managers in the name of the owners. The tenants argued that the apartment owners as principals were liable for the wrongful acts of the managers, their agents.*

The apartment managers were husband and wife and had managed the apartment complex for nearly four years. Prior to taking this position, they had lived in another state, where the husband had operated a bar and spent considerable time gambling. When they took the position at the apartment complex, the husband still owed about $18,000 in gambling debts and was under considerable pressure to pay them off.

The apartment managers were responsible for renting the apartments, collecting the rents, making deposits, and providing necessary maintenance. They had no authority to write checks on the account where the rent money was deposited.

Soon after the managers arrived, the husband devised a plan that permitted some tenants to pay a year's rent in advance, thereby receiving a small discount on their monthly payments. Rather than depositing that year's rent in the rent account, the husband deposited only one month's rent and kept the remainder, which he used to pay his gambling debts. As the advance rental payment plan spread among the

GUNN v. SCHAEFFER
Court of Civil Appeals of Texas, El Paso, 1978.
567 S.W.2d 30.

tenants, the managers had more and more advance money to use to pay the monthly rent of those tenants whose money they had pocketed in earlier months.

Since it was so easy to obtain advance rental money, and since their need for more funds increased to meet the monthly rental payments of those who had already paid in advance, the managers devised a plan to sell short-term savings certificates to the tenants. These certificates were issued in the name of the apartment complex and bore the name of the manager as well as a fictitious name signed by the manager as treasurer. The certificates provided for interest in excess of that paid by any bank or savings association.

The apartment managers were eventually indicted and convicted for felony violations. Meanwhile, the tenants held worthless savings certificates for which they had paid a great deal of money. Therefore, they sued the owners of the apartment complex, alleging both conspiracy and responsibility based on a principal-agent relationship.

The trial court found that no conspiracy existed. It also concluded that there was no reasonable basis for holding the apartment owners liable for the actions of their managers.

OSBORN, Justice.
* * *

On the issue of agency, the affidavit and deposition show that * * * [the apartment manager] had no actual authority to issue the certificates of indebtedness. Nevertheless, the issue as to the apparent authority must also be considered. We conclude that one employed to manage an apartment complex, with actual authority to collect and deposit rent, does not have any apparent authority to borrow money from the tenants and issue certificates of indebtedness in the name of the apartment complex. In *Bolin v. Pacific Finance Corporation*, 278 S.W.2d 879 (Tex.Civ.App.—Amarillo 1944, no writ), the Court stated the controlling rules with regard to determining an agent's authority as follows:

"When an apparent authority is claimed to arise from representations or conduct, the acts and statements of the principal must be looked to for the requisite foundation and not those of the agent; the former alone can give rise to authority of this character; the latter are never in themselves sufficient for that purpose. The principal must have affirmatively held the agent out as possessing sufficient authority to embrace the particular act in question, or else have voluntarily and in due awareness, actual or constructive, of the agent's assumption of power permitted him to act as if he had the requisite authority. The powers which the agent pretends to have, or assumes to exercise, are inoperative as a basis for ostensible authority when the principal is not affected by knowledge of them and does not validate them by acquiescence or assent; and no mere combination of circumstances which may, without the principal's participation, mislead third persons, however reasonably, into a false inference of authority affords a sufficient predicate for apparent authority * * *."

"One who deals with an agent of a corporation must exercise proper diligence to ascertain the authority with which the agent has been clothed and cannot rely on the acts and declarations of the agent alone."

With regard to the specific authority of an agent to borrow money in the name of the principal, the rule is set forth in *Guaranty Bank & Trust Co. v. Beaumont Cadillac Co.*, 218 S.W. 638 (Tex.Civ.App.—Beaumont 1920, writ dism'd), as follows:

" 'Power to borrow money is not to be inferred without clear evidence of such grant. Such authority must be expressly conferred or necessarily implied from the authority granted, and will not be inferred from a mere general authority, unless the character of the business or the duties of the agent are of such a nature that he is bound to borrow money * * * in order to carry out his instructions or the duties of his office.' "

It is pointed out in the comment under Restatement of Agency 2d, Sec. 73, that a manager has no power to borrow money in connection with the operation of the business or to issue negotiable instruments in the name of the principal, unless the business conducted is one involving the borrowing of money or the issuing of negotiable instruments such as banking and other financial business. Under the heading of "Authorization to Borrow," Section 74 says:

"Unless otherwise agreed, an agent is not authorized to borrow unless such borrowing is usually incident to the performance of acts which he is authorized to perform for the principal." The comment under this section notes that *the authority to borrow is not inferred unless it is practically indispensable to the continuance of the principal's business* or to prevent a very considerable loss to the principal and where it is impossible to communicate with the principal. [Emphasis added.] There is no suggestion in the record in this case that the principals were in the business of borrowing money, nor is there a suggestion that it was indispensable to the continuance of their business or to prevent a loss that made the borrowing by the manager necessary in this case.

The appellate court concluded that the owners were not liable to the tenants of the apartment complex for the money that they had paid for the worthless certificates from the apartment house managers. The appellate court affirmed the trial court's judgment.

JUDGMENT AND REMEDY

FORMATION OF THE AGENCY RELATIONSHIP

The following discussions will emphasize the usual form that an agency relationship takes. The contractual aspects of the formation and termination of agency are similar for employer-employee and independent contractor relationships. The distinctions among agent, employee, and independent contractor will become clearer in the chapter on liability.

The agency relationship is a *consensual* relationship; that is, it comes about by consent and agreement between the parties. The agreement need not be in writing, and consideration is not required.[3] The same basic rights and duties are involved whether it is a gratuitous agency or an agency for hire.

Generally, there are no formalities required to create an agency. The agency relationship can arise by acts of the parties in one of four ways: (1) by agreement, (2) by ratification, (3) by estoppel, or (4) by operation of law.

---

3. There are two main exceptions to oral agency agreements:

1. In many states, the Statute of Frauds requires that, whenever agency authority empowers the agent to enter into

Agency by Agreement

As stated earlier, agency is a consensual relationship. It must be based on some *affirmative* indication between the principal and the agent that the agent agrees to act for the principal and the principal agrees to have the agent so act.

An agency agreement can take the form of an express written contract. For example, P enters into a sales agreement with A, a realtor, to sell P's house. An agency relationship exists between P and A for the sale of the house. Express agreements can be oral. For example, P asks B, a gardener, to care for her lawn on a regular basis. B agrees. An agency relationship exists between P and B for the lawn care.

An agency agreement can be implied from conduct. For example, a hotel allows Jack Andrews to park cars, but Andrews has no employment contract there. He can infer from the hotel's conduct that he has authority to act as a valet. It can be implied that he is an agent for the hotel. His purpose is to provide valet parking services for hotel guests.

Agency by Ratification

When the principal's consent is given after an agent has acted, an agency can be created by ratification, in which case it has the same effect as if the consent were given before the action. For example, Alfred James, an employee of Anne Paul, contracts to purchase a tract of land in Paul's name without her authority to do so. Paul learns of James's actions and decides that the land is of great value and that she will go through with the sale. When a principal accepts the benefits or in some way affirms the conduct of one purporting to act on his behalf, an agency

relationship is created. In this case, Paul has *ratified* James's acts, thereby creating an agency relationship between them. (Note that the creation of the agency "relates" to the time of James's unauthorized act.)

Agency by Estoppel

When a principal causes a third person to believe that another person is his or her agent, and the third person deals with the supposed agent, the principal is "estopped to deny" the agency relationship. In these situations, the principal's actions create the appearance of "apparent authority," which does not in fact exist. For example: M accompanies P to call on a customer, S, the proprietor of the General Store. M has done sales work but is not employed by P at this time. P boasts to S that he wishes he had three more assistants "just like M." S has reason to believe from P's statements that M is an agent for P. S then places seed orders with M. If P does not correct the impression that M is an agent, P will be bound to fill the orders just as if M were really P's agent. P's representation to S created the "apparent authority" in M to carry out the usual and necessary sales agent transactions for which P will be bound. Note, however, that this authority generally cannot be established by acts or declarations of the purported agent.

The theory of apparent authority does not extend to all acts under all circumstances. The third person must prove that he or she *reasonably* believed that the agent had authority. Facts and circumstances must show that an ordinary, prudent person who is familiar with business practice and custom would be justified in concluding that the agent had authority. The law also is designed to protect third parties not privy to the original agreement.

Agency by Operation of Law

In some cases, the courts have found it desirable to find an agency relationship in the absence of a formal agreement. This often occurs in family relationships. For example, suppose a wife purchases certain basic necessities and charges

---

a contract that the Statute of Frauds requires to be in writing, then the agent's authority from the principal must likewise be in writing. This is known as the "Equal Dignity Rule." It occurs most frequently in contracts for the sale of an interest in land or contracts that cannot be performed within one year. The Statute of Frauds is discussed in Chapter 11.

2. A power of attorney is written authority conferred to an agent. It is conferred in a formal writing, usually acknowledged by a notary public, whose seal is attached to the formal document. A power of attorney can be general, giving the agent broad powers, or it can grant the agent only restricted authority.

them to her husband's account. If the husband has not supplied these goods, the courts will often rule that the husband is liable for their payment because of a social policy of promoting the general welfare of the wife. Also, the husband has a legal duty to supply necessities for his wife and children. Sometimes agency by operation of law is created, giving an agent emergency power to act under unusual circumstances that are not covered by the agreement when failure to act would cause a principal substantial loss. If the agent is unable to contact the principal, the courts will often grant this emergency power.

LEGAL CAPACITY

A principal must have legal capacity to enter contracts. The logic is simple. A person who cannot legally enter contracts directly should not be allowed to do it indirectly through an agent. An agent derives the authority to enter contracts from the principal, and a contract made by an agent is legally viewed as a contract of the principal. It is immaterial whether the agent personally has the legal capacity to make that contract. Thus, a minor can be an agent but cannot be a principal appointing an agent.[4] In the latter case, any resulting contracts will be voidable by the minor principal, but not by the adult third party.

Conversely, any person can be an agent, regardless of whether he or she has the capacity to contract. For example, newspaper delivery boys and girls can enroll newspaper subscriptions. Even a person who is legally incompetent can be appointed an agent if that person is capable of performing the required functions.

AGENCY POWER COUPLED WITH AN INTEREST

An agency *coupled with an interest* is a relationship created for the benefit of the agent (or

third person). The agent actually acquires a beneficial interest in the subject matter of the agency. Under these circumstances it is not equitable to permit a principal to terminate at will. Hence, this type of agency is "irrevocable."

For example, Sarah Roberts (principal) owns Blackacre. She needs some immediate cash, so she enters into an agreement with John Hartwell that Hartwell will lend her $10,000, and she will grant Hartwell a one-half interest in Blackacre and "the exclusive right to sell" it for $25,000 if she fails to repay the $10,000. The loan is to be repaid out of the sales proceeds. Hartwell's power to sell Blackacre is coupled with a beneficial interest of one-half ownership in Blackacre created at the time of the loan for the purpose of supporting it and securing its repayment. Hartwell's agency power is irrevocable.

An agency coupled with an interest should not be confused with situations in which the agent merely derives proceeds or profits from the sale of the subject matter. For example, an agent who merely receives a commission from the sale of real property does not have a beneficial interest in the property itself. Likewise, an attorney whose fee is a percentage of the recovery (a contingency fee) merely has an interest in the proceeds. These agency relationships are revocable by the principal, subject to any express contractual arrangements that the principal has with the agent.

Since, in an agency coupled with an interest, the interest is not created for the benefit of the principal, it is not really an agency power in the usual sense. Therefore, any attempt by the principal to revoke an agency normally has no legal force or effect. Finally, an agency coupled with an interest is not terminated by the death of either the principal or the agent.

TERMINATION OF AN AGENCY

Agency law is similar to contract law, and termination of agency occurs similarly to the termination of a contract—by act of the parties or by operation of law. Once the relationship

---

4. Exceptions have been granted by some courts to allow a minor to appoint an agent for the limited purpose of contracting for the minor's necessities of life. Casey v. Kastel, 237 N.Y. 305, 142 N.E. 671 (1924).

between the principal and the agent has ended, the agent no longer has the right to bind the principal. However, third persons also need to be notified that the agency has been revoked.

Termination by Act of the Parties

LAPSE OF TIME An agency agreement may specify the time period during which the agency relationship will exist. The agency simply ends when that time expires. For example, A signs an agreement of agency with P "beginning January 1, 1980, and ending December 31, 1985." The agency is automatically terminated on December 31, 1985. Of course, the parties can agree to continue the relationship, in which case the same terms will apply.

If no definite time is stated, then the agency continues for a reasonable time and can be terminated at will by either party. A "reasonable time" depends upon the circumstances and the nature of the agency relationship. For example, P asks A to sell P's car. After two years, if A has not sold P's car and there has been no communication between P and A, it is safe to assume that the agency relationship has terminated. A no longer has the authority to sell P's car.

PURPOSE ACHIEVED An agent can be employed to accomplish a particular objective such as the purchase of stock for a cattle rancher. The agency automatically ends upon the completion of the assignment—that is, after the cattle have been purchased.

If more than one agent is employed to accomplish the same purpose, such as the sale of real estate, the first agent to complete the sale terminates the agency relationship for all the others.

OCCURRENCE OF A SPECIFIC EVENT An agency can be created to terminate upon the happening of a certain event. For example, P

appoints A to handle her business affairs while she is away. When P returns, the agency automatically terminates.

Sometimes an aspect of the agent's authority terminates on the occurrence of a particular event. For example, P, a banker, permits A, the credit manager, to grant a credit line of $1,000 to certain depositors who maintain $1,000 in a savings account. If any customer's savings account falls below $1,000, A can no longer continue making the credit line available to that customer. But A's right to extend credit to the other customers maintaining the minimum balance will continue.

MUTUAL AGREEMENT Recall from basic contract law that parties can cancel (rescind) a contract by mutually agreeing to terminate the contractual relationship. The same result occurs in agency law regardless of whether the agency agreement is in writing or whether it is for a specific duration. For example, P no longer wishes A to be his agent, and A does not want to work for P any more. Either party can communicate to the other the intent to terminate the relationship. Such communication effectively relieves each of the rights, duties, and powers inherent in the relationship.

The agent's act is said to be a renunciation of authority. The principal's act is a revocation of authority.

TERMINATION BY ONE PARTY As a general rule, either party can terminate the agency relationship; but although both parties may have the *power* to terminate, they may not each possess the *right*. Wrongful termination can subject the canceling party to a suit for damages.

For example, A has a one-year employment contract with P for $12,000. P can discharge A before the contract period expires (P has the *power* to breach the contract); however, P will be liable to A for money damages because P has no *right* to breach the contract.

The next case involves the premature termination of an agency relationship.

BACKGROUND AND FACTS   *The plaintiff, D. H. McDonald, was hired as a real estate agent to find a buyer for Robert Davis's grocery store. The contract gave McDonald an exclusive right for six months to close a sale. One month after the contract had been signed, the store was leased, and a month later, the seller wrote to McDonald to take it off the market. McDonald sued for wrongful termination of an agency and for breach of contract.*

McDONALD v. DAVIS
Court of Civil Appeals of
Texas, 1965.
389 S.W.2d 494.

BELL, Chief Justice.
* * *

The contract which was dated November 17, 1962, reads as follows:

"To McDonald Realty

For and in consideration of your agreement to list and for your efforts to find a purchaser, I/we Douglas Robinson and Robert D. Davis, the undersigned, hereby authorize and give you, above named, the exclusive right, privilege, and agency for a period of 6 Mos. from this date, and thereafter until written notice of termination of this agreement is given, to sell at a price of $11,500, or any sum that I/we may accept, the property described as follows, to-wit: A Drive-in Grocery Located 5605 Spencer Hiway, Houston, Texas. Better known as D & D Grocery.

If said property is sold or exchanged during the term of this agreement, or if sold within three (3) months after the expiration of this agreement to any purchaser to whom it may have been submitted by you before the expiration of this agreement, I/we agree to pay you a commission of 10% of the sale price, at Houston, Texas.

I/we agree to furnish title policy and make proper conveyance of this property.

You are hereby authorized to place suitable signs on this property and remove other signs. Accepted:

    McDonald Realty   D. Robinson
                                    Owner
By: D. H. McDonald   Robert D. Davis
                                    Owner"

The principal may of course revoke an agent's authority where not coupled with an interest, but *there is a distinction between his power to revoke and his right to revoke.* [Emphasis added.] He at any time before full performance can revoke the authority of an agent so the agent will lose his authority to bring the principal into legal relations with a third party. However, if he has no right to revoke it, he will be liable for damages suffered by the agent by reason of the wrongful revocation. Where, as here, there is a bilateral contract, the principal has no right to revoke to the prejudice of the agent.

Where a principal breaches the contract, he becomes liable in damages. Where, as here, suit is for breach of a contract granting the agent the exclusive right for a definite period of time to sell property, the damages are for breach of contract and not for the commission promised if the agent sold. He is entitled to recover the reasonable profit he would have made.
* * *

"The loss suffered by the plaintiff is the measure of his damages. That loss is the amount as fixed by the contract which he would have earned but for the wrongful conduct of the defendants in preventing him from earning it. Upon establishing the contract, his readiness and willingness to perform it, and that he was denied opportunity to perform it through its wrongful breach by the defendants, rendering its performance by him impossible, the plaintiff made out his case; and prima facie was entitled as damages to the amount which under the contract he would, presumably, have earned if his rights had been respected. * * * * * *

JUDGMENT AND REMEDY   *Judgment was for the plaintiff (agent). The court awarded damages to McDonald because although the defendant had the power to revoke the agency, he wrongfully used that power by cancelling before the agreed-upon six month period had expired.*

COMMENTS   *Termination does not always give rise to liability for damages. Only wrongful termination incurs liability. If there are facts justifying the termination, such as misconduct, lack of cooperation, or some breach of duty, the breaching party can forfeit all claims of damages.*

Termination by Operation of Law

DEATH OR INSANITY The general rule is that death or insanity of either the principal or the agent automatically and immediately terminates the ordinary agency relationship. Knowledge of the death is not required[5]. Some states, however, have changed this common law by statute. For example, P sends A to the Far East to purchase a rare book. Before A makes the purchase, P dies, A's agent status is terminated at the moment of death, even though A does not know that P had died.

Agent's transactions that occur after the death of the principal are not binding on the principal's estate. Assume A is hired by P to collect a debt from T (a third party). P dies, but A still collects the money from T, not knowing of P's death. T's payment to A is no longer legally sufficient to discharge T's debt to P because A no longer has P's authority to collect the money. If A absconds with the money, T must again pay the debt to P's estate. There are, however, limits to this rule. They are discussed in the section on partnerships in Chapter 34.

UNFORESEEN CIRCUMSTANCES

Impossibility When the subject matter of an agency is destroyed or lost, the agency terminates. For example, P employs A to sell P's house. Prior to any sale, the premises are destroyed by fire. A's authority to sell P's house terminates. When it is impossible for the agent to perform the agency lawfully, because of war, or because of a change in the law, the authority of the agent terminates.

Changed Circumstances When an event occurs that has such an unusual effect on the subject matter of the agency that the agent can reasonably infer that the principal will not want the agent to continue, the agency terminates. P hires A to sell a tract of land for $10,000. Subsequently, A learns that there is oil under the land and that the land is therefore worth $1 million. A's authority to sell the land for $10,000 is terminated.

5. An exception to virtually all agency notice and termination rules occurs in an agency coupled with an interest, which is not automatically terminated by death or incapacity.

Bankruptcy Bankruptcy of the principal (or the agent) usually terminates the agency relationship.[6] Some situations, such as a serious financial loss, might indicate that future contracts should not be made.

Notice Required for Termination

When an agency terminates by operation of law due to death, insanity, or some other unforeseen circumstance, there is no duty to notify third persons.[7] However, if the parties themselves have terminated the agency, it is the principal's duty to inform any third parties who know of the existence of the agency that it has been terminated. Either the principal or another person can give the notice.

An agent's authority continues until the agent receives some notice of termination. No particular *form* of notice is required. The principal can actually notify the agent, or the agent can learn of the termination through some occur-

rence that gives the agent reason to know of the termination. For example, Marshall bids on a shipment of steel, and Smith is hired to arrange transportation of the shipment. When Smith learns that Marshall has lost the bid, Smith's authority to make the transportation arrangement terminates.

Notice to third parties, however, follows the general rule that an agent's *apparent authority* continues until the third person is notified (from any source of information) that authority has been terminated.

The principal is expected to notify directly any third person whom the principal knows has relied upon the agency because that person has dealt with the agent. For third persons who have merely heard about the agency in general but have not dealt with the agent, constructive notice will be sufficient.

If the agent's authority is written, it must be revoked in writing and sent to all persons to whom the agent might have shown the writing that initially established the agency relationship. Sometimes a written authorization (like that granting power of attorney) contains an expiration date. The passage of the expiration date is sufficient notice of termination for third parties.

Death or incapacity of the principal automatically and immediately terminates the agent's apparent authority. Under these circumstances, no notice is required to third parties unless the agent's power is coupled with an interest.

---

6. Insolvency, as distinguished from bankruptcy, will not necessarily terminate the relationship. Most states do not consider the appointment of a receiver grounds for terminating the agency.

7. There is an exception to this rule in banking. UCC Sec. 4-405 provides that the bank as the agent can continue to exercise specific types of authority even after the customer's death or insanity unless it has knowledge of the death or insanity. When it has knowledge of the customer's death, it has authority for ten days after the death to pay checks (but not notes or drafts) drawn by the customer unless the bank receives a stop payment order from someone who has an interest in the account, such as an heir. (This rule does not apply to insanity.)

QUESTIONS AND CASE PROBLEMS

1. Lionberger's Auto Parts leased out automobile utility trailers. Lionberger was a member of Nationwide Trailer Rental System, an association of rental operators. Nationwide's leasing system operated as follows. Each member rented trailers that it owned. Trailers that were rented for a one-way trip were

delivered at the point of destination to other members of Nationwide. The system was reciprocal in that members rented each other's trailers to customers. Uniformity in operation and administrative control was achieved through a system of rules implemented by Nationwide. A uniform lease agreement was used, and division of rental fees between the renter and the owner of one-way trailers was provided for in Nationwide's bylaws. When a trailer owned by Lionberger is rented out by another member of Nationwide, does a principal-agent relationship exist between Lionberger and the other member of Nationwide? Does a bailor-bailee relationship also exist? If so, does the latter relationship have any effect on the agency relationship? [Lionberger v. United States, 371 F.2d 831 (Ct. Cl. 1967)]

2. Miller sold insurance for Massachusetts Mutual Life Insurance Company under a contract that he renewed annually. Miller derived his income almost exclusively from the efforts of agents who worked under him. In connection with his job, Miller borrowed and invested large sums of money to promote sales by his agents. He was free to vary the terms of the contracts he had with them in regard to their rates and commissions. In addition, he could hire and fire them without Massachusetts Mutual's approval. Miller received a commission from Massachusetts Mutual for all the sales that he or his agents made. Is Miller an employee of Massachusetts Mutual or an independent contractor? [Massachusetts Mutual Life Ins. Co. v. Central Penn Nat. Bank, 372 F.Supp. 1027 (E.D. Penn. 1974)]

3. Holiday Inns operates its hotel chain on a franchise basis. Each hotel is owned by a franchisee who is responsible for operating and managing it. Holiday Inns, as franchisor, receives a small percentage of the profits of each franchised hotel. In exchange, each hotel uses the Holiday Inn name, follows certain business practices, and maintains certain standards set by the franchisor. Goynes was the night clerk in the Phenix City, Alabama, Holiday Inn. One evening, he was handed a Gulf Oil credit card by one of the hotel's customers. Noting that the card identification number was one that Gulf Oil had revoked, Goynes retained the card and refused to return it to the customer. The customer wished to sue for conversion. Since Goynes had no money, the customer had to look to one of Goynes's principals. What principal-agent relationship exists between Goynes and any of the other parties discussed above? [Wood v. Holiday Inns, Inc., 369 F.Supp. 82 (M.D. Ala. 1974)]

4. Roy Haven brought a medical malpractice action against his surgeon, Judson Randolph, M.D., and the hospital where the surgery had been performed. Haven claimed that the doctor's negligence caused him to suffer paralysis as a result of minor surgery. Haven also wished to hold the hospital responsible as Randolph's principal. Randolph was not employed by the hospital, and any services that the hospital provided were at Randolph's direction. Would Randolph be deemed an agent of the hospital? [Haven v. Randolph, 342 F.Supp. 538 (D.C.D.C. 1972)]

5. Crittendon took his Chevrolet to a service station operated by Mendenhall and discussed the problem of its faulty wheel bearings with him. During their conversation, Mendenhall stated that he had previously worked at a Chevrolet garage and was familar with the repair of Chevrolets. The service station at which Mendenhall worked was owned by State Oil Company and displayed two signs, each containing only the word *State*. Mendenhall leased the service station from State but received neither a salary nor repair tools from State. Crittendon left his car for Mendenhall to repair. After Mendenhall repaired it, he took it out for a test drive, went off the road, and damaged it extensively. Crittendon wished to establish an agency relationship between State and Mendenhall so he could recover from State. Does Crittendon have any grounds to argue for the existence of a principal-agent relationship? [Crittendon v. State Oil Co., 78 Ill. App.2d 112, 222 N.E.2d 561 (1966)]

6. Robert and Esther Levine purchased two airline tickets through Comet Travel Agency for an overseas flight with British Overseas Airways. Subsequent to the purchase but prior to the flight, the Levines found that they would not be able to make the trip and therefore returned the tickets directly to British Overseas Airways for a refund. Instead of mailing the refund to the Levines, BOA mailed it to Comet Travel Agency. The manager of Comet absconded with the funds, and the Levines tried to recover from BOA, which claimed that it was justified in sending the refund to Comet since Comet was the Levine's authorized agent. What argument would allow the Levines to recover from British Overseas Airways? [Levine v. British Overseas Airways Corp., 66 Misc. 2d 766, 322 N.Y.S.2d 119 (1971)]

7. Pro Golf manufactured and marketed golf equipment both in the U.S. and abroad. In 1961, Robert Wynn became Pro Golf's sales representative in the Far East. Wynn and Pro Golf did not have a formal contract, but letters exchanged between them indicated the type of relationship they had. In a 1970 letter from Pro Golf to Wynn, Pro Golf stated, "You will continue to have the exclusive right to import and promote the sale of golf equipment in the Far East market. However, this is not an irrevocable right but would remain in effect only so long as you did a satisfactory business in this market." Several years later, Pro Golf terminated Wynn's exclusive right, but first it gave Wynn five months' notice of its desire to terminate. Was Pro Golf's termination proper? What if Pro Golf had given Wynn no notice? [First Flight Associates, Inc. v. Professional Golf Co., 527 F.2d 931 (6th Cir. 1975)]

8. On October 11, 1973, John Gray, owner of a 50

percent interest in a government oil and gas lease, assigned 10 percent of the operating rights and working interest to John Tylle in consideration of Tylle's payment of $10,000. The assignment was in writing and stated: "Until further notice assignee hereby appoints and designates assignor as agent and operator of the said lease for the purpose of development and management." A few weeks later, John Gray died unexpectedly. Tylle filed a claim against Gray's estate, seeking to recover the $10,000 he paid Gray. In order for Tylle to be successful, he must show that the agency relationship between him and Gray had been terminated. Will Tylle be successful? [In the matter of the estate of Gray, 37 Colo. App. 47, 541 P.2d. 336 (1975)]

9. Selastomer, Inc., and P.S. & E. Inc. orally agreed in 1965 that P.S. & E. would become the exclusive selling agency for the seal rings and packing seals that Selastomer manufactured. P.S. & E. thereafter hired additional personnel, expended money for tooling, and used its staff to introduce Selastomer's products into the market. As a result, numerous prospective purchasers began to test and consider buying Selastomer's products. Shortly thereafter, Selastomer gave P.S. & E. notice that it intended to sell its products on its own; and three months after giving notice to P.S. & E., it began to invade P.S. & E.'s market. Is Selastomer in breach of the agency agreement? What damages, if any, should Selastomer pay P.S. & E.? [P.S. & E., Inc. v. Selastomer Detroit, Inc., 470 F.2d. 125 (7th Cir. 1972)]

10. In 1970, the Moulton-Niguel Water District hired an independent contractor to construct a water tank for the district. During the construction process, one of the contractor's employees was injured. Those in charge of the water district realized at the time they employed the independent contractor that construction of the water tank was particularly hazardous because of the type of construction and the tank's location. During construction, the contractor negligently failed to take certain precautions to protect its workers. Furthermore, the water district failed to demand that the contractor use certain safety precautions. Therefore, the contractor's employee was injured as a result of the contractor's negligence. Since the contractor was insolvent, the injured employee wants to sue the water district, but first he must prove a principal-agent relationship between himself and the water district. Will he succeed? [Stilson v. Moulton-Niguel Water District, 21 Cal. App. 3d. 928, 98 Cal. Rptr. 914 (1972)]

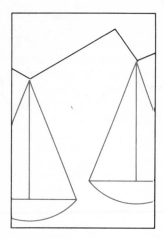

34

Agency and Employment
Duties of Agents and Principals

The principal-agent relationship is fiduciary—one of trust. In it, each party owes the other the duty to act with the utmost good faith. It is presumed that neither party will keep from the other information that has any bearing on their agency relationship. This chapter considers the duties that, in many cases, are simply specific applications of this general fiduciary obligation. It looks first at duties owed by the agent to the principal and then at duties owed by the principal to the agent.

THE AGENT'S DUTY TO THE PRINCIPAL

The duties that an agent owes to a principal are set out in the agency agreement, or they arise by operation of law. They are implied from the agency relationship whether or not the principal is known or disclosed to a third party. Chapter 35 will show the importance of whether or not the principal has been disclosed in its discussion of the liabilities of the agent and the principal.

Duty to Perform

An implied condition in every agency contract is the agent's agreement to use reasonable diligence and skill in performing the work. When an agent fails to perform his or her duties entirely, liability for breach of contract generally will occur. For example, an insurance agent who fails to obtain the insurance coverage requested by a principal is guilty of breach of contract. When an agent performs carelessly or negligently, the agent can be liable in tort as well.

In many situations, an agent who does not act for money (a gratuitous or free agent) can be subject to the same standards of care and duty to perform. A gratuitous agent cannot, however, be liable for breach of contract because there is no contract. A gratuitous agent is subject only to tort liability. However, once the agent has begun, the duty to continue to perform and to take care in rendering the performance is required. For example, Alex Paul's friend, Amy Foster, is a real estate broker. She (the agent) gratuitously offers to sell Paul's (the principal) farm, Black Acre. If she never attempts to sell Black Acre, Paul has no legal cause of action to force her to do so. But assume that Foster finds a buyer. She keeps promising the buyer to come up with the sales contract but fails to do so within a reasonable period of time. The buyer becomes disgruntled and seeks another property, and the sale ultimately falls through. Paul has a cause of action in tort for negligence—that is, failure to use the degree of care reasonably expected of real estate brokers.

Duty to Notify

A basic concept of agency law is that the agent is required to notify the principal of all matters that come to his or her attention concerning the subject matter of the agency. This means that *any facts disclosed to the agent are imputed to the principal.* It is not what the agent actually tells that is important; what the agent *should have told* is crucial. For example, A is P's agent for the purchase of certain property from X. In the course of dealing, A discovers that many years ago, Y obtained mineral rights to remove certain items from the subsurface. Thinking that this is unimportant, A neglects to tell P. The purchase of the land takes place subject to Y's right to mine on it. P does not have recourse against X; that is, P cannot rescind the sale or use the existence of Y's right to remove minerals as a defense to avoid going through with the sale. A had the duty to notify P. The fact that he failed to do so and breached his fiduciary duty cannot be allowed to prejudice the rights of the innocent third party, X. P, however, does have recourse against A.

Duty of Loyalty

An agent has a duty not to compete with his or her principal unless the agent fully discloses the competitive actions and the principal consents. Thus, a salesperson repesenting Avon products cannot sell products of a competing line at the same time unless Avon consents.

Agreements not to compete after termination of employment, if validly drawn, are acceptable. Certain information is deemed so confidential, however, that even termination of the employment relationship will not permit an agent to disclose it. For example, an agent can never disclose trade secrets or confidential information acquired in the course of employment. An agent can, however, use the skills and basic knowledge that were acquired while working for the principal.

Customer lists, like trade secrets, cannot be disclosed by present or former employees because substantial time and money are involved in compiling them. The following case involves customer lists.

BACKGROUND AND FACTS   *The corporation (the plaintiff) was on the brink of bankruptcy. It was involved in freight forwarding, which is a highly competitive business. Salespersons in this kind of business often expend considerable time soliciting prospective clients to ascertain their specialized needs. The corporation hired Robert Agnes as its president. A few years after Agnes became president, the corporation made a profit.*

ABC TRANS, ETC. v. AERONAUTICS FORWARDERS, INC.
Appellate Court of Illinois, 1978.
62 Ill.App.3d 671, 20 Ill.Dec. 160, 379 N.E.2d 1228.

Agnes made increasing salary demands and finally tendered his resignation, but not before copying customer lists and actively recruiting a vice-president, Brownstein, to lease and set up a competing air forwarding company (the defendant).

SULLIVAN, Presiding Justice:

* * *

While acting as an agent or employee of another, one owes the duty of fidelity and loyalty; accordingly, a fiduciary cannot act inconsistently with his agency or trust; *i.e.,* solicit his employer's customers for himself, entice coworkers away from his employer, or appropriate his employer's personal property. However, "[i]t is not necessarily a breach of duty for an agent to form a rival concern and purchase machinery for it while working for his principal, though it would be for an agent to continue to work for his principal after a rival corporation which he also served as agent begins business." Thus, as a means of fostering free enterprise, the employee who gains general skills and knowledge and forms relationships with customers and coworkers during the course of his employment may use such skills, knowledge and relationships to compete with his former employer once the employment is terminated but may not compete while still employed as his employer who, lulled by trust in the employee's fidelity and loyalty, is deprived of the opportunity to compete with that employee. Turning to the question of relief where a betrayal of confidence and trust has been demonstrated, we note that equity will prevent the continuance of such conduct in a proper case and will compel the former employee to turn over the gains to one equitably entitled thereto.

* * *

During January, 1978, plaintiff's facilities, funds and personal property had been used by its employees under the direction of [defendant] Brownstein to pre-stamp Aeronautics's air bills, to furnish office supplies and airline containers to Aeronautics, and to prepare Aeronautics's daily station report forms. Furthermore, Brownstein continued to meet with plaintiff's customers in order to obtain commitments for Aeronautics on the basis that plaintiff was in financial trouble and would suffer a massive employee walkout. He also had meetings with plaintiff's employees to inform them of the nationwide plan to leave work on a certain Friday, and to devastate plaintiff's ability to compete by simply reporting to Aeronautics on the following Monday morning.

Brownstein admitted securing equipment and supplies for Aeronautics while still employed by plaintiff but denied that plaintiff's funds were used for this purpose. He also admitted that he told plaintiff's staff he would be following Agnes; that he expressed the hope that circumstances would then allow him to ask them to join him; and that he had informed plaintiff's clients of its unhealthy financial prognosis and its management by untrustworthy executives while asking them for the opportunity to solicit their business once he had changed jobs.

JUDGMENT AND REMEDY

The appellate court awarded judgment for the plaintiff, reversing the trial court's earlier decision in favor of the defendant. The appellate court found that the defendant had breached the duty of loyalty to the plaintiff corporation and hence was liable for damages. ·

An agent's duty of loyalty does not require concealment of a principal's dishonest acts. For example, if a principal is cheating on contracts, an agent can tell a third party, and the third party can sue the principal for damages.

COMMENTS

CONFLICTS OF INTEREST An agent cannot take a position adverse to its principal. Anything an agent obtains by virtue of the employment relationship belongs to the principal. It is a breach of an agent's fiduciary duty to secretly retain benefits or profits that, by right, belong to the principal. Courts in this case will imply a *constructive trust:* The agent actually holds the money on behalf of the principal, and the principal can recover it in a lawsuit. For example, Andrews, a purchasing agent, gets cash rebates from a customer. If Andrews keeps the rebates, he violates his fiduciary duty to his principal, Metcalf. Upon finding out about the cash rebates, Metcalf can sue Andrews and recover them.

Personal purchases operate the same way. The rules against self-purchase prohibit an agent from taking advantage of the agency relationship to obtain goods or property that the principal wants to purchase. For example, Peterson (the principal) wants to purchase property in the suburbs. Cox, Peterson's agent, learns that a valuable tract of land has just become available. Cox cannot buy the land for herself. Peterson gets the right of first refusal. If Cox purchases the land for her benefit, the courts will impose a constructive trust on the land; that is, the land will be held for and on behalf of the principal despite the fact that the agent attempted to buy it in her own name.

In the following case, a real estate agent was supposedly acting on behalf of a landowner for the sale of a piece of property. The agent was also in the business of buying and holding land for resale. When the agent realized that the land was increasing in value, he decided to purchase the real estate for himself. The landowner agreed to sell the land to the agent for an agreed-upon price. A sales contract was drawn up but never consummated because the landowner later decided to sell the property to a third person. The agent attempted to sue the landowner for selling the property to the third party on the basis that the agent lost certain profits he would otherwise have made on the resale of the property. The trial court decided that the agent had no cause of action.

BACKGROUND AND FACTS *Ramsey, the plaintiff, was a licensed real estate broker and was also in the business of buying and holding land for resale. Gordon, the defendant, was the owner of approximately 181 acres of land. Gordon agreed to sell Ramsey the tract of land for $800 per acre. A contract of sale to convey the property was drawn up; but before the contract was executed, Gordon conveyed the property to a third party for the same price ($800 per acre).*

Meanwhile, Ramsey, acting for himself, began negotiating for the resale of that property to another customer for a price of $1,250 per acre. Naturally, when Ramsey learned that Gordon had conveyed the property to another buyer, he blamed Gordon for his lost profits. Ramsey claimed that he lost over $90,000 in profits on the resale of the property.

RAMSEY v. GORDON
Court of Civil Appeals of Texas, Waco, 1978.
567 S.W.2d 868.

HALL, Justice.
* * *

Ramsey [the plaintiff] testified that he operated two businesses, "Ramsey Realty" and "Ramsey Properties," that both are sole proprietorships owned by him, that under Ramsey Realty he acts as a real estate agent selling others' property for a commission, and that under Ramsey Properties he purchases property for himself. Although Ramsey now claims he was only a purchaser in the transaction with Gordon [the defendant], he testified on the trial that he was both agent and purchaser—that he was "a purchasing agent." Specifically, Ramsey testified again and again that under the contract he was Gordon's agent for the sale of the property. The trial court expressly found that he was Gordon's agent. The court also found that Ramsey knew the property was appreciating in value when the contract was made, and "up until and through January, 1974", that Ramsey failed to disclose that fact to Gordon; that he became personally interested in the property transaction by attempting to purchase the property himself, that the appreciation in value of the property from $800.00 per acre to $1,000.00 per acre was a material fact relating to the sale of the property; and that Ramsey failed to find a purchaser for Gordon for the best price available. Upon these findings the court concluded that Ramsey had breached his agency agreement and duties under the contract, and that the contract was therefore voidable at Gordon's election.

Ramsey does not challenge the finding that the property was increasing in value when the contract was being negotiated and made with Gordon, nor the findings that he knew the value was increasing and failed to disclose that fact to Gordon. Indeed, he may not do so because they are amply supported by the evidence and its inferences. His response to the conclusion that he breached his duties as Gordon's agent is to argue that he was only a purchaser and to cite Gordon's testimony that Gordon believed $800.00 per acre was a fair price when he made the contract. The over-all import of the record is that when it served Ramsey's purposes he would claim that under the contract he was Gordon's agent, but that in fact he used the contract to speculate with the property to his personal advantage without disclosure to Gordon. As we have said, the [trial] court found that Ramsey was Gordon's agent. Ramsey's testimony supports that finding.

Whenever an agent breaches his duty to his principal by becoming personally interested in an agency agreement, the contract is voidable at the election of the principal without full knowledge of all the facts surrounding the agent's interest. [Emphasis added.] * * * [It is a] "settled rule" that "an agent in dealing with a principal on his own account owes it to the principal not only to make no misstatements concerning the subject matter of the transaction, but also to disclose to him fully and completely all material facts known to the agent which might affect the principal; and that unless this duty on the part of the agent has been met, the principal cannot be held to have ratified the transaction."

JUDGMENT AND REMEDY   *The judgment of the trial court was affirmed. Ramsey was denied recovery because an agency relationship existed between Ramsey and Gordon, and Ramsey breached his duties under this relationship.*

Duties Owed by Subagents

If Paul (the principal) authorizes Andy (the agent) to hire subagents, then the subagents have the same duties to Paul as the agent has.

(The principal's authorization is needed for the hiring of subagents, except in emergencies.) Additionally, the agent is responsible to the principal for any subagent's wrongdoing. Of course, the subagents owe Andy the same duties that Andy owes Paul. Thus, an agent can recover from a subagent for the subagent's improper performance.

UNAUTHORIZED SUBAGENTS If an agent hires a subagent without the principal's authority, then the subagent has no legal relationship to the principal. Since the subagent and the principal have no agency relationship to one another, no duties arise between them. A principal will not be liable to third parties for that subagent's acts. However, the agent who hires the subagent without authority will be liable to the principal if the subagent acts wrongfully, and the agent will bear the loss.

Duty to Account

Unless an agent and a principal agree otherwise, the agent has the duty to keep and make available to the principal an account of all property, money, and so on received and paid out on behalf of the principal. The agent has a duty to maintain separate accounts for the principal's funds and for personal funds, and no intermingling of them is allowed. Agents often violate this duty. When a professional, such as an attorney, violates the duty to account, he or she is subject to disciplinary proceedings by the Bar, as well as being liable to the principal.

Rights and Benefits Acquired during Employment

Every business interest (except small gifts) acquired during an employment relationship belongs to the principal, to be held for and on behalf of the principal. From this rule arises the duty of an agent to account to a principal.

An interesting question occurs when an employee invents a product and the employer claims a right to the invention or patent. The rules operate as follows. When an employee is hired to develop patents or inventions, then all rights to such developments belong to the employer, unless there is an agreement to the contrary. But when an employee is hired for other duties and, incidental to the employment, perfects a patent or invention, the property is not necessarily that of the employer. The **shop right doctrine** provides that if a patent or invention is perfected on the employer's time using the employer's materials *and* if it relates to the employer's business, then the employer has a right to it. The employer's right is irrevocable even after the employment relationship ends.

Principal's Right to Indemnification

A principal can be sued by a third party for an agent's negligent conduct, and in certain situations the principal can sue the agent for an equal amount of damages. This is called **indemnification.** The same holds true if the agent violates the principal's instructions. For example, Lewis (the principal) tells his agent, Moore, who is a used car salesman, to make no warranties about the used cars. Moore is anxious to make a sale to Walters, the third party, and makes warranties about the car's engine anyway. Lewis is not absolved from liability to Walters for engine failure, but if Walters sues Lewis, Lewis can then sue Moore for indemnification for violating his instructions.

In the following case, an insurance agent issued a binder policy knowing that the insurance company policy would not normally insure a boat of the type mentioned in the case without first inspecting it. When the boat was destroyed, the company was held liable, and it demanded that the agent (and the agency that hired the agent) indemnify the insurer for its losses.

BACKGROUND AND FACTS *An employee of Buckingham-Wheeler, an independent insurance agency met with a boat owner, DiMicco, to discuss insuring a twenty-foot Chris Craft cruiser. The boat was sixteen years old at the time. After some discussion, the agency's employee advised DiMicco that he was issuing a binder policy on the boat and that*

CRAWFORD v. DiMICCO

District Court of Appeals of Florida, Fourth District, 1968. 216 So.2d 769.

DiMicco could from that moment forward consider the insurance coverage to be in effect. The agency's employee issued the binder policy despite the fact that he knew that the company would not insure a boat having a value of $5,000 or greater or a boat that was over three years old without first inspecting it. A few weeks later, the boat was damaged in a storm, and ultimately, it sank. DiMicco sought damages for the loss of his boat. Fidelity denied that insurance coverage had ever existed. Buckingham-Wheeler admitted issuing the binder, but contended that the coverage had been cancelled prior to the damage to the boat, and that DiMicco had been informed of this by a telephone call from an employee of Buckingham-Wheeler. The jury found that Fidelity was liable to DiMicco and that Fidelity could not recover from Buckingham-Wheeler.

CROSS, Judge.

* * *

[W]e are to determine if an insurance agent binds a contract of insurance which he is not authorized to do, is such agent liable to indemnify the company for its losses arising from the enforcement of the insurance contract so bound.

The facts as alluded to above are simple, and the law is equally so. It has long been well settled that an agent owes to his principal the obligation of high fidelity, and that he may not proceed without or beyond his authority, particularly where he has been forbidden to act and that so proceeding, his actions caused loss to his principal, the agent is fully accountable to the principal therefor.

An elementary factor in the principal-agent relationship is control. As stated in 2d Restatement of Agency, § 14B(f), "An agent acts for and on behalf of his principal and subject to his control. * * * The agent owes a duty of obedience to his principal."

The record in this case reveals that the agency through its employee proceeded without and went beyond its authority * * *.

The record further indicates that the agent's employee was informed on a prior occasion when dealing with insurance being placed on another vessel, that as a matter of course the insurer specifically instructed the agent's employee that a survey is required on vessels that are valued at $5,000 or over or are more than three years old, if the vessel was to be submitted to the insurer for insurance.

Under the facts of the instant case and the settled law applicable thereto, unless and until the principal with full knowledge of all the applicable facts waived the breach of its instructions, ratified or adopted the agent's act as its own, or facts otherwise raising an estoppel against the principal, the agent became and remained liable to the principal for the damages incurred in acting without authority to the disadvantage of its principal. The facts herein reveal no adoption, ratification or estoppel on the part of the principal-insurer.

The * * * agency through its employee, acted precipitatively, unreasonably and without authority. The testimony reveals vividly that the agency's employee admittedly and grievously breached his duty to the insurer by his initial unauthorized act in binding the vessel, and therefore the * * * agent cannot escape the loss or any part thereof and throw such loss upon the principal-insurer.

The court entered judgment in favor of the principal, holding the agency and its agent liable, and the agent had to indemnify the company for the amount of money it had paid out to the boat owner.   **JUDGMENT AND REMEDY**

LIMITS ON INDEMNIFICATION Sometimes it is difficult to distinguish between instructions of the principal that limit an agent's authority and those that are mere advice. For example, Willis (the principal) owns an office supply company; Jones (the agent) is the manager. Willis tells Jones, "Don't order any more supplies this month." Willis goes on vacation. A large order comes in from a local business, and the present inventory is insufficient to meet it. What is Jones to do? In this situation, Jones probably has the inherent power to order more supplies despite Willis' statement. It is unlikely that Jones would be required to indemnify Willis in the event that the local business subsequently cancelled the order.

PRINCIPAL'S REMEDIES FOR AGENT'S VIOLATION OF FIDUCIARY DUTY

A principal has contract remedies for breach of an agent's fiduciary duty and tort remedies for fraud committed by the agent. A principal can hold an agent accountable for damages proximately caused by the agent's actions. An agent can be required to give up secret profits or advantages obtained. If a principal can show malice or bad faith on the part of the agent, then punitive damages can also be awarded.

PRINCIPAL'S DUTIES TO AGENT

The principal's duties to an agent can be express, or they can be implied by law by virtue of the agency relationship.

Compensation and Reimbursement

Unless it is a gratuitous agency, the principal must pay agreed value (or reasonable value) for an agent's services. The principal must reimburse the agent for all expenses or losses in-

volved in carrying out the agent's authorized duties. Most states have laws that regulate the payment of wages to employees. When the agent is a sales agent entitled to commission, the principal incurs liability once the offer is accepted, regardless of whether the contract is subsequently breached. In the case of subagents, a principal is liable to pay wages only if the agent was authorized to hire the additional employees. If not, the subagent must look to the agent who hired him or her for compensation.

Duty of Cooperation

A principal has a duty to both cooperate with and assist an agent in performing his or her duties and to do nothing to prevent such performance. For example, when a principal grants an agent an exclusive territory, the principal cannot compete with that agent in violation of the **exclusive agency.** To do so exposes the principal to liability for the agent's lost sales or profits.

Duty to Provide Safe Working Conditions

The common law requires a principal to provide safe premises, equipment, and conditions for all employees. The principal has a duty to inspect and warn employees of any defects. Today, the employer's liability is frequently covered by workmen's compensation acts, which are the primary remedy for an agent injured on the job.

AGENT REMEDIES AGAINST PRINCIPAL

Indemnification by Principal

Subject to the terms of the agency agreement, a principal has a duty to indemnify an agent for authorized payments or liabilities incurred because of authorized and lawful acts and transactions and also for losses suffered because of the principal's failure to perform any duties. Additionally, the principal must indemnify the agent for the value of benefits that the agent confers upon the principal unofficially.

The amount of indemnification is usually specified in the agency contract. If it is not, the courts will look to the nature of the business and the type of loss.

Authorized subagents can recover from either the principal or the agent who hires them, since the subagent is in a fiduciary relationship to both. If the authorized subagent gets indemnification from the agent who does the hiring, the agent can then seek indemnification from the principal.

Agent's Lien against Principal's Property

An agent can obtain a lien against property in the principal's possession up to the amount of compensation or indemnity owed. Similarly, a subagent can obtain a lien against the hiring agent for services and expenses and against the principal for property in the principal's possession to the extent of the agent's right in such property.

Other Remedies

An agent can (1) withhold further performance, (2) counterclaim if the principal sues, and (3) demand that the principal give an accounting. These contract remedies are all for damages. Since the principal-agent relationship is deemed to be consensual in nature, an agent has no right to specific performance in an ordinary agency contract. An agent can recover for past services and future damages but cannot force the principal to allow him or her to continue acting as an agent.

QUESTIONS AND CASE PROBLEMS

1. On April 15, 1965, Probert became a sales agent for American Gypsum Company. Although no formal contract was drawn up, one of American Gypsum's officers signed a memorandum to Probert indicating the amount of commission he would make on each sale and indicating that American Gypsum would reimburse him for his auto and travel expenses and that he would be sales agent for three states (including Washington). About a year later, and somewhat as a result of Probert's efforts, American Gypsum made a large sale to a Washington-based lumber company. Probert claimed that American Gypsum owed him a commission on the sale even though he himself did not arrange the sale. Is Probert entitled to a commission? [Probert v. American Gypsum Div., 3 Wash. App. 112, 472 P.2d 604 (1970)]
2. Sam Kademenos was about to sell a $1 million life insurance policy to a prospective customer when he resigned from the company, Equitable Life. Before resigning, however, he had expended substantial company money and had utilized Equitable's medical examiners in order to procure the $1 million sale.

After resigning, Kademenos joined a competitor, Jefferson Life Insurance Company, and made the sale through it. Has he breached any duty to Equitable? [Kademenos v. Equitable Life Assurance Society, 513 F.2d. 1073 (3d Cir. 1975)]
3. HML Corporation and General Foods Corporation entered into an agreement under which General Foods agreed to buy for thirty-two months at least 85 percent of its salad dressing requirements in a designated area from HML. No minimum quantity was specified, and General Foods was to have exclusive rights to sell in the designated area. After attempting to promote HML's salad dressing for twelve months without success, General Foods informed HML that it would no longer require any salad dressing. What arguments based on agency law can HML assert to keep its contract with General Foods alive? Do you think HML will be successful? [HML Corp. v. General Foods Corp., 365 F.2d. 77 (3d Cir. 1966)]
4. Walter T. Zumpe was employed by Chase and Sanborne from 1946 to 1964. Because Zumpe's work afforded him access to information that Chase and Sanborne considered confidential, Zumpe signed two agreements, one in 1959 and the other in 1964, which provided that he was not to disclose any of Chase and Sanborne's manufacturing processes and techniques

to any of its competitors without Chase and Sanborne's express written permission. In 1964, Zumpe left Chase and Sanborne and joined one of its competitors. Chase and Sanborne sought to enjoin Zumpe from working for the competitor and from disclosing confidential information and trade secrets learned during his employment. Should a court issue such an injunction? [Standard Brands, Inc. v. Zumpe, 264 F.Supp. 254 (E.D. La. 1967)]

5. During the course of the administration of the estate of Baldwin M. Baldwin, it became necessary to sell a vast apartment complex owned by the estate, known as "Baldwin Hills Village." Skyline Realty, a real estate broker, was commissioned to make the sale. A number of prospective purchasers were contacted, and they were present at the private sale of Baldwin Hills Village. Lemby, a real estate broker, was also present. On a number of prior occasions, he had indicated to the executors of Baldwin's estate that he was interested in purchasing the property. At the private sale, Lemby outbid all others and bought Baldwin Hills Village. Lemby then sought his commission on the sale from the Baldwin estate. Will anything in agency law prevent Lemby from recovering? [In re Estate of Baldwin, 34 Cal.App.3d 596, 110 Cal.Rptr. 189 (1973)]

6. On December 3, 1962, Dorin, acting in his capacity as soliciting agent for Occidental Life Insurance Company, submitted Milton Silverstein's application for a life insurance policy in the sum of $50,000. The application, signed by both Silverstein and Dorin, contained the following question and answer: "Has any company declined to issue or renew, postponed or cancelled, any life or accident and sickness insurance on your life? No." Notwithstanding his knowledge that Silverstein had been denied life insurance with the Equitable Life Assurance Society on the ground of ill health, Dorin failed to disclose this information to Occidental. On December 22, Occidental issued a life insurance policy for $50,000 as applied for by Silverstein. On June 30, 1963 Silverstein died, and an investigation by Occidental revealed the false statements contained in the application. Occidental then demanded that Dorin refund the $2,200 commission he had earned on that policy. Is Occidental entitled to a refund from Dorin?

[Dorin v. Occidental Life Ins. Co., 132 Ill.App.2d 387, 270 N.E.2d. 515 (1971)]

7. For seven years, Bertha Hecht did business with the brokerage firm of Harris, Upham and Company. Hecht gave Harris unfettered discretion to trade on the stock market with funds she supplied. Subsequently, she became dissatisfied with Harris, Upham and brought a suit to recover for losses resulting from bad investments it had made. Assuming the brokerage firm believed in good faith that the investments it had made were sound ones, can Hecht recover? [Hecht v. Harris, Upham and Co., 283 F.Supp. 417 (N.D. Cal. 1968)]

8. Diamantopoulos, known as "Barber Bill," was a barber of modest means in the city of Milwaukee. In 1961, he was in failing health and was frequently hospitalized. Because of his failing health, Barber Bill executed a power of attorney in favor of his godson, Dakouras, that gave to Dakouras "full power and authority to do and perform all and every act and thing whatsoever required and necessary to be done as fully to all intents and purposes as I might or could do if personally present." At that time, Barber Bill had a bank account of $10,415. The bank book was delivered to Dakouras, and over the following ten-month period, Dakouras made four withdrawals, completely exhausting the account. None of this money was ever spent for Barber Bill's benefit. Has Dakouras breached any duty under agency law? [Alexopoulos v. Dakouras, 48 Wis.2d 32, 179 N.W.2d. 836 (1970)]

9. Roger Simpson paid Larkin Travel Service $3,800 for a round trip airline ticket on Compagnie Nationale Air France. In addition to purchasing the ticket for Simpson, Larkin planned Simpson's itinerary for the trip and arranged for hotel accommodations and sight-seeing tours. Prior to the trip, Simpson became ill, informed Larkin that he wished to cancel his trip, and asked for a refund. Larkin responded that the travel agency had undergone voluntary bankruptcy and could not refund Simpson's money. Simpson then wished to recover from Air France, but first, he had to prove an agency relationship between Air France and Larkin Travel Service. Will Simpson be successful? [Simpson v. Compagnie Nationale Air France, 42 Ill.2d 496, 248 N.E. 2d. 117 (1969)]

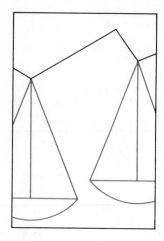

35

Agency and Employment
Liability of Principals and Agents

The first part of this chapter is concerned with the rights of third parties who contract with agents. Whether or not an agent's principal will be liable to the third party on a contract based on the agent's actions depends on a number of factors: (1) whether the agent had authority, (2) what kind of authority the agent had (that is, the source of the authority), and (3) how far that authority extended. If the agent lacked authority, it is necessary to determine whether the principal ratified the agent's acts. Once these issues are determined, the contractual duties of the principal and the agent can be established.

The second part of this chapter examines tort liability. Here the distinction between employer-employee, employer-independent contractor and principal-agent becomes important. Negligence liability usually arises in the employer-employee relationship based on the theory of *respondeat superior*. In the principal-agent relationship, the tort of misrepresentation is often the focus of lawsuits by third parties.

PRINCIPAL'S LIABILITY FOR CONTRACTS

A principal's liability based on a contract with a third party is rooted in the authority given to the agent to enter legally binding contracts on the principal's behalf. An agent's power to act comes from four sources: (1) actual authority, (2) apparent authority, (3) emergency, and (4) ratification.

Actual Authority

Actual authority is the power that the principal confers upon the agent to accomplish the purpose of the agency. The principal communicates actual authority directly to the agent, not to a third person. Actual authority can be *expressly* or *impliedly* conferred, but some manifestation from the principal must reach the agent and indicate that he or she is to act for the principal and is subject to the principal's command.

EXPRESS AUTHORITY   Express authority includes that which the principal has engaged the agent to do. It can be given orally or in writing. For example, giving an agent a power of attorney confers express authority.[1] The power of attorney is a written document and is usually notarized. Like all agency relationships, a power of attorney can be special—permitting the agent to do specified acts only—or it can be general—permitting the agent to transact all business dealings for the principal.

Equal dignity statutes in most states require that if the contract being executed is in writing, then the agent's authority must also be in writing.[2] Failure to comply with the equal dignity rule can make a contract voidable *at the option of the principal.* The law regards the contract at that point as a mere offer. If the principal decides to accept the offer, acceptance must be ratified in writing. For example, Palmer (the principal) asks Larkins (the agent) to sell a ranch that Palmer owns. Larkins finds a buyer and signs a sales contract on behalf of Palmer to sell the ranch. The buyer cannot enforce the contract unless Palmer subsequently ratifies Larkins' agency status *in writing.* Once ratified, either party can enforce rights under the contract.

The equal dignity rule does not apply when

---

1.   An agent who holds the power of attorney is called an attorney-in-fact for the principal.

2.   An exception to the equal dignity rule exists in modern business practice. An executive officer of a corporation, when acting for the corporation in an ordinary business situation, is not required to obtain written authority from the corporation.

an agent acts in the presence of a principal or when the agent's act of signing is merely perfunctory. For example, Lucas (the principal) negotiates a contract, but the day it is to be signed, Lucas is called out of town. Lucas authorizes Hilton to sign the contract. In that case, oral authorization is sufficient.

IMPLIED AUTHORITY   Implied authority is either conferred by custom or inferred by the principal's conduct if it leads the agent to believe that he or she possesses authority to act as an agent or authority reasonably necessary to carry out express authority. For example, Lester, a secretary (the agent), has purchased office supplies for years, and Henry (the principal) has always paid for them without any objection. Lester has implied authority to continue the purchases.

Mistakes can make agents out of the unwary. For example, Shaffer (the principal) goes to a stockbroker's office looking for Powell. Shaffer leaves a note on McPherson's desk, thinking it is Powell's desk. The note says, "I authorize you to sell my 100 shares of IBM stock at market price, signed Shaffer." Even though Shaffer intended the authorization for Powell, McPherson can act with valid authority to sell the stock.

Apparent Authority—Estoppel

Apparent authority is given when the principal tells *a third person* that a particular person is the principal's agent but does not tell the actual agent. If the third person reasonably believes and relies on the statements and deals with the purported agent, the principal will be bound to honor any contracts made by the agent. For example, Jones, a traveling salesman for ABC Company, has in his possession many samples of the company's goods. Any reasonable potential buyer will believe that ABC Company authorizes Jones to sell the goods. By allowing Jones to have the goods in his car, the company confers apparent authority on him. If the company tells Jones that some of the goods are defective and all should be returned, a potential buyer will have no way of knowing that Jones's actual authority has been expressly limited. Here ABC Company is liable for any defective goods Jones sells after the company expressly limits his authority. The basis of ABC's liability is not Jones's actual authority; it is Jones's apparent authority.

In some cases, it is not reasonable for a third person to believe or rely on the statements made by an agent. In fact, apparent authority can never be created by statements of the agent alone. This is especially true when a contract contains language indicating that it must be approved by the home office. When such information is disclosed, as in the following case, the agent's own statements or assurances will not overcome the express restriction on the agent's authority.

MID-STATE HOMES, INC. v. BERRY

Court of Civil Appeals of Alabama, 1978.
359 So.2d 401.

BACKGROUND AND FACTS *The plaintiffs signed a written contract for the purchase of a shell house. One of its provisions specifically stated that the terms of purchase were subject to the approval of a particular individual. The plaintiffs were aware of the provision and admitted that approval was never obtained. However, the plaintiffs maintained that the defendant corporation's agent assured them that their request would be approved and that the sale would go through. Thus, the plaintiffs went ahead and made certain repairs and improvements to the house while awaiting approval of the sales contract. Meanwhile, not only did the corporation refuse to convey the property, but the house was destroyed by fire.*

The trial court, sympathetic to the plaintiffs' plight, entered a judgment in their favor. The corporation appealed the judgment, arguing that the plaintiffs had no right to rely on the apparent authority of the agent, especially in light of the fact that the written contract clearly conditioned the sale upon corporate approval, and not upon the agent's approval.

WRIGHT, Presiding Judge.
* * *

Plaintiffs learned that [defendant] Mid-State Homes had repossessed an unfinished shell house located in Crenshaw County, Alabama, and was offering it for sale. They contacted the sales representative for Mid-State at his office in Montgomery.

They were informed of the conditions of the sale of the house and signed an instrument entitled an "agreement for deed." They gave the sales representative three hundred dollars as down payment. The instrument which the plaintiffs signed stated on its face that its terms were subject to the approval of Herb Clarkson [principal]. The Mid-State representative told plaintiff that the agreement would have to be forwarded to Tampa, Florida and signed and approved by Clarkson. * * * Upon examination there it was determined to contain errors. A corrected instrument, still containing the proviso of approval by Clarkson, was sent to the Montgomery representative. He secured plaintiffs' signatures on February 12, 1977 and returned it to Tampa.

According to plaintiffs' testimony, the representative of defendant told them he was sure the sale would go through and approved their request to make repairs and improvements to the house while awaiting the approval of the sale by Clarkson. Acting on such alleged assurance, plaintiffs did make improvements and performed labor on the house. * * *

On March 5, 1977, plaintiffs attempted to make the first scheduled payment on the house. They were informed that * * * no more money could be accepted until [the situation] was straightened out. A few days thereafter the house was destroyed by fire. Plaintiffs' down payment was returned to them.
* * *

We have carefully examined the evidence and discern no authority, apparent or otherwise, shown to have been possessed by the sales representative to enter into such a contract as that claimed by plaintiffs. The record is very clear that the representative expressly was without authority to execute a contract of sale of the property. That authority was expressly reserved to Herb Clarkson of the Tampa office by the written contract signed by plaintiffs. They stated they were aware of that provision in the contract. The evidence is undisputed that the contract to purchase the house * * * was never executed by defendant. The * * * contract stated the sale was subject to the approval of Clarkson. The complaint further says that in spite of the statement in the contract requiring its approval by Clarkson, plaintiffs were assured by defendant's agent that they could make improvements with safety and they did make improvements. The evidence of plaintiffs followed these allegations:
* * *

There was alleged only one contract between plaintiffs and defendant. Its existence was then nullified by proof that it required the approval of Clarkson. The assurances of safety to make improvements by the agent was not a contract. If plaintiffs' testimony as to such assurance is true, it amounts only to a representation or opinion by the agent which plaintiffs acted upon to make improvements upon defendant's property. The essence of the assurance was that the agent was sure that the contract would be approved by Clarkson, the sale consummated and the property become that of plaintiffs. There was no real authority in the agent to make such an assurance. It was directly opposed to the subjection stated on the face of the contract. An agent cannot negative by his own representation the express restriction of his authority known to the third party.

The evidence discloses no apparent authority. Apparent authority cannot come from the acts or declarations of the agent but arises from the action or declaration of the principal disclosed to the plaintiff.

Since there was no evidence to support the existence of a contract between the plaintiffs and the defendant, the plaintiffs could not recover for a breach of contract. The judgment was reversed, and the case was remanded to the trial court for it to determine whether the plaintiffs had the right to recover the cost of their labor and materials from the agent.

JUDGMENT AND REMEDY

FURTHER COMMENTS ON APPARENT AUTHORITY Sometimes a principal will go beyond merely making statements or performing actions that create the impression in a third party that a person is the agent for a particular purpose. If, for example, the principal has "clothed the agent" with both possession and apparent ownership of the principal's property, the agent will have very broad powers. The purported agent can deal with the property as if he or she were the true owner. For example, to deceive certain creditors, Baker (the principal) and Hunter (the agent) agree verbally that Hunter will hold certain stock certificates for Baker. Hunter's possession and apparent ownership of the stock certificates are such strong indications of ownership that a reasonable person would conclude that Hunter was the actual owner. If Hunter negotiates the stock certificates to a third person, Baker will be estopped from denying Hunter's authority to transfer the stock.

Where land is involved, courts have held that possession alone is *not* a sufficient indication of ownership. A reasonable person should realize that the possessor might be only a tenant or an adverse possessor. (See Chapter 52 for details.) However, if the agent also possesses the deed to the property and sells the property to an unsuspecting buyer, the principal cannot cancel the sale or assert a claim to title. Of course, the principal has a right to recover from the agent for violation of a fiduciary duty. The next case illustrates the operation of apparent authority to bind a principal.

WINEGARDNER v. BURNS

Supreme Court of Alabama, 1978. 361 So.2d 1054.

BACKGROUND AND FACTS *In August 1968, the Town House Motel closed, and the plaintiff, Winegardner, hired the defendant, Burns Patrol Service (the Agency), to provide security for the vacant building. The agreement between the parties was in writing. Later, the Agency's operations supervisor, Hancock, orally agreed to check the boiler pressure, temperature, and pump regularly. The Agency entered into both the written contract and this oral agreement by and through its agent, Hancock. The pipes burst. The Agency contended that Hancock never had the authority either to enter into the original contract or to modify the agreement orally.*

ALMON, Justice.
* * *

"The Agency argues that Hancock had no authority to contract and consequently could not bind the Agency. W. W. Casey, who was Hancock's immediate supervisor with the Agency, testified that he had authority to contract but Hancock did not. We quote from portion of the record of Casey's testimony:

"Q   Actually was Mr. Hancock an assistant manager?

A   No, sir.

Q   Assistant to you?

A   No, sir. He was—whatever.

Q   Operations supervisor?

A   Yes, sir.

* * *

Q   Is there anything that you were authorized to do that he wasn't authorized to?

A   Yes, sir.

Q   What was that?

A   Sign contracts.

Q   Now, did you sign the contract that started the service at the Town House Motel?

A   No, sir.

Q   Did anybody sign it?
A   This one is not signed. If course, I wouldn't remember whether it was signed or not, unless I saw my own signature on it.
* * *
Q   Well, right now, though, in your best judgment, did Mr. Hancock supervise the preparation?
A   The way Hancock did business, sent it out without having me sign it.
Q   That's what you mean, Hancock did it?
A   That's his way of doing business, that's the reason he was relieved."

It appears from the record that if Casey didn't approve the contract then it must have been approved by Hancock. The record is clear that Hancock was the only person with whom plaintiffs dealt. The contract was not signed by anyone from the Agency. The Agency admits the contract was binding, consequently it appears Hancock was the only person who could have bound the Agency. *If in fact Hancock did not have actual authority to contract for the Agency, then clearly under these circumstances he had apparent authority.* [Emphasis added.]

The appellate court affirmed the trial court's judgment for the plaintiff, Winegardner. The Agency was held liable for the damages resulting from the bursting pipes.   **JUDGMENT AND REMEDY**

Emergency Powers

An unforeseen emergency, where the agent is unable to communicate with the principal for some reason, gives rise to an agent's emergency power. The agent has the authority to do whatever is necessary to protect or preserve the property and rights of the principal.

For example, Fisher (the agent) is a brakeman on Pacific Railroad (the principal). While Fisher is acting within the scope of his employment, he falls under the train many miles from home and is severely injured. Davis, the conductor (also an agent), directs Thompson, a doctor, to give medical aid to Fisher. There is no express authority in Davis to bind Pacific Railroad for the services of Thompson. Yet, because of the emergency situation, the law recognizes this authority.

Ratification

In general, ratification is the affirmation of a previously unauthorized contract or act. Generally, only a principal can ratify. The principal must be aware of all material facts; otherwise, the ratification is not effective. Ratification binds the principal to the agent's acts and treats the acts or contracts as if they had been authorized by the principal *from the outset.* If the principal does not ratify, there is no contract, and the third party agreement with the agent is viewed merely as an unaccepted offer. The principal's acceptance (that is, the ratification) is binding only if the principal knows the terms of the contract accurately. If not, the principal can thereafter rescind ratification unless, of course, the third party has proceeded to change position in reliance on the contract.

For example, without authority, an agent contracts with a third person on behalf of a principal for repair work to the principal's office building. The principal learns of the contract from the agent and agrees to "some repair work," thinking that it will involve only patching and painting the exterior of the building. In fact, the contract includes resurfacing the parking lot, which the principal does not want done. Upon learning of the additional provision, the principal rescinds the contract. If the third party has made no preparations to do the work (such as purchasing materials, hiring additional workers, or renting equipment), then the principal can still rescind. But if the third party has, to his or her detriment, relied on the principal's ratification by making preparations, the principal must reimburse the third party for the cost of the preparations.

Two important points must be stressed. First, it is immaterial whether the principal's lack of knowledge results from the agent's fraud or is simply a mistake on the principal's part. If the third party has not changed position in reliance on the principal, the principal can repudiate the ratification. The unauthorized contract remains an offer, and the principal's acceptance is not valid because contract law provides that one cannot accept terms one does not know about. Second, the whole transaction must be ratified; a principal cannot affirm the desirable parts of a contract and reject the undesirable parts.

Death or incapacity of the third party *before* ratification will revoke an unauthorized contract. Most courts will also recognize intervening and extraordinary change of circumstances as a basis for setting aside a principal's ratification to permit a third party to revoke. Assume that A, without authority, enters into a contract with a third party who wants to purchase P's shopping center. The following night the shopping center is destroyed by fire. P's subsequent ratification will not be effective to bind the third party. The courts will reason that it is unjust to hold a third party liable in such a case and will permit the transaction to be avoided despite ratification.

EXPRESS RATIFICATION If a principal's statements or conduct express an intent to be bound, the prior unauthorized act will be ratified, and the principal will become a party to the contract. For example, Smith (the agent) negotiates the sale of a shipment of oranges to World Markets without the authorization of Samuelson (the principal). Samuelson sees the completed paperwork and tells Smith to go ahead with it. Samuelson thus ratifies the sale and is now bound to the terms of the sales contract.

IMPLIED RATIFICATION Implied ratification occurs most commonly when a principal decides to accept the benefits of a previously unauthorized transaction. In the example above, if Samuelson accepts World Markets' check in payment for the oranges, he ratifies the contract and is bound to its terms.

Ratification can be implied under certain circumstances. If Samuelson knows of the unauthorized acts and fails to repudiate or object to them within a reasonable time, the contract will be ratified.

A partnership is a special type of agency in which each partner is the agent of all the others. Therefore, the act of each partner (agent) is binding on all the others. In the following case, one of the partners in a Texas partnership executed a contract on behalf of the partnership for certain goods and services. Among the various provisions in the contract was an arbitration clause that required the partnership to go into arbitration over any contract dispute and not sue in a court of law. The partnership argued that the act of the individual partner who executed the contract on behalf of the partnership was unauthorized. Therefore, the binding arbitration agreement should not apply to them. However, since the partnership had already accepted and paid for the goods and services covered by the other provisions of the contract, the court held that the partnership could not affirm the desirable and reject the undesirable parts of the contract—that is, the arbitration provision.

WYDEL ASSOCIATES v. THERMASOL, LTD.
United States District Court, Western District of Texas, 1978.
452 F.Supp. 739.

BACKGROUND AND FACTS *The plaintiff is a Texas partnership, Wydel Associates, and the defendant is a Delaware corporation, Thermasol, Ltd. The plaintiff entered into a contract that was executed by only one of the partners in the partnership. The contract involved the delivery, installation, and maintenance of twenty-eight in-room steam* bath units to be provided by the defendant company. Although the plaintiff received and paid for the steam bath units, the plaintiff sought recovery for the defendant's alleged breach of contract, breach of warranty, and other violations under a state deceptive trade practices act.

The defendant argued that the plaintiff had no right to be in a court of law because the contract clearly contained a provision requiring that any disputes proceed to arbitration for settlement, not to a court of law. In fact, while the plaintiff was bringing this suit in federal court, the defendant proceeded to submit the dispute to an arbitrator under the arbitration provisions. The plaintiff declined to participate in the arbitration proceedings, awaiting the court's judgment as to whether or not there existed a valid and binding agreement to arbitrate under the circumstances of this case.

The plaintiff argued that since the contract was executed by only one partner of the Texas partnership, the contract's arbitration clause should not be binding upon the partnership because the executing partner exceeded the scope of his authority in executing that portion of the contract.

SPEARS, Chief Judge.
* * *

[I]t appears from the pleadings that under state law the plaintiff has clearly ratified the contract by accepting benefits under the contract and/or bringing the instant suit upon the contract. [Furthermore, the] pleadings reflect that the benefits under the contract were received when the steam bath systems were installed in the plaintiff's hotel. * * * [P]laintiff has ratified the contract by its acceptance of a payment for part of the goods and services covered by the contract. * * *

Texas law recognizes that a principal's institution of an action upon a contract as made by an agent is *ipso facto* a ratification of the contract. It has been held that in ratifying the acts of an agent, the principal assumes the burdens as well as the benefits of contracts made by the agent. *A contract cannot be adopted in part and rejected in part because the act of ratification extends to the entire contract.* [Emphasis added.]

JUDGMENT AND REMEDY

The court decided that it did not have the jurisdiction to settle the contract dispute because the arbitration clause was valid and binding on both the plaintiff and the defendant. Therefore, the arbitration proceedings that the defendant had initiated superseded any legal remedy. The court required that the plaintiff submit to the arbitration decision.

COMMENTS

The right to submit contract disagreements to binding arbitration rather than to the judgment of a court of law is recognized by both federal and state law. An arbitration decision is entitled to full faith and credit in a court of law, which means that it is binding to the extent that it determines the rights and liabilities of those particular parties under that particular contract. Unless an arbitration decision is wholly unreasonable and arbitrary, no court of law will upset it.

AGENT'S LIABILITY FOR CONTRACTS

Normally, an agent is not party to a contract that he or she makes with a third party on behalf of a disclosed principal because the contract is between the third person and the principal. The agent is not liable for the nonperformance of either party. However, an agent who gives a personal promise to perform will normally be liable. Whether or not the agent is considered to have made a personal promise depends on the interpretation of the transaction that is based on writings in connection with it and its background, including the knowledge of the other party about the relationship between the agent and the principal. Thus, an agent becomes personally liable to third parties when he or she (1) enters into a contract on behalf of an undisclosed or partially disclosed principal, (2) acts without authority or exceeds the scope of authority granted by the principal, or (3) personally guarantees performance by the principal. Whenever the agent lacks authority or exceeds the scope of authority, the agent's liability is based on the theory of breach of implied warranty of authority, not on breach of the contract itself.[3]

The agent's implied warranty of authority can be breached intentionally or by good faith mistake.[4] The agent's liability remains, *as long as* a third party has relied on agency status. Conversely, where the third party *knows* at the time of the contract that the agent is mistaken, or the agent indicates to the third party *uncertainty* about the extent of authority, the agent is not personally liable for breach of warranty.

Agent's Authorized Acts

An agent's acts are *authorized* if they are either within the scope of the agent's authority or

---

3. The agent's liability is not on the contract because the agent was never personally intended as a party to the contract.

4. If the agent intentionally misrepresents his or her authority, then the agent can also be liable in tort for misrepresentation.

---

subsequently ratified by the principal. However, the rules of liability differ on the basis of whether the principal's identity is disclosed or undisclosed to the third party.

UNDISCLOSED PRINCIPAL   When neither the fact of agency nor the identity of the principal is disclosed, a third party is deemed to be dealing with the agent personally, and the agent is liable as a party on the contract. For example, in a contract for the sale of a horse, a third party knows only that Scammon (the agent) wants to purchase the horse. The third party does not know that Scammon is actually negotiating for Johnson (the principal). Scammon signs a written contract in her own name, never indicating any agency relationship. She delivers the horse to Johnson, who is in fact the principal, but Johnson refuses to pay her. Scammon tries to return the horse to the third party, who refuses to take it. The third party is entitled to hold Scammon liable for payment. The agent's subjective intent is not relevant. The third party contracted with the agent on the basis of the *agent's* credit and reputation, not the undisclosed principal's. Therefore, the agent is liable.

However, in the example above, Scammon (the agent) has two possible means of recouping her losses. First, she can sue Johnson (the principal) for **indemnification.** There is an implied promise inherent in the agency relationship that the principal will perform any contract that the agent is authorized to enter on the principal's behalf.[5] Second, if Scammon can establish *actual* authority, once the principal's identity is revealed, the third party can hold either the principal or the agent liable on the contract.[6] Of course, the third party can obtain payment only once.

As a general rule, if a person is damaged by

---

5. If A is a gratuitous agent, and P accepts the benefits of A's contract with a third party, then P will be liable to A on the theory of quasi-contract.

6. The agent can never establish apparent authority because the principal has not previously been revealed and cannot, therefore, have informed the third party of an agency relationship.

the negligence of an agent, that person can sue the agent and the principal in the same lawsuit or in separate lawsuits. A recovery or a judgment against one will not bar separate suit against the other. In the following case, the plaintiff chose to proceed against the agent and did not name the principal as a party to the lawsuit.

BACKGROUND AND FACTS   *The plaintiff purchased a packaged tour for an African safari from a travel bureau, the defendant. The travel bureau failed to disclose that it was in fact a special agent for the tour's sponsor, World Trek. Prior to the purchase of the package, the plaintiff had direct contact with the travel bureau but never with the tour sponsor. Hence, the tour sponsor, World Trek, was an undisclosed principal.*

During the course of the trip, the tour itinerary had to be changed. The travel bureau failed to contact the plaintiff overseas, leaving the plaintiff stranded in Egypt for a week. The plaintiff sued the travel bureau for damages sustained. The travel bureau claimed that it was not liable since it was merely an agent for World Trek and that World Trek was the proper party to the lawsuit.

ROSEN v.
DEPORTER-BUTTERWORTH
TOURS, INC.
Appellate Court of Illinois, 1978.
62 Ill.App.3d 762, 19 Ill. Dec. 743,
379 N.E.2d 407.

BARRY, Presiding Justice.

* * *

The final issue presented for review is whether the trial court erred in finding defendant [the travel bureau] liable to the plaintiff for the price of the tour. Inherent in a decision of this issue is a determination of the relationship between plaintiff and defendant and defendant and the tour sponsor, World Trek.

* * *

[I]n the normal situation between a travel bureau and its traveler client a special agency relationship arises for the limited object of the one business transaction between the two parties. It is clear in the present case that the plaintiff employed the defendant travel bureau as his special agent for the limited purpose of arranging the African Safari Tour sponsored by World Trek.

Although the sponsor of the tour, World Trek, as advertised in the brochure, was not a party to this lawsuit, their relationship to the defendant is an important factor in deciding liability. The record contains a letter from defendant to World Trek as plaintiff's exhibit no. 4, which admits to defendant's selling of World Trek's tour to the plaintiff and hints of a principal-agency relationship between World Trek and the defendant. The evidence also disclosed that the defendant received a 10% commission from World Trek for selling its tour. *The legal principle that an agent is liable as a principal [to] a third party in the case of an undisclosed agency relationship* is well established and needs no citation for authority. [Emphasis added.] In the instant case the plaintiff was aware that World Trek was sponsoring the tour but was without knowledge as to whether the defendant was truly representing him as his special agent for arranging the tour or whether defendant was acting as an agent for World Trek in selling its tour to plaintiff.

The traditional relationship between a travel bureau, such as defendant, and the tour sponsors of the various tours sold has been categorized as one of agent and principal particularly in the field of tort liability of the travel bureau for injuries that occur to the traveler * * *. No sound reason exists for not finding the same principal-agent relationship between a tour sponsor and a travel bureau in the case of alleged liability for breach of an agreement involving the ultimate sale of the tour to an ordinary member of the traveling public, such as the plaintiff.
* * *

[But], *if an agent does not disclose the existence of an agency relationship and the identity of his principal, he binds himself to the third party with whom he acts as if he, himself, were the principal.* [Emphasis added.]
* * *

The fact that the plaintiff knew that World Trek and not defendant was the tour sponsor does not satisfy the necessary disclosure to prevent defendant from becoming liable as principal. * * *

JUDGMENT AND REMEDY *The travel bureau failed to exercise the degree of care required of it as the plaintiff's agent and was therefore liable for the damages that resulted.*

Negotiable Instruments   The agency rule for negotiable instruments is controlled by the Uniform Commercial Code, not agency law. UCC Sec. 3-401 provides that only the signer of negotiable paper can be held liable. Extrinsic evidence to show an agency relationship is not admissible. Therefore, if an agent signs the paper using his or her own name and not indicating any agency status, the agent is personally liable. For examples of proper signature form indicating agency, see UCC Sec. 3-403.

The Principal's Rights against the Agent   The undisclosed principal is nonetheless entitled to contract rights obtained on his or her behalf by an agent (regardless of whether the third party knows of the agency). The undisclosed principal is, in effect, the beneficiary of all contract rights.

An undisclosed principal bears the risk of the agent's dishonesty. If that principal gives money to be delivered to a third party to an agent and the agent absconds, the principal stands the loss. Likewise, if the third party gives money to an agent to be delivered to an undisclosed principal, and the agent absconds, the principal stands the loss.

The Third Party's Right to Rescind a Contract with an Undisclosed Principal   In some cases, nondisclosure of the existence and identity of a principal is a fraud upon the third person. For example, Knight and Jones are neighbors with adjoining property. They have been fighting for years because Jones will not sell Knight his property. Knight hires Short to buy the property. Short assures Jones that he is purchasing the land on his own behalf. Upon learning of the fraud, Jones can opt to rescind the sale or to complete it.[7]

The Third Party's Right to an Agent's Personal Performance   In certain instances involving undisclosed principals, the duties involved cannot be delegated under contract law. The third party can refuse to permit the principal's performance and can hold the agent liable for personal performance. Typical examples involve extensions of credit or highly personal service contracts.

7.   If Short's powers were coupled with an interest, the third party would not have a right to rescind. (See Chapter 33). Short's power coupled with an interest would be irrevocable, and his beneficial interest would be paramount over Knight, since the benefit of the agency relationship would really be for Short.

Partially Disclosed Principals

In some cases, an agent discloses his or her agency status, but the principal goes unnamed. When the principal is partially disclosed, the principal and agent can both be parties to a contract, or only one of them can be, depending on the agreement of the parties. The burden of proof is on the one who seeks to hold the agent as a party to the contract. In the absence of evidence otherwise, however, an agent for a partially disclosed principal is inferred as a party to a contract. In a contract where the agent has written his or her name plus the word *agent*, parol evidence can be introduced to show the intent of the parties. Consider an example. Casper, a manufacturer's representative, purchases supplies from a third party who knows that Casper is an agent but who does not know the identity of the manufacturer. Casper is a party to the contract. In many situations, she can be held personally liable to the third party. The third party intended to contract with Casper on the basis of her credit and reputation, not that of the undisclosed, unknown principal.

The unknown principal, *once revealed,* can obtain contract rights and be liable on the contract, subject to the same exceptions noted above for an undisclosed principal. Similarly, if a third party actually knows the principal's identity (perhaps through independent investigation), then even though the contract is made with the agent, the principal can be held as a party on the contract.

THE PRINCIPAL'S LIABILITY FOR TORTS OF AN AGENT

In general, a principal is liable for the tortious acts committed by his or her agents while acting within the scope of their authority. In general, an agent is personally liable for wrongful acts that injure or damage third parties whether or not these acts are authorized by the principal and whether or not the principal is liable. The following sections take up several broad headings of tort liability, including misrepresentation and negligence.

Misrepresentation

A principal is exposed to tort liability whenever a third person sustains loss due to the agent's misrepresentation. The key to a principal's liability is whether or not the agent was actually or apparently authorized to make representations at all.

Assume Lewis is a demonstrator for Moore's products. Moore sends Lewis to a home show to demonstrate the products and answer questions from consumers. Moore has given Lewis authority to make statements about the products. If Lewis makes only true representations, all is fine; but if he makes false claims, Moore will be liable for any injuries or damages sustained by third parties in reliance on Lewis's false representations.

To hold a principal liable, the injured party must establish only that the agent had the principal's authority to make statements about the subject matter involved. In the case of written contracts, a principal can insert a disclaimer clause—for example, "Representations not contained in this written contract are not part of the agreement and have no effect." This can limit a principal's tort liability resulting from an agent's fraudulent statements. However, a third party will retain basic contract remedies such as avoiding the contract if it is not performed or receiving money damages for losses sustained. (See Chapter 14 for details.)

An interesting series of cases have arisen on the theory that when a principal has placed an agent in a position to defraud a third party, the principal is liable for the agent's illegal acts. For example, Pratt is a loan officer at First Security Bank. In the ordinary course of the job, Pratt approves and services loans and has access to the credit records of all customers. Pratt falsely represents to a borrower, McMillan, that the bank feels insecure about McMillan's loan and intends to call it in unless McMillan provides additional collateral such as stocks and bonds. McMillan gives Pratt numerous stock certificates that Pratt keeps in his own possession, later using them to make personal investments. The bank is liable to McMillan for losses sustained on the stocks even though the bank had no direct role or knowledge of the fraudulent scheme.

The theory is that the agent's position conveys to third persons the impression that the agent has the authority to make statements and perform acts that are consistent with the ordinary duties that are within the scope of the position. When an agent appears to be acting within the scope of the authority that the position of agency confers but is actually taking advantage of a third party, the principal who placed the agent in that position is liable. In the example above, if a bank teller or security guard had told McMillan that the bank required additional security for a loan, McMillan would not be justified in relying on either person's authority to make that representation. However, McMillan could reasonably expect that the loan officer was telling the truth.

INNOCENT MISREPRESENTATION   Tort liability based on fraud requires proof that a material misstatement was made knowingly and with the intent to deceive. An agent's innocent mistakes occurring in a contract transaction or involving a warranty contained in the contract can provide grounds for the third party's rescission of the contract and the award of damages. Moreover, justice dictates that where a principal knows that an agent is not accurately advised of facts but does not correct either the agent's or the third party's impressions, the principal is directly responsible to the third party for resulting damages.

Negligence: Personal Injury

An employer (master) is liable for the physical harm caused by an employee (servant) who is acting within the scope of employment, because the employer has a legal right to control all the details of that physical performance. If a principal has the legal right to control the details of the physical performance of an agent, the principal becomes an employer (master). The principal-employer is liable for the physical harm of the agent-employee that occurs in the scope of the principal's authority and in furtherance of the principal's business.

THE DOCTRINE OF RESPONDEAT SUPERIOR   The theory of liability based on *respondeat superior* is that it imposes vicarious liability on the principal (that is, liability without regard to the personal fault of the master for torts committed by a servant in the course of employment).[8]

At early common law, a servant (employee) was viewed as the master's (employer's) property. The master was deemed to have absolute control over the servant's acts and was held strictly liable for them no matter how carefully the master supervised the servant. The rationale for the doctrine of *respondeat superior* is based on the principle of social duty. Every person shall manage his or her own affairs, whether alone or through agents or servants, so as not to injure another. Liability is imposed on employers or principals because they are deemed to be in better financial positions to bear the loss. The superior financial position carries with it the duty to be responsible for damages. Normally, the loss is shifted to the public by a price increase or covered by liability insurance.

Today the doctrine continues, but employers carry liability insurance and spread the cost of risk over the entire business enterprise. Public policy requires that an injured person be afforded effective relief, and recovery from the business enterprise is far more effective than recovery from an individual employee. Since liability rights exist under law and public policy for the protection of third parties, a master (employer) cannot contract with a servant (employee) to disclaim responsibilities for injuries resulting from the servant's acts. Such disclaimer provisions will not normally be effective because they are against public policy.[9]

---

8.   The doctrine of *respondeat superior* applies not only to master-servant relationships but also to principal-agent relationships as long as there is the right of control by the principal over the agent. The theory of *respondeat superior* is similar to the theory of strict liability covered in Chapter 21.

9.   This doctrine of *respondeat superior* may not apply if the principal or employer has sovereign or charitable organization immunity.

SUBSERVANTS If an agent is authorized to hire subservants (employees) for the employer, then the employer is liable for their acts. There is a slight difference in result if the agent hires for an undisclosed employer. In such a case, the agent is responsible for the employee in contract law for such things as wages. However, the undisclosed employer is generally held to be liable for tort injuries. The doctrine of *respondeat superior* imposes liability on the *true* master.

An agent's unauthorized hiring of a subagent or employee generally will not create any legal relationship between the principal and the subagent. However, an agent can use emergency power to hire a subagent where it is impossible to contact the principal and the situation requires immediate action to preserve the principal's property or interest. Here again, the principal can be held liable for negligent actions of the subagent in carrying out the job.

BORROWED SERVANTS Employers can lend the services of their employees to other employers. Suppose employer 1 (general employer) leases ground moving equipment to employer 2 (special employer) and sends along an employee to operate the machinery. Who is liable for injuries caused by the employee's negligent actions at the job site? Liability turns on which employer had the right to control the employee at the time. In general, employer 1 (the general employer), who rents the equipment, is presumed to retain control of the employee. However, if the rental is for a long period of time, control may be deemed to pass to employer 2. Naturally, if employer 2 specifically directs the employee in the performance of specific acts, then employer 2 assumes liability for the employee. However, the division of control over the employee may be such that the employers are jointly liable.

INDEPENDENT CONTRACTORS The doctrine of *respondeat superior* is limited to master-servant (employer-employee) and principal-agent relationships. Thus, the general rule concerning liability for the acts of an independent contractor is that the employer is not liable for physical harm caused to a third person by the negligent act of an independent contractor in the performance of the contract. An employer who has no legal right to control the details of the physical performance of a contract cannot be held liable. Here again the test is the *right to control*. Since an employer bargains with an independent contractor only for results and retains no control over the manner in which those results are achieved, the employer is generally not expected to bear the responsibility of torts committed by an independent contractor. A collection agency is a typical example of an independent contractor relationship. The creditor is generally not liable for the acts of the collection agency because collection is a distinct business occupation.

EXCEPTIONALLY HAZARDOUS ACTIVITIES The law categorizes certain activities as exceptionally hazardous. These acts are so inherently dangerous that an employer cannot be shielded from liability merely by using an independent contractor. Typical examples of such activities include blasting operations, transportation of highly volatile chemicals, or use of poisonous gases. Strict liability is imposed upon the employer as a matter of law.

DUTIES THAT CANNOT BE DELEGATED Certain employer duties cannot be delegated. For example, an owner has a duty to maintain his or her auto in a safe operating condition. Even though an employer may have had vehicles repaired at a reputable shop, the employer will be liable for any injury caused by the defective condition of a vehicle.

Scope of Employment

Once the master-servant (employer-employee) relationship is established, the tortious act must have been committed within the course and scope of employment in order for the employer to be held liable under the theory of *respondeat superior.*[10]

"FROLIC" BY AN EMPLOYEE   The act causing injury must have occurred as part of the employee's regular duties in employment. For example, Sutton (the agent) is a delivery driver for Schwartz (the principal). Schwartz provides Sutton with a vehicle and instructs him to use it for making company deliveries. Nevertheless, one day Sutton drives his own car instead of the company vehicle and negligently injures Walker. Even though Sutton's act (driving the car) was unauthorized, the negligence occurred as part of Sutton's regular duties of employment (making deliveries). Hence, Schwartz is still liable to Walker for the injuries caused by Sutton, even though Sutton used his own car contrary to Schwartz's instructions. Only if Sutton's acts exceed the scope of employment duties in a way that the employer would not reasonably expect to happen will Schwartz be relieved of liability.

An employee going to and from work or to and from meals is usually considered outside the scope of employment. All travel time of a traveling salesperson, however, is normally considered within the scope of employment for the duration of the business trip, including the return trip home.

When an employee goes on a frolic of his or her own—that is, departs from the employer's business to take care of personal affairs—is the employer liable? It depends. If the employee's activity is a substantial departure akin to an utter abandonment of the employer's business, then the employer is not liable.

For example, Susan is on an errand for Mary. Susan's house is a few blocks away. On the way back from the errand, Susan decides to drive home for a minute (that is, she takes a detour). On the way home, she negligently injures David. Susan's activity is probably not a substantial departure from Mary's business activity. Thus, Mary will be liable.

Assume, however, that Mary schedules Susan for a delivery route from Washington to New York City. The trip is expected to take two days. Susan departs; but instead of heading north, she decides to drive south to North Carolina to check out some property she wishes to buy there. Susan's plan is to call Mary with a false report of mechanical difficulties two days later to cover her extended absence. On the highway to North Carolina, Susan negligently collides with another vehicle, injuring James. Mary will probably not be liable for Susan's acts since Susan had substantially abandoned Mary's business purpose to pursue her own personal business.

The following case is a classic in agency law. Although it is nearly 150 years old, the legal principle for which it stands is still viable in the law of agency.

---

10. The Restatement, Second, Agency, Section 229 indicates the general factors that courts will consider in determining whether or not a particular act occurred within the course and scope of employment. They are (1) whether the act was authorized by the master; (2) the time, place, and purpose of the act; (3) whether the act was one commonly performed by employees on behalf of their employers; (4) the extent to which the employer's interest was advanced by the act; (5) the extent to which the private interests of the employee were involved; (6) whether the employer furnished the means or instrumentality (for example, a truck or a machine) by which the injury was inflicted; (7) whether the employer had reason to know that the employee would do the act in question and whether the employee had ever done it before; and (8) whether the act involved the commission of a serious crime.

JOEL v. MORISON

Court of Exchequer, England, 1834.

6 Carrington & Payne Reports 501.

BACKGROUND AND FACTS   *The plaintiff was walking across Bishopsgatestreet when he was knocked down by a cart driven negligently by a servant of the defendant. The plaintiff suffered a fractured leg and multiple injuries. The plaintiff took the position that the defendant was liable for his injuries because the defendant's servant was driving the cart that caused the injuries. The defendant argued that his cart was never* *driven in the neighborhood in which the plaintiff was injured. Moreover, it was suggested that the defendant's servant had gone out of his way for his own purposes and might have taken the cart at a time when it was not wanted for business purposes to pay a visit to some friends.*

PARKE, B. Judge.

* * *

His Lordship afterwards, in summing up, said—This is an action to recover damages for an injury sustained by the plaintiff, in consequence of the negligence of the defendant's servant. There is no doubt that the plaintiff has suffered the injury, and there is no doubt that the driver of the cart was guilty of negligence, and there is no doubt also that the master, if that person was driving the cart on his master's business, is responsible. If the servants, being on their master's business, took a detour to call upon a friend, the master will be responsible. If you think the servants lent the cart to a person who was driving without the defendant's knowledge, he will not be responsible. Or, if you think that the young man who was driving took the cart surreptitiously, and was not at the time employed on his master's business, the defendant will not be liable. The master is only liable where the servant is acting in the course of his employment. If he was going out of his way, against his master's implied commands, when driving on his master's business, he will make his master liable; but if he was going on a frolic of his own, without being at all on his master's business, the master will not be liable. As to the damages, the master * * * [although not himself] guilty of any offence, * * * is only responsible in law, therefore the amount should be reasonable.

JUDGMENT AND REMEDY

The verdict was for the plaintiff, and he was awarded damages of £30. In this case, the master was held liable for the acts of his servant.

COMMENTS

The Restatement, Second, Agency, Section 235 gives two illustrations of the concept of an agent's frolic:

While delivering gasoline for a principal, an agent lights a pipe and negligently throws the blazing match into a pool of gasoline that has dripped on the ground during the delivery process. The gasoline ignites, and the principal is subject to liability for the resulting harm.

While chauffeuring a principal, an agent negligently throws a lighted cigarette from the window of the car into a passing load of hay. The agent does not intend to ignite the hay, but is careless about where the cigarette falls. The principal is not liable for this act.

The difference in result between these two situations is that, in the former case, the negligence of the employee relates directly to the manner of conducting the business of delivering the goods for which the employee was hired. On the other hand, the negligence of the chauffeur is unrelated to the management or control of the car the chauffeur is driving.

Fellow-Servant Injuries

A key exception to *respondeat superior* is the fellow-servant rule: an employer is not liable for injuries inflicted by one employee upon another while both are engaged in the same general enterprise.

Traditionally, employees were expected to assume the risk of injury by fellow employees, and an employee was deemed as capable as an employer of self-protection from such danger on the job. So except in cases where the employer was negligent in hiring irresponsible personnel or where a supervisor injured a worker, the employer was held blameless.

Today, broad coverage is provided for on-the-job injuries for industrial workers under workmen's compensation statutes. These statutes broadly define the scope of employment and provide fixed compensation to insured workers who are injured in industrial accidents Workmen's compensation statutes create an absolute liability on the part of the employer at the sacrifice of all common law defenses. The employer can benefit because the employee cannot recover common law damages. Thus, workmen's compensation statutes eliminate contributory or comparative negligence and the fellow-servant rule, reducing the common law defenses based on risk taking.

Workmen's compensation, however, leaves large numbers of people in the labor force unprotected. For example, domestic workers, laborers, and independent contractors are not protected. Some industrial companies have very few employees who are covered. Finally, workmen's compensation will not cover injuries caused by willful misconduct of either the employer or a fellow employee. In these cases, the fellow-servant rule is still significant.

EMPLOYER'S LIABILITY FOR EMPLOYEE'S INTENTIONAL TORTS

Under *respondeat superior*, the employer is liable for intentional torts of the employee within the scope of employment, just as the employer is liable for negligence. For example, an employer is liable for an employee's assault and battery or an employee's false imprisonment within the scope of employment. Also, an employer is liable for permitting an employee to engage in reckless acts that can injure others. For example, an employer observes an employee smoking while filling containerized trucks with highly flammable liquids. Failure to stop the employee will cause the employer to be liable for any injuries that result.

An innocent employee acting at the employer's direction can nonetheless be liable as a tortfeasor along with the employer for committing the tortious act. For example, an employer directs an employee to burn out a field of crops. The employee does so, assuming that the field belongs to the employer, although the latter never said so. Both can be found liable to the owner of the field for damages.

EMPLOYER HAS A DUTY OF CARE IN HIRING EMPLOYEES An employer who knows or should know that an employee has a propensity for committing tortious acts is liable for the employee's acts even if they would not ordinarily be considered within the scope of employment. For example, the Blue Moon employs Joe Green as a bouncer, knowing that he has a history of assault and battery. While he is working one night within the scope of his employment, he viciously attacks a patron who "looks at him funny." The Blue Moon will bear the responsibility for Green's acts because it knew that he had a propensity toward committing tortious acts.

NOTICE OF DANGEROUS CONDITIONS The employer is charged with knowledge of all facts discovered by an employee and pertinent to the employment situation. To illustrate, a maintenance employee in M's apartment notices a lead pipe protruding from the ground. The employee neglects either to fix it or to inform the employer of the danger. X falls on the pipe and is injured. The employer is charged with knowledge of the dangerous condition regardless of whether or not the employee actually informed the employer. That knowledge is imputed to the employer by virtue of the agency relationship.

QUESTIONS AND
CASE PROBLEMS

1. Under the Fair Housing Act, racial discrimination in housing practices (including the renting of apartments) is prohibited. Leach owned two apartment complexes in Columbus, Mississippi, and employed Jenkins as office manager of the apartments. For the entire time that she managed the apartments, Jenkins did not rent to any blacks, even though blacks make up about 37 percent of the local population. The United States Attorney General brought suit against Leach for violations of the Fair Housing Act. Leach contended that Jenkins did all the renting and made all the decisions as to whom she rented the apartments. Will the government win its case against Leach? [United States v. Real Estate Development Corp., 347 F.Supp. 776 (N.D. Miss. 1972)]

2. Rausch hired Jones as a special agent and gave him the authority to negotiate a surety agreement on Rausch's behalf. Rausch's hiring of Jones was with the explicit understanding that Jones would not have to draw up the agreement unless Rausch qualified for a second mortgage from Citizens State Bank. If he did qualify, Jones was to draw up an agreement under which certain shares of stock owned by Rausch would be pledged to Citizens Bank. Jones thereafter negotiated an agreement with Citizens Bank that purported to make Citizens a pledgee of Rausch's stock. Rausch failed to qualify for the second mortgage, but Citizens Bank claimed that it was a pledgee of Rausch's stock under the agreement negotiated by Rausch's agent, Jones. Did Jones have the authority to make Citizens Bank a pledgee of Rausch's stock? [Citizens State Bank v. Rausch, 9 Ill.App.3d. 1004, 292 N.E.2d. 678 (1973)]

3. Hohenberg Brothers was a Memphis-based cotton merchandiser, and Killebrew was a Mississippi cotton farmer. Both parties were represented by D. T. Syle, Jr., a cotton agent. In February 1973, Killebrew signed and delivered to Syle a one-page purchase and sales agreement form covering the sale of Killebrew's 1973 cotton crop. All of the blanks in this document were completed, except for the name and signature of the purchaser, who was still unknown. On March 2, Syle secured an oral commitment that Hohenberg would purchase Killebrew's crop at the prices set forth in the one-page contract. Hohenberg immediately sent Syle its standard three-page purchase and sales agreement, the terms of which were identical to Syle's one-page document. Syle signed Killebrew's name and returned it to Hohenberg. Has Syle acted beyond the scope of his agency in signing Killebrew's name? [Hohenberg Brothers Co. v. Killebrew, 505 F.2d 643 (5th Cir. 1974)]

4. U-Vend Corporation was engaged in the business of leasing and servicing vending machines. Mel Williams was the manager of a local Radio Shack store, a retailer of electrical goods. On November 12, U-Vend delivered at Williams's request a hot drink machine and a soda dispensing machine to the Radio Shack that Williams managed. Williams signed a receipt for them as manager. Monthly lease payments were made by check to U-Vend, and the checks were signed either by Williams or by other Radio Shack employees. Williams's authority as manager of the local store was limited. He could not make purchases of stock or of any other items used in the store. He could not write checks for Radio Shack, and he did not have a Radio Shack checkbook in his possession. No payments on the lease were ever made by Radio Shack, and it knew nothing of the lease until Mel Williams left his position about seven months after he signed the contract with U-Vend. U-Vend wished to enforce the five-year lease agreement that Williams had signed. What authority, if any, can U-Vend argue that Williams had to bind Radio Shack? [Fairfield Lease Corp. v. Radio Shack Corp., 5 Conn. Cir. 460, 256 A.2d. 690 (1968)]

5. Lederer, a homeowner in the Chicago suburbs, hired Novera to care for the grounds around his home. One day Lederer mentioned to Novera that one of the maple trees in the backyard was in need of care and asked Novera to recommend someone for the job and to have that person talk to Lederer's wife. Three weeks later, Lederer and his wife left for vacation, and Novera brought in Wing's Tree Experts, which did extensive work pruning, clipping, and cutting down dead trees in Lederer's yard. When Lederer returned from vacation, he was presented with a bill by Wing. Must Lederer pay the bill? [Wing v. Lederer, 77 Ill.App.2d 413, 222 N.E.2d. 535 (1966)]

6. Roland "Cookie" Gomez began doing business as Cookie's Auto Sales in 1954 and continued operating as a sole proprietorship until May 29, 1963, at which time Cookie's Auto Sales became Cookie's Auto Sales, Inc. John Prevost did business with Cookie Gomez in a number of different capacities from the mid 1950s through the early 1970s. Prevost began working for University Volkswagen Inc. in January 1968, and in July of the same year, Gomez began

sending automobiles from his place of business to University Volkswagen for body work. Prevost handled Volkswagen accounts. Because of his long-time friendship with Gomez, Prevost made arrangements so that Gomez would not have to pay for work done by University Volkswagen until thirty days after the work was performed. Several years later, Gomez defaulted on his payments to University Volkswagen. The company wished to hold Gomez personally liable for the money that Gomez owed it. Gomez pointed out that since his business was incorporated, he could not be held personally liable because he was acting as an agent for "Cookie's Auto Sales Inc." Gomez also argued that Prevost should have realized that Cookie's Auto Sales was incorporated because all Gomez's ads were in the name of "Cookie's Auto Sales, Inc." Should Gomez be held personally liable? [Prevost v. Gomez, 251 So.2d. 470 (La. App. 1971)]

7. McQuade Travel Agency, Inc., agreed to sell two tickets for a European cruise aboard "HMS Riviera" to Harry and Viola Domeck. The Domecks paid McQuade Travel directly, and McQuade in turn sent the money, less the travel agent's 10 percent commission, to Caribbean Cruise Lines, Inc., which owned HMS Riviera and which employed McQuade Travel as its agent. Later the Domecks learned that their cruise was permanently cancelled because Caribbean Cruise Lines was in bankruptcy. The Domecks demanded their money back from McQuade, but McQuade defended on the ground that it was only an agent of Caribbean Cruise Lines and that the Domecks had to recover from it. McQuade also argued that the Domecks should have known that it was acting only as an agent of Caribbean Cruise Lines, even though it did not disclose the exact name of the principal, because it disclosed the name of Caribbean's ship. McQuade also argued that, in any event, it must have been obvious to the Domecks that McQuade could not afford to own a ship. Will the Domecks recover from McQuade Travel Agency? [E.A. McQuade Travel Agency, Inc. v. Domeck, 190 So.2d.3 (Fla. App. 1966)]

8. Dinkler Management Corporation engaged the Stein Printing Company, a partnership, to print menus for a Bahamian hotel company. Dinkler failed to disclose the name of the Bahamian company, but the name did appear on the menus. When Stein sought payment for the printing work done through Dinkler, Dinkler insisted that the Bahamian hotel owed the money. Can Stein recover from Dinkler? Can Stein recover from the Bahamian hotel? Can it recover from both? [Dinkler Management Corp. v. Stein, 115 Ga.App. 586, 155 S.E.2d. 442 (1967)]

9. For many years, Abell Company, publisher of the Sun newspaper in Baltimore City, ran advertisements for Warner and Company, a long-established and well-known haberdashery located in Baltimore City. Each February, two contracts were entered into; they provided that morning, evening, and Sunday editions would advertise the clothing store's merchandise. Skeen, Warner's advertising manager, was responsible for procuring the advertisements, and he always signed the contracts with his name followed by the words "Warner & Co." When Warner and Company went bankrupt, Abell argued that Skeen was personally responsible for the advertising debt owed by the company. Abell contended that the use of the name "Warner & Co." was not sufficient to indicate the corporate status of Warner, and thus Skeen should be held personally liable. Will Skeen be liable? [Abell Co. v. Skeen, 265 Md. 53, 288 A.2d. 596 (1972)]

10. Moore was employed by the federal government as an electronics engineer and was assigned to Edwards Air Force Base. He was ordered to travel from his base to another army base for certain electronics testings, and he was authorized to travel by commercial carrier or by his privately owned automobile. Travel by private automobile was "authorized between Edwards Air Force Base, California and El Centro, California, and return, only" and was to be reimbursed at the rate of $.10 per mile. While on his return trip, Moore negligently drove off the road and hit a pedestrian. Assuming that the accident occurred while Moore was utilizing the most direct route from El Centro to Edwards Air Force Base, can the injured party hold the federal government liable? What if Moore had deviated about a mile from the most direct route in order to visit a friend who lived just a short distance from Edwards Air Force Base? What if Moore had deviated more than ten miles? [United States v. Romitti, 363 F.2d. 662 (9th Cir. 1966)]

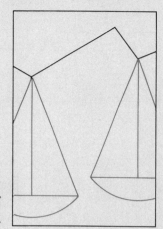

UNIT VII
Business Organizations

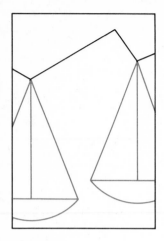

36

Forms of
Business Organization

There are basically three types of business organizations—sole proprietorships, partnerships, and corporations. Additionally, there are two types of partnerships—limited partnerships and unlimited, or general, partnerships—and various classifications of corporations, such as closely-held corporations and Subchapter S corporations. There are also joint stock companies, business trusts, joint ventures, and syndicates or investment groups. This chapter will first describe the form of these business organizations. Then it will compare a partnership with a corporation in more detail, for a person starting out in business most often chooses between these two forms when deciding how a business should be organized.

SOLE PROPRIETORSHIP

The simplest form of business is a sole proprietorship. The owner is the business. This form is used by anyone who does business without creating an organization. One usually associates a sole proprietorship with small enterprises, although this is not necessarily the case. The owner's personal estate is liable for his or her business debts.

PARTNERSHIP

A partnership arises from an agreement between two or more persons to carry on a business for profit. Partners are co-owners of a business and have joint control over its operation and the right to share in its profits. Partnership agreements are not always formal, although it is often desirable that they be formal. The Uniform Partnership Act (UPA), now adopted by most states, sets out the rules of operation of a partnership in the absence of any formal agreement and also includes areas not covered by formal agreements. Partnerships are typically not separate legal entities in most states, and the personal estates of partners are usually subject to partnership obligations. Chapter 37 treats in detail the creation and termination of partnerships. Chapter 39 treats the duties of the partners.

Limited Partnerships

The most popular special form of a partnership is the limited partnership, which is comprised of at least one general partner and one or more limited partners. The law treats the general partner exactly the same as a partner in any ordinary partnership, but the limited partner is treated as an investor only. The limited partner contributes capital, but not management or control. The personal estate of a limited partner is not liable for partnership obligations beyond the capital invested. This topic is treated in Chapter 39.

BUSINESS CORPORATIONS

The most important form of business organization is the corporation. A corporation comes into existence by an act of the state, and therefore it is a legal entity. It typically has perpetual existence. One of the key features of a corporation is that the liability of its owners is limited to their investments. Their personal estates are usually not liable for the obligations of the corporation.

Corporations consist of shareholders, who are the owners of the business. A board of directors, elected by the shareholders, manages the business. The board of directors normally employs officers to oversee day-to-day operations.

OTHER FORMS OF BUSINESS ORGANIZATION

There are a number of other, less common forms of business organization. They include joint ventures, syndicates or investment groups, joint stock companies, and business trusts.

Joint Ventures

When two or more persons combine their interest in a particular business enterprise and agree to share in losses or profits jointly or in proportion to their contribution, they are engaged in a joint venture. The joint venture, a less formal association than the partnership, is created in contemplation of a limited activity or a single transaction.

A joint venture is normally not a legal entity and therefore cannot be sued as such, but its members can be sued individually. Usually joint ventures are taxed like partnerships.

Syndicates or Investment Groups

A group of individuals getting together to finance a particular project like the building of a shopping center or the purchase of a professional basketball franchise is called a syndicate or an investment group. The form of such groups varies considerably. In some cases, the members merely own property jointly and have no legally recognized business arrangement.

Joint Stock Company

A joint stock company or association resembles a corporation but is normally treated like a partnership. Ownership is evidenced by shares of transferable stock. Each shareholder is liable for the joint stock company's obligations as if he or she were a partner in a partnership. A modern example is the American Express Company, which was a joint stock association until 1965.

Business Trusts

A business trust is created by a written trust agreement that sets forth the interests of the beneficiaries and the obligations and powers of the trustees. With a business trust, legal ownership and management of the property of the business stays with one or more of the trustees, and the profits are distributed to the beneficiaries. The business trust was started in Massachusetts in an attempt to obtain the limited liability advantage of corporate status while avoiding certain restrictions on a corporation's ownership and development of real property. In some states, the beneficiaries are treated as partners unless they are personally liable to business creditors; thus the limited liability advantage is eliminated. In a number of states, business trusts must pay corporate taxes. The business trust was more popular at the turn of the century than it is today. Its decline is a result of antitrust laws (discussed in detail in Chapter 50).

THE ADVANTAGES AND DISADVANTAGES OF A SOLE PROPRIETORSHIP

Advantages

One advantage of a sole proprietorship is that the proprietor receives all the profits because he or she takes all the risk. In addition, it is often easier and less costly to start a sole proprietorship than to start any other kind of business. Few legal forms must be completed, and since the proprietor makes all the decisions, the problem of reaching agreement among all the people involved is avoided. The sole proprietor is also free from corporate income taxes, paying only personal income taxes on profits. However, these taxes are not necessarily lower than those for a corporation.

Disadvantages

As sole owner, the proprietor bears the whole risk of losses. In addition, the proprietor's opportunity to raise capital is limited to personal funds and the funds of those who are willing to make loans. Additionally, and perhaps more importantly for many potential entrepreneurs, the sole proprietor has unlimited liability, or

legal responsibility, for all obligations incurred in doing business.

COMPARING A PARTNERSHIP WITH A CORPORATION

Exhibit 36-1 is an abbreviated comparison between a partnership and a corporation, giving the essential advantages and disadvantages of each.

Other Points of Comparison for Choosing a Form of Business

LIABILITY OF OWNERS   The form of organization—whether a sole proprietorship, partnership, or corporation—does not always determine the issue of owners' liability. For example, banks may be unwilling to lend money to small corporations with few shareholders, unless the owners agree to be personally liable for the loan. John Janks and several of his brothers own a small dry cleaning store. They have formed a corporation, and they now wish to start two more stores in a neighboring city. The local bank may require that each of them sign a note and be personally liable for the increased debt (often as a guarantor). The corporate form of business does not prevent them from having personal liability in such a case because they have assumed the liability voluntarily.

NEED FOR CAPITAL   One of the most common reasons for changing from a sole proprietorship or partnership to a corporation is the need for additional capital to finance expansion. A sole proprietor can seek partners. They will bring capital with them, and in some instances the partnership will be able to secure more funds than the sole proprietor could. But when a firm wants to expand greatly, simply increasing the number of partners can lead to too many partners for the firm to operate efficiently. Therefore, the corporation is the most logical choice for an expanding business organization. There are almost limitless possibilities for obtaining more capital by issuing shares of

EXHIBIT 36-1   COMPARING A PARTNERSHIP WITH A CORPORATION

CHARACTERISTIC	PARTNERSHIP	CORPORATION
1. Method Of Creation	Created by agreement of the parties.	Charter issued by state—created by statutory authorization.
2. Legal Position	Not a separate legal entity in many states.	Always a legal entity separate and distinct from its owners—a legal fiction for the purposes of owning property and being party to litigation.
3. Liability	Unlimited liability (except for limited partners in a limited partnership).	Limited liability of shareholders—shareholders are not liable for the debts of the corporation.
4. Duration	Terminated by agreement of the partners, by the death of one or more of the partners, by withdrawal of a partner, or by bankruptcy.	Can have perpetual existence.
5. Transferability Of Interest	Although partnership interest can be assigned, assignee does not have full rights of a partner.	Shares of stock can be transferred.
6. Management	Each general partner has a direct and equal voice in management unless expressly agreed otherwise in the partnership agreement. (Limited partner has no rights in management in a limited partnership.)	Shareholders elect directors who set policy and appoint officers.
7. Taxation	Each partner pays pro rata share of income taxes on net profits, whether or not they are distributed.	Double taxation—corporation pays income tax on net profits, with no deduction for dividends, and shareholders pay income tax on disbursed dividends they receive.
8. Organizational Fees, Annual License Fees, And Annual Reports	None.	All required.
9. Transaction Of Business In Other States	Generally no limitation.[a]	Normally must qualify to do business and obtain certificate of authority.

[a]A few states have enacted statutes requiring that foreign partnerships qualify to do businesss there—for example, 3 N.H. Rev. Stat. Ann. Chapter 305-A in New Hampshire.

stock. The original owners find that their share of the company is reduced, but they are able to expand at a much more rapid rate by selling shares in the company.

TAX CONSIDERATIONS Various tax considerations must be taken into account when comparing a partnership with a corporation. They are listed in Exhibit 36-2.

EXHIBIT 36-2   PARTNERSHIP VERSUS CORPORATION—TAX CONSIDERATIONS

TAX ASPECT	PARTNERSHIP	CORPORATION
1. Federal Income Tax	Partner is taxed on proportionate share of partnership income, even if not distributed; the partnership files information returns only.	Income of the corporation is taxed; stockholders are also taxed on distributed dividends. Must file corporate income tax forms.
2. Accumulation	Partners taxed on accumulated as well as distributed earnings.	Corporate stockholders not taxed on accumulated earnings. There is, however, a penalty tax, in some instances, that the corporation must pay for accumulations of income.
3. Capital Gains And Losses	All partners taxed on their proportionate share of capital gains and losses.	Corporation taxed on capital gains and losses. There is no special deduction to reduce taxes for any excess of long-term gains over short-term losses, but there is a special rate.
4. Exempt Interest	Partners are not taxed on exempt interest received from the firm.	Any exempt interest distributed by a corporation is fully taxable income to the stockholders. Exempt interest can come, for example, from municipal bonds.
5. Pension Plan	Partners are not eligible for an exempt pension trust. The firm cannot deduct payments for partners except under what is called a Keogh Plan.	Employees and officers who are also stockholders can be beneficiaries of a pension trust. The corporation can deduct its payments to the trust.
6. Social Security	Partners do not pay social security tax, but often must pay a self-employment tax.	All compensation to officers and employee stockholders subject to social security taxation up to the maximum.
7. Death Benefits (excluding those provided by insurance)	There is no exemption for payments to partners' beneficiaries.	Benefits up to $5,000 can be received tax-free by stockholders' and employees' beneficiaries.
8. State Taxes	In many states, the partnership is not subject to state income taxes.	The corporation is subject to state income taxes (although these taxes can be deducted on federal returns).

QUESTIONS AND
CASE PROBLEMS

1.   Suppose A, B, and C are college graduates, and A has come up with an idea for a new product that she believes could make the three of them very rich. Her idea is to manufacture beer dispensers for home use, and her goal is to market them to consumers throughout the Midwest. A's personal experience qualifies her to be both first line supervisor and general manager of the new firm. B is a born salesperson. C has little interest in sales or management but would like to invest a large sum of money that she has inherited from her aunt. What should A, B, and C consider in deciding which form of business organization to operate under?

2.   The limited liability aspect of the corporation is one of the most important reasons that firms choose to organize as corporations rather than as partnerships or sole proprietorships. Limited liability means that if a corporation is not able to meet its obligations with corporate assets, creditors will not be allowed to look to the owners (stockholders) of the corporation to satisfy their claims. Assume that A and B (from problem 1) do not have a wealthy friend like C who wishes to go into business with them and that therefore they must borrow money to start their business. A and B decide to incorporate. What do you think a lender will ask them when they seek a loan? What effect does this have on the "advantage" of limited liability under incorporation?

3.   Assume A and B have incorporated and have successfully operated their beer dispenser manufacturing firm for nine months. They employ twenty-five persons. One of the employees severs a finger while working with a metal bending machine, and a jury awards him $300,000. Total assets of the corporation are $275,000. If the employee sues the corporation, who will pay the difference?

4.   Assume that A and B have been in business for several years and are very successful. Seeing how successful they are, C now wishes to join the firm. A and B agree to sell C a one-third interest in the firm so that all three have an equal say in management. B and C both agree that manufacturing beer dispensers is not enough and that the firm should expand its operations to include manufacturing and distributing bar accessories. A vehemently disagrees, arguing that the market is already flooded with such items and that most companies that manufacture them are only marginally profitable. B and C outvote A with their two-thirds share and expand the business. How could this have been avoided if the business had been incorporated? Could it have been avoided if the firm had operated as a partnership? Explain.

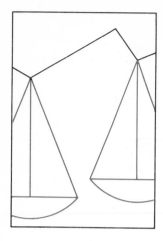

37

Partnerships
Creation and Termination

To a great extent, partnership law derives from agency law. Each partner is considered an agent of every other partner. Thus, the agency concepts of imputing knowledge and responsibility for acts done within the scope of the partnership relationship will apply.

Partnership law is distinct from agency law in an important way. A partnership is based upon a voluntary contract between two or more competent persons who agree to place some or all of their money, effects, labor, and skill in business with the understanding that there will be a proportional sharing of the profits and losses between them. An agent can be compensated from business profits but does not agree to bear the ordinary business losses and has no ownership interest in the business.

Partnership law in the United States is codified in the *Uniform Partnership Act (UPA)*. The UPA, which has been adopted in most states, replaces the body of common law principles dealing with partnerships.[1]

In the past, attempts to formulate a concrete definition of the term *partnership* caused endless controversy among judges, lawyers, and members of the business community. **Partnership** is defined by the UPA as "an association of two or more persons to carry on as co-owners a business for profit."[2] Therefore, three essential elements of a partnership are (1) a common ownership interest in a business, (2) sharing of the

---

1. The UPA was first passed in 1914 by Pennsylvania. To date, Louisiana, Georgia, and Mississippi have not adopted it.
2. UPA Sec. 6(1).

profits and losses of the business, and (3) the right to manage the operations of the partnership.

CHARACTERISTICS OF A PARTNERSHIP

A partnership is sometimes called a *firm*, a term that connotes an entity separate and apart from its aggregate members. Sometimes the law of partnership recognizes the independent entity, but for certain other purposes, the law treats it as an aggregate of individual partners. At common law, a partnership is never treated as a separate legal entity. Thus, a common law suit can never be brought by or against the firm in its own name; each individual partner has to sue or be sued. The UPA, on the other hand, recognizes a partnership as an entity (apart from its individual members) for limited purposes, including the capacity to sue or be sued, to collect judgments against the partnership in its own name, to proceed in federal bankruptcy courts, and to convey property.

Partnership as an Entity

LEGAL CAPACITY   States vary on how a partnership is viewed as a party in a legal suit. Some permit a partnership to sue and be sued in the firm name; others allow a partnership to be sued as an entity but not to sue others in its firm name (that is, the partnership must use the names of the individual partners). Federal courts recognize the partnership as an entity that can sue or be sued when a federal constitutional question is involved. Otherwise, federal courts follow the practice adopted by the state in which the federal court is located.

JUDGMENTS   Partnership liability is first paid out of partnership assets when a judgment is rendered *against the firm name*. In a general partnership, the personal assets of the individual members are subject to liability if the partnership's assets are inadequate. Even in limited partnerships, at least one of the partners—called a general partner—subjects his or her personal assets to liability for the partnership's obligations. Good legal practice dictates that where state law permits a firm to be sued, the partners should be joined as parties to the suit. This insures that a wide range of assets will be available for paying the judgment.

The general rule is that a judgment creditor of a partnership can execute the judgment against either partnership or individual property. [UPA Sec. 15] In some states, the judgment creditor must, however, exhaust the remedies against partnership property before proceeding to execute against the individual property of the partners.[3]

BANKRUPTCY   In federal court, an adjudication of bankruptcy *in the firm name* applies only to the partnership entity. It does not constitute personal bankruptcy for the partners. Similarly, the personal bankruptcy of an individual partner does not bring the partnership entity or its assets into bankruptcy.

CONVEYANCE OF PROPERTY   The title to real or personal property can be held in the firm name. This means that the partnership as an entity can own property apart from that owned by its individual members. As such, the property can be conveyed (transferred) without having each individual partner join in the transaction.

Under common law, title to real estate could not be held in a partnership's firm name. Each partner was regarded as a co-owner (known in legal terminology as a *tenant in partnership*). Each partner had to join in all conveyancing. Although the modern rule of partnership property ownership disregards the need for aggregate action in conveyancing, there are some practical difficulties to consider. Most states do not require public records to keep lists of members of a partnership, although

---

3. Under the doctrine of marshaling assets, this is the ranking, or arrangement, of assets in due order of administration. Marshaling of assets allows the proper application of the assets to various claims.

other states have statutes that require the filing of a certificate of copartnership. Hence, in determining the validity of a conveyance in a partnership name, it may be impossible to tell whether the person executing the deed is actually a partner and has authority to convey. Some states have passed laws requiring firms to file a statement of partnership. This list names members of the firm authorized to execute conveyances on behalf of the firm.

Aggregate Theory of Partnership

When the partnership is not regarded as a separate legal entity, it is treated as an *aggregate* of the individual partners. For example, for federal income tax purposes, a partnership is *not* a tax-paying entity. The income or losses incurred by it are "passed through" the partnership framework and attributed to the partners on their individual tax returns. The partnership as an entity has no tax identity or liability. It merely files an informational return with the IRS, indicating the profit and loss that each partner will report on his or her individual tax return.

FORMATION OF A PARTNERSHIP

A partnership is ordinarily formed by an explicit agreement among the parties. The law also recognizes another form of partnership —*partnership by estoppel*. This form arises

when persons who are not partners represent themselves as partners when dealing with third parties. The liability of partners by estoppel is covered later in the chapter.

This section will describe the requirements for the creation of a true partnership, including references to the liability of "alleged partners." The next section will deal with the process by which partnerships are terminated.

A partnership is a voluntary association of individuals. As such, a *true partnership* is generally based on agreement among the parties that reflects their intention to create a partnership, contribute capital, share profits, and participate in management. The partnership relationship involves a high degree of trust and reliance.

Parties cannot avoid partnership liability, even by *expressly* designating themselves as some other business form, if the evidence establishes the essential elements of a partnership. In the following case, a physician purchased an interest in a medical center along with numerous other doctors. The amount of money each doctor received for practicing at the center was based upon the billing for the services that each performed. The bills were collected in the name of the center. From the total billing, a percentage was deducted to cover expenses and profit sharing. The center's method of allocating expenses to the doctors bore no direct relationship to their actual expenses.

STUART v. OVERLAND
MEDICAL CENTER
Missouri Court of Appeals,
1978. 510 S.W.2d 494.

BACKGROUND AND FACTS *The plaintiff, a physician, sued to settle a dispute arising out of his withdrawal from a claimed professional partnership. The trial court concluded that the plaintiff practiced medicine in a partnership with the defendants at the Overland Medical Center. The court further determined that the partnership between the plaintiff and the defendants was dissolved by the plaintiff's lawsuit. The court evaluated the dollar amount of the plaintiff's interest in the partnership; and after deducting certain amounts due the defendants for expenses, the court awarded the plaintiff a judgment.*

The defendants not only challenged the formula used by the lower court in determining the value of the plaintiff's interest in the medical center, but they also challenged the court's conclusion that the relationship between the plaintiff and the defendants was a partnership. In support of their contention, the defendants tried to show that the relationshp was one of expense-sharing rather than partnership.

WEIER, Judge.

* * *

Under the Uniform Partnership Law which was adopted in this state in 1949, a partnership is defined as "an association of two or more persons to carry on as co-owners a business for profit." A partnership is defined judicially as "a contract of two or more competent persons to place their money, effects, labor and skill, or some or all of them, in lawful commerce or business and to divide the profits and bear the loss in certain proportions." The contract creating the partnership need not be written, but may be expressed orally or implied from the acts and conduct of the parties. The primary consideration in determining the existence of a partnership is whether the parties intended to carry on as co-owners a business for profit. With this general background in mind, we proceed:

* * *

The amount of money each doctor received for practicing his profession at the Center was based upon the billing for services performed by each doctor and collected by and in the name of the Center less a percent of the expenses. By way of illustration, if one doctor collected $1,000.00, and the amount collected by all the doctors was $10,000.00, the doctor who collected $1,000.00 would receive $1,000.00 less 10% of the expenses since the $1,000.00 was ten percent of the total amount collected by all the doctors. The amount of expenses to which each doctor's income was subject was determined by the same method used to allocate collections. Again by way of illustration, if the expenses of all the doctors totaled $2,000.00 for the year in which they collected $10,000.00, the doctor who collected $1,000.00 would be liable for ten percent of the expenses or $200.00. Thus, at the end of this hypothetical year, the doctor who collected the $1,000.00 would receive $800.00 as income. Defendants argue that since this method of allocating income is not a profit sharing arrangement but rather an expense sharing arrangement, the relationship between the doctors at the Center cannot be denominated a partnership. We find this argument unconvincing. Each doctor received compensation for the services he performed at the Center. The amount each doctor received as compensation may properly be called income or profit as the two terms are often used interchangeably and, for the most part, have the same meaning. Each doctor shared to some extent in the income or profit of the other doctors although the sharing was not the result of proportionally dividing the total amount of money collected by all the doctors without considering the amount of money each doctor collected individually. Rather, the profit sharing was accomplished by the Center's method of allocating the expenses to be deducted from each doctor's collections. For example, if the doctor referred to in our illustration above had actual expenses of $100.00, $100.00 of the $200.00 he had to pay as expenses was used to pay or help pay another doctor's expenses. It was in this manner that the doctors in the Center actually shared profits. Because the expenses each doctor had to pay bore no relationship to the actual expenses of each doctor, some doctors were receiving profits that otherwise might have been distributed to the doctor or doctors whose actual expenses were slight when compared to the actual expenses of other doctors.

Thus the evidence proved that plaintiff was practicing his profession with the other doctors in the Center as a co-owner of the Center's facilities for a profit. While co-ownership and the sharing of profits by those engaged in business are not factors which conclusively establish the parties' relationship as that of partnership, they are prima facie evidence of partnership. As such, the presumption of partnership prevails unless evidence sufficient to rebut the presumption is brought forward. In this case, defendants presented no evidence which would lead to the conclusion that the relationship between plaintiff and them was anything other than a partnership.

JUDGMENT AND REMEDY

The appellate court affirmed the trial court's judgment that the professional arrangement between the plaintiff and the defendants was a partnership. The plaintiff's interest in the partnership was evaluated by the trial court, and that determination of value was upheld by the appellate court.

COMMENTS

The rights and liabilities of the partners among themselves, although fixed by law, are subject to agreements between the parties insofar as such agreements—and intentions—can be ascertained. Even an oral agreement can be sufficient to establish a framework for a partnership. If there are sufficient circumstances to indicate the intent to carry on a business for profit as co-owners, and if the court can ascertain a method for determining the value of any partner's interest, then a partnership will be presumed unless otherwise disavowed.

Formalities

As a general rule, agreements to form a partnership can be oral, written, or implied by contract. Some partnership agreements, however, must be in writing to be legally enforceable within the Statute of Frauds. (See Chapter 11 for details.) For example, a partnership agreement that, by its terms, is to continue for more than one year or one that authorizes the partners to deal in real property transfers must be evidenced by a sufficient writing.

Practically speaking, it is far better to set out the provisions of any partnership agreement in writing. It is much harder to prove exactly what the terms of an oral agreement are because a court must evaluate oral testimony given by persons with an interest in the eventual decision. In addition, the drafting of a written agreement enables the partners to anticipate problems that they might not otherwise foresee if the agreement is made orally. For instance, Tomkins and Fredericks plan to enter into a partnership agreement to sell tires. Among the provisions to be included is that Tomkins is to provide two-thirds of the capital to start up the business and is to receive two-thirds of the profit in return. The agreement is made orally. Tomkins now sues because Fredericks claims that one-half the profits should be his. Without a writing, Tomkins may have a hard time overcoming the presumption that he is entitled to only one-half the profits of a two-person partnership.[4] A partnership agreement, called *articles of partnership*, usually specifies each partner's share of the profits and is binding regardless of how uneven the distribution appears to be.

Duration of Partnership

The partnership agreement can specify the duration of the partnership in terms of a specific date or with respect to the completion of a particular project. This is called a *partnership for term*. A dissolution without the consent of

---

4. The law assumes that members of a partnership share profits and losses equally unless a partnership agreement provides otherwise.

all the partners prior to the expiration of the partnership term constitutes a breach of the agreement, and the responsible partner can be liable for any losses resulting from it.

If no fixed duration is specified, the partnership is a *partnership at will*. This type of partnership can be dissolved any time by any partner without violating the agreement or incurring liability for resulting losses to other partners.

Capacity

Any person having the capacity to enter a contract can become a partner. A partnership contract entered into with a minor as a partner is voidable and can be disaffirmed by the minor. (See Chapter 8 for details.)

Lack of legal capacity due to insanity at the time of the agreement likewise allows the purported partner either to avoid the agreement or to enforce it. If a partner becomes insane and is adjudicated mentally incompetent during the course of the partnership, the partnership is not automatically dissolved.

The Corporation as Partner

Traditionally, there has been some disagreement as to whether a corporation can become a partner. A corporation is a legal entity authorized to engage in activities set out in its articles of incorporation and its bylaws, subject to general corporation statutes. One view is that a corporation cannot be a partner unless the corporation's articles of incorporation specifically empower it to enter into a partnership as a partner. The opposite view, which appears to prevail today, is contained in the Model Business Corporate Act. Basically, the capacity of corporations to contract is a question of corpora-

tion law. Many states have restrictions on corporations becoming partners, though such restrictions have become less common over the years. Many decisions in jurisdictions that do not permit corporate partners nevertheless validate the arrangements by characterizing them as joint ventures rather than partnerships.

Mutual Consent

A partnership is a voluntary association of co-owners. It cannot be forced upon anyone. The *intent* to associate is a key element of a partnership, and one cannot join a partnership unless *all* other partners consent.

Indications of Partnership

Parties commonly find themselves in conflict over whether their business enterprise is a legal partnership, especially in the absence of a formal written contract. To answer this question, the courts have developed broad guidelines for interpreting partnership status. The strongest indication of a partnership relationship is the presence of profit sharing. However, its existence is not the sole reason for the business relationship and should not be confused with profit sharing in the form of bonus or employee wages, rents, annuity payments, interest, or consideration for the sale of goodwill in a business.

Other indications that a partnership relationship is intended are more persuasive. They include contributing capital to the enterprise, joint ownership of property, and sharing of gross income. None of these factors alone is conclusive in proving that a partnership relationship exists. In the following case, a widow attempted to persuade the court that she and her late husband were business partners.

BACKGROUND AND FACTS *The plaintiff was a widow who, for tax reasons, attempted to establish that a partnership had existed between herself and her late husband. At the trial, she testified that her deceased husband asked her to marry him and move with him to another city to help run his nursery business. They married, and the plaintiff gave up*

MILLER v. CITY BANK & TRUST CO., N.A.

Court of Appeals of Michigan, 1978. 82 Mich.App. 120, 266 N.W.2d 687.

her well-paying job to move south with her new husband. Although the plaintiff did not make any capital contributions to the partnership, she held a management position in the nursery business, and she did physical labor. In addition, she kept all the books and hired and fired employees. She received periodic payments of $50 or $100. Whenever the plaintiff received a check, her husband also received one for the same amount. Money for household expenses was taken out of the business account.

Along with the nursery business, her husband had been engaged in making land sales. However, no land had ever been conveyed to the partnership.

The year after the plaintiff married her husband, a business registration certificate was filed for the nursery, indicating that the business was a partnership. Checking accounts, vehicles, and other equipment were bought and held under the business name. On the other hand, annual tax forms and schedules listed the business as a sole proprietorship and the plaintiff's occupation as housewife. A Michigan business activities form also indicated a sole proprietorship. Finally, in applying for a self-employment and pension and profit-sharing plan, the husband stated in his application that his business was a sole proprietorship.

There was never any formal written partnership agreement. The plaintiff, however, stated that her husband had described the relationship when he asked her to marry him and at all times since, as one of partnership. She was under the impression that they were business partners. Furthermore, the plaintiff testified that her husband told her that she was "the best partner he ever had."

DANHOF, Chief Judge.

* * *

On the basis of these facts, the trial court found that the plaintiff had not carried her burden of proof [to establish the existence of a partnership]. * * *

* * *

The burden of proof to show a partnership is on the one alleging the partnership, and the burden is stricter when relatives are the alleged partners. Also the fact that the alleged partner is deceased further raises the burden of proof * * *. The elements of a partnership are generally considered to include a voluntary association of two or more people with legal capacity in order to carry on, via co-ownership, a business for profit. Co-ownership of the business requires more than merely joint ownership of the property and is usually evidenced by joint control and the sharing of profits and losses. With the intentions of the party to form a partnership as our polestar we will review the trial court's finding.

It is not disputed that the parties were involved in a business venture for profit and had the legal capacity to form a partnership. However, the evidence relating to co-ownership does not indicate that a legal partnership was contemplated. Prior to the marriage, Mr. Miller [the plaintiff's husband] operated the business and owned all the property. Mrs. Miller [the plaintiff] made no capital contributions except her services. Even though plaintiff worked long and hard hours, this does not establish that the parties had an agreement to form a partnership. This evidence could also be viewed as consistent with an employee-employer relationship or that of a helpful wife who assisted her husband without them intending a legal partnership.

[The court then proceeded to evaluate other factors that might indicate the intent of the parties to form a partnership.]

Co-ownership is also indicated by profit sharing. In fact, profit sharing is prima facie evidence of a partnership. However, the [trial] court did not find an agreement to share profits and we cannot say that this was clearly erroneous.

[When an appellate court reviews a trial court's findings of fact, it will not disturb the resulting judgment unless there is absolutely no factual evidence to support the trial court's conclusion. In this case, the appellate court showed that there were many possible interpretations to be made from the fact that Mr. and Mrs. Miller each received monthly payments from the business.] That Mr. and Mrs. Miller each received monthly payments from the nursery checking account does not necessarily establish profit sharing. The payments could also be reasonably viewed as salary or wages. Another possible interpretation would be that Mr. Miller was withdrawing money from his sole proprietorship and was dividing it equally because he felt an obligation to share equally with his wife, as a wife rather than a business partner.

Another indicia of co-ownership is mutual agency and control. That Mrs. Miller kept the books, wrote checks, and hired and fired does not necessarily establish any control other than that which might be given to a trusted employee. However, it is not necessary that this control be exercised as long as it exists. In view of the absence of the exercise of control or mutual agency, evidence of an agreement in respect to the division of control is about the only way to prove mutual agency and control. However, no evidence of an agreement with respect to mutual control was presented.

The intention of the parties to enter into a partnership comprising the above-mentioned elements is the controlling issue in this case. The filing of the business registration papers listing the business as a partnership gives support to plaintiff's claim.

* * *

The trial court found that there was sufficient, competent evidence to rebut the presumption concerning the nursery business.

* * *

The evidence introduced against these claims indicated that the deceased did not intend to form a legal partnership with his wife. First, there is no written agreement and there is only plaintiff's testimony in support of an oral one. The income tax returns and schedules listed the business as a sole proprietorship, listed Mr. Miller's income as wages and Mrs. Miller's occupation as a housewife. In 1964, Mr. Miller applied for a self-employee retirement deduction plan as a sole proprietorship. Mr. Miller's social security forms listed the business as a sole proprietorship. All the capital contributions came from Mr. Miller and the property remained in his name (or his and his wife's name), and none was transferred to the partnership. Shortly before his death, Mr. Miller deeded his homestead to his wife and himself as tenants by the entirety and this would seem needless if they already owned it as partners. Although none of these facts are conclusive, they are all factors to be weighed in the decision.

JUDGMENT
AND REMEDY

After reviewing the entire trial court record, the appellate court agreed that the presumption of partnership established by the filing of business registration papers was rebutted by other competent evidence, which tended to show that Mr. Miller intended the business to be run as a sole proprietorship. The trial court's judgment that no partnership existed was affirmed.

Partnership by Estoppel

Parties who are not partners can hold themselves out as partners and make representations that third persons rely on in dealing with these alleged partners. The law of partnership imposes liability on the alleged partner or partners, but it does not confer any partnership rights on these persons.

There are two aspects of liability. The person representing to be a partner in an actual or alleged partnership is liable to any third person who extends credit in good faith reliance on such representations. Similarly, a person who expressly or impliedly consents to such misrepresentation of an alleged partnership relationship is also liable to third persons who extend credit in good faith reliance.

For example, Moore owns a small shop. Knowing that the Midland Bank will not make a loan on his credit alone, Moore represents that Lewis, a financially secure businesswoman, is a partner in Moore's business. Lewis knows of Moore's misrepresentation but fails to correct the bank's information. Midland Bank, relying on the strength of Lewis's reputation and credit, extends a loan to Moore. Moore will be liable to the bank for the loan repayment. Furthermore, in many states, Lewis would also be held liable to the bank in such a loan transaction. Lewis will normally be estopped from denying that Moore is her partner and will be regarded as if she were in fact a partner in Moore's business to the extent that this loan is concerned.

When a real partnership exists, and a partner represents that a nonpartner is a member of the firm, the nonpartner is regarded as an agent whose acts are binding on the partner. Middle Earth Movers has three partners—Johnson, Mathews, and Huntington. Mathews represents to the business community that Thompson is a partner. If Thompson negotiates a contract in Middle Earth Movers' name, the contract will be binding on Mathews, but normally not on Johnson and Huntington (unless, of course, Johnson and Huntington knew and consented to Mathews's representation).

PARTNERSHIP PROPERTY RIGHTS

For financial and credit reasons it is frequently necessary to distinguish between property belonging to the firm and property belonging to each individual partner, particularly in bankruptcy proceedings. A partnership can own any real or personal property, unless the partnership agreement contains some prohibition or limitation on what it can acquire. Holding property in the firm name can be merely a convenience, so *title alone is not conclusive* in establishing that a particular asset belongs to the partnership.

Factors Indicating Partnership Property

UPA Sec. 8(1) provides that "all property originally brought into the partnership's stock or subsequently acquired, by purchase or otherwise, *on account of the partnership,* is partnership property." (Emphasis added.) Indications that the asset was acquired with the intention that it be a partnership asset is the heart of the phrase *on account of the partnership.* Thus, the more closely an asset is associated with the business operations of the partnership, the more likely it is to be a partnership asset. Moreover, when such an asset is purchased with partnership funds, it will belong to the partnership unless a contrary intention is shown.

PROPERTY
RIGHTS OF PARTNERS

A partner has three property rights delineated in UPA Sec. 24: a right to specific partnership property, a right to an interest in the partnership, and a right to participation in the management of the partnership.

Rights to Specific
Partnership Property

Each partner holds partnership property as a *tenant in partnership* with all the other partners. Tenancy of ownership has several important effects. If a partner dies, the surviving partners have the right of survivorship. Because of principles of property law discussed in Chapter 52, the right of survivorship prevents the partnership's property from passing into the estate of the decedent. Surviving partners are entitled to possession, but they have a duty to account to the decedent's estate for the *value* of the deceased partner's interest in the partnership.

Rights to an Interest
in the Partnership

A partner's interest in the partnership is his or her share of the profits and surplus. It is viewed under the UPA as personal property.[5] A partner can assign the right to receive profits and capital to an assignee. This action neither dissolves the partnership nor creates any management rights in the assignee. After assignment, the partner (assignor) remains personally liable on all partnership debts and remains a partner.

Creditor Rights
against a Partnership

A partner's personal debts are not the debts of the partnership. A creditor cannot attach or

execute against true partnership assets to satisfy a partner's personal debts. Depending on state laws, a creditor can obtain a judgment against the partner and afterwards be granted a "charging order" against the partner's interest in the partnership. When this occurs, the creditor holds a lien against the partnership and is entitled to any future distribution of profits and assets ordinarily belonging to the debtor/partner until the judgment is satisfied. A firm's creditor, on the other hand, has rights to partnership property.

LIMITED PARTNERSHIPS

The limited partnership is a creature of statute. Most states have adopted some form of the Uniform Limited Partnership Act (ULPA), which codifies the law of limited partnerships. Limited partnerships are used most frequently in the context of commercial investment. A person willing to purchase the financial interest in a business might not want any management responsibility or personal liability for partnership debts. The limited partnership form meets this need, since only one general partner (who has unlimited liability) is necessary. In this case, the *general partner* assumes management responsibility of the partnership and takes full personal liability for all its debts. A *limited partner* contributes cash (or other property) and owns an interest in the firm but undertakes no management responsibilities and is not personally liable for partnership debts beyond the amount of his or her investment. This topic is treated in detail in Chapter 38.

TERMINATION

Introduction

Any change in the relations of the partners that demonstrates unwillingness or inability to carry on partnership business terminates the partnership. If any of the partners wish to continue the business, they are free to reorganize into a *new* partnership.

The termination of a partnership has two

---

5. For inheritance purposes, the distinction between personal and real property can be significant. This is especially important because even if the firm's assets are real property, the value of the interest paid to the estate is received and treated as personal property.

stages—dissolution and winding up. Both must take place before termination is complete.

Dissolution occurs when any partner (or partners) indicates an intention to disassociate from the partnership. *Winding up* is the actual process of collecting and distributing the partnership's assets.

Dissolution is the principal remedy of a partner against copartners. Events causing the dissolution can be grouped into three basic categories: (1) acts by partners, (2) operation of law, and (3) court decree.

Dissolution terminates the right of a partnership to exist as a going concern, but the partnership continues to exist long enough to wind up its affairs. When winding up is complete, the partnership's *legal* existence is terminated. The concepts of dissolution and winding up are discussed by the Supreme Court of Minnesota in the next case.

MARAS v.
STILINOVICH

Supreme Court of Minnesota,
1978. 268 N.W.2d 541.

BACKGROUND AND FACTS *The plaintiff, Mary Stilinovich, brought this appeal to contest the finding of a referee appointed to liquidate the assets of a partnership between herself and the defendant, Nick Maras. The referee ordered the dissolution of the partnership due to irreconcilable differences between the partners. The plaintiff and the defendant were a sister and brother who had formed a partnership by oral agreement with assets left to them by their deceased father. There were accusations of misappropriation on both sides, and the referee was appointed. Maras tendered a written offer to buy out his sister for $65,000. No such offer was submitted by the plaintiff. A hearing was held, and the referee ordered an accounting. After the accounting, he ordered the business to be sold to Maras for the $65,000. The plaintiff contended that the referee erred in his order.*

YETKA, Justice.

* * *

[This] was essentially a partnership dissolution in which the undivided two-thirds interest in the land and building was treated as a partnership asset. * * * [W]hether a sale could be ordered to one partner over the objection of the other [is contested. The parties stipulated that the assets were partnership assets and not subject to mere partition.] We find the stipulation is broad enough to allow sale to one partner where the other fails to tender a timely bid. * * *

After dissolution, a partnership continues until liquidated or wound up. Although dissolution of a partnership is usually followed by liquidation, a withdrawing partner may be paid his partnership contribution and share of accumulated profits and no liquidation need occur. Minn. [law] provides, in effect, that the partnership affairs must be wound up after dissolution unless otherwise agreed. Crane and Bromberg, Law of Partnership, § 86, suggests that the most logical buyers of a dissolved partnership are the remaining partners, and in the stipulation the parties agreed to one of the partners carrying on the business. Agreements for continuation of partnership business after dissolution are generally valid and enforceable. * * * Oral agreements are generally sufficient to establish a partnership relationship * * * and we hold that the oral agreement in this case was sufficient to establish the framework for dissolution of a partnership. The referee was clearly acting within the scope of his powers by ordering the sale to [defendant].

* * *

The method of conducting and confirming a judicial sale is within the discretion of the court, and the policy of the law should be to sustain judicial sales where no injustice occurs. Thus, if the parties were treated fairly and the rights of [plaintiff] were not prejudiced by the terms of the sale, then the trial court [judgment] should be affirmed.

* * *

The court examined the proceedings and concluded that dissolution was fair. The trial court judgment was therefore affirmed.

JUDGMENT AND REMEDY

Dissolution by Acts of the Partners

BY AGREEMENT A partnership can be dissolved if certain events stipulated in the partnership agreement occur. For example, when a partnership agreement expresses a fixed term or a particular business objective to be accomplished, the passing of the date or the accomplishment of the project dissolves the partnership. However, partners do not have to abide by the stipulations in the agreement. They can mutually agree to dissolve the partnership early or to extend it. If they agree to continue in the partnership, they become *partners at will*, with all the rights and duties remaining as originally agreed.

PARTNER'S POWER TO WITHDRAW A partnership is a personal legal relationship among co-owners. No person can be compelled either to be a partner or to remain one. Implicit in a partnership is each partner's *power* to disassociate from the partnership at any time. A and C form a partnership with no definite term or particular undertaking specified—that is, a partnership at will. Both A and C have the power and the right to withdraw from the partnership. The partnership continues for three years, until one day C announces that she no longer wishes to continue in the partnership. Assuming that C's sudden withdrawal will not do irreparable damage to the firm, her act is sufficient to begin the process of dissolution.

It is expected that a partner will attempt to dissolve in good faith. Bad faith is evidenced, for example, when a partner's election of dissolution is prompted by hopes of personal gain from a business opportunity that ordinarily would go to the partnership. In such a case, the partner will still have the *power* to withdraw and dissolve the partnership but will not have the *right* and therefore may be liable for resulting losses.

ADMISSION OF NEW PARTNERS Any change in the composition of the partnership, whether by withdrawal of a partner or by *admission of a new partner*, results in dissolution. In practice, this result is usually modified by providing that the remaining or new partners continue in the firm's business. Nonetheless, a new partnership arises. The new partnership carries over the debts of the dissolved partnership. Creditors of the prior partnership become creditors of the one that is continuing the business. [UPA Sec. 41]

TRANSFER OF A PARTNER'S INTEREST The UPA provides that voluntary transfer [6] or involuntary sale of a partner's interest for the benefit of creditors does not alone operate to dissolve the partnership. [UPA Sec. 28] However, either occurrence can ultimately lead to judicial dissolution of the partnership, as discussed below.

_____

6. UPA Sec. 27. A single partner cannot transfer his or her interest to another person and *make* that person a partner in the firm.

Dissolution by Operation of Law

DEATH A partnership is dissolved upon the death of any partner, even if the partnership agreement provides for carrying on the business with the executor of the decedent's estate. Any change in the composition among partners results in a new partnership. (But there is always the possibility of a reformation of the partnership upon the death of a partner.)

BANKRUPTCY Because a partner's credit reputation is an intrinsic part of his or her contribution to a partnership, the bankruptcy of a partner will dissolve a partnership in most cases. Insolvency alone will not result in dissolution. Naturally, bankruptcy of the firm itself will result in dissolution.

ILLEGALITY Any event that makes it unlawful for the partnership to continue its business or for any partner to carry on in the partnership will result in dissolution. Even if the illegality of the partnership business is a cause for dissolution, the partners can decide to change the nature of their business and continue in the partnership. For example, A and B enter a partnership agreement to run a tuna fishing business. Subsequently a maritime law prohibiting tuna fishing by private concerns is passed. A and B do not necessarily have to dissolve their partnership. They can choose to remain partners and fish for something that is not prohibited.

When the illegality applies to an individual partner, then dissolution *must* occur. For example, the state legislature passes a law making it illegal for magistrate judges to engage in the practice of law. Once an attorney in a law firm is appointed a magistrate, the partnership must be dissolved. The next case deals with dissolution of a partnership due to illegality.

WILLIAMS v. BURRUS

Court of Appeals of Washington, Division 1, 1978. 20 Wash. App. 494, 581 P.2d 164.

BACKGROUND AND FACTS *Williams sued the defendant, Burrus, for an accounting and dissolution of their partnership. The dissolution evolved out of a law that prevented certain people from being awarded a liquor license. Since Williams was within that class of people, Burrus bought the partnership asset, a restaurant, in his name alone. It was shown at trial that if disclosure of Williams's interest had been known, the license would have been denied. The only issue to be considered on appeal was whether the trial court erred in refusing to give Williams any relief in the form of his share of partnership assets.*

ANDERSEN, Judge.

* * *

Courts will not assist in the dissolution of an illegal partnership or entertain an action for an accounting or distribution of its assets. The trial court's decision was not erroneous.

Where, as here, no error is assigned to the findings of fact, our review is limited to determining whether the challenged conclusions of law are supported by the findings.

No state retail liquor license of any kind can be issued to a partnership unless all of the members thereof are qualified to obtain a license, and no licenseholder can allow any other person to use such a license.

Furthermore, a partnership is dissolved by any event which makes it unlawful for the business of the partnership to be carried on or for the members to carry it on in partnership.

The issue of illegality may be raised at any time.

Under the general rule that the courts will not aid either party to an illegal agreement where a partnership is formed to carry out an illegal business or to conduct a lawful business in an illegal manner, the courts will refuse to aid any of the parties thereto in an action against the other. * * *
* * *

The appellate court affirmed the trial court's holding that the partnership was illegal and refused to enforce any rights for any of the parties. The case was dismissed.

JUDGMENT AND REMEDY

Dissolution by Judicial Decree

Dissolution of a partnership can result from judicial decree. UPA Sec. 32 provides the following situations in which a court can dissolve a firm.

INSANITY A partnership can obtain judicial declaration of dissolution where a partner is adjudicated insane or is shown to be of unsound mind. This action often involves a series of complex tests and standards.

INCAPACITY When it appears that a partner has become incapable of performing his or her duties under the partnership agreement, a decree of dissolution may be required. It must appear that the incapacity is permanent and will substantially affect the partner's ability to discharge his or her duties to the firm.

BUSINESS IMPRACTICALITY When it becomes obvious that the firm's business can be operated only at a loss, judicial dissolution may be ordered.

IMPROPER CONDUCT A partner's impropriety involving partnership business (for example, fraud perpetrated upon the other partners) or improper behavior reflecting unfavorably upon the firm (for example, habitual drunkenness) will provide grounds for a judicial decree of dissolution.

Dissolution may also be granted when personal dissension between partners becomes so persistent and harmful as to undermine the confidence and cooperation necessary to carry on the firm's business. (In general, courts are reluctant to allow partners to sue each other except for dissolution.) This type of dissension is illustrated by the next case.

BACKGROUND AND FACTS *The plaintiff, First Western, sued for dissolution of its partnership with the defendant, Hotel Gearhart. On May 1, 1968, the plaintiff and the defendant agreed to purchase a motel and restaurant. They also agreed that the plaintiff would be responsible for financing the purchase and construction costs of building condominiums on the property. The defendant was to be responsible for operating the existing motel and restaurant. The profits were to be split, with 75 percent allocated to the plaintiff and 25 percent to the defendant. Thirty condominium units were built at a profit of $95,000. Shortly thereafter, dissension arose between the partners. The plaintiff charged the defendant with commingling partnership funds with his own funds and with failure to pay taxes. The defendant charged the plaintiff with failure to provide a complete accounting and with charging improper expenses.*

FIRST WESTERN MORTGAGE CO. v. HOTEL GEARHART, INC.
Supreme Court of Oregon, 1971.
260 Or. 196, 488 P.2d 450.

When the dissension reached a peak, the plaintiff filed this suit for dissolution. The trial court refused to dissolve the partnership on the ground that the disharmony between the partners was too trifling to justify termination.

HOWELL, Justice.
* * *

The plaintiff was entitled to a decree of dissolution. Although the parties were engaged in a joint venture, the law applicable to partnerships applies to joint ventures. Under [Oregon law] on application of a partner the court *shall* decree a dissolution for various reasons, including circumstances which render a dissolution equitable. In the instant case the parties had the right to dissolve the partnership by the express will of either party as the partnership had no definite term. * * * However, this does not preclude a partner from bringing a suit for dissolution by judicial decree. In such event, a court of equity may decree a dissolution because of any circumstances which render such dissolution just and equitable or where the interests of the partners will be best served by a dissolution. While a court of equity will not decree dissolution because of trifling disputes among the partners, *dissolution will be granted where the dissensions are so serious and persistent as to make continuance impracticable, or where all confidence and cooperation between the parties have been destroyed.* [Emphasis added.]

In the instant case the trial court refused dissolution on the ground that the disputes were trifling. We disagree. The evidence definitely establishes that serious disharmony exists between the parties. This fact is not disputed, and both parties want a termination of their joint venture. * * *

JUDGMENT AND REMEDY   *The decision of the trial court was reversed, and the case was remanded with directions to the trial court to grant the dissolution, to wind up the joint venture, and to direct an accounting.*

Notice of Dissolution

Dissolution ends the partnership as a going concern. Thereafter, it remains viable only for the purpose of winding up its affairs. In some circumstances, however, a partnership or a withdrawing partner can become bound to a contract made after dissolution has begun but before winding up is complete.

NOTICE TO PARTNERS   The intent to dissolve or withdraw from a firm must be communicated *clearly*. All partners will share liability for the acts of any partner who continues conducting business for the firm without knowing the partnership has been dissolved. For example, A, B, and C have a partnership. A tells B of her intent to withdraw. Before C learns of A's intentions, C enters a contract with a third party. The contract is equally binding on A, B, and C. Unless the other partners have notice, the withdrawing partner will continue to be bound as a partner to all contracts created for the firm.

NOTICE TO THIRD PARTIES   Dissolution of a partnership by the act of a partner requires notice to all affected third persons. The manner of giving notice depends upon the third person's relationship to the firm. Any third person who has dealt with the firm must receive *actual notice*. For all others, a newspaper or similar public notice is sufficient.

Dissolution resulting from operation of law requires *no notice* to third parties. However, surviving partners can be bound by communications sent to a deceased partner from a client who did not know of the partner's death.[7]

Winding Up

Once dissolution occurs and partners have been notified, they cannot create new obligations on behalf of the partnership. Their only authority is to complete transactions begun but not finished at the time of dissolution and to wind up the business of the partnership. Winding up includes collecting and preserving partnership assets, discharging liabilities (paying debts), and accounting to each partner for the value of his or her interest in the partnership.

Where dissolution is caused by a partner's act that violates the partnership agreement, the innocent partners may have rights to damages resulting from the dissolution. Also, the innocent partners have the right to buy out the offending partner and continue the business instead of winding up the partnership.

_____

7. Childers v. United States, 442 F.2d 1299 (5th Cir. 1971).

Dissolution resulting from the death of a partner vests all partnership assets in the surviving partners. The surviving partners act as a fiduciary in settling partnership affairs as quickly as practicable and in accounting to the estate of the deceased partner for the value of the decedent's interest in the partnership. The surviving partners are entitled to payment for their services in winding up the partnership as well as to reimbursement for any costs incurred in the process. [UPA Sec. 18(f)]

Distribution of Assets

Both creditors of the partnership and creditors of the individual partners can make claims on the partnership's assets. In general, creditors of the partnership have priority over creditors of individual partners in the distribution of partnership assets; the converse priority is usually followed in the distribution of individual partner assets.

The distribution of partners' assets is made after third party debts are paid. The priorities are as follows:

1. Refund of advances made to or for the firm by a partner.
2. Return of capital contribution to a partnership.
3. Distribution of the balance, if any, to partners in accordance with their respective interest in the partnership.

QUESTIONS AND CASE PROBLEMS

1. In April 1970, Harber, Pittman, and Calvert entered into an oral agreement to build and sell 235 houses. Following their agreement, Harber withdrew $6,000 in partnership funds and purchased three lots on which houses were to be built. The lots were purchased in his name, and after the homes were constructed, title was also in his name. When Harber sells the houses (at a profit) can he retain the proceeds

for himself? [Davis v. Pioneer Bank and Trust Co., 272 So.2d 430 (La.App. 1973)]
2. Prior to 1964, Dr. Cook was engaged in the practice of pathology in the city of Lake Charles. He owned a laboratory and worked at several local hospitals. Dr. Stevens, who had been practicing only a short time, moved to Lake Charles and entered into an agreement with Dr. Cook. The agreement provided that the two were to operate as partners. Dr. Cook agreed to furnish the use of his laboratory and equipment, which would remain in his own name; and each doctor agreed to devote his full working time to the partnership. Also, both agreed to perform,

as nearly as feasible, 50 percent of the work of the partnership. Neither doctor transferred ownership of any money or property, including medical equipment, to the partnership. The agreement also provided that all partnership assets would belong to Dr. Cook upon termination of the partnership. Is there a partnership? [Stevens v. Cook and Stevens, 245 So.2d 798 (La.App. 1971)]

3. Altman entered into an agreement with Young Lumber Company whereby Altman was to act as superintendent for a particular job that Young Lumber wished to contract as a subcontractor. The agreement also provided that Altman would estimate the job for Young Lumber and that he would receive 50 percent of the profits as his pay. There was no understanding, however, as to the sharing of losses. In addition, once work commenced, all necessary contracts were signed and all bills were paid in the name of Young Lumber. Is there a partnership between Altman and Young Lumber? [United States v. Young Lumber Co., 376 F.Supp. 1290 (D.C.S.C. 1974)]

4. Everett H. Johnson was a home builder. He had operated under the trade name of "Everett H. Johnson & Son" since 1952, when his son, Everett R., was in his early teens. Not long after Everett R. returned from the Korean War, he became an employee of his father. Less than a year later, Everett H. Johnson entered into a contract with Mr. and Mrs. Bragg. Most of the discussions about contract negotiations were held in the presence of both Johnson and his son. In addition, the contract was typed on stationery bearing the name "Everett H. Johnson & Son." When Johnson and his son talked to the Braggs, it became apparent to the Braggs that Everett R. was a neophyte in the business and was just learning the trade. At no time did the father state to the Braggs that his son was a partner. As a result of a subsequent dispute, the Braggs asserted that they believed that Johnson and his son were partners and that their final decision to enter into the contract was based upon their belief that the son was a partner. Would a court infer a partnership by estoppel under these circumstances? [Bragg v. Johnson, 229 A.2d 497 (Del.Super.Ct. 1966)]

5. In April 1964, Campbell and Miller agreed to go into the meat packing and processing business as a partnership. Campbell, who had experience in the meat packing business, promised Miller, who had experience in the construction business, that if Miller would plan and construct a meat packing building and draw a salary during the building's construction of only $75 per week, upon completion of the building

the two would operate the business as a partnership, sharing profits and losses on a 50/50 basis. The building was to be built with both parties' funds, and upon its completion, Miller was to retain ownership and lease the building to the partnership. Just prior to the completion of the building, Campbell backed out of the partnership. Can Miller recover from Campbell for breach of partnership agreement? [Campbell v. Miller, 274 N.C. 143, 161 S.E.2d 546 (1968)]

6. In 1969, Simon, Genia, and Ury Rapoport entered into an agreement with Morton, Gerome, and Burton Parnes to form the partnership known as 55 Perry Company. Each of the families owned 50 percent of the partnership interests. In December 1974, Simon and Genia Rapoport assigned a 10 percent interest of their share in the partnership to their adult children, Daniel and Kalia. An amended partnership certificate was filed in the county clerk's office, as required by law, indicating the addition of Daniel and Kalia as partners. However, when the Rapoports requested the Parneses to execute an amended partnership agreement reflecting this change in the partnership, the Parneses refused. In a court action by the Rapoports to force the Parnes to execute the amended partnership agreement, what will be the result? What interest in the partnership, if any, can Daniel and Kalia Rapoport take without the Parneses' consent? [Rapoport v. 55 Perry Co., 50 A.D.2d 54, 376 N.Y.S.2d 147 (1975)]

7. Lynne, Ernest, and Stanley Timmermann established a partnership in 1965 for the purpose of engaging in farming activities. In January 1969, Lynne stated to the other two partners that he no longer wished to be involved in the partnership. It was not until August 31, 1970, however, that Lynne ceased to participate in the farming activities of the partnership. In January 1972, Lynne attempted to bring about a forced liquidation of the partnership through a lawsuit. In January 1969, the value of the partnership was approximately $50,000. On August 31, 1970, the value of the partnership was slightly less than $10,000; and in January 1972, the value of the partnership was in excess of $300,000. Assuming Lynne had a one-third interest in the partnership, approximately how much should he receive when he withdraws? Explain your answer. [Timmermann v. Timmermann, 272 Or. 613, 538 P.2d 1254 (1975)]

8. On September 28, 1958, Reid and three others entered into a written partnership agreement for the purpose of leasing for profit certain real property located in Montgomery County, Pennsylvania. Reid was to manage the property, and the others were to

perform the physical labor necessary to maintain the premises in good condition. One year later, Reid notified the others that she was dissolving the partnership and requested that the partnership assets be liquidated as soon as possible. Has dissolution occurred? Assuming dissolution has occurred, can the other partners recover damages for breach of partnership agreement on the ground that the partnership was a partnership for a particular undertaking and hence not terminable at will? [Girard Bank v. Haley, 460 Pa. 237, 332 A.2d 443 (1975)]

9. A partnership, known as Mac Coal Company, was formed by Thomas Eddy and Carlo Teodori in 1964. Shortly thereafter, the partnership purchased a coal mine from North Star Coal Company, one-fourth of which was paid for with partnership funds and three-fourths of which was paid for with a mortgaged bank loan. One year later, Teodori withdrew from the partnership. Mortgage payments are due over the next nine years. Can Eddy, the remaining partner, continue paying the mortgage in the name of Mac Coal Company? [North Star Coal Co. v. Eddy, 442 Pa. 583, 277 A.2d 154 (1971)]

10. Respass and Sharp were partners who owned and managed a racing stable. In addition, they were engaged in bookmaking. At the time Sharp died, $4,724, representing the undistributed profits of the bookmaking business, was on deposit in Sharp's personal bank account. Respass, arguing that Sharp's death resulted in dissolution of the partnership, sought to recover one-half of the profits from the bookmaking business. What result? [Central Trust and Safe Co. v. Respass, 112 Ky. 606, 66 S.W. 421 (1902)]

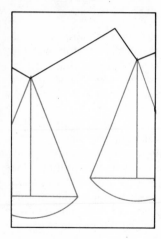

38

Partnerships
Operation and Duties

The rights and duties of partners are governed largely by the specific terms of their partnership agreement. In the absence of provisions to the contrary in the partnership agreement, the law imposes the rights and duties discussed in this chapter. The character and nature of the partnership business generally influence the application of these rights and duties.

RIGHTS AMONG PARTNERS

Management

"All partners have equal rights in the management and conduct of partnership business." [UPA Sec. 18(c)] Management rights belong to all partners in an ordinary partnership.[1] Each partner has one vote in management matters *regardless of the proportional size of his or her interest in the firm.* Often, partners will agree to delegate daily management responsibilities to a management committee made up of one or more partners.

---

1. Compare the management rights of general and limited partners in limited partnerships. The absence of management responsibility and the concomitant liability limitations are distinguishing characteristics of such partnerships. See the discussion on limited partnership in Chapter 39.

The majority rule controls decisions in ordinary matters connected with partnership business. However, unanimous consent of the partners is required to bind the firm in any of the following actions:

1. To alter the essential nature of the firm's business as expressed in the partnership agreement or to alter the capital structure of the partnership. [UPA Sec. 18(h)]
2. To admit new partners or enter a wholly new business.
3. To assign partnership property into a trust for the benefit of creditors.
4. To dispose of the partnership's goodwill.
5. To confess judgment against the partnership or submit partnership claims to arbitration.
6. To undertake any act that would make further conduct of partnership business impossible. [UPA Sec. 9(3)]

Each of these matters significantly affects the nature of the partnership.

INTEREST IN THE PARTNERSHIP Each partner is entitled to the proportion of business profits and losses that is designated in the partnership agreement. If the agreement does not apportion profits and losses, the partners share in them equally. For example, Browning and Lewis form a partnership. Browning contributes 60 percent of the capital and Lewis 40 percent. Unless their agreement reflects a 60-40 distribution, they will each obtain a 50 percent interest in the firm and share equally in both profits and losses. This point is raised in the following case.

BACKGROUND AND FACTS *Alfred Waagen, the plaintiff, and Karl Gerde, the defendant, ran a commercial fishing business and owned a fishing vessel named the Princess. During the first five years of the business, the Princess made a number of fishing trips along the Pacific coast looking for tuna, halibut, and salmon without any marked success. The defendant decided to try fishing for soupfin shark, so he bought some secondhand nets and began experimenting with them. He was able to catch some shark, but the nets soon became torn and useless. The defendant wrote to the plaintiff twice about using nets to catch shark. The plaintiff received the second letter, and although he never expressly agreed to the purchase of the netting, he never objected.*

The plaintiff and the defendant alternated every six months in running the fishing vessel and divided the profits in the following way. Two-thirds of each trip's catch went to the crew and one-third to the boat. The plaintiff and the defendant each received one-half of the boat's share.

When the defendant began netting for sharks, he retained all of the boat's one-third share of the catch. The defendant's theory was that since the plaintiff had not expressly authorized the purchase of the nets, they belonged exclusively to the defendant, and he was entitled to plaintiff's one-half share as rental for their use.

The Princess was subsequently sold, and the defendant disposed of the nets for $7,000, a sum that he retained in addition to the rental ($37,705.42) that he had charged against the boat's one-third share of the catch. The total profit resulting from the use and sale of these nets was $23,832.88, and the defendant kept it all. Furthermore, when the partnership was dissolved, the defendant failed to account for this sum of

WAAGEN v. GERDE
Supreme Court of Washington, 1950.
36 Wash. 2d 563, 219 P. 2d 595.

money. Therefore, the plaintiff claimed one-half of this sum, or $11,916.44.

In the trial court, the defendant argued that the shark netting venture was separate from the commercial fishing business in which he and the plaintiff had been partners. Therefore, he had no need to share half this sum with the plaintiff.

However, in submitting income tax returns for the partnership, the defendant had provided a sworn statement indicating the name of the partnership and its date of organization. Furthermore, the organization had been designated as a partnership. The defendant had also provided the name and address of both himself and the plaintiff as copartners. On the strength of this sworn statement, the trial court determined that a partnership existed and that the plaintiff and the defendant were to share equally in the partnership.

DONWORTH, Justice.

* * *

Coming back to the question of whether the shark nets were a separate venture of appellant and not a partnership activity, the judgment and decree contains this finding:

"It Further Appearing from the accounts and records of the partnership and the accounting thereof that the defendant Karl Gerde, during the life of the partnership, collected all of the proceeds of the partnership business, and from time to time accounted to the plaintiff, but that said accounting to the plaintiff was false and fraudulent, in that said defendant Gerde failed to advise the plaintiff that he was retaining one-half of the proceeds of all shark caught by the partnership for rental to himself for the use of the said nets, to-wit, the sum of $44,705.42; that said defendant charged to said gross amount the cost of said nets and the maintenance thereof, and credited and retained for his own account the sum of $23,832.88; that he fraudulently concealed from the plaintiff the fact that he retained said sums, and that said sums were deducted from the gross earnings of the M/V Princess, and led the plaintiff to believe that defendant had accounted fully for the earnings of said vessel; that plaintiff did not discover that the defendant Karl Gerde claimed these nets as his separate property and entitled to the earnings thereof until after * * * [dissolution of the partnership] * * *."

* * *

From the evidence above referred to, and other testimony and exhibits in the record, we are convinced that the findings of the trial court, that *the parties were partners in connection with the purchase and use of the shark nets, are fully sustained* * * *. [Emphasis added.]

This being so, the rule stated in Simich v. Culjak, 27 Wash.2d 403, 178 P.2d 336, 339, is applicable here: "It is the universal rule that partners are required to exercise the utmost good faith toward each other, and where an accounting is had, it is the duty of a partner who manages, conducts, or operates a partnership business, to render complete and accurate accounts of all of the partnership business. This rule is grounded upon the theory that the managing partner is acting as a trustee for his firm.

* * *

The general rule is clear that one partner is not entitled to extra compensation from the partnership, in the absence of an express or an implied agreement therefor. Each case must depend largely upon its own facts, and thus other cases are generally of little or no assistance in deciding the case at hand.

The exception to the general rule is well stated in 1 Rowley, Modern Law of Partnership 412, § 354, as follows: " 'Where it can be fairly and justly implied from the course of dealing between the partners, nor [or] from circumstances of equivalent force, that one partner is to be compensated for his services, his claim will be sustained.' 'The partnership may be of such a peculiar kind, and the arrangements and the course of dealing of the partners in regard to it may be such as pretty plainly to show an expectation and understanding, without an express agreement upon the subject, that certain services of a copartner should be paid for. Such cases, presenting unusual conditions, are exceptions to the general rule.' "

While appellant's ingenuity and industry were largely responsible for the success of the Princess in shark fishing, we cannot find anything in the record from which an agreement to pay him special compensation could be implied. Appellant did inform respondent that he was busy getting the nets ready and that it would "be lots of work to fix" them, but never at any time did he inform respondent what the work actually entailed or that he expected any compensation for it. Since respondent had so little knowledge of the conduct of the net operations, there could not be any implied agreement for compensation. The trial court found no factual basis for such an allowance, and we can find none in the record.

The facts as found by the trial court were adopted by the appellate court. The lower court correctly applied the legal principles involved, and the plaintiff was granted $11,916.44 as his share of the partnership profits.	**JUDGMENT AND REMEDY**
As a general rule, the filing of a partnership income tax return does not constitute an admission that a partnership exists. It raises the presumption of a partnership, but that presumption can be overcome by other evidence. In this case, the information contained in the partnership return did constitute an admission that the partnership existed because defendant gave certain pertinent information under oath.	**COMMENTS**

Compensation

A partner's time, skill, and energy on behalf of partnership business is a duty and generally not a compensable service. Partners can, of course, agree otherwise. For example, the managing partner of a law firm often receives a salary in addition to his share of profits for performing special administrative duties in office and personnel management. UPA Sec. 18(s) provides that a surviving partner is entitled to compensation for services in winding up partnership affairs (and reimbursement for expenses incurred in the process) above and apart from his or her share in the partnership profits.

Each partner impliedly promises to devote full time and render exclusive service to the partnership. Assume that Hunter, Brooks, and Palmer enter a partnership. Palmer undertakes independent consulting for an outside firm without the consent of Hunter and Brooks. Palmer's compensation from the outside firm is considered partnership income. A partner cannot engage in any independent competitive or even noncompetitive activities that involve the partnership's time. If Palmer engages in an activity that competes with the partnership, then Palmer has breached the fiduciary duty that he owes it. Even with a noncompetitive activity, Palmer can breach his fiduciary duty if the partnership suffers from the loss of his efforts. Of course, the partnership agreement or unanimous consent of the partners can permit a partner to engage in any activity.

Inspection of Books

Partnership books and records must be kept equally accessible to all partners. Each partner has the right to examine (and each partner has the corresponding duty to produce) full and complete information concerning the conduct of all aspects of partnership business. [UPA Sec. 20] Each firm retains books in which to record and secure such information. Partners contribute the information, and a bookkeeper typically has the duty to preserve it. The books must be kept at the firm's principal business office and cannot be removed without the consent of all the partners. [UPA Sec. 19] Every partner, whether active or inactive, is entitled to inspect all books and records upon demand and can make copies of the materials. The personal representative of a deceased partner's estate has the same right of access to partnership books and records that the decedent would have had.

Accounting

An accounting of partnership assets or profits is done to determine the value of each partner's proportionate share in the partnership. An accounting can be performed voluntarily, or it can be compelled by order of a court in equity.[2]

_____

2. The principal remedy of a partner against copartners is an equity suit for dissolution, an accounting, or both. With minor exceptions, a partner cannot maintain an action against other firm members for damages until partnership affairs are settled and an accounting is done. This rule is necessary because legal disputes between partners invariably involve conflicting claims to shares in the partnership. Logically, the value of each partner's share must first be determined by an accountant.

Formal accounting occurs by right in connection with dissolution proceedings, but a partner also has the right to a formal accounting in the following situations:

1. When the partnership agreement provides for a formal accounting.
2. When a partner is wrongfully excluded from the business, from access to the books, or both.
3. When any partner is withholding profits or benefits belonging to the partnership in breach of the fiduciary duty.
4. When circumstances "render it just and reasonable." [UPA Sec. 22]

Property Rights

There is an important legal distinction between a partner's rights in specific property belonging to the firm to be used for business purposes and a partner's right to share in the firm's earned profits to the extent of the partner's interest in the firm. No individual partner has a right to specific property of the firm. Chapter 37 discussed the factors that the courts use in determining property rights of partners in partnerships and the rights of creditors. A judgment creditor of an individual partner has no right to execute or attach specific partnership property, but he or she can obtain the partner's share of profits. A creditor of the firm can levy directly upon partnership property (discussed below).

PARTNER'S INTEREST IN THE FIRM A partner's interest in the firm is a personal asset consisting of a proportionate share of the profits earned and a return of capital after dissolution and winding up.

A partner's interest is susceptible to assignment or to a judgment creditor's lien. Neither an assignment nor a court's charging order entitling a creditor to receive a share of the partner's money will cause dissolution of the firm.

PARTNERSHIP PROPERTY Partners are "tenants in partnership" of all firm property. A partner has no right to sell, assign, or in any way deal with a particular item of partnership property as an exclusive owner. Nor is a partner's personal credit related to partnership property; creditors cannot use it to satisfy the personal debts of a partner. Partnership property is available only to satisfy partnership debts, to enhance the firm's credit, or to achieve other business purposes.

Every partner is a co-owner with all other partners of specific partnership property such as office equipment, paper supplies, and vehicles. Each partner has equal rights to possess partnership property for business purposes or in satisfaction of firm debts, but not for any other purpose without the consent of all the other partners. These principles are aptly illustrated by the next case.

BACKGROUND AND FACTS   *The plaintiff and the defendant who were partners in a real estate business dissolved the partnership by mutual agreement on May 1, 1975. The original agreement called for each partner to share equally in profits and losses. On November 29, 1972, the defendant made a down payment on a piece of property in his own name and reimbursed himself out of the partnership's checking account. The property was carried on the books of the partnership. At dissolution, the plaintiff wanted the defendant to turn over 50 percent of the rents and profits from that property. The trial court ruled for the plaintiff, and the defendant appealed.*

STAUTH v. STAUTH
Court of Appeals of Kansas, 1978.
—Kan.—,582 P.2d 1160.

SPENCER, Judge.
* * *

The evidence was conflicting as to whether defendant was to hold the property for the partnership. Defendant testified that sometime after he had signed the real estate purchase contract, but prior to closing, it was agreed between plaintiff and defendant that they would share profits on the sales of houses and lots as long as plaintiff supervised construction on the lots. The lots were then entered as assets on the partnership records as a matter of convenience, and if plaintiff was to share in the profits, the expenses should be paid by the partnership. Plaintiff testified that the agreement prior to closing was that the lots were to be partnership property, but that defendant told him the lots could be held in defendant's name alone as a convenience in making sales. In that way only defendant and his wife would be required to execute conveyances. Plaintiff stated that defendant told him that the attorney for the partnership had indicated that title to the real estate might be held in defendant's name alone as long as there was a written agreement that the lots were indeed partnership property.

In 60 Am.Jur.2d, *Partnership* § 93, pp. 22-23, it is stated:

"* * * An agreement that certain real estate should be part of the firm assets may be implied from the acts and conduct of the partners; the agreement need not be express.

"* * * [A]mong indicia of partnership ownership are the payment by the partnership of taxes * * *.

"Partnership books may also be considered to determine the question, as, for example, how the property was entered and carried on the books of the company. The manner in which the accounts are kept, whether the purchase money is severally charged to the members of the firm, or whether the accounts treat it the same as other firm property, may be controlling circumstances in determining such intention, and from these circumstances the agreement of the parties may be inferred."

From the record, it appears that the purchase of the real estate was entered on the partnership records prior to the closing of that transaction. Thereafter, abstract fees, taxes, and payments on the purchase money mortgage were paid by the partnership. Profits were reported as partnership income.

* * *

Did the partnership provide the purchase money or some part thereof? Defendant made the down payment from his personal account but was reimbursed from partnership funds on the day of closing the transaction. The purchase money was provided by a 100 percent loan obtained in the names of defendant and his wife and secured by a mortgage on the real estate. This loan was entered as a liability on the partnership records on the day that purchase was finalized. The partnership made all payments on the loan. * * * Even though funds for the purchase of the real estate were provided from another source, it is evident that the liability for repayment of those funds was assumed by the partnership, which thereafter did in fact make all payments that were made on the loan. There was evidence from which the trial court could properly find that the partnership paid the purchase money or some part thereof.

JUDGMENT AND REMEDY   *The appellate court affirmed the trial court's ruling that the defendant had to turn over 50 percent of the profits in rents from the disputed property to the plaintiff.*

DUTIES AND POWERS OF PARTNERS

Fiduciary Duty

Partners stand in a fiduciary relationship to one another the way that principals and agents do. (See Chapter 34.) It is a relationship of extraordinary trust and loyalty. The fiduciary duty imposes a responsibility upon each partner to act in good faith for the benefit of the partnership. It requires that each partner subordinate his or her personal interests in the event of conflict and consider the mutual welfare of all partners in partnership activities.

This fiduciary duty underlies the entire body of law pertaining to partnership and to agency. From it, certain other duties are commonly implied. Thus, a partner must account to the partnership for any personal profits or benefits derived without consent of all of the partners in any partnership transaction.[3] These include transactions among partners or with third parties connected with the formation, conduct, or liquidation of the partnership, or with any use of partnership property. [UPA Sec. 21]

Upon the death of a partner, the surviving partner is under a fiduciary duty to liquidate partnership assets without delay and credit the estate of the deceased partner for the value of the decedent's interest in the partnership. The fiduciary duty arises by implication in the personal representative of the deceased partner's estate as well. The principles of fiduciary duty and property rights are illustrated in the next case.

---

3. In this sense, "to account" to the partnership means not only to divulge the information but also to determine the value of any benefits or profits derived and to hold that money or property in trust on behalf of the partnership.

BACKGROUND AND FACTS *About 45 doctors, including Dr. Witlin, owned and operated a health center as partners. When Dr. Witlin died, the other doctors, in accordance with their partnership agreement, purchased his share of the center, paying his widow $65,228. The partnership agreement provided that on Witlin's death a management committee of the partnership was required to make a good faith determination of the fair market value of Witlin's share. The partnership had the option to offer this amount to Witlin's widow. The $65,228 offer, however, was based only on the book value of the partnership's assets. In addition, although the partnership was in the process of bargaining to sell the health center at a price which would have doubled Dr. Witlin's widow's proportionate share, the partnership did not inform her of that fact. Mrs. Witlin now seeks a greater amount for her husband's share, even though she has accepted the partnership's offer.*

ESTATE OF WITLIN
California Court of Appeal, 1978.
83 Cal. App. 3d 167, 147 Cal. Rptr. 723.

COBEY, Associate Justice.

* * *

Appellants [the forty-five doctors] owed such a duty to plaintiff as the widow and executrix of their deceased partner in purchasing from her their deceased partner's interest in the partnership. Throughout the transaction they were bound to act toward her "in the highest good faith" and they were forbidden to obtain any advantage over her in the matter by, among other things, the slightest concealment. Yet the management committee never revealed to plaintiff or her representative, King, that the basic value in their formula for determining the fair market value of the partnership was book value alone. Likewise, as already noted, the management committee did not mention to King the possibility that the hospital might be shortly sold.

This possibility of sale was quite real. It appears from plaintiff's improperly rejected offers of proof that the management committee reached in 1969 a tentative agreement with General Health Services to sell the partnership's assets to it for approximately $60,000 a percentage point, that between April and September 28, 1971, the management committee and the American Cyanamid Corporation were discussing a sale of the partnership to it for at least $93,000 a percentage point, and, as already noted from the evidence itself, that the partnership's assets were finally sold in June 1972 to Hospital Corporation of America for about $84,000 a percentage point.

The management committee knew all of this, but they apparently never breathed a word of it to either plaintiff or her attorney. It seems that in discussing the fair market value of the partnership they talked out of both sides of their mouths. They talked to plaintiff and her attorney in terms of $16,000 and $24,600 per percentage point while they were more or less simultaneously talking to conglomerates interested in purchasing the hospital and the other assets of the partnership in terms of selling prices ranging from $60,000 to $93,500 per percentage point. Given this situation, how could their offer of $24,600 per percentage point to plaintiff have been a good faith determination on their part of the fair market value of the partnership? Obviously the jury's verdict was correct and solidly supported in this respect.

JUDGMENT AND REMEDY *The judgment under appeal was affirmed. The partners were held to have breached their fiduciary duty to their deceased partner by failing to make a full and fair disclosure.*

General Agency Powers

Each partner is an *agent* of every other partner and acts as both a principal and an agent in any business transaction within the scope of the partnership agreement. Each partner is a general agent of the partnership to carry on the usual business of the firm. Thus, every partner's act in every contract and in every contract signed in the partnership name that furthers partnership business binds the firm. [UPA Sec. 9(1)]

The UPA affirms general principles of agency law that pertain to the authority of a partner to bind a partnership in contract or tort. When a partner is apparently carrying on partnership business with third persons in the usual way, both the partner and the firm share liability. It is only when third persons *know* that the partner has no such authority that the partnership is not liable. For example, P, a partner in Firm X, applies for a loan on behalf of the partnership without authorization from the other partners. The bank manager knows P has no authority. If the bank manager grants the loan, P will be personally bound, but the firm will not be liable.

JOINT LIABILITY Partners have only joint liability on all partnership debts and contracts. [UPA Sec. 15(b)] Partners are jointly and severally liable for tort actions and breaches of trust to third persons. [UPA Sec. 15(a)]

Joint liability means that the group of partners wins or loses as a group. One partner cannot be singled out to be sued. Every partner's name must be listed in the suit, and the individual assets of each partner are equally exposed to potential liability (although the actual contribution in the event of a judgment is calculated on each partner's proportionate share of the firm). If the court awards the claimant a judgment, the claimant is barred from further suits against the partners and against the firm, once satisfaction (that is, payment) of the judgment is made.

In states that allow a firm to be sued in its own name, a contract claimant or a creditor claimant can sue the firm as an *entity* without joining each partner. A judgment against the partnership binds only partnership assets. In such states, the better practice is to sue both the firm as an *entity* and all partners *jointly*. Then, judgment is enforceable against the assets of the partnership and the assets of the individual partners. The judgment rendered in such a case must be internally consistent. For example, if C sues Firm X and all its partners jointly for breach of contract and the court finds the firm liable, then it must hold the partners liable (and vice versa).

Joint and several liability means that a claimant can sue one partner without joining the others. Moreover, regardless of the outcome of the suit against the first partner, **res judicata** (a matter or thing settled by judgment in the courts) does not protect the other partners in subsequent suits filed against them.

Agency concepts relating to apparent authority, actual authority, and ratification are also applicable to partnerships. The extent of *implied authority* is generally broader for partners than for ordinary agents. The character and scope of the partnership business and the customary nature of the particular business operation determine the scope of implied powers. For example, the usual course of business in a trading or commercial partnership involves buying and selling commodities. Consequently, each partner in a trading firm has a wide range of implied powers to borrow money in the firm name and to extend the firm's credit in issuing or indorsing negotiable instruments.

In an ordinary partnership, firm members can exercise all implied powers reasonably necessary and customary to carry on that particular business. Some customarily implied powers include the authority to make warranties on goods in the sales business, the power to convey real property in the firm name where such conveyances are part of the ordinary course of partnership business, the power to enter contracts consistent with the firm's regular course of business, and the power to make admissions and representations concerning partnership affairs. [UPA Sec. 11]

Like the law of agency, the law of partnership imputes one partner's knowledge to all other partners because members of a partnership stand in a fiduciary relationship to one another. Such a relationship assumes that each partner willfully discloses to every other partner all relevant information pertaining to the business of the partnership. The same rule applies to members of a joint venture.

BACKGROUND AND FACTS *The plaintiff in this action, Mobil Oil Corp., leased some property. The lease contained certain restrictions against the sale of petroleum products on property adjoining the leased premises or within a thousand feet of the existing oil company station. The defendants leased the adjoining property and attempted to sell petroleum and petroleum products on the land. Mobil brought this action to enjoin (prohibit) the defendants from using the adjoining property as a service station for the duration of the lease.*

At the trial, the defendants argued that they had no knowledge of the lease restrictions against the sale of petroleum and petroleum products on that land. Mobil disputed the defendants' position, proving that one of the defendant partners had known of the restrictions and claiming that was sufficient to impute knowledge of the restriction to all the partners.

The trial court ruled in favor of the plaintiff, Mobil Oil Corp., and upheld the lease restrictions.

MOBIL OIL CORP. v. HURWITZ

Appellate Court of Illinois, 1978.

63 Ill. App. 3d 430, 20 Ill. Dec. 372, 380 N.E. 2d 49.

TRAPP, Justice.

* * *

Section 12 of the Uniform Partnership Act (Ill.Rev.Stat.1969, ch. 106½, par. 12) provided, as it now does:

> "Notice to any partner of any matter relating to partnership affairs, and the knowledge of the partner acting in the particular matter, acquired while a partner or then present to his mind, and the knowledge of any other partner who reasonably could and should have communicated it to the acting partner, operate as notice to or knowledge of the partnership, except in the case of a fraud on the partnership committed by or with the consent of that partner."

The context of the statute substantially coincides with language of the Supreme Court in *Greer v. Carter Oil Co.* (1940), 373 Ill. 168, 25 N.E.2d 805. Restrictions upon the use of this property are patently significant in the light of the value placed upon the property for commercial purposes. Accordingly, we conclude that the trial court did not err in imputing the knowledge of * * * [one partner] to * * * [another partner] during the course of the transaction.

The record shows strong reasons to impute knowledge of the respective covenant [restrictions on land] to the members of the joint venture. As noted, [the defendants] Sapp and Hurwitz were the founders of the joint venture. The record shows that on April 17, 1974, counsel for Sapp and Hurwitz by a letter addressed to each advised that as to a lease of another portion of the area, there were problems with restrictive covenants regarding the sale of petroleum products. In March 1973, a title commitment issued by the Chicago Title & Trust Company procured and paid for by Sapp noted the respective covenants of the Mobil lease. A sublease by Sapp and Hurwitz for a term of 25 years, executed September 7, 1973, contained the [same] restriction that no gasoline be sold. Thus, the record is clear that Sapp and Hurwitz had actual knowledge of the restriction at the time of forming the joint venture.

As a matter of law, the [other] members of a joint venture stand in a fiduciary relationship one with another. The relationship requires full disclosure to [all] the associates in a joint venture.

JUDGMENT AND REMEDY

The appellate court affirmed a permanent injunction entered in favor of Mobil Oil Corp. prohibiting the defendants from selling petroleum and petroleum products on the property adjoining the service station for the duration of their lease.

COMMENTS

Sometimes, land use restrictions are not enforceable because they impose or create an illegal restraint of trade. In such cases, the courts consider whether the restriction is so unreasonable that an individual cannot conduct a business or practice a profession. It must be demonstrated that the restriction seriously impairs the public interest as well. Indeed, to prove that a covenant is in violation of public policy, one must show that a perpetual injury to the public will result if the restrictions are enforced. If the covenant will not function in perpetuity, but is only for the life of the sublease, it will usually be held that the restriction does not injure the public interest.

Property Powers

A partner's power to sell partnership property bought for resale carries with it the implied powers to execute documents necessary to transfer title and make normal warranties. Hence, a partner in the tire business negotiating a contract for the sale of tires can warrant that "each lot of tires contains 1,000 radial tires, with white walls, 4 ply." The partner can also sign documents of title necessary for transporting the goods to the buyer. A partner does not have the power, however, to sell office equipment, fixtures, or other equipment used in the business without authorization from the other partners. A partner's power to purchase property for the partnership business carries with it the implied power to sign delivery acceptance documents for personal property, to accept title for real property, and to arrange payment of the purchase price in cash or upon the firm's credit.

Only if a firm is involved in the real estate business does a partner have the implied authority to convey partnership real estate. Otherwise, such a sale must be authorized.

QUESTIONS AND CASE PROBLEMS

1. A partnership agreement states the following: "The said partners have contributed to the partnership in the following proportions to-wit: John E. Craig, party of the first part, equipment, technical knowledge, skill, and experience in the proportion of 50 percent, Raymond L. Carney, party of the second part, equipment, technical knowledge, skill, and experience in the proportion of 50 percent, and John A. Hamilton, party of the third part, the sum of $20,000 cash to commence the business. It is agreed that the sum actually contributed by the party of the third part shall bear interest at the rate of 6 percent per annum." What proportion of profits or losses should be attributed to each of the partners? Would it make any difference if John Hamilton did not work in the business but the other two partners did? [Craig v. Hamilton, 213 Kan. 665, 518 P.2d 539 (1974)]

2. James and Edmund Bickett and William O'Brien entered into a written partnership agreement. Its express purpose was to buy a specific tract of timber land at a specific price. Contrary to this agreement, O'Brien purchased the land in his own name and with his own money. Can the Bicketts force O'Brien to convey the property to the partnership? Can they force O'Brien to convey two-thirds of the property to them personally? [O'Brien v. Bickett, 419 S.W.2d. 726 (Ky. App. 1967)]

3. A and B were brothers operating a dairy farm in North Carolina. In 1963, their assets were worth $100,000, and they had accumulated profits of $12,000. That year, C joined the partnership and contributed a $200,000 farm that he owned. In 1973, the partnership was dissolved. At that time, the assets were valued at $500,000, and accumulated profits totaled $12,000. How much is each partner entitled to upon dissolution? [Halsey v. Choate, 27 N.C. App. 49, 217 S.E.2d. 740 (1975)]

4. Summers, a partner in a two-person partnership, approached the other partner, Dooley, about hiring an additional employee. Dooley refused, stating that he did not believe the additional employee was needed. Nevertheless, Summers hired him. Dooley, who handled the payroll, objected to the hiring and refused to pay for the new employee out of partner-ship funds. After two months, Summers was finally forced to pay the man out of his own personal funds, and the man quit. Summers then sought reimbursement from the partnership. Can he recover? [Summers v. Dooley, 94 Idaho 87, 481 P.2d. 318 (1971)]

5. David Bell and Fred Herzog were partners in a real estate partnership. The partnership operated from August 1968 until August 1969, when Herzog notified Bell that he, Herzog, considered Bell's failure to devote his time and efforts to the real estate business and his failure to make payments required by the partnership agreement a breach of the agreement and that he was therefore terminating the partnership. Bell in turn wrote to Herzog, stating that he considered Herzog's letter to be the "last straw" and that he, Bell, was therefore terminating the partnership. Bell then sought an accounting of all the partnership's assets and liabilities. Herzog objected on the ground that Bell's failure to contribute to the management of the partnership constituted a breach of fiduciary duty, a breach of the partnership agreement, and a breach of the Uniform Partnership Act. Should Bell's demand for an accounting be denied? [Bell v. Herzog, 39 A.D.2d 813, 322 N.Y.S.2d. 501 (1972)]

6. Frances, Henry, and Reuben Barthuly were partners in a somewhat unsuccessful partnership. Frances and Henry together owned a one-half interest, and Reuben owned the other half. Under the partnership agreement, Henry had the authority to hire employees and to fix their salaries. The partnership was dissolved in 1966, but the winding up process took approximately four years. During that period, Henry hired Frances as the firm's book-keeper. Reuben became aware that Frances was drawing a salary from the partnership and that Henry had approved the salary so Reuben demanded an accounting. He objected to Frances's having collected a salary and demanded that she repay it into the partnership funds before the partnership's assets were divided. Can Frances keep the salary that she received? [Barthuly v. Barthuly, 192 Neb. 610, 223 N.W.2d. 429 (1974)]

7. Harestad and Weitzel entered into an oral agreement in August 1970 to be "partners in a real estate and building business," and each contributed equal amounts to the partnership. In October 1970, Weitzel purchased an apartment project in his own name with his own funds. Over the next two years, he oversaw the development and consummated the sale

of the apartment project for a handsome profit. Upon voluntary dissolution of the partnership by both parties, Harestad sought half the profit that Weitzel had made from his apartment project deal. Can she recover? [Harestad v. Weitzel, 272 Or. 199, 536 P.2d. 522 (1975)]

8. A patient sued a physician for medical malpractice and successfully recovered a money judgment. The patient did not sue the partnership to which the physician belonged and made no allegation against the partnership. Injury to the patient occurred in the course of partnership business. Can the physician now recover from his copartners for damages that he paid out of his personal funds? [Flynn v. Reaves, 135 Ga. App. 651, 218 S.E.2d. 661 (1975)]

9. Harris and Phillips were co-partners doing business as Dan's Used Cars. On his way home from work one evening, Harris struck Cook with his automobile, causing extensive injuries to Cook and damages to Cook's automobile. At the time, Harris was using a partnership car and was headed home on the most direct route from the partnership lot to his home. Harris testified that he had no set working hours and that he frequently traveled to and from his home and the used car lot. In addition, Harris stated that he was constantly on call by Phillips or his customers while at home. Can Cook recover from Dan's Used Cars in addition to recovering from Harris individually? [Phillips v. Cook, 239 Md. 215, 210 A.2d. 743 (1965)]

10. Walsh and O'Connor were copartners in a general partnership. Barneson joined them and contributed $10,000. Later, Barneson realized that the partnership had been insolvent when he joined and that the copartners, Walsh and O'Connor, were $20,000 in debt to their various creditors. The creditors all obtained judgments against the partnership of Walsh, O'Connor, and Barneson and wished to levy against Barneson's $10,000 contribution. Can the creditors reach this money? Since the $10,000 would be insufficient to satisfy the creditors, they also wish to levy against Barneson's personal assets. Can they reach these assets? [Ellingson v. Walsh, O'Connor and Barneson, 15 Cal. 2d 673, 104 P.2d. 507 (1940)]

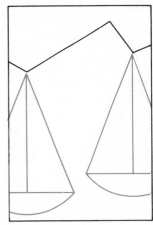

39

Partnerships
Limited Partnerships

This chapter will look in detail at the management, formation, and termination of limited partnerships. It will also look at some other, highly specialized forms of partnerships, such as limited partnership associations, mining partnerships, and subpartnerships.

DEFINITION OF LIMITED PARTNERSHIP

Limited partnerships are formed by compliance with statutory requirements. They consist of at least one general partner and one or more limited partners. The general partner (or partners) assumes management responsibility of the partnership and as such has full personal liability for all debts of the partnership. The limited partner (or partners) contributes cash (or other property) and owns an interest in the firm but does not undertake any management responsibilities and is not personally liable for partnership debts beyond the amount of his or her investment. A limited partner can forfeit limited liability by taking part in managing the business. In many respects, limited partnerships are like general partnerships, discussed in Chapter 37. They are sometimes referred to as special partnerships, in contrast to general partnerships.

HISTORY OF LIMITED PARTNERSHIPS

Business employs services and capital. A need therefore exists for a form of organization that permits capital investment without responsibility for management and without liability for losses beyond the initial investment. Such an organization should also allow the right to share in the profits with limited liability for losses. During the Middle Ages, this kind of organization was called a *commenda*.[1] In a commenda, the *commendator* supplied money to the *tractator* and received a major portion of the profits but was not liable for losses. If the tractator lost the capital investment, the commendator was liable only if proven negligent. This particular institution was sanctioned by the French Commercial Code in 1707, Sections 23-28. Over a century later, the first limited partnership acts were adopted in Connecticut and Pennsylvania in 1836 and in New York in 1882.

Limited Partnership Statutes—Early Versions

All states have enacted limited partnership statutes. The earlier versions of such acts displayed an obvious hostility toward limited liability that derived from the common law. Courts imposed full liability on limited partners when there were only trivial failures to comply with the law.

The Uniform Limited Partnership Act

The Uniform Limited Partnership Act was promulgated in 1916. It has been adopted by forty-eight states (not Delaware or Louisiana) and by the District of Columbia and the Virgin Islands. Its thirty-one sections are set forth in Appendix D of this book. The great virtue of the ULPA is that it expressly provides protection against technical defects if there has been a

1. W. Holdsworth, *History of English Law*, 195, Methuen and Co. Ltd., London (1956).

good faith attempt at compliance. [ULPA Secs. 2(2), 6, and 11] Under the ULPA, a limited partnership can conduct any business that can be carried on by a general partnership unless there is an exception in the state statutes. The most predominant exceptions are banking and insurance.

The Revised Uniform Limited Partnership Act

On August 5, 1976, the National Conference of Commissioners on Uniform State Laws approved a Revised Uniform Limited Partnership Act. It contains eleven articles and sixty-four sections (set forth in Appendix E), and it was made available to state legislatures in 1977. The articles are:

1. General Provisions.
2. Formation; Certificate of Limited Partnership.
3. Limited Partners.
4. General Partners.
5. Finance.
6. Distributions and Withdrawal.
7. Assignment of Partnership Interest.
8. Dissolution.
9. Foreign Limited Partnerships.
10. Derivative Actions.
11. Miscellaneous.

FORMATION

The creation of a limited partnership is a public and formal proceeding that must follow statutory requirements. Contrast this with the informal, private, and voluntary agreement that usually suffices for a general partnership as described in Chapter 37. There must be two or more partners, and they must sign a certificate that sets forth, at a minimum, the following information:

1. Firm name.
2. Character of the business.
3. Location of the principal place of business.
4. Name and place of residence of each mem-

ber and whether each is a general or a limited partner.

5.   Duration of the partnership.

6.   Amount of cash and a description and agreed-upon valuation of any other property contributed by each limited partner.

7.   Additional contributions (if any) to be made by each limited partner and the times at which they are to be made.

8.   Methods for changes in personnel (if any) and subsequent continuance of the business.

9.   Share of profits or other compensation that each limited partner is entitled to receive.

In essence, the content of the certificate and the method of filing it resemble those of the corporate charter. Often, there are private, informal agreements covering matters that do not have to be stated in the certificate, such as the profit shares of the general partners.

Where to File Certificates

The certificate must be filed with the designated state official. It is usually open to public inspection. The official is normally in the county where the principal business of the firm will be carried on. Some states require multiple filings if business is carried on in numerous counties. Others require only one filing, usually at the state capital. Constructive notice (by reason of law) does not usually exist for a certificate filed in another state. Thus, if a limited partnership chooses to do business where a certificate is not filed, a court can rule that its failure to file locally makes it a general partnership. This is similar to the qualification rules for foreign corporations. Some states require newspaper publication of certificates, or at least a summary of them, in addition to a filing.

NUMBER OF LIMITED PARTNERS Originally, limited partnerships were conceived to accommodate only a few limited partners. There seems, however, to be no statutory limit to their numbers, and in some cases, very large groups have been assembled. In a 1966 case, the limited partners of a real estate syndicate brought a class action suit against the general partners and some outsiders.[2] The limited partners numbered several hundred.

The Role of the Limited Partner and Liability

General partners conduct a business as if it were a general partnership. They are personally liable to the creditors; thus at least one general partner is necessary so that someone has personal liability. This policy can, nonetheless, be circumvented in states where a corporation can be the general partner in a partnership. Since the corporation has limited liability by virtue of corporate laws, no one in the limited partnership actually has personal liability.

Limited Partners Cannot Participate in Management

The exemptions and personal liability of the limited partners rest on their not participating in management. In other words, the contribution of a limited partner cannot be in services—it has to be in cash or other property. Also, the surname of a limited partner cannot be included in the partnership name. A violation of either of these provisions renders the limited partner just as liable as a general partner to any creditor who does not know that he or she is a limited partner. Note that no law expressly bars the participation of limited partners in the management of the partnership. Rather, the threat of personal liability deters their participation. How much actual review and advisement a limited partner can engage in before being exposed to liability is an unsettled question.[3]

The issue of the degree of control of the limited partner comes up in the following case.

---

2.   Lichtyger v. Franchard Corp., 18 N.Y.2d 528, 223 N.E. 2d 869 (1966).

3.   See Plasteel Products Corp. v. Helman, 271 F.2d 354 (1st Cir. 1959) (interpreting Massachusetts law).

HOLZMAN v. DE ESCAMILLA

District Court of Appeal, 4th District, 1948.

86 Cal. App.2d 858, 195 P.2d 833.

BACKGROUND AND FACTS *In 1943, Hacienda Farms, Ltd., was organized as a limited partnership. Ricardo de Escamilla was the general partner, and James Russell and H. W. Andrews were limited partners. The partnership went into bankruptcy in December 1943. Lawrence Holzman was appointed trustee of the estate. In 1944, he brought action to determine the actual status of Russell and Andrews. Holzman claimed that they were not really limited partners but were actually general partners and thus liable to the creditors of the partnership. The trial court agreed with Holzman and rendered judgment to that effect. Russell and Andrews appealed the verdict.*

MARKS, Justice.

* * *

The findings supporting the judgment are so fully supported by the testimony of certain witnesses, although contradicted by Russell and Andrews, that we need mention but a small part of it. We will not mention conflicting evidence as conflicts in the evidence are settled in the trial court and not here.

De Escamilla was raising beans on farm lands near Escondido at the time the partnership was formed. The partnership continued raising vegetable and truck crops which were marketed principally through a produce concern controlled by Andrews.

The record shows the following testimony of de Escamilla:

"A. We put in some tomatoes.

"Q. Did you have a conversation or conversations with Mr. Andrews or Mr. Russell before planting the tomatoes? A. We always conferred and agreed as to what crops we would put in. * * *

"Q. Who determined that it was advisable to plant watermelons? A. Mr. Andrews. * * *

"Q. Who determined that string beans should be planted? A. All of us. There was never any planting done—except the first crop that was put into the partnership as an asset by myself, there was never any crop that was planted or contemplated in planting that wasn't thoroughly discussed and agreed upon by the three of us; particularly Andrews and myself."

De Escamilla further testified that Russell and Andrews came to the farms about twice a week and consulted about the crops to be planted. He did not want to plant peppers or egg plant because, as he said, "I don't like that country for peppers or egg plant; no, sir," but he was overruled and those crops were planted. The same is true of the watermelons.

Shortly before October 15, 1943, Andrews and Russell requested de Escamilla to resign as manager, which he did, and Harry Miller was appointed in his place.

Hacienda Farms, Limited, maintained two bank accounts, one in a San Diego bank and another in an Escondido bank. It was provided that checks could be drawn on the signatures of any two of the three partners. It is stated in plaintiff's brief, without any contradiction (the checks are not before us) that money was withdrawn on twenty checks signed by Russell and Andrews and that all other checks except three bore the signatures of de Escamilla, the general partner, and one of the other defendants. The general partner had no power to withdraw money without the signature of one of the limited partners.

Section 2483 of the Civil Code provides as follows:

"A limited partner shall not become liable as a general partner, unless, in addition to the exercise of his rights and powers as a limited partner, he takes part in the control of the business."

The foregoing illustrations sufficiently show that Russell and Andrews both took "part in the control of the business." The manner of withdrawing money from the bank accounts is particularly illuminating. The two men had absolute power to withdraw all the partnership funds in the banks without the knowledge or consent of the general partner. Either Russell or Andrews could take control of the business from de Escamilla by refusing to sign checks for bills contracted by him and thus limit his activities in the management of the business. They required him to resign as manager and selected his successor. They were active in dictating the crops to be planted, some of them against the wish of Escamilla. This clearly shows they took part in the control of the business of the partnership and thus became liable as general partners.

The trial court's judgment was affirmed. The personal assets of Russell and Andrews could be charged by the creditors of Hacienda Farms. Ltd.   **JUDGMENT AND REMEDY**

LIABILITY TO CREDITORS   A limited partner is liable to creditors to the extent of any contribution that had been promised to the firm but not made and to the extent of any part of a contribution that was withdrawn from the firm.[4] If the firm is defectively organized, and the limited partner fails to renunciate (withdraw from the partnership) on discovery of the defect, the partner can be held liable to the firm's creditors. Note, though, that the ULPA and the Revised ULPA allow people to remain limited partners regardless of whether they comply with statutory technicalities. Liability for false statements in a partnership certificate runs in favor of persons relying on them and against members who sign the certificate knowing of the falsity.[5] A limited partnership is formed by good faith compliance with requirements for signing and filing the certificate even if it is incomplete or defective. When a limited partner discovers a defect in the formation of the limited partnership, he or she can obtain shelter from liability by renouncing an interest in the profits of the partnership.

Liability of Limited Partners   The liability of a limited partner is limited to the capital that he or she contributes or agrees to contribute to the partnership. By contrast, the liability of a general partner for partnership indebtedness is virtually unlimited.

---

4. See Kittredge v. Langley, 252 N.Y. 405, 169 N.E. 626 (1930).

5. See Walraven v. Ramsay, 335 Mich. 331, 55 N.W.2d 853 (1953).

CHEMICAL BANK OF ROCHESTER v. ASHENBURG

Supreme Court of Monroe County, 1978.
94 Misc. 2d 64, 405 N.Y.S.2d 175.

BACKGROUND AND FACTS *This case involved a suit by the Chemical Bank of New York (the plaintiff) against the limited partners of a partnership to recover funds advanced on a note. Stanndco Developers formed a partnership with eighteen others in which it was the sole general partner. On Stanndco's representation that a number of apartment units were to be transferred from Stanndco to the partnership, all the limited partners executed personal promissory notes to the partnership to pay for their "shares" in the partnership. The total came to $101,000. Three years later, Stanndco, as an individual, sought to borrow $101,000 from the bank using the partnership notes as collateral. The bank agreed to purchase the notes at a discount. Stanndco indorsed the notes to itself without the consent or ratification of the limited partners. The bank then sought to collect on the notes from the individuals (that is, from the limited partners).*

EMMETT J. SCHNEPP, Justice.
* * *

Plaintiff [bank] had knowledge that Stanndco was negotiating the instruments in a transaction for its own benefit, without authority, and in breach of its duty as a fiduciary. Plaintiff knew from the outset of the transaction, when Stanndco first approached it for a corporate loan, that the notes were not being used by Stanndco for a partnership purpose. * * * In the face of these facts, plaintiff acted in bad faith. Chemical Bank had actual knowledge or knowledge of facts sufficient to impute notice on the infirmities, defects and defenses to the instrument. In short, plaintiff, having taken the notes with notice and in bad faith, is not entitled to the rights of a holder in due course.
* * *

It is held that plaintiff takes subject to the defendants' claim that the notes were negotiated for the individual purpose of a general partner in breach of its fiduciary duty. Plaintiff, a non-holder in due course, may not recover on the notes against the defendant makers * * *.

* * * The defendants, as both makers of the notes and limited partners, had a legitimate expectation that the provisions of the Partnership Law would be followed. They had no cause to anticipate that a general partner would exceed his authority by assigning their rights in specific partnership property without their written consent or ratification and thus effectively terminate their right to have their contribution returned. It was the written consent or ratification of each defendant limited partner that was required for the proper negotiation of the notes—and this is what Stanndco failed to secure. Clearly, each defendant maker is offended and damaged by Stanndco's breach of duty, because each is a limited partner. * * * Plaintiff's conduct permitted the diversion of the partnership assets and it should not profit from its own wrongdoing. Under these circumstances it would be unconscionable not to permit the defendants to assert their claim as a defense against plaintiff.
* * *

The court dismissed Chemical Bank's lawsuit against the limited partners. Since Chemical Bank knew that Stanndco was transferring the notes other than for legitimate partnership purposes, it was not permitted to recover any money from the limited partners.

JUDGMENT AND REMEDY

RESTRICTIONS ON WHAT THE LIMITED PARTNER CAN DO As already mentioned, the limited partner cannot take control of the firm, cannot contribute services and cannot allow his or her name to appear in the firm name. Additionally, the limited partner has no authority to bind the firm, even though, in some sense, he or she is a "member" of it.

RIGHTS OF THE LIMITED PARTNER Subject to these limitations, limited partners have essentially the same rights as general partners: the right of access to partnership books, the right to an accounting of partnership business, and the right to participate in the dissolution winding up and distribution of partnership assets. They are entitled to a return of their contributions in accordance with the partnership certificate. They can also assign their interests subject to specific clauses in the certificate.

LIMITED PARTNER'S RIGHT TO SUE In jurisdictions that have considered the matter, courts seem to recognize fully the limited partner's right to sue, either individually or on behalf of the firm, for economic injury to the firm by the general partners or by outsiders. In addition, investor protection legislation, such as security laws (discussed in Chapter 43) may give some protection to limited partners.

THE USE OF A LIMITED PARTNERSHIP

The limited partnership is a less effective liability shield than the corporation. In many respects, the corporation is more flexible, and its charter does not require the frequent amendments that a limited partnership certificate does. The conclusion that one might draw is that limited partnerships have little utility, except for special reasons.

Before World War II, limited partnerships were used sparingly, but during and after the war, their number increased, largely because of high federal income tax rates, particularly on corporations. A limited partnership allows the limited partners to deduct expenses or losses against other income directly and to be protected from personal liability. These features make limited partnerships profitable for high income, high tax bracket individuals who invest in particularly high-risk enterprises, such as oil and gas drilling, Broadway plays, and the like. These advantages, combined with other tax benefits, such as deductions for intangible drilling expenses and percentage depletion in oil and gas ventures or accelerated depreciation in construction, make limited partnerships appealing.

DISSOLUTION

A limited partnership is dissolved in the same way as an ordinary partnership. The retirement, death, or insanity of a general partner can dissolve the partnership, but such circumstances do not do so if the business can be continued by one or more of the other general partners in accordance with their certificate or with the consent of all members. The death or assignment of interest of a limited partner does not dissolve the limited partnership. With respect to dissolution, limited partnerships resemble corporations more closely than they do general partnerships. This follows from the fact that there are public filings, passive investors, and limited liability, all of which are also features of corporations.

Causes of Dissolution

A limited partnership is dissolved by the expiration of its term or the completion of its undertaking. When there is no definite term or undertaking, the express will of any general partner will usually dissolve the partnership. Limited partners do not have the power to dissolve unless they have rightfully, but unsuccessfully demanded return of their contribution. (See ULPA Sec. 16) If, however, the general partners dissolve the partnership without the consent of the limited partners before the end of the term fixed by the certificate, this dissolution is considered a breach.

Illegality, expulsion, and bankruptcy dissolve a limited partnership, except that the bankruptcy of a limited partner does not dissolve the partnership unless it causes the bankruptcy of the firm.

The retirement of a general partner causes a dissolution unless the members consent to a continuation by the remaining general partners or unless this contingency is provided for in the certificate.

Consequences of Dissolution

The consequences of the dissolution of general partnerships apply to limited partnerships (see Chapter 37). Therefore, the firm continues in operation while winding up. The general partners of a limited partnership have the authority to wind up, as in an ordinary partnership. The representatives of general partners, not the limited partners, succeed the general partners. Limited partners have the right to obtain dissolution and winding up by a court decree.[6]

Assuming that the general partners continue the business, the limited partners generally have the right to be paid the value of their interests at dissolution, plus profits or interest on that value from dissolution until payment.

PRIORITIES IN DISTRIBUTION OF ASSETS

Upon dissolution, creditors' rights to distribu-

6. Klebanow v. New York Produce Exchange, 344 F.2d 294 (2d Cir. 1965).

tion of assets precede partners' rights, and limited partners' rights precede general partners' rights. Limited partners take both their share of profits and of contributed capital before general partners receive anything.

LIMITED PARTNERSHIP ASSOCIATIONS

Certain states allow the formation of limited partnership associations. They are legal hybrids that actually resemble corporations, although they are called partnership associations in some states. They originated in Pennsylvania in 1874, and the capital that was subscribed to the association was made the sole source responsible for its debts. In 1966, the Pennsylvania Act was repealed except for professions not permitted to incorporate. Three other states have similar laws: Michigan, New Jersey, and Ohio. (Virginia had one from 1874 to 1918.) This organization is seldom seen outside Pennsylvania and Michigan.

The organizational document is publicly filed and can be changed by amendment. It fixes the capital of the association, and there is no maximum or minimum amount. Each member contributes a designated part of the capital.

The association's life is restricted—usually to twenty years. There must be at least three members, and Ohio has established a maximum of twenty-five. The word *limited* must be the last word in the association's name, and it must be conspicuously used on advertisements, signs, and stationery. Dissolution of the limited partnership association occurs when the prescribed term expires or by a majority vote of the members.

An important difference between this type of association and corporations involves the transfer of shares. The shares are freely transferable, but the new transferee does not become a member in the association unless duly elected by the other members. When membership is refused, however, the transferee can recover the value of his or her shares from the association.

QUESTIONS AND
CASE PROBLEMS

1. A, B, C, and D entered into an oral partnership agreement under which A and B were to manage the firm and C and D were to contribute the funds necessary to start it up. The four also orally agreed that C and D would be limited partners. The partnership was formed in Pennsylvania, and under Pennsylvania's Uniform Partnership Act there is no requirement that a partnership agreement be in writing. Under Pennsylvania's Limited Partnership Act, however, limited partnerships must record a certificate of their establishment in the county clerk's office. A, B, C, and D failed to file such a certificate but operated as a limited partnership in that C and D exercised no control over management of the firm. Thereafter, one of the partnership's creditors sued, and, since the assets of the partnership were not sufficient to satisfy the partnership's debt, the creditor wished to attach C's and D's personal assets. Can he? [Ruth v. Crane, 392 F. Supp. 724 (E.D.Pa. 1975)]

2. The Ponderosa Land Company was a properly established limited partnership whose members were Harold Brown, Walter Brown, and W. D. Blaster. The Browns were general partners, and Blaster was the sole limited partner. His only contribution to the firm was providing it with start-up capital of $50,000. After a number of years of successful operation, Blaster decided to withdraw from the firm since he was badly in need of cash. He requested that the partnership return his capital contribution. Is the partnership dissolved? [Brown v. Brown, 15 Ariz. App. 333, 488 P.2d 689 (1971)]

3. Patricia Allen was a limited partner in a rather large firm that had been formed for the purpose of "ownership and promotion for development of a tract of land." A number of the general partners decided that it might be more profitable to mortgage the land owned by the partnership and make loans to small businesses. Thereafter the land was mortgaged, and the proceeds were loaned to numerous borrowers. In most cases the loans were unsecured. Patricia Allen objected to all of this but felt that, since she was merely a limited partner, her only option was to sell her investment and withdraw. Is any other recourse available to her? [Allen v. Steinberg, 244 Md. 119, 223 A.2d 240 (1966)]

4. Diversified Properties was a limited partnership that owned and operated several garden apartments and other real estate located mostly in Maryland. Weil was the only general partner; all the others were limited partners. The partnership was not well-managed and improvised from crisis to crisis. Kaye and Snider, two of the limited partners, took more and more of an interest in the affairs of the partnership as the partnership's financial condition worsened. On several occasions, both men gave Weil advice and suggestions on how to run the firm. In addition, Snider and Kaye often conferred between themselves and with Weil in attempts to salvage the enterprise and continue operations. Upon learning this, one of the partnership's creditors attempted to attach Snider's and Kaye's personal assets, claiming that their activities made them general partners. Do the facts support this claim? [Weil v. Diversified Properties, 319 F.Supp. 778 (D.C. D.C. 1970)]

5. Thirty-one limited partners with $202,000 invested in a real estate syndicate, River View Associates, brought suit against the managers and general partners of River View for breach of trust and breach of fiduciary duty. The limited partners alleged that the partnership built and leased a hotel to Sheridan Corporation. Sheridan managed the hotel, and the general partners of River View assumed the ownership responsibilities of the hotel. Initially, the hotel had been leased to another corporation, and rental from the lease was $590,000 a year. This gave the limited partners an 11 percent return on their investment. In 1963, however, the managing partners of River View decided to lease the hotel to Sheridan Corporation. Under the new lease, the rental was reduced by approximately $157,000 a year, leaving the limited partners with an 8 percent return on their investment. The rent, however, was "guaranteed" under a bond procured by Sheridan. Can the limited partners interfere with the decision of the general partners to enter into a new lease with Sheridan? [Lichtyger v. Franchard Corp., 18 N.Y.2d 528, 277 N.Y.S.2d 377, 223 N.E.2d 869 (1966)]

6. In 1970, John J. McMullen Associates was organized as a limited partnership with eight limited partners and one general partner for the purpose of managing and developing techniques and uses for liquefied natural gas. Several of the limited partners had technical skills and training with respect to natural gas uses. On occasion, one or more of the limited partners would appear at the various job sites where the partnership operated and would discuss technical problems that arose in the course of the

firm's work. Often, the limited partners would give advice, but the final decision always rested with the project manager (general partner). Will such activities cause a limited partner to be deemed a general partner? [Gast v. Petsinger, 228 Pa. Super. 394, 323 A.2d 371 (1974)]

7.   Fidelity Lease Limited, a limited partnership, had over twenty limited partners and one general partner. The general partner was a corporation, Interlease Corporation, and was managed by Sanders, Kahn, and Crombie, all three of whom happened to be limited partners of Fidelity Lease Limited. Assuming that in Texas, where this partnership was established, corporations are allowed to be partners in a partnership, what will the liability of Sanders, Kahn, and Crombie be in a suit against Fidelity Lease Limited? Will their liability be limited? [Delaney v. Fidelity Lease Limited, 517 S.W.2d 420 (Tex. Civ. App. 1974)]

40

Corporations
Nature and Formation

A BRIEF HISTORY OF THE CORPORATION

The corporation is the most widely used form of business organization. It can be owned by a single person, or it can have hundreds, even thousands, of shareholders. The shareholder form of business organization developed in Europe at the end of the seventeenth century. The firms were called joint stock companies, and they frequently collapsed because their organizers absconded with the funds or proved incompetent. The most famous collapse involved the South Sea Company, which assumed England's national debt in 1711 and obtained in return a monopoly over British trade with the South Sea Islands in South America plus an annual interest payment. The shares of the company were driven up by speculation, fraud was exposed, and a collapse followed. The event came to be known as the South Sea Bubble, and it led to the Bubble Act of 1720, a law that curtailed the use of joint stock companies in England for over a hundred years. Because of this history of fraud and collapse, organizations resembling corporations were regarded with suspicion in the United States during its early years.

In the eighteenth century, a typical U.S. corporation was a municipality. Although several business corporations were formed after the Revolutionary War, it was not until the nineteenth century that the corporation came into common use for private business. In 1811, New York passed a general incorporation law allowing businesses to incorporate. Incorporation was permissible by five or more persons for the manufacture of textiles, glass, metals, and paint. The corporation could have capital of only $100,000 and a life of twenty years.

The significance of the New York law was that it allowed voluntary incorporation using standard bureaucratic procedures rather than special acts of the legislature, which were usually available only to businesspersons with political influence. By the mid-nineteenth century, railroads predominated among corporations. After the Civil War, manufacturing corporations became numerous.

The Corporation as a Creature of Statute

The corporation is a creature of statute. Its existence depends generally upon state law, although some corporations, especially public organizations, can be created under federal law. Each state has its own body of corporate law, and these laws are not entirely uniform. The Model Business Corporation Act (often called the Model Act) is a codification of modern corporation law. It enunciates principles of corporate law that have been adopted to some degree or another by every state.

The key distinctions among the various organizational forms available to business involve: (1) the relationships among members of the organization, (2) the personal financial liability of members of the organization, (3) the control and continuity of the organization, (4) the establishment of credit and the acquisition of capital for the organization, and (5) the tax implications of the chosen organizational form.

THE NATURE OF A CORPORATION

The Corporation as a Legal "Person"

A **corporation** is a legal entity created and recognized by state law. It can consist of one or more *natural* persons identified under a common name. It is recognized under state and federal law as a "person," and it enjoys many, but not all, of the same rights and privileges that U.S. citizens enjoy.

The Bill of Rights guarantees citizens certain protections, and corporations are considered citizens in most instances. For example, a corporation has the same right as a natural person to equal protection of laws under the Fourteenth Amendment. It has the right of access to the courts as an entity that can sue or be sued. It also has the right of due process before denial of life, liberty, or property as well as the freedom from unreasonable search and seizures and from double jeopardy. However, the next case shows that corporations are not regarded as citizens entitled to *all* the privileges and immunities of state and federal laws.

WILD v. BREWER

United States Court of Appeals, Ninth Circuit, 1964. 329 F.2d 924.

BACKGROUND AND FACTS *Brewer, an IRS agent, served Wild with a summons requiring Wild to appear and testify about the tax liability of "Albert J. Wild, President, Air Conditioning Supply Company." The corporation was wholly owned by Wild. All books and records requested were those of the corporation. Wild appeared but refused to produce the records on the ground that they might tend to incriminate him and were thus protected by the Fifth Amendment. Wild was cited for contempt. He appealed. The majority of the appellate court affirmed, ordering Wild to produce the corporate books and records. One judge, however, found support for Wild's position.*

MADDEN, Judge (dissenting).
* * *

The privilege guaranteed by the Fifth Amendment, against the Government of the United States, "in any criminal case" not to be compelled to be a witness against one's self, is available not only to defendants in criminal trials but to witnesses in any kind of official proceeding under the auspices of the United States. It applies not only to the giving of oral testimony, but to the production from one's possession of incriminating documents or objects.

* * *

There is without question a general doctrine that an officer of a corporation who, as such officer, has custody of its records may not successfully refuse to produce those records in response to a subpoena [court ordered summons] issued to the corporation and served upon him as custodian, on the ground that the records contain material which would incriminate him. * * *

A corporation does not have the Constitutional privilege against self-incrimination. It therefore cannot, if its records are subpoenaed, assert the Fifth Amendment privilege. * * *

[But Wild] did not claim the privilege for the corporation, and could not have done so. He claims it for himself, and says that he, and not any artificial legal entity, will be the one to suffer the punishment if he is obliged to furnish to the Government the evidence which will bring about his conviction. * * *

Wild says that since he is the sole owner of his corporation, the corporation does embody the "purely private or personal interests of its [only] constituent(s),'' who is Wild himself.

[The dissenting judge was sympathetic to Wild's position. However, the majority decision was binding. A corporation does not enjoy the Fifth Amendment privilege against self-incrimination, even when it is claimed for the benefit of the sole owner.]

JUDGMENT AND REMEDY

The trial court ruling of contempt was affirmed. Wild was unable to invoke the Fifth Amendment to protect company records. He was required to produce the records in response to the IRS subpoena.

COMMENTS

A corporation is a legal fiction; that is, it is considered to be a person for most purposes under the law. However, certain constitutional privileges do not apply to a corporate person, although they do apply to a natural person. An unsettled area of corporation law has to do with the criminal acts of a corporation. It is obvious that a corporation cannot be sent to prison even though, under law, it is a person. Most courts hold a corporation that has violated the criminal statutes liable for fines. Where criminal conduct can be attributed to corporate officers or agents, those individuals, as natural persons, are held liable and can be imprisoned for their acts.

Characteristics of the Corporate Entity

A corporation is an artificial person, with its own corporate name, owned by individual shareholders. It is a legal entity with rights and responsibilities. The corporation substitutes itself for its shareholders in conducting corporate business and in incurring liability. Its authority to act and the liability for its actions are separate and apart from the individuals who own it, although in certain limited situations, the "corporate veil" can be pierced (that is, liability for the corporation's obligations can be extended to shareholders). In some instances, shareholders can voluntarily make themselves personally liable for some or all of the debts of the corporation. This is particularly true with smaller corporations that attempt to obtain financing.

Responsibility for overall management of the corporation is entrusted to the board of directors, which is elected by shareholders. Corporate officers and other employees are hired by the board of directors to run the daily business operations of the corporation.

SHAREHOLDERS The acquisition of a share of stock makes a person an owner or shareholder in a corporation. Unlike the members in a partnership, the body of shareholders can change constantly without affecting the continued existence of the corporation. Thus, a corporation is not affected by the death of a shareholder, whereas the death of a partner would dissolve a partnership.

As a general rule, a shareholder is not personally liable for the corporation's business debts; nor is the corporation responsible for a shareholder's personal debts. Each shareholder's liability is limited to the amount of the investment (that is, the money actually paid when the stock was acquired). Thus, if Paul Ginsberg purchases one hundred shares of Ace Manufacturing stock at $1 per share, and Ace Manufacturing goes bankrupt owing creditors millions of dollars, Ginsberg's loss is limited to the $100 purchase price that he originally paid for the shares. The converse is also true. If Ginsberg declares bankruptcy and owes creditors thousands of dollars, the Ace Manufacturing Company is not liable, and the creditors can claim only the one hundred shares of stock.

Shareholders have no legal title to corporate property vested in the corporation, such as buildings and equipment. They have only an *equitable* interest in the corporation. In a partnership, each general partner is a tenant in the partnership property. (See discussions in Chapter 39.) A limited partner, however, is like a shareholder in this regard—neither has ownership rights in business property.

A shareholder can sue the corporation, and the corporation can sue a shareholder. The shareholder's derivative suit and the special responsibility of majority shareholders of the corporation will be discussed in Chapter 41.

Shareholders are owners without direct control over the management of the corporation's business. Only through the election of the board of directors can they exercise influence over corporate policy. They are neither managers nor agents of the corporation. In a partnership, on the other hand, general partners have control and responsibility for the management of the business, and each partner is an agent who can bind all other partners in the course of business.

BOARD OF DIRECTORS A general rule in corporate law says, "Directors must direct the corporate business affairs." The board of directors is elected by shareholders and is periodically accountable to them for reelection.

The board is responsible for making decisions about overall policy. Directors declare dividends, authorize major corporate contracts, appoint or remove officers and set their salaries, issue authorized shares of stock, and recommend changes in the corporate charter. They delegate the day-to-day operation of corporate affairs to the officers and other employees of the corporation. The board can organize itself into executive committees and delegate these committees particular responsibilities to act on behalf of the entire board or to report back to it. Then, it acts as a unit.

OFFICERS AND OTHER EMPLOYEES Officers are agents of the corporation. They answer to the board of directors rather than to the shareholders directly, and they can be removed at any time by the board.

TAX CONSIDERATIONS Since a corporation is a separate legal entity, corporate profits are taxed by the state and federal governments. Corporations can do one of two things with corporate profits—retain them or pass them on to shareholders in the form of dividends. The corporation receives no tax deduction for dividends distributed to shareholders. When dividends are money payments, they are again taxable (except when they represent distributions of capital) as ordinary nonservice income to the shareholder receiving them. This double taxation feature of the corporate organization is one of its major disadvantages. On the other hand, retained earnings, if invested properly, will yield higher corporate profits in the future and thus cause the price of the company's stock to rise. Individual shareholders can then reap the benefits of these retained earnings in the gains they receive when they sell their shares. These gains are treated for tax purposes as capital gains. For many individuals, capital gains tax rates are lower than the tax rates applied to ordinary income.

Classification of Corporations

Corporations can be classified by location, sources of funds, objectives, corporate activities, and ownership arrangements. Some special corporate forms are discussed in the next chapter.

DOMESTIC AND FOREIGN CORPORATIONS A corporation must be incorporated in a particular state. The corporation is referred to as a *domestic* corporation by its home state (the state in which it incorporates). By contrast, a corporation operating in any other state is called a *foreign* corporation. This chapter is not concerned with international corporations, so the terms *domestic* and *foreign* apply only to status within the United States.

PUBLIC AND PRIVATE CORPORATIONS A public corporation is one formed by the government to meet some political or governmental purpose. Cities and towns that incorporate are common examples. In addition, many federal government organizations, such as the post office and Amtrak, are public corporations.

Private corporations are created either wholly or in part for private benefit. Most corporations are private, and it is these corporations that the chapter discusses. Private corporations can serve a public purpose, such as a public utility does, but they are nonetheless owned by private persons rather than the government.

NONPROFIT CORPORATIONS A familiar form of nonprofit corporation is the religious, charitable, or educational corporation. Its purpose is not to make a profit, but it is permitted to do so if the profit is left within the corporation. Nonprofit corporations are organized under state statutes that usually provide for different formation and operation policies. Such corporations can issue shares of stock but cannot pay out dividends to shareowners. Most nonprofit corporations are private.

PROFESSIONAL CORPORATIONS Professional corporations are relatively new in corporate law. Most of them are private corporations involving practitioners of professions such as law, accounting, or medicine. The professional corporation has become extremely popular because its tax benefits (pension plan, medical benefits, and so forth) are often more beneficial than those provided by a partnership form of organization.

CLOSE CORPORATIONS The "close corporation," or closely-held corporation is typically one in which the shares of stock are held either by a single shareholder or by a few shareholders (the actual number is usually controlled by state law). Close corporation shareholders manage the firm directly. The closely-held corporation is discussed more extensively in Chapter 42.

FORMATION OF A CORPORATION

Promoters' Activities

Before the corporation can become a reality, people must invest in it as original subscribers to stock. Specialized promoters often carry out the creation of corporations, taking the preliminary steps for corporate organization, issuing a prospectus, procuring subscriptions for stock, and arranging for the charter or articles of incorporation. In short, they analyze the economic feasibility of a proposed corporation and then set out to bring together the necessary resources and personnel.

It is not unusual for a promoter to purchase or lease property with a view to selling it to the corporation to be organized. In addition, the promoter enters into contracts with attorneys, accountants, architects, or other professionals whose services will be needed in planning for the proposed corporation. Finally, a promoter induces people to purchase stock in the corporation.

Some interesting legal questions arise in regard to the promoter's activities. The most important is whether the promoter is personally liable for contracts made on behalf of a corporation that does not yet have any legal existence. Moreover, once the corporation is formed, does it assume liability on these contracts, or is the promoter still personally liable? As a general rule, a promoter is held personally liable on pre-incorporation contracts. The courts have frequently found that promoters are not agents of a corporation to be formed. They are liable upon any contracts made for the proposed corporation unless the party with whom they have contracted agrees to hold only the corporation liable.

Obviously, promoters who make agreements in their own names without referring to the proposed corporation continue to be liable after incorporation unless the third party releases them. Even in cases where the third party has made the agreement in the name of or with reference to the proposed corporation, a number of courts still hold promoters personally liable after incorporation unless the third party clearly indicated at the time of signing the agreement an intent to release them after the formation of the corporation. Basically, the reasoning is that the promoter is acting as an agent for a nonexistent principal.

The promoter can be held personally liable for all contracts that he or she signs if the proposed corporation is not formed or if it is formed but does not adopt the promoter's signed agreements. There are exceptions, however. For example, the third party can release the promoter from liability. The agreement can also expressly release the promoter from liability in the event that the corporation is not formed or does not accept the agreement. Finally, if, on evidence, the court believes that the third party and the promoter entered into an agreement that would not hold the promoter personally liable should the corporation not come into being, then the promoter will not be held personally liable. Since there are substantial risks of personal liability, promoters should see an attorney before signing any pre-incorporation agreements.

In the following case, a corporation offered to purchase land. Its offer was signed by the promoter as president before the corporation came into existence. The sellers agreed to accept the offer under the erroneous belief that a corporation existed. When they learned that there was no corporation, the sellers withdrew their acceptance prior to the time the corporation became incorporated. The corporation then sought to have the contract for the sale of the land enforced.

MACY CORP. v. RAMEY

Court of Common Pleas of
Ohio, 1957.
144 N.E.2d 698.

BACKGROUND AND FACTS *An offer to purchase a forty-eight-acre parcel of land from the defendant, Ramey, was signed as follows:*

> "Macy Corporation
> by B. Ruben, Pres.
> Macy T. Block."

Ramey signed an acceptance of the offer to purchase made by Macy Corporation. At the time the offer was made, the corporation had not yet completed the process of incorporation.

Several weeks after the offer had been accepted, the defendant and her husband withdrew their acceptance of the offer and advised the plantiff that they would not perform their part of the agreement to sell. The withdrawal letter was mailed to "Macy Corporation, c/o Bernard R. Ruben," and copies were mailed to B. Ruben and Macy T. Block, the persons signing the offer. The articles of incorporation for the corporation were not filed until six days after the letter of repudiation had been received.

After receiving the notice, the corporation twice notified the defendant and her husband that it was ready, willing, and able to proceed according to the terms of the contract for sale. The defendant, however, refused to execute and deliver a deed to the premises.

The defendant's position was that she and her husband, Dr. Ramey (who died before the trial), signed the acceptance believing that they were dealing with a large corporation with plenty of money backing it. After they made their qualified acceptance of the offer, they learned that the corporation had not yet been formed. Thus the defendant argued that since one of the parties to the contract was a nonexistent corporation, the transaction lacked the parties essential to the execution of a contract, and it was not binding.

BARTLETT, Judge.
* * *

The Court is constrained to believe the testimony of Mrs. Ramey that she was led to believe that she and her husband were dealing with an existing company and this is supported by the signing of the offer of February 4, 1955, as "Macy Corporation, By B. Ruben, Pres." This was a false pretense, since there was no such corporation in existence at the time.

"Mutual consent is essential to every agreement and agreement is essential to every contract. There can be no binding contract where there is no real consent and it is no agreement where one party enters into the contract under a mistake as to the identity of the other party as where one party accepted an offer meant for another."
* * *

"In many cases it is said, * * * that the promoter is the agent of the corporation. But this is hardly true, at least until the corporation is actually organized, because until then no principal would be in existence, and the corporation would not be bound by contracts made before its existence."

"Attempt of promoter to bind corporation that is not in existence is contrary to public policy." Odenkirk v. Vretman, 7 Ohio Law Abst. 628.
* * *

"The difficulty surrounding the situation is that such a contract could not be made that would be binding upon anybody. How could two men make a contract that would bind a corporation which must have at least five directors in Ohio? Even if the two men owned all the stock except the qualifying shares for the directors, the directors could turn down and refuse to make such a contract, and the attempt to bind a corporation that was not in existence in my judgment is contrary to public policy and ought not to be tolerated and, in my view, the courts do not tolerate such contracts."

* * *

In the instant case there was no valid contract with the so-called "Macy Corporation" prior to its creation, since the transaction lacked the necessity of two parties to the execution of a contract.

There was at no time a contract with B. Ruben and Macy T. Block since they never made any promise that was binding on them, and moreover, the Rameys at all times believed they were making a contract with "Macy Corporation."

* * *

The Court finds that the Rameys had withdrawn from the arrangement and had so notified Mr. Ruben, Mr. Block and their embryo corporation, at least one week before the corporation came to life and made its attempt to accept the promise of the Rameys to sell their land at a certain price. Consequently, the acceptance was too late to effect a contract between the Rameys and the Macy Corporation.

* * *

"One who asks specific performance of a contract in the procurement of which he has practised deceit is always an unwelcome suitor in a court of equity and will generally be denied relief. Misrepresentation leading to the execution of a contract is likewise a ground for the refusal of a court of equity to grant specific performance."

The maxim, "He who comes into equity must come with clean hands," as a basis for the refusal of specific performance or other equitable relief, is as old as the equity courts themselves.

This transaction with the Rameys was conceived in deceit and misrepresentation. They were wilfully deceived into believing they were dealing with the "Macy Corporation" when there was no such entity; they were led to believe "B. Ruben was its president," and he never was; there was deceit practised in the adding of the name of "Macy T. Block" to the offer after it was accepted by the Rameys; and finally, on April 20, 1955, the Rameys were notified the Macy Corporation was ready, willing and able to proceed with arrangement to buy the land of the Rameys, when in truth and fact the corporation had not yet come into existence.

* * *

The deceit and misrepresentations in this case cannot be justified.

JUDGMENT AND REMEDY *The decree for specific performance requested by the plaintiff was denied. The defendant was not required to sell the land to the corporation.*

Subscribers and Subscriptions

Prior to the actual formation of the corporation, the promoter can contact potential individual investors and they can agree to purchase capital stock in the future corporation. This agreement is often called a subscription agreement, and the potential investor is called a subscriber. Subscribers become shareholders as soon as the corporation is formed. Thus, if the XYZ Corporation becomes insolvent, the trustee in bankruptcy can collect the consideration for any unpaid stock from a pre-incorporation subscriber.

Many courts view the pre-incorporation subscriptions as continuing offers to purchase corporate stock. On or after its formation the corporation can choose to accept the offer to purchase. In addition, the pre-incorporation subscriber can revoke the offer to purchase before acceptance. On the other hand, a majority of courts treat a subscription as a contract between the subscribers. It is therefore irrevocable except with the consent of *all* of the subscribers. Under Section 17 of the Model Act, a subscription can be revoked for a period of six months unless otherwise provided in the subscription agreement or unless all the subscribers agree to the revocation of the subscription.

There are various ways that a promoter can avoid the problem of revocation. One way is to set up a trust with the promoter as trustee and the corporation as beneficiary (under the law of trusts, a beneficiary need not exist at the creation of the trust). The promoter/trustee enters a contract with the subscriber. By the terms of the contract, the subscriber promises to buy the stock. If the subscriber fails to subscribe or fails to pay, he or she is liable to the promoter/trustee for breach of contract.

A typical problem in pre-incorporation subscription agreement cases is that the corporation actually formed differs from the corporation that the subscriber originally agreed to invest in. The rule of thumb is that if the departure is minimal (for example, merely a change in name), the agreement is likely to be upheld. But if the change is material (such as entering a different business entirely), the agreement will not be enforced against an unwilling investor. More important problems arise, however, when the corporation is not formed or it fails after formation.

Incorporation

Exact procedures for incorporation differ among states, but the basic requirements are relatively similar.

STATE CHARTERING Since state incorporation laws differ, individuals have found some advantage in looking for the states that offer the most advantageous tax or incorporation provisions. Delaware has historically had the least restrictive laws. Consequently, a significant number of corporations, including a number of the largest, have incorporated there. Delaware's statutes permit firms to incorporate in Delaware and carry out business and locate operating headquarters elsewhere. (Most other states now permit this.) On the other hand, closely-held corporations, particularly those of a professional nature, generally incorporate in the state where their principal stockholders live and work. In recent years, a number of policymakers have suggested that differences among state corporation statutes have led to some undesirable consequences. This has prompted various proposals, including a proposal for federal chartering with a more standardized and restrictive incorporation process.[1]

ARTICLES OF INCORPORATION The primary document needed to begin this phase of the incorporation process is called the charter, the articles, or the certificate of incorporation. The

1. See, for example, Symposium, Federal Chartering of Corporations, 61 Geo. L.J. 71 (1972); Carey, Federalism and Corporate Law: Reflections upon Delaware, 83 Yale L.J. 663 (1974).

articles include basic information about the corporation and serve as a primary source of authority for its future organizational and business functioning.

CORPORATE NAME Choice of a corporate name is subject to state approval to insure against duplication or deception. Fictitious name statutes usually require that the secretary of state run a check on the proposed name in the state of incorporation. Once cleared, a name can be reserved for a short time, pending the completion of the articles of incorporation. All corporate statutes require the corporation name to include the word *Corporation, Incorporated, Co., Corp.,* or *Inc.*

Some states require that the name of the corporation be expressed in English letters or characters. States usually require that a corporate name not be the same as or deceptively similar to the name of an existing corporation doing business within the state. For example, if an existing corporation is named General Dynamics, the state will not allow another corporation to be called General Dynamic. The corporate goodwill established by the original name might go in part to the second corporation because the similarity of its name might confuse people.

GENERAL NATURE AND PURPOSE The intended business activities of the corporation must be specified in the articles, and naturally, they must be lawful. A general statement of corporate purpose is usually sufficient to give rise to all of the powers necessary or convenient to the purpose of the organization. The corporate charter can state, for example, that the corporation is organized "to engage in the production and sale of agricultural products."

Some states have prohibitions against the incorporation of certain professionals, such as doctors or lawyers, except pursuant to a professional incorporation statute. In some states, certain industries, such as banks, insurance companies, or public utilities, cannot be operated in the general corporate form and are governed by special incorporation statutes.

DURATION A corporation can have perpetual existence under most state corporate statutes. However, a few states prescribe a maximum duration after which the corporation must formally renew its existence.

CAPITAL STRUCTURE The capital structure of the corporation is generally set forth in the articles. A few state statutes require a minimum capital investment for ordinary business corporations, while those engaged in insurance or banking can be required to have a greater capital investment. The number of shares of stock authorized for issuance, their par value, the various types or classes of stock authorized for issuance, and other relevant information concerning equity, capital, and credit must be outlined in those provisions of the articles. The range of possibilities is discussed in Chapter 43.

INTERNAL ORGANIZATION Whatever the internal management structure of the corporation, it should be described in the articles, although it can be included in bylaws adopted after the corporation is formed. The bylaws should not be confused with the articles of incorporation, which state the name of the corporation, its address, duration, purpose, number of shares, and so forth. The articles of incorporation commence the corporation; the bylaws are formed after commencement. Bylaws are subject to and cannot conflict with the incorporation statute or the corporation's charter. Section 27 of the Model Act provides that "the power to alter, amend, or repeal the bylaws or adopt new bylaws shall be vested in the board of directors unless reserved to the shareholders by the articles of incorporation." That section further indicates that the bylaws must be consistent with the articles of incorporation. Typical bylaw provisions describe the quorum and voting requirements for shareholders, the election of the board of directors, the methods of replacing directors, and the manner and time of fixing shareholder and board meetings.

PRINCIPAL OFFICE AND REGISTERED AGENT

The corporation must indicate the location and address of its principal office within the state. It must give the name and address of a specific person designated as *agent* to receive legal documents on behalf of the corporation.

INCORPORATORS

Each incorporator must be listed by name and must indicate an address. An incorporator is a person (or persons) who applies to the state on behalf of the corporation to obtain its corporate charter. The incorporator need not be a subscriber and need not have any interest at all in the corporation. States vary on the required number of incorporators; it can be as few as one or as many as three. Incorporators *must* sign the articles of incorporation when they are submitted to the state; often this is their only duty. In some states, they participate at the first organizational meeting of the corporation.

FIRST ORGANIZATIONAL MEETING

The first organizational meeting is provided for in the articles of incorporation but is held after the charter is actually granted. At this meeting, the incorporators elect the first board of directors and complete the routine business of incorporation (pass bylaws, issue stock, and so forth). Sometimes, the meeting is held after the election of the board of directors, and the business to be transacted depends upon the requirements of the state's incorporation statute, the nature of the business, the provisions made in the articles, and the desires of the promoters.

Adoption of bylaws is probably the most important purpose of the first organizational meeting. The bylaws are the internal rules of management for the corporation. The shareholders, directors, and officers must abide by them in conducting corporate business. Unless they have knowledge of the bylaws, corporation employees and third persons dealing with the corporation are not bound by them.

CORPORATE CHARTER

Once the articles of incorporation have been prepared, signed, and authenticated by the incorporators, they are sent to the appropriate state official, usually the secretary of state, along with the appropriate filing fee. In many states, the secretary of state then issues a *certificate of incorporation* representing the state's authorization for the corporation to conduct business. The certificate and a copy of the articles are returned to the incorporators, who then hold the initial organizational meeting that completes the details of incorporation.

IMPROPER INCORPORATION

The procedures for incorporation are very specific, and sometimes errors are made that form the basis for challenging the existence of the corporation. This can become important when, for example, a third person attempts to enforce a contract or bring suit for a tort injury and fortuitously learns of the defective incorporation. The plaintiff then seeks to make the would-be shareholders personally liable. The situation can also arise when the corporation seeks to enforce a contract against a defaulting party who learns of the defective incorporation and seeks to avoid liability on that ground. Courts have developed three theories to prevent the windfall that would occur in giving a contracting party the benefit of the stockholders' personal liability. The theories are *de jure* corporation, *de facto* corporation, and corporation by estoppel.

DE JURE CORPORATION

If there is at least substantial compliance with all conditions precedent to incorporation, the corporation is said to have *de jure* existence in law. This means that the corporation is properly formed, and neither the state nor a third party can attack its existence. To illustrate, Brown Motor Company, Inc., a domestic corporation, is being sued by a customer, Fred Muris, for an injury sustained at Brown's headquarters. Muris wants to challenge Brown's corporate status because he knows that the personal assets of the owners, Gary and Edward Brown, far exceed the company's assets. Muris discovers that the address of one of the incorporators is incorrectly listed in the articles and argues that this error means that the corporation was improperly formed. Hence it is not a duly authorized corporation and Gary and Edward Brown are personally liable. The law regards such inconsequential procedural defects as substantial compliance, and courts will uphold the *de jure* status of Brown Motor Company. Fred Muris can sue only Brown Motor Company as a corporate entity.

DE FACTO CORPORATIONS In some situations, there is a serious defect of compliance with statutory mandates—for example, the expiration of the corporation charter. In certain circumstances, the corporation is held to have *de facto* status, and its existence cannot be challenged by third persons (except for the State). The following elements are required for *de facto* status:

1. There must be a state statute under which the corporation can be incorporated validly.
2. The parties must have made a good faith attempt to comply with the statute.
3. The enterprise must have already undertaken to do business as a corporation.

Practically speaking, the concept of *de facto* status has limited utility in modern corporate law. The Model Act and most state statutes agree that the issuance of a certificate of incorporation (charter) by the secretary of state is *prima facie* evidence of corporate status (that is,

de jure corporation). However, the right of the state to command a corporation to correct irregularities in corporate formation can be enforced under the *de facto* doctrine.

CORPORATION BY ESTOPPEL Sometimes a corporation has neither *de jure* nor *de facto* status. When justice requires, the courts treat an alleged corporation as if it were an actual corporation for the purpose of determining the rights and liabilities involved in that particular situation. Corporation by estoppel is thus determined by the situation. It does not extend recognition of corporate status beyond the resolution of the problem at hand.

If an association which is neither an actual corporation nor a *de facto* or *de jure* corporation holds itself out as being a corporation, it will be estopped from denying corporate status in a lawsuit by such third party. This usually occurs when a third party contracts with an association which claims to be a corporation, but does not hold a certificate of incorporation. When the third party brings suit naming the "corporation" as the defendant, the association may not escape from liability on the ground that no corporation exists.

DISREGARDING THE CORPORATE ENTITY

In some unusual situations, a corporate entity is used by its owners to perpetrate a fraud, circumvent the law, or in some other way accomplish an illegitimate objective. In these cases, the court will ignore the corporate structure by "piercing the corporate veil" and will expose the shareholders to personal liability.

The next case involves an attempt by a tort victim to pierce the corporate veil when the funds of the corporation were insufficient to compensate him.

WALKOVSZKY v. CARLTON

Court of Appeals of New York, 1966. 18 N.Y.2d 414, 276 N.Y.S.2d 585, 223 N.E.2d 6.

BACKGROUND AND FACTS *The plaintiff was severely injured by a taxicab owned by defendant Seon Cab Corporation and negligently operated by defendant Marchese. Defendant Carlton was a stockholder of ten corporations, one of which was Seon. Each corporation had two cabs registered to its name, and each cab carried only the minimum*

liability insurance ($10,000) required by New York statute. The plaintiff
contended that these ten corporations were really a single entity and that
he was entitled to hold the stockholders personally liable for the damages
because the corporate structure was an attempt to defraud the general
public. The trial court dismissed the action, but the appellate court
reversed.

FULD, Judge.
* * *

The law permits the incorporation of a business for the very purpose of enabling
its proprietors to escape personal liability but, manifestly, the privilege is not
without its limits. Broadly speaking, the courts will disregard the corporate form,
or, to use accepted terminology, "pierce the corporate veil", whenever necessary
"to prevent fraud or to achieve equity". In determining whether liability should be
extended to reach assets beyond those belonging to the corporation, we are
guided, by "general rules of agency". In other words, whenever anyone uses
control of the corporation to further his own rather than the corporation's
business, he will be liable for the corporation's acts "upon the principle of
respondeat superior [master is liable] applicable even where the agent is a natural
person".
* * *

In the case before us, the plaintiff has explicitly alleged that none of the
corporations "had a separate existence of their own" and, as indicated above, all
are named as defendants. However, it is one thing to assert that a corporation is a
fragment of a larger corporate combine which actually conducts the business.

It is quite another to claim that the corporation is a "dummy" for its individual
stockholders who are in reality carrying on the business in their personal
capacities for purely personal rather than corporate ends.
* * *

Either the stockholder is conducting the business in his individual capacity or
he is not. If he is, he will be liable; if he is not, then, it does not matter—insofar as
his personal liability is concerned—that the enterprise is actually being carried on
by a larger "enterprise entity".
* * *

The individual defendant is charged with having "organized, managed,
dominated and controlled" a fragmented corporate entity but there are no
allegations that he was conducting business in his individual capacity. Had the
taxicab fleet been owned by a single corporation, it would be readily apparent that
the plaintiff would face formidable barriers in attempting to establish personal
liability on the part of the corporation's stockholders. The fact that the fleet
ownership has been deliberately split up among many corporations does not ease
the plaintiff's burden in that respect. The corporate form may not be disregarded
merely because the assets of the corporation, together with the mandatory
insurance coverage of the vehicle which struck the plaintiff, are insufficient to
assure him the recovery sought. If Carlton were to be held individually liable on
those facts alone, the decision would apply equally to the thousands of cabs which
are owned by their individual drivers who conduct their businesses through
corporations[.]
* * *

[W]e agree with the court at Special Term that, if the insurance coverage required by statute "is inadequate for the protection of the public, the remedy lies not with the courts but with the Legislature." It may very well be sound policy to require that certain corporations must take out liability insurance which will afford adequate compensation to their potential tort victims. However, the responsibility for imposing conditions on the privilege of incorporation has been committed by the Constitution to the Legislature (N.Y.Const. art. X,§ 1) and it may not be fairly implied, from any statute, that the Legislature intended, without the slightest discussion or debate, to require of taxi corporations that they carry automobile liability insurance over and above that mandated by the Vehicle and Traffic Law.

JUDGMENT AND REMEDY

The appeals court affirmed the trial court's dismissal of the law suit. The amended complaint was refiled and upheld. [287 N.Y.S.2d 546 Affirmed 23 N.Y. 2d 714] The case was then settled.

Adequate Capitalization

In other typical cases, a corporation may have insufficient capital at the time it is formed to meet its prospective debts or potential liabilities. Such "thin capitalization" is exacerbated when a corporation fails to obtain the amount of insurance that any reasonable business can be expected to have in the interest of public responsibility. Hence, victims who are injured may be able to reach the personal assets of stockholders to satisfy their claims.

MINTON v. CAVANEY
Supreme Court of California,
1961.
56 Cal. 2d 576, 15 Cal. Rptr. 641,
364 P.2d 473.

BACKGROUND AND FACTS *The plaintiff's daughter drowned in a public swimming pool operated by Seminole Hot Springs Corporation (Seminole). The defendant, Cavaney, was a director and the secretary-treasurer of Seminole. Cavaney stated that Seminole had never had any assets and had never functioned as a corporation. No stock was ever issued. The trial court entered a judgment for the plaintiff, Minton.*

TRAYNOR, Justice.

* * *

The figurative terminology "alter ego" and "disregard of the corporate entity" is generally used to refer to the various situations that are an abuse of the corporate privilege. The equitable owners of a corporation, for example, are personally liable when they treat the assets of the corporation as their own and add or withdraw capital from the corporation at will, when they hold themselves out as being personally liable for the debts of the corporation or when they provide inadequate capitalization and actively participate in the conduct of corporate affairs.

In the instant case the evidence is undisputed that there was no attempt to provide adequate capitalization. Seminole never had any substantial assets. It leased the pool that it operated, and the lease was forfeited for failure to pay the rent. Its capital was " 'trifling compared with the business to be done and the risks of loss' * * *."

SEPARATION OF PERSONAL AND CORPORATE INTEREST

Often, corporations are formed according to law by a single person or by a few family members. The corporate entity and the sole stockholder (or family member stockholders) must carefully preserve the separate status of the corporation and its owners. Certain practices indicate potential trouble for the one-person or family-owned corporation—the commingling of corporate and personal funds, the failure to hold and record minutes of board of directors' meetings, or the shareholders' continuous, personal use of corporate property (for example vehicles). When the corporate privilege is abused for personal benefit and the corporate business is treated in such a careless manner that the corporation and the shareholder in control are no longer separate entities, the court will require an owner to assume personal liability to creditors for the corporation's debts.

In short, where the facts show that great injustice would result from use of a corporation to avoid individual responsibility, a court of equity will look behind the corporate structure to the individual stockholder.

General corporation law has no specific prohibition against a shareholder lawfully lending money to his or her corporation. However, when an officer or director lends money and takes back security in the form of corporate assets, the courts will scrutinize the transaction closely. Any such transaction must be made in good faith and for fair value.

In the following case, two shareholders made a lawful loan of money to a corporation (which later became insolvent) and in return took a security interest in certain pieces of corporate property. When the corporation became insolvent, some creditors charged that the shareholders' loan transaction was not made in good faith and therefore that their security interest should be set aside.

BACKGROUND AND FACTS *The plaintiffs were creditors of the Olympic Homes Systems Corporation (Olympic). Two of its shareholders, Langley and Clayton, the defendants, had made a sizable loan to the corporation. In return, they took a security interest in certain corporate property.*

When the corporation became insolvent, the general creditors attempted to set aside the priority of the defendants' security interest. The defendants argued that the general creditors failed to show either that there was any fraud involved in making the loan or that the loan was not an "arm's length" transaction. Moreover, the general creditors did not establish that the defendants were in a fiduciary capacity with the corporation and that they showed a lack of good faith in the loan transaction. The trial court entered judgment for the general creditors, and the shareholders appealed.

INTERTHERM, INC. v.
OLYMPIC HOMES
SYSTEMS, INC.
Court of Appeals of Tennessee,
1978.
569 S.W.2d 467.

DROWOTA, Judge.
* * *

This is a suit by general creditors against an insolvent corporation and three of its shareholders. The issue is whether a security interest taken by two of the shareholders in personal property of the corporation is valid, and whether it entitles the two shareholders to priority over the general creditors as to the property covered by it.

* * *

It is true, in Tennessee as elsewhere, that there is no general prohibition against a good faith transaction between a shareholder and his corporation. Accordingly, a shareholder may lawfully loan money to his corporation and receive security therefor.

It is also generally held that officers and directors may, in good faith, lawfully loan money to the corporation they serve and take security therefor. This rule is clearly followed in Tennessee. The rule further provides, however, that "such transactions will invite the closest investigation by the courts, and must be characterized by the utmost good faith." The burden of proving such good faith is on the officer or director.

* * *

As a fiduciary, the officer or director has a strong influence on how the corporation conducts its affairs, and a correspondingly strong duty not to conduct those affairs to the unfair detriment of others, such as minority shareholders or creditors, who also have legitimate interests in the corporation but lack the power of the fiduciary.

It is also generally held * * * that courts will closely scrutinize the transactions of a majority, dominant, or controlling shareholder with his corporation, and will place the burden of proof upon the shareholder when the good faith and fairness of such a transaction is challenged. * * * It is obvious, however, that the reason for applying the rule to a shareholder is the same as the reason for applying it to an officer or director, that is, that he occupies a fiduciary position with regard to the corporation and those interested in it. Unless it is shown that a shareholder owns a majority of the stock or that he otherwise controls or dominates a corporation, however, a shareholder cannot be said to be a fiduciary and the reason for closely scrutinizing his transactions with the corporation disappears. Further, in reviewing the cases in which the courts have closely scrutinized transactions between a corporation and a shareholder and have put the burden of justifying them on the latter, we find that they almost invariably involve a majority, dominant, or controlling shareholder. Accordingly, it is clear that courts should apply the rule of close scrutiny and place the burden on the shareholder to justify a transaction with his corporation only when the shareholder owns a majority of stock, or is shown to dominate or control the corporation to a significant degree in some other way.

In the instant case, defendants contend that their secured loan to Olympic should be upheld under the general rule that shareholders may lawfully contract with their corporation. Plaintiffs, on the other hand, argue that this Court should scrutinize this transaction closely and put the burden of justifying it on defendants who, plaintiffs further argue, have failed to carry that burden. We hold that the instant transaction should not be subjected to close scrutiny, and that the burden of proof should not be on defendant shareholders, because plaintiffs have offered no evidence from which we could conclude that defendants owned a majority of Olympic's stock or otherwise dominated it in such a way as to justify imposing fiduciary responsibilities on them.

There is no evidence in this record that either defendant Langley or defendant Clayton was ever an officer or director of Olympic. The evidence is that each owned 15% of the capital stock of Olympic. It is clear that both were involved in setting up the corporation, but there is nothing to show that they participated in the business afterward. There is evidence that they did not intend to participate in the corporation's everyday affairs. * * * In short, there is no evidence of any degree of power or control by defendants over the corporation at any time. As far as we can tell from this record, defendants were simply two 15% shareholders who, although they participated in setting up the corporation, were not even its promoters. It is our conclusion that plaintiffs are required to present at least some evidence that defendant shareholders were also officers or directors, or that they in some significant way dominated the corporation, in order to invoke close scrutiny of the transaction and place the burden of justifying it on defendants. Plaintiffs have failed to do so here.

Plaintiffs, then, by failing to show that defendants Langley and Clayton had any fiduciary capacity with Olympic, have failed to shift from themselves the burden of proving fraud or absence of good faith in the loan transaction.
* * *

On the meager evidence in this record, then, we have no choice but to conclude that defendants were minority shareholders without control.
* * *

We hold that defendants Langley and Clayton have a valid security interest in the property of Olympic recited in the security agreement of September 18, 1973, and that no reason appears for subordinating that interest to the claims of Olympic's general creditors.

The Supreme Court of Tennessee reversed the lower court and held that the defendants, Langley and Clayton, held a valid security interest and were entitled to priority over the general creditors.	**JUDGMENT AND REMEDY**

QUESTIONS AND CASE PROBLEMS

1. During the early months of 1971, a number of persons began to organize a company later known as Timberjack of Alabama, Inc. On June 8, 1971, a day before the company was formally incorporated, it was assigned certain rights in collateral that was held by Eaton Yale, Ltd. On June 8, Timberjack repossessed the collateral, and on June 9, Timberjack was formally incorporated. Eaton then demanded that Timberjack return the collateral since the right to repossess it was in Timberjack, Inc., and Timberjack, Inc. did not exist on the day repossession took place. Can Eaton reclaim the goods? [In re Wilco Forest Machinery, Inc., 491 F.2d. 1041 (5th Cir. 1974)]

2. Johnson, Linder, and Green were promoters for a venture that was to own and operate an outdoor theater. It was agreed that they were to receive 75 percent of the stock of the new firm for performing the necessary work to open the theater, and Nychyk was to invest $60,000 for the remaining 25 percent. Nychyk's investment was to cover the cost of capital improvements for the theater. Green, who performed much of the design work and labor for the theater, paid himself a salary of $9,000 from the $60,000 as a salary to cover his living expenses, although there was never any agreement for Green to use any of these funds for his living expenses. When the venture failed, Nychyk sought to recover the $9,000 used by

Green. Can Nychyk recover? [Johnson v. Nychyk, 21 Ariz. App. 186, 517 P.2d. 1079 (1974)]

3. Watchie, an entrepreneur, acquired the rights to buy certain property that was later to be developed into a large shopping center. Watchie interested a group of Seattle investors, known as the Seattle Syndicate, in purchasing the land. Over the next two years, Watchie was the promoter of a corporation whose investors contributed approximately $1.5 million for the purchase of the land sold to the Seattle Syndicate. Watchie then convinced the Seattle Syndicate to sell the land to the newly formed corporation for $1,458,000 and convinced the investors that this was a good price. The Seattle Syndicate made a handsome profit on the sale, but Watchie shared in none of it. He was, however, paid a commission of $162,000 on the sale by the Seattle Syndicate. He failed to report this amount to the investors of the newly formed corporation. Can he retain it? [Park City Corp. v. Watchie, 249 Or. 493, 439 P.2d. 587 (1968)]

4. In December 1971, Hartmann and Daffern contacted Jones, an architect, about designing a lodge and restaurant building that Hartmann and Daffern wanted to construct. At this meeting, architects' fees and the general financing of the project were discussed. At the request of Hartmann and Daffern, Jones began work on schematic drawings. After each segment of work that he completed, he sent a bill to Hartmann. Hartmann paid the bills with personal checks. Jones was aware that Hartmann and Daffern intended to incorporate at some point but never inquired as to when the incorporation was to take place. At about the same time that Hartmann and Daffern became D.H.F. Corporation, Jones informed Hartmann that he was beginning the next phase of the project, the working drawings. Hartmann consented. Neither Hartmann nor Daffern informed Jones that the two had incorporated. Later, D.H.F. Corporation became insolvent, and Jones sought to recover for his work on the working drawings from Hartmann and Daffern individually. Are Hartmann and Daffern liable? [Jones v. Hartmann, 541 P.2d. 123 (Colo. App. 1975)]

5. Vodopich, a registered real estate broker, participated in a transaction involving the sale of land from Naples Bay Industries, Inc. to Basil F. Mulley. For his services, Vodopich was entitled to a 10 percent commission, but he subsequently agreed to forego his rights to the commission in consideration for the exclusive right to resell the property. This agreement was reached orally between Vodopich

and Mulley and other persons who were promoting the creation of a corporation that was to become Collier County Development, Inc. At the time the agreement was made, Vodopich was aware that the corporation did not yet exist. Subsequently, Collier County Development, Inc. was duly incorporated, but neither it nor Mulley lived up to the agreement with Vodopich concerning the exclusive resale rights. Who will be the successful party in a lawsuit between Vodopich and Mulley and between Vodopich and Collier County Development, Inc.? [Vodopich v. Collier County Development, Inc., 319 So.2d. 43 (Fla. App. 1975)]

6. Wesley Philpot and his wife engaged the services of Bob Childs Realty Company, Inc. to sell a tract of real estate. Childs Realty sold the property and demanded a commission from the Philpots. The Philpots refused to pay on the ground that Childs Realty had not complied with the Arkansas brokers' law, which required brokers to be incorporated before they could be licensed. Childs Realty argued that it should be deemed a corporation since its president had signed articles of incorporation, and it held itself out as a corporation by use of the designation "Inc." Has Bob Childs Realty Company complied with the Arkansas statute requiring licensed real estate brokers to be incorporated? [Childs v. Philpot, 253 Ark. 589, 487 S.W.2d. 637 (1972)]

7. New Liberty Medical and Hospital Corporation entered into an agreement with New Liberty Hospital District under which the hospital district agreed to purchase the hospital's debentures under the sole condition that the debentures be legally issued. The district then attempted to avoid its obligation under the agreement with the hospital claiming that, even though the hospital held a proper certificate of incorporation issued by the secretary of state of Missouri, it did not properly comply with all of the statutory requirements of nonprofit corporations. In a suit by the hospital against the district to enforce the agreement, can the district raise this defense? Explain. [New Liberty Medical and Hospital Corp. v. E.F.Hutton and Co., 474 S.W.2d. 1 (Mo. 1971)]

8. In a proceeding initiated by the Internal Revenue Service to seize certain records from Theodore Accounting Service, P.A., Charles Theodore, the company's vice-president, refused to turn over the records. He argued that since Theodore Accounting Service, P.A., never filed the articles of association required by South Carolina law, the partnership never became a valid corporation. The requested records, therefore, were the personal property of

Charles Theodore and entitled to Fifth Amendment protection. Theodore Accounting Service had used the notation "P.A." on its federal tax returns and had claimed tax status as a corporation for the past three years. Can the IRS seize the records it seeks? [United States v. Theodore, 479 F.2d. 749 (4th Cir. 1973)]

9. Slowek and Zamparelli are doing business under the assumed name of "New York Office of Consumer Interest" pursuant to a certificate duly filed in the Albany county clerk's office. Their firm is engaged in the business of soliciting advertising from contractors and home repair and improvement businesses for the purpose of publishing a booklet offering the prices of these advertisers. The booklet is called "Consumers' Home Improvement Guide." Should the attorney general for the state of New York take any action against Slowek and Zamparelli? [Lefkowitz v. Slowek, 79 Misc. 2d 1098, 362 N.Y.S.2d. 110 (1974)]

10. Rosenbloom was the promoter for a new corporation that was to be known as International Diversified Investments. In order to finance the corporation, Rosenbloom sought out Thomas and Dorothy Hidell as investors. The Hidells subscribed to one hundred shares of International Diversified stock at a price of $10 a share. This pre-incorporation subscription was signed and delivered to Rosenbloom on March 1, 1973. One month later, International Diversified Investments was duly incorporated under the laws of Delaware, but the articles of incorporation authorized only fifty shares of stock. International Diversified Investments became a highly successful company, and the Hidells wished to recover damages for the fifty shares of stock they never received. Can they recover? [Hidell v. International Diversified Investments, 520 F.2d. 529 (7th Cir. 1975)]

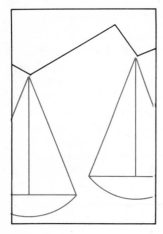

41

Corporations

Corporate Powers and Management

CORPORATE POWERS

Express Powers

The express powers of a corporation are found in its articles of incorporation, in the law of the state of incorporation, and in the state and federal constitutions. The order of priority used when conflicts arise among documents involving corporations is: (1) the U.S. Constitution, (2) state constitutions, (3) state statutes, (4) the certificate of incorporation (charter), (5) bylaws, and (6) resolutions of the board of directors.

It is important to keep in mind that the corporation is a "legal person." Under modern law, except as limited by charter, statutes, or constitution, a corporation can engage in all acts and enter into any contract available to a natural person *in order to accomplish the purposes for which it was created.*

Implied Powers

Certain inherent powers attach when a corporation is created. Barring express constitutional, statutory, or charter prohibitions, the corporation has the implied power to do all acts reasonably appropriate and necessary to accomplish its corporate purpose. For this reason, a corporation has the implied power to borrow money within certain limits, to lend money or extend credit to those with whom it has a legal or contractual relationship, and to make charitable contributions.[1]

---

1. The right of a corporation to make political contributions in federal elections is prohibited by the Federal Elections Campaign Act. [18 USC Sec. 321]

To borrow money, the corporation acts through its board of directors to authorize the execution of negotiable paper. Most often, the president or chief executive officer of the corporation will execute the necessary papers on behalf of the corporation. In so doing, corporate officers have the implied power to bind the corporation in matters directly connected with the ordinary business affairs of the enterprise. This is the issue in the next case.

BACKGROUND AND FACTS   *The plaintiff loaned $5,000 to the defendant corporation. The corporation, through its president, executed a promissory note for $5,000 plus interest. The promissory note became overdue. The plaintiff demanded payment from the defendant many times, but the defendant corporation refused to pay any part of the note.*

The corporation acknowledged that there was a note executed and delivered to the plaintiff by its president, Arne Poulsen, but it alleged that Poulsen had neither the power nor the authority to make or deliver the note on behalf of the corporation or to bind the corporation to the payment of such an obligation. Further, the corporation contended that Poulsen's act was not properly approved by the board of directors.

F.M. BENTALL v. KOENIG BROTHERS, INC.
Supreme Court of Montana, 1962.
140 Mont. 339, 372 P.2d 91.

JOHN C. HARRISON, Justice.
* * *

It is the defendant corporation's contention that the note in question was executed and delivered by the president, Arne Poulsen, without having been so directed or authorized by any order or resolution of the corporation's board of directors, and hence the authority for the execution and delivery thereof to the plaintiff must rest upon the evidence of the defendant corporation's alleged ratification of those acts by the board of directors or upon such general authority as must be ascribed to the president of the corporation who signed the note.

In the instant case, the defendant corporation's Articles of Incorporation provided for three members to act as directors of the corporation. At the time of the execution of the note in question, R. W. Brenneke, Alvin F. Koenig, and Arne Poulsen were its directors. It is undisputed that Alvin Koenig and Arne Poulsen authorized the execution of the note in question. They constituted a quorum and their action, which was not contrary to law nor contrary to the articles of incorporation or by-laws of the defendant corporation, was binding on the defendant corporation.

The defendant corporation, however, argues that "Arne Poulsen had a conflicting or adverse interest with respect to this loan, and therefore, could not be counted either as part of a quorum of the board of directors, or in any vote by said board, insofar as this loan was concerned."

It is true that a director of a corporation may not cast a vote upon an issue in which he has an adverse interest. However, here, Arne Poulsen, as a director of the defendant corporation, had *no* interest adverse to that of the defendant corporation.

First of all, * * * the $5,000, which is covered by the note in question, was a loan to the defendant corporation and, was not * * * [a personal loan to Poulsen].

Secondly, the record discloses that the defendant corporation, at the time the note to the plaintiff was executed, was in debt and in immediate need of money to cover current operating expenses. * * * When he [Poulsen] obtained the $5,000 loan from the plaintiff for the defendant corporation, he was acting as an agent of the defendant corporation.

* * *

In the case at bar, * * * two of the three directors of the defendant corporation, in the absence of the third director, authorized the execution of a promissory note *to a third party,* the plaintiff. These directors did not execute the note to themselves nor did they stand to profit from its execution.

Arne Poulsen, as president of the defendant corporation, not only had express authority to execute the note in question, but he also had *implied* authority.

In the absence of special authority, the president of a corporation has no power, merely by virtue of his office alone, to execute negotiable paper in the name of the corporation. "Where, however, such power is specially conferred upon him [president] * * * by the corporate charter or by a resolution or by-law of the board of directors, or, *where such power exists, by implication* from the nature of the agency or *by reason of his* * * * being held out by custom or course of dealing as having such authority, or being *intrusted with the conduct and management of the corporate affairs, which requires the use of such instruments in the ordinary course of the business, the president* * * * *may bind the corporation by the execution* * * * *of negotiable paper* * * *." (Emphasis added.)

The plaintiff's case does not here rest upon the proposition that Poulsen's authority to bind the corporation by promissory notes executed for it or in its name may be implied from the mere fact of his official position. To the proof of the fact that he was president, or chief executive officer of the defendant corporation, is added other evidence that he was also one of its three directors and the *manager* of its business. The entire corporation was made up of Poulsen, Alvin Koenig, and one R. W. Brenneke, who is not shown to have any active hand in the business. The record shows that Poulsen had and exercised "full management and control of the affairs of said corporation." The evidence as to the whole course of conduct of the directors and stockholders of the defendant corporation in allowing Poulsen such "full management and control" was sufficient to justify a finding that he was thereby vested with power to borrow money on the note of the corporation.

The defendant corporation was in debt and Poulsen, as a faithful servant intent on saving his corporation, did what the ordinary prudent business man would do in carrying on the affairs of the corporation (i.e., borrow money in the name of the corporation and bind it by a note evidencing the same) and, in so doing, violated no statute of this state, nor the articles of incorporation or any by-law of the defendant corporation. Poulsen was dealing with a matter directly connected with the ordinary business affairs of the defendant corporation and the promissory note to the plaintiff was such as was usual, proper, and necessary, under the circumstances, in the ordinary prosecution of the corporation's business.

JUDGMENT AND REMEDY   *The Supreme Court of Montana affirmed the lower court's decision that the corporation was liable on the $5,000 note.*

Ultra Vires Doctrine

The term *ultra vires* means "beyond the powers." In corporate law, acts of a corporation that are beyond the authority given to it under its charter or under the statutes by which it was incorporated are *ultra vires* acts.

Ultra vires acts can be understood only within the context of the particular purpose for which the corporation was organized. Acts in furtherance of the corporation's expressed purposes are within the corporate power; acts beyond the scope of corporate business as described in the charter are *ultra vires*.

A majority of cases dealing with *ultra vires* acts have involved contracts made for unauthorized purposes. For example, it is hard to know how a contract made by a plumbing company for the purchase of six thousand cases of vodka is reasonably related to the conduct and furtherance of the corporation's main purpose of providing plumbing installation and services. Hence, such a contract would probably be held *ultra vires*.

Corporate acts can be *ultra vires* simply in the sense of being beyond corporate powers. Such acts are not necessarily illegal; however, all illegal acts are inherently *ultra vires*.

In certain cases, the law recognizes the right of a shareholder to sue the board of directors for its alleged wrongful exercise of business judgment on behalf of the corporation. A stockholder can bring what is called a *derivative suit* against the corporation by first demanding that the directors correct the wrong. Failing that, the stockholder can ask the court to enforce the corporate right.

Certain acts of the board of directors can be unauthorized at the time they first occur but ratified later by a majority vote of the stockholders. Such ratification of the board of directors' actions by a majority of shareholders will ordinarily cure an otherwise voidable wrong. However, certain acts, such as waste of corporate assets, will usually require unanimous shareholder action for ratifying or condoning the wrong.

The Model Business Corporation Act essentially abolishes the *ultra vires* doctrine. Under Section 7 of the act, the doctrine cannot be asserted by the corporation as a means of avoiding its contractual obligations except in three very limited circumstances.

BACKGROUND AND FACTS   *In 1966 HFC, Inc. instituted an employee stock option plan as a means of retaining services of valued employees as well as obtaining services of new employees. In April 1974, due to a drop in the market price of HFC stock, HFC's board of directors adopted a resolution cancelling the 1966 plan and replacing it with a more favorable plan (i.e. one which allowed employees to purchase HFC stock for a lower price). This was done to ensure that the incentive value of the stock option plan be maintained. Michelson, a stockholder, brought a derivative suit against the corporation alleging that the board had violated its fiduciary duties to the corporation and its stockholders by the unauthorized modifications in the stock option plan. Prior to trial, the board's action was ratified by a majority of HFC's stockholders. The ratification, however, was not unanimous.*

MICHELSON v.
DUNCAN
Court of Chancery Delaware,
1978.
386 A.2d 1144.

HARTNETT, Vice Chancellor.
* * *

The issue to be determined therefore is whether the after-the-fact stockholder ratification in 1977 legally cured any possible legal challenges to the revisions of the Stock Option Plan and the waivers agreed to by the Board of Directors without prior stockholder approval.

As a general rule, stock option plans are an acceptable and necessary means by which corporations gain the services of new employees and retain the services of valued employees. Stock options are provided for in Delaware law, and every corporation may issue options, the terms of which must be either in the Certificate of Incorporation or in a resolution adopted by the Board of Directors. Furthermore, [Delaware law] provides *inter alia*:

> In the absence of actual fraud in the transaction, the judgment of the directors as to the consideration for the issuance of such rights or options and the sufficiency thereof shall be conclusive.

It is also a general rule of law that ratification by a majority of stockholders binds a corporation to unauthorized acts by a Board of Directors if such acts could have been authorized by the stockholders in the first instance, since ratification cures a voidable wrong. Ratification relates back to the time of the occurrence of the act which was ratified, and is thus equivalent to original authority.

Under most circumstances majority stockholder approval is all that is necessary; however, unanimous stockholder ratification must be obtained where it is alleged that there has been a waste or gift of corporate assets.

[Plaintiff] Michelson argues that the 1966 Plan, which was approved by the stockholders in 1977 was violated in 1973 and 1974 when the Board of Directors, without prior stockholder approval, made substantial amendments to the Plan. He argues that the 1973 and 1974 amendments to the Plan were contrary to the provisions of the Plan as approved by the stockholders in 1966. Michelson does not, however, argue that the amendments of the Plan constitute a corporate gift of assets.

* * *

Here the stockholders, after receiving a full disclosure of all germane facts, overwhelmingly ratified the acts of the Board of Directors in modifying certain stock option plans. There has been no allegation or showing of any gift or waste of corporate assets. The ratification of the stockholders is therefore binding.

JUDGMENT AND REMEDY *The stockholder ratification was upheld. The plaintiff-shareholder had no cause of action.*

COMMENTS *When officers or directors breach their duty to the corporation, the corporation has a claim against the wrongdoers and can seek damages for breach of duty. Since the corporation can act only through its officers and directors, it is unlikely that the wrongdoers will cause the corporation to bring suit against themselves. In certain instances, a shareholder has the right to bring suit on behalf of the corporation. This suit is called a derivative suit,[2] and any recovery from it goes to the corporation.[3]*

---

2. A derivative suit is different from a shareholder's individual suit, in which the plaintiff-shareholder claims that the wrongdoing directly injured a group of shareholders.

3. In the rare instances where recovery to the corporation would result in a windfall to a third party or to the wrongdoers, a court will award minority shareholders individual *pro rata* recovery. See Perlman v. Feldmann, 219 F.2d 173 (2d Cir., cert denied 349 U.S. 952, 75 S.Ct. 880 (1955).

Before a derivative action can be filed, a stockholder must make a demand to the directors that the corporation bring suit. This gives management a chance to investigate the claim, after which management can have the corporation file suit on its own behalf.[4]

----

4. In certain limited circumstances, a demand on the board will be excused. For example, if the alleged wrongdoers constituted a majority of the board of directors, a demand would be futile.

Judicial Treatment of *Ultra Vires*

The courts have treated *ultra vires* in a variety of ways. One treatment is based upon the common law principle of agency whereby an unauthorized contract made by an agent is void—no rights or duties arise for either party. Early decisions often held that *ultra vires* contracts were void.

The more modern approach is to uphold the validity of contracts that have been performed by all sides. In some states, when a contract is entirely executory, neither party having performed, a defense of *ultra vires* can be used by either party to prevent enforcement of the contract. The current trend in dealing with *ultra vires* contracts is embodied in statutory enactments similar to Section 7 of the Model Act, which upholds the validity and enforceability of an *ultra vires* contract as between the parties involved. However, the right of shareholders on behalf of the corporation, the right of the corporation itself to recover damages from the officers and directors who caused the transaction, and the right of the attorney general of the state to institute an injunction against the transaction or to institute dissolution proceedings against the corporation for *ultra vires* acts have been upheld.

BROAD STATEMENT OF PURPOSE Corporations are increasingly aware of the benefit of adopting a very broad statement of purpose to include virtually all conceivable activities. Corporate statutes in many states permit the expression "any lawful purpose" to be a legally sufficient stated purpose in the articles of incorporation.

Torts and Criminal Acts

A corporation is liable for the torts committed by its agents or officers within the course and scope of their employment. A corporation can act only through its agents and servants. This principle applies to a corporation exactly as it applies to the ordinary agency relationships discussed in Chapter 35. It follows the doctrine of *respondeat superior*.

At common law, a corporation could not be held liable for a crime, particularly one that required intent. However, under modern criminal law, a corporation can sometimes be held liable for the criminal acts of its agents and employees, provided the punishment can be applied to the corporation.

CORPORATE MANAGEMENT: SHAREHOLDERS

Shareholders' Position in the Corporation

SHAREHOLDER POWERS Shareholders must approve fundamental changes affecting the corporation. Hence, shareholders are empowered to amend the articles of incorporation (charter) and bylaws, merger, consolidation, dissolution, and the sale of all or substantially all of the corporation's assets *outside the ordinary course of business.*

Election and removal of the board of directors are accomplished by vote of the shareholders. The first board of directors is either named in the articles of incorporation or chosen by the incorporators to serve until the first shareholders' meeting. From that time on, selection and retention of directors are exclusively a shareholder function.

Directors usually serve their full term. If they are unsatisfactory, they are simply not reelected. Shareholders have the inherent power to remove a director from office *for cause* (breach of duty or misconduct) by a majority vote.[5] Some state statutes permit removal of directors without cause by the vote of a majority of the holders of outstanding shares entitled to vote.[6] Some corporate charters expressly provide that shareholders, by majority vote or larger than majority vote, can remove a director at any time *without cause.*

---

5.   A director can demand court review of removal for cause.

6.   Some states provide for cumulative voting for directors. In states in which voting for directors is by cumulative ballot, a director cannot be removed without cause over the negative vote which would be sufficient to elect that director in the first place. See, for example, California Corporate Code, Sec. 303A.

GRACE v. GRACE INSTITUTE

Court of Appeals of New York, 1967.
19 N.Y.2d 307, 279 N.Y.S.2d 721, 226 N.E.2d 531.

BACKGROUND AND FACTS   *The Grace Institute was incorporated by an act of the legislature of the state of New York to provide women with instruction in the trades and occupations and in branches of domestic arts and sciences. The corporation was formed under the general corporation law of New York. Three members of the Grace family and their successors were named original life members of the board of trustees. All the powers and privileges of the corporation were to be exercised by these three life members together with such other persons as they might select to be trustees.*

The plaintiff in this action, Michael P. Grace, II, was a successor to one of the original life members and, by virtue of that position, became a member of the board of trustees of the institute. During his tenure in office, he brought several lawsuits against the institute, all of which he lost. As a result of these unsuccessful lawsuits, certain charges were drawn up against him, and a hearing was held. Thereafter, he was removed as a trustee and life member of the Grace Institute, despite the fact that no provision in the incorporating statute or the bylaws of the corporation related to the removal of a life member. However, one section of the statute did provide that absence from three consecutive meetings constituted grounds for removal of a trustee.

KEATING, Judge.
* * *

The law is settled that a corporation possesses the inherent power to remove a member, officer or director for cause, regardless of the presence of a provision in the charter or by-laws providing for such removal.

The question with which we are presented in this case is whether there exists any triable issues relating to the manner in which this petitioner was removed from his position as a life member and trustee.

It has been the consistent policy of the courts of this State to avoid interference with the internal management and operation of corporations. Although we are dealing here with a charitable corporation over which the Supreme Court is vested with supervisory powers, the Legislature in creating it set up a governing board of trustees and vested in them the power and authority necessary for the management and operation of the Institute. That body, after hearings and deliberation, has decided that the petitioner's conduct was so inimical to the corporate interests as to require his removal. In reaching that conclusion, the trustees had before them evidence of a series of lawsuits commenced by the petitioner against the corporation in each of which he was unsuccessful and in none of which did any of the 13 jurists who took part find even so much as a single triable issue.

After reviewing each of these actions and after studying the entire record in this case, we have reached the conclusion that the evidence clearly supported the finding of the trustees that Michael had embarked on a course of conduct designed to involve the Institute in endless and costly litigation and that the suits were undertaken for the purpose of harassing the Institute and its members. Under these circumstances, courts should not substitute their judgment for the judgment of those charged by the Legislature with the responsibility of running the corporation and seeing to it that it fulfills the purposes for which it was created.

In addition, we have examined the procedure by which the petitioner was removed and we have concluded there is no question but that he was given a reasonable opportunity to be heard and to answer the charges leveled against him. At the hearing during which the charges were aired, he was represented by three attorneys and a law assistant. His attorneys were permitted to cross-examine one of the parties who had been instrumental in preparing the charges against Michael and they could have exercised their right to examine others. Yet despite this opportunity to be heard and to present evidence, Michael never took the stand and never even attempted to answer the charges. The objections of Michael to the hearing we find to be without merit. The things to which he objects in no way detracted from his opportunity to be heard or the validity of his removal.

Michael argues, however, that the position of life member was created by the Legislature and "only the Legislature has the power to change the rights and privileges specifically granted by the act of incorporation." Michael obviously misapprehends the nature of the rights and privileges accorded to him. The Legislature surely could not have intended that a life member retain his position regardless of the manner in which he acted and regardless of the manner in which he abused his trust. The petitioner may not be removed so long as he adheres to what must be regarded as an implied condition of his position—that is so long as he faithfully serves the Institute. Once he breaches that condition and engages in activities that obstruct and interfere with the operation of the corporation and the purposes for which the Legislature created it, he may be removed.

The New York Court of Appeals reached the conclusion that Michael P. Grace, II, had been rightfully removed from his position as a life member and trustee of the Grace Institute.   **JUDGMENT AND REMEDY**

THE RELATIONSHIP BETWEEN THE SHARE-HOLDER AND THE CORPORATION As a general rule, shareholders have no responsibility for the daily management of the corporation, but they are ultimately responsible for choosing the board of directors, which does have such control. Ordinarily, corporate officers and other employees owe no direct duty to individual stockholders. Their duty is to the corporation as a whole. However, a director is in a fiduciary relationship to the corporation and therefore serves the interests of the shareholders as a whole.

Generally, there is no legal relationship between shareholders and creditors of the corporation. Shareholders can, in fact, be creditors of the corporation and have the same rights of recovery against the corporation as any other creditor. The rights and liabilities of creditors and shareholders are discussed in Chapter 44.

SHAREHOLDERS' FORUM Commonly, shareholders' meetings occur annually, but special meetings can be called to take care of urgent matters. Since it is not practical for most small shareholders of publicly-traded corporations to attend the shareholders' meetings, they normally give third persons a written authorization to vote their shares at the meeting. This authorization, called a proxy, is often solicited by management.

Shareholders in a corporation enjoy both common law and statutory inspection rights. Shareholders at common law enjoyed qualified rights to inspect corporate books and records, such as the bylaws and minutes of the board of directors' executive committee, and shareholders' meetings, as well as any other documents, such as contracts, correspondence, and tax returns. They even had the right to inspect the corporate headquarters.

The shareholders' common law inspection rights exist concurrently with any rights created by statute. However, corporate statutes do not usually deal with shareholders' right to inspect the minutes of the board of directors' or shareholders' meetings, the bylaws, or other records. The shareholders' common law right of inspection operates in these cases.

Notice of Meetings The notice and time of meetings, including the day and the hour, is announced in writing to each shareholder a reasonable time [7] prior to the date of the shareholder meeting.[8] Special meeting notices must include a statement of the purpose of the meeting; business transacted at a special meeting is limited to that purpose.

Shareholder Voting In order for shareholders to act, a minimum number of them (in terms of number of shares held) must be present at a meeting. This minimum number, called a **quorum,** is generally more than 50 percent. Corporate business matters are presented in the form of *resolutions,* which shareholders vote to approve or disapprove. Some state statutes have set forth voting limits, and corporations, articles, or bylaws must remain within the statutory limitations. Some states provide that the unanimous written consent of shareholders is a permissible alternative to holding a shareholders' meeting.

Once a quorum is present, a majority vote of the shares represented at the meeting is usually required to pass resolutions. Assume that Midwestern Supply, Inc., has 10,000 outstanding shares of voting stock. Its articles set the quorum at 50 percent of outstanding shares and provide that a majority vote of shares present is necessary to pass on ordinary matters. At the shareholders' meeting a *quorum* of stockholders representing 5,000 outstanding shares must be present to conduct business, and

---

7. The shareholder can waive the requirement of written notice by signing a waiver form. A shareholder who did not receive written notice, but who learned of the meeting and attended without protesting the lack of notice, is said to have waived notice by such conduct.
8. State statutes and the bylaws typically set forth a minimum allowance notice requirement.

a vote of at least 2,501 of those shares represented at the meeting is needed to pass ordinary resolutions. If more than 5,000 are present, a larger vote will be needed.

At times, a larger than majority vote will be required either by statute or by corporation charter. Extraordinary corporate matters such as merger, consolidation, or dissolution of the corporation will require a higher percentage of the representatives of *all* corporate stock shares entitled to vote, not just a portion of those present at that particular meeting.

Voting Lists   Voting lists are prepared by the corporation prior to each shareholder meeting. Persons whose names appear on the corporation's stockholder records as the record owners of the shares are the persons ordinarily entitled to vote.[9] The voting list contains the name and address of each shareholder as shown on the corporate records on a given cutoff date (record date). It also includes the number of voting shares held by each owner. The list is usually kept at the corporate headquarters and is available for shareholder inspection.

Voting Techniques   Some states permit or require shareholders to elect directors by *cumulative voting*, a method of voting designed to insure minority representation on the board of directors.[10] Under cumulative voting, stockholders are permitted to accumulate their votes and cast them for one or more nominees for director. All nominees stand for election at the same time. To illustrate, Scott owns 100 shares of stock in White Machinery Corporation. There are two director positions to be filled at the annual shareholders' meeting. Three candidates—Joseph White, Bryan Field, and Debbee Marshall—are running for these two positions. Under ordinary voting procedures, Scott would cast one vote per share, or 100 votes for

each directorship to be filled. Under the cumulative voting method, Scott is permitted to cast the total number of votes to which he is entitled for all positions to be filled in the election (200 votes) and to distribute these votes among the candidates in any way he chooses. Thus, Scott can give all 200 votes to Joseph White, or he can give 190 votes to White and 10 votes to Field, or he can even give 50 votes to Field and 100 votes to Marshall and not vote 50 shares.

Cumulative voting is permitted by nearly every corporate statute if it is provided for in the corporation's charter. It is a mandatory method of voting for directors in a few states. In corporations not having cumulative voting, the entire board can be elected by stockholders voting a majority of those shares at the meeting.

SHAREHOLDER AGREEMENTS   A group of shareholders can agree in writing prior to the meeting to vote their shares together in a specified manner. The validity of shareholder voting agreements will not be discussed here.

PROXY VOTING   A shareholder can appoint a voting agent. A proxy is a written authorization to cast the shareholder's vote, and a person can solicit proxies from a number of shareholders in an attempt to concentrate voting power.

VOTING TRUST   Shareholders can enter an agreement (a trust contract) whereby legal title (record ownership on the corporate books) is transferred to a trustee who is responsible for voting the shares. The agreement can specify how the trustee is to vote, or it can allow the trustee to use his or her discretion. The trustee takes physical possession of the actual stock certificate and in return gives the shareholder a "voting trust certificate." The shareholder retains all rights of ownership (for example, the right to receive dividend payments) except the power to vote.

A voting trust is not the same thing as a proxy, for the latter can be revoked more easily.

9.   Where the legal owner is deceased, bankrupt, incompetent, or in some other way under a legal disability, his or her vote can be cast by a person designated by law to control and manage the owner's property.

10.   See, for example, the California Corporate Code, Sec. 708.

The holder of a proxy has neither legal title to the stock nor possession of the certificates, but voting trustees have both.[11]

CORPORATE MANAGEMENT: DIRECTORS

Position

Every corporation is governed by directors. Subject to statutory limitations, the number of directors is set forth in the corporation's articles or bylaws. Historically, the minimum number of directors has been three, but today many states permit fewer.

Few qualifications are legally required of directors. Only a handful of states retain minimum age and residency requirements. A director is sometimes a shareholder, but this is not a necessary qualification unless, of course, statutory provisions, corporate articles, or bylaws require ownership.

Compensation for directors is ordinarily specified in the corporate articles or bylaws. Because directors are in a *fiduciary* relationship to the shareholders and to the corporation, an express agreement or provision for compensation is necessary for them to receive money from the funds they control or for which they have responsibilities.

The first board of directors is normally appointed by the incorporators upon the creation of the corporation, or directors are named by the corporation itself in the articles. The first board serves until the first annual shareholders' meeting. Subsequent directors are elected by majority vote of the shareholders.

The term of office for a director is one year—from annual meeting to annual meeting. Longer and staggered terms are permissible under most state statutes. A board of directors can be divided into categories. A common practice is to have three classes, so that one-third of the board is elected each year for a three-year term. In this way, there is greater management continuity.[12]

---

11. Under Section 34 of the Model Act, the term of a voting trust cannot exceed ten years.
12. Of course, staggered boards defeat the purpose of cumulative voting.

Sometimes the board of directors itself can be empowered by the corporate articles or bylaws to remove a director *for cause*—even though it can *never* remove without cause. The board's action is subject to review by the shareholders.

When vacancies occur on the board of directors due to death or resignation, or when a new position is created through amendment of the articles or bylaws, either the shareholders or the board itself can fill the position, depending on state law or the provisions of the bylaws.

Management Responsibilities

Directors have responsibility for all policy-making decisions necessary to the management of all corporate affairs. Just as shareholders cannot act individually to bind the corporation, the directors must act as a body in carrying out routine corporate business. One director has one vote, and generally the majority rules.

The general areas of responsibility of the board of directors include:

1. Declaration and payment of corporate dividends to shareholders.
2. Authorization for major corporate policy decisions—for example, the initiation of proceedings for the sale or lease of corporate assets outside the regular course of business, the determination of new product lines, and the overseeing of major contract negotiations and major management-labor negotiations.
3. Appointment, supervision and removal of corporate officers and other managerial employees and the determination of their compensation.
4. Financial decisions involving such things as the issuance of authorized shares or bonds.

Directors' Liability

Honest mistakes of judgment and poor business actions on the part of the directors do not make them liable to the corporation for damages sustained. After all, directors are not insurers of the business success of the corporation. They must be loyal, honest, and reasonably careful, however. If directors (and officers) hire employees carefully, they are not personally liable for the willful wrongs and negligent acts of such employees; rather, the corporation is liable.

When, however, a director never attends board meetings nor examines records and books, he or she can be held liable for losses resulting from unsupervised acts of officers and employees. Also, when directors (and officers) allow the assets of the corporation to be diverted to objectives outside the charter or statutory powers, they may be held liable for damages to the corporation, to a trustee appointed for the corporation, or to the shareholders in a derivative suit.

The Board of Directors' Forum

The board of directors conducts business by holding formal meetings with recorded minutes.[13] The date upon which regular meetings are held is usually established in the articles and bylaws or by board resolution, and no further notice is customarily required. Special meetings can be called with notice sent to all directors.

Quorum requirements can vary among jurisdictions. Many states leave the decision to the corporate articles or bylaws. Voting is done *in person* (unlike voting at shareholders' meetings, which can be done by proxy).[14] The rule is one vote per director. Ordinary matters generally require a majority vote; certain extraordinary issues can require a larger than majority vote.

Delegation of Board of Directors' Powers

The board of directors can delegate some of its functions to an executive committee or to corporate officers. In doing so, the board does not avoid its responsibility for directing the affairs of the corporation. Rather, the daily responsibilities of corporate management are given over to corporate officers and managerial personnel, who are empowered to make decisions relating to *ordinary corporate affairs* within *well-defined guidelines*.

Executive Committee Most states permit the board of directors to elect an executive committee from among the directors to handle the interim management decisions between board of directors' meetings as provided in the bylaws. The *executive committee* is limited to making management decisions about ordinary business matters.

Corporate Officers The officers and other executive employees are hired by the board of directors or, in rare instances, by the shareholders. In addition to the duties that are articulated in the bylaws, corporate and managerial officers are agents of the corporation, and the ordinary rules of agency apply or have been applied to their employment (unlike the board of directors, whose powers are conferred by the state). Qualifications are determined, in the main, at the discretion of the corporation and are included in the articles or bylaws. In most states, a person can hold more than one office. Corporate officers can be removed by the board of directors at any time with or without cause and regardless of the terms of the employment contract, although the corporation can still be liable for breach of contract damages.

13. Michigan now has a corporate statute authorizing conference phone calls for a board of directors' meeting.
14. Except in Louisiana, where a director can vote by proxy under certain circumstances.

QUESTIONS AND CASE PROBLEMS

1. Woods, the president of Pecos Valley Gas Company, signed a contract with Greenspon Iron and Steel Company for the purchase of forty-five miles of gas pipe for sixty-one cents per foot. The board of directors of Pecos Valley, however, had instructed Woods not to sign the contract, and Pecos Valley refused to accept delivery of the pipe. Greenspon sued Pecos Valley for breach of contract, and Pecos Valley defended on the ground that Woods was not acting within the usual scope of his office, that in the past he had never had the authority to sign contracts for the company unless the board of directors ap-

proved. Greenspon had never done business with Pecos Valley before. Will Greenspon recover? [Joseph Greenspon's Sons Iron and Steel Co. v. Pecos Valley Gas Co., 156 A. 350 (Del. Super. Ct. 1931)]

2. Harris Lumber Company was a corporation organized under the law of the state of Arkansas. Harris was the president of the corporation; Nelson was its secretary and treasurer; and Jones was its remaining director and shareholder. Several years after its incorporation, Harris Lumber owed Merchants and Farmers Bank $4,500. A promissory note was executed for the amount of the debt, and a mortgage was executed on certain personal property owned by Harris Lumber to secure payment. Nelson, who at the time was general manager of Harris Lumber, signed both the note and the mortgage. Payments amounting to $2,150 were made over the next two and one-half years on the promissory note. At that point payment ceased, and Merchants Bank brought this suit to recover the balance of the sum owed. Harris Lumber Company never objected to the execution of the mortgage or the note or to any of the payments under the note until Merchants Bank filed this suit. However, at that point, Harris Lumber claimed that Nelson did not have the authority to sign promissory notes or to execute mortgages on behalf of Harris Lumber. In fact, neither the corporate charter nor any of the board of directors' resolutions vested the general manager with any authority to bind the corporation. Will Merchants Bank be successful in its suit against Harris Lumber Company? [Merchants and Farmers Bank v. Harris Lumber Co., 103 Ark. 283, 146 S.W. 508 (1912)]

3. Capital Electric Power Association, a utility, had 10,000 shares of stock authorized, issued, and outstanding. Capital's articles of incorporation provided that voters holding 50 percent of its outstanding shares constituted a quorum. At a shareholders' meeting, only two shareholders appeared. Each held exactly 2,000 shares, but one also had the proxies of 600 shareholders. Can any official action be undertaken at the shareholders' meeting? [McNair v. Capital Electric Ass'n., 324 So.2d. 234, (Miss. 1975)]

4. Monaghan Land Co. was organized by a number of incorporators to "buy, hold and sell" a one-half interest in a piece of land known as the Sicily Island Tract. A majority of the stockholders of Monaghan entered into a voting trust agreement under which trustees were given the right to vote all of the majority shares at all meetings and in all proceedings where stockholder consent was required by law. At a subsequent stockholders' meeting, the trustees voted to sell the Sicily Island Tract, which constituted substantially all of Monaghan's assets. Can the stockholders who parted with their voting rights object? [Clarke Memorial College v. Monaghan Land Co., 257 A.2d. 234 (Del. Ch. 1969)]

5. Edward Beresth, Gershon Weil, Nathan Weil, and Raymond Harrison comprised all the directors of Self Service Sales Corporation and were holders of a majority of its stock. On August 27, the above stockholders entered into a voting agreement under which they agreed to call a meeting to approve the following amendments to the bylaws: (1) that three directors would constitute a quorum and (2) that the stockholders would not thereafter vote to amend the bylaws "so adopted" without consent of all four of the signatories to the agreement. Thereafter, in an attempt to squeeze out Nathan Weil, the other three directors voted to *repeal* the bylaw that provided that three directors constituted a quorum and *replace* it with a bylaw establishing that two directors would constitute a quorum. Can Nathan Weil legally stop this? [Weil v. Beresth, 154 Conn. 12, 220 A.2d. 456 (1966)]

6. The capital stock of G.S.P. Corporation was owned by Plodzik, Ricketts, and Westbury, who were also the sole directors of the corporation. In 1965, Plodzik and Ricketts agreed to sell their company to Star Corporation. Since Plodzik and Ricketts constituted two-thirds of the shareholders of G.S.P. Corporation, as well as a majority of the board of directors, they took this action without consulting Westbury. Have Plodzik and Ricketts exceeded their authority? [Star Corp. v. General Screw Products Co., 501 S.W.2d. 374 (Tex. Civ. App. 1973)]

7. Orloff was both secretary and director of the Stott Realty Company. The majority of Stott Realty's board of directors directed the secretary to sign certain mortgage papers. Orloff refused, both as secretary and director, to sign them. Shortly thereafter, at a full meeting of the board of directors, she was removed from both offices, and T. P. Danahey was appointed to fill both vacancies. Was the board of directors' action proper? [Stott v. Stott Realty Co., 246 Mich. 267, 224 N.W.623 (1929)]

8. Scott N. Brown, the president of First Trust Company, was also president or controlling shareholder in a number of other companies. As president of First Trust, Brown authorized a number of loans to the companies that he dominated. The directors of First Trust knew of the loans and also knew that most were unsecured, but they never objected to any of the loans made by First Trust to Brown's companies; nor

did they examine the companies' financial reports. In fact, the directors virtually turned the entire management of First Trust over to Brown because of their faith in him as an entrepreneur. First Trust later became insolvent in large measure due to the loans that it had made to several of Brown's other companies. The trustee in bankruptcy of First Trust, representing First Trust's creditors, wished to recover from the directors of First Trust for the damages sustained as a result of the loans. Are the directors of First Trust liable? [Neese v. Brown, 218 Tenn. 686, 405 S.W.2d. 577 (1964)]

9. Free For All Missionary Baptist Church, Inc., by and through its pastors (who were also its president and secretary), leased from Southeastern Beverage and Ice Equipment Company, Inc., certain liquor dispensary equipment for use in an establishmer.t known as Soul On Top of Peachtree. The church made an initial payment of $1,575 and then defaulted on the monthly rental payments. Southeastern brought suit against the church corporation, seeking damages for the balance of the lease. The shareholders of the church corporation defended on the ground that the action by its president and secretary and by the church were all *ultra vires*. Is this a valid defense? [Free For All Missionary Baptist Church, Inc. v. Southeastern Beverage and Ice Equipment Co., Inc., 135 Ga. App. 498, 218 S.E.2d. 169 (1975)]

10. On July 1, 1924, Ralston Purina Company hired Harker under the terms of a five-year employment contract. The contract provided that Ralston was to sell Harker 290 shares of its capital stock immediately at $25 per share, which was substantially less than the actual value of the stock. The contract further provided that if Harker stopped working at Ralston for any reason other than his death within the next five years, Ralston would have the power to repurchase the stock from Harker at the price Harker paid. Prior to April 15, 1928, Harker completed payment of the purchase price of the stock, and on that date his employment for some reason came to an end. Ralston Purina wished to enforce the contract and repurchase the stock from Harker. Harker argued that such a repurchase would be *ultra vires* since a corporation could not enter into an agreement to repurchase its own stock from an employee. Is Harker's argument sound? [Harker v. Ralston Purina Co., 45 F.2d. 929 (7th Cir. 1930)]

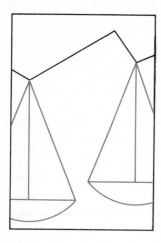

42

Corporations
Special Corporate Forms
and Benefits of Incorporating

Chapter 36 mentioned several specialized classifications of corporations, such as Subchapter S corporations, closely-held corporations, and professional corporations. This chapter will examine certain of these classifications in more detail. The last part of the chapter will look briefly at the costs and benefits of starting a corporation.

THE SUBCHAPTER S CORPORATION

Certain corporations can choose to qualify under Subchapter S of the Internal Revenue Code to avoid the imposition of income taxes at the corporate level while retaining all the advantages of a corporation, particularly limited legal liability. A Subchapter S corporation is sometimes known as a *tax option* corporation. Basically, it elects to be taxed in a manner similar to that of a partnership—to file only an informational return that allocates income among the shareholders regardless of dividend distributions. This is the way corporate taxes can be avoided. While the Subchapter S corporation has the advantages of the corporate form without the double taxation of income (corporate income is not taxed separately), it does have some disadvantages. One of the most important disadvantages relates to the amount of income that can be placed in pension plans that permit corporate shareholders to shelter income from personal federal income taxes.

Requirements for Subchapter S Qualification

There are numerous requirements for Subchapter S qualification. The following are some of the more important:

1.   The corporation must be a domestic corporation.
2.   The corporation must not be a member of an affiliated group of corporations.
3.   The shareholders of the corporation must be either individuals, estates, or certain trusts that are treated as owned by the grantor. Corporations and partnerships cannot be shareholders.
4.   For taxable years beginning after 1978, the corporation must have fifteen or fewer shareholders.
5.   The corporation can have only one class of stock; all shareholders have the same voting rights.
6.   The corporation must not derive more than 20 percent of its gross receipts from passive investment income.
7.   The corporation cannot derive more than 80 percent of its gross receipts from outside the United States.
8.   No shareholder of the corporation can be a nonresident alien.

Benefits of Electing Subchapter S

At times, it is beneficial for a regular corporation to elect Subchapter S status. Below are checklists of situations where Subchapter S election can be beneficial.

1.   When the corporation has losses, the Subchapter S election allows the shareholders to use them to offset other income.
2.   Whenever the stockholders are in a lower tax bracket than the corporation, the Subchapter S election causes their entire income to be taxed in the shareholders' bracket, whether or not it is distributed. This is particularly attractive when the corporation wants to accumulate earnings for some future business purpose.

3.   Taxable income of a Subchapter S corporation is taxable only to those who are shareholders at the end of the corporate year when that income is distributed.
4.   The Subchapter S corporation can choose a fiscal year that will permit it to defer some of its shareholders' taxes. This is important because undistributed earnings are not taxed to the shareholder until after the corporation's (not the shareholder's) year.
5.   The shareholder in a Subchapter S corporation can give some of his or her stock to other members of the family who are in a lower tax bracket.
6.   A Subchapter S corporation can still offer some tax-free corporate benefits. These fringe benefits can mean federal tax savings to the shareholders.

CLOSE CORPORATIONS

This section deals with close corporations—sometimes called closed corporations, closely-held corporations, family corporations, or privately-held corporations. A close corporation is one whose shares are closely held by members of a family or by relatively few persons. Usually, the members of the small group that is involved in a close corporation are personally known to each other. Because there is such a small number of shareholders, there is no trading market for the shares.

In practice, a close corporation is often operated like a partnership. A few states recognize this in the special statutory provisions that cover close corporations. Under these statutes, a number of the formalities and mechanics required of a regular corporation are waived. Under Maryland statute, for example, the close corporation can elect to eliminate the board of directors.

Close Corporation Statutes

In order to be eligible for small corporation status, a corporation has to have a limited number of shareholders, the transfer of corporation stock must be subject to certain restrictions, and the corporation must not make any public offering of its securities.[1] Close corporation statutes provide greater flexibility by expressly permitting electing corporations to vary significantly from traditional corporation law.[2]

Management

The close corporation has a single shareholder or a closely-knit group of shareholders who usually hold the positions of directors and officers. The management of a close corporation resembles that of a sole proprietorship or a partnership. In the eyes of the law, however, it is still a corporation and must meet the same legal requirements as other corporations subject to the special statutes mentioned above. In states where special statutes have not been enacted, close corporations have sometimes had to circumvent the law.

Consider an example where a state law requires that a corporation have two directors, and a close corporation has only one shareholder. In the articles of incorporation, the number of directors can be set at two, but the corporation can operate with a permanent vacancy on the board of directors. Alternatively, a disinterested person, usually a friend, can be convinced to put his or her name down as director.

Transfer of Shares

Since, by definition, a close corporation has a small number of shareholders, the transfer of shares of one shareholder to someone else can cause serious management problems. In other words, the other shareholders can find themselves required to share control with someone they either do not know or do not like. To avoid this problem, it is usually advisable for the close corporation with several shareholders to specify restrictions on the transferability of stock in its articles of incorporation.

Consider an example. Tom, Dick, and Harry Smith are the only shareholders of Smith Boat Company. Tom and Dick Smith do not want Harry to sell his shares to an unknown third person. The articles of incorporation might therefore restrict the transferability of shares to outside persons. For example, the restriction might require shareholders to offer their shares to the corporation or other shareholders first before going to an outside purchaser.

Another way that control of a close corporation can be stabilized is through the use of a shareholder agreement. Agreements among shareholders to vote their stock in a particular way are generally upheld. Shareholder agreements can also provide that when one of the original shareholders dies, his or her shares of stock in the corporation are divided in such a way that the proportionate holdings of the survivors, and thus their porportionate control, be maintained.

1. See, for example, 8 Del. Code Annotated, Sec. 342. This section provides that electing corporations must have a maximum limitation on the number of shareholders, not exceeding thirty.
2. For example, in some states, the close corporation need not have a board of directors.

GALLER v. GALLER
Supreme Court of Illinois, 1965.
32 Ill.2d 16, 203 N.E.2d 577.

BACKGROUND AND FACTS *Benjamin and Isadore Galler were brothers and 50 percent shareholders in a wholesale drug business that was incorporated under Illinois law as the Galler Drug Company.*

The corporation prospered, and in July 1955, Benjamin and Isadore and their wives entered into a carefully drafted agreement among themselves and the corporation. The written agreement purported to provide that, in the event of the death of either brother, the corporation would provide income for the support and maintenance of his immediate family. In addition, the family of the deceased brother would have equal control over the corporation.

Benjamin died in 1957. Shortly thereafter, his widow, Emma, requested that Isadore, the surviving brother, comply with the terms of the 1955 agreement. Isadore refused to cooperate. Emma sued, seeking specific performance of the 1955 agreement. The trial court agreed with Emma, holding that the shareholder agreement was valid. The intermediate appellate court subsequently held that the 1955 agreement was void on the ground of public policy. The Illinois Supreme Court reviewed the case.

UNDERWOOD, Justice.

* * *

The power to invalidate the agreements on the grounds of public policy is so far reaching and so easily abused that it should be called into action to set aside or annul the solemn engagement of parties dealing on equal terms only in cases where the corrupt or dangerous tendency clearly and unequivocally appears upon the face of the agreement itself or is the necessary inference from the matters which are expressed, and the only apparent exception to this general rule is to be found in those cases where the agreement, though fair and unobjectionable on its face, is a part of a corrupt scheme and is made to disguise the real nature of the transaction.

* * *

At this juncture it should be emphasized that we deal here with a so-called close corporation. Various attempts at definition of the close corporation have been made. For our purposes, a close corporation is one in which the stock is held in a few hands, or in a few families, and wherein it is not at all, or only rarely, dealt in by buying or selling. Moreover, it should be recognized that shareholder agreements similar to that in question here are often, as a practical consideration, quite necessary for the protection of those financially interested in the close corporation. While the shareholder of a public-issue corporation may readily sell his shares on the open market should management fail to use, in his opinion, sound business judgment, his counterpart of the close corporation often has a large total of his entire capital invested in the business and has no ready market for his shares should he desire to sell. He feels, understandably, that he is more than a mere investor and that his voice should be heard concerning all corporate activity. Without a shareholder agreement, specifically enforceable by the courts, insuring him a modicum of control, a large minority shareholder might find himself at the mercy of an oppressive or unknowledgeable majority. Moreover, as in the case at bar, the shareholders of a close corporation are often also the directors and officers thereof. With substantial shareholding interests abiding in each member of the board of directors, it is often quite impossible to secure, as in the large public-issue corporation, independent board judgment free from personal motivations concerning corporate policy. For these and other reasons too voluminous to enumerate here, often the only sound basis for protection is afforded by a lengthy, detailed shareholder agreement securing the rights and obligations of all concerned.

* * *

The Appellate Court correctly found many of the contractual provisions free from serious objection, and we need not prolong this opinion with a discussion of them here. That court did, however, find difficulties in the stated purpose of the agreement as it relates to its duration, the election of certain persons to specific offices for a number of years, the requirement for the mandatory declaration of stated dividends (which the Appellate Court held invalid), and the salary continuation agreement.

* * * While limiting voting trusts in 1947 to a maximum duration of 10 years, the [Illinois State] legislature has indicated no similar policy regarding straight voting agreements although these have been common since prior to 1870. In view of the history of decisions of this court generally upholding, in the absence of fraud or prejudice to minority interests or public policy, the right of stockholders to agree among themselves as to the manner in which their stock will be voted, we do not regard the period of time within which this agreement may remain effective as rendering the agreement unenforceable.

The clause that provides for the election of certain persons to specified offices for a period of years likewise does not require invalidation. * * *

We turn next to a consideration of the effect of the stated purpose of the agreement upon its validity. The pertinent provision is: "The said Benjamin A. Galler and Isadore A. Galler desire to provide income for the support and maintenance of their immediate families." Obviously, there is no evil inherent in a contract entered into for the reason that the persons originating the terms desired to so arrange their property as to provide post-death support for those dependent upon them. Nor does the fact that the subject property is corporate stock alter the situation so long as there exists no detriment to minority stock interests, creditors or other public injury.

JUDGMENT AND REMEDY

The Illinois Supreme Court held that the provisions of the shareholder agreement were enforceable.

PROFESSIONAL SERVICE ASSOCIATIONS— PROFESSIONAL CORPORATIONS

In the past, professional persons such as physicians, lawyers, dentists, and accountants could not incorporate. Today they can, and their corporations are typically called professional service associations or professional corporations. They can be identified by the letters S.C. (service corporation), P.C. (professional corporation), Inc. (incorporated), or P.A. (professional association). In general, a professional corporation is formed like an ordinary business corporation.

The Liability of Members of a Professional Corporation

Subject to certain exceptions, the shareholders of a professional corporation have limited liability.

MALPRACTICE OF AN ASSOCIATE The liability of a shareholder in a professional service association for the malpractice of another member is not clear. In a partnership, dentists X, Y, and Z are each unlimitedly liable for whatever malpractice liability is incurred by the others within the scope of the partnership. If the three formed a professional corporation, the orthodox corporate law rule would apply, and none of the dentists would be liable for the malpractice of the others. As far as statutory reference to malpractice liability is concerned, a conservative court might interpret the statutory preservation of malpractice liability, thus causing the individual shareholder in a professional association to be liable for the acts of his or her associates as if the professional corporation were a partnership.

ORDINARY TORT   Torts that are not related to malpractice are often treated differently from malpractice. A shareholder in a professional corporation is protected from the liability imposed because of torts committed by other members. If a secretary has been sent from the office to pick up tax forms from the IRS and, in the process, runs into another car, both the corporation and the secretary will be held liable. Ordinarily, the shareholder in a professional corporation will not be personally liable.

THE SHAREHOLDER CREATES LIABILITY Any shareholder of a professional corporation who engages in a negligent action and who is guilty of malpractice is *personally* liable for the damage caused. Basically, this is the same rule of law that applies to ordinary business corporations.

Tax Benefits of the Professional Corporation

The tax benefits of the professional corporation are basically those that apply to all corporations. One of the major benefits involves a pension and profit-sharing plan that can be set up. This is discussed under the subheading "Benefits of Incorporating."[3]

FOREIGN CORPORATIONS

As indicated earlier, a corporation is referred to as a *domestic corporation* by its home state; a

corporation organized in any other state is called a *foreign corporation*. Thus, a corporation holding a Washington state charter is a domestic corporation in Washington but a foreign corporation in all other states (and nations). Whether or not a corporation is domestic is determined by the state in which it is chartered, not by the state of residence of its shareholders and incorporators or the state in which it conducts its business.

Status and Rights of Foreign Corporations

A corporation incorporated in one state typically must obtain a certificate to do business as a foreign corporation within another state. Once this has occurred, the powers conferred upon a corporation by its home state can be exercised in the other state. Numerous states have specific local laws that are designed to regulate foreign corporations. Sometimes, local statutes relating to corporations in general will also apply to foreign corporations. When these statutes relate to internal corporate affairs, they normally do not apply to foreign corporations.

POSTING A BOND   Some jurisdictions require that a foreign corporation post a bond to insure performance of its contracts. Often a foreign corporation must comply with standards of financial responsibility before a certificate of authority to transact business will be issued.

JURISDICTION OVER FOREIGN CORPORATIONS   Before a state court can hear a dispute in which a foreign corporation is the defendant, the state court must have *jurisdiction* over the defendant. A state court only has jurisdiction over foreign corporations which have sufficient *contacts* with the state. A foreign corporation which has its home office within the state or has manufacturing plants in the state meets this "contacts" requirement. A foreign corporation whose only contact with the state is that one of its directors resides there does not

---

3.   See also R. A. Anderson, *Running a Professional Corporation* (Philadelphia, Pa.: Littoral Development Company, 1971).

have sufficient contact with the state for the state court to exercise jurisdiction over it.

In the following case, the defendant was a foreign corporation that manufactured a defective component part for a forklift vehicle that injured the plaintiff. The Florida court had to determine whether or not the foreign corporation had sufficient legal presence in the state of Florida to permit it to be the subject of a lawsuit in Florida.

HARLO PRODUCTS CORP. v. J.I. CASE CO.
District Court of Appeals of Florida, First District, 1978.
360 So.2d 1328.

BACKGROUND AND FACTS *A personal injury action was brought against a forklift owner (Case) when the arm of the forklift fell and injured someone. The accident occurred as a result of an allegedly defective forklift component manufactured by the defendant, Harlo. The forklift owner, Case, was engaged in business in Florida. Harlo was a foreign corporation with its principal place of business in Grandville, Michigan.*

At the trial, Case argued that a component part of the forklift that produced the injury was manufactured by Harlo and that other forklifts in Case's possession in Florida contained similar defective component parts, also manufactured by Harlo. Therefore, Case argued that the Florida courts had jurisdiction over Harlo. In its defense, Harlo argued that it was a Michigan corporation not licensed to do business in Florida and that it did not engage in business in Florida. Its only contact with Florida occurred when the forklifts that contained a component that it had manufactured found their way into the state. Therefore, Harlo moved to dismiss the action pending against it. The trial court refused, and Harlo immediately appealed the denial.

MILLS, Judge.
* * *

Harlo [the defendant] filed an affidavit stating that it was a Michigan corporation not licensed to do business in Florida, that it did not engage in business in Florida, and that it maintained no offices, agents, employees, bank accounts, books, records, telephone listings or other business activities in Florida. Case [plaintiff] filed a counter-affidavit stating that a component of the injury producing forklift was manufactured by Harlo and that other forklifts in its possession in Florida contained the component manufactured by Harlo.

Case contends that the facts alleged in its * * * complaint clearly bring [Harlo] within Florida Statutes Section 48.193(1)(f)2 (1977), which states:

"(1) Any person, whether or not a citizen or resident of this state, who personally or through an agent does any of the acts enumerated in this subsection thereby submits that person and, if he is a natural person, his personal representative to the jurisdiction of the courts of this state for any cause of action arising from the doing of any of the following: * * *

(f) Causes injury to persons or property within this state arising out of an act or omission outside of this state by the defendant, provided that at the time of the injury either: * * *

2. Products, materials, or things processed, serviced, or manufactured by the defendant anywhere were used or consumed within this state in the ordinary

course of commerce, trade, or use, and the use or consumption resulted in the injury."

[The court decided that Harlo came within the scope of the Florida statute because it manufactured a product that injured a person in the state of Florida. However, the mere presence in Florida of Harlo's product was not a sufficient contact for the assertion of personal jurisdiction over it by a Florida court.]

Before a state court can acquire personal jurisdiction over a foreign corporation, the foreign corporation must have certain minimum contacts with the forum state so that the maintenance of the suit does not offend traditional notions of fair play and substantial justice. It is necessary that there be some act by which the foreign corporation purposely avails itself of the privilege of conducting activities within the forum state, thus invoking the benefits and protection of its laws.

In *Dunn v. The Upjohn Co.*, we held that a Georgia pharmacist, who filled and delivered a prescription to a Florida resident in Georgia who was injured after using the prescription in Florida, was not subject to personal jurisdiction in Florida because the pharmacist did not purposely avail himself of the privilege of conducting activities in Florida and did not have minimum contacts with Florida.

In *Jack Pickard Dodge, Inc. v. Yarbrough*, we held that Section 48.193(1)(f)2 was unconstitutional as applied to a North Carolina automobile dealer, who serviced a car owned by Avis who later sold it at auction in Florida to a Florida resident who was injured in Florida * * *.

The facts in this case, although not the same, are sufficiently similar to warrant the same result. The only allegation connecting Harlo with Florida is that it manufactured a component of forklifts which are used throughout Florida. The statements in Harlo's affidavit that it was a Michigan corporation not licensed to do business in Florida, that it did not engage in business in Florida and that it maintained no offices, agents, employees, bank accounts, books, records, telephone listings or other business activities in Florida, are unrefuted by Case. There are no allegations showing that Harlo purposely availed itself of the privilege of carrying on business activities in Florida nor that it had minimum contacts with Florida.

The court dismissed the complaint against Harlo because the mere presence in Florida of its product was not a sufficient contact to constitutionally permit the assertion of personal jurisdiction over the foreign corporation by a Florida court.

JUDGMENT AND REMEDY

NONPROFIT CORPORATIONS

Some corporations are formed without a profit-making purpose. These are called nonprofit, not for profit, or eleemosynary corporations. They are sometimes (although not necessarily) private charities. They can be used in conjunction with an ordinary corporation to facilitate making contracts with the government. Private hospitals, private universities, and the like are frequently organized as nonprofit corporations.

Although shares of stock can be issued, dividends are not paid out to the members. Formation of nonprofit corporations often follows state statutes that are based on the Model Nonprofit Corporation Act. Eleven states plus the District of Columbia have adopted this act in at least modified form. In any event, the corporation statutes provide for the organization of nonprofit corporations in much the same way that other types of corporations are formed. The nonprofit corporation is a convenient form of organization that allows various groups to own property and to form contracts without the individual members being exposed to liability.

CORPORATE FORMATION AND ITS COSTS

This section will discuss the desirability of an individual's incorporating as a close corporation, a professional corporation, or a Subchapter S corporation. Incorporation for individuals with regular jobs is limited to those who also have substantial outside, "moonlighting" income that can be funneled through the corporation. This income cannot be salaried income; it must be in the form of payments that can go directly into a corporation. (Any checks that the individual receives from which social security and federal withholding taxes are deducted generally cannot be deposited into the corporation as corporate income.) A family cannot incorporate simply because it is a family; it must be engaged in a bona fide business from which it receives nonsalaried income.

The Costs of Incorporating

Just about anyone in any state can start a corporation. There are, however, numerous expenses associated with starting and running such a venture. Below is a list of the possible expenses:

1. *Lawyers' fees.* These can range from a minimum of $250 to as much as $3,000.
2. *Accountants' fees.* It can cost several hundred dollars to establish a bookkeeping system for a corporation.
3. *Fees to the state.* The state can require an annual corporate fee ranging from a few dollars to several hundred dollars.
4. *Unemployment insurance taxes.* Even if the corporation has only one employee, and it is clearly set up for tax reasons only, it must still pay unemployment insurance taxes, either to

the state in which it is registered or to the federal government.
5. *Employer's contribution to social security.* Even if a person is a salaried employee of some other company, as an employee of his or her own corporation, he or she must pay an employer's "contribution" to social security. This "contribution" is nonrefundable and seems to be on the rise.
6. *Annual legal and accounting fees.* Many forms must be filed for corporations in different states. In addition, corporate records and minute books must be maintained. Typically, an accountant or a lawyer does this. Annual fees for such services can run into many hundreds of dollars. Numerous forms must be filled out every year for retirement funds in particular.

The Benefits of Incorporating

One of the major benefits of incorporating is the tax benefit of starting a pension or profit-sharing plan and the tax-related benefits associated with fringe benefits.

PENSION AND PROFIT-SHARING PLANS The IRS routinely allows pension plans consisting of two parts—a 10 percent retirement plan and a 15 percent profit-sharing plan. The 10 percent and 15 percent numbers refer to the percentage of the gross salary paid to the corporation's individual employees in any one year. Assume that Leed has $50,000 of his income funneled through his close corporation and that he pays himself that $50,000 in salary. Leed could contribute $5,000 to his corporate pension plan and $7,500 to his corporate profit-sharing plan.

THE BENEFIT OF PENSION AND PROFIT-SHARING PLANS—A DIGRESSION The tax-sheltered pension or profit-sharing plan allows the individual to save before taxes as opposed to saving after-tax dollars. If the individual is in the 50 percent tax bracket, for example, a pension tax shelter will allow him or her to save twice as many before-tax dollars as after-tax dollars.

A tax-exempt savings plan does not, however, allow the individual to avoid paying taxes indefinitely on the savings put into the plan. Eventually, the individual will have to pay taxes, but they will be paid as they are taken out of the plan. Thus, the individual saves on taxes because he or she is usually in a lower tax bracket after retirement. Moreover, the individual puts off having to pay those taxes, allowing savings to grow at compounded rates. This is a key aspect of tax-exempt pension and profit-sharing plans. By deferring taxes until a future date, interest can be earned on those deferred taxes while they are not being paid (and the taxes on those earnings are deferred). In other words, the government loans the individual the taxes owed for a number of years and does not charge interest on the loan. It must be repaid, generally at retirement, but in the meantime, extra income can be earned. A simple numerical example follows to illustrate the point.

Compare two possibilities—a regular savings program in which the individual puts, say, $100 in a savings and loan account each year

and another program in which the individual sets up a retirement pension plan containing money that is not currently taxed. To simplify the arithmetic, assume that the individual is in the 50 percent tax bracket; thus, this individual can have the same after-tax income to spend during the year by placing $200 in the tax-exempt pension plan. Assume further that the same rate of return is earned in the pension plan as in the savings and loan association.

As Exhibit 42-1 indicates, the individual with the pension plan will have more retirement dollars to spend than the individual without it, although they both have the same after-tax income during their working years. In the example, the tax-exempt savings plan would have yielded $14.34 more than the other plan after five years. This does not sound like much, but it is equivalent to an increase in total savings of 12.7 percent. That percentage figure would increase dramatically in a comparison of a tax-sheltered plan over a thirty-year period to a plan that is not a tax shelter. Moreover, even 12.7 percent represents quite a difference if the sums of money involved are large. And they

---

EXHIBIT 42–1   THE BENEFITS OF A TAX-SHELTERED SAVINGS PLAN

	YEAR 1	YEAR 2	YEAR 3	YEAR 4	YEAR 5
PLAN 1—Not Tax Sheltered					
Principal	$100.00	$102.50	$105.06	$107.69	$110.382
Interest	5.00	5.125	5.253	5.384	5.519
Taxes	−2.50	−2.5625	−2.627	−2.692	−2.7596
After-tax total	$102.50	$105.06	$107.69	$110.38	$113.14

Net after-tax savings, end of 5 years = $113.14

PLAN 2—Tax Sheltered					
Principal	$200.00	$210.00	$220.50	$231.525	$242.826
Interest	10.00	10.50	11.025	11.57625	12.1413
Total	$210.00	$220.50	$231.53	$242.83	$254.97

Taxes paid at 50% at end of year 5 = 0.5 x $254.97 = $127.48
Net after-tax savings at end of 5 years = $254.97 − 127.48 = $127.49

certainly would be greater than those in our example for the average retirement plan. To repeat, the benefit of the pension plan is that the payment of taxes is deferred until some later date. Moreover, a person with a tax-exempt pension plan does not pay taxes on the interest earned until it is distributed later on.

Fringe Benefits

An individual who starts a corporation can take advantage of a number of fringe benefits that provide items that might otherwise have to be bought with after-tax dollars.

TERM LIFE INSURANCE An individual, through his or her own corporation, can purchase up to $50,000 of term life insurance every year with dollars out of the corporation. Because these dollars are a cost to the corporation, they are not taxable. If the person is in the 50 percent tax bracket, for example, that means that he or she is buying $50,000 of term insurance for "fifty-cent dollars." In this example, the cost of that insurance is essentially one-half what it would have been if it had been purchased outside the corporate structure.

A MEDICAL PLAN An individual can set up a completely comprehensive medical plan to cover virtually all kinds of medical expenses. Thus, the corporation can reimburse the individual with before-tax dollars for any payments made for medical insurance. The corporation can pay for all medicines, dental work,

and anything that relates to physical well-being. For someone with a large family, this comprehensive medical plan can mean substantial savings every year. If, in general, an individual spends $2,000 more each year in medical expenses than his or her medical insurance covers and if the individual is in the 50 percent tax bracket, he or she gets a "kickback" of $1,000.

The benefit of a medical plan is reduced by the availability of medical deductions that the individual could have taken off his or her income before figuring federal income taxes. Part of the person's medical insurance plus any medical expenses exceeding 3 percent of the adjusted gross income can be itemized as specific deductions on his or her personal federal income tax return. Essentially, then, a medical plan within the corporation for the individual and dependents eliminates the medical expenses that generally are not deductible.

The Revenue Act of 1978 requires that a medical plan not discriminate among employees. In other words, if it is made available for the president of the corporation, it must also be made available for all employees in the corporation.

DISABILITY INSURANCE An individual can purchase, with before-tax dollars, long-term disability insurance through the corporation. In other words, a person can buy a salary continuation policy with before-tax dollars that might otherwise have to be bought with after-tax dollars. Such policies pay a certain amount of money every month if the person becomes disabled and is unable to work.

QUESTIONS AND CASE PROBLEMS

1. Life Carpet and Tile Company, Inc. is incorporated in Florida and does all of its business in that state. Pace Carpet Mills, Inc. is a foreign corporation. Life Carpet filed a lawsuit against Pace Carpet Mills in a Florida court. In its complaint, it alleged that Pace

carried on its Florida business through a local distributor and that Pace exercised almost complete control over the distributor. Can the lawsuit be brought in Florida? [Pace Carpet Mills, Inc. v. Life Carpet and Tile Co., Inc., 365 So.2d. 445 (Fla. App. 1978)]

2. In Illinois, foreign corporations are subject to the Illinois Attachment Act. Under this act, a corporation that is not a state resident subjects its property in Illinois to court supervision during any lawsuits that are pending against it. Vinylweld, Inc., an Illinois

corporation, brought suit in Illinois against Metropolitan Greetings, Inc., a Massachusetts corporation. Prior to the suit, Metropolitan Greetings had complied with the registration provisions of Illinois's statutes that license corporations to do business in Illinois. Should Metropolitan Greetings be subject to Illinois's attachment statute? [Vinylweld, Inc. v. Metropolitan Greetings, Inc., 360 F.Supp. 1360 (N.D. Ill. 1973)]

3. Arthur B. and Eleanor L. Clemens, husband and wife, were the stockholders of Clemens Company, Inc., which was incorporated under the laws of California. After two years of fairly unsuccessful operation, the company finally began turning a profit. Arthur Clemens then filed with the IRS for treatment as a Subchapter S corporation because of the tax advantages. His wife, Eleanor, who was a 50 percent stockholder of the company, objected, but the firm began filing tax returns as a Subchapter S corporation in spite of her objection. Has Clemens Company properly become a Subchapter S corporation? [Clemens v. Commissioner of Internal Revenue, 453 F.2d. 869 (9th Cir. 1971)]

4. Shelborne Enterprises, Inc., a Florida corporation, had done business for a number of years before its shareholders unanimously decided to elect for Subchapter S tax treatment. The corporation's stock was divided into four categories, each having an unequal number of shares and each entitled to elect one director. Shelborne conducted its business and filed tax returns for the next three years as a Subchapter S corporation. The commissioner of the Internal Revenue Service then sought to recover past taxes beginning with the year that Shelborne first filed as a Subchapter S corporation. The IRS claimed that Shelborne improperly elected Subchapter S status. What result? [Pollack v. Commissioner of Internal Revenue, 392 F.2d. 409 (5th Cir. 1968)]

5. The Valley Loan Association was engaged in the financing of retail installment sales of consumer goods by loans and by purchase of retail installment sales contracts. Valley Loan elected for treatment as a Subchapter S corporation. The commissioner of Internal Revenue Service, however, challenged Valley Loan's election on the ground that Section 1372(e)(5) of Subchapter S denies the right of election to small business corporations whose gross receipts from dividends, interest, and so forth exceed 20 percent of their total gross receipts. Would it be a fair result to deny Valley Loan Association the right to elect under Subchapter S of the Internal Revenue Code? [Valley Loan Ass'n. v. United States, 258 F.Supp. 673 (D. Colo. 1966)]

6. Paul Hessler was the president of Hessler, Inc., a family corporation. Hessler controlled approximately 80 percent of the corporation's stock and completely dominated the management of its business. Matters of business, contracts, hiring, and firing were carried on by the president without action or approval of the directors. Farrel was employed by Hessler for forty years as Hessler's outdoor advertising business manager. During Farrel's employment, the firm's president repeatedly assured Farrel that upon retirement he would receive some kind of retirement benefits. Relying on this assurance, Farrel, over a course of years, declined several attractive offers of employment with other businesses. Farrel retired about five years after Hessler. Hessler, Inc., by and through its directors, refused to pay Farrel any retirement benefits, arguing that the board of directors never approved such benefits. Can Farrel recover? [Hessler, Inc. v. Farrel, 226 A.2d. 708 (Del. 1967)]

7. Shirley Botwin owned 25 percent of the stock of Central Structural Steel Company, Inc. Central was a closed corporation. Botwin's husband, along with two other persons, owned the remaining stock. When the Botwins decided to divorce, Shirley Botwin wished to examine corporate records in order to plan a divorce settlement. She was denied all information about the affairs of the corporation. Can she force Central to allow her to examine the corporate records? [Botwin v. Central Structural Steel Co., 28 A.D.2d 522, 279 N.Y.S.2d. 741 (1967)]

8. Donald McCallum, John Gray, and Lee Evans entered into a pre-incorporation agreement that provided: (1) the three-named persons would cause a corporation to be organized under the laws of Oregon with an authorized capital of a thousand shares, (2) each would receive one-third of the shares, and (3) no shareholder would sell, transfer, or in any way dispose of his shares unless and until he offered to sell the shares to the other shareholders. Subsequently, Lee Evans wished to withdraw from the corporation and offered his shares to both McCallum and Gray. Gray declined, but McCallum agreed to purchase all the shares. Thereafter, at a stockholders' meeting with McCallum and Gray both present, McCallum voted, over Gray's objections, to amend the bylaws allowing an additional thousand shares to be issued. Since Gray had no money to invest at the time, the shares would be purchased by outsiders. Gray objected to the dilution of his interest in the company. Does Gray have any legal grounds to object to McCallum's action? [McCallum v. Gray, 273 Or. 617, 542 P.2d. 1025 (1975)]

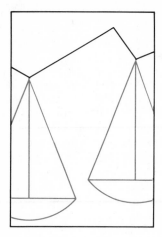

43

Corporations

Corporate Financing and Securities Regulation

In order to obtain financing, corporations issue **securities**—evidence of the obligation to pay money or of the right to participate in earnings and the distribution of corporate trusts and other property. The principal method of long-term and initial corporate financing is the issuance of stocks—**equity**—and bonds—**debt**—both of which are sold to investors. Stocks, or **equity securities,** represent the purchase of ownership in the business firm. Bonds (debentures), or **debt securities,** represent the lending of money by firms (and governments).[1]

CHARACTERISTICS OF BONDS

Bonds are issued by business firms and by government at all levels as evidence of the funds they are borrowing from investors. Bonds almost always have a designated maturity date—the date when the principal or face amount of the bond (or loan) is returned to the investor. Bonds are sometimes referred to as *fixed income securities* because their owners receive a fixed dollar interest payment during the period of time until maturity.

In the bond trade, the word *bond* refers specifically to a debenture

---

1. The term *bonds* is often used to describe both secured and unsecured obligations. Technically, however, bonds are secured by a lien or other security interest and debentures are unsecured.

with a face value of $1,000. Bonds can be sold below their face value at a *discount* or above their face value at a *premium*. Bonds sold at premiums have yields that are less than their coupon, or stated, rates; those sold at a discount have yields that are greater.

Corporate Bonds

The characteristics of corporate bonds vary widely, in part because corporations differ greatly in their ability to generate the earnings and cash flow necessary to make interest payments and to repay the principal amount of the bonds at maturity. Furthermore, corporate bonds are only part of the total debt and overall financial structure of corporate business.

Because debt financing represents a legal obligation on the part of the corporation, various features and terms of a particular bond issue are specified in a lending agreement called a **bond indenture.** A corporate trustee, often a commercial bank trust department, represents the collective well-being of all bondholders in insuring that the terms of the bond issue are met by the corporation. The bond indenture specifies the maturity date of the bond and the pattern of interest payments until maturity. Most corporate bonds pay semiannually a coupon rate of interest on the $1,000 face amount of the bond. For example, the owner of a 6 percent corporate bond would receive $30 interest every six months. The indenture indicates whether any portion of the bond is to be retired each year in a series of *sinking fund payments,* and it specifies any collateral for the bond issue, such as buildings or equipment. Additionally, the indenture indicates how the bondholder (and other creditors of the business firm) will fare if the firm gets into serious financial difficulty and is unable to meet all its legal obligations.

DEBENTURES No specific assets of the corporation are pledged as backing for debentures. Rather, they are backed by the general credit rating of the corporation, plus any assets that can be seized if the corporation allows the debentures to go into default.

MORTGAGE BONDS Mortgage bonds are secured by a mortgage on all or part of the corporate-owned real property. There are a variety of mortgage bonds, including first, second, and even third mortgage types. The first mortgage bonds are "senior" securities. Their owners have first claim to the mortgaged assets of the company if it defaults.

EQUIPMENT TRUST BONDS The collateral for the equipment trust bond (loan) is a specific piece of equipment. The title of the equipment is vested in a trustee, who holds it for the benefit of the bond owners.

COLLATERAL TRUST BONDS Collateral trust bonds are secured by intangibles. They can be shares of stock in another corporation or accounts receivable.

CONVERTIBLE BONDS Convertible bonds can be exchanged for a specified number of shares of common stock when and if the bondholder so desires. The rate of conversion is determined when the convertible bond is issued.

CALLABLE BONDS Callable bonds, which may be debentures or any other kind of bonds, may be called in and the principal repaid at any time. The callable provision is put into the bond when it is issued.

CHARACTERISTICS OF STOCKS

Issuing stocks is another way corporations obtain financing. Stocks represent ownership in a business firm; bonds represent borrowing by the firm. Government does not issue stocks because there is no ownership of government. Stocks are important because private enterprise society rests upon the concept of private ownership of the business organizations that produce and distribute the countless products and services purchased by consumers, business units, government, and other organizations.

A 1975 survey revealed that 25,270,000 individuals, representing 11.8 percent of the total United States population, owned corporate stock. The two major types of stock are preferred stock and common stock.

Preferred Stock

Preferred stock is "preferred" in the sense that its owners must be paid their dividends before common shareholders are paid theirs. Also, preferred shareholders generally have a higher claim on the assets of the corporation if the firm is liquidated. Preferred stock shareholders may or may not have the right to vote. There are a number of different types of preferred stock, which are defined below.

From an investment standpoint, preferred stock is more like bonds than like common stock. It is not included among the liabilities of a business because it is equity. Like all equity securities, preferred shares have no fixed maturity time when they must be retired by the firm. Occasionally, firms do retire preferred stock, but they are not legally obligated to do so. Preferred shareholders receive periodic dividend payments, usually established as a fixed percentage of the face amount of each preferred share. A 7 percent preferred stock with a face amount of $100 per share would pay its owner a $7 dividend each year. This is not a legal obligation on the part of the firm, but the interest payments due to bondholders are legal obligations.

CUMULATIVE PREFERRED STOCK Any dividend payment on cumulative preferred stock not made in a given year must be paid before any dividends can be paid to owners of common stock. In other words, the corporation is liable to the preferred shareholders for past dividends not yet paid (called dividend arrearages). If, for example, a corporation fails to pay dividends

for three years on a stock with a $100 par value and a $5 annual dividend preference, then the company must pay the cumulative preferred stockholders $15 per share at the end of the three years before any dividends can be paid to common stockholders. Sometimes there are limits as to how far back dividends have to be paid—for example, there may be three- or five-year cumulative limits.

PARTICIPATING PREFERRED STOCK With participating preferred stock, the owner can share to some extent in additional dividends that are paid by the firm. Usually, the preferred stockholders are paid their agreed-upon rate of, say, $5 per share (the dividend preference), and then common stockholders are paid an equal percentage rate, after which any additional dividends declared by the board of directors are distributed equally among preferred and common stockholders.

CONVERTIBLE PREFERRED STOCK The owner of shares of convertible preferred stock has an option of converting each share into a specified number of common shares. Sometimes convertible preferred stock can be exchanged for common stock in another company. In any event, the exchange ratio is determined when the convertible preferred shares of stock are issued. Hence, if there is an increase in the market value of the corporation's common stock, the market value of the convertible preferred stock also rises.

REDEEMABLE OR CALLABLE PREFERRED STOCK Redeemable or callable preferred stock is issued by a corporation under the express condition that the corporation has the right to buy back the shares of stock from the preferred stockholders at some future time. The terms of such a buy-back arrangement are specified when the preferred stock is issued. Corporations issue callable preferred so that they can call in the higher-cost preferred stock and reissue lower-cost shares if interest rates fall in the future.

THE CAUTIOUS POSITION OF THE PRE-FERRED SHAREHOLDER Preferred share-holders are investors who have assumed a rather cautious position in their relationship to the corporation. They have a stronger position than common shareholders with respect to dividends and claims on assets, but as a result, they will not share in the full prosperity of the firm if it grows successfully over time. A preferred shareholder receives fixed dividends periodically, and there may be changes in the market price of the shares. The return and the risk for a share of preferred stock lie somewhere between those of bonds and common stock. As a result, preferred stock is often categorized with corporate bonds as a fixed income security even though the legal status is not the same. Some experts even contend that preferred stock is more like bonds than like common stocks, even though preferred stock appears in the owner-ship section of the firm's balance sheet (finan-cial statements).

Common Stock

Common stock represents the true ownership of a corporation. Typically, each investor in a particular firm is entitled to one vote per com-mon share held. Voting rights in a corporation apply to election of the firm's board of directors and to any proposed changes in the ownership structure of the firm.[2] For example, a common shareholder generally has the right to vote in a decision on a proposed merger, since mergers can change the proportion of ownership. Many small investors in giant corporations probably feel, and rightly so, that their small number of votes has little impact on the business firm—particularly when incumbent management owns or obtains right-to-vote shares by proxy and thus has a significant and often controlling proportion of the total votes. Still, voting rights are an important characteristic of common stock and one that some investors take seriously.

There is no obligation to return a principal amount per share to each common stock share-

holder. No firm can insure that the market price per share of its common stock will not go down over time. Neither does the issuing firm guaran-tee a dividend; indeed, some business firms never pay dividends. Considering these nega-tive aspects, why would an individual even consider investing in common stock? The answer, of course, is that all owners are entitled to their proportional share of the corporation's after-tax earnings. If Janet Gray owns 100 shares (0.01 percent of 1 million shares out-standing) of a firm that earns $3 million after taxes, she will receive a proportional share of those earnings totaling $300. Earnings are the key to the benefits that an investor receives from common stock.

Either the earnings of a corporation are paid out in the form of cash dividends to share-holders, or they are retained in the business for the express purpose of enhancing future earn-ings. If the board of directors of Janet Gray's firm (and it is *her* firm because she is a common shareholder) declares a dividend of $1.20 per share, then $120 of her $300 earnings is received now as a tangible benefit, with the other $180 retained. Her other tangible benefit is the market price per share that she will receive if and when she ultimately sells part or all of her 100 common shares. But market price depends, among other things, on the recent earnings (and dividends) of the firm and, more importantly, on expectations for future earnings and dividends, as well as on the overall economic well-being of the country.

Common shareholders, then, are a group of investors who assume the *residual* position in the overall financial structure of a business. In terms of receiving payment for their investment, they are last in line. The earnings to which they are entitled also depend on all the other groups—suppliers, employees, managers, bankers, governments, bondholders, and preferred shareholders—being paid what is due them first. Once those groups are paid, however, common shareholders are entitled to *all* the remaining earnings. (But the board of directors is not normally under any duty to declare the remaining earnings as dividends.) This is the

---

2. State corporation law specifies the types of issues on which shareholder approval must be obtained.

central feature of ownership in any business, be it a corner newsstand, a retail store, an architectural firm, or a giant international oil corporation. In each instance, the common stock owners occupy the riskiest position, but they can expect a correspondingly greater return on their investment. Again, it can be seen why the return and risk pattern holds. As one moves from savings accounts and U.S. government bonds to corporate bonds with different ratings to preferred stock and, finally, to common stock, expected returns increase to compensate for the higher risks that are undertaken. Exhibit 43-1 is a comparison of stocks and bonds.

DIVIDENDS

A dividend is a distribution of property. It can be shares of stock or cash paid to the shareholders in proportion to their interests. In most cases, dividends are paid in cash. The sources of dividends are (1) retained earnings, (2) net profits (current earnings), or (3) surplus. Dividends are payable from limited funds as prescribed by various state statutes:

1. *Retained earnings.* All states allow dividends to be paid from the undistributed net profits earned by the corporation, including capital gains from the sale of fixed assets. The undistributed net profits are called earned surplus or retained earnings.

2. *Net profits.* A few state statutes allow dividends to be issued from current net profits without regard to deficits in prior years.

3. *Surplus.* A number of state statutes allow dividends to be paid out of any kind of surplus.

Limitations on Dividends

All states prohibit the payment of dividends when a corporation is or will become insolvent if it pays them (that is, if its liabilities exceed its assets or if the corporation is unable to pay its debts as they mature). Other states prohibit dividends if they impair the capital of the corporation. Various federal statutes (to be described below) place further limitations.

General principles of accounting are often relevant to the discussion of some of the legal rules governing the distribution of dividends. Many modern corporate statutes define the accounting terms used in their provisions. In short, the question of whether or not to declare and distribute a dividend is within the discretion of the board of directors, but the question of which account to use to make the payment is a question to be settled under the corporation law of the state.

EXHIBIT 43-1   HOW DO STOCKS AND BONDS DIFFER?

Common Stocks	Bonds
1. Stocks represent ownership.	1. Bonds represent owed debt.
2. Stocks (common) do not have a fixed dividend rate.	2. Interest on bonds must always be paid, whether or not any profit is earned.
3. Stockholders can elect a board of directors, which control the corporation.	3. Bondholders usually have no voice in or control over management of the corporation.
4. Stocks do not have a maturity date; the corporation does not usually repay the stockholder.	4. Bonds have a maturity date when the bondholder is to be repaid the face value of the bond.
5. All corporations issue or offer to sell stocks. This is the usual definition of a corporation.	5. Corporations do not necessarily issue bonds.
6. Stockholders have a claim against the property and income of a corporation after all creditors' claims have been met.	6. Bondholders have a claim against the property and income of a corporation that must be met before the claims of stockholders.

BACKGROUND AND FACTS   *Pierce Oil Corporation was organized in June 1913 under the laws of the state of Virginia and was dissolved in December 1940. A receiver was authorized to collect all outstanding accounts and to institute any legal action necessary to obtain a judgment for the recovery of accounts due the company.*

The receiver found that certain taxes had been paid to the Internal Revenue Service under protest. In an attempt to close out the corporation's books, the receiver filed suit against the United States of America to recover the taxes paid under protest on amounts that the corporation characterized as undistributed profits. The receiver made a claim with the IRS for a refund of $17,714.55. The IRS commissioner never took any action on this claim. Therefore, when the receiver presented the situation to the trial court, the court entered a judgment for the corporation, ordering the United States to refund the $17,714.55. The trial court noted that for a number of years preceding the taxable year 1937, the corporation's operations had been unsuccessful. For 1937, the corporation had sustained a deficit of $1,149,642.76, while its net earnings and profits were only $86,412.46. These earnings could not restore the corporation's capital deficit, and it did not declare a dividend in 1937 because its capital deficit exceeded its net assets. In fact, the corporation attempted to obtain a tax credit under the Internal Revenue Act of 1942. This act contains a provision for deficit corporations that are prohibited from paying dividends under state law while they have a deficit in accumulated earnings and profits.

The IRS in 1937 did not agree with the corporation's interpretation of the code provision or with its assertion that Virginia corporation law prohibited it from declaring a dividend because of its deficit. Therefore, under protest, the corporation paid the IRS the $17,714.55 as undistributed profits tax for 1937.

The trial court, believing that the corporation was correct in its position, declared that the $17,714.55 should be returned to the taxpayer.

DOBIE, Circuit Judge.

* * *

The Federal Revenue Act of 1936, c. 690, section 26(c) (3), as amended by section 501(a) (2) of the Revenue Act of 1942, c. 619, provides a credit for deficit corporations "if the corporation is prohibited by a provision of a law or of an order of a public regulatory body from paying dividends during the existence of a deficit in accumulated earning and profits * * *."

Section 3840 of the Virginia Code provides that the directors of a corporation shall "have power to declare and pay dividends upon the shares of its capital stock *out of net earnings, or out of its net assets in excess of its capital as hereinafter defined.*" (Court's emphasis.) This is immediately followed by a definition of the word "capital", as the sum of the consideration received by a corporation in payment for its shares of stock, or such amounts as from time to time may be transferred to capital, less such amounts as may be transferred from capital by reduction thereof.

UNITED STATES v. RIELY
Circuit Court of Appeals, Fourth Circuit, 1948.
169 F.2d 542.

The only question, then, that we are called upon to decide is whether or not, by this Virginia Statute, the taxpayer-corporation was prohibited from paying dividends from its net earnings of $86,412.46 for the year 1937, when these earnings were far from sufficient to restore its capital deficit. No Virginia case has been found interpreting or applying the instant provision of the Virginia Statute. The District Judge interpreted the Statute as prohibiting the declaration of dividends for the year 1937 and granted the refund sought by the taxpayer. In this, we think, he erred.

At the outset, it should be noted that no question of corporate insolvency is here involved and that corporate creditors play no part in the problem. When corporate creditors are fully satisfied, the funds of a dissolved corporation are distributed among the stockholders. Accordingly, whether or not a dividend is declared, or the funds are held for distribution, these funds, in either event, go to the stockholders.

If a pure analytical approach be employed, clearly there was here no prohibition of the declaration of dividends. The Statute is couched, not in the terms of a negative prohibition, but rather in the terms of positive authorization. Directors of a corporation are empowered to declare and pay dividends "out of net earnings, or out of its net assets in excess of its capital." Manifestly, net earnings (on the one hand) and excess of assets over capital (on the other hand) are utterly and absolutely distinct and separate. Either may exist, or not exist, as to a specified period, with, or without, the other.

* * *

Net earnings are defined in Webster's New International Dictionary as "Excess of earnings over expenses, sometimes including interest charges, *during a given period*." (Court's emphasis) In Ballentine's Law Dictionary we find: "The net earnings of a business have been defined as the gross receipts less the expenses of operating the business to earn such receipts." States Black's Law Dictionary (followed by a long citation of supporting cases): "Net earnings are the excess of the gross earnings over the expenditures defrayed in producing them, and aside from and exclusive of capital laid out in constructing or equipping the works or plant." In none of these definitions is any mention made of excess of assets over capital as an inseparable concomitant of, or even as having any relation to, net earnings.

* * *

JUDGMENT AND REMEDY

The circuit court of appeals held that the Virginia statute did not prohibit the corporation from paying dividends during the year in question. Therefore, the corporation was not entitled to a refund of the taxes paid under protest. The judgment of the district court was reversed, and the IRS retained the taxes.

Who Declares and Who Gets Dividends

Generally, dividends are declared at the discretion of the board of directors. Unless there has been bad faith or an obvious abuse of discretion, shareholders cannot compel distribution of dividends no matter how large the surplus in the corporation.

Cash dividends belong to the shareholders

"of record," as declared by the board of directors. The corporation can, for example, make the cash dividend payable to those who will be holders of record on a later date.

FEDERAL SECURITIES REGULATIONS

The sale and transfer of securities is heavily regulated by federal and state statutes and by government agencies. This is a complex area of the law, and the rest of this chapter will outline the nature of federal security regulations and their effect on the business world.

The most important federal security regulations are the Securities Act of 1933 and the Federal Securities Exchange Act of 1934. These acts and others are administered by the Securities and Exchange Commission.

Securities and Exchange Commission

Congress has delegated to the Securities and Exchange Commission (SEC) the responsibility of administering all federal securities laws. The SEC acts as an interpreter of federal statutes and as a rule maker. It also investigates alleged infractions of the laws. Violation of federal securities law involves both criminal and civil liability. The U.S. Attorney General, the Securities and Exchange Commission, and, in certain circumstances, the purchaser or seller of stock can bring suit. The SEC has regulatory authority over brokers, dealers, and stock exchanges.

The Securities Act of 1933

The Securities Act of 1933 was passed to avoid another stock market crash like the one of 1929.[3] The act was designed to prohibit various forms of fraud and to stabilize the securities industry by requiring that all essential information

concerning the issue of stocks be made available to the investing public. The 1933 law requires that a registration statement be filed with the SEC when certain securities are to be publicly offered. The public offering and sale of securities is generally accomplished with the aid of professional underwriters—investment bankers specializing in the sale and distribution of securities. Corporate management and the underwriters each retain a law firm specializing in securities law to assist them in complying with the law.

The 1933 act is basically a disclosure statute. It permits a corporation to sell junk to the public as long as appropriate disclosures are made. This is in contrast to several of the state securities statutes, which permit the registration (and sale) of only those securities offerings that are fair or equitable.

SOME REQUIREMENTS OF THE REGISTRATION STATEMENT The registration statement must include the following:

1. A description of the significant provisions of the security offered for sale, including the relationship between that security and the other capital securities of the registrant. Also, the corporation must disclose how it intends to use the proceeds of the sale.
2. A description of the registrant's properties and business.
3. A description of the management of the registrant, its security holdings, remuneration, and other benefits, including pensions and stock options. There must be disclosure of the interest of directors or officers in any material transactions with the corporation.
4. A financial statement certified by an independent public accounting firm.
5. A description of threatened or pending lawsuits.

EXEMPTIONS A corporation can avoid the high cost and complicated procedures associated with registration by taking advantage of certain exemptions. Transactions are exempt if they do not involve a public offering. Some

---

3. 15 USCA, Secs. 77A-77AA (1976) For a survey of the various provisions of the 1933 act, see David L. Ratner, *Securities Regulation in a Nutshell* (St. Paul: West Publishing Co., 1978) and Blumenthal, *Securities Law in Perspective* (1977).

exempt transactions are private offerings to a limited number of persons, offerings to an institution that has access to the required information,[4] and offerings restricted to residents of the state in which the issuing company is organized and doing business (but these are still subject to state law).[5] The SEC also has the power to exempt small issues under $500,000 from the registration requirement.[6]

The Securities Act of 1933 deals primarily with the initial distribution of securities by an issuer. It has two main parts, the registration and prospectus requirements and the antifraud provisions.

Under the registration and prospectus requirements, no security can be sold or offered for sale through the mails or through interstate commerce without filing a registration statement unless either the security is exempt or the transaction falls within one of the exempt categories.[7] The registration statement becomes a matter of public record, and the information it contains furnishes the basis for drawing up a prospectus that must be given to each purchaser or prospective purchaser of the securities.

The antifraud provisions of the 1933 act apply if either interstate commerce or the mails are involved in the offer or sale of corporate securities. Even though a security may fall into an exempt category, or the transaction may otherwise be exempt from registration, the civil and criminal liabilities for misrepresentation and fraud still apply.

A registration statement is first filed with the SEC. Then, a public selling campaign begins, making use of the written preliminary prospectus. However, the securities cannot be sold until after the effective date of the registration statement.[8] Federal legislation provides severe sanctions for engaging in transactions in securities that should have been registered and for making any false statements or material omissions in a registration statement or prospectus. Liability for false statements and omissions extends to every director of the issuer at the time of registration, every person who has signed the registration statement, every expert who provided expert information incorporated into the statement or prospectus, every underwriter, every person named as one who is about to become a director, and, of course, the issuer.

Violations of the 1933 act are not treated lightly. In the following case, the BarChris Construction Corporation was sued by the purchasers of the corporation's debentures under Section 11 of the Securities Act of 1933. Section 11 imposes liability when a registration statement or prospectus contains material false statements or material omissions.

---

4. Securities Act, Sec. 4(2), 15 USCA Sec. 77d(2).

5. Securities Act, Sec. 3(a)(11), 15 USCA Sec. 77c(a)(11).

6. Securities Act, Sec. 3(b), 15 USCA Sec. 77(b). For issues of less than $500,000, the commission has adopted a simplified registration process under Regulation A.

7. Not surprisingly, certain types of securities are exempted from the registration provisions, including securities issued by nonprofit corporations and securities issued by the federal government or state governments.

---

8. As a practical matter, the registration statement does not become effective until its effectiveness is ordered by the SEC. Theoretically, a registration statement becomes effective twenty days after the filing of the most recent amendment.

ESCOTT v. BARCHRIS CONSTR. CORP.
United States District Court, S.D. New York, 1968.
283 F.Supp. 643.

BACKGROUND AND FACTS *This lawsuit was brought by purchasers of BarChris debentures (bonds) under Section 11 of the Securities Act of 1933. The plaintiffs alleged that the registration statement filed with the Securities and Exchange Commission, which became effective on May 16, 1961, contained material false statements and material omissions.*

The defendants fell into three categories: (1) the persons who signed the registration statement, (2) the underwriters (consisting of eight investment banking firms), and (3) BarChris's auditors—Peat, Marwick, Mitchell & Company. Included in the group of defendants who signed the registration statement were: (1) BarChris's nine directors, (2) BarChris's controller, (3) one of BarChris's attorneys, (4) two investment bankers who were later named as directors of the BarChris Corporation, and (5) numerous other persons participating in the preparation of the registration statement.

BarChris grew out of a business started in 1946 as a bowling alley building company. The introduction of automatic pin setting machines in 1952 sparked rapid growth in the bowling industry. BarChris benefited from this increased interest in bowling, and its construction operations expanded rapidly. It was estimated that, in 1960, BarChris installed approximately 3 percent of all bowling lanes built in the United States. BarChris's sales increased dramatically between 1956 and 1960, and the company was recognized as a significant factor in the bowling construction industry.

BarChris was in constant need of cash to finance its operations, a need which grew more and more pressing as the operations expanded. In 1959, BarChris sold over a half million shares of its common stock to the public. By early 1961, it needed additional working capital, and this time it decided to sell debentures.

BarChris filed a registration statement of the debentures with the SEC and received the proceeds of the financing. Nevertheless, it experienced increasing financial difficulties, which, in time, became insurmountable. By early 1962, it was painfully apparent that BarChris was beginning to fail. In October, BarChris filed a petition for an arrangement under the bankruptcy act, and it defaulted on the interest due on the debentures in November.

The plaintiffs challenged the accuracy of the registration statement and charged that the text of the prospectus—including many of the figures—was false and that material information had been omitted.

The federal district court reviewed all of the figures and statements included in the prospectus.

McLEAN, District Judge.
* * *

The action is brought under Section 11 of the Securities Act of 1933. Plaintiffs allege that the registration statement [and the prospectus included in it] with respect to these debentures filed with the Securities and Exchange Commission, which became effective on May 16, 1961, contained material false statements and material omissions.
* * *

On the main issue of liability, the questions to be decided are (1) did the registration statement contain false statements of fact, or did it omit to state facts which should have been stated in order to prevent it from being misleading; (2) if so, were the facts which were falsely stated or omitted "material" within the meaning of the Act.
* * *

It is a prerequisite to liability under Section 11 of the Act that the fact which is falsely stated in a registration statement, or the fact that is omitted when it should have been stated to avoid misleading, be "material." The regulations of the Securities and Exchange Commission pertaining to the registration of securities define the word as follows:

"The term 'material', when used to qualify a requirement for the furnishing of information as to any subject, limits the information required to those matters as to which an average prudent investor ought reasonably to be informed before purchasing the security registered."

What are "matters as to which an average prudent investor ought reasonably to be informed"? It seems obvious that they are matters which such an investor needs to know before he can make an intelligent, informed decision whether or not to buy the security.

Early in the history of the Act, a definition of materiality was given in Matter of Charles A. Howard, which is still valid today. A material fact was there defined as:

"* * * a fact which if it had been correctly stated or disclosed would have deterred or tended to deter the average prudent investor from purchasing the securities in question."

The average prudent investor is not concerned with minor inaccuracies or with errors as to matters which are of no interest to him. The facts which tend to deter him from purchasing a security are facts which have an important bearing upon the nature or condition of the issuing corporation or its business.

Judged by this test, there is no doubt that many of the misstatements and omissions in this prospectus were material. This is true of all of them which relate to the state of affairs in 1961, i.e., the overstatement of sales and gross profit for the first quarter, the understatement of contingent liabilities as of April 30, the overstatement of orders on hand and the failure to disclose the true facts with respect to officers' loans, customers' delinquencies, application of proceeds and the prospective operation of several alleys.

* * *

JUDGMENT AND REMEDY   *BarChris Corporation itself and all the signers of the registration statement for the debentures, the underwriters, and the corporation's auditors were held liable.*

The Securities Exchange Act of 1934

The Securities Exchange Act provides for the regulation and registration of security exchanges, brokers, dealers, and national securities associations (such as NASD). It regulates the markets in which securities are traded by maintaining a continuous disclosure system for all corporations with securities on the security exchanges and for those companies that have assets in excess of $1 million and five hundred or more shareholders. These corporations are referred to as Section 12 companies, since they are required to register their securities under Section 12 of the 1934 act. The act regulates proxy solicitation for voting, and it allows the SEC to engage in market surveillance to regulate undesirable market practices such as fraud, market manipulation, misrepresentation, and stabilization. ("Stabilization" is a kind of market manipulating technique whereby securities underwriters bid for securities to stabilize their price during their issuance. See Rules 10b-6, 7, and 8.)

INSIDER TRADING One of the most important parts of the 1934 act relates to so-called insider trading. Because of their positions, corporate directors and officers often obtain advance inside information that can affect the future market value of the corporate stock. Obviously, their position can give them a trading advantage over the general public and shareholders. The 1934 Securities Exchange Act defines and extends liability to officers and directors in their personal transactions for taking advantage of such information when they know it is unavailable to the person with whom they are dealing. In addition, in order to deter the use of inside information, the 1934 act requires officers, directors, and certain large shareholders to turn over to the corporation all short-term profits realized on the purchase and sale of corporate stock.

SEC RULE 10b-5 Section 10(b) of the 1934 act and SEC Rule 10b-5 cover not only corporate officers, directors, and majority shareholders but also any persons having access to or receiving information of a nonpublic nature on which trading is based. Those persons to whom the material information is transmitted are known as *tippees*.

DISCLOSURE UNDER RULE 10b-5 Any material omission or misrepresentation of material facts in connection with the purchase or sale of a security may violate Section 10(b) and Rule 10b-5. The key to liability under this rule is whether the insider's information is "material."

Following are some examples of material facts calling for a disclosure under the rule:

1. A new ore discovery.
2. Fraudulent trading in the company stock by a broker/dealer.
3. A dividend change (whether up or down).
4. A contract for the sale of corporate assets.
5. A new discovery (process or product).
6. A significant change in the firm's financial condition.

WHEN MUST DISCLOSURE UNDER RULE 10b-5 BE MADE? Courts have struggled with the problem of when information becomes public knowledge. Clearly, when inside information becomes public knowledge, all insiders should be allowed to trade without disclosure. The courts have suggested that insiders should refrain from trading for a "reasonable waiting period" when the news is not readily translatable into investment action. Presumably, this gives the news time to filter down and to be evaluated by the investing public. What a reasonable waiting period is is not at all clear.

The following is one of the landmark cases interpreting Rule 10b-5. The SEC sued Texas Gulf Sulphur for issuing a misleading press release. The release underestimated the magnitude and value of a mineral discovery. The SEC also sued several of Texas Gulf Sulphur's directors, officers, and employees under Rule 10b-5 after these persons had purchased large amounts of the corporate stock prior to the announcement of the corporation's rich ore discovery.

BACKGROUND AND FACTS *Texas Gulf Sulphur Co. (TGS) drilled a hole on November 12, 1963, near Timmins, Ontario. It appeared to yield a core with exceedingly high mineral content. Since TGS did not own the mineral rights in the surrounding regions, it maintained secrecy about the results of the core sample. Evasive tactics were undertaken to camouflage the drill site, and a second hole was drilled. TGS completed an extensive land acquisition program and then began drilling this lucrative site. Rumors began to spread, and by early April 1964, a "tremendous staking rush [was] going on."*

On April 11, 1964, an unauthorized report of the extraordinary

SECURITIES AND EXCHANGE COMM. v. **TEXAS GULF SULPHUR CO.**

United States Court of Appeals, Second Circuit, 1968.
401 F.2d 833.

mineral find hit the papers. On April 12, TGS announced to the press a strike of at least 25 million tons of ore. Charles Fogarty, executive vice-president of TGS had already purchased 1,700 shares of stock during the month of November 1963 and an additional 300 shares in December. In March 1964, he bought 400 shares, and in April he bought 300 shares. Other TGS officials also purchased stock. They accepted stock options on February 20, 1964.

The Securities and Exchange Commission filed suit against TGS and several of its officers, directors, and employees to enjoin (prevent) TGS's continued violation of the Securities Exchange Act of 1934 and to compel the individual defendants to rescind the securities transactions they had made. The complaint alleged that, on the basis of material inside information concerning the results of TGS's drilling, the defendants either personally or through agents purchased TGS stock, while the information concerning the drill site remained undisclosed to the investing public. The SEC further charged that certain of the defendants (tippers) had divulged information to certain others (tippees) for their use in purchasing TGS stock before the information was disclosed to the public or to other sellers. In addition, certain defendants had accepted options to purchase TGS stock without disclosing material information about the progress of the drilling to either the stock option committee or the TGS board of directors. Finally, the complaint charged that TGS issued a deceptive press release on April 12, 1964.

The deceptive press release should be the focus in reading the following case. The trial court judge held that the issuance of the press release was lawful because it was not issued for the purpose of benefiting the corporation, and there was no evidence that any insider had used the information in the press release to personal advantage. Thus it was not "misleading or deceptive on the basis of the facts then known." The trial court went on to find that most of the defendants had not violated Rule 10b-5.

WATERMAN, Circuit Judge.
* * *

This action was commenced in the United States District Court for the Southern District of New York by the Securities and Exchange Commission (the SEC) pursuant to * * * the Securities Exchange Act of 1934 (the Act) against Texas Gulf Sulphur Company (TGS) and several of its officers, directors and employees, to enjoin certain conduct by TGS and the individual defendants said to violate Section 10(b) of the Act, * * * and Rule 10b-5 * * * (the Rule), promulgated thereunder.
* * *

I. THE INDIVIDUAL DEFENDANTS

A. *Introductory*

Rule 10b-5, 17 CFR 240.10b-5, on which this action is predicated, provides:

It shall be unlawful for any person, directly or indirectly, by the use of any means or instrumentality of interstate commerce, or of the mails, or of any facility of any national securities exchange,

(1)   to employ any device, scheme, or artifice to defraud,

(2)   to make any untrue statement of a material fact or to omit to state a material fact necessary in order to make the statements made, in the light of the circumstances under which they were made, not misleading, or

(3)   to engage in any act, practice, or course of business which operates or would operate as a fraud or deceit upon any person, in connection with the purchase or sale of any security.

Rule 10b-5 was promulgated pursuant to the grant of authority given the SEC by Congress in Section 10(b) of the Securities Exchange Act of 1934 (15 U.S.C. §78j(b)). By that Act Congress purposed to prevent inequitable and unfair practices and to insure fairness in securities transactions generally, whether conducted face-to-face, over the counter, or on exchanges. The Act and the Rule apply to the transactions here, all of which were consummated on exchanges. [T]he Rule is based in policy on the justifiable expectation of the securities marketplace that all investors trading on impersonal exchanges have relatively equal access to material information. The essence of the Rule is that anyone who, trading for his own account in the securities of a corporation has "access, directly or indirectly, to information intended to be available only for a corporate purpose and not for the personal benefit of anyone" may not take "advantage of such information knowing it is unavailable to those with whom he is dealing," i.e., the investing public. Insiders, as directors or management officers are, of course, by this Rule, precluded from so unfairly dealing, but the Rule is also applicable to one possessing the information who may not be strictly termed an "insider" within the meaning of Sec. 16(b) of the Act. Thus, anyone in possession of material inside information must either disclose it to the investing public, or, if he is disabled from disclosing it in order to protect a corporate confidence, or he chooses not to do so, must abstain from trading in or recommending the securities concerned while such inside information remains undisclosed. So, it is here no justification for insider activity that disclosure was forbidden by the legitimate corporate objective of acquiring options to purchase the land surrounding the exploration site; if the information was, as the SEC contends, material, its possessors should have kept out of the market until disclosure was accomplished.

B.   *Material Inside Information*

An insider is not, of course, always foreclosed from investing in his own company merely because he may be more familiar with company operations than are outside investors. An insider's duty to disclose information or his duty to abstain from dealing in his company's securities arises only in "those situations which are essentially extraordinary in nature and which are reasonably certain to have a substantial effect on the market price of the security if [the extraordinary situation is] disclosed." Fleischer, Securities Trading and Corporate Information Practices: The Implications of the Texas Gulf Sulphur Proceeding, 51 Va.L.Rev. 1271, 1289.

Nor is an insider obligated to confer upon outside investors the benefit of his superior financial or other expert analysis by disclosing his educated guesses or predictions. The only regulatory objective is that access to material information be enjoyed equally, but this objective requires nothing more than the disclosure of

basic facts so that outsiders may draw upon their own evaluative expertise in reaching their own investment decisions with knowledge equal to that of the insiders.
* * *

In each case, then, whether facts are material within Rule 10b-5 when the facts relate to a particular event and are undisclosed by those persons who are knowledgeable thereof will depend at any given time upon a balancing of both the indicated probability that the event will occur and the anticipated magnitude of the event in light of the totality of the company activity. Here, notwithstanding the trial court's conclusion that the results of the first drill core, * * * were "too 'remote' * * * to have had an significant impact on the market, i.e., to be deemed material," knowledge of the possibility, which surely was more than marginal, of the existence of a mine of the vast magnitude indicated by the remarkably rich drill core located rather close to the surface (suggesting mineability by the less expensive openpit method) within the confines of a large anomaly (suggesting an extensive region of mineralization) might well have affected the price of TGS stock and would certainly have been an important fact to a reasonable, if speculative, investor in deciding whether he should buy, sell, or hold. After all, this first drill core was "unusually good and * * * excited the interest and speculation of those who knew about it."
* * *

Finally, a major factor in determining whether the * * * discovery was a material fact is the importance attached to the drilling results by those who knew about it. In view of other unrelated recent developments favorably affecting TGS, participation by an informed person in a regular stock-purchase program, or even sporadic trading by an informed person, might lend only nominal support to the inference of the materiality of the * * * discovery; nevertheless, the timing by those who knew of it of their stock purchases and their purchases of short-term calls—purchases in some cases by individuals who had never before purchased calls or even TGS stock—virtually compels the inference that the insiders were influenced by the drilling results.
* * *

We hold, therefore, that all transactions in TGS stock or calls by individuals apprised of the drilling results * * * were made in violation of Rule 10b-5.[1] Inasmuch as the visual evaluation of that drill core (a generally reliable estimate though less accurate than a chemical assay) constituted material information, those advised of the results of the visual evaluation as well as those informed of the chemical assay traded in violation of law.

II. THE CORPORATE DEFENDANT
Introductory

At 3:00 P.M. on April 12, 1964, evidently believing it desirable to comment upon the rumors concerning the Timmins project, TGS issued the press release. * * * It read in pertinent part as follows:
* * *

---

1. Even if insiders were in fact ignorant of the broad scope of the Rule and acted pursuant to a mistaken belief as to the applicable law such an ignorance does not insulate them from the consequences of their acts. Tager v. SEC.

"Recent drilling on one property near Timmins has led to preliminary indications that more drilling would be required for proper evaluation of this prospect. The drilling done to date has not been conclusive, but the statements made by many outside quarters are unreliable and include information and figures that are not available to TGS.

"The work done to date has not been sufficient to reach definite conclusions and any statement as to size and grade of ore would be premature and possibly misleading. When we have progressed to the point where reasonable and logical conclusions can be made, TGS will issue a definite statement to its stockholders and to the public in order to clarify the Timmins project."
* * *

It does not appear to be unfair to impose upon corporate management a duty to ascertain the truth of any statements the corporation releases to its shareholders or to the investing public at large. Accordingly, we hold that Rule 10b-5 is violated whenever assertions are made, as here, in a manner reasonably calculated to influence the investing public, e.g., by means of the financial media, Fleischer, supra, 51 Va.L.Rev. at 1294-95, if such assertions are false or misleading or are so incomplete as to mislead irrespective of whether the issuance of the release was motivated by corporate officials for ulterior purposes. It seems clear, however, that if corporate management demonstrates that it was diligent in ascertaining that the information it published was the whole truth and that such diligently obtained information was disseminated in good faith, Rule 10b-5 would not have been violated.
* * *

We conclude, then, that, having established that the release was issued in a manner reasonably calculated to affect the market price of TGS stock and to influence the investing public, we must remand to the district court to decide whether the release was misleading to the reasonable investor and if found to be misleading, whether the court in its discretion should issue the injunction the SEC seeks.

JUDGMENT AND REMEDY

The appellate court's judgment was favorable to the SEC. The information contained in the press release was material, and the transaction in stock by the insiders who knew of it had violated Rule 10b-5. Thus, the options of the individual defendants were rescinded. However, the questions of whether the press release was misleading and what remedies should be imposed were remanded to the trial court for decision. The trial court is bound to apply the law as enunciated by the court of appeals in making this decision.

COMMENTS

Texas Gulf Sulphur Company was not only sued by the SEC, but numerous civil actions for damages were brought against it by plaintiff-investors who had sold their TGS stock as a result of the deceptively gloomy press release regarding the corporation's mineral exploration. All these suits were settled in 1972.[9] In a federal lawsuit filed against TGS some two years after the initial case, a court of appeals held that investors

9.   Cannon v. Texas Gulf Sulphur, 55 F.R.D. 308 (S.D.N.Y. 1972).

who had sold stock relying on the representations in the press release could recover damages from the corporation and the officers who drafted the release. The court went on to state that the proper measure of damages was the difference between the selling price and the price at which the investors could have reinvested within a reasonable period of time after they became aware of a curative press release made by TGS.

After TGS issued its curative press release, the court held that a diligent and reasonable investor would have become informed of it within four days, and investors who sold their stock more than four days after the second press release was issued could not recover under the Securities Exchange Act on the basis of reliance on the earlier, deceptive release.

WHEN DOES RULE 10b-5 APPLY? Rule 10b-5 applies in virtually all cases concerning the trading of securities, whether on organized exchanges, in over-the-counter markets, or in private transactions. The rule covers notes, bonds, certificates of interest and participation in any profit-sharing agreement, agreements to form a corporation, and joint venture agreements; in short, it covers just about any form of security. It is immaterial whether a firm has securities registered under the 1933 act for the 1934 act to apply.

Rule 10b-5 is applicable only when the requisites of federal jurisdiction, such as the use of the mails, of stock exchange facilities, or of any instrumentality of interstate commerce, are present. However, virtually no commercial transaction can be completed without such contact. In addition, the states have corporate securities laws, many of which include provisions similar to Rule 10b-5.

INSIDER REPORTING AND TRADING— SECTION 16 (b) Officers, directors, and certain large stockholders[10] of Section 12 corporations are required to file reports with the SEC concerning their ownership and trading of the corporation's securities.[11] In order to discourage such insiders from using nonpublic information about their company to their personal benefit in the stock market, Section 16(b) of the 1934 act provides for the recapture by the corporation of all profits realized by the insider on any purchase and sale or sale and purchase of the corporation's stock within any six-month period.[12] It is irrelevant whether the insider actually used inside information; all profits must be returned to the corporation.

Section 16(b) applies not only to stock but to warrants, options, and securities convertible into stock. In addition, the courts have fashioned complex rules for determining profits. Corporate insiders are well advised to seek competent counsel prior to trading in the corporation's stock. Exhibit 43-2 compares the effects of Rule 10b-5 and Section 16b.

PROXY STATEMENTS Section 14(a) of the Securities and Exchange Act of 1934 regulates the solicitation of proxies from shareholders of Section 12 companies. The SEC regulates the content of proxy statements sent to shareholders by corporate managers who are requesting authority to vote on behalf of the shareholders in a particular election on specified issues. Whoever solicits a proxy must fully and accurately disclose all facts that are pertinent to the matter to be voted on. SEC Rule 14a-9 is similar to the antifraud provisions of Rule 10b-5. Remedies for violation are extensive, ranging

---

10. Those stockholders owning 10 percent of the class of equity securities registered under Section 12 of the 1934 act.
11. 1934 Act, Sec. 16(a), 15 USCA Sec. 78

12. In a declining stock market, one can realize profits by selling at a high price and repurchasing at a later time at a lower price.

from injunctions to preventing a vote from being taken, to monetary damages.

Other Federal Securities Laws

There are numerous other federal securities laws, and they are briefly listed here:

1. The Public Utility Holding Company Act of 1935.
2. The Trust Indenture Act of 1939.
3. The Investment Company Act of 1940.
4. The Investment Advisors Act of 1940.
5. The Security Investors Protection Act of 1970.

In addition, miscellaneous federal statutes regulate the issue of securities. For example, the Interstate Commerce Commission regulates motor and rail carriers, the Federal Home Loan Bank Board regulates federal saving and loan associations, and the Comptroller of the Currency regulates national banks.

STATE SECURITIES LAWS

Today, all states have their own corporate securities laws that regulate the offer and sale of securities within individual state borders.[13] Often referred to as *blue sky laws*, they are designed to prevent "speculative schemes which have no more basis than so many feet of blue sky."

Since the adoption of the 1933 and 1934 securities acts, the state and federal governments have regulated securities concurrently. Indeed, both acts specifically preserve state securities laws. There are certain common

_____

13. These laws are catalogued and annotated in CCH, *Blue Sky Law Reporter*, a loose-leaf service.

EXHIBIT 43—2 COMPARISON OF COVERAGE APPLICATION AND LIABILITIES UNDER 10b-5 AND SECTION 16 (b)

	RULE 10-b-5	SECTION 16 (b)
1. Subject matter of transaction	Any security (does not have to be registered).	Any security (does not have to be registered).
2. Transactions covered	Purchase or sale.	Short swing purchase and sale or short swing sale and purchase.
3. Who is subject to liability?	Virtually anyone with inside information— including officers, directors, controlling stockholders, and tippees.	Officers, directors, and certain 10 percent stockholders.
4. Is omission, scheme or misrepresentation necessary for liability?	Yes.	No.
5. Any exempt transactions?	No.	Yes, there are a variety of exemptions.
6. Is direct dealing with the party necessary?	No.	No.
7. Who can bring an action?	A person transacting with an insider or the SEC or a purchaser or a seller damaged by a wrongful act.	Corporation and shareholder by derivative action.

features in the state blue sky laws. They have antifraud provisions, many of which are patterned after Rule 10b-5. Also, most state corporate securities laws regulate securities brokers and dealers.

Typically, these laws also provide for the registration or qualification of securities offered or issued for sale within the state. Unless an applicable exemption from registration is found, issuers must register or qualify their stock with the appropriate state official, often called a corporations commissioner. There is a difference in philosophy in the state statutes. Many are like the Securities Act of 1933 and mandate certain disclosures before registration is effective and a permit to sell the securities is issued. Others have fairness standards that a corporation must meet in order to offer or sell stock in the state. The Uniform Securities Act, which has been adopted in part by several states, was drafted to be acceptable to states with differing regulatory philosophies.

QUESTIONS AND CASE PROBLEMS

1. Maresh, an experienced geologist, owned certain oil and gas leases covering land in Nebraska. To raise money for the drilling of a test well, he undertook to sell fractional interests in the leases. He approached Garfield, a man with whom he had done business in the past. Garfield had mentioned that he would be interested in investing in some of Maresh's future oil ventures. Garfield had wide business experience in the stock market and in oil stocks. He felt that the investment in Maresh's gas leases could be lucrative. Based on Garfield's promise to wire the money promptly, Maresh began drilling. Soon after, when Maresh realized that the land was dry, Garfield refused to pay his share of the investment. Garfield claimed that he could rescind the agreement to invest since the investment offered by Maresh was a security within the meaning of the Securities Act of 1933, and it had not been registered. Did Maresh offer a security within the meaning of the 1933 act? [Garfield v. Strain, 320 F.2d. 116 (10th Cir. 1963)]

2. The Howey Company owned large tracts of citrus acreage in Lake County, Florida. For several years, it planted about five hundred acres annually, keeping half of the groves itself and offering the other half to the public to help finance additional development. Howey-in-the-Hills Service, Inc. was a service company engaged in cultivating and developing these groves, including the harvesting and marketing of the crops. Each prospective customer was offered both a land sales contract and a service contract after being told that it was not feasible to invest in a grove unless service arrangements were made. Of the acreage sold by Howey, 85 percent was sold with a service contract with Howey-in-the-Hills Service, Inc. Must Howey register the sales of these parcels of citrus groves with the Securities and Exchange Commission? [Securities and Exchange Comm. v. W. J. Howey Co., 328 U.S. 293, 66 S.Ct. 1100 (1946)]

3. Zabriskie purchased certain notes from Lewis in connection with a real estate venture that Lewis was trying to establish. The notes bore a maturity date of eight months after the date of purchase. The Securities Act of 1933 excludes from its definition of securities any note that has a maturity date not exceeding nine months at the time of issue. Knowing that the Securities Act is an attempt to control the sales of *investment* securities, can a better test be devised than this strict nine-month rule? [Zabriskie v. Lewis, 507 F.2d. 546 (10th Cir. 1974)]

4. Children's Hospital offered and sold a number of 8 percent mortgage bonds in order to raise enough money to begin operation. Its promoters solicited purchasers mainly through the mails and through local newspaper advertisements. Children's Hospital was to be a nonprofit medical organization established mainly to serve the needs of children in the local community. The promoters, however, expected to earn large profits from organizing the hospital. Must the promoters of Children's Hospital register the sale of the mortgage bonds with the Securities and Exchange Commission? [Securities and Exchange Comm. v. Children's Hospital, 214 F.Supp. 883 (D. Ariz. 1963)]

5. On September 1, 1971, the Ecological Science Corporation issued a press release stating, in part, that it had renegotiated the terms of approximately $14 million in loans from its prime lender and that, under the renegotiated agreement, $4 million was due upon demand and the remainder on a specified date. The press release, however, failed to mention that, on the

same date as the renegotiated loan agreement, an insurance and annuity association had refused to provide the corporation with the $4 million loan that it had planned to use to repay the demand loan. Moreover, while discussing its European prospects in the press release, Ecological Science Corporation failed to mention the proposed transfer of voting control among its European subsidiaries. Has Ecological Science Corporation violated any of the provisions of the Securities Act of 1934? [Securities and Exchange Comm. v. Koenig, 469 F.2d. 198 (2d Cir. 1972)]

6. Vincent Chiarella was employed by a printing house that specialized in printing financial statements for public companies. Chiarella thus had access to information about certain companies before the information was released to the general public. While doing some typesetting for the XYZ Corporation, Chiarella came across some information about XYZ that led him to conclude that its stock would be a worthwhile investment. Chiarella purchased several thousand shares of XZY Corporation stock and within nine months had made a profit of $30,000. Has Chiarella violated Rule 10b-5 of the 1934 securities act? [United States v. Chiarella, 588 F.2d. 1358 (2nd Cir. 1978)]

7. Emerson Electric Company owned 13.2 percent of Dodge Manufacturing Company's stock. Within six months of the purchase of this stock, Emerson sold enough shares to a broker to reduce its holding to 9.96 percent. One week later (but still less than six months after Emerson's initial purchase), Emerson sold its remaining shares of Dodge stock. The sole purpose of Emerson's initial sale of just over 3 percent of its Dodge stock was to avoid liability under Section 16 of the Securities Act of 1934, which prohibits short-swing trading. Assuming Emerson made no profit on the initial sale of stock but made substantial profits when it sold the remaining 9.96 percent of Dodge stock, must it disgorge the profits it made on the sale? [Reliance Electric Co. v. Emerson Electric Co., 404 U.S. 418, 92 S.Ct. 596 (1972)]

8. Repide owned three-quarters of the stock of the Philippine Sugar Estates Development Company, which in turn owned one-half of what were known as the "Friar Lands" in the Philippine Islands. The government wished to purchase the Friar Lands and made an offer to purchase them for approximately $6 million. Since the Philippine Sugar Company owned one-half the lands and the remaining lands were fractionally owned, the company had a strong say in whether or not the owners would jointly accept the government's offer. Repide, acting on behalf of the company, rejected the government's offer and informed the government that he believed the lands to be worth over $13 million. In fact, Repide knew that the lands were almost worthless, except for the fact that the government wanted to buy them. Meanwhile, Repide sought to purchase the remaining 25 percent of the outstanding shares of the Philippine Sugar Company from their owner, Strong. Instead of negotiating with Strong directly, Repide began negotiations with her agent, Jones, whom he knew was in possession of the stock. Repide never informed Jones or Strong of the government's offers for the Friar Lands and thereafter purchased Strong's shares for a very small amount. In fact, the purchase price was lower than Strong would have received if the government's original offer for the Friar Lands had been accepted. Subsequently, the government paid almost $8 million for the Friar Lands. What liability does Repide have to Strong, if any? (Strong v. Repide, 213 U.S. 419, 29 S.Ct. 521 (1909)]

9. Leston Nay owned 90 percent of the stock of First Securities Company. Between the years 1942 and 1966, Hochfelder sent large sums of money to Nay to be invested in escrow accounts of First Securities. The whole investment scheme was a fraud, and Nay converted the money sent by Hochfelder to his own use. Hochfelder then sued Ernst & Ernst, First Securities' auditor, for failing to use proper auditing procedures and thus negligently failing to discover the fraudulent scheme. Will Ernst & Ernst be found guilty of violating Section 10(b) and Rule 10b-5 of the 1934 Securities Act? [Ernst & Ernst v. Hochfelder, 425 U.S. 185, 96 S.Ct. 1375 (1976)]

10. Lakeside Plastics and Engraving Company was a close corporation incorporated in Minnesota. The company suffered losses from the time it was incorporated in 1946. Of its four shareholders, only one was involved in management of the firm. Notwithstanding its earlier difficulties, by 1954, it was apparent that the firm was about to become profitable. Without informing the other shareholders of this fact, the shareholder-manager bought out the remaining shareholders. He accomplished this by making numerous misrepresentations to them. Assuming the shareholder-manager used none of the instrumentalities of interstate commerce, including the mails or the telephone, in making these misrepresentations, can the remaining shareholders bring an action under Section 10(b) of the Securities Act of 1934? If not, do the remaining shareholders have any legal recourse? [Myzel v. Fields, 386 F.2d. 718 (8th Cir. 1967)]

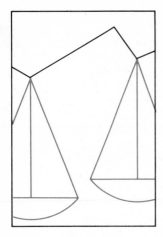

44

Corporations
Rights and Duties of Directors, Managers, and Shareholders

The corporation combines the efforts and resources of a large number of individuals to jointly produce greater returns than the individuals could obtain outside the corporation. Sometimes, actions that benefit the corporation as a whole do not coincide with the interests of the individual. This chapter focuses on the rights and duties of directors, managers, and shareholders and the resolution of conflicts among them.

THE ROLE OF OFFICERS AND DIRECTORS

Directors occupy a position of responsibility unlike that of other corporate personnel. Directors are sometimes inappropriately characterized as *agents* because they act for and on behalf of the corporation. However, no individual director can act as an agent to bind the corporation, and, as a group, directors collectively control the corporation in a way no agent can control a principal. Directors are often incorrectly characterized as *trustees* because they occupy positions of trust and control over the corporation. However, unlike trustees, they do not own or hold title to property for the use and benefit of others.

Directors manage the corporation through the officers who are selected by the board; these officers are agents of the corporation. Directors and officers are deemed *fiduciaries* of the corporation. Their relationship with the corporation and its shareholders is one of trust and confidence. The fiduciary duties of the directors and officers include the duty of care and the duty of loyalty.

702

The Duty of Care

Directors are obligated to be honest and reasonably careful to use prudent business judgment in the conduct of corporate affairs. The so-called business judgment rule does not require directors to insure the success of every venture that the corporation undertakes. The test is objective—the directors must exercise the same degree of care that reasonably prudent people use in the conduct of their own personal business affairs. Thus, corporate losses resulting merely from poor business judgment or an honest mistake of judgment will not normally result in the imposition of legal liability on directors.

BREACH OF THE DUTY OF CARE Directors can be held answerable to the corporation and to the shareholders for breach of their duty of care. When directors delegate work to corporate officers and employees, they are expected to use a reasonable amount of supervision. Otherwise, they will be held liable for *negligence* or *mismanagement* of corporate personnel. For example, a corporate bank director failed to attend any board of directors' meetings in five and a half years and never inspected any of the corporate books or records. Meanwhile, the bank president made various improper loans and permitted large overdrafts. The corporate director was held liable to the corporation for losses of nearly $20,000 resulting from the unsupervised actions of the bank president and the loan committee.

The standard of due care has been variously described and codified in many corporation codes.[1] The impact of the standard is to require that directors carry out their responsibility in an informed, business-like manner.

The standard also varies by the nature of the business. Directors and officers are often expected to act carefully in light of their own actual knowledge and training.

It is expected that directors attend board of directors' meetings and have their votes entered into the minutes of corporate meetings. Directors are also expected to keep themselves well informed on corporate matters and to familiarize themselves with corporate financial statements. Furthermore, they are expected to understand the legal advice rendered by corporate counsel. A director who is unable to carry out such responsibilities must resign. Even when the required duty of care has not been exercised, directors and officers are liable only for the damages caused to the corporation by their negligence.

Duty of Loyalty

The essence of the fiduciary duty requires subordination of self-interest to the interest of the entity to which the duty is owed. It presumes constant loyalty to the corporation on the part of the directors and officers. In general, the duty of loyalty prohibits directors from using corporate funds or confidential corporate information for personal advantage. It requires officers and directors to fully disclose any corporate opportunity or any possible conflict of interest that might occur in a transaction involving the directors and the corporation.

Cases dealing with fiduciary duty typically involve one or more of the following: (1) competing with the corporation, (2) usurping a corporate opportunity, (3) having an interest that conflicts with the interest of the corporation, (4) engaging in insider trading, (5) authorizing some corporate transaction that is detrimental to minority shareholders, and (6) sale of control of the corporation.

In the following case, the Alabama court reviewed a situation in which officers, directors, and shareholders attempted to secure advantages for themselves at the expense of the corporation.

---

1. See, for example, Section 36 of the Model Business Corporation Act, which provides that "a director shall perform his duties as a director, including his duties as a member of any committee of the board upon which he may serve, in good faith, in any manner he reasonably believes to be in the best interest of the corporation, and with such care as an ordinarily prudent person in a like position would use under similar circumstances."

MORAD v.
COUPOUNAS

Supreme Court of Alabama,
1978. 361 So.2d 6.

BACKGROUND AND FACTS *The defendants, Morad and Thomson, were officers, directors, and shareholders of Bio-Lab, Inc. Bio-Lab had one additional shareholder, the plaintiff, Coupounas. While serving as officers and directors of Bio-Lab, the defendants incorporated and operated a competing business, Med-Lab, Inc. The plaintiff brought a derivative suit on behalf of Bio-Lab against the defendants and Med-Lab, alleging that, in opening the competing business, they had usurped a corporate opportunity of Bio-Lab.*

FAULKNER, Justice.

* * *

"It is well settled that directors and other governing members of a corporation are so far agents of the corporation that in their dealings respecting corporate interests, they are subject to the rules which apply generally to persons standing in fiduciary relations and which forbid such persons to secure an advantage for themselves which fidelity to the trust reposed in them would carry to others whose interests they ought to represent.

* * *

"[I]n general the legal restrictions which rest upon such officers in their acquisitions are generally limited to property wherein the corporation has an interest already existing, or in which it has an expectancy growing out of an existing right, or to cases where the officers' interference will in some degree balk the corporation in effecting the purposes of its creation."

* * *

"[I]f there is presented to a corporate officer or director a business opportunity which the corporation is financially able to undertake, is, from its nature, in the line of the corporation's business and is of practical advantage to it, is one in which the corporation has an interest or a reasonable expectancy, and, by embracing the opportunity, the self-interest of the officer or director will be brought into conflict with that of his corporation, the law will not permit him to seize the opportunity for himself."

* * *

"[n]umerous factors are to be weighed, including the manner in which the offer was communicated to the officer; the good faith of the officer; the use of corporate assets to acquire the opportunity; the financial ability of the corporation to acquire the opportunity; the degree of disclosure made to the corporation; the action taken by the corporation with reference thereto; and the need or interest of the corporation in the opportunity. These, as well as numerous other factors, are weighed in a given case. The presence or absence of any single factor is not determinative of the issue of corporate opportunity."

* * *

Here the trial court specifically found that one of the corporate purposes of Bio-Lab was to expand into specific new areas, including Tuscaloosa. Ample evidence in the record supports this conclusion. Bio-Lab's certificate of incorporation declared that one of the purposes of the business was "to have one or more offices." * * *

* * *[T]estimony revealed that $44,000 had been required to establish Med-Lab. At the end of 1974 Bio-Lab had only $24,300 available for this purpose. But, Raburn [a certified public accountant, familiar with the books of both Med-Lab and Bio-Lab] also testified that in 1974 Bio-Lab had paid a "rather high" dividend of $20,000. His testimony indicated that the payment of dividends is often restricted when a corporation wishes to expand. Thus, if the dividend had not been paid, Bio-Lab clearly should have had the financial ability to expand to Tuscaloosa, with or without a loan. In light of this testimony the trial court's finding that defendants improperly formed Med-Lab to the detriment of Bio-Lab is clearly supportable and will not be disturbed by this Court on appeal.

JUDGMENT AND REMEDY

The Alabama Supreme Court determined that the appropriate remedy for the defendant's breach of duty and loyalty was for the court to impose a "constructive trust," which would require all profits of Med-Lab to be paid to Bio-Lab.

COMMENTS

Directors and officers of a corporation are expected to act with undivided loyalty. This rule restricts them from competing with the corporation, and, at the very least, it requires fiduciaries to offer business opportunities to the corporation.

Conflicts of Interest

Corporate directors often have many business affiliations, and they can even sit on the board of more than one corporation. Of course, they are precluded from entering into or supporting any business that operates in direct competition with the corporation. The fiduciary duty requires them to make full disclosure of any potential *conflicts of interest* that might arise in any corporate transaction.

Contracts between Director and Corporation

Sometimes the corporation will enter into a contract or engage in a transaction in which an officer or director has a material interest. The director or officer must make full disclosure of that interest and should abstain from voting on the proposed transaction.

For example, Pacific Business Corporation needs office space. Louis Allen, one of its five directors, owns the building adjoining the corporation. He negotiates a lease with Pacific Business for the space, making full disclosure to Pacific Business and the other four board directors. The lease arrangement is fair and reasonable, and it is unanimously approved by the corporation's board of directors. In such a case, the contract is valid. The rule is one of reason; otherwise directors would be prevented from ever giving financial assistance to the corporations they serve. The various state statutes contain different standards, but a contract will generally not be voidable if (1) it was fair and reasonable to the corporation at the time it was entered into, (2) there is full disclosure of the interest of the officers or directors in the transaction, and (3) the contract is approved by a majority of the disinterested directors or shareholders.

Contracts between Corporations Having Common Directors

Often, contracts are negotiated between corporations having one or more directors who are members of both boards. Care should be taken in these situations because they are often severely scrutinized by courts.

LIABILITIES OF CORPORATE OFFICERS

The duties of corporate officers are the same as the duties of directors because their respective corporate positions involve both of them in decision making and place them in similar control positions. Hence, they are viewed as having the same fiduciary duty of care and loyalty in their conduct of corporate affairs. Officers are subject to the same obligations concerning corporate opportunities and conflict of interest as are directors.

RIGHTS OF CORPORATE OFFICERS AND OTHER MANAGEMENT EMPLOYEES

Corporate officers and other high-level managers are employees of the company, and their rights are defined by employment contracts. Employee rights are outlined in Chapter 34.

DUTIES AND LIABILITIES OF MAJOR SHAREHOLDERS

In some cases, a majority shareholder is regarded as having a fiduciary duty to the corporation and to the minority shareholders. This occurs when a single shareholder (or a few acting in concert) own a sufficient number of shares to exercise de facto control over the corporation.

RIGHTS OF DIRECTORS

Right of Participation

A corporate director must have certain rights in order to function properly in the position—the main one being the right to be notified of board of director meetings and to participate in them.

Right of Inspection

A director must have access to all corporate books and records in order to make decisions and exercise the necessary supervision. This right is virtually absolute and cannot be restricted.

Right of Indemnification

It is not unusual for corporate directors to become involved in lawsuits by virtue of their position and their actions as directors. Under certain circumstances, most states (and the Model Act) permit a corporation to indemnify a director for legal costs, fees, and judgments involved in defending corporation related suits. The common law, however, has restricted the right to reimbursement of costs, even in successful litigation, without explicit insurance or the agreement of the corporation.

Right of Compensation

Historically, directors have had no inherent right to compensation for their services as directors. Officers receive compensation, and nominal sums are often paid as honoraria to directors. In many cases, directors are also chief corporate officers and receive compensation in their managerial positions. Most directors, however, gain through indirect benefits, such as business contacts, prestige, and other rewards.

There is a growing trend toward providing more than nominal compensation for directors, especially in large corporations where directorships can be enormous burdens in terms of time, work, effort, and risk. Many states permit the corporate articles or bylaws to authorize compensation for directors, and in some cases the board can set its own compensation unless the articles or bylaws provide otherwise.

SHAREHOLDER RIGHTS

Shareholders own the corporation. Their rights are established in the articles of incorporation and under the state's general incorporation law.

The Right to a Stock Certificate

A stock certificate evidences ownership, and shareholders have the right to demand that the corporation issue a certificate and record their names and addresses in the corporate stock record books. Stock is *intangible* personal property—the ownership right exists independently of the certificate itself. A stock certificate may be lost or destroyed, but ownership is not destroyed with it. Corporate records reflect ownership, although they do not determine it.

A new certificate can be issued to replace one that has been lost or destroyed.[2] Notice of shareholder meetings, dividends, and operational and financial reports are all distributed according to the recorded ownership listed in the corporation's books, not on the basis of possession of the certificate. Assume that Betty Anderson's corporate stock in Chrysler Corporation is destroyed in a fire on September 1. The corporation declares a dividend on September 5. According to corporate records, Betty Anderson is the "record owner" and receives the dividend even though she no longer has the certificate.

Of course, to sell or otherwise transfer the shares, indorsement and delivery of the actual certificate to the transferee are required.

Preemptive Rights

Preemption is a preference given to a shareholder over all other purchasers to subscribe to or purchase a prorated share of a new issue so the shareholder can maintain his or her portion of control, voting power, or financial interest in the corporation. Preemptive rights exist only if permitted by state statute, and they can be denied or limited by corporate articles. Generally, preemptive rights apply only to additional stock sold for cash. For example, Paula Smith purchases one hundred shares of National Clothing Corporation stock. A total of one thousand shares of that issue are outstanding. Subsequently, National Clothing decides to issue another thousand shares to increase its capital stock to a total of two thousand shares. If preemptive rights have been provided, Smith can purchase one additional share of the new stock being issued for each share currently

owned—or one hundred additional shares. Thus she can own two hundred of the two thousand shares outstanding, and her relative position as a shareholder will be maintained. If preemptive rights are not reserved, her proportionate control and voting power will be diluted from that of a 10 percent shareholder to that of a 5 percent shareholder because of the issuance of the additional one thousand shares.

Preemptive rights are far more significant in a close corporation because of the relatively few number of shares and the substantial interest each shareholder controls.

Stock Warrants

When preemptive rights exist and a corporation is issuing additional shares, each shareholder is usually given *stock warrants*. A **stock warrant** entitles each shareholder to buy a given number of shares within a limited time period (usually two weeks) at a stated price.

Dividend Rights

A dividend is a distribution of corporate profits *ordered by the directors* and paid to the shareholders in proportion to their respective shares in the corporation. Dividends can be paid in cash, property, stock of the corporation that is paying the dividends, or stock of other corporations.[3]

State laws vary, but every state controls the general legal requirements under which dividends are paid. Once declared, a dividend becomes a corporate debt enforceable at law like any other debt.[4]

When directors fail to declare a dividend, shareholders can ask a court of equity for an injunction to compel the directors to meet and to

---

2. To have a lost or destroyed certificate reissued, a shareholder is normally required to furnish an indemnity bond to protect the corporation against potential loss should the original certificate reappear at some future time in the hands of a bona fide purchaser. [UCC Secs. 8-302 and 8-405(2)]

3. Technically, dividends paid in stock are not dividends. They maintain each shareholder's proportional interest in the corporation. On one occasion a distillery declared and paid a "dividend" in bonded whiskey.

4. State laws prescribe the circumstances under which dividends can be paid. An insolvent corporation cannot declare a dividend. State laws also control the sources of revenue to be used. Only certain funds are legally available for paying dividends.

declare a dividend. It must be shown that the directors have acted so unreasonably in withholding the dividend that their conduct is an abuse of discretion. Often, large money reserves are accumulated for a bona fide purpose such as expansion, research, and other legitimate corporate goals. The mere fact that sufficient corporate earnings or surplus are available to pay a dividend will not be enough to compel directors to distribute funds that, in the board's opinion, should not be paid. The courts are circumspect about interfering with corporate operations and will not compel directors to declare dividends unless abuse of discretion is clearly shown. Directors are not ordinarily required to declare dividends to shareholders. A striking exception to this rule is exemplified by the following case.

DODGE v. FORD MOTOR CO.

Supreme Court of Michigan, 1919.
204 Mich. 459, 170 N.W. 668.

BACKGROUND AND FACTS *Ford Motor Company was formed in 1903. Henry Ford, the president and majority shareholder, attempted to run the corporation as if it were a one-man operation. The business expanded rapidly and, in addition to regular quarterly dividends, often paid special dividends. Sales and profits were:*

1910   18,664 cars $4,521,509 profit

1911   34,466 cars $6,275,031 profit

1912   68,544 cars $13,057,312 profit, $14,475,095 surplus

1913   168,304 cars $25,046,767 profit, $28,124,173 surplus

1914   248,307 cars $30,338,454 profit, $48,827,032 surplus

1915   264,351 cars $24,641,423 profit, $59,135,770 surplus

By 1916, surplus above capital was $111,960,907.

Originally, the Ford car sold for more than $900. From time to time, the price was reduced, and in 1916 it sold for $440. For the year beginning August 1, 1916, the price was reduced again, to $360. No special dividend was paid after October 1915 for reasons explained in the opinion that follows. The plaintiffs were minority stockholders, who owned one-tenth of the shares of the corporation. They petitioned the court to compel the directors to declare a dividend.

OSTRANDER, Chief Justice.
* * *

[I]t is charged that notwithstanding the earnings for the fiscal year ending July 31, 1916, the Ford Motor Company has not since that date declared any special dividends:

"And the said Henry Ford, president of the company, has declared it to be the settled policy of the company not to pay in the future any special dividends, but to put back into the business for the future all of the earnings of the company, other than the regular dividend of five per cent. (5%) monthly upon the authorized capital stock of the company—two million dollars ($2,000,000)."

This declaration of the future policy, it is charged in the bill, was published in the public press in the city of Detroit and throughout the United States in substantially the following language:

" 'My ambition,' declared Mr. Ford, 'is to employ still more men; to spread the benefits of this industrial system to the greatest possible number, to help them build up their lives and their homes. To do this, we are putting the greatest share of our profits back into the business.' "

It is charged further that the said Henry Ford stated to plaintiffs personally, in substance, that as all the stockholders had received back in dividends more than they had invested they were not entitled to receive anything additional to the regular dividend of 5 per cent a month, and that it was not his policy to have larger dividends declared in the future, and that the profits and earnings of the company would be put back into the business for the purpose of extending its operations and increasing the number of its employes, and that, inasmuch as the profits were to be represented by investment in plants and capital investment, the stockholders would have no right to complain. * * *
* * *

"It is a well-recognized principle of law that the directors of a corporation, and they alone, have the power to declare a dividend of the earnings of the corporation, and to determine its amount. Courts of equity will not interfere in the management of the directors unless it is clearly made to appear that they are guilty of fraud or misappropriation of the corporate funds, or refuse to declare a dividend when the corporation has a surplus of net profits which it can, without detriment to its business, divide among its stockholders, and when a refusal to do so would amount to such an abuse of discretion as would constitute a fraud, or breach of that good faith which they are bound to exercise towards the stockholders."
* * *

There is committed to the discretion of directors, a discretion to be exercised in good faith, the infinite details of business, including the wages which shall be paid to employes, the number of hours they shall work, the conditions under which labor shall be carried on, and the price for which products shall be offered to the public.
* * * [I]t is not within the lawful powers of a board of directors to shape and conduct the affairs of a corporation for the merely incidental benefit of shareholders and for the primary purpose of benefiting others, and no one will contend that, if the avowed purpose of the defendant directors was to sacrifice the interests of shareholders, it would not be the duty of the courts to interfere.
* * * Defendants say, and it is true, that a considerable cash balance must be at all times carried by such a concern. But, as has been stated, there was a large daily, weekly, monthly, receipt of cash. The output was practically continuous and was continuously, and within a few days, turned into cash. Moreover, the contemplated expenditures were not to be immediately made. The large sum appropriated for the smelter plant was payable over a considerable period of time. *So that, without going further, it would appear that, accepting and approving the plan of the directors, it was their duty to distribute on or near the 1st of August, 1916, a very large sum of money to stockholders.* [Emphasis added.]

In reaching this conclusion, we do not ignore, but recognize, the validity of the proposition that plaintiffs have from the beginning profited by, if they have not lately, officially, participated in, the general policy of expansion pursued by this corporation. We do not lose sight of the fact that it had been, upon an occasion, agreeable to the plaintiffs to increase the capital stock to $100,000,000 by a stock dividend of $98,000,000. These things go only to answer other contentions now made by plaintiffs, and do not and cannot operate to estop them to demand proper dividends upon the stock they own. It is obvious that an annual dividend of 60 per cent. upon $2,000,000, or $1,200,000, is the equivalent of a very small dividend upon $100,000,000, or more.

* * *

JUDGMENT AND REMEDY   *The defendant, Ford, was ordered by the court to declare a dividend.*

Right to Vote

Shareholders exercise ownership control through the power of their vote. In the early development of corporate law, each shareholder was entitled to one vote per share. This rule still holds today, but the voting techniques discussed in Chapter 43 (pooling agreements, voting trusts, cumulative voting methods, and so on) all enhance the power of the shareholder's vote.

Inspection Rights

Shareholders have the right to inspect and copy certain corporate books and records for any *proper purpose*, provided they make the request in advance. Either the shareholder can inspect in person, or an attorney, agent, accountant, or other assistant can do so.

The power of inspection is fraught with potential abuses, and the corporation is allowed to protect itself from them. For example, a shareholder can properly be denied access to corporate records to prevent harassment or to protect trade secrets or other confidential corporate information. Section 52 of the Model Act imposes various standard requirements on the shareholder's inspection right:

Any person who shall have been a holder of record shares * * * at least six months immediately preceding his [or her] demand or [who is] * * * the holder of * * * at least 5 percent of all the outstanding shares of the corporation, upon written demand stating the purpose thereof, shall have the right to examine, in person, or by agent or attorney, at any reasonable time or times, for any proper purpose its relevant books and records of accounts, minutes, and record of shareholders and to make extracts therefrom.

However, a corporation's improper refusal to allow access to its records can result in severe and costly liability to the corporation. Under Section 52 of the Model Act, the penalty is 10 percent the value of the shares owned by the shareholder who has been denied access to the books.

SKOURAS v. ADMIRALTY ENTERPRISES, INC.
Court of Chancery of Delaware, 1978.
386 A.2d 674.

BACKGROUND AND FACTS   *The plaintiff, Skouras, was the holder of 2,871 shares (between 4 and 5 percent) of common stock of a closely-held family corporation. The plaintiff demanded to inspect the corporate books and records so he could substantiate his fears of mismanagement and his fears that certain corporate acts that were detrimental to the corporation were occurring. Admiralty Enterprises, the defendant corporation, contended that the plaintiff's purpose was merely to harass the corporation and to attempt to force it to offer to buy out the plaintiff's shares at a premium price. The court, however, was persuaded that the plaintiff had acted in good faith and had established a proper purpose for demanding the right of inspection.*

MARVEL, Chancellor.

* * *

A proper purpose is defined in 8 Del.C. Section 220 as one which is "* * * reasonably related to such person's interest as a stockholder * * *", and it is clearly proper for a stockholder to ask leave to examine corporate books and records to follow up his suspicions of corporate mismanagement, thereby acting not only on his own behalf but on that of the corporation and its other stockholders. * * *

* * * [A]lthough the Court cannot, of course, read the thoughts of a stockholder, it must be satisfied that a plaintiff has successfully carried the burden of proving that the purpose behind his demand is proper. Once a proper purpose is established, it becomes irrelevant that the stockholder may have a secondary and perhaps questionable ulterior purpose behind his primary purpose.

A further qualification as to the right of inspection of books and records is that even if a proper purpose for a demand is demonstrated and such demand is shown to be reasonably related to a plaintiff's interest as a stockholder, nonetheless such demand must not be for a purpose adverse to the best interests of the corporation.

Whether or not a plaintiff is entitled to inspection of corporate books and records depends on whether or not a clear indication of wrong-doing on the part of corporate mismanagement has been established clearly as a result of a trial. Here plaintiff places great emphasis on the fact that Admiralty appears to be in a precarious financial condition, and at trial plaintiff sought to establish the existence of a number of improper transactions on the part of corporate management, including the making of loans by Admiralty not only of money but of stock for the personal benefit of directors, the improper purchase of stock from directors, and the payment of salaries to family members who performed little or no services for Admiralty or its affiliates.

* * *

Plaintiff concedes that many of the practices complained of have an ostensible business purpose but contends that the apparent precariousness of defendant's financial affairs coupled with its refusal to supply plaintiff with any information relating to the matters as to which he seeks to be informed clearly support the propriety of plaintiff's demand. * * *

Although it is clear that plaintiff has acted impetuously insofar as the affairs of Admiralty are concerned and could well have been less extravagant in his written complaints about Admiralty, I am satisfied that his basic purpose, in embarking on his present project, has its roots in his concern over the activities of and problems facing Admiralty rather than by a design merely to harass. Thus, letters put in evidence disclose that plaintiff as a minority stockholder was convinced that serious damage is being and has been inflicted upon the corporation by incumbent management. In short, a careful reading of the letters which are the basis of defendant's charge of harassment discloses that plaintiff was in fact seeking to rally support to his battle against what he believed to be corporate acts detrimental to Admiralty and consequently to himself as a minority stockholder of such corporation.

* * *

Finally, defendant is concerned that plaintiff may use information acquired by him as a result of an inspection of Admiralty's books and records for the purpose of doing harm to Admiralty rather than for his own benefit. However, as stated in 5 Fletcher Cyc. Corporations, Section 2275 (Perm. Ed.1972) "[i]t is clearly the rule of the cases discussing it that the mere possibility of such abuse or misuse is not grounds for any withholding or restriction of the right [of inspection]."

The present record does not, in my opinion, support defendant's present fears that confidential corporate matters will be divulged as a result of the inspection here granted. Plaintiff assured the Court at trial that he would not use any knowledge he might gain, were inspection to be granted, to defendant's detriment. However, upon a showing that plaintiff has breached his commitment and indeed duty not to harm his corporation by improperly using the knowledge gained from the inspection hereby granted, appropriate relief may be sought.

An appropriate form of order may be presented on notice.

JUDGMENT AND REMEDY *The chancery court ordered that the plaintiff be granted the right to inspect certain books and records as requested.*

Right to Transfer Shares

Corporate stock represents an ownership right in intangible personal property. The law generally recognizes the right of an owner to transfer property to another person unless there are valid restrictions on its transferability. Although stock certificates are negotiable instruments and freely transferable by indorsement and delivery, transfer of stock in closely-held corporations is generally restricted by contract, the bylaws, or a restriction stamped on the stock certificate. The existence of any restrictions on transferability should always be noted on the face of the stock certificate.

CLOSELY-HELD CORPORATIONS Sometimes, corporations impose restrictions on transfer. In a closely-held corporation, for example, the shareholders often actively manage and are intimately involved in the daily business operations of the corporation. Hence, a restriction on transfer of shares to third persons is a general practice.

RIGHT OF FIRST REFUSAL Sometimes, corporations or their shareholders restrict transferability by reserving the option to purchase any shares offered for resale by a shareholder. The option remains with the corporation or the shareholders only for a specified or reasonable time limit. Variations on the purchase option are possible. For example, a shareholder might be required to offer the shares to other shareholders or the corporation first.

CORPORATE RECORDS When shares are transferred, a new entry is made in the corporate stock book to indicate the new owner. Until the corporation is notified and the entry is complete, voting rights, notice of shareholder meetings, dividend distribution, and so forth are all held by the current record owner.

Rights upon Dissolution

When a corporation is dissolved and its outstanding debts and the claims of its creditors have been satisfied, the remaining assets are distributed pro rata among the shareholders. Certain classes of preferred stock can be given priority to the extent of their contractual preference. If no preferences to distribution of assets upon liquidation are given to any class of stock, then the stockholders share the remaining assets.

COMPELLING RECEIVERSHIP A minority shareholder does not simply have to watch the board of directors mishandle or waste corporate assets or to permit a deadlock to threaten or irreparably injure the corporation's finances. A minority shareholder can petition a court to appoint a receiver and to liquidate the business assets of the corporation. The Model Act, Section 97, permits any shareholder to institute such an action when it appears that (1) the directors are deadlocked in the management of corporate affairs, shareholders are unable to break that deadlock, and irreparable injury to the corporation is being suffered or threatened; (2) the acts of the directors or those in control of the corporation are illegal, oppressive, or fraudulent; or (3) corporate assets are being misapplied or wasted.

SHAREHOLDER LIABILITIES

One of the hallmarks of the corporate organization is that shareholders are not personally liable for the debts of the corporation. If the corporation fails, shareholders can lose their investment, but that is generally the limit of liability. In certain instances of fraud, undercapitalization, or careless observance of corporate formalities, a court will pierce the corporate veil (disregard the corporate entity) and hold the shareholders individually liable. But these situations are the exception, not the rule.

Illegal Dividends

Whenever a dividend is paid while the corporation is *insolvent*, it is automatically an illegal dividend, and shareholders can be liable for returning the payment to the corporation or its creditors.

Dividends are generally required by statute to be distributed only from certain authorized corporate accounts representing profits. Sometimes dividends are improperly paid from an unauthorized account, or their payment causes the corporation to become insolvent. Generally, shareholders must return illegal dividends only if they knew that the dividends were illegal when they received them.

In all cases of illegal and improper dividends, the board of directors can be held personally liable for the amount of the payment. However, when directors can show that a shareholder *knew* a dividend was illegal when it was received, they can recover their loss of that amount from the shareholder.

QUESTIONS AND CASE PROBLEMS

1. Alex, Brown and Sons was a Pennsylvania stockbroker that purchased and sold stock and owned stock in its own name for a number of companies, including Latrobe Steel Company. Upon learning that a large corporation was about to make a tender offer (that is, an offer to purchase stock from shareholders) to Latrobe's shareholders, Alex, Brown sought permission to inspect and obtain a copy of Latrobe's list of shareholders. Alex, Brown stood to make a substantial profit by way of commission for shares it could secure in conjunction with the tender offer. Should Alex, Brown be allowed to inspect and obtain the shareholder list from Latrobe? [Alex, Brown and Sons v. Latrobe Steel Co., 376 F.Supp. 1373 (W.D. Pa. 1974)]

2. Robertson and Tedder were directors and officers of the Plantation Golf Club. Together they made up the majority of shareholders in the company. Coleman was a minority shareholder. For the previous three years, Robertson and Tedder had fixed their own compensation for their services as officers of the corporation. Coleman felt that the salaries were excessive. Can he now object? [Coleman v. Plantation Golf Club, Inc., 212 So.2d. 806 (Fla. Dist. Ct. App. 1968)]

3. Grant and Martin were directors of Lincoln Stores, Inc. Both had worked for Lincoln Stores in other capacities—as store manager and as general manager, respectively. Hayley was one of the managers of the very successful Lincoln store that was located in Norwich, Connecticut. The Reid and Hughes Company owned a store several buildings down from the Lincoln store in Norwich. Reid and Hughes presented little competition to Lincoln. On April 27, Grant, Martin, and Hayley agreed to purchase the Reid and Hughes store, and Hayley resigned from Lincoln's employ to take charge of it.

Before he left, however, Hayley obtained certain confidential information that he later used to assist him in setting up operations at the Reid and Hughes store. Grant and Martin, desiring to continue in Lincoln's employ, concealed their ownership of the new store and continued as directors at Lincoln. Thereafter, the Reid and Hughes store became quite successful and competitive with Lincoln. Lincoln Stores then sued Grant, Martin, and Hayley for their breach of loyalty. Should it recover? If so, what should Lincoln be awarded as damages: lost profits? ownership of the competing store? [Lincoln Stores v. Grant, 309 Mass. 417, 34 N.E.2d. 704 (1941)]

4. Barnes-King Development Company, a Montana corporation, was voluntarily dissolved by order of the court on December 16, 1925. On December 20, 1968, some 43 years later, the trustee of Barnes-King filed a petition for distribution of the company's assets. The petition showed that, in 1968, the assets amounted to $42,000. At the time of dissolution in 1925, there were 400,000 shares of stock outstanding. At the time of distribution in 1970, only 185,000 shares of the assets of Barnes-King had been proportionately distributed to shareholders. These shareholders claimed that the remaining unclaimed shares had been abandoned and therefore should go to them. Under common law, abandoned property escheats to the state. Who gets the unclaimed assets? [Barnes-King Development Co. v. Corette, 156 Mont. 202, 478 P.2d. 868 (1971)]

5. Crothers, Williams, and Ross were the sole shareholders of Ross Transport, Inc. Each held approximately one-third of the company's stock. Without contacting Crothers, Williams and Ross, who were the directors of the company, had the company issue additional shares to themselves. Crothers sued, claiming that both his voting power and his right to share in dividends had been lessened. What theory should Crothers assert to be successful against Williams, Ross, and Ross Transport? [Ross Transport, Inc. v. Crothers, 185 Md. 573, 45 A.2d 267 (1946)].

6. Shubin and Surchin were codirectors of Approved Business Machines Company, Inc. Each owned a 20 percent interest in the company. The remaining 60 percent was owned by four persons,

each owning 15 percent. For a year, there was serious internal dissension between the two major shareholders, Shubin and Surchin. The corporation was a closed corporation, and the remaining shareholders were evenly divided in their support of one of the two directors. Surchin applied to the courts for a dissolution of the firm, since he felt that the disagreement among the shareholders was irreconcilable. Should a judge grant Surchin's request? [Application of Surchin, 55 Misc.2d 888, 286 N.Y.S.2d. 580 (1967)]

7. Engdahl was a 10 percent stockholder, a director, and the treasurer of Aero Drapery, Inc. In May of 1967 several Aero employees expressed to Engdahl their dissatisfaction with their employment with Aero. Later that month, at Engdahl's suggestion, Engdahl met with the employees and suggested that they join together and form a new enterprise. In early June they decided to go into the custom-drapery business in direct competition with Aero. Later that month the new business associates decided upon a location for the new business, contacted suppliers, and secured an advertisement in the Yellow Pages. In July, 1967, Engdahl tendered his resignation as Director and Treasurer of Aero Drapery, Inc. Has Engdahl breached any duty to Aero Drapery, Inc.? Would your answer be different if Engdahl had resigned early in May of 1967? (What additional fact do you need to know to answer the latter question?) Aero Drapery of Kentucky, Inc. v. Engdahl, 507 S.W. 2d 166 (Ky. App. 1974).

8. Hartung, Odle and Burke were architects. In 1971 they organized as a corporation. Their association, however, was riddled with dissent from the start. As it became apparent that the corporate turmoil would eventually result in reorganization of the corporation, Hartung began conferring with several clients of the firm informing them that he was willing to continue as their architect after his withdrawal from the corporation. The corporation was later dissolved, and several of its clients continued to do business with Hartung. Do Odle and Burke have any recourse against Hartung for his activities? Hartung vs. Architects Hartung/Odle/Burke, Inc., 301 N.E.2nd 240 (Ind. App. 1973).

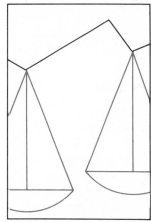

45

Corporations
Merger, Consolidation, and Termination

Corporations increase their holdings for a number of reasons. They may wish to enlarge their physical plants, increase their property or investment holdings, or acquire the assets, know-how, or goodwill of another corporation. Sometimes acquisition is motivated by a desire to eliminate a competitor, to accomplish diversification, or to insure adequate resources and markets for the acquiring corporation's product. Whatever the reason, the corporation typically extends its operations by combining with another corporation through (1) merger, (2) consolidation, (3) purchase of assets, or (4) purchase of a controlling interest of the other corporation.

This chapter will examine the various ways that merger or consolidation alters the fundamental structure of the corporation. The terms *merger* and *consolidation* are often used interchangeably, but they refer to two legally distinct proceedings. Whether a combination is in fact a merger or a consolidation, the rights and liabilities of shareholders, the corporation, and its creditors are the same.

Dissolution and liquidation are the combined processes by which a corporation terminates its existence. The last part of this chapter will discuss the typical reasons and methods for terminating a corporation.

MERGERS AND CONSOLIDATION

Mergers

A **merger** involves the legal combination of two or more corporations. After a merger, only one of the corporations continues to exist (the **surviving corporation**), and all the others cease to exist (disappearing corporations). For example, Corporation A and Corporation B decide to merge. It is agreed that A will absorb B, so, upon merger, B ceases to exist as a separate entity and A continues as the *surviving corporation*.

A merger can be represented symbolically as $A + B = A$. After the merger, A is recognized as a single corporation, possessing all the rights, privileges, and powers of itself and B. A automatically acquires all of B's property and assets without the necessity of formal transfer or deed. A becomes liable for all B's debts and obligations. Finally, A's articles of incorporation are deemed *amended* to include any changes that are stated in the articles of merger.

Consolidation

In the case of a **consolidation**, two or more corporations combine so that each corporation ceases to exist and a new one emerges. Corporation A and Corporation B consolidate to form an entirely new organization, Corporation C. In the process, A and B both terminate. C comes into existence as an entirely new entity.

A symbolic representation of consolidation, then, is $A + B = C$. The results of consolidation are essentially the same as the results of merger. C is recognized as a new corporation and a single entity; A and B cease to exist. C accedes to all the rights, privileges, and powers previously held by A and B. Title to any property and assets owned by A and B passes to C without formal transfer. C assumes liability for all debts and obligations owed by A and B. The articles of consolidation *take the place of* A's and B's original corporate articles and are thereafter regarded as C's corporate articles.

In both merger and consolidation, the surviving or newly formed corporation takes over the assets of the former corporations and assumes their liabilities. Further, the surviving or newly formed corporation issues new shares or pays some fair consideration to shareholders in exchange for the stock of the corporations that have ceased to exist.

In a merger, the surviving corporation is vested with the disappearing corporation's preexisting legal rights and obligations. For example, if the disappearing corporation had a right of action against a third party, after the merger, the surviving corporation could then bring suit to recover for the disappearing corporation's damages. The corporation statutes of many states provide that a successor (surviving) corporation inherit a *chose in action* (a right to sue for a debt or sum of money) from a merging corporation as a matter of law. So, too, the common law rule recognizes that a chose in action to enforce a property right upon merger will vest with the successor (surviving) corporation, and no right of action will remain with the disappearing corporation.

SUN PIPE LINE CO. v. ALTES

United States Court of Appeals, Eight Circuit, 1975.
511 F.2d 280.

BACKGROUND AND FACTS *Sun Pipe Line Company (Sun), merged with OMR, Inc. in August 1972. Sun, the plaintiff in this case was the surviving corporation. As part of the merger agreement, Sun succeeded to all of OMR's rights and liabilities. State law provided that surviving corporations were entitled to maintain legal actions for damages based on the disappearing corporation's rights and liabilities.*

The disappearing corporation, OMR, acquired a right-of-way to lay pipeline across certain property. The property was subsequently sold to the defendant, Altes. At the time he purchased the land in early 1972, Altes knew that there was an easement for the pipeline across it and that the pipeline did in fact exist.

Altes owned and operated a rock quarrying and landfill business which was conducted on the parcel of property in question. The operations consisted of removing rock from below the surface, crushing it, selling it, and then filling the excavation with trash and covering it with soil. Defendant Altes warned his workers not to conduct the quarrying operation in the area where the pipeline was buried. Nonetheless, on March 16, 1972, one of his employees did operate a front end loader in the vicinity of the pipeline and while digging into the soil, he punctured it. A considerable amount of gasoline being pumped at high pressure escaped through the hole, and the pipeline had to be shut down for repairs. There was no question that Altes's employee had been negligent and that this negligence was attributable to Altes.

At the time of the break in the pipeline, it was owned by OMR, but this litigation was initiated by Sun Pipe Line Company (the plaintiff) after its merger with OMR in August 1972.

The trial court refused to instruct the jury that Sun Pipe Line Company had the right, under state law, to bring this lawsuit. The jury was never instructed as to the law of merger. Instead, the trial judge merely told the members of the jury that it was up to them to determine the effect of the merger.

ROSS, Circuit Judge.

* * *

Sun Pipe Line Company (Sun), a Pennsylvania corporation with its principal place of business in Oklahoma, brought this diversity action against Robert Altes, a resident of Arkansas, seeking to recover in excess of $35,000 for damages incurred when one of Altes' employees, while operating an earth moving machine, punctured a pipeline [now] owned by Sun. After a trial in the district court the jury returned a verdict for defendant Altes, and judgment was entered accordingly. Sun appeals, alleging that the court erred in * * * refusing to instruct the jury that Sun had the right to bring this action.

[The] issue which developed at trial was whether Sun had a right to prosecute the action. It was revealed that at the time of the break the pipeline was owned by OMR, Inc., a successor firm to Oklahoma Mississippi River Products, Inc., but that the litigation was initiated by Sun after its merger with OMR in August, 1972, in which Sun was the surviving corporation. Evidence was received on this issue, including the articles of merger.

Since the issue of Sun's right to bring the action had been injected into the trial, Sun requested that the district judge instruct the jury that, in accordance with the merger agreement between Sun and OMR, Sun succeeded to all of OMR's rights and liabilities and was entitled to maintain an action for damages against Altes. The court refused to give this instruction.

During his closing argument Altes' attorney argued to the effect that, since OMR owned the pipeline at the time of the accident, Sun had failed to prove that it had sustained any damages. When Sun objected to this line of argument on the ground that it had the right to bring suit for damages to OMR as a matter of law, the trial judge merely told the jury that it is "for you to determine the effect of the merger." Altes' counsel continued to argue that Sun had sustained no damages.

The instruction requested by Sun was not given and neither was the jury informed as to the law of merger. On the other hand, the jury was told that, before it could award damages to Sun, it must find that Sun had sustained damages. Thus, the jury was left in the position of determining whether Sun could recover for damages to OMR. This was error.

Fed.R.Civ.P. 17(b) states that "[t]he capacity of a corporation to sue or be sued shall be determined by the law under which it was organized." Sun is a Pennsylvania corporation, so the law of that state determines whether it can sue to recover premerger damages to OMR.

Pa.Stat.Ann. tit. 15, § 1907 (1974 Supp.) deals with the effect of a merger or consolidation of corporations and provides:

All the property, real, personal, and mixed and franchises of each of the corporations parties to the plan of merger or consolidation, *and all debts due on whatever account to any of them, including subscriptions to shares and other choses in action belonging to any of them,* shall be taken and deemed to be transferred to and vested in the surviving or new corporation, as the case may be, without further act or deed. (Court's emphasis.)

This statute makes it explicitly clear that Sun, the surviving corporation, was vested with OMR's chose in action against Altes and could bring this lawsuit to recover for OMR's damages. In addition, we note that the merger agreement itself conformed to the Pennsylvania statute by providing that Sun would be vested with "all property, real, personal and mixed, and all debts due to each" of the corporations.

Finally, this Court has stated that statutes, such as Pennsylvania's, which provide that a successor corporation inherits a chose in action from a merging corporation as a matter of law merely serve to codify the common law rule "which recognizes that a chose in action to enforce a property right upon merger vests in the successor corporation and no right of action remains in the merging corporation."

In light of this well settled statutory and common law rule, the trial court should have given Sun's requested instruction. The effect of the court's instructions combined with the argument of Altes' attorney was to leave this question of law to the unfettered and unguided discretion of the jury, and this constituted prejudicial error.

JUDGMENT AND REMEDY

The circuit court reversed the district court ruling and held that the lower court erred in refusing to instruct the jury that, as a matter of law, Sun had the right to bring the suit. The case was returned to the trial court for further proceedings consistent with the principle of law that the surviving corporation inherits any claims for damages belonging to the disappearing corporation.

The Procedure

All states have statutes authorizing mergers and consolidations for *domestic* corporations, and most allow the combination of domestic (in-state) and foreign (out-of-state) corporations. Although the procedures vary somewhat among jurisdictions, they all contain the basic requirements outlined below:

1. The board of directors of *each* corporation involved must approve a merger or consolidation plan.
2. The shareholders of *each* corporation must

vote approval of the plan at a shareholders' meeting. Most state statutes require approval of a majority or two-thirds of the outstanding shares of voting stock. Frequently, statutes require that each class of stock approve the merger; thus, the holders of nonvoting stock must also approve the merger.

3. Once approved by *all* the boards of directors and the shareholders, the plan is filed, usually with the secretary of state.

4. When state formalities are satisfied, the state issues a certificate of merger (to the surviving corporation) or a certificate of consolidation (to the newly consolidated corporation).

Short-Form Merger Statutes (or Parent-Subsidy Mergers)

The Model Act in most states provides a simplified procedure for the merger of a substantially owned subsidiary corporation into its parent corporation. Under these provisions, a short-form merger can be accomplished *without approval of the shareholders* of either corporation.

The **short-form merger** can be utilized only when the parent corporation owns at least 90 to 95 percent of the outstanding shares of each class of stock of the subsidiary corporation. The simplified procedure requires that a plan for the merger be approved by the board of directors of the parent corporation before it is filed with the state.

Appraisal Rights

What if a shareholder disapproves of the merger or consolidation, but is outvoted by the other shareholders? The law recognizes that a dissenting shareholder should not be forced to become an unwilling shareholder in a corporation that is new or different from the one in which the shareholder originally invested. The shareholder has the right to dissent and is entitled to be paid fair value for the number of shares held on the date of the merger or consolidation.

A dissenting shareholder must protect his or her right to payment by adhering strictly to statutory procedures, which vary from state to state.

Valuation of shares is often a point of contention between the dissenting shareholder and the corporation. The Model Act provides that the "fair value of shares" is the value on the day prior to the date on which the vote was taken.[1] The corporation must make a written offer to purchase a dissenting shareholder's stock, accompanying the offer with a current balance sheet and income statement for the applicable (appropriate) corporation. If the shareholder and the corporation do not agree on the fair value, a court will determine it.

Shareholder Approval

Shareholders invest in a corporate enterprise with the expectation that the board of directors will manage the enterprise and will approve ordinary business matters. Actions taken on extraordinary matters must be authorized by the board of directors and the shareholders. Often, modern statutes will require that certain types of extraordinary matters be approved by a prescribed voter consent of the shareholders. Typically, matters requiring shareholder approval include sale, lease, or exchange of all or substantially all corporate assets outside of the corporation's regular course of business. Other examples include amendments to the articles of incorporation, transactions concerning merger or consolidation, and dissolution.

Hence, when any extraordinary matter arises, the corporation must proceed as authorized by law to obtain shareholder and board of director approval. Sometimes, a transaction can be characterized in such a way as not to require shareholder approval, but a court will use its equity powers to require such approval. In order to determine the nature of the transaction, the courts will look not only to the details of the transaction but also to its consequences. In the following case, a "reorganization agreement" seemed to be a guise for a merger.

---

1. Section 81 of the Model Act provides for excluding any appreciation or depreciation of the stock in anticipation of the approval.

FARRIS v. GLEN ALDEN CORP.

Supreme Court of
Pennsylvania, 1958.
393 Pa. 427, 143 A.2d 25.

BACKGROUND AND FACTS *The plaintiff, Farris, a shareholder, filed suit to enjoin the corporation and its officers from carrying out a reorganization agreement that would, in effect, transform Glen Alden Corporation, a coal mining company, into a diversified holding company with interests in motion pictures, textile companies, and other industries.*

At a shareholders' meeting, the shareholders approved the reorganization agreement. The plaintiff contended that approval by the shareholders at the annual meeting was invalid because the true intent and purpose of the reorganization was to effect a merger between Glen Alden, the defendant, and another corporation. Had the reorganization been a true merger, the shareholders of both corporations would have been entitled to appraisal rights, and management would have been forced to buy out dissenting shareholders. Instead, the agreement provided for a backward reorganization. Glen Alden, the smaller company, purchased the assets of the List Corporation, the larger company, in exchange for a large amount of Glen Alden stock. If Glen Alden had been the selling corporation, Pennsylvania law would have afforded Glen Alden shareholders appraisal rights. Farris, a Glen Alden shareholder, objected and claimed to be entitled to appraisal rights because the transfer was a de facto merger.

COHEN, Justice.

We are required to determine on this appeal whether, as a result of a "Reorganization Agreement" executed by the officers of Glen Alden Corporation and List Industries Corporation, and approved by the shareholders of the former company, the rights and remedies of a dissenting shareholder accrue to the plaintiff.

Glen Alden is a Pennsylvania corporation engaged principally in the mining of anthracite coal and lately in the manufacture of air conditioning units and fire-fighting equipment. In recent years the company's operating revenue has declined substantially, and in fact, its coal operations have resulted in tax loss carryovers of approximately $14,000,000. In October 1957, List, a Delaware holding company owning interests in motion picture theaters, textile companies and real estate, and to a lesser extent, in oil and gas operations, warehouses and aluminum piston manufacturing, purchased through a wholly owned subsidiary 38.5% of Glen Alden's outstanding stock. This acquisition enabled List to place three of its directors on the Glen Alden board.

* * *

Two days after the agreement was executed notice of the annual meeting of Glen Alden to be held on April 11, 1958, was mailed to the shareholders together with a proxy statement analyzing the reorganization agreement and recommending its approval as well as approval of certain amendments to Glen Alden's articles of incorporation and bylaws necessary to implement the agreement. At this meeting the holders of a majority of the outstanding shares, (not including those owned by List), voted in favor of a resolution approving the reorganization agreement.

On the day of the shareholders' meeting, plaintiff, a shareholder of Glen Alden, filed a complaint in equity against the corporation and its officers seeking to enjoin them temporarily until final hearing, and perpetually thereafter, from executing and carrying out the agreement.

The gravamen of the complaint was that the notice of the annual shareholders' meeting did not conform to the requirements of the Business Corporation Law, 15 P.S. § 2852-1 et seq., in three respects: (1) It did not give notice to the shareholders that the true intent and purpose of the meeting was to effect a merger or consolidation of Glen Alden and List; (2) It failed to give notice to the shareholders of their right to dissent to the plan of merger or consolidation and claim fair value for their shares, and (3) It did not contain copies of the text of certain sections of the Business Corporation Law as required.

By reason of these omissions, plaintiff contended that the approval of the reorganization agreement by the shareholders at the annual meeting was invalid and unless the carrying out of the plan were enjoined, he would suffer irreparable loss by being deprived of substantial property rights.

* * *

When use of the corporate form of business organization first became widespread, it was relatively easy for courts to define a "merger" or a "sale of assets" and to label a particular transaction as one or the other. But prompted by the desire to avoid the impact of adverse, and to obtain the benefits of favorable, government regulations, particularly federal tax laws, new accounting and legal techniques were developed by lawyers and accountants which interwove the elements characteristic of each, thereby creating hybrid forms of corporate amalgamation. Thus, it is no longer helpful to consider an individual transaction in the abstract and solely by reference to the various elements therein determine whether it is a "merger" or a "sale". Instead, to determine properly the nature of a corporate transaction, we must refer not only to all the provisions of the agreement, but also to the consequences of the transaction and to the purposes of the provisions of the corporation law said to be applicable. We shall apply this principle to the instant case.

* * *

We hold that the combination contemplated by the reorganization agreement, although consummated by contract rather than in accordance with the statutory procedure, is a merger within the protective purview of the corporation law. The shareholders of Glen Alden should have been notified accordingly and advised of their statutory rights of dissent and appraisal. The failure of the corporate officers to take these steps renders the stockholder approval of the agreement at the 1958 shareholders' meeting invalid. The lower court did not err in enjoining the officers and directors of Glen Alden from carrying out this agreement.

The appellate court held that the shareholders were entitled to appraisal rights.   **JUDGMENT AND REMEDY**

Purchase of Assets

When a corporation acquires all or substantially all of the assets of another corporation by direct purchase, the purchasing or *acquiring* corporation simply extends its ownership and control over more physical assets. Since no change in the legal entity occurs, the *acquiring corpora-*

tion is not required to obtain shareholder approval for the purchase.[2]

Although the acquiring corporation may not be required to obtain shareholder approval for an acquisition, the Department of Justice has issued guidelines that significantly constrain and often prohibit mergers for any acquisition, including takeover bids (discussed in the next section). These guidelines are part of the federal antitrust laws to enforce Section 7 of the Clayton Act (discussed in Chapters 50 and 51). The Department of Justice merger guidelines are given in Exhibit 45-1. A horizontal merger involves two firms in the same industry. A vertical merger involves two firms in different industries, where one supplies the other (such as an electricity company and a coal company). A conglomerate merger involves totally unrelated firms.

The corporation that is *selling* all its assets is substantially changing its business position and perhaps its ability to carry out its corporate purposes. For that reason, the corporation whose assets are *acquired* must obtain both board of director and shareholder approval. In some states, a dissenting shareholder of the selling corporation can demand appraisal rights.

A dissenting shareholder's appraisal remedy is essentially a statutory creation. Depending on the jurisdiction, the appraisal remedy will often apply to mergers, consolidations, and sales of substantially all corporate assets other than those made in the regular course of business.

---

2. If the acquiring corporation plans to pay for the assets with its own corporate stock and not enough authorized unissued shares are available, the shareholders must vote to approve issuance of additional shares by amendment of the corporate articles. Also, acquiring corporations whose stock is traded in a national stock exchange can be required to obtain their own shareholders' approval if they plan to issue a significant number of shares, such as 20 percent or more of the outstanding shares.

CAMPBELL v. VOSE

United States Court of Appeals,
Tenth Circuit, 1975.
515 F.2d 256.

BACKGROUND AND FACTS *This lawsuit was brought by a minority stockholder, Campbell, as a stockholders' derivative suit to assert his right as a dissenting shareholder when the defendant corporation sold substantially all its assets to a wholly-owned subsidiary. The plaintiff argued that he was entitled to shareholder appraisal rights under the Oklahoma statutes. The trial court entered a judgment adverse to the plaintiff.*

SETH, Circuit Judge.
* * *

The * * * Cause of Action in the complaint is directed to the rights of minority stockholders when the corporation is "reorganized" or when it sells "all" or "substantially all" of its assets. A remedy is provided in such circumstances by [Oklahoma statutes]. The trial court concluded as a matter of law that the creation of a wholly owned subsidiary corporation, and the transfer to it of the land and plant of the Cotton Oil Company without a stockholders' vote, was not an event under Oklahoma law which would give rise to rights in the dissenting stockholders to have their shares redeemed.

This issue of dissenters' rights was advanced by the plaintiff by asserting that the creation of the subsidiary with the transfer of assets to it by the Cotton Oil Company was a "sale, lease, exchange or other disposition of all or substantially all of its assets," as contemplated in [Oklahoma laws]. This [law] requires

EXHIBIT 45-1 DEPARTMENT OF JUSTICE MERGER GUIDELINES

HORIZONTAL
MERGERS

1. When the share of sales of the four largest firms in a market amounts to approximately 75 percent or more of industry sales, a merger will ordinarily be challenged between two firms with the following shares of the market:

Acquiring Firm	Acquired Firm
4% or more	4% or more
10% or more	2% or more
15% or more	1% or more

2. When the share of sales of the four largest firms in a market, amounts to less than approximately 75 percent of industry sales, a merger will ordinarily be challenged between two firms with the following shares of the market:

Acquiring Firm	Acquired Firm
5% or more	5% or more
10% or more	4% or more
15% or more	3% or more
20% or more	2% or more
25% or more	1% or more

3. Mergers occurring in a market in which there is a significant trend toward increased concentration are also likely to be challenged. The trend toward concentration is considered present when the market share of two of eight of the largest firms in that market has increased by 7 percent or more in the five or ten years prior to the merger. An acquisition by any of the eight largest firms of another firm that has a market share of approximately 2 percent or more will ordinarily be challenged.

VERTICAL MERGERS

1. When the supplying firm accounts for 10 percent or more of the sales in its market, and the purchasing firm accounts for 6 percent or more of the purchases in that market, the merger will ordinarily be challenged.

2. When the purchasing firm accounts for 6 percent or more of the purchases in the market and the supplying firm accounts for 10 percent or more of the sales in that market, the merger will ordinarily be challenged.

3. In some situations, mergers outside the above limits will be challenged.

CONGLOMERATE
MERGERS

1. When one of the firms: (1) has approximately 25 percent or more of the market, (2) is one of the two largest firms in a market where the two largest firms have a market share of 50 percent or more, (3) is one of the four largest firms in a market where the eight largest firms have a market share of approximately 75 percent or more and the acquired firm has a 10 percent market share, or (4) is one of the market's eight largest firms and the eight have a combined market share of approximately 75 percent, the merger will ordinarily be challenged.

2. When there is a danger that reciprocal buying might result, the merger will ordinarily be challenged.

3. When the acquisition might raise barriers to entry or increase the acquiring firm's market power, the merger will ordinarily be challenged.

shareholder approval of such a transaction, and * * * creates rights in the minority stockholders who do not consent.

The figures used by the trial court and in the corporate balance sheet at the time of transfer show that about one-third of all corporate assets were transferred to the subsidiary in exchange for stock and for debentures. The record shows that the land, buildings, machinery, inventory, and all tangibles of the company were transferred. The assets retained were bank balances, promissory notes, and the investment portfolio, consisting of common stocks. Thus all the operating property and tangibles that remained of the old Cotton Oil business were transferred. The surpluses and accumulated earnings were retained as represented in the investments and bank accounts. The record shows that the tangibles were instrumental in creating the current income of the corporation which had been a problem to management. This was removed by the transfer and the creation of the debt.

The appellees argue that the transfer was not a "sale" as urged by appellant. Appellees state in their brief that since the transferee was a wholly-owned subsidiary, the parent corporation still had enough "control" over the assets to prevent the transaction from being a sale. Thus the appellees in their brief say:

"In this case, the property which was transferred is still subject to the Company's use, possession and control since Machine Works is a wholly owned subsidiary of the Company."

It is difficult to see how there could be any real corporate entity for the subsidiary for any purpose if the assets transferred are in the present corporation's "possession," and within its control. [W]e assume on the basis of the trial court's findings, * * * [that] the parent divested itself of possession and title to the assets, and placed them in the possession and control of the subsidiary. Thus it looks more like a sale or "other disposition" under the statute than anything else. An exchange for stock and for evidence of indebtedness was made, and the indicia of ownership were held by the subsidiary. We must hold that the transaction did bring into play the statutory rights of dissenting shareholders, contrary to the trial court's conclusion.

The "all" or "substantially all" of the assets presents another issue, and is also a condition which must exist before the statute comes into play. The statute is in purely quantitive terms, but the appellant urges that other considerations exist because the assets transferred were all the "operating assets," and only money or investments remained. The record shows that the Cotton Oil Company had engaged in dual activities for several years, the plant operations (storage and machine shops) on one hand, and investments of the accumulated earnings on the other hand.

In the corporate resolution relating to the transfer, the recitation is made that the desire was to separate the "operating business activities from its investment activities." About this time, the Cotton Oil Company was changed into a personal holding company for tax purposes. The time that this took place is not clear from the record, but it was apparently related to the need for corporate changes to meet the problems arising from the accumulation of income. Such a change was substantial. Thus the corporate changes surrounding the creation of the subsidiary, the separation of the business activities with the result that the parent corporation has only investments, makes the transfer of assets have much different implications than it would ordinarily have. There is also the accompanying problem that really no values were established relating to the same standard, or related to current conditions. The consequences of the creation of the subsidiary discussed above with the fact all operating assets were transferred to it, together with the debt back makes the transaction a sale and results in a situation where for all practical purposes, "substantially" all of the assets were sold. All the effective operating assets were sold. The investment segment remaining was large in dollars but was the last and a large step in the change in the nature of corporate activity. In these circumstances, more than dollar values must be considered. It was another significant step also in the prevention of current income which was another aspect of the change in corporate purpose. *The transaction was thus one which required consideration by the stockholders, and gives rise to the rights of dissenting shareholders under the Oklahoma statutes.* [Emphasis added.]

The appellate court ruled that Campbell and other stockholders had the right to approve or disapprove of the sale of corporate assets. If they did not approve, as minority stockholders they were entitled to shareholder appraisal rights.

JUDGMENT AND REMEDY

Purchase of Stock

An alternative to the purchase of another corporation's assets is the purchase of a substantial number of the voting shares of its stock. This enables the acquiring corporation to control the acquired, or *target* corporation. The acquiring corporation deals directly with the shareholders in seeking to purchase the shares they hold.

A so-called "take-over bid" is subject to state and federal securities regulations. When the acquiring corporation makes a public offer to all shareholders of the target corporation, it is called a *tender offer* (an offer that is publicly advertised and addressed to all shareholders of the would-be target company). A tender offer is sometimes made when the acquiring firm believes that the target company is poorly managed. For this reason, the offer price is generally higher than the market price of the target stock prior to the announcement of the tender offer. The higher price induces shareholders to tender their shares to the acquiring firm. The tender offer can be conditional upon the receipt of a specified number of outstanding shares by a specified date. The offering corporation can

make an *exchange* tender offer in which it offers target stockholders its own securities in exchange for their target stock. In a cash tender offer, the offering corporation offers the target stockholders cash in exchange for their target stock.

Federal securities laws strictly control the terms, duration, and circumstances under which most tender offers are made. In addition, over thirty states have passed "take-over" statutes that impose additional regulations on tender offers.

The use of the tender offer as a method of gaining corporate control began in the mid-1960s. Highly contested legal battles and enormous expenses involved in complying with federal and state regulations have worked to discourage the use of tender offers as a vehicle for obtaining control of a corporation through stock purchase.

TERMINATION

Termination of a corporate life, like termination of a partnership, has two phases—liquidation and dissolution. **Liquidation** is the process by which corporate assets are converted into cash and distributed among creditors and shareholders according to specific rules of preference.[3] **Dissolution** is the legal death of the artificial "person" of the corporation.

Dissolution can be brought about in any of the following ways: (1) an act of a legislature in the state of incorporation; (2) the expiration of the time provided in the certificate of incorporation; (3) the voluntary approval of the shareholders and the board of directors; (4) unanimous action

3. Upon dissolution, the liquidated assets are first used to pay creditors. Any remaining assets are distributed to shareholders according to their respective stock rights; preferred stock has priority over common stock.

by all shareholders; or (5) court decree brought about by the attorney general of the state of incorporation for any of the following reasons— failure to comply with administrative requirements (for example, failure to pay annual franchise taxes or to submit an annual report or to have a designated registered agent), the procurement of a corporate charter through fraud or misrepresentation upon the state, the abuse of corporate powers (*ultra vires* acts), the violation of the state criminal code after the demand to discontinue has been made by the secretary of state, the failure to commence business operations, or the abandonment of operations before starting up.

GRUENBERG v. GOLDMINE PLANTATION, INC.

Court of Appeal of Louisiana, Fourth Circuit, 1978.
360 So.2d 884.

BACKGROUND AND FACTS *The plaintiff, Howard Gruenberg, a minority shareholder of a close corporation, instituted this action for involuntary dissolution. The defendant corporation was Goldmine Plantation, Inc. Goldmine's principal asset was a nine hundred acre tract of land fronting on the east bank of the Mississippi River. In 1941, the land was acquired for $65,000. In 1975, the property was appraised at $3,000 per acre, giving it a value of $2,700,000.*

The land had been used to grow sugar cane, and the mineral rights had been leased. Between 1966 and the present, various industrial enterprises expressed the desire to buy the land. The latest price offered was about $3,600 per acre net to vendor.

Although none of the attempts to purchase the land had taken the form of a written or binding offer, evidence presented at the trial court suggested that prospective offers were substantial, and a contract to sell could have materialized had the Goldmine board of directors expressed any interest. However, the board decided not to sell the real estate.

Minority shareholders, frustrated by the board's disinterest in selling the property and by low dividends from the sugar cane operations, petitioned the court for involuntary dissolution under the provisions of the state's corporate statute.

STOULIG, Judge.
* * *

In the light of this situation, we consider whether plaintiffs and intervenors have sustained the proof to support their demands for involuntary dissolution under [any grounds permitted by state law]:

"A. The court may entertain a proceeding for involuntary dissolution under its supervision when it is made to appear that:
* * *

(2) The objects of the corporation have wholly failed, or are entirely abandoned, or their accomplishment is impracticable; or

(3) It is beneficial to the interests of the shareholders that the corporation should be liquidated and dissolved; or

* * *

(7) The corporation has been guilty of gross and persistent ultra vires acts * * *."

First we hold the evidence does not support our concluding the objects of incorporation have "wholly failed" or "been abandoned" or that "their accomplishment is impracticable." [Thus the proof required by (A)(2) is lacking].

* * *

[Second], [i]t can be urged validly in this case that the low returns of the past have been more than offset by the appreciation of the corporate assets. With the completion of the river bridge at Luling within the next few years, the land value, according to Kuebel, should increase tremendously. Thus the proof required by (A)(3) is lacking.

Finally, we consider the contention that the majority shareholders and the board have been guilty of gross and persistent ultra vires acts. While we question the wisdom of the board's approach in reaching a decision not to sell the real estate, we conclude the action taken is within the scope of the board's authority and therefore legal.

"Unless it clearly appears that the act is an abuse of discretion, intra vires, legal and good faith acts of the board of directors, other corporate officers, or the majority stockholders, i.e., acts pertaining to the internal management, of the corporation, where they are not fraudulent or unfair to minority stockholders, will not be interfered with or remedied at the instance of minority stockholders, regardless of whether such acts are wise or expedient. In other words, to warrant the interposition of a court in favor of the minority shareholders in a corporation, as against the contemplated action of the majority, where such action is within the corporate powers, a case must be made out which plainly shows that such action is so far opposed to the true interests of the corporation itself as to lead to the clear inference that no one thus acting could have been influenced by any honest desire to secure such interests, but that he must have acted with an intent to subserve some outside purpose, regardless of the consequences to the company and in a manner inconsistent with its interests."

* * *

We appreciate the frustrations of the minority who are locked into a financial situation in which they have a substantial interest but no control. Appellants suggest the shareholders be equated to partners and be permitted to disengage from the corporation as they could were Goldmine operated as a partnership. Our substantive law provides for involuntary dissolution but offers no remedy for the minority shareholder with substantial holdings who is out of control and trapped in a closed corporation. We will not abrogate the legislative function to provide relief.

The judgment of the trial court was affirmed. The appellate court concluded that it would not permit the minority shareholder to force involuntary dissolution under the provisions of the statute and that the officers of the corporation had acted within the scope of their delegated authority. The objects of incorporation had not wholly failed, and dissolution was not essential to protect the minority shareholder's interests.

JUDGMENT AND REMEDY

QUESTIONS AND CASE PROBLEMS

1. Some of the stockholders of the Gulf Company, who were also shareholders of the Warrior Company, wished to have the former sell all its assets to the latter. Both the bylaws and the certificate of incorporation of the Gulf Company were silent on the matter of the sale of company assets, so the shareholders needed to find out how to proceed with the sale of assets. What three steps must they take? [Finch v. Warrior Cement Co., 16 Del. Ch. 44, 141 A. 54 (1928)]

2. For many years, Bellanca Corporation had been in the business of manufacturing airplanes, although in recent years it had engaged in no business operations, had been delisted by the American Stock Exchange, and had in fact become an "empty shell." In 1961, through a series of agreements, the majority shareholder of Bellanca agreed to purchase all the stock of seven California corporations engaged in the egg business and in turn agreed to sell his majority share in Bellanca to Dean and Glen Olson. Orzeck, a minority shareholder of Bellanca, objected to the entire transaction, but it was carried through in spite of her objections. Orzeck felt that she should have been given dissenting shareholders' appraisal rights, which are available when a minority shareholder objects to a company's merger. Should Orzeck be granted dissenters' appraisal rights? [Orzeck v. Englehart, 41 Del. Ch. 361, 195 A.2d. 375 (1963)]

3. The Delaware Racing Association owned 95 percent of the shares of Delaware Steeplechase Association. Pursuant to the Model Business Corporation Act, the Delaware Racing Association proceeded to merge with Steeplechase. The owner of the 5 percent remaining shares of Steeplechase objected to the merger and filed a petition with the court to prevent it. Can he prevent the merger? [Application of Delaware Racing Ass'n, 213 A.2d. 203 (Del. 1965)]

4. Assume in Question 3 above that the 5 percent shareholder elected to take cash for his shares instead of exchanging them for shares of the parent corporation. Should valuation be based on the liquidation value of Steeplechase, since Steeplechase will no longer exist after merging into Delaware Racing Association? On the other hand, should the minority shareholder be given the "going concern" value of his stock since he himself chose to withdraw from a going concern?

5. A owned two-thirds of the outstanding shares of United States Distributing Corporation, a Virginia corporation. B owned the remaining one-third. In United States Distributing's charter and on each of its stock certificates was the following provision: "In case of the liquidation or dissolution of this corporation, or a distribution of its assets, the assets of this corporation shall first be applied toward paying the holders of its stock all accrued and unpaid dividends thereon." The accumulative unpaid dividends on United States Distributing's stock amounted to $84 per share. At a shareholders' meeting, A voted in favor of a merger with Pittston Company, a Delaware corporation, and B dissented. After filing the proper written notice of his dissent, B demanded dissenting shareholders' appraisal rights. B argued that these rights included payment by the surviving corporation, the Pittston Company, of accumulated dividends out of the assets received from United States Distributing as provided in United States Distributing's charter. What result? [Adams v. United States Distributing Corp., 184 Va. 134, 34 S.E.2d. 244 (1945)]

6. Nevada Land and Mortgage Company was engaged in a variety of property transactions. Prior to 1965, it had suffered financial reverses causing its board of directors to contemplate merger or consolidation with or sale of assets to the Leroy Corporation. Lamb was a creditor of Nevada Land and Mortgage. If the two corporations merge, and Leroy is the surviving corporation, will Leroy be liable to Lamb? If the two consolidate, will the resulting corporation be liable to Lamb? If Leroy purchases the assets of Nevada Land and Mortgage, will it then be liable to Lamb? [Lamb v. Leroy Corp., 85 Nev. 276, 454 P.2d.24 (1969)]

7. Arthur Gerth owned 53 percent of the XYZ Corporation's common stock and half of its preferred stock. His brother, Harry, owned 1 percent of its common stock, and Kruger owned the remainder of its common and preferred stock. The XYZ Corporation was in the retail lumber business. Of the three shareholders, Gerth was the only employee of the corporation. As its president, he paid himself a combined salary and bonus of approximately $15,000 annually. This left less than $2,000 in profits to be distributed as dividends. Kruger brought suit to have XYZ Corporation dissolved on the ground that Gerth was drawing an excessive salary and bonus and was thus wasting corporate assets and leaving an insufficient amount available for dividends. Under Gerth's leadership, the XYZ Corporation had become

quite successful, and Gerth claimed that he deserved the salary and bonus because of his efforts. Should XYZ be dissolved? [Kruger v. Gerth, 22 A.D.2d 916, 255 N.Y.S.2d 498 (1964)]

8. Vulcan Manufacturing Company had been engaged in the manufacture of automobile jacks but went out of business in 1965. Vulcan's assets were auctioned off at a sheriff's sale about six months later. The bulk of the assets came into the hands of Great Lakes Distributing Company. Subsequently, Great Lakes rented the building in which Vulcan had previously conducted its business and began manufacturing and repairing automobile jacks. Comstock, who had been injured by one of the defective jacks manufactured by Vulcan in 1963, obtained a judgment against Vulcan that same year. Can Great Lakes Distributing Company be held liable on the judgment that Comstock obtained against Vulcan? Are there any additional facts that might make Great Lakes liable? [Comstock v. Great Lakes Distibuting Co., 209 Kan. 306, 496 P.2d 1308 (1973)]

9. Parker Laundry Company was an Illinois corporation owned and operated by Paul A. Parker. Its offices were in the city of Rock Island. In 1954, Parker, as sole director of Parker Laundry, filed the appropriate petition with the court for dissolution and dissolved the company. At the time, Parker Laundry's assets totaled $2,000, and its liabilities totaled approximately $4,000. Parker notified all the company's creditors except for the city of Rock Island, to which the company owed taxes of approximately $1,000. Two years later, after the city realized that the company had dissolved, it filed suit against Paul A. Parker personally for the $1,000 that Parker Laundry had owed in back taxes at the time of its dissolution. Can Paul Parker be held personally liable? If so, for how much? [People v. Parker, 30 Ill.2d 486, 197 N.E.2d 30 (1964)]

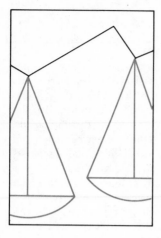

46

Corporations
Private Franchises

The Federal Trade Commission has defined *franchise* as "an arrangement in which the owner of a trademark, a trade name, or a copyright licenses others, under specified conditions or limitations, to use the trademark, trade name, or copyright in purveying goods or services." The franchise system has also been described as an organization composed of distributive units established and administered by a supplier as a medium for expanding and controlling the market of its products. Each franchise dealer is a legally independent but economically dependent unit of the integrated business system. The individual *franchisee* (the holder of the franchise) can operate as an independent business; yet it can obtain the advantages of a regional or national organizational affiliation to supply products, advertising, and other services.

The franchise system also provides the consumer public with an opportunity to obtain uniform products at numerous distribution points from small independent contractors. The system therefore seems good for the businessperson, good for the consumer, and good for the economy.

The use of franchises has expanded rapidly in recent years. The system began in the early part of the century. Between 1910 and 1940, early applications of franchising appeared in the automobile industry, sports, and the soft drink bottling industry. Franchises now account for about 25 percent of all retail sales and over 13 percent of gross national product in the United States. The franchise pattern of business development is a particularly appealing form of capitalistic enterprise. It has the advantage of enabling groups of individuals with small amounts of capital to become entrepreneurs.

THE LAW OF FRANCHISING

The growth in franchise operations has outdistanced the law of franchising. There has yet to be developed a solid body of appellate decisions under federal or state laws relating to franchise law. Because of the absence of law precisely addressed to franchising, the courts tend to apply general common law principles and the federal or state statutory definitions where they are applicable. The franchise relationship has characteristics associated with agency law, employment law, and independent contracting; yet it really does not fit into any of these traditional classifications.

About fifteen states currently have statutes dealing with franchise law. Although there is no real uniformity among the states' statutes, the following definition was adopted by two states to provide for a basic definition of franchising:

"Franchise" means a written agreement for a definite or indefinite period, in which a person grants to another person a license to use a trade name, trademark, service mark, or related characteristics, and in which there is a community of interest in the marketing of goods or services at wholesale, retail, by lease, agreement, or otherwise.[1]

TYPES OF FRANCHISES

There are three types of franchises: distributorships, chain-style businesses, and manufacturing or processing plants.

1. A *distributorship* relationship occurs where a manufacturing concern (franchisor) licenses a dealer (franchisee) to sell its product. Often, a distributorship covers an exclusive territory.
2. A *chain-style business* operation occurs when a franchisee operates under a franchisor's trade name and is identified as a member of a select group of dealers who engage in the franchisor's business. The franchisee is generally required to follow standardized or prescribed methods of operations. Often, the franchisor requires that minimum prices and standards of operation be maintained. In addition, sometimes the franchisee is obligated to deal exclusively with the franchisor to obtain materials and supplies.
3. A *manufacturing or processing plant arrangement* is one in which the franchisor transmits to the franchisee the essential ingredients or formula to make a particular product. The franchisee then markets it either at wholesale or at retail in accordance with the franchisor's standards.

ADVANTAGES OF THE FRANCHISE SYSTEM

A system of franchises allows a highly effective means of gaining rapid market expansion and exposure with a minimum of capital outlay by the franchisor. Because franchisees make their own investments in order to undertake business operations, they have a strong incentive to make a profit. In most cases, the contract is written so that both the franchisee and the franchisor make a profit.

The franchisee gets the benefit of all of the franchisor's trade names and trademarks. In addition, the franchise carries with it goodwill and customer acceptance as well as the benefits of the franchisor's national advertising. The franchisee can obtain guidance from an experienced organization in areas such as site selection, operational know-how, and bookkeeping. For the franchisee, a moderate investment can develop into a prosperous business.

In short, the franchisee pledges money and service; the franchisor pledges aid and protection. In an economic context, franchising systems are clearly desirable for both parties. But there are some shortcomings—especially for the franchisee. The following sections will attempt to outline some of the problems that have arisen in the franchise arrangement. Most problems occur *after* the franchise agreement

1. N.J. Rev. Stat. Sec. 56:10-3 (Supp.1972). Wash. Rev. Code Ann. Sec. 19.100.010 (Supp.1972).

has been entered into. Because there are usually a number of potential franchisees for every franchise operation, typical contract provisions favor the franchisor. The courts, hampered by a lack of case law or statutory law, have been very slow to protect the rights of the franchisee.

THE FRANCHISE AGREEMENT

The franchise relationship is defined by a contract between the franchisor and the franchisee. Each franchise relationship and each industry has its own characteristics, so it is difficult to describe the broad range of details a franchising contract will include. The following sections, however, will define the essential characteristics of the franchise relationship.

Entering the Franchise Relationship

Prospective franchisees must initially decide on the type of business they wish to undertake. Then, they must obtain information about the business from the franchisor. Usually, franchisors will have numerous statistics and market studies available for prospective franchisees to examine. Of course, people who acquire franchised businesses differ greatly in their grasp of business operations. Some purchasers are experienced businesspersons with a firm grasp of the economic realities of how to operate a franchise. Others want to own a business but have never had business experience. In the latter situation, the franchisee must rely heavily on the franchisor in evaluating and setting up the initial business organization.

Payment for Franchise

The franchisee ordinarily pays an initial fee for the franchise license (the privilege of being granted a franchise). This fee is separate from the various products that the franchisee purchases from or through the franchisor. In some industries, the franchisor relies heavily on the initial sale of the franchise for realizing a profit.

In other industries, the continued dealing between the parties brings profit to both.

In most situations, the franchisor will receive a stated percentage of the annual sales or annual volume of business done by the franchisee. The franchise agreement may also require the franchisee to pay a percentage of advertising costs and certain administrative expenses incurred throughout the franchise arrangement.

Location and Business Organization

Typically, the franchisor will determine the territory to be served. The franchise agreement can specify whether the premises for the business must be leased or purchased outright. In some cases, construction of a building is necessary to meet the terms of the franchise agreement. In addition, the agreement will specify whether the franchisor supplies equipment and furnishings for the premises or whether this is the responsibility of the franchisee. When the franchise is a service operation such as a motel, the contract often provides that the franchisor will establish certain standards for the facility and will make inspections to insure that the standards are being maintained in order to protect the franchise name and reputation.

The business organization of the franchisee is of great concern to the franchisor. Depending on the terms of the franchise agreement, the franchisor may specify particular requirements for the form and capital structure of the business. The franchise agreement can provide that standards of operation such as sales quotas, quality standards, or record keeping, be conducted by the franchisor. Furthermore, a franchisor may wish to retain stringent control over the training of personnel involved in the operation and over administrative aspects of the business. Although the day-to-day operation of the franchise business is normally left up to the franchisee, the franchise agreement can provide for whatever amount of supervision and control the parties agree upon.

Price and Quality Controls

Franchises provide the franchisor with an outlet for the firm's goods and services. Depending upon the nature of the business, the franchisor may require the franchisee to purchase products from the franchisor at an established price. Of course, without explicit statutory authorization, such as fair trade laws or their equivalent, a franchisor cannot set the prices at which the franchisee will resell the goods. A franchisor can suggest retail prices but cannot coerce the franchisee into selling at that particular price.

A franchisor can require franchisees to purchase supplies from it. In fact, in certain franchise arrangements there may be an obligation to deal exclusively with the franchisor. However, requiring a franchisee to purchase *exclusively* from the franchisor may violate federal antitrust laws. The implications of antitrust violations on territorial restrictions, restrictions on products sold, resale price fixing, and price discrimination will be discussed later.

As a general rule, there is no question of the validity of a franchise agreement provision that permits the franchisor to maintain certain quality standards. Since the franchisor has a legitimate interest in maintaining the quality of the product or service in order to protect its name and reputation, it can exercise greater control in this area than would otherwise be tolerated.

Termination of the Franchise Arrangement

The duration of the franchise is a matter to be determined between the parties. Generally, a franchise will start out for a short period, such as a year, so that the franchisee and the franchisor can determine whether they want to stay in business with one another. Usually the franchise agreement will specify that termination must be "for cause" such as death or disability of the franchisee, insolvency of the franchisee, breach of the franchise agreement, or failure to meet specified sales quotas. Most franchise contracts provide that notice of termination must be given. If no set time for termination is given, then a reasonable time with notice will be implied. A franchisee must be given reasonable time to wind up the business—that is, to do the accounting and return the copyright or trademark or any other property of the franchisor.

Much franchise litigation has arisen over termination provisions. Since the franchise agreement is normally a form contract drawn and prepared by the franchisor, and since in reality there is very little equality of bargaining power between the franchisee and the franchisor, the termination provisions of contracts are generally more favorable to the franchisor. The lack of statutory law and case law is felt most harshly by the franchisee in this area. In some states automobile dealer and gasoline station franchises have some statutory protection.

The franchisee normally invests a substantial amount of time and money in the franchise operation to make it successful. Despite this fact, the franchisee may receive little or nothing for the business upon termination. The franchisor owns the trademark and hence the business. The courts have often struggled to offer a terminated franchisee some kind of relief, as is illustrated in the next case.

BACKGROUND AND FACTS *The plaintiff, Atlantic Richfield Company (Arco), entered into a "dealer lease" with the defendant, Razumic, in 1953. The defendant expended $5,000 for inventory, equipment, and capital. Arco financed the initial supply of gasoline to get the service station on its feet, and the defendant opened for business. Over the years, the parties signed numerous agreements resembling the first dealer lease, as well as various forms concerning the use of Arco's promotional*

ATLANTIC RICHFIELD CO. v. RAZUMIC
Supreme Court of
Pennsylvania, 1978.
480 Pa., 366, 390 A.2d 736.

campaign materials, purchase of fuel, and credit card sale arrangements.

In 1970, Razumic moved into a new service station built by Arco and signed a three-year dealer lease. On June 29, 1973, Arco notified Razumic that the lease would not be renewed and directed Razumic to vacate the premises in thirty days. Razumic refused to leave, and Arco filed suit to force termination of the lease agreement. The trial court found for Arco, holding that the dealership agreement could be terminated at will for any reason.

ROBERTS, Justice.

* * *

In his pleadings, at trial, and on appeal to this Court, Razumic has urged that he and Arco were parties to a franchise agreement Arco could not terminate at will. Arco, on the other hand, has contended throughout that the dealership agreement could be terminated for any reason. We agree with Razumic.

We believe that the 1970 writing and its riders embody a franchise agreement.

"In its simplest terms, a franchise is a license from the owner of a trademark or trade name permitting another to sell a product or service under the name or mark. More broadly stated, the franchise has evolved into an elaborate agreement by which the franchisee undertakes to conduct a business or sell a product or service in accordance with methods and procedures prescribed by the franchisor, and the franchisor undertakes to assist the franchisee through advertising, promotion and other advisory services."

"[T]he cornerstone of a franchise system must be the trademark or trade name of a product. It is this uniformity of product and control of its quality and distribution which causes the public to turn to franchise stores for the product."

Given the comprehensive terms of the writing obligating Razumic to operate the Arco service station in a manner Arco determined would reflect favorably upon the public image of the Arco trademark, report and share gross receipts with Arco pursuant to a "FRANCHISE RENT SCHEDULE," and allow Arco to inspect the station to assure Razumic's continued compliance with the many provisions of the form writing, it is clear that Razumic was not pursuing solely his own business interests. Rather, Razumic conducted his business and sold his products in accordance with methods prescribed by Arco.

The writing provides Arco the right to terminate the "lease" should Razumic abandon the premises or close them "for a period of seventy-two hours." Razumic's negligence or willful misconduct causing damages to a substantial portion of the premises gives Arco "the right to terminate this lease without liability." Razumic's failure to make timely payment of rent, his death or insolvency, or governmental taking also permit Arco to terminate the "lease." Further, Razumic's "fail[ure] to comply with any of his other obligations" set forth in the writing permits Arco to terminate the agreement if Razumic fails to remedy the situation after fifteen days' notice of non-compliance.

The writing does not, however, contain any provision granting Arco the right to terminate the franchise agreement at will. In view of the provisions authorizing

Arco to terminate the parties' franchise agreement for limited, business reasons and an additional provision authorizing Razumic, upon giving "at least sixty days advance written notice," to terminate the agreement without reason upon the anniversary of a term where the stated term exceeds one year, the absence of a similar term authorizing Arco to terminate the agreement without reason is striking.

An Arco dealer has his own expectations. He knows that his good service will· in many instances produce regular customers. He also realizes, however, that much of his trade will be attracted because his station offers the products, services, and promotions of the well-established and well-displayed name "Arco." Unlike a tenant pursuing his own interests while occupying a landlord's property, a franchisee such as Razumic builds the goodwill of both his own business and Arco.

In exchange, an Arco dealer such as Razumic can justifiably expect that his time, effort, and other investments promoting the goodwill of Arco will not be destroyed as a result of Arco's arbitrary decision to terminate their franchise relationship. Consistent with these reasonable expectations, and Arco's obligation to deal with its franchisees in good faith and in a commercially reasonable manner, Arco cannot arbitrarily sever its franchise relationship with Razumic. A contrary conclusion would allow Arco to reap the benefits of its franchisees' efforts in promoting the goodwill of its name without regard for the franchisees' interests.

For the above reasons, the writing's leasehold terminology stating a three year term of occupancy does not govern the duration of the comprehensive contractual business relationship between Razumic and Arco. Rather, the language establishes a right of occupancy which the franchise Razumic can reasonably expect will not be abruptly halted. Consistent with Razumic's reasonable expectations, principles of good faith and commercial reasonableness, Arco may not arbitrarily recover possession of the service station and thereby summarily terminate the franchise relationship.

JUDGMENT AND REMEDY

The Supreme Court of Pennsylvania reversed the trial court's decision. Arco was prohibited from terminating the franchise agreement without good cause.

COMMENTS

The UCC requirements of good faith in contract dealings are often applied to ongoing franchise relationships when the franchise involves the sale of goods. However, the UCC provisions have ordinarily not been applied to franchise agreements that extend to the leasing of premises.

DETERMINATION OF RELIEF The courts and legal commentators have tried to apply many theories to protect a franchisee's rights upon termination. Some courts have held that every contract contains an implied covenant of good faith and fair dealing. Others have held that if a franchise investment is substantial and the relationship has been established for an indefinite duration, it cannot be terminated until after a reasonable period of time has elapsed.

What a reasonable time is will depend upon the circumstances in each case. Some of the circumstances that the courts consider are: (1) the amount of preliminary and promotional expenditures made, (2) the length of time the franchise has been in operation before notice of termination was given, (3) the prospects for forfeiture of profits, and (4) whether or not the franchise has been proven profitable during its actual operation.

If contract provisions allow for termination, even though they may be unfair to the franchisee, no cause of action can be found. The Uniform Commercial Code Sec. 2-302 has been used by some courts to find that termination provisions dispensing with notification are invalid if their effect is unconscionable. The courts have generally refused to find that franchises terminable by notice at any time or at the end of a specific time are unconscionable *per se*.

MEASURE OF DAMAGES The courts have also struggled to determine how best to measure damages to prevent injustice or unfairness when misconduct occurs in a franchise relationship. Since franchising is a rather peculiar form of capitalist enterprise, serious franchising problems warrant legislative attention. Congress enacted statutory requirements under the Automobile Dealers' Day in Court Act (15 USCA Sec. 1221). Thus, in some cases, a franchisee need not rely on common law principles to obtain protection in the courts from franchisor abuses.

CONSUMER AND FRANCHISEE PROTECTION The consumer protection movement and pressures from certain industries (primarily car dealers) have resulted in the passage of numerous statutes to protect franchisees from bad faith termination of their franchise contracts. For example, the Automobile Dealers' Day in Court Act (15 USCA Sec. 1221) allows an auto dealer who contends that the franchisor did not act in good faith and without coercion in terminating the franchise to take the matter to court for a judicial termination. Moreover, various states have passed laws in recent years that spell out certain conditions and circumstances under which a franchise can be terminated. However, these laws are subject to serious constitutional challenges under the impairment of contracts clause, the due process clause, and the interstate commerce clause of the U.S. Constitution.

The realities of the franchise industry demonstrate a need for uniform regulation. Common law theories and existing statutory remedies are really not very helpful in their application to franchising problems. The franchise system is a complex and unique business enterprise. It is growing so fast that it seems almost impossible that any regulatory scheme designed can be both comprehensive and flexible enough to meet the needs of franchises.

REA AND 22 FORD, INC. v. FORD MOTOR CO.
United States Court of Appeals, Third Circuit, 1977.
560 F.2d 554.

BACKGROUND AND FACTS *In this case, there was both an individual and a corporate plaintiff. Both plaintiffs filed this action to recover from the automobile manufacturer (franchisor) for damages based on alleged violations of the Automobile Dealers' Day in Court Act. The suit was under litigation for more than ten years. The basic controversy arose when the manufacturer required the plaintiff to resign his holdings in a competing manufacturer's dealership as a condition for obtaining a Ford franchise.*

In February 1964, the plaintiff, Rea, was given a franchise for a Ford dealership in Pennsylvania. At that time he was already a principal stockholder of an Oldsmobile dealership in Pennsylvania. Rea told Ford that he would acquire the assets needed to operate the Ford dealership by liquidating the Oldsmobile business, and Ford had him sign a letter committing him to taking that step.

Subsequently, Rea suggested to a Ford representative that the Oldsmobile operation might not be closed at all. The Ford representative then warned Rea that unless he got out of the Oldsmobile business, Ford might not ship him the cars needed to operate the Ford franchise. Shortly thereafter, Rea gave up his interest in the Oldsmobile franchise, kept part of its assets to be used in operating the Ford franchise, and sold the rest.

At the trial, it was established that the manufacturer's requirement was a violation of the Automobile Dealers' Day in Court Act. On appeal, the liability end of the act was upheld; the only issue remaining was the measure of damages.

JAMES HUNTER, III, Circuit Judge.

* * *

At the outset, Ford argues that the trial court erred in refusing to allow Ford to introduce evidence tending to establish that: (1) Ford's acts were not the proximate cause of the sale of Rea's Oldsmobile business; (2) Ford's acts were not the proximate cause of any loss in profits by Rea's corporate entities; and (3) Rea failed to "mitigate" damages and, therefore, Ford had not caused any real harm. These elements of causation, says Ford, go to damages alone and were not foreclosed by this court's affirmance of the finding of liability under the Automobile Dealers' Day in Court Act.

We do not agree. Causation is an element of liability. Our remand left open only the amount of damages, not the fact of damage.

[The court refused to allow Ford to challenge the question of liability. It then went on to discuss the elements of damage and the appropriate calculation.]

Ford also claims that the court below erred in including Rea's projected salary and bonuses at the last Oldsmobile franchise in the damage calculation.

[Ford continued to argue that Rea's compensation should be limited to what he would have received as a principal stockholder.]

Again, we do not agree. The corporate entity that suffered harm was the Oldsmobile franchise, which ceased to exist; the "dealer" for purposes of the action under the Auto Dealers' Act was Edward Rea in his capacity as a *Ford* dealer.

In that capacity, he personally suffered damage not only through loss of income as a shareholder of the Oldsmobile business Ford forced him to close, but also through loss of the salary and bonuses he could have earned in that business. Since Rea was injured in both respects by Ford's action, he can be made whole only by recovering both types of compensation.

Ford's last point of appeal is that the trial court erred in awarding Rea damages covering the period between Ford's successful first appeal and the retrial as to damages. Ford claims to have been "penalized" for taking an appeal.

We do not agree. The court merely exercised its ordinary powers. Lost profits are recoverable in an action for the destruction or interruption of an established business, whenever they are not merely speculative or conjectural. And, in general, a court has the power to award damages occurring up to the date of the ultimate judgment in the case. Ford does not claim that the damages were too speculative; indeed the fact that the injured party—Rea—had survived the intervening period meant precisely that any objection that he might not have lived to suffer "future damages"—those occurring after the first trial—was obviated. As for the supposed "penalty," Ford might likewise claim that it was "penalized" by defending the action at all, since that also prolonged the period for which lost profits might have been recovered.

[The court went on to evaluate certain other calculations. It found that certain deductions were properly made but certain others were improper, so it reversed the latter. After the court assessed the value of all of the assets involved, it arrived at its decision to adjust the award given by the district court.]

JUDGMENT AND REMEDY *The court of appeals upheld both the liability and damages award of the district court. However, the court recalculated the value of the assets and hence the damages suffered by the plaintiff and vacated the district court's judgment, remanding the case with instructions to the district court to add approximately $160,934 to the judgment awarded the plaintiff. In addition, the court of appeals determined that the Oldsmobile dealership as a corporate entity had no right of action. Only the individual plaintiff, Rea, could collect damages.*

REGULATION OF THE FRANCHISING INDUSTRY

Any industry that expands rapidly without a uniform regulatory scheme is likely to engage in certain abusive and destructive practices. The franchising industry is no exception. The Federal Trade Commission has recently begun investigations to determine whether illegal methods have been used to compel restaurant franchisees to purchase goods and services at artificially inflated prices. Other abusive practices have been discovered in the form of hidden markups on the capital assets and equipment that must be purchased by a franchisee either from the franchisor or from approved vendors. Cases of misrepresentation occur in the initial sale of many franchises. More than a few unsuspecting franchisees have learned after entering into the franchise contract that in order to operate the business and meet the established sales quotas they must work an inordinate number of hours a week.

The franchise relationship grows out of a contract. But because of the nature of the franchise system, the common law remedies that have been applied to contract and sales contract situations do not provide adequate relief. Furthermore, only about fifteen states have enacted statutory laws to govern franchise relationships. Thus, what is permissible in one state may not be permissible in another. Such lack of uniformity places a great hardship on franchise arrangements, especially when they are operated on a national scale. Within the last ten years, regulation of the franchise industry has finally begun at the federal level. Most federal remedies deal with violations of antitrust laws. Attempts at control using the federal securities laws have been less effective. The courts, the state legislatures, and the Congress are all attempting to develop uniform regulations for the franchising industry.

The Franchise Contract: Disclosure Protection

A franchise purchaser can suffer substantial loss if the franchisor has not provided full and complete information regarding the franchisor-franchisee relationship as well as the details of the contract under which the business will be operated. When misrepresentation permeates the initial sale of a franchise operation, the common law remedy of fraud in the inducement provides inadequate relief. In most cases, the franchisee has already paid the franchise purchase price and may also have incurred substantial losses in the initial operating phases of the business. The elements of fraud are exceedingly difficult to prove. Even the tort of intentional misstatement or misrepresentation of a material fact upon which the franchisee relied places a great burden on the franchisee to show that the franchisor's original offer was misleading or fraudulent.

Only a few of the states that have enacted legislation concerning franchising have included disclosure provisions. California was the first state to enact a franchise disclosure law, and it has served as a model for other disclosure statutes. The California Franchise Investment Law sets out twenty-two items that must be disclosed in a registration filed with the state. Some of the items of disclosure include: (1) the name and business address of the franchisor, (2) the business experience of any persons affiliated with the franchisor, (3) whether any person associated with the franchisor has been convicted of a felony, (4) a recent financial statement, (5) a typical franchise agreement, (6) a statement of all fees that the franchisee is required to pay, and (7) other information that the commissioner of corporations may reasonably require.[2]

Some courts have attempted to apply the Securities Act of 1933 and various state blue sky laws to franchise agreements. This has met with limited success. The franchise agreement could possibly be considered an "investment contract" within the meaning of blue sky laws and the 1933 Securities Act. Thus, it would be subject to the registration and disclosure requirements of the securities laws. It has been argued that a franchise arrangement is an investment contract that is a security under the Securities Act. This theory, however, has not met with much success on the federal level. The United States Supreme Court has defined an investment contract as "a contract, transaction or scheme whereby a person invests his (or her) money in a common enterprise and is led to expect profits solely from the efforts of the promoter or third party."[3] The typical franchise agreement fails this test for determining "investment contracts" because a franchisee must make an effort to make money. Thus, franchise agreements are usually *not* considered securities under the Securities Act.

Federal law prohibits mail fraud. According to 18 USCA Sec. 1341, the U.S. mails cannot be used to further a scheme to defraud. Like Section 5 of the FTC Act, the mail fraud provision penalizes misrepresentations made by use of the mails. In reality, this is not a very effective means for preventing fraud or misrepresentation in a franchisor's negotiations with a potential franchisee because it affords only an after the fact remedy. Similarly, the Federal Trade Commission, under Section 5 of the FTC Act, gives the FTC power to stop unfair or deceptive practices in commerce and to prohibit deceptive advertising. Both the FTC provisions and the mail fraud provisions lack the affirmative protection that disclosure laws would afford a potential purchaser of a franchise.

The FTC Franchise Rule

The FTC franchise rule was promulgated in response to widespread evidence of deception and unfair practices in connection with the resale of franchises and business opportunity ventures. This rule requires that, within a specified time, franchisors and franchise

---

2. Cal. Corp. Code Sec. 31001 (West Supp.1975). The California Franchise Investment Law provides: "California franchisees have suffered substantial losses where the franchisor or his (or her) representative has not provided full and complete information regarding the franchisor-franchisee relationship, the details of the contract between the franchisor and the franchisee, and the prior business experience of the franchisor." It is the intent of this law to provide each prospective franchisee with the information necessary to make an intelligent decision regarding the franchise being offered. Cal. Corp. Code Section 31001 (West Supp.1975). As cited in 59 Minn. Law Rev. 1027 (1975). Casenote: Franchise Regulation.

---

3. SEC v. W.J. Howey Co., 328 U.S. 293, 66 S.Ct. 1100 (1946).

brokers furnish the information that prospective franchisees need in order to make an informed decision about entering into a franchise relationship. The rule sets forth the circumstances under which a franchisor or broker can make claims about the projected sales income or profits of existing or potential outlets. The rule also imposes requirements that concern the establishment of the franchise relationship.

Franchisee's Relationship to Franchisor: Agent or Independent Contractor?

The mere licensing of a trade name does not create an agency relationship. However, the courts have determined that certain factors in the franchisor-franchisee relationship do indicate an agency relationship:

1. The terms of the agreement create an agency relationship.
2. The franchisor exercises a high degree of control over the franchisee's activities.

3. A third person looking at the relationship between the franchisor and the franchisee would reasonably believe that there is an agency relationship.
4. The franchisor derives an especially great benefit from the franchisee's activities. The greater the benefit, the more likely an agency relationship will be found.[4]

If these factors show a very close relationship between the franchisor and the franchisee, then their relationship will be deemed to be that of an employer-employee or principal-agent. If the factors show a high degree of independence between the franchisee and franchisor, then the franchisee will be deemed an independent contractor. The characterization of the relationship has tax implications and implications for the regulatory treatment of the business organization. In addition, if an agency relationship is found, the franchisor is liable for the franchisee's improper actions or injuries to third parties both in tort and in contract.

4. See Kuchta v. Allied Builders Corp., 21 Cal. App. 3d 541, 98 Cal. Rptr. 588 (1971).

QUESTIONS AND CASE PROBLEMS

1. Joseph and Gertrude Kuchta entered into a contract with Ralph Weiner under which Weiner was to build an outdoor patio and living area in the back yard of the Kuchta's home. The relationship between Weiner and his franchisor, Allied Builders, was such that Weiner performed all construction work and Allied controlled construction standards and approved the design and utility of all of Weiner's construction plans. Weiner drew up plans for the outdoor living area and submitted them to the Orange County Building and Safety Department. The plans were not approved since they violated certain zoning ordinances. Nevertheless, without informing the Kuchtas, Weiner proceeded with the construction. After the work was completed, the Kuchtas received a notice from the Orange County Building and Safety Department advising them that the roof and other

improvements violated the code and ordering their removal. The Kuchtas sought to recover both from Allied Builders and from Weiner. Since Weiner was insolvent, the Kuchtas' recovery depended upon their ability to sue Allied Builders. Can the Kuchtas sue Allied? Why or why not? [Kuchta v. Allied Builders Corp., 21 Cal. App. 3d 541, 98 Cal. Rptr. 588 (1971)]
2. Paul Rubenfeld and Mobil Oil Corporation signed a written agreement providing, among other things, that Rubenfeld had the right to use and occupy a service station owned by Mobil. Mobil required Rubenfeld to undergo a certain period of dealer training and granted him the right to use the Mobil trademark. In addition, Mobil had representatives visit Rubenfeld's service station to encourage the sale of Mobil's products, to inspect the station, and to make recommendations concerning the price at which Rubenfeld should sell his gasoline. Rubenfeld's rent and profits were both dependent upon the amount of gasoline he sold. Is the agreement between Rubenfeld and Mobil Oil Corporation one of lessor-lessee or franchisor-franchisee? [Mobil Oil Corp. v. Rubenfeld, 72 Misc. 2d 392, 339 N.Y.S. 2d. 623 (1972)]

3. Ger-Ro-Mar, Inc. was a manufacturer and distributor of lingerie and swimwear. Through its multi-level marketing program, Ger-Ro-Mar enlisted the services of men and women throughout the country to sell its products at wholesale and retail. Under the selling arrangement, franchisees were required to buy an inventory before they could participate in the program. A prospective franchisee could enter at any of three levels—key distributor, senior key, or supervisor. Entry at a particular level was based on the amount of inventory initially purchased by the franchisee. To induce individuals to become franchisees, Ger-Ro-Mar distributed various promotional materials that described the marketing system and illustrated how an individual could earn large sums of money by building a large personal group of salespeople through recruitment. The illustration in Ger-Ro-Mar's brochures promised that district managers could earn up to $56,000 and regional managers up to $90,000 yearly. Of the regional manager position, Ger-Ro-Mar's promotional brochure promised, "ANY ONE CAN ACHIEVE THIS LEVEL." An investigation by the FTC revealed that the success promised in the brochure was dependent upon the franchisee's recruitment of salespersons who in turn would recruit salespersons under them. Is there anything wrong with Ger-Ro-Mar's franchising scheme? Why might the FTC wish to order Ger-Ro-Mar to cease and desist distribution of its promotional brochure? [Ger-Ro-Mar, Inc. v. FTC, 518 F.2d. 33 (2nd Cir. 1975)]

4. In June 1963, Econo-Car granted Carl Taute a franchise to operate a rent-a-car business in Billings, Montana. Burko, an Econo-Car agent, told Taute at the time that as a result of a study for Burko, Econo-Car knew the three best locations for a rent-a-car business in Billings, that Burko would send three men to Billings to help Taute during his first few weeks, and that the entire franchise fee paid by Taute would be spent for three pages of newspaper advertisements during the grand opening. In August 1963, while the contract was still in its early stages of performance and very little time or money had been spent by either party, Taute learned that Burko's statements were false. Nevertheless, Taute continued with his preparations to go into business and, in fact, conducted business for about six months. Thereafter, Taute sued Econo-Car to rescind the franchise agreement, claiming that Econo-Car's agent fraudulently induced him into becoming a franchisee. Will Taute be successful in rescinding the franchise agreement? [Taute v. Econo-Car Int'l, Inc., 414 F.2d. 828 (9th Cir. 1969)]

5. Arthur Murray, Inc., was engaged in the business of licensing persons to operate dance studios using its registered trade name "Arthur Murray" along with the Arthur Murray method of dancing. A franchise agreement was entered into between Burkin, Inc., and Arthur Murray, Inc., granting Burkin a franchise to conduct a dance studio in San Diego, California. Under the franchise agreement, Burkin received the right to use the Arthur Murray name and method of dancing. Arthur Murray, Inc., had the right to control Burkin's employment practices, to fix the minimum tuition rates to be charged, to select the financial institution handling all pupil installment contracts, and to designate the location, layout, and decoration of Burkin's dance studio. Gertrude Nichols signed up for several dozen dancing lessons, all of which she paid for in advance. Shortly thereafter, Burkin became insolvent and closed its dance studio franchise. Can Nichols recover from Arthur Murray, Inc.? Would she be able to recover if none of the signs in Burkin's franchised studio and none of the contracts that she signed indicated that such a company as Arthur Murray, Inc., existed? [Nichols v. Arthur Murray, Inc., 248 Cal. App. 2d 610, 56 Cal. Rptr. 728 (1967)]

6. Terry Wilson owned a small stereo store in Eugene, Oregon. Charles Zimmerman was an agent for Soundarama Marketing Company. Zimmerman approached Wilson, offering to sell Wilson a Soundarama franchise under which Wilson would be allowed to sell Soundarama products and advertise its service. Wilson was unwilling to purchase a Soundarama franchise unless Soundarama's equipment was certified. Zimmerman assured Wilson that the equipment was certified by Underwriters Laboratory. It was unlawful to sell stereo equipment in Oregon unless it was certified. After purchasing the franchise from Zimmerman, Wilson learned that the Soundarama equipment was not certified by Underwriters Laboratory. Wilson informed Soundarama of his dissatisfaction and told them that if certification was not obtained within two weeks, he would rescind the franchise contract. Since Soundarama was a California corporation, it informed Wilson that it would be simpler for him to obtain certification and that it was his duty to have the equipment certified. When two weeks passed and Soundarama's equipment remained uncertified, Wilson brought suit to rescind the franchise agreement. Will he succeed? [Wilson v. Zimmerman, 261 Or. 528, 495 P.2d. 713 (1972)]

7. Geraldine Yarborough owned the Tastee Freeze Company. She entered into a contract with Roger

Harkey under which Harkey was granted a ten-year franchise to operate a Tastee Freeze in the city of Roswell, NewMexico. Harkey agreed to sell "on certain premises only the franchised products, or other such products as the franchise owner might approve." In addition, the franchise agreement provided that when Harkey ceased to sell the franchised products, the agreement would terminate. After three years, Harkey ceased selling Tastee Freeze products, removed all indication of the Tastee Freeze name and trademark, and began selling the product of a competitor. Can Yarborough stop Harkey from selling a competitor's product? (Hint: Consider what is the most commercially reasonable construction of the provisions of the franchise contract.) [Yarborough v. Harkey, 67 N.M. 204, 354 P.2d. 137 (1960)]

8. E.T. Runyan and Pacific Air Industries, Inc. entered into a written franchise agreement whereby, in consideration of Runyan's payment of $25,000, he was awarded an exclusive photogrammetric franchise for four southern California counties. Under the agreement, Pacific was obligated to train Runyan in the rudiments of photogrammetry, including twenty-five hours of sales and technical assistance for an initial period. In the meantime, Runyan resigned his position with Tidewater Oil Company. Since Runyan was entering a technical field in which he had no experience, he relied on Pacific's promise. Pacific's training program proved to be entirely inadequate. Runyan nevertheless attempted to oper-

ate his franchise, but when he realized that he was unable to do so, he attempted to rescind. Can Runyan rescind the franchise agreement? [Runyan v. Pacific Air Industries, Inc., 2 Cal. 3d 304, 85 Cal. Rptr. 138, 466 P.2d. 682 (1970)]

9. A franchise agreement entered into between Shakey's Incorporated, as franchisor, and Charles Martin, as franchisee, included the following provision: "Upon termination of this agreement, for a period of one year thereafter, the franchisee shall not engage in the production or sale of pizza products in a location within a radius of thirty miles from the franchised premises." After operating a Shakey's pizza franchise for several years, Martin ceased doing business as Shakey's, removed all indications of Shakey's trade name from the premises, and proceeded to do business as "Martin's Pizza Parlor." Has Martin violated his agreement not to compete? What protectable business interest does Shakey's have, if any? Is the agreement not to compete a reasonable one? [Shakey's Incorporated v. Martin, 91 Idaho 758, 430 P.2d. 504 (1967)]

10. Earl Lovelace was the owner of an H & R Block franchise. The franchise agreement between Lovelace and H & R Block included a covenant not to compete, which provided that "if Lovelace shall terminate or breach the franchise agreement, he shall not enter into competition directly or indirectly with H & R Block for a period of five years thereafter." Is this covenant reasonable? [H & R Block, Inc. v. Lovelace, 208 Kan. 538, 493 P.2d. 205 (1972)]

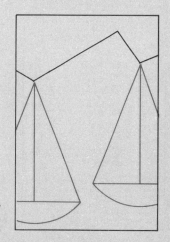

UNIT VIII

Government Regulation

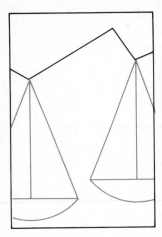

47

Government Regulation
Regulation and
Administrative Agencies

Regulation of private business activities was relatively minimal in the United States until the 1930s. The Great Depression was associated with many major changes in individuals' lives, one of which was the increased regulation of private activities. There was even talk about socializing all industrial activity. Regulation has always increased during major conflicts, such as World Wars I and II. However, in the last decade or so, business regulations have shifted from rules primarily evolved from the common law and from judicial interpretation of statutory regulations to more direct controls.

Furthermore, until recently, the functions and authority of many government agencies were primarily ministerial. Their actions were generally limited to carrying out specific activities mandated by legislatures. Thus, social security offices gave information and advice to individuals filing for benefits but possessed relatively few discretionary powers. Starting in the late 1960s, an increasing number of new rules and regulations were established along with new federal regulatory agencies. Probably, the current constraints placed on business transactions by regulatory authorities have more impact on the economy than those that stem from the common law and the courts. For example, seven new regulatory agencies, including the Occupational Safety and Health Administration (OSHA), the Consumer Product Safety Commission (CPSC), and the Environmental Protection Agency (EPA), were created in the early 1970s. The first four years of the 1970s saw a doubling of the number of pages in the Federal Register, the primary document for notification of federal rules and regulations.

INCREASING REGULATIONS

The scope of regulation has also expanded, going beyond the traditional judicial regulation of commerce, employment, transportation, health, and financial markets. For example, the Clean Air Act amendments of 1970 provide for setting air quality standards,[1] and the Consumer Product Safety Commission Act of 1972 establishes a commission with the power to set safety standards for consumer products and ban products with undue risk of injury.[2] The early 1970s also saw extensive controls over petroleum manufacturers emerge with the Emergency Petroleum Allocation Act of 1973.

Existing agencies have also expanded their activities. For example, Exhibit 47-1 shows that, by fiscal year (FY) 1979, the administrative costs of forty-one regulatory agencies are expected to be more than double what they were in FY 1974. In FY 1974, these agencies' costs were $2.2

billion. They are estimated to be $4.8 billion in FY 1979. Administrative costs, however, are very much smaller than the costs of compliance by business. In 1976, for example, the estimated total cost to business of federal regulation was approximately $65.5 billion; administrative costs represented only $3.2 billion, less than 5 percent of the total costs.

An important distinction between regulation created formally by government agencies and regulation that is established informally through the judicial system arises in the creation, promulgation, and enforcement of regulations. Administrative agencies possess a mixture of legislative and judicial authority as well as executive powers. In addition, procedural differences combined with the broader discretionary authority given to government agencies yield regulations that often differ significantly from those developed in the legislative and judicial process.[3] This chapter will investigate the general scope of regulatory actions and the activities that are subject to their control. In addition, it will emphasize regulatory powers and procedures and review the regulation process.

---

1. 42 USCA Sec. 7401 (1977)
2. 15 USCA Sec. 2051 et seq.

3. Murray Weidenbaum, "On Estimating Regulatory Costs," *Regulation* (May/June 1978): 14–17.

EXHIBIT 47-1 ADMINISTRATIVE COSTS OF FORTY-ONE FEDERAL REGULATORY AGENCIES (FISCAL YEARS, DOLLARS IN MILLIONS)

Year	1974	1975	1976	1977	1978 (revised)	1979 (proposed)	Increase 1974-79
Consumer Safety and Health	$1,302	$1,463	$1,613	$1,985	$2,582	$2,671	105%
Job Safety and other Working Conditions	310	379	446	· 492	562	626	102%
Energy and Environment	347	527	682	870	989	1,116	222%
Industry-Specific	245	269	270	309	340	341	39%
Financial Reporting, etc.	36	45	53	58	70	69	92%
Total	2,240	2,683	3,064	3,714	4,543	4,823	115%

Source: Murray Weidenbaum, "On Estimating Regulatory Costs," *Regulation* (May/June 1978): 15. Copyright 1978 American Enterprise Institute for Public Policy Research. Reprinted with permission.

ADMINISTRATIVE AGENCIES

Administrative agencies are the primary interpreters and enforcers of many legislative statutes that focus on business regulation. Sometimes, these agencies are part of a traditional administrative branch of the government. For example, the Justice Department enforces the Sherman Act, the Clayton Act, and other antitrust laws. The National Highway Traffic Safety Administration and the Department of Transportation enforce regulations regarding safety, emissions, controls, and fuel economy of automobiles. In other cases, Congress has established administrative agencies that are independent of the executive branch. For example, the Interstate Commerce Commission regulates most service transportation within the United States as well as the service transportation of foreign countries that takes place within the boundaries of the United States. Other independent agencies include the Federal Aviation Administration, the Civil Aeronautics Board, the Commodity Futures Trading Commission, the Equal Employment Opportunity Commission, the Export-Import Bank of the United States, the Federal Communications Commission, the Federal Energy Administration, the Federal Home Loan Bank Board, the Federal Maritime Commission, the Federal Power Commission, the Federal Trade Commission, the International Trade Commission, the National Labor Relations Board, the Securities and Exchange Commission, and the Small Business Administration.

REGULATORY POWERS AND PROCEDURES

Administrative agencies combine the duties and responsibilities of the judicial, executive, and legislative branches of the government. Heads of administrative agencies are generally appointed by the president with the consent of two-thirds of the Congress. Because Congress has delegated certain powers to agencies, they are able to combine the legislative and judicial powers that are traditionally separated under the Constitution. Thus, agencies are able to promulgate rules, and they have policing powers to insure compliance. They are also able to render judgments and impose penalties or remedies as prescribed by law if violations have occurred. Administrative decisions can be appealed to the courts, but since the subject matter is generally very specialized or technical in nature (and the agency has been given broad discretionary powers initially), the courts will not generally reverse agency actions unless they are arbitrary and capricious, or they are not supported by the record or not in accordance with legal precedent (or the law).

It is the province and duty of the judiciary to interpret the law, and it is the province of Congress to formulate legislative policy, to mandate programs and projects, and to establish their relative priority for the nation. Once Congress has exercised its legislative power and decided the order of priorities in a given area, the executive branch administers the law, and the courts (the judiciary) interpret and enforce it when enforcement is sought.

At times, Congress provides funds and authorizes programs for purposes that conflict with one another. In the following case, a conflict arose between the completion and operation of a federal dam project by the Tennessee Valley Authority and the explicit provision of the Endangered Species Act of 1973 that prohibited the operation of that dam because it would destroy the only known population of the snail darter, an endangered species. In such a case, the judiciary is called upon not to question the legislative policies, programs, and projects of Congress but to determine what the law is and to enforce it as necessary.

TENNESSEE VALLEY AUTHORITY v. HILL

Supreme Court of the United States, 1978. 437 U.S. 153, 98 S. Ct. 2297.

BACKGROUND AND FACTS *Environmental groups and others brought this action under the Endangered Species Act of 1973 to enjoin the Tennessee Valley Authority from completing a dam and impounding a section of land on the Little Tennessee River. The dam was virtually* *completed when the injunction was sought, and Congress continued to appropriate large sums of public money for the project even after congressional appropriations committees were advised of the project's apparent impact upon the survival of the snail darter, an endangered species.*

BURGER, Chief Justice.

We begin with the premise that operation of the Tellico Dam will either eradicate the known population of snail darters or destroy their critical habitat. Petitioner does not now seriously dispute this fact. In any event, the Secretary of the Interior is vested with exclusive authority to determine whether a species such as the snail darter is "endangered" or "threatened" and to ascertain the factors which have led to such a precarious existence. By § 4(d) Congress has authorized—indeed commanded—the Secretary to "issue such regulations as he deems necessary and advisable to provide for the conservation of such species." As we have seen, the Secretary promulgated regulations which declared the snail darter an endangered species whose critical habitat would be destroyed by creation of the Tellico Reservoir. Doubtless petitioner would prefer not to have these regulations on the books, but there is no suggestion that the Secretary exceeded his authority or abused his discretion in issuing the regulations. Indeed, no judicial review of the Secretary's determinations has ever been sought and hence the validity of his actions are not open to review in this Court.

Starting from the above premise, two questions are presented: (a) would TVA be in violation of the Act if it completed and operated the Tellico Dam as planned?; (b) if TVA's actions would offend the Act, is an injunction the appropriate remedy for the violation? For the reasons stated hereinafter, we hold that both questions must be answered in the affirmative.

It may seem curious to some that the survival of a relatively small number of three-inch fish among all the countless millions of species extant would require the permanent halting of a virtually completed dam for which Congress has expended more than $100 million. The paradox is not minimized by the fact that Congress continued to appropriate large sums of public money for the project, even after congressional appropriations committees were apprised of its apparent impact upon the survival of the snail darter. We conclude, however, that the explicit provisions of the Endangered Species Act require precisely that result.

One would be hard pressed to find a statutory provision whose terms were any plainer than those in § 7 of the Endangered Species Act. Its very words affirmatively command all federal agencies "to *insure* that actions *authorized, funded,* or *carried out* by them do not *jeopardize* the continued existence" of an endangered species or "*result* in the destruction or modification of habitat of such species * * *." (Emphasis added.) This language admits of no exception. Nonetheless, petitioner urges, as do the dissenters, that the Act cannot reasonably be interpreted as applying to a federal project which was well under way when Congress passed the Endangered Species Act of 1973. To sustain that position, however, we would be forced to ignore the ordinary meaning of plain language. It has not been shown, for example, how TVA can close the gates of the Tellico Dam without "carrying out" an action that has been "authorized" and "funded" by a federal agency. Nor can we understand how such action will *"insure"* that the snail darter's habitat is not disrupted. Accepting the Secretary's determinations, as we must, it is clear that TVA's proposed operation of the dam will have precisely the opposite effect, namely the *eradication* of an endangered species.

Concededly, this view of the Act will produce results requiring the sacrifice of the anticipated benefits of the project and of many millions of dollars in public funds. But examination of the language, history and structure of the legislation under review here indicates beyond doubt that Congress intended endangered species to be afforded the highest of priorities.

* * *

As it was finally passed, the Endangered Species Act of 1973 represented the most comprehensive legislation for the preservation of endangered species ever enacted by any nation.

* * *

It is against this legislative background that we must measure TVA's claim that the Act was not intended to stop operation of a project which, like Tellico Dam, was near completion when an endangered species was discovered in its path.

* * *

The plain intent of Congress in enacting this statute was to halt and reverse the trend toward species extinction, whatever the cost. This is reflected not only in the stated policies of the Act, but in literally every section of the statute. All persons, including federal agencies, are specifically instructed not to "take" endangered species, meaning that no one is "to harass, harm, pursue, hunt, shoot, wound, kill, trap, capture, or collect" such life forms. Agencies in particular are directed by the Act to "use *all methods* and procedures which are necessary" to preserve endangered species. (Emphasis added.) In addition, the legislative history undergirding § 7 reveals an explicit congressional decision to require agencies to afford first priority to the declared national policy of saving endangered species. The pointed omission of the type of qualifying language previously included in endangered species legislation reveals a conscious decision by Congress to give endangered species priority over the "primary missions" of federal agencies.

* * *

Our system of government is, after all, a tripartite one, with each Branch having certain defined functions delegated to it by the Constitution. While "[it] is emphatically the province and duty of the judicial department to say what the law is," *Marbury v. Madison* (1803), it is equally—and emphatically—the exclusive province of the Congress not only to formulate legislative policies, mandate programs and projects, but also to establish their relative priority for the Nation. Once Congress, exercising its delegated powers has decided the order of priorities in a given area, it is for the Executive to administer the laws and for the courts to enforce them when enforcement is sought.

* * *

But is that our function? We have no expert knowledge on the subject of endangered species, much less do we have a mandate from the people to strike a balance of equities on the side of the Tellico Dam. Congress has spoken in the plainest of words, making it abundantly clear that the balance has been struck in favor of affording endangered species the highest of priorities, thereby adopting a policy which it described as "institutionalized caution."

Our individual appraisal of the wisdom or unwisdom of a particular course consciously selected by the Congress is to be put aside in the process of interpreting a statute. Once the meaning of an enactment is discerned and its constitutionality determined, the judicial process comes to an end. We do not sit as a committee of review, nor are we vested with the power of veto. The lines ascribed to Sir Thomas More by Robert Bolt are not without relevance here:

> "The law, Roper, the law. I know what's legal, not what's right. And I'll stick to what's legal . . .. I'm *not* God. The currents and eddies of right and wrong, which you find such plain-sailing, I can't navigate, I'm no voyager. But in the thickets of the law, oh there I'm a forester. . . . What would you do? Cut a great road through the law to get after the Devil? . . . And when the last law was down, and the Devil turned round on you—where would you hide, Roper, the laws all being flat? This country's planted thick with laws from coast to coast—Man's laws, not God's—and if you cut them down . . . d'you really think you could stand upright in the winds that would blow then? Yes, I'd give the Devil benefit of law, for my own safety's sake." Bolt, A Man for All Seasons, Act I, at 147 (Heinemann ed. 1967).

We agree with the Court of Appeals that in our constitutional system the commitment to the separation of powers is too fundamental for us to pre-empt congressional action by jucidially decreeing what accords with "commonsense and the public weal." Our Constitution vests such responsibilities in the political Branches.

The Supreme Court held that the Endangered Species Act of 1973 prohibited the completion of the dam. The snail darter, as an endangered species, was protected from possible extinction even though the dam was virtually completed and large sums of public money had been appropriated for the project.

JUDGMENT AND REMEDY

Ministerial Powers

The legislative powers of administrators have grown considerably over time. Initially, their actions were more ministerial than legislative and were often explicitly specified by statute. Thus, administrators had the power to issue or renew licenses. Sometimes statutes required an administrator to accept or reject a commodity based on a congressionally established standard. Over the years, as society has become more complex, Congress has authorized administrators to formulate rules and guidelines under general authority granted to administrative agencies. Thus the safety and health administrator is authorized to make rules that protect the safety and health of individuals in certain circumstances, such as places of employment. The discretion given administrators effectively transmits legislative power to them. For example, they have been given the power to prohibit unfair methods of competition, to grant licenses "as public interest, convenience, or necessity requires," and to prevent or promote other generally specified goals.

Investigatory Powers

A number of administrative agencies generally have the power to investigate the records, practices, or premises of business organizations. For example, OSHA inspectors can obtain a warrant and enter a place of employment to determine if a violation of safety or health has occurred. In addition, Section 6B of the Federal Trade Commission Act grants the FTC broad investigatory powers to require the inspection of records, the completion of questionnaires, or other assistance to the commission in supplying information prior to a specific rule, complaint, or adjudicative action. Witnesses can also be subpoenaed and examined under oath by the agency.

Complaints

Complaints (or charges) can be initiated by private parties, including individuals and corporations, or by employees of the administrative agency. After a complaint is served on an alleged wrongdoer, the party is given an opportunity to answer. Eventually, the complaint is heard by an administrator appointed by the agency. The administrator makes a final decision and enters an order directing the party to cease (or engage) in certain acts if the party has engaged in misconduct as defined by the agency. Otherwise, the complaint is dismissed. Compliance with the order is usually enforced by a separate division of the administrative agency, and failure to comply can result in fines and other penalties. After the final hearing, the affected party can appeal to the courts. In some cases, the party can engage in an informal settlement process or agree to a **consent decree**—an agreement by the parties that carries the sanction of the court.

Rule-making Powers

General rule-making powers have been established by statute for a number of administrative agencies. Rule making often derives from evidence or facts obtained from investigatory activities. The process formally begins with notification, which can be in the form of a complaint to the party specifying the alleged misconduct. Usually the recipient of the com-

plaint is given an opportunity to file an answer. In the case of general rules, notification is made through public announcement (in the Federal Register if the rule is promulgated by one of the federal administrative agencies). The second stage of rule making involves a hearing. Then the administrator makes a decision and, in the case of an individual complaint, either enters an order or dismisses it. In some cases, the administrator has a right to alter actions prior to the hearing, provided certain conditions are met. At any time, of course, there can be an informal settlement with a stipulation, consent decree, or other agreement.

Compliance and Enforcement Powers

All final orders carry the weight of statutory law with prescribed penalties for violations unless invalidated by the courts, and failure to comply is treated like any other violation of the law. In most cases, violations are considered civil matters so that money damages must be paid or specific actions taken (such as the installation of pollution control equipment). In recent years, however, there has been a trend toward including criminal penalties as well. Thus, violators, including corporate officers, can be subject to jail sentences. For example, the Energy Policy and Conservation Act of 1976 makes the failure of any manufacturer to comply with any average fuel economy standard unlawful conduct.

Adjudicative Powers

Most final actions and orders of administrative agencies can be appealed to the courts. Judicial review is often provided to interpret the enabling statute or the validity of administrative agency procedures. The review, however, is generally limited and does not require a fullfledged rehearing to establish the validity of the facts. As noted earlier, unless the decision is a definite abuse, an arbitrary or capricious use of discretionary powers, or a question of law, review will often be denied. This has given administrators tremendous discretionary powers.

In the case of general rules, the administrative hearing can involve extensive presentations of evidence by employees of the administrative agency, by parties who are directly affected, and by the general public.[4] Economic evidence bearing on the potential consequences of the rule can be presented, and testimony can be given about the costs and benefits of the rule. For example, evidence on the prices of eyeglasses in localities with and without restrictions on price advertising was examined in the FTC hearings on ophthalmic goods.

In the case of a complaint, the agency enters, files an order, or dismisses the action. Agreement usually specifies the action that must be taken or stopped as well as penalties for not carrying out the provisions of the order. For general rules, the agency often modifies its initial policies to incorporate information ob-

tained in the hearing. In individual complaints and general rule making, public record of the agreement or issued rule is necessary.

In some cases, rule making can preempt state law. In 1978, the FTC adopted the final rule on the advertising of ophthalmic goods and services. This rule states that it is an unfair practice for states to enforce restrictions against advertising unless the ads are deceptive.

A reviewing agency or court is generally bound by the findings of fact reached during the initial administrative hearing. In general, the courts have ruled that administrators are presumed to have based their final orders on reasonable grounds, and the courts will not attempt to second guess the agency on questions with which the agency is more familiar.[5] The courts will not infer a basis other than that articulated and will not enforce an order on any ground not stated.

---

4. The trend in recent years has been to provide funds to the general public for participation at administrative hearings involving rule making.

5. Kesler and Sons Constr. Co. v. Utah State Div. of Health, 30 Utah 2d 90, 513 P.2d 1017 (1973).

BACKGROUND AND FACTS *The Federal Trade Commission issued a cease and desist order to Moog Industries, Inc., to stop illegal price discrimination. Moog argued that the order should not go into effect until its competitors, who were using the same practices, were also ordered to stop. Otherwise, the firm would have to go out of business. Moog appealed after the commission rejected this argument.*

MOOG INDUSTRIES INC. v. FEDERAL TRADE COMM.
Supreme Court of the United States, 1958.
355 U.S. 411, 78 S.Ct. 377.

Per Curian.
* * *

In view of the scope of administrative discretion that Congress has given the Federal Trade Commission, it is ordinarily not for courts to modify ancillary features of a valid Commission order. This is but recognition of the fact that in the shaping of its remedies within the framework of regulatory legislation, an agency is called upon to exercise its specialized, experienced judgment. Thus, the decision as to whether or not an order against one firm to cease and desist from engaging in illegal price discrimination should go into effect before others are similarly prohibited depends on a variety of factors peculiarly within the expert understanding of the Commission. Only the Commission, for example, is competent to make an initial determination as to whether and to what extent there is a relevant "industry" within which the particular respondent competes and whether or not the nature of that competition is such as to indicate identical treatment of the entire industry by an enforcement agency. Moreover, although an allegedly illegal practice may appear to be operative throughout an industry, whether such appearances reflect fact and whether all firms in the industry should be dealt with in a single proceeding or should receive individualized treatment are questions that call for discretionary determination by the administrative agency. It is clearly within the special competence of the Commission to appraise the adverse effect on competition that might result from postponing a particular order prohibiting continued violations of the law. Furthermore, the Commission alone is empowered to develop that enforcement policy best calculated to achieve the ends contemplated by Congress and to allocate its available funds and personnel in such a way as to execute its policy efficiently and economically.

The question, then, of whether orders such as those before us should be held in abeyance until the respondents' competitors are proceeded against is for the Commission to decide. If the question has not been raised before the Commission, as was the situation in No. 77, a reviewing court should not in any event entertain it. If the Commission has decided the question, its discretionary determination should not be overturned in the absence of a patent abuse of discretion. Accordingly, the judgment is affirmed. * * *

JUDGMENT AND REMEDY   *The agency judgment was affirmed. Moog Industries was ordered to stop its illegal price discrimination practices immediately, notwithstanding what its competitors were doing.*

OVERLAPPING REGULATION

Regulations originate in a large number of independent authorities that have overlapping jurisdiction, making the precise rule difficult, if not impossible, to interpret. Exhibit 47-2 shows more than a dozen agencies that have jurisdiction regarding the use of energy. In each case, some of the more important activities are listed along with their estimated expenditures in fiscal year 1979. The interstate transportation of petroleum is governed by regulations of the Department of Energy, the Department of the Interior, the Interstate Commerce Commission, and several other agencies, including the Internal Revenue Service.

TYPES OF REGULATION

Profit Regulation

One of the most important forms of regulation concerns the direct or indirect control of profits. Traditionally, profits have generally been unregulated. Not until the middle of the nineteenth century was the traditional **laissez-faire** doctrine challenged. Today, in addition to federal, state, and local taxation, the most important profit regulations arise where the government has granted exclusive rights to produce a commodity. Most electric and water public utilities fall into this category. In such situations, the regulatory form usually chosen is **rate making**. Rather than regulate profits directly, regulatory commissions or their equivalent set a rate of return on capital.

Price Regulation

A closely related form of regulation involves control of the actual prices that sellers can charge. Price regulation can take the form of a maximum, minimum, or uniform price. New York City, for example, establishes the maximum price that certain apartment owners can charge their tenants. The interstate movement of natural gas is also subject to a maximum price based on geographic location. Minimum prices

EXHIBIT 47-2 AGENCIES HAVING JURISDICTION OVER THE USE OF ENERGY

AGENCY	FUNCTION	ESTIMATED FY 1980 EXPENDITURES (MILLIONS OF DOLLARS)
Department of Energy	Energy information, regulation, and policy.	$1,003.0
Federal Energy Regulatory Commission	Oil, gas, hydro, and multiresource regulation.	73.9
Department of the Interior	Energy and minerals management, including leasing of offshore oil and gas and public land leasing for oil, gas, and coal fields.	92.1
Interstate Commerce Commission	Compliance, enforcement, and tariff examination. Includes regulation of oil and coal, slurry pipeline rates, and routes.	33.8
Environmental Protection Agency	Pollution abatement and control programs and their enforcement. Includes standards for vehicle and smokestack emissions.	814.0
Department of Transportation	Grants to state agencies to help fund gas pipeline safety programs.	2.8
Nuclear Regulatory Commission	Licensing of nuclear energy plants and control of nuclear fuel export.	57.0
Department of Commerce	Control of tanker construction and safety and establishment of marine sanctuaries.	112.5[a]
U.S. Coast Guard (Department of Transportation)	Inspection and monitoring of tankers and liquid natural gas carriers.	20.5[a]
National Highway Traffic Safety Administration (Department of Transportation)	Automotive fuel economy and consumer information.	12.5
Occupational Safety and Health Administration (Department of Labor)	Promulgation and enforcement of safety and health standards (includes energy related substances).	122.1
Consumer Product Safety Commission	Control of home structural products, including home insulation.	7.8
Federal Trade Commission	Litigation involving the energy industry.	—[b]
Department of Justice	Antitrust regulation.	43.6
Internal Revenue Service (Department of the Treasury)	Tax regulations affecting energy users and producers.	—[b]
Federal Trade Commission	Relief from import injury, including tariffs and quotas on energy imports.	—[b]

[a]FY 1979.
[b]Not available.
Source: Computed from Executive Office of the President, *Budget of the U.S. Government, Fiscal Year 1979 and 1980* (Washington D.C.: Government Printing Office, 1979), appendix.

are often established as floors for certain agricultural products, such as wheat. Price regulations can have substantial effects on the number of units sold, the quality of goods or associated services, and other terms of business transactions. For example, producers who find that the profit rates on price-controlled products are too low may decide to no longer produce the products. They will sell their existing supplies and cut out that particular line of production from their businesses. Sometimes, all prices (including those paid to workers) are controlled by national laws. In the early 1970s, for example, all wages and prices were controlled by the federal government.

Advertising

Restrictions on professional advertising have survived many constitutional challenges in the past, but they appear to be weakening today. The Supreme Court has held that commercial speech is entitled to certain protections under the First Amendment. A familiar phrase for all consumers is "truth in advertising." But beyond government concern for disclosure of information, consumers have a right to information that is helpful, and in many ways indispensable, to the formation of an intelligent decision on important private matters.

The public's right to become informed about the availability of legal services has been of particular concern in recent years. Each state individually controls its legal profession, defining professional and unprofessional conduct. The latter subjects attorneys to monetary penalties or the suspension or revocation of their licenses. For years, state statutes have effectively prevented advertising by members of the legal profession. In addition, the American Bar Association's code of professional responsibility prohibits advertising on ethical grounds. Advertising was always felt to have an adverse effect on professionalism because it suggests that a lawyer might be motivated merely by profit rather than by commitment to a client's welfare.

In the 1970s, the restraint upon attorney advertising was challenged on constitutional grounds as a violation of First Amendment rights and on the ground that it limited competition in violation of the Sherman Antitrust Act. The Supreme Court ultimately ruled that restraints on attorney advertising did not tend to limit competition. However, in a landmark decision, the Court held that price advertising of legal services was permissible within certain limitations, under the protection of the First Amendment.

BATES v. STATE BAR OF ARIZONA
Supreme Court of the United States, 1977.
433 U.S. 350, 97 S.Ct. 2691.

BACKGROUND AND FACTS *The appellants were licensed attorneys and members of the Arizona State Bar. They were charged by the state bar association with violating a professional disciplinary rule that prohibited attorneys from advertising in newspapers or other media. The attorneys had placed a newspaper advertisement for their "legal clinic," stating that they were offering "legal services at very reasonable fees." They listed their fees for certain services—in particular, uncontested divorces, uncontested adoptions, simple personal bankruptcies, and changes of name.*

At the trial, the Arizona State Supreme Court upheld the State Bar Committee's conclusion that these attorneys had violated the professional disciplinary rule.

BLACKMUN, Justice.
* * *

As part of its regulation of the Arizona Bar, the Supreme Court of that State has imposed and enforces a disciplinary rule that restricts advertising by attorneys.
* * *

In March 1974, appellants left the Society and opened a law office, which they call a "legal clinic," in Phoenix. Their aim was to provide legal services at modest fees to persons of moderate income who did not qualify for governmental legal aid. In order to achieve this end, they would accept only routine matters, such as uncontested divorces, uncontested adoptions, simple personal bankruptcies, and changes of name, for which costs could be kept down by extensive use of paralegals, automatic typewriting equipment, and standardized forms and office procedures. More complicated cases, such as contested divorces, would not be accepted. Because appellants set their prices so as to have a relatively low return on each case they handled, they depended on substantial volume.

After conducting their practice in this manner for two years, appellants concluded that their practice and clinical concept could not survive unless the availability of legal services at low cost was advertised and, in particular, fees were advertised. Consequently, in order to generate the necessary flow of business, that is, "to attract clients," appellants on February 22, 1976, placed an advertisement (reproduced in the margin) in the Arizona Republic, a daily newspaper of general circulation in the Phoenix metropolitan area. As may be seen, the advertisement stated that appellants were offering "legal services at very reasonable fees," and listed their fees for certain services.

[The appellants conceded that the advertisement constituted a clear violation of the disciplinary rules that regulated the conduct of all professional attorneys in the state.]

The disciplinary rule provides in part:

"(B) A lawyer shall not publicize himself, or his partner, or associate, or any other lawyer affiliated with him or his firm, as a lawyer through newspaper or magazine advertisements, radio or television announcements, display advertisements in the city or telephone directories or other means of commercial publicity, nor shall he authorize or permit others to do so in his behalf."

* * *

Numerous justifications are proffered for the restriction of such price advertising. We consider each in turn:

1. *The Adverse Effect on Professionalism.* Appellee places particular emphasis on the adverse effects that it feels price advertising will have on the legal profession. The key to professionalism, it is argued, is the sense of pride that involvement in the discipline generates. It is claimed that price advertising will bring about commercialization, which will undermine the attorney's sense of dignity and self-worth. The hustle of the marketplace will adversely affect the profession's service orientation, and irreparably damage the delicate balance between the lawyer's need to earn and his obligation selflessly to serve. Advertising is also said to erode the client's trust in his attorney: Once the client perceives that the lawyer is motivated by profit, his confidence that the attorney is acting out of a commitment to the client's welfare is jeopardized. And advertising is said to tarnish the dignified public image of the profession. At its core, the argument presumes that attorneys must conceal from themselves and from their clients the real-life fact that lawyers earn their livelihood at the bar. We suspect that few attorneys engage in such self-deception.

* * *

Moreover, the assertion that advertising will diminish the attorney's reputation in the community is open to question. Bankers and engineers advertise, and yet these professions are not regarded as undignified. In fact, it has been suggested that the failure of lawyers to advertise creates public disillusionment with the profession. The absence of advertising may be seen to reflect the profession's failure to reach out and serve the community: Studies reveal that many persons do not obtain counsel even when they perceive a need because of the feared price of services or because of an inability to locate a competent attorney. Indeed, cynicism with regard to the profession may be created by the fact that it long has publicly eschewed advertising, while condoning the actions of the attorney who structures his social or civic associations so as to provide contacts with potential clients. Since the belief that lawyers are somehow "above" trade has become an anachronism, the historical foundation for the advertising restraint has crumbled.

2. *The Inherently Misleading Nature of Attorney Advertising.* It is argued that advertising of legal services inevitably will be misleading (a) because such services are so individualized with regard to content and quality as to prevent informed comparison on the basis of an advertisement, (b) because the consumer of legal services is unable to determine in advance just what services he needs, and (c) because advertising by attorneys will highlight irrelevant factors and fail to show the relevant factor of skill.

We are not persuaded that restrained professional advertising by lawyers inevitably will be misleading. Although many services performed by attorneys are indeed unique, it is doubtful that any attorney would or could advertise fixed prices for services of that type. The only services that lend themselves to advertising are the routine ones: the uncontested divorce, the simple adoption, the uncontested personal bankruptcy, the change of name, and the like—the very services advertised by appellants. Although the precise service demanded in each task may vary slightly, and although legal services are not fungible, these facts do not make advertising misleading so long as the attorney does the necessary work at the advertised price. We thus find of little force the assertion that advertising is misleading because of an inherent lack of standardization in legal services.

The second component of the argument—that advertising ignores the diagnostic role—fares little better. It is unlikely that many people go to an attorney merely to ascertain if they have a clean bill of legal health. Rather, attorneys are likely to be employed to perform specific tasks. Although the client may not know the detail involved in performing the task, he no doubt is able to identify the service he desires at the level of generality to which advertising lends itself.

The third component is not without merit: Advertising does not provide a complete foundation on which to select an attorney. The alternative—the prohibition of advertising—serves only to restrict the information that flows to consumers. Moreover, the argument assumes that the public is not sophisticated enough to realize the limitations of advertising, and that the public is better kept in ignorance than trusted with correct but incomplete information. We suspect the argument rests on an underestimation of the public. In any event, we view as dubious any justification that is based on the benefits of public ignorance.

3. *The Adverse Effect on the Administration of Justice.* Advertising is said to have the undesirable effect of stirring up litigation. * * * Advertising, it is

argued, serves to encourage the assertion of legal rights in the courts, thereby undesirably unsettling societal repose. There is even a suggestion of barratry.

But advertising by attorneys is not an unmitigated source of harm to the administration of justice. * * * As the bar acknowledges, "the middle 70% of our population is not being reached or served adequately by the legal profession." ABA, Revised Handbook on Prepaid Legal Services 2 (1972). Among the reasons for this underutilization is fear of the cost, and an inability to locate a suitable lawyer. Advertising can help to solve this acknowledged problem: Advertising is the traditional mechanism in a free-market economy for a supplier to inform a potential purchaser of the availability and terms of exchange.

4. *The Undesirable Economic Effects of Advertising.* It is claimed that advertising will increase the overhead costs of the profession, and that these costs then will be passed along to consumers in the form of increased fees. Moreover, it is claimed that the additional cost of practice will create a substantial entry barrier, deterring or preventing young attorneys from penetrating the market and entrenching the position of the bar's established members.

These two arguments seem dubious at best. Although it is true that the effect of advertising on the price of services has not been demonstrated, there is revealing evidence with regard to products; where consumers have the benefit of price advertising, retail prices often are dramatically lower than they would be without advertising. It is entirely possible that advertising will serve to reduce, not advance, the cost of legal services to the consumer.

The entry-barrier argument is equally unpersuasive. In the absence of advertising, an attorney must rely on his contacts with the community to generate a flow of business. In view of the time necessary to develop such contacts, the ban in fact serves to perpetuate the market position of established attorneys. Consideration of entry-barrier problems would urge that advertising be allowed so as to aid the new competitor in penetrating the market.

5. *The Adverse Effect of Advertising on the Quality of Service.* It is argued that the attorney may advertise a given "package" of service at a set price, and will be inclined to provide, by indiscriminate use, the standard package regardless of whether it fits the client's needs.

Restraints on advertising, however, are an ineffective way of deterring shoddy work. An attorney who is inclined to cut quality will do so regardless of the rule on advertising.

6. *The Difficulties of Enforcement.* Finally, it is argued that the wholesale restriction is justified by the problems of enforcement if any other course is taken. Because the public lacks sophistication in legal matters, it may be particularly susceptible to misleading or deceptive advertising by lawyers. After-the-fact action by the consumer lured by such advertising may not provide a realistic restraint because of the inability of the layman to assess whether the service he has received meets professional standards. Thus, the vigilance of a regulatory agency will be required. But because of the numerous purveyors of services, the overseeing of advertising will be burdensome.

It is at least somewhat incongruous for the opponents of advertising to extol the virtues and altruism of the legal profession at one point, and, at another, to assert that its members will seize the opportunity to mislead and distort. We suspect that, with advertising, most lawyers will behave as they always have: They will abide by their solemn oaths to uphold the integrity and honor of their profession and of the legal system. For every attorney who overreaches through advertising, there will be thousands of others who will be candid and honest and straightforward. And, of course, it will be in the latter's interest, as in other cases of misconduct at the bar, to assist in weeding out those few who abuse their trust.

In sum, we are not persuaded that any of the proffered justifications rise to the level of an acceptable reason for the suppression of all advertising by attorneys.

In holding that advertising by attorneys may not be subjected to blanket suppression, and that the advertisement at issue is protected, we, of course, do not hold that advertising by attorneys may not be regulated in any way. We mention some of the clearly permissible limitations on advertising not foreclosed by our holding.

Advertising that is false, deceptive, or misleading of course is subject to restraint.

JUDGMENT AND REMEDY *The United States Supreme Court upheld a First Amendment protection applied to professional advertisements by attorneys, although the Court recognized that such advertisements were subject to certain limitations. Hence, the State of Arizona and every other state in the United States had a constitutional obligation to permit reasonable professional advertisements by attorneys in newspapers.*

Quotas and Duties

Another form of regulation is the establishment of quotas or duties on specific levels of production, imports, or sales. Petroleum companies, for example, are limited in the amount of petroleum products that they can bring into the country. In other cases, explicit import duties or taxes are applied to various products. Unlike price regulation, quotas establish a fixed level of output for sales, so their effects are often more stringent than those associated with duties and other price regulation. Both quotas and duties are often established to protect domestic industries from competition.

Licensing and Allocating Rights

Through their exercise of licensing power, agencies control entry into given economic activities. Thus, no rail, motor, or water carrier can extend its routes without a license from the Interstate Commerce Commission. The Federal Power Commission has similar authority over utilities, the Federal Communications Commis-

sion over radio and television broadcasters, and the Securities and Exchange Commission over the investment business. In recent years, there has been a trend toward deregulation, which limits the licensing power of agencies. For example, the Civil Aeronautics Board no longer has the power to license routes.

Standard Setting

Another form of regulation involves standard setting. The U.S. Department of Agriculture establishes a large number of standards for food products. It grades beef and issues standards for other meat and poultry products, for example. Such grading helps consumers in evaluating alternative selections of beef, although sometimes the labeling standards are difficult to understand. For example, food products that are labeled "beef with gravy" must contain at least 50 percent cooked beef, but if the ingredients are reversed so that the label reads "gravy with beef," only 35 percent of the contents must be beef.

Disclosure Requirements

In recent years, regulatory authorities have instituted a number of measures that require sellers to disclose certain information prior to the completion of a sale. In some cases, disclosures must be made in alternative forms. For example, if Martin Pontiac advertises on local television that a 1980 Pontiac can be paid for over the next thirty-six months, the down payment, the amount of monthly payment, and the annual percentage rate of interest must also be specified in the ad. Another disclosure requirement that was recently proposed concerns sales by used car dealers. If enacted, the regulations would require the disclosure of the nature and type of repairs performed on all used cars prior to resale.

Contract Revisions

Sometimes, regulatory agencies promulgate rules that limit the ability of parties to write contracts. For example, in recent years there have been movements to limit the remedies available to creditors for defaults on consumer loans. In some states, creditors are unable to attach wages or put liens on particular forms of property. Employers subject to the Wage and Hour Act cannot hire employees who agree to work for less than the minimum wage.

Materials and Process Regulations

Regulatory agencies can also specify the type of material that can be used in the manufacture of certain goods. The Food and Drug Administration (FDA), for example, has prohibited the use of red dye #2 in food and cosmetics. In other cases, regulatory action specifies the form of manufacturing or prohibits certain processes. The FDA also prohibits the use of a U-shaped assembly line in the manufacturing of pharmaceutical products. Firms must use an assembly line that has no bends.[6]

---

6.   21 CFR 211.42

Taxes and Subsidies

In many cases, taxes are imposed as a means of raising revenue for the government, but sometimes they are used as a means of changing economic behavior. For example, if taxes are imposed on inputs—the factors of production such as raw materials and labor—then firms that use those inputs will find them more costly and substitute lower-cost alternatives. Taxes on the final product will also cause consumers to switch purchases to lower-cost alternatives. In other cases, subsidies are provided to encourage the use of a particular input or the consumption of a particular commodity. Such regulation is not as restrictive as contraints on the final output, but behavior is often altered. An example of a particular subsidy is the investment tax credit that applies to capital equipment with a service life of three years or more. The credit is given to purchasers of business capital, and it effectively reduces the taxes they owe. Since the credit effectively lowers the price of the capital equipment, it encourages those in business to purchase more.

REGULATED ACTIVITIES

Virtually every economic activity is subject to some regulation at one stage or another in the process of manufacturing, wholesaling, retailing, or other activity. A few of those activities are discussed below.

Transportation

Virtually all forms of transportation—surface, air, and water—are subject to a multitude of government regulations. The commerce clause of the Constitution gives the federal government the power to regulate commerce and interstate trade. The Interstate Commerce Commission (ICC), created by the Act to Regulate Commerce in 1887, has regulated freight service transportation throughout the United States since that time. The major form of regulation concerns the rates that can be charged for different commodities as well as distance traveled.[7] In addition to rate regulation, the ICC prohibits carriers from carrying freight on back hauls (return trips) in a number of situations. Such prohibitions decrease the options of shippers, thereby generating higher prices for all shipping.

The ICC also regulates the lease rates on railroad freight cars and other rolling stock. In recent years, the price has not been permitted to rise, so individual firms have found that rail cars have become a cheaper means of storing merchandise. A significant shortage of railroad cars has been the main result of this regulation.

In some cases, the ICC's regulatory powers exceed those of other government agencies. For example, in United States v. Interstate Commerce Comm., the Justice Department attempted to block the commission's approval of the merger of the Great Northern Railway Company and the Northern Pacific Railway Company.[8] The department argued that the ICC failed to give sufficient weight to the diminution of competition between the lines and failed to balance antitrust objections and national transportation goals properly. By supporting the commission, the Court gave the ICC the right to approve mergers when the cost savings outweighed the anticompetitive consequences of the merger.

Utilities

Because of the specific monopoly status of utilities, local and state governments have regulated the provision of electrical power and water, gas, and phone service. In addition to setting the maximum rate that utilities can charge, regulatory commissions also institute requirements to serve new customers or to prohibit individuals from purchasing services. In Santa Barbara, California, for example, the local government placed a moratorium on new construction by prohibiting water and sewer hookups for new homes.

---

7. Thomas Gail Moore, "Freight Transportation Regulation: Service Freight and the Interstate Commerce Commission," AEI (1972).

8. 396 U.S. 491, 90 S.Ct. 708 (1970).

Communications

The most prominent form of regulation of communications is concerned with the right to transmit or broadcast signals in the electromagnetic spectrum. Various regulatory agencies, including the Department of Defense and the Federal Communications Commission, have the right to allocate the air waves. Licenses are generally granted for specific periods of time, and they regulate the mixture of programming that the station can offer its audience. Licenses also specify the station's maximum and minimum wattage power for transmission without interference. Despite these regulations, broadcast rights represent significant assets, so firms often devote considerable effort to obtaining them. Licensing renewal is sometimes affected by a station's record in hiring or promoting members of minority groups.

Consumer Products

Ultimately, consumer products are subject to a large number of regulations, since virtually every regulation has its final impact on the price of the commodity in the market. Some regulations, however, are more direct. The Consumer Product Safety Commission (CPSC) has jurisdiction over more than ten thousand products. The agency has been given the authority to establish mandatory safety standards, to require warnings by manufacturers, to require producers to give rebates to consumers, and to ban or recall products without a court hearing. In addition, it can impose criminal penalties so that executives in firms with violations can face jail sentences.[9]

Health and Safety

In 1970, Congress passed a comprehensive act to regulate occupational safety and health.[10] In response, the Department of Labor has issued

---

9. Consumer Product Safety Act, Public Law 92-573. 42 USCA Sec. 3142-1, 29 USCA Sec. 661.

10. Occupational Safety and Health Act of 1970.

various detailed rules and regulations specifying safety standards for almost every industry. There are standards that apply to fire extinguishers, electrical groundings, exits from buildings, guards for machines, and other resources or activities generally affecting production in industry. In addition, certain rules apply to particular work activities. For example, regulations can specify the times and locations when construction personnel must wear hard hats. The law imposes numerous record-keeping requirements concerning accidental injuries and job-related health problems.

Inspections must comply with statutory procedures. No examination that amounts to a warrantless search is permitted. The Constitution protects all citizens, including corporations, from unreasonable searches. Hence, health and safety inspections must meet constitutional requirements. This does not mean that surprise inspections cannot take place. It merely means that unless the agency conducting the inspection has obtained *consent* to inspect, an inspection cannot be made without a search warrant. In the following case, the Supreme Court described such a situation.

BACKGROUND AND FACTS *Prior to 1978, inspectors of the Occupational Safety and Health Administration were not required to obtain permission to enter the work areas of firms subject to OSHA's jurisdiction. In 1975, an OSHA inspector entered the customer service area of Barlow's Inc., an electrical and plumbing installation business. After showing his credentials, the inspector informed the president and general manager, Barlow, that he wished to conduct a search of the working areas of the business.*

Upon inquiry, Barlow learned that no complaint had been received about his company. The inspection was simply the result of a random selection process. On further questioning the inspector, Barlow learned that he did not have a search warrant. Thereupon, Barlow refused to permit the inspector to enter the working area of his business. He said that he was relying on his rights guaranteed by the Fourth Amendment of the United States Constitution.

OSHA filed suit in the United States District Court and was ultimately successful in having that court issue an order compelling Barlow to admit the inspector for purposes of conducting an occupational safety and health inspection.

Once again, this time with court order in hand, the OSHA inspector presented himself at Barlow's Inc., and Barlow again refused admission. This time, Barlow went to court seeking an injunction to prohibit the inspector from making a warrantless search on the ground that it violated the Fourth Amendment of the Constitution.

A court composed of three judges was convened, and it ruled in Barlow's favor, holding that the Fourth Amendment required a warrant for the type of search involved and that the statutory authorization for warrantless inspections under the OSHA statute was unconstitutional. Therefore, a permanent injunction against such searches or inspections was entered. This appeal challenged the validity of that injunction.

MARSHALL v. BARLOW'S INC.
Supreme Court of the United States, 1978.
436 U.S. 934, 98 S.Ct. 1816.

WHITE, Judge.

* * *

The Warrant Clause of the Fourth Amendment protects commercial buildings as well as private homes. To hold otherwise would belie the origin of that Amendment, and the American colonial experience. An important forerunner of the first 10 Amendments to the United States Constitution, the Virginia Bill of Rights, specifically opposed "general warrants, whereby an officer or messenger may be commanded to search suspected places without evidence of a fact committed." The general warrant was a recurring point of contention in the colonies immediately preceding the Revolution. The particular offensiveness it engendered was acutely felt by the merchants and businessmen whose premises and products were inspected for compliance with the several Parliamentary revenue measures that most irritated the colonists. "[T]he Fourth Amendment's commands grew in large measure out of the colonists' experience with the writs of assistance. . . [that] granted sweeping power to customs officials and other agents of the King to search at large for smuggled goods."

* * *

The Secretary urges that an exception from the search warrant requirement has been recognized for "pervasively regulated business[es]."

* * *

Invoking the Walsh-Healey Act of 1936, the Secretary attempts to support a conclusion that all businesses involved in interstate commerce have long been subjected to close supervision of employee safety and health conditions. But the degree of federal involvement in employee working circumstances has never been of the order of specificity and pervasiveness that OSHA mandates. It is quite unconvincing to argue that the imposition of minimum wages and maximum hours on employers who contracted with the government under the Walsh-Healey Act prepared the entirety of American interstate commerce for regulation of working conditions to the minutest detail. Nor can any but the most fictional sense of voluntary consent to later searches be found in the single fact that one conducts a business affecting interstate commerce; under current practice and law, few businesses can be conducted without having some effect on interstate commerce.

* * *

We conclude that the concerns expressed by the Secretary do not suffice to justify warrantless inspections under OSHA or vitiate the general constitutional requirement that for a search to be reasonable a warrant must be obtained.

JUDGMENT AND REMEDY *The permanent injunction was upheld. OSHA inspections conducted without warrants were held to be unconstitutional.*

Industrial Production

In addition to health and safety, government regulations specify many of the factors that influence the production of goods and services. The Energy Policy and Conservation Act of 1975, for example, specifies that oil refineries must establish certain stockpiles of crude oil suitable for use in emergency situations. In other cases, the actual production process is subject to regulation. For example, the Food and Drug Administration requires that all storage facilities used in the production of pharmaceutical products, including refrigerators, maintain at least a two-foot clearance between walls and stored items. In addition, various production processes must be isolated from one another by walls with double doors.

Employment

A number of regulations govern wage levels, hiring practices, pensions, and other conditions of employment. In most industries, employers are required to pay a minimum wage specified by Congress in the Fair Labor Standards Act. In 1980, the minimum wage for nonagricultural workers was $3.10. The act also prohibits the employment of children under the age of fourteen years, sets maximum hours, and specifies overtime pay provisions. Employers must also make a number of mandatory payments on behalf of employees. These include payments to social security for retirement (OASI), disability income (DI), unemployment compensation, and workmen's compensation (for work-related accidents).

A number of additional regulations govern hiring, promotion, and procedures for handling disputes between labor and management. Em-

ployers cannot, for example, discriminate against individuals because of age, race, sex, color, national origin, or religious beliefs. Since 1964, under Title VII of the Civil Rights Act, the Supreme Court has increasingly defined the limits of employment discrimination.

One of the objectives of Congress in enacting the Civil Rights Act was to achieve equality of employment opportunity and to remove barriers that operated in the past to favor identifiable groups of white employees over other employees. The Supreme Court has enforced the provisions of the Civil Rights Act pertaining to employment opportunities to prevent various employment practices that operated to disqualify minorities from advancement opportunities. The Civil Rights Act has been used to prohibit educational requirements from being invoked as a bar to promotion and transfer opportunities for minority employees when these requirements have no relationship to job performance. Even where employment practices are neutral on their face, but their impact is to maintain the status quo of prior discriminatory employment practices, the Civil Rights Act is a method for removing such barriers.

BACKGROUND AND FACTS *The defendant, Duke Power Company, was sued by a number of its black employees for practicing racial discrimination in hiring and assigning employees at its Dan River plant. The plant was organized into five operating departments: (1) labor, (2) coal handling, (3) operation, (4) maintenance, and (5) laboratory test. Blacks were employed only in the labor department, where the highest paying jobs paid less than the lowest paying jobs in the other four departments (which employed only whites). Promotions were normally made within each department on the basis of seniority. Transferees into a department usually began at the lowest position.*

In 1955, the company began to require a high school education for an initial assignment into any department except the labor department. In addition, it required a high school education for any transfer from the coal handling department to any inside department (operations, maintenance, or laboratory). For ten years, this company-wide policy was enforced.

In 1965, when the company abandoned its policy of restricting blacks to the labor department, a high school diploma was nevertheless made a prerequisite to transfer from the labor department into any other department.

GRIGGS v. DUKE POWER CO.

Supreme Court of the United States, 1971.

401 U.S. 424, 91 S.Ct. 849.

From the time the high school requirement was instituted in 1955 to the time the lawsuit was filed, white employees hired before the time of the high school education requirement continued to perform satisfactorily and to achieve promotions in the operating departments.

In 1965, the company added further requirements for any new employees. To qualify for placement in any but the labor department it became necessary to score satisfactorily on two professionally prepared aptitude tests as well as to have a high school education. Completion of high school alone continued to make employees eligible for transfer into the four desirable departments. Of course, blacks who had been employed prior to the time of this new requirement had been ineligible for transfer.

In September 1965, the company began to permit employees who lacked a high school education to qualify for transfer from the labor or coal handling department to an inside job by passing two tests—the Wonderlic Personnel test, which purported to measure general intelligence, and the Bennett Mechanical Comprehension test. Neither of these tests measured the ability to learn to perform a particular job or category of job. The requisite scores used both for initial hiring and for transfer approximated the national median for high school graduates. Enforcing the median standard screened out approximately half of all high school graduates across the country, not to mention those within the company attempting to pass with a sufficient score. Hence, these two requirements, the diploma and the test, rendered a markedly disproportionate number of blacks ineligible for employment advancement in the company.

The district court hearing the case initially found that while the company had followed a policy of overt racial discrimination prior to the passage of the Civil Rights Act, such conduct had since ceased. Consequently, the impact of prior inequities was beyond the reach of the corrective action authorized by the act. The court of appeals found that Duke Power Company had no discriminatory intent in adopting the diploma and test requirements and that the standards had been applied fairly to both whites and blacks. On this basis, it concluded that there was no violation of the Civil Rights Act.

BURGER, Chief Justice.

We granted the writ in this case to resolve the question whether an employer is prohibited by the Civil Rights Act of 1964, Title VII, from requiring a high school education or passing of a standardized general intelligence test as a condition of employment in or transfer to jobs when (a) neither standard is shown to be significantly related to successful job performance, (b) both requirements operate to disqualify Negroes at a substantially higher rate than white applicants, and (c) the jobs in question formerly had been filled only by white employees as part of a longstanding practice of giving preference to whites.

* * *

The objective of Congress in the enactment of Title VII is plain from the language of the statute. It was to achieve equality of employment opportunities and remove barriers that have operated in the past to favor an identifiable group of white employees over other employees. Under the Act, practices, procedures, or tests neutral on their face, and even neutral in terms of intent, cannot be maintained if they operate to "freeze" the status quo of prior discriminatory employment practices.

* * *

Congress did not intend by Title VII, however, to guarantee a job to every person regardless of qualifications. In short, the Act does not command that any person be hired simply because he was formerly the subject of discrimination, or because he is a member of a minority group. Discriminatory preference for any group, minority or majority, is precisely and only what Congress has proscribed. What is required by Congress is the removal of artificial, arbitrary, and unnecessary barriers to employment when the barriers operate invidiously to discriminate on the basis of racial or other impermissible classification.

* * *

The Act proscribes not only overt discrimination but also practices that are fair in form, but discriminatory in operation. The touchstone is business necessity. If an employment practice which operates to exclude Negroes cannot be shown to be related to job performance, the practice is prohibited.

On the record before us, neither the high school completion requirement nor the general intelligence test is shown to bear a demonstrable relationship to successful performance of the jobs for which it was used. Both were adopted, as the Court of Appeals noted, without meaningful study of their relationship to job-performance ability. Rather, a vice president of the Company testified, the requirements were instituted on the Company's judgment that they generally would improve the overall quality of the work force.

The evidence, however, shows that employees who have not completed high school or taken the tests have continued to perform satisfactorily and make progress in departments for which the high school and test criteria are now used. The promotion record of present employees who would not be able to meet the new criteria thus suggests the possibility that the requirements may not be needed even for the limited purpose of preserving the avowed policy of advancement within the Company. In the context of this case, it is unnecessary to reach the question whether testing requirements that take into account capability for the next succeeding position or related future promotion might be utilized upon a showing that such long-range requirements fulfill a genuine business need. In the present case the Company has made no such showing.

* * *

The U.S. Supreme Court found that the Duke Power Company had in fact violated Title VII of the Civil Rights Act. Accordingly, the company was prohibited from requiring a high school education or the passing of a standardized general intelligence test as a condition of employment or as a prerequisite to transferring from one job to another.

JUDGMENT AND REMEDY

Innovation

Many federal regulations indirectly affect investment and innovation. In some industries, however, the regulations are more closely applied to innovative actions and to the research and developmental process. For example, the 1962 Kefauver-Harris amendments to the Food, Drug and Cosmetic Act of 1938 effectively eliminated the time constraint for the Food and Drug Administration's approval of a new drug application. After 1962, the FDA could withhold a drug from the market indefinitely until the agency was satisfied that the drug was both safe and effective for its intended use. Currently, the FDA views its role as requiring the manufacturer to prove a drug safe, rather than requiring the agency to prove it unsafe. As a consequence, approval times for new drugs have gone from an average of six months to more than six years in many cases.

Energy

Energy is regulated by a large number of independent agencies, each of which promulgates numerous rules and regulations. More importantly, numerous studies have shown that these organizations have been extremely effective in altering economic activity in energy and related industries. For example, the Federal Power Commission (FPC) has regulated the price of natural gas for many years. The FPC uses a geographic area rate regulation procedure that is based on average regional accounting costs for establishing maximum prices. It set initial price ceilings close to market prices so the regulation had little or no effect. Throughout the 1960s, the FPC, in its determination to hold the line against increases in natural gas prices, failed to increase regional maximum prices to reflect real increases in demand and inflationary pressures. As a consequence, shortages appeared; in some cases, they represented extreme problems by the 1970s.[11]

---

11. Paul MacAvoy, "The Regulated Induced Shortage of Natural Gas," *Journal of Law and Economics* (April 1971): 167-200.

Patent and Copyright

The Constitution delegates powers "to promote the progress of science and useful arts, by securing limited times to authors and inventors concerning the exclusive right to their respective writings and discoveries * * *." As early as 1790, a number of statutes implementing this power were passed. The patent laws exclude others for a period of seventeen years from making, using, or selling inventions that are claimed and determined to be patentable. Patent laws are unique in that they permit a number of practices that are considered to be anticompetitive. For example, the owner of a patent can fix prices to at least one licensee—a per se violation of antitrust laws in the absence of a patent. Thus, the patent law deviates from the general policy of preventing monopolies in order to encourage the development and production of goods and services by offering economic protection for a limited period of time. In a similar manner, authors or their estates hold exclusive rights to the authors' published or unpublished works for life plus fifty years. For works that are anonymous or pseudonymous, protection is given for a minimum of seventy-five years from publication or one hundred years from creation.

Trademarks

Under common law, merchants acquire legal rights in the words or symbols they use to distinguish their goods from others by adoption and use. Congress, acting under the commerce clause of the Constitution, enacted legislation long ago to facilitate the acquisition and enforcement of trademark rights. In 1946, the Lanham Act permitted registration of any distinctive mark indicative of its source or origin. (Trademarks include "any word, name, symbol, or device, or any combination thereof adopted and used by the manufacturer [or] merchant to identify its goods and distinguish them from those manufactured or sold by others.") Existing law, however, has determined that if the trademark becomes associated as a generic term for the commodities and loses its association with a particular producer, then it is no longer valid. The trademarks linoleum and aspirin, for example, were lost when they became generally accepted as the generic name of the goods.

Financing

Many regulations have extensive impact on banking and other financial activities. For example, the Federal Reserve Board of Governors limits the maximum interest that banks can offer on checking and savings accounts.[12] This causes a significant differential between the amount that individuals can receive on checking and savings accounts relative to other forms of savings, especially during periods of extensive inflation. In addition, there are regulations regarding entry into banking promulgated by the Federal Reserve System and Federal Deposit Insurance Corporation. Among other things, these regulations require proof that there is sufficient need in the community for a new bank. Other government organizations, such as the Federal Housing Administration (FHA), also govern financial transactions. For example, the FHA has requirements concerning the extension of mortgage credit as a condition of underwriting loans.

PUBLIC REVIEW OF REGULATION

In recent years, there has been growing recognition of the broad discretionary powers given to administrative agencies. In response, the Federal government has attempted to impose new constraints on agencies as a means of limiting the number of ineffective or potentially harmful rules. For example, in 1978, President Carter issued an order requiring agencies to determine the possible economic impacts of regulations that have substantial economic effects.[13] The order required agencies that wished to promulgate rules that were expected to have major consequences to prepare a clear statement of the problem requiring action and an analysis of the economic consequences of the proposed regulation, along with alternative solutions to the problem. Congress has also begun to hold hearings on the costs of complying with regulations. In 1973, for example, Congress held hearings focusing just on the burden of federal paperwork. Exhibit 47-3 lists the compliance forms for a typical firm subject to government regulation. Furthermore, a 1979 study of forty-eight manufacturing firms by the Business Roundtable found that government regulations account for 10 percent of total capital expenditures.

Finally, the public can seek specific statutory override of administrative powers through the U.S. Congress and other legislative bodies. For example, Congress significantly limited the Civil Aeronautics Board's ability to regulate air fares in the Airline Deregulation Act of 1978.

12. Regulation Q. 12 CFR § 217 (1979).
13. Improving Government Regulations, Executive Order #12044.

EXHIBIT 47-3 GOVERNMENT FORMS REQUIRED OF GRAYMILLS CORPORATION

AGENCY	FORM OR SUBDIVISION	FORM NUMBER	TIME TO FILL OUT FORM
Federal			
Department of Commerce	Census of Manufacturers	MC-35M	8.0 hours
Office of Equal Employment Opportunity	Employer Information Report EEO-I	265-41	0.5
Federal Trade Commission	Division of Financial Statistics	MG-1	0.8

AGENCY	FORM OR SUBDIVISION	FORM NUMBER	TIME TO FILL OUT FORM
Department of Labor	Log of Occupational Injuries and Illnesses	100	1.0
Department of Labor	Supplementary Record of Occupational Injuries and Illnesses	101	0.5
Department of Labor	Summary—Occupational Injuries and Illnesses	102	1.0
Department of Labor	Wage Developments in Manufacturing	BLS 2675b	0.5
Department of Labor	Employee Welfare or Pension Benefit Plan Description	D-1	1.0
Department of Labor	Employee Welfare or Pension Benefit Plan Description Amendment	D-1A	1.0
Department of Labor	Employee Welfare or Pension Benefit Plan Annual Report	D-2	8.0
Department of Labor	Information on Employee Welfare or Pension Benefit Plan Covering Fewer than 100 Participants	D-3	—[a]
Department of the Treasury	Federal Tax Deposits— Withheld Income and FICA Taxes	501	104.0
Department of the Treasury	Unemployment Taxes	508	12.0
Department of the Treasury	Employer's Annual Federal Unemployment Tax Return	940	3.0
Department of the Treasury	Employee's Withholding Exemption Certificate	W-4	—[b]
Department of the Treasury	Reconciliation of Income Tax Withheld from Wages	W-3	24.0
Department of the Treasury	Report of Wages Payable under the Federal Insurance Contributions Act	941a	64.0
Department of the Treasury	Return of Employee's Trust Exempt from Tax	990-P	1.0
Department of the Treasury	U.S. Information Return for the Calendar Year 1971	1099	3.0

AGENCY	FORM OR SUBDIVISION	FORM NUMBER	TIME TO FILL OUT FORM
State of Illinois			
Industrial Commission	Application for Adjustment of Claim—Notice of Disputed Claims and Memorandum of Names and Addresses	None	—[c]
Industrial Commission	Employer's Report of Compensable Injury	None	—[c]
Industrial Commission	Memorandum of Names and Addresses for Service of Notices	None	—[c]
Industrial Commission	Notice of Filing Claim	77	—[c]
Employment Service	DOL-BES Form	None	—[d]
Division of Unemployment Compensation	Notice of Possible Ineligibility	UC (Ill.) Ben-22	—[e]
Division of Unemployment Compensation	Employer's Contribution Report	UC-3D	64.0
Department of Revenue	Retailers' Occupation Tax, Use Tax, County, Municipal Service Occupation and Service Use Tax Return	RR-1A	2.0
Department of Revenue	Employee's Illinois Withholding Exemption Certificate	Il-W-4	—[b]
Department of Revenue	Monthly State Income Tax Payment Form	Il-501	1.0
Department of Revenue	Application for Renewal of Resale Certificate Number	RR-490H	—[f]
State of California			
Department of Business Taxes	State, Local, and District Sales and Use Tax Return	BT 401C	2.0
State of New Jersey			
Division of Taxation	Resale Certificate	SF-3	—[f]
Division of Taxation	Blanket Exemption Certificate	1786 AC	—[f]
City of Chicago			
Commission on Human Relations	Contractor Employment Practices Report	None	1.0

AGENCY	FORM OR SUBDIVISION	FORM NUMBER	TIME TO FILL OUT FORM
Metropolitan Sanitary District	Industrial Waste Surcharge Certified Statement	Fl-235	2.0
Metropolitan Sanitary District	Report of Exemption Claim or Estimate of Liability for Surcharge	Fl-236	1.0
Metropolitan Santiary District	Computation of Initial Estimate of Liability for Surcharge	Fl-236A	2.0
City of Los Angeles			
Department of Building and Safety	Application and Agreement for Testing Electrical Equipment	B&S E-147	1.0
Department of Building and Safety	Application for Approval Labels	B&S R9	1.0

[a] Not available.
[b] 5 minutes per form.
[c] ½ hour each.
[d] 15 minutes per month.
[e] 15 minutes per form.
[f] 1 hour each.

Source: U.S. Senate, Hearings, Subcommittee on Government Regulation, *The Federal Paperwork Burden*, 92nd Congress, Part 1, pp. 124-128.

QUESTIONS AND CASE PROBLEMS

1. Article III of the Constitution provides that the judicial power shall reside in the Supreme Court of the United States and such inferior courts as the Congress shall from time to time create. Judicial power is the power to resolve disputes and includes the power to determine whether an individual has committed certain acts and whether the commission of such acts constitutes the breach of a duty owed to another or to society as a whole. Administrative agencies have the power to determine whether a person is guilty or innocent of violating agency rules and regulations. Does this contradict the mandate of Article III?

2. While courts have the power to review all agency decisions, they generally defer to the agency's findings of fact (especially where agency expertise is involved) but examine carefully the agency's findings of law. This, of course, is because courts deem *themselves* the experts on the law. Even in cases where agency expertise is not important, courts generally defer to the facts as found by the agency. For example, in a patent-related case investigated by the Federal Trade Commission, the commission made a certain finding of fact with respect to the testimony of Lidoff. The commission would not have made the finding if it had not found Lidoff to be a credible witness. Why might the reviewing court be unwilling to question the agency's determination with regard to Lidoff's credibility? [Charles Pfizer and Co. v. Federal Trade Comm., 401 F.2d. 574 (6th Cir. 1968)]

3. Administrative agencies act in the capacities of both lawmaker and judge, or fact finder. Under the Constitution, these two roles are distinctly divided

between the legislature and the courts. What advantages are there in combining the functions within an administrative agency? What disadvantages?

4. All actions taken by an administrative agency, whether legislative or judicial, are subject to review by the courts. The relevant test for review is whether the agency acted in an "arbitrary or capricious" manner in promulgating the rule.The Secretary of Commerce issued a flammability standard that required all mattresses, including crib mattresses, to pass a test that involved bringing the mattress in contact with a burning cigarette. The manufacturers of crib mattresses petitioned the court, asking it to hold that the flammability standard should not apply to crib mattresses. The manufacturers said that applying such a rule to crib mattresses would not only be unreasonable but arbitrary and capricious since infants do not smoke. How should the court rule? [Bunny Bear, Inc. v. Peterson, 473 F.2d. 1002 (5th Cir. 1973)]

5. If an administrative agency acts arbitrarily or capriciously, the reviewing court will strike down its rule. Agencies, however, are given wide latitude or discretion in formulating agency rules. Only when an agency abuses this discretion will a reviewing court reverse it. In Question 4 above, the administrative agency promulgated a single flammability standard for more than one type of mattress. If the crib mattress manufacturer had clearly demonstrated by proof that a flammability test used on infant mattresses in Europe was equally as satisfactory as the "cigarette test" and had been used with good results for years in Europe, would the Secretary of Commerce have abused his discretion in adopting the cigarette test? What if the crib mattress manufacturer proved that the flammability test used in Europe was better than the cigarette test? Would the Secretary of Commerce have abused his discretion?

6. The standard of review that applies to administrative adjudicatory procedures is somewhat higher than the one applied to the rule-making process. When an administrative agency decides whether an agency rule or regulation has been violated, it conducts a hearing somewhat similar to a nonjury trial. Why do courts require stronger support for agencies' adjudicatory decisions than for their rule-making decisions?

7. Reviewing courts readily support rules promulgated by administrative agencies, but they require ·

that the adjudicative findings of an agency be supported by "substantial evidence on the record." When an administrative agency conducts an adjudicative hearing, a record is made of all the evidence and testimony presented at the hearing. If the finding of the hearing is supported by the evidence contained in the record, a reviewing court will uphold the agency's finding. The Adolph Coors Company was accused by the FTC of engaging in certain price-fixing agreements in violation of the Sherman Antitrust Act. After a complete adjudicative hearing, the commission concluded that Coors had in fact engaged in illegal price-fixing. Substantial evidence was presented at the hearing in support of the commission's findings. But Coors also presented substantial evidence that it had never entered into any price-fixing arrangements. Should a reviewing court uphold the FTC's findings? [Adolph Coors Co. v. Federal Trade Comm., 497 F.2d. 1178 (10th Cir. 1974)]

8. Mary Burke Sprogis was employed by United Airlines as a stewardess. On June 19, 1966, she was discharged for violating a current company policy that required stewardesses to be unmarried. This rule had never been applied to any male employee. Sprogis sued United Airlines under Title 7 of the Civil Rights Acts of 1964, which prohibits, among other things, discrimination based on sex. Must United Airlines reinstate Sprogis? [Sprogis v. United Airlines, Inc. 444 F.2d. 1194 (7th Cir. 1971)]

9. Johnson & Johnson's trademark "shower to shower" was used as the label on body powder that it manufactured. The Colgate-Palmolive Company later adopted a similar trademark, "hour after hour," which it applied to its line of aerosol deodorants and antiperspirants. Johnson & Johnson sought to prevent Colgate-Palmolive from using the phrase "hour after hour" on the ground that it violated Johnson & Johnson's trademark. In determining whether one has adopted a phrase or name that violates another's trademark rights, courts look to the Lanham Trademark Act. The act provides that a product name violates another's trademark rights when the names are so similar that they are likely to deceive or confuse buyers. Under this test, has Colgate-Palmolive's "hour after hour" violated Johnson & Johnson's "shower to shower" trademark? [Johnson & Johnson v. Colgate-Palmolive Co., 345 F.Supp. 1216 (D.N.J. 1972)]

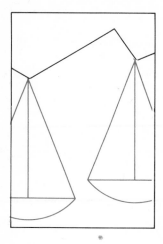

48

Government Regulation
Consumer Protection

Consumer grievances (usually limited to persons who purchase retail goods and services) regarding the price and terms of credit, repossession, warranties, defective or shoddy goods, and other aspects of the sale, financing, and service of consumer goods represent some of the more important problems facing individuals in society. There is no question that these grievances have been responsible for the ever-growing judicial, legislative, and administrative actions designed to give the consumer adequate protection in the selection, purchase, financing, and service of consumer goods in a seemingly impersonal urbanized marketplace.

Consumer protection arises from three distinct sources—from common law through judicial rulings; from simplification and codification of common law through federal, state, and local statutes, including the Uniform Commercial Code; and from administrative law through rule making and enforcement activities, such as the Federal Trade Commission's rule allowing consumers to keep unsolicited merchandise received through the mails.

Since parties who make contracts are generally given the right to specify the terms, consumer protection under the common law is sometimes limited. As Chapter 9 and Chapter 11 illustrated, the interests of consumers have often been important in judicial decisions. For example, the unconscionability doctrine (which deals with contracts that would be grossly unfair to enforce) protects consumers from certain pricing techniques for goods that are sold on credit. Consider the example of Williams, who made a series of purchases from Walker-Thomas Furniture Company from 1957 to 1962. Each of the time payment contracts that she signed contained the clause that all payments would be credited pro rata on all outstanding accounts. In 1962 she purchased furniture for $164, bringing her total purchases since 1957 to $1,800. The pro rata claim, however, meant that she still owed money on all items despite the fact that she had paid a total of $1,400 through 1962. A court found this clause to be unconscionable and unenforceable.[1]

CONSUMER PROTECTION SOURCES

A number of federal laws—such as the Consumer Credit Protection Act, the Uniform Consumer Sales Practices Act, and the Magnuson-Moss Warranty Act—have been passed to provide more explicit direction on the duty of sellers and the rights of consumers. In recent years, the pressure on Congress to enact further laws to protect consumers has increased. New regulations in this area are likely to be drafted in the future.

State Statutes

Various provisions of the Uniform Commercial Code provide consumer protection in commercial sales transactions.[2] Finally, a number of statutes in California, Florida, New York, and other states provide explicit protection to consumers. For example, the California Civil Code permits consumers to keep unsolicited goods. If they are billed for the goods, they can seek an injunction to stop billing, and they can collect reasonable attorneys' fees.[3] In New York, consumers who purchase goods at home must be aware of their rights to cancel the transaction prior to midnight of the third business day after the transaction.[4]

Administrative Agencies

Administrative agencies provide an important form of consumer protection. For example, the Federal Trade Commission will spend approximately 46 percent of its estimated $66.5 million budget for fiscal year 1979 for consumer protec-

tion activities. The FTC, which is headed by five commissioners appointed by the president for terms of seven years, has been given extensive enforcement responsibilities in a number of statutes, some of which are discussed below. The most important authority, however, is Section 5 of the original Federal Trade Commission Act of 1914 as amended in 1938. It permits the commission to stop "unfair or deceptive acts or practices" that influence, inhibit, or restrict consumers unfairly in their purchasing decisions. Many of these practices are prohibited by industry guidelines or trade regulation rules. Violations are punishable by law and can occur in two circumstances. A company can engage in a practice prohibited by a trade regulation, or it can violate a known cease and desist order issued against another party. For example, if the FTC issues a cease and desist order to Ford Motor Company that prohibits the advertising of fuel economy levels achieved when the automobiles are driven by professional drivers without disclosing that information, the FTC can impose civil penalties against another automobile producer if it advertises mileage tests without the disclosure.[5] The commission can also bring actions for consumers who have been injured. Other agencies of the federal government, such as the Department of Housing and Urban Development, are also engaged in consumer protection activities. HUD, for example, enforces provisions of the National Mobile Home Construction and Safety Standards Act of 1974, which require that periodic inspections and investigations be conducted to enforce federal standards. It also enforces the Interstate Land Sale Full Disclosure Act, which requires that sellers of subdivided lots provide certain statements of record that must include a legal description of the land, who has title to the land, and the present condition of the land.

1. Williams v. Walker-Thomas Furniture Co., 198 A.2d 914 (D.C.App. 1964).
2. The UCC is discussed more fully in the sections on sales and commercial transactions.
3. Section 1584.5
4. N.Y. Business Corporation Law, Sec. 1101 (McKinney 1964).
5. FTC Improvements Act of 1975.

The Courts

Finally, consumers themselves can use the courts to obtain remedies for their grievances. Since the time, embarrassment, and cost to consumers of private lawsuits can be prohibitive, various mechanisms have been developed to remove these barriers. They include prelegal services, small claims courts, and recovery of attorneys' fees in class actions. Attorneys' fees, however, are generally recoverable only when there is an express statutory authorization.[6] Class actions have become a relatively more common form of addressing consumer grievances, but these actions are subject to certain rules and limits that make them difficult to pursue, particularly by individuals.

Organization

Consumers also have access to the Better Business Bureau system, a national organization of independent nonprofit organizations financed by businesses to regulate themselves. The main organization, the Council of Better Business Bureau, Inc., has established the following priority projects:

1. Expanding and improving the services of BBB and seeking standardization and coordination among the parts of the network.
2. Establishing consumer arbitration as a means of achieving consumer justice.
3. Establishing a consumer education program to include the traditional information booklets, audio-visual material, school curriculum material, and programs tailored to meet the needs of minority, low income, and elderly groups.

4. Establishing a top level procedure for voluntary self-regulation of advertising.[7]

A consumer can also contact the local Chamber of Commerce for help in seeking methods of settling a grievance.

ADVERTISING

The basic protection afforded consumers against deceptive advertising derives more from statutory and administrative sources than from common law. Common law protection is based on fraud and requires proof of intent to misrepresent facts and other criteria. On the other hand, the statutory law and administrative regulations focus on whether the advertising is likely to be misleading, regardless of intent. Behind this approach is the notion that the purpose of prohibiting false advertising through legislation is to protect the consumer rather than to punish the seller or advertiser.

The Federal Trade Commission Act empowers the FTC to determine what constitutes a deceptive practice within the meaning of Section 5 of the act. The FTC's judgment can be appealed to a court, but it is accorded great weight by the reviewing court. When the commission renders an opinion or issues an order, appeal can be taken through judicial channels. The commission is responsible for enforcing the legislative policy of the act it administers, and the courts will recognize that the administrative agency that deals continually with cases in the area is often in a better position than the courts are to determine when a practice is deceptive within the meaning of the act.

---

6. See Alyeska Pipeline Service Co. v. The Wilderness Society, 421 U.S. 240, 95 S.Ct. 1612 (1975).

7. H. Bruce Palmer, *Association Management Magazine,* November 1970.

FEDERAL TRADE COMM. v. COLGATE-PALMOLIVE CO.
Supreme Court of the United States, 1965.
380 U.S. 374, 85 S.Ct. 1035.

BACKGROUND AND FACTS *The Federal Trade Commission issued a complaint against Colgate-Palmolive Company and Ted Bates & Company, Inc., an advertising agency, for using commercials that misrepresented the characteristics of Colgate's Rapid Shave. Bates had prepared TV commercials that showed how Rapid Shave could soften something as tough as sandpaper. In the commercial, Rapid Shave was applied to something that looked like sandpaper, and shortly thereafter a* razor shaved it clean. Unknown to the viewers, the "sandpaper" was actually a piece of plexiglass with sand on it.

Initially, a hearing examiner thought that Rapid Shave could shave sandpaper, although not as quickly as the advertisement suggested, so the examiner dismissed the complaint, saying that the misrepresentation was not a material one that would mislead the public.

The commission, however, reversed the hearing examiner, finding that, since Rapid Shave could not shave the sandpaper within the time depicted in the commercials, the product's moisturizing power had been misrepresented. In addition, the use of a plexiglass substitute for sandpaper was material misrepresentation because it misled viewers into believing that they had seen something which, in fact, they had not. As a result of these findings, the commission entered a cease and desist order against Colgate-Palmolive.

The court of appeals then set aside the order because it was so broadly written that it forbade all use of undisclosed simulations in television commercials. Five months later, the commission issued a revised order prohibiting Colgate-Palmolive from presenting advertisements depicting a test, experiment, or demonstration represented as actual proof of a product claim but not in fact constituting proof because of the use of an undisclosed mock-up.

Once again, the court of appeals set aside the commission's order, so the commission petitioned the Supreme Court to set forth a legal standard of the words, deceptive practice within the meaning of Section 5 of the Federal Trade Commission Act.

WARREN, Chief Justice.
* * *

The basic question before us is whether it is a deceptive trade practice, prohibited by §5 of the Federal Trade Commission Act, to represent falsely that a televised test, experiment, or demonstration provides a viewer with visual proof of a product claim, regardless of whether the product claim is itself true.

The case arises out of an attempt by respondent Colgate-Palmolive Company to prove to the television public that its shaving cream, "Rapid Shave," outshaves them all. Respondent Ted Bates & Company, Inc., an advertising agency, prepared for Colgate three one-minute commercials designed to show that Rapid Shave could soften even the toughness of sandpaper. Each of the commercials contained the same "sandpaper test." The announcer informed the audience that, "To prove Rapid Shave's super-moisturizing power, we put it right from the can onto this tough, dry sandpaper. It was apply * * * soak * * * and off in a stroke." While the announcer was speaking, Rapid Shave was applied to a substance that appeared to be sandpaper, and immediately thereafter a razor was shown shaving the substance clean.
* * *

In reviewing the substantive issues in the case, it is well to remember the respective roles of the Commission and the courts in the administration of the Federal Trade Commission Act. When the Commission was created by Congress in 1914, it was directed by §5 to prevent "[u]nfair methods of competition in commerce." Congress amended the Act in 1938 to extend the Commission's jurisdiction to include "unfair or deceptive acts or practices in commerce"—a significant amendment showing Congress' concern for consumers as well as for competitors. * * *

This statutory scheme necessarily gives the Commission an influential role in interpreting §5 and in applying it to the facts of particular cases arising out of unprecedented situations. * * *

We accept the Commission's determination that the commercials involved in this case contained three representations to the public: (1) that sandpaper could be shaved by Rapid Shave; (2) that an experiment had been conducted which verified this claim; and (3) that the viewer was seeing this experiment for himself. * * * For the purposes of our review, we can assume that the first two representations were true; the focus of our consideration is on the third, which was clearly false. The parties agree that §5 [of the Federal Trade Commission Act] prohibits the intentional misrepresentation of any fact which would constitute a material factor in a purchaser's decision whether to buy. They differ, however, in their conception of what "facts" constitute a "material factor" in a purchaser's decision to buy. Respondents submit, in effect, that the only material facts are those which deal with the substantive qualities of a product. The Commission, on the other hand, submits that the misrepresentation of any fact so long as it materially induces a purchaser's decision to buy is a deception prohibited by §5.

The Commission's interpretation of what is a deceptive practice seems more in line with the decided cases than that of respondents. This Court said in *Federal Trade Comm'n v. Algoma Lumber Co.*, "[T]he public is entitled to get what it chooses, though the choice may be dictated by caprice or by fashion or perhaps by ignorance." It has long been considered a deceptive practice to state falsely that a product ordinarily sells for an inflated price but that it is being offered at a special reduced price, even if the offered price represents the actual value of the product and the purchaser is receiving his money's worth. Applying respondents' arguments to these cases, it would appear that so long as buyers paid no more than the product was actually worth and the product contained the qualities advertised, the misstatement of an inflated original price was immaterial.

* * * [T]he present case is not concerned with a mode of communication, but with a misrepresentation that viewers have objective proof of a seller's product claim over and above the seller's word. Secondly, * * * the present case, deal[s] with methods designed to get a consumer to purchase a product, not with whether the product, when purchased, will perform up to expectations. * * *

It is generally accepted that it is a deceptive practice to state falsely that a product has received a testimonial from a respected source. * * *

* * * We find it an immaterial difference that in one case the viewer is told to rely on the word of a celebrity or authority he respects, in another on the word of a testing agency, and in the present case on his own perception of an undisclosed simulation.
* * *

We agree with the Commission, therefore, that the undisclosed use of plexiglass in the present commercials was a material deceptive practice, independent and separate from the other misrepresentation found. Respondents claim that it will be impractical to inform the viewing public that it is not seeing an actual test, experiment or demonstration, but we think it inconceivable that the ingenious advertising world will be unable, if it so desires, to conform to the Commission's insistence that the public be not misinformed. If, however, it becomes impossible or impractical to show simulated demonstrations on television in a truthful manner, this indicates that television is not a medium that lends itself to this type of commercial, not that the commercial must survive at all costs. * * * If the inherent limitations of a method do not permit its use in the way a seller desires, the seller cannot by material misrepresentation compensate for those limitations.

* * * [W]hen the commercial not only makes a claim, but also invites the viewer to rely on his own perception for demonstrative proof of the claim, the respondents will be aware that the use of undisclosed props in strategic places might be a material deception. * * *

The judgment of the court of appeals was reversed, and the case was remanded for entry of a judgment enforcing the commission's revised cease and desist order prohibiting Colgate-Palmolive from using the commercials.

JUDGMENT AND REMEDY

Bait and Switch

In some cases, the Federal Trade Commission has promulgated specific rules to govern advertising. One of its more important rules is called "Guides on Bait Advertising,"[8] and it is designed to prohibit advertisements that specify a very low price for a particular item. The low price is the bait to lure the consumer into the store. Then, the salesperson tries to switch the consumer to some other, more expensive item. According to the FTC guidelines, bait advertis-ing occurs if the seller refuses to show the advertised item, fails to have adequate quantities of it available, fails to promise or deliver the advertised item within a reasonable time, or discourages employees from selling the item.

Numerous techniques fall into the bait and switch category. In the following case, sales personnel not only were directed to engage in certain baiting practices but were rewarded for doing so.

_____

8.   16 CFR § 238 (1968).

BACKGROUND AND FACTS *All-State Industries, a producer of residential aluminum siding, storm windows, and other products used a bait and switch sales technique in selling its products. The "ADV" lower-cost grade of aluminum was featured in the company's ads, but salespersons, following the training manual, attempted to actually sell the "PRO" grade after contacting the customers. The Federal Trade Commission found this practice to be an "unfair and deceptive" practice under 5(b) of the FTC act and issued a cease and desist order. All-State Industries appealed.*

ALL-STATE INDUSTRIES OF NORTH CAROLINA, INC. v. FEDERAL TRADE COMM.

United States Court of Appeals, Fourth Cir., 1970.
423 F.2d 423.

BRYAN, Circuit Judge.

* * *

From the Hearing Examiner's findings of fact, the following account unfolds of how they vend their products. These are of two grades. The "ADV" is the cheaper. It is extensively advertised, primarily through mailouts to people whose names and addresses are culled from telephone directories. "PRO", the other grade, is of a higher quality and not so widely publicized.

Respondents' sales technique, or "pitch", is devised to create, first, a demand for the "ADV" product. Through inflated promotion it is presented as a "special offer" with "limited time" prices. But the Examiner found the "ADV" is actually priced uniformly and without time limit. He held as untrue All-State's claim that they deal directly from their factory with the output "100% guaranteed".

Inquiries or "leads" are answered by a supposed "sales manager". He attempts to pressure the prospect into signing a contract, a note and a deed, committing him to the purchase of "ADV" articles but leaving blank the monetary obligation. As soon as the contract is executed, the salesperson brings out a sample of the "ADV" and points out deficiencies in it, "whether real or imaginary". The "PRO" is then shown in contrast, to the detriment of the "ADV". Whenever possible the "PRO" is then sold "at the highest price obtainable from the individual customer". The salesmen have incentives to substitute the "PRO"— they receive no commission on "ADV" but only on "PRO" sales.

This "bait and switch" artifice, the Examiner discovered, was fully set forth in the sales force's training manual and was employed generally. He also reported that All-State's agents utilized "gimmicks whereby the original prices quoted for respondents' products can be reduced." For example, the representative would promise a potential buyer a special discount, even below the quoted sale price, if the latter would allow the use of his home for demonstration or display purposes. Rarely, however, would a patron's home be so utilized. It was found as a bare inducement to overcome "sales resistance at a higher price" and provide "some apparently reasonable basis for the reduction in price."

* * *

JUDGMENT AND REMEDY *The cease and desist order was enforced against All-State Industries as well as against each of All-State's sales agents.*

Corrective Advertising

If the Federal Trade Commission rules that a seller has made a false or deceptive advertising statement, the commission can require the seller to make additional advertisements that correct it. (Former statements are contradicted, and the correct statement is presented in the new ads.) For example, the FTC filed a complaint against Warner Lambert stating that the firm had misrepresented its product, Listerine, by adver-

tising that it would prevent and cure colds and sore throats. After determining through expert medical testimony that Listerine would neither cure nor prevent colds and that similar relief could be obtained through the use of warm salt water, the commission concluded that the firm had made deceptive statements about the medical benefits of its product. The commission then ordered corrective advertising. In addition to the actual corrective advertisement, the FTC can require that the statement "THIS ADVER-

TISEMENT IS PUBLISHED PURSUANT TO THE ORDER OF THE FEDERAL TRADE COMMISSION" in large capital letters be placed in the ad.

CERTIFICATION

Many products have one or more of their attributes tested against predetermined standards and certified if the standards are met. For example, a toaster might be tested by Underwriters Laboratory, a private laboratory that tests manufactured products for electrical safety.[9] Statements about certification are often included in advertisements, displayed on the product, noted by sales personnel, or included in the brochures that accompany the product. Sometimes, the entire product is approved by some independent organization. Certification represents a seal of approval, which means that the product will satisfy the demands of ordinary use.

Third party certification permits an independent body that is better qualified than the consumer and that does not have a direct interest in the sale of the product to examine the commodity. In some cases, such organizations are indirectly funded by manufacturers through testing associations. For example, many gas appliances are tested by the American Gas Association. On the other hand, some organizations, such as Consumers Union and Consumers' Research, do not certify or approve products but choose particular tests and report their findings to the consumer in monthly magazines and annual volumes.[10]

Guaranteed Third Party Approval

Approval by third parties can be limited to testing and certification, but some third party approval mechanisms include remedies as well. For example, Good Housekeeping Approval means that the magazine will refund the pur-

chase price or replace the purchased article if it should prove defective. Good Housekeeping Approval, however, is limited to the products that are advertised in the magazine and are tested to determine if the advertising statements are correct.

Guaranteed third party approval is generally limited to actual replacement of the product or refund of the money that was paid. Thus, Good Housekeeping Approval does not extend to damages incurred by using the product. Zayda Hanberry purchased shoes produced by Victor B. Handal and Brothers, Inc., from Akron, a retail store. The shoes were advertised as meeting the "Good Housekeeping Consumers' Guarantee Seal," which contains the promise, "If the product or performance is defective, Good Housekeeping guarantees replacement or refund to consumer." The day she bought the shoes, Hanberry slipped and fell on the vinyl floor of her kitchen. The shoes were defective because they had a low coefficient of friction on vinyl and certain other floor coverings until they were broken in. Despite this defect, the court found that *liability* for individually defective items cannot be extended through warranty or strict liability theories to a general endorser who has made no representation that each item has been examined and tested. Thus, Good Housekeeping was not liable for damages by endorsing the shoes.[11]

Labeling and Packaging

A number of federal and state laws that govern labeling and packaging have been passed to provide the consumer with accurate information or warnings about the use or possible misuse of the product. For example, the Fur Products Labeling Act, the Wool Products Labeling Act, the Cigarette Labeling and Advertising Act, the Food, Drug and Cosmetic Act, the Flammable Fabrics Act, the Fair Packaging and Labeling Act, and others have been enacted in part to reduce the amount of incorrect labeling

---

9. Underwriters Laboratory also investigates fire and other safety characteristics associated with the product.
10. Consumers Union produces *Consumer Reports*, and Consumers' Research produces *Consumer Bulletin*.

11. Hanberry v. Hearst Corp., 276 Cal.App.2d 680, 81 Cal.Rptr. 519 (1969).

and packaging in consumer products. In general, labels must be accurate, which means that they must use words as they are ordinarily understood by consumers. For example, a regular size box of cereal cannot be labeled "giant" if it would tend to exaggerate the amount of cereal. Labels often must specify the raw materials used in the product, such as the percent of cotton, nylon, or other fibers used in a shirt. The Fair Packaging Act requires that consumer goods have labels that identify the product, the manufacturer, the packer or distributor and its place of business, the net quantity of contents, and the quantity of each serving if the number of servings is stated.[12] Additional authority to add requirements governing words that are used to describe packages, terms that are associated with savings claims, information disclosure for ingredients in nonfood products, and standards for partial filling of packages is also included in this statute. The provisions are enforced by the Federal Trade Commission and the Department of Health, Education, and Welfare.

SALES

A number of statutes that protect the consumer in sales transactions concern the disclosure of certain terms in sales, rules governing home or door-to-door sales, mail order transactions, and referral sales. For example, the Federal Reserve Board of Governors has issued Regulation Z, which governs credit provisions associated with sales contracts, and numerous states have passed laws governing the remedies available to consumers in home sales. Furthermore, states have adopted a number of provisions as they have incorporated the UCC and the UCCC into their statutory codes. In 1968, Congress passed the first of a series of statutes regarding the content of information contained in written and oral messages. If, for example, certain credit terms are used in an advertisement, other credit information is also required. Thus, if Prolific Pontiac Sales states in a newspaper advertisement that individuals have thirty-six months to

pay, the firm must also include the cash price of the automobiles, the down payment, the amount of each periodic payment, and the annual percentage rate of interest.

Door-to-Door Sales

Door-to-door sales have often been singled out for special treatment in the laws of most states. The special treatment stems in part from the nature of the sales transaction if the salesperson is able to gain entrance. A door-to-door seller usually has a captive audience because many individuals are actually immobilized at home. Since repeat purchases are not as likely as they are in stores, the seller has little incentive to establish goodwill with the purchaser. Furthermore, the seller is unlikely to present alternative products and their prices. Thus, a number of states have passed statutes that permit the buyers of goods sold door-to-door to cancel their contracts within a specified period of time, usually two to three days after the sale. In addition, a Federal Trade Commission regulation makes it a Section 5 violation for door-to-door sellers to fail to give consumers three days to cancel any sale. This rule applies in addition to state statutes so that consumers are given the most favorable benefits of the FTC rule and their own state statute. In addition, the FTC rule requires that the notification be given in Spanish if the oral negotiation was in that language.

Mail Order Transactions

Consumers buying from mail order houses have typically been given less protection than when they purchase in stores. Many mail order houses are outside the state, and it is more costly to seek redress for grievances in that situation. In addition to the federal statute that prevents the use of mails to defraud individuals, several states have passed statutes governing certain practices by sellers, including insurance companies, that solicit through the mails. The state statutes parallel the federal statutes governing mail fraud.

---

12. 15 USCA Sec. 1451 et seq.

In some cases, the courts have found that transactions between consumers of one state and merchants who have offices located and organized under the law of another state can be regulated by the state where the transaction occurs. United Life Insurance Company, for example, was incorporated and maintained its offices outside California. The firm solicited sales of insurance policies by mail to California residents. The court held that the transactions made in California would be subject to the California Insurance Code.[13]

Referral Sales

Referral sales contain two agreements—one to purchase the goods or services and the other to compensate the consumer for each (potential) customer referred to the seller. In many cases the courts have ruled that referral sales fall under lottery laws, which govern transactions involving a chance for a prize, thus subjecting sellers to potential criminal penalties or injunctions. Furthermore, the UCCC prohibits the use of referral sales when the rebate is paid only when individuals whose names have been previously furnished become customers. In other states, the sale of goods on referral plans constitutes the sale of security as defined by the blue sky laws. If the seller is not licensed to sell securities, the sale will be void.

CREDIT

One of the more important areas of consumer protection concerns the rights of consumers in credit transactions. Credit has become the American way of life; nearly all major purchases are financed by some form of credit.

---

13. People v. United Nat. Life Ins., 66 Cal.2d 577, 58 Cal.Rptr. 599, 427 P.2d 199.

Most consumer installment credit is extended by commercial banks and finance companies, although credit unions, retail outlets, and various miscellaneous lenders also provide credit to employees and customers.[14] Of course, a large percentage of credit, especially for automobile sales, originates with retailers but is subsequently sold to banks and finance companies. Perhaps the most important new form of credit issued by commercial banks is the credit card (such as Master Charge or Visa). Holders of credit cards have open end accounts that can be used at thousands of stores and businesses throughout the world.

The credit industry is highly regulated and often subject to numerous state and federal licensing requirements. Nevertheless, state and federal legislators have found it necessary to pass laws governing those aspects of credit that have created the most significant consumer grievances.

In enacting the Truth in Lending Act, Congress provided that a credit card holder would be liable for a maximum of $50 in charges resulting from the unauthorized use of the card. The credit card holder must, of course, comply with the conditions set forth in the Truth in Lending Act in order to limit liability to $50. In the following case, the Alabama Court illustrates how this provision of the Truth in Lending Act applies when a "friend" abuses the credit card privilege.

---

14. Installment credit refers to all credit scheduled to be repaid in more than four payments and represents the predominant form of credit. The so-called Four Installment Rule has been codified into the Code of Federal Regulations under the designation Regulation Z, pursuant to the delegated powers under the Truth in Lending Act. The Four Installment Rule removes the creditor's incentive to bury credit charges. Consumer obligations that are payable in more than four installments require the disclosure of credit information even if no interest is being charged.

BACKGROUND AND FACTS *The appellant, Robert A. Martin, became an American Express credit card holder in 1972. Approximately three years later, in 1975, Martin gave his credit card to a business associate, E. L. McBride. McBride was supposed to use the card to make purchases for a business venture in which the two men were engaged. Martin*

MARTIN v. AMERICAN EXPRESS, INC.
Court of Civil Appeals of Alabama, 1978.
361 So.2d 597.

claimed that he orally authorized McBride to charge up to $500 on the credit card.

Martin gave the card to McBride in April. McBride returned it in May. In June, Martin received a statement from American Express indicating that the amount owed on his credit card account was $5,300. Martin refused to pay. American Express filed suit against Martin to obtain the money.

During the course of the proceedings, Martin admitted that he had given his credit card to McBride to use in a joint venture. Martin further stated that, although he did not know McBride very well, he was not concerned about giving up his card to McBride because he had told McBride not to charge more than $500. Martin was also relying on a letter that he had sent to American Express prior to giving his card to McBride. In this letter, he asked American Express not to allow the total charges on his account to exceed $1,000.

The trial court ultimately ruled in favor of American Express, holding Martin liable for the bills that had been charged to his account. Martin appealed arguing to the appellate court that his liability ought to be limited to $50 because McBride's actions constituted an "unauthorized use" under the Truth in Lending Act.

BRADLEY, Judge.

* * *

[The] issue is whether the use of a credit card by a person who has received the card and permission to utilize it from the cardholder constitutes "unauthorized use" under the Truth in Lending Act, 15 U.S.C.A. §1602(o) and §1643(a). We hold that in instances where a cardholder, who is under no compulsion by fraud, duress or otherwise, voluntarily permits the use of his (or her) credit card by another person, the cardholder has authorized the use of that card and is thereby responsible for any charges as a result of that use.

Section 1643(a), which is of principal concern in this case, limits a cardholder's liability to $50 for the "unauthorized use of a credit card." However, the statutory limitation on liability comes into play only where there is an "unauthorized use" of a credit card. And section 1602(o) defines "unauthorized use" as the "use of a credit card by a person other than the cardholder [a] who does not have actual, implied, or apparent authority for such use, and [b] from which the cardholder receives no benefit."

* * *

"A cardholder shall be liable for the unauthorized use of a credit card only if the card is an accepted credit card, the liability is not in excess of $50 . . ., and the unauthorized use occurs before the cardholder has notified the card issuer that an unauthorized use of the credit card has occurred or may occur as a result of loss, theft, or otherwise."

We believe Congress clearly indicated that "unauthorized use" of a card would occur only where there was no "actual, implied or apparent authority" for such use by the cardholder. In the present case Martin maintains that the actual, implied or apparent authority given by him to McBride was limited to the $500 amount which Martin told McBride not to exceed. Thus, Martin says he gave no authority for McBride to charge the large sum which eventually resulted in this suit. Furthermore, Martin asserts that prior to giving the card to McBride, he (Martin) wrote American Express and requested that its employees not allow the amounts charged to his credit card account to exceed $1,000. And since no such action was taken, Martin argues that any sum charged in excess of $1,000 constituted an "unauthorized" charge on his credit card.

We cannot accept either of the above contentions. McBride was actually authorized by Martin to use the latter's card. Martin admitted this fact. And the authority to use it, if not actual, remained apparent even after McBride ignored Martin's directions by charging over $500 to Martin's credit card account. Consequently, Martin was not entitled to rely on the provisions contained in section 1643(a) and he must be held responsible for any purchases made through the use of his card.

Nor are we aware of any requirement, either by statute, contract or trade usage, which would compel a credit card issuer to undertake a policy whereby the issuer would see to it that charges on a cardholder's account do not exceed a specified amount. Such a policy would place a difficult and potentially disastrous burden on the issuer. We know of no authority which requires a card issuer to perform services of this nature and Martin has provided us with none.

The express intent of Congress in enacting the Truth in Lending Act was to protect the consumer or cardholder against charges for the unauthorized use of his or her credit card and to limit his or her liability for such unauthorized use to a maximum of $50 providing, however, that the conditions set forth in the statute are complied with. We believe that §1643(a) clearly indicates that such protection is warranted where the card is obtained from the cardholder as a result of loss, theft or wrongdoing. However, we are not persuaded that section 1643(a) is applicable where a cardholder voluntarily and knowingly allows another to use his card and that person subsequently misuses the card.

Were we to adopt any other view, we would provide the unscrupulous and dishonest cardholder with the means to defraud the card issuer by allowing his or her friends to use the card, run up hundreds of dollars in charges and then limit his or her liability to $50 by notifying the card issuer. We do not believe such a result was either intended or sanctioned by Congress when it enacted section 1643(a).

* * *

The appellate court affirmed the trial court's judgment granting American Express an award for the total amount of charges made on Martin's card by McBride. McBride's conduct did not amount to an "unauthorized use" of Martin's card under the Truth in Lending Act.

JUDGMENT AND REMEDY

The Uniform Consumer Credit Code

In 1968, the National Conference of Commissioners on the Uniform State Laws promulgated the Uniform Consumer Credit Code (UCCC).

The UCCC has been controversial, but it has been adopted in approximately 25 percent of the states.[15] The UCCC is an attempt to promulgate a comprehensive body of rules governing the most important aspects of consumer credit. Sections of the UCCC, for example, focus on truth in lending, maximum credit ceilings, door-to-door sales, and referral sales. The UCCC is also concerned with materials contained in fine print clauses and various provisions of creditor remedies, including deficiency judgments (personal judgments for the amount of debt that is not secured by property) and garnishments (proceedings where property, money, or wages controlled by a third person are transferred to the court to satisfy a judgment). (See Chapter 31 for details.) For example, the UCCC limits creditor remedies to either repossession or suit for default if the purchase price is $1,000 or less; purchases over $1,000 are unaffected by the limitations of credit remedies. The UCCC applies to most types of sales, including real estate. It also replaces existing state consumer credit laws as well as installment loan, usury, and retail installment sale acts.

Since the UCCC prohibits a seller in consumer credit sales or leases from taking negotiable instruments, except checks, it places limits on holders in due course. Cooling off periods for door-to-door sales are also specified in the code. Some provisions, such as those governing interest rates, differ from the provisions of other statutes. For example, the UCCC establishes interest rate ceilings of 18 percent per year on unpaid balances of the principal rather than having mandatory disclosure requirements.

Consumer Credit Reports

Nearly every credit transaction is accompanied by a consumer report or an investigated report for the creditor. The former is more common and is largely concerned with the amount and location of individual bank accounts, savings accounts, and other assets. In addition, information on existing credit liabilities, such as charge accounts and mortgages, is included in consumer credit reports. Information on the consumer's credit background, bill paying habits, previous judgments, tax liens, bankruptcies,

and other related areas can also be provided. In some cases, these reports contain income, marital status, occupation, employment history, legal difficulties, and other personal information.

Investigative reports, on the other hand, are far more personalized than consumer reports and are usually used for either employment or insurance decisions. Extensive interviews with business associates, neighbors, and other contacts are usually included in such reports. Prior to the Fair Credit Reporting Act, consumers who applied for credit had relatively little access to the contents of the reports, and those who were denied credit had no right to know why. If the information in the reports was obsolete or wrong, the consumer could not change it.

The Fair Credit Reporting Act specifies that a consumer must be notified when an investigative report will be made. Upon request, the consumer can obtain the substance of all information in the consumer reporting agency's files, as well as the sources and recipients of information. The latter, however, is subject to certain time limits. Reports by one business to a credit reporting agency or to another business that relate only to that business's experience with the consumer do not constitute a consumer report.

More importantly, if the consumer disagrees with the information in the agency's file, the agency must reinvestigate, unless the complaint is unfounded. Inaccurate information must be deleted from the agency's file, and the consumer can submit a statement concerning any unresolved disputes. Other information usually stays in the file for seven years.[16] The Federal Trade Commission has been given the responsibility for administering and enforcing provisions of the Fair Credit Reporting Act.

DISCLOSURE Perhaps the most important consumer protection law concerning disclosure is Title I of the Consumer Credit Protection Act, which is often referred to as the Truth-in-Lending Act. The act was instituted as a

---

15. By 1974 the UCCC had undergone six redrafts. Furthermore, in those jurisdictions where the law has been adopted, it is not uniform among them.

16. 15 USCA Sec. 1681 et seq. (1972).

means of comparing different credit offers. For example, one creditor may offer a rate of 1.5 percent per month. Another creditor may specify the finance charges as an add-on so that the consumer will pay $8 per $100 borrowed for thirty months. Still another creditor may take the finance charges from the initial amount of the loan so that the proceeds to the consumer will be the face amount of the loan less interest deductions. A uniform method of presenting these alternatives, such as that specified in Title I, lowers the cost to consumers of choosing among alternative loan options.

The Truth-in-Lending Act covers a number of factors, including the amount and purpose of the credit, the status of the debtor, and the business of the creditor. But the most important provisions govern (1) the time of disclosure, (2) the finance charges, and (3) the annual percentage rate. Disclosure in a closed end credit transaction (that is, one that applies to the current purchase only) must be made before the credit is extended. For example, Mountain View Mortgage Company must provide Janet Martin with the cost of financing and the interest rate for the purchase of a home before the time of closing (the time the purchase is finalized). Disclosure must be made early enough that Martin can shop around. In addition, the consumer must be told of the nature of the finance charges, including interest, service on other transaction activity charges, loan fees, points, finders' fees, investigation or credit report fees, and other charges. Buried finance charges must also be revealed. The finance charge then becomes the difference between the installment prices and the cash price. For example, a stereo can be sold for $600 payable in ten monthly installments of $60, or $500 cash. The $100 is really a finance charge and must be disclosed.

The final significant form of disclosure regards the "annual percentage rate," a method of reducing all finance charges to a common comparable finance charge per unit of time. In general, unless items are explicitly tied to particular clauses of the credit contract (such as a fee for the credit report) and are reported in the disclosure statement, their price must be included in the calculation of the annual percentage rate. Thus, when Colonial Bank, which handled the financing for Ron Starks's purchase of a used automobile, failed to disclose a sales fee separately or to include its value in the annual percentage rate, a violation of Regulation Z of the Truth-in-Lending Act was found. The sales fee in this case was included on the sales order form and represented the costs of title and license registration. The figure, however, was not separately itemized or listed as part of the finance charge on the disclosure statement.[17]

OPEN END CREDIT   The key features to open end credit are (1) a plan by which the customer and the creditor enter into a series of consumer credit transactions and (2) discretion in the consumer to either pay in installments or pay the balance in full. American Express, Master Charge, Visa, and the typical department store revolving account are all examples of open end credit.

In contrast to open end credit, closed end credit is extended for a specific period of time. The total amounts, number of payments, and due dates are generally agreed upon by the creditor and the customer at the time of the transaction. Common examples of closed end credit include most consumer loans from finance companies; credit sales of large items such as cars, furniture, and major appliances; and real estate transactions. A typical statement includes the outstanding balance at the start of the billing period, amounts credited during the billing cycle, the amount of any finance charge, the periodic rate of interest, the annual percentage rate, the unpaid balance on which the finance charge was computed, the closing date of the billing cycle, and the outstanding balance, as well as the statement of the period in which payment must be made in order to avoid finance charges. Disclosure requirements also apply to real estate transactions.

---

17.   Starks v. Orleans Motors, Inc., 500 F.2d 1182 (5th Cir. 1974).

RATE REGULATION Laws regulating the maximum cost of credit, often referred to as usury laws, date back to the period when it was considered immoral to charge a borrower interest. Initially, regulated rates applied to all loans, but it became clear that since the typical consumer loan was much smaller than the commercial loan, the cost of extending credit to consumers was considerably higher per dollar of the loan. This substantially restricted credit and prompted a model consumer loan law in 1916. The law specified a maximum 3.5 percent per month interest rate, a rate approximately seven times larger than the prevailing commercial rate.[18] Usually compensation or other benefits received by the lender are classified as interest unless a specific charge is made to reimburse or compensate the seller for services other than extending credit. For example, expenses involved in opening a loan and closing expenses for appraising or recording fees can be excluded. Furthermore, charges paid by the debtor on

default or prepayment penalties are not considered finance charges when computing the interest rate for usury statute purposes.[19]

COLLECTION AND REPOSSESSION Repossession of goods and collection procedures have been the subject of a large number of consumer grievances in the past. A number of regulations and court decisions have been instituted to reduce the more serious problems facing consumers in these areas.

In 1965 (with amendments in 1968) the Federal Trade Commission established "Guides against Deceptive Debt Collection" in order to prevent the scare tactics used in the collection of debts. In addition, state statutes often prohibit bills or letters that give the consumer the impression that a lawsuit has actually been initiated. Threatening telephone calls to the consumer or to relatives can also be unlawful if they exceed all reasonable bounds of decency.

18. The Uniform Small Loan Law.

19. Glaire v. La Lanne-Parris-Health Spa, Inc., 12 Cal.3d 915, 117 Cal.Rptr. 541, 528 P.2d 357 (1975).

CALLARAMA v. ASSOCIATES DISCOUNT CORP. OF DELAWARE, INC.

Supreme Court, Monroe County, New York, 1972. 329 N.Y.S.2d 711, 69 Misc.2d 287.

BACKGROUND AND FACTS *The plaintiff, Alphonse F. Callarama, filed this lawsuit against the defendant, Associates Discount Corporation of Delaware, seeking compensatory and punitive damages for emotional distress and injuries suffered because of the abusive and harassing collection techniques that the defendant employed to collect an unpaid balance owed by the plaintiff on a retail installment contract.*

In June 1970, agents of the defendant made telephone calls to the plaintiff, the plaintiff's wife, and various relatives of the plaintiff. The language used was damaging, threatening, harassing, and malicious, obscene, and vicious. As a result the plaintiff suffered severe emotional distress, humiliation, psychic shock, and physical injuries, including a posterior myocardial infarction. The defendants moved to dismiss the complaint on the ground that there was no such cause of action recognized by the law.

SCHNEPP, Justice.

* * *

Recovery is sought in tort and the question is whether threatening and harassing statements combined with the use of obscene and opprobious language made maliciously and resulting in damage are actionable. Can there be a recovery for the malicious infliction of emotional distress resulting in personal injuries without proof of the breach of any duty other than the duty to refrain from inflicting it?

Intent or recklessness is an essential element in torts which is characterized as outrageous conduct causing mental disturbance. A malicious act requires a wrongful motive and an intent to harm. The word "malice" adds color to intent and embraces within its meaning an intent to do evil. The fact that the complaint does not contain the word "intent" so that it "does not fall plainly within the rule announced in some decided case does not require the dismissal of the complaint". Novel causes need not be dismissed because they are novel and torts are infinitely various and are not limited or confined. Redress should be provided for any demonstrated wrong. This rule that there must be a remedy for the commission of a cognizable wrong has been limited by various practical difficulties such as proliferation of claims, fraudulent claims, speculative damages or injuries, problems of unlimited liability, foreseeability, unduly burdensome liability and the difficulty of circumscribing the area of liability within tolerable limits. "Freedom from mental disturbance is now a protected interest in this State" and any objection against recovery due to any of the practical difficulties described above is offset by the fact that emotional upsets are marked by definite physical symptoms which are capable of proof. * * *

The plaintiffs must still prove the underlying cause of action; "* * * the question of proof in individual situations should not be the arbitrary basis upon which to bar all actions, and 'it is beside the point * * * in determining sufficiency of a pleading'". It will be for the trier of the facts here to determine whether the conduct of the defendant was threatening, harassing and malicious and whether in fact it was the proximate cause of the emotional distress and physical injuries claimed by plaintiff. The conduct must be more than mere insults, indignities, threats and annoyances and must be so shocking and outrageous as to exceed all reasonable bounds of decency. The Court has no knowledge of the quality and genuineness of the proof, and whether or not it will fit into that category cannot be passed upon by the Court at this stage. This applies also on the question of plaintiffs' ability to recover punitive damages, which requires the submission of proof as to the character of the employment of the agent, his fitness and authorization.
* * *

The court refused to grant the defendant's motion to dismiss, allowing the plaintiff the right to move ahead into trial to prove, under recognized principles of law, the elements of his cause of action.   **JUDGMENT AND REMEDY**

In 1977, Congress passed the Fair Debt Collection Practices Act. The purpose of the act is to regulate the debt collection practices of persons who collect debts from consumers arising out of purchases that are primarily for personal, family, or household purposes.

Billing errors have long represented problems to consumers, especially with credit cards and other open end installment credit options. Prior to 1975, a consumer who was billed incorrectly on a credit card statement might have received a series of computer-written letters threatening a bad credit rating in response to the consumer's letters asking that the statement be corrected. The Fair Credit Billing Act of 1975 establishes certain procedures for consumers who complain about billing errors and requires that creditors explain or correct the mistakes within thirty days.

For various reasons, debtors do not always make the required payments, and creditors seek judicial action. Collection of debts through the judicial system is usually dependent on the initial filing of legal action. In some cases, collection can be begun prior to judgment through the use of garnishment. Thus, if California Credit brings an action against Linda MacDonald to collect a debt and learns that Homestead Mortgage holds her property, California Credit can garnish this property. If California Credit is successful in its legal action against MacDonald, the judgment can be satisfied by MacDonald's property held by Homestead Mortgage. Furthermore, if Homestead Mortgage disposes of the property, California Credit can recover from Homestead directly. Some states have statutes that exempt certain property from the collection process, for example, personal property up to $750. Other states have homestead laws that protect the real property of the debtor. Purchase money mortgages and security interest are generally not protected by the homestead statute in most states.

Title 3 of the Consumer Credit Protection Act limits garnishment to either 25 percent of a person's disposable earnings or the amount that the disposable earnings exceed thirty times the minimum federal hourly wage, whichever is smaller. Creditors are also limited in their ability to repossess secured property without notice in some form of adversary hearing.

WARRANTIES

Warranties that accompany the sale of consumer products are governed by the Uniform Commercial Code in all states except Louisiana.

Under the UCC, express and implied warranties of merchantability and fitness are given. If a car dealer states that an automobile is new, this constitutes an express warranty and need not be in writing, although the statement must be an affirmation of fact or promise.[20] Every sale of goods by a merchant seller carries an implied warranty of merchantability, which means that the goods must be fit for the ordinary purposes for which goods are used. For example, there is an implied warranty of merchantability that hand lotion will not burn the skin.[21] Implied warranties of fitness arise whenever buyers rely on the merchant's skill and judgment to select suitable goods. For example, if a customer wants to see ski boats, and the boat dealer sells the customer an outboard that has insufficient power to pull a water skier, a breach of warranty has probably occurred. Other provisions regarding disclosure of warranties are also governed by the UCC.

In response to a perceived problem in consumer warranty protection, Congress passed the Magnuson-Moss Warranty Act of 1975. The act was designed to simplify warranty protection so that the average consumer could understand the limitations or inclusions of warranty protection. The statute governs disclosure of warranty. Under its provisions, manufacturers and sellers are not required to make express warranties. However, if a warranty is given, it must comply with the disclosure requirements of the act. For the most part, warranties must now be designated either *full* or *limited*. A full warranty means that the seller warrants *at least* the minimum federal standards set forth in Section 104 of the Act (e.g., the warrantor must remedy any defect within a reasonable time and without charge). A limited warranty means that the warranties listed in Section 104 are *not all* included.[22]

---

20. Additional actions that are likely to result in express warranties are covered by Section 2-313 of the UCC; they are described in Chapter 21.

21. Section 2-314 covers additional implied warranties of merchantability; it too is discussed in Chapter 21.

22. See Chapter 21.

QUESTIONS AND
CASE PROBLEMS

1. Norman's Health Club, Inc., was a chain of recreation centers located in St. Louis, Missouri. The health clubs sold lifetime memberships for $360; the fee could be paid either in full or in twenty-four installments of $15 each. The vast majority of persons joining the health clubs chose the installment plan. Under this plan, Norman's Health Club had prospective members sign installment notes, which in turn were sold to finance companies at discounts of between $85 and $165. Club members who paid cash were charged about 10 percent less than those who paid under the installment plan. Assuming that no disclosures about finance charges were made on the installment notes signed by the prospective club members, has Norman's Health Club violated the disclosure requirements of the Truth-in-Lending Act? Has there been any violation by the finance companies that purchased the notes? [Joseph v. Norman's Health Club, Inc., 532 F.2d 86 (8th Cir. 1976)]

2. In 1969, a door-to-door salesman for Family Publications Services, Inc., sold Leila Mourning a five-year subscription to four magazines. Mourning agreed to pay $3.95 immediately and to remit a similar amount monthly for thirty months. She also signed a form contract that contained a clause stating that the subscriptions could not be cancelled and providing that any default in an installment payment would render the entire balance due. The contract made no reference to service or finance charges. Mourning thereafter defaulted on one of her payments, and Family Publications threatened to bring suit for the balance due. Mourning defended on the ground that Family Publications failed to disclose the nature and amount of the finance charges in its installment contract. Family Publications contended that since no finance charges were involved, no disclosure was necessary. Assuming no finance charges were involved in the installment plan, has Family Publications Services, Inc. violated the Truth-in-Lending Act? [Mourning v. Family Publications Services Inc., 411 U.S. 356, 93 S.Ct. 1652 (1973)]

3. On July 16, Polly Ann Barber entered into a retail installment contract with Kimbrell's, Inc., for the purchase of various items of household furniture totaling $592. Barber later sued Kimbrell's for violating the Truth-in-Lending Act because Kimbrell's used the term *total time balance* in its disclosure document rather than *total of payments* as the act required. At the same time, Barber sued Furniture Distributors, Inc., claiming that it too was liable as a creditor under the act. Furniture Distributors, Inc. participated in the development and preparation of the standard contract form and distributed it for use in all the retail stores in the Kimbrell's chain. It was also the parent company of Kimbrell's and had extensive knowledge of the credit terms for all the consumer credit sales that Kimbrell's made. Each time one of the Kimbrell's stores made a consumer credit sale, the installment contract was sent to Furniture Distributors for review. If Kimbrell's is in violation of the Truth-in-Lending Act, can Barber also hold Furniture Distributors liable? [Barber v. Kimbrell's, Inc., 577 F.2d 216 (4th Cir. 1978)]

4. The W. T. Grant Company (Grants), a retailer, sold both on a cash basis and under Grants credit plans. A customer who entered into a credit contract with Grants was offered the opportunity to take out credit life insurance, health and accident insurance, and property insurance. The election of insurance coverage was purely voluntary and was evidenced by the customer's signature on the contract within the blocked-off "Insurance Agreement" segment. The insurance charges became part of the unpaid balance upon which the finance charge was computed. Must the insurance charges be disclosed as finance charges? [Welmaker v. W. T. Grant Co., 365 F.Supp. 531 (N.D.Ga. 1972)]

5. Under Georgia law, promissory notes signed by consumers must be notarized. Generally, a small fee is charged by notaries for their signatures. American Finance Company was engaged in the business of making consumer loans. The loan contracts complied with all of the requirements of the Truth-in-Lending Act but failed to mention that customers would be charged a fee for notarization. Buford brought suit against American Finance Company. He had signed one of American's promissory notes and claimed in the suit that failure to disclose the notary fee constituted a violation of the Truth-in-Lending Act. Is he correct? American Finance Company argued that Buford was incorrect and further argued that even if Buford was right, American Finance should not be held liable since the charge was a minimal one and was left off inadvertently. Assuming that American Finance did not intentionally omit the charge, is this a

valid defense? [Buford v. American Finance Co., 333 F.Supp. 1243 (N.D.Ga. 1971)]

6. Roseman was employed as a debit agent for the John Hancock Insurance Company. He resigned, following accusations that he had been dishonest with his company expense account. Before his resignation he reimbursed the account. Part of the information concerning Roseman's resignation was contained in a credit report held by the Retail Credit Company, Inc. Subsequently, Roseman was denied a position with another insurance company after it consulted the Retail Credit Company's report. Assuming that the information held by the Retail Credit Company was accurate, was its circulation of such information illegal?

Roseman felt that he was slighted by Retail Credit Company because there were two sides to the story of his resignation, and his side was not included in the company's files. He complained that Retail Credit Company should have informed him that it had such information, and he claimed further that he had the right to include a statement in the files setting forth his version of the circumstances surrounding his resignation. Is Roseman correct? [Roseman v. Retail Credit Co., Inc., 428 F.Supp. 643 (E.D.Pa. 1977)]

7. Harold Grey signed an installment contract as payment for membership in a European Health Spas Club. The disclosure documents that accompanied the installment loan contract were printed in regular type, with the exception of the words: "FINANCE CHARGE," "ANNUAL PERCENTAGE RATE," and "MEMBER ACKNOWLEDGES THAT HE HAS READ AND RECEIVED A FILLED-IN SIGNED COPY OF THIS AGREEMENT." In addition, at the top of the disclosure statement, the words "NOTICE TO BUYER" were printed. Under federal truth-in-lending regulations, the words *finance charge* and *annual percentage rate* must be printed conspicuously in the truth-in-lending disclosure statements. Otherwise, the creditor is deemed in violation of the act. Has the requirement of conspicuousness been met? [Grey v. European Health Spas Inc., 428 F.Supp. 841 (D.C.Conn. 1977)]

8. Roger Gonzalez purchased a Ford from Schmerler Ford on credit. The installment credit agreement that Gonzalez signed named Ford Motor Credit Corporation as the payee of the loan. Nowhere on the loan form or the disclosure documents did the name Schmerler Ford appear. Schmerler Ford,

however, helped Gonzalez fill out the loan forms and then forwarded them to Ford Motor Credit Corporation. Schmerler lacked the authority to negotiate the interest rate charged on the loan and lacked the ability to approve Gonzalez's loan. Gonzalez's loan was made solely by Ford Motor Credit Corporation. Later it was discovered that the loan forms failed to disclose all of the relevant information that was required under the Truth-in-Lending Act. Who can be held liable as having violated the act—Schmerler Ford, Ford Motor Credit Corporation, or both? [Gonzalez v. Schmerler Ford, 397 F.Supp. 323 (N.D.Ill. 1975)]

9. On December 7, 1973, Jerry Reed and his wife executed an installment sales contract for the purchase of a new 1974 mobile home from Washington Trailer Sales, Inc. The Reeds made a cash down payment of $863 and were to pay the balance on an installment basis. On December 13, 1973, Washington Trailer Sales assigned the sales contract to Commerce Union Bank, a bank with which it did business on an irregular basis. In fact, this was the first contract that Washington Trailer Sales had assigned to the bank within the last seven months. Commerce Union Bank played no part in the arranging for and extending of credit to the Reeds. Subsequently, the Reeds brought an action against Washington Trailer Sales and Commerce Union Bank on the ground that certain statements contained in the installment sales contract disclosure form were not conspicuous, as required by the Truth-in-Lending Act. If the technical violation of the act that the Reeds allege could not have been discerned by Commerce Union Bank after a reasonable inspection of the installment contract and disclosure form, would Commerce Union Bank be liable? [Reed v. Washington Trailer Sales, Inc., 393 F.Supp. 886 (M.D.Tenn. 1974)]

10. A garnishment proceeding was brought by Sterling Finance Company against Lawrence Thornhill pursuant to a judgment that Sterling Finance had against Thornhill. Under the Truth-in-Lending Act, which limits garnishment to 25 percent of the garnishee's disposable earnings, Sterling Finance could have obtained $66.25 from Thornhill. Under the law of Ohio, where the garnishment proceeding was brought, Sterling Finance was entitled to $192.52. How much of Thornhill's pay can Sterling Finance Company garnish? [Sterling Finance Co. v. Thornhill, 263 N.E.2d 925 (Mun.Ct. 1970)]

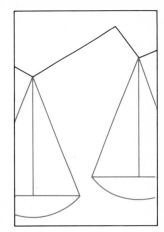

49

Government Regulation
Environmental Law

The traditional belief that air, water, and land will absorb all waste products without being harmed has been refuted by a considerable body of evidence. Furthermore, as society has become more urbanized, the concern for future degradation of the environment has strengthened. These forces, plus general economic growth, higher wealth, and the proliferation of synthetic products that resist decomposition, have caused policy makers and some individuals to seek methods to reduce or prevent pollution.

HISTORICAL BACKGROUND

In one sense, concerns about the environment are not new. The English Parliament, for example, passed a number of acts that regulated the burning of soft coal in medieval England. Moreover, through common law nuisance statutes, property owners were given relief from pollution in situations where the individual could identify a distinct harm separate from that affecting the general public. Thus, if a factory polluted the air and killed a farmer's crops, the farmer could seek an injunction against the factory.

Needless to say, nuisance suits that granted specific relief for individuals were inadequate when the harm from pollution could not be identified with groups separate from the public at large. Under the common law, citizens were denied *standing* (access to the courts) unless specific harm could be shown. Thus, a group of citizens who wished to stop a new development that would cause significant water pollution would be denied access to the courts on the ground that the harm to them did not differ from the harm borne by the general public.[1] A public authority, however, could sue for public nuisance.

The common law also limited relief from pollution in situations where the harm was caused by two or more independent sources. For example, if a number of firms were polluting the air, a harmed individual could sue any individual firm; however, until early in the twentieth century, the plaintiff was not able to sue all of the factories simultaneously. Thus, specific proof of damages and individual actions was often impossible. These difficulties in seeking relief in pollution cases, along with the forces creating additional pollution, have been largely responsible for the development of statutory regulations of environmental quality.

REGULATION BY ADMINISTRATIVE AGENCIES

Beginning in 1970, Congress passed a number of federal statutes directing administrative agencies to study the effects of pollution on the environment. On January 1, 1970, the National Environmental Policy Act created the Council of Environmental Quality and mandated that an environmental statement be prepared for every recommendation or report on legislation or major federal action that significantly affects the quality of the environment.[2] Since that time, the government has passed a number of acts, like the Clean Air Act, that govern air quality. In addition, a number of regulations have been promulgated for water quality. They include the Federal Water Pollution Control Act of 1965,[3]

the Marine Protection and Research and Sanctuaries Act of 1972,[4] and the Safe Drinking Water Act of 1974.[5] Additional regulations governing the use of pesticides,[6] radiation,[7] solid toxic substances,[8] and noise[9] have also been promulgated.

The federal government estimates that its total outlays in 1982 will approach $13.6 billion for environmental programs, an amount more than double that spent in 1975.[10] Furthermore, at least twenty federal agencies and departments are involved in enforcing regulations having an impact on environmental outcomes.[11] Their activities include, for example, research, development, and demonstration of the effective use of pesticide control methods and establishment and enforcement of standards.

Other federal environmental activities focus on the abatement of pollution from federal facilities and the employment and training of individuals involved with environmental pollution abatement activities.

ENVIRONMENTAL PROTECTION AGENCY

The Environmental Protection Agency (EPA) is a primary administrative organization for dealing with federal regulations concerning the environment. It employs approximately ten thousand individuals who carry out the direc-

---

1. Save the Bay Committee, Inc. v. Mayor, etc., of the City of Savannah, 227 Ga. 436, 181 S.E.2d 351 (1971).
2. National Environmental Policy Act of 1969, 42 USCA Sec. 4321 et seq.
3. Federal Water Pollution Control Act, 33 USCA Sec. 1151 (1965).
4. Marine Protection and Research and Sanctuaries Act of 1972, 16 USCA Sec. 1431 et seq; 33 USCA Sec. 1407 et seq.
5. Safe Drinking Waters Act, 21 USCA Sec. 349; 42 USCA Sec. 201, 300F et seq. (1974).
6. Federal Insecticide, Fungicide and Rodenticide Act of 1972. 7 USCA Sec. 135 et seq; (1947) as amended May 12, 1964.
7. Resource Conservation Recovery Act of 1976, 42 USCA Sec. 6901 et seq. (1976).
8. Toxic Substances Control Act of 1976. 15 USCA Sec. 2602 (1976).
9. Noise Control Act of 1972. 42 USCA Sec. 1604 (1972).
10. *Budget of the United States Government,* Fiscal Year 1980, (Washington, D.C.: Government Printing Office, 1979) p. 143.
11. *Budget of the United States Government, Special Analyses,* Fiscal Year 1980 (Washington, D.C.: Government Printing Office, 1979), p. 273.

tives of the numerous and complex regulations of federal statutes affecting the environment, including those described above.

Environmental Impact Statements

One of the important responsibilities of the EPA is seeing that all federal actions, including proposed legislation, affecting the quality of the human environment have their impact on the environment analyzed. The environmental impact statement has become an important instrument used by private citizens, consumer interests, businesses, and federal agencies in shaping the final outcome of regulatory actions. Even if an agency believes that the impact statement is unnecessary, a statement supporting this conclusion must be filed.[12]

_____

12. Arizona Public Service Co. v. Federal Power Comm., 483 F.2d 1275 (D.C.Cir. 1973).

BACKGROUND AND FACTS *The director of the Bureau of Land Management prepared an environmental impact statement in connection with the proposed sale of offshore oil lands by the Department of the Interior. The Natural Resources Defense Council claimed that the statement was inadequate and obtained an injunction against the proposed sale. The plaintiffs, Natural Resources Defense Council, Inc., argued that the environmental impact statement failed to adequately discuss the alternatives it contained. The government appealed, moving to dismiss the preliminary injunction.*

NATURAL RESOURCES DEFENSE COUNCIL INC. v. MORTON
United States Court of Appeals, District of Columbia Circuit, 1972.
458 F.2d 827.

LEVENTHAL, Circuit Judge.

This appeal raises a question as to the scope of the requirement of the National Environmental Policy Act (NEPA) that environmental impact statements contain a discussion of alternatives. * * *
* * *

Adjacent to the proposed lease area is the greatest estuarine coastal marsh complex in the United States, some 7.9 million acres, providing food, nursery habitat and spawning ground vital to fish, shellfish and wildlife, as well as food and shelter for migratory waterfowl, wading birds and fur-bearing animals. * * *

The coastal regions of Louisiana and Mississippi contain millions of acres suitable for outdoor recreation, with a number of state and federal recreation areas, and extensive beach shorelines (397 miles for Louisiana, and 100 miles for Mississippi). * * *
* * *

Oil pollution is the problem most extensively discussed in the Statement and its exposition of unavoidable adverse environmental effects. The Statement acknowledges that both short and long term effects on the environment can be expected from spillage, including in that term major spills (like that in the Santa Barbara Channel in 1969); minor spills from operations and unidentified sources; and discharge of waste water contaminated with oil.
* * *

The [District] Court finds that the defendants failed to comply with NEPA by failing to discuss some alternatives at all, such as meeting energy demands by federal legislation or administrative action freeing current onshore and state-controlled offshore production from state market demand prorationing or a change in the Federal Power Commission's natural gas pricing policies. In addition the defendants only superficially discussed the alternatives listed in their Final Impact Statement, and they failed to discuss in detail the environmental impacts of the alternatives they listed in the statement. The Court does not wish to give the impression that it believes the alternatives are better than the proposed lease sale, but it believes that these alternatives must be explored and discussed thoroughly in order to comport with the intent and requirements of Section 4332(2)(C) of NEPA.

* * *

Congress contemplated that the Impact Statement would constitute the environmental source material for the information of the Congress as well as the Executive, in connection with the making of relevant decisions, and would be available to enhance enlightenment of—and by—the public. The impact statement provides a basis for (a) evaluation of the benefits of the proposed project in light of its environmental risks, and (b) comparison of the net balance for the proposed project with the environmental risks presented by alternative courses of action.

* * *

We think the Secretary's Statement erred in stating that the alternative of elimination of oil import quotas was entirely outside its cognizance. Assuming, as the Statement puts it, that this alternative "involves complex factors and concepts, including national security, which are beyond the scope of this statement," it does not follow that the Statement should not present the environmental effects of that alternative. While the consideration of pertinent alternatives requires a weighing of numerous matters, such as economics, foreign relations, national security, the fact remains that, as to the ingredient of possible adverse environmental impact, it is the essence and thrust of NEPA that the pertinent Statement serve to gather in one place a discussion of the relative environmental impact of alternatives.

The Government also contends that the only "alternatives" required for discussion under NEPA are those which can be adopted and put into effect by the official or agency issuing the statement. The Government seeks to distinguish the kind of impact statement required for a major Federal action from that required with a legislative proposal. And it stresses that the objective of the Secretary's action was to carry out the directive in the President's clean energy message * * *.

While we agree with so much of the Government's presentation as rests on the assumption that the alternatives required for discussion are those reasonably available, we do not agree that this requires a limitation to measures the agency or official can adopt. * * *

When the proposed action is an integral part of a coordinated plan to deal with a broad problem, the range of alternatives that must be evaluated is broadened. While the Department of the Interior does not have the authority to eliminate or reduce oil import quotas, such action is within the purview of both Congress and the President, to whom the impact statement goes. The impact statement is not only for the exposition of the thinking of the agency, but also for the guidance of these ultimate decision-makers, and must provide them with the environmental effects of both the proposal and the alternatives, for their

consideration along with the various other elements of the public interest.
* * *

The need for continuing review of environmental impact of alternatives under NEPA cannot be put to one side on the ground of past determinations by Congress or the President. * * *
* * *

We reiterate that the discussion of environmental effects of alternatives need not be exhaustive. What is required is information sufficient to permit a reasoned choice of alternatives so far as environmental aspects are concerned. * * *

* * * In this as in other areas, the functions of courts and agencies, rightly understood, are not in opposition but in collaboration, toward achievement of the end prescribed by Congress. So long as the officials and agencies have taken the "hard look" at environmental consequences mandated by Congress, the court does not seek to impose unreasonable extremes or to interject itself within the area of discretion of the executive as to the choice of the action to be taken.

Informed by our judgment that discussion of alternatives may be required even though the action required lies outside the Interior Department, the Secretary will, we have no doubt, be able without undue delay to provide the kind of reasonable discussion of alternatives and their environmental consequences that Congress contemplated.
* * *

The court of appeals denied the government's motion. The Department of Interior was required to discuss alternatives in its environmental impact statement more fully. **JUDGMENT AND REMEDY**

WHO PREPARES THE STATEMENT Environmental impact statements are prepared by the agency with the responsibility for carrying out the project. Anything that will potentially affect the environment—such as urban renewal projects, new construction, or the introduction of new technology—requires an environmental impact statement.[13] Among other requirements, environmental impact statements must (1) identify the environmental impact of the proposed action, (2) discuss alternatives to it, (3) identify differences between short-term and long-term impacts, (4) identify unavoidable impacts of the proposed action, and (5) indicate all irreversible uses of resources.

The Environmental Protection Agency is also responsible for the primary enforcement of statutory regulations concerning the environ-

ment, and it is likely that the number of regulations enforced by the agency will continue to increase in the future.

PRIVATE LITIGATION

Private parties will continue to recover damages or obtain injunctions for environmental harms under a combination of statutory and common law provisions. The Clean Air Act Amendments of 1972, the Water Pollution and Prevention Control Act of 1972, and the Noise Control Act of 1972, for example, authorize private lawsuits for violations of air, water, and noise pollution standards. Furthermore, some courts have held that organizations can have standing in representing members' interests even if there is no direct organizational interest in the dispute.[14]

---

13.   Loveless v. Yantis, 82 Wash.2d 754, 513 P.2d 1023 (1973).

14.   Undergraduate Student Ass'n v. Peltason, 359 F.Supp. 320 (N.D.Ill. 1973).

On the other hand, some federal statutes give the government exclusive rights to lawsuits for violations of environmental protection regulations. For example, the Environmental Protection Agency is given the exclusive right to bring suits involving the violation of the Federal Water Pollution Control Act.

AIR POLLUTION

Federal involvement with air pollution goes back to the 1950s, when Congress authorized funds for air pollution research. In 1963, the federal government passed the Clean Air Act, which focused on multistate air pollution and provided assistance to states. Various amendments, particularly in 1970 and 1977,[15] strengthened the government's authority to regulate the quality of air. In total, these acts provide the regulatory basis for promulgating standards to control pollution, primarily automobile and stationary sources.

Automobile Pollution

Regulations governing air pollution from automobiles and other mobile sources specify pollution standards and time schedules. For example, the 1970 Clean Air Act required a

reduction of 90 percent in the amount of carbon monoxide and hydrocarbons emitted from automobiles by 1975.[16] Additional regulations that control air pollution indirectly focus on improved gas mileage for new automobiles and gasoline additives such as lead. Similar regulations for aircraft are administered by the Federal Aviation Administration. The Environmental Protection Agency also sets national air quality standards for major pollutants throughout the United States.

The 1977 amendments to the Clean Air Act establish multilevel standards by preventing the deterioration of air quality in areas where the existing quality exceeds that required by federal law. These air quality standards cover carbon monoxide, nitrogen dioxide, hydrocarbons, sulfur dioxide, and other harmful materials. Standards are specified at two levels. The highest, which is designed to protect human health, has general guidelines for protecting vegetation, climate, visibility, and certain economic conditions. The Department of Health, Education, and Welfare has divided the country into atmospheric areas for the purpose of preparing these controls, and each area is required to institute a plan for meeting the standards.

---

15. Clean Air Act Amendments of 1970, 42 USC Sec. 7521, Clean Air Act Amendments of 1977, 42 USC Secs. 7521-25, 7541-51.

16. Carbon monoxide, a colorless, odorless gas, can reduce mental performance and result in death if inhaled in sufficient quantities. Hydrocarbons are unburned fuel, one of the principal ingredients that generate smog.

ETHYL CORP. v.
ENVIRONMENTAL
PROTECTION
AGENCY

United States Court of Appeals,
District of Columbia Circuit,
1976. 541 F.2d 1.

BACKGROUND AND FACTS *Ethyl Corporation, a leading producer of "antiknock" compounds for increasing gasoline octane rating, filed for review of the Environmental Protection Agency order that required annual reductions in the lead content of gasoline. The Clean Air Act authorized the agency to regulate gasoline additives that are a danger to public health or welfare. The lower court found that the EPA's determination that lead emissions introduced a significant risk of harm to urban populations was not an abuse of discretion. The Ethyl Corporation appealed.*

WRIGHT, Circuit Judge.

* * *

Man's ability to alter his environment has developed far more rapidly than his ability to foresee with certainty the effects of his alterations. It is only recently that we have begun to appreciate the danger posed by unregulated modification of the world around us, and have created watchdog agencies whose task it is to warn us, and protect us, when technological "advances" present dangers unappreciated— or unrevealed—by their supporters. Such agencies, unequipped with crystal balls and unable to read the future, are nonetheless charged with evaluating the effects of unprecedented environmental modifications, often made on a massive scale. Necessarily, they must deal with predictions and uncertainty, with developing evidence, with conflicting evidence, and, sometimes, with little or no evidence at all. Today we address the scope of the power delegated one such watchdog, the Environmental Protection Agency (EPA). We must determine the certainty required by the Clean Air Act before EPA may act to protect the health of our populace from the lead particulate emissions of automobiles.

* * *

Hard on the introduction of the first gasoline-powered automobiles came the discovery that lead "antiknock" compounds, when added to gasoline, dramatically increase the fuel's octane rating. Increased octane allows for higher compression engines, which operate with greater efficiency. Since 1923 antiknocks have been regularly added to gasoline, and a large industry has developed to supply those compounds. Today, approximately 90 percent of motor gasoline manufactured in the United States contains lead additives, even though most 1975 and 1976 model automobiles are equipped with catalytic converters, which require lead-free gasoline. From the beginning, however, scientists have questioned whether the addition of lead to gasoline, and its consequent diffusion into the atmosphere from the automobile emission, poses a danger to the public health. * * *

* * *

On October 28, 1973, as a result of a motion filed in *Natural Resources Defense Council, Inc. v. EPA,* this court ordered EPA to reach within 30 days a final decision on whether lead additives should be regulated for health reasons. * * * [The EPA Document] candidly discusses the various scientific studies, both pro and con, underlying this information, and ultimately concludes that lead from automobile emissions will endanger the public health. * * * Under the final regulations, lead in all gasoline would be reduced over a five-year period to an average of 0.5 grams per gallon.

* * * Our scope * * * requires us to strike "agency action, findings, and conclusions" [only if] we find [them] to be "arbitrary, capricious, an abuse of discretion, or otherwise not in accordance with law." This standard of review is a highly deferential one. It presumes agency action to be valid. Moreover, it forbids the court's substituting its judgment for that of the agency * * *.

This is not to say, however, that we must rubber-stamp the agency decision as correct. To do so would render the appellate process a superfluous (although time-consuming) ritual. Rather, the reviewing court must assure itself that the agency decision was "based on a consideration of the relevant factors * * *."

Petitioners [Ethyl Corp.] vigorously attack both the sufficiency and the validity of the many scientific studies relied upon by the Administrator, while advancing for consideration various studies allegedly supportive of their position. The record in this case is massive—over 10,000 pages. Not surprisingly, evidence may be isolated that supports virtually any inference one might care to draw. * * *

Because of the importance of the issues raised, we have accorded this case the most careful and exhaustive consideration. We find that in this rule-making proceeding the EPA has complied with all the statutory procedural requirements and that its reasons as stated in its opinion provide a rational basis for its action. Since we reject all of petitioners' claims of error the Agency may enforce its low-lead regulations.

* * *

JUDGMENT AND REMEDY *The Environmental Protection Agency regulations were affirmed by the U.S. Court of Appeals. The EPA was permitted to enforce its low lead regulations.*

WATER POLLUTION

Federal regulations governing the pollution of water can be traced back nearly a century to the River and Harbor Act of 1886 as amended in 1899.[17] These regulations required a permit for discharging or depositing refuse in navigable waterways. The courts have even determined that hot water can be considered refuse.[18] In 1965, Congress passed the Federal Water Pollution Control Act, which strengthened the Environmental Protection Agency's enforcement powers.

Clean Water Regulation

Perhaps the most important regulations that govern the quality of water were instituted in 1972 by Congress. These regulations establish goals to (1) make waters safe for swimming, (2) protect fish and wildlife, and (3) eliminate the discharge of pollutants into the water. They set forth specific time schedules, which were extended by amendment in 1977. The 1972 Clean Water Act also specifies a number of regulations with time schedules for controlling industrial water pollution. Regulations for the most part specify that the best available tech-

nology be installed. Further, the act requires both municipal and industrial dischargers to apply for permits before they discharge wastes into the nation's navigable waters. Finally, the act establishes standing for citizens (or organizations) whose interests have been affected against parties who violate EPA or state standards and orders. Both injunctive relief and damages can be sought through claims under the act.

Other Regulations

In 1972, through the Marine Protection Research and Sanctuaries Act, Congress established a system of permits that regulate the discharge and introduction of materials into coastal waters and continuous marine areas. The Safe Drinking Water Act of 1974 established additional regulations governing drinking water standards. The rules, which are similar to those under the Clean Water Act, provide that states assume the primary responsibility for complying with national standards. The federal government assumes responsibility where states fail to institute or enforce drinking water standards. In most cases, explicit penalties are imposed on parties that pollute the water. The polluting party can also be required to clean up pollution or pay for the cost of doing so.

---

17. 33 USC Sec. 407.
18. 33 USC Sec. 1254(t).

BACKGROUND AND FACTS   *In this action, a number of oil companies, including Atlantic Richfield Company and Gulf Oil Co., were assessed monetary penalties that included paying for the cost of cleaning up oil discharges. The defendants (Atlantic Richfield) argued that the imposition of such penalties in an accidental oil spill when the reporting and cleaning requirements had been satisfied constituted a criminal action. Therefore, the defendants believed that they had the right to a jury trial. The court had to determine whether these penalties denied due process.*

Two cases were consolidated and heard by the District Court simultaneously. In one case, Atlantic Richfield Company (Arco) was the defendant; in the other, Gulf Oil Company was the defendant.

UNITED STATES OF AMERICA v. ATLANTIC RICHFIELD CO.

Eastern District of Pennsylvania 1977. 429 F.Supp. 830.

BECKER, District Judge.

* * *

These cases raise issues concerning the proper construction and the constitutionality of the "civil penalty" provision of the oil and hazardous substance sections of the Federal Water Pollution Control Act Amendments of 1972. * * * The constructional issues boil down to whether Congress intended to impose the civil penalty on persons who spill oil accidentally, report such spill to the appropriate authorities, and clean it up at their own expense (hereinafter "accidental, reporting self-cleaners"). * * *

Turning now to the operative facts, we note that the stipulations as to the relevant events in each of the cases before us track essentially the same pattern. In each case either Arco or Gulf owned or operated a vessel or facility from which oil was discharged in harmful quantity into the navigable waters of the United States. The discharges were "accidental" or "unintentional," but, perforce, they violated the prohibition on discharge of (b)(3); hence, without more, they subjected the owners (defendants) to liability for the civil penalty under (b)(6). However, the appropriate defendant (or its agent) promptly reported each spill and cleaned it up within the limits of technological feasibility and to the satisfaction of the Coast Guard. Despite defendants' compliance with their reporting and clean up duties, the Coast Guard, following the prescribed administrative procedure, assessed a civil penalty in each case. Upon defendants' refusal to pay, the government sued.

* * *

The first prong of defendants' argument goes as follows: The stipulated facts would not survive a motion to dismiss for failure to state a claim under the common law of negligence; *i. e.*, although the facts reveal "accidental" spills, they do not reveal a basis for inferring that defendants caused the spills through a lack of due care; but "negligence" is the lowest level of "fault" recognized by our law; *i. e.*, non-negligent conduct is reasonable conduct; therefore, if the spills were not negligent, we can infer that there was no reasonable means for defendants to prevent the spills.

We find that defendants' argument makes most sense when translated into simple economic terms. A rational owner of an oil facility, recognizing his potential liabilities for clean ups * * * (and for damages under common law damage remedies which §1321 [of the act] leaves untouched), will attempt to minimize the costs of spills. To accomplish this he will calculate the marginal costs of preventing spills and of potential liabilities. He will thereupon engage in prevention to the point where the marginal cost of prevention equals his marginal liability for spills. Because that point defines *reasonable* spill prevention, a reasonable person will spend money for just that much prevention and no more. To spend less would be negligent. * * * To spend more would be wasteful or inefficient. * * *

On this basis we can make some sense of defendants' argument that (b)(6) serves no regulatory purpose when applied to "faultless" spillers. But defendants move from the claim that they were "faultless" to the claim that no regulatory purpose would be served by imposing a (b)(6) penalty, an argument we reject because it proceeds from a faulty premise. While it is true that the stipulated facts about the spills themselves would not be sufficient to support an action in negligence, this is not such an action, but rather an action to enforce a penalty.

The elements of this statutory action are only that defendant violated (b)(3) and that the Coast Guard following the appropriate procedure assessed the (b)(6) penalty. The statute does not make "fault" an element of the cause of action, but rather a factor in the administrative penalty setting procedure. This is proper because there is no principle of law which requires that civil regulability through imposition of penalty be predicated upon a finding of fault. Moreover, a number of factors support civil regulability here in the absence of fault. First, as we explain more fully in our discussion of the Constitutional issues, *infra*, the principal goal of (b)(6) is to *deter* spills. Second, the Congressional purpose here was to impose a standard of conduct higher than that related just to economic efficiency. Additionally, the Congress obviously believed: (a) that no clean up effort could be complete because, after discharge, it is impossible to guarantee against residual harm from quantities of oil too small or too well dispersed to be detectable; and (b) that even the transitory pollution of waters was deleterious to the environment. * * *

In view of the foregoing analysis we must reject defendant's contention that, as applied to accidental, reporting, self-cleaners, (b)(6) is really criminal rather than civil because, (1) the statutory language is not ambiguous; and (2) even where defendants are not at fault, the penalty does not act only as a punishment but serves the ends of civil regulation. * * *

JUDGMENT AND REMEDY *The district court held that the penalties provided under the Federal Water Pollution Control Act Amendments of 1972 were civil, not criminal, penalties. Therefore, the government could continue to assess and collect them against Atlantic Richfield, Gulf, and other oil companies for accidental oil spills.*

NOISE POLLUTION

In 1972, Congress prescribed standards and regulations for the control of aircraft noise, including sonic booms, and for the control of emissions of railroad and motor vehicles involved in interstate commerce. The Noise Control Acts of 1970 and 1972 established the goal of creating an environment free from noise that is injurious to the health and welfare of the public. The courts have ruled that local control of noise is preempted when state regulations conflict with those established by federal statutes.[19]

Regulations promulgated by the noise control acts are administrated by the Federal Aviation Administration, the Environmental Protection Agency, and the Department of Transportation. The EPA, for example, is authorized to establish noise emission levels for equipment, motors, and engines. It also reviews production processes, verifies reports for compliance with the law, conducts audit tests, and makes inspections of manufacturer records.

TOXIC SUBSTANCES

The Toxic Substances Control Act was passed in 1976 to regulate chemicals and chemical compounds that are known to be toxic and to introduce procedures for investigating harmful effects from new chemical compounds. The regulations authorize the Environmental Protection Agency to insure that manufacturers, processors, and other organizations using chemicals determine their effect on human health and the environment before they are used by the public. The EPA also has the authority to regulate substances that potentially create a hazard or an unreasonable risk of injury.

PESTICIDE CONTROL

The use of chemical pesticides to kill insects and weeds has significantly increased agricultural productivity. On the other hand, there is a growing body of evidence that residuals from these chemicals have not been absorbed by the environment. In some cases, build-ups of residuals have killed animals, and some potential long-term effects detrimental to the public have also been identified. The original regulations governing pesticides were established by the Federal Insecticide, Fungicide and Rodenticide Act of 1947, as amended in 1972.[20] The Environmental Protection Agency has been given the authority to control the introduction of pesticides. Pesticides must be (1) registered before they can be sold, (2) certified and used only for approved applications, and (3) used in amounts that meet established limits when they are applied to crops that provide food for animals or people. The EPA also has the right to inspect manufacturing establishments. In some situations, the supply of pesticides is controlled to keep hazardous chemicals off the market. Those substances that have been identified as harmful are subject to suspension and cancellation of registration.

WASTE DISPOSAL

Waste disposal can occur on land, in the water, or in the air; thus regulations protecting these resources from pollution also apply to waste disposal. In 1970, Congress passed the Materials Policy Act, an act designed to reduce solid waste disposal by encouraging the recycling of waste and the reuse of materials by society. The Act also provides for pilot waste disposal projects utilizing modern technology. For example, the development and use of technology that converts garbage into useful products has been greatly encouraged by the solid waste programs of the Environmental Protection Agency. The EPA also carries out the provisions of the Resource Conservation and Recovery Act of 1976, which governs EPA studies and recommendations of solid waste disposal ranging from glass and plastic waste to airport landfill. The EPA is primarily concerned with issuing federal facility permits and reviewing the state permit system for the use of certain equipment. It conducts on-site inspections of hazardous waste generators and cites violators. The Solid Waste Disposal Act gives each state the power to enact its own hazardous waste standards.

Federal statutes also attempt to generate state and local community initiative for solving solid waste disposal problems by providing monies and expert guidance for state and local studies. A number of states have sought to reduce the problem of solid waste disposal by requiring recycling or reuse of various products.

19. Burbank v. Lockheed Air Terminal Inc., 411 U.S. 624, 93 S.Ct. 1854 (1973).

20. Federal Environmental Pesticide Control Act of 1972.

AMERICAN CAN CO. v.
OREGON LIQUOR
CONTROL COMM.

15 Or.App. 618, 517 P.2d 691
1974.

BACKGROUND AND FACTS *The State of Oregon adopted a law prohibiting the use of nonreturnable containers for beer and carbonated beverages. It also prohibited the sale of metal beverage containers that used detachable pull-top opening devices. The American Can Company instituted an action against the Oregon Liquor Control Commission as well as other administrative bodies of the State of Oregon and appealed the initial decision that upheld the law.*

TANZER, Judge.

* * *

The bottle bill, enacted by the Oregon legislature in 1971, became effective on October 1, 1972. The statute's principal provisions are as follows:

1. Every retailer of the covered beverages (beer or carbonated beverages) in Oregon is required to "accept from a consumer any empty beverage containers of the kind, common size and brand sold by the dealer" and to pay the consumer the statutory "refund value" of the container. * * *

* * *

Metal beverage containers, a part of which is wholly detachable in opening without a can opener ("pull top" cans), may not be sold at retail in Oregon.

* * *

The primary legislative purpose of the bottle bill is to cause bottlers of carbonated soft drinks and brewers to package their products for distribution in Oregon in returnable, multiple-use deposit bottles toward the goals of reducing litter and solid waste in Oregon and reducing the injuries to people and animals due to discarded "pull tops."

As bases for attacking the validity of the statute, plaintiffs [the American Can Company] invoke the Equal Protection and Due Process Clauses of the Fourteenth Amendment to the United States Constitution, and the Commerce Clause, art. 1, § 8, clause 3, of the United States Constitution. In addition, plaintiffs cite various provisions of the Oregon Constitution.

One of the plaintiffs' main objectives at trial was to show that the bottle bill would have an effect not only upon manufacturers of bottles and cans, but also upon an entire distribution chain including brewers, soft drink bottlers and canners, beer wholesalers, retailers and, ultimately, consumers. The evidence in this regard demonstrated that the consumption of malt beverages and soft drinks had increased greatly in the United States in recent years, and that a large part of this increase could be attributed to the use of convenient "one-way" packages, including both cans and non-returnable bottles. Plaintiffs assert that non-returnable containers are essential to the existence of national and regional beer markets, and that non-returnable containers are also essential to the continued existence of soft drink enterprises. The non-returnable containers were shown to have provided economies in the packaging and distribution of soft drinks and beer by eliminating the cost of shipping the containers both ways, thus causing an increase in feasible shipping distances and enlarging the market each manufacturer could cover. Among the effects of the bottle bill, plaintiffs' witnesses predicted, would be a substantial reduction in Oregon sales of soft drinks packaged outside Oregon, and impairment of the ability of distant brewers to compete in the Oregon market. The bottle bill would necessitate substantial changes in the structure of the industries involved in the manufacturing and merchandising of beer and soft drinks.

* * *

The Oregon legislature was persuaded that the economic benefit to the beverage industry brought with it deleterious consequences to the environment and additional cost to the public. The aggravation of the problems of litter in public places and solid waste disposal and the attendant economic and esthetic burden to the public outweighed the narrower economic benefit to the industry. Thus the legislature enacted the bottle bill over the articulate opposition of the industries represented by plaintiffs.

As with every change of circumstance in the market place, there are gainers and there are losers. Just as there were gainers and losers, with plaintiffs apparently among the gainers, when the industry adapted to the development of non-returnable containers, there will be new gainers and losers as they adapt to the ban. The economic losses complained of by plaintiffs in this case are essentially the consequences of readjustment of the beverage manufacturing and distribution systems to the older technology in order to compete in the Oregon market.

* * *

* * * The introduction of any new circumstance affecting competition will cause economic winners and economic losers throughout the industry as it readjusts to that new circumstance. The evidence is that plaintiffs expect to be among the losers, unless, of course, they are able to make marketing adjustments.

Economic loss restricted to certain elements of the beverage industry must be viewed in relation to the broader loss to the general public of the state of Oregon which the legislature sought, by enactment of the bottle bill, to avoid. The availability of land and revenues for solid waste disposal, the cost of litter collection on our highways and in our public parks, the depletion of mineral and energy resources, the injuries to humans and animals caused by discarded pull tops, and the esthetic blight on our landscape, are all economic, safety and esthetic burdens of great consequence which must be borne by every member of the public. The legislature attached higher significance to the cost to the public than they did to the cost to the beverage industry and we have no cause to disturb that legislative determination.

* * *

Plaintiffs' and intervenors' constitutional challenges having failed, we hold the bottle bill to be a valid exercise of Oregon's police power. In doing so, we acknowledge having had the benefit of an able analysis by the trial court.

* * *

The Supreme Court of Oregon affirmed the trial court's ruling that Oregon had legitimately exercised its state police power in passing laws concerning solid waste disposal. The additional cost to the beverage industry was recognized, but the court would not accept it as a justification for overturning a legislative enactment. Hence, the bottle bill was upheld.

JUDGMENT AND REMEDY

JUDICIAL LIMITS

In the first half of the 1970s, federal and state legislators enacted many statutes that regulate environmental quality. Judicial interpretations of these statutes have generally given the administrative agencies that carry out their directives broad discretionary powers. Beginning in the mid 1970s, however, the courts began to place stricter limits on administrative discretion. Recent court decisions that impose a cost-benefit standard on administrative decisions are likely to limit discretion in the environmental area as well.

In American Petroleum v. Occupational Safety and Health Administration, an OSHA regulation limiting benzine exposure in the workplace was invalidated by the Fifth Circuit Court of Appeals.[21] In 1977, OSHA promulgated regulations reducing permissible exposure by 90 percent from the 1971 standard. This action was based primarily on the results of three studies that showed an increased risk of leukemia in workers who had been exposed to benzine at levels in excess of one hundred times the 1977 permissible levels. The court interpreted the "reasonably necessary" language of the Occupational Safety and Health Act to require an estimate of the expected benefits of the regulation "in order to determine whether the benefits bear a reasonable relationship to the standard's demonstrably high costs."

---

21.   581 F.2d 493 (5th Cir. 1978).

QUESTIONS AND CASE PROBLEMS

1.   In April 1973, virtually all of the nation's railroads requested ICC authority for a rate increase of 5 percent. After an environmental study was completed, the ICC determined that the rate increase would not have a significant environmental impact. Thus, instead of publishing a complete environmental impact statement, the ICC published only a short statement giving its conclusions that no significant adverse environmental impact would result from the rate increase and giving the reasons for its determination. A number of interested parties brought suit to enjoin the rate increase on the ground that it would lead to higher costs for recycling materials and therefore have a significant adverse impact on the environment, since recycled materials would be priced out of the market. The ICC's published decision not to prepare a complete environmental impact statement documented the alleged effects of the rate increases on recyclable materials. Did the ICC comply with the Environmental Policy Act when it published an abbreviated statement? [Asphalt Roofing Mfg. Ass'n v. ICC, 567 F.2d 994 (D.C. Cir. 1977)]

2.   Citizens against Toxic Sprays, Inc. was an organization established to challenge the use of toxic sprays in places where they could be harmful to humans, animals, or vegetation. The group sought to enjoin the United States Forest Service from using the herbicide TCDD because of its hazardous effect on people who breathed it. TCDD was used only in national forests, not in any residential areas. Citizens against Toxic Sprays alleged that some of its members were affected by the use of TCDD in two of the national forests because they lived near them, worked in them, or used them for recreational activities. Does Citizens against Toxic Sprays have *standing* to sue the United States Forest Service? [Citizens Against Toxic Sprays, Inc. v. Bergland, 428 F.Supp. 908 (D.C.Or. 1977)]

3.   Virginia Dalsis, the proprietor of a small store in the city of Olean, New York, brought a suit to enjoin the construction of a mall because of its projected size. Dalsis alleged that the large size of the shopping center would have an adverse environmental effect on the downtown area, causing economic blight and deterioration to the section in which her business was located. Dalsis, however, did not bring the suit until three months after construction of the shopping mall had begun even though she was aware of the mall's potential size almost a year before construction started. Should Dalsis be allowed to enjoin the construction of the shopping mall? [Dalsis v. Hills, 424 F.Supp. 784 (W.D.N.Y. 1976)]

4.   The Government Services Administration (GSA) entered into an agreement with a private individual

under which the individual was to construct a building to GSA's specifications and lease it to the GSA. Under the contemplated lease provision, GSA would have use of the entire building for a five-year (renewable) period. As many as 2,300 government employees would be assigned to the building, and most would commute by automobile. Cost of the lease was approximately $11 million. GSA proceeded with its plans for the building without preparing any environmental impact statement. Was a statement necessary? [S.W. Neighborhood Assembly v. Eckard, 445 F.Supp. 1195 (D.C.D.C. 1978)]

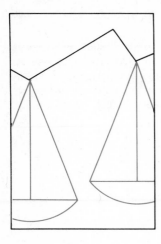

50

Government Regulation
Antitrust

Competition is the socially desired state of market organization in the United States today. Therefore, antitrust laws have been legislated and enforced to improve business behavior and to keep markets competitive. The next two chapters will look at the important developments in the field of antitrust law and how they affect business today. Chapter 50 will discuss those statutes that are enforced by the Department of Justice. Chapter 51 will investigate the enforcement of other statutes, such as the Robinson-Patman Act.

COMMON LAW ACTIONS

Today's antitrust laws are direct descendants of common law actions intended to limit restraints of trade. That is not to say, however, that a neat classification of trade restraints can be found in the common law.

The first recorded case about trade restraints in the common law involved a man named John Dyer and has become known as Dyer's Case.[1] Dyer had agreed not to "use his art of a dyer's craft within the town * * * for half a year." The court denied the plaintiff the ability to collect on a bond for Dyer's breach of his agreement. The effect of the agreement was to restrain trade, according to the common law. At that time, restraint of trade was defined as the failure to promote "fair" commercial activity.

1. Y.B. Pasch. 2 Hen. 5 f. 5, PL. 26 (1414).

The same issue arose on numerous occasions. A celebrated case occurred in 1711 when a man named Mitchell leased a baking shop for five years, subject to the condition that the lessor, Reynolds, who was also a baker, would not practice the baking art in the immediate area for the term of the lease. Thus, Mitchell was actually buying the use of a baking shop *and* the trade that went with it. The court rejected Mitchell's argument and ruled in favor of Reynolds.[2] This case is so celebrated because the court's opinion systematically classified trade restraints into those that were good and those that were bad. Lord Parker, who rendered the opinion, distinguished between general and particular restraints, the former being invalid and the latter valid. *General restraints* were used for the purpose of limiting competition. On the other hand, certain *particular restraints* that were supported by "good consideration" were acceptable. These *partial,* or *ancillary, restraints,* as they became known, were generally upheld if limited in time and place. Thus Mitchell v. Reynolds provided the basis for the modern formulation of the so-called "rule of reason" in which the court determines whether the restraint in question is reasonable. Since Mitchell v. Reynolds, the rule of reason has played an important role in antitrust litigation in this country. In order to find out whether a partial restraint is reasonable (i.e. legal), the courts inquire into its purpose and its probable effect.

Price Fixing Takes Over

The phrase *laissez-faire* refers to an economic philosophy that argues that government should leave the economy strictly alone. In England in the nineteenth century, as *laissez-faire* ideas became dominant, the courts expanded the concept of the rule of reason. They began to suggest, for example, that what was reasonable could best be judged by those involved in a contract, not by outsiders. Ultimately, *laissez-faire* theory gained such ascendancy that courts began to accept agreements among traders to

divide territories or to sell only at agreed-upon prices. By the second half of the nineteenth century, such transactions were generally held to be lawful where no element of coercion was involved.[3]

Common Law in the United States

Common law in the United States was not as receptive to restraints in trade as English law. In U.S. v. Addyston Pipe & Steel Co.,[4] Circuit Judge William Howard Taft concluded that apart from "reasonable" ancillary (partial) restraints, the common law condemned all other restraints of trade. Thus, contrary to the English rule, American courts did not apply a reasonableness test to certain forms of anticompetitive activity like price fixing, territorial divisions, or concerted refusals to deal. This view of the common law was adopted by the Supreme Court in its first interpretations of the Sherman Act, the mainstay of American antitrust law.

THE BEGINNING OF U.S. ANTITRUST LAW

With the growth of national markets after the Civil War, a number of small companies were combined to form large companies, and they started to engage in practices that were seen as monopolistic. Reported abusive practices by corporate giants in the second half of the nineteenth century finally led to legislation restricting the power of these so-called trusts. The first piece of legislation was the Interstate Commerce Act of 1887, and in 1890, the Sherman Act was passed. These acts were designed to prevent trusts from acting against the public interest.

The Formation of Trusts

Interestingly, *trusts* were a legal innovation that John D. Rockefeller's Standard Oil Company

---

2.   1 P. Wms. 181, 24 Eng. Rep 347 (1711).

3.   See, for example, Mogul Steamship Co. v. McGregor Gow & Co. [1892] A.C. 25 (1891).

4.   85 F. 271 (6th Cir. 1898) modified and affirmed 175 U.S. 211, 20 S.Ct. 10 (1899).

created. Standard's attorneys established an arrangement whereby owners of stock in several companies could transfer their stock to a set of trustees. In return, the owners received consideration in the form of certificates entitling them to a specified share in the pooled earnings of the jointly managed companies. In the late 1800s, the term *trust* was randomly applied to all forms of suspicious business combinations. There were trusts in oil, sugar, cotton, linseed oil, whiskey, and other industries, and the trusts seemed to absorb new enterprises at an expanding rate. Furthermore, it was felt that the process of consolidation was achieved by *predatory* tactics. Predatory business tactics advance the competitive position of one business by threatening to drive another business out of the market. In fact, the activities of the Standard Oil Company are given as the prime example of such tactics. Because of its size, Standard Oil was able to sell kerosene at a price below its cost. Standard's lower prices forced many competitors to sell or close down. As total industry output declined, Standard Oil raised the price and presumably obtained monopoly power.[5]

The 1890 Sherman Act was the response, and its purpose was to promote competition within the U.S. economy.[6] The author of the legislation, Senator Sherman, told Congress that the Sherman Act "does not announce a new principle of law, but applies old and well-recognized principles of the common law."[7] However, the common law was never very clear, and, indeed, it was certainly not very familiar to the legislators of the Fifty-first Congress of the United States. Actually, it appears that the Sherman Act was an attempt by Congress to get the federal courts to create a common body of federal antitrust law.

---

5. Not everyone agrees with this rendition of the facts. See, for example, John S. McGee, "Predatory Price Cutting: The Standard Oil (New Jersey) Case," *Journal of Law and Economics* 1 (1958). McGee finds that the facts are consistent with a competitive market with increased supply.

6. 26 Stat 209 (1890) as amended 15 USC Secs. 1-7.

7. 21 Congressional Record 2456 (1890).

The Main Provisions of the Sherman Antitrust Act

Sections I and II contain the main provisions of the Sherman Act. They are:

§ I: Every contract, combination in the form of trust or otherwise, or conspiracy, in restraint of trade or commerce among the several States, or with foreign nations, is hereby declared to be illegal [and is a misdemeanor punishable by fine and/or imprisonment]. * * *

§ II: Every person who shall monopolize, or attempt to monopolize, or combine or conspire with any other person or persons, to monopolize any part of the trade or commerce among the several States, or with foreign nations, shall be deemed guilty of a misdemeanor [and is similarly punishable]. * * *

Sections I and II Compared

The two main sections of the Sherman Act are quite different. Section I requires two or more persons, since a person cannot combine or conspire alone. Thus, the essence of the illegal activity is *the act of joining together*. Section II applies to both an individual person and several people because it states that "every person who * * *." Thus, unilateral conduct can result in a violation of Section II. The cases brought to court under Section I of the Sherman Act differ from those brought under Section II. Section I cases are often concerned with finding an agreement (written or oral) that leads to a restraint of trade. Section II cases deal with the structure of a monopoly that exists in the marketplace. Thus, Section I focuses on agreements that are restrictive—that is, agreements that have a wrongful purpose. Section II looks at the so-called misuse of monopoly power in the marketplace. However, both sections seek to curtail market industrial practices that result in undesired monopoly pricing and output behavior. Any case brought under Section II, however, must be one in which the "threshold" or "necessary" amount of monopoly power already exists.

The Proscriptive Nature of the Sherman Act

The Sherman Act does not tell businesses how they should act. It tells them how they should *not* act. In this sense, the act is *proscriptive* rather than *prescriptive*. It is the basis for *policing* rather than *regulating* business conduct.

Other Aspects of the Sherman Act

JURISDICTION The Sherman Act applies only to restraints that have a significant impact on commerce. In principle, only interstate commerce is affected because Congress can regulate only interstate commerce. If, however, a practice has a significant anticompetitive effect on commerce, the courts have construed the meaning of *interstate* more and more broadly. In principle, state regulation of anticompetitive practices covers purely local restraints on competition.

The Sherman Act extends to U.S. nationals abroad who are engaged in activities that will affect U.S. foreign commerce. It was applied, for example, in Continental Ore Co. v. Union Carbide and Carbon Corp.[8] In that case, the defendant, Union Carbide, tried to monopolize the Canadian market in Canada by excluding competitors. It did this by having its Canadian subsidiary, Electro-Met, initiate political action that resulted in the Canadian Metals Controller granting it an exclusive market in vanadium products. This effectively prohibited the U.S. plaintiff, Continental Ore Company, from entering Canadian markets.

STANDING The Department of Justice is not the only entity that can file suit under the Sherman Act. Some private parties can also sue for damages or other remedies. The courts have determined that the test of ability to sue depends on the directness of the injury suffered by the purported plaintiff. Thus, a person wishing to sue under the Sherman Act must

prove that (1) the antitrust violation either directly caused or was at least a substantial factor in causing the injury that was suffered, and (2) the unlawful actions of the purported defendant affected business activities of the plaintiff that were protected by the antitrust laws.

One of the unique features of the Sherman Antitrust Act is that it allows any person injured as a result of violations of the Act to bring a suit for treble damages against the defendants in addition to reasonable attorneys' fees. In the 1960s, General Electric Company, along with other major electrical equipment manufacturers, paid over $200 million in treble damage claims. Certain of the corporate officers were fined, and some of them even went to jail.

REMEDIES AND SANCTIONS Any person found guilty of violating either Section I or Section II of the Sherman Act is subject to criminal prosecution for a misdemeanor. Currently, upon conviction, a person can be fined up to $100,000 or imprisoned for three years, or both. A corporation can be fined $1 million. The Department of Justice can simultaneously institute civil proceedings to restrain the conduct that is in violation of the act.

The various remedies that the Justice Department has asked the court to impose include divestiture, dissolution, and divorcement, or making a company give up one of its operating functions. A group of meat packers, for example, can be forced to divorce themselves from controlling or owning butcher shops.

The Courts' Initial Reaction to the Sherman Act

Initially, the Sherman Act was stripped of any effectiveness because the courts interpreted it so narrowly. For example, five years after passage of the act, the Supreme Court refused to apply the Sherman Act to a sugar trust.[9] The

8.   370 U.S. 690, 82 S.Ct. 1404 (1962).

9.   United States v. E. C. Knight Co., 156 U.S. 1, 15 S.Ct. 249 (1895).

Court held that the law did not extend to restraints affecting *just* the manufacture of commodities. According to the Court, "commerce secedes to manufacturer, and is not a part of it." In other words, the manufacturer of a commodity does not control commerce and therefore cannot violate the Sherman Act.

Then the Court swung the other way. In essence, it significantly modified antitrust legislation by allowing no opportunity to adjust its decisions to practical necessities. In a series of opinions beginning with U.S. v. Trans-Missouri Freight Assn., the Court declared illegal certain price-fixing agreements and territorial divisions because Section I of the Sherman Act condemned *every* restraint of trade.[10] This absolute position clearly could not hold for long. The Court then retreated once again. It first condemned direct restraints.[11] It then came to the conclusion that restraints that were lawful at common law might not be prohibited by the Sherman Act.[12]

One of the great political victories, at least from President Theodore Roosevelt's and President William Howard Taft's points of view, was the ruling of the Supreme Court that *holding companies* were not exempt from the Sherman

Act. The case in point was Northern Securities Co. v. United States.[13] The court deemed the merger of two competing railroads an illegal restraint of trade. Two famous financiers, James J. Hill and J. P. Morgan, were successfully challenged by the judicial system.

The following case involves Standard Oil Company of New Jersey. In a landmark decision, the Supreme Court ordered the dissolution of the oil trust into approximately thirty companies.

Note that in this decision, the Court ruled that only those restraints whose character was *unreasonably* anticompetitive were outlawed by the Sherman Act. Critics of that decision contended that conservative federal judges would reduce the act to insignificance again. Other critics contended that if the court was to interpret the act as applying only to unreasonable restraints, then businesses should be told in advance which restraints were lawful.

10. 166 U.S. 290, 17 S.Ct. 540 (1897).
11. Hopkins v. United States, 171 U.S. 578, 19 S.Ct. 40 (1898).
12. United States v. Joint Traffic Ass'n, 171 U.S. 505, 19 S.Ct. 25 (1898).
13. 193 U.S. 197, 24 S.Ct. 436 (1904).

THE STANDARD OIL CO. OF NEW JERSEY v. UNITED STATES

221 U.S. 1, 31 S.Ct. 502 (1911).

BACKGROUND AND FACTS *Standard Oil Company of New Jersey and thirty-three other corporations, John D. Rockefeller, William Rockefeller, and five other individual defendants were the appellants in this case. They attempted to reverse a decree holding that they were conspiring "to restrain the trade and commerce in petroleum, commonly called 'crude oil', in refined oil, and in the other products of petroleum, among several States and Territories of the United States and District of Columbia and with foreign nations, and to monopolize the said commerce." The conspiracy was alleged to have been formed around 1870 by three of the individual defendants—John D. Rockefeller, William Rockefeller, and Henry M. Flagler.*

The government charged that John D. Rockefeller, William Rockefeller, and several other named individuals organized the Standard Oil Corporation of Ohio and soon afterwards became participants in an illegal plan to acquire substantially all of the oil refineries located in Cleveland, Ohio. Therefore, the government charged the original owners of the company with being in an illegal combination for the restraint and monopolization of all interstate commerce in petroleum products.

In addition, the government charged that there was a trust agreement in which the stock of over forty corporations, including Standard Oil of Ohio, was held for the benefit of the members of the combination. The trust agreement was adjudged void because it was in restraint of trade, and the trust was ordered dissolved. It is questionable whether the trust was actually dissolved as required by the decree, because the stock held by the trust was apparently shifted around and control of the companies was preserved in the same hands.

In the third phase of its case, the government charged that the individual defendants operated a holding company through Standard Oil Company of New Jersey. This company acquired the majority of stock in various other corporations engaging in the purchasing, transporting, refining, shipping, and selling of oil in the United States, the District of Columbia, and foreign nations. In short, the government attacked the Standard Oil trust, the Standard Oil Company, and the Standard Oil Company of New Jersey because the net effect of these organizations was to create a monopoly and restrain trade. The government sought an injunction to prevent the defendants from continuing their control over the subsidiary corporations.

WHITE, Chief Justice.
* * *

It is sufficient to say that, whilst admitting many of the alleged acquisitions of property, the formation of the so-called trust of 1882, its dissolution in 1892, and the acquisition by the Standard Oil Company of New Jersey of the stocks of the various corporations in 1899, * * * [the appellants] deny all the allegations respecting combinations or conspiracies to restrain or monopolize the oil trade; and particularly that the so-called trust of 1882, or the acquisition of the shares of the defendant companies by the Standard Oil Company of New Jersey in 1899, was a combination of *independent or competing* concerns or corporations. * * *

The [lower] court decided in favor of the United States. In the opinion delivered, all the multitude of acts of wrong-doing charged in the bill were put aside, in so far as they were alleged to have been committed prior to the passage of the Anti-trust Act, "except as evidence of their (the defendants') purpose, of their continuing conduct and of its effect."

By the decree which was entered it was adjudged that the combining of the stocks of various companies in the hands of the Standard Oil Company of New Jersey in 1899 constituted a combination in restraint of trade and also an attempt to monopolize and a monopolization under §2 of the Anti-trust Act. The decree was against seven individual defendants, the Standard Oil Company of New Jersey, thirty-six domestic companies and one foreign company which the Standard Oil Company of New Jersey controls by stock ownership; these 38 corporate defendants being held to be parties to the combination found to exist.
* * *

The Standard Oil Company of New Jersey was enjoined from voting the stocks or exerting any control over the said 37 subsidiary companies, and the subsidiary companies were enjoined from paying any dividends as to the

Standard Oil Company or permitting it to exercise any control over them by virtue of the stock ownership or power acquired by means of the combination. The individuals and corporations were also enjoined from entering into or carrying into effect any like combination which would evade the decree. Further, the individual defendants, the Standard Oil Company, and the 37 subsidiary corporations were enjoined from engaging or continuing in interstate commerce in petroleum or its products during the continuance of the illegal combination.

* * *

Giving to the facts just stated, the weight which it was deemed they were entitled to, in the light afforded by the proof of other cognate facts and circumstances, the court below held that the acts and dealings established by the proof operated to destroy the "potentiality of competition" which otherwise would have existed to such an extent as to cause the transfers of stock which were made to the New Jersey corporation and the control which resulted over the many and various subsidiary corporations to be a combination or conspiracy in restraint of trade in violation of the first section of the act, but also to be an attempt to monopolize and a monopolization bringing about a perennial violation of the second section.

We see no cause to doubt the correctness of these conclusions, considering the subject from every aspect, that is, both in view of the facts established by the record and the necessary operation and effect of the law as we have construed it upon the inferences deducible from the facts, for the following reasons:

a. Because the unification of power and control over petroleum and its products which was the inevitable result of the combining in the New Jersey corporation by the increase of its stock and the transfer to it of the stocks of so many other corporations, aggregating so vast a capital, gives rise, in and of itself, * * * to the *prima facie* presumption of intent and purpose to maintain the dominancy over the oil industry, not as a result of normal methods of industrial development, but by new means of combination which were resorted to in order that greater power might be added than would otherwise have arisen had normal methods been followed, the whole with the purpose of excluding others from the trade and thus centralizing in the combination a perpetual control of the movements of petroleum and its products in the channels of interstate commerce.

b. Because the *prima facie* presumption of intent to restrain trade, to monopolize and to bring about monopolization resulting from the act of expanding the stock of the New Jersey corporation and vesting it with such vast control of the oil industry, is made conclusive by * * * what was done under those agreements and the acts which immediately preceded the vesting of power in the New Jersey corporation as well as by * * * the modes in which the power vested in that corporation has been exerted and the results which have arisen from it.

* * * [W]e think no disinterested mind can survey the * * * question without being irresistibly driven to the conclusion that the very genius for commercial development and organization which it would seem was manifested from the beginning soon begot an intent and purpose to exclude others which was frequently manifested by acts and dealings wholly inconsistent with the theory that they were made with the single conception of advancing the development of business power by usual methods, but which on the contrary necessarily involved the intent to drive others from the field and to exclude them from their right to

trade and thus accomplish the mastery which was the end in view. And, considering the period from the date of the trust agreements of 1879 and 1882, up to the time of the expansion of the New Jersey corporation, the gradual extension of the power over the commerce in oil which ensued, the decision of the Supreme Court of Ohio [to dissolve the trust], the tardiness or reluctance in conforming to the commands of that decision, the method first adopted and that which finally culminated in the plan of the New Jersey corporation, all additionally serve to make manifest the continued existence of the intent which we have previously indicated and which among other things impelled the expansion of the New Jersey corporation. The exercise of the power which resulted from that organization fortifies the foregoing conclusions, since the development which came, the acquisition here and there which ensued of every efficient means by which competition could have been asserted, the slow but resistless methods which followed by which means of transportation were absorbed and brought under control, the system of marketing which was adopted by which the country was divided into districts and the trade in each district in oil was turned over to a designated corporation within the combination and all others were excluded, all lead the mind up to a conviction of a purpose and intent which we think is so certain as practically to cause the subject not to be within the domain of reasonable contention.

The inference that no attempt to monopolize could have been intended, and that no monopolization resulted from the acts complained of, since it is established that a very small percentage of the crude oil produced was controlled by the combination, is unwarranted. As substantial power over the crude product was the inevitable result of the absolute control which existed over the refined product, the monopolization of the one carried with it the power to control the other, and if the inferences which this situation suggests were developed, which we deem it unnecessary to do, they might well serve to add additional cogency to the presumption of intent to monopolize which we have found arises from the unquestioned proof on other subjects. * * *

The Supreme Court concluded that the decree issued by the lower court was right and should be affirmed. It forbade Standard Oil from engaging in any future combinations in violation of the Sherman Antitrust Act. In addition, it attempted to neutralize the effect of the monopoly that Standard Oil had created by commanding the dissolution of the combination (the trust) and causing the New Jersey corporation to divest itself of the numerous shares of stock that it controlled.	**JUDGMENT AND REMEDY**

THE DEVELOPMENT OF PER SE VIOLATIONS

According to the rule of reason, only unreasonable restraints were illegal at common law. Clearly, the rule was applied in the Standard Oil case. However, there really is no rule of reason explicitly stated in Section I of the Sherman Act. It does not matter, according to Section I, whether the guilty party was successful in fixing prices, dividing markets or restraining trade in any other way. Section I states very clearly that any *attempt* to restrain trade is illegal. Thus, certain kinds of restrictive contracts will be deemed inherently anticompetitive—that is, in restraint of trade *as a matter* of law. In such *per se violations* of Section I, there is no need to examine any other facts. Recall that in United States v. Trans-Missouri Freight Ass'n., the Court held that Section I condemned *every* restraint of trade. In 1897, the Court recognized no exceptions. The defendants in the case contended that they were exempt from the Sherman Act because they were regulated by the Interstate Commerce Act. Thus, the fixing of rates was legal because it was reasonable and therefore valid under common law. To the Court, the railroads were engaging in a per se violation of Section I of the Sherman Act.

The following case involved six leading producers of cast iron pipe who agreed among themselves to divide the southern and western markets into what turned out to be regional monopolies. The six companies instituted a complex system of fixed prices for each territory. According to the evidence, the prices fixed by these companies were sufficiently low to discourage entry by eastern manufacturers. The defense contended (1) that the arrangement was not a monopoly but the avoidance of ruinous price competition and (2) that the prices at which pipes were sold in each region were reasonable.

UNITED STATES v. ADDYSTON PIPE & STEEL CO.

Sixth Circuit, 1898.
29 C.C.A. 141, 85 F. 271

BACKGROUND AND FACTS *The defendants, several pipe and steel companies, entered into an association and agreed to divide up business and profits in the following manner. The bonuses on the first ninety thousand tons of pipe secured in any territory would be divided equally among the six companies. At increasing levels of tonnage, the companies would divide a percentage of the profits. As part of the agreement, the prices of various lengths and widths of pipe were standardized. As a result of the agreement, all the participating companies shared equally in the profits and no company in the industry was in a position to gain a price advantage over any other.*

TAFT, Circuit Judge.
* * *

Two questions are presented in this case for our decision: First. Was the association of the defendants a contract, combination, or conspiracy in restraint of trade, as the terms are to be understood in the act? Second. Was the trade thus restrained trade between the states?

The contention on behalf of defendants is that the association would have been valid at common law, and that the federal anti-trust law was not intended to reach any agreements that were not void and unenforceable at common law. * * * Contracts that were in unreasonable restraint of trade at common law were not unlawful in the sense of being criminal, or giving rise to a civil action for damages in favor of one prejudicially affected thereby, but were simply void, and were not enforced by the courts. * * * The effect of the act of 1890 is to render such contracts unlawful in an affirmative or positive sense, and punishable as a misdemeanor, and to create a right of civil action for damages in favor of those injured thereby, and a civil remedy by injunction in favor of both private persons and the public against the execution of such contracts and the maintenance of such trade restraints.

The argument for defendants is that their contract of association was not, and could not be, a monopoly, because their aggregate tonnage capacity did not exceed 30 per cent. of the total tonnage capacity of the country; that the restraints upon the members of the association, if restraints they could be called, did not embrace all the states, and were not unlimited in space; that such partial restraints were justified and upheld at common law if reasonable, and only proportioned to the necessary protection of the parties; that in this case the partial restraints were reasonable, because without them each member would be subjected to ruinous competition by the other, and did not exceed in degree of stringency or scope what was necessary to protect the parties in securing prices for their product that were fair and reasonable to themselves and the public; that competition was not stifled by the association because the prices fixed by it had to be fixed with reference to the very active competition of pipe companies which were not members of the association, and which had more than double the defendants' capacity; that in this way the association only modified and restrained the evils of ruinous competition, while the public had all the benefit from competition which public policy demanded.

* * *

This very statement of the rule implies that the contract must be one in which there is a main purpose, to which the covenant in restraint of trade is merely ancillary. The covenant is inserted only to protect one of the parties from the injury which, in the execution of the contract or enjoyment of its fruits, he may suffer from the unrestrained competition of the other. The main purpose of the contract suggests the measure of protection needed, and furnishes a sufficiently uniform standard by which the validity of such restraints may be judicially determined. In such a case, if the restraint exceeds the necessity presented by the main purpose of the contract, it is void for two reasons: First, because it oppresses the covenantor, without any corresponding benefit to the covenantee; and, second, because it tends to a monopoly. But where the sole object of both parties in making the contract as expressed therein is merely to restrain competition, and enhance or maintain prices, it would seem that there was nothing to justify or excuse the restraint, that it would necessarily have a tendency to monopoly, and therefore would be void. In such a case there is no measure of what is necessary to the protection of either party, except the vague and varying opinion of judges as to how much, on principles of political economy, men ought to be allowed to restrain competition. There is in such contracts no main lawful purpose, to subserve which partial restraint is permitted, and by which its reasonableness is measured, but the sole object is to restrain trade in order to avoid the competition which it has always been the policy of the common law to foster.

* * *

Upon this review of the [common] law and the authorities, we can have no doubt that the association of the defendants, however reasonable the prices they fixed, however great the competition they had to encounter, and however great the necessity for curbing themselves by joint agreement from committing financial suicide by ill-advised competition, was void at common law, because in restraint of trade, and tending to a monopoly. But the facts of the case do not require us to go so far as this, for they show that the attempted justification of this association on the grounds stated is without foundation.

* * *

Another aspect of this contract of association brings it within the term used in the statute, "a conspiracy in restraint of trade." A conspiracy is a combination of two or more persons to accomplish an unlawful end by lawful means or a lawful end by unlawful means. In the answer of the defendants, it is averred that the chief way in which cast-iron pipe is sold is by contracts let after competitive bidding invited by the intending purchaser. It would have much interfered with the smooth working of defendants' association had its existence and purposes become known to the public. A part of the plan was a deliberate attempt to create in the minds of the members of the public inviting bids the belief that competition existed between the defendants. Several of the defendants were required to bid at every letting, and to make their bids at such prices that the one already selected to obtain the contract should have the lowest bid. It is well settled that an agreement between intending bidders at a public auction or a public letting not to bid against each other, and thus to prevent competition, is a fraud upon the intending vendor or contractor, and the ensuing sale or contract will be set aside. * * * The largest purchasers of pipe are municipal corporations, and they are by law required to solicit bids for the sale of pipe in order that the public may get the benefit of competition. One of the means adopted by the defendants in their plan of combination was this illegal and fraudulent effort to evade such laws, and to deceive intending purchasers. No matter what the excuse for the combination by defendants in restraint of trade, the illegality of the means stamps it as a conspiracy, and so brings it within that term of the federal statute.
* * *

JUDGMENT AND REMEDY *The agreement was a price-fixing agreement prohibited by both common law and statute. The companies participating in the agreement were guilty of a per se violation for having built in a price-fixing arrangement to their agreement.*

COMMENTS *Obviously, the defense that was presented did not convince the circuit court. Taft wanted to build a per se prohibition of all price-fixing agreements. He read the common law as voiding all such agreements unless they were contingent to some legitimate cause. Therefore, the defense of "reasonableness" was deemed irrelevant.*

A few years after United States v. Addyston Pipe & Steel Co., the Supreme Court made it clear that no price-fixing agreement could be tempered by any reasonableness standard in United States v. Trenton Potteries Co. In this case, over 80 percent of the makers of toilets and bathroom products belonged to an association that fixed the prices of the pottery used. Moreover, the association limited the sales to so-called legitimate jobbers.

UNITED STATES v. TRENTON POTTERIES CO.
Supreme Court of the United States, 1927.
273 U.S. 392, 47 S.Ct. 377, 71 L.Ed. 700.

BACKGROUND AND FACTS *The trial court convicted twenty individuals and twenty-three corporations of violating the Sherman Antitrust Law. They were found guilty as charged for being a combination to fix and maintain uniform prices for the sale of sanitary pottery in restraint of interstate commerce. In addition, they were found guilty of being a combination to restrain interstate commerce by limiting the sale* *of pottery to a special group known to the association as "legitimate jobbers."*

The original convictions were set aside by the court of appeals on the ground that there were errors in the conduct of the trial. The case was ultimately heard by the Supreme Court.

STONE, Justice.

* * *

Respondents, engaged in the manufacture or distribution of 82 per cent. of the vitreous pottery fixtures produced in the United States for use in bathrooms and lavatories, were members of a trade organization known as the Sanitary Potters' Association. Twelve of the corporate respondents had their factories and chief places of business in New Jersey, one was located in California, and the others were situated in Illinois, Michigan, West Virginia, Indiana, Ohio, and Pennsylvania. Many of them sold and delivered their product within the Southern district of New York, and some maintained sales offices and agents there.

There is no contention here that the verdict was not supported by sufficient evidence that respondents, controlling some 82 per cent. of the business of manufacturing and distributing in the United States vitreous pottery of the type described, combined to fix prices and to limit sales in interstate commerce to jobbers.

The issues raised here by the government's specification of errors relate only to the decision of the Circuit Court of Appeals upon its review of certain rulings of the District Court made in the course of the trial. * * *

The trial court charged, in submitting the case to the jury that, if it found the agreements or combination complained of, it might return a verdict of guilty *without regard to the reasonableness of the prices fixed, or the good intentions of the combining units, whether prices were actually lowered or raised or whether sales were restricted to the special jobbers, since both agreements of themselves were unreasonable restraints.* [Emphasis added.] These instructions repeated in various forms applied to both counts of the indictment. The trial court refused various requests to charge that both the agreement to fix prices and the agreement to limit sales to a particular group, if found, did not in themselves constitute violations of law, unless it was also found that they unreasonably restrained interstate commerce. In particular the court refused the request to charge the following:

"The essence of the law is injury to the public. It is not every restraint of competition and not every restraint of trade that works an injury to the public; it is only an undue and unreasonable restraint of trade that has such an effect and is deemed to be unlawful."

* * *

The court below held specifically that the trial court erred in refusing to charge as requested and held in effect that the charge as given on this branch of the case was erroneous. * * *

This disposition of the matter ignored the fact that the trial judge plainly and variously charged the jury that the combinations alleged in the indictment, if found, were violations of the statute as a matter of law, saying:

"* * * The law is clear that an agreement on the part of the members of a combination controlling a substantial part of an industry, upon the prices which the members are to charge for their commodity, is in itself an undue and unreasonable restraint of trade and commerce. * * *" The question * * * to be considered here is whether the trial judge correctly withdrew from the jury the consideration of the reasonableness of the particular restraints charged.

* * *

The aim and result of every price-fixing agreement, if effective, is the elimination of one form of competition. The power to fix prices, whether reasonably exercised or not, involves power to control the market and to fix arbitrary and unreasonable prices. The reasonable price fixed today may through economic and business changes become the unreasonable price of to-morrow. Once established, it may be maintained unchanged because of the absence of competition secured by the agreement for a price reasonable when fixed. Agreements which create such potential power may well be held to be in themselves unreasonable or unlawful restraints, without the necessity of minute inquiry whether a particular price is reasonable or unreasonable as fixed and without placing on the government in enforcing the Sherman Law the burden of ascertaining from day to day whether it has become unreasonable through the mere variation of economic conditions. Moreover, in the absence of express legislation requiring it, we should hesitate to adopt a construction making the difference between legal and illegal conduct in the field of business relations depend upon so uncertain a test as whether prices are reasonable—a determination which can be satisfactorily made only after a complete survey of our economic organization and a choice between rival philosophies. * * *

The charge of the trial court, viewed as a whole, fairly submitted to the jury the question whether a price-fixing agreement as described in the first count was entered into by the respondents. Whether the prices actually agreed upon were reasonable or unreasonable was immaterial in the circumstances charged in the indictment and necessarily found by the verdict. The requested charge which we have quoted, and others of similar tenor, while true as abstract propositions, were inapplicable to the case in hand and rightly refused.

* * *

JUDGMENT AND REMEDY

The Supreme Court came out in strong support of the trial court's finding of a price-fixing agreement in violation of the Sherman Antitrust Act. The Court went on to clarify that the error allegedly committed by the trial court with regard to the jury charge was not a significant consideration because the existence of any price-fixing agreement, reasonable or unreasonable, constituted a violation of the Sherman Antitrust Act in its opinion.

COMMENTS

A literal interpretation of Justice Stone's ruling indicates that any proof of the mere existence of any price-fixing agreement establishes the defendant's illegal purpose. The prosecution need demonstrate nothing else.

The Effect of the Depression on Per Se Standards

During the Great Depression of the 1930s, a number of decisions tempered the Court's effort to establish per se violations. Prices fell dramatically during the depression, and a number of companies attempted to fix prices to prevent ruin. For example, when the price of bituminous coal fell 25 percent from 1929 to 1933, over 130 coal companies in the Appalachian region formed a new company that served as the exclusive selling agent for member firms. The agent was supposed to get the best price obtainable. If it could not sell all the output of all of the firms at that price, it allocated output to each firm in an orderly fashion. Thus, it was acting as a sales cartel, or a central sales agency, and clearly was in violation of the Sherman Act as interpreted prior to the depression. Nonetheless, the Supreme Court, in Appalachian Coals, Inc. v. United States, decided that the Sherman Act was to prevent "undue" restraints on interstate commerce.[14] With this decision, the Court returned to a rule of reason, even though it was using price-fixing language. Basically, the Court held that the issue of legality ultimately rested on the effect of the agreement on competition.

But the Court's return to the rule of reason did not survive the depression. In United States

_____

14.   288 U.S. 344, 53 S.Ct. 471 (1933):

v. Socony Vacuum Oil Co. [310 U.S. 150, 60 S. Ct. 811 (1940)], the Supreme Court returned to the rigid per se standard, condemning all price-fixing arrangements.

Additional Per Se Violations

In addition to the price-fixing agreements that violate Section I of the Sherman Act, two other types of violations are per se illegal.

HORIZONTAL MARKET DIVISIONS Dividing a territory for the sale of a specific product into two or more divisions allocated specifically to individual companies is also a per se violation of the Sherman Act. If two cement companies normally sell cement throughout the entire state of California, they cannot enter into an agreement in which one of them sells only in southern California and the other sells only in northern California. As a matter of law, this is illegal, even if it might seem "reasonable."

JOINT REFUSALS TO DEAL, OR GROUP BOYCOTTS If a single manufacturer or wholesaler of goods refuses to sell to a potential buyer or group of buyers, this is usually deemed a per se violation of the antitrust laws. In a classic case, General Motors attempted to prevent a group of discount sellers from selling General Motors cars.

BACKGROUND AND FACTS *Beginning in the late 1950s, "discount houses" and "referral services" began offering to sell new cars to the public at allegedly bargain prices. By 1960, about eighty-five Chevrolet dealers, without authorization from General Motors, furnished cars to the discount houses. As the volume of these sales grew, the nonparticipating Chevrolet dealers located near one or more of these discount outlets began to feel the financial pinch.*

The nonparticipating dealers became increasingly disgruntled. They began to flood the Chevrolet division of General Motors with letters and telegrams asking for help.

Within a month, General Motors had elicited from each dealer a promise not to do business with any discounters. But such agreements

UNITED STATES v. GENERAL MOTORS CORP.

384 U.S. 127, 86 S.Ct. 1321 (1966).

would require policing—a fact that had been anticipated. General Motors elicited the help of three of its associations and a number of individual dealers.

The associations made spot checks to assure that no Chevrolet dealer continued to supply a discounter with cars. They did this by hiring professional investigators to purchase cars from dealers suspected of cooperating with discounters. Each association contributed $5,000 to provide a fund with which the "professional" shopper would pay for the automobile.

Armed with information about violations obtained from the dealers or their associations, General Motors staff asked the offending dealer to come in and talk with them. The dealer was then confronted with the car purchased by the "professional shopper," the documents of the sale, and, in most cases, a tape recording of the transaction. In every instance, the embarrassed dealer repurchased the car, sometimes at a substantial loss, and promised to stop such sales in the future. The checks with which the cars were repurchased were made payable to an attorney acting jointly for the three associations.

The government charged that these practices were unlawful and that they constituted a conspiracy to restrain trade in violation of the Sherman Antitrust Act.

FORTAS, Justice.

* * *

Both the Government and the appellees urge the importance, for purposes of decision, of the "location clause" in the Dealer Selling Agreement which prohibits a franchised dealer from moving to or establishing "a new or different location, branch sales office, branch service station, or place of business * * * without the prior written approval of Chevrolet." The appellees contend that this contractual provision is lawful, and that it justifies their actions. They argue that General Motors acted lawfully to prevent its dealers from violating the "location clause," that the described arrangements with discounters constitute the establishment of additional sales outlets in violation of the clause, and that the individual dealers—and their associations—have an interest in uniform compliance with the franchise agreement, which interest they lawfully sought to vindicate.

The Government invites us to join in the assumption, only for purposes of this case, that the "location clause" encompasses sales by dealers through the medium of discounters. But it urges us to hold that, so construed, the provision is unlawful as an unreasonable restraint of trade in violation of the Sherman Act.

* * * We have here a classic conspiracy in restraint of trade: joint, collaborative action by dealers, the appellee associations, and General Motors to eliminate a class of competitors by terminating business dealings between them and a minority of Chevrolet dealers and to deprive franchised dealers of their freedom to deal through discounters if they so choose. Against this fact of unlawful combination, the "location clause" is of no avail. Whatever General Motors might or might not lawfully have done to enforce individual Dealer Selling Agreements by action within the borders of those agreements and the relationship which each defines, is beside the point. And, because the action taken constitutes a combination or conspiracy, it is not necessary to consider what might be the legitimate interest of a dealer in securing compliance by others with the "location clause," or the lawfulness of action a dealer might individually take to vindicate this interest.

* * * The error of the trial court lies in its failure to apply the correct and established standard for ascertaining the existence of a combination or conspiracy under §1 of the Sherman Act. See United States v. Parke, Davis & Co. The trial court attempted to justify its conclusion on the following reasoning: That each defendant and alleged co-conspirator acted to promote its own self-interest; that General Motors, as well as the defendant associations and their members, has a lawful interest in securing compliance with the "location clause" and in thus protecting the franchise system of distributing automobiles—business arrangements which the court deemed lawful and proper; and that in seeking to vindicate these interests the defendants and their alleged co-conspirators entered into no "agreements" among themselves, although they may have engaged in "parallel action."

These factors do not justify the result reached. It is of no consequence, for purposes of determining whether there has been a combination or conspiracy under §1 of the Sherman Act, that each party acted in its own lawful interest. Nor is it of consequence for this purpose whether the "location clause" and franchise system are lawful or economically desirable. * * *

Neither individual dealers nor the associations acted independently or separately. The dealers collaborated, through the associations and otherwise, among themselves and with General Motors, both to enlist the aid of General Motors and to enforce dealers' promises to forsake the discounters. The associations explicitly entered into a joint venture to assist General Motors in policing the dealers' promises, and their joint proffer of aid was accepted and utilized by General Motors.

* * * General Motors sought to elicit from all the dealers agreements, substantially interrelated and interdependent, that none of them would do business with the discounters. These agreements were hammered out in meetings between nonconforming dealers and officials of General Motors' Chevrolet Division, and in telephone conversations with other dealers. It was acknowledged from the beginning that substantial unanimity would be essential if the agreements were to be forthcoming. And once the agreements were secured, General Motors both solicited and employed the assistance of its alleged co-conspirators in helping to police them. What resulted was a fabric interwoven by many strands of joint action to eliminate the discounters from participation in the market, to inhibit the free choice of franchised dealers to select their own methods of trade and to provide multilateral surveillance and enforcement. This process for achieving and enforcing the desired objective can by no stretch of the imagination be described as "unilateral" or merely "parallel."
* * *

We note, moreover, that inherent in the success of the combination in this case was a substantial restraint upon price competition—a goal unlawful *per se* when sought to be effected by combination or conspiracy.

There is in the record ample evidence that one of the purposes behind the concerted effort to eliminate sales of new Chevrolet cars by discounters was to protect franchised dealers from real or apparent price competition. The discounters advertised price savings. Some purchasers found and others believed that discount prices were lower than those available through the franchise dealers. Certainly, complaints about price competition were prominent in the letters and telegrams with which the individual dealers and salesmen bombarded General Motors in November 1960. And although the District Court [trial court] found to the contrary, there is evidence in the record that General Motors itself was not unconcerned about the effect of discount sales upon general price levels.

The protection of price competition from conspiratorial restraint is an object of special solicitude under the antitrust laws. We cannot respect that solicitude by closing our eyes to the effect upon price competition of the removal from the market, by combination or conspiracy, of a class of traders. Nor do we propose to construe the Sherman Act to prohibit conspiracies to fix prices at which competitors may sell, but to allow conspiracies or combinations to put competitors out of business entirely.

* * *

JUDGMENT AND REMEDY *The Supreme Court found that, beyond question, these activities were a conspiracy to restrain trade in violation of Section I of the Sherman Act.*

THE CLAYTON ACT

In 1914, Congress attempted to strengthen federal antitrust laws by adopting the Clayton Act, which was aimed at specific monopolistic practices. The important sections of the Clayton Act are sections 2, 3, 7, 8.

Section 2: [It is illegal to] discriminate in price between different purchasers [except in cases where the differences are due to differences in selling or transportation costs].

Section 3: [Producers cannot sell] on the condition, agreement or understanding that the * * * purchaser thereof shall not use or deal in the goods * * * of a competitor or competitors of the seller.

Section 7: [Corporations cannot hold stock in another company] where the effect * * * may be to substantially lessen competition.

Section 8: * * * no person at the same time shall be a director in any two or more corporations, any one of which has capital, surplus, and undivided profits aggregating more than $1 million, engaged in whole or in part in commerce, other than banks, banking associations, trust companies, and common carriers.

The Clayton Act outlaws price discrimination, exclusive dealing and tying contracts, the purchase of enough stock in a competing corporation to reduce competition, and interlocking directorates (discussed in Chapter 51).

Enforcement of the Clayton Act

Enforcement of the Clayton Act is carried out simultaneously by the Department of Justice and the Federal Trade Commission. Those portions of the Clayton Act that strengthen Sections 1 and 8 of the Sherman Act are enforced primarily by the Justice Department, as are exclusive dealings, tying contracts, and sections 7 and 8 of the Clayton Act. There is, however, some overlap between the two. For example, Section 7 of the Clayton Act, which involves mergers, is also enforced by the FTC. Other portions; such as Section 2 of the Clayton Act, fall almost exclusively under the jurisdiction of the FTC.

EXEMPTIONS FROM ANTITRUST LAWS

In a sense, Congress's attention to the antitrust laws since the Clayton Act has focused primarily on writing *exceptions* to the coverage of the Sherman Act. The Clayton Act itself sought unsuccessfully to exempt unions from the antitrust law. The National Labor Relations Act of 1935 further protected them from antitrust legislation. Today, therefore, unions can lawfully engage in actions that are normally prohibited as long as they act in their self-interest and do not conspire or combine with nonlabor groups to accomplish their goals.

The Miller-Tydings Act

The Miller-Tydings Act was passed in 1937 as an amendment to Section I of the Sherman Act, and it allows fair-trade agreements. A fair-trade agreement occurs when a manufacturer can specify to all the people who sell his or her product that they cannot sell it below a listed, or fair-trade, price. This is called resale price maintenance. This type of fair-trade agreement would seem to violate antitrust laws aimed at preventing price-fixing. Nonetheless, the Miller-Tydings Act made this type of price-fixing legal.

On March 13, 1976, Congress repealed the Miller-Tydings Act. It had become clear by then that a major result of this exemption to the Sherman Act was the stifling of price competition among retailers.

Small Businesses

Small businesses are allowed to engage in certain concerted activities without violating the antitrust laws. This legislation started with the Small Business Act of 1953.

Labor and Agriculture

Labor and agricultural organizations are exempted from the Sherman Antitrust Act by Section 6 of the Clayton Act. Agriculture's exemption from antitrust legislation is further extended by the Capper-Volstead Act (1922), the Cooperative Marketing Act (1926), and certain provisions of the Robinson-Patman Act.

Labor's exemption was strengthened by the Norris-La Guardia Act of 1932.

Sports

Most commercial activities are subject to the antitrust laws, but there are exceptions. For example, baseball remains untouched by the antitrust laws; it was not thought to be commerce in the Sherman Act's original contemplation and is thus not commerce today. Baseball's exemption is anomalous, especially since no other professional sport receives such treatment.

Professionals

A current controversial topic in antitrust law is the regulation of professionals, such as lawyers and doctors. Professional organizations are no longer exempt from antitrust enforcement. They cannot establish minimum fee schedules or prohibit competitive bidding in any way. The traditional incantations about the maintenance of high quality no longer shield professionals from the antitrust laws.

Insurance

The McCarran-Ferguson Act exempts from the antitrust laws all activities that are in the "business of insurance." The primary element of the insurance business is the spreading and underwriting of policyholder risk. Thus, any such activity can be exempt from the antitrust laws by the McCarran-Ferguson Act if it is regulated by state law.

Government actions that hinder competition are exempt from antitrust laws. In Parker v. Brown, the Supreme Court upheld the activities of a California agency that fixed raisin production and prices, even though this was done at the request of and with the concurrence of a majority of growers.[15] The state regulation was not a burden on interstate commerce since it coincided with federal agricultural policy. Moreover, the Sherman Act's prohibition of contracts in restraint of trade by "any person" applied to private businesses, not government agencies.

---

15.   317 U.S. 341, 63 S.Ct. 307 (1943).

Foreign Trade

Sometimes the choice to exempt certain activities from antitrust actions is based upon a decision that certain goals can be better achieved through cartelization. For example, the Webb-Pomerene Act exempts acts or agreements made in the course of export trade by associations of producers formed solely for the purpose of engaging in export trade. Cartelization promotes an increased national investment in the covered activities, thereby aiding the nation's balance of payments.

QUESTIONS AND CASE PROBLEMS

1. Meister Brau, Inc., was engaged in the business of brewing beers, malts, and ales. It acquired the Berger Meister Beer Company through a purchase of the latter's common stock. Berger Meister sold the beer it brewed through distributors who operated as individual businesses separate from Berger Meister. Soon after Meister Brau acquired Berger Meister, it terminated some of Berger Meister's distributors. The distributors handled the products of a number of other breweries, but they complained that the reduced sales volume that would result from their being terminated by Meister Brau would drive them out of business. The distributors thus brought suit against Meister Brau, alleging that its agreement with its new subsidiary, Berger Meister, to terminate the distributors constituted a conspiracy in restraint of trade in violation of Section I of the Sherman Act. The distributors alleged that the terminations would reduce competition in a market that was already tending toward concentration. Has Meister Brau violated Section I of the Sherman Act? [Ricchetti v. Meister Brau, Inc., 431 F.2d 1211 (9th Cir. 1970)]

2. Since 1946, Bay Distributors, Inc., a Florida corporation located in the Tampa Bay area, had been engaged in the wholesale distribution and sale of various brands of wines and distilled spirits in approximately a thirteen-county area of the west coast of Florida. The wines that Bay sold included a line produced by United Vintners, Inc., most of which was marketed under the trade name "Italian Swiss Colony." Bay was the exclusive distributor in the Florida west coast area of United Vintners' wines. Between March 1965 and May 1970, Cal Distributing Company acted as Bay's subdistributor in the Sarasota area, which included two of the thirteen counties mentioned above. Cal sold no wine outside the Sarasota area. Although customers in the Sarasota area could have purchased United Vintners' products from either Cal or Bay, neither actually solicited customers from the other. About May 5, 1970, Bay notified Cal that it would no longer sell Cal United Vintners' wines. It would, however, continue to sell Cal all other wines for which Bay was the exclusive distributor. After Bay refused to sell United Vintners' products to Cal as a subdistributor, Bay started selling them directly to the retail businesses to which Cal had been selling them. Using these facts, along with the other facts given below, answer the following questions. [Cal Distributing Co. v. Bay Distributors, Inc., 337 F.Supp. 1154 (M.D.Fla. 1971)]

a. Which, if any, of the antitrust statutes discussed in this chapter might Bay have violated when it terminated Cal as its subdistributor? Be specific.

b. In order to establish a claim for relief from monopolization, Bay must be shown to possess *monopoly power* in the relevant market. In determining the relevant market, the court must determine the relevant *geographic* market and the relevant *product* market. Both before and after Bay's termination of Cal, at least six other companies distributed wine at wholesale in the Sarasota area from warehouses located in Tampa. Each of these competitors supplied wine along the entire west coast of Florida, including the Sarasota area, from offices and warehouses located in Tampa. The cost of transporting wine to retailers throughout the Florida west coast area is not such as to prevent wholesale distributors from supplying this area from Tampa. The "relevant geographic market" is the area that Bay would have to monopolize if it were to be deemed in violation of the antitrust laws. Is the relevant geographic market in this case the city of Sarasota, the west coast of Florida, the entire state of Florida, or some other area?

c. In determining whether Bay's act of discontinuing Cal shows monopoly power, the "relevant product market" must be determined. This involves analyzing the commodities reasonably interchangeable by consumers for the same purposes. For example, in one case, the Supreme Court held that even though the DuPont Company produced approximately 75 percent of the cellophane sold nationwide, the competition between cellophane and other flexible packaging materials was sufficient to prevent cellophane from constituting a separate relevant product market in itself. Using the DuPont case as an analogy, what is the relevant product market in this case—all United Vintners wines, all wines, all alcoholic beverage, or something else?

d. Gallo Wines provides the primary competition to United Vintners. However, both Gallo and United Vintners face direct competition from all other wines. This competition prevents Bay from raising its prices without losing business. The competition provided by Gallo was described by Calvin LaHurd, the president of Cal Distributing Company, as "very, very vigorous." In fact, sales of Gallo Wines at wholesale have exceeded Bay's sales of United Vintners continuously for each month since December 1968. In addition, since December 1968, the monthly sales of United Vintners have never exceeded 22 percent of the total volume of wine sold to retailers in the relevant geographic area. By way of comparison, the monthly sales of Gallo Wines by Tampa Wholesale Liquor Company, one of the area distributors, have averaged over 22 percent of monthly wholesale wine sales in the relevant geographic area during the same period. In order to be deemed in violation of the antitrust laws, Bay Distributors must be shown to possess the power to control prices or exclude competition in the relevant market. In order to establish this, Cal must show that there exists a dangerous probability of monopoly power over prices and competition within the relevant market, coupled with a specific intent to monopolize. On the basis of all the facts given, can Cal establish that Bay possessed the necessary *monopoly power* just described?

3. On August 5, 1969, at a hearing held before the Arizona Corporation Commission, the Arizona Water Company, a private corporation, sought and was granted the right to deliver water in a specified geographic area. Subsequently, the State of Arizona issued the company a "certificate of convenience and necessity," which confirmed the company's exclusive right to sell water in the specified area. In light of antitrust laws that prohibit the exercise of monopoly powers, should Arizona Water Company be granted this exclusive right? Under what conditions should the State of Arizona be allowed to withdraw the "certificate of convenience and necessity" that it awarded Arizona Water Company? [Fernandez v. Arizona Water Co., 21 Ariz.App. 107, 516 P.2d. 49 (1974)]

4. Buckeye and Lamb were competing to be the first to obtain a natural monopoly in the cable TV business in Toledo. To be first in obtaining a completed facility was crucial because in the cable TV business—like that of the electric, gas, and telephone utilities—it is not feasible to compete house-to-house for customers in the same area. Buckeye arranged construction of its cable TV facilities first, whereupon Lamb claimed that this violated the antitrust laws. In order to beat Lamb, Buckeye had to be the first to convince Bell Telephone to assist in the construction of a cable TV system along its telephone lines. Lamb objected to the contract between Bell Telephone and Buckeye, claiming that it was "an agreement in restraint of trade." What result? [Lamb Enterprises, Inc. v. Toledo Blade Co., 461 F.2d 506 (6th Cir. 1972)]

5. The Professional Golfers Association of America (PGA) was founded in 1916 as a voluntary, unincorporated, nonprofit association. It has some 4,300 members and sponsors or cosponsors substantially all of the professional golf tournaments held in the United States. In order to compete in these tournaments, a player must be either a member of the PGA, an approved tournament player, or one of a limited number of participants designated or invited by the local sponsor of the tournament. Because of the increasing popularity of professional tournament golf, some means had to be found to limit the number of golfers who could enter these tournaments. PGA rules limiting entry to the categories of persons named above and defining the qualifications necessary for nonmember entrance were intended to accomplish this purpose. PGA gives official recognition to many tournaments that it neither sponsors nor cosponsors. These "approved tournaments" are free from any PGA control; yet PGA plans its schedule around them and counts them in determining its official standings. Herbert C. Deesen was a professional golfer who competed for several years in PGA-sponsored tournaments. Deesen sued the PGA, alleging that its sheer size and vast control over professional golf tournaments in the United States amounted to monopoly control in violation of Section II of the Sherman Antitrust Act. Do the PGA's activities violate the Sherman Act? If so, how? [Deesen v. Professional Golfers Ass'n of America, 358 F.2d 165 (9th Cir. 1966)]

6. American Oil Company was a producer and distributor of oil, gas, and related products. Olson's was engaged in bulk distribution and retail sales of oil products. Early in 1967, American decided to acquire control of Olson's bulk distribution operations, and it

purchased substantially all of Olson's assets. Thereafter, American negotiated a contract with Lawrence McMullen under which McMullen was to assume control of the Olson operation. Under the agreement, McMullen was to take charge of the Olson plant and was to be paid on a commission basis for the bulk petroleum sales that he procured. In addition, the contract between American and McMullen imposed certain territorial limitations and price restrictions on sales by the operations that McMullen was to control. Could the agreement between McMullen and American Oil imposing price restrictions and territorial controls on the operations of which McMullen took charge constitute a violation of Section I of the Sherman Antitrust Act? Explain. [American Oil Co. v. McMullen, 508 F.2d 1345 (10th Cir. 1975)]

7. A relatively small number of companies are engaged in the manufacturing of corrugated containers in the United States. Corrugated containers are a fungible product for which demand is relatively inelastic. That is, changes in the price charged for the containers significantly affect demand for them. The dominant sellers in the corrugated container business agreed to give each other, on request, information about their most recent prices charged or quoted. This agreement stabilized corrugated container prices. At no time did the sellers agree to sell at fixed prices. Has a violation of the antitrust laws occurred? [United States v. Container Corp. of America, 393 U.S. 333, 89 S.Ct. 510 (1969)]

8. Klor's was a retail establishment that sold appliances. Broadway-Hale, a retail chain of department stores, operated a store next door that competed with Klor's in the sale of appliances. At Broadway-Hale's request, several manufacturers and distributors of the major brands of appliances agreed either not to sell to Klor's or to sell to it only at higher than normal prices. All the participants in this agreement admitted its existence. However, they justified their actions by stating that their participation in the agreement was the result of a private quarrel between Broadway-Hale and Klor's. Later, when Klor's sued both Broadway-Hale and these manufacturers and distributors, alleging that they participated in a "group boycott" against Klor's, the manufacturers and distributors asserted that Klor's was "just one small retailer" and therefore their actions could not be deemed in restraint of competition. Have the manufacturers and distributors presented any defense to the charge of group boycott that would stand up in court? [Klor's, Inc. v. Broadway-Hale Stores, Inc., 359 U.S. 207, 79 S.Ct. 705 (1959)]

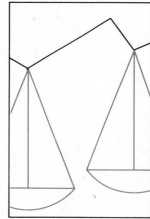

51

Government Regulation
The Federal Trade Commission
and Trade Regulation

This chapter is concerned with business regulation as it is prescribed by various federal statutes, and it will concentrate on the activities associated with the Federal Trade Commission. It is difficult to divide the activities of the Justice Department that regulate business activities from those of the FTC along any accepted theoretical grounds. Nevertheless, the activities of the commission do, in general, differ from those of the antitrust division of the Justice Department.

COMMISSION RESOURCES AND AUTHORITY

The estimated budget of the Federal Trade Commission for fiscal year (FY) 1980 is nearly $70 million, and total staff is estimated at about 1,800 individuals.[1] In addition to the consumer protection activities discussed in Chapter 48, the commission spends about half its total budget in efforts designed to maintain the competitive nature of the U.S. economy. This effort involves enforcing federal statutes that include, but are not limited to, the Federal Trade Commission Act,[2] Sections 2, 3, 7, and 8 of the Clayton Act[3] as amended by the Celler-Kefauver and Robinson-Patman Acts,[4] the Export Trade Act,[5] the Emergency Petroleum Allocation Act,[6]

1. *Budget of the U.S. Government, Fiscal Year 1980* (Washington, D.C.: Government Printing Office, 1979), appendix, p. 910.
2. 15 USCA Secs. 41-58.
3. 15 USCA Secs. 12-27, as amended.
4. 15 USCA Secs. 18, 21, 13c.
5. 15 USCA Secs. 61-65.
6. 15 USCA Sec. 755.

the Federal Trade Commission Improvement Act,[7] and the Hart-Scott-Rodino Antitrust Improvement Act.[8]

The Federal Trade Commission Act

In 1914, Congress passed the Federal Trade Commission Act, which created a bipartisan administrative agency headed by five commissioners, no more than three of whom could be of the same political party.[9] Section 5 of the act gives the FTC broad powers to prevent "unfair methods of competition in commerce and unfair or deceptive acts or practices in commerce." Amendments, particularly in 1975, have broadened the commission's powers.[10] The FTC also has the authority to conduct investigations relating to alleged violations of antitrust statutes and to make reports and recommendations to Congress regarding legislation. More importantly, the FTC can promulgate interpretive rules and general statements of policy with respect to unfair or deceptive acts or practices. It can also promulgate trade regulation rules, which *define* particular unfair or deceptive acts or practices including requirements for the purpose of preventing such acts or practices. The commission has issued guidelines defining unfair practices, but these guidelines are very broad, and many seemingly unfair practices are allowed.[11]

The FTC initiates most of its investigations because of oral or written communications from the general public and private business firms. The primary enforcement mechanism of the FTC is **cease and desist orders** (orders to stop certain activities or practices) against violations of the Federal Trade Commission Act. Furthermore, businesses that violate these orders are subject to fines of up to $10,000 per day for each

7. 15 USCA Sec. 230 *et seq.*
8. 15 USCA Sec. 18a.
9. 15 USCA Secs. 41-51 (1914)
10. Magnuson-Moss FTC Improvements Act of 1975.
11. The commission, for example, has indicated that a practice is "unfair" if it offends public policy or is immoral, unethical, oppressive, unscrupulous, or causes substantial injury to consumers.

day of continued violation. Cease and desist orders can be appealed to the courts. Unlike the Sherman Act, treble damage actions cannot be brought under Section 5 of the FCT Act.

Beginning in the early 1960s, the FTC issued a number of **trade regulation rules**. These rules define acceptable and unacceptable practices for various industries. For example, the FTC has promulgated trade regulation rules governing the pricing of eyeglasses and funerals. The commission considers a number of proposed trade regulation rules covering a wide range of industry practices each year. Violations of trade regulation rules, like violations of cease and desist orders, are subject to potential fines of up to $10,000 per day.

Additional Authority

Section 5 of the Federal Trade Commission Act overlaps a number of other antitrust statutes, including the Sherman Act, the Clayton Act, and other laws designed to reduce unfair methods of competition. The FTC initiates investigations and issues cease and desist orders particularly for violations of Sections 2, 3, 7, and 8 of the Clayton Act as amended by Celler-Kefauver, the Robinson-Patman, and other acts.

PRICE DISCRIMINATION   One of the more important activities of the Federal Trade Commission has been the detection and prohibition of **price discrimination** (that is, charging different prices to different purchasers for identical goods) when such discrimination lessens competition or tends to create a monopoly.

Subsequent judicial interpretation and responses by businesses effectively circumvented the original intent of Section 1 of the Clayton Act, so by 1936 Congress responded by enacting the Robinson-Patman Act. This act tightened the prohibition against price discrimination so that if goods of similar grade and quality were sold at different prices, and these differences could not be justified by differences in production costs, the practice would violate the Robinson-Patman Act. In addition, the act prohibited sellers from cutting prices to levels substantially below those charged by their competitors.[12]

In the following antitrust action, the plaintiff was a local company engaged in selling

---

12. Robinson-Patman Act, Subsection B.

frozen pies. The defendant was one of several national companies also engaged in selling frozen pies. The defendant cut the price of its frozen pies in a local market so that the price was below cost. The practice was found to be a violation of the Robinson-Patman Act.

BACKGROUND AND FACTS *The Utah Pie Company (the plaintiff) brought an antitrust action against the Continental Baking Company, the Carnation Company, and the Pet Milk Company for violations of the Robinson-Patman Act. Only the Continental Baking Company participated in this appeal to the Supreme Court. The Court had to determine whether the defendant had engaged in discriminatory price cutting by selling its frozen pies in a local market below its direct costs plus allocation for overhead, without having any justification. The lower court had found that the defendants had violated the statute by charging a different price to different customers for the same goods.*

UTAH PIE CO. v.
**CONTINENTAL
BAKING CO.**
Supreme Court of the United
States, 1967.
386 U.S. 685, 87 S.Ct. 1326

WHITE, Justice.
* * *

The product involved is frozen dessert pies—apple, cherry, boysenberry, peach, pumpkin, and mince. * * * Petitioner is a Utah corporation which for 30 years had been baking pies in its plant in Salt Lake City and selling them in Utah and surrounding States. It entered the frozen pie business in late 1957. It was immediately successful with its new line and built a new plant in Salt Lake City in 1958. The frozen pie market was a rapidly expanding one: 57,060 dozen frozen pies were sold in the Salt Lake City market in 1958, 111,729 dozen in 1959, 184,569 dozen in 1960, and 266,908 dozen in 1961. Utah Pie's share of this market in those years was 66.5%, 34.3%, 45.5%, and 45.3% respectively, its sales volume steadily increasing over the four years. Its financial position also improved. Petitioner is not, however, a large company. At the time of the trial, petitioner operated with only 18 employees, nine of whom were members of the Rigby family. * * *

Each of the respondents [defendants] is a large company and each of them is a major factor in the frozen pie market in one or more regions of the country. Each entered the Salt Lake City frozen pie market before petitioner began freezing dessert pies. None of them had a plant in Utah. * * * The Salt Lake City market was supplied by respondents chiefly from their California operations. They sold primarily on a delivered price basis.
* * *

The major competitive weapon in the Utah market was price. The location of petitioner's [Utah Pie] plant gave it natural advantages in the Salt Lake City marketing area and it entered the market at a price below the then going prices for respondents' [Continental Baking] comparable pies. For most of the period involved here its [Utah Pies] prices were the lowest in the Salt Lake City market.
* * * There was ample evidence [established at trial] to show that * * * the

respondents contributed to what proved to be a deteriorating price structure over the period covered by this suit, and * * * the respondents in the course of the ongoing price competition sold frozen pies in the Salt Lake market at prices lower than it sold pies of like grade and quality in other markets considerably closer to its plants. * * *

Petitioner's case against Continental is not complicated. Continental was a substantial factor in the market in 1957. But its sales of frozen 22-ounce dessert pies, sold under the "Morton" brand, amounted to only 1.3% of the market in 1958, 2.9% in 1959, and 1.8% in 1960. Its problems were primarily that of cost and in turn that of price, the controlling factor in the market. In late 1960 it worked out a co-packing arrangement in California by which fruit would be processed directly from the trees into the finished pie without large intermediate packing, storing, and shipping expenses. Having improved its position, it attempted to increase its share of the Salt Lake City market by utilizing a local broker and offering short-term price concessions in varying amounts. Its efforts for seven months were not spectacularly successful. Then in June 1961, it took the steps which are the heart of petitioner's complaint against it. Effective for the last two weeks of June it offered its 22-ounce frozen apple pies in the Utah area at $2.85 per dozen. It was then selling the same pies at substantially higher prices in other markets. The Salt Lake City price was less than its direct cost plus an allocation for overhead. Utah's going price at the time for its 24-ounce "Frost 'N' Flame" apple pie sold to Associated Grocers was $3.10 per dozen, and for its "Utah" brand $3.40 per dozen. At its new prices, Continental sold pies to American Grocers in Pocatello, Idaho, and to American Food Stores in Ogden, Utah. Safeway, one of the major buyers in Salt Lake City, also purchased 6,250 dozen, its requirements for about five weeks. Another purchaser ordered 1,000 dozen. Utah's response was immediate. It reduced its price on all of its apple pies to $2.75 per dozen. Continental refused Safeway's request to match Utah's price, but renewed its offer at the same prices [$2.85] effective July 31 for another two-week period. Utah filed suit on September 8, 1961. Continental's total sales of frozen pies increased from 3,350 dozen in 1960 to 18,800 dozen in 1961. Its market share increased from 1.8% in 1960 to 8.3% in 1961. * * *

* * * [A] competitor who is forced to reduce his price to a new all-time low in a market of declining prices will in time feel the financial pinch and will be a less effective competitive force.

      * * *

Section 2(a) [of the Robinson-Patman Act] does not forbid price competition which will probably injure or lessen competition by eliminating competitors, discouraging entry into the market or enhancing the market shares of the dominant sellers. But Congress has established some ground rules for the game. Sellers may not sell like goods to different purchasers at different prices if the result may be to injure competition in either the sellers' or the buyers' market unless such discriminations are justified as permitted by the Act. This case concerns the sellers' market. * * * The frozen pie market in Salt Lake City was highly competitive. At times Utah Pie was a leader in moving the general level of prices down, and at other times each of the respondents also bore responsibility for the downward pressure on the price structure. We believe that the Act reaches price discrimination that erodes competition as much as it does price discrimination that is intended to have immediate destructive impact. In this case, the evidence shows a drastically declining price structure which * * * could rationally [be] attribute[d] to continued or sporadic price discrimination. The jury was entitled to conclude that "the effect of such discrimination," [by the Continental Bakery] "may be substantially to lessen competition * * * or to injure, destroy, or prevent competition with any person who either grants or knowingly receives the benefit of such discrimination * * *." The statutory test is one that necessarily looks forward on the basis of proven conduct in the past. * * *

The Supreme Court found that the trial court was correct in holding the Continental Baking Company guilty of violating the Robinson-Patman Act for price discrimination without justification, with the effect of substantially lessening competition.

JUDGMENT AND REMEDY

EXCLUSIVE DEALINGS   Section 3 of the Clayton Act as amended prohibits exclusive dealing contracts when the effect of these contracts would be "to substantially lessen competition or tend to create a monopoly."[13]

Exclusive dealing contracts arise when a seller or manufacturer requires the buyer to *not* purchase the products of competitive sellers. Section 3 has also been interpreted by the courts to prohibit *tying contracts* where the seller of a commodity agrees to provide the commodity on the condition that the buyer purchase one or more other commodities offered by the seller.

13.   15 USCA Sec. 14 (1914).

Thus, an auto dealer is not allowed to require that a customer purchase insurance from the firm.

MERGERS   The FTC also enforces Section 7 of the Clayton Act as amended by the Celler-Kefauver Act, which provides merger guidelines. These guidelines prohibit acquisition of the stock of another corporation whenever the effect would be to restrain commerce or tend to create a monopoly. (Mergers were discussed more fully in Chapter 45.) The act was intended to preserve competition by arresting the continuous trend toward fewer and fewer small business owner-competitors.

BACKGROUND AND FACTS   *In 1958, Von's Grocery Company ranked third in retail sales in the Los Angeles area. Its largest direct competitor, Shopping Bag Food Stores, ranked sixth in retail sales for the same period. The merger of these two highly successful, expanding, and aggressive competitors created the second largest grocery chain in Los Angeles, with sales of almost $173 million annually. The number of small business owners operating single grocery stores in the Los Angeles retail grocery market had been dropping in the years prior to the merger, and after it, the number dropped still further. The grocery business in the Los Angeles area was being concentrated into the hands of fewer and fewer owners as small grocery companies were continually being absorbed by the larger firms through mergers.*

On March 25, 1960, the United States brought this action, charging that Von's Grocery Company's acquisition of its direct competitor,

UNITED STATES v. VON'S GROCERY CO.
Supreme Court of the United States, 1966.
384 U.S. 270, 86 S.Ct. 1478

*Shopping Bag Food Stores, violated Section 7 of the Clayton Act, which, as amended in 1950 by the Celler-Kefauver Anti-Merger Act, provides in relevant part: "That no corporation engaged in commerce * * * shall acquire the whole or any part of the assets of another corporation engaged also in commerce, where in any line of commerce in any section of the country, the effect of such acquisition may be substantially to lessen competition, or to tend to create a monopoly."*

On March 28, 1960, three days later, the district court refused to grant the government's motion for a temporary restraining order. Immediately, Von's took over all of Shopping Bag's capital stock and assets, including its thirty-six grocery stores in Los Angeles. After a hearing, the district court concluded that there was not a reasonable probability that the merger would tend "substantially to lessen competition" or "create a monopoly" in violation of Section 7. The government appealed directly to the Supreme Court of the United States.[1]

BLACK, Justice.

* * *

* * * The sole question here is whether the District Court properly concluded on the facts before it that the Government had failed to prove a violation of §7. * * *

From this country's beginning there has been an abiding and widespread fear of the evils which flow from monopoly—that is the concentration of economic power in the hands of a few. On the basis of this fear, Congress in 1890, when many of the Nation's industries were already concentrated into what it deemed too few hands, passed the Sherman Act in an attempt to prevent further concentration and to preserve competition among a large number of sellers. Several years later, in 1897, this Court emphasized this policy of the Sherman Act by calling attention to the tendency of powerful business combinations to restrain competition "by driving out of business the small dealers and worthy men whose lives have been spent therein, and who might be unable to readjust themselves to their altered surroundings." The Sherman Act failed to protect the smaller businessmen from elimination through the monopolistic pressures of large combinations which used mergers to grow ever more powerful. As a result in 1914 Congress, viewing mergers as a continuous, pervasive threat to small business, passed §7 of the Clayton Act which prohibited corporations under most circumstances from merging by purchasing the stock of their competitors. Ingenious businessmen, however, soon found a way to avoid §7 and corporations began to merge simply by purchasing their rivals' assets. This Court in 1926, over the dissent of Justice Brandeis, joined by Chief Justice Taft and Justices Holmes and Stone approved this device for avoiding §7 and mergers continued to concentrate economic power into fewer and fewer hands until 1950 when Congress passed the Celler-Kefauver Anti-Merger Act now before us.

Like the Sherman Act in 1890 and the Clayton Act in 1914, the basic purpose of the 1950 Celler-Kefauver Act was to prevent economic concentration in the American economy by keeping a large number of small competitors in their bill,

---

1. Direct appeal is authorized by Section 2 of the expediting act, 15 USC Sec. 29.

both of its sponsors, Representative Celler and Senator Kefauver, emphasized their fear, widely shared by other members of Congress, that this concentration was rapidly driving the small businessman out of the market. * * * "The dominant theme pervading congressional consideration of the 1950 amendments was a fear of what was considered to be a rising tide of economic concentration in the American economy." To arrest this "rising tide" toward concentration into too few hands and to halt the gradual demise of the small businessman, Congress decided to clamp down with vigor on mergers. It both revitalized §7 of the Clayton Act by "plugging its loophole" and broadened its scope so as not only to prohibit mergers between competitors, the effect of which "may be substantially to lessen competition, or to tend to create a monopoly" but to prohibit all mergers having that effect. By using these terms in §7 which look not merely to the actual present effect of a merger but instead to its effect upon future competition, Congress sought to preserve competition among many small businesses by arresting a trend toward concentration in its incipiency before that trend developed to the point that a market was left in the grip of a few big companies. Thus, where concentration is gaining momentum in a market, we must be alert to carry out Congress' intent to protect competition against ever-increasing concentration through mergers.

The facts of this case present exactly the threatening trend toward concentration which Congress wanted to halt. The number of small grocery companies in the Los Angeles retail grocery market had been declining rapidly before the merger and continued to decline rapidly afterwards. This rapid decline in the number of grocery store owners moved hand in hand with a large number of significant absorptions of the small companies by the larger ones. In the midst of this steadfast trend toward concentration, Von's and Shopping Bag, two of the most successful and largest companies in the area, jointly owning 66 grocery stores merged to become the second largest chain in Los Angeles. This merger cannot be defended on the ground that one of the companies was about to fail or that the two had to merge to save themselves from destruction by some larger and more powerful competitor. What we have on the contrary is simply the case of two already powerful companies merging in a way which makes them even more powerful than they were before. If ever such a merger would not violate §7, certainly it does when it takes place in a market characterized by a long and continuous trend toward fewer and fewer owner-competitors which is exactly the sort of trend which Congress, with power to do so, declared must be arrested.

Appellees' primary argument is that the merger between Von's and Shopping Bag is not prohibited by §7 because the Los Angeles grocery market was competitive before the merger, has been since, and may continue to be in the future. Even so, §7 "requires not merely an appraisal of the immediate impact of the merger upon competition, but a prediction of its impact upon competitive conditions in the future; this is what is meant when it is said that the amended §7 was intended to arrest anti-competitive tendencies in their 'incipiency.' " It is enough for us that Congress feared that a market marked at the same time by both a continuous decline in the number of small businesses and a large number of mergers would slowly but inevitably gravitate from a market of many small competitors to one dominated by one or a few giants, and competition would thereby be destroyed. Congress passed the Celler-Kefauver Act to prevent such a destruction of competition. * * *

JUDGMENT
AND REMEDY *The judgment of the district court was reversed and the case was remanded to the district court to order that Von's Grocery Company divest itself of Shopping Bag's capital stock and assets, including the thirty-six grocery stores in the Los Angeles area.*

INTERLOCKING DIRECTORATES *Interlocking directorates* occur when substantially the same people serve as officers and board members of different corporations. Section 8 of the Clayton Act prohibits *interlocking directorates* when elimination of competition among firms with such directorates would constitute a violation of the antitrust laws. (Corporations with capital, surplus, and undivided profits totaling less than $1 million are exempt.)

A number of statutes deal directly with *potential* competition in the economy. For example, the FTC is responsible for registering the articles of association or incorporation for associations that are organized under the Export Trade Act. It is also responsible for receiving and monitoring regulations governing mandatory allocations of crude oil, residual fuel oil, and refined petroleum products under the Emergency Petroleum Act of 1973. And it is responsible for working with the Justice Department in developing voluntary agreements under the International Energy Program. The Energy Policy and Conservation Act also creates responsibilities relating to automobile fuel economy, appliance efficiencies, and recycled oil.

FTC ACTIVITIES

The Federal Trade Commission organizes its trade regulation activities into the three general categories of competition, consumer protection, and economic activities rather than along specific lines of enforcing explicit statutes. Most FTC investigation and trade regulation activities can be put into the main categories shown in Exhibit 51-1, which also gives the percentage of

---

EXHIBIT 51-1   MAJOR FTC MAINTAINING COMPETITION MISSIONS AND PERCENT OF DIRECT TOTAL EFFORT

PROGRAM	PERCENT OF FISCAL YEAR 1979 RESOURCE ESTIMATES
Energy and petroleum industries	21.2
Health care	11.8
Food industries: Producer, manufacturer, distributor, and retailer	11.6
Transportation industries	11.0
Horizontal restraints	12.5
Mergers and joint ventures	8.4
Distributional restraints	7.2
Industry-wide matters	3.5
Compliance with competitive orders	4.3
Other	8.5
Total	100.0

Source: Federal Trade Commission, *Zero-Based Program Budget, FY1979* (Washington, D.C.: Government Printing Offices, 1978).

resources spent in maintaining competition for each of these major categories.

Transportation

Regulatory activities of the commission are also concerned with the transportation service and equipment industries to the extent that high profits in those industries reflect anticompetitive conditions. Factors that can impede development of major innovations are also under the scrutiny of the commission.

Health Care

A major activity of the commission is the ongoing investigation of health care facilities, including professional health services and suppliers of hospital services, drugs, and medical products. Potential practices that impede competition—such as accreditation of professional schools, licensing, codes of professional ethics, minimum fee schedules, joint practice clinics, malpractice and other insurance costs, and other factors that directly or indirectly influence the provision of professional health services—are under continued investigation. The commission is also investigating the institutions and practices that determine the prices for prescription drugs, patent medicines, and medical supplies.

Food

FTC food programs concern all stages of agricultural production and marketing. The commission is investigating the organization of the industry as well as existing regulations that include quotas, subsidies, support programs, or other methods of modifying market conditions. The investigation extends to the manufacturer-processor levels, where it is concentrating on barriers to entry that lessen competition. Similar activities are conducted at the distribution and retailing level.

Energy

The major activity in the energy area concerns the Exxon investigation, the single largest enforcement activity in the history of the Federal Trade Commission. Beginning with a 1973 complaint, it now involves eight major petroleum refining companies. The commission believes that these companies are monopolizing domestic petroleum refining and that they maintain anticompetitive market conditions in petroleum products in certain portions of the country. It hopes to determine whether there is access to petroleum supplies and facilities by independent producers and, if necessary, to seek remedies to enhance product or price competition. The commission is also investigating various methods of conducting and financing business operations in other energy-producing firms, including barriers to the development of new sources of fuel, delivery of existing energy supplies, or characteristics that can impede investment, exploration, development, production, transportation, or other aspects of conducting business in energy-producing firms.

A number of other industries are subject to FTC trade regulation rules, but they are generally categorized under particular forms of activity rather than by the services or goods they provide. Once the FTC has found a practice to be unacceptable, it is irrelevant whether the practice is permissible by state law. In the following case, the FTC ruled that advertisements used by a weight loss clinic were unacceptable, even though they had been reviewed by the attorney general of the state in accordance with a state health plan act and the attorney general had not disapproved of them.

BACKGROUND AND FACTS *The defendants operated a weight loss clinic in California. The FTC entered a cease and desist order prohibiting their continued use of an advertisement that failed to indicate that a drug used by the clinic was new and had not been approved for such use by the FDA (Food and Drug Administration).*

SIMEON MANAGEMENT CORP. v. FEDERAL TRADE COMM.
United States Court of Appeals, Ninth Circuit, 1978. 579 F.2d 1137.

The clinics utilized the Simeon method of weight reduction. After an initial physical examination by a licensed physician, patients were put on a four- to six-week treatment program, which generally included a five hundred calorie per day diet, daily medical counseling, and daily injections of human chorionic gonadotropin (HCG)—a prescription drug derived from the urine of pregnant women. The FDA declared that HCG was a new drug and approved it for some uses, but not for the treatment of obesity. The FDA found that there was no substantial evidence that HCG was safe or effective for such use.

As one of the principal means of promoting the business of their weight reduction clinics, the petitioners placed advertisements in newspapers, magazines, and other media. These advertisements represented that the treatment program utilized in the clinics was safe, effective, and medically approved. The advertisements did not mention HCG or that injection of a drug would be part of the treatment program.

The clinics were registered under the Health Plan Act that had been passed by the California legislature. The act required the clinics' advertisements to be reviewed by the attorney general's office prior to dissemination.

The FTC commenced administrative proceedings against the clinics. The advertisements were challenged as deceptive, unfair, and false because they failed to disclose that the treatments offered involved injections of HCG and that HCG was not approved by the FDA as safe and effective for use in weight control.

BURNS, District Judge.
* * *

Petitioners * * * contend that we should set aside the cease and desist order because, after reviewing the advertisements pursuant to the Knox-Mills Health Plan Act, the California Attorney General did not disapprove of their nature and contents. Petitioners argue that this failure to disapprove constitutes a prima facie determination that the advertisements are representative, fair and legal. They also argue that FTC regulation of their advertisements impermissibly interferes with the state regulation.

These contentions lack merit. Whether a state official has approved the advertisements or not is irrelevant to the operation of the federal regulatory scheme set forth in the FTCA. That scheme does not impermissibly intrude upon state regulation.

Petitioners contend that the FTC has no jurisdiction to encroach upon the confidential relationship between a physician and patient. They argue that, because HCG is administered by or under the supervision of a physician as part of the weight reduction program, the Commission has no jurisdiction to regulate the advertising used in promoting the clinics.

This contention also lacks merit. The Commission's order does not pretend to affect the right of a physician to prescribe or administer HCG for his or her patients as part of a course of weight reduction treatments. The order prevents petitioners from advertising their clinics and weight reduction program in a way which fails to disclose that the FDA has not approved HCG for such use and that there is no substantial evidence that HCG is effective in the treatment of obesity. The order in no way impinges upon the traditional physician-patient relationship. * * *

The Commission found that (1) some consumers will reasonably believe that the government exercises control over the promotion and use of prescription drugs; (2) this belief is intensified by the advertisements' representations that the weight loss treatments are safe, effective and medically approved; and (3) the representations may therefore reasonably lead consumers into the mistaken belief that the claims of safety and effectiveness are based, not on the advertiser's own opinion, but on a determination by the FDA. It further found that, in view of the public's belief that the government strictly regulates drugs, the fact that the treatments involve administration of a drug lacking FDA approval for such use may materially affect a consumer's decision to undergo the treatment. Accordingly, the Commission declared that the failure to disclose that the weight reduction treatments involve injection of a drug lacking FDA approval for such use renders the advertisements deceptive and thus in violation of §5 of the FTCA. * * *

The need for the courts to defer to the Commission's judgment results in part from the statutory scheme and in part from the weight of accumulated agency expertise. * * *

Once the Commission has found an advertisement to be deceptive, it is authorized, within the bounds of reason, to infer that the deceptive information would be a material factor in the consumer's decision to buy. *Colgate, supra,* 380 U.S. at 392, 85 S.Ct. 1035. The Commission found that the fact that the advertised treatments involve administration of a drug lacking FDA approval for such use might materially affect the consumer's decision to obtain such treatments. Again, in view of the extent of governmental regulation in this area, we cannot say that this determination is unreasonable. * * *

For the foregoing reasons, we hold that the Commission's determination that the petitioners' advertisements are deceptive in violation of §5 of the FTCA is supported by substantial evidence on the record as a whole and is not arbitrary, capricious, [nor] an abuse of discretion * * *. * * *

JUDGMENT AND REMEDY

The Supreme Court upheld the FTC order preventing the petitioners' use of the advertisements as deceptive and in violation of Section 5 of the Federal Trade Commission Act.

VERTICAL RESTRAINTS

FTC activities involving vertical restraints include resale price maintenance, mergers, price discrimination, and other practices among firms at various levels of production, distribution, or sales that can result in anticompetitive outcomes. Investigations into resale price maintenance, the establishment of uniform retail prices by producers, are likely to become less important by the repeal of the federal statute authorizing states to adopt fair trade laws.[14]

---

14. See the discussion of the Miller-Tydings Act in Chapter 50.

Vertical Mergers

Vertical mergers occur when a company at one stage of production acquires a company at a higher or lower stage of production. Thus, the acquisition of a tire plant by an automobile manufacturer would constitute a backward vertical integration, while acquisition of a car-renting agency would constitute a forward vertical integration. The FTC's approach to vertical mergers depends on a number of factors, including definition of the relevant product in geographic markets as well as the characteristics identified as impeding competition. For example, the commission will attack any vertical merger that keeps competitors of either party from the segment of the market that otherwise would be open to them. Thus, in Ashgrove Cement Co. v. Federal Trade Comm.,[15] the commission found that "foreclosure manifests a particularly anticompetitive character when it occurs as part of a trend toward forward integration in a concentrated market.[16] Thus, the potential entrant is faced with the choice of entering at the supply level and competing with a continually shrinking market or entering at both the supply and consumer levels, but incurring increased costs of entering. In such circumstances, the commission clearly has indicated that the potential entrant faces entry barriers.

Other Vertical Restraints

The commission also investigates other vertical restraints that promote unfair practices or impede competition. These restraints include, but are not limited to, long-term requirements contracts, territorial and customer restrictions,

vertical price fixing, and tying requirements, in which the seller ties the purchase of one commodity to another commodity supplied by the seller. The commission determined that requirements to buy all products of a seller (full-output purchase requirements) seriously reduce competition in suppliers' markets. Accordingly, it attacked a series of full-output purchase requirement contracts to purchase petroleum coke (a by-product of the refining process) that Great Lakes Carbon had with various refiners.[17] The initial terms of these contracts ranged from seven to twenty years, with extensions for five-year minimum periods. The commission also determined that territorial restrictions are illegal when the firm also attempts to fix prices. Thus, in Coors,[18] the commission found that territorial restrictions on Coors distributors with simultaneous wholesale and retail minimum prices reduced competition in the beer industry.

The commission has ruled that certain other exclusionary practices, such as tying arrangements and **reciprocal buying,** are unlawful. Reciprocal arrangements exist when the seller of one good is required to purchase one or more goods provided by the buyer of the initial good. Thus, if an automobile manufacturer sells to a leasing company, the leasing firm cannot require that employees of the automobile manufacturer rent cars from the firm.

---

15. 85 FTC 1123, 519 F. 2d 934 [D.C.Cir. 1975].
16. The law's current theory of injury to competition in vertical mergers is contained in the concept of foreclosure. For example, a manufacturer can acquire a retailer and force the new retail subsidiary to sell the manufacturer's parent product. This would "foreclose" rival manufacturers from the market.
17. 2582 FTC 1529 (1973).
18. 83 FTC 32 (1973).

FEDERAL TRADE COMM. v. CONSOLIDATED FOODS CORP.

Supreme Court of the United States, 1965.
380 U.S. 92, 85 S.Ct. 1220

BACKGROUND AND FACTS *Consolidated Foods owns a network of food processing plants, wholesale outlets, and retail food stores. It acquired Gentry, a producer of dehydrated onion and garlic products. The FTC maintained that this acquisition violated Section 7 of the Clayton Act because, through reciprocal buying, it gave Consolidated*

Foods the power to lessen competition in the dehydrated onion and garlic markets. Consolidated appealed the FTC ruling to the United States Court of Appeals, which reversed the FTC judgment. The case then went to the Supreme Court.

DOUGLAS, Justice.
* * *

Section 7 of the Clayton Act is concerned "with probabilities, not certainties." Reciprocity in trading as a result of an acquisition violates §7, if the probability of a lessening of competition is shown. We turn then to that, the principal, aspect of the present case.

Consolidated is a substantial purchaser of the products of food processors who in turn purchase dehydrated onion and garlic for use in preparing and packaging their food. Gentry * * * principally engaged in the manufacture of dehydrated onion and garlic, had * * * immediately prior to its acquisition by Consolidated, about 32% of the total sales of the dehydrated garlic and onion industry. * * *

After the acquisition Consolidated (though later disclaiming adherence to any policy of reciprocity) did undertake to assist Gentry in selling. An official of Consolidated wrote as follows to its distributing divisions:

"Oftentimes, it is a great advantage to know when you are calling on a prospect, whether or not that prospect is a supplier of someone within your own organization. Everyone believes in reciprocity providing all things are equal.

"Attached is a list of prospects for our Gentry products. We would like to have you indicate on the list whether or not you are purchasing any of your supplies from them. If so, indicate whether your purchases are relatively large, small or insignificant.
* * *

Food processors who sold to Consolidated stated they would give their onion and garlic business to Gentry for reciprocity reasons if it could meet the price and quality of its competitors' products. * * *
* * *

[T]he Commission concluded:
"With two firms accounting for better than 85% of both product lines for eleven successive years, maximum concentration short of monopoly has already been achieved. If it is desirable to prevent a trend toward oligopoly it is *a fortiori* desirable to remove, so far as possible, obstacles to the creation of genuinely competitive conditions in an oligopolistic industry. * * *"
* * *

The Court of Appeals, on the other hand, gave post-acquisition evidence almost conclusive weight. It pointed out that, while Gentry's share of the dehydrated onion market increased by some 7%, its share of the dehydrated garlic market decreased 12%. * * *

The Court of Appeals was not in error in considering the post-acquisition evidence in this case. But we think it gave too much weight to it. No group acquiring a company with reciprocal buying opportunities is entitled to a "free trial" period. To give it such would be to distort the scheme of §7. The "mere *possibility*" of the prohibited restraint is not enough. Probability of the proscribed evil is required, as we have noted. If the post-acquisition evidence were given conclusive weight or allowed to override all probabilities, then acquisitions would go forward willy-nilly, the parties biding their time until reciprocity was allowed fully to bloom. It is, of course, true that post-acquisition conduct may amount to a violation of §7 even though there is no evidence to establish probability *in limine.* But the force of §7 is still in probabilities, not in what later transpired. That must necessarily be the case, for once the two companies are united no one knows what the fate of the acquired company and its competitors would have been but for the merger.

Moreover, the post-acquisition evidence here tends to confirm, rather than cast doubt upon, the probable anti-competitive effect which the Commission found the merger would have. The Commission found that Basic's [Gentry's chief competitor] product was superior to Gentry's—as Gentry's president freely and repeatedly admitted. Yet Gentry, in a rapidly expanding market, was able to increase its share of onion sales by 7% and to hold its losses in garlic to a 12% decrease. Thus the Commission was surely on safe ground in reaching the following conclusion:

"If reciprocal buying creates for Gentry a protected market, which others cannot penetrate despite superiority of price, quality, or service, competition is lessened whether or not Gentry can expand its market share. It is for this reason that we reject respondent's argument that the decline in its share of the garlic market proves the ineffectiveness of reciprocity. We do not know that its share would not have fallen still farther, had it not been for the influence of reciprocal buying. This loss of sales fails to refute the likelihood that Consolidated's reciprocity power, which it has shown a willingness to exploit to the full, will not immunize a substantial segment of the garlic market from normal quality, price, and service competition."

* * * We do not go so far as to say that any acquisition, no matter how small, violates §7 if there is a probability of reciprocal buying. Some situations may amount only to *de minimis.* But where, as here, the acquisition is of a company that commands a substantial share of a market, a finding of probability of reciprocal buying by the Commission, whose expertise the Congress trusts, should be honored, if there is substantial evidence to support it.

* * *

JUDGMENT AND REMEDY   *The FTC order was upheld by the Supreme Court. Consolidated Foods was required to divest itself of Gentry.*

HORIZONTAL RESTRAINTS

In addition to mergers, horizontal restraints include all practices that potentially limit the competition among firms selling products of similar characteristics: industry practices, such as basing-point or delivered pricing schemes, cooperative associations that engage in price fixing, restrictions on advertising and price competition, and other restraints on trade.

Horizontal Mergers

The statutory authority for enforcing anticompetitive mergers is Section 6 of the Clayton Act.

This section was introduced because it was feared that concentration would potentially facilitate collusion among sellers in the market, and that such collusion would be difficult to detect. In general, the commission determines the legality of **horizontal mergers** by looking at the degree of concentration or market shares of merging firms, although the Court has indicated that it would look at the likely effects of the merger as well. Thus, if a merger facilitates horizontal collusion without increasing production or marketing efficiencies, it will be declared unlawful. Mergers will be permitted when they enhance consumer welfare by increasing efficiency if they do not increase the probability of horizontal collusion. Furthermore, mergers that facilitate and increase efficiency must be evaluated on the relative magnitude of the two facts. For example, in *Philadelphia National Bank*,[19] the Commission held that even in situations with low entry barriers, there may be a loss of actual competition. Thus, mergers can be declared illegal even where entry is relatively easy.

Other Horizontal Restraints

Over the years, the traditional methods for fixing prices by allocating territories or boycotting competitors have been rapidly disappearing. Consequently, the commission has revised its enforcement approach to focus more on the hidden forms of restricting competition. These may, for example, concern the exchange of information on prices or other characteristics as a means of enforcing a hidden restrictive agreement. Thus, the commission has paid particular attention to trade associations that disseminate trade information among producers and potential clients. It is argued that this can

provide a mechanism for enforcing informal agreements. The FTC has, for example, charged a lettuce produce cooperative with price fixing.[20] More importantly, the commission has turned to activities or practices that can constitute restraints on competition. For example, in the early 1970s, it began the first of a number of cases attacking shopping center leases that give major tenants a veto over other tenants. For example, in *Tysons Corner*,[21] the three major department stores were given lease arrangements that permitted them to disapprove prospective tenants who wished to rent space in the center. These clauses were ruled as prima facie evidence of unreasonable restraint of trade. The commission in this case ruled that agreements that create approval rights as broad as those involved in the *Tysons Corner* case are per se illegal and amount to an agreement to fix prices.

CONGLOMERATE MERGERS

Conglomerate mergers often extend product lines at the retail level, particularly among products that are complementary, although mergers can also occur among firms using similar suppliers.

A large number of conglomerate mergers, however, occur where the merging firms have no direct functional business link. In such mergers there are no changes in market structure, market shares, or concentration ratios. In many cases, conglomerate mergers serve to reduce overhead costs by spreading them over a larger range of output and reducing advertising and other promotional costs.

_____

19. FTC Docket No. 8986.

20. California Lettuce Producers Cooperative, FTC Docket No. 8970.

21. Tysons Corner Regional Shopping Center 85 FTC 970 (1975).

BACKGROUND AND FACTS   *The Federal Trade Commission argued that Procter & Gamble's acquisition of Clorox Chemical Company violated the Clayton Act and lessened competition in the household liquid bleach market. At the time of the merger, Clorox was the leading manufacturer of household bleach (49 percent of national sales) in a*

FEDERAL TRADE COMM. v. PROCTER & GAMBLE CO.
Supreme Court of the United States, 1967.
386 U.S. 568, 87 S.Ct. 1224

highly concentrated market. The commission found that extensive advertising expenditures could increase Clorox's market share. Purex, the major competitor, did not sell its product in some markets, primarily in the Northeast and Mid-Atlantic states. Procter & Gamble was a large, diversified producer of high-turnover household products primarily sold in grocery stores and drugstores. Through its large advertising budget, Procter & Gamble was able to obtain substantial price reductions. The commission argued that its acquisition of Clorox would discourage entry and competition in this market.

DOUGLAS, Justice.
* * *

At the time of the acquisition, Clorox was the leading manufacturer of household liquid bleach, with 48.8% of the national sales—annual sales of slightly less than $40,000,000. Its market share had been steadily increasing for the five years prior to the merger. Its nearest rival was Purex, which manufactures a number of products other than household liquid bleaches, including abrasive cleaners, toilet soap, and detergents. Purex accounted for 15.7% of the household liquid bleach market. The industry is highly concentrated; in 1957, Clorox and Purex accounted for almost 65% of the Nation's household liquid bleach sales, and, together with four other firms, for almost 80%. * * *

Since all liquid bleach is chemically identical, advertising and sales promotion are vital. In 1957 Clorox spent almost $3,700,000 on advertising, imprinting the value of its bleach in the mind of the consumer. * * * The Commission found that these heavy expenditures went far to explain why Clorox maintained so high a market share despite the fact that its brand, though chemically indistinguishable from rival brands, retailed for a price equal to or, in many instances, higher than its competitors.

Procter is a large, diversified manufacturer of low-price, high-turnover household products sold through grocery, drug, and department stores. Prior to its acquisition of Clorox, it did not produce household liquid bleach. * * * Procter has been marked by rapid growth and diversification. It has successfully developed and introduced a number of new products. Its primary activity is in the general area of soaps, detergents, and cleansers; in 1957, of total domestic sales, more than one-half * * * were in this field. Procter was the dominant factor in this area. * * *

In the marketing of soaps, detergents, and cleansers, as in the marketing of household liquid bleach, advertising and sales promotion are vital. * * * Due to its tremendous volume, Procter receives substantial discounts from the media. As a multi-product producer Procter enjoys substantial advantages in advertising and sales promotion. Thus, it can and does feature several products in its promotions, reducing the printing, mailing, and other costs for each product. It also purchases network programs on behalf of several products, enabling it to give each product network exposure at a fraction of the cost per product that a firm with only one product to advertise would incur.

Prior to the acquisition, Procter was in the course of diversifying into product lines related to its basic detergent-soap-cleanser business. Liquid bleach was a distinct possibility since packaged detergents—Procter's primary product line—and liquid bleach are used complementarily in washing clothes and fabrics, and in general household cleaning. * * *

The decision to acquire Clorox was the result of a study conducted by Procter's promotion department designed to determine the advisability of entering the liquid bleach industry. * * * Since a large investment would be needed to obtain a satisfactory market share, acquisition of the industry's leading firm was attractive. * * *

The final report confirmed the conclusions of the initial report and emphasized that Procter would make more effective use of Clorox's advertising budget and that the merger would facilitate advertising economies. A few months later, Procter acquired the assets of Clorox in the name of a wholly owned subsidiary, the Clorox Company, in exchange for Procter stock.

The Commission * * * found that the substitution of Procter with its huge assets and advertising advantages for the already dominant Clorox would dissuade new entrants and discourage active competition from the firms already in the industry due to fear of retaliation by Procter. * * *

The anticompetitive effects with which this product-extension merger is fraught can easily be seen: (1) the substitution of the powerful acquiring firm for the smaller, but already dominant, firm may substantially reduce the competitive structure of the industry by raising entry barriers and by dissuading the smaller firms from aggressively competing; (2) the acquisition eliminates the potential competition of the acquiring firm.

The liquid bleach industry was already oligopolistic before the acquisition, and price competition was certainly not as vigorous as it would have been if the industry were competitive. Clorox enjoyed a dominant position nationally, and its position approached monopoly proportions in certain areas. The existence of some 200 fringe firms certainly does not belie that fact. * * *

The FTC order that Procter & Gamble divest itself of the Clorox Company was upheld by the Supreme Court of the United States.   **JUDGMENT AND REMEDY**

INDUSTRY-WIDE MATTERS

The Federal Trade Commission investigates and enforces regulations in the context of industry-wide matters. Industry-wide problems may be indicated by high prices, profits, lack of product innovation, or the absence of entry by new firms. In such cases, the exact cause of reduced performance may not be readily identifiable. Determining the problem and selecting the appropriate remedy require a more extensive analysis than is necessary in other FTC investigations. Industry-wide matters include investigations of the petroleum and automobile industries as well as breakfast cereals as part of the food program investigation. Other matters under FTC investigation in the 1970s include the household detergent and appliance industries.[22] A typical investigation, such as that concerning the household detergent industry, might involve an initial specification that the industry is highly concentrated, has high profits, lacks price competition, and maintains high entry barriers that are caused by advertising

22. In addition, the commission has investigated office copiers, automobile crash parts, title insurance, and automobile rental industries .

and brand proliferation. In such cases, the commission remedy is likely to be diversification, although neither major violations nor specific remedies have been determined.

EXEMPTIONS TO FTC REGULATION ACTIVITIES

The major exemptions to FTC trade regulation activities are those firms or industries that are regulated under local, state, and other federal authorities. For example, public utilities have generally been exempt—if not by statute, then through appropriate defenses at early stages of the complaint, so that few public utility cases have been subject to the commission's authority.

For similar reasons, industries that are directly regulated by federal agencies, like the securities market, are also generally outside the scope of FTC investigations. There are, however, obvious exceptions, many of which are discussed in Chapter 48. For example, the FTC has engaged in explicit enforcement of specific credit protection statutes even though many credit markets are highly regulated by the Federal Reserve Board, the Federal Home Loan Bank Board, and other federal agencies. In addition, some of the activities under the jurisdiction of the Food and Drug Administration are also subject to FTC investigations. For example, provisions regarding the labeling of products are subject to both FTC and FDA regulatory practices.

QUESTIONS AND CASE PROBLEMS

1. In December 1964, Graflex, Inc. quoted a price to International Film Center, Inc. of $324 apiece for the sale of thirty-two sound projectors. International was to use the quoted price in its bid to supply projectors to the local school board. Graflex knew of International's intention to use its quoted price in its bid to the school board. Graflex also quoted a price of $275 to Rosenfeld for the same projectors. The school board accepted Rosenfeld's low bid to sell it projectors. International Film Center, learning of the difference between the two bids, complained to Graflex and was advised by letter that the difference had been inadvertent. In addition, Graflex apologized for the mistake and assured International that it would never happen again. It did not happen thereafter. International Film Center subsequently charged Graflex with price discrimination and brought a lawsuit against it for damages. Will it succeed? [International Film Center, Inc. v. Graflex, Inc., 427 F.2d 334 (3rd Cir. 1970)]

2. Richard Carroll was a commercial fisherman. Several years ago, he brought a personal injury action against his employer, a commercial fishing vessel owner. Because he brought the personal injury action, Carroll was blacklisted by the Protection Maritime Insurance Company and consequently

denied employment. Protection Maritime informed other companies of Carroll's personal injury suit, and Carroll was unable to buy insurance except at very high rates. Since commercial fishing vessels are required to insure their employees, Carroll found it impossible to obtain employment. Carroll believed that Protection Maritime Insurance committed "price discrimination" in violation of federal laws by charging him only the highest rates. Will Carroll's claim stand up in court? [Carroll v. Protection Maritime Ins. Co., Ltd., 512 F. 2d 4 (1st Cir. 1975)]

3. Febco, Inc., manufactured lawn and turf equipment. The Colorado Pump and Supply Company was a wholesale distributor of such equipment in the Colorado area. An important item that Colorado Pump distributed was a control device for sprinkling systems. Although Febco manufactured one of the better sprinkler controls, a number of other manufacturers competed in the field with competitive and satisfactory substitutes for the Febco controllers. In an agreement between Febco and Colorado Pump under which Colorado Pump was given the right to distribute Febco products, Colorado Pump was required to stock a complete line of Febco products. Industry data proved that, in this line of goods, it was important for distributors to protect the "goodwill" of manufacturers by carrying a complete line of a manufacturer's goods or none at all. Does the requirement by Febco that Colorado Pump stock an entire line of Febco products constitute an illegal tying arrangement? [Colorado Pump and Supply Co. v. Febco, Inc., 472 F.2d 637 (10th Cir. 1973)]

4. In 1972, the Federal Maritime Commission approved an agreement under which the world's two largest containership operators—Sea Land Service, Inc. and United States Lines, Inc.—would become subsidiaries of the same corporate parent—R. J. Reynolds Tobacco Company. The commission approved the acquisition agreement on condition that the subsidiaries would remain independent companies in competition with each other. The Federal Maritime Commission, however, does not have the power to immunize companies from the antitrust laws. Knowing this, does the agreement described above violate any of the antitrust statutes discussed in this chapter? [American Mail Line Limited v. Federal Maritime Comm., 503 F.2d 157 (D.C. Cir. 1974)]

5. Fedders Corporation was a manufacturer of air-conditioners and air-conditioning systems. Fedders claimed in its advertising that its air-conditioners were unique because they had "reserved cooling power," a term that Fedders admitted was intended to imply "an unusual ability to produce cold air under extreme conditions of heat and humidity." In fact, however, Fedders air-conditioners had no technical advantage over the equipment manufactured by its competitors. Accordingly, the Federal Trade Commission concluded that Fedders was engaging in misrepresentations in its advertising in violation of Section 5 of the Federal Trade Commission Act. Was the Federal Trade Commission's conclusion correct? [Fedders Corp. v. Federal Trade Comm., 529 F.2d 1398 (2nd Cir. 1976)]

6. Double Eagle Lubricants, Inc., was engaged in the business of marketing motor oil re-refined from previously used oil. It sold the oil in quart cans of the type normally used in the oil trade. The brand name appeared on the front panel, and the side panel contained the required statement disclosing the source of the oil. The cans were intended for display with the front panel facing the prospective customer. The Federal Trade Commission held a hearing to determine whether Double Eagle labeling was deceptive. At the hearing, Double Eagle produced an array of so-called public witnesses, who testified in effect that the labeling did not deceive them. No effort was made by the commission to counter this testimony. Nevertheless, the commission found that

placing the information that the oil was re-refined on the side panel was deceptive. Such information should have been included on the front panel. Was the FTC's finding correct? Would the finding made without the support of testimony of public witnesses withstand the scrutiny of a reviewing court? [Double Eagle Lubricants, Inc. v. Federal Trade Comm., 360 F.2d 268 (10th Cir. 1965)]

7. Tampa Electric is a public utility that serves a large area on the west coast of Florida. It entered into a contract with Nashville Coal Company under which it agreed to purchase all of the coal it would require over a twenty-year period for its station in Tampa. In addition, the agreement stated that Tampa Electric would purchase any additional coal it would require for other stations it might build during the term of the contract. Nashville Coal Company competed with approximately seven hundred producers in the "peninsular Florida" area. It was estimated that Tampa Electric would require 2.25 million tons of coal a year from Nashville Coal Company, an amount that would constitute 0.77 percent of the coal sold in peninsular Florida. Nashville Coal Company subsequently notified Tampa Electric that it could not perform as agreed since the contract was in violation of Section 3 of the Clayton Act. Is the contract enforceable? [Tampa Electric v. Nashville Coal Co., 365 U.S. 320, 81 S.Ct. 623 (1961)]

8. The Phillipsburg Bank and the Second National Bank both conducted business as full-service banks in the town of Phillipsburg. Five other full-service banks operated in the Lehigh Valley area, which encompasses Phillipsburg and half a dozen other cities. Phillipsburg Bank and the Second National Bank merged, leaving only two banks in Phillipsburg. In determining whether a violation of Section 7 of the Clayton Act had occurred, the key issue is whether the "relevant geographic market" was the town of Phillipsburg or the entire Lehigh Valley. If it can be determined that the merger lessened competition in the "relevant geographic market" then the merger will be held to violate Section 7. What is the "relevant geographic market" in this case? (Consider where people will most likely go to do their banking after the merger.) [United States v. Phillipsburg Nat. Bank, 399 U.S. 350, 90 S.Ct. 2035 (1970)]

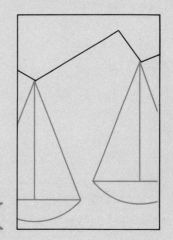

UNIT IX

Protection of Property and Other Interests

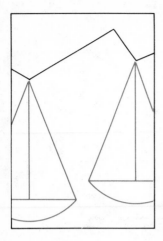

52

Nature and Ownership
of Real Property

Real property is land and the buildings and plants, trees, and crops it contains. Real property, also called real estate or realty, is immovable, whereas personal property is movable.

From earliest times, property has provided a means for survival. Primitive peoples lived off the fruits of the land, eating the vegetation and wildlife. Later, as the wildlife was domesticated and the vegetation cultivated, property provided pasturage and farmland. In the twelfth and thirteenth centuries, land was a symbol of the power of feudal lords. The more land they held, the more powerful they were. After the age of feudalism passed, property continued to be an indicator of family wealth and social position.

NATURE OF REAL PROPERTY

Real property usually means land, but there are other aspects of it that must be considered, such as subsurface and air rights, plant life and vegetation, and fixtures.

Land

Land includes the soil on the surface of the earth and natural or artificial structures that are attached to it. Land also includes all the waters contained on or under the surface and all the air space above it. The

848

exterior boundaries of land extend straight down to the center of the earth and straight up to the farthest reaches of the atmosphere (subject to certain qualifications).

Subsurface and Air Rights

The owner of real property has relatively exclusive rights to the air space above the land as well as the soil and minerals underneath it. Until fifty years ago, the right to use air space was not too significant, but today, commercial airlines and high rise office buildings and apartments use the air space regularly. Early cases involving air rights dealt with matters such as the right to run a telephone wire across a person's property when the wire did not touch any of the property[1] and whether a bullet shot over the person's land constituted trespass.[2] Today, cases involving air rights present questions such as the right of commercial and private planes to fly over property or the right of individuals to seed clouds and produce artificial rain. Flights over private land do not normally violate the property owners' rights unless they are low and frequent, causing a direct interference with the enjoyment and use of the land.[3] Likewise, if cloud seeding activities interfere with the enjoyment and use of the land, the property owner can sue to stop them. The owner of land is entitled to use the property without others causing unreasonable noise, pollution, or vibrations.

The property owner also owns all the subsurface of the land. The boundaries of the land extend straight down to the center of the earth. Any oil, minerals, and treasure found under the surface of the land belong to the landowner. Any intrusion into the subsurface of the land violates the rights of its owner. For example, suppose Homestake Mining Company has a mine directly adjoining Redland Company's land. Homestake digs a shaft several hundred feet deep and hits a rich vein of ore. Homestake begins mining operations and follows the vein up and across into Redland's property. Although Homestake does not intend to mine any of Redland's ore, it is still liable to Redland for trespass. Redland can recover damages for the ore taken from below the surface of its land.

Any limitations on either air rights or subsurface rights have to be indicated on the deed transferring title at the time of purchase. Where no such encumbrances are noted, a purchaser can expect unfettered right to possession of the property. If any preexisting covenant unknown to the purchaser interferes with these rights, the purchaser can sue for breach of warranty of title. However, most state statutes limit the time period in which the purchaser can sue. An alternative lawsuit is for breach of the covenant of quiet enjoyment. There is a limit on the time for bringing such a suit, but it does not begin to run until after the discovery of the breach.

Plant Life and Vegetation

Plant life, both natural and cultivated, is also considered to be real property. When a parcel of land is sold and the land has growing crops on it, the sale includes the crops, unless otherwise specified in the sales contract. When crops are sold by themselves, they are considered to be personal property or goods. Consequently, the sale of crops (whether they are severed by the buyer or the seller) is a sale of goods, and it is governed by the Uniform Commercial Code rather than by real property law. [UCC Sec. 2-107]

Fixtures

Certain personal property can become so closely associated with the real property to which it is attached that the law views it as real property. Such property is known as a **fixture**—a thing

1. Butler v. Frontier Telephone Co., 186 N.Y. 486, 79 N.E. 716 (1906). Stringing a wire across someone's property violates the air rights of that person. Leaning walls, buildings, projecting eave spouts and roofs also violate the air rights of the property owner.

2. Herrin v. Sutherland, 74 Mont. 587, 241 P. 328 (1925). Shooting over a person's land constitutes trespass.

3. United States v. Causby, 328 U.S. 256, 66 S.Ct. 1062 (1946).

affixed to realty. A thing is *affixed* to realty when it is attached to it by roots, embedded in it, or permanently attached by means of cement, plaster, bolts, nails, or screws. The fixture can be physically attached to real property, be attached to another fixture, or even be without any actual physical attachment to the land, as long as the owner *intends* the property to be a fixture.

Fixtures are included in the sale of land if the sales contract does not provide otherwise. The sale of a house includes the land and the house and garage on it as well as the cabinets, plumbing, and windows. Since these are permanently affixed to the property, they are considered a part of it. However, unless otherwise agreed, the curtains and throw rugs are not included. Items such as drapes and window-unit air-conditioners are difficult to classify. Thus, a contract for the sale of a house or commercial realty should indicate which items of this sort are included in the sale.

INTENTION   In order to determine whether or not a certain item is a fixture, the *intention* of the party who placed the fixture must be examined. If the person intended the item to be a fixture, then it will be a fixture. To illustrate: Suppose the owner of a house buys a workbench for the garage. The workbench is not bolted to the wall, but it cannot easily be removed. If the owner intended the workbench to become a fixture—part of the garage—then it is a fixture. If the owner plans to remove it after a couple of months, then it is not a fixture. The objective intention of the owner will control. For instance, certain items can only be attached to property permanently; such items are fixtures. The owner must have intended them to be since they had to be permanently attached to the property. A tile floor, cabinets, and carpeting are good examples of this type of fixture. Objectively, any persons seeing the owner install such items would assume that the owner intended them to become part of the property. When a piece of property is custom-made for installation on real property, such as storm windows, the property is usually classified as a

fixture. Again, any objective observer would assume that the owner intended the piece of property to become part of the real property.

TRADE FIXTURES   A **trade fixture** is any article placed in or attached to a rented building by the tenant in order to pursue the trade or business for which the tenant occupies the premises. Trade fixtures are generally removable without material alteration to the premises. Indeed, they are not fixtures at all, since the person who installs them intends to remove them eventually. In many cases, the item would be a fixture if the owner had installed it but not if the lessee installed it. For example, suppose Helen Getty rents a small structure located on a main highway and installs gas pumps and a storage tank. The pumps and tanks are trade fixtures, and Getty can remove them when the lease ends. Naturally, if any damages occur to the property when Getty removes the trade fixtures, she must pay the landlord for the damage.

OWNERSHIP INTEREST IN REAL PROPERTY—ESTATES IN LAND

Ownership of property is an abstract concept that cannot exist independent of the legal system. No one can actually possess or *hold* a piece of land, the air above, the earth below, and all the water contained on it. The legal system therefore recognizes certain rights and duties that constitute the ownership interest in real property.

Freehold Estates

Rights of ownership in real property, called **estates,** are classified according to their nature, quantity, and extent. Two major categories of estates are freehold estates, which are held indefinitely and less than freehold estates, which are held for a predetermined time. There are two kinds of freehold estates—estates in fee, and life estates.

THE FEE SIMPLE ABSOLUTE   The **fee simple absolute,** or fee simple, is the largest estate known to the law. It is limited absolutely to a person and his or her heirs and is assigned forever without limitation or condition. In a fee simple, the owner has the greatest aggregation of rights, privileges, and powers possible. The rights that accompany a fee simple include the right to use the land for whatever purpose the owner sees fit, subject to laws that prevent the owner from unreasonably interfering with another person's land. A fee simple is potentially infinite in duration and can be disposed of by will or by deed (by selling or giving it away). When the owner of a fee simple dies without a will, the fee simple passes to the owner's legal heirs. The owner of a fee simple absolute also has the rights of *exclusive* possession and waste. *Waste* means that the owner can use the land without replenishing what is used. If Albert Samuelson has fee simple absolute ownership of fifteen acres in the mountains, he can mine any ore on that land without replacing it. The term *waste* refers to injury done to the land by one rightfully in possession of the land.

At early common law, a fee simple absolute could be conveyed only by stating that the conveyance was "to A and his heirs." The words "and his heirs" denoted the fee simple as infinite in duration and distinguished it from other estates such as the *fee simple defeasible* (which is defined below). In the United States today, these so-called words of limitation have been eliminated and a conveyance "to A" as well as "to A and his heirs" will convey a fee simple.

THE FEE SIMPLE DEFEASIBLE   A **fee simple defeasible**[4] encompasses a number of estates that *almost* constitute absolute ownership.[5] Essentially, a fee simple defeasible is a fee simple that can end if a specified condition or event occurs. For example, a conveyance "to A and his heirs as long as the land is used for charitable purposes" creates a fee simple defeasible. In this type of conveyance the original owner retains a *partial* ownership interest. As long as the condition does not occur, A has full ownership rights, but if the specified condition does occur (for example, if the land ceases to be used for charitable purposes), then the land reverts, or returns, to the original owner.[6] The interest that the original owner retains is called a *future interest* since, if it arises, it will arise in the future.[7]

Consider another example. Simon deeds some land to XYZ Church "for as long as this land is used for church purposes and no longer." For two years, the land is used by the church for a playground for the children going to Sunday School. The church then sells the land to Smith, who intends to build an apartment building on it. As soon as Simon learns of the sale to Smith, he begins a court action to have himself declared the owner of the land.[8] Since Simon deeded a fee simple determinable to XYZ Church, he will succeed in his court action. The church has absolute ownership of the land as long as it is used for church purposes. XYZ Church can even sell the land or otherwise dispose of it to those who will also use it for church purposes. However, as soon as the land stops being used for the specified purpose, the fee simple determinable terminates and ownership reverts to Simon.

THE LIFE ESTATE   A **life estate** is an estate that lasts for the life of some specified in-

---

4. The word *defeasible* refers to an owner's ability to lose ownership of property, whether the loss is voluntary or involuntary.

5. The term *fee simple defeasible* encompasses the fee simple determinable, the fee simple subject to special limitation, the fee simple subject to condition subsequent, and the fee simple subject to an executory interest.

6. If the original owner is not living at the time, the land passes to his or her heirs. In other words, once the condition occurs, A is divested of rights regardless of whether the original owner to (or through) whom the land reverts is alive.

7. In the specific example given in the text, the future interest that the owner holds is known as a *possibility of reverter.* In the conveyance "to A, but if the premises are ever used for the sale of alcoholic beverages then to B," the original owner has conveyed the entire interest. The owner has conveyed a fee simple defeasible to A and all future interest to B.

8. Note that the instant the condition is broken, legal ownership automatically vests in Simon.

dividual. A conveyance "to A for his life" creates a life estate.[9] Estates for life can be created by an act of law or by an act of the parties. In a life estate, the life tenant has fewer rights of ownership than the holder of a fee simple defeasible. The life tenant has the right to use the land provided no waste (injury to the land) is committed. In other words, the life tenant cannot injure the land in a manner that would adversely affect the owner of the future interest in it. The life tenant can use the land to harvest crops or, if mines and oil wells are already on the land, can extract minerals and oil from it. But the life tenant cannot exploit the land by creating new wells or mines.

Consider some examples. Michaelson deeds land to Hitchcock for life. Oil is found under that land. Agents of Mobil Oil Company negotiate an oil and gas lease with Hitchcock, but Mobil never contacts Michaelson. It merely starts drilling an oil well. When Michaelson learns of this, he demands that Mobil stop drilling or negotiate a lease with him. Michaelson can enforce his demand because a life tenant alone cannot make a binding oil and gas lease upon the property if no drilling was taking place at the time the life estate was created. By the same token, Hitchcock cannot sell any of the timber that is on the land without Michaelson's approval, because the removal of standing timber will reduce the value of the land. On the other hand, if Hitchcock wants to use part of the land for grazing sheep, Michaelson will certainly have to allow him to do so, especially if the land on which the sheep will graze is poor land of no value for anything else.

The life tenant has the right to mortgage the life estate and create liens, easements, and leases; but none can extend beyond the life of the tenant. In addition, the owner of a life estate has exclusive right of possession during his or her life. Exclusive possession, however, is subject to the rights of the future interest holder to come onto the land and protect the future interest.

9. A less common type of life estate is created by the conveyance "to A for the life of B." This is known as an estate *pur autre vie*, or an estate for the life of another.

Along with these rights, the life tenant also has some *duties*—to keep the property in repair and to pay property taxes. In short, the owner of the life estate has the same rights as a fee simple owner except that the future interest of the land must be kept intact for the person who eventually will receive possession.

Nonfreehold Estates

The **less than freehold estates** are generally considered to be personal rather than real property. They are covered in this chapter for the sake of convenience because they relate to ownership of an interest in land. These estates include (1) the tenancy for years, (2) the tenancy from period to period, (3) the tenancy at will, and (4) the tenancy by sufferance. All involve the transfer of the right to possession for *a specified period of time*. The owner or lessor (landlord) conveys the property to the lessee (tenant) for a certain period of time. In every nonfreehold estate, the tenant has a *qualified* right to exclusive possession (qualified by the right of the landlord to enter upon the premises to assure that no waste is being committed). The tenant can use the land, for example, by harvesting crops, but cannot injure the land by such activities as cutting down timber for sale or extracting oil.

TENANCY FOR YEARS   A **tenancy for years** is created by express contract (which can sometimes be oral) by leasing the property for a specified period of time. For example, signing a lease to rent an apartment creates a tenancy for years. At the end of the period specified in the lease, the lease ends (without notice) and possession of the land returns to the lessor. If the tenant dies during the period of the lease, the lease passes to the tenant's heirs as personal property. Often, leases include renewal or extension provisions.

TENANCY FROM PERIOD TO PERIOD   A **tenancy from period to period** is created by a lease that does not specify how long it is to last but does specify that rent is to be paid at certain intervals. For example, a tenancy from period to period is created by a lease that states, "Rent is due on the tenth day of every month." This is a tenancy from month to month. This type of tenancy can also be from week to week or from year to year. A tenancy from period to period sometimes arises when a landlord allows a tenant under a tenancy for years to hold over and continue paying monthly or weekly rent. At common law, in order to terminate a tenancy from period to period, the landlord or tenant must give one period's notice to the other party. If the tenancy is month to month, one month's notice must be given. If the tenancy is week to week, one week's notice must be given. State statutes often define the required notice of termination in a tenancy from period to period.

Therefore, the particular statute in question should be referred to in order to determine the proper time for notice of termination.

As long as a tenancy exists, a landlord can collect rent in full regardless of whether the premises are actually occupied by the tenant. Thus, when a tenant wrongfully abandons the premises and refuses to pay rent, the landlord can either permit the premises to remain vacant or refuse to recognize the attempted surrender by the tenant and bring a lawsuit to collect the rent as it comes due. A tenant who wrongfully abandons the premises and refuses to pay rent cannot try to shift the burden onto the landlord to find someone to take the tenant's place. The issue of termination of tenancy is examined in the following case.

BACKGROUND AND FACTS *The plaintiff owned and operated an apartment house, and the defendant wished to rent an apartment in the plaintiff's building. The defendant wanted apartment 51; it was occupied at the time the defendant arrived but was soon to become vacant. In the meantime, it was agreed orally that the prospective tenant could occupy apartment 2 at a rental of $50 per month. On the day apartment 51 became available, the defendant vacated apartment 2 without notice and left the building for good. The defendant left the key on the plaintiff's office desk without explanation. The plaintiff's agent, Richards, used the key left by the defendant to clean apartment 2 and ready it for a new tenant.*

Subsequently, the plaintiff sought to recover rent from the day the defendant left until the apartment was finally rented, eight months later. Meanwhile, the defendant died, and her executor, Libby, defended the action. The trial court found for the plaintiff.

ENOCH C. RICHARDS CO. v. LIBBY

Supreme Judicial Court of Maine, 1940.
136 Me. 376, 10 A.2d 609.

THAXTER, Justice.
* * *

So long * * * as a tenancy exists the landlord may collect rent in full regardless of actual occupancy of the premises by the tenant. Such being the case it must follow that, where there is a wrongful abandonment of premises by a tenant and a refusal to pay rent, the landlord may at his election permit them to remain vacant, refuse to recognize the attempted surrender by the tenant, and bring suit to collect the rent as it comes due. The tenant can not by such action cast a burden on the landlord to find someone to take his place. Such is the overwhelming weight of authority.

[There can be wrongful abandonment of the premises only if the tenancy has not been terminated. In this case, however, the Supreme Judicial Court of Maine found sufficient indications that the relationship of landlord-tenant had been terminated because the plaintiff's agent, Richards, knew that the day the defendant left she intended to give up apartment 2. Moreover, every act of the landlord was inconsistent with the recognition that the tenancy of the defendant was continuing.]

The acts of the landlord can not, therefore, be explained on the theory that there was any obligation on its part to mitigate damages, and there is no evidence to indicate that the landlord claimed to be acting for the tenant. The question, therefore, is whether the acts of the parties constituted a termination of the tenancy by operation of law.

There is no doubt that the relationship of landlord and tenant may be terminated by the acts of the parties.

* * *

In the case before us it is apparent from the testimony of both Mrs. Stewart [the defendant] who acted as Mrs. Hodsdon's agent, and of Mrs. Richards, the manager and agent of the plaintiff, that Mrs. Richards knew that Mrs. Hodsdon, when she left, intended to give up apartment #2. There were complaints between the parties. Mrs. Richards said that apartment 51 was ready, Mrs. Stewart replied that they weren't going to take it. Mrs. Richards then found fault because she had not been given a month's notice; but at the same time gave no intimation that she intended to hold Mrs. Hodsdon as a tenant. The key was left on the office desk. Mrs. Richards took the key, entered the apartment, cleaned it, made it ready for a new tenant and showed it to prospective tenants from time to time . Her conduct was unequivocal; she made no attempt to qualify it. Every act done is inconsistent with the present claim that the tenancy of Mrs. Hodsdon continued.

Most significant is the response of Mrs. Richards to a question by the court as to whether she was holding an apartment for Mrs. Hodsdon if she decided to come back.

"The Court: Which apartment was it you said you would hold for her? A. I was holding, really, either one; because in the spring of the year that is a hard time to let apartments anyway. I couldn't hold one just separately for her and not rent it if I had a chance."

This language certainly shows that Mrs. Richards claimed the right after Mrs. Hodsdon left to put a new tenant in apartment #2 whenever she had the chance to do so. It is utterly inconsistent with the present contention of the plaintiff that Mrs. Hodsdon remained a tenant of that apartment during the succeeding months with the right to be given thirty days' notice before her tenancy could be terminated.

JUDGMENT AND REMEDY   *The Supreme Judicial Court of Maine reversed the trial court's finding of a tenancy. The court recognized that the plaintiff and the defendant had terminated their landlord-tenant relationship the day the defendant moved out. Hence, the defendant was not required to pay rent for the intervening eight months during which the plaintiff sought a new tenant.*

TENANCY AT WILL Suppose L, the landlord, rents an apartment to T "for as long as L wishes." In such a case, T receives a leasehold estate known as a **tenancy at will.** At common law, either party can terminate the tenancy without notice. This type of estate usually arises when a tenant who has been under a tenancy for years retains possession after the termination date of that tenancy with the landlord's consent. (This is called holding over.) Before the tenancy has been converted into a tenancy from period to period (by the periodic payment of rent), it is a tenancy at will terminable by either party without notice. The death of either party or the voluntary commission of waste by the tenant will terminate a tenancy at will.

TENANCY BY SUFFERANCE A **tenancy by sufferance** is not a tenancy at all. It is the mere possession of land without right. A tenancy by sufferance is not an estate, since it is created by a tenant *wrongfully* holding over. Whenever a life estate, tenancy for years, tenancy from period to period, or tenancy at will ends, and the tenant continues to retain possession of the premises without the owner's permission, a tenancy by sufferance is created. A tenancy by sufferance can be converted into a leasehold if a landlord accepts rent from the tenant. If the landlord does not accept rent and ultimately evicts the tenant, the tenant is liable to the landlord as if he or she were a trespasser.

RELATIONSHIP OF LANDLORD AND TENANT

Much real property is used by those who do not own it. A **lease** is a contract by which the owner—the landlord—grants the tenant an exclusive right to use and possess the land for an ascertainable period of time. The basic characteristic of this particular estate is that it continues for the ascertainable term and carries with it the obligation by the tenant to pay rent to the landlord. Usually, the creation of the leasehold estate by contract for terms longer than a year (or three years in some jurisdictions) must be in writing.

Duties and Warranties of the Landlord

When a landlord leases premises to a tenant, a *warranty of possession* and a *covenant of quiet enjoyment* are implied by law. Under the warranty of possession, the landlord warrants that the premises have been leased only to one tenant, but he does not have an obligation to actually deliver possession to the tenant. It is the new tenant's responsibility to evict a former tenant who wrongfully holds over.

Under the covenant of quiet enjoyment, a landlord essentially warrants that he or she will not *evict* the tenant. Generally, questions regarding breach of a covenant of quiet enjoyment arise not when a landlord actually evicts a tenant, but rather when the landlord's action (or inaction) affects the tenant's use and enjoyment of the premises in a way that constitutes a *constructive eviction*. For example, suppose Smith, a quiet minister, rents half of a duplex from Lawson. Lawson rents the other half of the duplex to three members of a rock band. The band rehearses in the duplex every night from about 11:00 in the evening to 5:00 in the morning. Smith complains to Lawson that strange people are constantly entering and leaving the premises and that the noise is unbearable. If Lawson fails to take any action, he has breached his covenant of quiet enjoyment to Smith and has *constructively evicted* him from the premises. Smith can probably rescind the rental agreement.

Under the common law, a landlord was under no duty to repair the premises rented by a tenant or to warrant that the premises were habitable or suitable for the particular purpose for which they were rented. An exception to this common law rule existed for furnished premises that were rented for short periods of time. Under most state statutes today, and under judicial decisions, a landlord of residential premises impliedly warrants that the premises are habitable and cannot disclaim this warranty unless the landlord and the tenant are of equal bargaining power. Additionally, a landlord is under an affirmative duty to repair and maintain the structure and all its *common areas* and fixtures. The landlord will be held liable for injuries resulting from negligent failure to maintain the rented premises.

Duties Owed by the Tenant

TENANT'S OBLIGATION TO PAY The tenant has an implied obligation to pay reasonable rent to the landlord. Most lease contracts contain an express promise, known as a covenant, that indicates that the tenant is to pay a specific amount at specified times. Generally, if the express promise is not in the lease agreement, then the tenant is obliged only to pay rent that is reasonable and only at the end of the term.

TERMINATING THE TENANT'S OBLIGATION TO PAY RENT

Whenever a tenant assigns his or her rights under a lease, the implied obligation to pay reasonable rent goes to the assignee. When there is an express agreement (a contract) for the tenant to pay rent of a specified sum at specified intervals, the tenant remains liable under this contract, even if he or she has assigned the leasehold estate to another. Note, however, that even though the assignee of the lease is bound to pay rent, the original tenant is not released from the contractual obligation to pay rent. Thus, whenever the assignee fails to pay, the landlord can look to the original tenant for compensation.

Many leases require that the right of assignment have the landlord's written consent, and an assignment that lacks consent can be avoided by the landlord. A landlord who knowingly accepts rent from the assignee, however, will be held to have waived the requirement. Once waived, it cannot later be revised.

Subleasing Subleasing involves a partial transfer of the original tenant's rights to the lease. An assignment can read that the original tenant assigns all rights, title, and interest in the lease to another person for a stated sum of money. If, however, the assignment indicates that the original tenant can reenter the premises whenever the assignee fails to pay the rent, most courts will then label such an agreement a sublease. This is because the original tenant has reserved the right of reentry and has, therefore, transferred less than the whole interest in the lease. By subleasing, the original tenant is not relieved of any obligations to the landlord under the lease. The lease may prohibit subleasing without the landlord's consent.

DESTRUCTION OF THE PREMISES AND THE OBLIGATION TO PAY RENT

Under common law, destruction by fire or flood of a whole building leased by a tenant did not relieve the tenant of the obligation to pay rent or permit the termination of the lease. The reasoning behind the common law rule was that the tenant's obligation to pay rent was an exchange for the *estate* in the land. At common law, the concept of estate was divorced from any economic benefits that went with it. Presumably, destruction of the leased building destroyed only part of the benefit. The tenant retained a nonfreehold interest in the land on which the building was constructed.

Today, state statutes have altered the common law rule. In most states, tenants who occupy only a portion of the building will not be covered under the rule. Thus, if the building burns down, apartment dwellers in most states are not continuously liable to the landlord for the payment of rent. Many leases contain clauses covering destruction of the building. For example, a clause can indicate that the landlord will repair and restore the building, and the tenant's obligation to pay rent will be suspended until the premises are restored, but only if the premises are wholly unsuitable for habitation.

CONCURRENT OWNERSHIP

Property owned by one person is said to be held severally. When two or more persons own property, it is said to be held concurrently. There are several types of **concurrent estates,** including tenancy in common, joint tenancy, and tenancy by entirety.

Tenancy in Common

The most common type of concurrent estate is a **tenancy in common.** Suppose Y conveys land "to A and B and C." This conveyance creates a tenancy in common among A, B, and C, whereby each takes a one-third interest. In a tenancy in common, each tenant has the right to convey his or her interest in the property. When one of the tenants dies, that tenant's interest passes to his or her heirs (or, by will, to someone else). Essentially, tenants in a tenancy in common each own an undivided fractional share of the property.

Joint Tenancy

In a **joint tenancy,** each tenant owns an undivided whole interest in the property. Thus, when one tenant dies, the others' interests "swallow up" the deceased's share and no property passes to the heirs of the deceased (even by will). Instead, all property of the deceased passes to the other joint tenants. This characteristic, which differs from tenancy in common, is known as *survivorship.*

A joint tenancy is transformed into a tenancy in common when one of the joint tenants transfers his or her interest to another party. A joint tenancy can also be transferred by *partition*; that is, the tenants can physically divide the property in equal parts. Since a joint tenant's interest is capable of being conveyed without the consent of the other joint tenants, it can be levied against by the tenant's creditors. This is also true of the tenancy in common.

Tenancy by the Entirety

A final type of concurrent estate is the **tenancy by the entirety**—a joint tenancy between a husband and wife. At common law, a tenancy by the entirety could be created in a husband and wife only where the conveyance was to, say, "Harriet and Daniel Campbell, husband and wife, and their heirs and assigns." A tenancy by the entirety differs from a joint tenancy and tenancy in common in that neither spouse can convey his or her interest without the express consent of the other. Since neither can voluntarily convey his or her interest, the creditors of one spouse cannot levy on the property. (However, if the spouses are jointly liable to the creditors, then the creditors can usually levy on the tenancy.) Divorce terminates a tenancy by the entirety and, in most states,

creates a tenancy in common. The tenancy by the entirety is not recognized in many states.[10]

Condominiums ("Real Estate in the Sky")

A condominium involves a form of ownership that combines elements of both individual and concurrent ownership. Prior to the 1960s, the condominium ownership form was virtually unknown in Anglo-American law. The National Housing Act of 1961 helped create incentives for this form of ownership by authorizing FHA mortgage insurance on single-family units in multi-family structures. Soon after this, state legislation paved the way for rapid development of condominiums. In a condominium, each unit is individually owned. The units vary from the size of a one or two bedroom apartment to the size of a very large home. (Condominiums are sometimes offices in commercial buildings.) Each owner has an undivided interest (tenancy in common) in the "common areas" of the condominium, including stairways, halls, elevators, recreational facilities, courtyards, and parking lots. Each owner pays an annual fee for the upkeep of these areas.

Several advantages accompany condominium ownership. First, it can provide tax deductions for interest on the mortgage and taxes that previously were available only to *owners* of real estate, not to tenants. Second, condominiums can be constructed in areas that previously were available only for apartment buildings. This gives the condominium owner greater flexibility in choosing where to live, since in some locations only apartment buildings are economically feasible. Third, condominiums generally provide greater security, since a large number of units are located on one parcel of land. Fourth, the normal upkeep of a house is eliminated, and the owners need pay only a small annual fee for upkeep of the common areas.

_____

10. See Dorf v. Tuscarora Pipeline Co., 48 N.J.Super. 26, 136 A.2d 778 (1957) and Lindenfelser v. Lindenfelser 396 Pa. 530, 153 A.2d 901 (1959). Some of the states that recognize tenancy by the entirety require express language to create it, thereby modifying the common law rule.

EXHIBIT 52-1
A TYPICAL DEED

Warranty Deed

This Indenture, *Made the*   *day of*   *, A.D. 19* *,*
BETWEEN   *,*

of the County of   *, and State of*   *, of the first part, and*

whose permanent address is   *, of the County of*
      , and State of   *, of the second part,*

Witnesseth, *That, the said part*   *of the first part, for and in consideration of the sum of*
                                               Dollars,
lawful money of the United States of America, to   *in hand paid by the said part*
of the second part, at or before the ensealing and delivery of these presents, the receipt whereof is
hereby acknowledged,   *granted, bargained, sold, aliened, remised, released, conveyed*
and confirmed, and by these presents do   *grant, bargain, sell alien, remise, release, convey*
and confirm unto the said part   *of the second part, and*   *heirs and assigns*
forever, all the following piece *, parcel* *or tract* *of land, situate, lying and being in the*
County of   *, State of*   *, and more*
particularly described as follows:

Together *with all and singular the tenements, hereditaments and appurtenances thereunto*
belonging or in anywise appertaining, and the reversion and reversions, remainder and remainders,
rents, issues and profits thereof, and also all the estate, right, title, interest, dower and right of
dower, separate estate, property, possession, claim and demand whatsoever, as well as in equity,
of the said part   *of the first part, of, in and to the same, and every part and parcel*
thereof, with the appurtenances.

To Have and To Hold   *the above granted, bargained and described premises, with the*
appurtenances, unto the said part   *of the second part,*   *heirs and*
assigns, to   *own proper use, benefit and behoof forever.*
     And the said part   *of the first part, for*   *and for*   *heirs, executors*
and administrators, do   *covenant, promise and agree to and with the said part*   *of*
the second part,   *heirs and assigns, that the said part*   *of the first part, at the*
time of the ensealing and delivery of these presents,   *lawfully seized of and in all*
and singular the above granted, bargained and described premises, with the appurtenances, and
     good right, full power and lawful authority to grant, bargain, sell and convey
the same in manner and form aforesaid. And the said part   *of the second part,*
heirs and assigns, shall and may at all times hereafter peaceably and quietly have, hold, use,
occupy, possess and enjoy the above granted premises and every part and parcel thereof, with
the appurtenances, without any let, suit, trouble, molestation, eviction or disturbance of the said
part   *of the first part,*   *heirs or assigns, or of any other person or persons lawfully*
claiming or to claim the same, by, through and under the grantor   *herein.*

Fifth, a condominium can amass large sums of money to spend on the common areas. There are also many disadvantages to condominiums; one is that there is no guarantee against escalation of upkeep fees.

TRANSFER OF OWNERSHIP

There are a number of ways ownership of real property can pass from one person to another.

They include deed, will, eminent domain, adverse possession, and inheritance. Conveyance by deed includes transfer by sale and by gift.

Conveyance by Deed

Possession and title to land are passed from person to person by means of a **deed**—the instrument of conveyance of real property. Deeds

And the said part   of the first part, for,   and for   heirs, warrants the above described and hereby granted and released premises, and every part and parcel thereof, with the appurtenances, unto the said part   of the second part, heirs and assigns, against the said part   of the first part,   heirs, and against all and every person or persons whomsoever lawfully claiming or to claim the same, by, through and under the grantor   herein, shall and will warrant and by these presents forever defend.

In Witness Whereof, The said part   of the first part   hereunto set hand   and seal   the day and year first above written.

Signed, sealed and delivered in presence of us:

_____   _____ (Seal)

_____   _____ (Seal)

State of Florida,

County of _____ } ss.

On this day personally appeared before me,
                              to me well known and known to me to be the individual   described in and who executed the foregoing deed of conveyance, and acknowledged that   executed the same for the purpose therein expressed, whereupon it is prayed that the same may be recorded.

In Witness Whereof, I have hereunto affixed my hand and official seal, this day of   , A.D. 19

(Seal)   _____

                                        NOTARY PUBLIC

My commission expires:_____

State of Florida,

County of _____ } ss.

I,   , a
in and for said County and State, do certify that on the   day of   , A.D. 19   , personally appeared before me,
          and
his wife, to me well known, and known to me to be the individual   described in and who executed the foregoing deed, and severally acknowledged that   executed the same for the purposes therein mentioned, and the said
                    , upon a separate and private examination, made separate and apart from her husband, then and there acknowledged before me that she executed the said deed for the purpose of conveying and relinquishing her dower and right of dower, homestead and separate estate in and to the land therein described, and also in token of having consented to the alienation of said described lands, and that she did the same freely and voluntarily, and without any constraint, apprehension, fear or compulsion of or from her said husband.

Given under my hand and official seal at   in said County and State, on this   day of   , A.D. 19   .

My commission expires: _____   _____

                                        NOTARY PUBLIC

are writings signed by the owner of property by which title to it is transferred to another. They must meet certain requirements. Exhibit 52-1 shows a deed.

REQUIREMENTS OF A VALID DEED Unlike contracts, a deed does not have to be supported by legally sufficient consideration. Gifts of real property are common, and they require deeds even though there is no consideration for the gift. The necessary requirements for a valid deed are: (1) the names of the buyer (grantee) and seller (grantor), (2) words evidencing an intent to convey (for example, "I hereby bargain, sell, grant, or give"), (3) a legally sufficient description of the land, (4) the grantor's (and usually the spouse's) signature, and (5) delivery of the deed.

Types of Deeds

GENERAL WARRANTY DEED   General warranty deeds warrant the greatest number of things. In most states, special language is required to make a general warranty deed. If the deed states that the seller is providing the "usual covenants," most courts will imply all of the following covenants (warranties) of title:

1. *A covenant of seisin and a covenant of the right to convey* warrant that the seller has title and the power to convey the estate that the deed describes. For example, if A, the owner of a life estate in Whiteacre, attempts to convey a fee simple to B, A's covenant of seisin will be breached. If B is damaged by A's breach, then B is entitled to recover from A.

2. *A covenant against encumbrances* guarantees that the property being sold or conveyed is not subject to any outstanding rights or interests that will diminish the value of the land, except as stated. Examples of common encumbrances include mortgages, liens, profits, easements, and private deed restrictions on the use of land. Unless the deed expressly states that the conveyance is subject to a particular encumbrance, a covenant against encumbrances will be breached if the buyer discovers an undisclosed encumbrance. Again, as in the case of a covenant of seisin, the buyer is entitled to recover for any damage caused by the breach of this covenant.

3. *A covenant for quiet enjoyment* guarantees that the grantee or buyer will not be disturbed in his or her possession of the land by the grantor or any third persons. For example, suppose Nancy Thomas sells her two-acre lot and office building by general warranty deed. Subsequently, a third person shows better title than Nancy had and proceeds to evict the buyer. Here the covenant for quiet enjoyment has been breached, and the buyer can recover the purchase price of the land plus any other damages incurred in being evicted.

BROWN v. LOBER

Court of Appeals of Illinois, 1978.

63 Ill.App.3d 727, 20 Ill.Dec. 286, 379 N.E.2d 1354.

BACKGROUND AND FACTS *The plaintiff, Brown, purchased real property in 1957 and received a warranty deed. The deed contained no list of encumbrances. In 1974, the plaintiff granted a call option to Consolidated Coal Company, permitting the company rights to subsurface coal. Consolidated paid the plaintiff $6,000 for these rights. In 1976, it was discovered that the plaintiff did not own the subsurface mineral rights free and clear as indicated by the warranty deed of 1957. Instead, the plaintiff owned only one-third of the rights. The rights to the remaining two-thirds had been deeded away in 1947 by a prior grantor.*

The plaintiff had already been paid $2,000 by the coal company for its one-third interest. The coal company would not pay the remaining $4,000. The plaintiff then filed this lawsuit, seeking the $4,000 in damages against the prior grantor, Lober, the defendant.

Lober asserted that the ten-year statute of limitations for covenant of seisin barred the lawsuit. Brown asserted that a right of action was permitted for breach of the covenant of quiet enjoyment. Brown argued that the period of limitations is not measured until after the discovery of the encumbrance.

The trial court found for Lober, deciding that the ten-year statute of limitations had run from the time the deed was issued in 1957. Brown appealed.

WINELAND, Justice.
* * *

In the instant case it is agreed by the parties that the plaintiffs had no knowledge of the previous grant of the sub-surface minerals until 1976. But if they did have it would have been of no moment because they could not have brought suit for breach of covenant of quiet enjoyment until they were actually or constructively evicted. It was at this time that the plaintiffs were advised by the coal company of the outstanding incumbrance in the underlying minerals. It was at this time that plaintiffs yielded as they had a right to do, to the paramount title to the two-thirds interest in the coal. The coal purchaser refused to pay them for the coal rights warranted to them by the Bosts. It would seem to be at this time that the covenant of quiet and peaceable possession was disturbed for the first time since 1957 and that this suit was brought. The Statute of Limitations could not be operative until plaintiffs' rights were disturbed in the possession of their title by the sale of the underlying coal.

In this case it would seem that a key question involves the 10 year Statute of Limitations. When did it start to run?
* * *

[H]ere even though the deed was made some 19 years previous to the suit, there was nothing done by the owner of the two-thirds coal interest to interfere with the grantee's rights. So far as the agreed state of facts shows no one attempted to assert paramount title to the underlying coal until 1976. It was not until then that the plaintiffs had any right to bring suit against the grantor on his covenant of warranty. At this point for the first time, according to the agreed statement of facts, the plaintiffs were compelled to yield up two-thirds of the consideration which was the *quid pro quo* for the subject of the warranty—the underlying coal interest. The statute could not possibly begin to run until this time and as the record shows they brought this suit immediately.
* * *

[Defendants] covenanted by their warranty deed that,
> "premises were free from all incumbrances; and they also warranted to the grantees, their heirs and assigns, the quiet and peaceable possession of such premises,"

furthermore, that they
> "will defend the title thereto against all persons who may lawfully claim the same. And such covenants shall be obligatory upon any grantor, his heirs and *personal representatives* * * *

* * *

The trial court judgment was vacated, and the case was remanded to be heard again, consistent with the appellate court's ruling on the law. The limitation period did not begin until the discovery of the encumbrance.

JUDGMENT AND REMEDY

SPECIAL WARRANTY DEED The general warranty deed gives all the covenants of title listed above, but the special warranty deed (also known as deed with covenant against grantor's acts) warrants only that the grantor or seller has not previously done anything to lessen the value of the real estate. If the special warranty deed discloses all liens or other encumbrances, the seller will not be liable to the buyer if a third person subsequently interferes with the buyer's ownership. However, if the third person's claim arises out of, or is related to, some act of the seller, the seller will be liable to the buyer for damages. Both the special warranty deed and the general warranty deed warrant that the seller has "marketable" title. Common defects that may render a title unmarketable include variations in the names of grantors and grantees, breaks in the chain of title, outstanding liens, and defectively executed deeds in the chain of title.

QUIT CLAIM DEED   A **quit claim** deed warrants less than any other deed. Essentially, it simply conveys to the grantee whatever interest the grantor had. In other words, if the grantor had nothing, then the grantee receives nothing. Naturally, if the grantor had a defective title, or no title at all, a conveyance by general warranty deed or special warranty deed will not cure the defects. However, such deeds will give the buyer a cause of action to sue the seller. A quit claim deed gives no cause of action. The buyer is simply left with whatever the seller had.

Quit claim deeds are often used to clear up past defects in the title. Suppose H and W own a parcel of land as tenants by the entirety.[11] They decide to sell it, and H makes out a deed in his name only. B, the buyer, keeps the property for several years and then wishes to sell it to C. C's attorney, while examining the title, notices that the deed from H and W was signed by H alone. Therefore, W has an outstanding interest in the property that creates a "cloud" over C's title. C's attorney induces W to convey any interest she may have by quit claim deed to either C or B before advising his client to make the purchase. Thus, the quit claim deed removes the cloud over the title, and C, after purchasing the land from B, becomes the fee simple owner of the land. Quit claims are often used among tenants in common where one tenant "releases" interest to another.

_____

11. An estate held in tenancy by the entirety cannot be conveyed unless both spouses sign the sales contract and deed.

Recording the Deed

Deeds are recorded in the presence of a notary public in the county where the property is located. Most statutes require that the deed be signed by the grantor in the presence of two attesting witnesses before it can be recorded. The grantor is then required to *acknowledge* the deed in the presence of a notary public. The purpose of recording the deed is to give notice to the world that a certain person is now the owner of a certain parcel of real estate. Putting everyone on notice as to the true owner means that the previous owners cannot fraudulently convey the land to a subsequent purchaser.

At common law, priorities as to titles were governed by a *first in time, first in right* rule. To illustrate: Suppose J sells Shady Acres to A. A receives the deed from J and is considered the true owner. If J subsequently attempts to convey the property to B, B will receive nothing, since A is the true owner.

Today this rule generally governs. However, in the example above, if B is a bona fide purchaser, he may prevail over A unless A has recorded the deed. A *bona fide purchaser* is a person who pays valuable consideration for the land, who acts in good faith, and who has no notice of a previous conveyance or sale.

Notice is accomplished by recording, so virtually every state has statutes defining the requirements of recording. Once the deed to Shady Acres is recorded, the records serve as notice to the whole world that A is the true owner. B cannot then be a bona fide purchaser, since the records give him *constructive* notice of the true owner. Before purchasing real estate, everyone is required to check the county records.

Warranty of Habitability

Under the common law the purchaser of a home was entitled to certain warranties with respect to title of the property purchased. However, the common law rule of *caveat emptor* ("let the buyer beware") held that the seller of a home made no warranties with respect to the soundness or fitness of the home

unless such a warranty was specifically included in the deed or contract of sale. While *caveat
emptor* is still the rule of law in many states,
there is currently a strong trend against it and in
favor of an implied warranty of habitability.
Under this new approach, the courts hold that
the seller of a new house warrants that it will be
fit for human habitation regardless of whether
any such warranty is included in the deed or
contract of sale. Essentially, under an implied
warranty of habitability, the seller warrants that
the house is in reasonable working order and is
of reasonably sound construction.

Historically, the protection afforded a new
home buyer under the doctrine of *caveat
emptor* has not been satisfactory since the buyer
of a new home would only recover for defective
workmanship if he or she could prove that the
seller (builder) of the home was *negligent* in
constructing the home. Recall from the chapter
on torts that proof of negligence requires a
plaintiff to prove the existence of a certain
standard of care, and the unreasonable violation of that standard. Such facts are not easily
proved in a court of law. Under an implied
warranty of habitability, the purchser is only
required to prove that the home he or she has
purchased was somehow defective and to prove
the damages which the defect caused. Thus,
under warranty of habitability theory, the seller
of a new home is in effect a guarantor of the
home's fitness.

Sale of Real Estate

Most transfers of ownership interest in real
property are accomplished by means of a sale.
The sale of real estate is similar to the sale of
goods. It involves a transfer of ownership, often
with certain warranties. However, in the sale of
real estate, certain formalities are observed that
are not required in the sale of goods. To meet
the requirements of law, a deed must be signed
and delivered.[12] In most states, the deed must

---

12. The phrase *signed, sealed, and delivered* used to refer
to the requirements for transferring title to real property by
deed. The seal has fallen from use, but signature and
delivery are still required.

also be recorded. In order to illustrate how a
transfer of ownership in real property is accomplished, a typical real estate transaction is
outlined below.

A Typical Procedure in the Sale of Real Estate

Suppose Janet Parker owns a parcel of real
estate—a two-acre lot with an office building.
Since her company is expanding to a new
location, she has decided to sell the property.
The first thing she will do is to attempt to locate
a buyer. This can be accomplished in different
ways. She can put the property up for sale
herself, or she can employ a real estate broker
or agent to help her locate a buyer.

LOCATING A BUYER   Brokers generally find
buyers because they can make a commission or
percentage of the selling price. The broker can
put Parker's property on an *open listing*. This
means that the broker must produce a buyer
who is ready, willing, and able to purchase the
real estate. The broker who is the first to
produce such a buyer is entitled to the commission. Alternatively, Parker can have an
exclusive agency with the broker. In this type of
arrangement, the broker has the exclusive right
as an agent to sell the property, although Parker
can employ another broker. If she does, the first
broker is still entitled to a commission. However, if Parker sells the property without the
assistance of the broker, she need not pay the
commission. Finally, Parker can give the broker
an *exclusive right to sell*. In this situation, the
broker is entitled to a commission no matter
who sells the real estate—Parker, this broker, or
another broker. An exclusive right to sell usually lasts for a specified period of time; after that
time, Parker is free to make arrangements with
another broker if the property has not yet been
sold.

CONTRACT OF SALE   Once a buyer is located,
a contract for the sale of the land must be
negotiated. See Exhibit 52-2 for a typical con-

EXHIBIT 52–2

A TYPICAL CONTRACT

SEEK THE SERVICE OF YOUR ATTORNEY PRIOR TO SIGNING.

CONTRACT FOR SALE AND PURCHASE

PARTIES: __John Seller and Jane Seller, his wife_____ , as "SELLER,"

of __Miami, Florida__ (Phone _____),

and __Tom Buyer and Tess Buyer, his wife__ , as "BUYER,"

of __Decatur, Georgia__ (Phone _____),

hereby agree that the Seller shall sell and the Buyer shall buy the following property upon the terms and conditions hereinafter set forth (INCLUDING THE STANDARDS ON THE REVERSE SIDE HEREOF), to-wit:

1. (a) Legal description of real estate located in __Dade__ County, Florida, to-wit:

Lot 1 of Block 3 of Happy Acres according to the plat thereof recorded in Plat Book 4, page 65, of the Public Records of Dade County, Florida, together with one G. E. refrigerator, Serial Number xxx, and one Fedders air conditioner, Serial Number xxxx, located therein. The purchase price includes $500 for the refrigerator and air conditioner.

(b) Personal property included, to-wit: one G. E. Refrigerator and one Fedders air conditioner

(c) Street address, if any, of the property being conveyed __1000 Underwater Drive, Juno, Florida__

II. PURCHASE PRICE	$ 21,500.00
PAYMENT:	
(a) Deposit to be held in trust by __Reel Tor__ in the amount of	$ 2,000.00
(b) Subject to AND assumption of Mortgage in favor of __Ace Federal__ bearing interest at __7½__ % per annum and payable as to principal and interest $ __144.00__ per month having an approximate present principal balance of	$ 15,300.00
(c) Purchase money mortgage and note bearing interest at __8__ % on terms set forth hereinbelow in the principal amount of	$ 3,000.00
(d) Other _____	$
(e) Balance to close (excluding deposit) subject to adjustments and prorations	$ 1,200.00
TOTAL	$ 21,500.00

III. EVIDENCE OF TITLE: In the event a base abstract to the subject property exists then the same shall be brought current as otherwise provided herein, but if such abstract does not exist then within __15__ days from the date of this Contract, the Seller shall, at his expense, deliver to the Buyer or his attorney, in accordance with Standard "A" on reverse side either (CHECK) ☒ (1) OR ☐ (2) (1) Abstract or (2) title guarantee commitment with fee owner's title policy premium payable by Seller at closing.

IV. TIME FOR ACCEPTANCE: If this Contract is not executed by both of the parties hereto on or before __September 1, 1974__, the aforesaid deposit shall be, at the option of the Buyer, returned to him and this agreement shall thereafter be null and void. The date of Contract shall be the date when the last one of the Seller and Buyer has signed this Contract.

V. CLOSING DATE: This transaction shall be closed and the deed and other closing papers delivered on the __10th__ day of __November__ 19__74__, unless extended by other provisions of this Contract.

VI. RESTRICTIONS, EASEMENTS, LIMITATIONS: The Buyer shall take title subject to: Zoning, restrictions, prohibitions and other requirements imposed by governmental authority; Restrictions and matters appearing on the plat or otherwise common to the subdivision; Public utility easements of record, provided said easements are located on the side or rear lines of the property and are not more than ten feet in width as to the rear line and seven and one half feet in width as to the side line, unless otherwise specified herein; Taxes for year of closing and subsequent years, assumed mortgages and purchase money mortgages, if any;

Other __and restrictions in deed recorded in Deed Book 65, page 235__

provided, however, that none of the foregoing shall prevent use of the property for the purpose of __a residence__

VII. POSSESSION: Seller covenants and warrants that there are no parties in possession other than the Seller, and if the property is rented, the tenant(s) disclosed pursuant to Standard "G" on reverse side. Seller agrees to deliver possession of said property at time of closing unless otherwise specified below. If possession is to be delivered prior to closing, Buyer assumes all risk of loss to the property from date of possession, shall be responsible and liable for maintenance thereof from date of possession, and shall be deemed to have accepted the property, real and personal, in its existing condition as of time of taking possession.

VIII. ASSIGNABILITY: (CHECK ONE) Buyer ☒ may assign ☐ may not assign this contract.

IX. TYPEWRITTEN OR HANDWRITTEN PROVISIONS: Typewritten or handwritten provisions inserted in this form or attached hereto as Addenda shall control all printed provision in conflict therewith.

X. FINANCING: If the purchase price or any part thereof is to be financed by a third party loan, this Contract is conditioned upon the Buyer obtaining a firm commitment for said loan within _____ days from date hereof, at an interest rate not to exceed _____%; term of _____ years; and in the principal amount of $ _____ Buyer agrees to use reasonable diligence to obtain said loan and failing the obtaining of the same within said time period, either party hereto may cancel this Contract.

XI. SPECIAL CLAUSES:

WITNESS: (Two are required) | Executed by Buyer on __August 15, 1974__
I. Witness _____ | s/ __Tom Buyer__ (SEAL)
U. Witness _____ | s/ __Tess Buyer__ (SEAL)

WITNESS: (Two are required) | Executed by Seller on __August 31, 1974__
H. Witness _____ | s/ __John Seller__ (SEAL)
S. Witness _____ | s/ __Jane Seller__ (SEAL)

Deposit received on __August 15, 1974__ to be held subject to this Contract; if check, subject to clearance.

By: __Reel Tor__ (SEAL)

Escrow Agent

tract. Here Parker must decide, inter alia, the cost of title examination and insurance, how to allocate property taxes, and what the actual purchase price will be. The contract for the sale of real estate must be in writing to be enforceable. The writing need not specify all the details of the transaction, but it should contain the essential terms of the bargain and be signed by

BROKER'S COMPENSATION: Seller agrees to pay the real estate broker named below, at time of closing, from the disbursements of the proceeds of sale, compensation in the amount of 5 % of gross purchase price for his services in effecting the sale. In the event Buyer fails to perform and deposit is retained, 50% thereof, but not exceeding the broker's compensation as above computed, shall be paid to the broker, as full consideration for broker's services including costs expended by broker, and the balance shall be applied first in payment of attorney's fees and other expenses incurred on behalf of Seller, and the remainder shall be paid to Seller. If the transaction shall not be closed because of refusal of Seller to perform, the Seller shall pay said commission in full to broker on demand.

s/ Reel Tor (SEAL)
Broker

s/ John Seller (SEAL)
Seller

By: ____________________

s/ Jane Seller (SEAL)

This form has been approved by ____________________

and ____________________

STANDARDS FOR REAL ESTATE TRANSACTIONS

A. EVIDENCE OF TITLE: (1) A base contract of title prepared or brought current by a reputable and existing abstract firm (if not existing then certified as correct by an existing firm) purporting to be an accurate synopsis of the instrument affecting the title to subject real property recorded in public records of the county wherein the land is situated, through date of this Contract. For purposes of this Contract a "base abstract" shall mean an abstract commencing with the earliest public records, or such later date as may be customary in the county wherein the land is situate, which has been last certified to a date within 35 years immediately preceding the date of this Contract. Seller shall convey a marketable title in accordance with the Standards adopted from time to time by The Florida Bar, subject only to liens, encumbrances, exceptions or qualifications set forth in this Contract and those which shall be discharged by Seller at or before closing. Upon closing of this transaction such abstract shall become the property of Buyer, subject to the right of retention thereof by first mortgagee until fully paid; or (2) A title guarantee commitment issued by a qualified title insuror agreeing to issue to Buyer, upon recording of the deed hereafter mentioned, an Owner's Guarantee in the amount of the purchase price, insuring title of the Buyer to the real property, subject only to liens, encumbrances, exceptions or qualifications set forth in this Contract and those which shall be discharged by Seller at or before closing. Buyer shall have thirty (30) days, if abstract, or five (5) days, if title guarantee, from date of receiving evidence of title, to examine same. If title is found defective, Buyer shall, within three (3) days thereafter, notify Seller in writing specifying defect(s). If said defects render title unmarketable, Seller shall have 120 days from receipt of notice within which to remove said defect(s), and if Seller is unsuccessful in removing them within said time, Buyer shall have the option of either (1) accepting the title as it then is, or (2) demanding a refund of all monies paid hereunder which shall forthwith be returned to Buyer and thereupon Buyer and Seller shall be released of all further obligations under the Contract; however, Seller agrees that he will, if title is found to be unmarketable, use diligent effort to correct the defects in title within the time limit provided therefor, including the bringing of necessary suits.

B. EXISTING MORTGAGES: The Seller shall obtain and furnish a statement from the mortgagee(s) setting forth principal balance, method of payment, interest rate, and whether the mortgage(s) is in good standing. In the event a mortgage requires acceptance or approval of Buyer by the mortgagee in order to avoid default, and mortgagee does not approve the Buyer, then Buyer, at his option, may rescind the contract and receive a return of all deposits made hereunder.

C. PURCHASE MONEY MORTGAGES: The purchase money note and mortgage, if any, shall provide for a thirty (30) day grace period in the event of default if it is a first mortgage and a 15 day grace period if a second mortgage; shall provide for right of prepayment in whole or in part without penalty; shall not provide for acceleration in event of resale of the property; and shall be otherwise in form and content required by Seller's attorney; provided, however, Seller shall not require clauses not customarily found in mortgages and mortgage notes generally utilized by savings and loan institutions in the county wherein the property is located. Said mortgage shall require the owner of the property encumbered to keep all prior liens and encumbrances in good standing and forbid the owner of the property from accepting modifications of or future advances under prior mortgage(s).

D. SURVEY: The Buyer, within time allowed for delivery of evidence of title and examination thereof, may have the property surveyed at his expense. If the survey, certified by a registered Florida surveyor, shows any encroachment on said property or that improvements intended to be located on the subject property in fact encroach on lands of others, or violate any of the Contract covenants, the same shall be treated as a title defect. Any survey prepared in connection with or as a consequence of this transaction may include a description of the property under the Florida Coordinate System as defined in Chapter 177, Florida Statutes.

E. TERMITE INSPECTION: Within ten (10) days from date of this Contract Buyer may have the improvements inspected at Buyer's expense by a licensed and bonded exterminator to determine whether there is any active terminate infestation or existing substantial damage from prior terminate infestation in the improvements. The consequence of said infestation or damage shall be that Seller shall pay all costs of treatment required to remedy such infestation or damage, including cost of repairing or replacing all portions of said improvement which are infested or damaged. However, in the event costs to be incurred are more than three percent (3%) of assessed valuation of improvements to the real property, based upon the most recent assessment by the County Tax Assessor, then Buyer shall have the option of cancelling this Contract within ten (10) days after receipt of the termite inspection report by giving written notice to Seller, or Buyer may elect to proceed with the transaction, in which event Buyer shall receive a credit at closing of an amount equal to three (3%) percent of said assessed valuation. "Termite" shall be deemed to include all wood destroying organisms.

F. INGRESS AND EGRESS: Seller covenants and warrants that there is ingress and egress to said property.

G. LEASES: Seller shall, not less than fifteen (15) days prior to closing, furnish to Buyer copies of all written leases and estoppel letters from each tenant specifying the nature and duration of said tenant's occupancy, rental rates and advanced rent and security deposits paid by tenant. In the event Seller is unable to obtain such letters from tenants, the same information shall be furnished by Seller to Buyer within said time period in the form of a Seller's affidavit, and Buyer may thereafter contact tenants to confirm such information. Seller shall deliver and assign all original leases to Buyer at closing.

H. LIENS: Seller shall, both as to the realty and personalty being sold hereunder, furnish to Buyer at time of closing an affidavit attesting to the absence, unless otherwise provided for herein, of any financing statements, claims of lien or potential lienors known to Seller and further attesting that there have been no improvements to the property for 90 days immediately preceding date of closing. If the property has been improved within said time, Seller shall deliver releases or waivers of all mechanic's liens, executed by general contractors, subcontractors, suppliers, and materialmen, in addition to Seller's lien affidavit, setting forth the names of all such general contractors, subcontractors, suppliers and materialmen and further reciting that in fact all bills for work to the subject property which could serve as a basis for a mechanic's lien have been paid or will be paid at closing.

I. PLACE OF CLOSING: Closing shall be held at office of Seller's attorney, if said office is located in the county wherein subject property is located; if not, then as otherwise agreed upon.

J. TIME: Time is of the essence of this Contract. Any reference herein to time periods of less than 6 days shall in the computation thereof exclude Saturdays, Sundays and legal holidays, and any time period provided for herein which shall end on a Saturday, Sunday or legal holiday shall extend to 5:00 p.m. of the next full business day.

K. DOCUMENTS FOR CLOSING: Seller's attorney shall prepare deed, mechanic's lien affidavit and any corrective instruments that may be required in connection with perfecting the title; Buyer's attorney will prepare closing statement, mortgage, mortgage note, and financing statements.

L. EXPENSES: State surtax and documentary stamps which are required to be affixed to the instrument of conveyance and cost of recording any corrective instruments shall be paid by Seller. Documentary stamps to be affixed to the note or notes secured by the purchase money mortgage, intangible tax on mortgage and cost of recording the deed, purchase money mortgage and financing statement shall be paid by Buyer.

M. PRORATION OF TAXES (REAL AND PERSONAL): Taxes shall be prorated based on the current year's tax with due allowance made for maximum allowable discount and homestead or other exemptions if allowed for said year. If closing occurs at a date when the current year's taxes are not fixed, and current year's assessment is available, taxes will be prorated based upon such assessment, and the prior year's millage. If current year's assessment is not available, then taxes will be prorated on the prior year's tax; provided, however, if there are completed improvements on the property by January 1st of year of closing, which improvements were not in existence on January 1st of the prior year, then taxes shall be prorated to date of closing based upon the prior year's millage and at an equitable assessment to be agreed upon between the parties, failing which, request will be made to the county tax assessor for an informal assessment taking into consideration homestead exemption, if any. However, any tax proration based on an estimate may at request of either party to the transaction, be subsequently readjusted upon receipt of tax bill and a statement to that effect is to be set forth in the closing statement.

N. SPECIAL ASSESSMENT LIENS: Certified, confirmed and ratified special assessment liens as of date of closing (and not as of date of Contract) are to be paid by Seller. Pending liens as of date of closing shall be assumed by Buyer, provided, however, that where the improvement has been substantially completed as of the date of Contract, such pending lien shall be considered as certified, confirmed or ratified and Seller shall, at closing, be charged an amount equal to the last estimate by the public body of the assessment for the improvement.

O. PERSONAL PROPERTY: The Seller represents and warrants that all major appliances, plumbing, electrical installations and machinery included in the sale shall be in working order and repair as of date of closing. Buyer may at his sole expense and on reasonable notice, cause an inspection to be made by a licensed firm or firms dealing in the repair and maintenance of such items with said inspections taking place within the period allowed for examination of the evidence of title or the taking of possession of subject property by Buyer, whichever event occurs first. Failure to object in writing to Seller within said time period shall be deemed a waiver of such right. Valid objections shall be resolved at cost of Seller with funds therefor being escrowed at closing. If a purchase money mortgage is taken by Seller, all personal property being conveyed will, at option of Seller, be subject to the lien of the mortgage note and evidenced by a recorded financing statement.

P. RISK OF LOSS: If the improvements are damaged by fire or other casualty prior to closing, and cost of restoring same does not exceed three percent (3%) of the assessed valuation of the improvements so damaged, cost of such restoration shall be an obligation of the Seller and closing shall proceed pursuant to the terms of the Contract. In the event the cost of repair of restoration shall be an amount equal to three (3%) percent or more of the assessed valuation of improvements so damaged, Buyer shall have the option of either taking the property as is, together with any insurance proceeds payable by virtue of such loss or damage, or of cancelling this Contract and receiving return of all deposits made hereunder.

Q. MAINTENANCE: Between date of contract and date of closing the property, including lawn, shrubbery and pool, if any, shall be maintained by Seller in the condition it existed as of date of Contract, ordinary wear and tear excepted.

R. PROCEEDS OF SALE AND CLOSING PROCEDURE: The deed shall be recorded and evidence of title continued at Buyer's expense, to show title in Buyer, without any encumbrances or change from the date of the last evidence which would render Seller's title unmarketable, and the cash proceeds of sale shall be held in escrow by Seller's attorney or by such other escrow agent as may be mutually agreed upon for a period of not longer than five (5) days. If Seller's title is rendered unmarketable, Buyer's attorney shall within said five (5) day period, notify Seller's attorney in writing of the defect and Seller shall have thirty (30) days from date of receipt of such notification to cure said defect. In the event Buyer fails to make timely demand for refund, he shall take title as is, waiving all rights against Seller as to such intervening defect except as may be available to Buyer by virtue of warranties, if any, contained in deed. In the event a portion of the purchase price is to be derived from institutional financing or re-financing, the requirements of the lending institution as to place, time and procedures for closing, and for disbursement of mortgage proceeds, shall control, anything in this Contract to the contrary notwithstanding.

the parties. The essential terms are: (1) an identification of the parties, (2) the description of the land to be conveyed, (3) the purchase price, and (4) the signature. In most cases, after the details of the transaction have been negotiated, an attorney will draw up a long, formal document that will be signed by both the seller and the buyer.

TITLE EXAMINATION After the sales contract has been negotiated, the buyer will begin the *title examination*. Essentially, a title examination is the examination of all past transfers and sales of the piece of property in question. Every county has a filing system where deeds, plats, and other instruments are recorded. A skilled examiner can determine from these records whether there are any liens, easements, profits, or other encumbrances on the land. These records, known as the chain of title, go back to the original grant or deed from the United States or the particular state where the land is located.[13] Usually, private abstract companies prepare what is known as an *abstract*. This document lists all of the records relating to a particular parcel of land. The attorney and title examiner do not have to search through the records themselves. The examiner then gives an opinion as to the validity of the title. Often, the sales contract requires a buyer to purchase *title insurance*—an insurance that protects both the seller and the buyer in the event that someone is shown to have a better title. Title insurance companies have their own staffs of attorneys and abstractors who examine titles on a full-time basis. Once a title insurance company's staff approves a title, the company will issue insurance on the property.

Along with the title examination, the sales contract may require the seller to make a survey of the land to check the exact boundaries and to make sure they coincide with the legal description contained in the deed and the county records. In addition, the survey makes sure no neighboring buildings or structures overlap onto the property.

OBTAINING A MORTGAGE Ordinarily most buyers do not have enough cash to buy real estate outright, so they arrange for a loan. To obtain the loan, the purchaser must put the property up as collateral. *Mortgages* are essentially liens against the property that enable the lender to foreclose and sell the real estate if the borrower fails to make timely payments. In most cases, a bank or savings and loan association is contacted for financing. In some cases, the seller may agree to loan the buyer the purchase price in exchange for the buyer's promissory note and mortgage. Either type of mortgage is known as a *(first) purchase money mortgage* because the seller or lender supplies the buyer with the *money* to *purchase* the house.

CLOSING The final stage of the sale is called the *closing*. The transaction is closed by the buyer paying the purchase price and the seller delivering the deed to the buyer. The closing is usually attended by the buyer, the seller, their attorneys, and the lender. When the property is being mortgaged, the lender ordinarily closes the mortgage deal, paying the seller for the property and receiving a lien (mortgage) on the property at the same time.

Transfer by Will or Inheritance

Property that is transferred on an owner's death is passed either by *will* or by *inheritance*. If the owner of land dies with a will, the land that the owner had prior to death passes according to the terms of the will. If the owner dies without a will, state statutes prescribe how and to whom the property will pass. Ordinarily, when the owner dies without a will, the property passes to the deceased's living heirs. This topic is discussed in Chapter 55.

Eminent Domain

Eminent domain (condemnation) is the power of the government to take land for public use. When a new public highway or railroad is to be built, the government must decide where to build it and how much land to condemn. The government then starts a condemnation pro-

---

13. Today the title search need not go back all the way to the grant from the government. Nearly every state has a marketable record title act that provides that the roots of title older than thirty or forty years are conclusively presumed to be valid. In other words, if the chain of title can be traced back thirty or forty years with no defects, no further search need be made.

ceeding in which the owner can show why the land should not be appropriated for public use and the government or agency involved can show why the public needs this particular parcel of land. Once the government determines that the land is to be condemned or taken for public use, another proceeding is held to determine the fair value of the land, which is usually approximately equal to its market value. The fair value is paid to the property owner as compensation for the taking of the property. Under federal and state constitutions, government is not allowed to take property without paying just compensation for it. A condemnation transfers title from the owner to the government. Then the government is considered the true owner and can use the land for whatever purpose was originally contemplated.

Adverse Possession

Adverse possession is a means of obtaining title to land without a deed being delivered. Essentially, when one person possesses the property of another for a certain statutory period of time, usually twenty or twenty-one years, that person (called the adverse possessor) acquires title to the land and cannot be removed from the land by the original owner. The adverse possessor is vested with a perfect title just as if there had been a conveyance by deed. Once title to the property has been obtained, if the new owner abandons the premises, title will not pass to the original owner. It will *escheat* to the state according to state law.

In order to hold property adversely, four elements must be satisfied. First, possession must be actual and exclusive; that is, the possessor must take sole physical occupancy of the property. Second, the possession must be open, visible, and notorious, not secret or clandestine. The possessor must occupy the land for all the world to see. Third, possession must be continuous and peaceable for the required period of time. This means that the possessor must not be interrupted in the occupancy by the true owner or by the courts. Being evicted or being served with an eviction notice will stop the statute of limitations from running and likewise stop the adverse possession. Finally, possession must be hostile and adverse. In other words, the possessor must claim the property as against the whole world. He or she cannot live on the property with the permission of the owner. Thus, a tenant who holds over is not holding adversely to the landlord, since the law presumes that the landlord is permitting the tenant to stay. Until the tenant repudiates the landlord-tenant relationship, he or she is not occupying the premises with hostility and adversity. Note that an adverse possessor cannot claim more land than he or she has continuously occupied (as by fencing in an area). Thus, someone living in a small shack on a thousand acre cattle farm cannot claim the whole thousand acres unless he or she has regularly and continuously used it.

QUESTIONS AND CASE PROBLEMS

1. Pabst Brewing Company purchased two adjoining lots from Jones. A brewery was located on one lot, and a very expensive residence was on the other lot. At the time of the purchase, Jones was the fee simple owner of the brewery, but unknown to either party, he owned only a life estate in the residence. After the purchase, the character of the real estate in the area changed. Factories and other breweries with railroad tracks made the area undesirable for a residence, and the house could not be rented profitably. Pabst removed the residence and graded down the property to fit it to commercial purposes, which greatly enhanced the property's value. Subsequently, Melms, who owned the remaining interest in the house sold by Jones, brought suit against Pabst to have himself declared owner of the property on which the residence stood and to recover damages for waste by Pabst. The waste claimed was the destruction of the residence and the grading down of the land to street level. Can Melms recover? [Melms v. Pabst Brewing Co., 104 Wis. 7, 79 N.W. 738 (1899)]

2. Waltz leased certain premises to Fetting Manufacturing Jewelry Company for five years at various

annual rentals payable in monthly installments. Near the end of the term, the parties attempted to negotiate a new lease, but they could not agree on terms. Fetting gave timely notice to Waltz that he was preparing to move, but he asked Waltz to extend the lease for a month or two. Although the parties were unable to agree on terms for an extension of the lease, Fetting continued to occupy the premises for one month after the expiration of the lease, without Waltz's consent. Then Fetting vacated the premises and refused to pay any further rent. Waltz sued, contending that the unauthorized holding over obligated Fetting to pay for another year. Can Waltz recover? [Fetting Mfg. Jewelry Co. v. Waltz, 160 Md. 50, 152 A. 434 (1930)]

3. United Homes Corporation owned and managed an apartment complex in the state of Washington. McCutcheon, one of the United Home's tenants, was injured when he fell down an unlighted interior stairway. The stairway was unlighted because United Homes had negligently failed to change the overhead lightbulbs. The stairway on which McCutcheon sustained his injury was located at the end of the hallway and was used by all the tenants in the apartment building. Will United Homes Corporation be liable for McCutcheon's injury? Explain. Would the answer be different if the lease signed by McCutcheon contained a clause stating that the lessor could not be held liable for injuries that the lessee sustained while entering or leaving the building? [McCutcheon v. United Homes Corp., 2 Wash.App. 618, 469 P.2d 997 (1970)]

4. Wilmore, the owner of a tract of land known as Robinson's Beach, periodically rented parcels of the land to various persons who built bungalows on them. The bungalows, built without the consent or interference of Wilmore, were placed on cinder blocks that in turn rested on top of the ground. Water and electrical hookups were made in a way that they could be readily removed. The bungalows were easily removable without injury either to them or to the land. Subsequently, Sigrol Realty Corporation purchased the land from Wilmore, but the purchase contract made no mention of the bungalows. Upon learning of the purchase, Valcich, the owner of several of the bungalows, began to remove them. Sigrol Realty brought an action to enjoin removal of the bungalows, claiming it purchased them as part of the realty. Should the injunction be issued? [Sigrol Realty Corp. v. Valcich, 12 App.Div.2d 430, 212 N.Y.S.2d 224 (1961)]

5. Piper and Mowris owned adjacent tracts of land.

Mowris had purchased his land from Thomas and Beatrice Carr in 1925. At the time the Carrs sold the land to Mowris, they owned an easement across Piper's land. When they sold their land to Mowris, they also sold him their easement. Over the next thirty years, Mowris seldom used the right of way over Piper's land, and it became overgrown "like a wilderness." Does Mowris still own an easement over Piper's land? Assume that, thirty years ago, Piper had built a fence along the boundary line dividing his and Mowris's property and that this fence obstructed Mowris's right of way. Has Mowris lost his easement? [Piper v. Mowris, 466 Pa. 89, 351 A.2d 635 (1976)]

6. The owners of the Seven Palms Motor Inn decided that their motel was in need of renovation. Accordingly, they ordered a large quantity of bedspreads, curtain rods, and drapes from Sears, Roebuck and Company. Thereafter, Seven Palms Motor Inn failed to pay its bill, which amounted to approximately $8,000, including installation. Under Missouri law, a supplier of fixtures can establish a lien on the land and building to which the fixtures become attached. Sears sought to establish such a lien to make it easier to recover the debt that Seven Palms owed it. Which, if any, of the above-named items will Sears be able to argue are fixtures? [Sears, Roebuck & Co. v. Seven Palms Motor Inn, 530 S.W.2d 695 (Mo.1975)]

7. X conveyed a life estate in certain land to her son, S, with the remainder to T. The deed was properly executed, signed by X, and delivered to S, but it was never recorded. X died one year later, leaving S her sole heir. Eighteen months later, S sold the land to P. The title records showed that the land was owned by X; therefore, P ascertained that S was X's sole heir. After the sale, T, who then occupied the land refused to relinquish possession to P. Who is entitled to the land? [Earle v. Fiske, 103 Mass. 491 (1870)]

8. Grow Investment and Mortgage Company conveyed to Larry Jones, by warranty deed, a residential lot located in Utah County. Among other things, the deed provided that the lot was subject to all "easements of record." Before Jones purchased the land, he inspected it and found an open irrigation ditch running down the east side and partly along the south side of the lot. It appeared to Jones that the ditch had at one time been used by the lot adjacent and to the north of the one that Jones was inspecting; it no longer seemed to be in use because it contained tree limbs, building refuse, weeds, and trash. After his inspection, Jones purchased the land from Grow Investment and later attempted to fill the ditch. The owners of the land in the lot adjacent and to the north of Jones's lot

were able to stop Jones from filling the ditch since they had a legally valid easement by prescription in the ditch. What can Jones do? [Jones v. Grow Investment and Mortgage Co., 11 Utah2d 326, 358 P.2d 909 (1961)]

9. Morton was a construction contractor of residential properties. One of the houses that Morton built was sold by his agent to a purchaser named Humber. The house was new when Humber purchased it. Shortly after the purchase, Humber lit a fire in the fireplace, and, because of a crack in the hearth, the house caught fire, and was damaged extensively. It was unclear whether the crack was the result of Morton's negligence, but Humber sought to recover from Morton under the theory that when Morton sold the house to Humber, he warranted that it was reasonably fit for human habitation. Morton argued that that was not the law and that the common law rule of *caveat emptor* ("let the buyer beware") governed the sale of realty. Who is correct? [Humber v. Morton, 426 S.W.2d 554 (Tex.1968)]

10. Smyth was the owner of a one-ninth interest in land. The other owners, who were cotenants, owned a combined eight-ninths interest in the property. Smyth and the other owners were tenants in common. The land was of considerable value, since large quantities of rock asphalt were just below its surface. Smyth mined one-ninth of the rock asphalt, sold it, and personally retained the profits. The other cotenants of the property sued Smyth, seeking a division of his profits from the mining operations among all the cotenants. Smyth claimed that since he took only one-ninth of the rock, which was his ownership share, he should not be divested of the profits. What result? [White v. Smyth, 147 Tex. 272, 214 S.W.2d 967 (1948)]

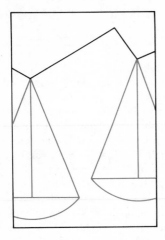

53

Future Interests, Nonpossessory Interests, and Land Use Control

The last chapter defined real property and then discussed the nature of an estate and how estates are acquired. Generally, the estates that were discussed were those in which the person having the estate (ownership interest) was also in *present* possession of the land. This chapter discusses estates and other types of interests in land that do not involve present possession by the owner. The last part of the chapter discusses encumbrances on land that affect the way land can be used.

FUTURE INTERESTS

A person can convey an estate that is limited by a specified period of time; the life of the grantor, grantee, or other person; or by an occurrence. The person to whom such an estate is conveyed has a *present possessory interest*. Life estates, terms for years, and fee simple determinable estates are examples of estates that carry present possessory interests, and which include a residuary interest that may or may not have been disposed of by the grantor. This residuary interest is a *future interest*, and it can take several forms. If it remains in the grantor, it is called a *reversion*, a *possibility of reverter*, or a *power of termination*. The first two are by far the more common residuary interests that a grantor retains. If the future interest is not retained by the grantor, then it is called either a *remainder* or an *executory interest*. Remainders can be either *vested* or *contingent*, depending upon the terms of the conveyance.

Reversionary Interests and Powers of Termination

When a grantor owns a fee simple estate in land and conveys an estate to another with a duration that is less than the duration of the estate that the grantor owns, there is an undisposed residue remaining in the grantor. That undisposed residue is called a **reversion**. For example, X owns a fee simple estate and conveys a life estate in Blackacre to A. X has not disposed of the interest in the land that remains after A's life. Therefore, X has automatically retained a reversion, and the reversion is a future interest. It is preceded by A's life estate, which is an estate in possession. X's reversion is created by operation of law. X does not have a present possessory interest in Blackacre but has a *vested* future interest—that is, an absolute right to possession of Blackacre at some point in the future, a right that X can convey in the present.

If X conveys Blackacre "to A and her heirs," he conveys a fee simple absolute. There is no future interest in Blackacre, since X has conveyed the entire estate to A. But what if X conveys a fee simple determinable, which is slightly less than a fee simple absolute? What has X retained? Suppose X conveys Blackacre "to A and her heirs as long as it is used for educational purposes." X has conveyed a fee simple determinable and, by operation of law, has retained a **possibility of reverter**—a future interest in favor of the grantor that is contingent on the happening of the event named in the conveyance. The conveyance of a determinable fee that gives rise to a possibility of reverter usually includes the words *so long as, until, while,* or *during.*

Powers of termination are also future interests retained by a grantor who is conveying an estate subject to a condition. Powers of termination are similar to possibilities of reverter except that future possession by the grantor requires an affirmative act. (That is, it does not occur automatically.) For example, suppose X conveys Blackacre "to A and her heirs, but if liquor is sold on the premises, the right to enter and terminate the estate is re-served." X has retained a power of termination and has the right to repossess the land in the future if liquor is sold on the premises and if X acts affirmatively to retake possession of Blackacre.

Remainders and Executory Interests

If the owner of real property conveys an estate that is less than a fee simple absolute and does not retain the residuary interest, then that interest will take the form of either a **remainder** or an **executory interest**. As mentioned above, a remainder can be either vested or contingent. Both are future interests, but the holder of a vested remainder has an absolute right to possession at the end of the prior estate. The owner of a contingent remainder has only a conditional right to possession when the prior estate ends. Both are estates in land in favor of persons other than the grantor, and both can be transferred to other persons (that is, purchased and sold, inherited, devised or bequeathed). Suppose X, the owner of Blackacre, transfers it "to A for ninety-nine years remainder to D." A has a present possessory interest in Blackacre in the form of a ninety-nine-year term. D has a future possessory interest in Blackacre, which is presently vested and which takes effect instantly at the end of ninety-nine years. Note the difference between D's vested remainder in this example and E's contingent remainder in the following example. X conveys Blackacre "to C for life remainder to E if and only if E marries within C's life." In this example, C has a present possessory interest in the form of a life estate, and E has a contingent remainder—a future possessory interest that is not vested at present. Its vesting is *contingent* upon E's marrying within C's lifetime. If E does not marry within C's lifetime, then the remainder that E would have taken *reverts* to X, who, by operation of law, retains a possibility of reverter at the time of the conveyance. If E does marry during C's lifetime, then E's future possessory interest *vests* immediately, but E still cannot take possession of Blackacre until the end of C's life estate.

Executory interests are future possessory interests in real property that are conveyed to persons other than the grantor at the time of a conveyance. These interests were not recognized at common law but are recognized in all states today. Executory interests are similar to vested and contingent remainders, with one important difference. Executory interests do not occur instantly at the end of a prior estate. In the examples of vested and contingent remainders above, note that D's and E's remainder interests become possessory interests as soon as the preceding estates terminate naturally. Executory interests take effect either before or after the natural termination of a preceding estate. To illustrate, X conveys Blackacre "to A for twenty years, but if A should divorce, then Blackacre is to pass immediately to C." C has a future interest in Blackacre that will become a present possessory interest if A becomes divorced. C's future interest, which can *cut short* A's interest, is known as a *shifting* executory interest. If X conveys Blackacre "to B for life and one year after B's death to D," B has a life estate, and D has an executory interest that will not arise until one year after the termination of B's life estate. Such an executory interest is known as a *springing* executory interest. By operation of law, X retains a reversion in Blackacre of one year, and D's executory interest then *springs* from X.

Rule Against Perpetuities

The purpose of the Rule Against Perpetuities is to prevent the tying up of property ownership. The Rule achieves this purpose by preventing *remoteness in vesting*. In its simplest form, the Rule is: No interest is good unless it must vest, if at all, not later than twenty-one years after some life in being at the creation of the interest (excluding periods of gestation). The Rule is not a perfect solution to the problem of tying up title, but it is stated in such precise terms that *any* conveyance that ties up title for a long period of time will be voided by the Rule. Unfortunately, some conveyances that do not tie up title are also voided by the rule. Before looking at any examples of the Rule in opera-

tion, the student should note that interests in land can be created either by deed (*inter vivos*) or by will (at the grantor's death). This is important in determining the identity of the life in being to which the rule refers. The first example is of a conveyance that is not voided by the Rule Against Perpetuities. Suppose X conveys Blackacre by deed "to B for life, then to C for life, then to D for life remainder to D's children." B, C, and D all have life estates, and D's children have a vested remainder in Blackacre. The Rule Against Perpetuities does not void the vested remainder of D's children, since their identity will be known at D's death (or within the period of gestation thereafter). Since X specifically names D in the conveyance, D must be alive at the creation of his or her interest and therefore is a life in being. The interests of D's children will vest, if at all, within twenty-one years of D's death, since their identities must be determined no later than nine months (the gestation period) after D's death. If D has no children, this will be known at D's death, and ownership of Blackacre will revert to X or X's heirs.

If X conveys Blackacre *by will* "to the first of my grandchildren to reach the age of twenty-one," this conveyance does not violate the Rule Against Perpetuities. Since the conveyance was by will, the interest in the first of X's grandchildren to reach twenty-one is not created until X's death. X's *children* will be deemed the "lives in being" under the Rule, since X can have no more children after death. Within twenty-one years of the death of any of X's children (the "lives in being"), the interest in X's *grandchildren* must vest, since no grandchild of X's can possibly reach the age of twenty-one more than twenty-one years after the death of the last of X's children (excluding periods of gestation). If X's will leaves Blackacre "to the first of my grandchildren to reach age thirty," the Rule Against Perpetuities will void any possible interest in X's grandchildren unless, at the time of X's death, one of the grandchildren is at least thirty years old. Even if, at X's death, X's oldest grandchild is five days short of thirty and in perfect health, he or she cannot obtain ownership of Blackacre under this latter version of X's will, since it is possible that he or she might die before age thirty and that none of X's other grandchildren will reach age thirty within twenty-one years of the death of X's last child. The Rule Against Perpetuities does not take into consideration probabilities of vesting; it considers only possible remoteness of vesting.

X may convey Blackacre *by deed* "to the first of my grandchildren to reach twenty-one." If, at the time of the conveyance, which is by deed, none of X's grandchildren is at least twenty-one years of age, then this conveyance will fail under the Rule Against Perpetuities. Again, even if several of X's grandchildren are between twenty and twenty-one years of age at the time of the conveyance (that is, at the time their contingent interest is created), there remains the possibility, however remote, that all of them will die, that X will then die, and that none of X's future grandchildren will reach twenty-one within twenty-one years of X's death. Note that in this example the "life in being" is not X's children but X. This is because the conveyance is by deed and because there is a period of time (twenty-one years) before the interest created by X might vest, during which X could outlive all of his or her children. Once again, the Rule Against Perpetuities is concerned not with the probability but with the possibility of this happening.

Suppose X conveys Blackacre *by will* "to the first baby born in Southern Methodist Hospital after my death." Even if two dozen babies are delivered each day at Southern Methodist Hospital, this conveyance by X is void, since it violates the Rule Against Perpetuities. Since the conveyance is by will, and the takers under the will are not X's descendants, it is impossible to determine a life in being. X could not serve as the life in being because X will be dead at the time his or her will takes effect. Since there is a possibility that no baby will be born at Southern Methodist Hospital within twenty-one years after X's death, the conveyance violates the Rule. X could have achieved the desired result and avoided the Rule by drafting the provision to read: "To the first baby born at Southern Methodist Hospital; but if none is born within twenty-one years of my death, then to my heirs."

It is most important to determine who the "life in being" is when deciding whether the Rule Against Perpetuities has been violated. The person whose life serves as the measuring rod need not be mentioned in the document creating the property interest at issue and need not take any interest in the property. Furthermore, the person need not be connected in any way with the property or the persons designated to take it.

BACKGROUND AND FACTS *Philomena Lux's will provided that some of her real estate be held in trust for her grandchildren and thereafter sold when the youngest reached twenty-one years of age. Other property was bequeathed directly to her grandchildren. Lux was survived by one son and five grandchildren ranging in age from two to eight. Lux's only surviving son, Anthony John Lux, Jr., was not to share in any part of the property that went to the grandchildren. The trial court summarily rejected any argument that since no life in being was named, the provisions violated the Rule Against Perpetuities.*

LUX v. LUX,
Supreme Court of Rhode Island, 1972.
109 R.I. 592, 288 A.2d 701.

KELLEHER, Justice.

* * *

The artless efforts of a draftsman have precipitated this suit which seeks the construction of and instructions relating to the will of Philomena Lux who died a resident of Cumberland on August 15, 1968. We hasten to add that the will was drawn by someone other than counsel of record.

Philomena Lux executed her will on May 9, 1966. She left her residuary estate to her husband, Anthony John Lux, and nominated him as the executor. Anthony predeceased his wife. His death triggered the following pertinent provisions of Philomena's will:

"Fourth: In the event that my said husband, Anthony John Lux, shall predecease me, then I make the following disposition of my estate:

* * *

"All the rest, residue and remainder of my estate, real and personal, of whatsoever kind and nature, and wherever situated, of which I shall die seized and possessed, or over which I may have power of appointment, or to which I may be in any manner entitled at my death, I give, devise and bequeath to my grandchildren, share and share alike.

"Any real estate included in said residue shall be maintained for the benefit of said grandchildren and shall not be sold until the youngest of said grandchildren has reached twenty-one years of age.

* * *

Philomena was survived by one son, Anthony John Lux, Jr., and five grandchildren whose ages range from two to eight. All the grandchildren were children of Anthony. * * * The Superior Court appointed a guardian ad litem to represent the interests of the grandchildren. It also designated an attorney to represent the rights of individuals who may have an interest under the will but who are at this time unknown, unascertained or not in being. * * *

Before determining the individuals who may benefit from Philomena's benevolence, it should be noted that the residuary devise to the grandchildren is a class gift which in no way violates the rule against perpetuities. The rule, in seeking to insure the free administration of property, requires that interest must vest within a life or lives in being at the time of the creation of the future interest plus twenty-one years thereafter including an allowance for the period of gestation in those instances where there is a posthumous birth. The person whose life serves as the measuring rod need not be mentioned in the will, nor need he take any interest in the property. He need not be connected in any way with the property or the persons designated to take it. Gray, Rule Against Perpetuities § 219.2, n. 2 (4th ed. 1942); Leach, Perpetuities in a Nutshell, 51 Harv.L.Rev. 638 (1938). The life in being is Philomena's son. No grandchild will be born to the testatrix once her son dies with a possible exception of an allowance being made for the gestation period. Hill v. Birmingham, 131 Conn. 174, 38 A.2d 604 (1944).

* * *

JUDGMENT AND REMEDY

The court held that distribution of the trust was to be made whenever the youngest of the grandchildren who were living at Philomena Lux's death attained the age of twenty-one. In reaching this decision, the appellate court held that the Rule Against Perpetuities had not been violated.

The Rule Against Perpetuities is in a state of transition. Because of the sometimes anomalous results obtained by a strict application of the rule, some jurisdictions have made slight modifications. The most notable of these are the *wait and see doctrine* and the *cy pres* doctrine. Under the wait and see doctrine, a period of time set by statute must pass before a conveyance is voided by the Rule. The example in which X conveyed Blackacre by will "to the first child born at Southern Methodist Hospital after my death" would likely be saved in a jurisdiction with a wait and see statute, since a child would surely be born at the hospital shortly after X's death. Literally translated, *cy pres* means "as nearly as possible." Under the *cy pres* doctrine, a conveyance that would violate the Rule against Perpetuities in its original form will be redrafted to conform to the intent of the grantor as nearly as possible without violating the rule. For example, if X conveys Blackacre by will "to the first of my grandchildren to reach twenty-five years of age," the age designated by the grantor will be reduced to twenty-one so that the conveyance will not be voided by the Rule.

NONPOSSESSORY INTERESTS

Ownership of land (freehold interests and interests less than freehold) is usually characterized by the owner's *possession* of the land. An owner of an interest in land can have a present right to possession, or, as in the case of future interests, can have a future right to possession. Some interests in land do not include any rights of possession. These interests, known as nonpossessory interests, include easements, profits, and licenses. Because easements and profits are similar, and the same rules apply to both, they will be discussed together.

Easements and Profits

An **easement** is the right of a person to make limited use of another person's property without taking anything from the property. For example, an easement can be the right to walk across another's property. A **profit** is the right to go onto land in possession of another and take away some part of the land itself or some product of the land. For example, R, the owner of Sandy View, gives A the right to go there and remove all the sand and gravel that A needs for her cement business. A has a profit. The differ-

ence between an easement and a profit is that an easement merely allows a person to use land without taking anything from it while a profit allows a person to take something from the land. Easements and profits can be classified as either *appurtenant* or *in gross*.

EASEMENT (OR PROFIT) APPURTENANT An easement or profit appurtenant arises where the owner of one piece of land has a right to go onto (or remove things from) an adjacent piece of land owned by another. Suppose W, the owner of Whiteacre, has a right to drive his or her car across G's land, Greenacre, which is adjacent to Whiteacre. This right of way over Greenacre is an easement appurtenant to Whiteacre and can be used only by the owner of Whiteacre. W can convey the easement when he or she conveys Whiteacre.

The outstanding feature of an easement appurtenant is that it involves two pieces of land owned by two different persons. The parcels of land and the persons who own them are known respectively as the *dominant tenement*, the *servient tenement*, the *dominant tenant*, and the *servient tenant*. In the example above, Whiteacre is the dominant tenement, since it is benefited by the easement, and Greenacre is the servient tenement, since it is burdened by the easement. In addition, W is the dominant tenant, since he or she is the owner of Whiteacre, and G is the servient tenant.

EASEMENT (OR PROFIT) IN GROSS An easement or profit in gross exists when the right to use or take things from another's land is not dependent upon the owner of the easement or profit also owning an adjacent tract of land. Suppose Z owns a parcel of land with a marble quarry. Z conveys to the XYZ Corporation, which owns no land, the right to come onto Z's land and remove up to five hundred pounds of marble per day. XYZ Corporation owns a profit in gross. An easement or profit in gross requires the existence of only one piece of land that must be owned by someone other than the owner of the easement or profit in gross.

Effect of Sale of Property

Whenever a parcel of land that is benefited by an easement or profit appurtenant is sold, the property carries the easement or profit along with it. Thus, if W sells Whiteacre to T and includes the appurtenant right-of-way across Greenacre in the deed to T, T will own both the property and the easement that benefits it.

When a piece of land that has the burden of an easement or profit appurtenant is sold, the new owner must recognize its existence only if he or she knew or should have known of it or if it was recorded in the appropriate office of the county. Thus, if W records his easement across Greenacre in the appropriate county office before G conveys the land, the new owner of Greenacre will have to allow W, or any subsequent owner of Whiteacre, to continue to use the path across Greenacre.

Creation of an Easement (or Profit)

Profits and easements can be created by *deed* or *will* or by *implication, necessity,* or *prescription.* Creation by deed or will simply involves delivery of a deed or disposition in a will by the owner of an easement stating that the grantee (the person receiving the profit or easement) is granted the rights in the easement or profit that the grantor had. An easement or profit is created by *implication* when the circumstances surrounding the division of a piece of property imply its creation. For example, suppose B divides a parcel of land that has only one well for drinking water and conveys the half without a well to D. Here, a profit by implication arises, since D needs drinking water. An easement by *necessity* does not require division of property for its existence. A person who rents an apartment by necessity has an easement in the private road leading up to it.

Easements and profits *by prescription* arise when one person uses another person's land for a period of time equal to the statute of limitations for recovery of property. If the owner of the land does not object to the use of the land for the required period of time, the person using the land has an easement or profit by prescription. Suppose Alfred Carin owns a plot of land with an old coal mine on it. Carin's neighbor, Max Beta, goes onto Carin's land every Sunday, Monday, and Tuesday and removes several wheelbarrows of coal for a period of seven years. The applicable statute of limitations for recovery of real property is five years. In this situation, Beta has a profit by prescription since he has openly taken coal for the limitations period without any objection from Carin, and Carin can no longer object. Beta owns the profit and can continue taking the coal as long as he wants. Of course, Beta cannot take substantially more coal than he took in the past. Thus, if he started a regular mining operation, Carin could stop him.

TERMINATION An easement or profit is terminated or extinguished in several ways. The simplest means of extinguishing it is deeding it back to the owner of the land that is burdened by it. Second, the owner of an easement or profit can abandon it and create evidence of his or her intent to relinquish the right to use it. Mere nonuse will not extinguish an easement or profit *unless it is accompanied by an intent to abandon.* Third, when the owner of an easement or profit becomes the owner of the property burdened by it, then it is merged into the property. Essentially, the individual now owns both the easement or profit and the land, so there is no need for the easement or profit to continue. The individual can simply use the land as owner in fee simple.

Licenses

A license is the revocable right of a person to come onto another person's land. It is a personal privilege that arises from the consent of the owner of the land and that can be revoked by the owner. Therefore, unlike easements or profits, a license cannot arise by prescription, since a prescriptive claim is, by definition, adverse to the rights of the property owner.

An example of a license is a ticket to attend a movie at a theater. A theater owner issues the ticket, which entitles the holder to enter onto the property of the owner. Another example of a license arises when a landowner sells personal property that is located on the land. For example, Ferguson purchases a tractor owned by Wilson that Wilson has left in the middle of his cornfield. Ferguson's purchase gives him the license to enter onto the cornfield to remove the tractor. A person who has property rights in the nature of a license can also have contractual rights. Since the rights of a licensee are revocable at the will of the licensor, a person should always look to the possible existence of an underlying contract to bolster his or her rights against the licensor.

LAND USE CONTROL

Land use control deals with the *limitations* placed upon property owners that either arise by agreement (covenants running with the land, equitable servitudes) or are imposed by the government (zoning).

Covenants
Running with the Land

A **covenant running with the land** is an agreement under which a landowner either acquires certain rights or is under certain obligations merely because he or she owns the land that is bound by the covenant. A covenant running with the land lies somewhere between a contract and an easement or profit appurtenant. Instead of binding person to person (as a contract does) or land to land (as an easement does), a covenant running with the land binds a person to land. Consider an example. Y is the owner of Grasslands, a twenty-acre estate whose northern half contains a small reservoir. Y wishes to convey the northern half to Arid City, but before she does, she digs an irrigation ditch connecting the reservoir with the lower ten acres that she uses as farmland. When Y conveys the northern ten acres to Arid City, she enters into an agreement with the city. The agreement, which is contained in the deed, states, "Arid City, its heirs and assigns, promise not to remove more than five thousand gallons of water per day from the Grasslands reservoir." Y has created a covenant running with the land under which Arid City and all future owners of the northern ten acres of Grasslands are limited to the amount of water they can draw from its reservoir.

Four requirements must be met for a covenant running with the land to be enforceable. If they are not met, a simple contract is created between the two original parties only.

1. The covenant running with the land must be created in a written agreement (covenant). It is usually contained in the document that conveys the land (deed or will).
2. The parties must intend that the covenant *run with the land*. In other words, the instrument that contains the covenant must state not only that the promissor is bound by the terms of the covenant but that all the promissor's "successors, heirs, or assigns" will be bound.
3. The covenant must *touch and concern* the land. The limitations on the activities of the owner of the burdened land must have some connection with the land. For example, a purchaser of land cannot be bound by a covenant requiring him or her to drive only Ford pickups, since such a restriction has no relation to the land purchased.
4. The original parties to the covenant must be in *privity of estate* at the time the covenant is created. This means that the relationship between them must be landlord-tenant, vendor-purchaser, testator-devisee, and so forth. Note that this is unlike an easement appurtenant, which can be created by two parties who merely own adjoining land and are not in privity of estate.

Equitable Servitudes

Because of the confusion over the meaning and application of the privity of estate requirement, covenants running with the land have not been a very effective device for guiding the development of residential and commercial land. Therefore, courts of equity have created an alternative means of private land use control known as **equitable servitudes**. Covenants running with the land and equitable servitudes are similar in their application and effect, but the requirements for enforcing an equitable servitude are somewhat less stringent. An equitable servitude is created by an instrument that complies with the Statute of Frauds, an intention that the use of land be restricted, and *notice* of the restriction to the person acquiring the burdened land. For example, A owns two adjacent lots, Brownacre and Redacre. A conveys Redacre to the city of Pleasantville, stipulating in the deed that it be utilized only as a wildlife sanctuary and that no buildings be built on it. A also records the restriction in the county land records office. Thereafter, when the Ace Construction Company purchases Redacre from Pleasantville with the intention of building office buildings on it, it is bound by the restrictions that A placed on the land even if the restrictions are not contained in the deed by which it obtains the land from Pleasantville. Because the restrictions are recorded in the appropriate county office, Ace Construction Company is deemed to be on *constructive notice* of the restrictions.

Developers generally utilize equitable servitudes when developing a large parcel of land and subdividing it into residences. The developer will file a **plat** in the county records office that describes the land being developed and the restrictions under which each subdivided lot is sold.[1]

Equitable servitudes and covenants running with the land have also been used to perpetuate neighborhood segregation. For example, property owners in entire neighborhoods sometimes joined together and conveyed

their homes to a straw man (usually a lawyer) who wrote in a restrictive covenant proscribing resale to minority groups. The straw man would then reconvey the property to the initial owners. In the Supreme Court case of Shelley v. Kraemer, such restrictive covenants were declared unconstitutional and could no longer be enforced in a court of law.[2] In addition, the Civil Rights Act of 1968 (also known as the Fair Housing Act) prohibits all discrimination based on race, color, religion, or national origin in the sale and leasing of housing.

Zoning

The government is by far the most potent force in guiding the development and use of land. State and local governments have far greater resources and enforcement powers than private individuals to control land use. Moreover, since, ideally, the government represents majority interests, it is in the best position to determine land uses that reflect the needs of society as a whole.

The state's power to control the use of land is derived from two sources: eminent domain and police power. Through eminent domain, the government can take land for public use, but it must pay just compensation, so this is an expensive method of land use control. Under its police power, however, the state can pass laws aimed at protecting public health, safety, morals, and general welfare. These laws can affect owners' rights and uses of land, but the state does not have to compensate the landowner. If the state's legislation restricts the landowner's property rights too much, the state's *regulation* will be deemed a *confiscation* and subject to the eminent domain requirements that just compensation be paid. For example, suppose Jones owns a large tract of land that she purchased with the intent to subdivide and develop into residential properties. At the time of the purchase, there were no zoning regulations restricting use of the land. If the state attempts to zone Jones's entire tract of land as "parkland only" and prohibits her from developing any part of it,

---

1. A plat, also called a plot, is a map or representation on paper of a piece of land subdivided into lots, with streets, alleys, and so forth usually drawn to scale. When filed with the appropriate records office, the plat contains the restrictions under which the subdivided lots have been sold.

2. 334 U.S. 1, 68 S.Ct. 836 (1948).

the action will be deemed confiscatory, since the government will be denying her the ability to use her property for any purpose for which it is reasonably suited. The state will have to compensate Jones, since it has effectively confiscated her land. However, if the state zones Jones's parcel of land as "three-fourths residential, one-fourth park area" after her purchase, this zoning regulation is not confiscatory since she will be able to use most of the property for building residences.

The state's power to regulate the use of land is limited in two other ways, both of which arise from the Fourteenth Amendment. First, the state cannot regulate the use of land arbitrarily or unreasonably, since this would be a denial of property without due process. There must be a *rational basis* for the classifications that the state imposes on the property. Note, however, that this limitation is not very stringent. Any act that is reasonably related to the health or general welfare of the public has a rational basis. Second, a state's regulation of land use control cannot be discriminatory. The state is prohibited from discriminating against any race, religion, or nationality. The state is also generally prohibited from discriminating against any other group as well. Discrimination on the basis of race, religion, or national origin is never justifiable. However, discrimination based on other factors (for example, low income versus high income groups) may be upheld if there is a rational basis for the discrimination.

Nonconforming Use

The problems associated with zoning are often the result of normal growing pains experienced by expanding suburban areas that once were rural in nature. John Gordon, a chicken farmer, has lived with his family in Charlesville and has been a chicken farmer all his life. Since Charlesville is located only eighty miles from Megalopolis, a booming sunbelt town, it is being invaded by suburbanites. Charlesville had never heard of zoning until the late 1960s, when its newly-elected zoning board decided that the 125 acres surrounding Gordon's 2 acre chicken farm were best suited for suburban residents.

Gordon appealed to the zoning board, claiming that his chicken farm, originally owned by his father, was located on the same 2 acres for seventy-five years. After hearing Gordon's plea, the zoning board gave him two years to close down and move his business. Gordon's chicken farm, which was in operation long before his area was zoned, is known as a **nonconforming use.** If the zoning ordinance called for Gordon's immediate removal, this would be confiscatory, and the government body promulgating the ordinance would have to pay just compensation for taking the farm. But as long as the nonconforming use is permitted to continue for a reasonable period of time, it is not deemed a taking of property, and therefore no compensation is necessary.

Floating Zones

Generally, the state agency charged with the responsibility of land use planning can take one of two approaches. The first is to designate, all at once, use restrictions on each parcel of land located within the entire area to be zoned (usually a city or town). Alternatively, the state agency can use "floating zones," deciding initially how much land should be designated for each of a variety of particular uses (commercial, residential, park, farming) and later assigning such designations at the request of landowners. Under the "floating zone" concept, the amount of land to be used for any one purpose is determined at the outset, but it is not assigned in what otherwise might be an arbitrary manner. This allows for flexibility in zoning.

Variance

A landowner whose land has been limited by a zoning ordinance to a particular use cannot make an alternative use of the land unless he or she first obtains a zoning variance. A landowner must meet three criteria to be entitled to a variance:

1. The landowner must find it impossible to realize a reasonable return on the land as zoned.

2.   The adverse effect of the zoning ordinance must be particular to the person seeking the variance and not one that has a similar effect on the other landowners within the same zone.

3.   A granting of the variance must not alter the essential character of the zoned area substantially.

By far the most important criterion used in granting a variance is whether it will alter the character of the neighborhood substantially. Courts tend to be rather lenient about the first two requirements. As the following case shows, courts also tend to defer to the discretion of zoning boards unless they have abused it.

CONNER v. HERD
Court of Appeals of Missouri,
1970. 452 S.W.2d 272.

BACKGROUND AND FACTS   *The city of Moline planned to build a new firehouse on land that was appropriately zoned for construction of a firehouse. However, the proposed firehouse was slightly larger than the zoning ordinances allowed. Thus, in April 1963, Moline filed with the Board of Zoning Adjustment of St. Louis County for variances from the set-back and building line provisions in the ordinance. Essentially, the city's plans called for construction of a building that would be set back about four feet farther than the zoning allowed. Alfred and Marie Conner, who owned adjacent property that faced the site of the new construction, objected to the variance. The variance was granted, and the Conners appealed the board's ruling to the courts.*

SMITH, Justice.
* * *
The genesis of the litigation was the filing by Moline in April, 1963, of an application to the Board for variances from the set-back and building line provisions. * * *

* * * [A]ppellants contend the findings of the Board were arbitrary and capricious and not based upon competent and substantial evidence. We take these in order.
* * *

"JURISDICTION AND POWERS.—The Board of Zoning Adjustment is hereby authorized to: (5) Permit a variation in the yard requirements of any Zoning District or the building and set back lines for Major Highways as provided by law where there are practical difficulties or unnecessary hardships in the carrying out of these provisions due to an irregular shape of the lot, topographical or other conditions, provided such variation will not seriously affect any adjoining property or the general welfare."

This provision, under which the Board acted here, empowers the Board to give variances under specified circumstances where strict enforcement of the regulations would be unjust. It imposes standards for the Board's action and is not a grant of legislative power.

This brings us to the heart of this appeal, appellants' contention that the action of the Board was not based on competent and substantial evidence and was arbitrary and capricious. Neither this court nor the trial court can substitute its judgment on the evidence for that of the Board. We may only determine whether the Board could reach the conclusion it did upon the evidence before it. We hold it could.
* * *

Having in mind the limited scope of our review of the findings of the Board we turn to the evidence which supports the Board's order. The property in question is on the northwest corner of Chambers Road and Clairmont Drive in an unincorporated portion of St. Louis County. Chambers Road is a major thoroughfare which was widened shortly before the application for variance. The land in question is owned by Moline and has been the site for its fire station since at least 1946. The old fire house complied with the Chambers Road set-back line but not with the Clairmont Drive building line upon which it encroached approximately 4½ feet as a pre-existing use.

* * *

The most efficient and satisfactory type of fire station for Moline's purposes is one where returning trucks can enter the back of the station from Clairmont Drive, remove the hoses and other equipment for cleaning, put clean equipment on the truck and move the truck into position for exit through the front onto Chambers Road for the next call. The lot in question is 165 feet in depth (after the widening of Chambers to 80 feet) and 80 feet in width. If the set-back line on Chambers Road, 80 feet, is adhered to there would not be enough room at the rear of the station (39 feet) for the large fire trucks to negotiate the turn from Clairmont Drive into the rear of the station. The entrance from Clairmont would also obviate the need for the trucks to back into the station from Chambers Road. There was also testimony that having the station located nearer the road than the old station would allow greater traffic safety in leaving the station in that both the dispatcher and the driver would have greater visibility along Chambers. This was based upon a difference in elevation of the property from front to rear of 6 feet, the front being higher. In view of testimony that regardless of where the station is located the trucks would have to slow down before entering Chambers Road to be sure the traffic was clear, we doubt that this evidence alone would be enough to establish a hardship based upon topographical conditions.

The width of the lot is such that a 2 foot variance on the building line of Clairmont Drive would be necessary to get the proposed fire station on the property if the regulation of a 6 foot side yard on the west (next to appellants) is met. The granted variance is less than the previously existing encroachment.

* * *

The Board could find here that in the absence of a variance Moline would be confronted with substantial additional expense, interruption of fire protection service during the period of construction, and unnecessary inconvenience if not outright danger to the residents of the district. The Board is not required to ignore the source of the funds available to the district (taxpayers) in determining that additional expense constitutes an unnecessary hardship. Under *Rosedale-Skinker, supra,* there exist sufficient "practical difficulties" and "unnecessary hardships" to the district to permit a variance and these arise from the inadequate size of the lot to contain a fire station. This was the essence of the Board's finding "that because of the requirements, the proposed new building and facilities cannot be erected as the eighty foot set back line on Chambers Road and the thirty foot building line on Clairmont Drive are intended."

Appellants contend that there is no evidence to support a conclusion that the variance will not "seriously affect any adjoining property." We do not agree. This contention must be judged only upon the effect of a variance, not upon the effect of a fire house. Appellants' contention is based solely upon the effect upon their property. The fire house to be constructed will be for the front 9 feet, one story in height. The remainder will be two stories. Some air conditioning equipment will be located on the roof of the one story section but the record does not require a conclusion that this will create an undue amount of noise or other disturbance affecting appellants' property, nor that any effect will be the result of the variance. Such equipment would actually be closer to appellants' home if the variance were not granted than if it were. It is also true that the proposed fire house will be 6 feet from appellants' property line and 13 feet from the edge of appellants' home. This, however, is not caused by the variance requested, for Moline could place the building that close without a variance. Appellants contend that the granting of the variance will reduce their view to the east. Appellant husband testified that he had paid $26,500 for his land and house and that "he felt" the proposed new fire house would damage him at least one-third to one-half the value of his property. He offered nothing to support his opinion, and could not state the fair market value of his home before or after the variance. Although such opinion evidence may be competent, its weight is for the trier of fact. Neither the Board, nor the trial court, nor this court is bound to accept such testimony as establishing the effect on appellants' property. Veal v. Leimkuehler, Mo.App., 249 S.W.2d 491 [9-12]. The Board had before it pictures of the area involved, taken from several different angles. It could determine from those pictures the degree to which appellants' view is reduced. It could take into account the improvement of traffic safety on Chambers Road, which would inure to appellants' benefit, which had been testified to. We do not doubt that there is some effect on appellants' property. That it is seriously affected we cannot hold as a matter of law on the record before us. Based upon the testimony and evidence before it, we cannot say there was no competent and substantial evidence to support the Board's finding in this regard.

The effect on general welfare finding is supported by the evidence of the need for the new building to render adequate fire protection to the district and by the testimony on the beneficial effect of the proposed construction upon traffic safety on Chambers Road, including the installation of a traffic light on Chambers Road to be controlled by the dispatcher when trucks leave the station.

JUDGMENT AND REMEDY	*The court found that the zoning board had enough evidence to grant the variance in accordance with the requirements of the zoning ordinance. The judgment of the circuit court, which had affirmed the action taken by the zoning board, was affirmed by the appellate court.*

QUESTIONS AND CASE PROBLEMS

1. Susan Barnard died in 1899. Her will created a trust for her son, Charles Barnard, and transferred certain assets that she owned at her death to a trustee. Her will further provided that the trustee "hold, manage, and keep invested one-third of the assets for

and during the life of my son Charles Inman Barnard: to pay the net income of such one-third in trust to my son Charles Inman Barnard for and during his life." The will went on to provide that the trust assets were to be transferred to Charles's issue (children), and "in default of such issue then to transfer said share to my granddaughter, Mary Curtis." Charles Barnard received the income from the trust during his life, but he died without marrying or having any children. Mary Curtis died before him. At the time the trust was created, what interest did Charles Barnard have?

What interest, if any, did Mary Curtis have? Does Mary Curtis's untimely death affect her interest? [Williams v. Welch, 358 Mass. 514, 265 N.E.2d 854 (1970)]

2. Dixie Gardens, Inc. was a developer in Pasco County, Florida. Henry Sloane purchased a lot and residence from a Dixie Gardens development. The deed read in part as follows: "If the developer or the Crestridge Utilities Corporation causes garbage collection service bi-weekly to be made available, the owner of each lot shall pay the developer or its assigns, the sum of $1.75 per month therefor." Sloane wished to employ another contractor for garbage collection, but Dixie Gardens argued that Sloane was bound by the provision quoted above, which amounted to a covenant running with the land. Is Dixie Gardens correct? [Sloane v. Dixie Gardens, Inc., 278 So.2d 309 (Fla. App. 1973)]

3. In 1961, Mary Schaefers divided her real property and conveyed it to her children, William, Elfreda, Julienne, and Rosemary. The deed from Mary Schaefers to her daughter Rosemary contained the following language: "It is further mutually agreed by and between the grantor and the grantee that as part of the consideration set out above, the grantee agrees to provide a permanent home for my daughter, Elfreda, should she desire or request one, and for my son, William Schaefers, should he desire or request one. Failure to perform the above will be considered a material breach of the consideration set out herein." In 1974, Rosemary conveyed her portion of her mother's property to Edward and Arthur Apel. Subsequently, William Schaefers attempted to prevent the sale to the Apels from taking place by telling them that the house was encumbered by a covenant running with the land and that if they purchased the house, they would be bound to provide a home for William and Elfreda Schaefers. Is Rosemary's promise to provide a home for William and Elfreda (should they demand one) a covenant running with the land? [Schaefers v. Apel, 295 Ala. 277, 328 So.2d 274 (1976)]

4. Charles W. Parker died leaving a valid will that placed his property in trust and paid the income from the trust to his wife, Emma, for the remainder of her life. The will provided that at Emma's death the trust assets were to be taken out of trust and given "to William H. Parker [Charles's brother]; but if William H. Parker is not living at the death of my wife, Emma, then his share should vest in the Presbyterian Church of Carlyle." What is the nature of Emma's interest? of William H Parker's interest? Of the Presbyterian Church of Carlyle's interest? [Presbyterian Church of Carlyle v. St. Louis Union Trust Co., 18 Ill.App.3d713, 310 N.E.2d 412 (1974)]

5. Plastics Company, Inc. was the lessor of certain premises in New Jersey that it used to store goods designated for shipment. Attached to the leased buildings was a loading platform, and in front of the loading platform was a short driveway leading to the street. After loading merchandise onto one of its trucks, Plastics Company left the truck in the driveway overnight and the next morning found that the goods had been stolen. Plastics Company sought to recover under its insurance policy with Travelers Indemnity Company. The insurance policy, however, applied only to goods in transit. The policy explicitly provided: "This policy does not insure property while it is located in or on premises, owned, leased, or occupied by the assured." The court determined that if the driveway on which the truck was parked at the time of the theft could be deemed an easement, then the truck would be deemed to be on "leased premises," and the insurance policy would not cover the theft. How could the lawyer for the Travelers Indemnity Company argue that the driveway constituted an easement? [Den Gre Plastics Co. v. Travelers Indem. Co., 107 N.J.Super. 535, 259 A.2d 485 (1969)]

6. Columbus Cosmetic Corporation and Shoppers Fair of South Bend, Inc. entered into an agreement whereby Shoppers Fair granted Columbus "an exclusive license to occupy 1,500 square feet of space in Shoppers Fair of South Bend for the purpose of selling drugs, cosmetics, etc." The agreement became effective in February 1960 and was to extend for a period of five years. Columbus had the right to renew for an additional five years provided it gave a one-year written notice. Shoppers Fair had the right to terminate the agreement after one year by giving written notice to Columbus at least sixty days before April in any year of the agreement, "but only if Columbus's sales during any lease year immediately preceding such notice are not more than 4 percent of the gross sales of the Shoppers Fair store." The agreement further provided that Columbus would pay Shoppers Fair 7 percent of its gross receipts or $9,600 each year, whichever was greater. Does Columbus's right to occupy floor space at Shoppers Fair constitute a license, or is it something more? [Columbus Cosmetic Corp. v. Shoppers Fair of South Bend, 26 App.Div.2d 391, 275 N.Y.S.2d 135 (1966)]

7. On November 21, 1967, North Clearlake Development Corporation entered into a contract with Clearlake Utilities Company that provided that "Clearlake Utilities Company shall have and is hereby granted the exclusive right to furnish water

and sewer service" to the approximately eighty acres of land that North Clearlake Development Corporation had developed and to "all owners and occupants of any part thereof for and during the entire term of this contract." At the time of the contract, North Clearlake Development Corporation owned a large tract of land that it had just begun developing. Will the contract between Clearlake Utilities and North Clearlake Development constitute a covenant running with the land, binding all persons who thereafter purchase lots and homes in the development? [Clearlake Apartments, Inc. v. Clearlake Utilities Co., 537 S.W.2d 48 (Tex.Civ.App. 1976)]

8.   In his will, Fletcher devised land to his granddaughter for life, then to the heirs of her body, if any, and if not, then to Fletcher's son, his heirs, and assigns. Assuming that at the time Fletcher dies, his only granddaughter is seven years old, what is the nature of her interest? What interest, if any, do the "heirs of her body" have? [Fletcher v. Hurdle, 259 Ark. 640, 536 S.W.2d 109 (1976)]

9.   Under a zoning ordinance enacted on November 14, 1960, and effective January 1, 1961, a 460-acre parcel of land in Ulster County was designated an "agricultural zone." Shortly before the effective date of the ordinance, Kart Wheelers Raceway, Inc. began construction of a two-acre go-cart raceway on a tract of land located on part of the area that was zoned for agriculture. Prior to the enactment of the ordinance, Kart Wheelers had expended the sum of $487 for work performed on the premises for the purpose of readying it for the raceway. The facilities were completed in August 1961 at a total cost of $33,000. The town of Lloyd then attempted to enforce the zoning ordinance against Kart Wheelers Raceway, seeking to have it remove the go-cart raceway *immediately*. Kart Wheelers claimed that the town could not force it to remove the raceway since the raceway constituted a "nonconforming use." Is Kart Wheelers correct in its assertion? [Town of Lloyd v. Kart Wheelers Raceway, 28 App.Div.2d 1015, 283 N.Y.S.2d 756 (1967)]

10.   Wilson owned a single-family home in a residentially zoned district in Harrison, Arkansas. Under local zoning ordinances, such a residence could be used for a home occupation, which the ordinance defined as one carried on solely by the inhabitants of the dwelling. Wilson sought permission from the Harrison zoning board to employ an outsider. The board granted the permission. The City of Harrison, however, appealed the board's decision on the ground that the board had authority only to grant a variance and that it had exceeded its power in authorizing a "nonconforming use." In addition, the city argued that, under the circumstances, the board should not have authorized Wilson to employ an outsider regardless of whether it had the authority to do so. Discuss the merits of the board's action and of the city's appeal. [City of Harrison v. Wilson, 248 Ark. 736, 453 S.W.2d 730 (1970)]

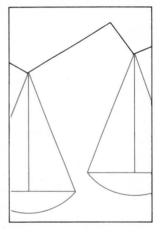

54

Insurance

THE NATURE OF INSURANCE

Insurance is a contract by which the insurance company (insurer) promises to pay a sum of money or give something of value to another (either the insured or the beneficiary) in the event that the insured is injured or sustains damage as the result of particular stated contingencies. Basically, insurance is an arrangement for *transferring and allocating risk*. In many cases, **risk** can be described as a prediction concerning potential loss, based on known and unknown factors. However, insurance involves much more than a game of chance, and insurers have an interest in seeing that risk is minimized. Many familiar safety devices are now commonplace because of insurance laws—automobile seat belts, fire escapes, train whistles, railroad crossing lights, reflecting road signs, and break-away highway lightposts, among others.

The Concept of Risk Pooling

All types of insurance use the principle of pooling of risk; that is, they spread the risk among a large number of people—the pool—to make the premiums small compared to the coverage offered. Consider life insurance. For any particular age group, only a small number of individuals will die in any one year. If a large percentage of this age group pays premiums to a life insurance company in exchange for a benefit payment in case of premature death, there will be a sufficient amount of money to pay the beneficiaries of the policyholders who do die. Given a long enough time for correction of data about the group and the particular disaster—in this case premature death—insurance companies can predict the total number of premature deaths in any one year with great accuracy. Thus, they can estimate the total amount they will have to pay if they insure the group, and they can predict the rates they will have to charge each member of the group in order to make the necessary payments and make a profit for the company.

Classification of Insurance

Insurance is classified according to the nature of the risk involved. For example, there is fire insurance, casualty insurance, life insurance, title insurance, and so forth. The persons and interests protected under each of these types of insurance policies differ. This is reasonable because, depending upon the nature of the activity, certain types of losses are expected, certain types are foreseeable, and certain others are unforeseeable.

Terminology

An insurance contract is called a **policy**; the consideration paid to the insurer is called a **premium**; and the insurance company is sometimes called an underwriter.

PARTIES   The *parties* to an insurance policy are the insurer (the insurance company) and the insured (the person obtaining the insurance policy and covered by its provisions). Insurance contracts are usually obtained through an *agent*, who ordinarily works for the insurance company, or a *broker*, who is ordinarily an independent contractor. When a broker deals with an applicant for insurance, the broker is, in effect, the applicant's agent. By contrast, an insurance agent is an agent of the insurance company. Thus, an insurance agent's relationship with the applicant for insurance is controlled by ordinary rules of agency law (see Chapter 34). As a general rule, the insurance company is bound by the acts of its agents when they act within the agency relationship. On the other hand, a

broker has no relationship with the insurance company and is an agent of the applicant for insurance. The status of agent or broker can be extremely important in determining liability. In most situations, state law determines the status of all parties writing or obtaining insurance. In some states, the broker and agent are treated identically, but in others they are not.

INSURABLE INTEREST   A person can insure anything in which he or she has an *insurable interest*. For example, a person has an insurable interest in his or her own health or life and in the health or life of his or her spouse. But a person cannot obtain fire insurance on the White House or auto insurance on A. J. Foyt's race cars. A person has an insurable interest in property if damage to or destruction of the property will cause that person a *direct pecuniary or monetary loss*. It is immaterial whether a person is a legal or equitable owner of the property being insured. If the person is in possession of the property, then he or she has an insurable interest. Thus, if A. J. Foyt lends someone one of his race cars for the weekend, that person has an insurable interest in the car for that period of time. (See the discussion of bailments in Chapter 16.) An insurable interest must exist at the time the loss occurs but not necessarily at the time the policy or contract of insurance is entered into, unless state statute provides otherwise. For example, B purchases an automobile, taking title in her name but intending the vehicle to be used by T. The insurance company issues a policy naming T as the insured. T uses the car for a period of time, decides to leave the state, and returns the car to B with no intention of ever using it again. Sometime later, B decides to sell the car. A potential buyer tests it and is involved in an accident. The insurance company can successfully defend against paying for the prospective buyer's accident. When T voluntarily abandoned the use of the vehicle, T's insurable interest ceased to exist.[1]

Insurable interest applying to life insur-

1.   See Universal C.I.T. v. Foundation Reserve Ins. Co., 79 N.M. 785, 450 P.2d 194 (1969).

ance is somewhat different. Every person has an insurable interest in his or her own life and can therefore insure it, naming anyone as beneficiary.

A person has an insurable interest in the life of another person if the person expects to receive some pecuniary gain from the fact that the other person's life continues or expects to suffer financial loss if the other person dies. Hence, a creditor can have an insurable interest in the life of a debtor because the death of the debtor may mean that the creditor will not be paid. In some instances, creditors do take out insurance policies on the life of debtors. However, if the creditor's insurance policy is unreasonably large—that is, substantially greater in amount than the debt—the policy may be void.

Consider two examples that illustrate the concept of insurable interest more clearly. James Jones insures his life for $100,000 with Continental Insurance Company, naming Henry Mason as beneficiary of the policy. When Jones dies, Continental Insurance cannot

refuse to pay Mason merely because he had no insurable interest in the life of Jones. The beneficiary of a life insurance policy need not have an insurable interest in the insured. Jones was actually insuring his own life for the benefit of Mason. Obviously, Jones has an insurable interest in his own life. On the other hand, if Jones bought a policy with Continental Insurance to insure the life of his next door neighbor, Robert Samuel, Continental Insurance could refuse to pay the face value of the policy upon Samuel's death because Jones had no insurable interest in Samuel's life.

The existence of an insurable interest is a primary concern when determining liability under an insurance policy. In the following case, the insurance company claimed that the policyholders had lost their insurable interest in certain real property by leasing the premises to a third party. Moreover, since the plaintiffs (the policyholders) had not demonstrated any actual loss, they had no interest in the property and, hence, no insurable interest. At trial, the judge agreed with the insurance company's argument.

BACKGROUND AND FACTS *In 1969, the plaintiffs purchased a $32,000 insurance policy against fire loss effective for three years. The property insured under the policy was a gas station. After they purchased the policy, the plaintiffs leased the service station and the land to Shell Oil Company for an initial term of fifteen years, with a renewal option of three additional five-year terms.*

Other parts of the lease provided that Shell could demolish and remove the existing building within one year and build a new ranch-style service station. In addition, Shell was obligated and exclusively entitled to insure any building it constructed during the term of the lease.

In 1971, the station was destroyed by fire. It had been scheduled for demolition but was still being used at the time of the fire. The court first examined the argument that the lease destroyed the plaintiffs' insurable interest in the property.

GENDRON v. PAWTUCKET MUT. INS. CO.
Supreme Judicial Court of Maine, 1978.
384 A.2d 694.

WERNICK, Justice.
* * *

The existence of an insured's insurable interest in property covered by a contract of insurance is determined by the relationship between the insured and the property insured—more specifically, by whether there is a relationship such that injury to the property will, as a natural consequence, result in a loss to the insured.

Since the question of insurable interest thus necessarily involves the insured's relationship to the property insured, we conclude that even if plaintiffs had purported by an executory contract to give a third person exclusive entitlement to place insurance on property already insured by plaintiffs, that fact is not by itself sufficient to terminate plaintiffs' insurable interest in the insured property. Plaintiffs had not, here, made an actual transfer of such of their rights in the insured property as would destroy their insurable interest; the mere leasing of property is not such an alienation of it as destroys insurable interest. This being so, defendant insurance company may not treat the "exclusive right to insure" provisions in the lease with Shell as a waiver or surrender by plaintiffs, capable of redounding to the benefit of defendant insurance company, of plaintiffs' insurable interest in the property they had insured with defendant. The insurer simply cannot thus benefit from collateral contractual relations between the insured and a third person so long as the insured retains legal title to the property.

We turn to the referee's other rationale of decision: that plaintiffs lacked insurable interest because the fire caused them no actual loss.

We take as settled principles of law in Maine that (1) insurable interest signifies such a relationship to property "as will necessarily entail a pecuniary loss in case of its injury [or] destruction" and (2) the term "actual cash value" in the fire insurance policy signifies the fair market value of the insured property, as measured by the usual test of what a willing buyer would offer and a willing seller accept in a cash sale on an open and free market.

Under the plain language of the instant policy (in accordance with Maine's standard form of fire insurance policy), the actual cash value of the insured property is its fair market value *as of the time of its destruction by fire.* True, particular circumstances might render a building utterly worthless by the time fire consumes it; for example, if the process of demolition has been commenced, or if the owner has abandoned the building. If, however, the building has not been "irrevocably committed to demolition or abandoned", the insured retains an insurable interest. And the mere existence of an executory contract for demolition does not destroy the value of the building or deprive the owner of an insurable interest.

These principles have *a fortiori* application, here. Plaintiffs continued to have legal title to the property they had insured with defendant and thus had rights to recover damages in the event Shell should commit a breach of the lease and demolition agreement. Moreover, special circumstances existed here tending to show affirmatively that the building was not worthless at the time of the fire. Plaintiff Dolard Gendron was still operating the gasoline service station as a sub-lessee, and under a separate contract with Shell plaintiffs had retained rights to the salvage value of the old station, potentially valued at approximately $10,000.00, intending to use the materials to build another garage at another location.

Lastly, that plaintiffs had the benefit of Shell's contractual obligation to build a new service station to replace the old structure cannot support defendant's assertion that thereby plaintiffs lost an insurable interest. An insured's entitlement to be compensated for the value of insured property from sources other than the insurance does not destroy insurable interest of the insured in the insured property.

The decision that the plaintiffs lacked an insurable interest was in error, so the appeal was sustained. The judgment for the defendant was set aside, and the case was remanded to the superior court for further proceedings.

JUDGMENT AND REMEDY

KEY MAN INSURANCE Key man insurance involves an organization insuring the life of a person who is important to the organization. Typically, a partnership will insure the life of each partner because the death of any one partner will legally dissolve the firm and cause some degree of loss to the partnership. So, too, a corporation has an insurable interest in the life expectancy of a key executive whose death would result in financial loss to the company.

WHEN MUST AN INSURABLE INTEREST EXIST? The insurable interest in life insurance must exist *at the time the policy is obtained.* This is exactly the opposite of property insurance, where the insurable interest must exist at the time the loss occurs and not necessarily when the policy is purchased. Because of this rule involving life insurance, in most states a divorce will not affect a policy. If the divorced spouse is named as beneficiary, the divorce action will not automatically divest that spouse's right to the proceeds or to an insurable interest.

An insured can assign the proceeds of his or her life insurance policy to a third person (beneficiary) who has no insurable interest, but the reverse is not true. Only those who have an insurable interest in the other person's life, such as a close relative, creditor, business associate, or employer, can take out a life insurance policy.

INDEMNITY

In fire insurance policies, insurance coverage is usually an *indemnity*; that is, the insurance pays only for what is actually lost. This is usually the replacement value of the property minus any depreciation. In addition, once payment is made, the insurance company is entitled to "stand in the shoes" of the insured in pursuing any lawsuits arising from the incident. This is called the right of subrogation.

THE RIGHT OF SUBROGATION

The right of subrogation allows the insured's insurance company to request reimbursement from the person who caused the loss or from that person's insurance company. Suppose that Sarah Washington's car is completely wrecked in an accident and that the issue of negligence is not clear-cut. Washington's insurance company might pay to have the car fixed or replaced, but under the right of subrogation, it can attempt to collect from the other person's insurance company if negligence is proven. Once Washington receives payment from her insurance company, the company is subrogated to any claim she may have against the wrongdoer. In other words, Washington cannot collect once from her own insurance company and once from the other person's insurance company.

OTHER INSURANCE CLAUSES

Suppose in the example above that Washington has both medical insurance on her automobile policy and Blue Cross health insurance through her employer, General Motors. Suppose also that she is injured in the auto accident, and her total medical bills amount to $2,000. Washington cannot be reimbursed simultaneously by her General Motors Blue Cross group health insurance policy and by her automobile insurance policy. Most group insurance policies have a so-called "other insurance" or coordination of benefits clause stating that any person with more than one insurance policy on property or health cannot collect more than the total financial losses sustained. Consider another example. Edward Johnson takes out fire insurance on his house from two different companies, with each policy having a face value of $50,000. If Johnson's house burns down he will not be paid $100,000 if the replacement value of the house is only $50,000. Each insurance company will pay Johnson a pro rata share of the loss—in this case, 50 percent.

STATE REGULATION OF INSURANCE

Each state has its own laws regulating domestic insurance companies. Statutes provide the method of incorporation, licensing, supervision, liquidation of insurers, and the licensing and supervision of agents and brokers. State law also regulates foreign insurance companies that conduct business within the state.

THE INSURANCE CONTRACT

An insurance contract is governed by the general principles of contract law. The application for insurance is usually attached to the policy and made part of the insurance contract. An insurance applicant is bound by any false statements that appear in the application (subject to certain exceptions). Because the insurance company evaluates the risk factors based on the information included in the insurance application, misstatements or misrepresentations can void a policy, especially if the insurance company can show that it would not have extended insurance if it had known the facts.

Timing

When an insurance contract comes into effect is important. In some instances, the insurance applicant is not protected until a formal written policy is issued. In other situations, the applicant is protected between the time the application is received and the time the insurance company either accepts or rejects it. Four situations should be kept in mind:

1. A broker is merely the agent of an applicant. Therefore, if the broker fails to procure a policy,

the customer is not insured. According to general principles of agency law, if the broker fails to obtain policy coverage and the applicant is damaged as a result, then the broker is liable to the damaged applicant/principal for the loss.

2. A person who seeks insurance from an insurance company's agent will usually be protected from the moment the application is made, provided some form of premium has been paid. Between the time the application is received and either rejected or accepted, the applicant is covered (possibly subject to certain conditions, such as successfully passing a medical examination). Usually the agent will write a memorandum or **binder** indicating that a policy is forthcoming and stating its essential terms.

3. If the parties agree that the policy will be issued and delivered at a later time, the contract is not effective until the policy is issued and delivered or sent to the applicant, depending upon the agreement. Thus, any loss sustained between the time of application and the delivery of the policy is not covered.

4. Parties can agree that a life insurance policy will be binding at the time the insured pays the first premium. The policy, however, can be *expressly contingent* upon the applicant's passing a physical examination. If the applicant pays the premium and passes the examination, then the policy coverage is continuously in effect. If the applicant pays the premium but dies before having the physical examination, then the applicant's estate must show that the applicant would have passed the examination had he or she not died.

Coverage on an insurance policy can begin when the policy is issued or, depending upon the terms of the contract, after a certain period of time has elapsed.

Interpreting Provisions of an Insurance Contract

The words used in an insurance contract have their ordinary meaning and are interpreted in light of the nature of the coverage involved. Where there is an ambiguity in the policy, the provision is interpreted against the insurance company. When it is unclear whether an insurance contract actually exists because the written policy has not been delivered, the uncertainty will be determined against the insurance company. The court will presume that the policy is in effect unless the company can show otherwise.

BACKGROUND AND FACTS *The plaintiff sued both the insurance company and its agent for their negligent failure to process and procure insurance coverage for plaintiff's fishing boat before it was destroyed by fire. The court looked at the type of insurance the plaintiff requested and the type of insurance the defendants would have provided if a policy had been in effect.*

KEDDIE v. BENEFICIAL INS. INC.
Supreme Court of Nevada, 1978.
___Nev.___,580 P.2d 955.

THOMPSON, Justice.
* * *

[The plaintiff] Keddie, a resident of Las Vegas, owned a thirty-two-foot, steel hulled, gas powered vessel moored in or operating from Bristol Bay, Alaska. From 1964 to 1967 he had used the boat for commercial fishing. In the Spring of 1970, Keddie contacted McDonald about insurance for that boat. * * * He did not request commercial fishing coverage for the Summer of 1970, nor did he advise McDonald that the vessel was a commercial fishing boat.

McDonald contacted an insurance broker in San Francisco who reponded by letter advising that additional information would be required before the application could be processed. An insurance application was enclosed with the letter. That application was forwarded to Keddie who filled it out and returned it. The application was for Yacht insurance applicable only to vessels not used for commercial purposes. Indeed, the application did not include certain items of equipment which would indicate a commercial use of the vessel.

Upon receipt of the completed application, the San Francisco broker quoted a yearly rate to McDonald who in turn advised Keddie. Keddie rejected this quotation since he preferred six months coverage to that of a year and asked McDonald to obtain a six-month quote. McDonald attempted to do so. Meanwhile, Keddie left Las Vegas for Alaska advising McDonald that any correspondence should be sent to his, Keddie's, Las Vegas post office box. From there it would be forwarded by a friend to Keddie in Naknek, Alaska.

By letter of May 25, 1970, the San Francisco broker notified McDonald that it would not write a six months policy. On June 2, 1970, by letter, McDonald notified Keddie of that fact. The letter was forwarded to Alaska where it remained unclaimed until it was returned to Las Vegas in August 1970. Beneficial Insurance never issued a policy to Keddie.

On July 6, 1970, while engaged in commercial fishing off Bristol Bay, Alaska, the vessel caught fire and was completely destroyed.

[The court then analyzed the legal issue.]

Once an agreement to procure insurance has been reached the insurance agent is obliged to use reasonable diligence to place the insurance and seasonably [within a reasonable amount of time] to notify the client if he is unable to do so.

The agreement to procure, however, must be one for a policy of insurance which would have covered the loss incurred. Had an insurance policy been issued pursuant to Keddie's application for Yacht Insurance, such policy would not have covered the loss incurred. Consequently, there is no basis for liability of either Beneficial Insurance or McDonald [the defendants] to Keddie [the plaintiff].

JUDGMENT AND REMEDY

The judgment of the trial court was affirmed. The trial court was correct in ruling for the defendants since the policy applied for by the plaintiff would not have covered the loss anyway.

COMMENTS

Another way to analyze this case is to say that an insurance contract was never formed because the plaintiff and the defendant did not agree on all essential terms. For example, the plaintiff wanted six months of coverage, but the defendant could obtain coverage only for a minimum of a year. If an acceptance modifies any of the essential terms of a contract, it is really a counter-offer and must then be accepted by the other party in order to create an enforceable contract of insurance. Here, the plaintiff applied for a six-month policy, which was, in essence, rejected by a counter-offer for one-year coverage. This counter-offer was never accepted; in fact, the plaintiff's boat was destroyed by fire before the last communication was received. Thus, no insurance contract was ever formed.

INTERPRETATION

The courts are increasingly cognizant of the fact that most people have no special training and therefore do not understand the intricate terminology used in insurance policies. The following case illustrates this problem.

ROY v. ALLSTATE INS. CO.

Superior Court of Connecticut, Appellate Session, 1978. 34 Conn.Sup. 650, 383 A.2d 637.

BACKGROUND AND FACTS *The insured (the plaintiff) was covered by an accidental death and dismemberment policy that provided full coverage in the event of "total and irrecoverable loss of entire sight of an eye." The plaintiff was in an accident and had a traumatic cataract surgically removed from his eye. After surgery, the plaintiff was fitted with a contact lens in his right eye. He had some amount of vision with the contact lens but could not tolerate wearing it. In effect, his eye was of little functional value, and there was no medical assurance that his eyesight could ever be regained. The insurance company (defendant) denied coverage under the policy.*

ARMENTANO, Judge.
* * *

"[A]n insurance policy is a contract to be interpreted and enforced in accordance with the real intent of the parties. The language used in the policy must be given its ordinary meaning unless some special or technical meaning is intended." In considering the meaning of the phrase "irrecoverable loss of sight," we must ascertain the meaning of the contract which the insured would reasonably expect and consider the intent of the insured in procuring the insurance.

It has been held generally that policies which insure against the total and irrecoverable loss of entire sight protect the insured against the irrecoverable loss of the practical use of sight. * * * Recently, the word "irrecoverable," as used in an insurance contract similar to the one in this case, was defined to mean "not able to regain, [put back to a former state, or recapture]." Therefore, we hold that an insured should recover under this kind of insurance contract if, within the [one year] period of time limited by the policy, he has, owing to an accident, lost the practical use of an eye which he will never be able to regain or recapture.

* * * [The Court then applied its definition of irrecoverable to this case.] Two doctors who examined the plaintiff concluded that he had sustained a permanent disability and that his right eye was of little functional value without the use of the contact lens. Without the contact lens which the plaintiff first started to wear in April or May, 1974, he had no vision in his right eye. The longest period of time during which the plaintiff could wear the contact lens in any given day in April or May, 1974, was four hours. Sometime after May 22, 1974, he stopped wearing the contact lens because he was unable to get used to it.

* * * In any event a continuous loss of functional use of the eye came about when the plaintiff concluded some time later, for reasons which are not challenged, that he could no longer wear the contact lens and stopped using it * * *. [T]he plaintiff could not continue to use the lens and * * * his loss of sight, which he previously may have thought could be regained by use of the lens, was never actually recoverable because of his inability to wear the lens. * * *

It is clear that the average man purchasing a policy similar to the one in this case would reasonably expect to be insured for an injury to his eye of the type involved in this case where, within the [one year] period of coverage, vision could be restored only to the limited extent that it was restored here. * * *

The trial court was correct in permitting the plaintiff to recover insurance benefits under the policy.   **JUDGMENT AND REMEDY**

CANCELLATION OF INSURANCE POLICIES

Under most state laws, once the initial premium on a policy has been paid, the policy does not automatically lapse if the next premium is not paid on the due date. Most policies allow a **grace period** of thirty or thirty-one days.

However, once there is a default in the payment of a premium, the insurer may be required to take certain steps before cancelling the policy. A default in the payment of a life insurance premium may require the insurer to issue a paid-up policy in a smaller amount than

originally contracted, to provide extended insurance for a period of time, or to pay the cash surrender value of the policy. These are alternatives to cancellation. When the insurance contract expressly declares that the insurance company cannot cancel the policy, these alternatives are important. When the insurance company can cancel the policy, contract provisions or state statutes usually require that the insurer give advance written notice of cancellation. Of course, an insurer cannot cancel a policy (or refuse to write a renewal policy) because of the national origin or the race of an applicant. Moreover, an insurance company cannot cancel a policy in order to penalize an insured who has just appeared as a witness in a case against the company.

DEFENSES AGAINST PAYMENT TO THE INSURED

An insurance company can raise any of the defenses that would be valid in any ordinary action on a contract and some defenses that do not apply in ordinary contract actions. If the insurance company can show that the policy was procured by fraud, misrepresentation, or violation of warranties, it may have a valid defense for its nonpayment on a claim. (The insurance company may also have the right to disaffirm or rescind the insurance contract.) Improper actions, such as those that are against public policy or are otherwise illegal, can give the insurance company a defense against payment of a claim or allow it to rescind the contract.

The following case involved the issue of liability for fire damage resulting from the actions of one of the insured persons under a contract of insurance. Because the insureds were married, the company claimed that the wrongful act of one spouse was attributable to the other, thereby preventing either from recovering fire insurance proceeds.

STEIGLER v. INS. CO. OF NORTH AMERICA
Supreme Court of Delaware, 1977.
384 A.2d 398.

BACKGROUND AND FACTS   *The plaintiffs sued on an insurance policy issued by Insurance Company of North America (INA) for fire damage to their home. The lower court denied the plaintiffs recovery. The plaintiffs were a husband and wife who owned the property as tenants in the entirety and who were insured under an INA policy. It was undisputed that the husband deliberately set fire to the house, that his actions constituted fraud under the terms of the policy, and that the policy was void and he could not recover under it. It was equally undisputed that the wife was not involved in any way in the act. The wife claimed that she was not barred from recovering under the policy since she was an innocent cotenant and was entitled to her pro rata share of the fire insurance proceeds.*

DUFFY, Justice.
* * *

As we have noted, the policy contained a standard fraud provision rendering the policy void "in case of any fraud * * * by the *insured* relating thereto" (emphasis added); and the policy insured two persons: "Herbert F. Steigler and Arlene R. Steigler."

The [first] critical question, of course, relates to the meaning of the word "insured" in the fraud provision. Does it mean one or both of the Steiglers? The answer is by no means clear because the word "insured" is singular while two persons are named as the "insured," i.e., Herbert F. Steigler and Arlene R. Steigler. Thus, construction of the term is required.

In resolving the ambiguity in the Steigler-INA contract we refer to two rules of construction. First, where ambiguous, the language of an insurance contract is always construed most strongly against the insurance company which has drafted it.

Second, "an insurance contract should be read to accord with the reasonable expectations of the purchaser so far as the language will permit."

Applying these principles, we hold that an "ordinary person owning an undivided interest in property, not versed in the nice distinctions of insurance law, would naturally suppose that his individual interest in the property was covered by a policy which named him without qualification as one of the persons insured."
* * *

In our judgment * * * Mrs. Steigler had an interest in the property, the policy named her without qualification as one of the persons insured and she should not be barred from recovering under the policy by the fraud of the other co-tenant.

INA contends that because the Steiglers are married the arson of the husband bars recovery by his wife. The theory is that the contract terms govern any claim, the contract is voided by fraud, and that husband and wife are one person, i. e., together and inseparably they hold the entire estate.

We are not persuaded that the "oneness" theory which is, to say the least, somewhat "quaint" in this day and age, should override the other principles at stake here. When two persons own property as tenants in common, it is generally recognized, as INA concedes, that the interests may be separable and, therefore, an innocent tenant in common can recover a *pro rata* [proportionate] share of fire insurance proceeds. Thus, for example, had the Steiglers owned the property and the policy as "co-habitants" rather than as spouses, the general rule would have permitted rather than have barred her recovery. Without pausing to explore the equal protection problems which such a result might raise, we conclude that barring a wife from recovering because she is a wife would be contrary to the public policy clearly mandated by the Married Women's Act.
* * *

The lower court ruling was reversed. The wife was entitled to half the insurance policy proceeds for the fire damage. The case was remanded to the trial court's jurisdiction under instruction to enter a ruling in the wife's favor and award her half the insurance proceeds.

JUDGMENT AND REMEDY

REBUTTAL OF THE DEFENSES OF THE INSURANCE COMPANY

There are certain ways in which the insurance company can be prevented from asserting some defenses that are normally available. State statutes and case law provide for such estoppel. For example, if a company tells an insured that information requested on a form is optional, and the insured provides it anyway, the company cannot use the information to avoid its contractual obligation under the insurance contract. In the life insurance field, certain clauses become incontestable after a stated period of time. For example, statements as to the age of the insured, even though incorrect, normally do not allow the insurance company to escape payment upon the death of the insured. Typically, the time period after which estoppel for such defenses occurs is two years.

TYPES OF INSURANCE

Insurance policies are often classified by the type of risk they insure—for example, dental insurance, automobile liability coverage, theft insurance, flood insurance. The remainder of this chapter will discuss the general aspects of four types of insurance: (1) life insurance, (2) fire and homeowner's insurance, (3) automobile insurance, and (4) accident and health insurance.

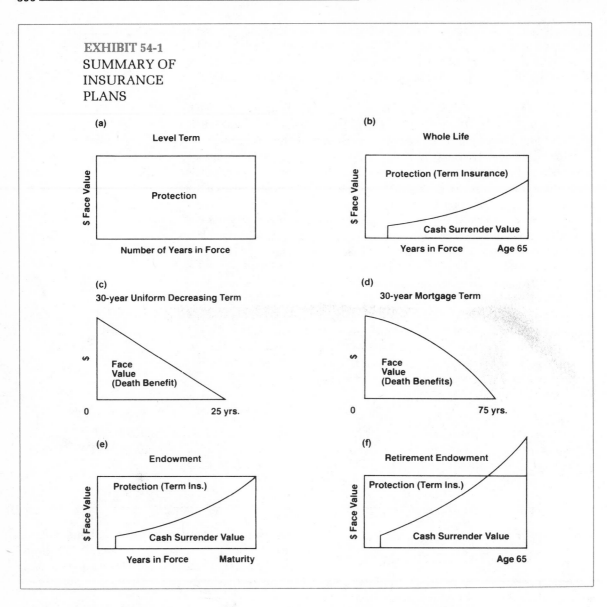

EXHIBIT 54-1
SUMMARY OF
INSURANCE
PLANS

TWO BASIC TYPES OF LIFE INSURANCE

There are basically two types of life insurance—term and whole life. **Term** offers "pure" protection. **Whole life**—also called straight life, ordinary life, or cash-value insurance—combines protection with a cash surrender value or saving fund. Exhibit 54-1 (panels a and b) illustrates the difference between term insurance and whole life insurance.

The Different Types of Term Insurance

There are three types of term insurance: (1) level, (2) decreasing, and (3) mortgage.

LEVEL TERM Premiums for level term insurance commonly increase at the end of each term, such as every five years, if the insured wishes to keep the same face value on the insurance policy. The increased premium reflects the rising probability of death as age increases.

DECREASING TERM Decreasing term insurance has a level premium but a decreasing face value, as illustrated in panel c of Exhibit 54-1.

MORTGAGE TERM Mortgage term insurance, or home protection plan, declines in face value an amount equal to the mortgage left to be paid. The idea is that if the insured dies, the home can be paid off with the proceeds. A mortgage term insurance policy decreases in uneven dollar amounts. (This type of insurance can insure other consumer debt also.)

Renewability and Convertibility

Term insurance policies often have other features. A term policy is called renewable if the coverage can be continued at the end of each period merely by paying the increased premium and without having a medical examination. Some policies are guaranteed renewable until the policyholder reaches retirement age.

Riders are often attached to term policies to permit the insured to convert the policy into whole life, for example, without having a medical examination. This convertibility feature of a term policy is often required by statute.

Whole Life Insurance

Whole life insurance premiums generally remain at the same level throughout the life of a policy. As a result, the policyholder pays more than is necessary to cover the insurance company's risk in the early years and less than is necessary to cover the company's risk in later years. Compared with term insurance, whole life is relatively more costly because it is a form of financial investment as well as insurance protection. The investment feature of the policy is known as its cash value.

LIVING BENEFITS Living benefits of a whole life policy include converting it into some sort of lump sum payment or stream of retirement income. When the insured reaches retirement age, premium payments on whole life can be discontinued and one of the following living benefit programs can be started:

1. Protection for the rest of the insured's life but at a lower face value.
2. Full protection but for a definite number of years in the future (extended term insurance).
3. A cash settlement that returns whatever savings and dividends have not been used to pay off the insurance company for excessive costs incurred for the particular age group of the insured (the cash surrender fund).
4. Conversion of a whole life policy into an annuity whereby the insured receives a specified amount of income each year for a certain number of years or for the rest of the insured's life.

BORROWING ON THE CASH VALUE OF THE POLICY One feature of a whole life insurance policy is that the insured can borrow on its cash value whenever needed. The interest rates on such loans are relatively favorable, as they should be, since the insured is in a sense borrowing his or her own money. Rates depend on the contract and the age of the policy. However, if the insured dies while the loan is outstanding, the sum paid to the beneficiary is reduced by the amount of the loan plus interest. In any event, this borrowing power can be considered as a cushion against financial emergencies.

DEATH BENEFITS In most life insurance policies, the insured specifies a beneficiary, who receives the death benefits of that policy. If Ken Kerr buys a $10,000 ordinary life policy and does not borrow any money on it, his beneficiary will receive $10,000 when he dies. However, there are certain options for settling a life insurance policy. The first plan involves a lump sum payment. In the second plan, the face value of the insurance policy is retained by the insurance company, but a small interest payment is made to the beneficiary for a certain number of years or for life. At the end of the specified period, the principal (face value) is then paid according to the terms in the contract. In the third plan, the face value is paid to the beneficiary in the form of annual, semiannual, quarterly, or monthly installments. The company makes regular payments of equal amounts until the fund is depleted. The insurance company guarantees a specific number of payments or payments that will total the face value of the policy. If, however, the beneficiary dies before the guaranteed payments have been made, the remainder goes to the estate of the beneficiary or as otherwise directed in the contract. This is sometimes called an annuity plan.

Other Types of Life Insurance Policies

There are numerous other types of life insurance policies. **Limited payment whole life** is a policy payable at the death of the insured, with little cash and surrender values. The premiums are paid for a stated number of years or until the insured reaches a certain age, such as sixty or sixty-five. An **endowment policy** offers a combination of temporary life insurance and a rapidly increasing cash surrender fund. It can be considered both a term insurance policy and a growing savings account. Exhibit 54-1, panel e, illustrates the main features of an endowment policy. A retirement endowment policy is one in which the insured continues paying until the cash surrender has exceeded the face value of the policy. This can be seen in panel f of Exhibit 54-1.

HOME, PROPERTY, AND LIABILITY INSURANCE POLICIES

There are basically two types of insurance policies for a home—standard fire insurance policies and homeowner's policies.

Standard Fire Insurance Policy

The standard fire insurance policy protects the homeowner against fire and lightning as well as damage from smoke and water caused by the fire or the fire department. Paying slightly more

will extend the coverage to damage caused by hail, windstorms, explosions, and so on. Personal theft and a comprehensive liability policy can also be added.

Homeowner's Policy

The homeowner's policy provides protection against a number of risks under a single policy, allowing the policyholder to save over the cost of buying each protection separately. In addition to a standard fire policy, liability coverage is also available.

There are basically two types of homeowner's policy coverage:

1. _Property coverage_ includes garage, house, and other private buildings on the policyholder's lot. It also includes the personal possessions and property of the policyholder at home, in traveling, or at work. It pays additional living expenses for living away from home because of a fire or some other covered peril.

2. _Liability coverage_ is for personal liability in case someone is injured on the insured's property, the insured damages someone else's property, or the insured injures someone else who is not in an automobile. It generally does not cover liability for professional malpractice.

Similar to liability coverage is coverage for medical payments for injury to others who are on the policyholder's property and for the property of others that is damaged by a member of the policyholder's family.

FORMS OF HOMEOWNER'S POLICIES   There are basically five forms of home and condominium owner's policies. Exhibit 54-2 describes each type. The basic form covers eleven perils, or risks; the broad form covers eighteen, and the comprehensive form covers those eighteen and all others.

Homeowners are not the only ones who take out insurance policies to cover losses. There is also renter's insurance, called "residence contents broad form" (HO-4). It covers personal possessions against the eighteen perils described in Exhibit 54-2. It also includes additional living expenses and liability coverage.

ADDING A PERSONAL ARTICLES FLOATER POLICY

An insured may wish to pay a slightly higher premium to insure specific personal articles—for example, cameras, musical instruments, works of art, jewelry, and other valuables. This is accomplished by adding a personal property or articles floater to a homeowner's policy. The insured submits a list of the things to be covered and some affidavits giving their current market value. Insuring under a floater provides all risk insurance, and the covered property can therefore be omitted from fire and theft policies.

PERSONAL EFFECTS FLOATER POLICY

A personal effects floater policy covers personal items when traveling. In most cases, it is not necessary because a regular homeowner's policy is sufficient coverage. This floater covers the articles only when they are taken off the insured's property. It does not cover theft from an unattended automobile unless there is evidence of forced entry, and even then, the company's liability is generally limited to 10 percent of the amount of insurance and to not more than $250 for all property in any one loss. This restriction in the policy can be removed by paying an additional premium.

COINSURANCE

As a general rule, 80 percent of the total value of a house should be insured— that is, 80 percent of its replacement value. If there is at least that much coverage, the full replacement cost of any damaged real property can be collected up to the limits of the policy. Say, for example, that the Perez roof is damaged in a fire, and it is going to cost Perez $2,500 to replace it. If he has at least 80 percent coverage on his house, his insurance company must pay him the full amount of the roof damage. But if his house is covered for less, he will get less— the amount of insurance in force divided by 80 percent of the replacement cost of the entire house times the loss on the roof.

Suppose Perez's house has a replacement value of $50,000 and he has insurance equal to $30,000. To find out what his insurance company pays, multiply the amount of loss for his roof in the preceding example ($2,500) by the amount of insurance in force over $40,000 (80 percent of total replacement value). Thus, his insurance company will pay

$$\$2,500 \quad x \quad \frac{\$30,000}{\$40,000} \quad = \quad \$1,875.$$

If he had had $40,000 worth of insurance coverage, he would have received the full $2,500 to replace the roof.

AUTOMOBILE INSURANCE

There are basically two kinds of automobile insurance: liability insurance and comprehensive and collision insurance.

Property Damage and Bodily Injury Liability

One kind of automobile insurance covers bodily injury and property damage liability. Liability limits are usually described by a series of three numbers, such as 25/50/5. This means that the policy will pay a maximum of $25,000 for bodily injury to one person, $50,000 to more than one person, and a maximum of $5,000 for property damage in one accident. Most insurance companies offer liability up to $300,000 and sometimes $500,000.

Individuals who are dissatisfied with the maximum liability limits offered by regular automobile insurance coverage can purchase a separate amount of coverage under an "umbrella policy". Umbrella limits sometimes go as high as $5 million. They also cover personal liability in excess of homeowner's liability limits.

Physical Damage Coverage

Another kind of automobile insurance covers damage to the insured's car in any type of collision. Usually, it is not advisable to purchase full collision coverage (otherwise known as zero deductible). The price per year is quite high

EXHIBIT 54-2

GUIDE TO PACKAGE POLICIES FOR HOMEOWNERS

These are the principal features of standard types of homeowners' insurance policies.

The amount of insurance provided for specific categories, such as personal property and comprehensive personal liability, can usually be increased by paying an additional premium.

The special limits of liability refer to the maximum amounts the policy will pay for the types of property listed in the notes. Usually, jewelry, furs, boats and other items subject to special limits have to be insured separately to obtain greater coverage. Adapted from New Jersey Insurance Department, *A Shopper's Guide to Homeowners Insurance*, 1977.

	BASIC FORM HOMEOWNERS HO-1	BROAD FORM HOMEOWNERS HO-2	SPECIAL FORM HOMEOWNERS HO-3	COMPREHENSIVE FORM HOMEOWNERS HO-5	HO-6 (FOR CONDOMINIUM OWNERS)
PERILS COVERED (see key below)	perils 1-11	perils 1-18	perils 1-18 on personal property except glass breakage; all risks, except those specifically excluded, on buildings	all risks except those specifically excluded	perils 1-18 except glass breakage
STANDARD AMOUNT OF INSURANCE ON: house, attached structures	based on property value; minimum $8,000	based on property value; minimum $8,000	based on property value; minimum $8,000	based on property value; minimum $15,000	$1,000 on owner's additions and alterations to unit
detached structures	10% of amount of insurance on house	10% of amount of insurance on house	10% of amount of insurance on house	10% of amount of insurance on house	no coverage

trees, shrubs, and plants	5% of amount of insurance on house; $250 maximum per item	5% of amount of insurance on house; $250 maximum per item	5% of amount of insurance on house; $250 maximum per item	5% of amount of insurance on house; $250 maximum per item	10% of personal property insurance; $250 maximum per item
personal property on premises	50% of insurance on house	50% of insurance on house	50% of insurance on house	50% of insurance on house	based on value of property; minimum $4,000
personal property away from premises	10% of personal property insurance (minimum $1,000)	10% of personal property insurance (minimum $1,000)	10% of personal property insurance (minimum $1,000)	50% of insurance on house	10% of personal property insurance (minimum $1,000)
additional living expense	10% of insurance on house	20% of insurance on house	20% of insurance on house	20% of insurance on house	40% of personal property insurance
SPECIAL LIMITS OF LIABILITY*	standard	standard	standard	standard	standard

KEY TO PERILS COVERED:

1. fire, lightning
2. damage to property removed from premises endangered by fire
3. windstorm, hail
4. explosion
5. riots
6. damage by aircraft
7. damage by vehicles not owned or operated by people covered by policy
8. damage from smoke
9. vandalism, malicious mischief
10. glass breakage
11. theft
12. falling objects
13. weight of ice, snow, sleet
14. collapse of building or any part of building
15. bursting, cracking, burning, or bulging of a steam or hot water heating system, or of appliances for heating water
16. leakage or overflow of water or steam from a plumbing, heating or air-conditioning system
17. freezing of plumbing, heating and air-conditioning systems and domestic appliances
18. injury to electrical appliances, devices, fixtures and wiring (excluding tubes, transistors and similar electronic components) from short circuits or other accidentally generated currents

*Special limits of liability: Money, bullion, numismatic property, bank notes-$100; securites, bills, deeds, tickets, etc.-$500; manuscripts-$1,000; jewelry, furs-$500 for theft; boats, including trailers and equipment-$500; trailers-$500.

because it is likely that small but costly repair jobs will be required each year. Most people take out $50 or $100 deductible coverage, which costs about one-fourth the price of zero deductible.

COMPREHENSIVE   Comprehensive insurance covers loss, damage, and destruction by fire, hurricane, hail, and vandalism. It is separate from collision insurance. Full comprehensive insurance is quite expensive. Again, $50 or $100 deductible is usually preferable.

Uninsured Motorist Coverage

Uninsured motorist coverage insures the driver and passengers against injury caused by any driver without insurance or by a hit-and-run driver. Certain states require that it be included in all insurance policies sold to drivers.

Accidental Death Benefits

Sometimes called double indemnity, accidental death benefits provide a lump sum to named beneficiaries if the policyholder dies in an automobile accident. It generally costs very little, but it may not be necessary if the insured has a sufficient amount of life insurance.

Medical Payment Coverage

Medical payments provided for in an auto insurance policy cover hospital and other medical bills and sometimes funeral expenses. This insurance protects all the passengers in the insured's car when the insured is driving.

No-Fault Auto Insurance

In May 1974, President Nixon wired the National Governors Conference that no-fault auto insurance was "an idea whose time has come." The president added, though, that the place for no-fault action was at the state, not the federal, level. Labor and consumer groups, however, were dissatisfied with the pace of state action and the lobbying tactics of no-fault opponents.

Therefore, pressure was brought upon Congress to institute a federal plan. Supporters of the plan indicate that eventually it will save motorists $1 billion a year in auto insurance premiums.

Under a no-fault insurance system, the insured's insurance company does not have to decide whose fault the accident was before payments are made for medical expenses resulting from the accident. In a traditional liability-based fault system, it must be determined who caused the accident. The insurer of the party deemed "at fault" then pays the bills—medical, lost earnings, pain and suffering, and automobile repairs—of the injured party.

No-fault insurance is not a new idea. Almost all other types of insurance are no-fault already. For example, life insurance companies pay without asking about fault (unless death is caused by suicide). The same is true of fire, homeowner's, and health and accident insurance. If a person breaks an ankle and is covered under a medical plan, the insurer does not ask whose fault it is before the medical bills are paid.

Original proponents of no-fault auto insurance believed it soon would be adopted by all states in the union. However, by 1977, only sixteen states had converted to pure no-fault.[2] Another eight states have passed some modified form of no-fault automobile insurance. In most no-fault states, the laws apply only to bodily injuries. Property damage claims are still settled by standard liability and collision sections of automobile insurance policies.

In no-fault states, the other party in an automobile accident can still be sued. Generally, certain "threshold" criteria must be satisfied before suit is allowed for pain and suffering, inconvenience, lost wages, and deprivation of the company of a spouse. The medical threshold level ranges from a few hundred dollars up to two thousand dollars in the sixteen no-fault states. In other states, serious injury or perma-

2.   The states are Colorado, Connecticut, Florida, Georgia, Hawaii, Kansas, Kentucky, Massachusetts, Michigan, Minnesota, Nevada, New Jersey, New York, North Dakota, Pennsylvania, and Utah.

nent disfigurement must be suffered before suits will be allowed.

ACCIDENT AND HEALTH INSURANCE

There are numerous types of prepaid medical insurance. A few are discussed here.

Hospital Expenses

Over 90 percent of all people in the United States are protected under some voluntary program that covers at least part of the medical care costs arising from illness and accidents. Hospital expense protection provides benefits for full or partial payment of room, board, and services any time the insured is in a hospital. It usually covers the use of the operating room, laboratories, x-rays, medicines, and incidental care.

Surgical Insurance

Almost everyone with some sort of hospital insurance also has surgical insurance, which pays for the services of a surgeon. Generally, there is a fee schedule that fixes a maximum amount. Any excess over the stipulated maximum must be paid by another type of insurance policy or by the patient.

Regular Medical Protection

Regular medical protection pays for doctor's office visits, as well as all x-ray, diagnostic, and laboratory expenses related to such visits. Generally, there is a maximum number of calls allowable for each sickness and a one-call deductible.

Major Medical

Major medical insurance covers all types of medical care. It does not provide for a fixed schedule of limits for each expense, as do the policies just discussed. Rather, it covers a fixed

percentage of all expenses, although some policies have limits on private nursing, extended care, hospital room and board, and outpatient psychiatric care. The contract includes a single lifetime maximum for each person covered. The limits range from $5,000 to $1 million. The lifetime limits normally restore themselves by fixed amounts per year if there is an automatic restoration clause.

THE DEDUCTIBLE The cost of any major medical policy is, in large part, a function of the deductible. The larger the amount of annual expenses a major medical policy does not cover, the smaller the premium.

COINSURANCE Most major medical policies have coinsurance structures. After the deductible, the policy may pay only 80 percent of all medical expenses for a single illness up to the lifetime maximum. The insured must pay the rest and thus becomes a coinsurer along with the insurance company.

Dental Insurance

An increasing number of companies offer dental insurance. It is usually provided only on a group basis through an employer or a union. Most dental insurance is a standard prepayment plan that usually covers 80 percent of the cost of treatment after some sort of deductible.

Disability Insurance

It is possible to insure against a loss of income by buying disability insurance or salary continuation insurance. If a plumber who has an auto accident can no longer use her hands, then a disability insurance policy would provide at least part of her lost income. Rates on these policies vary with the occupation of the individual. For example, office workers pay a lower premium per dollar of insurance than people in more hazardous occupations.

Homemaker's Disability

It is possible for the homemaker to buy insurance to replace the value of the household duties performed if the insured becomes incapacitated.

WAITING PERIOD The longer the insured agrees to wait before disability payments are started, the lower the premium. Typical waiting periods are 15, 30, 90, and 180 days.

Worker's Compensation

Worker's compensation insurance is a type of accident, health, and disability insurance that has been made mandatory by statutes in all states. It provides a system of compensation for workers who suffer losses in the course of their employment. It usually covers losses due to physical injury. Some states have enacted statutes that provide coverage for losses due to disease and illness. The geographical location and the type of industry in a particular jurisdiction dictate which type of disease losses are covered. For example, such statutes provide coverage for lung diseases in areas where coal mining is the major occupation.

The amount of compensation to be paid to the injured or ill worker is determined by a fixed schedule of payment benefits, based on three basic factors: (1) the wages that the injured party was earning, (2) the seriousness of the injury, and (3) the permanence of the injury. Suppose that Deel had an injury and was 10 percent permanently disabled. In such a case, if Deel was earning $200 per week, he would receive 10 percent of this figure, or $20 per week, for a predetermined time, according to the benefit schedule then in effect.

QUESTIONS AND CASE PROBLEMS

1. Thompson contracted with Occidental Life Insurance Company of California for an insurance policy on his life. The beneficiary of the policy was his wife. Before Occidental issued the policy to Thompson, Thompson filled out an application in which he was asked several questions regarding his health. One of the questions asked if Thompson had ever had pressure in his chest. Another asked if he had any disorder with his blood or blood vessels. Thompson entered negative answers to each of these questions since, earlier that morning, one of Occidental's physicians had asked him about these conditions. At that time, he had explained to the physician that two months earlier he had been treated for phlebitis (vein inflammation) and, at about the same time, had experienced minor chest pains. Thompson died in an accident shortly thereafter, and Occidental refused to pay on this life insurance policy, claiming that Thompson misrepresented facts on the application. Under these circumstances, is Thompson's wife entitled to Thompson's life insurance benefits? [Thompson v. Occidental Life Ins. Co., 109 Cal.Rptr. 473, 513 P.2d 353 (1973)]

2. Donald R. Noah was the beneficiary of three life insurance policies that insured the life of William L. Noah, Donald's brother. The insurer was Mutual Savings Life Insurance Company. While the policies were in force, William Noah drowned in Galveston, Texas. Mutual Savings Life refused to pay Donald Noah on the ground that he did not have an insurable interest in his brother's life. Donald Noah sued the company. Is Donald Noah entitled to collect under the policies? Would the answer be the same if William Noah had been Donald's cousin? What if he had been Donald's nephew? [Mutual Sav. Life Ins. Co. v. Noah, 291 Ala. 444, 282 So.2d 271 (1973)]

3. Cahn, Inc., an insurance brokerage firm, procured a homeowner's liability policy from the Michigan Millers Mutual Insurance Company at the request of Effye Lewis. The policy covered property owned by her and located on Dixwell Avenue in New Haven, Connecticut. In October, four years later, Lewis purchased other property on Read Street and obtained a liability insurance policy on this property from another insurer. About two months later, she moved from her Dixwell Avenue property to her Read Street property. In April of the following year, Lewis mailed Cahn a premium payment on the policy covering the Dixwell Avenue property. With the payment she enclosed a note requesting that her mail be sent to her Read Street property. Cahn interpreted the note to mean not only that she had moved but that

she desired to have her liability insurance coverage transferred to the Read Street property. With this in mind, Cahn requested and received an indorsement from the Michigan Millers Insurance Company transferring the insurance coverage to the Read Street property. Nine months later, a neighbor was injured on Lewis's Dixwell Avenue property. She requested Michigan Millers to defend the suit as required under the policy, but the insurance company declined, claiming that the Dixwell Avenue property was no longer insured. With a sharp attorney, Lewis was able to recover from Michigan Millers Insurance Company even though the injury occurred on uninsured property. How did Lewis's attorney manage to recover? [Lewis v. Michigan Millers Mut. Ins. Co., 154 Conn. 660, 228 A.2d 803 (1967)]

4. On January 24, 1961, Vulcan and Borden entered into an agreement whereby Vulcan agreed to render certain engineering and procurement services for Borden's chemical plant in Geismar, Louisiana. Part of the agreement provided: "All disputes shall be submitted to arbitration upon the demand of either party to the dispute." In 1962, several accidents occurred at the Borden plant, causing substantial damage. They were Vulcan's fault. Borden and its insurance company, Lumbermens Mutual Casualty, conducted lengthy negotiations regarding the extent to which Lumbermens would pay for the damages. After Borden and Lumbermens reached a settlement, Lumbermens brought suit against Vulcan to recover for the damage that Vulcan had caused. Vulcan objected to Lumbermens lawsuit on the ground that no disputes between Vulcan and Borden could be brought before a court before they were submitted to arbitration. Must Lumbermens Mutual submit to arbitration with Vulcan? [Lumbermens Mut. Cas. Co. v. Borden Co., 268 F.Supp. 303 (S.D.N.Y.1967)]

5. In February 1967, Gentry agreed orally to purchase a house and property owned by Irwin. The next day Gentry procured fire insurance from the Hanover Insurance Company for the home. On March 14, 1967, before the purchase transaction was completed, the house was destroyed by fire. Gentry sought to recover under the insurance policy from Hanover Insurance Company. Hanover refused to pay. Should Gentry be able to recover? [Gentry v. Hanover Ins. Co., 284 F.Supp. 626 (W.D.Ark.1968)]

6. Charles and Norma Watson asked the Dillingham Company, Ltd., to write an automobile insurance policy to cover the use of a 1965 Volkswagen by their minor son, Mark. The car was owned by Mark's mother. Since Mark had been involved in several accidents, Dillingham decided that it could obtain insurance only through the Automobile Assigned Risk Plan. Mark went to Dillingham's offices to apply for the Plan, partially filled out an application form, and signed the form and a blank duplicate. The application form provided in part that the insurance agent processing an assigned risk application was not the agent of the insurance company to which the application would be assigned. A Dillingham employee completed Mark's application form but expressly requested issuance of a "nonowner policy" even though Mark had indicated in the application that he was a seventeen-year-old living with his parents. The completed application was sent to the Plan's office. Subsequently, Mark was assigned to the United States Fidelity and Guaranty Company, to which he forwarded his first premium payment. The company issued a policy including an indorsement entitled "nonowner policy," which provided that the policy did not apply to "any automobile owned by the named insured or a member of the same household." Mark was involved in an accident while driving his mother's automobile. Is the United States Fidelity and Guaranty Company obligated to pay under the policy? [Watson v. United States Fidelity and Guaranty Co., 427 F.2d 1355 (9th Cir. 1970)]

7. Bunge Corporation was one of the holders of warehouse receipts on vegetable oils stored in the tanks of a warehousing subsidiary of the American Express Company. In late 1963, it was discovered that a massive fraud had been perpetrated by Tino de Angelis, president of a vegetable oil concern, and that there was little or no oil in the tanks. This scandal was popularly known as the "salad oil swindle." Bunge brought suit on a contract of insurance against its insurance company, London and Overseas Insurance, to recover its losses. Thereafter, Bunge entered into a settlement agreement with American Express, giving it a release from liability; that is, Bunge agreed not to sue American Express. London refused to pay anything to Bunge Corporation but proceeded to institute an action against American Express on the theory that its negligence was the cause of Bunge's loss. The court promptly threw out London's lawsuit, and the judge cited two reasons why London had no right to sue. What were they? [Bunge Corp. v. London and Overseas Ins. Co., 394 F.2d 496 (2d Cir. 1968)]

8. In June 1961, Groban contracted to purchase an inventory of Caterpillar tractor parts from SLDC. Before that purchase was concluded, Groban contracted to resell the inventory to Union. At Union's request, Groban agreed to obtain marine war risk insurance on the shipment at Union's expense. Groban subsequently purchased two contracts of

insurance, one naming itself as beneficiary and the second naming Union as beneficiary. The goods were destroyed during shipment. If Groban attempts to recover under the insurance policy, will it have an insurable interest? If Union attempts to recover, will it have an insurable interest? [Groban v. S. S. Pegu, 331 F.Supp. 883 (S.D.N.Y.1971)]

9. On June 8, 1966, a convent that had been constructed in 1877 burned to the ground. It was insured by Royal Insurance Company. At the time of the fire, the previous residents of the convent, the Sisters of Presentation, had abandoned the old building and moved into a new one. Under an agreement with the bishop, they had obligated themselves to surrender the old convent for demolition. They had already received new land and a new building in exchange for their contractual agreement that the old land would be occupied by an expanding high school. The Sisters of Presentation demanded recovery from Royal Insurance Company, but Royal refused to pay on the ground that the Sisters of Presentation had no insurable interest in the building. The Sisters of Presentation argued that, had their new building been destroyed by fire, they might have been forced to reoccupy the old convent even though it would not be habitable without an expenditure of approximately $120,000. Do the Sisters of Presentation have an insurable interest in the old convent? [Royal Ins. Co. v. Sisters of Presentation, 430 F.2d 759 (9th Cir. 1970)]

10. In 1950, Youse purchased a fire insurance policy from Employers Fire Insurance Company. The policy covered most of Youse's personal property and provided that the company would pay for "all direct loss or damage by fire." Youse accidentally lost his ring in a pile of trash near a trash burner. Youse later recovered it, but only after the trash had been burned. The ring was extensively damaged. Should Youse recover? Was this the type of fire that Employers Fire Insurance Company had in mind when it provided coverage for Youse's property? Should this matter? [Youse v. Employers Fire Ins. Co., 172 Kan. 111, 238 P.2d 472 (1951)]

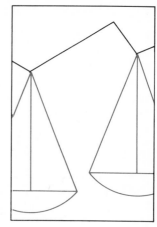

55

Wills, Trusts, and Estates

The laws of succession of property are a necessary corollary to the concept of private ownership of property. The law requires that upon death, title to the decedent's property must vest somewhere. The decedent can direct the passage of property after death by *will*, subject to certain limitations imposed by the state. If no valid will has been executed, the person is said to have died *intestate*, and state law prescribes the distribution of the property among heirs or next of kin. If no heirs or kin can be found, the property escheats (title is transferred) to the state.

In addition, a person can transfer property through a *trust*.[1] The owner (settlor) transfers legal title to the property to a *trustee*, who has a duty imposed by law to hold the property for the use or benefit of another (the beneficiary).

The following sections will describe how testamentary dispositions are made by *will*, by *statutes of descent and distribution*, or with *trusts*.

ORIGINS OF INHERITANCE LAWS

Under the common law, persons had no power to control the distribution of their property after death. This power is derived solely from statutes

---

1. Note that a "trust" can be set up by the property owner *during his or her life* (by a deed accompanied by a trust document) or *at his or her death* (by a will accompanied by a trust document). This chapter discusses both.

originating in feudal England, where the transfer of property at death was strictly controlled. The heir (the one who inherited) was required to pay the feudal lord a sum of money[2] for the privilege of succeeding to his or her ancestor's lands. When a tenant died without heirs, the land escheated (title passed) to the feudal lord of the manor.[3] Sweeping land reforms in England during the 1920s replaced inheritance payments and escheat to the feudal lord with the right of the crown to receive inheritance taxes and to take property of an intestate without heirs. Modern legislation has changed the terminology but not the result. In all states, title to land of persons dying intestate and without heirs vests in the state; the right to make a will and the way to make one are determined by state laws. Wills must follow rigid technical statutory requirements. Furthermore, taxes are imposed upon the transfer of property at death by the state and federal governments.

PURPOSES OF INHERITANCE LAWS

State regulation of inheritance has developed in response to certain desirable social and political goals. Four principles underlie U.S. inheritance and succession laws.[4]

1. *The concept of private property.* Any system of laws to regulate the passage of a decedent's estate must do so in the context of a firmly rooted tradition of private ownership of property.
2. *Effectuating the individual's testamentary intent.* The right to direct the distribution of one's own property to whomever one chooses (subject to the rights of the surviving spouse and

minor children) is often taken as a basic tenet of U.S. jurisprudence. Many formalities surround the court's duty to insure that when a will is offered for authentication, it is in fact the genuine and final expression of the decedent's wishes. The seriousness of this function is reflected in the highly publicized controversy over the numerous proffers of "authentic" wills belonging to billionaire Howard Hughes. The freedom of an individual to have his or her intentions satisfied after death is subject to limitations imposed by law.

3. *The policy favoring family.* Protection of the family has been a cornerstone of inheritance laws throughout history. As noted earlier, intestate succession is inheritance by heirs of the deceased. In contemporary law, this goal is reinforced by state statutes guaranteeing that an absolute portion of the decedent's estate will be allotted to the surviving spouse and minor children. Although laws differ from state to state, most provide a *homestead exemption* from taxation and creditors, a family allowance to provide funds to meet daily expenses until the estate is settled, and an exemption for household and personal effects.

4. *Reflection of societal interests.* State succession laws perpetuate certain social and political goals by: (1) protecting a decedent's family from absolute poverty against creditors' claims (and preventing the family's dependency on the state), (2) obtaining money through escheat (transfer of abandoned property to the state), (3) channeling the efficient and economic use of property by prohibiting wasteful bequests (devises), (4) encouraging educational and scientific research and other civic programs through estate tax exemptions or deductions, and (5) maintaining social stability and confidence in the legal system by adhering to traditional principles of law.

WILLS

Concept of a Will

A **will** is the final declaration of the disposition that a person desires to have made of his or her

---

2. The sum, called a relief, was usually equivalent to one year's rent.
3. It was not until 1925 that escheat for failure of heirs was abolished. C. J. Moynihan, *Introduction to the Law of Real Property* (St. Paul, Minn. West Publishing, 1962), p. 22.
4. For a discussion of the goals of succession laws and the need for increasing flexibility in applying these laws, see John T. Gaubatz, "Notes toward a Truly Modern Wills Act," *University of Miami Law Review* 31 (Spring 1977): 497.

property after death. It is a formal instrument that must follow the *exact* requirements of the Statute of Wills in order to be effective. The reasoning behind such a strict requirement is obvious. A will becomes effective only after death. No attempts to modify it after the death of the maker are allowed because the court cannot ask the maker to confirm the attempted modifications.

A will is *revocable* at any time before death. For example, Walt Harrison has a valid will. He decides to add a bequest to his niece. If he dies on the way to the lawyer's office, the current will takes effect without the intended gift to the niece. Although Harrison's will was not binding during his lifetime, it becomes binding upon his death.

VOCABULARY OF WILLS AND TRUSTS Every
area of law has its own special vocabulary, and wills and trusts are no exception. A man who makes out a will is known as a **testator**, and a woman who makes out a will is called a **testatrix.** The court responsible for administering any legal problems surrounding a will is called a **probate court.** When a person dies, a *personal representative* settles the affairs of the deceased. An **executor** or **executrix** is a personal representative named in the will; an **administrator** or **administratrix** is a personal representative appointed by the court for a decedent who dies without a will or who fails to name an executor in the will. A gift of real estate

by will is generally called a **devise**, and a gift of personal property under a will is called a **bequest.**

TYPES OF GIFTS Gifts by will can be *specific,
general,* or *residuary.* A *specific* devise or bequest describes particular property that can be distinguished from all the rest of the testator's property. For example, Johnson's will provides, "I give my nephew, Tom, my gold pocket watch with initials MTJ." A *general* gift does not single out any particular item of property, and any property of comparable nature will satisfy the gift. For example, "I give Dana $10,000." A specified sum of money is almost always a *general* gift. Sometimes a will provides that any assets remaining after specific gifts are made and debts are paid will be distributed through a residuary clause. A residuary provision is used because the exact amount to be distributed cannot be determined until all other gifts and payouts are made. A residuary estate can pose problems, however, when the will directs that only a portion of the money or assets be divided among named beneficiaries, leaving some assets still remaining. In such a case, if the court cannot determine the testator's intent, the remainder of the residuary passes according to laws of intestacy.

In the following case, the lower court tried to apply a distribution formula not actually provided by the terms of the will's "general residuary clause."

BACKGROUND AND FACTS *The Johnson will contained a residuary clause that provided a general remainder clause:*

"The remainder of my estate shall be divided as follows among the following people.

"FIFTH: I hereby give bequeath and devise one-quarter of the balance of my money and estate of which I may die seised and possessed, both real, personal and mixed, of every kind, character and description whatsoever and wheresoever situate to THE CANCER SOCIETY to be theirs absolutely and forever.

"SIXTH: I hereby give, bequeath and devise one-half (½) of the balance of my money to LILLIAN BUTLER to be hers absolutely and forever."

Only three-quarters of the residuary was disposed of by the terms of the will. One quarter remained. The lower court presumed that Johnson

KORTZ v. AMERICAN NAT. BANK OF CHEYENNE

Supreme Court of Wyoming, 1977.
571 P.2d 985.

intended one-third of the residuary for the American Cancer Society and two-thirds for Lillian Butler. Johnson's daughter and heir by intestacy objected. She claimed the one-quarter under the laws of intestate succession.

ROSE, Justice.

* * *

First, in the consideration of a will, the intention of the testator must govern. In ascertaining the testator's intention, it is not for us to read into the will something which the deceased did not place there. We can only glean decedent's intent and purpose from what his testament says. Under Wyoming law, the testator's intention is to be ascertained if at all possible from the meaning of all words used in the context of the entire will. We have declined to supply words for a testator where the will is clear and unambiguous.

* * *

The residuary clause, in the present case, does not make an express declaration that *all* of the testator's residuary estate was to be distributed to the listed legatees. It says, the remainder "shall be divided *as follows* among the following people," and then goes on to distribute only a portion of the residuary estate. The specific distributive clauses are not, therefore, wholly inconsistent with the general residuary clause and there is no ambiguity created by the plain wording of the instrument which authorizes such interpretation as is contended for by the appellee.

* * *

We hold that the language of the Johnson will is clear and unambiguous. As a result, the testator intended a portion of his residuary estate to pass by intestacy. The language of residuary paragraphs FIFTH and SIXTH discloses that the Cancer Society is to receive one-quarter of the *property and money* remaining after the payment of debts and specific bequests, or one-sixteenth of the estate. Lillian Butler, in turn, is to receive one-half of the *money*, if any, remaining after payment of debts, specific bequests and the Cancer Society bequest, or three thirty-seconds of the money remaining in the estate. This leaves three thirty-seconds of the money and three-sixteenths of all other property in the estate undistributed. We note a distinction between the assets bequeathed to these residuary legatees, since the bequest to Lillian Butler refers only to money. There is no basis for the trial court to vary these bequests, even though a portion of the testator's residuary estate must thereby pass by intestacy.

JUDGMENT AND REMEDY

The lower court was admonished by the appellate court for attempting to rewrite the testator's will. The case was returned to the trial court for entry of a judgment consistent with the principles of law articulated in this opinion. Johnson's daughter and heir was entitled to one-quarter of the residuary estate. One-quarter went to the American Cancer Society, and one-half to Lillian Butler.

OTHER PURPOSES OF A WILL A will can serve many purposes besides the distribution of property. It can appoint a guardian for minor children or incapacitated adults. It can appoint a personal representative to settle the affairs of the deceased. State laws vary in the types of powers and functions that they grant to personal representatives under the supervision of the probate court.

The Uniform Probate Code

Probate laws vary from state to state. In 1969, the American Bar Association and the National Conference of Commissions on Uniform State Laws approved the Uniform Probate Code (UPC). The UPC codifies general principles and procedures for the resolution of conflicts in settling estates and relaxes some of the requirements of a valid will found under earlier state laws. References to UPC provisions will be included where general practice in most states is consistent. However, since succession and inheritance laws vary widely among different states, one should always check the particular laws of the state involved.[5]

Testamentary Capacity

Not everyone who owns property necessarily qualifies to make a valid disposition of that property by will. *Testamentary capacity* requires the testator to be of *legal age* and *sound mind* at the time the will is made. The *legal age for executing* a will varies, but in most states and under the UPC, the minimum age is eighteen years. [UPC Sec. 2-501] Thus, a will of a

_____
5. For example, California law differs *substantially* from the UPC.

twenty-one-year-old decedent written when the person was twelve is *invalid.*

The concept of "being in sound mind" refers to the testator's ability to formulate and comprehend a personal plan for the disposition of property. Further, a testator must intend the document to be his or her will.

Courts have grappled with the requirement of *sound mind* for a long time and not always with consistent results. Mental incapacity is a highly subjective matter that is not easily measured. The general test for testamentary capacity has the following provisions:

1. The testator must comprehend and remember the "natural objects of his or her bounty" (usually family members, but including persons for whom the testator has affection).
2. The testator must comprehend the kind and character of the property being distributed.
3. The testator must understand and formulate a plan for disposing of the property to family members and friends.

Less mental ability is required to make a will than to manage one's own business affairs or to enter into a contract. Thus, a testator may be feeble, aged, eccentric, or offensive and still possess testamentary capacity. Moreover, a person can be judged insane or have insane delusions about certain subjects yet, during lucid moments, still be of *sound mind* to make a valid will.

In the following case, testamentary capacity appeared to be present even though the testator was diagnosed schizophrenic. The will was valid because, according to clear and convincing proof on the court record, it was executed during a lucid interval.

BACKGROUND AND FACTS *The testator, Darrell Elmer Gentry, had served in the United States Army but was ultimately discharged after confinement in the psychiatric ward at Walter Reed Hospital. In 1965, while still a patient at a veterans administration hospital, the testator was*

ESTATE OF GENTRY
Court of Appeals of Oregon, 1976.
32 Or.App. 45, 573 P.2d 322.

adjudicated incompetent to manage his own affairs. He was placed under the guardianship of Pioneer Trust Company.

During the course of his confinement, the testator executed a will naming his mother as sole beneficiary. The testator also had a daughter, but he disinherited her.

After the testator died, his daughter came forward to contest the validity of the will and to assert her right to her father's estate by virtue of intestate succession. The daughter challenged the will on the ground that her father lacked testamentary capacity to execute a valid will.

THORNTON, Judge.

* * *

Dr. Esperson, the ward physician under whose care the testator was placed while testator was at the Veterans Administration Hospital from 1967 to 1973, testified that testator suffered from a psychosis diagnosed as schizophrenia; that his mental illness was largely controllable by psychiatric medication; that he was generally lucid so long as he took his prescribed medication, but when allowed to leave the hospital for any extended period would stop taking his medicines and would shortly become psychotic and sometimes obstreperous; that he would then have to be returned to the hospital. The record shows that this pattern of behavior was repeated again and again almost from the beginning of testator's hospitalization at Roseburg until his death. Not infrequently testator would go AWOL from the hospital. Dr. Esperson expressed the opinion, however, that testator was mentally competent to execute a will if not in one of his deranged intervals, and that he was capable of executing the instant will.

In a letter received by Pioneer Trust Company September 29, 1969, three days before the challenged will was executed, testator wrote to Mr. E. F. Smith, a trust officer who was handling his financial affairs at Pioneer Trust Company, stating in part that "I want my mother to inherit my 4 or 5 thousand." This was reiterated by testator on other occasions, including in a letter to his mother postmarked October 6, 1969. In a letter dated September 30, 1969, apparently in response to the letter received from the testator, Trust Officer Smith wrote testator informing him that if he was serious about having his estate go to his mother he should go to some attorney in Roseburg and have him prepare a valid will, taking care to inform the attorney that he was "living currently at the Veterans Administration Hospital at Roseburg."

The will was prepared by a Roseburg attorney, and witnessed by the attorney and his secretary.

Respondent Pioneer Trust Company of Salem was the executor named in the will.

* * *

The attorney who drafted the will, and who was an attesting witness, testified by deposition pursuant to stipulation. He stated that testator came to him on October 2, apparently bearing the above described letter from Smith; that he, the attorney, spent approximately 25 to 30 minutes discussing the details with the testator, including the nature and extent of his property, the persons who were the natural objects of his bounty and the effect of his will prior to drafting the will; that he, the attorney, was fully aware that testator was under guardianship; that notwithstanding testator appeared to be mentally competent when the will was executed. The attorney's secretary, however, had no specific recollection of the testator or the circumstances. The attorney's rough notes of his consultation were received in evidence and correspond with his testimony and the provisions of the will.

Mental competency to make a will is determined at the precise moment the will is executed.

"The final test is whether the decedent was competent *at the time the will was executed*. Evidence of incapacitation prior or subsequent to the time of the will's execution is relevant but it lacks the probative value of evidence revealing his mental condition at the material time. Its value diminishes the more removed it is from the crucial date. Thus, the testimony of attesting witnesses and, next to them, of those present at the execution of the will is to be accorded 'great weight' in cases of this kind."

A will made by an insane person may be valid if made during a lucid interval.

Although the proponent of a will has the burden of proving the testamentary capacity of the testator, a duly executed will gives rise to a presumption of competency.

Where a testator is under guardianship at the time of the execution of the will and the guardianship was established because of the ward's mental incompetency, a presumption of mental incompetency arises. However, merely because the testator was under guardianship at the time of execution of the will is not conclusive of his mental incompetency at the time if the evidence shows that the testator possessed the requisite testamentary capacity at the time of the execution of the will.

After a de novo review of the record [de novo means that the court is reading the record and deciding its own interpretations of which facts and conclusions are true. De novo means *new review*—that is, just like a new trial. Ordinarily, the appellate court just checks the trial court to be sure that some substantiation exists for the trial court's conclusions and then reviews the application of law. Here, the appellate court does *both*—it reviews *facts* and conclusions and applies principles of *law*.], including the testator's voluminous medical records from the Veterans Administration, we conclude that the proponent established by clear and convincing evidence that despite the testator's admitted mental illness he was mentally competent at the time he executed the challenged will * * *.

The trial court's judgment was affirmed. The testator's mother was decreed the sole beneficiary of the estate. The will was valid because it was executed during a lucid moment. **JUDGMENT AND REMEDY**

FORMAL REQUIREMENTS OF A WILL

A will must comply with strict formalities designed to insure that the testator or testatrix understood his or her actions and to help prevent fraud. Unless statutory requirements are met, the will is declared void and the decedent's property is distributed according to the laws of intestacy of that state. The requirements are not uniform among the jurisdictions. However, most states uphold the following basic requirements for executing a will.

1. *A will must be in writing.* A written document is generally required, although in

some cases oral wills are found valid.[6] [UPC Sec. 2-502] The writing itself can be informal as long as it substantially complies with the statutory requirements. In some states a will can be handwritten in crayon or ink. It can be written on a sheet or scrap of paper, on a paper bag, or on a piece of cloth. A will in the handwriting of the testator is called **holographic** (or olographic). A will also can refer to a written memorandum that itself is not a will but that contains information necessary to carry out the will. For example, T's will provides that a certain sum of money be divided among a group of charities designated on a particular list T gave to the trustee *the same day the will was signed.* The written list will be "incorporated by reference" into the will only if it was in existence when the will was executed (signed) and if it is sufficiently described so that it can be identified.

2.   *A will must be signed by the testator.* It is a fundamental requirement in almost all jurisdictions that the testator or testatrix's signature appear, generally at the end of the will. Each jurisdiction dictates by statute and court decision what constitutes a signature. Initials, an "X" or other mark, and words like *Mom* have all been upheld as valid when it was shown that the testator intended them to be a signature.

3.   *A will must be witnessed.* A will must be attested by two and sometimes three witnesses. The number of witnesses, their qualifications, and the manner in which the witnessing must be done are generally set out in a statute.

A witness can be required to be disinterested—that is, not a beneficiary under the will. By contrast, the UPC provides that a will is valid even if it is attested by an interested witness. [UPC Sec. 2-505] There are no age requirements for witnesses, but they must be competent.

Witnesses function to verify that the testator actually executed (signed) the will and had the requisite intent and capacity at the time. A witness does not have to read the contents of the will. Usually, the testator and witnesses must all

sign in sight of one another, but the UPC deems it sufficient if the testator acknowledges his or her signature to the witnesses. [UPC Sec. 2-502] The UPC does not require all parties to sign in the presence of one another.

4.   *A will can be "published."* Publication is an oral declaration by the maker to the witnesses that the document they are about to sign is his or her "last will and testament." Publication is becoming an unnecessary formality in most states, and it is not required under the UPC.

Holographic Wills

Generally, strict compliance with the formalities listed above is required before a document is accepted as the decedent's will. The holographic will presents one of the few exceptions. A holographic will is one that is completely in the handwriting of the decedent. For a holographic will to be probated (validated), it must also be dated and signed by the decedent.

FRAUD, UNDUE INFLUENCE, AND MISTAKE

A valid will must represent the maker's intention to create a will that transfers and distributes his or her property. When it can be shown that the decedent's plan of distribution was the result of fraud or improper pressure brought by another person, the will is declared invalid.

Undue influence may be a factor if the testator or testatrix ignores blood relatives and names as beneficiary a nonrelative who is in constant close contact and in a position to influence the making of the will. For example, a nurse or friend caring for the deceased before death named as the beneficiary to the exclusion of all family members might well be challenged for undue influence.

Fraud will invalidate a will. Assume X dies leaving his property to B. B had convinced X that he was X's long lost son, but in fact he is not. The will is invalid.

REVOCATION OF WILLS

An executed will is revocable by the maker at any time during the maker's lifetime. Wills can

---

6.   *Nuncupative* is the legal name for an oral will. An oral will made by a soldier on active service or a sailor at sea is recognized as valid in many states for distributing *personal property,* but it will not transfer title to real property.

also be revoked by operation of law. Revocation can be partial or complete, and it must follow certain strict formalities.

Act of the Maker

REVOCATION BY PHYSICAL ACT The testator or testatrix may revoke a will by intentionally burning, tearing, cancelling, obliterating, or destroying it, or by having someone else do so in the presence of and at the maker's direction.[7] In some states, partial revocation by physical act of

---

7. The destruction cannot be inadvertent. It must show the maker's intent to revoke.

the maker is recognized. Thus, those portions of a will lined out or torn away are dropped, and the remaining parts of the will are valid. In no case, however, can a provision be crossed out and an additional or substitute provision written in. Such altered portions require reexecution (resigning) and reattestation (rewitnessing). This is commonly done by **codicil.**

To revoke a will by physical act, it is necessary to follow the mandates of a state statute exactly. Where a state statute prescribes the exact methods for revoking a will by physical act, those are the only methods that will revoke the will.

BACKGROUND AND FACTS *The decedent, Lisbeth R. Eglee, was a resident of Charlestown, Rhode Island. She died on November 11, 1973. Subsequently, the defendant, Donald R. Eglee, who was the stepson and an heir of Lisbeth R. Eglee, filed this petition with a local probate court, requesting that a written instrument, executed and dated by the decedent on March 7, 1966, be admitted to probate.*

The plaintiff, Milton Haller, successor in interest to Duna Haller, sister of Lisbeth, stipulated that the document offered by the defendant was executed as the decedent's will in compliance with the laws of the state of Connecticut, the place in which the will was executed. The decedent had made lines with a red pencil through every word and signature. In addition, diagonally across each clause of the instrument were the decedent's initials, the word "obliterated," and the date, September 19, 1973. The record indicated, however, that the entire document remained legible despite the defacement. The parties agreed that the will was free of markings, initials, and notation at the time of its execution.

The will was admitted to probate. The trial court found that although the decedent had demonstrated an intention to revoke her will, she had failed to comply with the precise methods of revocation required by state law. Therefore, the will had not been validly revoked and the legible portions did constitute a valid will.

ESTATE OF EGLEE
Supreme Court of Rhode Island, 1978.
—R.I.—, 383 A.2d 586.

BEVILACQUA, Chief Justice.

* * *

The issue before us is whether the decedent's actions constituted a sufficient revocation of her will. It is well settled that a will may be validly revoked if the testator, or some third person acting under the testator's direction and in his presence, performs a prescribed physical act with the specified intent of revoking the will. The revocation procedure in Rhode Island is set forth in [the statute] which reads:

> "No will or codicil or any part thereof shall be revoked otherwise than as provided in [the statute] or by another will or codicil executed in manner hereinbefore required, or by some writing declaring an intention to revoke the same and executed in the manner in which a will is hereinbefore required to be executed, or by *burning, tearing, or otherwise destroying* the same by the testator, or by some person in his presence and by his direction, with the intention of revoking the same." (Emphasis added.)

Thus, revocation of a validly executed will under [state statute] requires the intent to revoke coupled with the act of "burning, tearing, or otherwise destroying" the will.

The plaintiff contends that the phrase "otherwise destroying" in [the state statute] should be construed so as to include the acts of cancelling and obliterating. However, in interpreting such provisions our duty is very narrowly described. We must construe statutes, not redraft them. In so doing, we are bound to ascertain the intent of the Legislature and to effectuate that intent when it is lawful and within legislative competence. Specifically, where a statute prescribes the methods and acts by which a will may be revoked, no acts other than those mentioned in the statute can operate as a revocation, because statutes governing revocation are mandatory and must be strictly construed. The rationale for making statutory formalities governing revocation of a will mandatory is to prevent mistake, misrepresentation, and fraud.

Examining the legislative history of [the statute], we find that prior to 1896, our revocation statute omitted the phrase "otherwise destroying" and provided that a will could be revoked by "cancelling" or "obliterating" as well as by other enumerated methods. Public Statutes 1882, ch. 182, § 6. When the Legislature amended the revocation statute in 1896, it deleted the words "cancelling" and "obliterating" and inserted the phrase "otherwise destroying." Generally, the omission from a revocation statute of one of the modes of revocation previously included renders it impossible to revoke a will by the omitted method. 2 Bowe-Parker, *Page on the Law of Wills*, § 21.4 at 354. It is obvious that if, as plaintiff argues, the Legislature had intended that the term "otherwise destroying" were to include revocation by cancellation or obliteration, it would have framed the pertinent clause to read "or by burning, tearing, cancelling, obliterating, or otherwise destroying." To adopt plaintiff's construction would contravene both the mandatory method of revocation delineated by [the state statute] and the obvious intent of the Legislature in drafting that statute.

Courts that have considered statutes identical to [the Rhode Island statute] have held that when the Legislature, after mentioning specific acts such as "burning" and "tearing" as sufficient to revoke a will, speaks of "otherwise destroying" a will, it must be understood as intending by the latter some mode of destruction ejusdem generis, a destruction of the same kind or nature as by the methods previously mentioned. Therefore, we believe that the phrase "otherwise destroying" imports a destruction of both the substance and contents of the will. Anything short of a destruction of this degree is entirely ineffectual as a revocation, particularly where the original writing remains legible as in the instant case.

Because [the Rhode Island statute on revocation of a will by physical act] cannot be construed so as to include cancelling and obliterating as appropriate methods of revocation, and because the acts of the testator in this case did not constitute "otherwise destroying" the will, we must agree with the trial justice that despite the testator's obvious intent to revoke, the will was not validly revoked.

The testator failed to revoke her validly executed will under the requirements of the state statute. The will continued as a valid testamentary disposition despite the testator's obvious intent to revoke. The revocation was incorrectly done, hence invalid.

JUDGMENT AND REMEDY

REVOCATION IN ANOTHER WRITING A **codicil** is simply a separate written instrument that amends or revokes provisions in a will. It eliminates the necessity of redrafting the entire will merely to add to it or amend it. A codicil can also be used to revoke an entire will and must be executed with the same formalities required for a will. It must refer expressly to the will. In effect, it updates a will because the will is "incorporated by reference" into the codicil.

A *second will* can be executed that may or may not revoke the first or a prior will, depending upon the language used. The second will must specifically use words like, "This will hereby revokes all prior wills." If the second will is otherwise valid and properly executed, it will revoke all prior wills. If the express *declaration of revocation* is missing, then both wills are read together. If any of the dispositions made in the second will are inconsistent with the prior will, the second will controls.

Revocation by Operation of Law

MARRIAGE In general, a will written and executed before marriage will be revoked by the fact of marriage. Public policy provides that a person's new marital obligations change any prior decisions concerning the disposition of property. Under the Uniform Probate Code (UPC), a subsequent marriage *does not revoke* a will. [UPC Sec. 2-508] The new spouse is entitled to whatever share of the estate the law provides for testators who die without a will. The rest is passed under the will. [UPC Sec. 2-301]

DIVORCE OR ANNULMENT Under common law and the UPC, divorce does not necessarily revoke the entire will. A divorce or an annulment occurring after a will has been executed will revoke those dispositions of property made under the will to the former spouse.

CHILDREN BORN AFTER A WILL IS EXECUTED If a child is born after a will has been executed and if it appears that the testator would have made a provision for the child, then the child is entitled to receive whatever portion of the estate he or she is allowed under state intestate laws. Most state laws allow a child to receive some portion of the estate if no provision is made in a will, unless it appears from the terms of the will that the testator intended to disinherit the child. Under the UPC, the rule is the same. [UPC Sec. 2-302]

RIGHTS UNDER A WILL

The law imposes certain limitations on the way a person can dispose of property in a will. For example, a married person who makes a will cannot deny leaving a certain portion of the estate to the surviving spouse. In most states this is called a "forced share," and it is often one-third.

Beneficiaries under a will have rights as well. A beneficiary can renounce his or her share of the property given under a will.[8] Further, a surviving spouse can renounce the

---

8. Usually done for tax reasons or because the recipient would fare better by taking his or her elective share.

amount given under a will and elect to take the "forced share" if the forced share is larger than the amount of the gift. State statutes provide the methods by which a surviving spouse accomplishes renunciation. The purpose of these statutes is to allow the spouse to obtain whichever distribution would be most advantageous.

STATUTES OF DESCENT AND DISTRIBUTION

The rules of descent are statutory. That means each state can regulate how property shall be distributed when a person dies without a will. State laws attempt to carry out what would have been the wishes of the decedent.

The rules of descent vary widely from state to state. However, there is usually a special statutory provision for the rights of the surviving spouse and minor children. In addition, the law provides that the debts of the decedent must first be satisfied out of his or her estate. The remaining assets then pass to the surviving spouse and to the children. For example, A dies intestate and is survived by his wife, B, and his children, C and D. A's property passes according to **intestacy laws.** After A's outstanding debts are paid, B will receive the real estate (either in fee simple or as a life estate) and ordinarily a one-third to one-half interest in the property. B will probably also be entitled to one-half of A's personal property. The remaining real and personal property will pass to C and D in equal portions.

Distribution

State statutes of descent and distribution specify the order in which other descendants of an intestate share in the estate. When there are no surviving spouse or children, then grandchildren, brothers and sisters, and, in some states, parents of the decedent are the next in line to share. These relatives are usually called *lineal descendants.* If there are no lineal descendants, then *collateral heirs* are the next group to share. Collateral heirs include nieces, nephews, aunts, and uncles of the decedent. If there are still no

survivors in any of those groups of people related to the decedent, most statutes provide that the property shall be distributed among the next of kin of any of the collateral heirs. Stepchildren are not considered kin. However, legally adopted children are recognized as lawful heirs of their adoptive parents. Because state statutes differ so widely, very few generalizations can be made about the laws of descent and distribution. It is extremely important to refer to the exact terms of the applicable state statutes when addressing any problem of intestacy distribution.

Under the UPC, the surviving spouse is entitled to take an elective share of one-third of the decedent's estate. [UPC Sec. 2-201] In addition, the UPC provides that the surviving spouse is entitled to:

1. A homestead allowance of $5,000.
2. A household and personal effects exemption to a value not to exceed $3,500.
3. A family allowance for a period of up to one year after the death occurs to provide for daily expenses before the estate is settled, up to the amount of $6,000. [UPC Secs. 2-401, 402, 403, and 404]

THE PATTERN OF INTESTACY DISTRIBUTION When a person dies intestate, the statute of the state where the decedent died will govern descent and distribution except for real estate, which is governed by the laws of the state where the real property is located.

When there is a surviving spouse, that spouse usually receives a share of the estate—half if there is also a surviving child and one-third if there are two or more children. Only where no children or grandchildren survive the decedent will a surviving spouse succeed to the *entire* estate.

When an intestate is survived by descendants of deceased children, the question arises as to what share the descendants (that is, grandchildren of the intestate) will receive. **Per stirpes** is a method of dividing an intestate share where a class or group of distributees (for example, grandchildren) take the share that their deceased parent *would have been* entitled to inherit. This is best explained by an example: Smith has three children, #1, #2, and #3. Child #1 has one child, D. Child #2 has two children, E and F. Child #3 has no children. Child #1 and child #2 die before Smith (their father). Child #3 is still living when Smith dies. Smith's wife died before him. Had all children been living, child #1, child #2, and child #3 would each be entitled to one-third of Smith's estate. In a *per stirpes* distribution, the lineal descendants of the deceased children will inherit whatever share was owed to their parents. Thus, grandchild D will inherit the one-third share that would have gone to D's parent, Smith's child #1. Grandchildren E and F must divide the one-third share that would have gone to their parent, Smith's child #2. Thus, E and F each receive a sixth. Child #3, who is still alive, gets one-third. If child #3 had had children, it would not have affected the distribution. Child #3 would have received one-third, and his or her spouse and children would have received nothing. Another type of distribution of an estate is on a **per capita** basis. This means simply that each person takes an equal share of the estate. Thus, according to the above example, D, E, F, and child #3 would each have received a per capita share of one-quarter.

In most states and under the Uniform Probate Code, inlaws do not share in an estate. If a child dies before his or her parents, the child's spouse will not receive an inheritance. Thus, the surviving spouses of child #1 and child #2 of Smith in the example above are not entitled to any share of the estate. Only the grandchildren (D, E, and F) are entitled to share.

Whether or not an illegitimate child inherits depends on state statute. In all states, intestate succession between the mother and the child exists. In some states, intestate succession between the father and the child can occur only where the child is "legitimized" by ceremony or the child has been "acknowledged" by the father. The constitutionality of these illegitimacy statutes has recently been upheld by the Supreme Court.

TRUSTS

A trust involves real property or personal property. The *legal* title to the property is transferred to the trustee, who is charged with certain duties of dealing with the property for the benefit of another person, the beneficiary. If Sanford conveys his farm to South Miami First National Bank, to be held for the benefit of Sanford's daughters, Sanford has created a trust. Sanford is the settlor, South Miami First National Bank is the trustee, and Sanford's daughters are the beneficiaries.

Express Trusts

An express trust is one created by a written instrument. Two types of trusts will be discussed: *inter vivos* trusts and testamentary trusts.

INTER VIVOS TRUSTS   An **inter vivos trust** is a trust executed by a grantor during his or her lifetime. The grantor executes a "trust deed," and legal title to the trust property passes to the trustee. The trustee has a duty to administer the property as directed by the grantor for the benefit and in the interest of the beneficiaries. The trustee must preserve the trust property, make it productive, and, if required by the terms of the trust deed, pay income to the beneficiaries, all in accordance with the terms of the trust. Once the *inter vivos* trust is created, the grantor has, in effect, given over the property for the benefit of beneficiaries. There can be favorable tax-related considerations to setting up an *inter vivos* trust.

TESTAMENTARY TRUSTS   A **testamentary trust** is a trust created by will to come into existence upon the settlor's death. Although a testamentary trust has a trustee who maintains legal title to the trust property, actions of the trustee are subject to judicial approval. The trustee of a testamentary trust can be named in the will or be appointed by the court. Unlike the *inter vivos* trust, a testamentary trust will not fail because a trustee has not been named in the will. The legal responsibilities of the trustees are the same in both kinds of trust. If the will setting up a testamentary trust is invalid, then the trust will also be invalid. The property that was supposed to be in the trust will then pass according to intestacy laws, not according to the terms of the trust.

ORAL TRUSTS An oral *inter vivos* trust is recognized in law. Of course, the property involved must be such that the Statute of Frauds will not prevent its transfer. In other words, the subject matter of an oral trust should not involve the transfer of realty, because the Statute of Frauds requires that any contract concerning the transfer of realty must be in writing. However, oral trusts can be used to transfer personal property. For example, Appelton, a grantor, hands certain jewelry over to Tyms and says, "Keep this jewelry for my daughter and give it to her when she reaches twenty-one." Appelton has created a valid oral trust with Tyms as the trustee. Appelton's daughter is the beneficiary. Tyms is under a duty to hand the property over to the daughter when she reaches twenty-one.

Implied Trusts

If property has been transferred through an oral trust and the trustee does not perform his or her duties, a court of equity can impose trust obligations on the trustee. This is especially true when the trustee uses fraud, duress, or undue influence or abuses a confidential relationship in order to come into the trustee position. If a beneficiary can prove that an oral trust was created, then a court of equity will either require the trustee to act on behalf of the beneficiary or declare that no trust exists. In that case, the property must be returned to the general estate of the decedent, and it then passes to the beneficiaries.

ESTATE ADMINISTRATION

The orderly procedure used to collect assets, settle debts, and distribute the remaining assets when a person dies is the subject matter of estate administration. This section will look at the duties of the personal representative of the deceased.

Principle Duties of the Personal Representative

The rules and procedures for managing the estate of a deceased are controlled by statute. Thus, they vary from state to state. In every state, there is a special court, often called a "probate court," which oversees the management of estates of decedents.

The first step after a person dies is usually to determine whether or not the decedent left a will. Sometimes the decedent's attorney will have that information or at least know if a will was ever executed. Sometimes it is not known for some time whether a valid will exists. The personal papers of the deceased must be reviewed. If a will exists, it probably names a personal representative to administer the estate. If there is no will, or if the will fails to name a personal representative, then the court must appoint one. Under the UPC, the term *personal representative* includes the executor (person named in the will) and administrator (person appointed by the court). [UPC Sec. 1-201(30)]

The first duty of the personal representative is to inventory and collect the assets of the decedent. If necessary, the assets must be appraised to determine their value. Both the rights of creditors and the rights of beneficiaries must be protected during the estate administration proceedings. In addition, the personal representative is responsible for managing the assets of the estate during the administration period and not allowing them to be wasted or depleted unnecessarily. A decedent's property often seems to "disappear" shortly after his or her death—usually into the hands of friends and relatives.

The personal representative receives and pays valid claims of creditors and arranges for the estate to pay federal and state income taxes and estate taxes (or inheritance taxes, depending on the state). A personal representative is required to post a bond to insure honest and faithful performance. Usually the bond exceeds the estimated value of the personal estate of the decedent. In some cases, the will can specify that the personal representative need not post a bond.

Each step in the administration of the estate is determined by state statute. When the ultimate distribution of assets to beneficiaries is determined, the personal representative is responsible for distributing the estate pursuant to court order. Once the assets have been distributed, the estate is closed, and the personal representative is relieved of any further responsibility or liability for the estate. Exhibit 55-1 lists the duties of the personal representative.

Probate versus Nonprobate

To probate a will means to determine whether or not it is valid. The process of probate is time-consuming and costly, and the court is involved in every step of the proceedings.

EXHIBIT 55–1   THE DUTIES OF THE PERSONAL REPRESENTATIVE

It would be impossible to indicate all the duties the executor must perform, but here are some.

1. Managing the estate until it is settled, including
   a. Collecting debts due the estate.
   b. Managing real estate; arranging for maintenance and repairs.
   c. Registering securities in the name of the estate.
   d. Collecting insurance proceeds.
   e. Running family business, if necessary.
   f. Arranging for the family's support during probate.
   g. Properly insuring assets.

2. Collecting all assets and necessary records, including
   a. Locating the will, insurance policies, real estate papers, car registrations, and birth certificates.
   b. Filing claims for pension, Social Security, profit sharing and veterans benefits.
   c. Taking possession of bank accounts, real estate, personal effects, and safe deposit boxes.
   d. Obtaining names, addresses, and Social Security numbers of all heirs.
   e. Making an inventory of all assets.
   f. Setting up records and books.

3. Determining the estate's obligations, including
   a. Determining which claims are legally due.
   b. Obtaining receipts for all claims paid.
   c. Checking on mortgages and other loans.

4. Computing and then paying all death taxes due, which requires
   a. Selecting the most beneficial tax alternatives.
   b. Deciding which assets to sell to provide necessary funds.
   c. Paying taxes on time to avoid penalties.
   d. Opposing what you think are unfair evaluations established by governmental taxing authorities.

5. Computing beneficiaries' shares and then distributing the estate, which includes
   a. Determining who gets particular items and settling family disputes.
   b. Transferring title to real estate and other property.
   c. Selling off assets to pay cash legacies.
   d. Paying final estate costs.
   e. Preparing accountings for the court's approval.

Reprinted by permission from *Personal Finance Today*, p. 519. Copyright © Roger LeRoy Miller Inc., (West Publishing Co.: St. Paul) 1979.

Attorneys and personal representatives often become involved in probate.

Many states have statutes that allow for the distribution of assets without probate proceedings. Faster and less expensive methods are then used. For example, property can be transferred by affidavit, and problems or questions can be handled during an administrative hearing. In addition, some state statutes provide that title to cars, savings and checking accounts, and certain other property can be passed merely by filling out forms.

FAMILY SETTLEMENT AGREEMENTS A majority of states also provide for *family settlement agreements*, which are private agreements among the beneficiaries. Once a will is admitted to probate, the family members can agree to settle among themselves the distribution of the decedent's assets. Although a family settlement agreement will speed the settlement process, a court order is still needed to protect the estate from future creditors and to clear title to the assets involved.

IN RE McCREA

Supreme Court of
Pennsylvania, 1977.
475 Pa. 383, 380 A.2d 773.

BACKGROUND AND FACTS *Family settlement agreements often expedite estate settlement. In the following case, the estate lingered on for twelve years. Evidence failed to establish a family settlement supposedly agreed upon by the beneficiaries soon after the deceased had died.*

ROBERTS, Justice.

* * *

Katherine Jane Wiest McCrea (Mrs. McCrea), whose husband had predeceased her by some thirty years, died testate on March 24, 1961. Her will divided her estate among her six children, Katherine, William, Sarah, Elizabeth, Margaret and John. Her will named as executors John, William, and Sarah, all of whom were law school graduates. At her death, Mrs. McCrea owned several farms in Cumberland County. Some structures on the property were rental units, and others were converted into rental units by the executors. The will contained no authority to continue the operation of either the farms or the rental units and the executors did not request permission, as required by [Pennsylvania Law] to do so.

* * *

Appellants contend that after Mrs. McCrea's death, the beneficiaries entered into a family settlement agreement by which each daughter would receive cash and John and William would receive the real estate and stocks and assume the debts of the estate. The orphans' [probate] court found that no such agreement had been entered into.

Although family settlement agreements are favored because they avoid potentially divisive litigation, the existence of such an agreement must be clear and unambiguous, and the agreement must be binding on all parties. The orphans' court concluded that clear and unambiguous evidence of an agreement binding on all parties did not exist. This conclusion is supported by the testimony of the children of Mrs. McCrea. Sarah and Katherine testified that they had no recollection of an agreement among the devisees; appellant William's testimony, intended to demonstrate the existence of an agreement, in fact supported the conclusion of the orphans' court. According to William, Sarah and Katherine never agreed to the terms of the purported settlement.

"[I]n reviewing the decision of the orphans' court, our task is to assure that the record is free from legal error and to determine if the chancellor's findings are supported by competent and adequate evidence, and are not predicated upon capricious disbelief of competent and credible evidence." Thus the conclusion of the orphans' court that the evidence did not establish the existence of a settlement agreement may not be disturbed.

No family settlement agreement was found. The court held the executors **JUDGMENT**
liable for penalty charges for inexcusably delaying the settlement of the **AND REMEDY**
estate for twelve years.

SUMMARY PROCEDURES The use of summary procedures in estate administration can save time and money. The expense of a personal representative's commission, attorneys' fees, appraisers' fees, and so forth can be eliminated or at least minimized if the parties utilize summary administration procedures. But in situations—for example, where a guardian for minor children or an incompetent person must be appointed and a trust has been created to protect the minor or incompetent—probate procedures cannot be avoided. In the ordinary situation, a person can employ various will substitutes to avoid the cost of probate—for example, *inter vivos* trusts, life insurance policies with named beneficiaries, or joint tenancy arrangements. Not all methods are suitable for every estate, but there are alternatives to a complete probate administration.

THE TAXATION OF ESTATES*

In the past, gift taxes (those imposed on the grantor of the gift) were less than estate taxes. Thus, it was beneficial for older individuals to make parts of their estates gifts to their future heirs to reduce the total taxes on the estates. This is often not the case now. The Tax Reform Act of 1976 virtually rewrote the estate and gift tax code. Specifically, the deductions and

---

*The following material is adapted with permission from *Personal Finance Today*, pp. 514-517. Copyright© Roger LeRoy Miller Inc., (West Publishing Co.: St. Paul) 1979.

credits granted in the 1976 Tax Reform Act exempt all but the extremely rich from federal estate taxes. Thus, one basic reason for setting up trusts has been eliminated for almost all individuals in the United States. The tax rate, which is the same for gifts and estates, is given in the unified rate schedule in Exhibit 55-2.

Comparing the Old Law with the New

It is interesting to compare the old federal estate tax law with the new one. Under the old law, half the estate could be left to a spouse, tax-free; then an additional $60,000 was exempt from taxes. Now, half the estate *or* up to $250,000 (whichever is *greater*) can be left to a spouse, tax-free. The $60,000 additional exemption is increased by means of a tax credit to $175,000 by 1981. Exhibit 55-3 shows the taxes due at the first partner's death, including the marital deduction. These figures are for 1981 and beyond; the taxes due were slightly more in 1979 and 1980. Taxes due on the estate of a single person are also shown.

THE NUMBERS ARE SMALL

In 1981, 98 percent of all estates will pay no federal estate tax. Estates up to $425,000 can be passed on to heirs free of any estate and gift taxes. For a person who has yet to accumulate significant wealth, it hardly pays to try to grasp the intricacies of estate taxation.

EXHIBIT 55–2   UNIFIED RATE SCHEDULE

If the amount with respect to which the tentative tax is to be computed is:	The tentative tax is:
Not over $10,000	18% of such amount.
Over $10,000 but not over $20,000	$1,800, plus 20% of the excess of such amount over $10,000.
Over $20,000 but not over $40,000	$3,800, plus 22% of the excess of such amount over $20,000.
Over $40,000 but not over $60,000	$8,200, plus 24% of the excess of such amount over $40,000.
Over $60,000 but not over $80,000	$13,000, plus 26% of the excess of such amount over $60,000.
Over $80,000 but not over $100,000	$18,200, plus 28% of the excess of such amount over $80,000.
Over $100,000 but not over $150,000	$23,800, plus 30% of the excess of such amount over $100,000.
Over $150,000 but not over $250,000	$38,800, plus 32% of the excess of such amount over $150,000.
Over $250,000 but not over $500,000	$70,800, plus 34% of the excess of such amount over $250,000.
Over $500,000 but not over $750,000	$155,800, plus 37% of the excess of such amount over $500,000.
Over $750,000 but not over $1,000,000	$248,300, plus 39% of the excess of such amount over $750,000.
Over $1,000,000 but not over $1,250,000	$345,800, plus 41% of the excess of such amount over $1,000,000.
Over $1,250,000 but not over $1,500,000	$448,300, plus 43% of the excess of such amount over $1,250,000.
Over $1,500,000 but not over $2,000,000	$555,800, plus 45% of the excess of such amount over $1,500,000.
Over $2,000,000 but not over $2,500,000	$780,800, plus 49% of the excess of such amount over $2,000,000.
Over $2,500,000 but not over $3,000,000	$1,025,800, plus 53% of the excess of such amount over $2,500,000.
Over $3,000,000 but not over $3,500,000	$1,290,800, plus 57% of the excess of such amount over $3,000,000.
Over $3,500,000 but not over $4,000,000	$1,575,800, plus 61% of the excess of such amount over $3,500,000.
Over $4,000,000 but not over $4,500,000	$1,880,800, plus 65% of the excess of such amount over $4,000,000.
Over $4,500,000 but not over $5,000,000	$2,205,800, plus 69% of the excess of such amount over $4,500,000.
Over $5,000,000	$2,550,800, plus 70% of the excess of such amount over $5,000,000.

EXHIBIT 55–3   FEDERAL ESTATE TAXES IN 1981 AND AFTER

Adjusted Gross Estate (after subtracting debts, funeral expenses, administrative costs, etc.)	Taxes Due at First Partner's Death (includes marital deduction)	Taxes Due at Death (single persons)
$ 60,000	$ 0	$ 0
80,000	0	0
100,000	0	0
200,000	0	6,600
300,000	0	37,200
400,000	0	68,000
500,000	21,400	98,900
1,000,000	98,800	265,600

STATE INHERITANCE AND ESTATE TAXES

An **inheritance tax** is paid by those who receive the property; an estate tax is paid by the estate. Most states impose an inheritance tax, but some impose an estate tax instead. Others impose both. The state inheritance tax (or estate tax, if that is the case) usually is set at a lower rate than the federal estate tax, but state exemptions usually are smaller than federal exemptions. Thus, the actual state tax due can be, and often is, considerably higher than the federal tax due.

State inheritance taxes are based on the value of the assets inherited by the individual. They are owed to the state in which the inherited assets are located rather than the state in which the person inheriting them lives. In many cases, the state tax rate varies not only with the

EXHIBIT 55-4   STATE INHERITANCE TAX RATES

Source: Commerce Clearing House.

Selected Categories of Heirs as of September 1, 1976

	Rate (percent)			
State	Spouse, child or parent	Brother or sister	Other than relative	Maximum rate applies above (thousands)
California	3—14	6—20	10—24	$ 400
Colorado	2—8	3—10	10—19	500
Connecticut	2—8	4—10	8—14	1,000
Delaware	1—6	5—10	10—16	200
Hawaii	1.5—7.5	3.5—9	3.5—9	250
Idaho	2—15	4—20	8—30	500
Illinois	2—14	2—14	10—30	500
Indiana	1—10	5—15	7—20	1,500
Iowa	1—8	5—10	10—15	150
Kansas	.5—5	3—12.5	10—15	500
Kentucky	2—10	4—16	6—16	500
Louisiana	2—3	5—7	5—10	25
Maine	5—10	8—14	14—18	250
Maryland	1	10	10	
Massachusetts	1.8—11.8	5.5—19.3	8—19.3	1,000
Michigan	2—8	2—8	10—15	750
Minnesota	1.5—10	6—25	8—30	1,000
Missouri	1—6	3—18	5—30	400
Montana	2—8	4—16	8—32	100
Nebraska	1	1	6—18	60
New Hampshire		15	15	
New Jersey	1—16	11—16	15—16	3,200
North Carolina	1—12	4—16	8—17	3,000
Oregon	3—12	3—12	3—12	500
Pennsylvania	6	15	15	
Rhode Island	2—9	3—10	8—15	1,000
South Dakota		4—16	6—24	100
Tennessee	5.5—9.5	6.5—20	6.5—20	500
Texas	1—6	3—10	5—20	1,000
Virginia	1—5	2—10	5—15	1,000
Washington	1—10	3—20	10—25	500
West Virginia	3—13	4—18	10—30	1,000
Wisconsin	1.25—12.5	5—25	10—30	500
Wyoming	2	2	6	
District of Columbia	1—8	5—23	5—23	1,000

value of the assets but also with the relationship of the recipient to the deceased. Exhibit 55-4 lists state inheritance taxes.

The Pick Up Tax

Most states have an added estate tax, which is usually called a pick up tax. This tax is designed to insure that an amount at least equal to the maximum allowable federal estate tax credit is charged. Some states, such as Florida, establish an estate tax exactly equal to the maximum federal credit allowed for state estate taxes paid. This makes it attractive for people to move to these states when they retire. This tax does not, however, increase the *total* death taxes paid; it applies only when the amount due from other state death taxes is less than the allowable federal estate credit.

QUESTIONS AND CASE PROBLEMS

1. In December 1927, Brainard decided to trade on the stock market during 1928. He consulted a lawyer and was advised that it was possible for him to trade in trust for his children and other members of his family. Brainard discussed the matter with his wife and mother and stated to them that he declared a trust of his stock trading during 1928 "for the benefit of my family—my wife, mother, and my two children." During 1928, Brainard traded on the stock market, and, by the end of the year, he determined his compensation at slightly less than $10,000. Is there a valid trust? [Brainard v. Commissioner, 91 F.2d 880 (7th Cir. 1937)]

2. On August 3, 1942, Albert Gordon delivered fifteen policies of insurance on his own life to the Portland Trust Bank pursuant to the terms of a written trust agreement. The trust instrument, executed on the same date, stated that the bank as trustee would be the beneficiary of the life insurance policies and would have the duty to collect the proceeds at Gordon's death. The trust instrument further provided that the bank as trustee would distribute the income earned from the proceeds in monthly installments to Gordon's wife. Was there a valid trust? Who is the settlor? The trustee? The beneficiary? Does the fact that Gordon can revoke the life insurance policies at any time prior to his death affect the answer? [Gordon v. Portland Trust Bank, 201 Or. 648, 271 P.2d 653 (1954)]

3. Harris executed a written instrument in which he named Bishop as trustee of $17,000 in bonds, notes, mortgages, and money. The instrument declared that Harris was hereby transferring these assets to Bishop in trust for the benefit of the public library in Alexandria, Ohio. Thereafter, however, Harris received interest on some of the notes and still had access to the money and instruments that were the subject of the trust. Has Harris created a valid trust? Consider the requirements of making a valid gift. [Whitehead v. Bishop, 23 Ohio App. 315, 155 N.E. 565 (1925)]

4. In 1925, Campbell died, leaving a will whose ninth clause read as follows: "My good friends Clark and Smith I appoint as my trustees. Each of my trustees is competent by reason of familiarity with the property, my wishes and friendships, to wisely distribute some portion at least of said property. I therefore give and bequeath to my trustees all my property in trust to make disposal by the way of a momento from myself, of such articles to such of my friends as they, my trustees, shall select. All of said property, not so disposed of by them, my trustees are directed to sell and the proceeds of such sale or sales to become and be disposed of as a part of the residue of my estate." Valid trust? [Clark v. Campbell, 82 N.H. 281, 133 A. 166 (1926)]

5. Edwin L. Bunker died intestate. He was survived by the following persons: his son, James Bunker; his uncle Cyrus's legally adopted son, Walter Bunker; his aunt's illegitimate daughter; James M. Steele, a son of a half-brother of the intestate's mother; and three living children of another half-brother of the intestate's mother. There was $1 million in Edwin's estate when he died. Under the rules of intestacy, who takes what? What will the answer be if James Bunker is not living at the time of his father's death? [Estate of Bunker, 106 N.H. 391, 211 A.2d 902 (1965)]

6. H. W. Wolfe died at the age of sixty-seven, leaving personal property worth about $4,000 and more than five hundred acres of land. Just before he died on July 31, 1911, he properly executed a will that contained the following provision: "I, H. W. Wolfe, will and bequeath to Miss Mary Lilly Luffman, a tract of land near Roaring Gap Post Office, on State Road and South Fork, adjoining the lands of J. M. Royal and others, the land bought by me from H. D. Woodruff. Witness my hand and seal, this thirty first day of July, 1911." On August 14, 1911, Wolfe wrote another will that provided in part: "I, H. W. Wolfe, do make and declare this to be my last will and testament. I will and bequeath all my effects to my brothers and sisters, to be divided equally among them. Witness my hand and seal, this the fourteenth day of August, 1911." Both wills were properly signed and attested. Who is entitled to what under these wills? [In re Wolfe's Will, 185 N.C. 563, 117 S.E. 804 (1923)]

7. The will of Grace Bradley Walters was properly executed and was witnessed by Margaret Weldon and Richard Coleman Bradley, both of whom were also legatees. However, only Richard Coleman Bradley would take if the will was not probated because he was next of kin. Will Margaret Weldon be able to share in Grace Bradley Walters' estate? [In re Walters' Estate 285 N.Y. 158, 33 N.E.2d 72 (1941)]

8. Neptune Center Associates was a limited partner-

ship engaged mainly in the business of making investments. Office Buildings of America, Inc., was a corporation engageeed in the business of purchasing commercial buildings, acting primarily as a broker. The investing members of Neptune Center Associates decided to purchase the Neptune City shopping center. A representative of the association contacted Office Buildings of America to arrange the deal. Thereafter, Neptune Associates gave Office Buildings of America approximately $400,000 "to be utilized for the specific purpose of purchasing Neptune City shopping center." Office Buildings of America was not to make the purchase for a number of weeks. In the meantime, it used the money given it by Neptune Associates to pay some of its general business expenses. Has a trust been created here? If so, have any duties of the trust relationship been broken? [McGlynn v. Schultz, 95 N.J. Super. 412, 231 A.2d 386 (1967)]

9.   F. V. Richardson was the owner and operator of a service station in Franklin County, Florida. On May 1, 1968, Ken Watson drove his car into Richardson's service station, filled it up with gas, then told Richardson that he wanted someone to witness his will. Richardson, in the presence of Watson, asked Barbara Shiver, a customer, to witness the will also. She signed the will as a witness in the presence of Richardson and Watson. Richardson then signed the will as a witness and asked W. W. Cooper to sign it also. All this time, Watson stood very close by, watching each of the witnesses sign the will. Each of the witnesses was aware that this was Watson's will. Is Watson's will valid? [In re Estate of Watson, 226 So.2d 249 (Fla. App. 1969)]

10.   Jesse Butterfield Morris died on February 11, 1967. On April 6, 1967, the Security First National Bank offered a document for probate as Morris's holographic will. The document was entirely in Morris's handwriting, but it contained no signatures of witnesses. The document was dated (November 1, 1965), was addressed to the Security First National Bank, and contained the initials J. B. M. at the end. Should Morris's will be probated? [In re Estate of Morris, 268 Cal. App.2d 638, 74 Cal.Rptr. 32 (1969)]

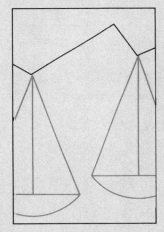

APPENDIX A
The Uniform
Commercial Code

1977 Official Text

(Adopted in 52 jurisdictions; all 50 States, although Louisiana has adopted only Articles 1, 3, 4, and 5; the District of Columbia, and the Virgin Islands.)

The Code consists of 10 Articles as follows:

Art.

1. GENERAL PROVISIONS

2. Sales

3. Commercial Paper

4. Bank Deposits and Collections

5. Letters of Credit

6. Bulk Transfers

7. Warehouse Receipts, Bills of Lading and Other Documents of Title

8. Investment Securities

9. Secured Transactions: Sales of Accounts, Contract Rights and Chattel Paper

10. Effective Date and Repealer

Article 1
GENERAL PROVISIONS

Part 1 Short Title, Construction, Application and Subject Matter of the Act

§ 1—101. Short Title.

This Act shall be known and may be cited as Uniform Commercial Code.

§ 1—102. Purposes; Rules of Construction; Variation by Agreement.

(1) This Act shall be liberally construed and applied to promote its underlying purposes and policies.

(2) Underlying purposes and policies of this Act are

(a) to simplify, clarify and modernize the law governing commercial transactions;

(b) to permit the continued expansion of commercial practices through custom, usage and agreement of the parties;

(c) to make uniform the law among the various jurisdictions.

(3) The effect of provisions of this Act may be varied by agreement, except as otherwise provided in this Act and except that the obligations of good faith, diligence, reasonableness and care prescribed by this Act may not be disclaimed by agreement but the parties may by agreement determine the standards by which the performance of such obligations is to be measured if such standards are not manifestly unreasonable.

(4) The presence in certain provisions of this Act of the words "unless otherwise agreed" or words of similar import does not imply that the effect of other provisions may not be varied by agreement under subsection (3).

(5) In this Act unless the context otherwise requires

(a) words in the singular number include the plural, and in the plural include the singular;

(b) words of the masculine gender include the feminine and the neuter, and when the sense so indicates words of the neuter gender may refer to any gender.

§ 1—103. Supplementary General Principles of Law Applicable.

Unless displaced by the particular provisions of this Act, the principles of law and equity, including the law merchant and the law relative to capacity to contract, principal and agent, estoppel, fraud, misrepresentation, duress, coercion, mistake, bankruptcy, or other validating or invalidating cause shall supplement its provisions.

§ 1—104. Construction Against Implicit Repeal.

This Act being a general act intended as a unified coverage of its subject matter, no part of it shall be deemed to be impliedly repealed by subsequent legislation if such construction can reasonably be avoided.

§ 1—105. Territorial Application of the Act; Parties' Power to Choose Applicable Law.

(1) Except as provided hereafter in this section, when a transaction bears a reasonable relation to this state and also to another state or nation the parties may agree that the law either of this state or of such other state or nation shall govern their rights and duties. Failing such agreement this Act applies to transactions bearing an appropriate relation to this state.

(2) Where one of the following provisions of this Act specifies the applicable law, that provision governs and a contrary agreement is effective only to the

extent permitted by the law (including the conflict of laws rules) so specified:

Rights of creditors against sold goods. Section 2—402.

Applicability of the Article on Bank Deposits and Collections. Section 4—102.

Bulk transfers subject to the Article on Bulk Transfers. Section 6—102.

Applicability of the Article on Investment Securities. Section 8—106.

Perfection provisions of the Article on Secured Transactions. Section 9—103.

§ 1—106. Remedies to Be Liberally Administered.

(1) The remedies provided by this Act shall be liberally administered to the end that the aggrieved party may be put in as good a position as if the other party had fully performed but neither consequential or special nor penal damages may be had except as specifically provided in this Act or by other rule of law.

(2) Any right or obligation declared by this Act is enforceable by action unless the provision declaring it specifies a different and limited effect.

§ 1—107. Waiver or Renunciation of Claim or Right After Breach.

Any claim or right arising out of an alleged breach can be discharged in whole or in part without consideration by a written waiver or renunciation signed and delivered by the aggrieved party.

§ 1—108. Severability.

If any provision or clause of this Act or application thereof to any person or circumstances is held invalid, such invalidity shall not affect other provisions or applications of the Act which can be given effect without the invalid provision or application, and to this end the provisions of this Act are declared to be severable.

§ 1—109. Section Captions.

Section captions are parts of this Act.

Part 2 General Definitions and Principles of Interpretation

§ 1—201. General Definitions

Subject to additional definitions contained in the subsequent Articles of this Act which are applicable to specific Articles or Parts thereof, and unless the context otherwise requires, in this Act:

(1) "Action" in the sense of a judicial proceeding includes recoupment, counterclaim, set-off, suit in equity and any other proceedings in which rights are determined.

(2) "Aggrieved party" means a party entitled to resort to a remedy.

(3) "Agreement" means the bargain of the parties in fact as found in their language or by implication from other circumstances including course of dealing or usage of trade or course of performance as provided in this Act (Sections 1—205 and 2—208). Whether an agreement has legal consequences is determined by the provisions of this Act, if applicable; otherwise by the law of contracts (Section 1—103). (Compare "Contract".)

(4) "Bank" means any person engaged in the business of banking.

(5) "Bearer" means the person in possession of an instrument, document of title, or certificated security payable to bearer or indorsed in blank.

(6) "Bill of lading" means a document evidencing the receipt of goods for shipment issued by a person engaged in the business of transporting or forwarding goods, and includes an airbill. "Airbill" means a document serving for air transportation as a bill of lading does for marine or rail transportation, and includes an air consignment note or air waybill.

(7) "Branch" includes a separately incorporated foreign branch of a bank.

(8) "Burden of establishing" a fact means the burden of persuading the triers of fact that the existence of the fact is more probable than its non-existence.

(9) "Buyer in ordinary course of business" means a person who in good faith and without knowledge that the sale to him is in violation of the ownership rights or security interest of a third party in the goods buys in ordinary course from a person in the business of selling goods of that kind but does not include a pawnbroker. All persons who sell minerals or the like (including oil and gas) at wellhead or minehead shall be deemed to be persons in the business of selling goods of that kind. "Buying" may be for cash or by exchange of other property or on secured or un-

secured credit and includes receiving goods or documents of title under a pre-existing contract for sale but does not include a transfer in bulk or as security for or in total or partial satisfaction of a money debt.

(10) "Conspicuous": A term or clause is conspicuous when it is so written that a reasonable person against whom it is to operate ought to have noticed it. A printed heading in capitals (as: NON-NEGOTIABLE BILL OF LADING) is conspicuous. Language in the body of a form is "conspicuous" if it is in larger or other contrasting type or color. But in a telegram any stated term is "conspicuous". Whether a term or clause is "conspicuous" or not is for decision by the court.

(11) "Contract" means the total legal obligation which results from the parties' agreement as affected by this Act and any other applicable rules of law. (Compare "Agreement".)

(12) "Creditor" includes a general creditor, a secured creditor, a lien creditor and any representative of creditors, including an assignee for the benefit of creditors, a trustee in bankruptcy, a receiver in equity and an executor or administrator of an insolvent debtor's or assignor's estate.

(13) "Defendant" includes a person in the position of defendant in a cross-action or counterclaim.

(14) "Delivery" with respect to instruments, documents of title, chattel paper, or certificated securities means voluntary transfer of possession.

(15) "Document of title" includes bill of lading, dock warrant, dock receipt, warehouse receipt or order for the delivery of goods, and also any other document which in the regular course of business or financing is treated as adequately evidencing that the person in possession of it is entitled to receive, hold and dispose of the document and the goods it covers. To be a document of title a document must purport to be issued by or addressed to a bailee and purport to cover goods in the bailee's possession which are either identified or are fungible portions of an identified mass.

(16) "Fault" means wrongful act, omission or breach.

(17) "Fungible" with respect to goods or securities means goods or securities of which any unit is, by nature or usage of trade, the equivalent of any other like unit. Goods which are not fungible shall be deemed fungible for the purposes of this Act to the extent that under a particular agreement or document unlike units are treated as equivalents.

(18) "Genuine" means free of forgery or counterfeiting.

(19) "Good faith" means honesty in fact in the conduct or transaction concerned.

(20) "Holder" means a person who is in possession of a document of title or an instrument or a certificated investment security drawn, issued, or indorsed to him or his order or to bearer or in blank.

(21) To "honor" is to pay or to accept and pay, or where a credit so engages to purchase or discount a draft complying with the terms of the credit.

(22) "Insolvency proceedings" includes any assignment for the benefit of creditors or other proceedings intended to liquidate or rehabilitate the estate of the person involved.

(23) A person is "insolvent" who either has ceased to pay his debts in the ordinary course of business or cannot pay his debts as they become due or is insolvent within the meaning of the federal bankruptcy law.

(24) "Money" means a medium of exchange authorized or adopted by a domestic or foreign government as a part of its currency.

(25) A person has "notice" of a fact when

   (a) he has actual knowledge of it; or

   (b) he has received a notice or notification of it; or

   (c) from all the facts and circumstances known to him at the time in question he has reason to know that it exists.

A person "knows" or has "knowledge" of a fact when he has actual knowledge of it. "Discover" or "learn" or a word or phrase of similar import refers to knowledge rather than to reason to know. The time and circumstances under which a notice or notification may cease to be effective are not determined by this Act.

(26) A person "notifies" or "gives" a notice or notification to another by taking such steps as may be reasonably required to inform the other in ordinary

course whether or not such other actually comes to know of it. A person "receives" a notice or notification when

(a) it comes to his attention; or

(b) it is duly delivered at the place of business through which the contract was made or at any other place held out by him as the place for receipt of such communications.

(27) Notice, knowledge or a notice or notification received by an organization is effective for a particular transaction from the time when it is brought to the attention of the individual conducting that transaction, and in any event from the time when it would have been brought to his attention if the organization had exercised due diligence. An organization exercises due diligence if it maintains reasonable routines for communicating significant information to the person conducting the transaction and there is reasonable compliance with the routines. Due diligence does not require an individual acting for the organization to communicate information unless such communication is part of his regular duties or unless he has reason to know of the transaction and that the transaction would be materially affected by the information.

(28) "Organization" includes a corporation, government or governmental subdivision or agency, business trust, estate, trust, partnership or association, two or more persons having a joint or common interest, or any other legal or commercial entity.

(29) "Party", as distinct from "third party", means a person who has engaged in a transaction or made an agreement within this Act.

(30) "Person" includes an individual or an organization (See Section 1—102).

(31) "Presumption" or "presumed" means that the trier of fact must find the existence of the fact presumed unless and until evidence is introduced which would support a finding of its non-existence.

(32) "Purchase" includes taking by sale, discount, negotiation, mortgage, pledge, lien, issue or re-issue, gift or any other voluntary transaction creating an interest in property.

(33) "Purchaser" means a person who takes by purchase.

(34) "Remedy" means any remedial right to which an aggrieved party is entitled with or without resort to a tribunal.

(35) "Representative" includes an agent, an officer of a corporation or association, and a trustee, executor or administrator of an estate, or any other person empowered to act for another.

(36) "Rights" includes remedies.

(37) "Security interest" means an interest in personal property or fixtures which secures payment or performance of an obligation. The retention or reservation of title by a seller of goods notwithstanding shipment or delivery to the buyer (Section 2—401) is limited in effect to a reservation of a "security interest". The term also includes any interest of a buyer of accounts or chattel paper which is subject to Article 9. The special property interest of a buyer of goods on identification of such goods to a contract for sale under Section 2—401 is not a "security interest", but a buyer may also acquire a "security interest" by complying with Article 9. Unless a lease or consignment is intended as security, reservation of title thereunder is not a "security interest" but a consignment is in any event subject to the provisions on consignment sales (Section 2—326). Whether a lease is intended as security is to be determined by the facts of each case; however, (a) the inclusion of an option to purchase does not of itself make the lease one intended for security, and (b) an agreement that upon compliance with the terms of the lease the lessee shall become or has the option to become the owner of the property for no additional consideration or for a nominal consideration does make the lease one intended for security.

(38) "Send" in connection with any writing or notice means to deposit in the mail or deliver for transmission by any other usual means of communication with postage or cost of transmission provided for and properly addressed and in the case of an instrument to an address specified thereon or otherwise agreed, or if there be none to any address reasonable under the circumstances. The receipt of any writing or notice within the time at which it would have arrived if properly sent has the effect of a proper sending.

(39) "Signed" includes any symbol executed or adopted by a party with present intention to authenticate a writing.

(40) "Surety" includes guarantor.

(41) "Telegram" includes a message transmitted by radio, teletype, cable, any mechanical method of transmission, or the like.

(42) "Term" means that portion of an agreement which relates to a particular matter.

(43) "Unauthorized" signature or indorsement means one made without actual, implied or apparent authority and includes a forgery.

(44) "Value". Except as otherwise provided with respect to negotiable instruments and bank collections (Sections 3—303, 4—208 and 4—209) a person gives "value" for rights if he acquires them

    (a) in return for a binding commitment to extend credit or for the extension of immediately available credit whether or not drawn upon and whether or not a chargeback is provided for in the event of difficulties in collection; or

    (b) as security for or in total or partial satisfaction of a pre-existing claim; or

    (c) by accepting delivery pursuant to a pre-existing contract for purchase; or

    (d) generally, in return for any consideration sufficient to support a simple contract.

(45) "Warehouse receipt" means a receipt issued by a person engaged in the business of storing goods for hire.

(46) "Written" or "writing" includes printing, typewriting or any other intentional reduction to tangible form.
Amended in 1962, 1972 and 1977.

§ 1—202. Prima Facie Evidence by Third Party Documents.

A document in due form purporting to be a bill of lading, policy or certificate of insurance, official weigher's or inspector's certificate, consular invoice, or any other document authorized or required by the contract to be issued by a third party shall be prima facie evidence of its own authenticity and genuineness and of the facts stated in the document by the third party.

§ 1—203. Obligation of Good Faith.

Every contract or duty within this Act imposes an obligation of good faith in its performance or enforcement.

§ 1—204. Time; Reasonable Time; "Seasonably".

(1) Whenever this Act requires any action to be taken within a reasonable time, any time which is not manifestly unreasonable may be fixed by agreement.

(2) What is a reasonable time for taking any action depends on the nature, purpose and circumstances of such action.

(3) An action is taken "seasonably" when it is taken at or within the time agreed or if no time is agreed at or within a reasonable time.

§ 1—205. Course of Dealing and Usage of Trade.

(1) A course of dealing is a sequence of previous conduct between the parties to a particular transaction which is fairly to be regarded as establishing a common basis of understanding for interpreting their expressions and other conduct.

(2) A usage of trade is any practice or method of dealing having such regularity of observance in a place, vocation or trade as to justify an expectation that it will be observed with respect to the transaction in question. The existence and scope of such a usage are to be proved as facts. If it is established that such a usage is embodied in a written trade code or similar writing the interpretation of the writing is for the court.

(3) A course of dealing between parties and any usage of trade in the vocation or trade in which they are engaged or of which they are or should be aware give particular meaning to and supplement or qualify terms of an agreement.

(4) The express terms of an agreement and an applicable course of dealing or usage of trade shall be construed wherever reasonable as consistent with each other; but when such construction is unreasonable express terms control both course of dealing and usage of trade and course of dealing controls usage of trade.

(5) An applicable usage of trade in the place where any part of performance is to occur shall be used in interpreting the agreement as to that part of the performance.

(6) Evidence of a relevant usage of trade offered by one party is not admissible unless and until he has given the other party such notice as the court finds sufficient to prevent unfair surprise to the latter.

§ 1—206. **Statute of Frauds for Kinds of Personal Property Not Otherwise Covered.**

(1) Except in the cases described in subsection (2) of this section a contract for the sale of personal property is not enforceable by way of action or defense beyond five thousand dollars in amount or value of remedy unless there is some writing which indicates that a contract for sale has been made between the parties at a defined or stated price, reasonably identifies the subject matter, and is signed by the party against whom enforcement is sought or by his authorized agent.

(2) Subsection (1) of this section does not apply to contracts for the sale of goods (Section 2—201) nor of securities (Section 8—319) nor to security agreements (Section 9—203).

§ 1—207. **Performance or Acceptance Under Reservation of Rights.**

A party who with explicit reservation of rights performs or promises performance or assents to performance in a manner demanded or offered by the other party does not thereby prejudice the rights reserved. Such words as "without prejudice", "under protest" or the like are sufficient.

§ 1—208. **Option to Accelerate at Will.**

A term providing that one party or his successor in interest may accelerate payment or performance or require collateral or additional collateral "at will" or "when he deems himself insecure" or in words of similar import shall be construed to mean that he shall have power to do so only if he in good faith believes that the prospect of payment or performance is impaired. The burden of establishing lack of good faith is on the party against whom the power has been exercised.

§ 1—209. **Subordinated Obligations**

An obligation may be issued as subordinated to payment of another obligation of the person obligated, or a creditor may subordinate his right to payment of an obligation by agreement with either the person obligated or another creditor of the person obligated. Such a subordination does not create a security interest as against either the common debtor or a subordinated creditor. This section shall be construed as declaring the law as it existed prior to the enactment of this section and not as modifying it. Added 1966.

Note: *This new section is proposed as an optional provision to make it clear that a subordination agreement does not create a security interest unless so intended.*

Article 2
SALES

Part 1
Short Title, Construction and Subject Matter

§ 2—101. **Short Title.**

This Article shall be known and may be cited as Uniform Commercial Code—Sales.

§ 2—102. **Scope; Certain Security and Other Transactions Excluded From This Article.**

Unless the context otherwise requires, this Article applies to transactions in goods; it does not apply to any transaction which although in the form of an unconditional contract to sell or present sale is intended to operate only as a security transaction nor does this Article impair or repeal any statute regulating sales to consumers, farmers or other specified classes of buyers.

§ 2—103. **Definitions and Index of Definitions.**

(1) In this Article unless the context otherwise requires

    (a) "Buyer" means a person who buys or contracts to buy goods.

    (b) "Good faith" in the case of a merchant means honesty in fact and the observance of reasonable commercial standards of fair dealing in the trade.

    (c) "Receipt" of goods means taking physical possession of them.

    (d) "Seller" means a person who sells or contracts to sell goods.

(2) Other definitions applying to this Article or to

specified Parts thereof, and the sections in which they appear are:

"Acceptance". Section 2—606.

"Banker's credit". Section 2—325.

"Between merchants". Section 2—104.

"Cancellation". Section 2—106(4).

"Commercial unit". Section 2—105.

"Confirmed credit". Section 2—325.

"Conforming to contract". Section 2—106.

"Contract for sale". Section 2—106.

"Cover". Section 2—712.

"Entrusting". Section 2—403.

"Financing agency". Section 2—104.

"Future goods". Section 2—105.

"Goods". Section 2—105.

"Identification". Section 2—501.

"Installment contract". Section 2—612.

"Letter of Credit". Section 2—325.

"Lot". Section 2—105.

"Merchant". Section 2—104.

"Overseas". Section 2—323.

"Person in position of seller". Section 2—707.

"Present sale". Section 2—106.

"Sale". Section 2—106.

"Sale on approval". Section 2—326.

"Sale or return". Section 2—326.

"Termination". Section 2—106.

(3) The following definitions in other Articles apply to this Article:

"Check". Section 3—104.

"Consignee". Section 7—102.

"Consignor". Section 7—102.

"Consumer goods". Section 9—109.

"Dishonor". Section 3—507.

"Draft". Section 3—104.

(4) In addition Article 1 contains general definitions and principles of construction and interpretation applicable throughout this Article.

§ 2—104. Definitions: "Merchant"; "Between Merchants"; "Financing Agency".

(1) "Merchant" means a person who deals in goods of the kind or otherwise by his occupation holds himself out as having knowledge or skill peculiar to the practices or goods involved in the transaction or to whom such knowledge or skill may be attributed by his employment of an agent or broker or other intermediary who by his occupation holds himself out as having such knowledge or skill.

(2) "Financing agency" means a bank, finance company or other person who in the ordinary course of business makes advances against goods or documents of title or who by arrangement with either the seller or the buyer intervenes in ordinary course to make or collect payment due or claimed under the contract for sale, as by purchasing or paying the seller's draft or making advances against it or by merely taking it for collection whether or not documents of title accompany the draft. "Financing agency" includes also a bank or other person who similarly intervenes between persons who are in the position of seller and buyer in respect to the goods (Section 2—707).

(3) "Between merchants" means in any transaction with respect to which both parties are chargeable with the knowledge or skill of merchants.

§ 2—105. Definitions: Transferability; "Goods"; "Future" Goods; "Lot"; "Commercial Unit".

(1) "Goods" means all things (including specially manufactured goods) which are movable at the time of identification to the contract for sale other than the money in which the price is to be paid, investment securities (Article 8) and things in action. "Goods" also includes the unborn young of animals and growing crops and other identified things attached to realty as described in the section on goods to be severed from realty (Section 2—107).

(2) Goods must be both existing and identified before any interest in them can pass. Goods which are not both existing and identified are "future" goods. A purported present sale of future goods or of any interest therein operates as a contract to sell.

(3) There may be a sale of a part interest in existing identified goods.

(4) An undivided share in an identified bulk of fungible goods is sufficiently identified to be sold although the quantity of the bulk is not determined. Any agreed proportion of such a bulk or any quantity thereof agreed upon by number, weight or other measure may to the extent of the seller's interest in the bulk be sold to the buyer who then becomes an owner in common.

(5) "Lot" means a parcel or a single article which is the subject matter of a separate sale or delivery, whether or not it is sufficient to perform the contract.

(6) "Commercial unit" means such a unit of goods as by commercial usage is a single whole for purposes of sale and division of which materially impairs its character or value on the market or in use. A commercial unit may be a single article (as a machine) or a set of articles (as a suite of furniture or an assortment of sizes) or a quantity (as a bale, gross, or carload) or any other unit treated in use or in the relevant market as a single whole.

§ 2—106. **Definitions: "Contract"; "Agreement"; "Contract for Sale"; "Sale"; "Present Sale"; "Conforming" to Contract; "Termination"; "Cancellation".**

(1) In this Article unless the context otherwise requires "contract" and "agreement" are limited to those relating to the present or future sale of goods. "Contract for sale" includes both a present sale of goods and a contract to sell goods at a future time. A "sale" consists in the passing of title from the seller to the buyer for a price (Section 2—401). A "present sale" means a sale which is accomplished by the making of the contract.

(2) Goods or conduct including any part of a performance are "conforming" or conform to the contract when they are in accordance with the obligations under the contract.

(3) "Termination" occurs when either party pursuant to a power created by agreement or law puts an end to the contract otherwise than for its breach. On "termination" all obligations which are still executory on both sides are discharged but any right based on prior breach or performance survives.

(4) "Cancellation" occurs when either party puts an end to the contract for breach by the other and its effect is the same as that of "termination" except that the cancelling party also retains any remedy for breach of the whole contract or any unperformed balance.

§ 2—107. **Goods to Be Severed From Realty: Recording.**

(1) A contract for the sale of minerals or the like (including oil and gas) or a structure or its materials to be removed from realty is a contract for the sale of goods within this Article if they are to be severed by the seller but until severance a purported present sale thereof which is not effective as a transfer of an interest in land is effective only as a contract to sell.

(2) A contract for the sale apart from the land of growing crops or other things attached to realty and capable of severance without material harm thereto but not described in subsection (1) or of timber to be cut is a contract for the sale of goods within this Article whether the subject matter is to be severed by the buyer or by the seller even though it forms part of the realty at the time of contracting, and the parties can by identification effect a present sale before severance.

(3) The provisions of this section are subject to any third party rights provided by the law relating to realty records, and the contract for sale may be executed and recorded as a document transferring an interest in land and shall then constitute notice to third parties of the buyer's rights under the contract for sale.

Part 2 **Form, Formation and Readjustment of Contract**

§ 2—201. **Formal Requirements; Statute of Frauds.**

(1) Except as otherwise provided in this section a contract for the sale of goods for the price of $500 or more is not enforceable by way of action or defense unless there is some writing sufficient to indicate that a contract for sale has been made between the parties and signed by the party against whom enforcement is sought or by his authorized agent or broker. A writing is not insufficient because it omits or incorrectly states a term agreed upon but the contract is not enforceable under this paragraph beyond the quantity of goods shown in such writing.

(2) Between merchants if within a reasonable time a writing in confirmation of the contract and sufficient against the sender is received and the party receiving it has reason to know its contents, it satisfies the requirements of subsection (1) against such party unless written notice of objection to its contents is given within ten days after it is received.

(3) A contract which does not satisfy the requirements of subsection (1) but which is valid in other respects is enforceable

(a) if the goods are to be specially manufactured for the buyer and are not suitable for sale to others in the ordinary course of the seller's business and the seller, before notice of repudiation is received and under circumstances which reasonably indicate that the goods are for the buyer, has made either a substantial beginning of their manufacture or commitments for their procurement; or

(b) if the party against whom enforcement is sought admits in his pleading, testimony or otherwise in court that a contract for sale was made, but the contract is not enforceable under this provision beyond the quantity of goods admitted; or

(c) with respect to goods for which payment has been made and accepted or which have been received and accepted (Sec. 2—606).

§ 2—202. **Final Written Expression: Parol or Extrinsic Evidence.**

Terms with respect to which the confirmatory memoranda of the parties agree or which are otherwise set forth in a writing intended by the parties as a final expression of their agreement with respect to such terms as are included therein may not be contradicted by evidence of any prior agreement or of a contemporaneous oral agreement but may be explained or supplemented

(a) by course of dealing or usage of trade (Section 1—205) or by course of performance (Section 2—208); and

(b) by evidence of consistent additional terms unless the court finds the writing to have been intended also as a complete and exclusive statement of the terms of the agreement.

§ 2—203. **Seals Inoperative.**

The affixing of a seal to a writing evidencing a contract for sale or an offer to buy or sell goods does not constitute the writing a sealed instrument and the law with respect to sealed instruments does not apply to such a contract or offer.

§ 2—204. **Formation in General.**

(1) A contract for sale of goods may be made in any manner sufficient to show agreement, including conduct by both parties which recognizes the existence of such a contract.

(2) An agreement sufficient to constitute a contract for sale may be found even though the moment of its making is undetermined.

(3) Even though one or more terms are left open a contract for sale does not fail for indefiniteness if the parties have intended to make a contract and there is a reasonably certain basis for giving an appropriate remedy.

§ 2—205. **Firm Offers.**

An offer by a merchant to buy or sell goods in a signed writing which by its terms gives assurance that it will be held open is not revocable, for lack of consideration, during the time stated or if no time is stated for a reasonable time, but in no event may such period of irrevocability exceed three months; but any such term of assurance on a form supplied by the offeree must be separately signed by the offeror.

§ 2—206. **Offer and Acceptance in Formation of Contract.**

(1) Unless other unambiguously indicated by the language or circumstances

(a) an offer to make a contract shall be construed as inviting acceptance in any manner and by any medium reasonable in the circumstances;

(b) an order or other offer to buy goods for prompt or current shipment shall be construed as inviting acceptance either by a prompt promise to ship or by the prompt or current shipment of conforming or nonconforming goods, but such a shipment of non-conforming goods does not constitute an acceptance if the seller seasonably notifies the buyer that the shipment is offered only as an accommodation to the buyer.

(2) Where the beginning of a requested performance is a reasonable mode of acceptance an offeror who is not notified of acceptance within a reasonable time may treat the offer as having lapsed before acceptance.

§ 2—207. **Additional Terms in Acceptance or Confirmation.**

(1) A definite and seasonable expression of accep-

tance or a written confirmation which is sent within a reasonable time operates as an acceptance even though it states terms additional to or different from those offered or agreed upon, unless acceptance is expressly made conditional on assent to the additional or different terms.

(2) The additional terms are to be construed as proposals for addition to the contract. Between merchants such terms become part of the contract unless:

  (a) the offer expressly limits acceptance to the terms of the offer;

  (b) they materially alter it; or

  (c) notification of objection to them has already been given or is given within a reasonable time after notice of them is received.

(3) Conduct by both parties which recognizes the existence of a contract is sufficient to establish a contract for sale although the writings of the parties do not otherwise establish a contract. In such case the terms of the particular contract consist of those terms on which the writings of the parties agree, together with any supplementary terms incorporated under any other provisions of this Act.

§ 2—208. **Course of Performance or Practical Construction.**

(1) Where the contract for sale involves repeated occasions for performance by either party with knowledge of the nature of the performance and opportunity for objection to it by the other, any course of performance accepted or acquiesced in without objection shall be relevant to determine the meaning of the agreement.

(2) The express terms of the agreement and any such course of performance, as well as any course of dealing and usage of trade, shall be construed whenever reasonable as consistent with each other; but when such construction is unreasonable, express terms shall control course of performance and course of performance shall control both course of dealing and usage of trade (Section 1—205).

(3) Subject to the provisions of the next section on modification and waiver, such course of performance shall be relevant to show a waiver or modification of

any term inconsistent with such course of performance.

§ 2—209. **Modification, Rescission and Waiver.**

(1) An agreement modifying a contract within this Article needs no consideration to be binding.

(2) A signed agreement which excludes modification or rescission except by a signed writing cannot be otherwise modified or rescinded, but except as between merchants such a requirement on a form supplied by the merchant must be separately signed by the other party.

(3) The requirements of the statute of frauds section of this Article (Section 2—201) must be satisfied if the contract as modifed is within its provisions.

(4) Although an attempt at modification or rescission does not satisfy the requirements of subsection (2) or (3) it can operate as a waiver.

(5) A party who has made a waiver affecting an executory portion of the contract may retract the waiver by reasonable notification received by the other party that strict performance will be required of any term waived, unless the retraction would be unjust in view of a material change of position in reliance on the waiver.

§ 2—210. **Delegation of Performance; Assignment of Rights.**

(1) A party may perform his duty through a delegate unless otherwise agreed or unless the other party has a substantial interest in having his original promisor perform or control the acts required by the contract. No delegation of performance relieves the party delegating of any duty to perform or any liability for breach.

(2) Unless otherwise agreed all rights of either seller or buyer can be assigned except where the assignment would materially change the duty of the other party, or increase materially the burden or risk imposed on him by his contract, or impair materially his chance of obtaining return performance. A right to damages for breach of the whole contract or a right arising out of the assignor's due performance of his entire obligation can be assigned despite agreement otherwise.

(3) Unless the circumstances indicate the contrary a

prohibition of assignment of "the contract" is to be construed as barring only the delegation to the assignee of the assignor's performance.

(4) An assignment of "the contract" or of "all my rights under the contract" or an assignment in similar general terms is an assignment of rights and unless the language or the circumstances (as in an assignment for security) indicate the contrary, it is a delegation of performance of the duties of the assignor and its acceptance by the assignee constitutes a promise by him to perform those duties. This promise is enforceable by either the assignor or the other party to the original contract.

(5) The other party may treat any assignment which delegates performance as creating reasonable grounds for insecurity and may without prejudice to his rights against the assignor demand assurances from the assignee (Section 2—609).

Part 3 General Obligation and Construction of Contract

§ 2—301. General Obligations of Parties.

The obligation of the seller is to transfer and deliver and that of the buyer is to accept and pay in accordance with the contract.

§ 2—302. Unconscionable Contract or Clause.

(1) If the court as a matter of law finds the contract or any clause of the contract to have been unconscionable at the time it was made the court may refuse to enforce the contract, or it may enforce the remainder of the contract without the unconscionable clause, or it may so limit the application of any unconscionable clause as to avoid any unconscionable result.

(2) When it is claimed or appears to the court that the contract or any clause thereof may be unconscionable the parties shall be afforded a reasonable opportunity to present evidence as to its commercial setting, purpose and effect to aid the court in making the determination.

§ 2—303. Allocation or Division of Risks.

Where this Article allocates a risk or a burden as between the parties "unless otherwise agreed", the agreement may not only shift the allocation but may also divide the risk or burden.

§ 2—304. Price Payable in Money, Goods, Realty, or Otherwise.

(1) The price can be made payable in money or otherwise. If it is payable in whole or in part in goods each party is a seller of the goods which he is to transfer.

(2) Even though all or part of the price is payable in an interest in realty the transfer of the goods and the seller's obligations with reference to them are subject to this Article, but not the transfer of the interest in realty or the transferor's obligations in connection therewith.

§ 2—305. Open Price Term.

(1) The parties if they so intend can conclude a contract for sale even though the price is not settled. In such a case the price is a reasonable price at the time for delivery if

    (a) nothing is said as to price; or

    (b) the price is left to be agreed by the parties and they fail to agree; or

    (c) the price is to be fixed in terms of some agreed market or other standard as set or recorded by a third person or agency and it is not so set or recorded.

(2) A price to be fixed by the seller or by the buyer means a price for him to fix in good faith.

(3) When a price left to be fixed otherwise than by agreement of the parties fails to be fixed through fault of one party the other may at his option treat the contract as cancelled or himself fix a reasonable price.

(4) Where, however, the parties intend not to be bound unless the price be fixed or agreed and it is not fixed or agreed there is no contract. In such a case the buyer must return any goods already received or if unable so to do must pay their reasonable value at the time of delivery and the seller must return any portion of the price paid on account.

§ 2—306. Output, Requirements and Exclusive Dealings.

(1) A term which measures the quantity by the output of the seller or the requirements of the buyer means such actual output or requirements as may occur in good faith, except that no quantity unreasonably

disproportionate to any stated estimate or in the absence of a stated estimate to any normal or otherwise comparable prior output or requirements may be tendered or demanded.

(2) A lawful agreement by either the seller or the buyer for exclusive dealing in the kind of goods concerned imposes unless otherwise agreed an obligation by the seller to use best efforts to supply the goods and by the buyer to use best efforts to promote their sale.

§ 2—307. **Delivery in Single Lot or Several Lots.**

Unless otherwise agreed all goods called for by a contract for sale must be tendered in a single delivery and payment is due only on such tender but where the circumstances give either party the right to make or demand delivery in lots the price if it can be apportioned may be demanded for each lot.

§ 2—308. **Absence of Specified Place for Delivery.**

Unless otherwise agreed

(a) the place for delivery of goods is the seller's place of business or if he has none his residence; but

(b) in a contract for sale of identified goods which to the knowledge of the parties at the time of contracting are in some other place, that place is the place for their delivery; and

(c) documents of title may be delivered through customary banking channels.

§ 2—309. **Absence of Specific Time Provisions; Notice of Termination.**

(1) The time for shipment or delivery or any other action under a contract if not provided in this Article or agreed upon shall be a reasonable time.

(2) Where the contract provides for successive performances but is indefinite in duration it is valid for a reasonable time but unless otherwise agreed may be terminated at any time by either party.

(3) Termination of a contract by one party except on the happening of an agreed event requires that reasonable notification be received by the other party and an agreement dispensing with notification is invalid if its operation would be unconscionable.

§ 2—310. **Open Time for Payment or Running of Credit; Authority to Ship Under Reservation.**

Unless otherwise agreed

(a) payment is due at the time and place at which the buyer is to receive the goods even though the place of shipment is the place of delivery; and

(b) if the seller is authorized to send the goods he may ship them under reservation, and may tender the documents of title, but the buyer may inspect the goods after their arrival before payment is due unless such inspection is inconsistent with the terms of the contract (Section 2—513); and

(c) if delivery is authorized and made by way of documents of title otherwise than by subsection (b) then payment is due at the time and place at which the buyer is to receive the documents regardless of where the goods are to be received; and

(d) where the seller is required or authorized to ship the goods on credit the credit period runs from the time of shipment but post-dating the invoice or delaying its dispatch will correspondingly delay the starting of the credit period.

§ 2—311. **Options and Cooperation Respecting Performance.**

(1) An agreement for sale which is otherwise sufficiently definite (subsection (3) of Section 2—204) to be a contract is not made invalid by the fact that it leaves particulars of performance to be specified by one of the parties. Any such specification must be made in good faith and within limits set by commercial reasonableness.

(2) Unless otherwise agreed specifications relating to assortment of the goods are at the buyer's option and except as otherwise provided in subsections (1) (c) and (3) of Section 2—319 specifications or arrangements relating to shipment are at the seller's option.

(3) Where such specification would materially affect the other party's performance but is not seasonably made or where one party's cooperation is necessary to the agreed performance of the other but is not seasonably forthcoming, the other party in addition to all other remedies

(a) is excused for any resulting delay in his own performance; and

(b) may also either proceed to perform in any reasonable manner or after the time for a material part of his own performance treat the failure to specify or to cooperate as a breach by failure to deliver or accept the goods.

§ 2—312. Warranty of Title and Against Infringement; Buyer's Obligation Against Infringement.

(1) Subject to subsection (2) there is in a contract for sale a warranty by the seller that

(a) the title conveyed shall be good, and its transfer rightful; and

(b) the goods shall be delivered free from any security interest or other lien or encumbrance of which the buyer at the time of contracting has no knowledge.

(2) A warranty under subsection (1) will be excluded or modified only by specific language or by circumstances which give the buyer reason to know that the person selling does not claim title in himself or that he is purporting to sell only such right or title as he or a third person may have.

(3) Unless otherwise agreed a seller who is a merchant regularly dealing in goods of the kind warrants that the goods shall be delivered free of the rightful claim of any third person by way of infringement or the like but a buyer who furnishes specifications to the seller must hold the seller harmless against any such claim which arises out of compliance with the specifications.

§ 2—313. Express Warranties by Affirmation, Promise, Description, Sample.

(1) Express warranties by the seller are created as follows:

(a) Any affirmation of fact or promise made by the seller to the buyer which relates to the goods and becomes part of the basis of the bargain creates an express warranty that the goods shall conform to the affirmation or promise.

(b) Any description of the goods which is made part of the basis of the bargain creates an express warranty that the goods shall conform to the description.

(c) Any sample or model which is made part of the basis of the bargain creates an express warranty that the whole of the goods shall conform to the sample or model.

(2) It is not necessary to the creation of an express warranty that the seller use formal words such as "warrant" or "guarantee" or that he have a specific intention to make a warranty, but an affirmation merely of the value of the goods or a statement purporting to be merely the seller's opinion or commendation of the goods does not create a warranty.

§ 2—314. Implied Warranty: Merchantability; Usage of Trade.

(1) Unless excluded or modified (Section 2—316), a warranty that the goods shall be merchantable is implied in a contract for their sale if the seller is a merchant with respect to goods of that kind. Under this section the serving for value of food or drink to be consumed either on the premises or elsewhere is a sale.

(2) Goods to be merchantable must be at least such as

(a) pass without objection in the trade under the contract description; and

(b) in the case of fungible goods, are of fair average quality within the description; and

(c) are fit for the ordinary purposes for which such goods are used; and

(d) run, within the variations permitted by the agreement, of even kind, quality and quantity within each unit and among all units involved; and

(e) are adequately contained, packaged, and labeled as the agreement may require; and

(f) conform to the promises or affirmations of fact made on the container or label if any.

(3) Unless excluded or modified (Section 2—316) other implied warranties may arise from course of dealing or usage of trade.

§ 2—315. Implied Warranty: Fitness for Particular Purpose.

Where the seller at the time of contracting has reason to know any particular purpose for which the goods are required and that the buyer is relying on the seller's skill or judgment to select or furnish suitable goods, there is unless excluded or modified under the next section an implied warranty that the goods shall be fit for such purpose.

§ 2—316. **Exclusion or Modification of Warranties.**

(1) Words or conduct relevant to the creation of an express warranty and words or conduct tending to negate or limit warranty shall be construed wherever reasonable as consistent with each other; but subject to the provisions of this Article on parol or extrinsic evidence (Section 2—202) negation or limitation is inoperative to the extent that such construction is unreasonable.

(2) Subject to subsection (3), to exclude or modify the implied warranty of merchantability or any part of it the language must mention merchantability and in case of a writing must be conspicuous, and to exclude or modify any implied warranty of fitness the exclusion must be by a writing and conspicuous. Language to exclude all implied warranties of fitness is sufficient if it states, for example, that "There are no warranties which extend beyond the description on the face hereof."

(3) Notwithstanding subsection (2)

(a) unless the circumstances indicate otherwise, all implied warranties are excluded by expressions like "as is", "with all faults" or other language which in common understanding calls the buyer's attention to the exclusion of warranties and makes plain that there is no implied warranty; and

(b) when the buyer before entering into the contract has examined the goods or the sample or model as fully as he desired or has refused to examine the goods there is no implied warranty with regard to defects which an examination ought in the circumstances to have revealed to him; and

(c) an implied warranty can also be excluded or modified by course of dealing or course of performance or usage of trade.

(4) Remedies for breach of warranty can be limited in accordance with the provisions of this Article on liquidation or limitation of damages and on contractual modification of remedy (Sections 2—718 and 2—719).

§ 2—317. **Cumulation and Conflict of Warranties Express or Implied.**

Warranties whether express or implied shall be construed as consistent with each other and as cumulative, but if such construction is unreasonable the intention of the parties shall determine which warranty is dominant. In ascertaining that intention the following rules apply:

(a) Exact or technical specifications displace an inconsistent sample or model or general language of description.

(b) A sample from an existing bulk displaces inconsistent general language of description.

(c) Express warranties displace inconsistent implied warranties other than an implied warranty of fitness for a particular purpose.

§ 2—318. **Third Party Beneficiaries of Warranties Express or Implied.**

Note: If this Act is introduced in the Congress of the United States this section should be omitted. (States to select one alternative.)

Alternative A

A seller's warranty whether express or implied extends to any natural person who is in the family or household of his buyer or who is a guest in his home if it is reasonable to expect that such person may use, consume or be affected by the goods and who is injured in person by breach of the warranty. A seller may not exclude or limit the operation of this section.

Alternative B

A seller's warranty whether express or implied extends to any natural person who may reasonably be expected to use, consume or be affected by the goods and who is injured in person by breach of the warranty. A seller may not exclude or limit the operation of this section.

Alternative C

A seller's warranty whether express or implied extends to any person who may reasonably be expected to use, consume or be affected by the goods and who is injured by breach of the warranty. A seller may not exclude or limit the operation of this section with respect to injury to the person of an individual to whom the warranty extends. As amended 1966.

§ 2—319. **F.O.B. and F.A.S. Terms.**

(1) Unless otherwise agreed the term F.O.B. (which means "free on board") at a named place, even though used only in connection with the stated price, is a delivery term under which

(a) when the term is F.O.B. the place of shipment, the seller must at that place ship the goods in the manner provided in this Article (Section 2—504) and bear the expense and risk of putting them into the possession of the carrier; or

(b) when the term is F.O.B. the place of destination, the seller must at his own expense and risk transport the goods to that place and there tender delivery of them in the manner provided in this Article (Section 2—503);

(c) when under either (a) or (b) the term is also F.O.B. vessel, car or other vehicle, the seller must in addition at his own expense and risk load the goods on board. If the term is F.O.B. vessel the buyer must name the vessel and in an appropriate case the seller must comply with the provisions of this Article on the form of bill of lading (Section 2—323).

(2) Unless otherwise agreed the term F.A.S. vessel (which means "free alongside") at a named port, even though used only in connection with the stated price, is a delivery term under which the seller must

(a) at his own expense and risk deliver the goods alongside the vessel in the manner usual in that port or on a dock designated and provided by the buyer; and

(b) obtain and tender a receipt for the goods in exchange for which the carrier is under a duty to issue a bill of lading.

(3) Unless otherwise agreed in any case falling within subsection (1) (a) or (c) or subsection (2) the buyer must seasonably give any needed instructions for making delivery, including when the term is F.A.S. or F.O.B. the loading berth of the vessel and in an appropriate case its name and sailing date. The seller may treat the failure of needed instructions as a failure of cooperation under this Article (Section 2—311). He may also at his option move the goods in any reasonable manner preparatory to delivery or shipment.

(4) Under the term F.O.B. vessel or F.A.S. unless otherwise agreed the buyer must make payment against tender of the required documents and the seller may not tender nor the buyer demand delivery of the goods in substitution for the documents.

§ 2—320. **C.I.F. and C. & F. Terms.**

(1) The term C.I.F. means that the price includes in a lump sum the cost of the goods and the insurance and freight to the named destination. The term C. & F. or C.F. means that the price so includes cost and freight to the named destination.

(2) Unless otherwise agreed and even though used only in connection with the stated price and destination, the term C.I.F. destination or its equivalent requires the seller at his own expense and risk to

(a) put the goods into the possession of a carrier at the port for shipment and obtain a negotiable bill or bills of lading covering the entire transportation to the named destination; and

(b) load the goods and obtain a receipt from the carrier (which may be contained in the bill of lading) showing that the freight has been paid or provided for; and

(c) obtain a policy or certificate of insurance, including any war risk insurance, of a kind and on terms then current at the port of shipment in the usual amount, in the currency of the contract, shown to cover the same goods covered by the bill of lading and providing for payment of loss to the order of the buyer or for the account of whom it may concern; but the seller may add to the price the amount of the premium for any such war risk insurance; and

(d) prepare an invoice of the goods and procure any other documents required to effect shipment or to comply with the contract; and

(e) forward and tender with commercial promptness all the documents in due form and with any indorsement necessary to perfect the buyer's rights.

(3) Unless otherwise agreed the term C. & F. or its equivalent has the same effect and imposes upon the seller the same obligations and risks as a C.I.F. term except the obligation as to insurance.

(4) Under the term C.I.F. or C. & F. unless otherwise agreed the buyer must make payment against tender

of the required documents and the seller may not tender nor the buyer demand delivery of the goods in substitution for the documents.

§ 2—321. **C.I.F. or C. & F.: "Net Landed Weights"; "Payment on Arrival"; Warranty of Condition on Arrival.**

Under a contract containing a term C.I.F. or C. & F.

(1) Where the price is based on or is to be adjusted according to "net landed weights", "delivered weights", "out turn" quantity or quality or the like, unless otherwise agreed the seller must reasonably estimate the price. The payment due on tender of the documents called for by the contract is the amount so estimated, but after final adjustment of the price a settlement must be made with commercial promptness.

(2) An agreement described in subsection (1) or any warranty of quality or condition of the goods on arrival places upon the seller the risk of ordinary deterioration, shrinkage and the like in transportation but has no effect on the place or time of identification to the contract for sale or delivery or on the passing of the risk of loss.

(3) Unless otherwise agreed where the contract provides for payment on or after arrival of the goods the seller must before payment allow such preliminary inspection as is feasible; but if the goods are lost delivery of the documents and payment are due when the goods should have arrived.

§ 2—322. **Delivery "Ex-Ship".**

(1) Unless otherwise agreed a term for delivery of goods "ex-ship" (which means from the carrying vessel) or in equivalent language is not restricted to a particular ship and requires delivery from a ship which has reached a place at the named port of destination where goods of the kind are usually discharged.

(2) Under such a term unless otherwise agreed

(a) the seller must discharge all liens arising out of the carriage and furnish the buyer with a direction which puts the carrier under a duty to deliver the goods; and

(b) the risk of loss does not pass to the buyer until the goods leave the ship's tackle or are otherwise properly unloaded.

§ 2—323. **Form of Bill of Lading Required in Overseas Shipment; "Overseas".**

(1) Where the contract contemplates overseas shipment and contains a term C.I.F. or C. & F. or F.O.B. vessel, the seller unless otherwise agreed must obtain a negotiable bill of lading stating that the goods have been loaded on board or, in the case of a term C.I.F. or C. & F., received for shipment.

(2) Where in a case within subsection (1) a bill of lading has been issued in a set of parts, unless otherwise agreed if the documents are not to be sent from abroad the buyer may demand tender of the full set; otherwise only one part of the bill of lading need be tendered. Even if the agreement expressly requires a full set

(a) due tender of a single part is acceptable within the provisions of this Article on cure of improper delivery (subsection (1) of Section 2—508); and

(b) even though the full set is demanded, if the documents are sent from abroad the person tendering an incomplete set may nevertheless require payment upon furnishing an indemnity which the buyer in good faith deems adequate.

(3) A shipment by water or by air or a contract contemplating such shipment is "overseas" insofar as by usage of trade or agreement it is subject to the commercial, financing or shipping practices characteristic of international deep water commerce.

§ 2—324. **"No Arrival, No Sale" Term.**

Under a term "no arrival, no sale" or terms of like meaning, unless otherwise agreed,

(a) the seller must properly ship conforming goods and if they arrive by any means he must tender them on arrival but he assumes no obligation that the goods will arrive unless he has caused the non-arrival; and

(b) where without fault of the seller the goods are in part lost or have so deteriorated as no longer to conform to the contract or arrive after the contract time, the buyer may proceed as if there had been casualty to identified goods (Section 2—613).

§ 2—325. **"Letter of Credit" Term; "Confirmed Credit".**

(1) Failure of the buyer seasonably to furnish an agreed letter of credit is a breach of the contract for sale.

(2) The delivery to seller of a proper letter of credit suspends the buyer's obligation to pay. If the letter of credit is dishonored, the seller may on seasonable notification to the buyer require payment directly from him.

(3) Unless otherwise agreed the term "letter of credit" or "banker's credit" in a contract for sale means an irrevocable credit issued by a financing agency of good repute and, where the shipment is overseas, of good international repute. The term "confirmed credit" means that the credit must also carry the direct obligation of such an agency which does business in the seller's financial market.

§ 2—326. Sale on Approval and Sale or Return; Consignment Sales and Rights of Creditors.

(1) Unless otherwise agreed, if delivered goods may be returned by the buyer even though they conform to the contract, the transaction is

(a) a "sale on approval" if the goods are delivered primarily for use, and

(b) a "sale or return" if the goods are delivered primarily for resale.

(2) Except as provided in subsection (3), goods held on approval are not subject to the claims of the buyer's creditors until acceptance; goods held on sale or return are subject to such claims while in the buyer's possession.

(3) Where goods are delivered to a person for sale and such person maintains a place of business at which he deals in goods of the kind involved, under a name other than the name of the person making delivery, then with respect to claims of creditors of the person conducting the business the goods are deemed to be on sale or return. The provisions of this subsection are applicable even though an agreement purports to reserve title to the person making delivery until payment or resale or uses such words as "on consignment" or "on memorandum". However, this subsection is not applicable if the person making delivery

(a) complies with an applicable law providing for a consignor's interest or the like to be evidenced by a sign, or

(b) establishes that the person conducting the business is generally known by his creditors to be

substantially engaged in selling the goods of others, or

(c) complies with the filing provisions of the Article on Secured Transactions (Article 9).

(4) Any "or return" term of a contract for sale is to be treated as a separate contract for sale within the statute of frauds section of this Article (Section 2—201) and as contradicting the sale aspect of the contract within the provisions of this Article on parol or extrinsic evidence (Section 2—202).

§ 2—327. Special Incidents of Sale on Approval and Sale or Return.

(1) Under a sale on approval unless otherwise agreed

(a) although the goods are identified to the contract the risk of loss and the title do not pass to the buyer until acceptance; and

(b) use of the goods consistent with the purpose of trial is not acceptance but failure seasonably to notify the seller of election to return the goods is acceptance, and if the goods conform to the contract acceptance of any part is acceptance of the whole; and

(c) after due notification of election to return, the return is at the seller's risk and expense but a merchant buyer must follow any reasonable instructions.

(2) Under a sale or return unless otherwise agreed

(a) the option to return extends to the whole or any commercial unit of the goods while in substantially their original condition, but must be exercised seasonably; and

(b) the return is at the buyer's risk and expense.

§ 2—328. Sale by Auction.

(1) In a sale by auction if goods are put up in lots each lot is the subject of a separate sale.

(2) A sale by auction is complete when the auctioneer so announces by the fall of the hammer or in other customary manner. Where a bid is made while the hammer is falling in acceptance of a prior bid the auctioneer may in his discretion reopen the bidding or declare the goods sold under the bid on which the hammer was falling.

(3) Such a sale is with reserve unless the goods are in explicit terms put up without reserve. In an auction with reserve the auctioneer may withdraw the goods at any time until he announces completion of the sale. In an auction without reserve, after the auctioneer calls for bids on an article or lot, that article or lot cannot be withdrawn unless no bid is made within a reasonable time. In either case a bidder may retract his bid until the auctioneer's announcement of completion of the sale, but a bidder's retraction does not revive any previous bid.

(4) If the auctioneer knowingly receives a bid on the seller's behalf or the seller makes or procures such a bid, and notice has not been given that liberty for such bidding is reserved, the buyer may at his option avoid the sale or take the goods at the price of the last good faith bid prior to the completion of the sale. This subsection shall not apply to any bid at a forced sale.

Part 4 Title, Creditors and Good Faith Purchasers

§ 2—401. **Passing of Title; Reservation for Security; Limited Application of This Section.**

Each provision of this Article with regard to the rights, obligations and remedies of the seller, the buyer, purchasers or other third parties applies irrespective of title to the goods except where the provision refers to such title. Insofar as situations are not covered by the other provisions of this Article and matters concerning title became material the following rules apply:

(1) Title to goods cannot pass under a contract for sale prior to their identification to the contract (Section 2—501), and unless otherwise explicitly agreed the buyer acquires by their identification a special property as limited by this Act. Any retention or reservation by the seller of the title (property) in goods shipped or delivered to the buyer is limited in effect to a reservation of a security interest. Subject to these provisions and to the provisions of the Article on Secured Transactions (Article 9), title to goods passes from the seller to the buyer in any manner and on any conditions explicitly agreed on by the parties.

(2) Unless otherwise explicitly agreed title passes to the buyer at the time and place at which the seller completes his performance with reference to the physical delivery of the goods, despite any reservation of a security interest and even though a document of title is to be delivered at a different time or place; and in particular and despite any reservation of a security interest by the bill of lading

(a) if the contract requires or authorizes the seller to send the goods to the buyer but does not require him to deliver them at destination, title passes to the buyer at the time and place of shipment; but

(b) if the contract requires delivery at destination, title passes on tender there.

(3) Unless otherwise explicitly agreed where delivery is to be made without moving the goods,

(a) if the seller is to deliver a document of title, title passes at the time when and the place where he delivers such documents; or

(b) if the goods are at the time of contracting already identified and no documents are to be delivered, title passes at the time and place of contracting.

(4) A rejection or other refusal by the buyer to receive or retain the goods, whether or not justified, or a justified revocation of acceptance revests title to the goods in the seller. Such revesting occurs by operation of law and is not a "sale".

§ 2—402. **Rights of Seller's Creditors Against Sold Goods.**

(1) Except as provided in subsections (2) and (3), rights of unsecured creditors of the seller with respect to goods which have been identified to a contract for sale are subject to the buyer's rights to recover the goods under this Article (Sections 2—502 and 2—716).

(2) A creditor of the seller may treat a sale or an identification of goods to a contract for sale as void if as against him a retention of possession by the seller is fraudulent under any rule of law of the state where the goods are situated, except that retention of possession in good faith and current course of trade by a merchant-seller for a commercially reasonable time after a sale or identification is not fraudulent.

(3) Nothing in this Article shall be deemed to impair the rights of creditors of the seller

(a) under the provisions of the Article on Secured Transactions (Article 9); or

(b) where identification to the contract or delivery is made not in current course of trade but in satisfaction of or as security for a pre-existing claim for money, security or the like and is made under circumstances which under any rule of law of the state where the goods are situated would apart from this Article constitute the transaction a fraudulent transfer or voidable preference.

§ 2—403. Power to Transfer; Good Faith Purchase of Goods; "Entrusting".

(1) A purchaser of goods acquires all title which his transferor had or had power to transfer except that a purchaser of a limited interest acquires rights only to the extent of the interest purchased. A person with voidable title has power to transfer a good title to a good faith purchaser for value. When goods have been delivered under a transaction of purchase the purchaser has such power even though

(a) the transferor was deceived as to the identity of the purchaser, or

(b) the delivery was in exchange for a check which is later dishonored, or

(c) it was agreed that the transaction was to be a "cash sale", or

(d) the delivery was procured through fraud punishable as larcenous under the criminal law.

(2) Any entrusting of possession of goods to a merchant who deals in goods of that kind gives him power to transfer all rights of the entruster to a buyer in ordinary course of business.

(3) "Entrusting" includes any delivery and any acquiescence in retention of possession regardless of any condition expressed between the parties to the delivery or acquiescence and regardless of whether the procurement of the entrusting or the possessor's disposition of the goods have been such as to be larcenous under the criminal law.

(4) The rights of other purchasers of goods and of lien creditors are governed by the Articles on Secured Transactions (Article 9), Bulk Transfers (Article 6) and Documents of Title (Article 7).

Part 5 Performance

§ 2—501. Insurable Interest in Goods; Manner of Identification of Goods.

(1) The buyer obtains a special property and an insurable interest in goods by identification of existing goods as goods to which the contract refers even though the goods so identified are non-conforming and he has an option to return or reject them. Such identification can be made at any time and in any manner explicitly agreed to by the parties. In the absence of explicit agreement identification occurs

(a) when the contract is made if it is for the sale of goods already existing and identified;

(b) if the contract is for the sale of future goods other than those described in paragraph (c), when goods are shipped, marked or otherwise designated by the seller as goods to which the contract refers;

(c) when the crops are planted or otherwise become growing crops or the young are conceived if the contract is for the sale of unborn young to be born within twelve months after contracting or for the sale of crops to be harvested within twelve months or the next normal harvest season after contracting whichever is longer.

(2) The seller retains an insurable interest in goods so long as title to or any security interest in the goods remains in him and where the identification is by the seller alone he may until default or insolvency or notification to the buyer that the identification is final substitute other goods for those identified.

(3) Nothing in this section impairs any insurable interest recognized under any other statute or rule of law.

§ 2—502. Buyer's Right to Goods on Seller's Insolvency.

(1) Subject to subsection (2) and even though the goods have not been shipped a buyer who has paid a part or all of the price of goods in which he has a special property under the provisions of the immediately preceding section may on making and keeping good a tender of any unpaid portion of their price recover them from the seller if the seller becomes insolvent within ten days after receipt of the first installment on their price.

(2) If the identification creating his special property has been made by the buyer he acquires the right to recover the goods only if they conform to the contract for sale.

§ 2—503. **Manner of Seller's Tender of Delivery.**

(1) Tender of delivery requires that the seller put and hold conforming goods at the buyer's disposition and give the buyer any notification reasonably necessary to enable him to take delivery. The manner, time and place for tender are determined by the agreement and this Article, and in particular

    (a) tender must be at a reasonable hour, and if it is of goods they must be kept available for the period reasonably necessary to enable the buyer to take possession; but

    (b) unless otherwise agreed the buyer must furnish facilities reasonably suited to the receipt of the goods.

(2) Where the case is within the next section respecting shipment tender requires that the seller comply with its provisions.

(3) Where the seller is required to deliver at a particular destination tender requires that he comply with subsection (1) and also in any appropriate case tender documents as described in subsections (4) and (5) of this section.

(4) Where goods are in the possession of a bailee and are to be delivered without being moved

    (a) tender requires that the seller either tender a negotiable document of title covering such goods or procure acknowledgment by the bailee of the buyer's right to possession of the goods; but

    (b) tender to the buyer of a non-negotiable document of title or of a written direction to the bailee to deliver is sufficient tender unless the buyer seasonably objects, and receipt by the bailee of notification of the buyer's rights fixes those rights as against the bailee and all third persons; but risk of loss of the goods and of any failure by the bailee to honor the non-negotiable document of title or to obey the direction remains on the seller until the buyer has had a reasonable time to present the document or direction, and a refusal by the bailee to honor the document or to obey the direction defeats the tender.

(5) Where the contract requires the seller to deliver documents

    (a) he must tender all such documents in correct form, except as provided in this Article with

respect to bills of lading in a set (subsection (2) of Section 2—323); and

    (b) tender through customary banking channels is sufficient and dishonor of a draft accompanying the documents constitutes non-acceptance or rejection.

§ 2—504. **Shipment by Seller.**

Where the seller is required or authorized to send the goods to the buyer and the contract does not require him to deliver them at a particular destination, then unless otherwise agreed he must

(a) put the goods in the possession of such a carrier and make such a contract for their transportation as may be reasonable having regard to the nature of the goods and other circumstances of the case; and

(b) obtain and promptly deliver or tender in due form any document necessary to enable the buyer to obtain possession of the goods or otherwise required by the agreement or by usage of trade; and

(c) promptly notify the buyer of the shipment.

Failure to notify the buyer under paragraph (c) or to make a proper contract under paragraph (a) is a ground for rejection only if material delay or loss ensues.

§ 2—505. **Seller's Shipment Under Reservation.**

(1) Where the seller has identified goods to the contract by or before shipment:

    (a) his procurement of a negotiable bill of lading to his own order or otherwise reserves in him a security interest in the goods. His procurement of the bill to the order of a financing agency or of the buyer indicates in addition only the seller's expectation of transferring that interest to the person named.

    (b) a non-negotiable bill of lading to himself or his nominee reserves possession of the goods as security but except in a case of conditional delivery (subsection (2) of Section 2—507) a non-negotiable bill of lading naming the buyer as consignee reserves no security interest even though the seller retains possession of the bill of lading.

(2) When shipment by the seller with reservation of a security interest is in violation of the contract for sale it constitutes an improper contract for transportation

within the preceding section but impairs neither the rights given to the buyer by shipment and identification of the goods to the contract nor the seller's powers as a holder of a negotiable document.

§ 2—506. **Rights of Financing Agency.**

(1) A financing agency by paying or purchasing for value a draft which relates to a shipment of goods acquires to the extent of the payment or purchase and in addition to its own rights under the draft and any document of title securing it any rights of the shipper in the goods including the right to stop delivery and the shipper's right to have the draft honored by the buyer.

(2) The right to reimbursement of a financing agency which has in good faith honored or purchased the draft under commitment to or authority from the buyer is not impaired by subsequent discovery of defects with reference to any relevant document which was apparently regular on its face.

§ 2—507. **Effect of Seller's Tender; Delivery on Condition.**

(1) Tender of delivery is a condition to the buyer's duty to accept the goods and, unless otherwise agreed, to his duty to pay for them. Tender entitles the seller to acceptance of the goods and to payment according to the contract.

(2) Where payment is due and demanded on the delivery to the buyer of goods or documents of title, his right as against the seller to retain or dispose of them is conditional upon his making the payment due.

§ 2—508. **Cure by Seller of Improper Tender or Delivery; Replacement.**

(1) Where any tender or delivery by the seller is rejected because non-conforming and the time for performance has not yet expired, the seller may seasonably notify the buyer of his intention to cure and may then within the contract time make a conforming delivery.

(2) Where the buyer rejects a non-conforming tender which the seller had reasonable grounds to believe would be acceptable with or without money allowance the seller may if he seasonably notifies the buyer have a further reasonable time to substitute a conforming tender.

§ 2—509. **Risk of Loss in the Absence of Breach.**

(1) Where the contract requires or authorizes the seller to ship the goods by carrier

    (a) if it does not require him to deliver them at a particular destination, the risk of loss passes to the buyer when the goods are duly delivered to the carrier even though the shipment is under reservation (Section 2—505); but

    (b) if it does require him to deliver them at a particular destination and the goods are there duly tendered while in the possession of the carrier, the risk of loss passes to the buyer when the goods are there duly so tendered as to enable the buyer to take delivery.

(2) Where the goods are held by a bailee to be delivered without being moved, the risk of loss passes to the buyer

    (a) on his receipt of a negotiable document of title covering the goods; or

    (b) on acknowledgment by the bailee of the buyer's right to possession of the goods; or

    (c) after his receipt of a non-negotiable document of title or other written direction to deliver, as provided in subsection (4)(b) of Section 2—503.

(3) In any case not within subsection (1) or (2), the risk of loss passes to the buyer on his receipt of the goods if the seller is a merchant; otherwise, the risk passes to the buyer on tender of delivery.

(4) The provisions of this section are subject to contrary agreement of the parties and to the provisions of this Article on sale on approval (Section 2—327) and on effect of breach on risk of loss (Section 2—510).

§ 2—510. **Effect of Breach on Risk of Loss.**

(1) Where a tender or delivery of goods so fails to conform to the contract as to give a right of rejection the risk of their loss remains on the seller until cure or acceptance.

(2) Where the buyer rightfully revokes acceptance he may to the extent of any deficiency in his effective insurance coverage treat the risk of loss as having rested on the seller from the beginning.

(3) Where the buyer as to conforming goods already identified to the contract for sale repudiates or is

otherwise in breach before risk of their loss has passed to him, the seller may to the extent of any deficiency in his effective insurance coverage treat the risk of loss as resting on the buyer for a commercially reasonable time.

§ 2—511. **Tender of Payment by Buyer; Payment by Check.**

(1) Unless otherwise agreed tender of payment is a condition to the seller's duty to tender and complete any delivery.

(2) Tender of payment is sufficient when made by any means or in any manner current in the ordinary course of business unless the seller demands payment in legal tender and gives any extension of time reasonably necessary to procure it.

(3) Subject to the provisions of this Act on the effect of an instrument on an obligation (Section 3—802), payment by check is conditional and is defeated as between the parties by dishonor of the check on due presentment.

§ 2—512. **Payment by Buyer Before Inspection.**

(1) Where the contract requires payment before inspection non-conformity of the goods does not excuse the buyer from so making payment unless

    (a) the non-conformity appears without inspection; or

    (b) despite tender of the required documents the circumstances would justify injunction against honor under the provisions of this Act (Section 5—114).

(2) Payment pursuant to subsection (1) does not constitute an acceptance of goods or impair the buyer's right to inspect or any of his remedies.

§ 2—513. **Buyer's Right to Inspection of Goods.**

(1) Unless otherwise agreed and subject to subsection (3), where goods are tendered or delivered or identified to the contract for sale, the buyer has a right before payment or acceptance to inspect them at any reasonable place and time and in any reasonable manner. When the seller is required or authorized to send the goods to the buyer, the inspection may be after their arrival.

(2) Expenses of inspection must be borne by the buyer but may be recovered from the seller if the goods do not conform and are rejected.

(3) Unless otherwise agreed and subject to the provisions of this Article on C.I.F. contracts (subsection (3) of Section 2—321), the buyer is not entitled to inspect the goods before payment of the price when the contract provides

    (a) for delivery "C.O.D." or on other like terms; or

    (b) for payment against documents of title, except where such payment is due only after the goods are to become available for inspection.

(4) A place or method of inspection fixed by the parties is presumed to be exclusive but unless otherwise expressly agreed it does not postpone identification or shift the place for delivery or for passing the risk of loss. If compliance becomes impossible, inspection shall be as provided in this section unless the place or method fixed was clearly intended as an indispensable condition failure of which avoids the contract.

§ 2—514. **When Documents Deliverable on Acceptance; When on Payment.**

Unless otherwise agreed documents against which a draft is drawn are to be delivered to the drawee on acceptance of the draft if it is payable more than three days after presentment; otherwise, only on payment.

§ 2—515. **Preserving Evidence of Goods in Dispute.**

In furtherance of the adjustment of any claim or dispute

    (a) either party on reasonable notification to the other and for the purpose of ascertaining the facts and preserving evidence has the right to inspect, test and sample the goods including such of them as may be in the possession or control of the other; and

    (b) the parties may agree to a third party inspection or survey to determine the conformity or condition of the goods and may agree that the findings shall be binding upon them in any subsequent litigation or adjustment.

Part 6 **Breach, Repudiation and Excuse**

§ 2—601. **Buyer's Rights on Improper Delivery.**

Subject to the provisions of this Article on breach in

installment contracts (Section 2—612) and unless otherwise agreed under the sections on contractual limitations of remedy (Sections 2—718 and 2—719), if the goods or the tender of delivery fail in any respect to conform to the contract, the buyer may

(a) reject the whole; or

(b) accept the whole; or

(c) accept any commercial unit or units and reject the rest.

§ 2—602. **Manner and Effect of Rightful Rejection.**

(1) Rejection of goods must be within a reasonable time after their delivery or tender. It is ineffective unless the buyer seasonably notifies the seller.

(2) Subject to the provisions of the two following sections on rejected goods (Sections 2—603 and 2—604),

(a) after rejection any exercise of ownership by the buyer with respect to any commercial unit is wrongful as against the seller; and

(b) if the buyer has before rejection taken physical possession of goods in which he does not have a security interest under the provisions of this Article (subsection (3) of Section 2—711), he is under a duty after rejection to hold them with reasonable care at the seller's disposition for a time sufficient to permit the seller to remove them; but

(c) the buyer has no further obligations with regard to goods rightfully rejected.

(3) The seller's rights with respect to goods wrongfully rejected are governed by the provisions of this Article on seller's remedies in general (Section 2—703).

§ 2—603. **Merchant Buyer's Duties as to Rightfully Rejected Goods.**

(1) Subject to any security interest in the buyer (subsection (3) of Section 2—711), when the seller has no agent or place of business at the market of rejection a merchant buyer is under a duty after rejection of goods in his possession or control to follow any reasonable instructions received from the seller with respect to the goods and in the absence of such instructions to make reasonable efforts to sell them for the seller's account if they are perishable or threaten to decline in value speedily. Instructions are

not reasonable if on demand indemnity for expenses is not forthcoming.

(2) When the buyer sells goods under subsection (1), he is entitled to reimbursement from the seller or out of the proceeds for reasonable expenses of caring for and selling them, and if the expenses include no selling commission then to such commission as is usual in the trade or if there is none to a reasonable sum not exceeding ten per cent on the gross proceeds.

(3) In complying with this section the buyer is held only to good faith and good faith conduct hereunder is neither acceptance nor conversion nor the basis of an action for damages.

§ 2—604. **Buyer's Options as to Salvage of Rightfully Rejected Goods.**

Subject to the provisions of the immediately preceding section on perishables if the seller gives no instructions within a reasonable time after notification of rejection the buyer may store the rejected goods for the seller's account or reship them to him or resell them for the seller's account with reimbursement as provided in the preceding section. Such action is not acceptance or conversion.

§ 2—605. **Waiver of Buyer's Objections by Failure to Particularize.**

(1) The buyer's failure to state in connection with rejection a particular defect which is ascertainable by reasonable inspection precludes him from relying on the unstated defect to justify rejection or to establish breach

(a) where the seller could have cured it if stated seasonably; or

(b) between merchants when the seller has after rejection made a request in writing for a full and final written statement of all defects on which the buyer proposes to rely.

(2) Payment against documents made without reservation of rights precludes recovery of the payment for defects apparent on the face of the documents.

§ 2—606. **What Constitutes Acceptance of Goods.**

(1) Acceptance of goods occurs when the buyer

(a) after a reasonable opportunity to inspect the goods signifies to the seller that the goods are conforming or that he will take or retain them in spite of their nonconformity; or

(b) fails to make an effective rejection (subsection (1) of Section 2—602), but such acceptance does not occur until the buyer has had a reasonable opportunity to inspect them; or

(c) does any act inconsistent with the seller's ownership; but if such act is wrongful as against the seller it is an acceptance only if ratified by him.

(2) Acceptance of a part of any commercial unit is acceptance of that entire unit.

§ 2—607. **Effect of Acceptance; Notice of Breach; Burden of Establishing Breach After Acceptance; Notice of Claim or Litigation to Person Answerable Over.**

(1) The buyer must pay at the contract rate for any goods accepted.

(2) Acceptance of goods by the buyer precludes rejection of the goods accepted and if made with knowledge of a non-conformity cannot be revoked because of it unless the acceptance was on the reasonable assumption that the non-conformity would be seasonably cured but acceptance does not of itself impair any other remedy provided by this Article for non-conformity.

(3) Where a tender has been accepted

(a) the buyer must within a reasonable time after he discovers or should have discovered any breach notify the seller of breach or be barred from any remedy; and

(b) if the claim is one for infringement or the like (subsection (3) of Section 2—312) and the buyer is sued as a result of such a breach he must so notify the seller within a reasonable time after he receives notice of the litigation or be barred from any remedy over for liability established by the litigation.

(4) The burden is on the buyer to establish any breach with respect to the goods accepted.

(5) Where the buyer is sued for breach of a warranty or other obligation for which his seller is answerable over

(a) he may give his seller written notice of the litigation. If the notice states that the seller may come in and defend and that if the seller does not do so he will be bound in any action against him by his buyer by any determination of fact common

to the two litigations, then unless the seller after seasonable receipt of the notice does come in and defend he is so bound.

(b) if the claim is one for infringement or the like (subsection (3) of Section 2—312) the original seller may demand in writing that his buyer turn over to him control of the litigation including settlement or else be barred from any remedy over and if he also agrees to bear all expense and to satisfy any adverse judgment, then unless the buyer after seasonable receipt of the demand does turn over control the buyer is so barred.

(6) The provisions of subsections (3), (4) and (5) apply to any obligation of a buyer to hold the seller harmless against infringement or the like (subsection (3) of Section 2—312).

§ 2—608. **Revocation of Acceptance in Whole or in Part.**

(1) The buyer may revoke his acceptance of a lot or commercial unit whose non-conformity substantially impairs its value to him if he has accepted it

(a) on the reasonable assumption that its non-conformity would be cured and it has not been seasonably cured; or

(b) without discovery of such non-conformity if his acceptance was reasonably induced either by the difficulty of discovery before acceptance or by the seller's assurances.

(2) Revocation of acceptance must occur within a reasonable time after the buyer discovers or should have discovered the ground for it and before any substantial change in condition of the goods which is not caused by their own defects. It is not effective until the buyer notifies the seller of it.

(3) A buyer who so revokes has the same rights and duties with regard to the goods involved as if he had rejected them.

§ 2—609. **Right to Adequate Assurance of Performance.**

(1) A contract for sale imposes an obligation on each party that the other's expectation of receiving due performance will not be impaired. When reasonable grounds for insecurity arise with respect to the performance of either party the other may in writing demand adequate assurance of due performance and

until he receives such assurance may if commercially reasonable suspend any performance for which he has not already received the agreed return.

(2) Between merchants the reasonableness of grounds for insecurity and the adequacy of any assurance offered shall be determined according to commercial standards.

(3) Acceptance of any improper delivery or payment does not prejudice the aggrieved party's right to demand adequate assurance of future performance.

(4) After receipt of a justified demand failure to provide within a reasonable time not exceeding thirty days such assurance of due performance as is adequate under the circumstances of the particular case is a repudiation of the contract.

§ 2—610. **Anticipatory Repudiation.**

When either party repudiates the contract with respect to a performance not yet due the loss of which will substantially impair the value of the contract to the other, the aggrieved party may

(a) for a commercially reasonable time await performance by the repudiating party; or

(b) resort to any remedy for breach (Section 2—703 or Section 2—711), even though he has notified the repudiating party that he would await the latter's performance and has urged retraction; and

(c) in either case suspend his own performance or proceed in accordance with the provisions of this Article on the seller's right to identify goods to the contract notwithstanding breach or to salvage unfinished goods (Section 2—704).

§ 2—611. **Retraction of Anticipatory Repudiation.**

(1) Until the repudiating party's next performance is due he can retract his repudiation unless the aggrieved party has since the repudiation cancelled or materially changed his position or otherwise indicated that he considers the repudiation final.

(2) Retraction may be by any method which clearly indicates to the aggrieved party that the repudiating party intends to perform, but must include any assurance justifiably demanded under the provisions of this Article (Section 2—609).

(3) Retraction reinstates the repudiating party's rights under the contract with due excuse and allowance to the aggrieved party for any delay occasioned by the repudiation.

§ 2—612. **"Installment Contract"; Breach.**

(1) An "installment contract" is one which requires or authorizes the delivery of goods in separate lots to be separately accepted, even though the contract contains a clause "each delivery is a separate contract" or its equivalent.

(2) The buyer may reject any installment which is non-conforming if the non-conformity substantially impairs the value of that installment and cannot be cured or if the non-conformity is a defect in the required documents; but if the non-conformity does not fall within subsection (3) and the seller gives adequate assurance of its cure the buyer must accept that installment.

(3) Whenever non-conformity or default with respect to one or more installments substantially impairs the value of the whole contract there is a breach of the whole. But the aggrieved party reinstates the contract if he accepts a non-conforming installment without seasonably notifying of cancellation or if he brings an action with respect only to past installments or demands performance as to future installments.

§ 2—613. **Casualty to Identified Goods.**

Where the contract requires for its performance goods identified when the contract is made, and the goods suffer casualty without fault of either party before the risk of loss passes to the buyer, or in a proper case under a "no arrival, no sale" term (Section 2—324) then

(a) if the loss is total the contract is avoided; and

(b) if the loss is partial or the goods have so deteriorated as no longer to conform to the contract the buyer may nevertheless demand inspection and at his option either treat the contract as avoided or accept the goods with due allowance from the contract price for the deterioration or the deficiency in quantity but without further right against the seller.

§ 2—614. **Substituted Performance.**

(1) Where without fault of either party the agreed berthing, loading, or unloading facilities fail or an agreed type of carrier becomes unavailable or the agreed manner of delivery otherwise becomes com-

mercially impracticable but a commercially reasonable substitute is available, such substitute performance must be tendered and accepted.

(2) If the agreed means or manner of payment fails because of domestic or foreign governmental regulation, the seller may withhold or stop delivery unless the buyer provides a means or manner of payment which is commercially a substantial equivalent. If delivery has already been taken, payment by the means or in the manner provided by the regulation discharges the buyer's obligation unless the regulation is discriminatory, oppressive or predatory.

§ 2—615. **Excuse by Failure of Presupposed Conditions.**

Except so far as a seller may have assumed a greater obligation and subject to the preceding section on substituted performance:

(a) Delay in delivery or non-delivery in whole or in part by a seller who complies with paragraphs (b) and (c) is not a breach of his duty under a contract for sale if performance as agreed has been made impracticable by the occurrence of a contingency the non-occurrence of which was a basic assumption on which the contract was made or by compliance in good faith with any applicable foreign or domestic governmental regulation or order whether or not it later proves to be invalid.

(b) Where the causes mentioned in paragraph (a) affect only a part of the seller's capacity to perform, he must allocate production and deliveries among his customers but may at his option include regular customers not then under contract as well as his own requirements for further manufacture. He may so allocate in any manner which is fair and reasonable.

(c) The seller must notify the buyer seasonably that there will be delay or non-delivery and, when allocation is required under paragraph (b), of the estimated quota thus made available for the buyer.

§ 2—616. **Procedure on Notice Claiming Excuse.**

(1) Where the buyer receives notification of a material or indefinite delay or an allocation justified under the preceding section he may by written notification to the seller as to any delivery concerned, and where the prospective deficiency substantially impairs the value of the whole contract under the provisions of this Article relating to breach of installment contracts (Section 2—612), then also as to the whole,

(a) terminate and thereby discharge any unexecuted portion of the contract; or

(b) modify the contract by agreeing to take his available quota in substitution.

(2) If after receipt of such notification from the seller the buyer fails so to modify the contract within a reasonable time not exceeding thirty days the contract lapses with respect to any deliveries affected.

(3) The provisions of this section may not be negated by agreement except in so far as the seller has assumed a greater obligation under the preceding section.

Part 7 **Remedies**

§ 2—701. **Remedies for Breach of Collateral Contracts Not Impaired.**

Remedies for breach of any obligation or promise collateral or ancillary to a contract for sale are not impaired by the provisions of this Article.

§ 2—702. **Seller's Remedies on Discovery of Buyer's Insolvency.**

(1) Where the seller discovers the buyer to be insolvent he may refuse delivery except for cash including payment for all goods theretofore delivered under the contract, and stop delivery under this Article (Section 2—705).

(2) Where the seller discovers that the buyer has received goods on credit while insolvent he may reclaim the goods upon demand made within ten days after the receipt, but if misrepresentation of solvency has been made to the particular seller in writing within three months before delivery the ten day limitation does not apply. Except as provided in this subsection the seller may not base a right to reclaim goods on the buyer's fraudulent or innocent misrepresentation of solvency or of intent to pay.

(3) The seller's right to reclaim under subsection (2) is subject to the rights of a buyer in ordinary course or other good faith purchaser under this Article (Section 2—403). Successful reclamation of goods excludes all other remedies with respect to them.

§ 2—703. **Seller's Remedies in General.**

Where the buyer wrongfully rejects or revokes acceptance of goods or fails to make a payment due on or before delivery or repudiates with respect to a part or the whole, then with respect to any goods directly affected and, if the breach is of the whole contract (Section 2—612), then also with respect to the whole undelivered balance, the aggrieved seller may

(a) withhold delivery of such goods;

(b) stop delivery by any bailee as hereafter provided (Section 2—705);

(c) proceed under the next section respecting goods still unidentified to the contract;

(d) resell and recover damages as hereafter provided (Section 2—706);

(e) recover damages for non-acceptance (Section 2—708) or in a proper case the price (Section 2—709);

(f) cancel.

§ 2—704. **Seller's Right to Identify Goods to the Contract Notwithstanding Breach or to Salvage Unfinished Goods.**

(1) An aggrieved seller under the preceding section may

(a) identify to the contract conforming goods not already identified if at the time he learned of the breach they are in his possession or control;

(b) treat as the subject of resale goods which have demonstrably been intended for the particular contract even though those goods are unfinished.

(2) Where the goods are unfinished an aggrieved seller may in the exercise of reasonable commercial judgment for the purposes of avoiding loss and of effective realization either complete the manufacture and wholly identify the goods to the contract or cease manufacture and resell for scrap or salvage value or proceed in any other reasonable manner.

§ 2—705. **Seller's Stoppage of Delivery in Transit or Otherwise.**

(1) The seller may stop delivery of goods in the possession of a carrier or other bailee when he discovers the buyer to be insolvent (Section 2—702) and may stop delivery of carload, truckload, planeload or larger shipments of express or freight when the buyer repudiates or fails to make a payment due before delivery or if for any other reason the seller

has a right to withhold or reclaim the goods.

(2) As against such buyer the seller may stop delivery until

(a) receipt of the goods by the buyer; or

(b) acknowledgment to the buyer by any bailee of the goods except a carrier that the bailee holds the goods for the buyer; or

(c) such acknowledgment to the buyer by a carrier by reshipment or as warehouseman; or

(d) negotiation to the buyer of any negotiable document of title covering the goods.

(3) (a) To stop delivery the seller must so notify as to enable the bailee by reasonable diligence to prevent delivery of the goods.

(b) After such notification the bailee must hold and deliver the goods according to the directions of the seller but the seller is liable to the bailee for any ensuing charges or damages.

(c) If a negotiable document of title has been issued for goods the bailee is not obliged to obey a notification to stop unitl surrender of the document.

(d) A carrier who has issued a non-negotiable bill of lading is not obliged to obey a notification to stop received from a person other than the consignor.

§ 2—706. **Seller's Resale Including Contract for Resale.**

(1) Under the conditions stated in Section 2—703 on seller's remedies, the seller may resell the goods concerned or the undelivered balance thereof. Where the resale is made in good faith and in a commercially reasonable manner the seller may recover the difference between the resale price and the contract price together with any incidental damages allowed under the provisions of this Article (Section 2—710), but less expenses saved in consequence of the buyer's breach.

(2) Except as otherwise provided in subsection (3) or unless otherwise agreed resale may be at public or private sale including sale by way of one or more contracts to sell or of identification to an existing contract of the seller. Sale may be as a unit or in parcels and at any time and place and on any terms but every aspect of the sale including the method, manner, time, place and terms must be commercially

reasonable. The resale must be reasonably identified as referring to the broken contract, but it is not necessary that the goods be in existence or that any or all of them have been identified to the contract before the breach.

(3) Where the resale is at private sale the seller must give the buyer reasonable notification of his intention to resell.

(4) Where the resale is at public sale

(a) only identified goods can be sold except where there is a recognized market for a public sale of futures in goods of the kind; and

(b) it must be made at a usual place or market for public sale if one is reasonably available and except in the case of goods which are perishable or threaten to decline in value speedily the seller must give the buyer reasonable notice of the time and place of the resale; and

(c) if the goods are not to be within the view of those attending the sale the notification of sale must state the place where the goods are located and provide for their reasonable inspection by prospective bidders; and

(d) the seller may buy.

(5) A purchaser who buys in good faith at a resale takes the goods free of any rights of the original buyer even though the seller fails to comply with one or more of the requirements of this section.

(6) The seller is not accountable to the buyer for any profit made on any resale. A person in the position of a seller (Section 2—707) or a buyer who has rightfully rejected or justifiably revoked acceptance must account for any excess over the amount of his security interest, as hereinafter defined (subsection (3) of Section 2—711).

§ 2—707. "Person in the Position of a Seller".

(1) A "person in the position of a seller" includes as against a principal an agent who has paid or become responsible for the price of goods on behalf of his principal or anyone who otherwise holds a security interest or other right in goods similar to that of a seller.

(2) A person in the position of a seller may as provided in this Article withhold or stop delivery (Section 2—705) and resell (Section 2—706) and recover incidental damages (Section 2—710).

§ 2—708. Seller's Damages for Non-Acceptance or Repudiation.

(1) Subject to subsection (2) and to the provisions of this Article with respect to proof of market price (Section 2—723), the measure of damages for non-acceptance or repudiation by the buyer is the difference between the market price at the time and place for tender and the unpaid contract price together with any incidental damages provided in this Article (Section 2—710), but less expenses saved in consequence of the buyer's breach.

(2) If the measure of damages provided in subsection (1) is inadequate to put the seller in as good a position as performance would have done then the measure of damages is the profit (including reasonable overhead) which the seller would have made from full performance by the buyer, together with any incidental damages provided in this Article (Section 2—710), due allowance for costs reasonably incurred and due credit for payments or proceeds of resale.

§ 2—709. Action for the Price.

(1) When the buyer fails to pay the price as it becomes due the seller may recover, together with any incidental damages under the next section, the price

(a) of goods accepted or of conforming goods lost or damaged within a commercially reasonable time after risk of their loss has passed to the buyer; and

(b) of goods identified to the contract if the seller is unable after reasonable effort to resell them at a reasonable price or the circumstances reasonably indicate that such effort will be unavailing.

(2) Where the seller sues for the price he must hold for the buyer any goods which have been identified to the contract and are still in his control except that if resale becomes possible he may resell them at any time prior to the collection of the judgment. The net proceeds of any such resale must be credited to the buyer and payment of the judgment entitles him to any goods not resold.

(3) After the buyer has wrongfully rejected or revoked acceptance of the goods or has failed to make a payment due or has repudiated (Section 2—610), a

seller who is held not entitled to the price under this section shall nevertheless be awarded damages for non-acceptance under the preceding section.

§ 2—710. **Seller's Incidental Damages.**

Incidental damages to an aggrieved seller include any commercially reasonable charges, expenses or commissions incurred in stopping delivery, in the transportation, care and custody of goods after the buyer's breach, in connection with return or resale of the goods or otherwise resulting from the breach.

§ 2—711. **Buyer's Remedies in General; Buyer's Security Interest in Rejected Goods.**

(1) Where the seller fails to make delivery or repudiates or the buyer rightfully rejects or justifiably revokes acceptance then with respect to any goods involved, and with respect to the whole if the breach goes to the whole contract (Section 2—612), the buyer may cancel and whether or not he has done so may in addition to recovering so much of the price as has been paid

(a) "cover" and have damages under the next section as to all the goods affected whether or not they have been identified to the contract; or

(b) recover damages for non-delivery as provided in this Article (Section 2—713).

(2) Where the seller fails to deliver or repudiates the buyer may also

(a) if the goods have been identified recover them as provided in this Article (Section 2—502); or

(b) in a proper case obtain specific performance or replevy the goods as provided in this Article (Section 2—716).

(3) On rightful rejection or justifiable revocation of acceptance a buyer has a security interest in goods in his possession or control for any payments made on their price and any expenses reasonably incurred in their inspection, receipt, transportation, care and custody and may hold such goods and resell them in like manner as an aggrieved seller (Section 2—706).

§ 2—712. **"Cover"; Buyer's Procurement of Substitute Goods.**

(1) After a breach within the preceding section the buyer may "cover" by making in good faith and without unreasonable delay any reasonable purchase of or contract to purchase goods in substitution for those due from the seller.

(2) The buyer may recover from the seller as damages the difference between the cost of cover and the contract price together with any incidental or consequential damages as hereinafter defined (Section 2—715), but less expenses saved in consequence of the seller's breach.

(3) Failure of the buyer to effect cover within this section does not bar him from any other remedy.

§ 2—713. **Buyer's Damages for Non-Delivery or Repudiation.**

(1) Subject to the provisions of this Article with respect to proof of market price (Section 2—723), the measure of damages for non-delivery or repudiation by the seller is the difference between the market price at the time when the buyer learned of the breach and the contract price together with any incidental and consequential damages provided in this Article (Section 2—715), but less expenses saved in consequence of the seller's breach.

(2) Market price is to be determined as of the place for tender or, in cases of rejection after arrival or revocation of acceptance, as of the place of arrival.

§ 2—714. **Buyer's Damages for Breach in Regard to Accepted Goods.**

(1) Where the buyer has accepted goods and given notification (subsection (3) of Section 2—607) he may recover as damages for any non-conformity of tender the loss resulting in the ordinary course of events from the seller's breach as determined in any manner which is reasonable.

(2) The measure of damages for breach of warranty is the difference at the time and place of acceptance between the value of the goods accepted and the value they would have had if they had been as warranted, unless special circumstances show proximate damages of a different amount.

(3) In a proper case any incidental and consequential damages under the next section may also be recovered.

§ 2—715. **Buyer's Incidental and Consequential Damages.**

(1) Incidental damages resulting from the seller's

breach include expenses reasonably incurred in inspection, receipt, transportation and care and custody of goods rightfully rejected, any commercially reasonable charges, expenses or commissions in connection with effecting cover and any other reasonable expense incident to the delay or other breach.

(2) Consequential damages resulting from the seller's breach include

(a) any loss resulting from general or particular requirements and needs of which the seller at the time of contracting had reason to know and which could not reasonably be prevented by cover or otherwise; and

(b) injury to person or property proximately resulting from any breach of warranty.

§ 2—716 **Buyer's Right to Specific Performance or Replevin.**

(1) Specific performance may be decreed where the goods are unique or in other proper circumstances.

(2) The decree for specific performance may include such terms and conditions as to payment of the price, damages, or other relief as the court may deem just.

(3) The buyer has a right of replevin for goods identified to the contract if after reasonable effort he is unable to effect cover for such goods or the circumstances reasonably indicate that such effort will be unavailing or if the goods have been shipped under reservation and satisfaction of the security interest in them has been made or tendered.

§ 2—717. **Deduction of Damages From the Price.**

The buyer on notifying the seller of his intention to do so may deduct all or any part of the damages resulting from any breach of the contract from any part of the price still due under the same contract.

§ 2—718. **Liquidation or Limitation of Damages; Deposits.**

(1) Damages for breach by either party may be liquidated in the agreement but only at an amount which is reasonable in the light of the anticipated or actual harm caused by the breach, the difficulties of proof of loss, and the inconvenience or nonfeasibility of otherwise obtaining an adequate remedy. A term

fixing unreasonably large liquidated damages is void as a penalty.

(2) Where the seller justifiably withholds delivery of goods because of the buyer's breach, the buyer is entitled to restitution of any amount by which the sum of his payments exceeds

(a) the amount to which the seller is entitled by virtue of terms liquidating the seller's damages in accordance with subsection (1), or

(b) in the absence of such terms, twenty per cent of the value of the total performance for which the buyer is obligated under the contract or $500, whichever is smaller.

(3) The buyer's right to restitution under subsection (2) is subject to offset to the extent that the seller establishes

(a) a right to recover damages under the provisions of this Article other than subsection (1), and

(b) the amount or value of any benefits received by the buyer directly or indirectly by reason of the contract.

(4) Where a seller has received payment in goods their reasonable value or the proceeds of their resale shall be treated as payments for the purposes of subsection (2); but if the seller has notice of the buyer's breach before reselling goods received in part performance, his resale is subject to the conditions laid down in this Article on resale by an aggrieved seller (Section 2—706).

§ 2—719. **Contractual Modification or Limitation of Remedy.**

(1) Subject to the provisions of subsections (2) and (3) of this section and of the preceding section on liquidation and limitation of damages,

(a) the agreement may provide for remedies in addition to or in substitution for those provided in this Article and may limit or alter the measure of damages recoverable under this Article, as by limiting the buyer's remedies to return of the goods and repayment of the price or to repair and replacement of non-conforming goods or parts; and

(b) resort to a remedy as provided is optional unless the remedy is expressly agreed to be exclusive, in which case it is the sole remedy.

(2) Where circumstances cause an exclusive or limited remedy to fail of its essential purpose, remedy may be had as provided in this Act.

(3) Consequential damages may be limited or excluded unless the limitation or exclusion is unconscionable. Limitation of consequential damages for injury to the person in the case of consumer goods is prima facie unconscionable but limitation of damages where the loss is commercial is not.

§ 2—720. **Effect of "Cancellation" or "Rescission" on Claims for Antecedent Breach.**

Unless the contrary intention clearly appears, expressions of "cancellation" or "rescission" of the contract or the like shall not be construed as a renunciation or discharge of any claim in damages for an antecedent breach.

§ 2—721. **Remedies for Fraud.**

Remedies for material misrepresentation or fraud include all remedies available under this Article for non-fraudulent breach. Neither rescission or a claim for rescission of the contract for sale nor rejection or return of the goods shall bar or be deemed inconsistent with a claim for damages or other remedy.

§ 2—722. **Who Can Sue Third Parties for Injury to Goods.**

Where a third party so deals with goods which have been identified to a contract for sale as to cause actionable injury to a party to that contract

(a) a right of action against the third party is in either party to the contract for sale who has title to or a security interest or a special property or an insurable interest in the goods; and if the goods have been destroyed or converted a right of action is also in the party who either bore the risk of loss under the contract for sale or has since the injury assumed that risk as against the other;

(b) if at the time of the injury the party plaintiff did not bear the risk of loss as against the other party to the contract for sale and there is no arrangement between them for disposition of the recovery, his suit or settlement is, subject to his own interest, as a fiduciary for the other party to the contract;

(c) either party may with the consent of the other sue for the benefit of whom it may concern.

§ 2—723. **Proof of Market Price: Time and Place.**

(1) If an action based on anticipatory repudiation comes to trial before the time for performance with respect to some or all of the goods, any damages based on market price (Section 2—708 or Section 2—713) shall be determined according to the price of such goods prevailing at the time when the aggrieved party learned of the repudiation.

(2) If evidence of a price prevailing at the times or places described in this Article is not readily available the price prevailing within any reasonable time before or after the time described or at any other place which in commercial judgment or under usage of trade would serve as a reasonable substitute for the one described may be used, making any proper allowance for the cost of transporting the goods to or from such other place.

(3) Evidence of a relevant price prevailing at a time or place other than the one described in this Article offered by one party is not admissible unless and until he has given the other party such notice as the court finds sufficient to prevent unfair surprise.

§ 2—724. **Admissibility of Market Quotations.**

Whenever the prevailing price or value of any goods regularly bought and sold in any established commodity market is in issue, reports in official publications or trade journals or in newspapers or periodicals of general circulation published as the reports of such market shall be admissible in evidence. The circumstances of the preparation of such a report may be shown to affect its weight but not its admissibility.

§ 2—725. **Statute of Limitations in Contracts for Sale.**

(1) An action for breach of any contract for sale must be commenced within four years after the cause of action has accrued. By the original agreement the parties may reduce the period of limitation to not less than one year but may not extend it.

(2) A cause of action accrues when the breach occurs, regardless of the aggrieved party's lack of knowledge of the breach. A breach of warranty occurs when tender of delivery is made, except that where a warranty explicitly extends to future performance of the goods and discovery of the breach must await the time of such performance the cause of action accrues

when the breach is or should have been discovered.

(3) Where an action commenced within the time limited by subsection (1) is so terminated as to leave available a remedy by another action for the same breach such other action may be commenced after the expiration of the time limited and within six months after the termination of the first action unless the termination resulted from voluntary discontinuance or from dismissal for failure or neglect to prosecute.

(4) This section does not alter the law on tolling of the statute of limitations nor does it apply to causes of action which have accrued before this Act becomes effective.

Article 3
COMMERCIAL PAPER

Part 1 Short Title, Form and Interpretation

§ 3—101. **Short Title.**

This Article shall be known and may be cited as Uniform Commercial Code—Commercial Paper.

§ 3—102. **Definitions and Index of Definitions.**

(1) In this Article unless the context otherwise requires

(a) "Issue" means the first delivery of an instrument to a holder or a remitter.

(b) An "order" is a direction to pay and must be more than an authorization or request. It must identify the person to pay with reasonable certainty. It may be addressed to one or more such persons jointly or in the alternative but not in succession.

(c) A "promise" is an undertaking to pay and must be more than an acknowledgment of an obligation.

(d) "Secondary party" means a drawer or endorser.

(e) "Instrument" means a negotiable instrument.

(2) Other definitions applying to this Article and the sections in which they appear are:
"Acceptance". Section 3—410.

"Accommodation party". Section 3—415.
"Alteration". Section 3—407.
"Certificate of deposit". Section 3—104.
"Certification". Section 3—411.
"Check". Section 3—104.
"Definite time". Section 3—109.
"Dishonor". Section 3—507.
"Draft". Section 3—104.
"Holder in due course". Section 3—302.
"Negotiation". Section 3—202.
"Note". Section 3—104.
"Notice of dishonor". Section 3—508.
"On demand". Section 3—108.
"Presentment". Section 3—504.
"Protest". Section 3—509.
"Restrictive Indorsement". Section 3—205.
"Signature". Section 3—401.

(3) The following definitions in other Articles apply to this Article:
"Account". Section 4—104.
"Banking Day". Section 4—104.
"Clearing House". Section 4—104.
"Collecting Bank". Section 4—105.
"Customer". Section 4—104.
"Depositary Bank". Section 4—105.
"Documentary Draft". Section 4—104.
"Intermediary Bank". Section 4—105.
"Item". Section 4—104.
"Midnight deadline". Section 4—104.
"Payor Bank". Section 4—105.

(4) In addition Article 1 contains general definitions and principles of construction and interpretation applicable throughout this Article.

§ 3—103. **Limitations on Scope of Article.**

(1) This Article does not apply to money, documents of title or investment securities.

(2) The provisions of this Article are subject to the provisions of the Article on Bank Deposits and Collections (Article 4) and Secured Transactions (Article 9).

§ 3—104. **Form of Negotiable Instruments; "Draft"; "Check"; "Certificate of Deposit"; "Note".**

(1) Any writing to be a negotiable instrument within this Article must

(a) be signed by the maker or drawer; and

(b) contain an unconditional promise or order to pay a sum certain in money and no other promise, order, obligation or power given by the maker or drawer except as authorized by this Article; and

(c) be payable on demand or at a definite time; and

(d) be payable to order or to bearer.

(2) A writing which complies with the requirements of this section is

(a) a "draft" ("bill of exchange") if it is an order;

(b) a "check" if it is a draft drawn on a bank and payable on demand;

(c) a "certificate of deposit" if it is an acknowledgment by a bank of receipt of money with an engagement to repay it;

(d) a "note" if it is a promise other than a certificate of deposit.

(3) As used in other Articles of this Act, and as the context may require, the terms "draft", "check", "certificate of deposit" and "note" may refer to instruments which are not negotiable within this Article as well as to instruments which are so negotiable.

§ 3—105. **When Promise or Order Unconditional.**

(1) A promise or order otherwise unconditional is not made conditional by the fact that the instrument

(a) is subject to implied or constructive conditions; or

(b) states its consideration, whether performed or promised, or the transaction which gave rise to the instrument, or that the promise or order is made or the instrument matures in accordance with or "as per" such transaction; or

(c) refers to or states that it arises out of a separate agreement or refers to a separate agreement for rights as to prepayment or acceleration; or

(d) states that it is drawn under a letter of credit; or

(e) states that it is secured, whether by mortgage, reservation of title or otherwise; or

(f) indicates a particular account to be debited or any other fund or source from which reimbursement is expected; or

(g) is limited to payment out of a particular fund or the proceeds of a particular source, if the instrument is issued by a government or governmental agency or unit; or

(h) is limited to payment out of the entire assets of a partnership, unincorporated association, trust or estate by or on behalf of which the instrument is issued.

(2) A promise or order is not unconditional if the instrument

(a) states that it is subject to or governed by any other agreement; or

(b) states that it is to be paid only out of a particular fund or source except as provided in this section.

§ 3—106. **Sum Certain.**

(1) The sum payable is a sum certain even though it is to be paid

(a) with stated interest or by stated installments; or

(b) with stated different rates of interest before and after default or a specified date; or

(c) with a stated discount or addition if paid before or after the date fixed for payment; or

(d) with exchange or less exchange, whether at a fixed rate or at the current rate; or

(e) with costs of collection or an attorney's fee or both upon default.

(2) Nothing in this section shall validate any term which is otherwise illegal.

§ 3—107. **Money.**

(1) An instrument is payable in money if the medium of exchange in which it is payable is money at the time the instrument is made. An instrument payable in "currency" or "current funds" is payable in money.

(2) A promise or order to pay a sum stated in a foreign currency is for a sum certain in money and, unless a different medium of payment is specified in the instrument, may be satisfied by payment of that number of dollars which the stated foreign currency will purchase at the buying sight rate for that currency on the day on which the instrument is payable or, if

payable on demand, on the day of demand. If such an instrument specifies a foreign currency as the medium of payment the instrument is payable in that currency.

§ 3—108. **Payable on Demand.**

Instruments payable on demand include those payable at sight or on presentation and those in which no time for payment is stated.

§ 3—109. **Definite Time.**

(1) An instrument is payable at a definite time if by its terms it is payable

(a) on or before a stated date or at a fixed period after a stated date; or

(b) at a fixed period after sight; or

(c) at a definite time subject to any acceleration; or

(d) at a definite time subject to extension at the option of the holder, or to extension to a further definite time at the option of the maker or acceptor or automatically upon or after a specified act or event.

(2) An instrument which by its terms is otherwise payable only upon an act or event uncertain as to time of occurrence is not payable at a definite time even though the act or event has occurred.

§ 3—110. **Payable to Order.**

(1) An instrument is payable to order when by its terms it is payable to the order or assigns of any person therein specified with reasonable certainty, or to him or his order, or when it is conspicuously designated on its face as "exchange" or the like and names a payee. It may be payable to the order of

(a) the maker or drawer; or

(b) the drawee; or

(c) a payee who is not maker, drawer or drawee; or

(d) two or more payees together or in the alternative; or

(e) an estate, trust or fund, in which case it is payable to the order of the representative of such estate, trust or fund or his successors; or

(f) an office, or an officer by his title as such in which case it is payable to the principal but the incumbent of the office or his successors may act as if he or they were the holder; or

(g) a partnership or unincorporated association, in which case it is payable to the partnership or association and may be indorsed or transferred by any person thereto authorized.

(2) An instrument not payable to order is not made so payable by such words as "payable upon return of this instrument properly indorsed."

(3) An instrument made payable both to order and to bearer is payable to order unless the bearer words are handwritten or typewritten.

§ 3—111. **Payable to Bearer.**

An instrument is payable to bearer when by its terms it is payable to

(a) bearer or the order of bearer; or

(b) a specified person or bearer; or

(c) "cash" or the order of "cash", or any other indication which does not purport to designate a specific payee.

§ 3—112. **Terms and Omissions Not Affecting Negotiability.**

(1) The negotiability of an instrument is not affected by

(a) the omission of a statement of any consideration or of the place where the instrument is drawn or payable; or

(b) a statement that collateral has been given to secure obligations either on the instrument or otherwise of an obligor on the instrument or that in case of default on those obligations the holder may realize on or dispose of the collateral; or

(c) a promise or power to maintain or protect collateral or to give additional collateral; or

(d) a term authorizing a confession of judgment on the instrument if it is not paid when due; or

(e) a term purporting to waive the benefit of any law intended for the advantage or protection of any obligor; or

(f) a term in a draft providing that the payee by indorsing or cashing it acknowledges full satisfaction of an obligation of the drawer; or

(g) a statement in a draft drawn in a set of parts (Section 3—801) to the effect that the order is effective only if no other part has been honored.

(2) Nothing in this section shall validate any term which is otherwise illegal.

§ 3—113. **Seal.**

An instrument otherwise negotiable is within this Article even though it is under a seal.

§ 3—114. **Date, Antedating, Postdating.**

(1) The negotiability of an instrument is not affected by the fact that it is undated, antedated or postdated.

(2) Where an instrument is antedated or postdated the time when it is payable is determined by the stated date if the instrument is payable on demand or at a fixed period after date.

(3) Where the instrument or any signature thereon is dated, the date is presumed to be correct.

§ 3—115. **Incomplete Instruments.**

(1) When a paper whose contents at the time of signing show that it is intended to become an instrument is signed while still incomplete in any necessary respect it cannot be enforced until completed, but when it is completed in accordance with authority given it is effective as completed.

(2) If the completion is unauthorized the rules as to material alteration apply (Section 3—407), even though the paper was not delivered by the maker or drawer; but the burden of establishing that any completion is unauthorized is on the party so asserting.

§ 3—116. **Instruments Payable to Two or More Persons.**

An instrument payable to the order of two or more persons

(a) if in the alternative is payable to any one of them and may be negotiated, discharged or enforced by any of them who has possession of it;

(b) if not in the alternative is payable to all of them and may be negotiated, discharged or enforced only by all of them.

§ 3—117. **Instruments Payable With Words of Description.**

An instrument made payable to a named person with the addition of words describing him

(a) as agent or officer of a specified person is payable to his principal but the agent or officer may act as if he were the holder;

(b) as any other fiduciary for a specified person or purpose is payable to the payee and may be negotiated, discharged or enforced by him;

(c) in any other manner is payable to the payee unconditionally and the additional words are without effect on subsequent parties.

§ 3—118. **Ambiguous Terms and Rules of Construction.**

The following rules apply to every instrument:

(a) Where there is doubt whether the instrument is a draft or a note the holder may treat it as either. A draft drawn on the drawer is effective as a note.

(b) Handwritten terms control typewritten and printed terms, and typewritten control printed.

(c) Words control figures except that if the words are ambiguous figures control.

(d) Unless otherwise specified a provision for interest means interest at the judgment rate at the place of payment from the date of the instrument, or if it is undated from the date of issue.

(e) Unless the instrument otherwise specifies two or more persons who sign as maker, acceptor or drawer or indorser and as a part of the same transaction are jointly and severally liable even though the instrument contains such words as "I promise to pay."

(f) Unless otherwise specified consent to extension authorizes a single extension for not longer than the original period. A consent to extension, expressed in the instrument, is binding on secondary parties and accommodation makers. A holder may not exercise his option to extend an instrument over the objection of a maker or acceptor or other party who in accordance with Section 3—604 tenders full payment when the instrument is due.

§ 3—119. **Other Writings Affecting Instrument.**

(1) As between the obligor and his immediate obligee or any transferee the terms of an instrument may be modified or affected by any other written agreement executed as a part of the same transaction, except that a holder in due course in not affected by any limitation of his rights arising out of the separate written agreement if he had no notice of the limitation when he took the instrument.

(2) A separate agreement does not affect the negotiability of an instrument.

§ 3—120. **Instruments "Payable Through" Bank.**

An instrument which states that it is "payable through" a bank or the like designates that bank as a collecting bank to make presentment but does not of itself authorize the bank to pay the instrument.

§ 3—121. **Instruments Payable at Bank.**

Note: If this Act is introduced in the Congress of the United States this section should be omitted.
(States to select either alternative)

Alternative A—

A note or acceptance which states that it is payable at a bank is the equivalent of a draft drawn on the bank payable when it falls due out of any funds of the maker or acceptor in current account or otherwise available for such payment.

Alternative B—

A note or acceptance which states that it is payable at a bank is not of itself an order or authorization to the bank to pay it.

§ 3—122. **Accrual of Cause of Action.**

(1) A cause of action against a maker or an acceptor accrues

(a) in the case of a time instrument on the day after maturity;

(b) in the case of a demand instrument upon its date or, if no date is stated, on the date of issue.

(2) A cause of action against the obligor of a demand or time certificate of deposit accrues upon demand, but demand on a time certificate may not be made until on or after the date of maturity.

(3) A cause of action against a drawer of a draft or an indorser of any instrument accrues upon demand following dishonor of the instrument. Notice of dishonor is a demand.

(4) Unless an instrument provides otherwise, interest runs at the rate provided by law for a judgment

(a) in the case of a maker, acceptor or other primary obligor of a demand instrument, from the date of demand;

(b) in all other cases from the date of accrual of the cause of action.

Part 2 **Transfer and Negotiation**

§ 3—201. **Transfer: Right to Indorsement.**

(1) Transfer of an instrument vests in the transferee such rights as the transferor has therein, except that a transferee who has himself been a party to any fraud or illegality affecting the instrument or who as a prior holder had notice of a defense or claim against it cannot improve his position by taking from a later holder in due course.

(2) A transfer of a security interest in an instrument vests the foregoing rights in the transferee to the extent of the interest transferred.

(3) Unless otherwise agreed any transfer for value of an instrument not then payable to bearer gives the transferee the specifically enforceable right to have the unqualified indorsement of the transferor. Negotiation takes effect only when the indorsement is made and until that time there is no presumption that the transferee is the owner.

§ 3—202. **Negotiation.**

(1) Negotiation is the transfer of an instrument in such form that the transferee becomes a holder. If the instrument is payable to order it is negotiated by delivery with any necessary indorsement; if payable to bearer it is negotiated by delivery.

(2) An indorsement must be written by or on behalf of the holder and on the instrument or on a paper so firmly affixed thereto as to become a part thereof.

(3) An indorsement is effective for negotiation only when it conveys the entire instrument or any unpaid residue. If it purports to be of less it operates only as a partial assignment.

(4) Words of assignment, condition, waiver, guaranty, limitation or disclaimer of liability and the like accompanying an indorsement do not affect its character as an indorsement.

§ 3—203. **Wrong or Misspelled Name.**

Where an instrument is made payable to a person under a misspelled name or one other than his own he may indorse in that name or his own or both; but signature in both names may be required by a person paying or giving value for the instrument.

§ 3—204. **Special Indorsement; Blank Indorsement.**

(1) A special indorsement specifies the person to

whom or to whose order it makes the instrument payable. Any instrument specially indorsed becomes payable to the order of the special indorsee and may be further negotiated only by his indorsement.

(2) An indorsement in blank specifies no particular indorsee and may consist of a mere signature. An instrument payable to order and indorsed in blank becomes payable to bearer and may be negotiated by delivery alone until specially indorsed.

(3) The holder may convert a blank indorsement into a special indorsement by writing over the signature of the indorser in blank any contract consistent with the character of the indorsement.

§ 3—205. **Restrictive Indorsements.**

An indorsement is restrictive which either

(a) is conditional; or

(b) purports to prohibit further transfer of the instrument; or

(c) includes the words "for collection", "for deposit", "pay any bank", or like terms signifying a purpose of deposit or collection; or

(d) otherwise states that it is for the benefit or use of the indorser or of another person.

§ 3—206. **Effect of Restrictive Indorsement.**

(1) No restrictive indorsement prevents further transfer or negotiation of the instrument.

(2) An intermediary bank, or a payor bank which is not the depositary bank, is neither given notice nor otherwise affected by a restrictive indorsement of any person except the bank's immediate transferor or the person presenting for payment.

(3) Except for an intermediary bank, any transferee under an indorsement which is conditional or includes the words "for collection", "for deposit", "pay any bank", or like terms (subparagraphs (a) and (c) of Section 3—205) must pay or apply any value given by him for or on the security of the instrument consistently with the indorsement and to the extent that he does so he becomes a holder for value. In addition such transferee is a holder in due course if he otherwise complies with the requirements of Section 3—302 on what constitutes a holder in due course.

(4) The first taker under an indorsement for the benefit of the indorser or another person (subparagraph (d) of Section 3—205) must pay or apply any value given by him for or on the security of the instrument consistently with the indorsement and to the extent that he does so he becomes a holder for value. In addition such taker is a holder in due course if he otherwise complies with the requirements of Section 3—302 on what constitutes a holder in due course. A later holder for value is neither given notice nor otherwise affected by such restrictive indorsement unless he has knowledge that a fiduciary or other person has negotiated the instrument in any transaction for his own benefit or otherwise in breach of duty (subsection (2) of Section 3—304).

§ 3—207. **Negotiation Effective Although It May Be Rescinded.**

(1) Negotiation is effective to transfer the instrument although the negotiation is

(a) made by an infant, a corporation exceeding its powers, or any other person without capacity; or

(b) obtained by fraud, duress or mistake of any kind; or

(c) part of an illegal transaction; or

(d) made in breach of duty.

(2) Except as against a subsequent holder in due course such negotiation is in an appropriate case subject to rescission, the declaration of a constructive trust or any other remedy permitted by law.

§ 3—208. **Reacquisition.**

Where an instrument is returned to or reacquired by a prior party he may cancel any indorsement which is not necessary to his title and reissue or further negotiate the instrument, but any intervening party is discharged as against the reacquiring party and subsequent holders not in due course and if his indorsement has been cancelled is discharged as against subsequent holders in due course as well.

Part 3 **Rights of a Holder**

§ 3—301. **Rights of a Holder.**

The holder of an instrument whether or not he is the owner may transfer or negotiate it and, except as otherwise provided in Section 3—603 on payment or satisfaction, discharge it or enforce payment in his own name.

§ 3—302. **Holder in Due Course.**

(1) A holder in due course is a holder who takes the instrument

(a) for value; and

(b) in good faith; and

(c) without notice that it is overdue or has been dishonored or of any defense against or claim to it on the part of any person.

(2) A payee may be a holder in due course.

(3) A holder does not become a holder in due course of an instrument:

(a) by purchase of it at judicial sale or by taking it under legal process; or

(b) by acquiring it in taking over an estate; or

(c) by purchasing it as part of a bulk transaction not in regular course of business of the transferor.

(4) A purchaser of a limited interest can be a holder in due course only to the extent of the interest purchased.

§ 3—303. **Taking for Value.**

A holder takes the instrument for value

(a) to the extent that the agreed consideration has been performed or that he acquires a security interest in or a lien on the instrument otherwise than by legal process; or

(b) when he takes the instrument in payment of or as security for an antecedent claim against any person whether or not the claim is due; or

(c) when he gives a negotiable instrument for it or makes an irrevocable commitment to a third person.

§ 3—304. **Notice to Purchaser.**

(1) The purchaser has notice of a claim or defense if

(a) the instrument is so incomplete, bears such visible evidence of forgery or alteration, or is otherwise so irregular as to call into question its validity, terms or ownership or to create an ambiguity as to the party to pay; or

(b) the purchaser has notice that the obligation of any party is voidable in whole or in part, or that all parties have been discharged.

(2) The purchaser has notice of a claim against the instrument when he has knowledge that a fiduciary has negotiated the instrument in payment of or as security for his own debt or in any transaction for his own benefit or otherwise in breach of duty.

(3) The purchaser has notice that an instrument is overdue if he has reason to know

(a) that any part of the principal amount is overdue or that there is an uncured default in payment of another instrument of the same series; or

(b) that acceleration of the instrument has been made; or

(c) that he is taking a demand instrument after demand has been made or more than a reasonable length of time after its issue. A reasonable time for a check drawn and payable within the states and territories of the United States and the District of Columbia is presumed to be thirty days.

(4) Knowledge of the following facts does not of itself give the purchaser notice of a defense or claim

(a) that the instrument is antedated or postdated;

(b) that it was issued or negotiated in return for an executory promise or accompanied by a separate agreement, unless the purchaser has notice that a defense or claim has arisen from the terms thereof;

(c) that any party has signed for accommodation;

(d) that an incomplete instrument has been completed, unless the purchaser has notice of any improper completion;

(e) that any person negotiating the instrument is or was a fiduciary;

(f) that there has been default in payment of interest on the instrument or in payment of any other instrument, except one of the same series.

(5) The filing or recording of a document does not of itself constitute notice within the provisions of this Article to a person who would otherwise be a holder in due course.

(6) To be effective notice must be received at such time and in such manner as to give a reasonable opportunity to act on it.

§ 3—305. **Rights of a Holder in Due Course.**

To the extent that a holder is a holder in due course he takes the instrument free from

(1) all claims to it on the part of any person; and

(2) all defenses of any party to the instrument with whom the holder has not dealt except

(a) infancy, to the extent that it is a defense to a simple contract; and

(b) such other incapacity, or duress, or illegality of the transaction, as renders the obligation of the party a nullity; and

(c) such misrepresentation as has induced the party to sign the instrument with neither knowledge nor reasonable opportunity to obtain knowledge of its character or its essential terms; and

(d) discharge in insolvency proceedings; and

(e) any other discharge of which the holder has notice when he takes the instrument.

§ 3—306. Rights of One Not Holder in Due Course.

Unless he has the rights of a holder in due course any person takes the instrument subject to

(a) all valid claims to it on the part of any person; and

(b) all defenses of any party which would be available in an action on a simple contract; and

(c) the defenses of want or failure of consideration, nonperformance of any condition precedent, nondelivery, or delivery for a special purpose (Section 3—408); and

(d) the defense that he or a person through whom he holds the instrument acquired it by theft, or that payment or satisfaction to such holder would be inconsistent with the terms of a restrictive indorsement. The claim of any third person to the instrument is not otherwise available as a defense to any party liable thereon unless the third person himself defends the action for such party.

§ 3—307. Burden of Establishing Signatures, Defenses and Due Course.

(1) Unless specifically denied in the pleadings each signature on an instrument is admitted. When the effectiveness of a signature is put in issue

(a) the burden of establishing it is on the party claiming under the signature; but

(b) the signature is presumed to be genuine or authorized except where the action is to enforce the obligation of a purported signer who has died or become incompetent before proof is required.

(2) When signatures are admitted or established, production of the instrument entitles a holder to recover on it unless the defendant establishes a defense.

(3) After it is shown that a defense exists a person claiming the rights of a holder in due course has the burden of establishing that he or some person under whom he claims is in all respects a holder in due course.

Part 4 Liability of Parties

§ 3—401. Signature.

(1) No person is liable on an instrument unless his signature appears thereon.

(2) A signature is made by use of any name, including any trade or assumed name, upon an instrument, or by any word or mark used in lieu of a written signature.

§ 3—402. Signature in Ambiguous Capacity.

Unless the instrument clearly indicates that a signature is made in some other capacity it is an indorsement.

§ 3—403. Signature by Authorized Representative.

(1) A signature may be made by an agent or other representative, and his authority to make it may be established as in other cases of representation. No particular form of appointment is necessary to establish such authority.

(2) An authorized representative who signs his own name to an instrument

(a) is personally obligated if the instrument neither names the person represented nor shows that the representative signed in a representative capacity;

(b) except as otherwise established between the immediate parties, is personally obligated if the instrument names the person represented but does not show that the representative signed in a representative capacity, or if the instrument does not name the person represented but does show that the representative signed in a representative capacity.

(3) Except as otherwise established the name of an organization preceded or followed by the name and office of an authorized individual is a signature made in a representative capacity.

§ 3—404. Unauthorized Signatures.

(1) Any unauthorized signature is wholly inoperative

as that of the person whose name is signed unless he ratifies it or is precluded from denying it; but it operates as the signature of the unauthorized signer in favor of any person who in good faith pays the instrument or takes it for value.

(2) Any unauthorized signature may be ratified for all purposes of this Article. Such ratification does not of itself affect any rights of the person ratifying against the actual signer.

§ 3—405. **Impostors; Signature in Name of Payee.**

(1) An indorsement by any person in the name of a named payee is effective if

(a) an impostor by use of the mails or otherwise has induced the maker or drawer to issue the instrument to him or his confederate in the name of the payee; or

(b) a person signing as or on behalf of a maker or drawer intends the payee to have no interest in the instrument; or

(c) an agent or employee of the maker or drawer has supplied him with the name of the payee intending the latter to have no such interest.

(2) Nothing in this section shall affect the criminal or civil liability of the person so indorsing.

§ 3—406. **Negligence Contributing to Alteration or Unauthorized Signature.**

Any person who by his negligence substantially contributes to a material alteration of the instrument or to the making of an unauthorized signature is precluded from asserting the alteration or lack of authority against a holder in due course or against a drawee or other payor who pays the instrument in good faith and in accordance with the reasonable commercial standards of the drawee's or payor's business.

§ 3—407. **Alteration.**

(1) Any alteration of an instrument is material which changes the contract of any party thereto in any respect, including any such change in

(a) the number or relations of the parties; or

(b) an incomplete instrument, by completing it otherwise than as authorized; or

(c) the writing as signed, by adding to it or by removing any part of it.

(2) As against any person other than a subsequent holder in due course

(a) alteration by the holder which is both fraudulent and material discharges any party whose contract is thereby changed unless that party assents or is precluded from asserting the defense;

(b) no other alteration discharges any party and the instrument may be enforced according to its original tenor, or as to incomplete instruments according to the authority given.

(3) A subsequent holder in due course may in all cases enforce the instrument according to its original tenor, and when an incomplete instrument has been completed, he may enforce it as completed.

§ 3—408. **Consideration.**

Want or failure of consideration is a defense as against any person not having the rights of a holder in due course (Section 3—305), except that no consideration is necessary for an instrument or obligation thereon given in payment of or as security for an antecedent obligation of any kind. Nothing in this section shall be taken to displace any statute outside this Act under which a promise is enforceable notwithstanding lack or failure of consideration. Partial failure of consideration is a defense pro tanto whether or not the failure is in an ascertained or liquidated amount.

§ 3—409. **Draft Not an Assignment.**

(1) A check or other draft does not of itself operate as an assignment of any funds in the hands of the drawee available for its payment, and the drawee is not liable on the instrument until he accepts it.

(2) Nothing in this section shall affect any liability in contract, tort or otherwise arising from any letter of credit or other obligation or representation which is not an acceptance.

§ 3—410. **Definition and Operation of Acceptance.**

(1) Acceptance is the drawee's signed engagement to honor the draft as presented. It must be written on the draft, and may consist of his signature alone. It becomes operative when completed by delivery or notification.

(2) A draft may be accepted although it has not been

signed by the drawer or is otherwise incomplete or is overdue or has been dishonored.

(3) Where the draft is payable at a fixed period after sight and the acceptor fails to date his acceptance the holder may complete it by supplying a date in good faith.

§ 3—411. **Certification of a Check.**

(1) Certification of a check is acceptance. Where a holder procures certification the drawer and all prior indorsers are discharged.

(2) Unless otherwise agreed a bank has no obligation to certify a check.

(3) A bank may certify a check before returning it for lack of proper indorsement. If it does so the drawer is discharged.

§ 3—412. **Acceptance Varying Draft.**

(1) Where the drawee's proffered acceptance in any manner varies the draft as presented the holder may refuse the acceptance and treat the draft as dishonored in which case the drawee is entitled to have his acceptance cancelled.

(2) The terms of the draft are not varied by an acceptance to pay at any particular bank or place in the United States, unless the acceptance states that the draft is to be paid only at such bank or place.

(3) Where the holder assents to an acceptance varying the terms of the draft each drawer and indorser who does not affirmatively assent is discharged.

§ 3—413. **Contract of Maker, Drawer and Acceptor.**

(1) The maker or acceptor engages that he will pay the instrument according to its tenor at the time of his engagement or as completed pursuant to Section 3—115 on incomplete instruments.

(2) The drawer engages that upon dishonor of the draft and any necessary notice of dishonor or protest he will pay the amount of the draft to the holder or to any indorser who takes it up. The drawer may disclaim this liability by drawing without recourse.

(3) By making, drawing or accepting the party admits as against all subsequent parties including the drawee the existence of the payee and his then capacity to indorse.

§ 3—414. **Contract of Indorser; Order of Liability.**

(1) Unless the indorsement otherwise specifies (as by such words as "without recourse") every indorser engages that upon dishonor and any necessary notice of dishonor and protest he will pay the instrument according to its tenor at the time of his indorsement to the holder or to any subsequent indorser who takes it up, even though the indorser who takes it up was not obligated to do so.

(2) Unless they otherwise agree indorsers are liable to one another in the order in which they indorse, which is presumed to be the order in which their signatures appear on the instrument.

§ 3—415. **Contract of Accommodation Party.**

(1) An accommodation party is one who signs the instrument in any capacity for the purpose of lending his name to another party to it.

(2) When the instrument has been taken for value before it is due the accommodation party is liable in the capacity in which he has signed even though the taker knows of the accommodation.

(3) As against a holder in due course and without notice of the accommodation oral proof of the accommodation is not admissible to give the accommodation party the benefit of discharges dependent on his character as such. In other cases the accommodation character may be shown by oral proof.

(4) An indorsement which shows that it is not in the chain of title is notice of its accommodation character.

(5) An accommodation party is not liable to the party accommodated, and if he pays the instrument has a right of recourse on the instrument against such party.

§ 3—416. **Contract of Guarantor.**

(1) "Payment guaranteed" or equivalent words added to a signature mean that the signer engages that if the instrument is not paid when due he will pay it according to its tenor without resort by the holder to any other party.

(2) "Collection guaranteed" or equivalent words added to a signature mean that the signer engages that if the instrument is not paid when due he will pay it according to its tenor, but only after the holder has reduced his claim against the maker or acceptor to judgment and execution has been returned unsatis-

fied, or after the maker or acceptor has become insolvent or it is otherwise apparent that it is useless to proceed against him.

(3) Words of guaranty which do not otherwise specify guarantee payment.

(4) No words of guaranty added to the signature of a sole maker or acceptor affect his liability on the instrument. Such words added to the signature of one of two or more makers or acceptors create a presumption that the signature is for the accommodation of the others.

(5) When words of guaranty are used presentment, notice of dishonor and protest are not necessary to charge the user.

(6) Any guaranty written on the instrument is enforcible notwithstanding any statute of frauds.

§ 3—417. **Warranties on Presentment and Transfer.**

(1) Any person who obtains payment or acceptance and any prior transferor warrants to a person who in good faith pays or accepts that

(a) he has a good title to the instrument or is authorized to obtain payment or acceptance on behalf of one who has a good title; and

(b) he has no knowledge that the signature of the maker or drawer is unauthorized, except that this warranty is not given by a holder in due course acting in good faith

(i) to a maker with respect to the maker's own signature; or

(ii) to a drawer with respect to the drawer's own signature, whether or not the drawer is also the drawee; or

(iii) to an acceptor of a draft if the holder in due course took the draft after the acceptance or obtained the acceptance without knowledge that the drawer's signature was unauthorized; and

(c) the instrument has not been materially altered, except that this warranty is not given by a holder in due course acting in good faith

(i) to the maker of a note; or

(ii) to the drawer of a draft whether or not the drawer is also the drawee; or

(iii) to the acceptor of a draft with respect to an alteration made prior to the acceptance if the holder in due course took the draft after the acceptance, even though the acceptance provided "payable as originally drawn" or equivalent terms; or

(iv) to the acceptor of a draft with respect to an alteration made after the acceptance.

(2) Any person who transfers an instrument and receives consideration warrants to his transferee and if the transfer is by indorsement to any subsequent holder who takes the instrument in good faith that

(a) he has a good title to the instrument or is authorized to obtain payment or acceptance on behalf of one who has a good title and the transfer is otherwise rightful; and

(b) all signatures are genuine or authorized; and

(c) the instrument has not been materially altered; and

(d) no defense of any party is good against him; and

(e) he has no knowledge of any insolvency proceeding instituted with respect to the maker or acceptor or the drawer of an unaccepted instrument.

(3) By transferring "without recourse" the transferor limits the obligation stated in subsection (2) (d) to a warranty that he has no knowledge of such a defense.

(4) A selling agent or broker who does not disclose the fact that he is acting only as such gives the warranties provided in this section, but if he makes such disclosure warrants only his good faith and authority.

§ 3—418. **Finality of Payment or Acceptance.**

Except for recovery of bank payments as provided in the Article on Bank Deposits and Collections (Article 4) and except for liability for breach of warranty on presentment under the preceding section, payment or acceptance of any instrument is final in favor of a holder in due course, or a person who has in good faith changed his position in reliance on the payment.

§ 3—419. **Conversion of Instrument; Innocent Representative.**

(1) An instrument is converted when

(a) a drawee to whom it is delivered for acceptance refuses to return it on demand; or

(b) any person to whom it is delivered for payment refuses on demand either to pay or to return it; or

(c) it is paid on a forged indorsement.

(2) In an action against a drawee under subsection (1) the measure of the drawee's liability is the face amount of the instrument. In any other action under subsection (1) the measure of liability is presumed to be the face amount of the instrument.

(3) Subject to the provisions of this Act concerning restrictive indorsements a representative, including a depositary or collecting bank, who has in good faith and in accordance with the reasonable commercial standards applicable to the business of such representative dealt with an instrument or its proceeds on behalf of one who was not the true owner is not liable in conversion or otherwise to the true owner beyond the amount of any proceeds remaining in his hands.

(4) An intermediary bank or payor bank which is not a depositary bank is not liable in conversion solely by reason of the fact that proceeds of an item indorsed restrictively (Sections 3—205 and 3—206) are not paid or applied consistently with the restrictive indorsement of an indorser other than its immediate transferor.

Part 5 Presentment, Notice of Dishonor and Protest

§ 3—501. **When Presentment, Notice of Dishonor, and Protest Necessary or Permissible.**

(1) Unless excused (Section 3—511) presentment is necessary to charge secondary parties as follows:

(a) presentment for acceptance is necessary to charge the drawer and indorsers of a draft where the draft so provides, or is payable elsewhere than at the residence or place of business of the drawee, or its date of payment depends upon such presentment. The holder may at his option present for acceptance any other draft payable at a stated date;

(b) presentment for payment is necessary to charge any indorser;

(c) in the case of any drawer, the acceptor of a draft payable at a bank or the maker of a note payable at a bank, presentment for payment is necessary, but failure to make presentment discharges such drawer, acceptor or maker only as stated in Section 3—502(1)(b).

(2) Unless excused (Section 3—511)

(a) notice of any dishonor is necessary to charge any indorser;

(b) in the case of any drawer, the acceptor of a draft payable at a bank or the maker of a note payable at a bank, notice of any dishonor is necessary, but failure to give such notice discharges such drawer, acceptor or maker only as stated in Section 3—502(1)(b).

(3) Unless excused (Section 3—511) protest of any dishonor is necessary to charge the drawer and indorsers of any draft which on its face appears to be drawn or payable outside of the states, territories, dependencies, and possessions of the United States, the District of Columbia and the Commonwealth of Puerto Rico. The holder may at his option make protest of any dishonor of any other instrument and in the case of a foreign draft may on insolvency of the acceptor before maturity make protest for better security.

(4) Notwithstanding any provision of this section, neither presentment nor notice of dishonor nor protest is necessary to charge an indorser who has indorsed an instrument after maturity.

§ 3—502. **Unexcused Delay; Discharge.**

(1) Where without excuse any necessary presentment or notice of dishonor is delayed beyond the time when it is due

(a) any indorser is discharged; and

(b) any drawer or the acceptor of a draft payable at a bank or the maker of a note payable at a bank who because the drawee or payor bank becomes insolvent during the delay is deprived of funds maintained with the drawee or payor bank to cover the instrument may discharge his liability by written assignment to the holder of his rights against the drawee or payor bank in respect of such funds, but such drawer, acceptor or maker is not otherwise discharged.

(2) Where without excuse a necessary protest is delayed beyond the time when it is due any drawer or indorser is discharged.

§ 3—503. **Time of Presentment.**

(1) Unless a different time is expressed in the instrument the time for any presentment is determined as follows:

(a) where an instrument is payable at or a fixed period after a stated date any presentment for acceptance must be made on or before the date it is payable;

(b) where an instrument is payable after sight it must either be presented for acceptance or negotiated within a reasonable time after date or issue whichever is later;

(c) where an instrument shows the date on which it is payable presentment for payment is due on that date;

(d) where an instrument is accelerated presentment for payment is due within a reasonable time after the acceleration;

(e) with respect to the liability of any secondary party presentment for acceptance or payment of any other instrument is due within a reasonable time after such party becomes liable thereon.

(2) A reasonable time for presentment is determined by the nature of the instrument, any usage of banking or trade and the facts of the particular case. In the case of an uncertified check which is drawn and payable within the United States and which is not a draft drawn by a bank the following are presumed to be reasonable periods within which to present for payment or to initiate bank collection:

(a) with respect to the liability of the drawer, thirty days after date or issue whichever is later; and

(b) with respect to the liability of an indorser, seven days after his indorsement.

(3) Where any presentment is due on a day which is not a full business day for either the person making presentment or the party to pay or accept, present-

ment is due on the next following day which is a full business day for both parties.

(4) Presentment to be sufficient must be made at a reasonable hour, and if at a bank during its banking day.

§ 3—504. **How Presentment Made.**

(1) Presentment is a demand for acceptance or payment made upon the maker, acceptor, drawee or other payor by or on behalf of the holder.

(2) Presentment may be made

(a) by mail, in which event the time of presentment is determined by the time of receipt of the mail; or

(b) through a clearing house; or

(c) at the place of acceptance or payment specified in the instrument or if there be none at the place of business or residence of the party to accept or pay. If neither the party to accept or pay nor anyone authorized to act for him is present or accessible at such place presentment is excused.

(3) It may be made

(a) to any one of two or more makers, acceptors, drawees or other payors; or

(b) to any person who has authority to make or refuse the acceptance or payment.

(4) A draft accepted or a note made payable at a bank in the United States must be presented at such bank.

(5) In the cases described in Section 4—210 presentment may be made in the manner and with the result stated in that section.

§ 3—505. **Rights of Party to Whom Presentment Is Made.**

(1) The party to whom presentment is made may without dishonor require

(a) exhibition of the instrument; and

(b) reasonable identification of the person making presentment and evidence of his authority to make it if made for another; and

(c) that the instrument be produced for acceptance or payment at a place specified in it, or if there be none at any place reasonable in the circumstances; and

(d) a signed receipt on the instrument for any

partial or full payment and its surrender upon full payment.

(2) Failure to comply with any such requirement invalidates the presentment but the person presenting has a reasonable time in which to comply and the time for acceptance or payment runs from the time of compliance.

§ 3—506. Time Allowed for Acceptance or Payment.

(1) Acceptance may be deferred without dishonor until the close of the next business day following presentment. The holder may also in a good faith effort to obtain acceptance and without either dishonor of the instrument or discharge of secondary parties allow postponement of acceptance for an additional business day.

(2) Except as a longer time is allowed in the case of documentary drafts drawn under a letter of credit, and unless an earlier time is agreed to by the party to pay, payment of an instrument may be deferred without dishonor pending reasonable examination to determine whether it is properly payable, but payment must be made in any event before the close of business on the day of presentment.

§ 3—507. Dishonor; Holder's Right of Recourse; Term Allowing Re-Presentment.

(1) An instrument is dishonored when

(a) a necessary or optional presentment is duly made and due acceptance or payment is refused or cannot be obtained within the prescribed time or in case of bank collections the instrument is seasonably returned by the midnight deadline (Section 4—301); or

(b) presentment is excused and the instrument is not duly accepted or paid.

(2) Subject to any necessary notice of dishonor and protest, the holder has upon dishonor an immediate right of recourse against the drawers and indorsers.

(3) Return of an instrument for lack of proper indorsement is not dishonor.

(4) A term in a draft or an indorsement thereof allowing a stated time for re-presentment in the event of any dishonor of the draft by nonacceptance if a time draft or by nonpayment if a sight draft gives the holder as against any secondary party bound by the term an option to waive the dishonor without affecting the liability of the secondary party and he may present again up to the end of the stated time.

§ 3—508. Notice of Dishonor.

(1) Notice of dishonor may be given to any person who may be liable on the instrument by or on behalf of the holder or any party who has himself received notice, or any other party who can be compelled to pay the instrument. In addition an agent or bank in whose hands the instrument is dishonored may give notice to his principal or customer or to another agent or bank from which the instrument was received.

(2) Any necessary notice must be given by a bank before its midnight deadline and by any other person before midnight of the third business day after dishonor or receipt of notice of dishonor.

(3) Notice may be given in any reasonable manner. It may be oral or written and in any terms which identify the instrument and state that it has been dishonored. A misdescription which does not mislead the party notified does not vitiate the notice. Sending the instrument bearing a stamp, ticket or writing stating that acceptance or payment has been refused or sending a notice of debit with respect to the instrument is sufficient.

(4) Written notice is given when sent although it is not received.

(5) Notice to one partner is notice to each although the firm has been dissolved.

(6) When any party is in insolvency proceedings instituted after the issue of the instrument notice may be given either to the party or to the representative of his estate.

(7) When any party is dead or incompetent notice may be sent to his last known address or given to his personal representative.

(8) Notice operates for the benefit of all parties who have rights on the instrument against the party notified.

§ 3—509. Protest; Noting for Protest.

(1) A protest is a certificate of dishonor made under the hand and seal of a United States consul or vice consul or a notary public or other person authorized to certify dishonor by the law of the place where

dishonor occurs. It may be made upon information satisfactory to such person.

(2) The protest must identify the instrument and certify either that due presentment has been made or the reason why it is excused and that the instrument has been dishonored by nonacceptance or nonpayment.

(3) The protest may also certify that notice of dishonor has been given to all parties or to specified parties.

(4) Subject to subsection (5) any necessary protest is due by the time that notice of dishonor is due.

(5) If, before protest is due, an instrument has been noted for protest by the officer to make protest, the protest may be made at any time thereafter as of the date of the noting.

§ 3—510. **Evidence of Dishonor and Notice of Dishonor.**

The following are admissible as evidence and create a presumption of dishonor and of any notice of dishonor therein shown:

(a) a document regular in form as provided in the preceding section which purports to be a protest;

(b) the purported stamp or writing of the drawee, payor bank or presenting bank on the instrument or accompanying it stating that acceptance or payment has been refused for reasons conconsistent with dishonor;

(c) any book or record of the drawee, payor bank, or any collecting bank kept in the usual course of business which shows dishonor, even though there is no evidence of who made the entry.

§ 3—511. **Waived or Excused Presentment, Protest or Notice of Dishonor or Delay Therein.**

(1) Delay in presentment, protest or notice of dishonor is excused when the party is without notice that it is due or when the delay is caused by circumstances beyond his control and he exercises reasonable diligence after the cause of the delay ceases to operate.

(2) Presentment or notice or protest as the case may be is entirely excused when

(a) the party to be charged has waived it expressly or by implication either before or after it is due; or

(b) such party has himself dishonored the in-

strument or has countermanded payment or otherwise has no reason to expect or right to require that the instrument be accepted or paid; or

(c) by reasonable diligence the presentment or protest cannot be made or the notice given.

(3) Presentment is also entirely excused when

(a) the maker, acceptor or drawee of any instrument except a documentary draft is dead or in insolvency proceedings instituted after the issue of the instrument; or

(b) acceptance or payment is refused but not for want of proper presentment.

(4) Where a draft has been dishonored by nonacceptance a later presentment for payment and any notice of dishonor and protest for nonpayment are excused unless in the meantime the instrument has been accepted.

(5) A waiver of protest is also a waiver of presentment and of notice of dishonor even though protest is not required.

(6) Where a waiver of presentment or notice or protest is embodied in the instrument itself it is binding upon all parties; but where it is written above the signature of an indorser it binds him only.

Part 6 **Discharge**

§ 3—601. **Discharge of Parties.**

(1) The extent of the discharge of any party from liability on an instrument is governed by the sections on

(a) payment or satisfaction (Section 3—603); or

(b) tender of payment (Section 3—604); or

(c) cancellation or renunciation (Section 3—605); or

(d) impairment of right of recourse or of collateral (Section 3—606); or

(e) reacquisition of the instrument by a prior party (Section 3—208); or

(f) fraudulent and material alteration (Section 3—407); or

(g) certification of a check (Section 3—411); or

(h) acceptance varying a draft (Section 3—412); or

(i) unexcused delay in presentment or notice of dishonor or protest (Section 3—502).

(2) Any party is also discharged from his liability on an instrument to another party by any other act or agreement with such party which would discharge his simple contract for the payment of money.

(3) The liability of all parties is discharged when any party who has himself no right of action or recourse on the instrument

(a) reacquires the instrument in his own right; or

(b) is discharged under any provision of this Article, except as otherwise provided with respect to discharge for impairment of recourse or of collateral (Section 3—606).

§ 3—602. **Effect of Discharge Against Holder in Due Course.**

No discharge of any party provided by this Article is effective against a subsequent holder in due course unless he has notice thereof when he takes the instrument.

§ 3—603. **Payment or Satisfaction.**

(1) The liability of any party is discharged to the extent of his payment or satisfaction to the holder even though it is made with knowledge of a claim of another person to the instrument unless prior to such payment or satisfaction the person making the claim either supplies indemnity deemed adequate by the party seeking the discharge or enjoins payment or satisfaction by order of a court of competent jurisdiction in an action in which the adverse claimant and the holder are parties. This subsection does not, however, result in the discharge of the liability

(a) of a party who in bad faith pays or satisfies a holder who acquired the instrument by theft or who (unless having the rights of a holder in due course) holds through one who so acquired it; or

(b) of a party (other than an intermediary bank or a payor bank which is not a depositary bank) who pays or satisfies the holder of an instrument which has been restrictively indorsed in a manner not consistent with the terms of such restrictive indorsement.

(2) Payment or satisfaction may be made with the consent of the holder by any person including a stranger to the instrument. Surrender of the in-

strument to such a person gives him the rights of a transferee (Section 3—201).

§ 3—604. **Tender of Payment.**

(1) Any party making tender of full payment to a holder when or after it is due is discharged to the extent of all subsequent liability for interest, costs and attorney's fees.

(2) The holder's refusal of such tender wholly discharges any party who has a right of recourse against the party making the tender.

(3) Where the maker or acceptor of an instrument payable otherwise than on demand is able and ready to pay at every place of payment specified in the instrument when it is due, it is equivalent to tender.

§ 3—605. **Cancellation and Renunciation.**

(1) The holder of an instrument may even without consideration discharge any party

(a) in any manner apparent on the face of the instrument or the indorsement, as by intentionally cancelling the instrument or the party's signature by destruction or mutilation, or by striking out the party's signature; or

(b) by renouncing his rights by a writing signed and delivered or by surrender of the instrument to the party to be discharged.

(2) Neither cancellation nor renunciation without surrender of the instrument affects the title thereto.

§ 3—606. **Impairment of Recourse or of Collateral.**

(1) The holder discharges any party to the instrument to the extent that without such party's consent the holder

(a) without express reservation of rights releases or agrees not to sue any person against whom the party has to the knowledge of the holder a right of recourse or agrees to suspend the right to enforce against such person the instrument or collateral or otherwise discharges such person, except that failure or delay in effecting any required presentment, protest or notice of dishonor with respect to any such person does not discharge any party as to whom presentment, protest or notice of dishonor is effective or unnecessary; or

(b) unjustifiably impairs any collateral for the instrument given by or on behalf of the party or any person against whom he has a right of recourse.

(2) By express reservation of rights against a party with a right of recourse the holder preserves

(a) all his rights against such party as of the time when the instrument was originally due; and

(b) the right of the party to pay the instrument as of that time; and

(c) all rights of such party to recourse against others.

Part 7 Advice of International Sight Draft

§ 3—701. **Letter of Advice of International Sight Draft.**

(1) A "letter of advice" is a drawer's communication to the drawee that a described draft has been drawn.

(2) Unless otherwise agreed when a bank receives from another bank a letter of advice of an international sight draft the drawee bank may immediately debit the drawer's account and stop the running of interest pro tanto. Such a debit and any resulting credit to any account covering outstanding drafts leaves in the drawer full power to stop payment or otherwise dispose of the amount and creates no trust or interest in favor of the holder.

(3) Unless otherwise agreed and except where a draft is drawn under a credit issued by the drawee, the drawee of an international sight draft owes the drawer no duty to pay an unadvised draft but if it does so and the draft is genuine, may appropriately debit the drawer's account.

Part 8
Miscellaneous

§ 3—801. **Drafts in a Set.**

(1) Where a draft is drawn in a set of parts, each of which is numbered and expressed to be an order only if no other part has been honored, the whole of the parts constitutes one draft but a taker of any part may become a holder in due course of the draft.

(2) Any person who negotiates, indorses or accepts a single part of a draft drawn in a set thereby becomes liable to any holder in due course of that part as if it were the whole set, but as between different holders in due course to whom different parts have been negotiated the holder whose title first accrues has all rights to the draft and its proceeds.

(3) As against the drawee the first presented part of a draft drawn in a set is the part entitled to payment, or if a time draft to acceptance and payment. Acceptance of any subsequently presented part renders the drawee liable thereon under subsection (2). With respect both to a holder and to the drawer payment of a subsequently presented part of a draft payable at sight has the same effect as payment of a check notwithstanding an effective stop order (Section 4—407).

(4) Except as otherwise provided in this section, where any part of a draft in a set is discharged by payment or otherwise the whole draft is discharged.

§ 3—802. **Effect of Instrument on Obligation for Which It Is Given.**

(1) Unless otherwise agreed where an instrument is taken for an underlying obligation

(a) the obligation is pro tanto discharged if a bank is drawer, maker or acceptor of the instrument and there is no recourse on the instrument against the underlying obligor; and

(b) in any other case the obligation is suspended pro tanto until the instrument is due or if it is payable on demand until its presentment. If the instrument is dishonored action may be maintained on either the instrument or the obligation; discharge of the underlying obligor on the instrument also discharges him on the obligation.

(2) The taking in good faith of a check which is not postdated does not of itself so extend the time on the original obligation as to discharge a surety.

§ 3—803. **Notice to Third Party.**

Where a defendant is sued for breach of an obligation for which a third person is answerable over under this Article he may give the third person written notice of the litigation, and the person notified may then give similar notice to any other person who is answerable over to him under this Article. If the notice states that the person notified may come in and defend and that if the person notified does not do so he will in any action against him by the person giving the notice be bound by any determination of fact common to the two litigations, then unless after seasonable receipt of the notice the person notified does come in and defend he is so bound.

§ 3—804. **Lost, Destroyed or Stolen Instruments.**

The owner of an instrument which is lost, whether by destruction, theft or otherwise, may maintain an action in his own name and recover from any party liable thereon upon due proof of his ownership, the facts which prevent his production of the instrument and its terms. The court may require security indemnifying the defendant against loss by reason of further claims on the instrument.

§ 3—805. **Instruments Not Payable to Order or to Bearer.**

This Article applies to any instrument whose terms do not preclude transfer and which is otherwise negotiable within this Article but which is not payable to order or to bearer, except that there can be no holder in due course of such an instrument.

Article 4
BANK DEPOSITS AND COLLECTIONS

Part 1 **General Provisions and Definitions**

§ 4—101. **Short Title.**

This Article shall be known and may be cited as Uniform Commercial Code—Bank Deposits and Collections.

§ 4—102. **Applicability.**

(1) To the extent that items within this Article are also within the scope of Articles 3 and 8, they are subject to the provisions of those Articles. In the event of conflict the provisions of this Article govern those of Article 3 but the provisions of Article 8 govern those of this Article.

(2) The liability of a bank for action or non-action with respect to any item handled by it for purposes of presentment, payment or collection is governed by the law of the place where the bank is located. In the case of action or non-action by or at a branch or separate office of a bank, its liability is governed by the law of the place where the branch or separate office is located.

§ 4—103. **Variation by Agreement; Measure of Damages; Certain Action Constituting Ordinary Care.**

(1) The effect of the provisions of this Article may be varied by agreement except that no agreement can disclaim a bank's responsibility for its own lack of good faith or failure to exercise ordinary care or can limit the measure of damages for such lack or failure; but the parties may by agreement determine the standards by which such responsibility is to be measured if such standards are not manifestly unreasonable.

(2) Federal Reserve regulations and operating letters, clearing house rules, and the like, have the effect of agreements under subsection (1), whether or not specifically assented to by all parties interested in items handled.

(3) Action or non-action approved by this Article or pursuant to Federal Reserve regulations or operating letters constitutes the exercise of ordinary care and, in the absence of special instructions, action or non-action consistent with clearing house rules and the like or with a general banking usage not disapproved by this Article, prima facie constitutes the exercise of ordinary care.

(4) The specification or approval of certain procedures by this Article does not constitute disapproval of other procedures which may be reasonable under the circumstances.

(5) The measure of damages for failure to exercise ordinary care in handling an item is the amount of the item reduced by an amount which could not have been realized by the use of ordinary care, and where there is bad faith it includes other damages, if any, suffered by the party as a proximate consequence.

§ 4—104. **Definitions and Index of Definitions.**

(1) In this Article unless the context otherwise requires

(a) "Account" means any account with a bank and includes a checking, time, interest or savings account;

(b) "Afternoon" means the period of a day between noon and midnight;

(c) "Banking day" means that part of any day on which a bank is open to the public for carrying on substantially all of its banking functions;

(d) "Clearing house" means any association of banks or other payors regularly clearing items;

(e) "Customer" means any person having an account with a bank or for whom a bank has agreed to collect items and includes a bank carrying an account with another bank;

(f) "Documentary draft" means any negotiable or nonnegotiable draft with accompanying documents, securities or other papers to be delivered against honor of the draft;

(g) "Item" means any instrument for the payment of money even though it is not negotiable but does not include money;

(h) "Midnight deadline" with respect to a bank is midnight on its next banking day following the banking day on which it receives the relevant item or notice or from which the time for taking action commences to run, whichever is later;

(i) "Properly payable" includes the availability of funds for payment at the time of decision to pay or dishonor;

(j) "Settle" means to pay in cash, by clearing house settlement, in a charge or credit or by remittance, or otherwise as instructed. A settlement may be either provisional or final;

(k) "Suspends payments" with respect to a bank means that it has been closed by order of the supervisory authorities, that a public officer has been appointed to take it over or that it ceases or refuses to make payments in the ordinary course of business.

(2) Other definitions applying to this Article and the sections in which they appear are:
"Collecting bank" Section 4—105.
"Depositary bank" Section 4—105.
"Intermediary bank" Section 4—105.
"Payor bank" Section 4—105.
"Presenting bank" Section 4—105.
"Remitting bank" Section 4—105.

(3) The following definitions in other Articles apply to this Article:
"Acceptance" Section 3—410.
"Certificate of deposit" Section 3—104.
"Certification" Section 3—411.
"Check" Section 3—104.
"Draft" Section 3—104.

"Holder in due course" Section 3—302.
"Notice of dishonor" Section 3—508.
"Presentment" Section 3—504.
"Protest" Section 3—509.
"Secondary party" Section 3—102.

(4) In addition Article 1 contains general definitions and principles of construction and interpretation applicable throughout this Article.

§ 4—105. **"Depositary Bank"; "Intermediary Bank"; "Collecting Bank"; "Payor Bank"; "Presenting Bank"; "Remitting Bank".**

In this Article unless the context otherwise requires:

(a) "Depositary bank" means the first bank to which an item is transferred for collection even though it is also the payor bank;

(b) "Payor bank" means a bank by which an item is payable as drawn or accepted;

(c) "Intermediary bank" means any bank to which an item is transferred in course of collection except the depositary or payor bank;

(d) "Collecting bank" means any bank handling the item for collection except the payor bank;

(e) "Presenting bank" means any bank presenting an item except a payor bank;

(f) "Remitting bank" means any payor or intermediary bank remitting for an item.

§ 4—106. **Separate Office of a Bank.**

A branch or separate office of a bank [maintaining its own deposit ledgers] is a separate bank for the purpose of computing the time within which and determining the place at or to which action may be taken or notices or orders shall be given under this Article and under Article 3.

Note: The brackets are to make it optional with the several states whether to require a branch to maintain its own deposit ledgers in order to be considered to be a separate bank for certain purposes under Article 4. In some states "maintaining its own deposit ledgers" is a satisfactory test. In others branch banking practices are such that this test would not be suitable.

§ 4—107. **Time of Receipt of Items.**

(1) For the purpose of allowing time to process items, prove balances and make the necessary entries on its books to determine its position for the day, a bank may fix an afternoon hour of two P.M. or later as a

cut-off hour for the handling of money and items and the making of entries on its books.

(2) Any item or deposit of money received on any day after a cut-off hour so fixed or after the close of the banking day may be treated as being received at the opening of the next banking day.

§ 4—108. **Delays.**

(1) Unless otherwise instructed, a collecting bank in a good faith effort to secure payment may, in the case of specific items and with or without the approval of any person involved, waive, modify or extend time limits imposed or permitted by this Act for a period not in excess of an additional banking day without discharge of secondary parties and without liability to its transferor or any prior party.

(2) Delay by a collecting bank or payor bank beyond time limits prescribed or permitted by this Act or by instructions is excused if caused by interruption of communication facilities, suspension of payments by another bank, war, emergency conditions or other circumstances beyond the control of the bank provided it exercises such diligence as the circumstances require.

§ 4—109. **Process of Posting.**

The "process of posting" means the usual procedure followed by a payor bank in determining to pay an item and in recording the payment including one or more of the following or other steps as determined by the bank:

(a) verification of any signature;

(b) ascertaining that sufficient funds are available;

(c) affixing a "paid" or other stamp;

(d) entering a charge or entry to a customer's account;

(e) correcting or reversing an entry or erroneous action with respect to the item.

Part 2 Collection of Items: Depositary and Collecting Banks

§ 4—201. **Presumption and Duration of Agency Status of Collecting Banks and Provisional Status of Credits; Applicability of Article; Item Indorsed "Pay Any Bank".**

(1) Unless a contrary intent clearly appears and prior to the time that a settlement given by a collecting bank for an item is or becomes final (subsection (3) of Section 4—211 and Sections 4—212 and 4—213) the bank is an agent or sub-agent of the owner of the item and any settlement given for the item is provisional. This provision applies regardless of the form of indorsement or lack of indorsement and even though credit given for the item is subject to immediate withdrawal as of right or is in fact withdrawn; but the continuance of ownership of an item by its owner and any rights of the owner to proceeds of the item are subject to rights of a collecting bank such as those resulting from outstanding advances on the item and valid rights of setoff. When an item is handled by banks for purposes of presentment, payment and collection, the relevant provisions of this Article apply even though action of parties clearly establishes that a particular bank has purchased the item and is the owner of it.

(2) After an item has been indorsed with the words "pay any bank" or the like, only a bank may acquire the rights of a holder

(a) until the item has been returned to the customer initiating collection; or

(b) until the item has been specially indorsed by a bank to a person who is not a bank.

§ 4—202. **Responsibility for Collection; When Action Seasonable.**

(1) A collecting bank must use ordinary care in

(a) presenting an item or sending it for presentment; and

(b) sending notice of dishonor or non-payment or returning an item other than a documentary draft to the bank's transferor [or directly to the depositary bank under subsection (2) of Section 4—212] *(see note to Section 4—212)* after learning that the item has not been paid or accepted as the case may be; and

(c) settling for an item when the bank receives final settlement; and

(d) making or providing for any necessary protest; and

(e) notifying its transferor of any loss or delay in transit within a reasonable time after discovery thereof.

(2) A collecting bank taking proper action before its midnight deadline following receipt of an item, notice or payment acts seasonably; taking proper action within a reasonably longer time may be seasonable but the bank has the burden of so establishing.

(3) Subject to subsection (1)(a), a bank is not liable for the insolvency, neglect, misconduct, mistake or default of another bank or person or for loss or destruction of an item in transit or in the possession of others.

§ 4—203. **Effect of Instructions.**

Subject to the provisions of Article 3 concerning conversion of instruments (Section 3—419) and the provisions of both Article 3 and this Article concerning restrictive indorsements only a collecting bank's transferor can give instructions which affect the bank or constitute notice to it and a collecting bank is not liable to prior parties for any action taken pursuant to such instructions or in accordance with any agreement with its transferor.

§ 4—204. **Methods of Sending and Presenting; Sending Direct to Payor Bank.**

(1) A collecting bank must send items by reasonably prompt method taking into consideration any relevant instructions, the nature of the item, the number of such items on hand, and the cost of collection involved and the method generally used by it or others to present such items.

(2) A collecting bank may send

(a) any item direct to the payor bank;

(b) any item to any non-bank payor if authorized by its transferor; and

(c) any item other than documentary drafts to any non-bank payor, if authorized by Federal Reserve regulation or operating letter, clearing house rule or the like.

(3) Presentment may be made by a presenting bank at a place where the payor bank has requested that presentment be made.

§ 4—205. **Supplying Missing Indorsement; No Notice from Prior Indorsement.**

(1) A depositary bank which has taken an item for collection may supply any indorsement of the customer which is necessary to title unless the item contains the words "payee's indorsement required" or the like. In the absence of such a requirement a statement placed on the item by the depositary bank to the effect that the item was deposited by a customer or credited to his account is effective as the customer's indorsement.

(2) An intermediary bank, or payor bank which is not a depositary bank, is neither given notice nor otherwise affected by a restrictive indorsement of any person except the bank's immediate transferor.

§ 4—206. **Transfer Between Banks.**

Any agreed method which identifies the transferor bank is sufficient for the item's further transfer to another bank.

§ 4—207. **Warranties of Customer and Collecting Bank on Transfer or Presentment of Items; Time for Claims.**

(1) Each customer or collecting bank who obtains payment or acceptance of an item and each prior customer and collecting bank warrants to the payor bank or other payor who in good faith pays or accepts the item that

(a) he has a good title to the item or is authorized to obtain payment or acceptance on behalf of one who has a good title; and

(b) he has no knowledge that the signature of the maker or drawer is unauthorized, except that this warranty is not given by any customer or collecting bank that is a holder in due course and acts in good faith

(i) to a maker with respect to the maker's own signature; or

(ii) to a drawer with respect to the drawer's own signature, whether or not the drawer is also the drawee; or

(iii) to an acceptor of an item if the holder in due course took the item after the acceptance or obtained the acceptance without knowledge that the drawer's signature was unauthorized; and

(c) the item has not been materially altered, except that this warranty is not given by any customer or collecting bank that is a holder in due course and acts in good faith

(i) to the maker of a note; or

(ii) to the drawer of a draft whether or not the drawer is also the drawee; or

(iii) to the acceptor of an item with respect to an alteration made prior to the acceptance if the holder in due course took the item after the acceptance, even though the acceptance provided "payable as originally drawn" or equivalent terms; or

(iv) to the acceptor of an item with respect to an alteration made after the acceptance.

(2) Each customer and collecting bank who transfers an item and receives a settlement or other consideration for it warrants to his transferee and to any subequent collecting bank who takes the item in good faith that

(a) he has a good title to the item or is authorized to obtain payment or acceptance on behalf of one who has a good title and the transfer is otherwise rightful; and

(b) all signatures are genuine or authorized; and

(c) the item has not been materially altered; and

(d) no defense of any party is good against him; and

(e) he has no knowledge of any insolvency proceeding instituted with respect to the maker or acceptor or the drawer of an unaccepted item.

In addition each customer and collecting bank so transferring an item and receiving a settlement or other consideration engages that upon dishonor and any necessary notice of dishonor and protest he will take up the item.

(3) The warranties and the engagement to honor set forth in the two preceding subsections arise notwithstanding the absence of indorsement or words of guaranty or warranty in the transfer or presentment and a collecting bank remains liable for their breach despite remittance to its transferor. Damages for breach of such warranties or engagement to honor shall not exceed the consideration received by the customer or collecting bank responsible plus finance charges and expenses related to the item, if any.

(4) Unless a claim for breach of warranty under this section is made within a reasonable time after the person claiming learns of the breach, the person

liable is discharged to the extent of any loss caused by the delay in making claim.

§ 4—208. **Security Interest of Collecting Bank in Items, Accompanying Documents and Proceeds.**

(1) A bank has a security interest in an item and any accompanying documents or the proceeds of either

(a) in case of an item deposited in an account to the extent to which credit given for the item has been withdrawn or applied;

(b) in case of an item for which it has given credit available for withdrawal as of right, to the extent of the credit given whether or not the credit is drawn upon and whether or not there is a right of charge-back; or

(c) if it makes an advance on or against the item.

(2) When credit which has been given for several items received at one time or pursuant to a single agreement is withdrawn or applied in part the security interest remains upon all the items, any accompanying documents or the proceeds of either. For the purpose of this section, credits first given are first withdrawn.

(3) Receipt by a collecting bank of a final settlement for an item is a realization on its security interest in the item, accompanying documents and proceeds. To the extent and so long as the bank does not receive final settlement for the item or give up possession of the item or accompanying documents for purposes other than collection, the security interest continues and is subject to the provisions of Article 9 except that

(a) no security agreement is necessary to make the security interest enforceable (subsection (1) (b) of Section 9—203); and

(b) no filing is required to perfect the security interest; and

(c) the security interest has priority over conflicting perfected security interests in the item, accompanying documents or proceeds.

§ 4—209. **When Bank Gives Value for Purposes of Holder in Due Course.**

For purposes of determining its status as a holder in due course, the bank has given value to the extent that it has a security interest in an item provided that the bank otherwise complies with the requirements of Section 3—302 on what constitutes a holder in due course.

§ 4—210. **Presentment by Notice of Item Not Payable by, Through or at a Bank; Liability of Secondary Parties.**

(1) Unless otherwise instructed, a collecting bank may present an item not payable by, through or at a bank by sending to the party to accept or pay a written notice that the bank holds the item for acceptance or payment. The notice must be sent in time to be received on or before the day when presentment is due and the bank must meet any requirement of the party to accept or pay under Section 3—505 by the close of the bank's next banking day after it knows of the requirement.

(2) Where presentment is made by notice and neither honor nor request for compliance with a requirement under Section 3—505 is received by the close of business on the day after maturity or in the case of demand items by the close of business on the third banking day after notice was sent, the presenting bank may treat the item as dishonored and charge any secondary party by sending him notice of the facts.

§ 4—211. **Media of Remittance; Provisional and Final Settlement in Remittance Cases.**

(1) A collecting bank may take in settlement of an item

(a) a check of the remitting bank or of another bank on any bank except the remitting bank; or

(b) a cashier's check or similar primary obligation of a remitting bank which is a member of or clears through a member of the same clearing house or group as the collecting bank; or

(c) appropriate authority to charge an account of the remitting bank or of another bank with the collecting bank; or

(d) if the item is drawn upon or payable by a person other than a bank, a cashier's check, certified check or other bank check or obligation.

(2) If before its midnight deadline the collecting bank properly dishonors a remittance check or authorization to charge on itself or presents or forwards for collection a remittance instrument of or on another bank which is of a kind approved by subsection (1) or

has not been authorized by it, the collecting bank is not liable to prior parties in the event of the dishonor of such check, instrument or authorization.

(3) A settlement for an item by means of a remittance instrument or authorization to charge is or becomes a final settlement as to both the person making and the person receiving the settlement

(a) if the remittance instrument or authorization to charge is of a kind approved by subsection (1) or has not been authorized by the person receiving the settlement and in either case the person receiving the settlement acts seasonably before its midnight deadline in presenting, forwarding for collection or paying the instrument or authorization,—at the time the remittance instrument or authorization is finally paid by the payor by which it is payable;

(b) if the person receiving the settlement has authorized remittance by a non-bank check or obligation or by a cashier's check or similar primary obligation of or a check upon the payor or other remitting bank which is not of a kind approved by subsection (1) (b),—at the time of the receipt of such remittance check or obligation; or

(c) if in a case not covered by sub-paragraphs (a) or (b) the person receiving the settlement fails to seasonably present, forward for collection, pay or return a remittance instrument or authorization to it to charge before its midnight deadline,—at such midnight deadline.

§ 4—212. **Right of Charge-Back or Refund.**

(1) If a collecting bank has made provisional settlement with its customer for an item and itself fails by reason of dishonor, suspension of payments by a bank or otherwise to receive a settlement for the item which is or becomes final, the bank may revoke the settlement given by it, charge back the amount of any credit given for the item to its customer's account or obtain refund from its customer whether or not it is able to return the items if by its midnight deadline or within a longer reasonable time after it learns the facts it returns the item or sends notification of the facts. These rights to revoke, charge-back and obtain refund terminate if and when a settlement for the item received by the bank is or becomes final (subsec-

tion (3) of Section 4—211 and subsections (2) and (3) of Section 4—213).

[(2) Within the time and manner prescribed by this section and Section 4—301, an intermediary or payor bank, as the case may be, may return an unpaid item directly to the depositary bank and may send for collection a draft on the depositary bank and obtain reimbursement. In such case, if the depositary bank has received provisional settlement for the item, it must reimburse the bank drawing the draft and any provisional credits for the item between banks shall become and remain final.]

Note: Direct returns is recognized as an innovation that is not yet established bank practice, and therefore, Paragraph 2 has been bracketed. Some lawyers have doubts whether it should be included in legislation or left to development by agreement.

(3) A depositary bank which is also the payor may charge-back the amount of an item to its customer's account or obtain refund in accordance with the section governing return of an item received by a payor bank for credit on its books (Section 4—301).

(4) The right to charge-back is not affected by

(a) prior use of the credit given for the item; or

(b) failure by any bank to exercise ordinary care with respect to the item but any bank so failing remains liable.

(5) A failure to charge-back or claim refund does not affect other rights of the bank against the customer or any other party.

(6) If credit is given in dollars as the equivalent of the value of an item payable in a foreign currency the dollar amount of any charge-back or refund shall be calculated on the basis of the buying sight rate for the foreign currency prevailing on the day when the person entitled to the charge-back or refund learns that it will not receive payment in ordinary course.

§ 4—213. **Final Payment of Item by Payor Bank; When Provisional Debits and Credits Become Final; When Certain Credits Become Available for Withdrawal.**

(1) An item is finally paid by a payor bank when the bank has done any of the following, whichever happens first:

(a) paid the item in cash; or

(b) settled for the item without reserving a right to revoke the settlement and without having such right under statute, clearing house rule or agreement; or

(c) completed the process of posting the item to the indicated account of the drawer, maker or other person to be charged therewith; or

(d) made a provisional settlement for the item and failed to revoke the settlement in the time and manner permitted by statute, clearing house rule or agreement.

Upon a final payment under subparagraphs (b), (c) or (d) the payor bank shall be accountable for the amount of the item.

(2) If provisional settlement for an item between the presenting and payor banks is made through a clearing house or by debits or credits in an account between them, then to the extent that provisional debits or credits for the item are entered in accounts between the presenting and payor banks or between the presenting and successive prior collecting banks seriatim, they become final upon final payment of the item by the payor bank.

(3) If a collecting bank receives a settlement for an item which is or becomes final (subsection (3) of Section 4—211, subsection (2) of Section 4—213) the bank is accountable to its customer for the amount of the item and any provisional credit given for the item in an account with its customer becomes final.

(4) Subject to any right of the bank to apply the credit to an obligation of the customer, credit given by a bank for an item in an account with its customer becomes available for withdrawal as of right

(a) in any case where the bank has received a provisional settlement for the item,—when such settlement becomes final and the bank has had a reasonable time to learn that the settlement is final;

(b) in any case where the bank is both a depositary bank and a payor bank and the item is finally paid,—at the opening of the bank's second banking day following receipt of the item.

(5) A deposit of money in a bank is final when made but, subject to any right of the bank to apply the deposit to an obligation of the customer, the deposit

becomes available for withdrawal as of right at the opening of the bank's next banking day following receipt of the deposit.

§ 4—214. **Insolvency and Preference.**

(1) Any item in or coming into the possession of a payor or collecting bank which suspends payment and which item is not finally paid shall be returned by the receiver, trustee or agent in charge of the closed bank to the presenting bank or the closed bank's customer.

(2) If a payor bank finally pays an item and suspends payments without making a settlement for the item with its customer or the presenting bank which settlement is or becomes final, the owner of the item has a preferred claim against the payor bank.

(3) If a payor bank gives or a collecting bank gives or receives a provisional settlement for an item and thereafter suspends payments, the suspension does not prevent or interfere with the settlement becoming final if such finality occurs automatically upon the lapse of certain time or the happening of certain events (subsection (3) of Section 4—211, subsections (1) (d), (2) and (3) of Section 4—213).

(4) If a collecting bank receives from subsequent parties settlement for an item which settlement is or becomes final and suspends payments without making a settlement for the item with its customer which is or becomes final, the owner of the item has a preferred claim against such collecting bank.

Part 3 **Collection of Items: Payor Banks**

§ 4—301. **Deferred Posting; Recovery of Payment by Return of Items; Time of Dishonor.**

(1) Where an authorized settlement for a demand item (other than a documentary draft) received by a payor bank otherwise than for immediate payment over the counter has been made before midnight of the banking day of receipt the payor bank may revoke the settlement and recover any payment if before it has made final payment (subsection (1) of Section 4—213) and before its midnight deadline it

(a) returns the item; or

(b) sends written notice of dishonor or nonpayment if the item is held for protest or is otherwise unavailable for return.

(2) If a demand item is received by a payor bank for credit on its books it may return such item or send notice of dishonor and may revoke any credit given or recover the amount thereof withdrawn by its customer, if it acts within the time limit and in the manner specified in the preceding subsection.

(3) Unless previous notice of dishonor has been sent an item is dishonored at the time when for purposes of dishonor it is returned or notice sent in accordance with this section.

(4) An item is returned:

(a) as to an item received through a clearing house, when it is delivered to the presenting or last collecting bank or to the clearing house or is sent or delivered in accordance with its rules; or

(b) in all other cases, when it is sent or delivered to the bank's customer or transferor or pursuant to his instructions.

§ 4—302. **Payor Bank's Responsibility for Late Return of Item.**

In the absence of a valid defense such as breach of a presentment warranty (subsection (1) of Section 4—207), settlement effected or the like, if an item is presented on and received by a payor bank the bank is accountable for the amount of

(a) a demand item other than a documentary draft whether properly payable or not if the bank, in any case where it is not also the depositary bank, retains the item beyond midnight of the banking day of receipt without settling for it or, regardless of whether it is also the depositary bank, does not pay or return the item or send notice of dishonor until after its midnight deadline; or

(b) any other properly payable item unless within the time allowed for acceptance or payment of that item the bank either accepts or pays the item or returns it and accompanying documents.

§ 4—303. **When Items Subject to Notice, Stop-Order, Legal Process or Setoff; Order in Which Items May Be Charged or Certified.**

(1) Any knowledge, notice or stop-order received by, legal process served upon or setoff exercised by a payor bank, whether or not effective under other rules of law to terminate, suspend or modify the

bank's right or duty to pay an item or to charge its customer's account for the item, comes too late to so terminate, suspend or modify such right or duty if the knowledge, notice, stop-order or legal process is received or served and a reasonable time for the bank to act thereon expires or the setoff is exercised after the bank has done any of the following:

(a) accepted or certified the item;

(b) paid the item in cash;

(c) settled for the item without reserving a right to revoke the settlement and without having such right under statute, clearing house rule or agreement;

(d) completed the process of posting the item to the indicated account of the drawer, maker or other person to be charged therewith or otherwise has evidenced by examination of such indicated account and by action its decision to pay the item; or

(e) become accountable for the amount of the item under subsection (1) (d) of Section 4—213 and Section 4—302 dealing with the payor bank's responsibility for late return of items.

(2) Subject to the provisions of subsection (1) items may be accepted, paid, certified or charged to the indicated account of its customer in any order convenient to the bank.

Part 4 Relationship Between Payor Bank and Its Customer

§ 4—401. When Bank May Charge Customer's Account.

(1) As against its customer, a bank may charge against his account any item which is otherwise properly payable from that account even though the charge creates an overdraft.

(2) A bank which in good faith makes payment to a holder may charge the indicated account of its customer according to

(a) the original tenor of his altered item; or

(b) the tenor of his completed item, even though the bank knows the item has been completed unless the bank has notice that the completion was improper.

§ 4—402. Bank's Liability to Customer for Wrongful Dishonor.

A payor bank is liable to its customer for damages proximately caused by the wrongful dishonor of an item. When the dishonor occurs through mistake liability is limited to actual damages proved. If so proximately caused and proved damages may include damages for an arrest or prosecution of the customer or other consequential damages. Whether any consequential damages are proximately caused by the wrongful dishonor is a question of fact to be determined in each case.

§ 4—403. Customer's Right to Stop Payment; Burden of Proof of Loss.

(1) A customer may by order to his bank stop payment of any item payable for his account but the order must be received at such time and in such manner as to afford the bank a reasonable opportunity to act on it prior to any action by the bank with respect to the item described in Section 4—303.

(2) An oral order is binding upon the bank only for fourteen calendar days unless confirmed in writing within that period. A written order is effective for only six months unless renewed in writing.

(3) The burden of establishing the fact and amount of loss resulting from the payment of an item contrary to a binding stop payment order is on the customer.

§ 4—404. Bank Not Obligated to Pay Check More Than Six Months Old.

A bank is under no obligation to a customer having a checking account to pay a check, other than a certified check, which is presented more than six months after its date, but it may charge its customer's account for a payment made thereafter in good faith.

§ 4—405. Death or Incompetence of Customer.

(1) A payor or collecting bank's authority to accept, pay or collect an item or to account for proceeds of its collection if otherwise effective is not rendered ineffective by incompetence of a customer of either bank existing at the time the item is issued or its collection is undertaken if the bank does not know of an adjudication of incompetence. Neither death nor incompetence of a customer revokes such authority to accept, pay, collect or account until the bank knows of

the fact of death or of an adjudication of incompetence and has reasonable opportunity to act on it.

(2) Even with knowledge a bank may for ten days after the date of death pay or certify checks drawn on or prior to that date unless ordered to stop payment by a person claiming an interest in the account.

§ 4—406. **Customer's Duty to Discover and Report Unauthorized Signature or Alteration.**

(1) When a bank sends to its customer a statement of account accompanied by items paid in good faith in support of the debit entries or holds the statement and items pursuant to a request or instructions of its customer or otherwise in a reasonable manner makes the statement and items available to the customer, the customer must exercise reasonable care and promptness to examine the statement and items to discover his unauthorized signature or any alteration on an item and must notify the bank promptly after discovery thereof.

(2) If the bank establishes that the customer failed with respect to an item to comply with the duties imposed on the customer by subsection (1) the customer is precluded from asserting against the bank

(a) his unauthorized signature or any alteration on the item if the bank also establishes that it suffered a loss by reason of such failure; and

(b) an unauthorized signature or alteration by the same wrongdoer on any other item paid in good faith by the bank after the first item and statement was available to the customer for a reasonable period not exceeding fourteen calendar days and before the bank receives notification from the customer of any such unauthorized signature or alteration.

(3) The preclusion under subsection (2) does not apply if the customer establishes lack of ordinary care on the part of the bank in paying the item(s).

(4) Without regard to care or lack of care of either the customer or the bank a customer who does not within one year from the time the statement and items are made available to the customer (subsection (1)) discover and report his unauthorized signature or any alteration on the face or back of the item or does not within three years from that time discover and report any unauthorized indorsement is precluded from

asserting against the bank such unauthorized signature or indorsement or such alteration.

(5) If under this section a payor bank has a valid defense against a claim of a customer upon or resulting from payment of an item and waives or fails upon request to assert the defense the bank may not assert against any collecting bank or other prior party presenting or transferring the item a claim based upon the unauthorized signature or alteration giving rise to the customer's claim.

§ 4—407. **Payor Bank's Right to Subrogation on Improper Payment.**

If a payor bank has paid an item over the stop payment order of the drawer or maker or otherwise under circumstances giving a basis for objection by the drawer or maker, to prevent unjust enrichment and only to the extent necessary to prevent loss to the bank by reason of its payment of the item, the payor bank shall be subrogated to the rights

(a) of any holder in due course on the item against the drawer or maker; and

(b) of the payee or any other holder of the item against the drawer or maker either on the item or under the transaction out of which the item arose; and

(c) of the drawer or maker against the payee or any other holder of the item with respect to the transaction out of which the item arose.

Part 5 Collection of Documentary Drafts

§ 4—501. **Handling of Documentary Drafts; Duty to Send for Presentment and to Notify Customer of Dishonor.**

A bank which takes a documentary draft for collection must present or send the draft and accompanying documents for presentment and upon learning that the draft has not been paid or accepted in due course must seasonably notify its customer of such fact even though it may have discounted or bought the draft or extended credit available for withdrawal as of right.

§ 4—502. **Presentment of "On Arrival" Drafts.**

When a draft or the relevant instructions require presentment "on arrival", "when goods arrive" or the like, the collecting bank need not present until in its judgment a reasonable time for arrival of the goods has expired. Refusal to pay or accept because the goods have not arrived is not dishonor; the bank must notify its transferor of such refusal but need not present the draft again until it is instructed to do so or learns of the arrival of the goods.

§ 4—503. Responsibility of Presenting Bank for Documents and Goods; Report of Reasons for Dishonor; Referee in Case of Need.

Unless otherwise instructed and except as provided in Article 5 a bank presenting a documentary draft

(a) must deliver the documents to the drawee on acceptance of the draft if it is payable more than three days after presentment; otherwise, only on payment; and

(b) upon dishonor, either in the case of presentment for acceptance or presentment for payment, may seek and follow instructions from any referee in case of need designated in the draft or if the presenting bank does not choose to utilize his services it must use diligence and good faith to ascertain the reason for dishonor, must notify its transferor of the dishonor and of the results of its effort to ascertain the reasons therefor and must request instructions.

But the presenting bank is under no obligation with respect to goods represented by the documents except to follow any reasonable instructions seasonably received; it has a right to reimbursement for any expense incurred in following instructions and to prepayment of or indemnity for such expenses.

§ 4—504. Privilege of Presenting Bank to Deal With Goods; Security Interest for Expenses.

(1) A presenting bank which, following the dishonor of a documentary draft, has seasonably requested instructions but does not receive them within a reasonable time may store, sell, or otherwise deal with the goods in any reasonable manner.

(2) For its reasonable expenses incurred by action under subsection (1) the presenting bank has a lien upon the goods or their proceeds, which may be foreclosed in the same manner as an unpaid seller's lien.

Article 5
LETTERS OF CREDIT

§ 5—101. Short Title.

This Article shall be known and may be cited as Uniform Commercial Code—Letters of Credit.

§ 5—102. Scope.

(1) This Article applies

(a) to a credit issued by a bank if the credit requires a documentary draft or a documentary demand for payment; and

(b) to a credit issued by a person other than a bank if the credit requires that the draft or demand for payment be accompanied by a document of title; and

(c) to a credit issued by a bank or other person if the credit is not within subparagraphs (a) or (b) but conspicuously states that it is a letter of credit or is conspicuously so entitled.

(2) Unless the engagement meets the requirements of subsection (1), this Article does not apply to engagements to make advances or to honor drafts or demands for payment, to authorities to pay or purchase, to guarantees or to general agreements.

(3) This Article deals with some but not all of the rules and concepts of letters of credit as such rules or concepts have developed prior to this act or may hereafter develop. The fact that this Article states a rule does not by itself require, imply or negate application of the same or a converse rule to a situation not provided for or to a person not specified by this Article.

§ 5—103. Definitions.

(1) In this Article unless the context otherwise requires

(a) "Credit" or "letter of credit" means an engagement by a bank or other person made at the request of a customer and of a kind within the scope of this Article (Section 5—102) that the issuer will honor drafts or other demands for payment upon compliance with the conditions specified in the credit. A credit may be either revocable or irrevocable. The engagement may be either an agreement to honor or a statement that the bank or other person is authorized to honor.

(b) A "documentary draft" or a "documentary demand for payment" is one honor of which is conditioned upon the presentation of a document or documents. "Document" means any paper including document of title, security, invoice, certificate, notice of default and the like.

(c) An "issuer" is a bank or other person issuing a credit.

(d) A "beneficiary" of a credit is a person who is entitled under its terms to draw or demand payment.

(e) An "advising bank" is a bank which gives notification of the issuance of a credit by another bank.

(f) A "confirming bank" is a bank which engages either that it will itself honor a credit already issued by another bank or that such a credit will be honored by the issuer or a third bank.

(g) A "customer" is a buyer or other person who causes an issuer to issue a credit. The term also includes a bank which procures issuance or confirmation on behalf of that bank's customer.

(2) Other definitions applying to this Article and the sections in which they appear are:
"Notation of Credit". Section 5—108.
"Presenter". Section 5—112(3).

(3) Definitions in other Articles applying to this Article and the sections in which they appear are:
"Accept" or "Acceptance". Section 3—410.
"Contract for sale". Section 2—106.
"Draft". Section 3—104.
"Holder in due course". Section 3—302.
"Midnight deadline". Section 4—104.
"Security". Section 8—102.

(4) In addition, Article 1 contains general definitions and principles of construction and interpretation applicable throughout this Article.

§ 5—104. **Formal Requirements; Signing.**

(1) Except as otherwise required in subsection (1) (c)

of Section 5—102 on scope, no particular form of phrasing is required for a credit. A credit must be in writing and signed by the issuer and a confirmation must be in writing and signed by the confirming bank. A modification of the terms of a credit or confirmation must be signed by the issuer or confirming bank.

(2) A telegram may be a sufficient signed writing if it identifies its sender by an authorized authentication. The authentication may be in code and the authorized naming of the issuer in an advice of credit is a sufficient signing.

§ 5—105. **Consideration.**

No consideration is necessary to establish a credit or to enlarge or otherwise modify its terms.

§ 5—106. **Time and Effect of Establishment of Credit.**

(1) Unless otherwise agreed a credit is established

(a) as regards the customer as soon as a letter of credit is sent to him or the letter of credit or an authorized written advice of its issuance is sent to the beneficiary; and

(b) as regards the beneficiary when he receives a letter of credit or an authorized written advice of its issuance.

(2) Unless otherwise agreed once an irrevocable credit is established as regards the customer it can be modified or revoked only with the consent of the customer and once it is established as regards the beneficiary it can be modified or revoked only with his consent.

(3) Unless otherwise agreed after a revocable credit is established it may be modified or revoked by the issuer without notice to or consent from the customer or beneficiary.

(4) Notwithstanding any modification or revocation of a revocable credit any person authorized to honor or negotiate under the terms of the original credit is entitled to reimbursement for or honor of any draft or demand for payment duty honored or negotiated

before receipt of notice of the modification or revocation and the issuer in turn is entitled to reimbursement from its customer.

§ 5—107. **Advice of Credit; Confirmation; Error in Statement of Terms.**

(1) Unless otherwise specified an advising bank by advising a credit issued by another bank does not assume any obligation to honor drafts drawn or demands for payment made under the credit but it does assume obligation for the accuracy of its own statement.

(2) A confirming bank by confirming a credit becomes directly obligated on the credit to the extent of its confirmation as though it were its issuer and acquires the rights of an issuer.

(3) Even though an advising bank incorrectly advises the terms of a credit it has been authorized to advise the credit is established as against the issuer to the extent of its original terms.

(4) Unless otherwise specified the customer bears as against the issuer all risks of transmission and reasonable translation or interpretation of any message relating to a credit.

§ 5—108. **"Notation Credit"; Exhaustion of Credit.**

(1) A credit which specifies that any person purchasing or paying drafts drawn or demands for payment made under it must note the amount of the draft or demand on the letter or advice of credit is a "notation credit".

(2) Under a notation credit

(a) a person paying the beneficiary or purchasing a draft or demand for payment from him acquires a right to honor only if the appropriate notation is made and by transferring or forwarding for honor the documents under the credit such a person warrants to the issuer that the notation has been made; and

(b) unless the credit or a signed statement that an appropriate notation has been made accompanies the draft or demand for payment the issuer may delay honor until evidence of notation has been procured which is satisfactory to it but its obligation and that of its customer continue for a reasonable time not exceeding thirty days to obtain such evidence.

(3) If the credit is not a notation credit

(a) the issuer may honor complying drafts or demands for payment presented to it in the order in which they are presented and is discharged pro tanto by honor of any such draft or demand;

(b) as between competing good faith purchasers of complying drafts or demands the person first purchasing has priority over a subsequent purchaser even though the later purchased draft or demand has been first honored.

§ 5—109. **Issuer's Obligation to Its Customer.**

(1) An issuer's obligation to its customer includes good faith and observance of any general banking usage but unless otherwise agreed does not include liability or responsibility

(a) for performance of the underlying contract for sale or other transaction between the customer and the beneficiary; or

(b) for any act or omission of any person other than itself or its own branch or for loss or destruction of a draft, demand or document in transit or in the possession of others; or

(c) based on knowledge or lack of knowledge of any usage of any particular trade.

(2) An issuer must examine documents with care so as to ascertain that on their face they appear to comply with the terms of the credit but unless otherwise agreed assumes no liability or responsibility for the genuineness, falsification or effect of any document which appears on such examination to be regular on its face.

(3) A non-bank issuer is not bound by any banking usage of which it has no knowledge.

§ 5—110. **Availability of Credit in Portions; Presenter's Reservation of Lien or Claim.**

(1) Unless otherwise specified a credit may be used

in portions in the discretion of the beneficiary.

(2) Unless otherwise specified a person by presenting a documentary draft or demand for payment under a credit relinquishes upon its honor all claims to the documents and a person by transferring such draft or demand or causing such presentment authorizes such relinquishment. An explicit reservation of claim makes the draft or demand non-complying.

§ 5—111. **Warranties on Transfer and Presentment.**

(1) Unless otherwise agreed the beneficiary by transferring or presenting a documentary draft or demand for payment warrants to all interested parties that the necessary conditions of the credit have been complied with. This is in addition to any warranties arising under Articles 3, 4, 7 and 8.

(2) Unless otherwise agreed a negotiating, advising, confirming, collecting or issuing bank presenting or transferring a draft or demand for payment under a credit warrants only the matters warranted by a collecting bank under Article 4 and any such bank transferring a document warrants only the matters warranted by an intermediary under Articles 7 and 8.

§ 5—112. **Time Allowed for Honor or Rejection; Withholding Honor or Rejection by Consent; "Presenter".**

(1) A bank to which a documentary draft or demand for payment is presented under a credit may without dishonor of the draft, demand or credit

(a) defer honor until the close of the third banking day following receipt of the documents; and

(b) further defer honor if the presenter has expressly or impliedly consented thereto.

Failure to honor within the time here specified constitutes dishonor of the draft or demand and of the credit [except as otherwise provided in subsection (4) of Section 5—114 on conditional payment].

Note: *The bracketed language in the last sentence of subsection (1) should be included only if the optional provisions of Section 5—114(4) and (5) are included.*

(2) Upon dishonor the bank may unless otherwise instructed fulfill its duty to return the draft or demand and the documents by holding them at the disposal of the presenter and sending him an advice to that effect.

(3) "Presenter" means any person presenting a draft or demand for payment for honor under a credit even though that person is a confirming bank or other correspondent which is acting under an issuer's authorization.

§ 5—113. **Indemnities.**

(1) A bank seeking to obtain (whether for itself or another) honor, negotiation or reimbursement under a credit may give an indemnity to induce such honor, negotiation or reimbursement.

(2) An indemnity agreement inducing honor, negotiation or reimbursement

(a) unless otherwise explicitly agreed applies to defects in the documents but not in the goods; and

(b) unless a longer time is explicitly agreed expires at the end of ten business days following receipt of the documents by, the ultimate customer unless notice of objection is sent before such expiration date. The ultimate customer may send notice of objection to the person from whom he received the documents and any bank receiving such notice is under a duty to send notice to its transferor before its midnight deadline.

§ 5—114. **Issuer's Duty and Privilege to Honor; Right to Reimbursement.**

(1) An issuer must honor a draft or demand for payment which complies with the terms of the relevant credit regardless of whether the goods or documents conform to the underlying contract for sale or other contract between the customer and the beneficiary. The issuer is not excused from honor of such a draft or demand by reason of an additional general term that all documents must be satisfactory to the issuer, but an issuer may require that specified documents must be satisfactory to it.

(2) Unless otherwise agreed when documents appear

on their face to comply with the terms of a credit but a required document does not in fact conform to the warranties made on negotiation or transfer of a document of title (Section 7—507) or of a certificated security (Section 8—306) or is forged or fraudulent or there is fraud in the transaction:

(a) the issuer must honor the draft or demand for payment if honor is demanded by a negotiating bank or other holder of the draft or demand which has taken the draft or demand under the credit and under circumstances which would make it a holder in due course (Section 3—302) and in an appropriate case would make it a person to whom a document of title has been duly negotiated (Section 7—502) or a bona fide purchaser of a certificated security (Section 8—302); and

(b) in all other cases as against its customer, an issuer acting in good faith may honor the draft or demand for payment despite notification from the customer of fraud, forgery or other defect not apparent on the face of the documents but a court of appropriate jurisdiction may enjoin such honor.

(3) Unless otherwise agreed an issuer which has duly honored a draft or demand for payment is entitled to immediate reimbursement of any payment made under the credit and to be put in effectively available funds not later than the day before maturity of any acceptance made under the credit.

[(4) When a credit provides for payment by the issuer on receipt of notice that the required documents are in the possession of a correspondent or other agent of the issuer

(a) any payment made on receipt of such notice is conditional; and

(b) the issuer may reject documents which do not comply with the credit if it does so within three banking days following its receipt of the documents; and

(c) in the event of such rejection, the issuer is entitled by charge back or otherwise to return of the payment made.]

[(5) In the case covered by subsection (4) failure to reject documents within the time specified in subparagraph (b) constitutes acceptance of the documents and makes the payment final in favor of the beneficiary.]

Amended in 1977.

Note: *Subsections (4) and (5) are bracketed as optional. If they are included the bracketed language in the last sentence of Section 5—112(1) should also be included.*

§ 5—115. **Remedy for Improper Dishonor or Anticipatory Repudiation.**

(1) When an issuer wrongfully dishonors a draft or demand for payment presented under a credit the person entitled to honor has with respect to any documents the rights of a person in the position of a seller (Section 2—707) and may recover from the issuer the face amount of the draft or demand together with incidental damages under Section 2—710 on seller's incidental damages and interest but less any amount realized by resale or other use or disposition of the subject matter of the transaction. In the event no resale or other utilization is made the documents, goods or other subject matter involved in the transaction must be turned over to the issuer on payment of judgment.

(2) When an issuer wrongfully cancels or otherwise repudiates a credit before presentment of a draft or demand for payment drawn under it the beneficiary has the rights of a seller after anticipatory repudiation by the buyer under Section 2—610 if he learns of the repudiation in time reasonably to avoid procurement of the required documents. Otherwise the beneficiary has an immediate right of action for wrongful dishonor.

§ 5—116. **Transfer and Assignment.**

(1) The right to draw under a credit can be transferred or assigned only when the credit is expressly designated as transferable or assignable.

(2) Even though the credit specifically states that it is nontransferable or nonassignable the beneficiary may before performance of the conditions of the credit assign his right to proceeds. Such an assignment is an assignment of an account under Article 9 on Secured Transactions and is governed by that Article except that

(a) the assignment is ineffective until the letter of credit or advice of credit is delivered to the assignee which delivery constitutes perfection of the security interest under Article 9; and

(b) the issuer may honor drafts or demands for

payment drawn under the credit until it receives a notification of the assignment signed by the beneficiary which reasonably identifies the credit involved in the assignment and contains a request to pay the assignee; and

(c) after what reasonably appears to be such a notification has been received the issuer may without dishonor refuse to accept or pay even to a person otherwise entitled to honor until the letter of credit or advice of credit is exhibited to the issuer.

(3) Except where the beneficiary has effectively assigned his right to draw or his right to proceeds, nothing in this section limits his right to transfer or negotiate drafts or demands drawn under the credit.

§ 5—117. **Insolvency of Bank Holding Funds for Documentary Credit.**

(1) Where an issuer or an advising or confirming bank or a bank which has for a customer procured issuance of a credit by another bank becomes insolvent before final payment under the credit and the credit is one to which this Article is made applicable by paragraphs (a) or (b) of Section 5—102(1) on scope, the receipt or allocation of funds or collateral to secure or meet obligations under the credit shall have the following results:

(a) to the extent of any funds or collateral turned over after or before the insolvency as indemnity against or specifically for the purpose of payment of drafts or demands for payment drawn under the designated credit, the drafts or demands are entitled to payment in preference over depositors or other general creditors of the issuer or bank; and

(b) on expiration of the credit or surrender of the beneficiary's rights under it unused any person who has given such funds or collateral is similarly entitled to return thereof; and

(c) a charge to a general or current account with a bank if specifically consented to for the purpose of indemnity against or payment of drafts or demands for payment drawn under the designated credit falls under the same rules as if the funds had been drawn out in cash and then turned over with specific instructions.

(2) After honor or reimbursement under this section the customer or other person for whose account the insolvent bank has acted is entitled to receive the documents involved.

Article 6
BULK TRANSFERS

§ 6—101. **Short Title.**

This Article shall be known and may be cited as Uniform Commercial Code—Bulk Transfers.

§ 6—102. **"Bulk Transfer"; Transfers of Equipment; Enterprises Subject to This Article; Bulk Transfers Subject to This Article.**

(1) A "bulk transfer" is any transfer in bulk and not in the ordinary course of the transferor's business of a major part of the materials, supplies, merchandise or other inventory (Section 9—109) of an enterprise subject to this Article.

(2) A transfer of a substantial part of the equipment (Section 9—109) of such an enterprise is a bulk transfer if it is made in connection with a bulk transfer of inventory, but not otherwise.

(3) The enterprises subject to this Article are all those whose principal business is the sale of merchandise from stock, including those who manufacture what they sell.

(4) Except as limited by the following section all bulk transfers of goods located within this state are subject to this Article.

§ 6—103. **Transfers Excepted From This Article.**

The following transfers are not subject to this Article:

(1) Those made to give security for the performance of an obligation;

(2) General assignments for the benefit of all the creditors of the transferor, and subsequent transfers by the assignee thereunder;

(3) Transfers in settlement or realization of a lien or other security interest;

(4) Sales by executors, administrators, receivers,

trustees in bankruptcy, or any public officer under judicial process;

(5) Sales made in the course of judicial or administrative proceedings for the dissolution or reorganization of a corporation and of which notice is sent to the creditors of the corporation pursuant to order of the court or administrative agency;

(6) Transfers to a person maintaining a known place of business in this State who becomes bound to pay the debts of the transferor in full and gives public notice of that fact, and who is solvent after becoming so bound;

(7) A transfer to a new business enterprise organized to take over and continue the business, if public notice of the transaction is given and the new enterprise assumes the debts of the transferor and he receives nothing from the transaction except an interest in the new enterprise junior to the claims of creditors;

(8) Transfers of property which is exempt from execution.

Public notice under subsection (6) or subsection (7) may be given by publishing once a week for two consecutive weeks in a newspaper of general circulation where the transferor had its principal place of business in this state an advertisement including the names and addresses of the transferor and transferee and the effective date of the transfer.

§ 6—104. **Schedule of Property, List of Creditors.**

(1) Except as provided with respect to auction sales (Section 6—108), a bulk transfer subject to this Article is ineffective against any creditor of the transferor unless:

    (a) The transferee requires the transferor to furnish a list of his existing creditors prepared as stated in this section; and

    (b) The parties prepare a schedule of the property transferred sufficient to identify it; and

    (c) The transferee preserves the list and schedule for six months next following the transfer and permits inspection of either or both and copying therefrom at all reasonable hours by any creditor of the transferor, or files the list and schedule in *(a public office to be here identified)*.

(2) The list of creditors must be signed and sworn to or affirmed by the transferor or his agent. It must contain the names and business addresses of all creditors of the transferor, with the amounts when known, and also the names of all persons who are known to the transferor to assert claims against him even though such claims are disputed. If the transferor is the obligor of an outstanding issue of bonds, debentures or the like as to which there is an indenture trustee, the list of creditors need include only the name and address of the indenture trustee and the aggregate outstanding principal amount of the issue.

(3) Responsibility for the completeness and accuracy of the list of creditors rests on the transferor, and the transfer is not rendered ineffective by errors or omissions therein unless the transferee is shown to have had knowledge.

§ 6—105. **Notice to Creditors.**

In addition to the requirements of the preceding section, any bulk transfer subject to this Article except one made by auction sale (Section 6—108) is ineffective against any creditor of the transferor unless at least ten days before he takes possession of the goods or pays for them, whichever happens first, the transferee gives notice of the transfer in the manner and to the persons hereafter provided (Section 6—107).

[§ 6—106. **Application of the Proceeds.**

In addition to the requirements of the two preceding sections:

(1) Upon every bulk transfer subject to this Article for which new consideration becomes payable except those made by sale at auction it is the duty of the transferee to assure that such consideration is applied so far as necessary to pay those debts of the transferor which are either shown on the list furnished by the transferor (Section 6—104) or filed in writing in the place stated in the notice (Section 6—107) within thirty days after the mailing of such notice. This duty of the transferee runs to all the holders of such debts, and may be enforced by any of them for the benefit of all.

(2) If any of said debts are in dispute the necessary sum may be withheld from distribution until the dispute is settled or adjudicated.

(3) If the consideration payable is not enough to pay all of the said debts in full distribution shall be made pro rata.]

Note: *This section is bracketed to indicate division of opinion as to whether or not it is a wise provision, and to suggest that this is a point on which State enactments may differ without serious damage to the principle of uniformity. In any State where this section is omitted, the following parts of sections, also bracketed in the text, should also be omitted, namely:*
Section 6—107(2)(c).
    6—108(3)(c).
    6—109(2).
In any State where this section is enacted, these other provisions should be also.

Optional Subsection (4)

[(4) The transferee may within ten days after he takes possession of the goods pay the consideration into the (specify court) in the county where the transferor had its principal place of business in this state and thereafter may discharge his duty under this section by giving notice by registered or certified mail to all the persons to whom the duty runs that the consideration has been paid into that court and that they should file their claims there. On motion of any interested party, the court may order the distribution of the consideration to the persons entitled to it.]

Note: *Optional subsection (4) is recommended for those states which do not have a general statute providing for payment of money into court.*

§ 6—107. The Notice.

(1) The notice to creditors (Section 6—105) shall state:

(a) that a bulk transfer is about to be made; and

(b) the names and business addresses of the transferor and transferee, and all other business names and addresses used by the transferor within three years last past so far as known to the transferee; and

(c) whether or not all the debts of the transferor are to be paid in full as they fall due as a result of the transaction, and if so, the address to which creditors should send their bills.

(2) If the debts of the transferor are not to be paid in full as they fall due or if the transferee is in doubt on that point then the notice shall state further:

(a) the location and general description of the property to be transferred and the estimated total of the transferor's debts;

(b) the address where the schedule of property and list of creditors (Section 6—104) may be inspected;

(c) whether the transfer is to pay existing debts and if so the amount of such debts and to whom owing;

(d) whether the transfer is for new consideration and if so the amount of such consideration and the time and place of payment; [and]

[(e) if for new consideration the time and place where creditors of the transferor are to file their claims.]

(3) The notice in any case shall be delivered personally or sent by registered or certified mail to all the persons shown on the list of creditors furnished by the transferor (Section 6—104) and to all other persons who are known to the transferee to hold or assert claims against the transferor.

§ 6—108. Auction Sales; "Auctioneer".

(1) A bulk transfer is subject to this Article even though it is by sale at auction, but only in the manner and with the results stated in this section.

(2) The transferor shall furnish a list of his creditors and assist in the preparation of a schedule of the property to be sold, both prepared as before stated (Section 6—104).

(3) The person or persons other than the transferor who direct, control or are responsible for the auction are collectively called the "auctioneer". The auctioneer shall:

(a) receive and retain the list of creditors and prepare and retain the schedule of property for the period stated in this Article (Section 6—104);

(b) give notice of the auction personally or by registered or certified mail at least ten days before it occurs to all persons shown on the list of creditors and to all other persons who are known to him to hold or assert claims against the transferor; [and]

[(c) assure that the net proceeds of the auction are applied as provided in this Article (Section 6—106).]

(4) Failure of the auctioneer to perform any of these duties does not affect the validity of the sale or the title of the purchasers, but if the auctioneer knows that the auction constitutes a bulk transfer such failure renders the auctioneer liable to the creditors of the transferor as a class for the sums owing to them from the transferor up to but not exceeding the net proceeds of the auction. If the auctioneer consists of several persons their liability is joint and several.

§ 6—109. **What Creditors Protected; [Credit for Payment to Particular Creditors].**

(1) The creditors of the transferor mentioned in this Article are those holding claims based on transactions or events occurring before the bulk transfer, but creditors who become such after notice to creditors is given (Sections 6—105 and 6—107) are not entitled to notice.

[(2) Against the aggregate obligation imposed by the provisions of this Article concerning the application of the proceeds (Section 6—106 and subsection (3) (c) of 6—108) the transferee or auctioneer is entitled to credit for sums paid to particular creditors of the transferor, not exceeding the sums believed in good faith at the time of the payment to be properly payable to such creditors.]

§ 6—110. **Subsequent Transfers.**

When the title of a transferee to property is subject to a defect by reason of his non-compliance with the requirements of this Article, then:

(1) a purchaser of any of such property from such transferee who pays no value or who takes with notice of such non-compliance takes subject to such defect, but

(2) a purchaser for value in good faith and without such notice takes free of such defect.

§ 6—111. **Limitation of Actions and Levies.**

No action under this Article shall be brought nor levy made more than six months after the date on which the transferee took possession of the goods unless the transfer has been concealed. If the transfer has been concealed, actions may be brought or levies made within six months after its discovery.

Note to Article 6: *Section 6—106 is bracketed to indicate division of opinion as to whether or not it is a wise provision,*

and to suggest that this is a point on which State enactments may differ without serious damage to the principle of uniformity.
In any State where Section 6—106 is not enacted, the following parts of sections, also bracketed in the text, should also be omitted, namely:
Sec. 6—107(2)(e).
    6—108(3)(c).
    6—109(2).
In any State where Section 6—106 is enacted, these other provisions should be also.

Article 7
Warehouse Receipts, Bills of Lading and Other Documents of Title

Part 1 General

§ 7—101. **Short Title.**

This Article shall be known and may be cited as Uniform Commercial Code—Documents of Title.

§ 7—102. **Definitions and Index of Definitions.**

(1) In this Article, unless the context otherwise requires:

(a) "Bailee" means the person who by a warehouse receipt, bill of lading or other document of title acknowledges possession of goods and contracts to deliver them.

(b) "Consignee" means the person named in a bill to whom or to whose order the bill promises delivery.

(c) "Consignor" means the person named in a bill as the person from whom the goods have been received for shipment.

(d) "Delivery order" means a written order to deliver goods directed to a warehouseman, carrier or other person who in the ordinary course of business issues warehouse receipts or bills of lading.

(e) "Document" means document of title as defined in the general definitions in Article 1 (Section 1—201).

(f) "Goods" means all things which are treated as

movable for the purposes of a contract of storage or transportation.

(g) "Issuer" means a bailee who issues a document except that in relation to an unaccepted delivery order it means the person who orders the possessor of goods to deliver. Issuer includes any person for whom an agent or employee purports to act in issuing a document if the agent or employee has real or apparent authority to issue documents, notwithstanding that the issuer received no goods or that the goods were misdescribed or that in any other respect the agent or employee violated his instructions.

(h) "Warehouseman" is a person engaged in the business of storing goods for hire.

(2) Other definitions applying to this Article or to specified Parts thereof, and the sections in which they appear are:

"Duly negotiate". Section 7—501.

"Person entitled under the document". Section 7—403(4).

(3) Definitions in other Articles applying to this Article and the sections in which they appear are:

"Contract for sale". Section 2—106.

"Overseas". Section 2—323.

"Receipt" of goods. Section 2—103.

(4) In addition Article 1 contains general definitions and principles of construction and interpretation applicable throughout this Article.

§ 7—103. **Relation of Article to Treaty, Statute, Tariff, Classification or Regulation.**

To the extent that any treaty or statute of the United States, regulatory statute of this State or tariff, classification or regulation filed or issued pursuant thereto is applicable, the provisions of this Article are subject thereto.

§ 7—104. **Negotiable and Non-Negotiable Warehouse Receipt, Bill of Lading or Other Document of Title.**

(1) A warehouse receipt, bill of lading or other document of title is negotiable

(a) if by its terms the goods are to be delivered to bearer or to the order of a named person; or

(b) where recognized in overseas trade, if it runs to a named person or assigns.

(2) Any other document is non-negotiable. A bill of lading in which it is stated that the goods are consigned to a named person is not made negotiable by a provision that the goods are to be delivered only against a written order signed by the same or another named person.

§ 7—105. **Construction Against Negative Implication.**

The omission from either Part 2 or Part 3 of this Article of a provision corresponding to a provision made in the other Part does not imply that a corresponding rule of law is not applicable.

Part 2 Warehouse Receipts: Special Provisions

§ 7—201. **Who May Issue a Warehouse Receipt; Storage Under Government Bond.**

(1) A warehouse receipt may be issued by any warehouseman.

(2) Where goods including distilled spirits and agricultural commodities are stored under a statute requiring a bond against withdrawal or a license for the issuance of receipts in the nature of warehouse receipts, a receipt issued for the goods has like effect as a warehouse receipt even though issued by a person who is the owner of the goods and is not a warehouseman.

§ 7—202. **Form of Warehouse Receipt; Essential Terms; Optional Terms.**

(1) A warehouse receipt need not be in any particular form.

(2) Unless a warehouse receipt embodies within its written or printed terms each of the following, the warehouseman is liable for damages caused by the omission to a person injured thereby:

(a) the location of the warehouse where the goods are stored;

(b) the date of issue of the receipt;

(c) the consecutive number of the receipt;

(d) a statement whether the goods received will be delivered to the bearer, to a specified person, or to a specified person or his order;

(e) the rate of storage and handling charges, except that where goods are stored under a field warehousing arrangement a statement of that fact is sufficient on a non-negotiable receipt;

(f) a description of the goods or of the packages containing them;

(g) the signature of the warehouseman, which may be made by his authorized agent;

(h) if the receipt is issued for goods of which the warehouseman is owner, either solely or jointly or in common with others, the fact of such ownership; and

(i) a statement of the amount of advances made and of liabilities incurred for which the warehouseman claims a lien or security interest (Section 7—209). If the precise amount of such advances made or of such liabilities incurred is, at the time of the issue of the receipt, unknown to the warehouseman or to his agent who issues it, a statement of the fact that advances have been made or liabilities incurred and the purpose thereof is sufficient.

(3) A warehouseman may insert in his receipt any other terms which are not contrary to the provisions of this Act and do not impair his obligation of delivery (Section 7—403) or his duty of care (Section 7—204). Any contrary provisions shall be ineffective.

§ 7—203. **Liability for Non-Receipt or Misdescription.**

A party to or purchaser for value in good faith of a document of title other than a bill of lading relying in either case upon the description therein of the goods may recover from the issuer damages caused by the non-receipt or misdescription of the goods, except to the extent that the document conspicuously indicates that the issuer does not know whether any part or all of the goods in fact were received or conform to the description, as where the description is in terms of marks or labels or kind, quantity or condition, or the receipt or description is qualified by "contents, condition and quality unknown", "said to contain" or the like, if such indication be true, or the party or purchaser otherwise has notice.

§ 7—204. **Duty of Care; Contractual Limitation of Warehouseman's Liability.**

(1) A warehouseman is liable for damages for loss of or injury to the goods caused by his failure to exercise such care in regard to them as a reasonably careful man would exercise under like circumstances but unless otherwise agreed he is not liable for damages which could not have been avoided by the exercise of such care.

(2) Damages may be limited by a term in the warehouse receipt or storage agreement limiting the amount of liability in case of loss or damage, and setting forth a specific liability per article or item, or value per unit of weight, beyond which the warehouseman shall not be liable; provided, however, that such liability may on written request of the bailor at the time of signing such storage agreement or within a reasonable time after receipt of the warehouse receipt be increased on part or all of the goods thereunder, in which event increased rates may be charged based on such increased valuation, but that no such increase shall be permitted contrary to a lawful limitation of liability contained in the warehouseman's tariff, if any. No such limitation is effective with respect to the warehouseman's liability for conversion to his own use.

(3) Reasonable provisions as to the time and manner of presenting claims and instituting actions based on the bailment may be included in the warehouse receipt or tariff.

(4) This section does not impair or repeal . . .

Note: *Insert in subsection (4) a reference to any statute which imposes a higher responsibility upon the warehouseman or invalidates contractual limitations which would be permissible under this Article.*

§ 7—205. **Title Under Warehouse Receipt Defeated in Certain Cases.**

A buyer in the ordinary course of business of fungible goods sold and delivered by a warehouseman who is also in the business of buying and selling such goods takes free of any claim under a warehouse receipt even though it has been duly negotiated.

§ 7—206. **Termination of Storage at Warehouseman's Option.**

(1) A warehouseman may on notifying the person on whose account the goods are held and any other person known to claim an interest in the goods require payment of any charges and removal of the goods from the warehouse at the termination of the period of storage fixed by the document, or, if no

period is fixed, within a stated period not less than thirty days after the notification. If the goods are not removed before the date specified in the notification, the warehouseman may sell them in accordance with the provisions of the section on enforcement of a warehouseman's lien (Section 7—210).

(2) If a warehouseman in good faith believes that the goods are about to deteriorate or decline in value to less than the amount of his lien within the time prescribed in subsection (1) for notification, advertisement and sale, the warehouseman may specify in the notification any reasonable shorter time for removal of the goods and in case the goods are not removed, may sell them at public sale held not less than one week after a single advertisement or posting.

(3) If as a result of a quality or condition of the goods of which the warehouseman had no notice at the time of deposit the goods are a hazard to other property or to the warehouse or to persons, the warehouseman may sell the goods at public or private sale without advertisement on reasonable notification to all persons known to claim an interest in the goods. If the warehouseman after a reasonable effort is unable to sell the goods he may dispose of them in any lawful manner and shall incur no liability by reason of such disposition.

(4) The warehouseman must deliver the goods to any person entitled to them under this Article upon due demand made at any time prior to sale or other disposition under this section.

(5) The warehouseman may satisfy his lien from the proceeds of any sale or disposition under this section but must hold the balance for delivery on the demand of any person to whom he would have been bound to deliver the goods.

§ 7—207. **Goods Must Be Kept Separate; Fungible Goods.**

(1) Unless the warehouse receipt otherwise provides, a warehouseman must keep separate the goods covered by each receipt so as to permit at all times identification and delivery of those goods except that different lots of fungible goods may be commingled.

(2) Fungible goods so commingled are owned in common by the persons entitled thereto and the warehouseman is severally liable to each owner for

that owner's share. Where because of overissue a mass of fungible goods is insufficient to meet all the receipts which the warehouseman has issued against it, the persons entitled include all holders to whom overissued receipts have been duly negotiated.

§ 7—208. **Altered Warehouse Receipts.**

Where a blank in a negotiable warehouse receipt has been filled in without authority, a purchaser for value and without notice of the want of authority may treat the insertion as authorized. Any other unauthorized alteration leaves any receipt enforceable against the issuer according to its original tenor.

§ 7—209. **Lien of Warehouseman.**

(1) A warehouseman has a lien against the bailor on the goods covered by a warehouse receipt or on the proceeds thereof in his possession for charges for storage or transportation (including demurrage and terminal charges), insurance, labor, or charges present or future in relation to the goods, and for expenses necessary for preservation of the goods or reasonably incurred in their sale pursuant to law. If the person on whose account the goods are held is liable for like charges or expenses in relation to other goods whenever deposited and it is stated in the receipt that a lien is claimed for charges and expenses in relation to other goods, the warehouseman also has a lien against him for such charges and expenses whether or not the other goods have been delivered by the warehouseman. But against a person to whom a negotiable warehouse receipt is duly negotiated a warehouseman's lien is limited to charges in an amount or at a rate specified on the receipt or if no charges are so specified then to a reasonable charge for storage of the goods covered by the receipt subsequent to the date of the receipt.

(2) The warehouseman may also reserve a security interest against the bailor for a maximum amount specified on the receipt for charges other than those specified in subsection (1), such as for money advanced and interest. Such a security interest is governed by the Article on Secured Transactions (Article 9).

(3) (a) A warehouseman's lien for charges and expenses under subsection (1) or a security interest under subsection (2) is also effective against any person who so entrusted the bailor with possession of

the goods that a pledge of them by him to a good faith purchaser for value would have been valid but is not effective against a person as to whom the document confers no right in the goods covered by it under Section 7—503.

(b) A warehouseman's lien on household goods for charges and expenses in relation to the goods under subsection (1) is also effective against all persons if the depositor was the legal possessor of the goods at the time of deposit. "Household goods" means furniture, furnishings and personal effects used by the depositor in a dwelling.

(4) A warehouseman loses his lien on any goods which he voluntarily delivers or which he unjustifiably refuses to deliver.

§ 7—210. **Enforcement of Warehouseman's Lien.**

(1) Except as provided in subsection (2), a warehouseman's lien may be enforced by public or private sale of the goods in bloc or in parcels, at any time or place and on any terms which are commercially reasonable, after notifying all persons known to claim an interest in the goods. Such notification must include a statement of the amount due, the nature of the proposed sale and the time and place of any public sale. The fact that a better price could have been obtained by a sale at a different time or in a different method from that selected by the warehouseman is not of itself sufficient to establish that the sale was not made in a commercially reasonable manner. If the warehouseman either sells the goods in the usual manner in any recognized market therefor, or if he sells at the price current in such market at the time of his sale, or if he has otherwise sold in conformity with commercially reasonable practices among dealers in the type of goods sold, he has sold in a commercially reasonable manner. A sale of more goods than apparently necessary to be offered to insure satisfaction of the obligation is not commercially reasonable except in cases covered by the preceding sentence.

(2) A warehouseman's lien on goods other than goods stored by a merchant in the course of his business may be enforced only as follows:

(a) All persons known to claim an interest in the goods must be notified.

(b) The notification must be delivered in person or sent by registered or certified letter to the last known address of any person to be notified.

(c) The notification must include an itemized statement of the claim, a description of the goods subject to the lien, a demand for payment within a specified time not less than ten days after receipt of the notification, and a conspicuous statement that unless the claim is paid within the time the goods will be advertised for sale and sold by auction at a specified time and place.

(d) The sale must conform to the terms of the notification.

(e) The sale must be held at the nearest suitable place to that where the goods are held or stored.

(f) After the expiration of the time given in the notification, an advertisement of the sale must be published once a week for two weeks consecutively in a newspaper of general circulation where the sale is to be held. The advertisement must include a description of the goods, the name of the person on whose account they are being held, and the time and place of the sale. The sale must take place at least fifteen days after the first publication. If there is no newspaper of general circulation where the sale is to be held, the advertisement must be posted at least ten days before the sale in not less than six conspicuous places in the neighborhood of the proposed sale.

(3) Before any sale pursuant to this section any person claiming a right in the goods may pay the amount necessary to satisfy the lien and the reasonable expenses incurred under this section. In that event the goods must not be sold, but must be retained by the warehouseman subject to the terms of the receipt and this Article.

(4) The warehouseman may buy at any public sale pursuant to this section.

(5) A purchaser in good faith of goods sold to enforce a warehouseman's lien takes the goods free of any rights of persons against whom the lien was valid, despite noncompliance by the warehouseman with the requirements of this section.

(6) The warehouseman may satisfy his lien from the proceeds of any sale pursuant to this section but must hold the balance, if any, for delivery on demand to

any person to whom he would have been bound to deliver the goods.

(7) The rights provided by this section shall be in addition to all other rights allowed by law to a creditor against his debtor.

(8) Where a lien is on goods stored by a merchant in the course of his business the lien may be enforced in accordance with either subsection (1) or (2).

(9) The warehouseman is liable for damages caused by failure to comply with the requirements for sale under this section and in case of willful violation is liable for conversion.

Part 3 Bills of Lading: Special Provisions

§ 7—301. Liability for Non-Receipt or Misdescription; "Said to Contain"; "Shipper's Load and Count"; Improper Handling.

(1) A consignee of a non-negotiable bill who has given value in good faith or a holder to whom a negotiable bill has been duly negotiated relying in either case upon the description therein of the goods, or upon the date therein shown, may recover from the issuer damages caused by the misdating of the bill or the non-receipt or misdescription of the goods, except to the extent that the document indicates that the issuer does not know whether any part of all of the goods in fact were received or conform to the description, as where the description is in terms of marks or labels or kind, quantity, or condition or the receipt or description is qualified by "contents or condition of contents of packages unknown", "said to contain", "shipper's weight, load and count" or the like, if such indication be true.

(2) When goods are loaded by an issuer who is a common carrier, the issuer must count the packages of goods if package freight and ascertain the kind and quantity if bulk freight. In such cases "shipper's weight, load and count" or other words indicating that the description was made by the shipper are ineffective except as to freight concealed by packages.

(3) When bulk freight is loaded by a shipper who makes available to the issuer adequate facilities for weighing such freight, an issuer who is a common carrier must ascertain the kind and quantity within a reasonable time after receiving the written request of the shipper to do so. In such cases "shipper's weight" or other words of like purport are ineffective.

(4) The issuer may by inserting in the bill the words "shipper's weight, load and count" or other words of like purport indicate that the goods were loaded by the shipper; and if such statement be true the issuer shall not be liable for damages caused by the improper loading. But their omission does not imply liability for such damages.

(5) The shipper shall be deemed to have guaranteed to the issuer the accuracy at the time of shipment of the description, marks, labels, number, kind, quantity, condition and weight, as furnished by him; and the shipper shall indemnify the issuer against damage caused by inaccuracies in such particulars. The right of the issuer to such indemnity shall in no way limit his responsibility and liability under the contract of carriage to any person other than the shipper.

§ 7—302. Through Bills of Lading and Similar Documents.

(1) The issuer of a through bill of lading or other document embodying an undertaking to be performed in part by persons acting as its agents or by connecting carriers is liable to anyone entitled to recover on the document for any breach by such other persons or by a connecting carrier of its obligation under the document but to the extent that the bill covers an undertaking to be performed overseas or in territory not contiguous to the continental United States or an undertaking including matters other than transportation this liability may be varied by agreement of the parties.

(2) Where goods covered by a through bill of lading or other document embodying an undertaking to be performed in part by persons other than the issuer are received by any such person, he is subject with respect to his own performance while the goods are in his possession to the obligation of the issuer. His obligation is discharged by delivery of the goods to another such person pursuant to the document, and does not include liability for breach by any other such persons or by the issuer.

(3) The issuer of such through bill of lading or other document shall be entitled to recover from the

connecting carrier or such other person in possession of the goods when the breach of the obligation under the document occurred, the amount it may be required to pay to anyone entitled to recover on the document therefor, as may be evidenced by any receipt, judgment, or transcript thereof, and the amount of any expense reasonably incurred by it in defending any action brought by anyone entitled to recover on the document therefor.

§ 7—303. **Diversion; Reconsignment; Change of Instructions.**

(1) Unless the bill of lading otherwise provides, the carrier may deliver the goods to a person or destination other than that stated in the bill or may otherwise dispose of the goods on instructions from

   (a) the holder of a negotiable bill; or

   (b) the consignor on a non-negotiable bill notwithstanding contrary instructions from the consignee; or

   (c) the consignee on a non-negotiable bill in the absence of contrary instructions from the consignor, if the goods have arrived at the billed destination or if the consignee is in possession of the bill; or

   (d) the consignee on a non-negotiable bill if he is entitled as against the consignor to dispose of them.

(2) Unless such instructions are noted on a negotiable bill of lading, a person to whom the bill is duly negotiated can hold the bailee according to the original terms.

§ 7—304. **Bills of Lading in a Set.**

(1) Except where customary in overseas transportation, a bill of lading must not be issued in a set of parts. The issuer is liable for damages caused by violation of this subsection.

(2) Where a bill of lading is lawfully drawn in a set of parts, each of which is numbered and expressed to be valid only if the goods have not been delivered against any other part, the whole of the parts constitute one bill.

(3) Where a bill of lading is lawfully issued in a set of parts and different parts are negotiated to different persons, the title of the holder to whom the first due negotiation is made prevails as to both the document and the goods even though any later holder may have received the goods from the carrier in good faith and discharged the carrier's obligation by surrender of his part.

(4) Any person who negotiates or transfers a single part of a bill of lading drawn in a set is liable to holders of that part as if it were the whole set.

(5) The bailee is obliged to deliver in accordance with Part 4 of this Article against the first presented part of a bill of lading lawfully drawn in a set. Such delivery discharges the bailee's obligation on the whole bill.

§ 7—305. **Destination Bills.**

(1) Instead of issuing a bill of lading to the consignor at the place of shipment a carrier may at the request of the consignor procure the bill to be issued at destination or at any other place designated in the request.

(2) Upon request of anyone entitled as against the carrier to control the goods while in transit and on surrender of any outstanding bill of lading or other receipt covering such goods, the issuer may procure a substitute bill to be issued at any place designated in the request.

§ 7—306. **Altered Bills of Lading.**

An unauthorized alteration or filling in of a blank in a bill of lading leaves the bill enforceable according to its original tenor.

§ 7—307. **Lien of Carrier.**

(1) A carrier has a lien on the goods covered by a bill of lading for charges subsequent to the date of its receipt of the goods for storage or transportation (including demurrage and terminal charges) and for expenses necessary for preservation of the goods incident to their transportation or reasonably incurred in their sale pursuant to law. But against a purchaser for value of a negotiable bill of lading a carrier's lien is limited to charges stated in the bill or the applicable tariffs, or if no charges are stated then to a reasonable charge.

(2) A lien for charges and expenses under subsection (1) on goods which the carrier was required by law to receive for transportation is effective against the consignor or any person entitled to the goods unless the carrier had notice that the consignor lacked

authority to subject the goods to such charges and expenses. Any other lien under subsection (1) is effective against the consignor and any person who permitted the bailor to have control or possession of the goods unless the carrier had notice that the bailor lacked such authority.

(3) A carrier loses his lien on any goods which he voluntarily delivers or which he unjustifiably refuses to deliver.

§ 7—308. **Enforcement of Carrier's Lien.**

(1) A carrier's lien may be enforced by public or private sale of the goods, in bloc or in parcels, at any time or place and on any terms which are commercially reasonable, after notifying all persons known to claim an interest in the goods. Such notification must include a statement of the amount due, the nature of the proposed sale and the time and place of any public sale. The fact that a better price could have been obtained by a sale at a different time or in a different method from that selected by the carrier is not of itself sufficient to establish that the sale was not made in a commercially reasonable manner. If the carrier either sells the goods in the usual manner in any recognized market therefor or if he sells at the price current in such market at the time of his sale or if he has otherwise sold in conformity with commercially reasonable practices among dealers in the type of goods sold he has sold in a commercially reasonable manner. A sale of more goods than apparently necessary to be offered to ensure satisfaction of the obligation is not commercially reasonable except in cases covered by the preceding sentence.

(2) Before any sale pursuant to this section any person claiming a right in the goods may pay the amount necessary to satisfy the lien and the reasonable expenses incurred under this section. In that event the goods must not be sold, but must be retained by the carrier subject to the terms of the bill and this Article.

(3) The carrier may buy at any public sale pursuant to this section.

(4) A purchaser in good faith of goods sold to enforce a carrier's lien takes the goods free of any rights of persons against whom the lien was valid, despite noncompliance by the carrier with the requirements of this section.

(5) The carrier may satisfy his lien from the proceeds of any sale pursuant to this section but must hold the balance, if any, for delivery on demand to any person to whom he would have been bound to deliver the goods.

(6) The rights provided by this section shall be in addition to all other rights allowed by law to a creditor against his debtor.

(7) A carrier's lien may be enforced in accordance with either subsection (1) or the procedure set forth in subsection (2) of Section 7—210.

(8) The carrier is liable for damages caused by failure to comply with the requirements for sale under this section and in case of willful violation is liable for conversion.

§ 7—309. **Duty of Care; Contractual Limitation of Carrier's Liability.**

(1) A carrier who issues a bill of lading whether negotiable or non-negotiable must exercise the degree of care in relation to the goods which a reasonably careful man would exercise under like circumstances. This subsection does not repeal or change any law or rule of law which imposes liability upon a common carrier for damages not caused by its negligence.

(2) Damages may be limited by a provision that the carrier's liability shall not exceed a value stated in the document if the carrier's rates are dependent upon value and the consignor by the carrier's tariff is afforded an opportunity to declare a higher value or a value as lawfully provided in the tariff, or where no tariff is filed he is otherwise advised of such opportunity; but no such limitation is effective with respect to the carrier's liability for conversion to its own use.

(3) Reasonable provisions as to the time and manner of presenting claims and instituting actions based on the shipment may be included in a bill of lading or tariff.

Part 4 **Warehouse Receipts and Bills of Lading: General Obligations**

§ 7—401. **Irregularities in Issue of Receipt or Bill or Conduct of Issuer.**

The obligations imposed by this Article on an issuer

apply to a document of title regardless of the fact that

(a) the document may not comply with the requirements of this Article or of any other law or regulation regarding its issue, form or content; or

(b) the issuer may have violated laws regulating the conduct of his business; or

(c) the goods covered by the document were owned by the bailee at the time the document was issued; or

(d) the person issuing the document does not come within the definition of warehouseman if it purports to be a warehouse receipt.

§ 7—402. **Duplicate Receipt or Bill; Overissue.**

Neither a duplicate nor any other document of title purporting to cover goods already represented by an outstanding document of the same issuer confers any right in the goods, except as provided in the case of bills in a set, overissue of documents for fungible goods and substitutes for lost, stolen or destroyed documents. But the issuer is liable for damages caused by his overissue or failure to identify a duplicate document as such by conspicuous notation on its face.

§ 7—403. **Obligation of Warehouseman or Carrier to Deliver; Excuse.**

(1) The bailee must deliver the goods to a person entitled under the document who complies with subsections (2) and (3), unless and to the extent that the bailee establishes any of the following:

(a) delivery of the goods to a person whose receipt was rightful as against the claimant;

(b) damage to or delay, loss or destruction of the goods for which the bailee is not liable [, but the burden of establishing negligence in such cases is on the person entitled under the document];

Note: The brackets in (1)(b) indicate that State enactments may differ on this point without serious damage to the principle of uniformity.

(c) previous sale or other disposition of the goods in lawful enforcement of a lien or on warehouseman's lawful termination of storage;

(d) the exercise by a seller of his right to stop delivery pursuant to the provisions of the Article on Sales (Section 2—705);

(e) a diversion, reconsignment or other disposition pursuant to the provisions of this Article (Section 7—303) or tariff regulating such right;

(f) release, satisfaction or any other fact affording a personal defense against the claimant;

(g) any other lawful excuse.

(2) A person claiming goods covered by a document of title must satisfy the bailee's lien where the bailee so requests or where the bailee is prohibited by law from delivering the goods until the charges are paid.

(3) Unless the person claiming is one against whom the document confers no right under Sec. 7—503(1), he must surrender for cancellation or notation of partial deliveries any outstanding negotiable document covering the goods, and the bailee must cancel the document or conspicuously note the partial delivery thereon or be liable to any person to whom the document is duly negotiated.

(4) "Person entitled under the document" means holder in the case of a negotiable document, or the person to whom delivery is to be made by the terms of or pursuant to written instructions under a non-negotiable document.

§ 7—404. **No Liability for Good Faith Delivery Pursuant to Receipt or Bill.**

A bailee who in good faith including observance of reasonable commercial standards has received goods and delivered or otherwise disposed of them according to the terms of the document of title or pursuant to this Article is not liable therefor. This rule applies even though the person from whom he received the goods had no authority to procure the document or to dispose of the goods and even though the person to whom he delivered the goods had no authority to receive them.

Part 5 **Warehouse Receipts and Bills of Lading: Negotiation and Transfer**

§ 7—501. **Form of Negotiation and Requirements of "Due Negotiation".**

(1) A negotiable document of title running to the order of a named person is negotiated by his indorsement and delivery. After his indorsement in blank or

to bearer any person can negotiate it by delivery alone.

(2) (a) A negotiable document of title is also negotiated by delivery alone when by its original terms it runs to bearer.

(b) When a document running to the order of a named person is delivered to him the effect is the same as if the document had been negotiated.

(3) Negotiation of a negotiable document of title after it has been indorsed to a specified person requires indorsement by the special indorsee as well as delivery.

(4) A negotiable document of title is "duly negotiated" when it is negotiated in the manner stated in this section to a holder who purchases it in good faith without notice of any defense against or claim to it on the part of any person and for value, unless it is established that the negotiation is not in the regular course of business or financing or involves receiving the document in settlement or payment of a money obligation.

(5) Indorsement of a non-negotiable document neither makes it negotiable nor adds to the transferee's rights.

(6) The naming in a negotiable bill of a person to be notified of the arrival of the goods does not limit the negotiability of the bill nor constitute notice to a purchaser thereof of any interest of such person in the goods.

§ 7—502. **Rights Acquired by Due Negotiation.**

(1) Subject to the following section and to the provisions of Section 7—205 on fungible goods, a holder to whom a negotiable document of title has been duly negotiated acquires thereby:

(a) title to the document;

(b) title to the goods;

(c) all rights accruing under the law of agency or estoppel, including rights to goods delivered to the bailee after the document was issued; and

(d) the direct obligation of the issuer to hold or deliver the goods according to the terms of the document free of any defense or claim by him except those arising under the terms of the docu-

ment or under this Article. In the case of a delivery order the bailee's obligation accrues only upon acceptance and the obligation acquired by the holder is that the issuer and any indorser will procure the acceptance of the bailee.

(2) Subject to the following section, title and rights so acquired are not defeated by any stoppage of the goods represented by the document or by surrender of such goods by the bailee, and are not impaired even though the negotiation or any prior negotiation constituted a breach of duty or even though any person has been deprived of possession of the document by misrepresentation, fraud, accident, mistake, duress, loss, theft or conversion, or even though a previous sale or other transfer of the goods or document has been made to a third person.

§ 7—503. **Document of Title to Goods Defeated in Certain Cases.**

(1) A document of title confers no right in goods against a person who before issuance of the document had a legal interest or a perfected security interest in them and who neither

(a) delivered or entrusted them or any document of title covering them to the bailor or his nominee with actual or apparent authority to ship, store or sell or with power to obtain delivery under this Article (Section 7—403) or with power of disposition under this Act (Sections 2—403 and 9—307) or other statute or rule of law; nor

(b) acquiesced in the procurement by the bailor or his nominee of any document of title.

(2) Title to goods based upon an unaccepted delivery order is subject to the rights of anyone to whom a negotiable warehouse receipt or bill of lading covering the goods has been duly negotiated. Such a title may be defeated under the next section to the same extent as the rights of the issuer or a transferee from the issuer.

(3) Title to goods based upon a bill of lading issued to a freight forwarder is subject to the rights of anyone to whom a bill issued by the freight forwarder is duly negotiated; but delivery by the carrier in accordance with Part 4 of this Article pursuant to its own bill of lading discharges the carrier's obligation to deliver.

§ 7—504. Rights Acquired in the Absence of Due Negotiation; Effect of Diversion; Seller's Stoppage of Delivery.

(1) A transferee of a document, whether negotiable or non-negotiable, to whom the document has been delivered but not duly negotiated, acquires the title and rights which his transferor had or had actual authority to convey.

(2) In the case of a non-negotiable document, until but not after the bailee receives notification of the transfer, the rights of the transferee may be defeated

(a) by those creditors of the transferor who could treat the sale as void under Section 2—402; or

(b) by a buyer from the transferor in ordinary course of business if the bailee has delivered the goods to the buyer or received notification of his rights; or

(c) as against the bailee by good faith dealings of the bailee with the transferor.

(3) A diversion or other change of shipping instructions by the consignor in a non-negotiable bill of lading which causes the bailee not to deliver to the consignee defeats the consignee's title to the goods if they have been delivered to a buyer in ordinary course of business and in any event defeats the consignee's rights against the bailee.

(4) Delivery pursuant to a non-negotiable document may be stopped by a seller under Section 2—705, and subject to the requirement of due notification there provided. A bailee honoring the seller's instructions is entitled to be indemnified by the seller against any resulting loss or expense.

§ 7—505. Indorser Not a Guarantor for Other Parties.

The indorsement of a document of title issued by a bailee does not make the indorser liable for any default by the bailee or by previous indorsers.

§ 7—506. Delivery Without Indorsement: Right to Compel Indorsement.

The transferee of a negotiable document of title has a specifically enforceable right to have his transferor supply any necessary indorsement but the transfer

becomes a negotiation only as of the time the indorsement is supplied.

§ 7—507. Warranties on Negotiation or Transfer of Receipt or Bill.

Where a person negotiates or transfers a document of title for value otherwise than as a mere intermediary under the next following section, then unless otherwise agreed he warrants to his immediate purchaser only in addition to any warranty made in selling the goods

(a) that the document is genuine; and

(b) that he has no knowledge of any fact which would impair its validity or worth; and

(c) that his negotiation or transfer is rightful and fully effective with respect to the title to the document and the goods it represents.

§ 7—508. Warranties of Collecting Bank as to Documents.

A collecting bank or other intermediary known to be entrusted with documents on behalf of another or with collection of a draft or other claim against delivery of documents warrants by such delivery of the documents only its own good faith and authority. This rule applies even though the intermediary has purchased or made advances against the claim or draft to be collected.

§ 7—509. Receipt or Bill: When Adequate Compliance With Commercial Contract.

The question whether a document is adequate to fulfill the obligations of a contract for sale or the conditions of a credit is governed by the Articles on Sales (Article 2) and on Letters of Credit (Article 5).

Part 6 Warehouse Receipts and Bills of Lading: Miscellaneous Provisions

§ 7—601. Lost and Missing Documents.

(1) If a document has been lost, stolen or destroyed, a

court may order delivery of the goods or issuance of a substitute document and the bailee may without liability to any person comply with such order. If the document was negotiable the claimant must post security approved by the court to indemnify any person who may suffer loss as a result of non-surrender of the document. If the document was not negotiable, such security may be required at the discretion of the court. The court may also in its discretion order payment of the bailee's reasonable costs and counsel fees.

(2) A bailee who without court order delivers goods to a person claiming under a missing negotiable document is liable to any person injured thereby, and if the delivery is not in good faith becomes liable for conversion. Delivery in good faith is not conversion if made in accordance with a filed classification or tariff or, where no classification or tariff is filed, if the claimant posts security with the bailee in an amount at least double the value of the goods at the time of posting to indemnify any person injured by the delivery who files a notice of claim within one year after the delivery.

§ 7—602. **Attachment of Goods Covered by a Negotiable Document.**

Except where the document was originally issued upon delivery of the goods by a person who had no power to dispose of them, no lien attaches by virtue of any judicial process to goods in the possession of a bailee for which a negotiable document of title is outstanding unless the document be first surrendered to the bailee or its negotiation enjoined, and the bailee shall not be compelled to deliver the goods pursuant to process until the document is surrendered to him or impounded by the court. One who purchases the document for value without notice of the process or injunction takes free of the lien imposed by judicial process.

§ 7—603. **Conflicting Claims; Interpleader.**

If more than one person claims title or possession of the goods, the bailee is excused from delivery until he has had a reasonable time to ascertain the validity of the adverse claims or to bring an action to compel all claimants to interplead and may compel such interpleader, either in defending an action for non-delivery of the goods, or by original action, whichever is appropriate.

Article 8
INVESTMENT SECURITIES

Part 1 Short Title and General Matters

§ 8—101. **Short Title.**

This Article shall be known and may be cited as Uniform Commercial Code—Investment Securities.

§ 8—102. **Definitions and Index of Definitions.**

(1) In this Article, unless the context otherwise requires:

(a) A "certificated security" is a share, participation, or other interest in property of or an enterprise of the issuer or an obligation of the issuer which is

(i) represented by an instrument issued in bearer or registered form;

(ii) of a type commonly dealt in on securities exchanges or markets or commonly recognized in any area in which it is issued or dealt in as a medium for investment; and

(iii) either one of a class or series or by its terms divisible into a class or series of shares, participations, interests, or obligations.

(b) An "uncertificated security" is a share, participation, or other interest in property or an enterprise of the issuer or an obligation of the issuer which is

(i) not represented by an instrument and the transfer of which is registered upon books maintained for that purpose by or on behalf of the issuer;

(ii) of a type commonly dealt in on securities exchanges or markets; and

(iii) either one of a class or series or by its terms divisible into a class or series of shares, participations, interests, or obligations.

(c) A "security" is either a certificated or an uncertificated security. If a security is certificated, the terms "security" and "certificated security" may mean either the intangible interest, the instrument representing that interest, or both, as the context requires. A writing that is a certificated security is governed by this Article and not by Article 3, even though it also meets the requirements of that Article. This Article does not apply to money. If a certificated security has been retained by or surrendered to the issuer or its transfer agent for reasons other than registration of transfer, other temporary purpose, payment, exchange, or acquisition by the issuer, that security shall be treated as an uncertificated security for purposes of this Article.

(d) A certificated security is in "registered form" if

(i) it specifies a person entitled to the security or the rights it represents; and

(ii) its transfer may be registered upon books maintained for that purpose by or on behalf of the issuer, or the security so states.

(e) A certificated security is in "bearer form" if it runs to bearer according to its terms and not by reason of any indorsement.

(2) A "subsequent purchaser" is a person who takes other than by original issue.

(3) A "clearing corporation" is a corporation registered as a "clearing agency" under the federal securities laws or a corporation:

(a) at least 90 percent of whose capital stock is held by or for one or more organizations, none of which, other than a national securities exchange or association, holds in excess of 20 percent of the capital stock of the corporation, and each of which is

(i) subject to supervision or regulation pursuant to the provisions of federal or state banking laws or state insurance laws,

(ii) a broker or dealer or investment company registered under the federal securities laws, or

(iii) a national securities exchange or association registered under the federal securities laws; and

(b) any remaining capital stock of which is held by individuals who have purchased it at or prior to the time of their taking office as directors of the corporation and who have purchased only so much of the capital stock as is necessary to permit them to qualify as directors.

(4) A "custodian bank" is a bank or trust company that is supervised and examined by state or federal authority having supervision over banks and is acting as custodian for a clearing corporation.

(5) Other definitions applying to this Article or to specified Parts thereof and the sections in which they appear are:

"Adverse claim". Section 8—302.
"Bona fide purchaser". Section 8—302.
"Broker". Section 8—303.
"Debtor". Section 9—105.
"Financial intermediary". Section 8—313.
"Guarantee of the signature". Section 8—402.
"Initial transaction statement". Section 8—408.
"Instruction". Section 8—308.
"Intermediary bank". Section 4—105.
"Issuer". Section 8—201.
"Overissue". Section 8—104.
"Secured Party". Section 9—105.
"Security Agreement". Section 9—105.

(6) In addition, Article 1 contains general definitions and principles of construction and interpretation applicable throughout this Article.

Amended in 1962, 1973 and 1977.

§ 8—103. **Issuer's Lien.**

A lien upon a security in favor of an issuer thereof is valid against a purchaser only if:

(a) the security is certificated and the right of the issuer to the lien is noted conspicuously thereon; or

(b) the security is uncertificated and a notation of the right of the issuer to the lien is contained in the initial transaction statement sent to the purchaser or, if his interest is transferred to him other than by registration of transfer, pledge, or release, the initial transaction statement sent to the registered owner or the registered pledgee.

Amended in 1977.

§ 8—104. **Effect of Overissue; "Overissue".**

(1) The provisions of this Article which validate a security or compel its issue or reissue do not apply to the extent that validation, issue, or reissue would result in overissue; but if:

(a) an identical security which does not constitute an overissue is reasonably available for purchase, the person entitled to issue or validation may compel the issuer to purchase the security for him and either to deliver a certificated security or to register the transfer of an uncertificated security to him, against surrender of any certificated security he holds; or

(b) a security is not so available for purchase, the person entitled to issue or validation may recover from the issuer the price he or the last purchaser for value paid for it with interest from the date of his demand.

(2) "Overissue" means the issue of securities in excess of the amount the issuer has corporate power to issue.

Amended in 1977.

§ 8—105. **Certificated Securities Negotiable; Statements and Instructions Not Negotiable; Presumptions.**

(1) Certificated securities governed by this Article are negotiable instruments.

(2) Statements (Section 8—408), notices, or the like, sent by the issuer of uncertificated securities and instructions (Section 8—308) are neither negotiable instruments nor certificated securities.

(3) In any action on a security:

(a) unless specifically denied in the pleadings, each signature on a certificated security, in a necessary indorsement, on an initial transaction statement, or on an instruction, is admitted;

(b) if the effectiveness of a signature is put in issue, the burden of establishing it is on the party claiming under the signature, but the signature is presumed to be genuine or authorized;

(c) if signatures on a certificated security are admitted or established, production of the security entitles a holder to recover on it unless the defendant establishes a defense or a defect going to the validity of the security;

(d) if signatures on an initial transaction statement are admitted or established, the facts stated in the statement are presumed to be true as of the time of its issuance; and

(e) after it is shown that a defense or defect exists, the plaintiff has the burden of establishing that he or some person under whom he claims is a person against whom the defense or defect is ineffective (Section 8—202).

Amended in 1977.

§ 8—106. **Applicability.**

The law (including the conflict of laws rules) of the jurisdiction of organization of the issuer governs the validity of a security, the effectiveness of registration by the issuer, and the rights and duties of the issuer with respect to:

(a) registration of transfer of a certificated security;

(b) registration of transfer, pledge, or release of an uncertificated security; and

(c) sending of statements of uncertificated securities.

Amended in 1977.

§ 8—107. **Securities Transferable; Action for Price.**

(1) Unless otherwise agreed and subject to any applicable law or regulation respecting short sales, a person obligated to transfer securities may transfer any certificated security of the specified issue in bearer form or registered in the name of the transferee, or indorsed to him or in blank, or he may transfer an equivalent uncertificated security to the transferee or a person designated by the transferee.

(2) If the buyer fails to pay the price as it comes due under a contract of sale, the seller may recover the price of:

(a) certificated securities accepted by the buyer;

(b) uncertificated securities that have been transferred to the buyer or a person designated by the buyer; and

(c) other securities if efforts at their resale would be unduly burdensome or if there is no readily available market for their resale.

Amended in 1977.

§ 8—108. **Registration of Pledge and Release of Uncertificated Securities.**

A security interest in an uncertificated security may be evidenced by the registration of pledge to the secured party or a person designated by him. There can be no more than one registered pledge of an uncertificated security at any time. The registered owner of an uncertificated security is the person in whose name the security is registered, even if the security is subject to a registered pledge. The rights of a registered pledgee of an uncertificated security under this Article are terminated by the registration of release.

Added in 1977.

Part 2 Issue—Issuer

§ 8—201. **"Issuer"**

(1) With respect to obligations on or defenses to a security, "issuer" includes a person who:

(a) places or authorizes the placing of his name on a certificated security (otherwise than as authenticating trustee, registrar, transfer agent, or the like) to evidence that it represents a share, participation, or other interest in his property or in an enterprise, or to evidence his duty to perform an obligation represented by the certificated security;

(b) creates shares, participations, or other interests in his property or in an enterprise or undertakes obligations, which shares, participations, interests, or obligations are uncertificated securities;

(c) directly or indirectly creates fractional interests in his rights or property, which fractional interests are represented by certificated securities; or

(d) becomes responsible for or in place of any other person described as an issuer in this section.

(2) With respect to obligations on or defenses to a security, a guarantor is an issuer to the extent of his guaranty, whether or not his obligation is noted on a certificated security or on statements of uncertificated securities sent pursuant to Section 8—408.

(3) With respect to registration of transfer, pledge, or release (Part 4 of this Article), "issuer" means a person on whose behalf transfer books are maintained.

Amended in 1977.

§ 8—202. **Issuer's Responsibility and Defenses; Notice of Defect or Defense.**

(1) Even against a purchaser for value and without notice, the terms of a security include:

(a) if the security is certificated, those stated on the security;

(b) if the security is uncertificated, those contained in the initial transaction statement sent to such purchaser or, if his interest is transferred to him other than by registration of transfer, pledge, or release, the initial transaction statement sent to the registered owner or registered pledgee; and

(c) those made part of the security by reference, on the certificated security or in the initial transaction statement, to another instrument, indenture, or document or to a constitution, statute, ordinance, rule, regulation, order or the like, to the extent that the terms referred to do not conflict with the terms stated on the certificated security or contained in the statement. A reference under this paragraph does not of itself charge a purchaser for value with notice of a defect going to the validity of the security, even though the certificated security or statement expressly states that a person accepting it admits notice.

(2) A certificated security in the hands of a purchaser for value or an uncertificated security as to which an initial transaction statement has been sent to a purchaser for value, other than a security issued by a government or governmental agency or unit, even though issued with a defect going to its validity, is valid with respect to the purchaser if he is without notice of the particular defect unless the defect involves a violation of constitutional provisions, in which case the security is valid with respect to a subsequent purchaser for value and without notice of

the defect. This subsection applies to an issuer that is a government or governmental agency or unit only if either there has been substantial compliance with the legal requirements governing the issue or the issuer has received a substantial consideration for the issue as a whole or for the particular security and a stated purpose of the issue is one for which the issuer has power to borrow money or issue the security.

(3) Except as provided in the case of certain unauthorized signatures (Section 8—205), lack of genuineness of a certificated security or an initial transaction statement is a complete defense, even against a purchaser for value and without notice.

(4) All other defenses of the issuer of a certificated or uncertificated security, including nondelivery and conditional delivery of a certificated security, are ineffective against a purchaser for value who has taken without notice of the particular defense.

(5) Nothing in this section shall be construed to affect the right of a party to a "when, as and if issued" or a "when distributed" contract to cancel the contract in the event of a material change in the character of the security that is the subject of the contract or in the plan or arrangement pursuant to which the security is to be issued or distributed.

Amended in 1977.

§ 8—203. **Staleness as Notice of Defects or Defenses.**

(1) After an act or event creating a right to immediate performance of the principal obligation represented by a certificated security or that sets a date on or after which the security is to be presented or surrendered for redemption or exchange, a purchaser is charged with notice of any defect in its issue or defense of the issuer if:

 (a) the act or event is one requiring the payment of money, the delivery of certificated securities, the registration of transfer of uncertificated securities, or any of these on presentation or surrender of the certificated security, the funds or securities are available on the date set for payment or exchange, and he takes the security more than one year after that date; and

 (b) the act or event is not covered by paragraph (a) and he takes the security more than 2 years after the date set for surrender or presentation or the date on which performance became due.

(2) A call that has been revoked is not within subsection (1).

Amended in 1977.

§ 8—204. **Effect of Issuer's Restrictions on Transfer.**

A restriction on transfer of a security imposed by the issuer, even if otherwise lawful, is ineffective against any person without actual knowledge of it unless:

(a) the security is certificated and the restriction is noted conspicuously thereon; or

(b) the security is uncertificated and a notation of the restriction is contained in the initial transaction statement sent to the person or, if his interest is transferred to him other than by registration of transfer, pledge, or release, the initial transaction statement sent to the registered owner or the registered pledgee.

Amended in 1977.

§ 8—205. **Effect of Unauthorized Signature on Certificated Security or Initial Transaction Statement.**

An unauthorized signature placed on a certificated security prior to or in the course of issue or placed on an initial transaction statement is ineffective, but the signature is effective in favor of a purchaser for value of the certificated security or a purchaser for value of an uncertificated security to whom the initial transaction statement has been sent, if the purchaser is without notice of the lack of authority and the signing has been done by:

(a) an authenticating trustee, registrar, transfer agent, or other person entrusted by the issuer with the signing of the security, of similar securities, or of initial transaction statements or the immediate preparation for signing of any of them; or

(b) an employee of the issuer, or of any of the foregoing, entrusted with responsible handling of the security or initial transaction statement.

Amended in 1977.

§ 8—206. **Completion or Alteration of Certificated Security or Initial Transaction Statement.**

(1) If a certificated security contains the signatures necessary to its issue or transfer but is incomplete in any other respect:

(a) any person may complete it by filling in the blanks as authorized; and

(b) even though the blanks are incorrectly filled in, the security as completed is enforceable by a purchaser who took it for value and without notice of the incorrectness.

(2) A complete certificated security that has been improperly altered, even though fraudulently, remains enforceable, but only according to its original terms.

(3) If an initial transaction statement contains the signatures necessary to its validity, but is incomplete in any other respect:

(a) any person may complete it by filling in the blanks as authorized; and

(b) even though the blanks are incorrectly filled in, the statement as completed is effective in favor of the person to whom it is sent if he purchased the security referred to therein for value and without notice of the incorrectness.

(4) A complete initial transaction statement that has been improperly altered, even though fraudulently, is effective in favor of a purchaser to whom it has been sent, but only according to its original terms.

Amended in 1977.

§ 8—207. Rights and Duties of Issuer With Respect to Registered Owners and Registered Pledgees.

(1) Prior to due presentment for registration of transfer of a certificated security in registered form, the issuer or indenture trustee may treat the registered owner as the person exclusively entitled to vote, to receive notifications, and otherwise to exercise all the rights and powers of an owner.

(2) Subject to the provisions of subsections (3), (4), and (6), the issuer or indenture trustee may treat the registered owner of an uncertificated security as the person exclusively entitled to vote, to receive notifications, and otherwise to exercise all the rights and powers of an owner.

(3) The registered owner of an uncertificated security that is subject to a registered pledge is not entitled to registration of transfer prior to the due presentment to the issuer of a release instruction. The exercise of conversion rights with respect to a convertible uncertificated security is a transfer within the meaning of this section.

(4) Upon due presentment of a transfer instruction from the registered pledgee of an uncertificated security, the issuer shall:

(a) register the transfer of the security to the new owner free of pledge, if the instruction specifies a new owner (who may be the registered pledgee) and does not specify a pledgee;

(b) register the transfer of the security to the new owner subject to the interest of the existing pledgee, if the instruction specifies a new owner and the existing pledgee; or

(c) register the release of the security from the existing pledge and register the pledge of the security to the other pledgee, if the instruction specifies the existing owner and another pledgee.

(5) Continuity of perfection of a security interest is not broken by registration of transfer under subsection (4)(b) or by registration of release and pledge under subsection (4)(c), if the security interest is assigned.

(6) If an uncertificated security is subject to a registered pledge:

(a) any uncertificated securities issued in exchange for or distributed with respect to the pledged security shall be registered subject to the pledge;

(b) any certificated securities issued in exchange for or distributed with respect to the pledged security shall be delivered to the registered pledgee; and

(c) any money paid in exchange for or in redemption of part or all of the security shall be paid to the registered pledgee.

(7) Nothing in this Article shall be construed to affect the liability of the registered owner of a security for calls, assessments, or the like.

Amended in 1977.

§ 8—208. Effect of Signature of Authenticating Trustee, Registrar, or Transfer Agent.

(1) A person placing his signature upon a certificated

security or an initial transaction statement as authenticating trustee, registrar, transfer agent, or the like, warrants to a purchaser for value of the certificated security or a purchaser for value of an uncertificated security to whom the initial transaction statement has been sent, if the purchaser is without notice of the particular defect, that:

(a) the certificated security or initial transaction statement is genuine;

(b) his own participation in the issue or registration of the transfer, pledge, or release of the security is within his capacity and within the scope of the authority received by him from the issuer; and

(c) he has reasonable grounds to believe the security is in the form and within the amount the issuer is authorized to issue.

(2) Unless otherwise agreed, a person by so placing his signature does not assume responsibility for the validity of the security in other respects.

Amended in 1962 and 1977.

Part 3 **Transfer**

§ 8—301. **Rights Acquired by Purchaser.**

(1) Upon transfer of a security to a purchaser (Section 8—313), the purchaser acquires the rights in the security which his transferor had or had actual authority to convey unless the purchaser's rights are limited by Section 8—302(4).

(2) A transferee of a limited interest acquires rights only to the extent of the interest transferred. The creation or release of a security interest in a security is the transfer of a limited interest in that security.

Amended in 1977.

§ 8—302. **"Bona Fide Purchaser"; "Adverse Claim"; Title Acquired by Bona Fide Purchaser.**

(1) A "bona fide purchaser" is a purchaser for value in good faith and without notice of any adverse claim:

(a) who takes delivery of a certificated security in

bearer form or in registered form, issued or indorsed to him or in blank;

(b) to whom the transfer, pledge, or release of an uncertificated security is registered on the books of the issuer; or

(c) to whom a security is transferred under the provisions of paragraph (c), (d)(i), or (g) of Section 8—313(1).

Amended in 1977.

§ 8—303. **"Broker".**

"Broker" means a person engaged for all or part of his time in the business of buying and selling securities, who in the transaction concerned acts for, buys a security from, or sells a security to, a customer. Nothing in this Article determines the capacity in which a person acts for purposes of any other statute or rule to which the person is subject.

§ 8—304. **Notice to Purchaser of Adverse Claims.**

(1) A purchaser (including a broker for the seller or buyer, but excluding an intermediary bank) of a certificated security is charged with notice of adverse claims if:

(a) the security, whether in bearer or registered form, has been indorsed "for collection" or "for surrender" or for some other purpose not involving transfer; or

(b) the security is in bearer form and has on it an unambiguous statement that it is the property of a person other than the transferor. The mere writing of a name on a security is not such a statement.

(2) A purchaser (including a broker for the seller or buyer, but excluding an intermediary bank) to whom the transfer, pledge, or release of an uncertificated security is registered is charged with notice of adverse claims as to which the issuer has a duty under Section 8—403(4) at the time of registration and which are noted in the initial transaction statement sent to the purchaser or, if his interest is transferred to him other than by registration of transfer, pledge, or release, the initial transaction statement sent to the registered owner or the registered pledgee.

(3) The fact that the purchaser (including a broker for

the seller or buyer) of a certificated or uncertificated security has notice that the security is held for a third person or is registered in the name of or indorsed by a fiduciary does not create a duty of inquiry into the rightfulness of the transfer or constitute constructive notice of adverse claims. However, if the purchaser (excluding an intermediary bank) has knowledge that the proceeds are being used or the transaction is for the individual benefit of the fiduciary or otherwise in breach of duty, the purchaser is charged with notice of adverse claims.

Amended in 1977.

§ 8—305. **Staleness as Notice of Adverse Claims.**

An act or event that creates a right to immediate performance of the principal obligation represented by a certificated security or sets a date on or after which a certificated security is to be presented or surrendered for redemption or exchange does not itself constitute any notice of adverse claims except in the case of a transfer:

(a) after one year from any date set for presentment or surrender for redemption or exchange; or

(b) after 6 months from any date set for payment of money against presentation or surrender of the security if funds are available for payment on that date.

Amended in 1977.

§ 8—306. **Warranties on Presentment and Transfer of Certificated Securities; Warranties of Originators of Instructions.**

(1) A person who presents a certificated security for registration of transfer or for payment or exchange warrants to the issuer that he is entitled to the registration, payment, or exchange. But, a purchaser for value and without notice of adverse claims who receives a new, reissued, or re-registered certificated security on registration of transfer or receives an initial transaction statement confirming the registration of transfer of an equivalent uncertificated security to him warrants only that he has no knowledge of any unauthorized signature (Section 8—311) in a necessary indorsement.

(2) A person by transferring a certificated security to a purchaser for value warrants only that:

(a) his transfer is effective and rightful;

(b) the security is genuine and has not been materially altered; and

(c) he knows of no fact which might impair the validity of the security.

(3) If a certificated security is delivered by an intermediary known to be entrusted with delivery of the security on behalf of another or with collection of a draft or other claim against delivery, the intermediary by delivery warrants only his own good faith and authority, even though he has purchased or made advances against the claim to be collected against the delivery.

(4) A pledgee or other holder for security who redelivers a certificated security received, or after payment and on order of the debtor delivers that security to a third person, makes only the warranties of an intermediary under subsection (3).

(5) A person who originates an instruction warrants to the issuer that:

(a) he is an appropriate person to originate the instruction; and

(b) at the time the instruction is presented to the issuer he will be entitled to the registration of transfer, pledge, or release.

(6) A person who originates an instruction warrants to any person specially guaranteeing his signature (subsection 8—312(3)) that:

(a) he is an appropriate person to originate the instruction; and

(b) at the time the instruction is presented to the issuer

(i) he will be entitled to the registration of transfer, pledge, or release; and

(ii) the transfer, pledge, or release requested in the instruction will be registered by the issuer free from all liens, security interests, restrictions, and claims other than those specified in the instruction.

(7) A person who originates an instruction warrants to a purchaser for value and to any person guaranteeing the instruction (Section 8—312(6)) that:

(a) he is an appropriate person to originate the instruction;

(b) the uncertificated security referred to therein is valid; and

(c) at the time the instruction is presented to the issuer

(i) the transferor will be entitled to the registration of transfer, pledge, or release;

(ii) the transfer, pledge, or release requested in the instruction will be registered by the issuer free from all liens, security interests, restrictions, and claims other than those specified in the instruction; and

(iii) the requested transfer, pledge, or release will be rightful.

(8) If a secured party is the registered pledgee or the registered owner of an uncertificated security, a person who originates an instruction of release or transfer to the debtor or, after payment and on order of the debtor, a transfer instruction to a third person, warrants to the debtor or the third person only that he is an appropriate person to originate the instruction and, at the time the instruction is presented to the issuer, the transferor will be entitled to the registration of release or transfer. If a transfer instruction to a third person who is a purchaser for value is originated on order of the debtor, the debtor makes to the purchaser the warranties of paragraphs (b), (c)(ii) and (c)(iii) of subsection (7).

(9) A person who transfers an uncertificated security to a purchaser for value and does not originate an instruction in connection with the transfer warrants only that:

(a) his transfer is effective and rightful; and

(b) the uncertificated security is valid.

(10) A broker gives to his customer and to the issuer and a purchaser the applicable warranties provided in this section and has the rights and privileges of a purchaser under this section. The warranties of and in favor of the broker, acting as an agent are in addition to applicable warranties given by and in favor of his customer.

Amended in 1962 and 1977.

§ 8—307. **Effect of Delivery Without Indorsement; Right to Compel Indorsement.**

If a certificated security in registered form has been delivered to a purchaser without a necessary indorsement he may become a bona fide purchaser only as of the time the indorsement is supplied; but against the transferor, the transfer is complete upon delivery and the purchaser has a specifically enforceable right to have any necessary indorsement supplied.

Amended in 1977.

§ 8—308. **Indorsements; Instructions.**

(1) An indorsement of a certificated security in registered form is made when an appropriate person signs on it or on a separate document an assignment or transfer of the security or a power to assign or transfer it or his signature is written without more upon the back of the security.

(2) An indorsement may be in blank or special. An indorsement in blank includes an indorsement to bearer. A special indorsement specifies to whom the security is to be transferred, or who has power to transfer it. A holder may convert a blank indorsement into a special indorsement.

(3) An indorsement purporting to be only of part of a certificated security representing units intended by the issuer to be separately transferable is effective to the extent of the indorsement.

(4) An "instruction" is an order to the issuer of an uncertificated security requesting that the transfer, pledge, or release from pledge of the uncertificated security specified therein be registered.

(5) An instruction originated by an appropriate person is:

(a) a writing signed by an appropriate person; or

(b) a communication to the issuer in any form agreed upon in a writing signed by the issuer and an appropriate person.

If an instruction has been originated by an appropriate person but is incomplete in any other respect, any person may complete it as authorized and the issuer may rely on it as completed even though it has been completed incorrectly.

(6) "An appropriate person" in subsection (1) means the person specified by the certificated security or by special indorsement to be entitled to the security.

(7) "An appropriate person" in subsection (5) means:

(a) for an instruction to transfer or pledge an uncertificated security which is then not subject to a registered pledge, the registered owner; or

(b) for an instruction to transfer or release an

uncertificated security which is then subject to a registered pledge, the registered pledgee.

(8) In addition to the persons designated in subsections (6) and (7), "an appropriate person" in subsections (1) and (5) includes:

(a) if the person designated is described as a fiduciary but is no longer serving in the described capacity, either that person or his successor;

(b) if the persons designated are descirbed as more than one person as fiduciaries and one or more are no longer serving in the described capacity, the remaining fiduciary or fiduciaries, whether or not a successor has been appointed or qualified;

(c) if the person designated is an individual and is without capacity to act by virtue of death, incompetence, infancy, or otherwise, his executor, administrator, guardian, or like fiduciary;

(d) if the persons designated are described as more than one person as tenants by the entirety or with right of survivorship and by reason of death all cannot sign, the survivor or survivors;

(e) a person having power to sign under applicable law or controlling instrument; and

(f) to the extent that the person designated or any of the foregoing persons may act through an agent, his authorized agent.

(9) Unless otherwise agreed, the indorser of a certificated security by his indorsement or the originator of an instruction by his origination assumes no obligation that the security will be honored by the issuer but only the obligations provided in Section 8—306.

(10) Whether the person signing is appropriate is determined as of the date of signing and an indorsement made by or an instruction originated by him does not become unauthorized for the purposes of this Article by virtue of any subsequent change of circumstances.

(11) Failure of a fiduciary to comply with a controlling instrument or with the law of the state having jurisdiction of the fiduciary relationship, including any law requiring the fiduciary to obtain court approval of the transfer, pledge, or release, does not render his indorsement or an instruction originated

by him unauthorized for the purposes of this Article.
Amended in 1962 and 1977.

§ 8—309. **Effect of Indorsement Without Delivery.**

An indorsement of a certificated security, whether special or in blank, does not constitute a transfer until delivery of the certificated security on which it appears or, if the indorsement is on a separate document, until delivery of both the document and the certificated security.

Amended in 1977.

§ 8—310. **Indorsement of Certificated Security in Bearer Form.**

An indorsement of a certificated security in bearer form may give notice of adverse claims (Section 8—304) but does not otherwise affect any right to registration the holder possesses.

Amended in 1977.

§ 8—311. **Effect of Unauthorized Indorsement or Instruction.**

Unless the owner or pledgee has ratified an unauthorized indorsement or instruction or is otherwise precluded from asserting its ineffectiveness:

(a) he may assert its ineffectiveness against the issuer or any purchaser, other than a purchaser for value and without notice of adverse claims, who has in good faith received a new, reissued, or re-registered certificated security on registration of transfer or received an initial transaction statement confirming the registration of transfer, pledge, or release of an equivalent uncertificated security to him; and

(b) an issuer who registers the transfer of a certificated security upon the unauthorized indorsement or who registers the transfer, pledge, or release of an uncertificated security upon the unauthorized instruction is subject to liability for improper registration (Section 8—404).

Amended in 1977.

§ 8—312. **Effect of Guaranteeing Signature, Indorsement or Instruction.**

(1) Any person guaranteeing a signature of an indorser of a certificated security warrants that at the time of signing:

(a) the signature was genuine;

(b) the signer was an appropriate person to indorse (Section 8—308); and

(c) the signer had legal capacity to sign.

(2) Any person guaranteeing a signature of the originator of an instruction warrants that at the time of signing:

(a) the signature was genuine;

(b) the signer was an appropriate person to originate the instruction (Section 8—308) if the person specified in the instruction as the registered owner or registered pledgee of the uncertificated security was, in fact, the registered owner or registered pledgee of the security, as to which fact the signature guarantor makes no warranty;

(c) the signer had legal capacity to sign; and

(d) the taxpayer identification number, if any, appearing on the instruction as that of the registered owner or registered pledgee was the taxpayer identification number of the signer or of the owner or pledgee for whom the signer was acting.

(3) Any person specially guaranteeing the signature of the originator of an instruction makes not only the warranties of a signature guarantor (subsection (2)) but also warrants that at the time the instruction is presented to the issuer:

(a) the person specified in the instruction as the registered owner or registered pledgee of the uncertificated security will be the registered owner or registered pledgee; and

(b) the transfer, pledge, or release of the uncertificated security requested in the instruction will be registered by the issuer free from all liens, security interests, restrictions, and claims other than those specified in the instruction.

(4) The guarantor under subsections (1) and (2) or the special guarantor under subsection (3) does not otherwise warrant the rightfulness of the particular transfer, pledge, or release.

(5) Any person guaranteeing an indorsement of a certificated security makes not only the warranties of a signature guarantor under subsection (1) but also warrants the rightfulness of the particular transfer in all respects.

(6) Any person guaranteeing an instruction request-ing the transfer, pledge, or release of an uncertificated security makes not only the warranties of a special signature guarantor under subsection (3) but also warrants the rightfulness of the particular transfer, pledge, or release in all respects.

(7) No issuer may require a special guarantee of signature (subsection (3)), a guarantee of indorsement (subsection (5)), or a guarantee of instruction (subsection (6)) as a condition to registration of transfer, pledge, or release.

(8) The foregoing warranties are made to any person taking or dealing with the security in reliance on the guarantee, and the guarantor is liable to the person for any loss resulting from breach of the warranties. Amended in 1977.

§ 8—313. **When Transfer to Purchaser Occurs; Financial Intermediary as Bona Fide Purchaser; "Financial Intermediary".**

(1) Transfer of a security or a limited interest (including a security interest) therein to a purchaser occurs only:

(a) at the time he or a person designated by him acquires possession of a certificated security;

(b) at the time the transfer, pledge, or release of an uncertificated security is registered to him or a person designated by him;

(c) at the time his financial intermediary acquires possession of a certificated security specially indorsed to or issued in the name of the purchaser;

(d) at the time a financial intermediary, not a clearing corporation, sends him confirmation of the purchase and also by book entry or otherwise identifies as belonging to the purchaser

(i) a specific certificated security in the financial intermediary's possession;

(ii) a quantity of securities that constitute or are part of a fungible bulk of certificated securities in the financial intermediary's possession or of uncertificated securities registered in the name of the financial intermediary; or

(iii) a quantity of securities that constitute or are part of a fungible bulk of securities shown on the account of the financial intermediary on the books of another financial intermediary;

(e) with respect to an identified certificated security to be delivered while still in the possession of a third person, not a financial intermediary, at the time that person acknowledges that he holds for the purchaser;

(f) with respect to a specific uncertificated security the pledge or transfer of which has been registered to a third person, not a financial intermediary, at the time that person acknowledges that he holds for the purchaser;

(g) at the time appropriate entries to the account of the purchaser or a person designated by him on the·books of a clearing corporation are made under Section 8—320;

(h) with respect to the transfer of a security interest where the debtor has signed a security agreement containing a description of the security, at the time a written notification, which, in the case of the creation of the security interest, is signed by the debtor (which may be a copy of the security agreement) or which, in the case of the release or assignment of the security interest created pursuant to this paragraph, is signed by the secured party, is received by

   (i) a financial intermediary on whose books the interest of the transferor in the security appears;

   (ii) a third person, not a financial intermediary, in possession of the security, if it is certificated;

   (iii) a third person, not a financial intermediary, who is the registered owner of the security, if it is uncertificated and not subject to a registered pledge; or

   (iv) a third person, not a financial intermediary, who is the registered pledgee of the security, if it is uncertificated and subject to a registered pledge;

(i) with respect to the transfer of a security interest where the transferor has signed a security agreement containing a description of the security, at the time new value is given by the secured party; or

(j) with respect to the transfer of a security interest where the secured party is a financial intermediary and the security has already been transferred to the financial intermediary under paragraphs (a), (b), (c), (d), or (g), at the time the transferor has signed a security agreement containing a description of the security and value is given by the secured party.

(2) The purchaser is the owner of a security held for him by a financial intermediary, but cannot be a bona fide purchaser of a security so held except in the circumstances specified in paragraphs (c), (d)(i), and (g) of subsection (1). If a security so held is part of a fungible bulk, as in the circumstances specified in paragraphs (d)(ii) and (d)(iii) of subsection (1), the purchaser is the owner of a proportionate property interest in the fungible bulk.

(3) Notice of an adverse claim received by the financial intermediary or by the purchaser after the financial intermediary takes delivery of a certificated security as a holder for value or after the transfer, pledge, or release of an uncertificated security has been registered free of the claim to a financial intermediary who has given value is not effective either as to the financial intermediary or as to the purchaser. However, as between the financial intermediary and the purchaser the purchaser may demand transfer of an equivalent security as to which no notice of adverse claim has been received.

(4) A "financial intermediary" is a bank, broker, clearing corporation, or other person (or the nominee of any of them) which in the ordinary course of its business maintains security accounts for its customers and is acting in that capacity. A financial intermediary may have a security interest in securities held in account for its customer.

Amended in 1962 and 1977.

§ 8—314. **Duty to Transfer, When Completed**

(1) Unless otherwise agreed, if a sale of a security is made on an exchange or otherwise through brokers:

   (a) the selling customer fulfills his duty to transfer at the time he:

      (i) places a certificated security in the possession of the selling broker or a person designated by the broker;

      (ii) causes an uncertificated security to be registered in the name of the selling broker or a person designated by the broker;

(iii) if requested, causes an acknowledgment to be made to the selling broker that a certificated or uncertificated security is held for the broker; or

(iv) places in the possession of the selling broker or of a person designated by the broker a transfer instruction for an uncertificated security, providing the issuer does not refuse to register the requested transfer if the instruction is presented to the issuer for registration within 30 days thereafter; and

(b) the selling broker, including a correspondent broker acting for a selling customer, fulfills his duty to transfer at the time he:

(i) places a certificated security in the possession of the buying broker or a person designated by the buying broker;

(ii) causes an uncertificated security to be registered in the name of the buying broker or a person designated by the buying broker;

(iii) places in the possession of the buying broker or of a person designated by the buying broker a transfer instruction for an uncertificated security, providing the issuer does not refuse to register the requested transfer if the instruction is presented to the issuer for registration within 30 days thereafter; or

(iv) effects clearance of the sale in accordance with the rules of the exchange on which the transaction took place.

(2) Except as provided in this section or unless otherwise agreed, a transferor's duty to transfer a security under a contract of purchase is not fulfilled until he:

(a) places a certificated security in form to be negotiated by the purchaser in the possession of the purchaser or of a person designated by the purchaser;

(b) causes an uncertificated security to be registered in the name of the purchaser or a person designated by the purchaser; or

(c) if the purchaser requests, causes an acknowledgment to be made to the purchaser that a certificated or uncertificated security is held for the purchaser.

(3) Unless made on an exchange, a sale to a broker purchasing for his own account is within subsection (2) and not within subsection (1).

Amended in 1977.

§ 8—315. **Action Against Transferee Based Upon Wrongful Transfer**

(1) Any person against whom the transfer of a security is wrongful for any reason, including his incapacity, as against anyone except a bona fide purchaser, may:

(a) reclaim possession of the certificated security wrongfully transferred;

(b) obtain possession of any new certificated security representing all or part of the same rights;

(c) compel the origination of an instruction to transfer to him or a person designated by him an uncertificated security constituting all or part of the same rights; or

(d) have damages.

(2) If the transfer is wrongful because of an unauthorized indorsement of a certificated security, the owner may also reclaim or obtain possession of the security or a new certificated security, even from a bona fide purchaser, if the ineffectiveness of the purported indorsement can be asserted against him under the provisions of this Article on unauthorized indorsements (Section 8—311).

(3) The right to obtain or reclaim possession of a certificated security or to compel the origination of a transfer instruction may be specifically enforced and the transfer of a certificated or uncertificated security enjoined and a certificated security impounded pending the litigation.

Amended in 1977.

§ 8—316. **Purchaser's Right to Requisites for Registration of Transfer, Pledge, or Release on Books**

Unless otherwise agreed, the transferor of a certificated security or the transferor, pledgor, or pledgee of an uncertificated security on due demand must supply his purchaser with any proof of his authority to transfer, pledge, or release or with any other requisite necessary to obtain registration of the

transfer, pledge, or release of the security; but if the transfer, pledge, or release is not for value, a transferor, pledgor, or pledgee need not do so unless the purchaser furnishes the necessary expenses. Failure within a reasonable time to comply with a demand made gives the purchaser the right to reject or rescind the transfer, pledge, or release.
Amended in 1977.

§ 8—317. **Creditors' Rights**

(1) Subject to the exceptions in subsections (3) and (4), no attachment or levy upon a certificated security or any share or other interest represented thereby which is outstanding is valid until the security is actually seized by the officer making the attachment or levy, but a certificated security which has been surrendered to the issuer may be reached by a creditor by legal process at the issuer's chief executive office in the United States.

(2) An uncertificated security registered in the name of the debtor may not be reached by a creditor except by legal process at the issuer's chief executive office in the United States.

(3) The interest of a debtor in a certificated security that is in the possession of a secured party not a financial intermediary or in an uncertificated security registered in the name of a secured party not a financial intermediary (or in the name of a nominee of the secured party) may be reached by a creditor by legal process upon the secured party.

(4) The interest of a debtor in a certificated security that is in the possession of or registered in the name of a financial intermediary or in an uncertificated security registered in the name of a financial intermediary may be reached by a creditor by legal process upon the financial intermediary on whose books the interest of the debtor appears.

(5) Unless otherwise provided by law, a creditor's lien upon the interest of a debtor in a security obtained pursuant to subsection (3) or (4) is not a restraint on the transfer of the security, free of the lien, to a third party for new value; but in the event of a transfer, the lien applies to the proceeds of the transfer in the hands of the secured party or financial intermediary, subject to any claims having priority.

(6) A creditor whose debtor is the owner of a security is entitled to aid from courts of appropriate jurisdiction, by injunction or otherwise, in reaching the security or in satisfying the claim by means allowed at law or in equity in regard to property that cannot readily be reached by ordinary legal process.
Amended in 1977.

§ 8—318. **No Conversion by Good Faith Conduct**

An agent or bailee who in good faith (including observance of reasonable commercial standards if he is in the business of buying, selling, or otherwise dealing with securities) has received certificated securities and sold, pledged, or delivered them or has sold or caused the transfer or pledge of uncertificated securities over which he had control according to the instructions of his principal, is not liable for conversion or for participation in breach of fiduciary duty although the principal had no right so to deal with the securities.
Amended in 1977.

§ 8—319. **Statute of Frauds**

A contract for the sale of securities is not enforceable by way of action or defense unless:

(a) there is some writing signed by the party against whom enforcement is sought or by his authorized agent or broker, sufficient to indicate that a contract has been made for sale of a stated quantity of described securities at a defined or stated price;

(b) delivery of a certificated security or transfer instruction has been accepted, or transfer of an uncertificated security has been registered and the transferee has failed to send written objection to the issuer within 10 days after receipt of the initial transaction statement confirming the registration, or payment has been made, but the contract is enforceable under this provision only to the extent of the delivery, registration, or payment;

(c) within a reasonable time a writing in confirmation of the sale or purchase and sufficient against the sender under paragraph (a) has been received by the party against whom enforcement is sought and he has failed to send written objection to its contents within 10 days after its receipt; or

(d) the party against whom enforcement is sought admits in his pleading, testimony, or otherwise in court that a contract was made for the sale of a stated quantity of described securities at a defined or stated price.
Amended in 1977.

§ 8—320. **Transfer or Pledge Within Central Depository System**

(1) In addition to other methods, a transfer, pledge, or release of a security or any interest therein may be effected by the making of appropriate entries on the books of a clearing corporation reducing the account of the transferor, pledgor, or pledgee and increasing the account of the transferee, pledgee, or pledgor by the amount of the obligation or the number of shares or rights transferred, pledged, or released, if the security is shown on the account of a transferor, pledgor, or pledgee on the books of the clearing corporation; is subject to the control of the clearing corporation; and

> (a) if certificated,
>
>> (i) is in the custody of the clearing corporation, another clearing corporation, a custodian bank, or a nominee of any of them; and
>>
>> (ii) is in bearer form or indorsed in blank by an appropriate person or registered in the name of the clearing corporation, a custodian bank, or a nominee of any of them; or
>
> (b) if uncertificated, is registered in the name of the clearing corporation, another clearing corporation, a custodian bank, or a nominee of any of them.

(2) Under this section entries may be made with respect to like securities or interests therein as a part of a fungible bulk and may refer merely to a quantity of a particular security without reference to the name of the registered owner, certificate or bond number, or the like, and, in appropriate cases, may be on a net basis taking into account other transfers, pledges, or releases of the same security.

(3) A transfer under this section is effective (Section 8—313) and the purchaser acquires the rights of the transferor (Section 8—301). A pledge or release under this section is the transfer of a limited interest. If a pledge or the creation of a security interest is intended, the security interest is perfected at the time when both value is given by the pledgee and the appropriate entries are made (Section 8—321). A transferee or pledgee under this section may be a bona fide purchaser (Section 8—302).

(4) A transfer or pledge under this section is not a registration of transfer under Part 4.

(5) That entries made on the books of the clearing corporation as provided in subsection (1) are not appropriate does not affect the validity or effect of the entries or the liabilities or obligations of the clearing corporation to any person adversely affected thereby.

Added in 1962; amended in 1977.

§ 8—321. **Enforceability, Attachment, Perfection and Termination of Security Interests**

(1) A security interest in a security is enforceable and can attach only if it is transferred to the secured party or a person designated by him pursuant to a provision of Section 8—313(1).

(2) A security interest so transferred pursuant to agreement by a transferor who has rights in the security to a transferee who has given value is a perfected security interest, but a security interest that has been transferred solely under paragraph (i) of Section 8—313(1) becomes unperfected after 21 days unless, within that time, the requirements for transfer under any other provision of Section 8—313(1) are satisfied.

(3) A security interest in a security is subject to the provisions of Article 9, but:

> (a) no filing is required to perfect the security interest; and
>
> (b) no written security agreement signed by the debtor is necessary to make the security interest enforceable, except as provided in paragraph (h), (i), or (j) of Section 8—313(1). The secured party has the rights and duties provided under Section 9—207, to the extent they are applicable, whether or not the security is certificated, and, if certificated, whether or not it is in his possession.

(4) Unless otherwise agreed, a security interest in a security is terminated by transfer to the debtor or a person designated by him pursuant to a provision of Section 8—313(1). If a security is thus transferred, the security interest, if not terminated, becomes unperfected unless the security is certificated and is delivered to the debtor for the purpose of ultimate sale or exchange or presentation, collection, renewal, or registration of transfer. In that case, the security interest becomes unperfected after 21 days unless, within that time, the security (or securities for which it has been exchanged) is transferred to the secured

party or a person designated by him pursuant to a provision of Section 8—313(1).

Added in 1977.

Part 4 Registration

§ 8—401. **Duty of Issuer to Register Transfer, Pledge, or Release**

(1) If a certificated security in registered form is presented to the issuer with a request to register transfer or an instruction is presented to the issuer with a request to register transfer, pledge, or release, the issuer shall register the transfer, pledge, or release as requested if:

(a) the security is indorsed or the instruction was originated by the appropriate person or persons (Section 8—308);

(b) reasonable assurance is given that those indorsements or instructions are genuine and effective (Section 8—402);

(c) the issuer has no duty as to adverse claims or has discharged the duty (Section 8—403);

(d) any applicable law relating to the collection of taxes has been complied with; and

(e) the transfer, pledge, or release is in fact rightful or is to a bona fide purchaser.

(2) If an issuer is under a duty to register a transfer, pledge, or release of a security, the issuer is also liable to the person presenting a certificated security or an instruction for registration or his principal for loss resulting from any unreasonable delay in registration or from failure or refusal to register the transfer, pledge, or release.

Amended in 1977.

§ 8—402. **Assurance that Indorsements and Instructions Are Effective**

(1) The issuer may require the following assurance that each necessary indorsement of a certificated security or each instruction (Section 8—308) is genuine and effective:

(a) in all cases, a guarantee of the signature (Section 8—312(1) or (2)) of the person indorsing a certificated security or originating an instruction including, in the case of an instruction, a warranty of the taxpayer identification number or, in the

absence thereof, other reasonable assurance of identity;

(b) if the indorsement is made or the instruction is originated by an agent, appropriate assurance of authority to sign;

(c) if the indorsement is made or the instruction is originated by a fiduciary, appropriate evidence of appointment or incumbency;

(d) if there is more than one fiduciary, reasonable assurance that all who are required to sign have done so; and

(e) if the indorsement is made or the instruction is originated by a person not covered by any of the foregoing, assurance appropriate to the case corresponding as nearly as may be to the foregoing.

(2) A "guarantee of the signature" in subsection (1) means a guarantee signed by or on behalf of a person reasonably believed by the issuer to be responsible. The issuer may adopt standards with respect to responsibility if they are not manifestly unreasonable.

(3) "Appropriate evidence of appointment or incumbency" in subsection (1) means:

(a) in the case of a fiduciary appointed or qualified by a court, a certificate issued by or under the direction or supervision of that court or an officer thereof and dated within 60 days before the date of presentation for transfer, pledge, or release; or

(b) in any other case, a copy of a document showing the appointment or a certificate issued by or on behalf of a person reasonably believed by the issuer to be responsible or, in the absence of that document or certificate, other evidence reasonably deemed by the issuer to be appropriate. The issuer may adopt standards with respect to the evidence if they are not manifestly unreasonable. The issuer is not charged with notice of the contents of any document obtained pursuant to this paragraph (b) except to the extent that the contents relate directly to the appointment or incumbency.

(4) The issuer may elect to require reasonable assurance beyond that specified in this section, but if it does so and, for a purpose other than that specified in

subsection (3)(b), both requires and obtains a copy of a will, trust, indenture, articles of co-partnership, by-laws, or other controlling instrument, it is charged with notice of all matters contained therein affecting the transfer, pledge, or release.

Amended in 1977.

§ 8—403. **Issuer's Duty as to Adverse Claims**

(1) An issuer to whom a certificated security is presented for registration shall inquire into adverse claims if:

(a) a written notification of an adverse claim is received at a time and in a manner affording the issuer a reasonable opportunity to act on it prior to the issuance of a new, reissued, or re-registered certificated security, and the notification identifies the claimant, the registered owner, and the issue of which the security is a part, and provides an address for communications directed to the claimant; or

(b) the issuer is charged with notice of an adverse claim from a controlling instrument it has elected to require under Section 8—402(4).

(2) The issuer may discharge any duty of inquiry by any reasonable means, including notifying an adverse claimant by registered or certified mail at the address furnished by him or, if there be no such address, at his residence or regular place of business that the certificated security has been presented for registration of transfer by a named person, and that the transfer will be registered unless within 30 days from the date of mailing the notification, either:

(a) an appropriate restraining order, injunction, or other process issues from a court of competent jurisdiction; or

(b) there is filed with the issuer an indemnity bond, sufficient in the issuer's judgment to protect the issuer and any transfer agent, registrar, or other agent of the issuer involved from any loss it or they may suffer by complying with the adverse claim.

(3) Unless an issuer is charged with notice of an adverse claim from a controlling instrument which it has elected to require under Section 8—402(4) or receives notification of an adverse claim under subsection (1), if a certificated security presented for

registration is indorsed by the appropriate person or persons the issuer is under no duty to inquire into adverse claims. In particular:

(a) an issuer registering a certificated security in the name of a person who is a fiduciary or who is described as a fiduciary is not bound to inquire into the existence, extent, or correct description of the fiduciary relationship; and thereafter the issuer may assume without inquiry that the newly registered owner continues to be the fiduciary until the issuer receives written notice that the fiduciary is no longer acting as such with respect to the particular security;

(b) an issuer registering transfer on an indorsement by a fiduciary is not bound to inquire whether the transfer is made in compliance with a controlling instrument or with the law of the state having jurisdiction of the fiduciary relationship, including any law requiring the fiduciary to obtain court approval of the transfer; and

(c) the issuer is not charged with notice of the contents of any court record or file or other recorded or unrecorded document even though the document is in its possession and even though the transfer is made on the indorsement of a fiduciary to the fiduciary himself or to his nominee.

(4) An issuer is under no duty as to adverse claims with respect to an uncertificated security except:

(a) claims embodied in a restraining order, injunction, or other legal process served upon the issuer if the process was served at a time and in a manner affording the issuer a reasonable opportunity to act on it in accordance with the requirements of subsection (5);

(b) claims of which the issuer has received a written notification from the registered owner or the registered pledgee if the notification was received at a time and in a manner affording the issuer a reasonable opportunity to act on it in accordance with the requirements of subsection (5);

(c) claims (including restrictions on transfer not imposed by the issuer) to which the registration of transfer to the present registered owner was subject and were so noted in the initial transaction statement sent to him; and

(d) claims as to which an issuer is charged with notice from a controlling instrument it has elected to require under Section 8—402(4).

(5) If the issuer of an uncertificated security is under a duty as to an adverse claim, he discharges that duty by:

(a) including a notation of the claim in any statements sent with respect to the security under Sections 8—408(3), (6), and (7); and

(b) refusing to register the transfer or pledge of the security unless the nature of the claim does not preclude transfer or pledge subject thereto.

(6) If the transfer or pledge of the security is registered subject to an adverse claim, a notation of the claim must be included in the initial transaction statement and all subsequent statements sent to the transferee and pledgee under Section 8—408.

(7) Notwithstanding subsections (4) and (5), if an uncertificated security was subject to a registered pledge at the time the issuer first came under a duty as to a particular adverse claim, the issuer has no duty as to that claim if transfer of the security is requested by the registered pledgee or an appropriate person acting for the registered pledgee unless:

(a) the claim was embodied in legal process which expressly provides otherwise;

(b) the claim was asserted in a written notification from the registered pledgee;

(c) the claim was one as to which the issuer was charged with notice from a controlling instrument it required under Section 8—402(4) in connection with the pledgee's request for transfer; or

(d) the transfer requested is to the registered owner.

Amended in 1977.

§ 8—404. Liability and Non-Liability for Registration

(1) Except as provided in any law relating to the collection of taxes, the issuer is not liable to the owner, pledgee, or any other person suffering loss as a result of the registration of a transfer, pledge, or release of a security if:

(a) there were on or with a certificated security the necessary indorsements or the issuer had received an instruction originated by an appropriate person (Section 8—308); and

(b) the issuer had no duty as to adverse claims or has discharged the duty (Section 8—403).

(2) If an issuer has registered a transfer of a certificated security to a person not entitled to it, the issuer on demand shall deliver a like security to the true owner unless:

(a) the registration was pursuant to subsection (1);

(b) the owner is precluded from asserting any claim for registering the transfer under Section 8—405(1); or

(c) the delivery would result in overissue, in which case the issuer's liability is governed by Section 8—104.

(3) If an issuer has improperly registered a transfer, pledge, or release of an uncertificated security, the issuer on demand from the injured party shall restore the records as to the injured party to the condition that would have obtained if the improper registration had not been made unless:

(a) the registration was pursuant to subsection (1); or

(b) the registration would result in overissue, in which case the issuer's liability is governed by Section 8—104.

Amended in 1977.

§ 8—405. Lost, Destroyed, and Stolen Certificated Securities

(1) If a certificated security has been lost, apparently destroyed, or wrongfully taken, and the owner fails to notify the issuer of that fact within a reasonable time after he has notice of it and the issuer registers a transfer of the security before receiving notification, the owner is precluded from asserting against the issuer any claim for registering the transfer under Section 8—404 or any claim to a new security under this section.

(2) If the owner of a certificated security claims that the security has been lost, destroyed, or wrongfully taken, the issuer shall issue a new certificated security or, at the option of the issuer, an equivalent

uncertificated security in place of the original security if the owner:

(a) so requests before the issuer has notice that the security has been acquired by a bona fide purchaser;

(b) files with the issuer a sufficient indemnity bond; and

(c) satisfies any other reasonable requirements imposed by the issuer.

(3) If, after the issue of a new certificated or uncertificated security, a bona fide purchaser of the original certificated security presents it for registration of transfer, the issuer shall register the transfer unless registration would result in overissue, in which event the issuer's liability is governed by Section 8—104. In addition to any rights on the indemnity bond, the issuer may recover the new certificated security from the person to whom it was issued or any person taking under him except a bona fide purchaser or may cancel the uncertificated security unless a bona fide purchaser or any person taking under a bona fide purchaser is then the registered owner or registered pledgee thereof.

Amended in 1977.

§ 8—406. Duty of Authenticating Trustee, Transfer Agent, or Registrar

(1) If a person acts as authenticating trustee, transfer agent, registrar, or other agent for an issuer in the registration of transfers of its certificated securities or in the registration of transfers, pledges, and releases of its uncertificated securities, in the issue of new securities, or in the cancellation of surrendered securities:

(a) he is under a duty to the issuer to exercise good faith and due diligence in performing his functions; and

(b) with regard to the particular functions he performs, he has the same obligation to the holder or owner of a certificated security or to the owner or pledgee of an uncertificated security and has the same rights and privileges as the issuer has in regard to those functions.

(2) Notice to an authenticating trustee, transfer agent, registrar or other agent is notice to the issuer with respect to the functions performed by the agent.

Amended in 1977.

§ 8—407. Exchangeability of Securities

(1) No issuer is subject to the requirements of this section unless it regularly maintains a system for issuing the class of securities involved under which both certificated and uncertificated securities are regularly issued to the category of owners, which includes the person in whose name the new security is to be registered.

(2) Upon surrender of a certificated security with all necessary indorsements and presentation of a written request by the person surrendering the security, the issuer, if he has no duty as to adverse claims or has discharged the duty (Section 8—403), shall issue to the person or a person designated by him an equivalent uncertificated security subject to all liens, restrictions, and claims that were noted on the certificated security.

(3) Upon receipt of a transfer instruction originated by an appropriate person who so requests, the issuer of an uncertificated security shall cancel the uncertificated security and issue an equivalent certificated security on which must be noted conspicuously any liens and restrictions of the issuer and any adverse claims (as to which the issuer has a duty under Section 8—403(4)) to which the uncertificated security was subject. The certificated security shall be registered in the name of and delivered to:

(a) the registered owner, if the uncertificated security was not subject to a registered pledge; or

(b) the registered pledgee, if the uncertificated security was subject to a registered pledge.

Added in 1977.

§ 8—408. Statements of Uncertificated Securities

(1) Within 2 business days after the transfer of an uncertificated security has been registered, the issuer shall send to the new registered owner and, if the security has been transferred subject to a registered pledge, to the registered pledgee a written statement containing:

(a) a description of the issue of which the uncertificated security is a part;

(b) the number of shares or units transferred;

(c) the name and address and any taxpayer identification number of the new registered owner and, if the security has been transferred subject to a registered pledge, the name and address and any taxpayer identification number of the registered pledgee;

(d) a notation of any liens and restrictions of the issuer and any adverse claims (as to which the issuer has a duty under Section 8—403(4)) to which the uncertificated security is or may be subject at the time of registration or a statement that there are none of those liens, restrictions, or adverse claims; and

(e) the date the transfer was registered.

(2) Within 2 business days after the pledge of an uncertificated security has been registered, the issuer shall send to the registered owner and the registered pledgee a written statement containing:

(a) a description of the issue of which the uncertificated security is a part;

(b) the number of shares or units pledged;

(c) the name and address and any taxpayer identification number of the registered owner and the registered pledgee;

(d) a notation of any liens and restrictions of the issuer and any adverse claims (as to which the issuer has a duty under Section 8—403(4)) to which the uncertificated security is or may be subject at the time of registration or a statement that there are none of those liens, restrictions, or adverse claims; and

(e) the date the pledge was registered.

(3) Within 2 business days after the release from pledge of an uncertificated security has been registered, the issuer shall send to the registered owner and the pledgee whose interest was released a written statement containing:

(a) a description of the issue of which the uncertificated security is a part;

(b) the number of shares or units released from pledge;

(c) the name and address and any taxpayer identification number of the registered owner and the pledgee whose interest was released;

(d) a notation of any liens and restrictions of the issuer and any adverse claims (as to which the issuer has a duty under Section 8—403(4)) to which the uncertificated security is or may be subject at the time of registration or a statement that there are none of those liens, restrictions, or adverse claims; and

(e) the date the release was registered.

(4) An "initial transaction statement" is the statement sent to:

(a) the new registered owner and, if applicable, to the registered pledgee pursuant to subsection (1);

(b) the registered pledgee pursuant to subsection (2); or

(c) the registered owner pursuant to subsection (3).

Each initial transaction statement shall be signed by or on behalf of the issuer and must be identified as "Initial Transaction Statement".

(5) Within 2 business days after the transfer of an uncertificated security has been registered, the issuer shall send to the former registered owner and the former registered pledgee, if any, a written statement containing:

(a) a description of the issue of which the uncertificated security is a part;

(b) the number of shares or units transferred;

(c) the name and address and any taxpayer identification number of the former registered owner and of any former registered pledgee; and

(d) the date the transfer was registered.

(6) At periodic intervals no less frequent than annually and at any time upon the reasonable written request of the registered owner, the issuer shall send to the registered owner of each uncertificated security a dated written statement containing:

(a) a description of the issue of which the uncertificated security is a part;

(b) the name and address and any taxpayer identification number of the registered owner;

(c) the number of shares or units of the uncertificated security registered in the name of the registered owner on the date of the statement;

(d) the name and address and any taxpayer identification number of any registered pledgee and the number of shares or units subject to the pledge; and

(e) a notation of any liens and restrictions of the issuer and any adverse claims (as to which the issuer has a duty under Section 8—403(4)) to which the uncertificated security is or may be subject or a statement that there are none of those liens, restrictions, or adverse claims.

(7) At periodic intervals no less frequent than annually and at any time upon the reasonable written request of the registered pledgee, the issuer shall send to the registered pledgee of each uncertificated security a dated written statement containing:

(a) a description of the issue of which the uncertificated security is a part;

(b) the name and address and any taxpayer identification number of the registered owner;

(c) the name and address and any taxpayer identification number of the registered pledgee;

(d) the number of shares or units subject to the pledge; and

(e) a notation of any liens and restrictions of the issuer and any adverse claims (as to which the issuer has a duty under Section 8—403(4)) to which the uncertificated security is or may be subject or a statement that there are none of those liens, restrictions, or adverse claims.

(8) If the issuer sends the statements described in subsections (6) and (7) at periodic intervals no less frequent than quarterly, the issuer is not obliged to send additional statements upon request unless the owner or pledgee requesting them pays to the issuer the reasonable cost of furnishing them.

(9) Each statement sent pursuant to this section must bear a conspicuous legend reading substantially as follows: "This statement is merely a record of the rights of the addressee as of the time of its issuance. Delivery of this statement, of itself, confers no rights on the recipient. This statement is neither a negotiable instrument nor a security."

Added in 1977.

Article 9
Secured Transactions; Sales of Accounts and Chattel Paper

Note: *The adoption of this Article should be accompanied by the repeal of existing statutes dealing with conditional sales, trust receipts, factor's liens where the factor is given a non-possessory lien, chattel mortgages, crop mortgages, mortgages on railroad equipment, assignment of accounts and generally statutes regulating security interests in personal property.*

Where the state has a retail installment selling act or small loan act, that legislation should be carefully examined to determine what changes in those acts are needed to conform them to this Article. This Article primarily sets out rules defining rights of a secured party against persons dealing with the debtor; it does not prescribe regulations and controls which may be necessary to curb abuses arising in the small loan business or in the financing of consumer purchases on credit. Accordingly there is no intention to repeal existing regulatory acts in those fields by enactment or re-enactment of Article 9. See Section 9—203(4) and the Note thereto.

Part 1 Short Title, Applicability and Definitions

§ 9—101. **Short Title.**

This Article shall be known and may be cited as Uniform Commercial Code—Secured Transactions.

§ 9—102. **Policy and Subject Matter of Article.**

(1) Except as otherwise provided in Section 9—104 on excluded transactions, this Article applies

(a) to any transaction (regardless of its form) which is intended to create a security interest in personal property or fixtures including goods, documents, instruments, general intangibles, chattel paper or accounts; and also

(b) to any sale of accounts or chattel paper.

(2) This Article applies to security interests created by contract including pledge, assignment, chattel mortgage, chattel trust, trust deed, factor's lien, equipment trust, conditional sale, trust receipt, other lien or title retention contract and lease or consignment intended as security. This Article does not apply to statutory liens except as provided in Section 9—310.

(3) The application of this Article to a security interest in a secured obligation is not affected by the fact that

the obligation is itself secured by a transaction or interest to which this Article does not apply. Amended in 1972.

§ 9—103. **Perfection of Security Interest in Multiple State Transactions**

(1) Documents, instruments and ordinary goods.

(a) This subsection applies to documents and instruments and to goods other than those covered by a certificate of title described in subsection (2), mobile goods described in subsection (3), and minerals described in subsection (5).

(b) Except as otherwise provided in this subsection, perfection and the effect of perfection or non-perfection of a security interest in collateral are governed by the law of the jurisdiction where the collateral is when the last event occurs on which is based the assertion that the security interest is perfected or unperfected.

(c) If the parties to a transaction creating a purchase money security interest in goods in one jurisdiction understand at the time that the security interest attaches that the goods will be kept in another jurisdiction, then the law of the other jurisdiction governs the perfection and the effect of perfection or non-perfection of the security interest from the time it attaches until thirty days after the debtor receives possession of the goods and thereafter if the goods are taken to the other jurisdiction before the end of the thirty-day period.

(d) When collateral is brought into and kept in this state while subject to a security interest perfected under the law of the jurisdiction from which the collateral was removed, the security interest remains perfected, but if action is required by Part 3 of this Article to perfect the security interest,

(i) if the action is not taken before the expiration of the period of perfection in the other jurisdiction or the end of four months after the collateral is brought into this state, whichever period first expires, the security interest becomes unperfected at the end of that period and is thereafter deemed to have been unperfected as against a person who became a purchaser after removal;

(ii) if the action is taken before the expiration of the period specified in subparagraph (i), the security interest continues perfected thereafter;

(iii) for the purpose of priority over a buyer of consumer goods (subsection (2) of Section 9—307), the period of the effectiveness of a filing in the jurisdiction from which the collateral is removed is governed by the rules with respect to perfection in subparagraphs (i) and (ii).

(2) Certificate of title.

(a) This subsection applies to goods covered by a certificate of title issued under a statute of this state or of another jurisdiction under the law of which indication of a security interest on the certificate is required as a condition of perfection.

(b) Except as otherwise provided in this subsection, perfection and the effect of perfection or non-perfection of the security interest are governed by the law (including the conflict of laws rules) of the jurisdiction issuing the certificate until four months after the goods are removed from that jurisdiction and thereafter until the goods are registered in another jurisdiction, but in any event not beyond surrender of the certificate. After the expiration of that period, the goods are not covered by the certificate of title within the meaning of this section.

(c) Except with respect to the rights of a buyer described in the next paragraph, a security interest, perfected in another jurisdiction otherwise than by notation on a certificate of title, in goods brought into this state and thereafter covered by a certificate of title issued by this state is subject to the rules stated in paragraph (d) of subsection (1).

(d) If goods are brought into this state while a security interest therein is perfected in any manner under the law of the jurisdiction from which the goods are removed and a certificate of title is issued by this state and the certificate does not show that the goods are subject to the security interest or that they may be subject to security interests not shown on the certificate, the security interest is subordinate to the rights of a buyer of the goods who is not in the business of selling goods of that kind to the extent that he gives value and receives delivery of the goods after issuance of the certificate and without knowledge of the security interest.

(3) Accounts, general intangibles and mobile goods.

(a) This subsection applies to accounts (other than an account described in subsection (5) on minerals) and general intangibles (other than uncertificated securities) and to goods which are mobile and which are of a type normally used in more than one jurisdiction, such as motor vehicles, trailers, rolling stock, airplanes, shipping containers, road building and construction machinery and commercial harvesting machinery and the like, if the goods are equipment or are inventory leased or held for lease by the debtor to others, and are not covered by a certificate of title described in subsection (2).

(b) The law (including the conflict of laws rules) of the jurisdiction in which the debtor is located governs the perfection and the effect of perfection or non-perfection of the security interest.

(c) If, however, the debtor is located in a jurisdiction which is not a part of the United States, and which does not provide for perfection of the security interest by filing or recording in that jurisdiction, the law of the jurisdiction in the United States in which the debtor has its major executive office in the United States governs the perfection and the effect of perfection or non-perfection of the security interest through filing. In the alternative, if the debtor is located in a jurisdiction which is not a part of the United States or Canada and the collateral is accounts or general intangibles for money due or to become due, the security interest may be perfected by notification to the account debtor. As used in this paragraph, "United States" includes its territories and possessions and the Commonwealth of Puerto Rico.

(d) A debtor shall be deemed located at his place of business if he has one, at his chief executive office if he has more than one place of business, otherwise at his residence. If, however, the debtor is a foreign air carrier under the Federal Aviation Act of 1958, as amended, it shall be deemed located at the designated office of the agent upon whom service of process may be made on behalf of the foreign air carrier.

(e) A security interest perfected under the law of the jurisdiction of the location of the debtor is perfected until the expiration of four months after a change of the debtor's location to another jurisdiction, or until perfection would have ceased by the law of the first jurisdiction, whichever period first expires. Unless perfected in the new jurisdiction before the end of that period, it becomes unperfected thereafter and is deemed to have been unperfected as against a person who became a purchaser after the change.

(4) Chattel paper.

The rules stated for goods in subsection (1) apply to a possessory security interest in chattel paper. The rules stated for accounts in subsection (3) apply to a non-possessory security interest in chattel paper, but the security interest may not be perfected by notification to the account debtor.

(5) Minerals.

Perfection and the effect of perfection or non-perfection of a security interest which is created by a debtor who has an interest in minerals or the like (including oil and gas) before extraction and which attaches thereto as extracted, or which attaches to an account resulting from the sale thereof at the wellhead or minehead are governed by the law (including the conflict of laws rules) of the jurisdiction wherein the wellhead or minehead is located.

(6) Uncertificated securities.

The law (including the conflict of laws rules) of the jurisdiction of organization of the issuer governs the perfection and the effect of perfection or non-perfection of a security interest in uncertificated securities.

Amended in 1972 and 1977.

§ 9—104. **Transactions Excluded From Article.**

This Article does not apply

(a) to a security interest subject to any statute of the United States, to the extent that such statute governs the rights of parties to and third parties affected by transactions in particular types of property; or

(b) to a landlord's lien; or

(c) to a lien given by statute or other rule of law for services or materials except as provided in Section 9—310 on priority of such liens; or

(d) to a transfer of a claim for wages, salary or other compensation of an employee; or

(e) to a transfer by a government or governmental subdivision or agency; or

(f) to a sale of accounts or chattel paper as part of a sale of the business out of which they arose, or an assignment of accounts or chattel paper which is for the purpose of collection only, or a transfer of a right to payment under a contract to an assignee who is also to do the performance under the contract or a transfer of a single account to an assignee in whole or partial satisfaction of a preexisting indebtedness; or

(g) to a transfer of an interest in or claim in or under any policy of insurance, except as provided with respect to proceeds (Section 9—306) and priorities in proceeds (Section 9—312); or

(h) to a right represented by a judgment (other than a judgment taken on a right to payment which was collateral); or

(i) to any right of set-off; or

(j) except to the extent that provision is made for fixtures in Section 9—313, to the creation or transfer of an interest in or lien on real estate, including a lease or rents thereunder; or

(k) to a transfer in whole or in part of any claim arising out of tort; or

(l) to a transfer of an interest in any deposit account (subsection (1) of Section 9—105), except as provided with respect to proceeds (Section 9—306) and priorities in proceeds (Section 9—312).

Amended in 1972.

§ 9—105. Definitions and Index of Definitions

(1) In this Article unless the context otherwise requires:

(a) "Account debtor" means the person who is obligated on an account, chattel paper or general intangible;

(b) "Chattel paper" means a writing or writings which evidence both a monetary obligation and a security interest in or a lease of specific goods, but a charter or other contract involving the use or hire of a vessel is not chattel paper. When a transaction is evidenced both by such a security agreement or a lease and by an instrument or a series of instruments, the group of writings taken together constitutes chattel paper;

(c) "Collateral" means the property subject to a security interest, and includes accounts and chattel paper which have been sold;

(d) "Debtor" means the person who owes payment or other performance of the obligation secured, whether or not he owns or has rights in the collateral, and includes the seller of accounts or chattel paper. Where the debtor and the owner of the collateral are not the same person, the term "debtor" means the owner of the collateral in any provision of the Article dealing with the collateral, the obligor in any provision dealing with the obligation, and may include both where the context so requires;

(e) "Deposit account" means a demand, time, savings, passbook or like account maintained with a bank, savings and loan association, credit union or like organization, other than an account evidenced by a certificate of deposit;

(f) "Document" means document of title as defined in the general definitions of Article 1 (Section 1—201), and a receipt of the kind described in subsection (2) of Section 7—201;

(g) "Encumbrance" includes real estate mortgages and other liens on real estate and all other rights in real estate that are not ownership interests;

(h) "Goods" includes all things which are movable at the time the security interest attaches or which are fixtures (Section 9—313), but does not include money, documents, instruments, accounts, chattel paper, general intangibles, or minerals or the like (including oil and gas) before extraction. "Goods" also includes standing timber which is to be cut and removed under a conveyance or contract for sale, the unborn young of animals, and growing crops;

(i) "Instrument" means a negotiable instrument (defined in Section 3—104), or a certificated security (defined in Section 8—102) or any other writing which evidences a right to the payment of money and is not itself a security agreement or lease and is of a type which is in ordinary course of business transferred by delivery with any necessary indorsement or assignment;

(j) "Mortgage" means a consensual interest created by a real estate mortgage, a trust deed on real estate, or the like;

(k) An advance is made "pursuant to commitment" if the secured party has bound himself to make it, whether or not a subsequent event of default or other event not within his control has relieved or may relieve him from his obligation;

(l) "Security agreement" means an agreement which creates or provides for a security interest;

(m) "Secured party" means a lender, seller or other person in whose favor there is a security interest, including a person to whom accounts or chattel paper have been sold. When the holders of obligations issued under an indenture of trust, equipment trust agreement or the like are represented by a trustee or other person, the representative is the secured party;

(n) "Transmitting utility" means any person primarily engaged in the railroad, street railway or trolley bus business, the electric or electronics communications transmission business, the transmission of goods by pipeline, or the transmission or the production and transmission of electricity, steam, gas or water, or the provision of sewer service.

(2) Other definitions applying to this Article and the sections in which they appear are:

"Account". Section 9—106.
"Attach". Section 9—203.
"Construction mortgage". Section 9—313(1).
"Consumer goods". Section 9—109(1).
"Equipment". Section 9—109(2).
"Farm products". Section 9—109(3).
"Fixture". Section 9—313(1).
"Fixture filing". Section 9—313(1).
"General intangibles". Section 9—106.
"Inventory". Section 9—109(4).
"Lien creditor". Section 9—301(3).
"Proceeds". Section 9—306(1).
"Purchase money security interest". Section 9—107.
"United States". Section 9—103.

(3) The following definitions in other Articles apply to this Article:

"Check". Section 3—104.
"Contract for sale". Section 2—106.
"Holder in due course". Section 3—302.
"Note". Section 3—104.
"Sale". Section 2—106.

(4) In addition Article 1 contains general definitions and principles of construction and interpretation applicable throughout this Article.

Amended in 1966, 1972 and 1977.

§ 9—106. **Definitions: "Account"; "General Intangibles".**

"Account" means any right to payment for goods sold or leased or for services rendered which is not evidenced by an instrument or chattel paper, whether or not it has been earned by performance. "General intangibles" means any personal property (including things in action) other than goods, accounts, chattel paper, documents, instruments, and money. All rights to payment earned or unearned under a charter or other contract involving the use or hire of a vessel and all rights incident to the charter or contract are accounts. Amended in 1966, 1972.

§ 9—107. **Definitions: "Purchase Money Security Interest".**

A security interest is a "purchase money security interest" to the extent that it is

(a) taken or retained by the seller of the collateral to secure all or part of its price; or

(b) taken by a person who by making advances or incurring an obligation gives value to enable the debtor to acquire rights in or the use of collateral if such value is in fact so used.

§ 9—108. **When After-Acquired Collateral Not Security for Antecedent Debt.**

Where a secured party makes an advance, incurs an obligation, releases a perfected security interest, or otherwise gives new value which is to be secured in whole or in part by after-acquired property his security interest in the after-acquired collateral shall be deemed to be taken for new value and not as security for an antecedent debt if the debtor acquires his rights in such collateral either in the ordinary course of his business or under a contract of purchase made pursuant to the security agreement within a reasonable time after new value is given.

§ 9—109. Classification of Goods; "Consumer Goods"; "Equipment"; "Farm Products"; "Inventory".

Goods are

(1) "consumer goods" if they are used or bought for use primarily for personal, family or household purposes;

(2) "equipment" if they are used or bought for use primarily in business (including farming or a profession) or by a debtor who is a non-profit organization or a governmental subdivision or agency or if the goods are not included in the definitions of inventory, farm products or consumer goods;

(3) "farm products" if they are crops or livestock or supplies used or produced in farming operations or if they are products of crops or livestock in their unmanufactured states (such as ginned cotton, wool-clip, maple syrup, milk and eggs), and if they are in the possession of a debtor engaged in raising, fattening, grazing or other farming operations. If goods are farm products they are neither equipment nor inventory;

(4) "inventory" if they are held by a person who holds them for sale or lease or to be furnished under contracts of service or if he has so furnished them, or if they are raw materials, work in process or materials used or consumed in a business. Inventory of a person is not to be classified as his equipment.

§ 9—110. Sufficiency of Description.

For purposes of this Article any description of personal property or real estate is sufficient whether or not it is specific if it reasonably identifies what is described.

§ 9—111. Applicability of Bulk Transfer Laws.

The creation of a security interest is not a bulk transfer under Article 6 (see Section 6—103).

§ 9—112. Where Collateral Is Not Owned by Debtor.

Unless otherwise agreed, when a secured party knows that collateral is owned by a person who is not the debtor, the owner of the collateral is entitled to

receive from the secured party any surplus under Section 9—502(2) or under Section 9—504(1), and is not liable for the debt or for any deficiency after resale, and he has the same right as the debtor

(a) to receive statements under Section 9—208;

(b) to receive notice of and to object to a secured party's proposal to retain the collateral in satisfaction of the indebtedness under Section 9—505;

(c) to redeem the collateral under Section 9—506;

(d) to obtain injunctive or other relief under Section 9—507(1); and

(e) to recover losses caused to him under Section 9—208(2).

§ 9—113. Security Interests Arising Under Article on Sales.

A security interest arising solely under the Article on Sales (Article 2) is subject to the provisions of this Article except that to the extent that and so long as the debtor does not have or does not lawfully obtain possession of the goods

(a) no security agreement is necessary to make the security interest enforceable; and

(b) no filing is required to perfect the security interest; and

(c) the rights of the secured party on default by the debtor are governed by the Article on Sales (Article 2).

§ 9—114. Consignment.

(1) A person who delivers goods under a consignment which is not a security interest and who would be required to file under this Article by paragraph (3) (c) of Section 2—326 has priority over a secured party who is or becomes a creditor of the consignee and who would have a perfected security interest in the goods if they were the property of the consignee, and also has priority with respect to identifiable cash proceeds received on or before delivery of the goods to a buyer, if

   (a) the consignor complies with the filing provision of the Article on Sales with respect to consignments (paragraph (3) (c) of Section 2—326) before the consignee receives possession of the goods; and

   (b) the consignor gives notification in writing to

the holder of the security interest if the holder has filed a financing statement covering the same types of goods before the date of the filing made by the consignor; and

(c) the holder of the security interest receives the notification within five years before the consignee receives possession of the goods; and

(d) the notification states that the consignor expects to deliver goods on consignment to the consignee, describing the goods by item or type.

(2) In the case of a consignment which is not a security interest and in which the requirements of the preceding subsection have not been met, a person who delivers goods to another is subordinate to a person who would have a perfected security interest in the goods if they were the property of the debtor. Added in 1972.

Part 2 Validity of Security Agreement and Rights of Parties Thereto

§ 9—201. **General Validity of Security Agreement.**

Except as otherwise provided by this Act a security agreement is effective according to its terms between the parties, against purchasers of the collateral and against creditors. Nothing in this Article validates any charge or practice illegal under any statute or regulation thereunder governing usury, small loans, retail installment sales, or the like, or extends the application of any such statute or regulation to any transaction not otherwise subject thereto.

§ 9—202. **Title to Collateral Immaterial.**

Each provision of this Article with regard to rights, obligations and remedies applies whether title to collateral is in the secured party or in the debtor.

§ 9—203. **Attachment and Enforceability of Security Interest; Proceeds; Formal Requisites**

(1) Subject to the provisions of Section 4—208 on the security interest of a collecting bank, Section 8—321 on security interests in securities and Section 9—113 on a security interest arising under the Article on Sales, a security interest is not enforceable against the debtor or third parties with respect to the collateral and does not attach unless:

(a) the collateral is in the possession of the secured party pursuant to agreement, or the debtor has signed a security agreement which contains a description of the collateral and in addition, when the security interest covers crops growing or to be grown or timber to be cut, a description of the land concerned;

(b) value has been given; and

(c) the debtor has rights in the collateral.

(2) A security interest attaches when it becomes enforceable against the debtor with respect to the collateral. Attachment occurs as soon as all of the events specified in subsection (1) have taken place unless explicit agreement postpones the time of attaching.

(3) Unless otherwise agreed a security agreement gives the secured party the rights to proceeds provided by Section 9—306.

(4) A transaction, although subject to this Article, is also subject to . . . . *, and in the case of conflict between the provisions of this Article and any such statute, the provisions of such statute control. Failure to comply with any applicable statute has only the effect which is specified therein.

Amended in 1972 and 1977.

Note: *At * in subsection (4) insert reference to any local statute regulating small loans, retail installment sales and the like.*

The foregoing subsection (4) is designed to make it clear that certain transactions, although subject to this Article, must also comply with other applicable legislation.

This Article is designed to regulate all the "security" aspects of transactions within its scope. There is, however, much regulatory legislation, particularly in the consumer field, which supplements this Article and should not be repealed by its enactment. Examples are small loan acts, retail installment selling acts and the like. Such acts may provide for licensing and rate regulation and may prescribe particular forms of contract. Such provisions should remain in force despite the enactment of this Article. On the other hand if a retail installment selling act contains provisions on filing, rights on default, etc., such provisions should be repealed as inconsistent with this Article except that inconsistent provisions as to deficiencies, penalties, etc., in the Uniform Consumer Credit Code and other recent related legislation should remain because those statutes were drafted after the substantial enactment of the Article and with the intention of modifying certain provisions of this Article as to consumer credit.

§ 9—204. **After-Acquired Property; Future Advances.**

(1) Except as provided in subsection (2), a security agreement may provide that any or all obligations covered by the security agreement are to be secured by after-acquired collateral.

(2) No security interest attaches under an after-acquired property clause to consumer goods other than accessions (Section 9—314) when given as additional security unless the debtor acquires rights in them within ten days after the secured party gives value.

(3) Obligations covered by a security agreement may include future advances or other value whether or not the advances or value are given pursuant to commitment (subsection (1) of Section 9—105). Amended in 1972.

§ 9—205. **Use or Disposition of Collateral Without Accounting Permissible.**

A security interest is not invalid or fraudulent against creditors by reason of liberty in the debtor to use, commingle or dispose of all or part of the collateral (including returned or repossessed goods) or to collect or compromise accounts or chattel paper, or to accept the return of goods or make repossessions, or to use, commingle or dispose of proceeds, or by reason of the failure of the secured party to require the debtor to account for proceeds or replace collateral. This section does not relax the requirements of possession where perfection of a security interest depends upon possession of the collateral by the secured party or by a bailee. Amended in 1972.

§ 9—206. **Agreement Not to Assert Defenses Against Assignee; Modification of Sales Warranties Where Security Agreement Exists.**

(1) Subject to any statute or decision which establishes a different rule for buyers or lessees of consumer goods, an agreement by a buyer or lessee that he will not assert against an assignee any claim or defense which he may have against the seller or lessor is enforceable by an assignee who takes his assignment for value, in good faith and without notice of a claim or defense, except as to defenses of a type which may be asserted against a holder in due course of a negotiable instrument under the Article on Commercial Paper (Article 3). A buyer who as part of one transaction signs both a negotiable instrument and a security agreement makes such an agreement.

(2) When a seller retains a purchase money security interest in goods the Article on Sales (Article 2) governs the sale and any disclaimer, limitation or modification of the seller's warranties. Amended in 1962.

§ 9—207. **Rights and Duties When Collateral is in Secured Party's Possession.**

(1) A secured party must use reasonable care in the custody and preservation of collateral in his possession. In the case of an instrument or chattel paper reasonable care includes taking necessary steps to preserve rights against prior parties unless otherwise agreed.

(2) Unless otherwise agreed, when collateral is in the secured party's possession

(a) reasonable expenses (including the cost of any insurance and payment of taxes or other charges) incurred in the custody, preservation, use or operation of the collateral are chargeable to the debtor and are secured by the collateral;

(b) the risk of accidental loss or damage is on the debtor to the extent of any deficiency in any effective insurance coverage;

(c) the secured party may hold as additional security any increase or profits (except money) received from the collateral, but money so received, unless remitted to the debtor, shall be applied in reduction of the secured obligation;

(d) the secured party must keep the collateral identifiable but fungible collateral may be commingled;

(e) the secured party may repledge the collateral upon terms which do not impair the debtor's right to redeem it.

(3) A secured party is liable for any loss caused by his failure to meet any obligation imposed by the preceding subsections but does not lose his security interest.

(4) A secured party may use or operate the collateral for the purpose of preserving the collateral or its value or pursuant to the order of a court of appropriate jurisdiction or, except in the case of consumer goods, in the manner and to the extent provided in the security agreement.

§ 9—208. **Request for Statement of Account or List of Collateral.**

(1) A debtor may sign a statement indicating what he believes to be the aggregate amount of unpaid indebtedness as of a specified date and may send it to the secured party with a request that the statement be approved or corrected and returned to the debtor. When the security agreement or any other record kept by the secured party identifies the collateral a debtor may similarly request the secured party to approve or correct a list of the collateral.

(2) The secured party must comply with such a request within two weeks after receipt by sending a written correction or approval. If the secured party claims a security interest in all of a particular type of collateral owned by the debtor he may indicate that fact in his reply and need not approve or correct an itemized list of such collateral. If the secured party without reasonable excuse fails to comply he is liable for any loss caused to the debtor thereby; and if the debtor has properly included in his request a good faith statement of the obligation or a list of the collateral or both the secured party may claim a security interest only as shown in the statement against persons misled by his failure to comply. If he no longer has an interest in the obligation or collateral at the time the request is received he must disclose the name and address of any successor in interest known to him and he is liable for any loss caused to the debtor as a result of failure to disclose. A successor in interest is not subject to this section until a request is received by him.

(3) A debtor is entitled to such a statement once every six months without charge. The secured party may require payment of a charge not exceeding $10 for each additional statement furnished.

Part 3 Rights of Third Parties; Perfected and Unperfected Security Interests; Rules of Priority

§ 9—301. **Persons Who Take Priority Over Unperfected Security Interests; Rights of "Lien Creditor".**

(1) Except as otherwise provided in subsection (2), an unperfected security interest is subordinate to the rights of

(a) persons entitled to priority under Section 9—312;

(b) a person who becomes a lien creditor before the security interest is perfected;

(c) in the case of goods, instruments, documents, and chattel paper, a person who is not a secured party and who is a transferee in bulk or other buyer not in ordinary course of business or is a buyer of farm products in ordinary course of business, to the extent that he gives value and receives delivery of the collateral without knowledge of the security interest and before it is perfected;

(d) in the case of accounts and general intangibles, a person who is not a secured party and who is a transferee to the extent that he gives value without knowledge of the security interest and before it is perfected.

(2) If the secured party files with respect to a purchase money security interest before or within ten days after the debtor receives possession of the collateral, he takes priority over the rights of a transferee in bulk or of a lien creditor which arise between the time the security interest attaches and the time of filing.

(3) A "lien creditor" means a creditor who has acquired a lien on the property involved by attachment, levy or the like and includes an assignee for benefit of creditors from the time of assignment, and a trustee in bankruptcy from the date of the filing of the petition or a receiver in equity from the time of appointment.

(4) A person who becomes a lien creditor while a security interest is perfected takes subject to the security interest only to the extent that it secures advances made before he becomes a lien creditor or within 45 days thereafter or made without knowledge of the lien or pursuant to a commitment entered into without knowledge of the lien. Amended in 1972.

§ 9—302. **When Filing Is Required to Perfect Security Interest; Security Interests to Which Filing Provisions of This Article Do Not Apply**

(1) A financing statement must be filed to perfect all security interests except the following:

(a) a security interest in collateral in possession of the secured party under Section 9—305;

(b) a security interest temporarily perfected in instruments or documents without delivery under Section 9—304 or in proceeds for a 10 day period under Section 9—306;

(c) a security interest created by an assignment of a beneficial interest in a trust or a decedent's estate;

(d) a purchase money security interest in consumer goods; but filing is required for a motor vehicle required to be registered; and fixture filing is required for priority over conflicting interests in fixtures to the extent provided in Section 9—313;

(e) an assignment of accounts which does not alone or in conjunction with other assignments to the same assignee transfer a significant part of the outstanding accounts of the assignor;

(f) a security interest of a collecting bank (Section 4—208) or in securities (Section 8—321) or arising under the Article on Sales (see Section 9—113) or covered in subsection (3) of this section;

(g) an assignment for the benefit of all the creditors of the transferor, and subsequent transfers by the assignee thereunder.

(2) If a secured party assigns a perfected security interest, no filing under this Article is required in order to continue the perfected status of the security interest against creditors of and transferees from the original debtor.

(3) The filing of a financing statement otherwise required by this Article is not necessary or effective to perfect a security interest in property subject to

(a) a statute or treaty of the United States which provides for a national or international registration or a national or international certificate of title or which specifies a place of filing different from that specified in this Article for filing of the security interest; or

(b) the following statutes of this state; [list any certificate of title statute covering automobiles, trailers, mobile homes, boats, farm tractors, or the like, and any central filing statute.]; but during any period in which collateral is inventory held for sale by a person who is in the business of selling goods of that kind, the filing provisions of this Article (Part 4) apply to a security interest in that collateral created by him as debtor; or

(c) a certificate of title statute of another jurisdiction under the law of which indication of a security interest on the certificate is required as a condition of perfection (subsection (2) of Section 9—103).

(4) Compliance with a statute or treaty described in subsection (3) is equivalent to the filing of a financing statement under this Article, and a security interest in property subject to the statute or treaty can be perfected only by compliance therewith except as provided in Section 9—103 on multiple state transactions. Duration and renewal of perfection of a security interest perfected by compliance with the statute or treaty are governed by the provisions of the statute or treaty; in other respects the security interest is subject to this Article.

Amended in 1972 and 1977.

§ 9—303. **When Security Interest Is Perfected; Continuity of Perfection.**

(1) A security interest is perfected when it has attached and when all of the applicable steps required for perfection have been taken. Such steps are specified in Sections 9—302, 9—304, 9—305 and 9—306. If such steps are taken before the security interest attaches, it is perfected at the time when it attaches.

(2) If a security interest is originally perfected in any way permitted under this Article and is subsequently perfected in some other way under this Article, without an intermediate period when it was unperfected, the security interest shall be deemed to be perfected continuously for the purposes of this Article.

§ 9—304. **Perfection of Security Interest in Instruments, Documents, and Goods Covered by Documents; Perfection by Permissive Filing; Temporary Perfection Without Filing or Transfer of Possession**

(1) A security interest in chattel paper or negotiable documents may be perfected by filing. A security interest in money or instruments (other than certificated securities or instruments which constitute part of chattel paper) can be perfected only by the secured party's taking possession, except as provided

in subsections (4) and (5) of this section and subsections (2) and (3) of Section 9—306 on proceeds.

(2) During the period that goods are in the possession of the issuer of a negotiable document therefor, a security interest in the goods is perfected by perfecting a security interest in the document, and any security interest in the goods otherwise perfected during such period is subject thereto.

(3) A security interest in goods in the possession of a bailee other than one who has issued a negotiable document therefor is perfected by issuance of a document in the name of the secured party or by the bailee's receipt of notification of the secured party's interest or by filing as to the goods.

(4) A security interest in instruments (other than certificated securities) or negotiable documents is perfected without filing or the taking of possession for a period of 21 days from the time it attaches to the extent that it arises for new value given under a written security agreement.

(5) A security interest remains perfected for a period of 21 days without filing where a secured party having a perfected security interest in an instrument (other than a certificated security), a negotiable document or goods in possession of a bailee other than one who has issued a negotiable document therefor

(a) makes available to the debtor the goods or documents representing the goods for the purpose of ultimate sale or exchange or for the purpose of loading, unloading, storing, shipping, transshipping, manufacturing, processing or otherwise dealing with them in a manner preliminary to their sale or exchange, but priority between conflicting security interests in the goods is subject to subsection (3) of Section 9—312; or

(b) delivers the instrument to the debtor for the purpose of ultimate sale or exchange or of presentation, collection, renewal or registration of transfer.

(6) After the 21 day period in subsections (4) and (5) perfection depends upon compliance with applicable provisions of this Article.

Amended in 1972 and 1977.

§ 9—305. **When Possession by Secured Party Perfects Security Interest Without Filing**

A security interest in letters of credit and advices of credit (subsection (2) (a) of Section 5—116), goods, instruments (other than certificated securities), money, negotiable documents, or chattel paper may be perfected by the secured party's taking possession of the collateral. If such collateral other than goods covered by a negotiable document is held by a bailee, the secured party is deemed to have possession from the time the bailee receives notification of the secured party's interest. A security interest is perfected by possession from the time possession is taken without a relation back and continues only so long as possession is retained, unless otherwise specified in this Article. The security interest may be otherwise perfected as provided in this Article before or after the period of possession by the secured party.

Amended in 1972 and 1977.

§ 9—306. **"Proceeds"; Secured Party's Rights on Disposition of Collateral.**

(1) "Proceeds" includes whatever is received upon the sale, exchange, collection or other disposition of collateral or proceeds. Insurance payable by reason of loss or damage to the collateral is proceeds, except to the extent that it is payable to a person other than a party to the security agreement. Money, checks, deposit accounts, and the like are "cash proceeds". All other proceeds are "non-cash proceeds".

(2) Except where this Article otherwise provides, a security interest continues in collateral notwithstanding sale, exchange or other disposition thereof unless the disposition was authorized by the secured party in the security agreement or otherwise, and also continues in any identifiable proceeds including collections received by the debtor.

(3) The security interest in proceeds is a continuously perfected security interest if the interest in the original collateral was perfected but it ceases to be a perfected security interest and becomes unperfected ten days after receipt of the proceeds by the debtor unless

(a) a filed financing statement covers the original collateral and the proceeds are collateral in which a security interest may be perfected by filing in the office or offices where the financing statement has been filed and, if the proceeds are acquired with cash proceeds, the description of collateral in the financing statement indicates the types of property constituting the proceeds; or

(b) a filed financing statement covers the original collateral and the proceeds are identifiable cash proceeds; or

(c) the security interest in the proceeds is perfected before the expiration of the ten day period.

Except as provided in this section, a security interest in proceeds can be perfected only by the methods or under the circumstances permitted in this Article for original collateral of the same type.

(4) In the event of insolvency proceedings instituted by or against a debtor, a secured party with a perfected security interest in proceeds has a perfected security interest only in the following proceeds:

(a) in identifiable non-cash proceeds and in separate deposit accounts containing only proceeds;

(b) in identifiable cash proceeds in the form of money which is neither commingled with other money nor deposited in a deposit account prior to the insolvency proceedings;

(c) in identifiable cash proceeds in the form of checks and the like which are not deposited in a deposit account prior to the insolvency proceedings; and

(d) in all cash and deposit accounts of the debtor in which proceeds have been commingled with other funds, but the perfected security interest under this paragraph (d) is

(i) subject to any right to set-off; and

(ii) limited to an amount not greater than the amount of any cash proceeds received by the debtor within ten days before the institution of the insolvency proceedings less the sum of (I) the payments to the secured party on account of cash proceeds received by the debtor during such period and (II) the cash proceeds received by the debtor during such period to which the secured party is entitled under paragraphs (a) through (c) of this subsection (4).

(5) If a sale of goods results in an account or chattel paper which is transferred by the seller to a secured party, and if the goods are returned to or are repossessed by the seller or the secured party, the following rules determine priorities:

(a) If the goods were collateral at the time of sale, for an indebtedness of the seller which is still unpaid, the original security interest attaches again to the goods and continues as a perfected security interest if it was perfected at the time when the goods were sold. If the security interest was originally perfected by a filing which is still effective, nothing further is required to continue the perfected status; in any other case, the secured party must take possession of the returned or repossessed goods or must file.

(b) An unpaid transferee of the chattel paper has a security interest in the goods against the transferor. Such security interest is prior to a security interest asserted under paragraph (a) to the extent that the transferee of the chattel paper was entitled to priority under Section 9—308.

(c) An unpaid transferee of the account has a security interest in the goods against the transferor. Such security interest is subordinate to a security interest asserted under paragraph (a).

(d) A security interest of an unpaid transferee asserted under paragraph (b) or (c) must be perfected for protection against creditors of the transferor and purchasers of the returned or repossessed goods.

Amended in 1972.

§ 9—307. **Protection of Buyers of Goods.**

(1) A buyer in ordinary course of business (subsection (9) of Section 1—201) other than a person buying farm products from a person engaged in farming operations takes free of a security interest created by his seller even though the security interest is perfected and even though the buyer knows of its existence.

(2) In the case of consumer goods, a buyer takes free of a security interest even though perfected if he buys without knowledge of the security interest, for value and for his own personal, family or household purposes unless prior to the purchase the secured party has filed a financing statement covering such goods.

(3) A buyer other than a buyer in ordinary course of business (subsection (1) of this section) takes free of a security interest to the extent that it secures future advances made after the secured party acquires knowledge of the purchase, or more than 45 days

after the purchase, whichever first occurs, unless made pursuant to a commitment entered into without knowledge of the purchase and before the expiration of the 45 day period. Amended in 1972.

§ 9—308. **Purchase of Chattel Paper and Instruments.**

A purchaser of chattel paper or an instrument who gives new value and takes possession of it in the ordinary course of his business has priority over a security interest in the chattel paper or instrument

(a) which is perfected under Section 9—304 (permissive filing and temporary perfection) or under Section 9—306 (perfection as to proceeds) if he acts without knowledge that the specific paper or instrument is subject to a security interest; or

(b) which is claimed merely as proceeds of inventory subject to a security interest (Section 9—306) even though he knows that the specific paper or instrument is subject to the security interest.

Amended in 1972.

§ 9—309. **Protection of Purchasers of Instruments, Documents and Securities**

Nothing in this Article limits the rights of a holder in due course of a negotiable instrument (Section 3—302) or a holder to whom a negotiable document of title has been duly negotiated (Section 7—501) or a bona fide purchaser of a security (Section 8—302) and the holders or purchasers take priority over an earlier security interest even though perfected. Filing under this Article does not constitute notice of the security interest to such holders or purchasers.
Amended in 1977.

§ 9—310. **Priority of Certain Liens Arising by Operation of Law.**

When a person in the ordinary course of his business furnishes services or materials with respect to goods subject to a security interest, a lien upon goods in the possession of such person given by statute or rule of law for such materials or services takes priority over a perfected security interest unless the lien is statutory and the statute expressly provides otherwise.

§ 9—311. **Alienability of Debtor's Rights: Judicial Process.**

The debtor's rights in collateral may be voluntarily or involuntarily transferred (by way of sale, creation of a security interest, attachment, levy, garnishment or other judicial process) notwithstanding a provision in the security agreement prohibiting any transfer or making the transfer constitute a default.

§ 9—312. **Priorities Among Conflicting Security Interests in the Same Collateral**

(1) The rules of priority stated in other sections of this Part and in the following sections shall govern when applicable: Section 4—208 with respect to the security interests of collecting banks in items being collected, accompanying documents and proceeds; Section 9—103 on security interests related to other jurisdictions; Section 9—114 on consignments.

(2) A perfected security interest in crops for new value given to enable the debtor to produce the crops during the production season and given not more than three months before the crops become growing crops by planting or otherwise takes priority over an earlier perfected security interest to the extent that such earlier interest secures obligations due more than six months before the crops become growing crops by planting or otherwise, even though the person giving new value had knowledge of the earlier security interest.

(3) A perfected purchase money security interest in inventory has priority over a conflicting security interest in the same inventory and also has priority in identifiable cash proceeds received on or before the delivery of the inventory to a buyer if

(a) the purchase money security interest is perfected at the time the debtor receives possession of the inventory; and

(b) the purchase money secured party gives notification in writing to the holder of the conflicting security interest if the holder had filed a financing statement covering the same types of inventory (i) before the date of the filing made by the purchase money secured party, or (ii) before the beginning of the 21 day period where the purchase money security interest is temporarily perfected without filing or possession (subsection (5) of Section 9—304); and

(c) the holder of the conflicting security interest receives the notification within five years before the debtor receives possession of the inventory; and

(d) the notification states that the person giving the notice has or expects to acquire a purchase money security interest in inventory of the debtor, describing such inventory by item or type.

(4) A purchase money security interest in collateral other than inventory has priority over a conflicting security interest in the same collateral or its proceeds if the purchase money security interest is perfected at the time the debtor receives possession of the collateral or within ten days thereafter.

(5) In all cases not governed by other rules stated in this section (including cases of purchase money security interests which do not qualify for the special priorities set forth in subsections (3) and (4) of this section), priority between conflicting security interests in the same collateral shall be determined according to the following rules:

(a) Conflicting security interests rank according to priority in time of filing or perfection. Priority dates from the time a filing is first made covering the collateral or the time the security interest is first perfected, whichever is earlier, provided that there is no period thereafter when there is neither filing nor perfection.

(b) So long as conflicting security interests are unperfected, the first to attach has priority.

(6) For the purposes of subsection (5) a date of filing or perfection as to collateral is also a date of filing or perfection as to proceeds.

(7) If future advances are made while a security interest is perfected by filing, the taking of possession, or under Section 8—321 on securities, the security interest has the same priority for the purposes of subsection (5) with respect to the future advances as it does with respect to the first advance. If a commitment is made before or while the security interest is so perfected, the security interest has the same priority with respect to advances made pursuant thereto. In other cases a perfected security interest has priority from the date the advance is made.

Amended in 1972 and 1977.

§ 9—313. **Priority of Security Interests in Fixtures.**

(1) In this section and in the provisions of Part 4 of this Article referring to fixture filing, unless the context otherwise requires

(a) goods are "fixtures" when they become so related to particular real estate that an interest in them arises under real estate law

(b) a "fixture filing" is the filing in the office where a mortgage on the real estate would be filed or recorded of a financing statement covering goods which are or are to become fixtures and conforming to the requirements of subsection (5) of Section 9—402

(c) a mortgage is a "construction mortgage" to the extent that it secures an obligation incurred for the construction of an improvement on land including the acquisition cost of the land, if the recorded writing so indicates.

(2) A security interest under this Article may be created in goods which are fixtures or may continue in goods which become fixtures, but no security interest exists under this Article in ordinary building materials incorporated into an improvement on land.

(3) This Article does not prevent creation of an encumbrance upon fixtures pursuant to real estate law.

(4) A perfected security interest in fixtures has priority over the conflicting interest of an encumbrancer or owner of the real estate where

(a) the security interest is a purchase money security interest, the interest of the encumbrancer or owner arises before the goods become fixtures, the security interest is perfected by a fixture filing before the goods become fixtures or within ten days thereafter, and the debtor has an interest of record in the real estate or is in possession of the real estate; or

(b) the security interest is perfected by a fixture filing before the interest of the encumbrancer or owner is of record, the security interest has priority over any conflicting interest of a predecessor in title of the encumbrancer or owner, and the debtor has an interest of record in the real estate or is in possession of the real estate; or

(c) the fixtures are readily removable factory or office machines or readily removable replacements of domestic applicances which are consumer goods, and before the goods become fixtures the security interest is perfected by any method permitted by this Article; or

(d) the conflicting interest is a lien on the real estate obtained by legal or equitable proceedings after the security interest was perfected by any method permitted by this Article.

(5) A security interest in fixtures, whether or not perfected, has priority over the conflicting interest of an encumbrancer or owner of the real estate where

(a) the encumbrancer or owner has consented in writing to the security interest or has disclaimed an interest in the goods as fixtures; or

(b) the debtor has a right to remove the goods as against the encumbrancer or owner. If the debtor's right terminates, the priority of the security interest continues for a reasonable time.

(6) Notwithstanding paragraph (a) of subsection (4) but otherwise subject to subsections (4) and (5), a security interest in fixtures is subordinate to a construction mortgage recorded before the goods become fixtures if the goods become fixtures before the completion of the construction. To the extent that it is given to refinance a construction mortgage, a mortgage has this priority to the same extent as the construction mortgage.

(7) In cases not within the preceding subsections, a security interest in fixtures is subordinate to the conflicting interest of an encumbrancer or owner of the related real estate who is not the debtor.

(8) When the secured party has priority over all owners and encumbrancers of the real estate, he may, on default, subject to the provisions of Part 5, remove his collateral from the real estate but he must reimburse any encumbrancer or owner of the real estate who is not the debtor and who has not otherwise agreed for the cost of repair of any physical injury, but not for any diminution in value of the real estate caused by the absence of the goods removed or by any necessity of replacing them. A person entitled to reimbursement may refuse permission to remove until the secured party gives adequate security for the performance of this obligation. Amended in 1972.

§ 9—314. **Accessions.**

(1) A security interest in goods which attaches before they are installed in or affixed to other goods takes priority as to the goods installed or affixed (called in this section "accessions") over the claims of all persons to the whole except as stated in subsection (3) and subject to Section 9—315(1).

(2) A security interest which attaches to goods after they become part of a whole is valid against all persons subsequently acquiring interests in the whole except as stated in subsection (3) but is invalid against any person with an interest in the whole at the time the security interest attaches to the goods who has not in writing consented to the security interest or disclaimed an interest in the goods as part of the whole.

(3) The security interests described in subsections (1) and (2) do not take priority over

(a) a subsequent purchaser for value of any interest in the whole; or

(b) a creditor with a lien on the whole subsequently obtained by judicial proceedings; or

(c) a creditor with a prior perfected security interest in the whole to the extent that he makes subsequent advances

if the subsequent purchase is made, the lien by judicial proceedings obtained or the subsequent advance under the prior perfected security interest is made or contracted for without knowledge of the security interest and before it is perfected. A purchaser of the whole at a foreclosure sale other than the holder of a perfected security interest purchasing at his own foreclosure sale is a subsequent purchaser within this section.

(4) When under subsections (1) or (2) and (3) a secured party has an interest in accessions which has priority over the claims of all persons who have interests in the whole, he may on default subject to the provisions of Part 5 remove his collateral from the whole but he must reimburse any encumbrancer or owner of the whole who is not the debtor and who has not otherwise agreed for the cost of repair of any physical injury but not for any diminution in value of the whole caused by the absence of the goods removed or by any necessity for replacing them. A person entitled to reimbursement may refuse permission to remove until the secured party gives adequate security for the performance of this obligation.

§ 9—315. **Priority When Goods Are Commingled or Processed.**

(1) If a security interest in goods was perfected and subsequently the goods or a part thereof have become part of a product or mass, the security interest continues in the product or mass if

(a) the goods are so manufactured, processed, assembled or commingled that their identity is lost in the product or mass; or

(b) a financing statement covering the original goods also covers the product into which the goods have been manufactured, processed or assembled.

In a case to which paragraph (b) applies, no separate security interest in that part of the original goods which has been manufactured, processed or assembled into the product may be claimed under Section 9—314.

(2) When under subsection (1) more than one security interest attaches to the product or mass, they rank equally according to the ratio that the cost of the goods to which each interest originally attached bears to the cost of the total product or mass.

§ 9—316. **Priority Subject to Subordination.**

Nothing in this Article prevents subordination by agreement by any person entitled to priority.

§ 9—317. **Secured Party Not Obligated on Contract of Debtor.**

The mere existence of a security interest or authority given to the debtor to dispose of or use collateral does not impose contract or tort liability upon the secured party for the debtor's acts or omissions.

§ 9—318. **Defenses Against Assignee; Modification of Contract After Notification of Assignment; Term Prohibiting Assignment Ineffective; Identification and Proof of Assignment.**

(1) Unless an account debtor has made an enforceable agreement not to assert defenses or claims arising out of a sale as provided in Section 9—206 the rights of an assignee are subject to

(a) all the terms of the contract between the account debtor and assignor and any defense or claim arising therefrom; and

(b) any other defense or claim of the account debtor against the assignor which accrues before the account debtor receives notification of the assignment.

(2) So far as the right to payment or a part thereof under an assigned contract has not been fully earned by performance, and notwithstanding notification of the assignment, any modification of or substitution for the contract made in good faith and in accordance with reasonable commercial standards is effective against an assignee unless the account debtor has otherwise agreed but the assignee acquires corresponding rights under the modified or substituted contract. The assignment may provide that such modification or substitution is a breach by the assignor.

(3) The account debtor is authorized to pay the assignor until the account debtor receives notification that the amount due or to become due has been assigned and that payment is to be made to the assignee. A notification which does not reasonably identify the rights assigned is ineffective. If requested by the account debtor, the assignee must seasonably furnish reasonable proof that the assignment has been made and unless he does so the account debtor may pay the assignor.

(4) A term in any contract between an account debtor and an assignor is ineffective if it prohibits assignment of an account or prohibits creation of a security interest in a general intangible for money due or to become due or requires the account debtor's consent to such assignment or security interest. Amended in 1972.

Part 4 Filing

§ 9—401. **Place of Filing; Erroneous Filing; Removal of Collateral.**

First Alternative Subsection (1)

(1) The proper place to file in order to perfect a security interest is as follows:

(a) when the collateral is timber to be cut or is minerals or the like (including oil and gas) or accounts subject to subsection (5) of Section 9—103, or when the financing statement is filed as a fixture filing (Section 9—313) and the collateral is goods which are or are to become fixtures, then in the office where a mortgage on the real estate would be filed or recorded;

(b) in all other cases, in the office of the [Secretary of State].

Second Alternative Subsection (1)

(1) The proper place to file in order to perfect a security interest is as follows:

(a) when the collateral is equipment used in farming operations, or farm products, or accounts or general intangibles arising from or relating to the sale of farm products by a farmer, or consumer goods, then in the office of the . . . . in the county of the debtor's residence or if the debtor is not a resident of this state then in the office of the . . . . in the county where the goods are kept, and in addition when the collateral is crops growing or to be grown in the office of the . . . . in the county where the land is located;

(b) when the collateral is timber to be cut or is minerals or the like (including oil and gas) or accounts subject to subsection (5) of Section 9—103, or when the financing statement is filed as a fixture filing (Section 9—313) and the collateral is goods which are or are to become fixtures, then in the office where a mortgage on the real estate would be filed or recorded;

(c) in all other cases, in the office of the [Secretary of State].

Third Alternative Subsection (1)

(1) The proper place to file in order to perfect a security interest is as follows:

(a) when the collateral is equipment used in farming operations, or farm products, or accounts or general intangibles arising from or relating to the sale of farm products by a farmer, or consumer goods, then in the office of the . . . . in the county of the debtor's residence or if the debtor is not a resident of this state then in the office of the . . . . in the county where the goods are kept, and in addition when the collateral is crops growing or to be grown in the office of the . . . . in the county where the land is located;

(b) when the collateral is timber to be cut or is minerals or the like (including oil and gas) or accounts subject to subsection (5) of Section 9—103, or when the financing statement is filed as a fixture filing (Section 9—313) and the collateral is goods which are or are to become fixtures, then

in the office where a mortgage on the real estate would be filed or recorded;

(c) in all other cases, in the office of the [Secretary of State] and in addition, if the debtor has a place of business in only one county of this state, also in the office of . . . . of such county, or, if the debtor has no place of business in this state, but resides in the state, also in the office of . . . . of the county in which he resides.

Note: *One of the three alternatives should be selected as subsection (1).*

(2) A filing which is made in good faith in an improper place or not in all of the places required by this section is nevertheless effective with regard to any collateral as to which the filing complied with the requirements of this Article and is also effective with regard to collateral covered by the financing statement against any person who has knowledge of the contents of such financing statement.

(3) A filing which is made in the proper place in this state continues effective even though the debtor's residence or place of business or the location of the collateral or its use, whichever controlled the original filing, is thereafter changed.

Alternative Subsection (3)

[(3) A filing which is made in the proper county continues effective for four months after a change to another county of the debtor's residence or place of business or the location of the collateral, whichever controlled the original filing. It becomes ineffective thereafter unless a copy of the financing statement signed by the secured party is filed in the new county within said period. The security interest may also be perfected in the new county after the expiration of the four-month period; in such case perfection dates from the time of perfection in the new county. A change in the use of the collateral does not impair the effectiveness of the original filing.]

(4) The rules stated in Section 9—103 determine whether filing is necessary in this state.

(5) Notwithstanding the preceding subsections, and subject to subsection (3) of Section 9—302, the proper place to file in order to perfect a security interest in collateral, including fixtures, of a transmitting utility is the office of the [Secretary of State]. This filing constitutes a fixture filing (Section 9—313) as to the

collateral described therein which is or is to become fixtures.

(6) For the purposes of this section, the residence of an organization is its place of business if it has one or its chief executive office if it has more than one place of business. Amended in 1962 and 1972.

Note: *Subsection (6) should be used only if the state chooses the Second or Third Alternative Subsection (1).*

§ 9—402. **Formal Requisites of Financing Statement; Amendments; Mortgage as Financing Statement.**

(1) A financing statement is sufficient if it gives the names of the debtor and the secured party, is signed by the debtor, gives an address of the secured party from which information concerning the security interest may be obtained, gives a mailing address of the debtor and contains a statement indicating the types, or describing the items, of collateral. A financing statement may be filed before a security agreement is made or a security interest otherwise attaches. When the financing statement covers crops growing or to be grown, the statement must also contain a description of the real estate concerned. When the financing statement covers timber to be cut or covers minerals or the like (including oil and gas) or accounts subject to subsection (5) of Section 9—103, or when the financing statement is filed as a fixture filing (Section 9—313) and the collateral is goods which are or are to become fixtures, the statement must also comply with subsection (5). A copy of the security agreement is sufficient as a financing statement if it contains the above information and is signed by the debtor. A carbon, photographic or other reproduction of a security agreement or a financing statement is sufficient as a financing statement if the security agreement so provides or if the original has been filed in this state.

(2) A financing statement which otherwise complies with subsection (1) is sufficient when it is signed by the secured party instead of the debtor if it is filed to perfect a security interest in

(a) collateral already subject to a security interest in another jurisdiction when it is brought into this state, or when the debtor's location is changed to this state. Such a financing statement must state that the collateral was brought into this state or that the debtor's location was changed to this state under such circumstances; or

(b) proceeds under Section 9—306 if the security interest in the original collateral was perfected. Such a financing statement must describe the original collateral; or

(c) collateral as to which the filing has lapsed; or

(d) collateral acquired after a change of name, identity or corporate structure of the debtor (subsection (7)).

(3) A form substantially as follows is sufficient to comply with subsection (1):

Name of debtor (or assignor)...................................

Address...

Name of secured party (or assignee)......................

Address...

1. This financing statement covers the following types (or items) of property:

(Describe)...

2. (If collateral is crops) The above described crops are growing or are to be grown on:

(Describe Real Estate).......................................

3. (If applicable) The above goods are to become fixtures on *

*Where appropriate substitute either ''The above timber is standing on . . . . '' or ''The above minerals or the like (including oil and gas) or accounts will be financed at the wellhead or minehead of the well or mine located on . . . . .''

(Describe Real Estate).......................................

and this financing statement is to be filed [for record] in the real estate records. (If the debtor does not have an interest of record) The name of a record owner is...

4. (If products of collateral are claimed) Products of the collateral are also covered.

(use	....
whichever	Signature of Debtor (or Assignor)
is	....
applicable)	Signature of Secured Party (or Assignee)

(4) A financing statement may be amended by filing a writing signed by both the debtor and the secured

party. An amendment does not extend the period of effectiveness of a financing statement. If any amendment adds collateral, it is effective as to the added collateral only from the filing date of the amendment. In this Article, unless the context otherwise requires, the term "financing statement" means the original financing statement and any amendments.

(5) A financing statement covering timber to be cut or covering minerals or the like (including oil and gas) or accounts subject to subsection (5) of Section 9—103, or a financing statement filed as a fixture filing (Section 9—313) where the debtor is not a transmitting utility, must show that it covers this type of collateral, must recite that it is to be filed [for record] in the real estate records, and the financing statement must contain a description of the real estate [sufficient if it were contained in a mortgage of the real estate to give constructive notice of the mortgage under the law of this state]. If the debtor does not have an interest of record in the real estate, the financing statement must show the name of a record owner.

(6) A mortgage is effective as a financing statement filed as a fixture filing from the date of its recording if

(a) the goods are described in the mortgage by item or type; and

(b) the goods are or are to become fixtures related to the real estate described in the mortgage; and

(b) the mortgage complies with the requirements for a financing statement in this section other than a recital that it is to be filed in the real estate records; and

(d) the mortgage is duly recorded.

No fee with reference to the financing statement is required other than the regular recording and satisfaction fees with respect to the mortgage.

(7) A financing statement sufficiently shows the name of the debtor if it gives the individual, partnership or corporate name of the debtor, whether or not it adds other trade names or names of partners. Where the debtor so changes his name or in the case of an organization its name, identity or corporate structure that a filed financing statement becomes seriously misleading, the filing is not effective to perfect a security interest in collateral acquired by the debtor more than four months after the change, unless a new appropriate financing statement is filed before the expiration of that time. A filed financing statement remains effective with respect to collateral transferred by the debtor even though the secured party knows of or consents to the transfer.

(8) A financing statement substantially complying with the requirements of this section is effective even though it contains minor errors which are not seriously misleading. Amended in 1972.

Note: *Language in brackets is optional.*

Note: *Where the state has any special recording system for real estate other than the usual grantor-grantee index (as, for instance, a tract system or a title registration or Torrens system) local adaptations of subsection (5) and Section 9—403(7) may be necessary. See Mass.Gen.Laws Chapter 106, Section 9—409.*

§ 9—403. What Constitutes Filing; Duration of Filing; Effect of Lapsed Filing; Duties of Filing Officer.

(1) Presentation for filing of a financing statement and tender of the filing fee or acceptance of the statement by the filing officer constitutes filing under this Article.

(2) Except as provided in subsection (6) a filed financing statement is effective for a period of five years from the date of filing. The effectiveness of a filed financing statement lapses on the expiration of the five year period unless a continuation statement is filed prior to the lapse. If a security interest perfected by filing exists at the time insolvency proceedings are commenced by or against the debtor, the security interest remains perfected until termination of the insolvency proceedings and thereafter for a period of sixty days or until expiration of the five year period, whichever occurs later. Upon lapse the security interest becomes unperfected, unless it is perfected without filing. If the security interest becomes unperfected upon lapse, it is deemed to have been unperfected as against a person who became a purchaser or lien creditor before lapse.

(3) A continuation statement may be filed by the secured party within six months prior to the expiration of the five year period specified in subsection (2). Any such continuation statement must be signed by the secured party, identify the original statement by

file number and state that the original statement is still effective. A continuation statement signed by a person other than the secured party of record must be accompanied by a separate written statement of assignment signed by the secured party of record and complying with subsection (2) of Section 9—405, including payment of the required fee. Upon timely filing of the continuation statement, the effectiveness of the original statement is continued for five years after the last date to which the filing was effective whereupon it lapses in the same manner as provided in subsection (2) unless another continuation statement is filed prior to such lapse. Succeeding continuation statements may be filed in the same manner to continue the effectiveness of the original statement. Unless a statute on disposition of public records provides otherwise, the filing officer may remove a lapsed statement from the files and destroy it immediately if he has retained a microfilm or other photographic record, or in other cases after one year after the lapse. The filing officer shall so arrange matters by physical annexation of financing statements to continuation statements or other related filings, or by other means, that if he physically destroys the financing statements of a period more than five years past, those which have been continued by a continuation statement or which are still effective under subsection (6) shall be retained.

(4) Except as provided in subsection (7) a filing officer shall mark each statement with a file number and with the date and hour of filing and shall hold the statement or a microfilm or other photographic copy thereof for public inspection. In addition the filing officer shall index the statement according to the name of the debtor and shall note in the index the file number and the address of the debtor given in the statement.

(5) The uniform fee for filing and indexing and for stamping a copy furnished by the secured party to show the date and place of filing for an original financing statement or for a continuation statement shall be $.......... if the statement is in the standard form prescribed by the [Secretary of State] and otherwise shall be $.........., plus in each case, if the financing statement is subject to subsection (5) of Section 9—402, $........... The uniform fee for each name more than one required to be indexed shall be

$........... The secured party may at his option show a trade name for any person and an extra uniform indexing fee of $.......... shall be paid with respect thereto.

(6) If the debtor is a transmitting utility (subsection (5) of Section 9—401) and a filed financing statement so states, it is effective until a termination statement is filed. A real estate mortgage which is effective as a fixture filing under subsection (6) of Section 9—402 remains effective as a fixture filing until the mortgage is released or satisfied of record or its effectiveness otherwise terminates as to the real estate.

(7) When a financing statement covers timber to be cut or covers minerals or the like (including oil and gas) or accounts subject to subsection (5) of Section 9—103, or is filed as a fixture filing, [it shall be filed for record and] the filing officer shall index it under the names of the debtor and any owner of record shown on the financing statement in the same fashion as if they were the mortgagors in a mortgage of the real estate described, and, to the extent that the law of this state provides for indexing of mortgages under the name of the mortgagee, under the name of the secured party as if he were the mortgagee thereunder, or where indexing is by description in the same fashion as if the financing statement were a mortgage of the real estate described. Amended in 1972.

Note: *In states in which writings will not appear in the real estate records and indices unless actually recorded the bracketed language in subsection (7) should be used.*

§ 9—404. **Termination Statement.**

(1) If a financing statement covering consumer goods is filed on or after ...., then within one month or within ten days following written demand by the debtor after there is no outstanding secured obligation and no commitment to make advances, incur obligations or otherwise give value, the secured party must file with each filing officer with whom the financing statement was filed, a termination statement to the effect that he no longer claims a security interest under the financing statement, which shall be identified by file number. In other cases whenever there is no outstanding secured obligation and no commitment to make advances, incur obligations or otherwise give value, the secured party must on written demand by the debtor send the debtor, for

each filing officer with whom the financing statement was filed, a termination statement to the effect that he no longer claims a security interest under the financing statement, which shall be identified by file number. A termination statement signed by a person other than the secured party of record must be accompanied by a separate written statement of assignment signed by the secured party of record complying with subsection (2) of Section 9—405, including payment of the required fee. If the affected secured party fails to file such a termination statement as required by this subsection, or to send such a termination statement within ten days after proper demand therefor, he shall be liable to the debtor for one hundred dollars, and in addition for any loss caused to the debtor by such failure.

(2) On presentation to the filing officer of such a termination statement he must note it in the index. If he has received the termination statement in duplicate, he shall return one copy of the termination statement to the secured party stamped to show the time of receipt thereof. If the filing officer has a microfilm or other photographic record of the financing statement, and of any related continuation statement, statement of assignment and statement of release, he may remove the originals from the files at any time after receipt of the termination statement, or if he has no such record, he may remove them from the files at any time after one year after receipt of the termination statement.

(3) If the termination statement is in the standard form prescribed by the [Secretary of State], the uniform fee for filing and indexing the termination statement shall be $......, and otherwise shall be $......, plus in each case an additional fee of $...... for each name more than one against which the termination statement is required to be indexed. Amended in 1972.

Note: *The date to be inserted should be the effective date of the revised Article 9.*

§ 9—405. **Assignment of Security Interest; Duties of Filing Officer; Fees.**

(1) A financing statement may disclose an assignment of a security interest in the collateral described in the financing statement by indication in the financing statement of the name and address of the assignee or by an assignment itself or a copy thereof on the face or back of the statement. On presentation to the filing officer of such a financing statement the filing officer shall mark the same as provided in Section 9—403(4). The uniform fee for filing, indexing and furnishing filing data for a financing statement so indicating an assignment shall be $...... if the statement is in the standard form prescribed by the [Secretary of State] and otherwise shall be $......, plus in each case an additional fee of $...... for each name more than one against which the financing statement is required to be indexed.

(2) A secured party may assign of record all or part of his rights under a financing statement by the filing in the place where the original financing statement was filed of a separate written statement of assignment signed by the secured party of record and setting forth the name of the secured party of record and the debtor, the file number and the date of filing of the financing statement and the name and address of the assignee and containing a description of the collateral assigned. A copy of the assignment is sufficient as a separate statement if it complies with the preceding sentence. On presentation to the filing officer of such a separate statement, the filing officer shall mark such separate statement with the date and hour of the filing. He shall note the assignment on the index of the financing statement, or in the case of a fixture filing, or a filing covering timber to be cut, or covering minerals or the like (including oil and gas) or accounts subject to subsection (5) of Section 9—103, he shall index the assignment under the name of the assignor as grantor and, to the extent that the law of this state provides for indexing the assignment of a mortgage under the name of the assignee, he shall index the assignment of the financing statement under the name of the assignee. The uniform fee for filing, indexing and furnishing filing data about such a separate statement of assignment shall be $...... if the statement is in the standard form prescribed by the [Secretary of State] and otherwise shall be $......, plus in each case an additional fee of $...... for each name more than one against which the statement of assignment is required to be indexed. Notwithstanding the provisions of this subsection, an assignment of record of a security interest in a fixture contained in a mortgage effective as a fixture filing (subsection (6) of

Section 9—402) may be made only by an assignment of the mortgage in the manner provided by the law of this state other than this Act.

(3) After the disclosure or filing of an assignment under this section, the assignee is the secured party of record. Amended in 1972.

§ 9—406. Release of Collateral; Duties of Filing Officer; Fees.

A secured party of record may by his signed statement release all or a part of any collateral described in a filed financing statement. The statement of release is sufficient if it contains a description of the collateral being released, the name and address of the debtor, the name and address of the secured party, and the file number of the financing statement. A statement of release signed by a person other than the secured party of record must be accompanied by a separate written statement of assignment signed by the secured party of record and complying with subsection (2) of Section 9—405, including payment of the required fee. Upon presentation of such a statement of release to the filing officer he shall mark the statement with the hour and date of filing and shall note the same upon the margin of the index of the filing of the financing statement. The uniform fee for filing and noting such a statement of release shall be $...... if the statement is in the standard form prescribed by the [Secretary of State] and otherwise shall be $......, plus in each case an additional fee of $...... for each name more than one against which the statement of release is required to be indexed. Amended in 1972.

[§ 9—407. Information From Filing Officer].

[(1) If the person filing any financing statement, termination statement, statement of assignment, or statement of release, furnishes the filing officer a copy thereof, the filing officer shall upon request note upon the copy the file number and date and hour of the filing of the original and deliver or send the copy to such person.]

[(2) Upon request of any person, the filing officer shall issue his certificate showing whether there is on file on the date and hour stated therein, any presently effective financing statement naming a particular debtor and any statement of assignment thereof and if there is, giving the date and hour of filing of each such statement and the names and addresses of each secured party therein. The uniform fee for such a certificate shall be $...... if the request for the certificate is in the standard form prescribed by the [Secretary of State] and otherwise shall be $....... Upon request the filing officer shall furnish a copy of any filed financing statement or statement of assignment for a uniform fee of $...... per page.] Amended in 1972.

Note: *This section is proposed as an optional provision to require filing officers to furnish certificates. Local law and practices should be consulted with regard to the advisability of adoption.*

§ 9—408. Financing Statements Covering Consigned or Leased Goods.

A consignor or lessor of goods may file a financing statement using the terms "consignor," "consignee," "lessor," "lessee" or the like instead of the terms specified in Section 9—402. The provisions of this Part shall apply as appropriate to such a financing statement but its filing shall not of itself be a factor in determining whether or not the consignment or lease is intended as security (Section 1—201(37)). However, if it is determined for other reasons that the consignment or lease is so intended, a security interest of the consignor or lessor which attaches to the consigned or leased goods is perfected by such filing. Added in 1972.

Part 5 Default

§ 9—501. Default; Procedure When Security Agreement Covers Both Real and Personal Property.

(1) When a debtor is in default under a security agreement, a secured party has the rights and remedies provided in this Part and except as limited by subsection (3) those provided in the security agreement. He may reduce his claim to judgment, foreclose or otherwise enforce the security interest by any available judicial procedure. If the collateral is documents the secured party may proceed either as to the documents or as to the goods covered thereby. A secured party in possession has the rights, remedies and duties provided in Section 9—207. The rights and remedies referred to in this subsection are cumulative.

(2) After default, the debtor has the rights and remedies provided in this Part, those provided in the security agreement and those provided in Section 9—207.

(3) To the extent that they give rights to the debtor and impose duties on the secured party, the rules stated in the subsections referred to below may not be waived or varied except as provided with respect to compulsory disposition of collateral (subsection (3) of Section 9—504 and Section 9—505) and with respect to redemption of collateral (Section 9—506) but the parties may by agreement determine the standards by which the fulfillment of these rights and duties is to be measured if such standards are not manifestly unreasonable:

(a) subsection (2) of Section 9—502 and subsection (2) of Section 9—504 insofar as they require accounting for surplus proceeds of collateral;

(b) subsection (3) of Section 9—504 and subsection (1) of Section 9—505 which deal with disposition of collateral;

(c) subsection (2) of Section 9—505 which deals with acceptance of collateral as discharge of obligation;

(d) Section 9—506 which deals with redemption of collateral; and

(e) subsection (1) of Section 9—507 which deals with the secured party's liability for failure to comply with this Part.

(4) If the security agreement covers both real and personal property, the secured party may proceed under this Part as to the personal property or he may proceed as to both the real and the personal property in accordance with his rights and remedies in respect of the real property in which case the provisions of this Part do not apply.

(5) When a secured party has reduced his claim to judgment the lien of any levy which may be made upon his collateral by virtue of any execution based upon the judgment shall relate back to the date of the perfection of the security interest in such collateral. A judicial sale, pursuant to such execution, is a foreclosure of the security interest by judicial procedure within the meaning of this section, and the secured party may purchase at the sale and thereafter hold the collateral free of any other requirements of this Article. Amended in 1972.

§ 9—502. **Collection Rights of Secured Party.**

(1) When so agreed and in any event on default the secured party is entitled to notify an account debtor or the obligor on an instrument to make payment to him whether or not the assignor was theretofore making collections on the collateral, and also to take control of any proceeds to which he is entitled under Section 9—306.

(2) A secured party who by agreement is entitled to charge back uncollected collateral or otherwise to full or limited recourse against the debtor and who undertakes to collect from the account debtors or obligors must proceed in a commercially reasonable manner and may deduct his reasonable expenses of realization from the collections. If the security agreement secures an indebtedness, the secured party must account to the debtor for any surplus, and unless otherwise agreed, the debtor is liable for any deficiency. But, if the underlying transaction was a sale of accounts or chattel paper, the debtor is entitled to any surplus or is liable for any deficiency only if the security agreement so provides. Amended in 1972.

§ 9—503. **Secured Party's Right to Take Possession After Default.**

Unless otherwise agreed a secured party has on default the right to take possession of the collateral. In taking possession a secured party may proceed without judicial process if this can be done without breach of the peace or may proceed by action. If the security agreement so provides the secured party may require the debtor to assemble the collateral and make it available to the secured party at a place to be designated by the secured party which is reasonably convenient to both parties. Without removal a secured party may render equipment unusable, and may dispose of collateral on the debtor's premises under Section 9—504.

§ 9—504. **Secured Party's Right to Dispose of Collateral After Default; Effect of Disposition.**

(1) A secured party after default may sell, lease or otherwise dispose of any or all of the collateral in its then condition or following any commercially reasonable preparation or processing. Any sale of goods is

subject to the Article on Sales (Article 2). The proceeds of disposition shall be applied in the order following to

(a) the reasonable expenses of retaking, holding, preparing for sale or lease, selling, leasing and the like and, to the extent provided for in the agreement and not prohibited by law, the reasonable attorneys' fees and legal expenses incurred by the secured party;

(b) the satisfaction of indebtedness secured by the security interest under which the disposition is made;

(c) the satisfaction of indebtedness secured by any subordinate security interest in the collateral if written notification of demand therefor is received before distribution of the proceeds is completed. If requested by the secured party, the holder of a subordinate security interest must seasonably furnish reasonable proof of his interest, and unless he does so, the secured party need not comply with his demand.

(2) If the security interest secures an indebtedness, the secured party must account to the debtor for any surplus, and, unless otherwise agreed, the debtor is liable for any deficiency. But if the underlying transaction was a sale of accounts or chattel paper, the debtor is entitled to any surplus or is liable for any deficiency only if the security agreement so provides.

(3) Disposition of the collateral may be by public or private proceedings and may be made by way of one or more contracts. Sale or other disposition may be as a unit or in parcels and at any time and place and on any terms but every aspect of the disposition including the method, manner, time, place and terms must be commercially reasonable. Unless collateral is perishable or threatens to decline speedily in value or is of a type customarily sold on a recognized market, reasonable notification of the time and place of any public sale or reasonable notification of the time after which any private sale or other intended disposition is to be made shall be sent by the secured party to the debtor, if he has not signed after default a statement renouncing or modifying his right to notification of sale. In the case of consumer goods no other notification need be sent. In other cases notification shall be sent to any other secured party from whom the secured party has received (before sending his notification to the debtor or before the debtor's renunciation of his rights) written notice of a claim of an interest in the collateral. The secured party may buy at any public sale and if the collateral is of a type customarily sold in a recognized market or is of a type which is the subject of widely distributed standard price quotations he may buy at private sale.

(4) When collateral is disposed of by a secured party after default, the disposition transfers to a purchaser for value all of the debtor's rights therein, discharges the security interest under which it is made and any security interest or lien subordinate thereto. The purchaser takes free of all such rights and interests even though the secured party fails to comply with the requirements of this Part or of any judicial proceedings

(a) in the case of a public sale, if the purchaser has no knowledge of any defects in the sale and if he does not buy in collusion with the secured party, other bidders or the person conducting the sale; or

(b) in any other case, if the purchaser acts in good faith.

(5) A person who is liable to a secured party under a guaranty, indorsement, repurchase agreement or the like and who receives a transfer of collateral from the secured party or is subrogated to his rights has thereafter the rights and duties of the secured party. Such a transfer of collateral is not a sale or disposition of the collateral under this Article. Amended in 1972.

§ 9—505. Compulsory Disposition of Collateral; Acceptance of the Collateral as Discharge of Obligation.

(1) If the debtor has paid sixty per cent of the cash price in the case of a purchase money security interest in consumer goods or sixty per cent of the loan in the case of another security interest in consumer goods, and has not signed after default a statement renouncing or modifying his rights under this Part a secured party who has taken possession of collateral must dispose of it under Section 9—504 and if he fails to do so within ninety days after he takes possession the debtor at his option may recover in conversion or under Section 9—507(1) on secured party's liability.

(2) In any other case involving consumer goods or

any other collateral a secured party in possession may, after default, propose to retain the collateral in satisfaction of the obligation. Written notice of such proposal shall be sent to the debtor if he has not signed after default a statement renouncing or modifying his rights under this subsection. In the case of consumer goods no other notice need be given. In other cases notice shall be sent to any other secured party from whom the secured party has received (before sending his notice to the debtor or before the debtor's renunciation of his rights) written notice of a claim of an interest in the collateral. If the secured party receives objection in writing from a person entitled to receive notification within twenty-one days after the notice was sent, the secured party must dispose of the collateral under Section 9—504. In the absence of such written objection the secured party may retain the collateral in satisfaction of the debtor's obligation. Amended in 1972.

§ 9—506. **Debtor's Right to Redeem Collateral.**

At any time before the secured party has disposed of collateral or entered into a contract for its disposition under Section 9—504 or before the obligation has been discharged under Section 9—505(2) the debtor or any other secured party may unless otherwise agreed in writing after default redeem the collateral by tendering fulfillment of all obligations secured by the collateral as well as the expenses reasonably incurred by the secured party in retaking, holding and preparing the collateral for disposition, in arranging for the sale, and to the extent provided in the agreement and not prohibited by law, his reasonable attorneys' fees and legal expenses.

§ 9—507. **Secured Party's Liability for Failure to Comply With This Part.**

(1) If it is established that the secured party is not proceeding in accordance with the provisions of this Part disposition may be ordered or restrained on appropriate terms and conditions. If the disposition has occurred the debtor or any person entitled to notification or whose security interest has been made known to the secured party prior to the disposition has a right to recover from the secured party any loss caused by a failure to comply with the provisions of this Part. If the collateral is consumer goods, the debtor has a right to recover in any event an amount

not less than the credit service charge plus ten per cent of the principal amount of the debt or the time price differential plus 10 per cent of the cash price.

(2) The fact that a better price could have been obtained by a sale at a different time or in a different method from that selected by the secured party is not of itself sufficient to establish that the sale was not made in a commercially reasonable manner. If the secured party either sells the collateral in the usual manner in any recognized market therefor or if he sells at the price current in such market at the time of his sale or if he has otherwise sold in conformity with reasonable commercial practices among dealers in the type of property sold he has sold in a commercially reasonable manner. The principles stated in the two preceding sentences with respect to sales also apply as may be appropriate to other types of disposition. A disposition which has been approved in any judicial proceeding or by any bona fide creditors' committee or representative of creditors shall conclusively be deemed to be commercially reasonable, but this sentence does not indicate that any such approval must be obtained in any case nor does it indicate that any disposition not so approved is not commercially reasonable.

Article 10
EFFECTIVE DATE AND REPEALER

§ 10—101. **Effective Date.**

This Act shall become effective at midnight on December 31st following its enactment. It applies to transactions entered into and events occurring after that date.

§ 10—102. **Specific Repealer; Provision for Transition.**

(1) The following acts and all other acts and parts of acts inconsistent herewith are hereby repealed:
(Here should follow the acts to be specifically repealed including the following:

    Uniform Negotiable Instruments Act
    Uniform Warehouse Receipts Act
    Uniform Sales Act
    Uniform Bills of Lading Act
    Uniform Stock Transfer Act

Uniform Conditional Sales Act
Uniform Trust Receipts Act
 Also any acts regulating:
Bank collections
Bulk sales
Chattel mortgages
Conditional sales
Factor's lien acts
Farm storage of grain and similar acts
Assignment of accounts receivable)

(2) Transactions validly entered into before the effective date specified in Section 10—101 and the rights, duties and interests flowing from them remain valid thereafter and may be terminated, completed, consummated or enforced as required or permitted by any statute or other law amended or repealed by this Act as though such repeal or amendment had not occurred.

Note *Subsection (1) should be separately prepared for each state. The foregoing is a list of statutes to be checked.*

§ 10—103. **General Repealer.**

Except as provided in the following section, all acts and parts of acts inconsistent with this Act are hereby repealed.

§ 10—104. **Laws Not Repealed.**

(1) The Article on Documents of Title (Article 7) does not repeal or modify any laws prescribing the form or contents of documents of title or the services or facilities to be afforded by bailees, or otherwise regulating bailees' businesses in respects not specifically dealt with herein; but the fact that such laws are violated does not affect the status of a document of title which otherwise complies with the definition of a document of title (Section 1—201).

[(2) This Act does not repeal . . . . *, cited as the Uniform Act for the Simplification of Fiduciary Security Transfers, and if in any respect there is any inconsistency between that Act and the Article of this Act on investment securities (Article 8) the provisions of the former Act shall control.]

Note: *At * in subsection (2) insert the statutory reference to the Uniform Act for the Simplification of Fiduciary Security Transfers if such Act has previously been enacted. If it has not been enacted, omit subsection (2).*

Article 11
(REPORTERS' DRAFT)
EFFECTIVE DATE AND
TRANSITION PROVISIONS

This material has been numbered Article 11 to distinguish it from Article 10, the transition provision of the 1962 Code, which may still remain in effect in some states to cover transition problems from pre-Code law to the original Uniform Commercial Code. Adaptation may be necessary in particular states. The terms "[old Code]" and "[new Code]" and "[old U.C.C.]" and "[new U.C.C.]" are used herein, and should be suitably changed in each state.

Note: *This draft was prepared by the Reporters and has not been passed upon by the Review Committee, the Permanent Editorial Board, the American Law Institute, or the National Conference of Commissioners on Uniform State Laws. It is submitted as a working draft which may be adapted as appropriate in each state.*

§ 11—101. **Effective Date.**

This Act shall become effective at 12:01 A.M. on ——, 19—.

§ 11—102. **Preservation of Old Transition Provision.**

The provisions of [here insert reference to the original transition provision in the particular state] shall continue to apply to [the new U.C.C.] and for this purpose the [old U.C.C. and new U.C.C.] shall be considered one continuous statute.

§ 11—103. **Transition to [New Code]—General Rule.**

Transactions validly entered into after [effective date of old U.C.C.] and before [effective date of new U.C.C.], and which were subject to the provisions of [old U.C.C.] and which would be subject to this Act as amended if they had been entered into after the effective date of [new U.C.C.] and the rights, duties and interests flowing from such transactions remain valid after the latter date and may be terminated, completed, consummated or enforced as required or permitted by the [new U.C.C.]. Security interests arising out of such transactions which are perfected when [new U.C.C.] becomes effective shall remain perfected until they lapse as provided in [new

U.C.C.], and may be continued as permitted by [new U.C.C.], except as stated in Section 11—105.

§ 11—104. Transition Provision on Change of Requirement of Filing.

A security interest for the perfection of which filing or the taking of possession was required under [old U.C.C.] and which attached prior to the effective date of [new U.C.C.] but was not perfected shall be deemed perfected on the effective date of [new U.C.C.] if [new U.C.C.] permits perfection without filing or authorizes filing in the office or offices where a prior ineffective filing was made.

§ 11—105. Transition Provision on Change of Place of Filing.

(1) A financing statement or continuation statement filed prior to [effective date of new U.C.C.] which shall not have lapsed prior to [the effective date of new U.C.C.] shall remain effective for the period provided in the [old Code], but not less than five years after the filing.

(2) With respect to any collateral acquired by the debtor subsequent to the effective date of [new U.C.C.], any effective financing statement or continuation statement described in this section shall apply only if the filing or filings are in the office or offices that would be appropriate to perfect the security interests in the new collateral under [new U.C.C.].

(3) The effectiveness of any financing statement or continuation statement filed prior to [effective date of new U.C.C.] may be continued by a continuation statement as permitted by [new U.C.C.], except that if [new U.C.C.] requires a filing in an office where there was no previous financing statement, a new financing statement conforming to Section 11—106 shall be filed in that office.

(4) If the record of a mortgage of real estate would have been effective as a fixture filing of goods described therein if [new U.C.C.] had been in effect on the date of recording the mortgage, the mortgage shall be deemed effective as a fixture filing as to such goods under subsection (6) of Section 9—402 of the [new U.C.C.] on the effective date of [new U.C.C.].

§ 11—106. Required Refilings.

(1) If a security interest is perfected or has priority

when this Act takes effect as to all persons or as to certain persons without any filing or recording, and if the filing of a financing statement would be required for the perfection or priority of the security interest against those persons under [new U.C.C.], the perfection and priority rights of the security interest continue until 3 years after the effective date of [new U.C.C.]. The perfection will then lapse unless a financing statement is filed as provided in subsection (4) or unless the security interest is perfected otherwise than by filing.

(2) If a security interest is perfected when [new U.C.C.] takes effect under a law other than [U.C.C.] which requires no further filing, refiling or recording to continue its perfection, perfection continues until and will lapse 3 years after [new U.C.C.] takes effect, unless a financing statement is filed as provided in subsection (4) or unless the security interest is perfected otherwise than by filing, or unless under subsection (3) of Section 9—302 the other law continues to govern filing.

(3) If a security interest is perfected by a filing, refiling or recording under a law repealed by this Act which required further filing, refiling or recording to continue its perfection, perfection continues and will lapse on the date provided by the law so repealed for such further filing, refiling or recording unless a financing statement is filed as provided in subsection (4) or unless the security interest is perfected otherwise than by filing.

(4) A financing statement may be filed within six months before the perfection of a security interest would otherwise lapse. Any such financing statement may be signed by either the debtor or the secured party. It must identify the security agreement, statement or notice (however denominated in any statute or other law repealed or modified by this Act), state the office where and the date when the last filing, refiling or recording, if any, was made with respect thereto, and the filing number, if any, or book and page, if any, of recording and further state that the security agreement, statement or notice, however denominated, in another filing office under the [U.C.C.] or under any statute or other law repealed or modified by this Act is still effective. Section 9—401 and Section 9—103 determine the proper place to file

such a financing statement. Except as specified in this subsection, the provisions of Section 9—403(3) for continuation statements apply to such a financing statement.

§ 11—107. **Transition Provisions as to Priorities.**

Except as otherwise provided in [Article 11], [old U.C.C.] shall apply to any questions of priority if the positions of the parties were fixed prior to the effective date of [new U.C.C.]. In other cases questions of priority shall be determined by [new U.C.C.].

§ 11—108. **Presumption that Rule of Law Continues Unchanged.**

Unless a change in law has clearly been made, the provisions of [new U.C.C.] shall be deemed declaratory of the meaning of the [old U.C.C.]

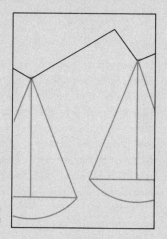

APPENDIX B

Uniform Consumer
Credit Code

1974 Act

An Act

Relating to certain consumer and other credit transactions and constituting the uniform consumer credit code; consolidating and revising certain aspects of the law relating to consumer and other loans, consumer and other sales of goods, services and interests in land, and consumer leases; revising the law relating to usury; relating certain practices relating to insurance in consumer credit transactions; providing for administrative regulation of certain consumer and other credit transactions; imposing fees making uniform the law with respect thereto; and repealing inconsistent legislation.

The Code consists of 9 Articles as follows:

1. General Provisions and Definitions

2. Finance Charges and Related Provisions

3. Regulation of Agreements and Practices

4. Insurance

5. Remedies and Penalties

6. Administration

7. [Reserved for Future Use]

8. [Reserved for Future Use]

9. Effective Date and Repealer

Article 1
GENERAL PROVISIONS AND DEFINITIONS

Part 1 Short Title, Construction, General Provisions

Section 1.101 [Short Title]

This Act shall be known and may be cited as Uniform Consumer Credit Code.

Section 1.102 [Purposes; Rules of Construction]

(1) This Act shall be liberally construed and applied to promote its underlying purposes and policies.

(2) The underlying purposes and policies of this Act are:

(a) to simplify, clarify, and modernize the law governing consumer credit and usury;

(b) to provide rate ceilings to assure an adequate supply of credit to consumers;

(c) to further consumer understanding of the terms of credit transactions and to foster competition among suppliers of consumer credit so that consumers may obtain credit at reasonable cost;

(d) to protect consumers against unfair practices by some suppliers of consumer credit, having due regard for the interests of legitimate and scrupulous creditors;

(e) to permit and encourage the development of fair and economically sound consumer credit practices;

(f) to conform the regulation of disclosure in consumer credit transactions to the Federal Truth in Lending Act; and

(g) to make uniform the law, including administrative rules, among the various jurisdictions.

(3) A reference to a requirement imposed by this Act includes reference to a related rule of the Administrator adopted pursuant to this Act.

Section 1.103 [Supplementary General Principles of Law Applicable]

Unless displaced by the particular provisions of this Act, the Uniform Commercial Code and the principles of law and equity, including the law relative to capacity to contract, principal and agent, estoppel, fraud, misrepresentation, duress, coercion, mistake, bankruptcy, or other validating or invalidating cause supplement its provisions. In the event of inconsistency between the Uniform Commercial Code and this Act the provisions of this Act control.

Section 1.104 [Construction Against Implicit Repeal]

This Act being a general act intended as a unified coverage of its subject matter, no part of it shall be construed to be impliedly repealed by subsequent legislation if that construction can reasonably be avoided.

Section 1.105 **[Severability]**

If any provision of this Act or the application thereof to any person or circumstances is held invalid, the invalidity does not affect other provisions or applications of this Act which can be given effect without the invalid provision or application, and to this end the provisions of this Act are severable.

Section 1.106 **[Adjustment of Dollar Amounts]**

(1) From time to time the dollar amounts in this Act designated as subject to change shall change, as provided in this section, according to and to the extent of changes in the Consumer Price Index for Urban Wage Earners and Clerical Workers: U.S. City Average, All Items, 1967=100, compiled by the Bureau of Labor Statistics, United States Department of Labor, and hereafter referred to as the Index. The Index for December of the year preceding the year in which this Act becomes effective is the Reference Base Index.

(2) The designated dollar amounts shall change on July 1 of each even-numbered year if the percentage of change, calculated to the nearest whole percentage point, between the Index at the end of the preceding year and the Reference Base Index is ten per cent or more, but

(a) the portion of the percentage change in the Index in excess of a multiple of ten per cent shall be disregarded and the dollar amounts shall change only in multiples of ten per cent of the amounts appearing in this Act on the date of enactment; and

(b) the dollar amounts shall not change if the amounts required by this section are those currently in effect pursuant to this Act as a result of earlier application of this section.

(3) If the Index is revised, the percentage of change pursuant to this section shall be calculated on the basis of the revised Index. If a revision of the Index changes the Reference Base Index, a revised Reference Base Index shall be determined by multiplying the Reference Base Index then applicable by the rebasing factor furnished by the Bureau of Labor Statistics. If the Index is superseded, the Index referred to in this section is the one represented by the Bureau of Labor Statistics as reflecting most accurately changes in the purchasing power of the dollar for consumers.

(4) The Administrator shall adopt a rule announcing

(a) on or before April 30 of each year in which dollar amounts are to change, the changes in dollar amounts required by subsection (2); and

(b) promptly after the changes occur, changes in the Index required by subsection (3) including, if applicable, the numerical equivalent of the Reference Base Index under a revised Reference Base Index and the designation or title of any index superseding the Index.

(5) A person does not violate this Act with respect to a transaction otherwise complying with this Act if he relies on dollar amounts either determined according to subsection (2) or appearing in the last rule of the Administrator announcing the then current dollar amounts.

Section 1.107 **[Waiver; Agreement to Forego Rights; Settlement of Claims]**

(1) Except as otherwise permitted in this Act, a consumer may waive or agree to forego rights or benefits under this Act only in settlement of a bona fide dispute.

(2) A claim by a consumer against a creditor for an excess charge, any other violation of this Act, a civil penalty, or a claim against a consumer for a default or breach of a duty imposed by this Act, if disputed in good faith, may be settled by agreement.

(3) A claim against a consumer, whether or not disputed, may be settled for less value than the amount claimed.

(4) A settlement in which the consumer waives or agrees to forego rights or benefits under this Act is invalid if the court as a matter of law finds the settlement to have been unconscionable at the time it was made. The competence of the consumer, any deception or coercion practiced upon him, the nature and extent of the legal advice received by him, and the value of the consideration are relevant to the issue of unconscionability.

Section 1.108 [Effect of Act on Powers of Organizations]

(1) This Act prescribes maximum charges for all creditors, except lessors and those excluded (Section 1.202), extending credit in consumer credit transactions (subsection (13) of Section 1.301), and displaces existing limitations on the powers of those creditors based on maximum charges.

(2) With respect to sellers of goods or services, small loan companies, licensed lenders, consumer and sales finance companies, industrial banks and loan companies, and commercial banks and trust companies, this Act displaces existing limitations on their powers based solely on amount or duration of credit.

(3) Except as provided in subsection (1) [and in the Article on Effective Date and Repealer (Article 9)], this Act does not displace limitations on powers of credit unions, savings banks, savings and loan associations, or other thrift institutions whether organized for the profit of shareholders or as mutual organizations.

(4) Except as provided in subsections (1) and (2) [and in the Article on Effective Date and Repealer (Article 9)], this Act does not displace:

(a) limitations on powers of supervised financial organizations (subsection (41) of Section 1.301) with respect to the amount of a loan to a single borrower, the ratio of a loan to the value of collateral, the duration of a loan secured by an interest in land, or other similar restrictions designed to protect deposits, or

(b) limitations on powers an organization is authorized to exercise under the laws of this State or the United States.

Section 1.109 [Transactions Subject to Act by Agreement]

Parties to a credit transaction or modification thereof that is not a consumer credit transaction (subsection (13) of Section 1.301) may agree in a writing signed by them that the transaction is subject to the provisions of this Act applying to consumer credit transactions. If the parties so agree the transaction is a consumer credit transaction for the purposes of this Act.

Section 1.110 [Obligation of Good Faith]

(1) Every contract or duty within this Act imposes an obligation of good faith in its performance or enforcement.

(2) "Good faith" means honesty in fact in the conduct or transaction concerned.

Part 2 Scope and Jurisdiction

Section 1.201 [Territorial Application]

(1) Except as otherwise provided in this section, this Act applies to a consumer credit transaction entered into in this State. For the purposes of this Act, a consumer credit transaction is entered into in this State if:

(a) pursuant to other than open-end credit, either a signed writing evidencing the obligation or offer of the consumer is received by the creditor in this State, or the creditor induces the consumer who is a resident of this State to enter into the transaction by face-to-face solicitation in this State; or

(b) pursuant to open-end credit, either the consumer's communication or his indication of intention to establish the open-end credit arrangement is received by the creditor in this State or, if no communication or indication of intention is given by the consumer before the first transaction, the creditor's communication notifying the consumer of the privilege of using the arrangement is mailed in this State.

(2) With respect to a consumer loan to which this Act does not otherwise apply, if a consumer who is a resident of this State, pursuant to solicitation in this State, sends a signed writing evidencing the obligation or offer of the consumer to a creditor in another state and receives the cash proceeds of the loan in this State:

(a) the creditor may not contract for or receive charges exceeding those permitted by the Article on Finance Charges and Related Provisions (Article 2); and

(b) the provisions on Powers and Functions of Administrator (Part 1) of the Article on Administration (Article 6) apply as though the loan were entered into in this State.

(3) The Part on Limitations on Creditors' Remedies (Part 1) of the Article on Remedies and Penalties (Article 5) applies to actions or other proceedings

brought in this State to enforce rights arising from consumer credit transactions or extortionate extensions of credit, wherever entered into.

(4) Except as provided in subsection (2), a consumer credit transaction to which this Act does not apply entered into with a person who is a resident of this State at the time of the transaction is valid and enforceable in this State to the extent that it is valid and enforceable under the laws of another jurisdiction, but:

(a) a creditor may not collect through actions or other proceedings in this State an amount exceeding the total amount permitted if the Article on Finance Charges and Related Provisions (Article 2) were applicable; and

(b) a creditor may not enforce rights against the consumer in this State with respect to the provisions of agreements that violate the provisions on Limitations on Agreements and Practices (Part 3) and Limitations on Consumers' Liabilities (Part 4) of the Article on Regulation of Agreements and Practices (Article 3).

(5) Except as provided in subsections (2), (3), and (4), a consumer credit transaction entered into in another jurisdiction is valid and enforceable in this State according to its terms to the extent that it is valid and enforceable under the laws of the other jurisdiction.

(6) For the purposes of this Act, the residence of a consumer is the address given by him as his residence in a writing signed by him in connection with a consumer credit transaction until he notifies the creditor of a different address as his residence, and is then the different address.

(7) Notwithstanding other provisions of this section:

(a) except as provided in subsection (3), this Act does not apply if the consumer is not a resident of this State at the time of a consumer credit transaction and the parties have agreed that the law of his residence applies; and

(b) this Act applies if the consumer is a resident of this State at the time of a consumer credit transaction and the parties have agreed that the law of his residence applies.

(8) Each of the following agreements or provisions of an agreement by a consumer who is a resident of this State at the time of a consumer credit transaction is

invalid with respect to the transaction:

(a) that the law of another jurisdiction apply;

(b) that the consumer consents to be subject to the process of another jurisdiction;

(c) that the consumer appoints an agent to receive service of process;

(d) that fixes venue; and

(e) that the consumer consents to the jurisdiction of the court that does not otherwise have jurisdiction.

(9) The following provisions of this Act specify the applicable law governing certain cases:

(a) applicability (Section 6.102) of the Part on Powers and Functions of Administrator (Part 1) of the Article on Administration (Article 6); and

(b) applicability (Section 6.201) of the Part on Notification and Fees (Part 2) of the Article on Administration (Article 6).

Section 1.202 **[Exclusions]**

This Act does not apply to:

(1) extensions of credit to organizations;

(2) except as otherwise provided in the Article on Insurance (Article 4), the sale of insurance if the insured is not obligated to pay instalments of the premium and the insurance may terminate or be cancelled after non-payment of an instalment of the premium;

(3) transactions under public utility or common carrier tariffs if a subdivision or agency of this State or of the United States regulates the charges for the services involved, the charges for delayed payment, and any discount allowed for early payment;

(4) transactions in securities or commodities accounts with a broker-dealer registered with the Securities and Exchange Commission; [or]

(5) except with respect to the provisions on compliance with the Federal Truth in Lending Act (Section 3.201), [civil liability for violation of disclosure provisions (Section 5.203), criminal penalties for disclosure violations (Section 5.302)], and powers and functions of the Administrator with respect to disclosure violations (Part 1 of Article 6), pawnbrokers who are licensed and whose rates and charges are regulat-

ed under or pursuant to ordinances or other statutes or

(6) ceilings on rates or limits on loan maturities of credit extended by a credit union organized under the laws of this State or of the United States if these ceilings or limits are established by these laws or by applicable regulations].

Note 1. If the enacting State wishes to apply for an exemption from the Federal Truth in Lending Act, the brackets before and after Sections 5.203 and 5.302 should be deleted and those sections enacted, and the brackets in subsection (5) preceding and following references to those sections should be omitted; otherwise, delete the brackets and the language enclosed within them, and delete the references to Sections 5.203 and 5.302 in the Table of Articles, Parts, and Sections.

Note 2. If subsection (6) is included by the enacting State, delete "[or]" at the end of subsection (4), the opening bracket at the end of subsection (5), and the closing bracket at the end of subsection (6). If subsection (6) is not included by the enacting State, delete the brackets before and after "or" at the end of subsection (4).

Section 1.203 **[Jurisdiction [and Service of Process]]**

[(1)] The [   ] court of this State may exercise jurisdiction over any creditor with respect to any conduct of the creditor subject to this Act or with respect to any claim arising from a transaction subject to this Act.

[(2) In addition to any other method provided by [rule] [statute], personal jurisdiction over a creditor may be acquired in a civil action or proceeding instituted in the [   ] court by service of process in the manner provided in this section. If a creditor is not a resident of this State or is a corporation not authorized to do business in this State and engages in any conduct in this State subject to this Act or in a transaction subject to this Act, he may designate an agent upon whom service of process may be made in this State. The agent shall be a resident of this State or a corporation authorized to do business in this State. The designation shall be in a writing and filed with the Secretary of State. If a designation is not made and filed or if process cannot be served in this State upon the designated agent, process may be served upon the Secretary of State, but service upon him is not effective unless the plaintiff or petitioner forthwith mails a copy of the process and pleading by registered or certified mail to the defendant or respondent at his last reasonably ascertainable address. An affidavit of compliance with this section shall be filed with the clerk of the court on or before the return day of the process, if any, or within any further time the court allows.]

Note: If the enacting State has an adequate long arm statute, the bracketed words "and Service of Process" in the section heading, the bracketed "(1)," and all of subsection (2) may be omitted.

Part 3 **Definitions**

Section 1.301 **[General Definitions]**

(1) "Actuarial method" means the method of allocating payments made on a debt between the amount financed and the finance charge pursuant to which a payment is applied first to the accumulated finance charge and any remainder is subtracted from, or any deficiency is added to, the unpaid balance of the amount financed. The Administrator may adopt rules not inconsistent with the Federal Truth in Lending Act further defining the term and prescribing its application.

(2) "Administrator" means the Administrator designated in the Article (Article 6) on Administration (Section 6.103).

(3) "Agreement" means the bargain of the parties in fact as found in their language or by implication from other circumstances including course of dealing, usage of trade, or course of performance.

(4) "Agricultural purpose" means a purpose related to the production, harvest, exhibition, marketing, transportation, processing, or manufacture of agricultural products by a natural person who cultivates, plants, propagates, or nurtures the agricultural products. "Agricultural products" includes agricultural, horticultural, viticultural, and dairy products, livestock, wildlife, poultry, bees, forest products, fish and shellfish, and products thereof, including processed and manufactured products, and products raised or produced on farms and processed or manufactured products thereof.

(5) "Amount financed" means the total of the following items:

(a) in the case of a sale, the cash price of the goods, services, or interest in land, less the amount of any down payment made in cash or in property traded in, and the amount actually paid or to be paid by the seller pursuant to an agreement with the buyer to discharge a security interest in, a lien on, or a debt with respect to property traded in;

(b) in case of a loan, the net amount paid to, receivable by, or paid or payable for the account of the debtor, plus the amount of any discount excluded from the finance charge (paragraph (b)(iii) of subsection (20)); and

(c) in the case of a sale or loan, to the extent that payment is deferred and the amount is not otherwise included and is authorized and disclosed to the consumer as required by law:

(i) amounts actually paid or to be paid by the creditor for registration, certificate of title, or license fees, and

(ii) permitted additional charges (Section 2.501).

(6) "Billing cycle" means the time interval between periodic billing statement dates.

(7) "Card issuer" means a person who issues a credit card.

(8) "Cardholder" means a person to whom a credit card is issued or who has agreed with the card issuer to pay obligations arising from the issuance to or use of the card by another person.

(9) "Cash price" of goods, services, or an interest in land means the price at which they are offered for sale by the seller to cash buyers in the ordinary course of business and may include (a) the cash price of accessories or services related to the sale, such as delivery, installation, alterations, modifications, and improvements, and (b) taxes to the extent imposed on a cash sale of the goods, services, or interest in land. The cash price stated by the seller to the buyer in a disclosure statement required by law is presumed to be the cash price.

(10) "Conspicuous":

A term or clause is "conspicuous" when it is so written that a reasonable person against whom it is to operate ought to have noticed it. Whether or not a term or clause is conspicuous is for decision by the court.

(11) "Consumer" means the buyer, lessee, or debtor to whom credit is granted in a consumer credit transaction.

(12) "Consumer credit sale":

(a) Except as provided in paragraph (b), "consumer credit sale" means a sale of goods, services, or an interest in land in which:

(i) credit is granted either pursuant to a seller credit card or by a seller who regularly engages as a seller in credit transactions of the same kind;

(ii) the buyer is a person other than an organization;

(iii) the goods, services, or interest in land are purchased primarily for a personal, family, household, or agricultural purpose;

(iv) the debt is payable in instalments or a finance charge is made; and

(v) with respect to a sale of goods or services, the amount financed does not exceed $25,000.

(b) A "consumer credit sale" does not include:

(i) a sale in which the seller allows the buyer to purchase goods or services pursuant to a lender credit card, or

(ii) unless the sale is made subject to this Act by agreement (Section 1.109), a sale of an interest in land if the finance charge does not exceed 12 per cent per year calculated according to the actuarial method on the assumption that the debt will be paid according to the agreed terms and will not be paid before the end of the agreed term.

(c) The amount of $25,000 in paragraph (a)(v) is subject to change pursuant to the provisions on adjustment of dollar amounts (Section 1.106).

(13) "Consumer credit transaction" means a consumer credit sale or consumer loan or a refinancing or consolidation thereof, or a consumer lease.

(14) "Consumer lease":

(a) "Consumer lease" means a lease of goods:

(i) which a lessor regularly engaged in the business of leasing makes to a person, except an organization, who takes under the lease primarily for a personal, family, household, or agricultural purpose;

(ii) in which the amount payable under the lease does not exceed $25,000;

(iii) which is for a term exceeding four months; and

(iv) which is not made pursuant to a lender credit card.

(b) The amount of $25,000 in paragraph (a)(ii) is subject to change pursuant to the provisions on adjustment of dollar amounts (Section 1.106).

(15) "Consumer loan":

(a) Except as provided in paragraph (b), "consumer loan" means a loan made by a creditor regularly engaged in the business of making loans in which:

(i) the debtor is a person other than an organization;

(ii) the debt is incurred primarily for a personal, family, household, or agricultural purpose;

(iii) the debt is payable in instalments or a finance charge is made; and

(iv) the amount financed does not exceed $25,000 or the debt, other than one incurred primarily for an agricultural purpose, is secured by an interest in land.

(b) A "consumer loan" does not include:

(i) a sale or lease in which the seller or lessor allows the buyer or lessee to purchase or lease pursuant to a seller credit card, or

(ii) unless the loan is made subject to this Act by agreement (Section 1.109), a loan secured by an interest in land if the security interest is bona fide and not for the purpose of circumvention or evasion of this Act and the finance charge does not exceed 12 per cent per year calculated according to the actuarial method on the assumption that the debt will be paid according to the agreed terms and will not be paid before the end of the agreed term.

(c) A loan that would be a consumer loan if the lender were regularly engaged in the business of making loans is a consumer loan if the loan is arranged for a commission or other compensation by a person regularly engaged in the business of arranging those loans and the lender is not regularly engaged in the business of making loans. The arranger is deemed to be the creditor making the loan.

(d) The amount of $25,000 in paragraph (a)(iv) is subject to change pursuant to the provisions on adjustment of dollar amounts (Section 1.106).

(16) "Credit" means the right granted by a creditor to a consumer to defer payment of debt, to incur debt and defer its payment, or to purchase property or services and defer payment therefor.

(17) "Credit card" means a card or device issued under an arrangement pursuant to which a card issuer gives to a cardholder the privilege of obtaining credit from the card issuer or other person in purchasing or leasing property or services, obtaining loans, or otherwise. A transaction is "pursuant to a credit card" only if credit is obtained according to the terms of the arrangement by transmitting information contained on the card or device orally, in writing, by mechanical or electronic methods, or in any other manner. A transaction is not "pursuant to a credit card" if the card or device is used solely in that transaction to:

(a) identify the cardholder or evidence his creditworthiness and credit is not obtained according to the terms of the arrangement;

(b) obtain a guarantee of payment from the cardholder's deposit account, whether or not the payment results in a credit extension to the cardholder by the card issuer; or

(c) effect an immediate transfer of funds from the cardholder's deposit account by electronic or other means, whether or not the transfer results in a credit extension to the cardholder by the card issuer.

(18) "Creditor" means the person who grants credit in a consumer credit transaction or, except as otherwise provided, an assignee of a creditor's right to payment, but use of the term does not in itself impose on an assignee any obligation of his assignor. In case of credit granted pursuant to a credit card, "creditor" means the card issuer and not another person honoring the credit card.

(19) "Earnings" means compensation paid or payable by an employer to an employee or for his account for personal services rendered or to be rendered by him, whether denominated as wages, salary, commission, bonus, or otherwise, and includes periodic payments pursuant to a pension, retirement, or disability program.

(20) "Finance charge":

(a) Except as provided in paragraph (b), "finance charge" means the sum of all charges payable directly or indirectly by the consumer and imposed directly or indirectly by the creditor as an incident to or as a condition of the extension of credit, including any of the following types of charges which are applicable:

(i) interest or any amount payable under a point, discount, or other system of charges, however denominated;

(ii) time-price differential, credit service, service, carrying, or other charge, however denominated;

(iii) premium or other charge for any guarantee or insurance protecting the creditor against the consumer's default or other credit loss; and

(iv) charges incurred for investigating the collateral or credit-worthiness of the consumer or for commissions or brokerage for obtaining the credit, irrespective of the person to whom the charges are paid or payable, unless the creditor had no notice of the charges when the credit was granted.

(b) The term does not include:

(i) charges as a result of default or delinquency if made for actual unanticipated late payment, delinquency, default, or other like occurrence, unless the parties agree that these charges are finance charges; a charge is not made for actual unanticipated late payment, delinquency, default or other like occurrence if imposed on an account that is or may be debited from time to time for purchases or other debts and, under its terms, payment in full or of a specified amount is required when billed, and in the ordinary course of business the consumer is permitted to continue to have purchases or other debts debited to the account after imposition of the charge;

(ii) additional charges (Section 2.501) or deferral charges (Section 2.503); or

(iii) a discount, if a creditor purchases or satisfies obligations of a cardholder pursuant to a credit card and the purchase or satisfaction is made at less than the face amount of the obligation.

(21) "Goods" includes goods not in existence at the time the transaction is entered into and merchandise certificates, but excludes money, chattel paper, documents of title, and instruments.

(22) "Insurance premium loan" means a consumer loan that (a) is made for the sole purpose of financing the payment by or on behalf of an insured of the premium on one or more policies or contracts issued by or on behalf of an insurer, (b) is secured by an assignment by the insured to the lender of the unearned premium on the policy or contract, and (c) contains an authorization to cancel the policy or contract financed.

(23) Except as otherwise provided, "lender" includes an assignee of a lender's right to payment, but use of the term does not in itself impose on an assignee any obligation of the lender.

(24) "Lender credit card" means a credit card issued by a supervised lender.

(25) "Loan":

(a) Except as provided in paragraph (b), "loan" includes:

(i) the creation of debt by the lender's payment of or agreement to pay money to the debtor or to a third person for the account of the debtor;

(ii) the creation of debt pursuant to a lender credit card in any manner, including a cash advance or the card issuer's honoring a draft or similar order for the payment of money drawn or accepted by the debtor, paying or agreeing to pay the debtor's obligation, or purchasing or otherwise acquiring the debtor's obligation from the obligee or his assignees;

(iii) the creation of debt by a cash advance to a debtor pursuant to a seller credit card;

(iv) the creation of debt by a credit to an account with the lender upon which the debtor is entitled to draw immediately; and

(v) the forbearance of debt arising from a loan.

(b) "Loan" does not include:

(i) a card issuer's payment or agreement to pay money to a third person for the account of a debtor if the debt of the debtor arises from a sale or lease and results from use of a seller credit card; or

(ii) the forbearance of debt arising from a sale or lease.

(26) "Merchandise certificate" means a writing not redeemable in cash and usable in its face amount in lieu of cash in exchange for goods or services.

(27) "Official fees" means:

(a) fees and charges prescribed by law which actually are or will be paid to public officials for determining the existence of or for perfecting, releasing, terminating, or satisfying a security interest related to a consumer credit transaction; or

(b) premiums payable for insurance in lieu of perfecting a security interest otherwise required by the creditor in connection with the transaction, if the premium does not exceed the fees and charges described in paragraph (a) which would otherwise be payable.

(28) "Open-end credit" means an arrangement pursuant to which:

(a) a creditor may permit a consumer, from time to time, to purchase or lease on credit from the creditor or pursuant to a credit card, or to obtain loans from the creditor or pursuant to a credit card;

(b) the amounts financed and the finance and other appropriate charges are debited to an account;

(c) the finance charge, if made, is computed on the account periodically; and

(d) either the consumer has the privilege of paying in full or in instalments or the creditor periodically imposes charges computed on the account for delaying payment and permits the consumer to continue to purchase or lease on credit.

(29) "Organization" means a corporation, government or governmental subdivision or agency, trust, estate, partnership, cooperative, or association.

(30) "Payable in instalments" means that payment is required or permitted by agreement to be made in more than four periodic payments, excluding a downpayment. If any periodic payment other than the downpayment under an agreement requiring or

permitting two or more periodic payments is more than twice the amount of any other periodic payment, excluding a downpayment, a consumer credit transaction is "payable in instalments."

(31) "Person" includes a natural person or an individual, and an organization.

(32) "Person related to" with respect to an individual means (a) the spouse of the individual, (b) a brother, brother-in-law, sister, sister-in-law of the individual, (c) an ancestor or lineal descendant of the individual or his spouse, and (d) any other relative, by blood or marriage, of the individual or his spouse who shares the same home with the individual. "Person related to" with respect to an organization means (a) a person directly or indirectly controlling, controlled by, or under common control with the organization, (b) an officer or director of the organization or a person performing similar functions with respect to the organization or to a person related to the organization, (c) the spouse of a person related to the organization, and (d) a relative by blood or marriage of a person related to the organization who shares the same home with him.

(33) "Precomputed consumer credit transaction" means a consumer credit transaction, other than a consumer lease, in which the debt is a sum comprising the amount financed and the amount of the finance charge computed in advance. A disclosure required by the Federal Truth in Lending Act does not in itself make a finance charge or transaction precomputed.

(34) "Presumed" or "presumption" means that the trier of fact must find the existence of the fact presumed unless and until evidence is introduced which would support a finding of its non-existence.

(35) "Sale of goods" includes an agreement in the form of a bailment or lease of goods if the bailee or lessee pays or agrees to pay as compensation for use a sum substantially equivalent to or in excess of the aggregate value of the goods involved and it is agreed that the bailee or lessee will become, or for no other or a nominal consideration has the option to become, the owner of the goods upon full compliance with the terms of the agreement.

(36) "Sale of an interest in land" includes a lease in which the lessee has an option to purchase the interest and all or a substantial part of the rental or

other payments previously made by him are applied to the purchase price.

(37) "Sale of services" means furnishing or agreeing to furnish services and includes making arrangements to have services furnished by another.

(38) "Seller" includes, except as otherwise provided, an assignee of the seller's right to payment, but use of the term does not in itself impose on an assignee any obligation of the seller.

(39) "Seller credit card" means either:

(a) a credit card issued primarily for the purpose of giving the cardholder the privilege of using the card to purchase or lease property or services from the card issuer, persons related to the card issuer, or persons licensed or franchised to do business under the card issuer's business or trade name or designation, or both from any of these persons and from other persons; or

(b) a credit card issued by a person except a supervised lender primarily for the purpose of giving the cardholder the privilege of using the credit card to purchase or lease property or services from at least 100 persons not related to the card issuer.

(40) "Services" includes (a) work, labor, and other personal services, (b) privileges with respect to transportation, hotel and restaurant accommodations, education, entertainment, recreation, physical culture, hospital accommodations, funerals, cemetery accommodations, and the like, and (c) insurance.

(41) "Supervised financial organization" means a person, except an insurance company or other organization primarily engaged in an insurance business:

(a) organized, chartered, or holding an authorization certificate under laws of this State or of the United States that authorizes the person to make loans and to receive deposits, including a savings, share, certificate or deposit account, and

(b) subject to supervision by an official or agency of this State or of the United States.

(42) "Supervised lender" means a person authorized to make or take assignments of supervised loans, under a license issued by the Administrator (Section 2.301) or as a supervised financial organization (subsection (41)).

(43) "Supervised loan" means a consumer loan, including a loan made pursuant to open-end credit, in which the rate of the finance charge, calculated according to the actuarial method, exceeds 18 per cent per year.

Section 1.302 [Definition: "Federal Truth in Lending Act"]

In this Act, as applicable, "Federal Truth in Lending Act" means Title I of the Consumer Credit Protection Act (Public Law 90-321; 82 Stat. 146; 15 U.S.C. § 1601 et seq.; as amended), except for the provisions concerning issuance, liability of holders, and fraudulent use of credit cards (Sections 132-134, as added by Public Law 90-321; 84 Stat. 1126; 15 U.S.C. §§ 1642-1644), and includes regulations issued by the Board of Governors of the Federal Reserve System pursuant to that Act except those relating to the excepted provisions.

Section 1.303 [Other Defined Terms]

Other defined terms in this Act and the sections in which they appear are:
"Closing costs" Section 2.501(1)
"Computational period" Section 2.503(1)
"Deferral" Section 2.503(1)
"Deferral period" Section 2.503(1)
"Disposable earnings" Section 5.105
"Garnishment" Section 5.105
"Home solicitation sale" Section 3.501
"Interval" Section 2.503(1)
"Periodic balance" Section 2.503(1)
"Pursuant to a credit card" Section 1.301(17)
"Residence" Section 1.201(6)
"Rule of 78" Section 2.503(1)
"Standard deferral" Section 2.503(1)
"Sum of the balances method" Section 2.503(1)
"Transaction" Section 2.503(1)

Article 2
FINANCE CHARGES AND RELATED PROVISIONS

Part 1 General Provisions

Section 2.101 [Short Title]

This Article shall be known and may be cited as Uniform Consumer Credit Code—Finance Charges and Related Provisions.

Section 2.102 [Scope]

Part 2 of this Article applies to consumer credit sales. Parts 3 and 4 apply to consumer loans, including loans made by supervised lenders. Part 5 applies to other charges and modifications with respect to consumer credit transactions. Part 6 applies to other credit transactions.

Part 2 Consumer Credit Sales: Maximum Finance Charges

Section 2.201 [Finance Charge for Consumer Credit Sales Not Pursuant to Open-End Credit]

(1) With respect to a consumer credit sale, except a sale pursuant to open-end credit, a creditor may contract for and receive a finance charge not exceeding that permitted in this section.

(2) The finance charge, calculated according to the actuarial method, may not exceed the equivalent of the greater of either of the following:

(a) the total of:

(i) 36 per cent per year on that part of the unpaid balances of the amount financed which is $300 or less;

(ii) 21 per cent per year on that part of the unpaid balances of the amount financed which exceeds $300 but does not exceed $1,000; and

(iii) 15 per cent per year on that part of the unpaid balances of the amount financed which exceeds $1,000; or

(b) 18 per cent per year on the unpaid balances of the amount financed.

(3) This section does not limit or restrict the manner of calculating the finance charge whether by way of add-on, discount, single annual percentage rate, or otherwise, so long as the rate of the finance charge does not exceed that permitted by this section. The finance charge may be contracted for and earned at the single annual percentage rate that would earn the same finance charge as the graduated rates when the debt is paid according to the agreed terms and the calculations are made according to the actuarial method. If the sale is a precomputed consumer credit transaction:

(a) the finance charge may be calculated on the assumption that all scheduled payments will be made when due, and

(b) the effect of prepayment is governed by the provisions on rebate upon prepayment (Section 2.510).

(4) For purposes of this section, the term of a sale agreement commences with the date the credit is granted or, if goods are delivered or services performed ten days or more after that date, with the date of commencement of delivery or performance. Any month may be counted as 1/12th of a year, but a day is counted as 1/365th of a year. Subject to classifications and differentiations the seller may reasonably establish, a part of a month in excess of 15 days may be treated as a full month if periods of 15 days or less are disregarded and that procedure is not consistently used to obtain a greater yield than would otherwise be permitted. The Administrator may adopt rules not inconsistent with the Federal Truth in Lending Act with respect to treating as regular other minor irregularities in amount or time.

(5) Subject to classifications and differentiations the seller may reasonably establish, he may make the same finance charge on all amounts financed within a specified range. A finance charge so made does not violate subsection (2) if:

(a) when applied to the median amount within each range, it does not exceed the maximum permitted by subsection (2), and

(b) when applied to the lowest amount within each range, it does not produce a rate of finance charge exceeding the rate calculated according to paragraph (a) by more than eight per cent of the rate calculated according to paragraph (a).

(6) Notwithstanding subsection (2), the seller may contract for and receive a minimum finance charge of not more than $5 when the amount financed does not exceed $75, or $7.50 when the amount financed exceeds $75.

(7) The amounts of $300 and $1,000 in subsection (2) are subject to change pursuant to the provisions on adjustment of dollar amounts (Section 1.106).

Section 2.202 **[Finance Charge for Consumer Credit Sales Pursuant to Open-End Credit]**

(1) With respect to a consumer credit sale pursuant to open-end credit, a creditor may contract for and receive a finance charge not exceeding that permitted in this section.

(2) For each billing cycle a finance charge may be made which is a percentage of an amount not exceeding the greatest of:

(a) the average daily balance of the open-end account in the billing cycle for which the charge is made, which is the sum of the amount unpaid each day during that cycle, divided by the number of days in that cycle; the amount unpaid on a day is determined by adding to any balance unpaid as of the beginning of that day all purchases and other debits and deducting all payments and other credits made or received as of that day;

(b) the balance of the open-end account at the beginning of the first day of the billing cycle [after deducting all payments and credits made in the cycle except credits attributable to purchases charged to the account during the cycle]; or

(c) the median amount within a specified range including the balance of the open-end account not exceeding that permitted by paragraph (a) or (b); a finance charge may be made pursuant to this paragraph only if the creditor, subject to classifications and differentiations he may reasonably establish, makes the same charge on all balances within the specified range and if the percentage when applied to the median amount within the range does not produce a charge exceeding the charge resulting from applying that percentage to the lowest amount within the range by more than eight per cent of the charge on the median amount.

(3) If the billing cycle is monthly, the finance charge may not exceed an amount equal to two per cent of that part of the maximum amount pursuant to subsection (2) which is $500 or less and one and one-half per cent of that part of the maximum amount which is more than $500. If the billing cycle is not monthly, the maximum charge for the billing cycle shall bear the same relation to the applicable monthly maximum

charge as the number of days in the billing cycle bears to 365 divided by 12. A billing cycle is monthly if the closing date of the cycle is the same date each month or does not vary by more than four days from the regular date. Without regard to the length of the billing cycle, the finance charge may be computed at a daily rate that does not exceed 1/365ths of 12 times the monthly charge permitted by this section for a billing cycle that is monthly.

(4) If the finance charge determined pursuant to subsection (3) is less than 50 cents, a finance charge may be made which does not exceed 50 cents if the billing cycle is monthly or longer, or the pro rata part of 50 cents which bears the same relation to 50 cents as the number of days in the billing cycle bears to 365 divided by 12 if the billing cycle is shorter than monthly.

(5) The amounts of $500 in subsection (3) are subject to change pursuant to the provisions on adjustment of dollar amounts (Section 1.106).

Part 3 Consumer Loans: Supervised Lenders

Section 2.301 [Authority to Make Supervised Loans]

Unless a person is a supervised financial organization or has obtained a license from the Administrator authorizing him so to do, he may not engage in the business of:

(1) making supervised loans, or

(2) taking assignments of and undertaking direct collection of payments from or enforcement of rights against consumers arising from supervised loans, but he may collect and enforce for three months without a license if he promptly applies for a license and his application has not been denied.

Section 2.302 [License to Make Supervised Loans]

(1) The Administrator shall receive and act on all applications for licenses to make supervised loans under this Act. Applications shall be in the form and filed in the manner prescribed by the Administrator and contain or be accompanied by the information the Administrator requires by rule.

(2) The Administrator may not issue a license unless upon investigation he finds that the financial responsibility, character, and fitness of the applicant, and of

the members thereof if the applicant is a partnership or association or of the officers and directors thereof if the applicant is a corporation, warrant belief that the business will be operated honestly and fairly within the purposes of this Act. In determining the financial responsibility of an applicant proposing to engage in making insurance premium loans, the Administrator shall consider the liabilities the lender may incur for erroneous cancellation of insurance.

(3) Upon written request, the applicant is entitled to a hearing on the question of his qualifications for a license if (a) the Administrator notifies the applicant in writing that his application has been denied, or (b) the Administrator does not issue a license within 60 days after the application for the license was filed. A request for a hearing may not be made more than 15 days after the Administrator mails a writing to the applicant notifying him that the application has been denied and stating in substance the Administrator's findings supporting denial of the application.

(4) The Administrator shall issue additional licenses to the same licensee upon compliance with all the provisions of this Act governing issuance of a single license. A separate license is required for each place of business. Each license remains in full force and effect until surrendered, suspended, or revoked.

(5) A licensee may not change the location of any place of business without giving the Administrator at least 15 days prior written notice.

(6) A licensee may conduct the business of making supervised loans only at or from a place of business for which he holds a license and only under the name in the license. Credit granted pursuant to a lender credit card does not violate this subsection.

Section 2.303 [Revocation or Suspension of License]

(1) The Administrator may issue to a person licensed to make supervised loans an order to show cause why his license with respect to one or more specific places of business should not be suspended for a period not in excess of six months or be revoked. The order shall set a place for a hearing and a time therefor that is no less than ten days from the date of the order. After the hearing the Administrator shall revoke or suspend the license or, if there are mitigating circumstances, may accept an assurance of discontinuance (Section 6.109) and allow retention of the license, if he finds that:

(a) the licensee has repeatedly and intentionally violated this Act or any rule or order lawfully made pursuant to this Act, or has violated an assurance of discontinuance; or

(b) facts or conditions exist which clearly would have justified the Administrator in refusing to grant a license for that place or those places of business were these facts or conditions known to exist at the time the application for the license was made.

(2) A revocation or suspension of a license is not lawful unless the Administrator, before instituting proceedings, gives notice to the licensee of the facts or conduct which warrant the intended action, and the licensee is afforded an opportunity to show compliance with all lawful requirements for retention of the license.

(3) If the Administrator finds that probable cause for revocation of a license exists and that enforcement of this Act requires immediate suspension of the license pending investigation, he, after a hearing upon five days' written notice, may enter an order suspending the license for not more than 30 days.

(4) Whenever the Administrator revokes or suspends a license, he shall enter an order to that effect and forthwith notify the licensee of the revocation or suspension. Within five days after entry of the order he shall deliver to the licensee a copy of the order and the findings supporting the order.

(5) A person holding a license to make supervised loans may relinquish the license by notifying the Administrator in writing of its relinquishment, but the relinquishment does not affect his liability for acts previously committed.

(6) Revocation, suspension, or relinquishment of a license does not impair or affect the obligation of any preexisting lawful contract between the licensee and any consumer.

(7) The Administrator may reinstate a license, terminate a suspension, or grant a new license to a person whose license has been revoked or suspended if no fact or condition then exists which clearly would have justified the Administrator in refusing to grant a license.

Section 2.304 [Records; Annual Reports]

(1) Every licensee shall maintain records in confor-

mity with generally accepted accounting principles and practices in a manner that will enable the Administrator to determine whether the licensee is complying with this Act. The record keeping system of a licensee is sufficient if he makes the required information reasonably available. The records need not be kept in the place of business where supervised loans are made, if the Administrator is given free access to the records wherever located. The records pertaining to any loan need not be preserved for more than two years after making the final entry relating to the loan, but in the case of open-end credit the two years are measured from the date of each entry.

(2) On or before April 15 each year every licensee shall file with the Administrator a composite annual report in the form prescribed by the Administrator relating to all supervised loans made by him. The Administrator shall consult with comparable officials in other states for the purpose of making the kinds of information required in annual reports uniform among the states. Information contained in annual reports shall be confidential and may be published only in composite form.

Section 2.305 [Examinations and Investigations]

(1) The Administrator shall examine periodically at intervals he deems appropriate the loans, business, and records of every licensee. In addition, for the purpose of discovering violations of this Act or securing information lawfully required, the Administrator or the official or agency to whose supervision the organization is subject (Section 6.105) at any time may investigate the loans, business, and records of any lender. For these purposes he shall have free and reasonable access to the offices, places of business, and records of the lender.

(2) If the lender's records are located outside this State, the lender at his option shall make them available to the Administrator at a convenient location within this State, or pay the reasonable and necessary expenses for the Administrator or his representative to examine them where they are located. The Administrator may designate representatives, including comparable officials of the state in which the records are located, to inspect them on his behalf.

(3) For purposes of this section, the Administrator may administer oaths or affirmations, and upon request of a party or his own motion may subpoena witnesses, compel their attendance, adduce evidence, and require the production of any matter which is relevant to the investigation, including the existence, description, nature, custody, condition, and location of any books, documents, or other tangible things and the identity and location of persons having knowledge of relevant facts, or any other matter reasonably calculated to lead to the discovery of admissible evidence.

(4) Upon failure without lawful excuse to obey a subpoena or to give testimony and upon reasonable notice to all persons affected thereby, the Administrator may apply to the [   ] court for an order compelling compliance.

Section 2.306 [Application of [Administrative Procedure Act] [Part on Administrative Procedure and Judicial Review] to Part]

Except as otherwise provided, the [State Administrative Procedure Act] [Part on Administrative Procedure and Judicial Review (Part 4) of the Article on Administration (Article 6)] applies to and governs all administrative action taken by the Administrator pursuant to this Part.

Section 2.307 [Restrictions on Interest in Land as Security]

(1) A lender may contract for an interest in land as security, except to secure a supervised loan in which the amount financed is $1,000 or less. A security interest taken in violation of this section is unenforceable to the extent of that loan.

(2) The amount of $1,000 in subsection (1) is subject to change pursuant to the provisions on adjustment of dollar amounts (Section 1.106).

Section 2.308 [Regular Schedule of Payments; Maximum Loan Term]

(1) Supervised loans, not made pursuant to open-end credit and in which the amount financed is $1,000 or less, shall be scheduled to be payable in substantially equal instalments at substantially equal periodic intervals except to the extent that the schedule of payments is adjusted to the seasonal or irregular income of the debtor, and

(a) over a period not exceeding 37 months if the amount financed exceeds $300, or

(b) over a period not exceeding 25 months if the amount financed is $300 or less.

(2) The amounts of $300 and $1,000 in subsection (1) are subject to change pursuant to the provisions on adjustment of dollar amounts (Section 1.106).

Section 2.309 [No Other Business for Purpose of Evasion]

A supervised lender may not carry on other business for the purpose of evasion or violation of this Act at a location where he makes supervised loans.

Part 4 Consumer Loans: Maximum Finance Charges

Section 2.401 [Finance Charge for Consumer Loans]

(1) With respect to a consumer loan, including a loan pursuant to open-end credit, a lender who is not a supervised lender may contract for and receive a finance charge, calculated according to the actuarial method, not exceeding 18 per cent per year. With respect to a consumer loan made pursuant to open-end credit, the finance charge shall be deemed not to exceed 18 per cent per year if the finance charge contracted for and received does not exceed a charge for each monthly billing cycle which is one and one-half per cent of the average daily balance of the open-end account in the billing cycle for which the charge is made. The average daily balance of the open-end account is the sum of the amount unpaid each day during that cycle divided by the number of days in the cycle. The amount unpaid on a day is determined by adding to any balance unpaid as of the beginning of that day all purchases, loans, and other debits and deducting all payments and other credits made or received as of that day. If the billing cycle is not monthly, the finance charge shall be deemed not to exceed 18 per cent per year if the finance charge contracted for and received does not exceed a percentage which bears the same relation to one and one-half per cent as the number of days in the billing cycle bears to 365 divided by 12. A billing cycle is monthly if the closing date of the cycle is the same date each month or does not vary by more than four days from the regular date.

(2) With respect to a consumer loan, including a loan pursuant to open-end credit, a supervised lender may contract for and receive a finance charge, calculated

according to the actuarial method, not exceeding the equivalent of the greater of either of the following:

(a) the total of:

(i) 36 per cent per year on that part of the unpaid balances of the amount financed which is $300 or less;

(ii) 21 per cent per year on that part of the unpaid balances of the amount financed which exceeds $300 but does not exceed $1,000; and

(iii) 15 per cent per year on that part of the unpaid balances of the amount financed which exceeds $1,000; or

(b) 18 per cent per year on the unpaid balances of the amount financed.

(3) This section does not limit or restrict the manner of calculating the finance charge, whether by way of add-on, discount, single annual percentage rate, or otherwise, so long as the rate of the finance charge does not exceed that permitted by this section. The finance charge may be contracted for and earned at the single annual percentage rate that would earn the same finance charge as the graduated rates when the debt is paid according to the agreed terms and the calculations are made according to the actuarial method. If the loan is a precomputed consumer credit transaction:

(a) the finance charge may be calculated on the assumption that all scheduled payments will be made when due, and

(b) the effect of prepayment is governed by the provisions on rebate upon prepayment (Section 2.510).

(4) Except as provided in subsection (6), the term of a loan for purposes of this section commences on the day the loan is made. Any month may be counted as 1/12th of a year, but a day is counted as 1/365th of a year. Subject to classifications and differentiations the lender may reasonably establish, a part of a month in excess of 15 days may be treated as a full month if periods of 15 days or less are disregarded and that procedure is not consistently used to obtain a greater yield than would otherwise be permitted. The Administrator may adopt rules not inconsistent with the Federal Truth in Lending Act with respect to treating as regular other minor irregularities in amount or time.

(5) Subject to classifications and differentiations the lender may reasonably establish, he may make the same finance charge on all amounts financed within a specified range. A finance charge so made does not violate subsection (1) or (2) if:

(a) when applied to the median amount within each range, it does not exceed the maximum permitted by the applicable subsection, and

(b) when applied to the lowest amount within each range, it does not produce a rate of finance charge exceeding the rate calculated according to paragraph (a) by more than eight per cent of the rate calculated according to paragraph (a).

(6) With respect to an insurance premium loan, the term of the loan commences on the earliest inception date of a policy or contract of insurance payment of the premium on which is financed by the loan.

(7) The amounts of $300 and $1,000 in subsection (2) are subject to change pursuant to the provisions on adjustment of dollar amounts (Section 1.106).

Part 5 Consumer Credit Transactions: Other Charges and Modifications

Section 2.501 [Additional Charges]

(1) In addition to the finance charge permitted by the parts of this Article on maximum finance charges for consumer credit sales and consumer loans (Parts 2 and 4), a creditor may contract for and receive the following additional charges:

(a) official fees and taxes;

(b) charges for insurance as described in subsection (2);

(c) annual charges, payable in advance, for the privilege of using a credit card which entitles the cardholder to purchase or lease goods or services from at least 100 persons not related to the card issuer, under an arrangement pursuant to which the debts resulting from the purchases or leases are payable to the card issuer;

(d) with respect to a debt secured by an interest in land, the following "closing costs," if they are bona fide, reasonable in amount, and not for the purpose of circumvention or evasion of this Act:

(i) fees or premiums for title examination,

abstract of title, title insurance, surveys, or similar purposes,

(ii) fees for preparation of a deed, settlement statement, or other documents, if not paid to the creditor or a person related to the creditor,

(iii) escrows for future payments of taxes, including assessments for improvements, insurance, and water, sewer and land rents, and

(iv) fees for notarizing deeds and other documents, if not paid to the creditor or a person related to the creditor; and

(e) charges for other benefits, including insurance, conferred on the consumer, if the benefits are of value to him and if the charges are reasonable in relation to the benefits, are of a type that is not for credit, and are authorized as permissible additional charges by rule adopted by the Administrator.

(2) An additional charge may be made for insurance written in connection with the transaction:

(a) with respect to insurance against loss of or damage to property, or against liability arising out of the ownership or use of property, if the creditor furnishes a clear, conspicuous, and specific statement in writing to the consumer setting forth the cost of the insurance if obtained from or through the creditor and stating that the consumer may choose the person through whom the insurance is to be obtained;

(b) with respect to consumer credit insurance providing life, accident, or health coverage, if the insurance coverage is not required by the creditor, and this fact is clearly and conspicuously disclosed in writing to the consumer, and if, in order to obtain the insurance in connection with the extension of credit, the consumer gives specific, dated, and separately signed affirmative written indication of his desire to do so after written disclosure to him of the cost thereof; and

(c) with respect to vendor's single interest insurance, but only (i) to the extent that the insurer has no right of subrogation against the consumer, and (ii) to the extent that the insurance does not duplicate the coverage of other insurance under which loss is payable to the creditor as his interest may appear, against loss of or damage to property for which a separate charge is made to the consumer pursuant to paragraph (a), and (iii) if a clear, conspicuous, and specific statement in writing is furnished by the creditor to the consumer setting forth the cost of the insurance if obtained from or through the creditor and stating that the consumer may choose the person through whom the insurance is to be obtained.

Section 2.502 [Delinquency Charges]

(1) With respect to a precomputed consumer credit transaction, the parties may contract for a delinquency charge on any instalment not paid in full within ten days after its due date, as originally scheduled or as deferred, in an amount, not exceeding $5, which is not more than five per cent of the unpaid amount of the instalment.

(2) A delinquency charge under subsection (1) may be collected only once on an instalment however long it remains in default. No delinquency charge may be collected with respect to a deferred instalment unless the instalment is not paid in full within ten days after its deferred due date. A delinquency charge may be collected at the time it accrues or at any time thereafter.

(3) A delinquency charge under subsection (1) may not be collected on an installment paid in full within ten days after its scheduled or deferred installment due date even though an earlier maturing installment or a delinquency or deferral charge on an earlier installment has not been paid in full. For purposes of this subsection a payment is deemed to have been applied first to any installment due in the computational period (paragraph (a) of subsection (1) of Section 2.503) in which it is received and then to delinquent installments and charges.

(4) If two installments or parts thereof of a precomputed consumer loan are in default for ten days or more, the lender may elect to convert the loan from a precomputed loan to one in which the finance charge is based on unpaid balances. In this event he shall make a rebate pursuant to the provisions on rebate upon prepayment (Section 2.510) as if the date of prepayment were one day before the maturity date of a delinquent installment, and thereafter may make a finance charge as authorized by the provisions on finance charge for consumer loans by lenders not

supervised lenders (subsection (1) of Section 2.401) or finance charge for consumer loans by supervised lenders (subsection (2) of Section 2.401), whichever is appropriate. The amount of the rebate shall not be reduced by the amount of any permitted minimum charge (Section 2.510). If the creditor proceeds under this subsection, any delinquency or deferral charges made with respect to installments due at or after the maturity date of the first delinquent installment shall be rebated, and no further delinquency or deferral charges shall be made.

(5) The amount of $5 in subsection (1) is subject to change pursuant to the provisions on adjustment of dollar amounts (Section 1.106).

Section 2.503 [Deferral Charges]

(1) In this section and in the provisions on rebate upon prepayment (Section 2.510) the following defined terms apply with respect to a precomputed consumer credit transaction:

(a) "Computational period" means (i) the interval between scheduled due dates of installments under the transaction if the intervals are substantially equal or, (ii) if the intervals are not substantially equal, one month if the smallest interval between the scheduled due dates of installments under the transaction is one month or more, and, otherwise, one week.

(b) "Deferral" means a postponement of the scheduled due date of an installment as originally scheduled or as previously deferred.

(c) "Deferral period" means a period in which no instalment is scheduled to be paid by reason of a deferral.

(d) The "interval" between specified dates means the interval between them including one or the other but not both of them; if the interval between the date of a transaction and the due date of the first scheduled installment does not exceed one month by more than 15 days when the computational period is one month, or does not exceed 11 days when the computational period is one week, the interval may be considered by the creditor as one computational period.

(e) "Periodic balance" means the amount scheduled to be outstanding on the last day of a computational period before deducting the instalment, if any, scheduled to be paid on that day.

(f) "Standard deferral" means a deferral with respect to a transaction made as of the due date of an installment as scheduled before the deferral by which the due dates of that installment and all subsequent installments as scheduled before the deferral are deferred for a period equal to the deferral period. A standard deferral may be for one or more full computational periods or a portion of one computational period or a combination of any of these.

(g) "Sum of the balances method," also known as the "Rule of 78," means a method employed with respect to a transaction to determine the portion of the finance charge attributable to a period of time before the scheduled due date of the final instalment of the transaction. The amount so attributable is determined by multiplying the finance charge by a fraction the numerator of which is the sum of the periodic balances included within the period and the denominator of which is the sum of all periodic balances under the transaction. According to the sum of the balances method the portion of the finance charge attributable to a specified computational period is the difference between the portions of the finance charge attributable to the periods of time including and excluding, respectively, the computational period, both determined according to the sum of the balances method.

(h) "Transaction" means a precomputed consumer credit transaction unless the context otherwise requires.

(2) Before or after default in payment of a scheduled instalment of a transaction, the parties to the transaction may agree in writing to a deferral of all or part of one or more unpaid instalments and the creditor may make at the time of deferral and receive at that time or at any time thereafter a deferral charge not exceeding that provided in this section.

(3) A standard deferral may be made with respect to a transaction as of the due date, as originally scheduled or as deferred pursuant to a standard deferral, of an instalment with respect to which no delinquency charge (Section 2.502) has been made or, if made, is

deducted from the deferral charge computed according to this subsection. The deferral charge for a standard deferral may equal but not exceed the portion of the finance charge attributable to the computational period immediately preceding the due date of the earliest maturing instalment deferred as determined according to the sum of the balances method multiplied by the whole or fractional number of computational periods in the deferral period, counting each day as 1/30th of a month without regard to differences in lengths of months when the computational period is one month or as 1/7th of a week when the computational period is one week. A deferral charge computed according to this subsection is earned pro rata during the deferral period and is fully earned on the last day of the deferral period.

(4) With respect to a transaction as to which a creditor elects not to make and does not make a standard deferral or a deferral charge for a standard deferral, a deferral charge computed according to this subsection may be made as of the due date, as scheduled originally or as deferred pursuant to either subsection (3) or this subsection, of an instalment with respect to which no delinquency charge (Section 2.502) has been made or, if made, is deducted from the deferral charge computed according to this subsection. A deferral charge pursuant to this subsection may equal but not exceed the rate of finance charge required to be disclosed to the consumer pursuant to law applied to each amount deferred for the period for which it is deferred computed without regard to differences in lengths of months, but proportionately for a part of a month, counting each day as 1/30th of a month or as 1/7th of a week. A deferral charge computed according to this subsection is earned pro rata with respect to each amount deferred during the period for which it is deferred.

(5) In addition to the deferral charge permitted by this section, a creditor may make and receive appropriate additional charges (Section 2.501), and any amount of these charges which is not paid may be added to the deferral charge computed accor ding to subsection (3) or to the amount deferred for the purpose of computing the deferral charge computed according to subsection (4).

(6) The parties may agree in writing at the time of a transaction that, if an instalment is not paid within ten

days after its due date, the creditor may unilaterally grant a deferral and make charges as provided in this section. A deferral charge may not be made for a period after the date that the creditor elects to accelerate the maturity of the transaction.

Section 2.504 **[Finance Charge on Refinancing]**

With respect to a consumer credit transaction except a consumer lease, the creditor by agreement with the consumer may refinance the unpaid balance and contract for and receive a finance charge based on the amount financed resulting from the refinancing at a rate not exceeding that permitted by the provisions on finance charge for consumer credit sales other than open-end credit (Section 2.201) if a consumer credit sale is refinanced, or for consumer loans (subsection (1) or (2) of Section 2.401, whichever is appropriate) if a consumer loan is refinanced. For the purpose of determining the finance charge permitted, the amount financed resulting from the refinancing comprises the following:

(1) if the transaction was not precomputed, the total of the unpaid balance and the accrued charges on the date of the refinancing, or, if the transaction was precomputed, the amount which the consumer would have been required to pay upon prepayment pursuant to the provisions on rebate upon prepayment (Section 2.510) on the date of refinancing, but for the purpose of computing this amount no minimum charge is permitted; and

(2) appropriate additional charges (Section 2.501), payment of which is deferred.

Section 2.505 **[Finance Charge on Consolidation]**

(1) In this section, "consumer credit transaction" does not include a consumer lease.

(2) If a consumer owes an unpaid balance to a creditor with respect to a consumer credit transaction and becomes obligated on another consumer credit transaction with the same creditor, the parties may agree to a consolidation resulting in a single schedule of payments. If the previous consumer credit transaction was not precomputed, the parties may agree to add the unpaid amount of the amount financed and accrued charges on the date of consolidation to the amount financed with respect to the subsequent consumer credit transaction. If the previous consumer credit transaction was precomputed, the

parties may agree to refinance the unpaid balance pursuant to the provisions on refinancing (Section 2.504) and to consolidate the amount financed resulting from the refinancing by adding it to the amount financed with respect to the subsequent consumer credit transaction. In either case the creditor may contract for and receive a finance charge as provided in subsection (3) based on the aggregate amount financed resulting from the consolidation.

(3) If the debts consolidated arise exclusively from consumer credit sales, the transaction is a consolidation with respect to a consumer credit sale and the creditor may make a finance charge not exceeding that permitted by the provisions on finance charge for consumer credit sales other than open-end credit (Section 2.201). If the debts consolidated include a debt arising from a prior or contemporaneous consumer loan, the transaction is a consolidation with respect to a consumer loan and the creditor may make a finance charge not exceeding that permitted by the provisions on finance charge for consumer loans by lenders not supervised lenders (subsection (1) of Section 2.401) or for consumer loans by supervised lenders (subsection (2) of Section 2.401), whichever is appropriate.

(4) If a consumer owes an unpaid balance to a creditor with respect to a consumer credit transaction arising out of a consumer credit sale, and becomes obligated on another consumer credit transaction arising out of another consumer credit sale by the same seller, the parties may agree to a consolidation resulting in a single schedule of payments either pursuant to subsection (2) or by adding together the unpaid balances with respect to the two sales.

Section 2.506 **[Advances to Perform Covenants of Consumer]**

(1) If the agreement with respect to a consumer credit transaction other than a consumer lease contains covenants by the consumer to perform certain duties pertaining to insuring or preserving collateral and the creditor pursuant to the agreement pays for performance of the duties on behalf of the consumer, he may add the amounts paid to the debt. Within a reasonable time after advancing any sums, he shall state to the consumer in writing the amount of sums advanced, any charges with respect to this amount, and any revised payment schedule and, if the duties

of the consumer performed by the creditor pertain to insurance, a brief description of the insurance paid for by the creditor including the type and amount of coverages. Further information need not be given.

(2) A finance charge may be made for sums advanced pursuant to subsection (1) at a rate not exceeding the rate of finance charge required to be stated to the consumer pursuant to law in a disclosure statement, but with respect to open-end credit the amount of the advance may be added to the unpaid balance of the debt and the creditor may make a finance charge not exceeding that permitted by the appropriate provisions on finance charge for consumer credit sales pursuant to open-end credit (Section 2.202) or for consumer loans (subsection (1) or (2) of Section 2.401), whichever is appropriate.

Alternative A:

Section 2.507 [Attorney's Fees]

With respect to a consumer credit transaction, the agreement may not provide for payment by the consumer of attorney's fees. A provision in violation of this section is unenforceable.

Alternative B:

Section 2.507 [Attorney's Fees]

(1) With respect to a consumer loan in which the finance charge calculated according to the actuarial method is more than 18 per cent per year, the agreement may not provide for payment by the consumer of attorney's fees:

(a) if the loan is not pursuant to open-end credit and the amount financed is $1,000 or less; or

(b) if the loan is pursuant to open-end credit and the balance of the account at the time of default is $1,000 or less.

A provision in violation of this subsection is unenforceable.

(2) With respect to any other consumer credit transaction, the agreement may provide for payment by the consumer of reasonable attorney's fees not in excess of 15 per cent of the unpaid debt after default and referral to an attorney not a salaried employee of the creditor. A provision in violation of this subsection is unenforceable.

(3) The amounts of $1,000 in subsection (1) are subject to change pursuant to the provisions on adjustment of dollar amounts (Section 1.106).

Section 2.508 [Conversion to Open-End Credit]

The parties may agree at or within ten days before the time of conversion to add the unpaid balance of a consumer credit transaction, except a consumer lease, not made pursuant to open-end credit to the consumer's open-end credit account with the creditor. The unpaid balance so added is an amount equal to the amount financed determined according to the provisions on finance charge on refinancing (Section 2.504).

Section 2.509 [Right to Prepay]

Subject to the provisions on rebate upon prepayment (Section 2.510), the consumer may prepay in full the unpaid balance of a consumer credit transaction, except a consumer lease, at any time without penalty.

Section 2.510 [Rebate Upon Prepayment]

(1) Except as otherwise provided in this section, upon prepayment in full of a precomputed consumer credit transaction, the creditor shall rebate to the consumer an amount not less than the unearned portion of the finance charge computed according to this section. If the rebate otherwise required is less than $1, no rebate need be made.

(2) Upon prepayment of a consumer credit transaction, whether or not precomputed, except a consumer lease or one pursuant to open-end credit, the creditor may collect or retain a minimum charge not exceeding $5 in a transaction which had an amount financed of $75 or less, or not exceeding $7.50 in a transaction which had an amount financed of more than $75, if the minimum charge was contracted for and the finance charge earned at the time of prepayment is less than the minimum charge contracted for.

(3) In the following subsections these terms have the meanings ascribed to them in subsection (1) of Section 2.503: computational period, deferral, deferral period, periodic balance, standard deferral, sum of the balances method, and transaction.

(4) If, with respect to a transaction payable according to its original terms in no more than [48] instalments, the creditor has made either:

(a) no deferral or deferral charge, the unearned

portion of the finance charge is no less than the portion thereof attributable according to the sum of the balances method to the period from the first day of the computational period following that in which prepayment occurs to the scheduled due date of the final instalment of the transaction; or

(b) a standard deferral and a deferral charge pursuant to the provisions on a standard deferral, the unpaid balance of the transaction includes any unpaid portions of the deferral charge and any appropriate additional charges incident to the deferral, and the unearned portion of the finance charge is no less than the portion thereof attributable according to the sum of the balances method to the period from the first day of the computational period following that in which prepayment occurs except that the numerator of the fraction is the sum of the periodic balances, after rescheduling to give effect to any standard deferral, scheduled to follow the computational period in which prepayment occurs. A separate rebate of the deferral charge is not required unless the unpaid balance of the transaction is paid in full during the deferral period, in which event the creditor shall also rebate the unearned portion of the deferral charge.

(5) In lieu of computing a rebate of the unearned portion of the finance charge as provided in subsection (4) of this section, the creditor:

(a) shall, with respect to a transaction payable according to its original terms in more than [48] instalments, and a transaction payable according to its original terms in no more than [48] instalments as to which the creditor has made a deferral other than a standard deferral, and

(b) may, in other cases,

recompute or redetermine the earned finance charge by applying, according to the actuarial method, the annual percentage rate of finance charge required to be disclosed to the consumer pursuant to law to the actual unpaid balances of the amount financed for the actual time that the unpaid balances were outstanding as of the date of prepayment, giving effect to each payment, including payments of any deferral and delinquency charges, as of the date of the payment. The Administrator shall adopt rules to simplify the calculation of the unearned portion of the finance charge, including allowance of the use of tables or other methods derived by application of a percentage rate which deviates by not more than one-half of one per cent from the rate of the finance charge required to be disclosed to the consumer pursuant to law, and based on the assumption that all payments were made as originally scheduled or as deferred.

(6) Except as otherwise provided in subsection (5), this section does not preclude the collection or retention by the creditor of delinquency charges (Section 2.502).

(7) If the maturity is accelerated for any reason and judgment is entered, the consumer is entitled to the same rebate as if payment had been made on the date judgment is entered.

(8) Upon prepayment in full of a precomputed consumer credit transaction by the proceeds of consumer credit insurance (Section 4.103), the consumer or his estate is entitled to the same rebate as though the consumer had prepaid the agreement on the date the proceeds of insurance are paid to the creditor, but no later than 20 business days after satisfactory proof of loss is furnished to the creditor.

Part 6 **Other Credit Transactions**

Section 2.601 **[Charges for Other Credit Transactions]**

(1) Except as provided in subsection (2), with respect to a credit transaction other than a consumer credit transaction, the parties may contract for payment by the debtor of any finance or other charge.

(2) With respect to a credit transaction which would be a consumer credit transaction if a finance charge were made, a charge for delinquency may not exceed amounts allowed for finance charges for consumer credit sales pursuant to open-end credit (Section 2.202).

Article 3
REGULATION OF AGREEMENTS AND PRACTICES

Part 1 **General Provisions**
Section 3.101 **[Short Title]**

This Article shall be known and may be cited as

Uniform Consumer Credit Code—Regulation of Agreements and Practices.

Section 3.102 [Scope]

Part 2 of this Article applies to disclosure with respect to consumer credit transactions. The provision on compliance with the Federal Truth in Lending Act (Section 3.201) applies to a sale of an interest in land or a loan secured by an interest in land, without regard to the rate of finance charge, if the sale or loan is otherwise a consumer credit sale or consumer loan. Parts 3 and 4 of this Article apply, respectively, to limitations on agreements and practices, and limitations on consumers' liabilities with respect to certain consumer credit transactions. Part 5 applies to home solicitation sales.

Part 2 Disclosure

Section 3.201 [Compliance with Federal Truth in Lending Act]

(1) A person upon whom the Federal Truth in Lending Act imposes duties or obligations shall make or give to the consumer the disclosures, information, and notices required of him by that Act and in all respects comply with that Act. To the extent the Federal Truth in Lending Act does not impose duties or obligations upon a person in a credit transaction, except a consumer lease, that is a consumer credit transaction under this Act, the person shall make or give to the consumer disclosures, information, and notices in accordance with the Federal Truth in Lending Act with respect to the credit transaction.

(2) The Federal Truth in Lending Act is deemed to apply to a credit transaction which is a consumer credit transaction under this Act, notwithstanding its inclusion in a class of transactions within this State which, by regulation of the Board of Governors of the Federal Reserve System, is exempt from the Federal Truth in Lending Act.

Section 3.202 [Consumer Leases]

(1) With respect to a consumer lease the lessor shall give to the lessee the following information:

(a) brief description or identification of the goods;

(b) amount of any payment required at the inception of the lease;

(c) amount paid or payable for official fees, registration, certificate of title, or license fees or taxes;

(d) amount of other charges not included in the periodic payments and a brief description of the charges;

(e) brief description of insurance to be provided or paid for by the lessor, including the types and amounts of the coverages;

(f) number of periodic payments, the amount of each payment, the due date of the first payment, the due dates of subsequent payments or interval between payments, and the total amount payable by the lessee;

(g) statement of the conditions under which the lessee may terminate the lease before the end of the term; and

(h) statement of the liabilities the lease imposes upon the lessee at the end of the term.

(2) The disclosures required by this section:

(a) shall be made clearly and conspicuously in writing, a copy of which shall be delivered to the lessee;

(b) may be supplemented by additional information or explanations supplied by the lessor, but none shall be stated, utilized, or placed so as to mislead or confuse the lessee or contradict, obscure, or detract attention from the information required to be disclosed by this section;

(c) need be made only to the extent applicable;

(d) shall be made on the assumption that all scheduled payments will be made when due and will comply with this section although rendered inaccurate by an act, occurrence, or agreement after the required disclosure; and

(e) shall be made before the lease transaction is consummated, but may be made in the lease to be signed by the lessee.

Section 3.203 [Notice to Consumer]

The creditor shall give to the consumer a copy of any writing evidencing a consumer credit transaction, except one pursuant to open-end credit, if the writing requires or provides for the signature of the consumer. The writing evidencing the consumer's obligation to pay the debt shall contain a clear and conspicuous notice informing the consumer that he should not sign it before reading it, that he is entitled to a copy of it, and, except in case of a consumer lease, that he is entitled to prepay the unpaid balance at any time without penalty and may be entitled to receive a refund of unearned charges in accordance with law. The following notice if clear and conspicuous complies with this section:

NOTICE TO CONSUMER:

1. Do not sign this paper before you read it.

2. You are entitled to a copy of this paper.

3. You may prepay the unpaid balance at any time without penalty and may be entitled to receive a refund of unearned charges in accordance with law.

Section 3.204 [Notice of Assignment]

A consumer may pay the original creditor until he receives notification of assignment of rights to payment pursuant to a consumer credit transaction and that payment is to be made to the assignee. A notification which does not reasonably identify the rights assigned is ineffective. If requested by the consumer, the assignee shall seasonably furnish reasonable proof that the assignment has been made and unless he does so the consumer may pay the original creditor.

Section 3.205 [Change in Terms of Open-End Credit Accounts]

(1) Whether or not a change is authorized by prior agreement, a creditor may change the terms of an open-end credit account applying to any balance incurred before or after the effective date of the change. If the change increases the rate of the finance charge or of additional charges, alters the method of determining the balance upon which charges are made so that increased charges may result, or imposes or increases minimum charges, the change is effective with respect to a balance incurred before the effective date of the change only if the consumer after receiving disclosure of the change agrees to it in writing or the creditor delivers or mails to the consumer two written disclosures of the change, the first at least three months before the effective date of the change and the second at a later time before the effective date of the change.

(2) A disclosure provided for in subsection (1) is mailed to the consumer when mailed to him at his address used by the creditor for mailing him periodic billing statements.

(3) If a creditor attempts to change the terms of an open-end credit account as provided in subsection (1) without complying with this section, any additional cost or charge to the consumer resulting from the change is an excess charge and is subject to the remedies available to the consumer (Section 5.201) and to the Administrator (Section 6.113).

Section 3.206 [Receipts; Statements of Account; Evidence of Payment]

(1) The creditor shall deliver or mail to the consumer, without request, a written receipt for each payment by coin or currency on an obligation pursuant to a consumer credit transaction. A periodic statement showing a payment received by mail complies with this subsection.

(2) Upon written request of a consumer, the person to whom an obligation is owed pursuant to a consumer credit transaction, except one pursuant to open-end credit, shall provide a written statement of the dates and amounts of payments made within the 12 months preceding the month in which the request is received and the total amount unpaid as of the end of the period covered by the statement. The statement shall be provided without charge once during each year of the term of the obligation. If additional statements are requested the creditor may charge not in excess of [$_____] for each additional statement.

(3) After a consumer has fulfilled all obligations with respect to a consumer credit transaction, except one pursuant to open-end credit, the person to whom the obligation was owed, upon request of the consumer, shall deliver or mail to the consumer written evidence acknowledging payment in full of all obligations with respect to the transaction.

Section 3.207 [Form of Insurance Premium Loan Agreement]

An agreement pursuant to which an insurance premium loan is made shall contain the names of the insurance agent or broker negotiating each policy or contract and of the insurer issuing each policy or contract, the number and inception date of, and premium for, each policy or contract, the date on which the term of the loan begins, and a clear and conspicuous notice that each policy or contract may be cancelled if payment is not made in accordance with the agreement. If a policy or contract has not been issued by the time the agreement is signed, the agreement may provide that the insurance agent or broker may insert the appropriate information in the agreement and, if he does so, shall furnish the information promptly in writing to the insured.

Section 3.208 [Notice to Co-Signers and Similar Parties]

(1) A natural person, other than the spouse of the consumer, is not obligated as a co-signer, co-maker, guarantor, indorser, surety, or similar party with respect to a consumer credit transaction, unless before or contemporaneously with signing any separate agreement of obligation or any writing setting forth the terms of the debtor's agreement, the person receives a separate written notice that contains a completed identification of the debt he may have to pay and reasonably informs him of his obligation with respect to it.

(2) A clear and conspicuous notice in substantially the following form complies with this section:

NOTICE

You agree to pay the debt identified below although you may not personally receive any property, services, or money. You may be sued for payment although the person who receives the property, services, or money is able to pay. This notice is not the contract that obligates you to pay the debt. Read the contract for the exact terms of your obligation.

IDENTIFICATION OF DEBT
YOU MAY HAVE TO PAY

_____

(Name of Debtor)

_____

(Name of Creditor)

_____

(Date)

_____

(Kind of Debt)

I have received a copy of this notice.

_____

(Date)

_____

(Signed)

(3) The notice required by this section need not be given to a seller, lessor, or lender who is obligated to an assignee of his rights.

(4) A person entitled to notice under this section shall also be given a copy of any writing setting forth the terms of the debtor's agreement and of any separate agreement of obligation signed by the person entitled to the notice.

Section 3.209 [Advertising]

(1) A seller, lessor, or lender may not advertise, print, display, publish, distribute, broadcast, or cause to be advertised, printed, displayed, published, distributed, or broadcast in any manner any statement or representation with regard to the rates, terms, or conditions of credit with respect to a consumer credit transaction that is false, misleading, or deceptive.

(2) Advertising that complies with the Federal Truth in Lending Act does not violate this section.

(3) This section does not apply to the owner or personnel, as such, of any medium in which an advertisement appears or through which it is disseminated.

Part 3 Limitations on Agreements and Practices

Section 3.301 [Security in Sales and Leases]

(1) With respect to a consumer credit sale, a seller may take a security interest in the property sold. In addition, a seller may take a security interest in goods upon which services are performed or in which goods sold are installed or to which they are annexed, or in land to which the goods are affixed or which is maintained, repaired or improved as a result of the sale of the goods or services, if in the case of a security interest in land the debt secured is $1,000 or more, or, in the case of a security interest in goods the debt secured is $300 or more. The seller may also take a security interest in property to secure the debt arising from a consumer credit sale primarily for an agricultural purpose. Except as provided with respect to cross-collateral (Section 3.302) a seller may not otherwise take a security interest in property to secure the debt arising from a consumer credit sale.

(2) With respect to a consumer lease, except one primarily for an agricultural purpose, a lessor may not

take a security interest in property to secure the debt arising from the lease. This subsection does not apply to a security deposit for a consumer lease.

(3) A security interest taken in violation of this section is void.

(4) The amounts of $1,000 and $300 in subsection (1) are subject to change pursuant to the provisions on adjustment of dollar amounts (Section 1.106).

Section 3.302 [Cross-Collateral]

(1) In addition to contracting for a security interest pursuant to the provisions on security in sales and leases (Section 3.301), a seller in a consumer credit sale may secure the debt arising from the sale by contracting for a security interest in other property if as a result of a prior sale the seller has an existing security interest in the other property. The seller may also contract for a security interest in the property sold in the subsequent sale as security for the previous debt.

(2) If the seller contracts for a security interest in other property pursuant to this section, the rate of finance charge thereafter on the aggregate unpaid balances so secured may not exceed that permitted if the balances so secured were consolidated pursuant to the provisions on finance charge on consolidation (subsection (2) of Section 2.505). The seller has a reasonable time after so contracting in which to make any adjustments required by this section.

Section 3.303 [Debt Secured by Cross-Collateral]

(1) If debts arising from two or more consumer credit sales, except sales primarily for an agricultural purpose or pursuant to open-end credit, are secured by cross-collateral (Section 3.302) or consolidated into one debt payable on a single schedule of payments, and the debt is secured by security interests taken with respect to one or more of the sales, payments received by the seller after the taking of cross-collateral or the consolidation are deemed, for the purpose of determining the amount of the debt secured by the various security interests, to have been applied first to the payment of the debts arising from the sales first made. To the extent debts are paid according to this section, security interests in items of property terminate as the debt originally incurred with respect to each item is paid.

(2) Payments received by the seller upon an open-end credit account are deemed, for the purpose of determining the amount of the debt secured by the various security interests, to have been applied first to the payment of finance charges in the order of their entry to the account and then to the payment of debts in the order in which the entries to the account showing the debts were made.

(3) If the debts consolidated arose from two or more sales made on the same day, payments received by the seller are deemed, for the purpose of determining the amount of the debt secured by the various security interests, to have been applied first to the payment of the smallest debt.

Section 3.304 [Use of Multiple Agreements]

(1) A creditor may not use multiple agreements with respect to a single consumer credit transaction with intent to obtain a higher finance charge than otherwise would be permitted by the provisions of the Article on Finance Charges and Related Provisions (Article 2).

(2) The excess amount of finance charge resulting from a violation of subsection (1) is an excess charge for the purposes of the provisions on rights of parties (Section 5.201) and the provisions on civil actions by Administrator (Section 6.113).

Section 3.305 [No Assignment of Earnings]

(1) A creditor may not take an assignment of earnings of the consumer for payment or as security for payment of a debt arising out of a consumer credit transaction. An assignment of earnings in violation of this section is unenforceable by the assignee of the earnings and revocable by the consumer. This section does not prohibit a consumer from authorizing deductions from his earnings in favor of his creditor if the authorization is revocable, the consumer is given a complete copy of the writing evidencing the authorization at the time he signs it, and the writing contains on its face a conspicuous notice of the consumer's right to revoke the authorization.

(2) A sale of unpaid earnings made in consideration of the payment of money to or for the account of the seller of the earnings is deemed to be a loan to him secured by an assignment of earnings.

Section 3.306 [Authorization to Confess Judgment Prohibited]

A consumer may not authorize any person to confess judgment on a claim arising out of a consumer credit transaction. An authorization in violation of this section is void.

Section 3.307 [Certain Negotiable Instruments Prohibited]

With respect to a consumer credit sale or consumer lease, [except a sale or lease primarily for an agricultural purpose,] the creditor may not take a negotiable instrument other than a check dated not later than ten days after its issuance as evidence of the obligation of the consumer.

Section 3.308 [Balloon Payments]

(1) Except as provided in subsection (2), if any scheduled payment of a consumer credit transaction is more than twice as large as the average of earlier scheduled payments, the consumer has the right to refinance, without penalty, the amount of that payment at the time it is due. The terms of the refinancing shall be no less favorable to the consumer than the terms of the original transaction.

(2) This section does not apply to:

(a) a consumer lease;

(b) a transaction pursuant to open-end credit;

(c) a transaction primarily for an agricultural purpose;

(d) a transaction to the extent that the payment schedule is adjusted to the seasonal or irregular income or scheduled payments or obligations of the consumer; or

(e) a transaction of a class defined by rule of the Administrator as not requiring for the protection of the consumer his right to refinance as provided in this section.

Section 3.309 [Referral Sales and Leases]

With respect to a consumer credit sale or consumer lease, the seller or lessor may not give or offer to give a rebate or discount or otherwise pay or offer to pay value to the consumer as an inducement for a sale or lease for the consumer giving to the seller or lessor the names of prospective buyers or lessees, or otherwise aiding the seller or lessor in making a sale or lease to another person, if the earning of the rebate, discount or other value is contingent upon the occurrence of an event after the time the consumer agrees to buy or lease. If a consumer is induced by a violation of this section to enter into a consumer credit sale or consumer lease, the agreement is unenforceable by the seller or lessor and the consumer, at his option, may rescind the agreement or retain the property delivered and the benefit of any services performed, without any obligation to pay for them. A sale or lease that would be a referral sale or lease if credit were extended by the seller or lessor is nonetheless so because the property or services are paid for in whole or in part by use of a credit card or by a consumer loan with respect to which the lender is subject to claims and defenses arising from the sale or lease (Section 3.405), and the consumer has the same rights against the card issuer or lender that he has against the seller or lessor under this section.

Part 4 Limitations on Consumers' Liabilities

Section 3.401 [Restriction on Liability in Consumer Lease]

The obligation of a lessee upon expiration of a consumer lease [, except one primarily for an agricultural purpose,] may not exceed twice the average payment allocable to a monthly period under the lease. This limitation does not apply to charges for damages to the leased property or for other default.

Section 3.402 [Limitation on Default Charges]

Except for reasonable expenses incurred in realizing on a security interest, the agreement with respect to a consumer credit transaction other than a consumer lease may not provide for any charges as a result of default by the consumer except those authorized by this Act. A provision in violation of this section is unenforceable.

Section 3.403 [Card Issuer Subject to Claims and Defenses]

(1) This section neither limits the liability of nor imposes liability on a card issuer as a manufacturer, supplier, seller, or lessor of property or services sold

or leased pursuant to the credit card. This section may subject a card issuer to claims and defenses of a cardholder against a seller or lessor arising from sales or leases made pursuant to the credit card.

(2) A card issuer is subject to claims and defenses of a cardholder against the seller or lessor arising from the sale or lease of property or services by a seller or lessor licensed, franchised, or permitted by the card issuer or a person related to the card issuer to do business under the trade name or designation of the card issuer or a person related to the card issuer, to the extent of the original amount owing to the card issuer with respect to the sale or lease of the property or services as to which the claim or defense arose.

(3) Except as otherwise provided in this section, a card issuer, including a lender credit card issuer, is subject to all claims and defenses of a cardholder against the seller or lessor arising from the sale or lease of property or services pursuant to the credit card:

(a) if the original amount owing to the card issuer with respect to the sale or lease of the property or services as to which the claim or defense arose exceeds $50;

(b) if the residence of the cardholder and the place where the sale or lease occurred are [in the same state or] within 100 miles of each other;

(c) if the cardholder has made a good faith attempt to obtain satisfaction from the seller or lessor with respect to the claim or defense; and

(d) to the extent of the amount owing to the card issuer with respect to the sale or lease of the property or services as to which the claim or defense arose at the time the card issuer has notice of the claim or defense. Notice of the claim or defense may be given before the attempt specified in paragraph (c). Oral notice is effective unless the card issuer requests written confirmation when or promptly after oral notice is given and the card-holder fails to give the card issuer written confir-mation within the period of time, not less than 14 days, stated to the cardholder when written confirmation is requested.

(4) For the purpose of determining the amount owing to the card issuer with respect to a sale or lease upon an open-end credit account, payments received for the account are deemed to have been applied first to the payment of finance charges in the order of their entry to the account and then to the payment of debts in the order in which the entries of the debts are made to the account.

(5) An agreement may not limit or waive the claims or defenses of a cardholder under this section.

Section 3.404 **[Assignee Subject to Claims and Defenses]**

(1) With respect to a consumer credit sale or con-sumer lease [, except one primarily for an agricultural purpose], an assignee of the rights of the seller or lessor is subject to all claims and defenses of the consumer against the seller or lessor arising from the sale or lease of property or services, notwithstanding that the assignee is a holder in due course of a negotiable instrument issued in violation of the provisions prohibiting certain negotiable instruments (Section 3.307).

(2) A claim or defense of a consumer specified in subsection (1) may be asserted against the assignee under this section only if the consumer has made a good faith attempt to obtain satisfaction from the seller or lessor with respect to the claim or defense and then only to the extent of the amount owing to the assignee with respect to the sale or lease of the property or services as to which the claim or defense arose at the time the assignee has notice of the claim or defense. Notice of the claim or defense may be given before the attempt specified in this subsection. Oral notice is effective unless the assignee requests written confirmation when or promptly after oral notice is given and the consumer fails to give the assignee written confirmation within the period of time, not less than 14 days, stated to the consumer when written confirmation is requested.

(3) For the purpose of determining the amount owing to the assignee with respect to the sale or lease:

(a) payments received by the assignee after the consolidation of two or more consumer credit sales, except pursuant to open-end credit, are deemed to have been applied first to the payment of the sales first made; if the sales consolidated arose from sales made on the same day, payments are deemed to have been applied first to the smallest sale; and

(b) payments received for an open-end credit account are deemed to have been applied first to the payment of finance charges in the order of their entry to the account and then to the payment of debts in the order in which the entries of the debts are made to the account.

(4) An agreement may not limit or waive the claims or defenses of a consumer under this section.

Section 3.405 [Lender Subject to Claims and Defenses Arising from Sales and Leases]

(1) A lender, except the issuer of a lender credit card, who, with respect to a particular transaction, makes a consumer loan to enable a consumer to buy or lease from a particular seller or lessor property or services [, except primarily for an agricultural purpose,] is subject to all claims and defenses of the consumer against the seller or lessor arising from that sale or lease of the property or services if:

(a) the lender knows that the seller or lessor arranged for the extension of credit by the lender for a commission, brokerage, or referral fee;

(b) the lender is a person related to the seller or lessor, unless the relationship is remote or is not a factor in the transaction;

(c) the seller or lessor guarantees the loan or otherwise assumes the risk of loss by the lender upon the loan;

(d) the lender directly supplies the seller or lessor with the contract document used by the consumer to evidence the loan, and the seller or lessor has knowledge of the credit terms and participates in preparation of the document;

(e) the loan is conditioned upon the consumer's purchase or lease of the property or services from the particular seller or lessor, but the lender's payment of proceeds of the loan to the seller or lessor does not in itself establish that the loan was so conditioned; or

(f) the lender, before he makes the consumer loan, has knowledge or, from his course of dealing with the particular seller or lessor or his records, notice of substantial complaints by other buyers or lessees of the particular seller's or lessor's failure or refusal to perform his contracts with them and of the particular seller's or lessor's failure to remedy his defaults within a reasonable time after notice to him of the complaints.

(2) A claim or defense of a consumer specified in subsection (1) may be asserted against the lender under this section only if the consumer has made a good faith attempt to obtain satisfaction from the seller or lessor with respect to the claim or defense and then only to the extent of the amount owing to the lender with respect to the sale or lease of the property or services as to which the claim or defense arose at the time the lender has notice of the claim or defense. Notice of the claim or defense may be given before the attempt specified in this subsection. Oral notice is effective unless the lender requests written confirmation when or promptly after oral notice is given and the consumer fails to give the lender written confirmation within the period of time, not less than 14 days, stated to the consumer when written confirmation is requested.

(3) For the purpose of determining the amount owing to the lender with respect to the sale or lease:

(a) payments received by the lender after consolidation of two or more consumer loans, except pursuant to open-end credit, are deemed to have been applied first to the payment of the loans first made; if the loans consolidated arose from loans made on the same day, payments are deemed to have been applied first to the smallest loan; and

(b) payments received for an open-end credit account are deemed to have been applied first to the payment of finance charges in the order of their entry to the account and then to the payment of debts in the order in which the entries of the debts are made to the account.

(4) An agreement may not limit or waive the claims or defenses of a consumer under this section.

Part 5 Home Solicitation Sales

Section 3.501 [Definition: "Home Solicitation Sale"]

"Home solicitation sale" means a consumer credit sale of goods or services, except primarily for an agricultural purpose, in which the seller or a person acting for him personally solicits the sale, and the buyer's agreement or offer to purchase is given to the seller or a person acting for him, at a residence. It does not include a sale made pursuant to a pre-existing open-end credit account with the seller or pursuant to prior negotiations between the parties at a business establishment at a fixed location where goods or services are offered or exhibited for sale, a transaction conducted and consummated entirely by mail or telephone, or a sale which is subject to the provisions of the Federal Truth in Lending Act on the consumer's right to rescind certain transactions. A sale that would be a home solicitation sale if credit were extended by the seller is nonetheless so because the goods or services are paid for in whole or in part by use of a credit card or by a consumer loan with respect to which the lender is subject to claims and defenses arising from the sale (Section 3.405), and the buyer has the same rights against the card issuer or lender that he has against the seller under this Part.

Section 3.502 [Buyer's Right to Cancel]

(1) Except as provided in subsection (5), in addition to any right otherwise to revoke an offer, the buyer may cancel a home solicitation sale until midnight of the third business day after the day on which the buyer signs an agreement or offer to purchase which complies with this Part.

(2) Cancellation occurs when the buyer gives written notice of cancellation to the seller at the address stated in the agreement or offer to purchase.

(3) Notice of cancellation, if given by mail, is given when it is properly addressed with postage prepaid and deposited in a mailbox.

(4) Notice of cancellation given by the buyer need not take a particular form and is sufficient if it indicates by any form of written expression the intention of the buyer not to be bound by the home solicitation sale.

(5) The buyer may not cancel a home solicitation sale if, by a separate dated and signed statement that is not as to its material provisions a printed form and describes an emergency requiring immediate remedy, the buyer requests the seller to provide goods or services without delay in order to safeguard the health, safety, or welfare of natural persons or to prevent damage to property the buyer owns or for which he is responsible, and

(a) the seller in good faith makes a substantial beginning of performance of the contract before the buyer gives notice of cancellation, and

(b) in the case of goods, they cannot be returned to the seller in substantially as good condition as when received by the buyer.

Section 3.503 [Form of Agreement or Offer; Statement of Buyer's Rights]

(1) In a home solicitation sale, unless the buyer requests the seller to provide goods or services without delay in an emergency (subsection (5) of Section 3.502), the seller shall present to the buyer and obtain his signature to a written agreement or offer to purchase that designates as the date of the transaction the date on which the buyer actually signs and contains a statement of the buyer's rights that complies with subsection (2). A copy of any writing required by this subsection to be signed by the buyer, completed at least as to the date of the transaction and the name and mailing address of the seller, shall be given to the buyer at the time he signs the writing.

(2) The statement shall either:

(a) comply with any notice of cancellation or similar requirement of any trade regulation rule of the Federal Trade Commission which by its terms applies to the home solicitation sale; or

(b) appear under the conspicuous caption: "BUYER'S RIGHT TO CANCEL," and read as follows: "If you decide you do not want the goods or services, you may cancel this agreement by mailing a notice to the seller. The notice must say that you do not want the goods or services and must be mailed before midnight of the third business day after you sign this agreement. The notice must be mailed to: _____ ."
(insert name & mailing address of seller)

(3) Until the seller has complied with this section the buyer may cancel the home solicitation sale by notifying the seller in any manner and by any means of his intention to cancel.

Section 3.504 [Restoration of Down Payment]

(1) Within ten days after a notice of cancellation has been received by the seller or an offer to purchase has been otherwise revoked, the seller shall tender to the buyer any payments made by the buyer, any note or other evidence of indebtedness, and any goods traded in. A provision permitting the seller to keep all or any part of any goods traded in, payment, note, or evi-

dence of indebtedness is in violation of this section and unenforceable.

(2) If the down payment includes goods traded in, the goods shall be tendered in substantially as good condition as when received by the seller. If the seller fails to tender the goods as provided by this section, the buyer may elect to recover an amount equal to the trade-in allowance stated in the agreement.

(3) Until the seller has complied with the obligations imposed by this section the buyer may retain possession of goods delivered to him by the seller and has a lien on the goods in his possession or control for any recovery to which he is entitled.

Section 3.505 [Duty of Buyer; No Compensation for Services Before Cancellation]

(1) Except as provided by the provisions on retention of goods by the buyer (subsection (3) of Section 3.504), and allowing for ordinary wear and tear or consumption of the goods contemplated by the transaction, within a reasonable time after a home solicitation sale has been cancelled or an offer to purchase revoked, the buyer upon demand shall tender to the seller any goods delivered by the seller pursuant to the sale, but he is not obligated to tender at any place other than his residence. If the seller fails to demand possession of goods within a reasonable time after cancellation or revocation, the goods become the property of the buyer without obligation to pay for them. For the purpose of this section, a reasonable time is presumed to be 40 days.

(2) The buyer shall take reasonable care of the goods in his possession before cancellation or revocation and for a reasonable time thereafter, during which time the goods are otherwise at the seller's risk.

(3) If a home solicitation sale is cancelled, the seller is not entitled to compensation for any services he performed pursuant to it.

Article 4
INSURANCE

Part 1 Insurance in General

Section 4.101 [Short Title]

This Article shall be known and may be cited as Uniform Consumer Credit Code—Insurance.

Section 4.102 [Scope [; Relation to Credit Insurance Act; Applicability to Parties]]

[(1)] This Article applies to insurance provided or to be provided in relation to a consumer credit transaction.

[(2) This Article supplements and does not repeal the Credit Insurance Act but to the extent of inconsistency between this Act and the Credit Insurance Act this Act controls. The provisions of this Act concerning administrative controls, liabilities, and penalties do not apply to persons acting as insurers, and the similar provisions of the Credit Insurance Act do not apply to creditors and debtors.]

Section 4.103 [Definition[s]: "Consumer Credit Insurance" [; "Credit Insurance Act"]]

In this Act:

[(1)] "Consumer credit insurance" means insurance, except insurance on property, by which the satisfaction of debt in whole or in part is a benefit provided, but does not include

(a) insurance provided in relation to a consumer credit transaction in which a payment is scheduled more than ten years after the extension of credit;

(b) insurance issued by an insurer as an isolated transaction not related to an agreement or plan for insuring consumers of or from the creditor; or

(c) insurance indemnifying the creditor against loss due to the consumer's default.

[(2) "Credit Insurance Act" means [NAIC Model Act, or any similar statute].]

Section 4.104 [Creditor's Provision of and Charge for Insurance; Excess Amount of Charge]

(1) Except as otherwise provided in this Article and subject to the provisions on additional charges (Section 2.501) and maximum finance charges (Parts 2 and 4 of Article 2), a creditor may agree to provide insurance, and may contract for and receive a charge for insurance separate from and in addition to other charges. A creditor need not make a separate charge for insurance provided or required by him. This Act does not authorize the issuance of the insurance prohibited under any statute, or rule thereunder, governing the business of insurance.

(2) The excess amount of a charge for insurance provided for in agreements in violation of this Article is an excess charge for purposes of the provisions of the Article on Remedies and Penalties (Article 5) as to effect of violations on rights of parties (Section 5.201) and of the provisions of the Article on Administration (Article 6) as to civil actions by the Administrator (Section 6.113).

Section 4.105 [Conditions Applying to Insurance to be Provided by Creditor]

If a creditor agrees with a consumer to provide insurance:

(1) the insurance shall be evidenced by an individual policy or certificate of insurance delivered to the consumer, or mailed to him at his address as stated by him, within 30 days after the term of the insurance commences under the agreement between the creditor and consumer, or the creditor shall promptly notify the consumer of any failure or delay in providing the insurance; and

(2) the creditor shall pay to the consumer or his estate all proceeds of consumer credit or property insurance received by the creditor in excess of the amount to which the creditor is entitled within ten days after receipt by the creditor of the proceeds.

Section 4.106 [Unconscionability]

(1) In applying the provisions of this Act on unconscionability (Sections 5.108 and 6.111) to a separate charge for insurance, consideration shall be given, among other factors, to:

(a) potential benefits to the consumer including the satisfaction of his obligations;

(b) the creditor's need for the protection provided by the insurance; and

(c) the relation between the amount and terms of credit granted and the insurance benefits provided.

(2) If consumer credit insurance otherwise complies with this Article and other applicable law, neither the amount nor the term of the insurance nor the amount of a charge therefor is in itself unconscionable.

Section 4.107 [Maximum Charge by Creditor for Insurance]

(1) Except as provided in subsection (2), if a creditor contracts for or receives a separate charge for insur-

ance, the amount charged to the consumer for the insurance may not exceed the premium to be charged by the insurer, as computed at the time the charge to the consumer is determined, conforming to any rate filings required by law and made by the insurer with the [Commissioner] of Insurance.

(2) A creditor who provides consumer credit insurance in relation to open-end credit may calculate the charge to the consumer in each billing cycle by applying the current premium rate to the balance in the manner permitted with respect to finance charges by the provisions on finance charge for consumer credit sales pursuant to open-end credit (Section 2.202).

Section 4.108 [Refund Required; Amount]

(1) Upon prepayment in full of a consumer credit transaction other than a consumer lease by the proceeds of consumer credit insurance, the consumer or his estate is entitled to a refund of any portion of a separate charge for insurance which by reason of prepayment is retained by the creditor or returned to him by the insurer, unless the charge was computed from time to time on the basis of the balances of the consumer's account.

(2) This Article does not require a creditor to grant a refund to the consumer if all refunds due to him under this Article amount to less than $1 and, except as provided in subsection (1), does not require the creditor to account to the consumer for any portion of a separate charge for insurance because:

(a) the insurance is terminated by performance of the insurer's obligation;

(b) the creditor pays or accounts for premiums to the insurer in amounts and at times determined by the agreement between them; or

(c) the creditor receives directly or indirectly under any policy of insurance a gain or advantage not prohibited by law.

(3) Except as provided in subsection (2), the creditor shall promptly make or cause to be made an appropriate refund to the consumer with respect to any separate charge made to him for insurance if:

(a) the insurance is not provided or is provided for a shorter term than that for which the charge to the consumer for insurance was computed; or

(b) the insurance terminates before the end of the

term for which it was written because of prepayment in full or otherwise.

(4) A refund required by subsection (3) is appropriate as to amount if it is computed according to a method prescribed or approved by the [Commissioner] of Insurance or a formula filed by the insurer with the [Commissioner] of Insurance at least 30 days before the consumer's right to a refund becomes determinable, unless the method or formula is employed after the [Commissioner] of Insurance notifies the insurer that he disapproves it.

Section 4.109 [Existing Insurance; Choice of Insurer]

If a creditor requires insurance, upon notice to him the consumer has the option of providing the required insurance through an existing policy of insurance owned or controlled by the consumer, or through a policy to be obtained and paid for by the consumer, but the creditor for reasonable cause may decline the insurance provided by the consumer.

Section 4.110 [Charge for Insurance in Connection with a Deferral, Refinancing, or Consolidation; Duplicate Charges]

(1) A creditor may not contract for or receive a separate charge for insurance in connection with a deferral (Section 2.503), a refinancing (Section 2.504), or a consolidation (Section 2.505), unless:

(a) the consumer agrees at or before the time of the deferral, refinancing, or consolidation that the charge may be made;

(b) the consumer is or is to be provided with insurance for an amount or a term, or insurance of a kind, in addition to that to which he would have been entitled had there been no deferral, refinancing, or consolidation;

(c) the consumer receives a refund or credit on account of any unexpired term of existing insurance in the amount required if the insurance were terminated (Section 4.108); and

(d) the charge does not exceed the amount permitted by this Article (Section 4.107).

(2) A creditor may not contract for or receive a separate charge for insurance which duplicates insurance with respect to which the creditor has previously contracted for or received a separate charge.

Section 4.111 [Cooperation Between Administrator and [Commissioner] of Insurance]

The Administrator and the [Commissioner] of Insurance shall consult and assist one another in maintaining compliance with this Article. They may jointly pursue investigations, prosecute suits, and take other official action they deem appropriate if either of them is otherwise empowered to take the action. If the Administrator is informed of a violation or suspected violation by an insurer of this Article, or of the insurance laws, rules, and regulations of this State, he shall inform the [Commissioner] of Insurance of the circumstances.

Section 4.112 [Administrative Action of [Commissioner] of Insurance]

[(1) To the extent that his responsibility under this Article requires, the [Commissioner] of Insurance shall adopt rules with respect to insurers, and with respect to refunds (Section 4.108), forms, schedules of premium rates and charges (Section 4.203), and his approval or disapproval thereof and, in case of violation, may make an order for compliance.

(2)] [The State administrative procedure act] [Each provision of the Part on Administrative Procedure and Judicial Review (Part 4) of the Article on Administration (Article 6) that applies to and governs administrative action taken by the Administrator also] applies to and governs all administrative action taken by the [Commissioner] of Insurance pursuant to this section.

Part 2 Consumer Credit Insurance

Section 4.201 [Term of Insurance]

(1) Consumer credit insurance provided by a creditor may be subject to the furnishing of evidence of insurability satisfactory to the insurer. Whether or not the evidence is required, the term of the insurance shall commence no later than when the consumer becomes obligated to the creditor or when the consumer applies for the insurance, whichever is later, except as follows:

(a) if any required evidence of insurability is not furnished until more than 30 days after the term otherwise would commence, the term may commence on the date the insurer determines the evidence to be satisfactory; or

(b) if the creditor provides insurance not previously provided covering debts previously created, the term may commence on the effective date of the policy.

(2) The originally scheduled term of consumer credit insurance shall extend at least until the due date of the last scheduled payment of the debt, except as follows:

(a) if the insurance relates to an open-end credit account, the term need extend only until payment of the debt under the account and may be sooner terminated after at least 30 days' notice to the consumer; or

(b) if the consumer is informed in writing that the insurance will be written for a specified shorter time, the term need extend only until the end of the specified time.

(3) The term of consumer credit insurance may not extend more than 15 days after the originally scheduled due date of the last scheduled payment of the debt, unless it is extended without additional cost to the consumer or as an incident to a deferral, refinancing, or consolidation.

Section 4.202 [Amount of Insurance]

(1) Except as provided in subsection (2):

(a) in the case of consumer credit insurance providing life coverage, the amount of insurance may not initially exceed the debt and, if the debt is payable in instalments, may not exceed at any time the greater of the scheduled or actual amount of the debt; or

(b) in the case of any other consumer credit insurance, the total amount of periodic benefits payable may not exceed the total of scheduled unpaid instalments of the debt, and the amount of any periodic benefit may not exceed the original amount of debt divided by the number of periodic instalments in which it is payable.

(2) If consumer credit insurance is provided in connection with an open-end credit account, the amounts payable as insurance benefits may be reasonably commensurate with the amount of debt as

it exists from time to time. If consumer credit insurance is provided in connection with a commitment to grant credit in the future, the amounts payable as insurance benefits may be reasonably commensurate with the total from time to time of the amount of debt and the amount of the commitment. If the debt or the commitment is primarily for an agricultural purpose and there is no regular schedule of payments, the amounts payable as insurance benefits may equal the total of the initial amount of debt and the amount of the commitment.

Section 4.203 [Filing and Approval of Rates and Forms]

(1) A creditor may not use a form or a schedule of premium rates or charges, the filing of which is required by this section, if the [Commissioner] of Insurance has disapproved the form or schedule and has notified the insurer of his disapproval. A creditor may not use a form or schedule unless:

(a) the form or schedule has been on file with the [Commissioner] of Insurance for 30 days, or has earlier been approved by him; and

(b) the insurer has complied with this section with respect to the insurance.

(2) Except as provided in subsection (3), all policies, certificates of insurance, notices of proposed insurance, applications for insurance, endorsements, and riders relating to consumer credit insurance delivered or issued for delivery in this State, and the schedules of premium rates or charges pertaining thereto, shall be filed by the insurer with the [Commissioner] of Insurance. Within 30 days after the filing of any form or schedule, he shall disapprove it if the premium rates or charges are unreasonable in relation to the benefits provided under the form, or if the form contains provisions which are unjust, unfair, inequitable, or deceptive, encourage misrepresentation of the coverage, or are contrary to any provision of the [Insurance Code] or of any rule or regulation promulgated thereunder.

(3) If a group policy of consumer credit insurance has been delivered in another state, the forms to be filed by the insurer with the [Commissioner] of Insurance are the group certificates and notices of proposed insurance. He shall approve them if:

(a) they provide the information that would be

required if the group policy were delivered in this State; and

(b) the applicable premium rates or charges do not exceed those established by his rules or regulations.

Part 3 Property and Liability Insurance

Section 4.301 [Property Insurance]

(1) A creditor may not contract for or receive a separate charge for insurance against loss of or damage to property, unless:

(a) the insurance covers a substantial risk of loss of or damage to property related to the credit transaction;

(b) the amount, terms, and conditions of the insurance are reasonable in relation to the character and value of the property insured or to be insured; and

(c) the term of the insurance is reasonable in relation to the terms of credit.

(2) The term of the insurance is reasonable if it is customary and does not extend substantially beyond a scheduled maturity.

(3) With respect to a transaction, except pursuant to open-end credit, a creditor may not contract for or receive a separate charge for insurance against loss of or damage to property, unless the amount financed exclusive of charges for the insurance is $300 or more and the value of the property is $300 or more.

(4) With respect to a transaction pursuant to open-end credit, the Administrator may adopt rules consistent with the principles set out in subsections (1) and (2) prescribing whether, and the conditions under which, a creditor may contract for or receive a separate charge for insurance against loss of or damage to property.

(5) The amounts of $300 in subsection (3) are subject to change pursuant to the provisions on adjustment of dollar amounts (Section 1.106).

Section 4.302 [Insurance on Creditor's Interest Only]

If a creditor contracts for or receives a separate charge for insurance against loss of or damage to property, the risk of loss or damage not willfully caused by the consumer is on the consumer only to the extent of any deficiency in the effective coverage of the insurance, even though the insurance covers only the interest of the creditor.

Section 4.303 [Liability Insurance]

A creditor may not contract for or receive a separate charge for insurance against liability unless the insurance covers a substantial risk of liability arising out of the ownership or use of property related to the credit transaction.

Section 4.304 [Cancellation by Creditor]

This section does not apply to an insurance premium loan. A creditor may request cancellation of a policy of property or liability insurance only after the consumer's default or in accordance with a written authorization by the consumer. In either case the cancellation does not take effect until written notice is delivered to the consumer or mailed to him at his address as stated by him. The notice shall state that the policy may be cancelled on a date not less than ten days after the notice is delivered, or, if the notice is mailed, not less than 13 days after it is mailed. A cancellation may not take effect until those times.

Article 5
REMEDIES AND PENALTIES

Part 1 Limitations on Creditors' Remedies

Section 5.101 [Short Title]

This Article shall be known and may be cited as Uniform Consumer Credit Code—Remedies and Penalties.

Section 5.102 [Scope]

This Part applies to actions or other proceedings to enforce rights arising from consumer credit transactions, to extortionate extensions of credit (Section 5.107), and to unconscionability (Section 5.108).

Section 5.103 [Restrictions on Deficiency Judgments]

(1) This section applies to a deficiency on a consumer credit sale of goods or services and on a consumer loan in which the lender is subject to claims and

defenses arising from sales and leases (Section 3.405). A consumer is not liable for a deficiency unless the creditor has disposed of the goods in good faith and in a commercially reasonable manner.

(2) If the seller repossesses or voluntarily accepts surrender of goods that were the subject of the sale and in which he has a security interest, the consumer is not personally liable to the seller for the unpaid balance of the debt arising from the sale of a commercial unit of goods of which the cash sale price was $1,750 or less, and the seller is not obligated to resell the collateral unless the consumer has paid 60 per cent or more of the cash price and has not signed after default a statement renouncing his rights in the collateral.

(3) If the seller repossesses or voluntarily accepts surrender of goods that were not the subject of the sale but in which he has a security interest to secure a debt arising from a sale of goods or services or a combined sale of goods and services and the cash price of the sale was $1,750 or less, the consumer is not personally liable to the seller for the unpaid balance of the debt arising from the sale, and the seller's duty to dispose of the collateral is governed by the provisions on disposition of collateral (Part 5 of Article 9) of the Uniform Commercial Code.

(4) If the lender takes possession or voluntarily accepts surrender of goods in which he has a purchase money security interest to secure a debt arising from a consumer loan in which the lender is subject to claims and defenses arising from sales and leases (Section 3.405) and the net proceeds of the loan paid to or for the benefit of the consumer were $1,750 or less, the consumer is not personally liable to the lender for the unpaid balance of the debt arising from that loan and the lender's duty to dispose of the collateral is governed by the provisions on disposition of collateral (Part 5 of Article 9) of the Uniform Commercial Code.

(5) For the purpose of determining the unpaid balance of consolidated debts or debts pursuant to open-end credit, the allocation of payments to a debt shall be determined in the same manner as provided for determining the amount of debt secured by various security interests (Section 3.303).

(6) The consumer may be held liable in damages to the creditor if the consumer has wrongfully damaged

the collateral or if, after default and demand, the consumer has wrongfully failed to make the collateral available to the creditor.

(7) If the creditor elects to bring an action against the consumer for a debt arising from a consumer credit sale of goods or services or from a consumer loan in which the lender is subject to claims and defenses arising from sales and leases (Section 3.405), when under this section he would not be entitled to a deficiency judgment if he took possession of the collateral, and obtains judgment:

(a) he may not take possession of the collateral, and

(b) the collateral is not subject to levy or sale on execution or similar proceedings pursuant to the judgment.

(8) The amounts of $1,750 in subsections (2), (3) and (4) are subject to change pursuant to the provisions on adjustment of dollar amounts (Section 1.106).

Section 5.104 [No Garnishment Before Judgment]

Before entry of judgment in an action against a consumer for debt arising from a consumer credit transaction, the creditor may not attach unpaid earnings of the consumer by garnishment or like proceedings.

Section 5.105 [Limitation on Garnishment]

(1) For purposes of this Part:

(a) "disposable earnings" means that part of the earnings of an individual remaining after the deduction from those earnings of amounts required by law to be withheld; and

(b) "garnishment" means any legal or equitable procedure through which earnings of an individual are required to be withheld for payment of a debt.

(2) The maximum part of the aggregate disposable earnings of an individual for any workweek which is subjected to garnishment to enforce payment of a judgment arising from a consumer credit transaction may not exceed the lesser of:

(a) 25 per cent of his disposable earnings for that week, or

(b) the amount by which his disposable earnings

for that week exceed 40 times the Federal minimum hourly wage prescribed by Section 6(a)(1) of the Fair Labor Standards Act of 1938, U.S.C. tit. 29, §206(a)(1), in effect at the time the earnings are payable.

In case of earnings for a pay period other than a week, the Administrator shall prescribe by rule a multiple of the Federal minimum hourly wage equivalent in effect to that set forth in paragraph (b).

(3) No court may make, execute, or enforce an order or process in violation of this section.

(4) At any time after entry of a judgment in favor of a creditor in an action against a consumer for debt arising from a consumer credit transaction, the consumer may file with the court his verified application for an order exempting from garnishment pursuant to that judgment, for an appropriate period of time, a greater portion or all of his aggregate disposable earnings for a workweek or other applicable pay period than is provided for in subsection (2). He shall designate in the application the portion of his earnings not exempt from garnishment under this section and other law, the period of time for which the additional exemption is sought, describe the judgment with respect to which the application is made, and state that the designated portion as well as his earnings that are exempt by law are necessary for the maintenance of him or a family supported wholly or partly by the earnings. Upon filing a sufficient application under this subsection, the court may issue any temporary order necessary under the circumstances to stay enforcement of the judgment by garnishment, shall set a hearing on the application not less than [five] nor more than [ten] days after the date of filing of the application, and shall cause notice of the application and the hearing date to be served on the judgment creditor or his attorney of record. At the hearing, if it appears to the court that all or any portion of the earnings sought to be additionally exempt are necessary for the maintenance of the consumer or a family supported wholly or partly by the earnings of the consumer for all or any part of the time requested in the application, the court shall issue an order granting the application to that extent; otherwise it shall deny the application. The order is subject to modification or vacation upon further application of any party to it upon a showing of changed circumstances after a hearing upon notice to all interested parties.

Section 5.106 [No Discharge From Employment for Garnishment]

An employer may not discharge an employee for the reason that a creditor of the employee has subjected or attempted to subject unpaid earnings of the employee to garnishment or like proceedings directed to the employer for the purpose of paying a judgment arising from a consumer credit transaction.

Section 5.107 [Extortionate Extensions of Credit]

(1) If it is the understanding of the creditor and the consumer at the time an extension of credit is made that delay in making repayment or failure to make repayment could result in the use of violence or other criminal means to cause harm to the person, reputation, or property of any person, the repayment of the extension of credit is unenforceable through civil judicial processes against the consumer.

(2) If it is shown that an extension of credit was made at an annual rate exceeding 45 per cent calculated according to the actuarial method and that the creditor then had a reputation for the use or threat of use of violence or other criminal means to cause harm to the person, reputation, or property of any person to collect extensions of credit or to punish the non-repayment thereof, there is prima facie evidence that the extension of credit was unenforceable under subsection (1).

Section 5.108 [Unconscionability; Inducement by Unconscionable Conduct; Unconscionable Debt Collection]

(1) With respect to a transaction that is, gives rise to, or leads the debtor to believe will give rise to, a consumer credit transaction, if the court as a matter of law finds:

(a) the agreement or transaction to have been unconscionable at the time it was made, or to have been induced by unconscionable conduct, the court may refuse to enforce the agreement; or

(b) any term or part of the agreement or transaction to have been unconscionable at the time it was made, the court may refuse to enforce the agreement, enforce the remainder of the agreement without the unconscionable term or part, or so limit the application of any unconscionable term or part as to avoid any unconscionable result.

(2) With respect to a consumer credit transaction, if the court as a matter of law finds that a person has engaged in, is engaging in, or is likely to engage in unconscionable conduct in collecting a debt arising from that transaction, the court may grant an injunction and award the consumer any actual damages he has sustained.

(3) If it is claimed or appears to the court that the agreement or transaction or any term or part thereof may be unconscionable, or that a person has engaged in, is engaging in, or is likely to engage in unconscionable conduct in collecting a debt, the parties shall be afforded a reasonable opportunity to present evidence as to the setting, purpose, and effect of the agreement or transaction or term or part thereof, or of the conduct, to aid the court in making the determination.

(4) In applying subsection (1), consideration shall be given to each of the following factors, among others, as applicable:

(a) belief by the seller, lessor, or lender at the time a transaction is entered into that there is no reasonable probability of payment in full of the obligation by the consumer or debtor;

(b) in the case of a consumer credit sale or consumer lease, knowledge by the seller or lessor at the time of the sale or lease of the inability of the consumer to receive substantial benefits from the property or services sold or leased;

(c) in the case of a consumer credit sale or consumer lease, gross disparity between the price of the property or services sold or leased and the value of the property or services measured by the price at which similar property or services are readily obtainable in credit transactions by like consumers;

(d) the fact that the creditor contracted for or received separate charges for insurance with respect to a consumer credit sale or consumer loan with the effect of making the sale or loan, considered as a whole, unconscionable; and

(e) the fact that the seller, lessor, or lender has knowingly taken advantage of the inability of the consumer or debtor reasonably to protect his interests by reason of physical or mental infirmities, ignorance, illiteracy, inability to understand the language of the agreement, or similar factors.

(5) In applying subsection (2), consideration shall be given to each of the following factors, among others, as applicable:

(a) using or threatening to use force, violence, or criminal prosecution against the consumer or members of his family;

(b) communicating with the consumer or a member of his family at frequent intervals or at unusual hours or under other circumstances so that it is a reasonable inference that the primary purpose of the communication was to harass the consumer;

(c) using fraudulent, deceptive, or misleading representations such as a communication which simulates legal process or which gives the appearance of being authorized, issued, or approved by a government, governmental agency, or attorney at law when it is not, or threatening or attempting to enforce a right with knowledge or reason to know that the right does not exist;

(d) causing or threatening to cause injury to the consumer's reputation or economic status by disclosing information affecting the consumer's reputation for credit-worthiness with knowledge or reason to know that the information is false; communicating with the consumer's employer before obtaining a final judgment against the consumer, except as permitted by statute or to verify the consumer's employment; disclosing to a person, with knowledge or reason to know that the person does not have a legitimate business need for the information, or in any way prohibited by statute, information affecting the consumer's credit or other reputation; or disclosing information concerning the existence of a debt known to be disputed by the consumer without disclosing that fact; and

(e) engaging in conduct with knowledge that like conduct has been restrained or enjoined by a court in a civil action by the Administrator against any person pursuant to the provisions on injunctions against fraudulent or unconscionable agreements or conduct (Section 6.111).

(6) If in an action in which unconscionability is claimed the court finds unconscionability pursuant to subsection (1) or (2), the court shall award reasonable fees to the attorney for the consumer or debtor. If the court does not find unconscionability and the consumer or debtor claiming unconscionability has brought or maintained an action he knew to be groundless, the court shall award reasonable fees to the attorney for the party against whom the claim is made. In determining attorney's fees, the amount of the recovery on behalf of the consumer is not controlling.

(7) The remedies of this section are in addition to remedies otherwise available for the same conduct under law other than this Act, but double recovery of actual damages may not be had.

(8) For the purpose of this section, a charge or practice expressly permitted by this Act is not in itself unconscionable.

Section 5.109 **[Default]**

An agreement of the parties to a consumer credit transaction with respect to default on the part of the consumer is enforceable only to the extent that:

(1) the consumer fails to make a payment as required by agreement; or

(2) the prospect of payment, performance, or realization of collateral is significantly impaired; the burden of establishing the prospect of significant impairment is on the creditor.

Section 5.110 **[Notice of Consumer's Right to Cure]**

(1) With respect to a consumer credit transaction, after a consumer has been in default for ten days for failure to make a required payment and has not voluntarily surrendered possession of goods that are collateral, a creditor may give the consumer the notice described in this section. A creditor gives notice to the consumer under this section when he delivers the notice to the consumer or mails the notice to him at his residence (subsection (6) of Section 1.201).

(2) Except as provided in subsection (3), the notice shall be in writing and conspicuously state: the name, address, and telephone number of the creditor to whom payment is to be made, a brief identification of the credit transaction, the consumer's right to cure the

default, and the amount of payment and date by which payment must be made to cure the default. A notice in substantially the following form complies with this subsection:

(name, address, and telephone number of creditor)

(account number, if any)

(brief identification of credit transaction)

(date) _____ is the LAST DAY FOR PAYMENT

(amount) _____ is the AMOUNT NOW DUE

You are late in making your payment(s). If you pay the AMOUNT NOW DUE (above) by the LAST DAY FOR PAYMENT (above), you may continue with the contract as though you were not late. If you do not pay by that date, we may exercise our rights under the law.

If you are late again in making your payments, we may exercise our rights without sending you another notice like this one. If you have questions, write or telephone the creditor promptly.

(3) If the consumer credit transaction is an insurance premium loan, the notice shall conform to the requirements of subsection (2) and a notice in substantially the form specified in that subsection complies with this subsection, except for the following:

(a) in lieu of a brief identification of the credit transaction, the notice shall identify the transaction as an insurance premium loan and each insurance policy or contract that may be cancelled;

(b) in lieu of the statement in the form of notice specified in subsection (2) that the creditor may exercise his rights under the law, the statement that each policy or contract identified in the notice may be cancelled; and

(c) the last paragraph of the form of notice specified in subsection (2) shall be omitted.

Section 5.111 **[Cure of Default]**

(1) With respect to a consumer credit transaction, except as provided in subsection (2), after a default consisting only of the consumer's failure to make a required payment, a creditor, because of that default, may neither accelerate maturity of the unpaid balance of the obligation, nor take possession of or otherwise enforce a security interest in goods that are collateral until 20 days after a notice of the consumer's right to cure (Section 5.110) is given, nor, with

respect to an insurance premium loan, give notice of cancellation as provided in subsection (4) until 13 days after a notice of the consumer's right to cure (Section 5.110) is given. Until expiration of the minimum applicable period after the notice is given, the consumer may cure all defaults consisting of a failure to make the required payment by tendering the amount of all unpaid sums due at the time of the tender, without acceleration, plus any unpaid delinquency or deferral charges. Cure restores the consumer to his rights under the agreement as though the defaults had not occurred.

(2) With respect to defaults on the same obligation other than an insurance premium loan and subject to subsection (1), after a creditor has once given a notice of consumer's right to cure (Section 5.110), this section gives the consumer no right to cure and imposes no limitation on the creditor's right to proceed against the consumer or goods that are collateral. For the purpose of this section, in open-end credit, the obligation is the unpaid balance of the account and there is no right to cure and no limitation on the creditor's rights with respect to a default that occurs within 12 months after an earlier default as to which a creditor has given a notice of consumer's right to cure (Section 5.110).

(3) This section and the provisions on waiver, agreements to forego rights, and settlement of claims (Section 1.107) do not prohibit a consumer from voluntarily surrendering possession of goods which are collateral and the creditor from thereafter accelerating maturity of the obligation and enforcing the obligation and his security interest in the goods at any time after default.

(4) If a default on an insurance premium loan is not cured, the lender may give notice of cancellation of each insurance policy or contract to be cancelled. If given, the notice of cancellation shall be in writing and given to the insurer who issued the policy or contract and to the insured. The insurer, within two business days after receipt of the notice of cancellation together with a copy of the insurance premium loan agreement if not previously given to him, shall give any notice of cancellation required by the policy, contract, or law and, within ten business days after the effective date of the cancellation, pay to the lender any premium unearned on the policy or contract as of that effective date. Within ten business

days after receipt of the unearned premium, the lender shall pay to the consumer indebted upon the insurance premium loan any excess of the unearned premium received over the amount owing by the consumer upon the insurance premium loan.

Section 5.112 **[Creditor's Right to Take Possession After Default]**

Upon default by a consumer with respect to a consumer credit transaction, unless the consumer voluntarily surrenders possession of the collateral to the creditor, the creditor may take possession of the collateral without judicial process only if possession can be taken without entry into a dwelling and without the use of force or other breach of the peace.

Section 5.113 **[Venue]**

An action by a creditor against a consumer arising from a consumer credit transaction shall be brought in the [county] of the consumer's residence (subsection (6) of Section 1.201), unless an action is brought to enforce an interest in land securing the consumer's obligation, in which case the action may be brought in the [county] in which the land or a part thereof is located. If the [county] of the consumer's residence has changed, the consumer upon motion may have the action removed to the [county] of his current residence. If the residence of the consumer is not within this State, the action may be brought in the [county] in which the sale, lease, or loan was made. If the initial papers offered for filing in the action on their face show noncompliance with this section, the [clerk] shall not accept them.

Section 5.114 **[Complaint; Proof]**

(1) In an action brought by a creditor against a consumer arising from a consumer credit transaction, the complaint shall allege the facts of the consumer's default, the amount to which the creditor is entitled, and an indication of how that amount was determined.

(2) A default judgment may not be entered in the action in favor of the creditor unless the complaint is verified by the creditor or sworn testimony, by affidavit or otherwise, is adduced showing that the creditor is entitled to the relief demanded.

Section 5.115 [Stay of Enforcement of or Relief from Default Judgment]

At any time after entry of a default judgment in favor of a creditor and against a consumer in an action arising from a consumer credit transaction, the court which rendered the judgment, for cause including lack of jurisdiction to render the judgment, and upon motion of a party or its own motion, with notice as the court may direct, may stay enforcement of or relieve the consumer from the judgment by order upon just and equitable conditions.

Section 5.116 [Limitation on Enforcement of Security for Supervised Loan]

(1) Except as to a purchase money security interest, this section applies to a security interest in an item of goods other than a motor vehicle which (a) is possessed by a consumer, (b) is being used by him or a member of a family wholly or partly supported by him, (c) is or may be claimed to be exempt from execution on a money judgment under the laws of this State, and (d) is collateral for a supervised loan.

(2) Unless the consumer, after written notice to him of his rights under this section, voluntarily surrenders to the lender possession of any item of goods to which this section applies, the lender, without an order or process of the [   ] court may not take possession of the item or otherwise enforce the security interest according to its terms. The notice to the consumer shall conform to any rule adopted by the Administrator.

(3) The court may order or authorize process respecting an item of goods to which this section applies only after a hearing upon notice to the consumer of the hearing and his rights at it. The notice shall be as directed by the court. The order or authorization may prescribe appropriate conditions as to payments upon the debt secured or otherwise. The court may not order or authorize process respecting the item if it finds upon the hearing both that the consumer lacks the means to pay all or part of the debt secured and that continued possession and use of the item is necessary to avoid undue hardship for the consumer or a member of a family wholly or partly supported by him.

(4) The court, upon application of the lender or the consumer and notice to the other, and after a hearing and a finding of changed circumstances, may vacate or modify an order or authorization pursuant to this section.

Part 2 Consumers' Remedies

Section 5.201 [Effect of Violations on Rights of Parties]

(1) If a creditor has violated any provision of this Act applying to collection of an excess charge or amount or enforcement of rights (subsections (2) and (4) of Section 1.201), authority to make supervised loans (Section 2.301), restrictions on interests in land as security (Section 2.307), limitations on the schedule of payments on loan terms for supervised loans (Section 2.308), attorney's fees (Section 2.507), charges for other credit transactions (Section 2.601), disclosure with respect to consumer leases (Section 3.202), notice to consumers (Section 3.203), receipts, statements of account, and evidences of payment (Section 3.206), form of insurance premium loan agreement (Section 3.207), notice to co-signers and similar parties (Section 3.208), security in sales and leases (Section 3.301), no assignments of earnings (Section 3.305), authorizations to confess judgment (Section 3.306), certain negotiable instruments prohibited (Section 3.307), referral sales and leases (Section 3.309), limitations on default charges (Section 3.402), card issuer subject to claims and defenses (subsection (5) of Section 3.403), assignees subject to claims and defenses (subsection (4) of Section 3.404), lenders subject to claims and defenses arising from sales and leases (subsection (4) of Section 3.405), limitation on enforcement of security for supervised loan (Section 5.116), or assurance of discontinuance (Section 6.109), the consumer has a [claim for relief] [cause of action] to recover actual damages and also a right in an action other than a class action, to recover from the person violating this Act a penalty in an amount determined by the court not less than $100 nor more than $1,000. With respect to violations arising from sales or loans made pursuant to open-end credit, no action pursuant to this subsection may be brought more than two years after the violations occurred. With respect to violations arising from other consumer credit transactions, no action pursuant to this subsection may be brought more than one year after the scheduled or accelerated maturity of the debt.

(2) A consumer is not obligated to pay a charge in excess of that allowed by this Act and has a right of refund of any excess charge paid. A refund may not be made by reducing the consumer's obligation by the amount of the excess charge, unless the creditor has notified the consumer that the consumer may request a refund and the consumer has not so requested within 30 days thereafter. If the consumer has paid an amount in excess of the lawful obligation under the agreement, the consumer may recover the excess amount from the person who made the excess charge or from an assignee of that person's rights who undertakes direct collection of payments from or enforcement of rights against consumers arising from the debt.

(3) If a creditor has contracted for or received a charge in excess of that allowed by this Act, or if a consumer is entitled to a refund and a person liable to the consumer refuses to make a refund within a reasonable time after demand, the consumer may recover from the creditor or the person liable in an action other than a class action a penalty in an amount determined by the court not less than $100 nor more than $1,000. With respect to excess charges arising from sales or loans made pursuant to open-end credit, no action pursuant to this subsection may be brought more than two years after the violation or passage of a reasonable time for refund occurs. With respect to excess charges arising from other consumer credit transactions no action pursuant to this subsection may be brought more than one year after the scheduled or accelerated maturity of the debt. For purposes of this subsection, a reasonable time is presumed to be 30 days.

(4) Except as otherwise provided, a violation of this Act does not impair rights on a debt.

(5) If an employer discharges an employee in violation of the provisions prohibiting discharge (Section 5.106), the employee within [   ] days may bring a civil action for recovery of wages lost as a result of the violation and for an order requiring reinstatement of the employee. Damages recoverable shall not exceed lost wages for six weeks.

(6) A creditor is not liable for a penalty under subsection (1) or (3) if he notifies the consumer of a violation before the creditor receives from the consumer written notice of the violation or the

consumer has brought an action under this section, and the creditor corrects the violation within 45 days after notifying the consumer. If the violation consists of a prohibited agreement, giving the consumer a corrected copy of the writing containing the violation is sufficient notification and correction. If the violation consists of an excess charge, correction shall be made by an adjustment or refund. The Administrator and any official or agency of this State having supervisory authority over a supervised financial organization shall give prompt notice to a creditor of any violation discovered pursuant to an examination or investigation of the transactions, business, records, and acts of the creditor (Sections 2.305, 6.105 and 6.106).

(7) A creditor may not be held liable in an action brought under this section for a violation of this Act if the creditor shows by a preponderance of evidence that the violation was not intentional and resulted from a bona fide error notwithstanding the maintenance of procedures reasonably adapted to avoid the error.

(8) In an action in which it is found that a creditor has violated this Act, the court shall award to the consumer the costs of the action and to his attorneys their reasonable fees. In determining attorney's fees, the amount of the recovery on behalf of the consumer is not controlling.

Section 5.202 [Damages or Penalties as Set-Off to Obligation]

Damages or penalties to which a consumer is entitled pursuant to this Part may be set off against the consumer's obligation, and may be raised as a defense to an action on the obligation without regard to the time limitations prescribed by this Part.

[Section 5.203 [Civil Liability for Violation of Disclosure Provisions]

(1) Except as otherwise provided in this section, a creditor who, in violation of the provisions of the Federal Truth in Lending Act other than its provisions concerning advertising of credit terms, fails to disclose information to a person entitled to it under this Act is liable to that person in an amount equal to the sum of:

(a) twice the amount of the finance charge in

connection with the transaction, but the liability under this paragraph shall be not less than $100 or exceed $1,000; and

(b) in the case of a successful action to enforce the liability under paragraph (a), the costs of the action together with reasonable attorney's fees as determined by the court.

(2) A creditor has no liability under this section, if within 15 days after discovering an error, and before the institution of an action under this section or the receipt of written notice of the error, the creditor notifies the person concerned of the error and makes adjustments in the appropriate account as necessary to assure that the person will not be required to pay a finance charge in excess of the amount or percentage rate actually disclosed. The Administrator and any official or agency of this State having supervisory authority over a supervised financial organization shall give prompt notice to a creditor of any error discovered pursuant to an examination or investigation of the transactions, business, records, and acts of the creditor (Sections 2.305, 6.105 and 6.106).

(3) A creditor may not be held liable in any action brought under this section for a violation of this Act if the creditor shows by a preponderance of evidence that the violation was not intentional and resulted from a bona fide error notwithstanding the maintenance of procedures reasonably adapted to avoid the error.

(4) Any action which may be brought under this section against the original creditor in a credit transaction involving a security interest in land may be maintained against any subsequent assignee of the original creditor, if the assignee, its subsidiaries, or affiliates were in a continuing business relationship with the original creditor at the time the credit was extended or at the time of the assignment, unless the assignment was involuntary, or the assignee shows by a preponderance of evidence that it did not have reasonable grounds to believe that the original creditor was engaged in violations of this Act and that it maintained procedures reasonably adapted to apprise it of the existence of the violations.

(5) An obligor or consumer has all rights under this Act that he has under the Federal Truth in Lending Act concerning a right of rescission as to certain transactions. A creditor or other person has all liabilities and defenses under this section that he has under the Federal Truth in Lending Act.

(6) In this section, creditor includes a person who in the ordinary course of business regularly extends or arranges for the extension of credit, or offers to arrange for the extension of credit, and the seller of an interest in land and the lender who makes a loan secured by an interest in land if, but for the rate of the finance charge made in the transaction, the sale or loan would be a consumer credit sale or consumer loan.

(7) An action may not be brought under this section more than one year after the date of the occurrence of the violation.

(8) The liability of a creditor under this section is in lieu of and not in addition to his liability under the Federal Truth in Lending Act. An action by a person with respect to a violation may not be maintained pursuant to this section if a final judgment has been rendered for or against that person with respect to the same violation pursuant to the Federal Truth in Lending Act. If a final judgment has been rendered in favor of a person pursuant to this section and thereafter a final judgment with respect to the same violation is rendered in favor of the same person pursuant to the Federal Truth in Lending Act, a creditor liable under both judgments has a [claim for relief] [cause of action] against that person for appropriate relief to the extent necessary to avoid double liability with respect to the same violation.

(9) The Administrator shall adopt rules to keep this section in harmony with the Federal Truth in Lending Act. These rules supersede any provisions of this section which are inconsistent with the Federal Truth in Lending Act.]

Part 3 Criminal Penalties

Section 5.301 [Willful and Knowing Violations]

(1) A supervised lender who willfully and knowingly makes charges in excess of those permitted by the Article on Finance Charges and Related Provisions (Article 2) applying to supervised loans (Part 4) is guilty of a misdemeanor and upon conviction may be [sentenced to pay a fine not exceeding $ [   ], or to imprisonment not exceeding one year, or both].

(2) A person who, in violation of the provisions of this Act applying to authority to make supervised loans (Section 2.301), willfully and knowingly engages without a license in the business of making supervised loans, or of taking assignments of and undertaking direct collection of payments from and enforcement of rights against consumers arising from supervised loans, is guilty of a misdemeanor and upon conviction may be [sentenced to pay a fine not exceeding $ [   ], or to imprisonment not exceeding one year or both].

(3) A person who willfully and knowingly engages in the business of entering into consumer credit transactions, or of taking assignments of rights against consumers arising therefrom and undertaking direct collection of payments or enforcement of these rights, without complying with the provisions of this Act concerning notification (Section 6.202) or payment of fees (Section 6.203), is guilty of a misdemeanor and upon conviction may be [sentenced to pay a fine not exceeding $100].

[Section 5.302 **[Disclosure Violations]**

(1) A person is guilty of a [misdemeanor] and upon conviction may be sentenced to pay a fine not exceeding $5,000, or to imprisonment not exceeding one year, or both, if he willfully and knowingly:

    (a) gives false or inaccurate information or fails to provide information which he is required to disclose under the Federal Truth in Lending Act;

    (b) uses any rate table or chart, the use of which is authorized by the provisions of the Federal Truth in Lending Act, in a manner which consistently understates the annual percentage rate determined according to those provisions; or

    (c) otherwise fails to comply with any requirement of the provisions on disclosure of the Federal Truth in Lending Act.

(2) The criminal liability of a person under this section is in lieu of and not in addition to his criminal liability under the Federal Truth in Lending Act; no prosecution of a person with respect to the same violation may be maintained pursuant to both this section and the Federal Truth in Lending Act.]

Article 6
ADMINISTRATION

Part 1 Powers and Functions of Administrator

Section 6.101 [Short Title]

This Article shall be known and may be cited as Uniform Consumer Credit Code—Administration.

Section 6.102 [Applicability and Scope]

This Part applies to persons who in this State:

(a) enter into, solicit, or participate in consumer credit transactions; or lead a debtor to believe that a transaction will give rise to a consumer credit transaction;

(b) directly collect payments from or enforce rights against consumers arising from consumer credit transactions, wherever they are entered into; or

(c) enter into a sale of an interest in land or a loan secured by an interest in land if, but for the rate of the finance charge, the sale or loan would be a consumer credit sale or consumer loan, but only for the purpose of authorizing the Administrator to enforce the provisions on compliance with the Federal Truth in Lending Act (Section 3.201).

Section 6.103 [Administrator]

"Administrator" means [   ].

Section 6.104 [Powers of Administrator; Reliance on Rules; Duty to Report]

(1) In addition to other powers granted by this Act, the Administrator within the limitations provided by law may:

    (a) receive and act on complaints, take action designed to obtain voluntary compliance with this Act, or commence proceedings on his own initiative;

    (b) counsel persons and groups on their rights and duties under this Act;

    (c) establish programs for the education of consumers with respect to credit practices and problems;

    (d) make studies appropriate to effectuate the purposes and policies of this Act and make the results available to the public; [and]

(e) adopt, amend, and repeal rules to carry out the specific provisions of this Act, but not with respect to unconscionable agreements or fraudulent or unconscionable conduct [;

(f) maintain offices within this State; and]

[(g) appoint any necessary attorneys, hearing examiners, clerks, and other employees and agents and fix their compensation, and authorize attorneys appointed under this section to appear for and represent the Administrator in court].

(2) In addition to other powers granted by this Act, the Administrator shall enforce the Federal Truth in Lending Act, except to the extent otherwise provided by law.

(3) To keep the Administrator's rules in harmony with the rules of administrators in other jurisdictions that enact substantially the Uniform Consumer Credit Code, the Administrator, so far as is consistent with the purposes, policies, and provisions of this Act, shall:

(a) before adopting, amending, and repealing rules, advise and consult with administrators in other jurisdictions that enact substantially the Uniform Consumer Credit Code; and

(b) in adopting, amending, and repealing rules, take into consideration the rules of administrators in other jurisdictions that enact substantially the Uniform Consumer Credit Code.

(4) Except for refund of an excess charge, no liability is imposed under this Act for an act done or omitted in conformity with a rule, interpretation, or declaratory ruling of the Administrator, notwithstanding that after the act or omission the rule, interpretation, or ruling is amended or repealed or is determined by judicial or other authority to be invalid for any reason.

(5) The Administrator shall report [annually on or before January 1] to the [Governor and Legislature] on the operation of his office, the use of consumer credit in this State, and the problems of persons of small means obtaining credit from persons regularly engaged in extending sales or loan credit. For the purpose of making the report, the Administrator may conduct research and make appropriate studies. The report shall include a description of the examination and investigation procedures and policies of his office, a statement of policies followed in deciding whether to investigate or examine the offices of credit suppliers subject to this Act, a statement of the number and percentages of offices which are periodically investigated or examined, a statement of the types of consumer credit problems of both creditors and consumers which have come to his attention through his examinations and investigations and the disposition of them under existing law, a statement of the extent to which rules of the Administrator pursuant to this Act are not in harmony with the rules of administrators in other jurisdictions that enact substantially the Uniform Consumer Credit Code and the reasons for these variations, and a general statement of the activities of his office and of others to promote the purposes of this Act. The report may not identify the creditors against whom action is taken by the Administrator.

Section 6.105 [Administrative Powers with Respect to Supervised Financial Organizations]

(1) With respect to supervised financial organizations, the powers of examination and investigation (Sections 2.305 and 6.106) and administrative enforcement (Section 6.108) shall be exercised by the official or agency to whose supervision the organization is subject. All other powers of the Administrator under this Act may be exercised by him with respect to a supervised financial organization.

(2) If the Administrator receives a complaint or other information concerning noncompliance with this Act by a supervised financial organization, he shall inform the official or agency having supervisory authority over the organization concerned. The Administrator may request information about supervised financial organizations from the officials or agencies supervising them.

(3) The Administrator and any official or agency of this State having supervisory authority over a supervised financial organization shall consult and assist one another in maintaining compliance with this Act. They may jointly pursue investigations, prosecute actions, and take other official action, as they deem

appropriate, if either of them otherwise is empowered to take the action.

Section 6.106 [Investigatory Powers]

(1) If the Administrator has cause to believe that a person has engaged in conduct or committed an act that is subject to action by the Administrator, he may make an investigation to determine whether the person has engaged in the conduct or committed the act. To the extent necessary for this purpose, he may administer oaths or affirmations, and, upon his own motion or upon request of any party, subpoena witnesses, compel their attendance, adduce evidence, and require the production of, or testimony as to, any matter relevant to the investigation, including the existence, description, nature, custody, condition, and location of any books, documents, or other tangible things and the identity and location of persons having knowledge of relevant facts, or any other matter reasonably calculated to lead to the discovery of admissible evidence.

(2) If the person's records are located outside this State, the person at his option shall make them available to the Administrator at a convenient location within this State or pay the reasonable and necessary expenses for the Administrator or his representative to examine them where they are located. The Administrator may designate representatives, including comparable officials of the State in which the records are located, to inspect them on his behalf.

(3) Upon application by the Administrator showing failure without lawful excuse to obey a subpoena or to give testimony, and upon reasonable notice to all persons affected thereby, the [   ] court shall grant an order compelling compliance.

(4) The Administrator may not make public the name or identity of a person whose acts or conduct he investigates under this section or the facts disclosed in the investigation, but this subsection does not apply to disclosures in actions or enforcement proceedings pursuant to this Act.

Section 6.107 [Application of [Administrative Procedure Act][Part on Administrative Procedure and Judicial Review]]

Except as otherwise provided, the [State Administrative Procedure Act] [Part on Administrative Procedure and Judicial Review (Part 4) of this Article] applies to and governs all administrative action taken by the Administrator pursuant to this Article.

Section 6.108 [Administrative Enforcement Orders]

(1) After notice and hearing the Administrator may order a creditor or a person acting in his behalf to cease and desist from violating this Act. A respondent aggrieved by an order of the Administrator may obtain judicial review of the order and the Administrator may obtain an order of the court for enforcement of his order in the [   ] court. The proceeding for review or enforcement is initiated by filing a petition in the court. Copies of the petition shall be served upon all parties of record.

(2) Within 30 days after service of the petition for review upon the Administrator, or within any further time the court allows, the Administrator shall transmit to the court the original or a certified copy of the entire record upon which the order is based, including any transcript of testimony, which need not be printed. By stipulation of all parties to the review proceeding, the record may be shortened. After hearing, the court may (a) reverse or modify the order if the findings of fact of the Administrator are clearly erroneous in view of the reliable, probative, and substantial evidence on the whole record, (b) grant any temporary relief or restraining order it deems just, and (c) enter an order enforcing, modifying, and enforcing as modified, or setting aside in whole or in part the order of the Administrator, or remanding the case to the Administrator for further proceedings.

(3) An objection not urged at the hearing shall not be considered by the court unless the failure to urge the objection is excused for good cause shown. A party may move the court to remand the case to the Administrator in the interest of justice for the purpose of adducing additional specified and material evidence and seeking findings thereon upon good cause shown for the failure to adduce this evidence before the Administrator.

(4) The jurisdiction of the court shall be exclusive and its final judgment or decree is subject to review by the [   ] court in the same manner and form and with the same effect as in appeals from a final judgment or decree in a [special proceeding]. The Administrator's copy of the testimony shall be avail-

able at reasonable times to all parties for examination without cost.

(5) A proceeding for review under this section shall be initiated within 30 days after a copy of the order of the Administrator is received. If no proceeding is so initiated, the Administrator may obtain an order of the court for enforcement of his order upon showing that his order was issued in compliance with this section, that no proceeding for review was initiated within 30 days after a copy of the order was received, and that the respondent is subject to the jurisdiction of the court.

(6) With respect to unconscionable agreements or fraudulent or unconscionable conduct by the respondent, the Administrator may not issue an order pursuant to this section but may bring a civil action for an injunction (Section 6.111).

Section 6.109 [Assurance of Discontinuance]

If it is claimed that a person has engaged in conduct which could be subject to an order by the Administrator (Sections 2.303 and 6.108) or by a court (Sections 6.110, 6.111, and 6.112), the Administrator may accept an assurance in writing that the person will not engage in the same or similar conduct in the future. The assurance may include any of the following: stipulations for the voluntary payment by the creditor of the costs of investigation or of an amount to be held in escrow as restitution to debtors aggrieved by past or future conduct of the creditor or to cover costs of future investigation, or admissions of past specific acts by the creditor or that those acts violated this Act or other statutes. A violation of an assurance of discontinuance is a violation of this Act.

Section 6.110 [Injunctions Against Violations of Act]

The Administrator may bring a civil action to restrain any person from violating this Act and for other appropriate relief including but not limited to the following: to prevent a person from using or employing practices prohibited by this Act, to reform contracts to conform to this Act and to rescind contracts into which a creditor has induced a consumer to enter by conduct violating this Act, even though a consumer is not a party to the action. An action under this section may be joined with an action under the provisions on civil actions by Administrator (Section 6.113).

Section 6.111 [Injunctions Against Unconscionable Agreements and Fraudulent or Unconscionable Conduct Including Debt Collection]

(1) The Administrator may bring a civil action to restrain a person to whom this Part applies from engaging in a course of:

(a) making or enforcing unconscionable terms or provisions of consumer credit transactions;

(b) fraudulent or unconscionable conduct in inducing consumers to enter into consumer credit transactions;

(c) conduct of any of the types specified in paragraph (a) or (b) with respect to transactions that give rise to or that lead persons to believe will give rise to consumer credit transactions; or

(d) fraudulent or unconscionable conduct in the collection of debts arising from consumer credit transactions.

(2) In an action brought pursuant to this section the court may grant relief only if it finds:

(a) that the respondent has made unconscionable agreements or has engaged or is likely to engage in a course of fraudulent or unconscionable conduct;

(b) that the respondent's agreements have caused or are likely to cause or the conduct of the respondent has caused or is likely to cause injury to consumers or debtors; and

(c) that the respondent has been able to cause or will be able to cause the injury primarily because the transactions involved are credit transactions.

(3) In applying subsection (1)(a), (b), and (c), consideration shall be given to each of the factors specified in the provisions on unconscionability with respect to a transaction that is, gives rise to, or that a person leads the debtor to believe will give rise to, a consumer credit transaction (subsection (4) of Section 5.108), among others.

(4) In applying subsection (1)(d), consideration shall be given to each of the factors specified in the provisions on unconscionability with respect to the collection of debts arising from consumer credit transactions (subsection (5) of Section 5.108), among others.

(5) In an action brought pursuant to this section, a

charge or practice expressly permitted by this Act is not in itself unconscionable.

Section 6.112 [Temporary Relief]

With respect to an action brought to enjoin violations of the Act (Section 6.110) or unconscionable agreements or fraudulent or unconscionable conduct (Section 6.111), the Administrator may apply to the court for appropriate temporary relief against a defendant, pending final determination of the action. The court may grant appropriate temporary relief.

Section 6.113 [Civil Actions by Administrator]

(1) After demand, the Administrator may bring a civil action against a creditor to recover actual damages sustained and excess charges paid by one or more consumers who have a right to recover explicitly granted by this Act. In a civil action under this subsection, penalties may not be recovered by the Administrator. The court shall order amounts recovered under this subsection to be paid to each consumer or set off against his obligation. A consumer's action, except a class action, takes precedence over a prior or subsequent action by the Administrator with respect to the claim of that consumer. A consumer's class action takes precedence over a subsequent action by the Administrator with respect to claims common to both actions, but the Administrator may intervene. An Administrator's action on behalf of a class of consumers takes precedence over a consumer's subsequent class action with respect to claims common to both actions. Whenever an action takes precedence over another action under this subsection, the latter action may be stayed to the extent appropriate while the precedent action is pending and dismissed if the precedent action is dismissed with prejudice or results in a final judgment granting or denying the claim asserted in the precedent action. A defense available to a creditor in a civil action brought by a consumer is available to him in a civil action brought under this subsection.

(2) The Administrator may bring a civil action against a creditor or a person acting in his behalf to recover a civil penalty of no more than $5,000 for repeatedly and intentionally violating this Act. A civil penalty pursuant to this subsection may not be imposed for a violation of this Act occurring more than two years before the action is brought or for making uncon-

scionable agreements or engaging in a course of fraudulent or unconscionable conduct.

(3) The Administrator may bring a civil action against a creditor for failure to file notification in accordance with the provisions on notification (Section 6.202) or to pay fees in accordance with the provisions on fees (Section 6.203) to recover the fees the defendant has failed to pay and a civil penalty in an amount determined by the court not exceeding the greater of three times the amount of fees the defendant has failed to pay or $1,000.

Section 6.114 [Jury Trial]

The Administrator has no right to trial by jury in an action brought by him under this Act.

Section 6.115 [Consumer's Remedies not Affected]

The grant of powers to the Administrator in this Article does not affect remedies available to consumers under this Act or under other principles of law or equity.

[Section 6.116 [Venue]

The Administrator may bring actions or proceedings in a court in a [county] in which an act on which the action or proceeding is based occurred or in a [county] in which respondent resides or transacts business.]

Part 2 Notification and Fees

Section 6.201 [Applicability]

This Part applies to a creditor engaged in entering into consumer credit transactions in this State and to a creditor having an office or place of business in this State who takes assignments and undertakes direct collection of payments from or enforcement of rights against consumers arising from these transactions.

Section 6.202 [Notification]

(1) Persons subject to this Part shall file notification with the Administrator within 30 days after commencing business in this State, and, thereafter, on or before January 31 of each year. The notification shall state:

(a) name of the person;

(b) name in which business is transacted if different from (a);

(c) address of principal office, which may be outside this State;

(d) address of all offices or retail stores, if any, in this State at which consumer credit transactions are entered into, or in case of a person taking assignments of obligations, the offices or places of business within this State at which business is transacted;

(e) if consumer credit transactions are entered into otherwise than at an office or retail store in this State, a brief description of the manner in which they are entered into;

(f) address of designated agent upon whom service of process may be made in this State; and

(g) whether supervised loans are made.

(2) If information in a notification becomes inaccurate after filing, no further notification is required until the following January 31.

Section 6.203 **[Fees]**

(1) A person required to file notification shall pay to the [Administrator] an annual fee of $10. The fee shall be paid with the filing of the first notification and on or before January 31 of each year thereafter.

(2) Except as provided in subsection (4), a person required to file notification who is a seller, lessor, or lender shall pay at the time and in the manner stated in subsection (1) an additional fee of [$10] for each $100,000 or part thereof exceeding [$10,000], of the average unpaid balances, including unpaid scheduled periodic payments under consumer leases, of obligations arising from consumer credit transactions entered into by him in this State and held on the last day of each calendar month during the preceding calendar year and held either by the seller, lessor, or lender or by his immediate or remote assignee who has not filed notification. The unpaid balances of assigned obligations held by an assignee who has not filed notification are presumed to be the unpaid balances of the assigned obligations at the time of their assignment by the seller, lessor, or lender.

(3) Except as provided in subsection (4), a person required to file notification who is an assignee shall pay at the time and in the manner stated in subsection (1) an additional fee of [$10] for each $100,000, or part thereof exceeding [$10,000], of the average unpaid balances, including unpaid scheduled periodic

payments payable by lessees, of obligations arising from consumer credit transactions entered into in this State taken by him by assignment and held by him by assignment and held by him on the last day of each calendar month during the preceding calendar year.

(4) A supervised financial organization is exempt from 50 per cent of the fees prescribed by subsections (2) and (3) to take account of its obligation to pay other fees or charges to officials or agencies to whose supervision it is also subject.

(5) To the extent that a seller, lessor, or lender, or his immediate or remote assignee is obligated to pay and pays fees to another state or official thereof pursuant to provisions similar but not necessarily identical to subsections (2) and (3), he is entitled to an exemption from the fees prescribed by subsections (2) and (3).

(6) The [Administrator] may collect a charge not exceeding [$25] from each person required to pay fees under this section with respect to fees not paid in full within 90 days after they are due.

Part 3 Council of Advisors on Consumer Credit

Section 6.301 [Council of Advisors on Consumer Credit]

(1) The Council of Advisors on Consumer Credit is created consisting of [sixteen] members appointed by the Governor. The Governor shall designate one of the Advisors as Chairman. In appointing members of the Council, the Governor shall seek to achieve a fair representation from the various segments of the consumer credit industry and the public.

(2) The term of office of each member of the Council is [four] years. Of those members first appointed, [four] shall be appointed for a term of [one] year, [four] for a term of [two] years, [four] for a term of [three] years, and [four] for a term of [four] years. A member chosen to fill a vacancy arising otherwise than by expiration of term shall be appointed for the unexpired term of the member whom he is to succeed. A member of the Council is eligible for reappointment.

(3) Members of the Council shall serve without compensation, but are entitled to reimbursement of expenses reasonably incurred in the performance of their duties.

Section 6.302 [Function of Council; Conflict of Interest]

The Council shall advise and consult with the Administrator concerning the exercise of his powers under this Act and may make recommendations to him. Members of the Council may assist the Administrator in obtaining compliance with this Act. Since it is an objective of this Part to obtain competent representatives of creditors and the public to serve on the Council and to assist and cooperate with the Administrator in achieving the objectives of this Act, service on the Council does not in itself constitute a conflict of interest regardless of the occupations or associations of the members.

Section 6.303 [Meetings]

The Council and the Administrator shall meet together at a time and place designated by the Chairman at least twice each year. The Council may hold additional meetings when called by the Chairman.

[Part 4] [Administrative Procedure and Judicial Review]

[Section 6.401 [Applicability and Scope]

This Part applies to the Administrator, prescribes the procedures to be observed by him in exercising his powers under this Act, and supplements the provisions of the Part on Powers and Functions of Administrator (Part 1) of this Article and of the Part on Supervised Lenders (Part 3) of the Article on Finance Charges and Related Provisions (Article 2).]

[Section 6.402 [Definitions in Part: "Contested Case"; "License"; "Licensing"; "Party"; "Rule"]

In this Part:

(1) "Contested case" means a proceeding, including but not restricted to one pursuant to the provisions on administrative enforcement orders (subsection (1) of Section 6.108) and licensing, in which the legal rights, duties, or privileges of a party are required by law to be determined by the Administrator after an opportunity for hearing.

(2) "License" means a license authorizing a person to make supervised loans pursuant to the provisions on authority to make supervised loans (Section 2.301).

(3) "Licensing" includes the Administrator's process

respecting the grant, denial, revocation, suspension, annulment, withdrawal, or amendment of a license.

(4) "Party" means the Administrator and each person named or admitted as a party, or who is aggrieved by action taken and seeks to be admitted as a party.

(5) "Rule" means each rule specifically authorized by this Act that applies generally and implements, interprets, or prescribes law or policy, or each statement by the Administrator that applies generally and describes the Administrator's procedure or practice requirements or the organization of his office. The term includes the amendment or repeal of a prior rule, but does not include:

(a) statements concerning only the internal management of the Administrator's office and not affecting private rights or procedures available to the public; [or]

(b) declaratory rulings issued pursuant to the provisions on declaratory rulings by Administrator (Section 6.409) [; or

(c) intra-office memoranda].]

[Section 6.403 [Public Information; Adoption of Rules; Availability of Rules and Orders]

(1) In addition to other rule-making requirements imposed by law, the Administrator shall:

(a) adopt as a rule a description of the organization of his office, stating the general course and method of the operations of his office and the methods whereby the public may obtain information or make submissions or requests;

(b) adopt rules of practice setting forth the nature and requirements of all formal and informal procedures available, including a description of all forms and instructions used by the Administrator or his office;

(c) make available for public inspection all rules and all other written statements of policy or interpretations formulated, adopted, or used by the Administrator in the discharge of his functions; and

(d) make available for public inspection all final orders, decisions, and opinions.

(2) A rule, order, or decision of the Administrator is not valid or effective against any person or party, nor .

may it be invoked by the Administrator for any person, until it has been made available for public inspection as herein required. This provision does not apply in favor of any person or party who has actual knowledge thereof.]

[Section 6.404 **[Procedure for Adoption of Rules]**

(1) Prior to the adoption, amendment, or repeal of any rule, the Administrator shall:

(a) give at least 30 days' notice of his intended action. The notice shall include a statement of either the terms or substance of the intended action or a description of the subjects and issues involved, and the time, place, and manner in which interested persons may present their views thereon. The notice shall be mailed to all persons who have made timely request of the Administrator for advance notice of his rule-making proceedings and be published in [here insert the medium of publication appropriate for the adopting State];

(b) afford all interested persons reasonable opportunity to submit data, views, or arguments, orally or in writing. In case of substantive rules, opportunity for oral hearing shall be granted if requested by 25 persons, a governmental subdivision or agency, or an association having not fewer than 25 members. The Administrator shall consider fully all written and oral submissions respecting the proposed rule. Upon adoption of a rule the Administrator, if requested to do so by an interested person before adoption or within 30 days thereafter, shall issue a concise statement of the principal reasons for and against its adoption, incorporating therein his reasons for overruling the considerations urged against its adoption.

(2) A rule is not valid unless adopted in substantial compliance with this section. A proceeding to contest any rule on the ground of non-compliance with the procedural requirements of this section shall be commenced within two years from the effective date of the rule.]

[Section 6.405 **[Filing and Taking Effect of Rules]**

(1) The administrator shall file in the office of the [Secretary of State] a certified copy of each rule adopted by him. The [Secretary of State] shall keep a permanent register of the rules open to public inspection.

(2) Each rule hereafter adopted is effective 20 days after filing, except that a later effective date may be specified in the rule.]

[Section 6.406 **[Publication of Rules]**

(1) The [Secretary of State] shall compile, index, and publish all effective rules adopted by the Administrator. Compilations shall be supplemented or revised as often as necessary.

(2) Compilations shall be made available upon request to [agencies and officials of this State] free of charge and to other persons at prices fixed by the [Secretary of State] to cover mailing and publication costs.]

[Section 6.407 **[Petition for Adoption of Rules]**

An interested person may petition the Administrator requesting the adoption, amendment, or repeal of a rule. The Administrator shall prescribe by rule the form for petitions and the procedure for their submission, consideration, and disposition. Within 30 days after submission of a petition, the Administrator either shall deny the petition in writing (stating his reasons for the denials) or initiate rule-making proceedings in accordance with the provisions on procedure for adoption of rules (Section 6.404).]

[Section 6.408 **[Declaratory Judgment on Validity or Applicability of Rules]**

The validity or applicability of a rule may be determined in an action for declaratory judgment in the [   ] court if it is alleged that the rule, or its threatened application, interferes with or impairs, or threatens to interfere with or impair, the legal rights or privileges of the plaintiff. The Administrator shall be made a party to the action. A declaratory judgment may be rendered whether or not the plaintiff has requested the Administrator to pass upon the validity or applicability of the rule in question.]

[Section 6.409 **[Declaratory Rulings by Administrator]**

The Administrator shall provide by rule for the filing and prompt disposition of petitions for declaratory rulings as to the applicability of any statutory provision or of any rule of the Administrator. Rulings disposing of petitions have the same status as decisions or orders in contested cases.]

[Section 6.410 **[Contested Cases; Notice; Hearing; Records]**

(1) In a contested case, all parties shall be afforded an opportunity for hearing after reasonable notice.

(2) The notice shall include:

(a) a statement of the time, place, and nature of the hearing;

(b) a statement of the legal authority and jurisdiction under which the hearing is to be held;

(c) a reference to the particular provisions of the statutes and rules involved; and

(d) a short and plain statement of the matters asserted. If the Administrator or other party is unable to state the matters in detail at the time the notice is served, the initial notice may be limited to a statement of the issues involved. Thereafter upon application a more definite and detailed statement shall be furnished.

(3) Opportunity shall be afforded all parties to respond and present evidence and argument on all issues involved.

(4) Unless precluded by law, informal disposition may be made of a contested case by stipulation, agreed settlement, consent order, or default.

(5) The record in a contested case shall include:

(a) pleadings, motions, and intermediate rulings;

(b) evidence received or considered;

(c) a statement of matters officially noticed;

(d) questions and offers of proof, objections, and rulings thereon;

(e) proposed findings and exceptions;

(f) any decision, opinion, or report by the officer presiding at the hearing; and

(g) staff memoranda or data submitted to the hearing officer or members of the office of the Administrator in connection with their consideration of the case.

(6) Oral proceedings or any part thereof shall be transcribed on request of any party [, but at his expense].

(7) Findings of fact shall be based exclusively on the evidence and on matters officially noticed.]

[Section 6.411 **[Rules of Evidence; Official Notice]**

In contested cases:

(1) irrelevant, immaterial, or unduly repetitious evidence shall be excluded. The rules of evidence as applied in [nonjury] civil cases in the [   ] court of this State shall be followed. If necessary to ascertain facts not reasonably susceptible of proof under those rules, evidence not admissible thereunder may be admitted (except where precluded by statute) if it is of a type commonly relied upon by reasonably prudent men in the conduct of their affairs. The Administrator shall give effect to the rules of privilege recognized by law. Objections to evidentiary offers may be made and shall be noted in the record. Subject to these requirements, if a hearing will be expedited and the interests of the parties will not be prejudiced substantially, any part of the evidence may be received in written form;

[(2) documentary evidence may be received in the form of copies or excerpts, if the original is not readily available. Upon request, parties shall be given an opportunity to compare the copy with the original;]

(3) a party may conduct cross-examinations required for a full and true disclosure of the facts;

(4) notice may be taken of judicially cognizable facts. In addition, notice may be taken of generally recognized technical or scientific facts within the Administrator's specialized knowledge. Parties shall be notified either before or during the hearing, or by reference in preliminary reports or otherwise, of the material noticed, including any staff memoranda or data, and they shall be afforded an opportunity to contest the material so noticed. The Administrator's experience, technical competence, and specialized knowledge may be utilized in the evaluation of the evidence.]

[Section 6.412 **[Decisions and Orders]**

A final decision or order adverse to a party in a contested case shall be in writing or stated in the record. A final decision shall include findings of fact and conclusions of law, separately stated. Findings of fact, if set forth in statutory language, shall be accompanied by a concise and explicit statement of the underlying facts supporting the findings. If, in accordance with rules of the Administrator, a party submitted proposed findings of fact, the decision shall include a ruling upon each proposed finding. Parties shall be notified either personally or by mail of any decision or order. Upon request a copy of the decision or order shall be delivered or mailed forthwith to each party and to his attorney of record.]

[Section 6.413 **[Licenses]**

(1) Whenever the grant or denial of a license is required to be preceded by notice and opportunity for hearing, the provisions of this Part concerning contested cases apply.

(2) A revocation, suspension, annulment, or withdrawal of a license is unlawful unless the Administrator, before instituting proceedings, gives notice by mail to the licensee of facts or conduct which warrant the intended action, and the licensee was afforded an opportunity to show compliance with all lawful requirements for retention of the license.]

[Section 6.414 **[Judicial Review of Contested Cases]**

(1) A person who has exhausted all administrative remedies available before the Administrator and is aggrieved by a final decision in a contested case is entitled to judicial review under this Part. This section does not limit utilization of or the scope of judicial review available under other means of review, redress, relief, or trial de novo provided by law. A preliminary, procedural, or intermediate action or ruling of the Administrator is immediately reviewable if review of the final decision of the Administrator would not provide an adequate remedy.

(2) Proceedings for review are instituted by filing a petition in the [   ] court within [30] days after [mailing notice of] the final decision of the Administrator or, if a rehearing is requested, within [30] days after the decision thereon. Copies of the petition shall be served upon the Administrator and all parties of record.

(3) The filing of the petition does not itself stay enforcement of the decision of the Administrator. The Administrator may grant, or the reviewing court may order, a stay upon appropriate terms.

(4) Within [30] days after service of the petition, or

within further time allowed by the court, the Administrator shall transmit to the reviewing court the original or a certified copy of the entire record of the proceeding under review. By stipulation of all parties to the review proceedings, the record may be shortened. A party unreasonably refusing to stipulate to limit the record may be taxed by the court for the additional costs. The court may require or permit subsequent corrections or additions to the record.

(5) If, before the date set for hearing, application is made to the court for leave to present additional evidence, and it is shown to the satisfaction of the court that the additional evidence is material and there were good reasons for failure to present it in the proceeding before the Administrator, the court may order that the additional evidence be taken before the Administrator upon conditions determined by the court. The Administrator may modify his findings and decision by reason of the additional evidence and shall file that evidence and any modifications, new findings, or decisions with the reviewing court.

(6) The review shall be confined to the record and be conducted by the court without a jury. In cases of alleged irregularities in procedure before the Administrator, not shown in the record, proof thereon may be taken in the court. The court, upon request, shall hear oral argument and receive written briefs.

(7) The court may not substitute its judgment for that of the Administrator as to the weight of the evidence on questions of fact. The court may affirm the decision of the Administrator or remand the case for further proceedings. The court may reverse or modify the decision if substantial rights of the appellant have been prejudiced because the administrative findings, inferences, conclusions, or decisions are:

(a) in violation of constitutional or statutory provisions;

(b) in excess of the statutory authority of the Administrator;

(c) made upon unlawful procedure;

(d) affected by other error of law;

(e) clearly erroneous in view of the reliable, probative, and substantial evidence on the whole record; or

(f) arbitrary or capricious or characterized by

abuse of discretion or clearly unwarranted exercise of discretion.]

[Section 6.415 **[Appeals]**

An aggrieved party may obtain a review of any final judgment of the [   ] court under this Part by appeal to the [   ] court. The appeal shall be taken as in other civil cases.]

Article 7

Reserved for Future Use

Article 8

Reserved for Future Use

Article 9
EFFECTIVE DATE AND REPEALER

Section 9.101 **[Time of Taking Effect; Provisions for Transition]**

(1) Except as otherwise provided in this section, this Act takes effect at 12:01 a.m. on [   ].

(2) To the extent appropriate to permit the Administrator to prepare for operation of this Act when it takes effect and to act on applications for licenses to make supervised loans under this Act (subsection (1) of Section 2.302), the Part on Supervised Lenders (Part 3) of the Article on Finance Charges and Related Provisions (Article 2), and the Article on Administration (Article 6) take effect [   ].

Note: Insert in lieu of brackets at the end of subsection (2) either "immediately" or the earliest time possible under the constitutional or statutory requirements of the enacting State.

(3) Transactions entered into before this Act takes effect and the rights, duties, and interests flowing from them thereafter may be terminated, completed, consummated, or enforced as required or permitted by any statute, rule of law, or other law amended, repealed, or modified by this Act as though the repeal, amendment, or modification had not occurred; but this Act applies to:

> (a) refinancings, consolidations, and deferrals made after this Act takes effect as to sales, leases, and loans whenever entered into;

> (b) sales or loans entered into after this Act takes effect pursuant to open-end credit entered into, arranged, or contracted for before this Act takes effect; and

> (c) all credit transactions entered into before this Act takes effect insofar as the Article on Remedies and Penalties (Article 5) limits the remedies of creditors.

Section 9.102 **[Continuation of Licensing]**

All persons licensed or otherwise authorized under [list statutes] on the effective date of this Act are licensed to make supervised loans under this Act pursuant to the Part on Supervised Lenders (Part 3) of the Article on Finance Charges and Related Provisions (Article 2), and that Part applies to the persons so previously licensed or authorized. The Administrator may, but is not required to, deliver evidence of licensing to the persons so previously licensed or authorized.

Section 9.103 **[Specific Repealer and Amendments]**

(1) The following acts and parts of acts are repealed:

> (a)

> (b)

> (c) [and so on]

(2) The following acts and parts of acts are amended:

> (a)

> (b)

> (c) [and so on]

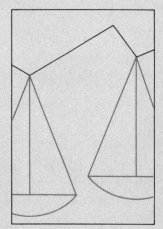

APPENDIX C
The Uniform
Partnership Act

(Adopted in 47 States, all except Georgia, Louisiana, and Mississippi; the District of Columbia, the Virgin Islands, and Guam. The adoptions by Alabama and Nebraska do not follow the official text in every respect, but are substantially similar, with local variations.)

The Act consists of 7 Parts as follows:

I. Preliminary Provisions

II. Nature of Partnership

III. Relations of Partners to Persons Dealing with the Partnership

IV. Relations of Partners to One Another

V. Property Rights of a Partner

VI. Dissolution and Winding Up

VII. Miscellaneous Provisions

An Act to make uniform the Law of Partnerships Be it enacted, etc.:

Part I Preliminary Provisions

Sec. 1. **Name of Act.**

This act may be cited as Uniform Partnership Act.

Sec. 2. **Definition of Terms.**

In this act, "Court" includes every court and judge having jurisdiction in the case.

"Business" includes every trade, occupation, or profession.

"Person" includes individuals, partnerships, corporations, and other associations.

"Bankrupt" includes bankrupt under the Federal Bankruptcy Act or insolvent under any state insolvent act.

"Conveyance" includes every assignment, lease, mortgage, or encumbrance.

"Real property" includes land and any interest or estate in land.

Sec. 3. **Interpretation of Knowledge and Notice.**

(1) A person has "knowledge" of a fact within the meaning of this act not only when he has actual knowledge thereof, but also when he has knowledge of such other facts as in the circumstances shows bad faith.

(2) A person has "notice" of a fact within the meaning of this act when the person who claims the benefit of the notice

(a) States the fact to such person, or

(b) Delivers through the mail, or by other means of communication, a written statement of the fact to such person or to a proper person at his place of business or residence.

Sec. 4. **Rules of Construction.**

(1) The rule that statutes in derogation of the common law are to be strictly construed shall have no application to this act.

(2) The law of estoppel shall apply under this act.

(3) The law of agency shall apply under this act.

(4) This act shall be so interpreted and construed as to effect its general purpose to make uniform the law of those states which enact it.

(5) This act shall not be construed so as to impair the obligations of any contract existing when the act goes into effect, nor to affect any action or proceedings begun or right accrued before this act takes effect.

Sec. 5. **Rules for Cases Not Provided for in this Act.**

In any case not provided for in this act the rules of law and equity, including the law merchant, shall govern.

Part II Nature of Partnership

Sec. 6. **Partnership Defined.**

(1) A partnership is an association of two or more persons to carry on as co-owners a business for profit.

(2) But any association formed under any other statute of this state, or any statute adopted by authority, other than the authority of this state, is not a partnership under this act, unless such association would have been a partnership in this state prior to the adoption of this act; but this act shall apply to limited partnerships except in so far as the statutes relating to such partnerships are inconsistent herewith.

Sec. 7. **Rules for Determining the Existence of a Partnership.**

In determining whether a partnership exists, these rules shall apply:

(1) Except as provided by Section 16 persons who are not partners as to each other are not partners as to third persons.

(2) Joint tenancy, tenancy in common, tenancy by the entireties, joint property, common property, or part ownership does not of itself establish a partnership, whether such co-owners do or do not share any profits made by the use of the property.

(3) The sharing of gross returns does not of itself establish a partnership, whether or not the persons sharing them have a joint or common right or interest in any property from which the returns are derived.

(4) The receipt by a person of a share of the profits of a business is prima facie evidence that he is a partner in the business, but no such inference shall be drawn if such profits were received in payment:

(a) As a debt by installments or otherwise,

(b) As wages of an employee or rent to a landlord,

(c) As an annuity to a widow or representative of a deceased partner,

(d) As interest on a loan, though the amount of payment vary with the profits of the business.

(e) As the consideration for the sale of a good-will of a business or other property by installments or otherwise.

Sec. 8. **Partnership Property.**

(1) All property originally brought into the partnership stock or subsequently acquired by purchase or otherwise, on account of the partnership, is partnership property.

(2) Unless the contrary intention appears, property acquired with partnership funds is partnership property.

(3) Any estate in real property may be acquired in the partnership name. Title so acquired can be conveyed only in the partnership name.

(4) A conveyance to a partnership in the partnership name, though without words of inheritance, passes the entire estate of the grantor unless a contrary intent appears.

Part III **Relations of Partners to Persons Dealing with the Partnership**

Sec. 9. **Partner Agent of Partnership as to Partnership Business.**

(1) Every partner is an agent of the partnership for the purpose of its business, and the act of every partner, including the execution in the partnership name of any instrument, for apparently carrying on in the usual way the business of the partnership of which he is a member binds the partnership, unless the partner so acting has in fact no authority to act for the partnership in the particular matter, and the person with whom he is dealing has knowledge of the fact that he has no such authority.

(2) An act of a partner which is not apparently for the carrying on of the business of the partnership in the usual way does not bind the partnership unless authorized by the other partners.

(3) Unless authorized by the other partners or unless they have abandoned the business, one or more but less than all the partners have no authority to:

(a) Assign the partnership property in trust for creditors or on the assignee's promise to pay the debts of the partnership,

(b) Dispose of the good-will of the business,

(c) Do any other act which would make it impossible to carry on the ordinary business of a partnership,

(d) Confess a judgment,

(e) Submit a partnership claim or liability to arbitration or reference.

(4) No act of a partner in contravention of a restriction on authority shall bind the partnership to persons having knowledge of the restriction.

Sec. 10. **Conveyance of Real Property of the Partnership.**

(1) Where title to real property is in the partnership name, any partner may convey title to such property by a conveyance executed in the partnership name; but the partnership may recover such property unless the partner's act binds the partnership under the provisions of paragraph (1) of section 9 or unless such property has been conveyed by the grantee or a person claiming through such grantee to a holder for value without knowledge that the partner, in making the conveyance, has exceeded his authority.

(2) Where title to real property is in the name of the partnership, a conveyance executed by a partner, in his own name, passes the equitable interest of the partnership, provided the act is one within the

authority of the partner under the provisions of paragraph (1) of section 9.

(3) Where title to real property is in the name of one or more but not all the partners, and the record does not disclose the right of the partnership, the partners in whose name the title stands may convey title to such property, but the partnership may recover such property if the partners' act does not bind the partnership under the provisions of paragraph (1) of section 9, unless the purchaser or his assignee, is a holder for value, without knowledge.

(4) Where the title to real property is in the name of one or more or all the partners, or in a third person in trust for the partnership, a conveyance executed by a partner in the partnership name, or in his own name, passes the equitable interest of the partnership, provided the act is one within the authority of the partner under the provisions of paragraph (1) of section 9.

(5) Where the title to real property is in the names of all the partners a conveyance executed by all the partners passes all their rights in such property.

Sec. 11. **Partnership Bound by Admission of Partner.**

An admission or representation made by any partner concerning partnership affairs within the scope of his authority as conferred by this act is evidence against the partnership.

Sec. 12. **Partnership Charged with Knowledge of or Notice to Partner.**

Notice to any partner of any matter relating to partnership affairs, and the knowledge of the partner acting in the particular matter, acquired while a partner or then present to his mind, and the knowledge of any other partner who reasonably could and should have communicated it to the acting partner, operate as notice to or knowledge of the partnership, except in the case of a fraud on the partnership committed by or with the consent of that partner.

Sec. 13. **Partnership Bound by Partner's Wrongful Act.**

Where, by any wrongful act or omission of any partner acting in the ordinary course of the business of the partnership or with the authority of his copartners, loss or injury is caused to any person, not being a partner in the partnership, or any penalty is incurred, the partnership is liable therefor to the same extent as the partner so acting or omitting to act.

Sec. 14. **Partnership Bound by Partner's Breach of Trust.**

The partnership is bound to make good the loss:

(a) Where one partner acting within the scope of his apparent authority receives money or property of a third person and misapplies it; and

(b) Where the partnership in the course of its business receives money or property of a third person and the money or property so received is misapplied by any partner while it is in the custody of the partnership.

Sec. 15. **Nature of Partner's Liability.**

All partners are liable

(a) Jointly and severally for everything chargeable to the partnership under sections 13 and 14.

(b) Jointly for all other debts and obligations of the partnership; but any partner may enter into a separate obligation to perform a partnership contract.

Sec. 16. **Partner by Estoppel.**

(1) When a person, by words spoken or written or by conduct, represents himself, or consents to another representing him to any one, as a partner in an existing partnership or with one or more persons not actual partners, he is liable to any such person to whom such representation has been made, who has, on the faith of such representation, given credit to the actual or apparent partnership, and if he has made such representation or consented to its being made in a public manner he is liable to such person, whether the representation has or has not been made or communicated to such person so giving credit by or with the knowledge of the apparent partner making the representation or consenting to its being made.

(a) When a partnership liability results, he is liable as though he were an actual member of the partnership.

(b) When no partnership liability results, he is liable jointly with the other persons, if any, so consenting to the contract or representation as to incur liability, otherwise separately.

(2) When a person has been thus represented to be a partner in an existing partnership, or with one or more persons not actual partners, he is an agent of the persons consenting to such representation to bind them to the same extent and in the same manner as though he were a partner in fact, with respect to persons who rely upon the representation. Where all the members of the existing partnership consent to the representation, a partnership act or obligation results; but in all other cases it is the joint act or obligation of the person acting and the persons consenting to the representation.

Sec. 17. **Liability of Incoming Partner.**

A person admitted as a partner into an existing partnership is liable for all the obligations of the partnership arising before his admission as though he had been a partner when such obligations were incurred, except that this liability shall be satisfied only out of partnership property.

Part IV **Relations of Partners to One Another**

Sec. 18. **Rules Determining Rights and Duties of Partners.**

The rights and duties of the partners in relation to the partnership shall be determined, subject to any agreement between them, by the following rules:

(a) Each partner shall be repaid his contributions, whether by way of capital or advances to the partnership property and share equally in the profits and surplus remaining after all liabilities, including those to partners, are satisfied; and must contribute towards the losses, whether of capital or otherwise, sustained by the partnership according to his share in the profits.

(b) The partnership must indemnify every partner in respect of payments made and personal liabilities reasonably incurred by him in the ordinary and proper conduct of its business, or for the preservation of its business or property.

(c) A partner, who in aid of the partnership makes any payment or advance beyond the amount of capital which he agreed to contribute, shall be paid interest from the date of the payment or advance.

(d) A partner shall receive interest on the capital contributed by him only from the date when repayment should be made.

(e) All partners have equal rights in the management and conduct of the partnership business.

(f) No partner is entitled to remuneration for acting in the partnership business, except that a surviving partner is entitled to reasonable compensation for his services in winding up the partnership affairs.

(g) No person can become a member of a partnership without the consent of all the partners.

(h) Any difference arising as to ordinary matters connected with the partnership business may be decided by a majority of the partners; but no act in contravention of any agreement between the partners may be done rightfully without the consent of all the partners.

Sec. 19. **Partnership Books.**

The partnership books shall be kept, subject to any agreement between the partners, at the principal place of business of the partnership, and every partner shall at all times have access to and may inspect and copy any of them.

Sec. 20. **Duty of Partners to Render Information.**

Partners shall render on demand true and full information of all things affecting the partnership to any partner or the legal representative of any deceased partner or partner under legal disability.

Sec. 21. **Partner Accountable as a Fiduciary.**

(1) Every partner must account to the partnership for any benefit, and hold as trustee for it any profits derived by him without the consent of the other partners from any transaction connected with the formation, conduct, or liquidation of the partnership or from any use by him of its property.

(2) This section applies also to the representatives of a deceased partner engaged in the liquidation of the affairs of the partnership as the personal representatives of the last surviving partner.

Sec. 22. **Right to an Account.**

Any partner shall have the right to a formal account as to partnership affairs:

(a) If he is wrongfully excluded from the partnership

business or possession of its property by his co-partners,

(b) If the right exists under the terms of any agreement,

(c) As provided by section 21,

(d) Whenever other circumstances render it just and reasonable.

Sec. 23. **Continuation of Partnership Beyond Fixed Term.**

(1) When a partnership for a fixed term or particular undertaking is continued after the termination of such term or particular undertaking without any express agreement, the rights and duties of the partners remain the same as they were at such termination, so far as is consistent with a partnership at will.

(2) A continuation of the business by the partners or such of them as habitually acted therein during the term, without any settlement or liquidation of the partnership affairs, is prima facie evidence of a continuation of the partnership.

Part V **Property Rights of a Partner**

Sec. 24. **Extent of Property Rights of a Partner.**

The property rights of a partner are (1) his rights in specific partnership property, (2) his interest in the partnership, and (3) his right to participate in the management.

Sec. 25. **Nature of a Partner's Right in Specific Partnership Property.**

(1) A partner is co-owner with his partners of specific partnership property holding as a tenant in partnership.

(2) The incidents of this tenancy are such that:

(a) A partner, subject to the provisions of this act and to any agreement between the partners, has an equal right with his partners to possess specific partnership property for partnership purposes; but he has no right to possess such property for any other purpose without the consent of his partners.

(b) A partner's right in specific partnership property is not assignable except in connection with the assignment of rights of all the partners in the same property.

(c) A partner's right in specific partnership property is not subject to attachment or execution, except on a claim against the partnership. When partnership property is attached for a partnership debt the partners, or any of them, or the representatives of a deceased partner, cannot claim any right under the homestead or exemption laws.

(d) On the death of a partner his right in specific partnership property vests in the surviving partner or partners, except where the deceased was the last surviving partner, when his right in such property vests in his legal representative. Such surviving partner or partners, or the legal representative of the last surviving partner, has no right to possess the partnership property for any but a partnership purpose.

(e) A partner's right in specific partnership property is not subject to dower, curtesy, or allowances to widows, heirs, or next of kin.

Sec. 26. **Nature of Partner's Interest in the Partnership.**

A partner's interest in the partnership is his share of the profits and surplus, and the same is personal property.

Sec. 27. **Assignment of Partner's Interest.**

(1) A conveyance by a partner of his interest in the partnership does not of itself dissolve the partnership, nor, as against the other partners in the absence of agreement, entitle the assignee, during the continuance of the partnership to interfere in the management or administration of the partnership business or affairs, or to require any information or account of partnership transactions, or to inspect the partnership books; but it merely entitles the assignee to receive in accordance with his contract the profits to which the assigning partner would otherwise be entitled.

(2) In case of a dissolution of the partnership, the assignee is entitled to receive his assignor's interest and may require an account from the date only of the last account agreed to by all the partners.

Sec. 28. **Partner's Interest Subject to Charging Order.**

(1) On due application to a competent court by any judgment creditor of a partner, the court which

entered the judgment, order, or decree, or any other court, may charge the interest of the debtor partner with payment of the unsatisfied amount of such judgment debt with interest thereon; and may then or later appoint a receiver of his share of the profits, and of any other money due or to fall due to him in respect of the partnership, and make all other orders, directions, accounts and inquiries which the debtor partner might have made, or which the circumstances of the case may require.

(2) The interest charged may be redeemed at any time before foreclosure, or in case of a sale being directed by the court may be purchased without thereby causing a dissolution:

(a) With separate property, by any one or more of the partners, or

(b) With partnership property, by any one or more of the partners with the consent of all the partners whose interests are not so charged or sold.

(3) Nothing in this act shall be held to deprive a partner of his right, if any, under the exemption laws, as regards his interest in the partnership.

Part VI Dissolution and Winding up

Sec. 29. **Dissolution Defined.**

The dissolution of a partnership is the change in the relation of the partners caused by any partner ceasing to be associated in the carrying on as distinguished from the winding up of the business.

Sec. 30. **Partnership Not Terminated by Dissolution.**

On dissolution the partnership is not terminated, but continues until the winding up of partnership affairs is completed.

Sec. 31. **Causes of Dissolution.**

Dissolution is caused:

(1) Without violation of the agreement between the partners,

(a) By the termination of the definite term or particular undertaking specified in the agreement,

(b) By the express will of any partner when no definite term or particular undertaking is specified,

(c) By the express will of all the partners who have not assigned their interests or suffered them to be charged for their separate debts, either before or after the termination of any specified term or particular undertaking.

(d) By the explusion of any partner from the business bona fide in accordance with such a power conferred by the agreement between the partners;

(2) In contravention of the agreement between the partners, where the circumstances do not permit a dissolution under any other provision of this section, by the express will of any partner at any time;

(3) By any event which makes it unlawful for the business of the partnership to be carried on or for the members to carry it on in partnership;

(4) By the death of any partner;

(5) By the bankruptcy of any partner or the partnership;

(6) By decree of court under section 32.

Sec. 32. **Dissolution by Decree of Court.**

(1) On application by or for a partner the court shall decree a dissolution whenever:

(a) A partner has been declared a lunatic in any judicial proceeding or is shown to be of unsound mind,

(b) A partner becomes in any other way incapable of performing his part of the partnership contract,

(c) A partner has been guilty of such conduct as tends to affect prejudicially the carrying on of the business,

(d) A partner wilfully or persistently commits a breach of the partnership agreement, or otherwise so conducts himself in matters relating to the partnership business that it is not reasonably practicable to carry on the business in partnership with him,

(e) The business of the partnership can only be carried on at a loss,

(f) Other circumstances render a dissolution equitable.

(2) On the application of the purchaser of a partner's interest under sections 27 or 28:

(a) After the termination of the specified term or particular undertaking,

(b) At any time if the partnership was a partnership at will when the interest was assigned or when the charging order was issued.

Sec. 33. **General Effect of Dissolution on Authority of Partner.**

Except so far as may be necessary to wind up partnership affairs or to complete transactions begun but not then finished, dissolution terminates all authority of any partner to act for the partnership,

(1) With respect to the partners,

(a) When the dissolution is not by the act, bankruptcy or death of a partner; or

(b) When the dissolution is by such act, bankruptcy or death of a partner, in cases where section 34 so requires.

(2) With respect to persons not partners, as declared in section 35.

Sec. 34. **Right of Partner to Contribution From Copartners After Dissolution.**

Where the dissolution is caused by the act, death or bankruptcy of a partner, each partner is liable to his copartners for his share of any liability created by any partner acting for the partnership as if the partnership had not been dissolved unless

(a) The dissolution being by act of any partner, the partner acting for the partnership had knowledge of the dissolution, or

(b) The dissolution being by the death or bankruptcy of a partner, the partner acting for the partnership had knowledge or notice of the death or bankruptcy.

Sec. 35. **Power of Partner to Bind Partnership to Third Persons After Dissolution.**

(1) After dissolution a partner can bind the partnership except as provided in Paragraph (3)

(a) By any act appropriate for winding up partnership affairs or completing transactions unfinished at dissolution;

(b) By any transaction which would bind the partnership if dissolution had not taken place, provided the other party to the transaction

(I) Had extended credit to the partnership prior to dissolution and had no knowledge or notice of the dissolution; or

(II) Though he had not so extended credit, had nevertheless known of the partnership prior to dissolution, and, having no knowledge or notice of dissolution, the fact of dissolution had not been advertised in a newspaper of general circulation in the place (or in each place if more than one) at which the partnership business was regularly carried on.

(2) The liability of a partner under paragraph (1b) shall be satisfied out of partnership assets alone when such partner had been prior to dissolution

(a) Unknown as a partner to the person with whom the contract is made; and

(b) So far unknown and inactive in partnership affairs that the business reputation of the partnership could not be said to have been in any degree due to his connection with it.

(3) The partnership is in no case bound by any act of a partner after dissolution

(a) Where the partnership is dissolved because it is unlawful to carry on the business, unless the act is appropriate for winding up partnership affairs; or

(b) Where the partner has become bankrupt; or

(c) Where the partner has no authority to wind up partnership affairs; except by a transaction with one who

(I) Had extended credit to the partnership prior to dissolution and had no knowledge or notice of his want of authority; or

(II) Had not extended credit to the partnership prior to dissolution, and, having no knowledge or notice of his want of authority, the fact of his want of authority has not been advertised in the manner provided for advertising the fact of dissolution in paragraph (1bII).

(4) Nothing in this section shall affect the liability under section 16 of any person who after dissolution represents himself or consents to another representing him as a partner in a partnership engaged in carrying on business.

Sec. 36. **Effect of Dissolution on Partner's Existing Liability.**

(1) The dissolution of the partnership does not of itself discharge the existing liability of any partner.

(2) A partner is discharged from any existing liability upon dissolution of the partnership by an agreement to that effect between himself, the partnership creditor and the person or partnership continuing the business; and such agreement may be inferred from the course of dealing between the creditor having knowledge of the dissolution and the person or partnership continuing the business.

(3) Where a person agrees to assume the existing obligations of a dissolved partnership, the partners whose obligations have been assumed shall be discharged from any liability to any creditor of the partnership who, knowing of the agreement, consents to a material alteration in the nature or time of payment of such obligations.

(4) The individual property of a deceased partner shall be liable for all obligations of the partnership incurred while he was a partner but subject to the prior payment of his separate debts.

Sec. 37. **Right to Wind Up.**

Unless otherwise agreed the partners who have not wrongfully dissolved the partnership or the legal representative of the last surviving partner, not bankrupt, has the right to wind up the partnership affairs; provided, however, that any partner, his legal representative or his assignee, upon cause shown, may obtain winding up by the court.

Sec. 38. **Rights of Partners to Application of Partnership Property.**

(1) When dissolution is caused in any way, except in contravention of the partnership agreement, each partner as against his co-partners and all persons claiming through them in respect of their interests in the partnership, unless otherwise agreed, may have the partnership property applied to discharge its liabilities, and the surplus applied to pay in cash the net amount owing to the respective partners. But if dissolution is caused by expulsion of a partner, bona fide under the partnership agreement and if the expelled partner is discharged from all partnership liabilities, either by payment or agreement under section 36(2), he shall receive in cash only the net amount due him from the partnership.

(2) When dissolution is caused in contravention of the partnership agreement the rights of the partners shall be as follows:

(a) Each partner who has not caused dissolution wrongfully shall have,

(I) All the rights specified in paragraph (1) of this section, and

(II) The right, as against each partner who has caused the dissolution wrongfully, to damages for breach of the agreement.

(b) The partners who have not caused the dissolution wrongfully, if they all desire to continue the business in the same name, either by themselves or jointly with others, may do so, during the agreed term for the partnership and for that purpose may possess the partnership property, provided they secure the payment by bond approved by the court, or pay to any partner who has caused the dissolution wrongfully, the value of his interest in the partnership at the dissolution, less any damages recoverable under clause (2aII) of the section, and in like manner indemnify him against all present or future partnership liabilities.

(c) A partner who has caused the dissolution wrongfully shall have:

(I) If the business is not continued under the provisions of paragraph (2b) all the rights of a partner under paragraph (1), subject to clause (2aII), of this section,

(II) If the business is continued under paragraph (2b) of this section the right as against his co-partners and all claiming through them in respect of their interests in the partnership, to have the value of his interest in the partnership, less any damages caused to his co-partners by the dissolution, ascertained and paid to him in cash, or the payment secured by bond approved by the court, and to be released from all existing liabilities of the partnership; but in ascertaining the value of the partner's interest the value of the good-will of the business shall not be considered.

Sec. 39. **Rights Where Partnership is Dissolved for Fraud or Misrepresentation.**

Where a partnership contract is rescinded on the ground of the fraud or misrepresentation of one of the parties thereto, the party entitled to rescind is, without prejudice to any other right, entitled,

(a) To a lien on, or right of retention of, the surplus of the partnership property after satisfying the partnership liabilities to third persons for any sum of money paid by him for the purchase of an interest in the partnership and for any capital or advances contributed by him; and

(b) To stand, after all liabilities to third persons have been satisfied, in the place of the creditors of the partnership for any payments made by him in respect of the partnership liabilities; and

(c) To be indemnified by the person guilty of the fraud or making the representation against all debts and liabilities of the partnership.

Sec. 40. **Rules for Distribution.**

In settling accounts between the partners after dissolution, the following rules shall be observed, subject to any agreement to the contrary:

(a) The assets of the partnership are:

(I) The partnership property,

(II) The contributions of the partners necessary for the payment of all the liabilities specified in clause (b) of this paragraph.

(b) The liabilities of the partnership shall rank in order of payment, as follows:

(I) Those owing to creditors other than partners,

(II) Those owing to partners other than for capital and profits,

(III) Those owing to partners in respect of capital,

(IV) Those owing to partners in respect of profits.

(c) The assets shall be applied in the order of their declaration in clause (a) of this paragraph to the satisfaction of the liabilities.

(d) The partners shall contribute, as provided by section 18(a) the amount necessary to satisfy the liabilities; but if any, but not all, of the partners are insolvent, or, not being subject to process, refuse to contribute, the other parties shall contribute their share of the liabilities, and, in the relative proportions in which they share the profits, the additional amount necessary to pay the liabilities.

(e) An assignee for the benefit of creditors or any person appointed by the court shall have the right to enforce the contributions specified in clause (d) of this paragraph.

(f) Any partner or his legal representative shall have the right to enforce the contributions specified in clause (d) of this paragraph, to the extent of the amount which he has paid in excess of his share of the liability.

(g) The individual property of a deceased partner shall be liable for the contributions specified in clause (d) of this paragraph.

(h) When partnership property and the individual properties of the partners are in possession of a court for distribution, partnership creditors shall have priority on partnership property and separate creditors on individual property, saving the rights of lien or secured creditors as heretofore.

(i) Where a partner has become bankrupt or his estate is insolvent the claims against his separate property shall rank in the following order:

(I) Those owing to separate creditors,

(II) Those owing to partnership creditors,

(III) Those owing to partners by way of contribution.

Sec. 41. **Liability of Persons Continuing the Business in Certain Cases.**

(1) When any new partner is admitted into an existing partnership, or when any partner retires and assigns (or the representative of the deceased partner assigns) his rights in partnership property to two or more of the partners, or to one or more of the partners and one or more third persons, if the business is continued without liquidation of the partnership affairs, creditors of the first or dissolved partnership are also creditors of the partnership so continuing the business.

(2) When all but one partner retire and assign (or the representative of a deceased partner assigns) their rights in partnership property to the remaining partner, who continues the business without liquidation of partnership affairs, either alone or with others,

creditors of the dissolved partnership are also creditors of the person or partnership so continuing the business.

(3) When any partner retires or dies and the business of the dissolved partnership is continued as set forth in paragraphs (1) and (2) of this section, with the consent of the retired partners or the representative of the deceased partner, but without any assignment of his right in partnership property, rights of creditors of the dissolved partnership and of the creditors of the person or partnership continuing the business shall be as if such assignment had been made.

(4) When all the partners or their representatives assign their rights in partnership property to one or more third persons who promise to pay the debts and who continue the business of the dissolved partnership, creditors of the dissolved partnership are also creditors of the person or partnership continuing the business.

(5) When any partner wrongfully causes a dissolution and the remaining partners continue the business under the provisions of section 38(2b), either alone or with others, and without liquidation of the partnership affairs, creditors of the dissolved partnership are also creditors of the person or partnership continuing the business.

(6) When a partner is expelled and the remaining partners continue the business either alone or with others, without liquidation of the partnership affairs, creditors of the dissolved partnership are also creditors of the person or partnership continuing the business.

(7) The liability of a third person becoming a partner in the partnership continuing the business, under this section, to the creditors of the dissolved partnership shall be satisfied out of partnership property only.

(8) When the business of a partnership after dissolution is continued under any conditions set forth in this section the creditors of the dissolved partnership, as against the separate creditors of the retiring or deceased partner or the representative of the deceased partner, have a prior right to any claim of the retired partner or the representative of the deceased partner against the person or partnership continuing the business, on account of the retired or deceased partner's interest in the dissolved partnership or on account of any consideration promised for such interest or for his right in partnership property.

(9) Nothing in this section shall be held to modify any right of creditors to set aside any assignment on the ground of fraud.

(10) The use by the person or partnership continuing the business of the partnership name, or the name of a deceased partner as part thereof, shall not of itself make the individual property of the deceased partner liable for any debts contracted by such person or partnership.

Sec. 42. **Rights of Retiring or Estate of Deceased Partner When the Business is Continued.**

When any partner retires or dies, and the business is continued under any of the conditions set forth in section 41 (1, 2, 3, 5, 6), or section 38(2b), without any settlement of accounts as between him or his estate and the person or partnership continuing the business, unless otherwise agreed, he or his legal representative as against such persons or partnership may have the value of his interest at the date of dissolution ascertained, and shall receive as an ordinary creditor an amount equal to the value of his interest in the dissolved partnership with interest, or, at his option or at the option of his legal representative, in lieu of interest, the profits attributable to the use of his right in the property of the dissolved partnership; provided that the creditors of the dissolved partnership as against the separate creditors, or the representative of the retired or deceased partner, shall have priority on any claim arising under this section, as provided by section 41(8) of this act.

Sec. 43. **Accrual of Actions.**

The right to an account of his interest shall accrue to any partner, or his legal representative, as against the winding up partners or the surviving partners or the person or partnership continuing the business, at the date of dissolution, in the absence of any agreement to the contrary.

Part VII Miscellaneous Provisions

Sec. 44. **When Act Takes Effect.**

This act shall take effect on the _____ day of _____ one thousand nine hundred and _____.

Sec. 45. **Legislation Repealed.**

All acts or parts of acts inconsistent with this act are hereby repealed.

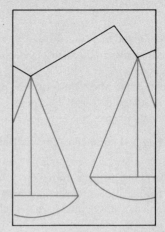

APPENDIX D

Uniform Limited Partnership Act

(Adopted in 48 States, all except Delaware and Louisiana; also in the District of Columbia, and the Virgin Islands.)

An Act to Make Uniform the Law Relating to Limited Partnerships

Be it enacted, etc., as follows:

Sec. 1. **Limited Partnership Defined.**

A limited partnership is a partnership formed by two or more persons under the provisions of Section 2, having as members one or more general partners and one or more limited partners. The limited partners as such shall not be bound by the obligations of the partnership.

Sec. 2. **Formation.**

(1) Two or more persons desiring to form a limited partnership shall

(a) Sign and swear to a certificate, which shall state

I. The name of the partnership,

II. The character of the business,

III. The location of the principal place of business,

IV. The name and place of residence of each member; general and limited partners being respectively designated,

V. The term for which the partnership is to exist,

VI. The amount of cash and a description of and the agreed value of the other property contributed by each limited partner,

VII. The additional contributions, if any, agreed to be made by each limited partner and the times at which or events on the happening of which they shall be made,

VIII. The time, if agreed upon, when the contribution of each limited partner is to be returned,

IX. The share of the profits or the other compensation by way of income which each limited partner shall receive by reason of his contribution,

X. The right, if given, of a limited partner to substitute an assignee as contributor in his place, and the terms and conditions of the substitution,

XI. The right, if given, of the partners to admit additional limited partners,

XII. The right, if given, of one or more of the limited partners to priority over other limited partners, as to contributions or as to compensation by way of income, and the nature of such priority,

XIII. The right, if given, of the remaining general partner or partners to continue the business on the death, retirement or insanity of a general partner, and

XIV. The right, if given, of a limited partner to demand and receive property other than cash in return for his contribution.

(b) File for record the certificate in the office of [here designate the proper office].

(2) A limited partnership is formed if there has been substantial compliance in good faith with the requirements of paragraph (1).

Sec. 3. **Business Which May Be Carried On.**

A limited partnership may carry on any business which a partnership without limited partners may carry on, except [here designate the business to be prohibited].

Sec. 4. **Character of Limited Partner's Contribution.**

The contributions of a limited partner may be cash or other property, but not services.

Sec. 5. **A Name Not to Contain Surname of Limited Partner; Exceptions.**

(1) The surname of a limited partner shall not appear in the partnership name, unless

(a) It is also the surname of a general partner, or

(b) Prior to the time when the limited partner became such the business had been carried on under a name in which his surname appeared.

(2) A limited partner whose name appears in a partnership name contrary to the provisions of paragraph (1) is liable as a general partner to partnership creditors who extend credit to the partnership without actual knowledge that he is not a general partner.

Sec. 6. **Liability for False Statements in Certificate.**

If the certificate contains a false statement, one who

suffers loss by reliance on such statement may hold liable any party to the certificate who knew the statement to be false.

(a) At the time he signed the certificate, or

(b) Subsequently, but within a sufficient time before the statement was relied upon to enable him to cancel or amend the certificate, or to file a petition for its cancellation or amendment as provided in Section 25(3).

Sec. 7. **Limited Partner Not Liable to Creditors.**

A limited partner shall not become liable as a general partner unless, in addition to the exercise of his rights and powers as a limited partner, he takes part in the control of the business.

Sec. 8. **Admission of Additional Limited Partners.**

After the formation of a limited partnership, additional limited partners may be admitted upon filing an amendment to the original certificate in accordance with the requirements of Section 25.

Sec. 9. **Rights, Powers and Liabilities of a General Partner.**

(1) A general partner shall have all the rights and powers and be subject to all the restrictions and liabilities of a partner in a partnership without limited partners, except that without the written consent or ratification of the specific act by all the limited partners, a general partner or all of the general partners have no authority to

(a) Do any act in contravention of the certificate,

(b) Do any act which would make it impossible to carry on the ordinary business of the partnership,

(c) Confess a judgment against the partnership,

(d) Possess partnership property, or assign their rights in specific partnership property, for other than a partnership purpose,

(e) Admit a person as a general partner,

(f) Admit a person as a limited partner, unless the right so to do is given in the certificate,

(g) Continue the business with partnership property on the death, retirement or insanity of a general partner, unless the right so to do is given in the certificate.

Sec. 10 **Rights of a Limited Partner.**

(1) A limited partner shall have the same rights as a general partner to

(a) Have the partnership books kept at the principal place of business of the partnership, and at all times to inspect and copy any of them,

(b) Have on demand true and full information of all things affecting the partnership, and a formal account of partnership affairs, whenever circumstances render it just and reasonable, and

(c) Have dissolution and winding up by decree of court.

(2) A limited partner shall have the right to receive a share of the profits or other compensation by way of income, and to the return of his contribution as provided in Sections 15 and 16.

Sec. 11. **Status of Person Erroneously Believing Himself a Limited Partner.**

A person who has contributed to the capital of a business conducted by a person or partnership erroneously believing that he has become a limited partner in a limited partnership, is not, by reason of his exercise of the rights of a limited partner, a general partner with the person or in the partnership carrying on the business, or bound by the obligations of such person or partnership; provided that on ascertaining the mistake he promptly renounces his interest in the profits of the business, or other compensation by way of income.

Sec. 12. **One Person Both General and Limited Partner.**

(1) A person may be a general partner and a limited partner in the same partnership at the same time.

(2) A person who is a general, and also at the same time a limited partner, shall have all the rights and powers and be subject to all the restrictions of a general partner; except that, in respect to his contribution, he shall have the rights against the other members which he would have had if he were not also a general partner.

Sec. 13. **Loans and Other Business Transactions with Limited Partner.**

(1) A limited partner also may loan money to and transact other business with the partnership, and, unless he is also a general partner, receive on account

of resulting claims against the partnership, with general creditors, a pro rata share of the assets. No limited partner shall in respect to any such claim

(a) Receive or hold as collateral security any partnership property, or

(b) Receive from a general partner or the partnership any payment, conveyance, or release from liability, if at the time the assets of the partnership are not sufficient to discharge partnership liabilities to persons not claiming as general or limited partners.

(2) The receiving of collateral security, or a payment, conveyance, or release in violation of the provisions of paragraph (1) is a fraud on the creditors of the partnership.

Sec. 14. **Relation of Limited Partners Inter Se.**

Where there are several limited partners the members may agree that one or more of the limited partners shall have a priority over other limited partners as to the return of their contributions, as to their compensation by way of income, or as to any other matter. If such an agreement is made it shall be stated in the certificate, and in the absence of such a statement all the limited partners shall stand upon equal footing.

Sec. 15. **Compensation of Limited Partner.**

A limited partner may receive from the partnership the share of the profits or the compensation by way of income stipulated for in the certificate; provided, that after such payment is made, whether from the property of the partnership or that of a general partner, the partnership assets are in excess of all liabilities of the partnership except liabilities to limited partners on account of their contributions and to general partners.

Sec. 16. **Withdrawal or Reduction of Limited Partner's Contribution.**

(1) A limited partner shall not receive from a general partner or out of partnership property any part of his contribution until

(a) All liabilities of the partnership, except liabilities to general partners and to limited partners on account of their contributions, have been paid or there remains property of the partnership sufficient to pay them,

(b) The consent of all members is had, unless the return of the contribution may be rightfully demanded under the provisions of paragraph (2), and

(c) The certificate is cancelled or so amended as to set forth the withdrawal or reduction.

(2) Subject to the provisions of paragraph (1) a limited partner may rightfully demand the return of his contribution

(a) On the dissolution of a partnership, or

(b) When the date specified in the certificate for its return has arrived, or

(c) After he has given six months' notice in writing to all other members, if no time is specified in the certificate either for the return of the contribution or for the dissolution of the partnership.

(3) In the absence of any statement in the certificate to the contrary or the consent of all members, a limited partner, irrespective of the nature of his contribution, has only the right to demand and receive cash in return for his contribution.

(4) A limited partner may have the partnership dissolved and its affairs wound up when

(a) He rightfully but unsuccessfully demands the return of his contribution, or

(b) The other liabilities of the partnership have not been paid, or the partnership property is insufficient for their payment as required by paragraph (1a) and the limited partner would otherwise be entitled to the return of his contribution.

Sec. 17. **Liability of Limited Partner to Partnership.**

(1) A limited partner is liable to the partnership

(a) For the difference between his contribution as actually made and that stated in the certificate as having been made, and

(b) For any unpaid contribution which he agreed in the certificate to make in the future at the time and on the conditions stated in the certificate.

(2) A limited partner holds as trustee for the partnership

(a) Specific property stated in the certificate as contributed by him, but which was not contributed or which has been wrongfully returned, and

(b) Money or other property wrongfully paid or conveyed to him on account of his contribution.

(3) The liabilities of a limited partner as set forth in this section can be waived or compromised only by the consent of all members; but a waiver or compromise shall not affect the right of a creditor of a partnership, who extended credit or whose claim arose after the filing and before a cancellation or amendment of the certificate, to enforce such liabilities.

(4) When a contributor has rightfully received the return in whole or in part of the capital of his contribution, he is nevertheless liable to the partnership for any sum, not in excess of such return with interest, necessary to discharge its liabilities to all creditors who extended credit or whose claims arose before such return.

Sec. 18. **Nature of Limited Partner's Interest in Partnership.**

A limited partner's interest in the partnership is personal property.

Sec. 19. **Assignment of Limited Partner's Interest.**

(1) A limited partner's interest is assignable.

(2) A substituted limited partner is a person admitted to all the rights of a limited partner who has died or has assigned his interest in a partnership.

(3) An assignee, who does not become a substituted limited partner, has no right to require any information or account of the partnership transactions or to inspect the partnership books; he is only entitled to receive the share of the profits or other compensation by way of income, or the return of his contribution, to which his assignor would otherwise be entitled.

(4) An assignee shall have the right to become a substituted limited partner if all the members (except the assignor) consent thereto or if the assignor, being thereunto empowered by the certificate, gives the assignee that right.

(5) An assignee becomes a substituted limited partner when the certificate is appropriately amended in accordance with Section 25.

(6) The substituted limited partner has all the rights and powers, and is subject to all the restrictions and liabilities of his assignor, except those liabilities of which he was ignorant at the time he became a limited partner and which could not be ascertained from the certificate.

(7) The substitution of the assignee as a limited partner does not release the assignor from liability to the partnership under Sections 6 and 17.

Sec. 20. **Effect of Retirement, Death or Insanity of a General Partner.**

The retirement, death or insanity of a general partner dissolves the partnership, unless the business is continued by the remaining general partners

(a) Under a right so to do stated in the certificate, or

(b) With the consent of all members.

Sec. 21. **Death of Limited Partner.**

(1) On the death of a limited partner his executor or administrator shall have all the rights of a limited partner for the purpose of settling his estate, and such power as the deceased had to constitute his assignee a substituted limited partner.

(2) The estate of a deceased limited partner shall be liable for all his liabilities as a limited partner.

Sec. 22. **Rights of Creditors of Limited Partner.**

(1) On due application to a court of competent jurisdiction by any judgment creditor of a limited partner, the court may charge the interest of the indebted limited partner with payment of the unsatisfied amount of the judgment debt; and may appoint a receiver, and make all other orders, directions, and inquiries which the circumstances of the case may require.

In those states where a creditor on beginning an action can attach debts due the defendant before he has obtained a judgment against the defendant it is recommended that paragraph (1) of this section read as follows:

On due application to a court of competent jurisdiction by any creditor of a limited partner, the court may charge the interest of the indebted limited partner with payment of the unsatisfied amount of such claim; and may appoint a receiver, and make all other orders, directions, and inquiries which the circumstances of the case may require.

(2) The interest may be redeemed with the separate property of any general partner, but may not be redeemed with partnership property.

(3) The remedies conferred by paragraph (1) shall not be deemed exclusive of others which may exist.

(4) Nothing in this act shall be held to deprive a limited partner of his statutory exemption.

Sec. 23. **Distribution of Assets.**

(1) In settling accounts after dissolution the liabilities of the partnership shall be entitled to payment in the following order:

(a) Those to creditors, in the order of priority as provided by law, except those to limited partners on account of their contributions, and to general partners,

(b) Those to limited partners in respect to their share of the profits and other compensation by way of income on their contributions,

(c) Those to limited partners in respect to the capital of their contributions,

(d) Those to general partners other than for capital and profits,

(e) Those to general partners in respect to profits,

(f) Those to general partners in respect to capital.

(2) Subject to any statement in the certificate or to subsequent agreement, limited partners share in the partnership assets in respect to their claims for capital, and in respect to their claims for profits or for compensation by way of income on their contributions respectively, in proportion to the respective amounts of such claims.

Sec. 24. **When Certificate Shall be Cancelled or Amended.**

(1) The certificate shall be cancelled when the partnership is dissolved or all limited partners cease to be such.

(2) A certificate shall be amended when

(a) There is a change in the name of the partnership or in the amount or character of the contribution of any limited partner,

(b) A person is substituted as a limited partner,

(c) An additional limited partner is admitted,

(d) A person is admitted as a general partner,

(e) A general partner retires, dies or becomes insane, and the business is continued under section 20,

(f) There is a change in the character of the business of the partnership,

(g) There is a false or erroneous statement in the certificate,

(h) There is a change in the time as stated in the certificate for the dissolution of the partnership or for the return of a contribution,

(i) A time is fixed for the dissolution of the partnership, or the return of a contribution, no time having been specified in the certificate, or

(j) The members desire to make a change in any other statement in the certificate in order that it shall accurately represent the agreement between them.

Sec. 25. **Requirements for Amendment and for Cancellation of Certificate.**

(1) The writing to amend a certificate shall

(a) Conform to the requirements of Section 2(1a) as far as necessary to set forth clearly the change in the certificate which it is desired to make, and

(b) Be signed and sworn to by all members, and an amendment substituting a limited partner or adding a limited or general partner shall be signed also by the member to be substituted or added, and when a limited partner is to be substituted, the amendment shall also be signed by the assigning limited partner.

(2) The writing to cancel a certificate shall be signed by all members.

(3) A person desiring the cancellation or amendment of a certificate, if any person designated in paragraphs (1) and (2) as a person who must execute the writing refuses to do so, may petition the [here designate the proper court] to direct a cancellation or amendment thereof.

(4) If the court finds that the petitioner has a right to have the writing executed by a person who refuses to do so, it shall order the [here designate the responsible official in the office designated in Section 2] in the office where the certificate is recorded to record the cancellation or amendment of the certificate; and where the certificate is to be amended, the court shall also cause to be filed for record in said office a certified copy of its decree setting forth the amendment.

(5) A certificate is amended or cancelled when there is filed for record in the office [here designate the office designated in Section 2] where the certificate is recorded

(a) A writing in accordance with the provisions of paragraph (1), or (2) or

(b) A certified copy of the order of court in accordance with the provisions of paragraph (4).

(6) After the certificate is duly amended in accordance with this section, the amended certificate shall thereafter be for all purposes the certificate provided for by this act.

Sec. 26. **Parties to Actions.**

A contributor, unless he is a general partner, is not a proper party to proceedings by or against a partnership, except where the object is to enforce a limited partner's right against or liability to the partnership.

Sec. 27. **Name of Act.**

This act may be cited as The Uniform Limited Partnership Act.

Sec. 28. **Rules of Construction.**

(1) The rule that statutes in derogation of the common law are to be strictly construed shall have no application to this act.

(2) This act shall be so interpreted and construed as to effect its general purpose to make uniform the law of those states which enact it.

(3) This act shall not be so construed as to impair the obligations of any contract existing when the act goes into effect, nor to affect any action on proceedings begun or right accrued before this act takes effect.

Sec. 29. **Rules for Cases Not Provided for in this Act.**

In any case not provided for in this act the rules of law and equity, including the law merchant, shall govern.

Sec. 30.[1] **Provisions for Existing Limited Partnerships.**

(1) A limited partnership formed under any statute of this state prior to the adoption of this act, may become a limited partnership under this act by complying with the provisions of Section 2; provided the certificate sets forth

(a) The amount of the original contribution of each limited partner, and the time when the contribution was made, and

(b) That the property of the partnership exceeds the amount sufficient to discharge its liabilities to persons not claiming as general or limited partners by an amount greater than the sum of the contributions of its limited partners.

(2) A limited partnership formed under any statute of this state prior to the adoption of this act, until or unless it becomes a limited partnership under this act, shall continue to be governed by the provisions of [here insert proper reference to the existing limited partnership act or acts], except that such partnership shall not be renewed unless so provided in the original agreement.

Sec. 31.[1] **Act [Acts] Repealed.**

Except as affecting existing limited partnerships to the extent set forth in Section 30, the act (acts) of [here designate the existing limited partnership act or acts] is (are) hereby repealed.

[1]Sections 30, 31, will be omitted in any state which has not a limited partnership act.

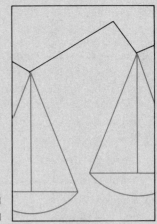

APPENDIX E

Revised Uniform
Limited Partnership Act

(Adopted August 5, 1976, by the National Conference of Commissioners on Uniform State Laws, subject to style changes; it is intended that it will replace the existing Uniform Limited Partnership Act (Appendix D); as of publication, it had not been adopted in any jurisdiction.)

The Act consists of 11 Articles as follows:

1. General Provisions
2. Formation; Certificate of Limited Partnership
3. Limited Partners
4. General Partners
5. Finance
6. Distribution and Withdrawal
7. Assignment of Partnership Interests
8. Dissolution
9. Foreign Limited Partnerships
10. Derivative Actions
11. Miscellaneous

Article 1
GENERAL PROVISIONS

Sec. 101. **Definitions.**

As used in this Act:

(1) "Certificate of limited partnership" means the certificate referred to in Section 201, as that certificate is amended from time to time.

(2) "Contribution" means any cash, property, or services rendered, or a promissory note or other binding obligation to contribute cash or property or to perform services, which a partner contributes to a limited partnership in his capacity as a partner.

(3) "Event of withdrawal of a general partner" means an event that causes a person to cease to be a general partner as provided in Section 402.

(4) "Foreign limited partnership" means a partnership formed under the laws of any state other than this State and having as partners one or more general partners and one or more limited partners.

(5) "General partner" means a person who has been admitted to a limited partnership as a general partner in accordance with the partnership agreement and who is named in the certificate of limited partnership as a general partner.

(6) "Limited partner" means a person who has been admitted to a limited partnership as a limited partner in accordance with the partnership agreement and who is named in the certificate of limited partnership as a limited partner.

(7) "Limited partnership" and "domestic limited partnership" mean a partnership formed by 2 or more persons under the laws of this State and having one or more general partners and one or more limited partners.

(8) "Partner" means any limited partner or general partner.

(9) "Partnership agreement" means the agreement, written or, to the extent not prohibited by law, oral or both, of the partners as to the affairs of a limited partnership and the conduct of its business.

(10) "Partnership interest" has the meaning specified in Section 701.

(11) "Person" means a natural person, partnership, limited partnership (domestic or foreign), trust, estate, association, or corporation.

(12) "State" means a state, territory, or possession of the United States, the District of Columbia, or the Commonwealth of Puerto Rico.

Sec. 102. **Name.**

The name of each limited partnership as set forth in its certificate of limited partnership:

(1) shall contain the words "limited partnership" in full;

(2) may not contain the name of a limited partner unless (i) it is also the name of a general partner or (ii) the business of the limited partnership had been carried on under that name before the admission of that limited partner;

(3) may not contain any word or phrase indicating or implying that it is organized other than for a purpose stated in its certificate of limited partnership;

(4) may not be the same as, or deceptively similar to, the name of any corporation or limited partnership organized under the laws of this State or licensed or registered as a foreign corporation or limited partnership in this State; and

(5) may not contain the following words [here insert prohibited words].

Sec. 103. **Reservation of Name.**

(a) The exclusive right to the use of a name may be reserved by:

(1) any person intending to organize a limited partnership under this Act and to adopt that name;

(2) any domestic limited partnership or any foreign limited partnership registered in this State which, in either case, intends to adopt that name;

(3) any foreign limited partnership intending to register in this State and to adopt that name; and

(4) any person intending to organize a foreign limited partnership and intending to have it registered in this State and to adopt that name.

(b) The reservation shall be made by filing with the Secretary of State an application, executed by the applicant, to reserve a specified name. If the Secretary of State finds that the name is available for use by a domestic or foreign limited partnership, he shall reserve the name for the exclusive use of the applicant for a period of 120 days. Once having reserved a name, the same applicant may not again reserve the same name until more than 60 days after the expiration of the last 120-day period for which that applicant had reserved that name. The right to the exclusive use of a name so reserved may be transferred to any other person by filing in the office of the Secretary of State a notice of the transfer, executed by the applicant for whom the name was reserved and specifying the name and address of the transferee.

Sec. 104. **Specified Office and Agent.**

Each limited partnership shall continuously maintain in this State:

(1) an office, which may but need not be a place of its business in this State, at which shall be kept the records required to be maintained by Section 105; and

(2) an agent for service of process on the limited partnership, which agent must be an individual resident of this State, a domestic corporation, or a foreign corporation authorized to do business in this State.

Sec. 105. **Records to be Kept.**

Each limited partnership shall keep at the office referred to in Section 104(1) the following: (1) a current list of the full name and last-known business address of each partner set forth in alphabetical order, (2) a copy of the certificate of limited partnership and all certificates of amendment thereto, together with executed copies of any powers of attorney pursuant to which any certificate has been executed, (3) copies of the limited partnership's federal, state, and local income tax returns and reports, if any, for the 3 most recent years, and (4) copies of any then effective written partnership agreements and of any financial statements of the limited partnership for the 3 most recent years. These records shall be available for inspection and copying at the reasonable request, and at the expense, of any partner during ordinary business hours.

Sec. 106. **Nature of Business.**

A limited partnership may carry on any business that a partnership without limited partners may carry on except [here designate prohibited activities].

Sec. 107. **Business Transactions of Partner with the Partnership.**

Except as otherwise provided in the partnership agreement, a partner may lend money to and transact other business with the limited partnership and, subject to other applicable provisions of law, has the same rights and obligations with respect thereto as a person who is not a partner.

Article 2
FORMATION; CERTIFICATE OF LIMITED PARTNERSHIP

Sec. 201. **Certificate of Limited Partnership.**

(a) Two or more persons desiring to form a limited partnership shall execute a certificate of limited partnership. The certificate shall be filed in the office of the Secretary of State and shall set forth:

(1) the name of the limited partnership;

(2) the general character of its business;

(3) the address of the office and the name and

address of the agent for service of process required to be maintained by Section 104;

(4) the name and the business address of each partner (specifying the general partners and limited partners separately);

(5) the amount of cash and a description and statement of the agreed value of the other property or services contributed by each partner and which each partner has agreed to contribute in the future;

(6) the times at which or events on the happening of which any additional contributions agreed to be made by each partner are to be made;

(7) any power of a limited partner to grant an assignee of any part of his partnership interest the right to become a limited partner, and the terms and conditions of the power;

(8) if agreed upon, the time at which or the events on the happening of which a partner may terminate his membership in the limited partnership and the amount of, or the method of determining, the distribution to which he may be entitled respecting his partnership interest, and the terms and conditions of the termination and distribution;

(9) any right of a partner to receive distributions of property including cash from the limited partnership;

(10) any right of a partner to receive, or of a general partner to make, distributions to a partner which include a return of all or any part of the partner's contribution;

(11) any time at which or events upon the happening of which the limited partnership is to be dissolved and its affairs wound up;

(12) any right of the remaining general partners to continue the business on the happening of an event of withdrawal of a general partner; and

(13) any other matters the partners, in their sole discretion, determine to include therein.

(b) A limited partnership is formed at the time of the filing of the certificate of limited partnership in the office of the Secretary of State or at any later time specified in the certificate of limited partnership if, in each case, there has been substantial compliance with the requirements of this section.

Sec. 202. **Amendments to Certificate.**

(a) A certificate of limited partnership is amended by filing a certificate of amendment thereto in the office of the Secretary of State. The certificate shall set forth:

(1) the name of the limited partnership;

(2) the date of filing of the certificate; and

(3) the amendments to the certificate.

(b) Within 30 days after the happening of any of the following events an amendment to a certificate of limited partnership reflecting the occurrence of the event or events shall be filed:

(1) a change in the amount or character of the contribution of any partner, or in any partner's obligation to make a contribution;

(2) the admission of a new partner;

(3) the withdrawal of a partner; and

(4) the continuation of the business under Section 801 after an event of withdrawal of a general partner.

(c) A certificate of limited partnership must be amended promptly by any general partner upon becoming aware that any statement therein was false when made or that any arrangements or other facts described have changed, making the certificate inaccurate in any respect, but amendments to show changes of addresses of limited partners need be filed only once every 12 months.

(d) A certificate of limited partnership may be amended at any time for any other proper purpose the general partners may determine.

(e) No person shall have any liability because an amendment to a certificate of limited partnership has not been filed to reflect the occurrence of any event referred to in subsection (b) of this section if the amendment is filed within the 30-day period specified in subsection (b).

Sec. 203. **Cancellation of Certificate.**

A certificate of limited partnership shall be cancelled upon the dissolution and the commencement of winding up of the limited partnership and at any other time there are no remaining limited partners. A certificate of cancellation shall be filed in the office of the Secretary of State and shall set forth:

(1) the name of the limited partnership;

(2) the date of filing of its certificate of limited partnership;

(3) the reason for filing the certificate of cancellation;

(4) the effective date (which shall be a date certain) of cancellation if it is not to be effective upon the filing of the certificate; and

(5) any other information the general partners filing the certificate may determine.

Sec. 204. **Execution of Certificates.**

(a) Each certificate required by this Article to be filed in the office of the Secretary of State shall be executed in the following manner:

(1) each original certificate of limited partnership must be signed by each partner named therein;

(2) each certificate of amendment must be signed by at least one general partner and by each other partner who is designated in the certificate as a new partner or whose contribution is described as having been increased; and

(3) each certificate of cancellation must be signed by each general partner.

(b) Any person may sign a certificate by an attorney-in-fact, but any power of attorney to sign a certificate relating to the admission or increased contribution of a partner must specifically describe the admission or increase.

(c) The execution of a certificate by a general partner constitutes an affirmation under the penalties of perjury that the facts stated therein are true.

Sec. 205. **Amendment or Cancellation by Judicial Act.**

If the persons required by Section 204 to execute any certificate of amendment or cancellation fail or refuse to do so, any other partner, and any assignee of a partnership interest, who is adversely affected by the failure or refusal, may petition the [here designate the proper court] to direct the amendment or cancellation. If the court finds that the amendment or cancellation is proper and that the persons so designated have failed or refused to execute the certificate, it shall order the Secretary of State to record an appropriate certificate of amendment or cancellation.

Sec. 206. **Filing in the Office of the Secretary of State.**

(a) Two signed copies of the certificate of limited partnership and of any certificates of amendment or cancellation (or of any judicial decree of amendment or cancellation) shall be delivered to the Secretary of State. A person who executes a certificate as an agent or fiduciary need not exhibit evidence of his authority as a prerequisite to filing. Unless the Secretary of State finds that any certificate does not conform to law, upon receipt of all filing fees required by law the Secretary of State shall:

(1) endorse on each duplicate original the word "Filed" and the day, month, and year of the filing thereof;

(2) file one duplicate original in his office; and

(3) return the other duplicate original to the person who filed it or his representative.

(b) Upon the filing of a certificate of amendment (or judicial decree of amendment) in the office of the Secretary of State, the certificate of limited partnership shall be amended as set forth therein, and upon the effective date of a certificate of cancellation (or a judicial decree thereof), the certificate of limited partnership shall be cancelled.

Sec. 207. **Liability for False Statement in Certificate.**

If any certificate of limited partnership or certificate of amendment or cancellation contains a false statement, one who suffers loss by reliance on the statement may recover damages for the loss from:

(1) any person actually executing, or causing another to execute on his behalf, the certificate who knew, and any general partner who knew or should have known, the statement to be false at the time the certificate was executed; and

(2) any general partner who thereafter knew or should have known that any arrangements or other facts described in the certificate have changed, making the statement inaccurate in any respect, within a sufficient time before the statement was relied upon to have reasonably enabled that general

partner to cancel or amend the certificate, or to file a petition for its cancellation or amendment under Section 205.

Sec. 208. **Constructive Notice.**

The fact that a certificate of limited partnership is on file in the office of the Secretary of State is constructive notice that the partnership is a limited partnership and that the persons designated therein as limited partners are limited partners, but is not constructive notice of any other fact.

Sec. 209. **Delivery of Certificates to Limited Partners.**

Upon the return by the Secretary of State pursuant to Section 206 of any certificate marked "Filed," the general partners shall promptly deliver or mail a copy of the certificate to each limited partner unless the partnership agreement provides otherwise.

Article 3
LIMITED PARTNERS

Sec. 301. **Admission of Additional Limited Partners.**

(a) After the filing of a limited partnership's original certificate of limited partnership, a person may be admitted as a new limited partner:

(1) in the case of a person acquiring a partnership interest directly from the limited partnership, upon compliance with the partnership agreement or, if the partnership agreement does not so provide, upon the written consent of all partners; and

(2) in the case of an assignee of a partnership interest of a partner who has the power, as provided in Section 704, to grant the assignee the right to become a limited partner, upon the exercise of that power and compliance with any conditions limiting the grant or exercise of the power.

(b) In each case under subsection (a), the person acquiring the partnership interest becomes a limited partner only upon amendment of the certificate of limited partnership reflecting that fact.

Sec. 302. **Voting.**

Subject to the provisions of Section 303, the partnership agreement may grant to all or a specified group of the limited partners the right to vote (on a per capita or any other basis) upon any matter.

Sec. 303. **Liability to Third Parties.**

(a) Except as provided in subsection (d), a limited partner as such is not liable for the obligations of a limited partnership unless, in addition to the exercise of his rights and powers as a limited partner, he takes part in the control of the business. But the limited partner's participation in the control of the business is not substantially the same as the exercise of the powers of a general partner, he is liable only to persons who transact business with the limited partnership with actual knowledge of his participation in control.

(b) A limited partner does not participate in the control of the business within the meaning of subsection (a) solely by doing one or more of the following:

(1) being a contractor for or an agent or employee of the limited partnership or of a general partner;

(2) consulting with and advising a general partner with respect to the business of the limited partnership;

(3) acting as surety for the limited partnership;

(4) approving or disapproving an amendment to the partnership agreement; and

(5) voting on one or more of the following matters:

(i) the dissolution and winding up of the limited partnership;

(ii) the sale, exchange, lease, mortgage, pledge, or other transfer of all or substantially all of the assets of the limited partnership other than in the ordinary course of its business;

(iii) the incurrence of indebtedness by the limited partnership other than in the ordinary course of its business;

(iv) a change in the nature of the business; or

(v) the removal of a general partner.

(c) The enumeration in subsection (b) shall not be construed to mean that the possession or exercise of any other powers by a limited partner constitutes participation by him in the business of the limited partnership.

(d) A limited partner who knowingly permits his name to be used in the name of the limited partnership, except under circumstances permitted by Section 102(2)(i), is liable to creditors who extend credit to the limited partnership without actual knowledge that the limited partner is not a general partner.

Sec. 304. **Person Erroneously Believing Himself a Limited Partner.**

(a) Except as provided in subsection (b) a person who makes a contribution to a business enterprise and erroneously and in good faith believes that he has become a limited partner in the enterprise is not a general partner in the enterprise and is not bound by its obligations by reason of making the contribution, receiving distributions from the enterprise, or exercising any rights of a limited partner, if, on ascertaining the mistake, he:

(1) causes an appropriate certificate of limited partnership or a certificate of amendment to be executed and filed; or

(2) withdraws from future equity participation in the enterprise.

(b) Any person who makes a contribution of the kind described in subsection (a) is liable as a general partner to any third party who transacts business with the enterprise (i) before the person withdraws and an appropriate certificate if any is filed to show the withdrawal, or (ii) before an appropriate certificate is filed to show his status as a limited partner and, in the case of an amendment, after expiration of the 30-day period for filing an amendment relating to the person as a limited partner under Section 202, but in each case only if the third party actually believed in good faith that the person was a general partner at the time of the transaction.

Sec. 305. **Information.**

Each limited partner has the right to:

(1) inspect and copy any of the partnership records required to be maintained by Section 105; and

(2) obtain from the general partners from time to time upon reasonable demand (i) true and full information regarding the state of the business and financial condition of the limited partnership, (ii) promptly after becoming available, a copy of the limited partnership's federal, state, and local income tax return for each year, and (iii) any other information regarding the affairs of the limited partnership as is just and reasonable.

Article 4
GENERAL PARTNERS

Sec. 401. **Admission.**

After the filing of a limited partnership's original certificate of limited partnership, new general partners may be admitted only with the specific written consent of each partner.

Sec. 402. **Events of Withdrawal.**

Except as otherwise approved by the specific written consent at the time of all partners, a person ceases to be a general partner of a limited partnership upon the happening of any of the following events:

(1) the general partner withdraws from the limited partnership as provided in Section 602;

(2) the general partner ceases to be a member of the limited partnership as provided in Section 702;

(3) the general partner is removed as a general partner in accordance with the partnership agreement;

(4) unless otherwise provided in the certificate of limited partnership, the general partner: makes an assignment for the benefit of creditors; files a voluntary petition in bankruptcy; is adjudicated a bankrupt or insolvent; files any petition or answer seeking for himself any reorganization, arrangement, composition, readjustment, liquidation, dissolution, or similar relief under any statute, law, or regulation; files any answer or other pleading admitting or failing to contest the material allegations of a petition filed against him in any proceeding of this nature; or seeks, consents to, or acquiesces in the appointment of any trustee, receiver, or liquidator of the general partner or of all or any substantial part of his properties;

(5) unless otherwise provided in the certificate of limited partnership, [120] days after the commencement of any proceeding against the general partner seeking any reorganization, arrangement, composition, readjustment, liquidation, dissolution, or similar

relief under any statute, law, or regulation, the proceeding has not been dismissed, or if, within [90] days after the appointment without his consent or acquiescence of any trustee, receiver, or liquidator of the general partner or of all or any substantial part of his properties, the appointment is not vacated or stayed, or if, within [90] days after the expiration of any stay, the appointment is not vacated;

(6) in the case of a general partner who is a natural person

    (i) his death; or

    (ii) the entry by a court of competent jurisdiction adjudicating him incompetent to manage his person or his property;

(7) in the case of a general partner who is acting as such in the capacity of a trustee of a trust, the termination of the trust (but not merely the substitution of a new trustee);

(8) in the case of a general partner that is a partnership, the dissolution and commencement of winding up of the partnership;

(9) in the case of a general partner that is a corporation, the filing of a certificate of dissolution, or its equivalent, for the corporation or the revocation of its charter; and

(10) in the case of an estate, the distribution by the fiduciary of all the estate's interest in the partnership.

Sec. 403. **General Powers and Liabilities.**

Except as otherwise provided in this Act and in the partnership agreement, a general partner of a limited partnership has all the rights and powers and is subject to all the restrictions and liabilities of a partner in a partnership without limited partners.

Sec. 404. **Contributions by a General Partner.**

A general partner may make contributions to a limited partnership and share in the profits and losses of, and in distributions from, the limited partnership as a general partner. A general partner may also make contributions to and share in profits, losses, and distributions as a limited partner. A person who is both a general partner and a limited partner has all the rights and powers, and is subject to all the restrictions and liabilities, of a general partner and also has, except as otherwise provided in the partnership agreement, all powers, and is subject to the

restrictions, of a limited partner to the extent he is participating in the partnership as a limited partner.

Sec. 405. **Voting.**

The partnership agreement may grant to all or a specified group of general partners the right to vote (on a per capita or any other basis), separately or with all or any class of the limited partners, on any matter.

Article 5
FINANCE

Sec. 501. **Form of Contributions.**

The contribution of a partner may be in cash, property, or services rendered, or a promissory note or other obligation to contribute cash or property or to perform services.

Sec. 502. **Liability for Contributions.**

(a) Except as otherwise provided in the certificate of limited partnership, a partner is obligated to the limited partnership to perform any promise to contribute cash or property or to perform services regardless of whether he is unable to perform because of death, disability or any other reason. If a partner does not make the required contribution of property or services, he is obligated at the option of the limited partnership to contribute cash equal to that portion of the value (as stated in the certificate of limited partnership) of the stated contribution that has not been made.

(b) Unless otherwise provided in the partnership agreement, the obligation of a partner to make a contribution or return money or other property paid or distributed in violation of this Act may be compromised only by consent of all of the partners. Notwithstanding a compromise so authorized, a creditor of a limited partnership who extends credit, or whose claim arises, after the filing of the certificate of limited partnership or an amendment thereto which, in either case, reflects the obligation and before the amendment or cancellation thereof to reflect the compromise may enforce the precompromise obligation.

Sec. 503. **Sharing of Profits and Losses.**

The profits and losses of a limited partnership shall

be allocated among the partners, and among classes of partners, in the manner provided in the partnership agreement. If the partnership agreement does not so provide, profits and losses shall be allocated on the basis of the value (as stated in the certificate of limited partnership) of the contributions actually made by each partner to the extent they have not been returned.

Sec. 504. **Sharing of Distributions.**

Distributions of cash or other assets of a limited partnership shall be allocated among the partners, and among classes of partners, in the manner provided in the partnership agreement. If the partnership agreement does not so provide, distributions shall be made on the basis of the value (as stated in the certificate of limited partnership) of the contributions actually made by each partner to the extent they have not been returned.

Article 6
DISTRIBUTIONS AND WITHDRAWAL

Sec. 601. **Interim Distributions.**

Except as otherwise provided in this Article, a partner is entitled to receive distributions from a limited partnership before his withdrawal from the limited partnership and before the dissolution and winding up thereof:

(1) to the extent and at the times or upon the happening of the events specified in the partnership agreement; and

(2) if any distribution constitutes a return of any part of his contribution under Section 608(b), to the extent and at the times or upon the happening of the events specified in the certificate of limited partnership.

Sec. 602. **Withdrawal of General Partner.**

A general partner may withdraw from a limited partnership at any time by giving written notice to the other partners, but if the withdrawal violates the partnership agreement, the limited partnership may recover from the withdrawing general partner damages for breach of the partnership agreement and offset the damages against the amount otherwise distributable to him.

Sec. 603. **Withdrawal of Limited Partner.**

A limited partner may withdraw from a limited partnership at the time or upon the happening of the events specified in the certificate of limited partnership and in accordance with any procedures provided in the partnership agreement. If the certificate of limited partnership does not specify the time or the events upon the happening of which a limited partner may withdraw from the limited partnership or a definite time for the dissolution and winding up of the limited partnership, a limited partner may withdraw from the limited partnership upon not less than 6 months' prior written notice to each general partner at his address on the books of the limited partnership at its office in this State.

Sec. 604. **Distributions Upon Withdrawal.**

Except as provided in this Article, upon withdrawal any withdrawing partner is entitled to receive any distributions to which he is entitled under the partnership agreement and, if not provided, he is entitled to receive, within a reasonable time after withdrawal, the fair value of his interest in the limited partnership as of the date of withdrawal, based upon his right to share in distributions from the limited partnership.

Sec. 605. **Distributions in Kind.**

Except as provided in the certificate of limited partnership, a partner, regardless of the nature of his contribution, has no right to demand and receive any distribution from a limited partnership in any form other than cash. Except as provided in the partnership agreement, a partner may not be compelled to accept a distribution of any asset in kind from a limited partnership to the extent that the percentage of the asset distributed to him exceeds a percentage of that asset which is equal to the percentage in which he shares in distributions from the limited partnership.

Sec. 606. **Right to Distributions.**

At the time a partner becomes entitled to receive a distribution, he has the status of, and is entitled to all of the remedies available to, a creditor of the limited partnership with respect to the distribution.

Sec. 607. **Limitations on Distributions.**

A partner may not receive a distribution from a limited partnership to the extent that, after giving effect to the distribution, all liabilities of the limited partnership other than liabilities to partners on account of their partnership interests, exceed the fair value of the partnership's assets.

Sec. 608. **Liability Upon Return of Contributions.**

(a) If a partner has received the return of any part of his contribution without violation of the partnership agreement or this Act, for a period of one year thereafter he is liable to the limited partnership for the amount of his contribution returned, but only to the extent necessary to discharge the limited partnership's liabilities to creditors who extended credit to the limited partnership during the period the contribution was held by the partnership.

(b) If a partner has received the return of any part of his contribution in violation of the partnership agreement or this Act, for a period of 6 years thereafter he is liable to the limited partnership for the amount of the contribution wrongfully returned.

(c) A partner has received a return of his contribution to the extent that a distribution to him reduces his share of the fair value of the net assets of the limited partnership below the value (as set forth in the certificate of limited partnership) of his contributions which have not theretofore been distributed to him.

Article 7
ASSIGNMENT OF PARTNERSHIP INTERESTS

Sec. 701. **Nature of Partnership Interest.**

A partnership interest is a partner's share of the profits and losses of a limited partnership and the right to receive distributions of partnership assets. A partnership interest is personal property.

Sec. 702. **Assignment of Partnership Interest.**

Except as otherwise provided in the partnership agreement, a partnership interest is assignable in whole or in part. An assignment of a partnership interest does not dissolve a limited partnership nor entitle the assignee to become a partner or to exercise any of the rights thereof. An assignment only entitles the assignee to receive, to the extent assigned, any distributions to which the assignor would be entitled. Except as otherwise provided in the partnership

agreement, a partner ceases to be a partner upon assignment of all his partnership interest.

Sec. 703. **Rights of Creditors.**

On due application to a court of competent jurisdiction by any judgment creditor of a partner, the court may charge the partnership interest of the partner with payment of the unsatisfied amount of the judgment debt with interest thereon. To the extent so charged, the judgment creditor has only the rights of an assignee of the partnership interest. This Act shall not be construed to deprive any partner of the benefit of any exemption laws applicable to his partnership interest.

Sec. 704. **Right of Assignee to Become Limited Partner.**

(a) An assignee of a partnership interest, including an assignee of a general partner, may become a limited partner if and to the extent that (1) the assignor gives the assignee that right in accordance with authority described in the certificate of limited partnership or, (2) in the absence of that authority, all other partners consent.

(b) An assignee who has become a limited partner has, to the extent assigned, all the rights and powers, and is subject to all the restrictions and liabilities, of a limited partner under the partnership agreement and this Act. An assignee who becomes a limited partner is also liable for the obligations of his assignor to make and return contributions as provided in Article 6, but the assignee is not obligated for liabilities unknown to the assignee at the time he became a limited partner and which could not be ascertained from the certificate of limited partnership.

(c) If an assignee of a partnership interest becomes a limited partner, the assignor is not released from the liability to the limited partnership under Sections 207 and 502.

Sec. 705. **Power of Estate of Deceased or Incompetent Partner.**

If a partner who is a natural person dies or a court of competent jurisdiction adjudges him to be incompetent to manage his person or his property, the partner's executor, administrator, guardian, conservator, or other legal representative may exercise all of the partner's rights for the purpose of settling his estate or administering his property, including any power the partner had to give an assignee the right to become a limited partner. If a partner that is a corporation, trust, or other entity other than a natural person is dissolved or terminated, those powers may be exercised by the legal representative or successor of the partner.

Article 8
DISSOLUTION

Sec. 801. **Nonjudicial Dissolution.**

A limited partnership is dissolved and its affairs shall be wound up upon the happening of the first to occur of the following:

(1) at the time or upon the happening of the events specified in the certificate of limited partnership;

(2) upon the unanimous written consent of all partners;

(3) upon the happening of an event of withdrawal of a general partner unless at the time there is at least one other general partner and the certificate of limited partnership permits the business of the limited partnership to be carried on by the remaining general partner and he does so, but the limited partnership shall not be dissolved or wound up by reason of any event of withdrawal if, within 90 days after the withdrawal, all partners agree in writing to continue the business of the limited partnership and to the appointment of one or more new general partners if necessary or desired; or

(4) upon entry of a decree of judicial dissolution in accordance with Section 802.

Sec. 802. **Dissolution by Decree of Court.**

On application by or for a partner the [here designate the proper court] court may decree a dissolution of a limited partnership whenever it is not reasonably practicable to carry on the business in conformity with the partnership agreement.

Sec. 803. **Winding Up.**

Unless otherwise provided in the partnership agreement, the general partners who have not wrongfully dissolved the limited partnership or, if none, the limited partners, may wind up the limited partnership's affairs; but any partner, his legal representative

or his assignee, upon cause shown, may obtain winding up by the [here designate the proper court] court.

Sec. 804. **Distribution of Assets.**

Upon the winding up of a limited partnership, the assets shall be distributed as follows:

(1) to creditors, including partners who are creditors (to the extent otherwise permitted by law), in satisfaction of liabilities of the limited partnership other than liabilities for distributions to partners pursuant to Section 601 or 604;

(2) except as otherwise provided in the partnership agreement, to partners and ex-partners in satisfaction of liabilities for distributions pursuant to Section 601 or 604; and

(3) except as otherwise provided in the partnership agreement, to partners *first* for the return of their contributions and *second* respecting their partnership interests, in the proportions in which the partners share in distributions.

Article 9
FOREIGN LIMITED PARTNERSHIPS

Sec. 901. **Law Governing.**

Subject to the constitution and public policy of this State, the laws of the state under which a foreign limited partnership is organized govern its organization and internal affairs and the liability of its limited partners, and a foreign limited partnership may not be denied registration by reason of any difference between those laws and the laws of this State.

Sec. 902. **Registration.**

Before transacting business in this State, a foreign limited partnership shall register with the Secretary of State. In order to register, a foreign limited partnership shall submit to the Secretary of State in duplicate an application for registration as a foreign limited partnership, signed and sworn to by a general partner and setting forth:

(1) the name of the foreign limited partnership and, if different, the name under which it proposes to transact business and register in this State;

(2) the state and date of its formation;

(3) the general character of the business it proposes to transact in this State;

(4) the name and address of any agent for service of process on the foreign limited partnership whom the foreign limited partnership desires to appoint, which agent must be an individual resident of this State, a domestic corporation, or a foreign corporation authorized to do business in this State; and with a place of business in this State;

(5) a statement that the Secretary of State is appointed the agent of the foreign limited partnership for service of process if no agent has been appointed pursuant to paragraph (4) or, if appointed the agent's authority has been revoked or the agent cannot be found or served with the exercise of reasonable diligence;

(6) the address of the office required to be maintained in the state of its organization by the laws of that state or, if not so required, of the principal office of the foreign limited partnership; and

(7) if the certificate of limited partnership filed in the foreign limited partnership's state of organization is not required to include the names and business addresses of the partners, a list of the names and addresses.

Sec. 903. **Issuance of Registration.**

(a) If the Secretary of State finds that an application for registration conforms to law and all requisite fees have been paid, he shall:

(1) endorse on the application the word "Filed", and the month, day, and year of the filing thereof;

(2) file in his office one of the duplicate originals of the application; and

(3) issue a certificate of registration to transact business in this State.

(b) The certificate of registration, together with one duplicate original of the application, shall be returned to the person who filed the application or his representative.

Sec. 904. **Name.**

A foreign limited partnership may register with the Secretary of State under any name (whether or not it is the name under which it is registered in its state of organization) that includes the words "limited part-

nership" and that could be registered by a domestic limited partnership.

Sec. 905. **Changes and Amendments.**

If any statement in a foreign limited partnership's application for registration was false when made or any arrangements or other facts described have changed, making the application inaccurate in any respect, the foreign limited partnership shall promptly file in the office of the Secretary of State a certificate, signed and sworn to by a general partner, correcting the statement.

Sec. 906. **Cancellation of Registration.**

A foreign limited partnership may cancel its registration by filing with the Secretary of State a certificate of cancellation signed and sworn to by a general partner. A cancellation does not terminate the authority of the Secretary of State to accept service of process on the foreign limited partnership with respect to [claims for relief] [causes of action] arising out of the transaction of business in this State.

Sec. 907. **Transaction of Business Without Registration.**

(a) A foreign limited partnership transacting business in this State without registration may not maintain any action, suit, or proceeding in any court of this State until it has registered.

(b) The failure of a foreign limited partnership to register in this State does not impair the validity of any contract or act of the foreign limited partnership, and does not prevent the foreign limited partnership from defending any action, suit, or proceeding in any court of this State.

(c) A limited partner of a foreign limited partnership is not liable as a general partner of the foreign limited partnership solely by reason of the foreign limited partnership's transacting business in this State without registration.

(d) A foreign limited partnership, by transacting business in this State without registration, appoints the Secretary of State as its agent for service of process with respect to [claims for relief] [causes of action] arising out of the transaction of business in this State.

Sec. 908. **Action by [Appropriate Official].**

The [appropriate official] may bring an action to

restrain a foreign limited partnership from transacting business in this State in violation of this Article.

Article 10
DERIVATIVE ACTIONS

Sec. 1001. **Right of Action.**

A limited partner may bring an action in the right of a limited partnership to recover a judgment in its favor if the general partners having authority to do so have refused to bring the action or an effort to cause those general partners to bring the action is not likely to succeed.

Sec. 1002. **Proper Plaintiff.**

In a derivative action, the plaintiff must be a partner at (1) the time of bringing the action, and (2) at the time of the transaction of which he complains or his status as a partner must have devolved upon him by operation of law or pursuant to the terms of the partnership agreement from a person who was a partner at the time of the transaction.

Sec. 1003. **Pleading.**

In any derivative action, the complaint shall set forth with particularity the effort of the plaintiff to secure initiation of the action by a general partner having authority to do so or the reasons for not making the effort.

Sec. 1004. **Expenses.**

If a derivative action is successful, in whole or in part, or anything is received by the plaintiff as a result of a judgment, compromise, or settlement of an action or claim, the court may award the plaintiff reasonable expenses, including reasonable attorney's fees, and shall direct him to account to the limited partnership for the remainder of the proceeds so received by him.

Article 11
MISCELLANEOUS

Sec. 1101. **Savings Clause.**

Sec. 1102. **Name of Act.**
This Act may be cited as the Uniform Limited Partnership Act.

Sec. 1103. **Construction and Application.**
This Act shall be so construed and applied to effect its general purpose to make uniform the law with respect to the subject of this Act among states enacting it.

Sec. 1104. **Rules for Cases Not Provided for in This Act.**
In any case not provided for in this Act the provisions of the Uniform Partnership Act govern.

Sec. 1105. **Act Repealed.**
Except as affecting existing limited partnerships to the extent set forth in Section   , the Act of [here designate the existing limited partnership act or acts] is hereby repealed.

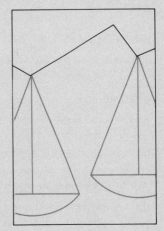

APPENDIX F

The Model Business Corporation Act

§ 1. **Short Title***

This Act shall be known and may be cited as the
". . . . .† Business Corporation Act."

§ 2. **Definitions**

As used in this Act, unless the context otherwise
requires, the term:

(a) "Corporation" or "domestic corporation" means a
corporation for profit subject to the provisions of this
Act, except a foreign corporation.

(b) "Foreign corporation" means a corporation for
profit organized under laws other than the laws of
this State for a purpose or purposes for which a
corporation may be organized under this Act.

(c) "Articles of incorporation" means the original or
restated articles of incorporation or articles of
consolidation and all amendments thereto including
articles of merger.

(d) "Shares" means the units into which the proprie-
tary interests in a corporation are divided.

(e) "Subscriber" means one who subscribes for
shares in a corporation, whether before or after
incorporation.

(f) "Shareholder" means one who is a holder of
record of shares in a corporation. If the articles of
incorporation or the by-laws so provide, the board of
directors may adopt by resolution a procedure
whereby a shareholder of the corporation may certify
in writing to the corporation that all or a portion of the
shares registered in the name of such shareholder are
held for the account of a specified person or persons.
The resolution shall set forth (1) the classification of
shareholder who may certify, (2) the purpose or
purposes for which the certification may be made, (3)
the form of certification and information to be
contained therein, (4) if the certification is with
respect to a record date or closing of the stock transfer
books within which the certification must be received
by the corporation and (5) such other provisions with
respect to the procedure as are deemed necessary or
desirable. Upon receipt by the corporation of a
certification complying with the procedure, the
persons specified in the certification shall be deemed,
for the purpose or purposes set forth in the certification, to be the holders of record of the number of
shares specified in place of the shareholder making
the certification.

(g) "Authorized shares" means the shares of all
classes which the corporation is authorized to issue.

(h) "Treasury shares" means shares of a corporation
which have been issued, have been subsequently
acquired by and belong to the corporation, and have
not, either by reason of the acquisition or thereafter,
been cancelled or restored to the status of authorized
but unissued shares. Treasury shares shall be deemed
to be "issued" shares, but not "outstanding" shares.

(i) "Net assets" means the amount by which the total
assets of a corporation exceed the total debts of the
corporation.

(j) "Stated capital" means, at any particular time, the
sum of (1) the par value of all shares of the corporation having a par value that have been issued, (2) the
amount of the consideration received by the corporation for all shares of the corporation without par value
that have been issued, except such part of the consideration therefor as may have been allocated to
capital surplus in a manner permitted by law, and (3)
such amounts not included in clauses (1) and (2) of this
paragraph as have been transferred to stated capital
of the corporation, whether upon the issue of shares
as a share dividend or otherwise, minus all reductions
from such sum as have been effected in a manner
permitted by law. Irrespective of the manner of
designation thereof by the laws under which a foreign
corporation is organized, the stated capital of a
foreign corporation shall be determined on the same
basis and in the same manner as the stated capital of a

---

*[By the Editor] The Model Business Corporation Act
prepared by the Committee on Corporate Laws (Section of
Corporation, Banking and Business Law) of the American
Bar Association was originally patterned after the Illinois
Business Corporation Act of 1933. It was first published as a
complete act in 1950. In subsequent years several revisions,
addenda and optional or alternative provisions were added.
The Act was substantially revised and renumbered in 1969.
This Act should be distinguished from the Model Business
Corporation Act promulgated in 1928 by the Commissioners
on Uniform State Laws under the name "Uniform Business
Corporation Act" and renamed Model Business Corporation
Act in 1943. This Uniform Act was withdrawn in 1957.
The Model Business Corporation Act has been influential in
the codification of corporation statutes in more than 35 states.
However, there is no state that has totally adopted it in its
current form. Moreover, since the Model Act itself has been
substantially modified from time to time, there is considerable variation among the statutes of the states that used this
Act as a model.

†Insert name of State.

domestic corporation, for the purpose of computing fees, franchise taxes and other charges imposed by this Act.

(k) "Surplus" means the excess of the net assets of a corporation over its stated capital.

(l) "Earned surplus" means the portion of the surplus of a corporation equal to the balance of its net profits, income, gains and losses from the date of incorporation, or from the latest date when a deficit was eliminated by an application of its capital surplus or stated capital or otherwise, after deducting subsequent distributions to shareholders and transfers to stated capital and capital surplus to the extent such distributions and transfers are made out of earned surplus. Earned surplus shall include also any portion of surplus allocated to earned surplus in mergers, consolidations or acquisitions of all or substantially all of the outstanding shares or of the property and assets of another corporation, domestic or foreign.

(m) "Capital surplus" means the entire surplus of a corporation other than its earned surplus.

(n) "Insolvent" means inability of a corporation to pay its debts as they become due in the usual course of its business.

(o) "Employee" includes officers but not directors. A director may accept duties which make him also an employee.

§ 3. **Purposes**

Corporations may be organized under this Act for any lawful purpose or purposes, except for the purpose of banking or insurance.

§ 4. **General Powers**

Each corporation shall have power:

(a) To have perpetual succession by its corporate name unless a limited period of duration is stated in its articles of incorporation.

(b) To sue and be sued, complain and defend, in its corporate name.

(c) To have a corporate seal which may be altered at pleasure, and to use the same by causing it, or a facsimile thereof, to be impressed or affixed or in any other manner reproduced.

(d) To purchase, take, receive, lease, or otherwise acquire, own, hold, improve, use and otherwise deal in and with, real or personal property, or any interest therein, wherever situated.

(e) To sell, convey, mortgage, pledge, lease, exchange, transfer and otherwise dispose of all or any part of its property and assets.

(f) To lend money and use its credit to assist its employees.

(g) To purchase, take, receive, subscribe for, or otherwise acquire, own, hold, vote, use, employ, sell, mortgage, lend, pledge, or otherwise dispose of, and otherwise use and deal in and with, shares or other interests in, or obligations of, other domestic or foreign corporations, associations, partnerships or individuals, or direct or indirect obligations of the United States or of any other government, state, territory, governmental district or municipality or of any instrumentality thereof.

(h) To make contracts and guarantees and incur liabilities, borrow money at such rates of interest as the corporation may determine, issue its notes, bonds, and other obligations, and secure any of its obligations by mortgage or pledge of all or any of its property, franchises and income.

(i) To lend money for its corporate purposes, invest and reinvest its funds, and take and hold real and personal property as security for the payment of funds so loaned or invested.

(j) To conduct its business, carry on its operations and have offices and exercise the powers granted by this Act, within or without this State.

(k) To elect or appoint officers and agents of the corporation, and define their duties and fix their compensation.

(l) To make and alter by-laws, not inconsistent with its articles of incorporation or with the laws of this State, for the administration and regulation of the affairs of the corporation.

(m) To make donations for the public welfare or for charitable, scientific or educational purposes.

(n) To transact any lawful business which the board of directors shall find will be in aid of governmental policy.

(o) To pay pensions and establish pension plans, pension trusts, profit sharing plans, stock bonus plans, stock option plans and other incentive plans for any or all of its directors, officers and employees.

(p) To be a promoter, partner, member, associate, or

manager of any partnership, joint venture, trust or other enterprise.

(q) To have and exercise all powers necessary or convenient to effect its purposes.

§ 5. Indemnification of Officers, Directors, Employees and Agents

(a) A corporation shall have power to indemnify any person who was or is a party or is threatened to be made a party to any threatened, pending or completed action, suit or proceeding, whether civil, criminal, administrative or investigative (other than an action by or in the right of the corporation) by reason of the fact that he is or was a director, officer, employee or agent of the corporation, or is or was serving at the request of the corporation as a director, officer, employee or agent of another corporation, partnership, joint venture, trust or other enterprise, against expenses (including attorneys' fees), judgments, fines and amounts paid in settlement actually and reasonably incurred by him in connection with such action, suit or proceeding if he acted in good faith and in a manner he reasonably believed to be in or not opposed to the best interests of the corporation, and, with respect to any criminal action or proceeding, had no reasonable cause to believe his conduct was unlawful. The termination of any action, suit or proceeding by judgment, order, settlement, conviction, or upon a plea of nolo contendere or its equivalent, shall not, of itself, create a presumption that the person did not act in good faith and in a manner which he reasonably believed to be in or not opposed to the best interest of the corporation, and, with respect to any criminal action or proceeding, had reasonable cause to believe that his conduct was unlawful.

(b) A corporation shall have power to indemnify any person who was or is a party or is threatened to be made a party to any threatened, pending or completed action or suit by or in the right of the corporation to procure a judgment in its favor by reason of the fact that he is or was a director, officer, employee or agent of the corporation, or is or was serving at the request of the corporation as a director, officer, employee or agent of another corporation, partnership, joint venture, trust or other enterprise against expenses (including attorneys' fees) actually and reasonably incurred by him in connection with the defense or settlement of such action or suit if he acted in good faith and in a manner he reasonably believed to be in or not opposed to the best interests of the corporation and except that no indemnification shall be made in respect of any claim, issue or matter as to which such person shall have been adjudged to be liable for negligence or misconduct in the performance of his duty to the corporation unless and only to the extent that the court in which such action or suit was brought shall determine upon application that, despite the adjudication of liability but in view of all circumstances of the case, such person is fairly and reasonably entitled to indemnity for such expenses which such court shall deem proper.

(c) To the extent that a director, officer, employee or agent of a corporation has been successful on the merits or otherwise in defense of any action, suit or proceeding referred to in subsections (a) or (b), or in defense of any claim, issue or matter therein, he shall be indemnified against expenses (including attorneys' fees) actually and reasonably incurred by him in connection therewith.

(d) Any indemnification under subsections (a) or (b) (unless ordered by a court) shall be made by the corporation only as authorized in the specific case upon a determination that indemnification of the director, officer, employee or agent is proper in the circumstances because he has met the applicable standard of conduct set forth in subsections (a) or (b). Such determination shall be made (1) by the board of directors by a majority vote of a quorum consisting of directors who were not parties to such action, suit or proceeding, or (2) if such a quorum is not obtainable, or, even if obtainable a quorum of disinterested directors so directs, by independent legal counsel in a written opinion, or (3) by the shareholders.

(e) Expenses (including attorneys' fees) incurred in defending a civil or criminal action, suit or proceeding may be paid by the corporation in advance of the final disposition of such action, suit or proceeding as authorized in the manner provided in subsection (d) upon receipt of an undertaking by or on behalf of the director, officer, employee or agent to repay such amount unless it shall ultimately be determined that he is entitled to be indemnified by the corporation as authorized in this section.

(f) The indemnification provided by this section shall

not be deemed exclusive of any other rights to which those indemnified may be entitled under any by-law, agreement, vote of shareholders or disinterested directors or otherwise, both as to action in his official capacity and as to action in another capacity while holding such office, and shall continue as to a person who has ceased to be a director, officer, employee or agent and shall inure to the benefit of the heirs, executors and administrators of such a person.

(g) A corporation shall have power to purchase and maintain insurance on behalf of any person who is or was a director, officer, employee or agent of the corporation, or is or was serving at the request of the corporation as a director, officer, employee or agent of another corporation, partnership, joint venture, trust or other enterprise against any liability asserted against him and incurred by him in any such capacity or arising out of his status as such, whether or not the corporation would have the power to indemnify him against such liability under the provisions of this section.

§ 6. Right of Corporation to Acquire and Dispose of Its Own Shares

A corporation shall have the right to purchase, take, receive or otherwise acquire, hold, own, pledge, transfer or otherwise dispose of its own shares, but purchases of its own shares, whether direct or indirect, shall be made only to the extent of unreserved and unrestricted earned surplus available therefor, and, if the articles of incorporation so permit or with the affirmative vote of the holders of a majority of all shares entitled to vote thereon, to the extent of unreserved and unrestricted capital surplus available therefor.

To the extent that earned surplus or capital surplus is used as the measure of the corporation's right to purchase its own shares, such surplus shall be restricted so long as such shares are held as treasury shares, and upon the disposition or cancellation of any such shares the restriction shall be removed pro tanto.

Notwithstanding the foregoing limitation, a corporation may purchase or otherwise acquire its own shares for the purpose of:

(a) Eliminating fractional shares.

(b) Collecting or compromising indebtedness to the corporation.

(c) Paying dissenting shareholders entitled to payment for their shares under the provisions of this Act.

(d) Effecting, subject to the other provisions of this Act, the retirement of its redeemable shares by redemption or by purchase at not to exceed the redemption price.

No purchase of or payment for its own shares shall be made at a time when the corporation is insolvent or when such purchase or payment would make it insolvent.

§ 7. Defense of Ultra Vires

No act of a corporation and no conveyance or transfer of real or personal property to or by a corporation shall be invalid by reason of the fact that the corporation was without capacity or power to do such act or to make or receive such conveyance or transfer, but such lack of capacity or power may be asserted:

(a) In a proceeding by a shareholder against the corporation to enjoin the doing of any act or the transfer of real or personal property by or to the corporation. If the unauthorized act or transfer sought to be enjoined is being, or is to be, performed or made pursuant to a contract to which the corporation is a party, the court may, if all of the parties to the contract are parties to the proceeding and if it deems the same to be equitable, set aside and enjoin the performance of such contract, and in so doing may allow to the corporation or to the other parties to the contract, as the case may be, compensation for the loss or damage sustained by either of them which may result from the action of the court in setting aside and enjoining the performance of such contract, but anticipated profits to be derived from the performance of the contract shall not be awarded by the court as a loss or damage sustained.

(b) In a proceeding by the corporation, whether acting directly or through a receiver, trustee, or other legal representative, or through shareholders in a representative suit, against the incumbent or former officers or directors of the corporation.

(c) In a proceeding by the Attorney General, as provided in this Act, to dissolve the corporation, or in a proceeding by the Attorney General to enjoin the corporation from the transaction of unauthorized business.

§ 8. **Corporate Name**

The corporate name:

(a) Shall contain the word "corporation," "company," "incorporated" or "limited," or shall contain an abbreviation of one of such words.

(b) Shall not contain any word or phrase which indicates or implies that it is organized for any purpose other than one or more of the purposes contained in its articles of incorporation.

(c) Shall not be the same as, or deceptively similar to, the name of any domestic corporation existing under the laws of this State or any foreign corporation authorized to transact business in this State, or a name the exclusive right to which is, at the time, reserved in the manner provided in this Act, or the name of a corporation which has in effect a registration of its corporate name as provided in this Act, except that this provision shall not apply if the applicant files with the Secretary of State either of the following: (1) the written consent of such other corporation or holder of a reserved or registered name to use the same or deceptively similar name and one or more words are added to make such name distinguishable from such other name, or (2) a certified copy of a final decree of a court of competent jurisdiction establishing the prior right of the applicant to the use of such name in this State.

A corporation with which another corporation, domestic or foreign, is merged, or which is formed by the reorganization or consolidation of one or more domestic or foreign corporations or upon a sale, lease or other disposition to or exchange with, a domestic corporation of all or substantially all the assets of another corporation, domestic or foreign, including its name, may have the same name as that used in this State by any of such corporations if such other corporation was organized under the laws of, or is authorized to transact business in, this State.

§ 9. **Reserved Name**

The exclusive right to the use of a corporate name may be reserved by:

(a) Any person intending to organize a corporation under this Act.

(b) Any domestic corporation intending to change its name.

(c) Any foreign corporation intending to make application for a certificate of authority to transact business in this State.

(d) Any foreign corporation authorized to transact business in this State and intending to change its name.

(e) Any person intending to organize a foreign corporation and intending to have such corporation make application for a certificate of authority to transact business in this State.

The reservation shall be made by filing with the Secretary of State an application to reserve a specified corporate name, executed by the applicant. If the Secretary of State finds that the name is available for corporate use, he shall reserve the same for the exclusive use of the applicant for a period of one hundred and twenty days.

The right to the exclusive use of a specified corporate name so reserved may be transferred to any person or corporation by filing in the office of the Secretary of State a notice of such transfer, executed by the applicant for whom the name was reserved, and specifying the name and address of the transferee.

§ 10. **Registered Name**

Any corporation organized and existing under the laws of any state or territory of the United States may register its corporate name under this Act, provided its corporate name is not the same as, or deceptively similar to, the name of any domestic corporation existing under the laws of this State, or the name of any foreign corporation authorized to transact business in this State, or any corporate name reserved or registered under this Act.

Such registration shall be made by:

(a) Filing with the Secretary of State (1) an application for registration executed by the corporation by an officer thereof, setting forth the name of the corporation, the state or territory under the laws of which it is incorporated, the date of its incorporation, a statement that it is carrying on or doing business, and a brief statement of the business in which it is engaged, and (2) a certificate setting forth that such corporation is in good standing under the laws of the state or territory wherein it is organized, executed by the Secretary of State of such state or territory or by such other official as may have custody of the records pertaining to corporations, and

(b) Paying to the Secretary of State a registration fee in the amount of . . . . for each month, or fraction thereof, between the date of filing such application and December 31st of the calendar year in which such application is filed.

Such registration shall be effective until the close of the calendar year in which the application for registration is filed.

§ 11. Renewal of Registered Name

A corporation which has in effect a registration of its corporate name, may renew such registration from year to year by annually filing an application for renewal setting forth the facts required to be set forth in an original application for registration and a certificate of good standing as required for the original registration and by paying a fee of . . . . A renewal application may be filed between the first day of October and the thirty-first day of December in each year, and shall extend the registration for the following calendar year.

§ 12. Registered Office and Registered Agent

Each corporation shall have and continuously main-tain in this State:

(a) A registered office which may be, but need not be, the same as its place of business.

(b) A registered agent, which agent may be either an individual resident in this State whose business office is identical with such registered office, or a domestic corporation, or a foreign corporation authorized to transact business in this State, having a business office identical with such registered office.

§ 13. Change of Registered Office or Registered Agent

A corporation may change its registered office or change its registered agent, or both, upon filing in the office of the Secretary of State a statement setting forth:

(a) The name of the corporation.

(b) The address of its then registered office.

(c) If the address of its registered office is to be changed, the address to which the registered office is to be changed.

(d) The name of its then registered agent.

(e) If its registered agent is to be changed, the name of its successor registered agent.

(f) That the address of its registered office and the address of the business office of its registered agent, as changed, will be identical.

(g) That such change was authorized by resolution duly adopted by its board of directors.

Such statement shall be executed by the corporation by its president, or a vice president, and verified by him, and delivered to the Secretary of State. If the Secretary of State finds that such statement conforms to the provisions of this Act, he shall file such statement in his office, and upon such filing the change of address of the registered office, or the appointment of a new registered agent, or both, as the case may be, shall become effective.

Any registered agent of a corporation may resign as such agent upon filing a written notice thereof, executed in duplicate, with the Secretary of State, who shall forthwith mail a copy thereof to the corporation at its registered office. The appointment of such agent shall terminate upon the expiration of thirty days after receipt of such notice by the Secretary of State.

If a registered agent changes his or its business address to another place within the same . . . .,* he or it may change such address and the address of the registered office of any corporation of which he or it is registered agent by filing a statement as required above except that it need be signed only by the registered agent and need not be responsive to (e) or (g) and must recite that a copy of the statement has been mailed to the corporation.

*Supply designation of jurisdiction, such as county, etc., in accordance with local practice.

§ 14. Service of Process on Corporation

The registered agent so appointed by a corporation shall be an agent of such corporation upon whom any process, notice or demand required or permitted by law to be served upon the corporation may be served.

Whenever a corporation shall fail to appoint or maintain a registered agent in this State, or whenever its registered agent cannot with reasonable diligence be found at the registered office, then the Secretary of State shall be an agent of such corporation upon whom any such process, notice, or demand may be served. Service on the Secretary of State of any such process, notice, or demand shall be made by delivering to and leaving with him, or with any clerk having charge of the corporation department of his office, duplicate copies of such process, notice or demand. In the event any such process, notice or demand is served on the Secretary of State, he shall immediately cause one of the copies thereof to be forwarded by registered mail, addressed to the corporation at its registered office. Any service so had on the Secretary of State shall be returnable in not less than thirty days.

The Secretary of State shall keep a record of all processes, notices and demands served upon him under this section, and shall record therein the time of such service and his action with reference thereto.

Nothing herein contained shall limit or affect the right to serve any process, notice or demand required or permitted by law to be served upon a corporation in any other manner now or hereafter permitted by law.

§ 15. **Authorized Shares**

Each corporation shall have power to create and issue the number of shares stated in its articles of incorporation. Such shares may be divided into one or more classes, any or all of which classes may consist of shares with par value or shares without par value, with such designations, preferences, limitations, and relative rights as shall be stated in the articles of incorporation. The articles of incorporation may limit or deny the voting rights of or provide special voting rights for the shares of any class to the extent not inconsistent with the provisions of this Act.

Without limiting the authority herein contained, a corporation, when so provided in its articles of incorporation, may issue shares of preferred or special classes:

(a) Subject to the right of the corporation to redeem any of such shares at the price fixed by the articles of incorporation for the redemption thereof.

(b) Entitling the holders thereof to cumulative, noncumulative or partially cumulative dividends.

(c) Having preference over any other class or classes of shares as to the payment of dividends.

(d) Having preference in the assets of the corporation over any other class or classes of shares upon the voluntary or involuntary liquidation of the corporation.

(e) Convertible into shares of any other class or into shares of any series of the same or any other class, except a class having prior or superior rights and preferences as to dividends or distribution of assets upon liquidation, but shares without par value shall not be converted into shares with par value unless that part of the stated capital of the corporation represented by such shares without par value is, at the time of conversion, at least equal to the aggregate par value of the shares into which the shares without par value are to be converted or the amount of any such deficiency is transferred from surplus to stated capital.

§ 16. **Issuance of Shares of Preferred or Special Classes in Series**

If the articles of incorporation so provide, the shares of any preferred or special class may be divided into and issued in series. If the shares of any such class are to be issued in series, then each series shall be so designated as to distinguish the shares thereof from the shares of all other series and classes. Any or all of the series of any such class and the variations in the relative rights and preferences as between different series may be fixed and determined by the articles of incorporation, but all shares of the same class shall be identical except as to the following relative rights and preferences, as to which there may be variations between different series:

(A) The rate of dividend.

(B) Whether shares may be redeemed and, if so, the redemption price and the terms and conditions of redemption.

(C) The amount payable upon shares in the event of voluntary and involuntary liquidation.

(D) Sinking fund provisions, if any, for the redemption or purchase of shares.

(E) The terms and conditions, if any, on which shares may be converted.

(F) Voting rights, if any.

If the articles of incorporation shall expressly vest authority in the board of directors, then, to the extent that the articles of incorporation shall not have established series and fixed and determined the variations in the relative rights and preferences as between series, the board of directors shall have authority to divide any or all of such classes into series and, within the limitations set forth in this section and in the articles of incorporation, fix and determine the relative rights and preferences of the shares of any series so established.

In order for the board of directors to establish a series, where authority so to do is contained in the articles of incorporation, the board of directors shall adopt a resolution setting forth the designation of the series and fixing and determining the relative rights and preferences thereof, or so much thereof as shall not be fixed and determined by the articles of incorporation.

Prior to the issue of any shares of a series established by resolution adopted by the board of directors, the corporation shall file in the office of the Secretary of State a statement setting forth:

(a) The name of the corporation.

(b) A copy of the resolution establishing and designating the series, and fixing and determining the relative rights and preferences thereof.

(c) The date of adoption of such resolution.

(d) That such resolution was duly adopted by the board of directors.

Such statement shall be executed in duplicate by the corporation by its president or a vice president and by its secretary or an assistant secretary, and verified by one of the officers signing such statement, and shall be delivered to the Secretary of State. If the Secretary of State finds that such statement conforms to law, he shall, when all franchise taxes and fees have been paid as in this Act prescribed:

(1) Endorse on each of such duplicate originals the word "Filed," and the month, day, and year of the filing thereof.

(2) File one of such duplicate originals in his office.

(3) Return the other duplicate original to the corporation or its representative.

Upon the filing of such statement by the Secretary of State, the resolution establishing and designating the series and fixing and determining the relative rights and preferences thereof shall become effective and shall constitute an amendment of the articles of incorporation.

§ 17. Subscriptions for Shares

A subscription for shares of a corporation to be organized shall be irrevocable for a period of six months, unless otherwise provided by the terms of the subscription agreement or unless all of the subscribers consent to the revocation of such subscription.

Unless otherwise provided in the subscription agreement, subscriptions for shares, whether made before or after the organization of a corporation, shall be paid in full at such time, or in such installments and at such times, as shall be determined by the board of directors. Any call made by the board of directors for payment on subscriptions shall be uniform as to all shares of the same class or as to all shares of the same series, as the case may be. In case of default in the payment of any installment or call when such payment is due, the corporation may proceed to collect the amount due in the same manner as any debt due the corporation. The by-laws may prescribe other penalties for failure to pay installments or calls that may become due, but no penalty working a forfeiture of a subscription, or of the amounts paid thereon, shall be declared as against any subscriber unless the amount due thereon shall remain unpaid for a period of twenty days after written demand has been made therefor. If mailed, such written demand shall be deemed to be made when deposited in the United States mail in a sealed envelope addressed to the subscriber at his last post-office address known to the corporation, with postage thereon prepaid. In the event of the sale of any shares by reason of any forfeiture, the excess of proceeds realized over the amount due and unpaid on such shares shall be paid to the delinquent subscriber or to his legal representative.

§ 18. Consideration for Shares

Shares having a par value may be issued for such consideration expressed in dollars, not less than the par value thereof, as shall be fixed from time to time by the board of directors.

Shares without par value may be issued for such consideration expressed in dollars as may be fixed from time to time by the board of directors unless the articles of incorporation reserve to the shareholders the right to fix the consideration. In the event that such right be reserved as to any shares, the shareholders shall, prior to the issuance of such shares, fix the consideration to be received for such shares, by a vote of the holders of a majority of all shares entitled to vote thereon.

Treasury shares may be disposed of by the corporation for such consideration expressed in dollars as may be fixed from time to time by the board of directors.

That part of the surplus of a corporation which is transferred to stated capital upon the issuance of shares as a share dividend shall be deemed to be the consideration for the issuance of such shares.

In the event of the issuance of shares upon the conversion or exchange of indebtedness or shares, the consideration for the shares so issued shall be (1) the principal sum of, and accrued interest on, the indebtedness so exchanged or converted, or the stated capital then represented by the shares so exchanged or converted, and (2) that part of surplus, if any, transferred to stated capital upon the issuance of shares for the shares so exchanged or converted, and (3) any additional consideration paid to the corporation upon the issuance of shares for the indebtedness or shares so exchanged or converted.

§ 19. Payment for Shares

The consideration for the issuance of shares may be paid, in whole or in part, in cash, in other property, tangible or intangible, or in labor or services actually performed for the corporation. When payment of the consideration for which shares are to be issued shall have been received by the corporation, such shares shall be deemed to be fully paid and non-assessable.

Neither promissory notes nor future services shall constitute payment or part payment for the issuance of shares of a corporation.

In the absence of fraud in the transaction, the judgment of the board of directors or the shareholders, as the case may be, as to the value of the consideration received for shares shall be conclusive.

§ 20. Stock Rights and Options

Subject to any provisions in respect thereof set forth in its articles of incorporation, a corporation may create and issue, whether or not in connection with the issuance and sale of any of its shares or other securities, rights or options entitling the holders thereof to purchase from the corporation shares of any class or classes. Such rights or options shall be evidenced in such manner as the board of directors shall approve and, subject to the provisions of the articles of incorporation, shall set forth the terms upon which, the time or times within which and the price or prices at which such shares may be purchased from the corporation upon the exercise of any such right or option. If such rights or options are to be issued to directors, officers or employees as such of the corporation or of any subsidiary thereof, and not to the shareholders generally, their issuance shall be approved by the affirmative vote of the holders of a majority of the shares entitled to vote thereon or shall be authorized by and consistent with a plan approved or ratified by such a vote of shareholders. In the absence of fraud in the transaction, the judgment of the board of directors as to the adequacy of the consideration received for such rights or options shall be conclusive. The price or prices to be received for any shares having a par value, other than treasury shares to be issued upon the exercise of such rights or options, shall not be less than the par value thereof.

§ 21. Determination of Amount of Stated Capital

In case of the issuance by a corporation of shares having a par value, the consideration received therefor shall constitute stated capital to the extent of the par value of such shares, and the excess, if any, of such consideration shall constitute capital surplus.

In case of the issuance by a corporation of shares without par value, the entire consideration received therefor shall constitute stated capital unless the corporation shall determine as provided in this section that only a part thereof shall be stated capital. Within a period of sixty days after the issuance of any shares without par value, the board of directors may allocate to capital surplus any portion of the consideration received for the issuance of such shares. No such allocation shall be made of any portion of the consideration received for shares without par value having a preference in the assets of the corporation in the event of involuntary liquidation except the amount, if any, of such consideration in excess of such preference.

If shares have been or shall be issued by a corporation in merger or consolidation or in acquisition of all or substantially all of the outstanding shares or of the property and assets of another corporation, whether domestic or foreign, any amount that would otherwise constitute capital surplus under the foregoing provisions of this section may instead be allocated to earned surplus by the board of directors of the issuing corporation except that its aggregate earned surplus shall not exceed the sum of the earned surpluses as defined in this Act of the issuing corporation and of all other corporations, domestic or foreign, that were merged or consolidated or of which the shares or assets were acquired.

The stated capital of a corporation may be increased from time to time by resolution of the board of directors directing that all or a part of the surplus of the corporation be transferred to stated capital. The board of directors may direct that the amount of the surplus so transferred shall be deemed to be stated capital in respect of any designated class of shares.

§ 22. Expenses of Organization, Reorganization and Financing

The reasonable charges and expenses of organization or reorganization of a corporation, and the reasonable expenses of and compensation for the sale or underwriting of its shares, may be paid or allowed by such corporation out of the consideration received by it in payment for its shares without thereby rendering such shares not fully paid or assessable.

§ 23. Shares Represented by Certificates and Uncertified Shares

The shares of a corporation shall be represented by certificates or shall be uncertificated shares. Certificates shall be signed by the chairman or vice-chairman of the board of directors or the president or a vice president and by the treasurer or an assistant treasurer or the secretary or an assistant secretary of the corporation, and may be sealed with the seal of the corporation or a facsimile thereof. Any of or all the signatures [of the president or vice president and the secretary of assistant secretary] upon a certificate may be a facsimile. [s if the certificate is manually signed on behalf of a transfer agent or a registrar, other than the corporation itself or an employee of the corporation.] In case any officer, transfer agent or registrar who has signed or whose facsimile signature has been placed upon such certificate shall have ceased to be such officer, transfer agent or registrar before such certificate is issued, it may be issued by the corporation with the same effect as if he were such officer, transfer agent or registrar at the date of its issue.

Every certificate representing shares issued by a corporation which is authorized to issue shares of more than one class shall set forth upon the face or back of the certificate, or shall state that the corporation will furnish to any shareholder upon request and without charge, a full statement of the designations, preferences, limitations, and relative rights of the shares of each class authorized to be issued, and if the corporation is authorized to issue any preferred or special class in series, the variations in the relative rights and preferences between the shares of each such series so far as the same have been fixed and determined and the authority of the board of directors to fix and determine the relative rights and preferences of subsequent series.

Each certificate representing shares shall state upon the face thereof:

(a) That the corporation is organized under the laws of this State.

(b) The name of the person to whom issued.

(c) The number and class of shares, and the designation of the series, if any, which such certificate represents.

(d) The par value of each share represented by such certificate, or a statement that the shares are without par value.

No certificate shall be issued for any share until such share is fully paid.

Unless otherwise provided by the articles of incorporation or by-laws, the board of directors of a corporation may provide by resolution that some or all of any or all classes and series of its shares shall be uncertificated shares, provided that such resolution shall not apply to shares represented by a certificate until such certificate is surrendered to the corporation. Within a reasonable time after the issuance or transfer of uncertificated shares, the corporation shall send to the registered owner thereof a written notice containing the information required to be set forth or stated on certificates pursuant to the second and third paragraphs of this section. Except as otherwise expressly provided by law, the rights and obligations of the holders of uncertificated shares and the rights and obligations of the holders of certificates representing shares of the same class and series shall be identical.

§ 24. Fractional Shares

A corporation may (1) issue fractions of a share, either

represented by a certificate or uncertificated, (2) arrange for the disposition of fractional interests by those entitled thereto, (3) pay in cash the fair value of fractions of a share as of a time when those entitled to receive such fractions are determined, or (4) issue scrip in registered or bearer form which shall entitle the holder to receive a certificate for a full share or an uncertificated full share upon the surrender of such scrip aggregating a full share. A certificate for a fractional share or an uncertificated fractional share shall, but scrip shall not unless otherwise provided therein, entitle the holder to exercise voting rights, to receive dividends thereon, and to participate in any of the assets of the corporation in the event of liquidation. The board of directors may cause scrip to be issued subject to the condition that it shall become void if not exchanged for certificates representing full shares or uncertificated full shares before a specified date, or subject to the condition that the shares for which scrip is exchangeable may be sold by the corporation and the proceeds thereof distributed to the holders of scrip, or subject to any other conditions which the board of directors may deem advisable.

§ 25. **Liability of Subscribers and Shareholders**

A holder of or subscriber to shares of a corporation shall be under no obligation to the corporation or its creditors with respect to such shares other than the obligation to pay to the corporation the full consideration for which such shares were issued or to be issued.

Any person becoming an assignee or transferee of shares or of a subscription for shares in good faith and without knowledge or notice that the full consideration therefor has not been paid shall not be personally liable to the corporation or its creditors for any unpaid portion of such consideration.

An executor, administrator, conservator, guardian, trustee, assignee for the benefit of creditors, or receiver shall not be personally liable to the corporation as a holder of or subscriber to shares of a corporation but the estate and funds in his hands shall be so liable.

No pledgee or other holder of shares as collateral security shall be personally liable as a shareholder.

§ 26. **Shareholders' Preemptive Rights**

The shareholders of a corporation shall have no preemptive right to acquire unissued or treasury shares of the corporation, or securities of the corporation convertible into or carrying a right to subscribe to or acquire shares, except to the extent, if any, that such right is provided in the articles of incorporation.

§ 26A. **Shareholders' Preemptive Rights [Alternative]**

Except to the extent limited or denied by this section or by the articles of incorporation, shareholders shall have a preemptive right to acquire unissued or treasury shares or securities convertible into such shares or carrying a right to subscribe to or acquire shares.

Unless otherwise provided in the articles of incorporation,

(a) No preemptive right shall exist

(1) to acquire any shares issued to directors, officers or employees pursuant to approval by the affirmative vote of the holders of a majority of the shares entitled to vote thereon or when authorized by and consistent with a plan theretofore approved by such a vote of shareholders; or

(2) to acquire any shares sold otherwise than for cash.

(b) Holders of shares of any class that is preferred or limited as to dividends or assets shall not be entitled to any preemptive right.

(c) Holders of shares of common stock shall not be entitled to any preemptive right to shares of any class that is preferred or limited as to dividends or assets or to any obligations, unless convertible into shares of common stock or carrying a right to subscribe to or acquire shares of common stock.

(d) Holders of common stock without voting power shall have no preemptive right to shares of common stock with voting power.

(e) The preemptive right shall be only an opportunity to acquire shares or other securities under such terms and conditions as the board of directors may fix for the purpose of providing a fair and reasonable opportunity for the exercise of such right.

§ 27. **By-Laws**

The initial by-laws of a corporation shall be adopted by its board of directors. The power to alter, amend or repeal the by-laws or adopt new by-laws, subject to repeal or change by action of the shareholders, shall be vested in the board of directors unless reserved to the shareholders by the articles of incorporation. The by-laws may contain any provisions for the regulation and management of the affairs of the corporation not inconsistent with law or the articles of incorporation.

§ 27A. **By-Laws and Other Powers in Emergency [Optional]**

The board of directors of any corporation may adopt emergency by-laws, subject to repeal or change by action of the shareholders, which shall, notwithstanding any different provision elsewhere in this Act or in the articles of incorporation or by-laws, be operative during any emergency in the conduct of the business of the corporation resulting from an attack on the United States or any nuclear or atomic disaster. The emergency by-laws may make any provision that may be practical and necessary for the circumstances of the emergency, including provisions that:

(a) A meeting of the board of directors may be called by any officer or director in such manner and under such conditions as shall be prescribed in the emergency by-laws;

(b) The director or directors in attendance at the meeting, or any greater number fixed by the emergency by-laws, shall constitute a quorum; and

(c) The officers or other persons designated on a list approved by the board of directors before the emergency, all in such order of priority and subject to such conditions, and for such period of time (not longer than reasonably necessary after the termination of the emergency) as may be provided in the emergency by-laws or in the resolution approving the list shall, to the extent required to provide a quorum at any meeting of the board of directors, be deemed directors for such meeting.

The board of directors, either before or during any such emergency, may provide, and from time to time modify, lines of succession in the event that during such an emergency any or all officers or agents of the corporation shall for any reason be rendered incapable of discharging their duties.

The board of directors, either before or during any such emergency, may, effective in the emergency, change the head office or designate several alternative head offices or regional offices, or authorize the officers so to do.

To the extent not inconsistent with any emergency by-laws so adopted, the by-laws of the corporation shall remain in effect during any such emergency and upon its termination the emergency by-laws shall cease to be operative.

Unless otherwise provided in emergency by-laws, notice of any meeting of the board of directors during any such emergency may be given only to such of the directors as it may be feasible to reach at the time and by such means as may be feasible at the time, including publication or radio.

To the extent required to constitute a quorum at any meeting of the board of directors during any such emergency, the officers of the corporation who are present shall, unless otherwise provided in emergency by-laws, be deemed, in order of rank and within the same rank in order of seniority, directors for such meeting.

No officer, director or employee acting in accordance with any emergency by-laws shall be liable except for willful misconduct. No officer, director or employee shall be liable for any action taken by him in good faith in such an emergency in furtherance of the ordinary business affairs of the corporation even though not authorized by the by-laws then in effect.

§ 28. **Meetings of Shareholders**

Meetings of shareholders may be held at such place within or without this State as may be stated in or fixed in accordance with the by-laws. If no other place is stated or so fixed, meetings shall be held at the registered office of the corporation.

An annual meeting of the shareholders shall be held at such time as may be stated in or fixed in accordance with the by-laws. If the annual meeting is not held within any thirteen-month period the Court of . . . . may, on the application of any shareholder, summarily order a meeting to be held.

A special meeting of the shareholders may be called by the board of directors, the holders of not less than one-tenth of all the shares entitled to vote at the meeting, or such other persons as may be authorized in the articles of incorporation or the by-laws.

§ 29. **Notice of Shareholders' Meetings**

Written notice stating the place, day and hour of the meeting and, in case of a special meeting, the purpose or purposes for which the meeting is called, shall be delivered not less than ten nor more than fifty days before the date of the meeting, either personally or by mail, by or at the direction of the president, the secretary, or the officer or persons calling the meeting, to each shareholder of record entitled to vote at such meeting. If mailed, such notice shall be deemed to be delivered when deposited in the United States mail addressed to the shareholder at his address as it appears on the stock transfer books of the corporation, with postage thereon prepaid.

§ 30. Closing of Transfer Books and Fixing Record Date

For the purpose of determining shareholders entitled to notice of or to vote at any meeting of shareholders or any adjournment thereof, or entitled to receive payment of any dividend, or in order to make a determination of shareholders for any other proper purpose, the board of directors of a corporation may provide that the stock transfer books shall be closed for a stated period but not to exceed, in any case, fifty days. If the stock transfer books shall be closed for the purpose of determining shareholders entitled to notice of or to vote at a meeting of shareholders, such books shall be closed for at least ten days immediately preceding such meeting. In lieu of closing the stock transfer books, the by-laws, or in the absence of an applicable by-law the board of directors, may fix in advance a date as the record date for any such determination of shareholders, such date in any case to be not more than fifty days and, in case of a meeting of shareholders, not less than ten days prior to the date on which the particular action, requiring such determination of shareholders, is to be taken. If the stock transfer books are not closed and no record date is fixed for the determination of shareholders entitled to notice of or to vote at a meeting of shareholders, or shareholders entitled to receive payment of a dividend, the date on which notice of the meeting is mailed or the date on which the resolution of the board of directors declaring such dividend is adopted, as the case may be, shall be the record date for such determination of shareholders. When a determination of shareholders entitled to vote at any meeting of shareholders has been made as provided in this section, such determination shall apply to any adjournment thereof.

§ 31. Voting Record

The officer or agent having charge of the stock transfer books for shares of a corporation shall make a complete record of the shareholders entitled to vote at such meeting or any adjournment thereof, arranged in alphabetical order, with the address of and the number of shares held by each. Such record shall be produced and kept open at the time and place of the meeting and shall be subject to the inspection of any shareholder during the whole time of the meeting for the purposes thereof.

Failure to comply with the requirements of this section shall not affect the validity of any action taken at such meeting.

An officer or agent having charge of the stock transfer books who shall fail to prepare the record of shareholders, or produce and keep it open for inspection at the meeting, as provided in this section, shall be liable to any shareholder suffering damage on account of such failure, to the extent of such damage.

§ 32. Quorum of Shareholders

Unless otherwise provided in the articles of incorporation, a majority of the shares entitled to vote, represented in person or by proxy, shall constitute a quorum at a meeting of shareholders, but in no event shall a quorum consist of less than one-third of the shares entitled to vote at the meeting. If a quorum is present, the affirmative vote of the majority of the shares represented at the meeting and entitled to vote on the subject matter shall be the act of the shareholders, unless the vote of a greater number or voting by classes is required by this Act or the articles of incorporation or by-laws.

§ 33. Voting of Shares

Each outstanding share, regardless of class, shall be entitled to one vote on each matter submitted to a vote at a meeting of shareholders, except as may be otherwise provided in the articles of incorporation. If the articles of incorporation provide for more or less than one vote for any share, on any matter, every reference in this Act to a majority or other proportion of shares shall refer to such a majority or other proportion of votes entitled to be cast.

Neither treasury shares, nor shares held by another corporation if a majority of the shares entitled to vote for the election of directors of such other corporation is held by the corporation, shall be voted at any meeting or counted in determining the total number of outstanding shares at any given time.

A shareholder may vote either in person or by proxy executed in writing by the shareholder or by his duly authorized attorney-in-fact. No proxy shall be valid after eleven months from the date of its execution, unless otherwise provided in the proxy.

[Either of the following prefatory phrases may be inserted here: "The articles of incorporation may provide that" or "Unless the articles of incorporation otherwise provide"] . . . at each election for directors every shareholder entitled to vote at such election shall have the right to vote, in person or by proxy, the number of shares owned by him for as many persons as there are directors to be elected and for whose election he has a right to vote, or to cumulate his votes by giving one candidate as many votes as the number of such directors multiplied by the number of his shares shall equal, or by distributing such votes on the same principle among any number of such candidates.

Shares standing in the name of another corporation, domestic or foreign, may be voted by such officer, agent or proxy as the by-laws of such other corporation may prescribe, or, in the absence of such provision, as the board of directors of such other corporation may determine.

Shares held by an administrator, executor, guardian or conservator may be voted by him, either in person or by proxy, without a transfer of such shares into his name. Shares standing in the name of a trustee may be voted by him, either in person or by proxy, but no trustee shall be entitled to vote shares held by him without a transfer of such shares into his name.

Shares standing in the name of a receiver may be voted by such receiver, and shares held by or under the control of a receiver may be voted by such receiver without the transfer thereof into his name if authority so to do be contained in an appropriate order of the court by which such receiver was appointed.

A shareholder whose shares are pledged shall be entitled to vote such shares until the shares have been transferred into the name of the pledgee, and thereafter the pledgee shall be entitled to vote the shares so transferred.

On and after the date on which written notice of redemption of redeemable shares has been mailed to the holders thereof and a sum sufficient to redeem such shares has been deposited with a bank or trust company with irrevocable instruction and authority to pay the redemption price to the holders thereof upon surrender of certificates therefor, such shares shall not be entitled to vote on any matter and shall not be deemed to be outstanding shares.

§ 34. Voting Trusts and Agreements Among Shareholders

Any number of shareholders of a corporation may create a voting trust for the purpose of conferring upon a trustee or trustees the right to vote or otherwise represent their shares, for a period of not to exceed ten years, by entering into a written voting trust agreement specifying the terms and conditions of the voting trust, by depositing a counterpart of the agreement with the corporation at its registered office, and by transferring their shares to such trustee or trustees for the purposes of the agreement. Such trustee or trustees shall keep a record of the holders of voting trust certificates evidencing a beneficial interest in the voting trust, giving the names and addresses of all such holders and the number and class of the shares in respect of which the voting trust certificates held by each are issued, and shall deposit a copy of such record with the corporation at its registered office. The counterpart of the voting trust agreement and the copy of such record so deposited with the corporation shall be subject to the same right of examination by a shareholder of the corporation, in person or by agent or attorney, as are the books and records of the corporation, and such counterpart and such copy of such record shall be subject to examination by any holder of record of voting trust certificates, either in person or by agent or attorney, at any reasonable time for any proper purpose.

Agreements among shareholders regarding the voting of their shares shall be valid and enforceable in accordance with their terms. Such agreements shall not be subject to the provisions of this section regarding voting trusts.

§ 35. Board of Directors

All corporate powers shall be exercised by or under authority of, and the business and affairs of a corporation shall be managed under the direction of, a board of directors except as may be otherwise provided in this Act or the articles of incorporation. If any such provision is made in the articles of incorporation, the powers and duties conferred or imposed upon the board of directors by this Act shall be exercised or performed to such extent and by such person or persons as shall be provided in the articles of incorporation. Directors need not be residents of this State or shareholders of the corporation unless the articles of incorporation or by-laws so require. The articles of incorporation or by-laws may prescribe other qualifications for directors. The board of directors shall have authority to fix the compensation of directors unless otherwise provided in the articles of incorporation.

A director shall perform his duties as a director, including his duties as a member of any committee of the board upon which he may serve, in good faith, in a manner he reasonably believes to be in the best interests of the corporation, and with such care as an ordinarily prudent person in a like position would use under similar circumstances. In performing his duties, a director shall be entitled to rely on information, opinions, reports or statements, including financial statements and other financial data, in each case prepared or presented by:

(a) one or more officers or employees of the corporation whom the director reasonably believes to be reliable and competent in the matters presented,

(b) counsel, public accountants or other persons as to matters which the director reasonably believes to be within such person's professional or expert competence, or

(c) a committee of the board upon which he does not serve, duly designated in accordance with a provision of the articles of incorporation or the by-laws, as to matters within its designated authority, which committee the director reasonably believes to merit confidence,

but he shall not be considered to be acting in good faith if he has knowledge concerning the matter in question that would cause such reliance to be unwarranted. A person who so performs his duties shall have no liability by reason of being or having been a director of the corporation.

A director of a corporation who is present at a meeting of its board of directors at which action on any corporate matter is taken shall be presumed to have assented to the action taken unless his dissent shall be entered in the minutes of the meeting or unless he shall file his written dissent to such action

with the secretary of the meeting before the adjournment thereof or shall forward such dissent by registered mail to the secretary of the corporation immediately after the adjournment of the meeting. Such right to dissent shall not apply to a director who voted in favor of such action.

§ 36. **Number and Election of Directors**

The board of directors of a corporation shall consist of one or more members. The number of directors shall be fixed by, or in the manner provided in, the articles of incorporation or the by-laws, except as to the number constituting the initial board of directors, which number shall be fixed by the articles of incorporation. The number of directors may be increased or decreased from time to time by amendment to, or in the manner provided in, the articles of incorporation or the by-laws, but no decrease shall have the effect of shortening the term of any incumbent director. In the absence of a by-law providing for the number of directors, the number shall be the same as that provided for in the articles of incorporation. The names and addresses of the members of the first board of directors shall be stated in the articles of incorporation. Such persons shall hold office until the first annual meeting of shareholders, and until their successors shall have been elected and qualified. At the first annual meeting of shareholders and at each annual meeting thereafter the shareholders shall elect directors to hold office until the next succeeding annual meeting, except in case of the classification of directors as permitted by this Act. Each director shall hold office for the term for which he is elected and until his successor shall have been elected and qualified.

§ 37. **Classification of Directors**

When the board of directors shall consist of nine or more members, in lieu of electing the whole number of directors annually, the articles of incorporation may provide that the directors be divided into either two or three classes, each class to be as nearly equal in number as possible, the term of office of directors of the first class to expire at the first annual meeting of shareholders after their election, that of the second class to expire at the second annual meeting after their election, and that of the third class, if any, to expire at the third annual meeting after their election.

At each annual meeting after such classification the number of directors equal to the number of the class whose term expires at the time of such meeting shall be elected to hold office until the second succeeding annual meeting, if there be two classes, or until the third succeeding annual meeting, if there be three classes. No classification of directors shall be effective prior to the first annual meeting of shareholders.

§ 38. Vacancies

Any vacancy occurring in the board of directors may be filled by the affirmative vote of a majority of the remaining directors though less than a quorum of the board of directors. A director elected to fill a vacancy shall be elected for the unexpired term of his predecessor in office. Any directorship to be filled by reason of an increase in the number of directors may be filled by the board of directors for a term of office continuing only until the next election of directors by the shareholders.

§ 39. Removal of Directors

At a meeting of shareholders called expressly for that purpose, directors may be removed in the manner provided in this section. Any director or the entire board of directors may be removed, with or without cause, by a vote of the holders of a majority of the shares then entitled to vote at an election of directors.

In the case of a corporation having cumulative voting, if less than the entire board is to be removed, no one of the directors may be removed if the votes cast against his removal would be sufficient to elect him if then cumulatively voted at an election of the entire board of directors, or, if there be classes of directors, at an election of the class of directors of which he is a part.

Whenever the holders of the shares of any class are entitled to elect one or more directors by the provisions of the articles of incorporation, the provisions of this section shall apply, in respect to the removal of a director or directors so elected, to the vote of the holders of the outstanding shares of that class and not to the vote of the outstanding shares as a whole.

§ 40. Quorum of Directors

A majority of the number of directors fixed by or in the manner provided in the by-laws or in the absence of a by-law fixing or providing for the number of directors, then of the number stated in the articles of incorporation, shall constitute a quorum for the transaction of business unless a greater number is required by the articles of incorporation or the by-laws. The act of the majority of the directors present at a meeting at which a quorum is present shall be the act of the board of directors, unless the act of a greater number is required by the articles of incorporation or the by-laws.

§ 41. Director Conflicts of Interest

No contract or other transaction between a corporation and one or more of its directors or any other corporation, firm, association or entity in which one or more of its directors are directors or officers or are financially interested, shall be either void or voidable because of such relationship or interest or because such director or directors are present at the meeting of the board of directors or a committee thereof which authorizes, approves or ratifies such contract or transaction or because his or their votes are counted for such purpose, if:

(a) the fact of such relationship or interest is disclosed or known to the board of directors or committee which authorizes, approves or ratifies the contract or transaction by a vote or consent sufficient for the purpose without counting the votes or consents of such interested directors; or

(b) the fact of such relationship or interest is disclosed or known to the shareholders entitled to vote and they authorize, approve or ratify such contract or transaction by vote or written consent; or

(c) the contract or transaction is fair and reasonable to the corporation.

Common or interested directors may be counted in determining the presence of a quorum at a meeting of the board of directors or a committee thereof which authorizes, approves or ratifies such contract or transaction.

§ 42. Executive and Other Committees

If the articles of incorporation or the by-laws so provide, the board of directors, by resolution adopted by a majority of the full board of directors, may designate from among its members an executive committee and one or more other committees each of which, to the extent provided in such resolution or in the articles of incorporation or the by-laws of the corporation, shall have and may exercise all the authority of the board of directors, except that no such committee shall have authority to (i) declare dividends or distributions, (ii) approve or recommend to shareholders actions or proposals required by this Act to be approved by shareholders, (iii) designate candidates for the office of director, for purposes of proxy solicitation or otherwise, or fill vacancies on the board of directors or any committee thereof, (iv) amend the by-laws, (v) approve a plan of merger not requiring shareholder approval, (vi) reduce earned or capital surplus, (vii) authorize or approve the reacquisition of shares unless pursuant to a general formula or method specified by the board of directors, or (viii) authorize or approve the issuance or sale of, or any contract to issue or sell, shares or designate the terms of a series of a class of shares, provided that the board of directors, having acted regarding general authorization for the issuance or sale of shares, or any contract therefor, and, in the case of a series, the designation thereof, may, pursuant to a general formula or method specified by the board by resolution or by adoption of a stock option or other plan, authorize a committee to fix the terms of any contract for the sale of the shares and to fix the terms upon which such shares may be issued or sold, including, without limitation, the price, the dividend rate, provisions for redemption, sinking fund, conversion, voting or preferential rights, and provisions for other features of a class of shares, or a series of a class of shares, with full power in such committee to adopt any final resolution setting forth all the terms thereof and to authorize the statement of the terms of a series for filing with the Secretary of State under this Act.

Neither the designation of any such committee, the delegation thereto of authority, nor action by such committee pursuant to such authority shall alone constitute compliance by any member of the board of directors, not a member of the committee in question, with his responsibility to act in good faith, in a manner he reasonably believes to be in the best interests of the corporation, and with such care as an ordinarily prudent person in a like position would use under similar circumstances.

§ 43. Place and Notice of Directors' Meetings; Committee Meetings

Meetings of the board of directors, regular or special, may be held either within or without this State.

Regular meetings of the board of directors or any committee designated thereby may be held with or without notice as prescribed in the by-laws. Special meetings of the board of directors or any committee designated thereby shall be held upon such notice as is prescribed in the by-laws. Attendance of a director at a meeting shall constitute a waiver of notice of such meeting, except where a director attends a meeting for the express purpose of objecting to the transaction of any business because the meeting is not lawfully called or convened. Neither the business to be transacted at, nor the purpose of, any regular or special meeting of the board of directors or any committee designated thereby need be specified in the notice or waiver of notice of such meeting unless required by the by-laws.

Except as may be otherwise restricted by the articles of incorporation or by-laws, members of the board of directors or any committee designated thereby may participate in a meeting of such board or committee by means of a conference telephone or similar communications equipment by means of which all persons participating in the meeting can hear each other at the same time and participation by such means shall constitute presence in person at a meeting.

§ 44. Action by Directors Without a Meeting

Unless otherwise provided by the articles of incorporation or by-laws, any action required by this Act to be taken at a meeting of the directors of a corporation, or any action which may be taken at a meeting of the directors or of a committee, may be taken without a meeting if a consent in writing, setting forth the action so taken, shall be signed by all of the directors, or all of the members of the committee, as the case may be. Such consent shall have the same effect as a unanimous vote.

§ 45. Dividends

The board of directors of a corporation may, from time to time, declare and the corporation may pay dividends in cash, property, or its own shares, except when the corporation is insolvent or when the payment thereof would render the corporation insolvent or when the declaration or payment thereof would be contrary to any restriction contained in the articles of incorporation, subject to the following provisions:

(a) Dividends may be declared and paid in cash or property only out of the unreserved and unrestricted earned surplus of the corporation, except as otherwise provided in this section.

[Alternative] (a) Dividends may be declared and paid in cash or property only out of the unreserved and unrestricted earned surplus of the corporation, or out of the unreserved and unrestricted net earnings of the current fiscal year and the next preceding fiscal year taken as a single period, except as otherwise provided in this section.

(b) If the articles of incorporation of a corporation engaged in the business of exploiting natural resources so provide, dividends may be declared and paid in cash out of the depletion reserves, but each such dividend shall be identified as a distribution of such reserves and the amount per share paid from such reserves shall be disclosed to the shareholders receiving the same concurrently with the distribution thereof.

(c) Dividends may be declared and paid in its own treasury shares.

(d) Dividends may be declared and paid in its own authorized but unissued shares out of any unreserved and unrestricted surplus of the corporation upon the following conditions:

> (1) If a dividend is payable in its own shares having a par value, such shares shall be issued at not less than the par value thereof and there shall be transferred to stated capital at the time such dividend is paid an amount of surplus equal to the aggregate par value of the shares to be issued as a dividend.

> (2) If a dividend is payable in its own shares without par value, such shares shall be issued at such stated value as shall be fixed by the board of directors by resolution adopted at the time such dividend is declared, and there shall be transferred to stated capital at the time such dividend is

paid an amount of surplus equal to the aggregate stated value so fixed in respect of such shares; and the amount per share so transferred to stated capital shall be disclosed to the shareholders receiving such dividend concurrently with the payment thereof.

(e) No dividend payable in shares of any class shall be paid to the holders of shares of any other class unless the articles of incorporation so provide or such payment is authorized by the affirmative vote or the written consent of the holders of at least a majority of the outstanding shares of the class in which the payment is to be made.

A split-up or division of the issued shares of any class into a greater number of shares of the same class without increasing the stated capital of the corporation shall not be construed to be a share dividend within the meaning of this section.

§ 46. **Distributions from Capital Surplus**

The board of directors of a corporation may, from time to time, distribute to its shareholders out of capital surplus of the corporation a portion of its assets, in cash or property, subject to the following provisions:

(a) No such distribution shall be made at a time when the corporation is insolvent or when such distribution would render the corporation insolvent.

(b) No such distribution shall be made unless the articles of incorporation so provide or such distribution is authorized by the affirmative vote of the holders of a majority of the outstanding shares of each class whether or not entitled to vote thereon by the provisions of the articles of incorporation of the corporation.

(c) No such distribution shall be made to the holders of any class of shares unless all cumulative dividends accrued on all preferred or special classes of shares entitled to preferential dividends shall have been fully paid.

(d) No such distribution shall be made to the holders of any class of shares which would reduce the remaining net assets of the corporation below the aggregate preferential amount payable in event of involuntary liquidation to the holders of shares having preferential rights to the assets of the corporation in the event of liquidation.

(e) Each such distribution, when made, shall be identified as a distribution from capital surplus and the amount per share disclosed to the shareholders receiving the same concurrently with the distribution thereof.

The board of directors of a corporation may also, from time to time, distribute to the holders of its outstanding shares having a cumulative preferential right to receive dividends, in discharge of their cumulative dividend rights, dividends payable in cash out of the capital surplus of the corporation, if at the time the corporation has no earned surplus and is not insolvent and would not thereby be rendered insolvent. Each such distribution when made, shall be identified as a payment of cumulative dividends out of capital surplus.

§ 47. Loans to Employees and Directors

A corporation shall not lend money to or use its credit to assist its directors without authorization in the particular case by its shareholders, but may lend money to and use its credit to assist any employee of the corporation or of a subsidiary, including any such employee who is a director of the corporation, if the board of directors decides that such loan or assistance may benefit the corporation.

§ 48. Liability of Directors in Certain Cases

In addition to any other liabilities, a director shall be liable in the following circumstances unless he complies with the standard provided in this Act for the performance of the duties of directors:

(a) A director who votes for or assents to the declaration of any dividend or other distribution of the assets of a corporation to its shareholders contrary to the provisions of this Act or contrary to any restrictions contained in the articles of incorporation, shall be liable to the corporation, jointly and severally with all other directors so voting or assenting, for the amount of such dividend which is paid or the value of such assets which are distributed in excess of the amount of such dividend or distribution which could have been paid or distributed without a violation of the provisions of this Act or the restrictions in the articles of incorporation.

(b) A director who votes for or assents to the purchase of the corporation's own shares contrary to the provisions of this Act shall be liable to the corporation, jointly and severally with all other directors so voting or assenting, for the amount of consideration paid for such shares which is in excess of the maximum amount which could have been paid therefor without a violation of the provisions of this Act.

(c) A director who votes for or assents to any distribution of assets of a corporation to its shareholders during the liquidation of the corporation without the payment and discharge of, or making adequate provision for, all known debts, obligations, and liabilities of the corporation shall be liable to the corporation, jointly and severally with all other directors so voting or assenting, for the value of such assets which are distributed, to the extent that such debts, obligations and liabilities of the corporation are not thereafter paid and discharged.

Any director against whom a claim shall be asserted under or pursuant to this section for the payment of a dividend or other distribution of assets of a corporation and who shall be held liable thereon, shall be entitled to contribution from the shareholders who accepted or received any such dividend or assets, knowing such dividend or distribution to have been made in violation of this Act, in proportion to the amounts received by them.

Any director against whom a claim shall be asserted under or pursuant to this section shall be entitled to contribution from the other directors who voted for or assented to the action upon which the claim is asserted.

§ 49. Provisions Relating to Actions by Shareholders

No action shall be brought in this State by a shareholder in the right of a domestic or foreign corporation unless the plaintiff was a holder of record of shares or of voting trust certificates therefor at the time of the transaction of which he complains, or his shares or voting trust certificates thereafter devolved upon him by operation of law from a person who was a holder of record at such time.

In any action hereafter instituted in the right of any domestic or foreign corporation by the holder or holders of record of shares of such corporation or of voting trust certificates therefor, the court having jurisdiction, upon final judgment and a finding that the action was brought without reasonable cause, may require the plaintiff or plaintiffs to pay to the parties named as defendant the reasonable expenses, including fees of attorneys, incurred by them in the defense of such action.

In any action now pending or hereafter instituted or maintained in the right of any domestic or foreign corporation by the holder or holders of record of less than five per cent of the outstanding shares of any class of such corporation or of voting trust certificates therefor, unless the shares or voting trust certificates so held have a market value in excess of twenty-five thousand dollars, the corporation in whose right such action is brought shall be entitled at any time before final judgment to require the plaintiff or plaintiffs to give security for the reasonable expenses, including fees of attorneys, that may be incurred by it in connection with such action or may be incurred by other parties named as defendant for which it may become legally liable. Market value shall be determined as of the date that the plaintiff institutes the action or, in the case of an intervenor, as of the date that he becomes a party to the action. The amount of such security may from time to time be increased or decreased, in the discretion of the court, upon showing that the security provided has or may become inadequate or is excessive. The corporation shall have recourse to such security in such amount as the court having jurisdiction shall determine upon the termination of such action, whether or not the court finds the action was brought without reasonable cause.

§ 50. **Officers**

The officers of a corporation shall consist of a president, one or more vice presidents as may be prescribed by the by-laws, a secretary, and a treasurer, each of whom shall be elected by the board of directors at such time and in such manner as may be prescribed by the by-laws. Such other officers and assistant officers and agents as may be deemed necessary may be elected or appointed by the board of directors or chosen in such other manner as may be prescribed by the by-laws. Any two or more offices may be held by the same person, except the offices of president and secretary.

All officers and agents of the corporation, as between themselves and the corporation, shall have such authority and perform such duties in the management of the corporation as may be provided in the by-laws, or as may be determined by resolution of the board of directors not inconsistent with the by-laws.

§ 51. **Removal of Officers**

Any officer or agent may be removed by the board of directors whenever in its judgment the best interests of the corporation will be served thereby, but such removal shall be without prejudice to the contract rights, if any, of the person so removed. Election or appointment of an officer or agent shall not of itself create contract rights.

§ 52. **Books and Records**

Each corporation shall keep correct and complete books and records of account and shall keep minutes of the proceedings of its shareholders and board of directors and shall keep at its registered office or principal place of business, or at the office of its transfer agent or registrar, a record of its shareholders, giving the names and addresses of all shareholders and the number and class of the shares held by each. Any books, records and minutes may be in written form or in any form capable of being converted into written form within a reasonable time.

Any person who shall have been a holder of record of shares or of voting trust certificates therefor at least six months immediately preceding his demand or shall be the holder of record of, or the holder of record of voting trust certificates for, at least five percent of all the outstanding shares of the corporation, upon written demand stating the purpose thereof, shall have the right to examine, in person, or by agent or attorney, at any reasonable time or times, for any proper purpose its relevant books and records of accounts, minutes, and record of shareholders and to make extracts therefrom.

Any officer or agent who, or a corporation which, shall refuse to allow any such shareholder or holder of voting trust certificates, or his agent or attorney, so to examine and make extracts from its books and records of account, minutes, and record of shareholders, for any proper purpose, shall be liable to such shareholder or holder of voting trust certificates in a penalty of ten per cent of the value of the shares owned by such shareholder, or in respect of which such voting trust certificates are issued, in addition to any other damages or remedy afforded him by law. It shall be a defense to any action for penalties under this section that the person suing therefor has within two years sold or offered for sale any list of shareholders or of holders of voting trust certificates for shares of such corporation or any other corporation or has aided or abetted any person in procuring any list of shareholders or of holders of voting trust certificates for any such purpose, or has improperly used any information secured through any prior examination of the books and records of account, or minutes, or record of shareholders or of holders of voting trust certificates for shares of such corporation or any other corporation, or was not acting in good faith or for a proper purpose in making his demand.

Nothing herein contained shall impair the power of any court of competent jurisdiction, upon proof by a shareholder or holder of voting trust certificates of proper purpose, irrespective of the period of time during which such shareholder or holder of voting trust certificates shall have been a shareholder of record or a holder of record of voting trust certificates, and irrespective of the number of shares held by him or represented by voting trust certificates held by him, to compel the production for examination by such shareholder or holder of voting trust certificates of the books and records of account, minutes and record of shareholders of a corporation.

Upon the written request of any shareholder or holder of voting trust certificates for shares of a corporation, the corporation shall mail to such shareholder or holder of voting trust certificates its most recent financial statements showing in reasonable detail its assets and liabilities and the results of its operations.

§ 53. Incorporators

One or more persons, or a domestic or foreign corporation, may act as incorporator or incorporators of a corporation by signing and delivering in duplicate to the Secretary of State articles of incorporation for such corporation.

§ 54. Articles of Incorporation

The articles of incorporation shall set forth:

(a) The name of the corporation.

(b) The period of duration, which may be perpetual.

(c) The purpose or purposes for which the corporation is organized which may be stated to be, or to include, the transaction of any or all lawful business for which corporations may be incorporated under this Act.

(d) The aggregate number of shares which the corporation shall have authority to issue; if such shares are to consist of one class only, the par value of each of such shares, or a statement that all of such shares are without par value; or, if such shares are to be divided into classes, the number of shares of each class, and a statement of the par value of the shares of each such class or that such shares are to be without par value.

(e) If the shares are to be divided into classes, the designation of each class and a statement of the preferences, limitations and relative rights in respect of the shares of each class.

(f) If the corporation is to issue the shares of any preferred or special class in series, then the designation of each series and a statement of the variations in the relative rights and preferences as between series insofar as the same are to be fixed in the articles of incorporation, and a statement of any authority to be vested in the board of directors to establish series and fix and determine the variations in the relative rights and preferences as between series.

(g) If any preemptive right is to be granted to shareholders, the provisions therefor.

(h) Any provision, not inconsistent with law, which the incorporators elect to set forth in the articles of incorporation for the regulation of the internal affairs of the corporation, including any provision restricting the transfer of shares and any provision which under this Act is required or permitted to be set forth in the by-laws.

(i) The address of its initial registered office, and the name of its initial registered agent at such address.

(j) The number of directors constituting the initial board of directors and the names and addresses of the persons who are to serve as directors until the first annual meeting of shareholders or until their successors be elected and qualify.

(k) The name and address of each incorporator.

It shall not be necessary to set forth in the articles of incorporation any of the corporate powers enumerated in this Act.

§ 55. Filing of Articles of Incorporation

Duplicate originals of the articles of incorporation shall be delivered to the Secretary of State. If the Secretary of State finds that the articles of incorporation conform to law, he shall, when all fees have been paid as in this Act prescribed:

(a) Endorse on each of such duplicate originals the word "Filed," and the month, day and year of the filing thereof.

(b) File one of such duplicate originals in his office.

(c) Issue a certificate of incorporation to which he shall affix the other duplicate original.

The certificate of incorporation, together with the duplicate original of the articles of incorporation affixed thereto by the Secretary of State, shall be returned to the incorporators or their representative.

§ 56. Effect of Issuance of Certificate of Incorporation

Upon the issuance of the certificate of incorporation, the corporate existence shall begin, and such certificate of incorporation shall be conclusive evidence that all conditions precedent required to be performed by the incorporators have been complied with and that the corporation has been incorporated under this Act, except as against this State in a proceeding to cancel or revoke the certificate of incorporation or for involuntary dissolution of the corporation.

§ 57. Organization Meeting of Directors

After the issuance of the certificate of incorporation an organization meeting of the board of directors named in the articles of incorporation shall be held, either within or without this State, at the call of a majority of the directors named in the articles of incorporation, for the purpose of adopting by-laws, electing officers and transacting such other business as may come before the meeting. The directors calling the meeting shall give at least three days' notice thereof by mail to each director so named, stating the time and place of the meeting.

§ 58. Right to Amend Articles of Incorporation

A corporation may amend its articles of incorporation, from time to time, in any and as many respects as may be desired, so long as its articles of incorporation as amended contain only such provisions as might be lawfully contained in original articles of incorporation at the time of making such amendment, and, if a change in shares or the rights of shareholders, or an exchange, reclassification or cancellation of shares or rights of shareholders is to be made, such provisions as may be necessary to effect such change, exchange, reclassification or cancellation.

In particular, and without limitation upon such general power of amendment, a corporation may amend its articles of incorporation, from time to time, so as:

(a) To change its corporate name.

(b) To change its period of duration.

(c) To change, enlarge or diminish its corporate purposes.

(d) To increase or decrease the aggregate number of shares, or shares of any class, which the corporation has authority to issue.

(e) To increase or decrease the par value of the authorized shares of any class having a par value, whether issued or unissued.

(f) To exchange, classify, reclassify or cancel all or any part of its shares, whether issued or unissued.

(g) To change the designation of all or any part of its shares, whether issued or unissued, and to change the preferences, limitations, and the relative rights in respect of all or any part of its shares, whether issued or unissued.

(h) To change shares having the par value, whether issued or unissued, into the same or a different number of shares without par value, and to change shares without par value, whether issued or unissued, into the same or a different number of shares having a par value.

(i) To change the shares of any class, whether issued or unissued, and whether with or without par value, into a different number of shares of the same class or into the same or a different number of shares, either with or without par value, of other classes.

(j) To create new classes of shares having rights and preferences either prior and superior or subordinate and inferior to the shares of any class then authorized, whether issued or unissued.

(k) To cancel or otherwise affect the right of the holders of the shares of any class to receive dividends which have accrued but have not been declared.

(l) To divide any preferred or special class of shares, whether issued or unissued, into series and fix and determine the designations of such series and the variations in the relative rights and preferences as between the shares of such series.

(m) To authorize the board of directors to establish, out of authorized but unissued shares, series of any preferred or special class of shares and fix and determine the relative rights and preferences of the shares of any series so established.

(n) To authorize the board of directors to fix and determine the relative rights and preferences of the authorized but unissued shares of series theretofore established in respect of which either the relative rights and preferences have not been fixed and determined or the relative rights and preferences theretofore fixed and determined are to be changed.

(o) To revoke, diminish, or enlarge the authority of the board of directors to establish series out of authorized but unissued shares of any preferred or special class and fix and determine the relative rights and preferences of the shares of any series so established.

(p) To limit, deny or grant to shareholders of any class the preemptive right to acquire additional or treasury shares of the corporation, whether then or thereafter authorized.

§ 59. Procedure to Amend Articles of Incorporation

Amendments to the articles of incorporation shall be made in the following manner:

(a) The board of directors shall adopt a resolution setting forth the proposed amendment and, if shares have been issued, directing that it be submitted to a vote at a meeting of shareholders, which may be either the annual or a special meeting. If no shares have been issued, the amendment shall be adopted by resolution of the board of directors and the provisions for adoption by shareholders shall not apply. The resolution may incorporate the proposed amendment in restated articles of incorporation which contain a statement that except for the designated amendment the restated articles of incorpora-

tion correctly set forth without change the corresponding provisions of the articles of incorporation as theretofore amended, and that the restated articles of incorporation together with the designated amendment supersede the original articles of incorporation and all amendments thereto.

(b) Written notice setting forth the proposed amendment or a summary of the changes to be effected thereby shall be given to each shareholder of record entitled to vote thereon within the time and in the manner provided in this Act for the giving of notice of meetings of shareholders. If the meeting be an annual meeting, the proposed amendment of such summary may be included in the notice of such annual meeting.

(c) At such meeting a vote of the shareholders entitled to vote thereon shall be taken on the proposed amendment. The proposed amendment shall be adopted upon receiving the affirmative vote of the holders of a majority of the shares entitled to vote thereon, unless any class of shares is entitled to vote thereon as a class, in which event the proposed amendment shall be adopted upon receiving the affirmative vote of the holders of a majority of the shares of each class of shares entitled to vote thereon as a class and of the total shares entitled to vote thereon.

Any number of amendments may be submitted to the shareholders, and voted upon by them, at one meeting.

§ 60. Class Voting on Amendments

The holders of the outstanding shares of a class shall be entitled to vote as a class upon a proposed amendment, whether or not entitled to vote thereon by the provisions of the articles of incorporation, if the amendment would:

(a) Increase or decrease the aggregate number of authorized shares of such class.

(b) Increase or decrease the par value of the shares of such class.

(c) Effect an exchange, reclassification or cancellation of all or part of the shares of such class.

(d) Effect an exchange, or create a right of exchange,

of all or any part of the shares of another class into the shares of such class.

(e) Change the designations, preferences, limitations or relative rights of the shares of such class.

(f) Change the shares of such class, whether with or without par value, into the same or a different number of shares, either with or without par value, of the same class or another class or classes.

(g) Create a new class of shares having rights and preferences prior and superior to the shares of such class, or increase the rights and preferences or the number of authorized shares, of any class having rights and preferences prior or superior to the shares of such class.

(h) In the case of a preferred or special class of shares, divide the shares of such class into series and fix and determine the designation of such series and the variations in the relative rights and preferences between the shares of such series, or authorize the board of directors to do so.

(i) Limit or deny any existing preemptive rights of the shares of such class.

(j) Cancel or otherwise affect dividends on the shares of such class which have accrued but have not been declared.

§ 61. Articles of Amendment

The articles of amendment shall be executed in duplicate by the corporation by its president or a vice president and by its secretary or an assistant secretary, and verified by one of the officers signing such articles, and shall set forth:

(a) The name of the corporation.

(b) The amendments so adopted.

(c) The date of the adoption of the amendment by the shareholders, or by the board of directors where no shares have been issued.

(d) The number of shares outstanding, and the number of shares entitled to vote thereon, and if the shares of any class are entitled to vote thereon as a class, the designation and number of outstanding shares entitled to vote thereon of each such class.

(e) The number of shares voted for and against such amendment, respectively, and, if the shares of any class are entitled to vote thereon as a class, the number of shares of each such class voted for and against such amendment, respectively, or if no shares have been issued, a statement to that effect.

(f) If such amendment provides for an exchange, reclassification or cancellation of issued shares, and if the manner in which the same shall be effected is not set forth in the amendment, then a statement of the manner in which the same shall be effected.

(g) If such amendment effects a change in the amount of stated capital, then a statement of the manner in which the same is effected and a statement, expressed in dollars, of the amount of stated capital as changed by such amendment.

§ 62. Filing of Articles of Amendment

Duplicate originals of the articles of amendment shall be delivered to the Secretary of State. If the Secretary of State finds that the articles of amendment conform to law, he shall, when all fees and franchise taxes have been paid as in this Act prescribed:

(a) Endorse on each of such duplicate originals the word "Filed," and the month, day and year of the filing thereof.

(b) File one of such duplicate originals in his office.

(c) Issue a certificate of amendment to which he shall affix the other duplicate original.

The certificate of amendment, together with the duplicate original of the articles of amendment affixed thereto by the Secretary of State, shall be returned to the corporation or its representative.

§ 63. Effect of Certificate of Amendment

The amendment shall become effective upon the issuance of the certificate of amendment by the Secretary of State, or on such later date, not more than thirty days subsequent to the filing thereof with the Secretary of State, as shall be provided for in the articles of amendment.

No amendment shall affect any existing cause of action in favor of or against such corporation, or any pending suit to which such corporation shall be a party, or the existing rights of persons other than shareholders; and, in the event the corporate name shall be changed by amendment, no suit brought by or against such corporation under its former name shall abate for that reason.

§ 64. Restated Articles of Incorporation

A domestic corporation may at any time restate its articles of incorporation as theretofore amended, by a resolution adopted by the board of directors.

Upon the adoption of such resolution, restated articles of incorporation shall be executed in duplicate by the corporation by its president or a vice president and by its secretary or assistant secretary and verified by one of the officers signing such articles and shall set forth all of the operative provisions of the articles of incorporation as theretofore amended together with a statement that the restated articles of incorporation correctly set forth without change the corresponding provisions of the articles of incorporation as theretofore amended and that the restated articles of incorporation supersede the original articles of incorporation and all amendments thereto.

Duplicate originals of the restated articles of incorporation shall be delivered to the Secretary of State. If the Secretary of State finds that such restated articles of incorporation conform to law, he shall, when all fees and franchise taxes have been paid as in this Act prescribed:

(1) Endorse on each of such duplicate originals the word "Filed," and the month, day and year of the filing thereof.

(2) File one of such duplicate originals in his office.

(3) Issue a restated certificate of incorporation, to which he shall affix the other duplicate original.

The restated certificate of incorporation, together with the duplicate original of the restated articles of incorporation affixed thereto by the Secretary of State, shall be returned to the corporation or its representative.

Upon the issuance of the restated certificate of incorporation by the Secretary of State, the restated articles of incorporation shall become effective and shall supersede the original articles of incorporation and all amendments thereto.

§ 65. Amendment of Articles of Incorporation in Reorganization Proceedings

Whenever a plan of reorganization of a corporation has been confirmed by decree or order of a court of competent jurisdiction in proceedings for the reorganization of such corporation, pursuant to the provisions of any applicable statute of the United States relating to reorganizations of corporations, the articles of incorporation of the corporation may be amended, in the manner provided in this section, in as many respects as may be necessary to carry out the plan and put it into effect, so long as the articles of incorporation as amended contain only such provisions as might be lawfully contained in original articles of incorporation at the time of making such amendment.

In particular and without limitation upon such general power of amendment, the articles of incorporation may be amended for such purpose so as to:

(A) Change the corporate name, period of duration or corporate purposes of the corporation;

(B) Repeal, alter or amend the by-laws of the corporation;

(C) Change the aggregate number of shares or shares of any class, which the corporation has authority to issue;

(D) Change the preferences, limitations and relative rights in respect of all or any part of the shares of the corporation, and classify, reclassify or cancel all or any part thereof, whether issued or unissued;

(E) Authorize the issuance of bonds, debentures or other obligations of the corporation, whether or not convertible into shares of any class or bearing warrants or other evidences of optional rights to purchase or subscribe for shares of any class, and fix the terms and conditions thereof; and

(F) Constitute or reconstitute and classify or reclassify the board of directors of the corporation, and appoint directors and officers in place of or in addition to all or any of the directors or officers then in office.

Amendments to the articles of incorporation pursuant to this section shall be made in the following manner:

(a) Articles of amendment approved by decree or order of such court shall be executed and verified in duplicate by such person or persons as the court shall designate or appoint for the purpose, and shall set forth the name of the corporation, the amendments of the articles of incorporation approved by the court, the date of the decree or order approving the articles of amendment, the title of the proceedings in which the decree or order was entered, and a statement that such decree or order was entered by a court having jurisdiction of the proceedings for the reorganization of the corporation pursuant to the provisions of an applicable statute of the United States.

(b) Duplicate originals of the articles of amendment shall be delivered to the Secretary of State. If the Secretary of State finds that the articles of amendment conform to law, he shall, when all fees and franchise taxes have been paid as in this Act prescribed:

(1) Endorse on each of such duplicate originals the word "Filed," and the month, day and year of the filing thereof.

(2) File one of such duplicate originals in his office.

(3) Issue a certificate of amendment to which he shall affix the other duplicate original.

The certificate of amendment, together with the duplicate original of the articles of amendment affixed thereto by the Secretary of State, shall be returned to the corporation or its representative.

The amendment shall become effective upon the issuance of the certificate of amendment by the Secretary of State, or on such later date, not more than thirty days subsequent to the filing thereof with the Secretary of State, as shall be provided for in the articles of amendment without any action thereon by the directors or shareholders of the corporation and with the same effect as if the amendments had been adopted by unanimous action of the directors and shareholders of the corporation.

§ 66. Restriction on Redemption or Purchase of Redeemable Shares

No redemption or purchase of redeemable shares shall be made by a corporation when it is insolvent or when such redemption or purchase would render it insolvent, or which would reduce the net assets below the aggregate amount payable to the holders of shares having prior or equal rights to the assets of the corporation upon involuntary dissolution.

§ 67. Cancellation of Redeemable Shares by Redemption or Purchase

When redeemable shares of a corporation are redeemed or purchased by the corporation, the redemption or purchase shall effect a cancellation of such shares, and a statement of cancellation shall be filed as provided in this section. Thereupon such shares shall be restored to the status of authorized but unissued shares, unless the articles of incorporation provide that such shares when redeemed or purchased shall not be reissued, in which case the filing of the statement of cancellation shall constitute an amendment to the articles of incorporation and shall reduce the number of shares of the class so cancelled which the corporation is authorized to issue by the number of shares so cancelled.

The statement of cancellation shall be executed in duplicate by the corporation by its president or a vice president and by its secretary or an assistant secretary, and verified by one of the officers signing such statement, and shall set forth:

(a) The name of the corporation.

(b) The number of redeemable shares cancelled through redemption or purchase, itemized by classes and series.

(c) The aggregate number of issued shares, itemized by classes and series, after giving effect to such cancellation.

(d) The amount, expressed in dollars, of the stated capital of the corporation after giving effect to such cancellation.

(e) If the articles of incorporation provide that the cancelled shares shall not be reissued, the number of shares which the corporation will have authority to issue itemized by classes and series, after giving effect to such cancellation.

Duplicate originals of such statement shall be delivered to the Secretary of State. If the Secretary of State finds that such statement conforms to law, he shall, when all fees and franchise taxes have been paid as in this Act prescribed:

(1) Endorse on each of such duplicate originals the word "Filed," and the month, day and year of the filing thereof.

(2) File one of such duplicate originals in his office.

(3) Return the other duplicate original to the corporation or its representative.

Upon the filing of such statement of cancellation, the stated capital of the corporation shall be deemed to be reduced by that part of the stated capital which was, at the time of such cancellation, represented by the shares so cancelled.

Nothing contained in this section shall be construed to forbid a cancellation of shares or a reduction of stated capital in any other manner permitted by this Act.

§ 68. Cancellation of Other Reacquired Shares

A corporation may at any time, by resolution of its board of directors, cancel all or any part of the shares of the corporation of any class reacquired by it, other than redeemable shares redeemed or purchased, and in such event a statement of cancellation shall be filed as provided in this section.

The statement of cancellation shall be executed in duplicate by the corporation by its president or a vice president and by its secretary or an assistant secretary, and verified by one of the officers signing such statement, and shall set forth:

(a) The name of the corporation.

(b) The number of reacquired shares cancelled by resolution duly adopted by the board of directors, itemized by classes and series, and the date of its adoption.

(c) The aggregate number of issued shares, itemized by classes and series, after giving effect to such cancellation.

(d) The amount, expressed in dollars, of the stated capital of the corporation after giving effect to such cancellation.

Duplicate originals of such statement shall be delivered to the Secretary of State. If the Secretary of State finds that such statement conforms to law, he shall, when all fees and franchise taxes have been paid as in this Act prescribed:

(1) Endorse on each of such duplicate originals the word "Filed," and the month, day and year of the filing thereof.

(2) File one of such duplicate originals in his office.

(3) Return the other duplicate original to the corporation or its representative.

Upon the filing of such statement of cancellation, the stated capital of the corporation shall be deemed to be reduced by that part of the stated capital which was, at the time of such cancellation, represented by the shares so cancelled, and the shares so cancelled shall be restored to the status of authorized but unissued shares.

Nothing contained in this section shall be construed to forbid a cancellation of shares or a reduction of stated capital in any other manner permitted by this Act.

§ 69. Reduction of Stated Capital in Certain Cases

A reduction of the stated capital of a corporation, where such reduction is not accompanied by any action requiring an amendment of the articles of incorporation and not accompanied by a cancellation of shares, may be made in the following manner:

(A) The board of directors shall adopt a resolution setting forth the amount of the proposed reduction and the manner in which the reduction shall be effected, and directing that the question of such reduction be submitted to a vote at a meeting of shareholders, which may be either an annual or a special meeting.

(B) Written notice, stating that the purpose or one of the purposes of such meeting is to consider the question of reducing the stated capital of the corporation in the amount and manner proposed by the board of directors, shall be given to each shareholder of record entitled to vote thereon within the time and in the manner provided in this Act for the giving of notice of meetings of shareholders.

(C) At such meeting a vote of the shareholders entitled to vote thereon shall be taken on the question of approving the proposed reduction of stated capital, which shall require for its adoption the affirmative vote of the holders of a majority of the shares entitled to vote thereon.

When a reduction of the stated capital of a corporation has been approved as provided in this section, a statement shall be executed in duplicate by the corporation by its president or a vice president and by its secretary or an assistant secretary, and verified by one of the officers signing such statement, and shall set forth:

(a) The name of the corporation.

(b) A copy of the resolution of the shareholders approving such reduction, and the date of its adoption.

(c) The number of shares outstanding, and the number of shares entitled to vote thereon.

(d) The number of shares voted for and against such reduction, respectively.

(e) A statement of the manner in which such reduction is effected, and a statement, expressed in dollars, of the amount of stated capital of the corporation after giving effect to such reduction.

Duplicate originals of such statement shall be delivered to the Secretary of State. If the Secretary of State finds that such statement conforms to law, he shall, when all fees and franchise taxes have been paid as in this Act prescribed:

(1) Endorse on each of such duplicate originals the word "Filed," and the month, day and year of the filing thereof.

(2) File one of such duplicate originals in his office.

(3) Return the other duplicate original to the corporation or its representative.

Upon the filing of such statement, the stated capital of the corporation shall be reduced as therein set forth.

No reduction of stated capital shall be made under the provisions of this section which would reduce the amount of the aggregate stated capital of the corporation to an amount equal to or less than the aggregate preferential amounts payable upon all issued shares having a preferential right in the assets of the corporation in the event of involuntary liquidation, plus the aggregate par value of all issued shares having a par value but no preferential right in the assets of the corporation in the event of involuntary liquidation.

§ 70. Special Provisions Relating to Surplus and Reserves

The surplus, if any, created by or arising out of a reduction of the stated capital of a corporation shall be capital surplus.

The capital surplus of a corporation may be increased from time to time by resolution of the board of directors directing that all or a part of the earned surplus of the corporation be transferred to capital surplus.

A corporation may, by resolution of its board of directors, apply any part or all of its capital surplus to the reduction or elimination of any deficit arising from losses, however incurred, but only after first eliminating the earned surplus, if any, of the corporation by applying such losses against earned surplus and only to the extent that such losses exceed the earned surplus, if any. Each such application of capital surplus shall, to the extent thereof, effect a reduction of capital surplus.

A corporation may, by resolution of its board of directors, create a reserve or reserves out of its earned surplus for any proper purpose or purposes, and may abolish any such reserve in the same manner. Earned surplus of the corporation to the extent so reserved shall not be available for the payment of dividends or other distributions by the corporation except as expressly permitted by this Act.

§ 71. Procedure for Merger

Any two or more domestic corporations may merge into one of such corporations pursuant to a plan of merger approved in the manner provided in this Act.

The board of directors of each corporation shall, by resolution adopted by each such board, approve a plan of merger setting forth:

(a) The names of the corporations proposing to merge, and the name of the corporation into which they propose to merge, which is hereinafter designated as the surviving corporation.

(b) The terms and conditions of the proposed merger.

(c) The manner and basis of converting the shares of each corporation into shares, obligations or other securities of the surviving corporation or of any other corporation or, in whole or in part, into cash or other property.

(d) A statement of any changes in the articles of incorporation of the surviving corporation to be effected by such merger.

(e) Such other provisions with respect to the proposed merger as are deemed necessary or desirable.

§ 72. Procedure for Consolidation

Any two or more domestic corporations may consolidate into a new corporation pursuant to a plan of consolidation approved in the manner provided in this Act.

The board of directors of each corporation shall, by a resolution adopted by each such board, approve a plan of consolidation setting forth:

(a) The names of the corporations proposing to consolidate, and the name of the new corporation into which they propose to consolidate, which is hereinafter designated as the new corporation.

(b) The terms and conditions of the proposed consolidation.

(c) The manner and basis of converting the shares of each corporation into shares, obligations or other securities of the new corporation or of any other corporation or, in whole or in part, into cash or other property.

(d) With respect to the new corporation, all of the statements required to be set forth in articles of incorporation for corporations organized under this Act.

(e) Such other provisions with respect to the proposed consolidation as are deemed necessary or desirable.

§ 72A. **Procedure for Share Exchange**

All the issued or all the outstanding shares of one or more classes of any domestic corporation may be acquired through the exchange of all such shares of such class or classes by another domestic or foreign corporation pursuant to a plan of exchange approved in the manner provided in this Act.

The board of directors of each corporation shall, by resolution adopted by each such board, approve a plan of exchange setting forth:

(a) The name of the corporation the shares of which are proposed to be acquired by exchange and the name of the corporation to acquire the shares of such corporation in the exchange, which is hereinafter designated as the acquiring corporation.

(b) The terms and conditions of the proposed exchange.

(c) The manner and basis of exchanging the shares to be acquired for shares, obligations or other securities of the acquiring corporation or any other corporation, or, in whole or in part, for cash or other property.

(d) Such other provisions with respect to the proposed exchange as are deemed necessary or desirable.

The procedure authorized by this Section shall not be deemed to limit the power of a corporation to acquire all or part of the shares of any class or classes of a corporation through a voluntary exchange or otherwise by agreement with the shareholders.

§ 73. **Approval by Shareholders**

First, second and third paragraphs of Section 73 are designated subsections (a), (b) and (c), respectively, and fourth subsection (d) is added, as follows:

(d) (1) Notwithstanding the provisions of subsections (a) and (b), submission of a plan of merger to a vote at a meeting of shareholders of a surviving corporation shall not be required if—

(i) the articles of incorporation of the surviving corporation do not differ except in name from those of the corporation before the merger,

(ii) each holder of shares of the surviving corporation which were outstanding immediately before the effective date of the merger is to hold the same number of shares with identical rights immediately after,

(iii) the number of voting shares outstanding immediately after the merger, plus the number of voting shares issuable on conversion of other securities issued by virtue of the terms of the merger and on exercise of rights and warrants so issued, will not exceed by more than 20 percent the number of voting shares outstanding immediately before the merger, and

(iv) the number of participating shares outstanding immediately after the merger, plus the number of participating shares issuable on conversion of other securities issued by virtue of the terms of the merger and on exercise of rights and warrants so issued, will not exceed by more than 20 percent the number of participating shares outstanding immediately before the merger.

(2) As used in this subsection—

(i) "voting shares" means shares which entitle their holders to vote unconditionally in elections of directors;

(ii) "participating shares" means shares which entitle their holders to participate without limitation in distribution of earnings or surplus.

At each such meeting, a vote of the shareholders shall be taken on the proposed plan. The plan shall be approved upon receiving the affirmative vote of the holders of a majority of the shares entitled to vote thereon of each such corporation, unless any class of shares of any such corporation is entitled to vote thereon as a class, in which event, as to such corporation, the plan shall be approved upon receiving the affirmative vote of the holders of a majority of the shares of each class of shares entitled to vote thereon as a class and of the total shares entitled to vote thereon. Any class of shares of any such corporation shall be entitled to vote as a class if any such plan contains any provision which, if contained in a proposed amendment to articles of incorporation, would entitle such class of shares to vote as a class and, in the case of an exchange, if the class is included in the exchange.

After such approval by a vote of the shareholders of each such corporation, and at any time prior to the filing of the articles of merger, consolidation or exchange, the merger, consolidation or exchange may be abandoned pursuant to provisions therefor, if any, set forth in the plan.

§ 74. Articles of Merger or Consolidation or Exchange

First paragraph of Section 74 is designated as subsection (a), and is amended to read as follows:

(a) Upon receiving the approvals required by Sections 71, 72 and 73, articles of merger or articles of consolidation shall be executed in duplicate by each corporation by its president or a vice president and by its secretary or an assistant secretary, and verified by one of the officers of each corporation signing such articles, and shall set forth:

(1) The plan of merger or the plan of consolidation;

(2) As to each corporation, either (i) the number of shares outstanding, and, if the shares of any class are entitled to vote as a class, the designation and number of outstanding shares of each such class or (ii) a statement that the vote of shareholders is not required by virtue of subsection 73(d);

(3) As to each corporation the approval of whose shareholders is required, the number of shares voted for and against such plan, respectively, and, if the shares of any class are entitled to vote as a class, the number of shares of each such class voted for and against such plan, respectively.

The second and third paragraphs of Section 74 are designated subsections (b) and (c), respectively.

§ 75. Merger of Subsidiary Corporation

Any corporation owning at least ninety per cent of the outstanding shares of each class of another corporation may merge such other corporation into itself without approval by a vote of the shareholders of either corporation. Its board of directors shall, by resolution, approve a plan of merger setting forth:

(A) The name of the subsidiary corporation and the name of the corporation owning at least ninety per cent of its shares, which is hereinafter designated as the surviving corporation.

(B) The manner and basis of converting the shares of the subsidiary corporation into shares, obligations or other securities of the surviving corporation or of any other corporation or, in whole or in part, into cash or other property.

A copy of such plan of merger shall be mailed to each shareholder of record of the subsidiary corporation.

Articles of merger shall be executed in duplicate by the surviving corporation by its president or a vice president and by its secretary or an assistant secretary, and verified by one of its officers signing such articles, and shall set forth:

(a) The plan of merger;

(b) The number of outstanding shares of each class of the subsidiary corporation and the number of such shares of each class owned by the surviving corporation; and

(c) The date of the mailing to shareholders of the subsidiary corporation of a copy of the plan of merger.

On and after the thirtieth day after the mailing of a copy of the plan of merger to shareholders of the subsidiary corporation or upon the waiver thereof by the holders of all outstanding shares duplicate originals of the articles of merger shall be delivered to the Secretary of State. If the Secretary of State finds that such articles conform to law, he shall, when all fees and franchise taxes have been paid as in this Act prescribed:

(1) Endorse on each of such duplicate originals the word "Filed," and the month, day and year of the filing thereof,

(2) File one of such duplicate originals in his office, and

(3) Issue a certificate of merger to which he shall affix

the other duplicate original.

The certificate of merger, together with the duplicate original of the articles of merger affixed thereto by the Secretary of State, shall be returned to the surviving corporation or its representative.

§ 76. Effect of Merger or Consolidation

A merger, consolidation or exchange shall become effective upon the issuance of a certificate of merger, consolidation or exchange by the Secretary of State, or on such later date, not more than thirty days subsequent to the filing thereof with the Secretary of State, as shall be provided for in the plan.

When a merger or consolidation has been effective:

(a) The several corporations parties to the plan of merger or consolidation shall be a single corporation, which, in the case of a merger, shall be that corporation designated in the plan of merger as the surviving corporation, and, in the case of a consolidation, shall be the new corporation provided for in the plan of consolidation.

(b) The separate existence of all corporations parties to the plan of merger or consolidation, except the surviving or new corporation, shall cease.

(c) Such surviving or new corporation shall have all the rights, privileges, immunities and powers and shall be subject to all the duties and liabilities of a corporation organized under this Act.

(d) Such surviving or new corporation shall thereupon and thereafter possess all the rights, privileges, immunities, and franchises, of a public as well as of a private nature, of each of the merging or consolidating corporations; and all property, real, personal and mixed, and all debts due on whatever account, including subscriptions to shares, and all other choses in action, and all and every other interest of or belonging to or due to each of the corporations so merged or consolidated, shall be taken and deemed to be transferred to and vested in such single corporation without further act or deed; and the title to any real estate, or any interest therein, vested in any of such corporations shall not revert or be in any way impaired by reason of such merger or consolidation.

(e) Such surviving or new corporation shall thenceforth be responsible and liable for all the liabilities and obligations of each of the corporations so merged or consolidated; and any claim existing or action or proceeding pending by or against any of such corporations may be prosecuted as if such merger or consolidation had not taken place, or such surviving or new corporation may be substituted in its place. Neither the rights of creditors nor any liens upon the property of any such corporation shall be impaired by such merger or consolidation.

(f) In the case of a merger, the articles of incorporation of the surviving corporation shall be deemed to be amended to the extent, if any, that changes in its articles of incorporation are stated in the plan of merger; and, in the case of a consolidation, the statements set forth in the articles of consolidation and which are required or permitted to be set forth in the articles of incorporation of corporations organized under this Act shall be deemed to be the original articles of incorporation of the new corporation.

When a merger, consolidation or exchange has become effective, the shares of the corporation or corporations party to the plan that are, under the terms of the plan, to be converted or exchanged, shall cease to exist, in the case of a merger or consolidation, or be deemed to be exchanged in the case of an exchange, and the holders of such shares shall thereafter be entitled only to the shares, obligations, other securities, cash or other property into which they shall have been converted or for which they shall have exchanged, in accordance with the plan, subject to any rights under Section 80 of this Act.

§ 77. Merger or Consolidation of Domestic and Foreign Corporations

One or more foreign corporations and one or more domestic corporations may be merged or consolidated, or participate in an exchange, in the following manner, if such merger, consolidation or exchange is permitted by the laws of the state under which each such foreign corporation is organized:

(a) Each domestic corporation shall comply with the provisions of this Act with respect to the merger, consolidation or exchange, as the case may be, of domestic corporations and each foreign corporation shall comply with the applicable provisions of the laws of the state under which it is organized.

(b) If the surviving or new corporation in a merger or consolidation is to be governed by the laws of any state other than this State, it shall comply with the provisions of this Act with respect to foreign corporations if it is to transact business in this State, and in every case it shall file with the Secretary of State of this State:

(1) An agreement that it may be served with process in this State in any proceeding for the enforcement of any obligation of any domestic corporation which is a party to such merger or consolidation and in any proceeding for the enforcement of the rights of a dissenting shareholder of any such domestic corporation against the surviving or new corporation;

(2) An irrevocable appointment of the Secretary of State of this State as its agent to accept service of process in any such proceeding; and

(3) An agreement that it will promptly pay to the dissenting shareholders of any such domestic corporation, the amount, if any, to which they shall be entitled under provisions of this Act with respect to the rights of dissenting shareholders.

§ 78. Sale of Assets in Regular Course of Business and Mortgage or Pledge of Assets

The sale, lease, exchange, or other disposition of all, or substantially all, the property and assets of a corporation in the usual and regular course of its business and the mortgage or pledge of any or all property and assets of a corporation whether or not in the usual and regular course of business may be made upon such terms and conditions and for such consideration, which may consist in whole or in part of cash or other property, including shares, obligations or other securities of any other corporation, domestic or foreign, as shall be authorized by its board of directors; and in any such case no authorization or consent of the shareholders shall be required.

§ 79. Sale of Assets Other Than in Regular Course of Business

A sale, lease, exchange, or other disposition of all, or substantially all, the property and assets, with or without the good will, of a corporation, if not in the usual and regular course of its business, may be made upon such terms and conditions and for such consideration, which may consist in whole or in part of cash or other property, including shares, obligations

or other securities of any other corporation, domestic or foreign, as may be authorized in the following manner:

(a) The board of directors shall adopt a resolution recommending such sale, lease, exchange, or other disposition and directing the submission thereof to a vote at a meeting of shareholders, which may be either an annual or a special meeting.

(b) Written notice shall be given to each shareholder of record, whether or not entitled to vote at such meeting, not less than twenty days before such meeting, in the manner provided in this Act for the giving of notice of meetings of shareholders, and, whether the meeting be an annual or a special meeting, shall state that the purpose, or one of the purposes is to consider the proposed sale, lease, exchange, or other disposition.

(c) At such meeting the shareholders may authorize such sale, lease, exchange, or other disposition and may fix, or may authorize the board of directors to fix, any or all of the terms and conditions thereof and the consideration to be received by the corporation therefor. Such authorization shall require the affirmative vote of the holders of a majority of the shares of the corporation entitled to vote thereon, unless any class of shares is entitled to vote thereon as a class, in which event such authorization shall require the affirmative vote of the holders of a majority of the shares of each class of shares entitled to vote as a class thereon and of the total shares entitled to vote thereon.

(d) After such authorization by a vote of shareholders, the board of directors nevertheless, in its discretion, may abandon such sale, lease, exchange, or other disposition of assets, subject to the rights of third parties under any contracts relating thereto, without further action or approval by shareholders.

§ 80. Right of Shareholders to Dissent and Obtain Payment for Shares

(a) Any shareholder of a corporation shall have the right to dissent from, and to obtain payment for his shares in the event of, any of the following corporate actions:

(1) Any plan of merger or consolidation to which the corporation is a party, except as provided in subsection (c);

(2) Any sale or exchange of all or substantially all of the property and assets of the corporation not made in the usual or regular course of its business, including a sale in dissolution, but not including a sale pursuant to an order of a court having jurisdiction in the premises or a sale for cash on terms requiring that all or substantially all of the net proceeds of sale be distributed to the shareholders in accordance with their respective interests within one year after the date of sale;

(3) Any plan of exchange to which the corporation is a party as the corporation the shares of which are to be acquired;

(4) Any amendment of the articles of incorporation which materially and adversely affects the rights appurtenant to the shares of the dissenting shareholder in that it—

(i) alters or abolishes a preferential right of such shares;

(ii) creates, alters or abolishes a right in respect of the redemption of such shares, including a provision respecting a sinking fund for the redemption or repurchase of such shares;

(iii) alters or abolishes a preemptive right of the holder of such shares to acquire shares or other securities;

(iv) excludes or limits the right of the holder of such shares to vote on any matter, or to cumulate his votes, except as such right may be limited by dilution through the issuance of shares or other securities with similar voting rights; or

(5) Any other corporate action taken pursuant to a shareholder vote with respect to which the articles of incorporation, the bylaws, or a resolution of the board of directors directs that dissenting shareholders shall have a right to obtain payment for their shares.

(b) (1) A record holder of shares may assert dissenters' rights as to less than all of the shares registered in his name only if he dissents with respect to all the shares beneficially owned by any one person, and discloses the name and address of the person or persons on whose behalf he dissents. In that event, his rights shall be determined as if the shares as to which he has dissented and his other shares were registered in the names of different shareholders.

(2) A beneficial owner of shares who is not the record holder may assert dissenters' rights with respect to shares held on his behalf, and shall be treated as a dissenting shareholder under the terms of this section and Section 81 if he submits to the corporation at the time of or before the assertion of these rights a written consent of the record holder.

(c) The right to obtain payment under this section shall not apply to the shareholders of the surviving corporation in a merger if a vote of the shareholders of such corporation is not necessary to authorize such merger.

(d) A shareholder of a corporation who has a right under this section to obtain payment for his shares shall have no right at law or in equity to attack the validity of the corporate action that gives rise to his right to obtain payment, nor to have the action set aside or rescinded, except when the corporate action is unlawful or fraudulent with regard to the complaining shareholder or to the corporation.

§ 81. **Procedures for Protection of Dissenters' Rights**

(a) As used in this section—

(1) "Dissenter" means a shareholder or beneficial owner who is entitled to and does assert dissenters' rights under Section 80, and who has performed every act required up to the time involved for the assertion of such rights.

(2) "Corporation" means the issuer of the shares held by the dissenter before the corporate action, or the successor by merger or consolidation of that issuer.

(3) "Fair value" of shares means their value immediately before the effectuation of the corporate action to which the dissenter objects, excluding any appreciation or depreciation in anticipation of such corporate action unless such exclusion would be inequitable.

(4) "Interest" means interest from the effective date of the corporate action until the date of payment, at the average rate currently paid by the corporation on its principal bank loans, or, if none, at such rate as is fair and equitable under all the circumstances.

(b) If a proposed corporate action which would give rise to dissenters' rights under Section 80(a) is submitted to a vote at a meeting of shareholders, the notice of meeting shall notify all shareholders that they have or may have a right to dissent and obtain payment for their shares by complying with the terms of this Section, and shall be accompanied by a copy of Sections 80 and 81 of this Act.

(c) If the proposed corporate action is submitted to a vote at a meeting of shareholders, any shareholder who wishes to dissent and obtain payment for his shares must file with the corporation, prior to the vote, a written notice of intention to demand that he be paid fair compensation for his shares if the proposed action is effectuated, and shall refrain from voting his shares in approval of such action. A shareholder who fails in either respect shall acquire no right to payment for his shares under this section or Section 80.

(d) If the proposed corporate action is approved by the required vote at a meeting of shareholders, the corporation shall mail a further notice to all shareholders who gave due notice of intention to demand payment and who refrained from voting in favor of the proposed action. If the proposed corporate action is to be taken without a vote of shareholders, the corporation shall send to all shareholders who are entitled to dissent and demand payment for their shares a notice of the adoption of the plan of corporate action. The notice shall (1) state where and when a demand for payment must be sent and certificates of certificated shares must be deposited in order to obtain payment, (2) inform holders of uncertificated shares to what extent transfer of shares will be restricted from the time that demand for payment is received, (3) supply a form for demanding payment which includes a request for certification of the date on which the shareholder, or the person on whose behalf the shareholder dissents, acquired beneficial ownership of the shares, and (4) be accompanied by a copy of Sections 80 and 81 of this Act. The time set for the demand and deposit shall be not less than 30 days from the mailing of the notice.

(e) A shareholder who fails to demand payment, or fails (in the case of certificated shares) to deposit certificates, as required by a notice pursuant to

subsection (d) shall have no right under this section or Section 80 to receive payment for his shares. If the shares are not represented by certificates, the corporation may restrict their transfer from the time of receipt of demand for payment until effectuation of the proposed corporate action, or the release of restrictions under the terms of subsection (f). The dissenter shall retain all other rights of a shareholder until these rights are modified by effectuation of the proposed corporate action.

(f)(1) Within 60 days after the date set for demanding payment and depositing certificates, if the corporation has not effectuated the proposed corporate action and remitted payment for shares pursuant to paragraph (3), it shall return any certificates that have been deposited, and release uncertificated shares from any transfer restrictions imposed by reason of the demand for payment.

(2) When uncertificated shares have been released from transfer restrictions, and deposited certificates have been returned, the corporation may at any later time send a new notice conforming to the requirements of subsection (d), with like effect.

(3) Immediately upon effectuation of the proposed corporate action, or upon receipt of demand for payment if the corporate action has already been effectuated, the corporation shall remit to dissenters who have made demand and (if their shares are certificated) have deposited their certificates the amount which the corporation estimates to be the fair value of the shares, with interest if any has accrued. The remittance shall be accompanied by—

> (i) the corporation's closing balance sheet and statement of income for a fiscal year ending not more than 16 months before the date of remittance, together with the latest available interim financial statements;

> (ii) a statement of the corporation's estimate of fair value of the shares; and

> (iii) a notice of the dissenter's right to demand supplemental payment, accompanied by a copy of Sections 80 and 81 of this Act.

(g)(1) If the corporation fails to remit as required by subsection (f), or if the dissenter believes that the amount remitted is less than the fair value of his shares, or that the interest is not correctly determined, he may send the corporation his own estimate of the value of the shares or of the interest, and demand payment of the deficiency.

(2) If the dissenter does not file such an estimate within 30 days after the corporation's mailing of its remittance, he shall be entitled to no more than the amount remitted.

(h) (1) Within 60 days after receiving a demand for payment pursuant to subsection (g), if any such demands for payment remain unsettled, the corporation shall file in an appropriate court a petition requesting that the fair value of the shares and interest thereon be determined by the court.

(2) An appropriate court shall be a court of competent jurisdiction in the county of this state where the registered office of the corporation is located. If, in the case of a merger or consolidation or exchange of shares, the corporation is a foreign corporation without a registered office in this state, the petition shall be filed in the county where the registered office of the domestic corporation was last located.

(3) All dissenters, wherever residing, whose demands have not been settled shall be made parties to the proceeding as in an action against their shares. A copy of the petition shall be served on each such dissenter; if a dissenter is a nonresident, the copy may be served on him by registered or certified mail or by publication as provided by law.

(4) The jurisdiction of the court shall be plenary and exclusive. The court may appoint one or more persons as appraisers to receive evidence and recommend a decision on the question of fair value. The appraisers shall have such power and authority as shall be specified in the order of their appointment or in any amendment thereof. The dissenters shall be entitled to discovery in the same manner as parties in other civil suits.

(5) All dissenters who are made parties shall be entitled to judgment for the amount by which the fair value of their shares is found to exceed the amount previously remitted, with interest.

(6) If the corporation fails to file a petition as provided in paragraph (1) of this subsection, each dissenter who made a demand and who has not already settled his claim against the corporation shall be paid by the corporation the amount demanded by him, with interest, and may sue therefor in an appropriate court.

(i) (1) The costs and expenses of any proceeding under subsection (h), including the reasonable compensation and expenses of appraisers appointed by the court, shall be determined by the court and assessed against the corporation, except that any part of the costs and expenses may be apportioned and assessed as the court may deem equitable against all or some of the dissenters who are parties and whose action in demanding supplemental payment the court finds to be arbitrary, vexatious, or not in good faith.

(2) Fees and expenses of counsel and of experts for the respective parties may be assessed as the court may deem equitable against the corporation and in favor of any or all dissenters if the corporation failed to comply substantially with the requirements of this section, and may be assessed against either the corporation or a dissenter, in favor of any other party, if the court finds that the party against whom the fees and expenses are assessed acted arbitrarily, vexatiously, or not in good faith in respect to the rights provided by this Section and Section 80.

(3) If the court finds that the services of counsel for any dissenter were of substantial benefit to other dissenters similarly situated, and should not be assessed against the corporation, it may award to these counsel reasonable fees to be paid out of the amounts awarded to the dissenters who were benefitted.

(j) (1) Notwithstanding the foregoing provisions of this section, the corporation may elect to withhold the remittance required by subsection (f) from any dissenter with respect to shares of which the dissenter (or the person on whose behalf the dissenter acts) was not the beneficial owner on the date of the first announcement to news media or to shareholders of the terms of the proposed corporate action. With respect to such shares, the corporation shall, upon effectuating the corporate action, state to each dissenter its estimate of the fair value of the shares, state the rate of interest to be used (explaining the basis thereof), and offer to pay the resulting amounts on receiving the dissenter's agreement to accept them in full satisfaction.

(2) If the dissenter believes that the amount offered is less than the fair value of the shares and interest determined according to this section, he may within 30 days after the date of mailing of the corporation's offer, mail the corporation his own estimate of fair value and interest, and demand their payment. If the dissenter fails to do so, he shall be entitled to no more than the corporation's offer.

(3) If the dissenter makes a demand as provided in paragraph (2), the provisions of subsections (h) and (i) shall apply to further proceedings on the dissenter's demand. [See subsections (c) and (d), supra.]

§ 82. Voluntary Dissolution by Incorporators

A corporation which has not commenced business and which has not issued any shares, may be voluntarily dissolved by its incorporators at any time in the following manner:

(a) Articles of dissolution shall be executed in duplicate by a majority of the incorporators, and verified by them, and shall set forth:

(1) The name of the corporation.

(2) The date of issuance of its certificate of incorporation.

(3) That none of its shares has been issued.

(4) That the corporation has not commenced business.

(5) That the amount, if any, actually paid in on subscriptions for its shares, less any part thereof disbursed for necessary expenses, has been returned to those entitled thereto.

(6) That no debts of the corporation remain unpaid.

(7) That a majority of the incorporators elect that the corporation be dissolved.

(b) Duplicate originals of the articles of dissolution shall be delivered to the Secretary of State. If the Secretary of State finds that the articles of dissolution conform to law, he shall, when all fees and franchise taxes have been paid as in this Act prescribed:

(1) Endorse on each of such duplicate originals the word "Filed," and the month, day and year of the filing thereof.

(2) File one of such duplicate originals in his office.

(3) Issue a certificate of dissolution to which he shall affix the other duplicate original.

The certificate of dissolution, together with the duplicate original of the articles of dissolution affixed thereto by the Secretary of State, shall be returned to the incorporators or their representative. Upon the issuance of such certificate of dissolution by the Secretary of State, the existence of the corporation shall cease.

§ 83. Voluntary Dissolution by Consent of Shareholders

A corporation may be voluntarily dissolved by the written consent of all of its shareholders.

Upon the execution of such written consent, a statement of intent to dissolve shall be executed in duplicate by the corporation by its president or a vice president and by its secretary or an assistant secretary, and verified by one of the officers signing such statement, which statement shall set forth:

(a) The name of the corporation.

(b) The names and respective addresses of its officers.

(c) The names and respective addresses of its directors.

(d) A copy of the written consent signed by all shareholders of the corporation.

(e) A statement that such written consent has been signed by all shareholders of the corporation or signed in their names by their attorneys thereunto duly authorized.

§ 84. Voluntary Dissolution by Act of Corporation

A corporation may be dissolved by the act of the corporation, when authorized in the following manner:

(a) The board of directors shall adopt a resolution recommending that the corporation be dissolved, and directing that the question of such dissolution be submitted to a vote at a meeting of shareholders, which may be either an annual or a special meeting.

(b) Written notice shall be given to each shareholder of record entitled to vote at such meeting within the time and in the manner provided in this Act for the giving of notice of meetings of shareholders, and, whether the meeting be an annual or special meeting, shall state that the purpose, or one of the purposes, of such meeting is to consider the advisability of dissolving the corporation.

(c) At such meeting a vote of shareholders entitled to vote thereat shall be taken on a resolution to dissolve the corporation. Such resolution shall be adopted upon receiving the affirmative vote of the holders of a majority of the shares of the corporation entitled to vote thereon, unless any class of shares is entitled to vote thereon as a class, in which event the resolution shall be adopted upon receiving the affirmative vote of the holders of a majority of the shares of each class of shares entitled to vote thereon as a class and of the total shares entitled to vote thereon.

(d) Upon the adoption of such resolution, a statement of intent to dissolve shall be executed in duplicate by the corporation by its president or a vice president and by its secretary or an assistant secretary, and verified by one of the officers signing such statement, which statement shall set forth:

(1) The name of the corporation.

(2) The names and respective addresses of its officers.

(3) The names and respective addresses of its directors.

(4) A copy of the resolution adopted by the shareholders authorizing the dissolution of the corporation.

(5) The number of shares outstanding, and, if the shares of any class are entitled to vote as a class, the designation and number of outstanding shares of each such class.

(6) The number of shares voted for and against the resolution, respectively, and, if the shares of any class are entitled to vote as a class, the number of shares of each such class voted for and against the resolution, respectively.

§ 85. Filing of Statement of Intent to Dissolve

Duplicate originals of the statement of intent to dissolve, whether by consent of shareholders or by act of the corporation, shall be delivered to the Secretary of State. If the Secretary of State finds that such statement conforms to law, he shall, when all fees and franchise taxes have been paid as in this Act prescribed:

(a) Endorse on each of such duplicate originals the word "Filed," and the month, day and year of the filing thereof.

(b) File one of such duplicate originals in his office.

(c) Return the other duplicate original to the corporation or its representative.

§ 86. Effect of Statement of Intent to Dissolve

Upon the filing by the Secretary of State of a statement of intent to dissolve, whether by consent of shareholders or by act of the corporation, the corporation shall cease to carry on its business, except insofar as may be necessary for the winding up thereof, but its corporate existence shall continue until a certificate of dissolution has been issued by the Secretary of State or until a decree dissolving the corporation has been entered by a court of competent jurisdiction as in this Act provided.

§ 87. Procedure after Filing of Statement of Intent to Dissolve

After the filing by the Secretary of State of a statement of intent to dissolve:

(a) The corporation shall immediately cause notice thereof to be mailed to each known creditor of the corporation.

(b) The corporation shall proceed to collect its assets, convey and dispose of such of its properties as are not to be distributed in kind to its shareholders, pay, satisfy and discharge its liabilities and obligations and do all other acts required to liquidate its business and affairs, and, after paying or adequately providing for the payment of all its obligations, distribute the remainder of its assets, either in cash or in kind, among its shareholders according to their respective rights and interests.

(c) The corporation, at any time during the liquidation of its business and affairs, may make application to a court of competent jurisdiction within the state and judicial subdivision in which the registered office or principal place of business of the corporation is situated, to have the liquidation continued under the supervision of the court as provided in this Act.

§ 88. Revocation of Voluntary Dissolution Proceedings by Consent of Shareholders

By the written consent of all of its shareholders, a

corporation may, at any time prior to the issuance of a certificate of dissolution by the Secretary of State, revoke voluntary dissolution proceedings theretofore taken, in the following manner:

Upon the execution of such written consent, a statement of revocation of voluntary dissolution proceedings shall be executed in duplicate by the corporation by its president or a vice president and by its secretary or an assistant secretary, and verified by one of the officers signing such statement, which statement shall set forth:

(a) The name of the corporation.

(b) The names and respective addresses of its officers.

(c) The names and respective addresses of its directors.

(d) A copy of the written consent signed by all shareholders of the corporation revoking such voluntary dissolution proceedings.

(e) That such written consent has been signed by all shareholders of the corporation or signed in their names by their attorneys thereunto duly authorized.

§ 89. Revocation of Voluntary Dissolution Proceedings by Act of Corporation

By the act of the corporation, a corporation may, at any time prior to the issuance of a certificate of dissolution by the Secretary of State, revoke voluntary dissolution proceedings theretofore taken, in the following manner:

(a) The board of directors shall adopt a resolution recommending that the voluntary dissolution proceedings be revoked, and directing that the question of such revocation be submitted to a vote at a special meeting of shareholders.

(b) Written notice, stating that the purpose or one of the purposes of such meeting is to consider the advisability of revoking the voluntary dissolution proceedings, shall be given to each shareholder of record entitled to vote at such meeting within the time and in the manner provided in this Act for the giving of notice of special meetings of shareholders.

(c) At such meeting a vote of the shareholders entitled to vote thereat shall be taken on a resolution to revoke the voluntary dissolution proceedings,

which shall require for its adoption the affirmative vote of the holders of a majority of the shares entitled to vote thereon.

(d) Upon the adoption of such resolution, a statement of revocation of voluntary dissolution proceedings shall be executed in duplicate by the corporation by its president or a vice president and by its secretary or an assistant secretary, and verified by one of the officers signing such statement, which statement shall set forth:

(1) The name of the corporation.

(2) The names and respective addresses of its officers.

(3) The names and respective addresses of its directors.

(4) A copy of the resolution adopted by the shareholders revoking the voluntary dissolution proceedings.

(5) The number of shares outstanding.

(6) The number of shares voted for and against the resolution, respectively.

§ 90. Filing of Statement of Revocation of Voluntary Dissolution Proceedings

Duplicate originals of the statement of revocation of voluntary dissolution proceedings, whether by consent of shareholders or by act of the corporation, shall be delivered to the Secretary of State. If the Secretary of State finds that such statement conforms to law, he shall, when all fees and franchise taxes have been paid as in this Act prescribed:

(a) Endorse on each of such duplicate originals the word "Filed," and the month, day and year of the filing thereof.

(b) File one of such duplicate originals in his office.

(c) Return the other duplicate original to the corporation or its representative.

§ 91. Effect of Statement of Revocation of Voluntary Dissolution Proceedings

Upon the filing by the Secretary of State of a statement of revocation of voluntary dissolution proceedings, whether by consent of shareholders or by act of the corporation, the revocation of the voluntary dissolution proceedings shall become effective and the corporation may again carry on its business.

§ 92. Articles of Dissolution

If voluntary dissolution proceedings have not been revoked, then when all debts, liabilities and obligations of the corporation have been paid and discharged, or adequate provision has been made therefor, and all of the remaining property and assets of the corporation have been distributed to its shareholders, articles of dissolution shall be executed in duplicate by the corporation by its president or a vice president and by its secretary or an assistant secretary, and verified by one of the officers signing such statement, which statement shall set forth:

(a) The name of the corporation.

(b) That the Secretary of State has theretofore filed a statement of intent to dissolve the corporation, and the date on which such statement was filed.

(c) That all debts, obligations and liabilities of the corporation have been paid and discharged or that adequate provision has been made therefor.

(d) That all the remaining property and assets of the corporation have been distributed among its shareholders in accordance with their respective rights and interests.

(e) That there are no suits pending against the corporation in any court, or that adequate provision has been made for the satisfaction of any judgment, order or decree which may be entered against it in any pending suit.

§ 93. Filing of Articles of Dissolution

Duplicate originals of such articles of dissolution shall be delivered to the Secretary of State. If the Secretary of State finds that such articles of dissolution conform to law, he shall, when all fees and franchise taxes have been paid as in this Act prescribed:

(a) Endorse on each of such duplicate originals the word "Filed," and the month, day and year of the filing thereof.

(b) File one of such duplicate originals in his office.

(c) Issue a certificate of dissolution to which he shall affix the other duplicate original.

The certificate of dissolution, together with the duplicate original of the articles of dissolution affixed

thereto by the Secretary of State, shall be returned to the representative of the dissolved corporation. Upon the issuance of such certificate of dissolution the existence of the corporation shall cease, except for the purpose of suits, other proceedings and appropriate corporate action by shareholders, directors and officers as provided in this Act.

§ 94. Involuntary Dissolution

A corporation may be dissolved involuntarily by a decree of the . . . . court in an action filed by the Attorney General when it is established that:

(a) The corporation has failed to file its annual report within the time required by this Act, or has failed to pay its franchise tax on or before the first day of August of the year in which such franchise tax becomes due and payable; or

(b) The corporation procured its articles of incorporation through fraud; or

(c) The corporation has continued to exceed or abuse the authority conferred upon it by law; or

(d) The corporation has failed for thirty days to appoint and maintain a registered agent in this State; or

(e) The corporation has failed for thirty days after change of its registered office or registered agent to file in the office of the Secretary of State a statement of such change.

§ 95. Notification to Attorney General

The Secretary of State, on or before the last day of December of each year, shall certify to the Attorney General the names of all corporations which have failed to file their annual reports or to pay franchise taxes in accordance with the provisions of this Act, together with the facts pertinent thereto. He shall also certify, from time to time, the names of all corporations which have given other cause for dissolution as provided in this Act, together with the facts pertinent thereto. Whenever the Secretary of State shall certify the name of a corporation to the Attorney General as having given any cause for dissolution, the Secretary of State shall concurrently mail to the corporation at its registered office a notice that such certification has been made. Upon the receipt of such certification, the Attorney General shall file an action in the name of the State against such corporation for its dissolution.

Every such certificate from the Secretary of State to the Attorney General pertaining to the failure of a corporation to file an annual report or pay a franchise tax shall be taken and received in all courts as prima facie evidence of the facts therein stated. If, before action is filed, the corporation shall file its annual report or pay its franchise tax, together with all penalties thereon, or shall appoint or maintain a registered agent as provided in this Act, or shall file with the Secretary of State the required statement of change of registered office or registered agent, such fact shall be forthwith certified by the Secretary of State to the Attorney General and he shall not file an action against such corporation for such cause. If, after action is filed, the corporation shall file its annual report or pay its franchise tax, together with all penalties thereon, or shall appoint or maintain a registered agent as provided in this Act, or shall file with the Secretary of State the required statement of change of registered office or registered agent, and shall pay the costs of such action, the action for such cause shall abate.

§ 96. **Venue and Process**

Every action for the involuntary dissolution of a corporation shall be commenced by the Attorney General either in the . . . . court of the county in which the registered office of the corporation is situated, or in the . . . . court of . . . . county. Summons shall issue and be served as in other civil actions. If process is returned not found, the Attorney General shall cause publication to be made as in other civil cases in some newspaper published in the county where the registered office of the corporation is situated, containing a notice of the pendency of such action, the title of the court, the title of the action, and the date on or after which default may be entered. The Attorney General may include in one notice the names of any number of corporations against which actions are then pending in the same court. The Attorney General shall cause a copy of such notice to be mailed to the corporation at its registered office within ten days after the first publication thereof. The certificate of the Attorney General of the mailing of such notice shall be prima facie evidence thereof. Such notice shall be published at least once each week for two successive weeks, and the first publication thereof may begin at any time after the summons has been returned. Unless a corporation shall have been served with summons, no default shall be taken against it earlier than thirty days after the first publication of such notice.

§ 97. **Jurisdiction of Court to Liquidate Assets and Business of Corporation**

The . . . . courts shall have full power to liquidate the assets and business of a corporation:

(a) In an action by a shareholder when it is established:

(1) That the directors are deadlocked in the management of the corporate affairs and the shareholders are unable to break the deadlock, and that irreparable injury to the corporation is being suffered or is threatened by reason thereof; or

(2) That the acts of the directors or those in control of the corporation are illegal, oppressive or fraudulent; or

(3) That the shareholders are deadlocked in voting power, and have failed, for a period which includes at least two consecutive annual meeting dates, to elect successors to directors whose terms have expired or would have expired upon the election of their successors; or

(4) That the corporate assets are being misapplied or wasted.

(b) In an action by a creditor:

(1) When the claim of the creditor has been reduced to judgment and an execution thereon returned unsatisfied and it is established that the corporation is insolvent; or

(2) When the corporation has admitted in writing that the claim of the creditor is due and owing and it is established that the corporation is insolvent.

(c) Upon application by a corporation which has filed a statement of intent to dissolve, as provided in this Act, to have its liquidation continued under the supervision of the court.

(d) When an action has been filed by the Attorney General to dissolve a corporation and it is established

certificate of authority under this Act shall, until a certificate of revocation or of withdrawal shall have been issued as provided in this Act, enjoy the same, but no greater, rights and privileges as a domestic corporation organized for the purposes set forth in the application pursuant to which such certificate of authority is issued; and, except as in this Act otherwise provided, shall be subject to the same duties, restrictions, penalties and liabilities now or hereafter imposed upon a domestic corporation of like character.

§ 108. **Corporate Name of Foreign Corporation**

No certificate of authority shall be issued to a foreign corporation unless the corporate name of such corporation:

(a) Shall contain the word "corporation," "company," "incorporated," or "limited," or shall contain an abbreviation of one of such words, or such corporation shall, for use in this State, add at the end of its name one of such words or an abbreviation thereof.

(b) Shall not contain any word or phrase which indicates or implies that it is organized for any purpose other than one or more of the purposes contained in its articles of incorporation or that it is authorized or empowered to conduct the business of banking or insurance.

(c) Shall not be the same as, or deceptively similar to, the name of any domestic corporation existing under the laws of this State or any foreign corporation authorized to transact business in this State, or a name the exclusive right to which is, at the time, reserved in the manner provided in this Act, or the name of a corporation which has in effect a registration of its name as provided in this Act, except that this provision shall not apply if the foreign corporation applying for a certificate of authority files with the Secretary of State any one of the following:

(1) a resolution of its board of directors adopting a fictitious name for use in transacting business in this State which fictitious name is not deceptively similar to the name of any domestic corporation or of any foreign corporation authorized to transact business in this State or to any name reserved or registered as provided in this Act, or

(2) the written consent of such other corporation or holder of a reserved or registered name to use

the same or deceptively similar name and one or more words are added to make such name distinguishable from such other name, or

(3) a certified copy of a final decree of a court of competent jurisdiction establishing the prior right of such foreign corporation to the use of such name in this State.

§ 109. **Change of Name by Foreign Corporation**

Whenever a foreign corporation which is authorized to transact business in this State shall change its name to one under which a certificate of authority would not be granted to it on application therefor, the certificate of authority of such corporation shall be suspended and it shall not thereafter transact any business in this State until it has changed its name to a name which is available to it under the laws of this State or has otherwise complied with the provisions of this Act.

§ 110. **Application for Certificate of Authority**

A foreign corporation, in order to procure a certificate of authority to transact business in this State, shall make application therefor to the Secretary of State, which application shall set forth:

(a) The name of the corporation and the state or county under the laws of which it is incorporated.

(b) If the name of the corporation does not contain the word "corporation," "company," "incorporated," or "limited," or does not contain an abbreviation of one of such words, then the name of the corporation with the word or abbreviation which it elects to add thereto for use in this State.

(c) The date of incorporation and the period of duration of the corporation.

(d) The address of the principal office of the corporation in the state or country under the laws of which it is incorporated.

(e) The address of the proposed registered office of the corporation in this State, and the name of its proposed registered agent in this State at such address.

(f) The purpose or purposes of the corporation which it proposes to pursue in the transaction of business in this State.

(g) The names and respective addresses of the directors and officers of the corporation.

(h) A statement of the aggregate number of shares which the corporation has authority to issue, itemized by classes, par value of shares, shares without par value, and series, if any, within a class.

(i) A statement of the aggregate number of issued shares itemized by classes, par value of shares, shares without par value, and series, if any, within a class.

(j) A statement, expressed in dollars, of the amount of stated capital of the corporation, as defined in this Act.

(k) An estimate, expressed in dollars, of the value of all property to be owned by the corporation for the following year, wherever located, and an estimate of the value of the property of the corporation to be located within this State during such year, and an estimate, expressed in dollars, of the gross amount of business which will be transacted by the corporation during such year, and an estimate of the gross amount thereof which will be transacted by the corporation at or from places of business in this State during such year.

(l) Such additional information as may be necessary or appropriate in order to enable the Secretary of State to determine whether such corporation is entitled to a certificate of authority to transact business in this State and to determine and assess the fees and franchise taxes payable as in this Act prescribed.

Such application shall be made on forms prescribed and furnished by the Secretary of State and shall be executed in duplicate by the corporation by its president or a vice president and by its secretary or an assistant secretary, and verified by one of the officers signing such application.

§ 111. **Filing of Application for Certificate of Authority**

Duplicate originals of the application of the corporation for a certificate of authority shall be delivered to the Secretary of State, together with a copy of its articles of incorporation and all amendments thereto, duly authenticated by the proper officer of the state or country under the laws of which it is incorporated.

If the Secretary of State finds that such applica-

tion conforms to law, he shall, when all fees and franchise taxes have been paid as in this Act prescribed:

(a) Endorse on each of such documents the word "Filed," and the month, day and year of the filing thereof.

(b) File in his office one of such duplicate originals of the application and the copy of the articles of incorporation and amendments thereto.

(c) Issue a certificate of authority to transact business in this State to which he shall affix the other duplicate original application.

The certificate of authority, together with the duplicate original of the application affixed thereto by the Secretary of State, shall be returned to the corporation or its representative.

§ 112. **Effect of Certificate of Authority**

Upon the issuance of a certificate of authority by the Secretary of State, the corporation shall be authorized to transact business in this State for those purposes set forth in its application, subject, however, to the right of this State to suspend or to revoke such authority as provided in this Act.

§ 113. **Registered Office and Registered Agent of Foreign Corporation**

Each foreign corporation authorized to transact business in this State shall have and continuously maintain in this State:

(a) A registered office which may be, but need not be, the same as its place of business in this State.

(b) A registered agent, which agent may be either an individual resident in this State whose business office is identical with such registered office, or a domestic corporation, or a foreign corporation authorized to transact business in this State, having a business office identical with such registered office.

§ 114. **Change of Registered Office or Registered Agent of Foreign Corporation**

A foreign corporation authorized to transact business in this State may change its registered office or change its registered agent, or both, upon filing in the office of the Secretary of State a statement setting forth:

(a) The name of the corporation.

(b) The address of its then registered office.

(c) If the address of its registered office be changed, the address to which the registered office is to be changed.

(d) The name of its then registered agent.

(e) If its registered agent be changed, the name of its successor registered agent.

(f) That the address of its registered office and the address of the business office of its registered agent, as changed, will be identical.

(g) That such change was authorized by resolution duly adopted by its board of directors.

Such statement shall be executed by the corporation by its president or a vice president, and verified by him, and delivered to the Secretary of State. If the Secretary of State finds that such statement conforms to the provisions of this Act, he shall file such statement in his office, and upon such filing the change of address of the registered office, or the appointment of a new registered agent, or both, as the case may be, shall become effective.

Any registered agent of a foreign corporation may resign as such agent upon filing a written notice thereof, executed in duplicate, with the Secretary of State, who shall forthwith mail a copy thereof to the corporation at its principal office in the state or country under the laws of which it is incorporated. The appointment of such agent shall terminate upon the expiration of thirty days after receipt of such notice by the Secretary of State.

If a registered agent changes his or its business address to another place within the same ....*, he or it may change such address and the address of the registered office of any corporation of which he or it is registered agent by filing a statement as required above except that it need be signed only by the registered agent and need not be responsive to (e) or (g) and must recite that a copy of the statement has been mailed to the corporation.

*Supply designation of jurisdiction, such as county, etc. in accordance with local practice.

§ 115. **Service of Process on Foreign Corporation**

The registered agent so appointed by a foreign corporation authorized to transact business in this State shall be an agent of such corporation upon whom any process, notice or demand required or permitted by law to be served upon the corporation may be served.

Whenever a foreign corporation authorized to transact business in this State shall fail to appoint or maintain a registered agent in this State, or whenever any such registered agent cannot with reasonable diligence be found at the registered office, or whenever the certificate of authority of a foreign corporation shall be suspended or revoked, then the Secretary of State shall be an agent of such corporation upon whom any such process, notice, or demand may be served. Service on the Secretary of State of any such process, notice or demand shall be made by delivering to and leaving with him, or with any clerk having charge of the corporation department of his office, duplicate copies of such process, notice or demand. In the event any such process, notice or demand is served on the Secretary of State, he shall immediately cause one of such copies thereof to be forwarded by registered mail, addressed to the corporation at its principal office in the state or country under the laws of which it is incorporated. Any service so had on the Secretary of State shall be returnable in not less than thirty days.

The Secretary of State shall keep a record of all processes, notices and demands served upon him under this section, and shall record therein the time of such service and his action with reference thereto.

Nothing herein contained shall limit or affect the right to serve any process, notice or demand, required or permitted by law to be served upon a foreign corporation in any other manner now or hereafter permitted by law.

§ 116. **Amendment to Articles of Incorporation of Foreign Corporation**

Whenever the articles of incorporation of a foreign corporation authorized to transact business in this State are amended, such foreign corporation shall, within thirty days after such amendment becomes effective, file in the office of the Secretary of State a copy of such amendment duly authenticated by the proper officer of the state or country under the laws of which it is incorporated; but the filing thereof shall not of itself enlarge or alter the purpose or purposes which such corporation is authorized to pursue in the transaction of business in this State, nor authorize such corporation to transact business in this State under any other name than the name set forth in its certificate of authority.

§ 117. Merger of Foreign Corporation Authorized to Transact Business in This State

Whenever a foreign corporation authorized to transact business in this State shall be a party to a statutory merger permitted by the laws of the state or country under the laws of which it is incorporated, and such corporation shall be the surviving corporation, it shall, within thirty days after such merger becomes effective, file with the Secretary of State a copy of the articles of merger duly authenticated by the proper officer of the state or country under the laws of which such statutory merger was effected; and it shall not be necessary for such corporation to procure either a new or amended certificate of authority to transact business in this State unless the name of such corporation be changed thereby or unless the corporation desires to pursue in this State other or additional purposes than those which it is then authorized to transact in this State.

§ 118. Amended Certificate of Authority

A foreign corporation authorized to transact business in this State shall procure an amended certificate of authority in the event it changes its corporate name, or desires to pursue in this State other or additional purposes than those set forth in its prior application for a certificate of authority, by making application therefor to the Secretary of State.

The requirements in respect to the form and contents of such application, the manner of its execution, the filing of duplicate originals thereof with the Secretary of State, the issuance of an amended certificate of authority and the effect thereof, shall be the same as in the case of an original application for a certificate of authority.

§ 119. Withdrawal of Foreign Corporation

A foreign corporation authorized to transact business in this State may withdraw from this State upon procuring from the Secretary of State a certificate of withdrawal. In order to procure such certificate of withdrawal, such foreign corporation shall deliver to the Secretary of State an application for withdrawal, which shall set forth:

(a) The name of the corporation and the state or country under the laws of which it is incorporated.

(b) That the corporation is not transacting business in this State.

(c) That the corporation surrenders its authority to transact business in this State.

(d) That the corporation revokes the authority of its registered agent in this State to accept service of process and consents that service of process in any action, suit or proceeding based upon any cause of action arising in this State during the time the corporation was authorized to transact business in this State may thereafter be made on such corporation by service thereof on the Secretary of State.

(e) A post-office address to which the Secretary of State may mail a copy of any process against the corporation that may be served on him.

(f) A statement of the aggregate number of shares which the corporation has authority to issue, itemized by classes, par value of shares, shares without par value, and series, if any, within a class, as of the date of such application.

(g) A statement of the aggregate number of issued shares, itemized by classes, par value of shares, shares without par value, and series, if any, within a class, as of the date of such application.

(h) A statement, expressed in dollars, of the amount of stated capital of the corporation, as of the date of such application.

(i) Such additional information as may be necessary or appropriate in order to enable the Secretary of State to determine and assess any unpaid fees or franchise taxes payable by such foreign corporation as in this Act prescribed.

The application for withdrawal shall be made on forms prescribed and furnished by the Secretary of State and shall be executed by the corporation by its president or a vice president and by its secretary or an assistant secretary, and verified by one of the officers signing the application, or, if the corporation is in the hands of a receiver or trustee, shall be executed on behalf of the corporation by such receiver or trustee and verified by him.

§ 120. Filing of Application for Withdrawal

Duplicate originals of such application for withdrawal shall be delivered to the Secretary of State. If the Secretary of State finds that such application conforms to the provisions of this Act, he shall, when all fees and franchise taxes have been paid as in this Act prescribed:

(a) Endorse on each of such duplicate originals the word "Filed," and the month, day and year of the filing thereof.

(b) File one of such duplicate originals in his office.

(c) Issue a certificate of withdrawal to which he shall affix the other duplicate original.

The certificate of withdrawal, together with the duplicate original of the application for withdrawal affixed thereto by the Secretary of State, shall be returned to the corporation or its representative. Upon the issuance of such certificate of withdrawal, the authority of the corporation to transact business in this State shall cease.

§ 121. Revocation of Certificate of Authority

The certificate of authority of a foreign corporation to transact business in this State may be revoked by the Secretary of State upon the conditions prescribed in this section when:

(a) The corporation has failed to file its annual report within the time required by this Act, or has failed to pay any fees, franchise taxes or penalties prescribed by this Act when they have become due and payable; or

(b) The corporation has failed to appoint and maintain a registered agent in this State as required by this Act; or

(c) The corporation has failed, after change of its registered office or registered agent, to file in the office of the Secretary of State a statement of such change as required by this Act; or

(d) The corporation has failed to file in the office of the Secretary of State any amendment to its articles of incorporation or any articles of merger within the time prescribed by this Act; or

(e) A misrepresentation has been made of any material matter in any application, report, affidavit, or other document submitted by such corporation pursuant to this Act.

No certificate of authority of a foreign corporation

shall be revoked by the Secretary of State unless (1) he shall have given the corporation not less than sixty days' notice thereof by mail addressed to its registered office in this State, and (2) the corporation shall fail prior to revocation to file such annual report, or pay such fees, franchise taxes or penalties, or file the required statement of change of registered agent or registered office, or file such articles of amendment or articles of merger, or correct such misrepresentation.

§ 122. Issuance of Certificate of Revocation

Upon revoking any such certificate of authority, the Secretary of State shall:

(a) Issue a certificate of revocation in duplicate.

(b) File one of such certificates in his office.

(c) Mail to such corporation at its registered office in this State a notice of such revocation accompanied by one of such certificates.

Upon the issuance of such certificate of revocation, the authority of the corporation to transact business in this State shall cease.

§ 123. Application to Corporations Heretofore Authorized to Transact Business in this State

Foreign corporations which are duly authorized to transact business in this State at the time this Act takes effect, for a purpose or purposes for which a corporation might secure such authority under this Act, shall, subject to the limitations set forth in their respective certificates of authority, be entitled to all the rights and privileges applicable to foreign corporations procuring certificates of authority to transact business in this State under this Act, and from the time this Act takes effect such corporations shall be subject to all the limitations, restrictions, liabilities, and duties prescribed herein for foreign corporations procuring certificates of authority to transact business in this State under this Act.

§ 124. Transacting Business Without Certificate of Authority

No foreign corporation transacting business in this State without a certificate of authority shall be permitted to maintain any action, suit or proceeding in any court of this State, until such corporation shall have obtained a certificate of authority. Nor shall any action, suit or proceeding be maintained in any court of this State by any successor or assignee of such corporation on any right, claim or demand arising out of the transaction of business by such corporation in this State, until a certificate of authority shall have been obtained by such corporation or by a corporation which has acquired all or substantially all of its assets.

The failure of a foreign corporation to obtain a certificate of authority to transact business in this State shall not impair the validity of any contract or act of such corporation, and shall not prevent such corporation from defending any action, suit or proceeding in any court of this State.

A foreign corporation which transacts business in this State without a certificate of authority shall be liable to this State, for the years or parts thereof during which it transacted business in this State without a certificate of authority, in an amount equal to all fees and franchise taxes which would have been imposed by this Act upon such corporation had it duly applied for and received a certificate of authority to transact business in this State as required by this Act and thereafter filed all reports required by this Act, plus all penalties imposed by this Act for failure to pay such fees and franchise taxes. The Attorney General shall bring proceedings to recover all amounts due this State under the provisions of this Section.

§ 125. Annual Report of Domestic and Foreign Corporations

Each domestic corporation, and each foreign corporation authorized to transact business in this State, shall file, within the time prescribed by this Act, an annual report setting forth:

(a) The name of the corporation and the state or country under the laws of which it is incorporated.

(b) The address of the registered office of the corporation in this State, and the name of its registered agent in this State at such address, and, in case of a foreign corporation, the address of its principal office in the state or country under the laws of which it is incorporated.

(c) A brief statement of the character of the business in which the corporation is actually engaged in this State.

(d) The names and respective addresses of the directors and officers of the corporation.

(e) A statement of the aggregate number of shares which the corporation has authority to issue, itemized by classes, par value of shares, shares without par value, and series, if any, within a class.

(f) A statement of the aggregate number of issued shares, itemized by classes, par value of shares, shares without par value, and series, if any, within a class.

(g) A statement, expressed in dollars, of the amount of stated capital of the corporation, as defined in this Act.

(h) A statement, expressed in dollars, of the value of all the property owned by the corporation, wherever located, and the value of the property of the corporation located within this State, and a statement, expressed in dollars, of the gross amount of business transacted by the corporation for the twelve months ended on the thirty-first day of December preceding the date herein provided for the filing of such report and the gross amount thereof transacted by the corporation at or from places of business in this State. If, on the thirty-first day of December preceding the time herein provided for the filing of such report, the corporation had not been in existence for a period of twelve months, or in the case of a foreign corporation had not been authorized to transact business in this State for a period of twelve months, the statement with respect to business transacted shall be furnished for the period between the date of incorporation or the date of its authorization to transact business in this State, as the case may be, and such thirty-first day of December. If all the property of the corporation is located in this State and all of its business is transacted at or from places of business in this State, or if the corporation elects to pay the annual franchise tax on the basis of its entire stated capital, then the information required by this subparagraph need not be set forth in such report.

(i) Such additional information as may be necessary or appropriate in order to enable the Secretary of State to determine and assess the proper amount of franchise taxes payable by such corporation.

Such annual report shall be made on forms prescribed and furnished by the Secretary of State, and the information therein contained shall be given as of the date of the execution of the report, except as to the information required by subparagraphs (g), (h) and (i) which shall be given as of the close of business on the thirty-first day of December next preceding the date herein provided for the filing of such report. It shall be executed by the corporation by its president, a vice president, secretary, an assistant secretary, or treasurer, and verified by the officer executing the report, or, if the corporation is in the hands of a receiver or trustee, it shall be executed on behalf of the corporation and verified by such receiver or trustee.

§ 126. Filing of Annual Report of Domestic and Foreign Corporations

Such annual report of a domestic or foreign corporation shall be delivered to the Secretary of State between the first day of January and the first day of March of each year, except that the first annual report of a domestic or foreign corporation shall be filed between the first day of January and the first day of March of the year next succeeding the calendar year in which its certificate of incorporation or its certificate of authority, as the case may be, was issued by the Secretary of State. Proof to the satisfaction of the Secretary of State that prior to the first day of March such report was deposited in the United States mail in a sealed envelope, properly addressed, with postage prepaid, shall be deemed a compliance with this requirement. If the Secretary of State finds that such report conforms to the requirements of this Act, he shall file the same. If he finds that it does not so conform, he shall promptly return the same to the corporation for any necessary corrections, in which event the penalties hereinafter prescribed for failure to file such report within the time hereinabove provided shall not apply, if such report is corrected to conform to the requirements of this Act and returned to the Secretary of State within thirty days from the date on which it was mailed to the corporation by the Secretary of State.

§ 127. Fees, Franchise Taxes and Charges to be Collected by Secretary of State

The Secretary of State shall charge and collect in accordance with the provisions of this Act:

(a) Fees for filing documents and issuing certificates.

(b) Miscellaneous charges.

(c) License fees.

(d) Franchise taxes.

§ 128. Fees for Filing Documents and Issuing Certificates

The Secretary of State shall charge and collect for:

(a) Filing articles of incorporation and issuing a certificate of incorporation, ... dollars.

(b) Filing articles of amendment and issuing a certificate of amendment, ... dollars.

(c) Filing restated articles of incorporation, ... dollars.

(d) Filing articles of merger or consolidation and issuing a certificate of merger or consolidation, ... dollars.

(e) Filing an application to reserve a corporate name, ... dollars.

(f) Filing a notice of transfer of a reserved corporate name, ... dollars.

(g) Filing a statement of change of address of registered office or change of registered agent, or both, ... dollars.

(h) Filing a statement of the establishment of a series of shares, ... dollars.

(i) Filing a statement of cancellation of shares, ... dollars.

(j) Filing a statement of reduction of stated capital, ... dollars.

(k) Filing a statement of intent to dissolve, ... dollars.

(l) Filing a statement of revocation of voluntary dissolution proceedings, ... dollars.

(m) Filing articles of dissolution, ... dollars.

(n) Filing an application of a foreign corporation for a certificate of authority to transact business in this State and issuing a certificate of authority, ... dollars.

(o) Filing an application of a foreign corporation for an amended certificate of authority to transact business in this State and issuing an amended certificate of authority, ... dollars.

(p) Filing a copy of an amendment to the articles of incorporation of a foreign corporation holding a certificate of authority to transact business in this State, ... dollars.

(q) Filing a copy of articles of merger of a foreign corporation holding a certificate of authority to transact business in this State, ... dollars.

(r) Filing an application for withdrawal of a foreign corporation and issuing a certificate of withdrawal, ... dollars.

(s) Filing any other statement or report, except an annual report, of a domestic or foreign corporation, ... dollars.

§ 129. **Miscellaneous Charges**

The Secretary of State shall charge and collect:

(a) For furnishing a certified copy of any document, instrument, or paper relating to a corporation, ... cents per page and .... dollars for the certificate and affixing the seal thereto.

(b) At the time of any service of process on him as agent of a corporation, ... dollars, which amount may be recovered as taxable costs by the party to the suit or action causing such service to be made if such party prevails in the suit or action.

§ 130. **License Fees Payable by Domestic Corporations**

The Secretary of State shall charge and collect from each domestic corporation license fees, based upon the number of shares which it will have authority to issue or the increase in the number of shares which it will have authority to issue, at the time of:

(a) Filing articles of incorporation;

(b) Filing articles of amendment increasing the number of authorized shares; and

(c) Filing articles of merger or consolidation increasing the number of authorized shares which the surviving or new corporation, if a domestic corporation, will have the authority to issue above the aggregate number of shares which the constituent domestic corporations and constituent foreign corporations authorized to transact business in this State had authority to issue.

The license fees shall be at the rate of .... cents per share up to and including the first 10,000 authorized shares, ... cents per share for each authorized share in excess of 10,000 shares up to and including 100,000

shares, and .... cents per share for each authorized share in excess of 100,000 shares, whether the shares are of par value or without par value.

The license fees payable on an increase in the number of authorized shares shall be imposed only on the increased number of shares, and the number of previously authorized shares shall be taken into account in determining the rate applicable to the increased number of authorized shares.

§ 131. **License Fees Payable by Foreign Corporations**

The Secretary of State shall charge and collect from each foreign corporation license fees, based upon the proportion represented in this State of the number of shares which it has authority to issue or the increase in the number of shares which it has authority to issue, at the time of:

(a) Filing an application for a certificate of authority to transact business in this State;

(b) Filing articles of amendment which increased the number of authorized shares; and

(c) Filing articles of merger or consolidation which increased the number of authorized shares which the surviving or new corporation, if a foreign corporation, has authority to issue above the aggregate number of shares which the constituent domestic corporations and constituent foreign corporations authorized to transact business in this State had authority to issue.

The license fees shall be at the rate of .... cents per share up to and including the first 10,000 authorized shares represented in this State, ... cents per share for each authorized share in excess of 10,000 shares up to and including 100,000 shares represented in this State, and .... cents per share for each authorized share in excess of 100,000 shares represented in this State, whether the shares are of par value or without par value.

The license fees payable on an increase in the number of authorized shares shall be imposed only on the increased number of such shares represented in this State, and the number of previously authorized shares represented in this State shall be taken into account in determining the rate applicable to the increased number of authorized shares.

The number of authorized shares represented in this State shall be that proportion of its total authorized shares which the sum of the value of its property located in this State and the gross amount of business transacted by it at or from places of business in this State bears to the sum of the value of all of its property, wherever located, and the gross amount of its business, wherever transacted. Such proportion shall be determined from information contained in the application for a certificate of authority to transact business in this State until the filing of an annual report and thereafter from information contained in the latest annual report filed by the corporation.

§ 132. Franchise Taxes Payable by Domestic Corporations

The Secretary of State shall charge and collect from each domestic corporation an initial franchise tax at the time of filing its articles of incorporation at the rate of one-twelfth of one-half of the license fee payable by such corporation under the provisions of this Act at the time of filing its articles of incorporation, for each calendar month, or fraction thereof, between the date of the issuance of the certificate of incorporation by the Secretary of State and the first day of July of the next succeeding calendar year.

The Secretary of State shall charge and collect from each domestic corporation an annual franchise tax, payable in advance for the period from July 1 in each year to July 1 in the succeeding year, beginning July 1 in the calendar year in which such corporation is required to file its first annual report under this Act, at the rate of .... of .... per cent of the amount represented in this State of the stated capital of the corporation, as disclosed by the latest report filed by the corporation with the Secretary of State.

The amount represented in this State of the stated capital of the corporation shall be that proportion of its stated capital which the sum of the value of its property located in this State and the gross amount of business transacted by it at or from places of business in this State bears to the sum of the value of all of its property, wherever located, and the gross amount of its business, wherever transacted, except as follows:

(a) If the corporation elects in its annual report in any year to pay its annual franchise tax on its entire stated capital, all franchise taxes accruing against the corporation after the filing of such annual report shall be assessed accordingly until the corporation elects otherwise in an annual report for a subsequent year.

(b) If the corporation fails to file its annual report in any year within the time prescribed by this Act, the proportion of its stated capital represented in this State shall be deemed to be its entire stated capital, unless its annual report is thereafter filed and its franchise tax thereafter adjusted by the Secretary of State in accordance with the provisions of this Act, in which case the proportion shall likewise be adjusted to the same proportion that would have prevailed if the corporation had filed its annual report within the time prescribed by this Act.

§ 133. Franchise Taxes Payable by Foreign Corporations

The Secretary of State shall charge and collect from each foreign corporation authorized to transact business in this State an initial franchise tax at the time of filing its application for a certificate of authority at the rate of one-twelfth of one-half of the license fee payable by such corporation under the provisions of this Act at the time of filing such application, for each month, or fraction thereof, between the date of the issuance of the certificate of authority by the Secretary of State and the first day of July of the next succeeding calendar year.

The Secretary of State shall charge and collect from each foreign corporation authorized to transact business in this State an annual franchise tax, payable in advance for the period from July 1 in each year to July 1 in the succeeding year, beginning July 1 in the calendar year in which such corporation is required to file its first annual report under this Act, at the rate of .... per cent of the amount represented in this State of the stated capital of the corporation, as disclosed by the latest annual report filed by the corporation with the Secretary of State.

The amount represented in this State of the stated capital of the corporation shall be that proportion of its stated capital which the sum of the value of its property located in this State and the gross amount of business transacted by it at or from places of business in this State bears to the sum of the value of all of its property, wherever located, and the gross amount of its business, wherever transacted, except as follows:

(a) If the corporation elects in its annual report in any year to pay its annual franchise tax on its entire stated capital, all franchise taxes accruing against the corporation after the filing of such annual report shall be assessed accordingly until the corporation elects otherwise in an annual report for a subsequent year.

(b) If the corporation fails to file its annual report in any year within the time prescribed by this Act, the proportion of its stated capital represented in this State shall be deemed to be its entire stated capital, unless its annual report is thereafter filed and its franchise tax thereafter adjusted by the Secretary of State in accordance with the provisions of this Act, in which case the proportion shall likewise be adjusted to the same proportion that would have prevailed if the corporation had filed its annual report within the time prescribed by this Act.

§ 134. **Assessment and Collection of Annual Franchise Taxes**

It shall be the duty of the Secretary of State to collect all annual franchise taxes and penalties imposed by, or assessed in accordance with, this Act.

Between the first day of March and the first day of June of each year, the Secretary of State shall assess against each corporation, domestic and foreign, required to file an annual report in such year, the franchise tax payable by it for the period from July 1 of such year to July 1 of the succeeding year in accordance with the provisions of this Act, and, if it has failed to file its annual report within the time prescribed by this Act, the penalty imposed by this Act upon such corporation for its failure so to do; and shall mail a written notice to each corporation against which such tax is assessed, addressed to such corporation at its registered office in this State, notifying the corporation (1) of the amount of franchise tax assessed against it for the ensuing year and the amount of penalty, if any, assessed against it for failure to file its annual report; (2) that objections, if any, to such assessment will be heard by the officer making the assessment on or before the fifteenth day of June of such year, upon receipt of a request from the corporation; and (3) that such tax and penalty shall be payable to the Secretary of State on the first day of July next succeeding the date of the notice. Failure to receive such notice shall not relieve the corporation of its obligation to pay the tax and any penalty assessed, or invalidate the assessment thereof.

The Secretary of State shall have power to hear and determine objections to any assessment of franchise tax at any time after such assessment and, after hearing, to change or modify any such assess-

ment. In the event of any adjustment of franchise tax with respect to which a penalty has been assessed for failure to file an annual report, the penalty shall be adjusted in accordance with the provisions of this Act imposing such penalty.

All annual franchise taxes and all penalties for failure to file annual reports shall be due and payable on the first day of July of each year. If the annual franchise tax assessed against any corporation subject to the provisions of this Act, together with all penalties assessed thereon, shall not be paid to the Secretary of State on or before the thirty-first day of July of the year in which such tax is due and payable, the Secretary of State shall certify such fact to the Attorney General on or before the fifteenth day of November of such year, whereupon the Attorney General may institute an action against such corporation in the name of this State, in any court of competent jurisdiction, for the recovery of the amount of such franchise tax and penalties, together with the cost of suit, and prosecute the same to final judgment.

For the purpose of enforcing collection, all annual franchise taxes assessed in accordance with this Act, and all penalties assessed thereon and all interest and costs that shall accrue in connection with the collection thereof, shall be a prior and first lien on the real and personal property of the corporation from and including the first day of July of the year when such franchise taxes become due and payable until such taxes, penalties, interest, and costs shall have been paid.

§ 135. **Penalties Imposed upon Corporations**

Each corporation, domestic or foreign, that fails or refuses to file its annual report for any year within the time prescribed by this Act shall be subject to a penalty of ten per cent of the amount of the franchise tax assessed against it for the period beginning July 1 of the year in which such report should have been filed. Such penalty shall be assessed by the Secretary of State at the time of the assessment of the franchise tax. If the amount of the franchise tax as originally assessed against such corporation be thereafter adjusted in accordance with the provisions of this Act, the amount of the penalty shall be likewise adjusted to ten per cent of the amount of the adjusted franchise tax. The amount of the franchise tax and the amount of the penalty shall be separately stated in any notice to the corporation with respect thereto.

If the franchise tax assessed in accordance with the provisions of this Act shall not be paid on or before the thirty-first day of July, it shall be deemed to be delinquent, and there shall be added a penalty of one per cent for each month or part of month that the same is delinquent, commencing with the month of August.

Each corporation, domestic or foreign, that fails or refuses to answer truthfully and fully within the time prescribed by this Act interrogatories propounded by the Secretary of State in accordance with the provisions of this Act, shall be deemed to be guilty of a misdemeanor and upon conviction thereof may be fined in any amount not exceeding five hundred dollars.

§ 136. **Penalties Imposed upon Officers and Directors**

Each officer and director of a corporation, domestic or foreign, who fails or refuses within the time prescribed by this Act to answer truthfully and fully interrogatories propounded to him by the Secretary of State in accordance with the provisions of this Act, or who signs any articles, statement, report, application or other document filed with the Secretary of State which is known to such officer or director to be false in any material respect, shall be deemed to be guilty of a misdemeanor, and upon conviction thereof may be fined in any amount not exceeding .... dollars.

§ 137. **Interrogatories by Secretary of State**

The Secretary of State may propound to any corporation, domestic or foreign, subject to the provisions of this Act, and to any officer or director thereof, such interrogatories as may be reasonably necessary and proper to enable him to ascertain whether such corporation has complied with all the provisions of this Act applicable to such corporation. Such interrogatories shall be answered within thirty days after the mailing thereof, or within such additional time as shall be fixed by the Secretary of State, and the answers thereto shall be full and complete and shall be made in writing and under oath. If such interrogatories be directed to an individual they shall be answered by him, and if directed to a corporation they shall be answered by the president, vice president, secretary or assistant secretary thereof. The Secretary of State need not file any document to which such interrogatories relate until such interrogatories be answered as herein provided, and not then if the answers thereto disclose that such document is not in conformity with the provisions of this Act. The Secretary of State shall certify to the Attorney General, for such action as the Attorney General may deem appropriate, all interrogatories and answers thereto which disclose a violation of any of the provisions of this Act.

§ 138. **Information Disclosed by Interrogatories**

Interrogatories propounded by the Secretary of State and the answers thereto shall not be open to public inspection nor shall the Secretary of State disclose any facts or information obtained therefrom except insofar as his official duty may require the same to be made public or in the event such interrogatories or the answers thereto are required for evidence in any criminal proceedings or in any other action by this State.

§ 139. **Powers of Secretary of State**

The Secretary of State shall have the power and authority reasonably necessary to enable him to administer this Act efficiently and to perform the duties therein imposed upon him.

§ 140. **Appeal from Secretary of State**

If the Secretary of State shall fail to approve any articles of incorporation, amendment, merger, consolidation or dissolution, or any other document required by this Act to be approved by the Secretary of State before the same shall be filed in his office, he shall, within ten days after the delivery thereof to him, give written notice of his disapproval to the person or corporation, domestic or foreign, delivering the same, specifying the reasons therefor. From such disapproval such person or corporation may appeal to the .... court of the county in which the registered office of such corporation is, or is proposed to be, situated by filing with the clerk of such court a petition setting forth a copy of the articles or other document sought to be filed and a copy of the written disapproval thereof by the Secretary of State; whereupon the matter shall be tried de novo by the court, and the court shall either sustain the action of the Secretary of State or direct him to take such action as the court may deem proper.

If the Secretary of State shall revoke the certificate of authority to transact business in this State of any foreign corporation, pursuant to the provisions of this Act, such foreign corporation may likewise appeal to the .... court of the county where the registered office of such corporation in this State is situated, by filing with the clerk of such court a petition setting forth a copy of its certificate of authority to transact business in this State and a copy of the notice of revocation given by the Secretary of State; whereupon the matter shall be tried de novo by the court, and the court shall either sustain the action of the Secretary of State or direct him to take such action as the court may deem proper.

Appeals from all final orders and judgments entered by the .... court under this section in review of any ruling or decision of the Secretary of State may be taken as in other civil actions.

§ 141. Certificates and Certified Copies to be Received in Evidence

All certificates issued by the Secretary of State in accordance with the provisions of this Act, and all copies of documents filed in his office in accordance with the provisions of this Act when certified by him, shall be taken and received in all courts, public offices, and official bodies as prima facie evidence of the facts therein stated. A certificate by the Secretary of State under the great seal of this State, as to the existence or non-existence of the facts relating to corporations shall be taken and received in all courts, public offices, and official bodies as prima facie evidence of the existence or non-existence of the facts therein stated.

§ 142. Forms to be Furnished by Secretary of State

All reports required by this Act to be filed in the office of the Secretary of State shall be made on forms which shall be prescribed and furnished by the Secretary of State. Forms for all other documents to be filed in the office of the Secretary of State shall be furnished by the Secretary of State on request therefor, but the use thereof, unless otherwise specifically prescribed in this Act, shall not be mandatory.

§ 143. Greater Voting Requirements

Whenever, with respect to any action to be taken by the shareholders of a corporation, the articles of incorporation require the vote or concurrence of the holders of a greater proportion of the shares, or of any class or series thereof, than required by this Act with respect to such action, the provisions of the articles of incorporation shall control.

§ 144. Waiver of Notice

Whenever any notice is required to be given to any shareholder or director of a corporation under the provisions of this Act or under the provisions of the articles of incorporation or by-laws of the corporation, a waiver thereof in writing signed by the person or persons entitled to such notice, whether before or after the time stated therein, shall be equivalent to the giving of such notice.

§ 145. Action by Shareholders Without a Meeting

Any action required by this Act to be taken at a meeting of the shareholders of a corporation, or any action which may be taken at a meeting of the shareholders, may be taken without a meeting if a consent in writing, setting forth the action so taken, shall be signed by all of the shareholders entitled to vote with respect to the subject matter thereof.

Such consent shall have the same effect as a unanimous vote of shareholders, and may be stated as such in any articles or document filed with the Secretary of State under this Act.

§ 146. Unauthorized Assumption of Corporate Powers

All persons who assume to act as a corporation without authority so to do shall be jointly and severally liable for all debts and liabilities incurred or arising as a result thereof.

§ 147. Application to Existing Corporations

The provisions of this Act shall apply to all existing corporations organized under any general act of this State providing for the organization of corporations for a purpose or purposes for which a corporation might be organized under this Act, where the power has been reserved to amend, repeal or modify the act under which such corporation was organized and where such act is repealed by this Act.

§ 148. Application to Foreign and Interstate Commerce

The provisions of this Act shall apply to commerce with foreign nations and among the several states only insofar as the same may be permitted under the provisions of the Constitution of the United States.

§ 149. **Reservation of Power**

The ....* shall at all times have power to prescribe such regulations, provisions and limitations as it may deem advisable, which regulations, provisions and limitations shall be binding upon any and all corporations subject to the provisions of this Act, and the ....* shall have power to amend, repeal or modify this Act at pleasure.

*Insert name of legislative body.

§ 150. **Effect of Repeal of Prior Acts**

The repeal of a prior act by this Act shall not affect any right accrued or established, or any liability or penalty incurred, under the provisions of such act, prior to the repeal thereof.

§ 151. **Effect of Invalidity of Part of this Act**

If a court of competent jurisdiction shall adjudge to be invalid or unconstitutional any clause, sentence, paragraph, section or part of this Act, such judgment or decree shall not affect, impair, invalidate or nullify the remainder of this Act, but the effect thereof shall be confined to the clause, sentence, paragraph, section or part of this Act so adjudged to be invalid or unconstitutional.

§ 152. **Repeal of Prior Acts**

(Insert appropriate provisions).........

GLOSSARY

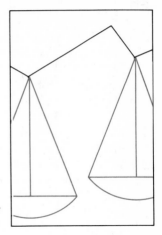

A

abandoned property   Property which the owner has parted with no intention of recovering it.

abuse of discretion   Clearly erroneous judgment; usually used in reference to action taken by an administrative agency which has no foundation in fact or in law.

acceleration clause   Clauses in contracts for rent, or for installment payments, which provide that all future payments will become due immediately upon the failure to tender timely payment on any one installment. (see *installment contracts, tender, severable contracts.*)

acceptance   The offeree's notification to the offeror that he agrees to be bound by the terms of the offeror's proposal. Although, historically acceptance had to be in the exact manner specified by the offeror, the trend is to allow acceptance by any means which will reasonably notify the offeror of the acceptance.

accession   1) The changing (through manufacturing) of one good into a new good (*i.e.,* flour into bread). 2) The right to all that which one's property produces (*i.e.,* fruit from trees) or to that which becomes added to or incorporated to that property (*i.e.,* buildings on one's land). 3) The right, upon payment for the original materials, to keep an article manufactured out of goods which were innocently converted. (see *conversion*)

accommodation party   A person who indorses a note, but is to receive no payment from it, nor consideration for his indorsement. Unless he uses a qualified indorsement, he is liable as a surety (secondarily liable) on the note.

accord An agreement between two persons, one of whom has a right of action against the other, to settle the dispute.

accord and satisfaction An agreement and payment between two parties, one of whom has a right of action against the other. After the agreement has been made, and payment has been tendered the "accord and satisfaction" is complete.

account 1) An intangible concept of individualized funds maintained by banks for each depositor. 2) A legal action, asking for a setting out of revenues, expenses, etc.

actual authority Power of an agent to bind its principal where such power derives either from express or implied agreement between principal and agent.

actus reus The "guilty act." As opposed to the mens rea, the *actus reus* is the physical aspect of a crime whereas the mens rea involves the psychological or intent factor.

adhesion contracts Standard "form" contracts, such as those between a large retailer and a consumer.

administrative law The rules under which administrative agencies such as the SEC and FTC carry out their duties and responsibilities. This law can initially be enforced by these agencies, outside the judicial process.

administrative process Methods prescribed by the Legislature which govern an agency's powers and procedure in enforcement of administrative law.

administrator (trix) One who is appointed by a court to handle the probate (disposition) of a person's estate if that person dies intestate. (see *estate, will, intestacy laws*)

adverse possession The acquisition of title to real property by occupying it, with the knowledge of the owner, for a period of time specified by state statutes.

affirmative defense A response to a plaintiff's claim which attacks the plaintiff's *legal* right to bring an action as opposed to attacking the truth of the claim. Running of the statute of limitations is an example of an affirmative defense.

agency A relationship between two persons whereby agreement or otherwise, one is bound by the words and acts of the other. The former is a *principal*; the latter is an *agent*.

agreement Synonym for contract.

allonge A piece of paper attached to a negotiable instrument, upon which transferees can make indorsements if there is no room left on the instrument itself.

answer The defendant's response to the complaint. Filing of the complaint and answer are governed by rules of procedure.

anticipatory breach or **anticipatory repudiation** The assertion by a party that he will not perform an obligation which he is contractually obligated to perform at a future time.

apparent authority Such authority as a reasonable person would assume an agent has in light of the conduct of the principal. Apparent authority cannot be established solely by the conduct of the agent and must be chargeable to the principal.

appellant The party who invokes the appellate jurisdiction of a superior court, after that party has lost in the inferior court. May be either the plaintiff or defendant.

appellee The party who won in the inferior court; the party against whom the appeal is taken.

arbitrary and capricious Without basis in fact or law. Without a rational basis.

arbitration The settling of a dispute by submitting it to a disinterested third party other than a court.

arbitration clauses Clauses in a contract which provide that in case of dispute the parties will determine their rights by means of compromise *outside* the judicial system.

arson The malicious burning of another's dwelling. Some statutes have expanded this to include any building, and to destruction by other means, *i.e.,* exploding.

articles of incorporation The instrument under which a corporation is formed which serves as a request to the state to be treated as a corporation under its laws.

articles of partnership The written contract by which parties enter into a partnership, to be governed by the terms set forth in the contract.

artisan's lien A possessory lien given to a person who has made improvements and added value to another person's personal property. This is given a security for services performed.

assault Any word or action intended to cause the

person to whom it is directed to be in fear of immediate physical harm; a reasonably believable threat. (see *battery*)

assault and battery An intentional threat of bodily harm and the carrying out of the threat.

assignment The act of transferring to another all or part of one's property, interest, or rights. In contract, one can assign to another his right to receive the performance of the other obligated party.

assignment of rights See *assignment*.

assumption of risk The bargained for transfer of any underlying risks in a contract (e.g., theft losses) from the party who otherwise would naturally or legally bear the losses flowing from such risks to the other party.

attachment In a secured transaction, the process by which a security interest in the property of another becomes enforceable. Attachment may occur upon the taking possession of the property or upon the signing of a security agreement by the person pledging the property as collateral.

B

bailee One to whom goods are entrusted by a bailor, for the bailor's benefit.

bailment Agreement to entrust goods of one person (bailor) to another (bailee).

bailor One who entrusts his goods to another, for his (bailor's) benefit.

bankruptcy Proceedings under law, initiated either by an "insolvent" person or business entity or by its creditors seeking to have the court adjudge it a *bankrupt*. Bankruptcy also includes the process of administering the bankrupt's assets and/or dividing its assets among its creditors.

battery The unprivileged intentional touching of another. (see *assault*)

bearer paper In the law of commercial paper, any instrument which runs to the bearer. It includes instruments payable to the bearer or to "cash."

beneficiary One who holds equitable title to property being held in trust, such property being cared for by the trustee. (see *fiduciary duty*)

bequest A gift by will of personal property. (verb— to bequeath)

bilateral contract A contract which includes the exchange of a promise for a promise. (as opposed to unilateral contract)

bill of lading A document which serves both to evidence the receipt of goods for shipment and to pass title of the goods.

binder A written, temporary insurance policy. (see *policy*)

"Blue Sky" laws Another name for state laws which regulate the offer and sale of securities.

bond An instrument which evidences a corporate debt. It is a security which involves no ownership interest in the issuing corporation.

bond indenture An instrument of indebtedness issued by a corporation.

breach See breach of contract.

breach of contract Failure of a promisor to substantially perform the obligations of a contract.

burglary The unlawful entry, at night, into a building with the intent to commit theft. Some state statutes expand this to include the intent to commit any felony. (see *felony*)

bylaws The rules which a business firm adopts in order to control the conduct of its internal affairs.

C

capital stock The amount of money or property contributed by shareholders to be used as a corporation's financial foundation. The total amount of stock to be issued in return for capital contributions is limited by the corporation's charter. (see *charter*)

cashier's check A negotiable instrument drawn by a bank on itself.

causa mortis gifts A gift made because the giver (donor) contemplates his imminent death. If the donor does not die of that ailment, the gift is revoked, because the intent was to give it upon death. No title transfers until the donor's death.

cause of action A legal right of redress against another; it includes both the right to sue and the right to recover in a court of law.

caveat emptor (Latin) Literally, "let the buyer beware."

cease and desist order Administrative or judicial order commanding a business firm to cease conducting the activities which the agency or court has deemed "unfair or deceptive trade practices."

certified check A check drawn by an individual on his own account but bearing a guarantee by a bank that the bank will pay the check regardless of whether the drawer's account contains adequate funds at the time the check is presented.

charter The basic document under which a corporation is organized, setting forth the corporation's and shareholders' rights and duties.

chattel Tangible personal property.

chattel paper Any instrument which evidences both a security interest in collateral and a money obligation with respect to the collateral.

check An unconditional order to pay a sum certain to bearer or to whom the check is made out. The check is drawn on a bank, signed by the drawer, and payable on demand.

civil law 1) That branch of law which deals with the definition and enforcement of all private or public rights, as opposed to criminal matters. 2) The law compiled by the early Roman jurists, which is still in force in many Western European states, and is the foundation for the law in Louisiana.

class action suit A legal action in which a group of persons (usually more than thirty) are represented by one or a few persons. The class can be either a plaintiff or a defendant.

close corporation A corporation whose shareholders are limited to a small group of persons, often including only family members. Shareholders of a close corporation usually reserve *preemptive* rights with respect to the shares of all other shareholders.

codicil A written supplement or modification of a will. Codicils must be executed with the same formalities as a will.

collateral Those goods which the secured party has an interest in, as security in case of nonpayment by the debtor.

collecting bank Any bank handling an item for collection, except the payor bank.

commercial paper Negotiable instruments, which are signed writings by which the maker promises (unconditionally) to pay a certain amount of money to the bearer of the paper (*i.e.*, checks, promissory notes).

common law That body of law developed in English and American courts, not attributable to a legislature.

common stock Shares of ownership in a corporation which are lowest in priority with respect to payment of dividends and distribution of the corporation's assets upon dissolution.

comparative negligence Concept in tort law whereby liability for injuries resulting from negligent acts is shared by all persons who were guilty of negligence, including the injured party, on a basis proportionate to each person's carelessness.

compensatory damages Money damages equivalent to the actual value of the performance promised to defendant/breaching party by plaintiff, or the loss sustained by plaintiff.

complaint The charge made by a plaintiff or by the state to a judicial officer alleging wrongdoing on the part of the defendant. Thus, the plaintiff is also referred to as the complainant.

concurrent conditions Conditions which must occur or be performed at the same time; they are mutually dependent. No obligations arise until the simultaneous performance of these conditions.

concurrent estates Estates in land of equal quantity and quality held by two or more persons simultaneously.

condition A qualification on a contractual agreement. The obligation to perform can be varied, depending on whether the conditions are met or not.

condition precedent A qualification on a contractual agreement which must be met before the other party's obligations arise. If the condition is not met, the (conditional) obligation never arises. There can be no breach until the condition is met.

condition subsequent A qualification on a contract which, if met, discharges the (conditional) obligation of the other party. If the condition never arises, the other party's obligation is absolute.

confusion The mixing together of two or more goods so that the independent goods cannot be identified.

conglomerate mergers Mergers between firms which do not compete with each other because they are in different industries as opposed to horizontal and vertical mergers.

consent decree A judgment entered, by a court, by the consent of the parties. In a consent decree neither party admits guilt or wrongdoing.

consequential damages Special damages, which compensate for loss that is indirect or mediate (*i.e.*, lost profits). The special damages must have been reasonably foreseeable at the time the breach or injury occurred, in order for the plaintiff to collect them.

consideration   That which motivates the exchange of promises in a contractual agreement. The consideration, which must be present to make the contract legally binding, must be lawful in itself. It is a flexible term, and can refer to anything of value. (see *contract*)

consolidation   A contractual and statutory process whereby two or more corporations join to become a completely new corporation. The original corporations cease to exist, and the new corporation acquires all their assets and liabilities (*i.e.*, A + B = C).

constructive delivery   The recognition of the act of intending that title to property be transferred to someone else, even though actual, physical delivery of the property is not made (because of difficulty, impossibility) (*i.e.*, the transfer of a key to a safe constructively delivers the contents of the safe).

constructive/implied conditions   Conditions or qualifications to a promise which arise from the very nature of the promise and which the law recognizes as conditioning the promise even though not expressly stated.

consumer goods   Goods which are purchased primarily for personal use.

contract   A set of promises constituting an agreement between parties, giving each a legal duty to the other and also the right to seek a remedy for the breach of the promises/duties owed to each. (see *specific performance, injunction*) The elements of an enforceable contract are competent parties, a proper subject matter, consideration (an exchange of promises/duties), and mutuality of agreement and of obligation. (see *consideration*)

contracts implied-in-law   Promises which the law imposes upon contracting parties in general, as opposed to contracts implied-in-fact which have as their basis the underlying facts and circumstances of a particular contractual situation.

contracts under seal   Formal agreements in which the seal is a substitute for *consideration*. A court will not invalidate a contract under seal for lack of consideration.

contractual capacity   The threshold mental capacity required by the law for a party who enters into a contract to be bound by that contract. Contractual capacity will not be found where one is forced to sign a contract under duress or is insane.

contributory negligence   Any wrongful or negligent act by a complaining party which contributed to or enhanced the complaining party's injuries. Contributory negligence is an absolute bar to recovery in some jurisdictions. (see *negligence, affirmative defense*)

conversion   The wrongful taking or retaining possession of property which belongs to another.

corporation   An association of persons, usually entered into to carry out business endeavors. The law treats the corporation itself as a person which can sue and be sued. The corporation is distinct from the individuals who compose it (shareholders). The corporation survives the death of its investors, as the shares can usually be transferred. Created under state corporation statutes.

counterclaim   A pleading by a defendant against the plaintiff in which the defendant states a claim for damages resulting from allegedly wrongful acts of the plaintiff. The counterclaim need not arise out of the same facts and circumstances as the plaintiff's claim.

counter-offer   An offeree's response to an offeror in which the offeree proposes different or additional terms than were contained in the original offer. Acceptance of a counter-offer constitutes a contract, and a counter-offer itself constitutes a rejection of the original offer.

course of dealing   The understandings which arise between two parties with respect to time and quality of performance expected and which develop over a period of time and number of transactions between the two parties.

course of performance   The understandings and standards of time and quality of performance which develop between two parties during the performance of an executory contract.

covenant of quiet enjoyment   A promise by the landlord to the tenant, implied in law, that the landlord will not cause the tenant to be evicted.

covenant running with the land   An executory promise made between a promisor and promisee but which binds them as landowners and binds subsequent owners of the land bound by the covenant.

creditor beneficiary   A third person, who is not a

party to a contract to whom one of the parties owes a prior obligation. As a part of the contract, the other party obligates himself to honor the prior debt to the beneficiary. The beneficiary can enforce the debt against either party.

crime   A broad term for violations of law which are punishable by the state or nation. Crimes are codified by legislatures and their objective is the protection of the public. (see *civil law, criminal law*)

crimes mala in se   Acts which are morally wrong/wrong in themselves whether prohibited by human laws or not. (see *crimes mala prohibita*)

crimes mala prohibita   Acts which are prohibited by human law, but are not necessarily wrong in themselves. (see *crimes mala in se*)

criminal law   Governs and defines those actions which subject the convicted offender to punishment imposed by the state.

cure   The right of a party who tenders non-conforming performance to reform his performance within a reasonable time.

cy pres   Doctrine in the law of trusts and wills under which a grantor's (or testator's) wishes will be carried out "as nearly as possible" even though the grant (bequest or devise) is illegal in its original form.

D

damages   Money sought as a remedy for a breach of contract action or for tortious acts.

debt securities   Securities which are of such duration that they evidence an obligation of the corporation to repay the holder, rather than evidencing an investment by the holder in exchange for stock.

debtor   A person who owes a sum of money or other obligations to another.

deceit   A false representation of facts made recklessly, maliciously, or with knowledge of its falsity, with the intent to cause the injured person to rely on the misrepresentation. (see *fraud*)

deed   A document by which title to property (usually real property) is passed.

de facto corporation   A business which holds itself out as a corporation but which has not been organized in substantial compliance with state corporation law.

defamation   Anything published or publicly spoken which causes injury to another's good name, reputation or character. (see *slander, libel*)

defendant   The party against whom the action is brought.

defense of property   The legally recognized privilege of a person to do limited harm to another in defending his or her property. One may only use the amount of force necessary to protect his or her property, as the use of even slightly greater force will be deemed wrongful.

de jure corporation   A corporation which has been organized substantially in compliance with state corporation laws.

delegation   The act of transferring to another all or part of one's duties arising under a contract.

demurrer   A pleading in which a defendant admits to the facts as alleged by the plaintiff but asserts that the plaintiff's claim fails to state a cause of action (i.e., has no basis in law).

depositary bank   The first bank to which an item is transferred for collection even though it may also be the payor bank.

devise   To make a gift of real property by will.

disaffirmance   The repudiation of an obligation.

discharge   Termination of one's obligation. In contract law, discharge occurs when the promisor has fully performed his or her promised performance or when a party to a contract has substantially breached the contract (then the other party is discharged).

discharge in bankruptcy   The release of a bankrupt from all debts which are provable, except those specifically excepted from discharge by statute.

discovery   A method by which opposing parties may obtain information from each other, to narrow down the issues to be presented at trial. Generally governed by rules of procedure, but may be controlled by the court.

dishonor   The refusal to pay or accept an instrument which has been properly presented.

dissolution   The formal disbanding of a partnership. Can take place by agreement of the parties, death of a partner, or court order. (see *partnership for term, partnership at will*)

dividend (a)   A distribution of profits to corporate shareholders, disbursed in proportion to the number of shares held.

dividend (b)   Share of the proceeds of a bankrupt's estate received by a general creditor.

documents of title   Documents exchanged in the regular course of business which evidence the right to possession of goods (e.g., bills of lading, warehouse receipts, etc.).

domestic corporation   In any given state, a corporation which is doing business and is organized under the laws of the state.

donee beneficiary   A person not a party to a contract but to whom the benefits of a contract flow as a result of the promisee's intention to make a gift to that person.

draft   Any negotiable instrument drawn on any person (including a bank) which orders that person to pay a certain sum of money.

drawee   The person who is ordered to pay on an instrument. With a check, the bank is always the drawee.

drawer   A person who initiates a draft (including a check) thereby ordering the drawee to pay.

due process   An individual's right not to be deprived of life, liberty, or property without a hearing.

duress   Any unlawful threat or coercion used by a person to induce another to act or refrain from acting in a manner he or she otherwise would.

E

easement   The right to use another's property in a manner established either by express or implied agreement.

easement appurtenant   An easement on a "servient estate," which serves a "dominant estate."

easement in gross   The right to use another's land which is not dependent upon ownership of land by the holder of the easement.

embezzlement   The fraudulent appropriation of money or other property by a person to whom the money or property has been entrusted.

eminent domain   The power of a government to take land from private citizens for a fair compensation.

endowment policy   In life insurance, a policy which is payable when the insured reaches a given age, or upon his death, if that occurs earlier.

equitable servitude   A restriction on the use of land enforceable in a court of equity.

equity   The system of remedial justice, separate from the common law, based upon settled rules of fairness, justice and honesty.

equity of redemption   The right of mortgager to redeem or purchase property which the mortgagor forfeited by breaching the mortgage agreement.

equity securities   Securities with no repayment terms or with repayment terms of such long duration

that they represent an ownership interest in a corporation rather than debt.

estate   Full ownership interest in land.

estray statutes   State laws dealing with person's rights in property whose ownership is unknown.

exclusive dealing contract   An agreement under which a producer of goods agrees to sell its goods exclusively through one distributor.

exculpatory contract or clause   A contract or contract clause which releases one of the parties from liability for his or her negligent acts.

executed contract   An agreement which has been substantially (or completely) performed by both parties.

executor (trix)   A person either expressly or by implication appointed by a testator to see that his will is administered appropriately. (see *will, testator*)

executory contract   A contract calling for continual performance by one or both of the parties.

executory interest   A future interest not held by the grantor which either cuts short (shifting) or begins some time after (springing) the natural termination of the preceding estate.

express condition   A qualification or condition upon which a promise is based and which is stated in the body of the contract.

express contract   A contract which is either oral or written. (As opposed to *implied contract*.)

express warranty   A promise, ancillary to an underlying sales agreement which is included in the written or oral terms of the sales agreement and under which the promisor assures the quality of the goods.

ex-ship   Words in a contract denoting that the seller may choose the shipper, and that risk of loss shall pass to the buyer upon the goods leaving the ship. Buyer is also responsible for any subsequent landing charges.

F

F.A.S.   "Free alongside ship"; delivery term under which the seller is obligated to deliver goods to a specified loading dock and bears all risk of loss up to that point.

factual causation   In tort law, the physical connection between a person's act or failure to act and the resulting injury to another or damage to property.

fee simple absolute   An estate or interest in land with no time or use limitations whatsoever.

fee simple defeasible   An estate which can be taken

away (by the prior grantor) upon the occurrence or non-occurrence of a specified event.

felony Crime which carries the most severe sanctions, usually ranging from one year in prison to the forfeiture of one's life (*i.e.*, arson, murder, rape, robbery).

fiduciary duty A duty to act for someone else's benefit, while subordinating one's personal interests to that of the other person. It is the highest standard of duty implied by law (*i.e.*, trustee, guardian).

financing statement A document setting out a lienholder's security interest in goods. When the document is filed with the appropriate government agency, all potential lenders are put on constructive notice of the security interest.

firm offers A signed writing which promises to keep an offer open for a specified time. Unlike an option, no consideration need by given to make the offer non-revocable. (see *merchant's firm offer*)

fixture A thing which was once personal property, but has become attached to real property in such a way that it takes on the characteristics of real property and becomes part of that real property. (see *chattel*, *personal property*, *real property*)

floating lien A security interest in varying assets (e.g., inventory).

floating zone A concept in zoning whereby land use is predetermined by assigning specified portions of an entire area to particular uses while not immediately assigning particular parcels to a certain use.

F.O.B. "Free on board"; the seller in a commercial contract which contains the term F.O.B. has the duty to load the goods for shipment without expense to the buyer. Once loaded properly, the buyer assumes the risk of loss in case the goods are damaged.

forebearance Refraining from doing something that one has a legal right to do.

foreclosure A proceeding in equity whereby a mortgagee either takes title to or forces the sale of the mortgagor's property in satisfaction of a debt.

foreign corporation In any given state, a corporation which does business in the state without being incorporated therein.

forgery The false or unauthorized signature of a document, or the false making of a document, with the intent to defraud. (see *fraud*)

form An agreement which places the risks and burdens normally associated with the underlying exchange on one of the parties and which leaves no room for bargaining over these terms.

formal contract An agreement which the law requires be executed under seal or in the presence of witnesses or both.

fraud Any misrepresentation either by misstatement or omission knowingly made with the intention of defrauding another and on which a reasonable person would and does rely to his detriment.

frustration of purpose doctrine Court created doctrine under which a party to a contract will be relieved of his or her duty to perform when the objective purpose for performance no longer exists (due to reasons beyond that party's control).

fungible goods Goods which cannot be distinguished from other goods of the same type (*i.e.*, bushels of wheat, apples of the same brand).

future interest A present interest in land in which the right of enjoyment or possession is in the future.

G

garnishment A process whereby a creditor legally appropriates the debtor's property or wages which are in the hands of a third party.

gift Any transfer of property to another which is without consideration, past or present.

gift causa mortis See causa mortis gift.

good faith Honesty in fact as well as honesty in the conduct or transaction concerned.

goods Any tangible personal property which can be traded in the marketplace.

grace period A span of time, after insurance policy premium (payment) was due, during which the policy remains in effect. (see *policy*)

grand jury A body of people (usually 23) selected to conduct fact finding hearings for the purpose of issuing true bills for criminal offenses. The grand jury does not adjudicate, it only accuses. The grand jurors need only find probable cause to indict someone, as opposed to the exclusion of reasonable doubt standard which is necessary to convict someone of a crime. In certain situtations, the state or U.S. prosecutor can issue an information, rather than seek a grand-jury indictment. (see *information*, *true bill*)

grantor One who transfers real property by deed.

guaranty An agreement in which the guarantor agrees to satisfy the debt of another (the debtor). The guarantor is responsible only if and when the debtor fails to repay; he is secondarily liable.

H

holder   A person who is in possession of a document or negotiable instrument which runs to him.

holder in due course   A person who is a holder of an instrument and who took it in good faith, for value, and without notice that the instrument is overdue or has been dishonored or that any defense or claim exists against it.

holder through a holder in due course   One who acquires the rights of a holder in due course by taking the instrument through him in good faith.

holographic document   A document written entirely in the signer's handwriting.

homestead exemption   Law allowing a householder/head of a family to designate his house and adjoining land a homestead, and exempting it from liability for his general debts.

horizontal merger   A merger between two companies which compete in the marketplace.

I

identification   Proof that a thing is what it is purported or represented to be.

implied authority   The power of an agent to act on behalf of his principal which is inferred from the responsibilities imposed on the agent in his employment.

implied-in-fact contract   A promise which the law deems as part of an overall agreement because the underlying facts and circumstances logically infer the existence of such a promise.

implied warranty   A guarantee which the law implies either through the situation of the parties or the nature of the transaction. (see *usage of trade, course of dealing*)

implied warranty of merchantability   See warranty of merchantability.

impossibility of performance   Doctrine under which a party to a contract is relieved of his or her duty to perform since performance has become impossible or totally impracticable (through no fault of the party).

impracticability (commercial impracticability)   Broadened interpretation of the doctrine of impossibility which holds that a party to a business related contract will be relieved of his or her duty to perform when premise (e.g., existence of certain goods) on which the contract was based no longer exists due to unforeseeable events.

incidental beneficiary   A person who indirectly receives, or will receive, a benefit as the result of a contract entered into by other parties. Since the incidental beneficiary is neither a donee beneficiary nor a creditor beneficiary he has no right to enforce the contract.

indemnification   The right of an employer/principal to recover (be indemnified) from an employee/agent anything paid out to satisfy claims arising from the employee/agent's negligence within the scope of his employment/agency. (see *respondeat superior, power of attorney*)

indictment   A charge by a grand jury that a named person has committed an unlawful act.

indorsement   A signature placed on an instrument or a document of title for the purpose of transferring one's ownership in the instrument or document of title.

informal contract   An agreement which is valid regardless of whether it is witnessed or sealed.

information   A formal accusation or complaint issued in certain types of actions by a prosecuting attorney or other law officer. The types of actions are set forth in the rules of states or the Federal Rules of Criminal Procedure. (see *grand jury, true bill*)

injunction   An order by a court requiring a person to act or refrain from acting in a certain manner.

insolvency   The financial state of a person when his liabilities exceed the value of his assets *or* when, due to the non-liquidity of his assets he is unable or unwilling to pay his debts as they come due.

installment contract   An executory agreement whereby either property purchased or payments due, or both, are made periodically.

insurable interest   An interest either in a person's life or well-being or in property which is sufficiently substantial that insuring against injury to the person or damage to the property will not amount to a mere wagering contract.

intangible property   A property right, usually represented by a document or certificate which has no intrinsic value but which evidences a valuable ownership interest.

intermediary bank   Any bank to which an item is

transferred in the course of collection, except the depositary or payor bank.

inter vivos gift   A gift made by a living person which is not in contemplation of death.

inter vivos trust   A trust in which the grantor (settlor) is a living person. (*i.e.*, a trust not established by a will)

intestacy laws   State laws determining the way in which an intestate's (one who dies with no will) estate is divided.

intestate   (Dying) without a valid will.

inventory   Goods held for sale or lease or to be furnished under contracts of service, including work in process and materials used or consumed in a business. Inventory of a person is not to be classified as his equipment.

invitee   Person who, either expressly or impliedly, is privileged to enter upon another's land. The inviter owes the invitee the duty to exercise reasonable care to protect an individual from harm (*i.e.*, a customer in a store, the postman).

involuntary bankruptcy   A proceeding against an insolvent debtor which is initiated by the debtor's creditors.

issue   The first delivery of an instrument to a holder or a remitter.

J

joint and several liability   Liability of a group of persons for the same act (or failure to act) whereby a claimant may sue one or more of the parties separately or all of them together at his option.

joint liability   Liability of a group of persons for the same wrongful act (or failure to act) whereby when one is sued, he can insist that the others be sued with him.

joint tenancy   The ownership interest of two or more co-owners of property whereby each owns an undivided portion of the property. The key feature of joint tenancy is the "right of survivorship" whereby, upon the death of one of the joint tenants, his interest automatically passes to the others and cannot be transferred in his will.

judgment creditor   A person in whose favor a money judgment has been entered by a court of law and who has not yet been paid.

judgment debt   A monetary obligation which is either evidenced by a written record, or brought about by legal action against the debtor.

jurisdiction   The authority of a court to hear and decide a specific action.

jurisprudence   The science of philosophy of law.

L

laissez-faire   Doctrine advocating government restraint in regulation of business.

larceny   Act of taking another's personal property unlawfully. Burglary carried to its logical conclusion. Some states classify larceny as either Grand or Petit, depending on the property's value. (see *burglary*)

law   Rules of social conduct to be followed by citizens of a society, as pronounced by that society's government.

law merchant   Relates chiefly to the transactions of merchants, mariners, and other commercial traders. Consists chiefly of the general customs of the trades, which remain law unless displaced by specific statutes (see *Uniform Commercial Code*).

lease   A transfer by the landlord/lessor of real or personal property to the tenant/lessee for a period of time, for a consideration (usually the payment of rent). At the end of the period, the land reverts to the lessor.

legality   Lawfulness.

legally sufficient consideration   That type of consideration which the law recognizes as *legally* adequate to support a contract. Legal sufficiency does not deal with monetary value of consideration (e.g., "love and affection" is not legally sufficient consideration).

lessee   A person who pays for the use or possession of another's property.

lessor   A property owner who allows others to use his property in exchange for payment of rent.

letters of credit   A written instrument, usually issued by a bank on behalf of a buyer, in which the issuer promises to pay the bearer of the instrument (seller) upon proper delivery of goods, or at a specified time thereafter.

libel   A written defamation. The press is, to a certain degree, protected from libel actions by the First Amendment.

license   A revocable privilege to enter on the land of another.

lien   An encumbrance upon a property, to satisfy or protect a claim for payment of a debt.

life estate   An interest in land which exists only for

the duration of the life of some person, usually the holder of the estate.

limited liability Concept in corporation law whereby shareholders' liability for debts incurred by the corporation are limited to the money which the shareholders invested in their stock.

limited partnership A partnership consisting of one or more general partners, who carry on the business as well as contribute assets and are liable to the full extent of their personal assets for debts of the partnership, and one or more limited partners, who just contribute assets and are liable only up to the amount contributed by them. (see *partnership by contract*)

liquidated damages An amount, stipulated in the contract, which the parties believe to be a reasonable estimation of the damages which will occur in the event of a breach.

liquidated debt A debt which is for a known or ascertainable sum of money, the amount of which cannot be disputed by either the debtor or creditor.

liquidation Sale of the assets of a corporation for cash and distribution of the cash received to creditors and then to shareholders.

lost property Property which the owner has involuntarily parted with and does not know where to find or recover it.

M

maker One who issues a promissory note (*i.e.*, one who promises to pay a certain sum to the holder of the note which he executes).

mechanic's lien A lien which a creditor has in property which is in his possession and which has been increased in value by the creditor through the application of his labor and materials.

merchant A person who deals in goods of the kind or holds himself out as having knowledge or skills peculiar to the trade or goods involved, or to whom such skills can be attributed because of the nature of his employment.

merchant's firm offer A signed, written offer to buy or sell goods, which by its terms will be held open for a certain time, without requiring consideration. The U.C.C. limits merchant's firm offers to a maximum of three months. (see *firm offer*, U.C.C.)

merger A statutory and contractual process by which one corporation (surviving corporation) acquires all the assets and liabilities of another corpora-

tion (merged corporation). The shareholders of the merged corporation receive either payment for their shares or shares in the surviving corporation (*i.e.*, A + B = A).

misdemeanors Lessor crime, punishable by more severe sanctions than a disturbance of the peace, but not as severe as felonies.

mislaid property Property which the owner has voluntarily parted with, with the intention of retrieving later, but which cannot now be found. Does not include intentionally hidden property.

mortgage A written instrument giving some person (the mortgagee), usually a creditor, an interest (lien) in the debtor's (mortgagor's) property as security for a debt.

mortgagee The person who takes the security interest under the mortgage agreement.

mortgagor The person who pledges collateral in a mortgage agreement.

mutual assent Agreement by both parties to a contract to any particular term.

N

necessaries Goods and services, such as food, shelter, clothing and employment, which are deemed necessary or essential for a person's well being.

negative easement A burden on land whereby the landowner is restricted under an easement agreement not to use his property in a certain way. (e.g., not to build a building higher than four stories so as to preserve an adjacent landholder's view.)

negligence Conduct which falls below that standard of care which would be exercised by the "reasonable man," in relation to the protection of others. A legal duty is inherent in negligence. (see *tort*) Negligence is a lesser disregard of duty than recklessness or willfulness.

negotiable instruments A written and signed unconditional promise to pay a specified sum of money at a specified time. (see *commercial paper*)

negotiation The transferring of an instrument to another in a manner that will vest the transferee with the right to enforce the instrument.

nominal damages An award of damages whereby a court recognizes that there has been a technical breach of duty but has found that no financial loss or injury has resulted from the breach of duty.

note Same as *promissory note*.

novation The release of an old debt or debtor with the substitution of a new one in its/his place.

nuisance An act which interferes with a person's possession or ability to use his or her property.

O

objective theory of contracts The view taken by American law that contracting parties shall only be bound by terms which can be objectively inferred from promises made. Contract law does not examine a contracting party's subjective intent or underlying motive.

offer A proposal to do something by an offeree which creates in the offeror a legal power to bind the offeree to the terms of his proposal by accepting the offer.

offeree One to whom an offer is made.

offeror Person who makes an offer.

option contract A contract whereby the offeror cannot revoke his offer for a stipulated time period, and the offeree can accept or reject during this period without fear of the offer being put to another person. Here, the offeree must give consideration for the option (the non-revocable offer), as well as for the further contractual promises, if he accepts.

order paper An instrument which is payable to the payee or to any person the payee by his indorsement designates.

ordinary bailment A transfer of goods to the bailee in trust for the bailor, with benefits going to both parties. In exchange for a fee, the bailee agrees to safely keep the property until the bailor recovers it. The bailee is responsible for exercising due care toward the goods.

output contract A binding agreement where one party agrees to deliver/sell his entire output of a good (an unspecified amount at the time of agreement) to another party, and the other agrees to accept all of the goods supplied.

P

pari delicto At equal fault.

parol evidence rule Substantive rule of contracts under which a court will not receive into evidence oral or written statements made prior to or contemporaneous with a written agreement where the court finds that the written agreement was intended by the parties to be a final and complete expression of their agreement.

partnership Two or more persons associated for the purpose of carrying on a business for profit.

partnership at will A partnership which, by the terms of the Articles of Partnership, may be dissolved at any time by any of the partners.

partnership by estoppel Two or more persons which associate in a cooperative business enterprise and hold themselves out as partners.

payee Person to whom a negotiable instrument is made payable.

payor bank A bank by which an item is payable as drawn (or is payable as accepted).

penalties Amounts stipulated to in the contract, but either not being a reasonable estimation of the damages, or motivated solely by a desire to deter a breach. The agreement as to the amount will not be enforced, and recovery will be limited to actual damages.

per capita The manner of distribution of property whereby the heirs to an intestate's estate share and share alike. As opposed to *per stirpes*.

perfect tender rule Strict doctrine, whereby tender of performance/goods which does not exactly conform to the contract can properly be rejected. (see *tender, substantial performance*)

perfection The method by which a secured party obtains a guarantee that his security interest cannot be challenged by a subsequent secured party. Usually accomplished by filing a financing statement at a location set out in the state statute. (see *secured party, security interest, financing statement*)

periodic tendency Interest in land created by the payment of rent at a fixed interval.

personal property Property which is movable; any property which is not real property. (see *real property*)

per stirpes Manner of distribution of property whereby a class or group of distributees take the share which their deceased would have been entitled to (e.g., A dies leaving one son, B, and two grandchildren of deceased daughter C. B takes one-half and the two grandchildren each take one-quarter).

piercing the corporate veil A court's act of ignoring the separate legal existence of the corporation and thereby holding the corporation's officers personally liable for their wrongdoings.

plaintiff The party bringing an action.

plat A chart or map, usually filed with a municipal

or county agency, which delineates the parcels into which a large tract of land has been subdivided.

pleadings Statements by the plaintiff and the defendant which detail the facts, charges, and defenses. Modern rules simplify common law pleading, often requiring only the complaint, answer, and sometimes a reply to the answer.

pledge That which is offered as security for the payment of a debt.

policy The contract encompassing an insurance agreement.

pooling agreement A procedure whereby shareholders can increase their voting power, which is directly related to the number of shares held.

possibility of reverter A future interest in land which a grantor retains after conveying property subject to a condition subsequent. (see *future interest*)

power of attorney A writing authorizing another to act as one's agent or attorney.

power of termination A future interest in land which results when a grantor conveys land subject to a condition subsequent but also conditions the reversion of the land on the affirmative retaking of possession either by himself or his heirs.

precedent A case which furnishes an example or authority for deciding subsequent cases in which identical or similar facts are presented.

preemptive right A shareholder's right to purchase newly issued stock of a corporation, before it is •offered to any outside buyers, on a pro rata basis, thereby allowing the shareholder to maintain his proportionate share and voice in the corporation.

preferential transfer A transfer by one who is insolvent to one or more of his creditors within 90 days of bankruptcy whereby the creditor to whom the property was transferred is put in a better position than other creditors with respect to their priority claims to the assets of the insolvent.

preferred stock Classes of stock which have priority over common stock both as to payment of dividends and distribution of assets upon the corporation's dissolution.

prenuptial agreement An agreement made by the parties to a marriage prior to the marriage. If the consideration for the agreement is the forthcoming marriage, there must be a signed writing to make the agreement enforceable. (see *Statute of Frauds*)

prescription The acquiring of an easement (or profit) by continuous and open use of land owned by another for a prescribed statutory period.

presentment Demand by a holder of commercial paper for payment (or acceptance).

presentment warranty A guarantee that, when presented by a holder for payment, the instrument will be honored.

prima facie (Latin) "at first sight." Something that is considered true because, on the face of it, it appears to be true.

principal A person who, by agreement or otherwise, authorizes an agent to act on his behalf such that acts of the agent become binding on the principal.

privilege In tort law, the ability to act contrary to another person's right without that person having legal redress for such acts. Privilege is usually raised as a defense, such as where A attacks B, B has a privilege to fight back to reasonably protect himself; but for A's assault in battery, B's battery would contravene A's rights.

privity of contract The relationship which exists between the promisor and promisee of a contract.

probable cause Reasonable ground to believe the existence of facts warranting acts such as search or arrest of a person.

probate The process of proving and validating a will.

probate court A special court, in some jurisdictions, having jurisdiction of proceedings concerning the settlement of a person's estate. (see *jurisdiction*, *estate*)

procedure The manner by which parties and courts must act when bringing an action, whether civil, criminal, or administrative. Includes pleading, process, evidence, and practice.

procedural law That law which deals with the manner of bringing an action.

profit The right to enter upon and remove things from the property of another. (e.g., the right to enter onto a person's land and remove sand and gravel therefrom.)

promisee Person to whom a contractual duty is owed.

promisor Person who is under a contractual duty to another.

promissory estoppel A legal principle whereby a party is not allowed (estopped) to deny certain relevant facts, because of statements they made, or because they made procedural errors. (*i.e.*, a defendant who does not plead an affirmative defense is estopped from doing so at trial.) (see *affirmative defense*)

promissory note A written instrument signed by a maker promising to pay a sum certain in money to a payee or a holder on a specified date.

promoter An entrepreneur who, utilizing his own capital, purchases or leases facilities and equipment for, and participates in the organization of a newly formed corporation. Promoters generally assume substantial risks in organizing new corporations, but also stand to realize significant profits from their efforts.

property Anything subject to being used, possessed, and disposed of; need not be tangible ("rights" are property).

proximate cause The "next" or "substantial" cause; in tort law, a concept used to determine whether a plaintiff's injury was the result of a defendant's negligent act. If the negligent act of a defendant was the sole cause or was a substantial cause of injuries to a plaintiff, the defendant will be liable to the plaintiff.

proxy An agreement between a stockholder and another under which the stockholder authorizes the other to vote the stockholder's shares in a certain manner.

punitive damages Compensation in excess of actual or consequential damages. They are awarded in order to punish the wrongdoer, and will be awarded only in cases involving willful or malicious misconduct. Also called "smart money."

purchase money security interest A security interest which the seller of goods retains when it "lends" the purchase price to the purchaser of the goods. Such a security interest is automatically perfected.

Q

qualified indorsement An indorsement on a negotiable instrument under which the indorser disclaims secondary liability on the instrument; under a qualified indorsement, however, an indorser still gives warranties of title. The most common qualified indorsement is "without recourse."

quasi-contracts A quasi-contract is not a contract at all, but a *remedy* afforded to a person who renders services or delivers goods to another who accepts the goods or services without payment for them.

quasi-judicial power The power of an administra-

tive agency to adjudicate the rights of individuals before it.

quasi-legislative The power of an administrative agency to engage in rule-making.

quitclaim deed A deed conveying title to real property, but guaranteeing nothing, not even the transferor's title, to the purchaser.

quorum The number of persons who must be present at a meeting of a corporation's stockholders in order for action taken at the meeting to be valid.

R

rate making power Government power to determine and set rates for business (*i.e.*, wage rate, prices).

ratification In contract, the act of adopting or confirming an act which does not meet the contractual obligation, or carried out by one without the authority to do so (or was incompetent at the time the contract was made). The act of ratification causes the ratifier to give up his right to sue for a performance which does not otherwise conform with the contract.

real property Property consisting of land and building thereupon, which are stationary, as opposed to personal property, which can be moved. Real property includes things growing on land before they are severed (such as timber) as well as fixtures.

reality of assent Consideration of whether a person to a contract *actually* or only *impliedly* "accepts" each and every proposed term.

reasonable doubt The standard used to determine the guilt or innocence of a person criminally charged. To be guilty of a crime, one must be proved guilty "beyond and to the exclusion of every reasonable doubt."

reciprocal contract A bilateral contract.

recognizance An obligation to return or reappear before a court.

reformation A court ordered correction of a written instrument, to cause it to reflect the true intentions of the parties.

rejection An offeree's communication to the offeror that the offeree does not accept the terms of the proposal made by the offeror.

remainder A future interest in property held by a person other than a grantor which occurs at the natural termination of the preceding estate. A remainder is a present right to future possession and can either be vested or contingent.

remand   The act of an appellate court sending a case back to the trial court ordering it to conduct either limited new hearings or an entire new trial.

replevin   An action in equity brought to recover possession of goods unlawfully taken by another; as opposed to recovering the value of the goods. (see *conversion*)

reply   Procedurally, a plaintiff's response to a defendant's answer.

repudiation   Rejection of a contract involving the unconditional refusal by one of the parties to perform.

requirements contracts   An agreement under which a promisor promises to supply the promisee with all the goods and/or services the promisee might require from period to period. While such contracts were at one time void for indefiniteness of amount, they are now universally valid.

res judicata   A rule that prohibits the same factual dispute between two parties to be retried by a court after final judgment has been entered by a trial court and all appeals have been exhausted (or the time for appeal has passed).

rescission   A remedy whereby the contract is cancelled and the parties are returned to the positions they occupied before the contract was made. May be done through mutual consent of the parties, by their conduct, or by the decree of a court of equity.

respondeat superior   A principle of law which says that an employer is liable for the negligent acts of his employees while they are working within the scope of their employment.

restitution   An equitable remedy under which a person who has rendered services to another, but where no valid contract between the two exists, will be reimbursed for the costs of his acts but will not be awarded profits; as opposed to an action for breach of contract.

restrictive indorsement   Any indorsement of a negotiable instrument which purports to prohibit further transfer of the instrument. As against banks, such indorsements are usually ineffective.

reversion   A future interest under which a grantor retains a present right to future interest of property which he conveys to another; usually the residue of a life estate, the reversion is always a vested property interest.

robbery   Theft from a person, accompanied by assault and/or battery. (see *assault, battery*)

rule against perpetuities   Rule against remoteness in vesting which states: "no interest in property is good unless it must vest, if at all, not later than 21 years, plus a period of gestation, after some life or lives in being at the time of creation of the interest."

S

sale   The passing of title from the seller to the buyer for a price.

satisfaction   The tender of substitute performance in return for the relinquishment of the right of action on a prior obligation. (see *accord and satisfaction*)

scope of employment   The activities in which an employee engages in the carrying out of his employer's business which are reasonably foreseeable by the employer.

secured party   Anyone who has an interest in a good, which they can exercise upon the occurrence or nonoccurrence of an event, and receive possession of the good.

secured transaction   Any transaction, regardless of its form, which is intended to create a security interest in personal property or fixtures including goods, documents, and other intangibles.

securities   Stock certificates or bonds given as evidence of a contribution to the assets of a corporation under which the security holder receives either an ownership interest in the corporation or a promise of repayment by the corporation.

security agreement   An agreement which creates or provides for a security interest.

security interest   An interest in personal property or fixtures which secures payment or performance of an obligation.

self-defense   The legally recognized privilege to protect one's self or one's property against injury by another. The privilege of self-defense only protects acts which are reasonably necessary to protect one's self or one's property.

severable contract   A contract which includes two or more promises which can be acted on separately such that the failure to perform one promise does not necessarily put the promisor in breach of the entire agreement.

shareholder   The holder of an ownership interest in a corporation.

shipment contract   Any agreement for the sale of goods under which the seller is authorized or required only to bear the expense of putting the goods in the hands of a common carrier and bears the risk of loss only up to that point. A contract for the sale of goods which is silent on a delivery term is presumed to be a shipment contract.

shop right doctrine An employer's privilege to use an invention developed by an employee, without compensating that employee.

short-swing profits Profits made on the purchase and sale of stock of a corporation within a six-month period.

sight draft A draft which is payable upon proper presentment.

signature The name or mark of a person, written by himself, or at his direction. In commercial law, any word or mark used with the intention of indorsing an instrument constitutes a signature. (see *indorsement*)

slander An oral defamation.

sole proprietorship A business which is owned and operated by a single person (or his or her immediate family) which is not incorporated under the laws of the domiciliary state.

special bailment Any of a number of relationships, including gratuitous bailments, for the benefit of the bailor only; involuntary bailments, which arise by the accidental leaving of property with another (the bailee need exercise only "ordinary care"); and constructive bailments, where one person holds another's goods in such a manner that the law imposes a bailment situation.

special indorsement An indorsement (signature of the transferor in a negotiation) specifying to whom the instrument is payable.

specific performance An equitable remedy, whereby the court orders one of the parties to a contract to perform his duties under the contract. Usually granted when money damages would be an inadequate remedy (e.g., purchase and sale of real property).

stale check A check, other than a certified check, which is presented more than six months after its date.

stare decisis A flexible doctrine of the courts, recognizing the value of following prior decisions (precedent) in cases similar to the one now before the court—the practice of a court's being consistent with prior decisions based on similar facts.

Statute of Frauds Statutory requirement (based on English common law) requiring that certain types of contracts be written to be enforceable. (e.g., contracts for the sale of goods over $500; contracts for the sale of land; contracts which cannot, by their terms, be performed within a year.)

statute of limitations Statutes of the federal government and the various states setting maximum time periods during which certain actions can be tried. After the time period set out in the applicable statute of limitations has run, no legal action can be brought regardless of whether any cause of action ever existed.

statutory law Laws which are enacted by a legislative body. (As opposed to constitutional law, administrative law or case law.)

stop payment order An order by a drawer of a check directing his bank not to pay a check.

strict liability Liability regardless of fault. Under tort law, strict liability is imposed on any person who introduces into commerce any good which is unreasonably dangerous when in a defective condition.

Subchapter S corporation A corporation which, because it has filed as a Subchapter S and because it has met certain requirements as set out by the internal revenue code qualifies for special income tax treatment. Essentially, a Subchapter S corporation is taxed the same as a partnership while at the same time allowing the corporation's owners to enjoy the privilege of limited liability.

sublease A lease executed by the lessee of land to a third person, conveying the same interest which the lessee enjoys, but for a shorter term than that for which the lessee holds.

subrogation The substitution of one person in the place of another giving the former the same legal rights which the latter had. Subrogation appears most frequently in construction contracts, insurance contracts and in negotiable instrument law.

substantial performance A doctrine of commercial reasonableness which recognizes that the rendering of a performance which does not exactly meet the terms of the agreement will be looked upon as fulfillment of the obligation less the damages which result from any deviation from the promised performance.

substantive law Laws which define the rights and duties of individuals with respect to each other, as opposed to procedural law which defines the manner in which these rights and duties may be enforced.

substituted agreement   A contract whereby the parties to an already existing contract agree that the existing contract is no longer binding and that a new contract or agreement will take its place.

summary judgment   A judgment entered by a trial court which is based upon the valid assertion by a defendant that the plaintiff does not have a cause of action.

surety   One who agrees to pay the debt of another. The surety is liable to the debtor even if the creditor does not seek to collect from the principal (original debtor) first. (see *suretyship*)

suretyship   The relationship among three parties whereby one person (the surety) guarantees payment of a debtor's debt for performance of an obligor's duties to a creditor or obligee.

surviving corporation   The corporation which, through a merger, acquires the assets and liabilities of another corporation.

T

tangible personal property   Property, which can be moved, which has physical substance and can be distinguished by the five senses; corporeal property.

tenancy at sufferance   Maintenance of occupancy by someone who has no estate in the land. He occupies only because the person entitled to eject him has not; he has no estate or title.

tenancy at will   The right of a tenant to remain in possession of land until either he or the landlord chooses to terminate the tenancy.

tenancy by the entirety   The joint ownership of property by husband and wife. Five "unities" must be present: time, title, interest, possession, and person (under common law, husband and wife were one person). Neither party can alienate or encumber the property, it is inherited by the survivor of the two, and dissolution of marriage transforms it to tenancy in common.

tenancy for years   A non-freehold estate/lease for a specified number of years, at which time the interest reverts to the grantor. The lease can be renewed or not at the end of the term of years.

tenancy from period to period   (periodic tenancy) A non-freehold estate/lease which exists for a period of one year or less, and can be renewed or not at the end of each period (*i.e.*, monthly).

tenancy in common   Co-ownership of property whereby each tenant owns an undivided fractional part of the property, and none owns the whole as in joint tenancy.

tender   A timely offer, or expression of willingness, to pay a debt or perform an obligation.

testamentary trust   A trust which is created by will, and therefore does not take effect until the death of the testator.

testate   Leaving a valid will; when a person dies leaving a valid will he dies testate.

testator (trix)   One who makes and executes a will. (see *will*)

title   The right to full ownership of property.

title insurance   An insurance policy which insures against defects in the title of property (usually real property).

tort   Civil wrongs (as opposed to criminal) not arising from a breach of contract; a breach of a legal duty owed by the defendant to the plaintiff. That breach must be the proximate cause of the harm done to plaintiff. (see *proximate cause, negligence*)

tortfeasor   One who commits a personal wrong (or a tort).

trade acceptance   A bill of exchange/draft drawn by the seller of goods on the purchaser, and accepted by such purchaser. It represents the purchaser's promise to pay.

trade fixture   Articles placed in or attached to buildings by the tenant, to carry on the tenant's business. They are generally removable without material harm to the real property.

trademark   A word or symbol which has become sufficiently associated with a good (common law) or has been registered with a government agency; once established, the person using the trademark has the right to bring a legal action against those who infringe upon the protection given the trademark. The remedy may be criminal, money damages, or an injunction against the defendant. (see *injunction*)

trespass   Any transgression or offense against the property of another.

trespass to land   The mere intentional or unintentional passing over another person's land uninvited, regardless whether any physical damage was done to the land.

trespass to personalty   Same as trespass.

traveler's check   A check drawn by the issuing bank upon itself which is accepted by the act of issuance.

Like a cashier's check, the bank is secondarily liable as drawee; additionally, it is primarily liable as acceptor.

true bill   Often called an indictment, the true bill is issued by the grand jury after a finding of probable cause to accuse a person of a criminal offense. (see *information, grand jury*)

trustee   One who holds legal title to property "in trust" for the benefit of another person (beneficiary), and who must carry out specific duties with regard to the property. The trustee owes a fiduciary duty to the beneficiary. (see *fiduciary duty*)

trustee in bankruptcy   The person appointed to oversee the estate of a bankrupt.

tying agreement   A requirement in a contract between a buyer and seller whereby the buyer of a specific good is obligated to purchase additional connected products.

U

ultra vires   Activities of a corporation's managers which are outside the scope of the power granted them by the corporation.

unconscionable contracts   A contract which is void as against public policy because one party, as a result of his disproportionate bargaining power, is forced to accept terms which are unfairly burdensome to him and which unfairly benefit the dominating party.

undue influence   Abuse of one's position of influence or relationship with another person to persuade that person to act or refrain from acting in a certain manner; usually involves breach of a fiduciary duty.

unilateral contract   A contract under which promise of payment or performance is given in exchange for performance by the other party (as opposed to a promise to perform by the other party).

unliquidated debt   An obligation which has not been reduced to a specific money amount; also, there may be a dispute between the parties as to this undetermined amount.

usage of trade   The prevailing, accepted customs within a particular trade or industry. It is implied that merchants are cognizant of the usage of their trade.

usury   Charging interest on a debt above the statutory maximum, as defined by various state statutes. A contract which includes a usurious interest rate is illegal, and therefore unenforceable.

V

venue   The geographical district in which the action is tried and from which the jury is selected. (see *jurisdiction*)

vertical merger   A combining of two firms, one of which purchases goods for resale from the other. If a producer or wholesaler acquires a retailer it is a *forward* merger. If a retailer or distributor acquires its producer it is a *backward* merger. (see *merger*)

vertical price-fixing contract   An agreement to maintain prices between producers and wholesalers or distributors, between producers and retailers, or between wholesalers or distributors and retailers.

vicarious liability   Responsibility for someone else's actions, arising out of some legal relationship. (see *respondeat superior, power of attorney*)

void   Having no legal force or binding effect.

voidable   That which may be legally annulled at the option of one of the parties.

voluntary bankruptcy   A bankruptcy proceeding which is initiated by the debtor.

voting trust   The entrusting of shares of a corporation to a trustee who is authorized to vote the shares so that certain persons remain directors, and thus in control of the corporation.

W

waiver   An intentional, knowing relinquishment of a legal right. (see *accord, satisfaction, novation*)

warehouseman   A person engaged in the business of storing goods for hire.

warehouse receipt   A receipt issued by a person engaged in the business of storing goods for hire; it is a document of title.

warranty   A guarantee by one party to the other that certain facts or conditions actually exist as represented, thus relieving the promisee of a duty to ascertain those facts himself. Under the U.C.C., three types of warranty exist. (see *promisee*)

warranty deed   A deed under which the grantor guarantees to the grantee that he (the grantor) has title to the property conveyed in the deed and that there are no encumbrances on the property other than what the grantor has represented.

warranty of merchantability   A promise by the seller of goods that they are reasonably fit for the general purpose for which they are sold.

watered stock   Stock issued by a corporation as fully

paid for, when in fact the entire par value has not been paid.

whole life A life insurance policy in which the insured pays a level premium for his or her entire life and in which there is a constantly accumulating cash value which the insured can withdraw or borrow against.

will An instrument directing what is to be done with a person's property upon his death, made by that person and revocable during his lifetime. No interests pass until the testator dies. (see *testator*)

winding up The settling of accounts and liquidation of assets or a partnership or corporation just prior to dissolution.

writ A written court order or a judicial process, directing that a sheriff, judge, or other judicial officer do what is commanded by the writ. Thus, a "writ of certiorari" commands the inferior court to send the record of the case to the issuing court, which will take appellate jurisdiction.

writ of certiorari Court order giving jurisdiction to an appellate court, on that court's discretion after a review of the petition, which is submitted by a party to the action. Many cases reach the U.S. Supreme Court this way, since there is no absolute right to Supreme Court review. (see *writ*)

writ of execution A writ which puts in force a court's decree.

Z

zoning The division of the land of an entire city or county by a legislature whereby the legislature prescribes certain general or particular uses for various segments of the land.

INDEX

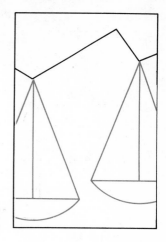

ABANDONED PROPERTY
See Personal Property

ACCEPTANCE
See Agreement; Sales

ACCESSION
See Personal Property

ACCOMMODATION PARTY
See Commercial Paper, Liability

ACCORD AND SATISFACTION
See Contracts, Discharge by accord and
satisfaction

ACTION
In personam, 12
In rem, 12
Quasi in rem, 12

ADMINISTRATIVE AGENCIES
Generally, 744-771
Administrative law,
Defined, 6
Administrative process,
Judicial process, compared with, 6
Agriculture, Department of, 758
Civil Aeronautics Board, 758
Congress, role of, 746

Consent decree, 750
Consumer Product Safety Commission,
744, 745, 753, 760
Costs,
Exhibit, 745
Courts, role of, 746-749
Energy,
Jurisdiction over use of, exhibit, 753
Environmental Protection Agency, 744,
753, 792-793
Federal Communications Commission,
758
Federal Housing Administration, 767
Federal Power Commission, 766
Federal Trade Commission, 750-753, 773,
774-778
See also Trade Regulation
Food and Drug Administration, 759, 762,
766
Forms required of corporation, exhibit,
767-770
Interstate Commerce Commission, 752,
753, 758-760
Labor, Department of, 760-761
Occupational Safety and Health Adminis-
tration, 744, 750, 753, 761-762
Powers and procedures, 746-752
Adjudicative powers, 750-752
Compliance and enforcement powers,
750

Complaints, 750
Investigatory powers, 749-750
Ministerial powers, 749
Rule-making powers, 750
Procedures,
See Powers and procedures, this topic
Regulated activities, 759-767
Advertising, 754-758
Communications, 760
Consumer products, 760
See also Consumer Protection
Employment, 763-765
Financing, 767
Health and safety, 760-762
Industrial production, 762-763
Innovation, 766
Transportation, 759-760
Utilities, 760
Regulation,
Contract revisions, 759
Disclosure requirements, 759
Licensing and allocating rights, 758
Materials and process, 759
Overlapping, 752
Price, 752, 754
Profit, 752
Public review of, 767
Quotas and duties, 758
Rate making, 752
Scope, expansion of, 745
Standard setting, 758
Taxes, 759
Types, 752-759
Regulations,
Source of law, 6
Securities and Exchange Commission,
689, 758
Subsidies, 759
Tennessee Valley Authority, 746-749
Types,
Administrative branch of government,
746
Independent of executive branch, 746

ADMINISTRATIVE LAW
See Administrative Agencies

ADVERSARY SYSTEM OF JUSTICE
American and English courts, followed in,
18

ADVERSE POSSESSION
See Real Property

ADVERTISING
See Administrative Agencies, Regulated
activities; Consumer Protection;
Federal Trade Commission

AGENCY
Generally, 544-569
Accounting by principal, agent's demand
for, 568
Agreement, by, 552

Agreements not to compete, 561
Authority,
Actual,
Agent's authorized acts, 578-580
Apparent, compared, 549-551
Express, 571
Implied, 571
Apparent, 571-575
Actual, compared, 549-551
"Clothed the agent," 573
Termination, 557
Commercial paper,
Indorsement, 415
Signature of original instrument, 433-
436
Conflicts of interest, 563-564
Corporations,
Torts and criminal acts, liability for, 661
Coupled with an interest, 553
Customer lists, 561-563
Defined, 544
Duties,
Agent to principal, 545, 560-567
Account, to, 565
Loyalty, duty of, 561-564
Notify, duty to, 561
Perform, duty to, 560-561
Subagents, 564-565
Unauthorized, 565
Employer,
Duty of care in hiring employees, 586
Nondelegatable, 583
Principal to agent, 545, 567
Compensation and reimbursement,
567
Cooperation, duty of, 567
Safe working conditions, duty to
provide, 567
Emergency powers, 575
Employee,
Defined, 545-546
Employer,
Employer-employee relationship, 545-
546
Liability for employee's intentional
torts,
Duty of care in hiring, 586
Notice of dangerous conditions, 586
Employment,
Rights and benefits acquired during,
565
Equal dignity statutes, 571
Estoppel, 552, 571-575
Exceptionally hazardous activities, 583
Fellow-servant rule, 586
Formation of agency relationship, 551-553
"Frolic" by employee, 584-585
Gratuitous or free agent, 561
Indemnification,
Agent's right to, 567-568, 578
Principal's right to, 565-567
Limits on, 567
Independent contractor, 546-548, 583
Insurance,

Agent's relationship with applicant, 886
Kinds of agents, 545-548
Legal capacity, 553
Liability,
  Agent, of,
    Contracts, 578-581
  Principal, of,
    Contracts, 570-577
    Torts, 581-586
      Intentional, 586
Lien of agent against principal's property, 568
Master-servant relationship, 545-546
Misrepresentation, 581-582
  Innocent, 582
Mutual,
  Partnership law, 544
Nature of, 544-545
Negligence, 582-583
Negotiable instruments, 580
Operation of law, by, 552-553
Partially disclosed principal, 581
Personal injury, 582-583
Principal-agent relationship, 545
Purpose, 545
Ratification, 575-577
  Agency by, 552
  Defined, 575
  Express, 576
  Implied, 576-577
Remedies,
  Agent's remedies against principal, 567-568
  Principal's remedies for agent's violation of fiduciary duty, 567
Respondeat superior, 582-583
Scope of employment, 549-551, 583-585
Servants,
  Borrowed, 583
  Subservants, 583
Specific performance,
  Agent cannot normally seek, 568
Termination of, 553-557
  Act of parties,
    Lapse of time, 554
    Mutual agreement, 554
    One party, by, 554-556
    Purpose achieved, 554
    Specific event, occurrence of, 554
  Apparent authority, 557
  Notice required, 557
  Operation of law, 556-557
    Death or insanity, 556
    Unforeseen circumstances, 556-557
      Bankruptcy, 557
      Changed circumstances, 556
      Impossibility, 556
  Premature, 554-556
Undisclosed principal, 578-580
  Negotiable instruments, 580
  Principal's rights against agent, 580
  Third party's rights,
    Personal performance of agent, 580
    Rescind contract, 580

AGREEMENT
  See also Duress; Fraud; Mistake
  Generally, 79-103
Acceptance, 98-101
  Communication of, 100
  Conditions, effect of, 99
  Defined, 98
  Mailbox rule, 101
  Silence as, 99-100
  Timing, rules on, 101
  Unequivocal, 99
  Who can accept, 99
Implication of reasonable terms, 80
Incidental or collateral terms,
  Uncertainty or indefiniteness of, 80
Indefiniteness of terms, 80
Mutual assent, 79-80
Offer,
  Agreements to agree, 86
  Auctions, 86
  Communication of, 92-94
  Counter offer,
    Termination of offer, operates as, 98
  Definiteness, 86-92
    Output and requirements contracts, 92
    Part performance, indefiniteness cured by, 89
    Uniform Commercial Code, relaxation of definiteness under, 89
  Firm offers, 97, 120-121
  Intention, 80-86
    Advertisements, catalogues and circulars, 83-85
    Opinion, expressions of, 81
    Preliminary negotiations, 81, 83
    Statements of, 81-82
  Requirements of, 80-94
  Rewards, 92-94
  Sham transactions, 86
  Social affairs, 86
  Termination of, 94-98
    Counter offer by offeree, 98
    Death or incompetency, 95-96, 97
    Destruction of subject matter, 95
    Law, operation of, 94-96
    Option contracts, 96-97
    Parties, action of, 96-98
    Rejection of offer by offeree, 98
    Revocation of offer by offeror, 96-98
      Firm offers, 97
      Option contract, 96-97
      Reliance to offeree's detriment, 97
      Unlimited contract, 98
    Supervening illegality, 96
    Time, lapse of, 94-95

ALIENS
See Capacity

ANTICIPATORY REPUDIATION
See Contracts, Discharge by breach of contract

ANTITRUST
    See also Federal Trade Commission
    Generally, 806-826
Agriculture, 823
Clayton Act, 831-834
    Enforcement of, 822
    Text, 822
Common law actions, 806-807
Exclusive dealing contracts, 831
Exemption from antitrust laws, 822-824
Fair-trade agreements, 823
Foreign trade, 824
Group boycotts, 819-822
Holding companies,
    Sherman Act and, 810
Horizontal restraints, 819, 840-841
Insurance, 823
Interlocking directorates, 834
Joint refusals to deal, 819-822
Labor, 823
McCarran-Ferguson Act, 823
Mergers, 831-834
    See also Corporations
    Clayton Act, 831-834
    Conglomerate, 841
    Horizontal, 840-841
    Vertical, 838
Miller-Tydings Act, 823
Price discrimination, 828-831
Professionals, 823
Reciprocal arrangements, 838
Resale price maintenance, 823
Restraint of trade, 806-807
    Defined, 806
Sherman Act,
    Courts' initial reaction to, 809-813
    Jurisdiction, 809
    Per se standard, 813-822
        Depression, effect of, 819
        Development of, 813-818
    Proscriptive nature, 809
    Remedies and sanctions, 809
    Rule of reason, 807, 813, 816, 819
    Sections I and II compared, 808
    Standing, 809
    Text, 808
    Treble damages, 809
Small Business Act of 1953, 823
Sports, 823
Standard Oil case, 810-813
Trusts,
    Formation of, 807-808
Tying contracts, 831
United States,
    Beginning of U.S. antitrust law, 807-813
    Common law, 807
Vertical restraints, 837-840

APPEAL
    Generally, 23-24
Abstract, 23
Appellant, 23
Appellee, 23

Intermediate and higher appeals courts, 24
Remand, 24

APPRAISAL RIGHTS
See Corporations, Mergers and consolidation

ARBITRATION
See Contracts

ARRANGEMENTS
See Bankruptcy and Reorganization

ARREST
See Criminal Procedure

ARSON
See Criminal Law

ASSAULT
See Torts

ASSIGNMENT
    See also Commercial Paper
    Generally, 193-203
Anti-assignment clauses, 198-201
Consideration, 196
Defined, 193
Delegation of duties, 193, 201-203
    Duties that can be delegated, 201
    Effect of, 202-203
    Form of, 201
Notice of, 201
Novation, compared, 193
Rights, assignable, 196-198
Statute of Frauds, 196

ATTACHMENT
    Generally, 508-511
Defined, 508
Enforceable right, 510
Wrongful attachment, 510-511

ATTORNEYS
Advertising, 754-758
Work product, discovery of, 28

AUCTIONS
See Agreement, Offer

BAILMENTS
    Generally, 261-278
Agreement, 266
Bailee,
    Bailments for sole benefit of, 267
    Defined, 261
    Duties of,
        Care, 268
        Negligence, presumption of, 268-270
        Relinquish property, 270-271
    Involuntary, 254, 255
    Rights of,

Compensation, 268
Possession, 267
Use of bailed property, 268
Risk of loss, 308-309
Bailor,
Bailments for sole benefit of, 266-267
Defined, 261
Duties of, 271-273
Rights of, 271
Common carriers, 274-275
Connecting carriers, 275
Shipper's loss, 275
Contractual bailments, 267
Defined, 261
Delivery of possession, 262-266
Constructive, 264
Misdelivery, 264-266
Elements, 261-266
Exclusive possession, 263
Exculpatory clauses, 273-274
Fungible goods, 266
Gratuitous, 266-267
Identical goods, return of, 266
Innkeepers,
Guests' automobiles, 276
Regular business, 276
Statutory changes, 276
Personal property requirement, 261
Special (extraordinary) bailments, 274-276
Termination of, 274
Types, 266-267
Warehouse companies, 275
Warranty liability,
Implied warranty of fitness, 271-273

BANKRUPTCIES AND REORGANIZATION
Generally, 526-541
Adjustment of debts of individual with regular income (wage earner plan), 538-540
Arrangements, 540
Bankruptcy Reform Act of 1978, 526-527
Commercial paper,
Bankruptcy as defense, 446
Concurrent jurisdiction, 527
Contracts,
Consideration, lack of, 121
Debts and claims, 531-536
Costs incurred in lawsuits, 532
Enforceable contracts, 532
Fixed liabilities evidenced by a judgment, 531
Lease, breach of contract action on unexpired, 532
Liquidated or for a sum certain, 531-532
Open accounts, 532
Provable claims, 531-532
Not dischargeable, 532
Workmen's compensation awards, 532
Written instruments, 531
Discharge,
Denial of, 532-535

Dividend, 532
Estate, defining the bankrupt's, 536-537
Exempt property, 536
Fraud,
Grounds for denying discharge, 533-535
Fraudulent conveyance,
See Voidable transfers, this topic
Goals of bankruptcy law, 527
Individual repayment plans, 537-538
Involuntary, 527-528
Non-liquidation proceedings, 537-540
Partnerships, 597
Priority of payment of claims, 535-536
Procedures, 528-531
Creditors' first meeting, 528-531
Naming a receiver, 528
Order for relief, 528
Receiver, 528
Reorganization,
Chapter XI, 540
Corporate, 538
Trustee in bankruptcy, 528
Types, 527-528
Voidable transfers, 536-537
Fraudulent conveyance, 537
Lien on debtor's property, 537
Preference, 536
Voidable rights, 536
Voluntary, 527
Wage earner plan, 538-540

BANKS
Accepting deposits, 468-471
Altered checks, payment on, 467-468
Automated clearing houses, 470-471
Bank-customer relationship, 457
Check clearing technology, 470-471
Check collection process, 468-470
Customers of different banks, 469-470
Customers of same bank, 469
Checks and the banking system, 452-473
Collecting bank, 468
Collection, 411
Death or incompetence of customer, 461
Depository bank, 468
Duties, 457-471
Electronic funds transfer systems (EFTS), 470, 471
Banks' liability, 471
Federal Reserve System, 470
Forged instrument, payment on, 464-467
Customer's duty to discover and report, 464-467
Forged signature of drawer, payment on, 463-464
Customer negligence, 463
Timely examination, 463-464
Honoring checks, 457-459
Indorsement by bank for customer, 415
Intermediary banks, 411, 469
Overdrafts, 463
Payor bank, 468
Restrictive indorsements, liability for, 411

Stale checks, 459-461
Stop payment orders, 461-463
   Exhibit, 461
Teller machines, 470
Unindorsed order paper, 415

BATTERY
See Torts

BETTER BUSINESS BUREAU SYSTEM
See Consumer Protection

"BLUE SKY" LAWS
See Contracts; Securities Regulation

BONDS
See Corporate Financing

BREACH
See Commercial Paper; Contracts; Sales

BULK SALES LAW
Commercial paper, 429
Notice and publication requirements, 515

BURGLARY
See Criminal Law

BUSINESS CRIMES
See Criminal Law

BUSINESS ORGANIZATIONS
   See also Corporations; Limited Part-
      nerships; Partnerships
Generally, 590 et seq.
Capital, need for, 593-594
Forms of, 590-594
Liability of owners, 593
Tax considerations,
   Exhibit, 594

BUSINESS TORTS
   Generally, 42-44
Contractual relations, interference with,
   44
Malicious injury to business, 42-44
Trademark, 42, 258, 766-767
Unfair competition, 42

BUSINESS TRUSTS
Defined, 591, 593

CAPACITY
   Generally, 124-139
Aliens, 137
Convicts, 136
Insane persons, 136
Intoxicated persons, 133-136
   Ratification, avoidance of, 136
Married women, 137
Minors, 124-133
   Disaffirmance, 124-132
   Insurance, 132

Loans, 132
Misrepresentation of age, effect of,
   130-131
Necessaries, liability for, 128-130
Nonvoidable contracts, 132-133
Parents' liability, 133
Ratification, 132
   Express, 132
   Implied, 132
Restitution, duty of, 125
Restoration, duty of, 125-128

CASE LAW
   See also Stare Decisis; West Publishing
      Company
Source of law, 7

CASE OR CONTROVERSY
See Federal Courts

CAVEAT EMPTOR
Real property, 862-863
Sales contract law, prior philosophy in,
   336

CHARITABLE SUBSCRIPTIONS
See Consideration

CHATTEL
See Personal Property

CHECKS
See Banks; Commercial Paper

CIVIL LAW
Defined, 9

CIVIL RIGHTS ACT OF 1964
Employment discrimination, 763-765

CLASS ACTIONS
See Consumer Protection

CLAYTON ACT
   See also Antitrust; Federal Trade Com-
      mission; Mergers
Exclusive dealing contracts, prohibition
   of, 831

COLLATERAL
See Secured Transactions

COMMERCIAL LAW
Codification of, 7-8
   See also Commercial Paper; Sales;
      Secured Transactions; Uniform
      Commercial Code
Defined, 7

COMMERCIAL PAPER
   Generally, 387-473
Accommodation party, 438-439
Agents or officers,

Indorsement, 415
Signature of original instrument, 433-436
Undisclosed principal, 580
Alteration, material, 446
Assignment, 406
Mere use of word "assign," 414
Order paper, transfer of without indorsement, 415
Bank drafts, 390
Bankruptcy, discharge in, 446
Bank's liability,
Restrictive indorsements, 41
Basic concepts, 387-393
Bearer instrument, 404
Holders, 418
Negotiation, 407
Bills of exchange, 387, 388
Exhibit, 389
Breach of contract, 442
Bulk transfer, 429
Certificates of deposit, 390
Exhibit, 391
Promises to pay, 390-391
Checks,
See also Banks
Banking system and, 452-473
Cashier's, 453
Exhibit, 453
Certified, 454-455
Alteration, 455-456
Certification
Drawer's request, 455
Holder's request, 455
Revocation, 455
Checking accounts, 390
Defined, 452
Drawee, 453
Drawer, 452-453
Holder, 453
Negotiability, 453
Orders to pay, 390
Payee, 453
Poorly filled out, exhibit of, 468
Traveler's, 453-454
Exhibit, 454
Contract law vs. law of commercial paper, 417-418
Defenses, 442-447
Personal, 442-446
Real or universal, 446-447
Defined, 387
Demand instruments, 390
Discharge, 447-449
Cancellation, 449
Impairment of recourse of collateral, 449
Payment or cancellation, 445, 447-449
Instruments acquired by theft or restrictively endorsed, 447-449
Reacquisition, 449
Discounting, 388
Drafts, 388

Orders to pay, 390
Drawee, 392
Drawer, 392
Duress, extreme, 445, 447
Estate, acquisition when taking over, 429
Fictitious payees, 414
Forged indorsements,
See Indorsements, this topic
Forgery, defense of, 446
Fraud,
In the execution (in factum), 446
In the inducement, 442-445
Functions and purposes, 387-388
Credit device, 388
Substitute for money, 387-388
Holders, 392-393, 418
Holder through a holder in due course, 393, 429
Rights of, 418
Holders in due course, 393, 417-431
Good faith, 424-426
Purchaser vs. transferor, 424
Negotiation, 407
Notice, 426-429
Claims against or defenses to an instrument, 427-429
Incomplete instruments, 427
Irregular instruments, 427-428
Payee as HDC, 428-429
Voidable obligations, 428
Fact, 426
Overdue or dishonored instruments, 426-427
Demand, 427
Time, 426-427
Requirements, 419-429
Shelter provision, 429
Value, 419-424
Agreed consideration performed, 421
Antecedent claim, 421
Check deposits and withdrawals, 424
Negotiable instrument, 421-424
Illegality, 445, 446-447
Imposter rule, 412-414
Indorsees, 392
Indorsements, 407-415
Additional language of transfer, 414
Agents or officers, 415
Allonge, 407
Bank's indorsement for customer, 415
Blank, 408
Exhibit, 408
Conditional, 409
Exhibit, 409
Correction of name, 414-415
Deposit or collection, for, 409-410
Forged or unauthorized indorsements, 411-414
Imposter rule, 412-414
Multiple payees, 415
Payable in the alternative, 415
Payable jointly, 415
Prohibiting further indorsement, 409

Qualified vs. unqualified, 408-409
 Exhibit of qualified indorsement, 408
 "Without recourse," 408-409
Restrictive vs. unrestrictive, 409-411
Special, 408
 Exhibit, 408
Trust or agency, 410-411
Types, 407-411
Unindorsed order paper, 415
Indorsers, 392
Judicial sale, 429
Legal process, taking under, 429
Liability, 432-442
 Accommodation party, 438-439
 Contractual, 436-439
 Forger, of, 436
 Primary and secondary, 436-438
 Signatures, based on, 432-439
  Agent, 433-436
   Sample signatures, 436
  Signature, defined, 432, 433
  Unauthorized signature, 433, 436
 Warranty, 439-442
Makers, 392
Mental incapacity, 445, 447
Negotiability, 395-405
 Money and no other promise, 402
 Omissions not affecting, 404
 Payable on demand or at a definite
  time, 402-403
  Acceleration clauses, 403
  Extension clauses, 403
 Payable to order or bearer, 404
 Promise or order, 396-397
 Requirements, 395-404
 Signed by maker or drawer, 396
  Placement of signature, 396
  What constitutes a signature, 396
 Sum certain in money, 400-402
  Finance charge, 401
  Money and no other promise, 402
  Sum certain, 400-401
 Unconditional promise or order, 396-
  400
  Consideration, statements of, 397-398
  Implied or constructive conditions,
   397
  Mortgage, secured by, 399
  Other agreements,
   Reference to, 398
   Subject to, 398-399
  Particular funds or accounts, indica-
   tion of, 399-400
 Writing, 396
  Permanence, 396
  Portability, 396
Negotiation,
 Bearer paper, 407
 Defined, 406 n. 1, 407
 Transferability and, 406-416
Nondelivery, 446
Notes,
 See Promissory notes, this topic
Order instrument, 404

Holders, 418
Negotiation, 407
Transfer without indorsement, 415
Orders to pay vs. promises to pay, 390
Parties, 391-392
Promises to pay vs. orders to pay, 390-391
Promissory notes, 390
 Exhibit, 391
 Promises to pay, 390-391
Shelter provision,
 See Holders in due course, this topic
Time and sight drafts, 388
Time instruments, 390
Trade acceptances, 388-389
 Exhibit, 389
Transferability and negotiation, 406-416
Types, 388-390
Unauthorized completion of incomplete
 instrument, 445-446
Unauthorized indorsements,
 See Indorsements, this topic
Unauthorized signatures,
 See Liability, signatures, based on, this
  topic
Undue influence, 445
Warranties, 439-442
 Presentment, 440-441
 Transfer, 440

COMMON LAW
Beginning of, 4
Source of law, 7

COMPLAINT
See Trial

CONDITIONS
See Contracts

CONDOMINIUMS
See Real Property

CONFUSION
See Personal Property

CONSIDERATION
 Generally, 104-123
Adequacy of, 107-109
Assignment, 196
Charitable subscriptions, 118-120
Construction contracts,
 Unforeseen or substantial difficulty in
  performance, 113-115
Debts
 New promises to pay barred,
  Bankruptcy, 121
  Statute of limitations, 121
 Settlement of,
  Liquidated vs. unliquidated, 113
Defined, 104
Exclusive dealing contracts, 116
Illegal act, promise to perform, 112
Illusory promise, 112
Legal sufficiency, 104-107

Detriment or benefit vs. bargained for, 105

"Good consideration" and, 107

Modification of control,
UCC change of common law rule, 294

Moral obligation or "good consideration," 107, 110-112

Output and requirements contracts, 116

Past consideration, 109-111

Pre-existing duty, promise to perform, 112

Promises enforceable without consideration, 116-120

Promissory estoppel, 116-118

Uniform Commercial Code, exceptions under, 120-121
Commercial paper, 121
Firm offers, 120-121
Letters of credit, 121
Modification, 121
Waiver or renunciation of claim, 121

CONSOLIDATION

See Corporations, Mergers and consolidation

CONSTITUTION

Case involving issues of constitutional law, 25-28

Source of law, 5-6

CONSUMER PROTECTION

See also Products Liability

Generally, 772-790

Administrative agencies, 773
See also Administrative Agencies, this index

Advertising, 774-779
Bait and switch, 777-778
Corrective, 778-779
Deceptive, 774-777

Better business bureau system, 774

Certification, 779-780

Class actions, 774

Common law, 772-773

Consumer Product Safety Act, 363-364

Consumer Product Safety Commission, 744, 745, 753, 760

Courts, use of, 774

Credit, 781-788
Collection and repossession, 786-788
Consumer credit reports, 784 et seq.
Credit cards, 781-783
Open end credit, 785
Rate regulation, 786
Uniform Consumer Credit Code, 519-521, 783-784

Debt collection, 786-788

Fair Debt Collection Practices Act, 787

Federal Trade Commission, 773
See also Administrative Agencies; Federal Trade Commission; Trade Regulation
Deceptive practices, 774-777

Guaranteed third party approval, 779

Housing and Urban Development, Department of, 773

Labeling and packaging, 779-780

Magnuson-Moss Warranty Act, 342-343, 788

Organization, 774

Sales, 780-781
Door-to-door, 780
Mail order, 780-781
Referral, 781

Sources, 773-774

Statutes
Federal, 773
State, 773

Truth in Lending Act (Consumer Credit Protection Act), 781-785
Class actions, 517-519
Disclosure, 516-517, 784-785
Who is subject to, 517

Unconscionability doctrine, 772-773

Warranties, 788
See also Warranty, this index

CONTRACTS

See also Agreement; Assignment; Capacity; Consideration; Duress; Parol Evidence Rule; Mistake; Products Liability; Specific Performance; Statute of Frauds; Third Party Beneficiary Contracts; Undue Influence

Generally, 68-245

Accord and satisfaction,
See Discharge by accord and satisfaction, this topic

Adhesion contracts, 169

Arbitration, 153

Bilateral vs. unilateral, 73-75

"Blue Sky" laws, 154

Breach,
See Discharge by breach of contract, this topic

Commercial paper, law of, compared, 417-418

Compromise or settlement agreement, 212-214

Conditions, 205-207
Breach of contract vs. occurrence or nonoccurrence of a condition, 205-206
Defined, 205
Types of,
Concurrent, 206-207
Constructive, 207
Expressed, 206-207
Implied, 206-207
Precedent, 206
Subsequent, 206

Construction contracts, 113-115

Crime or tort, contracts for the commission of, 150

Damages, 227-234
Compensatory, 228-231
Construction contracts, 228-231

Sale of goods, 228
Sale of land, 228
Consequential (special), 231-233
Mitigation of, 234
Nominal, 228, 234
Punitive (examplary), 233
Types of, 228-234
Defined, 70
Discharge by accord and satisfaction, 214-215
Discharge by agreement, 211-215
Discharge by breach of contract, 216-221
Anticipatory breach (anticipatory repudiation), 216-221
Breach. defined, 227
Material breach, 216
Discharge by impossibility of performance, 221-224
Commercial impracticability, 224
Frustration of purpose, 223
Temporary impossibility, 224
Discharge by operation of law, 215-216
Alteration of the contract, 215
Bankruptcy, 216
Statute of limitations, 215-216
Discharge by performance, 207-211
Constructive condition and substantial performance, 209-210
Degree of performance required, 208-210
Express condition and full performance, 208-209
Time for performance, 210-211
Discriminatory contracts, 154
Election of remedies, 240-241
Elements, 69-70
Essential terms, 80
Exclusive dealing contracts, 116
Exculpatory clauses, 149-150, 242-243
Adhesion contracts, 243
Executed vs. executory, 76
Express vs. implied, 70-73
Formal vs. informal, 75
Freedom of contract and freedom from contract, 69
Frustration of purpose, 223
Function, 69
Gambling, 141-144
Illegality, effect of,
In pari delicto, 155
Protected classes, enforcement for benefit of, 154-155
Severable contracts containing legal and illegal portions, 154
Implied vs. express, 70-73
Implied-in-law vs. implied-in-fact, 75
Impossibility of performance,
See Discharge by impossibility of performance, this topic
Informal vs. formal, 75
Legal process, agreements obstructing, 151-154

Forum selection and arbitration clauses, 153-154
Legality of, 140-156
Licensing statutes, 144-145
Limitation of liability clauses, 242-243
Uniform Commercial Code, 243
Liquidated damages vs. penalty provisions, 234
Minors,
See Capacity
Nonmarried couples, agreements as to earnings and property rights, 145-146
Novation, 211-212
See also Assignment
Objective theory, 71
Options, 96-97
Output contracts, 92, 116
Parents, liability of, 133
Part performance,
Indefiniteness of offer cured by, 89
Public policy, contrary to, 145-154
Public service, contracts injuring, 150-151
Quantum meruit,
See Quasi-contracts, this topic
Quasi-contracts (implied in law), 75-77, 238-240
Limitation on, 77
Quantum meruit, 238
Unjust enrichment, 239-240
Reciprocal, 73
Recognizance, 75
Reformation, 237-238
Requirements contracts, 92, 116
Rescission and restitution, 211, 234-235
Restraint of trade, 146-149
Agreements not to compete, 147-149
Resale price maintenance agreements, 147
Seal, under, 75
Severable contracts,
Legal and illegal portions, 154
Simple, 75
Statutory prohibitions, 140-145
Substituted agreement, 212
Sunday laws, 144
Tender, 207-208
Types, 70-78
Unconscionable, 149-150, 169, 235
Undue influence,
Fiduciary relationships, 168
Unenforceable, 76-77
Unilateral vs. bilateral, 73-75
Unjust enrichment,
See Quasi-contracts, this topic
Usury, 140-141
Exceptions, 141
Installment sales, 141
Valid, 76
Void, 76
Voidable, 76, 124-137
Waiver of breach, 241-242
Writing,

Requirement of (Statute of Frauds), 172-184
Sufficiency of, 184

CONVERSION
See Torts

CONVICTS
See Capacity

COPYRIGHTS
Generally, 258-259, 766
Common law copyright, 258
Defined, 258
Duration, 259
Exclusive use, 259
Fair use, 259
Library reproduction, 259
New copyright law,
Purposes, 258-259
Works "for hire," 259

CORPORATE FINANCING
Generally, 682 et seq.
Bonds, 682-683
Callable, 683
Collateral trust, 683
Convertible, 683
Equipment trust, 683
Mortgage, 683
Stocks, compared,
Exhibit, 686
Debentures, 683
Dividends, 686-688
Limitations on, 686-688
Who declares and who gets, 688-689
Stocks, 683-686
Bonds, compared,
Exhibit, 686
Common, 685-686
Preferred, 684-685

CORPORATIONS
See also Corporate Financing; Franchises
Alter ego, 650
Appraisal rights,
See Mergers and consolidation, this topic
Articles of incorporation, 645-646
Board of directors,
See Directors, this topic
Capital structure, 646
Capitalization,
Adequate, 650
Charter, 647
State chartering, 645
Classification, 641, 670 et seq.
Close, 641, 671-675
Management, 672
Statutes, 671-672
Transfer of shares, 672-674

Conflicts of interest, 705
Consolidation,
See Mergers and consolidation, this topic
Contracts,
Corporations having common directors, between, 705
Director and corporation, between, 705
Corporate entity, characteristics of, 639-641
Criminal acts of agents or officers, 661
Cumulative voting, 665
De facto, 648
De jure, 647-648
Defined, 591, 638
Directors,
See also Conflicts of interest; Contracts; Duty of care; Duty of loyalty; all this topic
Compensation, 666
Delegation of powers, 667
Forum, 667
Meetings, 667
Qualifications, 666
Removal, 661-663
Responsibilities, 640, 666
Rights,
Compensation, 706
Indemnification, 706
Inspection, 706
Participation, 706
Role of, 640, 702 et seq.
Term of office, 666
Voting, 667
Disregarding the corporate entity,
See Piercing of corporate veil, this topic
Dissolution, 726-727
Defined, 726
Procedure, 726
Dividends,
Illegal, 713
Domestic, 641
Duration, 646
Duty of care, 703
Duty of loyalty, 703-705
Estoppel, corporation by, 648
Executive committee, 667
Fifth Amendment protection, no, 638-639
Foreign, 641, 675-677
Bond, posting, 675
Jurisdiction over, 675-677
Formation, 641-648
Fringe benefits, 679
History, 637-638
Incorporation, 645-648
Benefits of, 678-680
Costs of, 678
Improper, 647
Incorporators, 647
Insurance,
Disability, 680
Key man, 889

Term life, 680
Internal organization, 646-647
Legal "person," corporation as, 638-639
Liability, 666-667
Liquidation, defined, 725-726
Management, 661-667
  Directors, 666-667
  Shareholders' position, 661-666
    See also Shareholders, this topic
Medical plan, 680
Mergers and consolidation, 716-725
  Appraisal rights, 719-722, 724-725
  Consolidation,
    Defined, 716
  Disappearing corporation, 716-718
  Mergers,
    Conglomerate, 722-723
    Defined, 716
    Department of Justice guidelines,
      exhibit, 733
    Horizontal, 722-723
    Short-form mergers (parent-subsidy
      mergers), 719
    Vertical, 722-723
  Procedure, 718-719
  Purchase of assets, 721-722, 724-725
  Purchase of stock, 725
  Shareholder approval, 719, 722, 724-725
  Surviving corporation, 716-718
  Tender offer, 725
Model Business Corporation Act, 638
Name, 646
Nature and purpose, statement of, 646
  Ultra vires doctrine, 661
Nature of, 638-641
Nonprofit, 641, 677-678
Officers, 640, 667
  Liabilities of, 706
  Rights of, 706
  Role, 702 et seq.
Organizational meeting, first, 647
Partnerships,
  Compared with corporations, 593-594
    Tax considerations, exhibit, 594
Pension and profit-sharing plans, 678-679
  Exhibit, 679
Personal and corporate interests, separa-
  tion of, 651-653
Piercing of corporate veil, 639-640,
  648-650
Powers, 656-661
  Express, 656
  Implied, 656-658
Principal office, 647
Private, 641
Professional, 641, 674-675
  Liability of members,
    Malpractice of associate, 674-675
    Ordinary torts by other members, 675
Promoters' activities, 641-644
Proxy voting, 665
Public, 641
Registered agent, 647
Service associations, professional, 674
Shareholders,

Corporation, relationship between
  shareholder and, 664
Forum, 664
Liabilities, 640, 713
Major,
  Duties and liabilities, 706
Meetings,
  Notice of, 664
  Quorum, 664-665
  Voting, 664-665
Powers, 640, 661-663
Quorum, 664
Rights, 640, 706-712
  Dissolution, upon, 712-713
    Compelling receivership, 712-
      713
  Dividends, 707-710
  Inspection, 710-712
  Preemptive, 707
  Stock certificate, 706-707
  Stock warrants, 707
  Transfer shares,
    Closely-held corporations, 712
    First refusal, 712
  Vote, 710
Voting, 664-666
  Lists, 665
  Proxy, 665
  Shareholder agreements, 665
  Techniques, 665
  Trust, 665-666
Subchapter S, 670-671
  Benefits, 671
  Qualification, requirements for, 671
Subscribers and subscriptions, 645
Surviving corporation,
  See Mergers and consolidation, this
    topic
Tax considerations, 640-641, 678-680
Tax option corporation, 670
Tender offer, 725
  See also Mergers and consolidation, this
    topic
Termination, 725-727
Thin capitalization, 650
Torts of agents or officers, 661
Ultra vires doctrine, 659-661
  Judicial treatment, 661
  Torts and criminal acts, 661
Voting,
  See also Shareholders, this topic
  Voting trust, 665-666

COURT OPINIONS
See also West Publishing Company
Reporting of,
  Federal Rules Decisions (F.R.D.), 24-25
  National reporter system, 24-25
  State opinions, 24
  Supreme Court of the United States,
    Lawyer's Edition (L.Ed.), 25
    Supreme Court Reporter (S.Ct.), 25, 27
    United States Supreme Court Reports
      (U.S.), 25

COURTS
Defined, 11
Establishment of, 4

**COVENANT RUNNING WITH THE
LAND**
See Land Use Control

CREDIT
See Consumer Protection

CREDIT CARDS
See Consumer Protection, Credit; Debtor,
    Protection of

CREDITORS' RIGHTS
    See also Attachment; Bulk Sales Law;
        Garnishment; Guaranty; Liens;
        Mortgage Foreclosure on Real
        Property; Suretyship; Writ of
        Execution
Laws assisting creditors, 506-515

CRIMINAL LAW
    Generally, 51-66
Actus reas, 53
Arson, 63-64
    Insurers, burning to defraud, 64
Burglary, 61
Business, crimes affecting, 60-65
Consent, defense of, 56
Corporate crimes, 65
Crime,
    Defined, 52
    Nature of, 51-52
Defenses, 54-59
Defined, 9
Duress, defense of, 56-57
Embezzlement, 61
    Trust funds, misapplication of, 61-63
Entrapment, defense of, 57-59
False measures, labels, and weights, 64
False pretenses, obtaining goods by, 64
Federal crimes, 53
Felonies, 52
Forgery, 60
Immunity, 59
Infancy, defense of, 54
Insanity, defense of, 56
Intoxication, defense of, 54-55
Justifiable use of force, defense of, 57
Larceny, 61
    Grand vs. petit, 61
    Property, what constitutes, 61
Lotteries, 64
Mails, use of to defraud, 64
Mala in se vs. mala prohibita, 52
Mens rea, 53-54
Misdemeanors, 52
Misrepresentation, 64
Mistake, defense of, 56
Organized crime, 53
Perjury, subornation of, 64
Punishment, 51-52
Receiving stolen goods, 64

Robbery, 60-61
Statute of limitations, 59
Victimless crime, 53
White collar crime, 53

CRIMINAL PROCEDURE
    Generally, 59-60
Arrest, 60
    Probable cause, defined, 60
Constitutional safeguards, 59-60
Indictment and information, 60
"Reasonable doubt" test, 60

CURIA REGIS (KING'S COURT)
Common law, beginning of, 4

DEBENTURES
See Corporate Financing

DEBTOR, PROTECTION OF
    Generally, 515-523
Consumer Credit Protection Act (Truth-
    in-Lending Act), 516-519
    Class actions, 517-519
    Disclosure requirements, 516-517
    Who is subject to, 517
Credit cards, 521, 781-783
    Lost or stolen, 521
Credit reports and collection practices,
    521-523
Debt collection, 522-523
Exemptions from debts, 515-516
    Garnishment, limitations on, 516, 519
    Homestead exemption, 516
Fair Credit Billing Act, 521
Fair Debt Collection Practices Act,
    522-523
Real estate transactions, 523
    Interstate Sales Full Disclosure Act, 523
    Real Estate Settlement Procedures Act,
    523
Uniform Consumer Credit Code (UCCC),
    519-521, 783-784
Garnishment, limitations on, 519
Holder-in-due-course doctrine, altera-
    tion of, 520-521
    Payment by check, 520
    Penalties, 520

DECEIT
See Torts, Misrepresentation

DEEDS
See Real Property

DEFAMATION
See Torts

DEPOSITION
See Discovery

**DESCENT AND DISTRIBUTION, STAT-
UTES OF**
See Inheritance

DIRECTED VERDICT, MOTION FOR
See Trial

DIRECTORS
See Corporations

DISCOVERY
Generally, 20-21
Admissions, request for, 21
Defined, 20
Depositions, 21
Documents, objects, and entry upon land, 21
Interrogatories, 21
Physical and mental examination, 21
Work product, attorney's, 28

DISMISSALS AND JUDGMENTS BEFORE TRIAL
Generally, 19-20
Demurrer, 20
Dismiss, motion to, 20
Judgment on the pleadings, 20
Summary judgment, motion for, 20

DISSOLUTION
See Corporations; Partnerships

DISTRIBUTORSHIPS
See Franchises

DIVIDENDS
See Corporate Financing; Corporations

DURESS
See also Commercial Paper; Criminal Law
Defined, 168
Economic need, 169

EASEMENT
See Nonpossessory Interests

EMBEZZLEMENT
See Criminal Law

EMINENT DOMAIN
See Real Property

EMPLOYMENT
See Agency

ENERGY
See Administrative Agencies; Federal Trade Commission

ENTRAPMENT
See Criminal Law

ENVIRONMENTAL LAW
Generally, 791-805
Air pollution, 796-798
Automobile pollution, 796-798
Clean Air Act, 796

Clean Water Act, 798
Council of Environmental Quality, 792
Environmental impact statements, 793-795
Who prepares, 795
Environmental Protection Agency, 744, 753, 792-793
Federal statutes and regulations, 792
Historical background, 791-792
Judicial limits, 804
National Environmental Policy Act, 792
Noise pollution, 800-801
Pesticide control, 801
Private litigation, 795-796
Toxic substances, 801
Waste disposal, 801-803
Water pollution, 798-800

EQUITABLE SERVITUDES
See Land Use Control

EQUITY
Courts of equity, 9-10
Remedies in law vs. remedies in equity, 9-10

ESTATES
Estate administration, 920-923
Family settlement agreements, 922-923
Personal representative, 909, 920-921
Duties of, 920-921
Exhibit, 921
Probate vs. nonprobate, 921-923
Summary procedures, 923
Taxation of,
States, by,
Estate tax, 824
Inheritance tax, 824-825
Exhibit, 825
Pick up tax, 925
Tax Reform Act of 1976, 923-924
Exhibits, 924

ESTOPPEL
See Agency

EXECUTIVE PRIVILEGE
President Nixon's claim of, 5-6

FAIR-TRADE AGREEMENTS
See Antitrust

FALSE IMPRISONMENT
See Torts

FEDERAL COURTS
Generally, 14 et seq.
District courts, 14
Federal supplement, 24
Intermediate courts of review, 14
Jurisdiction,
Case or controversy, 27
Concurrent vs. exclusive, 17
Diversity of citizenship, 16-17

Federal questions, 16
Standing, 27
Organization chart, 15
Specialized courts, 14

FEDERAL SYSTEM
Problems of duplication, 28

FEDERAL TRADE COMMISSION
Generally, 827-845
Activities, 834-837
Maintaining competition missions, exhibit, 834
Advertising, 835-837
Cease and desist orders, 828
Clayton Act, 831-834
Energy, 835
Exclusive dealing contracts, 831
Exemptions to regulated activities, 844
Federal Trade Commission Act, 828
Food, 835
Health care, 835
Horizontal restraints, 840-841
Industry-wide investigations, 843-844
Mergers, 831-834
Conglomerate, 841
Horizontal, 840-841
Vertical, 838
Price discrimination, 828-831
Reciprocal buying, 838-840
Resources and authority, 827-834
Robinson-Patman Act, 828-831
Trade regulation rules, 828
Transportation, 835
Tying contracts, 831
Vertical restraints, 837-840

FINANCING STATEMENT
See Secured Transactions

FIXTURES
Defined, 849-850
Intention, 850
Trade fixtures, 850
Uniform Commercial Code,
Deliberate failure to use the word "fixtures," 282, n. 2

FORECLOSURE
See Mortgage Foreclosure on Real Property; Secured Transactions, Strict foreclosure

FORGERY
See Commercial Paper; Criminal Law

FRANCHISES
Generally, 730-742
Advantages, 731-732
Business organization, 732
Chain-style businesses, 731
Defined, 730, 731
Disclosure protection, 738-739
Distributorships, 731

FTC franchise rule, 739-740
Franchise agreement, 732 et seq.
Franchisee's relationship to franchisor, 740
Law, absence of, 731
Location, 732
Manufacturing or processing plants, 731
Payment, 732
Price and quality controls, 733
Regulation, 738-740
Statutes, 731
Termination, 733-738
Consumer and franchisee protection, 736
Damages, measure of, 736-738
Relief, determination of, 735-736
Types, 731

FRAUD
Generally, 161-169
Elements of, 161
Injury to innocent party, 166-169
Innocent misrepresentation, 165
Intent to deceive, 165
Knowledge of falsehood, 165
Misrepresentation of facts, 161-165
Concealment and silence, compared, 164-165
Misrepresentation of law, compared, 164
Reliance on the misrepresentation, 165-166

FUTURE INTERESTS
Generally, 870-875
Executory interest, 870, 871-872
Shifting, 872
Springing, 872
Possibility of reverter, 851, n. 7, 870, 871
Power of termination, 870, 871
Remainder,
Contingent, 870, 871
Vested, 870, 871
Reversion, 870, 871
Rule against perpetuities, 872-875
Cy pres doctrine, 874-875
Wait and see doctrine, 874-875

GAMBLING
See Contracts

GARNISHMENT
Generally, 511-514
Defined, 511
Limitations on, 516, 519
Ownership of garnished property, 513-514
Renewal, 511-512

GIFTS
Generally, 250-253
Acceptance, 251
Causa mortis, 253
Delivery, 250-252
Donative intent, 251

Inter vivos, 253
Tax Reform Act of 1976, 923-924

GOODS
See Sales; Secured Transactions

GOVERNMENT REGULATION
See also Administrative Agencies; Antitrust; Consumer Protection; Environmental Law; Federal Trade Commission
Generally, 744-845

GUARANTY
Suretyship, compared, 514

HOLDERS IN DUE COURSE
See Commercial Paper

HOLDING COMPANIES
See Antitrust

INDEMNIFICATION
See Agency

INDEMNITY
See Insurance

INDORSEMENTS
See Commercial Paper

INHERITANCE
See also Estates; Trusts; Wills
Collateral heirs, 918
Descent and distribution, statutes of, 918-919
Intestacy,
Administrator or administratrix, 909, 920
Distribution, pattern of, 918-919
Per capita, 919
Per stirpes, 918-919
Laws,
Origins of, 907-908
Purposes of, 908
Lineal descendants, 918
Uniform Probate Code, 911, 918-919
Surviving spouse, 918-919

INJUNCTIONS
Defined, 10

INSANITY
See Criminal Law

INSURANCE
See also Antitrust
Generally, 885-906
Accident and health, 903-904
Agent, 886
Automobile, 899-903
Accidental death benefits, 902
Comprehensive, 902
Medical payment coverage, 902

No-fault, 902-903
Physical damage coverage, 899, 902
Property damage and bodily injury liability, 899
Uninsured motorist coverage, 902
Binder, 890
Broker, 886
Cancellation, 893-894
Classification, 886, 895-897
Exhibit, 896
Contract, 890-893
Interpreting provisions, 890-893
Timing, 890
Co-ordination of benefits clauses, 889-890
Defenses, 894-895
Rebuttal of defenses, 895
Defined, 885
Dental, 903
Disability, 903-904
Homemaker's, 904
Waiting period, 904
Endowment, 898
Fire insurance, 898
Homeowner's, 898-899
Coinsurance, 899
Exhibit, 900-901
Floater policies, 899
Liability coverage, 898
Property coverage, 898
Hospital expenses, 903
Indemnity, 889
Insurable interest, 141, 886-888
Sales, 316
Medical,
Major, 903
Regular, 903
"Other insurance" clauses, 889-890
Policy, 886
Parties, 886
Premium, 886
Renewability and convertibility, 897
Risk,
Defined, 885
Pooling, 885-886
State regulation, 890
Subrogation, 889
Surgical, 903
Term, 896-897
Decreasing, 897
Level, 896-897
Mortgage, 897
Underwriter, 886
Whole life, 897-898
Borrowing on cash value, 897
Death benefits, 897-898
Limited payment, 898
Living benefits, 897
Workman's compensation, 904

INTERROGATORIES
See Discovery

INTOXICATION
See Capacity; Criminal Law

INVESTMENT GROUPS
Defined, 591

JOINT STOCK COMPANY
Defined, 591

JOINT VENTURES
Defined, 591

JUDGE
Court, synonymous use of in legal literature, 11

JUDGMENT N.O.V. (NOTWITHSTANDING THE VERDICT)
See Trial

JUDICIAL PROCESS
Administrative process, compared with, 6

JUDICIAL REVIEW
Establishment of, 5

JURISDICTION
See also Federal Courts
Defined, 11
In personam, 12
Long-arm statute, 12
Subject matter, 12
Venue, compared, 12

JURISPRUDENTIAL THOUGHT, SCHOOLS OF
See Legal Thought, Schools of

JURY INSTRUCTIONS
See Trial, Charges (Instructions to jury)

JURY TRIAL
Right to, 21-22

KING'S COURT
See Curia Regis (King's Court)

LAISSEZ-FAIRE
Price fixing, 807

LAND
See Real Property

LAND USE CONTROL
Generally, 877-882
Covenants running with the land, 877
Equitable servitudes, compared, 878
Equitable servitudes, 877-878
Covenants running with the land, compared, 878
Plat, 878
Zoning, 878-882
Floating zones, 879
Nonconforming use, 879
Variance, 879-880
Zoning boards, discretion of, 880-882

LANDLORD AND TENANT
Generally, 852-856
Destruction of premises, 856
Landlord,
Duties and warranties, 855
Lease,
Assignments, 856
Defined, 855
Subleasing, 856
Tenancies,
Period to period, 852-854
Suffrance, at, 855
Will, at, 854-855
Years, for, 852
Tenant,
Duties, 855-856
Obligation to pay rent, 855-856
Terminating tenant's obligation to pay rent, 856

LANHAM ACT
Tradename regulation, 766-767

LARCENY
See Criminal Law

LAW
American,
History of, 4-5
Sources of, 4-7
Civil vs. criminal, 9
Classification of, 8-10
Defined, 2-3
Equity and law compared, 9-10
How to find, 24-25
Public vs. private, 9
Study of, approaches to
Environmental, 2-3
Traditional, 2
Substantive vs. procedural, 8-9

LAW MERCHANT (LEX MERCATORIA)
Merchant courts, operation of, 7
Sales law, modern, 280

LAWSUIT
Chart of, 23

LEASE
See Landlord and Tenant

LEGAL THOUGHT, SCHOOLS OF
Analytical, 3-4
Historical, 3
Legal realists, 4
Natural law, 3

LETTERS OF CREDIT
Contract, type of, 75

LIBEL
See Torts

LICENSES

See Nonpossessory Interests

LIENS
Artisan's lien on personal property, 507
Mechanic's lien on real property, 506-507

LIMITED PARTNERSHIPS
Generally, 627-636
Defined, 591, 627
Dissolution, 633-634
Causes, 634
Consequences, 634
Distribution of assets, priorities in, 634
Formation, 628-629
Where to file certificates, 629
General partner,
Role, 605
History, 628
Liability to creditors, 631
Limited partners,
Liability, 629, 631-633
Management, cannot participate in, 629-631
Number of, 629
Restrictions on, 629-631, 633
Rights of, 633
Right to sue, 633
Role, 605, 629
Limited partnership associations, 634
Management,
Partnership, compared, 614 n. 1
Uniform Limited Partnership Act, 605, 1121-1128 (Appendix D)
Uniform Limited Partnership Act, 628
Revised act, 628, 1129-1142 (Appendix E)
Use of, 633

LIQUIDATED DAMAGES
See Contracts; Sales, Remedies

LIQUIDATION
See Corporations

LONG-ARM STATUTE
See Jurisdiction

LOST PROPERTY
See Personal Property

LOTTERIES
See Criminal Law

MARSHALING ASSETS
Partnerships, 597 n. 3

MASTER-SERVANT RELATIONSHIP
See generally Agency

MERCHANT
See Law Merchant (Lex Mercatoria); Sales

MERGERS
See Antitrust; Corporations

MINORS
See Capacity

MISLAID PROPERTY
See Personal Property

MISREPRESENTATION
See Criminal Law; Torts

MISTAKE
Generally, 157-161
Mutual mistake of material fact, 158-161,
Identity vs. value, 159
Unilateral, 157-158

MODEL BUSINESS CORPORATION ACT
See Uniform Acts

MORTGAGE FORECLOSURE ON REAL PROPERTY
Equity of redemption, 515
Foreclosure, 515
Mortgagee, 515
Mortgagor, 514

MORTGAGES
See Foreclosure on Real Property; Statute of Frauds, Land; Third Party Beneficiary Contracts

NATIONAL APPELLATE COURT
Establishment of, 17

NATIONAL REPORTER SYSTEM
See West Publishing Company

NEGLIGENCE
See Torts

NEGOTIABILITY
See Commercial Paper

NEGOTIABLE INSTRUMENTS
See generally Commercial Paper
Contract, type of, 75

NONPOSSESSORY INTERESTS
Generally, 875-877
Easements and profits, 875-876
Appurtenant, 875
Creation of,
Deed or will, 876
Implication, 876
Necessity, 876
Prescription, 876
Easement, defined, 875
Profit, defined, 875
Sale of property, effect of, 876
Tenants,
Dominant, 875
Servient, 875
Tenement,
Dominant, 875

Servient, 875
Termination, 876
Licenses, 876-877

NOVATION
See Assignment; Contracts

OFFER
See Agreement; Sales

OPTIONS
See Contracts

ORDINANCES
Source of law, 6

PAROL EVIDENCE RULE
See also Sales
Defined, 184
Exceptions, 184-185, 187
Integration or merger clause, 185-187

PARTNERSHIPS
Accounting, 618
Agency law,
Partnership law compared, 596
Agency powers, 622-624
Implied authority, 622
Aggregate theory, 598
Articles of partnership, 600
Bankruptcy, 597
Capacity,
Legal capacity of partnership as entity, 597
Partners, required of, 601
Characteristics, 597-598
Compensation, 617-618
Conveyance of property, 597-598
Corporations,
As partner, 601
Compared with partnerships, 593-594
Tax considerations, exhibit, 594
Defined, 590-591, 596-597
Dissolution, 606-611
Acts of partners, by,
Admission of new partners, 607
Agreement, 607
Power to withdraw, 607
Transfer of a partner's interest, 607
Judicial decree, by,
Business impracticality, 609
Improper conduct, 609-610
Incapacity, 609
Insanity, 609
Notice of,
Partners, to, 610
Third parties, to, 610-611
Operation of law, by,
Bankruptcy, 608
Death, 608
Illegality, 608-609
Winding up, compared, 606
Duration, 600-601
Duties and powers of partners, 620-624

Entity, partnership as, 597-598
Estoppel, partnership by, 598, 604
Fiduciary duty, 620-621
Formation, 598-604
Formalities, 600
Indications of, 601-604
Inspection of books, 618
Insurance,
Key man, 889
Interest in the partnership, 615-617, 618
Judgments, 597
Knowledge, imputed, 623
Liability,
Joint, 622
Joint and several, 622
Management, 614-615
Mutual agency, 544
Mutual consent, 601
Personal debts of a partner,
Creditor's rights against partnership, 605, 618
Powers and duties of partners, 620-624
Property powers, 624
Property rights, 604-605, 618-620
Partnership property rights, 604
Factors indicating partnership property, 604
Property rights of partners,
Interest in partnership, 605, 618
Specific partnership property, 605, 618, 620
Rights among partners, 614-620
Term, partnership for, 600
Termination, 605-611
See also Dissolution; Winding up; both this topic
Distribution of assets, 611
Winding up, 611
Dissolution, compared, 606

PATENTS
Generally, 766
Computer programs, 258
Design, 258
Plants, 258

PER SE STANDARD
See Antitrust, Sherman Act

PERJURY, SUBORNATION OF
See Criminal Law

PERSONAL PROPERTY
See also Bailments; Gifts
Generally, 248-260
Abandoned property, 257-258
Treasure trove, 257
Accession, 253
Acquiring and transferring ownership of, 249-253
Bequest,
See Wills
Chattel, 249
Confusion,

Defined, 253-254
Intentional or negligent, 254
Defined, 248
Expanding nature of, 249
Goods,
    Chattel, compared, 249
Intangible, 248-249
Lost property, 255-257
    Estray statutes, 255
Mislaid property, 254-255, 256
Possession, 249
Production, 250
Property, defined, 248
Purchase, 250
Real property, compared, 248
Tangible, 248
Wild animals, 249

PLEADINGS
See Trial

POLLUTION
See generally Environmental Law

PRELIMINARY NEGOTIATIONS
See Agreement, Offer, intention

PRETRIAL HEARING
Purpose of, 21

PRICE DISCRIMINATION
See Federal Trade Commission

PRINCIPAL
See generally Agency

PRIVACY
See Torts

PRIVATE LAW
Defined, 9

PROBABLE CAUSE
See Criminal Procedure, Arrest

PROBATE
See generally Estates; Inheritance; Wills

PROCEDURAL LAW
Defined, 8

PROCEDURE
Defined, 18
Federal rules of procedure, 18

PRODUCTS LIABILITY
    See also Consumer Protection
Generally, 356-366
Consumer Product Safety Act, 363-364
Fraud, 361
Misrepresentation, 361
Negligence, 357-361
    Privity of contract not required, 360-361
    Statutory duty, violation of, 361

Strict liability, 361-363
    Bystanders, 363
    Crash-worthiness doctrine, 363
    Defenses, 362-363
    Lessors, 363
    Limitations on recovery, 362
    Requirements of, 362
    Restatement of torts rule, 362
    Suppliers of component parts, 363
Warranty theory, 356-357
    See also Warranty
    Privity of contract, 357
    Third party beneficiaries, 357

PROFIT
See Nonpossessory Interests

PROMISSORY ESTOPPEL
See Consideration

PROMOTERS
See Corporations

PROPERTY
See generally Bailments; Gifts; Personal
    Property; Real Property

PROPRIETORSHIP, SOLE
Defined, 590

PROXIMATE CAUSE
See Torts, Causation

PUBLIC LAW
Defined, 9

QUANTUM MERUIT
See Contracts, Quasi-contracts

REAL PROPERTY
    See also Future Interests; Land Use
        Control; Landlord and Tenant;
        Mortgage Foreclosure on Real
        Property; Nonpossessory Inter-
        ests; Statute of Frauds, Land
Generally, 848-869
Adverse possession, 867
Air rights, 849
Caveat emptor, 862-863
Concurrent ownership, 856-858
    Joint tenancy, 857
    Tenancy by the entirety, 857
    Tenancy in common, 856-857
Condominiums, 857-858
Deed, 858-862
    Covenants,
        Encumbrances, against, 860
        Quiet enjoyment, 860
        Right to convey, 860
        Seisin, 860
    Quit claim, 862
    Recording, 862
        Bona fide purchaser, 862
        Constructive notice, 867

Requirements, 589
Types, 860-862
Warranty,
    Exhibit, 858-859
    General, 860-861
    Special, 861-862
Defined, 848
Devise,
    See Wills
Eminent domain, 866-867
Estates, 850-855
    Freehold, 850-852
    Nonfreehold, 852-855
Fee simple,
    Absolute, 851
    Defeasible, 851
Fixtures, 849-850
    See also Fixtures
Interstate Sales Full Disclosure Act, 523
Land,
    Defined, 848-849
Life estate, 851-852
    Pur autre vie, 852 n. 9
Nature of, 848-850
Personal property, compared, 248
Plant life, 849
Real Estate Settlement Procedures Act,
    523
Sale of, 863-866
    Broker,
        Exclusive agency, 863
        Exclusive right to sell, 863
        Open listing, 863
    Buyer, locating a, 863
    Closing, 866
    Contract of sale, 863-865
        Exhibit, 866-865
    Mortgage, obtaining a, 866
    Title examination, 866
Subsurface rights, 849
Survivorship, 857
Tenancies,
    Period to period, 852-854
    Suffrance, at, 855
    Will, at, 854-855
    Years, for, 852
Transfer of ownership, 858-862
Warranty of habitability, 862-863
Will or inheritance, transfer by, 866
    See also Inheritance; Wills

RECOGNIZANCE
See Contracts

REGULATORY AGENCIES
See generally Administrative Agencies;
    Antitrust; Consumer Protection;
    Environmental Law; Federal Trade
    Commission

REMEDIES
    See also Equity; Sales
Defined, 9
Remedies at law, 9

REORGANIZATION
See Bankruptcies and Reorganization

REPLEVIN
See Sales, Remedies

RESCISSION
See Contracts

RESPONDEAT SUPERIOR
See Agency

RESTITUTION
See Contracts, Rescission and restitution

RESTRAINT OF TRADE
See Antitrust; Contracts; Federal Trade
    Commission

REWARDS
See Agreement, Offer

RISK OF LOSS
See Sales

ROBBERY
See Criminal Law

ROBINSON-PATMAN ACT
Price discrimination, 828-831

RULE OF REASON
See Antitrust, Sherman Act

SALES
    See also Contracts; Products Liability
    Generally, 280-385
Acceptance
    Generally, 291-294
    Additional terms, 292-293
        Rules between merchants, 292-293
    Methods of, 291-292, 330
    Partial, 332-333
    Revocation of, 330-333
        Notice, requirement of, 332
Anticipatory repudiation, 333
Breach,
    Material, defined, 370
    Notification of seller by buyer, 376
Bulk transfers, 312
Buyer's obligations, 329 et seq.
C.I.F. contracts, 323
Commercial reasonableness, 319
Consideration,
    Modification of contract, 294
        Writing, when required, 294
Cover,
    See Remedies, Buyer, this topic
Cure, 324
Damages,
    See Remedies, this topic
Destination contracts, 323
Entrusting, 315
Ex-ship contracts, 323

F.A.S. contracts, 323
F.O.B. contracts, 323
Formation of a sales contract, 286-299
Good faith, 319-321
Goods,
  Animals, unborn young of, 283
  Crops, 849
  Defined, 282-283
  Everyday purchases, 280
  Money as a commodity, 283
  Movable, 282
  Rare coins, 283
  Real estate, associated with, 282
  Services, compared, 282
  Tangible, 282
Imperfect title, 312-316
Inspection, right of, 330
  C.O.D. shipments, 330
  Documents of title, payment due on
    receipt of, 330
Installment contracts, 324-329
  Defined, 324-325
Insurable interest,
  Buyer's, 316
  Seller's, 316
Lex Mercantoria (Law Merchant), 7, 280
Liquidated damages,
  See Remedies, this topic
Merchant,
  Dealer in goods of kind involved, 283
  Defined, 283-285
  Employer of broker, agent or other
    intermediary, 283
  Holding out as having pertinent knowl-
    edge or skill, 283
Mirror-image rule of offer and acceptance
  rejected, 292
Offer,
  Generally, 286-291
  Merchant's firm offer, 291
  Ongoing contract, duration of, 290
  Open terms, 286-291
    Assortment term omitted, 290
    Open delivery term, 289-290
    Open payment term, 290-291
    Open price term, 286-288
    Shipping arrangements, 290
Parol evidence, 296-299
  See also Parol Evidence Rule
  Consistent additional terms, 296
  Course of dealing and usage of trade,
    296-299
  Course of performance, 299
Payment, 330
Performance,
  Generally, 319-329
  Concurrent conditions, 321
  Delivery,
    Place of,
      Carrier cases, 322-323
      Non-carrier cases, 322
    Tender of, 321-322
  Perfect tender rule, 323
    Exceptions,

Agreement of parties, 323-329
Commercial   impracticability,
  327-329
Cure, 324
Destruction of identified goods,
  329
Inappropriate shipping arrange-
  ments, 324
Installment contracts, 324-326
Substitution of carriers, 324
Remedies, 367-385
  Buyer, 372-379
    Acceptance, right to revoke, 373-375
      Opportunity for cure required, 375
    Cancel, right to, 377-379
    Damages,
      Warranty, breach of, 376
    Fraud of seller, 379
    Identified goods, right to recover from
      insolvent seller, 376-377
    Nonconforming   or   improperly
      delivered goods, right to reject,
      373
    Nondelivery or repudiation, right to
      recover for, 375-376
      Cover, right of, 375-376
    Replevy goods, right to, 377
    Security interest in the goods, right to
      retain and enforce, 377
    Specific performance, right to obtain,
      377
    Suit by customer of buyer resulting
      from seller's breach of warranty,
      376
  Limitation of, 380-383
    Consequential damages, 383
  Liquidated damages, 380
  Seller, 367-372
    Cancel the sales contract, right to,
      370-372
    Delivery of goods,
      Right to stop carrier or bailee
        from delivering to insolvent
        buyer, 368-369
      Right to withhold, 368
    Identify goods to the contract after
      buyer has breached, right to, 369
    Purchase price plus incidental
      damages, right to recover, 370
    Reclaim goods in possession of insol-
      vent buyer, right to, 369
    Repossession of goods, 372
    Resell goods, right to, 369-370
    Seller's lien, 367-368
Rescind,
  Two meanings, 336 n. 1
Risk of loss,
  Generally, 304-312
  Bailees, 308-309
  Breach of contract,
    Absence of, 304-309
    Presence of, 309-312
      Buyer's breach, 310-312
      Seller's breach, 309

Bulk transfers, 312
Carrier cases, 304-306
    Destination contracts, 304-306
    Shipment contracts, 304
Non-carrier cases, 307-308
    Merchant seller, 307
    Non-merchant seller, 307-308
Sale on approval, 309
Sale or return, 309
Sale,
    Defined, 280, 282
    Goods, of, 281-286
    Transactions in goods, contrasted, 282
Seller's retention of sold goods, 315-316
Shipment contracts, 322
Statute of Frauds, 294-296
    Exceptions, 295-296
    Relaxed requirements for sufficiency of
        the writing, 295
    Written confirmation sufficient if
        between merchants, 295
Statute of limitations, 379
Title, passage of, 303-304
    Agreement, 303
    Delivery,
        Destination contracts, 303-304
        Documents of title, 304
        Non-document of title cases, 304
        Shipment contracts, 303
    Goods, existence of, 303
    Identification, 303
    Sales contracts vs. contracts to sell, 303
Unconscionability, 299
Uniform Commercial Code,
    Summary of rules, 287
Void title, 312
Voidable title, 312-315
Waiver of defenses, 383

SECURED TRANSACTIONS
Generally, 474-503
Accounts, 476
After-acquired property, 491
Attachments, 477, 478
Chattel paper, 476
Collateral,
    See also Default; Description of col-
        lateral, both this topic
    Defined, 475
    Moved to another jurisdiction, 492
    Reasonable care, 496
    Release, 496
Debtor, 475
Default, 496-501
    Basic remedies, 497
    Common elements, 497
    Disposal of collateral, 498-501
        Consumer goods, 500
        Procedures, 500
        Proceeds, 501
        Retention of collateral, 500
    Possession, secured party's right to take,
        497
        Assembling the collateral, 498

Breach of the peace, 497
    Reasonable care of the collateral, 498
    Stipulation of conditions, 496
Defined, 474
Description of collateral, 478-483
Documents of title, 746
Effective time for perfection, 492
Filing, 478, 483-487
    Where, 483-487
        Classification of collateral, 486-487
Financing statement,
    Amendment, 496
    Defined, 476
Floating lien, 491-492
    Exhibit, 491
Future advances, 491
General intangibles, 476
Goods, 475-476
Information request by creditors, 495-496
Perfection,
    Automatic, 487
    Defined, 476
    Methods,
        Filing, 478
        Purchase money security interest in
            consumer goods, 478
        Transfer of collateral, 478
    Possession, 487
    Proceeds (temporary automatic perfec-
        tion), 487
Priorities, 492-495
    Conflicting perfected security interests,
        492
    Conflicting unperfected security inter-
        ests, 492-493
    Exceptions to perfection priority rules,
        Buyers in the ordinary course of busi-
            ness, 493
        Buyers of chattel paper, 495
        Secondhand goods, 439-495
Proceeds, 491
Purchase money security interest, 477-478
Secured party,
    Defined, 475
Security agreement, 475
Security interest,
    Assignment, 496
    Creation of, 476-477
        Debtor has rights in collateral, 477
        Value given to debtor, 477
        Written agreement, 477
    Defined, 475
    Enforceable, 477
Status of debt, debtor's request for infor-
    mation on, 496
Strict foreclosure, 498
Termination, 501
Uniform Commercial Code,
    Excluded transactions, 477
    Prior law, 475
    Simplification of terminology, 475
Unperfected security interest,
    Parties that prevail over,
        Buyers in ordinary course, 490-491

Lien creditors, 490
Perfected security interest, 490

SECURITIES REGULATION
Generally, 689-700
"Blue Sky" laws, 699
Federal, 689-699
Miscellaneous federal statutes, 699
Registration,
Exemptions, 689-690
Statement,
Material false statements or material omissions, 690
Requirements, 689
Securities Act of 1933, 689-692
Antifraud provisions, liability under, 690-692
Securities and Exchange Commission, 689, 758
Securities Exchange Act of 1934, 692-700
Insider reporting and trading, 693, 695-696, 698
Proxy statements, 698-699
Rule 10b-5, 693-698
Disclosure under, 693-698
Section 16(b), exhibit comparing, 699
When applied, 698
Section 16(b), 698
Rule 10b-5, exhibit comparing, 699
Stabilization, 692
State securities laws, 699-700

SHAREHOLDERS
See Corporations

SHERMAN ACT
See Antitrust

SLANDER
See Torts

SOLE PROPRIETORSHIP
Advantages and disadvantages, 593
Defined, 590

SPECIFIC PERFORMANCE
See also Agency
Generally, 235-237
Order of, defined, 10
Personal services contract, 237
Sale of land, 237

STANDING
See Federal Courts

STARE DECISIS
Defined, 4
Functions, 4
Precedent,
Conflicting or none, 5
Departure from, 4

STATE COURT SYSTEM
Generally, 12-14
Appellate courts, 13-14

Inferior trial courts, 12-13
National reporter system, 24
Trial courts of general jurisdiction, 13

STATUTE OF FRAUDS
Generally, 172-184
Administrator or executor's promise to personally pay estate debts, 182
Assignment, 196
Contracts not performable within one year, 178-180
Debt or duty of another, promise to answer for, 180-182
Goods over $500, sale of, 294-296
Exceptions, 295-296
Relaxed requirements for sufficiency of the writing, 295
Written confirmation sufficient if between merchantes, 295
Land,
Easements, 176
Leases, 176
Life estates, 173-174
Mortgages, 174-176
Partial performance, 176
Sale of, 173
Will, promise to leave property in a, 176-178
Marriage, promise made in consideration of, 182
Uniform Commercial Code,
Intangibles, 184
Sale of goods, 183
Securities, 184
Security agreements, 184
Writing, sufficiency of, 184

STATUTE OF LIMITATIONS
See Consideration, Debts, new promises to pay barred; Criminal Law; Sales

STATUTES
Source of law, 6

STOCKS
See Corporate Financing

SUBROGATION
See Insurance

SUBSTANTIVE LAW
Defined, 8

SUMMONS
See Trail

SUNDAY LAWS
See Contracts

SUPREME COURT
Generally, 14 et seq.
Appeal, 17-18
Certiorari, writ of, 18, 27
Opinions, 25-28

See also Court Opinions; West Publishing Company

SURETYSHIP
Defined, 514
Indemnity, compared, 514
Rights of surety, 514

SYNDICATES
Defined, 591

TAX REFORM ACT OF 1976
See Estates, Taxation of

TENANCY IN COMMON
See Real Property, Concurrent ownership

TENDER OFFER
See Corporations

THIRD PARTY BENEFICIARY CONTRACTS
Generally, 189-193
Creditor beneficiaries, 190-191
Donee beneficiaries, 191-192
Incidental beneficiaries, 192
Mortgage assumption, 191
Vesting of third party rights, 192-193

TITLE, PASSAGE OF
See Sales

TORTS
See also Business Torts; Fraud; Products Liability
Generally, 29-50
Assault, 35
    Defenses, 35
    Defined, 35
Battery, 34-35
    Defenses, 35
    Defined, 34
Causation,
    Factual, 30-31
        "But for" test, 31
        "Substantial factor" test, 31
    Proximate, 31-33
Conversion, 42, 255, 264-266
Defamation, 38
    Computer, by, 39
    Defenses, 38
    Defined, 29
Disparagement of goods, 38-39
Duty,
    Breach of, 34
    Care, of, 33-34
Elements, 30-34
False imprisonment, 35-37
Injury, 30
Intentional,
    Wrongs against the person, 34-39
    Wrongs against property, 39-42
Kinds, 34
Libel, 38

Mental distress, infliction of, 37-38
Misrepresentation, 39
    See also Fraud
Negligence, 44-47
    Defenses,
        Assumption of risk, 46
        Contributory and comparative negligence, 46-47
        Supersed, intervening forces, 45-46
    Products liability, 357-361
Privacy, invasion of right to, 39
Property, defense of, 35
Proximate cause, 31-33
    Foreseeability, 33
Reasonable person standard, 34, 44
Scope of, 30
Self-defense, 35
Slander, 38
Slander of title, 38-39
Strict liability, 47-49
    Abnormally dangerous activities, 47-49
    Products liability, 361-363
    Workmen's compensation, 49
Trespass,
    Land, 39-41
    Personal property, 41-42

TRADE REGULATION
See Federal Trade Commission

TRADEMARKS
Generally, 766-767
Defined, 42, 258

TRESPASS
See Torts

TRIAL
See also Appeal; Discovery; Dismissals and Judgments Before Trial; Pretrial Hearing
Affirmative defense, 19
Answer, 19
Charges (instructions to jury), 22
Closing argument, 22
Complaint, 19
Counterclaim, 19
Cross-examination, 22
Direct examination, 22
Directed verdict, motion for, 22
Judgment n.o.v. (notwithstanding the verdict), 22-23
Jury trial, right to, 21-22
Opening statements, 22
Pleadings, 19
Rebuttal, 22
Recross-examination, 22
Redirect examination, 22
Rejoinder, 22
Reply, 19
Summons,
    Defined, 19
    Service of, 19

TRUSTS
See also Antitrust; Business Trusts
Implied, 920
Inter vivos, 919
Oral, 920
Testamentary, 919-920

TRUTH-IN-LENDING ACT
See Consumer Protection; Debtor, Protector of, Consumer Credit Protection Act

TYING CONTRACTS
See Federal Trade Commission

ULTRA VIRES DOCTRINE
See Corporations

UNCONSCIONABILITY
See Consumer Protection; Contracts; Sales

UNFAIR COMPETITION
See Business Torts

UNIFORM ACTS
See also Uniform Commercial Code
Model Business Corporation Act, 638
Text, 1143
Uniform Consumer Credit Code (UCCC), 519-521, 783-784
Text, 1055
Uniform Limited Partnership Act, 605, 628
Revised act, 628
Text, 1129
Text, 1121
Uniform Negotiable Instruments Law, 281, 388
History, 388
Uniform Partnership Act, 596
Text, 1109
Uniform Probate Code, 911
Uniform Sales Act, 281
Uniform Securities Act, 700

UNIFORM COMMERCIAL CODE
See also Agreement; Commercial Paper; Consideration; Contracts; Sales; Secured Transactions
Adoption process, 8
Article Three,
Uniform Negotiable Instruments Law, relation to, 388
Article Two,
Scope of, 281-285
Bulk Sales Law, 515
Debtors and creditors, rights and duties, 495-496
Function of, 8
Origins of, 7-8
Sale of goods,
UCC rules summarized, 287
Summary of, 281
Text, 929

UNJUST ENRICHMENT
See also Contracts, Quasi-contract
Quasi-contract, relation to, 75, 77

USURY
See Contracts

VENUE
Defined, 12

WAGE EARNER PLAN
See Bankruptcy and Reorganization

WARRANTY
Generally, 336-357
Commercial paper, 439-442
Consumer protection, 788
Disclaimers, 347-353
Buyer's refusal to inspect, 348
Express, 347
Implied, 347-348
Fitness, 348
Merchantability, 348
Unconscionability and, 348-353
Usage of trade, 348
Express, 338-343
Basis of the bargain, 338-340
Opinion and value, statements of, 340-342
Formal words (warranty or guarantee), use of not required, 340
Full warranty, 342
Implied, 343-347
Fitness for a particular purpose, 271-273, 345-347
Merchantability, 343-345
Limited warranty, 342
Magnuson-Moss Warranty Act, 342-343, 788
Overlapping, 347
Products liability, 357
Puffing, 340
Quality, 338-353
Real property,
Warranty of habitability, 862-863
Title,
Disclaimer of, 338
Good title, 337
No infringements, 337-338
No liens, 337

WEALTH TRANSFER
See Estates, Taxation of

WEST PUBLISHING COMPANY
National reporter system,
Federal Reporter (F. or F.2d), 24
Federal Rules Decisions (F.R.D.), 24-25
Federal Supplement, 24
State decisions (by geographic area), 24
Supreme Court Reporter (S.Ct.), 25, 27

WILLS
See also Estates; Inheritance; Trusts

Generally, 908-918
Bequest, 909
Codicil, 915, 917
Defined, 908-909
Devise, 909
Executor or executrix, 909
    Administrator or administratrix, compared, 909
Forced share, 917-918
Formal requirements, 913-914
Fraud, 914
General gift, 909
Gifts, types of, 909-910
Holographic, 914
Probate court, 909
Purposes, 911
Renunciation of rights, 917-918
Residuary provision, 909-910
Revocation, 909, 914-917
    Another writing, by, 917
    Operation of law,
        Afterborn children, 917
        Divorce or annulment, 917
        Marriage, 917

Physical act, by, 915-917
Rights under, 917-918
Specific devise or bequest, 909
Statute of Frauds,
    Promise to devise real property, 176-178
Testamentary capacity, 911-913
Testator or testatrix, 909
Undue influence, 914
Uniform Probate Code, 911

WINDING UP
See Partnership

WORKMEN'S COMPENSATION
    See also Insurance; Torts, Strict liability
Bankruptcy, 532
Fellow-servant rule, elimination of, 586

WRIT OF EXECUTION
Defined, 507

ZONING
See Land Use Control

✝